W9-BPS-685

Ounces	9 x 12 envelope, 9 x 12 SASE number of pages	9 x 12 SASE (for return trips) number of pages	First Class Postage	Third Class Postage	Postage from U.S. to Canada
under 2	...	1 to 2	$.39*	$.39*	$.63*
2	1 to 4	3 to 8	.52	.52	.73
3	5 to 10	9 to 12	.75	.75	.86
4	11 to 16	13 to 19	.98	.98	1.09
5	17 to 21	20 to 25	1.21	1.21	1.32
6	22 to 27	26 to 30	1.44	1.21	1.55
7	28 to 32	31 to 35	1.67	1.33	1.78
8	33 to 38	36 to 41	1.90	1.33	2.01
9	39 to 44	42 to 46	2.13	1.44	2.24
10	45 to 49	47 to 52	2.36	1.44	2.47
11	50 to 55	53 to 57	2.59	1.56	2.70
12-32	56 to 99	58 to 101	2.90	1.56	2.80

* This cost includes a 10¢ assessment for oversized mail that is light in weight.

1994
Writer's Market

Where & How
To Sell What You Write

Editor: Mark Garvey

Assistant Editor: Roseann S. Biederman

WRITER'S DIGEST BOOKS
Cincinnati, Ohio

Distributed in Canada by
McGraw-Hill Ryerson
300 Water St.
Whitby, Ontario L1N 9B6

Distributed in Australia by
Kirby Book Co.
Private Bag No. 19
Alexandria NSW 2015

Managing Editor, Market Books Department:
Constance J. Achabal

Writer's Market. *Copyright © 1993 by Writer's Digest Books. Published by F&W Publications, 1507 Dana Ave., Cincinnati, Ohio 45207. Printed and bound in the United States of America. All rights reserved. No part of this book may be reproduced in any form or by any electronic or mechanical means including information storage and retrieval systems without written permission from the publisher. Reviewers may quote brief passages to be printed in a magazine or newspaper.*

This edition of Writer's Market *features a "self-jacket" that eliminates the need for a separate dust jacket. It provides sturdy protection for your book while it saves paper, trees and energy.*

Library of Congress Catalog Number
31-20772
International Standard Serial Number
0084-2729
International Standard Book Number
0-89879-607-5

U.S. Postage by the Page by Carolyn Hardesty
Canadian Postage by the Page by Barbara Murrin

Contents

Getting Published

Before Your First Sale 5

If you are new to the writing business, or would like to brush up on the basics of selling your writing, this section will point you in the right direction. First-time authors L. Warren Douglas and E.P. Jones talk about the road to publication and the satisfactions of "telling your story."

Targeting Your Magazine Submissions, by John Wood 24

A senior editor at Modern Maturity *offers a four-point plan for getting the right article ideas in front of the right editors — solid advice that will show you how to sell more of your writing.*

Selling Your Book Proposal, 31

In order to interest an editor in your book, you must convince him a substantial audience is waiting to buy it. In this article, you'll learn how to sell your proposal to an editor by proving a viable market exists for it. Interviews with writer Harvey Rachlin and editors James Cohee of Sierra Club Books and Ron Powers of TAB/McGraw-Hill offer an inside look at how publishing decisions are made and how writers can most effectively sell their ideas.

The Business of Writing

Current Trends in Publishing, by Roseann Beiderman 39

The book and magazine publishing industries are in constant flux. This look at recent publishing trends will bring you up to date on the kinds of books and magazines that are currently hot — and give you valuable advice to help you stay on top of the trends. Author Alec Wilkinson talks about writing literary nonfiction.

How Much Should I Charge? 46

Setting your freelance writing fees can be a real headache. Our suggestions for determining your fees — along with our list of hundreds of freelance jobs and typical fees — will help take some of the guesswork out of it.

Minding the Details *61*

From contracts to rights, copyright, money and taxes, this section will help you negotiate and secure fair agreements, keep track of your intellectual property rights, and handle your earnings responsibly and legally.

The Markets

Book Publishers *73*

Hundreds of places to sell your book ideas. The introduction to this section includes current information about the book publishing industry as well as interviews with Loompanics Unlimited's Steve O'Keefe and University of Texas Press' Theresa May.

Canadian and International Book Publishers *227*

Subsidy/Royalty Publishers *244*

Small Presses *264*

Book Producers *275*

Consumer Magazines *282*

Match your interests to the hundreds of magazines listed in this section. Current magazine publishing trends are discussed in the introduction, and interviews with Marlane Liddell of Smithsonian *and Carol Wiley Lorente of* Vegetarian Times *offer inside tips on approaching the magazine market.*

Trade, Technical and Professional Journals *679*

The magazines in this section serve a multitude of trades and professions. The introduction, by business and trade writer Jack Neff, gives valuable tips for working with these highly-specialized publications—and advice from trade magazine editor Steve Shapiro of Pacific Fishing.

Scriptwriting 829

In his introduction to this section, Hollywood insider Kerry Cox tells you how to increase your chances of getting your scripts and plays published.

Syndicates 872

Newspaper syndicates distribute writers' works around the nation and the world. In this section, you'll hear from writer Mark Powell about the challenges of writing for newspapers, and syndicate executive Anita Tobias on the best way to approach a syndicate.

Greeting Cards & Gift Ideas 887

The greeting card and gift markets are viable outlets for many styles of writing. Current, Inc.'s Nan Stine offers good advice for freelancers interested in working for the greeting card industry.

Resources

Contests and Awards 899

Organizations of Interest 945

Publications of Interest 947

Glossary 949

Book Publishers Subject Index 954

General Index 981

From the Editors

Most freelance writers work alone. Most wouldn't have it any other way. Our writing is one part of our lives that admits no compromise. That's the glory and attraction of it: The work we do is so completely our own. We write first for ourselves—to tell our story, to share our enthusiasms, to coax meaning from the world around us—and only secondarily for an audience, for prestige or for a paycheck. And since most of the effort involved in writing takes place inside our own heads, freelancing can sometimes seem a lonely endeavor.

Yet the solitary nature of the act of writing belies the fact that there are thousands of us doing it. Taken together with the thousands of publishers and editors plying their arts, we form a culture of individuals dedicated to the creation and dissemination of the written word.

One of the most appealing aspects of our jobs, as editors of *Writer's Market*, is the opportunity we have to observe the writing/publishing community from a vantage point that few enjoy. From our perspective (lodged somewhere between the two halves of that community) we get a good view of the dynamics of writer/publisher relationships. We listen to writers talk about editors, editors talk about writers, and both of them talk about the frustrations and joys of the publishing process. And year after year, we do our best to bring the two halves of the writing/publishing community together.

This year, as always, we've assembled the most current information on the best markets for your freelance writing. The publishers who have chosen to list in this year's *Writer's Market* are interested in receiving submissions. Like lumber to carpenters, freelance submissions are the raw material of the publishing industry. Without a steady influx of new material, publishers would die on the vine. But it's a buyer's market. The flow of material across editors' desks is more than just steady—it's a deluge. Some of the larger book publishers and consumer magazines receive literally thousands of unsolicited submissions every week. Cause for concern? Definitely. Cause for surrender? Never.

To rise above the tide of submissions flowing into editors' offices, you need an advantage, an edge that will distinguish your submission from the flood of mediocre material they're used to seeing. That edge is information: information about the particular kinds of material publishers want to see and how they wish to be contacted as well as information about how to present your writing professionally—in short, the kind of information you'll find in the pages of *Writer's Market*.

In addition to the thousands of market listings for everything from books to greeting cards, we have included articles and other special features to help you use those listings to your best advantage. Articles such as Before Your First Sale, Targeting Your Magazine Submissions and Selling Your Book Proposal give you solid, fundamental information to help you deal professionally and successfully with the publishing world.

Current Trends in Publishing, How Much Should I Charge? and Minding the Details offer more advanced information for writers who know the basics but need up-to-date details about the publishing climate, fee structures and handling the business details of a writing career.

Interviews with experts in the field continue to be an important part of our lineup. This year we talk with authors and editors from a wide variety of writing and publishing backgrounds. These "Insider Reports" offer insightful comments and good advice for freelancers hoping to crack new markets.

We hope your experiences in the writing community in 1994 are positive, successful—and financially rewarding. See you in '95.

Mark Garvey
Editor

Roseann S. Biederman
Assistant Editor

How to Get the Most Out of Writer's Market

Writer's Market is here to assist you in deciding where and how to submit your writing to appropriate markets. Each individual listing contains information about the editorial focus of the market, how they prefer material to be submitted, payment information and other helpful tips.

Where to start

A quick look at the Table of Contents will familiarize you with the arrangement of *Writer's Market*. The three largest sections of the book are the market listings of Book Publishers; Consumer Magazines; and Trade, Technical and Professional Journals. Within each category, the markets are listed alphabetically. You will also find sections for scriptwriting markets, greeting card publishers and syndicates. Be sure to read the introduction for each section before you turn to the listings. The section introductions contain specific information about trends, submission methods and other helpful resources for the material included in that section.

Narrowing your search

After you've identified the market categories you're interested in, you can begin researching specific markets within each section.

Publishers listed in the Book Publishers section are categorized, in the Book Publishers Subject Index, according to types of books they are interested in. If, for example, you plan to write a book on a religious topic, simply turn to the Book Publishers Subject Index and look under Religion subhead in Nonfiction for the names and page numbers of companies that publish such books.

Consumer Magazines and Trade, Technical and Professional Journals are categorized by subject to make it easier for you to identify markets for your work. If you want to publish an article dealing with some aspect of retirement, you could look under the Retirement category of Consumer Magazines to find an appropriate market. You would want to keep in mind, however, that magazines in other categories might also be open to your article (for example, women's magazines publish such material as well). Keep your antennae up while studying the markets: less obvious markets often offer the best opportunities.

Interpreting the markets

Once you've identified companies or publications that cover the subjects you're interested in, you can begin evaluating specific listings to pinpoint the markets most receptive to your work and most beneficial to you.

In evaluating an individual listing, first check the location of the company, the types of material it is interested in seeing, submission requirements, and rights and payment policies. Depending upon your personal concerns, any of these items could be a deciding factor as you determine which markets you plan to approach. In addition to this information, many listings also include a reporting time. This lets you know how long it will typically take for the publisher to respond to your initial query or submission. (We suggest that you allow an additional month for a response, just in case your submission is under further review or the publisher is backlogged.)

Check the Glossary at the back of the book for unfamiliar words. Specific symbols and abbreviations are explained in the table on page 72. The most important abbreviation is SASE—self-addressed, stamped envelope. Always enclose one when you send unsolicited queries, proposals or manuscripts. This requirement is not included in most of the individual market listings because it is a "given" that you must follow if you expect to receive a reply.

A careful reading of the listings will reveal many editors are very specific about their needs. Your chances of success increase if you follow directions to the letter. Often companies do not accept unsolicited manuscripts and return them unread. Read each listing closely, heed the tips given, and follow the instructions. Work presented professionally will normally be given more serious consideration.

Whenever possible, obtain writer's guidelines before submitting material. You can usually obtain them by sending a SASE to the address in the listing. You should also familiarize yourself with the company's publications. Many of the listings contain instructions on how to obtain sample copies, catalogs or market lists. The more research you do upfront, the better your chances of acceptance, publication and payment.

Additional help

This year's book contains articles on selling to magazines, pitching a book proposal, current trends in book and magazine publishing and much more. "Insider Reports"—interviews with writers and editors—offer advice and an inside look at publishing.

Minding the Details offers valuable information about rights, taxes and other practical matters. New or unpublished writers should also read Before Your First Sale. There is also a helpful section titled How Much Should I Charge? that offers guidance for setting your freelance writing fees.

Getting Published

Before Your First Sale

Whether you're a new writer interested in learning the ins and outs of the publishing world for the first time or an experienced writer who is considering trying to publish in new areas, this section is for you.

Every writer who publishes regularly has, at some point or other, come to the realization that writing for publication is not simply a matter of having a talent for writing. Your writing ability will help you complete that novel or article, but that talent will not get your work published. The difference between writers who publish and writers who don't is largely a matter of education. Those who take the time to learn how the publishing industry works, publish more often than those who don't.

If there is an overall impression we would like you to carry away from this article it is this: Success in getting published is not mysterious; it is not an impossible dream; and it does not happen by accident.

Selling your writing involves more than randomly selecting a publisher and sending out your query or manuscript. It involves following professional guidelines, submitting your work carefully and dealing courteously with editors. Business savvy can never replace writing talent, but a combination of both will help you succeed.

You may think that a previously unpublished writer has a difficult time breaking into the field. As with any profession, experience is valued, but that doesn't mean publishers are closed to new writers. While it is true that some editors are partial to working with certain writers, most are open to professional submissions and good ideas from any writer, and quite a few magazine editors like to feature different styles and "voices" in their publications.

In nonfiction book publishing, experience in writing or in a particular subject area is valued by editors as an indicator of the author's ability and expertise in the subject. Again, as with magazines, the idea is paramount, and new authors break in every year with good, timely ideas.

As you work in the writing field, you may read articles or talk to writers and editors who give conflicting advice. There are some norms in the business, but in a field of creative people, these are few. You'll probably hear as many different routes to publication as writers you talk to, and they'll tell you about the same number of taboos they encountered. You could easily drive yourself crazy trying to do, or not do, everything you're told.

The following information on submissions should be used as a guideline for what has worked for many other writers, not as the *only* method you can follow. It's easy to get wrapped up in the specifics of submitting (should my name go at the top left or right of the manuscript?) and fail to consider weightier matters (is this idea appropriate for this market?). Let common sense and courtesy be your guides as you work with editors, and eventually you'll develop a style all your own.

Targeting your ideas

Writers often think of an interesting story, complete the manuscript and then begin to look for a suitable publisher or magazine. While this approach is common for literary fiction, poetry and screenwriting, it reduces your chances of success in many other writing areas. Instead, try choosing categories that interest you and study those sections in *Writer's Market*. Select several listings that you consider good prospects for your type of writing. Sometimes the individual listings will even help you generate ideas.

Next, make a list of the potential markets for each idea. Make the initial contact with markets using the method stated in the market listings. If you exhaust your list of possibilities, don't give up. Reevaluate the idea, revise it or try another angle. Continue developing ideas and approaching markets with them. Identify and rank potential markets for an idea and continue the process, but don't approach a market a second time until you receive a response to your first submission.

Prepare for rejection and the sometimes lengthy wait. When a submission is returned, check your file folder of potential markets for that idea. Cross off the market that rejected the idea and immediately mail an appropriate submission to the next market on your list. If the editor has given you suggestions or reasons as to why the manuscript was not accepted, you might want to incorporate these when revising your manuscript.

Don't take rejection personally. A rejection only means that your particular piece did not fit the needs of the publisher at that time. Most editors do not have the time to respond individually and will simply return your submission in your self-addressed, stamped envelope. Others will send a form rejection letter, sometimes with a check-off list of possible reasons the query or manuscript was rejected. This is not a sign of disrespect for your work. It's a response method in publishing that reflects the huge number of submissions received and the inability of the editor to respond personally to all of them. If you receive a rejection slip or letter that, while rejecting your idea, offers helpful hints or encourages future submissions, consider that market carefully. Although it's discouraging whenever an idea is rejected, a personalized response means the editor believes your submission warranted an individual note and perhaps a longer explanation of the reason for rejecting the piece.

But be careful not to read too much into a personalized rejection. Some editors suggest changes when rejecting manuscripts. If you believe those changes will make the manuscript better, implement them, but do not assume the editor will now automatically accept your revised manuscript. It may happen, but suggested changes are just that, and implementing them does not guarantee acceptance.

Query and cover letters

A query letter is a brief but detailed letter written to interest an editor in your manuscript. It is a tool for selling both magazine articles and nonfiction books. With a magazine query you are attempting to interest an editor in your writing an article for her periodical. A book query's job is to get an editor interested enough to ask you to send in either a full-blown proposal or the entire manuscript. [Note: Some book editors accept proposals on first contact. Refer to individual listings for contact guidelines.] Some beginners are hesitant to query, thinking an editor can more fairly judge an idea by seeing the entire manuscript. Actually, most editors of nonfiction prefer to be queried.

Do your best writing when you sit down to compose your query. There is no query formula that guarantees success, but there are some points to consider when you begin:

● Queries are single-spaced business letters, usually limited to one page. Address the current editor by name. (If you cannot tell whether an editor is male or female from the name in the listing, address the editor by a full name: Dear Chris Baker.) Don't show unwarranted familiarity by immediately addressing an editor by a first name; follow the editor's lead when responding to your correspondence.

● Grab the editor's interest with a strong opening. Some queries begin with a paragraph that approximates the lead of the intended article.

● Briefly detail the structure of the article. Give some facts and perhaps an anecdote and mention people you intend to interview. Give editors enough information to make them want to know more, but don't feel the need to give them details of the whole story.

● If photos are available to accompany the manuscript, let the editor know, but never send original photos, transparencies or artwork on your initial contact with a publisher. Send photocopies or contact sheets instead. You should always have duplicates, so if your material is lost, you haven't lost your only copy.

INSIDER REPORT

Commitment and professionalism pay off for first-time novelist

"I was at a point in my life where my career was shot; everything else was shot; and the only way I had to use the kind of talent and training I had was to write," says first-time novelist L. Warren Douglas, author of *A Plague of Change* (Del Rey, 1993). "Over the past approximately 20 years, I'd been vegetating in manual labor jobs and things like that. And I'd finally just had enough—it was do or die. And I love science fiction, so that was my logical choice. It's really important that a person makes a commitment to it. It doesn't matter if it's fulltime or part time or whatever, but they have to have that drive and that commitment to keep doing it and not just get tired and stop sending out query letters."

To attract the interest of editors, Douglas polished a one-page query letter that eventually got his phone

L. Warren Douglas

ringing. "I sent out a query letter that I rewrote at least 20 times," says Douglas. "And I sent *just* the query letter, hoping to pique editorial interest and not cost too much. Someone once told me that in your query letter you should describe the entire book in the first sentence, and then elaborate on it in your first paragraph. Previous credits or anything like that can be in another paragraph, but the query should definitely never go over that short, non-threatening one-page limit. I would advise anyone to do it that way."

The first editor to respond to Douglas' query wrote back with a thoughtful, four-page critique. "After she wrote, I sat down and literally rewrote the book working 12- and 14-hour days and shipped it back to her in a matter of weeks, having addressed her concerns and having written her a letter telling her exactly how I had addressed her concerns." Though that editor was not the one who eventually bought the manuscript, Douglas believes it is important to listen closely to editors' suggestions and strive to be as reliable and professional as possible in your dealings with them. "I realized that these people are in business," he says. "They want somebody who isn't all infatuated with his own book. You have to apply yourself in a business-like manner"

• Mention any special training or experience that qualifies you to write the article—either as an assignment or on speculation. If you have prior writing experience, you should mention it; if not, there's no need to call attention to the fact. Some editors will also ask to look at clips or tearsheets—actual pages or photocopies of your published work. If possible, submit something related to your idea, either in topic or style.

● Your closing paragraph should include a direct request to do the article. It may specify the date the manuscript can be completed and an approximate length. Don't discuss fees or request advice from the editor at this time. Treat the query like a short introductory job interview. You wouldn't presume to discuss money at this early a stage in a job interview; treat the query the same way.

Fiction is sometimes queried, but most fiction editors don't like to make a final decision until they see the complete manuscript. (This is also true for many humor and opinion pieces.) The majority of editors will want to see a synopsis and sample chapters for a book, and a complete manuscript of a short story. If a fiction editor does request a query, briefly describe the main theme and story line, including the conflict and resolution of your story.

Some writers state politely in their query letters that after a specified date (slightly beyond the listed reporting time), they will assume the editor is not currently interested in their topic and will submit the query elsewhere. It's a good idea to do this only if your topic is a timely one that will suffer if not considered quickly.

For more information about writing query letters and biographical notes, read *How to Write Irresistible Query Letters*, by Lisa Collier Cool (Writer's Digest Books).

A brief single-spaced cover letter enclosed with your manuscript is helpful in personalizing a submission. If you have previously queried the editor on the article or book, the cover letter should be a brief reminder: "Here is the piece on digital recording technology, which we discussed previously. I look forward to hearing from you at your earliest convenience." Don't use the letter to make a sales pitch. Your manuscript must stand on its own at this point.

If you are submitting to a market that considers unsolicited complete manuscripts, your cover letter should tell the editor something about your manuscript and about you — your publishing history and any particular qualifications you have for writing the enclosed manuscript.

Once your manuscript has been accepted, you may offer to get involved in the editing process, but policy on this will vary from magazine to magazine. Most magazine editors don't send galleys to authors before publication, but if they do, you should return the galleys as promptly as possible after you've reviewed them. Book publishers will normally involve you in rewrites whether you like it or not.

Book proposals

Most nonfiction books are sold by book proposal, a package of materials that details what your book is about, who its intended audience is, and how

R.J. Anderson
844 Leffler St.
Hamilton, NY 13346
(315)555-2367

June 6, 1994

Robert Baker
Articles Editor
Recorded Music Magazine
54 S.R. 309 West
Chicago, IL 60605

Dear Mr. Baker:

Today's recording studios are magical places. They use the very latest in electronic technology to perform unbelievable feats of legerdemain and sculpt the aural illusions that make up modern music. High-end recording studios can house literally millions of dollars worth of equipment and require the expert hand of a well-trained recording engineer — a technological magician — to use them to their fullest potential. Buck Mann, one of pop music's most sought-after recording engineers, is such a magician.

I would like to write an interview/profile of Buck Mann for *Recorded Music*. After honing his engineering chops in the commercial music houses of Dallas and Los Angeles, Buck came to New York where he has engineered award-winning albums for artists ranging from Kyle Miller to The Yellow Club. His knowledge is astounding; his techniques are unique; his results are world-renowned. Buck is currently engineering the next Trillionaires CD in New York City.

I believe your readers will be enlightened by glimpsing Buck Mann's studio methods and entertained by his stories about working with the "stars."

A recording engineer myself, I have worked with Buck in the past as an assistant on various studio projects. As a journalist I have covered the New York recording scene since 1985. I have full access to Buck Mann both inside the studio and out.

I can deliver the completed article, at any desired length from 1,000 to 4,000 words, two months after assignment. Photos can be included if you so desire. I look forward to hearing from you.

Sincerely,

R.J. Anderson

Sample magazine query.

you intend to write it. Most fiction is sold either by complete manuscript, especially for first-time authors, or by two or three sample chapters.

The nonfiction book proposal includes some combination of a cover or query letter, an overview, an outline, author's information sheet and sample chapters. Editors also want to see information about the audience for your book and about titles that compete with your proposed book.

Take a look at individual listings to see what submission method editors prefer. If they have not specified, send as much of the following information as you can.

• The cover or query letter should be a short introduction to the material you include in the proposal.

• An overview is a brief summary of your book. For nonfiction, it should detail your book's subject and give an idea of how that subject will be developed. If you're sending a synopsis of a novel, cover the basic plot.

• An outline covers your book chapter by chapter. The outline should include all major points covered in each chapter. Some outlines are done in traditional outline form, but most are written in paragraph form.

• An author's information sheet should — as succinctly and clearly as possible — acquaint the editor with your writing background and convince her of your qualifications to write about the subject.

• Many editors like to see sample chapters, especially for a first book. In fiction it's essential. In nonfiction, sample chapters show the editor how well you write and develop the ideas from your outline.

• Marketing information is now expected to accompany every book proposal. If you can provide information about the audience for your book and ways the book publisher can reach those people, you will increase your chances of acceptance. For more information on compiling market information for your nonfiction book proposal, see Selling Your Book Proposal, on page 31.

Editors also want to know what books in the marketplace compete with yours. Look in the *Subject Guide* to *Books in Print* for titles on the topic of your book. Then check out those titles and write a one- or two-sentence synopsis for each. Be sure to mention how your book will be different from the other titles.

A word about agents

An agent represents a writer's work to publishers, often negotiates publishing contracts, follows up to see that contracts are fulfilled and generally handles the business affairs while leaving the writer free to write. Effective agents are valued for their contacts in the publishing industry, their savvy about which publishers and editors to approach with which ideas, their ability to guide an author's career and their astute business sense.

While most book publishers listed in *Writer's Market* publish books by un-agented writers, some of the larger ones are reluctant to consider submissions

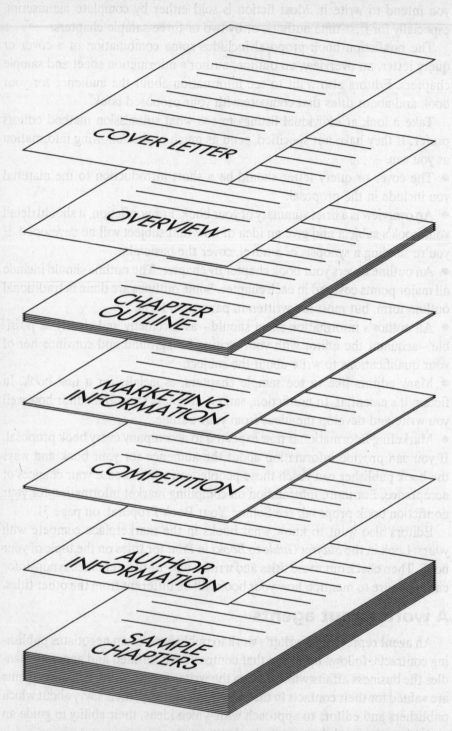

COVER LETTER

OVERVIEW

CHAPTER OUTLINE

MARKETING INFORMATION

COMPETITION

AUTHOR INFORMATION

SAMPLE CHAPTERS

A nonfiction book proposal will usually consist of the elements illustrated above. Their order is less important than the fact that you have addressed each component.

The outline

The outline included in your proposal package should most often be the kind known as a "chapter outline." A "formal outline," the kind with Roman and Arabic numerals and upper and lower case letters that we all learned in high school, may be useful for your own purposes when you sit down to write the book, but the chapter outline will be more effective at quickly giving an editor a sense of the scope of your material and how you plan to develop it.

In a chapter outline, you simply describe in clear prose, as succinctly and lucidly as possible, the content and thrust of each chapter—forgoing the formal outline's hierarchical arrangement of subheads. If you like, you can devote one page of your chapter outline to each chapter.

that have not reached them through a literary agent. Companies with such a policy are so noted in the listings.

For more information about finding and working with a literary agent, see *Guide to Literary Agents and Art/Photo Reps* (Writer's Digest Books). The *Guide* offers listings of agents and artists' representatives as well as helpful articles written by professionals in the field.

Writing tools

Like anyone involved in a trade or business, you need certain tools and supplies to produce your product or provide your service. While writers compose their work in a variety of ways—ranging from pencil and legal pad to personal computers—there are some basics you'll need for your writing business. We've also included information about some you may want in the future.

Typewriter. Many writers use electric or electronic typewriters that produce either pica or elite type. Pica type has 10 characters to a horizontal inch and elite has 12; both have six single-spaced, or three double-spaced lines to a vertical inch. The slightly larger pica type is easier to read and many editors prefer it, although they don't object to elite.

Editors do dislike, and often refuse to read, manuscripts that are single-spaced, typed in all caps or in an unusual type style such as script or italic. These manuscripts are hard on the eyes. Strive for clean, easy-to-read manuscripts and correspondence that reflect a professional approach to your work and consideration for your reader.

Use a good black typewriter ribbon and clean the keys frequently. Even the best typists make errors. *Occasional* retyping over erasures is acceptable, but strikeovers give your manuscript a sloppy, careless appearance. Hiding typos with large splotches of correction fluid makes your work look amateurish; use it sparingly. Some writers prefer to use typing correction film for final drafts. Better yet, a self-correcting electric typewriter with a correction tape makes typo corrections nearly invisible. Whatever method you use, it's best to retype a page that has several noticeable corrections. Sloppy typing is taken by many editors as a sign of sloppy work habits—and the possibility of careless research and writing.

Personal computers and word processors. More writers are working on personal computers than ever before. A personal computer can make a writer's work much more efficient. Revising and editing are faster and easier on a computer than on a typewriter, and there is no need to retype. Writers can also rely on their computers to give them fresh, readable copy as they revise rough drafts into finished manuscripts. For some writers, a fairly inexpensive word processor is adequate to produce manuscripts and letters; others may have additional uses and want computers with more capabilities.

When a manuscript is written on a computer, it can come out of the computer in three ways: as hard copy from the computer's printer; stored on a removable 5¼" floppy disk or 3½" diskette that can be read by other computers; or as an electronic transfer over telephone lines using a modem (a device that allows one computer to transmit to another).

Disk and computer printout submissions are sent to editors in the following ways:

● Hard copy—Computer printout submissions are fine to submit as long as they look like neatly-typed manuscripts. Some older and cheaper printers produce only a low-quality dot-matrix printout with hard-to-read, poorly shaped letters and numbers. Many editors are not willing to read these manuscripts. (In addition, most editors dislike copy with even, or justified, right margins.) New dot-matrix and ink jet printers, however, produce near letter-quality (NLQ) printouts that are almost indistinguishable from a typewritten manuscript. These are acceptable to editors, as are true letter-quality submissions. Remember that readability is the key. Whether you use a $100 24-pin dot-matrix printer or a $1,000 laser printer doesn't matter to the editor. He just wants to be able to read your manuscript easily.

When you submit hard copy to an editor, be sure to use quality paper. Some computer printers use standard bond paper that you'd use in a typewriter. Others are equipped with a tractor-feed that pulls continuous form paper with holes along the edges through the machine. If you use continuous form paper, be sure to remove the perforated tabs on each side and separate the pages before you send the manuscript for consideration.

● Disk—You'll find that more publishers are accepting or even requesting submissions on disk. A few publishers pay more (up to 15%) for electronic submissions, and some won't accept anything but submissions on disk. Eventually, industry observers say, electronic submissions will be the norm, just as

About electronic submissions

Publishers that accept submissions by disk or modem have this phrase in their listings: Query for electronic submissions. We give the information this way because you'll need to speak with someone before you send anything by these methods. Also, many magazines and publishers change system requirements as equipment and software are updated. Instead of listing information that you may find is outdated when you begin to send the submission, we have put general information in the listing.

Be prepared when you discuss your submission to note the operating system and software you used. Most publishers can work with DOS or Macintosh files, but it will expedite matters to get this clear up front.

typewritten submissions became the norm over handwritten manuscripts earlier in the century.

● Modem—Some publishers who accept submissions on disk also will accept electronic submissions by modem. This is a faster method of getting your manuscript to the publisher electronically. When you receive an assignment, ask about the editor's computer requirements. You'll need to work out submission information before you send something by modem, but you'll probably find that even computer systems you thought were incompatible can communicate easily by modem.

Because most editors also want hard copy along with an electronic submission, you may wonder why you should even consider using a disk or modem. Editors like electronic submissions because they can revise manuscripts quickly as well as save typesetting expenses. Most want backup hard copy in case there is a problem with a computer submission, but some prefer to edit the hard copy first, then have the writer make revisions and send the final version electronically. If you have a particularly timely topic or a manuscript that needs to be submitted quickly, a disk or modem submission is an asset that also can save you and the editor time on deadline.

Fax machines and boards. We have included publishers' facsimile machine numbers in the listings. Fax machines transmit copy across phone lines. Those publishers who wanted to list their facsimile machine numbers have done so.

Between businesses, the fax has come into standard daily use for materials that have to be sent quickly. In addition, some public fax machines are being installed in airports, hotels, libraries and even grocery stores.

The fax information we have included in listings is not to be used to transmit queries or entire manscripts to editors, unless they specifically request it. Although some machines transmit on regular bond paper, most still use a cheaper grade that is difficult to write on, making it unsuitable for editing. In most cases, this paper also fades with time, an undesirable characteristic for a manuscript. Writers should continue to use traditional means for sending manuscripts and queries and use the fax number we list only when an editor asks to receive correspondence by this method.

Some computer owners also have fax boards installed to allow transmissions to their computer screens or computer printers. Unless the fax board can operate independently from the computer's main processor, an incoming fax forces the user to halt whatever work is in process until the transmission ends. You should never send anything by this method without calling or arranging with the editor for this type of transmission.

Stationery and business cards. The paper you use for manuscripts and correspondence must measure 8½ × 11 inches. That's a standard size and editors are adamant—they don't want unusual colors or sizes. There's a wide range of white 8½ × 11 papers. The cheaper ones are made from wood pulp and will suffice, but are not recommended. Editors also discourage the use of erasable bond for manuscripts; typewriter ribbon ink on erasable bond tends to smear when handled and is difficult to write on. Don't use less than a 16 lb. bond paper; 20 lb. is preferred. Your best bet is paper with a 25% cotton fiber content. Its texture shows type neatly and it holds up under erasing and corrections.

You don't need fancy letterhead for your correspondence with editors. Plain bond paper is fine. Just type your name, address, phone number and the date at the top of the page—centered or in the right-hand corner. If you want letterhead, make it as simple and businesslike as possible. Many quick print shops have standard typefaces and can supply letterhead stationery at a relatively low cost.

Never use letterhead for typing your manuscripts. Only the first page of queries, cover letters and other correspondence should be typed on letterhead.

Business cards can be a useful tool for some writers, but many feel presumptuous using them. If you offer other editorial services such as copyediting or proofreading in addition to writing, you may want to have business cards. Or if you specialize in an area of nonfiction or work with business clients, you may want to invest in some. Again, simplicity is the key. Briefly list your name, services, address, phone and fax numbers. Don't feel it is mandatory to invest in business cards to have a professional image. Publishing operates fairly informally and a significant number of writers find they never need business cards.

Assorted supplies. Where will you put all your manuscripts and correspondence? A two- or four-drawer filing cabinet with file folders is a good choice, but some writers find they can make do with manila envelopes and cardboard boxes. It's important to organize and label your correspondence, manuscripts, ideas, submission records, clippings, etc., so you can find them when you need them. See Recording Submissions in this section for other helpful hints on keeping records.

You will also need stamps and envelopes. See Mailing Submissions in this section and the U.S. and Canadian Postage by the Page tables on the front and back inside covers of the book. If you decide to invest in a camera to increase your sales, you'll find details on submitting and mailing photos in the section on Mailing Submissions.

Manuscript format

When submitting a manuscript for possible publication, you can increase its chances of making a favorable impression by adhering to some fairly standard matters of physical format. Many professional writers use the format described here. Of course, there are no "rules" about what a manuscript must look like. These are just guidelines—some based on common sense, others more a matter of convention—that are meant to help writers display their work to best advantage. Strive for easy readability in whatever method you choose and adapt your style to your own personal tastes and those of the editors to whom you submit. Complete information on formats for books, articles, scripts, proposals and cover letters, with illustrated examples, is available in *The Writer's Digest Guide to Manuscript Formats*, by Dian Dincin Buchman and Seli Groves (Writer's Digest Books).

Most manuscripts do not use a cover sheet or title page. Use a binder only if you are submitting a play or a television or movie script. Use a paper clip to hold pages together, not staples. This allows editors to separate the pages easily for editing.

The upper corners of the first page of an article manuscript contain important information about you and your manuscript. This information should be single-spaced. In the upper *left* corner list your name, address, phone number and Social Security number (publishers must have this to file accurate payment records with the government). If you are using a pseudonym for your byline, your legal name still must appear in this space. In the upper *right* corner, indicate the approximate word count of the manuscript, the rights you are offering for sale and your copyright notice (© 1994 Patrick Jones). A handwritten copyright symbol is acceptable. [For more information about rights and copyright, see Minding the Details on page 63.] For a book manuscript include the same information with the exception of rights. Do not number the first page of your manuscript.

Center the title in capital letters one-third of the way down the page. Set your typewriter to double-space. Type "by" centered one double-space under your title, and type your name or pseudonym centered one double-space beneath that.

After the title and byline, drop down two double-spaces, paragraph indent, and begin the body of your manuscript. Always double-space your manuscript and use standard paragraph indentations of five spaces. Margins should be about 1½ inches on all sides of each full page of typewritten manuscript.

On every page after the first, type your last name, a dash and the page number in either the upper left or right corner. The title of your manuscript may, but need not, be typed on this line or beneath it. Page number two would read: Jones—2. If you are using a pseudonym, type your real name, followed by your pen name in parentheses, then the page number: Jones (Smith)—2. Then drop down two double-spaces and continue typing. Follow this format throughout your manuscript.

If you are submitting novel chapters, leave the top one-third of the first page of each chapter blank before typing the chapter title. Subsequent pages should include the author's last name, the page number, and a shortened form of the book's title: Jones—2—Skating. (In a variation on this, some authors place the title before the name on the left side and put the page number on the right-hand margin.)

When submitting poetry, the poems should be typed single-spaced (double-space between stanzas), one poem per page. For a long poem requiring more than one page, paper clip the pages together. You may want to write "continued" at the bottom of the page, so if the pages are separated, editors, typesetters and proofreaders won't assume your poem ends at the bottom of the first page.

Estimating word count

Many computers will provide you with a word count of your manuscript. Don't be surprised if your editor does another count after editing the manuscript. While your computer is counting characters, an editor or production editor is more concerned with the amount of space the text will occupy on a page. If you have several small headlines, or subheads, for instance, they will be counted the same by your computer as any other word of text. An editor may count them differently to be sure enough space has been estimated for larger type.

For short manuscripts, it's often quickest to count each word on a representative page and multiply by the number of pages. You can get a very rough count by multiplying the number of pages in your manuscript by 250 (the average number of words on a double-spaced typewritten page). Do not count words for a poetry manuscript or put the word count at the top of the manuscript.

To get a more precise count, add the number of characters and spaces in an average line and divide by 6 for the average words per line. Then count the number of lines of type on a representative page. Multiply the words per line by the lines per page to find out the average number of words per page.

INSIDER REPORT

Telling the story of a life

E. P. Jones had a story to tell. Her first book, *Where is Home?: Living Through Foster Care* (Four Walls Eight Windows, 1990) is the record of her life growing up in the foster care system of New York. It is a chronicle of her experiences within that bureaucracy and a testament to her own will and strength of character.

"I was raised in foster care starting at the age of six," says Jones. "My mother was an alcoholic and my father had abandoned me." She was working in New York as a bookkeeper and had not seriously considered telling her story until a chance meeting with a journalist convinced her that it was a story worth sharing. "My first reaction," says Jones, "was 'I'm a bookkeeper. I do accounting. I don't write!' But she encouraged me, so I just spat it out."

© 1990 Moyra Davey

E.P. Jones

Jones' previous status as a ward of the state meant there were state-controlled records in existence that would help in the reconstruction and telling of her story. Getting access to those files, however, proved to be the first major hurdle to overcome. "I wanted my material to be as true to life as possible, so I tried to get those records. I wound up having to sue the city of New York to obtain them. I sued under the Freedom of Information Act and eventually received the records." The judge who released the records stipulated they had to be quoted accurately. "Verbatim," says Jones. "We could not alter them." In the book, direct quotations from the state's files are juxtaposed with Jones' own recollections about the circumstances of her upbringing, providing both a reminder of the story's truthfulness and an interesting objective counterpoint to her intensely personal narrative.

The second major hurdle was the writing of the book itself. The nature of the material, and the author's closeness to it, made the writing process painful. "I was writing about things I had never revealed to anyone. It was like opening myself up to the entire world. It was like taking a part of your body or your person and removing it. It took me a good two years to get it all out."

Three years after the publication of *Where is Home?*, Jones works for the interests of foster care children and the foster care system. "At present I am an independent consultant and trainer for child welfare agencies. I do it locally and nationally. I conduct workshops for youngsters in care, for social workers and for child care staff." And she is not finished writing about foster care. "I would like very much to do yet another book on this topic," she says. "I just have to find the time."

Then count the number of manuscript pages (fractions should be counted as fractions, except in book manuscript chapter headings, which are counted as a full page). Multiply the number of pages by the number of words per page you already determined. This will give you the approximate number of words in the manuscript.

Photographs and slides

The availability of good quality photos can be a deciding factor when an editor is considering a manuscript. Many publications also offer additional pay for photos accepted with a manuscript. When submitting black-and-white prints, editors usually want to see 8×10 glossy photos, unless they indicate another preference in the listing. The universally accepted format for transparencies is 35mm; few buyers will look at color prints. Don't send any transparencies or prints with a query; wait until an editor indicates interest in seeing your photos.

On all your photos and slides, you should stamp or print your copyright notice and "Return to:" followed by your name, address and phone number. Rubber stamps are preferred for labeling photos since they are less likely to cause damage. You can order them from many stationery or office supply stores. If you use a pen to write this information on the back of your photos, be careful not to damage the print by pressing too hard or by allowing ink to bleed through the paper. A felt tip pen is best, but you should take care not to put photos or copy together before the ink dries or it will smear.

Captions can be typed on a sheet of paper and taped to the back of the prints. Some writers, when submitting several transparencies or photos, number the photos and type captions (numbered accordingly) on a separate 8½×11 sheet of paper.

Submit prints rather than negatives or consider having duplicates made of your slides or transparencies. Don't risk having your original negative or slide lost or damaged when you submit it.

Photocopies

Make copies of your manuscripts and correspondence before putting them in the mail. Don't learn the hard way, as many writers have, that manuscripts get lost in the mail and that publishers sometimes go out of business without returning submissions.

You might want to make several copies of your manuscript while it is still clean. Some writers keep their original manuscript as a file copy and submit good quality photocopies. Submitting copies can save you the expense and effort of retyping a manuscript if it becomes lost in the mail.

Some writers include a self-addressed postcard with a photocopied submission and suggest in the cover letter that if the editor is not interested in the manuscript, it may be tossed out and a reply returned on the postcard. This practice is recommended when dealing with international markets. If you find that your personal computer generates copies more cheaply than you can pay to have them returned, you might choose to send disposable manuscripts. Submitting a disposable manuscript costs the writer some photocopy or computer printer expense, but it can save on large postage bills.

Mailing submissions

No matter what size manuscript you're mailing, always include sufficient return postage and a self-addressed envelope large enough to contain your manuscript if it is returned.

A manuscript of fewer than six pages may be folded in thirds and mailed as if it were a letter using a #10 (business-size) envelope. The enclosed SASE can be a #10 folded in thirds (though these are sometimes torn when a letter opener catches in one of the folds), or a #9 envelope which will slip into the mailing envelope without being folded. Some editors also appreciate the convenience of having a manuscript folded into halves in a 6 × 9 envelope.

For manuscripts of six pages or longer, use 9 × 12 envelopes for both mailing and return. The return SASE may be folded in half.

A book manuscript should be mailed in a sturdy, well-wrapped box. Enclose a self-addressed mailing label and paper clip your return postage stamps or International Reply Coupons to the label.

Always mail photos and slides First Class. The rougher handling received by Fourth Class mail could damage them. If you are concerned about losing prints or slides, send them certified or registered mail. For any photo submission that is mailed separately from a manuscript, enclose a short cover letter of explanation, separate self-addressed label, adequate return postage and an envelope. Never submit photos or slides mounted in glass.

To mail up to 20 prints, you can buy photo mailers that are stamped "Photos—Do Not Bend" and contain two cardboard inserts to sandwich your prints. Or use a 9 × 12 manila envelope, write "Photos—Do Not Bend" and make your own cardboard inserts. Some photography supply shops also carry heavy cardboard envelopes that are reusable.

When mailing a number of prints, say 25-50 for a book with illustrations, pack them in a sturdy cardboard box. A box for typing paper or photo paper is an adequate mailer. If, after packing both manuscript and photos, there's empty space in the box, slip in enough cardboard inserts to fill the box. Wrap the box securely.

To mail transparencies, first slip them into protective vinyl sleeves, then mail as you would prints. If you're mailing a number of sheets, use a cardboard box as for photos.

Types of mail service

● First Class is the most expensive way to mail a manuscript, but many writers prefer it. First Class mail generally receives better handling and is delivered more quickly. Mail sent First Class is also forwarded for one year if the addressee has moved, and is returned automatically if it is undeliverable.

• Fourth Class rates are available for packages, but be sure to pack your materials carefully because they will be handled roughly. To make sure your package will be returned to you if it is undeliverable, print "Return Postage Guaranteed" under your address.

• Certified Mail must be signed for when it reaches its destination. If requested, a signed receipt is returned to the sender. There is a $1 charge for this service, in addition to the required postage, and a $1 charge for a return receipt.

• Registered Mail is a high-security method of mailing. The package is signed in and out of every office it passes through, and a receipt is returned to the sender when the package reaches its destination. This service begins at $4.40 in addition to the postage required for the item. If you obtain insurance for the package, the cost begins at $4.50.

• United Parcel Service may be slightly cheaper than First Class postage if you drop the package off at UPS yourself. UPS cannot legally carry First Class mail, so your cover letter needs to be mailed separately. Check with UPS in your area for current rates. The cost depends on the weight of your package and the distance to its destination.

• If you're in a hurry to get your material to your editor, you have a lot of choices these days. In addition to fax and modem technologies mentioned earlier, overnight and two-day mail services are provided by both the U.S. Postal Service and several private firms. More information on next day service is available from the U.S. Post Office in your area, or check your Yellow Pages under "Delivery Services."

Other correspondence details

Use money orders if you are ordering sample copies or supplies and do not have checking services. You'll have a receipt, and money orders are traceable. Money orders for up to $35 can be purchased from the U.S. Postal Service for a 75¢ service charge; the cost is $1 for a maximum $700 order. Banks, savings and loans, and some commercial businesses also carry money orders; their fees vary. *Never* send cash through the mail for sample copies.

Insurance is available for items handled by the U.S. Postal Service but is payable only on typing fees or the tangible value of the item in the package—such as typing paper—so your best insurance when mailing manuscripts is to keep a copy of what you send. Insurance is 75¢ for $50 or less and goes up to a $5 maximum charge.

When corresponding with publications and publishers in other countries, International Reply Coupons (IRCs) must be used for return postage. Surface rates in other countries differ from those in the U.S., and U.S. postage stamps are of use only within the U.S. Currently, one IRC costs 95¢ and is sufficient for one ounce traveling at surface rate; two must be used for airmail return. Canadian writers pay $1.50 for an IRC.

Because some post offices don't carry IRCs (or because of the added expense), many writers dealing with international mail send photocopies and tell the publisher to dispose of them if the manuscript is not appropriate. When you use this method, it's best to set a deadline for withdrawing your manuscript from consideration, so you can market it elsewhere.

International money orders are also available from the post office for a $3 charge. See U.S. and Canadian Postage by the Page on the inside covers for specific mailing costs. All charges were current at press time but are subject to change during the year.

Recording submissions

Your job is not over once you've submitted your manuscript. Don't just sit around and wait for the phone to ring. Manage your writing business by keeping copies of all manuscripts and correspondence, and by recording the dates of submissions.

One way to keep track of your manuscripts is to use a record of submissions that includes the date sent, title, market, editor and enclosures (such as photos). You should also note the date of the editor's response, any rewrites that were done, and, if the manuscript was accepted, the publication date and payment information. You might want to keep a similar record just for queries.

Also remember to keep a separate file for each manuscript or idea along with its list of potential markets. You may want to keep track of expected reporting times on a calendar, too. Then you'll know if a market has been slow to respond and you can follow up on your query or submission. It will also also provide you with a detailed look at your sales over time.

Targeting Your Magazine Submissions

by John Wood

You have in your hands *Writer's Market* — the writer's "bible," the freelancer's Rand-McNally, the literary telescope in your hunt for the rarest of all lettered species, *Editorus quos payus maximus*. For those of you just starting out, the jungle of freelance writing probably never looked so inviting — or intimidating.

I know what some of you are thinking: "So many magazines, so little time. There's enough to go around for everybody." You view the marketplace the way a lion gazes at a herd of wildebeests. Well, as you'll soon learn, don't be so quick to lick your chops.

I also know what some others are thinking: "So many magazines, where do I start? I'm not going to wade through all this." How can you cull from a herd in which every wildebeest looks the same? Well, as you'll also learn, that task isn't as difficult as you may think.

Either way you look at it, though, you'll have to send your idea to one of these magazines sooner or later. When you do, it will be read by an editor who will decide whether or not to assign it. The problem is, most query letters are inappropriate, incomplete, unprofessional, bland, and read like they came from an assembly-line. It's as if they were all written by the same graduate from the "How to Write for Magazines" correspondence class from hell. If your query fits into this category, you will get a rejection letter, which unfortunately won't explain why your idea was rejected or suggest what you could have done differently or better.

That's where I come in. I'm an editor with 10 years experience reading freelancers' query letters. I don't want to read any more of them. Any more bad ones, that is. So I've developed a four-step plan on how to upgrade the quality and presentation of your queries *before* you send them out; in short, how to write an irresistible query letter. In this article you'll learn how to:
- Develop an idea that's right for you.
- Find the right magazines for your idea.
- Distribute your mailings for maximum exposure and effect.
- Sell yourself and your idea in ways guaranteed to grab an editor's attention.

John Wood *is a senior editor at* Modern Maturity, *the largest circulation magazine in the United States.*

Master these four basics and you'll not only remove yourself from a magazine's slush pile but become a fixture in its accounting department. (Hint: That's where they make out the checks.)

So let's get started!

What should I write about?

Professional writers choose ideas that interest them. Beginning writers ask, "Whatcha got?" There's a big difference. Poring over *Writer's Market* to see what magazines grab you is like perusing the personals for a spouse. Decide what you want to write about *before* you worry about which magazine to approach.

How do you do that? Start by examining what subjects fascinate you. Sports? People? Health? Humor? What is your writing style? Sarcastic? Upbeat? Descriptive? Cynical? What kind of articles do you prefer? Short or long? How-to's or essays? Q&As or profiles? And what can you realistically do? Are you really up to *New Yorker* quality at this point in your career? Can you really have the article you're contemplating ready in three weeks? Do you really know what it takes to interview Clint Eastwood?

Once you've analyzed your writing style and abilities, review your non-writing talents. What do you know how to do? Are you a backpacker? Cook? Stand-up comedian? Then think ahead. What will be timely a year from now that you could approach an editor about now? Historical anniversary? Seasonal event? Movie opening? Book publication?

Tip 1: Narrow the focus of your story idea as much as you can. A query about osteoporosis, for example, is too broad, too unwieldy, doesn't say anything. Take one aspect of the subject and zoom in on just that: New studies show calcium may prevent osteoporosis. Then take *that* angle and break it down even farther: Calcium won't help older people prevent osteoporosis, by then the damage is already done. And so on.

Tip 2: Never propose personal experiences (if it's negative, you're liable to be too biased; if it's positive, no editor will care unless you're a celebrity— trust me).

Okay, you can put your clothes back on now, your self-examination is complete. If you were honest with yourself, you should have produced one ideal topic to pursue. Your next step: Find the right magazines for it.

Who should I pitch it to?

Start with the book you're holding now. That's not a plug, it's a fact. But notice I said *start*. Always begin your research with *Writer's Market*, but never end with it.

To find which magazines are right for your idea, search *Writer's Market* listings for six to ten magazines that publish articles similar to the topic you've chosen to write about. Get several recent issues of each magazine from your local library or bookstore. Study the issues in depth—from the departments to the features, the visual elements to the ads. Does it slant its pieces a certain way? Is the magazine elegant, avant-garde, cerebral, lightweight? What style and length does it prefer (note the dissimilarities among *Spy*, *Ms.*, *People* and *Reader's Digest*, for example).

What you're looking for is a match. Which magazines publish topics you like to write about; prefer your type and style of writing; want writers with your kind of nonwriting expertise; and need articles about your favorite hobbies and activities? The better you match up, the better your odds will be for a sale.

Unfortunately, many new writers—believing in the theory that if you toss enough pencils at a ceiling, one will stick—send their travel queries, for example, to every travel magazine in the country hoping one will hit. But that's like grocery shopping blindfolded for a finicky eater. Sure the person needs food, but that doesn't mean he'll eat just anything. Editors are the same way; they buy what they're accustomed to buying. Only by thoroughly researching a magazine beforehand will you know if your material belongs there. You may find your idea is right for only one magazine, or a dozen. However many matches you find, that's how many you should target—and no more.

Why do all this extra work, you ask? Why hole up in a library studying issues of *Carpentry Corner* while your competitors are keeping the postal service afloat with their blizzard of manuscript submissions? Because your competitors' queries are already on their way back—before the editors have even seen them. They were doomed from the start, I guarantee you. When your letters arrive, on the other hand, they will be read, pondered and passed around because they'll be tailor-made for that magazine. The difference may not seem that great to you, but to an editor it is everything. You will have made the final cut.

Tip 3: Don't waste your time writing for sample copies—unless the magazine is obscure, local, or your area doesn't have it. Ditto for writer's guidelines. They're often out of date, woefully incomplete, no substitute for your own research, and not much different than what's in *Writer's Market* anyway.

Tip 4: Never send your query to a name on a masthead—especially the top one—unless you've confirmed first that the person is the correct one for your topic. *This is very important!* Otherwise your material will end up in the slush pile. Instead, call the magazine and ask for "Editorial." Say you want to send something you've written and need the name of the editor who handles that subject area ("To Your Health" department, investment advice, movie reviews). Do not accept an answer like, "Oh, just send it in; I'm sure it will be read." This person isn't an editor and doesn't understand the system. It will be bounced if you "just send it in." Demand to speak to someone who knows which editor handles travel or gardening or whatever.

Whew—you're halfway home! You've discovered the perfect topic, the best magazines for it, and the right editor to send it to. Before you drop it in the mail, though, read the next section.

How should I circulate it?

There are two ways you can send your proposal—the honorable way or the smart way. The honorable way is to send one query to one magazine and wait until the idea is accepted or rejected (several months later, assuming you hear back at all) before you send it to a second magazine. This is done out of fear of alienating editors who despise "simultaneous submissions."

I favor the smart way: Shotgun the sucker to everybody at the same time and don't worry about the fallout—you're the one trying to sell your article, not the editor. That doesn't mean sending the same letter to 20 different editors, though. The same *idea*, yes, but never the same letter.

How do you do that? Customize your pitch to each magazine so each publication gets its own personal angle on the topic. That computer article you want to write for *Money* will be different than the one for *Parade*, even though your core research for both may be the same. This method takes more effort, but it will turn each article idea into dozens and dozens of sales opportunities.

Tip 5: Never tip off that you're a beginning writer. If you present yourself professionally, note your qualifications for writing the piece, and slant your idea to the magazine's needs, who would know you're a new writer? Your query will look exactly like that of a seasoned pro, which is all you want it to do. *The key is to avoid the slush pile.* Editors want to move the junk off their desks quickly and get to the good stuff. Keep them reading and you stay alive. If you haven't sold anything yet or you've only sold to small or local publications, don't mention it—unless you're querying same.

Tips 6: Never offer an article on spec. Many new writers believe this will appeal to an editor's pocketbook by offering her a free look at their finished product.

Number one, it labels your piece as damaged goods. An editor will assume you're trying to unload an article killed or rejected by another magazine.

Number two, it labels you as desperate. "I'm so unworthy, I'll do all the work upfront, show it to you for no obligation, and even let you toss it in the circular file and keep my SASE stamps if you don't like it. Deal?"

And number three, it labels you as naive. Do you honestly believe you can write an article first and then hope you conceived the precise topic, angle, sources, structure, style, and length the editor would have wanted—without any input beforehand?

Your query letter is now ready to send out, right? Wrong. Before you press "type" on that word processor, you need to complete one final step. You've done everything up to now to sell yourself and your idea to an editor. Now you've got to get his attention. So pick up your two-by-four and read on.

How should I sell it?

Do editors read query letters completely? (Most don't.) Do they get excited reading query letters? (Most don't.) Do they place them in their "Promising Ideas" file or, better yet, snatch up the phone, call the writers, and ask how they want their name spelled on the check? (Most . . . you guessed it.)

Your goal, therefore, is to make your query letter sing; make a positive impression that lasts, show 'em something they've never seen before. In short, **STAND OUT**. Even if you get shot down, *go down in flames*. What have you got to lose? This is your audition before the director. The spotlight's on and the audience has hushed. This is your 15 minutes (more like 15 seconds) of fame Andy Warhol said everybody gets once in their life.

How do you stand out? Do something different. *Playboy* interviewer Larry Grobel recalls what happened when he referred a beginning writer to an editor he knew at an airline magazine. "She wrote him a kind of crazy note and then put it on tangerine paper. It intrigued him enough to call me up and say, 'Can she really write?' She now writes regularly for *Esquire* and others."

Grobel remembers how the late novelist Bernard Wolfe used to send out manuscripts. "He wrote the editor's name and address in HUGE letters—they literally covered the entire envelope. Then he underlined everything. I asked him if he always did that, and he said, 'It gets their attention.' And he was a professional writer."

Be advised, though, that oddball stationery and anything smacking of amateur theatrics can just as easily backfire. Some editors are like the pro football coach who told a player who had just done a victory dance after scoring a touchdown: "Son, next time you get in the end zone, act like you've been there before."

What are some other ways to stand out?

Devise a catchy headline and descriptive blurb for your idea.

Target a particular department in the magazine. I always sit up when a query recommends a specific section; it shows the writer actually sat down, read my magazine, and gave the idea some thought. Departments are also the easiest place to break in and build a reputation with an editorial staff.

Pitch your idea like a Hollywood screenwriter. You think you have it rough. These poor souls, if they're lucky enough to even get an audience with a producer, have only a few moments to pitch their plot. What they've found works best is to devise a brief, sweeping image to "hook" the listener into wanting more: Godfather meets the Terminator, Sleeping Beauty set in the Wild West, Thelma and Louise as men.

Consider subject matter that magazines rarely get (but which editors are dying for):

Humor.

Quizzes.

Celebrity Q&As/profiles.

Advice from well-known experts.

Checklists ("Top 10 Ways to Spot a Scam").

Fiction. This is far and away the most difficult genre to write and sell. Consequently, it's also treasured most by editors. (One telling statistic: Last year only 23 fiction pieces were submitted for National Magazine Award consideration *from a total of 328 magazines and 1,367 entries!*)

Give editors more than one reason to say yes. A single idea presented one way to each magazine is like having only one dart and getting only one chance to hit a bull's eye. Earlier I suggested customizing your ideas to each magazine. Now go one step further: Devise more than one place for each idea and more than one way to do it. Rather than just propose a general financial feature you think would be right for *Smart Money*, for example, also mention that your notion could work, with some alterations, as a filler for its "Collecting" department, as a profile for its "Me & My Money" column, or as a financial quiz for its "Back Page" feature. Never assume editors will be alert enough to think of such obvious spinoffs.

And finally, nudge hesitant editors by creating other elements to accompany your idea. Proposing an article about African-American political pundits for *Essence* may be fine, but think how much more attractive your package would be if you also offered a sidebar on "The African-American Spokesperson Hall of Fame," a quiz on "10 Questions You're Sure to Be Asked on *Nightline*," and a graph showing the difference between the number of whites and people of color used as fixtures on CNN, *MacNeil/Lehrer NewsHour* and *This Week with David Brinkley*.

Tip 7: Empty your guns. If you've done similar articles, say so. If you have a special "in" with the subject you're proposing, elaborate. If you know of anything — no matter how trivial or farfetched — that might help convince an editor you deserve this assignment, mention it. This is no time to be modest.

Tip 8: Show you care. Sharp editors have a keen eye. They can read between the lines of a query and sense whether the writer is just farming out the idea for bucks — or is truly passionate about it. So if you're truly excited and inspired to write your article — if you honestly believe you are the most qualified, the most well-prepared, the most experienced, the *only* person who can nail the essence of your idea and bring it home (and you should be or you shouldn't be proposing it) — then let there be no doubt on the page. Give us no alternative but to say, "Yes!"

Now. It's time. You're ready to send out your query. This may have seemed like a lot of work — maybe much more than you expected — but that's what professional writing is all about. Writing for magazines is serious business; it is not a hobby. Every query an editor receives is a potential costly investment and every writer a potential business partner.

As your "consultant" in this business endeavor, I will make the following prediction: If you faithfully adopt the steps I've outlined into your future writing practice, you will not only elevate yourself above 95 percent of all freelance writers out there, you will evolve into the second rarest of lettered species, *Writerus quos getus humungus buckus*.

When that glorious day comes, it will be our enviable but difficult task to hunt *you* down. I only pray I'll be able to afford you.

Selling Your Book Proposal

This is it. You've finally hit on the book idea of a lifetime. And, in order to give it its best chance in the publishing marketplace, you have crafted your proposal with careful attention to every detail. In your proposal package, you've told your prospective editor all she could possibly want to know in order to make the decision to publish. You've given her an overview of the subject of the book and explained how you intend to develop your material. You've included a chapter outline that clearly lays out the structure of the book and the contents of each chapter. Your author information sheet has told the editor just enough about you to let her know that you're knowledgable and qualified to write the book. And your sample chapter will serve as more than adequate evidence of your writing and research capabilities. Once the editor has read and assimilated the overwhelming display of evidence arrayed before her, why would she possibly say no? Only one reason, really: You forgot to mention whether anyone at all might be interested in actually *buying* copies of your book.

The last bit of evidence that's going to tip the scales in your favor—given that the rest of your proposal is in great shape—is to convince the editor that there is an audience waiting to buy your book.

Commercial Darwinism

Today, perhaps more than ever, editors and publishers are asking tough marketing-related questions about every query and proposal they consider. The decision to publish a book involves a substantial financial commitment from publishers. They need to feel as though they stand a reasonable chance of not only recouping their investment but making a profit as well. When considering whether to publish a book, publishers ask themselves variations of these questions: Is there a sizable book-buying audience for this book? Will that audience be accessible through our promotional and publicity efforts? Is this the kind of book on this subject that the targeted audience is likely to buy (i.e., is it better than others on the same subject)? In the publishing world (as is true of businesses in general), the most marketable ideas—if not necessarily the most skillfully executed—do seem to rise to the top. Call it commercial Darwinism. The books that survive are those for which a specific audience can be identified and targeted.

Editors and marketing

While editors still delight in authors, books, reading and writing (all the reasons they got into publishing in the first place), the fact is, the modern editor's life is not what many writers imagine it to be. The tasks most people think of when they think of editing—reading manuscripts, providing guidance for authors at work, generally fiddling around with the written word—take up a relatively small portion of the editor's work week. Any one acquiring editor may be responsible for handling a couple dozen books (or more) in various stages at any one time. The editor spends his day not lovingly poring over manuscripts, but mainly in attending meetings. There are proposal board meetings, title meetings, cover and interior design meetings, jacket and catalog copy meetings and other meetings related to publicity and promotional efforts. So the truly "editorial" part of editing is either delegated to associates and assistants or is squeezed in between meetings or after hours, at home.

You will note that the largest portion of an editor's work day is taken up with various marketing concerns of one kind or another. The motive force behind nearly every decision an editor makes about his books is really a question of marketing: Who are the people who will want this book and what are the most efficient and effective ways to convince them to buy it?

As a writer, you are in the position of having to convince an editor that publishing your book will be a good financial decision for her company. That is your challenge. The image you want to conjure—the notion you want to dangle before the editor's mind's eye—is that of a book that's timely, well-written and for which a substantial, *reachable* audience exists. Whether that audience is widely or narrowly defined (*Finding Meaning in Your Job* vs. *Canoeing the Colorado River*, for example), the editor must feel—it's your job to *make* her feel—that enough people will buy this book to make it profitable for her company. For a commercial publisher, all other concerns about your proposal are secondary to its prospects in the marketplace.

Convincing an editor

As we've seen, an editor will be expecting your assessment of the market for your book as a part of your proposal package. This will be based on your own research drawn from any number of sources, but it will be most forceful if it is specific and backed by objective information.

Let's assume, as an example, that you would like to write a how-to book about cutting hair. You have been giving the members of your family their haircuts for ten years, and you feel that you could write a clear, step-by-step guide that would lead the novice successfully through the process. In the marketing section of your proposal for *The Family Barber*, you will want to make points similar to the following:

Marketing considerations are "essential ingredients"

James Cohee, senior editor at Sierra Club Books, says market information and assessment of the competition for your book are "essential ingredients in preparing a proposal."

Cohee says that Sierra Club Books operates somewhat like a university press — and, as is the case with most university presses in today's economic environment, success in the trade (as opposed to among a strictly academic audience) is important. "Our work is subsidized by the Sierra Club, and yet we're a commercial publisher. Our books are sold by Random House, and they have to live or die in the trade. I think that's true of many of the larger university presses. They're subsidized by a state budget or a private budget, and a part of their list is sold through the trade." And success in the trade comes from publishing books with a specific audience in mind — and reaching that audience.

Every project that's approved for publication by Sierra Club Books has to first make it through a two-level proposal process. In both proposal meetings, audience and competition are key factors under consideration. "We do marketing research," says Cohee. "When an editor has a proposal, it goes first to a weekly editorial meeting chaired by the publisher; the marketing director is also there. We talk about the prospects for this book and certainly questions about who's going to buy it and what the size of the market is come up there. But we also have a second, oversight committee: a committee that meets twice a year and is made up of publishing professionals and some Sierra Club activists who sit on the committee and advise the Sierra Club. This committee reviews every proposal we have. They have to review it before we can contract for it. And one of the factors that committee weighs is marketing considerations."

Authors should anticipate the scrutiny with which publishers will pore over their proposal and provide as much audience-related information as possible up front. "Every proposal should discuss the market and it should list and comment on the major competition," says Cohee. "That's something we want to know, and it's something we will find out. We not only go to the bookstores to check it out, but we frequently send the proposal to our sales reps and ask them to comment on the market."

"Do it yourself" **has become the credo of the 90s.** To bolster this assertion, point to trends in recent magazine articles (and even entire magazines) that espouse the stay-at-home and handle-it-yourself ethics. Name specific magazines and specific articles. An editor who can see that topics such as home canning, gardening and clothes-making are more popular now than they used to be will probably agree with you that there may be a substantial audience for a book on cutting hair at home. Trends in book publishing move a little

slower, but can be used to make your point too. *Publishers Weekly*'s annual report on book sales (usually published in March) is a good source of broad-brush information about general trends in book publishing. You should also be watching *PW*'s weekly bestseller lists to see what's currently hot.

A large audience exists that is interested in accomplishing necessary tasks on a budget. To give some indication of the size of the audience for *The Family Barber*, point to sales figures for books that have a similar audience in mind. In the past year, several books have been published offering advice for living and raising a family on a limited budget. Some of the most successful ones will have their sales histories emblazoned on their covers ("Over 500,000 sold!"). Use those figures to make the case for your own book. Sales figures for books that don't have the numbers on their covers may be a little harder to gather. *Publishers Weekly*'s annual report will give specific sales ranges for books that have done well in the past year, but that information may be too old to do you much good. Most publishers will be reluctant to share sales figures for specific books, but it may be worth your while to ask (it certainly can't hurt). When you call, ask to speak to someone in marketing.

Special outlets are available for a book of this type. Not all sales of books are through bookstores. For a large percentage of their profits, publishers rely on what are known as "special sales." These include such outlets as book clubs, direct marketing campaigns, non-book retail stores, corporate purchases, catalog sales and more. Any information you can dig up about special sales opportunities for your book will grab an editor's attention. With our example, *The Family Barber*, there may be multiple special sales opportunities. *Literary Market Place* (available in libraries) lists book clubs, some of which may be devoted to family-related or child-rearing topics. These would be natural outlets for this book. It may also do well if marketed through a special-interest mail order catalog. To locate a mail-order catalog that might be right for your topic, check your local library's copy of *Directory of Mail Order Catalogs* (Grey House Publishing) or *The National Directory of Catalogs* (Oxbridge Communications). You can also locate special-interest groups that may be interested in bulk purchases of your book or that may be able to provide you with other useful information regarding your prospective market by consulting *The Encyclopedia of Associations* (Gale). Some authors are, themselves, "special outlets." If you are actively engaged in speaking or teaching on the subject of your book at seminars, conferences or the like, you are in a position to sell books. That will appeal to any potential publisher.

What about the competition?

The marketability of a book depends, in great part, on the competition it faces in bookstores. Part of convincing an editor that your book will sell is

INSIDER REPORT

Authors should offer specific marketing strategies

Ron D. Powers is the editorial director of the Professional Book Group for TAB/McGraw-Hill, Inc. Publishing a wide variety of books for professionals working in various trades and businesses, the Professional Book Group is interested in seeing proposals that accurately target the audiences they serve. Here Powers talks about the proposal process and the need for prospective authors to accurately assess the market for their books.

Ron D. Powers

"When queried for the first time by a new author," says Powers, "and by new I mean either unpublished or having never published with us, we like to see an annotated outline of the proposal and a succinct cover letter stating the concept of the book and its proposed audience. We also need to see the author's resume, curriculum vitae, or biography, and list of significant achievements. A list of previous publications is also very helpful."

Since good ideas can come from anywhere, Powers encourages the submission of unsolicited book proposals. "We will review any proposal we receive," he says, adding this caveat, "but in all honesty, the majority never make it past the acquiring editor's evaluation for any number of reasons. Occasionally an excellent book comes in over the transom. We will return proposal materials to an author upon request in the cover letter and with the enclosure of a SASE by the sender."

As with any other publisher, TAB/McGraw-Hill pays particular attention to the marketability of the unsolicited book ideas they receive. All proposals go through an approval process that includes review by several editors and an editorial review board, with input from marketing groups. Powers says, "The majority of our publications are geared toward professionals in specific industries, so we are fairly confident when approaching a project that we can reach the potential reader using existing marketing channels. Proposals are reviewed by all of our marketing channels, including the trade group, direct marketing, book club marketing, international marketing, and our special sales group to ascertain the salability of the book in each of those channels. To some degree, we measure the potential of a new proposal based on how well we have sold similar titles to that audience in the past."

But, Powers stresses, they also expect writers to inject whatever marketing savvy they possess into the project. And the more specifics the writer can offer, the better. He says, "We depend on the author to help us define the potential audiences for his proposed book. More is always better, and specific names, lists, and organizations to contact are better yet. Vague allusions to an untargeted group of individuals or an all-encompassing profession should be avoided."

showing him how it will stand apart from other, similar books both in its content and in your treatment of it.

If you can show an editor that you've taken a close and careful look at your competition, you will make a greater impression than the writer who simply asserts: "Other books on my subject are all lousy." Your mission, then, is to find out what similar books are available and compare them critically (and as objectively as possible) to your own proposed book.

If, after sussing out the competition, you discover that your angle or treatment is *not* clearly different and better, then your proposal should probably be re-worked or perhaps scrapped in favor of a topic that will stand a better chance in bookstores.

There are several ways to find out about competing books, but two of the easiest are to consult *Books In Print* and to haunt your local bookstores.

Books In Print

Books In Print, a multi-volume reference set published annually by R.R. Bowker, lists nearly every book currently in print. It indexes books by author, by title and by subject. The *Subject Guide* volumes will be of most use to you as you compile your list of competing titles. Bowker's arrangement of heads and subheads within the subject guide allows you to search for titles in very specific subject areas. Your local library should have current copies of all *Books In Print* volumes available for reference use.

Bowker also offers a subscription service to the *Books In Print* database on CD-ROM. This allows for quick, computerized searching of titles, authors and subject matter. With its ability to search by keyword (for example, type in "astral projection" and you get a list of every book in the database whose description contains that phrase—type in "astral projection" and "baseball" and you'll see those books whose descriptions contain both of those terms) *Books In Print* on CD-ROM is an efficient and sophisticated search tool. If your local library doesn't subscribe to the *Books In Print* on CD-ROM database, ask if they know of any other libraries nearby that might have it. You may be able to find a local university library that subscribes.

Off to the bookstore

What do you do with the information you dig up from *Books In Print*? The listings in *BIP* will give you basic information, such as the publisher's name, the book's page count and price and the author's name. It's a starting point, but you're going to need more complete information (ideally you want to see a copy of the book, but that's not always possible) before you judge how each book listed compares to yours. If the publisher's name is one you recognize as being a major publisher, the book will likely be available for your perusal at a local bookstore. If it's not on the shelf, the store will usually order a copy for you with no obligation to buy. If the book you're interested in seeing has been published by a smaller house that is not serviced by the large book distributors, you can always write to the publisher and ask for a copy of their catalog. Publishers' addresses can be found in the *Publishers* volume of *Books In Print* or in *Literary Market Place*.

While you're at the bookstore, check out every section under which you might expect to find a book such as yours. Pull out competing titles and give them a good going-over. Take a small notebook with you to the bookstore to jot down your thoughts about specific competing titles.

Some questions you will want to ask yourself as you peruse competing books are:

- Does this book cover the topic thoroughly? Are there areas this author has missed?
- If this is a how-to book, does the reader really know "how-to" after reading it?
- Could the information be presented in a more reader-friendly way?
- Is this author as knowledgable in this field as I am?

When presenting your findings about competing books in your proposal, resist the urge to denigrate them across the board. Coming across as though your book is the only viable one and all others are garbage will not do your case any good. Be objective. Point out the good along with the bad. And remember that just because there is competition in the marketplace for your book does not mean there's not room for one more book on the subject. In fact, some activity in a given subject area might be an indication of the subject's popularity and reason enough to publish another book on the topic. If that's the case, then your job is to establish a slightly new angle on the topic — an angle that offers more than the competition or is developed differently.

The crucial difference

Researching your book's market potential may not sound like the most exciting part of being a writer (although some *do* enjoy the process), but in today's market, editors and publishers are looking at this kind of information as an essential component of every proposal they consider.

Showing an editor that you have carefully considered your market and are well aware of the size of your audience and the best ways to reach them may mean the difference between having your proposal tossed aside and being offered a book contract.

Authors must be promoters, too

Harvey Rachlin has been writing nonfiction books for over 15 years. His subject matter is broad and eclectic. His varied interests have taken him from songwriting (*The Songwriter's Handbook*—Funk & Wagnalls, 1977) to police work (*The Making of a Cop*—Pocket Books, 1991). In between, he has written books about money, the television and movie industries, the Kennedy family and more. While Rachlin writes on subjects that he personally finds interesting, he is well aware that it takes more than just interest in the topic—and more than sheer writing talent—to sell a book publisher on a proposal.

Harvey Rachlin

"You want to convince a publisher that: A) you have a great idea, B) you can execute it, and C) there is a large potential audience for that book," says Rachlin. "When you're writing your proposal, you've got to do your homework. It's not just a matter of proving you can write. You also have to put on a business hat and demonstrate that from the publisher's point of view it would make sense for them to publish your book."

According to Rachlin, the most convincing evidence of all is numbers. "Publishers love numbers," he says. "If you can, you need to provide some idea of the potential number of people who might be interested in buying your book." The numbers can come from a variety of sources. For his book *The TV and Movie Business*, Rachlin did plenty of research upfront in order to show the book's potential. "I contacted the television and movie business trade and professional associations, guilds and unions—SAG, AFTRA, Actor's Equity, Director's Guild of America and many others. I asked how many members they had and if they had any idea of the total number of people (nonmembers) who had an interest in or were practicing that profession. In the library, I found directories that listed institutions, colleges and schools and private associations—any entity that might be a potential consumer of the book. A lot of schools have courses in media and this book was a prime candidate for use as a text in those schools." After amassing his estimate of the potential audience size and the information on special markets he had contacted, Rachlin plugged this information into his proposal. The proposal was accepted, and the book was published by Crown/Harmony in 1991.

Rachlin is also a proponent of authors doing whatever they can to help in the effort to market their books. "As the author, you need to hustle a little and be creative. Offer to speak or run workshops on your subject at local libraries and schools. Promote yourself in local media by sending out press releases. When you become a writer, you're not *just* a writer, you're a promoter too.'"

The Business of Writing

Current Trends in Publishing

by Roseann Biederman

Book publishing

Like many industries in the 1980s, book publishing succumbed to excess. Astronomical print runs for books with limited audiences, and exorbitant advances paid to big-name authors, reflected the over-confidence that prevailed in the industry. Hard-hit by the recession, publishers have been forced to take a more conservative approach in the 1990s. Consequently, we are witnessing a decrease in the number of titles published and their print runs, as in the case of Price Stern Sloan. According to Associate Editor Cindy Chang, "We've cut back on the number of titles we're publishing—such as publishing one title to see how it sells before committing to a series, or doing fewer titles in a series, such as two instead of four. We're also having much smaller print runs."

The outlook for books

Despite the bad news, book sales have been increasing steadily over the past five years. *Publishers Weekly* recently forecasted an average annual increase of 3.5% in book shipments over the next five years. This growth is attributed to the end of the recession, an increase in disposable income, and expanding school and library budgets.

While this figure translates into a healthy market for book sales in the 1990s, it may be slightly deceptive. A recent article in the *Wall Street Journal* speculates that the apparently flourishing book sales may be more the result of rising prices than an increase in the actual number of books sold. Publishers are still concerned with the bottom line and are not likely to take risks on books they suspect will be anything but top sellers.

INSIDER REPORT

Alec Wilkinson on literary nonfiction

Alec Wilkinson

Alec Wilkinson writes a kind of nonfiction that is as gripping, rich and skillful as the best fiction, yet which resonates all the deeper for its truthfulness. His latest, *A Violent Act* (Knopf, 1993), is a dissection of a one-man criminal rampage and its effects on the innocents whose lives were seared by a fateful brush with the killer, Mike Jackson.

"Most of the fiction writers I know get absorbed by the idea of what might have happened; I feel more absorbed and gripped by the idea of what *did* happen," Wilkinson says. "To me, the world represents a mystery that, just by my nature, I am constantly trying to penetrate. That seems to me a cast of mind that lends itself to observing the world in the way that, say, a figurative painter does—and in the way that a writer of fiction does *not*." Wilkinson says that investigating and reporting on reality is his way of coming to terms with the world around him.

Wilkinson's writing career began in New York, where he moved after getting "slightly fixed on" the idea of writing for the *New Yorker*. "I just thought I would try to start where I really wanted to be, and if I was disappointed, I would figure out something else from there. I did it just the way anybody does it. I wrote a letter to the *New Yorker* and said I wanted to work there." He pursued his goal by turning in spec pieces for the magazine's "Talk of the Town" section—one a week over the course of one winter. Finally, the editors accepted a piece, and Wilkinson eventually went on to a staff position at the famed weekly.

The nonfiction Wilkinson admires—he speaks most reverently of *New Yorker* legend Joseph Mitchell—is characterized by clear reporting, telling dialogue and a skew on reality that results when the writer filters his subject through his own worldview. Wilkinson's own writing is typified by close observation of the people he writes about and a style of character development that relies more on what the characters say than on anything Wilkinson might say about them. The people in his books sometimes talk for pages at a time. "A very effective way to make someone come alive on the page is to let them talk," he says. "It's like a soliloquy on stage; it's just absorbing. If they can say it better than I can write it, I'll let 'em talk."

He feels strongly about the value of the kind of writing he does, writing that has been called "literary nonfiction." "I don't understand why painters are thought of as either figurative painters or abstract painters and writers are thought of as either fiction or *non*fiction writers. If you can write as well as Joseph Mitchell, you're not *non* anything. You are doing something that very few people are doing—or are able to do."

—*Mark Garvey*

Certainly one way to stay ahead of the competition is to be apprised of what kinds of books are popular now. As the trends we will be looking at relate primarily to nonfiction, see *Novel & Short Story Writer's Market* (Writer's Digest Books) for information on current trends in fiction.

Nonfiction front-runners

Presently, the strongest nonfiction categories include biography, sports (especially golf, with *Harvey Penick's Little Red Book*, published by Simon & Schuster, being the top-selling sports book of all time), health and fitness, ecology and the environment, business and the economy.

Other popular nonfiction subjects are ethnic/multicultural issues, gardening, cooking and parenting. According to Craig Walker, editor-in-chief at Grosset & Dunlap, "Top nonfiction sellers fall into two subject areas generally: contemporary biography and natural history/endangered species." Issues that are important to the population's major demographic group, namely the baby boomer generation, are often reflected in current nonfiction titles. Certainly, with a renewed interest in espousing 'simpler values' and an increased focus on home and family (consider the success of Martha Stewart's lifestyle, how-to and cooking books, published by Clarkson Potter), books in these areas should continue to be popular.

The wave of children's publishing

Another area that continues to be strong is children's publishing. Chang reports that, while Price Stern Sloan's primary line of lifestyle books continues to be strong, juvenile titles are the top-sellers. "Our children's nonfiction titles, such as our Wee Sing line of children's musical videos, and books and audiocassettes, continue to be our best-selling line as parents and teachers alike look to supplement traditional learning with fun," she says.

Paula Wiseman, editor-in-chief at Philomel Books, a division of Putnam, offers this perspective on the success of the children's book market: "The opening up of the universe of children's books — knowledgable independent bookstores, literature-based curriculum, increased media exposure to children's books — has made more of a diverse audience," she says. "This audience has allowed publishers more freedom in what they publish simply because there are more readers with more interests." Without question, writing juvenile nonfiction that conveys information to youngsters in fresh new ways that make learning fun, is a special talent. As schools continue to move away from traditional textbook-based curriculum in favor of literature-based curriculum, this talent will be increasingly sought. For more information about children's book publishing, consult *Children's Writer's & Illustrator's Market*, published by Writer's Digest Books.

Room for niche titles

What does all this mean for the writer who has just completed an obscure history of glassblowing or a book on poisonous lizards, subjects not likely to procure bestseller status? Is there a market for highly specialized nonfiction titles? According to Wiseman, there is. "I am often surprised by the subjects of nonfiction books that become very successful," she says. "A seemingly obscure and dry subject like cathedrals can become instantly fascinating in the hands of the right author or illustrator. The success of nonfiction, I would say, is the chemistry between the creator and the subject. If it's right and the publisher understands what the book is and how it should best be presented, there is every chance it will be a top book. It's a matter of letting a talented person follow his or her fire." Specialized books are finding more room in the marketplace these days, too. With the rise of "superstores" (bookstores carrying many more titles than the average bookstore), more shelf space is opening up for special interest titles. Clearly, this is good news for publishers and writers of narrowly-targeted books.

Becoming market-wise

Current information on the nonfiction market doesn't end here. Another invaluable source is your local bookseller, who truly has his finger on the pulse of the market. He knows what is selling and what isn't, and is, of necessity, abreast of current trends. Keep in mind, however, that a trendy topic does not always guarantee publication. If you want to write a book about Elvis and there are already 30 books in publication covering that subject, you'd better be prepared to substantiate that your angle is truly unique and will stand up to or surpass the competition. It is also worth noting that, since publication can occur as much as two years after acceptance of a manuscript, the trend you're trying to jump on may be passed. Study the current edition of *Books In Print*, available at your library, to assess your competition. For more information on researching the competition for your nonfiction book, see Selling Your Book Proposal on page 31.

Trade journals covering the publishing industry are also important resources for the nonfiction writer. *Publishers Weekly, Library Journal* and *The American Bookseller*, to name a few, chart book sales and industry trends. *Book Industry Trends*, published by Book Industry Study Group, makes projections regarding how the book publishing industry will perform in the years ahead. Finally, writers' groups and professional organizations serve dual roles as information sources and support networks. Check out the writing clubs in your area, or look into one of the national groups such as the National Writer's Club which have regional chapters. Armed with these resources, you'll be savvy to the market and ready to forge ahead.

Consumer magazines

Change is a constant in the consumer magazine industry. New publications sprout up as quickly as existing ones go under. What might be a hot topic today and, consequently, an area of growth due to new titles, could very well be history next year. *Samir Husni's Guide to New Consumer Magazines*, reports that, in 1992 alone, a record 679 new consumer magazines were launched. Many of the titles that have survived the recession have done so at the expense of a decrease in number of pages per issue and number of issues published per year. Advertising has also suffered during the past few years, although ad pages do seem to be increasing. Changes in consumer magazine publishing reflect consumer lifestyle changes, as evident in the trends that follow.

As the trends we will be looking at are specific to the consumer magazine industry, please see the introduction to Trade Journals for more information about that segment of magazine publishing. Trade journals by nature tend to be more stable than consumer ones, with less flux in start-ups and declines. They serve to provide information to the specific trades/industries they represent. And while writing for trade journals usually means less pay and prestige than writing for consumer magazines, it can provide a viable means of building your clips and reputation. In fact, many writers with expertise in certain industries develop trade magazine writing into successful careers, without ever delving into the world of mass-circulation publications.

What's hot

As in nonfiction book publishing, the magazine industry is experiencing a surge of growth in the niche and special interest areas, to the point that these publications may be gaining on their mass-circulation counterparts. With less disposable income and free time to devote to purchasing and reading a variety of magazines, perhaps consumers are streamlining their spending habits and buying only those publications that specifically address what they are most interested in.

Just what are consumers interested in right now? The hottest publications are those addressing lifestyle, parenting, health and fitness, food, shelter (specifically espousing a "country" style), and, yes, sex. In fact, magazine expert Samir Husni recently reported in *Folio* that the number of sex magazines launched annually has exceeded those in all other categories for the past four years. Husni suggests that they are "fantasy vehicles," offering a safe alternative in the age of AIDS.

Another area that is holding steady is retirement publications. As baby boomers move into the over-50 age group in the not-too-distant future, this market promises future growth. A. June Lang, office editor at *Alive!*, a magazine for Christian seniors, says that this success can be attributed not only to these magazines' appeal to the fastest growing age group in America, but also to their ability to adapt as senior lifestyles change. "Seniors have better health now and are retiring at an earlier age, and Christian magazines have increased their awareness of the needs and abilities of seniors." Perhaps with the recent launch of a title as specific as *Senior Golfer*, we will see increased specialization among retirement publications. According to Marjorie P. Groves, Ph.D., editor of *Mature Outlook*, this specialization will be by level of health rather than by major topics such as health or travel. "For example," she says, "*Mature Outlook* magazine is for active people interested in maintaining or improving their general health; others are for a specific ailment or specific aspect of health. Several publications focus on travel information for people 50+ and are segmented within the travel field. The possibilities seem endless."

With seven new listings in the Child Care and Parental Guidance section of this edition of *Writer's Market*, sustained growth in this area is evident. Perhaps the success of parenting magazines lies in their ability to tap into societal change. Most address changes in family structure, such as divorce, single parenting and working mothers, and many (including *Child* and *Healthy Kids*) offer customized editions to address the concerns of parents of children in specific age groups.

Home improvement and how-to titles continue to flourish, particularly those dealing with gardening, woodworking and home decorating. *Folio* recently highlighted the success of shelter magazines espousing the "country" lifestyle, which focuses on traditional living and decorating. With over two-dozen of these titles in publication, this category is clearly holding steady, appealing to the millions of Americans seeking a return to simpler values and affordable lifestyles in the wake of a tenuous economy, and particularly to aging baby boomers dreaming of a retirement home in the country. While there is a clear distinction between "country decorating" and "country living" publications, there may be some overlap between the two, says Bruce Woods, a columnist (writing under a pen name) for *Back Home* magazine and the editor of *Writer's Digest*. "Country decorating presents an opportunity for people to reflect in their habitat their interest in the country life. The difference is that readers of country living magazines demand more authenticated how-to information," he says.

The health and fitness category continues to impact the consumer magazine industry, with a plethora of titles available to suit every healthy lifestyle, from *Men's Health* to *Sober Times*. *Advertising Age* reports that, with the health trend of the 1990s, advertising and circulation in this category is showing gains.

The market for freelancers

Magazine editors use freelancers for various reasons. They may depend on them because, due to budget restraints and small staffs, they are forced to look outside for quality writing to fill editorial space. Other publications may use freelance writing sporadically to inject a fresh perspective into their traditional editorial. Mike Diegel, editor of *Outdoor America*, admits that, while freelance opportunities at the magazine are limited, "there will always be room for different writers who present compelling, tightly focused proposals." "For that," he says, "I'll make space." Even if freelance writing opportunities for a particular magazine are confined only to columns or even fillers, don't write these markets off. Even short pieces written for a magazine you admire contribute to your portfolio of published clips and can lead to higher-profile assignments in the future.

It is important to tailor your writing to a specific publication. Many editors, including Laura Burns of *MICROpendium*, complain about writers submitting "recycled" material, which immediately clues them in to the writer's unfamiliarity with their magazine. Burns says that, while *MICROpendium* is a good market for freelancers, they must be familiar with the specific computer (the TI99/4A) which is the magazine's focus. "This is more important than their being good writers," she says. "People are always trying to get general interest articles to fit a specialized publication. They must know the magazine first."

Keeping with the trends

It is evident that consumer magazine publishing is a volatile industry, and for that reason, successful writers must stay on top of changes and trends. By regularly visiting libraries, bookstores and newsstands, you can apprise yourself of happenings in the industry. Trade publications such as *Folio*, *Writer's Digest* and *Advertising Age* report on consumer magazine trends, start-ups and shut-downs, as well as on the status of advertising, circulation and single-copy sales. Perhaps your most important research will be to obtain a few issues of a publication you are interested in submitting work to. After you have familiarized yourself with its editorial content, write to the magazine requesting its editorial calendar and writer's guidelines. Having taken these steps, you have laid the foundation for your magazine writing career, with an eye on the future as you continue to watch trends.

How Much
Should I Charge?

Establishing your own pay rates can be a tricky business, as there are many factors involved in the decision. These determinants must be weighed carefully to produce an arrangement that is satisfying to both you and your client.

Keep in mind that every situation and client is unique, and that rates vary in different locations. Generally, you can charge more in metropolitan areas than you can in small towns, and more on the East and West Coasts than in the central parts of the U.S. The nature of your client's business should also be taken into account. A nonprofit organization, for example, may not be able to afford the same fee for a copywriter as a large corporation. Similarly, most newspapers do not usually pay as much for feature articles as do magazines. Finally, the size of your client is a factor to be weighed: Smaller companies seldom pay as much as large corporations.

Network with other freelancers in your area to find out how much they are charging. You'll want to make sure you aren't selling yourself short, but you'll also want to ensure that you aren't pricing yourself out of the market. In preparing for a bid, first look at the range of fees listed for that particular service. Then try to assess how much you think the client is willing to pay for your services. If you are unsure, ask them what they have budgeted for the project and start from there.

It is especially difficult to set your own fees if you are in unfamiliar territory. If you secure an assignment in an area of business that is new to you, you may want to start by charging an hourly rate for your services rather than a flat fee. One way to establish this rate is to determine what an annual salary might be for a staff person to do the same job you are bidding on. Base your hourly wage on that. If, for example, you think the buyer would have to pay a staff person $26,000 per year, divide that by 2,000 (approximately 40 hours per week for 50 weeks) and you will arrive at $13 per hour.

Next, add another 33% to cover the cost of fringe benefits that an employer normally pays (but that you must now absorb) in Social Security, unemployment insurance, hospitalization, retirement funds, etc. This figure varies from employer to employer, of course. The U.S. Chamber of Commerce reports that the U.S. average paid by employers is 37.6% of the employee's salary.

Then add another dollars-per-hour figure to cover your actual overhead expense for office space, equipment, supplies; plus time spent on professional meetings, researching and writing unsuccessful proposals. (To get this figure, add up one year's expenses and divide by the number of hours per year you work on freelancing. In the beginning—when you may have large one-time expenses, such as a computer—you may have to adjust this figure to avoid pricing yourself out of the market. Finally, you may wish to figure in a profit percentage to be used for capital investments or future growth.

Here's an example:
  $26,000 (salary) ÷ 2,000 (hours) = $13.00 per hour
                                    + 4.29 (33% to cover fringe benefits, taxes, etc.)
                                    + 2.50 (overhead based on annual expenses of $5,000)
                                    + 1.30 (10% profit margin)

                                    $21.09 per hour charge

Once you have worked repeatedly for a particular client or have established a specific area of expertise, you will get a feel for the time and effort involved. Then you may feel more comfortable charging a flat fee for projects rather than an hourly rate. Businesses are sometimes more likely to agree to flat fees because they like to know ahead of time how much a project will cost.

Reservations about hourly rates can be alleviated through effective communication. Be sure to get a letter of agreement signed by both parties covering the work to be done and the fee (or rate) to be paid. If there is any question about how long the project will take you, be sure the agreement indicates that you are estimating the time and that your project fee is based on a certain number of hours. If more time is required, you should be able to renegotiate with the client. If you quote a flat fee up front, you should stipulate in your original agreement that a higher rate will be charged for any overtime hours or late changes in the project. Another solution is to require partial payment as parts of the job are completed, so both you and the client have a better idea of the time involved.

Sometimes it is worth working for lower rates if it means gaining valuable experience or establishing your reputation in a certain field. If you are trying to establish yourself as an expert in a specific area, it may be important for you simply to get published clips. You may also agree to a low-paying assignment if it supports a cause that you believe in.

Keep in mind that certain industries have payment procedures that are fairly standard. For example, greeting card companies pay a flat fee per idea, rather than an hourly rate. We have indicated such specifications where they apply. In markets where payment methods vary, both kinds of rates are given so you have as many pricing options as possible. Please note that the categories often encompass a wide range due to responses from various locations and from writers with various levels of experience. For further confirmation in setting your rates, contact professional organizations in your area. They may have rates surveys to help you, and may also provide you with valuable freelance contacts.

Advertising, Copywriting & PR

Advertising copywriting: Advertising agencies and the advertising departments of large companies need part-time help in rush seasons. Newspapers, radio and TV stations also need copywriters for their small business customers who do not have agencies. Depending on the client, the locale and the job, the following rates could apply: $20-100 per hour, $250 and up per day, $500 and up per week, $1,000-2,000 as a monthly retainer. Flat-fee-per-ad rates could range from $100 and up per page depending upon size and kind of client.

Book jacket copywriting: From $100-600 for front cover jacket plus flaps and back jacket copy summarizing content and tone of the book.

Brochures: $20-600 per published page or $100-7,500 and up per project depending on client (small nonprofit organization to large corporation), length and complexity of job.

Consultation for communications: *See Business & Technical Writing.*

Copyediting for advertising: $25 per hour.

Copywriting for book club catalogs: $85-200.

Direct-mail catalog copy: $75-200 per item; $150-1,000 per page.

Direct-mail packages: Copywriting direct mail letter, response card, etc., $500-30,000 depending on writer's skill, reputation and the client.

Direct response card on a product: $250-500.

Events promotion: $20-30 per hour. *See also Shopping mall promotion (this section).*

Flyers for tourist attractions, small museums, art shows: $50 and up for writing a brief bio, history, etc.

Fundraising campaign brochure: $5,000 for 20 hours' research and 30 hours to write a major capital campaign brochure, get it approved, lay out and produce with a printer. For a standard fundraising brochure, many fundraising executives hire copywriters for $50-75 an hour to do research which takes 10-15 hours and 20-30 hours to write/produce.

New product release: $300-500 plus expenses.

News release: *See Press release (this section).*

Picture editing: *See Editorial/Design Packages.*

Political writing: *See Public relations and Speechwriting (this section).*

Press background on a company: $500-1,200 for 4-8 pages.

Press kits: $500-3,000.

Press release: 1-3 pages, $25-500.

Print advertisement: $200 per project.

Product literature: Usually paid per hour or day: $60 per hour; $400 per day. Per page, $100-300.

Promotional materials: *See Brochures (this section).*

Proofreading corporate publications and documents: $15-25 per hour.

Public relations for business: $250-600 per day plus expenses; up to $1,750 for large corporations.

Public relations for conventions: $500-2,500 flat fee.

Public relations for libraries: Small libraries, $5-10 per hour; larger cities, $35 per hour and up.

Public relations for nonprofit or proprietary organizations: Small towns, $100-500 monthly retainers.

Public relations for politicians: Small town, state campaigns, $10-50 per hour; incumbents, congressional, gubernatorial, and other national campaigns, $25-100 per hour; up to 10% of campaign budget.

Public relations for schools: $15-20 per hour and up in small districts; larger districts have full-time staff personnel.

Radio advertising copy: $20-100 per script; $200-225 per week for a four- to six-hour day; larger cities, $250-400 per week.

Recruiting brochure: 8-12 pages, $500-2,500.

Rewriting: Copy for a local client, $25-100 per hour, depending on the size of the project.

Sales brochure: 12-16 pages, $750-3,000. Up to $500 per page.

Sales letter for business or industry: $350-1,000 for one or two pages.

Services brochure: 12-18 pages, $1,250-2,000.

Shopping mall promotion: $500-1000 monthly retainer up to 15% of promotion budget for the mall.

Speech, editing and evaluation: $18 per hour and up.

Speech for government official: $4,000 for 20 minutes plus up to $1,000 travel and miscellaneous expenses.

Speech for local political candidate: $250 for 15 minutes; for statewide candidate, $375-500.

Speech for national congressional candidate: $1,000 and up.

Speech for owner of a small business: $100 for 6 minutes.

Speech for owners of larger businesses: $500-3,000 for 10-30 minutes.

Speech for statewide candidate: $500-800.

Speechwriting (general): $20-75 per hour.

Trade journal ad copywriting: $250-500.

TV commercial: $60-375 per finished minute; $10-2,000 per finished project.

TV home shopping: Local ad copy: $6 per hour. Writing, miscellaneous freelance: $15-85 per hour; 50-$1 per word.

Audiovisuals & Electronic Communications

Audiocassette scripts: $10-50 per scripted minute, assuming written from existing client materials, with no additional research or meetings; otherwise $75-100 per minute, $750 minimum.

Audiovisuals: For writing, $250-350 per requested scripted minute; includes rough draft, editing conference with client, and final shooting script. For consulting, research, producing, directing, soundtrack oversight, etc., $400-600 per day plus travel and expenses. Writing fee is sometimes 10% of gross production price as billed to client. Some charge flat fee of 1,500-2,100 per package.

Book summaries for film producers: $50-100 per book. *Note: You must live in the area where the business is located to get this kind of work.*

Copyediting audiovisuals: $20 per hour.

Industrial product film: $125-150 per minute; $500 minimum flat fee.

Novel synopsis for film producer: $150 for 5-10 pages typed, single-spaced.

Radio advertising copy: *See Advertising, Copywriting & PR.*

Radio continuity writing: $5 per page to $150 per week, part-time.

Radio copywriting: *See Advertising, Copywriting & PR.*

Radio documentaries: $258 for 60 minutes, local station.

Radio editorials: $10-30 for 90-second to two-minute spots.

Radio interviews: For National Public Radio, up to 3 minutes, $25; 3-10 minutes, $40-75; 10-60 minutes, $125 to negotiable fees. Small radio stations would pay approximately 50% of the NPR rate; large stations, double the NPR rate.

Script synopsis for business: $40 per hour.

Script synopsis for agent or film producer: $75 for 2-3 typed pages, single-spaced.

Scripts for nontheatrical films for education, business, industry: Prices vary among producers, clients, and sponsors and there is no standardization of rates in the field. Fees include $75-120 per minute for one reel (10 minutes) and corresponding increases with each successive reel; approximately 10% of the production cost of films that cost the producer more than $1,500 per release minute.

Screenwriting: $6,000 and up per project.

Slide presentation: Including visual formats plus audio, $150-600 for 10-15 minutes.

Slide/single image photos: $75 flat fee.

Slide/tape script: $75-100 per minute, $750 minimum.

TV commercial: *See Advertising, Copywriting & PR.*

TV copywriting: *See Advertising, Copywriting & PR.*

TV documentary: 30-minute 5-6 page proposal outline, $1,839 and up; 15-17 page treatment, $1,839 and up; less in smaller cities.

TV editorials: $35 and up for 1-minute, 45 seconds (250-300 words).

TV home shopping, local ad copy: *See Advertising, Copywriting & PR.*

TV information scripts: Short 5- to 10-minute scripts for local cable TV stations, $10-15 per hour.

TV instruction taping: *See Educational & Literary Services.*

TV news film still photo: $3-6 flat fee.

TV news story: $16-25 flat fee.

TV filmed news and features: From $10-20 per clip for 30-second spot; $15-25 for 60-second clip; more for special events.

TV, national and local public stations: $35-100 per minute down to a flat fee of $5,186 and up for a 30- to 60-minute script.

TV scripts: (Teleplay only), 60 minutes; network prime time, Writers Guild rates: $14,048; 30 minutes, $10,414.

Books

Abstracting and abridging: Up to $75/hour for nonfiction; $30/hour for reference material.

Anthology editing: Variable advance plus 3-15% of royalties. Advance should cover reprint fees or fees handled by publisher. Flat-fee-per-manuscript rates could range from $500-5,000 or more if it consists of complex, technical material.

Book proposal consultation: $20-75 per hour, or flat rate, $100-250.

Book proposal writing: $175-3,000 depending on length and whether client provides full information or writer must do some research, and whether sample chapter is required. Also up to $150 per page.

Book query critique: $50 for letter to publisher and outline.

Book summaries for book clubs: $50-100 per book.

Consultant to publishers: $25-75 per hour.

Content editing: $12-50 per hour; $600-5,000 per manuscript, based on size and complexity of the project. *See also Manuscript criticism (this section).*

Copyediting: $10-35 per hour. Rates generally on lower end of scale for juvenile books, mid-range for adult trade, and higher for reference material.

Ghostwriting, as told to: Author gets full advance and 50% of author's royalties; subject gets 50%. Hourly rate for subjects who are self-publishing ($25-50 per hour).

Ghostwriting without as-told-to credit: For clients who are either self-publishing or have no royalty publisher lined up, $5,000 to $35,000 (plus expenses) with one-fourth down payment, one-fourth when book half finished, one-fourth at three quarters mark and last fourth of payment when manuscript completed; or chapter by chapter; or $100 per page.

Ghostwriting a corporate book: *See Business & Technical Writing.*

Indexing: $15-40 per hour; charge higher hourly rate if using computer indexing software programs that take fewer hours; $1.50-6 per printed book page; 40-70 per line of index; or flat fee of $250-500, depending on length.

Ghostwriting a religious book: $6,000-15,000. 50% of flat fee in advance and 50% upon completion of accepted ms.

Jacket copywriting: *See Advertising, Copywriting & PR.*

Manuscript criticism: $160 for outline and first 20,000 words; $300-500 for up to 100,000 words. Also $15-35 per hour for trade books, slightly lower for nonprofit.

Movie novelization: $3,500-15,000, depending on writer's reputation, amount of work to be done, and amount of time writer is given.

Novel synopsis for literary agent: $150 for 5-10 pages typed, single-spaced.

Packaging consultation: $75 per hour.

Picture editing: *See Editorial/Design Packages.*

Production editing: $22-30 per hour; for reference/professional books, up to $50 per hour.

Proofreading: $12-25 per hour and up; sometimes $1.50-3 per page.

Research for writers or book publishers: $15-40 an hour and up; $15-200 per day and all expenses. Some quote a flat fee of $300-500 for a complete and complicated job.

Rewriting: $18-50 per hour; sometimes $5 per page. Some writers have combination ghostwriting and rewriting short-term jobs for which the pay could be $350 per day and up. Some participate in royalties on book rewrites.

Science writing, textbook: *See Business & Technical Writing.*

Science writing, encyclopedias: *See Business & Technical Writing.*

Textbook copyediting: $15-20 per hour, depending on whether el-hi, college, technical or non-technical.

Textbook editing: $15-30 per hour.

Textbook proofreading: $13-20 per hour.

Textbook writing: $15-50 per hour.

Translation, literary: $25 per hour; also $95-125 per 1,000 English words.

Business & Technical Writing

Annual reports: A brief report with some economic information and an explanation of figures, $20-35 per hour; 12-page report, $600-1,500; a report that must meet Securities and Exchange Commission (SEC) standards and reports that use legal language could bill at $40-75 per hour. Some writers who provide copywriting and editing services charge flat fees ranging from $5,000-10,000.

Associations: Miscellaneous writing projects, small associations, $15-25 per hour; larger groups, up to $85 per hour; or a flat fee per project, such as

$550-1,000 for 2,000-word magazine articles, or $1,200-1,800 for a 10-page booklet.

Audiovisuals/audiocassette scripts: *See Audiovisuals & Electronic Communications.*

Book, ghostwritten, as told to: *See Books.*

Book summaries for business people: 4-8 printed pages, $400.

Brochures: *See Advertising, Copywriting & PR.*

Business booklets, announcement folders: Writing and editing, $100-1,000 depending on size, research, etc.

Business content editing: $20-35 per hour.

Business facilities brochure: 12-16 pages, $1,000-4,000.

Business letters: Such as those designed to be used as form letters to improve customer relations, $100 per letter for small businesses; $500 and up per form letter for corporations.

Business meeting guide and brochure: 4 pages, $200; 8-12 pages, $400. *See also Advertising, Copywriting & PR.*

Business plan: $1 per word; $175 per manuscript page; or $50-1,500 per project.

Business writing: On the local or national level, this may be advertising copy, collateral materials, speechwriting, films, public relations or other jobs — see individual entries on these subjects for details. General business writing rates could range from $25-60 per hour; $100-200 per day, plus expenses.

Business writing seminars: $250 for a half-day seminar, plus travel expenses. *See also Educational & Literary Services.*

Catalogs for business: $25-40 per hour or $25-600 per printed page; more if many tables or charts must be reworked for readability and consistency. *See also Advertising, Copywriting & PR.*

Collateral materials for business: *See Catalogs for business (this section).*

Consultation on communications: $250 per day plus expenses for nonprofit, social service and religious organizations; $400 per day to others.

Commercial reports for businesses, insurance companies, credit agencies: $6-10 per page; $5-20 per report on short reports.

Company newsletters and inhouse publications: Writing and editing 2-4 pages, $200-500; 4-8 pages, $500-1,000; 12-48 pages, $1,000-2,500. Writing, $20-60 per hour; editing, $15-40 per hour. *See also Editorial/Design Packages.*

Consultation to business: On writing, PR, $25-60 per hour.

Consumer complaint letters: $25 each.

Copyediting for business: $20-50 per manuscript page.

Copyediting for nonprofit organizations: $15-30 per hour.

Corporate comedy: Half-hour show, $300-800.

Corporate history: $1,000-20,000, depending on length, complexity and client resources.

Corporate periodicals, editing: $50-60 per hour.

Corporate periodicals, writing: $25-100 per hour, depending on size and nature of corporation. Also $1 per word.

Corporate profile: Up to 3,000 words, $1,250-2,500.

Editing/manuscript evaluation for trade journals: $20-25 per hour.

Executive biography: Based on a resume, but in narrative form, $100.

Financial presentation for a corporation: 20-30 minutes, $1,500-4,500.

Fundraising campaign brochure: *See Advertising, Copywriting & PR.*

Ghostwriting, general: $25-100 per hour; $200 per day plus expenses.

Ghostwriting article for a physician: $2,500-3,000.

Ghostwriting a corporate book: 6 months' work, $20,000-40,000.

Government public information officer: Part-time, with local governments, $25 per hour; or a retainer for so many hours per period.

Government research: $35 per hour.

Grant appeals for local non-profit organizations: $50 per hour or flat fee.

Grant proposals: $40-100 per hour. Also $500-1,000 each.

Handbooks: $50-100 per hour; $25 per hour for nonprofit.

Indexing for professional journals: $15-40 per hour.

Industrial manual: $50-100 per manuscript page or $4,000 per 50 pages.

Industrial product film: *See Audiovisuals & Electronic Communications.*

Industrial promotions: $15-40 per hour.

Job application letters: $20-40.

Manuals/documentation: $25-60 per hour.

Market research survey reports: $15-30 per hour; writing results of studies or reports, $500-1,200 per day; also $500-2,000 per project.

Medical editing: $25-65 per hour.

Medical proofreading: $12-30 per hour.

Medical writing: $25-100 per hour; manuscript for pharmaceutical company submitted to research journal, $4,500-5,000.

Newsletters, abstracting: $30 per hour.

Newsletters, editing: $50-500 per issue (up to $850 per issue if includes writing); also $25-150 per published page. Some writers who do this charge regularly on a monthly basis. *See also Company newsletters (this section) and Desktop publishing (Editorial/Design Packages).*

Newsletter writing: $10-800 per published page (depending on type of client); also $500-5,000 per issue. Also $250-400 per article. *See also Company newsletters and Retail business newsletters (this section) and Desktop publishing (Editorial/Design Packages).*

Opinion research interviewing: $4-6 per hour or $15-25 per completed interview.

Picture editing: *See Editorial/Design Packages.*

Production editing: $10-30 per hour.

Programmed instruction consultant fees: *See Educational & Literary Services.*

Programmed instruction materials for business: *See Educational & Literary Services.*

Proofreading: $15-50 per hour; $20 per hour limit for nonprofit.

Public relations for business: *See Advertising, Copywriting & PR.*

Resume writing: $25-500 per resume.

Retail business newsletters for customers: $175-300 for writing 4-page publications. Also $100 per page. Some writers work with a local printer and handle production details as well, billing the client for the total package. Some writers also do their own photography. *See also Editorial/Design Packages.*

Sales letter for business or industry: *See Advertising, Copywriting & PR.*

Science writing: For newspapers $150-600; magazines $2,000-5,000; encyclopedias $1 per line; textbook editing $40 per hour; professional publications $500-1,500 for 1,500-3,000 words.

Scripts for nontheatrical films for business & industry: *See Audiovisuals & Electronic Communications.*

Services brochure: *See Advertising, Copywriting & PR.*

Software manual writing: $35-50 per hour for research and writing.

Special news article for trade publication: *See Magazines & Trade Journals.*

Speech for business owner: *See Advertising, Copywriting & PR.*

Teaching business writing to company employees: *See Educational & Literary Services.*

Technical editing: $15-60 per hour.

Technical typing: $1-5 per double-spaced page.

Technical writing: $35 per ms page or $35-75 per hour, depending on degree of complexity and type of audience.

Translation, commercial: Final draft from one of the common European languages, $115-120 per 1,000 words.

Translation for government agencies: Up to $125 per 1,000 foreign words into English.

Translation through translation agencies: Less 33⅓% (average) for agency commission.

Translation, technical: $125 per 1,000 words.

Editorial/Design Packages

Business catalogs: *See Business & Technical Writing.*

Demo software: $70 per hour.

Desktop publishing: For 1,000 dots-per-inch type, $10-15 per camera-ready page of straight type; $30 per camera-ready page with illustrations, maps, tables, charts, photos; $100-150 per camera-ready page for oversize pages with art. Also $20-40 per hour depending on graphics, number of photos, and amount of copy to be typeset. Packages often include writing, layout/ design, and typesetting services.

Fundraising campaign brochure: *See Advertising, Copywriting & PR.*

Greeting cards ideas (with art included): Anywhere from $30-300, depending on size of company.

Newsletters: *See Desktop Publishing (this section) and Newsletters (Business & Technical Writing).*

Picture editing: $20-35.

Photo brochures: $700-15,000 flat fee for photos and writing.

Photo research: $12-25 per hour.

Photography: $5-150 per b&w photo; $10-300 per color photo; also $800 per day.

Printers' camera-ready typeset copy: Usually negotiated with individual printers. *See also Manuscript typing (Miscellaneous).*

Educational & Literary Services

Business writing seminars: *See Business & Technical Writing.*

Copyediting for theses/dissertations: $15-20 per hour.

Educational consulting and educational grant and proposal writing: $250-750 per day or $25-75 per hour.

English teachers, lay reading for: $6 per hour.

Lectures at national conventions by well-known authors: $2,500-20,000 and up, plus expenses; less for panel discussions.

Lectures at regional writers' conferences: $300 and up, plus expenses.

Lectures to local librarians or teachers: $50-100.

Lectures to school classes: $25-75; $150 per day; $250 per day if farther than 100 miles.

Indexing for scholarly journals: $12 per hour.

Manuscript evaluation for scholarly journals: $15 per hour.

Manuscript evaluation for theses/dissertations: $15-30 per hour.

Programmed instruction consultant fees: $300-700 per day; $50 per hour.

Programmed instruction materials for business: $50 per hour for inhouse writing and editing; $500-700 per day plus expenses for outside research and writing. Alternate method: $2,000-5,000 per hour of programmed training provided, depending on technicality of subject.

Public relations for schools: *See Advertising, Copywriting & PR.*

Readings by poets, fiction writers: $25-600 depending on the author.

Scripts for nontheatrical films for education: *See Audiovisuals & Electronic Communications.*

Short story manuscript critique: 3,000 words, $40-60.

Teaching adult education course: $10-60 per class hour; fee usually set by school, not negotiated by teachers.

Teaching adult seminar: $350 plus mileage and per diem for a 6- or 7-hour day; plus 40% of the tuition fee beyond the sponsor's break-even point.

Teaching business writing to company employees: $60 per hour.

Teaching college course or seminar: $15-70 per class hour.

Teaching creative writing in school: $15-70 per hour of instruction, or $1,500-2,000 per 12-15 week semester; less in recessionary times.

Teaching elementary and middle school teachers how to teach writing to students: $75-120 for a 1-1½ hour session.

Teaching home-bound students: $5-15 per hour.

Teaching journalism in high school: Proportionate to salary scale for full-time teacher in the same school district.

Tutoring: $25 per 1-1½ hour private session.

TV instruction taping: $150 per 30-minute tape; $25 residual each time tape is sold.

Writer-in-schools: Arts council program, $130 per day; $650 per week. Personal charges plus expenses vary from $25 per day to $100 per hour depending on school's ability to pay.

Writer's workshop: Lecturing and seminar conducting, $50-150 per hour to $750 per day plus expenses; local classes, $35-50 per student for 10 sessions.

Writing for scholarly journals: $75 per hour.

Magazines & Trade Journals

Abstracting: $20-30 per hour for trade and professional journals; $8 per hour for scholarly journals.

Article manuscript critique: 3,000 words, $40.

Arts reviewing: Regional arts events summaries for national trade magazines, $35-100.

Book reviews: $50-300.

Consultation on magazine editorial: $1,000-1,500 per day plus expenses.

Copyediting: $13-30 per hour.

Editing: General, $25-500 per day or $250-2,000 per issue; Religious publications, $200-500 per month or $15-30 per hour.

Fact checking: $17-25 per hour.

Feature articles: Anywhere from 20¢ to $4 per word; or $200-2000 per 2,000 word article, depending on size (circulation) and reputation of magazine.

Feature article for an association: *See Business & Technical Writing.*

Ghostwriting articles (general): Up to $2 per word; or $300-3,000 per project.

Ghostwritten professional and trade journal articles under someone else's byline: $400-4,000.

Ghostwriting article for physician: $2,500-3,000.

Indexing: $15-40 per hour.

Magazine, city, calendar of events column: $150.

Magazine column: 200 words, $40; 800 words, $400. Also $1 per word. Larger circulation publications pay fees related to their regular word rate.

Manuscript consultation: $25-50 per hour.

Manuscript criticism: $40-60 per article or short story of up to 3,000 words. Also $20-25 per hour.

Picture editing: *See Editorial/Design Packages.*

Permission fees to publishers to reprint article or story: $75-500; 10-15 per word; less for charitable organizations.

Production editing: $15-25 per hour.

Proofreading: $12-20 per hour.

Poetry criticism: $25 per 16-line poem.

Research: $12-20 per hour.

Rewriting: Up to $80 per manuscript page; also $100 per published page.

Science writing for magazines: $2,000-5,000 per article. *See also Business & Technical Writing.*

Short story manuscript critique: 3,000 words, $40-60; $1.25 and up per page.

Special news article: For a business's submission to trade publication, $250-500 for 1,000 words.

Stringing: 20¢-$1 per word based on circulation. Daily rate: $150-250 plus expenses; weekly rate: $900 plus expenses. Also $10-35 per hour plus expenses; $1 per column inch.

Trade journal ad copywriting: *See Advertising, Copywriting & PR.*

Trade journal feature article: For business client, $400-1,000. Also $1 per word.

Translation: $17 per hour.

Newspapers

Ads for small business: $25 for a small, one-column ad, or $10 per hour and up. *See also Advertising, Copywriting & PR.*

Arts reviewing: For weekly newspapers, $15-35; for dailies, $45 and up; for Sunday supplements, $100-400.

Book reviews: For small newspapers, byline and the book only; for larger publications, $35-200.

Column, local: $10-20 for a weekly; $15-30 for dailies of 4,000-6,000 circulation; $30-50 for 7,000-10,000 dailies; $40-75 for 11,000-25,000 dailies; and $100 and up for larger dailies.

Copyediting: $10-30 per hour; up to $40 per hour for large daily paper.

Copywriting: *See Advertising, Copywriting & PR.*

Dance criticism: $25-400 per article.

Drama criticism: Local, newspaper rates; non-local, $50 and up per review.

Editing/manuscript evaluation: $25 per hour.

Fact checking: *See Magazines & Trade Journals.*

Feature: $25-35 per article plus mileage for a weekly; $40-500 for a daily (depending on size of paper). Also 10-20¢ per word.

Feature writing, part-time: $2,000 a month for an 18-hour week.

Obituary copy: Where local newspapers permit lengthier than normal notices paid for by the funeral home (and charged to the family), $15-20. Writers are engaged by funeral homes.

Picture editing: *See Editorial/Design Packages.*

Proofreading: $20 per hour.

Science writing for newspapers: *See Business & Technical Writing.*

Stringing: Sometimes flat rate of $20-35 to cover meeting and write article; sometimes additional mileage payment.

Syndicated column, self-promoted: $5-10 each for weeklies; $10-25 per week for dailies, based on circulation.

Miscellaneous

Church history: $200-1,000 for writing 15 to 50 pages.

College/university history: $35 per hour for research through final ms.

Comedy writing for night club entertainers: Gags only, $5-25 each. Routines, $100-1,000 per minute. Some new comics may try to get a 5-minute routine for $150; others will pay $2,500 for a 5-minute bit from a top writer.

Comics writing: $35-50 per page and up for established comics writers.

Contest judging: Short manuscripts, $5 per entry; with one-page critique, $15-25. Overall contest judging: $100-500.

Copyediting and content editing for other writers: $10-50 per hour or $2-5 per page.

Craft ideas with instructions: $50-200 per project.

Encyclopedia articles: Entries in some reference books, such as biographical encyclopedias, 500-2,000 words; pay ranges from $60-80 per 1,000 words. Specialists' fees vary.

Greeting card verse: Anywhere from $25 up to $300 per sentiment, depending on the size of the company. Rates generally run higher for humorous material than for traditional. *See also Editorial/Design Packages.*

Genealogical research: $25 per hour.

Histories, family: Fees depend on whether the writer edits already prepared notes or does extensive research and writing; and the length of the work, $500-15,000.

Histories, local: Centennial history of a local church, $25 per hour for research through final manuscript for printer.

Manuscript criticism, poetry: $25 per 16 line poem.

Manuscript typing: Depending on ms length and delivery schedule, $1.25-2 per page with one copy; $15 per hour.

Party toasts, limericks, place card verses: $1.50 per line.

Research for individuals: $5-30 per hour, depending on experience, geographic area and nature of the work.

Restaurant guide features: Short article on restaurant, owner, special attractions, $20; interior, exterior photos, $25.

Special occasion booklet: Family keepsake of a wedding, anniversary, Bar Mitzvah, etc., $120 and up.

Minding the Details

While the recession may be getting better, it doesn't seem to be in any hurry. Writers are affected by today's stagnant economy just like everyone else. Of course, some would say that the "economy" of the writing industry has been stagnant for many years. Except for a small minority of blockbuster writers, average book advances don't climb dramatically from one year to the next; magazine payment rates don't keep up with inflation. This is a business in which one of the leading magazine industry trade journals unabashedly published an article entitled "Getting Good Writers Without Paying." The average freelance writer is said to make less than $10,000 a year. Against odds like those, freelance writers need to arm themselves with as much business knowledge and savvy as they can muster.

Each of the following sections discusses a writing business topic that affects anyone selling his writing. Of first importance to every freelance writer are the contracts and agreements that license a publisher to use the writer's work. With that in mind, we'll talk about contract points and a closely related topic — rights. We'll take a look at the writer's rights and sort out some potentially confusing terminology. We'll also demystify the subject of copyright by answering some of the questions writers ask most often about the subject of protecting their creations. And for those of you who are already making money with your writing, we'll offer advice on keeping track of financial matters and staying on top of your tax liabilities. The act of writing may be miles away from the mundane concerns of commerce and industry, but once you endeavor to publish your work and make money from your writing, you are working in the writing *business* — and you incur a variety of legal and tax-related responsibilities.

Some creative types approach the world of business details with an enthusiasm usually reserved for writer's block or oral surgery. But these topics don't have to be simply tolerated as necessary evils. Looked at in a different light, they can be seen as important keys to a successful writing career and interesting in their own right. One thing is sure: The more you know about the business side of a writing career, the longer yours is likely to last.

Our treatment of the business topics that follow is necessarily limited. Look for complete information on each subject at your local bookstore or library — both in books (some of which are mentioned below) and periodicals aimed at writers. Information is also available from the federal government, as indicated later in this article.

Contracts and agreements

If you've been freelancing even a short time, you know that contracts and agreements vary considerably from one publisher to another. Some magazine editors work only by verbal agreement; others have elaborate documents you must sign in triplicate and return before you begin the assignment. As you evaluate any contract or agreement, consider carefully what you stand to gain and lose by signing. Did you have another sale in mind that selling all rights the first time will negate? Does the agreement provide the publisher with a number of add-ons (advertising rights, reprint rights, etc.) for which they won't have to pay you again?

A contract is rarely a take-it-or-leave-it proposition. If an editor tells you that his company will allow *no* changes on the contract, you will then have to decide how important the assignment is to you. But most editors are open to negotiation, and you should learn to compromise on points that don't matter to you while maintaining your stand on things that do.

When it's not specified, most writers assume that a magazine publisher is buying one-time rights. Some writers' groups can supply you with a sample magazine contract to use when the publisher doesn't supply one, so you can document your agreement in writing. Members of The Authors Guild are given a sample book contract and information about negotiating when they join. For more information about contracts and agreements, see *Business and Legal Forms for Authors & Self-Publishers*, by Tad Crawford (Allworth Press, 1990); *From Printout to Published*, by Michael Seidman (Carroll & Graf, 1992) or *The Writer's Guide to Contract Negotiations*, by Richard Balkin (Writer's Digest Books, 1985), which is out of print but should be available in libraries.

Rights and the writer

A creative work can be used in many different ways. As the originator of written works, you enjoy full control over how those works are used; you are in charge of the rights that your creative works are "born" with. When you strike an agreement to have your work published, you are giving the publisher the right to use your work in one or more ways. Whether that right is simply to publish the work for the first time in a periodical or to publish it as many times as he likes and in whatever form he likes is up to you — it all depends on the terms of the contract or agreement the two of you arrive at. As a general rule, the more rights you license away, the less control you have over your work and the more money you should be paid for the license. We find that writers and editors sometimes define rights in different ways. To eliminate any misinterpretations, read Types of Rights and you'll see the definitions upon which editors updated the information in their listings.

Occasionally, we hear from a writer who is confused because an editor claims never to acquire or buy rights. The truth is, any time an editor buys a story or asks you for permission to publish a story, even without payment, the editor is asking you for rights. In some cases, however, editors will reassign those rights to the author after publishing the story.

Sometimes editors simply don't take the time to specify the rights they are buying. If you sense that an editor is interested in getting stories but doesn't seem to know what his and the writer's responsibilities are regarding rights, be wary. In such a case, you'll want to explain what rights you're offering (preferably one-time rights only) and that you expect additional payment for subsequent use of your work.

You should strive to keep as many rights to your work as you can from the outset, otherwise, your attempts to resell your writing may be seriously hampered.

The Copyright Law that went into effect Jan. 1, 1978, said writers were primarily selling one-time rights to their work (plus any revision of that collective work and any later collective work in the same series) unless they—and the publisher—agreed otherwise in writing. Book rights are covered fully by the contract between the writer and the book publisher.

Types of rights

● First Serial Rights—First serial rights means the writer offers the newspaper or magazine the right to publish the article, story or poem for the first time in any periodical. All other rights to the material belong to the writer. Variations on this right are, for example, first North American serial rights. Some magazines use this purchasing technique to obtain the right to publish first in both the U.S. and Canada because many U.S. magazines are circulated in Canada. If an editor had purchased only first U.S. serial rights, a Canadian magazine could come out with prior or simultaneous publication of the same material.

When material is excerpted from a book scheduled to be published and it appears in a magazine or newspaper prior to book publication, this is also called first serial rights.

● One-Time Rights—This differs from first serial rights in that the buyer has no guarantee he will be the first to publish the work. See also Simultaneous Rights.

● Second Serial (Reprint) Rights—This gives a newspaper or magazine the opportunity to print an article, poem or story after it has already appeared in another newspaper or magazine.

The term also refers to the sale of part of a book to a newspaper or magazine after the book has been published, whether or not there has been any first serial publication. Income derived from second serial rights to book material is often shared 50/50 by author and book publisher.

● All Rights—Some magazines buy all rights because of the top prices they pay for material or the exclusive nature of the publication; others have book publishing interests or foreign magazine connections. (Some will call this world rights.) A writer who sells an article, story or poem to a magazine under these terms forfeits the rights to use his material in its present form elsewhere. If he signs a work-for-hire agreement, he signs away all rights and the copyright to the company making the assignment.

If you think you may want to use the material later (perhaps in book form), you must avoid submitting to such markets or refuse payment and withdraw your material. Ask the editor whether he is willing to buy first rights instead of all rights before you agree to an assignment or sale. Some editors will reassign rights to a writer after a given period, such as one year. It's worth an inquiry in writing.

● Simultaneous Rights—This term covers articles and stories sold to publications (primarily religious magazines) that do not have overlapping circulations. A Catholic publication, for example, might be willing to buy simultaneous rights to a Christmas story they like very much, even though they know a Presbyterian magazine may be publishing the same story in its Christmas issue. Publications that buy simultaneous rights indicate this fact in their listings in *Writer's Market*.

Always advise an editor when the material you are sending is a simultaneous submission to another market. Some writers put the information in their cover letters while others also add it to the upper right-hand corner of the first page of the manuscript under the word count.

● Foreign Serial Rights—Can you resell a story you had published in the U.S. or North America to an international magazine? If you sold only first U.S. serial rights or first North American rights, yes, you are free to market your story abroad. Of course, you must contact a magazine that buys material that has previously appeared in the U.S. or North American periodicals. You can find such markets in *International Literary Market Place*, by R.R. Bowker, and *International Writers' and Artists' Yearbook*, by A&C Black Ltd.

● Syndication Rights—This is a division of serial rights. For example, a book publisher may sell the rights to a newspaper syndicate to print a book in 123 installments in each of 20 U.S. newspapers. If they did this after book publication, they would be syndicating second serial rights to the book. The syndicate would take a commission on the sales it made to newspapers, and the remaining percentage would be split between author and publisher.

● Subsidiary Rights—These are the rights, other than book publication rights, that should be specified in a book contract. These may include various serial rights; movie, television, audiotape and other electronic rights; translation rights, etc. The contract lists what percentage of these sales goes to the author and what percentage to the publisher. Be careful when signing away these rights. If the publisher is unlikely to market them, you may be able to retain them and market them yourself or through an agent.

● Dramatic, Television and Motion Picture Rights—This means the writer is selling his material for use on the stage, in television or in the movies. Often a one-year option to buy such rights is offered (generally for 10% of the total price). The interested party then tries to sell the idea to other people—actors, directors, studios or television networks, etc. Some properties are optioned over and over again, but most fail to become dramatic productions. In such cases, the writer can sell his rights again and again—as long as there is interest in the material. Though dramatic, TV and motion picture rights are more important to the fiction writer than the nonfiction writer, producers today are increasingly interested in nonfiction material; many biographies, topical books and true stories are being dramatized.

Copyrighting your writing

Copyright law is sometimes complex, but it exists to perform a very simple function: to protect creators of original works. It is engineered to encourage creative expression and aid in the progress of the arts and sciences by ensuring that artists and authors hold the rights by which they can profit from their labors.

The copyright law protects your writing, unequivocally recognizes you (its creator) as its owner, and grants you all the rights, benefits and privileges that come with ownership.

In other words, the moment you finish a piece of writing—whether it is a short story, article, novel or poem—the law recognizes that only you can decide how it is to be used.

The following are common copyright questions writers ask.

● *What rights do I have under copyright law?* The law gives you, as creator of your work, the right to print, reprint and copy the work; to sell or distribute copies of the work; to prepare "derivative works"—dramatizations, translations, musical arrangement, novelizations, etc.; to record the work; and to perform or display literary, dramatic or musical works publicly. These rights give you control over how your work is used, and assure you (in theory) that you receive payment for any use of your work.

If, however, you create the work as a "work for hire," you do not own any of these rights. The person or company that commissioned the work for hire owns the copyright.

● *When does copyright law take effect, and how long does it last?* A piece of writing is copyrighted the moment it is put to paper and you indicate your authorship. Protection lasts for the life of the author plus 50 years, thus allowing your heirs to benefit from your work. For material written by two or more people, protection lasts for the life of the last survivor plus 50 years. The life-plus-50 provision applies if the work was created or registered with the Copyright Office after Jan. 1, 1978, when the updated copyright law took effect. The old law protected works for a 28-year term and gave the copyright owner the option to renew the copyright for an additional 28 years at the end of that term. Works copyrighted under the old law that are in their second 28-year term automatically receive an additional 19 years of protection (for a total of 75 years). Works in their first term also receive the 19-year extension beyond the 28-year second term, but must still be renewed when the first term ends.

If you create a work anonymously or pseudonymously, protection lasts for 100 years after the work's creation, or 75 years after its publication, whichever is shorter. The life-plus-50 coverage takes effect, however, if you reveal your identity to the Copyright Office any time before the original term of protection runs out.

Works created on a for-hire basis are also protected for 100 years after the work's creation or 75 years after its publication, whichever is shorter. But the copyright is held by the publisher, not the writer.

● *Do I have to register my work with the Copyright Office to receive protection?* No. Your work is copyrighted whether or not you register it, although registration offers certain advantages. For example, you must register the work before you can bring an infringement suit to court. You can register the work *after* an infringement has taken place, and *then* take the suit to court, but registering after the fact removes certain rights from you. You can sue for actual damages (the income or other benefits lost as a result of the infringement), but you can't sue for statutory damages and you can't recover attorney's fees unless the work has been registered with the Copyright Office *before* the infringement took place. Registering before the infringement also allows you to make a stronger case when bringing the infringement to court. A bill known as the Copyright Reform Act of 1993 was introduced into Congress in February, 1993. If it becomes law, the act would make it possible to claim attorney's fees and punitive damages in infringement cases even if the work has not been formally registered.

If you suspect that someone might infringe on your work, register it. If you doubt that an infringement is likely (and infringements are rare), you might save yourself the time and money involved in registering the material.

● *I have an article that I want to protect fully. How do I register it?* Request the proper form from the Copyright Office. Send the completed form, the registration fee, and one copy (if the work is unpublished; two if it's published) of the work to the Register of Copyrights, Library of Congress, Washington DC 20559. You needn't register each work individually. A group of articles can be registered simultaneously if they meet these requirements: They must be assembled in orderly form (simply placing them in a notebook binder is sufficient); they must bear a single title ("Works by Patrick Jones," for example); they must represent the work of one person (or one set of collaborators); and they must be the subject of a single claim to copyright. No limit is placed on the number of works that can be copyrighted in a group.

● *If my writing is published in a "collective work"—such as a magazine—does the publication handle registration of the work?* Only if the publication owns the piece of writing. Although the copyright notice carried by the magazine covers its contents, you must register any writing to which *you* own the rights if you want the additional protection registration provides.

Collective works are publications with a variety of contributors. Magazines, newspapers, encyclopedias, anthologies, etc., are considered collective works. If you sell something to a collective work, state in writing what rights you're selling. If you don't specify rights, the law allows one-time rights plus publication in any revision of the collective work and any later collective work in the same series. For example, a publishing company could reprint a contribution from one issue in a later issue of its magazine without paying you. The same is true for other collective works, so always detail in writing what rights you are selling before actually making the sale.

When contributing to a collective work, ask that your copyright notice be placed on or near your published manuscript (if you still own the manuscript's rights). Prominent display of your copyright notice on published work has two advantages: It signals to readers and potential reusers of the piece that it belongs to you, and not to the collective work in which it appears; and it allows you to register all published work bearing such notice with the Copyright Office as a group for a single fee. A published work *not* bearing notice indicating you as copyright owner can't be included in a group registration.

Display of copyright notice is especially important when contributing to an uncopyrighted publication—that is, a publication that doesn't display a copyright symbol and doesn't register with the Copyright Office. When the United States joined the Berne Copyright Convention on March 1, 1989, mandatory notice of copyright was no longer required and failure to place a notice of copyright on copies no longer results in loss of copyright. It can still be important to display a copyright notice so no one will innocently infringe on your copyright, however.

Official notice of copyright consists of the symbol ©, the word "Copyright," or the abbreviation "Copr."; the name of the copyright owner or owners; and the year date of the first publication (for example, "© 1994 by Patrick Jones"). A hand-drawn copyright symbol is acceptable.

● *How do I transfer copyright?* A transfer of copyright, like the sale of any property, is simply an exchange of the property for payment. The law stipulates, however, that the transfer of any exclusive rights (and the copyright is the most exclusive of rights) must be made in writing to be valid. Various types of exclusive rights exist, as outlined in Types of Rights. Usually it is best not to sell your copyright. If you do, you lose control over the use of the manuscript and forfeit future income from its use.

- *What does "work for hire" mean to me?* This is a work that another party commissions you to do. Two types of work-for-hire works exist: Work done as a regular employee of a company, and commissioned work that is specifically called "work for hire" in writing at the time of assignment. The phrase "work for hire" or something close must be used in the written agreement, though you should watch for similar phrasings. The work-for-hire provision was included in the new copyright law so that no writer could unwittingly sign away his copyright. The phrase "work for hire" is a bright red flag warning you that signing the agreement will result in loss of rights to any material created under the agreement.

Some editors offer work-for-hire agreements when making assignments and expect writers to sign them routinely. By signing them, you forfeit the potential for additional income from a manuscript through reprint sales or sale of other rights. Be careful, therefore, in signing away your rights in a "work-for-hire" agreement. Many articles written as works for hire or to which all rights have been sold are never resold. If, however, you retain the copyright, you might try to resell the article—something you couldn't do if you forfeited your rights to the piece.

- *Can I get my rights back if I sell all rights to a manuscript or if I sell the copyright itself?* Yes. You or your heirs can terminate the transfer of rights 40 years after the grant was made or, in the case of publication, 35 years after publication—whichever comes first. You can do this by serving written notice, within specified time limits, to the person to whom you transferred rights. Consult the Copyright Office for the procedural details.

- *Do all copyright transfers have to be in writing to be legal?* Only work-for-hire agreements and transfers of exclusive rights *must* be in writing. However, getting any agreement in writing before the sale is wise. Beware of other statements about what rights the buyer purchases that may appear on checks, writer's guidelines or magazine mastheads. If the publisher makes such a statement elsewhere, you might insert a phrase such as "No statement pertaining to purchase of rights other than the one detailed in this letter—including masthead statements or writer's guidelines—applies to this agreement" into the letter that outlines your rights agreement.

- *Are ideas and titles copyrightable?* No. Nor can facts be copyrighted. Only the actual expression of ideas or information can be copyrighted. You can't copyright the idea to do a solar energy story, and you can't copyright lists of materials for building solar energy converters. But you can copyright the article that results from that idea and that information.

- *Where can I get more information about copyright?* Write to the Copyright

Office (Library of Congress, Washington DC 20559) for a free Copyright Information Kit. To get answers to specific questions about copyright (but not legal advice), call (not collect) the Copyright Public Information Office at (202)707-3000 weekdays between 8:30 a.m. and 5 p.m. (Eastern Standard Time). To order copyright forms by telephone, call (202)707-9100. A good overview of basic copyright concerns for writers can be found in Stephen Fishman's *The Copyright Handbook: How to Protect and Use Written Works* (Nolo Press, 1992) and Ellen Kozak's *Every Writer's Guide to Copyright & Publishing* (Henry Holt, 1990).

Reprint sales

One of the easiest ways to make additional freelance money is through selling the rights for a publication to reprint your work. First, you need to be sure you have retained the right to reprint. Then check out prospective listings in the Consumer and Trade sections; those interested in buying reprints will state that in their listings. Editors who consider reprints for publication have been asked what type of material (fiction or nonfiction) they consider; the method of submission they prefer (typed manuscript, photocopy or tearsheet); and the percentage they pay (based on the amount paid for an original article). This will help you determine the best market for your reprint sales.

Finances

You probably didn't become a writer for the thrill of handling accounting, taxes and bookkeeping, but they are a necessary part of running a small business. If you dislike handling these tasks, you can always employ someone else to do them for a fee. If you do employ a professional, you must still keep the original records with an eye to providing the professional with the appropriate information. You may even be able to find another small business owner for whom you can do some professional writing or editing in exchange for his work.

If you decide to handle these tasks yourself—or if you just want to know what to expect of the person you employ—consider these tips:

Accurate records are essential, and the easiest way to keep them is to separate your writing income and expenses from your personal ones. Most professionals find that separate checking accounts and credit cards help them provide the best and easiest records.

The best financial forms are the ones that get used, and usually the simpler the form, the more likely it will be used regularly. Get in the habit of recording every transaction related to your writing. You can start at any time; you don't need to begin on January 1. Because you're likely to have expenses before you have income, start keeping your records whenever you make your first purchase related to writing—such as this copy of *Writer's Market.*

Your bookkeeping system. For most freelance writers, a simple type of single-entry bookkeeping is adequate. The heart of the single-entry system is the journal, an accounting book available at any stationery or office supply store. You record all of the expenses and income of your writing business in the journal.

The single-entry journal's form is similar to a standard check register. Instead of withdrawals and deposits, you record expenses and income. You'll need to describe each transaction clearly—including the date; the source of the income (or the vendor of your purchase); a description of what was sold or bought; whether the payment was by cash, check or credit card; and the amount of the transaction.

Your receipt file. Keep all documentation pertaining to your writing expenses or income. This is true whether you have started a bookkeeping journal or not. For every payment you receive, you should have a check stub from the publisher's check, a letter of agreement or contract stating the amount of payment, or your own bank records of the deposit. For every check you write to pay business expenses, you should have a record in your check register as well as a cancelled check. Keep credit card receipts, too. And for every cash purchase, you should have a receipt from the vendor—especially if the amount is over $25. For small expenses, you can usually keep a list if you don't record them in a journal.

Tax information

Freelance writers, artists and photographers have a variety of concerns about taxes that employees don't have, including deductions, self-employment tax and home office credits. Many freelance expenses can be deducted in the year in which they are incurred (rather than having to be capitalized, or depreciated, over a period of years). For details, consult the IRS publications mentioned below. Keep in mind that to be considered a business (and not a hobby) by the IRS you need to show a profit in three of the past five years. Hobby losses are deductible only to the extent of income produced by the activity.

There also is a home office deduction that can be claimed if an area in your home is used *exclusively* and *regularly* for business. Contact the IRS for information on requirements and limitations for this deduction. If your freelance income exceeds your expenses, regardless of the amount, you must declare that profit. If the profit is $400 or more, you also must pay quarterly Self-Employment Social Security Tax by filing the required self-employment tax form (Schedule SE) along with your 1040 form.

While we cannot offer you tax advice or interpretations, we can suggest several sources for the most current information.

● Call your local IRS office. Look in the white pages of the telephone directory under U.S. Government—Internal Revenue Service. Someone will be able to respond to your request for IRS publications and tax forms or other information. Ask about the IRS Tele-tax service, a series of recorded messages you can hear by dialing on a touch-tone phone. If you need answers to complicated questions, ask to speak with a Taxpayer Service Specialist.

● Obtain the basic IRS publications. You can order them by phone or mail from any IRS office; most are available at libraries and some post offices. Start with *Your Federal Income Tax* (Publication 17) and *Tax Guide for Small Business* (Publication 334). These are both comprehensive, detailed guides— you'll need to find the regulations that apply to you and ignore the rest. There are many IRS publications relating to self-employment and taxes; Publication 334 lists many of these publications—such as *Business Use of Your Home* (Publication 587) and *Self-Employment Tax* (Publication 533).

● Consider other information sources. Many public libraries have detailed tax instructions available on tape. Some colleges and universities offer free assistance in preparing tax returns. And if you decide to consult a professional tax preparer, the fee is a deductible business expense on your tax return.

Important Listing Information

- *Listings are based on editorial questionnaires and interviews. They are not advertisements; publishers do not pay for their listings. The markets are not endorsed by* Writer's Market *editors.*
- *All listings have been verified before publication of this book. If a listing has not changed from last year, then the editor told us the market's needs have not changed and the previous listing continues to accurately reflect its policies.*
- Writer's Market *reserves the right to exclude any listing.*
- *When looking for a specific market, check the index. A market may not be listed for one of these reasons.*
  1. *It doesn't solicit freelance material.*
  2. *It doesn't pay for material.*
  3. *It has gone out of business.*
  4. *It has failed to verify or update its listing for the 1994 edition.*
  5. *It was in the middle of being sold at press time, and rather than disclose premature details, we chose not to list it.*
  6. *It hasn't answered* Writer's Market *inquiries satisfactorily. (To the best of our ability, and with our readers' help, we try to screen out fraudulent listings.)*
  7. *It buys few manuscripts, thereby constituting a very small market for freelancers.*
- *See the index of additional markets at the end of each major section for specific information on individual markets not listed.*

Keys to Symbols and Abbreviations

‡ *New listing in all sections*
* *Subsidy book publisher or small press*
□ *Cable TV market in Scriptwriting section*
ms-*manuscript;* mss-*manuscripts*
b&w-*black and white (photo)*
SASE-*self-addressed, stamped envelope*
SAE-*self-addressed envelope*
IRC-*International Reply Coupon, for use on reply mail in countries other than your own.*

See Glossary for definitions of words and expressions used in writing/ publishing.

The Markets

Book Publishers 74

Book Publishers

The book publishing industry is enjoying relatively good health these days. Having weathered the recent recession successfully, the industry is setting sales records and, by aggressively seeking to exploit cutting-edge electronic technology, seems poised for an extended period of growth well into the next century. Booksellers, too, are in a dynamic growth spurt. The large bookselling chains and "superstores" (if there's not one near you, just wait a day or two) are moving publishers' products in ever-greater quantities and providing customers with greater title selection than ever before. With this marriage of high technology and expanded channels of distribution, we are, perhaps, witnessing a watershed moment in American publishing and bookselling.

But of course, no industry moves forward without drawing fire from some quarters. With the entry of book publishers into the computer/electronic arena some hear the death knell for the printed page. The rapid growth of chains and superstores is the cause of dismay among many owners of independent bookstores and their patrons. And there is some question of just how many square feet of bookstore space the American public can reasonably be expected to support.

In light of the increased attention being paid to profitability and the "bottom line," some complain that the art of publishing and bookselling is losing its soul. Many writers (and readers) assume that the race for profit describes the totality of American publishing today. Far from it. The beauty (and strength) of the current publishing scene is in its diversity. For every publisher out there (and in here) who seems blinded by the "blockbuster" mentality, there are a dozen who are seeking thoughtful, provocative and important works with little regard for hitting the bestseller lists. That's not to say these publishers are not interested in making a profit; they are. It's just that many of them pursue a publishing philosophy based first on the importance and quality of the work and only secondarily on its profitability. Publishers who do that successfully have found ways to contain costs and thrive on lower profit margins than the "blockbuster" publishers.

What's hot

The fiction bestseller lists continue to be dominated by top-name authors. Stephen King, Danielle Steel, Mary Higgins Clark, Judith Krantz, and their ilk all continue to make regular appearances. In a relatively short period of time, John Grisham has taken his place among that coterie with his phenome-

INSIDER REPORT

Publishing outside the mainstream

Loompanics Unlimited has a near-twenty-year tradition of publishing books that test the limits of propriety, conformity and, some would argue, good taste. Loompanics has taken our Constitution's First Amendment to heart. Steve O'Keefe, editorial director at Loompanics, calls their books "hard core nonfiction: do-it-yourself with an edge." Offering titles such as *Sneak it Through: Smuggling Made Easier*; *Kitchen Improvised Plastic Explosives*; and *Selling Yourself to Science: The Complete Guide to Selling Your Organs, Body Fluids, Bodily Functions and Being a Human Guinea Pig*, Loompanics has thrived by providing quirky books to an audience that the mainstream publishers have either ignored or carefully avoided.

Photograph by Storm O'Keefe

Steve O'Keefe

"We're not really competing with mainstream publishers," says O'Keefe. "For example, we're not interested in carving out a piece of the true crime market or part of the textbook business. Where are you going to shelve *How to Start Your Own Country* or *Successful Armed Robbery*? We are driven more by the manuscripts we receive than by the market. A lot of our sales are through direct mail, and you need unusual material to succeed in direct mail," says O'Keefe, "Both our market and our personal tastes favor well-written books on offbeat subjects."

Unlike the Byzantine and often maddeningly slow proposal process at the larger publishing houses, decision-making at Loompanics is refreshingly simple: "We don't do any [market] research," says O'Keefe. "It's a judgment call, gut instinct. If we like an idea, we ask to see the manuscript. If we like the manuscript, we do the book. It's that simple. No committees, no focus groups; it's very clean."

Writers interested in publishing with Loompanics should make the effort to familiarize themselves with the company's catalog before contacting them. "More than half the submissions we receive are totally inappropriate for our company. Yet not a week goes by that we don't receive unsolicited poetry, fiction or inspirational stuff. If these writers even glanced at our catalog, they would never waste their money sending us this material. Writers should get a copy of our catalog and study it before sending anything. You can learn a lot about what a publisher is trying to do by reading their catalog. What do they give the most space to? What sort of books are they publishing this year? How do they talk about the books they publish? Study the catalog; then, in your cover letter, make an *explicit* connection between what you're writing and what we're publishing. If you show us that you've spent at least a little time getting familiar with our business, we're much more likely to spend a little time considering your proposal."

If you think you've got a book for Loompanics, O'Keefe says, "We like a detailed outline and a sample chapter or two."

nally successful thrillers. But the word is not all bad for newcomers: *Publishers Weekly* reports that 10-15% of top-selling fiction authors in 1992 (industry statistics typically run one year behind) were new to the bestseller lists and that five sold more than 100,000 copies.

Nonfiction had a strong 1992 and that trend continued through 1993. Rush Limbaugh's *The Way Things Ought to Be* enjoyed sales in excess of two million copies in hardcover. The success of General Norman Schwarzkopf's *It Doesn't Take a Hero* was indicative of the popularity of biographies in general. Books on Truman, Princess Di, Ted Kennedy, John F. Kennedy, Magic Johnson and Sam Walton all found success. Other nonfiction categories currently doing well include inspirational, self-help, cooking and diet, humor, computers and home care.

How to publish your book

The markets in this year's book publisher section offer opportunities in nearly every area of publishing. Large, commercial houses are here as are their smaller counterparts; large and small "literary" houses are represented as well. In addition, you'll find university presses, industry-related publishers, textbook houses and more.

The Book Publishers Subject Index is the place to start. You'll find it before the General Index. Subject areas for both fiction and nonfiction are broken out for the more than 800 total book publisher listings. Not all of them buy the kind of book you've written, but this Index will tell you which ones do.

When you have compiled a list of publishers interested in books in your subject area, read the detailed listings. Pare down your list by cross-referencing two or three subject areas and eliminating the listings only marginally suited to your book. When you have a good list, send for those publishers' catalogs and any writer's guidelines available. You want to make sure your book idea is not a duplicate of something they've already published. Visit bookstores and libraries to see if their books are well represented. When you find a couple of books they have published that are similar to yours, write or call the company to find out who edited these books. This last, extra bit of research could be the key to getting your proposal to precisely the right editor.

Publishers prefer different kinds of submission on first contact. Most like to see a one-page query with SASE, especially for nonfiction. Others will accept a brief proposal package that might include an outline and/or a sample chapter. Some publishers will accept submissions from agents only. Virtually no publisher wants to see a complete manuscript on initial contact, and sending one when they prefer another method will signal the publisher "this is an amateur's submission." Editors do not have the time to read an entire manuscript, even editors at small presses that receive fewer submissions. Perhaps the only exceptions to this rule are children's book manuscripts and

University presses seek a larger presence in the trade

"A common misconception about university presses is that they publish only scholarly works," says Theresa May, assistant director and executive editor at the University of Texas Press. "While it is true that the majority of titles on any of our lists will be scholarly in nature, almost all university presses these days publish trade titles as well. Some publish original fiction or literature in translation; some publish regional trade titles. Some publish cookbooks and practical books in a wide range of areas. In short, any university house is almost sure to have on every seasonal list some books of interest to non-academic audiences."

Theresa May

Just as every book published by a university press is not necessarily a scholarly work, not every author is necessarily active in the academic community. Ms. May: "Many of our most successful books, in financial terms, are written by non-faculty authors. Because we publish regional natural history, guidebooks, etc., we see a great many manuscripts from non-academics with regional avocational interests. While all these manuscripts must be vetted for factual accuracy and must survive the same review process as any other manuscript submitted to a university press, they are frequently written by authors who have few or no direct ties to the academic community."

Scholarly publishing's push toward the trade (the publishing of more general interest titles) has come as a result of the rocky economy of the past few years, says May. University presses, thanks to stretched budgets, have become more willing to take on books of wider general interest which can be counted on to generate more immediate cash than scholarly books. "In response to the economy," says May, "scholarly houses are looking more like serious trade houses in some ways.

"However," says May, "the goals of trade and scholarly publishing will always, I think, be distinct. While economics may produce superficial similarities between the two, university publishers feel strongly that their primary mission is to advance knowledge, and that mission will continue to drive university press list building."

poetry manuscripts, which take only as much time to read as an outline and sample chapter anyway.

In your one-page query, give an overview of your book, mention the intended audience, the competition (check *Books in Print*), and what sets your book apart. Detail any previous publishing experience or special training relevant to the subject of your book. All of this information will help your cause; you will look professional in your approach. Above all do not claim to have written the next number one bestseller, even if you think you have. One slip like that and your proposal will sink for sure. For more on "selling" your proposals, see page 31.

Only one in a thousand writers will sell a book to the first publisher they query, especially if the book is the writer's first effort. Make a list of a dozen or so publishers that might be interested in your book. Try to learn as much about the books they publish and their editors as you can. Research, knowing the specifics of your subject area, and openness to editing suggestions are often the difference between acceptance and rejection. You are likely to receive at least a few rejections, however, and when that happens, don't give up. Rejection is as much a part of publishing, if not more, than signing royalty checks. Send your query to the next publisher on your list. You may be able to speed up the process at this early stage by sending simultaneous queries, but do so only to publishers who state they accept them.

Personalize your queries by addressing them individually and mentioning what you know about a company from its catalog or books you've seen. Never send a form letter as a query. Envelopes addressed to "Editor" or "Editorial Department" end up in the dreaded slush pile, a remote region in the mail room of publishing houses from which few or no books emerge, especially at the larger companies.

If a publisher offers you a contract, you may want to seek advice before signing and returning it. An author's agent will very likely take 15% if you employ one, but you could be making 85% of a larger amount. For more information on literary agents, contact the Association of Author's Representatives, 3rd Floor, 10 Astor Place, New York NY 10003, (212)353-3709. Also check the current edition of *Guide to Literary Agents and Art/Photo Reps* (Writer's Digest Books). Attorneys will only be able to tell you if everything is legal, not if you are getting a good deal, unless they have prior experience with literary contracts. If you have a legal problem, you might consider contacting Volunteer Lawyers for the Arts, 6th Floor, 1 E. 53rd St., New York NY 10022, (212)319-2787.

Special notice about subsidy publishing

Starting with our 1993 edition, we created a separate section within Book Publishers entitled Subsidy/Royalty Publishers. We did this so writers wanting to deal solely with royalty publishers will be able to find them exclusively in the main Book Publishers section.

Subsidy publishing involves paying money to a publishing house to publish a book. The source of the money could be a government, foundation or university grant, or it could be the author of the book. When a book publisher has informed us that it considers author-subsidy arrangements, we have placed that publisher in the Subsidy/Royalty section. For more information on subsidy publishing, see the introduction to Subsidy/Royalty Book Publishers on page 244.

Writer's Market is primarily a reference tool to help you sell your writing, and we encourage you to work with publishers that pay a royalty. You will find over 700 such book publishers in the following section. If one of them offers you an author-subsidy arrangement (sometimes called "cooperative publishing" or "co-publishing"), or asks you to pay for all or part of the cost of any aspect of publishing (printing, advertising, etc.), or asks you to guarantee the purchase of any number of the books yourself, we would like you to let us know about that company immediately.

Publishers are offering more author-subsidy arrangements than ever before. Some publishers feel they must seek them to expand their lists beyond the capabilities of their limited resources. While this may be true, and you may be willing to agree to it, we would like to keep subsidy publishers and royalty publishers separate, so that you will be able to choose more easily between them.

Publishers that publish fewer than four books per year, but not more than 50% of them on an author-subsidy basis, are still listed in Small Presses with an asterisk (*). Author-subsidy publishers in Canada are also denoted with an asterisk (*), and are listed in Canadian and International Book Publishers.

For a list of publishers according to their subjects of interest, see the nonfiction and fiction sections of the Book Publishers Subject Index. Information on some book publishers and producers not included in this edition of *Writer's Market* can be found in Book Publishers and Producers/Changes '93-'94.

A.R.E. PRESS, 68th St. and Atlantic Ave., P.O. Box 656, Virginia Beach VA 23451-0656. Fax: (804)422-6921. Editor-in-Chief: Joseph W. Dunn, Jr. Publishes hardcover and trade paperback originals. Publishes 12 titles/year. Receives 600 proposals and mss/year. 75% of books from first-time authors, 95% from unagented writers. Pays 10-15% royalty on net receipts after returns and discounts. Offers $2,000 maximum advance. Publishes book approximately 18 months after acceptance of ms. Reports in 6 weeks on queries. *Writer's Market* recommends allowing 2 months for reply. "We do not accept unsolicited mss." Book catalog and ms guidelines for #10 SASE.
Nonfiction: All book proposals must be compatible with and connected to the material in the Edgar Cayce psychic readings "We would like to see more books that tell the stories of people who have applied the Cayce spiritual principles successfully in their lives. We currently seek the personal, as opposed to the academic or analytical perspective. Mistakes are made when writers do not follow our Author Guidelines, and are not familiar with the thrust of the Cayce material." Query or submit chapter outline with 3 sample chapters, including cover letter and brief synopsis.
Recent Nonfiction Title: *And the Night Shall be No More,* by Glenn Sandefur; *Beyond the Ashes: Cases of Reincarnation from the Holocaust,* by Rabbi Yonassan Gershom; *Arctic Rendezvous,* by Graham McGill; *Passports to Change,* by Mary Lu McFall; *On Wings of Spirit,* by Aron Abrahamsen.
Fiction: "We reject anything that has come to be identified as 'occult.' We will consider fiction that has an uplifting slant, but it should be spiritual or metaphysical compatible with the Cayce philosophy." Query first.
Tips: "Our audience is comprised of people of all ages, races and religious persuasions who are seeking deeper insights into themselves, their spirituality, and their connection to God. Keep your queries and proposals brief and to the point. Please don't send superfluous material with your proposal."

AASLH, American Association for State and Local History, Suite 600, 530 Church St., Nashville TN 37219-2325. (615)255-2971. Fax: (615)255-2979. Estab. 1940. Publishes paperback originals and reprints. Averages approximately 6 titles/year; receives 20-30 submissions annually. 50% of books from first-time authors; 100%

of books from unagented writers. Query for royalty rates. Publishes book an average of 1 year after acceptance. Reports in 3 months on submissions. Free book catalog.

Nonfiction: How-to, reference, collections, preservation, and textbook. "We publish books, mostly technical, that help people do effective work in historical societies, sites and museums, or do research in, or teach, history. No manuscripts on history itself—that is, on the history of specific places, events, people." Write for ms guidelines for submitting manuscripts.

Recent Nonfiction Title: *Ideas And Images: Developing Interpretative History Exhibits*, edited by Kenneth Ames, Barbara Franco and L. Thomas Frye.

Tips: "The American Association for State and Local History provides leadership for and service to those who practice and support history in North America: historical societies, museums, historic sites, parks, libraries, archives, historic preservation organizations, schools, colleges, and other educational organizations."

ABBOTT, LANGER & ASSOCIATES, 548 1st St., Crete IL 60417-2199. (708)672-4200. President: Dr. Steven Langer. Estab. 1967. Publishes trade paperback originals and loose-leaf books. Averages 18 titles/year; receives 25 submissions annually. 15% of books from first-time authors; 100% of books from unagented writers. Pays 10-15% royalty; no advance. Publishes book an average of 18 months after acceptance. Query for electronic submissions. Book catalog for 6×9 SAE with 2 first class stamps. Reports in 1 month on queries; 3 months on mss.

Nonfiction: How-to, reference, technical on some phase of personnel administration, industrial relations, sales management, etc. Especially needs "a very limited number (3-5) of books dealing with very specialized topics in the field of personnel management, wage and salary administration, sales compensation, training, recruitment, selection, labor relations, etc." Publishes for personnel directors, wage and salary administrators, training directors, sales/marketing managers, security directors, etc. Query with outline. Reviews artwork/photos.

Tips: "A writer has the best chance selling our firm a how-to book in personnel management, sales/marketing management or security management."

ABINGDON PRESS, Imprint of The United Methodist Publishing House, P.O. Box 801, Nashville TN 37202-0801. (615)749-6301. Fax: (615)748-6512. President & Publisher: Robert K. Feaster. Editorial Director: Neil M. Alexander. Managing Editor/Assistant Editorial Director: Michael E. Lawrence. Senior Editor General Interest Books & Resources Books: Mary Catherine Dean. Senior Editor Academic Books: Rex Mathews. Senior Editor United Methodist Book & Resources: J.Richard Peck. Editor Professional Books: Paul Franklyn. Editor Reference Books: Jack Keller. Estab. 1789. Publishes hardcover and paperback originals and reprints; church supplies. Averages 100 titles/year. Receives approximately 2,500 submissions annually. Few books from first-time authors; 90-95% of books from unagented writers. Average print order for a writer's first book is 4,000-5,000. Pays royalty. Publishes book an average of 3 months after acceptance. Query for electronic submissions. Ms guidelines for SASE. Reports in 3 months.

Nonfiction: Religious-lay and professional, children's religious books and academic texts. Length: 32-300 pages. Query with outline and samples only.

Recent Nonfiction Title: *Can Homophobia Be Cured: Wrestling With Questions That Challenge The Church*, by Bruce Hilton.

‡ACADEMY CHICAGO, 213 W. Institute Place, Chicago IL 60610-3125. (312)751-7302. Fax: (312)751-7306. Editorial Director/Senior Editor: Anita Miller. Estab. 1975. Publishes hardcover and paperback originals and reprints. Averages 25–30 titles/year; receives approximately 2,000 submissions annually. Average print order for a writer's first book is 1,500-5,000. Pays 7-10% royalty; modest advances. Publishes book an average of 18 months after acceptance. Book catalog for 9×12 SAE with 3 first class stamps; guidelines for #10 SASE. Submit cover letter with first four chapters. Reports in 2 months.

Nonfiction: Adult, travel, true crime and historical. No how-to, cookbooks, self-help, etc. Query and submit first four consecutive chapters.

Recent Nonfiction Title: *The Iron Gates of Santo Tomas*, by Emily Jan Sickle.

Fiction: "Mysteries, mainstream novels." No "romantic," children's, young adult, religious or sexist fiction; nothing avant-garde.

Recent Fiction Title: *Murder on the 13th*, by A.E. Eddenden.

Tips: "At the moment, we are looking for good nonfiction; we certainly want excellent original fiction, but we are swamped."

ACCELERATED DEVELOPMENT INC., 3808 Kilgore Ave., Muncie IN 47304-4896. (317)284-7511. Fax: (317)284-2535. President: Dr. Joseph W. Hollis. Executive Vice President: Marcella Hollis. Estab. 1973. Publishes textbooks, paperback originals and tapes. Averages 10-15 titles/year; receives 170 submissions annually. 50% of books from first-time authors; 100% of books from unagented writers. Query for electronic submissions. Pays 6-15% royalty on net price. Publishes book an average of 1 year after acceptance. Reports in 3 months. Book catalog for 6½×9½ SAE with 3 first class stamps.

Nonfiction: Reference books and textbooks on psychology, counseling, guidance and counseling, teacher education and death education. "Especially needs psychologically-based textbook or reference materials, death education material, theories of counseling psychology, techniques of counseling, and gerontological counseling." Publishes for professors, counselors, teachers, college and secondary students, psychologists, death educators, psychological therapists, and other health-service providers. "Write for the graduate level student and at elementary and secondary school level in the affective domain." Submit outline, 2 sample chapters, prospectus, and author's resume. Reviews artwork/photos.

Recent Nonfiction Title: *Psychopathology and Psychotherapy: From Diagnosis to Treatment*, by Len Sperry, MD, PhD, and Jon Carlson, EdD, PsyD.

Tips: "Freelance writers should be aware of American Psychological Association style of preparing manuscripts."

ACCENT PUBLICATIONS, (formerly Accent Books), P.O. Box 15337, Denver CO 80215. (303)988-5300. Managing Editor: Mary B. Nelson. Estab. 1947. Publishes evangelical Christian education and church resource products. Guidelines available for #10 SASE. 100% of books from unagented writers. Pays royalty on cover price or purchases outright. Publishes book an average of 1 year after acceptance. Query or submit 3 sample chapters with a brief synopsis and chapter outline. Do not submit full ms unless requested. Reports in 3 months. Book catalog for 9 × 12 SAE with 6 first class stamps.

● No longer considers fiction.

Nonfiction: "We are currently soliciting only nonfiction proposals in the areas of Christian education and Church Resources. C.E. products are teaching tools designed for the layman or professional Christian leadership to use in the church's education process. Church Resources are products that can be used in any aspect of the local church ministry. We would consider Bible studies, study guides, teacher helps, ministry aids, quiz books (by age level), puzzle books (by age level), and other C.E. products. We do not consider fiction for children, youth, or adults. We do not consider devotionals, poetry, biographies, autobiographies, personal experience stories, mss. with a charismatic emphasis, or general Christian living books. We also consider books for the professional and volunteer in church ministries."

‡ACCORD COMMUNICATIONS, LTD., (formerly Romar Books, Ltd.), Suite B, 18002 15th Ave. NE, Seattle WA 98155. (206)368-8164. Managing Editor: Karen Duncan. Imprints are Evergreen Pacific Publishing, Larry Reynolds, Managing Editor; A.K.A. Books, Karen Duncan, Managing Editor. Publishes hardcover and trade paperback originals and mass market paperback reprints. Publishes 3 titles/year. Receives 150 queries, 25-30 mss/year. 98% from first-time authors, 100% from unagented writers. Pays royalty, "standard but negotiable," or outright purchase "may be considered." Advance varies widely. Publishes ms 1-2 years after acceptance. Simultaneous submissions OK. Reports in 2 weeks on queries, 2 months on proposals, 3 months on mss.

Nonfiction: How-to (marine-related), reference, atlases and guides, recreation (boating and fishing), mystery fiction, mystery criticism and history. Query. Reviews artwork/photos as part of freelance ms package.

Recent Nonfiction Title: *A.B. Seas*, by Laurie Kimpton-Lorence (how-to-sail).

Fiction: Suspense and mystery. Submit synopsis with 3 sample chapters.

ACE SCIENCE FICTION, Imprint of The Berkley Publishing Group, 200 Madison Ave., New York NY 10016. (212)686-9820. Assistant Editor: Laura Anne Gilman. Estab. 1953. Publishes paperback originals and reprints. Averages 96 titles/year. Reports in 3-6 months. Writer's guidelines for #10 SASE.

Fiction: Science fiction and fantasy. Query with synopsis and first 3 chapters.

Recent Fiction Title: *Far-Seer*, by Robert J. Sawyer.

ACTA PUBLICATIONS, 4848 N. Clark St., Chicago IL 60640. Co-Publisher: Gregory F. Augustine Pierce. Estab. 1958. Publishes trade paperback originals. Publishes 10 titles/year. Receives 50 queries and 15 mss/ year. 50% of mss from first-time authors, 100% from unagented writers. Pays 7½-12½% royalty on wholesale price. Publishes book 1 year after acceptance of ms. No simultaneous submissions. Reports in 2 months on proposals. Book catalog and author guidelines free on request.

Nonfiction: Religion. "We publish non-academic, practical books aimed at the mainline religious market." Submit outline and 1 sample chapter. Reviews artwork/photos as part of freelance ms package. Writers should send photocopies.

Fiction: Religious. "Looking for innovative, practical fiction aimed at mainline religious market." Submit synopsis and 1 sample chapter.

Tips: "Don't send a submission unless you have read our catalog or one of our books."

AGLOW PUBLICATIONS, Women's Aglow Fellowship International, P.O. Box 1548, Lynnwood WA 98046-1548. (206)775-7282. Acquisitions Editor: Karen E. Anderson. Estab. 1969. Publishes trade paperback originals. Averages 6-8 titles/year; receives 300 submissions annually. "A few" books from first-time authors; 90% of books from unagented writers. Average print order of a writer's first book is 10,000. Pays up to 10% royalty on retail price plus advance. Publishes book 1 year after acceptance. Reports in 2 months on queries with outline and synopsis. Book catalog and guidelines for 9 × 12 SAE with 2 first class stamps.

Nonfiction: Biblically-oriented support group books, self-help and inspirational. Subjects include self-help, how to grow in Christian faith, glorify Christ and encourage others – primarily women. No fiction, children's, personal testimony, devotionals, poetry, cookbooks. Familiarize yourself first with our published books and discover ours is a specific target market. Query with outline and synopsis.

Recent Nonfiction Title: *Inside A Woman*, by Jane Hansen.

Tips: "We are looking for books that address the practical aspects of the Christian life and, at the same time, nurture readers to discover their true identity in Jesus Christ through the power of the Holy Spirit. Material needs a strong biblical base, as well as strong research on your subject. We want meaty manuscripts with the milk of human kindness."

ALASKA NORTHWEST BOOKS, Imprint of Graphic Arts Center Publishing. Editorial offices: Suite 300, 2208 NW Market St., Seattle WA 98107. (206)784-5071. Fax: (206)784-5316. Contact: Acquisitions Editor. Estab. 1959. Publishes hardcover and trade paperback originals and reprints. Firm averages 15 titles/year. Receives hundreds of submissions/year. 50% of books from first-time authors. 80% from unagented writers. Pays 10-15% royalty on wholesale price. Buys mss outright (rarely). Offers advance. Publishes book an average of 1 year after acceptance. Simultaneous submissions OK. Reports in 6 months on queries. Book catalog and ms guidelines for 9 × 12 SAE with 3 first class stamps.

Nonfiction: "All written for a general readership, not for experts in the subject." Subjects include nature and environment, travel, cookbooks, Native American culture, adventure, outdoor recreation and sports, the arts, and children's books. "Our book needs are as follows: one-quarter Alaskan focus, one-quarter Northwest, one-quarter Pacific coast, one-quarter national (looking for logical extensions of current subjects)." Submit outline/synopsis and sample chapters.

Recent Nonfiction Title: *The Hidden Coast: Kayak Explorations from Alaska to Mexico*, by Joel W. Rogers.

Tips: "Book proposals that are professionally written and polished, with a clear market receive our most careful consideration. We are looking for originality. We publish a wide range of books for a wide audience. Some of our books are clearly for travelers, others for those interested in outdoor recreation or various regional subjects. If I were a writer trying to market a book today, I would research the competition (existing books) for what I have in mind, and clearly (and concisely) express why my idea is different and better. I would describe the bookbuyers (and readers) – where they are, how many of them are there, how they can be reached (organizations, publications), why they would want or need my book."

THE ALBAN INSTITUTE, INC., 4125 Nebraska Ave. NW, Washington DC 20016. (202)244-7320. Editor-in-Chief: Celia A. Hahn. Publishes trade paperback originals. Averages 9 titles/year; receives 100 submissions annually. 100% of books from unagented writers. Pays 7-10% royalty on books; $50-100 on publication for 450-3,600 word articles relevant to congregational life – practical – ecumenical. Publishes book an average of 1 year after acceptance. Reports in 2 months. Proposals must be submitted. No unsolicited manuscripts. Book catalog and ms guidelines for 9 × 12 SAE with 3 first class stamps.

Nonfiction: Religious – focus on local congregation – ecumenical. Must be accessible to general reader. Research preferred. Needs mss on the task of the ordained leader in the congregation, the career path of the ordained leader in the congregation, problems and opportunities in congregational life, and ministry of the laity in the world and in the church. No sermons, devotional, children's titles, inspirational or prayers. Query for guidelines.

Tips: "Our audience is comprised of intelligent, probably liberal mainline Protestant and Catholic clergy and lay leaders, executives and seminary administration/faculty – people who are concerned with the local church at a practical level and new approaches to its ministry. We are looking for titles on Problems and Opportunities in Congregational Life, The Clergy Role and Career, and The Ministry of the Laity in the Church and in the World."

ALLEN PUBLISHING CO., 7324 Reseda Blvd., Reseda CA 91335. (818)344-6788. Owner/Publisher: Michael Wiener. Estab. 1979. Publishes mass market paperback originals. Firm averages 4 titles/year. Receives 50-100 submissions/year. 50% of books from first-time authors. 90% from unagented writers. Buys mss outright for negotiable sum. Publishes book an average of 6 months after acceptance. Simultaneous submissions OK. Reports in 2 weeks. *Writer's Market* recommends allowing 2 months for reply. Book catalog and writer guidelines for #10 SASE.

Nonfiction: How-to and self-help. Subjects include how to start various businesses and how to improve your financial condition. "We want self-help material, 25,000 words approximately, aimed at wealth-builders, opportunity seekers, aspiring entrepreneurs. We specialize in material for people who are relatively inexperienced in the world of business and have little or no capital to invest. Material must be original and authoritative, not rehashed from other sources. All our books are marketed exclusively by mail, in soft-cover, 8½ × 11 format. We are a specialty publisher and will not consider anything that does not exactly meet our needs." Query. Reviews artwork/photos as part of ms package.

Recent Nonfiction Title: *A Consumer's Guide to Multi Level Marketing*.

Tips: "We are a specialty publisher, as noted above. If your subject does not match our specialty, do not waste your time and ours by submitting a query we cannot possibly consider."

‡ALLWORTH PRESS, 10 E. 23rd St., New York NY 10010. Publisher: Tad Crawford. Publishes hardcover and trade paperback originals. Publishes 10 titles/year. Pays 6-7 1/2% royalty (for paperback) on retail price. Reports in 1 month on queries and proposals, 2 months on mss. Book catalog and ms guidelines free on request.
Nonfiction: How-to and reference. Subjects include art/architecture, business and economics, photography and legal. "We are trying to give ordinary people advice to better themselves in practical ways—as well as helping creative people in the fine and commercial arts." Query.

ALMAR PRESS, 4105 Marietta Dr., Vestal NY 13850-4032. (607)722-0265. Fax: (607)722-0265. Editor-in-Chief: A.N. Weiner. Managing Editor: M.F. Weiner. Estab. 1977. Publishes hardcover and paperback originals and reprints. Averages 8 titles/year; receives 200 submissions annually. 75% of books from first-time authors; 100% of books from unagented writers. Average print order for a writer's first book is 2,000. Pays 10% royalty, no advance. Publishes book an average of 6 months after acceptance. Prefers exclusive submissions; however, simultaneous (if so indicated) submissions OK. Query for electronic submissions. Reports in 2 months. Book catalog for #10 SAE with 2 first class stamps. *"Submissions must include SASE for reply."*
Nonfiction: Publishes business, technical, regional and consumer books and reports. "These main subjects include general business, financial, travel, career, technology, personal help, Northeast regional, hobbies, general medical, general legal, and how-to. *Almar Reports* are business and technology subjects published for management use and prepared in 8½×11 book format. Reprint publications represent a new aspect of our business." Submit outline and sample chapters. Reviews artwork/photos as part of ms package.
Tips: "We're adding a new series of postcard books for various topics where the picture postcards are illustrated and the captions describe the scene on the postcard and the history related to it. Approximately 225 illustrations per book. We are open to any suggested topic. This type of book will be important to us. We look for timely subjects. The type of book the writer has the best chance of selling to our firm is something different or unusual—*no* poetry or fiction, also *no* first-person travel or family history. The book must be complete and of good quality."

‡AMACOM BOOKS, Imprint of American Management Association, 135 W. 50th, New York NY 10020. (212)903-8081. Director: Weldon P. Rackley. Publishes hardcover and trade paperback originals and trade paperback reprints. Firm averages 65 titles/year. Receives 200 submissions/year. 50% of books from first-time authors. 90% from unagented writers. Pays 10-15% royalty on net receipts by the publisher. Publishes book an average of 9 months after acceptance. Query for electronic submissions. Reports in 2-3 weeks on queries. Free book catalog and manuscript guidelines.
Nonfiction: How-to, reference, self-help, textbook and retail bookstore market. Subjects include business, computers, business education, business books of all types. Query. Submit outline/synopsis and sample chapters.
Tips: "Our audience consists of people in the business sector looking for very applied books on business."

‡AMERICA WEST PUBLISHERS, P.O. Box 2208, Carson City NV 89702-2208. (702)885-0700. Fax: 885-0713. Review Editor: George Green. Estab. 1985. Publishes hardcover and trade paperback originals and hardcover and trade paperback reprints. Averages 20 titles/year. Receives 50 submissions/year. 30% of books from first-time authors, 90% from unagented writers. Pays 10% on wholesale price. Offers $300 average advance. Publishes book an average of 6 months after acceptance. Simultaneous submissions OK. Reports in 1 month. Free book catalog and manuscript guidelines.
Nonfiction: UFO—metaphysical. Subject includes health/medicine (holistic self-help), political (including cover-up), economic. Submit outline/synopsis and sample chapters. Reviews artwork/photos as part of ms package.
Recent Nonfiction Title: *Committee of 300*, by John Coleman.
Tips: "We currently have materials in all bookstores that have areas of UFO's and also political and economic nonfiction."

AMERICAN ASTRONAUTICAL SOCIETY, Univelt, Inc., Publisher, P.O. Box 28130, San Diego CA 92198. (619)746-4005. Editorial Director: Robert H. Jacobs. Estab. 1970. Publishes hardcover originals. Averages 8 titles/year; receives 12-15 submissions annually. 5% of books from first-time authors; 5% of books from unagented writers. Average print order for a writer's first book is 600-2,000. Pays 10% royalty on actual sales, no advance. Publishes book an average of 4 months after acceptance. Simultaneous submissions OK. Reports in 1 month. *Writer's Market* recommends allowing 2 months for reply. Book catalog and ms guidelines for 9×12 SAE with 3 first class stamps.
Nonfiction: Proceedings or monographs in the field of astronautics, including applications of aerospace technology to Earth's problems. "Our books must be space-oriented or space-related. They are meant for technical libraries, research establishments and the aerospace industry worldwide." Submit outline and 1-2 sample chapters. Reviews artwork/photos as part of ms package.
Recent Nonfiction Title: *Space Business Opportunities*, edited by Wayne J. Essen and Don K. Tomajan.

‡**AMERICAN BAR ASSOCIATION, PUBLICATIONS PLANNING & MARKETING,** 750 N. Lake Shore Dr., Chicago IL 60611. (312)988-6104. Manager, Book Development: Susan Yessne. Publishes hardcover and trade paperback originals and trade paperback reprints. Publishes 50 titles/year. Receives 100+ queries/year. Pays royalties; "varies a great deal." Publishes book 6 months after acceptance of ms. Simultaneous submissions OK. Query for electronic submission: prefers disk; WordPerfect or Microsoft Word software. Reports in 2 months on queries and proposals, 3 months on mss. Manuscript guidelines free on request.
Nonfiction: Law. Subjects include law practice. "All proposals should be for books that will help lawyers practice law better—no treatises, no memoirs, no philosophical meanderings. Writers should avoid not thinking of the audience; not meeting the needs of the reader; not writing well about practical matters." Query with outline and 1 sample chapter.
Recent Nonfiction Title: *The Law of Parent-Child Relations*, by Scott Friedman (law).
Tips: "We mainly serve lawyers. The best authors for us have an idea of what the law is about and, in fact, are probably teaching or practicing law."

AMERICAN CATHOLIC PRESS, 16160 S. Seton Dr., South Holland IL 60473-1863. (312)331-5845. Editorial Director: Fr. Michael Gilligan, Ph.D. Estab. 1967. Publishes hardcover originals and hardcover and paperback reprints. "Most of our sales are by direct mail, although we do work through retail outlets." Averages 4 titles/year. Pays by outright purchase of $25-100; no advance. Publishes book an average of 8 months after acceptance. Simultaneous submissions OK. Reports in 2 months.
Nonfiction: "We publish books on the Roman Catholic liturgy—for the most part, books on religious music and educational books and pamphlets. We also publish religious songs for church use, including Psalms, as well as choral and instrumental arrangements. We are interested in new music, meant for use in church services. Books, or even pamphlets, on the Roman Catholic Mass are especially welcome. We have no interest in secular topics and are not interested in religious poetry of any kind." Query.

AMERICAN CORRECTIONAL ASSOCIATION, 8025 Laurel Lakes Ct., Laurel MD 20707-5075. (301)206-5100. Fax: (301)206-5061. Managing Editor: Elizabeth Watts. Publishes hardcover and trade paperback originals. Firm averages 18 titles/year. Receives 20 submissions/year. 90% of books from first-time authors. 100% from unagented writers. Pays 10% royalty on net sales. Publishes book an average of 9 months after acceptance. Query for electronic submissions. Reports in 3 months. Free book catalog and ms guidelines.
Nonfiction: How-to, reference, technical, textbook, correspondence courses. "We are looking for practical, how-to texts or training materials written for the corrections profession. No true-life accounts of current or former inmates or correctional officers, theses or dissertations." Query. Reviews artwork/photos as part of ms package.
Recent Nonfiction Title: *The Effective Correctional Officer.*
Tips: "People in the field want practical information, as do academics to a certain extent. Our audience is made up of criminal justice students and corrections professionals. If I were a writer trying to market a book today, I would contact publishers while developing my manuscript to get a better idea of the publishers' needs."
● This publisher advises out-of-town freelance editors and proofreaders to refrain from requesting work from them.

‡**AMERICAN EAGLE PUBLICATIONS INC.,** P.O. Box 41401, Tuscon AZ 85717. (602)888-4957. Publisher: Mark Ludwig. Firm produces hardcover and trade paperback originals and reprints. Averages 8 titles/year. 50% of mss from first-time authors; 100% from unagented writers. Pays 5-12% royalty on retail price. Offers $1,000 average advance. Publishes book 6 months after acceptance of ms. Simultaneous submissions OK. Query for electronic submissions. Reports in 2 months. Catalog for #10 SASE.
Nonfiction: Biography and technical. Subjects include computers and electronics (security), military/war and science (computers and artificial intelligence). "We are highly specialized in nonfiction. Writers should call and discuss what they have first." Query. Reviews artwork/photos as part of freelance ms package. Writers should send photocopies.
Recent Nonfiction Title: *The Captive*, by M. Rowlandson (biography).
Tips: Audience is "scholarly, university profs, (some used as textbooks) very technical programmers and researchers, military, very international."

AMERICAN HOSPITAL PUBLISHING, INC., American Hospital Association, 737 N. Michigan Ave., Chicago IL 60611-2615. (312)440-6800. Fax: (312)951-8491. Vice President, Books: Brian Schenk. Estab. 1979. Publishes trade paperback originals. Firm averages 20-30 titles/year. Receives 75-100 submissions/year. 20% of books from first-time authors; 100% from unagented writers. Pays 10-12% royalty on retail price. Offers

 The double dagger before a listing indicates that the listing is new in this edition. New markets are often more receptive to freelance submissions.

$1,000 average advance. Publishes book an average of 1 year after acceptance. Reports in 2 months. Book catalog and manuscript guidelines for 9×12 SAE with 7 first class stamps.

Nonfiction: Reference, technical, textbook. Subjects include business and economics (specific to health care institutions); health/medicine (never consumer oriented). Need field-based, reality-tested responses to changes in the health care field directed to hospital CEO's, planners, boards of directors, or other senior management. No personal histories, untested health care programs or clinical texts. Query.

Tips: "The successful proposal demonstrates a clear understanding of the needs of the market and the writer's ability to succinctly present practical knowledge of demonstrable benefit that comes from genuine experience that readers will recognize, trust and accept. The audience is senior and middle management of health care institutions. These days we're a little more cautious in what we choose to publish."

AMERICAN LIBRARY ASSOCIATION, 50 E. Huron St., Chicago IL 60611-2795. (312)944-6780. Fax: (312)280-3255. Senior Editor-Acquisitions: Herbert Bloom. Estab. 1896. Publishes hardcover and trade paperback originals. Averages 35 titles/year. Pays royalty. Free book catalog and manuscript guidelines.

Nonfiction: Reference and library science. Query. Curriculum material based on library resources.

Recent Nonfiction Title: *Major U.S. Government Statistical Series,* by Stratford and Stratford.

‡**AMERICAN NURSES PUBLISHING,** #100 W. 600 Maryland Ave. SW, Washington DC 20024. (202)554-4444, ext. 184. Publications Editor: Beth Gyorgy. Firm produces trade paperback originals and reprints. Averages 12-15 titles/year. Receives 20 queries and 10 mss/year. 75% of mss from first-time authors; 100% from unagented writers. Pays 10% royalty on retail price. Publishes book 8-16 months after acceptance of ms. Reports in 6 months on proposals and mss. Free catalog and ms guidelines.

Nonfiction: Biography, how-to, illustrated book, reference, technical and textbook. Subjects include business and economics, education, health/medicine, money/finance, psychology, science, women's issues/studies and nursing. Submit outline and 1 sample chapter. Reviews artwork/photos as part of freelance ms package. Writers should send photocopies.

Recent Nonfiction Title: *Innovation at the Work Site,* by Barbara Burges (ref./text).

Tips: Audience is nurses.

AMERICAN PRESS, 520 Commonwealth Ave., Boston MA 02215-2605. Editor: Marcy Taylor. Publishes college textbooks. Publishes 25 titles/year. Receives 350 queries and 100 mss/year. 50% of mss from first-time authors, 90% from unagented writers. Pays 5-15% royalty on wholesale price. Publishes book 9 months after acceptance of ms. Reports in 3 months. Book catalog free on request.

Nonfiction: Technical and textbook. Subjects include agriculture/horticulture, anthropology/archaeology, art/architecture, business and economics, education, government/politics, health/medicine, history, music/dance, psychology, science, sociology and sports. "We prefer that our authors actually teach courses for which the manuscripts are designed." Do not send complete manuscript. Query or submit outline with tentative table of contents.

Recent Nonfiction Title: *Weight Training,* by O'Connor (textbook).

THE AMERICAN PSYCHIATRIC PRESS, INC., 1400 K St. NW, Washington DC 20005. (202)682-6268. Editor-in-Chief: Carol C. Nadelson, M.D. Estab. 1981. Publishes hardcover and trade paperback originals. Averages 50 titles/year, 2-4 trade books/year; receives about 300 submissions annually. About 10% of books from first-time authors; 95% of books from unagented writers. Pays 10% minimum royalty based on all money actually received, maximum varies; offers average $3,000-5,000 advance. Publishes book an average of 9 months after acceptance. Simultaneous submissions OK (if made clear in cover letter). Query for electronic submissions. Reports in 6 weeks "in regard to an *initial* decision regarding our interest. A *final* decision requires more time." *Writer's Market* recommends allowing 2 months for reply. Author questionnaire and proposal guidelines available for SASE.

Nonfiction: Reference, technical, textbook and general nonfiction. Subjects include psychiatry and related subjects. Authors must be well qualified in their subject area. No first-person accounts of mental illness or anything not clearly related to psychiatry. Query with outline and sample chapters.

Recent Nonfiction Title: *Dr. Silver's Advice to Parents on Attention-Deficit Hyperactivity Disorder,* by Larry B. Silver, M.D.

Tips: "Because we are a specialty publishing company, books written by or in collaboration with a psychiatrist have the best chance of acceptance. Make it authoritative and professional."

AMERICAN SOCIETY OF CIVIL ENGINEERS, ASCE Press, 345 E. 47th St., New York NY 10017-2398. (212)705-7689. Book Acquisitions Editor: Zoe G. Foundotos. Estab. 1988. Imprint averages 5-10 titles/year. 80% of books from first-time authors; 100% from unagented writers. Pays 10% royalty. No advances available. Simultaneous submissions OK. Query for electronic submissions. Reports in 2 months.

Nonfiction: Civil engineering. "We are looking for topics that are useful and instructive to the engineering practitioner." Query with outline and sample chapters.

Tips: "ASCE is a not-for-profit organization, so we've always been cost conscious. The recession has made us *more* conscious and much more cautious about our spending habits."

‡**AMERICAN VETERINARY PUBLICATIONS, INC.,** 5782 Thornwood Dr., Goleta CA 93117. Publisher: Dr. Paul W. Pratt. Publishes hardcover and trade paperback originals. Publishes 2-4 titles/year. Receives 6 queries, 2-3 mss/year. 100% from unagented writers. Pays royalty on net price. Publishes book 1-4 years after acceptance. No simultaneous submissions. Reports in 1 month on queries, 2 months on proposals and mss. Book catalog/ms guidelines free on request.
Nonfiction: Reference, technical, textbook, health/medicine and science. "We publish highly technical books on veterinary medicine *only*. No pet books." Query. Reviews artwork/photos as part of ms package; send photocopies.

AMHERST MEDIA, 418 Homecrest Dr., Amherst NY 14226-1219. (716)874-4450. Fax: (716)874-4450. Publisher: Craig Alesse. Estab. 1974. Publishes hardcover and trade paperback originals and reprints. Averages 7 titles/year. Receives 20 submissions/year. 80% of books from first-time authors; 100% from unagented writers. Pays 5-8% royalty. Publishes book an average of 3-6 months after acceptance. Simultaneous submissions OK. Reports in 1 month. *Writer's Market* recommends allowing 2 months for reply. Book catalog for #10 SAE with 3 first class stamps. Manuscript guidelines free on request.
Nonfiction: How-to. Subjects include photography, business, sales, marketing, astronomy and video. We are looking for well-written and illustrated photo, video and astronomy books. Query. Reviews artwork/photos as part of ms package.
Tips: "Our audience is made up of beginning to advanced photographers. If I were a writer trying to market a book today, I would fill the need of a specific audience and edit in a tight manner."

ANCESTRY INCORPORATED, P.O. Box 476, Salt Lake City UT 84110-0476. (801)531-1790. Fax: (801)531-1798. Managing Editor: Ted Naanes. Estab. 1983. Publishes hardcover, trade and paperback originals. Averages 10 titles/year; receives 10-20 submissions annually. 70% of books from first-time authors; 100% of books from unagented writers. Pays 8-12% royalty or purchases mss outright. Advances are discouraged but considered if necessary. Publishes book an average of 1 year after acceptance. Simultaneous submissions OK. Query for electronic submissions. Reports in 2 months. Book catalog for 9 × 12 SAE with 2 first class stamps.
Nonfiction: How-to, reference and genealogy. Subjects include Americana; history (family and local); and hobbies (genealogy). "Our publications are aimed exclusively at the genealogist. We consider everything from short monographs to book length works on immigration, migration, record collections and heraldic topics." No mss that are not genealogical or historical. Query, or submit outline/synopsis and sample chapters. Reviews artwork/photos.
Recent Nonfiction Title: *Kentucky Ancestry,* by Roseann Reinemuth Hogan.
Tips: "Genealogical reference, how-to, and descriptions of source collections have the best chance of selling to our firm. Be precise in your description. Please, no family histories or genealogies."

‡**ANCHORAGE PRESS, INC.,** P.O. Box 8067, New Orleans LA 70182-8067. (504)283-8868. Fax: (504)866-0500. Editor: Orlin Corey. Publishes hardcover originals. Estab. 1935. Firm averages 10 titles/year. Receives 450-900 submissions/year. 50% of books from first-time authors. 80% from unagented writers. Pays 10-15% royalty on retail price. Playwrights also receive 50-70% royalties. Publishes book an average of 1 year after acceptance. Reports in 3 weeks on queries; 4 months on mss. Free book catalog and ms guidelines.
Nonfiction: Textbook and plays. Subjects include education, language/literature and plays. "We are looking for play anthologies; and texts for teachers of drama/theater (middle school and high school.)" Query. Reviews artwork/photos as part of ms package.
Recent Nonfiction Title: *Wish In One Hand, Spit in the Other,* an anthology of plays by Suzan Zeder, edited by Susan Pearson David.
Fiction: Plays of juvenile/young people's interest. Query.

AND BOOKS, 702 S. Michigan, South Bend IN 46618. (219)219-3134. Editor: Janos Szebedinszky. Estab. 1980. Publishes trade paperback originals. Averages 10 titles/year. Receives 1,000 submissions/year. 50% of books from first-time authors. 90% of books from unagented writers. Pays 6-10% royalty on retail price. Simultaneous submissions OK. Publishes book an average of 1 year after acceptance. Query for electronic submissions. Reports in up to 3 months. Book catalog for #10 SASE.
Nonfiction: Subjects include computers (consumer-level), current affairs, social justice, psychology and religion, music: jazz, blues, classical. Especially needs books on computers and electronic publishing. No biography, humor or diet books.
Tips: "Attempt to get an intro or foreword by a respected authority on your subject. Include comments by others who have reviewed your material. Research the potential market and include the results with your proposal. In other words, make every effort to communicate your knowledge of the publishing process. A little preliminary legwork and market investigation can go a long way to influence a potential publisher. No longer interested in books on sports or law."

ANDREWS AND McMEEL, 4900 Main St., Kansas City MO 64112. Editorial Director: Donna Martin. Publishes hardcover and paperback originals. Averages 30 titles/year. Pays royalty on retail price. "Query only. No unsolicited manuscripts. Areas of specialization include humor, how-to, and consumer reference books, such as *The Universal Almanac*, edited by John W. Wright." Reports in 2 months.

APPALACHIAN MOUNTAIN CLUB BOOKS, 5 Joy St., Boston MA 02108. (617)523-0636. Fax: (617)523-0722. Editor: Gordon Hardy. Estab. 1876. Publishes hardcover and trade paperback originals. Averages 8 titles/ year; receives 100 submissions annually. 50% of books from first-time authors; 95% of books from unagented writers. Publishes book an average of 6 months after receipt of acceptable ms. Simultaneous submissions OK. Query for electronic submissions. Reports in 4 months. Book brochure for 8½ × 11 SAE.
Nonfiction: How-to, reference, field guides and guidebooks. Subjects include history (Northeast, mountains), nature, outdoor recreation, conservation and travel. "We want manuscripts about the environment, mountains and their history and culture, and outdoor recreation (such as hiking, climbing, skiing, canoeing, kayaking). Destination focus on Northeast U.S." No physical fitness manuals. Query or submit outline/ synopsis and sample chapters.
Tips: "We are expanding into conservation and outdoor how-to throughout the Northeast U.S. that offers opportunities for outdoor recreation. We also will consider children's books on outdoor recreation, nature, and environmentally related subjects. Supply illustration sample for children's books."

‡APPLAUSE BOOKS, 211 W. 71st St., New York NY 10023. Managing Editor: Jonathan Dodd. Publishes hardcover and trade paperback originals and trade paperback reprints. Publishes 25 titles/year. Receives 500 queries and 400 ms/year. Pays royalty. Publishes book 8 months after acceptance of ms. Reports in 1 month on queries, 2 months on proposals, 3 months on mss. Book catalog free on request.
Nonfiction: Performing arts. All unsolicited mss returned unopened.
Recent Nonfiction Title: *Acting in Film*, by Michael Caine.

APPLEZABA PRESS, P.O. Box 4134, Long Beach CA 90804. (213)591-0015. Publisher: D.H. Lloyd. Estab. 1977. Publishes hardcover and trade paperback originals. Firm averages 4 titles/year. Receives 1,000 submissions/year. 5% of books from first-time authors; 95% from unagented writers. Pays 8-15% royalty on retail price. Publishes book average of 3 years after acceptance. Simultaneous submissions OK. Reports in 2 months. Free book catalog; ms guidelines for #10 SASE.
Nonfiction: Cooking, foods and nutrition. Query. Reviews artwork/photos as part of ms package.
Fiction: Literary and short story collections. Query or submit outline/synopsis and sample chapters.

‡ARCADE PUBLISHING, 141 Fifth Ave., New York NY 10010. (212)475-2633. Publisher: Richard Seaver. Publishes hardcover originals and trade paperback reprints. Publishes 40 titles/year. 5% of mss from first-time authors, 5% from unagented writers. Pays royalty on retail price. Offers $3,000-100,000 advance. Publishes book 12-18 months after acceptance of ms. Simultaneous submissions OK. Query for electronic submissions: "via disk—but only if accompanied by a printout." Prefers Mac compatible. Reports in 2-3 months on queries.
Nonfiction: Biography, cookbook, children's/juvenile and general nonfiction. Subjects include cooking, foods & nutrition, government/politics, history, nature/environment and travel. Query. Reviews artwork/photos as part of freelance ms package. Writers should send photocopies.
Recent Nonfiction Title: *The Struggle and the Triumph*, by Lech Walesa (autobiography/politics).
Fiction: Ethnic, historical, humor, literary, mainstream/contemporary, mystery, short story collections and suspense. Query. Agented submissions only.
Recent Fiction Title: *Texas Summer*, by Terry Southern (contemporary novel).
Poetry: "We do not publish poetry as rule; in our three-and-half years we have published only one volume of poetry." Query.
Recent Poetry Title: *The Mirrored Clubs of Hell*, by Gerrit Henry.

ARCHITECTURAL BOOK PUBLISHING CO., INC., 268 Dogwood Lane, Stamford CT 06903. (203)322-1460. Editor: Walter Frese. Estab. 1891. Averages 10 titles/year; receives 400 submissions annually. 80% of books from first-time authors; 95% of books from unagented writers. Average print order for a writer's first book is 5,000. Royalty is percentage of retail price. Publishes book an average of 10 months after acceptance. Prefers queries, outlines and 2 sample chapters with number of illustrations. Reports in 2 weeks. *Writer's Market* recommends allowing 2 months for reply.
Nonfiction: Publishes architecture, decoration, and reference books on city planning and industrial arts. Accepts nonfiction translations. Also interested in history, biography, and science of architecture and decoration. Query with outline and 2 sample chapters. Enclose SASE for return of materials.

ARCHIVES PUBLICATIONS, (formerly The Archives Press Incorporated), 334 State St., Los Altos CA 94022. (800)373-1897. Contact: Phil Wycliff. Imprints are Archives Press. Contact: Phil Wycliff; Epona Media, Contact: Hazel Pathon; Book Processor, Contact: Donna Maria Cordoba. Publishes hardcover and trade paperback originals and reprints. Publishes 15 titles/year. Each imprint publishes 2/year. Receives 200 queries/year. 70% of mss from first-time authors, 100% from unagented writers. Pays 7½-10% royalty on retail price or make outright purchase (negotiable). Offers $500-5,000 advance. Publishes book 6 months after acceptance of ms. No simultaneous submissions. Query for electronic submission. Reports in 1 month. *Writer's*

Market recommends allowing 2 months for reply. Book catalog and ms guidelines free on request.
Nonfiction: Biography, cookbook, how-to, children's/juvenile and reference. Subjects include anthropology/archaelology, art/architecture, cooking, foods and nutrition, history (Irish only), music/dance, psychology, astronomy and literary. "We are deeply committed to excellence in literature, both fiction and nonfiction. If you're not a deep thinker don't bother us." Query by mail only or submit proposal package, including 1-2 sample chapters. All unsolicited manuscripts returned unopened. No response unless queried first.
Fiction: Adventure, erotica, historical, literary, occult, religious (new age-mystical), sports and equestrian. "We take a serious look at all well presented fiction *after* query. No science fiction." Query by mail only. All unsolicited manuscripts are returned unread.
Tips: "All prospective authors subscribe to our newsletter, *The Independent Publisher*, which gives guidelines, changes, new titles and important tidbits on our style and publications philosophy. The newsletter comes out three times a year and costs $5. We can fax it to you if you prefer. Do not send a SASE. Send loose stamps and a 3×5 card or a check or money order for $3 for each submission. This defrays the cost of reading it and sending it back. Stick to the topics. We publish equestrian, rock and roll, archaeology, astronomy, anthropology and Celtica. No New Age. We emphasize Irish topics. No explicit sex or UFOs."

ARCHWAY PAPERBACKS/MINSTREL BOOKS, Imprint of Pocket Books, (formerly Archway/Minstrel Books), Dept. WM, 1230 Avenue of the Americas, New York NY 10020. (212)698-7268. Editorial Director: Patricia MacDonald. Publishes mass market paperback originals and reprints. Averages 60 titles/year. Receives 1,000 submissions/year. Pays royalty. Publishes book an average of 2 years after acceptance. Reports in 3 months. SASE for all material necessary or query not answered.
Nonfiction: Middle grade and young adult. Subjects include current popular subjects or people, sports. Query with SASE. Submit outline/synopsis and sample chapters. Reviews artwork/photos as part of ms package.
Fiction: Middle grade, young adult. Suspense thrillers for YA; mysteries, school stories, funny/scary stories, animal stories for middle grade readers. No picture books. Query/SASE. Submit outline/synopsis and sample chapters.
Recent Fiction Title: *My Teacher Is An Alien*, by Bruce Grille (young reader novel).

‡ARCsoft PUBLISHERS, P.O. Box 179, Hebron MD 21830. (410)742-9009. Publisher: Anthony R. Curtis. Estab. 1980. Publishes trade paperback originals. Averages 20 titles/year. "We now offer only 'buyout' contracts in which all rights are purchased. Typically, an advance of 20 percent is paid at contract signing and 80 percent at acceptable completion of work. Royalties are no longer offered because writers suffer under royalty contracts for small-volume technical books." Offers variable advance. Publishes book an average of 6 months after acceptance. Reports in 1 month on queries; 10 weeks on mss. Free book catalog.
Nonfiction: Technical. "We publish technical books including space science, desktop publishing, personal computers and hobby electronics, especially for beginners." Accepts nonfiction translations. Query or submit outline/synopsis and 1 sample chapter. Reviews artwork/photos as part of ms package.
Recent Nonfiction Title: *Space Almanac*, by A.R. Curtis.
Tips: "We look for the writer's ability to cover our desired subject thoroughly, writing quality and interest."

JASON ARONSON, INC., 230 Livingston St., Northvale NJ 07647-1726. (201)767-4093. Fax: (201)767-4330. Vice President: Arthur Kurzweil. Estab. 1967. Publishes hardcover originals and reprints. 90% of books are originals; 10% are reprints. Firm averages 50 titles/year. 50% of books from first-time authors. 95% from unagented writers. Pays 10-15% royalty on retail price. Publishes book an average of 1 year after acceptance. Reports in 1 month on queries. *Writer's Market* recommends allowing 2 months for reply. Free book catalog.
Nonfiction: How-to, reference, technical. Subjects include psychology and religion. "We publish in two fields: psychotherapy and Judaica. We are looking for high quality books in both fields." Query. Reviews artwork/photos as part of ms package.

ART DIRECTION BOOK COMPANY, 6th Floor, 10 E. 39th St., New York NY 10016. (212)889-6500. Editorial Director: Dan Barron. Senior Editor: Loren Bliss. Imprint is Infosource Publications. Publishes hardcover and paperback originals. Publishes 12 titles/year. Pays 10% royalty on retail price; offers average $1,000 advance. Publishes book an average of 1 year after acceptance. Reports in 3 months. Book catalog for 6×9 SASE.
Nonfiction: Commercial art, ad art how-to and textbooks. "We are interested in books for the professional advertising art field—books for art directors, designers, etc.; also entry level books for commercial and advertising art students in such fields as typography, photography, paste-up, illustration, clip-art, design, layout and graphic arts." Query with outline and 1 sample chapter. Reviews artwork/photos as part of ms package.
Recent Nonfiction Title: *American Corporate Identity #8*, by D.E. Carter.

ASIAN HUMANITIES PRESS, P.O. Box 3523, Fremont CA 94539. (510)659-8272. Fax: (510)659-0501. Editor: Lew Lancaster. Other imprint is Jain Publishing Co. (for non-Asian subjects). Estab. 1976. Publishes hardcover and trade paperback originals and reprints. Firm averages 10 titles/year. Receives 200 submissions/

year. 90% of books from unagented authors. Pays up to 6-10% royalty on net sale. Publishes book an average of 1 year after acceptance. Query for electronic submissions. Reports on queries in 1 month. Book catalog for 6×9 SAE with 2 first class stamps.

Nonfiction: Reference, textbooks and general trade books. Subjects include Asian classics (fiction and nonfiction), language/literature/poetry (Asian), philosophy/religion (Asian and East-West), psychology/spirituality (Asian and East-West), art/culture (Asian and East-West). Submit proposal package, including vita and a list of prior publications with SASE. Reviews artwork/photos as part of ms package. Writers should send photocopies.

Recent Nonfiction Title: *The Bhagavad Gita: A Scripture for the Future,* by Sacheindra K. Majundar.

ASM INTERNATIONAL, Materials Park OH 44073-0002. (216)338-5151. Fax: (216)338-4634. Acquisitions Editor: Mary Thomas Haddad. Publishes hardcover originals. Averages 25 titles/year. Pays royalty on gross revenue. Publishes book 6 months after acceptance of ms. Simultaneous submissions OK but not preferred. Query for electronic submissions. Reports in 3 months on proposals. Book catalog and ms guidelines free on request (mostly technical style issues).

Nonfiction: Technical. Subjects include engineering materials and processes and testing. Query with outline.

Tips: "We are one of the world's leading publishers of materials reference books."

ASTRO COMMUNICATIONS SERVICES, INC., (formerly ACS Publications, Inc.) P.O. Box 34487, San Diego CA 92163-4487. (619)297-9203. Editorial Director: Maritha Pottenger. Estab. 1973. Publishes trade paperback originals and reprints. Averages 8 titles/year; receives 400 submissions annually. 50% of books from first-time authors; 95% of books from unagented writers. Average print order for a writer's first book is 3,000. Pays 15% royalty "on monies received through wholesale and retail sales." No advance. Publishes book an average of 2 years after acceptance. Query for electronic submissions. Reports in 3 months. Book catalog and guidelines for 9×12 SAE with 3 first class stamps.

Nonfiction: New Age. Subjects include astrology, useful metaphysics. "Our most important market is astrology. We are seeking pragmatic, useful, immediately applicable contributions to field; prefer psychological approach. Specific ideas and topics should enhance people's lives. Research also valued. No determinism ('Saturn made me do it.'). No autobiographies. No airy-fairy 'space cadet' philosophizing. Keep it grounded, useful, opening options (not closing doors) for readers." Query or submit outline and 3 sample chapters.

Tips: "The most common mistake writers make when trying to get their work published is to send works to inappropriate publishers. We get too many submissions outside our field or contrary to our world view."

ATHENEUM CHILDREN'S BOOKS, Imprint of Macmillan, Inc., 866 3rd Ave., New York NY 10022. (212)702-7894. Vice President and editorial director: Jonathan J. Lanman. Editors: Marcia Marshall and Jean Karl. Publishes hardcover originals. Averages 60 titles/year; receives 7,000-8,000 submissions annually. 8-12% of books from first-time authors; 50% of books from unagented writers. Pays 10% royalty on retail price; offers average $2,000-3,000 advance. Publishes book an average of 18 months after acceptance. Reports in up to 3 months on outline and sample chapters. Book catalog and ms guidelines for 9½×12½ SAE with 2 first class stamps.

Nonfiction: Biography, how-to, humor, illustrated book, juvenile (pre-school through young adult) and self-help, all for juveniles. Subjects include: Americana, animals, art, business and economics, cooking and foods, health, history, hobbies, music, nature, philosophy, photography, politics, psychology, recreation, religion, sociology, sports, and travel, all for young readers. "Do remember, most publishers plan their lists as much as two years in advance. So if a topic is 'hot' right now, it may be 'old hat' by the time we could bring it out. It's better to steer clear of fads. Some writers assume juvenile books are for 'practice' until you get good enough to write adult books. Not so. Books for young readers demand just as much 'professionalism' in writing as adult books. So save those 'practice' manuscripts for class, or polish them before sending them." Query, submit outline and sample chapters.

Fiction: Adventure, ethnic, experimental, fantasy, gothic, historical, horror, humor, mainstream, mystery, romance, science fiction, suspense, and western, all in juvenile versions. "We have few specific needs except for books that are fresh, interesting and well written. Again, fad topics are dangerous, as are works you haven't polished to the best of your ability. (The competition is fierce.) We've been inundated with dragon stories (misunderstood dragon befriends understanding child), unicorn stories (misunderstood child befriends understanding unicorn), and variations of 'Ignatz the Egg' (Everyone laughs at Ignatz the egg [giraffe/airplane/accountant] because he's square [short/purple/stupid] until he saves them from the eggbeater [lion/storm/I.R.S. man] and becomes a hero). Other things we don't need at this time are safety pamphlets, ABC books, and rhymed narratives. In writing picture book texts, avoid the coy and 'cutesy.'" Query, submit outline/synopsis and sample chapters for novels; complete ms for picture books. Please do not send illustrations.

Recent Fiction Title: *One of the Boys,* by Scott Johnson.

Poetry: "At this time there is a growing market for children's poetry. However, we don't anticipate needing any for the next year or two, especially rhymed narratives."

Tips: "Our books are aimed at children from pre-school age, up through high school. We no longer publish Argo Books."

ATHENEUM PUBLISHERS, Imprint of Macmillan, Inc., Dept. WM, 866 3rd Ave., New York NY 10022. Publisher: Mr. Lee Goerner. Receives 10,000 submissions annually. 5% of books from first-time authors; 1% of books from unagented writers. Average print order for a writer's first book is 7,000. Publishes book an average of 1 year after acceptance. Simultaneous submissions OK. Electronic submissions OK, but requires hard copy also. Reports in 2 months on queries.

Nonfiction: General trade material dealing with politics, psychology, history, sports, biographies and general interest. Length: 40,000 words minimum. Query or submit outline/synopsis and a sample chapter. Include SASE.

AVALON BOOKS, Imprint of Thomas Bouregy & Co., Inc., 401 Lafayette St., New York NY 10003-7014. Vice President and Publisher: Marcia Markland. Estab. 1950. Publishes 60 titles/year.

Fiction: "We publish wholesome romances, mysteries and westerns that are sold to libraries throughout the country. Our books are read by adults as well as teenagers, and their characters are all adults. All the romances and mysteries are contemporary; all the westerns are historical." Length: 40,000 to 50,000 words. Submit first chapter and a brief, but complete summary of the book. Enclose sufficient SASE.

Tips: "We are looking for contemporary characters and fresh, contemporary plots and storylines. Every heroine should have an interesting career or profession. We do accept unagented manuscripts, and we do publish first novels. Right now we are concentrating on finding talented new mystery and romantic suspense writers."

AVANYU PUBLISHING INC., P.O. Box 27134, Albuquerque NM 87125. (505)266-6128. Fax: (505)256-9243. President: J. Brent Ricks. Estab. 1984. Publishes hardcover and trade paperback originals and reprints. Firm averages 4 titles/year. Receives 40 submissions/year. 30% of books from first-time authors. 90% from unagented writers. Pays 8% maximum royalty on wholesale price. No advance. Publishes book an average of 1 year after acceptance. Query for electronic submissions. Reports in 6 weeks. *Writer's Market* recommends allowing 2 months for reply. Book catalog for #10 SASE.

Nonfiction: Biography, illustrated book, reference, Southwest Americana. Subjects include Americana, anthropology/archaeology, art/architecture, ethnic, history, photography, regional, sociology. Query. Reviews artwork/photos as part of ms package.

Fiction: Adventure, historical, Western. Query.

Tips: "Writers have the best chance selling us history oriented books with lots of pictures, or contemporary Indian/Western art. Our audience consists of libraries, art collectors and history students."

AVERY PUBLISHING GROUP, 120 Old Broadway, Garden City Park NY 11040. (516)741-2155. Fax: (516)742-1892. Contact: Managing Editor. Estab. 1976. Publishes hardcover and trade paperback originals. Averages 40 titles/year. Receives 200-300 submissions/year. 90% of books from first-time authors; 95% from unagented writers. Pays 10% royalty on wholesale price. Publishes book an average of 1 year after acceptance. Simultaneous submissions OK. Reports in 1 week. *Writer's Market* recommends allowing 2 months for reply. Book catalog free on request.

Nonfiction: Cookbook, how-to, reference and textbook. Subjects include business and economics, child guidance/parenting, cooking, foods and nutrition, health/medicine, history, military/war, nature/environment, child birth and alternative health. Query.

Recent Nonfiction Title: *Juicing for Life*, by Cherie Calbom & Maureen Keane.

AVON BOOKS, Division of the Hearst Corp., 1350 Avenue of the Americas, New York NY 10019. (212)261-6800. Fax: (212)532-2172. Vice President/Publisher, trade paperbacks: Mark Gompertz. Vice President/Editor-in-Chief: Robert Mecoy. Estab. 1941. Publishes trade and mass market paperback originals and reprints. Averages 400 titles/year. Pay and advance are negotiable. Publishes ms an average of 2 years after acceptance. Simultaneous submissions OK. Reports in 2 months. Book catalog for SASE.

Nonfiction: How-to, popular psychology, self-help, health, history, war, sports, business/economics, biography and politics. No textbooks. Query only.

Recent Nonfiction Title: *Don't Know Much About History* (trade).

Fiction: Romance (contemporary), historical romance, science fiction, fantasy, men's adventure, suspense/thriller, mystery, and western. Submit query letter only.

Recent Fiction Title: *See Jane Run*, by Joy Fielding (mass market).

AVON FLARE BOOKS, Young Adult Imprint of Avon Books, Division of the Hearst Corp., 1350 Avenue of the Americas, New York NY 10019. (212)261-6817. Fax: (212)261-6895. Editorial Director: Ellen Krieger. Publishes mass market paperback originals and reprints. Imprint publishes 18-20 new titles annually. 25% of books from first-time authors; 15% of books from unagented writers. Pays 6-8% royalty; offers minimum $2,500 advance. Publishes book an average of 15 months after acceptance. Simultaneous submissions OK. Reports in 4 months. Book catalog and manuscript guidelines for 8×10 SAE with 5 first class stamps.

Nonfiction: General. Submit outline/synopsis and sample chapters. "*Very* selective with young adult nonfiction."

Fiction: Adventure, ethnic, humor, mainstream, mystery, romance, suspense and contemporary. "Very selective with mystery." Mss appropriate to ages 12-18. Query with sample chapters and synopsis.

Recent Fiction Title: *Live From New York*, by Alan Gelb.

Tips: "The YA market is not as strong as it was 5 years ago. We are very selective with young adult fiction. Avon does not publish picture books, nor do we use freelance readers."

BACKCOUNTRY PUBLICATIONS, Imprint of The Countryman Press, Inc., P.O. Box 175, Woodstock VT 05091. (802)457-1049. Managing Editor: Robin Dutcher-Bayer. Estab. 1973. Publishes trade paperback originals. Averages 12 titles/year. 50% of books from first-time authors; 95% from unagented writers. Pays 5-10% royalty on retail price. Offers $750 average advance. Publishes book average of 9 months after acceptance. Simultaneous submissions OK. Reports in 2 months. Free book catalog.

Nonfiction: Reference. Subjects include recreation. "We're looking for regional guides to hiking, walking, bicycling, cross-country skiing, canoeing, and fishing for all parts of the country." Submit outline and sample chapters. Reviews artwork/photos as part of ms package.

Recent Nonfiction Title: *In Rhode Island*, by Adam Fry.

Tips: "No unsolicited manuscripts please! No material is returned without SASE."

BAEN PUBLISHING ENTERPRISES, Distributed by Simon & Schuster, P.O. Box 1403, Riverdale NY 10471-0671. (212)548-3100. Editor-in-Chief: Jim Baen. Executive Editor: Toni Weisskopf. Consulting Editor: Josepha Sherman. Estab. 1983. Publishes mass market paperback originals and reprints. Averages 80-100 titles/year; receives 5,000 submissions annually. 10% of books from first-time authors; 25% of books from unagented writers. Pays 6-8% royalty on cover price. Reports in 2 weeks on partials, 1-4 months on complete mss. Queries not necessary. Ms guidelines for #10 SASE.

Fiction: Fantasy and science fiction. Submit outline/synopsis and sample chapters or (preferred) synopsis and complete ms.

Recent Fiction Title: *Prince of Sparta*, by Jerry Pournelle and S.M. Stirling.

Tips: "Our audience includes those who are interested in *hard* science fiction and quality fantasy pieces that engage the mind as well as entertain."

BAKER BOOK HOUSE COMPANY, P.O. Box 6287, Grand Rapids MI 49516-6287. Fax: (616)676-9573. Director of Publications: Allan Fisher. Assistant to the Director of Publications: Jane Dekker. Estab. 1939. Publishes hardcover and trade paperback originals. Averages 120 titles/year. 10% of books from first-time authors; 85% of books from unagented writers. Queries and proposals only. No unsolicited mss. Pays 14% royalty on net receipts. Publishes book within 1 year after acceptance. Simultaneous submissions (if so identified) OK. Reports in 2 months. Book catalog for 9×12 SAE with 6 first class stamps.

Nonfiction: Contemporary issues, women's concerns, parenting, singleness, seniors' concerns, self-help, children's books, Bible study, Christian doctrine, reference books, books for pastors and church leaders, textbooks for Christian colleges and seminaries. Query with proposal.

Recent Nonfiction Title: *Beyond Charity: A Community-Development Handbook for Christians*, by John M. Perkins.

Fiction: Novels focusing on women's concerns, mysteries. Query.

Recent Fiction Title: *A Multitude of Sins: A Suspense Novel*, by Virginia Stem Owens.

Tips: "Most of our authors and readers are evangelical Christians, and our books are purchased from Christian bookstores, mail-order retailers, and school bookstores."

● In June, 1992, Baker Book House Company purchased stock and rights to Gleneida Publishing Group. Total sales in 1992 were 50% higher than in 1991.

BALE BOOKS, Division of Bale Publications, P.O. Box 2727, New Orleans LA 70176. Editor-in-Chief: Don Bale, Jr. Estab. 1963. Publishes hardcover and paperback originals and reprints. Averages 10 titles/year; receives 25 submissions annually. 50% of books from first-time authors; 90% of books from unagented writers. Average print order for a writer's first book is 1,000. Offers standard 10-12½-15% royalty contract on wholesale or retail price; sometimes purchases mss outright for $500. Offers no advance. Publishes book an average of 3 years after acceptance. Reports in 3 months. Book catalog for #10 SAE with 2 first class stamps.

Nonfiction: Numismatics. "Our specialties are coin and stock market investment books; especially coin investment books and coin price guides. Most of our books are sold through publicity and ads in the coin newspapers. We are open to any new ideas in the area of numismatics. The writer should write for a teenage through adult level. Lead the reader by the hand like a teacher, building chapter by chapter. Our books

A bullet introduces comments by the editor of Writer's Market *indicating special information about the listing.*

sometimes have a light, humorous treatment, but not necessarily. We look for good English, construction and content, and sales potential." Submit outline and 3 sample chapters.

BALLANTINE BOOKS, See listing for Random House, Inc.

‡**BANDANNA BOOKS**, 319-B Anacapa St., Santa Barbara CA 93101. (805)962-9915. Publisher: Sasha Newborn. Imprints are Humanist Classics, Wordbooks. Firm publishes trade paperback originals and reprints. Publishes 4 titles/year. Receives 50 queries, 20 mss/year. 20% of mss from first-time authors, 100% from unagented writers. Pays 5-10% royalty on retail price (a few books gratis). Offers $50-200 advance. Publishes book 9 months after acceptance. Simultaneous submissions OK. Query for electronic submissions. Reports in 1 month on proposals. Book catalog free on request.
Nonfiction: Illustrated book and textbook. Subjects include education, government/politics, history, language/literature, philosophy, translation and women's issues/studies. "Bandanna Books seeks to humanize the classics and language-learning materials in non-sexist, modernized translations and plain-English texts, suitable for advanced high-school and college classes." Submit outline and 1 or 2 sample chapters. Reviews artwork/photos as part freelance ms package. Writers should send photocopies.
Tips: "Our readers are age 16-22, high school or college age, liberal arts orientation. A well-thought-out proposal is important, even if unconventional. Read the classics."

‡**B&B PUBLISHING, INC.**, P.O. Box 393, Fontana WI 53125. (414)275-9474. Contact: Jean Blashfield Black. Publishes hardcover and trade paperback originals. Publishes 15 titles/year. Receives 200 queries, 100 mss/year. 10% of mss from first-time authors; 100% from unagented writers. Pays 2½-5% royalty on wholesale price or makes outright purchase for $2,000-5,000. Offers $2,000 advance. Publishes book 1 year after acceptance. Simultaneous submissions OK. Query for electronic submissions; disk only. Prefers Macintosh or PC in Microsoft Word. SASE. Reports in 1 month on queries and proposals, 3 months on mss. Book catalog/ms guidelines free on request.
Nonfiction: Children's/juvenile, reference, Americana, history, military/war, nature/environment, science and trivia. "We are seeking nonfiction environment-related material with series potential." Query. Reviews artwork/photos as part of ms package. Writers should send photocopies.
Recent Nonfiction Title: *Cars, An Environmental Challenge*, by Terri Willis and Wallace B. Black (environmental/juvenile).
Tips: Audience is general trade schools and public library.

BANKS-BALDWIN LAW PUBLISHING CO., 1904 Ansel Rd., Cleveland OH 44106. (216)721-7373. Fax: (216)721-8055. Editor-in-Chief: P.J. Lucier. Acquisitions Supervisor: Eve Greene. Estab. 1804. Publishes law books and services in a variety of formats. Averages 10 new titles/year; receives 10-15 submissions annually. 5% of books from first-time authors; 90% of books from unagented writers. "Most titles include material submitted by outside authors." Pays 8-16% on net revenue, or fee. Offers advance not to exceed 25% of anticipated royalty or fee. Publishes book an average of 18 months after acceptance, 3 months after receipt of ms. Query for electronic submissions. Reports in 3 weeks on queries. *Writer's Market* recommends allowing 2 months for reply. Free book catalog; ms guidelines for SASE.
Nonfiction: Reference, law/legal. Query.
Tips: "We publish books for attorneys, government officials and professionals in allied fields. Trends in our field include more interest in handbooks, less in costly multi-volume sets; electronic publishing. A writer has the best chance of selling us a book on a hot new topic of law. Check citations and quotations carefully."

BANTAM BOOKS, Subsidiary of Bantam Doubleday Dell, Dept. WM, 1540 Broadway, New York NY 10036. (212)354-6500. Imprints are Spectra, Crime Lane, New Age, Domain, Fanfair, Bantam Classics, Bantam New Fiction, Loveswept, New Sciences, Books for Young Readers. Publishes hardcover, trade paperback and mass market paperback originals, trade paperback, mass market paperback reprints and audio. Publishes 400 titles/year. Buys no books from unagented writers. Pays 4-15% royalty. Publishes book an average of 1 year after ms is accepted. Simultaneous submissions OK. Reports in 2 months.
Nonfiction: Biography, coffee table book, how-to, cookbook, humor, illustrated book, juvenile and self-help. Subjects include Americana, anthropology/archaelogy, business/economics, child guidance/parenting, computers and electronics, cooking, foods and nutrition, gay/lesbian, government/politics, health/medicine, history, language/literature, military/war, money/finance, music/dance, philosophy, psychology, religion, science, sociology, sports and travel. Query or submit outline/synopsis. All unsolicited mss are returned unopened.
Recent Nonfiction Title: *It Doesn't Take a Hero*, by General H. Norman Schwarzkopf.
Fiction: Adventure, fantasy, feminist, gay/lesbian, historical, horror, juvenile, literary, mainstream/contemporary, mystery, romance, science fiction, suspense, western, young adult. Query or submit outline/synopsis. All unsolicited mss are returned unopened.
Recent Fiction Title: *The Scorpio Illusion*, by Robert Ludlum.

BANTAM DOUBLEDAY DELL, 1540 Broadway, New York NY 10036. Divisions include Bantam Books, Doubleday Books, and Dell Books. Imprints include Doubleday Books for Young Readers, Delacorte Press, and Delta Books.

BARRON'S EDUCATIONAL SERIES, INC., 250 Wireless Blvd., Hauppauge NY 11788. Fax: (516)434-3723. Director of Acquisitions: Grace Freedson. Publishes hardcover and paperback originals and software. Publishes 170 titles/year. 10% of books from first-time authors; 90% of books from unagented writers. Pays royalty, based on both wholesale and retail price. Publishes book an average of 1 year after acceptance. Simultaneous submissions OK. Reports in 6-8 months. Free catalog.
Nonfiction: Adult education, art, business, cookbooks, crafts, foreign language, review books, guidance, pet books, travel, literary guides, parenting, health, juvenile, young adult sports, test preparation materials and textbooks. Reviews artwork/photos as part of package. Query or submit outline/synopsis and 2-3 sample chapters. Accepts nonfiction translations.
Recent Nonfiction Title: *Career Selector 2001*, by James Gonyea.
Tips: "The writer has the best chance of selling us a book that will fit into one of our series."

BAYWOOD PUBLISHING CO., INC., 26 Austin Ave., Amityville NY 11701. (516)691-1270. Fax: (516)691-1770. Publishes 25 titles/year. Pays 7-15% royalty on retail price. Publishes book 1 year after acceptance of ms. Book list and ms guidelines free on request.
Nonfiction: Technical and scholarly. Subjects include anthropology/archaeology, computers and electronics, gerontology, imagery, labor relations, education, death and dying, drug, nature/environment, psychology, public health/medicine, sociology, technical communications and women's issues/studies. Submit outline/synopsis and sample chapters.

‡BEACON HILL PRESS OF KANSAS CITY, Book division of Nazarene Publishing House, 6401 The Paseo, Kansas City MO 64131. Fax: (816)333-1748. Coordinator: Bonnie Perry. Estab. 1912. Publishes hardcover and paperback originals. Averages 50-60 titles/year. Offers "standard contract (sometimes flat rate purchase). Advance royalty (10% of retail) is paid on first 1,000 copies at publication date. On standard contract, pays 12% on net sales on first 10,000 copies and 14% on subsequent copies at the end of each calendar year." Publishes book an average of 1½-2 years after acceptance. Reports in up to 6 months unless immediately returned. "Book Committee meets quarterly to select from the manuscripts which will be published."
Nonfiction: Inspirational, Bible-based. Doctrinally must conform to the evangelical, Wesleyan tradition. Conservative view of Bible. No autobiography, poetry, devotional collections, or children's picture books. Accent on holy living; encouragement in daily Christian life. Contemporary issues. Popular style books usually under 128 pages. Query. Textbooks "almost exclusively done on assignment." Full ms or outline/sample chapters. Length: 20,000-40,000 words.
Recent Nonfiction Title: *How to Go to Work on Your Faith*, by Jerry Ramey with Ed Stewart.
Fiction: Limited wholesome, inspirational fiction.
Recent Fiction Title: *Father of the Fatherless*, by Margaret E. Kelehner.

BEACON PRESS, 25 Beacon St., Boston MA 02108. (617)742-2110. Fax: (617)723-3097. Director: Wendy J. Strothman. Estab. 1854. Publishes hardcover originals and paperback reprints. Averages 50 titles/year; receives 4,000 submissions annually. 10% of books from first-time authors; 70% of books from unagented writers. Average print order for a writer's first book is 3,000. Offers royalty on net retail price; advance varies. Publishes book an average of 1 year after acceptance. Simultaneous submissions OK. Return of materials not guaranteed without SASE. Reports in 2 months.
Nonfiction: General nonfiction including works of original scholarship, religion, women's studies, philosophy, current affairs, anthropology, environmental concerns, African-American studies, gay and lesbian studies. Query or submit outline/synopsis and sample chapters.
Recent Nonfiction Title: *Race Matters*, Cornel West.
Tips: "We probably accept only one or two manuscripts from an unpublished pool of 4,000 submissions per year. No fiction, children's book, or poetry submissions invited. Authors should have academic affiliation."

BEAR AND CO., INC., P.O. Box 2860, Santa Fe NM 87504-2860. (505)983-9868. Vice President, Editorial: Barbara Clow. Estab. 1978. Publishes trade paperback originals. Averages 12 titles/year. Receives 6,000 submissions/year. 20% of books from first-time authors; 90% of books from unagented writers. Pays 10% royalty on net. Publishes book an average of 18 months after acceptance. Query for electronic submissions. Reports in 1 month on queries. *Writer's Market* recommends allowing 2 months for reply. "No response without SASE." Book catalog for 9×12 SAE with 3 first class stamps.
Nonfiction: Illustrated books, science, theology, mysticism, religion and ecology. "We publish books to 'heal and celebrate the earth.' Our interest is in New Age, western mystics, new science, ecology. We are not interested in how-to, self-help, etc. Our readers are people who are open to new ways of looking at the world. They are spiritually oriented but not necessarily religious; interested in healing of the earth, peace issues, and receptive to New Age ideas." Query or submit outline and sample chapters. Reviews artwork/photos as part of ms package.

Recent Nonfiction Title: *Bringers of the Dawn*, by Barbara Maaciniak.
Tips: "We have continued to publish 12 titles/year, instead of going to 15-20 at this point. We have *increased* publicity and marketing work, and our sales have not dropped."

BEHRMAN HOUSE INC., 235 Watchung Ave., W. Orange NJ 07052-9827. (201)669-0447. Fax: (201)669-9769. Projects Editor: Adam Siegel. Managing Editor: Adam Bengal. Estab. 1921. Publishes Jewish nonfiction-history, Bible, philosophy, holidays, ethics—for children and adults. Averages 20 titles/year. Receives 200 submissions/year. 20% of books from first-time authors; 95% from unagented writers. Pays 2-10% on wholesale price or retail price. Buys some mss outright for $500-10,000. Offers $1,000 average advance. Publishes book an average of 18 months after acceptance. Simultaneous submissions OK. Reports in 2 months. Free book catalog.
Nonfiction: Juvenile (1-18), reference and textbook. Subjects include religion. "We want Jewish textbooks for the El-Hi market." Query with outline and sample chapters.

‡FREDERIC C. BEIL, PUBLISHER, INC., 414 Tattnall St., Savannah GA 31401. (912)233-2446. Editor: Mary Ann Bowman. Publishes hardcover originals and reprints. Publishes 11 titles/year. Receives 200 queries and 9 mss/year. 15% of mss from first-time authors, 100% from unagented writers. Pays 7½% royalty on retail price. Publishes book 20 months after acceptance. Simultaneous submissions OK. Query for electronic submissions. Reports in 1 month on queries. Book catalog free on request.
Nonfiction: Biography, illustrated book, general trade and reference. Subjects include art/architecture, history, language/literature, book arts, regional and religion. Query. Reviews artwork/photos as part of freelance mss package. Writers should send photocopies.
Recent Nonfiction Title: *Savannah: A History of Her People Since 1733*, by Preston Russell and Barbara Hines (history).
Fiction: Historical and literary. Query.
Recent Fiction Title: *A Memoir of Mary Ann*, Flannery O'Connor.

THE BENJAMIN COMPANY, INC., 21 Dupont Ave., White Plains NY 10605-3537. (914)997-0111. Fax: (914)997-7214. President: Ted Benjamin. Estab. 1953. Publishes hardcover and paperback originals. Averages 5-10 titles/year. 90-100% of books from unagented writers. "Usually commissions author to write specific book; seldom accepts proffered manuscripts." Publishes book an average of 6 months after acceptance. Buys mss by outright purchase. Offers advance. Simultaneous submissions OK. Query for electronic submissions. Reports in 2 months.
Nonfiction: Business/economics, cookbooks, cooking and foods, health, hobbies, how-to, self-help, sports and consumerism. "Ours is a very specialized kind of publishing—for clients (industrial and association) to use in promotional, PR, or educational programs. If an author has an idea for a book and close connections with a company that might be interested in using that book, we will be very interested in working together with the author to 'sell' the program and the idea of a special book for that company. Once published, our books often get trade distribution through a distributing publisher, so the author generally sees the book in regular book outlets as well as in the special programs undertaken by the sponsoring company. We do not encourage submission of manuscripts. We usually commission an author to write for us. The most helpful thing an author can do is to let us know what he or she has written, or what subjects he or she feels competent to write about. We will contact the author when our needs indicate that the author might be the right person to produce a needed manuscript." Query.
Recent Nonfiction Title: *GoldStar Micro-Convection Cookbook; Pepper People*, (for McCormick & Company).

ROBERT BENTLEY, INC., Automotive Publishers, 1000 Massachusetts Ave., Cambridge MA 02138. (617)547-4170. Publisher: Michael Bentley. Estab. 1949. Publishes hardcover and trade paperback originals and reprints. Publishes 15-20 titles/year. 20% of books are from first-time authors; 95% from unagented writers. Pays 10-15% royalty on net price; or makes outright purchase. Advances negotiable. Publishes book an average of 1 year after acceptance. Query for electronic submissions. Reports in 3-6 weeks. Book catalog and ms guidelines for 8½×11 SAE with 4 first class stamps.
Nonfiction: How-to, technical, theory of operation, coffee table. Automotive subjects only; this includes motor sports. Query or submit outline and sample chapters. Reviews artwork/photos as part of manuscript package.
Recent Nonfiction Title: *The Jeep Owner's Bible: A Hands-on Guide to Getting the Most From Your Jeep*, by Moses Ludel (automotive).
Tips: "We are excited about the possibilities and growth in the automobile enthusiast book market. Our audience is composed of serious and intelligent automobile, sports car, or racing enthusiasts, automotive technicians and high performance tuners."

THE BERKLEY PUBLISHING GROUP, Publishers of Berkley/Berkley Trade Paperbacks/Jove/Diamond/Pacer/Ace Science Fiction, 200 Madison Ave., New York NY 10016. (212)951-8800. Editor-in-Chief: Leslie Gelbman. Publishes paperback originals and reprints. Publishes approximately 800 titles/year. Pays 4-10% royalty

on retail price; offers advance. Publishes book an average of 2 years after acceptance.
Nonfiction: How-to, family life, business, health, nutrition and true crime.
Fiction: Mystery, historical, mainstream, suspense, western, romance and science fiction. Submit outline/synopsis and first 3 chapters for Ace Science Fiction only. No other unsolicited mss accepted.
Tips: "No longer seeking adventure or occult fiction."

‡BERKSHIRE HOUSE PUBLISHERS, INC., P.O. Box 297, Stockbridge MA 01262. President: Jean J. Rousseau. Publishes 12-15 titles/year. Receives 100+ queries and 6 mss/year. 50% of mss from first-time authors, 100% from unagented writers. Pays 5-10% royalty on retail price. Offers $500-5,000 advance. Publishes book 6-12 months after acceptance. Simultaneous submissions OK. Query for electronic submissions. Reports in 1 month on proposals. Book catalog free on request.
Nonfiction: Biography, cookbook. Subjects include Americana, history, nature/environment, recreation (outdoors), wood crafts and regional. "All our books have a strong Berkshires or New England orientation—no others, please. To a great extent, we choose our topics then commission the authors, but we don't discourage speculative submissions. We just don't accept many. Don't overdo it; a well-written outline proposal is more useable than a full manuscript. Also, include a c.v. with other writing credits." Submit outline proposal and c.v. with writing credits.
Tips: "Our readers are literate, active, prosperous, interested in travel, especially in selected 'Great Destinations' areas and outdoor activities and cooking."

BETHEL PUBLISHING, Subsidiary of Missionary Church, Inc., 1819 S. Main St., Elkhart IN 46516-4299. (219)293-8585. Fax: (219)522-5670. Executive Director: Rev. Richard Oltz. Estab. 1903. Publishes trade paperback originals and reprints. Averages 5 titles/year. Receives 250 submissions/year. 80% of books from first-time authors, 90% from unagented writers.Pays 5-10% royalties. Offers $250 average advance. Publishes book an average of 1 year after acceptance. Simultaneous submissions OK. Reports in 2 months. Book catalog for 9×12 SAE with 3 first class stamps.
Nonfiction: Reference. Subjects include religion. Reviews artwork/photos as part of ms package. Query.
Fiction: Adventure, religious, suspense, young adult. Books must be evangelical in approach. No occult, gay/lesbian or erotica. Query.
Tips: "Our audience is made up of Christian families with children. If I were a writer trying to market a book today, I would find out what publisher specializes in the type of book I have written."

BETTER HOMES AND GARDENS BOOKS, Division of the Meredith Corporation, 1100 Walnut St., Des Moines IA 50309-3400. Fax: (515)284-2446. Editorial Director and Vice President: Elizabeth P. Rice. Estab. 1930. Publishes hardcover and trade paperback originals. Averages 40 titles/year. "Although many of our books are produced by on-staff editors, we often buy book-length manuscripts from outside authors. We also use freelance writers on assignment for sections or chapters of books already in progress." Reports in 6 weeks. *Writer's Market* recommends allowing 2 months for reply.
Nonfiction: "We publish nonfiction in many family and home-service categories, including gardening, decorating and remodeling, crafts, money management, handyman's topics, cooking and nutrition, Christmas activities, and other subjects of home-service value. Emphasis is on how-to and on stimulating people to action. We require concise, factual writing. Audience is comprised of readers with home and family as their main center of interest. Style should be informative and lively with a straightforward approach. Stress the positive. Emphasis is entirely on reader service. Because most of our books are produced by on-staff editors, we're less interested in book-length manuscripts than in hearing from freelance writers with solid expertise in gardening, do-it-yourself, health/fitness, and home decorating. We have no need at present for cookbooks or craft books. The Executive Editor recommends careful study of specific Better Homes and Gardens Books titles before submitting material." Prefers outline and sample chapters. *"Please include SASE with appropriate return postage."*
Tips: "Writers often fail to familiarize themselves with the catalog/backlist of the publishers to whom they are submitting. We expect heavier emphasis on health/fitness, gardening and do-it-yourself titles. But, again, we're most interested in hearing from freelance writers with subject expertise in these areas or in receiving queries for book-length manuscripts. Queries/mss may be routed to other editors in the publishing group."

BETTERWAY BOOKS, (formerly Betterway Publications, Inc.), Imprint of F&W Publications, 1507 Dana Ave., Cincinnati OH 45207. (513)531-2222. Editors: David Lewis, William Brohaugh. Estab. 1982. Publishes hardcover and trade paperback originals, and trade paperback reprints. Averages 30 titles/year. Pays 10% royalty on net receipts. Simultaneous (if so advised) submissions OK. Publishes book an average of 12-18 months after acceptance. Reports in 2 months. Book catalog for 9×12 SAE with 6 first-class stamps.
Nonfiction: How-to, illustrated book, reference and self-help in eight categories. Direct queries for these categories to David Lewis: home building and remodeling, woodworking, small business and personal finance, and hobbies and collectibles. Direct queries for these categories to William Brohaugh: sports and recreation, reference books and handbooks (including genealogy), lifestyle (including home organization), and theater and the performing arts. "Betterway books are instructional books that are to be *used*. We like specific step-by-step advice, charts, illustrations, and clear explanations of the activities and projects the books describe.

We are interested mostly in original material, but we will consider republishing self-published nonfiction books and good instructional or reference books that have gone out of print before their time. Send a sample copy, sales information, and reviews, if available. If you have a good idea for a reference book that can be updated annually, try us. We're willing to consider freelance compilers of such works." No cookbooks, diet/exercise, psychology self-help, health or parenting books. Query or submit outline and sample chapters. Reviews artwork/photos as part of ms package.

● Betterway was formerly located in Crozet, Virginia, but was recently purchased by F&W Publications. Betterway no longer publishes juvenile books under its Shoe Tree Press imprint.

Recent Nonfiction Title: *How to Have a Fabulous, Romantic Honeymoon on a Budget,* by Diane Warner.

Tips: "Keep the imprint name well in mind when submitting ideas to us. What is the 'better way' you're proposing? How will readers benefit *immediately* from the instruction and information you're giving them?"

‡BICYCLE BOOKS, INC., P.O. Box 2038, Mill Valley CA 94942. (415)381-2515. Editor: Rob van der Plas. Estab. 1985. Publishes hardcover and trade paperback originals. Firm averages 6 titles/year. Receives 20 submissions/year. 20% of books are from first-time authors. 50% from unagented writers. Pays 7½-15% royalty. Publishes book an average of 1 year after acceptance. Simultaneous submissions OK. Query for electronic submissions. Reports in 2 months. Book catalog free on request.

Nonfiction: How-to and technical. Subjects include recreation, sports, travel and bicycle-related titles only. "Bicycle travel manuscripts must include route descriptions and maps. Please, do not send anything outside the practical how-to field." Submit complete ms. Artwork/photos essential as part of the freelance manuscript package.

Tips: "Writers have a good chance selling us books with better and more illustrations and a systematic treatment of the subject. Our audience: sports/health/fitness conscious adults; cyclists and others interested in technical aspects. If I were a writer trying to market a book today, I would first check what is on the market and ask myself whether I am writing something that is not yet available and wanted."

‡BLACK SPARROW PRESS, 24 10th St., Santa Rosa CA 95401. (707)579-4011. Assistant to Publisher: Michele Filshie. Estab. 1966. Publishes hardcover and trade paperback originals and reprints. Averages 12 titles/year. 15% of books from first-time authors; 75% from unagented writers. Pays 5-10% royalty on retail price. Publishes book an average of 1 year after acceptance. Simultaneous submissions OK. Reports in 1 month on queries; 2 months on mss. Book catalog free on request.

Nonfiction: Subjects include language/literature. No how-to, cookbook, juvenile, self-help. Query.

Recent Nonfiction Title: *Looking for Genet,* by Alfred Chester (literary essays and reviews).

Fiction: Literary, feminist, gay/lesbian, short story collections. We generally solicit from authors we are interested in. "We only publish 12 new books a year so our schedule is quickly filled." No genre such as romance, westerns, etc. Query.

Recent Fiction Title: *A Brief History of Camouflage,* by Thaisa Frank (stories).

Poetry: "We generally solicit from authors we are interested in." No light verse, nonsense verse, limmerick, traditional rhymed verse. Submit 5 samples.

Recent Poetry Title: *According to Her Contours,* by Nancy Boutilier.

JOHN F. BLAIR, PUBLISHER, 1406 Plaza Dr., Winston-Salem NC 27103-1470. (919)768-1374. Fax: (919)768-9194. Editor: Carolyn Sakowski. Estab. 1954. Publishes hardcover originals and trade paperbacks. Receives 2,000 submissions annually. 20-30% of books from first-time authors; 90% of books from unagented writers. Average print order for a writer's first book is 3,500-5,000. Royalty negotiable. Publishes book an average of 1-1½ years after acceptance. Query for electronic submissions. Reports in 3 months. Book catalog and ms guidelines for 9 × 12 SAE with 5 first class stamps.

Nonfiction: Especially interested in well-researched adult biography and history books dealing with the Southeastern United States. Also interested in environment, civil war, outdoors, travel and Americana; query on other nonfiction topics. Looks for utility and significance. Submit outline and first 3 chapters. Reviews artwork/photos as part of ms package.

Fiction: "We are interested only in material related to the Southeastern United States." No category fiction, juvenile fiction, picture books or poetry.

‡BLOCKBUSTER BOOKS, INC., 2131 Hollywood Blvd., Hollywood FL 33020-6750. (305)925-5242. Fax: (305)925-5244. Acquisitions Editor: George Sheldon. Estab. 1943. Imprints include Fell Publishers, Inc., Compact Books, Inc. Publishes trade paperback originals and hardcover and trade paperback reprints. Firm averages 20 titles/year. Receives 2,000 submissions/year. 50% of books from first-time authors. 75% from unagented writers. Pays 6-10% royalty. Publishes book an average of 1 year after acceptance. Reports in 3-6 months on queries. Book catalog for 9 × 12 SAE with 4 first class stamps. Manuscript guidelines for #10 SASE.

Nonfiction: Coffee table book, cookbook, how-to, self-help. Subjects include animals, business and economics, child guidance/parenting, cooking, foods & nutrition, money/finance, religion, sports. "Blockbuster has published over 1,500 books to date. We are looking for mass market topics published in trade format. We are interested only in the eight topics of specialization that Blockbuster is known for." Reviews artwork/photos as part of freelance ms package.

Recent Nonfiction Title: *Help Your Child Excel in Math*, by Margaret Borge and Phillip Gibbons (Education/Family).

‡**BLUE BIRD PUBLISHING**, #306, 1713 E. Broadway, Tempe AZ 85282. (602)968-4088. Fax: (602)831-1829. Publisher: Cheryl Gorder. Estab. 1985. Publishes trade paperback originals. Firm averages 6 titles/year. 50% of books from first-time authors. 100% from unagented writers. Pays 10% royalty on wholesale price; 15% on retail price. Publishes book an average of 9 months after acceptance. Simultaneous submissions OK. Reports in 3 months. Book catalog and ms guidelines for #10 SASE.
Nonfiction: How-to and reference. Subjects include child guidance/parenting, education (especially home education) and sociology (current social issues). "The home schooling population in the U.S. is exploding. We have a strong market for anything that can be targeted to this group: home education manuscripts, parenting guides, curriculum ideas. We would also like to see complete nonfiction manuscripts in current issues, how-to topics." Submit complete ms. Reviews artwork/photos as part of ms package.
Recent Nonfiction Title: *Survival Guide to Step-Parenting*.
Tips: "We are interested if we see a complete manuscript that is aimed toward a general adult nonfiction audience. We are impressed if the writer has really done his homework and the manuscript includes photos, artwork, graphs, charts, and other graphics." Please do not send fiction or short stories.

BLUE DOLPHIN PUBLISHING, INC., P.O. Box 1908, Nevada City CA 95959-1908. (916)265-6925. Fax: (916)265-0787. Imprint is Pelican Pond Publishing (health and ecology titles). Publisher: Paul M. Clemens. Estab. 1985. Publishes hardcover and trade paperback originals. Firm averages 8 titles/year. Receives over 3,000 submissions/year. 75% of books from first-time authors. 90% from unagented writers. Pays 10% on wholesale price. Publishes book an average of 6-9 months after acceptance. Simultaneous submissions OK. Query for electronic submissions. Reports in 1 month on queries; "longer with books we're considering more closely." Please send SASE with query. Free book catalog.
Nonfiction: Biography, cookbook, how-to, humor and self-help. Subjects include anthropology/archaeology, cooking, foods and nutrition, ecology, education, health/medicine, psychology and comparative religion. "We are interested primarily in self-help psychology, health and the environment, comparative spiritual traditions, including translations." Submit outline and sample chapters with SASE. Reviews artwork as part of package.
Recent Nonfiction Title: *Mary's Message to the World*, by Annie Kirkwood.
Poetry: "We will only consider previously published authors of some merit or translations of noted works." Submit complete ms.
Tips: "Our audience is the concerned person interested in self-growth and awareness for oneself and the planet."

‡**BLUE POPPY PRESS**, 1775 Linden Ave., Boulder CO 80304. (303)442-0796. Editor-in-Chief: Bob Flaws. Publishes trade paperback originals. Publishes 8-10 titles/year. Receives 6-10 queries and 5-8 mss/year. 10-15% of mss from first-time authors; 100% from unagented writers. Pays 10-15% royalty "of sales price at all discount levels." Publishes book 6-10 months after acceptance. Simultaneous submissions OK. Query for electronic submissions. Prefers WordPerfect 3.5″ disks. Reports in 1 month. Book catalog free on request. Manuscript guidelines for #10 SASE.
Nonfiction: Self-help, technical, textbook, health/medicine, women's issues/studies. "Books must be related to Chinese/Oriental medicine, philosophy, history, culture, etc." Submit outline and 1 sample chapter. Reviews artwork/photos as part of ms package "if part of the whole, or necessary to an understanding of the overall project."
Recent Nonfiction Title: *The Medical I Ching*, by Mike Shima (I Ching for use by healthcare practioners).
Tips: Audience is "people interested in alternatives in healthcare, preventive medicine, Chinese philosophy and medicine."

BNA BOOKS, Division of The Bureau of National Affairs, Inc., 1250 23rd St. NW, Washington DC 20037-1165. (202)833-7470. Fax: (202)833-7490. Contact: Acquisitions Manager. Estab. 1929. Publishes hardcover and softcover originals. Averages 35 titles/year. Receives 200 submissions/year. 20% of books from first-time authors; 95% of books from unagented writers. Pays 5-15% royalty on net cash receipts; offers $500 average advance. Simultaneous submissions OK. Publishes book an average of 1 year after acceptance. Reports in 3 months on queries. Free book catalog and ms guidelines.
Nonfiction: Reference and professional/scholarly. Subjects include business law and regulation, environment and safety, legal practice, labor relations and human resource management. No biographies, bibliographies, cookbooks, religion books, humor or trade books. Submit detailed table of contents or outline.
Tips: "Our audience is made up of practicing lawyers and business executives; managers, federal, state, and local government administrators; unions; and libraries. We look for authoritative and comprehensive works on subjects of interest to executives, professionals, and managers, that relate to the interaction of government and business."

THE BOLD STRUMMER LTD., 20 Turkey Hill Circle, P.O. Box 2037, Westport CT 06880-2037. (203)259-3021. Fax: (203)259-7369. Contact: Nicholas Clarke. Publishes hardcover and trade paperback originals and reprints. Publishes 6-8 titles/year. Receives 5 queries and 2 mss/year. 50% of mss from first-time authors, 100% from unagented writers. Pays 10% royalty on retail price. Publishes book 6 months after acceptance of ms. Query for electronic submissions. Book catalog and ms guidelines free on request.
Nonfiction: Music with an emphasis on guitar and piano-related books. Query. Writers should send photocopies.
Tips: "The Bold Strummer Ltd, or our associate publisher Pro/Am Music resources, publishes most good quality work that is offered in our field(s). BSL publishes guitar and related instrument books (guitar, violin, drums). Bold Strummer has also become a leading source of books about Flamenco. Pro/AM specializes in piano books, composer biography, etc. Very narrow niche publishers."

BONUS BOOKS, INC., 160 E. Illinois St., Chicago IL 60611. (312)467-0580. Associate Editor: Ann Barthel. Estab. 1985. Publishes hardcover and trade paperback originals and reprints. Averages 30 titles/year. Receives 400-500 submissions/year. 40% of books from first-time authors; 60% from unagented writers. Pays 6-10% royalty on wholesale price. Advances are not frequent. Publishes book an average of 8 months after acceptance. Simultaneous submissions OK "if informed they are such." Query for electronic submissions. Reports in 2 months on queries. Book catalog free on request. All submissions and queries must include SASE.
Nonfiction: Biography, coffee table book, how-to. Subjects include business and economics, foods and nutrition, government/politics, health/medicine, money/finance, recreation, true crime, sports and women's issues/studies. Query with outline and sample chapters. Reviews artwork/photos as part of ms package.
Recent Nonfiction Title: *Ron Santo: For Love of Ivy*, by Ron Santo with Randy Minkoff (sports autobiography).

BOOKCRAFT, INC., 1848 W. 2300 S., Salt Lake City UT 84119. (801)972-6180. Editorial Manager: Cory H. Maxwell. Estab. 1942. Publishes mainly hardcover originals and reprints. Pays standard 7½-10-12½-15% royalty on retail price; rarely gives advance. Averages 40-45 titles/year; receives 500-600 submissions annually. 20% of books from first-time authors; virtually 100% of books from unagented writers. Publishes book an average of 6 months after acceptance. Reports in about 3 months. Will send general information to prospective authors on request; ms guidelines for #10 SASE.
Nonfiction: "We publish for members of The Church of Jesus Christ of Latter-Day Saints (Mormons) and do not distribute to the national market. All our books are closely oriented to the faith and practices of the LDS church, and we will be glad to review such mss. Those which have merely a general religious appeal are not acceptable. Ideal book lengths range from about 100 to 300 pages or so, depending on subject, presentation, and age level. We look for a fresh approach—rehashes of well-known concepts or doctrines not acceptable. Mss should be anecdotal unless truly scholarly or on a specialized subject. We do not publish anti-Mormon works. We also publish short and moderate length books for children and young adults, and fiction as well as nonfiction. These reflect LDS principles without being 'preachy'; must be motivational. 30,000-45,000 words is about the right length, though good, longer mss are not ruled out. We publish only 5 or 6 new juvenile titles annually. No poetry, plays, personal philosophizings, or family histories." Query. "Include contents page with manuscript."
Fiction: Should be oriented to LDS faith and practices.
Recent Fiction Title: *The Work and the Glory: Truth Will Prevail*, by Gerald N. Land.
Tips: "The competition in the area of fiction is much more intense than it has ever been before. We receive two or three times as many quality fiction manuscripts as we did even as recently as five years ago."

‡THE BORGO PRESS, P.O. Box 2845, San Bernardino CA 92406-2845. (714)884-5813. Fax: (909)888-4942. Publisher: Robert Reginald. Associate Publisher: Mary A. Burgess. Editor: Daryl F. Mallett. Estab. 1975. Publishes hardcover and paperback originals. Averages 150 titles/year, of which 120 are imported or distributed books; receives 500 submissions annually. 5% of books from first-time authors; 100% of books from unagented writers. Pays royalty on retail price: "10% of gross." No advance. Publishes book an average of 3 years after acceptance. "99% of our sales go to the academic library market; we do not sell to the trade (i.e., bookstores)." Query for electronic submissions. Reports in 3 months. Book catalog and writer's guidelines for 9 × 12 SAE with 6 first class stamps.
Nonfiction: Publishes literary critiques, bibliographies, historical research, film critiques, theatrical research, interview volumes, biographies, social studies, political science, and reference works for the academic library market only. Query with letter or outline/synopsis and 1 sample chapter. "All of our proprietary books,

Market conditions are constantly changing! If this is 1995 or later, buy the newest edition of Writer's Market *at your favorite bookstore or order directly from Writer's Digest Books.*

without exception, are published in open-ended, numbered, monographic series. Do not submit proposals until you have looked at actual copies of recent Borgo Press publications (*not our catalog*). We are *not* a market for fiction, poetry, popular nonfiction, artwork, or anything else except scholarly monographs in the humanities and social sciences. We discard unsolicited manuscripts from outside of our subject fields that are not accompanied by SASE. The vast majority of proposals we receive are clearly unsuitable and are a waste of both our time and the prospective author's."

Recent Nonfiction Title: *The Catholic Priest*, by Bishop Karl Prüter.

Tips: "We are currently buying comprehensive, annotated bibliographies of twentieth-century writers; these must be produced to a strict series format (available for SASE and 3 first class stamps). Proposals for *The Milford Series: Popular Writers of Today* series of literary critiques should go to the series editor, Dr. Dale Salwak, Dept. of English, Citrus College, 1000 W. Foothill Blvd., Glendora CA 91740. Many of our other series now have outside series editors."

BOWLING GREEN STATE UNIVERSITY POPULAR PRESS, Bowling Green State University, Bowling Green OH 43403-1000. (419)372-7866. Fax: (419)372-8095. Editor: Ms. Pat Browne. Estab. 1967. Publishes hardcover and trade paperback originals and reprints. Averages 25-30 titles/year. Receives 150-200 submissions/year. 50% of books from first-time authors; 95% from unagented writers. Pays 5-12½% royalty on wholesale price or buys mss outright. Publishes book an average of 1 year after acceptance. Reports in 3 months. Book catalog and manuscript guidelines free on request.

Nonfiction: Biography, reference and textbook. Subjects include Americana, anthropology/archaeology, art/architecture, history, language/literature, photography, regional, religion, sociology, sports and women's issues/studies. Submit outline and sample chapters.

Tips: "Our audience includes university professors, students, and libraries."

‡THE BOXWOOD PRESS, 183 Ocean View Blvd., Pacific Grove CA 93950. (408)375-9110. Editor: Dr. Ralph Buchsbaum. Imprints include Viewpoint Books, Free Spirit Books. Publishes hardcover and trade paperback originals. Firm averages 5 titles/year. Receives 25 submissions/year. Subsidy publishes 25% of books. Determines subsidy by high merit; low market. Pays 10% royalty. Publishes book an average of 10 months after acceptance. Query for electronic submissions. Reports in 6 weeks on queries; 2 months on mss. Book catalog free on request.

Nonfiction: Biography, technical and textbook. Subjects include biology (plants and animals), health/medicine, history, nature/environment, philosophy, psychology, regional or area studies and other science. Submit complete ms. Reviews artwork/photos as part of ms package.

Tips: "Writers have the best chance selling us sound science and natural history books. Our audience is high school and college, general and educated. If I were a writer trying to market a book today, I would know my subject, readership and do my clearest writing."

‡BOYD & FRASER PUBLISHING COMPANY, Division of South-Western Publishing Company, One Corporate Place, Ferncroft Village, Danvers MA 01923-4001. (508)777-9069. Senior Acquisitions Editor: James H. Edwards. Publishes hardcover and paperback originals primarily for the college textbook market; some trade sales of selected titles. Averages 25-30 titles/year. Receives 100 submissions/year. 50% of books from first-time authors; 100% from unagented writers. Pays 15% royalty on wholesale price. Advance is negotiated individually. Publishes book an average of 1 year after acceptance. Simultaneous submissions OK. Query for electronic submissions. Reports in 1 month on queries; 2 months on mss. Book catalog and manuscript guidelines free on request.

Nonfiction: Textbook. Subjects include computer information systems and application software. Query or submit outline/synopsis first; unsolicited mss not invited. Reviews artwork/photos as part of ms package.

Recent Nonfiction Title: *Principles of Information Systems*, by Ralph Stair.

Tips: "Writers have the best chance sending us proposals for college-level textbooks in computer education. Our audience consists of students enrolled in business-oriented courses on computers or computer application topics."

BOYDS MILLS PRESS, Subsidiary of *Highlights for Children*, 815 Church St., Honesdale PA 18431-1895. (717)253-1164. Imprint is Wordsong—publishes works of poetry. Manuscript Coordinator: Beth Troop. Estab. 1990. Publishes hardcover originals. Publishes 70 titles/year. Receives 8,600 queries and mss/year. 20% of books are from first-time authors; 75% from unagented writers. Pays varying royalty on retail price. Offers varying advance. Simultaneous submissions OK. Reports in 1 month. *Writer's Market* recommends allowing 2 months for reply. Free book catalog and ms guidelines.

Nonfiction: Juvenile on all subjects. "Boyds Mills Press is not interested in mss depicting violence, explicit sexuality, racism of any kind or which promotes hatred." Submit outline and sample chapters. Reviews artwork/photos as part of ms package.

Recent Nonfiction Title: *Sea Snakes*, by Sneed B. Collard III.

Fiction: Juvenile in all genres. Also publishes boardbooks, puzzle books, gamebooks and poetry. Submit outline/synopsis and sample chapters or complete ms.

Recent Fiction Title: *Smart Dog*, by Ralph Leemis.

Tips: "Our audience is pre-school to young adult. Concentrate first on your writing. Polish it. Then — and only then — select a market." Needs primarily picture book material.

BRANDEN PUBLISHING CO., INC., 17 Station St., Box 843, Brookline Village MA 02147. Editor: Adolph Caso. Estab. 1965. Subsidiaries include International Pocket Library and Popular Technology, Four Seas and Brashear. Publishes hardcover and trade paperback originals, reprints and software. Averages 15 titles/year; receives 1,000 submissions annually. 80% of books from first-time authors; 90% of books from unagented writers. Average print order for a writer's first book is 3,000. Pays 5-10% royalty on net; offers $1,000 maximum advance. Publishes book an average of 10 months after acceptance. Query for electronic submissions. Reports in 1 month. *Writer's Market* recommends allowing 2 months for reply.

Nonfiction: Biography, illustrated book, juvenile, reference, technical and textbook. Subjects include Americana, art, computers, health, history, music, photography, politics, sociology, software and classics. Especially looking for "about 10 manuscripts on national and international subjects, including biographies of well-known individuals." No religion or philosophy. Prefers paragraph query with author's vita and SASE; no unsolicited mss. No telephone inquiries. Reviews artwork/photos as part of ms package.

Recent Nonfiction Title: *Michael Jackson, The King of Pop!*.

Fiction: Ethnic (histories, integration); mainstream (emphasis on youth and immigrants); religious (historical-reconstructive); romance (novels with well-drawn characters). No science, mystery or pornography. Paragraph query with author's vita and SASE; no unsolicited mss. No telephone inquiries!

Tips: "Branden publishes only manuscripts determined to have a significant impact on modern society. Our audience is a well-read general public, professionals, college students, and some high school students. If I were a writer trying to market a book today, I would thoroughly investigate the number of potential readers interested in the content of my book. We like books by or about women."

BRASSEY'S (US), Imprint of Macmillan Publishing Company (New York), 1st Floor, 8000 Westpark Dr., McLean VA 22102-3101. (703)442-4535. Fax: (703)790-9063. Associate Director of Publishing: Don McKeon. Publishes hardcover and trade paperback originals and reprints. Publishes 30 titles/year. Receives 100-150 queries/year. 50% of mss from first-time authors, 85% from unagented writers. Pays 6-18% royalty on wholesale price. Offers $50,000 maximum advance. Publishes book 8½ months after acceptance of ms. Simultaneous submissions OK. SASE required. Query for electronic submissions. Reports in 2 months on proposals. Book catalog and ms guidelines free on request.

Nonfiction: Biography, coffee table book, reference and textbook. Subjects include government/politics, history, military/war and intelligence studies. "We are seeking to build our biography and military history lists." When submitting nonfiction, be sure to include sufficient biographical information (e.g., track records of previous publications), and "make clear in proposal how your work might differ from other such works already published and with which yours might compete." Submit outline and 1 sample chapter (not complete ms), and proposal package, including biographical information, analysis of book's competition and return postage. Reviews artwork/photos as part of freelance ms package. Send photocopies.

Fiction: Historical. "Submissions must be related to history, military, or intelligence topics." Submit synopsis and 1 sample chapter.

Tips: "Our audience consists of military personnel, government policymakers, and laypersons with an interest in military history, biography, defense issues and intelligence studies."

BREVET PRESS, INC., P.O. Box 1404, Sioux Falls SD 57101. Publisher: Donald P. Mackintosh. Managing Editor: Peter E. Reid. Estab. 1972. Publishes hardcover and paperback originals and reprints. Receives 40 submissions annually. 50% of books from first-time authors; 100% of books from unagented writers. Average print order for a writer's first book is 5,000. Pays 5% royalty; advance averages $1,000. Publishes book an average of 1 year after acceptance. Simultaneous submissions OK. Reports in 2 months. Free book catalog.

Nonfiction: Specializes in business management, history, place names, and historical marker series. Americana (A. Melton, editor); business (D.P. Mackintosh, editor); history (B. Mackintosh, editor); and technical books (Peter Reid, editor). Query; "after query, detailed instructions will follow if we are interested." Reviews artwork/photos; send copies if photos/illustrations are to accompany ms.

Tips: "Write with market potential and literary excellence. Keep sexism out of the manuscripts by male authors."

BRICK HOUSE PUBLISHING CO., #4 Limbo Lane, P.O. Box 266, Amherst NH 03031. (603)672-5112. Publisher: Robert Runck. Estab. 1976. Publishes hardcover and trade paperback originals. Averages 12 titles/year; receives 200 submissions annually. 20% of books from first-time authors; 100% of books from unagented writers. Pays 10% royalty on wholesale price. Publishes book an average of 6 months after acceptance. Simultaneous submissions OK. Query for electronic submissions. Reports in 6 weeks on queries. *Writer's*

Market recommends allowing 2 months for reply. Book catalog and ms guidelines for 9 × 12 SAE with 4 first class stamps.

Nonfiction: How-to, reference, technical and textbook. Subjects include Northeast regional, business, self-help, sane public policy, renewable energy, energy conservation, and environmental concerns.

Tips: "Authors should address the following questions in their query/proposals: What are my qualifications for writing this book? What distinguishes it from other books on the same topic. What can I do to promote the book?"

‡BRIGHTON PUBLICATIONS, INC., P.O. Box 120706, St. Paul MN 55112-0706. (612)636-2220. Editor: Sharon E. Dlugosch. Publishes trade paperback originals. Publishes 4 titles/year. Receives 20 queries and 4 mss/year. 50% of mss from first-time authors; 100% from unagented writers. Pays 10% royalty on wholesales price. Publishes book 6 months after acceptance. Simultaneous submissions OK. Query for electronic submissions. Reports in 2 months on queries, 3 months on mss. Book catalog/ms guidelines for #10 SASE.

Nonfiction: How-to, business, tabletop, party themes, home making. "We're interested in topics telling how to live any part of life well. Specifically, we're developing business how-to, celebration themes, and home making." Query. Submit outline and 2 sample chapters.

BRISTOL PUBLISHING ENTERPRISES, INC., P.O. Box 1737, San Leandro CA 94577. (415)895-4461. Imprints include Nitty Gritty Cookbooks. Chairman: Patricia J. Hall. President: Brian Hall. Estab. 1988. Publishes 12-14 titles/year. Receives 1,000 proposals/year. 15% of books from first-time authors; 100% from unagented writers. Pays 6-9% royalty on wholesale price. Average advance $100. Publishes within 1 year of acceptance. Reports in 3-4 months. Book catalog for SAE with 2 first class stamps.

Nonfiction: Cookbooks. Nonfiction books for readers over 50 years of age. Submit outline and sample chapters.

BRITISH AMERICAN PUBLISHING, 19B British American Blvd., Latham NY 12110-1420. (518)786-6000. Estab. 1987. Imprint is The Paris Review Editions. Publishes hardcover and trade paperback originals and hardcover reprints. Firm averages 15 titles/year. Receives 1,000 submissions/year. 10% of books from first-time authors. 10% from unagented writers. Pays royalties. Publishes book an average of 1 year after acceptance. Simultaneous submissions OK. Reports in 2 months. Ms guidelines for #10 SASE.

Nonfiction: Biography, humor, self-help, how-to. Subjects include business and economics, child guidance/parenting, cooking, foods and nutrition, education, government/politics, history, language/literature, psychology, recreation, regional, sports and travel. Submit complete ms, competitive title information, and SASE. *Writer's Market* recommends query with SASE first.

Recent Nonfiction Title: *Just Let Me Play*, by Charlie Sifford.

Fiction: Adventure, confession, experimental, fantasy, feminist, historical, horror, humor, literary, mainstream/contemporary, mystery, religious, romance, short story collections and suspense. Submit complete ms and SASE. *Writer's Market* recommends query with SASE first.

Poetry: Submit complete ms.

Tips: "We have more interest in nonfiction this year than last."

BROADMAN & HOLMAN PRESS, (formerly Broadman Press), 127 9th Ave. N, Nashville TN 37234. Publishes hardcover and paperback originals (85%) and reprints (15%). Averages 48 titles/year. Royalty rates are negotiable. Reports in 2 months. Writer's guidelines for #10 SAE with 2 first class stamps.

Nonfiction: Religion. "We are open to freelance submissions in all areas. Materials in these areas must be suited for a conservative Protestant readership. No poetry, biography, sermons, or anything outside the area of the Protestant tradition." Query, submit outline/synopsis and sample chapters. Reviews artwork/photos as part of ms package.

Fiction: Religious. "We publish almost no fiction—less than five titles per year. For our occasional publication we want not only a very good story, but also one that sets forth Christian values. Nothing that lacks a positive Christian emphasis; nothing that fails to sustain reader interest." Submit complete ms with synopsis.

Tips: "Textbook and family material are becoming an important forum for us—Bible study is very good for us, but our publishing is largely restricted in this area to works that we enlist on the basis of specific author qualifications. Preparation for the future and living with life's stresses and complexities are trends in the subject area."

BROADWAY PRESS, P.O. Box 1037, Shelter Island NY 11964-1037. (516)749-3266. Fax: (516)749-3267. Publisher: David Rodger. Estab. 1985. Publishes trade paperback originals. Averages 2-3 titles/year; receives 50-75 submissions annually. 50% of books from first-time authors; 75% of books from unagented writers. Pays negotiable royalty. Publishes book an average of 18 months after acceptance. Simultaneous submissions OK. Reports in 3 months on queries.

Nonfiction: Reference and technical. Subjects include theatre, film, television and the performing arts. "We're looking for professionally-oriented and authored books." Submit outline and sample chapters.

Recent Nonfiction Title: *Photometrics Handbook*, by Robert Mumm.

Tips: "Our readers are primarily professionals in the entertainment industries. Submissions that really grab our attention are aimed at that market."

BROWNDEER PRESS, Imprint of Harcourt Brace & Company Children's Books, P.O. Box 80160, Portland OR 97280-1160. Editorial Director: Linda Zuckerman. Publishes hardcover originals. Averages 14 titles/year; receives 4,000 submissions annually. 25% of books from first-time authors; 25% of books from unagented writers. Pays royalty on retail price. Advance negotiable. Publishes book an average of 2 years after acceptance. Simultaneous submissions OK. Reports in 3 months. "Mss, queries, or art samples without SASE will not receive a response or be returned. No certified mail, please." Does not accept applications for freelance readers. Guidelines for #10 SASE.

Nonfiction: Juvenile. Query only. Submit resume. Reviews artwork/photos as part of ms package.

Fiction: Juvenile, middle grade and young adult. Picture books. Submit synopsis, 3 sample chapters, resume and cover letter.

Poetry: Submit complete ms.

Tips: "We are not accepting easy readers, chapter books or middle grade biographies at this time. Read contemporary children's books at all age levels; try to take some writing or children's literature courses; join a critique group; talk to children's librarians and booksellers in children's bookstores; read *Horn Book, Booklist, School Library Journal* and *Publishers Weekly.*"

‡*BUDDHA ROSE PUBLICATIONS, P.O. Box 548, Hermosa Beach CA 90254. Director: Scott Shaw. Imprint is Baker & Taylor. Editor-in-Chief: Elliot Sebastian. Publishes hardcover and trade paperback originals. Publishes 25 titles/year. Receives 1,000 queries and 350 mss/year. 10% of mss from first-time authors, 10% from unagented writers. Subsidy publishes 20% of books. Determines whether an author should be subsidy published by material and its marketability. Pays 15% royalty on wholesale price. Offers $100-10,000 advance. Publishes book 4-6 months after acceptance of ms. Simultaneous submissions OK. Reports in 1 month. Book catalog for SAE with 5 first class stamps. Manuscript guidelines free on request.

Nonfiction: Reference, self-help and textbook. Subjects include anthropology/archaeology, art/architecture, ethnic, government/politics, history, nature/environment, philosophy, psychology, religion, science, sociology and travel. Submit entire text. Reviews artwork/photos as part of the freelance ms package. Writers should send transparencies.

Fiction: Experimental and literary. Submit entire ms.

Poetry: "Make your poetry scream of experience—forget boring rhymes." Submit 5 sample poems.

Tips: Live what you write; be it fiction, poetry or cultural, for this is the only place where knowledge is born.

‡BUSINESS NEWS PUBLISHING COMPANY, P.O. Box 2600, Troy MI 48007. (313)362-3700. Publisher: Joanna Turpin. Publishes hardcover and trade paperback originals and reprints. Publishes 8 titles/year. Receives 35 queries and 15 mss/year. 30% of mss from first-time authors, 100% from unagented writers. Pays 10-15% royalty on wholesale price (net receipts) or on retail price. Offers $500-1,000 advance. Publishes book 12 months after acceptance of ms. Simultaneous submissions OK. Query for electronic submissions. Reports in 1 month. Book catalog and ms guidelines free on request.

Nonfiction: How-to, reference, technical and textbook. Subjects include heating, ventilating, air conditioning, refrigeration and plumbing. "We are looking for books that incorporate theory, practical applications and troubleshooting as related to heating/ventilating/air conditioning/refrigeration/plumbing." Submit outline and 1 sample chapter, or submit proposal package, including summary, comparison, outline and sample chapter. Reviews artwork/photos as part of freelance ms package. Writers should send photocopies.

Recent Nonfiction Title: *Refrigeration Licenses Unlimited*, by Carrico (reference).

Tips: Audience is students, contractors, technicians, engineers.

C Q INC., Imprint of Congressional Quarterly, Inc., 1414 22nd St. NW, Washington DC 20037. (202)887-8642. Acquisitions Editor: Jeanne Ferris. Publishes 30-40 hardcover and paperback titles/year. 95% of books from unagented writers. Pays royalties on net receipts. Sometimes offers an advance. Publishes book an average of 6-12 months after acceptance. Simultaneous submissions OK. Reports in 3 months. Free book catalog.

Nonfiction: Reference books, information directories and monographs on federal and state governments, national elections, politics and governmental issues. Public affairs paperbacks on developing issues and events. Submit prospectus, writing sample and curriculum vitae.

Tips: "Our books present important information on American government and politics, and related issues, with careful attention to accuracy, thoroughness and readability."

C Q PRESS, Imprint of Congressional Quarterly, Inc., 1414 22nd St. NW, Washington DC 20037. (202)887-8641. Acquisitions Editor: Brenda Carter. Publishes 20-30 hardcover and paperback original titles annually. 95% of books from unagented writers. Pays standard college royalty on wholesale price; offers college text advance. Publishes book an average of 6 months after acceptance of final ms. Simultaneous submissions OK. Reports in 3 months. Free book catalog.

Nonfiction: College text. All levels of political science texts. "We are one of the most distinguished publishers in the areas of American government, public administation and international relations textbooks." Submit proposal, outline and sample chapter.

Recent Nonfiction Title: *The Third House: Lobbyists and Lobbying in the States*, by Alan Rosenthal.

CADDO GAP PRESS, Suite 275, 3145 Geary Blvd., San Francisco CA 94118. (415)750-9978. Publisher: Alan H. Jones. Estab. 1989. Publishes trade paperback originals and educational journals and newsletters. Publishes 4 titles/year. Receives 20 queries and 10 mss/year. 50% of mss from first-time authors, 100% from unagented writers. Pays 10% royalty on wholesale price. Publishes book 1 year after acceptance of ms. Simultaneous submissions OK. Query for electronic submissions. Reports in 2 months on proposals. Book catalog free on request.
Nonfiction: Subjects limited to teacher education, the social foundations of education, and multicultural education, with particular focus on California. Query.
Recent Nonfiction Title: *In the First Person Singular: The Foundations of Education*, by R. Freeman Butts.

CALGRE PRESS, Subsidiary of Calgre, Inc., P.O. Box 711, Antioch CA 94509. (510)945-8210. Editor: Diane Power. Estab. 1988. Publishes hardcover and trade paperback originals. Firm averages 4 titles/year. 70% of books from first-time authors; 90% from unagented writers. Pays 5-15% royalty on retail price. Publishes book an average of 9 months after acceptance. Simultaneous submissions OK. Reports in 2 months. Book catalog and manuscript guidelines for #10 SASE.
Nonfiction: How-to, reference, self-help. Subjects include child guidance/parenting, education. Submit outline/synopsis and sample chapters. Reviews artwork/photos as part of ms package.
Tips: "The writer has the best chance with how-to and self-help books, also books dealing with education and our educational system. Our audience includes adults, parents, teachers, business oriented adults in search of behavior motivation for higher productivity. If I were a writer trying to market a book today, I would contact small publishing firms specializing in the field that my book covers. An alternative is to contact literary agents hoping that they'll accept it for one of their big publishers."

CALIFORNIA STATE UNIVERSITY PRESS, California State University at Fresno, Fresno CA 93740-0099. (209)278-3056. Fax: (209)278-6758. Managing Editor: Carla Millar. Publishes hardcover and trade paperback originals. Firm averages 5 titles/year. Receives 75 submissions/year. 50% of books from first-time authors. 100% from unagented writers. Pays 10-25% royalty based upon gross sales. Offers $1,000 average advance. Publishes book an average of 6 months after acceptance. Simultaneous submissions OK. Reports in 1 month. *Writer's Market* recommends allowing 2 months for reply. Free book catalog.
• There is presently a 2 year moratorium on accepting new manuscripts.
Nonfiction: Biography and coffee table book. Subjects include Americana, art/architecture, business and economics, government/politics, language/literature and music/dance. "We are looking for books of general interest to an educated audience. We have published books on architecture (seven by Frank Lloyd Wright), art, music, film, business, city politics and culture, New Age politics and drama." Submit outline and sample chapters. Reviews artwork/photos as part of ms package.
Recent Nonfiction Title: *Surviving the Storms: Memory of Stalin's Tyranny*, by Helen Dmitriew.
Tips: "Our audience is made up of educated individuals with broad interests."

‡CAMBRIDGE EDUCATIONAL, (formerly Cambridge Career Products), P.O. Box 2153, Charleston WV 25328-2153. (800)468-4227. Fax: (304)744-9351. Subsidiaries include: Cambridge Home Economics, Cambridge Physical Education and Health. President: Edward T. Gardner, Ph.D. Estab. 1980. Publishes hardcover and trade paperback originals. Firm averages 12 titles/year. Receives 20 submissions/year. 20% of books from first-time authors. 90% from unagented writers. Pays 6-15% on wholesale price, $1,500-18,500 outright purchase. Offers $1,200 average advance. Publishes book an average of 8 months after acceptance. Simultaneous submissions OK. "No report unless interested." Free book catalog and manuscript guidelines.
Nonfiction: How-to, young adult (13-24) and self-help. Subjects include child guidance/parenting, cooking, foods and nutrition, education, health/medicine, money/finance, recreation and sports. "We need high quality books written for young adults (13 to 24 years old) on job search, career guidance, educational guidance, personal guidance, home economics, physical education, coaching, recreation, health, personal development, substance abuse, and sports. We are looking for script writers in the same subject area and age group. We only publish books written for young adults and primarily sold to libraries, schools, etc. We do not seek books targeted to adults or written at high readability levels." Query or submit outline/synopsis and sample chapters or send complete ms. Reviews artwork/photos as part of ms package.
Tips: "We encourage the submission of high-quality books on timely topics written for young adult audiences at moderate to low readability levels. Call and request a copy of all our current catalogs, talk to the management about what is timely in the areas you wish to write on, thoroughly research the topic, and write a manuscript that will be read by young adults without being overly technical. Low to moderate readibility yet entertaining, informative and accurate."

CAMBRIDGE UNIVERSITY PRESS, 40 W. 20th St., New York NY 10011. Editorial Director: Sidney Landau. Estab. 1534. Publishes hardcover and paperback originals. Publishes 1,300 titles/year; receives 1,000 submissions annually. 50% of books from first-time authors; 99% of books from unagented writers. Subsidy publishes (nonauthor) 8% of books. Pays 10% royalty on receipts; 8% on paperbacks; no advance. Publishes book an average of 1 year after acceptance. Query for electronic submissions. Reports in 4 months.

Nonfiction: Anthropology, archeology, economics, life sciences, mathematics, psychology, physics, art history, upper-level textbooks, academic trade, scholarly monographs, biography, history, and music. Looking for academic excellence in all work submitted. Department Editors: Frank Smith (history, social sciences); Mary Vaughn (English as second language); Deborah Goldblatt (English as a second language); Sidney Landau (reference); Lauren Cowles (mathematics, computer science); Scott Parris (economics); Julia Hough (developmental and social psychology, cognitive science); Alex Holzman (politics, sociology, history of science); Beatrice Rehl (fine arts, film studies); Robin Smith (life sciences); Alan Harvey, (applied mathematics); Florence Padgett, (engineering, materials science); and Terence Moore (philosophy); Julie Greenblatt (American literature, Latin American literature); Rachael Winfree (sociology, East Asian studies). Query. Reviews artwork/photos.
Recent Nonfiction Title: *The Life of Isaac Newton*, by Richard S. Westfall.

CAMDEN HOUSE, INC., P.O. 2025, Columbia SC 29202. (803)788-8689. Editor: J. Bruno. Publishes hardcover originals and reprints. Publishes 25-30 titles/year. 75% of books from first-time authors. Pays 5-10% royalties on retail price. Publishes ms an average of 10 months after acceptance. Query for electronic submissions. Reports in 1 month on queries "no phone calls, please." *Writer's Market* recommends allowing 2 months for reply.
Nonfiction: "Reference works, especially local history published under the aegies of civic organizations." Query. SASE a necessity. Reviews artwork/photos as part of ms package.
Recent Nonfiction Title: *Music, Love, Death and Mann's Doctor Faustus*, by John Fetzer (literary criticism).
   • The editor does not want to see any fiction or poetry submissions.

CAMELOT BOOKS, Children's Book Imprint of Avon Books, Division of the Hearst Corp., Dept. WM, 1350 Avenue of the Americas, New York NY 10019. (212)261-6800. Fax: (212)261-6895. Editorial Director: Ellen Krieger. Publishes paperback originals and reprints. Averages 60-70 titles/year; receives 1,000-1,500 submissions annually. 10-15% of books from first-time authors; 50% of books from unagented writers. Pays 6-8% royalty on retail price; offers minimum advance of $2,000. Publishes book an average of 2 years after acceptance. Simultaneous submissions OK. Reports in 10 weeks. Free book catalog and ms guidelines for 8×10 SAE and 5 first class stamps.
Fiction: Subjects include adventure, fantasy, humor, juvenile (Camelot, 8-12 and Young Camelot, 7-10) mainstream, mystery, ("very selective with mystery and fantasy") and suspense. Avon does not publish picture books. Submit entire ms or 3 sample chapters and a brief "general summary of the story, chapter by chapter."
Recent Fiction Title: *Saving Casey*, by Karen Mueller Coombs.

CAMINO BOOKS, INC., P.O. Box 59026, Philadelphia PA 19102. (215)732-2491. Publisher: E. Jutkowitz. Estab. 1987. Publishes hardcover and trade paperback originals. Averages 5 titles/year. Receives 500 submissions/year. 20% of books from first-time authors. Pays 6-12% royalty on net price. Offers $1,000 average advance. Publishes book an average of 1 year after acceptance. Reports in 2 weeks on queries. *Writer's Market* recommends allowing 2 months for reply.
Nonfiction: Biography, cookbook, how-to, humor and juvenile. Subjects include agriculture/horticulture, Americana, art/architecture, child guidance/parenting, cooking, foods and nutrition, ethnic, gardening, government/politics, history, regional and travel. Query or submit outline/synopsis and sample chapters. Include SASE.
Recent Nonfiction Title: *In Search of Ghosts: Haunted Places in the Delaware Valley*, by Elizabeth Hoffman.
Tips: "The books must be of interest to readers in the Middle Atlantic states."

C&T PUBLISHING, #1, 5021 Blum Rd., Martinez CA 94553. (510)370-9600. Fax: (510)370-1576. Editor-in-Chief: Diane Pedersen. Technical Editor: Liz Aneloski. Estab. 1983. Publishes hardcover and trade paperback originals. Publishes 6-8 titles/year; receives 24 submissions/year. Buys 10% from first-time authors; 100% from unagented writers. Pays 5-10% royalty on retail price. Offers $1,000 average advance. Publishes book an average of 9 months after acceptance. Simultaneous submissions OK. Reports in 1 month. *Writer's Market* recommends allowing 2 months for reply. Free book catalog and ms guidelines.
Nonfiction: Quilting books, primarily how-to, occasional quilt picture books, children's books relating to quilting, quilt-related crafts, wearable art, other books relating to fabric crafting. "Please submit ms with color photos of your work."
Recent Nonfiction Title: *Christmas Traditions From The Heart*, by Margaret Peters.
Tips: "In our industry, we find that how-to books have the longest selling life. The art quilt is coming into its own as an expression by women. Quiltmakers, sewing enthusiasts and fiber artists are our audience."

CAPRA PRESS, P.O. Box 2068, Santa Barbara CA 93120. (805)966-4590. Contact: Noel Young. Estab. 1970. Publishes hardcover and trade paperback originals. Firm averages 15 titles/year. Receives 4,000 submissions/year. 1% of books from first-time authors. 20% from unagented writers. Pays 10-15% royalty on wholesale price. Offers $1,000 average advance. Publishes book an average of 18 months after acceptance. Simultaneous submissions OK. Query for electronic submissions. Reports in 2 months. Book catalog for 6×9 SAE and 2 first class stamps.

Nonfiction: Biography, how-to, self-help and natural history. Subjects include animals, art/architecture, gardening, language/literature, nature/environment, recreation, regional and sociology. "We are looking for general trade titles with focus on the West." No juvenile books, code books or poetry. Query or submit outline and sample chapters. Reviews artwork/photos as part of ms package.

Recent Nonfiction Title: *California Gardens*, by Carole Leigh.

Fiction: Historical (western states), literary (from established authors), mainstream/contemporary and short story collections (only if stories have been in periodicals previously). No experimentals, fantasy, or genre fiction. Submit complete ms.

Recent Fiction Title: *Final Fate of the Alligators*, by Edward Hoagland.

Tips: "Writers have the best chance selling us nonfiction relating to architecture, natural history (birds, animals) or environmental subjects."

CAPSTONE PRESS, INC., 2440 Fernbrook Lane, Minneapolis MN 55447. (507)387-4492. Contact: Acquisitions Editor. Publishes hardcover originals. Firm averages 48-96 titles/year. Buys by outright purchase. Publishes book an average of 6 months after acceptance. Reports in 2 weeks. *Writer's Market* recommends allowing 2 months for reply. Book catalog free on request.

Nonfiction: Juvenile *only*. Subjects include Americana, animals, history, hobbies, science, sports and travel. Query. Reviews artwork/photos as part of ms package.

CARADIUM PUBLISHING, # 435, 2503 Del Prado Blvd S, Cape Coral FL 33904. (813)574-1799. Product Evaluation: Troy Dunn. Publishes hardcover originals and trade and mass market paperback originals. Publishes 15-20 titles/year. Receives 300 queries and 250 mss/year. 50% of mss from first-time authors, 90% from unagented writers. Pays 15-20% royalty on retail price or outright purchase, $100 minimum. Offers $0-5,000 advance. Publishes book 3 months after acceptance of ms. Simultaneous submissions are OK. Does not return submissions. Books remain on file or destroyed. Reports on queries in 2 months.

Nonfiction: Business related: how-to, reference and self-help. Subjects include business and economics (motivation and how-to) and money/finance. "We specialize in infomercials for our products." Query with outline and 3 sample chapters. Reviews artwork/photos as part of freelance ms package. Writers should send photocopies.

Recent Nonfiction Title: *The Locator*, by Klunder & Dunn.

Fiction: Erotica and lesbian. Query or submit 3 sample chapters.

Tips: "Know the market you want to reach statistically and be creative in your submissions."

CARDOZA PUBLISHING, 132 Hastings St., Brooklyn NY 11235. (718)743-5229. Acquisitions Editor: Rose Smith. Estab. 1981. Imprints are Gambling Research Institute and Word Reference Library. Publishes trade paperback originals and reprints and mass market paperback originals. Publishes 10 titles/year. Receives 50 queries and 12 mss/year. 50% of mss from first-time authors, 100% from unagented writers. Pays 5% royalty on retail price. Offers $500-2,000 advance. Publishes book 6 months after acceptance of ms. Simultaneous submissions OK. Reports in 2 months on queries.

Nonfiction: How-to and reference. Subjects include recreation, sports and travel. "The presentation should be typed and professional looking. Sample writing a must. Our specialities are reference (words), gambling (games)." Submit outline with 1 or 2 sample chapters.

CAREER PUBLISHING, INC., P.O. Box 5486, Orange CA 92613-5486. (714)771-5155. Fax: (714)532-0180. Editor-in-Chief: Marilyn M. Martin. Publishes paperback originals and software. Averages 6-20 titles/year; receives 300 submissions annually. 80% of books from first-time authors; 90% of books from unagented writers. Average print order for a writer's first book is 5,000-10,000. Pays 10% royalty on actual amount received; no advance. Publishes book an average of 6 months after acceptance. Simultaneous submissions OK (if so informed with names of others to whom submissions have been sent). Query for electronic submissions. Reports in 2 months. Book catalog and ms guidelines for 9 × 12 SAE and 2 first class stamps.

Nonfiction: Microcomputer material, educational software, word processing, guidance material, allied health, dictionaries, etc. "Textbooks should provide core upon which class curriculum can be based: textbook, workbook or kit with 'hands-on' activities and exercises, and teacher's guide. Should incorporate modern and effective teaching techniques. Should lead to a job objective. We also publish support materials for existing courses and are open to unique, marketable ideas with schools in mind. Reading level should be controlled appropriately—usually 8th-9th grade equivalent for vocational school and community college level courses. Any sign of sexism or racism will disqualify the work. No career awareness masquerading as career training." Submit outline, 2 sample chapters and table of contents. Reviews artwork/photos as part of ms package. If material is to be returned, enclose SAE and return postage.

Recent Nonfiction Title: *HyperCard Authoring Tool*, by Dennis Myers and Annette Lamb.

Tips: "Authors should be aware of vocational/career areas with inadequate or no training textbooks and submit ideas and samples to fill the gap. Trends in book publishing that freelance writers should be aware of include education—especially for microcomputers."

CAROL PUBLISHING, 120 Enterprise Ave., Secaucus NJ 07094. (201)866-0490. Publisher: Steven Schraggas. Imprints include Lyle Stuart, Birch Lane Press, Citadel Press and University Books. Firm publishes hardcover originals, and trade paperback originals and reprints. Firm averages 80 titles/year. Receives 1,000 submissions/year. 5% of books from first-time authors; 5% from unagented writers. Pays 10-15% royalty on retail price. Publishes book an average of 1 year after acceptance. Simultaneous submissions OK. Reports in 2 months.

Nonfiction: Biography, how-to, humor, illustrated book and self-help. Subjects include Americana, animals, art/architecture, business and economics, child guidance/parenting, computers and electronics, cooking, foods and nutrition, ethnic, gay/lesbian, health/medicine, history, hobbies, money/finance, music/dance, nature/environment, philosophy, psychology, recreation, regional, science, sports, travel and women's issues/studies. Submit outline/synopsis and sample chapters.

Recent Nonfiction Title: *A Woman Named Jackie,* by C. David Heymann.

Fiction: Adventure, confession, fantasy, horror, humor, literary, mystery, science fiction. Submit outline/synopsis and sample chapters.

Recent Fiction Title: *A Reasonable Madness,* by Fran Borf.

CAROLRHODA BOOKS, INC., 241 1st Ave. N., Minneapolis MN 55401. (612)332-3344. Submissions Editor: Rebecca Poole. Estab. 1969. Publishes hardcover originals. Averages 50-60 titles/year. Receives 1,500 submissions/year. 15% of books from first-time authors; 95% of books from unagented writers. Pays 4-6% royalty on wholesale price, makes outright purchase, or negotiates cents per printed copy. Publishes book an average of 18 months after acceptance. Simultaneous submissions OK. Reports in 4 months. Book catalog and ms guidelines for 9 × 12 SASE with 4 first class stamps.

Nonfiction: Publishes only children's books. Subjects include biography, animals, art, history, music and nature. Needs "biographies in story form on truly creative individuals — 25 manuscript pages in length." Send full ms. Reviews artwork/photos as part of ms package. No originals, please.

Recent Nonfiction Title: *Mammolina: A Story About Maria Montessori,* by Barbara O'Connor. Illustrations by Sara Campitelli.

Fiction: Children's historical. No anthropomorphized animal stories. Submit complete ms.

Recent Fiction Title: *The Rainmakers,* by E.J. Bird.

Tips: "Our audience consists of children ages four to eleven. We publish very few picture books. Nonfiction science topics, particularly nature, do well for us, as do biographies, photo essays, and easy readers. We prefer manuscripts that can fit into one of our series. Spend time developing your idea in a unique way or from a unique angle; avoid trite, hackneyed plots and ideas."

CARROLL & GRAF PUBLISHERS, INC., 260 5th Ave., New York NY 10001. (212)889-8772. Contact: Kent Carroll. Publishes hardcover, trade and mass market paperback originals, and trade and mass market paperback reprints. Averages 125 titles/year; receives 1,000 submissions annually. 10% of books from first-time authors; 10% of books from unagented writers. Pays 6-15% royalty on retail price. Publishes book an average of 9 months after acceptance. Reports in 1 month. *Writer's Market* recommends allowing 2 months for reply. Book catalog for 6 × 9 SASE.

Nonfiction: Biography, history, psychology, current affairs. Query with SASE. Reviews artwork/photos as part of ms package.

Fiction: Literary, erotica, mainstream, mystery, science fiction, horror/fantasy and suspense. Query with SASE.

CARSTENS PUBLICATIONS, INC., Hobby Book Division, P.O. Box 700, Newton NJ 07860-0700. (201)383-3355. Publisher: Harold H. Carstens. Estab. 1933. Publishes paperback originals. Averages 8 titles/year. 100% of books from unagented writers. Pays 10% royalty on retail price; offers advance. Publishes book an average of 1 year after acceptance. Query for electronic submissions. *Writer's Market* recommends allowing 2 months for reply. Book catalog for SASE.

Nonfiction: Model railroading, toy trains, model aviation, railroads and model hobbies. "We have scheduled or planned titles on several railroads as well as model railroad and model airplane books. Authors must know their field intimately because our readers are active modelers. Our railroad books presently are primarily photographic essays on specific railroads. Writers cannot write about somebody else's hobby with authority. If they do, we can't use them." Query. Reviews artwork/photos as part of ms package.

Tips: "No fiction. We need lots of good b&w photos. Material must be in model, hobby, railroad and transportation field only."

CASSANDRA PRESS, P.O. Box 868, San Rafael CA 94915. (415)382-8507. Fax: (415)382-7758. President: Gurudas. Estab. 1985. Publishes trade paperback originals. Averages 6 titles/year. Receives 200 submissions/year. 50% of books from first-time authors; 50% from unagented writers. Pays 6-8% maximum royalty on retail price. Advance rarely offered, but to $4,000 when one is offered. Publishes book an average of 1 year after acceptance. Simultaneous submissions OK. Reports in 3 weeks on queries, 2-3 months on manuscripts. Free book catalog and manuscript guidelines.

Nonfiction: Children's/juvenile, and self-help. Subjects include bereavement. "We accept only manuscripts dealing with grief." Submit complete ms. *Writer's Market* recommends query with SASE first.
Fiction: Grief. Submit complete ms.
   ● This press is not interested in seeing novels or personal stories.

CENTERSTREAM PUBLICATIONS, P.O. Box 5450, Fullerton CA 92635. (714)779-9390. Owner: Ron Middlebrook. Publishes hardcover and mass market paperback originals and trade paperback and mass market paperback reprints. Publishes 12 titles/year. Receives 15 queries and 15 mss/year. 80% of mss from first-time authors, 100% from unagented writers. Pays royalty on wholesale price. Offers $300-3,000 advance. Publishes book 8 months after acceptance of ms. Simultaneous submissions OK. Query for electronic submissions. Reports in 1 month on queries. *Writer's Market* recommends allowing 2 months for reply. Book catalog free on request.
Nonfiction: Currently only publishing music history.

CHARLESBRIDGE PUBLISHING, 85 Main St., Watertown MA 02172. (617)926-0329. Managing Editor: Elena Dworkin Wright. Estab. 1980. Publishes school programs and hardcover and trade paperback originals. Receives 1,000 submissions/year. 10% of books from first-time authors; 100% from unagented writers. Publishes books an average of 1 year after acceptance. Reports in 2 months.
Nonfiction: Picture books. "We look for nature/science books that teach about the world from a perspective that is relevant to a young child." Submit complete mss with written description proposing art.
Fiction: Multicultural picturebooks.
Recent Fiction Title: *Woodhoopoe Willie*, by Virginia Kroll.
Tips: "Markets through schools, book stores and specialty stores at museums, science centers, etc."

CHATHAM PRESS, Box A, Old Greenwich CT 06870. Fax: (203)622-6688. Contact: Editor. Estab. 1971. Publishes hardcover and paperback originals, reprints and anthologies. Averages 15 titles/year; receives 50 submissions annually. 25% of books from first-time authors; 75% of books from unagented writers. Subsidy publishes mainly poetry or ecological topics (nonauthor) 10% of books. "Standard book contract does not always apply if the book is heavily illustrated. Average advance is low." Publishes book an average of 6 months after acceptance. Query for electronic submissions. Reports in 2 weeks. *Writer's Market* recommends allowing 2 months for reply. Book catalog and ms guidelines for 6×9 SAE with 6 first class stamps.
Nonfiction: "Publishes mostly regional history and natural history, involving mainly Northeast seaboard to the Carolinas, mostly illustrated, with emphasis on conservation and outdoor recreation." Accepts nonfiction translations from French and German. Query with outline and 3 sample chapters. Reviews artwork/photos as part of ms package.
Tips: "Illustrated New England-relevant titles have the best chance of being sold to our firm. We have a slightly greater (15%) skew towards cooking and travel titles."
   ● Due to the current economy this press indicates its need for freelance material has lessened.

CHELSEA GREEN, P.O. Box 130, Post Mills VT 05058-0130. (802)333-9073. Editor: Ian Baldwin Jr. Assistant Editor: Helen Whybrow. Estab. 1984. Publishes hardcover and paperback trade originals. Averages 6 titles/year. Reports in 3 months.
Nonfiction: Biography, nature, politics, travel, environmental issues and sustainable lifestyle.
   ● No longer considering fiction, poetry, art or history books. Query only and include SASE.
Recent Nonfiction Title: *Beyond The Limits*, by Dunella Meadows et alia.
Tips: "We do not accept unsolicited mss and we are reviewing very few submissions." Looking for authors with a background in writing published articles/books; also likes advance sale contacts from author.

CHESS ENTERPRISES, 107 Crosstree Rd., Caraopolis PA 15108. Fax: (412)262-2138. Owner: Bob Dudley. Estab. 1981. Publishes trade paperback originals. Publishes 10 titles/year. Receives 35 queries and 14 mss/year. 20% of mss from first-time authors, 100% from unagented writers. Makes outright purchase — totally dependent upon author and subject. Offers 50% advance. Publishes book 4 months after acceptance of ms. Simultaneous submissions OK. Query for electronic submissions. Reports in 1 month on queries. *Writer's Market* recommends allowing 2 months for reply. Book catalog free on request.
Nonfiction: Game of chess only. Query.
Tips: "Books are targeted to chess tournament players, book collectors."

CHICAGO REVIEW PRESS, 814 N. Franklin, Chicago IL 60610-3109. (312)337-0747. Editorial Director: Amy Teschner. Estab. 1973. Imprints are Lawrence Hill Books, A Capella Books and Ziggurat Books. Publishes hardcover and trade paperback originals. Averages 15 titles/year; receives 500 submissions annually. 50% of books from first-time authors; 75% of books from unagented writers. Pays 7½-12½% royalty. Offers average $1,000 advance. Publishes book an average of 15 months after acceptance. Simultaneous submissions OK. Query for electronic submissions. Reports in 2 months on queries. Book catalog for 9×12 SAE with 7 first class stamps.

Nonfiction: How-to, guidebooks, architecture, specialty cookbooks, popular science, adoption, Midwest gardening, urban issues, feminism, recreation, regional titles. Needs regional Chicago and the Midwest material and how-to, popular science, and nonfiction project books in the arts and sciences for ages 10 and up.
- No longer looking for books on Native American culture. Query or submit outline and sample chapters. Reviews artwork/photos.

Recent Nonfiction Title: *A Handbook to the Universe: Explorations of Matter, Energy, Space and Time*, by Richard Paul.

Tips: "The audience we envision for our books is comprised of adults and young people 15 and older, educated readers with special interests, do-it-yourselfers. Right now, we also are very excited about our series called Ziggurat Books, hands-on books for kids 10 and up on subjects such as astronomy, architecture and photography."

CHILD WELFARE LEAGUE OF AMERICA, Suite 310, 440 1st St. NW, Washington DC 20001. (202)638-2952. Director, Publications: Susan Brite. Publishes hardcover and trade paperback originals. Publishes 10-12 titles/year. Receives 60-100 submissions/year. 95% of writers are unagented. 50% of books are nonauthor subsidy published. Pays 0-10% royalty on net domestic sales. Publishes book an average of 1 year after acceptance. Query for electronic submissions. Reports on queries in 3 months. Free book catalog and manuscript guidelines.

Nonfiction: Child welfare. Subjects include child guidance/parenting, sociology. Submit outline and sample chapters.

Tips: "Our audience is child welfare workers, administrators, agency executives, parents, etc. We also publish training curricula, including videos."

CHILDREN'S PRESS, 5440 N. Cumberland Ave., Chicago IL 60656. (312)693-0800. Publishes hardcover originals. Publishes 120-140 titles/year. Receives 1,800 queries from first-time authors and 900 mss/year. 10% of mss from first-time authors, 100% from unagented writers. Makes outright purchase for $500-1,000. Publishes book an average of 20 months after acceptance. Simultaneous submissions OK. Reports in 3 months on queries. Book catalog and ms guidelines free on request.

Nonfiction: Children's/juvenile. Subjects include animals, anthropology/archaeology, art/archetecture, ethnic, health/medicine, history, hobbies, music/dance, nature/environment, science and sports. "We publish nonfiction books that supplement the elementary school curriculum." Submit outline with 1 sample chapter and return SASE. Sometimes reviews artwork/photos as part of freelance ms package. Writers should send photocopies.

Recent Nonfiction Title: *Extraordinary American Indians*.

Fiction: Historical, juvenile and picture books. "Focus of picture books will be on early childhood topics and emergent literary programs." Submit synopsis and 1 sample chapter.

Recent Fiction Title: *Bear and Alligator Tales*.

Tips: "Fiction is selected for the beginning reader—ages 4,5,6; nonfiction for either the 8-9 year old or the 11-12 year old."

CHINA BOOKS & PERIODICALS, INC., 2929 24th St., San Francisco CA 94110. (415)282-2994. Fax: (415)282-0994. Senior Editor: Wendy K. Lee. Estab. 1960. Publishes hardcover and trade paperback originals. Firm averages 5 titles/year. Receives 300 submissions/year. 10% of books from first-time authors. 95% from unagented writers. Pays 10-12% royalty on net receipts. Offers $1,500 average advance. Publishes book an average of 1 year after acceptance. Simultaneous submissions OK. Query for electronic submissions. Reports in 1 month on queries. *Writer's Market* recommends allowing 2 months for reply. Book catalog free on request. Manuscript guidelines for #10 SASE.

Nonfiction: "*Important: All* books *must* be on topics related to China or East Asia, or Chinese-Americans. Books on China's history, politics, environment, women, art, architecture; language textbooks, acupuncture and folklore." Biography, coffee table book, cookbook, how-to, juvenile, self-help, textbook. Subjects include agriculture/horticulture, art/architecture, business and economics, cooking, foods and nutrition, ethnic, gardening, government/politics, history, language/literature, nature/environment, religion, sociology, translation, travel, women's issues studies. Query. Submit outline and sample chapters. Reviews artwork/photos as part of ms package.

Fiction: Ethnic, experimental, feminist, gay/lesbian, historical, literary, religious. "*Must* have Chinese, Chinese-American or East Asian theme. We are looking for high-quality fiction with a Chinese or East Asian theme or translated from Chinese that makes a genuine literary breakthrough and seriously treats life in contemporary China or Chinese-Americans. No fiction that is too conventional in style or treats hackneyed subjects. No fiction without Chinese or Chinese-American or East Asian themes, please." Query and submit outline/synopsis and sample chapters.

Recent Fiction Title: *The Banker*, by Cheng Naishan.

Tips: "We have a very much stronger need for writers and illustrators to work in children's nonfiction with a Chinese theme. We look for a well-researched, well-written book on China or East Asia that contains fresh insights and appeals to the intelligent reader. Our audience consists of educated and curious readers of trade books, academics, students, travelers, government officials, business people and journalists. I would also make sure to submit queries to the *smaller* publishers, especially those in your home region, because they will treat your work more seriously."

CHOSEN BOOKS PUBLISHING CO., LTD., Baker Book House, Box 6287, Grand Rapids MI 49516-6287. Editor: Jane Campbell. Estab. 1971. Publishes hardcover and trade paperback originals. Averages 12-16 titles/year; receives 600 submissions annually. 15% of books from first-time authors; 99% of books from unagented writers. Pays royalty on retail price. Publishes book an average of 1-2 years after acceptance. Simultaneous submissions OK. Reports in 2 months. Manuscript guidelines for #10 SASE.

Nonfiction: How-to, self-help, and a very limited number of first-person narratives. "We publish books reflecting the current acts of the Holy Spirit in the world, books with a charismatic Christian orientation." No New Age, poetry, fiction, academic or children's books. Submit synopsis, chapter outline, two sample chapters and SASE. No complete mss. No response without SASE.

Recent Nonfiction Title: *Possessing the Gates of the Enemy,* by Cindy Jacobs.

Tips: "In expositional books we look for solid, practical advice for the growing and maturing Christian from authors with professional or personal experience platforms. Narratives must have a strong theme and reader benefits. No conversion accounts or chronicling of life events, please. State the topic or theme of your book clearly in your cover letter."

CHRONICLE BOOKS, Chronicle Publishing Co., 275 5th St., San Francisco CA 94103. (415)777-7240. Fax: (415)777-8887. Associate Publishers: Nion McEvoy and Caroline Herter. Editor, fiction: Jay Schaefer. Editor, cookbooks: Bill LeBlond. Editor, children's: Victoria Rock. Publishes hardcover and trade paperback originals. Averages 200 titles/year; receives 2,500 submissions annually. 10% of books from first-time authors; 15% of books from unagented writers. Pays 5-8% royalty on retail price or makes outright purchase for $500-5,000. Publishes book an average of 1½ years after acceptance. Simultaneous submissions OK. Reports in 2 months on queries. Book catalog for 11 × 14 SAE with 5 first class stamps.

Nonfiction: Coffee table book, cookbook, and regional California on art, design, gardening, health, nature, photography, recreation, and travel. Query or submit outline/synopsis and sample chapters. Reviews artwork/photos with ms package.

Fiction: Juvenile, picture books, novels, novellas, and short story collections. Query or submit outline/synopsis and sample chapters.

CHRONIMED PUBLISHING, (formerly DCI Publishing), Suite 250, 13911 Ridgedale Dr., Minneapolis MN 55343. (612)541-0239. Fax: (612)541-4969. Associate Publisher: David Wexler. Estab. 1986. Publishes hardcover and trade paperback originals. Firm averages 16-20 titles/year. Receives 300 submissions/year. 30% of books are from first-time authors. 60% from unagented writers. Pays 8-15% royalties on net price. Publishes ms an average of 6 months after acceptance. Simultaneous submissions OK. Query for electronic submissions. Reports in up to 3 months. Book catalog and ms guidelines free.

Nonfiction: Cookbook and self-help. Subjects include cooking, foods and nutrition, health/medicine and psychology. "We are seeking anything relating to health, from fitness to family psychology from authoritative sources. No New Age material." Submit outline and sample chapters.

Recent Nonfiction Title: *The Label Reader's Pocket Dictionary of Food Additives,* by Mike Lapchick with Cindy Applaseth, R.Ph.

CHURCH GROWTH INSTITUTE, P.O. Box 4404, Lynchburg VA 24502-9985. (804)525-0022. Fax: (804)525-0608. Editor/Public Relations Coordinator: Cindy Spear. Director of Research and Development: Marvin Osborn. Estab. 1984. Publishes trade paperback originals. Publishes 8 titles/year. Pays 5% on retail price or makes outright purchase. Publishes book 1 year after acceptance of ms. Simultaneous submissions OK. Reports in 2 months on queries. Book catalog for 9 × 12 SAE and 4 first class stamps. Manuscript guidelines given after query and outline is received.

Nonfiction: How-to and textbook. Subjects include religious education (church-growth related). "Material should originate from a conversative Christian view and cover topics that will help churches grow, through leadership training, new attendance or stewardship programs, and new or unique ministries. Accepted manuscripts will be adapted to our resource packet format. All material must be practical and easy for the *average* Christian to understand." Query or submit outline and brief explanation of what the packet will accomplish in the local church and whether it is leadership or lay-oriented. Reviews artwork/photos as part of freelance ms package. Writers should send photocopies or transparencies.

‡**CIRCLET PRESS, INC.**, P.O. Box 15143, Boston MA 02215. Publisher/Editor: Cecilia Tan. Publishes hardcover and trade paperback originals. Publishes 6 titles/year. Receives 50-100 queries and 40-60 mss/year. 50% of mss from first-time authors; 90% from unagented writers. Pays 4-12% royalty on retail price or outright purchase (depending on rights); also pays in books if author prefers. Offers $100-300 advance. Publishes book 3-12 months after acceptance. Simultaneous submissions OK. Query for electronic submissions. Prefers Macintosh DD disk 3.5, queries via e-mail to "ctan@world.std.com". Reports in 1 month on queries. Book catalog for #10 SASE. Manuscript guidelines free on request for #10 SASE.

Fiction: Erotica, fantasy if erotic, feminist if science fiction, gay/lesbian if science fiction, science fiction if erotic, short story collections. "Fiction must combine both the erotic and the fantastic. The erotic content needs to be an integral part of a science fiction story, and vice versa. Writers should not assume that any sex is the same as erotica." Query. Submit synopsis and 2 sample chapters. Queries only via e-mail to "ctan@world.std.com".

Recent Fiction Title: *Telepaths Don't Need Safewords*, by Cecilia Tan (short stories of erotic science fiction).

Tips: "Our audience is adults who enjoy science fiction and fantasy, especially the works of Anne Rice, Storm Constantine, Samuel Delany, who enjoy vivid storytelling and erotic content. Seize your most vivid fantasy, your deepest dream and set it free onto paper. That is at the heart of all good speculative fiction. Then if it has an erotic theme as well as a science fictional one, send it to me."

CITADEL PRESS, Imprint of Carol Publishing Group, 120 Enterprise, Secaucus NJ 07094. Fax: (201)866-8159. Editorial Director: Allan J. Wilson. Estab. 1945. Other imprints are Lyle Stuart, Birch Lane Press and University Books. Publishes hardcover originals and paperback reprints. Averages 60-80 titles/year. Receives 800-1,000 submissions annually. 7% of books from first-time authors; 50% of books from unagented writers. Average print order for a writer's first book is 5,000. Pays 10% royalty on hardcover, 5-7% on paperback; offers average $10,000 advance. Publishes book an average of 1 year after acceptance. Simultaneous submissions OK. Reports in 2 months. Book catalog for $1.

Nonfiction and Fiction: Biography, film, psychology, humor and history. Also seeks "off-beat material, but no poetry, religion, politics." Accepts nonfiction and fiction translations. Query or submit outline/synopsis and 3 sample chapters. Reviews artwork/photos as part of ms package.

Tips: "We concentrate on biography, popular interest, and film, with limited fiction (no romance, religion, poetry, music)."

CLARION BOOKS, Imprint of Houghton Mifflin Company, 215 Park Ave. S., New York NY 10003. Editor and Publisher: Dorothy Briley. Executive Editor: Dinah Stevenson. Senior Editor: Nina Ignatowicz. Estab. 1965. Publishes hardcover originals. Averages 50 titles/year. Pays 5-10% royalty on retail price; advances from $2,500, depending on whether project is a picture book or a longer work for older children. Prefers no multiple submissions. Reports in 2 months. Publishes book an average of 18 months after acceptance. Ms guidelines for #10 SASE.

Nonfiction: Americana, biography, history, holiday, humor, nature, photo essays and word play. Prefers books for younger children. Reviews artwork/photos as part of ms package. Query.

Recent Nonfiction Title: *Eleanor Roosevelt: A Life of Discovery*, by Russell Freedman.

Fiction: Adventure, humor, mystery, strong character studies, and suspense. "We would like to see more distinguished short fiction for readers 7 to 10." Accepts fiction translations. Send complete ms. Looks for "freshness, enthusiasm—in short, life" (fiction and nonfiction).

Recent Fiction Title: *The Real Plato Jones*, by Nina Bowden.

CLARKSON POTTER, Imprint of Crown Publishers, Division of Random House, 201 E. 50th St., New York NY 10022. (212)572-6162. Fax: (212)572-6192. Editor-in-Chief: Lauren Shakely, associate publisher, Crown. Publishes hardcover and trade paperback originals. Averages 55 titles/year; receives 1,500 submissions annually. 18% of books from first-time authors, "but many of these first-time authors are well-known and have had media coverage." Pays 10% royalty on hardcover; 5-7½% on paperback; 5-7% on illustrated hardcover, varying escalations; advance depends on type of book and reputation or experience of author. No unagented mss can be considered. *Writer's Market* recommends allowing at least 2 months for reply. No manuscript guidelines available.

Nonfiction: Publishes art, autobiography, biography, cooking and foods, design, how-to, humor, juvenile, nature, photography, self-help, style and annotated literature. Accepts nonfiction translations. "Manuscripts must be cleanly typed on 8½×11 nonerasable bond; double-spaced. *Chicago Manual of Style* is preferred." Reviews artwork/photos as part of ms package.

● Published a winner of the 18th annual National Book Critics Circle Award—Carol Brightman's *Mary McCarthy and Her World*.

Fiction: Will consider "quality fiction."

CLEAR LIGHT PUBLISHERS, 823 Don Diego, Santa Fe NM 87501. (505)989-9590. Publisher: Harmon Houghton. Estab. 1981. Publishes hardcover and trade paperback originals. Publishes 12 titles/year. Receives 36 queries/year. 10% of mss from first-time authors, 50% from unagented writers. Pays 10% royalty on wholesale price. Offers advance: 50% of gross potential. Publishes book 1 year after acceptance of ms. Simultaneous submissions OK. Query for electronic submissions. Reports in 3 months on queries. Book catalog free on request.

ALWAYS enclose a self-addressed, stamped envelope (SASE) with all your queries and correspondence.

Nonfiction: Biography, coffee table book, cookbook and humor. Subjects include Americana, anthropology/archaelogy, art/architecture, cooking, foods and nutrition, ethnic, history, nature/environment, philosophy, photography and regional (Southwest). Query. Reviews artwork/photos as part of freelance ms package. Send photocopies.

CLEIS PRESS, P.O. Box 14684, San Francisco CA 94114-0684. Fax: (415)864-3385. Acquisitions Coordinator: Frederique Delacoste. Estab. 1980. Publishes trade paperback originals and reprints. Publishes 10 titles/year. 20% of books are from first-time authors; 75% from unagented writers. Royalties vary on retail price. Publishes book an average of 1 year after acceptance. Simultaneous submissions OK "only if accompanied by an original letter stating where and when ms was sent." No electronic submissions. Reports in 2 months. Book catalog for #10 SAE and 2 first class stamps.
Nonfiction: Human rights, feminist. Subjects include gay/lesbian, government/politics, sociology (of women), women's issues/studies. "We are interested in books that: will sell in feminist and progressive bookstores, and will sell in Europe (translation rights). We are interested in books by and about women in Latin America; on lesbian and gay rights; and other feminist topics which have not already been widely documented. We do not want religious/spiritual tracts; we are not interested in books on topics which have been documented over and over, unless the author is approaching the topic from a new viewpoint." Query or submit outline and sample chapters.
Recent Nonfiction Title: *Madonnarama as in Sex and Popular Culture*, edited by Lisa Frank and Paul Smith.
Fiction: Feminist, gay/lesbian, literary. "We are looking for high quality novels by women. We are especially interested in translations of Latin American women's fiction. No romances!" Submit complete ms.
Recent Fiction Title: *In the Garden of Dead Cars*, by Sybil Claiborne.
Tips: "An anthology project representing the work of a very diverse group of women ... an anthology on a very hot, very unique, risk-taking theme. These books sell well for us; they're our trademark. If I were trying to market a book today, I would become very familiar with the presses serving my market. More than reading publishers' catalogs, I think an author should spend time in a bookstore whose clientele closely resembles her intended audience; be absolutely aware of her audience; have researched potential market; present fresh new ways of looking at her topic; avoid 'PR' language in query letter."

CLEVELAND STATE UNIVERSITY POETRY CENTER, R.T. 1815, Cleveland State University, Cleveland OH 44115. (216)687-3986. Fax: (216)687-9366. Editor: Leonard M. Trawick. Estab. 1962. Publishes trade paperback and hardcover originals. Averages 5 titles/year; receives 400 queries, 900 mss annually. 60% of books from first-time authors; 100% of books from unagented writers. 30% of titles subsidized by CSU, 30% by government subsidy. CSU poetry series pays one-time, lump-sum royalty of $200-400 plus 50 copies; Cleveland Poetry Series (Ohio poets only) pays 100 copies. $1,000 prize for best manuscript each year. No advance. Publishes book an average of 1 year after acceptance. Simultaneous submissions OK. Reports in 2 weeks on queries; 6 months on mss. Book catalog for 6×9 SAE with 2 first class stamps; ms guidelines for SASE.
Poetry: No light verse, "inspirational," or greeting card verse. ("This does not mean that we do not consider poetry with humor or philosophical/religious import.") Query—ask for guidelines. Submit only December-February. Reviews artwork/photos if applicable (e.g., concrete poetry).
Tips: "Our books are for serious readers of poetry, i.e. poets, critics, academics, students, people who read *Poetry, Field, American Poetry Review, Antaeus*, etc. Trends include movement away from 'confessional' poetry; greater attention to form and craftsmanship. Try to project an interesting, coherent personality; link poems so as to make coherent unity, not just a miscellaneous collection. Especially needs poems with *mystery*, i.e., poems that suggest much, but do not tell all."

CLIFFS NOTES, INC., P.O. Box 80728, Lincoln NE 68501. (402)423-5050. General Editor: Michele Spence. Notes Editor: Gary Carey. Imprint is Centennial Press. Estab. 1958. Publishes trade paperback originals. Averages 20 titles/year. 100% of books from unagented writers. Pays royalty on wholesale price. Buys majority of mss outright; "full payment on acceptance of ms." Publishes book an average of 1 year after acceptance. Reports in 1 month. *Writer's Market* recommends allowing 2 months for reply. "We provide specific guidelines when a project is assigned."
Nonfiction: Self-help and textbook. "We publish self-help study aids directed to junior high through graduate school audience. Publications include *Cliffs Notes, Cliffs Test Preparation Guides, Cliffs StudyWare*, and other study guides. Most authors are experienced teachers, usually with advanced degrees. Some books also appeal to a general lay audience. Query.
Recent Nonfiction Title: *A Raisin in the Sun* Notes, Cliffs *Advanced Practice for the TOEFL*.

COBBLEHILL BOOKS, Affiliate of Dutton Children's Books, 375 Hudson St., New York NY 10014. (212)366-2000. Editorial Director: Joe Ann Daly. Senior Editor: Rosanne Lauer. Pays royalty. Publishes fiction and nonfiction for young readers, middle readers and young adults, and picture books. Query for mss longer than picture book length; submit complete ms for picture books. Reports in 1 month. Simultaneous submissions OK if so noted.

COFFEE HOUSE PRESS, Suite 400, 27 N. 4th St., Minneapolis MN 55401. (612)338-0125. Fax: (612)338-4004. Editorial Assistant: Michael L. Wiegers. Estab. 1984. Publishes trade paperback originals. Publishes 10-12 titles/year; receives 2,000 queries and mss/year. 95% of books are from unagented writers. Pays 8% royalty on retail price. Offers average $500 advance. Publishes book an average of 18 months after acceptance. Reports in 1 month on queries. *Writer's Market* recommends allowing 2 months for reply. Reports in 6 months for mss. Free book catalog; ms guidelines for #10 SASE and 2 first class stamps (52¢).
Fiction: Ethnic, literary, short story collections. Looking for novels, but not genre. *Writer's Market* recommends query with SASE first.
Tips: "We are looking for more women writers."

‡COLLECTOR BOOKS, Division of Schroeder Publishing Co., Inc., 5801 Kentucky Dam Rd., P.O. Box 3009, Paducah KY 42002-3009. Editor: Lisa Stroup. Estab. 1974. Publishes hardcover and paperback originals. Publishes 35 titles/year. 50% of books from first-time authors; 100% of books from unagented writers. Average print order for a writer's first book is 5,000-10,000. Pays 5% royalty on retail; no advance. Publishes book an average of 8 months after acceptance. Reports in 1 month. Book catalog for 9×12 SAE and 4 first class stamps. Ms guidelines for #10 SASE.
Nonfiction: "We only publish books on antiques and collectibles. We require our authors to be very knowledgeable in their respective fields and have access to a large representative sampling of the particular subject concerned." Query. Accepts outline and 2-3 sample chapters. Reviews artwork/photos as part of ms package.
Tips: "Common mistakes writers make include making phone contact instead of written contact and assuming an accurate market evaluation."

THE COLLEGE BOARD, Imprint of College Entrance Examination Board, 45 Columbus Ave., New York NY 10023-6917. (212)713-8000. Director of Publications: Carolyn Trager. Publishes trade paperback originals. Firm publishes 30 titles/year; imprint publishes 12 titles/year. Receives 20-30 submissions/year. 25% of books from first-time authors; 50% from unagented writers. Pays royalty on retail price of books sold through bookstores. Offers advance based on anticipated first year's earnings. Publishes book an average of 9 months after acceptance. Reports in 1 month on queries. *Writer's Market* recommends allowing 2 months for reply. Book catalog free on request.
Nonfiction: Education-related how-to, reference, self-help. Subjects include college guidance, education, language/literature, science. "We want books to help students make a successful transition from high school to college." Query or send outline and sample chapters. Reviews artwork/photos as part of ms package.
Tips: "Our audience consists of college-bound high school students, beginning college students and/or their parents."

COLONIAL PRESS, 1237 Stevens Rd. SE, Bessemer AL 35023. (205)428-2146. President: Bradley Twitty. Estab. 1956. Publishes hardcover and trade paperback originals and reprints. Publishes 10-50 titles/year. Receives 100 queries/year. 50% of mss from first-time authors, 100% from unagented writers. Pays 10-50% net wholesale. Publishes book 3 months after acceptance of ms. Simultaneous submissions OK. Reports in 3 months on queries. Book catalog free on request. Manuscript guidelines for #10 SASE.
Nonfiction: Biography, cookbook, humor, illustrated book, children's/juvenile, self-help, technical and textbook (pre-school to college). Subjects include business and economics, cooking, foods and nutrition, education, ethnic, government/politics, history, language/literature, music/dance, philosophy, psychology, regional, science, sociology and translation. Query. Reviews artwork/photos as part of the freelance ms package. Writers should send photocopies.
Fiction: Ethnic, historical, humor, juvenile, occult, picture books, plays, short story collections, young adult and gerontology and nutrition. "We are sympathetic and willing to look and see before we say no." Query.
Poetry: "We insist on what we publish being poetry. We do publish verse. We do not call it poetry. Just send us a little sample – two to five poems. Short biographical sketch and telephone number." Query.
Recent Poetry Title: *Koan America*, by David Starkey.
Tips: "We publish more textbooks than any other type. We like lab manuals and worktext. We need material for ages 3 and up. We are a small company; but, we pioneered authentic children's drawings in textbooks. We welcome good writers. If a writer wants to make big bucks writing – we are not the one. If a good writer has a fresh idea and cannot find a publisher – contact us."

COMPASS AMERICAN GUIDES INC., 6051 Margarido Dr., Oakland CA 94618. Managing Editor: Kit Duahe. Publisher: Christopher Burt. Publishes hardcover and trade originals and paperback originals. Publishes 8 titles/year. Receives 100 queries and 10 mss/year. 50% of mss from first-time authors, 90% from unagented writers. Simultaneous submissions OK. Query for electronic submissions. Reports in 3 months on proposals. Book catalog free on request.
Nonfiction: Travel guides. Submit proposals based on format only, for guides to states not yet covered. Authors must reside in state. "We cannot guarantee the return of any submissions."
• Query this publisher about their suggested format.

COMPCARE PUBLISHERS, division of Comprehensive Care Corp., Suite 100, 3850 Annapolis Ln., Minneapolis MN 55447. (612)559-4800. Fax: (612)559-2415. Editorial Director: Linda Christensen. Publishes trade paperback originals and reprints. Firm publishes 20 titles per year. Receives 800 queries and 300 ms/year. 30% of mss from first-time authors, 80% from unagented writers. Pays 10% royalty on net price. Offers advance based on projected sales. Publishes book 18 months after acceptance of ms. Simultaneous submissions OK. Reports in 6 months. Book catalog and ms guidelines free on request.
Nonfiction: Humor, self-help, positive living, relationships/family, gift, psychology, sociology. "We publish for the general market reader in areas of positive living and continued personal growth. No personal stories." Query with outline, 4 sample chapters, and proposal including author bio, comparisons with competitive markets, and description of tarket market. Reviews artwork/photos as part of freelance ms package. Writers should send photocopies.
Recent Nonfiction Title: *Can't Buy Me Love*, Sally Coleman and Nancy Hull-Mast.
Tips: "Our audience is a general adult readership, often referred to our books by counselors and therapists."

COMPUTE BOOKS, General Media Company, 324 W. Wendover Ave., Greensboro NC 27408. (919)275-9809. Editor-in-Chief: Stephen Levy. Estab. 1979. Publishes trade paperback originals. Averages 16 titles/year. Pays royalties based on gross wholesale receipts. Simultaneous submissions OK if noted in cover letter. Publishes ms an average of 8 months after acceptance. Query for electronic submissions. Reports in 4 months.
Nonfiction: Books on computers. "We publish books for the home and business computer user and are always looking for PC and video game books. We are also interested in entertainment programs; educational programs; and Nintendo and Sega Genesis related books. Submit outline and synopsis with sample chapters. "Writers who are known to us through articles in *Compute Magazine* already have our trust—we know they can come through with the right material—but we have often bought from writers we did not know, and from writers who had never published anything before."
Tips: "If I were trying to create a marketable computer book today, I would become intimately familiar with one computer, then define a specific area to explain to less-familiar computer users, and write a clear, concise outline of the book I meant to write, along with a sample chapter from the working section of the book (not the introduction). Then send that proposal to a publisher whose books you believe are excellent and who targets the same audience you are aiming at. Once the proposal was in the mail, I'd forget about it. Keep learning more about the computer and develop another book proposal. *Don't write a book without a go-ahead from a publisher.* The chances are too great that you will spend 6 months writing a book, only to discover that there are nine on the market with the same concept by the time your manuscript is ready to send out."

CONARI PRESS, Suite B, 1144 65th St., Emeryville CA 94608. (510)596-4040. Executive Editor: Mary Jane Ryan. Estab. 1987. Publishes hardcover and trade paperback originals. Firm averages 10 titles/year. Receives 200 submissions/year. 50% of books from first-time authors. 50% from unagented writers. Pays 8-12% royalty on list price. Offers $1,500 average advance. Publishes book an average of 9 months after acceptance. Simultaneous submissions OK. Query for electronic submissions. Reports in 3 months. Book catalog and ms guidelines for #10 SASE.
Nonfiction: Psychology/self-help, women's issues. Submit outline and sample chapters. Reviews artwork/photos as part of ms package.
Tips: "Writers should send us well-targeted, specific and focused manuscripts."

CONCORDIA PUBLISHING HOUSE, 3558 S. Jefferson Ave., St. Louis MO 63118-3968. (314)268-1000. Fax: (314)268-1329. Chief Editor: Rev. David V. Koch. Editorial Associate: Doris M. Schraer. Estab. 1869. Publishes hardcover and trade paperback originals. Averages 50 titles/year. Receives 1,200 submissions/year. 10% of books from first-time authors; 95% from unagented writers. Pays royalty or buys by outright purchase. Publishes book an average of 1 year after acceptance. Simultaneous submissions OK. Query for electronic submissions. Reports in 2 months on queries. Manuscript guidelines for #10 SASE.
Nonfiction: Juvenile, adult. Subjects include child guidance/parenting (in Christian context), inspirational, how-to, religion. "We publish Protestant, inspirational, theological, family and juveniles. All manuscripts must conform to the doctrinal tenets of The Lutheran Church—Missouri Synod. Authors should query before submitting a manuscript." Query.
Fiction: Juvenile. "We will consider preteen and children's fiction and picture books. All books must contain Christian content. No adult Christian fiction." Query.
Tips: "Our needs have broadened to include writers of books for lay adult Christians and of Christian novels (low-key, soft-sell) for pre-teens and teenagers."

THE CONSULTANT PRESS, #201, 163 Amsterdam Ave., New York NY 10023-5001. (212)838-8640. Fax: (212)838-8640. Publisher: Bob Persky. Imprint is The Photographic Arts Center. Estab. 1980. Publishes trade paperback originals. Firm averages 7 titles/year; Receives 10 submissions/year. 20% of books from first-time authors. 75% from unagented writers. Pays 7-12% royalty on wholesale price. Offers $500 average advance. Publishes book an average of 6 months after acceptance. Simultaneous submissions OK. Reports in 2 months. Free book catalog.

Nonfiction: How-to, reference, art/architecture, business and economics, and photography. "Our prime areas of interest are books on the business of art and photography. Writers should check *Books In Print* for competing titles." Submit outline and 2 sample chapters.

Tips: "Artists, photographers, galleries, museums, curators and art consultants are our audience."

‡CONSUMER REPORTS BOOKS, Subsidiary of Consumers Union, 101 Truman Ave., Yonkers NY 10703-1057. Fax: (914)378-2903. Contact: Sarah Uman. Estab. 1936. Publishes trade hardcover and paperback originals and reprints. Averages 30-35 titles/year; receives 1,000 submissions annually. Most of books from agented writers. Pays variable royalty on retail price; buys some mss outright. Publishes book an average of 1½ years after acceptance. Simultaneous submissions OK. Reports in 6 weeks on queries; 2 months on mss. Free book list and writer's manuscript guidelines on request.

Nonfiction: Cookbook, how-to, reference, self-help and automotive. Subjects include money and finance, cooking and foods, health and medicine, automotive, consumer guidance, home owners reference. Submit outline/synopsis and 1-2 sample chapters.

CONTEMPORARY BOOKS, INC., Suite 1200, 2 Prudential Plaza, 180 N. Stetson Ave, Chicago IL 60601-6790. (312)540-4500. Associate Publisher: Nancy J. Crossman. Estab. 1947. Publishes hardcover originals and trade paperback originals and reprints. Averages 65 titles/year; receives 2,500 submissions annually. 10% of books from first-time authors; 25% of books from unagented writers. Pays 6-15% royalty on retail price. Publishes book an average of 10 months after acceptance. Query for electronic submissions. Simultaneous submissions OK. Reports in 3 weeks. *Writer's Market* recommends allowing 2 months for reply. Manuscript guidelines for SASE.

Nonfiction: Biography, cookbook, how-to, humor, reference and self-help. Subjects include business, finance, cooking, health, fitness, psychology, sports, real estate, nutrition, popular culture and women's studies. Submit outline and sample chapters. Reviews artwork/photos as part of ms package.

Tips: "The New Age market has become saturated. Also, competition in cookbooks means we need professional, accomplished cooks instead of amateurs to write them."

‡COOL HAND COMMUNICATIONS, INC., 235 Goolsby Blvd., Deerfield Beach FL 33442. (305)429-3347. Publisher: Chris K. Hedrick. Publishes hardcover, trade paperback and mass market paperback originals. Publishes 15-20 titles/year. Receives 1,000 queries/year. 40% of mss from first-time authors; 80% from unagented writers. Pays 6-15% royalty on wholesale price. Advance varies. Publishes book 12-18 months after acceptance. Simultaneous submissions OK. Query for electronic submissions. Prefers IBM-MS-DOS ASCII text or WordPerfect V5.1. Reports in 2-4 weeks on queries, 2 months on mss. Manuscript guidelines for 9 × 12 SAE with 4 first class stamps.

Nonfiction: Biography, coffee table book, cookbook, how-to, humor, illustrated book, self-help, books on important issues, animals, art/architecture, business and economics, cooking, foods and nutrition, government/politics, health/medicine, history, hobbies, music/dance, nature/environment, philosophy, psychology, recreation, sociology, sports, travel, true crime. "We're looking for books that can make a positive difference in the lives of readers and society as a whole—novel, innovative approaches to the important issues of our times—the environment, poverty, race relations, animal and human abuse, drugs, crime, etc. We don't want to see anything so specialized that the subject matter limits the size of the potential audience. Nothing too esoteric—we prefer practical, useful information and material that offers concrete solutions to difficult problems. We seek positive, uplifting books that educate and entertain. We don't want lists of questions—we want answers." Query. Reviews artwork/photos as part of ms package.

Recent Nonfiction Title: *Creative Costumes*, by Mark Walker (how-to).

Fiction: Adventure, historical (no historical romance), horror, humor, maintream/contemporary, mystery, religious, suspense. "We're in the market for fiction with great story lines and strong characters. Subject matter isn't nearly as important as the quality of the writing and whether the work has soul—it has to make the reader feel as well as think. And if the book succeeds in communicating a positive message, so much the better. No science fiction or fantasy, and we're not big for historical romance or *anything* with galacious sex, unwarranted violence or material intended to shock simply for shock's sake. No children's books, either, unless text and graphics are of superior quality and virtually press-ready."

CORNELL MARITIME PRESS, INC., P.O. Box 456, Centreville MD 21617-0456. (410)758-1075. Managing Editor: Charlotte Kurst. Estab. 1938. Publishes hardcover originals and quality paperbacks for professional mariners and yachtsmen. Averages 7-9 titles/year; receives 150 submissions annually. 41% of books from first-time authors; 99% of books from unagented writers. Payment is negotiable but royalties do not exceed 10% for first 5,000 copies, 12½% for second 5,000 copies, 15% on all additional. Royalties for original paperbacks are invariably lower. Revised editions revert to original royalty schedule. Publishes book an average of 1 year after acceptance. Query for electronic submissions. Send queries first, accompanied by writing samples and outlines of book ideas. Reports in 1 month. *Writer's Market* recommends allowing 2 months for reply. Book catalog for 10 × 13 SAE with 5 first class stamps.

Nonfiction: Marine subjects (highly technical); manuals; and how-to books on maritime subjects. Tidewater imprint publishes books on regional history, folklore and wildlife of the Chesapeake Bay and the Delmarva Peninsula.

Recent Nonfiction Title: *Learn to Navigate by the Tutorial System Developed at Harvard*, by Charles A. Whitney and Frances W. Wright.

CORWIN PRESS, INC., 2455 Teller Rd., Newbury Park CA 91320. (805)499-9734. Project Development Editor: Ann McMartin. Publishes hardcover and paperback originals. Publishes 30 titles/year. Pays 10% royalty on net sales. Publishes book 7 months after acceptance of ms. Simultaneous submissions OK. Reports on queries in 1 month. *Writer's Market* recommends allowing 2 months for reply. Book catalog and ms guidelines for #10 SASE.
Nonfiction: Professional-level publications. Subjects include educational policy, educational administration and educational evaluation primarily in K-12. Query.

‡COTTONWOOD PRESS, INC., Suite 398, 305 West Magnolia, Fort Collins CO 80521. Editor: Cheryl Thurston. Publishes trade paperback originals. Publishes 2-8 titles/year. Receives 50 queries and 400 mss/year. 50% of mss from first-time authors, 100% from unagented writers. Pays 10-12% royalty on net sales. Publishes book 1 year after acceptance. Simultaneous submissions OK (if notified). Reports in 1 month on queries and proposals, 3 months on mss. Book catalog for 6×9 SAE and 2 first class stamps. Manuscript guidelines for #10 SASE.
Nonfiction: Textbook. Subjects include: education and language/literature. "We publish *only* supplemental textbooks for English/language arts teachers, grades 5-12, with an emphasis upon middle school and junior high materials. Don't assume we publish educational materials for all subject areas. We do not. Never submit anything to us before looking at our catalog. We have a very narrow focus and a distinctive style. Writers who don't understand that are wasting their time." Query with outline and 1-3 sample chapters.
Recent Nonfiction Title: *Writing Your Life*, by Mary Borg (supplemental textbook).

COUNCIL FOR INDIAN EDUCATION, 517 Rimrock Rd., Billings MT 59102. (406)252-7451. Editor: Hap Gilliland. Estab. 1963. Publishes hardcover and trade paperback originals. Publishes 6 titles/year. Receives 200 queries/year. 75% of mss from first-time authors, 100% from unagented writers. Pays 10% (book mss) on wholesale price or makes outright purchase of short stories. Publishes book 1 year after acceptance of ms. Simultaneous submissions OK. Reports in 3 months on queries. Book catalog and ms guidelines for #10 SASE.
Nonfiction: Biography, how-to, humor, illustrated book and children's/juvenile. Subjects include anthropology/archaeology, education, ethnic, history, hobbies, nature/environment and recreation related to Indian life. Query. Reviews artwork/photos as part of the freelance ms package. Writers should send photocopies.
Fiction: Adventure, ethnic, historical, humor, juvenile, mystery, picture books, short story collections and Western. All must be Indian related. Submit synopsis or complete mss.
Poetry: "We publish one poetry book per year—all poems related to Indian life must be upbeat, positive—no complaining." Submit individual poems or submit complete ms.
Tips: "Our books are for students, kindergarten through high school. Many are American Indian. We buy *only* books related to Native American Life and culture, suitable for use in schools (all levels). We accept no mss. June thru September."

THE COUNTRYMAN PRESS, INC., P.O. Box 175, Woodstock VT 05091. (802)457-1049. Managing Editor: Robin Dutcher-Bayer. Estab. 1973. Imprints include Foul Play Press and Backcountry Publications. Publishes hardcover and trade paperback originals and paperback reprints. Publishes 20-25 titles/year. Receives 2,500 submissions/year. 50% of books from first-time authors; 75% from unagented writers. Pays 5-10% royalty on retail price. Offers $750 average advance. Publishes book an average of 1 year after acceptance. Simultaneous submissions OK. Reports in 1 month on queries. *Writer's Market* recommends allowing 2 months for reply. No material returned w/o SASE; no unsolicited mss *please!* Free book catalog.
Nonfiction: Cookbook, how-to, travel guides. Subjects include cooking, foods and nutrition, adult fitness, history, nature/environment, recreation, fishing, regional (New England, especially Vermont), travel. "We want good 'how-to' books, especially those related to rural life; also nature/environmental issues." Submit outline and sample chapters. Reviews artwork/photos as part of ms package.
Recent Nonfiction Title: *Wilderness Ethics*, by Laura and Guy Waterman.
Fiction: Mystery. Submit inquiries, or outline, sample chapter and SASE. No unsolicited mss *please!*
Recent Fiction Title: *The Only Game*, by Patrick Ruell.

CRAFTSMAN BOOK COMPANY, 6058 Corte Del Cedro, Carlsbad CA 92009-9974. (619)438-7828 or (800)829-8123. FAX (619)438-0398. Editorial Manager: Laurence D. Jacobs. Estab. 1957. Publishes paperback originals. Averages 12 titles/year; receives 50 submissions/year. 85% of books from first-time authors; 98% of books from unagented writers. Pays 7½-12½% royalty on wholesale price or retail price. Publishes book an average of 18 months after acceptance. Simultaneous submissions OK. Query for electronic submissions. Reports in 1 month on queries. *Writer's Market* recommends allowing 2 months for reply. Free book catalog and ms guidelines.

Nonfiction: How-to and technical. All titles are related to construction for professional builders. Query. Reviews artwork/photos as part of ms package.

Tips: "The book should be loaded with step-by-step instructions, illustrations, charts, reference data, forms, samples, cost estimates, rules of thumb, and examples that solve actual problems in the builder's office and in the field. The book must cover the subject completely, become the owner's primary reference on the subject, have a high utility-to-cost ratio, and help the owner make a better living in his chosen field."

CREATIVE PUBLISHING CO., The Early West, Box 9292, College Station TX 77842-0292. (409)775-6047. Contact: Theresa Earle. Estab. 1978. Publishes hardcover originals. Receives 20-40 submissions/year. 50% of books from first-time authors; 100% from unagented writers. Royalty varies on wholesale price. Publishes book an average of 8 months after acceptance. *Writer's Market* recommends allowing 2 months for reply. Free book catalog.

Nonfiction: Biography. Subjects include Americana (western), history. No mss other than 19th century western America. Query. Reviews artwork/photos as part of ms package.

‡CRISP PUBLICATIONS, INC., 1200 Hamilton Ct., Menlo Park CA 94025-1427. (415)323-6100. Managing Editor: Kathleen Barcos. Publishes trade paperback originals. Firm averages 25-30 titles/year. Pays royalty on retail price. Publishes book an average of 6 months after acceptance. Free book catalog.

Nonfiction: How-to and self-help. Subjects include art/architecture, business and economics, education, health/medicine and money/finance. Submit outline/synopsis and sample chapters.

CROSS CULTURAL PUBLICATIONS, INC., P.O. Box 506, Notre Dame IN 46556. General Editor: Cyriac Pullapilly. Publishes hardcover originals. Publishes 4-5 titles/year. Receives 300 queries and 100 mss/year. 25% of mss from first-time authors; 100% from unagented writers. Pays 10% royalty on wholesale price. Publishes book 6 months after acceptance of ms. Simultaneous submissions OK. Reports in 1 month on queries. *Writer's Market* recommends allowing 2 months for reply. Book catalog free on request.

Nonfiction: Biography. Subjects include government/politics, history, philosophy, religion, sociology and scholarly. "We publish scholarly books that deal with intercultural topics—regardless of discipline." Query.

THE CROSSING PRESS, 97 Hangar Way, Watsonville CA 95076. (408)722-0711. Co-Publishers: Elaine Goldman Gill, John Gill. Publishes hardcover and trade paperback originals. Averages 40 titles/year; receives 1,600 submissions annually. 10% of books from first-time authors; 75% of books from unagented writers. Pays royalty. Publishes book an average of 18 months after acceptance. Simultaneous submissions OK. Reports in 6 weeks on queries. *Writer's Market* recommends allowing 2 months for reply. Free book catalog.

Nonfiction: Cookbook, how-to, men's studies, literary and feminist. Subjects include cooking, health, gays, mysteries, sci-fi. Submissions to be considered for the feminist series must be written by women. Submit outline and sample chapter.

Fiction: Good literary material. Submit outline and sample chapter.

Tips: "Simple intelligent query letters do best. No come-ons, no cutes. It helps if there are credentials. Authors should research the press first to see what sort of books it publishes."

CROSSWAY BOOKS, Imprint of Good News Publishers, 1300 Crescent St., Wheaton IL 60187-5800. Fax: (708)682-4785. Editorial Director: Leonard G. Goss. Estab. 1938. Publishes hardcover and trade paperback originals. Averages 50 titles/year; receives 3,000 submissions annually. 5% of books from first-time authors; 90% of books from unagented writers. Average print order for a writer's first book is 5,000. Pays negotiable royalty; offers negotiable advance. Publishes book an average of 1 year after acceptance. No phone queries! Reports in up to 9 months. Book catalog and ms guidelines for 9 × 12 SAE and 6 first class stamps.

Nonfiction: Subjects include issues on Christianity in contemporary culture, Christian doctrine, and church history. "All books must be written out of Christian perspective or world view." Query with outline.

Recent Nonfiction Title: *Ethics for a Brave New World*, by John S. Feinberg and Paul Feinberg.

Fiction: Contemporary; science fiction; fantasy (genuinely creative in the tradition of C.S. Lewis, J.R.R. Tolkien and Madeleine L'Engle); and juvenile (10-14; 13-16). No formula romance, short stories, poetry, true stories, children's illustrated. Also, no horror novels or "Issue" novels. Query with synopsis. "All fiction must be written from a genuine Christian perspective."

Recent Fiction Title: *Prophet*, by Frank E. Peretti.

Tips: "The writer has the best chance of selling our firm a book which, through fiction or nonfiction, shows the practical relevance of biblical doctrine to contemporary issues and life."

CROWN PUBLISHING GROUP, Division of Random House, 201 E. 50th St., New York NY 10022. "Prefers not to share information."

DANCE HORIZONS, Imprint of Princeton Book Co., Publishers, P.O. Box 57, 12 W. Delaware Ave., Pennington NJ 08534. (609)737-8177. Fax: (609)737-1869. Managing Editor: Debi Elfenbein. Estab. 1976. Publishes hardcover and paperback originals and paperback reprints on dance only. Averages 10 titles/year; receives 25-30 submissions annually. 50% of books from first-time authors; 98% of books from unagented writers.

Pays 10% royalty on net receipts; offers no advance. Publishes book an average of 10 months after acceptance. Simultaneous submissions OK. Reports in 3 months. Free book catalog.

Nonfiction: Dance-related subjects only. Query first. Reviews artwork/photos.

Recent Nonfiction Title: *Jazz Dance Class, Beginning Thru Advanced*, by Gus Giordano.

Tips: "We're very careful about the projects we take on. They have to be, at the outset, polished, original and cross-marketable."

JOHN DANIEL AND COMPANY, PUBLISHERS, Imprint of Daniel & Daniel, Publishers Inc., P.O. Box 21922, Santa Barbara CA 93121-0121. (805)962-1780. Publisher: John Daniel. Estab. 1985. Publishes trade paperback originals. Averages 5 titles/year; receives 1,500-3,000 submissions annually. 50% of books from first-time authors; 100% of books from unagented writers. Pays 10% royalty on wholesale price. Publishes book an average of 1 year after acceptance. Simultaneous submissions OK. Query for electronic submissions. Reports in 2 months. Book catalog and ms guidelines for #10 SASE.

Nonfiction: Autobiography, biography, literary memoir and essays. "We'll look at anything, but are particularly interested in books in which literary merit is foremost—as opposed to books that simply supply information. No libelous, obscene, poorly written or unintelligent manuscripts." Query or submit outline and sample chapters.

Recent Nonfiction Title: *My Well-Balanced Life on a Wooden Leg*, by Al Capp (memoir).

Fiction: Novels and short story collections. "We do best with books by authors who have demonstrated a clear, honest, elegant style. No libelous, obscene, poorly written, or boring submissions." Query or submit synopsis and sample chapters.

Recent Fiction Title: *The Year of the Buck*, by Susan Harper (stories).

Poetry: "We're open to anything, but we're very cautious. Poetry's hard to sell." Submit complete ms.

Recent Poetry Title: *Mind and Blood*, by John Finlay.

Tips: "If fame and fortune are what you're after, you should aim for the major leagues, the big time publishers, and I wish you luck. But in the meantime, remember there is a friendlier, smaller, more approachable market among small press magazines and book publishers. The small press has been around since Guttenberg, and is still alive and well. It has given us the first works of Herman Melville, Mark Twain, James Joyce, Virginia Woolf, Anais Nin, Raymond Chandler, and a host of other stars that light up the literary heavens."

DANTE UNIVERSITY OF AMERICA PRESS, INC., P.O. Box 843, Brookline VA 02147-0843. President: Adolph Caso. Estab. 1975. Publishes hardcover originals and reprints, and trade paperback originals and reprints. Averages 5 titles/year; receives 50 submissions annually. 50% of books from first-time authors; 50% of books from unagented writers. Average print order for a writer's first book is 3,000. Pays royalty; offers negotiable advance. Publishes book an average of 10 months after acceptance. Simultaneous submissions OK. Query for electronic submissions. Reports in 2 months.

Nonfiction: Biography, reference, reprints, and translations from Italian and Latin. Subjects include general scholarly nonfiction, Renaissance thought and letter, Italian language and linguistics, Italian-American history and culture, and bilingual education. Query first with SASE. Reviews artwork/photos as part of ms package.

Fiction: Translations from Italian and Latin. Query first with SASE.

Poetry: "There is a chance that we would use Renaissance poetry translations."

MAY DAVENPORT, PUBLISHERS, 26313 Purissima Rd., Los Altos Hills CA 94022. (415)948-6499. Editor/Publisher: May Davenport. Estab. 1976. Imprint is md Books (nonfiction and fiction). Publishes hardcover and trade paperback originals. Averages 4 titles/year; receives 1,000-2,000 submissions annually. 95% of books from first-time authors; 5% from professional writers. Pays 15% royalty on retail price; no advance. Publishes book an average of 1-3 years after acceptance. Reports in 1 month. *Writer's Market* recommends allowing 2 months for reply. Ms guidelines for #10 SASE.

Nonfiction: Juvenile (13-17). Subject art, music to interest ages 13-17. "Our readers are students in elementary and secondary public school districts, as well as correctional institutes of learning, etc. No hack writing." Query.

Recent Nonfiction Title: *Leroy, The Lizard*, by Claudia Cherness.

Fiction: Adventure, fantasy. "We're overstocked with picture books and first readers; prefer literature for TV-oriented teenagers. Be entertaining while informing." No sex or violence. Query with SASE.

Recent Fiction Title: *Tug of War*, by Barbara A. Scott.

Tips: "Imagine yourself a teen narrator in today's complex computer world with problems and solutions teens face uninhibitedly, so other teens will laugh and read your tale. . . .if you can't, forget it."

JONATHAN DAVID PUBLISHERS, INC., 68-22 Eliot Ave., Middle Village NY 11379-1194. Fax: (718)894-2818. Editor-in-Chief: Alfred J. Kolatch. Publishes hardcover and trade paperback originals and reprints. Publishes 20-25 titles/year. 50% of ms from first-time authors, 90% from unagented writers. Pays royalty or makes outright purchase. Offers $1,000-5,000 advance. Publishes book 18 months after acceptance of ms. Reports in 1 month on queries. *Writer's Market* recommends allowing 2 months for reply. Book catalog for 6×9 SAE and 4 first class stamps.

Nonfiction: Cookbook, how-to, reference and self-help. Subjects include religion and sports. "We specialize in Judaica." Submit outline and 1 sample chapter.

HARLAN DAVIDSON, INC., 3110 N. Arlington Heights Rd., Arlington Heights IL 60004-1592. (708)253-9720. Fax: (708)253-9728. Editor-in-Chief: Maureen G. Hewitt. Estab. 1972. Additional Imprint is Forum Press, Inc. Publishes college texts, both hardcover and paperback. Publishes 15 titles/year. Receives 200 queries and 25 mss/year. 100% of mss from unagented writers. Mss are contracted as work for hire. Pays royalty on net. Publishes book 10 months after acceptance of ms. Simultaneous submissions OK. Query for electronic submissions. Reports in 3 months on proposals. Book catalog free on request.
Nonfiction: Subjects include business, education, government, history (main list), biographical history, literature, philosophy, regional state histories, sociology, ethnic history and women's issues/studies. "Because we are a college textbook publisher, academic credentials are extremely important. We usually find our own authors for a need in the field that we identify, but we are also receptive to ideas brought to us by qualified professionals, in history, especially." Submit outline and proposal package, including brief description of proposed book and its market and competition; and a recent vita.
Recent Nonfiction Title: *African Americans in the Early Republic, 1789-1831*, by Donald R. Wright.

DAVIS PUBLICATIONS, INC., 50 Portland St., Worcester MA 01608. (508)754-7201. Fax: (508)753-3834. Managing Editor: Wyatt Wade. Acquisitions Editor: Martha Siegel. Estab. 1901. Averages 5-10 titles/year. Pays 10-12% royalty. Publishes book an average of 1 year after acceptance. *Writer's Market* recommends allowing 2 months for reply. Book catalog for 9 × 12 SAE with 2 first class stamps. Write for copy of guidelines for authors.
Nonfiction: Publishes technique-oriented art, design and craft books for the educational market. Accepts nonfiction translations. "Keep in mind the intended audience. Our readers are visually oriented. All illustrations should be collated separately from the text, but keyed to the text. Photos should be good quality transparencies and black and white photographs. Well-selected illustrations should explain, amplify, and enhance the text. We average 2-4 photos/page. We like to see technique photos as well as illustrations of finished artwork, by a variety of artists, including students. Recent books have been on papermaking, airbrush painting, jewelry, design, puppets, and watercolor painting." Submit outline, sample chapters and illustrations. Reviews artwork/photos as part of ms package.
Recent Nonfiction Title: *Computers in the Artroom*, by Deborah Greh.

W.S. DAWSON CO., P.O. Box 62823, Virginia Beach VA 23466. (804)499-6271. Fax: (804)490-0922. Publisher: C.W. Tazewell. Publishes hardcover and trade paperback originals. Publishes 10 titles/year. Receives 16 queries and 6 mss/year. Pays negotiated royalty. Publishes book 6 months after acceptance of ms. Simultaneous submissions OK. Query for electronic submissions. Reports in 1 month on queries. *Writer's Market* recommends allowing 2 months for reply. Book catalog free on request.
Nonfiction: Biography and humor. Subjects include history, regional. "Most publications are Virginia local history, genealogy and biography, and in particular Eastern Virginia. Advance approval is requested before sending mss, etc." Query. Reviews artwork/photos as part of ms package. Writers should send photocopies.
Recent Nonfiction Title: *Bricks and Mortar: What's New in Old Princess Ann County and New Virginia Beach.*

‡DEACONESS PRESS, 2450 Riverside Ave. S., Minneapolis MN 55454. (612)672-4180. Senior Editors: Jay Johnson, Jack Caravela. Firm produces hardcover and trade paperback originals. Averages 10 titles/year. 30% of mss from first-time authors; 50% from unagented writers. Pays 6-15% royalty on wholesale price. Offers $1,000-2,500 advance. Publishes book 6 months after acceptance of ms. Simultaneous submissions OK. Query for electronic submissions. Reports in 2 months on proposals. Book catalog free on request.
Nonfiction: Self-help and social issues. Subjects include child guidance/parenting, health/medicine, psychology, sociology and young adult self-help. "We publish nonfiction titles which promote healthy living for teens and adults, with an emphasis on how physical health, mental health, and relationship issues affect the family." Query, or submit proposal package, including outline, sample chapters (2-3), marketing information, rationale, and information on competitive titles.
Tips: Audience is "individuals and families facing physical health issues, mental health issues, and other stresses and changes in their lives. Learn about titles competitive to your work and be prepared to tell us how your manuscript is different and/or better than what has already been written about the subject."

DEARBORN FINANCIAL PUBLISHING, INC., 520 N. Dearborn St., Chicago IL 60610-4354. (312)836-4400. Fax: (312)836-1021. Senior Vice President: Anita Constant. Estab. 1959. Imprints are Dearborn/R&R Newkirk (contact: Anne Shropshire), Enterprise/Dearborn (contact: Kathleen A. Welton) and Real Estate Education Co. (contact Carol Luitjens). Publishes hardcover and paperback originals. Averages 200 titles/year. Receives 200 submissions/year. 50% of books from first-time authors. 50% from unagented writers. Pays 1-15% on wholesale price. Publishes book an average of 6 months after acceptance. Simultaneous submissions OK. Query for electronic submissions. Reports in 1 month. *Writer's Market* recommends allowing 2 months for reply. Free book catalog and manuscript guidelines.

Nonfiction: How-to, reference and textbooks. Subjects include small business, real estate, insurance, banking, securities and money/finance. Query.
Tips: "People seeking real estate, insurance, broker's licenses are our audience; also business professionals interested in information on managing their finances, and people starting and running a small business."

DEATH VALLEY NATURAL HISTORY ASSOCIATION, P.O. Box 188, Death Valley CA 92328. (619)786-2331. Executive Director: Esy Feilds. Publishes hardcover and trade paperback originals and reprints. Publishes 5 titles/year. Receives 10 queries and 10 mss/year. 80% of mss from first-time authors, 80% from unagented writers. Pays royalty or makes outright purchase. Publishes book 9 months after acceptance of ms. Query for electronic submissions. Reports in 6 months on proposals. Book catalog and mss guidelines for #10 SASE.
Nonfiction: Biography, coffee table book, children's/juvenile, technical and textbook. Subjects include history (regional) and nature/environment (regional). "All our publishing relates to Death Valley and the Mojave Desert." All unsolicited mss are returned unopened.

IVAN R. DEE, INC., 1332 N. Halstead St., Chicago IL 60622-2632. (312)787-6262. Fax: (312)787-6269. President: Ivan R. Dee. Estab. 1988. Imprint is Elephant Paperbacks. Publishes hardcover originals and trade paperback originals and reprints. Averages 25 titles/year. 10% of books from first-time authors; 75% from unagented writers. Pays royalty. Publishes book an average of 9 months after acceptance. Reports in 1 month on queries. *Writer's Market* recommends allowing 2 months for reply. Book catalog free on request.
Nonfiction: History, literature and letters, biography, politics, contemporary affairs, theater. Submit outline and sample chapters. Reviews artwork/photos as part of ms package.
Recent Nonfiction Title: *Hard Choices, Lost Voices,* by Donald P. Judges.
Tips: "We publish for an intelligent lay audience and college course adoptions."

DEL REY BOOKS, Imprint of Ballantine Books, Division of Random House, 201 E. 50th St., New York NY 10022. (212)572-2677. Executive Editor: Shelly Shapiro. Senior Editor: Veronica Chapman. Estab. 1977. Publishes hardcover, trade paperback and mass market originals and mass market paperback reprints. Averages 60 titles/year; receives 1,900 submissions annually. 10% of books from first-time authors; 40% of books from unagented writers. Pays royalty on retail price. Offers competitive advance. Publishes book an average of 1 year after acceptance. Reporting time slow. Writer's guidelines for #10 SASE.
Fiction: Fantasy ("should have the practice of magic as an essential element of the plot") and science fiction ("well-plotted novels with good characterization, exotic locales, and detailed alien cultures."). Submit complete ms or detailed outline and first three chapters.
 • With the launch of their "Discovery" program in 1992, Del Rey emphasized their commitment to developing and promoting new science fiction writers.
Recent Fiction Title: *Domes of Fire,* by David Eddings.
Tips: "Del Rey is a reader's house. Our audience is anyone who wants to be pleased by a good entertaining novel. Pay particular attention to plotting and a satisfactory conclusion. It must be/feel believable. That's what the readers like."

DELACORTE PRESS, Imprint of Dell Books, Division of Bantam Doubleday Dell, 666 5th Ave., New York NY 10103. (212)765-6500. Editor-in-Chief: Leslie Schnur. Publishes hardcover originals. Publishes 36 titles/year. Royalty and advance vary. Publishes book an average of 2 years after acceptance, but varies. Simultaneous submissions OK. Reports in 2 months. Book catalog and guidelines for 9×12 SASE.
Nonfiction and Fiction: *Query, outline, first 3 chapters or brief proposal.* No mss for children's or young adult books accepted in this division.

DELL BOOKS, Division of Bantam Doubleday Dell, 666 5th Ave., New York NY 10103. "Prefers not to share information."

DELPHI PRESS, INC., P.O. Box 1538, Oak Park IL 60304. (708)524-7900. Fax: (708)524-7902. Publisher: Karen Jackson. Estab. 1989. Publishes trade paperback originals and reprints. Publishes 10-12 titles/year. Receives 50-100 queries and 20-30 mss/year. 95% of mss from first-time authors, 95% from unagented writers. Pays 7½-12% royalty on wholesale price. Publishes book within 1 year after acceptance of ms. Simultaneous submissions OK. Query for electronic submissions. Reports in 1 month on proposals. *Writer's Market* recommends allowing 2 months for reply. Book catalog and ms guidelines free on request.
Nonfiction: Delphi Press focuses on women's spirituality, men's mysteries; Wicca, witchcraft and pagan practice; ritual, healing, divination and magick; nature/earth religions and deep ecology; sacred psychology and inner development especially utilizing magick or psychic techniques. Submit complete ms or outline and 3 sample chapters.
Poetry: Query or submit complete ms.
Tips: "Audience is educated-up-scale women interested in women's spirituality and personal power."

THE DENALI PRESS, P.O. Box 021535, Juneau AK 99802-1535. (907)586-6014. Fax: (907)463-6780. Editorial Director: Alan Schorr. Editorial Associate: Sally Silvas-Ottumwa. Estab. 1986. Publishes trade paperback originals. Averages 5 titles/year. Receives 120 submissions/year. 50% of books from first-time authors; 80% from unagented writers. Pays 10% royalty on wholesale price; buys some mss by outright purchase. Publishes book an average of 9-12 months after acceptance. Simultaneous submissions OK. Query for electronic submissions. Reports in 2 months. Author must contact us prior to sending manuscripts. Prefer letter of inquiry. Book catalog free on request.
Nonfiction: Reference. Subjects include Americana, Alaskana, anthropology, ethnic, government/politics, history, recreation, regional, sports and travel. "We need reference books—ethnic, refugee and minority concerns. Also interested in developing more titles in our travel series." Query with outline and sample chapters; all unsolicited mss are returned unopened.
Tips: "We have expanded our travel and family guide series. Just published reference guide to raising children in Los Angeles and in 1994 will publish guide on relocating in Paris."

T.S. DENISON & CO., INC., 9601 Newton Ave. S., Minneapolis MN 55431-2590. (612)888-3831. Fax: (612)888-9641. Editor-in-Chief: Sherrill B. Flora. Acquisitions Editor: Baxter Brings. Estab. 1876. Publishes teacher aid materials; receives 500 submissions annually. 90% of books from first-time authors; 100% of books from unagented writers. Average print order for a writer's first book is 3,000. Royalty varies; no advance. Publishes book an average of 1-2 years after acceptance. Reports in 2 months. Book catalog and ms guidelines for 9×12 SAE with 3 first class stamps.
Nonfiction: Specializes in early childhood and elementary school teaching aids. Send prints if photos are to accompany ms. Submit complete ms. *Writer's Market* recommends query with SASE first. Reviews artwork/photos as part of ms package.
Recent Nonfiction Title: *Let's Meet Famous Artists*, by Harriet Kinghorn.
Recent Fiction Title: *Everyday Songs*, by Connie Walters.

DENLINGERS PUBLISHERS, LTD., P.O. Box 2300, Centreville VA 22020-2300. (703)830-4646. Fax: (703)830-5303. Publisher: William W. Denlinger. Estab. 1926. Publishes hardcover and trade paperback originals and reprints. Averages 12 titles/year; receives 250 submissions annually. 10% of books from first-time authors; 85% of books from unagented writers. Average print order for a writer's first book is 3,000. Pays variable royalty. No advance. Publishes book an average of 1 year after acceptance. Simultaneous submissions OK. Query for electronic submissions. Reports in 1 week on queries. *Writer's Market* recommends allowing 2 months for reply. Book catalog for SASE.
Nonfiction: How-to and technical books; dog-breed books only. Query. Reviews artwork/photos as part of ms package.
Recent Nonfiction Title: *Proction Dogs*, by Weiss and Rose.

DEVYN PRESS, Subsidiary of Baron Barclay Bridge Suppliers, Suite 230, 3600 Chamberlain Ln., Louisville KY 40241. (502)426-0410. President: Randy Baron. Publishes hardcover and trade paperback originals and reprints. Publishes 10 titles/year. Receives 40 queries and 20 mss/year. 50% of mss from first-time authors, 90% from unagented writers. Pays 5-10% royalty on wholesale price. Offers $500-1,000 advance. Publishes book 6 months after acceptance of ms. Simultaneous submissions OK. Query for electronic submissions. Reports in 2 months on queries. Book catalog and ms guidelines free on request.
Nonfiction: How-to, self-help. Subjects include sports and games/bridge. "We are the world's largest publisher of books on the game of bridge." Query. Reviews artwork/photos as part of freelance ms package. Writers should send photocopies.

DISCIPLESHIP RESOURCES, 1908 Grand Ave., Box 840, Nashville TN 37202. (615)340-7068. Fax: (615)340-7006. Editor: Craig B. Gallaway. Publishes trade paperback originals and reprints. Publishes 30 titles/year. Receives 300 queries and 150 mss/year. 20% from first-time authors, 40% from unagented writers. Pays 5-10% royalty on retail price or makes outright purchase of $250-1,500. Offers $250 advance. Publishes book 6 months after acceptance of ms. Query for electronic submissions. Reports in 2 months on queries. Book catalog free on request. Manuscript guidelines for #10 SASE.
Nonfiction: Subjects include theology of ministry, evangelism, worship, stewardship, ministry of laity, family ministry, Christian education, ethnic (church), history (Methodist/church), music/dance (religious), nature/environment (ecology), recreation (leisure ministry), Christian biography (ecclesiastical). "Materials must be focused on specific ministries of the church, in particular the United Methodist Church, but we also work with ecumenical resources." Query or submit proposal package, including outline, sample chapter, description of audience! Reviews artwork/photos as part of freelance mss package. Writers should send photocopies.
Tips: "Focus on ministry, write simply, and do more research."

DORAL PUBLISHING, INC., P.O. Box 596, Wilsonville OR 97070. (503)694-5707. Editor-in-Chief: Luana Luther. Imprints are Golden Boy Press, Marketing Coordinator: Lynn Grey; Swan Valley Press, Editor: Joan Bailey. Adele Publications, Publisher: William Cusick. Publishes hardcover and trade paperback originals, Publishes 7 titles/year. Receives 16 queries and 12 mss/year. 60% of mss from first-time authors, 85% from unagented writers. Pays 10-17% royalty on wholesale price. Publishes book 4 months after acceptance of ms. Query for electronic submissions. *Writer's Market* recommends allowing 2 months for reply. Book catalog free on request. Manuscript guidelines for #10 SASE.

Nonfiction: How-to, children's/juvenile, reference. Subjects include animals (dogs). "We publish only books about Pure Bred Dogs. No flowery prose." Submit outline and 2 sample chapters. Reviews artwork/photos as part of the freelance ms package. Writers should send photocopies.

DORLING KINDERSLEY, INC., 232 Madison Ave., New York NY 10016. Senior Editor, children's books: B. Alison Weir. Executive Editor, adult books: Jeanette Mall. Publishes hardcover originals. Publishes 70 titles/year. Receives 300 queries and 1,000 mss/year. Pays royalty. "As of 2/15/93, only agented mss will be considered." Simultaneous submissions OK. Reports in 3 months. Book catalog and ms guidelines free on request.

Nonfiction: Coffee table book, cookbook, how-to, illustrated book and reference. Subjects include agriculture/horticulture, animals, art/architecture, guidance, cooking, foods and nutrition, gardening, health/medicine, hobbies, nature/environment, photography, recreation and travel. Submit proposal package. Reviews artwork/photos as part of ms package.

Recent Nonfiction Title: Eyewitness Science series.

Fiction: Juvenile division only.

Recent Fiction Title: *Bon Appetit, Bertie!,* by Joan Knight.

DOUBLEDAY, A division of Bantam Doubleday Dell, Publishing Group, Inc., 666 5th Ave., New York NY 10103. (212)765-6500. Imprints are Anchor Books, Nan A. Talese, Image, Currency Books, Perfect Crime, Main Street Books, DD Western, Loveswept and Perfect Crime. Publishes hardcover and trade paperback originals. Offers royalty on retail price and variable advance. Doubleday accepts fiction and nonfiction through agents. Will not read unsolicited material. Send proposal/synopsis to above imprints as appropriate. Sufficient postage for return via fourth class mail must accompany ms.

DOWN EAST BOOKS, Division of Down East Enterprise, Inc., P.O. Box 679, Camden ME 04843-0679. Managing Editor: Karin Womer. Estab. 1954. Publishes hardcover and trade paperback originals and trade paperback reprints. Averages 10-14 titles/year; receives 300 submissions annually. 50% of books from first-time authors; 90% of books from unagented writers. Average print order for a writer's first book is 3,000. Pays 10-15% on receipts. Offers average $200 advance. Publishes book an average of 1 year after acceptance. Simultaneous submissions OK. Reports in 2 months. Ms guidelines for 9 × 12 SAE with 3 first class stamps.

Nonfiction: Books about the New England region, Maine in particular. Subjects include Americana, history, nature, guide books, crafts and recreation. "All of our books must have a Maine or New England emphasis." Query. Reviews artwork/photos as part of ms package.

Recent Nonfiction Title: *Cape Cod,* by Alan Nyivi.

Fiction: "We generally publish no fiction except for an occasional juvenile title (average 1/year) but are now keeping alert for good general-audience novels—same regional criteria apply."

DRAMA BOOK PUBLISHERS, 260 Fifth Ave., New York NY 10001. (212)725-5377. Fax: (212)725-8506. Managing Editor: Judith Durant. Estab. 1967. Publishes hardcover and paperback originals and reprints. Averages 4-15 titles/year; receives 420 submissions annually. 70% of books from first-time authors; 90% of books from unagented writers. Royalty varies; advance varies; negotiable. Publishes book an average of 18 months after acceptance. Reports in 2 months.

Nonfiction: Texts, guides, manuals, directories, reference—for and about performing arts theory and practice: acting, directing; voice, speech, movement, music, dance, mime; makeup, masks, wigs; costumes, sets, lighting, sound; design and execution; technical theatre, stagecraft, equipment; stage management; producing; arts management, all varieties; business and legal aspects; film, radio, television, cable, video; theory, criticism, reference; playwriting; theatre and performance history. Accepts nonfiction, drama and technical works in translations also. *Query;* accepts 1-3 sample chapters; no complete mss. Reviews artwork/photos as part of ms package.

‡DUKE PRESS, Subsidiary of Duke Communications International. 221 E. 29th St., Loveland CO 80538. (303)663-4700. Manager, Editorial Product Development: David R. Bernard. Publishes trade paperback originals. Publishes 8 titles/year. Receives 12 queries and 8 mss/year. Pays 8-12% royalty on retail price. Offers $500-2,000 advance. Publishes book 9 months after acceptance. Query for electronic submissions. SASE. Reports in 1 month on proposals. Book catalog and ms guidelines free on request.

> *For information on book publishers' areas of interest, see the nonfiction and fiction sections in the Book Publishers Subject Index.*

Nonfiction: How-to, technical and textbook. Subjects include IBM AS/400 midrange computer. Submit outline and 2 sample chapters.

Tips: "Readers are MIS managers, programmers, and system operators working on an IBM AS/400 midrange computer. Authors must have technical knowledge and experience on an IBM AS/400."

DUQUESNE UNIVERSITY PRESS, 600 Forbes Ave., Pittsburgh PA 15282-0101. (412)434-6610. Fax: (412)434-5780. Contact: Acquisitions Editor. Estab. 1927. Averages 9 titles/year; receives 400 submissions annually. 25% of books from first-time authors; 100% of books from unagented writers. Average print order for a writer's first book is 1,000. Subsidy publishes (nonauthor) 20% of books. Pays 10% royalty on net sales; no advance. Publishes book an average of 1 year after acceptance. Query for electronic submissions. Query. Reports in 3 months. Book catalog for 9×12 SAE with 2 first class stamps.

Nonfiction: Scholarly books in the humanities, social sciences for academics, libraries, college bookstores and educated laypersons. Looks for scholarship. No unsolicited mss. Query.

Recent Nonfiction Title: *The Birth of Popular Culture,* by Tom Hayes.

DURST PUBLICATIONS LTD., 29-28 41st Ave., Long Island City NY 11101. (718)706-0303. Fax: (718)706-0891. Owner: Sanford Durst. Publishes hardcover and trade paperback originals and reprints. Averages 20 titles/year; receives 100 submissions annually. Average print order for first book is 2,500. Pays variable royalty. Publishes book an average of 6 months after acceptance. Reports in 1 month. *Writer's Market* recommends allowing 2 months for reply. Book catalog for 6×9 SAE and 4 first class stamps.

Nonfiction: How-to and reference. Subjects include Americana, art, business and economics, cooking and foods, hobbies—primarily coin collecting, stamp collecting, antiques and legal. Especially needs reference books and how-to on coins, medals, tokens, paper money, art, antiques—illustrated with valuations or rarities, if possible. Publishes for dealers, libraries, collectors and attorneys. Submit outline and sample chapters. Reviews artwork/photos as part of ms package.

Recent Nonfiction Title: *Buying & Selling Country Land,* by D. Reisman (practical/legal).

Tips: "Write in simple English. Do not repeat yourself. Present matter in logical, orderly form. Try to illustrate."

DUSTBOOKS, Box 100, Paradise CA 95967. (916)877-6110. Publisher: Len Fulton. Publishes hardcover and paperback originals. Averages 7 titles/year. Offers 15% royalty. Simultaneous submissions OK if so informed. Reports in 2 months. Free book catalog; writer's guidelines for #10 SASE.

Nonfiction: Our specialty is directories of small presses, poetry publishers, and two monthly newsletters on small publishers (*Small Press Review* and *Small Magazine Review*)." Publishes annual *International Directory of Little Magazines & Small Presses.*

DUTTON CHILDREN'S BOOKS, Division of Penguin USA, 375 Hudson St., New York NY 10014. (212)366-2000. Editor-in-Chief: Lucia Monfried. Estab. 1852. Firm publishes hardcover originals. Publishes 70 titles/year. 15% from first-time authors. Pays royalty on retail price. Simultaneous submissions OK. Reports in 1 month on queries. *Writer's Market* recommends allowing 2 months for reply. Book catalog for 9½×11 SAE with 6 first class stamps. Ms guidelines for #10 SASE. *"Please send query letter first on all except picture book manuscripts."*

Nonfiction: For preschoolers to middle-graders; including animals/nature, U.S. history, general biography, science and photo essays.

Recent Nonfiction Title: *Monarch Butterflies: Mysterious Travelers,* by Bianca Lavies.

Fiction: Dutton Children's Books has a complete publishing program that includes picture books; easy-to-read books; and fiction for all ages, from "first-chapter" books to young adult readers.

Recent Fiction Title: *Fortune Tellers,* by Lloyd Alexander.

EAGLE'S VIEW PUBLISHING, 6756 N. Fork Rd., Liberty UT 84310. Editor-in-Chief: Denise Knight. Estab. 1982. Publishes trade paperback originals. Publishes 4-6 titles/year. Receives 40 queries and 20 mss/year. 90% of mss from first-time authors, 100% from unagented writers. Pays 8-10% royalty on wholesale price. Publishes book 1 year after acceptance of ms. Simultaneous submissions OK. Query for electronic submissions. Reports on proposals in 4 months. Book catalog and ms guidelines for $1.50.

Nonfiction: How-to, Indian and mountain man and American frontier (history and craft). Subjects include anthropology/archaeology (native American crafts), ethnic (native American), history (American frontier), hobbies (crafts, especially beadwork, earrings), sports (sports car racing and autocross). "We are expanding from our Indian craft base to more general crafts." Submit outline and 1 or 2 sample chapters. Reviews artwork/photos as part of freelance ms package. Writers should send photocopies or sample illustrations. "We prefer to do photography in house."

EAST COAST PUBLISHING, P.O. Box 2829, Poughkeepsie NY 12603-0888. (800)327-4212. Vice President: K.K. Makris. Estab. 1987. Publishes hardcover and trade paperback originals. Firm averages 5 titles/year. Receives more than 100 submissions/year. 50% of books from first-time authors. 100% from unagented writers. Pays 10% on wholesale price or outright purchase of $1,000. Publishes book an average of 1 year

after acceptance. Simultaneous submissions OK. Query for electronic submissions. Reports in 2 months on queries. Book catalog for 9×12 SAE and 3 first class stamps. Manuscript guidelines for #10 SASE.
Nonfiction: How-to, reference, technical. Subjects include business and economics, government/politics and law. "The publisher is interested in reviewing manuscripts which deal with technical legal and business areas, including banking, in a manner which withstands the scrutiny of the industry, but appeals to the lay person reader. No biographies, autobiographies, cookbooks, art-related books, juvenile, alternative/New Age, religion, self-help psychology or humor books please." Reviews artwork/photos as part of ms package.
Recent Nonfiction Title: *Notary Public Handbook: A Guide for Florida*, by Piombino, A.E. (law).
Tips: "When considering a ms, the most essential element evaluated is the ability of the writer to impart the information in clear, concise language, creating an elegant delivery of the subject matter. Our audience consists of both the professional and general public communities. If I were a writer trying to market a book today, I would allow my editor to prevail in implementing revisions which will ultimately result in a better ms. Unless the editing is fatal to the originally intended thought, the writer should allow the editor to polish and fine tune the ms."

EASTERN NATIONAL PARK & MONUMENT ASSOCIATION, 446 W. Lane, Conshohocken PA 19428. (215)832-0555. Vice President of Marketing: Chesley Moroz. Estab. 1948. Imprint is Eastern Acorn Press. Publishes trade paperback originals and reprints. Publishes 50-60 titles/year. Receives 20 queries and 10 mss/year. 5% of mss from first-time authors, 50% from unagented writers. Pays 1-10% royalty on retail price or makes outright purchase of $6,000 maximum. Publishes book 1-2 years after acceptance of ms. Reports in 1 month on queries. *Writer's Market* recommends allowing 2 months for reply. Book catalog free on request.
Nonfiction: Biography, children's/juvenile. Subjects include Americana, history, military/war and nature/environment. "Requests for editorial plans are only accepted from member agencies." Query. All unsolicited mss are returned unopened.

‡THE EDUCATION CENTER, INC., Product Development Division, 1607 Battleground Ave., Greensboro NC 27408. Development Manager: Charlotte Perkins. Estab. 1973. Publishes supplementary resource books for elementary teachers: preschool/grade 6. Publishes 25 titles/year. Receives 100 queries and 50 mss/year. Less than 5% of mss from first-time authors, 100% from unagented writers. Pays 2-6% royalty on wholesale price (on books sold through dealers); 2-6% royalty on retail price (on books sold through direct mail). "Payment schedule and amount negotiated when contract signed." Publishes book 2-12 months after acceptance of ms (depending on condition of ms). Query for electronic submissions. Prefers Macintosh. Reports in 2 months on proposals. Book catalog and ms guidelines for 9×12 SASE.
Nonfiction: Teacher resource/supplementary materials. Subjects include education P/K-6 and language/literature. "We place a strong emphasis on materials that teach the basic language arts and math skills. We are also seeking materials for teaching science and geography, literature-based activities for the whole language classroom, cooperative learning ideas and multicultural materials. Technical, complex or comprehensive manuscripts (such as textbooks) are not accepted." Submit outline with 1 sample chapter.
Recent Nonfiction Title: *Kinder Capers*, by Enid Milhouse, Vera Refles (thematic teaching units).

‡ELLIOTT & CLARK PUBLISHING, INC., Suite 21, 1638 R Street NW, Washington DC 20009. Publisher: Carolyn M. Clark. Publishes hardcover and trade paperback originals. Publishes 7 titles/year. 50% of mss from first-time authors, 90% from unagented writers. Pays royalty on wholesale price. Offers $1,000-7,500 advance. Publishes book 15 months after acceptance. Simultaneous submissions OK. Reports in 2 months on proposals. Book catalog for #10 SASE. Manuscript guidelines free on request.
Nonfiction: Biography, coffee table book and self-help. Subjects include Americana, art/architecture, gardening, history, nature/environment and photography. "We specialize in illustrated histories—need to think of possible photography/illustration sources to accompany manuscript. Submit an analysis of audience or a discussion of possible sales avenues beyond traditional book stores (such as interest groups, magazines, associations, etc.)." Submit proposal package, including possible illustrations (if applicable), outline, sales avenues. Reviews artwork/photos as part of freelance ms package. Writers should send transparencies.
Recent Nonfiction Titles: *Thirty Plants That Can Save Your Life*, Douglas Schar (health/gardening paperback).
Tips: "We prefer proactive authors who are interested in providing marketing and the rights leads."

‡ELYSIUM GROWTH PRESS, 5436 Fernwood Ave., Los Angeles CA 90027. (310)455-1000. Fax: (310)455-2007. Publishes hardcover and paperback originals and reprints. Averages 4 titles/year; receives 20 submissions/year. 20% of books from first-time authors; 100% of books from unagented writers. Pays $3,000 average advance. Publishes book an average of 18 months after acceptance. Query for electronic submissions. Reports in 1-2 months on queries; 2 months on submissions. Book catalog free on request.
Nonfiction: Illustrated book, self-help and textbook. Subjects include health, nature, philosophy, photography, psychology, recreation, sociology and travel. A nudist, naturist, special niche publisher. Needs books on "body self-image, body self-appreciation, world travel and subjects depicting the clothing-optional lifestyle." Query. All unsolicited mss are returned unopened. Reviews artwork/photos as part of ms package.
Recent Nonfiction Title: *Therapy, Nudity & Joy*, by Dr. Aileen Goodson.

ENSLOW PUBLISHERS INC., Bloy St. and Ramsey Ave., P.O. Box 777, Hillside NJ 07205. (908)964-4116. Editor: Brian D. Enslow. Estab. 1977. Publishes hardcover and paperback originals. Averages 50 titles/year. 30% require freelance illustration. Pays royalty on net price; offers $500-5,000 advance. Publishes book an average of 8 months after acceptance. Reports in 2 weeks. *Writer's Market* recommends allowing 2 months for reply. Book catalog for $2, check and 9 × 12 SAE with 3 first class stamps.

Nonfiction: Interested in manuscripts for young adults and children. Some areas of special interest are science, social issues, biography, reference topics and recreation. Query with information on competing titles and writer's resume.

• This publisher is especially interested in ideas for series.

PAUL S. ERIKSSON, PUBLISHER, Battell-on-the-Otter, Suite 208, Middlebury VT 05753-1441. (802)388-7303; Summer: Forest Dale VT 05745. (802)247-8415. Publisher/Editor: Paul S. Eriksson. Associate Publisher/Co-Editor: Peggy Eriksson. Estab. 1960. Publishes hardcover and paperback trade originals and paperback trade reprints. Averages 5-10 titles/year; receives 1,500 submissions annually. 25% of books from first-time authors; 95% of books from unagented writers. Average print order for a writer's first book is 3,000-5,000. Pays 10-15% royalty on retail price; advance offered if necessary. Publishes book an average of 6 months after acceptance. *Writer's Market* recommends allowing 2 months for reply. Catalog for #10 SASE.

Nonfiction: Americana, birds (ornithology), art, biography, business/economics, cookbooks/cooking/foods, health, history, hobbies, how-to, humor, nature, politics, psychology, recreation, self-help, sociology, sports and travel. Query with SASE.

Fiction: Serious, literary. Query with SASE. No simultaneous submissions.

Recent Fiction Title: *The Headmaster's Papers*, by Richard A. Hawley.

Tips: "We look for intelligence, excitement and salability. We are now looking for more serious, literary fiction, not mainstream fiction."

ETC PUBLICATIONS, 700 E. Vereda Sur, Palm Springs CA 92262-4816. (619)325-5352. Editorial Director: LeeOna S. Hostrop. Senior Editor: Dr. Richard W. Hostrop. Estab. 1972. Publishes hardcover and paperback originals. Averages 6-12 titles/year; receives 100 submissions annually. 75% of books from first-time authors; 90% of books from unagented writers. Average print order for a writer's first book is 2,500. Offers 5-15% royalty, based on wholesale and retail price. No advance. Publishes book an average of 9 months after acceptance. Reports in 3 weeks. *Writer's Market* recommends allowing 2 months for reply.

Nonfiction: Educational management, gifted education, futuristics and textbooks. Accepts nonfiction translations in above areas. Submit complete ms with SASE. *Writer's Market* recommends query first with SASE. Reviews artwork/photos as part of ms package.

Tips: "ETC will seriously consider textbook manuscripts in any knowledge area in which the author can guarantee a first-year adoption of not less than 500 copies. Special consideration is given to those authors who are capable and willing to submit their completed work in camera-ready, typeset form."

M. EVANS AND CO., INC., 216 E. 49 St., New York NY 10017-1502. Fax: (212)486-4544. Editor-in-Chief: George C. deKay. Estab. 1960. Publishes hardcover originals. Royalty schedule to be negotiated. Averages 30-40 titles/year. 5% of books from unagented writers. Publishes book an average of 8 months after acceptance. "No mss should be sent unsolicited. A letter of inquiry is essential." Reports in 2 months. Book catalog for 9 × 12 SAE with 3 first class stamps.

Nonfiction and Fiction: "We publish a general trade list of adult fiction and nonfiction, cookbooks and semireference works. The emphasis is on selectivity because we publish only 30 titles a year. Our general fiction list, which is very small, represents an attempt to combine quality with commercial potential. We also publish westerns. Our most successful nonfiction titles have been related to health and the behavioral sciences. No limitation on subject. A writer should clearly indicate what his book is all about, frequently the task the writer performs least well. His credentials, although important, mean less than his ability to convince this company that he understands his subject and that he has the ability to communicate a message worth hearing." Reviews artwork/photos.

Tips: "Writers should review our book catalog or the *Publishers Trade List Annual* before making submissions."

FABER & FABER, INC., Division of Faber & Faber, Ltd., London, England; 50 Cross St., Winchester MA 01890. (617)721-1427. Contact: Publishing Assistant. Estab. 1976. Publishes hardcover and trade paperback originals, and trade paperback reprints. Averages 30 titles/year; receives 1,200 submissions annually. 10% of books from first-time authors; 25% of books from unagented writers. Pays 10% royalty on wholesale or retail price; advance varies. Publishes book an average of 1 year after acceptance. Simultaneous submissions OK. Reports in 3 months on queries. Book catalog for 9 × 12 SAE and 4 first class stamps; writer's guidelines for #10 SASE.

Nonfiction: Anthologies, biography, contemporary culture, film and screenplays, history and natural history. Subjects include Americana, animals, pop/rock music, New England and sociology. Query with synopsis and outline with SASE. Reviews artwork/photos as part of ms package.

Recent Nonfiction Title: *The Hottest Water in Chicago*, by Pemberton.

Fiction: Collections, ethnic, experimental and regional. No historical/family sagas or mysteries. Query with synopsis and outline with SASE.

Recent Fiction Title: *The Loop*, by Joe Coomer.

Tips: "Subjects that have consistently done well for us include popular culture; serious, intelligent rock and roll books; anthologies; and literary, somewhat quirky fiction. Please do not send entire ms; include SASE for reply."

FACTS ON FILE, INC., 460 Park Ave. S., New York NY 10016-7382. (212)683-2244. Editorial Director: Susan Schwartz. Estab. 1941. Publishes hardcover originals and reprints. Averages 125 titles/year; receives approximately 2,000 submissions annually. 25% of books from unagented writers. Pays 10-15% royalty on retail price. Offers average $10,000 advance. Simultaneous submissions OK. Query for electronic submissions. No submissions returned without SASE. Reports in 2 months on queries. Free book catalog.

Nonfiction: Reference and other informational books on business and economics, cooking and foods (no cookbooks), health, history, hobbies (but no how-to), entertainment, natural history, philosophy, psychology, recreation, religion, language, sports and multicultural studies. "We need serious, informational books for a targeted audience. All our books must have strong library interest, but we also distribute books effectively to the book trade." No computer books, technical books, cookbooks, biographies (except YA), pop psychology, humor, do-it-yourself crafts, fiction or poetry. Query or submit outline and a sample chapter.

Tips: "Our audience is school and public libraries for our more reference-oriented books and libraries, schools and bookstores for our less reference-oriented informational titles."

FAIRLEIGH DICKINSON UNIVERSITY PRESS, 285 Madison Ave., Madison NJ 07940. (201)593-8564. Fax: (201)593-8543. Director: Harry Keyishian. Estab. 1967. Publishes hardcover originals. Averages 30 titles/year; receives 300 submissions annually. 33% of books from first-time authors; 100% of books from unagented writers. Average print order for a writer's first book is 1,000. "Contract is arranged through Associated University Presses of Cranbury, New Jersey. We are a *selection* committee only." Subsidy publishes (nonauthor) 2% of books. Publishes book an average of 1 year after acceptance. Reports in 2 weeks on queries. *Writer's Market* recommends allowing 2 months for reply.

Nonfiction: Reference and scholarly books. Subjects include art, business and economics, Civil War, film, history, Jewish studies, literary criticism, music, philosophy, politics, psychology, sociology and women's studies. Looking for scholarly books in all fields. No nonscholarly books. Query with outline and sample chapters. Reviews artwork/photos as part of ms package.

Tips: "Research must be up to date. Poor reviews result when authors' bibliographies and notes don't reflect current research. We follow *Chicago Manual of Style* style in scholarly citations."

THE FAMILY ALBUM, Rt. 1, Box 42, Glen Rock PA 17327. (717)235-2134. Fax: (717)235-8042. Contact: Ron Lieberman. Estab. 1969. Publishes hardcover originals and reprints and software. Averages 2 titles/year; receives 150 submissions annually. 30% of books from first-time authors; 100% of books from unagented writers. Average print order for a writer's first book is 1,000. Pays royalty on wholesale price. Publishes book an average of 10 months after acceptance. Simultaneous submissions OK. Query for electronic submissions. Reports in 2 months.

Nonfiction: "Significant works in the field of (nonfiction) bibliography. Worthy submissions in the field of Pennsylvania history, biography, folk art and lore. We are also seeking materials relating to books, literacy, and national development. Special emphasis on Third World countries, and the role of printing in international development." No religious material. Submit outline and sample chapters.

FARRAR, STRAUS AND GIROUX, INC., 19 Union Square W., New York NY 10003. Publisher, Books for Young Readers: Stephen Roxburgh. Editor-in-Chief, Books for Young Readers: Margaret Ferguson. Publishes hardcover originals. Receives 5,000 submissions annually. Pays royalty; offers advance. Publishes book an average of 18 months after acceptance. Reports in 3 months. Catalog for 6×9 SAE and 3 first class stamps.

Nonfiction and Fiction: "We are primarily interested in fiction picture books and novels for children and middle readers, but do some nonfiction—both picture book and longer formats." Submit outline/synopsis and sample chapters. Reviews copies of artwork/photos as part of ms package.

Recent Nonfiction Title: *Jake: A Labrador Puppy at Work and Play*, by Robert F. Jones.

Recent Fiction Title: *For The Life of Laetitia*, by Merle Hodge.

Recent Picture Book Title: *The Return of Freddy Legrand*, by Jon Agee.

Tips: "Study our style and our list."

FAWCETT JUNIPER, Imprint of Ballantine/Del Rey/Fawcett/Ivy, Division of Random House, 201 E. 50th St., New York NY 10022. (212)751-2600. Editor-in-Chief, Vice President: Leona Nevler. Publishes 24 titles/year. Pays royalty. Publishes book an average of 1 year after acceptance. Simultaneous submissions OK. Reports in 2 months on queries.

Nonfiction: Adult books.
Recent Nonfiction Title: *My Life: Magic Johnson*, by Magic Johnson.
Fiction: Mainstream/contemporary, young adult (12-18). No children's books. Query.
Recent Fiction Title: *The Secret History*, by Donna Tartt.

THE FEMINIST PRESS AT THE CITY UNIVERSITY OF NEW YORK, 2nd Floor, 311 E. 94th St., New York NY 10128. (212)360-5790. Senior Editor: Susannah Driver. Publishes hardcover and trade paperback originals and reprints. Publishes 8-10 titles/year. Receives 500 queries/mss/year. 20% of mss from first-time authors, 90% from unagented writers. Pays royalty on net price. Offers $100 average advance. Simultaneous submissions OK. Query for electronic submissions. Reports in 4 months on proposals. Book catalog and ms guidelines free on request.
Nonfiction: "The Feminist Press's primary mission is to publish works committed to the eradication of gender-role stereotyping that are multi-cultural in focus. Persons should write for our guidelines for submission and catalog; note that we generally publish for the college classroom." Biography, children's/juvenile, primary materials for the humanities and social science classroom and general readers. Subjects include ethnic, gay/lesbian, government/politics, health/medicine, history, language/literature, music/dance, sociology, translation, women's issues/studies and peace, memoir, international. Send proposal package, including materials requested in our guidelines. Reviews artwork/photos as part of freelance ms package. Writers should send photocopies and SASE.
Recent Nonfiction Title: *Fault Lines: A Memoir*, by Meena Alexander.
Fiction: "The Feminist Press publishes fiction reprints only. No original fiction is considered."
Tips: "Our audience consists of college students, professors, general readers."

J.G. FERGUSON PUBLISHING COMPANY, Suite 250, 200 W. Monroe, Chicago IL 60606. Editorial Director: C.J. Summerfield. Estab. 1940. Publishes hardcover originals. Firm averages 4-8 titles/year. Pays by project. Reports in 3 months on queries.
Nonfiction: Reference. "We publish work specifically for the high school/college library reference market. Nothing is a single-author project. They are encyclopedic in nature. We mainly publish medical and career encyclopedias. No mass market, scholarly, or juvenile books, please." Query or submit outline and one sample chapter.

DONALD I. FINE, INC., 19 W. 21st St., New York NY 10010. (212)727-3270. Imprints include Primus Library of Contemporary Americana. Publishes hardcover originals and trade paperback originals and reprints. Firm averages 45-60 titles/year. Receives 1,000 submissions/year. 30% of books from first-time authors. Pays royalty on retail price. Advance varies. Publishes book an average of 1 year after acceptance. Book catalog for 6×9 SASE.
 • Donald L. Fine, Inc. is currently accepting only agented mss.
Nonfiction: Biography, cookbook, humor, self-help. Subjects include history, military/war and sports. All unsolicited mss are returned unopened. Reviews artwork/photos as part of ms package.
Recent Nonfiction Title: *Merchant of Dreams: Louis B. Mayer, M.G.M. and the Secret Hollywood*, by Charles Higham.
Fiction: Adventure, ethnic, fantasy, historical, horror, humor, literary, mainstream/contemporary, mystery, science fiction, suspense and western. All unsolicited mss are returned unopened.
Recent Fiction Title: *Inadmissible Evidence*, by Philip Friedman.

FIREBRAND BOOKS, 141 The Commons, Ithaca NY 14850. (607)272-0000. Publisher: Nancy K. Bereano. Estab. 1985. Publishes hardcover and trade paperback originals. Averages 8-10 titles/year; receives 300-400 submissions annually. 50% of books from first-time authors; 90% of books from unagented writers. Pays 7-9% royalty on retail price, or makes outright purchase. Publishes book an average of 18 months after acceptance. Simultaneous submissions OK "with notification." Reports in 1 month on queries. *Writer's Market* recommends allowing 2 months for reply. Free book catalog.
Nonfiction: Criticism and essays. Subjects include feminism and lesbianism. Submit complete ms.
Fiction: Will consider all types of feminist and lesbian fiction.
Tips: "Our audience includes feminists, lesbians, ethnic audiences, and other progressive people."

FISHER BOOKS, P.O. Box 38040, Tucson AZ 85740-8040. (602)292-9080. Fax: (602)292-0431. Contact: Editorial Submissions Director. Estab. 1987. Publishes trade paperback originals and reprints. Firm averages 8 titles/year. 25% of books from first-time authors; 75% from unagented writers. Pays 10-15% royalty on wholesale price. Simultaneous submissions OK. Reports in 1 month. *Writer's Market* recommends allowing 2 months for reply. Book catalog for 3 first class stamps.
Nonfiction: Subjects include cooking, automotive, foods and nutrition, regional gardening, family health, self-help/parenting. Submit outline and sample chapters, not complete ms. Include return postage.
Recent Nonfiction Title: *Life After Loss*, by Bob Deits.

J. FLORES PUBLICATIONS, P.O. Box 830131, Miami FL 33283-0131. Editor: Eli Flores. Estab. 1982. Publishes trade paperback originals and reprints. Averages 10 titles/year. 99% of books from unagented writers. Pays 10-15% royalty on net sales; no advance. Publishes book an average of 1 year after acceptance. Simultaneous submissions OK. Reports in 1 month on queries. *Writer's Market* recommends allowing 2 months for reply. Book catalog and ms guidelines for 9 × 12 SAE with 2 first class stamps.

Nonfiction: How-to, illustrated book and self-help. "We need original nonfiction manuscripts on outdoor adventure, military science, weaponry, current events, self-defense, true crime and personal finance/careers. How-to manuscripts are given priority." Query with outline and 2-3 sample chapters. Reviews artwork/photos. "Photos are accepted as part of the manuscript package and are strongly encouraged."

Recent Nonfiction Title: *How To Be Your Own Detective*, by Kevin Sherlock.

Tips: "Trends include illustrated how-to books on a specific subject. Be thoroughly informed on your subject and technically accurate."

FOCAL PRESS, Subsidiary of Butterworth Heinemann, Division of Reed Elsevier (USA) Inc., 80 Montvale Ave., Stoneham MA 02180. (617)438-8464. Publishing Director: Karen M. Speerstra. Estab. U.S., 1981; UK, 1938. Imprint publishes hardcover and paperback originals and reprints. Averages 30-35 UK-US titles/year; entire firm averages 100 titles/year; receives 500-700 submissions annually. 25% of books from first-time authors; 90% of books from unagented writers. Pays 10-12% royalty on wholesale price; offers $1,500 average advance. Publishes book an average of 1 year after acceptance. Simultaneous submissions OK. Reports in 2 months. Free book catalog and ms guidelines.

Nonfiction: How-to, reference, technical and textbooks in media arts: photography, film and cinematography, broadcasting, theater and performing arts. High-level scientific/technical monographs are also considered. "We do not publish collections of photographs or books composed primarily of photographs. Our books are text-oriented, with artwork serving to illustrate and expand on points in the text." Query preferred, or submit outline and sample chapters. Reviews artwork/photos as part of ms package.

Recent Nonfiction Title: *Digital Nonlinear Editing*, by Thomas A. Ohanian.

Tips: "We are publishing fewer photography books. Our advances and royalties are more carefully determined with an eye toward greater profitability for all our publications."

‡FOCUS ON THE FAMILY BOOK PUBLISHING, 420 N. Cascade, Colorado Springs CO 80903. Managing Editor: Gwen Weising. Publishes hardcover and trade paperback originals. Publishes 15-20 titles/year. Receives 120 mss/year. 25% of mss from first-time authors, 25% from unagented writers. Pays royalty. Offers advance. Publishes book 1 year after acceptance of ms. Simultaneous submissions OK. Query for electronic submissions. Reports in 1 month on queries, 2 months on proposals. Book catalog free on request. Manuscript guidelines for #10 SASE.

Nonfiction: How-to, children's/juvenile and self-help. Subjects include child guidance/parenting, money/finance and women's issues/studies. "We are the publishing arm of Focus on the Family, an evangelized Christian organization. Authors need to be aware that our book publishing is closely related to the focus of the organization, which is the strengthening and preservation of family and marriages." Query.

Recent Nonfiction Title: *Finding the Love of Your Life*, by Neil Warren (self-help).

Tips: "Our audience is families and the people who make up families. Know what we publish before submitting query."

FOUR WALLS EIGHT WINDOWS, P.O. Box 548, New York NY 10014. Office: 39 W. 14th St., Room 503, New York NY 10011. Estab. 1987. Publishes hardcover and trade paperback originals and trade paperback reprints. Averages 16 titles/year. Receives 1,500 submissions/year. 10% of books from first-time authors. 70% from unagented writers. Pays royalty (depends — negotiated contract) on retail price. Offers $2,000 average advance. Publishes book an average of 12 months after acceptance. Reports in 1 month on queries. *Writer's Market* recommends allowing 2 months for reply. Book catalog for 6 × 9 SAE with 3 first class stamps.

Nonfiction: Political, investigative. Subjects include art/architecture, cooking, foods and nutrition, government/politics, history, language/literature, nature/environment, science, travel. "We do not want New Age works." Query first. Submit outline with SASE. All sent without SASE discarded.

Recent Nonfiction Title: *The Superpollsters; How They Measure and Manipulate Public Opinion in America*, by David W. Moore (current affairs).

Fiction: Ethnic, experimental, feminist, literary, mystery. "No romance, popular." Query first. Submit outline/synopsis with SASE.

Tips: "Send us something original, unusual, off-beat, possibly 'alternative.'"

‡FPMI COMMUNICATIONS, INC., 707 Fiber St., NW, Huntsville AL 35801-5833. (205)539-1850. Fax: (205)539-0911. President: Ralph Smith. Publishes trade paperback originals. Averages 4-6 titles/year. Receives 4-5 submissions/year. 60% of books from first-time authors; 100% from unagented writers. Pays 15% on retail price. Publishes book an average of 1 year after acceptance. Simultaneous submissions OK. Query for electronic submissions. Reports in 3 weeks on queries; 2 months on mss. Free book catalog.

Nonfiction: Technical. Subjects include government/politics, labor relations and personnel issues. "We will be publishing books for government and business on topics such as sexual harassment, drug testing, and how to deal with leave abuse by employees. Our books are practical, how-to books for a supervisor or manager. Scholarly theoretical works do not interest our audience." Submit outline/synopsis and sample chapters or send complete ms.

Recent Nonfiction Title: *The Federal Managers Guide to Liability*, by William B. Wiley, Attorney at Law.

Tips: "We are interested in books that are practical, easy-to-read and less than 150 pages. Primary audience is federal managers and supervisors—particularly first and second level. If I were a writer trying to market a book today, I would emphasize practical topics with plenty of examples in succinct, concrete language."

THE FREE PRESS, Division of Macmillan, 866 3rd Ave., New York NY 10022. President/Publisher: Erwin A. Glikes. Estab. 1947. Imprint is Lexington Books (Managing Director: Dino Battista). Averages 120 titles/year; receives 3,000 submissions annually. 15% of books from first-time authors; 50% of books from un-agented writers. Royalty schedule varies. Publishes book an average of 11 months after acceptance. Reports in 2 months.

Nonfiction: Publishes adult nonfiction, professional books and college texts in the social sciences, humanities and business. Reviews artwork/photos as part of ms package "but we can accept no responsibility for photos or art. Looks for identifiable target audience, evidence of writing ability." Accepts nonfiction translations. Send 1-3 sample chapters, outline, and query letter before submitting mss.

FRIENDS UNITED PRESS, 101 Quaker Hill, Richmond IN 47374. (317)962-7573. Fax: (317)966-1293. Editor/Manager: Ardith Talbot. Publishes 12 titles/year. Receives 100 queries and 80 mss/year. 50% of mss from first-time authors; 99% from unagented authors. Pays 7½% royalty. Publishes ms 1 year after acceptance of ms. Simultaneous submissions OK. Query for electronic submissions. Reports in 7 months. Book catalog and ms guidelines free on request.

Nonfiction: Biography, humor, children's/juvenile, reference and textbook. Subjects include religion. "Authors should be Quaker and should be familiar with Quaker history, spirituality and doctrine." Submit proposal package. Reviews artwork/photos as part of ms package. Writers should send photocopies.

Fiction: Historical, juvenile and religious. "Must be Quaker-related." Query.

Tips: "Spirituality mss must be in agreement with Quaker spirituality."

GALLAUDET UNIVERSITY PRESS, 800 Florida Ave. NE, Washington DC 20002. (202)651-5488. Imprints include Kendall Green Publications, Clerc Books and Gallaudet University Press. Managing Editor: Ivey Pittle Wallace. Estab. 1980. Publishes hardcover and paperback originals and reprints. Averages 15 titles/year. Pays 10-15% royalty on wholesale price (net). Simultaneous submissions OK. Query for electronic submissions. Reports in 3 months. Free manuscript guidelines.

Nonfiction: Scholarly and serious books on deafness and hearing loss. Topics include audiology, biography, education, health/medicine, history, linguistics, literature, parenting, psychology, sign language, sociology, and sports. Submit outline/synopsis and sample chapters or complete ms. Reviews artwork/photos as part of ms. package.

Recent Nonfiction Title: *Deaf History Unveiled*, by John Vikrey.

Tips: "Individuals in our audience come from many walks of life and include every age group. The common denominator among them is an interest and/or openness to learn more about deafness."

GARRETT PARK PRESS, P.O. Box 190, Garret Park MD 20896. Publisher: Robert Calvert. Estab. 1967. Publishes trade paperback originals. Firm averages 6 titles/year. Receives 80 submissions/year. 20% of books from first-time authors. 100% from unagented writers. Pays 10-15% royalty on wholesale or retail price. Publishes book an average of 8 months after acceptance. Reports in 1 month on queries. *Writer's Market* recommends allowing 2 months for reply. Free book catalog.

Nonfiction: Reference. Subjects include employment, education, ethnic. Query.

Tips: "We publish books on careers only."

GAY SUNSHINE PRESS AND LEYLAND PUBLICATIONS, P.O. Box 410690, San Francisco CA 94141-0690. (707)996-6082. Editor: Winston Leyland. Estab. 1970. Publishes hardcover and trade paperback originals and trade paperback reprints. Averages 6-8 titles/year. Pays royalty or makes outright purchase. Reports in 6 weeks on queries. Book catalog for $1.

Nonfiction: How-to and gay lifestyle topics. "We're interested in innovative literary nonfiction which deals with gay lifestyles." No long personal accounts, academic or overly formal titles. Query. "After query is returned by us, submit outline and sample chapters. Enclose SASE. All unsolicited mss are returned unopened."

Fiction: Erotica, ethnic, experimental, historical, mystery, science fiction and gay fiction in translation. "Interested in well-written novels on gay themes; also short story collections. We have a high literary standard for fiction." Query. "After query is returned by us, submit outline/synopsis and sample chapters. Enclose SASE. All unsolicited mss are returned unopened."

GEM GUIDES BOOK COMPANY, Suite F, 315 Cloverleaf Dr., Baldwin Park CA 91706-6510. (818)855-1611. Fax: (818)855-1610. Imprints include Gembooks. Editor: Robin Shepherd. Publishes trade paperback originals. Averages 6-8 titles/year. Receives 40 submissions/year. 30% of books from first-time authors. 100% from unagented writers. Pays 6-10% royalty on wholesale price. Offers $1,000 average advance. Publishes book an average of 4 months after acceptance. Simultaneous submissions OK. Reports in 1 month. *Writer's Market* recommends allowing 2 months for reply.

Nonfiction: Regional books for the Western U.S. Subjects include cooking, foods and nutrition, hobbies, nature/environment, recreation, travel. We are looking for books on bicycling in the southwest and nature books, also travel/local interest titles for the Western U.S. Query. Submit outline/synopsis and sample chapters. Reviews artwork/photos as part of ms package.

Recent Nonfiction Title: *The Old West Trivia Book*, by Don Bullis.

Tips: "Authors have the best chance selling us books about rocks, minerals, and recreational opportunities in the Western U.S. We have a general audience of people interested in recreational activities. Publishers plan and have specific books lines in which they specialize. Learn about the publisher and submit materials compatible with that publisher's product line."

GIFTED EDUCATION PRESS, The Reading Tutorium, 10201 Yuma Ct., P.O. Box 1586, Manassas VA 22110. (703)369-5017. Publisher: Maurice D. Fisher. Estab. 1981. Publishes paperback originals for school districts and libraries. Averages 5 titles/year; receives 50 submissions annually. 100% of books from first-time authors; 100% of books from unagented writers. Pays royalty of $1 per book. Publishes book an average of 6 months after acceptance. Simultaneous submissions OK. Reports in 4 months. Book catalog for #10 SAE with 2 first class stamps. Send letter of inquiry first. No unsolicited mss will be accepted.

Nonfiction: How-to. Subjects include philosophy, psychology, education of the gifted, the humanities, science and technology; and how to teach adults to read. "Need books on how to educate gifted children—both theory and practice, and adult literacy. Also, we are searching for books on using computers with the gifted, and teaching the sciences to the gifted. Need rigorous books on procedures, methods, and specific curriculum for the gifted. We need individuals to write brief book reviews and 'blurbs' for our Gifted Ed. News Page. *Send letter of inquiry only.* Do not send manuscripts or parts of manuscripts. Unsolicited manuscripts will be promptly returned without being read!"

Tips: "If I were a writer trying to market a book today, I would develop a detailed outline based upon intensive study of my field of interest. Present creative ideas in a rigorous fashion. Be knowledgeable about and comfortable with ideas. We are looking for books on using computers with gifted students; books on science and humanities education for the gifted; and books on how to teach adults to read."

GLENBRIDGE PUBLISHING LTD., 6010 W. Jewell Ave., Denver CO 80232-7106. Fax: (303)987-9037. Editor: James A. Keene. Estab. 1986. Publishes hardcover originals and reprints, and trade paperback originals. Publishes 6 titles/year. Pays 10% royalty. Publishes book an average of 1 year after acceptance. Simultaneous submissions OK. Reports in 2 months on queries. Book catalog for 6×9 SAE with 2 first class stamps. Ms guidelines for #10 SASE.

Nonfiction: Reference and textbook. Subjects include Americana, business and economics, history, music, philosophy, politics, psychology and sociology. Query or submit outline/synopsis and sample chapters. Include SASE.

Recent Nonfiction Title: *Spring Winds of Beijing*, by Gail Copeland.

GLOBAL PRESS WORKS, P.O. Box 71886, Marietta GA 30009. Publisher: Jami Schwartz-Edelheit. Publishes trade paperback originals and reprints. Publishes 6 titles per year. Receives 30 queries and 20 mss/year. 30% of mss from first time authors; 50% from unagented writers. Pays royalty or makes outright purchase. Advance varies per project. Publishes book 6 months after acceptance. Query for electronic submissions. Reports in on proposals. Manuscript guidelines for #10 SASE. Manuscripts not accepted without prior solicitation.

Nonfiction: How-to, children's/juvenile, self-help, child guidance/parenting, education, nature/environment. "We focus on submissions that directly relate to environmental and self-esteem issues with children. All subject matter must be appropriate to educators, schools, libraries, and parents." Submit proposal package including outline and 3 sample chapters. Reviews artwork/photos as part of freelance ms package. Writers should send photocopies.

Tips: "We are looking for writers who combine creativity, knowledge and dedication to the education of children in the fields of self-esteem and environmental awareness."

THE GLOBE PEQUOT PRESS, INC., P.O. Box 833, Old Saybrook CT 06475-0833. (203)395-0440. Fax: (203)395-0312. Managing Editor: Bruce Markot. Imprints are Voyager Books and East Woods Books. Publishes hardcover and paperback originals and paperback reprints. Averages 70 titles/year; receives 1,500 submissions annually. 30% of books from first-time authors; 60% of books from unagented writers. Average print order for a writer's first book is 5,000-7,500. Offers 7½-10% royalty on net price; offers advances. Publishes book an average of 1 year after acceptance of ms. Simultaneous submissions OK. Reports in 3 months. Book catalog for 9×12 SASE.

Nonfiction: Travel guidebooks (regional OK), natural history, outdoor recreation, business, careers, gardening, carpentry, how-to, Americana and cookbooks. No doctoral theses, fiction, genealogies, memoirs, poetry or textbooks. Submit outline, table of contents, sample chapter, and resume/vita. Reviews artwork/photos.

‡**DAVID R. GODINE, PUBLISHER, INC.**, Horticultural Hall, 300 Massachusetts Ave., Boston MA 02115. Editorial Director: Mark Polizzotti. Publishes hardcover and trade paperback originals and reprints. Publishes 40 titles/year. Receives 5,000 queries and 3,000 mss/year. 10% of mss from first-time authors, 40% from unagented writers. Pays royalty on retail price. Publishes book 3 years after acceptance of ms. Simultaneous submissions OK. Reports in 3 months on queries. Book catalog for 9×6 SAE with 2 first class stamps. Manuscript guidelines for #10 SASE.
Nonfiction: Biography, coffee table book, cookbook, humor, illustrated book and children's/juvenile. Subjects include agriculture/horticulture, Americana, art/architecture, gardening, nature/environment, photography and translation. Query with 3 sample chapters. Reviews artwork/photos as part of the freelance ms package. Writers should send photocopies. NO ORIGINALS.
Recent Nonfiction Title: *Joseph Banks: A Life*, by Patrick O'Brian (biography).
Fiction: Adventure, feminist, historical, humor, juvenile, literary, mystery, short story collection and young adult. "Currently, we are over-committed with [fiction] manuscripts under contract, and we are not considering any new manuscripts."
Recent Fiction Title: *Intimates*, by David Huddle (stories).
Poetry: "Our poetry list is filled through 1994."
Recent Poetry Title: *Powers of Congress*, by Alice Fulton.
Tips: Our audience is "open-minded and serious readers with varied tastes. When submitting to Godine, be familiar with what kind of books we publish. We do not want manuscripts that are purely commercially motivated. First-time authors should try to get published in a journal or periodical before attempting to publish a book."

‡**GOLDEN WEST BOOKS**, Box 80250, San Marino CA 91118. (213)283-3446. Editor-in-Chief: Donald Duke. Managing Editor: Vernice Dagosta. Publishes hardcover and paperback originals. Averages 4 titles/year. Receives 50 submissions annually. 50% of books from first-time authors; 100% of books from unagented writers. Pays 10% royalty contract; no advance. Publishes book an average of 3 months after acceptance. Simultaneous submissions OK. Reports in 1 month. Free book catalog.
Nonfiction: Publishes selected Western Americana and transportation Americana. Query or submit complete ms. "Illustrations and photographs will be examined if we like manuscript."

GOVERNMENT INSTITUTES, INC., Suite 200, 4 Research Place, Rockville MD 20850. (301)921-2355. Director of Acquisitions: Roland W. Schumann III. Estab. 1973. Publishes hardcover and softcover originals. Averages 45 titles/year; receives 20 submissions annually. 50% of books from first-time authors; 100% of books from unagented writers. Pays royalty or fee. No advance. Publishes book an average of 2 months after acceptance. Simultaneous submissions OK with notification. Reports in 1 month on queries. *Writer's Market* recommends allowing 2 months for reply. Book catalog available on request.
Nonfiction: Reference and technical. Subjects include environmental law, employment law, FDA matters, industrial hygiene, safety and real estate with an environmental slant. Needs professional-level titles in those areas. Also looking for international environmental topics. Submit outline and at least one sample chapter.
Recent Nonfiction Title: *The Greening of American Business*, edited by Thomas F.P. Sullivan.
Tips: "We also conduct courses. Authors frequently serve as instructors."

‡**GRAPEVINE PUBLICATIONS, INC.**, P.O. Box 2449, Corvallis OR 97339-2449. (503)754-0583. Fax: (503)754-6508. Managing Editor: Christopher M. Coffin. Estab. 1983. Publishes trade paperback originals. Averages 6-10 titles/year; receives 200-300 submissions/year. 20% of books from first-time authors; 100% of books from unagented writers. Pays 6-9% royalty on retail price. Publishes book an average of 6 months after acceptance. Simultaneous submissions OK. Query for electronic submissions. Reports in 1 month on queries; 1-2 months on mss.
Nonfiction: Tutorials on technical subjects written for the layperson, innovative curricula or resources for math and science teachers. Subjects include math, science, computers, calculators, software, video, audio and other technical tools. Submit complete ms.
Recent Nonfiction Title: *HP 48G/GX Algebra/Calculus*, by Coffin.
Fiction: Children's picture books and juvenile fiction.
Recent Fiction Title: *Aaron's Clock Works*, by Coffin.
Tips: "We place heavy emphasis on readability, visual presentation, clarity, and reader participation. We will insist on numerous diagrams and illustrations, loosely-spaced text, large, easy-to-read formats, friendly, conversational writing, but tight, well-designed instruction. We disguise top-flight teaching as merely refreshing reading. The writer must be first and foremost a teacher who holds an engaging one-on-one conversation with the reader through the printed medium."

GRAPHIC ARTS CENTER PUBLISHING CO., 3019 NW Yeon Ave., P.O. Box 10306, Portland OR 97210-1519. (503)226-2402. Fax: (503)223-1410. General Manager: Douglas Pfeiffer. Managing Editor: Jean Andrews. Estab. 1968. Publishes hardcover originals. Makes outright purchase, averaging $3,000. Reports in 6 months. Book catalog for 9×12 SAE with 3 first class stamps.

● Graphic Arts Center publishing has bought the imprint Alaska Northwest Books.

Nonfiction: "All titles are pictorials with text. Text usually runs separately from the pictorial treatment. Authors must be previously published and are selected to complement the pictorial essay." Query.

Recent Nonfiction Title: *National Parks of America*, by Randal and Stewart Udall.

Tips: "Our subject areas include international, national, regional and state subjects. Working in conjunction with an established professional photographer to submit an idea is an excellent approach."

GRAPHIC ARTS TECHNICAL FOUNDATION, 4615 Forbes Ave., Pittsburgh PA 15213-3796. (412)621-6941. Fax: (412)621-3049. Editor-in-Chief: Thomas M. Destree. Technical Editor: Pamela J. Groff. Estab. 1924. Publishes trade paperback originals and hardcover reference texts. Firm averages 10 titles/year. Receives 15 submissions/year. 50% of books from first-time authors; 100% from unagented writers. Pays 5-15% royalty on average price. Publishes book an average of 1 year after acceptance. Query for electronic submissions. Reports in 1 month on queries. *Writer's Market* recommends allowing 2 months for reply. Book catalog for 9×12 SAE with 2 first class stamps; manuscript guidelines for #10 SASE.

Nonfiction: How-to, reference, technical and textbook. Subjects include printing/graphic arts. "We want textbook/reference books about printing and related technologies, providing that the content does not overlap appreciably with any other GATF books in print or in production. Although original photography is related to printing, we do not anticipate publishing any books on that topic." Query or submit outline and sample chapters. All queries and samples submitted must include ample return postage and appropriate return envelope to ensure a response. Reviews artwork/photos as part of ms package.

Recent Nonfiction Title: *Binding and Finishing*, by Ralph Lyman.

Tips: "Company has become more 'bottom-line' oriented. Thus we are less likely to accept manuscripts that require a lot of work. Recently, we had an author prepare the entire manuscript for us—all the way up to plate-ready films. The idea is to get it in and out as a marketable product as quickly as we can. We are more likely to work with authors who can bring a ms in quickly. More work is done in-house. We are encouraged to spend less time on projects and authors."

GRAYWOLF PRESS, Suite 203, 2402 University Ave., St. Paul MN 55114. Fax: (612)641-0036. Editor: Anne Czarniecki. Estab. 1974. Publishes hardcover and trade paperback originals and reprints. Averages 12-16 titles/year. Receives 2,000 submissions/year. 20% of books from first-time authors. Pays 6-12½% royalty on retail price; royalty advance varies. Publishes book an average of 9 to 18 months after acceptance. Simultaneous submissions OK but discouraged. Reports in 3 months on queries. Free book catalog.

Nonfiction: Literary essays and memoirs. "We do not publish mainstream romance novels, thrillers, science fiction, or mysteries." Query first.

Fiction: Literary novels and short story collections. Query first.

Recent Fiction Title: *Cloudstreet*, by Tim Winton.

GREAT NORTHWEST PUBLISHING AND DISTRIBUTING COMPANY, INC., P.O. Box 21-2383, Anchorage AK 99521-2383. (907)373-0122. President: Marvin H. Clark Jr. Estab. 1979. Imprint is Alaska Outdoor Books. Publishes hardcover and trade paperback originals. Averages 5 titles/year; receives 22-25 submissions annually. 30% of books from first-time authors; 100% of books from unagented writers. Pays 10% royalty. Publishes book an average of 1 year after acceptance. Simultaneous submissions OK. Query for electronic submissions. Reports in 2 weeks on queries. *Writer's Market* recommends allowing 2 months for reply. Free book catalog.

Nonfiction: Biography and how-to. Subjects include Alaska and hunting. "Alaskana and hunting books by very knowledgeable hunters and residents of the Far North interest our firm." Query.

Tips: "Pick a target audience first, subject second. Provide crisp, clear journalistic prose."

GREENHAVEN PRESS, INC., P.O. Box 289009, San Diego CA 92198-0009. Managing Editor: Bonnie Szumski. Estab. 1970. Publishes hard and softcover educational supplementary materials and (nontrade) juvenile nonfiction. Averages 10 juvenile manuscripts published/year; all are works for hire; receives 100 submissions/year. 50% of juvenile books from first-time authors; 100% of juvenile books from unagented writers. Makes outright purchase for $1,000-3,000. Publishes book an average of 1 year after acceptance. Does not accept unsolicited mss. Book catalog for 9×12 SAE with 3 first class stamps.

Nonfiction: Juvenile. "We produce tightly formatted books for young people grades 4-6. Series has specific requirements: Opposing Viewpoints Juniors (5th-6th grade). Potential writers should familiarize themselves with our catalog and senior high material. No unsolicited manuscripts."

GROSSET & DUNLAP PUBLISHERS, Imprint of the Putnam Berkley Publishing Group, 200 Madison Ave., New York NY 10016. Publisher/Vice President: Jane O'Connor. Estab. 1898. Imprints are Tuffy Books and Platt & Munk. Publishes hardcover and paperback originals. Averages 75 titles/year; receives more than

3,000 submissions annually. Publishes book an average of 18 months after acceptance. Simultaneous submissions OK. Reports in 2 months.

Nonfiction: Juveniles. Submit proposal or query first. Nature and science are of interest. Looks for new ways of looking at the world of a child.

Fiction: Juveniles, picture books for 3-7 age group and some higher. Submit proposal or query first.

Tips: "Nonfiction that is particularly topical or of wide interest in the mass market; a new concept for novelty format for preschoolers; and very well-written fiction on topics that appeal to parents of preschoolers have the best chance of selling to our firm. We want something new—a proposal for a new series for the ordinary picture book. You have a better chance if you have new ideas."

GROVE WIEDENFELD, Division of Grove Press Inc., 841 Broadway, New York NY 10003-4793. "Prefers not to share information."

GRYPHON PUBLICATIONS, P.O. Box 209, Brooklyn NY 11228. Owner/Publisher: Gary Lovisi. Imprints are: Paperback Parade Magazine; Hardboiled Magazine; Other Worlds Magazine; Gryphon Books & Gryphon Doubles. Publishes hardcover originals and trade paperback originals and reprints. Publishes 12 titles/year. Receives 500 queries and 1,000 mss/year. 60% of mss from first-time authors, 90% from unagented writers. Makes outright purchase by contract, price varies. Publishes book 12-18 months after acceptance of ms. Query for electronic submissions. Reports in 2 weeks on queries. *Writer's Market* recommends allowing 2 months for reply. Book catalog and ms guidelines for #10 SASE.

Nonfiction: Reference and bibliography. Subjects include hobbies, literature and book collecting. "We need well-written, well-researched articles, but query first on topic and length. Mistakes writers often make when submitting nonfiction are submitting not fully developed/researched material." Query. Reviews artwork/photos as part of freelance ms package. Writers should send photocopies (slides, transparencies may be necessary later).

Fiction: Adventure, fantasy, mystery, science fiction, suspense and urban horror and hardboiled fiction. "We want cutting-edge fiction, under 3,000 words with impact!" Query or submit complete ms.

Tips: "We are very particular about novels and book-length work. A first-timer has a better chance with a short story or article."

GYLANTIC PUBLISHING COMPANY, P.O. Box 2792, Littleton CO 80161-2792. Fax: (303)727-4279. Editor: Julie Baker. Estab. 1991. Publishes hardcover and trade paperback originals. Publishes 5 titles/year. Receives 600 queries and mss/year. 50% of mss from first-time authors, 100% from unagented writers. Pays 7½-12½% royalty on retail price. Publishes book 1 year after acceptance of ms. Simultaneous submissions OK. Reports in 2 months. No unsolicited manuscripts. Manuscript guidelines for #10 SASE.

Nonfiction: Subjects include child guidance/parenting, gay/lesbian, health/medicine, history, money/finance, women's issues/studies and men's issues/studies. "We are looking for self-help and information books concerning young adults, aging America, men's issues, women's issues and minorities. No 'slice of life,' autobiographical, new age, mystical, technically scientific, religious, art or music." Query.

Tips: "If I were a writer trying to market a book today, I would learn how to write a good proposal, have my work professionally edited, select an appropriate publisher for my subject, and study the market of my subject."

HALF HALT PRESS, INC., 6416 Burkittsville Rd., Middletown MD 21769-7006. (301)371-9110. Fax: (301)371-9211. Publisher: Elizabeth Carnes. Estab. 1986. Publishes hardcover and trade paperback originals and reprints (90% originals, 10% reprints). Firm averages 8 titles/year. Receives 25 submissions/year. 50% of books from first-time authors. 50% from unagented authors. Pays 10-12½% royalty on retail price. Offers advance by agreement. Publishes book an average of 1 year after acceptance. Reports in 1 month on queries. *Writer's Market* recommends allowing 2 months for reply. Book catalog for 6×9 SAE with 2 first class stamps.

Nonfiction: Instructional: Horse and equestrian related subjects only. We need serious instructional works by authorities in the field on horse-related topics, broadly defined. Query. Reviews artwork/photos as part of ms package.

Tips: "Writers have the best chance selling us well written, unique works that teach serious horse people how to do something better. If I were a writer trying to market a book today, I would offer a straightforward presentation, letting work speak for itself, without hype or hard sell. Allow publisher to contact writer, without frequent calling to check status. They haven't forgotten the writer but may have many different proposals at hand; frequent calls to 'touch base,' multiplied by the number of submissions, become an annoyance. As the publisher/author relationship becomes close and is based on working well together, early impressions may be important, even to the point of being a consideration in acceptance for publication."

For explanation of symbols, see the Key to Symbols and Abbreviations on page 72. For unfamiliar words, see the Glossary.

‡ALEXANDER HAMILTON INSTITUTE, 197 W. Spring Valley Ave., Maywood NJ 07607. (201)587-7050. Editor-in-Chief: Brian L.P. Zevnik. Estab. 1909. Publishes 3-ring binder and paperback originals. Averages 18 titles/year; receives 150 submissions annually. 40% of books from first-time authors; 90% of books from unagented writers. "We pay advance against negotiated royalty or straight fee (no royalty)." Offers average $3,000 advance. Publishes book an average of 10 months after acceptance. Simultaneous submissions OK. Reports in 1 month on queries; 2 months on mss.

Nonfiction: Executive/management books for two audiences. One is overseas, upper-level manager. "We need how-to and skills building books. *No* traditional management texts or academic treatises." The second audience is U.S. personnel executives and high-level management. Subject is legal personnel matters. "These books combine court case research and practical application of defensible programs." Query or submit outline or synopsis. Preferred form is outline, three paragraphs on each chapter, examples of lists, graphics, cases.

Tips: "We sell exclusively by direct mail to managers and executives around the world. A writer must know his/her field and be able to communicate practical systems and programs."

HANCOCK HOUSE PUBLISHERS LTD., 1431 Harrison Ave., Box X1, Blaine WA 98231. (604)538-1114. Fax: (604)538-2262. Publisher: David Hancock. Estab. 1971. Publishes hardcover and trade paperback originals and reprints. Averages 12 titles/year; receives 400 submissions annually. 50% of books from first-time authors; 100% of books from unagented writers. Pays 10% maximum royalty on wholesale price. Simultaneous submissions OK. Publishes book an average of 6 months after acceptance. Reports in 6 months. Book catalog free on request.

Nonfiction: Biography, how-to and self-help. Subjects include Americana, popular science, history (Northwest coast Indians), nature, recreation (sports handbooks for teachers), sports, and investment guides. Query with outline and sample chapters. Reviews artwork/photos.

Recent Nonfiction Title: *Pheasants of the World*, 350 color photos.

HARCOURT BRACE & COMPANY, (formerly Harcourt Brace Jovanovich), Children's Books Division, 1250 6th Ave., San Diego CA 92101. (619) 699-6810. Contact: Manuscript Submissions. Imprints include Harcourt Brace Children's Books, Gulliver Books, Browndeer Press, Voyager and Odyssey Paperbacks, and Jane Yolen Books. Publishes hardcover originals and trade paperback reprints. Division publishes 75 hardcover originals/year and 40-50 paperback reprints/year. Royalty varies. Advance varies. Publishes ms an average of 2 years after acceptance. Reports in 6 weeks on queries; 2 months on mss. Book catalog for 9 × 12 SAE with 3 first class stamps. Manuscript guidelines for #10 SASE.

Nonfiction: Juvenile. Query. Reviews artwork/photos as part of ms package "but requests that no originals are sent."

Fiction: Query or submit outline/synopsis and sample chapters for middle-grade and young-adult novels; or complete ms for picture books.

HARCOURT BRACE & COMPANY, (formerly Harcourt Brace Jovanovich), 6277 Sea Harbor Dr., Orlando FL 32887. Divisions include Harcourt Brace Children's Books Division and Holt, Rinehart & Winston. Did not want a listing for their Adult Trade Books Division. "The trade division of Harcourt Brace & Company does *not* accept any unsolicited manuscripts. The children's division is the only one open to unsolicited submissions."

• HB published the nonfiction winner of 1992's National Book Award, *Becoming a Man: Half a Life Story*, by Paul Monette.

HARPER SAN FRANCISCO, Division of HarperCollins, 3rd Floor, 1160 Battery St., San Francisco CA 94111-1213. (415)477-4400. Fax: (415)477-4444. Publisher: Thomas Grady. Estab. 1817. Firm publishes hardcover and trade paperback originals and trade paperback reprints. Publishes 180 titles/year. Receives about 10,000 submissions/year. 5% of books from first-time authors; 50% from unagented writers. Pays royalty. Publishes book an average of 18 months after acceptance. Simultaneous (if notified) submissions OK. Reports in 2 months on queries. Free book catalog and ms guidelines.

Nonfiction: Biography, how-to, reference, self-help. Subjects include addiction/recovery, philosophy, psychology, religion, women's issues/studies, theology, New Consciousness, anthropology, spirituality, gay and lesbian studies. Query or submit outline and sample chapters.

Recent Nonfiction Title: *Men and the Water of Life*, by Michael Meade.

HARPERCOLLINS PUBLISHERS, 10 E. 53rd St., New York NY 10022. (212)207-7000. Managing Editor: Tracy Behar. Imprints include Harper San Francisco (religious books only); Harper Perennial Library; Harper Reference, Basic Books, Harper Business and Harper Torchbooks. Publishes hardcover and paperback originals, and paperback reprints. Trade publishes more than 400 titles/year. Pays standard royalties; advances negotiable. *No unsolicited queries or mss.* Reports on solicited queries in 6 weeks. *Writer's Market* recommends allowing 2 months for reply.

Nonfiction: Americana, animals, art, biography, business/economics, cookbooks, health, history, how-to, humor, music, nature, philosophy, politics, psychology, reference, religion, science, self-help, sociology, sports and travel.
Recent Nonfiction Title: *Upon This Rock.*
Fiction: Adventure, fantasy, gothic, historical, mystery, science fiction, suspense, western and literary. "We look for a strong story line and exceptional literary talent."
Recent Fiction Title: *Power in The Blood.*
Tips: "Strongly suggest that you go through a literary agent before submitting any ms. Any unsolicited query or ms will be returned unread."

HARTLEY & MARKS, P.O. Box 147, Point Roberts WA 98281. (206)945-2017. Editorial Director: Sue Tauber. Estab. 1974. Publishes hardcover and trade paperback originals. Averages 8-10 titles/year. Receives 700 submissions/year. 80% of books from first-time authors; 100% from unagented writers. Pays 7-10% royalty on retail price. Reports in 2 months. Free book catalog.
Nonfiction: How-to, self-help and technical. Subjects include agriculture/gardening (organic), building, healthy lifestyles, holistic medicine, aging, practical crafts, nature/environment (practical how-to), psychology self-help, typography, translations of aforementioned subjects. No metaphysical books, autobiography or recipe books. Query or submit outline and sample chapters.
Recent Nonfiction Title: *The Whole Way to Allergy Relief & Prevention: A Doctor's Complete Guide to Treatment & Self-Care*, by Jacqueline Krohn, M.D.

THE HARVARD COMMON PRESS, 535 Albany St., Boston MA 02118-2500. (617)423-5803. Fax: (617)695-9794. President: Bruce P. Shaw. Managing Editor: Dan Rosenberg. Imprint is Gambit Books. Estab. 1976. Publishes hardcover and trade paperback originals and reprints. Averages 8 titles/year. Receives 1,000 submissions annually. 75% of books from first-time authors; 75% of books from unagented writers. Average print order for a writer's first book is 7,500. Pays royalty; offers average $2,000 advance. Publishes book an average of 9 months after acceptance. Simultaneous submissions OK. Reports in 2 months. Book catalog for 9×12 SAE and 3 first class stamps; ms guidelines for SASE.
Nonfiction: Travel, cookbook, how-to, health, reference and self-help. Emphasis on travel, family matters and cooking. "We want strong, practical books that help people gain control over a particular area of their lives, whether it's family matters, business or financial matters, health, careers, food or travel. An increasing percentage of our list is made up of books about family matters; in this area we are looking for authors who are knowledgeable, if not experts, and who can offer a different approach to the subject. We are open to good nonfiction proposals that show evidence of strong organization and writing, and clearly demonstrate a need in the marketplace. First-time authors are welcome." Accepts nonfiction translations. Submit outline and 1-3 sample chapters. Reviews artwork/photos.
Recent Nonfiction Title: *You and Your New Baby*, by Linda Todd (parenting).

HARVEST HOUSE PUBLISHERS, 1075 Arrowsmith, Eugene OR 97402-9197. (503)343-0123. Fax: (503)342-6410. Vice President of Editorial: Eileen L. Mason. Manuscript Coordinator: LaRae Weikert. Estab. 1974. Publishes hardcover, trade paperback and mass market originals and reprints. Averages 70-80 titles/year; receives 3,500 submissions annually. 10% of books from first-time authors; 90% of books from unagented writers. Pays 14-18% royalty on wholesale price. Publishes book an average of 1 year after acceptance. Simultaneous submissions OK. Reports in 10 weeks. Book catalog for 9×12 SAE with 2 first class stamps; manuscript guidelines for SASE.
Nonfiction: Juvenile (picture books ages 2-8; ages 9-12), self-help, counseling, current issues, women's and family on Evangelical Christian religion. No cookbooks, theses, dissertations, music, or poetry. Query or submit outline and sample chapters.
Recent Nonfiction Title: *Christianity in Crisis*, by Hank Hanegraaff.
Fiction: Historical, mystery and religious. No short stories. Query or submit outline/synopsis and sample chapters.
Recent Fiction Title: *The Tapestry*, by MaryAnn Minatra.
Tips: "Audience is women ages 25-40 and high school youth—evangelical Christians of all denominations."

HASTINGS HOUSE, Eagle Publishing Corp., 141 Halstead Ave., Mamaroneck NY 10543. (914)835-4005. Editor/Publisher: Hy Steirman. Publishes hardcover and trade paperback originals and reprints. Publishes 12 titles/year. Receives 350 queries and 125 mss/year. 5% of mss from first-time authors, 40% from unagented writers. Pays 8-10% royalty on retail price. Offers $1,000-10,000 advance. Publishes book 10 months after acceptance of ms. Reports in 1 month. *Writer's Market* recommends allowing 2 months for reply. Book catalog free on request.
Nonfiction: Biography, coffee table book, cookbook, how-to, humor, children's/juvenile, reference, self-help and consumer. Subjects include business and economics, cooking, foods and nutrition, health/medicine, psychology, travel and writing. "We are looking for books that address consumer needs." Query or submit outline.
Recent Nonfiction Title: *Living Will Handbook*, by Alan Lieberson, MD, JD (consumer legal/medical).

‡THE HAWORTH PRESS, INC., 10 Alice St., Binghampton NY 13904. (607)722-5857. Managing Editor: Bill Palmer. Imprints are: Harrington Park Press; Food Products Press; Pharmaceutical Products Press; International Business Press; The Haworth Medical Press; The Haworth Pastoral Press. Publishes hardcover and trade paperback originals. Publishes 75 titles/year. Each imprint publishes 5-10 titles/year. Receives 110 queries and 46 mss/year. 20% of mss from first-time authors, 98% from unagented writers. Pays 7½-12% royalty on wholesale price. Publishes book 16 months after acceptance of ms. Reports in 2 months on mss. Book catalog and ms guidelines free on request.

Nonfiction: Reference, textbook and popular trade. Subjects include agriculture/horticulture, business and economics, cooking/foods/nutrition, gay/lesbian, health/medicine, psychology, religion, sociology, women's issues/studies and pharmacy. Submit outline and 3 sample chapters. Reviews artwork/photos as part of freelance ms package. Writers should send camera-ready artwork, b&w photos.

Recent Nonfiction Title: *Reproductive Hazards in the Workplace*, by Regina Kenen (popular trade, women's studies).

HAY HOUSE, INC., P.O. Box 6204, Carson CA 90749-6204. (310)605-0601. Editorial Director: Dan Olmos. Estab. 1985. Imprint is Lulu's Library (children's division). Publishes hardcover and trade paperback originals, and trade paperback reprints. Firm averages 10 titles/year; imprint averages 10 titles/year. Receives approximately 250 submissions/year. 20% of books are from first-time authors. 25% from unagented writers. Pays 8-12% royalty. Offers $0-5,000 average advance. Publishes book an average of 8-15 months after acceptance. Simultaneous submissions OK. Reports in 1 month. *Writer's Market* recommends allowing 2 months for reply. Free book catalog.

Nonfiction: Biography, how-to, humor, juvenile, reference and self-help. Subjects include ecology, healing power of pets, business and economics/self-help, cooking, foods and nutrition, education/self-help, gardening/environment, gay/lesbian, health/medicine, money/finance/self-help, nature/environment/ecology, philosophy/New Age, psychology/self-help, recreation, religion, science/self-help, sociology/self-help and women's issues/studies. "Hay House is interested in a variety of subjects so long as they have a positive self-help/metaphysical slant to them. No poetry or negative concepts that are not conducive to helping/healing ourselves or our planet." Query or submit outline and sample chapters. Reviews artwork/photos as part of ms package if duplicate.

Tips: "Our audience is concerned with ecology, our planet, the healing properties of love, self-help, and teaching children loving principles. Hay House has noticed that our reader is interested in taking more control of his/her life. A writer has a good chance of selling us a book with a unique, positive, and healing message. If I were a writer trying to market a book today, I would research the market thoroughly to make sure that there weren't already too many books on the subject I was interested in writing about. Then I would make sure that I had a unique slant on my idea."

HEALTH ADMINISTRATION PRESS, Foundation of the American College of Healthcare Executives, 1021 E. Huron St., Ann Arbor MI 48104-9990. (313)764-1380. Fax: (313)763-1105. Director: Daphne M. Grew. Acquisitions Editor: E. Kobrinski. Estab. 1972. Imprints are Health Administration Press, Association for Health Services Research/Health Administration Press, AUPHA Press/Health Administration Press, and ACHE Management Series. Publishes hardcover and trade paperback originals. Publishes 14 titles/year. Pays 10-15% royalty on net revenue from sale of book. Occasionally offers small advance. Publishes book an average of 10 months after acceptance. Query for electronic submissions. Reports in 6 weeks on queries. *Writer's Market* recommends allowing 2 months for reply. Book catalog free on request.

Nonfiction: Professional or textbook. Subjects include business and economics, government/politics, health/medicine, sociology, health administration. "We are always interested in good, solid texts and references, and we are adding to our management series; books in this series offer health services CEOs and top managers immediately useful information in an accessible format." Submit outline and sample chapters.

Tips: "We publish books primarily for an audience of managers of health care institutions and researchers and scholars in health services administration. The books we like to see have something to say and say it to our audience."

HEALTH COMMUNICATIONS, INC., 3201 SW 15th St., Deerfield Beach FL 33442-8190. (305)360-0909. Fax: (305)360-0034. Senior Editor: Marie Stilkind. Estab. 1982. Publishes trade paperback originals. Publishes 35 titles/year. Receives 520 submissions/year. 20% of books from first-time authors. 90% from unagented writers. Pays 15% royalty on wholesale price. Publishes book an average of 9 months after acceptance. Reports in 1 month on queries. *Writer's Market* recommends allowing 2 months for reply. Free book catalog and ms guidelines with SAE.

Nonfiction: Self-help recovery. Subjects include adult child and co-dependent issues, psychology and recovery/addiction. We are looking for recovery trends in self-help format. Submit outline and sample chapters. Reviews artwork/photos as part of ms package.

Tips: "Our new areas of interest are spirituality, self-esteem, and wellness."

HENDRICK-LONG PUBLISHING CO., INC., P.O. Box 25123, Dallas TX 75225-1123. (214)358-4677. Contact: Joann Long. Estab. 1969. Publishes hardcover and trade paperback originals and hardcover reprints. Firm averages 8 titles/year. Receives 500 submissions/year. 90% from unagented writers. Pays royalty on selling price. Publishes book an average of 18 months after acceptance. Reports in 1 month on queries, 2 months if more than query sent. *Writer's Market* recommends allowing 2 months for reply. Book catalog for 9 × 12 SAE with 4 first class stamps. Manuscript guidelines for #10 SASE.
Nonfiction: Biography and juvenile. Subject mainly Texas focused material for children and young adults. Query or submit outline and 2 sample chapters. Reviews artwork/photos as part of ms package; copies of material are acceptable. Do not send original art.
Recent Nonfiction Title: *Santa Anna: Patriot or Scoundrel*, by Ruby C. Tolliver.
Fiction: Adventure (Texas juvenile), historical (Texas juvenile), mystery (Texas juvenile) and western (Texas juvenile). Query or submit outline/synopsis and 2 sample chapters.
Recent Fiction Title: *Shipwrecked on Padre Island*, by Isabell R. Marvin.

HENDRICKSON PUBLISHERS, INC., 137 Summit St., P.O. Box 3473, Peabody MA 01961-3473. Acquisitions Editor: Phil Anderson. Estab. 1983. Publishes hardcover and trade paperback originals and reprints. Averages 8-12 titles/year; receives 100-125 submissions annually. 3% of books from first-time authors; 100% of books from unagented writers. Publishes book an average of 8 months after acceptance. Simultaneous (if so notified) submissions OK. Reports in 2 months. Free book catalog. Ms guidelines for SASE.
Nonfiction: Religious, principally academic. "We will consider any quality mss within the area of religion specifically related to biblical studies and related fields. Popularly written manuscripts, poetry, plays or fiction are not acceptable." Submit outline and sample chapters.

VIRGIL W. HENSLEY, INC., 6116 E. 32nd St., Tulsa OK 74135-9927. (918)664-8520. Editor: Terri Kalfas. Estab. 1965. Publishes hardcover and paperback originals. Publishes 5-10 titles/year Receives 450 submissions/year. 50% of books from first-time authors; 50% from unagented writers. Pays 5% minimum royalty on gross sales or outright purchase of $250 minimum for study aids. Publishes ms an average of 18 months after acceptance. Reports in 2 months on queries. Ms guidelines for #10 SAE.
Nonfiction: Bible study curriculum. Subjects include child guidance/parenting, money/finance, religion, women's issues/studies. "We look for subjects that lend themselves to long-term Bible studies – prayer, prophecy, family, faith, etc. We do not want to see anything non-Christian." Actively seeking nonfiction other than Bible studies. No new age, poetry, plays, sermon collections. Query with synopsis and sample chapters.
Recent Nonfiction Title: *Exploring the New Testament: The Four Gospels*, by Chip Ricks.
Fiction: Actively seeking Christian fiction. Christianity must be germane to the plot without sermonizing.
Tips: "Submit something that crosses denominational lines directed toward the large Christian market, not small specialized groups. We serve an interdenominational market – all Christian persuasions. No new age."

HERALD PRESS, Imprint of Mennonite Publishing House, 616 Walnut Ave., Scottdale PA 15683-1999. (412)887-8500. Fax: (412)887-3111. Book Editor: David Garber. Estab. 1908. Publishes hardcover, trade paperback originals and reprints. Averages 30 titles/year; receives 900 submissions annually. 15% of books from first-time authors. 95% of books from unagented writers. Pays minimum royalty of 10% retail, maximum of 12% retail. Advance seldom given. Publishes book an average of 14 months after acceptance. Query for electronic submissions. Reports in 2 months. Book catalog 50¢.
Nonfiction: Christian inspiration, Bible study, current issues, missions and evangelism, peace and justice, family life, Christian ethics and theology, ethnic (Amish, Mennonite), self-help and juveniles (mostly ages 8-14). No drama or poetry. Query or submit outline and 2 sample chapters. Reviews artwork/photos as part of ms package.
Recent Nonfiction Title: *Sexual Abuse in Christian Homes and Churches*, by Carolyn Holderread Heggen.
Fiction: Religious. Needs some fiction for youth and adults reflecting themes similar to those listed in nonfiction, also "compelling stories that treat social and Christian issues in a believable manner." No fantasy. Query or submit outline/synopsis and sample chapters.
Recent Fiction Title: *Andy*, by Mary Christner Borntrager.
Tips: "We currently have a surplus of juvenile book proposals. We have been more selective to make sure of market for proposed book."

‡HERALD PUBLISHING HOUSE, Division of Reorganized Church of Jesus Christ of Latter Day Saints, 3225 S. Noland Rd., P.O. Box 1770, Independence MO 64055. (816)252-5010. Fax: (816)252-3976. Editorial Director: Roger Yarrington. Estab. 1860. Imprints include Independence Press and Graceland Park Press. Estab. 1860. Publishes hardcover and trade paperback originals and reprints. Averages 30 titles/year; receives 700 submissions annually. 20% of books from first-time authors; 100% of books from unagented writers. Pays 5% maximum royalty on retail price. Offers average $400 advance. Publishes book an average of 14 months after acceptance. Reports in 3 weeks on queries; 2 months on mss. Book catalog for 9 × 12 SASE.
Nonfiction: Self-help and religious (RLDS Church). Subjects include Americana, history and religion. Herald House focus: history and doctrine of RLDS Church. Independence Press focus: regional studies (Midwest, Missouri). No submissions unrelated to RLDS Church (Herald House) or to Midwest regional studies (Inde-

pendence Press). Query. Use *Chicago Manual of Style*. Reviews artwork/photos as part of ms package.
Tips: "The audience for Herald Publishing House is members of the Reorganized Church of Jesus Christ of Latter Day Saints; for Independence Press, persons living in the Midwest or interested in the Midwest; for Graceland Park Press, readers interested in academic and exploratory studies on religious topics."

HERITAGE BOOKS, INC., 1540-E Pointer Ridge Place, Bowie MD 20716-1859. (301)390-7708. Editorial Director: Karen Ackermann. Estab. 1978. Publishes hardcover and paperback originals and reprints. Averages 100 titles/year; receives 300 submissions annually. 25% of books from first-time authors; 100% from unagented writers. Pays 10% royalty on retail price; no advance. Publishes book an average of 6 months after acceptance. Simultaneous submissions OK. Reports in 1 month. *Writer's Market* recommends allowing 2 months for reply. Book catalog for SAE.
Nonfiction: "We particularly desire nonfiction titles dealing with history and genealogy including how-to and reference works, as well as conventional histories and genealogies. Ancestries of contemporary people are not of interest. The titles should be either of general interest or restricted to Eastern U.S. and Midwest Material dealing with the present century is usually not of interest. We prefer writers to query or submit an outline." Reviews artwork/photos.
Recent Nonfiction Title: *Fauquier County, Virginia, Deeds, 1778-1785*, by John K. Gott.
Tips: "The quality of the book is of prime importance; next is its relevance to our fields of interest."

‡HEYDAY BOOKS, Box 9145, Berkeley CA 94709. (415)549-3564. Publisher: Malcolm Margolin. Publishes hardcover and trade paperback originals, trade paperback reprints. Averages 4-9 titles/year; receives 200 submissions annually. 50% of books from first-time authors; 75% of books from unagented writers. Pays 8-10% royalty on retail price. Publishes book an average of 8 months after acceptance. Reports in 1 week on queries; up to 5 weeks on mss. Book catalog for 7×9 SAE and 2 first class stamps.
Nonfiction: Books about California only; how-to and reference. Subjects include Americana, history, nature and travel. "We publish books about native Americans, natural history, history, and recreation, with a strong California focus." Query with outline and synopsis. Reviews artwork/photos.
Tips: "Give good value, and avoid gimmicks. We are accepting *only* nonfiction books with a California focus."

‡HIGH PLAINS PRESS, P.O. Box 123, 539 Cassa Rd., Glendo WY 82213. Publisher: Nancy Curtis. Publishes hardcover and trade paperback originals. Publishes 4 titles/year. Receives 300 queries and 200 mss/year. 80% of mss from first-time authors; 95% from unagented writers. Pays 10-15% royalty on wholesale price. Offers $100-300 advance. Publishes book 2 years after acceptance. Simultaneous submissions OK. Query for electronic submissions. Prefers Mac Word. Reports in 1 month on queries; 1 month on proposals; 3 months on mss. Book catalog free on request, mss guidelines for #10 SASE.
Nonfiction: Biography, Western Americana, Americana, art/architecture, history, nature/environment, regional, travel. "We plan to focus on books of the American West, particularly history." Submit outline. Reviews artwork/photos as part of freelance ms package. Writer should send photocopies.
Recent Nonfiction Title: *Steamboat, Legendary Bucking Horse*, by Candy & Flossie Moulton (Western history).
Poetry: "We only seek poetry closely tied to the Rockies. Poets should not submit single poems." Query; submit complete ms.
Recent Poetry Title: *No Roof But Sky*, by Jane Candia Coleman (Western, free verse).

HIPPOCRENE BOOKS INC., 171 Madison Ave., New York NY 10016. (212)685-4371. President: George Blagowidow. Estab. 1971. Publishes hardcover and trade paperback originals. Averages 100 titles/year. Receives 250 submissions annually. 10% of books from first-time authors; 95% of books from unagented writers. Pays 6-10% royalty on retail price. Offers $2,000 dollar advance. Publishes book an average of 16 months after acceptance. Simultaneous submissions OK. Reports in 2 months. Book catalog for 9×12 SAE with 5 first class stamps. Ms guidelines for #10 SASE.
Nonfiction: Reference. Subjects include foreign language, travel, military history and dictionaries. Submit outline and 2 sample chapters.
Recent Nonfiction Titles: *Terrible Innocence*, by Mark Coburn.
Tips: "Our recent successes in publishing general books considered midlist by larger publishers is making us more of a general trade publisher. We continue to do well with travel books and reference books like dictionaries, atlases and language studies. We ask for proposal, sample chapter, and table of contents. We then ask for material if we are interested."

HOLIDAY HOUSE, 425 Madison Ave., New York NY 10017. (212)688-0085. Editor-in-Chief: Margery Cuyler. Estab. 1935. Publishes hardcover originals and hardcover and trade paperback reprints. Firm averages 60 titles/year. Receives 3,000 submissions/year. 20% of books from first-time authors. 50% from unagented writers. Pays royalty. Publishes book an average of 1 year after acceptance. Simultaneous submissions OK. Reports in 2 weeks on queries. *Writer's Market* recommends allowing 2 months for reply. Book catalog for 9×12 SAE with 7 first class stamps. Manuscript guidelines for #10 SASE.

Nonfiction: Illustrated book, juvenile. Submit outline and sample chapters or complete ms for picture books only. Reviews artwork/photos as part of ms package.

Fiction: Adventure, ethnic, fantasy, historical, humor, juvenile, mystery, picture books, science fiction, suspense and western. "We are interested in all juvenile fiction up to 8-12 year old novels. No young adult novels with sex, violence or drugs as subject matter." Submit outline/synopsis and 3 sample chapters or complete ms for picture books only.

Recent Fiction Title: *The Battle for the Castle*, by Elizabeth Winthrop.

Tips: "We are interested in short chapter books for 8-12 year olds, and are currently *not* seeking to acquire more picture books."

HOLLOW EARTH PUBLISHING, P.O. Box 1355, Boston MA 02205-1355. (603)433-8735. Fax: (603)433-8735. Editor/Publisher: Helian Yvette Grimes. Publishes hardcover, trade and mass market paperback originals and reprints. Firm averages 6 titles/year. Receives 40 submissions/year. 30% of books from first-time authors. 100% from unagented writers. Pays 5-15% royalty on wholesale price. Publishes book an average of 6 months after acceptance. Simultaneous submissions OK. Query for electronic submissions. Reports on queries in 3 weeks. *Writer's Market* recommends allowing 2 months for reply. Book catalog for 9 × 12 SAE with 3 first class stamps. Manuscript guidelines for #10 SASE.

Nonfiction: How-to, reference, technical (computer) and mythology. Subjects include architecture, computers and electronics, photography, religion/mythology and travel. "We are currently interested in books on technical aspects of photography and computer books on object-oriented programming." Query. All unsolicited mss are returned unopened. Reviews artwork/photos as part of ms package.

Fiction: Fantasy, literary, mystery, science fiction. Submit outline/synopsis and sample chapters. All unsolicited mss are returned unopened.

Tips: "Computer books are fairly easy to publish because they can be marketed specifically."

HOLMES & MEIER PUBLISHERS, INC., 30 Irving Place, New York NY 10003-2303. (212)254-4100. Fax: (212)254-4104. Publisher: Miriam H. Holmes. Editor: Sheila Friedling. Managing Editor: Katharine Turok. Estab. 1969. Imprint is Africana Publishing Co. Publishes hardcover and paperback originals. Publishes 30 titles/year. Pays royalty. Publishes book an average of 18 months after acceptance. Reports in up to 6 months. Send SASE. Free book catalog.

Nonfiction: Africana, art, biography, business/economics, history, Judaica, Latin American studies, literary criticism, politics, reference and women's studies. Accepts translations. "We are noted as an academic publishing house and are pleased with our reputation of excellence in the field. However, we are also expanding our list to include books of more general interest." Query first and submit outline, sample chapters, curriculum vitae and idea of intended market/audience.

Recent Nonfiction Title: *A Political Biography*, by Wayne Northcutt.

HOLT, RINEHART & WINSTON, Division of Harcourt Brace, 6277 Sea Harbor Dr., Orlando FL 32887. "Prefers not to share information."

HOME EDUCATION PRESS, P.O. Box 1083, Tonasket WA 98855. (509)486-1351. Publisher: Helen Hegener. Publishes trade paperback originals. Publishes 6-8 titles/year. Receives 20-40 queries and 10-12 mss/year. 95% of mss from first-time authors, 95% from unagented writers. Pays 10-20% royalty on retail price. Publishes book 1 year after acceptance of ms. Query for electronic submissions. Reports in 1 month on queries. *Writer's Market* recommends allowing 2 months for reply. Book catalog free on request. Manuscript guidelines for #10 SASE.

Nonfiction: How-to and education; specifically homeschooling. Subjects include child guidance/parenting, education and home schooling. Query. Reviews artwork/photos as part of the freelance ms package as appropriate. Writers should send photocopies.

Tips: "We are not interested in any books not directly relating to homeschooling." Mistakes writers often make when submitting nonfiction is "submitting curriculum or 'how to teach. . .' books. We are *not* interested in new ideas for teaching kids to read or write. We're more interested in real life experiences than academic expertise."

HOMESTEAD PUBLISHING, Box 193, Moose WY 83102. Editor: Carl Schreier. Publishes hardcover and trade paperback originals and trade paperback reprints. Averages 10 titles/year; receives 1,000 submissions annually. 30% of books from first-time authors. 90% of books from unagented writers. Pays 8-12% royalty on net receipts; offers $1,000 average advance. Publishes book an average of 1 year after acceptance. Query for electronic submissions. Reports in 2 months. Book catalog for #10 SAE with 2 first class stamps.

Nonfiction: Biography, coffee table book, illustrated book, juvenile and reference. Subjects include animals, art, history, nature, photography and travel. Especially needs natural history and nature books for children. No textbooks. Query or submit outline and sample chapters. Reviews artwork/photos as part of ms package. Submit SASE for return of material.

Tips: "Illustrated books on natural history are our specialty. Our audiences include professional, educated people with an interest in natural history, conservation, national parks, and western art. Underneath the visual aspects, a book should be well written, with a good grasp of the English language. We are looking for professional work and top quality publications."

HOUGHTON MIFFLIN CO., Adult Trade Division, 222 Berkeley St., Boston MA 02116-3764. (617)351-5912. Fax: (617)351-1109. "We no longer accept unsolicited manuscripts or proposals."

HOUGHTON MIFFLIN CO., Children's Trade Books, 222 Berkeley St., Boston MA 02116. Editor: Michele Ganter. Estab. 1864. Publishes hardcover originals and trade paperback reprints (some simultaneous hard/soft). Averages 60 titles/year. Pays standard royalty; offers advance. Reports in 2 months. Enclose SASE.
Nonfiction: Submit outline/synopsis and sample chapters. Reviews artwork/photos as part of ms package.
Recent Nonfiction Title: *Christopher Columbus: How He Did It*, by Charlotte & David Yue.
Fiction: Submit complete ms.
Recent Fiction Title: *When The Road Ends*, by Jean Thesman.

HOWELL PRESS, INC., 1147 River Rd., Bay 2, Charlottesville VA 22901-4172. (804)977-4006. President: Ross A. Howell Jr. Estab. 1985. Firm averages 6 titles/year. Receives 500 submissions/year. 10% of books from first-time authors. 80% from unagented writers. Pays 5-7% on net retail price. "We generally offer an advance, but amount differs with each project and is generally negotiated with authors on a case-by-case basis." Publishes book an average of 18 months after acceptance. Reports in 2 months. Book catalog for 9×12 SAE with 4 first class stamps.
Nonfiction: Illustrated books and historical texts. Subjects include aviation, military history, cooking, maritime history, motorsports, gardening. "Generally open to most ideas, as long as writing is accessible to average adult reader. Our line is targeted, so it would be advisable to look over our catalog before querying to better understand what Howell Press does." Query. Submit outline and sample chapters. Reviews artwork/photos as part of ms package. Mss submitted without return postage will not be returned.
Recent Nonfiction Title: *Aviation: A History Through Art*, by Philip Handleman and The American Society of Aviation Artists.
Tips: "Focus of our program has been illustrated books, but we will also consider nonfiction manuscripts that would not be illustrated. Selections limited to history, transportation, cooking and gardening."

HOWELLS HOUSE, Box 9546, Washington DC 20016-9546. (202)333-2182. Publisher: W.D. Howells. Imprints are The Compass Press; Whalesback Books. Publishes hardcover and trade paperback originals and reprints. Publishes 4 titles/year. Each imprint publishes 2-3 titles/year. Receives 50 queries and 50 mss/year. 50% of mss from first-time authors, 60% from unagented writers. Pays 15-20% net royalty; or makes outright purchase. May offer advance. Publishes book 6 months after ms development completed. Reports in 2 months on proposals.
Nonfiction: Biography, coffee table book, illustrated book and textbook. Subjects include Americana, anthropology/archaeology, art/architecture, business and economics, education, government/politics, history, military/war, photography, science, sociology and translation. Query.
Recent Nonfiction Title: *War in the Woods*, by Taar (history).
Fiction: Historical, humor, literary and mainstream/contemporary. Query.
Tips: "Our interests will focus on institutions and institutional change."

HRD PRESS, INC., 22 Amherst Rd., Amherst MA 01002. (413)253-3488. Fax: (413)253-3490. Publisher: Robert W. Carkhuff. Estab. 1970. Publishes hardcover and trade paperback originals. Averages 15-20 titles/year. Receives 300-400 submissions/year. 25% of books from first-time authors. 100% from unagented writers. Pays 10-15% royalty on wholesale price. Offers $1,000 average advance. Publishes book an average of 6 months after acceptance. Simultaneous submissions OK. Reports in 1 month on queries. *Writer's Market* recommends allowing 2 months for reply. Free book catalog and ms guidelines.
Nonfiction: Reference, software, technical. Subjects include business. "We are looking for mostly business oriented titles, training and the development of human resources. Submit outline and samples chapters.
Recent Nonfiction Title: *Polarity Management: Identifying and Managing Unsolvable Problems*, by Barry Johnson, Ph.D.
Tips: "We are no longer seeking juvenile nonfiction or psychology titles."

HUDSON HILLS PRESS, INC., Suite 1308, 230 5th Ave., New York NY 10001-7704. (212)889-3090. President/Editorial Director: Paul Anbinder. Estab. 1978. Publishes hardcover and paperback originals. Averages 10 titles/year; receives 50-100 submissions annually. 15% of books from first-time authors; 90% of books from unagented writers. Average print order for a writer's first book is 3,000. Offers royalties of 4-6% on retail price. Average advance: $3,500. Publishes book an average of 1 year after acceptance. Simultaneous submissions OK. Reports in 2 months. Book catalog for 6×9 SAE with 2 first class stamps.

Nonfiction: Art and photography. "We are only interested in publishing books about art and photography, including monographs." Query first, then submit outline and sample chapters. Reviews artwork/photos as part of ms package.

HUMAN KINETICS PUBLISHERS, INC., P.O. Box 5076, Champaign IL 61825-5076. (217)351-5076. Fax: (217)351-2674. Publisher: Rainer Martens. Director, Trade: Ted Miller. Director, Academic: Rick Frey. Imprints are HK Trade, HK Academic. Estab. 1974. Publishes hardcover and paperback text and reference books and trade paperback originals. Averages 80 titles/year; receives 300 submissions annually. 50% of books from first-time authors; 97% of books from unagented writers. Pays 10-15% royalty on net income. Publishes book an average of 18 months after acceptance. Simultaneous submissions OK. Query for electronic submissions. Reports in 2 months. Free book catalog.
Nonfiction: How-to, reference, self-help, technical and textbook. Subjects include health, recreation, sports, sport sciences and sports medicine, and physical education. Especially interested in books on fitness; books on all aspects of sports technique or how-to books and coaching books; books which interpret the sport sciences and sports medicine, including sport physiology, sport psychology, sport pedagogy and sport bio-mechanics. No sport biographies, sport record or statistics books or regional books. Submit outline and sample chapters. Reviews artwork/photos as part of ms package.
Recent Nonfiction Title: *In-Line Skating,* by Mark Powell and John Svensson.
Tips: "Books which accurately interpret the sport sciences and health research to coaches, athletes and fitness enthusiasts have the best chance of selling to us."

‡**HUMAN SERVICES INSTITUTE, INC.,** P.O. Box 14610, Bradenton FL 34280-4610. (813)746-7088. Senior Editor: Dr. Lee Marvin Joiner. Estab. 1988. Publishes hardcover and trade paperback originals. Firm averages 10-12 titles/year. Receives 100 submissions/year. 95% of books are from first-time authors. 100% from un-agented writers. Pays 7-15% royalty on wholesale price. Publishes book an average of 9 months after acceptance. Query for electronic submissions. Reports in 2 weeks on queries, 1 month on mss. Free book catalog and ms guidelines.
Nonfiction: Self-help. Subjects include child guidance/parenting, psychology and women's issues/studies. "We are looking for books on divorce, cocaine, cults, sexual victimization, alternative medicine, mental health, secular recovery and violence. No autobiographical accounts." Query or submit outline/synopsis and sample chapters.
Recent Nonfiction Title: *Broken Boys/Mending Men,* by Grugman-Black.
Tips: "Our audience is made up of clinics, hospitals, prisons, mental health centers, human service profession-als and general readers. If I were a writer trying to market a book today, I would write a video script (30 minute) first. This should contain the book's message in a compressed format."

HUMANICS PUBLISHING GROUP, 1482 Mecaslin St. NW, Atlanta GA 30309. Fax: (404)874-1976. Acquisi-tions Editor: W. Arthur Bligh. Estab. 1976. Publishes softcover, educational and trade paperback originals. Averages 24 titles/year; receives 500 submissions annually. 20% of books from first-time authors; 100% of books from unagented writers. Average print order for a writer's first book is 5,000. Pays average 8% royalty on net sales; buys some mss outright. Publishes book an average of 1 year after acceptance. Reports in 3 months. Book catalog and ms guidelines for SASE.
Nonfiction: Self-help, teacher resource books and psychological assessment instruments for early education. Subjects include health, psychology, sociology, education, business and New Age. Submit outline and at least 3 sample chapters. Reviews artwork/photos as part of ms package.
• This publisher is especially interested in books on child development, business and health.
Recent Nonfiction Title: *Balance of Body, Balance of Mind,* by Will Johnson.
Tips: "Be resourceful, bold and creative. But be sure to have the facts and expertise in hand to back up your work."

‡**HUMDINGER BOOKS,** 1889 Preston White Dr., Reston VA 22091. (703)620-1100. Publisher: Jennifer Kuchta. Publishes hardcover, trade paperback and mass market paperback originals. Publishes 6-10 titles/year. Payment "negotiated profit sharing—case-by-case." Publishes book 3-6 months after acceptance of ms. Simultaneous submissions OK. Query for electronic submissions. Reports in 1 month. Book catalog not available.
Nonfiction: Personal development, self-help, small business and entrepreneurialism. "We are looking for unique works with a niche appeal." Query. All unsolicited mss are returned unopened.
Recent Nonfiction Title: *Soar . . . If You Dare,* by James R. Ball (personal development).

‡**HUNTER PUBLISHING, INC.,** 300 Raritan Center Pkwy., Edison NJ 08818. President: Michael Hunter. Estab. 1985. Averages 100 titles/year; receives 300 submissions annually. 10% of books from first-time au-thors. 75% of books from unagented writers. Pays royalty; offers $0-2,000 average advance. Publishes book on average 9 months after acceptance. Simultaneous submissions OK. Query for electronic submissions. Reports in 3 weeks on queries; 1 month on submissions. *Writer's Market* recommends allowing 2 months for reply. Book catalog for #10 SAE with 4 first class stamps.

Nonfiction: Reference. Subjects include travel. "We need travel guides to areas covered by few competitors: Caribbean Islands, Pacific Islands, Canada, Mexico, regional U.S. from an active 'adventure' perspective. Walking guides to all areas—from Australia to India." No personal travel stories or books not directed to travelers. Query or submit outline/synopsis and sample chapters. Reviews artwork/photos as part of ms package.

Tips: "Study what's out there, pick some successful models, and identify ways they can be made more appealing. We need active adventure-oriented guides and more specialized guides for travelers in search of the unusual."

HUNTINGTON HOUSE PUBLISHERS, P.O. Box 53788, Lafayette LA 70505-3788.(318)237-7049. Editor-in-Chief: Mark Anthony. Estab. 1982. Publishes hardcover, trade paperback, and mass market paperback originals, trade paperback reprints. Averages 25-30 titles/year; receives 1,500 submissions annually. 25% of books from first-time authors; 90% of books from unagented writers. Average print order for a writer's first book is 5,000-10,000. Pays up to 10% royalty on sale price. Publishes book an average of 1 year after acceptance. Simultaneous submissions OK. Query for electronic submissions. Reports in 4 months. Free book catalog and ms guidelines.

Nonfiction: Current social and political issues, biographies, self-help, inspirational and children's books. Query with descriptive outline.

Tips: "Write clear, crisp and exciting mss that grab the reader. The company's goal is to educate and keep readers abreast of critical current events. Published authors should expect a heavy publicity schedule."

ICS PUBLICATIONS, Institute of Carmelite Studies, 2131 Lincoln Rd. NE, Washington DC 20002. (202)832-8489. Editorial Director: Steven Payne, O.C.D. Publishes hardcover and trade paperback originals and reprints. Publishes 8 titles/year. Receives 10-20 queries and 10 mss/year. 10% of mss from first-time authors, 90-100% from unagented writers. Pays 2-6% royalty on retail price or makes outright purchase. Offers $500 advance. Publishes book an average of 1-2 years after acceptance. Accepts simultaneous submissions if so noted. Query for electronic submissions. Reports in 2 months on proposals. Book catalog for 7x10 SAE and 2 first class stamps; writer's guidelines for #10 SASE.

Nonfiction: Religious (should relate to Carmelite spirituality and prayer). "We are looking for significant works on Carmelite history, spirituality, and main figures (Saints Theresa, John of the Cross, Therese of Lisieux, etc.). Also open to more general works on prayer, spiritual direction, etc. Too often we receive proposals for works that merely repeat what has already been done, or are too technical for a general audience, or have little to do with the Carmelite tradition and spirit." Query or submit outline with 1 sample chapter.

Tips: "Our audience consists of those interested in the Carmelite tradition or in developing their life of prayer and spirituality."

IDEALS PUBLISHING CORP., Suite 800, 565 Marriott Dr., Nashville TN 37210-8000. (615)885-8270. Publisher: Patricia Pingry. Publishes highly illustrated seasonal and nostalgic hardbound books. Uses short prose and poetry. Also publishes *Ideals Magazine*. Firm averages 4 hardbound, 8 *Ideals*, 1-2 others titles/year. Payment varies. Simultaneous submissions OK. Publishes reprints of previously published articles or short stories. Send information about when and where the article previously appeared. Reports in 2 months. Manuscript guidelines free on request.

Nonfiction: Coffee table book. Query. Reviews artwork/photos as part of ms package.
● No longer publishing children's titles.

ILR PRESS, Division of the School of Industrial and Labor Relations, Cornell University, Ithaca NY 14853-3901. (607)255-3061. Director: E. Benson. Estab. 1945. Publishes hardcover and trade paperback originals and reprints. Averages 5-10 titles/year. Pays royalty. Reports in 2 months on queries. Free book catalog.

Nonfiction: All titles relate to industrial and labor relations, including relevant work in the fields of history, sociology, political science, economics, human resources, and organizational behavior. Book manuscript needs for the next year include "manuscripts on workplace problems, employment policy, women and work, personnel issues, current history, and dispute resolution that will interest academics and practitioners." Query or submit outline and sample chapters.

Recent Nonfiction Title: *Women and Unions: Forging a Partnership*, edited by Dorothy Sue Cobble.

Tips: "We are interested in manuscripts that address topical issues in industrial and labor relations that concern both academics and the general public. These must be well documented to pass our editorial evaluation, which includes review by academics in the industrial and labor relations field."

IMAGINE, INC., P.O. Box 9674, Pittsburgh PA 15226. (412)921-8777. President: Bob Michelucci. Estab. 1982. Publishes trade paperback originals. Averages 3-5 titles/year; receives 50 submissions annually. 50% of books from first-time authors; 75% of books from unagented writers. Pays 6-10% royalty on retail price. Offers average $500 advance. Publishes book an average of 1 year after acceptance. Reports in up to 3 months. SASE's are a *must* for all replies.

Nonfiction: Coffee table book, how-to, illustrated book and reference. Subjects include films, science fiction, fantasy and horror films. Submit outline and sample chapters with illustrations and/or photos.
Recent Nonfiction Title: *Bruno Sammartino, An Autobiography of Wrestling's Living Legend*, by Bob Michelucci and Paul McCullough.
Tips: "If I were a writer trying to market a book today, I would research my subject matter completely before sending a manuscript. Our audience is between ages 18-45 and interested in film, science fiction, fantasy and the horror genre. We do not solicit nor publish fiction *novels*, please don't submit fiction mss."

INCENTIVE PUBLICATIONS, INC., 3835 Cleghorn Ave., Nashville TN 37215-2532. (615)385-2934. Editor: Jan Keeling. Estab. 1970. Publishes paperback originals. Averages 25-30 titles/year; receives 350 submissions annually. 25% of books from first-time authors; 95% of books from unagented writers. Pays royalty or makes outright purchase. Publishes book an average of 1 year after acceptance. Reports in 1 month on queries. *Writer's Market* recommends allowing 2 months for reply. Book catalog and ms guidelines for 3 first-class stamps.
Nonfiction: Teacher resources and books on educational areas relating to children. Query with synopsis and detailed outline.
Recent Nonfiction Title: *The Early Childhood Teacher's Every-Day-All-Year-Long Book* (early childhood units, activities, patterns and more).

INDIANA UNIVERSITY PRESS, 601 N. Morton St., Bloomington IN 47404-3797. (812)337-4203. Fax: (812)855-7931. Director: John Gallman. Estab. 1951. Publishes hardcover and paperback originals and paperback reprints. Averages 175 titles/year. 30% of books from first-time authors. 98% from unagented writers. Average print order for a writer's first book varies depending on subject. Subsidy publishes (nonauthor) 9% of books. Pays maximum 10% royalty on retail price; offers occasional advance. Publishes book an average of 1 year after acceptance. Reports in 2 months. Free book catalog and ms guidelines.
Nonfiction: Scholarly books on humanities, history, philosophy, religion, Jewish studies, Black studies, criminal justice, translations, semiotics, public policy, film, music, philanthropy, social sciences, regional materials, African studies, Soviet and East European Studies, women's studies, and serious nonfiction for the general reader. Query or submit outline and sample chapters. "Queries should include as much descriptive material as is necessary to convey scope and market appeal to us." Reviews artwork/photos.
Recent Nonfiction Title: *Charles Sanders Peirce: A Life*, by Joseph Brent.
Tips: "We have been a bit more cautious about specialized monographs."

INDUSTRIAL PRESS INC., 200 Madison Ave., New York NY 10016-4078. (212)889-6330. Fax: (212)545-8327. Editorial Director: Woodrow Chapman. Estab. 1884. Publishes hardcover originals. Averages 12 titles/year; receives 25 submissions annually. 2% of books from first-time authors; 100% of books from unagented writers. Publishes book an average of 1 year after acceptance of finished ms. Query for electronic submissions. Reports in 1 month. *Writer's Market* recommends allowing 2 months for reply. Free book catalog.
Nonfiction: Reference and technical. Subjects include business and economics, science and engineering. "We envision professional engineers, plant managers, on-line industrial professionals responsible for equipment operation, professors teaching manufacturing, engineering, technology related courses as our audience." Especially looking for material on manufacturing technologies and titles on specific areas in manufacturing and industry. Computers in manufacturing are a priority. No energy-related books or how-to books. Query.

INFORMATION RESOURCES PRESS, Division of Herner and Company, Suite 550, 1110 N. Glebe Rd., Arlington VA 22201. (703)558-8270. Fax: (703)558-4979. Estab. 1970. Publishes hardcover originals. Averages 6 titles/year; receives 25 submissions annually. 80% of books from first-time authors; 100% of books from unagented writers. Pays 10-15% royalty on net cash receipts after returns and discounts. Publishes book an average of 1 year after acceptance. Simultaneous submissions OK. Query for electronic submissions. Reports in 2 weeks on queries. *Writer's Market* recommends allowing 2 months for reply. Free book catalog available.
Nonfiction: Reference, technical and textbook. Subjects include health and library and information science. Needs basic or introductory books on information science, library science, and health planning that lend themselves for use as textbooks. Preferably, the mss will have been developed from course notes. No works on narrow research topics (nonbasic or introductory works). Submit outline and sample chapters.
Tips: "Our audience includes libraries (public, special, college and university); librarians, information scientists, college-level faculty; schools of library and information science; health planners, graduate-level students of health planning, and administrators; economists. Our marketing program is slanted toward library and information science and health planning, and we can do a better job of marketing in these areas."

***ALWAYS** enclose a self-addressed, stamped envelope (SASE) with all your queries and correspondence.*

INITIATIVES PUBLISHING CO., 800 Sailview Rd., Knoxville TN 37922-4754. Publisher: Jason Harriman. Estab. 1988. Publishes hardcover originals and trade paperback originals and reprints. Publishes 6-10 titles/ year. Receives 350 queries and 50 mss/year. 80% of mss from first-time authors, 90% from unagented writers. Pays 4-12% royalty on wholesale price or makes outright purchase for $2,500-5,000. Publishes book 10 months after acceptance of ms. Query for electronic submissions. Reports in 2 months on proposals. Book catalog and ms guidelines free on request.

Nonfiction: How-to, reference, self-help and technical. Subjects include business and economics, government/politics and money/finance (primary focus). Submit outline and 1 sample chapter or proposal package, including proposed market. Reviews artwork/photos as part of freelance ms package. Writers should send photocopies.

● The publisher reports that submissions with solid marketing proposals get more consideration.

Tips: "We plan to adopt a strong advocacy position in favor of those wishing to improve the prosperity of their lives, through planning, education, working smarter (no self-help or financial fads). The biggest mistake that writers often make is failure to consider a broad enough market to warrant investment necessary to produce and market a book."

INNER TRADITIONS INTERNATIONAL, P.O. Box 388, 1 Park St., Rochester VT 05767. (802)767-3174. Fax: (802)767-3726. Editor-in-Chief: (Ms.) Leslie Colket. Estab. 1975. Imprints are Inner Traditions, Destiny Books, Healing Arts Press, and Park Street Press. Publishes hardcover and trade paperback originals and reprints. Averages 40 titles/year. Receives 1,500 submissions/year. 5% of books from first-time authors. 5% from unagented writers. Pays 8-10% royalty on net receipts. Offers $1,000 average advance. Publishes book an average of 1 year after acceptance. Reports in 3 months on queries, 3-6 months on mss. Free book catalog and ms guidelines.

Nonfiction: Coffee table book, cookbook, illustrated book, self-help. Subjects include anthropology/archaeology, art, natural foods, cooking, nutrition, health/alternative medicine, history and mythology, indigenous cultures, music/dance, nature/environment, esoteric philosophy, psychology, world religions, women's issues/ studies, New Age. Query or submit outline and sample chapters with return postage. Reviews artwork/photos as part of ms package.

Tips: "No longer looking for biography, textbooks, business/economics books. We are also not as eager to produce expensive art books as we once were. We are interested in the spiritual and transformative aspects of the above subjects, especially as they relate to world cultures. We are not inclined to take on autobiographical stories of self-transformation."

INSIGHT BOOKS, Imprint of Plenum Publishing Corp., 233 Spring St., New York NY 10013-1578. (212)620-8000. Fax: (212)463-0742. Editor: Frank K. Darmstadt. Estab. 1946. Publishes trade hardcover and paperback originals. Averages 12 titles/year. Receives 500 submissions/year. 50% of books from first-time authors. 75% from unagented writers. Pays royalty. Advance varies. Publishes book an average of 18 months to 2 years after acceptance. Simultaneous submissions OK. Query for electronic submissions. Reports in 2 months. Free book catalog.

Nonfiction: Self-help, how-to, treatises, essays, biography. Subjects include anthropology/archaeology, art/ architecture, business and economics, child rearing and development, education, ethnic, gay and lesbian studies, government/politics, health/medicine, language/literature, money/finance, nature/environment, psychology, parenting, science, sociology and women's issues/studies. Submit outline and sample chapters. *Single Parents by Choice: A Growing Trend in Family Life*, by Naomi Miller.

Tips: "Writers have the best chance selling authoritative, quality, well-written, serious information in areas of health, mental health, social sciences, education and child-rearing and development. Our audience consists of informed general readers as well as professionals and students in human, life and social sciences. If I were a writer trying to market a book today, I would say something interesting, important and useful, and say it well."

INTERCULTURAL PRESS, INC., P.O. Box 700, Yarmouth ME 04096. (207)846-5168. Fax: (802)685-4842. Contact Editor-in-Chief: David S. Hoopes, 130 North Rd., Vershire VT 05079. (802)685-4448. Estab. 1980. Publishes hardcover and trade paperback originals. Averages 5-7 titles/year; receives 50-80 submissions annually. 50% of books from first-time authors; 95% of books from unagented writers. Pays royalty; occasionally offers small advance. Publishes book an average of 2 years after acceptance. Simultaneous submissions OK. Reports in 2 months. Free book catalog and ms guidelines.

Nonfiction: How-to, reference, self-help, textbook and theory. Subjects include business and economics, philosophy, politics, psychology, sociology, travel, or "any book with an international or domestic intercultural, multicultural or cross-cultural focus, i.e., a focus on the cultural factors in personal, social, political or economic relations. We want books with an international or domestic intercultural or multicultural focus, especially those on business operations (how to be effective in intercultural business activities) and education (textbooks for teaching intercultural subjects, for instance). Our books are published for educators in the intercultural field, business people who are engaged in international business, managers concerned with cultural diversity in the workplace, and anyone else who works in an occupation where cross-cultural communication and adaptation are important skills. No manuscripts that don't have an intercultural focus." Accepts

nonfiction translations. Query "if there is any question of suitability (we can tell quickly from a good query)," or submit outline. Do not submit mss unless invited.
Recent Nonfiction Title: *Understanding Cultural Differences*, by Edward T. Hall and Mildred Reed Hall.

INTERLINK PUBLISHING GROUP, INC., 99 7th Ave., Brooklyn NY 11215. (718)797-4292. Fax: (718)855-7329. Publisher: Michel Moushabeck. Imprints are Interlink Books, Crocodile Books, USA, Olive Branch Press. Publishes hardcover and trade paperback originals. Averages 30 titles/year. Receives 200 submissions/year. 30% of books from first-time authors; 50% from unagented writers. Pays 5-7% royalty on retail price. Publishes book an average of 18 months after acceptance. Simultaneous submissions OK. Reports in 1 month on queries. *Writer's Market* recommends allowing 2 months for reply. Free book catalog and manuscript guidelines.
Nonfiction: Coffee table book, cookbook, how-to, illustrated book and juvenile. Subjects include art/architecture, child guidance/parenting, cooking, foods and nutrition, ethnic, gardening, government/politics, history, nature/environment, religion, travel, women's issues/studies and third world literature and criticism. Submit outline and sample chapters for adult nonfiction; complete ms for juvenile titles. Reviews artwork/photos as part of ms package.
Fiction: Ethnic, feminist, juvenile, picture books and short story collections (only third world). Adult fiction – We are looking for translated works relating to the Middle East, Africa or Latin America. Juvenile/Picture Books – Our list is full for the next two years. No science fiction, romance, plays, erotica, fantasy, horror. Submit outline/synopsis and sample chapters.
Tips: "Any submissions that fit well in our International Folktale Series series will receive careful attention."

INTERNATIONAL FOUNDATION OF EMPLOYEE BENEFIT PLANS, P.O. Box 69, Brookfield WI 53008-0069. (414)786-6700. Fax: (414)786-2990. Director of Publications: Dee Birschel. Estab. 1954. Publishes hardcover and trade paperback originals. Averages 10 titles/year; receives 20 submissions annually. 15% of books from first-time authors. 80% of books from unagented writers. Pays 5-15% royalty on wholesale and retail price. Publishes book an average of 1 year after acceptance. Reports in 3 months on queries. Book catalog free on request; ms guidelines for SASE.
Nonfiction: Reference, technical, consumer information and textbook. Subjects include health care, pensions, retirement planning, business and employee benefits. "We publish general and technical monographs on all aspects of employee benefits – pension plans, health insurance, etc." Query with outline.
Tips: "Be aware of interests of employers and the marketplace in benefits topics, for example, how AIDS affects employers, health care cost containment."

‡INTERNATIONAL INFORMATION ASSOCIATES, INC., P.O. Box 773, Morrisville PA 19067. (215)493-9214. Vice President/Publisher: Richard Bradley. Publishes trade paperback originals. Publishes 4-6 titles/year. Receives 25 queries and 6 mss/year. 98% of mss from first-time authors, 100% from unagented writers. Pays 10-12% royalty on retail price. Publishes book 12-14 months after acceptance. Simultaneous submissions OK. Query for electronic submissions. Prefers "any major MS-DOS or ASCII." Reports in 1 month on queries. Book catalog free on request. Manuscript guidelines for #10 SASE.
Nonfiction: How-to, reference, self-help, technical and textbook. Subjects include business and economics, health/medicine, money/finance, psychology and science. "Writers should be qualified in some way to write the text, if not by academic background then by experience." Query. Reviews artwork/photos as part of freelance ms package. Writers should send photocopies.
Tips: "Our audience is the professional at work in a particular field – on an international basis. Please remember that *anything* you write us will be used to judge *how* you write. Whether an author can write is as important as the topic."

INTERNATIONAL MARINE PUBLISHING CO., Division of TAB Books, Inc., McGraw-Hill Company, P.O. Box 220, Camden ME 04843. Fax: (207)236-6314. Imprints are Seven Seas and Ragged Mountain Press. Acquisitions Editor: James R. Babb. Vice President, Editorial: Jonathan Eaton. Estab. 1971. Publishes hardcover and paperback originals. Averages 40 titles/year; receives 500-700 submissions annually. 30% of books from first-time authors; 80% of books from unagented writers. Pays standard royalties, based on net price, with advances. Publishes book an average of 1 year after acceptance. Reports in 2 months. Book catalog and ms guidelines for SASE.
Nonfiction: "Mostly marine nonfiction but a wide range of subjects within that category: boatbuilding, boat design, yachting, seamanship, boat maintenance, maritime history, etc." All books are illustrated. "Material in all stages welcome. We prefer queries first with outline and 2-3 sample chapters." Reviews artwork/photos as part of ms package.
Tips: "We no longer consider fiction submissions. Freelance writers should be aware of the need for clarity, accuracy and interest. Many progress too far in the actual writing, with an unsalable topic."

‡INTERNATIONAL MEDICAL PUBLISHING, 404 Second St., Alexandria VA 22314. (703)519-0807. Fax: (703)519-0806. Editor: Thomas Masterson, MD. Publishes mass market paperback originals. Publishes 11 titles/year. Receives 5 queries and 2 mss/year. 100% of mss from first-time authors, 100% from unagented writers. Pays royalty on retail price. Publishes book 8 months after acceptance. Query for electronic submissions. Prefers disk. Reports in 2 months on queries. Book catalog free on request.

Nonfiction: Reference and textbook. Subjects include health/medicine. "We distribute only through medical and scientific bookstores. Look at our books. Think about practical material for doctors-in-training. We are interested in handbooks. Writers should avoid lack of clarity in writing. Keep prose simple when dealing with very technical subjects." Query with outline. Writers should send photocopies.

Recent Nonfiction Title: *The ER Intern Pocket Survival Guide*, by Rothenhaus (handbook).

Tips: Audience is medical students and physicians.

‡INTERNATIONAL PUBLISHERS CO., INC., P.O. Box 3042, New York NY 10116. (212)366-9816. Fax: (212)366-9820. President: Betty Smith. Estab. 1924. Publishes hardcover and trade paperback originals and trade paperback reprints. Averages 10-15 titles/year; receives 100 submissions annually. 10% of books from first-time authors. Pays 5-7½% royalty on paperbacks; 10% royalty on cloth. No advance. Publishes book an average of 6 months after acceptance. Simultaneous submissions OK. Reports in 1 month on queries (send SASE), 6 months on mss. Book catalog and ms guidelines for SASE with 2 first class stamps.

Nonfiction: Biography, reference and textbook. Subjects include Americana, economics, history, philosophy, politics, social sciences, and Marxist-Leninist classics. "Books on labor, black studies and women's studies based on Marxist science have high priority." Query or submit outline and sample chapters. Reviews artwork/photos as part of ms package.

Recent Nonfiction Title: *Reversing Discrimination: The Case for Affirmative Action*, by Prof. Gerald Horne.

Fiction: "We publish very little fiction. Do not submit poetry." Query or submit outline and sample chapters.

‡INTERNATIONAL WEALTH SUCCESS, P.O. Box 186, Merrick NY 11566-0186. (516)766-5850. Editor: Tyler G. Hicks. Estab. 1967. Averages 10 titles/year; receives 100 submissions annually. 100% of books from first-time authors; 100% of books from unagented writers. Average print order for a writer's first book "varies from 500 and up, depending on the book." Pays 10% royalty on wholesale or retail price. Buys all rights. Usual advance is $1,000, but this varies, depending on author's reputation and nature of book. Publishes book 4 months after acceptance. Query for electronic submissions. Reports in 1 month. Book catalog and ms guidelines for 9 × 12 SAE with 3 first class stamps.

Nonfiction: Self-help and how-to. "Techniques, methods, sources for building wealth. Highly personal, how-to-do-it with plenty of case histories. Books are aimed at the wealth builder and are highly sympathetic to his and her problems." Financing, business success, venture capital, etc. Length: 60,000-70,000 words. Query. Reviews artwork/photos as part of ms package.

Tips: "With the mass layoffs in large and medium-size companies there is an increasing interest in owning your own business. So we will focus on more how-to hands-on material on owning—and becoming successful in—one's own business of any kind. Our market is the BWB—Beginning Wealth Builder. This person has so little money that financial planning is something they never think of. Instead, they want to know what kind of a business they can get into to make some money without a large investment. Write for this market and you have millions of potential readers. Remember—there are a lot more people *without* money than *with* money."

INTERVARSITY PRESS, Division of InterVarsity Christian Fellowship, P.O. Box 1400, Downers Grove IL 60515-0700. (708)964-5700. Fax: (708)964-1251. Editorial Director: Andrew T. LePeau. Imprints are Saltshaker Books (Contact: Don Stephenson), and Life Guides (Contact: Cindy Bunch-Hotaling). Estab. 1947. Publishes hardcover and paperback originals and reprints. Averages 70 titles/year; receives 1,200 submissions annually. 25% of books from first-time authors; 95% of books from unagented writers. Subsidy publishes (nonauthor) 6% of books. Pays average 10% royalty on retail price; negotiable advance. Sometimes makes outright purchase for negotiable amount. Publishes book an average of 1 year after acceptance of final draft. "Indicate simultaneous submissions." Reports in 3 months. Book catalog for 9 × 12 SAE with 5 first class stamps. Writer's guidelines for SASE.

Nonfiction: "InterVarsity Press publishes books geared to the presentation of Biblical Christianity in its various relations to personal life, art, literature, sociology, psychology, philosophy, history and so forth. Though we are primarily publishers of trade books, we are cognizant of the textbook market at the college, university and seminary level within the general religious field. The audience for which the books are published is composed primarily of adult Christians. Stylistic treatment varies from topic to topic and from fairly simple popularizations to scholarly works primarily designed to be read by scholars." Accepts nonfiction translations. Query or submit outline and 2 sample chapters.

Recent Nonfiction Title: *The Contemporary Christian*, by John Stott.

Fiction: Fantasy, humor, mainstream, murder mysteries, religious, science fiction. "Typically our fiction is explicitly Christian and arises out of a Christian perspective."

Recent Fiction Title: *Stolen Identity*, by Brian Regrut (suspense).

Tips: "Religious publishing has become overpublished. Books that fill niches or give a look at a specific aspect of a broad topic (such as marriage or finances or Christian growth) are doing well for us. Also, even thoughtful books need lower reading levels, more stories and illustrative materials. If I were a writer trying to market a book today, I would read William Zinsser's *On Writing Well* and do as he says. Writers commonly send us types of mss that we don't publish, and act as if we should publish their work—being too confident of their ideas and ability. We are more open to fiction and humor submissions than in the past."

INTERWEAVE PRESS, 201 E. 4th St., Loveland CO 80537. (303)669-7672. Book Coordinator: Barbara Liebler. Estab. 1975. Firm publishes hardcover and trade paperback originals. Publishes 8 titles/year; receives 50 submissions/year. 60% from first-time authors; 98% from unagented writers. Pays 10% royalty on net receipts. Offers $500 average advance. Publishes book an average of 1 year after acceptance. Simultaneous (if clearly identified) submissions OK. Query for electronic submissions. Reports in 2 months. Free book catalog and ms guidelines.
Nonfiction: How-to, technical. Subjects include fiber arts—basketry, spinning, knitting, dyeing and weaving. Submit outline/synopsis and sample chapters. Reviews artwork/photos as part of ms package.
Tips: "We are looking for very clear, informally written, technically correct manuscripts, generally of a how-to nature, in our specific fiber fields. Our audience includes a variety of creative self-starters who like fibers and appreciate inspiration and clear instruction. They are often well educated and skillful in many areas."

IOWA STATE UNIVERSITY PRESS, 2121 S. State Ave., Ames IA 50010-8300. (515)292-0140. Fax: (515)292-3348. Acquisitions Editor: Gretchen Van Houten. Editor-in-Chief: Bill Silag. Estab. 1924. Hardcover and paperback originals. Averages 45 titles/year; receives 450 submissions annually. 98% of books from unagented writers. Average print order for a writer's first book is 1,200. Subsidy publishes (nonauthor) some titles, based on sales potential of book and contribution to scholarship on trade books. Pays 10% royalty for trade books on wholesale price; no advance. Publishes book an average of 1 year after acceptance. Simultaneous submissions OK, if advised. Query for electronic submissions. Reports in up to 6 months. Free book catalog; ms guidelines for SASE.
Nonfiction: Publishes agriculture, engineering, history, scientific/technical textbooks, food and nutrition, economics, aviation, journalism and veterinary sciences. Accepts nonfiction translations. Submit outline and several sample chapters, preferably not in sequence; must be double-spaced throughout. Looks for "unique approach to subject; clear, concise narrative; and effective integration of scholarly apparatus." Send contrasting b&w glossy prints to illustrate ms.
Tips: "We have reduced the number of titles published annually."

ISHIYAKU EUROAMERICA, INC., (IEA Publishers), 716 Hanley Industrial Court, St. Louis MO 63144-1904. (314)644-4322 or (800)633-1921. Fax: (314)644-9532. Editor-in-Chief: Dr. Gregory Hacke. Estab. 1983. Publishes hardcover originals. Averages 15 titles/year; receives 50 submissions annually. 75% of books from first-time authors; 100% of books from unagented writers. Average print order for a writer's first book is 3,000. Pays 10% minimum royalty on retail price or pays 35% of all foreign translation rights sales. Offers average $1,000 advance. Simultaneous submissions OK. Query for electronic submissions. Reports in 2 weeks on queries. *Writer's Market* recommends allowing 2 months for reply. Free book catalog; ms guidelines for SASE.
Nonfiction: Reference and medical/nursing textbooks. Subjects include health (medical and dental); psychology (nursing); and psychiatry. Especially looking for "all phases of nursing education, administration and clinical procedures." Query, or submit outline and sample chapters. Reviews artwork/photos as part of ms package.
Tips: "Medical authors often feel that their incomplete works deserve to be published; dental authors have a tendency to overstress facts, thereby requiring considerable editing. We prefer the latter to the former. We are looking for more medical therapists, particularly surgeons dealing with the latest techniques."

ITALICA PRESS, Suite 605, 595 Main St., New York NY 10044-0047. (212)935-4230. Fax: (212)838-7812. Publisher: Eileen Gardiner. Publishes trade paperback originals. Receives 75 queries and 20 mss/year. 50% of mss from first-time authors, 100% from unagented writers. Pays 7-15% royalty on wholesale price. Publishes book 1 year after acceptance of ms. Simultaneous submissions OK. Query for electronic submissions. Reports in 1 month on queries. *Writer's Market* recommends allowing 2 months for reply. Book catalog free on request.
Nonfiction: Biography, art/architecture, ethnic, history, language/literature, philosophy, religion, translation and travel. "We publish *only* English translations of medieval and Renaissance source materials." Query. Reviews artwork/photos as part of freelance ms package. Writers should send photocopies.
Tips: "We are interested in considering a wide variety of medieval and Renaissance topics (not historical fiction), and for modern works we are only interested in translations from Italian fiction."

JAIN PUBLISHING CO., P.O. Box 3523, Fremont CA 94539. (510)659-8272. Fax: (510)659-0501. Editor-in-chief: M.K. Jain. Imprint is Asian Humanities Press. Publishes hardcover and trade paperback originals and reprints. Publishes 10 titles/year. Receives 250 queries/year. 20% of mss from first-time authors; 90% from unagented writers. Pays 6-10% royalty on net sales or makes outright purchase of $1,000-3,000. Offers occasional $1,000-2,000 advance. Publishes book approximately 1 year after acceptance. Query for electronic submissions. Reports in 3 months on mss. Book catalog for 6×9 SAE and 2 first class stamps; manuscript guidelines for #10 SASE.

Nonfiction: Self-help (motivational/inspirational), how-to, cooking, foods and nutrition (vegetarian), health/medicine (holistic/alternative), nature/environment, personal and organizational development, money and personal finance, computer books (general purpose). "Manuscripts should be related to our subjects and written in an 'easy to read' and understandable format. Preferably between 40,000-80,000 words." Submit proposal package, including curriculum vitae and list of prior publications with SASE. Reviews artwork/photos as part of freelance package. Writers should send photocopies.
Tips: "We're interested more in user-oriented books than general treatises."

JIST WORKS, INC., 720 N. Park Ave., Indianapolis IN 46202-3431. (317)264-3709. Fax: (317)264-3709. Managing Editor: Sara Hall. Estab. 1981. Publishes trade paperback originals and reprints. Receives 30-50 submissions/year. 60% of books from first time authors; 100% from unagented writers. Pays 5-12% royalty on wholesale price or outright purchase (negotiable). Publishes ms an average of 6-12 months after acceptance. Simultaneous submissions OK. Query for electronic submissions. Reports in 2 months on queries. Book catalog and ms guidelines for 9×12 SAE and 4 first class stamps.
Nonfiction: How-to, career, reference, self-help, software, textbook. Specializes in job search, self-help and career related topics. "We want text/workbook formats that would be useful in a school or other institutional setting. We also publish trade titles. All reading levels. Will consider books for professional staff and educators, appropriate software and videos." *Writer's Market* recommends query with SASE first. Reviews artwork/photos as part of ms package.
Tips: "Institutions and staff who work with people of all reading and academic skills, making career and life decisions or who are looking for jobs are our primary audience, but we're focusing more on trade topics for consumers."

‡JOHNSON BOOKS, Johnson Publishing Co., 1880 S. 57th Ct., Boulder CO 80301. (303)443-9766. Fax: (303)443-1679. Estab. 1979. Editorial Director: Walter R. Bornemen. Imprints are Spring Creek Press and Cordillera Press. Publishes hardcover and paperback originals and reprints. Publishes 10-12 titles/year; receives 500 submissions annually. 30% of books from first-time authors; 90% of books from unagented writers. Average print order for a writer's first book is 5,000. Royalties vary. Publishes book an average of 1 year after acceptance. Reports in 2 months. Book catalog and ms guidelines for 9×12 SAE with 5 first class stamps.
Nonfiction: General nonfiction, books on the West, environmental subjects, natural history, paleontology, geology, archaeology, travel, guidebooks, and outdoor recreation. Accepts nonfiction translations. "We are primarily interested in books for the informed popular market, though we will consider vividly written scholarly works. As a small publisher, we are able to give every submission close personal attention." Query first or call. Accepts outline/synopsis and 3 sample chapters. Looks for "good writing, thorough research, professional presentation and appropriate style. Marketing suggestions from writers are helpful." Reviews artwork/photos.
Tips: "We are looking for nature titles with broad national, not just regional, appeal. We have recently acquired Cordillera Press and are now publishing more titles than ever. We are trying to include more outdoor recreation books in addition to our other areas listed."

‡BOB JONES UNIVERSITY PRESS, Greenville SC 29614. Acquisitions Editor: Mrs. Gloria Repp. Publishes trade paperback originals and reprints. Publishes 10 titles/year. Receives 50 queries and 300 mss/year. 40% of mss from first-time authors, 100% from unagented writers. Makes outright purchase of $500-1,250. Publishes book 1 year after acceptance. Simultaneous submissions OK. Query for electronic submissions. Reports in 2 months on mss. Book catalog and ms guidelines free on request.
Nonfiction: Biography (for teens) and children's/juvenile. Subjects include animals, gardening, health/medicine, history, nature/environment and sports. "We're looking for concept books on almost any subject suitable for children. We also like biographies." Submit outline and 3 sample chapters.
Recent Nonfiction Title: *With Daring Faith*, by Rebecca Davis (biography).
Fiction: Juvenile and young adult. "We're looking for well-rounded characters and plots with plenty of action." Submit synopsis and 5 sample chapters or complete ms.
Recent Fiction Title: *In Search of Honor*, by Donna Hess (historical fiction for teens).
Tips: "Our readers are children ages 2 and up, teens and young adults. We're looking for high-quality writing that reflects a Christian perspective and features well-developed characters in a convincing plot. Most open to: first chapter books; adventure; biography."

JUDSON PRESS, P.O. Box 851, Valley Forge PA 19482-0851. (215)768-2118. Publisher: Harold W. Rast. Estab. 1824. Publishes hardcover and paperback originals. Averages 10-15 titles/year; receives 750 queries annually. Average print order for a writer's first book is 5,000. Pays royalty or flat fee. Publishes book an

For information on setting your freelance fees, see How Much Should I Charge?

average of 15 months after acceptance. Simultaneous submissions acceptable. Reports in 6 months. Enclose return postage. Book catalog for 9 × 12 SAE and 4 first class stamps; ms guidelines for #10 SASE.

Nonfiction: Adult religious nonfiction of 30,000-80,000 words. "Our audience is mostly church members who seek to have a more fulfilling personal spiritual life and want to serve Christ in their churches and other relationships." Query with outline and 1 sample chapter.

Tips: "Writers have the best chance selling us practical books assisting clergy or laypersons in their ministry and personal lives. Our audience consists of Protestant church leaders and members. Be sensitive to our workload and adapt to the market's needs. Books on multicultural issues are very welcome."

‡**KALMBACH PUBLISHING CO.**, 21027 Crossroads Circle, P.O. Box 1612, Waukesha WI 53187-9951. Fax: (414)796-1383. Books Managing Editor: Terry Spohn. Publishes hardcover and paperback originals and paperback reprints. Averages 15-20 titles/year; receives 100 submissions annually. 85% of books from first-time authors; 100% of books from unagented writers. Offers 5-8% royalty on retail price. Average advance is $1,000. Publishes book an average of 18 months after acceptance. Reports in 2 months.

Nonfiction: Hobbies, how-to, amateur astronomy and recreation. "Our book publishing effort is in amateur astronomy, railroading and hobby how-to-do-it titles *only*." Query first. "I welcome telephone inquiries. They save me a lot of time, and they can save an author a lot of misconceptions and wasted work." In written query, wants to see "a detailed outline of two or three pages and a complete sample chapter with photos, drawings, and how-to text." Reviews artwork/photos as part of ms package.

Recent Nonfiction Title: *The Spirit of Railroading*, by Gary Dolzall & Mike Dahneman.

Tips: "Our books are about half text and half illustrations. Any author who wants to publish with us must be able to furnish good photographs and rough drawings before we'll consider contracting for his book."

KAR-BEN COPIES INC., 6800 Tildenwood Ln., Rockville MD 20852-4371. (301)984-8733 or 1-800-4KAR-BEN. Fax: (301)881-9195. President: Judye Groner. Contact: Madeline Wikler. Estab. 1975. Publishes hardcover and trade paperback originals. Averages 8-10 titles/year; receives 150 submissions annually. 25% of books from first-time authors; 100% from unagented writers. Average print order for a writer's first book is 5,000. Pays 6-8% royalty on net receipts; makes negotiable outright purchase; offers average $1,000 advance. Publishes book an average of 1 year after acceptance. Reports in 2 months. Book catalog and ms guidelines for 9 × 12 SAE with 2 first class stamps.

Nonfiction: Jewish juvenile (ages 1-12). Especially looking for books on Jewish life-cycle, holidays, and customs for children – "early childhood and elementary." Send only mss with Jewish content. Query with outline and sample chapters. Reviews artwork/photos as part of ms package.

Fiction: Adventure, fantasy, historical and religious (all Jewish juvenile). Especially looking for Jewish holiday and history-related fiction for young children. Submit outline/synopsis and sample chapters or complete ms.

Recent Fiction Title: *The Kingdom of Singing Birds*, by Miriam Aroner.

Tips: "We envision Jewish children and their families, and juveniles interested in learning about Jewish subjects, as our audience."

KENT STATE UNIVERSITY PRESS, P.O. Box 5190, Kent OH 44242-0001. (216)672-7913. Fax: (216)672-3104. Director: John T. Hubbell. Senior Editor: Julia Morton. Estab. 1965. Publishes hardcover and paperback originals and some reprints. Averages 20-25 titles/year. Subsidy publishes (nonauthor) 20% of books. Standard minimum book contract on net sales; rarely offers advance. "Always write a letter of inquiry before submitting manuscripts. We can publish only a limited number of titles each year and can frequently tell in advance whether or not we would be interested in a particular manuscript. This practice saves both our time and that of the author, not to mention postage costs. If interested we will ask for complete manuscript. Decisions based on in-house readings and two by outside scholars in the field of study." Reports in 3 months. Enclose return postage. Free book catalog.

Nonfiction: Especially interested in "scholarly works in history and literary studies of high quality, any titles of regional interest for Ohio, scholarly biographies, archaeological research, the arts, and general nonfiction."

Tips: "We are cautious about publishing heavily illustrated manuscripts."

MICHAEL KESEND PUBLISHING, LTD., 1025 5th Ave., New York NY 10028. (212)249-5150. Director: Michael Kesend. Editor: Judy Wilder. Estab. 1979. Publishes hardcover and trade paperback originals and reprints. Averages 4-6 titles/year; receives 150 submissions annually. 50% of books from first-time authors; 50% of books from unagented writers. Pays 3-12½% royalty on wholesale price or retail price, or makes outright purchase for $500 minimum. Advance varies. Publishes book an average of 18 months after acceptance. Reports in 2 months on queries. Guidelines for #10 SASE.

Nonfiction: Biography, how-to, illustrated book, self-help and sports. Subjects include animals, health, history, hobbies, nature, sports, travel, the environment, and guides to several subjects. Needs sports, health self-help and environmental awareness guides. No photography mss. Submit outline and sample chapters. Reviews artwork/photos as part of ms package.

Fiction: No science fiction or romance. No simultaneous submissions. Submit outline/synopsis and 2-3 sample chapters.

Tips: "We are now more interested in nature-related topics, regional guides, outdoor travel guides and sports nonfiction. Very little fiction is being published by us."

KINSEEKER PUBLICATIONS, P.O. Box 184, Grawn MI 49637-0184. (616)276-6745. Editor: Victoria Wilson. Estab. 1986. Publishes trade paperback originals. Averages 6 titles/year. 100% of books from unagented writers. Pays 10-25% royalty on retail price. Publishes book an average of 8 months after acceptance. Simultaneous submissions OK. Reports in 3 months. Book catalog and ms guidelines for #10 SASE.

Nonfiction: Reference books. Subjects are local history and genealogy. Query or submit outline and sample chapters. Reviews artwork/photos as part of ms package.

B. KLEIN PUBLICATIONS, P.O. Box 8503, Coral Springs FL 33075-8503. (305)752-1708. Fax: (305)752-2547. Editor-in-Chief: Bernard Klein. Estab. 1946. Publishes hardcover and paperback originals. Specializes in directories, annuals, who's who books, bibliography, business opportunity, reference books. Averages 5 titles/year. Pays 10% royalty on wholesale price, "but we're negotiable. Advance depends on many factors." Markets books by direct mail and mail order. Simultaneous submissions OK. Reports in 2 months. Book catalog for #10 SASE.

Nonfiction: Business, hobbies, how-to, reference, self-help, directories and bibliographies. Query or submit outline and sample chapters.

Recent Nonfiction Title: *Mail Order Business Directory,* by Bernard Klein.

ALFRED A. KNOPF, INC., Division of Random House, 201 E. 50th St., New York NY 10022. (212)940-7742. Submit manuscripts to Senior Editor or Children's Book Editor. Publishes hardcover and paperback originals. Averages 200 titles annually. 15% of books from first-time authors; 30% of books from unagented writers. Royalty and advance vary. Publishes book an average of 12 months after acceptance. Simultaneous (if so informed) submissions OK. Reports in 3 months. Book catalog for 7½ × 10½ SAE with 5 first class stamps.

Nonfiction: Book-length nonfiction, including books of scholarly merit. Preferred length: 50,000-150,000 words. "A good nonfiction writer should be able to follow the latest scholarship in any field of human knowledge, and fill in the abstractions of scholarship for the benefit of the general reader by means of good, concrete, sensory reporting." Query. Reviews artwork/photos as part of ms package.

Recent Nonfiction Title: *The Evolution of Useful Things,* by Henry Petroski (technology).

Fiction: Publishes book-length fiction of literary merit by known or unknown writers. Length: 40,000-150,000 words. *Writer's Market* recommends writers query with sample chapters.

Recent Fiction Title: *All the Pretty Horses,* by Cormac McCarthy.

• This title was the winner of the 18th annual National Book Critics Circle Award.

KNOWLEDGE BOOK PUBLISHERS, Suite 100, 3863 SW Loop 820, Fort Worth TX 76133-2063. (817)292-4270. Fax: (817)294-2893. Editor/Publisher: Dr. O.A. Battista. Estab. 1976. Publishes hardcover, trade paperback and mass market paperback originals. Firm averages 4-6 titles/year. Receives 50-100 submissions/year. 75% of books from first-time authors. 0% from unagented writers. Pays 10-15% royalty on wholesale price. Advance varies. Publishes book an average of 1 year after acceptance. Query for electronic submissions. Reports in 1 month on queries. *Writer's Market* recommends allowing 2 months for reply. Manuscript guidelines for #10 SASE.

Nonfiction: How-to, humor, juvenile, technical. Subjects include Americana, health/medicine, science. Submit through agent only.

Fiction: Juvenile. Submit through agent only.

Tips: "Our audience is a general audience interested in *new* knowledge useful in everyday life. If I were a writer trying to market a book today, I would do intense research on a new knowledge data that the general public can use to their *personal* benefit in everyday life."

KNOWLEDGE INDUSTRY PUBLICATIONS, INC., 701 Westchester Ave., White Plains NY 10604. (914)328-9157. Fax: (914)328-9093. Senior Vice President: Janet Moore. Publishes hardcover and paperback originals. Averages 10 titles/year; receives 30 submissions annually. 25% of books from first-time authors; 100% of books from unagented writers. Average print order for a writer's first book is 2,500. Offers negotiable advance. Publishes book an average of 1 year after acceptance. Query for electronic submissions. Reports in 3 months. Free book catalog; ms guidelines for SASE.

Nonfiction: Business and economics, also corporate, industrial video, interactive video. Especially needs TV and video. Query first, then submit outline and sample chapters. Reviews artwork/photos as part of ms package.

KODANSHA AMERICA, INC., (formerly Kodansha International U.S.A.), 114 5th Ave., New York NY 10011. (212)727-6460. Contact: Editorial Department. Estab. (in U.S.) 1989. Publishes hardcover and trade paperback originals (70%); and reprints (30%). Averages 20-30 titles/year. Receives 3,000 submissions/year. 10% of books from first-time authors; 30% from unagented writers. Pays 6-15% royalty on retail price. Offers

$5,000 average advance. Publishes book an average of 9 months after acceptance. Simultaneous submissions OK. Reports in up to 3 months. Book catalog for 9 × 12 SAE with 6 first class stamps.

Nonfiction: Biography, topical books-current events. Subjects include anthropology/archaeology, art/architecture, business and economics, cooking, ethnic, gardening, government/politics, history, craft, language, nature/environment, philosophy, psychology, religion, science, sociology, translation, travel and Asian subjects. We are looking for distinguished critical books on international subjects. No pop psychology, how-to, true crime, regional. Query with sample. SASE. Reviews artwork/photos as part of ms package.

Recent Nonfiction Title: *Hope Dies Last: The Autobiography of Alexander Dubcek.*

Tips: "Our focus is on nonfiction titles of an international and cross-cultural nature, well-researched, written with authority, bringing something of a world view to the general reading public. We are especially interested in titles with staying power, which will sell as well in five years' time as now. Potential authors should be aware of what comparable titles are on the market, and from whom."

KRIEGER PUBLISHING CO., P.O. Box 9542, Melbourne FL 32902-9542. (407)724-9542. FAX (407)951-3671. Executive Assistant: Marie Bowles. Imprints are Orbit Series, Anvil Series and Public History. Publishes hardcover and paperback originals and reprints. Averages 120 titles/year; receives 50-60 submissions annually. 30% of books from first-time authors; 100% of books from unagented writers. Pays royalty on net realized price. Publishes book an average of 8 months after acceptance. Reports in 1 month. *Writer's Market* recommends allowing 2 months for reply. Free book catalog.

Nonfiction: College reference, technical, and textbook. Subjects include history, music, philosophy, psychology, space science herpetology, chemistry, physics, engineering and medical. Query. Reviews artwork/photos as part of ms package.

Recent Nonfiction Title: *Education in the Rural American Community,* by Michael W. Galbraith.

LARK BOOKS, Altamont Press, 50 College St., Asheville NC 28801. Publisher: Rob Pulleyn. Estab. 1976. Imprints are: Lark Books; Sterling/Lark Books. Publishes hardcover and trade paperback originals and reprints. Publishes 20 titles/year. Sterling publishes 6; Lark publishes 14. Receives 100 queries and 50 mss/year. 80% of mss from first-time authors, 100% from unagented writers. Pays 5-20% royalty on gross income or makes outright purchase. Offers up to $2,500 advance. Publishes book 1 year after acceptance of ms. Simultaneous submissions OK. Query for electronic submissions. Reports in 2 months.

Nonfiction: Coffee table book, cookbook, how-to, illustrated book and children's/juvenile. Subjects include cooking, foods and nutrition, gardening, hobbies, nature/environment and crafts. "We publish high quality, highly illustrated books, primarily in the crafts/leisure markets. We work closely with bookclubs. Our books are either how-to, 'gallery' or combination books." Submit outline and 1 sample chapter or proposal package, including sample projects, table of contents. Reviews artwork/photos as part of the freelance ms package. Writers should send transparencies if possible.

LARSON PUBLICATIONS/PBPF, 4936 Rt. 414, Burdett NY 14818-9729. (607)546-9342. Director: Paul Cash. Estab. 1982. Publishes hardcover and trade paperback originals. Averages 4-5 titles/year. Receives 1,000 + submissions/year. 5% of books from first-time authors. Pays 7½% royalty on retail price; or 10% cash received. Rarely offers advance. Publishes book an average of 1 year after acceptance. Simultaneous submissions OK. Reports in 4 months on queries. Unsolicited mss not accepted; queries only. Book catalog for 9 × 12 SAE with 3 first class stamps.

Nonfiction: Spiritual philosophy. Subjects include philosophy, psychology and religion. We are looking for studies of comparative spiritual philosophy or personal fruits of independent (transsectarian viewpoint) spiritual research/practice. Query or submit outline and sample chapters. Reviews artwork/photos as part of ms package.

Recent Nonfiction Title: *Standing in Your Own Way,* by Anthony Damiani.

‡MERLOYD LAWRENCE BOOKS, Imprint of Addison Wesley, 102 Chestnut St., Boston MA 02108. President: Merloyd Lawrence. Estab. 1982. Publishes hardcover and trade paperback originals. Averages 7-8 titles/year. Receives 400 submissions/year. 25% of books from first-time authors. 20% from unagented writers. Pays royalty on retail price. Publishes book an average of 1 year after acceptance. Simultaneous submissions OK. Reports in 3 weeks on queries; no unsolicited ms read. All queries with SASE read and answered. Book catalog available from Addison Wesley.

Nonfiction: Biography. Subjects include child development/parenting, health/medicine, nature/environment, psychology. Query with SASE.

‡SEYMOUR LAWRENCE INC., Houghton Mifflin Co., 215 Park Ave. S., New York NY 10003. (212)420-5825. Publisher: Seymour Lawrence. Publishes hardcover originals. Publishes 6-8 titles/year. Receives 20-30 queries and 200 mss/year. Pays royalty on retail price. Offers $7,500-300,000 advance. Publishes book 9 months after acceptance of ms. Simultaneous submissions OK. Query for electronic submissions. Reports in 1 month on mss. Book catalog free on request.

Nonfiction: Biography. Subjects include nature/environment. Seeking literary biography. Submit outline and 2-3 sample chapters.
Recent Nonfiction Title: *Notes From Montana*, by Rick Bass (nature).
Fiction: Literary. Submit complete ms.
Recent Fiction Title: *Folly*, by Susan Minot (novel).
Tips: Audience is readers of quality fiction, contemporary literature.

LAWYERS & JUDGES PUBLISHING CO., P.O. Box 30040, Tucson AZ 85751-0040. (602)751-1500. President: Steve Weintraub. Publishes trade paperback originals. Publishes 10 titles/year. Receives 15 queries and 10 mss/year. 5% of mss from first-time authors, 100% from unagented writers. Pays 7-10% royalty on retail price. Publishes book 5 months after acceptance of ms. Simultaneous submissions OK. Query for electronic submissions. Reports in 2 months. Book catalog free on request.
Nonfiction: Reference. Subjects include legal/insurance. "We are a highly specific publishing company, reaching the legal and insurance fields and accident reconstruction. Unless a writer is an expert in these areas, we are not interested." Submit proposal package, including full or *very* representative ms. *Writer's Market* recommends query with SASE first.
Recent Nonfiction Title: *Bicycle Accident Reconstruction*, by James Garriott.

LEADERSHIP PUBLISHERS, INC., Talented and Gifted Education, P.O. Box 8358, Des Moines IA 50301-8358. (515)278-4765. Fax: (575)270-8303. Editorial Director: Lois F. Roets. Estab. 1982. Publishes trade paperback originals. Publishes 5 titles/year. Receives 25 queries and 10 mss/year. Pays 10% royalty of sales. Publishes book 1 year after acceptance of ms. Reports in 3 months. Book catalog and ms guidelines for 9×12 SAE and 3 first class stamps.
Nonfiction: Textbook. Subjects include education. "We publish enrichment/supplementary educational programs and teacher reference books." Submit outline and 2 sample chapters. Reviews artwork/photos as part of ms package. Writers should send photocopies.

LEHIGH UNIVERSITY PRESS, Linderman Library, Lehigh University, 30 Library Dr., Bethlehem PA 18015-3067. (215)758-3933. Fax: (215)758-5605. Director: Philip A. Metzger. Publishes hardcover originals. Publishes 10 titles/year. Receives 30 queries and 25 mss/year. 70% of mss from first-time authors, 100% from unagented writers. Pays royalty. Publishes book 18 months after acceptance of ms. Simultaneous submissions OK. Reports in 3 months. Book catalog and ms guidelines free on request.
Nonfiction: Biography, reference and academic. Subjects include Americana, art/architecture, history, language/literature and science. "We are an academic press publishing scholarly monographs. We are especially interested in works on 18th century studies and the history of technology, but consider works of quality on a variety of subjects." Submit 1 sample chapter and proposal package.

LEISURE BOOKS, Division of Dorchester Publishing Co., Inc., Suite 1008, 276 5th Ave., New York NY 10001-0112. (212)725-8811. Editorial Assistant: Kim Mattson. Estab. 1970. Publishes mass market paperback originals and reprints. Averages 160 titles/year; receives thousands of submissions annually. 20% of books from first-time authors; 20% of books from unagented writers. Pays royalty on retail price. Advance negotiable. Publishes book an average of 18 months after acceptance. Reports in 1 month on queries. *Writer's Market* recommends allowing 2 months for reply. Book catalog and ms guidelines for #10 SASE.
Nonfiction: "Our needs are minimal as we publish perhaps two nonfiction titles a year." Query.
Fiction: Historical romance (115,000 words); time-travel romance (90,000 words); futuristic romance (90,000 words). "We are strongly backing historical romance. No sweet romance, science fiction, western, erotica, contemporary women's fiction, mainstream or male adventure." Query or submit outline/synopsis and sample chapters. "No material will be returned without SASE."
● Leisure Books has started a new line, Love Spell, which will publish all romance titles.
Recent Fiction Title: *Terms of Surrender*, by Shirl Henke.
Tips: "Historical romance is our strongest category. We are no longer seeking Gothic romances; now seeking time-travel romances."

‡LERNER PUBLICATIONS COMPANY, 241 First Ave. N., Minneapolis MN 55401. (612)332-3344. Submissions Editor: Jennifer Martin. Imprints are: Runestone Press; First Avenue Editions. Firm produces hardcover originals. Averages 75-100 titles/year. Receives 1,000 queries and 300 mss/year. 50% of mss from first-time authors; 90% from unagented writers. Royalty or outright purchase negotiable. Offers $200-1,000 advance. Publishes book 18-24 months after acceptance of ms. Simultaneous submissions OK. Query for electronic submissions. Reports in 2 months on proposals. Catalog for 9×12 SAE with 4 first class stamps. Ms guidelines for #10 SAE.
Nonfiction: Children's/juvenile. Subjects include animals, anthropology/archaeology, art/architecture, business and economics, computers and electronics, cooking/foods/nutrition, ethnic, government/politics, health/medicine, history, language/literature, money/finance, music/dance, nature/environment, recreation, science, sports, biography and geography. "We are interested in multicultural work by authors of the focus ethnic groups. Picture books or any work clearly intended for adults (parents and teachers) are not of interest to

us. We also do not publish video or audio cassettes. Our main audience consists of children in grades 3 through 9." Submit proposal package, including introductory letter, outline, 1-2 sample chapters, resume, SASE.

Fiction: Young adult and middle grade. "We publish very little fiction—usually only one or two titles per year—mainly in the mystery and/or multicultural issues areas. We do not publish adult fiction, picture books, 'Babysitters Club'-type series." Query.

Recent Fiction Title: *Mystery in Miami Beach*, by Harriet K. Feder (mystery-juvenile).

‡**LEXIKOS,** P.O. Box 296, Lagunitas CA 94938. (415)488-0401. Editor: Mike Witter. Estab. 1981. Imprint is Don't Call It Frisco Press. Publishes hardcover and trade paperback originals and trade paperback reprints. Averages 8 titles/year; receives 200 submissions annually. 50% of books from first-time authors; 90% of books from unagented writers. Average print order for a writer's first book is 5,000. Royalties vary from 8-12½% according to books sold. "Authors asked to accept lower royalty on high discount (50% plus) sales." Offers average $1,000 advance. Publishes book an average of 10 months after acceptance. Simultaneous submissions OK. Reports in 1 month. Book catalog and ms guidelines for 6×9 SAE with 2 first class stamps.

Nonfiction: Coffee table book, illustrated book. Subjects include regional, outdoors, oral histories, Americana, history and nature. Especially looking for 50,000-word "city and regional histories, anecdotal in style for a general audience; books of regional interest about *places*; adventure and wilderness books; annotated reprints of books of Americana; Americana in general." No health, sex, European travel, diet, broad humor, fiction, quickie books (we stress backlist vitality), religion, children's or nutrition. Submit outline and sample chapters. Reviews artwork/photos as part of ms package.

Recent Nonfiction Title: *A River Went Out Of Eden*, by Chana Cox.

Tips: "A regional interest or history book has the best chance of selling to Lexikos. Submit a short, cogent proposal; follow up with letter queries. Give the publisher reason to believe you will help him *sell* the book (identify the market, point out the availability of mailing lists, distinguish your book from the competition). Avoid grandiose claims."

LIBRARIES UNLIMITED, P.O. Box 6633, Englewood CO 80155-6633. Fax: (303)220-8843. Editor-in-Chief: Bohdan S. Wynar. Estab. 1964. Imprints are Teacher Ideas Press and Ukranian Academic Press. Publishes hardcover and paperback originals. Averages 60 titles/year; receives 100-200 submissions annually. 10-20% of books from first-time authors. Average print order for a writer's first book is 2,000. 10% royalty on net sales; advance averages $500. Publishes book an average of 1 year after acceptance. Reports in 2 months. Free book catalog and ms guidelines.

Nonfiction: Publishes reference and library science textbooks, teacher resource and activity books, also software. Looks for professional experience. Query or submit outline and sample chapters; state availability of photos/illustrations with submission. All prospective authors are required to fill out an author questionnaire.

Recent Nonfiction Title: *Reference Guide to Science Fiction*, by Michael Burgess.

LIBRARY RESEARCH ASSOCIATES, INC., RD #5, Box 41, Dunderberg Rd., Monroe NY 10950-3703. (914)783-1144. President: Matilda A. Gocek. Editor: Dianne D. McKinstrie. Estab. 1968. Publishes hardcover and trade paperback originals. Averages 4 titles/year; receives about 300 submissions annually. 100% of books from first-time authors; 100% of books from unagented writers. Pays 10% maximum royalty on retail price. Offers 20 copies of the book as advance. Publishes book an average of 14 months after acceptance. Reports in 3 months. Book catalog free on request.

Nonfiction: Biography, how-to, reference, technical and American history. Subjects include Americana, business and economics, history and politics. "Our nonfiction book manuscript needs for the next year or two will include books about historical research of some facet of American history, and definitive works about current or past economics or politics." No astrology, occult, sex, adult humor or gay rights. Submit outline and sample chapters.

Recent Nonfiction Title: *Sailors, Waterways and Tugboats I Have Known*, by Capt. Fred G. Godfrey.

Tips: "Our audience is adult, over age 30, literate and knowledgeable in business or professions. The writer has the best chance of selling our firm historical nonfiction texts. Fiction has been eliminated from our lists. We now consider American historical and political works and legal ms."

LIFETIME BOOKS, INC., 2131 Hollywood Blvd., Hollywood FL 33020. (305)925-4252. Editor: George Sheldon. Publishes hardcover and trade paperback originals and reprints. Firm averages 20 titles/year. Receives 1,000 submissions/year. 50% of books from first-time authors. 80% from unagented writers. Pays royalty on wholesale price. Publishes book an average of 1 year after acceptance. Simultaneous submissions OK. Query for electronic submissions. Reports in 3 months on queries. Book catalog for 9×12 SAE with 5 first class stamps. Free manuscript guidelines.

Nonfiction: Biography, coffee table book, cookbook, how-to, illustrated book, reference and self-help. Subjects include Americana, animals, business and economics, child guidance/parenting, computers and electronics, cooking, foods and nutrition, education, gardening, health/medicine, hobbies, military/war, money/finance, nature/environment, philosophy, psychology, regional, religion, sports, travel and women's issues/studies. "We are interested in material on business, finance, health and fitness, self-improvement and medicine. We will not consider topics that only appeal to a small, select audience." Query.

Recent Nonfiction Title: *Make A Great Presentation in Two Hours,* by Frank Paola (business).

Fiction: "We are currently publishing very little fiction." Submit outline/synopsis and sample chapters.

Tips: "We are most interested in well-written, timely nonfiction with strong sales potential. Our audience is very general. Learn markets and be prepared to help with sales and promotion."

LION PUBLISHING, 1705 Hubbard Ave., Batavia IL 60510. (708)879-0707. Assistant Editor: Robert Bittner. Estab. 1971. Publishes hardcover and trade paperback originals. Firm averages 15 titles/year. Pays royalty. Publishes book an average of 18 months after acceptance. Reports in 3 months. Book catalog for 9 × 12 SAE with 4 first class stamps. Manuscript guidelines for #10 SAE with 1 first class stamp.

Nonfiction: Subjects include child guidance/parenting, social concerns, biography and religion. "We are especially interested in manuscripts on relationships and on spirituality. We do not want Bible studies or sermons." Query or submit outline and sample chapters.

Fiction: Fantasy, literary historical, and YA. "Give us a story that anyone would be intrigued with—and write it from a Christian perspective." Submit complete ms. *Writer's Market* recommends query with SASE first.

Recent Fiction Title: *The Endless Knot,* by Stephen Lawhead.

Tips: "All Lion books are written from a Christian perspective. However, they must speak primarily to a general audience. Because Lion's approach is unique, potential authors must request our guidelines. Half of our titles are children's books, yet we receive few mss of publishable quality and almost no nonfiction (say, for 8-12 year olds) of any kind. In short, we need high-quality nonfiction of all types that fit our guidelines."

‡LITTLE, BROWN AND COMPANY, CHILDREN'S BOOK DIVISION, 34 Beacon St., Boston MA 02108. (617)227-0730. Editorial Assistant: Lauren Adams. Publishes hardcover originals. Publishes 100 titles/year. Receives 1,500 queries and 5,000 mss/year. 5% of mss from first-time authors, 50% from unagented writers. Pays royalty on retail price. Offers advance to be negotiated individually. Publishes book 2 years after acceptance of ms. Simultaneous submissions OK "if indicated as such." Reports in 1 month on queries, 3 months on proposals and mss. Book catalog for 8 × 10 SAE with 3 first class stamps. Manuscript guidelines free on request.

Nonfiction: Children's/juvenile. Subjects include animals, art/architecture, cooking/foods/nutrition, ethnic, gay/lesbian, history, hobbies, nature/environment, recreation, science and sports. "We have published and will continue to publish books on a wide variety of nonfiction topics which may be of interest to children and are looking for strong writing and presentation, but no predetermined topics." Writers should avoid "looking for the 'issue' they think publishers want to see, choosing instead topics they know best and are most enthusiastic about/inspired by." Submit outline and 3 sample chapters "including first and last if possible" or proposal package, including "most complete outline possible, samples and background info (if project is not complete due to necessary research)." Reviews artwork/photos as part of freelance package. Writers should include photocopies (color if possible).

Recent Nonfiction Title: *Voices from the Fields: Children of Migrant Farmworkers Tell Their Stories,* by S. Beth Atkin (middle grade photo essay).

Fiction: All juvenile/young adult. Categories include adventure, ethnic, fantasy, feminist, gay/lesbian, historical, humor, mystery, picture books, science fiction, short story collections and suspense. "We are looking for strong fiction for children of all ages in any area, including multicultural. We always prefer full manuscripts for fiction."

Recent Fiction Title: *Kinda Blue,* by Ann Grifalconi (picture book).

Tips: "Our audience is children of all ages, from preschool through young adult. We are looking for quality material that will work in hardcover—send us your best."

LITTLE, BROWN AND CO., INC., Division of Time Warner Inc., 34 Beacon St., Boston MA 02108. (617)227-0730. Contact: Editorial Department, Trade Division. Estab. 1837. Imprint is Bullfinch Press. Publishes hardcover and paperback originals and paperback reprints. Averages 100 titles/year. "Royalty and advance agreements vary from book to book and are discussed with the author at the time an offer is made. Submissions *only* from authors who have had a book published or have been published in professional or literary journals, newspapers or magazines."

Nonfiction: "Some how-to books, distinctive cookbooks, biographies, history, popular science and nature, and sports." Query *only.* Will not accept unsolicited mss or proposals.

Recent Nonfiction Title: *The Cat and the Curmudgeon,* by Cleveland Avery.

Fiction: Contemporary popular fiction as well as fiction of literary distinction. Query *only.* Will not accept unsolicited mss or proposals.

Recent Fiction Title: *The Last Voyage of Somebody the Sailor,* by John Barth.

LLEWELLYN PUBLICATIONS, Subsidiary of Llewellyn Worldwide, Ltd., P.O. Box 64383, St. Paul MN 55164-0383. (612)291-1970. Fax: (612)291-1908. Acquisitions Manager: Nancy J. Mostad. Estab. 1901. Publishes trade and mass market paperback originals. Averages 60 titles/year. Receives 500 submissions/year. 30% of books from first-time authors; 90% from unagented writers. Pays 10% royalty on moneys received both wholesale and retail. Publishes book an average of 1 year after acceptance. Simultaneous submissions OK. Query for electronic submissions. Reports in 2 months. Book catalog for 9 × 12 SAE with 4 first class stamps. Manuscript guidelines free on request.

Nonfiction: How-to and self-help. Subjects include nature/environment, health and nutrition, metaphysical/magic, psychology and women's issues/studies. Submit outline and sample chapters. Reviews artwork/photos as part of ms package.

Recent Nonfiction Title: *The Family Wicca Book*, by Ashleen O'Gaea.

Fiction: Metaphysical/occult.

LOCUST HILL PRESS, P.O. Box 260, West Cornwall CT 06796-0260. (203)672-0060. Fax: (203)672-4968. Publisher: Thomas C. Bechtle. Publishes hardcover originals. Publishes 12 titles/year. Receives 50 queries and 20 mss/year. 100% of mss from unagented writers. Pays 12-18% royalty on retail price. Publishes book 6 months after acceptance of ms. Simultaneous submissions OK. Query for electronic submissions. Reports in 2 months on queries. Book catalog free on request.

Nonfiction: Reference. Subjects include art/architecture, business and economics, ethnic, language/literature, music/dance, philosophy, psychology, religion, science and women's issues/studies. "Since our audience is exclusively college and university libraries (and the occasional specialist), we are less inclined to accept manuscripts in 'popular' (i.e., public library) fields. While bibliography has been and will continue to be a specialty, our Locust Hill Literary Studies is gaining popularity as a series of essay collections and monographs in a wide variety of literary topics." Query.

Tips: "Remember that this is a small, very specialized academic publisher with no distribution network other than mail contact with most academic libraries worldwide. Please shape your expectations accordingly. If your aim is to reach the world's scholarly community by way of its libraries, we are the correct firm to contact. But *please*: no fiction, poetry, or personal memoirs."

LODESTAR BOOKS, Affiliate of Dutton Children's Books, division of Penguin Books USA, 375 Hudson St., New York NY 10014. (212)366-2627. Editorial Director: Virginia Buckley. Senior Editor: Rosemary Brosnan. Publishes hardcover originals. Publishes juveniles, young adults, fiction and nonfiction; and picture books. Averages 25-30 titles/year; receives 1,000 submissions annually. 10-20% of books from first-time authors; 25-30% of books from unagented writers. Average print order for a writer's first novel or nonfiction is 5,000-6,000; picture book print runs are higher. Pays royalty on invoice list price; advance offered. Publishes book an average of 18 months after acceptance. Reports in 4 months. Ms guidelines for SASE.

Nonfiction: Query or submit outline and 2-3 sample chapters including "theme, chapter-by-chapter outline, and 1 or 2 completed chapters." State availability of photos and/or illustrations. Queries/mss may be routed to other editors in the publishing group. Reviews artwork/photos as part of ms package.

Recent Nonfiction Title: *Playing America's Game*, by Michael Cooper.

Fiction: Publishes for young adults (middle grade) and juveniles (ages 5-17): multicultural, adventure, fantasy, historical, humorous, contemporary, mystery, science fiction, suspense and western books, also picture books. Submit complete ms.

Recent Fiction Title: *Out of Here*, by Sandy Asher.

Tips: "A young adult or middle-grade novel that is literary, fast-paced, well-constructed (as opposed to a commercial novel); well-written nonfiction on contemporary issues, photographic essays, and nonfiction picture books have been our staples. We do only a select number of picture books, which are very carefully chosen."

LONE EAGLE PUBLISHING CO., Suite 9, 2337 Roscomare Rd., Los Angeles CA 90077-1851. (310)471-8066. Fax: (310)471-4969. Toll Free: 1-800-FILMBKS. President: Joan V. Singleton. Estab. 1982. Publishes hardcover and trade paperback originals. Averages 8 titles/year; receives 20-30 submissions annually. 100% of books from unagented writers. Pays 10% royalty minimum on net income wholesale and retail. Offers $250-500 average advance. Publishes a book an average of 1 year after acceptance. Simultaneous submissions OK. Query for electronic submissions. Reports in 1 month on queries. *Writer's Market* recommends allowing 2 months for reply. Book catalog for #10 SAE with 2 first class stamps.

Nonfiction: Technical, how-to, and reference. Subjects include films and television. "We are looking for technical books in film and television. No unrelated topics or biographies." Submit outline and sample chapters. Reviews artwork/photos as part of ms package.

Recent Nonfiction Title: *The Hollywood Job-Hunter's Survival Guide*, by Hugh Taylor.

Tips: "A well-written, well-thought-out book on some technical aspect of the motion picture (or video) industry has the best chance: for example, script supervising, editing, special effects, costume design, production design. Pick a subject that has not been done to death, make sure you know what you're talking about, get someone well-known in that area to endorse the book and prepare to spend a lot of time publicizing the book."

LONELY PLANET PUBLICATIONS, Suite 251, 155 Filbert St., Oakland CA 94607. Sales and Marketing Director: Eric Kettunen. Publishes trade paperback originals. Publishes 30 titles/year. Receives 500 queries and 100 mss/year. 5% of mss from first-time authors, 50% from unagented writers. Makes outright purchase or negotiated fee — ⅓ on contract, ⅓ on submission, ⅓ on approval. Publishes book 1-2 years after acceptance of ms. Simultaneous submissions OK. Query for electronic submissions. Reports in 3 months on queries. Book catalog free on request.

Nonfiction: Travel guides and travel phrasebooks exclusively. "Writers should request our catalog first to make sure we don't already have a book similar to what they have written or would like to write. Also they should call and see if a similar book is on our production schedule. Lonely Planet publishes travel guides and phrasebooks, period." Submit outline or proposal package. Reviews artwork/photos as part of ms package. Writers should send photocopies. "Don't send unsolicited transparencies!"

LONGMAN PUBLISHING GROUP, 10 Bank St., White Plains NY 10606-1951. (914)993-5000. Fax: (914)997-8115. Contact: Barbara McIntosh. Estab. 1974. Publishes hardcover and paperback originals. Publishes 200 titles/year. Pays variable royalty; offers variable advance. Reports in 2 months.

Nonfiction: Textbooks only (elementary/high school, college and professional): history, political science, economics, communications, social sciences, social work, education, English, Latin, foreign languages, English as a second language. No trade, art or juvenile.

LONGMEADOW PRESS, 201 High Ridge Rd., Box 10218, Stamford CT 06904. (203)352-2110. Senior Editor: Pam Lislander. Publishes hardcover and trade paperback originals and reprints. Publishes 200 titles/year. Pays royalty or makes outright purchase. Simultaneous submissions OK.

Nonfiction: Biography, coffee table book, cookbook, how-to, humor, illustrated book, children's/juvenile, reference and self-help. Subjects include Americana, animals, art/architecture, business and economics, child guidance/parenting, cooking, foods and nutrition, education, ethnic, government/politics, health/medicine, history, hobbies, language/literature, military/war, money/finance, music/dance, nature/environment, photography, psychology, recreation, regional, science, sociology, sports, travel and women's issues/studies. Submit outline. Reviews artwork/photos as part of ms package.

Recent Nonfiction Title: *How to Get the Job You Want in 30 Days*, by Wendy Stehling Drumm.

Fiction: Adventure, confession, ethnic, historical, horror, humor, juvenile, mainstream/contemporary, mystery, occult, romance, suspense, Western and young adult. Query.

Recent Fiction Title: *Missing in Manhattan*, by Adams Roundtable.

LONGSTREET PRESS, INC., Suite 118, 2140 Newmarket Parkway, Marietta GA 30067. (404)980-1488. Associate Editor: Suzanne Bell. Estab. 1988. Publishes hardcover and trade paperback originals. Averages 30 titles/year. Receives 250 submissions/year. 25-30% of books from first-time authors. 60% from unagented writers. Pays royalty. Publishes book an average of 1 year after acceptance. Simultaneous submissions OK. Reports in 3 months. No electronic submissions via disk or modem. Book catalog for 9 × 12 SAE with 4 first class stamps. Manuscript guidelines for #10 SASE.

Nonfiction: Biography, coffee table book, cookbook, humor, illustrated book, reference. Subjects include Americana, cooking, foods and nutrition, gardening, history, language/literature, nature/environment, photography, regional, sports, women's issues/studies. "We want serious journalism-oriented nonfiction on subjects appealing to a broad, various audience. No poetry, how-to, religious or inspirational, scientific or highly technical, textbooks of any kind, erotica." Query or submit outline and sample chapters. Reviews artwork as part of ms package.

Fiction: Literary, mainstream/contemporary. "We are looking for solid literary fiction with appeal to a general reader. No juvenile or young adult literature, science fiction, mysteries, supernatural/horror, action/adventure/thriller, romance, historical fiction and romances." Query or submit outline/synopsis and sample chapters.

Tips: "Midlist books have a harder time making it. The nonfiction book, serious or humorous, with a clearly defined audience has the best chance. The audience for our books has a strong sense of intellectual curiosity and a functioning sense of humor. If I were a writer trying to market a book today, I would do thorough, professional work aimed at a clearly defined and reachable audience."

LOOMPANICS UNLIMITED, P.O. Box 1197, Port Townsend WA 98368. President: Michael Hoy. Estab. 1975. Publishes trade paperback originals. Publishes 20 titles/year; receives 500 submissions annually. 40% of books from first-time authors; 100% of books from unagented writers. Average print order for a writer's first book is 1,000. Pays 7½-15% royalty on wholesale or retail price or makes outright purchase of $100-1,200. Offers average $500 advance. Publishes book an average of 1 year after acceptance. Simultaneous submissions OK. Reports in 2 months. Free author guidelines. Book catalog is $5, postpaid.

Nonfiction: How-to, reference and self-help. Subjects include the underground economy, privacy, weapons, self-sufficiency, anarchism and "beat the system" books. "We are looking for how-to books in the fields of espionage, investigation, the underground economy, police methods, how to beat the system, crime and criminal techniques. No cookbooks, inspirational, travel, management or cutesy-wutesy stuff." Query, or submit outline/synopsis and sample chapters. Reviews artwork/photos.

Tips: "Our audience is young males looking for hard-to-find information on alternatives to 'The System.' "

● Look for the Insider Report with Loompanics' Steve O'Keefe in the introduction of this section.

LOTHROP, LEE & SHEPARD BOOKS, Imprint of William Morrow & Company, 1350 Avenue of the Americas, New York NY 10019. (212)261-6500. Fax: (212)261-6648. Editor-in-Chief: Susan Pearson. Estab. 1859. Other children's imprints are Morrow Junior Books, Greenwillow Books and Tambourine Books. Publishes hardcover original children's books only. Royalty and advance vary according to type of book. Averages 60 titles/year. Fewer than 2% of books from first-time authors; 25% of books from unagented writers. Average print order for a writer's first book is 6,000. Publishes book an average of 2 years after acceptance. Does *not* accept unsolicitied manuscripts. Reports in 3 months.
Fiction and Nonfiction: Publishes picture books, general nonfiction, and novels. Juvenile fiction emphasis is on novels for the 8-12 age group. Looks for "organization, clarity, creativity, literary style." Query *only.* Does *not* read unsolicited manuscripts.
Recent Nonfiction Title: *Kangaroos: On Location*, by Kathy Darling; photos by Tara Darling.
Tips: "Trends in book publishing that freelance writers should be aware of include the demand for books for children under age three and the shrinking market for young adult books, especially novels."

LOUISIANA STATE UNIVERSITY PRESS, Baton Rouge LA 70894-5053. (504)388-6294. Editor-in-Chief: Margaret Fisher Dalrymple. Estab. 1935. Publishes hardcover originals and hardcover and trade paperback reprints. Averages 60-70 titles/year. Receives 500 submissions/year. 33% of books from first-time authors. 90% from unagented writers. Pays royalty on wholesale price. Publishes book an average of 1 year after acceptance. Reports in 3 weeks on queries. *Writer's Market* recommends allowing 2 months for reply. Free book catalog and ms guidelines.
Nonfiction: Biography. Subjects include anthropology/archaeology, art/architecture, ethnic, government/politics, history, language/literature, military/war, music/dance, philosophy, photography, regional, sociology, women's issues/studies. Query or submit outline and sample chapters.
Fiction: Literary, novels, poetry collections and short story collections. Query. Submit outline/synopsis and sample chapters.
Tips: "Our audience includes scholars, intelligent laymen, general audience."

LOVE CHILD PUBLISHING, Suite 318, 6565 Sunset Blvd., Hollywood CA 90028-7206. (213)960-5490. Publisher/Editor: Tanya-Monique Kersey. Publishes trade paperback originals. Publishes 5-7 titles/year. Receives 20 queries and 5 ms/year. 90% of mss from first-time authors; 100% from unagented writers. Pays 5-12% royalty. Terms are negotiable. Advance varies. Publishes book 1 year after acceptance. Simultaneous submissions OK. Reports in 3 months on queries. Book catalog and manuscript guidelines for #10 SASE.
Nonfiction: How-to, reference, performing arts, and entertainment. "We publish career publications (books, guides, directories, monologue/scene books) for African Americans and other minorities in the entertainment industry (in front of and behind the camera talent). We also publish some career publications that are not specifically for minorities." Submit outline with 1-2 sample chapters.
Recent Nonfiction Title: *Original Monologues for African American Actors*, by Sabrina Norma.
Tips: "Know the entertainment industry!"

LOYOLA UNIVERSITY PRESS, 3441 N. Ashland Ave., Chicago IL 60657-1397. (312)281-1818. Fax: (312)281-0555. Editorial Director: Rev. Joseph F. Downey. Estab. 1927. Imprints are Campion Books, Values & Ethics. Publishes hardcover and trade paperback originals and reprints. Averages 12 titles/year; receives 150 submissions annually. 60% of books from first-time authors; 95% of books from unagented writers. Pays 10% royalty on net price, retail and wholesale; offers no advance. Publishes book an average of 1 year after acceptance. Simultaneous submissions acceptable. Query for electronic submissions. Reports in 2 months. Book catalog for 6×9 SASE.
Nonfiction: Biography and textbook. Subjects include art (religious); history (church); and religion. The four subject areas of Campion Books include Jesuitica (Jesuit history, biography and spirituality); Literature-Theology interface (books dealing with theological or religious aspects of literary works or authors); contemporary Christian concerns (books on morality, spirituality, family life, pastoral ministry, prayer, worship, etc.); and Chicago/art (books dealing with the city of Chicago from historical, artistic, architectural, or ethnic perspectives, but with religious emphases). Values and Ethics Series favors mss of a more scholarly and interdisciplinary bent. Query before submitting ms. Reviews artwork/photos.
Recent Nonfiction Titles: *Japan's Hidden Christians*, by Ann M. Harrington.
Tips: "Our audience is principally the college-educated reader with a religious, theological interest."

LUCENT BOOKS, P.O. Box 289011, San Diego CA 92198-9011. (619)485-7424. Managing Editor: Bonnie Szumski. Publishes hardcover originals and reprints. Publishes 50 titles/year. 50% from first-time authors; 90% from unagented writers. Does not accept unsolicited manuscripts. *Writing by assignment only.* Buys by outright purchase of $2,000-3,000. Offers average advance of 1/3 of total fee. Publishes book an average of 9 months after acceptance. Book catalog and ms guidelines for 9×12 SAE with 3 first class stamps.
Nonfiction: Juvenile. Subjects include controversial issues, discoveries and inventions, anthropology/archaelogy, business and economics, computers and electronics, government/politics, history, military/war, nature/environment, science, sports, women's issues/studies, biographies and histories. All on the juvenile level. Absolutely publishes *no* fiction or *anything* resembling fiction. All unsolicited mss are returned unopened.

Tips: "Please do not send material inappropriate to a company's list. In our case, no unsolicited manuscripts are accepted and no fiction is published. When writers send inappropriate material, they can make a lifetime enemy of the publisher."

LURAMEDIA, P.O. Box 261668, San Diego CA 92196-1668. (619)578-1948. Fax: (619)578-7560. Editorial Director: Lura Jane Geiger, Ph.D. Estab. 1982. Publishes trade paperback originals. Averages 6-8 titles/year; receives 250 submissions annually. 60% of books from first-time authors. 90% of books from unagented writers. Pays 10% royalty on wholesale price. Publishes book an average of 15 months after acceptance. Proposals only; no unsolicited mss. Reports in 3 months. Book catalog and ms guidelines for 9 × 12 SAE with 2 first class stamps.
Nonfiction: "Books for Healing & Hope, Balance & Justice. We publish books that contribute to spiritual, emotional and physical renewal. Our subjects include health of body and mind, woman's issues, relationships, prayer/meditation, creativity, journaling, relational group work, creative biblical education, values for children/family, aging, justice, alternative life-styles, ecology, experience of minorities, social issues. We especially favor approaches that utilize self disclosure, personal reflection, journal writing, stories/fables/parables, essays, meditations, sermons and prayers. We are looking for books that are well-thought out, books that encourage creative thinking rather than giving all the answers."
Recent Nonfiction Title: *I Sit Listening to the Wind: Woman's Encounter Within Herself*, by Judith Duerk.
Tips: "Our audience includes people who want to grow and change; who want to get in touch with their spiritual side; who want to relax; who are creative and want creative ways to live."

LYONS & BURFORD, PUBLISHERS, INC., 31 W. 21 St., New York NY 10010. (212)620-9580. Fax: (212)929-1836. Publisher: Peter Burford. Estab. 1984. Publishes hardcover and trade paperback originals and reprints. Averages 40-50 titles/year. 50% of books from first-time authors. 75% from unagented writers. Pays varied royalty on retail price. Publishes book an average of 1 year after acceptance. Simultaneous submissions OK. Reports in 2 weeks on queries. *Writer's Market* recommends allowing 2 months for reply. Free book catalog.
Nonfiction: Subjects include agriculture/horticulture, Americana, animals, art/architecture, cooking, foods and nutrition, gardening, hobbies, nature/environment, science, sports and travel. Query.
Recent Nonfiction Title: *The Great Bear Almanac*, by Gary Browa.
Tips: "We want practical, well written books on any aspect of the outdoors."

McDONALD & WOODWARD PUBLISHING CO., P.O. Box 10308, Blacksburg VA 24062-0308. (703)951-9465. Managing Partner: Jerry N. McDonald. Estab. 1986. Publishes hardcover and trade paperback originals. Publishes 5 titles/year. Receives 30 queries and 10 mss/year. 50% of mss from first-time authors, 100% from unagented writers. Pays 10% royalty on net receipts. Publishes book 1 year after acceptance of ms. Simultaneous submissions OK. Query for electronic submissions. Reports in 2 months. Book catalog free on request.
Nonfiction: Biography, coffee table book, how-to, illustrated book and self-help. Subjects include Americana, animals, anthropology, ethnic, history, nature/environment, science and travel. "We are especially interested in additional titles in our 'Guides to the American Landscape' series. Should consult titles in print for guidance. We want well organized, clearly written, substantive material." Query or submit outline and sample chapters. Reviews artwork/photos as part of freelance ms package. Writers should send photocopies.

MARGARET K. McELDERRY BOOKS, Imprint of Macmillan Children's Book Group, Inc., 866 3rd Ave., New York NY 10022. Fax: (212)605-3045. Editor: Margaret K. McElderry. Estab. 1971. Publishes hardcover originals. Publishes about 25 titles/year; receives 4,000 submissions annually. 8% of books from first-time authors; 50% of books from unagented writers. The average print order is 6,000-7,500 for a writer's first teen book; 10,000-15,000 for a writer's first picture book. Pays royalty on retail price. Publishes book an average of 1½ years after acceptance. Reports in 3 months. Catalog for 9 × 12 SAE with 4 first class stamps. Manuscript guidelines for #10 SASE.
Nonfiction and Fiction: Quality material for preschoolers to 16-year-olds, but publishes only a few YAs. Looks for "originality of ideas, clarity and felicity of expression, well-organized plot and strong characterization (fiction) or clear exposition (nonfiction); quality." *Writer's Market* recommends query with SASE first. Reviews artwork/photos as part of ms package.
Recent Title: *Randall's Wall*, by Carol Fenner.
Tips: "There is not a particular 'type' of book that we are interested in above others, though we always look for humor. Rather, we look for superior quality in both writing and illustration. Freelance writers should be aware of the swing away from teen-age novels to books for younger readers and of the growing need for beginning chapter books for children just learning to read on their own."

McFARLAND & COMPANY, INC., PUBLISHERS, P.O. Box 611, Jefferson NC 28640. (919)246-4460. Fax: (919)246-5018. President and Editor-in-Chief: Robert Franklin. Vice President: Rhonda Herman. Editors: Lisa Camp and Steve Wilson. Estab. 1979. Publishes mostly hardcover and a few "quality" paperback originals; a non-"trade" publisher. Averages 115 titles/year; receives 1,000 submissions annually. 70% of books from first-time authors; 95% of books from unagented writers. Average first print order for a book is 1,000.

Pays 10-12½% royalty on net receipts; no advance. Publishes book an average of 9 months after acceptance. Reports in 2 weeks. *Writer's Market* recommends allowing 2 months for reply.

Nonfiction: Reference books and scholarly, technical and professional monographs. Subjects include Americana, art, business, chess, drama/theatre, cinema/radio/TV (very strong), health, history, librarianship (very strong), music, sociology, sports/recreation (very strong) women's studies (very strong), and world affairs (very strong). "We will consider *any* scholarly book—with authorial maturity and competent grasp of subject." Reference books are particularly wanted—fresh material (i.e., not in head-to-head competition with an established title). "We don't like manuscripts of fewer than 200 pages. Our market consists mainly of libraries." No New Age material, memoirs, poetry, children's books, devotional/inspirational works or personal essays. Query or submit outline and sample chapters. Reviews artwork/photos as part of ms package.

Recent Nonfiction Title: *Women Prime Ministers and Presidents, 1960-1992*, by Olga S. Opfell.

Tips: "We do *not* accept novels or fiction of any kind or personal Bible studies. What we want is well-organized *knowledge* of an area in which there is not good information coverage at present, plus reliability so we don't feel we have to check absolutely everything."

McGRAW-HILL INC., 1221 Avenue of the Americas, New York NY 10020. Divisions include McGraw-Hill Ryerson (Canada), Osborne/McGraw-Hill, and TAB Books. Declined a listing for their Adult Trade Books Division.

‡MCGUINN & MCGUIRE PUBLISHING, P.O. Box 20603, Bradenton FL 34203. Managing Editor: Christopher Carroll. Publishes hardcover and trade paperback originals. Publishes 6 titles/year. Receives 150 queries and 75 mss/year. 50% of mss from first-time authors, 100% from unagented writers. Pays 10-15% royalty on wholesale price. Offers $250-500 advance. Publishes book 1 year after acceptance of ms. Simultaneous submissions OK. Query for electronic submissions. Reports in 1 month on queries and proposals, 2 months on mss. Book catalog and ms guidelines for #10 SASE.

Nonfiction: Biography, how-to, self-help and technical. Subjects include business and economics, health/medicine, history, nature/environment, science and women's issues/studies. "We are not interested in religious materials, memoirs, books relating to a personal philosophy, or diet books. Author should be able to demonstrate that his/her book fills a void in the market." Query or submit outline and 3 sample chapters. Reviews artwork/photos as part of the freelance ms package. Writers should send photocopies.

Recent Nonfiction Title: *The Confident Speaker*, by Ray Harlan (business/public speaking).

Tips: Audience is educated adults.

MACMILLAN PUBLISHING COMPANY, 866 3rd Ave., New York NY 10022. Imprints include Atheneum, Bradbury Press, Charles Scribner's Sons, Margaret K. McElderry Books, Four Winds Press, Macmillan USA Children's Books, Dillon Press, New Discovery, Crestwood House, Aladdin, and Collier Books.

● Macmillan is changing its imprints this year and will probably be sold.

MADISON BOOKS, 4720 Boston Way, Lanham MD 20706. (301)459-5308. Fax: (301)459-2118. Publisher: James E. Lyons. Managing Editor: Jennifer Smith. Estab. 1984. Publishes hardcover originals and trade paperback originals and reprints. Averages 40 titles/year. Receives 1,200 submissions/year. 15% of books from first-time authors; 50% from unagented writers. Pays 10-15% royalty on net price. Publishes ms an average of 1 year after acceptance. *Writer's Market* recommends allowing 2 months for reply. Book catalog and manuscript guidelines for 9 × 12 SAE and 4 first class stamps.

Nonfiction: History, biography, contemporary affairs, popular culture and trade reference. Query or submit outline and sample chapter. No complete mss.

MADISON HOUSE PUBLISHERS, INC., P.O. Box 3100, Madison WI 53704. (608)244-6210. Director: Gregory M. Britton. Publishes hardcover and trade paperback originals and reprints. Publishes 7 titles/year. Receives 40 queries and 10 mss/year. 40% of mss from first-time authors, 95% from unagented writers. Pays 5-15% royalty on wholesale price. Publishes book 6 months after acceptance of ms. Simultaneous submissions OK. Reports on queries and proposals in 3 weeks. *Writer's Market* recommends allowing 2 months for reply. Book catalog and ms guidelines free on request.

Nonfiction: Biography, reference and textbook. Subjects include Americana, government/politics and history. "We are an independent academic press focused in early American and constitutional history." Submit outline or proposal package including vitae or resume.

Recent Nonfiction Title: *Race and Revolution*, by Gary B. Nash (scholarly/history).

M&H PUBLISHING CO., INC., P.O. Box 268, LaGrange TX 78945-0268. (409)968-9508. President: Helen Ingalls. Publishes hardcover and mass market paperback originals. Averages 6 titles/year. Receives 12 queries and 6 mss/year. 25% from first-time authors; 100% from unagented writers. Pays 7% royalty on retail price. Publishes book 4 months after acceptance. Simultaneous submissions OK. Query for electronic submissions. Reports in 1 month on queries. *Writer's Market* recommends allowing 2 months for reply. Book catalog free on request.

Nonfiction: Technical, health/medicine. "Writers must be totally current with federal regulations." Query. Reviews artwork/photos as part of freelance ms package.

Tips: "Our audience is long term care and health care workers; nurses, etc."

MARKETSCOPE BOOKS, 119 Richard Ct., Aptos CA 95003. (408)688-7535. Editor-in-Chief: Ken Albert. Estab. 1985. Publishes hardcover and trade paperback originals. Firm averages 10 titles/year. 50% of books from first-time authors. 50% from unagented writers. Pays 10-15% royalty on wholesale price. Publishes book an average of 6-12 months after acceptance. Simultaneous submissions OK. Reports in 1 months on queries. *Writer's Market* recommends allowing 2 months for reply.

Nonfiction: Biography, how-to, humor, self-help. Subjects include anthropology/archaeology, child guidance/parenting, sexuality, health/medicine, hobbies, money/finance, nature/environment, recreation, regional, religion, sociology. Submit query letter. Reviews artwork/photos as part of the freelance ms package.

MARLOR PRESS, INC., 4304 Brigadoon Dr., St. Paul MN 55126. (612)484-4600. Editorial Director: Marlin Bree. Estab. 1981. Publishes mostly quality trade paperback originals and a few hardcover books. Averages 6 titles/year; receives 100 submissions annually. Pays 10% royalty on net sales. Publishes book an average of 1 year after final acceptance. Reports in 3 months on personal queries.

Nonfiction: Travel guide books, problem-solving books oriented to the family, and, in particular, children's books. No unsolicited materials. Please query first, and submit outline with sample chapters only when requested. Do not send full ms. Reviews artwork/photos as part of ms package.

Tips: "We are interested in practical, problem-solving books relating to family and family relationships. We are broadening our line to include some nonfiction children's books, such as *Kid's Book to Welcome a New Baby*, by Barbara J. Collman. We are not interested in esoteric advice, personal reminiscences, or anecdotal materials. We want books that are pragmatic, straight-forward and problem-solving that fill a need in today's family and in the market."

‡MASTERS PRESS, A Division of Howard W. Sams & Co., 2647 Waterfront Pkwy. E. Dr., Indianapolis IN 46214-2041. (317)298-5706. Managing Editor: Mark Montieth. Imprint is Spalding Sports Library. Publishes trade paperback originals. Publishes 30-40 titles/year. Imprint publishes 20 titles/year. Receives 75 queries and 50 mss/year. 80% of mss from first-time authors, 80% from unagented writers. Pays royalty. Publishes book 6-9 months after acceptance. Simultaneous submissions OK. Query for electronic submission: prefers WordPerfect 5.1 or ASCII DOS. Reports in 2 months on proposals. Book catalog free on request.

Nonfiction: Sports. Submit proposal package, including outline, sample chapters, author information.

Recent Nonfiction Title: *The Spalding Book of Rules and 1993 Sports Almanac*, by Bing Broido (sports reference).

Tips: "Our audience is athletes, coaches, fans and participants of various sports."

MAVERICK PUBLICATIONS, P.O. Box 5007, Bend OR 97708. (503)382-6978. Fax: (503)382-4831. Publisher: Gary Asher. Estab. 1968. Publishes trade paperback originals and reprints. Averages 10 titles/year; receives 100 submissions annually. Pays 15% royalty on wholesale price. Publishes book an average of 1 year after acceptance. Simultaneous submissions OK. Reports 2 months.

Nonfiction: Pacific Northwest only: aviation, cooking, history, hobby, how-to, marine, native American, nature and environment, recreation, reference, sports and travel. Submit proposal.

Recent Nonfiction Title: *The Oregon Trail Cookbook*, by Leslie Whipple.

MEADOWBROOK PRESS, 18318 Minnetonka Blvd., Deephaven MN 55391. (612)473-5400. Contact: Submissions Editor. Estab. 1975. Publishes trade paperback originals and reprints. Averages 12 titles/year. Receives 250 queries annually. 25% of books from first-time authors. 75% of books from unagented writers. Pays 5-7½% royalty; offers $2,000 average advance. Publishes book an average of 1 year after acceptance. Simultaneous submissions OK. Reports in 2 months on queries. Book catalog and ms guidelines for #10 SASE.

Nonfiction: How-to, humor, juvenile, illustrated book and reference. Subjects include baby and childcare, senior citizen's, children's activities, travel, relationships, business, cooking. No academic, autobiography, semi-autobiography or fiction. Query with outline and sample chapters. "We prefer a query first; then we will request an outline and/or sample material."

Recent Nonfiction Title: *The Joy of Parenthood*, by Jan Blaustone.

Tips: "We like how-to books in a simple, accessible format and any new advice on parenting. We look for a fresh approach to overcoming traditional problems (e.g. potty training)."

‡MEDIA FORUM INTERNATIONAL, LTD., RFD 1, P.O. Box 107, W. Danville VT 05873. (802)592-3444. Or P.O. Box 65, Peacham VT 05862. (802)592-3310. Managing Director: D.K. Bognár. Estab. 1969. Imprint: Media Forum Books; Division: Ha' Penny Gourmet. Publishes hardcover and trade paperback originals. Averages 4 titles/year. Pays 10% minimum royalty.

Nonfiction: Biography, cookbook (occasional), humor and reference. Subjects include cooking, ethnic, broadcast/film and drama. "*All mss are assigned.*"
Recent Nonfiction Title: *The Language of Broadcasting and Film. A Comprehensive, International Dictionary of Radio, Television and Film*, was projected for 1993.

MEDIA PUBLISHING/MIDGARD PRESS, Division of Westport Publishers, Inc., Suite 202, 2444 O Street, Lincoln NE 68510. (402)474-2676. Fax: (402)474-5104. President: Paul C. Temme. Publishes hardcover originals and trade paperback originals and reprints. Averages 4 titles/year. Receives 125 submissions/year. 60% of books from first-time writers; 95% from unagented writers. Pays royalty based on net sales. Makes some work-for-hire assignments. "Midgard Press is contract publishing; Media Publishing is trade publishing." Publishes book an average of 6 months after acceptance. Simultaneous submissions OK. Reports in 2 months. Submit query or ms with SASE.
Nonfiction: Biography, how-to, reference, self-help, textbook. Subjects include Americana, history and regional studies. Query or submit outline and sample chapters. Reviews artwork/photos as part of ms package.
Recent Nonfiction Title: *Guns Gold and Glory*, by Larry Underwood.

MENASHA RIDGE PRESS, INC., 3169 Cahaba Heights Rd., Birmingham AL 35243. (205)967-0566. Publisher: R.W. Sehlinger. Senior Acquisitions Editor: Leslie Cummins. Estab. 1982. Publishes hardcover and trade paperback originals. Averages 10-15 titles/year; receives 600-800 submissions annually. 50% of books from first-time authors; 90% of books from unagented writers. Average print order for a writer's first book is 4,000. Pays 10% royalty on wholesale price or purchases outright; offers average $1,000 advance. Publishes book an average of 1 year after acceptance. Simultaneous submissions OK. Query for electronic submissions. Reports in 2 months. Book catalog for 9 × 12 SAE and 4 first class stamps.
Nonfiction: How-to, reference, self-help, consumer, outdoor recreation, travel guides and small business. Subjects include business and economics, health, hobbies, recreation, adventure sports, travel and consumer advice. No biography or religious copies. Submit outline. Reviews artwork/photos.
Tips: "Audience: age 25-60, 14-18 years' education, white collar and professional, $30,000 median income, 75% male, 75% east of Mississippi River."

MERIWETHER PUBLISHING LTD., 885 Elkton Dr., Colorado Springs CO 80907-3557. (303)594-4422. Editors: Arthur or Theodore Zapel. Estab. 1968. Publishes hardcover and trade paperback originals and reprints. Firm publishes 5-10 books/year; 45-60 plays/year. Receives 1,200 submissions/year. 50% of books from first-time authors; 90% from unagented writers. Pays 10% royalty on retail price or outright purchase of $250-2,500. Publishes book an average of 6 months after acceptance. Simultaneous submissions OK. Reports in 1 month. Book catalog and ms guidelines available for $1 and SASE.
Nonfiction: How-to, reference, educational, humor and inspirational. Also textbooks. Subjects include art/theatre/drama, music/dance, recreation, religion. "We're looking for unusual textbooks or trade books related to the communication or performing arts. We are not interested in religious titles with fundamentalist themes or approaches – we prefer mainstream religion titles." Query or submit outline/synopsis and sample chapters.
Fiction: Plays. "Plays only – humorous, mainstream, mystery, religious, suspense."
Tips: "Our educational books are sold to teachers and students at college and high school levels. Our religious books are sold to youth activity directors, pastors and choir directors. Our trade books are directed at the public with a sense of humor. Another group of buyers is the professional theatre, radio and TV category. We will focus more on books of plays and acting texts."

METAMORPHOUS PRESS, P.O. Box 10616, Portland OR 97210. (503)228-4972. Fax: (503)223-9117. Publisher: David Balding. Acquisitions Editor: Nancy Wyatt-Kelsey. Estab. 1982. Publishes hardcover and trade paperback originals and reprints. Averages 4-5 titles/year; receives 1,500 submissions annually. 90% of books from first-time authors; 90% of books from unagented writers. Average print order for a writer's first book is 2,000-5,000. Pays minimum 10% profit split on wholesale prices. No advance. Publishes book an average of 1 year after acceptance. Simultaneous submissions OK. Query for electronic submissions. Reports in 3 months. Book catalog and ms guidelines for 9 × 12 SAE with 3 first class stamps.
Nonfiction: How-to, illustrated book, reference, self-help, technical and textbook – all related to behavioral science and personal growth. Subjects include business and sales, health, psychology, sociology, education, science and new ideas in behavioral science. "We are interested in any well-proven new idea or philosophy in the behavioral science areas. Our primary editorial screen is 'will this book further define, explain or support the concept that we are responsible for our reality or assist people in gaining control of their lives.'" Submit idea, outline, and table of contents only. Reviews artwork/photos as part of ms package.
Recent Nonfiction Title: *Professional Act*, by Mary Stark.

The double dagger before a listing indicates that the listing is new in this edition. New markets are often more receptive to freelance submissions.

‡**METEOR PUBLISHING CORPORATION**, 3369 Progress Dr., Bensalem PA 19020. (215)245-1489. Editor-in-Chief: Kate Duffy. Imprint is Kismet. Publishes mass market paperback originals. Publishes 72 titles/year. Receives 700 queries and 1,500 mss/year. 40% of mss from first-time authors, 60% from unagented writers. Offers advance (negotiable). Publishes book 1 year after acceptance of ms. Simultaneous submissions OK. Reports in 3 months on mss. Manuscript guidelines for #10 SASE.
Fiction: Romance. "We publish category, contemporary series romance." If unpublished in contemporary romance, submit complete ms; published authors may submit partials.
Recent Fiction Title: *Midnight Sun*, by Vella Munn (contemporary romance).
Tips: Audience is readers of romance fiction.

MICHIGAN STATE UNIVERSITY PRESS, Room 25, 1405 S. Harrison Rd., East Lansing MI 48823-5202. (517)355-9543. Fax: (800)678-2120. Director: Fred Bohm. Editor-in-Chief: Julie Loehr. Estab. 1947. Publishes hardcover and softcover originals. Averages 20 titles annually. Receives 400 submissions/year. 75% of books from first-time writers; 100% from unagented writers. Pays 10% royalty on net sales. Publishes ms an average of 9 months after acceptance. Query for electronic submissions. *Writer's Market* recommends allowing 2 months for reply. Book catalog and manuscript guidelines for 9 × 12 postmarked envelope.
Nonfiction: Reference, technical, and scholarly. Subjects include African Studies, agriculture, American Studies, business and economics, Canadian Studies, history, literature, philosophy, politics and world religion. Looking for "scholarship that addresses the social and political concerns of the late 20th century." Query with outline and sample chapters. Reviews artwork/photos.
Recent Nonfiction Title: *An Enchanting Darkness: The American Vision of Africa in the Twentieth Century*, by Dennis Hickey and Kenneth Wylie.

MICROTREND BOOKS, Imprint of Slawson Communications, Inc., Suite E, 2075 Corte Del Nogal, Carlsbad CA 92009-1414. (619)929-1979. Fax: (619)929-1008. Editorial Director: Lance A. Leventhal, Ph.D. Estab. 1963. Publishes only computer books as trade paperback originals. Imprint averages 12 titles/year. Receives 75 submissions/year. 50% of books from first-time authors; 80% from unagented writers. Pays 12-15% royalty on net price. Advance amount determined by subject. Publishes book an average of 4 months after acceptance. Simultaneous submissions OK. Reports in 2 weeks. *Writer's Market* recommends allowing 2 months for reply. Book catalog for $2.
Nonfiction: Technical. Subjects include computers and electronics. No entry level computer book manuscripts. Query or submit outline and sample chapters. Reviews artwork/photos as part of ms package.
Recent Nonfiction Title: *Unix User's Handbook*, by Tim Parker (computer).
Tips: "Our audience is made up of mid to advanced computer users. If I were a writer trying to market a book today, I would know the computer trade. The key point is to provide obvious value to the reader in an attractive, comprehensible form."

MILKWEED EDITIONS, Suite 400, 1st Ave. N, Minneapolis MN 55401. (612)332-3192. Editor: Emilie Buchwald. Estab. 1980. Publishes hardcover originals and paperback originals and reprints. Averages 10-12 titles/year. Receives 1,560 submissions/year. 30% of books from first-time authors; 70% from unagented writers. Pays 10% royalty on wholesale price. Offers average advance of $500. Publishes work an average of 1 year after acceptance. Simultaneous submissions OK. Reports in 1-6 months. Book catalog for 2 first class stamps; ms guidelines for SASE.
Nonfiction: Subjects include anthropology/archaeology, art/architecture, government/politics, history, language/literature, nature/environment, photography, regional, sports, women's issues/studies. Query.
Fiction: Literary. Query.
Recent Fiction Title: *The Boy Without a Flag*, by Abraham Rodriguez, Jr.
Children's: Novels and biographies for readers aged 8-14. High literary quality.
Recent Children's: *I am Lavinia Cumming*, by Susan Lowell.
Tips: "We are looking for excellent writing in fiction, nonfiction and poetry. Write for our fiction contest guidelines. Twelve books were chosen for our 1993 list."

THE MILLBROOK PRESS, INC., 2 Old New Milford Rd., Brookfield CT 06804. Manuscript Coordinator: Tricia Bauer. Estab. 1989. Publishes hardcover originals. Publishes 120 titles/year. Pays 5-7½% royalty on wholesale price or makes outright purchase. Advance varies. Publishes book 1 year after acceptance of ms. Reports on queries and proposals in 1 month. Book catalog for 9 × 12 SAE with 4 first class stamps. Manuscript guidelines for #10 SASE.
Nonfiction: Children's/juvenile. Subjects include animals, anthropology/archaeology, government/politics, ethnic, health/medicine, history, hobbies, nature/environment, science and sports. "We publish curriculum-related nonfiction for the school/library market. Mistakes writers most often make when submitting nonfiction are failure to research competing titles and failure to research school curriculum." Query or submit outline with 1 sample chapter.

MILLS & SANDERSON, PUBLISHERS, Suite 201, 41 North Rd., Bedford MA 01730-1021. (617)275-1410. Fax: (617)275-1713. Publisher: Jan H. Anthony. Estab. 1986. Publishes trade paperback originals. Publishes 6-8 titles/year; receives 500 submissions annually. 50% of books from first-time authors; 80% of books from unagented writers. Pays 12½% royalty on net price; offers standard $1,000 advance. Publishes book 1 year after acceptance. Simultaneous submissions OK. Reports in 2-4 months. Ms guidelines for #10 SASE.

Nonfiction: Family problem solving. No religion, travel, photography or fiction. Query first.

Recent Nonfiction Title: *Give Back the Pain: Emotional Healing Through Source Completion Therapy*, by Robert T. Bleck, Ph.D.

Tips: "We are currently publishing **only** nonfiction titles dealing with widely-shared, specific problems faced by today's families. Manuscript must cover an interesting subject with broad appeal, be written by an author whose credentials indicate he/she knows a lot about the subject. There must be a certain uniqueness about it. We have discontinued our travel and health/fitness books."

MINNESOTA HISTORICAL SOCIETY PRESS, Minnesota Historical Society, 345 Kellogg Blvd. West, St. Paul MN 55102-1906. (612)296-2264. Managing Editor: Ann Regan. Imprint is Borealis Books (reprints only). Contact: Sarah Rubinstein, editor. Firm publishes hardcover and trade paperback originals and trade paperback reprints. Averages 10 titles/year (4 for each imprint). Receives 50 queries and 25 mss/year. 8% of mss from first-time authors; 100% from unagented writers. Pays 5% royalty on net income. Publishes book 14 months after acceptance. Query for electronic submissions. Reports in 1 month on queries. *Writer's Market* recommends allowing 2 months for reply. Book catalog free on request.

Nonfiction: Biography, coffee table book, cookbook, illustrated book, reference, anthropology/archaeology, art/architecture, history, photography, regional, women's issues/studies, Native American studies. Query with proposal package including letter, outline, vita, and sample chapter. Reviews artwork/photos as part of freelance mss package. Writer should send photocopies.

Recent Nonfiction Title: *What This Awl Means: Feminist Archaeology at a Wahpeton Dakota Village*, by Janet Spector (archaeology, women's studies).

MIS PRESS, subsidiary of Henry Holt & Co., 115 W. 18th St., New York NY 10011.(212)886-9210. Publisher: Steven Berkowitz. Publishes trade paperback originals. Publishes 30 titles/year. Receives 150 queries/year. 20% of mss from first-time authors; 50% from unagented writers. Pays 5-15% royalty on wholesale price, or makes outright purchase of $5,000-20,000. Offers $7,000 advance. Publishes book an average of 4 months after acceptance. Simultaneous submissions OK. Query for electronic submissions. Book catalog and manuscript guidelines free on request.

Nonfiction: Technical, computer and electronic. "Submissions should be about or related to computer software or hardware." Submit outline and proposal package.

MODERN LANGUAGE ASSOCIATION OF AMERICA, Dept. WM, 10 Astor Place, New York NY 10003. (212)475-9500. Fax: (212)477-9863. Director of Book Acquisitions and Development: Joseph Gibaldi. Estab. 1883. Publishes hardcover and paperback originals. Averages 15 titles/year; receives 125 submissions annually. 100% of books from unagented writers. Pays 5-10% royalty on net proceeds. Publishes book an average of 1 year after acceptance. Query for electronic submissions. Reports in 3 weeks on mss. Book catalog free on request.

Nonfiction: Scholarly and professional. Subjects include language and literature. Publishes mss on current issues in literary and linguistic research and teaching of language and literature at postsecondary level. No critical monographs. Query or submit outline/synopsis and sample chapters.

MONITOR BOOK CO., INC., Box 9078, Palm Springs CA 92263. (619)323-2270. Editor-in-Chief: Alan F. Pater. Publishes hardcover originals. Pays 10% minimum royalty or by outright purchase, depending on circumstances; no advance. Reports in 4 months. Book catalog for SASE.

Nonfiction: Americana, biographies (only of well-known personalities), law and reference books. Send prints if photos and/or illustrations are to accompany ms.

MOON PUBLICATIONS, INC., #1, 330 Wall St. Chico CA 95928-5629. (916)345-5473. Fax: (916)345-6751. Senior Editor: Taran March. Estab. 1973. Publishes trade paperback originals. Publishes average of 15 titles/year; receives 100-200 submissions/year. 50% of books from first-time authors; 95% from unagented writers. Pays royalty on wholesale price; offers advance of up to $10,000. Publishes book an average of 18 months after acceptance. Simultaneous submissions OK. Query for electronic submissions. Reports in 1 month. *Writer's Market* recommends allowing 2 months for reply. Book catalog and proposal guidelines for 7½ × 10½ SAE with 2 first class stamps.

Nonfiction: "We specialize in travel guides to Asia and the Pacific Basin, the United States, Canada, the Caribbean, and Latin America, but are open to new ideas. Our guides include in-depth cultural and historical background, as well as recreational and practical travel information. We prefer comprehensive guides to entire countries, states, and regions over more narrowly defined areas such as cities, museums, etc. Writers should write first for a copy of our guidelines. Query with outline, table of contents, and writing sample. Author should also be prepared to provide photos, artwork and base maps. No fictional or strictly narrative travel writing; no how-to guides." Reviews artwork/photos as part of ms package.

Recent Nonfiction Title: *Thailand Handbook*, by Carl Parkes.
Tips: "Moon Travel Handbooks are designed by and for independent travelers seeking the most rewarding travel experience possible. Our Handbooks appeal to all travelers because they are the most comprehensive and honest guides available."

MOREHOUSE PUBLISHING CO., 871 Ethan Allen Hwy., Ridgefield CT 06877-2801. Fax: (203)431-3964. Publisher: E. Allen Kelley. Senior Editor: Deborah Grahame-Smith. Estab. 1884. Publishes hardcover and paperback originals. Averages 20 titles/year; receives 500 submissions annually. 40% of books from first-time authors; 75% of books from unagented writers. Pays 6-10% royalty on retail price. Publishes book an average of 8 months after acceptance. Book catalog for 9 × 12 SAE with 5 first class stamps.
Nonfiction: Specializes in Christian publishing (with an Anglican emphasis). Theology, ethics, church history, pastoral counseling, liturgy, religious education activity and gift books, and children's books (preschool-teen). No poetry or drama. Accepts outline/synopsis and 1-2 sample chapters. Reviews artwork/photos as part of ms package.
Recent Nonfiction Title: *The Saints Among Us*, by George H. Gallup, Jr., and Timothy Jones.

WILLIAM MORROW AND CO., 1350 Avenue of the Americas, New York NY 10019. (212)261-6500. Fax: (212)261-6595. Editorial Director: Adrian Zackheim. Managing Editor: Debbie Mercer-Sullivan. Imprints include Beech Tree Books (juvenile), Amy Cohn, editor-in-chief. Greenwillow Books (juvenile), Susan Hirschman, editor-in-chief. Hearst Books (trade), Ann Bramson, editorial director. Hearst Marine Books (nautical), Ann Bramson, editor. Lothrop, Lee & Shepard (juvenile), Susan Pearson, editor-in-chief. Morrow Junior Books (juvenile), David Reuther, editor-in-chief. Mulberry Books (juvenile), Paulette Kaufmann, editor-in-chief. Quill Trade Paperbacks, Andrew Dutter, editor. Tambourine Books (juvenile), Amy Cohn, editor-in-chief. Estab. 1926. Publishes 200 titles/year. Receives 10,000 submissions annually. 30% of books from first-time authors; 5% of books from unagented writers. Payment is on standard royalty basis on retail price. Advance varies. Publishes book an average of 1-2 years after acceptance. Reports in 3 months. Query letter on all books. *No unsolicited mss or proposals.*
Nonfiction and Fiction: Publishes adult fiction, nonfiction, history, biography, arts, religion, poetry, how-to books and cookbooks. Length: 50,000-100,000 words. Query only; mss and proposals should be submitted only through an agent.

MORROW JUNIOR BOOKS, Division of William Morrow and Co., 1350 Avenue of the Americas, New York NY 10019. (212)261-6691. Editor-in-Chief: David L. Reuther. Executive Editor: Meredith Charpentier. Senior Editor: Andrea Curley. Publishes hardcover originals. Publishes 50 titles/year. All contracts negotiated separately; offers variable advance. Book catalog and guidelines for 9 × 12 SAE with 2 first class stamps.
Nonfiction: Juveniles (trade books). No textbooks.
Fiction: Juveniles (trade books). Query.
Tips: "We are no longer accepting unsolicited manuscripts."

MOTHER COURAGE PRESS, 1667 Douglas Ave., Racine WI 53404-2721. (414)637-2227. Fax: (414)637-8242. Publisher: Barbara Lindquist. Estab. 1981. Publishes trade paperback and hardcover originals. Averages 4 titles/year; receives 800-900 submissions annually. 100% of books from first-time authors; 100% of books from unagented writers. Pays 10-15% royalty on wholesale; offers $250 average advance. Publishes book an average of 1 year after acceptance. Simultaneous submissions OK. Query for electronic submissions. Reports in 3 months. Book catalog for #10 SASE.
Nonfiction: How-to and self-help. Subjects include sexual abuse, psychology, sociology and spirituality. "We are looking for books on women's spirituality, Native American with women's emphasis feminist issues, humor and books about courageous women." Submit outline and sample chapters. Reviews artwork/photos as part of ms package.
Fiction: Lesbian fiction of any genre. "Don't send male-oriented fiction of any kind." Submit outline/synopsis and sample chapters.
Tips: "We like to do books that have 'Women of Courage' as the theme. Do not send anything unsolicited by registered or certified mail. Call us with your proposal—we will give you our answer immediately."

MOTORBOOKS INTERNATIONAL, 275 S. Third St., Stillwater MN 55082. Fax: (612)439-5627. Director of Publications: Tim Parker. Editor-in-Chief: Michael Dregni. Estab. 1973. Hardcover and paperback originals. Averages 100 titles/year. 95% of books from unagented writers. Offers 12% royalty on net receipts. Offers $3,000 average advance. Publishes book an average of 1 year after acceptance. Simultaneous submissions OK. Query for electronic submissions. Reports in 3 months. Free book catalog; ms guidelines for #10 SASE.
Nonfiction: Biography, history, how-to, photography (as they relate to cars, trucks, motorcycles, motor sports, aviation—domestic, foreign and military). Accepts nonfiction translations. Submit outline, 1-2 sample chapters and sample of illustrations. "State qualifications for doing book." Reviews artwork/photos as part of ms package.
Recent Nonfiction Title: *Chaparral*, by Falcomer w/Nye.

MOUNTAIN PRESS PUBLISHING COMPANY, P.O. Box 2399, Missoula MT 59806-2399. (406)728-1900. Fax: (406)728-1635. History Editor: Daniel Greer. Natural History Editor: Kathleen Ort. Estab. 1948. Imprints are Roadside Geology Series, Roadside History Series, Classics of the Fur Trade. Publishes hardcover and trade paperback originals. Averages 15 titles/year. Receives 250 submissions/year. 50% of books from first-time authors. 90% of books from unagented writers. Pays 7-15% on wholesale price. Publishes book an average of 1 year after acceptance. Query for electronic submissions. Reports in 1 month on queries. *Writer's Market* recommends allowing 2 months for reply. Free book catalog.

Nonfiction: Western history and Americana, nature/environment, regional, earth science, travel. "We are expanding our Roadside Geology and Roadside History series (done on a state by state basis). We are interested in how-to books (about horses) and well-written regional outdoor guides—plants, flowers and birds. No personal histories or journals." Query or submit outline and sample chapters. Reviews artwork/photos as part of ms package.

Tips: "It is obvious that small- to medium-size publishers are becoming more important, while the giants are becoming harder and less accessible. If I were a writer trying to market a book today, I would find out what kind of books a publisher was interested in and tailor my writing to them. Research markets and target my audience. Research other books, on the same subjects. Make yours different. Don't present your manuscript to a publisher—*sell* it to him. Give him the information he needs to make a decision on a title."

THE MOUNTAINEERS BOOKS, Suite 107, 1011 SW Klickitat Way, Seattle WA 98134-1162. (206)223-6303. Director: Donna DeShazo. Estab. 1961. Publishes hardcover and trade paperback originals (95%) and reprints (5%). Averages 25 titles/year; receives 150-250 submissions annually. 25% of books from first-time authors; 98% of books from unagented writers. Average print order for a writer's first book is 5,000-7,000. Offers royalty based on net sales. Offers advance on occasion. Publishes book an average of 1 year after acceptance. Reports in 2 months. Book catalog and ms guidelines for 9 × 12 SAE with 3 first class stamps.

Nonfiction: Adventure travel, recreation, natural history, conservation/environment, non-competitive self-propelled sports, and outdoor how-to books. "We specialize in books dealing with mountaineering, hiking, backpacking, skiing, snowshoeing, canoeing, bicycling, etc. These can be either how-to-do-it or where-to-do-it (guidebooks)." Does *not* want to see "anything dealing with hunting, fishing or motorized travel." Submit author bio, outline and minimum of 2 sample chapters. Accepts nonfiction translations. Looks for "expert knowledge, good organization." Also interested in nonfiction adventure narratives. Ongoing award—The Barbara Savage/"Miles from Nowhere" Memorial Award for outstanding adventure narratives is offered.

Fiction: "We might consider an exceptionally well-done book-length manuscript on mountaineering." Does *not* want poetry or mystery. Query first.

Tips: "The type of book the writer has the best chance of selling our firm is an authoritative guidebook (*in our field*) to a specific area not otherwise covered; or a how-to that is better than existing competition (again, *in our field*)."

MUSEUM OF NORTHERN ARIZONA PRESS, Rt. 4, Box 720, Flagstaff AZ 86001. (602)774-5211. Fax: (602)779-1527. Publisher: Diana Clark Lubick. Editorial Assistant: D.A. Boyd. Estab. 1926. Publishes hardcover and trade paperback originals, and quarterly magazine. Averages 10-12 titles/year; receives 35 submissions annually. 10% of books from first-time authors; 100% of books from unagented writers. Subsidy publishes (nonauthor) 15% of books. Pays one-time fee on acceptance of ms. No advance. Publishes book an average of 1 year after acceptance. Queries only. Query for electronic submissions. Reports in 2 months. Book catalog for 9 × 12 SAE and ms guidelines for #10 SASE.

Nonfiction: Coffee table book, reference and technical. Subjects include Southwest, art, nature, science. "Especially needs manuscripts on the Colorado Plateau that are written for a well-educated general audience." Query or submit outline and 3-4 sample chapters. Reviews artwork/photos as part of ms package.

Recent Nonfiction Title: *Canyon Country*, by Wayne Ranney.

MUSTANG PUBLISHING CO., P.O. Box 3004, Memphis TN 38173-0004. (901)521-1406. President: Rollin Riggs. Estab. 1983. Publishes nonfiction hardcover and trade paperback originals. Averages 8 titles/year; receives 1,000 submissions annually. 50% of books from first-time authors; 90% of books from unagented writers. Pays 6-8% royalty on retail price. Publishes book an average of 1 year after acceptance. Simultaneous submissions OK. No electronic submissions. No phone calls, please. Reports in 1 month. *Writer's Market* recommends allowing 2 months for reply. SASE a must. Book catalog for #10 SASE and $1.

Nonfiction: How-to, humor and self-help. Subjects include Americana, hobbies, recreation, sports and travel. "Our needs are very general—humor, travel, how-to, etc.—for the 18-to 40-year-old market." Query or submit outline and sample chapters.

Recent Nonfiction Title: *"Working in T.V. News: The Insider's Guide,"* by Carl Filoreto with Lynn Setzer.

Tips: "From the proposals we receive, it seems that many writers never go to bookstores and have no idea what sells. Before you waste a lot of time on a nonfiction book idea, ask yourself, 'How often have my friends and I actually *bought* a book like this?' Know the market, and know the audience you're trying to reach."

THE MYSTERIOUS PRESS, Subsidiary of Warner Books, 1271 6th Ave., New York NY 10020. (212)522-5144. Fax: (212)522-7990. Editor-in-Chief: William Malloy. Publishes hardcover originals, trade paperback reprints and mass market paperback reprints. Averages 40-50 titles/year; receives 750 submissions annually. 10% of books from first-time authors. *Accepts no unagented mss.* Pays standard, but negotiable, royalty on retail price; amount of advance varies widely. Publishes book an average of 1 year after acceptance. Reports in 2 months.
Nonfiction: Reference books on criticism and history of crime fiction. Submit complete ms. *Writer's Market* recommends query with SASE first. Reviews artwork/photos as part of ms package.
Recent Nonfiction Title: *Sleep with the Devil, A Jim Thompson Biography*, by Michael McCauley.
Fiction: Mystery, suspense and espionage. "We will consider publishing any outstanding crime/espionage/suspense/detective novel that comes our way. No short stories." Submit complete mss. *Writer's Market* recommends query with SASE first.
Recent Fiction Title: *Kissing the Gunner's Daughter*, by Ruth Randell.
Tips: "We no longer read unagented material. Agents only, please."

N.A.L. DUTTON, Imprint of Penguin USA, 375 Hudson St., New York NY 10014. (212)366-2000. Publisher: Elaine Koster. Estab. 1852. Publishes hardcover originals. Firm averages 120 titles/year. *Editor's note: Reads agented material only.* Does not read unsolicited manuscripts.
Nonfiction: Biography, self-help, serious nonfiction, politics, psychology, science.
Fiction: Mainstream/contemporary. "We don't publish genre romances or westerns."

THE NAIAD PRESS, INC., P.O. Box 10543, Tallahassee FL 32302. (904)539-5965. Fax: (904)539-9731. Editorial Director: Barbara Grier. Estab. 1973. Publishes paperback originals. Averages 24 titles/year; receives over 1,000 submissions annually. 20% of books from first-time authors; 99% of books from unagented writers. Average print order for a writer's first book is 12,000. Pays 15% royalty on wholesale or retail price; no advance. Publishes book an average of 18 months after acceptance. Reports in 4 months. Book catalog and ms guidelines for #10 SAE and 2 first class stamps.
Fiction: "We publish lesbian fiction, preferably lesbian/feminist fiction. We are not impressed with the 'oh woe' school and prefer realistic (i.e., happy) novels. We emphasize fiction and are now heavily reading manuscripts in that area. We are working in a lot of genre fiction — mysteries, short stories, fantasy — all with lesbian themes, of course." Query.
Recent Fiction Title: *Flashpoint*, by Katherine V. Forrest.
Tips: "There is tremendous world-wide demand for lesbian mysteries from lesbian authors published by lesbian presses, and we are doing several such series. We are no longer seeking science fiction. Manuscripts under 60,000 words have twice as good a chance as over 60,000."

NASW PRESS, (formerly National Association of Social Workers), Suite 700, 750 1st St., NE, Washington DC 20002-4241. Fax: (202)336-8312. Contact: Director of Publications. Averages 8-10 titles/year; receives 100 submissions annually. 20% of books from first-time authors. 100% of books from unagented writers. Pays 10-15% royalty on net prices. Publishes book an average of 1 year after acceptance. Reports in 3 months on submissions. Free book catalog and ms guidelines.
Nonfiction: Textbooks of interest to professional social workers. "We're looking for books on social work in health care, mental health and occupational social work. Books must be directed to the professional social worker and build on the current literature." Submit outline and sample chapters. Rarely reviews artwork/photos as part of ms package.
Recent Nonfiction Title: *Interactional Supervision*, by Lawrence Shulman.
Tips: "Our audience includes social work practitioners, educators, students and policy makers. They are looking for practice-related books that are well grounded in theory. The books that do well are those that have direct application to the work our audience does. New technology, AIDS, welfare reform and health policy will be of increasing interest to our readers. We are particularly interested in manuscripts for fact-based practice manuals that will be very user-friendly."

NATIONAL PRESS BOOKS, INC., Suite 212, 7200 Wisconsin Ave., Bethesda MD 20814. (301)657-1616. Editorial Director: G. Edward Smith. Estab. 1984. Publishes hardcover and trade paperback originals. Firm averages 23 titles/year. Receives 1,500 submissions/year. 40% of books are from first-time authors. 80% from unagented writers. Pays 5-10% royalty on wholesale or retail price. Also makes outright purchases. Offers flexible average advance. Publishes book an average of 8 months after acceptance. Simultaneous submissions OK. Reports in 4 months. Book catalog and manuscript guidelines for 7½ × 10½ SAE and 4 first class stamps.
Nonfiction: Biography, cookbook and self-help. Subjects include business and economics, child guidance/parenting, cooking, foods and nutrition, government/politics, history, money/finance, psychology, regional and sports. Query or submit outline and sample chapters. Reviews artwork/photos as part of ms package.

NATIONAL TEXTBOOK CO., Imprint of NTC Publishing Group, 4255 W. Touhy Ave., Lincolnwood IL 60646. (708)679-5500. Fax: (708)679-2494. Vice President/Publisher: Richard L. Smith. Publishes originals for education and trade market, and software. Averages 100-150 titles/year; receives 200 submissions annually. 10% of books from first-time authors; 80% of books from unagented writers. Mss purchased on either royalty

or buy-out basis. Publishes book an average of 1 year after acceptance. Reports in 4 months. Book catalog and ms guidelines for 6×9 SAE and 2 first class stamps.
Nonfiction: Textbooks. Major emphasis being given to foreign language and language arts classroom texts, especially secondary level material, and business and career subjects (marketing, advertising, sales, etc.). John T. Nolan, Language Arts Executive Editor; N. Keith Fry, Executive Editor/Foreign Language and ESL; Anne Knudsen, Executive Editor/NTC Business Books and VGM Career Guidance; and Passport Books. Send sample chapter and outline or table of contents.
Recent Nonfiction Title: *The Career Book*, by Joyce Lain Kennedy.

THE NAUTICAL & AVIATION PUBLISHING CO., 8 W. Madison St., Baltimore MD 21201. (410)659-0220. Fax: (410)539-8832. President/Publisher: Jan Snouck-Hurgronje. Editor: Christine Connor. Estab. 1979. Publishes hardcover originals and reprints. Averages 8-10 titles/year. Receives 20-25 submissions/year. Pays 10-15% royalty on net selling price. Offers $500-1,000 average advance. Simultaneous submissions OK. *Writer's Market* recommends allowing 1 month for reply. Free book catalog.
Nonfiction: Reference. Subjects include history, military/war. Submit synopsis and cover letter, or a maximum of 3 chapters. Reviews artwork/photo as part of package.
Recent Nonfiction Title: *The Battle for Lundy's Lane: On the Niagara in 1814*, by Donald E. Granes.
Fiction: Historical. Submit outline/synopsis and sample chapters.
Recent Fiction Title: *Checkfire!*, by Adm. Mack.
Tips: "Please note that we are publishers of *military* history only—our name is misleading, and we often get inquiries on general nautical or aviation books. We generally do not publish fiction titles. We are primarily and increasingly a nonfiction publishing house."

NAVAL INSTITUTE PRESS, Imprint of U.S. Naval Institute, Annapolis MD 21402-5035. Executive Editor: Paul Wilderson. Press Director: Thomas F. Epley. Contact: Anne Collier Rehill, assistant acquisitions editor; Shannon Becker, associate acquisitions editor. Estab. 1873. Averages 50 titles/year; receives 400-500 submissions annually. 60% of books from first-time authors; 75% of books from unagented writers. Average print order for a writer's first book is 3,000. Pays 14-21% royalty based on net sales; advance. Publishes book an average of 1 year after acceptance. Query letter strongly recommended. *Writer's Market* recommends allowing 3 months for reply. Free book catalog; ms guidelines for SASE.
Nonfiction: "We are interested in naval and maritime subjects and in broad far-reaching military topics, including government policy and funding. Specific subjects include: tactics, strategy, navigation, naval history, biographies, naval aviation and others." Reviews artwork/photos as part of ms package.
Recent Nonfiction Title: *Storm Center*, by Will and Sharon Rogers with Gene Gregston.
Fiction: Limited, very high quality fiction on naval and maritime themes.
Recent Fiction Title: *The Right Kind of War*, by John McCormick.

NAVPRESS, Division of The Navigators, P.O. Box 35001, Colorado Springs CO 80935-3500. (719)531-3551. Submissions Editor: Deborah Weaver. Estab. 1975. Imprint is Pinon Press. Publishes hardcover and trade paperback originals and software. Averages 40 titles/year. Receives 600-700 submissions/year. 10% of books from first-time authors; 75% from unagented writers. Pays royalty on wholesale price. Publishes book an average of 18 months after acceptance. Simultaneous submissions OK. Reports in 2 months. Free book catalog and manuscript guidelines for 9×12 SAE with 5 first class stamps.
Nonfiction: Christian instruction. Subjects include business and economics, child guidance/parenting, money/finance, religion and women's issues/studies. Query with outline.
Tips: "We want fresh insights on the relevancy of the Christian faith in contemporary society; books that creatively respond to felt needs. Aggressively study existing books and seek to find niches in the market where specific needs of significant groups of readers are not being met."

NEAL-SCHUMAN PUBLISHERS, INC., 100 Varick St., New York NY 10013. (212)925-8650. Director, Editorial: Margo Hart. Publishes hardcover and trade paperback originals. Firm averages 30-40 titles/year. Receives 100 submissions/year. 50% of books from first-time authors. 95% from unagented writers. Pays 10-15% royalty on net sales. Publishes book an average of 9 months after acceptance. Query for electronic submissions. Reports in 2 weeks on queries. *Writer's Market* recommends allowing 2 months for reply. Free book catalog and ms guidelines.
Nonfiction: How-to, reference, software, technical, textbook, texts and professional books in library and information science. Subjects include library and information science. "We are looking for reference books in business and health-related sciences." Submit outline and sample chapters. Reviews artwork/photos as part of ms package if submitted.
Recent Nonfiction Title: *Dictionary of AIDS Related Terminology*.

THOMAS NELSON PUBLISHERS, Nelson Place at Elm Hill Pike, P.O. Box 141000, Nashville TN 37214-1000. (615)889-9000. Managing Editor: Darryl F. Winburne. Estab. 1798. Imprints are Oliver-Nelson, Janet Thoma, and Jan Dennis Books. Publishes hardcover and paperback originals and reprints. Averages 250 titles/year. Pays royalty or makes outright purchase. Publishes book an average of 1 year after acceptance. Send proposal

to Book Editorial. Reports in 2 months. SASE must accompany submissions or unable to return proposals.
Nonfiction: Adult inspirational/motivational Christian trade books and reference books on the Bible and Christianity. Accepts outline/synopsis and 3 sample chapters.
Fiction: Seeking high quality novels with Christian themes for adults and teens.

NELSON-HALL PUBLISHERS, 111 N. Canal St., Chicago IL 60606. (312)930-9446. Editorial Director: Harold Wise, Ph.D. Estab. 1909. Publishes hardcover and paperback originals. Averages 50 titles/year. 90% of books submitted by unagented writers. Pays 15% maximum royalty on retail price; offers average advance. Reports in 1 month. *Writer's Market* recommends allowing 2 months for reply. Free book catalog.
Nonfiction: College textbooks and general scholarly books in the social sciences. Query.
Recent Nonfiction Title: *The Rich Get Richer*, by Denny Braun, Ph.D.

NEW DIRECTIONS PUBLISHING CORPORATION, 80 Eighth Ave., New York NY 10011. (212)255-0230. Manuscripts Editor: Stephen Moran. Publishes hardcover and trade paperback originals and and reprints. Publishes 30 titles/year. Receives 400 queries and 800 mss/year. 50% of mss from first-time authors, 60% from unagented writers. Pays 7½-15% royalty. Offers $500 advance. Publishes book 1 year after acceptance of ms. Simultaneous submissions OK. Query for electronic submissions. Reports in 4 months on queries. Book catalog free on request.
Fiction: Experimental, literary and short story collections. Submit 1-2 sample chapters.
Poetry: Submit 3-4 sample poems.

THE NEW ENGLAND PRESS, INC., P.O. Box 575, Shelburne VT 05482. (802)863-2520. Fax: (802)863-1570. President: Alfred Rosa. Managing Editor: Mark Wanner. Estab. 1978. Publishes hardcover and trade paperback originals and trade paperback reprints. Averages 6-12 titles/year; receives 200 submissions annually. 25% of books from first-time authors; 75% of books from unagented writers. Pays 10-15% royalty on wholesale price. Publishes ms an average of 1 year after acceptance. Reports in 3 months. Catalog for 6×9 SAE and 4 first class stamps.
Nonfiction: Biography, how-to, nature and illustrated book. Subjects include Americana (Vermontiana and New England); history (New England orientation); and essays (New England orientation). No juvenile or psychology. Query or submit outline and sample chapters. Reviews artwork/photos.
Fiction: Historical (New England orientation). No novels. Query.

‡**NEW LEAF PRESS, INC.**, P.O. Box 311, Green Forest AR 72638. Fax: (501)438-5120. Contact: Editorial Board. Estab. 1975. Publishes hardcover and paperback originals. Publishes 15-20 titles/year; receives 400 submissions annually. 15% of books from first-time authors; 90% of books from unagented writers. Average print order for a writer's first book is 10,000. Pays 10% royalty on first 10,000 copies, paid once per year; no advance. Send photos and illustrations to accompany ms. Publishes book an average of 10 months after acceptance. Simultaneous submissions OK. Reports in 3 months. Book catalog and guidelines for 9×12 SAE with 5 first class stamps.
Nonfiction: Biography and self-help. Charismatic books; life stories, and how to live the Christian life. Length: 100-400 pages. Submit complete ms. Reviews artwork/photos as part of ms package.
Recent Nonfiction Title: *Integrity: How I Lost it, and My Journey Back*, by Richard Dortch.
Tips: "Biographies, relevant nonfiction, and Bible-based fiction have the best chance of being sold to our firm. Honest and real-life experience help make a book or query one we can't put down."

NEW READERS PRESS, Publishing Division of Laubach Literacy International, P.O. Box 131, Syracuse NY 13210-0131. Fax: (315)422-6369. Editorial Director: Marianne Ralbovsky. Estab. 1959. Publishes paperback originals. Averages 70 titles/year; receives 500 submissions/year. 40% of books by first-time authors; 95% of books by unagented writers. Average print order for a writer's first book is 5,000. "Most of our sales are adult basic education programs, volunteer literacy programs, private human services agencies, prisons, and libraries with literacy outreach programs." Pays royalty on retail price, or by outright purchase. Rate varies according to type of publication and length of ms. Advance is "different in each case, but does not exceed projected royalty for first year." Publishes book an average of 1 year after acceptance. Query for electronic submissions. Reports in 3 months. Free book catalog and authors' brochure.
Nonfiction: "Our audience is adults with limited reading skills (8th grade level and below). We publish basic education and ESL literacy materials in reading and writing, math, social studies, health, science, and English as a second language. We are particularly interested in materials that fulfill curriculum requirements in these areas. Manuscripts must be not only easy to read (0 to 6th grade level) but mature in tone and concepts. We are not interested in anything at all written for children or teenagers." Write for guidelines or submit outline and 1-3 sample chapters.

Fiction: Short novels (7,500-10,000 words) at third grade reading level on themes of interest to adults and older teenagers. Write for guidelines or submit synopsis.
Tips: "We have a structured library of fiction and nonfiction titles for pleasure reading that need to follow specific guidelines."

NEW RIVERS PRESS, Suite 910, 420 N. 5th St., Minneapolis MN 55401. Managing Editor: Katherine Maehr. Publishes trade paperback originals. Publishes 10-14 titles/year. Receives 500 queries and 450 mss/year. 95% of mss from first-time authors, 99.9% from unagented writers. Pays royalty or makes outright purchase. Publishes book 14 months after acceptance of ms. Reports in 6 months. Book catalog free on request. Manuscript guidelines for #10 SASE.
Nonfiction: Memoirs. "We publish memoirs, essay collections, and other forms of creative nonfiction." Query. Reviews artwork/photos as part of freelance ms package, but not usually.
Fiction: Literary and short story collections. Query or submit synopsis and 2 sample chapters.
Poetry: Query or submit 10-15 sample poems.

NEW VICTORIA PUBLISHERS, P.O. Box 27, Norwich VT 05055. (802)649-5297. Editor: Claudia Lamperti. Estab. 1976. Publishes trade paperback originals. Averages 5-6 titles/year; receives 100 submissions/year. 50% of books from first-time authors; most books from unagented writers. Pays 10% royalty on wholesale price. Publishes book an average of 1 year after acceptance. Prefers electronic submissions. Reports on queries in 1 month. *Writer's Market* recommends allowing 2 months for reply. Free book catalog. .
Nonfiction: History. "We are interested in feminist history or biography and interviews with or topics relating to lesbians. No poetry." Submit outline and sample chapters.
Recent Nonfiction Title: *A Perilous Advantage*, by Natalie Barney, translated by Anna Livia (essays and epigrams).
Fiction: Adventure, erotica, fantasy, historical, humor, mystery, romance, science fiction and western. "We will consider most anything if it is well written and appeals to lesbian/feminist audience." Submit outline/synopsis and sample chapters.
Recent Fiction Title: *Other World*, by Sarah Dreher (mystery).
Tips: "Try to appeal to a specific audience and not write for the general market."

‡**NEW YORK NICHE PRESS**, Suite 2646, 175 5th Ave., New York NY 10010. (212)675-3699. Publisher: Michael Danowski. Publishes trade paperback originals and newsletters. Publishes 4 titles/year. Receives 4 queries/year. 50% of mss from first-time authors, 100% from unagented writers. Simultaneous submissions OK.
Nonfiction: Regional and travel. Subjects include recreation and travel (New York City). "Timely information should be balanced with useful material that will not date the work. Should be street-smart in style." Submit outline with 1 sample chapter. Reviews artwork/photos as part of freelance ms package. Writers should send photocopies.
Recent Nonfiction Title: *Dim Sum: How About Some? A Guide to NYC's Liveliest Chinese Dining & How To Make A Day of It*, by Wanda Chin and Michael P. Danowski (New York restaurant/travel guide).
Tips: "Our readers are New York residents and enthusiastic visitors to NYC. We use material with the 'New York attitude.' We are considering fiction about and for New York."

NEW YORK ZOETROPE, INC., 838 Broadway, New York NY 10003. (212)420-0590. Fax: (212)529-3330. Contact: Susan Schenker. Publishes hardcover and trade paperback originals, reprints and software. Averages 10 titles/year; receives 100 submissions annually. 25% of books from first-time authors; 75% of books from unagented writers. Subsidy publishes (nonauthor) 3% of books. Pays 10-20% royalty on wholesale prices or makes outright purchase of $500-1,000. Offers average $1,000 advance. Publishes book an average of 9 months after acceptance. Simultaneous submissions OK. Query for electronic submissions. Reports in 2 months. Book catalog and guidelines for 6×9 SAE.
Nonfiction: Reference, technical and textbook. Subjects include film, TV, entertainment industry and media. Interested especially in film and television. No fiction. Query with synopsis and outline.
Recent Nonfiction Title: *Emotion Picture Guide Annual*, by Baseline editors.
Tips: "Film- or media-oriented (academic and popular) subjects have the best chance of selling to our firm. Media books (reference) are our strongest line."

NEWCASTLE PUBLISHING CO., INC., 13419 Saticoy, N. Hollywood CA 91605. (213)873-3191. Fax: (213)780-2007. Editor-in-Chief: Alfred Saunders. Estab. 1970. Publishes trade paperback originals and reprints. Averages 10 titles/year; receives 300 submissions annually. 70% of books from first-time authors; 95% of books

A bullet introduces comments by the editor of Writer's Market indicating special information about the listing.

from unagented writers. Average print order for a writer's first book is 3,000-5,000. Pays 5-10% royalty on retail price; no advance. Publishes book an average of 8 months after acceptance. Simultaneous submissions OK. Reports in 1 month. *Writer's Market* recommends allowing 2 months for reply. Free book catalog; ms guidelines for SASE.

Nonfiction: How-to, self-help, metaphysical, New Age and practical advice for older adults. Subjects include health (physical fitness, diet and nutrition), psychology and religion. "Our audience is made up of college students and college-age nonstudents; also, adults ages 25 and up and older adults of above average education. They are of above average intelligence and are fully aware of what is available in the bookstores." No biography, travel, children's books, poetry, cookbooks or fiction. Query or submit outline and sample chapters. Looks for "something to grab the reader so that he/she will readily remember that passage."

Tips: "Check the shelves in the larger bookstores on the subject of the manuscript being submitted. A book on life extension, holistic health, or stress management has the best chance of selling to our firm along with books geared for older adults on personal health issues, etc."

THE NOBLE PRESS, INC., Suite 508, 213 W. Institute Place, Chicago IL 60610. (312)642-1168. Executive Editor: Douglas Seibold. Estab. 1988. Firm publishes hardcover and trade paperback originals. Publishes 15 titles/year; receives 1,500 submissions/year. 50% of books from first-time authors; 80% from unagented writers. Pays 5-15% royalty on retail price. Advance varies. Publishes book an average of 8 months after acceptance. Simultaneous submissions OK. Reports in 6 weeks. *Writer's Market* recommends allowing 2 months for reply. Manuscript guidelines for 1 first class stamp.

Nonfiction: Subjects include education, ethnic, government/politics, history, nature/environment, philosophy, sociology, women's issues/studies. No cookbooks, technical manuals, or texts in full. Query or submit outline and 1 sample chapter.

Recent Nonfiction Title: *Eco-Journeys*, by Stephen Foehr.

Tips: "The writer has the best chance of selling us a nonfiction book that addresses contemporary issues of importance to our society. Many of our books take subjects often explored in academic arenas, and we translate them in such a way that mainstream readers can understand and become involved in them."

NORDICPRESS, NordicTrack, Inc., 104 Peavey Rd., Chaska MN 55318-2234. (612)368-2545. Publishing Director: Charles Wetherall. Estab. 1976. Publishes trade paperback originals. Averages 6-8 titles/year. Pays 6-10% royalty on wholesale or retail price, or offers outright purchase for $2,500-5,000. Offers average $2,500 advance. Publishes book an average of 9 months after acceptance of ms. Simultaneous submissions OK. Reports in 2 months.

Nonfiction: Cookbook, how-to, self-help. Subjects include physical fitness, weight loss, nutrition, health/medicine, and recreation. "We're looking for books that promote the fitness lifestyle and our message of balanced fitness programs." Submit outline and sample chapters. Reviews artwork/photos as part of ms package.

Recent Nonfiction Title: *Maximizing Your Energy & Personal Productivity.*

NORTH LIGHT BOOKS, Imprint of F&W Publications, 1507 Dana Ave., Cincinnati OH 45207. Editorial Director: David Lewis. Publishes hardcover and trade paperback originals. Averages 30-35 titles/year. Pays 10% royalty on net receipts. Offers $3,000 advance. Simultaneous submissions OK. Reports in 2 months. Book catalog for 9×12 SAE with 6 first class stamps.

Nonfiction: Art and graphic design instruction books. Interested in books on watercolor painting, oil painting, basic drawing, pen and ink, airbrush, markers, basic design, computer graphics, desktop publishing, desktop design, color, layout and typography. Do not submit coffee table art books without how-to art instruction. Query or submit outline and examples of artwork (transparencies and photographs OK).

Recent Nonfiction Titles: *Making a Good Layout.*

NORTHERN ILLINOIS UNIVERSITY PRESS, DeKalb IL 60115-2854. (815)753-1826/753-1075. Fax: (815)753-1845. Director: Mary L. Lincoln (history). Acquisitions Editor: Dan Coran (literature). Estab. 1965. Pays 10-15% royalty on wholesale price. Free book catalog.

Nonfiction: "The NIU Press publishes mainly history, social sciences, philosophy, literary criticism and regional studies. We do not consider collections of previously published articles, essays, etc., nor do we consider unsolicited poetry." Accepts nonfiction translations. Query with outline and 1-3 sample chapters.

Recent Nonfiction Title: *World Historians and Their Goals: Twentieth-Century Answers to Modernism*, by Paul Costello.

‡NORTHLAND PUBLISHING CO., INC., P.O. Box 1389, Flagstaff AZ 86002-1389. (602)774-5251. Fax: (602)774-0592. Assistant Editor: Erin Murphy. Estab. 1958. Publishes hardcover and trade paperback originals. Firm averages 20 titles/year. Receives 1,500 submissions/year. 30% of books from first-time authors. 75% from unagented writers. Pays 8-15% royalty (on net receipts), depending upon terms. Offers $1,000 average advance. Publishes book an average of 14 months after acceptance. Simultaneous submissions OK. Reports in 1 month on queries; 2 months on mss. Free book catalog and manuscript guidelines.

Nonfiction: Subjects include animals, anthropology/archaeology, art/architecture, cooking, history, nature/environment, photography and regional (American West/Southwest). "We are seeking authoritative, well-written manuscripts on natural history subjects. We do not want to see poetry, general fiction, or New Age/science fiction material." Query or submit outline/synopsis and sample chapters. Reviews artwork/photos as part of ms package.

Recent Nonfiction Title: *Cougar: The American Lion*, by Kevin Hansen, in association with the Mountain Lion Foundation.

Fiction: Unique children's stories, especially those with Southwest/West regional theme; Native American folktales (retold by Native Americans only, please); natural history subjects. Manuscripts should be no shorter than 350 words, no longer than 1,500. We do not want to see chapter books or "mainstream" stories.

Recent Fiction Title: *Antelope Woman: An Apache Folktale*, retold and illustrated by Michael Lacapa.

Tips: "In general, our audience is composed of general interest readers and those interested in specialty subjects such as Native American culture and crafts. It is not necessarily a scholarly market, but is sophisticated."

NORTHWORD PRESS, INC., P.O. Box 1360, Minocqua WI 54548. (715)356-9800. Editor: Gregory Linder. Imprint: Heartland Press. Publishes hardcover and trade paperback originals. Estab. 1984. Firm averages 20 titles/year; imprint averages 5 titles/year. Receives 500 submissions/year. 50% of books are from first time authors. 90% are from unagented writers. Pays 5-15% royalty on wholesale price. Offers $1,500 average advance. Publishes book an average of 9 months. Simultaneous submissions OK. Query for electronic submissions. Reports in 3 weeks on queries. *Writer's Market* recommends allowing 2 months for reply. Book catalog for 9 × 12 SAE with 2 first class stamps. Manuscript guidelines for SASE.

Nonfiction: Coffee table book, how-to, illustrated book, juvenile. Subjects include nature/environment (exclusive). "We are seeking nature topics only with special attention to wildlife. Environmental issue (green books) a new area of interest." Submit outline and sample chapters. Reviews artwork/photos as part of ms package.

Recent Nonfiction Title: *True North*, by Stephen J. Krasemann (nature photography and text).

Tips: "Think nature and wildlife. That's exclusively what we publish."

W.W. NORTON CO., INC., 500 5th Ave., New York NY 10110. (212)354-5500. "Prefers not to share information."

NOYES DATA CORP., 120 Mill Rd., Park Ridge NJ 07656. Fax: (201)391-6833. Estab. 1959. Publishes hardcover originals. Averages 40 titles/year. Pays 10%-12% royalty on retail price; advance varies, depending on author's reputation and nature of book. Reports in 2 weeks. Free book catalog.

Nonfiction: Noyes Publications and Noyes Data Corp. publish technical books on practical industrial processing, science, economic books pertaining to chemistry, chemical engineering, food, textiles, energy, electronics, pollution control—primarily of interest to the business executive. Length: 50,000-250,000 words. Query the Editorial Department.

NTC PUBLISHING GROUP, 4255 W. Touhy Ave., Lincolnwood IL 60646-1975. (708)679-5500. Fax: (708)679-2494. Imprints include National Textbook Company, Passport Books, NTC Business Books, VGM Career Books. Foreign Language and English as a Second Language/Senior Editor: Tim Rogus. Language Arts Executive Editor: John Nolan. Passport Books Editor: Don Spinella. NTC Business Books Executive Editor: Anne Knudsen. VGM Career Books Editor: Mark Beyer. Estab. 1960. Publishes hardcover and trade paperback originals and reprints. Averages 150 titles/year. Receives 800 submissions/year. 98% of books from unagented writers. Pays royalty or buys by outright purchase. Offers varying advance. Publishes book an average of 8 months after acceptance. Simultaneous submissions OK. Query for electronic submissions. Reports in 2 months. Book catalog free on request.

Nonfiction: Textbook, travel, foreign language, reference, advertising and marketing busines books. Subjects include business, education, language/literature, photography, travel. Query. Reviews artwork/photos as part of ms package.

Recent Nonfiction Title: *English as a Second Language, International*.

OCTAMERON ASSOCIATES, 1900 Mt. Vernon Ave., Alexandria VA 22301. (703)836-5480. Editorial Director: Karen Stokstad. Estab. 1976. Publishes trade paperback originals. Averages 15 titles/year; receives 100 submissions annually. 10% of books from first-time authors; 100% of books from unagented writers. Average print order for a writer's first book is 8,000-10,000. Pays 7½% royalty on retail price. Publishes book an average of 6 months after acceptance. Simultaneous submissions OK. Query for electronic submissions. Reports in 2 months. Book catalog for #10 SAE with 2 first class stamps.

Nonfiction: Reference, career and post-secondary education subjects. Especially interested in "paying-for-college and college admission guides." Query or submit outline and 2 sample chapters. Reviews artwork/photos as part of ms package.

ODDO PUBLISHING, INC., P.O. Box 68, Fayetteville GA 30214-0068. (404)461-7627. Contact: Managing Editor. Estab. 1964. Publishes hardcover, paperback originals and coloring/activity books. Averages 4 titles/year; receives 600 submissions annually. 25% of books from first-time authors; 100% of books from unagented writers. Average print order for a writer's first book is 3,500. Makes outright purchase. "We judge all scripts independently." Royalty considered for special scripts only. Publishes book an average of 2-3 years after acceptance. Reports in up to 4 months. Book catalog for 9×12 SAE with 5 first class stamps.
Nonfiction and Fiction: Publishes juvenile books (ages 4-10) in language arts, workbooks in math, writing (English), photophonics, science (space and oceanography), and social studies for schools, libraries, and trade. Interested in children's supplementary readers in the areas of language arts, math, science, geography, social studies, etc. "Texts run from 1,500 to 3,500 words. Ecology, space, patriotism, oceanography and pollution are subjects of interest. Manuscripts must be easy to read, general, and not set to outdated themes. They must lend themselves to full color illustration. No stories of grandmother long ago. No love angle, permissive language, or immoral words or statements." Submit complete ms. *Writer's Market* recommends query with SASE first. Reviews artwork/photos as part of ms package.
Tips: "We are currently expanding our line to include materials more acceptable in the trade market. To do so, we are concentrating on adding titles to our top selling series in lieu of developing new series; our publishing schedule has been set for the next 18-24 months."

‡OPEN COURT PUBLISHING COMPANY, Carus Publishing, Suite 2000, 332 S. Michigan Ave., Chicago IL 60604. Editorial Director: David Ramsey Steele. Publishes hardcover and trade paperback originals. Publishes 15 titles/year. Receives 400 queries and 200 mss/year. 20% of mss from first-time authors, 65% from unagented writers. Pays royalty on wholesale price. Offers $1,000-2,000 advance. Publishes book 1 year after acceptance of ms. Reports in 3 months on queries and proposals, 6 months on mss. Book catalog free on request.
Nonfiction: Textbook and academic philosophy. Subjects include education, philosophy, psychology, religion, women's issues/studies and Eastern thought. "We market to academic and intelligent lay readers. We are interested in manuscripts on feminist thought, cognition, Taoist thought, Buddhist thought, comparative religion, Jungian psychology, academic philosophy—any area, learning and reading as related to elementary education. When submitting nonfiction, writers often fail to specify the market for their books. It is not enough to list all the groups of people who *should* be interested." Submit outline and 2 sample chapters or proposal package, including prospectus, sample chapters, vita. Reviews artwork/photos as part of the freelance ms package. Writers should send photocopies.
Tips: Audience is academics and intelligent lay readers.

ORCHISES PRESS. P.O. Box 20602, Alexandria VA 22320-1602. (703)683-1243. Editor-in-Chief: Roger Lathbury. Publishes hardcover and trade paperback originals and reprints. Publishes 4-5 titles/year. Receives 200 queries and 100 mss/year. 1% of mss from first-time authors, 95% from unagented writers. Pays 36% of receipts after Orchises has recouped its costs. Publishes book 1 year after acceptance of ms. Simultaneous submissions OK. Query for electronic submissions. Reports in 3 months. Book catalog for #10 SASE.
Nonfiction: Biography, how-to, humor, reference, technical and textbook. No real restrictions on subject matter. Query. Reviews artwork/photos as part of the freelance ms package. Writers should send photocopies.
Poetry: Poetry must have been published in respected literary journals. Although we publish free verse, have strong formalist preferences. Query or submit 5 sample poems.
Recent Poetry Title: *After Oz*, by Michael Bugeja.
Tips: "Audience is professional, literate and academic. Show some evidence of appealing to a wider audience than simply people you know."

‡OREGON HISTORICAL SOCIETY PRESS, Oregon Historical Society, 1200 SW Park, Portland OR 97205-2483. (503)222-1741. Fax: (503)221-2035. Director—Publications & Special Projects: Bruce Taylor Hamilton. Estab. 1873. Publishes hardcover originals, trade paperback originals and reprints and a quarterly historical journal, *Oregon Historical Quarterly*. Publishes 2-4 titles/year. Receives 300 submissions/year. 75% of books from first-time authors; 100% from unagented writers. Pays royalty on wholesale price or makes outright purchase. Publishes book an average of 18 months after acceptance. Simultaneous submissions OK. Query for electronic submissions. Reports in 1 week on queries; 3 months on mss. Free book catalog. Ms guidelines for #10 SASE.
Nonfiction: Subjects include Americana, art/architecture, biography, business history, ethnic, government/politics, history, nature/environment, North Pacific Studies, photography, reference, regional juvenile, women's. Query or submit outline/synopsis and sample chapters or submit complete ms. Reviews artwork/photos as part of ms package.

ALWAYS enclose a self-addressed, stamped envelope (SASE) with all your queries and correspondence.

Recent Nonfiction Title: *So Far From Home: An Army Bride on the Western Frontier, 1865-1869*, Julia Gilliss, edited by Priscilla Knuth.

OREGON STATE UNIVERSITY PRESS, 101 Waldo Hall, Corvallis OR 97331-6407. (503)737-3166. Managing Editor: Jo Alexander. Estab. 1965. Publishers hardcover and paperback originals. Averages 6 titles/year; receives 100 submissions annually. 75% of books from first-time authors; 100% of books from unagented writers. Average print order for a writer's first book is 1,500. Pays royalty on net receipts. No advance. Publishes book an average of 1 year after acceptance. Query for electronic submissions. Reports in 1 month. *Writer's Market* recommends allowing 2 months for reply. Book catalog for 6 × 9 SAE with 2 first class stamps.
Nonfiction: Publishes scholarly books in history, biography, geography, literature, life sciences and natural resource management, with strong emphasis on Pacific or Northwestern topics. Submit outline and sample chapters.

‡O'REILLY & ASSOCIATES, 103 Morris St., Sebastopol CA 95472. (707)829-0515. Publisher: Tim O'Reilly. Publishes hardcover and trade paperback originals. Publishes 30 titles/year. Receives 200 queries and 30 mss/year. Pays 10% royalty on net. Offers $3,000-5,000 advance. Publishes book 6 months after acceptance. Simultaneous submissions OK. Query for electronic submissions. Prefers modem. Reports in 1 month. *Writer's Market* recommends allowing 2 months for reply. Book catalog and ms guidelines free on request.
Nonfiction: Technical. Subjects include chiefly computers and electronics. "We publish books that interest our editors. They tend to be books that are useful as opposed to theoretical, 'state of the art' technology, can become the definitive work on a topic." Query with 1 sample chapter and proposal package, including your credentials. Reviews artwork/photos as part of freelance ms package.

ORYX PRESS, 4041 N. Central Indian School Rd., Phoenix AZ 85012. (602)265-2651. President: Phyllis B. Steckler. Acquisitions Editor: Tracy Moore. Estab. 1975. Publishes hardcover and paperback originals. Averages 55 titles/year; receives 300 submissions annually. 40% of books from first-time authors; 95% of books from unagented writers. Average print order for a writer's first book is 1,500. Pays 10% royalty on net receipts; no advance. Publishes book an average of 9 months after acceptance. Query for electronic submissions. Reports in 3 months. Free book catalog and ms guidelines.
Nonfiction: Bibliographies, directories, general reference, library and information science, education, business reference, health care, gerontology, automation, and agriculture monographs. Publishes nonfiction for public, college and university, junior college, school and special libraries; agriculture specialists, health care deliverers; and managers. Query or submit outline/synopsis and 1 sample chapter. Queries/mss may be routed to other editors in the publishing group.
Recent Nonfiction Title: *The Dictionary of Bias-Free Usage: A Guide to Non-Discriminatory Language*, by Rosalie Maggio.

OSBORNE/MCGRAW-HILL, Subsidiary of McGraw-Hill Inc., Dept. WM, 2600 10th St., Berkeley CA 94710. (510)548-2805. (800)227-0900. Editor-in-Chief: Jeff Pepper. Estab. 1979. Publishes trade paperback originals. Averages 65 titles/year. Receives 120 submissions/year. 30% of books from first-time authors; 99% from unagented writers. Pays 10-15% royalty on wholesale price. Offers $5,000 average advance. Publishes book an average of 6 months after acceptance. Simultaneous submissions OK. Query for electronic submissions. Reports in 2 months. Book catalog and manuscript free on request.
Nonfiction: Software and technical. Subjects include computers. Query with outline and sample chapters. Reviews artwork/photos as part of ms package.

OUR SUNDAY VISITOR, INC., 200 Noll Plaza, Huntington IN 46750. (219)356-8400. President/Publisher: Robert Lockwood. Editor: Jacquelyn Murphy. Estab. 1912. Publishes paperback originals and reprints. Averages 20-30 titles a year; receives over 100 submissions annually. 10% of books from first-time authors; 90% of books from unagented writers. Pays variable royalty on net receipts; offers average $1,000 advance. Publishes book an average of 1 year after acceptance. Query for electronic submissions. Reports in 3 months on most queries and submissions. Author's guide and catalog for SASE.
Nonfiction: Catholic viewpoints on current issues, reference and guidance, Bibles and devotional books, and Catholic heritage books. Prefers to see well-developed proposals as first submission with "annotated outline, three sample chapters, and definition of intended market." Reviews artwork/photos as part of ms package.
Tips: "Solid devotional books that are not first person, well-researched church histories or lives of the saints and self-help for those over 55, have the best chance of selling to our firm. Make it solidly Catholic, unique, without pious platitudes."

THE OVERLOOK PRESS, Distributed by Viking/Penguin, 149 Wooster St., New York NY 10012. Contact: Editorial Department. Imprint is Tusk Books. Publishes hardcover and trade paperback originals and hardcover reprints. Averages 40 titles/year; receives 300 submissions annually. Pays 3-15% royalty on wholesale or retail price. Submissions accepted only through literary agents. Reports in 2 months. Free book catalog.

Nonfiction: Art, architecture, design, film, history, biography, current events, popular culture, and New York State regional. No pornography.
Fiction: Literary fiction, fantasy, and foreign literature in translation. "We tend not to publish commercial fiction."

‡**PACIFIC BOOKS, PUBLISHERS**, P.O. Box 558, Palo Alto CA 94302-0558. (415)965-1980. Editor: Henry Ponleithner. Estab. 1945. Averages 6-12 titles/year. Royalty schedule varies with book. No advance. Send complete ms. Reports "promptly." Book catalog and guidelines for 9×12 SASE.
Nonfiction: General interest, professional, technical and scholarly nonfiction trade books. Specialties include western Americana and Hawaiiana. Looks for "well-written, documented material of interest to a significant audience." Also considers text and reference books for high school and college. Accepts artwork/photos and translations.
Recent Nonfiction Title: *California in the Year 2000: A Look Into the Future of the Golden State as it Approaches the Millennium*, by Charles F. Adams.

PACIFIC PRESS PUBLISHING ASSOCIATION, Book Division, Seventh-day Adventist Church, P.O. Box 7000, Boise ID 83707. (208)465-2595. Fax: (208)465-2531. Vice President for Editorial Development: B. Russell Holt. Acquisitions Editor: Marvin Moore. Estab. 1874. Publishes hardcover and trade paperback originals and reprints. Averages 35 titles/year; receives 600 submissions and proposals annually. Up to 50% of books from first-time authors; 100% of books from unagented writers. Pays 8-16% royalty on wholesale price. Offers average $300-500 advance depending on length. Publishes books an average of 6-10 months after acceptance. Query for electronic submissions. Reports in 2-3 months. Ms guidelines for #10 SASE.
Nonfiction: Biography, cookbook (vegetarian), how-to, juvenile, self-help and textbook. Subjects include cooking and foods (vegetarian only), health, nature, religion, and family living. "We are an exclusively religious publisher. We are looking for practical, how-to oriented manuscripts on religion, health, and family life that speak to human needs, interests and problems from a Biblical perspective. We can't use anything totally secular or written from other than a Christian perspective." Query or submit outline and sample chapters. Reviews artwork/photos as part of ms package.
Recent Nonfiction Title: *Deceived by the New Age*, by Will Baron.
Tips: "Our primary audiences are members of our own denomination (Seventh-day Adventist), the general Christian reading market, and the secular or nonreligious reader. Books that are doing well for us are those that relate the Biblical message to practical human concerns and those that focus more on the experiential rather than theoretical aspects of Christianity. We are assigning more titles, using less unsolicited material — although we still publish manuscripts from freelance and proposals."

PALADIN PRESS, P.O. Box 1307, Boulder CO 80306-1307. (303)443-7250. Fax: (303)442-8741. President/Publisher: Peder C. Lund. Editorial Director: Jon Ford. Estab. 1970. Publishes hardcover and paperback originals and paperback reprints. Averages 36 titles/year. 50% of books from first-time authors; 100% of books from unagented writers. Pays 10-12-15% royalty on net sales. Publishes book an average of 1 year after acceptance. Simultaneous submissions OK. Reports in 2 months. Free book catalog.
Nonfiction: "Paladin Press primarily publishes original manuscripts on military science, weaponry, self-defense, personal privacy, espionage, police science, action careers, guerrilla warfare, fieldcraft and 'creative revenge' humor. How-to manuscripts are given priority. Manuals on building weapons, when technically accurate and clearly presented, are encouraged. If applicable, send sample photographs and line drawings with complete outline and sample chapters." Query or submit outline and sample chapters.
Recent Nonfiction Title: *The Ultimate Sniper: An Advanced Training Manual for Military; Police Snipers*, by Major John Plaster, USAR (Ret.).
Tips: "We need lucid, instructive material aimed at our market and accompanied by sharp, relevant illustrations and photos. As we are primarily a publisher of 'how-to' books, a manuscript that has step-by-step instructions, written in a clear and concise manner (but not strictly outline form) is desirable. No fiction, first-person accounts, children's, religious or joke books. We are also interested in serious, professional videos."

‡**PANDEMIC INTERNATIONAL PUBLISHERS INC.**, P.O. Box 61849, Vancouver WA 98666. (503)281-0339. Editor: Ann Fishburn. Publishes hardcover and trade paperback originals. Publishes 12 titles/year. Receives 20 queries and 5 mss/year. 50% of mss from first-time authors, 50% from unagented writers. Pays 6-10% royalty on retail price. Publishes book 3 months after acceptance of ms. Simultaneous submissions OK. Query for electronic submissions. Reports in 1 month on queries and proposals, 2 months on mss. Book catalog free on request. Manuscript guidelines for #10 SASE.
Nonfiction: Reference and foreign language. Subjects include travel and phrase books (foreign language). Query.
Recent Nonfiction Title: *Do You Speak Doctor?*, by Gregg. M. Cox (reference/Spanish/medical).
Tips: "Our readers are travelers who seek independent vacations, away from the usual tourist areas. Those who wish to improve their language skills. Travel guides should be based on *your* experience. Most important of all, how will your guide help others have a better and easier trip? Unusual locations are the key and language information will improve your chances."

PANTHEON BOOKS, Division of Random House, Inc., 25th Floor, 201 E. 50th St., New York NY 10022. Publishes quality fiction and nonfiction. Send query letter first, addressed to Adult Editorial Department.

‡**PARENTING PRESS**, P.O. Box 75267, Seattle WA 98125. Managing Editor: Alice Cummiskey. Imprints are: Earth Friendly Press; Polar Books. Firm produces hardcover and trade paperback originals. Averages 6-8 titles/year. Receives 150 queries and 300 mss/year. 75% of mss from first-time authors; 100% from unagented writers. Pays royalty on wholesale price. Publishes book 18 months after acceptance of ms. Simultaneous submissions OK. Reports in 3 months. Catalog and ms guidelines free on request.
Nonfiction: Biography, children's/juvenile and parenting. Subjects include child guidance/parenting. "We do not publish 'complete' parenting books. We look for books that offer choices to different parenting topics." Query, submit outline with 1 sample chapter, or proposal package, including marketing info. Reviews artwork/photos as part of freelance ms package. Writers should send photocopies.
Tips: "Request submission guideline first."

PARKSIDE PUBLISHING CORPORATION, Subsidiary of Parkside Medical Services Corp., 205 W. Touhy Ave., Park Ridge IL 60068. (708)698-4700. Fax: (708)318-0966. Subsidiaries include Parkside; Fireside/Parkside. Vice President/Publisher: John Small. Estab. 1986. Publishes hardcover, trade paperback and mass market paperback originals. Averages 6-10 titles/year. Receives 200 submissions/year. 50% of books from first-time authors; 50% from unagented writers. Pays 7-10% royalty on retail price. Average advance varies. Publishes book an average of 1 year after acceptance. Reports in 2 months on queries. Book catalog and manuscript guidelines free on request.
Nonfiction: Self-help, health/medicine, addiction and recovery, aging. "We need books on addiction and recovery (alcoholism, drug abuse, eating disorders, incest, mental health) for recovering individuals and families." Also interested in books on aging and life stages. No fiction or poetry. Query or submit outline and sample chapters. Reviews artwork/photos as part of ms package.
Tips: "Our audience is generally people who are interested in improving their life. Try to write a high-quality book with a clearly-defined niche in the field of addiction and recovery, general self-help, or aging and personal growth."

PASSPORT PRESS, P.O. Box 1346, Champlain NY 12919-1346. (514)937-3868. Publisher: Jack Levesque. Estab. 1975. Publishes trade paperback originals. Averages 4 titles/year. 25% of books from first-time authors; 100% from unagented writers. Pays 6% royalty on retail price. Publishes book an average of 9 months after acceptance. *Send 1-page query only. Unsolicited manuscripts or samples and non-travel material will not be returned even if accompanied by postage.*
Nonfiction: Travel books only, not travelogues. Especially looking for manuscripts on practical travel subjects and travel guides on specific countries. Query. Reviews artwork/photos as part of ms package.

PAULIST PRESS, 997 Macarthur Blvd., Mahwah NJ 07430. (201)825-7300. Fax: (201)825-8345. Editor: Rev. Kevin A. Lynch. Managing Editor: Donald Brophy. Estab. 1865. Publishes hardcover and paperback originals and paperback reprints. Averages 90-100 titles/year; receives 500 submissions annually. 5-8% of books from first-time authors; 95% of books from unagented writers. Subsidy publishes (nonauthor) 1-2% of books. Pays royalty on retail price. Usually offers advance. Publishes book an average of 10 months after acceptance. Reports in 2 months. Query for electronic submissions.
Nonfiction: Philosophy, religion, self-help and textbooks (religious). Accepts nonfiction translations from German, French and Spanish. "We would like to see theology (Catholic and ecumenical Christian), popular spirituality, liturgy, and religious education texts." Submit outline and 2 sample chapters. Reviews artwork/photos as part of ms package.
Recent Nonfiction Title: *A Way Without Words*, by Marsha Sinetar.

PBC INTERNATIONAL INC., 1 School St., Glen Cove NY 11542. (516)676-2727. Fax: (516)676-2738. Publisher: Mark Serchuck. Editorial Manager: Kevin Clark. Estab. 1980. Imprints are Library of Applied Design (nonfiction), Architecture & Interior Design Library (nonfiction), Great Graphics Series (nonfiction), Design In Motion Series (nonfiction), and Showcase Edition (nonfiction). Publishes hardcover and paperback originals. Averages 18 titles/year; receives 100-200 submissions annually. Most of books from first-time authors and unagented writers done on assignment. Pays royalty and/or flat fees. Simultaneous submissions OK. *Writer's Market* recommends allowing 2 months for reply. Book catalog for 9 × 12 SASE.
Nonfiction: Subjects include design, graphic art, architecture/interior design, packaging design, marketing design, product design. No submissions not covered in the above listed topics. Query with outline and sample chapters. Reviews artwork/photos as part of ms package.
Recent Nonfiction Title: *Designing With Light: Residential Interiors.*
Tips: "PBC International is the publisher of full-color visual idea books for the design, marketing and graphic arts professional."

‡**PEACHPIT PRESS**, 2414 6th St., Berkeley CA 94710. (510)548-4393. Managing Editor: Roslyn Bullas. Publishes trade paperback originals. Publishes over 30 titles/year. Receives 250 queries and 6 mss/year. 10% of mss from first-time authors, 90% from unagented writers. Pays 12-20% royalty on wholesale price. Offers

$3,000-10,000 advance. Publishes book 6 months after acceptance of ms. Simultaneous submissions OK. Query for electronic submissions. Reports in 1 month on proposals. Book catalog free on request.
Nonfiction: How-to, reference and technical. Subjects include computers and electronics. "We prefer no phone calls." Submit short, 1-page proposal (preferred) or outline. Reviews artwork/photos as part of the freelance ms package. Writers should send photocopies.
Recent Nonfiction Title: *Ecolinking*, by Don Rittner (online environmental info).

PEACHTREE PUBLISHERS, LTD., 494 Armour Circle NE, Atlanta GA 30324-4888. (404)876-8761. Contact: Managing Editor. Estab. 1977. Publishes hardcover and trade paperback originals. Averages 15-20 titles/year; receives up to 10,000 submissions annually. 25% of books from first-time authors; 75% of books from unagented writers. Average print order for a writer's first book is 5,000-10,000. Publishes book 1 to 2 years after acceptance. Reports in 6 months on queries. Book catalog for 9 × 12 SAE with 3 first class stamps.
Nonfiction: General and humor. Subjects include art, juvenile, cooking and foods, history, recreation and travel. No technical, reference or animals. Submit outline and sample chapters. Reviews artwork/photos as part of ms package.
Recent Nonfiction Title: *About Birds*, by Cathryn and John Sill (children's).
Fiction: Literary, humor, juvenile and mainstream. "We are particularly interested in fiction with a Southern feel." No fantasy, science fiction or romance. Submit sample chapters.
Recent Fiction Title: *Orange Cheeks*, by Jay O'Callahan (children's).
Tips: "We're looking for mainstream fiction and nonfiction of general interest. Although our books are sold throughout North America, we consider ourselves the national publisher with a Southern voice."

PELICAN PUBLISHING COMPANY, 1101 Monroe St., P.O. Box 3110, Gretna LA 70053. (504)368-1175. Editor: Nina Kooij. Estab. 1926. Publishes hardcover, trade paperback and mass market paperback originals and reprints. Averages 40 titles/year; receives 5,500 submissions annually. 45% of books from first-time authors; 70% of books from unagented writers. Pays royalty on publisher's actual receipts. Publishes book an average of 18 months after acceptance. Reports in 1 month on queries. *Writer's Market* recommends allowing 2 months for reply. Writer's guidelines for SASE.
Nonfiction: Travel, biography, coffee table book (limited), cookbook, how-to, humor, illustrated book, juvenile, self-help, motivational, inspirational, and Scottish. Subjects include Americana (especially Southern regional, Ozarks, Texas and Florida); business and economics (popular how-to and motivational); cooking and food; health; history; music (American artforms: jazz, blues, Cajun, R&B); politics (special interest in conservative viewpoint); recreation; religion (for popular audience mostly, but will consider others); and travel. *Travel*: Regional and international (especially areas in Pacific). *Motivational*: with business slant. *Inspirational*: author must be someone with potential for large audience. *Cookbooks*: "We look for authors with strong connection to restaurant industry or cooking circles, i.e. someone who can promote successfully." *How-to*: will consider broad range. Query. "We require that a query be made first. This greatly expedites the review process and can save the writer additional postage expenses." Does not consider multiple queries or submissions. Reviews artwork/photos as part of ms package; absolutely no art originals—copies only.
Recent Nonfiction Title: *The Maverick Guide to Berlin*, by Jay Brunhouse.
Fiction: Historical, humor, mainstream, Southern, and juvenile. "Fiction needs are *very* limited. We are most interested in Southern novels." No young adult, romance, science fiction, fantasy, gothic, mystery, erotica, confession, horror, sex or violence. Submit outline/synopsis and 2 sample chapters.
Recent Fiction Title: *When the Great Canoes Came*, by Mary Louise Clifford.
Tips: "We do extremely well with travel, motivational and cookbooks. We will continue to build in these areas. The writer must have a clear sense of the market and this includes knowledge of the competition. A query letter should describe the project briefly, give the author's writing and professional credentials, and promotional ideas. Include SASE."

‡PENDAYA PUBLICATIONS, INC., 510 Woodvine Ave., Metairie LA 70005. (504)834-8151. Manager: Earl J. Mathes. Publishes hardcover originals. Publishes 1 or 2 titles/year. Receives 6-8 queries and 3-4 mss/year. 100% of mss from unagented writers. Pays 4-8% royalty on retail price (varies). Offers $500-3,000 advance. Publishes book 9 months after acceptance. Reports in 6 months on mss.
Nonfiction: Coffee table book and illustrated book. Subjects include anthropology/archaeology, art/architecture, photography, travel and design. Submit proposal package. Writers should send transparencies.
Recent Nonfiction Title: *Seeing What I Like & Liking What I See*, by Charles Colbert (photo/coffee table/design philosophy).

PENGUIN USA, 375 Hudson St., New York NY 10014. Imprints include Dial Books for Young Readers, Dutton, Dutton Juvenile, Dutton/New American Library, and Viking. "Prefers not to share information."

PENNSYLVANIA HISTORICAL AND MUSEUM COMMISSION, Imprint of the Commonwealth of Pennsylvania, P.O. Box 1026, Harrisburg PA 17108-1026. (717)787-8099. Fax: (717)783-1073. Chief, Publications and Sales Division: Diane B. Reed. Estab. 1913. Publishes hardcover and paperback originals and reprints. Averages 6-8 titles/year; receives 25 submissions annually. Pays 5-10% royalty on retail price. May make outright purchase of $500-1,000; sometimes makes special assignments; may offer $350 average advance. Publishes book an average of 18 months after acceptance. Simultaneous submissions OK. Query for electronic submissions. Reports in 6 weeks. *Writer's Market* recommends allowing 2 months for reply. Manuscripts prepared according to the *Chicago Manual of Style*.

Nonfiction: All books must be related to Pennsylvania, its history or culture: biography, coffee table, how-to, illustrated book, cookbook, reference, technical, visitor attractions and historic travel guidebooks. "The Commission seeks manuscripts on Pennsylvania in general, but more specifically on archaeology, history, art (decorative and fine), politics, travel, photography, nature, sports history and cooking." Query or submit outline and sample chapters. Guidelines and proposal forms available.

Recent Nonfiction Title: *Guide to the State Historical Markers of Pennsylvania*, by George R. Beyer.

Tips: "Our audience is diverse—students, specialists and generalists—all of them interested in one or more aspects of Pennsylvania's history and culture. Manuscripts must be well researched and documented (footnotes not necessarily required depending on the nature of the manuscript) and interestingly written. Because of the expertise of our reviewers, manuscripts must be factually accurate, but in being so, writers must not sacrifice style. We have a tradition of publishing scholarly and reference works, as well as more popularly styled books that reach an even broader audience."

THE PERMANENT PRESS/SECOND CHANCE PRESS, 4170 Noyac Rd., Sag Harbor NY 11963. (516)725-1101. Fax: (516)725-1101. Editor: Judith Shepard. Estab. 1978. Publishes hardcover originals and reprints. Permanent Press publishes literary fiction. Second Chance Press devotes itself exclusively to re-publishing fine books that are out of print and deserve continued recognition. Averages 10 titles/year; receives 3,000 submissions annually. 35% of books from first-time authors; 75% of books from unagented writers. Average print order for a writer's first book is 2,000. Pays 10% royalty on wholesale price; offers $1,000 advance for Permanent Press books and royalty only on Second Chance Press titles. Publishes book an average of 18 months after acceptance. Simultaneous submissions OK. Reports in 3 months on queries. Book catalog for 7 first class stamps.

Nonfiction: Biography, autobiography and historical. No scientific and technical material or academic studies. Query.

Fiction: Adventure, ethnic, historical, humor, mainstream, mystery, and suspense. Especially looking for high line literary fiction, "original and arresting." No mass market romance. Query.

Recent Fiction Title: *Upstate*, by Sallie Bingham.

Tips: "We are no longer looking for the following types of fiction: confession, experimental, science fiction and fantasy."

PERSPECTIVES PRESS, P.O. Box 90318, Indianapolis IN 46290-0318. (317)872-3055. Publisher: Pat Johnston. Estab. 1982. Publishes hardcover and trade paperback originals. Averages 4 titles/year; receives 200 queries annually. 95% of books from first-time authors. 95% of books from unagented writers. Pays 5-15% royalty on net sales. Publishes book an average of 1 year after acceptance. Simultaneous submissions OK. Reports in 2 weeks on queries. *Writer's Market* recommends allowing 2 months for reply. Book catalog and writer's guidelines for #10 SAE and 2 first class stamps.

Nonfiction: How-to, juvenile and self-help books on health, psychology and sociology—all related to adoption or infertility. Query.

Recent Nonfiction Title: *A Child's Journey Through Placement*, by Vera Fahlberg M.D.

Fiction: Adoption/infertility for adults or children. Query.

Recent Fiction Title: *Lucy's Feet*, by Stephanie Stein.

Tips: "For adults we are seeking infertility and adoption decision-making materials, books dealing with adoptive or foster parenting issues, books to use with children, books to share with others to help explain infertility or adoption or foster care, special programming or training manuals, etc. For children we will consider adoption or foster care related fiction manuscripts that are appropriate for preschoolers and for early elementary children. We do not consider YA. Nonfiction manuscripts are considered for all ages. No autobiography. While we would consider a manuscript from a writer who was not personally or professionally involved in these issues, we would be more inclined to accept a manuscript submitted by an infertile person, an adoptee, a birthparent, an adoptive parent, a professional working with any of these."

PETER PAUPER PRESS, INC., 202 Mamaroneck Ave., White Plains NY 10601-5376. (914)681-0144. Fax: (914)681-0389. Co-Publisher: Nick Beilenson. Estab. 1928. Publishes hardcover originals. Averages 24 titles/year; receives 200 submissions annually. Buys some mss outright for $1,000. Offers no advance. Publishes ms an average of 9 months after acceptance. Simultaneous submissions OK. Reports in 1 month. *Writer's Market* recommends allowing 2 months for reply. Book catalog for #10 SAE with 2 first class stamps.

Nonfiction: Subjects include compilations of quotes, Americana, humor, holidays and inspirational. *No* cookbooks, religious fiction, or children's books. Submit complete ms. *Writer's Market* recommends query with SASE first. Reviews artwork as part of ms package.

Recent Nonfiction Title: *For My Friend*, compiled by Nick Beilenson.

Tips: "We are looking especially for collections of quotes."

PETERSON'S, P.O. Box 2123, Princeton NJ 08543-2123. (800)338-3282. President: Peter W. Hegener. Publisher: Carole Cushmore. Managing Editor: A.J. Hollander. Estab. 1966. Publishes trade and reference books. Averages 55-75 titles/year. Receives 200-250 submissions annually. 30% of books from first-time authors; 90% from unagented writers. Average print order for a writer's first book is 10,000-15,000. Pays 6-8% royalty on net sales; offers advance. Publishes book an average of 1 year after acceptance. Reports in 2 months. Free catalog.
Nonfiction: Career (self-help and how-to) books, as well as educational and career directories. Submit complete ms or detailed outline and sample chapters. *Writer's Market* recommends query with SASE first. Looks for "appropriateness of contents to our market, accuracy of information, author's credentials, and writing style suitable for audience." Reviews artwork/photos as part of ms package.
Recent Nonfiction Title: *The Three Career Couple: His Job, Her Job, and Their Job Together.*

‡PFEIFFER & COMPANY, 8517 Production Ave., San Diego CA 92121. (619)578-5900. Fax: (619)578-2042. President: J. William Pfeiffer. Estab. 1968. Publishes paperback and hardback originals and reprints. Averages 80 titles/year. Specializes in practical materials for human resource development, consultants, etc. Pays average 10% royalty; no advance. Publishes book an average of 6 months after acceptance. Markets books by direct mail and through bookstores. Simultaneous submissions OK. Reports in 4 months. Book catalog and guidelines for SASE.
Nonfiction: Richard Roe, Vice President, Publications. Publishes (in order of preference) human resource development and group-oriented material, management education, personal growth, and business. No materials for grammar school or high school classroom teachers. Use *American Psychological Association Style Manual*. Query. Send prints or completed art or rough sketches to accompany ms.
Recent Nonfiction Title: *The 1993 Annual: Developing Human Resources*, J.W. Pfeiffer, editor.

PHANES PRESS, P.O. Box 6114, Grand Rapids MI 49516. (616)456-5740. Editor/Publisher: David Fideler. Publishes hardcover and trade paperback originals and reprints. Publishes 10-15 titles/year. Receives 30 queries and 24 mss/year. 100% of mss are from unagented writers. Pays 5-10% royalty on retail price. Publishes book an average of 18 months after acceptance. Simultaneous submissions OK. Query for electronic submissions. Reports in 3 months. Book catalog free on request.
Nonfiction: Art/architecture, history, music/dance, nature/environment, philosophy, religion, science. "We only publish manuscripts that fit within our specialized niche. Please request a free catalog before sending a proposal to verify that your subject matter coincides with our other publications." Submit outline and 2 sample chapters.
Recent Nonfiction Title: *The Mystery of the Seven Vowels*, by Joscelyn Godwin (spiritual studies/music).
Tips: "We have an intelligent audience interested in the cosmological, spiritual and philosophical traditions of the Western world."

PHILOMEL BOOKS, Division of The Putnam Publishing Group, 200 Madison Ave., New York NY 10016. (212)951-8700. Editor-in-Chief: Paula Wiseman. Editorial Director: Patricia Lee Gauch. Editorial Assistant: Laura Walsh. Estab. 1980. Publishes hardcover originals. Publishes 35-40 titles/year; receives 2,600 submissions annually. 15% of books from first-time authors; 30% of books from unagented writers. Pays standard royalty. Advance negotiable. Publishes book an average of 1-2 years after acceptance. Reports in 3 months on queries. Book catalog for 9×12 SAE with 4 first class stamps. Request book catalog from marketing department of Putnam Publishing Group.
Nonfiction: Young adult and children's picture books (ages 2-17). No alphabet books or workbooks. Query first. Always include SASE. Looks for quality writing, unique ideas, suitability to our market.
Fiction: Young adult and children's books (ages 2-17) on any topic. Particularly interested in fine regional fiction and quality picture books. Query to department.
Tips: "We prefer a very brief synopsis that states the basic premise of the story. This will help us determine whether or not the manuscript is suited to our list. If applicable, we'd be interested in knowing the author's writing experience or background knowledge. We are always looking for beautifully written manuscripts with stories that engage. We try to be less influenced by the swings of the market than in the power, value, essence of the manuscript itself."

PICCADILLY BOOKS, Java Publishing Co., P.O. Box 25203, Colorado Springs CO 80936-5203. (719)548-1844. Publisher: Bruce Fife. Estab. 1985. Publishes hardcover and trade paperback originals and trade paperback reprints. Publishes 3-8 titles/year; receives 120 submissions/year. 70% of books from first-time authors; 95% from unagented writers. Pays 5-10% royalty on retail price. Offers $250 average advance. Publishes book an average of 9 months after acceptance. Simultaneous submissions OK. Reports in 2 months. Book catalog for 6×9 SAE and 2 first class stamps; ms guidelines for #10 SASE.
Nonfiction: Biography, how-to, humor, self-help. Subjects include games, business, children's humor, recreation, entertainment and performing arts. Submit complete ms. *Writer's Market* recommends query with SASE first. Reviews artwork/photos as part of ms package.
Fiction: Short, one-act humorous plays for children. No novels accepted. Submit complete ms.

THE PICKERING PRESS, P.O. Box 331531, Miami FL 33233-1531. (305)444-8784. Fax: (305)444-8784. President: Brenda Beck. Estab. 1986. Publishes hardcover and trade paperback originals and trade paperback reprints. Firm averages 3-4 titles/year. Receives 25 submissions/year. 10% of books from first-time authors; 100% from unagented writers. Pays 6-15% on wholesale price. Buys mss outright for $2,500. Publishes book an average of 9 months after acceptance. Query for electronic submissions. Reports in 2 months on queries. Free book catalog.
Nonfiction: How-to, illustrated book and self-help. Subjects include art/architecture, history and regional. Looking for regional/Florida history ms. No regional books outside of Florida. Submit query or outline and sample chapters. Reviews artwork/photos as part of ms package.
Tips: "Nonfiction and regional history have the best chance of being sold to our firm. If I were a writer trying to market a book today, I would clearly define the market for my book prior to approaching publishers, and be prepared to offer non-book trade suggestions in addition to traditional techniques."

THE PILGRIM PRESS, United Church Board for Homeland Ministries, 700 Prospect Ave. E., Cleveland OH 44115-1100. (216)736-3703. Editorial Director: Richard E. Brown. Publishes trade paperback originals. Firm averages 20 titles/year. 40% of books from first-time authors. 100% from unagented writers. Pays standard royalties and advances where appropriate. Publishes book an average of 18 months after acceptance. Reports in 6 months on queries. Book catalog and ms guidelines free on request.
Nonfiction: Ethics, social issues with a strong commitment to justice—addressing such topics as public policy, sexuality and gender, economics, medicine, gay and lesbian concerns, human rights, minority liberation and the environment—primarily in a Christian context, but not exclusively. Also, publishes books on American religious history.
Recent Nonfiction Title: *Troubled Voices: Stories of Ethics and Illness*, by Richard Zaner.
Tips: "We are concentrating more on academic/scholarly submissions. Writers should send books about contemporary social issues in a Christian context. Our audience is liberal, open-minded, socially aware, feminist, educated lay church members and clergy, teachers and seminary professors."

PILOT BOOKS, 103 Cooper St., Babylon NY 11702-2319. (516)422-2225. Fax: (516)422-2227. President: Sam Small. Estab. 1959. Publishes paperback originals. Averages 20-30 titles/year; receives 100-200 submissions annually. 20% of books from first-time authors; 90% of books from unagented writers. Average print order for a writer's first book is 3,000. Offers standard royalty contract based on wholesale or retail price. Usual advance is $250, but this varies, depending on author's reputation and nature of book. Publishes book an average of 8 months after acceptance. Reports in 1 month. *Writer's Market* recommends allowing 2 months for reply. Book catalog and guidelines for #10 SASE.
Nonfiction: Financial, business, travel, career, personal guides and training manuals. "Our training manuals are utilized by America's major corporations as well as the government. Directories and books on travel and moneymaking opportunities. Wants clear, concise treatment of subject matter." Length: 8,000-30,000 words. Send outline. Reviews artwork/photos as part of ms package.
Recent Nonfiction Title: *The Senior Citizen's Guide To Starting A Part-Time, Home-Based Business*, by Judy Kerr.

PINEAPPLE PRESS, INC., P.O. Box 16008, Southside Station, Sarasota FL 34239. (813)952-1085. Editor: June Cussen. Estab. 1982. Publishes hardcover and trade paperback originals. Averages 12 titles/year; receives 1,500 submissions annually. 20% of books from first-time authors; 80% of books from unagented writers. Pays 6½-15% royalty on retail price. Seldom offers advance. Publishes book an average of 1 year after acceptance. Simultaneous submissions OK. Reports in 3 months. Book catalog for 9×12 SAE and 2 first class stamps.
Nonfiction: Biography, how-to, reference, nature. Subjects include animals, history, gardening and nature. "We will consider most nonfiction topics. We are seeking quality nonfiction on diverse topics for the library and book trade markets." No pop psychology or autobiographies. Query or submit outline/brief synopsis and sample chapters with SASE.
Recent Nonfiction Title: *Keep the Money Coming*, by Christine Graham.
Fiction: Literary, historical and mainstream. No romance, science fiction, or children's. Submit outline/brief synopsis and sample chapters.
Recent Fiction Title: *Riders of the Suwannee*, by Lee Gramling.
Tips: "If I were a writer trying to market a book today, I would learn everything I could about book publishing and book publicity and agree to actively participate in promoting my book. A query on a novel without a brief sample seems useless."

PIPPIN PRESS, 229 E. 85th St., P.O. Box 92, Gracie Station, New York NY 10028. (212)288-4920. Fax: (212)563-5703. Publisher/President: Barbara Francis. Estab. 1987. Publishes hardcover originals. Publishes 4-6 titles/year; receives 4,500 queries/year. 80% of queries from unagented writers. Pays royalty. Publishes book an average of 18-24 months after acceptance. Reports in 3 weeks on queries. Do *not* send mss. "We do not accept unsolicited mss, but we welcome queries (with SASE)." *Writer's Market* recommends allowing 2 months for reply. Book catalog for 6×9 SASE; ms guidelines for #10 SASE.

Nonfiction: Children's books: biography, humor, juvenile, picture books. Animals, history, language/literature, nature, science. General nonfiction for children ages 4-10. Query only. Reviews copies of artwork/photos as part of ms package.

Recent Nonfiction Title: *James Madison and Dolley Madison and Their Times*, by Robert Quackenbush (humorous).

Fiction: Adventure, fantasy, historical, humor, juvenile, mystery, picture books, suspense. Wants humorous fiction for ages 7-11. Query only.

Recent Fiction Title: *Evil Under the Sea: A Miss Mallard Mystery*, written and illustrated by Robert Quackenbush.

Tips: "Read as many of the best children's books published in the last five years as you can. We are looking for multi-ethnic fiction and nonfiction for ages 7-10, as well as general fiction for this age group. I would pay particular attention to children's books favorably reviewed in *School Library Journal*, *The Booklist*, *The New York Times Book Review*, and *Publishers Weekly*."

PLAYERS PRESS, INC., P.O. Box 1132, Studio City CA 91614-0132. (818)789-4980. Vice President, Editorial: Robert W. Gordon. Estab. 1965. Publishes hardcover and trade paperback originals, and trade paperback reprints. Averages 25-35 titles/year; receives 200-1,000 submissions annually. 10% of books from first-time authors; 80% of books from unagented writers. Pays royalty on wholesale price. Publishes book an average of 20 months after acceptance. Reports on queries in 1-3 weeks, on manuscripts up to 1 year. Book catalog and guidelines for 9 × 12 SAE and 4 first class stamps.

Nonfiction: Juvenile and theatrical drama/entertainment industry. Subjects include the performing arts, theater and film crafts. Needs quality plays and musicals, adult or juvenile. Query. Reviews artwork/photos as part of package.

Fiction: Subject matter of plays include adventure, confession, ethnic, experimental, fantasy, historical, horror, humor, mainstream, mystery, religious, romance, science fiction, suspense and western. Submit complete ms for theatrical plays only. "No novels or story books are accepted. We publish plays, musicals and books on theatre, film and television, only."

Tips: "Plays, entertainment industry texts, theater, film and television books have the only chances of selling to our firm."

PLENUM PUBLISHING, 233 Spring St., New York NY 10013-1578. (212)620-8000. Senior Editor, Trade Books: Linda Greenspan Regan. Estab. 1946. Publishes hardcover originals. Averages 350 titles/year; Plenum Trade publishes 12. Receives 250 submissions annually. 25% of books from first-time authors. 35% of books from unagented writers. Publishes book an average of 8 months after acceptance. Simultaneous submissions OK. Query for electronic submissions. Reports in several months on queries.

Nonfiction: Subjects include trade science, criminology, sociology, psychology, and health. "We are seeking high quality, popular books in the sciences and social sciences." Query only.

Tips: "Our audience consists of intelligent laymen and professionals. Authors should be experts on subject matter of book. They must compare their books with competitive works, explain how theirs differs, and define the market for their books."

PLEXUS PUBLISHING, INC., 143 Old Marlton Pike, Medford NJ 08055-8750. (609)654-6500. Fax: (609)654-4309. Editorial Director: Thomas Hogan. Estab. 1977. Publishes hardcover and paperback originals. Averages 4-5 titles/year; receives 10-20 submissons annually. 70% of books from first-time authors; 90% of books from unagented writers. Pays 10-20% royalty on wholesale price; buys some booklets outright for $250-1,000. Offers $500-1,000 advance. Simultaneous submissions OK. Reports in 3 months. Book catalog and guidelines for 10 × 13 SAE with 4 first class stamps.

Nonfiction: Biography (of naturalists) and reference. Subjects include plants, animals, nature and life sciences. "We will consider any book on a nature/biology subject, particularly those of a reference (permanent) nature that would be of lasting value to high school and college audiences, and/or the general reading public (ages 14 and up). Authors should have authentic qualifications in their subject area, but qualifications may be by experience as well as academic training." No gardening; no philosophy or psychology; generally not interested in travel but will consider travel that gives sound ecological information. Also interested in mss of about 20-40 pages in length for feature articles in *Biology Digest* (guidelines available with SASE). Query. Reviews artwork/photos as part of ms package.

Tips: "We will give serious consideration to well-written manuscripts that deal even indirectly with biology/nature subjects. For example, *Exploring Underwater Photography* (a how-to for divers) and *The Literature of Nature* (an anthology of nature writings for college curriculum) were accepted for publication."

POCKET BOOKS, Division of Paramount Publishing, Dept. WM, 1230 Avenue of the Americas, New York NY 10020. Imprints include Pocket Star Books, Washington Square Press (high-quality mass market), Archway and Minstrel (juvenile/YA imprints). Publishes paperback originals and reprints, mass market and trade paperbacks and hardcovers. Averages 450 titles/year; receives 750 submissions annually. 15% of books from first-time authors. 100% of submissions are from agented writers. Pays royalty on retail price. Publishes book an average of 1 year after acceptance. *No unsolicited mss or queries.* "All submissions must go through a literary agent."

Nonfiction: History, biography, reference and general nonfiction, cookbooks, humor, calendars.

Fiction: Adult (mysteries, thriller, psychological suspense, Star Trek ® novels, romance, westerns).

‡**POGO PRESS, INCORPORATED**, 4 Cardinal Lane, St. Paul MN 55127. Vice President: Leo J. Harris. Publishes trade paperback originals. Publishes 2 titles/year. Receives 10 queries and 10 mss/year. 100% of mss from unagented writers. Pays royalty on wholesale price. Publishes mss 6 months after acceptance. Query for electronic submissions; "negotiable." Reports in 1 month on queries. Book catalog free on request.

Nonfiction: "We limit our publishing to Breweriana and popular culture. Our books are heavily illustrated." Query. Reviews artwork/photos as part of freelance mss package. Writers should send photocopies. "We do not publish fiction."

Recent Nonfiction Title: *San Francisco Murals*, by T. Drescher; *World's Fair Notes*, by M. Shaw; *Monumental Minnesota*, by M. Harris.

POSEIDON PRESS, Division of Simon & Schuster, 1230 Avenue of the Americas, New York NY 10020. (212)698-7290. Vice President/Publisher: Ann E. Patty. Publishes hardcover and trade paperback originals. Averages 20 titles/year; receives 1,000 submissions annually. 20% of books from first-time authors; none from unagented writers. Pays 10-15% royalty on hardcover retail price. Publishes book an average of 1 year after acceptance. Does not accept unsolicited material.

Nonfiction: Autobiography, biography, economics, culture, history, politics, psychology. No religious/inspirational, cookbooks, diet or exercise. *Writer's Market* recommends query with SASE first.

Recent Nonfiction Title: *The Queen's Throat*, by Wayne Koestenbaum.

Fiction: Literary, historical, contemporary and mainstream. *Writer's Market* recommends query with SASE first.

Recent Fiction Title: *Arc d'Y*, by Steve Erickson.

‡**POTENTIALS DEVELOPMENT FOR HEALTH & AGING SERVICES**, 775 Main St., Buffalo NY 14203-1387. (716)842-2658. Editor: J.A. Elkins. Estab. 1978. Publishes paperback originals. Averages 1 title/year; receives 20-30 submissions annually. 90% of books from first-time authors; 100% of books from unagented writers. Average print order for a writer's first book is 500. Pays 5% royalty on sales of first 3,000 copies; 8% thereafter. Publishes book an average of 1 year after acceptance. Reports in 3 months. Book catalog and ms guidelines for #10 SASE.

Nonfiction: "We seek material of interest to those working with elderly people in the community and in institutional settings. We need tested, innovative and practical ideas." Query or submit outline/synopsis and 3 sample chapters. Looks for "suitable subject matter, writing style and organization."

Tips: "The writer has the best chance of selling us materials of interest to those working with elderly people in nursing homes, senior and retirement centers. Our major market is activity directors. Give us good reasons why activity directors would want or need the material submitted."

PRAEGER PUBLISHERS, Imprint of the Greenwood Publishing Group, Inc., 88 Post Road West, Westport CT 06881. (203)226-3571. Fax: (203)226-6009. General Manager: Ron Chambers. Estab. 1950. Publishes hardcover originals and reprints and trade paperback originals. Averages 280 titles/year. Receives 1,200 submissions/year. 5% of books from first-time authors; 90% from unagented writers. Pays 6½-15% royalty on net sales. Advance offered varies. Publishes book an average of 9 months after acceptance. Simultaneous submissions OK. Reports in 1 month. *Writer's Market* recommends allowing 2 months for reply. Book catalog and manuscript guidelines free on request.

Nonfiction: "We are looking for women's studies, sociology, psychology, education, contemporary history, military studies, political science, business, economics, international relations, philosophy. No language and literature." Query or submit outline and sample chapters.

Recent Nonfiction Title: *An American Paradox: Censorship in a Nation of Free Speech*, by Patrick Garry.

PRAKKEN PUBLICATIONS, INC., P.O. Box 8623, Ann Arbor MI 48107-8623. (313)769-1211. Fax: (313)769-8383. Publisher: George Kennedy. Estab. 1934. Publishes educational hardcover and paperback originals as well as educational magazines. Averages 4 book titles/year; receives 50 submissions annually. 20% of books from first-time authors; 95% of books from unagented writers. Pays 10% royalty on net price of book (negotiable, with production costs). Publishes book an average of 6 months after acceptance. Simultaneous submissions OK. Reports in 1 month on queries if reply requested and SASE furnished. *Writer's Market* recommends allowing 2 months for reply. Book catalog for #10 SASE.

Nonfiction: Industrial, vocational and technology education and related areas, and general educational reference. "We are interested in manuscripts with broad appeal in any of the specific subject areas of industrial arts, vocational-technical education, and reference for the general education field." Submit outline and sample chapters. Reviews artwork/photos as part of ms package.

Recent Nonfiction Title: *Chisels on a Wheel: A Comprehensive Reference to Modern Woodworking Tools and Materials.*

Tips: "We have a continuing interest in magazine and book manuscripts which reflect emerging issues and trends in education, especially vocational, industrial, and technical education."

PRECEPT PRESS, Subsidiary of Teach'em Inc., 160 E. Illinois St., Chicago IL 60611. Associate Editor: Anne Barthel. Publishes hardcover and trade paperback originals. Publishes 20 titles/year. Receives 200 queries and 100 mss/year. 25% of mss from first-time authors, 90% from unagented writers. Pays royalty. Publishes book 8 months after acceptance of ms. Simultaneous submissions OK. Query for electronic submissions. Reports in 3 months on proposals. All submissions and queries must include SASE. Manuscript guidelines for #10 SASE.

Nonfiction: Reference, technical and textbook. Subjects include business and economics, health/medicine and science. Query.

THE PRESERVATION PRESS, Imprint of the National Trust for Historic Preservation, 1785 Massachusetts Ave. NW, Washington DC 20036. Fax: (202)673-4172. Director: Buckley C. Jeppson. Estab. 1975. Publishes nonfiction books on historic preservation (saving and reusing the "built environment"). Averages 20 titles/ year; receives 150 submissions annually. 20% of books from first-time authors; 50% of books from unagented writers. Books are often commissioned by the publisher. Publishes book an average of 1 year after acceptance. Query for electronic submissions. *Writer's Market* recommends allowing 2 months for reply. Book catalog for 9×12 SASE.

Nonfiction: Subject matter encompasses architecture and architectural history, building restoration and historic preservation, architectural and historical guide books. No local history. Looks for "relevance to national history-aware audience; educational or instructional value; depth; uniqueness; need in field." Query. Reviews artwork/photos as part of ms package.

Tips: "The writer has the best chance of selling our press a book clearly related to our mission—historic preservation—that covers new ideas and is unique and practical. If it fills a clear need, we will know immediately. Currently looking especially for juvenile books."

PRESIDIO PRESS, Suite 300, 505B San Marin Dr., Novato CA 94945-1340. (415)898-1081. Fax: (415)898-0383. Editor-in-Chief: Dale Wilson. Estab. 1974. Imprint is Lyford Books. Publishes hardcover originals and reprints. Firm averages 25 titles/year. Receives 700 submissions/year. 10% of books from first-time authors. 30% from unagented writers. Pays 15-20% royalty on net receipts. Offers various advances. Publishes book an average of 1 year after acceptance. Reports in 2 months on queries. Free book catalog and manuscript guidelines for 7½×10½ SAE with 4 first class stamps.

Nonfiction: Subjects include military history and military affairs. Query or submit outline and sample chapters. Reviews artwork/photos as part of ms package. "Prefer photocopies with initial submission, not originals."

Recent Nonfiction Title: *Scatterpath*, by Maralys Wills.

Fiction: Men's action-adventure, thriller, mystery, military and historical. Query or submit outline/synopsis and sample chapters.

Recent Fiction Title: *Saving the Breakout*, by Alwyn Featherspon.

Tips: "Our audience consists of readers with interest in military history and military affairs as well as trade fiction. If I were a writer trying to market a book today, I would study the market. Find out what publishers are publishing, what they say they want and so forth. Then write what the market seems to be asking for, but with some unique angle that differentiates the work from others on the same subject. We feel that readers of hardcover fiction are looking for works no less than 100,000 words."

THE PRESS AT CALIFORNIA STATE UNIVERSITY, FRESNO, Shaw and Cedar Avenues, Fresno CA 93740-0099. (209)278-3056. Fax: (209)278-6758. General Manager: Carla Millar. Publishes hardcover and trade paperback originals. Averages 5 titles/year; receives 75 submissions/year. 50% of books from first-time authors; 100% from unagented writers. Offers average $1,000 advance. Publishes book an average of 6 months after acceptance. Simultaneous submissions OK. Reports in 2 weeks. *Writer's Market* recommends allowing 2 months for reply. Free book catalog.

● There is presently a 2-year moratorium on accepting new mss.

Nonfiction: Biography, coffee table book, scholarly books. Subjects include art/architecture, business and economics, government/politics, history, music/dance, film. "We are looking for mss of significant general interest that are competently and professionally done. We have published books on art, architecture, music, film, drama, business and New Age politics." Query or submit outline and sample chapters. Reviews artwork/photos as part of ms package.

Recent Nonfiction Title: *Surviving the Storms: Memory of Stalin's Tyranny*, by Helen Dmitriew.

PRICE STERN SLOAN, INC., PUBLISHERS, 11150 Olympic Blvd., Los Angeles CA 90064-1823. Juvenile submissions to Associate Editor: Cindy Chang. Adult trade/humor/calendars submissions to Assistant Editor: Cindy Eng Alvarez. Cookery submissions to Cookery Editorial Director: Jeanette Egan. Estab. 1963. Im-

prints: HP Books, Troubador Press and Wonder Books. Subsidiaries: Tallfellow Press. Divisions: HP Books, Special Product. Publishes trade paperback originals. Averages 150 titles a year; receives 3,000 submissions annually. 20% from first-time authors; 20% from unagented writers. Pays royalty and (small) advance on wholesale prices or by outright purchase. Publishes book an average of 1 year after acceptance. Reports in 2-3 months. Manuscript guideline for SASE; catalog for 9×12 SAE with five first class stamps.
Nonfiction: Subjects include cookbooks, humor, calendars and satire (limited). Juveniles (all ages). Query *only*, please. Reviews artwork/photos as part of ms package. Please do not send *original* artwork or ms. "Most titles are unique in concept as well as execution."

PRIMA PUBLISHING, P.O. Box 1260, Rocklin CA 95677-1260. (916)768-0426. Publisher: Ben Dominitz. Contact: Jennifer Basye. Imprint is Prima Computer Books (contact: Roger Stewart). Estab. 1984. Publishes hardcover and trade paperback originals and trade paperback reprints. Publishes 120 titles/year. Receives 750 queries/year. Buys 10% of books from first-time authors; 30% from unagented writers. Pays 15-20% royalty on wholesale price. Advance varies. Publishes books an average of 6-9 months after acceptance. Simultaneous submissions OK. Query for electronic submissions. Reports in 3 months. Catalog for 9×12 SAE with 8 first class stamps; writer's guidelines for #10 SASE.
Nonfiction: Biography, cookbook, how-to, self-help and travel. Subjects include business and economics, cooking and foods, health, music, politics and psychology. "We want books with originality, written by highly qualified individuals. No fiction at this time." Query.
Tips: "Prima strives to reach the primary and secondary markets for each of its books. We are known for promoting our books aggressively. Books that genuinely solve problems for people will always do well if properly promoted. Try to picture the intended audience while writing the book. Too many books are written to an audience that doesn't exist."

PRINCETON BOOK COMPANY, PUBLISHERS, P.O. Box 57, Pennington NJ 08534. (609)737-8177. President: Charles H. Woodford. Estab. 1976. Imprint is Dance Horizons. Publishes hardcover originals, trade paperback originals and reprints. Firm averages 10 titles/year. Receives 100 submissions/year. 25% of books from first-time authors. 100% from unagented writers. Pays 10% royalty on wholesale price. Publishes book an average of 10 months after acceptance. Simultaneous submissions OK. Reports in 1 month. *Writer's Market* recommends allowing 2 months for reply. Free book catalog.
Nonfiction: How-to, reference, self-help and textbook. Subjects include dance. Query or submit outline and sample chapters. Reviews artwork/photos as part of manuscript package.
Recent Nonfiction Title: *The Search for Isadora: The Legend and Legacy of Isadora Duncan,* by Lillian Loewenthal.
Tips: "Books that have appeal to both trade and text markets are of most interest to us. Our audience is made up of dance professors, students and professionals. If I were a writer trying to market a book today, I would write with a clear notion of the market in mind. Don't produce a manuscript without first considering what is needed in your field."

PROBUS PUBLISHING CO., 1925 N. Clybourn St., Chicago IL 60614. (312)868-1100. Fax: (312)868-6250. VP/ Editorial Director: James M. McNeil. Estab. 1983. Imprints are Probus Trade, Bankers Publishing Co., Probus/Mortgage Bankers Association, Probus/Healthcare Financial Management Association. Publishes hardcover and paperback originals and trade paperback reprints. Averages 115 titles/year; receives 250 submissions annually. 60% of books from first-time authors; 95% of books from unagented writers. Pays 10-15% royalty on wholesale price; advance varies. Publishes book an average of 5 months after acceptance. Simultaneous submissions OK. Reports in 2 weeks. *Writer's Market* recommends allowing 2 months for reply. Free book catalog; ms guidelines for SASE.
Nonfiction: How-to and technical. Subjects include banking, investment, corporate finance, small business, marketing, futures/options trading. Query or submit outline and sample chapters.

PROFESSIONAL PUBLICATIONS, INC., 1250 5th Ave., Belmont CA 94002-3863. (415)593-9119. Fax: (415)592-4519. Acquisitions Editor: Gerald Galbo. Estab. 1975. Publishes hardcover and paperback originals. Averages 12 titles/year; receives 100-200 submissions annually. Pays 8-12% royalty on wholesale price; offers $1,000 average advance. Sometimes makes outright purchase for $1,000-2,000. Publishes book an average of 6-18 months after acceptance. Simultaneous submissions OK. Query for electronic submissions. Reports in 2 weeks on queries. *Writer's Market* recommends allowing 2 months for reply. Free book catalog. Free ms guidelines for authors.
Nonfiction: Reference, technical and textbook. Subjects include business and economics, mathematics, engineering, accounting, architecture, interior design, law, contracting and building. Especially needs "licensing examination review books for general contractors and lawyers." Query or submit outline and sample chapters. Reviews artwork/photos as part of ms package.
Recent Nonfiction Title: *Engineering Your Start-Up: A Guide For Hi-Tech Entrepreneurs,* by Michael Baird.
Tips: "We specialize in books for working professionals: engineers, architects, contractors, accountants, etc. The more technically complex the manuscript is the happier we are. We love equations, tables of data, complex illustrations, mathematics, etc. In technical/professional book publishing, it isn't always obvious to

us if a market exists. We can judge the quality of a ms, but the author should make some effort to convince us that a market exists. Facts, figures, and estimates about the market—and marketing ideas from the author—will help sell us on the work. Besides our interest in highly technical materials, we will be trying to broaden our range of titles in each discipline. Specifically, we will be looking for career guides for accountants and architects, as well as for engineers."

PROLINGUA ASSOCIATES, 15 Elm St., Brattleboro VT 05301. (802)207-7779. Senior Editor: Raymond C. Clark. Publisher: Arthur A. Burrows. Estab. 1980. Publishes paperback originals. Averages 6 titles/year; receives 30-50 submissions annually. 25% of books from first-time authors. 100% of books from unagented writers. Pays 5-10% royalty on wholesale price; offers $200 average advance. Publishes book an average of 1 year after acceptance. Simultaneous submissions OK. Reports in 2 weeks on queries. *Writer's Market* recommends allowing 2 months for reply. Book catalog for 9 × 12 SAE with 4 first class stamps.
Nonfiction: Reference and textbook. Subjects include English as a second language, French and Spanish. "We are always willing to consider innovative language texts and language teacher resources which fit with our approach to language teaching. Also interested in intercultural training." Query or submit outline and sample chapters.
Recent Nonfiction Title: *The ESL Miscellany*, 2nd, Revised Edition, by Clark, Burrows, and Moran (reference).
Tips: "Get a catalog of our books, take a couple of books by ProLingua out of the library or from a nearby language department, ask about ProLingua, and in general try to determine whether your book would fit into ProLingua's list."

PRUETT PUBLISHING, 2928 Pearl St., Boulder CO 80301. (303)449-4919. Publisher: Jim Pruett. Editor: Dianne Russell. Estab. 1959. Publishes hardcover originals and trade paperback originals and reprints. Firm averages 10-12 titles/year. 60% of books are from first-time authors. 100% from unagented writers. Pays 10-12% royalty on net income. Publishes book an average of 18 months after acceptance. Simultaneous submissions OK. Reports in 2 months on queries. Free book catalog and manuscript guidelines.
Nonfiction: Biography, illustrated book and textbook. Subjects include agriculture/horticulture (western), Americana (western), animals (western), archaeology (Native American), cooking, foods and nutrition, ethnic (Native American), gardening (western), history, nature/environment, recreation (outdoor), regional, sports (cycling, hiking, flyfishing). *No longer seeking coffee table books, child guidance/parenting books, travel books or railroad histories.* "We are looking for nonfiction manuscripts and guides that focus on the Rocky Mountain West." Reviews artwork/photos as part of ms package.
Tips: "There has been a movement away from large publisher's mass market books and towards small publisher's regional interest books, and in turn distributors and retail outlets are more interested in small publishers. Author's don't need to have a big-name to have a good publisher. Look for similar books that you feel are well produced—consider design, editing, overall quality and contact those publishers. Get to know several publishers, and find the one that feels right—trust your instincts."

PSI RESEARCH, 300 N. Valley Dr., Grants Pass OR 97526. (503)479-9464. Fax: (503)476-1479. Contact: Acquisitions Editor. Estab. 1975. Imprint is Oasis Press. Firm publishes hardcover, trade paperback and binder originals. Publishes 20-30 books/year; receives 90 submissions/year. 60% from first-time authors; 90% from unagented writers. Pays royalty. Publishes ms an average of 6-12 months after acceptance. Simultaneous submissions OK. Reports in 2 weeks (initial feedback) on queries. *Writer's Market* recommends allowing 2 months for reply. Free book catalog and ms guidelines.
Nonfiction: How-to, reference, self-help, textbook. Subjects include business and economics, computers and electronics, education, money/finance, retirement, exporting, franchise, finance, marketing and public relations, relocations. Needs information-heavy, readable manuscripts written by professionals in their subject fields. Interactive where appropriate. Authorship credentials less important than hands-on experience qualifications. Must relate to either small business or to individuals who are entrepreneurs, owners or managers of small business (1-300 employees). Query for unwritten material or to check current interest in topic and orientation. Submit outline/synopsis and sample chapters. Reviews artwork/photos as part of freelance ms package.
Recent Nonfiction Title: *Essential Corporation*, by Carl Sniffen.
Tips: "Best chance is with practical, step-by-step manuals for operating a business, with worksheets, checklists. The audience is made up of entrepreneurs of all types: small businesses and those who would like to be; attorneys, accountants and consultants who work with small businesses; college students; dreamers. Make sure your information is valid and timely for its audience, also that by virtue of either its content quality or viewpoint, it distinguishes itself from other books on the market."

PUBLISHERS ASSOCIATES, P.O. Box 140361, Las Colinas TX 75014-0361. (214)686-5332. Senior Editor: Belinda Buxjom. Estab. 1979. Imprints are Hercules Press, The Liberal Press, Liberal Arts Press, Minuteman Press, Monument Press, Nichole Graphics, Scholars Books, Tagelwüld. Publishes trade paperback originals. Receives 1,500 submissions/year. 40% of books from first-time authors. 100% from unagented writers. Pays 4% and up royalty on retail price. Publishes book an average of 4 months after acceptance. Reports in up to

4 months. Book catalog for 6×9 SAE with 4 first class stamps. Manuscript guidelines for #10 SAE with 2 first class stamps.

Nonfiction: Textbook (scholarly). Subjects include gay/lesbian, government politics (liberal), history, religion (liberation/liberal) and women's issues/studies. "We are looking for gay/lesbian history, pro-choice/feminist studies and liberal politics. Quality researched gay/lesbian history will have beginning royalty of 7% and up. Academics are encouraged to submit. No biographies, evangelical fundamentalism/bible, conservative politics, New Age studies or homophobic. No fiction or poetry." Query. Reviews artwork/photos as part of ms package.

Recent Nonfiction Title: *Homophobia and the Judaeo-Christian Tradition*, by Stemmeler and Clark (religion/gay/lesbian).

Tips: "Writers have the best chance with gender free/nonsexist, liberal academic studies. We sell primarily to libraries and to scholars. Our audience is highly educated, politically and socially liberal, if religious they are liberational. If I were a writer trying to market a book today, I would compare my manuscript with books already published by the press I am seeking to submit to."

PURDUE UNIVERSITY PRESS, Bldg. B, 1532 South Campus Courts, West Lafayette IN 47907-1532. (317)494-2038. Director: David Sanders. Managing Editor: Margaret Hunt. Publishes hardcover and trade paperback originals and trade paperback reprints. Averages 12 titles/year; receives 150 submissions annually. Royalties vary. No advance. Publishes book an average of 15 months after acceptance. Reports in 2 months. Book catalog and ms guidelines for 9×12 SASE.

Nonfiction: Biography, scholarly and regional. Subjects include Americana (especially Indiana), scholarly studies in history, philosophy, politics, religion, sociology, theories of biology and literary criticism. "The writer must present good credentials, demonstrate good writing skills, and above all explain how his/her work will make a significant contribution to scholarship/regional studies. Our purpose is to publish scholarly and regional books. We are looking for manuscripts on these subjects: theory of biography, Balkan and Danubian studies, interdisciplinary, regional (Midwest) interest, horticulture, history, literature, history of philosophy, criticism, and effects of science and technology on society. No cookbooks, nonbooks, textbooks, theses/dissertations, manuals/pamphlets, fiction, or books on how-to, fitness/exercise or fads. Submit prospectus."

Recent Nonfiction Title: *Reconstructing Illness: Studies in Pathography*, by Anne Hunsaker Hawkins.

PUSH/PULL/PRESS, Imprint of JSA Publications, Inc., P.O. Box 37175, Oak Park, MI 48334-2945. (313)546-9123. Director: Joe Ajlouny. "Push/Pull/Press publishes original illustrated humor books." Other imprints include Scrivener Press (travel) and Compositional Arts (creative nonfiction). Firm publishes trade paperback and mass market paperback originals. Averages 8 titles/year (each imprint publishes 2-3 titles/year). Receives 400 queries and 50 mss/year. 75% of mss from first-time authors; 75% from unagented writers. Pays 7-10% royalty on retail price. Offers $500-3,000 advance. Publishes book 10 months after acceptance. Simultaneous submissions OK. Reports in 1 month. *Writer's Market* recommends allowing 2 months for reply. Manuscript guidelines for #10 SASE.

Nonfiction: How-to, humor, music, Americana, history, hobbies, philosophy, psychology, sociology, sports, travel. Submit proposal package including illustration samples (photocopies).

Recent Nonfiction Titles: *The Politically Incorrect Joke Book*, by Four White Males; *Gifts I Almost Got You*, by Dusty Rumsey.

Tips: "Your submissions must be clever!"

THE PUTNAM BERKLEY GROUP, Divisions include Ace Science Fiction & Fantasy, Berkley Books, and Grosset & Dunlap. See The Berkley Publishing Group.

Q.E.D. PUBLISHING GROUP, P.O. Box 812070, Wellesley MA 02181-2070. (617)237-5656. Fax: (617)235-0826. President: Edwin F. Kerr. Estab. 1971. Publishes computer books and reports for MIS professionals. Averages 30 titles/year. Pays 10-15% royalty on net sales. Publishes book an average of 4-6 months after acceptance. Query for electronic submissions. Reports in 1 month. Free book catalog.

Nonfiction: Technical. Subjects include computers, systems development, personal computing, and database technology. "Our books are read by data processing managers and professionals." Submit outline and 2 sample chapters. Reviews artwork/photos as part of ms package.

Recent Nonfiction Title: *OS/2 Workplace Shell: The User's Guide and Tutorial*.

‡QUARRY PRESS, P.O. Box 1061, Kingston, Ontario K7K 1S2 Canada. Publisher: Bob Hilderley. Firm produces hardcover and trade paperback originals. Average 18-22 titles/year. Works with 10-20% first-time authors; 95% unagented writers. Pays royalty on retail price based on Writers' Union of Canada basic contract (rates vary). Offers variable advance. Publishes book 6-12 months after acceptance of ms. Submissions from abroad (i.e., U.S. and overseas) must have International Reply Coupons. Reports in 6 months. Catalog for 9×12 SAE with sufficient IRC (International Reply Coupons) for return.

Nonfiction: Biography, coffee table book, humor, illustrated book, children's/juvenile and reference. Subjects include animals, art/architecture, history (local), language/literature, photography, regional, biography and poetry. "Check our catalogue to see what we publish and remember we are a *Canadian* publishing house." Submit outline or proposal package, including cover letter, outline/synopsis/20 pg. text. Rarely reviews artwork/photos as part of freelance ms package.

Recent Nonfiction Title: *Bowering's Guide to Eastern Ontario*, Ian Bowering, ed. (local/travel).

Fiction: Experimental, gay/lesbian, literary and picture books. Submit synopsis and 20 pages of text.

Recent Fiction Title: *In Christ There is No East or West*, by Kent Nussey (short stories).

Tips: "*Don't* get an agent. Enclose self addressed postcard with sufficient IRCs for return so we can notify you when your ms arrives."

QUILL, Imprint of William Morrow and Co., Inc., 1350 Avenue of the Americas, New York NY 10019. (212)261-6500. Editor: Andrew Dutter. Publishes trade paperback originals and reprints. Averages 40 titles/year; receives over 2,000 submissions annually. 25% of books from first-time authors; 5% of books from unagented writers. Pays royalty on retail price. Offers variable advance. Publishes ms an average of 1 year after acceptance. Simultaneous submissions OK. No unsolicited mss or proposals; mss and proposals should be submitted through a literary agent. Reports in 3 months.

Nonfiction: Biography and trade books. Subjects include history, music, psychology, science, light reference and military history. Needs nonfiction trade paperbacks with enduring importance; books that have backlist potential and appeal to educated people with broad intellectual curiosities. No fiction, poetry, fitness, diet, how-to, self-help or humor. *Query only*.

Recent Nonfiction Title: *A Forest of Kings: The Untold Story of the Ancient Maya*, by Linda Schele and David Freidel.

RAGGED MOUNTAIN PRESS, Imprint of International Marine/McGraw-Hill, P.O. Box 220, Camden ME 04843. (207)236-4837. Fax: (207)236-6314. Acquisitions Editors: James R. Babb, Dorcas Susan Millee. Estab. 1971. Publishes hardcover and trade paperback originals and reprints. Publishes 40 titles/year. Imprint publishes 12 (Ragged Mountain), remainder are International Marine. Receives 200 queries and 100 mss/year. 30% of mss from first-time authors; 90% from unagented writers. Pays 10-15% royalty on wholesale price. Offers $500-5,000 advance. Publishes book 1 year after acceptance of ms. Simultaneous submissions OK. Query for electronic submissions. Reports in 1 month on queries. *Writer's Market* recommends allowing 2 months for reply. Book catalog for 9 × 12 SAE and 10 first class stamps. Manuscript guidelines for #10 SASE.

Nonfiction: Biography, cookbook and how-to, humor, illustrated book and technical (all outdoor related). Subjects include animals, cooking (outdoor related), fishing, camping, climbing, kayaking, government/politics (environmental issues only), hobbies, photography (outdoor), recreation (outdoor) and travel (alternative and adventure travel). "Ragged Mountain publishes nonconsumptive outdoor, environmental issue, and alternative travel books of literary merit or unique appeal. Be familiar with the existing literature. Find a subject that hasn't been done, or has been done poorly, then explore it in detail and from all angles." Query or submit outline with 3 sample chapters. Reviews artwork/photos as part of freelance ms package. Writers should send photocopies.

Recent Nonfiction Title: *The Complete Book of Fly Fishing*, by Tom McNally.

RAINBOW BOOKS, P.O. Box 430, Highland City FL 33846-0430. Phone/Fax: (813)648-4420. Editorial Director: B. A. Lampe. Estab. 1979. Publishes hardcover, trade paperback originals, video (VHS) and audio tapes and does book packaging. Averages 10-15 titles/year; receives 600 submissions annually. 70% of books from first-time authors; 90% of books from unagented writers. Publishes book an average of 8 months after acceptance. Reports in 2 weeks on queries. Reports in 2 months on mss. Book catalog for 6 × 9 SAE with 75¢ postage; ms guidelines for #10 SASE.

Nonfiction: Self-help, how-to, travel, business, science and resource books. Require query first on all books. Does not accept proposals. Interested in all nonfiction books.

Recent Nonfiction Title: *An Illustrated Diet Book For Humans*, by Carlos Pestana.

Tips: "No SASE, no response. We do not accept proposals and we do not want to see religious titles with a doomsday thrust."

RANDOM HOUSE, INC., Subsidary of Advance Publications, 11th Floor, 201 E. 50th St., New York NY 10022. (212)940-7742. Random House Trade Division publishes 120 titles/year; receives 3,000 submissions annually. Imprints include Random House, Alfred A. Knopf, Ballantine, Crown, Del Rey, Fawcett, Modern Library, Pantheon, Clarkson N. Potter, Villard, and Vintage. Pays royalty on retail price. Simultaneous submissions OK. Reports in 2 months. Free book catalog; ms guidelines for #10 SASE.

● Not every imprint is listed. Some asked not to be listed.

Nonfiction: Biography, cookbook, humor, illustrated book, self-help. Subjects include Americana, art, business and economics, classics, cooking and foods, health, history, music, nature, politics, psychology, religion, sociology and sports. No juveniles or textbooks (separate division). Query with outline and at least 3 sample chapters.

Fiction: Adventure, confession, experimental, fantasy, historical, horror, humor, mainstream, mystery, and suspense. Submit outline/synopsis and at least 3 sample chapters.

Tips: "If I were a writer trying to market a book today, I would get an agent. Enclose SASE for reply or return of materials."

RANDOM HOUSE, INC. JUVENILE BOOKS, 201 E. 50th St., New York NY 10022. (212)940-7742. Subsidiaries include Knopf Children's Books, Knopf Children's Paperbacks (Bullseye Books, Dragonfly Books and Borzoi Sprinters), Random House Children's Books, Crown Children's Books. Juvenile Division: J. Schulman, Publisher. Managing Editor: R. Abend. Alfred A. Knopf: S. Spinner, Executive Editor. Random House Juvenile: S. Spinner. Crown: S. Boughton, Executive Editor. Kate Klimo, Editor-in-Chief. Firm publishes hardcover, trade paperback and mass market paperback originals, and mass market paperback reprints. Publishes 300 titles/year. Simultaneous submissions OK.

Nonfiction: Biography, humor, illustrated book, juvenile. Subjects include animals, nature/environment, recreation, science, sports. Query or submit outline and sample chapters. Submit ms through agent only.

Recent Nonfiction Title: *175 More Science Experiments to Amuse and Amaze Your Friends*, by T. Cash and B. Taylor.

Fiction: Adventure, confession (young adult), fantasy, historical, horror, humor, juvenile, mystery, picture books, science fiction (juvenile/young adult), suspense, young adult. Submit through agent only.

Recent Fiction Title: *Aliens for Lunch*, by J. Etra and S. Spinner.

Tips: "Books for children 6 months to 15 years old."

REFERENCE SERVICE PRESS, Suite 9, 1100 Industrial Rd., San Carlos CA 94070-4131. (415)594-0743. Fax: (415)594-0411. Acquisitions Editor: Stuart Hauser. Estab. 1977. Publishes hardcover originals. Firm averages 5 titles/year. 100% of books from unagented writers. Pays 10% or higher royalty. Publishes book an average of 3-6 months after acceptance. Simultaneous submissions OK. Query for electronic submissions. Reports in 2 months. Book catalog for #10 SASE.

Nonfiction: Reference. Subjects include education, ethnic, military/war, women's issues/studies and disabled. We are interested only in directories and monographs dealing with financial aid. Submit outline and sample chapters.

Tips: "Our audience consists of librarians, counselors, researchers, students, reentry women, scholars and other fundseekers."

RELIGIOUS EDUCATION PRESS, 5316 Meadow Brook Rd., Birmingham AL 35242-3315. (205)991-1000. Fax: (205)991-9669. Contact Editor: Dr. Nancy J. Vickers. Estab. 1974. Publishes trade paperback and hardback originals. Averages 5 titles/year; receives 280 submissions annually. 40% of books from first-time authors; 100% of books from unagented writers. Pays 10% royalty on actual selling price. "Many of our books are work for hire. We do not have a subsidy option." Offers no advance. Query for electronic submissions. Reports in 2 months. Free book catalog.

Nonfiction: Technical and textbook. Scholarly subjects on religion and religious education. "We publish serious, significant and scholarly books on religious education and pastoral ministry." No mss under 200 pages, no poetry, books on Biblical interpretation, or "popular" books. Query. Reviews artwork/photos as part of ms package.

Tips: "Write clearly, reason exactly and connectively, and meet deadlines. We do not return unsolicited mss unless accompanied by return postage."

RENAISSANCE HOUSE PUBLISHERS, Subsidiary of Jende-Hagan, Inc., 541 Oak St., P.O. Box 177, Frederick CO 80530-0177. (303)833-2030. Fax: (303)833-2030. Editor: Eleanor Ayer. Publishes an ongoing series of 48-page guidebooks of travel-related interest. Averages 8 titles/year; receives 125 submissions annually. 60% of books from first-time authors; 75% of books from unagented writers. Pays 8-10% royalty on net receipts. Offers average advance of 10% of anticipated first printing royalties. May consider work for hire by experts in specific fields of interest. Publishes book an average of 18 months after acceptance. Query for electronic submissions. Reports in 1 month on queries. *Writer's Market* recommends allowing 2 months for reply.

Nonfiction: Subjects include regional guidebooks. No fiction, personal reminiscences, general traditional philosophy, books on topics totally unrelated to subject areas specified above. Please—no inquiries outside the topic of regional guidebooks! We publish to a very specific formula. *Writer's Market* recommends query with SASE first.

Tips: "We rely exclusively on in-house generation of book concepts and then find authors who will write for hire to our specifications. We are continually adding to our American Traveler Guidebooks series."

REVIEW AND HERALD PUBLISHING ASSOCIATION, 55 West Oak Ridge Dr., Hagerstown MD 21740-7390. Acquisitions Editor: Penny Estes Wheeler. Estab. 1849. Publishes hardcover and paperback originals. Specializes in religious-oriented books. Averages 30-40 titles/year; receives 300-400 submissions annually. 15% of books from first-time authors; 100% of books from unagented writers. Average print order for a writer's first book is 5,000-7,500. Pays 14% of retail price, hardcover; 12% of retail price, softcover; offers average $500 advance. Publishes book an average of 18 months after acceptance. Query for electronic submissions. Reports in 4 months. Free brochure; ms guidelines for SASE.

Nonfiction: Juveniles (religious-oriented only), nature, and religious, 128 pages average. Query or submit outline and 2-3 sample chapters. Prefers to do own illustrating. Looks for "literary style, constructive tone, factual accuracy, compatibility with Adventist theology and lifestyle, and length of manuscript." Reviews artwork/photos as part of ms package.

• Not accepting music, poetry, puzzles or games, and very few children's mss.
Recent Nonfiction Title: *His Guiding Hand*, by Dorothy Davenport.
Recent Fiction Title: *Tough Guy*, by Andy Demsky.
Tips: "Familiarize yourself with Adventist theology because Review and Herald Publishing Association is owned and operated by the Seventh-day Adventist Church. We are accepting fewer but better-written manuscripts. Most of our books were written on assignment."

RICHBORO PRESS, P.O. Box 947, Southampton PA 18966-0947. (215)364-2212. Fax: (215)364-2212. Editor: George Moore. Estab. 1979. Publishes hardcover, trade paperback originals and software. Averages 4 titles/ year. Receives 500 submissions annually. 90% of books from unagented writers. Pays 10% royalty on retail price. Publishes book an average of 1 year after acceptance. Electronic submissions preferred. Reports in 2 months on queries. Free book catalog; ms guidelines $1 for #10 SASE.
Nonfiction: Cookbook, how-to and gardening. Subjects include cooking and foods. Query.

‡**RISING TIDE PRESS**, 5 Kivy St., Huntington Station NY 11746-2042. (516)427-1289. Editor/Publisher: Lee Boojamra. Publishes trade paperback originals. Publishes 10-20 titles/year. Receives 500 queries and 150 mss/year. 75% of mss from first-time authors, 100% from unagented writers. Pays 10-15% royalty on wholesale price. Publishes book 12-15 months after acceptance. Query for electronic submissions: prefers any major IBM compatible WP program on 5¼" or 3½" disk. Reports in 1 week on queries, 1 months on proposals and 2 months on mss. Book catalog $1. Writer's guidelines for #10 SASE.
Nonfiction: Lesbian nonfiction. Subjects include gay/lesbian. Submit outline. Query with proposal including entire ms with *large* SASE. Reviews artwork/photos as part of freelance ms package. Writers should include photocopies.
Fiction: "Lesbian fiction only." Adventure, erotica, fantasy, historical, horror, humor, literary, mainstream/ contemporary, mystery, occult, romance, science fiction, suspense, mixed genres. "Major characters must be lesbian. Primary plot must have lesbian focus and sensibility." Query, submit synopsis or entire ms.
Recent Fiction Title: *Return to Isis*, by Jean Stewart (science fiction).
Tips: "Our books are for, by and about lesbian lives. We welcome unpublished authors. We do *not* consider agented authors. Any material submitted should be proofed."

THE RIVERDALE COMPANY, PUBLISHERS, P.O. Box 2679, Westwood MA 02090-0004. (617)446-7134. President: John Adams. Vice President: Adele Adams. Estab. 1984. Publishes hardcover originals. Averages 8-10 titles/year; receives 50 submissions annually. 20% of books from first-time authors; 100% of books from unagented writers. Pays 0-15% royalty on wholesale price. Publishes book an average of 8 months after acceptance. Reports in 2 months.
Nonfiction: "We publish technical and social science books for scholars, students, policymakers; and tour, restaurant and recreational guides for the mass market." Subjects include economics, history, humanities, politics, psychology, sociology and travel. Especially needs social science and travel mss on South Asia or Africa. Will consider college text proposals in economics and Third World studies; travel guides of any sort. Query. Accepts outline and 2-3 sample chapters.
Recent Nonfiction Title: *A Woman's Guide to Carefree Travel Abroad*, by Joanne Turpin.

ROCKY TOP PUBLICATIONS, P.O. Box 33, Stamford NY 12167-0033. President/Publisher: Joseph D. Jennings. Contact: Emerson Bach. Estab. 1982. Publishes hardcover and paperback originals. Averages 4-6 titles/ year. 70% of books from first-time authors; 95% of books from unagented writers. Pays 4-10% royalty (may vary) on wholesale price. Publishes book an average of 6 months after acceptance. Reports in up to 6 months.
Nonfiction: How-to, reference, self-help and technical. Subjects include animal health, health, hobbies (crafts), medical, nature, philosophy (Thoreau or environmental only) and science. No autobiographies, biographies, business "get rich quick" or fad books. Query.
Tips: "No unsolicited manuscripts."

ROUTLEDGE, INC., (formerly Routledge, Chapman & Hall, Inc.), 29 W. 35th St., New York NY 10001-2299. (212)244-3336. Editorial Director (New York): William P. Germano, editor for media, literary criticism, cultural studies, classical studies, and theater arts. Editor for philosophy and psychoanalysis: Maureen MacGrogan. Editor for history and politics: Cecelia Cancellaro. Editor for education and sociology: Jayne Fargnoli. Editor for anthropology: Max Zutty. Science books published under Chapman & Hall. Humanities and social sciences published under Routledge. Imprints include Theatre Arts Books. Routledge list includes

Market conditions are constantly changing! If this is 1995 or later, buy the newest edition of Writer's Market *at your favorite bookstore or order directly from* Writer's Digest Books.

humanities, social sciences, business and economics, reference. Monographs, reference works, hardback and paperback upper-level texts, academic general interest. Averages 800 titles/year; receives 5,000 submissions annually. 10% of books from first-time authors; 95% of books from unagented authors. Average royalty 10% net receipts; advances. No simultaneous submissions. Reports in 6 weeks on queries. *Writer's Market* recommends allowing 2 months for reply. Do not send mss at initial stage. No replies to unsolicited inquiries without SASE.

Nonfiction: Academic subjects include philosophy, literary criticism, psychoanalysis, social sciences, business and economics, history, psychology, women's studies, lesbian and gay studies, race and ethnicity, political science, anthropology, geography development, education, reference.

Tips: "We have 30 subject editors in the U.K. as well."

‡ROXBURY PUBLISHING CO., P.O. Box 491044, Los Angeles CA 90049. (213)653-1068. Executive Editor: Claude Teweles. Publishes hardcover and paperback originals and reprints. Averages 10 titles/year. Pays royalty. Simultaneous submissions OK. Reports in 2 months.

Nonfiction: College-level textbooks only. Subjects include business and economics, humanities, speech, English, developmental studies, social sciences and sociology. Query, submit outline/synopsis and sample chapters, or submit complete ms.

RUSSELL SAGE FOUNDATION, 112 E. 64th St., New York NY 10021. (212)750-6037. Fax: (212)371-4761. Director of Publications: Lisa Nachtigall. Estab. 1907. Publishes hardcover and paperback originals. Averages 20 titles/year. Unsolicited manuscripts not accepted for publication. Publishes book an average of 9 months after acceptance. *Writer's Market* recommends allowing 2 months for reply.

Nonfiction: Social science research. Subjects include business and economics, education, ethnic, government, history, psychology, sociology, women's issues/studies, public policy. Query or submit outline and sample chapters.

Recent Nonfiction Title: *Uneven Tides*, edited by Sheldon Danziger and Peter Gottschalk (economic inequality, economics, public policy).

‡RUTGERS UNIVERSITY PRESS, 109 Church St., New Brunswick NJ 08901. (908)932-7762. Associate Director and Editor-in-Chief: Marlie Wasserman. Publishes hardcover and trade paperback originals and trade paperback reprints. Publishes 70 titles/year. Receives up to 1,500 queries and up to 300 mss/year. Up to 30% of mss from first-time authors, 70% from unagented writers. Pays 7½-12% royalty on retail price. Offers $1,000-4,000 advance. Publishes book 1 year after acceptance of ms. Simultaneous submissions OK (with notification that it is simultaneous). Query for electronic submissions. Reports in 1 month on proposals. Book catalog free on request.

Nonfiction: Biography, textbook and books for use in undergraduate courses. Subjects include Americana, anthropology/archaeology, education, gay/lesbian, government/politics, health/medicine, history, language/literature, nature/environment, regional, science, sociology, translation and women's issues/studies. "Our press aims to reach audiences beyond the academic community. Writing should be accessible." Submit outline and 2-3 sample chapters. Reviews artwork/photos as part of the freelance ms package. Writers should send photocopies.

Recent Nonfiction Title: *Gender Play: Girls and Boys in School*, by Barrie Thorne.

Fiction: Experimental, feminist, gay/lesbian, historical and literary. "The majority of the fiction we accept is literary. Our fiction list is small so we are very selective. We rarely publish short story collections from unknown writers. Writers often submit fiction that is too commercial in terms of writing style." Submit synopsis and 2-3 sample chapters.

Recent Fiction Title: *The Sleeper Wakes: Harlem Renaissance Stories by Women*, Marcy Knopf, ed.

Poetry: "We *rarely* publish poetry."

Tips: Both academic and general audiences. "Many of our books have potential for undergraduate course use. We are more trade-oriented than most university presses. We are looking for intelligent, well-written and accessible books. Avoid overly narrow topics."

RUTLEDGE HILL PRESS, 211 7th Ave. N., Nashville TN 37219. (615)244-2700. Fax: (615)244-2978. President: Lawrence Stone. Vice President: Ron Pitkin. Estab. 1982. Publishes hardcover and trade paperback originals and reprints. Averages 25 titles/year; receives 600 submissions annually. 40% of books from first-time authors; 90% of books from unagented writers. Pays 10-20% royalty on wholesale price. Publishes book an average of 1 year after acceptance. Reports in 3 months. Book catalog for 9 × 12 SAE and 3 first class stamps.

Nonfiction: Biography, cookbook, humor, reference and self-help. "The book must have an identifiable market, preferably one that is geographically limited." Submit outline and sample chapters. Reviews artwork/photos as part of ms package.

ST. ANTHONY MESSENGER PRESS, 1615 Republic St., Cincinnati OH 45210-1298. (513)241-5615. Fax: (513)241-0399. Editor-in-Chief: The Rev. Norman Perry, O.F.M. Managing Editor: Lisa Biedenbach. Estab. 1970. Publishes paperback originals. Averages 14 titles/year; receives 250 submissions annually. 10% of books from first-time authors; 100% of books from unagented writers. Pays 10-12% royalty on net receipts of sales.

Offers $600 average advance. Publishes book an average of 1 year after acceptance. Books are sold in bulk to groups (study clubs, high school or college classes, and parishes) and in bookstores. No simultaneous submissions. Query for electronic submissions. Reports in 2 months. Book catalog and ms guidelines for 9 × 12 SAE with 2 first-class stamps.

Nonfiction: Religion. "We try to reach the Catholic market with topics near the heart of the ordinary Catholic's belief. We want to offer insight and inspiration and thus give people support in living a Christian life in a pluralistic society. We are not interested in an academic or abstract approach. Our emphasis is on popular writing with examples, specifics, color and anecdotes." Length: 25,000-40,000 words. Query or submit outline and 2 sample chapters. Reviews artwork/photos as part of ms package.

Recent Nonfiction Title: *Why Be Catholic? Understanding Our Experience and Tradition*, by Richard Rohr and Joseph Martos.

Tips: "We are looking for aids to parish ministry, prayer, spirituality, scripture, liturgy and the sacraments. Also, we are seeking manuscripts that deal with Catholic identity—explaining it, identifying it, understanding it. The book cannot be the place for the author to think through a subject. The author has to think through the subject first and then tell the reader what is important to know. Style uses anecdotes, examples, illustrations, human interest, 'colorful' quotes, fiction techniques of suspense, dialogue, characterization, etc. Address practical problems, deal in concrete situations, free of technical terms and professional jargon. We do not publish fiction, poetry, autobiography, personal reflections, academic studies, art or coffee-table books."

ST. BEDE'S PUBLICATIONS, Subsidiary of St. Scholastica Priory, P.O. Box 545, Petersham MA 01366-0545. (508)724-3407. Fax: (508)724-3574. Editorial Director: Sr. Scholastica Crilly, OSB. Estab. 1978. Publishes hardcover originals, trade paperback originals and reprints. Averages 8-12 titles/year; receives 100 submissions annually. 30-40% of books from first-time authors; 90% of books from unagented writers. Subsidy publishes (nonauthor) 10% of books. Pays 5-10% royalty on wholesale price or retail price. No advance. Publishes book an average of 2 years after acceptance. Simultaneous submissions OK. Query for electronic submissions. Unsolicited mss are not returned unless accompanied by sufficient return postage. Reports in 2 months. Book catalog and ms guidelines for 9 × 12 SAE and 2 first class stamps.

Nonfiction: Textbook (theology), religion, prayer, spirituality, hagiography, theology, philosophy, church history and related lives of saints fields. "We are always looking for excellent books on prayer, spirituality, liturgy, church or monastic history. Theology and philosophy are important also. We publish English translations of foreign works in these fields if we think they are excellent and worth translating." No submissions unrelated to religion, theology, spirituality, etc. Query or submit outline and sample chapters.

● No longer seeking fiction.

Tips: "There seems to be a growing interest in monasticism among lay people and we will be publishing more books in this area. For our theology/philosophy titles our audience is scholars, colleges and universities, seminaries, etc. For our other titles (i.e. prayer, spirituality, lives of saints, etc.) the audience is above-average readers interested in furthering their knowledge in these areas."

‡ST. CLAIR PRESS, St. Clair Ave., Beverly Shores IN 46301-0527. Vice President: Flossy McNally. Subsidiary of Little Stirrup Cay, Ltd. Publishes hardcover originals. Each publish 1-3 titles/year. Pays 7.5-12% royalty on retail price. Simultaneous submissions OK. Reports in 3 months.

Nonfiction: Science and technology. Submit outline and sample chapter(s).

Fiction: Adventure and mainstream/contemporary. Submit synopsis and sample chapter(s).

Recent Fiction Title: *The Shallow Sea*, by Neil Ruzic (adventure/suspense).

ST. MARTIN'S PRESS, 175 5th Ave., New York NY 10010. "Prefers not to share information."

ST. PAUL BOOKS AND MEDIA, Daughters of St. Paul, 50 St. Paul's Ave., Boston MA 02130. (617)522-8911. Fax: (617)541-9805. Director, Editorial Department: Sister Anne Eileen, FSP. Estab. 1948. Firm publishes hardcover, trade paperback originals, and reprints. Average 20 titles/year; receives approximately 900 proposals/year. Pays authors 7-12% royalty on net sales. Publishes ms an average of 1-2 years after acceptance. Reports in 2 months. Book catalog for 9 × 12 SAE with 4 first class stamps.

Nonfiction: Biography, juvenile, self-help. Subjects include child guidance/parenting, psychology and religion. "No strictly secular manuscripts." Query only. No unsolicited mss, without prior query.

Recent Nonfiction Title: *5 Steps to Post-Abortion Healing*, by Holly Francis.

Fiction: Juvenile. Query only. No unsolicited mss, without prior query.

Tips: "We are more interested in books of religious (Catholic) doctrine and moral teachings, less interested in spirituality. Always interested in books of Christian formation for families. No New Age books, please."

SAN FRANCISCO PRESS, INC., P.O. Box 42680, San Francisco CA 94142-6800. (510)524-1000. President: Terry Gabriel. Founded 1959. Publishes hardcover originals and trade paperback originals and reprints. Averages 5-10 titles/year. Receives over 100 submissions/year. 50% of books from first-time authors. 90% from unagented writers. Pays 10-15% on wholesale price. Publishes book an average of 6 months after acceptance. Simultaneous submissions OK. Reports in 1 month on queries. *Writer's Market* recommends allowing 2 months for reply. Book catalog for #10 SAE and 1 first-class stamp.

Nonfiction: Technical, college textbook. Subjects include computers and electronics, biotechnology, public health, history of technology, musicology, and science. Submit outline and sample chapters.

● This press has been overwhelmed with music book mss when their need is for musicology.

Recent Nonfiction Title: *Electricity and Magnetism in Biology and Medicine*, Ed. Martin Blank.

Tips: "Our books are aimed at specialized audiences; we do not publish works intended for the general public."

SANDHILL CRANE NATURE BOOKS, (formerly Sandhill Crane Press, Inc.), P.O. Box 147050, Gainesville FL 32614-7050. (904)375-6610. Fax: (904)371-0962. Publisher: Dr. W. Backhuys. Estab. 1947. Imprints are Flora & Fauna Publications and Universal Book Services (Warmonderweg 80, 2341 KZ Oegstgeest, The Netherlands. 071-170208. Fax: +31-71-171-856). Publishes hardcover and trade paperback originals. Firm publishes 10-12 titles/year; receives 70 submissions annually. 50% of books from first-time authors; 100% of books from unagented writers. Average print order for a writer's first book is 500. Pays 10% royalty on list price; negotiable advance. Publishes book an average of 1 year after acceptance. Query for electronic submissions. Reports in 2 months on queries.

Nonfiction: Reference, technical, textbook, and directories. Subjects include plants and animals (for amateur and professional biologists), and natural history. Looking for "books dealing with kinds of plants and animals; new nature guide series underway. No nature stories or 'Oh My' nature books." Query with outline and 2 sample chapters. Reviews artwork/photos as part of ms package.

Tips: "Well-documented books, especially those that fit into one of our series, have the best chance of selling to our firm—biology, natural history, usually no garden books."

SANDLAPPER PUBLISHING, INC., P.O. Box 730, Orangeburg SC 29116-0730. (803)531-1658. Fax: (803)534-5223. Acquisitions: Frank N. Handal. Estab. 1982. Publishes hardcover and trade paperback originals and reprints. Averages 6 titles/year; receives 200 submissions annually. 80% of books from first-time authors; 95% of books from unagented writers. Pays 15% maximum royalty on net receipts. Publishes book on average of 20 months after acceptance. Simultaneous submissions OK if informed. Reports in 2 months. Book catalog and ms guidelines for 9 × 12 SAE with 4 first class stamps.

Nonfiction: History, biography, illustrated books, humor, cookbook, juvenile (ages 9-14), reference and textbook. Subjects are limited to history, culture and cuisine of the Southeast and especially South Carolina. "We are looking for manuscripts that reveal underappreciated or undiscovered facets of the rich heritage of our region. If a manuscript doesn't deal with South Carolina or the Southeast, the work is probably not appropriate for us. We don't do self-help books, children's books about divorce, kidnapping, etc., and absolutely no religious manuscripts." Query or submit outline and sample chapters "if you're not sure it's what we're looking for, otherwise complete ms." *Writer's Market* recommends query with SASE first. Reviews artwork/photos as part of ms package.

Fiction: We do not need fiction submissions at present, "and will not consider any horror, romance or religious fiction." Query or submit outline/synopsis and sample chapters. "Do check with us on books dealing with regional nature, science and outdoor subjects."

Tips: "Our readers are South Carolinians, visitors to the region's tourist spots, and friends and family that live out-of-state. We are striving to be a leading regional publisher for South Carolina. We will be looking for more history and biography."

SAS INSTITUTE INC., SAS Campus Dr., Cary NC 27513-8000. (919)677-8000. Fax: (916)677-8166. Acquisitions Editor: David D. Baggett. Estab. 1976. Publishes hardcover and trade paperback originals. Firm averages 40 titles/year. Receives 10 submissions/year. 50% of books from first-time authors. 100% from unagented writers. Payment negotiable. Offers negotiable advance. Query for electronic submissions. Reports in 2 weeks on queries. *Writer's Market* recommends allowing 2 months for reply. Free book catalog and ms guidelines.

Nonfiction: Software, technical, textbook and statistics. "SAS Institute's Publications Division publishes books developed and written in-house. Through the Books by Users program, we also publish books by SAS users on a variety of topics relating to SAS software. We want to provide our users with additional titles to supplement our primary documentation and to enhance the users' ability to use the SAS System effectively. We're interested in publishing manuscripts that describe or illustrate using any of SAS Institute's software products. Books must be aimed at SAS software users, either new or experienced. Tutorials are particularly attractive, as are descriptions of user-written applications for solving real-life business, industry, or academic problems. Books on programming techniques using the SAS language are also desirable. Manuscripts must reflect current or upcoming software releases, and the author's writing should indicate an understanding of the SAS System and the technical aspects covered in the manuscript." Query. Submit outline/synopsis and sample chapters. Reviews artwork/photos as part of ms package.

Recent Nonfiction Title: *SAS Software Solutions: Basic Data Processing*, by Tom Miron.

Tips: "Our readers are SAS software users, both new and experienced. If I were a writer trying to market a book today, I would concentrate on developing a manuscript that teaches or illustrates a specific concept or application that SAS software users will find beneficial in their own environments or can adapt to their own needs."

SASQUATCH BOOKS, 1931 2nd Ave., Seattle WA 98101. (206)441-6202. Fax: (206)441-6213. Managing Editor: Anne Depue. Estab. 1975. Firm publishes regional hardcover and trade paperback originals. Averages 10-15 titles/year. 25% of books from first-time authors; 95% from unagented writers. Pays authors royalty on cover price. Offers wide range of advances. Publishes ms an average of 6 months after acceptance. No simultaneous submissions. Query first. Reports in 2 months. Book catalog for 9×12 SAE with 2 first class stamps.

Nonfiction: Subjects include regional art/architecture, children's books, cooking, foods, gardening, history, nature/environment, recreation, sports and travel. "We are seeking quality nonfiction works about the Pacific Northwest and West Coast regions. In this sense we are a regional publisher, but we do distribute our books nationally." Submit outline and sample chapters.

Recent Nonfiction Title: *My Cousin Has Eight Legs.*

Tips: "We sell books through a range of channels in addition to the book trade. Our audience consists of active, literate residents of the Pacific Northwest."

SCARECROW PRESS, INC., Division of Grolier, 52 Liberty St., P.O. Box 4167, Metuchen NJ 08840-1279. Fax: (908)548-5767. President: Albert W. Daub. Vice President, Editorial: Norman Horrocks. Estab. 1950. Publishes hardcover originals. Averages 110 titles/year; receives 600-700 submissions annually. 70% of books from first-time authors; 100% of books from unagented writers. Average print order for a writer's first book is 1,000. Pays 10% royalty on net of first 1,000 copies; 15% of net price thereafter. 15% initial royalty on camera-ready copy. Offers no advance. Publishes book 6-18 months after receipt of ms. Query for electronic submissions. Reports in 1 month. *Writer's Market* recommends allowing 2 months for reply. Book catalog for 9×12 SAE and 4 first class stamps.

Nonfiction: Needs reference books and meticulously prepared annotated bibliographies, indexes and books on women's studies, music, movies and stage. Query. Occasionally reviews artwork/photos as part of ms package.

Tips: "Essentially we consider any scholarly title likely to appeal to libraries. Emphasis is on reference material, but this can be interpreted broadly, provided author is knowledgeable in the subject field."

SCHIFFER PUBLISHING LTD., 77 Lower Valley Rd., Atglen PA 19310. (215)593-1777. Fax: (215)593-2002. President: Peter Schiffer. Estab. 1972. Imprint is Whitford Press. Publishes hardcover and trade paperback originals and reprints. Firm averages 100 titles/year; imprint averages 40 titles/year. Receives 500 submissions/year. 90% of books from first-time authors. 95% from unagented writers. Royalty on wholesale price. Publishes book an average of 6 months after acceptance. Simultaneous submissions OK. Reports in 2 weeks on queries. Free book catalog.

Nonfiction: Coffee table book, how-to, illustrated book, reference and textbook. Subjects include Americana, art/architecture, aviation, history, hobbies, military/war and regional. "We want books on collecting, hobby carving, military, architecture, aeronautic history and natural history." Query with SASE. Submit outline and sample chapters. Reviews artwork/photos as part of ms package.

SCHIRMER BOOKS, Imprint of Macmillan Publishing Co., 866 3rd Ave., New York NY 10022. Fax: (212)605-9368. Editor-in-Chief: Maribeth Anderson Payne. Editor: Jonathan Wiener. Assistant Editor: Soo Mee Kwon. Publishes hardcover and paperback originals, related audio recordings, paperback reprints and some software. Averages 20 books/year; receives 250 submissions annually. 25% of books from first-time authors; 75% of books from unagented writers. Submit photos and/or illustrations only "if central to the book, not if decorative or tangential." Publishes book an average of 1 year after acceptance. Query for electronic submissions. Reports in 4 months. Book catalog and ms guidelines for SASE.

Nonfiction: Publishes college texts, biographies, scholarly, reference, and trade on the performing arts specializing in music, film and theatre. Submit outline/synopsis and sample chapters and current vita. Reviews artwork/photos as part of ms package.

Recent Nonfiction Title: *Black and Blue: The Life and Lyrics of Andy Razof,* by Barry Singer.

Tips: "The writer has the best chance of selling our firm a music book with a clearly defined, reachable audience, either scholarly or trade. Must be an exceptionally well-written work of original scholarship prepared by an expert in the field who has a thorough understanding of correct manuscript style and attention to detail (see the *Chicago Manual of Style*)."

SCHOLASTIC, INC., 730 Broadway, New York NY 10003. (212)505-3000. Editorial Director: Bonnie Verburg. Estab. 1920. Publishes trade paperback originals and hardcovers. Pays royalty on retail price. Reports in 3 months. Ms guidelines for #10 SASE.

Nonfiction: Publishes general nonfiction. Query.

Recent Nonfiction Title: *One More River to Cross,* by Jim Haskins.

Fiction: Family stories, mysteries, school, and friendships for ages 8-12, 35,000 words. YA fiction, romance, family and mystery for ages 12-15, 40,000-45,000 words for average to good readers. Query. Not accepting unsolicited mss at this time.

Tips: Queries may be routed to other editors in the publishing group.

SCHOLASTIC PROFESSIONAL BOOKS, 730 Broadway, New York NY 10003. Publishing Director: Claudia Cohl. Editor-in-Chief: Terry Cooper. Editorial Coordinator: Jaime Lucero. Buys 35-40 manuscripts/year from published or unpublished writers. "Writer should have background working in the classroom with elementary or middle school children and developing quality, appropriate, and innovative learning experiences and/or solid background in developing supplementary educational materials for these markets." Offers standard contract. Reports in 2 months. Book catalog for 9 × 12 SAE.

Nonfiction: Elementary and middle-school level enrichment — all subject areas, whole language, theme units, integrated materials, writing process, management techniques, teaching strategies based on personal/professional experience in the classroom. Models and strategies for restructuring, site-based management, shared decision-making. Production is limited to printed matter: resource and activity books, professional development materials, reference titles. Length: 6,000-12,000 words. Query should include table of contents.

CHARLES SCRIBNER'S SONS, Children's Books Department, Imprint of Macmillan Publishing Co., 866 3rd Ave., New York NY 10022. (212)702-7885. Editorial Director, Children's Books: Clare Costello. Estab. 1846. Other children's book imprints are Atheneum, Margaret K. McElderry Books, Bradbury Press, Four Winds, Crestwood and Aladdin. Publishes hardcover originals. Averages 20-25 titles/year. Pays royalty on retail price; offers advance. Publishes book an average of 1 year after acceptance. Reports in 1 month on queries. *Writer's Market* recommends allowing 2 months for reply. Free book catalog and ms guidelines.

Nonfiction: Subjects include animals, biography, health, history, nature, science, self-help, sports for ages 3-14. Query. Reviews artwork/photos as part of ms package.

Recent Nonfiction Title: *We Shall Overcome*, by Fred Powledge.

Fiction: Adventure, fantasy, historical, humor, mystery, picture books, science fiction and suspense. Submit outline/synopsis and sample chapters.

Recent Fiction Title: *Letters From a Slave Girl*, by Mary E. Lyons.

‡SERVANT PUBLICATIONS, 840 Airport Blvd., P.O. Box 8617, Ann Arbor MI 48107. (313)761-8505. Editorial Director: Ann Spangler. Estab. 1972. Imprint is Vine Books, "especially for evanglical Protestant readers." Publishes hardcover, trade and mass market paperback originals and trade paperback reprints. Averages 40 titles/year. 5% of books from first-time authors; 85% of books from unagented writers. Publishes book an average of 1 year after acceptance. Reports in 2 months. Free book catalog for 9 × 12 SASE.

Nonfiction: "We're looking for practical Christian teaching, biblical psychology, scripture, current problems facing the Christian church, and inspiration." No heterodox or non-Christian approaches. Query or submit brief outline/synopsis and 1 sample chapter. All unsolicited queries and mss are returned unopened. Only accept queries from agents or from published authors.

Recent Nonfiction Title: *Rediscovering Holiness*, by James I. Packer.

Fiction: Historical fiction; will accept unsolicited queries. Submit brief outline/synopsis and 1 sample chapter.

Recent Fiction Title: *The Bird in the Tree*, by Elizabeth Goudge.

SEVGO PRESS, 1955 22nd St., Northport AL 35476-4250. Publisher: John Seymour. Publishes hardcover and trade paperback originals. Publishes 6 titles/year (nonsubsidy). Receives 30 queries and 20 mss/year. 90% of books from first-time authors; 90% from unagented writers. We no longer do subsidy publishing. Determined by marketability. Pays 10% royalty on wholesale price. Publishes book 6 months after ms is accepted. Reports in 1 month on queries. *Writer's Market* recommends allowing 2 months for reply. Book catalog for #10 SASE with 2 first class stamps. Manuscript guidelines for #10 SASE.

Nonfiction: Biography, cookbook, how-to and textbook. Subjects include cooking, foods and nutrition, education, history (local), military/war and regional. Query.

Fiction: Humor, drama and juvenile. Query.

HAROLD SHAW PUBLISHERS, 388 Gundersen Dr., P.O. Box 567, Wheaton IL 60189. (708)665-6700. Director of Editorial Services: Ramona Cramer Tucker. Estab. 1967. Publishes mostly trade paperback originals and reprints. Averages 32 titles/year; receives 4,000 submissions annually. 10% of books from first-time authors; 90% of books from unagented writers. Offers 5-10% royalty on retail price. Sometimes makes outright purchase for $1,000-2,500. Publishes book an average of 12-15 months after acceptance. Reports in 1 month on queries. *Writer's Market* recommends allowing 2 months for reply. Book catalog and ms guidelines for 9 × 12 SAE with 5 first class stamps.

Nonfiction and Fiction: Subjects include marriage, family and parenting, self-help and spiritual growth and Bible study. "We are looking for general nonfiction, with different twists — self-help manuscripts on issues and topics with fresh insight and colorful, vibrant writing style. No autobiographies or biographies accepted. Must have an evangelical Christian perspective for us even to review the ms." Query. Reviews artwork/photos as part of ms package.

Recent Nonfiction Title: *Finding Your Place After Divorce: Help and Hope for Women Who Are Starting Again*, by Carole Sanderson Streeter.

Tips: "Get an editor who is not a friend or a spouse who will tell you honestly whether your book is marketable. It will save a lot of your time and money and effort. Then do an honest evaluation. Who would actually read the book other than yourself? If it won't sell at least 5,000 copies, it's not very marketable and most publishers wouldn't be interested."

SIERRA CLUB BOOKS, Dept. WM, 100 Bush St., San Francisco CA 94104. (415)291-1600. Fax: (415)291-1602. Senior Editor: James Cohee. Estab. 1962. Publishes hardcover and paperback originals and reprints. Averages 20 titles/year; receives 1,000 submissions annually. 50% of books from unagented writers. Royalties vary by project. Offers average $3,000-15,000 advance. Publishes book an average of 12-18 months after acceptance. Reports in 2 months. Free book catalog.

Nonfiction: Animals; health; history (natural); how-to (outdoors); juveniles; nature; philosophy; photography; recreation (outdoors, nonmechanical); science; sports (outdoors); and travel (by foot or bicycle). "The Sierra Club was founded to help people to explore, enjoy and preserve the nation's forests, waters, wildlife and wilderness. The books program looks to publish quality trade books about the outdoors and the protection of natural resources. Specifically, we are interested in literary natural history, environmental issues such as nuclear power, self-sufficiency, politics and travel, and juvenile books with an ecological theme." Does *not* want "proposals for large color photographic books without substantial text; how-to books on building things outdoors; books on motorized travel; or any but the most professional studies of animals." Query first, submit outline and sample chapters. Reviews artwork/photos ("duplicates, not originals") as part of ms package.

Fiction: Adventure, historical, mainstream and ecological fiction. "We do very little fiction, but will consider a fiction manuscript if its theme fits our philosophical aims: the enjoyment and protection of the environment. Does *not* want any manuscript with animals or plants that talk; apocalyptic plots." Query first, submit outline/synopsis and sample chapters.

SIGNATURE BOOKS, Suite G4, 350 S. 400 E., Salt Lake City UT 84111. (801)531-1483. Fax: (801)531-1488. Publisher: Gary Bergera. Publishes hardcover originals and trade and mass market paperback originals. Publishes 12 titles/year. Receives 100 queries and 100 mss/year. 10% of mss from first-time authors, 100% from unagented writers. Pays royalty. Publishes book 1 year after acceptance of ms. Simultaneous submissions OK. Query for electronic submissions. Reports in 6 months on proposals. Book catalog and ms guidelines free on request.

Nonfiction: Biography, humor and essays. Subjects include Americana (western), gay/lesbian, history, religion (predominantly Mormon) and women's issues/studies. "We prefer manuscripts in Utah/western studies. Familiarize yourself with our backlist before submitting a proposal." Submit proposal package, including 2-3 sample chapters. Reviews artwork/photos as part of freelance ms package. Writers should send photocopies.

Fiction: Historical, humor or religious. Query or submit synopsis.

Poetry: Submit complete ms.

Tips: "We have a general adult audience that is somewhat Mormon-oriented."

SILHOUETTE BOOKS, 300 E. 42nd St., New York NY 10017. (212)682-6080. Fax: (212)682-4539. Editorial Director, Silhouette Books, Harlequin historicals: Isabel Swift. Estab. 1979. Other divisions are Harlequin Books, Gold Eagle Books and Worldwide Library. Publishes mass market paperback originals. Averages 316 titles/year; receives 4,000 submissions annually. 10% of books from first-time authors; 25% of books from unagented writers. Pays royalty. Publishes book an average of 1 year after acceptance. No unsolicited mss. Send query letter, 2 page synopsis and SASE to head of imprint. Ms guidelines for #10 SASE.

Imprints: Silhouette Romances (contemporary adult romances), Anne Canadeo, Senior Editor; 53,000-58,000 words. Silhouette Special Editions (contemporary adult romances), Tara Gavin, Senior Editor; 75,000-80,000 words. Silhouette Desires (contemporary adult romances), Lucia Macro, Senior Editor; 55,000-60,000 words. Silhouette Intimate Moments (contemporary adult romances), Silhouette Shadows (contemporary adult gothic romances), Leslie Wainger, Senior Editor and Editorial Coordinator; 80,000-85,000 words. Harlequin Historicals (adult historical romances), Tracy Farrell, Senior Editor; 95,000-105,000 words.

Fiction: Romance (contemporary and historical romance for adults). "We are interested in seeing submissions for all our lines. No manuscripts other than the types outlined above. Ms should follow our general format, yet have an individuality and life of its own that will make it stand out in the readers' minds."

Recent Fiction Title: *Dragonslayer*, by Emilie Richards.

Tips: "The romance market is constantly changing, so when you read for research, read the latest books and those that have been recommended to you by people knowledgeable in the genre. We are actively seeking new authors for all our lines, contemporary and historical."

SIMON & SCHUSTER, Trade Books Division, 1230 Avenue of the Americas, New York NY 10020. Imprints and divisions include Pocket Books, Prentice Hall, and Silver Burdett Press. "We do not accept unsolicited manuscripts. Only manuscripts submitted by agents will be considered."

Nonfiction and Fiction: General adult fiction, history, biography, science, philosophy, the arts and popular culture, running 50,000 words or more. "Our program does not, however, include school textbooks, extremely technical or highly specialized works, or, as a general rule, poetry or plays. Exceptions have been made, of course, for extraordinary manuscripts of great distinction or significance."
● Published a winner of the 18th annual National Book Critics Circle Award—Gary Wills' *Lincoln at Gettysburg: The Words that Remade America*.

‡SKY PUBLISHING CORP., 49 Bay State Rd., Cambridge MA 02138. (617)864-7360. Director, Books & Products Division: Stephen Peters. Publishes hardcover and trade paperback originals. Publishes 6 titles/year. Receives 25 queries and 12 mss/year. 20% of mss from first-time authors, 95% from unagented writers. Pays 10-15% royalty on retail price. Publishes book 6 months after acceptance of ms. Query for electronic submissions. Reports in 2 months on proposals. Book catalog free on request.
Nonfiction: Biography, coffee table book, how-to, illustrated book, reference, technical and textbook. Subjects include hobbies (amateur astronomy), nature/environment, photography and science (astronomy/space). "Sky Publishing specializes in books on astronomy and space science, for all ages and levels of experience. Writers should have a clear idea of the audience or market for the book." Submit outline and 1 sample chapter or proposal package, including outline of chapters, brief description of book, resume. Reviews artwork/photos as part of the freelance ms package. Writers should send art/illustration plan.
Recent Nonfiction Title: *Starhopping for Backyard Astronomers*, by Mac Robert (how-to guide).

SLAWSON COMMUNICATIONS, INC., Suite E, 2075 Corte Del Nogal, Carlsbad CA 92009-1414. (619)929-1979. Subsidiaries include Microtrend®. CEO: Leslie S. Smith. Computer Book Editor: Lance A. Leventhal. Estab. 1983. Publishes trade paperback originals. Firm averages 24 titles/year. Receives 100 submissions/year. 60% of books are from first-time authors. 90% from unagented writers. Pays 10-15% royalty on wholesale price. Offers $1,000-10,000 average advance. Publishes book an average of 6 months after acceptance. Simultaneous submissions OK. Reports in 2 weeks on queries. *Writer's Market* recommends allowing 2 months for reply. Book catalog for $2.50.
Nonfiction: Software, technical, programming and application books. Subjects include computers. Submit outline and sample chapters. Reviews artwork/photos as part of ms package.
Recent Nonfiction Title: *C/C++ Programmer's Guide to Using PC BIOS*.

GIBBS SMITH, PUBLISHER, Dept. WM, P.O. Box 667, Layton UT 84041. (801)544-9800. Editorial Director: Madge Baird. Estab. 1969. Imprint is Peregrine Smith Books. Publishes hardcover and paperback originals and reprints. Averages 25-30 titles/year; receives 2,000 submissions annually. 25% of books from first-time authors; 40% of books from unagented writers. Average print order for a writer's first book is 3,000-4,000. Starts at 8% royalty on wholesale price. Offers average $1,000 advance. Publishes book an average of 1½ years after acceptance. Reports in 2 months. Book catalog for 6×9 SAE and 3 first class stamps; ms guidelines for #10 SASE.
Nonfiction: Subjects include cowboy western, western American history, natural history, architecture, art history, and fine arts. "We consider biographical, historical, and descriptive studies in all of the above. Emphasis is also placed on pictorial content." Query. Reviews artwork/photos as part of ms package.
Recent Nonfiction Title: *The Cowboy Boot Book*, text by Tyler Beard, photos by Jim Arndt.
Tips: "We are interested in work with a broad general appeal or a strong regional western interest: We want to publish books that have strong gift appeal."

THE SMITH, The Generalist Association, Inc., 69 Joralemon St., Brooklyn NY 11201. (718)834-1212. Publisher: Harry Smith. Estab. 1964. Publishes hardcover and trade paperback originals. Averages 5 titles/year. Receives 2,500 queries/year. 50% of mss from first-time authors; more than 90% from unagented writers. Pays royalty. Offers $500-1,000 advance. Publishes book 9 months after acceptance. Simultaneous submissions OK. Reports in 3 months. Book catalog free on request.
Nonfiction: Literary essays, language and literature. "The 'how' is as important as the 'what' to us. Don't bother to send anything if the prose is not outstanding itself. We don't publish anything about how to fix your car or your soul." Query or submit proposal package including outline and sample chapter. Reviews artwork/photos as part of freelance ms package. Writers should send photocopies.
Recent Nonfiction Title: *Crank Letters*, by Kirby Congdon (letters).
Fiction: Experimental, fantasy, feminist, literary, science fiction. "Emphasis is always on artistic quality. A synopsis of almost any novel sounds stupid." Query or submit 1 sample chapter.
Recent Fiction Title: *The Cleveland Indian*, by Luke Salisbury.
Poetry: "No greeting card sentiments, no casual jottings. Do not send complete ms." Submit 7-10 sample poems.
Recent Poetry Title: *Matriarch*, by Glenna Luschei.

SOCIAL SCIENCE EDUCATION CONSORTIUM, Suite 240, 3300 Mitchell Lane, Boulder CO 80301-2272. (303)492-8154. Fax: (303)449-3925. Managing Editor: Laurel R. Singleton. Estab. 1963. Publishes trade paperback originals. Publishes 8 titles/year. 25% of mss from first-time authors, 100% from unagented writers.

Pays 8-12% royalty, net sales (retail price minus average discount). Publishes book 6 months after acceptance of ms. Simultaneous submissions OK. Query for electronic submissions. Reports in 1 month on proposals. *Writer's Market* recommends allowing 2 months for reply.

Nonfiction: Teacher resources. Subjects include education, government/politics and history. "We publish titles of interest to social studies teachers particularly; we do not generally publish on such broad educational topics as discipline, unless there is a specific relationship to the social studies/social sciences." Submit outline and 1-2 sample chapters.

SOHO PRESS, INC., 853 Broadway, New York NY 10003. (212)260-1900. Editor-in-Chief: Juris Jurjevics. Estab. 1986. Publishes hardcover and trade paperback originals. Firm averages 25 titles/year. Receives 4,000 submissions/year. 75% of books from first-time authors. 50% of books from unagented writers. Pays 10-15% on retail price. Publishes book an average of 1 year after acceptance. Simultaneous submissions OK. Reports in 2 months. Book catalog for 6×9 SAE with 2 first class stamps.

Nonfiction: Biography. "We want literary nonfiction: travel, autobiography, biography, etc. No self-help." Submit outline and sample chapters.

Recent Nonfiction Title: *O Come Ye Back to Ireland*, by Niall Williams and Christine Breen (travel and biography).

Fiction: Adventure, ethnic, feminist, historical, literary, mainstream/contemporary, mystery and suspense. Submit complete ms with SASE. *Writer's Market* recommends query with SASE first.

Recent Fiction Title: *The Woman Who Married a Bear*, by John Straley.

SOUNDPRINTS, Division of Trudy Management Corporation, P.O. Box 679, Norwalk CT 06856. Contact: Editor. Publishes hardcover originals. Publishes 9-12 titles/year. Receives 50 queries and unsolicited ms/year. 90% of mss from unagented writers. Makes outright purchase or pays royalty on wholesale price. Publishes book 1-2 years after acceptance of ms. Simultaneous submissions OK. Reports on queries in 1 month. *Writer's Market* recommends allowing 2 months for reply. Book catalog free on request. Manuscript guidelines for #10 SASE.

Nonfiction: Children's/juvenile, animals. "We focus on North American wildlife and ecology. Subject animals must be portrayed realistically and must not be anthropomorphic. Meticulous research is required." Query. Reviews artwork/photos as part of freelance ms package, although we usually contract with a separate illustrator. (All of our books are now being illustrated in full color.)

Fiction: Juvenile. "When we publish juvenile fiction, it will be about wildlife and all information in the book *must* be accurate." Query.

Tips: "Our books are written for children from ages 4-8. Our most successful authors can craft a wonderful story which is derived from authentic wildlife facts. First inquiry to us should ask about our interest in publishing a book about a specific animal."

SOURCEBOOKS, INC., (formerly Financial Sourcebooks), P.O. Box 313, Naperville IL 60566. (312)961-2161. Publisher: Dominique Raccah. Estab. 1987. Publishes hardcover and trade paperback originals. Firm averages 15 titles/year. 50% of books from first-time authors; 100% from unagented writers. Pays 5-15% royalty on wholesale price, or buys mss outright. Publishes book an average of 6 months after acceptance. Simultaneous submissions OK. Query for electronic submissions. Reports in 3 months on queries. "We do not want to see complete mss." Book catalog and ms guidelines free for 8×10 SASE.

Nonfiction: *Small Business Sourcebooks:* books for small business owners, entrepreneurs and students. "A key to submitting books to us is to explain *how* your book helps the reader, *why* it is different from the books already out there (please do your homework) and the *author's credentials* for writing this book." *Financial Sourcebooks:* economics, finance, banking and insurance, directories and reference materials for financial executives. *Sourcebook Trade:* self-help and how to. "Books likely to succeed with us are self-help, New Age, psychology, women's issues, how-to, house and home, gift books or books with strong artwork." Query or submit outline and sample chapters (2-3 chapters, not the first). Reviews artwork/photos as part of ms package.

Recent Nonfiction Title: *Future Vision: The 189 Most Important Trends of the 1990s.*

Tips: "Executives today are bombarded with information in most every form through much of their working day. Writers can easily sell us books that will help a busy professional deal with the workload more productively. That means books that 1.) compile otherwise difficult to obtain (but useful) information; or 2.) develop new concepts or ideas that will help executives 'work smarter'; or 3.) reformat concepts or information executives need into some more useful or digestible form (e.g., graphics, tutorials, etc.)."

SOUTH END PRESS, 116 Saint Botolph St., Boston MA 02115. (617)266-0629. Fax: (617)266-1595. Contact: Dionne Brooks. Publishes hardcover and trade paperback originals and reprints. Publishes 15 titles/year. Receives 400 queries and 100 mss/year. 50% of mss from first-time authors, 95% from unagented writers. Pays 10% royalty on wholesale price. Occasionally offers $500-2,500 advance. Publishes book 9 months after acceptance of ms. Simultaneous submissions OK. Query for electronic submissions. Reports in up to 3 months on queries and proposals. Book catalog and ms guidelines free on request.

Nonfiction: Subjects include economics, education, ethnic, gay/lesbian, government/politics, health/medicine, history, military/war, music/dance, nature/environment, philosophy, science, sociology, women's issues/studies and political. "We publish books with a new left/feminist multi-cultural perspective." Query or submit 2 sample chapters including intro or conclusion. Reviews artwork/photos as part of the freelance ms package. Writers should send photocopies.
Recent Nonfiction Title: *Year 501*, by Noam Chomsky (political).

‡**SOUTH WIND PUBLISHING**, 342 Overdale St., Morgantown WV 26505. (304)291-1748. Editorial Assistant: Jenny Dunkerly. Publishes trade paperback originals. Publishes 5-10 titles/year. Pays 5-10% royalty on wholesale/retail price. Sometimes offers very small advance. Publishes book 6-18 months after acceptance of ms. Simultaneous submissions OK. Query for electronic submissions: prefers IBM formatted disk (either size); ASCII format. Reports in 1 month on queries, 2 months on proposals, 3 months on mss. Book catalog and ms guidelines for #10 SASE.
Nonfiction: Biography, history, illustrated book, children's/juvenile. Subjects include regional history, nature/environment, recreation and travel. "We will consider diverse nonfiction titles and plan to branch out into juvenile nonfiction in the coming years." Query with outline and 2 sample chapters or submit proposal package, including resume, writing samples, 2 sample chapters or detailed outline. Reviews artwork/photos as part of freelance ms package. Writers should send photocopies. "Do not send original manuscript, photos or artwork. We do not guarantee safe return of these."
Recent Nonfiction Title: *The Complete Guide to West Virginia Inns*, by Mary Furbee (travel guide).
Fiction: Regional/Appalachia. "We might consider regional fiction. Query first." Send query only.
Tips: "Our audience is interested in the culture, history, and natural world of West Virginia and the Appalachian mountains. We are looking for extremely well-written books that are detailed, practical, entertaining, informative, descriptive and/or well-organized."

SOUTHERN ILLINOIS UNIVERSITY PRESS, P.O. Box 3697, Carbondale IL 62901-3697. (618)453-2281. Fax: (618)453-1221. Director: TBA. Editorial Director: Curtis Clark. Averages 60 titles/year; receives 500 submissions annually. 50% of books from first-time authors; 99% of books from unagented writers. Publishes book an average of 1 year after acceptance. Reports in 2 months. Free book catalog.
Nonfiction: "We are interested in scholarly nonfiction on the humanities, social sciences and contemporary affairs. No dissertations or collections of previously published articles." Accepts nonfiction translations from French, German, Scandinavian and Hebrew. Query.
Recent Nonfiction Title: *Shattered Applause: The Lives of Eva Le Gallienne*, by Robert A. Schanke.

‡**SOUTHERN METHODIST UNIVERSITY PRESS**, P.O. Box 415, Dallas TX 75275. Senior Editor: Kathryn Lang. Publishes hardcover and trade paperback originals and reprints. Publishes 10-15 titles/year. Receives 500 queries and 500 mss/year. 75% of mss from first-time authors, 95% from unagented writers. Pays up to 10% royalty on wholesale price. Offers $500 advance. Publishes book 1 year after acceptance of ms. Query for electronic submissions. Reports in 1 month on queries and proposals, 3 months on mss.
Nonfiction: Biography. Subjects include medical ethics/human values, history (regional), language/literature and regional. "We are seeking works on the following areas: theology; film/theater; regional; medical ethics/human values." Query with outline, 3 sample chapters and table of contents. Reviews artwork/photos as part of the freelance ms package. Writers should send photocopies.
Recent Nonfiction Title: *Images of Australia*, by Neil Rattigan (film study).
Fiction: Literary and short story collections. Query.
Tips: Audience is general educated readers of quality fiction and nonfiction.

‡**SOUTHPARK PUBLISHING GROUP, INC.**, Suite 156-359, 4041 W. Wheatland Rd., Dallas TX 75237-9991. (214)296-5657. Managing Editor: Ms. Susan Watson. Publishes trade paperback originals. Publishes 6+ titles/year. Receives 50+ queries/year and 10 mss/year. 25% of mss from first-time authors, 100% from unagented writers. Pays 10-15% royalty on retail price. Publishes book 9 months after acceptance. Simultaneous submissions OK. Reports on queries in 2 months. Book catalog and ms guidelines for #10 SASE.
Nonfiction: How-to, self-help, travel guides. Subjects include hobbies, recreation, travel for and by disabled people. "Our intent is to publish a series of domestic and international travel, how-to and self-help guidebooks." Query. Reviews artwork/photos as part of freelance ms package (upon request).
Recent Nonfiction Title: *Handicapped in Walt Disney World*, by Peter Smith (guidebook).
Tips: "Our audience is the general public."

‡**SOUTHWEST PUBLISHING COMPANY OF ARIZONA**, #194, 9666 E. Riggs Rd., Sun Lakes AZ 85248. (602)895-7995. Editor: Barbara DeBolt. Imprints are: Gold Star (for senior market); Midnight Star (mysteries); Western Star (westerns/sagas); Native Star (Native Americans). Publishes trade and mass market paperback originals. Publishes 15-20 titles/year. Receives 500 queries and 400-500 mss/year. 99% of mss from first-time authors, 100% from unagented writers. Pays 10-20% royalty on wholesale or retail price. Query for electronic submissions. Reports in 1 month on queries, 2 months on proposals, 4 months on mss. Book catalog free on request. Manuscript guidelines for #10 SASE.

Nonfiction: How-to and self-help. Subjects include philosophy and religion (metaphysical). "As a small press we prefer not to have a lot of photographs for inclusion in publications as they are expensive to print. We do very little nonfiction at this time but are always looking." Query. Reviews artwork/photos as part of the freelance ms package. Writers should send photocopies.

Recent Nonfiction Title: *How To Write a Bestseller in 40 Days or Less!*, by Barbara DeBolt (how-to).

Fiction: Adventure, fantasy, gothic, historical, mainstream/contemporary, mystery, occult, religious (metaphysical), romance (not genre), science fiction (UFOs), suspense and western. "As a small press, we are doing everything possible for our authors with regard to distribution, etc. Some authors come to us knowing we are small yet expect celebrity results." Query or submit synopsis and 3 sample chapters.

Recent Fiction Title: *Treasure in the Jungle Mist*, by Bill J. Harrison (adventure/mystery).

Tips: Audience is "general, senior (retired), 30+. Know our no-advance policy beforehand and know our guidelines. No response ever without a SASE. Absolutely no phone queries."

THE SPEECH BIN, INC., 1965 25th Ave., Vero Beach FL 32960. (407)770-0007. Fax: (407)770-0006. Senior Editor: Jan Binney. Estab. 1984. Publishes trade paperback originals. Publishes 10-20 titles/year. Receives 200-250 manuscripts per year. 50% of books from first-time authors; 90% from unagented writers. Pays negotiable royalty on wholesale price. Publishes ms average of 6 months after acceptance. Query for electronic submissions. Do not Fax manuscripts. Reports in up to 3 months. Book catalog for 9×12 SASE.

Nonfiction: How-to, illustrated book, juvenile (preschool-teen), reference, textbook, educational material and games for both children and adults. Subjects include health, communication disorders and education for handicapped persons. Query or submit outline and sample chapters. Reviews artwork/photos as part of ms package. Do not send original artwork; photocopies only, please.

Recent Nonfiction Title: *Articu-Action*, by Denise Grigas.

Fiction: "Booklets or books for children and adults about handicapped persons, especially with communication disorders." Query or submit outline/synopsis and sample chapters. "This is a potentially new market for The Speech Bin."

Tips: "Our audience is made up of special educators, speech-language pathologists and audiologists, parents, caregivers, and teachers of children and adults with developmental and post-trauma disabilities. Books and materials must be research-based, clearly presented, well written, competently illustrated, and unique. We'll be adding books and materials for use by occupational and physical therapists and other allied health professionals. We are also looking for more materials for use in treating adults and very young children with communication disorders. Please do not fax manuscripts to us."

SPINSTERS INK, (formerly Spinsters Book Company), P.O. Box 300170, Minneapolis MN 55403. (612)377-0287. Editor: Kelly Kager. Estab. 1978. Publishes trade paperback originals and reprints. Averages 6-8 titles/year; receives 200 submissions annually. 50% of books from first-time authors; 95% of books from unagented writers. Pays 7-11% royalty on retail price. Publishes book an average of 18 months after acceptance. Reports in 2 months. Free book catalog; ms guidelines for SASE.

Nonfiction: Self-help and feminist analysis for positive change. Subjects include women's issues. "We are interested in books that not only name the crucial issues in women's lives, but show and encourage change and growth. We do not want to see work by men, or anything that is not specific to women's lives (humor, childrens' books, etc.)." Query. Reviews artwork/photos as part of ms package.

Recent Nonfiction Title: *Lesbians at Midlife*.

Fiction: Ethnic, women's, lesbian. "We do not publish poetry or short fiction. We are interested in fiction that challenges language, that is feminist, that treats lesbian lifestyles with the diversity and complexity they deserve. We are also interested in genre fiction, especially mysteries." Submit outline/synopsis and sample chapters.

Recent Fiction Title: *The Two-Bit Tango*, by Elizabeth Pincus (lesbian mystery).

ST PUBLICATIONS, INC., Signs of the Times Publishing Co., Book Division, 407 Gilbert Ave., Cincinnati OH 45202. (513)421-2050. Fax: (513)421-5144. Book Division Publisher: Tod Swormstedt. Estab. 1957. Publishes hardcover and trade paperback originals and hardcover reprints. Averages 6 titles/year. 50% of books from first-time authors; 100% of books from unagented writers. Pays royalty on wholesale price: 10% until recovery of production costs; 12½% thereafter; and 15% on straight reprints. Publishes book an average of 9 months after acceptance. Reports in 6 weeks on queries. *Writer's Market* recommends allowing 2 months for reply. Free book catalog and ms guidelines.

Nonfiction: "We need technical how-to books for professionals in three specific industries: the sign industry, including outdoor advertising, electric and commercial signs; the screen printing industry, including the printing of paper products, fabrics, ceramics, glass and electronic circuits; and the visual merchandising and store design industry. We are not interested in submissions that do not relate specifically to those three fields." Submit outline and sample chapters. Reviews artwork/photos as part of ms package.

Recent Nonfiction Title: *Sign Design Gallery*.

Tips: "The writer has the best chance of selling our firm how-to books related to our industries: signs, screen printing, and visual merchandising. These are the fields our marketing and distribution channels are geared to. Request copies of, and thoroughly absorb the information presented in, our trade magazines (*Signs of the*

Times, Identity, VM&SD, Screenplay and *Screen Printing*). Our books are permanent packages of this type of information. We are taking a closer look at submissions that we can sell outside our primary range of customers, yet still confining our subject interests to sign painting and design, visual merchandising, display and store design, and screen printing (both technical and art aspects)."

STACKPOLE BOOKS, Company of Commonwealth Communications Services, P.O. Box 1831, Harrisburg PA 17105. Fax: (717)234-1359. Editorial Director: Judith Schnell. Estab. 1935. Publishes hardcover and paperback originals. Publishes 70 titles/year. Publishes book an average of 1 year after acceptance. Reports in 1 month. *Writer's Market* recommends allowing 2 months for reply.
Nonfiction: Outdoor-related subject areas — fishing, hunting, wildlife, adventure, outdoor skills, gardening, decoy carving/woodcarving, outdoor sports, crafts, military guides and history. Submit proposal. Reviews artwork/photos as part of ms package.
Recent Nonfiction Title: *The Canoe Handbook*, by Slim Ray.
Tips: "Stackpole seeks well-written, authoritative manuscripts for specialized and general trade markets. Proposals should include chapter outline, sample chapter and illustrations and author's credentials."

STANDARD PUBLISHING, Division of Standex International Corp., 8121 Hamilton Ave., Cincinnati OH 45231. (513)931-4050. Publisher/Vice President: Eugene H. Wigginton. Estab. 1866. Publishes hardcover and paperback originals and reprints. Specializes in religious books for children. Publishes book an average of 18 months after acceptance. Reports in 3 months. Ms guidelines for #10 SASE.
• Standard has developed a new series of early readers for 1st and 2nd graders.
Nonfiction: Publishes how-to; crafts (to be used in Christian education); juveniles; Christian education; quiz; puzzle. All mss must pertain to religion. Query.
Recent Nonfiction Title: *Great Ideas V.B.S.*, by John Cetshall.
Fiction: Religious, contemporary for ages 8-11 or 12-15.
Recent Fiction Title: *A Place in the Palace*, by Carol Reinsma.
Tips: "Children's books (picture books, ages 4-7), juvenile fiction (8-11 and 12-15), Christian education, activity books, and helps for Christian parents and church leaders are the types of books writers have the best chance of selling to our firm."

STANFORD UNIVERSITY PRESS, Stanford CA 94305-2235. (415)723-9598. Editor-in-Chief: Norris Pope. Estab. 1925. Averages 75 titles/year; receives 1,500 submissions annually. 40% of books from first-time authors. 95% of books from unagented writers. Subsidy (nonauthor) publishes 65% of books. Pays up to 15% royalty ("typically 10%, often none"); sometimes offers advance. Publishes book an average of 1 year after receipt of final manuscript. Query for electronic submissions. Reports in 6 weeks. Free book catalog.
Nonfiction: Scholarly books in the humanities, social sciences, and natural sciences: history and culture of China, Japan, and Latin America; European history; biology, natural history, and taxonomy; anthropology, linguistics, and psychology; literature, criticism, and literary theory; political science and sociology; archaeology and geology; and medieval and classical studies. Also high-level textbooks and books for a more general audience. Query. "We like to see a prospectus and an outline." Reviews artwork/photos as part of ms package.
Tips: "The writer's best chance is a work of original scholarship with an argument of some importance."

STAR BOOKS INC., 408 Pearson St., Wilson NC 27893-1850. (919)237-1591. President: Allen W. Harrell. Estab. 1982. Firm averages 9-15 titles/year. 90% of books from first-time authors. 100% from unagented writers. Pays 10-15% royalty on retail price. Offers no advance. Publishes book an average of 1 year after acceptance. Reports in 4 months.
• No book length mss for now.
Nonfiction: Biography, humor, juvenile, self-help. Subjects include abortion, alcoholism, biography, Christian testimony, cartoons (Christian), devotionals, divorce, personal experiences (specifically Christian), prayer (devotional books), rape. "We are looking for first-person accounts (testimonies) by persons who have found God's answers for the difficult problems of life. No third-person, impersonal, researched material." Submit complete ms. *Writer's Market* recommends query with SASE first. Reviews artwork/photos (b&w only) as part of ms package.
Fiction: Adventure, confession, ethnic, fantasy, humor, juvenile, picture books (b&w only), poetry (with Christian focus), novels (biblical or contemporary Christian), short stories (Christian), religious, romance, short story collections, young adult. All must have strong Christian focus. "We don't want to see anything that is not specifically Christian or is too esoteric." Submit complete ms. *Writer's Market* recommends query with SASE first. No simultaneous submissions.

STARBURST PUBLISHERS, P.O. Box 4123, Lancaster PA 17604. (717)293-0939. Editorial Director: Ellen Hake. Estab. 1982. Publishes hardcover and trade paperback originals and trade paperback reprints. Averages 10-15 titles/year. Receives 1,000 submissions/year. 60% of books by first-time authors; 90% from unagented writers. Pays 6-15% royalty on net price to retailer. Publishes book an average of 1 year after acceptance. Reports in 1 month on queries. Book catalog for 9 × 12 SAE with 4 first class stamps. Manuscript guidelines for #10 SASE.

Nonfiction: General nonfiction, how-to, self-help, Christian. Subjects include business/economics, child guidance/parenting, cooking/foods/nutrition, counseling/career guidance, educational, gardening, health/medicine, juvenile (Bible-based teaching picture books), money/finance, nature and environment, psychology, real estate, recreation, religion. No poetry. "We are looking for contemporary issues facing Christians and today's average American." Submit outline, 3 sample chapters, bio, photo and SASE. Reviews artwork/photos as part of freelance ms package.

Recent Nonfiction Title: *Allergy Cooking With Ease*, by Nicolette M. Dumke (cooking/foods/nutrition).

Fiction: Adventure, fantasy, historical, mainstream/contemporary, romance, western. "We are looking for good, wholesome Christian fiction." Submit outline/synopsis, 3 sample chapters, bio, photo and SASE.

Recent Fiction Title: *The Nuworld Chronicles*, by Gilbert Morris (historical/fantasy).

Tips: "60% our line goes into the Christian marketplace; 40% into the general marketplace. We are one of the few publishers that has *direct sales representation* into both the Christian and general marketplace. Write on an isslue that slots you on talk shows and thus establish your name as an expert and writer."

STEMMER HOUSE PUBLISHERS, INC., 2627 Caves Rd., Owings Mills MD 21117-2998. (410)363-3690. President: Barbara Holdridge. Estab. 1975. Publishes hardcover originals. Averages 12 titles/year; receives 500 submissions annually. 10% of books from first-time authors; 90% of books from unagented writers. Average print order for a writer's first book is 4,000-10,000. Pays royalty on wholesale price. Publishes book an average of 1 year after acceptance. Reports in 2 months. Book catalog for 9 × 12 SAE with 4 first class stamps.

Nonfiction: Biography, cookbook, illustrated book, juvenile (ages 4-14) and design books. Subjects include Americana, animals, art, cooking and foods, history and nature. Especially looking for "quality biography, history, and art and design." No humor. Query or submit outline and sample chapters with cover letter and SASE.

Recent Nonfiction Title: *Elizabeth I*, by Rosalind K. Marshall.

Fiction: Ethnic, historical, mainstream and philosophical. No longer seeking adventure fiction. "We want only manuscripts of sustained literary merit. No popular-type manuscripts written to be instant bestsellers." Query.

Recent Fiction Title: *The Fringe of Heaven*, by Margaret Sutherland (contemporary novel).

● Currently Stemmer House is publishing very little fiction, focusing primarily on nonfiction.

Tips: "We are interested in finding original manuscripts on gardens and gardening. If I were a writer trying to market a book today, I would not imitate current genres on the bestseller lists, but strike out with a subject of intense interest to me. Freelancer has best chance of selling a book with a universal theme, either for adults or children, exceptionally well written, and marketable internationally. Our goal is a list of perennial sellers of which we can be proud."

STERLING PUBLISHING, 387 Park Ave. S., New York NY 10016. (212)532-7160. Acquisitions Manager: Sheila Anne Barry. Estab. 1949. Publishes hardcover and paperback originals and reprints. Averages 175 titles/year. Pays royalty; offers advance. Publishes book an average of 8 months after acceptance. Reports in 2 months. Guidelines for SASE.

Nonfiction: Alternative lifestyle, fiber arts, games and puzzles, health, how-to, business, hobbies, how-to, children's humor, children's science, nature and activities, militaria, pets, recreation, reference, sports, technical, wine and woodworking, crafts, history, medieval, Celtic subjects, . No longer seeking New Age. Query or submit complete chapter list, detailed outline and 2 sample chapters with photos if applicable. Reviews artwork/photos as part of ms package.

Recent Nonfiction Title: *Cars Europe Never Built*, by Gregory Janicki.

STILL WATERS PRESS, 112 W. Duerer St., Galloway NJ 08201-9402. (609)652-1790. Editor: Shirley Warren. Publishes trade paperback originals. Publishes 7 titles/year. Receives 300 queries and 500 mss/year. 75% of mss from first-time authors, 100% from unagented writers. Pays 10% royalty on wholesale and retail price, or pays in copies—initial press run 10%; subsequent runs 10%. Author receives 50% discount purchasing her own books. Publishes book 4 months after acceptance of ms. Simultaneous submissions OK. Reports in 1 month on queries. *Writer's Market* recommends allowing 2 months for reply. Book catalog and ms guidelines for #10 SASE.

Nonfiction: How-to (for poets only), humor and fine essays. Subjects include language/literature and women's issues/studies. "We publish small books only, no manuscript over 10 typewritten pages will be read. Mistakes writers often make when submitting nonfiction are: 'soap-boxing' instead of presenting valid, supported argument for their point. Using too much sentimentality; not enough sentiment and having a patriarchal attitude." Query.

Recent Nonfiction Title: *The Poet & Her Persona*, by Shirley Warren.

Fiction: Short-short fiction. "Mistakes writers most often make when submitting fiction: Not compelling, characters boring, descriptions nondescript, storyline too soft." Submit short-short only; maximum 10 typewritten double-spaced pages.

Poetry: Length: Maximum 24 pages. No "abused childhood" works or poems about writing or teaching poetry. Prefers American settings and single-spaced poetry. "Mistakes poets most often make when submitting poetry: Spelling errors, patriarchal attitude, twisted syntax to achieve weak rhyme, lines way too long for our format, poems about dead poets, settings in the past rather than present." Submit 5 sample poems.

Recent Poetry Title: *Natural Selections*, by Jeff Worley & Lance Olsen.

Tips: "We want our poetry books to be accessible to all human beings; our writer's guides to be references poets consult most often; and our humor to tickle anyone who reads it. Advise writers to read other poets, both contemporary and traditional; attend some workshops, establish rapport with your local peers, attend readings. We prefer to publish people who are actively engaged in the literary life of their own community—writers' groups, readings, arts festivals, etc. Keep your best work in circulation—someone out there is looking for you."

STILLPOINT PUBLISHING, Division of Stillpoint International, Inc., P.O. Box 640, Walpole NH 03608. (603)756-9281. Fax: (603)756-9282. Managing Editor: Charmaine Wellington. Publishes hardcover originals and trade paperback originals and reprints. Averages 8-10 titles/year. Receives 500 submissions/year. 50% of books from first-time authors; 90% from unagented writers. Pays royalty. Publishes book an average of 9-15 months after acceptance. Simultaneous submissions OK. Reports in 6 weeks. *Writer's Market* recommends allowing 2 months for reply. Manuscript guidelines free on request with SASE.

Nonfiction: Spiritual growth; personal growth/recovery; body/mind/spirit health for individual and global well-being; nature/sacred ecology. "Stillpoint specializes in books that approach personal and planetary issues from their spiritual core. We are looking for manuscripts that apply spiritual values—expressed in mainstream, non-denominational terms—to personal and global well-being in today's world." Query or submit outline and sample chapters.

Recent Nonfiction Title: *Spiritual Crisis: What's Really Behind Loss, Disease and Life's Major Hurts*, by Meredith Young-Sowers (spiritual growth/healing).

Tips: "Writers have the best chance of acceptance if they submit nonfiction that offers a unique perspective gained from life experience and/or research that addresses the spiritual foundations of a current area of personal, social or environmental change. The work needs to be insightful, practical and reflect a level of spiritual values. If I were a writer trying to market a book today, I would choose a publisher who understands my book's unique message."

STIPES PUBLISHING CO., 10-12 Chester St., Champaign IL 61824-0526. (217)356-8391. Fax: (217)356-5753. Contact: Robert Watts. Estab. 1925. Publishes hardcover and paperback originals. Averages 15-30 titles/year; receives 150 submissions annually. 50% of books from first-time authors; 100% of books from unagented writers. Pays 15% maximum royalty on retail price. Publishes book an average of 4 months after acceptance. Reports in 2 months.

Nonfiction: Technical (some areas), textbooks on business and economics, music, chemistry, agriculture/horticulture, environmental education, and recreation and physical education. "All of our books in the trade area are books that also have a college text market. No books unrelated to educational fields taught at the college level." Submit outline and 1 sample chapter.

Recent Nonfiction Title: *Keyboard Musicianship Book I* (6th edition), by James Lyke, Tony Caramia, Reid Alexanader, and Ron Elliston.

STOEGER PUBLISHING COMPANY, 55 Ruta Court, S. Hackensack NJ 07606-1799. (201)440-2700. Fax: (201)440-2707. Publisher: Robert E. Weise. Estab. 1925. Publishes trade paperback originals. Averages 12-15 titles/year. Royalty varies, depending on ms. Simultaneous submissions OK. Reports in 1 month on queries. *Writer's Market* recommends allowing 2 months for reply. Book catalog for #10 SAE and 2 first class stamps.

Nonfiction: Specializing in reference and how-to books that pertain to hunting, fishing and appeal to gun enthusiasts. Submit outline and sample chapters.

Recent Nonfiction Title: *Rifle Guide*, by Sam Fadala.

STONEYDALE PRESS, 205 Main St., Stevensville MT 59870. (406)777-2729. Publisher: Dale A. Burk. Estab. 1976. Publishes hardcover and trade paperback originals. Publishes 4-6 titles/year. Receives 40-50 queries and 6-8 mss/year. 90% of mss from unagented writers. Pays 12-15% royalty. Publishes book 18 months after acceptance of ms. Reports in 1 month on queries and proposals. *Writer's Market* recommends allowing 2 months for reply. Book catalog available.

Nonfiction: How-to hunting books. "We are interested only in hunting books." Query.

‡STOREY COMMUNICATIONS/GARDEN WAY PUBLISHING, Schoolhouse Rd., Pownal VT 05261. (802)823-5200. Senior Editor/Director of Acquisitions: Gwen Steege. Publishes hardcover and trade paperback originals and reprints. Publishes 25 titles/year. Receives 300 queries and 150 mss/year. 30% of mss from first-time

---

For information on book publishers' areas of interest, see the nonfiction and fiction sections in the Book Publishers Subject Index.

authors, 80% from unagented writers. Pays royalty or makes outright purchase. Publishes book 2 years after acceptance of ms. Simultaneous submissions OK. Query for electronic submissions. Reports in 1 month on queries, 3 months on proposals and mss. Book catalog and ms guidelines free on request.

Nonfiction: Cookbook, how-to and children's/juvenile. Subjects include agriculture/horticulture, animals, cooking/foods/nutrition, gardening, hobbies and nature/environment. Submit proposal package, including outline, sample chapter, competitive books, author resume. "Occasionally" reviews artwork/photos as part of the freelance ms package.

Recent Nonfiction Title: *The Able Gardener*, by Kathy Yeomans (gardening).

SUCCESS PUBLISHING, P.O. Box 30965, Palm Beach Gardens FL 33420. (407)626-4643. Fax: (407)775-1693. President: Allan H. Smith. Submission Manager: Robin Garretson. Estab. 1982. Publishes trade paperback originals. Averages 6 titles/year. Receives 200 submissions annually. 75% of books from first-time authors. 100% of books from unagented writers. Pays 7% royalty. Publishes book an average of 3 months after acceptance. Simultaneous submissions OK. Reports in 2 months on queries. Book catalog and manuscript guidelines for #10 SAE and 2 first class stamps.

Nonfiction: How-to, humor and self-help. Business and economics, hobbies and money/finance. "We are looking for books on how-to subjects such as home business and sewing." Query.

• Success Publishing is looking for ghostwriters.

Recent Nonfiction Title: *How To Write A "How To" Book*, by Smith (how-to).

Tips: "Our audience is made up of housewives, hobbyists and owners of home-based businesses. If I were a writer trying to market a book today, I would read books about how to market a self-written book."

SUNBELT MEDIA, INC., P.O. Box 90159, Austin TX 78709-0159. (512)288-1771. Imprints are Eakin Press and Nortex Press. Editorial Director: Edwin M. Eakin. Publishes hardcover and paperback originals and reprints. Averages 25 titles/year; receives 500 submissions annually. 80% of books from first-time authors; 90% of books from unagented writers. Average print order for a writer's first book is 2,000-5,000. Pays 10-12-15% on net sales as royalty. Publishes book an average of 12-18 months after acceptance. Simultaneous submissions OK. Query for electronic submissions. Reports in 3 months. Book catalog and ms guidelines for #10 SAE with 4 first class stamps.

Nonfiction: Adult nonfiction categories include Western Americana, business, sports, biographies, Civil War, cookbooks, regional Texas history. Juvenile nonfiction includes biographies of historic personalities, prefer with Texas or regional interest, or nature studies. Easy read illustrated books for grades one through three. *Writer's Market* recommends query with SASE first.

Recent Nonfiction Title: *The Magnificient Barbarians: Little told tales of the Texas Revolution*, by Bill and Marjorie Walraven.

Fiction: No longer publishes adult fiction. Juvenile fiction for grades four through seven, preferably relating to Texas and the southwest or contemporary. Query or submit outline/synopsis and sample chapters.

SUNFLOWER UNIVERSITY PRESS, Subsidiary of Journal of the West, Inc., 1531 Yuma, Box 1009, Manhattan KS 66502-4228. (913)539-1888. Publisher: Carol A. Williams. Publishes trade paperback originals and reprints. Averages 12 titles/year. Receives 250 submissions/year. 75% of books from first-time authors. 90% of books from unagented writers. Pays 10% royalty after first printing. Publishes book an average of 8 months after acceptance and contract. Reports in 3 months. Free book catalog.

Nonfiction: Biography, illustrated books, reference. Subjects include agriculture/horticulture, Americana, anthropology/archaeology, business and economics, ethnic, government/politics, health/medicine, history, language/literature, military/war, money/finance, music/dance, nature/environment, photography, recreation, regional, religion, science, sociology, sports, women's issues/studies. Our field of specialization lies in memoirs and histories of the West, and of the military, naval, and air fields; perhaps some specialized collectors' books. Query or submit 2-3 sample chapters. Reviews artwork/photos as part of the ms package (photocopies acceptable).

Fiction: Historical, western, military. We need narratives that are historically accurate and shed light on historical incidents or events. No X-rated, juvenile, stream of consciousness. Query or submit 2-3 sample chapters.

Tips: "Our audience is the informed aviation, military, or Western American history enthusiast."

SUNSTONE PRESS, Imprint of Sunstone Corporation. P.O. Box 2321, Santa Fe NM 87504-2424. (505)988-4418. Fax: (505)988-1025. President: James C. Smith Jr. Estab. 1971. Other imprint is Sundial Publications. Publishes paperback originals; few hardcover originals. Averages 20 titles/year; receives 400 submissions annually. 70% of books from first-time authors; 100% of books from unagented writers. Average print order for writer's first book is 2,000-5,000. Pays royalty on wholesale price. Publishes book an average of 1 year after acceptance. Reports in 2 months. Book catalog for 9×12 SAE with 3 first class stamps.

Nonfiction: How-to series craft books. Books on the history and architecture of the Southwest. "Looks for strong regional appeal (Southwestern)." *Writer's Market* recommends query with SASE first. Reviews artwork/photos as part of ms package.

Recent Nonfiction Title: "Kachina Tales from the Indian Pueblos" by Gene Hodge.
Fiction: Publishes material with Southwestern theme. *Writer's Market* recommends query with SASE first.
Recent Fiction Title: *Tubar*, by John Tilley.

SYBEX, INC., 2021 Challenger Dr., Alameda CA 94501. (415)523-8233. Fax: (510)523-2373. Editor-in-Chief: Dr. Rudolph S. Langer. Acquisitions Manager: Dianne King. Acquisitions Editor: David J. Clark. Estab. 1976. Publishes paperback originals. Averages 100 titles/year. Royalty rates vary. Offers average $3,000 advance. Publishes book an average of 3 months after acceptance. Simultaneous submissions OK. Query for electronic submissions. Reports in up to 6 months. Free book catalog.
Nonfiction: Computers and computer software. "Manuscripts most publishable in the field of personal computers, desktop computer business applications, hardware, programming languages, and telecommunications." Submit outline and 2-3 sample chapters. Looks for "clear writing; technical accuracy; logical presentation of material; and good selection of material, such that the most important aspects of the subject matter are thoroughly covered; well-focused subject matter; and well-thought-out organization that helps the reader understand the material." Reviews artwork/photos as part of ms package.
Tips: Queries/mss may be routed to other editors in the publishing group.

SYRACUSE UNIVERSITY PRESS, 1600 Jamesville Ave., Syracuse NY 13244-5160. (315)443-5534. Fax: (315)443-5545. Executive Editor: Cynthia Maude-Gembler. Estab. 1943. Averages 30 titles/year; receives 400 submissions annually. 40% of books from first-time authors; 95% of books from unagented writers. Subsidy publishes (nonauthor) 20% of books. Pays royalty on net sales. Publishes book an average of 15 months after acceptance. Simultaneous submissions discouraged. Reports in 2 months. Book catalog and ms guidelines for 9×12 SAE with 3 first class stamps.
Nonfiction: "Special opportunity in our nonfiction program for freelance writers of books on New York state. We have published regional books by people with limited formal education, but authors were thoroughly acquainted with their subjects, and they wrote simply and directly about them. Provide precise descriptions about subjects, along with background description of project. The author must make a case for the importance of his or her subject." Query. Accepts outline and at least 2 sample chapters. Reviews artwork/photos as part of ms package.

SYSTEMS CO., P.O. Box 876, Graham WA 98338-0876. (206)847-5775. President: Frank L. Bouquet. Estab. 1981. Publishes hardcover and mass market paperback originals. Averages 4 titles/year. Receives 10 queries and 3 mss/year. Pays 10-30% royalty (varies with book type). Publishes book approximately 3 months after acceptance. Reports in 3 months. Book catalog for #10 SASE; manuscript guidelines for $1.
Nonfiction: Cookbook, how-to, humor, self-help, technical, textbook, and specialized books: engineering, radiation, autos, bicycles. Query or submit outline with 1 sample chapter. Writers should send photocopies.
Fiction: Humor. Submit synopsis with 1 sample chapter.
Poetry: Query or submit 1 sample poem.

‡T.F.H. BOOKS, T.F.H. Publications, Inc., 1 TFH Plaza, Neptune City NJ 07753. Managing Editor: Neal Pronek. Publishes hardcover and mass market paperback originals. Publishes 50 titles/year. Receives 100 queries and 50 mss/year. 10% of mss from first-time authors, 100% from unagented writers. Makes outright purchase for $500-1,000+. Publishes book 1 year after acceptance of ms. Reports in 1 month on queries. Book catalog and ms guidelines free on request.
Nonfiction: Coffee table book, how-to, children's/juvenile, reference and hobby. Subjects include animals, hobbies and nature/environment. "TFH publishes guides to the care of pets of all types. Avoid sending unprofessional, amateurish treatment of the subject." Query. Reviews artwork/photos as part of the freelance ms package. Writers should send transparencies.

TAB BOOKS, Imprint of McGraw-Hill, Inc., Blue Ridge, Summit PA 17294-0850. (717)794-2191. Fax: (717)794-5344. Editorial Director: Ron Powers. Estab. 1964. Imprint is Windcrest computer books (Contact: Brad Schepp). Publishes hardcover and paperback originals and reprints. Publishes 275 titles/year; receives 600 submissions annually. 50% of books from first-time authors; 85% of books from unagented writers. Average print order for writer's first book is 10,000. Pays variable royalty; buys some mss outright for a negotiable fee. Offers advance. Query for electronic submissions. Reports in 3 months. Write for free book catalog and ms guidelines.
Nonfiction: TAB publishes titles in such fields as computer hardware, computer software, business, startup guides, with marine line, aviation, automotive, construction and mechanical trades, electronics, electrical and electronics repair, amateur radio, shortwave listening, calculators, robotics, telephones, TV servicing, audio, recording, hi-fi and stereo, electronic music, electric motors, electrical wiring, electronic test equipment, video programming, CATV, MATV and CCTV, broadcasting, appliance servicing and repair, license study guides, mathematics, reference books, schematics and manuals, small gasoline engines, two-way radio and CB. Accepts unsolicited proposals. Query with outline. Reviews artwork/photos as part of ms package.

Tips: "Many writers believe that a cover letter alone will describe their proposed book sufficiently; it rarely does. The more details we receive, the better the chances are that the writer will get published by us. We expect a writer to tell us what the book is about, but many writers actually fail to do just that."

TAMBOURINE BOOKS, Imprint of William Morrow & Co., Inc., 1350 Ave. of the Americas, New York NY 10019. (212)261-6500. Publishes hardcover originals. Publishes 50 titles/year. Receives 300 queries and 1,300 mss/year. 10% of mss from first-time authors, 25% from unagented writers. Publishes book 18 months after acceptance of ms. Simultaneous submissions OK. Reports in 1 month on queries. *Writer's Market* recommends allowing 2 months for reply. Book catalog for 9×12 SAE. Manuscript guidelines for #10 SASE.
Nonfiction and Fiction: Children's trade books, preschool through young adult. Primary emphasis on picture books and fiction. Reviews artwork/photos as part of freelance ms package. Writers should send photocopies (8½×11 color copies).
Recent Nonfiction Title: *The Bear Family*, by Dieter Betz (nature/animal).
Recent Fiction Title: *The Circus*, by Heidi Goennel (picture book).

TAYLOR PUBLISHING COMPANY, 1550 W. Mockingbird Ln., Dallas TX 95235. (214)819-8100. Contact: Editorial Assistant, Trade Books Division. Estab. 1981. Publishes hardcover and softcover originals. Averages 30 titles/year; receives 1,000 submissions annually. 25% of books from first-time authors; 25% of books from unagented writers. Buys some mss outright. Publishes book 1½ years after acceptance. Simultaneous submissions OK. Reports in 1 month. *Writer's Market* recommends allowing 2 months for reply. Book catalog and ms guidelines for 9×12 SASE.
Nonfiction: Gardening, coffee table books, nature/outdoors, sports, popular culture, parenting, health and home improvement. Submit outline and sample chapters. Also submit author bio as it pertains to the proposed subject matter. Reviews artwork/photos as part of ms package.
   ● No longer seeking true crime, cook-books, humor, self-help or trivia.
Recent Nonfiction Title: *How I Played the Game*, by Byron Nelson.

TEACHERS COLLEGE PRESS, 1234 Amsterdam Ave., New York NY 10027. (212)678-3929. Fax: (212)678-4149. Director: Carole P. Saltz. Executive Acquisitions Editor: Sarah Biondello. Estab. 1904. Publishes hardcover and paperback originals and reprints. Averages 40 titles/year. Pays royalty. Publishes book an average of 1 year after acceptance. Reports in 2 months. Free book catalog.
Nonfiction: "This university press concentrates on books in the field of education in the broadest sense, from early childhood to higher education: good classroom practices, teacher training, special education, innovative trends and issues, administration and supervision, film, continuing and adult education, all areas of the curriculum, computers, guidance and counseling and the politics, economics, philosophy, sociology and history of education. We have recently added women's studies to our list. The Press also issues classroom materials for students at all levels, with a strong emphasis on reading and writing and social studies." Submit outline and sample chapters.
Recent Nonfiction Title: *Cultural Diversity, Families, and the Special Education System: Communication and Empowerment*, by Beth Harry.

TEMPLE UNIVERSITY PRESS, Broad and Oxford Sts., Philadelphia PA 19122. (215)204-8787. Fax: (215)204-4719. Editor-in-Chief: Michael Ames. Publishes 70 titles/year. Pays royalty of up to 10% on wholesale price. Publishes book an average of 1 year after acceptance. Query for electronic submissions. Reports in 2 months. Free book catalog.
Nonfiction: American history, sociology, women's studies, health care, philosophy, labor studies, photography, urban studies, law, Latin American studies, Afro-American studies, Asian American studies, public policy and regional (Philadelphia area). "All books should be scholarly. Authors are generally connected with a university. No memoirs, fiction or poetry." Uses *Chicago Manual of Style*. Reviews artwork/photos as part of ms package. Query.

TEN SPEED PRESS, P.O. Box 7123, Berkeley CA 94707. (510)845-8414. Acquisitions Editor: Nichole Geiger. Estab. 1971. Imprints are Celestial Arts and Double Elephant Books. Publishes trade paperback originals and reprints. Firm averages 60 titles/year; imprint averages 20 titles/year. 25% of books from first-time authors. 50% from unagented writers. Pays 8-12% royalty on retail price. Offers $2,500 average advance. Publishes book an average of 1 year after acceptance. Simultaneous submissions OK. Reports in 2 months on queries. Book catalog for 9×12 SAE with 6 first class stamps. Manuscript guidelines for #10 SASE.
Nonfiction: Cookbook, how-to, reference and self-help. Subjects include business and career, child guidance/parenting, cooking, foods and nutrition, gardening, health/medicine, money/finance, nature/environment, recreation and science. "We mainly publish innovative how-to books. We are always looking for cookbooks from proven, tested sources—successful restaurants, etc. *Not* 'grandma's favorite recipes.' Books about the 'new science' interest us. No biographies or autobiographies, first-person travel narratives, fiction or humorous treatments of just about anything." Query or submit outline and sample chapters.

Recent Nonfiction Title: *How to Start a Business Without Quitting Your Job*, by Philip Holland (business/career).

Tips: "We like books from people who really know their subject, rather than people who think they've spotted a trend to capitalize on. We like books that will sell for a long time, rather than nine-day wonders. Our audience consists of a well-educated, slightly weird group of people who like food, the outdoors and take a light but serious approach to business and careers. If I were a writer trying to market a book today, I would really study the backlist of each publisher I was submitting to, and tailor my proposal to what I perceive as their needs. Nothing gets a publisher's attention like someone who knows what he or she is talking about, and nothing falls flat like someone who obviously has no idea who he or she is submitting to."

TEXAS A&M UNIVERSITY PRESS, Drawer C, College Station TX 77843-4354. (409)845-1436. Fax: (409)847-8752. Director: John F. Stetter. Editor-in-Chief: Noel Parsons. Estab. 1974. Publishes 30 titles/year. Subsidy publishes (nonauthor) 25% of books. Pays in royalties. Publishes book an average of 1 year after acceptance. Query for electronic submissions. Reports in 3 months on queries. Free book catalog.
Nonfiction: Natural history, American history, environmental history, military history, women's studies, economics and regional studies. *Writer's Market* recommends query with SASE first.
Recent Nonfiction Title: *Bale o' Cotton! The Mechanical Art of Cotton Ginning*, by Karen Gerhardt Britton.

TEXAS CHRISTIAN UNIVERSITY PRESS, P.O. Box 30783, TCU, Fort Worth TX 76129. (817)921-7822. Fax: (817)921-7333. Director: Judy Alter. Editor: A.T. Row. Estab. 1966. Publishes hardcover originals, some reprints. Averages 8 titles/year; receives 100 submissions annually. 10% of books from first-time authors; 75% of books from unagented writers. Subsidy publishes (nonauthor) 10% of books. Pays royalty. Publishes book an average of 16 months after acceptance. Reports in 1 month on queries. *Writer's Market* recommends allowing 2 months for reply.
Nonfiction: American studies, juvenile (Chaparral Books, 10 and up), Texana, literature and criticism. "We are looking for good scholarly monographs, other serious scholarly work and regional titles of significance." Query. Reviews artwork/photos as part of ms package.
Fiction: Adult and young adult regional fiction. Query.
Tips: "Regional and/or Texana nonfiction or fiction have best chance of breaking into our firm."

‡**TEXAS TECH UNIVERSITY PRESS**, Mail Stop 1037, Lubbock TX 79409-1037. (800)832-4042. Fax: (806)742-2979. Managing Editor: Carole Young. Publishes hardcover and trade paperback originals and reprints. Publishes 12 titles/year. Receives 200+ queries and mss/year. 10% of mss from first-time authors, 80% from unagented writers. Subsidy publishes 50% of books. Decision to subsidy publish is based upon size of the market and cost of production. Pays 5-20% royalty on wholesale price. Publishes book 18 months after acceptance of ms. No multiple submissions. Photocopied submissions OK. Query for electronic submissions. Reports in 1 month on queries, 6 months on mss. Book catalog free on request.
Nonfiction: "Coffee table" book, illustrated book, technical, memoirs, scholarly works; medical books. Subjects include Americana, animals, art/architecture, ethnic, health/medicine, history, language/literature, music/dance, nature/environment, regional (Texas/New Mexico) and science. "We will consider all manuscripts that meet our requirements. Competition is stiff, however, and we suggest that authors present well-researched, amply documented, well-written manuscripts. No philosophy, psychology, or business and economics." Query with outline/synopsis and sample chapters or complete ms. Reviews artwork/photos as part of freelance ms package.
Recent Nonfiction Title: *The Roadrunner*, by Wyman Meinzer (trade natural history).
Poetry: "We only consider submissions that were finalists or winners in one of the national poetry contests. We also host an invitation-only poetry contest for first book authors." Submit complete ms.
Recent Poetry Title: *All That Matters*, by Walt McDonald (contemporary).
Tips: "Our trade books are for general audiences. Our scholarly books are directed toward specific disciplines."

TEXAS WESTERN PRESS, Imprint of The University of Texas at El Paso, El Paso TX 79968-0633. (915)747-5688. Fax: (915)747-5111. Director: Dale L. Walker. Estab. 1952. Imprint is Southwestern Studies. Publishes hardcover and paperback originals. Publishes 7-8 titles/year. "This is a university press, 40 years old; we offer a standard 10% royalty contract on our hardcover books and on some of our paperbacks as well. We try to treat our authors professionally, produce handsome, long-lived books and aim for quality, rather than quantity of titles carrying our imprint." Reports in 2 months. Free book catalog and ms guidelines.
Nonfiction: Scholarly books. Historic and cultural accounts of the Southwest (West Texas, New Mexico, northern Mexico and Arizona). Occasional technical titles. "Our *Southwestern Studies* use manuscripts of up to 30,000 words. Our hardback books range from 30,000 words up. The writer should use good exposition in his work. Most of our work requires documentation. We favor a scholarly, but not overly pedantic, style. We specialize in superior book design." Query with outline. Follow *Chicago Manual of Style*.
Tips: "Texas Western Press is interested in books relating to the history of Hispanics in the U.S., will experiment with photo-documentary books, and is interested in seeing more 'popular' history and books on Southwestern culture/life."

THEATRE ARTS BOOKS, Imprint of Routledge, Inc., 29 W. 35th St., New York NY 10001-2299. (212)244-3336. Editorial Director: William P. Germano. Publishes hardcover and trade paperback originals. Pays royalty. Publishes ms an average of 1 year after acceptance. Reports in 6 weeks. Use *Chicago Manual of Style* for ms guidelines.

Nonfiction: Drama and theater. Subjects include acting, directing, lighting, costume, dance, staging, etc. "We publish only books of broad general interest to actors, directors and theater technicians, especially books that could be useful in college classrooms. Most of our authors have had long experience in professional theater. Topics that are very narrowly focused (a costume book on women's shoes in the eighteenth century, for example) would not be acceptable. We no longer publish original plays." Query with outline, synopsis and author's qualifications.

THE THEOSOPHICAL PUBLISHING HOUSE, Subsidiary of The Theosophical Society in America, 306 W. Geneva Rd., Wheaton IL 60187-0270. (708)665-0130. Fax: (708)665-8791. Senior Editor: Brenda Rosen. Estab. 1968. Imprint is Quest Books. Publishes trade paperback originals. Averages 12 titles/year; receives 750-1,000 submissions annually. 20% of books from first-time authors; 95% of books from unagented writers. Average print order for a writer's first book is 5,000. Pays 12½% royalty on net price; offers average $3,000 advance. Publishes book an average of 9 months after acceptance. Simultaneous submissions OK. Reports in 2 months. Free book catalog; ms guidelines for SASE.

Nonfiction: Subjects include self-development, self-help, philosophy (holistic), psychology (transpersonal), Eastern and Western religions, theosophy, comparative religion, men's and women's spirituality, Native American spirituality, holistic implications in science, health and healing, yoga, meditation and astrology. "TPH seeks works that are compatible with the theosophical philosophy. Our audience includes the 'New Age' community, seekers in all religions, general public, professors, and health professionals. No submissions that do not fit the needs outlined above." Accepts nonfiction translations. Query or submit outline and sample chapters. Reviews artwork/photos as part of ms package.

Recent Nonfiction Title: *Life Force: The Psycho-Historical Recovery of the Self,* by Jean Houston, Ph.D.

Tips: "The writer has the best chance of selling our firm a book that illustrates a connection between spiritually-oriented philosophy or viewpoint and some field of current interest."

‡THOMAS PUBLICATIONS, Subsidiary of Thomas Graphics, Inc., Box 33244, Austin TX 78764. (512)832-0355. Contact: Ralph D. Thomas. Publishes trade paperback originals and reprints. Averages 8-10 titles/year; receives 20-30 submissions annually. 90% of books from first-time authors; 90% of books from unagented writers. Pays 10-15% royalty on wholesale or retail price, or makes outright purchase of $500-2,000. Publishes book an average of 1 year after acceptance. Simultaneous submissions OK. Reports in 2 weeks on queries; 1 month on mss. Book catalog $1.

Nonfiction: How-to, reference and textbook. Subjects include sociology and investigation and investigative techniques. "We are looking for hardcore investigative methods books, manuals on how to make more dollars in private investigation, private investigative marketing techniques, and specialties in the investigative professions." Query or submit outline/synopsis and sample chapters. Reviews artwork/photos as part of ms package.

Tips: "Our audience includes private investigators, those wanting to break into investigation, related trades such as auto repossessors, private process servers, news reporters, and related security trades."

THREE CONTINENTS PRESS, 1901 Pennsylvania Ave. NW, Washington DC 20006. Publisher/Editor-in-Chief: Donald E. Herdeck. General Editor: Harold Ames, Jr. Estab. 1973. Publishes hardcover and paperback originals and reprints. Averages 20-30 titles/year. Receives 200 submissions annually. 15% of books from first-time authors; 100% of books from unagented writers. Average print order for a writer's first book is 1,000. Subsidy publishes (nonauthor) 5% of books. Pays 10% royalty; advance "only on delivery of complete manuscript which is found acceptable; usually $300." Simultaneous submissions OK. State availability of photos/illustrations. Reports in 3 months.

Nonfiction and Fiction: Specializes in African, Caribbean, Middle Eastern (Arabic and Persian) and Asian-Pacific literature, criticism and translation, Third World literature and history. Scholarly, well-prepared mss; creative writing. Fiction, poetry, criticism, history and translations of creative writing. "We search for books that will make clear the complexity and value of non-Western literature and culture, including bilingual texts (Arabic language/English translations). We are always interested in genuine contributions to understanding non-Western culture." Length: 50,000-125,000 words. Query. "Please do not submit manuscript unless we ask for it. We prefer an outline, and an annotated table of contents, for works of nonfiction; and a synopsis, a plot summary (one to three pages), for fiction. For poetry, send two or three sample poems." Reviews artwork/photos as part of ms package.

Recent Nonfiction Title: *The Imperishable Empire: A Study of British Fiction on India,* by Rashna B. Singh.

Recent Fiction Title: *Fields of Fig and Olive,* by Kathyrn Abdoul-Baki (short story collection).

Tips: "We need a *polished* translation, or original prose or poetry by non-Western authors *only.*"

THUNDER'S MOUTH PRESS, 7th Floor, 632 Broadway, New York NY 10012. (212)226-0277. Publisher: Neil Ortenberg. Estab. 1982. Publishes hardcover and trade paperback originals and reprints, almost exclusively nonfiction. Averages 15-20 titles/year; receives 1,000 submissions annually. 10% of books from unagented writers. Average print order for a writer's first book is 7,500. Pays 5-10% royalty on retail price; offers average $5,000 advance. Publishes book an average of 8 months after acceptance. Reports in 3 months on queries. Does not consider unsolicited manuscripts.
Nonfiction: Biography, politics, popular culture. *Writer's Market* recommends query with SASE first.
Fiction: Query only.

TIARE PUBLICATIONS, P.O. Box 493, Lake Geneva WI 53147. President: Gerry L. Dexter. Estab. 1986. Publishes trade paperback originals. Publishes 6-12 titles/year. Receives 25 queries and 10 mss/year. 40% of mss from first-time authors, 100% from unagented writers. Pays 15% royalty on retail/wholesale price. Publishes book 3 months after acceptance of ms. Query for electronic submission. Reports in 1 month on queries. Book catalog for $1.
Nonfiction: Technical. "We are always looking for new ideas in the areas of amateur radio, shortwave listening, scanner radio monitoring, monitoring satellite transmissions—how to, equipment, techniques, etc." Query.
Recent Nonfiction Title: *Citizens Guide to Scanning*, by Laura E. Quarantello.

TICKNOR & FIELDS, Imprint of Houghton-Mifflin, 215 Park Ave. S., New York NY 10003. (212)420-5800. Editorial Director: John Herman. Associate Editors: Jane Von Mehren and Cindy Spiegel. Estab. 1980. Publishes hardcover originals. Imprint averages 20 titles/year. Receives 500 submissions/year. 10% of books from first-time authors; 100% of submissions from agents. Does *not* accept unsolicited mss. Pays royalty. Reports in 3 months.
Nonfiction and Fiction: General subjects. Query.
Recent Nonfiction Title: *The Best American Essays 1992*.

TIDEWATER PUBLISHERS, Imprint of Cornell Maritime Press, Inc., P.O. Box 456, Centreville MD 21617-0456. (410)758-1075. Managing Editor: Charlotte Kurst. Estab. 1938. Publishes hardcover and paperback originals. Imprint averages 7-9 titles/year. Receives 150 submissions/year. 41% of books from first-time authors. 99% from unagented writers. Pays 7½-15% royalty on retail price. Publishes book an average of 1 year after acceptance. Reports in 1 month. *Writer's Market* recommends allowing 2 months for reply. Book catalog for 10×13 SAE with 5 first class stamps.
Nonfiction: Cookbook, history, illustrated book, juvenile, reference. Subjects are all regional. Query or submit outline and sample chapters. Reviews artwork/photos as part of ms package.
Recent Nonfiction Title: *Chesapeake Bay Schooners*, by Quentin Snediker and Ann Jensen.
Fiction: Regional juvenile fiction only. Query or submit outline/synopsis and sample chapters.
Recent Fiction Title: *Broken Wings Will Fly*, by Mick Blackistone; illustrated by Jennifer Heyd Wharton.
Tips: "Our audience is made up of readers interested in works that are specific to the Chesapeake Bay and Delmarva Peninsula area."

TIMBER PRESS, INC., 9999 SW Wilshire, Portland OR 97225-5091. (503)292-0745. Fax: (503)292-6607. Publisher: Robert B. Conklin. Dr. Dale Johnson, acquisitions in horticulture and botany. Dr. Reinhard Pauly, acquisitions in music. Estab. 1976. Imprints are Timber Press (horticulture), Dioscorides Press (botany), and Amadeus Press (music). Publishes hardcover and paperback originals. Publishes 40 titles/year; receives 300-400 submissions annually. 75% of books from first-time authors; 95% of books from unagented writers. Pays 10% royalty; sometimes offers advance to cover costs of artwork and final ms completion. Publishes book an average of 2 years after acceptance. Query for electronic submissions. Reports in 2 months. Book catalogs for 9×12 SAE with 5 first class stamps.
Nonfiction: Horticulture, botany, plant sciences, natural history, Northwest regional material, classical and traditional music. Accepts nonfiction translations from all languages. Query or submit outline and 3-4 sample chapters. Reviews artwork/photos as part of ms package.
Recent Nonfiction Title: *Gardening with Perennials Month by Month*, by Joseph Hudak.
Tips: "The writer has the best chance of selling our firm good books on botany, plant science, horticulture, or serious music."

TIMES BOOKS, Imprint of Random House, Inc., 201 E. 50 St., New York NY 10022. (212)872-8110. Vice President and Publisher: Peter Osnos. Editorial Director: Steve Wasserman. Publishes hardcover and paperback originals and reprints. Publishes 50-60 titles/year. Pays royalty; average advance. Publishes book an average of 1 year after acceptance. *Writer's Market* recommends allowing 2 months for reply.
Nonfiction: Business/economics, science and medicine, history, biography, women's issues, the family, cookbooks and current affairs. Accepts only solicited manuscripts. *Writer's Market* recommends query with SASE first. Reviews artwork/photos as part of ms package.
Recent Nonfiction Title: *Nobody Nowhere: The Extraordinary Autobiography of an Autistic*, by Donna Williams.

TOR BOOKS, Subsidiary of St. Martin's Press, 14th Floor, 175 5th Ave., New York NY 10010. (212)388-0100. Fax: (212)388-0191. Publisher: Tom Doherty. Assistant Editor: Natalia Aponte. Estab. 1980. Publishes mass market, hardcover and trade paperback originals and reprints. Averages 250 books/year. Pays 6-8% royalty; offers negotiable advance. Reports in 4 months. Book catalog for 9×12 SAE with 2 first class stamps.
 • TOR publishes selected nonfiction. Query first.
Fiction: Science fiction, fantasy, horror, technothrillers, "women's" suspense, American historicals. "We prefer an extensive chapter-by-chapter synopsis and the first 3 chapters complete." Prefers agented mss or proposals.
Recent Fiction Title: *The Shadow Rising,* by Robert Jordan.
Tips: "We're never short of good sci fi or fantasy, but we're always open to solid, technologically knowledgeable hard science fiction or thrillers by writers with solid expertise."

TRANSPORTATION TRAILS, Imprint of National Bus Trader, Inc., 9698 W. Judson Rd., Polo IL 61064-9015. (815)946-2341. Fax: (815)946-2347. Editor: Larry Plachno. Estab. 1977. Publishes hardcover, trade paperback and mass market paperback originals. Firm averages 8 titles/year. Receives 10 submissions/year. 50% of books from first-time authors. 100% from unagented writers. Pays 10-15% on retail price. Publishes book an average of 1 year after acceptance. Simultaneous submissions OK. Reports in 1 month. *Writer's Market* recommends allowing 2 months for reply. Free book catalog and manuscript guidelines.
Nonfiction: "We are interested in transportation history—prefer electric interurban railroads or trolley lines but will consider steam locomotives, horsecars, buses, aviation and maritime." Query. Reviews artwork/photos as part of ms package.
 • This publisher is also interested in books on family cohesion and the need for Christian values in America.
Recent Nonfiction Title: *Sunset Lines—The Story of the Chicago Aurora and Elgin Railroads,* by Larry Plachno.
Tips: "We are not interested in travel nonfiction."

‡TREND BOOK DIVISION, P.O. Box 611, St. Petersburg FL 33731-0611. (813)821-5800. Fax: (813)822-5083. Chairman: Andrew Barnes. President: Andrew Corty. Publisher: Lynda Keever. Estab. 1958. Publishes paperback originals and reprints. Specializes in books on Florida—all categories. Pays royalty; no advance. Books are marketed through *Florida Trend* magazine. Publishes book an average of 8 months after acceptance. Reports in 1 month.
Nonfiction: Business, economics, history, law, politics, reference, textbooks and travel. "All books pertain to Florida." Query. Reviews artwork/photos as part of ms package.
Tips: "We are shifting to more emphasis on books of a Florida business/economics nature."

TSR, INC., P.O. Box 756, Lake Geneva WI 53147. (414)248-3625. Estab. 1975. Imprints are TSR™ Books, Dungeons & Dragons Books, Dragonlance® Books, Forgotten Realms™ Books, Spelljammer™ Books, Ravenloft™ Books, and Dark Sun™ Books. Publishes trade paperback originals. Firm averages 70-80 titles/year; imprint averages 20-25 titles/year. Receives 700 submissions/year. 30-40% of books from first-time authors. 5% from unagented authors. Pays 4% royalty on retail price. Offers $4,000 average advance. Publishes book an average of 1 year after acceptance. Simultaneous submissions OK. Send to submissions editor. Reports in 10-12 weeks on queries; 6 weeks on mss.
Nonfiction: "All of our nonfiction books are generated in-house."
Fiction: Fantasy and science fiction. "We have a very small market for good science fiction and fantasy for the TSR Book line, but also need samples from writers willing to do work-for-hire for our other lines. We do not need occult, new age, or adult theme fiction. Nor will we consider mystery or excessively violent or gory fantasy, science fiction or horror." Query and write for guidelines. Submit outline/synopsis and sample chapters.
Recent Fiction Title: *The Ring of Winter,* by James Lowder.
Tips: "Our audience is comprised of highly imaginative 12-40 year-old males."

TWIN PEAKS PRESS, P.O. Box 129, Vancouver WA 98666-0129. (206)694-2462. President: Helen Hecker. Estab. 1984. Publishes hardcover and trade paperback originals and reprints. Averages 7-10 titles/year. Receives 1,000 submissions/year. 25% of books from first-time authors. 100% from unagented writers. Payment varies by individual agreement. Publishes book an average of 6 months after acceptance. Simultaneous submissions OK. *Does not report unless interested.* Do *not* send unsolicited mss.
Nonfiction: Cookbook, how-to, reference and self-help. Subjects include business and economics, cooking, foods and nutrition, health/medicine, hobbies, recreation, sociology, sports and travel. Query with outline in writing only.
Recent Nonfiction Title: *Travel for the Disabled.*

TYNDALE HOUSE PUBLISHERS, INC., 351 Executive Dr., P.O. Box 80, Wheaton IL 60189-0080. (708)668-8300. Vice President, Editorial: Ronald Beers. Contact: Marilyn Dellorto. Estab. 1962. Publishes hardcover and trade paperback originals and mass paperback reprints. Averages 100 titles/year. 5-10% of books from first-time authors. Average first print order for a writer's first book is 5,000-10,000. Royalty and advance negotiable. Publishes book an average of 12-18 months after acceptance. Send query and synopsis, not whole ms. Will review solicited mss only. Reports in up to 3 months. Book catalog and ms guidelines for 9 × 12 SAE with 9 first class stamps.

Nonfiction: "Practical, user-friendly Christian books: home and family, Christian growth/self-help, devotional/inspirational, theology/Bible doctrine, children's nonfiction, contemporary/critical issues." Query.

Fiction: "Biblical, historical and other Christian themes. No short story collections. Children's books: character building stories with Christian perspective. Especially interested in ages 6-12." Query.

ULYSSES PRESS, Suite 1, 3286 Adeline St., Berkeley CA 94703. (510)601-8301. Editorial Director: Leslie Henriques. Estab. 1982. Publishes trade paperback originals. Averages 15 titles/year. 25% of titles from first-time authors; 75% from unagented writers. Pays 12-16% royalty on wholesale price. Offers $2,000-6,000 advance. Publishes book 6 months after acceptance. Simultaneous submissions OK. Query for electronic submissions. Reports in 2 months on proposals. Book catalog free on request.

Nonfiction: Travel and health. Submit proposal package including outline, 2 sample chapters, and market analysis. Reviews artwork/photos as part of freelance ms package. Writers should send photocopies.

Recent Nonfiction Title: Publishes three series of travel guidebooks—*Hidden, Ultimate* and the *Virago Woman's Travel Series*. Also publishes the Dr. Art Ulene health book series.

UMBRELLA BOOKS, Imprint of Epicenter Press Inc., 18821 64th Ave. NE, Seattle WA 98155-3334. (206)485-6822. President: Kent Sturgis. Estab. 1988. Publishes 4-6 titles/year. Pays royalty on net price. Publishes book an average of 1 year after acceptance. Query for electronic submissions. Reports in 3 months on queries. Manuscript guidelines for #10 SASE.

Nonfiction: Travel (West Coast and Alaska). Query; do *not* send photos.

UNITED RESOURCE PRESS, 4521 Campus Dr. #388, Irvine CA 92715. General Manager: Sally Black. Publishes trade paperback and mass market paperback originals. Publishes 6 titles/year. 50% of books from first-time authors. 50% from unagented writers. Pays 3-7% royalty on retail price. Publishes book an average of 1 year after acceptance. Simultaneous submissions OK. Query for electronic submissions. Reports in 2 months.

Nonfiction: "For next two years we will focus on personal finance (primarily)." Submit outline and sample chapters.

Recent Nonfiction Title: *Marriage and Money.*

UNIVELT, INC., P.O. Box 28130, San Diego CA 92198. (619)746-4005. Publisher: Robert H. Jacobs. Estab. 1970. Imprints are American Astronautical Society, National Space Society, and Lunar & Planetary Institute. Publishes hardcover originals. Averages 8 titles/year; receives 20 submissions annually. 5% of books from first-time authors; 5% of books from unagented writers. Subsidy publishes (nonauthor) 10% of books. Average print order for a writer's first book is 1,000-2,000. Pays 10% royalty on actual sales; no advance. Publishes book an average of 4 months after acceptance. Reports in 1 month. *Writer's Market* recommends allowing 2 months for reply. Book catalog and ms guidelines for SASE.

Nonfiction: Publishes in the field of aerospace, especially astronautics and technical communications, but including application of aerospace technology to Earth's problems, also astronomy. Submit outline and 1-2 sample chapters. Reviews artwork/photos as part of ms package.

Recent Nonfiction Title: *Men and Women of Space,* by Douglas B. Hawthorne.

Tips: "Writers have the best chance of selling manuscripts on the history of astronautics (we have a history series) and astronautics/spaceflight subjects. We publish for the American Astronautical Society. Queries may be routed to other editors in the publishing group."

UNIVERSITY OF ALABAMA PRESS, P.O. Box 870380, Tuscaloosa AL 35487-0380. Director: Malcolm MacDonald. Estab. 1945. Publishes hardcover originals. Averages 40 titles/year; receives 200 submissions annually. 80% of books from first-time authors; 100% of books from unagented writers. "Pays maximum 10% royalty on wholesale price; no advance." Publishes book an average of 16 months after acceptance. *Writer's Market* recommends allowing 2 months for reply. Free book catalog; ms guidelines for SASE.

Nonfiction: Biography, history, politics, religion, literature and archaeology. Considers upon merit almost any subject of scholarly interest, but specializes in speech communication, political science and public administration, literary criticism and biography, and history. Accepts nonfiction translations. Reviews artwork/photos as part of ms package.

Tips: "The University Press does not commission projects with freelance writers. Some who submit their manuscripts to us are independent scholars who have written on speculation, but they are not freelancers in the commonly accepted meaning of that word."

UNIVERSITY OF ALASKA PRESS, 1st Floor, Gruening Bldg., UAF, Fairbanks AK 99775-1580. (907)474-6389. Fax: (907)474-7225. Manager: Debbie Van Stone. Editorial Assistant: Pam Odom. Estab. 1967. Imprints are Ramuson Library Historical Translation Series, Oral Biographies, and Classic Reprints. Publishes hardcover originals and trade paperback originals and reprints. Averages 5-10 titles/year. Receives 100 submissions/year. 0% of books from first-time authors; 100% from unagented writers. Pays 7½-10% royalty on net sales. Publishes book an average of 2 years after acceptance. Query for electronic submissions. Reports in 2 months. Book catalog free on request.

Nonfiction: Biography, reference, technical, textbook, scholarly nonfiction relating to Alaska-circumpolar north. Subjects include agriculture/horticulture, Americana (Alaskana), animals, anthropology/archaeology, art/architecture, education, ethnic, government/politics, health/medicine, history, language, military/war, nature/environment, regional, science and translation. Nothing that isn't northern or circumpolar. Query or submit outline. Reviews copies of artwork/photos as part of ms package.

Recent Nonfiction Title: *The Aurora Watcher's Handbook*, by Neil Davis (reference).

Tips: "Writers have the best chance with scholarly nonfiction relating to Alaska, the circumpolar north and North Pacific Rim. Our audience is made up of scholars, historians, students, libraries, universities, individuals."

UNIVERSITY OF ARIZONA PRESS, 1230 N. Park Ave., #102, Tucson AZ 85719-4140. (602)621-1441. Fax: (602)621-8899. Director: Stephen Cox. Senior Editor: Joanne O'Hare. Estab. 1956. Publishes hardcover and paperback originals and reprints. Averages 50 titles/year; receives 300-400 submissions annually. 30% of books from first-time authors; 95% of books from unagented writers. Average print order is 1,500. Royalty terms vary; usual starting point for scholarly monograph is after sale of first 1,000 copies. Publishes book an average of 1 year after acceptance. Query for electronic submissions. Reports in three months. Book catalog for 9×12 SAE; ms guidelines for #10 SASE.

Nonfiction: Scholarly books about anthropology, Arizona, American West, archaeology, environmental science, global change, Latin America, Native Americans, natural history, space sciences and women's studies. Query and submit outline, list of illustrations and sample chapters. Reviews artwork/photos as part of ms package.

Tips: "Perhaps the most common mistake a writer might make is to offer a book manuscript or proposal to a house whose list he or she has not studied carefully. Editors rejoice in receiving material that is clearly targeted to the house's list, 'I have approached your firm because my books complement your past publications in . . .,' presented in a straightforward, businesslike manner."

THE UNIVERSITY OF ARKANSAS PRESS, 201 Ozark Ave., Fayetteville AR 72701-1201. (501)575-3246. Fax: (501)575-6044. Director: Miller Williams. Acquisitions Editor: Scott Danforth. Estab. 1980. Publishes hardcover and trade paperback originals and reprints. Averages 36 titles/year; receives 4,000 submissions annually. 30% of books from first-time authors; 90% of books from unagented writers. Pays 10% royalty on net receipts from hardcover; 6% on paper. Publishes book an average of 1 year after acceptance. Simultaneous (if so informed) submissions OK. Query for electronic submissions. Reports in up to 3 months. Book catalog for 9×12 SAE with 5 first class stamps; ms guidelines for #10 SAE and 2 first class stamps.

Nonfiction: Americana, history, humanities, nature, general politics and history of politics, and sociology. "Our current needs include literary criticism—especially on contemporary authors, history and biography. We won't consider manuscripts for texts, juvenile or religious studies, or anything requiring a specialized or exotic vocabulary." Query or submit outline and sample chapters.

Recent Nonfiction Title: *Encyclopedia of the Blues*, by Gérard Herzhaft.

Fiction: "Works of high literary merit; short stories; rarely novels. No genre fiction." Query.

Recent Fiction Title: *The Laughing Man of Woodmont Coves*, by Tom T. Hall.

Poetry: "Because of small list, query first." Arkansas Poetry Award offered for publication of first book. Write for contest rules.

Recent Poetry Title: *A New Geography of Poets*, edited by Edward Field, Gerald Locklin, and Charles Stetler.

UNIVERSITY OF CALIFORNIA PRESS, 2120 Berkeley Way, Berkeley CA 94720. Director: James H. Clark. Assistant Director: Lynne E. Withey. Estab. 1893. Los Angeles office: 405 Hilgard Ave., Los Angeles CA 90024-1373. New York office: Room 513, 50 E. 42 St., New York NY 10017. UK office: University Presses of California, Columbia, and Princeton, 1 Odlands Way, Bognor Regis, W. Sussex PO22 9SA England. Publishes hardcover and paperback originals and reprints. "On books likely to do more than return their costs, a standard royalty contract beginning at 7% on net receipts is paid; on paperbacks it is less." Publishes 180 titles/year. Queries are always advisable, accompanied by outlines or sample material. Accepts nonfiction translations. Send to Berkeley address. Reports vary, depending on the subject. *Writer's Market* recommends allowing 2 months for reply. Enclose return postage.

Nonfiction: "Most of our publications are hardcover nonfiction written by scholars." Publishes scholarly books including history, art, literary studies, social sciences, natural sciences and some high-level popularizations. No length preferences. *Writer's Market* recommends query with SASE first.

Fiction and Poetry: Publishes fiction and poetry only in translation.

‡UNIVERSITY OF IDAHO PRESS, 16 Brink Hall, Moscow ID 83844-1107. (208)885-7564. Imprints are: Northwest Folklife; Idaho Yesterdays; Northwest Naturalist Books. Director: Peggy Pace. Publishes hardcover and trade paperback originals and reprints. Publishes 8-10 titles/year. Receives 150-250 queries and 25-50 mss/

year. 100% of mss from unagented writers. Pays up to 10% royalty on net sales. Publishes book 1 year after acceptance of ms. Query for electronic submissions. Reports in 5 months. Book catalog and ms guidelines free on request.

Nonfiction: Biography, reference, technical and textbook. Subjects include agriculture/horticulture, Americana, anthropology/archaeology, ethnic, history, language/literature, military/war, nature/environment, recreation, regional and women's issues/studies. "Writers should contact us to discuss projects in advance and refer to our catalog to see the types of projects we are publishing. Avoid being unaware of the constraints of scholarly publishing, and avoid submitting queries and mss in areas we don't publish in." Query or submit proposal package, incuding sample chapter, contents, vita. Reviews artwork/photos as part of the freelance ms package. Writers should send photocopies.

Tips: Audience is educated readers, scholars.

UNIVERSITY OF ILLINOIS PRESS, 54 E. Gregory, Champaign IL 61820-6680. (217)333-0950. Fax: (217)244-8082. Director/Editor-in-Chief: Richard L. Wentworth. Estab. 1918. Publishes hardcover and trade paperback originals and reprints. Averages 100-110 titles/year. 50% of books from first-time authors; 95% of books from unagented writers. Subsidy publishes (nonauthor) 20% of books. Pays 0-10% royalty on net sales; offers average $1,000-1,500 advance (rarely). Publishes book an average of 1 year after acceptance. Query for electronic submissions. Reports in 1 month. *Writer's Market* recommends allowing 2 months for reply. Book catalog for 9 × 12 SAE and 2 first class stamps.

Nonfiction: Biography, reference and scholarly books. Subjects include Americana, history (especially American history), music (especially American music), politics, sociology, philosophy, sports and literature. Always looking for "solid scholarly books in American history, especially social history; books on American popular music, and books in the broad area of American studies." Query with outline.

Recent Nonfiction Title: *Thunder Below! The USS Barb Revolutionizes Submarine Warfare in World War II,* by Admiral Eugene B. Fluckey.

Fiction: Ethnic, experimental and mainstream. "We publish 2-3 collections of stories by individual writers each year and topical anthologies. We do not publish novels." Query.

Recent Fiction Title: *Middle Murphy,* by Mark Costello (stories).

Tips: "Serious scholarly books that are broad enough and well-written enough to appeal to non-specialists are doing well for us in today's market."

UNIVERSITY OF IOWA PRESS, 119 W. Park Rd., Iowa City IA 52242. (319)335-2000. Fax: (319)335-2055. Director: Paul Zimmer. Estab. 1969. Publishes hardcover and paperback originals. Averages 30 titles/year; receives 300-400 submissions annually. 30% of books from first-time authors; 95% of books from unagented writers. Average print order for a writer's first book is 1,200-1,500. Pays 7-10% royalty on net price. "We market mostly by direct mailing of flyers to groups with special interests in our titles and by advertising in trade and scholarly publications." Publishes book an average of 1 year after acceptance. Query for electronic submissions. Reports within 4 months. Free book catalog and ms guidelines.

Nonfiction: Publishes anthropology, archaeology, British and American literary studies, history (Victorian, U.S., regional Latin American), aviation history, history of photography and natural history. Looks for evidence of original research; reliable sources; clarity of organization, complete development of theme with documentation and supportive footnotes and/or bibliography; and a substantive contribution to knowledge in the field treated. Query or submit outline. Use *Chicago Manual of Style.* Reviews artwork/photos as part of ms package.

Recent Nonfiction Title: *Salem Is My Dwelling Place*

Fiction and Poetry: Currently publishes the Iowa Short Fiction Award selections. Please query regarding poetry or fiction before sending manuscript.

Tips: "Now seeking regional history instead of German and medieval history."

UNIVERSITY OF MAINE PRESS, 51 Public Affairs Building, Orono ME 04469. (207)581-1408. Contact: Director. Publishes hardcover and trade paperback originals and reprints. Publishes 4 titles/year. Receives 50 queries and 25 mss/year. 10% of mss from first-time authors, 90% from unagented writers. Publishes book 1 year after acceptance of ms. Simultaneous submissions OK. Query for electronic submissions. *Writer's Market* recommends allowing 2 months for reply.

Nonfiction: "We are an academic book publisher, interested in scholarly works on regional history, regional life sciences, Franco-American studies. Authors should be able to articulate their ideas on the potential market for their work." Query.

Fiction: "The University of Maine Press publishes primarily regional fiction: Maine, New England, Canadian Maritimes." Query.

UNIVERSITY OF MASSACHUSETTS PRESS, P.O. Box 429, Amherst MA 01004. (413)545-2217. Fax: (413)545-1226. Director: Bruce Wilcox. Estab. 1963. Publishes hardcover and paperback originals, reprints and imports. Averages 30 titles/year; receives 600 submissions annually. 20% of books from first-time authors; 90% of books from unagented writers. Average print order for a writer's first book is 1,500. Royalties generally 10% of net income. Advance rarely offered. No author subsidies accepted. Publishes book an average of 1 year after acceptance. Query for electronic submissions. Preliminary report in 1 month. *Writer's Market* recommends allowing 2 months for reply. Free book catalog.

Nonfiction: Publishes African-American studies, art and architecture, biography, criticism, history, natural history, philosophy, poetry, public policy, sociology and women's studies in original and reprint editions. Accepts nonfiction translations. Submit outline and 1-2 sample chapters. Reviews artwork/photos as part of ms package.

Recent Nonfiction Title: *Black Yankees: The Development of an Afro-American Subculture in Eighteenth-Century New England*, by William D. Piersen.

UNIVERSITY OF MICHIGAN PRESS, Dept. WM, 839 Greene St., Ann Arbor MI 48106. (313)764-4388. Fax: (313)936-0456. Director: Colin Day. Editors: Mary C. Erwin, LeAnn Fields, Joyce Harrison, Ellen Bauerle, Malcolm Litchfield. Estab. 1930. Imprint is Ann Arbor Paperbacks. Publishes hardcover and paperback originals and reprints. Averages 110 titles/year. Pays royalty on net price; offers advance. Query for electronic submissions. Reports in 2 months. Free book catalog.

Nonfiction: Archaeology, advanced textbooks, anthropology, classics, economics, English as a second language, Great Lakes regional, history, law, literary criticism, music, political science, reference, theater, women's studies. Query first.

UNIVERSITY OF MISSOURI PRESS, 2910 LeMone Blvd., Columbia MO 65201. (314)882-7641. Director: Beverly Jarrett. Publishes hardcover and paperback originals and paperback reprints. Averages 50 titles/year; receives 500 submissions annually. 25-30% of books from first-time authors; 90% of books from unagented writers. Average print order for a writer's first book is 1,000-1,500. Pays up to 10% royalty on net receipts; no advance. Publishes book an average of 1 year after acceptance. Query for electronic submissions. Reports in 6 months. Free book catalog; ms guidelines for SASE.

Nonfiction: Scholarly publisher interested in history, literary criticism, political science, social science and some art history. Also regional books about Missouri and the Midwest. No mathematics or hard sciences. Query or submit outline and sample chapters. Consult *Chicago Manual of Style*.

Fiction: "Collections of short fiction are considered throughout the year; the press does not publish novels. Inquiries should be directed to Clair Willcox, Editor, and should include a table of contents and a brief description of the ms that notes its length."

Recent Fiction Title: *Thief of Lives*, by Kit Reed.

UNIVERSITY OF NEBRASKA PRESS, Dept. WM, 901 N. 17th St., Lincoln NE 68588-0520. (402)472-3581. Editor-in-Chief: Willis G. Regier. Estab. 1941. Publishes hardcover and paperback originals and reprints. Specializes in scholarly nonfiction, some regional books; reprints of Western Americana; and natural history. Averages 50 new titles, 50 paperback reprints (*Bison Books*)/year; receives more than 1,000 submissions annually. 25% of books from first-time authors; 95% of books from unagented writers. Average print order for a writer's first book is 1,000. Royalty is usually graduated from 10% on wholesale price for original books; no advance. Reports in 4 months. Book catalog and guidelines for 9 × 12 SAE with 5 first class stamps.

Nonfiction: Publishes Americana, biography, history, nature, photography, psychology, sports, literature, agriculture and American Indian themes. Accepts nonfiction and fiction translations but no original fiction. Query. Accepts outline/synopsis, 2 sample chapters and introduction. Looks for "an indication that the author knows his/her subject thoroughly and interprets it intelligently." Reviews artwork/photos as part of ms package.

Recent Nonfiction Title: *Billy the Kid*, by Robert Utley.

Recent Fiction Title: *Mad Love*, by André Breton (translation).

UNIVERSITY OF NEVADA PRESS, Reno NV 89557-0076. (702)784-6573. Fax: (702)784-6200. Director: Thomas R. Radko. Editor-in-Chief: Nick Cady. Estab. 1961. Publishes hardcover and paperback originals and reprints. Averages 22 titles/year. 20% of books from first-time authors; 99% of books from unagented writers. Average print order for a writer's first book is 2,000. Pays average of 10% royalty on net price. Publishes book an average of 1 year after acceptance. Preliminary report in 2 months. Free book catalog and ms guidelines.

Nonfiction: Specifically needs regional history and natural history, literature, current affairs, ethnonationalism, gambling and gaming, anthropology, biographies and Basque studies. "We are the first university press to sustain a sound series on Basque studies—New World and Old World." No juvenile books. Submit complete ms. *Writer's Market* recommends query with SASE first. Reviews photocopies of artwork/photos as part of ms package.

Recent Nonfiction Title: *Survival of the Spirit: Chiricahua Apache in Captivity*, by H. Henrietta Stockel.

UNIVERSITY OF NEW MEXICO PRESS, 1720 Lomas Blvd. NE, Albuquerque NM 87131-1591. (505)277-2346. Contact: Editor. Estab. 1929. Publishes hardcover originals and trade paperback originals and reprints. Firm averages 50 titles/year. Receives 500 submissions/year. 12% of books from first-time authors. 90% from unagented writers. Pays up to 15% royalty on wholesale price. Publishes book an average of 1 year after acceptance. Reports in 2 weeks on queries. *Writer's Market* recommends allowing 2 months for reply. Free book catalog.

Nonfiction: Biography, illustrated book and scholarly books. Subjects include anthropology/archaeology, art/architecture, ethnic, history and photography. "No how-to, humor, juvenile, self-help, software, technical or textbooks." Query. Reviews artwork/photos as part of ms package. Prefers to see photocopies first.

Tips: "Most of our authors are academics. A scholarly monograph by an academic has a better chance than anything else. Our audience is a combination of academics and interested lay readers."

THE UNIVERSITY OF NORTH CAROLINA PRESS, P.O. Box 2288, Chapel Hill NC 27515-2288. (919)966-3561. Director: Kate Douglas Torrey. Publishes hardcover and paperback originals and occasionally, paperback reprints. Specializes in scholarly books and regional trade books. Averages 65 titles/year. 70% of books from first-time scholarly authors; 90% of books from unagented writers. Royalty schedule "varies." Occasional advances. Query for electronic submissions. Publishes book an average of 1 year after acceptance. Reports in 5 months. Free book catalog; ms guidelines for SASE.

Nonfiction: "Our major fields are American history, American studies and Southern studies." Also, scholarly books in legal history, Civil War history, literary studies, classics, gender studies, oral history, folklore, political science, religious studies, historical sociology, Latin American studies. In European studies, focus is on history of the Third Reich, 20th-century Europe, and Holocaust history. Special focus on general interest books on the lore, crafts, cooking, gardening and natural history of the Southeast. Submit outline/synopsis and sample chapters; must follow *Chicago Manual of Style*. Looks for "intellectual excellence and clear writing. We do *not* publish poetry or original fiction." Reviews artwork/photos as part of ms package.

Recent Nonfiction Title: *Walking the Blue Ridge: A Guide to the Trails of the Blue Ridge Parkway*, by Leonard M. Adkins.

UNIVERSITY OF NORTH TEXAS PRESS, P.O. Box 13856, Denton TX 76203-3856. Fax: (817)565-4590. Director: Frances B. Vick. Publishes hardcover and trade paperback originals and reprints. Publishes 10 titles/year. Receives 300 queries and mss/year. 99% of mss from unagented writers. Pays 7½-10% royalty of net. Publishes book 1 year after acceptance of ms. Simultaneous submissions OK. Query for electonic submissions. Reports in 2 months on queries. Book catalog free on request.

Nonfiction: Biography, coffee table book and reference. Subjects include agriculture/horticulture, Americana, computers and electronics, ethnic, government/politics, history, language/literature, military/war, nature/environment and regional. "We have a series called War and the Southwest; Environmental Philosophy Series; Texas Folklore Society Publications series. Poetry series—Texas poets; literary biographies of Texas writers series." Query. Reviews artwork/photos as part of freelance ms package. Writers should send photocopies.

Fiction: Literary and short story collections. Submit sample chapters.

Poetry: Only publish Texas poets, or poets with Texas connections at this time. Query.

UNIVERSITY OF OKLAHOMA PRESS, 1005 Asp Ave., Norman OK 73019-0445. (405)325-5111. Fax: (405)325-4000. Editor-in-Chief: John Drayton. Estab. 1928. Imprint is Oklahoma Paperbacks. Publishes hardcover and paperback originals and reprints. Averages 70 titles/year. Pays royalty comparable to those paid by other publishers for comparable books. Publishes book an average of 12-18 months after acceptance. Query for electronic submissions. Reports in 3 months. Book catalog $1 with 9 × 12 SAE and 6 first class stamps.

Nonfiction: Publishes American Indian studies, Western U.S. history, literary theory, and classical studies. No unsolicited poetry and fiction. Query, including outline, 1-2 sample chapters and author résumé. Use *Chicago Manual of Style* for ms guidelines. Reviews artwork/photos as part of ms package.

UNIVERSITY OF PENNSYLVANIA PRESS, 418 Service Dr., Philadelphia PA 19104-6097. (215)898-6261. Fax: (215)898-0404. Editorial Director: Timothy Clancy. Estab. 1860. Publishes hardcover and paperback originals and reprints. Averages 70 titles/year; receives 650 submissions annually. 10-20% of books from first-time authors; 99% of books from unagented writers. Subsidy publishes (nonauthor) 4% of books. Subsidy publishing is determined by evaluation obtained by the press from outside specialists; approval by Faculty Editorial Committee and funding organization. Royalty determined on book-by-book basis. Publishes book an average of 9 months after delivery of completed ms. Query for electronic submissions. Reports in 3 months. Book catalog for 9 × 12 SAE with 6 first class stamps. Do not send unsolicited mss.

Nonfiction: Publishes Americana, literature, business, economics, history, medicine, biological sciences, law, anthropology, folklore, art history, architecture. "Serious books that serve the scholar and the professional." Follow the *Chicago Manual of Style*. Query with outline and letter describing project, state availability of photos and/or illustrations to accompany ms, with copies of illustrations. Do not send ms with query. Include resume or vita.

Recent Nonfiction Title: *Dangerous Men and Adventurous Women: Romance Writers on the Appeal of the Romance*, edited by Jayne Ann Krentz.

Tips: "Queries/mss may be routed to other editors in the publishing group."

UNIVERSITY OF PITTSBURGH PRESS, Dept. WM, 127 N. Bellefield Ave., Pittsburgh PA 15260. (412)624-4110. Fax: (412)624-7380. Editor-in-Chief: Catherine Marshall. Estab. 1936. Publishes hardcover and trade paperback originals and reprints. Averages 55 titles/year. 5% of books from first-time authors; 99% from unagented writers. Pays royalties on net sales (per contract). Publishes books an average of 1 year after acceptance. Query for electronic submissions. Reports in 2 months. Book catalog free on request. Manuscript guidelines for contests for #10 SASE.

Nonfiction: Biography, reference, textbook, scholarly monographs. Subjects include anthropology/archaeology, art/architecture, business and economics, ethnic, government/politics, health/medicine, history, language/literature, music/dance, philosophy, regional, Latin American studies, Russian and East European studies, social and labor history, Milton studies. Query. Reviews artwork/photos as part of ms package.

Recent Nonfiction Title: *The Puzzle People: Memoirs of a Transplant Surgeon*, by Thomas E. Starzl.

Fiction: Literary. "One title per year, winner of the Drue Heinz Literature Prize." No novels. Submit complete ms via contest; send SASE for rules.

Recent Fiction Title: *Director of the World and Other Stories*, by Jane McCafferty.

Poetry: 6 titles per year; 1 from previously unpublished author. Submit complete ms via contest; send SASE for rules; authors with previous books send direct to press in Sept. and Oct.

Recent Poetry Title: *The Company of Heaven*, by Jeffrey Skinner.

UNIVERSITY OF SCRANTON PRESS, University of Scranton, Scranton PA 18510. Fax: (717)941-4309. Director: Richard Rousseau. Imprint is Ridge Row Press. Publishes hardcover originals. Publishes 8 titles/year. Receives 200 queries and 45 mss/year. 60% of mss from first-time authors, 100% from unagented writers. Pays 10% royalty. Publishes book 1 year after acceptance of ms. Query for electronic submissions. Reports in 2 weeks on queries. *Writer's Market* recommends allowing 2 months for reply. Book catalog and ms guidelines free on request.

Nonfiction: Scholarly monographs. Subjects include art/architecture, language/literature, philosophy, religion and sociology. Looking for clear editorial focus: Theology/religious studies; philosophy/philosophy of religion; scholarly treatments; the culture of northwestern Pennsylvania. Query or submit outline and 2 sample chapters.

Recent Nonfiction Title: *The Jesuit Tradition in Education and Missions: A 450 Year Perspective* (theology/church history).

Poetry: Only poetry related to northeastern Pennsylvania.

THE UNIVERSITY OF TENNESSEE PRESS, 293 Communications Bldg., Knoxville TN 37996-0325. Fax: (615)974-3724. Acquisitions Editor: Meredith Morgan. Estab. 1940. Averages 30 titles/year; receives 300 submissions annually. 50% of books from first-time authors; 99% of books from unagented writers. Average print order for a writer's first book is 1,250. Subsidy publishes (nonauthor) 10% of books. Pays negotiable royalty on net receipts. Publishes book an average of 1 year after acceptance. Reports in 2 months. Book catalog for 12×16 SAE and 2 first class stamps; ms guidelines for SASE.

Nonfiction: American history, cultural studies, religious studies, vernacular architecture and material culture, literary criticism, African-American studies, women's studies, Caribbean, anthropology, folklore and regional studies. Prefers "scholarly treatment and a readable style. Authors usually have Ph.D.s." Submit outline, author vita, and 2 sample chapters. No fiction, poetry or plays. Reviews artwork/photos as part of ms package.

Recent Nonfiction Title: *American Home Life, 1880-1930: A Social History of Spaces and Services*, edited by Jessica H. Foy and Thomas J. Schlereth.

Tips: "Our market is in several groups: scholars; educated readers with special interests in given scholarly subjects; and the general educated public interested in Tennessee, Appalachia and the South. Not all our books appeal to all these groups, of course, but any given book must appeal to at least one of them."

UNIVERSITY OF TEXAS PRESS, P.O. Box 7819, Austin TX 78713-7819. Fax: (512)320-0668. Executive Editor: Theresa May. Estab. 1952. Averages 60 titles/year; receives 1,000 submissions annually. 50% of books from first-time authors; 99% of books from unagented writers. Average print order for a writer's first book is 1,000. Pays royalty usually based on net income; occasionally offers advance. Publishes book an average of 18 months after acceptance. Query for electronic submissions. Reports in up to 3 months. Free book catalog and writer's guidelines.

Nonfiction: General scholarly subjects: astronomy, natural history, American, Latin American and Middle Eastern studies, native Americans, classics, films, biology, contemporary architecture, archeology, anthropology, geography, ornithology, ecology, Chicano studies, linguistics, 20th-century and women's literature. Also uses specialty titles related to Texas and the Southwest, national trade titles, and regional trade titles. Accepts nonfiction and fiction translations (Middle Eastern or Latin American fiction). Query or submit outline and 2 sample chapters. Reviews artwork/photos as part of ms package.

Recent Nonfiction Title: *Bat Bomb: World War II's Other Secret Weapon*, by Jack Couffer.

Recent Fiction Translation: *A World For Julius*, by Alfredo Bryce Echenique (translation from Spanish).

Tips: "It's difficult to make a manuscript over 400 double-spaced pages into a feasible book. Authors should take special care to edit out extraneous material. Looks for sharply focused, in-depth treatments of important topics."

• See the interview with Theresa May in the introduction to this section.

‡UNIVERSITY PRESS OF AMERICA, INC., 4720 Boston Way, Lanham MD 20706. (301)459-3366. Publisher: James E. Lyons. Estab. 1975. Publishes hardcover and paperback originals and reprints. Averages 450 titles/year. Pays 5-15% royalty on net receipts; occasional advance. Reports in 6 weeks. Book catalog and guidelines for SASE.

Nonfiction: Scholarly monographs, college, and graduate level textbooks in history, economics, business, psychology, political science, African studies, Black studies, philosophy, religion, sociology, music, art, literature, drama and education. No juvenile, elementary or high school material. Submit outline or request proposal questionnaire.

Recent Nonfiction Title: *The Use of Force: Military Power and International Politics*, fourth edition, edited by Robert J. Art and Kenneth N. Waltz (political science).

‡UNIVERSITY PRESS OF COLORADO, P.O. Box 849, Niwot CO 80544. (303)530-5337. Director: Luther Wilson. Estab. 1965. Publishes hardcover and paperback originals. Averages 30 titles/year; receives 500 submissions annually. 50% of books from first-time authors; 99% of books from unagented writers. Average print order for a writer's first book is 1,500-2,000. Pays 10-12½-15% royalty contract on net price; no advances. Publishes book an average of 9 months after acceptance. Electronic submissions encouraged. Reports in 3 months. Free book catalog.

Nonfiction: Scholarly, regional and environmental subjects. Length: 250-500 pages. Query first with table of contents, preface or opening chapter. Reviews artwork/photos as part of ms package.

Recent Nonfiction Title: *Moctezuma's Mexico*, by David Carrasco and Eduardo Matos Moctezuma.

Tips: "Books should be solidly researched and from a reputable scholar, because we are a university press. We have a new series on world resources and environmental issues."

UNIVERSITY PRESS OF KENTUCKY, 663 S. Limestone, Lexington KY 40508-4008. (606)257-2951. Contact: Editor-in-Chief. Estab. 1951. Publishes hardcover originals and hardcover and trade paperback reprints. Averages 45 titles/year. Payment varies: no advance. Publishes ms an average of 1 year after acceptance. Reports in 1 month on queries. *Writer's Market* recommends allowing 2 months for reply. Free book catalog.

Nonfiction: Biography, reference and monographs. Subjects include Americana, history, politics and sociology. "We are a scholarly publisher, publishing chiefly for an academic and professional audience. Strong areas are history, literature, political science, folklore, anthropology, and sociology. No textbooks, genealogical material, lightweight popular treatments, how-to books; and generally books not related to our major areas of interest." Query. Reviews artwork/photos, but generally does not publish books with extensive number of photos.

Recent Nonfiction Title: *John Marshall Harlan: The Last Whig Justice*, by Loren Beth.

Tips: "Most of our authors are drawn from our primary academic and professional audience. We are probably not a good market for the usual freelance writer."

UNIVERSITY PRESS OF MISSISSIPPI, 3825 Ridgewood Rd., Jackson MS 39211-6492. (601)982-6205. Fax: (601)982-6217. Director: Richard Abel. Associate Director and Editor-in-Chief: Seetha Srinivasan. Estab. 1970. Imprint is Muscadine Books (regional trade). Publishes hardcover and paperback originals and reprints. Averages 45 titles/year; receives 500 submissions annually. 20% of books from first-time authors; 95% of books from unagented writers. "Competitive royalties and terms." Publishes book an average of 1 year after acceptance. Reports in up to 3 months. Book catalog for 9 × 12 SAE with 3 first class stamps.

Nonfiction: Americana, biography, history, politics, folklife, literary criticism, ethnic/minority studies, natural sciences and popular culture with scholarly emphasis. Interested in southern regional studies and literary studies. Submit outline and sample chapters and *curriculum vita* to Acquisitions Editor. "We prefer a proposal that describes the significance of the work and a chapter outline." Reviews artwork/photos as part of ms package.

Fiction: Commissioned trade editions by prominent writers.

For explanation of symbols, see the Key to Symbols and Abbreviations on page 72. For unfamiliar words, see the Glossary.

UNIVERSITY PRESS OF NEW ENGLAND, (Includes Wesleyan University Press), 23 S. Main St., Hanover NH 03755-2048. (603)643-7100. Fax: (603)643-1540. Director: Thomas L. McFarland. Editors: Jeanne West, Michael Lowenthal, David Caffry and Terry Cochran. Estab. 1970. "University Press of New England is a consortium of university presses. Some books—those published for one of the consortium members—carry the joint imprint of New England and the member: Wesleyan, Dartmouth, Brandeis, Brown, Tufts, Universities of Connecticut, New Hampshire, Vermont, Rhode Island and Middlebury." Publishes hardcover and trade paperback originals and trade paperback reprints. Averages 60 titles/year. Subsidy publishes (nonauthor) 80% of books. Pays standard royalty; occasionally offers advance. Query for electronic submissions. Reports in 2 months. Book catalog and guidelines for 9 × 12 SAE with 5 first class stamps.
Nonfiction: Americana (New England), art, biography, history, music, nature, politics, psychology, reference, science, sociology, and regional (New England). No festschriften, memoirs, unrevised doctoral dissertations, or symposium collections. Submit outline and 1-2 sample chapters.
Fiction: Regional (New England) novels and reprints.

UTAH STATE UNIVERSITY PRESS, Logan UT 84322-7800. (801)750-1362. Fax: (801)750-1541. Contact: Director. Publishes hardcover and trade paperback originals and reprints. Averages 6 titles/year; receives 170 submissions annually. 8% of books from first-time authors. Average print order for a writer's first book is 1,000. Subsidy publishes (nonauthor) 45% of books. Pays royalty on net price; no advance. Publishes book an average of 18 months after acceptance. Query for electronic submissions. Reports in 2 weeks on queries. *Writer's Market* recommends allowing 2 months for reply. Free book catalog; ms guidelines for SASE.
Nonfiction: Biography, reference and textbook on folklore, Americana (history and politics). "Particularly interested in book-length scholarly manuscripts dealing with folklore, Western history, Western literature. All manuscript submissions must have a scholarly focus." Submit complete ms. *Writer's Market* recommends query with SASE first. Reviews artwork/photos as part of ms package.
Poetry: "At the present time, we have accepted several poetry manuscripts and will not be reading poetry submissions for one year."

VANDAMERE PRESS, Subsidiary of AB Associates, P.O. Box 5243, Arlington VA 22205. Acquisitions Editor: Jerry Frank. Publishes hardcover and trade paperback originals and reprints. Publishes 8 titles/year. Receives 500 queries and 500 ms/year. 75% of mss from first-time authors, 90% from unagented writers. Pays royalty on revenues generated. Publishes book 6-36 months after acceptance of ms. Simultaneous submissions OK. Reports in 3 months.
Nonfiction: Biography, coffee table book, children's/juvenile and self-help. Subjects include Americana, child guidance/parenting, education, gardening, history, military/war, recreation, regional, travel and career guide. Submit outline and 1 or 2 sample chapters. Reviews artwork/photos as part of the freelance ms package. Writers should send photocopies.
Fiction: Adventure, erotica, humor, mystery and suspense. Submit synopsis and 5-10 sample chapters.
Tips: "Authors who can provide endorsements from significant published writers, celebrities, etc. will *always* be given serious consideration. Clean, easy-to-read, *dark* copy is essential. Patience in waiting for replies is essential. All unsolicited work is looked at but as a last priority." No response without SASE.

THE VESTAL PRESS, LTD., P.O. Box 97, Vestal NY 13850-0097. (607)797-4872. Fax: (607)797-4898. Publisher: Grace L. Houghton. Estab. 1961. Publishes hardcover and trade paperback originals and reprints. Averages 6-8 titles/year; receives 50-75 submissions annually. 20% of books from first-time writers; 95% of books from unagented authors. Pays 10% maximum royalty on net sales. Publishes books an average of 1 year after acceptance. Simultaneous submissions OK. Reports in up to 6 months. Book catalog for $2 with 6 × 9 SAE and 2 first class stamps.
Nonfiction: Technical antiquarian hobby topics in antique radio, mechanical music (player pianos, music boxes, etc.), reed organs, carousels, antique phonographs, early cinema history, regional history based on postcard collections. Also publishes titles in woodcarving. Query or submit outline and sample chapters.
Recent Nonfiction Title: *Where's the Fire: American Firefighters in Picture Postcards circa 1910.*

VGM CAREER HORIZONS, Imprint of NTC Publishing Group, 4255 W. Touhy Ave., Lincolnwood IL 60646-1975. (708)679-5500. Fax: (708)679-2494. Editorial Director: Anne Knudsen. Estab. 1963. Publishes hardcover and paperback originals. Averages 40-45 titles/year; receives 150-200 submissions annually. 15% of books from first-time authors; 95% of books from unagented writers. Pays royalty or makes outright purchase. Advance varies. Publishes book an average of 1 year after acceptance. Simultaneous submissions OK. Query for electronic submissions. Reports in 3 months. Book catalog and ms guidelines for 9 × 12 SAE with 5 first class stamps.
Nonfiction: Textbook and general trade on careers in medicine, business, environment, etc. Query or submit outline and sample chapters. Reviews artwork/photos as part of ms package.
Recent Nonfiction Title: *Joyce Lain Kennedy's Career Book.*
Tips: "Our audience is made up of job seekers, career planners, job changers, and students and adults in education and trade markets. Study our existing line of books before sending proposals."

VICTOR BOOKS, Division of Scripture Press Publications, Inc. 1825 College Ave., Wheaton IL 60187. Contact: Acquisitions Editor. Estab. 1934. Publishes hardcover and trade paperback originals. Firm averages 100 titles/year. Receives 1,500 submissions/year. Royalty on all books, advances on some. Simultaneous submissions OK if specified. Reports in 1 month on queries. *Writer's Market* recommends allowing 2 months for reply. Ms guidelines for #10 SASE; specify general, children's adult novels or academic (Bridge Point). Catalog and guidelines for 4 first class stamps.
Tips: "All books must in some way be Bible-related by authors who themselves are evangelical Christians. Victor, therefore, is not a publisher for everybody. Only a small fraction of the manuscripts received can be seriously considered for publication. Most books result from contacts that acquisitions editors make with qualified authors, though from time to time an unsolicited proposal triggers enough excitement to result in a contract."

VIKING PENGUIN, Division of Penguin USA, 375 Hudson St., New York NY 10014. "Prefers not to share information."
• This publisher is accepting only agented submissions.

VILLARD BOOKS, Random House, 201 E. 50th St., New York NY 10022. (212)572-2720. Publisher and Editor-in-Chief: Diane Reverand. Contact: Melanie Ceclca. Estab. 1983. Publishes hardcover and trade paperback originals. Averages 55-60 titles/year. 95% of books are agented submissions. Pays varying advances and royalties; negotiated separately. Simultaneous submissions OK. Query for electronic submissions. *Writer's Market* recommends allowing 2 months for reply.
Nonfiction and Fiction: Looks for commercial nonfiction and fiction. Submit outline/synopsis and up to 50 pages in sample chapters. No unsolicited submissions.

‡**VISTA PUBLICATIONS,** P.O. Box 661447, Miami Springs FL 33166. Owner: Helen Brose. Publishes trade and mass market paperback originals. Publishes 2 titles/year. Receives 5 queries/year. 50% of mss from first-time authors, 50% from unagented writers. Pays 10-15% royalty on retail price. Publishes book 1 year after acceptance. Simultaneous submissions OK. Query for electronic submissions. Prefers diskette—3½"; IBM compatible. Reports in 1 month on proposals. Book catalog and ms guidelines free on request.
Nonfiction: Subjects include anthropology/archaeology, cooking, foods and nutrition, government/politics, history, language/literature, regional and travel. "We specialize in books about Guatemala, Central America, and/or by Guatemalan authors in English or Spanish." Submit synopsis and 1 sample chapter.
Recent Nonfiction Title: *The Rulers of Tikal*, by Genevieve Michel (archaeology).
Fiction: "We are open to any work as long as it relates in some way to Guatemala." Query. Submit synopsis and 1 sample chapter.
Recent Fiction Title: *El Salvador de Buques*, by Rodrigo Rey Rosa (novel).
Tips: "Our audience consists of people interested in works about Guatemala or by Guatemalan authors. The topic of the manuscript should be within our guidelines of publishing works relating to Guatemala."

VOYAGEUR PRESS, 123 N. 2nd St., Stillwater MN 55082. (612)430-2210. Acquisitions Editor: Tom Lebovsky. Publishes hardcover and trade paperback originals. Publishes 20 titles/year. Receives 1,200 queries and 500 mss/year. 10% of mss from first-time authors, 90% from unagented writers. Pays royalty. Publishes book 1 year after acceptance of ms. Simultaneous submissions OK. Reports in 3 months. Book catalog and ms guidelines free on request.
Nonfiction: Coffee table book (and smaller format photographic essay books), cookbook, how-to (photography) and children's/juvenile. Subjects include natural history, nature/environment, photography, outdoor recreation, regional and travel. Query or submit outline and proposal package. Reviews artwork/photos as part of the freelance ms package. Photographers should send transparencies—duplicates only please and tearsheets.
Tips: "Our audience includes readers interested in wildlife biology and natural history and tourists wishing to learn more about wilderness or urban areas. Please present as focused an idea as possible in a brief submission (1 page cover letter; 2 page outline or proposal). Note your credentials for writing the book. Tell all you know about the market niche and marketing possibilities for proposed book."

‡**WAITE GROUP PRESS,** 200 Tamal Plaza, Corte Madera CA 94925. Editorial Director: Scott Calamar. Publishes trade paperback originals. Publishes 25 titles/year. Receives 50 queries and 35 mss/year. 25% of mss from first-time authors, 100% from unagented writers. Pays royalty on wholesale price or makes outright purchase. Publishes book 4 months after acceptance of ms. Query for electronic submissions. Reports in 2 months. Book catalog free on request.
Nonfiction: How-to, reference, self-help and technical. Subjects include computers and software. "We prefer cutting-edge topics." Query or submit outline.
Recent Nonfiction Title: *Virtual Reality Playhouse*, by Nicholas Larroff (computer).
Tips: Audience is "those interested in having fun and learning about their PCs and Macintoshes. We emphasize new technologies and graphics. Agents are not necessary or preferable. Know your subject and please be patient!"

J. WESTON WALCH, PUBLISHER, P.O. Box 658, Portland ME 04104-0658. (207)772-2846. Fax: (207)772-3105. Editor-in-Chief: Richard S. Kimball. Editor: Jane Carter. Math/Science Editor: Eric Olson. Computer Editor: Robert Crepeau. Estab. 1927. Publishes paperback originals and software. Averages 75 titles/year; receives 300 submissions annually. 10% of books from first-time authors; 95% of books from unagented writers. Average print order for a writer's first book is 700. Offers 10-15% royalty on gross receipts; buys some titles by outright purchase for $100-2,500. No advance. Publishes book an average of 18 months after acceptance. Query for electronic submissions. Reports in 2 months. Book catalog for 9×12 SAE with 5 first class stamps; ms guidelines for #10 SASE.

Nonfiction: Subjects include art, business, computer education, economics, English, foreign language, government, health, history, mathematics, middle school, music, psychology, science, social science, sociology and special education. "We publish only supplementary educational material for grades six to twelve in the U.S. and Canada. Formats include books, posters, blackline masters, card sets, cassettes, microcomputer courseware, video and mixed packages. Most titles are assigned by us, though we occasionally accept an author's unsolicited submission. We have a great need for author/artist teams and for authors who can write at third- to tenth-grade levels. We do *not* want basic texts, anthologies or industrial arts titles. Most of our authors—but not all—have secondary teaching experience. *Query first.* Looks for sense of organization, writing ability, knowledge of subject, skill of communicating with intended audience." Reviews artwork/photos as part of ms package.

Recent Nonfiction Title: *Recycling! Ways to Manage Household Waste*, by Kathy Sammis.

WALKER AND CO., Division of Walker Publishing Co., 720 5th Ave., New York NY 10019. Fax: (212)307-1764. Contact: Submissions Editor. Estab. 1959. Publishes hardcover and trade paperback originals and reprints of British books. Averages 150 titles/year; receives 4,500 submissions annually. 50% of books from first-time authors; 50% of books from unagented writers. Pays varying royalty or makes outright purchase. Advance averages from $1,000-3,000 "but could be higher or lower." Do not telephone submissions editors. Material without SASE will not be returned. *Writer's Market* recommends allowing 4 months for reply. Book catalog and guidelines for 9×12 SAE with 3 first class stamps.

Nonfiction: Biography, business, histories, science and natural history, health, music, nature and environment, parenting, reference, popular science, and self-help books. Query or submit outline and sample chapter. Reviews photos as part of ms package. Do not send originals.

Fiction: Mystery/suspense, juvenile (ages 5 and up), western.

Tips: "We also need preschool to young adult nonfiction, science fiction, historical novels, biographies and middle-grade novels. Query."

‡WARD HILL PRESS, P.O. Box 04-0424, Staten Island NY 10304. (718)816-9449. Editorial Director: Elizabeth Davis. Publishes trade paperback originals. Publishes 4-6 titles/year. Receives 50 or more queries and 25 mss/year. 75% of mss from first-time authors, 90% from unagented writers. Pays 6-12% royalty on retail price. Offers $800-1,600 advance. Publishes book 6 months after acceptance. Query for electronic submissions. Prefers disk. Reports in 1-2 months on queries. Book catalog and ms guidelines free on request.

Nonfiction: Biography, how-to and children's/juvenile. Subjects include ethnic, history and women's issues/studies (young adult), and automotive how-to (adult). "We publish multicultural books for young adults—specifically, biographies of people not yet covered by more mainstream publishers. We also publish a small line of car-care books and monographs for adults." Query. Reviews artwork/photos as part of freelance ms package. "Query first." Writers should send photocopies.

Recent Nonfiction Title: *Zora Neale Hurston: A Storyteller's Life*, by Yates (bio).

WARNER BOOKS, Warner Publishing Inc., Time & Life Bldg., 1271 Avenue of the Americas, New York NY 10020. (212)522-7200. Publisher, Warner Paperbacks: Mel Parker. Publishes hardcover, trade and mass market paperback originals and reprints. Does not accept unsolicited mss or proposals.

‡WARREN PUBLISHING HOUSE, INC., P.O. Box 2250, Everett WA 98203-0250. (206)353-3100. Editorial Manager: Kathleen Cubley. Publishes educational paperback originals and hardcover and paperback children's picture books/easy-readers. Publishes 12-14 titles/year. Receives 200 queries and 1,000+ mss/year. 50% of mss from first-time authors, 100% from unagented writers. Makes outright purchase plus copy of book/newsletter author's material appears in. Simultaneous submissions OK. Reports in 1 month. Book catalog and mss guidelines free on request.

Nonfiction: Cookbook, illustrated activity book, children's/juvenile and textbook. Subjects include agriculture/horticulture, animals, art/architecture, child guidance/parenting, cooking, foods & nutrition, education, ethnic, gardening, health/medicine, history, hobbies, language/literature, music/dance, nature/environment and science. "We consider activity ideas that are appropriate for people (teacher/parents) who work with children two to six years old." Query.

Recent Nonfiction Title: *Exploring Wood,* by Jean Warren.

Fiction: Adventure, ethnic, fantasy, juvenile and original stories and songs that have learning values for children ages 2 to 6. Query.

Recent Fiction Title: *Huff and Puff on Halloween,* by Jean Warren (children's picture book/easy-reader).

Poetry: Query.

Recent Poetry Title: *1-2-3 Rhymes, Stories & Songs,* by Jean Warren (educational poetry).

Tips: "Our audience is teachers (and parents) who work with children ages 2 to 6. Write for submission requirements."

WASHINGTON STATE UNIVERSITY PRESS, Pullman WA 99164-5910. (800)354-7360. Fax: (509)335-8568. Director: Thomas H. Sanders. Editor: Glen Lindeman. Estab. 1928. Publishes hardcover originals, trade paperback originals and reprints. Averages 6-10 titles/year; receives 75-150 submissions annually. 50% of books from first-time writers; 100% of books from unagented authors. Subsidy publishes 20% of books. "The nature of the manuscript and the potential market for the manuscript determine whether it should be subsidy published." Pays 10% royalty on second printing. Publishes book an average of 18 months after acceptance. Query for electronic submissions. Reports on queries in 1 month. *Writer's Market* recommends allowing 2 months for reply.

Nonfiction: Biography, academic and scholarly. Subjects include Americana, art, business and economics, ethnic studies history (especially of the American West and the Pacific Northwest), nature, philosophy, politics, psychology, and sociology. "Needs for the next year are quality manuscripts that focus on the development of the Pacific Northwest as a region, and on the social and economic changes that have taken place and continue to take place as the region enters the 21st century. No romance novels, historical fiction, how-to books, gardening books, or books specifically written as classroom texts." Submit outline and sample chapters. Reviews artwork/photos as part of ms package.

Tips: "Our audience consists of scholars, specialists and informed general readers who are interested in well-documented research presented in an attractive format. Writers have the best chance of selling to our press completed manuscripts on regional history. We have developed our marketing in the direction of regional and local history and have attempted to use this as the base around which we hope to expand our publishing program. In regional history, the secret is to write a good narrative—a good story—that is substantiated factually. It should be told in an imaginative, clever way. Have visuals (photos, maps, etc) available to help the reader envision what has happened. Tell the local or regional history story in a way that ties it to larger, national, and even international events. Weave it into the large pattern of history."

FRANKLIN WATTS, INC., Division of Grolier, Inc., 95 Madison Ave., New York NY 10016. (212)686-7070. Editorial Director: John Selfridge. Publishes both hardcover and softcover originals for middle schoolers and young adults. Entire firm publishes 200 titles/year, about 30% from first-time authors; 20-40% of books from unagented writers. Simultaneous queries OK. Reports in 1-3 months on queries. Free book catalog.

Nonfiction: History, science, social issues and biography. Subjects include American and world history, politics, natural and physical sciences. Multicultural, curriculum-based lists published twice a year. Strong also in the area of contemporary problems and issues facing young people. No humor, coffee table books, cookbooks or gardening books. Query. No calls or unsolicited mss.

WAYFINDER PRESS, P.O. Box 217, Ridgeway CO 81432-02170. (303)626-5452. Owner: Marcus E. Wilson. Estab. 1980. Publishes trade paperback originals. Firm averages 3 titles/year. Receives 80 submissions/year. 30% of books are from first-time authors. 90% from unagented writers. Pays 8-12% royalty on retail price. Publishes book an average of 6 months after acceptance. Simultaneous submissions OK. Reports in 2 weeks on queries. Return postage must be included.

Nonfiction: Biography, illustrated book, reference. Subjects include Americana, government/politics, history, nature/environment, photography, recreation, regional, sociology and travel. "We are looking for books on western Colorado: history, sociology, nature, recreation, photo, and travel. No books on subjects outside our geographical area of specialization." Query or submit outline/synopsis and sample chapters. Reviews artwork/photos as part of ms package.

Recent Nonfiction Title: *Ouray Hiking Guide,* by Kelvin Kent.

Fiction: Adventure, historical, humor, mystery, picture books. "We are looking for fiction with a specific Colorado perspective." Query or submit outline/synopsis and sample chapters.

Tips: "Writers have the best chance selling us tourist oriented books. The local population and tourists comprise our audience."

SAMUEL WEISER, INC., P.O. Box 612, York Beach ME 03910. (207)363-4393. Editor: Eliot Stearns. Estab. 1956. Publishes hardcover originals and trade paperback originals and reprints. Publishes 18-20 titles/year; receives 200 submissions annually. 50% of books from first-time authors; 98% of books from unagented writers. Pays 10% royalty on wholesale or retail price; offers average $500 advance. Publishes book an average of 1½ years after acceptance. Query for electronic submissions. Reports in 3 months. Free book catalog.

Nonfiction: How-to and self-help. Subjects include health, music, philosophy, psychology and religion. "We look for strong books in our specialty field—written by teachers and people who know the subject. Don't want a writer's rehash of all the astrology books in the library, only texts written by people with strong background in field. No poetry or novels." Submit complete ms. *Writer's Market* recommends query with SASE first. Reviews artwork/photos as part of ms package.

Recent Nonfiction Title: *Helping Heaven Happen*, by Dr. David Curtis.

Tips: "Most new authors do not check permissions, nor do they provide proper footnotes. If they did, it would help. We specialize in oriental philosophy, metaphysics, esoterica of all kinds (tarot, astrology, qabalah, magic, etc.). We look at all manuscripts submitted to us. We are interested in seeing freelance art for book covers."

WESCOTT COVE PUBLISHING CO., P.O. Box 130, Stamford CT 06904. President: Julius M. Wilensky. Estab. 1968. Publishes trade paperback originals and reprints. Publishes 4 titles/year. Receives 20 queries and 8 mss/year. 50% of mss from first-time authors, 100% from unagented writers. Pays 10% royalty on retail price. Offers $1,500 advance. Publishes book 8 months after acceptance of ms. Simultaneous submissions OK. Reports in 1 month on queries. *Writer's Market* recommends allowing 2 months for reply. Book catalog free on request.

Nonfiction: Cruising guides and nautical books. "Our authors must be longtime expert sailors, familiar with the area they write about." Query with outline and 1 or 2 sample chapters.

WESTERN PUBLISHING, 1220 Mound Ave., Racine WI 53404. "Prefers not to share information."

‡WESTERNLORE PRESS, P.O. Box 35305, Tucson AZ 85740. Editor: Lynn R. Bailey. Publishes 6-12 titles/year. Pays standard royalties on retail price "except in special cases." Query. Reports in 2 months. Enclose return postage with query.

Nonfiction: Publishes Western Americana of a scholarly and semischolarly nature: anthropology, history, biography, historic sites, restoration, and ethnohistory pertaining to the greater American West. Re-publication of rare and out-of-print books. Length: 25,000-100,000 words.

WESTPORT PUBLISHERS, INC., #310, 4050 Pennsylvania, Kansas City MO 64111-3051. (816)756-1490. Fax: (816)756-0159. Editor: Bear Lamble. Estab. 1982. Subsidiaries include Media Publishing, Midgard Press (author—subsidy division), Media Periodicals, and Test Corporation of America. Publishes hardcover and trade paperback originals. Averages 5-6 titles/year. Receives 125 submissions/year. 50% of books from first-time authors. 100% from unagented writers. Pays royalty. Publishes book an average of 9 months after acceptance. Reports in 2 months on queries. Send SASE with queries and mss.

Nonfiction: Subjects include child guidance/parenting, cooking, foods and nutrition, psychology and regional studies. "Topics to consider are child guidance/parenting; psychology related; regional topics; family and 'sandwich' generation issues." Submit complete ms with SASE. *Writer's Market* recommends query with SASE first. Reviews artwork/photos as part of ms package.

Recent Nonfiction Title: *Beyond Discipline: Parenting that Lasts a Lifetime*, by Edward R. Christopher.

Tips: "Books with a well-defined audience have the best chance of succeeding. An author must have demonstrated expertise in the topic on which he or she is writing."

WHITE CLIFFS MEDIA COMPANY, P.O. Box 433, Tempe AZ 85280-0433. (602)921-8039. Owner: Lawrence Aynesmith. Estab. 1985. Publishes hardcover and trade paperback originals. Averages 5-10 titles/year. 75% of books from first-time authors; 75% from unagented writers. Pays 5-12% royalty. Publishes book an average of 1 year after acceptance. Query for electronic submissions. Reports in 3 months. Book catalog for #10 SASE.

Nonfiction: Biography, textbook. Subjects include anthropology, education, ethnic, music/dance, sociology. "We are looking for ethnic music performance, music sociology/biography (more pop/mass oriented), books on computer/desktop publishing." Query. Reviews artwork/photos as part of ms package.

Tips: "Distribution is more difficult due to the large number of publishers. Writers should send proposals that have potential for mass markets as well as college texts, and that will be submitted and completed on schedule. Our audience reads college texts, general interest trade publications. If I were a writer trying to market a book today, I would send a book on music comparable in quality and mass appeal to a book like Stephen Hawking's *A Brief History of Time*."

‡ALBERT WHITMAN AND CO., 6340 Oakton St., Morton Grove IL 60053-2723. (708)581-0033. Editor-in-Chief: Kathleen Tucker. Estab. 1919. Publishes hardcover originals and paperback reprints. Firm averages 30 titles/year. Receives 2,000 submissions/year. 20% of books from first-time authors. 70% from unagented writers. Pays 10% royalty. Publishes book an average of 18 months after acceptance. Simultaneous submissions OK. Reports in 5 months. Book catalog for 8 × 10 SAE and 2 first class stamps. Manuscript guidelines for #10 SASE.

Nonfiction: "All books are for ages 2-12." Biography and concept books which are about special problems children have. Other subjects include agriculture/horticulture, animals, anthropology/archaeology, art/architecture, computers and electronics, cooking, foods and nutrition, ethnic, gardening, health/medicine, history, hobbies, language/literature, music/dance, nature/environment, photography, recreation, religion, science, sports and travel. "We are looking for picture books for young children. No adult subjects, please." Submit complete ms (picture books). Reviews artwork/photos as part of ms package. "We may accept the manuscript and reject the artwork."

Fiction: "All books are for ages 2-12." Adventure, ethnic, fantasy, historical, humor, mystery, picture books and concept books (to help children deal with problems and concerns). "We need historical fiction and picture books. No young adult and adult books." Submit outline/synopsis and sample chapters (novels) and complete ms (picture books).

Recent Fiction Title: *Two of Everything*, by Lily Toy Hong (folktale).

Tips: "There is a trend toward highly visual books. The writer can most easily sell us a strong picture book text that has good illustration possibilities. We sell mostly to libraries, but our bookstore sales are growing. The books are all for children somewhere between the ages of 2 and 12. If I were a writer trying to market a book today, I would study published picture books."

THE WHITSTON PUBLISHING CO., P.O. Box 958, Troy NY 12181-0958. (518)283-4363. Fax: (518)283-4363. Editorial Director: Jean Goode. Estab. 1969. Publishes hardcover originals. Averages 20 titles/year; receives 100 submissions annually. 50% of books from first-time authors; 100% of books from unagented writers. Pays 10% royalty on price of book (wholesale or retail) after sale of 500 copies. Publishes book an average of 30 months after acceptance. Reports in up to 6 months. Book catalog for $1.

Nonfiction: "We publish scholarly and critical books in the arts, humanities and some of the social sciences. We also publish bibliographies and indexes. We will consider author bibliographies. We are interested in scholarly monographs and collections of essays." Query. Reviews artwork/photos as part of ms package.

WILDERNESS ADVENTURE BOOKS, P.O. Box 968, Fowlerville MI 48836-0968. Fax: (517)223-8290. Editor: Erin Sims Howarth. Estab. 1983. Publishes hardcover and trade paperback originals and reprints. Firm averages 6 titles/year. Receives 250 submissions/year. 90% of books from first-time authors. 90% from unagented writers. Pays 5-10% royalty on retail price. Offers $100 average advance. Publishes book an average of 10 months after acceptance. Simultaneous submissions OK. Reports in 1 month. *Writer's Market* recommends allowing 2 months for reply. Free book catalog.

Nonfiction: Biography, how-to and illustrated book. Subjects include Americana, animals, history, nature/environment, regional, non-competitive sports and travel. Query. Reviews artwork/photos as part of ms package.

Fiction: Adventure, historical and young adult. Query.

Tips: "We are no longer seeking poetry or children's stories."

WILDERNESS PRESS, 2440 Bancroft Way, Berkeley CA 94704-1676. (510)843-8080. Fax: (510)548-1355. Editorial Director: Thomas Winnett. Estab. 1967. Publishes paperback originals. Averages 5 titles/year; receives 150 submissions annually. 20% of books from first-time authors; 95% of books from unagented writers. Average print order for a writer's first book is 5,000. Pays 8-10% royalty on retail price; offers average $1,000 advance. Publishes book an average of 8 months after acceptance. Reports in 1 month. *Writer's Market* recommends allowing 2 months for reply. Book catalog for 9×12 SASE.

Nonfiction: "We publish books about the outdoors. Most of our books are trail guides for hikers and backpackers, but we also publish how-to books about the outdoors. The manuscript must be accurate. The author must thoroughly research an area in person. If he is writing a trail guide, he must walk all the trails in the area his book is about. The outlook must be strongly conservationist. The style must be appropriate for a highly literate audience." Query or submit outline and sample chapters demonstrating "accuracy, literacy, and popularity of subject area." Reviews artwork/photos as part of ms package.

Recent Nonfiction Title: *Oahu Trails*, by Kathy Morey.

JOHN WILEY & SONS, 605 3rd Ave., New York NY 10158. "Prefers not to share information."

WILLIAMSON PUBLISHING CO., P.O. Box 185, Church Hill Rd., Charlotte VT 05445. (802)425-2102. Editorial Director: Susan Williamson. Estab. 1983. Publishes trade paperback originals. Averages 12 titles/year; receives 1,000 submissions annually. 50% of books from first-time authors; 80% of books from unagented writers. Average print order for a writer's first book is 10,000. Pays 10% royalty on sales dollars received. Advance negotiable. Publishes book an average of 1 year after acceptance. Simultaneous submissions OK. Reports in 2-4 months on queries with SASE. Book catalog for 8×10 SAE and 4 first class stamps.

Nonfiction: Subjects include children's activity books, education, gardening, careers, psychology, home crafts, parenting, building, animals, cooking and foods, hobbies, nature, landscaping, and children. "Our areas of concentration are children's interactive books, people-oriented business and psychology books, women's issues, cookbooks, international marketing, gardening, small-scale livestock raising, family housing (all aspects), health and education." No children's fiction books, no picture books, photography, politics, religion, history, art or biography. Query with outline and sample chapters.

Recent Nonfiction Title: *The Kids' Multicultural Art Book*, by Alexandra M. Terzian.

Tips: "We're most interested in authors who are experts in their fields—doers, not researchers. Give us a good, solid manuscript with original ideas and we'll work with you to refine the writing. We also have a highly skilled staff to develop the high quality graphics and design of our books."

‡WILLOWISP PRESS, INC., Subsidiary of Pages, Inc., 801 94th Ave.. North, St. Petersburg FL 33702-2426. (813)578-7600. Contact: Acquisitions Editor. Publishes trade paperback originals. 10% of books are from first-time authors. 80% from unagented writers. Pays royalty or buys by outright purchase. Offers varying average advance. Publishes book an average of 9-18 months after acceptance. Simultaneous submissions OK. Electronic submissions "only upon request." Reports in 5 weeks on queries; 2 months on mss. Book catalog for 9×12 SAE with 5 first class stamps. Manuscript guidelines for #10 SASE.

Nonfiction: Illustrated book and juvenile. Subjects include animals, science, sports, environmental, etc. Query with outline. Reviews artwork/photos as part of ms package "rarely."

Recent Nonfiction Title: *A Look Around Rain Forests*, by Ed Perez.

Fiction: (K through Middle School only). Adventure, humor, juvenile, literary, contemporary, mystery, picture books, romance, science fiction, short story collections, suspense and young adult. "3-6 grade level a prime market for both fiction and nonfiction. Nothing directed at high school; no poetry or religious orientation."

Recent Fiction Titles: *The Haunted Underwear*, by Janet Adele Bloss (humor, family); *Dead Wrong*, by Alida E. Young (contemporary, in our "Lifelines" line).

WILSHIRE BOOK CO., 12015 Sherman Rd., N. Hollywood CA 91605. (818)765-8579. Publisher: Melvin Powers. Senior Editor: Marcia Grad. Estab. 1947. Publishes trade paperback originals and reprints. Publishes 50 titles/year; receives 5,000 submissions annually. 80% of books from first-time authors; 75% of books from unagented writers. Average print order for a writer's first book is 5,000. Pays standard royalty; offers variable advance. Publishes book an average of 9 months after acceptance. Reports in 1 month. *Writer's Market* recommends allowing 2 months for reply.

Nonfiction: Self-help, motivation, inspiration, psychology, recovery, how-to, entrepreneurship, mail order and horsemanship. "We are always looking for books such as *Psycho-Cybernetics*, *The Magic of Thinking Big*, *Guide to Rational Living*; and *Think and Grow Rich*. We also need manuscripts teaching mail order and entrepreneur techniques. All I need is the concept of the book to determine if project is viable. I welcome phone calls to discuss manuscripts or book ideas with authors." Synopsis or detailed chapter outline, 3 chapters and SASE required. Reviews artwork/photos as part of ms package.

Fiction: Adult fables that teach principles of psychological growth or offer guidance in living.

Tips: "We are looking for such books as *Illusions*, *The Little Prince*, and *The Greatest Salesman in the World*."

WINDSOR BOOKS, Subisidary of Windsor Marketing Corp., P.O. Box 280, Brightwaters NY 11718-0280. (516)321-7830. Managing Editor: Stephen Schmidt. Estab. 1968. Publishes hardcover and trade paperback originals, reprints, and very specific software. Averages 8 titles/year; receives approximately 40 submissions annually. 60% of books from first-time authors; 90% of books from unagented writers. Pays 10% royalty on retail price; 5% on wholesale price (50% of total cost); offers variable advance. Publishes book an average of 6 months after acceptance. Simultaneous submissions OK. Reports in 2 weeks on queries. *Writer's Market* recommends allowing 2 months for reply. Free book catalog and ms guidelines.

Nonfiction: How-to and technical. Subjects include business and economics (investing in stocks and commodities). Interested in books on strategies, methods for investing in the stock market, options market, and commodity markets. Query or submit outline and sample chapters. Reviews artwork/photos as part of ms package.

Tips: "Our books are for serious investors; we sell through direct mail to our mailing list and other financial lists. Writers must keep their work original; this market tends to have a great deal of information overlap among publications."

WINDWARD PUBLISHING, INC., P.O. Box 371005, Miami FL 33137-1005. (305)576-6232. Vice President: Jack Zinzow. Estab. 1973. Publishes trade paperback originals. Publishes 6 titles/year. Receives 50 queries and 10 mss/year. 35% of mss from first-time authors, 100% from unagented writers. Pays 10-15% royalty on wholesale price. Publishes book 14 months after acceptance of ms. Simultaneous submissions OK. Query for electronic submissions. Reports in 2 weeks on queries. *Writer's Market* recommends allowing 2 months for reply. Book catalog free on request.

Nonfiction: Cookbook, how-to, illustrated book, children's/juvenile and handbooks. Subjects include agriculture/horticulture, animals, gardening, nature/environment, recreation (fishing, boating, diving, camping) and science. Query. Reviews artwork/photos as part of the freelance ms package.

Recent Nonfiction Title: *Sea Mammals*, by Larry Brown.

‡WINE APPRECIATION GUILD LTD., 155 Connecticut St., San Francisco CA 94107. (415)864-1202. Fax: (415)864-0377. Director: Maurice Sullivan. Estab. 1973. Imprints are Vintage Image and Wine Advisory Board (nonfiction). Publishes hardcover and trade paperback originals, trade paperback reprints, and soft-

ware. Averages 12 titles/year; receives 30-40 submissions annually. 30% of books from first-time authors; 100% of books from unagented writers. Pays 5-15% royalty on wholesale price or makes outright purchase. Publishes book an average of 18 months after acceptance. Simultaneous submissions OK. Query for electronic submissions. Reports in 2 months. Book catalog for $2.

Nonfiction: Cookbook and how-to—wine related. Subjects include wine, cooking and foods and travel. Must be wine-related. Submit outline/synopsis and sample chapters. Reviews artwork/photos as part of ms package.

Tips: "Our books are read by wine enthusiasts—from neophytes to professionals, and wine industry and food industry people. We are interested in anything of a topical and timely nature connected with wine, by a knowledgeable author. We do not deal with agents of any type. We prefer to get to know the author as a person and to work closely with him/her."

WINGBOW PRESS, Subsidiary of Bookpeople, 7900 Edgewater Dr., Oakland CA 94621-2004. (510)632-4700. Editor: Randy Fingland. Estab. 1971. Publishes trade paperback originals. Averages 2 titles/year; receives 450 submissions annually, "mostly fiction and poetry, which we aren't even considering." 50% of books from first-time authors; 90% of books from unagented writers. Pays 7-10% royalty on retail price; offers average $250 advance. Publishes book an average of 18 months after acceptance. Query for electronic submissions. Reports in 2 months.

Nonfiction: Reference and self-help. Subjects include psychology, health and women's issues. "We are currently looking most seriously at women's studies, health, psychology and personal development. No business/finance how-to." Query or submit outline and sample chapters.

Recent Nonfiction Title: *Massage for Healthier Children*, by Marybetts Sinclair.

Tips: "This year we've been even more careful about what we're publishing."

WOODBINE HOUSE, 5615 Fishers Ln., Rockville MD 20852. (301)468-8800. Fax: (301)468-5784. Editor: Susan Stokes. Estab. 1985. Publishes hardcover and trade paperback books from first-time authors; 80% of books from unagented writers. Pays royalty. Publishes book an average of 18 months after acceptance. Simultaneous submissions OK. Query for electronic submissions. Reports in 2 months. Book catalog and ms guidelines for 6×9 SAE and 3 first class stamps.

Nonfiction: Primarily publishes books for and about children with disabilities, but will consider other nonfiction books that would appeal to a clearly defined audience. No personal accounts or general parenting guides. Submit outline and sample chapters. Reviews artwork/photos as part of ms. package.

Recent Nonfiction Title: *Children With Tourette Syndrome*, edited by Tracy Haerle.

Tips: "Before querying, familiarize yourself with the types of books we publish and put some thought into how your book could be marketed (aside from in bookstores). Keep cover letters concise and to the point; if it's a subject that interests us, we'll ask to see more."

WOODBRIDGE PRESS, P.O. Box 6189, Santa Barbara CA 93160. (805)965-7039. Editor: Howard Weeks. Estab. 1971. Publishes hardcover and trade paperback originals. Firm averages 4-5 titles/year. Receives 500 submissions/year. 60% of books from first-time authors. 80% from unagented writers. Pays 10-15% on wholesale price. Publishes book an average of 8 months after acceptance. Simultaneous submissions OK. Reports as expeditiously as possible with SASE. *Writer's Market* recommends allowing 2 months for reply. Free book catalog.

Nonfiction: Cookbook (vegetarian) and self-help. Subjects include agriculture/horticulture, cooking, foods and nutrition, gardening, health and psychology (popular). Query. Reviews artwork/photos as part of ms package.

Recent Nonfiction Title: *Hydroponic Tomatoes for Home Gardeners*, by Howard M. Rosh.

WOODLAND HEALTH BOOKS, P.O. Box 1422, Provo UT 84603. Publisher: Mark Lisonbee. Publishes hardcover and trade paperback originals. Publishes 5 titles/year. Receives 25 queries and 15 mss/year. 50% of mss from first-time authors, 100% from unagented writers. Publishes book 6 months after acceptance of ms. Simultaneous submissions OK. Query for electronic submissions. Reports in 1 month on proposals. *Writer's Market* recommends allowing 2 months for reply. Book catalog free on request.

Nonfiction: Subjects include health/alternative medicine. "Our readers are interested in herbs and other natural health topics. Most of our books are sold through health food stores." Query.

Recent Nonfiction Title: *An Introduction to Natural Health*, by Deanne Tenney.

WRITER'S DIGEST BOOKS, Imprint of F&W Publications, 1507 Dana Ave., Cincinnati OH 45207. Editorial Director: William Brohaugh. Estab. 1920. Publishes hardcover and paperback originals. Averages 16 titles/year. Pays 10% royalty on net receipts. Simultaneous (if so advised) submissions OK. Publishes book an average of 12-18 months after acceptance. Enclose return postage. *Writer's Market* recommends allowing 2 months for reply. Book catalog for 9×12 SAE with 6 first class stamps.

Nonfiction: Instructional books for writers. "We're seeking how-to books by authors who can write from successful experience. Our books stress results and how very specifically to achieve them. Should be well-researched, yet lively and readable. Our books concentrate on writing techniques over marketing techniques. We do *not* want to see books telling readers how to crack specific nonfiction markets: *Writing for the Computer*

Market or *Writing for Trade Publications*, for instance. Concentrate on broader writing topics. Books must be instructional; books whose primary purpose is to inspire writers don't work here. In the offices here we refer to a manuscript's 4T value—manuscripts must have information writers can Take To The Typewriter. We don't talk *about* writing. We instruct. Query or submit outline and sample chapters. Be prepared to explain how the proposed book differs from existing books on the subject." No fiction or poetry. "Writer's Digest Books also publishes instructional books for photographers, songwriters and musicians, but the main thrust is on writing books. The same philosophy applies to songwriting and photography books: they must instruct about the creative craft, as opposed to instructing about marketing." Writer's Digest Books in years past has published books for general audiences, particularly in the area of home organization. These books will now be published under WDB's Betterway Books imprint; see the Betterway listing for details.

• Among WDB's recent awards are the Hugo for Orson Scott Card's *Writing and Selling Science Fiction and Fantasy* and the ASCAP-Deems Taylor Award for Journalism for Randy Poe's *Music Publishing: A Songwriter's Guide*.

Recent Nonfiction Title: *The Complete Guide to Writing Magazine Articles*, by John M. Wilson.

WRS PUBLISHING, 701 N. New Rd., Waco TX 76710. (817)776-6461. Acquisitions Director: Ann Page. Estab. 1967. Publishes hardcover, trade and mass market paperback originals. Firm averages 20-25 titles/year. Receives 600 submissions/year. 10% of books from first-time authors. 90% from unagented writers. Pays 15-20% royalty on wholesale price. Advance negotiable. Publishes book an average of 1 year after acceptance. Simultaneous submissions OK if such is stated. Query for electronic submissions. Reports in 1 month on queries. Free book catalog and ms guidelines with SASE.
Nonfiction: Subjects include "primarily inspirational stories of ordinary people with extraordinary potential. We are looking for stories which have received extensive, spontaneous publicity on TV, radio and in newspapers. Ideally, subjects of these books should be active on the speaking circuit after the book is published." Query or submit outline and samples chapters. Submit artwork/photos as part of ms package with SASE.
Recent Nonfiction Title: *Blind Courage*, by Bill Irwin and *I'm Not Dead Yet*, by Randy Bird.
Tips: "We are primarily interested in inspiring stories which fit the bookstore market and library needs. Our books appeal primarily to educated persons with an interest in improving their general lifestyle. If I were a writer trying to market a book today, I would first consider the appeal of the story to the mass media (TV, newspapers, magazines). Publicity is almost always indispensable in successfully marketing a book, and if a book can't be promoted, it should seldom be published."

‡XENOS BOOKS, Box 52152, Riverside CA 92517-3152. (909)370-2229. Editor: Karl Kvitko. Estab. 1986. Publishes hardcover and trade paperback originals. Publishes 2-5 titles/year. Reeives 20-30 queries and 20-25 mss/year. 10% of mss from first-time authors, 100% from unagented writers. Subsidy publishes 20% of books. Pays 15% maximum royalty after recovery of production costs. May pay in copies of book. Publishes book 6 months after acceptance of ms. Simultaneous submissions OK. Query for electronic submissions: prefers 5¼" floppy disK, text in WordPerfect. Reports in 1 month. *Writer's Market* recommends allowing 2 months for reply. Manuscript guidelines free on request.
Nonfiction: Biography, illustrated book, reference, textbook, autobiography, literary criticism, social comment, philosophy, etc. Subjects include animals, anthropology/archaeology, art/architecture, ethnic, government/politics, history, language/literature, philosophy, psychology, religion, science, sociology, translation. "Originality in all areas is the chief criterion. We want works that speak to the mind and the heart, not university exercises that speak to neither. Writers should not send articles or short pieces. We want only book-length works." Query first or send outline and complete work. Writers should send photocopies.
Fiction: Experimental, fantasy, historical, literary, mainstream/contemporary, picture books, plays, science fiction and short story collections. "We do not like standard genres. We are more interested in imaginative fiction that big publishers reject as 'not quite right for us.' Literature in the old sense." Query first or submit synopsis plus full ms.
Poetry: "If Rilke, Lorca, Tsvetaeva, Kolmar, Yeats mean something to you, we're in the same category. We like foreign languages, translations. Writers should not send two or three poems. We want collections." Submit complete mss.
Tips: "We think there are people who are repelled by mass-media products and seek out original writing. We publish for them. If you submit your work to Xenos Books, understand that we are very small and cannot do what a big publisher does. But on a much smaller scale we can sometimes do better."

‡YANKEE BOOKS, Imprint of Rodale Press, 33 E. Minor St., Emmaus PA 18098. Associate Editor: Sarah Dunn. Publishes hardcover originals and trade paperback originals and reprints. Publishes 10 titles/year. Receives 600 queries and 100 mss/year. 5% of mss from first-time authors, 50% from unagented writers. Pays 5-6½% royalty on retail price. Offers $2,000-5,000 advance. Publishes book 1 year after acceptance. Simultaneous submissions OK. Query for electronic submissions; prefers IBM compatible disks. Reports in 1 month on queries, 3 months on proposals and 6 months on mss. Manuscript guidelines for #10 SASE.
Nonfiction: Cookbook, how-to and humor. Subjects include cooking, foods and nutrition, nature/environment, regional, travel and New England lore. "Keep the subject matter specific to New England." Submit outline and 1 sample chapter, or submit proposal package, including bio of author, 1-page summary of topic.

Reviews artwork/photos as part of freelance ms package. Writers should send photocopies.
Recent Nonfiction Title: *The Fishmonger Cookbook*, by Dorothy Butchelder (cookbook).
Tips: "Our audience is New England residents and visitors to New England, New England-philes. Submit proposals only. Please do not send unsolicited manuscripts."

‡**ZEBRA** and **PINNACLE BOOKS**, 475 Park Ave. S., New York NY 10016. (212)889-2299. Publisher: Ruth Harris. Publishes hardcover, trade paperback and mass market paperback originals; trade paperback and mass market paperback reprints. Zebra publishes 360 titles/year; Pinnacle publishes 120 titles/year. Pays royalty. "Rarely" makes outright purchase. Publishes book 2 years after acceptance of ms. Simultaneous submissions OK. Reports in 3 months on proposals. Manuscript guidelines for #10 SASE.
Nonfiction: Biography, how-to, humor and self-help. Subjects include business and economics, health/medicine, military/war and money/finance. Submit outline with 3 sample chapters.
Fiction: Adventure, erotica, fantasy, gothic, historical, horror, humor, literary, mainstream/contemporary, mystery, occult, romance, short story collections, suspense, western and young adult. Submit synopsis with 3 sample chapters.

ZOLAND BOOKS, INC., 384 Huron Ave., Cambridge MA 02138-6828. (617)864-6252. Fax: (617)661-4998. Publisher/Editor: Roland Pease, Jr. Assistant Editor: Paul Karns. Marketing Director: Christine Alaimo. Estab. 1987. Publishes hardcover and trade paperback originals. Averages 8-15 titles/year. Receives 400+ submissions/year. 15% of books from first-time authors. 60% from unagented writers. Pays 7% royalty on retail price. Publishes book an average of 1½ years after acceptance. Reports in 6 months. Book catalog for 6½×9½ SAE with 2 first class stamps.
Nonfiction: Biography, coffee table book. Subjects include art/architecture, language/literature, nature/environment, photography, regional, translation, travel, women's issues/studies. Query. Reviews artwork/photos as part of ms package.
Fiction: Literary and short story collections. Submit complete ms. *Writer's Market* recommends query with SASE first.
Recent Fiction Title: *Whistling and Other Stories*, by Myra Goldberg.
Tips: "We are most likely to publish books which provide original, thought-provoking ideas, books which will captivate the reader, and are evocative."

ZONDERVAN PUBLISHING HOUSE, 5300 Patterson SE, Grand Rapids MI 49530. (616)698-6900. Contact: Manuscript Review. Estab. 1931. Publishes hardcover and trade paperback originals and reprints. Averages 130 titles/year; receives 3,000 submissions annually. 20% of books from first-time authors; 80% of books from unagented writers. Average print order for a writer's first book is 5,000. Pays royalty of 14% of the net amount received on sales of cloth and softcover trade editions and 12% of net amount received on sales of mass market paperbacks. Offers variable advance. Reports in 3 months on proposals. SASE required. Recommend ms guidelines for #10 SASE. To receive a recording about submission call (616)698-3447.
Nonfiction and Fiction: Biography, autobiography, self-help, devotional, contemporary issues, Christian living, Bible study resources, references for lay audience; some adult fiction; youth and children's ministry, teens and children. Academic and Professional Books: college and seminary textbooks (biblical studies, theology, church history, the humanities); preaching, counseling, discipleship, worship, and church renewal for pastors, professionals, and lay leaders in ministry; theological and biblical reference books. All from religious perspective (evangelical). Immediate needs listed in guidelines. Submit outline/synopsis, 1 sample chapter, and SASE for return of materials.
Recent Nonfiction Title: *Descending into Greatness*, by Bill Hybles.
Recent Fiction Title: *The Shining Face*, by Harold Myra.

Canadian and International Book Publishers

This section lists book publishers whose addresses of principal contact lie outside the United States. Some of the publishers listed in this section also have offices in the U.S. A few of the publishers listed in the previous section have offices worldwide, and are certainly "international" in the subjects of the books they publish and distribute.

The Canadian and International Book Publishers section is intended for writers whose ideas and books are better suited for the Canadian or international marketplace. Writers should be aware that the requirements of these publishers are quite different from those of their U.S. counterparts. Some publishers listed here concentrate solely on subjects and authors from their own countries (or landed immigrants) and do not accept queries, proposals or manuscripts from American writers.

There is more government support of book publishing in Canada than in the U.S. A number of national and provincial arts councils subsidize book publishing. Most subsidy arrangements with Canadian publishers involve such an agency, not the author, as the source of the subsidy. However, there are a few author-subsidy publishers in Canada and writers should proceed with caution when they are made this offer. We have denoted partial author-subsidy publishers with an asterisk (*).

Despite a healthy book publishing industry, Canada is still dominated by publishers from the United States. Two out of every three books found in Canadian bookstores are published in the U.S. These odds have made some Canadian publishers even more determined to concentrate on Canadian authors and subjects. Writers interested in additional Canadian book publishing markets should consult *Literary Market Place* (R.R. Bowker & Co.), *The Canadian Writer's Guide* (Fitzhenry & Whiteside) and *The Canadian Writer's Market* (McClelland & Stewart).

International mail

Whatever your nation of residence may be, enclose International Reply Coupons (IRCs) with all correspondence to publishers outside your country. Postage stamps from your country are not valid on letters and parcels originating elsewhere. Publishers receiving SASEs and manuscripts with stamps from other countries are not likely to return or respond to the material, as international mailing costs are a considerable expense.

To defer a portion of this expense otherwise paid by you, consider sending disposable (photocopies or computer generated) outlines, synopses, sample chapters or manuscripts. This eliminates the cost of having an entire manuscript package returned to you. One IRC will cover the cost of the publisher's reply. They are available at post offices all over the world and can be redeemed for stamps of any country. Please note that the cost for items such as catalogs is expressed in the currency of the country in which the publisher is located.

For a list of publishers according to their subjects of interest, see the nonfiction and fiction sections of the Book Publishers Subject Index. Information on some book publishers and producers not included in this edition of *Writer's Market* can be found in Book Publishers and Producers/Changes '93-'94.

AQUARIAN PRESS, Imprint of HarperCollins, 77-85 Fulham Palace Rd., Hammersmith, London W6 8JB England. Fax: 081-307-4440. Publishing Director: Eileen Campbell. Estab. 1952. Other imprints are Pandora and Thorsons. Publishes paperback originals. Firm averages 50-60 titles/year. Pays 7½-10% royalty. Reports in 2 months. Free book catalog.
Nonfiction: Publishes a broad-based New Age list covering the Western tradition, astrology, divination, psychic awareness, psychology and therapy, religion and spirituality, philosophy and the new science.

ARSENAL PULP PRESS, 100-1062 Homer St., Vancouver British Columbia V6B 2W9 Canada. (604)687-4233. Editor: Linda Field. Imprint is Tillacum Library. Publishes hardcover and trade paperback originals. Publishes 12 titles/year. Each imprint publishes 1-2 titles/year. Receives 300 queries and 200 mss/year. 25% of books from first-time authors; 100% from unagented writers. Pays royalty. Publishes book 1 year after acceptance of ms. Simultaneous submissions OK. Query for electronic submissions. Reports in 2 months on queries, with exceptions. Book catalog and ms guidelines free on request.
Nonfiction: Biography, coffee table book and humor. Subjects include ethnic, history, regional (British Columbia) and sociology. Submit outline and 1 sample chapter.
Fiction: Ethnic, feminist, gay/lesbian, humor, literary and short story collections. Submit 1 sample chapter.
Tips: "We *very* rarely publish American authors."

BALLANTINE BOOKS OF CANADA, Division of Random House of Canada, Ltd., 1265 Aerowood Dr., Mississauga, Ontario L4W 1B9, Canada. "Prefers not to share information."

BANTAM BOOKS CANADA, INC., Subsidiary of Bantam Doubleday Dell Publishing Group, 105 Bond St., Toronto, Ontario M5B 1Y3, Canada. "Prefers not to share information."

BEACH HOLME PUBLISHERS LTD., 4252 Commerce Circle, Victoria, British Columbia V8Z 4M2 Canada. (604)727-6514. Managing Editor: Guy Chadsey. Estab. 1971. Publishes trade paperback originals. Averages 12 titles/year; receives 300 submissions annually. 40% of books from first-time authors. 70% of books from unagented writers. Pays 10% royalty on retail price; offers $600 average advance. Publishes ms an average of 1½ years after acceptance. Simultaneous (if so advised) submissions OK. Reports in 3 months.
Nonfiction: Biography (regional), juvenile and young adult. Subjects include history (regional) and regional (Pacific Northwest). Interested only in areas mentioned above. Submit outline and sample chapters.
Recent Nonfiction Title: *Custodian of Yellow Point*, by Marilyn McGinnon (regional biography).
Fiction: Experimental, science fiction, young adult and speculative fiction. "Anticipate no need for fiction in next year."
Recent Fiction Title: *The Maerlande Chronicles*, by Elisabeth Vonasburg, translated by Jane Breily.
Tips: "Make sure the manuscript is well written. We see so many mss that only the unique and excellent can't be put down."

BLACK MOSS PRESS, P.O. Box 143, Station A, Windsor, Ontario N9A 6L7 Canada. Editor: Kristina Russelo. Publishes trade paperback originals. Publishes 12 titles/year. Receives 300 queries and 1,200 mss/year. 85% of mss from first-time authors, 100% from unagented writers. Pays 5-10% royalty or 10% of the print run. Publishes book 30 months after acceptance of ms. Reports in 1 month. *Writer's Market* recommends allowing 2 months for reply. Book catalog free on request. Manuscript guidelines for #10 SAE with one IRC.

Fiction: Historical, humor, juvenile, literary and short story collections. Our adult fiction titles are novellas only. Submit synopsis and 3 sample chapters (first, last and middle).
- Black Moss Press currently has a large backlog of mss.

Poetry: Looking for 64-page collections of *previously published* (at least in magazines) poets. Query.

Recent Poetry Title: *Blue Panic*, by Rosemary Sullivan (contemporary).

Tips: "We publish *only* Canadian citizens or landed immigrants."

BOREALIS PRESS, LTD., 9 Ashburn Dr., Nepean, Ontario K2E 6N4 Canada. Editorial Director: Frank Tierney. Senior Editor: Glenn Clever. Estab. 1972. Imprint is The Tecumseh Press. Publishes hardcover and paperback originals. Averages 4 titles/year; receives 400-500 submissions annually. 80% of books from first-time authors; 95% of books from unagented writers. Pays 10% royalty on retail price; no advance. Publishes book an average of 18 months after acceptance. "No multiple submissions or electronic printouts on paper more than 8½ inches wide." Reports in 2 months. Book catalog $2 with SAE and IRCs.

Nonfiction: "Only material Canadian in content." Query. Reviews artwork/photos as part of freelance ms package. Looks for "style in tone and language, reader interest, and maturity of outlook."

Recent Nonfiction Title: *Vagrants of the Barren*, by Charles G.D. Roberts, ed. Martin Wars (animal).

Fiction: "Only material Canadian in content and dealing with significant aspects of the human situation." Query.

Recent Fiction Title: *An Index to the Contents of the Periodical* **Canadian Literature**, *Volume Nos. 1-102.*, Comp. Glenn Clever (reference).

Tips: "Ensure that creative writing deals with consequential human affairs, not just action, sensation, or cutesy stuff."

THE BOSTON MILLS PRESS, 132 Main St., Erin, Ontario N0B 1T0 Canada. (519)833-2407. Fax: (519)833-2195. President: John Denison. Estab. 1974. Publishes hardcover and trade paperback originals. Averages 16 titles/year; receives 100 submissions annually. 75% of books from first-time authors; 90% from unagented writers. Pays 6-10% royalty on retail price; no advance. Publishes book an average of 8 months after acceptance. Simultaneous submissions OK. Query for electronic submissions. Reports in 1 month. *Writer's Market* recommends allowing 2 months for reply. Free book catalog.

Nonfiction: Illustrated book. Subjects include history. "We're interested in anything to do with Canadian or American history—especially transportation. We like books with a small, strong market." No autobiographies. Query. Reviews artwork/photos as part of freelance ms package.

Recent Nonfiction Title: *Next Stop Grand Central*, by Stan Fischler (railway history).

Tips: "We can't compete with the big boys so we stay with short-run specific market books that bigger firms can't handle. We've done well this way so we'll continue in the same vein."

*BROADVIEW PRESS LTD., P.O. Box 1243, Peterborough, Ontario K9J 7H5 Canada. (705)743-8990. Senior Editor: Don LePan. Estab. 1985. Publishes hardcover and trade paperback originals. Firm averages 10-12 titles/year. Receives 250 submissions/year. 40% of books from first-time authors; 100% from unagented writers. Subsidy pubishes 5%. Subsidy determined "if the market is minimal and the book has scholarly significance." Royalty varies and negotiable. Advance negotiable. Publishes book 3-12 months after acceptance. Simultaneous submissions OK. Query for electronic submissions. Reports in 4 months. Free book catalog.

Nonfiction: Biography, reference, self-help, textbook, general nonfiction. Subjects include anthropology/archaeology, art/architecture, business and economics, government/politics, health/medicine, history, language/literature, money/finance, nature/environment, philosophy, psychology, sports, travel, women's issues/studies. "We specialize in university/college supplementary textbooks which often have both a trade and academic market. Nothing in the form of a nonfiction novel." Submit outline and sample chapters. Sometimes reviews artwork/photos as part of freelance ms package.

Recent Nonfiction Title: *The Train Doesn't Stop Here Any More: An Illustrated History of Railway Stations in Canada*, by Ron Brown (history/coffee table).

Tips: "Publishing has become more concentrated in specific areas, with small print runs and more cost effective production. The days of large advances and long runs are over."

ALWAYS submit unsolicited manuscripts or queries with a self-addressed, stamped envelope (SASE) within your country or a self-addressed envelope with International Reply Coupons (IRC) purchased from the post office for other countries.

THE CAITLIN PRESS, P.O. Box 2387 Station B, Prince George, British Columbia V2N 2S6 Canada. (604)964-4953. Contact: Cynthia Wilson. Publishes trade paperback originals. Publishes 4-5 titles/year. Receives 105-120 queries and 50 mss/year. 100% of books from unagented writers. Pays 15% royalty on wholesale price. Publishes book 18 months after acceptance of ms. Simultaneous submissions OK. Reports in 1 month on queries. *Writer's Market* recommends allowing 2 months for reply. Book catalog for #10 SASE.

Nonfiction: Biography and cookbook. Subjects include history, photography and regional. "We publish books about the British Columbia interior or by people from the interior. We are not interested in mss that do not reflect a British Columbia influence." Submit outline and proposal package. Reviews artwork/photos as part of freelance ms package. Writers should send photocopies.

Fiction: Adventure, historical, humor, mainstream/contemporary, short story collections and young adult. Submit ms only. *Writer's Market* recommends query with SASE first.

Poetry: Submit sample poems or complete ms.

Tips: "We publish mainly for the local market. If the book is not about the BC interior or written by someone from the interior, we're not interested."

CAMDEN HOUSE PUBLISHING, Telemedia Communications Inc., 7 Queen Victoria Rd., Camden East, Ontario K0K 1J0 Canada. (613)378-6661. Fax: (613)378-6123. Imprint is Old Bridge Press. Editor: Tracy Read. Estab. 1976. Publishes hardcover originals and reprints. Averages 4-8 titles/year. Receives 75-100 submissions annually. 20% of books from first-time authors; 90% from unagented writers. Pays 7-10% royalty on retail price. Offers average $5,000 advance. Publishes book an average of 18 months after acceptance. Reports in 2 months. Free book catalog.

Nonfiction: Cookbooks, how-to, juvenile, reference. Subjects include agriculture/horticulture, animals, natural history, cooking, foods and nutrition, gardening, hobbies, nature/environment, photography, recreation, travel. No New Age material. Submit outline and sample chapters. Reviews artwork/photos as part of freelance ms package.

Recent Nonfiction Title: *The Backyard Astronomer's Guide*, by Terence Dickinson and Alan Dyer (extensive reference for amateur astronomers).

Tips: "Old Bridge copublishes books with American publishers seeking access to the Canadian marketplace. We will arrange for distribution and commit to a print run. Same categories of interest as Camden House."

*CANADIAN PLAINS RESEARCH CENTER, University of Regina, Regina, Saskatchewan S4S 0A2 Canada. (306)585-4795. Fax: (306)586-9862. Coordinator: Brian Mlazgar. Estab. 1974. Publishes scholarly paperback originals and some casebound originals. Averages 5-6 titles/year; receives 10-15 submissions annually. 35% of books from first-time authors. Subsidy publishes 80% (nonauthor) of books. Determines whether an author should be subsidy published through a scholarly peer review. Publishes book an average of 2 years after acceptance. Query for electronic submissions. Reports in 2 months. Free book catalog and ms guidelines. Also publishes *Prairie Forum*, a scholarly journal.

Nonfiction: Biography, coffee table book, illustrated book, technical, textbook and scholarly. Subjects include animals, business and economics, history, nature, politics and sociology. "The Canadian Plains Research Center publishes the results of research on topics relating to the Canadian Plains region, although manuscripts relating to the Great Plains region will be considered. Material *must* be scholarly. Do not submit health, self-help, hobbies, music, sports, psychology, recreation or cookbooks unless they have a scholarly approach. For example, we would be interested in acquiring a pioneer manuscript cookbook, with modern ingredient equivalents, if the material relates to the Canadian Plains/Great Plains region." Submit complete ms. *Writer's Market* recommends query with SASE first. Reviews artwork/photos as part of freelance ms package.

Recent Nonfiction Title: *The Administration of Dominion Lands, 1870-1930*, by Kirk N. Lambrecht.

Tips: "Pay great attention to manuscript preparation and accurate footnoting, according to the *Chicago Manual of Style*."

COACH HOUSE PRESS, Suite 107, 50 Prince Arthur St., Toronto, Ontario M5R 1B5 Canada. (416)979-7374. Fax: (416)979-7006. Publisher: Margaret McClintock. Unsols Editor: Diane Martin. Estab. 1964. Publishes trade paperback originals. Averages 16 titles/year. Pays 10-15% royalty on retail price. Publishes book an average of 1 year after acceptance. Simultaneous submissions OK. Reports on mss in approximately 6 months. Free book catalog.

An asterisk preceding a listing indicates that subsidy publishing or co-publishing (where author pays part or all of publishing costs) is available. Firms whose subsidy programs comprise more than 50% of their total publishing activities are listed at the end of the Subsidy/Royalty Publishers section.

Nonfiction: Illustrated book, criticism and essays. Subjects include art, social commentary, language/literature. *Submit ms through agent only.*

Fiction: Drama, poetry, experimental, feminist, gay/lesbian, literary, short story collections.

Tips: "We prefer proposals only, with one sample chapter, due to a HUGE increase in unsolicited mss received."

COTEAU BOOKS, Imprint of Thunder Creek Publishing Cooperative, Suite 401, 2206 Dewdney Ave., Regina, Saskatchewan S4R 1H3 Canada. (306)777-0170. Fax: (306)522-5152. Managing Editor: Shelley Sopher. Estab. 1975. Publishes hardcover, trade paperback and mass market paperback originals. Publishes 10 titles/year; receives approximately 1,000 queries and mss/year. 20% of books from first-time authors; 95% from unagented writers. Pays 10% royalty on retail price or outright purchase of $50-200 for anthology contributors. Publishes book an average of 18-24 months after acceptance. Reports in 2 months on queries. Reports in 4 months on average on mss. Book catalog free with SASE or IRC.

Nonfiction: Reference, desk calendars. Subjects include language/literature, regional and women's issues/studies. "We publish only Canadian authors; **we will consider NO American manuscripts.** We are interested in history for our region and books on multicultural themes pertaining to our region." Reviews artwork/photos as part of freelance ms package.

Recent Nonfiction Title: *On Air: Radio in Saskatchewan,* by Wayne Schmalz.

Fiction: Ethnic, feminist, humor, juvenile, literary, mainstream/contemporary, picture books, plays, short story collections. "No popular, mass market sort of stuff. We are a literary press." Submit complete ms. **We only publish fiction and poetry from Canadian authors.**

Recent Fiction Title: *The Crew,* by Jim Dickinson.

Tips: "For children's and Y.A. manuscripts, we are only considering the work of Canadian Prairie (Alberta, Saskatchewan and Manitoba) authors."

HARRY CUFF PUBLICATIONS LIMITED, 94 LeMarchant Rd., St. John's, Newfoundland, Labrador A1C 2H2 Canada. (709)726-6590. Fax: (709)726-0902. Editor: Harry Cuff. Managing Editor: Robert Cuff. Estab. 1980. Publishes hardcover and trade paperback originals. Averages 10 titles/year; receives 50 submissions annually. 50% of books from first-time authors; 100% of books from unagented writers. Pays 10% royalty on retail price. No advance. Publishes book an average of 8 months after acceptance. Reports in 6 months on mss. Book catalog for 6×9 SASE.

Nonfiction: Biography, humor, reference, technical, and textbook, all dealing with Newfoundland, Labrador. Subjects include history, photography, politics and sociology. Query.

Recent Nonfiction Title: *Prime Ministers of Newfoundland* by Michael Harrington.

Fiction: Ethnic, historical, humor and mainstream. Needs fiction by Newfoundlanders or about Newfoundland, Labrador. Submit complete ms. *Writer's Market* recommends query with SASE first.

Recent Fiction Title: *Princes,* by Tom Finn.

Tips: "We are currently dedicated to publishing books about Newfoundland, Labrador, but we will accept other subjects by Newfoundland, Labrador authors. We will return 'mainstream' manuscripts from the U.S. unread."

DOUBLEDAY CANADA LIMITED, 105 Bond St., Toronto, Ontario M5B 1Y3, Canada. "Prefers not to share information."

DUNDURN PRESS LTD., 2181 Queen St. E., Toronto, Ontario M4E 1E5 Canada. (416)698-0454. Fax: (416)698-1102. Publisher: Kirk Howard. Estab. 1972. Publishes hardcover and trade paperback originals and reprints. Averages 20 titles/year; receives 500 submissions annually. 45% of books from first-time authors; 90% from unagented writers. Average print order for a first book is 2,000. Pays 10% royalty on retail price; 8% royalty on some paperback children's books. Publishes book an average of 1 year after acceptance. Query for electronic submissions. Reports in 3 months.

Nonfiction: Biography, coffee table books, juvenile (12 and up), literary and reference. Subjects include Canadiana, art, history, hobbies, Canadian history and literary criticism. Especially looking for Canadian biographies. No religious or soft science topics. Query with outline and sample chapters. Reviews artwork/photos as part of ms package.

Tips: "Publishers want more books written in better prose styles. If I were a writer trying to market a book today, I would visit bookstores and watch what readers buy and what company publishes that type of book 'close' to my manuscript."

*ECW PRESS, 1980 Queen St. E., 2nd Floor, Toronto, Ontario M4L 1J2 Canada. (416)694-3348. Fax: (416)698-9906. President: Jack David. Estab. 1979. Publishes hardcover and trade paperback originals. Publishes 20-25 titles/year; receives 120 submissions annually. 50% of books from first-time authors; 80% from unagented writers. Subsidy publishes (nonauthor) up to 5% of books. Pays 10% royalty on retail price. Simultaneous submissions OK. Query for electronic submissions. Reports in 2 months. Free book catalog.

Nonfiction: Reference and Canadian literary criticism. "ECW is interested in all Canadian literary criticism aimed at the undergraduate and graduate university market." Query. Reviews artwork/photos as part of freelance ms package.
Tips: "The writer has the best chance of selling literary criticism to our firm because that's our specialty and the only thing that makes us money. ECW does not publish fiction or poetry."

FITZHENRY & WHITESIDE, LTD., 195 Allstate Parkway, Markham, Ontario L3R, 4T8 Canada. (416)764-0030. Fax: (416)764-7156. Senior Vice President: Robert Read. Estab. 1966. Publishes hardcover and paperback originals and reprints. Royalty contract varies; advance negotiable. Publishes 25 titles/year, text and trade. Reports in 3 months. Enclose return postage.
Nonfiction: "Especially interested in topics of interest to Canadians, and by Canadians." Textbooks for elementary and secondary schools, also biography, history, health, fine arts and children's books. Submit outline and one sample chapter. Length: open.
Recent Title: *Treasures from Fred Renner's Place, When Heaven Smiled On Our Earth.*

GENERAL PUBLISHING CO., LTD., 30 Lesmill Rd., Don Mills, Ontario M3B 2T6, Canada. "Prefers not to share information."

GOOSE LANE EDITIONS, 469 King St., Fredericton, New Brunswick E3B 1E5 Canada. Acquisitions Editor: Laurel Boone. Firm averages 12-14 titles/year. Receives 350 submissions/year. 20% of books from first-time authors; 75-100% from unagented writers. Pays royalty on retail price. Reports in 2 months. Book catalog and ms guidelines free with SASE. Please use Canadian stamps or IRCs.
Nonfiction: Biography, illustrated book, literary history (Canadian). Subjects include art/architecture, history, language/literature, nature/environment, photography, translation, women's issues/studies. Query first. Reviews photocopied artwork/photos as part of freelance ms package.
Fiction: Experimental, feminist, historical, literary and short story collections. "Our needs in fiction never change: substantial, character-centred literary fiction (either as novel or collection of short stories) which shows more interest in the craft of writing (i.e. use of language, credible but clever plotting, shrewd characterization) than in cleaving to tired, mainstream genre-conventions." No mainstream, mass market, genre, mystery, thriller, confessional or sci-fi fiction, please." Query or submit complete ms.
Tips: "Trends we have noticed are continuing cutbacks, close-downs, belt-tightening, and drying-up of funds and government support for the arts. Writers should send us books that show a very well-read author who has thought long and deeply about the art of writing and, in either fiction or nonfiction, has something of Canadian relevance to offer. We almost never publish books by non-Canadian authors. Our audience is literate, thoughtful, well-read, non-mainstream. If I were a writer trying to market a book today, I would contact the targeted publisher with a query letter and synopsis, and request a book catalog and ms guidelines. Purchase a recent book from the publisher in a relevant area, if possible. Never send a complete ms blindly to a publisher. **Never** send a ms or sample without IRCs or sufficient return postage in Canadian stamps."

*GUERNICA EDITIONS, Box 633, Station N.D.G., Montreal, Quebec H4A 3R1 Canada. (514)987-7411. Fax: (514)982-9793. Editor/Publisher: Antonio D'Alfonso. Estab. 1978. Publishes trade paperback originals, reprints and software. Averages 20 titles/year; receives 1,000 submissions annually. 5% of books from first-time authors. Average print order for a first book is 1,000. Subsidy publishes (nonauthor) 50% of titles. "Subsidy in Canada is received only when the author is established, Canadian-born and active in the country's cultural world. The others we subsidize ourselves." Pays 3-10% royalty on retail price. Makes outright purchase of $200-5,000. Offers 10¢/word advance for translators. IRCs required. "American stamps are of no use to us in Canada." Reports in 3 months. Book catalog for SASE.
Nonfiction: Biography, art, film, history, music, philosophy, politics, psychology, religion, literary criticism, ethnic history, and multicultural comparative literature.
Fiction: Ethnic and translations. "We wish to open up into the fiction world and focus less on poetry. Also specialize in European, especially Italian, translations." Query.
Poetry: "We wish to have writers in translation. Any writer who has translated Italian poetry is welcomed. Full books only. Not single poems by different authors, unless modern, and used as an anthology. First books will have no place in the next couple of years." Submit samples.
Recent Poetry Title: *Croton Elegies*, by Antonio Barolini; translated by Helen Barolini.
Tips: "We are seeking less poetry, more prose, essays, novels, and translations into the English or French."

HARCOURT BRACE CANADA, INC., Subsidiary of Harcourt Brace, Inc., 55 Horner Ave., Toronto, Ontario M8Z 4X6, Canada. "Prefers not to share information."

HARLEQUIN ENTERPRISES, LTD., Subsidiary of Torstar Corporation, Home Office: 225 Duncan Mill Rd., Don Mills, Ontario M3B 3K9 Canada. (416)445-5860. President and Chief Executive Officer: Brian E. Hickey. Editorial divisions: Harlequin Books (Editorial Director: Karin Stoecker); Silhouette Books (Editorial Director: Isabel Swift; for editorial requirements, see separate listing, under Silhouette Books); and Worldwide Library/Gold Eagle Books (Editorial Director: Randall Toye; see separate listing under Worldwide Library). Imprints: Harlequin Romance and Harlequin Presents (Paula Eykelhof, Editor); Harlequin Superromance (Marsha Zinberg, Senior Editor); Harlequin Temptation (Birgit Davis-Todd, Senior Editor); Harlequin Regency Romance (Maureen Stonehouse, Editor); Harlequin Intrigue and Harlequin American Romance (Debra Matteucci, Senior Editor and Editoriaᵢ Coordinator); Harlequin Historicals (Tracy Farrell, Senior Editor). Estab. 1949. Submissions for Harlequin Intrigue, Harlequin American Romance and Harlequin Historicals should be directed to the designated editor and sent to Harlequin Books, 300 E. 42nd St., New York NY 10017. (212)682-6080. All other submissions should be directed to the Canadian address. Publishes mass market paperback originals. Averages 780 titles/year; receives 10,000 submissions annually. 10% of books from first-time authors; 20% from unagented writers. Pays royalty. Offers advance. Publishes book an average of 1 year after acceptance. Reports in 2 weeks on queries. *Writer's Market* recommends allowing 2 months for reply. Free writer's guidelines.

Fiction: Adult contemporary and historical romance, including novels of romantic suspense (Intrigue), short contemporary romance (Presents and Romance), long contemporary romance (Superromance), short contemporary sensuals (Temptation), period historical (Regency) and adult historical romance (Historicals). "We welcome submissions to all of our lines. Know our guidelines and be familiar with the style and format of the line you are submitting to. Stories should possess a life and vitality that makes them memorable for the reader."

Tips: "Harlequin's readership comprises a wide variety of ages, backgrounds, income and education levels. The audience is predominantly female. Because of the high competition in women's fiction, readers are becoming very discriminating. They look for a quality read. Read as many recent romance books as possible in all series to get a feel for the scope, new trends, acceptable levels of sensuality, etc."

HARPERCOLLINS PUBLISHERS LTD., Suite 2900, 55 Avenue Rd., Hazleton Lanes, Toronto, Ontario M5R 3L2, Canada. "Prefers not to share information."

*HERALD PRESS CANADA, Subsidiary of Mennonite Publishing House, 490 Dutton Dr., Waterloo, Ontario N2L 6H7 Canada. (412)887-8500. Fax: (412)887-3111. Book Editor: S. David Garber. Estab. 1908. Firm publishes hardcover and trade paperback originals and reprints. Firm averages 34 titles/year (a few are by Congregational Literature Division); division publishes 30 titles/year. Receives 900 submissions/year. 15% of books are from first-time authors; 98% from unagented writers. Subsidy publishes 5% of books, "not an option for an individual author, only for a church agency." Pays 10-12% royalty on retail price. Publishes book an average of 1 year after acceptance. Accepts electronic submissions only with hard copy. SASE. Reports in 3 weeks on queries. *Writer's Market* recommends allowing 2 months for reply. Book catalog 60¢. Manuscript guidelines free on request.

Nonfiction: Coffee table book, cookbook, illustrated book, juvenile, reference, self-help, textbook. Subjects include child guidance/parenting, cooking, foods and nutrition, education, Christian, ethnic, Mennonite, Amish, history, language/literature, money/finance, stewardship, nature/environment, psychology, counseling, self-help, recreation, lifestyle, missions, justice, peace. "We will be seeking books on Christian inspiration, medium-level Bible study, current issues of peace and justice, family life, Christian ethics and lifestyle, and earth stewardship." Does not want to see war, politics, or the end of the world. Query or submit outline and sample chapters. Reviews artwork/photos as part of freelance ms package.

Recent Nonfiction Title: *Facing the Brokenness,* by K.C. Ridings (meditations for parents of sexually abused children).

Fiction: Ethnic (Mennonite/Amish), historical (Mennonite/Amish), humor, juvenile (Christian orientation), literary, picture books, religious, romance (Christian orientation), short story collections and young adult. Does not want to see war, gangsters, drugs, explicit sex, or cops and robbers. Query or submit outline/synopsis and sample chapters.

Recent Fiction Title: *Joseph,* by James R. Shott (Bible-based).

HMS PRESS, P.O. Box 340, Station B, London, Ontario N6A 4W1 Canada. President: Wayne Ray. Imprint is Spare Time Editions (Editor: Joe Blades). Publishes trade paperback originals. Firm averages 6 titles/year. Receives 5 queries and 2 mss/year. Pays 10% royalty on retail price, or pays in books. No advance. Publishes books 3-6 months after acceptance. Simultaneous submissions OK. Query for electronic submissions. Reports in 1 month on queries. Book catalog and mss guidelines free on request.

Nonfiction: Biography, how-to, gardening, history, language/literature, military/war. Query or submit outline with 2 sample chapters. Reviews artwork/photos as part of freelance ms package. Writer should submit b&w prints.

Fiction: Literary. Query.

Poetry: Query or submit 6 sample poems.

Recent Poetry Title: *Under The Jasmine Moon,* by Geri Rosengweig.

HOUGHTON MIFFLIN CANADA LTD., Subsidiary of Houghton Mifflin Co., 150 Steelcase Rd. W., Markham, Ontario L3R 3J9, Canada. "Prefers not to share information."

HOUNSLOW PRESS, Subsidiary of Anthony R. Hawke Limited, 124 Parkview Ave., Willowdale, Ontario M2N 3Y5 Canada. (416)225-9176. President: Tony Hawke. Estab. 1972. Publishes hardcover and trade paperback originals. Firm averages 8 titles/year. Receives 250 submissions/year. 10% of books from first-time authors; 95% from unagented writers. Pays 10-12½% royalty on retail price. Offers $500 average advance. Publishes book an average of 1 year after acceptance. Reports in 2 months on queries. Free book catalog.
Nonfiction: Biography, coffee-table book, cookbook, how-to, humor, illustrated book and self-help. Subjects include animals, art/architecture, business and economics, child guidance/parenting, cooking, foods and nutrition, health/medicine, history, money/finance, photography, translation and travel. "We are looking for controversial manuscripts and business books." Query.
Fiction: Literary and suspense. "We really don't need any fiction for the next year or so." Query.
Tips: "If I were a writer trying to market a book today, I would try to get a good literary agent to handle it."

JESPERSON PRESS LTD., 39 James Lane, St. John's, Newfoundland A1E 3H3 Canada. (709)753-0633. Fax: (709)753-5507. Publishing Assistant: Albert Johnson. Estab. 1973. Publishes hardcover and trade paperback originals. Firm averages 10 titles/year. Receives 30 submissions/year. 100% of books from unagented writers. Pays 10% royalty. Publishes book an average of 9 months after acceptance. Simultaneous submissions OK. Query for electronic submissions. Reports in 2 months on queries. Free book catalog.
Nonfiction: Biography, cookbook, humor, illustrated book, juvenile, reference, technical and textbook. Subjects include animals, cooking, foods and nutrition, education, ethnic, history, language/literature, military/war, music/dance, nature/environment, regional, religion and translation. "We deal mainly with mss centering around the Newfoundland culture. No books on the history of flying in Newfoundland or Canada." Submit complete ms. *Writer's Market* recommends query with SASE first. "Prefers to receive all photos/artwork after acceptance of mss."
Recent Nonfiction Title: *Some Fine Times!*, by Ed Smith (humor).
Fiction: Adventure, historical, humor, mainstream/contemporary, mystery, romance, short story collections and young adult. "We, for the most part, publish Newfoundland authors." Submit complete ms. *Writer's Market* recommends query with SASE first.
Recent Fiction Title: *Daddy's Back*, by Barbara Ann Lane (young adult/supernatural).

LONE PINE PUBLISHING, #206 10426 81st Ave., Edmonton, Alberta T6E 1X5 Canada. (403)433-9333. Editor-in-Chief: Glenn Rollans. Estab. 1980. Imprints are Lone Pine, Home World, Pine Candle and Pine Cone. Publishes hardcover and trade paperback originals and reprints. Averages 12-20 titles/year. Receives 200 submissions/year. 45% of books from first-time authors; 95% from unagented writers. Pays royalty. Simultaneous submissions OK. Reports in 2 months on queries. Free book catalog.
Nonfiction: Biography, how-to, juvenile and nature/recreation guide books. Subjects include animals, anthropology/archaeology, art/architecture, business and economics, gardening, government/politics, history, nature/environment ("this is where most of our books fall"), photography, sports, travel ("another major category for us). We publish recreational and natural history titles, and some historical biographies. Most of our list is set for the next year and a half, but we are interested in seeing new material." Submit outline and sample chapters. Reviews artwork/photos as part of ms package.
Recent Nonfiction Title: *Lois Hole's Northern Vegetable Gardening*, by Lois Hole.
Tips: "Writers have their best chance with recreational or nature guidebooks and popular history. Most of our books are strongly regional in nature. We are mostly interested in books for Western Canada and Ontario, with some limited interest in the U.S. Pacific Northwest. If I were a writer trying to market a book today, I would query first, to save time and money, and contact prospective publishers before the book is completed. Always send material with SASE (Canadian postage) or IRCs, and make the ms clean and easy to read."

McGRAW-HILL RYERSON LIMITED, Division of McGraw-Hill, 300 Water St., Whitby, Ontario L1N 9B6 Canada. Fax: (416)430-5020. Publishes hardcover and trade paperback originals and trade paperback reprints. 75% of books are originals; 25% are reprints. Firm averages 25-30 new titles/year. 15% of books from first-time authors; 85% from unagented writers. Pays 7½-15% royalty on retail price. Offers $2,000 average advance. Publishes book an average of 1 year after acceptance. Simultaneous submissions OK. Reports in 2 months on queries.
Nonfiction: Cookbook, how-to, reference, self-help, professional. Subjects include Canadiana, business and economics, military/war, money/finance, sports, aviation. "We are looking for books on Canadian small business and personal finance. No books and proposals that are primarily American in focus. We publish for the Canadian market." Query. Submit outline and sample chapters.
Recent Nonfiction Title: *The Evaders: True Stories of Downed Canadian Airmen and their Helpers in World War II*, by Emerson Lavender and Norman Sheffe (aviation history and reference).
Tips: "Writers have the best chance of selling us well-priced nonfiction, usually trade paper format. Our audience consists of consumers who need current information. If I were a writer trying to market a book today, I would test market ideas and research relevant potential publishers."

THE MERCURY PRESS, Imprint of Aya Press, 137 Birmingham St., Stratford, Ontario N5A 2T1 Canada. Editor: Beverley Daurio. Estab. 1978. Publishes trade paperback originals and reprints. Averages 9 titles/year. Receives 200 submissions/year. 10% of books from first-time authors; 99% from unagented writers. Pays 10% royalty on retail price. Publishes book an average of 1 year after acceptance. Query for electronic submissions. Reports in 2 months. Free book catalog. We publish *only* Canadian writers.
Nonfiction: Biography. Subjects include art/architecture, government/politics, history, language/literature, music/dance, sociology and women's issues/studies. Query.
Recent Nonfiction Title: *Frontiers: Essays on Race and Culture,* by Marlene Nourbese Philip.
Fiction: Feminist, literary, mainstream/contemporary and short story collections. No genre fiction except Canadian murder mysteries, published under the Midnight Originals imprint. Submit complete ms with SASE.
Poetry: No unsolicited mss until 1995. No traditional, rhyme, confessional.
Tips: "If I were a writer trying to publish a book today, I would study markets objectively, listen to feedback, present mss professionally, and use IRCs plus SAE for submissions to Canada."

NETHERLANDIC PRESS, P.O. Box 396, Station A, Windsor, Ontario N9A 6L7 Canada. (519)944-2171. Editor: Hendrika Ruger. Publishes various nonfiction, fiction and poetry by and about Dutch-Canadians.

NEWEST PUBLISHERS LTD., #310, 10359 Whyte Ave., Edmonton, Alberta T6E 1Z9 Canada. (403)432-9427. Fax: (403)432-9429. General Manager: Liz Grieve. Estab. 1977. Publishes trade paperback originals. Averages 8 titles/year. Receives 100 submissions/year. 40% of books from first-time authors; 90% from unagented writers. Pays 10% royalty. Publishes book an average of 2 years after acceptance. Simultaneous submissions OK. Reports in 2 weeks on queries. *Writer's Market* recommends allowing 2 months for reply. Book catalog for 9 × 12 SAE and 4 first class stamps.
Nonfiction: Literary/essays. Subjects include art/architecture, ethnic, government/politics (Western Canada), history (Western Canada) and Canadiana. Query.
Fiction: Literary and short story collections. We are looking for Western Canadian authors. Submit outline/synopsis and sample chapters.
Recent Fiction Title: *A Whiter Shade of Pale/Becoming Emma,* by Caterina Edwards.
Tips: "Our audience consists of people interested in the west and north of Canada; teachers, professors. Trend is towards more nonfiction submissions. Would like to see more full-length literary fiction."

NIGHTWOOD EDITIONS, Harbour Publishing, P.O. Box 411, Madeira Park, British Columbia V0N 2H0 Canada. (604)883-2730. Contact: Kim La Fave. Publishes hardcover and trade paperback originals. Publishes 4 titles/year. Receives 200 queries and 100 mss/year. 30% of books from first-time authors; 90% from unagented writers. Pays 7½-20% royalty on wholesale price. Publishes book 3 months after acceptance of ms. Simultaneous submissions OK. No fax submissions. Reports in 1 month on queries. *Writer's Market* recommends allowing 2 months for reply. Book catalog for 9 × 12 SAE with 2 IRCs.
Nonfiction: Children's/juvenile. "We are only interested in children's or young adult books that cover Canadian subjects." Query. Reviews artwork/photos as part of freelance ms package. Writers should send photocopies.
Recent Nonfiction Title: *Bear Stories,* by H. Evans (children's).
Fiction: Juvenile, no YA. "We are only looking for children's fiction." Query.
Tips: "Our audience consists of young people on Canada's west coast."

*OISE PRESS, Subsidiary of Ontario Institute for Studies in Education, 252 Floor W., Toronto, Ontario M5S 1V6 Canada. (416)923-6641, ext. 2531. Fax: (416)926-4725. Editor-in-Chief: Hugh Oliver. Estab. 1965. Publishes paperback originals for the education market. Averages 25 titles/year; receives 100 submissions annually. 20% of books from first-time authors; 90% from unagented writers. Subsidy publishes (nonauthor) 5% of books. Pays 10-15% royalty; rarely offers an advance. Simultaneous submissions OK. Query for electronic submissions. Reports in up to 4 months. Free book catalog and guidelines.
Nonfiction: Textbooks and educational books. "Our audience includes educational scholars; educational administrators, principals and teachers and students. In the future, we will be publishing fewer scholarly books and more books for teachers and students." Submit complete ms. *Writer's Market* recommends query with SASE first. Reviews artwork/photos as part of freelance ms package.
Recent Nonfiction Title: *Our Present: Their Future—A Resource Book for Personal and Global Futures,* by Barbara Dixon and Lillian Lane.

OOLICHAN BOOKS, P.O. Box 10, Lantzville, British Columbia V0R 2H0 Canada. (604)390-4839. Publisher: Ron Smith. Estab. 1974. Publishes hardcover originals and trade paperback originals and reprints. 99% of books are originals; 1% are reprints. Firm averages 10 titles/year. Receives 1,000 submissions/year. 40% of books from first-time authors; 90% from unagented writers. Pays 6-10% royalty on retail price. Publishes book an average of 18 months after acceptance. "At present, we are booked two years in advance." Simultaneous submissions OK. Query for electronic submissions. Reports in 2 months on queries. Book catalog for 9 × 12 SAE and 2 IRCs. Manuscript guidelines for #10 SASE.

Nonfiction: Biography and history. Subjects include ethnic, government/politics, history, language/literature, regional western Canadian, religion, translation and native issues. "We are interested in considering western Canadian regional history and autobiography. However, our list is now booked two years in advance (to the end of 1994, at present). Any manuscripts we accepted would not be published until at least 1995. No how-to books, including cookbooks; no military, Americana, art/architecture, or business." Query or submit outline and sample chapters. Reviews artwork/photos as part of freelance ms package occasionally.

Recent Nonfiction Title: *Aboriginal Self-Determination*, Edited by Frank Cassidy (Native issues).

Fiction: Ethnic, experimental, feminist, humor, literary and short story collections. "Our list is now booked two years in advance. However, we are always interested in new fiction, either short story collections or novels. We are no longer publishing children's, juvenile, or young adult titles." Query or submit outline/synopsis and sample chapters.

Recent Fiction Title: *White Buick*, by Greg Hollingshead (short story collection).

Poetry: "We are seeking contemporary poetry—poets should be aware of current aesthetics. Our list is booked two years in advance; any manuscripts considered would be for publication in 1995 or 1996. We do not want to see doggerel, card verse, or verse that proselytizes." Submit 10-15 samples.

Recent Poetry Title: *Swimming Out of History*, by Florence McNeil.

Tips: "Oolichan is a literary press interested in fiction, poetry and regional history. Our decision to publish is ultimately based on the quality of the writing."

ORCA BOOK PUBLISHERS LTD., P.O. Box 5626 Station B., Victoria, British Columbia V8R 6S4 Canada. (604)380-1229. Publisher: R. Tyrrell. Children's Book Editor: Ann Featherstone. Estab. 1984. Publishes hardcover and trade paperback originals. Publishes 15-20 titles/year; receives 500-600 submissions/year. 50% from first-time authors; 80% from unagented writers. Pays 10-12½% royalty on retail price. Offers average $1,000 advance. Publishes ms an average of 9-12 months after acceptance. Reports in 3 weeks on queries. *Writer's Market* recommends allowing 2 months for reply. Book catalog for 9×12 SAE and $1 (Canadian) postage; ms guidelines for SASE or IRCs.

Nonfiction: Biography, illustrated book, travel guides, children's. Subjects include history, nature/environment, recreation, sports, and travel. Needs history (*west coast Canadian*) and young children's book. Query or submit outline and sample chapters. All unsolicited mss are returned unopened. Reviews artwork/photos as part of ms package. *Publishes Canadian material only.*

Fiction: Juvenile, literary, mainstream/contemporary. Needs west coast Canadian contemporary fiction; illustrated children's books, 4-8-year-old range older juvenile and ya. Query or submit outline/synopsis and sample chapters. All unsolicited mss are returned unopened.

Recent Fiction Title: *Belle's Journey*, by Marilyn Reynolds.

OUTCROP, THE NORTHERN PUBLISHERS, Box 1350, Yellowknife, Northwest Territories X1A 2N9 Canada. (403)920-4652. Publisher: Ronne Heming. Publishes trade paperback originals. Publishes 4 titles/year. Receives 20 queries and 10 mss/year. 90% of mss from first-time authors, 100% from unagented writers. Pays 8-10% on retail price. Publishes book 10 months after acceptance of ms. Reports in 3 months on queries and proposals. Book catalog free on request.

Nonfiction: Biography, cookbook and reference. Subjects include anthropology/archaelogy, business and economics, ethnic, government/politics, history, nature/environment, science and travel. Looking for books with "specific Northwest Territories/Yukon focus." Query or submit outline and 3 sample chapters. Reviews artwork/photos as part of freelance package. Writers should send photocopies.

Recent Nonfiction Title: *Barrenland Beauties*, by Page Burt.

PANDORA PRESS, Imprint of HarperCollins, 77-85 Fulham Palace Rd., Hammersmith, London W6 8JB England. Fax: 081-307-4440. Publishing Director: Eileen Campbell. Commissioning Editor: Karen Molosn. Publishes hardcover and paperback originals. Firm averages 10-20 titles/year. Pays 7 1/2-10% royalty. Reports in 2 months. Free book catalog.

• No longer publishes fiction.

Nonfiction: Wide-ranging list of feminist writing includes subjects on culture and media, health, lifestyle and sexuality, biography and reference, and women's issues/studies.

‡PEGUIS PUBLISHERS LIMITED, 520 Hargrave St., Winnipeg, Manitoba R3A 0X8 Canada. (204)956-1486. Fax: (204)947-0080. Acquisitions, Managing Editor: Annalee Greenberg. Educational paperback originals. Averages 8 titles/year. Receives 150 submissions/year. 50% of books from first-time authors; 100% from unagented writers. Pays 10% average royalty on educational net (trade less 20%). Publishes book an average of 1-2 years after acceptance. Simultaneous submissions OK. Electronic submissions only if accompanied by hard copy. Reports in 3 months on queries; 1 month on mss if quick rejection, up to 1 year if serious consideration. Free book catalog.

Nonfiction: Educational (focusing on teachers' resource material for primary education, integrated whole language). Submit outline/synopsis and sample chapters or complete ms.

Recent Nonfiction Title: *Together is Better: Collaborative Assessment, Evaluation and Reporting*, by Davies, Cameron, Politano, and Gregory.

Fiction: None.

Tips: "Writers have the best chance selling us quality educational resource materials. Our audience consists of educators (teachers, administrators and professors of education)."

PENGUIN BOOKS CANADA LTD., Subsidiary of The Penguin Publishing Co., Ltd., Suite 300, 10 Alcorn Ave., Toronto, Ontario M4V 3B2 Canada. "Prefers not to share information."

PLAYWRIGHTS CANADA PRESS, Imprint of Playwrights Union of Canada, 54 Wolseley St., 2nd floor, Toronto, Ontario M5T 1A5 Canada. (416)947-0201. Fax: (416)947-0159. Managing Editor: Tony Hamill. Estab. 1972. Publishes paperback originals and reprints of plays by Canadian citizens or landed immigrants, whose plays have been professionally produced on stage. Receives 100 member submissions/year. 50% of plays from first-time authors; 50% from unagented authors. Pays 10% royalty on list price. Publishes about 1 year after acceptance. Simultaneous submissions OK. Reports in up to 1 year. Free play catalog and ms guidelines. Non-members should query. Accepts children's plays.

THE PRAIRIE PUBLISHING CO., P.O. Box 2997, Winnipeg, Manitoba R3C 4B5 Canada. (204)885-6496. Publisher: Ralph E. Watkins. Publishes fiction and children's books with regional themes (Manitoba).

PRENTICE-HALL CANADA, INC., College Division, Subsidiary of Simon & Schuster, 1870 Birchmount Rd., Scarborough, Ontario M1P 2J7 Canada. (416)293-3621. Fax: (416)299-2539. Editorial Director: C.J. Newman. Estab. 1961. Publishes hardcover and paperback textbooks and software. Averages 50 titles/year. Receives 200-300 submissions annually. 30-40% of books from first-time authors; 100% from unagented writers. Pays 10-15% royalty on net price. Publishes book an average of 14 months after acceptance. Query for electronic submissions. Reports in 2 months.

Nonfiction: The College Division publishes textbooks suitable for the community college and large university market. Most submissions should be designed for existing courses in all disciplines of study. Will consider software in most disciplines, especially business, technology and sciences. Canadian content is important. The division also publishes textbooks and reference books in computer science, technology and mathematics. *Writer's Market* recommends query with SASE first.

Tips: "Manuscripts of interest to Canadians and/or by authors resident in Canada should be forwarded to above address. All other manuscripts should be sent to Prentice-Hall, Inc., Englewood Office, NJ 07632."

PRENTICE-HALL CANADA, INC., School Division, Subsidiary of Simon & Schuster, 1870 Birchmount Rd., Scarborough, Ontario M1P 2J7 Canada. (416)293-3621. Fax: (416)299-2539. President: Rob Greenaway. Director of Publishing and Marketing: MaryLynne Meschino. Estab. 1960. Imprint is Globe/Modern Curriculum Press. Averages 30 titles annually. *Writer's Market* recommends allowing 2 months for reply.

Nonfiction: Publishes texts, workbooks, and instructional media including computer courseware, video disks, and filmstrips for elementary grades and junior and senior high schools. Subjects include geography, history, language arts, science, social studies, health and French as a second language. Query.

Recent Nonfiction Title: *The Law in Canada*, by Barnhorst/Zetzl.

PRENTICE-HALL CANADA, INC., Trade Division, Subsidiary of Simon & Schuster, 1870 Birchmount Rd., Scarborough, Ontario M1P 2J7 Canada. (416)293-3621. Managing Editor: Tanya Long. Estab. 1960. Publishes hardcover and trade paperback originals. Averages about 20 titles/year; receives 750-900 submissions annually. 30% of books from first-time authors; 40% from unagented writers. Negotiates royalty and advance. Publishes book an average of 9 months after acceptance. Query for electronic submissions. Reports in 3 months. Manuscript guidelines for #10 SAE with 1 IRC.

Nonfiction: Subjects of Canadian and international interest: politics and current affairs, business, health and food. Send outline and sample chapters. Reviews artwork/photos as part of freelance ms package.

Recent Nonfiction Title: *A Century of Canadian Home Cooking*, by Carol Ferguson and Margaret Fraser.

Tips: "Present a clear, concise thesis, well-argued with a thorough knowledge of existing works with strong Canadian orientation. Needs general interest nonfiction books on topical subjects."

PRESS GANG PUBLISHERS, Feminist Co-Operative, 603 Powell St., Vancouver, British Columbia V6A 1H2 Canada. (604)253-2537. Fax: (604)253-7870. Editor: Barbara Kuhne. Publishes nonfiction, fiction and poetry, giving priority to Canadian women, women of color and lesbian writers.

‡PRODUCTIVE PUBLICATIONS, P.O. Box 7200 Station A, Toronto, Ontario M5W 1X8 Canada. Owner: Iain Williamson. Publishes trade paperback originals. Publishes 21 titles/year. Receives 10 queries and 5 mss/year. 80% of mss from first-time authors, 100% from unagented writers. Pays 5-25% royalty on wholesale price.

Publishes book 3 months after acceptance of ms. Query for electronic submissions. Reports in 1 month on queries and proposals, 3 months on mss. Book catalog free on request.

Nonfiction: How-to, reference, self-help and technical. Subjects include business and economics, health/medicine, hobbies and software (business). "We are interested in small business/entrepreneurship/employment/self-help (business)/how-to/health and wellness — 100 pages +." Submit outline. Reviews artwork/photos as part of the freelance ms package. Writers should send photocopies.

Recent Nonfiction Title: *Your Guide to Starting & Self-Financing Your Own Business in Canada*, by Iain Williamson (business).

Tips: "We are looking for books written by *knowledgable, experienced experts* who can express their ideas *clearly* and *simply*."

QUÉBEC/AMÉRIQUE, 425 St. Jean-Baptiste, Montreal, Quebec H2Y 2Z7 Canada. (514)393-1450. Contact: Johanne Parrot. Publishes trade and mass market paperback originals. Publishes 50 titles/year. Receives 500 queries and 500 mss/year. 50% of mss from first-time authors, 95% from unagented writers. Pays 10-14% royalty on retail price. Publishes book 8 months after acceptance of ms. Simultaneous submissions OK. Query for electronic submissions. Reports in 4 months. Book catalog free on request. *Does not publish English language mss.*

Nonfiction: Illustrated book, children's/juvenile, reference, self-help, government/politics, health/medicine, language/literature and technical. Submit complete mss. *Writer's Market* recommends query with SASE first. Reviews artwork/photos as part of freelance ms package. Writers should send transparencies.

Fiction: Adventure, juvenile, literary, mainstream/contemporary, picture books, science fiction, short story collections, young adult. Submit complete mss. *Writer's Market* recommends query with SASE first.

RANDOM HOUSE OF CANADA LTD., Subsidiary of Random House, Inc., 1265 Aerowood Dr., Mississauga, Ontario L4W 1B9, Canada. "Prefers not to share information."

‡*REIDMORE BOOKS, INC., 1200 Energy Square, 10109-106 Street, Edmonton, Alberta T5J 3L7 Canada. (403)488-5091. Director of Sales: Janet Mayfield. Director of Marketing: Cathie Crooks. Publishes hardcover originals. Firm averages 10-12 titles/year. Receives 18-20 submissions/year. 60% of books from first-time authors. 100% from unagented writers. Subsidy publishes 5-10% of books. Pays royalty. Offers $1,500 average advance. Publishes book an average of 8 months after acceptance. Query for electronic submissions. Reports in 1-3 months on queries. Free book catalog.

Nonfiction: Textbook. Subjects include ethnic, government/politics, history. Query. All unsolicited mss are returned unopened. Reviews artwork/photos as part of ms package.

Recent Nonfiction Title: *Greece: Discovering the Past*, by Jim Parsons, John Ewing and Alec Newhart (educational text).

RUBICON PUBLISHING INC., Suite #1, 116 Thomas St., Oakville, Ontario L6J 3A8 Canada. Fax: (416)849-7579. Editorial Assistant: Pamela Wyatt. Publishes trade paperback originals. Publishes 4 titles/year. Receives 100 queries/year. 50% of mss from first-time authors; 100% from unagented writers. Pays 5-10% royalty on wholesale price. Publishes book 14 months after acceptance of ms. Simultaneous submissions OK. Reports in 3 months on proposals.

Nonfiction: Children's/juvenile, reference and textbook. Subjects include education and multiculturalism, ESL materials, etc. (will consider other subjects with a detailed proposal). Prefers Canadian material. Hope to develop more nonfiction for children in the next few years. Submit proposal package, including mention of target audience, competition on the market, writer's qualifications for subject, outline and 1 sample chapter. Reviews artwork/photos as part of the freelance ms package. Writers should send photocopies only.

Recent Nonfiction Title: *A Sound of Thunder*, by Ian Mills (educational).

Fiction: Adventure, historical especially Canadian, juvenile, literary, mainstream/contemporary, picture books and young adult. Prefers Canadian writers and/or settings; also interested in young adult fiction that could also be used for novel study in schools. Submit synopsis and 1-2 sample chapters.

Recent Fiction Title: *Looking for a Hero*, by David Boyd (young adult).

SELF-COUNSEL PRESS, 1481 Charlotte Rd., North Vancouver, British Columbia V7J 1H1 Canada. (604)986-3366. Also 1704 N. State Street, Bellingham, WA 98225. (206)676-4530. Managing Editor: Ruth Wilson. Publishes trade paperback originals. Averages 15-20 titles/year. Receives 1,000 submissions/year. 80% of books from first-time authors; 95% from unagented writers. Average print run for first book is 6,000. Pays 10% royalty on gross receipts. Publishes book an average of 9 months after acceptance. Simultaneous submissions OK. Query for electronic submissions. Reports in 2 months. Book catalog and manuscript guidelines free on request for 9 × 12 SAE.

Nonfiction: How-to, self-help. Subjects include law, business, psychology, reference. Query or submit outline and sample chapters.

Recent Nonfiction Title: *Managing Growth* (self-help business).

Tips: "The self-counsel author is an expert in his or her field and capable of conveying practical, specific information to those who are not. We look for manuscripts full of useful information that will allow readers to take the solution to their needs or problems into their own hands and succeed."

SIMON & PIERRE PUBLISHING CO. LTD., Suite 404, 815 Danforth Ave., Toronto, Ontario M4J 1L2 Canada. (416)463-0313. Director of Operations: Jean Paton. Publishes hardcover and trade paperback originals and reprints. Firm averages 6-10 titles/year. Receives 300 submissions/year. 50% of books are from first-time authors; 85% from unagented writers. Trade book royalty 10% sliding to 15% on retail price. Education royalty is 8% of net. Offers $500 average advance. Publishes book an average of 1 year after acceptance. Simultaneous submissions OK. Reports in 3 weeks on queries. *Writer's Market* recommends allowing 3 months for reply. Free book catalog and ms guidelines.

Nonfiction: *Canadian authors only.* Biography, reference, drama, language/literature, music/dance (drama), Sherlockian literature and criticism. "We are looking for Canadian drama and drama related books." Query or submit outline and sample chapters. Sometimes reviews artwork/photos as part of ms package.

Fiction: Adventure, historical, literary, mainstream/contemporary, mystery, plays (Canadian, must have had professional production), short story collections and young adult. "No romance, sci-fi or experimental." Query or submit outline/synopsis and sample chapters.

Recent Fiction Title: *Found: A Body*, by Betsy Struthers (novel).

Recent Poetry Title: *I Want to Lasso Time*, by George Swede.

Tips: "We are looking for Canadian themes by Canadian authors. Special interest in drama and dramarelated topics; also Sherlockian. If I were a writer trying to market a book today, I would check carefully the types of books published by a publisher before submitting manuscript; books can be examined in bookstores, libraries, etc.; should look for a publisher publishing the type of book being marketed. Clean manuscripts essential; if work is on computer disk, give the publisher that information. Send information on markets for the book, and writer's resume, or at least why the writer is an expert in the field. Covering letter is important first impression."

SONO NIS PRESS, 1745 Blanshard St., Victoria, British Columbia V8W 2J8 Canada. Editor: Angela Addison. Publishes hardcover and trade paperback originals and reprints. Receives hundreds of queries/year. 5-10% of mss from first-time authors, 100% from unagented writers. Pays 10-12 royalty on retail price. Publishes book 8 months after acceptance of ms. Simultaneous submissions OK. Query for electronic submissions. Reports in 1 month on queries. *Writer's Market* recommends allowing 2 months for reply. Book catalog for 9 × 12 SAE and 3 IRCs.

Nonfiction: Biography and reference. Subjects include history (British Columbia), hobbies (trains), regional (British Columbia) and maritime (British Columbia) transportation (western Canada). Query or submit outline and 3 sample chapters. Reviews artwork/photos as part of the freelance ms package. Writers should send photocopies.

Recent Nonfiction Title: *Logging By Rail: The B.C. Story*, by Robert Turner.

Poetry: Query.

Recent Poetry Title: *Postcards Home*, by Christopher Wiseman.

THEYTUS BOOKS LTD., Box 20040, Penticton, British Columbia V2A 8K3 Canada. Manager: Greg Young-Ing. Publishes hardcover and trade paperback originals and reprints. Firm averages 5 titles/year. Receives 30 submissions/year. Pays royalty. No advance. Publishes book an average of 1 year after acceptance. Simultaneous submissions OK. Query for electronic submissions. Reports on queries in 10 weeks. Free book catalog and manuscript guidelines.

Nonfiction: Biography, coffee table book, how-to, illustrated book, textbook. Subjects include education, government/politics, history, philosophy, women's issues/studies and native studies. Submit outline and sample chapters.

Fiction: Ethnic, experimental, feminist, historical, literary, religious, native studies. Submit outline/synopsis and sample chapters.

Poetry: "We are looking for poetry by native authors." Submit 10 samples.

Tips: "We are interested in native authors, as our audience consists of native people."

THISTLEDOWN PRESS, 633 Main St., Saskatoon, Saskatchewan S7H 0J8 Canada. (306)244-1722. Editor-in-Chief: Patrick O' Rourke. Estab. 1975. Publishes trade paperback originals by resident Canadian authors *only*. Averages 10-12 titles/year; receives 350 submissions annually. 10% of books from first-time authors; 90% from unagented writers. Average print order for a first poetry book is 500; fiction is 1,000. Pays standard royalty on retail price. Publishes book an average of 18-24 months after acceptance. Reports in 2 months. Book catalog and guidelines for #10 SASE.

Some Canadian publishers will consider book proposals by Canadian authors only. Please check each listing carefully for this restriction.

Fiction: Juvenile (ages 8 and up), literary. Interested in fiction mss from resident Canadian authors only. Minimum of 30,000 words. Accepts no unsolicited work. Query first.
Recent Fiction Title: *Nights in the Yungas*, by Stephen Heninghan (short fiction).
Poetry: "The author should make him/herself familiar with our publishing program before deciding whether or not his/her work is appropriate." No poetry by people *not* citizens and residents of Canada. Prefers poetry mss that have had some previous exposure in literary magazines. Accepts no unsolicited work. Query first.
Recent Poetry Title: *Old Habits*, by Rhona McAdam.
Tips: "We prefer to receive a query letter first before a submission. We're looking for quality, well-written literary fiction—for children and young adults and for our adult fiction list as well. Increased emphasis on fiction (short stories and novels) for young adults, aged 12 to 18 years."

THORSONS, Imprint of HarperCollins, 77-85 Fulham Palace Rd., Hammersmith, London W6 8JB, England. Fax: 081-307-4440. Publishing Director: Eileen Campbell. Estab. 1930. Other imprints are Pandora and Aquarian Press. Publishes hardcover and paperback originals. Firm averages 80-90 titles/year. Pays 7½-10% royalty. Reports in 2 months. Free book catalog.
Nonfiction: Publishes books on health and lifestyle, environmental issues, business, popular psychology, self-help, and positive thinking.

TUNDRA BOOKS INC., Suite 604, 345 Victoria Ave., Montreal, Quebec H3Z 2N2 Canada. (514)932-5434. Associate Editor: Arjun Basu. Publishes hardcover and trade paperback originals. Publishes 12-15 titles/year. Receives 100 queries and 250-300 mss/year. 10% of mss from first-time authors; 100% from unagented writers. Pays 3.5-10% royalty on wholesale price. Offers $1,500-3,000 advance. Publishes book 15 months after acceptance of ms. Simultaneous submissions OK. Reports in 3 months. Manuscript guidelines free on request.
• Tundra is not accepting unsolicited ms until December 1994.
Fiction: Juvenile, picture book and young adult. "Look at our books. We are not a trendy company. We work with artists primarily. Our motto is: Children's books as works of art." Query.
Tips: "*Always* query. Our audience consists of kids and their parents."

TURNSTONE PRESS, 607-100 Arthur St., Winnipeg, Manitoba R3B 1H3 Canada. (204)947-1555. Managing Editor: Pat Sanders. Publishes trade paperback originals. Publishes 8 titles/year. Receives 600-800 mss/year. 25% of mss from first-time authors; 75% from unagented writers. Pays 10% royalty on retail price. Offers $100-500 advance. Publishes book 1 year after acceptance of ms. Query for electronic submissions. Reports in 3 months. Book catalog free on request.
Fiction: Adventure, ethnic, experimental, feminist, humor, literary, mainstream/contemporary, mystery and short story collections. Submit full ms. *Writer's Market* recommends query with SASE (Canadian postage) first.
Recent Fiction Title: *Fox*, by M. Sweatman.
Poetry: Submit complete ms.
Recent Poetry Title: *This Only Home*, by D. Cooley.
Tips: "We publish only Canadian citizens or landed immigrants."

ULYSSES TRAVEL PUBLICATIONS, Ulysses Book and Maps, 4176 St. Denis, Montreal, Quebec H2W 2M5 Canada. (514)843-9882. Fax: (514)843-9448. Editor: Claude Morneau. Publishes trade paperback originals. Publishes 20 titles/year. Receives 20 queries and 15 mss/year. 40% of mss from first-time authors, 100% from unagented writers. Pays 3-8% royalty on retail price. Offers $1,000 advance. Publishes book 6 months after acceptance of ms. Simultaneous submissions OK. Query for electronic submissions. Does not return submissions. Reports in 6 months. Book catalog and ms guidelines free on request.
Nonfiction: Self-help. Subjects include business and economics and travel. Send complete manuscript. *Writer's Market* recommends query with SASE (Canadian postage) first.
Recent Nonfiction Title: *Best Bed and Breakfasts in Québec*, (travel).

‡THE UNIVERSITY OF ALBERTA PRESS, 141 Athabasca Hall, Edmonton, Alberta T6G 2E8 Canada. (403)492-3662. Fax: (403)492-0719. Director: Norma Gutteridge. Estab. 1969. Subsidiary/imprint is Pica Pica Press. Publishes hardcover and trade paperback originals and trade paperback reprints. Averages 10 titles/year; receives 100-200 submissions annually. 60% of books from first-time authors; majority from unagented writers. Average print order for a first book is 1,000. Pays 10% royalty on retail price. Publishes book an average of 1 year after acceptance. Query for electronic submissions. Reports in 1 week on queries; 3 months on mss. Free book catalog and ms guidelines.
Nonfiction: Biography, how-to, reference, technical, textbook, and scholarly. Subjects include art, history, nature, philosophy, politics, and sociology. Especially looking for "biographies of Canadians in public life, and works analyzing Canada's political history and public policy, particularly in international affairs. No pioneer reminiscences, literary criticism (unless in Canadian literature), reports of narrowly focused studies, unrevised theses." Submit complete ms. Reviews artwork/photos as part of freelance ms package.
Tips: "We are interested in original research making a significant contribution to knowledge in the subject."

*THE UNIVERSITY OF CALGARY PRESS, 2500 University Dr. NW, Calgary, Alberta T2N 1N4 Canada. (403)220-7578. Fax: (403)282-0085. Acting Director: Shirley Onn. Estab. 1981. Publishes scholarly hardcover and paperback originals. Averages 12-18 titles/year; receives 175 submissions annually. Less than 5% of books from first-time authors; 99% from unagented authors. "As with all Canadian University Presses, UCP does not have publication funds of its own. Money must be found to subsidize each project. We do not consider publications for which there is no possibility of subvention." Publishes book average of 1 year after acceptance. Pays negotiable royalties. "Manuscript must pass a two tier review system before acceptance." Query for electronic submissions. Reports on 2 weeks on queries. *Writer's Market* recommends allowing 2 months for reply. Book catalog and guidelines for 9 × 12 SAE with 2 IRCs.

Nonfiction: "UCP has developed an active publishing program that includes up to 18 new scholarly titles each year and 7 scholarly journals. (For UCP's purposes works of scholarship are usually required to be analytical in nature with unity of purpose and unfolding argument and aimed primarily at an audience of specialists.) UCP publishes in a wide variety of subject areas and is willing to consider any innovative scholarly manuscript. The intention is not to restrict the publication list to specific areas."

Recent Nonfiction Title: *Galapagos: A Natural History*, by M.H. Jackson.

Tips: "If I were trying to interest a scholarly publisher, I would prepare my manuscript on a word processor and submit a completed prospectus, including projected market, to the publisher."

UNIVERSITY OF MANITOBA PRESS, 244-106 Curry Place, Winnipeg, Manitoba R3T 2N2 Canada. Director: Patricia Dowdall. Publishes hardcover and trade paperback originals. Publishes 4-6 titles/year. Pays 5-15% royalty on wholesale price.

Nonfiction: Scholarly. Subjects include history, regional, religion, women's issues/studies and native. Query.

‡*THE UNIVERSITY OF OTTAWA PRESS, 542 King Edward, Ottawa, Ontario K1N 6N5 Canada. (613)564-2270. Fax: (613)564-9284. Editor, English Publications: Suzanne Bossé. Firm averages 25 titles/year; 12 titles/year in English. Receives 100 submissions/year. 20% of books from first-time authors; 95% from unagented writers. Determines subsidy by preliminary budget. Pays 5-10% royalty on net price. Publishes book an average of 1 year after acceptance. Reports in 2 months on queries; 4 months on mss. Free book catalog and ms guidelines.

Nonfiction: Reference, textbook, scholarly. Subjects include education, Canadian government/politics, Canadian history, language/literature, nature/environment, philosophy, religion, sociology, translation, women's issues/studies. "We are looking for scholarly mss by academic authors resident in Canada." No trade books. Submit outline/synopsis and sample chapters.

Recent Nonfiction Title: *How to Write an Executive Summary*, by Ed and Judi Jewinski (self-help for government and business).

Tips: "Envision audience of academic specialists and (for some books) educated public."

UNIVERSITY OF TORONTO PRESS, Suite 700, 10 St. Mary St., Toronto, Ontario M4Y 2W8, Canada. "Prefers not to share information."

VANWELL PUBLISHING LIMITED, 1 Northrup Crescent, P.O. Box 2131, St. Catharines, Ontario L2M 6P5 Canada. (416)937-3100. Fax: (416)937-1760. General Editor: Ms. Lynn J. Hunt. Estab. 1983. Publishes trade originals and reprints. Firm averages 5-7 titles/year. Receives 100 submissions/year. 85% of books from first-time authors; 100% from unagented writers. Pays 8-15% royalty on wholesale price. Offers $200 average advance. Publishes book an average of 1 year after acceptance. Query for electronic submissions. Reports in 1 month on queries. *Writer's Market* recommends allowing 2 months for reply. Free book catalog.

Nonfiction: Biography. Subjects include military/war. All military/history related. *Writer's Market* recommends query with SASE first. Reviews artwork/photos as part of freelance ms package.

Tips: "The writer has the best chance of selling a manuscript to our firm which is in keeping with our publishing program, well written and organized. Our audience: older male, history buff, war veteran; regional tourist; students. Military/aviation and Canadian military/history have the best chance with us. However, we have reduced our publishing program for the next few years."

VEHICULE PRESS, Box 125, Place du Parc Station, Montreal, Quebec H2W 2M9 Canada. (514)844-6073. Fax: (514)844-7543. President/Publisher: Simon Dardick. Imprints include Signal Editions (poetry) and Dossier Quebec (history, memoirs). Publishes trade paperback originals by Canadian authors *only*. Averages 13 titles/year; receives 250 submissions annually. 20% of books from first-time authors; 95% from unagented writers. Pays 10-15% royalty on retail price; offers $200-500 advance. Publishes book an average of 1 year after acceptance. Query for electronic submissions. Reports in 2 months on queries. Book catalog for 9 × 12 SAE with IRCs.

Nonfiction: Biography and memoir. Subjects include Canadiana, feminism, history, politics, social history and literature. Especially looking for Canadian social history. Query. Reviews artwork/photos as part of freelance ms package.

Recent Nonfiction Title: *Half the Kingdom: Seven Jewish Feminists*, edited by Francine Zuckerman.
Poetry: Contact Michael Harris, editor. Looking for Canadian authors *only*. Submit complete ms.
Recent Poetry Title: *Fortress of Chains*, by Elisabeth Harvor.
Tips: "We are only interested in Canadian authors."

*VESTA PUBLICATIONS, LTD., Box 1641, Cornwall, Ontario K6H 5V6 Canada. (613)932-2135. Fax: (613)932-7735. President: Ajay Gill. Estab. 1976. Publishes trade paperback and mass market paperback originals. Pays 10% minimum royalty on wholesale price. Subsidy publishes 5% of books. "We ask a writer to subsidize a part of the cost of printing; normally, it is 50%. We do so when we find that the book does not have a wide market, as in the case of university theses and the author's first collection of poems. The writer gets 25 free copies and 10% royalty on paperback editions." No advance. Publishes 4 titles/year; receives 350 submissions annually. 100% of books from unagented writers. Simultaneous submissions OK if so informed. Query for electronic submissions. Reports in 1 month. *Writer's Market* recommends allowing 2 months for reply. "Phone us before submission and save time." Send SAE with IRCs. Free book catalog.
Nonfiction: Publishes Americana, biography, ethnic, government/politics, philosophy, language/literature, money/finance, reference, and religious books. Accepts nonfiction translations. Query. Looks for knowledge of the language and subject. State availability of photos and/or illustrations to accompany ms.
Fiction: Ethnic and literary. Query.
Poetry: Submit 5-6 samples.

*WALL & EMERSON, INC., 6 O'Connor Dr., Toronto, Ontario M4K 2K1 Canada. (416)467-8685. Fax: (416)696-2460. President: Byron E. Wall. Vice President: Martha Wall. Imprints are Wall & Thompson and Wall & Emerson. Publishes hardcover and trade paperback originals and reprints. Firm averages 5 titles/year. 50% of books from first-time authors; 100% from unagented writers. Subsidy publishes 10% of books. Only subsidies provided by external granting agencies accepted. Generally these are for scholarly books with a small market. Pays royalty of 8-15% on wholesale price. Publishes book an average of 1 year after acceptance. Simultaneous submissions OK. Prefers electronic submissions. Reports in 2 months on queries.
Nonfiction: Reference and textbook. Subjects include adult education, health/medicine, philosophy, psychology, science and mathematics. "We are looking for any undergraduate college text that meets the needs of a well-defined course in colleges in the U.S. and Canada." *Editor's note: No longer seeking business and economics, computers and electronics, government/politics, history, language/literature, nature/environment or sociology.* Submit outline and sample chapters.
Recent Nonfiction Title: *Calculus: The Analysis of Functions*, by Peter D. Taylor.
Tips: "We are most interested in textbooks for college courses; books that meet well defined needs and are targeted to their audiences are best. Our audience consists of college undergraduate students and college libraries. If I were a writer trying to market a book today, I would identify the audience for the book and write directly to the audience throughout the book. I would then approach a publisher that publishes books specifically for that audience."

WEIGL EDUCATIONAL PUBLISHERS LTD., 2114 College Ave., Regina, Saskatchewan S4S 3Y9 Canada. (306)569-0766. Publisher: Linda Weigl. Estab. 1979. Publishes hardcover originals and reprints. Firm averages 6-7 titles/year. Receives 50-100 submissions/year. 30% of books from first-time authors; 100% from unagented writers. Pays 5-12% royalty on retail price. Publishes book an average of 2 years after acceptance. Query for electronic submissions. Reports in up to 4 months. Free book catalog.
Nonfiction: K-12 student and teacher materials: social studies, language arts, science/environmental studies, life skills, multicultural texts: Canadian focus. Submit outline and sample chapters. Reviews artwork/photos as part of freelance ms package.
Recent Nonfiction Title: *Canadian Citizenship in Action*.
Fiction: Juvenile educational: multicultural and environmental.
Tips: "Audience is school students and teachers. Curriculum fit is very important."

‡WHITECAP BOOKS LTD., 1086 W. 3rd St., North Vancouver, British Columbia V7P 3J6 Canada. (604)980-9852. Fax: (604)980-8197. Editorial Director: Pat Crowe. Publishes hardcover and trade paperback originals. Publishes 24 titles/year. Receives 150 queries and 50 mss/year. 20% of mss from first-time authors, 90% from unagented writers. Pays 10% royalty on retail price. Offers $500-2,000 advance. Publishes book 8 months after acceptance of ms. Simultaneous submissions OK. Query for electronic submissions. Reports in 2 months on proposals. Book catalog free on request.
Nonfiction: Biography, coffee table book, cookbook and children's/juvenile. Subjects include animals, art/architecture, gardening, history, hobbies, nature/environment, recreation, regional and travel. "We require an annotated outline. Writers should also take the time to research our list through our catalogue." Submit outline, 2 sample chapters, table of contents. Reviews artwork/photos as part of the freelance ms package. Writers should send photocopies, transparencies, relevant material.
Recent Nonfiction Title: *Guardians of the Whales*, by Bruce Obee (natural history).
Tips: "Our readership is a general audience."

WOLSAK AND WYNN PUBLISHERS LTD., P.O. Box 316, Don Mills, Ontario M3C 2S7 Canada. President: Heather Cadsby. Secretary/Treasurer: Maria Jacobs. Publishes trade paperback originals. Publishes 5 titles/ year. Receives 75 queries/year. 50% of books from first-time authors; 100% from unagented writers. Pays 10% royalty on retail price. Publishes book 1 year after acceptance of ms. Query for electronic submissions. Reports in 4 months on queries. Book catalog and ms guidelines free on request.
Poetry: Submit 10 sample poems. Include SAE and IRCs.

WORLDWIDE LIBRARY, Division of Harlequin Enterprises Ltd., 225 Duncan Mill Rd., Don Mills, Ontario M3B 3K9 Canada. (416)445-5860. Editorial Director: Randall Toye. Senior Editor: Feroze Mohammed. Estab. 1949. Imprints are Gold Eagle and Worldwide Mystery. Publishes mass market paperback originals; mysteries are a reprint program. Averages 72 titles/year; receives 1,100 submissions annually. 20% of books from first-time authors; 25% from unagented writers. Offers negotiable royalty on retail price; offers average $2,000-5,000 advance. Publishes book an average of 1 year after acceptance. Reports in 2 months.
Fiction: Action-adventure and near-future fiction. Query first; will accept synopsis and first 3 chapters.
Recent Fiction Title: *Time Raider*, by John Barnes.
Tips: "We are an excellent market for action-adventure and near-future fiction."

YORK PRESS LTD., P.O. Box 1172, Fredericton, New Brunswick E3B 5C8 Canada. (506)458-8748. General Manager/Editor: Dr. S. Elkhadem. Estab. 1975. Publishes trade paperback originals. Averages 10 titles/year; receives 50 submissions annually. 10% of books from first-time authors; 100% of books from unagented writers. Pays 10-20% royalty on wholesale price. Publishes book an average of 6 months after acceptance. Reports in 2 weeks. *Writer's Market* recommends allowing 2 months for reply. Free book catalog; ms guidelines for $2.50.
Nonfiction and Fiction: Reference, textbook and scholarly. Especially needs literary criticism, comparative literature and linguistics and fiction of an experimental nature by well-established writers. Query.
Recent Nonfiction Title: *Tennessee Williams: Life, Work and Criticism*, by F. Londré.
Recent Fiction Title: *Red White & Blue*, by Ben Stoltzfus.
Tips: "If I were a writer trying to market a book today, I would spend a considerable amount of time examining the needs of a publisher *before* sending my manuscript to him. Scholarly books and creative writing of an experimental nature are the only kinds we publish. The writer must adhere to our style manual and follow our guidelines exactly."

Subsidy/Royalty Book Publishers

In this section you'll find listings for U.S. book publishers that publish even a small percentage of their books on an author-subsidy basis.

The number of publishers seeking author-subsidy, "co-publishing" or "co-operative publishing" arrangements with authors has increased in the past few years. Also known as "vanity presses," they offer services ranging from printing your book to distributing and promoting it. Their prices can run as high as $25,000.

Letters making subsidy offers sometimes are the first and only encouraging correspondence writers receive about their book proposals. You should read with a grain of salt how much a publisher loves your book if they are asking you to pay for its production, marketing and/or distribution. Other letters express how much a publisher would like to publish a writer's book, if only they had sufficient funds. They ask if you, the author, would consider investing in a portion of the cost of the book's publication. These letters are often persuasive, and perhaps you will decide that co-publishing may be the route you want to take. Just be certain you know what you're getting into.

Full subsidy publishers often argue that the current economic climate necessitates authors paying the costs of publishing. Because subsidy publishers make a profit on simply producing 1,000 or so bound books, they don't have a stake in marketing the books they publish. Royalty publishers, on the other hand, must sell books to make money because they pay the publishing costs.

Before agreeing to a subsidy contract, ask yourself some questions. What would you do with 1,000 or even 500 copies of your book, if the distribution were left to you? How many do you realistically think you could sell? Few bookstores deal with individuals selling single books. Talk to a local bookstore owner before you sign a contract to see if they stock any titles by the publisher who wants to print your book.

In a co-publishing arrangement, the publisher will usually market its co-published books because it has paid part of the production cost, but writers have other concerns. How do you know the 50% you are paying is truly 50% of the total cost? If you are unsure, call a printer in your area and ask for an estimated cost of printing the type and number of books the publisher has proposed to you. If the printer's quote is significantly lower than the original figure you received, contact the publisher to discuss the matter.

Also at issue is your royalty arrangement. Often a writer is asked for up to half the cost to publish a book, and yet offered a royalty of less than 15%. Authors eager to have their books published find themselves adding up the number of sales they would need to break even. They forget that bookstores take 40-50% of the cover price for each copy they sell, and there are other charges: distributors, shippers and wholesalers all must be paid as well. Stay realistic about what you think you could make back, and proceed cautiously.

Don't bow to pressure from any subsidy publisher who claims you must "act now" or the offer to publish may be withdrawn. Don't confuse subsidy publishers with royalty publishers. Unlike the relationship you might have with a royalty publisher, in which you attempt to earn their favor, you are a subsidy publisher's *customer*, not a supplicant. And as a customer, you should approach the relationship as you would when considering the purchase of any other service—with a dose of skepticism and clear ideas about the contractual assurances you want to see. It is recommended that you consult with an attorney before signing any publishing contract.

If you are truly committed to your book and think there is a market for it, consider self-publishing as an option. It generally costs less than subsidy publishing for essentially the same services, and you have much more control over what is done with your book. For more information on self-publishing, take a look at *The Complete Guide to Self-Publishing*, by Tom and Marilyn Ross (Writer's Digest Books) or *The Publish It Yourself Handbook*, by Bill Henderson (Pushcart Press). In any case, proceed with caution any time a publisher is asking you to finance all or part of the cost of publication.

While we encourage writers to sell their work to royalty publishers, we have listed other book publishing options here. Publishers with the longer listings publish at least 50% of their books on a royalty basis. The shorter listings at the end of this section are the names and addresses of publishers producing more than 50% of their books on an author-subsidy basis.

For a list of publishers according to their subjects of interest, see the nonfiction and fiction sections of the Book Publishers Subject Index. Information on some book publishers and producers not included in this edition of *Writer's Market* **can be found in Book Publishers and Producers/Changes '93-'94.**

‡ACTAEON PUBLISHING, P.O. Box 98, Wayne WV 25570-0098. (304)525-3361. Managing Editor: Todd Vaughn. Estab. 1992. Publishes hardcover, trade paperback and mass market paperback originals. Publishes 6-10 titles/year. 90% of mss from first time authors, 100% from unagented writers. Subsidy publishes 20% of books. Pays 15-20% royalty on wholesale and retail price. Publishes book 6 months after acceptance of ms. Simultaneous submissions OK. Query for electronic submission: prefers WordStar or WordPerfect. Reports in 2 weeks on queries. Book catalog for #10 SASE. Manuscript guidelines for #10 SASE.
Nonfiction: Biography, cookbook, how-to, humor, illustrated book, children's/juvenile, reference, self-help, technical, textbook. Subjects include Americana, animals, anthropology/archaeology, business and economics, child guidance/parenting, computers and electronics, cooking, foods & nutrition, education, ethnic, gardening, gay/lesbian, government/politics, health/medicine, history, hobbies, language/literature, military/war, money/finance, music/dance, nature/environment, philosophy, photography, psychology, recreation, regional, religion, science, sociology, software, sports, translation, travel, women's issues/studies. "We do not publish, nor will we consider, racially offensive or pornographic manuscripts." Query with outline and 2-3 sample

chapters. Reviews artwork/photos as part of freelance ms package. Writers should send photocopies.

Fiction: Adventure, confession, ethnic, fantasy, feminist, gothic, historical, horror, humor, juvenile, literary, mainstream/contemporary, mystery, religious, romance, science fiction, short story collections, suspense, western and young adult. Racially offensive or pornographic mss will not be considered. Query. Submit 3 sample chapters. Complete ms is preferred.

Recent Fiction Title: *The Great Fish*, by Latisha Isaacs Herrold (children's fiction).

Tips: "Breaking into the literary market is very difficult. I would try the small presses and put all my efforts into marketing my work. Many writers become discouraged after being rejected by the large publishers. Believe in yourself and your work."

ALPINE PUBLICATIONS, INC., 225 S. Madison Ave., Loveland CO 80537-7027. (303)667-9317. Publisher: B.J. McKinney. Estab. 1975. Publishes hardcover and trade paperback originals. Averages 6 titles/year. Subsidy publishes 2% of books when "book fits into our line but has a market so limited (e.g., rare dog breed) that we would not accept it on royalty terms." Occasional advances. Pays 7-15% royalty. Publishes book an average of 18 months after acceptance. Reports in 3 months. Writer's guidelines for #10 SAE with 2 first class stamps.

Nonfiction: How-to books about companion animals. "We need comprehensive breed books on the more popular AKC breeds, books on showing, breeding, genetics, gait, care, new training methods, and cat and horse books. No fiction or fictionalized stories of real animals; no books on reptiles; no personal experience stories except in case of well-known professional in field." Submit outline and sample chapters. Reviews artwork/photos as part of ms package.

Recent Nonfiction Title: *Backpacking With Your Dog*, by LaBelle.

‡AMERICAN MEDIA, P.O. Box 4646, Westlake Village CA 91359. (805)496-1649. President: G. Edward Griffin. Publishes hardcover, trade paperback and mass market paperback originals. Publishes 3 titles/year. Receives 60 queries and 25 mss/year. 75% of books from first-time authors; 100% from unagented writers. Subsidy publishes 10% of books. "Marketability determines whether author should be subsidy published." Pays 5-15% royalty on retail price. Publishes book 4 months after acceptance of ms. Simultaneous submissions OK. SASE. Reports in 1 month. Book catalog free on request.

Nonfiction: Biography, coffee table book, cookbook, reference and documentaries. Subjects include anthropology/archaeology, business and economics, cooking, foods & nutrition, education, government/politics, health/medicine, history, military/war and money/finance. Query with outline and 1 sample chapter. Reviews artwork/photos as part of ms package. Writers should send photocopies.

ASHGATE PUBLISHING COMPANY, Old Post Rd., Brookfield VT 05036. (802)276-3162. Fax: (802)276-3837. President: James W. Gerard. Estab. 1978. Imprints include Ashgate, Avebury, Avebury Technical, Scolar, and Varorium. Publishes hardcover originals and reprints and trade paperback originals. Averages 250 titles/year. Receives 100 submissions/year. 25% of books from first-time authors; 100% from unagented writers. Subsidy publishes 10% of books. Pays royalty on retail price or buys mss outright. Publishes book an average of 3 months after acceptance. Simultaneous submissions OK. Query for electronic submissions. Reports in 2 months. Free book catalog and manuscript guidelines.

Nonfiction: Reference, technical and textbook. Subjects include art/architecture, business and economics, government/politics, money/finance, philosophy, religion and sociology. Submit outline and sample chapters.

‡ASTRO COMMUNICATIONS SERVICES (ACS Publications), P.O. Box 34487, San Diego CA 92163. Editorial Director: Marithe Pottenger. Publishes hardcover and trade paperback originals and reprints. Publishes 6 titles/year. Receives 300 queries and 60 mss/year. 60% of mss from first-time authors, 95% from unagented writers. Subsidy publishes 5% of books. Pays 15-20% royalty on monies *received*. Publishes book 1 year after acceptance. Simultaneous submissions OK. Query for electronic submissions. Reports in 1-2 months on queries. Book catalog and ms guidelines for 9×12 SAE with 2 first class stamps.

Nonfiction: Astrology only. "Material must be helpful, practical (no "airy-fairy"). Must emphasize personal power and responsibility (No "Saturn made me do it"). Help people lead fuller, happier lives. Don't send totally unsuitable material (e.g. fiction, poetry, autobiographies). We do *astrology only*!" Query.

Recent Nonfiction Title: *Astro Essentials*, by Maritha Pottenger (astrology).

ASYLUM ARTS PUBLISHING, P.O. Box 6203, Santa Maria CA 93456. Publisher: Greg Boyd. Publishes hardcover and trade paperback originals. Publishes 6-10 titles/year. Receives 100 queries and 50 mss/year. 10% of books from first-time authors; 100% from unagented writers. Subsidy publishes 20% of books. Subsidized

Market conditions are constantly changing! If this is 1995 or later, buy the newest edition of Writer's Market *at your favorite bookstore or order directly from Writer's Digest Books.*

projects must be of the same literary quality as other titles and must "fit" our list—subsidized books are usually in difficult to sell genres, i.e. poetry, drama. Pays 7-10% royalty on wholesale price. Publishes book 18 months after acceptance of ms. Query for electronic submissions. Reports on mss in 4 months. Book catalog free on request.

Fiction: Erotica, experimental, literary, plays, short story collections. "Writers should be able to recognize our preferences by familiarizing themselves with the kind of work published in *Asylum Annual* magazine. We lean toward post-modern fiction and translations of 19th century French texts, as well as translations of contemporary authors." Query.

Poetry: Writers and poets should be familiar with our books and with the contents of *Asylum Annual* magazine. Poets should be forewarned that we can afford to publish very few poetry titles. We do not consider chapbook-length manuscripts. Query.

Tips: Audience is libraries, college students and faculty, sophisticated readers of contemporary literature. "Writers should always query before sending a manuscript that may be totally inappropriate for our list."

‡BEAVER POND PUBLISHING & PRINTING, P.O. Box 224, Greenville PA 16125. (412)588-3492. Owner: Richard E. Faler, Jr. Estab. 1989. Publishes 95% mass market paperback originals, 5% reprints. Averages 5 titles/year. Receives 20 submissions/year. 20% of books from first-time authors. 20% from unagented writers. Subsidy publishes 10% of books. Determines subsidy "if we don't wish to take on the book as publisher, but the author still wants us to print it." Pays 8-10% royalty on net sales. Buys mss outright for $100-1,000 on booklets. Publishes book an average of 11 months after acceptance. Simultaneous submissions OK. Reports in 1 month. Manuscript guidelines for #10 SASE.

Nonfiction: How-to. Subjects include animals, natural history of wildlife, hobbies particularly on exotic pets (snakes instead of dogs), nature/environment, photography especially of wildlife, recreation, hunting, fishing. "We want to see manuscripts suitable for 24 page booklet-200 page books that are written with authority on very specific topics and that are how-to. Example: "Photographing Birds in Flight." Query. Submit outline/synopsis and sample chapters and complete ms. Reviews artwork/photos as part of ms package.

Tips: "We're looking for very specific topics in both consumptive and non-consumptive animal use that are too specific for larger publishers. There are experts out there with valuable information. We want to make that information available. Our primary audiences are hunters, fishermen and photographers. If I were a writer trying to market a book today, I would look for a niche, fill that niche, and attempt to fill it with a work that would be difficult, if not impossible, for someone to duplicate or do better. We are particularly interested in 3,000-7,000 word booklet mss at this time."

BERGH PUBLISHING, INC., Subsidiary of Bergh & Bergh Verlagsanstalt GmbH, Switzerland, Suite 715, 276 Fifth Ave., New York NY 10001. (212)686-8551. Contact: Sven-Erik Bergh. Publishes hardcover originals and reprints. Firm averages 10-15 titles/year. Receives 74 submissions/year. 40% of books from first-time authors; 60% from unagented writers. Subsidy publishes 2% of books. Pays 10-15% on wholesale price. Preliminary letter with SASE required.

Nonfiction: Biography, cookbook, illustrated book and juvenile. Subjects include animals, cooking, foods and nutrition, government/politics. Query.

Recent Nonfiction Title: *Christmas at New England Favorite Inns.*

BINFORD & MORT PUBLISHING, 1202 NW 17th Ave., Portland OR 97209-2405. (503)221-0866. Publisher: James Gardenier. Editor: James Roberts. Estab. 1891. Publishes hardcover and paperback originals and reprints. Receives 500 submissions annually. 60% of books from first-time authors; 90% of books from unagented writers. Average print order for a writer's first book is 5,000. Pays 10% royalty on retail price; offers variable advance (to established authors). Publishes about 10-12 titles annually. Occasionally does some subsidy publishing (10%), at author's request. Publishes book an average of 1 year after acceptance. Reports in 4 months.

Nonfiction: Books about the Pacific Coast and the Northwest. Subjects include Western Americana, biography, history, nature, maritime, recreation, reference, and travel. Query with sample chapters and SASE. Reviews artwork/photos as part of ms package.

Recent Nonfiction Title: *The House at Bridal Veil,* by Anita Birt.

‡BLACK HAT PRESS, Box 12, Goodhue MN 55027. (612)923-4590. Editor/Publisher: Beverly Voldseth. Publishes poetry. Is "open to any good writing." Also publishes *Rag Mag,* a semiannual literary magazine.

‡BLUE HORIZON PRESS, #206, 21301 Powerline Rd. #206, Boca Raton FL 33433-2388. (407)487-8823. Director: Clint Nangle. Editor: Denny Smela. Estab. 1992. Subsidiary of Gulfstream Equity Management. **Tips:** "Looking for top recognized experts, particularly in recovery subjects and international investing. We are looking for premium information that will sell for a premium price."

BRIARCLIFF PRESS PUBLISHERS, 11 Wimbledon Ct., Jericho NY 11753. Editorial Director: Trudy Settel. Senior Editor: J. Frieman. Estab. 1980. Publishes hardcover and paperback originals. Averages 5-7 titles/year; receives 250 submissions annually. 10% of books from first-time authors; 60% from unagented writers.

Average print order for a writer's first book is 5,000. Subsidy publishes 20% of books. Pays $4,000-5,000 for outright purchase; offers average of $1,000 advance. Publishes book an average of 6 months after acceptance. Reports in 2 months. Catalog for 9 × 12 SAE and 3 first class stamps.

Nonfiction: How-to, cookbooks, sports, travel, fitness/health, business and finance, diet, gardening and crafts. "We want our books to be designed to meet the needs of specific businesses." Accepts nonfiction translations from French, German and Italian. Query or submit outline and 2 sample chapters. Reviews artwork/photos as part of ms package.

Tips: "We do not use unsolicited manuscripts. Ours are custom books prepared for businesses, and assignments are initiated by us."

‡CAREER ADVANCEMENT CENTER, P.O. Box 436, Woodmere NY 11598. President: Eric Gelb. Publishes trade paperback originals. Publishes 2-3 titles/year. 50% of mss from first-time authors, 80% from unagented writers. Pays 6-10% royalty on retail price. Publishes book 8-10 months after acceptance. Simultaneous submissions OK. "Prefer hard copy." Word perfect 3½" disk. Book catalog and ms guidelines for #10 SASE.

Nonfiction: How-to and self-help. Subjects include business and economics, money/finance and career development. "Get in touch with the (intended) target market and make sure the book fits." Submit outline and 3 sample chapters, query, or send complete ms. Responds in 3 months. Include resume. Reviews artwork/photos as part of freelance ms package. Writers should send photocopies "if applicable."

Recent Nonfiction Title: *Personal Budget Planner*, by Eric Gelb (how-to).

Tips: "Audience is mass market. We are a marketing firm. We publish user-friendly how-to books which are easy to read. Usually anecdotal! We expect our authors to actively market their books with (if we publish them)."

‡THE CHARLES PRESS, PUBLISHERS., P.O. Box 15715, Philadelphia PA 19103. (215)925-3995. Also 1238 Callowhill St., Philadelphia PA 19123. Managing Editor: Lauren Meltzer. Publishes hardcover and trade paperback originals and reprints. Publishes 12-15 titles/year. Receives 300 queries and 100 mss/year. 20% of mss from first-time authors, all from unagented writers. Subsidy publishes 1% of books "but we plan to increase this. If the project is for one reason or another, very high risk, then we would address this." Pays 10-12% royalty on retail price. Publishes book 3-8 months after acceptance of ms. Simultaneous submissions OK. Query for electronic submission: prefers IBM-compatible — WordPerfect/MicroSoft Word. Reports in 1 month on proposals.

Nonfiction: How-to and self-help. Subjects include animals, health/medicine, psychology and sociology. Query.

Recent Nonfiction Title: *The Cruelest Death: The Enigma of Adolescent Suicide*, by David Lester, PhD.; *Questions and Answers about Depression and its Treatment*, by Ivan Goldberg, MD.

THE CHRISTOPHER PUBLISHING HOUSE, 24 Rockland St., Commerce Green, Hanover MA 02339-2226. (617)826-7474. Fax: (617)826-5556. Managing Editor: Nancy Lucas. Estab. 1910. Publishes hardcover and trade paperback originals. Averages 10-20 titles/year; receives 400-500 submissions annually. 30% of books from first-time authors; 100% of books from unagented writers. Subsidy publishes 15% of books. Pays 5-30% royalty on net proceeds; offers no advance. Publishes book an average of 12-15 months after acceptance. Simultaneous submissions OK. Query for electronic submissions. Reports in 2 months. Book catalog for #10 SAE with 2 first class stamps; ms guidelines for SASE.

Nonfiction: Biography, how-to, reference, self-help, textbook and religious. Subjects include Americana, animals, art, business and economics, cooking and foods (nutrition), health, history, philosophy, politics, psychology, religion, sociology and travel. "We will be glad to review all nonfiction manuscripts, particularly college textbook and religious-oriented." Submit complete ms. *Writer's Market* recommends query with SASE first. Reviews artwork/photos as part of ms package.

Poetry: "We will review all forms of poetry." Submit complete ms.

Recent Poetry Title: *The Sea Cries Over My Shoulder*, by Jonathan Russell.

Tips: "Our books are for a general audience, slanted toward college-educated readers. There are specific books targeted toward specific audiences when appropriate."

‡ARTHUR H. CLARK CO. , P.O. Box 14707, Spokane WA 99214-0707. (509)928-9540. Editorial Director: Robert A. Clark. Estab. 1902. Publishes hardcover originals. Averages 8 titles/year; receives 40 submissions annually. 40% of books from first-time authors; 100% of books from unagented writers. Subsidy publishes 15% of books based on whether they are "high-risk sales." Subsidy publishes (nonauthor) 5% of books. Pays 10% minimum royalty on wholesale price. Publishes book an average of 9 months after acceptance. Reports in 1 week on queries; 6 months on mss. Book catalog for 6 × 9 SAE.

Nonfiction: Biography, reference and historical nonfiction. Subjects include Americana and history. "We're looking for documentary source material in Western American history." Query or submit outline/synopsis with SASE. Looks for "content, form, style." Reviews artwork/photos as part of ms package.

Tips: "Western Americana (nonfiction) has the best chance of being sold to our firm."

CLEANING CONSULTANT SERVICES, INC., P.O. Box 1273, Seattle WA 98111. (206)682-9748. President: William R. Griffin. Publishes trade paperback originals and reprints. Averages 4-6 titles/year; receives 15 submissions annually. 75% of books from first-time authors; 100% from unagented writers. Subsidy publishes 5% of books. "If they (authors) won't sell it and won't accept royalty contract, we offer our publishing services and often sell the book along with our books." Pays 5-15% royalty on retail price or outright purchase, $100-2,500, depending on negotiated agreement. Publishes book an average of 6-12 months after acceptance. Reports in 6 weeks on queries. *Writer's Market* recommends allowing 2 months for reply. Free book catalog; ms guidelines for SASE.
Nonfiction: How-to, illustrated book, reference, self-help, technical, textbook and directories. Subjects include business, health, and cleaning and maintenance. Needs books on anything related to cleaning, maintenance, self-employment or entrepreneurship. Query or submit outline and sample chapters. Reviews artwork/photos as part of ms package.
Tips: "Our audience includes those involved in cleaning and maintenance service trades, opportunity seekers, schools, property managers, libraries — anyone who needs information on cleaning and maintenance. How-to and self-employment guides are doing well for us in today's market. We are now seeking books on fire damage restoration and also technical articles for *Cleaning Business Magazine*, a quarterly. We are also interested in video or audio tapes, software and games that are specific to the cleaning industry."

COLLEGE PRESS PUBLISHING CO., INC., P.O. Box 1132, Joplin MO 64802-1132. (417)623-6280. Fax: (417)623-8250. Contact: John M. Hunter. Estab. 1958. Publishes hardcover and trade paperback originals and reprints. Publishes 25 titles/year. Receives 150 submissions/year. 25% of books are from first-time authors; 100% from unagented writers. Subsidy publishes 5% of books. Subsidy considered "if we really want to publish a book, but don't have room in schedule at this time or funds available." Pays 10% royalty on net receipts. Publishes book an average of 1 year after acceptance. Simultaneous submissions OK. Reports on queries in 2 months. Book catalog for 9 × 12 SAE with 5 first class stamps.
Nonfiction: Bible commentaries, topical Bible studies. (Christian church, Church of Christ.) Query.
Recent Nonfiction Title: *Intimacy with God*, by John Caldwell.
Fiction: Religious. Query.
Tips: "Topical Bible study books have the best chance of being sold to our firm. Our audience consists of Christians interested in reading and studying Bible-based material."

‡CONSORTIUM PUBLISHING, 640 Weaver Hill Rd., West Greenwich RI 02817. Chief of Publications: John Carlevale. Publishes 10-12 titles/year. Receives 30 queries and 25 mss/year. 50% of mss from first-time authors, 90% from unagented writers. Subsidy publishes 5% of books. Pays royalty. Publishes book 2-3 months after acceptance. Simultaneous submissions OK. Query for electronic submissions. Reports in 1 month on queries, 1-2 months on proposals or mss. Book catalog and ms guidelines free on request.
Nonfiction: Biography, self-help, technical and textbook. Subjects include child guidance/parenting, education, health/medicine, language/literature, music/dance, psychology, science and sociology. Query. Writers should send photocopies.
Recent Nonfiction Title: *Who's Who in RI Jazz*, by Kaplan and Petteruti (biographical/essay).
Fiction: Juvenile. Query.

CREATIVE ARTS BOOK COMPANY, 833 Bancroft Way, Berkeley CA 94710. (415)848-4777. Publisher: Donald S. Ellis. Senior Editor: George Samsa. Estab. 1976. Publishes hardcover and paperback originals and paperback reprints. Averages 20 titles/year; receives 800-1,000 submissions annually. 10% of books from first-time authors; 20% from unagented writers. Subsidy publishes 5% of books. Pays 5-15% royalty on retail price. Offers minimum $500 advance. Publishes book an average of 12-18 months after acceptance. Simultaneous submissions OK. Reports in 9 weeks. Free book catalog.
Nonfiction: Biographies and essays. Especially interested in music and works on California. *Writer's Market* recommends query with SASE first.
Fiction: "Looking for serious literary fiction of broad appeal," especially books by and/or about women and crime fiction. *Writer's Market* recommends query with SASE first.

CSS PUBLISHING COMPANY, P.O. Box 4503, Lima OH 45802-4503. (419)227-1818. Editorial Director: Fred Steiner. Estab. 1970. Imprint is Fairway Press (contact: Ellen Shockey). Publishes trade paperback originals. Publishes 50 titles/year. Receives 300 mss/year. 65% of books from first-time authors; 100% from unagented writers. Subsidy publishes 20%. "If books have limited market appeal and/or deal with basically same subject matter as title already on list, we will consider subsidy option." Pays outright purchase of $25-400. Publishes book 1-2 years after acceptance. Simultaneous submissions OK. Query for electronic submissions. Reports on mss in 6 months. Book catalog free on request; ms guidelines for #10 envelope and stamp.
Nonfiction: "We are looking for innovative Christian resources for mainline Protestant denominations; some Catholic resources. We are interested in worship resources, preaching illustrations, collections of short stories based on modern adaptations of scripture, Advent-Christmas dramas for congregations, Lent-Easter season dramas for congregations."

Recent Nonfiction Title: *A Night In Shining Darkness*, by Lynda Pujado.
Tips: "Books that sell well for us are seasonal sermon and worship resources; books aimed at clergy on professional growth and survival; also books of children's object lessons; seasonal plays (Christmas/Lent/ Easter etc.). Our primary market is the clergy in all mainline denominations; others include church leaders, education directors, Sunday school teachers, women's groups, youth leaders; to a certain extent we publish for the Christian layperson. Write something that makes Christianity applicable to the contemporary world, something useful to the struggling, searching Christian. The treatment might be humorous, certainly unique. We have published a few titles that other houses would not touch—with some degree of success. We are open to new ideas and would be pleased to see anything new, different, creative, and well-written that fits our traditional markets."

DELTA SALES PUBLISHING CO., Suite 520, 4195 Chino Hills Pkwy, Chino Hills CA 91709. (714)393-9737. President: Dick Bathurst. Estab. 1991. Publishes hardcover and trade and mass market paperback originals. 100% of books are original. Firm averages 5 titles/year. Receives 3 submissions/year. 25% of books from first-time authors; 100% from unagented writers. Subsidy publishes 25% of books. Determines subsidy on case by case basis. Pays 10-15% royalty on wholesale price. Publishes book an average of 6 months after acceptance. Simultaneous submissions OK. Reports in 3 months. Catalog for 9 × 12 SAE.
Nonfiction: How-to, humor, self-help and leadership. Subjects include business and economics, money/ finance and psychology. "We are looking for books on creativity, self-help and success-oriented topics. No sex-related material." Query or submit outline and sample chapters. Reviews artwork/photos as part of ms package.
Recent Nonfiction Title: *Passionate Leadership*, by Tony Vercillo (self-help).
Fiction: Fantasy, humor, mystery and science fiction. Query or submit synopsis and sample chapters.
Tips: "We would like to see self-help material that is geared toward 21-45 year old people. Our audience consists of students and entry-level and middle level managers. If I were a writer trying to market a book today, I would focus on books that have 'catchy' titles and wide-spread appeal."

‡DEVIN-ADAIR PUBLISHERS, INC., 6 N. Water St., Greenwich CT 06830. (203)531-7755. Editor: Jane Andrassi. Estab. 1911. Imprints are Patriot Press, Flag Press, Irish Book Society, and Photography Associates. Publishes hardcover and paperback originals, reprints and software. Averages 20 titles/year; receives up to 500 submissions annually. 30% of books from first-time authors; 70% from unagented writers. Average print order for a writer's first book is 7,500. Subsidy publishes 5% of books. Royalty on sliding scale, 5-25%; "average advance is low." Publishes book an average of 9 months after acceptance. No simultaneous submissions. Query for electronic submissions. Book catalog and guidelines for 6 × 9 SAE and 5 first class stamps.
Nonfiction: Publishes Americana, business, how-to, conservative politics, history, medicine, nature, economics, sports and travel books. New line: photography books. Accepts translations. Query or submit outline/ synopsis and sample chapters. Looks for "early interest, uniqueness, economy of expression, good style, and new information." Reviews artwork/photos as part of ms package.
Tips: "We seek to publish books of high quality manufacture. We spend 8% more on production and design than necessary to ensure a better quality book. Trends include increased specialization and a more narrow view of a subject. General overviews are now a thing of the past. Better a narrow subject in depth than a wide superficial one."

‡DISCOVERY ENTERPRISES, LTD., Suite 210, 134 Middle St., Lowell MA 01852. (508)459-1720./ Executive Director: JoAnne B. Weisman. Publishes hardcover and trade paperback originals. Publishes 6-8 titles/year. Receives 500 queries and 100 mss/year. 25% of mss from first-time authors, 100% from unagented writers. Subsidy publishes 10% of books. Pays 6-10% royalty. Offers $400-1,500 advance. Publishes book 6 months after acceptance. Simultaneous submissions OK. Reports in 3 months on queries. Book catalog and mss guidelines for #10 SASE.
Nonfiction: Biography (illustrated biographies for ages 10-15), illustrated book, children's/juvenile, textbook and educational manuals and classroom plays for grades 3-6 (historical only). Subjects include education (teachers curriculum guides in social studies), history (American history series, including primary and secondary source materials—ages 10-18) and global studies classroom materials for ages 8-12. "We're interested in biographies which are sophisticated—reading level for kids ages 10-15; 10-12,000 words well documented. Do not provide illustrations other than photos, as we hire illustrators independently. Include documentation of research. Do not "write down to children. Include a C.V. (curriculum vitae or resumé) with submission." Query with outline and 2 sample chapters. Writers should send photocopies.
Recent Nonfiction Title: *The New England Transcendentalists: Life of The Mind and of the Spirit*, by Ellen Hansen (64 page paperback with primary and secondary sources, notes and bibliography).
Tips: "Query first, and then if asked, send sample chapters. Work must be neat, double-spaced, and must have a post-paid return envelope."

‡DUNAMIS HOUSE, 19801 SE 123rd St., Issaquah WA 98027. Editor: Bette Filley. Publishes trade paperback originals. Publishes 3-4 titles/year. Imprint publishes 3-4 titles/year. Receives 12-15 queries and 6 mss/year. 50% of mss from first-time authors, 100% from unagented writers. Subsidy publishes 50% of books. "The

estimated demand for the book" determines whether an author should be subsidy published. Pay negotiated depending on author's participation. Publishes book 12-15 months after acceptance. Simultaneous submission OK. Prefers IBM-compatible. Reports in 1 month on queries. Book catalog and ms guidelines for #10 SASE.
Nonfiction: How-to and Northwest mountaineering books and trail guides. Subjects include nature/environment. "We are interested only in Washington and Oregon mountaineering books and trail guides. We want manuscripts on Mount Rainier, Mount Hood and 'popular' Northwest mountains." Query with outline and 1 or 2 sample chapters. Reviews artwork/photos as part of freelance ms package. Writers should send photocopies. "Be sure to include adequate postage if you want the mss returned."
Recent Nonfiction Title: *Discovering The Wonders of the Wonderland Trail Encircling Mount Rainier*, by Bette Filley (trail guide).
Tips: "Include a list of your qualifications or how you came about your mountaineering expertise. Our readers are very knowledgable."

EDICIONES UNIVERSAL, P.O. Box 450353, Miami FL 33245-0353. (305)642-3355. Fax: (305)642-7978. Director: Juan M. Salvat. General Manager: Martha Salvat-Golik. Estab. 1965. Publishes trade paperback originals in Spanish. Publishes 50 titles/year; receives 150 submissions/year. 40% of books from first-time authors; 90% from unagented writers. Subsidy publishes 10% of books. Pays 5-10% royalty on retail price. Publishes book an average of 9 months after acceptance. Simultaneous submissions OK. Reports in 1 month on queries. *Writer's Market* recommends allowing 2 months for reply. Book catalog free on request.
Nonfiction: Biography, cookbook, humor and reference. Subjects include cooking and foods, philosophy, politics, psychology and sociology. "We specialize in Cuban topics." All manuscripts must be in Spanish. Submit outline and sample chapters. Reviews artwork/photos as part of freelance ms package.
Recent Nonfiction Title: *Cultura Afro Cubana, Vol. 3.*
Fiction: "We will consider everything as long as it is written in Spanish." Submit synopsis and sample chapters.
Recent Fiction Title: *Viaje a la Habana*, by Reinaldo Arenas.
Poetry: "We will consider any Spanish-language poetry." Submit 3 or more poems.
Recent Poetry Title: *Antologia De Poesia Infantil*, by Ana Rosa Nunez.
Tips: "Our audience is composed entirely of Spanish-language readers. This is a very limited market. Books on Cuban or Latin American topics have the best chance of selling to our firm."

‡EDUCATION ASSOCIATES, Division of The Daye Press, Inc., P.O. Box 8021, Athens GA 30603. (404)542-4244. Editor, Text Division: D. Keith Osborn. Estab. 1974. Publishes hardcover and trade paperback originals. Averages 2-6 titles/year; receives 300 submissions annually. 1% of books from first-time authors; 100% from unagented writers. Subsidy publishes 5% of books. "We may publish a college study guide that has a very limited audience and is appropriate for a specific college course." Buys mss "on individual basis." Publishes book an average of 9 months after acceptance. Do not send mss; query first. No response without SASE. Reports in 1 month on queries.
Nonfiction: How-to, textbook, lab manuals. Subjects include psychology and education. "Books in the fields of early childhood and middle school education. No basic textbooks. Rather, are interested in more specific areas of interest in above fields. We are more interested in small runs on topics of more limited nature than general texts." Query only with one-page letter. If interested will request synopsis and sample chapters. Absolutely no reply unless SASE is enclosed. No phone queries.
Recent Nonfiction Title: *Family Studies Guide*, by M. Coleman.
Tips: "We are not taking any unsolicited college textbook manuscripts for the coming year. We will consider small runs of college study guides or study manuals that are used by a professor at his/her own college or university. Will consider any college academic field for a small run lab manual."

WILLIAM B. EERDMANS PUBLISHING CO., 255 Jefferson Ave. SE, Grand Rapids MI 49503. (616)459-4591. Fax: (616)459-6540. Editor-in-Chief: Jon Pott. Assistant to the Editor: Ina Vondiziano. Managing Editor: Charles Van Hof. Children's Book Editor: Amy Eerdmans. Estab. 1911. Publishes hardcover and paperback originals and reprints. Averages 65-70 titles/year; receives 3,000-4,000 submissions annually. 25% of books from first-time authors; 95% from unagented writers. Average print order for a writer's first book is 4,000. Subsidy publishes 1% of books. Pays 7½-10% royalty on retail price; usually no advance. Publishes book an average of 1 year after acceptance. Simultaneous submissions OK if noted. Reports in 3 weeks for queries. *Writer's Market* recommends allowing 2 months for reply. Free book catalog.
Nonfiction: Religious, reference, textbooks, monographs, and children's books. Subjects include children's religious literature, history, philosophy, psychology, religion, sociology, regional history and geography. "Approximately 80% of our publications are religious—specifically Protestant—and largely of the more academic or theological variety (as opposed to the devotional, inspirational or celebrity-conversion books). Our history and social studies titles aim, similarly, at an academic audience; some of them are documentary histories. We prefer that writers take the time to notice if we have published anything at all in the same category as their manuscript before sending it to us." Accepts nonfiction translations. Query. Include SASE for return of ms. Accepts outline and 2-3 sample chapters. Reviews artwork/photos.

Recent Nonfiction Title: *A Dictionary of Biblical Tradition in English Literature*, ed. by David Lyle Jeffrey.
Tips: "We look for quality and relevance."

FALCON PRESS PUBLISHING CO., INC., P.O. Box 1718, Helena MT 59624. (406)442-6597. Fax: (406)442-2995. Publisher: Bill Schneider. Editorial Director: Chris Cauble. Estab. 1978. Imprint is Skyhouse Publications (subsidy publisher; contact: Rick Newby). Publishes hardcover and trade paperback originals. Averages 60-70 titles/year. Subsidy publishes 20% of books. Pays 8-15% royalty on net price or pays flat fee. Publishes book an average of 6 months after ms is in final form. Reports in 1 month on queries. *Writer's Market* recommends allowing 2 months for reply. Free book catalog.
Nonfiction: "We're primarily interested in ideas for recreational guidebooks and books on regional outdoor subjects for either adults or children. We can only respond to submissions that fit these categories." No fiction or poetry. Query only; do not send ms.
Recent Nonfiction Title: *Arizona Scenic Drives.*
Tips: "We are concentrating even more on seeking people with outdoor recreational writing experience to write our guidebooks for fishing, hiking, scenic driving, rockhounding wildlife watching and birding. Especially interested in Rockhound's guides to Western states, and hiking guides to Eastern and Southern states."

FILTER PRESS, P.O. Box 5, Palmer Lake CO 80133-0005. (719)481-2523. President: Gilbert L. Campbell. Estab. 1956. Publishes trade paperback originals and reprints. Firm averages 2-3 titles/year. Receives 100 mss/year. 25% of books are from first-time authors; 100% from unagented writers. Subsidy publishes 10% of books, "if the book has merit, but it is not one we would commission." Pays 6-10% royalties on wholesale price. Publishes ms an average of 6-8 months after acceptance. SASE. Reports in 2 months.
Nonfiction: Cookbook and how-to. Subjects include Americana, anthropology/archaeology, cooking, foods and nutrition, ethnic, hobbies, regional and travel. "We will consider some Western Americana, up to 72 pages. We do not want family diaries. Most of our works are reprints of 19th century published things on Indians, Gold rushes, western exploration, etc. Very rarely do we use unsolicited material. I dream up a project, find an author in 90% of them." Query. Reviews artwork/photos as part of ms package.
Recent Nonfiction Title: *Kokopelli, Casanova of the Cliff Dwellers*; and *Coyote and the Fish, a trickster legend.*
Tips: "We are cutting back to 2-3 new titles, and *none* over 72 pages."

‡GALLERIE PUBLICATIONS, 2901 Panorama Dr., North Vancouver British Columbia V7G 2A4 Canada. (604)929-8706. Editor: Caffyn Kelley. Publishes trade paperback originals. Publishes 6 titles/year. Receives 15 queries/year. 85% of mss from first-time authors. Subsidy publishes 15% of books. Makes outright purchase of $250. Publishes book 3 months after acceptance. Simultaneous submissions OK. Reports in 2 months on proposals.
Nonfiction: Autobiography, philosophy. Subjects include art/architecture and gay/lesbian. "Take a look at our catalogue. We are specialty publishers of books by women artists." Submit proposal package, including summary and sample illustrations. Reviews artwork/photos as part of freelance ms package.
Tips: "Our readers are women concerned with social issues. We do *welcome* unsolicited submissions, queries, phone calls from people *familiar* with our books."

‡THE GRADUATE GROUP, 86 Norwood Rd., West Hartford CT 06117-2236. (203)232-3100. President: Mara Whitman. Publishes 25 titles/year. Receives 10 queries/year. Subsidy publishes 5% of books. Flyers free on request.
Nonfiction: Reference and career/internships. Subjects include career/internship. Query.
Recent Nonfiction Title: *New Internships for 1992-1993*, by Robert Whitman.
Tips: "Our audience is career planning offices and college and law school libraries. We are a small publishing company that specializes in career planning and internship-related publications. Reference books that help students with their career."

GULF PUBLISHING CO., Book Division, P.O. Box 2608, Houston TX 77252-2608. (713)529-4301. Fax: (713)520-4438. Vice President: C.A. Umbach Jr. Editor-in-Chief: William J. Lowe. Contact: Kathleen Daily. Estab. 1916. Imprints include Gulf, (sci-tech, business/management, and HRD/adult education), Lone Star Books (regional Texas books, gardening, cookbooks, and travel guides) and Pisces Books, (travel and outdoor recreation line). Publishes hardcover and large format paperback originals and software. Averages 40 titles/year; receives 250 submissions annually. 30% of books from first-time authors; 100% from unagented writers. Subsidy publishes 5% of books. Pays 10% royalty on net income. Publishes book an average of 1 year after acceptance. Simultaneous submissions OK. Query for electronic submissions. Reports in 2 months. Book catalog for 9×12 SAE with 3 first class stamps. ms guidelines for SASE.
Nonfiction: Popular science, business, management, reference, regional trade (including gardening, cookbooks, regional travel guides), scientific and technical. Submit outline and 1-2 sample chapters. Reviews artwork/photos as part of freelance ms package.
Recent Nonfiction Title: *Transcultural Leadership*, 2nd Edition.
Tips: "Common mistakes writers make include calling first, not having a marketing plan of their own, and not matching publishers with their subject. Tell us the market, and how it can be reached at *reasonable* cost. In the last year, we have been more careful to research market potential of titles to be published."

HAMPTON ROADS PUBLISHING COMPANY, INC., 891 Norfolk Sq., Norfolk VA 23502-3209. (804)459-2453. Fax: (804)766-8907. Publisher: Robert S. Friedman. Vice President: Frank DeMarco. Publishes hardcover and trade paperback originals and reprints. Publishes 20 titles/year. Receives 400 queries and 325 mss/year. 25% of mss from first-time authors, 50% from unagented writers. Subsidy publishes 10% of books. Determined by market risk. Pays 8-15% royalty on wholesale/retail price. Offers advance. Publishes book 3-4 months after acceptance of ms. Simultaneous submissions OK. Query for electronic submissions. Does not return submissions without SASE. Reports in 1-3 months on queries. Book catalog for 9 × 12 SAE and 2 first class stamps.

Nonfiction: Cookbook, how-to, illustrated book and self-help. Subjects include child guidance/parenting, cooking, foods and nutrition, health/medicine, money/finance, new age and regional. Submit proposal package, including outline. Reviews artwork/photos as part of freelance ms package. Writers should send photocopies.

Recent Nonfiction Title: *Whispered Wisdom*, by Mary Summer Rain (inspirational).

Fiction: Literary, mainstream/contemporary and occult. Submit synopsis and 3 sample chapters.

HARIAN CREATIVE BOOKS, 47 Hyde Blvd., Ballston Spa NY 12020-1607. (518)885-7397. Publisher: Dr. Harry Barba. Estab. 1967. Imprints include Barba-cue Specials, What's Cookin, The Harian Press. Estab. 1967. Publishes hardcover originals, trade paperback originals, mass market paperback originals and reprints. Firm averages 3-5 titles/year. Receives 300-500 submissions/year. Subsidy publishes 10% of books. Pays 10-15% on retail price. Publishes book an average of 1 year after acceptance. Simultaneous submissions OK. Reports in 1 month on queries. *Writer's Market* recommends allowing 2 months for reply. Book catalog materials and sample copy of book: $10. Manuscript guidelines for #10 SASE.

Nonfiction: Coffee table book, cookbook, humor and self-help. Subjects include Americana, education, language/literature, recreation and regional. Query with SASE.

Fiction: Adventure, experimental, humor, literary, mainstream/contemporary, romance and short story collections. Query with SASE.

Recent Fiction Title: *Round Trip to Byzantium*, by Harry Barba (novel).

HARMONY HOUSE PUBLISHERS, 1008 Kent Rd., Goshen KY 40026. (502)228-4446. Fax: (502)228-2010. Contact: William Strode. Estab. 1980. Publishes hardcover originals. Publishes 20 titles/year. Subsidy publishes 8% of books. Pays royalty; advance. Publishes book 18 months after acceptance of ms. Simultaneous submissions OK. Query for electronic submissions. Reports in 2 months on proposals.

Nonfiction: Coffee table book, cookbook and illustrated book. Subjects include animals, education, military/war, nature/environment, photography and sports. Query. Reviews artwork/photos as part of ms package. Writers should send photocopies or transparencies.

HAWKES PUBLISHING, INC., 5947 South 350 West, Murray UT 84107. (801)266-5555. President/Editor: John Hawkes. Estab. 1965. Publishes hardcover and trade paperback originals. Averages 24 titles/year; receives 200 submissions annually. 70% of books from first-time authors; 90% from unagented writers. Subsidy publishes 25-50% of books/year based on "how promising they are." Pays varying royalty of 10% on retail price to 10% on wholesale; no advance. Publishes book an average of 6 months after acceptance. Letters preferred describing book. Reports in 1 month on queries. *Writer's Market* recommends allowing 2 months for reply. Free book catalog.

Nonfiction: Cookbook, how-to and self-help. Subjects include cooking and foods, health, history, hobbies and psychology. Query or submit outline and sample chapters. Reviews artwork/photos.

HEART OF THE LAKES PUBLISHING, P.O. Box 299, Interlaken NY 14847-0299. (607)532-4997. Fax: (607)532-4684. Contact: Walter Steesy. Estab. 1976. Imprints include Empire State Books and Windswept Press. Publishes hardcover and trade paperback originals and reprints. Averages 20-25 titles/year; receives 200 submissions annually. 100% of books from unagented writers. Average print order for a writer's first book is 500-1,000. Subsidy publishes 10% of books, "depending on type of material and potential sales." 15% author subsidized; 35% nonauthor subsidized. Payment is "worked out individually." Publishes book an average of 1-2 years after acceptance. Simultaneous submissions OK. Query for electronic submissions. Reports in 1 month. *Writer's Market* recommends allowing 2 months for reply. Current books flyer for #10 SAE and 2 first class stamps.

Nonfiction: New York state and regional, history and genealogy source materials. Query. Reviews artwork/photos.

Fiction: Done only at author's expense.

For explanation of symbols, see the Key to Symbols and Abbreviations on page 72. For unfamiliar words, see the Glossary.

‡HOPE PUBLISHING HOUSE, P.O. Box 60008, Pasadena CA 91116. Publisher: Faith A. Sand. Imprint is New Paradigm Books, Susan L. Parry, Assistant Editor. Publishes hardcover originals and reprints. Publishes 6 titles/year. Imprints publish 4 (Hope); 2 (New Paradigan). Receives 120 queries and 30 mss/year. 20% of books from first-time authors; 100% from unagented writers. Subsidy publishes 20% of books (by foundation or church organizations wanting us to publish a certain work for their use). Pays 10% royalty on net. Publishes book 9 months after acceptance. Query for electronic submissions. Reports in 2 months on queries. Book catalog and ms guidelines for #10 SASE.

Nonfiction: Biography, how-to, children's/juvenile, reference, technical and textbook. Subjects include Americana, anthropology/archaeology, child guidance/parenting, education, ethnic, government/politics, heath/medicine, language/literature, military/war, nature/environment, philosophy, psychology, religion, sociology, translation, travel and women's issues/studies. "We are a nonprofit program unit of the Southern California Ecumenical Council dedicated to publishing books that are of service to the faith community on religious and current social issues." Query. Reviews artwork/photos as part of freelance ms package. Writers should send photocopies.

Recent Nonfiction Title: *The Elephant in the Bedroom: Automobile Dependence and Denial* (the economy and the environment).

Poetry: "Needs to be of interest to religious community."

Recent Poetry Title: Journey, by Justine Merritt (social changes and religious conversion).

Tips: "Our readers are part of the faith community and are interested in current social issues."

‡HUMANITIES PRESS INTERNATIONAL, INC., 165 1st Ave., Atlantic Highlands NJ 07716-1289. (908)872-1441. Fax: (908)872-0717. President: Keith M. Ashfield. Estab. 1951. Imprints are Humanities Press and Ashfield Press. Publishes hardcover originals and trade paperback originals and reprints. Averages 35-50 titles/year. Receives 500 submissions/year. 5% of books from first-time authors; 80% from unagented writers. Subsidy publishes 2% of books. Pays 5-12½% royalty on retail price. Offers $500 average advance. Publishes book an average of 1 year after acceptance. Reports in 3 weeks on queries; 10 weeks on mss. Free book catalog.

Nonfiction: Subjects include politics (international/theory), philosophy (continental, cultural theory), history (European Early Modern to Modern), and sociology. "We want books for senior level undergraduates and upward."

Recent Nonfiction Title: *Racial Formation/Critical Transformations: Articulations of Power in Ethnic and Racial Studies in the United States*, by E. San Juan, Jr.

Tips: "We want well-written contributions to scholarly investigation or syntheses of recent thought. Serious students and scholars are our audience."

HUNTER HOUSE INC., PUBLISHERS, P.O. Box 2914, Alameda CA 94501-2914. Fax: (510)865-4295. Publisher: K.S. Rana. Editor: Lisa E. Lee. Estab. 1978. Publishes trade paperback and hardcover originals. Averages 12 titles/year; receives 200 submissions annually. 60% of books from first-time authors; 60% from unagented writers. "We will consider whether an author should be subsidy published based upon subject matter, quality of the work, and if a subsidy is available." Pays 12-15% royalty on net price. Offers modest advance. Publishes book an average of 1-2 years after acceptance and receipt of final ms. Simultaneous submissions OK. Reports in 2 months. Book catalog and ms guidelines for 9 × 12 SAE with 2 first class stamps.

Nonfiction: Health, social issues, young adult, and self-help. Subjects include family, health, women's health, self-help, psychology, spiritual. Needs mss on new healthcare and treatment, older people and intergenerational concerns. No evangelical, overly political, Americana, esoteric or erotica. Looking specifically for women's health titles and titles concerning natural healing. Query or submit outline and sample chapters. Reviews artwork/photos. "Please enclose return postage for material."

Tips: "Manuscripts on family, health, psychology and social/women's issues for an *aware* public do well for us. Write simply, with established credentials and imagination. Submit queries with an overview, outline, sample chapters, foreword, testimonials from people in the field, marketing information, competition and anything unique about your work. We respect writers and do not mistreat them. We ask for the same consideration."

IEEE PRESS, Subsidiary of The Institute of Electrical and Electronics Engineers, P.O. Box 1331, Piscataway NJ 08855-1331. (908)562-3969. Director of Book Publishing: Dudley R. Kay. Estab. 1971. Publishes hardcover and softcover originals and reprints. Averages 35-40 titles/year. Receives 80-100 submissions/year. 70% of books from first-time authors; 100% from unagented writers. Subsidy publishes 10% of books. Pays 5-18% royalty on wholesale price. Publishes book an average of 6-9 months after acceptance. Simultaneous submissions OK. Query for electronic submissions. Reports in 2 months. Free book catalog and ms guidelines.

Nonfiction: Technical reference and textbooks. Subjects include computers and electronics. "We need advanced texts and references in electrical engineering but we're also recently interested in more accessible "understanding technology" books for the non-specialist, as well as historical aspects of electro-technology. *Major* push is on original, authored works rather than edited collections and reprints. No trade/consumer orientation books in electronics and computers. We publish for the professional and advanced student in engineering." Query. Submit outline and sample chapters.

Recent Nonfiction Title: *Writing and Speaking in the Technology Professions*, by D. Beer.

Tips: "Professional reference books have flourished due to changing technologies and need to keep current. However, technical writers are few. Engineers and scientists should consider trained technical writers as co-authors. We are now more open to 'entry-level' overviews of a technical specialty. Our audience consists of engineers—largely at management and project leader levels. If I were a writer trying to market a book today, I would work with a good agent or other experienced writer with contacts and knowledge of the 'system.' Authors expend too much energy, and endure unnecessary frustration, because they don't know how to match a good idea and respectable proposal with the *appropriate* publishers."

INFO NET PUBLISHING, Suite C, 34188 Coast Hwy., Dana Point CA 92629. (714)489-9292. Fax: (714)489-9595. President: Herb Wetenkamp. Estab. 1985. Publishes trade and mass market paperback originals. Firm averages 4 titles/year. Receives 50-60 submissions/year. 85% of books from first-time authors; 85% from unagented writers. Subsidy publishes 5%, "subsidy determined case by case." Pays 5-10% on wholesale price. Buys mss outright for $850 and up. Combination purchase/royalty. Publishes book an average of 1 year after acceptance. Simultaneous submissions OK. Reports in 2-4 months on queries.

Nonfiction: Cookbook, how-to, reference, self-help, bicycling, skiing and technical. Subjects include business and economics, cooking, foods and nutrition, history, hobbies, recreation, sports, travel and small retailer. "We are seeking specialty authors in vertical market how-tos, specific industry oriented overviews and senior how-tos and self-helps. No cookbooks without a theme, or travel books with too much goo. We are open to unique adventure and/or history first person accounts. No romance." Query. Submit outline and sample chapters. Reviews artwork/photos as part of ms package.

Recent Nonfiction Title: *Principles of Bicycle Retailing III*, by Randy W. Kirk (retail how-to).

Tips: "We have noticed an increase in audience served by specialty pubishers, more targeted marketing, vertical publishing. If I were a writer trying to market a book today, I would expect to participate fully in *marketing* the book. No author can expect to be successful unless he/she *sells* the book after writing it."

INTERSTATE PUBLISHERS, INC., 510 N. Vermilion St., P.O. Box 50, Danville IL 61834-0050. (217)446-0500. Fax: (217)446-9706. Acquisitions/Vice President-Editorial: Ronald L. McDaniel. Estab. 1914. Hardcover and paperback originals and software. Publishes about 30 titles/year. 50% of books from first-time authors; 100% of books from unagented writers. Usual royalty is 10%; no advance. Markets books by mail and exhibits. Publishes book an average of 9-12 months after acceptance. Reports in 4 months. Book catalog for 9×12 SAE with 4 first class stamps. "Our guidelines booklet is provided only to persons who have submitted proposals for works in which we believe we might be interested. If the booklet is sent, no self-addressed envelope or postage from the author is necessary."

Nonfiction: Publishes high school and undergraduate college-level texts and related materials in agricultural education (production agriculture, agriscience and technology, agribusiness, agrimarketing, horticulture). "We wish to expand our line of *AgriScience* textbooks and related materials for grades 9-12." Also publishes items in correctional education (books for professional training and development and works for use by and with incarcerated individuals in correctional facilities). "We favor, but do not limit ourselves to, works that are designed for class-quantity rather than single-copy sale." Query or submit outline and 2-3 sample chapters. Reviews artwork/photos as part of freelance ms package.

Recent Nonfiction Title: *Dairy Cattle Science*, 3rd ed., by M. E. Ensminger.

Tips: "Freelance writers should be aware of strict adherence to the use of nonsexist language; fair and balanced representation of the sexes and of minorities in both text and illustrations; and discussion of computer applications and career opportunities wherever applicable. Writers commonly fail to identify publishers who specialize in the subject areas in which they are writing. For example, a publisher of textbooks isn't interested in novels, or one that specializes in elementary education materials isn't going to want a book on auto mechanics."

‡JORDAN ENTERPRISES PUBLISHING CO., Subsidiary of ScoJtia, Publishing Co., P.O. Box 15111, St. Louis MO 63110. Managing Editor: Patrique Quintahlen. Publishes hardcover and trade paperback originals and reprints. Publishes 3 titles/year. Imprint publishes 2 titles/year. Receives 3,000 queries and 2,000 mss/year. 50% of books from first-time authors; 5% from unagented writers. Subsidy publishes 1% of books. "We subsidy publish on books of poetry: subjects family, love, philosophy." Pays 10-15% royalty on retail price or makes outright purchase of $200-5,000. Offers $500-5,000 advance. Publishes book 1 year after acceptance. Simultaneous submissions OK. Query for electronic submissions. Prefers Macintosh compatible. Reports in 2 months on queries and proposals, 6-12 months on mss. Manuscript guidelines for #10 SASE.

Nonfiction: Biography, how-to, humor, illustrated book, children's/juvenile, reference, self-help, technical and textbook. Subjects include animals, art/architecture, child guidance/parenting, cooking, foods & nutrition, education, ethnic, gardening, health/medicine, history, hobbies, language/literature, money/finance, music/dance, nature/environment, philosophy, photography, psychology, recreation, regional, religion, science, sociology, sport, translation, travel and women's issues/studies. "We plan to publish more biographies and how-to, self-help books for children in upcoming seasons. Writers should send nonfiction submissions to

Scojtia division of our company." Query with outline and 3 sample chapters. Writers should send photocopies. "Tearsheets are preferred, kept on file."

Recent Nonfiction Title: *Ten Hour Publishing Consultations*, by Patrick Miller (writers reference); *The Golden Time*, by Shamel Dezjordyn (history); and *Roommates, College Sublets, and Living in the Dorm*, by Prentiss Van Daves (how-to college reference).

Fiction: Adventure, fantasy, juvenile, literary, mainstream/contemporary, mystery, picture books, romance, science fiction, suspense and young adult. "We plan to publish picture book fantasies, and juvenile and young adult fantasy novels from new unpublished writers." Submit synopsis and 3 sample chapters.

Recent Fiction Title: *The Strawberry Fox*, by Prentiss Van Daves (middle reader); *The Christmas Toy Welcome*, by Prentiss Van Daves (picture book) and *Tumbling In The Stumbling Stone Kingdom*, by Prentiss Van Daves (picture book).

Poetry: "We plan to publish more poetry for the new American Family. Writers must submit fifty poems to be considered for publication." Query. Submit complete ms.

Tips: "We publish books for children around the globe, who look to books for joy and inspiration between fun times at play, with imagination and art."

KUMARIAN PRESS, INC., Suite 119, 630 Oakwood Ave., W. Hartford CT 06110-1529. (203)953-0214. Editor: Trish Reynolds. Estab. 1977. Publishes hardcover and paperback originals and paperback reprints. Averages 8-12 titles/year. Receives 100-150 submissions/year. 10% of books from first-time authors; 100% from unagented writers. Subsidy publishes 25% of books. Determines subsidy by financial viability. Pays 0-10% royalty on net. Publishes book an average of 9 months after acceptance. Query for electronic submissions. Reports in 2 months. Free book catalog and ms guidelines.

Nonfiction: Professional. Subjects include agriculture/horticulture, business and economics, government/politics, nature/environment, religion, sociology, women's issues/studies, international development. "We are looking for mss that address the practical needs of international development community; specific topics include: women in development, natural resource management, private vs. voluntary organizations, and effective and accountable public service. We have begun a new series entitled Kumarian Press Books for a World that Works. The books in this series will be less academic in form and content than our traditional book and geared toward people who frequent independent bookstores, a more informed audience so to speak. We want these books to be more journalistic in style and to be 64,000 to 76,000 words in length."

Recent Nonfiction Title: *Voices From the Amazon*, by Binka Le Breton.

Tips: "Authors have the best chance selling us well written mss that are specifically targeted to addressing the issues faced by the international development community. Our audience is the international development community, university students and the informed reader on world affairs."

PETER LANG PUBLISHING, Subsidiary of Verlag Peter Lang AG, Bern, Switzerland, 62 W. 45th St., New York NY 10036-4208. (212)302-6740. Fax: (212)302-7574. Managing Director: Christopher S. Myers; Senior Acquisitions Editor: Michael Flamini. Estab. 1952. Publishes mostly hardcover originals. Averages 200 titles/year. 75% of books from first-time authors; 98% from unagented writers. Subsidy publishes 25% of books. All subsidies are guaranteed repayment plus profit (if edition sells out) in contract. Subsidy published if ms is highly specialized and author relatively unknown. Pays 10-20% royalty on net price. Translators get flat fee plus percentage of royalties. No advance. Publishes book an average of 1 year after acceptance. Reports in 2 months. Free book catalog.

Nonfiction: General nonfiction, reference works, and scholarly monographs. Subjects include literary criticism, Germanic and Romance languages, art history, business and economics, American and European political science, history, music, philosophy, psychology, religion, sociology and biography. All books are scholarly monographs, textbooks, reference books, reprints of historic texts, critical editions or translations. "We are expanding and are receptive to any scholarly project in the humanities and social sciences." No mss shorter than 200 pages. Submit complete ms. *Writer's Market* recommends query with SASE first. Fully refereed review process.

Fiction and Poetry: "We do not publish original fiction or poetry. We seek scholarly and critical editions only. Submit complete ms."

Tips: "Besides our commitment to specialist academic monographs, we are one of the few US publishers who publish books in most of the modern languages. A major advantage for Lang authors is international marketing and distribution of all titles. Translation rights sold for many titles."

LIBRA PUBLISHERS, INC., Suite 383, 3089C Clairemont Dr., San Diego CA 92117-6892. (619)571-1414. Contact: William Kroll. Estab. 1960. Publishes hardcover and paperback originals. Specializes in the behavioral sciences. Averages 15 titles/year; receives 300 submissions annually. 60% of books from first-time authors; 85% from unagented writers. 10-15% royalty on retail price; no advance. "We will also offer our services to authors who wish to publish their own works. The services include editing, proofreading, production, artwork, copyrighting, and assistance in promotion and distribution." Publishes book an average of 8 months after acceptance. Reports in 2 weeks. *Writer's Market* recommends allowing 2 months for reply. Free book catalog; writer's guidelines for #10 SASE.

Nonfiction: Mss in all subject areas will be given consideration, but main interest is in the behavioral sciences. Prefers complete manuscript but will consider outline and 3 sample chapters. Reviews artwork/photos as part of freelance ms package.
Recent Nonfiction Title: *Behind the Therapists' Notes*, by Theodore C. Kent, Ph.D.; and *Emotional Abuse of the Child*, by Dory Renn, Ph.D.
Recent Fiction Title: *Dear Ruth*, by Christine Kyle; and *The Long Wind*, by Beverly Lauderdale.

LONGSTREET HOUSE, P.O. Box 730, Hightstown NJ 08520-0730. (609)448-1501. Editor: Dr. David Martin. Estab. 1985. Publishes hardcover and trade paperback originals and reprints. Publishes 5 titles/year. Receives 15 queries and 10 mss/year. 40% of mss from first-time authors; 100% from unagented writers. Subsidy publishes 25% of books. Pays 8-12% royalty on retail price. Publishes book 18 months after acceptance of ms. Simultaneous submissions OK. Reports in 2 months on proposals. Book catalog free on request.
Nonfiction: Biography and history. Subjects include history, military/war (Civil War) and regional. Submit outline. Reviews artwork/photos as part of freelance ms package. Writers should send photocopies.
Recent Nonfiction Title: *Jersey Cavaliers*, by Longacre (Civil War history).

MASEFIELD BOOKS, Suite B-54, 7210 Jordan Ave., Canoga Park CA 91303. Fax: (818)703-6087. Publisher: Ken Fermoyle. Publishes nonfiction: education, government/politics, history, psychology and sociology. A modest subsidy program is available for those books with extremely limited markets.

‡NEW FALCON PUBLICATIONS, Subsidiary of J.W. Brown, Inc., 655 E. Thunder Bird, Phoenix AZ 85022. Editor: Frank Martin. Publishes hardcover and trade paperback originals and reprints. Publishes 25 titles/year. Receives 200 queries and 50 mss/year. 20% of mss from first-time authors, 20% from unagented writers. Subsidy publishes 8% of books. Pays 6-12% royalty on retail price; on subsidy—by agreement. Offers $0-5,000 advance. Publishes book 18 months after acceptance. Simultaneous submissions OK. Query for electronic submissions. SASE. Reports in 2 months on queries and proposals, 3 months on mss. Book catalog free on request.
Nonfiction: Biography, how-to, self-help and textbook. Subjects include anthropology/archaeology, education, gay/lesbian, health/medicine, philosophy, psychology, religion, sociology, occult and metaphysical. Submit outline and 3 sample chapters.
Recent Nonfiction Title: *The Unhealed Healer*, by J. Marvin Spiegelman (psychology).
Fiction: Erotica, experimental, fantasy, gay/lesbian, horror, occult, religious and science fiction. Submit 3 sample chapters.
Recent Fiction Title: *Illuminati of Immortality*, by W. Saalman (fantasy/sci-fi).
Tips: "Be polite, be timely, have patience, be neat. Include short resume."

‡NORTH COUNTRY BOOKS, INC., Imprints are Pine Tree Press, North Country Books, 18 Irving Place, Utica NY 13501. (315)733-2482. Publisher: Sheila Orlin. Publishes hardcover and trade paperback originals and reprints. Publishes 6-20 titles/year. Imprint publishes 5-10 titles/year. Receives 300-500 queries and 200-300 mss/year. 80% of mss from first-time authors, 100% from unagented writers. Pays 8% royalty on retail price. Publishes book 1-2 years after acceptance. Simultaneous submissions OK. Reports in 6-8 months on mss. Book catalog free on request.
Nonfiction: New York State regional history, biography, field guides, stories, coffee table, children's, etc. Submit proposal package including completed ms, number of photos/artwork, any pertinent information. Photocopies of photos/artwork helpful, but not imperative. An outline with 2-3 sample chapters would be read, but completed ms preferred.
Recent Nonfiction Title: *The Constables*, by Edith Pilcher (biographical sketch); *Mammals of the Adirondacks*, by Wm. Chapman (field guide); and *Oneida Lake*, by Jack Henke (history of place names).
Fiction: Seldom publishes fiction. Adventure, mystery, romance and suspense. Submit synopsis and 2-3 sample chapters (completed ms preferred).
Tips: "We are a New York State regional publisher appealing to a general trade market of people interested in NY State."

ORION RESEARCH, #330, 14555 N. Scottsdale Rd., Scottsdale AZ 85254-3457. (602)951-1114. Publisher: Roger Rohrs. Imprint is Orion Blue Books. Publishes hardcover originals. Publishes 14 titles/year. Receives 10 queries and 10 mss/year. 50% of mss from first-time authors; 50% from unagented writers. Subsidy publishes 5% of books. Pays royalty on wholesale price. Simultaneous submissions OK. Query for electronic submissions. Reports in 2 months on proposals. Book catalog and ms guidelines for #10 SASE.
Nonfiction: How-to, reference and textbook. Subjects include computers and electronics, education and photography. Query.

PACIFIC BOATING ALMANAC, P.O. Box 2749, Rancho Mirage CA 92270. (310)287-2831. Editor: Peter L. Griffes. Publishes four annual boating guides along the West Coast. Since 1964.
Nonfiction: Almanac's include Coast Piloting, facilities information, history of harbors and miscellaneous information. Review photo's and written material as it pertains to the areas.

PENDRAGON PRESS, Subsidiary of Camelot Publishing Co., Inc., R.R. 1, Box 159, Ferry Rd., Stuyvesant NY 12173-9720. (518)828-3008. Fax: (518)828-2368. Managing Editor: Robert Kessler. Estab. 1972. Publishes hardcover originals and reprints. Averages 12-15 titles/year. Receives 100 submissions/year. 50% of books from first-time authors; 99.9% from unagented writers. Subsidy publishes 20% of books. "If the book is of such special interest that sales will not cover publishing expenses, we subsidy publish." Pays 8-12% royalty on sales price. Publishes book an average of 15 months after acceptance. Simultaneous submissions OK. Query for electronic submissions. Reports in 3 months. Book catalog and manuscript guidelines free on request.

Nonfiction: Reference. Subjects include music/dance and sociology (of music). "We deal specifically with scholarly material, for study and research." Submit outline and sample chapters. Reviews artwork/photos as part of freelance ms package.

Recent Nonfiction Title: *Nadia Boulanger*, by Jerôme Spycket (musicology).

Tips: "In our field, music history, there is a trend toward exploring interdisciplinary studies, such as aesthetics in music, sociology of music, ethnomusicology, etc."

PICKWICK PUBLICATIONS, 4137 Timberlane Dr., Allison Park PA 15101-2932. Fax: (412)487-8862. Editorial Director: Dikran Y. Hadidian. Estab. 1982. Publishes paperback originals and reprints. Averages 6-8 titles/year; receives 10 submissions annually. 50% of books from first-time authors; 90% from unagented writers. Subsidy publishes 10% of books. Publishes book an average of 18-24 months after acceptance. Reports in 4 months. Book catalog for 6×9 SAE with 3 first class stamps.

Nonfiction: Religious and scholarly mss in Biblical archeology, Biblical studies, church history and theology. Also reprints of outstanding out-of-print titles and original texts and translations. Accepts nonfiction translations from French or German. No popular religious material. Query or submit outline and 2 sample chapters. Consult *The Chicago Manual of Style*.

Recent Nonfiction Title: *Calvin's Concept of the Law*, by I. John Hesselink.

PMN PUBLISHING, GFA Management, Inc., Box 47024, Indianapolis IN 46247. Publisher: George Allen. Estab. 1988. Publishes trade and mass market paperback originals and trade paperback reprints. Publishes 5-6 titles/year. Receives 24 queries and 24 mss/year. 50% of books from first-time authors; 75% from unagented writers. Subsidy publishes 25% of books. Subsidy determined by size of the market to which the work is targeted. Pays 5-10% royalty on retail price. Publishes book 18 months after acceptance of ms. Simultaneous submissions OK. Reports in 2 months on queries and proposals. Book catalog free on request.

Nonfiction: How-to, reference, self-help, technical and textbook. Subjects include business and economics, military/war, money/finance, religion and real estate. "Strongest interest is in real estate management, mobile home park management." Query or submit outline.

‡PRINCETON ARCHITECTURAL PRESS, 37 E. 7th St., New York NY 10003. (212)995-9620. Fax: (212)995-9454. Estab. 1981. Publishes hardcover and trade paperback originals and hardcover reprints. Averages 30 titles/year; receives 200 submissions annually. 50% of books from first-time authors; 100% from unagented writers. Pays 6-10% royalty on wholesale price. Simultaneous submissions OK. Query for electronic submissions. Reports in 2-3 months. Book catalog and guidelines for 9×12 SAE with 3 first class stamps. "Manuscripts will not be returned unless SASE is enclosed."

Nonfiction: Illustrated book and textbook. Subjects include architecture, landscape architecture, graphic design, urban planning and design. Needs texts on architecture, landscape architecture, architectural monographs, and texts to accompany a possible reprint, architectural history and urban design. Submit outline/synopsis and sample chapters or complete ms. Reviews artwork/photos as part of ms package.

Tips: "Our audience consists of architects, designers, urban planners, architectural theorists, and architectural-urban design historians, and many academicians and practitioners. We are still focusing on architecture and architectural history but would like to increase our list of books on design."

‡PROCLAIM PUBLISHING, #2610, 1117 Marquette Ave., Minneapolis MN 55403. Publisher/Editor: Jo Reaves. Publishes hardcover, trade paperback and mass market paperback originals. Publishes 12-24 titles/year. Receives 50 queries/year; 90% of books from first-time authors; 90% from unagented writers. Subsidy publishes 90% of books, "first time authors mostly." Pays 10-25% royalty on retail price. Publishes book 2-6 months after acceptance. Simultaneous submissions OK. Query for electronic submissions. Prefers Macintosh-Microsoft Word software. Reports in 1-2 month. Manuscript guidelines free on request for #10 SASE.

Nonfiction: Illustrated book, children's/juvenile, self-helf and textbook. Subjects include child guidance/parenting, health/medicine, language/literature, religion, women's issues/studies and poetry. "For the most part, books are written to be of interest to the Christian market and distributed to Christian bookstores." Submit outline, 2-3 sample chapters and proposal package, including "info on the writer's educational background and qualifications, comparison with other books on market, audience directed to, when book will be ready and if it is a simultaneous submission." Reviews artwork/photos as part of freelance ms package. Writers should send photocopies.

Fiction: Juvenile, literary, mainstream/contemporary, picture books, religious, short story collections, young adult and poetry. "Our target is the Christian market." Submit synopsis and 2-3 sample chapters.
Poetry: Submit 3-4 sample poems.
Recent Poetry Title: *Choose Life*, by Dale Stone (rhymed-couplets Christian orientation).

‡PROSTAR PUBLICATIONS, LTD., (formerly Pacific Boating Almanac), P.O. Box 67571, Los Angeles CA 90067. (310)287-2833. Editor: Peter L. Griffes. Publishes trade paperback originals and reprints. Publishes 7-8 titles/year. Receives 10 queries and 30 mss/year. 20% of books from first-time authors; 80% from un-agented writers. Subsidy publishes 5% of books; depends on title subject and time of publication. Pays 15% royalty on wholesale price. Publishes book 6 months after acceptance of ms. Simultaneous submissions OK. Query for electronic submissions. Reports in 2 months. Book catalog free on request. Manuscript guidelines for #10 SASE.
Nonfiction: How-to, technical, textbook (marine titles). Subjects include recreation (marine titles) and sports (sailing). Submit proposal package. Sometimes reviews artwork/photos as part of freelance ms package. Writers should send photocopies.
Recent Nonfiction Title: *Powerboating Illustrated*, by Pat Royce (nautical).

QED PRESS, Subsidiary of Comp-type, Inc., 155 Cypress St., Fort Bragg CA 95437. (707)964-9520. Fax: (707)964-7531. Senior Editor: John Fremont. Estab. 1985. Publishes hardcover originals and trade paperback originals and reprints. Averages 10 titles/year; *will publish only 5 titles in 1993.* Receives 2,000 submissions/year. 75% of books from first-time authors; 75% from unagented writers. Subsidy publishes 10% of books. Decision made upon evaluation of ms. Pays 6-12% royalty on retail price. Publishes ms an average of 1 year after acceptance. Simultaneous submissions OK. Query for electronic submissions. Reports in 2 months. Book catalog for 9 × 12 SAE and 2 first class stamps.
Nonfiction: Biography, cookbook, how-to, humor, self-help. "We seek books on the aging process, coping with aging, careers for older people, investments, etc." No juvenile, illustrated, photography, travel. Submit outline and sample chapters.
Fiction: Adventure, ethnic, experimental, fantasy, feminist, historical, literary, mainstream/contemporary, mystery, science fiction, short story collections, suspense. "Our thrust will be the acquisition of translated fiction by contemporary European, African and South American authors." Submit outline/synopsis and sample chapters.
Poetry: Minimal needs for poetry. No traditional, religious, rhymed or derivative poetry. Submit 3 samples.
Tips: "Our audience is older, literary, literate, involved and politically aware."

R&E PUBLISHERS, P.O. Box 2008, Saratoga CA 95070. (408)866-6303. Fax: (408)866-0825. Publisher: R. Reed. Estab. 1967. Publishes hardcover and trade paperback originals. Averages 40 titles/year. Receives 3,000 submissions/year. 80% of books from first-time authors; 80% from unagented writers. Subsidy publishes 5% of books. Pays 10-20% on wholesale price. Publishes book an average of 6 months after acceptance. Simultaneous submissions OK. Query for electronic submissions. Reports in 3 months. Free book catalog and manuscript guidelines for #10 SASE.
Nonfiction: How-to, humor, illustrated book, reference, self-help, software, technical and textbook. Subjects include business and economics, child guidance/parenting, computers, cooking, foods and nutrition, education, ethnic, government/politics, health/medicine, history, money/finance, music/dance, nature/environment, philosophy, psychology, regional, science, sociology, travel and women's issues/studies. Query or submit outline and sample chapters. Reviews artwork as part of freelance ms package.
Recent Nonfiction Title: *Talking Justice: 602 Ways to Promote Racial Harmony*, by T. Trotter and J. Allen.

‡RED APPLE PUBLISHING, P.O. Box 101, Gig Harbor WA 98335. (206)265-6595. 1(800)245-6595. Fax: (206)265-6596. Contact: Peggy J. Meyer. Publishes paperback originals. Publishes 5 titles/year. Receives 20 queries and 10 mss/year. 100% of books from first-time authors; 100% from unagented writers. Subsidy publishes 100% of books. Publishes book 3 months after acceptance. Simultaneous submissions OK. Query for electronic submissions. Prefers Wordperfect. Reports in 1 month on queries. Book catalog and mss guidelines free on request.
Nonfiction: Autobiography, biography, history and Americana. Query. Reviews artwork/photos as part of freelance ms package. Writers should send photocopies.
Recent Nonfiction Title: *The Great Depression*, by Duval A. Edwards (history/autobiography); *Tales of a Country Doctor*, by Dr. Brandt A. Bede (history of medicine in Lewis County WA); *Tales From the Woodshed*, by Fred Austin (logger's autobiography); and *Conrad and Me*, by Lillian Claunch (childhood tales).
Tips: Audience is senior/elder writers.

RESOURCE PUBLICATIONS, INC., Suite 290, 160 E. Virginia St., San Jose CA 95112-5876. Editorial Director: Kenneth E. Guentert. Estab. 1973. Publishes paperback originals. Publishes 14 titles/year; receives 100-200 submissions annually. 30% of books from first-time authors; 99% from unagented writers. Average print order for a first book is 3,000. Subsidy publishes 10% of books. "If the author can present and defend a personal publicity effort or otherwise demonstrate demand and the work is in our field, we will consider it."

Pays 8% royalty; occasionally offers advance in the form of books. Publishes book an average of 18 months after acceptance. Query for electronic submissions. Reports in 3 months.

Nonfiction: "We look for imaginative but practical books relating to ministry, counseling, and education. We are looking particularly for educational resources in the prevention field." Query or submit outline and sample chapters. Prepare a clear outline of the work and an ambitious schedule of public appearances to help make it known and present both as a proposal to the publisher. Accepts translations. Reviews artwork/ photos as part of freelance ms package.

Recent Nonfiction Title: *Tutoring and Mentoring: Two Peer Helping Programs for Elementary School*; and *Moms: A Personal Journal*.

Fiction: "We are not interested in novels or collections of short stories in the usual literary sense. But we look for storytelling resources and collections of short works in the area of drama, dance, song, and visual art, especially if related to education or ministry." Query or submit outline/synopsis and sample chapters.

Tips: "Books that provide readers with practical, usable suggestions and ideas pertaining to worship, celebration, education, and the arts have the best chance of selling to our firm. We are hoping to build on a strong list of peer-helping books with additional resources on the prevention of drug abuse, domestic violence, and other social ills."

S.P.I. BOOKS, (formerly Shapolsky Publishers), 136 W. 22nd St., New York NY 10011. (212)633-2022. Fax: (212)633-2123. Acquisitions Editor: Ron L. Smith. Estab. 1983. Publishes hardcover and paperback originals and reprints; 75% originals and 25% reprints. Subsidy publishes 5% of books. Pays 5-10% royalty on retail price. Offers average $1,000 advance. Publishes ms an average of 10 months after acceptance. Simultaneous submissions OK. Reports on queries with SASE in 3 months. No unsolicited mss will be read.

Nonfiction: "The major thrust of our list is true crime and entertainment, humor and sports. No memoirs." Query or submit outline/synopsis and sample chapters. Reviews artwork/photos as part of freelance ms package.

Recent Nonfiction Title: *More of Hollywood's Unsolved Mysteries*, by John Austin.

Tips: "90% of our books are general interest; 10% are Jewish interest."

SKIDMORE-ROTH PUBLISHING, INC., 7730 Trade Center Dr., El Paso TX 79912. (915)877-4455. President: Linda Roth. Contact: Brenda Goodner. Estab. 1987. Firm averages 10 titles/year. Receives 250 submissions/ year. 50% of books first-time authors; 100% from unagented writers. Pays 5-12½% royalty on wholesale price. Publishes book an average of 9 months after acceptance. Simultaneous submissions OK. Reports in 1 month. *Writer's Market* recommends allowing 2 months for reply. Also offers subsidy arrangements.

Nonfiction: Technical, textbook. Subjects include nursing, allied health and health/medicine. We a re currently searching for m anuscripts in the following areas: nursing and allied health. Nothing on religion, hi story, music/dance, travel, spo rts, agriculture, computers, military, politics, gay/lesbian or literature. Query. Rev iews artwork/photos as part of freelance ms package.

● No longer seeking self-help, child guidance/parenting, psychology, consumer-health, or self-improvement.

Recent Nonfiction Title: *Geriatric Nursing Care Plans*, by Marie Jaffe, R.N., M.S.

Tips: "Anything on nursing is more likely to be published. Our audience is largely professionals in the field of medicine, nursing, allied health. If I were a writer trying to market a book today, I would look for an area that has been completely overlooked by other writers and write on that subject."

STARBOOKS PRESS, Imprint of Woldt Corp., P.O. Box 2737, Sarasota FL 34230-2737. (813)957-1281. Editor: Patrick J. Powers. Estab. 1980. Publishes trade paperback originals. Imprint averages 10-12 titles/year. Receives 30-50 submissions/year. 10% of books from first-time authors; 100% from unagented writers. Subsidy publishes 10% of books. "Subsidy deals are based on marketability and quality of work. Poetry is in this category." Pays 15% royalty based on wholesale price or buys outright for up to $150. Offers 50% average advance. Publishes book an average of 2 months after acceptance. Simultaneous submissions OK. Query for electronic submissions. Reports in up to 2 months. Free book catalog. Manuscript guidelines for 6×9 SAE with 2 first class stamps.

Nonfiction: Subjects include gay and lesbian. Query or submit outline and sample chapters. Reviews artwork/ photos as part of freelance ms package.

Fiction: Erotica, gay/lesbian. "We need to produce at least ten new titles per year. Only gay and lesbian genre will be considered." Submit outline/synopsis and sample chapters (first and last pages vital).

Poetry: All poetry contracts are offered on a subsidy basis. Submit complete ms.

Tips: "Submission for one of our anthologies is in an ideal beginning. Our audience consists of gay males. We will publish our first lesbian anthology in 1993. If I were a writer trying to market a book today, I would keep trying to improve my work and recognize this is a business for the publisher; time is limited and suggestions should be accepted and acted upon. So often we get manuscripts which the author says cannot be edited in any way."

TRANSACTION BOOKS, Rutgers University, New Brunswick NJ 08903. (201)932-2280. Fax: (201)932-3138. President: I.L. Horowitz. Publisher: Scott Bramson. Book Division Director: Mary E. Curtis. Publishes hardcover and paperback originals and reprints. Specializes in scholarly social science books. Averages 135 titles/year; receives 800 submissions annually. 15% of books from first-time authors; 85% of books from unagented writers. Average print order for a first book is 1,000. Subsidy publishes 10% of books. "Royalty depends on individual contract; we've gone anywhere from 2% edited to 15% authored." No advance. Publishes book an average of 10 months after acceptance. Electronic submissions OK, but requires hard copy also. Reports in 4 months. Book catalog and ms guidelines for SASE.
Nonfiction: Americana, biography, economics, history, law, medicine and psychiatry, music, philosophy, politics, psychology, reference, scientific, sociology, technical and textbooks. "All must be scholarly social science or related." Strong emphasis on applied social research. Query or submit outline. "Do not submit sample chapters. We evaluate complete manuscripts only." Accepts nonfiction translations. Use *Chicago Manual of Style.* Looks for "scholarly content, presentation, methodology, and target audience." State availability of photos/illustrations and send one photocopied example.

‡UAHC PRESS, Union of American Hebrew Congregations, 838 5th Ave., New York NY 10021. (212)249-0100. Managing Director: Stuart L. Benick. Trade Acquisitions Editor: Aron Hirt-Manheimer. Text Acquisitions Editor: David Kasakove. Estab. 1873. Publishes hardcover and trade paperback originals. Averages 15 titles/year. 60% of books from first-time authors; 90% from unagented writers. Subsidy publishes 40% of books. Pays 5-15% royalty on wholesale price. Publishes book an average of 9 months after acceptance. Simultaneous submissions OK. Book catalog and ms guidelines for SASE.
Nonfiction: Illustrated, juvenile and Jewish textbooks. "Looking for authors that can share an enthusiasm about Judaism with young readers. We welcome first-time authors." Reviews artwork/photos as part of freelance ms package.
Tips: "We publish books that teach values."

‡VISTA PUBLISHING INC., 473 Broadway, Long Branch NJ 07740. (908)229-6500. President: Carolyn Zagury. Publishes trade paperback originals. Publishes 6 titles/year. Receives 25 queries and 20 mss/year. 95% of books from first-time authors; 100% from unagented writers. Subsidy publishes 5% of books. "Decision to subsidy publish based on overall estimated market and shared risk factors." Pays 30-50% royalty on percentage of total net sales. Publishes book 6 months after acceptance. Simultaneous submissions OK. Query for electronic submissions. Prefers disk. Reports in 2 months on mss. Book catalog and ms guidelines free on request.
Nonfiction: Biography, how-to, humor, reference, self-help and textbook. Subjects include business and economics, health/medicine, psychology and women's issues/studies. Query. Submit proposal package, including complete ms. Writers should send photocopies.
Recent Nonfiction Title: *To Live and Die With Dignity: A Guide to Living Wills*, by Samuel L. Peluso, Esq. (reference); *Nurse Entrepreneur*, by Carolyn Zagury, MS, RN, CPC (self-help); and *Nurse Leadership Development*, by Laura McCarthy, MS, RN and Carolyn Zagury, MS, RN, CPC (training manual).
Fiction: Adventure, feminist, humor, mainstream/contemporary, mystery, short story collections and suspense. Query with complete ms.
Recent Nonfiction Title: *Fluff My Pillow, Bend My Straw: The Evolution and Undoing Of A Nurse*, by Joan Brady, RN, BSN (fiction novel).
Poetry: "We prefer a mix of humor and serious poetry." Submit complete ms.
Tips: Audience is nursing professionals, healthcare providers, women. "Be willing to take a chance and submit a ms for consideration. Our small press was developed to assist writers in successfully publishing. We seek the talent of nurses, healthcare providers and women authors."

WESTERN BOOK/JOURNAL PRESS, Subsidiary of Journal Lithograph Co., 1470 Woodberry, San Mateo CA 94403. (415)573-8877. Executive Editor: Marie T. Mollath. Estab. 1960. Publishes hardcover and trade paperback originals and reprints. Publishes 16 titles/year. Receives 10 queries and 30 mss/year. 70% of mss from first-time authors. Subsidy publishes 15% of books. Pays 10-22% royalty. Publishes book 14 months after acceptance of ms. Query for electronic submissions. Reports in 1 month on queries. *Writer's Market* recommends allowing 2 months for reply. Book catalog and ms guidelines free on request.
Nonfiction: Biography, self-help and technical. Subjects include architecture, government/politics, regional, science and historical biographies. Submit proposal package, including entire ms. *Writer's Market* recommends query with SASE first. Reviews artwork/photos as part of freelance ms package. Writers should send photocopies.
Recent Nonfiction Title: *Expanding Geospheres*, by C. Warren Hunt.

‡WOODSONG GRAPHICS, INC., P.O. Box 304, Lahaska PA 18931-0304. (215)794-8321. Editor: Ellen P. Bordner. Estab. 1977. Publishes hardcover and trade paperback originals. Averages 6-8 titles/year; receives 2,500-3,000 submissions annually. 40-60% of books from first-time authors; 100% of books from unagented writers. Average print order for writer's first book is 2,500-5,000. Will occasionally consider subsidy publishing based on "quality of material, motivation of author in distributing his work, and cost factors (which depend on the type of material involved), plus our own feelings on its marketability." Subsidy publishes 50% of books. Pays royalty on net price; offers average $100 advance. Publishes book an average of 1 year after acceptance. Simultaneous submissions OK. Reports in 1 month on queries; reports on full mss *can* take several months, depending on the amount of material already in house. "We do everything possible to facilitate replies, but we have a small staff and want to give every manuscript a thoughtful reading." Book catalog for #10 SASE. "Manuscripts not returned unless SASE enclosed."

Nonfiction: Biography, cookbook, how-to, humor, illustrated book, juvenile, reference, and self-help. Subjects include cooking and foods, hobbies, philosophy and psychology. "We're happy to look at anything of good quality, but we're not equipped to handle lavish color spreads at this time. Our needs are very open, and we're interested in seeing any subject, provided it's handled with competence and style. Good writing from unknowns is also welcome." No pornography; only minimal interest in technical manuals of any kind. Query or submit outline/synopsis and at least 2 sample chapters. Reviews artwork/photos as part of ms package.

Fiction: Adventure, experimental, fantasy, gothic, historical, humor, mainstream, mystery, romance, science fiction, suspense and western. "In fiction, we are simply looking for books that provide enjoyment. We want well-developed characters, creative plots, and good writing style." No pornography or "sick" material. Submit outline/synopsis and sample chapters.

Tips: "Good nonfiction with an identified target audience and a definite slant has the best chance of being sold to our firm. We rarely contract in advance of seeing the completed manuscript. We prefer a synopsis, explaining what the thrust of the book is without a chapter-by-chapter profile. If the query is interesting enough, we'll look at the full manuscript for further details. Partial subsidy program available for authors with a serious interest in promoting their own books."

YE GALLEON PRESS, P.O. Box 287, Fairfield WA 99012-0287. (509)283-2422. Owner: Glen C. Adams. Estab. 1937. Firm averages 25 titles/year. Subsidy publishes 25% of books. "Subsidy based on sales probabilities." Pays 5-10% royalties based on moneys actually received. No advance. Publishes book an average of 9 months after acceptance. Reports in 2 weeks on queries. *Writer's Market* recommends allowing 2 months for reply. Free book catalog.

Nonfiction: Biography (if sponsored). Subjects include Americana and history. Query. Reviews artwork/photos as part of freelance ms package.

Fiction: Historical. "I print historical fiction only if paid to do so and even then it needs to be pretty good." Query.

Tips: "We are looking for books on native Americans written from an Indian point of view. Our audience is general. A probable reader is male, college educated, middle-aged or past, wearing glasses or collector of rare western U.S. history. We are not likely to take any more manuscripts on a royalty basis this year as we are offered more work than we can handle."

‡YES INTERNATIONAL PUBLISHERS, 1317 Summit Ave., St. Paul MN 55105-2602. (612)645-6808. President: Theresa King. Publishes trade paperback originals. Publishes 3 titles/year. Receives 10 queries and 3 mss/year. 10% of books from first-time authors; 100% from unagented writers. Subsidy publishes 60% of books. Pays 4-12% royalty on retail price. Offers $100-1,000 advance. Publishes book 1 year after acceptance. Reports in 1 month on queries and proposals, 1-2 months on mss. Book catalog free on request. Manuscript guidelines for #10 SASE.

Nonfiction: How-to and self-help. Subjects include health/medicine (holistic), philosophy (transformational), psychology (transpersonal), regional (spirituality) and women's issues/studies (spirituality). "We have a small budget and accept only very well written manuscripts of about 20,000 to 35,000 words. Writers often do not check the type of work we publish and try to convince us to publish theirs whether it fits our line or not." Query with outline and 2 sample chapters. Reviews artwork/photos as part of freelance manuscript package. Writers should send photocopies.

Recent Nonfiction Title: *Pigs Eat Wolves: Going Into Partnership With Your Dark Side*, by Charles Bates (psychology); *The Wellness Tree*, by Justin O'Brien (wellness); and *The Spiral Path*, by Theresa King (women's spirituality).

Tips: "Our audience is college-educated adults."

Subsidy Publishers

The following companies publish more than 50% of their books on an author-subsidy basis.

Aegina Press, Inc.
59 Oak Lane
Spring Valley, Huntington WV 25704

American Literary Press
Suite 10, 11419 Cronridge Dr.
Owings Mills MD 21117

American Society for Nondestructive Testing
P.O. Box 28518
Columbus OH 43228

Authors' Unlimited
3324 Barham Blvd.
Los Angeles CA 90068

Automobile Quarterly
15040 Kutztown Rd., Box 348
Kutztown PA 19530

‡Barney Press
#60, 8300 Kern Canyon Rd.
Bakersfield CA 93306

Brunswick Publishing Company
P.O. Box 555
Lawrenceville VA 23868

Carlton Press, Inc.
11 W. 32nd St.
New York NY 10001

Dorrance Publishing Co., Inc.
643 Smithfield St.
Pittsburgh PA 15222

Evanston Publishing, Inc.
1216 Hinman Ave.
Evanston IL 60202

Fairway Press
628 S. Main St.
Lima OH 45804

Fithian Press
P.O. Box 1525
Santa Barbara CA 93102

‡Give Books Away
2525 McKinnon Dr.
Decatur GA 30030

The Golden Quill Press
Avery Rd.
Francestown NH 03043

Harbor House (West) Publishers, Inc.
40781 Smoke Tree Lane
Rancho Mirage CA 92270

Lucky Books
P.O. Box 1415
Winchester VA 22601

‡Poetry On Wings, Inc.
P.O. Box 1000
Pear Blossom CA 93553

Peter Randall Publisher
P.O. Box 4726
Portsmouth NH 03802

Reflected Images Publishers
P.O. Box 314
Medford OR 97501

Rivercross Publishing, Inc.
Dept. WM, 127 E. 59th St.
New York NY 10022

Treehaus Communications, Inc.
906 W. Loveland Ave.
Loveland OH 45140

Vantage Press
516 W. 34th St.
New York NY 10001

‡Wildstar Publishing
1550 California St.
San Francisco CA 94109

Small Presses

"Small press" is a relative term. Compared to the 15 or 16 conglomerates, the rest of the book publishing world may seem to be comprised of small presses. Several of the publishers listed in the Book Publishers section consider themselves small presses and cultivate the image. For our purpose of classification, the publishers listed in this section are called small presses because they publish three or fewer books per year.

The publishing opportunities are slightly more limited with the companies listed here when compared to the larger Book Publishers section. Small presses tend not to be able to market their books as effectively as larger publishers. Their print runs and royalty arrangements are usually smaller. It boils down to money, what a publisher can afford, and in that area, small presses simply can't compete with conglomerates.

However, realistic small press publishers don't try to compete with Simon & Schuster. They realize everything about their efforts operates on a smaller scale. Most small press publishers get into book publishing for the love of it, not the profit. Of course, every publisher, small or large, wants successful books. But small press publishers often measure success in different ways.

They tend to have more personal relationships with their writers, and for that reason, many writers actually prefer to work with small presses over their conglomerate counterparts. What small presses lack in financial ability, they often make up in enthusiasm, personal attention in the writer-editor relationship, and confidence in a book. If a book doesn't sell for a major publisher, it is swiftly replaced by one the publisher hopes will sell. A great many midlist books go out of print every year, even books published in the same calendar year. This rarely happens with a small press, which can't afford to replace books the way a conglomerate can. Small presses make every effort to build a backlist by keeping their books in print for as long as possible.

Books in Print lists approximately 26,000 publishers, 10,000 having started since 1982. The desktop publishing revolution of the last decade and the emergence of short run printers have created a climate in which small presses can thrive. Small companies interested in publishing for a small market no longer have to rely on high cost typesetting and large print runs. The result has been the publication of a book for nearly every niche market. "Small publishers often have a much keener sense of the market than their larger counterparts," says John F. Baker, editorial director of *Publishers Weekly*. "They also tend to be more open to minority books and subjects."

Just because they publish three or fewer titles per year does not mean small press editors have the time to look at complete manuscripts. In fact, because most small presses are understaffed, the editors have even less time for submissions. The procedure for contacting a small press with your book idea is exactly the same as it is for a larger publisher. Send a one-page query with SASE first. If the press is interested in your proposal, be ready to send an outline or synopsis, and/or a sample chapter or two. Be patient with their reporting times; small presses are usually slower to respond than larger companies. You might consider simultaneous queries, as long as you note them, to compensate for the waiting game.

Virtually all the submission and contract procedures are alike for every publisher. The terms vary widely, but the steps are the same. For more information on small presses, see *Novel & Short Story Writer's Market* and *Poet's Market* (Writer's Digest Books), and *Small Press Review* and *The International Directory of Little Magazines and Small Presses* (Dustbooks).

For a list of publishers according to their subjects of interest, see the nonfiction and fiction sections of the Book Publishers Subject Index. Information on some book publishers and producers not included in this edition of *Writer's Market* can be found in Book Publishers and Producers/Changes '93-'94.

ACME PRESS, P.O. Box 1702, Westminster MD 21158-1702. (410)848-7577. Managing Editor: Ms. E.G. Johnston. Estab. 1991. Publishes humor. "We accept submissions on any subject as long as the material is humorous; prefer full-length novels. No cartoons or art (text only). No pornography. SASE mandatory."

ACORN PUBLISHING, 1063 S. Talmadge, Waverly NY 14892. (607)565-4486. Fax: (607)565-4486. Editor: Mary O. Robb. Estab. 1985. Publishes trade paperback originals on health, recreation, sports and general fitness.

‡AEGIS PUBLISHING GROUP, 796 Aquidneck Ave., Newport RI 02840-5201. (401)849-4200. Publisher: Robert Mastin. Estab. 1992. Reports in 2 months. "Our specialty is home business how-to books that will help a start-up home business entrepreneur succeed. Author must be an experienced authority in the subject, and the material must be very specific with helpful step-by-step advice. No fiction."

AHSAHTA PRESS, Boise State University, Dept. of English, 1910 University Dr., Boise ID 83725-1525. (208)385-1999. Fax: (208)385-4373. Co-Editor: Tom Trusky. Estab. 1974. Publishes Western American poetry in trade paperback. Reads SASE samplers annually, January through March.

ANIMA PUBLICATIONS, Imprint of Anima Books, 1053 Wilson Ave., Chambersburg PA 17201-1247. (717)267-0087. Managing Editor: Barbara D. Rotz. "Our books are read at the undergraduate level as texts in religious studies programs and by the general reading audience with an interest in Asian religions."

‡ANOTHER CHICAGO PRESS, P.O. Box 11223, Chicago IL 60610. Publisher: Lee Webster. Publishes fiction: ethnic, literary and short story collections.

APU PRESS, Subsidiary of Alaska Pacific University, 4101 University Dr., Anchorage AK 99508. (907)564-8304. Editor: Cherrill Mears. Estab. 1963. Reports in 2 months. "We publish books relating to Alaska and The Pacific Rim."

 A bullet introduces comments by the editor of* Writer's Market *indicating special information about the listing.

‡ARCUS PUBLISHING COMPANY, P.O. Box 228, Sonoma CA 95476. (707)996-9529. Contact: Judith Stephenson. Publishes holistic, New Age, personal growth books in the area of health, nature, psychology, evolution, spiritual/symbology and personal relationship to the environment. "We have recently changed our focus. We will be publishing books which encourage self-exploration and look toward the future. Expertise, high energy, compassion, humanitarian values and a commitment to high quality will be appreciated." Send for guidelines. Send query letter first.

‡ARIADNE PRESS, 4817 Tallahassee Ave., Rockville MD 20853. (301)949-2514. President: Carol Hoover. Adventure, feminist, historical, humor, literary and mainstream/contemporary.

AUTO BOOK PRESS, P.O. Bin 711, San Marcos CA 92079-0711. (619)744-3582. Editorial Director: William Carroll. Estab. 1955. Publishes hardcover and paperback originals. Automotive material only: technical or definitive how-to.

B&B PUBLISHING, INC., P.O. Box 393, Fontana WI 53125. (414)275-9474. President: Jean Blashfield Black. "Looking for books related to the environment, supplementary science and social studies materials for schools and libraries and general nonfiction in the areas of the environment, business and trivia."
   • This small press is also a book producer.

BARN OWL BOOKS, P.O. Box 226, Vallecitos NM 87581. (505)582-4226. Publisher: Gina Covina. Estab. 1983. Imprint is Amazon Press. Nonfiction and fiction on women's, gay/lesbian, feminist and mainstream topics. Query first.

BIDDLE PUBLISHING CO., #103, P.O. Box 1305, Brunswick ME 04011. President: Julie Zimmerman. Publishes general nonfiction, including health, peace and social concerns, autobiography, history.

‡BLACK TIE PRESS, P.O. Box 440004, Houston TX 77244-0004. (713)789-5119. Publisher/Editor: Peter Gravis. Estab. 1986. Imprints are Deluxe, Matineé and Plain Editions. Publishes fiction and poetry. We publish books not individual poems, articles, or stories

‡BORDER BOOKS, INC., (formerly Out West Publishing), P.O. Box 80780, Albuquerque NM 87198-0780. (505)266-8322. Publisher: Dave DeWitt. Editor: Melissa T. Jackson. Estab. 1992. Publishes books on cooking, travel, gardening and the Southwest. Written query first, please.

BOTTOM DOG PRESS, INC., %Firelands College, Huron OH 44839. (419)433-5560. Director: Larry Smith. Estab. 1984. "We do fiction and nonfiction by Midwesterners and about the Midwest. Query first."

BRETT BOOKS, INC., P.O. Box 290-637, Brooklyn NY 11229-0011. Publisher: Barbara J. Brett. Estab. 1993. Publishes general interest nonfiction books on timely subjects. Submit query letter only. Include SASE.

CALYX BOOKS, P.O. Box B, Corvallis OR 97339. (503)753-9384. Also publishes *Calyx, A Journal of Art & Literature by Women.* Editors: Margarita Donnelly and Bev McFarland et. al. Estab. 1986 for Calyx Books 1976 for Calyx, Inc. Publishes fine literature by women, fiction, nonfiction and poetry. Please query with SASE for submission deadlines and guidelines.

‡CAROLINA WREN PRESS, 120 Morris St., Durham NC 27701. (919)560-2738. Managing Editor: Richard Morrison. "We are interested in poetry, fiction, nonfiction, biography, autobiography, literary nonfiction work by and/or about people of color, women, gay/lesbian issues."

CAROUSEL PRESS, P.O. Box 6061, Albany CA 94706-0061. (510)527-5849. Editor/Publisher: Carole T. Meyers. Estab. 1976. Publishes nonfiction, family-oriented travel books.

CHALLENGER PRESS, Suite 8, 540 Alisal Rd., Solvang CA 93463. (805)688-4439. Fax: (805)686-1340. Editor: Adryan Russ. Estab. 1989. Publishes self-help books.

‡CHICORY BLUE PRESS, 795 East St North, Goshen NY 06756. (203)491-2271. Publisher: Sondra Zeidenstein. Publishes trade paperback originals. "Query first. Focus of press is on chapbook-length manuscripts, in any genre, by women past 60."

CLARITY PRESS INC., 3277 Roswell Rd. NE, #469, Atlanta GA 30305. (404)231-0649. Fax: (404)231-3899. Editorial Committee Contact: Annette Gordon. Estab. 1984. Publishes manuscripts on minorities, human rights in US, Middle East and Africa. No fiction. Responds *only* if interested so do *not* enclose SASE.

CLOTHESPIN FEVER PRESS, Suite 34, 655 Fourth Ave., San Diego CA 92101. (619)234-2656. Publisher: Jenny Wrenn. Estab. 1986. Publishes lesbian fiction and nonfiction. We are looking at non-lesbian works in the nonfiction field.

‡THE COTTAGE PRESS, Box 135, Lincoln Center MA 01773. (617)259-8771. Publisher: MaryAnn Hales. Imprints are Heritage House, Publishers (subsidy publishing). "We publish personal narrative and are also interested in unpublished diaries or letters."

CREATIVE WITH WORDS PUBLICATIONS, P.O. Box 223226, Carmel CA 93922. Publisher/Editor: Brigitta Geltrich. Staff Editor: Bert Hower. Estab. 1975. Publishes poetry and prose, modern fairytales and folkloristic themes. SASE for guidelines and themes. Sample copies $5 with large mailing envelope.

DELANCEY PRESS, P.O. Box 40285, Philadelphia PA 19106. (215)238-9103. Editorial Director: Wesley Morrison. Estab. 1990. "We are open to reviewing all types of nonfiction and fiction. No scripts, short stories or westerns. Queries by *letter* only; no initial contact by phone."

‡DIAMOND PRESS, Box 2458, Doylestown PA 18901. (215)345-6094. Fax: (215)345-6692. Marketing Director: Paul Johnson. Estab. 1985. Publishes trade paperback originals on softball and antiques. "We are now more interested in baseball, fast pitch softball and slow pitch softball books."

DICKENS PUBLICATIONS, 1703 Taylor St. N.W., Washington DC 20011. President: Nathaniel A. Dickens. Estab. 1982. "Publishes nonfiction related to education, history, finance and various forms of fiction."

*DIMI PRESS, 3820 Oak Hollow Lane SE, Salem OR 97302-4774. (503)364-7698. Fax: (503)364-9727. President: Dick Lutz. Estab. 1981. Trade paperback originals of health and psychology, also certain other nonfiction titles. Subsidy publishing.

‡DISKOTECH, INC., Suite 210, 7930 State Line, Prairie Village KS 66208. (913)432-8606. Director: John Slegman. Estab. 1989. "Diskotech, Inc. is interested in publishing multimedia works. We are especially interested in computerized video autobiographies, biographies and how-to books as well as computerized video novels. Diskotech, Inc. has published a new form of the novel—a computerized video novel (CVN). It is a multimedia form that uses three media—printed text, video, software. We also publish computerized greeting cards. We are looking for computer graphics, games, animation and virtual reality programs that could be used for this purpose."

DRAGON'S DEN PUBLISHING, Imprint of GMS Publications, 11659 Doverwood Dr., Riverside CA 92505-3216. Publisher: G. Michael Short. Estab. 1988. Publishes fantasy, science fiction, mystery, horror. No longer considering western fiction. Needs more science fiction submissions. No writer guidelines available.

DUSTY DOG REVIEWS, (formerly Dusty Dog Chapbook Series), 1904-A Gladden, Gallup NM 87301. (505)863-2398. Editor: John Pierce. Estab. 1991. Features over 75 honest and evaluative poetry book/chapbook reviews as well as literary magazine reviews from small and midrange presses in each issue. Subscription price: $4.50/yr/3 issues. Single copy price: $2. Each press editor and/or magazine editor will receive 1 free copy of the issue in which the review appears. Published 250 poetry book/chapbooks reviews in 1992. Expected to publish 250-300 book reviews in 1993.

E.J.M. PUBLISHING, INC., Suite 127, 976 Murfreesboro Rd., Nashville TN 37217. (615)781-8835. President: Kimberly A. Warren. Editor: Rod Warren. Looking for human interest especially men's rights, step-parenting, child abuse, especially any from children's point of view, paranormal and U.F.O. (must be eyewitness accounts).

E.M. PRESS, INC., Box 4057, Manassas VA 22119. (703)368-9828. Editor/Publisher: Beth Miller. Estab. 1991. "We are looking for quality mainstream literature (biographies, historical events, life-experience, literary fiction) from first-time writers and veterans alike. We will consider how-to, hobby and sports material. No textbooks." Reports in 2 months.

EASTERN CARIBBEAN INSTITUTE, Box 1338, Frederiksted, Virgin Islands 00841-1338. (809)772-1011. Fax: (809)772-3665. President/Publisher: S.B. Jones-Hendrickson. Estab. 1982. Publishes nonfiction: biography, technical and textbook. Subjects include education, ethnic, government/politics, philosophy and economics. Fiction: ethnic, literary, plays and young adult as they pertain to the Caribbean and/or the Third World.

EASTERN PRESS, P.O. Box 881, Bloomington IN 47402-0881. Publisher: Don Lee. Estab. 1981. Publishes academic books on Asian subjects.

‡EXCALIBUR PUBLISHING, #790, 434 Ave. of Americas, New York NY 10011. (212)777-1790. Publisher: Sharon Good. "We are interested in performing arts titles."

FIESTA CITY PUBLISHERS, P.O. Box 5861, Santa Barbara CA 93150-5861. (805)733-1984. President: Frank E. Cooke. Estab. 1982. Publishes how-to, health cookbooks, music books and books for children. "Financial and economic considerations require that we consider books with simple illustrations; books with commercial appeal; mss which are original, interesting and understandable. We are looking at less material and fewer mss. As with many firms, we are tightening wherever possible."

FORD-BROWN & CO., PUBLISHERS, P.O. Box 2764, Boston MA 02208-2764. Publisher: Steven Ford Brown. Estab. 1975. Publishes poetry and poetry criticism. Reports in 2 months.

FRANCISCAN PRESS, Quincy University, 1800 College Ave., Quincy IL 62301-2670. (217)228-5670. Fax: (217)228-5672. Director: Dr. Terrence J. Riddell. Estab. 1991. Publishes nonfiction books on religion.

FREE SPIRIT PUBLISHING INC., Suite 616, 400 1st Ave. N., Minneapolis MN 55401-1724. (612)338-2068. President: Judy Galbraith. Editorial Assistant: M. Elizabeth Salzmann. Estab. 1983. Publishes psychology and self-help materials for children and teens, educational/parenting books for adults.

FRONT ROW EXPERIENCE, 540 Discovery Bay Blvd., Byron CA 94514-9454. (510)634-5710. Fax: (510)634-5710. Editor: Frank Alexander. Estab. 1974. Imprint is Kokono. Publishes teacher/educator edition paperback originals. Only wants submissions for "Movement Education," special education and related areas.

‡GEMINI PUBLISHING COMPANY, Suite 120, 11543 Gullwood Dr., Houston TX 77089. (713)484-2424. President: Don Diebel. "We are seeking books, cassettes and videos on meeting, attracting and becoming intimate with women." Catalog $1.

GMS PUBLICATIONS, 11659 Doverwood Dr., Riverside CA 92505-3216. Publisher: G. Michael Short. Estab. 1988. Imprints are Dragon's Den Publishing, DDP Deluxe Editions and New Horizons Press. Publishes business, mail order, advertising, how-to and cookbooks. "No writer guidelines available."

GRYPHON HOUSE, INC., 3706 Otis St., Box 275, Mt. Rainier MD 20712. (301)779-6200. Editor-in-Chief: Kathy Charner. Publishes trade paperback originals of how-to and creative educational activities for teachers to do with preschool children ages 1-5.

HELIX PRESS, 4410 Hickey, Corpus Christi TX 78413. (512)852-8834. Editor: Aubrey R. McKinney. Estab. 1984. Publishes hardcover originals on science for adults.

HEMINGWAY WESTERN STUDIES SERIES, Boise State University, 1910 University Dr., Boise ID 83725. (208)385-1999. Editor: Tom Trusky. Publishes Rocky Mountain multiple edition artist's books which deal with political, social and environmental issues. Write for author's guidelines and catalog.

HILLBROOK HOUSE, Imprint of Publishing Enterprises of Nashville, P.O. Box 24443, Nashville TN 37202. (615)256-6099. Publisher: Joanne Jaworski. "Publishes only through PEN's book consultation services."

‡IDEALS PUBLISHING CORP., Suite 800, 565 Marriott Dr., Nashville TN 37210. (615)885-8270. Publisher: Patricia Pingry. Publishes highly illustrated hardbound books. Uses short prose and poetry. Also publishes *Ideals Magazine*. Firm averages 12-16 titles/year. Payment varies. Simultaneous submissions OK. Reports in 2 months. Manuscript guidelines free on request.

‡ILLUMINATIONS PRESS, #B, 2110 9th St., Berkeley CA 94710-2141. (510)849-2102. Editor/Publisher: Norm Moser. Estab. 1965. Publishes poetry, plays and fiction. "Contributor must subscribe to the 90s Book series (current rate, $37), plus pay 50% or less of overall costs—any profits are shared 50-50."

IN PRINT PUBLISHING, Suite F-2, 65 Verde Valley School Rd., Sedona AZ 86336-9048. (602)284-1370. Publisher/Editor: Tomi Keitlen. Estab. 1991. "We are interested in books that will give people hope: biographies of those that have overcome physical and mental disadvantages. No violence or sex or poetry. Particularly interested in metaphysical how-to books."

‡INDEPENDENCE PUBLISHER, INC., 4771 E. Conway Dr., Atlanta GA 30327. (404)843-8084. Associate Editor: Walter Sturdivant. "We seek nonfiction on social issues and biographies. We accept the work of both new writers and published writers."

INDIANA HISTORICAL SOCIETY, 315 W. Ohio St., Indianapolis IN 46202-3299. (317)232-1882. Director of Publications: Thomas A. Mason. Estab. 1830. "We seek book-length manuscripts that are solidly researched and engagingly written on topics related to the history of Indiana." Reports in 6 months.

‡INTERTEXT, 2633 East 17th Ave., Anchorage AK 99508-3207. Editor: Sharon Ann Jaeger.

INVERTED-A, INC., 401 Forrest Hill, Grand Prairie TX 75051. (214)264-0066. Editors: Amnon Katz and Aya Katz. Estab. 1977. Publishes nonfiction books on a range of subjects, novellas, short story collections and poetry.

‡ITHACA PRESS, P.O. Box 853, Lowell MA 01853. General Editor: Charles E. Ziavras. Publishes historical and mainstream/contemporary fiction.

JAMENAIR LTD., P.O. Box 241957, Los Angeles CA 90024-9757. (310)470-6688. Publisher: P.K. Studner. Estab. 1986. Publishes originals and reprints on business and economics, computers and electronics, education and career-advancement/job search.

ALICE JAMES BOOKS, Imprint of Alice James Poetry Cooperative, 33 Richdale Ave., Cambridge MA 02140. (617)354-1408. Program Administrator: Jean Amaral. Estab. 1973. Books of poetry.

LAHONTAN IMAGES, P.O. Box 1093, Susanville CA 96130-1093. (916)257-6747. Owner: Tim I. Purdy. Estab. 1986. Publishes books pertaining to northeastern California and western Nevada. Reports in 2 months.

LAUGHING BEAR PRESS, P.O. Box 36159, Denver CO 80236-0159. (303)744-3624. Editor: Tom Person. Estab. 1976. Publishes books of experimental poetry, *Laughing Bear Newsletter* on independent and self-publishing, and *The Newsletter Consultant* for small professional offices. Send SASE for sample issue of *Laughing Bear Newsletter*.

LAWCO LTD., P.O. Box 2009, Manteca CA 95336-1209. (209)239-6006. Imprints are Money Tree and Que House. Senior Editor: Bill Thompson. Publishes nonfiction books on billiards industry.

LEE & LOW BOOKS, 14th Floor, 228 E. 45th St., New York NY 10017. (212)867-6155. Publisher: Philip Lee. Editor-in-Chief: Elizabeth Szabla. Estab. 1991. "We focus on multicultural children's books. Of special interest are stories set in contemporary America. We are interested in fiction as well as nonfiction." Titles released in 1993 include *Abuela's Weave* by Omar S. Castaneda; *Baseball Saved Us* by Ken Mochizuki; *Joshua's Masai Mask* by Dakari Hru.

LIBERTY BELL PRESS, Suite 3-183, 4700 S. 900 E, Salt Lake City UT 84117. (801)943-8573. Estab. 1988. Publisher: Ron Jorgenson. Editor: Lee Richardson. Estab. 1988. Actively seeking input from lawyers, judges or those with legal expertise to submit mss on "beating the present divorce laws of the 50 states. Looking for how-to formats."

‡LINCOLN SPRINGS PRESS, P.O. Box 269, Franklin Lakes NJ 07417. Contact: M. Gabrielle. Estab. 1987. Nonfiction subjects include Americana, ethnic, government/politics, history, language/literature, military/war, sociology and women's issues/studies. Fiction: ethnic, feminist, gothic, historical, literary, mainstream/contemporary, mystery, romance, short story collections.

LINTEL, P.O. Box 8609, Roanoke VA 24014-8609. (703)345-2886. Editorial Director: Walter James Miller. Estab. 1978. Publishes experimental fiction, art poetry and selected nonfiction.

‡LOLLIPOP POWER BOOKS, (formerly Lollipop Books), 120 Morris St., Durham NC 27701. (919)560-2738. Editor: Ruth A. Smullin. Imprint of Carolina Wren Press. Imprint publishes trade paperback originals.
Fiction: "Current publishing pointers are 1) Books with African-American, Latino or native American charcacters 2) Bi-lingual Books (English/Spanish) 3) Books that show gay men or lesbian women as ordinary people who can raise children."

LORIEN HOUSE, P.O. Box 1112, Black Mountain NC 28711-1112. (704)669-6211. Owner/Editor: David A. Wilson. Estab. 1969. Publishes nonfiction: how-to and technical. Subjects include Americana, history, nature/environment, philosophy and science. "I need only a few ms at any time and therefore am very selective."

MADWOMAN PRESS, P.O. Box 690, Northboro MA 01532-0690. (508)393-3447. Editor and Publisher: Diane Benison. Estab. 1991. Publishes lesbian fiction and nonfiction. Query for further information.

‡MARABOU PUBLISHING, P.O. Box 1682, New York NY 10013-1682. Also 31-69 35st Astoria, NY, 11106. (718)274-6315. Publishes sports. "We are looking for nonfiction sports books which are geared for the historically aware. Those stories that deal with little-written about subjects will receive the most attention. Query only."

‡MAUPIN HOUSE PUBLISHING, P.O. Box 90148, Gainesville FL 32607. (904)373-5588. Co-Publisher: Julia Graddy. Publishes nonfiction books on horticulture, education, regional (Florida), travel, holistic health and wellness.

MERRY MEN PRESS, 274 Roanoke Rd., El Cajon CA 92020-4023. Contact: Robin Hood. Estab. 1984. Publishes science fiction/fantasy, erotica in a book anthology. Deadline Dec. 31 of each year. Reads year round. **Pays upon acceptance.** Please send for guidelines.

METAL POWDER INDUSTRIES FEDERATION, 105 College Rd. E., Princeton NJ 08540. (609)452-7700. Fax: (609)987-8523. Publications Manager: Mary D. Stoner. Estab. 1946. "Contact Publications Manager before submittal of a manuscript; work must relate to powder metallurgy or particulate materials. We publish monographs, textbooks, handbooks, design guides, conference proceedings, standards, and general titles in this field."

MEYERBOOKS, PUBLISHER, P.O. Box 427, Glenwood IL 60425-0427. (708)757-4950. Publisher: David Meyer. Estab. 1976. Imprint is David Meyer Magic Books. History, reference and self-help works published on subjects of Americana, cooking and foods, health and nature. Reports in 3 months.

MID-LIST PRESS, Subsidiary of Jackson, Hart & Leslie, 4324 12th Ave S., Minneapolis MN 55407-3218. Acquisitions Editor: Maria Ahrens. "We are trying to provide a forum for first novelists with our First Novel Award series."

MOSAIC PRESS MINIATURE BOOKS, 358 Oliver Rd., Cincinnati OH 45215. (513)761-5977. Publisher: Miriam Irwin. Estab. 1977. "Publishes one nonfiction book per year. Subjects range widely. Please query."

MOUNTAIN AUTOMATION CORPORATION, P.O. Box 6020, Woodland Park CO 80866-6020. (719)687-6647. President: Claude Wiatrowski. Estab. 1976. Publishes illustrated souvenir books and videos for specific tourist attractions.

MYSTIC SEAPORT MUSEUM, 50 Greenmanville Ave., Mystic CT 06355-0990. (203)572-0711. Fax: (203)572-5328. Imprint is American Maritime Library. Publications Director: Joseph Gribbins. "We need serious, well-documented biographies, studies of economic, social, artistic, or musical elements of American maritime (not naval) history; books on traditional boat and ship types and construction (how-to)." Reports in 2 months.

NAR PUBLICATIONS, P.O. Box 233, Barryville NY 12719-0233. (914)557-8713. Fax: (914)557-6770. Editor: Monique E. Dubacher. Estab. 1977. Imprints are Teacher Update and Education Guild. Publishes trade paperback originals on business and economics, child guidance/parenting, education, gardening, government/politics, health/medicine, hobbies, money/finance, recreation, sports and consumer.

NATIONAL PUBLISHING COMPANY, P.O. Box 8386, Philadelphia PA 19101-8386. (215)732-1863. Fax: (215)735-5399. Editor: Peter F. Hewitt. Estab. 1863. Publishes Bibles, New Testament and foreign language New Testaments.

NATUREGRAPH PUBLISHERS, INC., P.O. Box 1075, Happy Camp CA 96039. (916)493-5353. Editor: Barbara Brown. Estab. 1946. Primarily publishes nonfiction for the layman in 7 general areas: natural history (biology, geology, ecology, astronomy); American Indian (historical and contemporary); outdoor living (backpacking, wild edibles, etc.); land and gardening (modern homesteading); crafts and how-to; holistic health (natural foods and healing arts).

NATURE'S DESIGN, P.O. Box 255, Davenport CA 95017-0255. (408)426-8205. Publisher/Editor: Frank S. Balthis. Estab. 1980. Publishes guides to parks and books on nature, wildlife and the environment. Query with SASE. Reports in 6 months.
  • Especially needs natural history and travel mss to be used with photographs by Frank S. Balthis.

NEW HORIZONS PRESS , Imprint of GMS Publications, 11659 Doverwood Dr., Riverside CA 92505-3216. Publisher: G. Michael Short. Estab. 1988. Publishes New Age books *only*. "No writer's guidelines available."

NEWSAGE PRESS, Suite 150, 825 NE 20th Ave., Portland OR 97232. (503)232-6794. Fax: (503)232-6891. Publisher: Maureen Michelson. Estab. 1985. Publishes hardcover and trade paperback originals.

NIGHTSHADE PRESS, P.O. Box 76, Troy ME 04987-0076. (207)948-3427. Co-Editors: Carolyn Page and Roy Zarucchi. Estab. 1988. Publishes *Potato Eyes*, a semi-annual literary magazine and 5 poetry collections/year. Query first for info. Reports in 2 months.
• Poetry ms selection is based on the Nightshade Annual Chapbook Award Competition.

OHIO BIOLOGICAL SURVEY, Subsidiary of The Ohio State University College of Biosciences, Museum of Biological Diversity, 1315 Kinnear Rd., Columbus OH 43212-1192. (614)292-9645. Editor: Veda M. Cafazzo. "Topics limited to information about Ohio's biota."

C. OLSON & CO., P.O. Box 5100, Santa Cruz CA 95063-5100. (408)458-3365. Owner: C. Olson. Estab. 1981. "We are looking for nonfiction books that can be sold at natural food stores and small independent bookstores on health and on how to live a life which improves the earth's environment." Query first only, and please enclose SASE.

‡OMEGA PUBLICATIONS, RD 1 Box 1030E, New Lebanon NY 12125.(518)794-8181. Contact: Abi'l-Khayr. "We are interested in any material related to sufism, and only that."

OPTIMUS PUBLISHING, Suite 318, 13931 N. Central Expwy., Dallas TX 75243. (214)294-2101. Managing Editor: Bill McMurray. Estab. 1990. "We are soliciting for our 'exclusive report' product line which features leisure time activities, self-help and fitness topics. All reports are of a 'how-to' nature and are 10,000-12,000 words in length."

‡OUR CHILD PRESS, 800 Maple Glen Lane, Wayne PA 19087. (215)964-0606. Editor: Carol Hallenbeck. "We publish only adoption-related materials. Query first." Recent titles: *Is That Your Sister? A True Story About Adoption* and *Oliver: A Story About Adoption*.

PAPIER-MACHE PRESS, 795 Via Manzana, Watsonville CA 95076. (408)726-3105. Fax: (408)726-1255. Owner/Editor: Sandra Martz. Publishes mostly fiction and poetry about women's issues. Query first.

PARTNERS IN PUBLISHING, P.O. Box 50374, Tulsa OK 74150-0374. (918)584-5906. Editor: P.M. Fielding. Estab. 1976. Publishes biography, how-to, reference, self-help, technical and textbooks on learning disabilities, special education.

PAX PUBLISHING, P.O. Box 22564, San Francisco CA 94122-2564. (415)759-5658. Senior Editor: James Arden. Publishes nonfiction books; areas include how-to, humor, self-help, business, computers, education, health/medicine, money/finance, philosophy and psychology.

*‡PERIVALE PRESS, 13830 Erwin St., Van Nuys CA 91401. (818)785-4671. Managing Editor: Barbara Rhys-Davies. Publishes criticism, fiction and poetry. 20% of books are subsidy published.

POPULAR MEDICINE PRESS, P.O. Box 1212, San Carlos CA 94070-1212. (415)594-1855. Fax: (415)594-1855. Vice President: John Bliss. Estab. 1986. Publishes books on nutrition, health and medicine. "We're less active this year and expect minimal activity in 1993."

‡PRIMER PUBLISHERS, 5738 N. Central Ave., Phoenix AZ 85012. (602)234-1574. "Query first. Trade paperback books, mostly regional subjects; travel, outdoor recreation, history, etc."

PROBE BOOKS, Subsidiary of Probe Ministries International, #100, 1900 Firman Dr., Richardson TX 75081-6796. (214)480-0240. Fax: (214)644-9664. Senior Editor: Louis D. Whitworth. Estab. 1973. Publishes academic, political, and cultural issues from a Christian perspective. Please query by letter or phone. Reports in 2 months.

PUBLISHERS SYNDICATION INTERNATIONAL, Suite 856, 1377 K Street NW, Washington DC 73069-5120. President/Editor: A.P. Samuels. Estab. 1971. Publishes books on military history.

PUCKERBRUSH PRESS, 76 Main St., Orono ME 04473. (207)581-3832 or 866-4808. Publisher/Editor: Constance Hunting. Estab. 1971. Publishes trade paperback originals of literary fiction and poetry.
• Constance Hunting was the subject of a Close-up in the 1992 edition, in which she says she is "not interested in commercial works."

REDBRICK PRESS, P.O. Box 2184, Reston VA 22090. (703)476-6420. Publisher: Jack Erickson. Estab. 1987. "RedBrick Press currently is publishing only books on microbreweries and specialty beers. We will expand in 1994 to include food and travel related titles."

RESOLUTION BUSINESS PRESS, Suite 208, 11101 NE 8th St., Bellevue WA 98004. (206)455-4611. Editor: Karen Strudwick. Estab. 1987. "We publish computer industry reference books, including *Northwest High Tech*, an annual guide to the computer industry of the Pacific Northwest and Silicon Valley and the *UNIX Universal Dictionary*."

RHOMBUS PUBLISHING CO., P.O. Box 806, Corrales NM 87048-0806. (505)897-3700. Editor/Publisher: Jeff Radford. Estab. 1984. Publishes nonfiction books on anthropology/archaeology, biography, government/politics, nature/environment, regional and travel.

ROCKBRIDGE PUBLISHING CO., P.O. Box 70, Natural Bridge Station VA 24579-0070. (703)291-1063. Fax: (703)291-1346. Publisher: Katherine Tennery. Estab. 1989. "We are developing a series of travel guides to the country roads in various Virginia counties. The self-guided tours include local history, identify geographic features, etc. We are also looking for material about the Civil War and the settlement/expansion of the American West."
  • Publisher is no longer accepting fiction.

ST. JOHN'S PUBLISHING, INC., 6824 Oaklawn Ave., Edina MN 55435. (612)920-9044. President: Donna Montgomery. Estab. 1986. Publishes nonfiction books on parenting.

‡SAKURA PRESS, 36787 Sakura Lane, Pleasant Hill OR 97455. Manager: Seiko Huntington. "We publish books on Japanese language and culture, learning aids, books and workbooks for young children (K-6). Also juvenile stories in Japanese for young children (K-6)."

SAND RIVER PRESS, 1319 14th St., Los Osos CA 93402. (805)528-7347. Publisher: Bruce Miller. Estab. 1987. Publishes mostly nonfiction titles on cooking, history, literature, Native Americans, regional (California) and some literary fiction.

SANDPIPER PRESS, P.O. Box 286, Brookings OR 97415-0028. (503)469-5588. Editor: Marilyn Riddle. Estab. 1979. Query.

‡THE SAVANT GARDE WORKSHOP, Subsidiary of The Savant Garde Institute Ltd., 6 Union St., P.O. Box 1650, Sag Harbor NY 11963. (516)725-1414. Artistic Director: Artemis Smith. "We publish books of philosophy, philosophy as literature, and avant garde thought. We are only interested in Nobel-prize-level material of extreme competence and originality. We are not a commercial publisher and are affiliated to a nonprofit educational foundation."

‡SCOTS PLAID PRESS, 22-B Pine Lake Dr., Whispering Pines NC 28327. Editor/Publisher: MaryBelle Campbell. Perfectbound, aesthetic chapbooks, archival limited editions. Publishes biography, how-to, humor, illustrated book and textbook. Subjects include anthropology/archaeology, language/literature, nature/environment, philosophy, psychology, regional, sociology, translation and travel nonfiction. Experimental, mainstream, historical and literary fiction, novels, plays and short story collections. Also free verse and narrative verse poetry.

‡SEACOAST PUBLICATIONS OF NEW ENGLAND, Suite 165, 2800A Lafayette Rd., Portsmouth NH 03801. Founder: Paul Jesep. Estab. 1992. Publishes trade paperback originals. "Books for children or adult nonfiction material all with a unique New England theme." Query. Reviews artwork/photos as part of freelance ms package.

SHOREWOOD BOOKS, INC., P.O. Box 461, Excelsior MN 55331-0461. (612)474-4043. Editor: Belinda Eaves. Estab. 1991. "Subjects can include any business related topic that will be of interest to executives, managers and entrepreneurs. We need books that tell small business owners how to cope with hard times. Our books are sold primarily to targeted business markets via mail order and therefore, must appeal to a wide audience." Query first with SASE.

SILVERCAT PUBLICATIONS, Suite C, 4070 Goldfinch St., San Diego CA 92103-1865. (619)299-6774. Editor: Robert Outlaw. Estab. 1988. Publishes consumer-oriented nonfiction on topics of current interest. Responds in 2 months.
  • They have expanded their interests to include books relating to quality-of-life issues.

ALWAYS enclose a self-addressed, stamped envelope (SASE) with all your queries and correspondence.

SKIPPINGSTONE PRESS, INC., P.O. Box 22105, Denver CO 80222. (303)377-0046. Fax: (303)333-1946. President: Mike Mancarella. Estab. 1988. "We publish literature-based whole language activity books for teachers, (grades 2-6) in the areas of readers' theater, clip art sources, US geography. We also have a text for evaluation and improved instruction for accomplished readers using basal readers (by Barbara Swaby). Our board games cover humor, dinosaurs, and friendship."

SOUND VIEW PRESS, 170 Boston Post Rd., Madison CT 06443. President: Peter Hastings Falk. Estab. 1985. Publishes hardcover and trade paperback originals, dictionaries, exhibition records, and price guides on 19th-mid 20th century American art.

‡SPACE AND TIME, 138 West 70th St., (4B), New York NY 10023-4432. Editor: Gordon Linzner. Publishes fantasy, horror, occult and science fiction. "We prefer mixed genre, i.e., horror-western, gay-science fiction, etc."

‡SPHERIC HOUSE, Subsidiary of Southwest H.E.R.M. Inc., P.O. Box 40877, Tucson AZ 85717-0877. (602)623-5577. Editors: Seth Linthicum/John Linthicum. Estab. 1985. Publishes a variety of nonfiction, children's fiction and poetry. Reports in 3 months.

STONE BRIDGE PRESS, P.O. Box 8208, Berkeley CA 94707-8208. (510)524-8732. Fax: (510)524-8711. Publisher: Peter Goodman. Estab. 1989. Publishes books on working and communicating with the Japanese, Japanese garden and design related books, Japan related literary fiction, language learning, travel and translations.

STONE WALL PRESS, INC., 1241 30th St. NW, Washington DC 20007. President/Publisher: Henry Wheelwright. Estab. 1972. Publishes hardcover and trade paperback originals of how-to, natural history, adventure travel, environmental/outdoor instruction and literature.

STORMLINE PRESS, P.O. Box 539, Urbana IL 61801. (217)328-2665. Publisher: Raymond Bial. Estab. 1985. "Publishes fiction and nonfiction, generally with a Midwest connection. Needs photography and regional works of the highest literary quality, especially those having to do with rural and small town themes. Stormline prefers works which are rooted in a specific place and time, such as *Silent Friends: A Quaker Quilt* by Margaret Lacey. The Press considers queries (with SASE only) during November and December. We do not consider unsolicited manuscripts."

‡STUDENT COLLEGE AID PUBLISHING DIVISION, 7950 N. Stadium Dr. #229, Houston TX 77030. Owner: Edward Rosenwasser. "We publish books about college financial aid and careers. Any book that is informative and interesting will be considered."

‡THE SUGAR HILL PRESS, 129 Sugar Hill Est. Rd., Weare NH 03281-4315. Publisher: L. Bickford. "We publish technical manuals for users of school administrative software *only*. (These are supplemental materials, not the manuals which come in the box.) A successful writer will combine technical expertise with crystal-clear prose."

THE SYSTEMSWARE CORPORATION, 973C Russell Ave., Gaithersburg MD 20879. (301)948-4890. Fax: (301)926-4243. Technical Editor: Julie Walker. "We specialize in innovative books and periodicals on Knowledge Engineering or Applied Artificial Intelligence and Knowledge Based Systems. We also develop software packages."

TAMBRA PUBLISHING, Suite D-122, 4375 W. Desert Inn, Las Vegas NV 89102. Fax: (702)876-5252. Editor: Tambra Campbell. Estab. 1985. Publishes how-to books on handwriting analysis and screenwriting/screenplays.

TECHNICAL ANALYSIS OF STOCKS & COMMODITIES, Technical Analysis, Inc., 3517 SW Alaska St., Seattle WA 98126-2730. (206)938-0570. Editor: Thom Hartle. Technical Editor: John Sweeney. Estab. 1982. Publishes business and economics books and software about using charts and computers to trade stocks, options, mutual funds or commodity futures. Reports in 3 months.

‡THOMAS ORGANIZATION, P.O. Box 641, Jamaica NY 11431. (212)856-8763 or 89-66 134th St., Richmond Hill NY 11418 (718)657-0384. Fax: (212)856-8660. Publisher: T. Ajayi Thomas. "Submit fiction acceptable to general audience/readers."

‡TICKET TO ADVENTURE, INC., P.O. Box 41005, St. Petersburg FL 33743. Administrative Vice President: Anne Wright. Target audience is females age 17-35, college students and career changers. Publishes specific, detailed 'how to gain employment' books such as *How to Get a Job with a Cruise Line*. Writers submitting nonfiction should avoid sketchy proposal (unclear objective) and lack of demonstration of market/buyer/audience.

‡TIMES CHANGE PRESS, P.O. Box 1380, Ojai CA 93024. (805)646-8595. Publisher: Lamar Hoover. "Our books are small format (5½×7), and nondogmatic in their approach to such topics as ecology and earth-consciousness, personal liberation, feminism, etc. We are not publishing poetry or fiction at this time."

TRAFALGAR SQUARE PUBLISHING, P.O. Box 257, N. Pomfret VT 05053-0257. (802)457-1911. Editor: Caroline Robbins. Contact: Martha Cook. Publishes nonfiction books about horses.

‡TURTLE PRESS, P.O. Box 290206, Wethersfield CT 06129-0206. (203)529-7770. Subsidiary of S.K. Productions, Inc.

UCLA-AMERICAN INDIAN STUDIES CENTER, 3220 Campbell Hall, 405 Hilgard Ave., Los Angeles CA 90024-1548. (213)825-7315. Editor: Duane Champagne. Estab. 1972. Publishes nonfiction how-to and reference books on anthropology, education, ethnic, government/politics, history, language/literature and sociology themes. Publishes poetry on Native American themes, a newsletter and academic journal.

UNIVERSITY OF CALIFORNIA LOS ANGELES CENTER FOR AFRO-AMERICAN STUDIES, 160 Haines Hall, 405 Hilgard Ave., Los Angeles CA 90024-1545. (310)825-3528. Fax: (310)206-3421. Managing Editor: Toyomi Igus. "Seeking nonfiction book-length manuscripts that have mainstream as well as scholarly or academic appeal and that focus on the African-American experience."

VALIANT PRESS, INC., P.O. Box 330568, Miami FL 33133. (305)665-1889. President: Charity Johnson. Estab. 1991. "We are interested in nonfiction books on Florida subjects."

VIRGINIA STATE LIBRARY AND ARCHIVES, Division of Publications and Cultural Affairs, 11th St. at Capitol Square, Richmond VA 23219-3491. (804)786-2311. Fax: (804)391-6909. Division Director: Sandra Gioia Treadway. Estab. 1823. "The Virginia State Library and Archives seeks material on the history and culture of Virginia, from the age of exploration to 1945. Submit outline and one sample chapter. Manuscripts should be restricted to a Virginia topic, and include notes and bibliography."

VOLCANO PRESS, INC., P.O. Box 270, Volcano CA 95689-0270. (209)296-3445. Fax: (209)296-4515. Publisher: Ruth Gottstein. "We publish women's health and social issues books, and muti-cultural books for children that are non-racist and non-sexist."

WASATCH PUBLISHERS, 4460 Ashford Dr., Salt Lake City UT 84124-2506. (801)278-5826. Publisher: John Veranth. Estab. 1974. Publishes books on outdoor recreation in the intermountain west.
  • Publisher has informed us they are "not taking on so many new books." Focus is on regional topics only.

WATERFRONT BOOKS, 85 Crescent Rd., Burlington VT 05401. (802)658-7477. Publisher: Sherrill N. Musty. Estab. 1983. Publishes books on children's issues, books that empower children, books on prevention, mental health and environmental concerns.

‡WESTERN TANAGER PRESS, 1111 Pacific Ave., Santa Cruz CA 95060. (408)425-1111. Fax: (408)425-0171. Publisher: Hal Morris. Estab. 1979. Publishes historical biography, hiking and biking guides and regional history hardcover and trade paperback originals and reprints.

WHOLE NOTES PRESS, (formerly Daedalus Press), Imprint of *Whole Notes Magazine*, P.O. Box 1374, Las Cruces NM 88004-1374. (505)382-7446. Editor: Nancy Peters Hastings. Estab. 1988. Publishes poetry chapbooks. Submit a sampler of 3-8 poems, along with SASE.

WORLD LEISURE, 177 Paris St., Boston MA 02128-3058. (617)569-1966. Fax: (617)561-7654. President: Charles Leocha. "We will be publishing annual updates to *Ski Europe* and *Skiing America*. Writers planning any ski stories should contact us for possible add-on assignments at areas not covered by our staff. We also will publish general travel titles such as *Travelers' Rights*, children's travel guides, guidebooks about myths and legends and self/help books such as *Getting to Know You, How to Write a Successful Personal Ad*."

YMAA PUBLICATION CENTER, 38 Hyde Park Ave., Jamaica Plain MA 02130. (617)524-9673. Fax: (617)524-4184. Contact: David Ripianzi. "We publish exclusively: Chinese philosophy, health, meditation, massage, recovery, martial arts."

Book Producers

Book producers provide services for book publishers, ranging from hiring writers to editing and delivering finished books. Writers who write for book producers are normally experts in specific subject areas. Book producers are usually not interested in publishing a writer's proposed manuscript, but they are interested in finding writers for manuscript ideas they have in development. If a book publisher has contracted a book producer to develop a book on boat building, the producer will seek out a writer with experience in that area.

Most often a book producer starts with a proposal, contacts writers, editors and illustrators, assembles the book, and sends it back to the publisher. The level of involvement and the amount of work to be done on a book by the producer is negotiated in individual cases. A book publisher may simply require the specialized skill of a particular writer or editor, or a producer could put together the entire book, depending on the terms of the agreement.

Writers have a similar working relationship with book producers. Their involvement depends on how much writing the producer has been asked to provide. Writers are then paid by the hour, by the word, or in some manner other than on a royalty basis. No matter how well or poorly a book sells, writers working for book producers earn flat fees. Writers may not receive credit (a byline in the book, for example) for their work, either. Most of the contracts require work for hire, and writers must realize they do not own the rights to the writing published under this arrangement.

The opportunities are good, though, especially for writing-related work, such as fact checking, research and editing. Writers don't have to worry about good sales. Their pay is secured under contract. Finally, writing for a book producer is a good way to broaden experience in publishing. Every book to be produced is different, and the chance to work on a range of books in a number of capacities may be the most interesting aspect of all.

Book producers most often want to see a query detailing writing experience. They keep this information on file and occasionally even share it with other producers. When they are contracted to develop a book that requires a particular writer's experience, they contact the writer. There are well over 100 book producers, but most prefer to seek writers on their own. The book producers listed in this section have expressed interest in being contacted by writers. For a list of more producers, contact the American Book Producers Association, Suite 604, 160 5th Ave., New York NY 10010, or look in *Literary Market Place* (R.R. Bowker).

For a list of publishers according to their subjects of interest, see the nonfiction and fiction sections of the Book Publishers Subject Index. Information on some book publishers and producers not included in this edition of *Writer's Market* can be found in Book Publishers and Producers/Changes '93-'94.

B&B PUBLISHING, INC., P.O. Box 393, Fontana WI 53125-0393. (414)275-9474. Fax: (414)275-9530. President: Jean B. Black. Vice President: Wallace B. Black. Publishes hardcover and trade paperback originals. Publishes 12-15 titles/year. 10% of books from first-time authors, 100% from unagented writers. Pays 5-10% royalty on net receipts, or makes outright purchase of $1,000. Offers $1,000 advance. Query for electronic submissions. Reports in 1 month. Promo sheets (listing titles) available for #10 SASE. Mss guidelines free on request.
   • This company is also listed in small presses.
Nonfiction: Query. Reviews artwork/photos as part of freelance mss package.

BLACKBIRCH GRAPHICS, INC., 1 Bradley Rd. #205, Woodbridge CT 06525. Fax: (203)389-1596. Editor-in-Chief: Bruce Glassman. Estab. 1979. Imprint is Blackbirch Press. Firm produces hardcover originals. Averages 70 titles/year. 20% of books from first-time authors, 85% from unagented writers. Pays 5-10% on net receipts. Makes outright purchase for $1,000-5,000. Offers $1,500 average advance. Query for electronic submissions. Does *not* return submissions, even those accompanied by SASE. Reports in 2 months. No phone calls, please.
Nonfiction: Biography, self-help, illustrated books, juvenile, how-to and reference. Subjects include women, African-Americans, Native Americans, and nature/environment. Submit proposal. Reviews artwork/photos as part of freelance ms package.
Tips: "Young adult publishing offers *series* work quite often. This means small advances and tight budgets on a *per book* basis but can allow authors to get commitments on 4-8 titles at a time."

BOOK CREATIONS INC., Schillings Crossing Rd., Canaan NY 12029. (518)781-4171. Fax: (518)781-4170. Editor-in-Chief: Paul Block. Estab. 1973. Produces trade paperback and mass market paperback orginals, primarily historical fiction. Averages 20-30 titles/year. 10% of books from first-time authors; 75% unagented writers. Pays royalty on net receipts or outright purchase. Advance varies with project. Reports in up to 3 months.
Nonfiction: Self-help. Subjects include cooking, foods and nutrition, health and recreation. Submit resume, publishing history and clips.
Fiction: Historicals, frontier, young adult, mystery, romance. Submit proposal and 50 pages of the work in progress.
Recent Fiction Title: *Edge of the World*, by William Sarabende.

‡BOOKWORKS, INC., 119 S. Miami St., West Milton OH 45383. (513)698-3619. Fax: (513)698-3651. President: Nick Engler. Estab. 1984. Firm averages 6 titles/year. Receives 1-10 submissions/year. less than 10% of books from first-time authors; 100% from unagented writers. Pays 2½-5% royalty on retail price. Buys mss outright for $3,000-10,000. Advance negotiable, varies. Publishes book an average of 8-18 months after acceptance. Simultaneous submissions OK. Reports in 6 weeks on queries; 2 months on mss.
Nonfiction: How-to. Subjects include woodworking and home improvement. Nothing other than woodworking/home improvement. Query or submit outline/synopsis and sample chapters. Reviews artwork/photos as part of manuscript package.
Tips: "We will not consider manuscripts unless written by experienced, competent craftsmen with firsthand knowledge of the subject. We publish how-to books for do-it-yourselfers, hobbyists and craftsmen."

CARPENTER PUBLISHING HOUSE, Suite 4602, 175 E. Delaware Place, Chicago IL 60611-1748. (312)787-3569. President: Allan Carpenter. Estab. 1962. Develops hardcover originals. "We develop our products or theirs on contract for major publishers. We assign work to authors and artists." Negotiates fee. Reports promptly on queries.
Nonfiction: Biography, juvenile, reference and supplementary texts. Subjects include Americana, history and directory/resource annuals. "We do not solicit mss. We specialize in books in large series." Query. All unsolicited mss are returned unopened.
Recent Nonfiction Title: *World Almanac of the U.S.A.*, for World Almanac Co.
   • If you have expertise on the provinces and cities of the People's Republic of China, Carpenter Publishing may be interereested in hearing from you.

‡CHANTICLEER PRESS, INC., 6th Floor, 575 Broadway, New York NY 10012. (212)941-2958. Managing Editor: Janice Easton. Trade paperback originals. Publishes 6-10 titles/year. Receives 150 queries and 50 mss/year. 10% of books from first-time authors; 95% from unagented writers. Pays royalty or makes outright

purchase. Publishes book 1-2 years after acceptance. Simultaneous submissions OK. Query for electronic submissions. Prefers DOS, Wordperfect 5.1. Reports in 1 month on proposals.
Nonfiction: Illustrated book, field guide and nature guide. Subjects include gardening and nature/environment. Submit outline and 2 sample chapters.
Recent Nonfiction Title: *Audubon Society Field Guides:* (1)Night Sky, by Mark R. Chartrand; (2)Weather, by David M. Ludlum (field guides); *Audubon Society Pocket Guide to Familiar Dinosaurs*, by Joseph Wallace (pocket guide).

‡CRACOM CORPORATION, Suite 109, 12131 Dorsett Rd., Maryland Heights MO 63043. (314)291-3988. Publisher and Editorial Director: Barbara Norwitz. Firm produces hardcover and trade paperback originals. Averages 6-10 titles/year. 80% of mss from first-time authors; 100% from unagented writers. Pays 10-15% royalty on wholesale price. Offers variable advance. Publishes book 5 months-2 years after acceptance of ms. Simultaneous submissions OK. Query for electronic submissions. Reports in 3 months. Ms guidelines free on request.
Nonfiction: Cookbook, children's/juvenile, self-help and technical. Subjects include cooking/foods/nutrition, education, health/medicine and child abuse/incest. Submit proposal package, including description of publication, intended market, outline, and 2 sample chapters. Reviews artwork/photos as part of freelance ms package. Writers should send photocopies, transparencies or prints.
Recent Nonfiction Title: *Just a Matter of Thyme*, by Roxie Kelley and Friends (cookbook).

HELENA FROST ASSOCIATES, Maple Rd. RR #9, Brewster NY 10509. (914)279-7923 or 301 E. 21st St., New York NY 10010. (914)279-7413. Fax: (212)353-2984. President: Helena Frost. Estab. 1986. Packages approximately 50 titles/year. Receives approximately 100 queries/year. Authors paid by flat or hourly fees or on freelance assignments. Query for electronic submissions. Reports in 3 weeks. Manuscript guidelines available per project.
Nonfiction: Textbook ancillaries, some general trade titles. Subjects include business and economics, education, government/politics, health/medicine, history, language/literature, psychology. Query.
Tips: "We are not interested in over-the-transom mss, but we do request writers' and editors' resumes with publication history and will review school-related proposals and outlines for submission to major publishers."

THE K S GINIGER COMPANY INC., Suite 519, 250 W. 57th St., New York NY 10107-0599. (212)570-7499. President: Kenneth S. Giniger. Estab. 1964. Publishes hardcover, trade paperback and mass paperback originals. Averages 8 titles/year; receives 250 submissions annually. 25% of books from first-time authors; 75% from unagented writers. Pays 5-15% royalty on retail price. Offers $3,500 average advance. Publishes book an average of 18 months after acceptance. Reports in 6 weeks on queries.
Nonfiction: Biography, coffee table, illustrated book, reference and self-help. Subjects include business and economics, health, history and travel. "No religious books, cookbooks, personal histories or personal adventure." Query with SASE. All unsolicited mss are returned unread (if postage enclosed for return of ms).
Recent Nonfiction Title: *Future Wars*, by Trevor N. Dupuy.
Tips: "We look for a book whose subject interests us and which we think can achieve success in the marketplace. Most of our books are based on ideas originating with us by authors we commission, but we have commissioned books from queries submitted to us."

GREENE COMMUNICATIONS, P.O. Box 8003, Cynthiana KY 41031-8003. (606)234-3266. Fax: (606)234-8071. Editorial Director: Randall Elisha Greene. Estab. 1987. Produces hardcover and trade paperback originals. Averages 2 titles/year. 50% of books from first-time authors; 10% from unagented writers. "Authors are paid by the publisher, rather than through our firm." Query for electronic submissions. Reports in 2 months. Serves some clients as their literary agent. Also provides services on a fee basis as manuscript editors.
Nonfiction: Autobiography, coffee table book, illustrated book, self-help, business history. Subjects include agriculture, Americana, art, business, government/politics, history, language/literature, music/dance, psychology, regional, religion, women's issues/studies. Query.
Recent Nonfiction Title: *Refuse to Stand Silently By*, by B. Eliot Wigginton, ed. (New York: Doubleday, 1992), (oral history, social activism).
Fiction: Adventure, ethnic, literary, mainstream, religious, short stories. Query.
Recent Fiction Title: *The Convention: A Parable*, by Will D. Campbell, for Peachtree (mainstream, religious).
Tips: "The trend involving firms such as ours is for book producers to provide trade houses with various services—from concept development through the finished-book stage. As a result, our company may only edit a book, copyedit, or provide any combination of services, as needed by the author and publisher. To contact us, authors may phone or write queries, but we avoid unsolicited material."

‡GREEY DE PENCIER BOOKS, Suite 302, 56 The Esplanade, Toronto, Ontario M5E 1A7 Canada. Editor-in-Chief: Sheba Meland. Firm produces hardcover and trade paperback originals. Averages 12 titles/year. Receives 100 queries and 500 mss/year. 15% of mss from first-time authors; 80% from unagented writers. Pays royalty on retail price. Publishes book 18 months after acceptance of ms. Simultaneous submissions OK.

Query for electronic submissions. Reports in 1-3 months. Catalog and ms guidelines for #10 SAE.

Nonfiction: Children's/juvenile. Subjects include animals, hobbies,, nature/environment and science. "We are closely affiliated with the discovery-oriented children's magazines *Owl* and *Chickadee*, and concentrate on fresh, innovative nonfiction and picture books with nature/science themes, and quality children's craft/how-to titles." Submit outline and 3 sample chapters, or proposal package, including outline, vita. Reviews artwork/photos as part of freelance ms package. Writers should send photocopies or transparencies (not originals).

Recent Nonfiction Title: *Real Live Science*, by Jay Ingram (activities).

Fiction: Picture books. Submit complete ms.

Recent Fiction Title: *A Tree in a Forest*, by Jan Thornhill (picture book).

Tips: "To get a feeling for our style of children's publishing, take a look at some of our recent books and at *Owl* and *Chickadee* magazines. We publish Canadian authors in the main, but will occasionally publish a work from outside Canada if it strikingly fits our list."

LAING COMMUNICATIONS INC., 16250 NE 80th St., Redmond WA 98052-3821. (206)869-6313. Fax: (206)869-6318. Vice President/Editorial Director: Christine Laing. Estab. 1985. Imprint is Laing Research Services (industry monographs). Firm produces hardcover and trade paperback originals. Averages 6-10 titles/year. 20% of books from first-time authors; 100% from unagented writers. Payment "varies dramatically since all work is sold to publishers as royalty-inclusive package." Reports in 1 month. *Writer's Market* recommends allowing 2 months for reply.

Nonfiction: Biography, coffee table book, cookbook, how-to, illustrated book, juvenile, reference, software, technical, textbook. Subjects include Americana, corporate histories, business and economics, computers/electronics, history, science. Query. Reviews artwork/photos as part of freelance ms package. The company also manages book divisions for three firms, producing 8-12 titles annually in technical and health care fields.

Recent Nonfiction Titles: *The World's Columbian Exposition*, for Preservation Press (history).

LAMPPOST PRESS INC., P.O. Box 7042, New York NY 10128-1213. (212)876-9511. President: Roseann Hirsch. Estab. 1987. Firm produces hardcover, trade paperback and mass market paperback originals. Averages 25 titles/year. 50% of books from first-time authors; 85% from unagented writers. Pays 50% royalty or by outright purchase.

Nonfiction: Biography, cookbook, how-to, humor, illustrated book, juvenile, self-help. Subjects include child guidance/parenting, cooking, foods and nutrition, gardening, health, money/finance, women's issues. Query or submit proposal. Reviews artwork/photos as part of freelance ms package.

Recent Nonfiction Titles: *Spinning Straw Into Gold: Your Emotional Recovery from Breast Cancer*, by Ronnie Kay (Simon & Schuster).

   ● No longer looking for fiction.

LUCAS-EVANS BOOKS INC., 1123 Broadway, New York NY 10010. (212)929-2583. Contact: Barbara Lucas. Estab. 1984. Packages hardcover, trade paperback originals and mass market paperback originals for major publishers. Averages 12 titles/year. 20% of books from first-time authors. Pays 1-10% royalty, "depending on our contract agreement with publisher." Makes work-for-hire assignments. Offers $3,000 and up average advance. Reports in 2 months.

Nonfiction: "We are looking for series proposals and selected single juvenile books: preschool through high school." Submit query letter with credentials, discussing proposed subject.

Fiction: Preschool through high school. Prefers picture books and early chapter books.

MEGA-BOOKS OF NEW YORK, INC., 116 E. 19th St., New York NY 10003. (212)598-0909. Fax: (212)979-5074. President: Pat Fortunato. Firm produces trade paperback originals and mass market paperback originals. Averages 95 titles/year. 30% of books from first-time authors; 75% from unagented writers. Makes outright purchase for $3,000 and up. Offers 50% average advance. Free ms guidelines.

Fiction: Juvenile, mystery and young adult. Submit resume, publishing history and clips.

Recent Fiction Titles: Nancy Drew and Hardy Boys series.

Tips: "Please be sure to obtain a current copy of our writers guidelines before writing. Please do not submit an unsolicited completed manuscript."

NEW ENGLAND PUBLISHING ASSOCIATES, INC., P.O. Box 5, Chester CT 06412. (203)345-4976. Fax: (203)345-3660. President: Elizabeth Frost Knappman. Vice President/Treasurer: Edward W. Knappman. Associate: Kathryn Cudlen-Dupont. Estab. 1983. Firm originates hardcover and trade paperback originals. 25% of books from first-time authors. Reports in 1 month. *Writer's Market* recommends allowing 2 months for reply.

Recent Nonfiction Title: *Facts to Blow Your Mind* (Price, Stern, Sloan).

Tips: "We prefer a phone call first, followed by writing samples or resumes. If you specialize in any area, let us know."

PARACHUTE PRESS, INC., #325, 156 5th Ave., New York NY 10010. (212)691-1421. Fax: (212)645-8769. Administrative Assistant: A. Leach. Firm produces hardcover, trade paperback and mass market paperback originals. Averages 50 titles/year. Pays 3-4% royalty or makes outright purchase. Offers $3,000 average advance. Returns rejected submissions when time permits. Reports in 2 months.
Nonfiction: Juvenile. Subjects include animals, cooking, foods and nutrition and sports. Query. Reviews artwork/photos as part of freelance ms package.
Fiction: Horror, juvenile and young adult. Submit proposal, resume, publishing history and clips.

RETAIL REPORTING CORP., 302 5th Ave., New York NY 10001-3604. (212)279-7000. Fax: (212)279-7014. Publisher: Larry Fuersich. Estab. 1939. Firm produces hardcover originals. 30% of books from first-time authors; 50% from unagented writers. Pays royalty or makes outright purchase. Offers $1,000-3,000 average advance. Query for electronic submissions. Reports in 2 months. Free catalog.
Nonfiction: Technical. Subjects include art/architecture, business and economics, design and graphic. Submit proposal. Reviews artwork/photos as part of freelance ms package.

SACHEM PUBLISHING ASSOCIATES, INC., P.O. Box 412, Guilford CT 06437. (203)453-4328. Fax: (203)453-4320. President: Stephen P. Elliott. Estab. 1974. Firm produces hardcover originals. Averages 3 titles/year. 25% of books from first-time authors; 100% from unagented writers. Pays royalty or makes outright purchase. Query for electronic submissions. Reports in 1 month.
Nonfiction: Reference. Subjects include Americana, government/politics, history and military/war. Submit resume and publishing history.
Recent Nonfiction Titles: *Reference Guide to U.S. Military History*, 5 vols., for Facts On File.

T.F.H. PUBLICATIONS, INC., 1 T.F.H. Plaza; Third and Union Avenues; Neptune City NJ 07753. Imprint is Paganiniana Publications. (201)988-8400. Managing Editor: Neal Pronek. Estab. 1952. Publishes hardcover originals. Averages 100 titles/year; receives 200 submissions annually. 80% of books from first-time authors; 95% from unagented writers. Royalty varies, depending on type of book, etc. Usually makes outright purchase of up to $20 per page. Normally pays half on acceptance, half on publication. Publishes book an average of 1 year after acceptance. Simultaneous submissions OK. Query for electronic submissions. Reports in 3 weeks.
Nonfiction: Coffee table book, how-to, illustrated book, reference, technical and textbook. Subjects include pets. "Our nonfiction book manuscript needs are for books that deal with specific guidelines for people who own or are interested in purchasing a particular type of pet. No books exclusively devoted to personal experiences with a particular pet, for example, *My Pet Sam*." Submit outline and sample chapters. No fiction or general nature studies. Reviews artwork/photos as part of ms package.
Recent Nonfiction Title: *Pot-bellied Pigs as Your New Family Pet*.
Tips: "Our audience is any and everyone who owns a pet. We do well with books that have a lot of color photographs combined with good sound advice about caring for a particular type of pet."

TENTH AVENUE EDITIONS, 625 Broadway, New York NY 10012. (212)529-8900. Fax: (212)529-7399. Managing Editor: Clive Giboire. Estab. 1984. Firm produces hardcover, trade paperback and mass market paperback originals. Averages 6 titles/year. Pays advance paid by publisher less our commission. Query for electronic submissions. Reports in 3 months.
Nonfiction: Biography, how-to, illustrated book, juvenile, catalogs. Subjects include music/dance, photography, women's issues/studies, art. *Queries only*. Reviews artwork/photos as part of freelance ms package.
Recent Nonfiction Titles: *Ira Clackens, A Memoir*.
Tips: "Send query with publishing background. Return postage a must."

DANIEL WEISS ASSOCIATES, INC., 33 W. 17th St., New York NY 10011. Assistant Editor: Laura Burns. Estab. 1987. Firm produces hardcover and mass market paperback originals. Averages 120 titles/year. 20% of books from first-time authors; 20% from unagented writers. Pays 1-4% royalty on retail price; or outright purchase $2,500 minimum "depending on author's experience." Offers $4,000 average advance. Reports in up to 3 months. Guidelines for #10 SASE.
Nonfiction: Juvenile. Submit proposal. Reviews artwork/photos as part of freelance ms package.
Fiction: Juvenile, young adult. Query.

THE WHEETLEY COMPANY, INC., Suite 1100, 4709 Golf Rd., Skokie IL 60076-1261. (708)675-4443. Fax: (708)675-4489. Human Resources Director: Linda Rogers. Estab. 1986. Firm produces hardcover originals for publishers of school, college and professional titles. Pays by the project. Query for electronic submissions. Does *not* return submissions, even those accompanied with SASE.

For information on setting your freelance fees, see How Much Should I Charge?

Nonfiction: Technical, textbook. Subjects include animals, anthropology, art/architecture, business and economics, child guidance/parenting, computers/electronics, cooking, foods and nutrition, education, government/politics, health, history, language/literature, money/finance, music/dance, nature/environment, philosophy, psychology, recreation, regional, religion, science, sociology, sports, translation. Submit resume and publishing history. Reviews artwork/photos as part of freelance ms package.

WIESER & WIESER, INC., 118 E. 25th St. New York NY 10010. (212)260-0860. Estab. 1976. Producer: George J. Wieser. Estab. 1976. Firm produces hardcover, trade paperback and mass market paperback originals. Averages 25 titles/year. 10% of books from first-time authors; 90% from unagented writers. Makes outright purchase for $5,000 or other arrangement. Offers $5,000 average advance. Reports in 2 weeks. *Writer's Market* recommends allowing 2 months for reply.
Nonfiction: Coffee table book. Subjects include Americana, cooking, foods and nutrition, gardening, health, history, hobbies, military/war, nature/environment, photography, recreation, sports and travel. Query. Reviews artwork/photos only as part of freelance book package.
Recent Nonfiction Title: *The Wall: A Day at the Vietnam Veterans Memorial* for St. Martin's Press.
Tips: "Have an original idea and develop it completely before contacting us."

Book Publishers and Producers/Changes '93-'94

The following book publishers and producers were listed in the 1993 edition but do not have listings in this edition of *Writer's Market*. The majority did not respond to our request to update their listings or return a questionnaire for a new listing. If a reason was given for their exclusion, we have included it in parentheses after the listing name.

A Capella Books
Abbey Press
ABC-Clio
Harry N. Abrams
ACA Books
Access Publishers (asked to be deleted)
Acropolis Books, Ltd.
Bob Adams
Alyson Publications
American Atheist Press
American Business Consultants
Amethyst Press
The Amwell Press
Anderson Publishing Co.
Apollo Books
Archetype Press, Inc.
M. Arman Publishing, Inc.
Arrow Publications
Artech House, Inc.
ASA, Aviation Supplies & Academics
Aztex Corp.,
Back to the Bible
Bascom Communications
Beau Lac Publishers
Between the Lines Inc. (does not accept American writers)
Beynch Press Publishing Co.
Black Bear Publications
Blue Heron Publishing
Bradbury Press
Bucknell University Press
Bull Publishing Co.
Camelot Publishing Co. (asked to be deleted)
Aristide D. Caratzas, Publisher
The Career Press (not considering new works)
Cassell Publications

Cay-Bel Publishing Co.
Cedi Publications
Charter House Publishers (overstocked)
Cliffhanger Press (asked to be deleted)
Consumer's Press
Copyright Information Services
Dalkey Archive Press (no longer considering freelance submissions)
Dayspring Press (removed because of complaints)
DDP Deluxe Editions
Delta Books
Dial Books for Young Readers
Distinctive Publishing Corporation
Dream Publishers
Editions Logiques/Logical Publishing
EES Publications
Lawrence Erlbaum Associates, Inc. (overwhelmed by submissions)
Evergreen Publications (out of business)
Far Corner Books (no new works this year)
Samuel French, Inc.
Michael Friedman Publishing Group
Fromm International (overstocked)
Gardner Press, Inc. (asked to be deleted)
Garland Publishing
Genealogical Publishing Co., Inc.
General Hall, Inc.
The J. Paul Getty Museum
Glencoe Division

Globe Press Books (moving)
Gollehon Press, Inc. (asked to be deleted)
Gospel Publishing House
Warren H. Green, Inc.
Gurze Books
Harbinger House, Inc. (works only with agents)
Harrow and Heston (does not use freelancers)
Haypenny Press (suspended)
James H. Heineman, Inc.
Hightext Publications, Inc.
W.D. Hoard & Sons Co.
Carl Hungness Publishing
Institute of Psychological Research Inc./Institut de Recherches Psychologiques, Inc.
International Self-Counsel Press, Ltd. (merged with Self-Counsel Press)
Jalmar Press/B.L. Winch & Associates
Lake Publishing Co.
Lavender Tapes
Leisure Press
Liberty Hall Press (no longer acquiring books)
Liberty Publishing Co., Inc.
Linch Publishing, Inc.
Los Hombres Press (only publishes haiku)
McClelland & Stewart (asked to be deleted)
McCutchan Publishing Corporation
Charles B. McFadden Co., Inc.
Macmillan Children's Books
Mallard Publishing (no new works)
Manic D Press

Markgraf Publications Group
Markowski International Publishers (not currently publishing)
Marquand Books, Inc.
Maxwell Macmillan Canada, Inc.
Mayfield Publishing Co.
Misty Hill Press
Mountain House Press
Multnomah Press (acquired by Questar)
Mute Swan Editions (no longer an HMS imprint)
Nichols Publishing
Northwest Publishing Inc.
Ohara Publications, Inc.
Ohio Psychology Publications, Inc.
Ohio State University Press
Ortho Information Services
Paradise Publications
Paragon House Publishers
Peacock Books
Perfection Learning Corp.
The Pilgrim Press
Pioneer Books (out of business)
Polestar Press Ltd. (only publishes Canadian writers)
Pollard Press
Porter Sargent Publishers, Inc.

(does not use freelance writing)
Prairie Oak Press
Prentice Hall Press (merged into Simon Schuster)
Prevention Health Books
Product Concept, Inc.
Que Corporation
Reference Publications, Inc.
Rockwell Publishing Co.
Rydal Press
Saterston Productions, Inc.
Semaphore Press
Sentinel Books
Seven Wolves Publishing
The Sheep Meadow Press
Shoe Tree Press
Shoestring Press
Silver Burdett Press
Silver Press Inc.
Skillpath Publications, Inc. (asked to be deleted)
Smooth Stone Press (too many inappropriate submissions)
Spectre Publications, Inc.
Starrhill Press
Starwood Publishing
Gareth Stevens, Inc.
Tafford Publishing
Theytus Books Ltd.
Time-Life Books, Inc. (too

many policy and editorial changes)
Transnational Publishers, Inc.
Travel Keys (no longer publishing books)
Charles E. Tuttle Publishing Co., Inc.
Undena Publications
Universe Books
University of Wisconsin Press (asked to be deleted)
University Press of Kansas (asked to be deleted)
Verso (NY)
Verso (UK)
Victory Press
Viking Penguin
Vortex Communications
Wayfarer Books
Weatherhill, Inc.
Webb Research Group (asked to be deleted)
Weidner & Sons, Publishing
Welcome Enterprises, Inc.
Whitehorse Press
Willow Creek Press (out of business)
Wingra Woods Press
Wizards Bookshelf (asked to be deleted)
Wordware Publishing, Inc.

Consumer Magazines

Consumer Magazines

The economy continues to keep the consumer magazine industry guessing. With readers clinging as tightly as ever to their discretionary "entertainment" dollars, magazine publishers have been striving to create special interest publications for ever narrower segments of the population. The hope is that readers who might be reluctant to spend money on a general interest magazine may be more inclined to purchase one that's tailored to their specific interests and lifestyles.

When a periodical succeeds in finding its audience, it attracts advertisers hoping to reach that same audience. According to industry figures, up to 50% of some consumer magazines' earnings come from ad sales; the remainder is from subscriptions and single copy sales. As long as enough advertisers find a particular magazine useful in reaching their customers, that magazine will thrive. If the magazine fails in its editorial mission – if its content does not match the interests of its supposed audience – it will lose readers and advertisers and it will fold.

Another reason for the success of niche publications – aside from the well-defined customers they deliver to advertisers – is the fact that by appealing to readers on the basis of a special interest, with information they are unlikely to find from another source, such magazines avoid competing for readers head to head with larger circulation, more general interest magazines.

Special interest magazines and the freelance writer

From *National Review* to *Mushing* (yes, dog sledding), there is a magazine published to match nearly every interest, viewpoint or lifestyle. The current abundance of special interest magazines means a greater opportunity to match your own special interests with theirs and, with a little luck and a lot of hard work, increase your frequency of publication.

While the temptation, especially for new writers, may be to immediately target the very largest and most well-known magazines, the surer, faster path to publication (and a writing career) begins with the smaller circulation, niche-market magazines. Begin by writing about things that interest you and targeting magazines that reflect those interests.

Before submitting

Each of the magazines listed in this section has been given the chance to state as clearly as possible what kind of material they are seeking and how

INSIDER REPORT

Target special interest publications with careful study and a good query letter

"One reason [for the proliferation of special interest magazines] is that consumers don't have time to read anymore – and maybe they don't have as much money to spend on magazines as they did once upon a time – so they narrow their choices to what they're vitally interested in," says Carol Wiley Lorente, managing editor of *Vegetarian Times* magazine.

Lorente sees the trend of specialization as good news for freelance writers. "I think that writers who tap into that niche market will see their opportunities increasing as the market grows. Remember that as the market grows, pages grow, and there have to be words to fill those pages. As a result, magazines add more features and departments – and someone has to write them!"

Carol Wiley Lorente

For writers interested in contributing to *Vegetarian Times*, she counsels: "Study our magazine for tone and content. Contribute articles on timely topics, and learn how to write a good query letter. Most of the query letters I receive are of the 'I'd like to write a story on this topic' variety, rather than a good intro of the story being proposed and some samples to show us the writer can do it."

Studying past issues of the magazine is crucial, says Lorente. "I'm constantly receiving queries for stories we published within the last year, or that are inappropriate to our focus. For example, if writers truly studied our magazine, they would know we stopped publishing 'Why I Became a Vegetarian' stories about 10 years ago."

they like writers to contact them. You stand the best chance of succeeding when you follow the guidelines set out in the listings. Time and again, editors have told us that the biggest problem they have with freelancers is that many submit material that is inappropriate for their magazine – either it's a subject the magazine doesn't cover or the tone or treatment is off the mark. The simplest and most effective remedy for this problem is to familiarize yourself with the magazine before submitting articles or ideas. If you make the effort to read at least two recent issues of a publication you're interested in writing for and request a copy of the publication's guidelines, you will place yourself well ahead of the pack of writers who are simply shotgunning material to any and every market. For a more detailed discussion of how to sell to magazines, be sure to read Targeting Your Magazine Submissions on page 24, by John Wood, a senior editor at *Modern Maturity*. Additional information on magazine submissions can be found in Getting Published.

What editors want

In nonfiction, editors continue to look for short feature articles covering specialized topics. They want crisp writing and expertise. If you are not an expert in the area about which you are writing, make yourself one through research.

Always query by mail before sending your manuscript package, but keep in mind that once a piece has been accepted, many publishers now prefer to receive your submission via disk or modem so they can avoid re-keying the manuscript.

Fiction editors prefer to receive complete short story manuscripts. Writers must keep in mind marketing fiction is very competitive and editors receive far more material than they can publish. For this reason, they often do not respond to submissions unless they are interested in using the story. Before submitting material, check the market's listing for fiction requirements to ensure your story is appropriate for that market. More comprehensive information on fiction markets can be found in *Novel & Short Story Writer's Market* (Writer's Digest Books). For a look at current trends in magazine publishing, see page 43.

Regardless of the type of writing you do, try to keep current on trends and changes in the industry. Trade magazines such as *Magazine Week*, *Folio* and *Writer's Digest* will keep you abreast of start-ups and shut downs and other writing business trends.

Payment

Writers make their living by developing a good eye for detail. When it comes to marketing their material, the one detail of interest to almost every writer is the question of payment. Most magazines listed herein have indicated pay rates; some give very specific payment-per-word rates while others state a range. Any agreement you come to with a magazine, whether verbal or written, should specify the payment you are to receive and when you are to receive it. Some magazines pay writers only after the piece in question has been published. Others pay as soon as they have accepted a piece and are sure they are going to use it.

In *Writer's Market*, those magazines that pay on acceptance have been highlighted with the phrase—"**pays on acceptance**"—set in bold type. Payment

Freshness, enthusiasm and competence are keys to an effective query

Marlane Liddell is the articles editor and a member of the board of editors at *Smithsonian Magazine*. She sees thousands of queries from freelance writers every year and describes the kinds of queries that catch her attention: "What we need from freelance writers is a query that surprises the editors. If we are entertained, we believe our readers will be too. I look for fresh ideas presented with enthusiasm and energy that make me want to read more. We try to surprise our readers, hoping that when they turn the page they find a new topic or an unexpected treatment of an old, familiar one." She echoes Carol Wiley Lorente's concern that writers study her magazine closely before querying. "*Smithsonian Magazine* receives some 12,000 unsolicited proposals and manuscripts a year. Many of them are rejected because it is obvious the

Marlane Liddell

writer has never read the magazine closely," she says. "It is vital to study the magazine and send a proposal that has been written specifically for us."

Many queries fall short by not providing enough information about how the writer is planning to develop the article. "Some writers don't include enough information in a proposal about how they would handle a story. I continually receive proposals on subjects that might work if I were given a more detailed query. If the writer has good credits one of us might request another proposal, but that takes time. We have a small staff—a freelancer has a much better chance with us if they send a good query the first time through."

In addition to providing a detailed description of how you would develop the story, Ms. Liddell recommends making the most of any previous publishing credits in your query. "On a practical level," she says, "it is important to give credits and copies of published articles that indicate you have the skills to write a 4,000-word article in a stylish manner."

Because of *Smithsonian Magazine*'s small staff, Liddell says they are dependent on freelance writers. "We can't possibly stay on top of all the subject areas we cover. Freelancers keep us up to date on people and places our readers want to know about." Those writers will do best, she says, who can "find a good subject, do some research, write an entertaining and informative query that is irresistible to an editor who has had a long day and can't believe there is any subject that hasn't been through before."

from these markets should reach you faster than from those who pay "on publication." There is, however, some variance in the industry as to what constitutes payment "on acceptance"—some writers have told us of two- and three-month waits for checks from markets that supposedly pay "on acceptance." It is never out of line to ask an editor when you might expect to receive payment for an accepted article.

So what is a good pay rate? There are no standards; the principle of supply and demand operates at full throttle in the business of writing and publishing. As long as there are more writers than there are opportunities for publication, wages for freelancers will never skyrocket. Rates vary widely from one market to the next, however, and the news is not entirely bleak. One magazine industry source puts the average pay rate for consumer magazine feature writing at $1.25 a word, with "stories that require extensive reporting . . . more likely to be priced at $2.50 a word." In our opinion, those estimates are on the high side of current pay standards. Smaller circulation magazines and some departments of the larger magazines will pay a lower rate. As your reputation grows (along with your clip file), you may be able to command higher rates.

Information on some publications not included in *Writer's Market* may be found in Consumer Magazines/Changes '93-'94, located at the end of this section.

Animal

The publications in this section deal with pets, racing and show horses, and other pleasure animals and wildlife. Magazines about animals bred and raised for the market are classified in the Farm category of Trade, Technical and Professional Journals. Publications about horse racing can be found in the Sports section.

AMERICAN FARRIERS JOURNAL, P.O. Box 624, Brookfield WI 53008-0624. (414)782-4480. Fax: (414)782-1252. Editor: Frank Lessiter. Published 7 times/year. Magazine covering horseshoeing and horse health, related to legs and feet of horses for a professional audience of full-time and part-time horseshoers, veterinarians and horseowners. Estab. 1975. Circ. 10,000. Pays on publication. Byline given. Buys all rights. Submit material 3 months in advance. Writer's guidelines for #10 SASE.
Nonfiction: Book excerpts, general interest, historical/nostalgic, how-to, interview/profile, new product, personal experience, photo feature and technical. Buys 50 mss/year. Send complete ms. Length: 800-3,000 words. Pays 30¢ per published line.
Photos: Send photos with ms. Reviews b&w contact sheets, b&w negatives, 35mm color transparencies and 8×10 b&w or color prints. Pays $10/published photo. Captions and identification of subjects required. Buys one-time rights.

AMERICA'S EQUESTRIAN, Garri Publications, Inc., 114 West Hills Rd., P.O. Box 249, Huntington Station NY 11746. (516)423-0620. Fax: (516)423-0567. Editorial Director: Dennis Garetano. 75% freelance written. Bimonthly magazine about horses. Estab. 1978. Circ. 16,500. Pays on publication. Byline given. Buys first North American serial rights. Submit seasonal/holiday material 6 months in advance. Query for electronic submissions. Reports in 3 months on queries. Sample copy for 9×12 SAE with 6 first class stamps. Writer's guidelines for #10 SASE.

Nonfiction: "Anything horse-related (see topics listed in columns/departments section below)." Buys 25 mss/year. Query with published clips. Length: 100-2,000 words. Pays $5-200.

Photos: State availability of photos with submission or send photos with submission. Reviews 5×7 prints. Offers $20/photo. Captions, model releases and identification of subjects required. Buys one-time rights. "No name on front of photo; give credit line." Cover: equine/sporting art. Send chromes, slides, or color photos. No payment.

Columns/Departments: Stable Management/Horse Care, Puzzles, Equine Spotlight, Equestrian Spotlight, Celebrity Corner, Diet/Health/Fitness, Horoscopes, The Judge's Corral, From The Horse's Mouth, Paddock Talk. "Remember these must all be related to horses or horse people." Features: Horse Show, Driving, Dressage, Racing, Eventing, Breeding, Gift Mart, Grand Prix, Western/Stable Management, Fencing, Transportation, Fashion. Query with published clips. Length: 500-1,000 words. Pays $25-75 maximum.

Fillers: Cartoons, gags to be illustrated by cartoonist. Buys 18/year. Pays $5.

Tips: "We are an information center for horse people. Write for guidelines."

‡ANIMALS, Massachusetts Society for the Prevention of Cruelty to Animals, 350 S. Huntington Ave., Boston MA 02130. (617)522-7400. Fax: (617)522-4885. Editor: Joni Praded. Managing Editor: Paula Abend. 90% freelance written. Bimonthly magazine publishing "articles on wildlife (American and international), domestic animals, balanced treatments of controversies involving animals, conservation, animal welfare issues, pet health and pet care." Circ. 100,000. **Pays on acceptance.** Publishes ms an average of 5 months after acceptance. Byline given. Offers negotiable kill fee. Buys one-time rights or makes work-for-hire assignments. Submit seasonal/holiday material 6 months in advance. Reports in 6 weeks. Sample copy $2.50 for 9×12 SAE with 4 first class stamps. Writer's guidelines for #10 SASE.

Nonfiction: Expose, general interest, how-to, opinion and photo feature on animal and environmental issues and controversies, plus practical pet-care topics. "*Animals* does not publish breed-specific domestic pet articles or 'favorite pet' stories. Poetry and fiction are also not used." Buys 50 mss/year. Query with published clips. Length: 3,000 words maximum. "Payment for features usually starts at $350." Sometimes pays the expenses of writers on assignment.

Photos: State availability of photos with submission, if applicable. Reviews contact sheets, 35mm transparencies and 5×7 or 8×10 prints. Payment depends on usage size and quality. Captions, model releases and identification of subjects required. Buys one-time rights.

Columns/Departments: Books (book reviews of books on animals and animal-related subjects), 300 words. Buys 18 mss/year. Query with published clips. Length: 300 words maximum. "Payment usually starts at $75."

Tips: "Present a well-researched proposal. Be sure to include clips that demonstrate the quality of your writing. Stick to categories mentioned in *Animals'* editorial description. Combine well-researched facts with a lively, informative writing style. Feature stories are written almost exclusively by freelancers. We continue to seek proposals and articles that take a humane approach. Articles should concentrate on how issues affect animals, rather than humans."

AQUARIUM FISH MAGAZINE, Fancy Publications, Box 6050, Mission Viejo CA 92690. (714)855-8822. Fax: (714)855-3045. Editor: Edward Bauman. 100% freelance written. Monthly magazine on aquariums, tropical fish, ponds and pond fish. "We need well-written feature articles, preferably with color transparencies, dealing with all aspects of the hobby and directed toward novices and experienced hobbyists." Estab. 1988. Circ. 70,000. Pays on publication. Buys first North American serial rights. ASCII files by disk or modem. Reports in 1 month on queries; 2 months on mss. Sample copy $3.50. Free writer's guidelines.

Nonfiction: "Articles on biology, care and breeding of aquarium and pond fish; pond and aquarium set-up and maintenance. No pet fish stories." Buys 45-60 mss/year. Query. Length: 1,500-3,500 words. Pays $100-300 for assigned articles.

Photos: Send slides with submission. Reviews contact sheets and transparencies. Offers $50-150 for color; up to $25 for b&w. Buys one-time rights.

Tips: "Know the subject; write tight, well-organized copy. Avoid 'my first aquarium' type of articles. Too many writers avoid adequate research. Many readers are knowledgeable about hobby and want solid information."

ARABIAN HORSE TIMES, Adams Corp., 1050 8th St. NE, Waseca MN 56093. (507)835-3204. Fax: (507)835-5138. Editor: Ruth James. 20% freelance written. Works with a small number of new/unpublished writers each year. Monthly magazine about Arabian horses. Editorial format includes hard news (veterinary, book reports, etc.), lifestyle and personality pieces and bloodline studies. Estab. 1969. Circ. 22,000. Pays on publication. Publishes ms an average of 6 months after acceptance. Byline given. Buys first serial rights. Submit seasonal/holiday material 3 months in advance. Simultaneous queries OK. Reports in 2 months. Sample copy $5. Writer's guidelines upon request.

 The double dagger before a listing indicates that the listing is new in this edition. New markets are often more receptive to freelance submissions.

Nonfiction: General interest, how-to, interview/profile and photo feature. Buys at least 12 mss/year. Query with published clips. Length: 1,000-3,000 words.

Photos: Prefers color prints. Payment depends on circumstances. Captions and identification of subjects required. Buys one-time rights.

Fiction: Will look at anything about Arabians except erotica or poetry. Buys 1-2 mss/year. Send complete ms. Length: 1,500-5,000 words.

Tips: "As our periodical is specific to Arabian horses, we are interested in anyone who can write well and tightly about them. Send us something timely. Also, narrow your topic to a specific horse, event, incident, person or problem. 'Why I Love Arabians' will not work."

‡**CALIFORNIA HORSE REVIEW**, P.O. Box 1238, Rancho Cordova CA 95741-1238. (916)638-1519. Fax: (916)638-1784. Editor: Jennifer Meyer. Associate Editor: Lisa Wolters. Monthly magazine covering equestrian interests. "*CHR* covers a wide spectrum—intensive veterinary investigation, trainer 'how-to' tips, breeding research updates and nutritional guidance. Editorial also devotes effort to reporting news and large state and national show results." Estab. 1963. Circ. 10,000. **Pays on acceptance.** Byline given. Buys first North American serial rights. Previously published submissions OK. Sample copy and writer's guidelines with SASE.

Nonfiction: General interest (West Coast equine emphasis), how-to (training, breeding, horse care, riding) and technical (riding, training). "No fiction or anything *without* a strong focal point of interest for *West Coast equestrians* in the major performance/show English and Western disciplines." Buys 25-40 mss/year. Query with published clips. Length: 500-2,500 words. Pays $50-175 for assigned articles; $25-150 for unsolicited articles. Sometimes pays telephone expenses of writers on assignment.

Photos: Send photos with submission. Reviews 3×5 or larger prints. Offers no additional payment for photos accepted with ms. Captions required. Buys one-time rights.

Tips: "Be accurate, precise and knowledgable about horses. Our readers are not beginners but sophisticated equestrians. Elementary, overly-basic how-to's are not appropriate for us."

CAT FANCY, Fancy Publications, Inc., Box 6050, Mission Viejo CA 92690. (714)855-8822. Editor: Debbie Phillips-Donaldson. 80-90% freelance written. Monthly magazine for men and women of all ages interested in all phases of cat ownership. Estab. 1974. Circ. 303,000. Pays on publication. Publishes ms an average of 6 months after acceptance. Buys first North American serial rights. Byline given. Absolutely no simultaneous submissions. Submit seasonal/holiday material 4 months in advance. Reports in 6-8 weeks. Sample copy $4.50. Writer's guidelines for SASE.

Nonfiction: Historical, medical, how-to, humor, informational, personal experience, photo feature and technical; must be cat-oriented. Buys 5-7 mss/issue. Query first. Length: 500-3,000 words. Pays $35 to $400; special rates for photo/story packages.

Photos: Photos purchased with or without accompanying ms. Pays $35 minimum for 8×10 b&w glossy and $50 minimum for color prints; $50-200 for 35mm or 2¼×2¼ color transparencies; occasionally pays more for particularly outstanding or unusual work. Send SASE for photo guidelines. Then send prints and transparencies. Model release required.

Fiction: Adventure, fantasy, historical and humorous. Nothing written with cats speaking or from cat's point of view. Buys 3-5 ms/year. Query first. Length: 500-3,000 words. Pays $50-400.

Fillers: Newsworthy or unusual; items with photos. Buys 25/year. Length: 500-1,000 words. Pays $35-100.

Tips: "Most of the articles we receive are profiles of the writers' own cats or profiles of cats that have recently died. We reject almost all of these stories. What we need are well-researched articles that will give our readers the information they need to better care for their cats. Please review past issues and notice the informative nature of articles before querying us with an idea."

CATS MAGAZINE, Cats Magazine Inc., P.O. Box 290037, Port Orange FL 32129-0037. (904)788-2770. Fax: (904)788-2710. Editor: Linda J. Walton. 50% freelance written. Monthly magazine for cat enthusiasts of all types, veterinarians, breeders and exhibitors. Estab. 1945. Circ. 149,000 and growing rapidly. Pays on publication. Byline given. Buys one-time rights. Submit seasonal/holiday material well in advance. Sample copy and writer's guidelines for 9×12 SAE with $2 postage.

Nonfiction: General interest (concerning cats); how-to (care, etc. for cats); health-related; humor; interview/profile (on cat-owning personalities); personal experience; and stories about cats that live in remarkable circumstances, or have had a remarkable experience (can be historical). No talking cats, please. Send complete ms with SASE. Length 400-2,000 words. Pays $25-450.

Photos: "Professional quality photographs that effectively illustrate the chosen topic are accepted with all submissions. However, it is the perogative of the art director to choose whether or not to use the photographs along with the printed piece." Photos that accompany an article should be in the form of color slides, 2¼ transparencies or glossy prints no smaller than 5×7. Pays $50-150 total depending on size used. To be considered for a cover shot, photos should be in the form of a transparency no smaller than 2¼. Pays $150-250. Clear, color prints are accepted for the picture of the month contest. Pays $25. Identification of subjects required. Buys one-time rights.

Fiction: Fantasy, historical, mystery, science fiction, slice-of-life vignettes and suspense. Only used occasionally. All fiction must involve a cat or the relationship of a cat and humans, etc. No talking cats, please. Send complete ms. Length: 800-1,500 words. Pays $25-200.

Poetry: Free verse, light verse and traditional. Length: 4-64 lines. Pays $10-40.

Tips: "Writer must show an affinity for cats. Articles critical of cats, unless obviously tongue-in-cheek will not be used. Extremely well-written, thoroughly researched, carefully thought out articles have the best chance of being accepted. Innovative topics or a new twist on an old subject are always welcomed."

THE CHRONICLE OF THE HORSE, P.O. Box 46, Middleburg VA 22117-0046. (703)687-6341. Fax: (703)687-3937. Editor: John Strassburger. Managing Editor: Nancy Comer. 80% freelance written. Weekly magazine about horses. "We cover English riding sports, including horse showing, grand prix jumping competitions, steeplechase racing, foxhunting, dressage, endurance riding, handicapped riding and combined training. We are the official publication for the national governing bodies of many of the above sports. We feature news, how-to articles on equitation and horse care and interviews with leaders in the various fields." Estab. 1937. Circ. 23,000. **Pays for features on acceptance**; news and other items on publication. Publishes ms an average of 4 months after acceptance. Byline given. Buys first North American rights and makes work-for-hire assignments. Submit seasonal/holiday material 3 months in advance. Reports in 1 month. Sample copy $2 for 9 × 12 SAE. Writer's guidelines for #10 SASE.

Nonfiction: General interest; historical/nostalgic (history of breeds, use of horses in other countries and times, art, etc.); how-to (trailer, train, design a course, save money, etc.); humor (centered on living with horses or horse people); interview/profile (of nationally known horsemen or the very unusual); technical (horse care, articles on feeding, injuries, care of foals, shoeing, etc.); and news (of major competitions, clear assignment with us first). Special issues include Steeplechasing, Grand Prix Jumping, Combined Training, Dressage, Hunt Roster, Junior and Pony and Christmas. No Q&A interviews, clinic reports, Western riding articles, personal experience or wild horses. Buys 300 mss/year. Query or send complete ms. Length: 300-1,225 words. Pays $25-200.

Photos: State availability of photos. Accepts prints or color slides. Accepts color for b&w reproduction. Pays $15-30. Identification of subjects required. Buys one-time rights.

Columns/Departments: Dressage, Combined Training, Horse Show, Horse Care, Racing over Fences, Young Entry (about young riders, geared for youth), Horses and Humanities, and Hunting. Query or send complete ms. Length: 300-1,225 words. Pays $25-200.

Poetry: Light verse and traditional. No free verse. Buys 30/year. Length: 5-25 lines. Pays $15.

Fillers: Anecdotes, short humor, newsbreaks and cartoons. Buys 300/year. Length: 50-175 lines. Pays $10-25.

Tips: "Get our guidelines. Our readers are sophisticated, competitive horsemen. Articles need to go beyond common knowledge. Freelancers often attempt too broad or too basic a subject. We welcome well-written news stories on major events, but clear the assignment with us."

THE EQUINE MARKET, Midwest Outdoors, 111 Shore Dr., Hinsdale IL 60521. (708)887-7722. Editor: Kandee Haertel. 90% freelance written. Monthly tabloid covering equestrian interests. Estab. 1970. Circ. 5,000. Pays on publication. Byline given. Buys all rights or makes work-for-hire assignments. Submit seasonal/holiday material 2 months in advance. Reprints OK; send photocopy of article, typed ms with rights for sale noted, and information about where and when the article previously appeared. Reports in 2 months. Free sample copy and writer's guidelines.

Nonfiction: Essays, general/interest, historical/nostalgic, how-to (horse care), inspirational, interview/profile, new product, opinion, personal experience, photo feature, show reporting, technical and travel. Special upcoming issues: holiday (November-December), farm (June) and tack shop (September). Buys 70 mss/year. Send complete ms. Length: 500-3,000 words. Pays $25-35 for assigned articles; $25 for unsolicited articles; or may trade articles for advertising.

Photos: Send photos with submission. Reviews negatives and 3 × 5 prints. Offers no additional payment for photos accepted with ms. Captions and identification of subjects required.

Fiction: Adventure, humorous and mainstream. Buys 15/year. Send complete ms. Length 500-3,000 words. Pays $25.

THE GREYHOUND REVIEW, P.O. Box 543, Abilene KS 67410. (913)263-4660. Fax: (913)263-4689. Editor: Gary Guccione. Managing Editor: Tim Horan. 20% freelance written. Monthly magazine covering greyhound breeding, training and racing. Estab. 1911. Circ. 7,000. **Pays on acceptance.** Byline given. Buys first rights. Submit seasonal/holiday material 2 months in advance. Query for electronic submissions. Reports in 2 weeks on queries; 1 month on mss. *Writer's Market* recommends allowing 2 months for reply. Sample copy $2.50. Free writer's guidelines.

Nonfiction: How-to, interview/profile and personal experience. "Articles must be targeted at the greyhound industry: from hard news, special events at racetracks to the latest medical discoveries." Do not submit gambling systems. Buys 24 mss/year. Query. Length: 1,000-10,000 words. Pays $85-150. Sometimes pays the expenses of writers on assignment.

Photos: State availability of photos with submission. Reviews 35mm transparencies and 8 × 10 prints. Offers $10-50/photo. Identification of subjects required. Buys one-time rights.

‡HORSEMEN'S YANKEE PEDLAR NEWSPAPER, 785 Southbridge St., Auburn MA 01501-1399. (508)832-9638. Fax: (508)832-9638. Publisher: Nancy L. Khoury. Managing Editor: Jane Sullivan. 40% freelance written. "All-breed monthly newspaper for horse enthusiasts of all ages and incomes, from one-horse owners to large commercial stables. Covers region from New Jersey to Maine." Circ. 15,000. Pays on publication. Buys all rights for one year. Publishes reprints of previously published articles. Send photocopy of article, including information about when and where the article previously appeared. For reprints, pays 100% of the amount paid for an original article. Submit seasonal/holiday material 3 months in advance of issue date. Query for electronic submissions. Publishes ms an average of 5 months after acceptance. Reports in 1 month. Sample copy $3.75.
Nonfiction: Humor, educational and interview about horses and the people involved with them. Pays $2/published inch. Buys 100 mss/year. Query or submit complete ms or outline. Length: 1,500 words maximum.
Photos: Purchased with ms. Captions and photo credit required. Submit b&w prints; for return include SASE. Pays $5.
Columns/Departments: Area news column. Buys 85-95/year. Length: 1,200-1,400 words. Query.
Tips: "Query with outline of angle of story, approximate length and date when story will be submitted. Stories should be people-oriented and horse-focused. Send newsworthy, timely pieces, such as stories that are applicable to the season, for example: foaling in the spring or how to keep a horse healthy through the winter. We like to see how-tos, features about special horse people and issues affecting horsemen."

HORSEPLAY, Box 130, Gaithersburg MD 20877. (301)840-1866. Fax: (301)840-5722. Editor: Cordelia Doucet. 50% freelance written. Works with published/established writers and a small number of new/unpublished writers each year. Monthly magazine covering horses and English horse sports for a readership interested in horses, show jumping, dressage, combined training, hunting and driving. 60-80 pages. Circ. 55,000. Pays at end of publication month. Buys all, first North American serial and second serial (reprint) rights. Offers kill fee. Byline given. Deadline 2 months prior to issue date. Nothing returned without SASE. Reports in 1 month. Sample copy for 10×13 SASE. Writer's and photographer's guidelines for #10 SASE.
Nonfiction: Instruction (various aspects of horsemanship, course designing, stable management, putting on horse shows, etc.); competitions; interview; photo feature; profile and technical. Query first. Preferred length: 1,500 words or less. Pays 10¢/word, all rights; 9¢/word, first North American serial rights; 7¢/word, second rights. Reprints OK; send tearsheet of article and information about when and where the article previously appeared.
Photos: Cordelia Doucet, editor. Purchased on assignment. Write captions on separate paper attached to photo. Query or send contact sheet, prints or transparencies.
Tips: Don't send fiction, Western riding, or racing articles.

HORSES ALL, Box 9, Hill Spring Alberta T0K 1E0 Canada. (403)626-3344. Fax: (403)626-3600. Editor: Renae French. 30% freelance written. Eager to work with new/unpublished writers. Monthly tabloid for horse owners, 75% rural, 25% urban. Circ. 11,200. Pays on publication. Publishes ms an average of 6 months after acceptance. Buys one-time rights. Phone queries OK. Submit seasonal material 3 months in advance. Simultaneous and previously published submissions OK. Reports on queries in 5 weeks; 6 weeks on mss. Sample copy $2 for 9×12 SAE.
Nonfiction: Interview, humor and personal experience. Query. Pays $20-100. Sometimes pays the expenses of writers on assignment.
Photos: State availability of photos. Captions required.
Columns/Departments: Open to suggestions for new columns/departments. Send query to Doug French. Length: 1-2 columns.
Fiction: Historical and western. Query. Pays $20-100.
Tips: "We use more short articles. The most frequent mistakes made by writers in completing an article assignment for us are poor research, wrong terminology and poor (terrible) writing style."

I LOVE CATS, I Love Cats Publishing, 16th Floor, 950 3rd Ave., New York NY 10022-2705. (212)888-1855. Editor: Lisa Sheets. 75% freelance written. Bimonthly magazine covering cats. "*I Love Cats* is a general interest cat magazine for the entire family. It caters to cat lovers of all ages. The stories in the magazine include fiction, nonfiction, how-to, humorous and columns for the cat lover." Estab. 1989. Circ. 200,000. Pays on publication. Publishes ms an average of 1 year after acceptance. Byline given. No kill fee. Buys all rights. Submit seasonal material 8 months in advance. Query for electronic submissions; IBM compatible. Reports in 2 months. Sample copy $3. Writer's guidelines for #10 SASE.

Market conditions are constantly changing! If this is 1995 or later, buy the newest edition of Writer's Market at your favorite bookstore or order directly from Writer's Digest Books.

Nonfiction: Essays, how-to, humor, inspirational, interview/profile, opinion, personal experience and photo feature. No poetry. Buys 100 mss/year. Send complete ms. Length: 100-1,300 words. Pays $40-250, contributor copies or other premiums "if requested." Sometimes pays expenses of writers on assignment. Send photos with submission. Offers no additional payment for photos accepted with ms. Identification of subjects required. Buys all rights.

Fiction: Adventure, fantasy, historical, humorous, mainstream, mystery, novel excerpts, slice-of-life vignettes and suspense. "This is a family magazine. No graphic violence, pornography or other inappropriate material. *I Love Cats* is strictly 'G-rated.' " Buys 50 mss/year. Send complete ms. Length: 500-1,500 words. Pays $40-250.

Fillers: Gags to be illustrated by cartoonist and short humor. Buys 10/year. Pays $10-35.

Tips: "Please keep stories short and concise. Send complete ms with photos, if possible. I buy lots of first-time authors. Nonfiction pieces w/color photos are always in short supply. With the exception of the standing columns, the rest of the magazine is open to freelancers. Be witty, humorous or take a different approach to writing."

LONE STAR HORSE REPORT, P.O. Box 14767, Fort Worth TX 76117. (817)838-8642. Editor: Henry L. King. 15-20% freelance written. Monthly magazine on horses and horse people in and around Dallas/Ft. Worth metroplex. Estab. 1983. Circ. 7,500. Pays on publication. Publishes ms an average of 2 months after acceptance. Byline given. Buys first and second serial (reprint) rights to material originally published elsewhere. Submit seasonal/holiday material 2 months in advance. Previously published submissions OK. Reports in 2 weeks on queries; 1 month on mss. *Writer's Market* recommends allowing 2 months for reply. Sample copy $1. Writer's guidelines for #10 SASE.

Nonfiction: Interview/profile (horsemen living in trade area); photo feature (horses, farms, arenas, facilities, people in trade area). Buys 30-40 mss/year. Query with published clips or send complete ms. Length: 200-2,000 words. Pays $15-60. Sometimes pays the expenses of writers on assignment.

Photos: State availability of photos. Pays $5 for 5×7 b&w or color prints. Buys one-time rights.

Tips: "We need reports of specific horse-related events in north Texas area such as trail rides, rodeos, play days, shows, etc., and also feature articles on horse farms, outstanding horses and/or horsemen. Since Texas now has pari-mutuel horse racing, more emphasis will be placed on coverage of racing and racehorse breeding. We report on the actions of the racing commission, locations of tracks, construction and ownership of those tracks, and the economic impact of the racing industry as new breeding farms and training facilities are established."

MUSHING, Stellar Communications, Inc., P.O. Box 149, Ester AK 99725-0149. (907)479-0454. Fax: (907)479-0454. Publisher: Todd Hoener. Managing Editor: Diane Herrmann. Bimonthly magazine on "all aspects of dog driving activities. We include information (how-to), nonfiction (entertaining), health, ethics, news and history stories." Estab. 1987. Circ. 6,000. Pays on publication. Publishes ms an average of 4 months after acceptance. Byline given. Buys first North American serial and second serial (reprint) rights. Submit seasonal/holiday material 4 months in advance. Query for electronic submissions. Reports in 1-6 months. Sample copy $3.50. Free writer's guidelines. Call for information.

Nonfiction: Historical, how-to, humor, interview/profile, new product, personal experience, photo feature, technical, travel. Themes are: November/December—Christmas, races and places, skiing, winter trips; January/February—travel, main dog sled race, recreation and work season; March/April—breeding, puppies, breakup; May/June—health and nutrition; July/August—dog packing, carting, musher interviews; September/October—equipment, events calendar, getting geared up for winter. Query with or without published clips, or send complete ms. Length: 500-3,000 words. Pays $50-250 for articles. Payment depends on quality, deadlines, experience. Sometimes pays expenses of writers on assignment.

Photos: Send photos with submission. Reviews contact sheets, transparencies, prints. Offers $20-150/photo. Captions, model releases, identification of subjects required. Buys one-time and second reprint rights. We look for good b&w and quality color for covers and specials.

Fillers: Anecdotes, facts, cartoons, newsbreaks, short humor. Length: 100-250 words. Pays $20-35.

Tips: "Read our magazine. Know something about dog-driven, dog-powered sports."

PAINT HORSE JOURNAL, American Paint Horse Association, P.O. Box 961023, Fort Worth TX 76161. (817)439-3400, ext. 210. Fax: (817)439-3484. Assoc. Editor: Dan Streeter. 10% freelance written. Works with a small number of new/unpublished writers each year. Monthly magazine for people who raise, breed and show Paint horses. Estab. 1966. Circ. 15,000. **Pays on acceptance.** Publishes ms an average of 3 months after acceptance. Buys first North American serial rights plus reprint rights occasionally. Pays negotiable kill fee. Byline given. Phone queries OK, but prefers written query. Submit seasonal/holiday material 3 months in advance. Reprints OK; send typed ms with rights for sale noted and information about when and where the article previously appeared. Pays 30% of their fee for an original article. Reports in 1 month. Sample copy for 9×12 SAE with 5 first class stamps. Writer's guidelines for #10 SASE.

Nonfiction: General interest (personality pieces on well-known owners of Paints); historical (Paint horses in the past—particular horses and the breed in general); how-to (train and show horses); photo feature (Paint horses). Now seeking informative well-written articles on recreational riding. Buys 4-5 mss/issue. Send complete ms. Pays $25-250.

Photos: Send photos with ms. Offers no additional payment for photos accepted with accompanying ms. Uses 3×5 or larger b&w or color glossy prints; 35mm or larger color transparencies. Captions required. Photos must illustrate article and must include Paint Horses.

Tips: "*PHJ* needs breeder-trainer articles, Paint horse marketing and timely articles from areas throughout the US and Canada. We are looking for more recreational and how-to articles. We are beginning to cover equine activity such as trail riding, orienteering and other outdoor events. Photos with copy are almost always essential. Well-written first person articles are welcomed. Submit items that show a definite understanding of the horse business. Be sure you understand precisely what a Paint horse is as defined by the American Paint Horse Association. Use proper equine terminology and proper grounding in ability to communicate thoughts."

PETS MAGAZINE, Moorshead Publications, 797 Don Mills Rd., Don Mills, Ontario M3C 3S5 Canada. (416)696-5488. Fax: (416)696-7395. Editor: Edward Zapletal. Editorial Director/Veterinarian: Dr. Tom Frisby. 50% freelance written. Bimonthly magazine on pets. Circ. 56,000 distributed by vet clinics; 7,000 personal subscriptions. Pays on publication. Publishes ms an average of 4 months after acceptance. Buys all rights. Submit seasonal/holiday material 4 months in advance. Previously published submissions OK (sometimes). Query for electronic submissions. Sample copy for #10 SAE with 95¢ IRC or Canadian stamps. Free writer's guidelines.

Nonfiction: General interest, historical, how-to (train, bathe/groom, build dog houses, make cat toys and photograph pets), breed profile and photo feature. No "I remember Fluffy. No poetry, no fiction." Buys 40 mss/year. Query with outline. Length: 300-2,000 words. Pays 10-18¢ (Canadian)/ word.

Photos: State availability of photos with submission. Reviews prints 3×5 and larger, b&w preferred. Offers $25 maximum/photo. Identification of subjects required. Buys all rights.

Fillers: Facts. Query with samples. Buys 1-2/year. Length: 100-400 words. Pays 10-15¢(Canadian)/word.

Tips: "Always call or send topic outline first; we always have a backlog of freelance articles waiting to be run. Prefers factual, information pieces, not anecdotal or merely humorous, but can be written with humor; we do not cover controversial areas such as product testing, vivisection, puppy mills, pound seizure."

PURE-BRED DOGS/AMERICAN KENNEL GAZETTE, American Kennel Club, 51 Madison Ave., New York NY 10010-1603. (212)696-8331. Fax: (212)696-8299. Features Editor: Dominique C. Davis. 80% freelance written. Monthly association publication on pure-bred dogs. "Material is slanted to interests of fanciers of pure-bred dogs as opposed to commercial interests." Estab. 1889. Circ. 58,000. **Pays on acceptance.** Publishes ms an average of 6 months after acceptance. Byline given. Offers 30% kill fee. Buys first North American serial rights. Submit seasonal/holiday material 6 months in advance. Reports in up to 6 months. Sample copy and writer's guidelines for 9×12 SAE with 11 first class stamps.

Nonfiction: General interest, historical, how-to, humor, photo feature, travel. No profiles, poetry, tributes to individual dogs, or fiction. Buys about 75 mss/year. Query with or without published clips or send complete ms. Length: 1,000-2,500 words. Pays $100-300. Sometimes pays expenses of writers on assignment.

Photos: Send photos with submission. Reviews transparencies and prints. Offers $25-100/photo. Captions required. Buys one-time rights. (Photo contest guidelines for #10 SASE.)

Fiction: Annual short fiction contest only. Guidelines for #10 SASE. Twelve annual contest winners are anthologized in separate booklet.

Tips: "Contributors should be involved in dog fancy or be expert in the area they write about (veterinary, showing, field trialing, obedience, training, dogs in legislation, dog art or history or literature). All submissions are welcome but the author must be credible. Veterinary articles must be written by or with veterinarians. Humorous features are personal experiences relative to pure-bred dogs. For features generally, know the subject thoroughly and be conversant with jargon peculiar to dog sport."

THE QUARTER HORSE JOURNAL, P.O. Box 32470, Amarillo TX 79120. (806)376-4811. Fax: (806)376-8364. Editor-in-Chief: Audie Rackley. Editor: Jim Jennings. 20% freelance written. Prefers to work with published/ established writers. Monthly official publication of the American Quarter Horse Association. Estab. 1948. Circ. 65,000. **Pays on acceptance.** Publishes ms an average of 3 months after acceptance. Buys first North American serial rights. Submit seasonal/holiday material 2 months in advance. Reports in 2 months. Free sample copy and writer's guidelines.

Nonfiction: Historical ("those that retain our western heritage"); how-to (fitting, grooming, showing, or anything that relates to owning, showing, or breeding); informational (educational clinics, current news); interview (feature-type stories—must be about established horses or people who have made a contribution to the business); personal opinion; and technical (equine updates, new surgery procedures, etc.). Buys 20 mss/year. Length: 800-2,500 words. Pays $50-250.

Photos: Purchased with accompanying ms. Captions required. Send prints or transparencies. Uses 5×7 or 8×10 b&w glossy prints; 2¼×2¼, 4×5 or 35 mm color transparencies. Offers no additional payment for photos accepted with accompanying ms.
Tips: "Writers must have a knowledge of the horse business."

REPTILE & AMPHIBIAN MAGAZINE, RD3, Box 3709A, Pottsville PA 17901-9219. (717)622-6050. Fax: (717)622-5858. Editor: Norman Frank, D.V.M. 80% freelance written. Full-color digest size bimonthly magazine covering reptiles and amphibians. Devoted to the amateur herpetologist who is generally college-educated and familiar with the basics of herpetology. Estab. 1989. Circ. 10,000. **Pays on acceptance.** Publishes ms an average of 4-6 months after acceptance. Byline given. Buys first North American serial, one-time and (occasionally) second serial (reprint) rights. Send photocopy of article or short story and information about when and where the article previously appeared. For reprints, pays 100% of the amount paid for an original article. Previously published submissions OK. Reports in 2 months. Sample copy $4. Writer's guidelines for #10 SASE.
Nonfiction: General interest, photo feature and technical. Publishes articles on life cycles of various reptiles and amphibians, natural history, captive care and breeding. No first-person narrative, "me-and-Joe" stories or articles by writers unfamiliar with the subject matter. "Readers are already familiar with the basics of herpetology and are usually advanced amateur hobbyists." Buys 30 mss/year. Query or send complete ms. Length: 1,500-2,000 words. Pays $75-100. Sometimes pays expenses of familiar or regular writer on assignment. Occasionally publishes reprints. Send photocopy of article with information about where and when it previously appeared. Pays same as for original articles.
Photos: Send photos with submission whenever possible. Reviews 35mm slide transparencies, 4×6, 5×7 and 8×10 glossy prints. Offers $10 for b&w, $25 for color photos. Captions, model releases and identification of subjects required. Animals should be identified by common and/or scientific name. Buys one-time rights.
Columns/Departments: Photo Dept./Herp●Art Dept., 750-1,000 words; Book Review, 750-1,000 words. Buys 12 mss/year. Send complete ms. Pays $50-75.
Tips: "Note your personal qualifications, such as experience in the field or advanced education. Writers have the best chance selling us feature articles—know your subject and supply high quality color photos."

TROPICAL FISH HOBBYIST, "The World's Most Widely Read Aquarium Monthly," TFH Publications, Inc., 211 W. Sylvania Ave., Neptune City NJ 07753. (908)988-8400. Editor: Ray Hunziker. Managing Editor: Neal Pronek. Assistant Editor: Mary Sweeney. 75% freelance written. Monthly magazine covering the tropical fish hobby. "We favor articles well illustrated with good color slides and aimed at both the neophyte and veteran tropical fish hobbyist." Estab. 1952. Circ. 60,000. **Pays on acceptance.** Publishes ms an average of 4 months after acceptance. Byline given. Buys all rights. Submit seasonal/holiday material 4 months in advance. Reports in 1 month. Sample copy $3 for 9×12 SAE with 6 first class stamps. Writer's guidelines for #10 SASE.
Nonfiction: General interest, how-to, photo feature, technical, and articles dealing with beginning and advanced aspects of the aquarium hobby. No "how I got started in the hobby" articles that impart little solid information. Buys 40-50 mss/year. Length: 500-2,500 words. Pays $25-100.
Photos: State availability of photos or send photos with ms. Pays $10 for 35mm transparencies. Identification of subjects required. "Originals returned to owner, who may market them elsewhere."
Fiction: "On occasion, we will review a fiction piece relevant to the aquarium hobby."
Tips: "We cater to a specialized readership—people knowledgable in fish culture. Prospective authors should be familiar with subject; photography skills are a plus. It's a help if an author we've never dealt with queries first or submits a short item."

THE WESTERN HORSEMAN, World's Leading Horse Magazine Since 1936, Western Horseman, Inc., P.O. Box 7980, Colorado Springs CO 80933-7980. (719)633-5524. Editor: Pat Close. 50% freelance written. Works with a small number of new/unpublished writers each year. Monthly magazine. Estab. 1936. Circ. 210,000. **Pays on acceptance.** Publishes ms an average of 5 months after acceptance. Buys one-time and North American serial rights. Byline given. Submit seasonal/holiday material 6 months in advance. Reports in 3 weeks. Sample copy $5. Writer's guidelines for #10 SASE.
Nonfiction: How-to (horse training, care of horses, tips, ranch/farm management, etc.) and informational (on rodeos, ranch life, historical articles of the West emphasizing horses). Buys 100 mss/year. Length: 500-2,000 words. Payment begins at $35-300; "sometimes higher by special arrangement."
Photos: Send photos with ms. Offers no additional payment for photos. Uses 5×7 or 8×10 b&w glossy prints and 35mm transparencies. Captions required.
Tips: "Submit clean copy with professional quality photos. All copy, including computer copy, should be double-spaced. Stay away from generalities. Writing style should show a deep interest in horses coupled with a wide knowledge of the subject."

Art and Architecture

Listed here are publications about art, art history, specific art forms and architecture written for art patrons, architects, artists and art enthusiasts. Publications addressing the business and management side of the art industry are listed in the Art, Design and Collectibles category of the Trade section. Trade publications for architecture can be found in Building Interiors and Construction and Contracting sections.

‡**AIRBRUSH ACTION**, Airbrush Action, Inc., P.O. Box 2052, Lakewood NJ 08701. (908)364-2111. Editor: Cliff Stieglitz. Managing Editor: Lawrence Gottried. Contact: Cliff Stieglitz. 75% freelance written. Bimonthly magazine for airbrushing in illustration, textiles, signs, fine art. "*Airbrush Action*, is edited for art professionals and beginners in all applications of airbrushing. We require mostly how-to technical editorial and artist profiles." Estab. 1985. Circ. 50,000. Pays on publication. Publishes ms an average of 1-2 months after acceptance. Byline given. Offers 50% kill fee. Buys all rights. Editorial lead time 2-10 months. Submit seasonal material 3-6 months in advance. Query for electronic submissions. Sample copy and writer's guidelines free on request.
Nonfiction: How-to and technical airbrushing. Query. Pays $100 minimum. Sometimes negotiates payment in contributor's copies. Sometimes pays expenses of writers on assignment (limit agreed upon in advance).
Photos: State availability of photos with submission. Reviews 4 × 5 35mm transparencies. Negotiates payment individually. Captions, model releases and identification of subjects required. Buys one time rights.
Columns/Departments: Q&A (Questions & Answers); Tech Corner (technical aspects of airbrushing); Airbrush Report (special interest/unusual uses of airbrushing). Query. Pays $50-150.
Fillers: Anecdotes, facts, gags to be illustrated by cartoonist. Pays $25-75.
Tips: "Writers approaching us should have good technical knowledge of airbrushing. We are most open to how-to's. Provide/submit clear how-to on a particular airbrush technique or painting."

THE AMERICAN ART JOURNAL, Kennedy Galleries, Inc. 40 W. 57th St., 5th Floor, New York NY 10019. (212)541-9600. Fax: (212)333-7451. Editor-in-Chief: Jayne A. Kuchna. Prefers to work with published/established writers; works with a small number of new/unpublished writers each year. Semiannual scholarly magazine of American art history of the 17th, 18th, 19th and 20th centuries, including painting, sculpture, architecture, decorative arts, etc., for people with a serious interest in American art, and who are already knowledgeable about the subject. Readers are scholars, curators, collectors, students of American art, or persons with a strong interest in Americana. Circ. 2,000. **Pays on acceptance.** Publishes ms an average of 6 months after acceptance. Buys all rights, but will reassign rights to writer. Byline given. Reports in 2 months. Sample copy $11.
Nonfiction: "All articles are about some phase or aspect of American art history." No how-to articles or reviews of exhibitions. No book reviews or opinion pieces. No human interest approaches to artists' lives. No articles written in a casual or "folksy" style. *Writing style must be formal and serious*. Buys 15-20 mss/year. Submit complete ms "with good cover letter." No queries. Length: 2,500-8,000 words. Pays $300-600.
Photos: Purchased with accompanying ms. Captions required. Uses b&w only. Offers no additional payment for photos accepted with accompanying ms.
Tips: "Articles *must be* scholarly, thoroughly documented, well-researched, well-written and illustrated. Whenever possible, all manuscripts must be accompanied by b&w photographs which have been integrated into the text by the use of numbers."

AMERICAN INDIAN ART MAGAZINE, American Indian Art, Inc., 7314 E. Osborn Dr., Scottsdale AZ 85251-6417. (602)994-5445. Editor: Roanne P. Goldfein. 97% freelance written. Works with a small number of new/unpublished writers each year. Quarterly magazine covering Native American art, historic and contemporary, including new research on any aspect of Native American art north of the US/Mexico border. Estab. 1975. Circ. 20,000. Pays on publication. Publishes ms an average of 3 months after acceptance. Byline given. Buys one-time and first rights. Simultaneous queries OK. Reports in 3 weeks on queries; 3 months on mss. Writer's guidelines for #10 SASE.
Nonfiction: New research on any aspect of Native American art. No previously published work or personal interviews with artists. Buys 12-18 mss/year. Query. Length: 1,000-2,500 words. Pays $75-300.
Tips: "The magazine is devoted to all aspects of Native American art. Some of our readers are knowledgeable about the field and some know very little. We seek articles that offer something to both groups. Articles reflecting original research are preferred to those summarizing previously published information."

ART OF CALIFORNIA, 1125 Jefferson St., Napa CA 94559. (707)226-1776. Editor: Gregory Saffell. Executive Editor: Monica E. Thow. 70% freelance written. Bimonthly magazine that covers visual fine arts in CA and the art and artists of the state. "As the only national and international source of information on the visual fine arts of California, the magazine includes scholarly and engaging articles that discuss the art of California from its blossoming in the 19th century through the vibrant and active movements of today. Readers include collectors, critics and art lovers." Estab. 1988. Circ. 20,000 Pays on publication. Publishes ms an average of 9 months after acceptance. Byline given. No kill fee. Buys first rights. Reports in 9 months. Sample copy $5 with 9 × 12 SAE and 10 first class stamps.

Nonfiction: Essays, general interest, interview/profile and photo feature. "It is imperative that prospective writers familiarize themselves with our magazine. Articles written without any direct knowledge of our publication will most likely not be appropriate." Buys approximately 24 mss/year. Query with published clips, or send complete ms. Length: 300-1,500 words. Pays $100-400 for assigned articles. Sometimes pays writers with contributor copies or other premiums rather than a cash payment upon agreement with author.

Photos: State availability of photos with submission or send photos with submission. Reviews 4×5 transparencies. Offers no additional payment for photos accepted with ms. Identification of subjects required. Buys one-time rights.

Tips: "*Art of California* magazine is a glossy, four-color publication featuring scholarly, yet engaging and understandable editorial specifically covering the art and artists of CA. We do not feature commercial art; we focus on the fine arts (i.e. painting, sculpture, furniture, photography, architecture, etc.). Writers need a background in the arts and/or writing about the arts. They cannot be merely journalists with no understanding or appreciation of the arts."

ART TIMES, A Cultural and Creative Journal, P.O. Box 730, Mount Marion NY 12456-0730. (914)246-6944. Fax: (914)246-6944. Editor: Raymond J. Steiner. 10% freelance written. Prefers to work with published/established writers; works with a small number of new/unpublished writers each year. Monthly tabloid covering the arts (visual, theatre, dance, etc.). "*Art Times* covers the art fields and is distributed in locations most frequented by those enjoying the arts. Our copies are sold at newsstands and are distributed throughout upstate New York counties as well as in most of the galleries in Soho, 57th Street and Madison Avenue in the metropolitan area; locations include theaters, galleries, museums, cultural centers and the like. Our readers are mostly over 40, affluent, art-conscious and sophisticated." Estab. 1984. Circ. 15,000. Pays on publication. Publishes ms an average of 1 year after acceptance. Byline given. Buys first serial rights. Submit seasonal/holiday material 8 months in advance. Simultaneous queries and simultaneous submissions OK. Reports in 3 months on queries; 6 months on mss. Sample copy for 9×12 SAE with 6 first class stamps. Writer's guidelines for #10 SASE.

Fiction: "We're looking for short fiction that aspires to be *literary*. No excessive violence, sexist, off-beat, erotic, sports, or juvenile fiction." Buys 8-10 mss/year. Send complete ms. Length: 1,500 words maximum. Pays $15 maximum (honorarium) and 1 year's free subscription.

Poetry: Poet's Niche. Avant-garde, free verse, haiku, light verse and traditional. "We prefer well-crafted 'literary' poems. No excessively sentimental poetry." Buys 30-35 poems/year. Submit maximum 6 poems. Length: 20 lines maximum. Offers contributor copies and 1 year's free subscription.

Tips: "Be advised that we are presently on an approximate two year lead. We are now receiving 300-400 poems and 40-50 short stories per month. We only publish 2-3 poems and one story each issue. Be familiar with *Art Times* and its special audience. *Art Times* has literary leanings with articles written by a staff of scholars knowledgeable in their respective fields. Although an 'arts' publication, we observe no restrictions (other than noted) in accepting fiction/poetry other than a concern for quality writing—subjects can cover anything and not specifically arts."

THE ARTIST'S MAGAZINE, F&W Publications, Inc., 1507 Dana Ave., Cincinnati OH 45207-1005. Editor: Greg Albert. 80% freelance written. Works with a small number of new/unpublished writers each year. Monthly magazine covering primarily two-dimensional art instruction for working artists. "Ours is a highly visual approach to teaching the serious amateur artist techniques that will help him improve his skills and market his work. The style should be crisp and immediately engaging." Circ. 250,000. **Pays on acceptance.** Publishes ms an average of 4 months after acceptance. Bionote given for feature material. Offers 20% kill fee. Buys first North American serial and second serial (reprint) rights. Simultaneous queries and previously published submissions OK "as long as noted as such." Reports in 2 months. Sample copy $3 for 9×12 SAE with 3 first class stamps. Writer's guidelines for #10 SASE.

• Writers must have working knowledge of art techniques. This magazine's most consistent need is for instructional articles written in the artist's voice. They often ask writers to forsake a byline.

Nonfiction: Instructional only—how an artist uses a particular technique, how he handles a particular subject or medium or how he markets his work. "The emphasis must be on how the reader can learn some method of improving his artwork or the marketing of it." No unillustrated articles; no seasonal/holiday material; no travel articles; no profiles of artists (except for "The Artist's Life," below). Buys 60 mss/year. Query first; all queries must be accompanied by slides, transparencies, prints or tearsheets of the artist's work as well as the artist's bio, and the writer's bio and clips. Length: 1,000-2,500 words. Pays $100-350 and up. Sometimes pays the expenses of writers on assignment.

Photos: "Transparencies are required with every accepted article since these are essential for our instructional format. Full captions must accompany these." Buys one-time rights.

Departments: Three departments are open to freelance writers. Strictly Business (articles dealing with the business and legal end of selling art: taxes, recordkeeping, copyright, contracts, etc.). Query first. Length: 1,800 word limit. Pays $150 and up. The Artist's Life and P.S. The Artist's Life (profiles and brief items about artists and their work; also, art-related games, puzzles and poetry). Query first with samples of artist's work for profiles; send complete ms for other items. Length: 600 words maximum. Pays $50 and up for profiles;

up to $25 for brief items and poetry. P.S. (a humorous look at art from the artist's point of view, or at least sympathetic to the artist). Send complete ms. Pays $50 and up.
Tips: "Look at several current issues and read the author's guidelines carefully. Remember that our readers are fine and graphic artists."

EQUINE IMAGES, The National Magazine of Equine Art, Equine Images Ltd., P.O. Box 916, Fort Dodge IA 50501. (800)247-2000, ext. 213. Fax: (800)247-2000, ext. 217. Editor: Paula Hauser. Publisher: Michael McCormick. 80% freelance written. Bimonthly magazine of equine art. "*Equine Images* serves collectors and equine art enthusiasts. We write for a sophisticated, culturally-oriented audience." Estab. 1986. Circ. 35,000. Pays on publication. Byline given. Buys first rights and makes work-for-hire assignments. Previously published submissions OK. Reports in 1 month. Sample copy $10 for 9 × 12 SAE. Writer's guidelines for #10 SASE.
Nonfiction: Historical/nostalgic (history of the horse in art), how-to (art collections), interview/profile (equine artists, galleries, collectors), personal experience (of equine artists and collectors) and photo feature (artworks or collections). "No articles about horses in general—just horse art." Buys 8-10 mss/year. Query with published clips. Length: 500-3,000 words. Pays $150-400 for assigned articles; $100-350 for unsolicited articles. Reprints OK; send photocopy of article and information about when and where the article previously appeared. Pays 50% of their fee for an original article.
Photos: State availability of photos with submission. Writer responsible for sending visuals with finished manuscript. Reviews contact sheets, transparencies, prints. Offers no additional payment for photos accepted with ms. Identification of subjects required. Buys one-time rights.
Tips: "We are interested only in art-related subjects. We are looking for stories that help art collectors better understand, expand or protect their collections. The most promising categories for writers are profiles of prominent artists and equine galleries or museums. Send a good query letter with accompanying visuals, along with published clips or writing samples."

THE ORIGINAL ART REPORT, P.O. Box 1641, Chicago IL 60690-1641. Editor and Publisher: Frank Salantrie. Newsletter emphasizing "visual art conditions from the visual artists' and general public's perspectives." Estab. 1967. Pays on publication. Reports in 2 weeks. Sample copy $1.50 with 1 first class stamp.
Nonfiction: Expose (art galleries, government agencies ripping off artists, or ignoring them); historical (perspective pieces relating to now); humor (whenever possible); informational (material that is unavailable in other art publications); inspirational (acts and ideas of courage); interview (with artists, other experts; serious material on visual art conditions; no profiles); personal opinion; technical (brief items to recall traditional methods of producing art); travel (places in the world where artists are welcomed and honored); philosophical, economic, aesthetic, and artistic. "We would like to receive investigative articles on government and private arts agencies, and nonprofits, too, perhaps hiding behind status to carry on for business entities. Exclusive interest in visual fine art condition as it affects individuals, society and artists and as they affect it. Must take advocacy position. Prefer controversial subject matter and originality of treatment. Also artist's position on non-art topics. No vanity profiles of artists, arts organizations and arts promoters' operations." Buys 4-5 mss/year. Query or submit complete ms. Length: 1,000 words maximum. Pays 1¢/word.
Columns/Departments: In Back of the Individual Artist. Artists express their views about non-art topics. After all, artists are in this world, too. WOW (Worth One Wow), Worth Repeating, and Worth Repeating Again. Basically, these are reprint items with introduction to give context and source, including complete name and address of publication. Looking for insightful, succinct commentary. Submit complete ms. Length: 500 words maximum and copy of item. Pays ½¢/word.
Tips: "We have a stronger than ever emphasis on editorial opinion or commentary, based on fact, of the visual art condition: economics, finances, politics and manufacture of art and the social and individual implications of and to fine art."

SOUTHWEST ART, CBH Publishing, P.O. Box 460535, Houston TX 77256-0535. (713)850-0990. Fax: (713)850-1314. Editor-in-Chief: Susan H. McGarry. Managing Editor: Jacqueline M. Pontello. 60% freelance written. Monthly fine arts magazine. "*SWA* is directed to art collectors interested in artists, market trends and art history of the American West." Estab. 1971. Circ. 72,000. **Pays on acceptance.** Publishes ms an average of 1 year after acceptance. Byline given. Offers $125 kill fee. Submit seasonal/holiday material 8 months in advance. Reports in 3-6 months. Free sample copy and writer's guidelines.
Nonfiction: Book excerpts, interview/profile and opinion. No fiction or poetry. Buys 84 mss/year. Query with published clips. Length 1,600-1,800 words. Pays $400 for assigned articles. Send photos with submission. Reprints OK; send tearsheet with information about when and where the article previously appeared.
Photos: Reviews transparencies (35mm, 2¼, 4 × 5) and 8 × 10 prints. Captions and identification of subjects required. Buys all rights.

THEDAMU, The Black Arts Magazine, Detroit Black Arts Alliance, 13217 Livernois, Detroit MI 48238-3162. (313)931-3427. Editor: David Rambeau. Managing Editor: Titilaya Akanke. Art Director: Charles Allen. 20% freelance written. Monthly literary magazine on the arts. "We publish Afro-American feature articles on local artists." Estab. 1965. Circ. 4,000. Pays on publication. Publishes 4 months after acceptance. Byline given. Buys one-time rights. Submit seasonal/holiday material 4 months in advance. Simultaneous and previously published submissions OK. Query for electronic submissions. Reprints OK; send photocopy of article and information about when and where the article previously appeared. Pays 50% of their fee for an original article. Reports in 1 month on queries; 3 months on mss. Sample copy $2 for 6×9 SAE with 4 first class stamps. Writer's guidelines for #10 SASE.

Nonfiction: Essays and interview/profile. Buys 20 mss/year. Send complete ms. Length: 500-1,500 words. Pays $10-25 for unsolicited articles. Pays with contributor copies or other premiums if writer agrees.

Photos: State availability of photos with submission. Reviews 5×7 prints. Offers no additional payment for photos accepted with ms. Captions, model releases and identification of subjects required. Buys one-time rights.

Tips: "Send a resume and sample ms. Query for fiction, poetry, plays and film/video scenarios. Especially interested in Afro-centric cartoonists for special editions and exhibitions."

WESTART, P.O. Box 6868, Auburn CA 95604. (916)885-0969. Editor-in-Chief: Martha Garcia. Semimonthly tabloid emphasizing art for practicing artists and artists/craftsmen; students of art and art patrons. 20 pages. Estab. 1961. Circ. 5,000. Pays on publication. Buys all rights. Byline given. Phone queries OK. Free sample copy and writer's guidelines.

Nonfiction: Informational, photo feature and profile. No hobbies. Buys 6-8 mss/year. Query or submit complete ms. Include SASE for reply or return. Length: 700-800 words. Pays 50¢/column inch.

Photos: Purchased with or without accompanying ms. Send b&w prints. Pays 50¢/column inch.

Tips: "We publish information which is current — that is, we will use a review of an exhibition only if exhibition is still open on the date of publication. Therefore, reviewer must be familiar with our printing and news deadlines."

WILDLIFE ART NEWS, The International Magazine of Wildlife Art, Pothole Publications, Inc., 4725 Hwy. 7, P.O. Box 16246, St. Louis Park MN 55416-0246. (612)927-9056. Fax: (612)927-9353. Editor: Robert Koenke. Senior Editor: Rebecca Hakala Rowland. 80% freelance written. Bimonthly magazine of wildlife art and conservation. "*Wildlife Art News* is the world's largest wildlife art magazine. Features cover interviews on living artists as well as wildlife art masters, illustrators and conservation organizations. Audience is publishers, collectors, galleries, museums, show promoters worldwide." Estab. 1982. Circ. 51,000. **Pays on acceptance.** Publishes ms an average of 6 months after acceptance. Byline given. Negotiable kill fee. Buys second serial (reprint) rights. Reports in 4-6 months. Sample copy for 9×12 SAE with 10 first class stamps. Writer's guidelines for #10 SASE.

Nonfiction: Buys 40 mss/year. Query with published clips. Length: 800-5,000 words. Pays $150-1,000 for assigned articles.

Columns/Departments: Buys up to 6 mss/year. Pays $100-300.

WOMEN ARTISTS NEWS, Midmarch Arts Press, 300 Riverside, New York NY 10025-5239. Editor: Judy Seigel. 70-90% freelance written. Eager to work with new/unpublished writers. Annual magazine for "artists and art historians, museum and gallery personnel, students, teachers, crafts personnel, art critics and writers." Estab. 1975. Circ. 5,000. "Token payment as funding permits." Publishes ms an average of 2 months after acceptance. Byline given. Submit seasonal material 2 months in advance. Reports in 1 month. *Writer's Market* recommends allowing 2 months for reply. Sample copy $3.

Nonfiction: Features, historical, interview, book reviews and photo feature. Query or submit complete ms. Length: 500-2,500 words.

Photos: Used with or without accompanying ms. Query or submit contact sheet or prints. Pays $5 for 5×7 b&w prints when money is available. Captions required.

Associations

Association publications allow writers to write for national audiences while covering local stories. If your town has a Kiwanis, Lions or Rotary Club chapter, one of its projects might merit a story in the club's magazine. If you are a member of the organization, find out before you write an article if the publication pays members for stories; some associations do not. In addition, some association publications gather their own club information and rely on freelancers solely for outside features. Be sure to find out what these policies are before you submit a manuscript. Club-financed magazines that carry material not directly related to the group's activities are classified by their subject matter in the Consumer and Trade sections.

THE ASSOCIATION EXECUTIVE, An Independent News Magazine Serving Association, Hospitality and Meeting Executives, Special Editions Publishing, Inc. 765 Douglas Ave., Altamonte Springs FL 32714-2541. Editor: Paul Singletary. 1% freelance written. Monthly tabloid on association and hospitality news. "We are primarily a news magazine, with special sections for features and news features. Our magazine is read by people who run associations and plan meetings. They are interested in things that affect their members and their associations." Circ. 4,600. Pays on publication on an individual basis. Byline given. Submit seasonal/holiday material 2 months in advance. Simultaneous and previously published submissions OK. Query for electronic submissions. Reports in 1 month on queries and mss. Sample copy and writer's guidelines for 9 × 12 SAE with 4 first class stamps.

Nonfiction: Opinion (the effect of current affairs on the association industry), travel (especially cities with convention facilities) and legislative. Feature sections on convention facilities: May: the Carolinas; July: Downtown Facilities; August: Georgia; October: Florida; November: Tennessee; and December: Virginia. Buys 1 ms/year. Query with or without published clips or send complete ms. Length: 500-2,500 words. Pays $1-50 for unsolicited articles.

Photos: Send photos with submission. Reviews transparencies (1 × 1¼) and 4 × 5 prints. Offers no additional payment for photos accepted with ms. Buys all rights.

Columns/Departments: Executive to Executive (ways and ideas for effective managament). Buys 1 ms/year. Send complete ms. Length: 500-1,500 words. Pays $1-50.

Tips: "Our magazine is easy to break into. Phone call will be answered right away, with explanations on our readers interests. Make sure that it relates to the interests of the association or convention planning industries."

COMEDY WRITERS ASSOCIATION NEWSLETTER, P.O. Box 023304, Brooklyn NY 11202-0066. (718)855-5057. Editor: Robert Makinson. 10% freelance written. Quarterly newsletter on comedy writing for association members. Estab. 1989. **Pays on acceptance.** Publishes ms an average of 3 months after acceptance. Byline given. Buys all rights. Reports in 2 weeks on queries; 1 month on mss. Sample copy $4. Writer's guidelines for #10 SASE.

Nonfiction: How-to, humor, opinion and personal experience. "No exaggerations about the sales that you make and what you are paid. Be accurate." Query. Length: 250-500 words. Pays 3¢/word.

Photos: State availability of photos with submission. Offers no additional payment for photos with ms.

Fillers: Facts. Length: 100 words maximum. Pays 3¢/word.

Tips: "The easiest way to be mentioned in the publication is to submit short jokes. (Payment is $1-3 per joke.)"

DISCOVERY YMCA, YMCA of the USA, 101 N. Wacker Dr., Chicago IL 60606-7386. (312)269-0523. Managing Editor: Mary Pyke. 40% freelance written. Quarterly magazine covering the YMCA movement in 50 states. "We concentrate on how YMCAs overcome obstacles and help solve pressing social problems." Estab. 1982. Circ, 95,000. **Pays on acceptance.** Publishes ms an average of 1-2 months after acceptance. Byline given. No kill fee. Makes work-for-hire assignments. Rarely accepts unsolicited submissions. Writer's guidelines for #10 SASE.

Nonfiction: Almost exclusively features/photo essays focusing on how local YMCAs meet community service needs. "No testimonies on how wonderful the YMCA is." Buys 10-12 mss/year. Query. Length: 2,500-15,000 words. Pays $550 for assigned articles; $300 for unsolicited articles. Pays expenses of writers on assignment.

Tips: "Send 3 or 4 pieces that you are really proud of having written. I don't need to see breadth of coverage but style and complete grasp of the subject. We are trying to diversify our pool of freelancers. We very much encourage writers of color to contact us. The YMCA is an incredibly diverse organization to match."

THE ELKS MAGAZINE, 425 W. Diversey, Chicago IL 60614-6196. Editor: Fred D. Oakes. Managing Editor: Judith L. Keogh. 50% freelance written. Prefers to work with published/established writers. Magazine published 10 times/year emphasizing general interest with family appeal. Estab. 1922. Circ. 1.5 million. **Pays on acceptance.** Buys first North American serial rights. Reports in 6-8 weeks. Sample copy and writer's guidelines for 9 × 12 SAE with 85¢ postage.

Nonfiction: Articles of information, business, contemporary life problems and situations, nostalgia, or just interesting topics, ranging from medicine, science and history to sports. "The articles should not just be a rehash of existing material. They must be fresh, thought-provoking, well-researched and documented." No fiction, political articles, travel, fillers or verse. Buys 2-3 mss/issue. Query; no phone queries. Length: 1,500-3,000 words. Pays from $100.

Tips: "Requirements are clearly stated in our guidelines. Loose, wordy pieces are not accepted. A submission, following a query letter go-ahead, should include several b&w prints if the piece lends itself to illustration. We offer no additional payment for photos accepted with manuscripts. We expect to continue targeting our content to an older (50+) demographic."

FEDCO REPORTER, A Publication Exclusively for FEDCO Members, Box 2605, Terminal Annex, Los Angeles CA 90051. (310)946-2511, ext. 3321. Editor: John Bregoli. 90% freelance written. Works with a small number of new/unpublished writers each year. Monthly catalog/magazine for FEDCO department store members. Estab. 1940. Circ. 2 million. **Pays on acceptance.** Publishes ms an average of 4 months after acceptance. Byline given. Offers $50 kill fee. Buys all rights. Query for electronic submissions. Reports in 6 weeks. Sample copy for 9 × 12 SAE with 4 first class stamps. Writer's guidelines for SASE.

Nonfiction: The magazine publishes material on historical events, personalities, anecdotes, little-known happenings and seasonal stories (especially relating to California) and stories about Southern California wildlife. No first person narrative. Buys 85 mss/year. Query with or without published clips or send complete manuscript. Length: 450 words. Pays $125.

Photos: State availability of photos. Reviews b&w and color slides. Pays $25.

Tips: "We publish tightly written, well-researched stories relating to the history of Southern California, regardless of prior writing experience."

KIWANIS, 3636 Woodview Trace, Indianapolis IN 46268. Fax: (317)879-0204. Executive Editor: Chuck Jonak. 85% of feature articles freelance written. Buys about 50 manuscripts annually. Magazine published 10 times/year for business and professional persons and their families. Estab. 1915. Circ. 285,000. **Pays on acceptance.** Buys first serial rights. Pays 40% kill fee. Publishes ms an average of 6 months after acceptance. Byline given. Reports within 2 months. Sample copy and writer's guidelines for 9 × 12 SAE with 5 first class stamps.

Nonfiction: Articles about social and civic betterment, small-business concerns, science, education, religion, family, youth, health, recreation, etc. Emphasis on objectivity, intelligent analysis and thorough research of contemporary issues. Positive tone preferred. Concise, lively writing, absence of cliches, and impartial presentation of controversy required. When applicable, include information and quotations from international sources. Avoid writing strictly to a US audience. "We have a continuing need for articles of international interest. In addition, we are very interested in proposals that concern helping youth, particularly prenatal through age five: day care, developmentally appropriate education, early intervention for at-risk children, parent education, safety and pediatric trauma." Length: 2,500-3,000 words. Pays $600-1,000. "No fiction, personal essays, profiles, travel pieces, fillers or verse of any kind. A light or humorous approach is welcomed where the subject is appropriate and all other requirements are observed." Usually pays the expenses of writers on assignment. Query first. Must include SASE for response.

Photos: "We accept photos submitted with manuscripts. Our rate for a manuscript with good photos is higher than for one without." Model release and identification of subjects required. Buys one-time rights.

Tips: "We will work with any writer who presents a strong feature article idea applicable to our magazine's audience and who will prove he or she knows the craft of writing. First, obtain writer's guidelines and a sample copy. Study for general style and content. When querying, present detailed outline of proposed manuscript's focus, direction, and editorial intent. Indicate expert sources to be used for attribution, as well as article's tone and length. Present a well-researched, smoothly written manuscript that contains a 'human quality' with the use of anecdotes, practical examples, quotations, etc."

‡THE LION, 300 22nd St., Oak Brook IL 60521-8842. (708)571-5466. Fax: (703)571-8890. Editor-in-Chief: Mark C. Lukas. Senior Editor: Robert Kleinfelder. 35% freelance written. Works with a small number of new/unpublished writers each year. Monthly magazine covering service club organization for Lions Club members and their families. Estab. 1917. Circ. 600,000. **Pays on acceptance.** Publishes ms an average of 5 months after acceptance. Buys all rights. Byline given. Phone queries OK. Reports in 6 weeks. Free sample copy and writer's guidelines.

Nonfiction: Informational (stories of interest to civic-minded individuals) and photo feature (must be of a Lions Club service project). No travel, biography, or personal experiences. No sensationalism. Prefers anecdotes in articles. Buys 4 mss/issue. Query. Length: 500-2,200. Pays $50-750. Sometimes pays the expenses of writers on assignment.

Photos: Purchased with or without accompanying ms or on assignment. Captions required. Query for photos. Black and white and color glossies at least 5 × 7 or 35mm color slides. Total purchase price for ms includes payment for photos accepted with ms. "Be sure photos are clear and as candid as possible."

Tips: "Incomplete details on how the Lions involved and actually carried out a project and poor quality photos are the most frequent mistakes made by writers in completing an article assignment for us. We are geared increasingly to an international audience."

THE NEIGHBORHOOD WORKS, Resources for Urban Communities, Center for Neighborhood Technology, 2125 West North Ave., Chicago IL 60647. (312)278-4800. Fax: (312)278-3840. Editor: Patti L. Wolter. 50% freelance written. Bimonthly magazine focusing on community organizing around issues of housing, energy, environment, transportation and economic development. "Writers must understand the importance of empowering people in low- and moderate-income city neighborhoods to solve local problems in housing, environment and local economy." Estab. 1978. Circ. 2,500. Pays on publication. Publishes ms an average of 2-4 months after acceptance. Byline given. Buys all rights. Submit seasonal/holiday material 4 months in advance. Previously published submissions OK. Reports in 2 months on queries; 2 months on mss. Sample copy and writer's guidelines for 9 × 12 SAE with 3 first class stamps.

Nonfiction: Exposes; historical (neighborhood history); how-to (each issue has "reproducible feature" on such topics as organizing a neighborhood recycling program); interview/profile ("of someone active on one of our issues"); personal experience ("in our issue areas, e.g, community organizing") and technical (on energy conservation and alternative energy, environmental issues). Buys about 10 mss/year. Query with resume and published clips or send complete ms. Length: 750-2,000 words. Pays $100-500. "We pay professional writers (people who make a living at it). We don't pay nonprofessionals and students but offer them a free subscription." Pays expenses of writers on assignment by previous agreement. Please include contact names, addresses and phone numbers of people interviewed in stories. Reprints OK; send photocopy of article.

Photos: State availability of photos with submission. Reviews contact sheets and prints. Offers $10-35/photo. Captions and identification of subjects required. Buys one-time rights.

Columns/Departments: Reproducible features (how-to articles on issues of interest to neighborhood organizations), 1,000-2,000 words. Query with published clips. Pays $100-250. Around the Nation, (300-word briefs on organizing efforts), pays $35.

Tips: "We are increasingly interested in stories from cities other than Chicago (our home base)."

THE OPTIMIST MAGAZINE, Optimist International, 4494 Lindell Blvd., St. Louis MO 63108. (314)371-6000. Fax: (314)371-6006. Editor: Gary S. Bradley. 10% freelance written. Magazine published 9 times/year about the work of Optimist clubs and members for members of the Optimist clubs in the United States and Canada. Circ. 165,000. **Pays on acceptance.** Publishes ms an average of 4 months after acceptance. Buys first North American serial rights. Submit seasonal material 3 months in advance. Reports in 1 week. Sample copy and writer's guidelines for 9×12 SAE with 4 first class stamps.

Nonfiction: "We want articles about the activities of local Optimist clubs. These volunteer community-service clubs are constantly involved in projects, aimed primarily at helping young people. With over 4,000 Optimist clubs in the US and Canada, writers should have ample resources. Some large metropolitan areas boast several dozen clubs. We are also interested in feature articles on individual club members who have in some way distinguished themselves, either in their club work or their personal lives. Good photos for all articles are a plus and can mean a bigger check." Buys 1-2 mss/issue. Query. "Submit a letter that conveys your ability to turn out a well-written article and tells exactly what the scope of the article will be." Length: 1,000-1,500 words. Pays $200 and up.

Photos: State availability of photos. Payment negotiated. Captions preferred. Buys all rights. "No mug shots or people lined up against the wall shaking hands."

Tips: "Find out what the Optimist clubs in your area are doing, then find out if we'd be interested in an article on a specific club project. All of our clubs are eager to talk about what they're doing. Just ask them and you'll probably have an article idea."

PERSPECTIVE, Pioneer Clubs, P.O. Box 788, Wheaton IL 60189-0788. (708)293-1600. Fax: 708-293-3053. Editor: Rebecca Powell Parat. 15% freelance written. Works with a number of new/unpublished writers each year. Triannual magazine for "volunteer leaders of clubs for girls and boys in grades K-12. Clubs are sponsored by local churches throughout North America." Magazine published three times a year. Estab. 1939. Circ. 24,000. **Pays on acceptance.** Publishes ms an average of 6 months after acceptance. Buys full rights for assigned articles, first North American serial rights for unsolicited manuscripts, and second serial (reprint) rights to material originally published elsewhere. Submit seasonal/holiday material 9 months in advance. Reprints OK. Send photocopy of article or typed ms with rights for sale noted. Pays 50% of their fee for an original article. Reports in 6 weeks. Writer's guidelines and sample copy $1.75 for 9×12 SAE with 6 first class stamps.

Nonfiction: Informational (relationship skills, leadership skills); inspirational (stories of leaders and children in Pioneer Clubs); interview (Christian education leaders, club leaders); and personal experience (of club leaders). Buys 8-12 mss/year. Byline given. Query. Length: 500-1,500 words. Pays $25-75. Sometimes pays expenses of writers on assignment.

Columns/Departments: Storehouse (game, activity, outdoor activity, service project suggestions—all related to club projects for any age between grades K-12). Buys 4-6 mss/year. Submit complete ms. Length: 150-250 words. Pays $8-15.

Tips: "We only assign major features to writers who have previously proven that they know us and our constituency. Submit articles directly related to club work, practical in nature, i.e., ideas for leader training in communication, discipline, teaching skills. They must have practical application. We want substance—not ephemeral ideas. In addition to a summary of the article idea and evidence that the writer has knowledge of the subject, we want evidence that the author understands our purpose and philosophy. Writers who have contact with Pioneer Clubs in a church in their area and who are interested in working on assignment are welcome to contact us."

‡THE PILOT LOG, Pilot International, P.O. Box 4844, Macon GA 31213-0599. (912)743-7403. Editor: Paige Henson. Bimonthly magazine for Pilot club news. Estab. 1937. Circ. 19,000. **Pays on acceptance.** Publishes ms an average of 6 months after acceptance. Offers 50% kill fee. Buys one-time rights. Editorial lead time 2 months. Submit seasonal material 6 months in advance. Accepts previously published submissions. Reports in 3 weeks on queries; 1 month on mss. Sample copy for 9×12 SAE and 3 first class stamps.

Nonfiction: General interest, how-to, inspirational (but not religious), interview/profile, personal experience and photo feature. "Nothing relating to aviation as we are a volunteer service organization founded in 1921 and named for the intrepid riverboat pilots of that day." Buys 3-4 mss/year. Send complete ms. Length: 750-1,500 words. Pays $200 minimum for assigned articles, $100 for unsolicited articles.

Photos: State availability of photos with submission. Reviews 4×5 prints. Offers $10-25 maximum/photo. Identification of subjects required. Buys one-time rights.

Fillers: Anecdotes, gags to be illustrated by cartoonists and short humor. Length: 125-250 words. Pays $10-25.

Tips: "Our audience comprises mostly women, yet we are trying to gear material to both genders. A special focus for service is brain-related disorders, but we'd rather have 'how-tos' on incorporating volunteerism into an already busy lifestyle; articles on volunteering in clubs vs single-issue volunteering; features which are uplifting to our readers; articles which address the needs and desires of the *modern*, busy volunteer. We are open to general features, cartoons and fillers, and gentle humor geared mostly to women."

RECREATION NEWS, Official Publication of the League of Federal Recreation Associations, Inc., Icarus Publishers, Inc., P.O. Box 32335, Washington DC 20007-0635. (202)965-6960. Editor: Sam Polson. 85% freelance written. Monthly guide to leisure-time activities for federal workers covering outdoor recreation, travel, fitness and indoor pastimes. Estab. 1979. Circ. 100,000. Pays on publication. Publishes ms an average of 8 months after acceptance. Byline given. Buys first rights and second serial (reprint) rights. Submit seasonal/holiday material 8 months in advance. Simultaneous queries and simultaneous and previously published submissions OK. Send photocopy of article with information about where and when it previously appeared. Pays $50 for reprints. Reports in 1-2 months. Sample copy and writer's guidelines for 9×12 SAE with $1.05 postage.

Nonfiction: Articles Editor. Leisure travel (no international travel); sports; hobbies; historical/nostalgic (Washington-related); and personal experience (with recreation, life in Washington). Special issues: skiing (December); education (August). Query with clips of published work. Length: 800-2,000 words. Pays from $50-300.

Photos: Photo editor. State availability of photos with query letter or ms. Uses b&w and color prints. Pays $25 for each print used. Uses color transparency on cover only. Pays $50-125 for transparency. Captions and identification of subjects required.

Tips: "Our writers generally have a few years of professional writing experience and their work runs to the lively and conversational. We like more manuscripts in a wide range of recreational topics, including the offbeat. The areas of our publication most open to freelancers are general articles on travel and sports, both participational and spectator, also historic in the DC area."

REVIEW, A Publication of North American Benefit Association, 1338 Military St., P.O. Box 5020, Port Huron MI 48061-5020. (313)985-5191, ext. 29. Editor: Janice U. Whipple. Associate Editor: Patricia J. Samar. 30% freelance written. Works only with published/established writers. Quarterly magazine published for NABA's primarily women-membership to help them care for themselves and their families. Estab. 1895. Circ. 40,000. **Pays on acceptance.** Publishes ms an average of 1 year after acceptance. Byline given. Not copyrighted. Buys one-time, simultaneous and second serial (reprint) rights. Submit seasonal/holiday material 6 months in advance. Simultaneous and previously published submissions OK. Send tearsheet or photocopy of article with information about when and where it previously appeared; or send ms with rights for sale noted. Reports in 2 months. Sample copy for 9×12 SAE with 4 first class stamps. Writer's guidelines for #10 SASE.

Nonfiction: Looking for general interest or how-to stories of interest to women aged 25-44, such as career/employment and/or juggling work and family responsibilities in the 90s; health and fitness (mental and physical); parenting children of all ages as a parent of any age; parenting your parents; and other relevant issues. Also interested in objective news/feature stories about current events and issues pertaining to women and issues of concern to them. Profiles of outstanding prominent women—particularly those whose prominence is related to volunteerism—are also sought. Buys 4-10 mss/year. Send complete ms. Length: 1,000 to 2,000 words. Pays $150 to $500 per ms.

Photos: Not interested in photos at this time, unless accompanied by a ms. Model release and identification of subjects required.

Tips: "We are interested in expanding our bank of freelance writers who are available on an as-needed assignment basis. Also we are very interested in covering a wide variety of women's issues. Please do not hesitate to query with an idea that is fresh and contemporary. Give background of writer as to education and credits. Manuscripts will be carefully considered, but received only with the understanding that North American Benefit Association shall not be responsible for loss or injury."

THE ROTARIAN, Rotary International, 1560 Sherman Ave., Evanston IL 60201. (708)866-3000. Fax: (708)328-8554 or (708)866-9732. Editor: Willmon L. White. Managing Editor: Charles W. Pratt. Associate Editor: Jo Nugent. 40% freelance written. Monthly magazine for Rotarian business and professional men and women and their families, schools, libraries, hospitals, etc. "Articles should appeal to an international audience and in some way help Rotarians help other people. The organization's rationale is one of hope, encouragement

and belief in the power of individuals talking and working together." Estab. 1911. Circ. 530,435. **Pays on acceptance.** Byline sometimes given. Kill fee negotiable. Buys one-time or all rights. Accepts previously published submissions. Reports in 2 weeks on queries and mss. Sample copy for 9 × 12 SAE with 6 first class stamps. Writer's guidelines for #10 SASE.
Nonfiction: Essays, general interest, humor, inspirational, photo feature, travel, business and environment. No fiction, religious or political articles. Query with published clips. Negotiates payment.
Photos: State availability of photos with submission. Reviews contact sheets and transparencies. Usually buys one-time rights.
Columns/Departments: Manager's Memo (business), Executive Health, Executive Lifestyle, Earth Diary and Trends. Length: 800 words. Query.
Fillers: Jokes for humor page. Buys 10/year. Length: 50 words maximum.
Tips: "Study issues, then query with SASE."

THE SAMPLE CASE, The Order of United Commercial Travelers of America, 632 N. Park St., Box 159019, Columbus OH 43215-8619. (614)228-3276. Associate Editor: Anne Pelok. Bimonthly magazine covering news for members of the United Commercial Travelers. Emphasizes fraternalism for its officers and active membership. Estab. 1888. Circ. 140,000. Pays on publication. Buys one-time rights. Reports in 3 months. Submit seasonal/holiday material 6 months in advance. Simultaneous queries and submissions OK. Reprints OK; send tearsheet or photocopy of article with information about where and when the article previously appeared or ms with rights for sale noted. Pays same for reprints as for original articles.
Nonfiction: Articles on travel in the US and Canada; food/cuisine; health/fitness/safety; family; hobbies/ entertainment; fraternal/civic activities; business finance/insurance.
Photos: David Knapp, Art Director. State availability of photos with ms. Prefers color prints. Pay negotiable. Captions required.

SCOUTING, Boy Scouts of America, 1325 W. Walnut Hill Lane, P.O. Box 75015, Irving TX 75015-2079. (214)580-2355. Fax: (214)580-2079. Editor: Ernest Doclar. Executive Editor: Jon Halter. 90% freelance written. Bimonthly magazine on Scouting activities for adult leaders of the Boy Scouts. Estab. 1913. Circ. 1 million. **Pays on acceptance.** Publishes ms an average of 4 months after acceptance. Byline given. Buys first North American serial rights. Submit seasonal/holiday material 4 months in advance. Reports in 2 weeks. Sample copy $1 for #10 SAE with 4 first class stamps. Writer's guidelines for #10 SASE.
Nonfiction: Buys 60 mss/year. Query with published clips. Length: 1,500-2,000 words. Pays $400-600 for assigned articles; pays $200-500 for unsolicited articles. Pays expenses of writers on assignment.
Photos: State availability of photos with submission. Reviews contact sheets and transparencies. Identification of subjects required. Buys one-time rights.
Columns/Departments: Family Quiz (quiz on topics of family interest), 1,000 words; Way it Was (Scouting history), 1,200 words. Buys 6 mss/year. Query. Pays $200-300.

THE SONS OF NORWAY VIKING, Sons of Norway, 1455 W. Lake St., Minneapolis MN 55408. (612)827-3611. Fax: (612)827-0658. Editor: Karin B. Miller. 50% freelance written. Prefers to work with published/ established writers. Monthly membership magazine for the Sons of Norway, a fraternal and cultural organization, covering Norwegian culture, heritage, history, Norwegian-American topics, modern Norwegian society, genealogy and travel. "Our audience is Norwegian-Americans (middle-aged or older) with strong interest in their heritage and anything Norwegian. Many have traveled to Norway." Estab. 1903. Circ. 70,000. **Pays on acceptance.** Publishes ms an average of 8 months after acceptance. Byline given. Offers 25% kill fee. Buys first North American serial and second serial (reprint) rights. Submit seasonal/holiday material 6 months in advance. Previously published submissions OK. Reports in 4 months. Free sample copy and writer's guidelines on request.
Nonfiction: General interest, historical/nostalgic, humor, interview/profile, and travel—all having a Norwegian angle. "Articles should not be personal impressions nor strictly factual but well-researched and conveyed in a warm and audience-involving manner. Does it entertain *and* inform?" Buys 30 mss/year. Query. Length: 1,500-2,000 words. Generally pays $100-350. Reprints OK; send tearsheet. Pays 25% of original article fee for reprints.
Photos: Reviews transparencies and prints. Pays $10-20/photo; pays $100 for cover color photo. Identification of subjects required. Buys one-time rights.
Tips: "Show familiarity with Norwegian culture and subject matter. Our readers are somewhat knowledgeable about Norway and quick to note misstatements. Articles about modern Norway are most open to freelancers—the society, industries—but historical periods also okay. Write before a scheduled trip to Norway to discuss subjects to research or interview while there."

THE TOASTMASTER, Toastmasters International, 23182 Arroyo Vista, Rancho Santa Margarita CA 92688-7052 or P.O. Box 9052, Mission Viejo, CA 92690-7052. (714)858-8255. Fax: (714)858-1207. Editor: Suzanne Frey. Associate Editor: Kathy O'Connell. 50% freelance written. Monthly magazine on public speaking, leadership and club concerns. "This magazine is sent to members of Toastmasters International, a nonprofit educational association of men and women throughout the world who are interested in developing their communication and leadership skills. Members range from novice speakers to professional orators and come from a wide variety of backgrounds." Estab. 1932. Circ. 170,000 (avg.). **Pays on acceptance.** Publishes ms an average of 8-10 months after acceptance. Byline given. Buys second serial (reprint), first-time or all rights. Submit seasonal/holiday material 3 months in advance. Simultaneous and previously published submissions OK. Query for electronic submissions. Reports in 6 weeks on queries; 1 month on mss. Sample copy for 9 × 12 SAE with 4 first class stamps. Writer's guidelines for #10 SASE.

Nonfiction: Book excerpts, how-to (communications related), humor (only if informative; humor cannot be off-color or derogatory), interview/profile (only if of a very prominent member or former member of Toast-masters International or someone who has a valuable perspective on communication and leadership). Buys 50 mss/year. Query. Length: 1,000-2,500 words. Pays $75-250. Sometimes pays expenses of writers on assignment. "Toastmasters members are requested to view their submissions as contributions to the organization. Some-times asks for book excerpts and reprints without payment, but original contribution from individuals outside Toastmasters will be paid for at stated rates."

Photos: Reviews b&w prints. Offers no additional payment for photos accepted with ms. Captions are required. Buys all rights.

Tips: "We are looking primarily for 'how-to' articles on subjects from the broad fields of communications and leadership which can be directly applied by our readers in their self-improvement and club programming efforts. Concrete examples are useful. Avoid sexist or nationalist language."

VFW MAGAZINE, Veterans of Foreign Wars of the United States, 406 W. 34th St., Kansas City MO 64111. (816)756-3390. Fax: (816)968-1169. Editor: Rich Kolb. 40% freelance written. Monthly magazine on veterans' affairs, military history, patriotism, defense and current events. "*VFW Magazine* goes to its members world-wide, all having served honorably in the armed forces overseas from World War II through the Persian Gulf War." Circ. 2.1 million. **Pays on acceptance.** Publishes ms 6 months after acceptance. Offers 50% kill fee on commissioned article. Buys first rights. Submit seasonal/holiday material 6 months in advance. Wants detailed query letters, resume and sample clips. Reports in 2 months. Sample copy for 9 × 12 SAE and 5 first class stamps.

• *VFW Magazine* is becoming more current events oriented.

Nonfiction: Interview/profile and veterans' affairs. Buys 25-30 mss/year. Query. Length: 1,500 words. Pays $500 maximum unless otherwise negotiated.

Photos: Send photos with submission. Reviews contact sheets, negatives, transparencies and prints. Captions, model releases and identification of subjects required. Buys first North American rights.

WOODMEN, 1700 Farnam St., Omaha NE 68102. (402)271-7211. Fax: (402)271-7269. Communications Man-ager: Scott Darling. Assistant Editor: Billie Jo Forist. 10% freelance written. Works with a small number of new/unpublished writers each year. Bimonthly magazine published by Woodmen of the World Life Insurance Society for "people of all ages in all walks of life. We have both adult and child readers from all types of American families." Circ. 498,000. Not copyrighted. Buys 2-3 mss/year. **Pays on acceptance.** Byline given. Buys one-time rights. Publishes ms an average of 2 months after acceptance. Will consider simultaneous submissions. Submit seasonal material 3 months in advance. Reports in 5 weeks. Free sample copy. Writer's guidelines for #10 SASE.

Nonfiction: "General interest articles which appeal to the American family—travel, history, art, new prod-ucts, how-to, sports, hobbies, food, home decorating, family expenses, etc. We want more 'consumer type' articles, humor, historical articles, think pieces, nostalgia, photo articles." Submit complete ms. Length: 1,500 words or less. Pays $10 minimum, 10¢/word.

Photos: Purchased with or without mss; captions optional "but suggested." Uses 8 × 10 glossy prints, 4 × 5 transparencies ("and possibly down to 35mm"). Payment "depends on use." Color and b&w prices vary according to use and quality.

Fiction: Humorous and historical short stories. Length: 1,500 words or less. Pays "$10 minimum or 10¢/word."

Astrology, Metaphysical and New Age

Magazines in this section carry articles ranging from the occult to holistic healing. The following publications regard astrology, psychic phenomena, metaphysical experiences and related subjects as sciences or as objects of serious study. Each has an individual personality and approach to these phe-nomena. If you want to write for these publications, be sure to read them carefully before submitting.

FATE, Llewellyn Worlwide, Ltd., P.O. Box 64383, St. Paul MN 55164-0383. Fax: (612)291-1908. Editor: Phyllis Galde. 70% freelance written. Estab. 1901. Buys all rights; occasionally first serial rights only. Byline given. Pays on publication. Sample copy and writer's guidelines $3 for 9 × 12 SAE with 5 first class stamps. Query. Reports in 3 months.

Nonfiction and Fillers: Personal psychic and mystical experiences, 300-500 words. Pays $25. Articles on parapsychology, Fortean phenomena, cryptozoology, parapsychology, spiritual healing, flying saucers, new frontiers of science, and mystical aspects of ancient civilizations, 2,000-3,000 words. Must include complete authenticating details. Prefers interesting accounts of single events rather than roundups. "We very frequently accept manuscripts from new writers; the majority are individual's first-person accounts of their own psychic/mystical/spiritual experiences. We do need to have all details, where, when, why, who and what, included for complete documentation. We ask for a notarized statement attesting to truth of the article." Pays 10¢/word. Fillers must be be fully authenticated also, and on similar topics. Length: 100-300 words.

Photos: Buys good glossy prints with mss. Pays $10.

HEART DANCE, 473 Miller Ave., Mill Valley CA 94941. (415)383-2525. Editor: Ms. Randy Peyser. The largest monthly New Age calendar of events for Northern California. Monthly magazine focusing on New Age spirituality and contemporary human awareness. Estab. 1990. Circ. 50,000. Pays on publication, $25 full page articles, $5-10 quotes or excerpts, plus many copies to impress your friends with. Publishes ms an average of 1-12 months after acceptance. Byline given. You keep the copyright. Buys one-time rights. Accepts simultaneous submissions, but don't overwhelm them. Reports back within 1 month on all submissions. Sample copy and writer's guidelines for 9 × 12 SASE with 98¢ postage.

Nonfiction: The focus—personal experience stories, near-death experiences, or experiences of having been touched by something greater than what we normally perceive. Humor is also welcomed. Not interested in how-to articles, or articles that refer to a specific self-help technique, specific type of spirituality or a specific religion. Not interested in poetry, UFO's, or any form of divination—astrology, numerology, etc. Articles *must be* a real heart-sharing.

Tips: We publish the kind of articles that people cut out and put on their refrigerators, or make copies and send to their friends; articles that inspire, that really touch people's hearts and make a difference in the quality of their lives. Pub your name/address/phone number on every page you submit. Extra points for typed submissions. Please send us a copy, not your original. Contact us and share your greatest gifts!

‡NEW FRONTIER, Magazine of Transformation, New Frontier Education Society, 101 Cuthbert St., Philadelphia PA 19106. Editor: Sw. Virato. 80% freelance written. Monthly New Age magazine. "*New Frontier* magazine writers should embody a sense of oneness with the universe. They should come from a basic spiritual model, and essentially be a New Age person. They should see the universe and all life from a holistic view." Estab. 1980. Circ. 60,000. Pays on publication. Publishes ms an average of 6 months after acceptance. Byline given. Offers 20% kill fee or $25. Buys first North American serial, first, one-time or second serial (reprint) rights or makes work-for-hire assignments. Editorial lead time is 3 months. Submit seasonal material 4 months in advance. Query for electronic submissions. MS/DOS format, MicroSoft Word, 5¼ floppy. Reports in 6 weeks on queries. Sample copy $2. Writer's guidelines for #10 SASE.

Nonfiction: Book excerpts, essays, expose, general interest, historical/nostalgic, how-to, humor, inspirational, interview/profile, new product, opinion, personal experience, photo feature and "anything with awareness. Nothing dealing with hate, violence, attack, war, crime, drugs, superficial sex, pornography, meat products or unconsciousness in general." Buys 15 mss/year. Query with published clips. Length: 1,500-4,000 words. Pays $100 minimum for assigned articles, $50 for unsolicited articles. Sometimes pays expenses of writers on assignment (limit agreed upon in advance).

Photos: State availability of photos with submission. Reviews contact sheets and 5 × 7 prints. Negotiates payment individually. Buys one-time rights.

Fillers: Newsbreaks. Buys 20/year. Length: 100-300 words. Pays $10-25.

Tips: "Our writers must have an awareness of the subject, and the subject must deal with a transformation of human consciousness in any of the following areas: astrology, ecology, spirituality, self-help, holistic health, metaphysics, health food, Eastern philosophy, yoga, cosmic consciousness, social responsibility, altered states, etc."

‡PARABOLA, The Magazine of Myth and Tradition, The Society for the Study of Myth and Tradition, 656 Broadway, New York NY 10012. (212)505-6200. Editors: Ellen Draper/Virginia Baron. Quarterly magazine on mythology, tradition and comparative religion. "*Parabola* is devoted to the exploration of the quest for meaning as expressed in the myths, symbols, and tales of the religious traditions. Particular emphasis is on the relationship between this wisdom and contemporary life." Estab. 1976. Circ. 40,000. Pays on publication.

 The double dagger before a listing indicates that the listing is new in this edition. New markets are often more receptive to freelance submissions.

Publishes ms 4 months after acceptance. Byline given. Offers kill fee for assigned articles only (usually $100). Buys first North American serial, first, one-time or second serial (reprint) rights. Editorial lead time is 4 months. Simlultaneous submissions OK. Query for electronic submissions. IBM-compatible WordPerfect or Macintosh M S Word disks. Requires hard copy accompanying disk. Reports in 2-3 weeks on queries; on mss "variable — depends on how early we receive it." Sample copy $6 current issue; $8 back issue. Writers guidelines and list of themes free on request.

Nonfiction: Book excerpts, essays, inspirational, personal experience, photo feature and religious. 1993 — "The Call," deadline Oct. 15; 1994 — "Twins," deadline Jan. 15. No articles not related to specific themes. Buys 4-8 mss/year. Query. Length: 2,000-4,000 words. Pays $200 minimum. Sometimes pays expenses of writers on assignment.

Photos: State availability of photos with submission. Reviews contact sheets, any transparencies and prints. Identification of subjects required. Buys one-time rights.

Columns/Departments: Contact: David Appelbaum (book reviews); Ellen Draper/Virginia Baron (Tangents, Epicycles). Tangents (reviews of film, exhibits, dance, theater, video, music relating to theme of issue), 2,000-4,000 words; Book Reviews (reviews of current books in religion, spirituality, mythology and tradition), 500 words; Epicycles (retellings of myths and folk tales of all cultures—no fiction or made-up mythology!), under 2,000 words. Buys 2-6 unsolicited mss/year. Query. Pays $75-300.

Fiction: "We *very* rarely publish fiction; must relate to upcoming theme. Query recommended."

Poetry: Free verse, traditional (must relate to theme). Buys 2-4 poems/year. Pays $50-75.

RAINBOW CITY EXPRESS, Adventures on the Spiritual Path, P.O. Box 8447, Berkeley CA 94707. Editor: Helen B. Harvey. 75-95% freelance written. Semi-annual magazine on "spiritual awakening and evolving consciousness, especially feminist spirituality, creative self-expression and women's issues. We take an eclectic, mature and innovative approach to the topics of spiritual awakening and evolution of consciousness. A positive, constructive, healing tone is required, not divisive, separatist slant." Estab. 1988. Circ. 1,000. Pays on publication. Byline given. Buys first North American serial or second serial (reprint) rights. Submit seasonal/holiday material 4-6 months in advance. Previously published submissions OK (only if full publishing information accompanies ms showing where previously published). Reports in 2 months on mss. Sample copy $7 postpaid. Writer's guidelines for #10 SAE with 2 first class stamps.

Nonfiction: Book excerpts, essays, general interest, historical/nostalgic, how-to, humor, inspirational, interview/profile, opinion, personal experience, religious, travel. "No get-rich-quick or how-to channel spirits, how-to manipulate the cosmos/others, occult/voodoo/spellcasting diatribes and no glorification of victimization/scapegoating or addictions." Buys 50-100 mss/year. Send complete ms (no book-length items, please). Length: 250-1,500 words. Pays token honorariums by individual arrangement only.

Columns/Departments: Book Reviews (spirituality, goddess consciousness, New Age topics), 250-500 words; Healing Forum. Acquires 30 mss/year. Send complete ms. Pays in contributor copies.

Fiction: Adventure, fantasy, historical, religious. "Fiction should relate directly to our slant which is about spiritual/consciousness evolution. No science fiction, thriller, sex, drugs or violence mss." Acquires about 12 mss/year. Query. Length: 500-1,000 words. Pays in contributor copies.

Poetry: Avant-garde, free verse, haiku, light verse, traditional. *No* rhyming poetry! Acquires about 30/year. Submit 3 poems maximum. Length: 8-30 lines.

Fillers: Anecdotes, short humor. "Fillers must relate to our spirituality slant."

Tips: "We feature true life experiences and insights related to spiritual awakenings and consciousness evolution. Readers/writers who have experienced some of these phenomena and know what they're talking about are likely to be well received. We are particularly interested in actual experiences with Kundalini activation and archetypal stirring. We aim to demonstrate the often-unsuspected connections between spiritual awakening and everyday realities. Note: *Please* obtain and study sample copy prior to submitting mss! No mss read or returned without SASE."

‡SHAMAN'S DRUM, A Journal of Experiential Shamanism, Cross-Cultural Shamanism Network, P.O. Box 430, Willits CA 95490. (707)459-0486. Editor: Timothy White. Associate Editor: Karen Eng. 75% freelance written. Quarterly educational magazine of cross-cultural shamanism. "*Shaman's Drum* seeks contributions directed toward a general but well-informed audience. Our intent is to expand, challenge, and refine our readers' and our understanding of shamanism in practice. Topics include indigenous medicineway practices, contemporary shamanic healers and healing practices, ecstatic spiritual practices, and contemporary shamanic psychotherapies. Our overall focus is cross-cultural, but our editorial approach is culture-specific—we prefer that authors focus on specific ethnic traditions or personal practices about which they have significant firsthand experience. We are looking for examples of not only how shamanism has transformed individual lives but also practical ways it can help ensure survival of life on the planet. We want material that captures the heart and feeling of shamanism and that can inspire people to direct action and participation, and to explore shamanism in greater depth." Estab. 1985. Circ. 18,500. Publishes ms 6 months after acceptance. Buys first North American serial and first rights. Editorial lead time 1 year. Reports in 3 months. Sample copy $5. Writer's guidelines for #10 SASE.

Nonfiction: Book excerpts, essays, interview/profile (please query), opinion, personal experience and photo feature. *No fiction, poetry or fillers.* Buys 16 mss/year. Send complete ms. Length: 3,000-8,000. "We pay 5-10¢ per word, depending on how much we have to edit. We generally pay 2 copies and tearsheets in addition to cash payment."

Photos: Send photos with submission. Reviews contact sheets, transparencies and all sizes prints. Offers $40-50/photo. Identification of subjects required. Buys one-time rights.

Columns/Departments: Contact: Judy Wells, Earth Circles Editor. Earth Circles (news format, concerned with issues, events, organizations related to shamanism, indigenous peoples and caretaking Earth. Relevant clippings also sought. Clippings paid with copies and credit line), 500-1,500 words. Buys 8 mss/year. Send complete ms. Pays 5-10¢/word. Reviews: contact Karen Eng, Associate Editor (in-depth reviews of books, records/tapes/CD's about shamanism or closely related subjects such as indigenous lifestyles, ethnobotany, transpersonal healing and ecstatic spirituality), 500-1,500 words. "Please query us first and we will send *Reviewer's Guidelines.*" Pays 5-10¢/word.

Tips: "All articles must have a clear relationship to shamanism, but may be on topics which have not traditionally been defined as shamanic. We prefer original material that is based on, or illustrated with, first-hand knowledge and personal experience. Articles should be well documented with descriptive examples and pertinent background information. Photographs and illustrations of high quality are always welcome and can help sell articles."

TRANSFORMATION TIMES, Life Resources Unlimited, P.O. Box 425, Beavercreek OR 97004-0425. (503)632-7141. Fax: (503)632-3502. Editor: Connie L. Faubel. Managing Editor: E. James Faubel. 100% freelance written. Tabloid covering new age, metaphysics, and natural health, published 10 times/year. Estab. 1983. Circ. 8,000. Pays on publication. Publishes ms an average of 2 months after acceptance. Byline given. Buys one-time rights. Submit seasonal/holiday material 2 months in advance. Simultaneous and previously published submissions OK. Send photocopy of article or short story and information about when and where the article previously appeared. For reprints, negotiates the amount paid. Query for electronic submissions. Sample copy and writer's guidelines $2.

Nonfiction: Book excerpts, inspirational, interview/profile, women's issues, metaphysical. "No articles with emphasis on negative opinions and ideas." Buys 60 mss/year. Send complete ms. Length: 500-1,000 words. Pays 1¢/word. Reprints OK; send typed ms with rights for sale noted.

Photos: Send photos with submission. Reviews 3×5 prints. Captions and identification of subjects required. Buys one-time rights.

Columns/Departments: Woman's Way (women's issues) 500-1,000 words. Buys 10 mss/year. Send complete ms. Pays 1¢/word.

Tips: "In addition to present interests, we plan on adding articles on environmental quality issues and socially responsible investing."

‡UFO MAGAZINE, A Forum on Extraordinary Theories and Phenomena, UFO Media Group, P.O. Box 1053, Sunland CA 91041. (818)951-1250. 50% freelance written. Bimonthly magazine covering UFO phenomena, events and theories. "*UFO Magazine* is the only newsstand-quality publication applying journalistic standards to the UFO subject. It is the most legitimate vehicle for UFO news and information now available to the general public." Pays on publication. Publishes ms 2-6 months after acceptance. Byline given. No kill fee. Buys one-time rights. Submit seasonal/holiday material 6 months in advance. Previously published submissions OK. Prefer electronic submissions. IBM-compatible, ASCII. Reports in 2 months on queries. Does not return unsolicited mss. Sample copy $5.45. Free writer's guidelines.

Nonfiction: Vicki Cooper, Editor. Book excerpts, essays, expose, general interest, historical/nostalgic, interview/profile, opinion, personal experience, photo feature and technical. "Please, no fiction or fanatical material!" Buys 15-20 mss/year. Query. Length: 500-3,500 words. Pays $25-100 for assigned articles, or "more in some cases;" $25 maximum for unsolicited articles. "Previously unpublished UFO researchers are paid with copies unless other arrangements are made." Sometimes pays expenses of writers on assignment.

Photos: Send photos with submission. Reviews contact sheets, transparencies and 5×7 prints. Offers no additional payment for photos accepted with ms from writers. Offers $5-25 per photo from professional photographers only. "Reprints can be given with credit to *UFO Magazine.*"

Columns/Departments: Forum (opinion pieces based on factual UFO cases), 500-2,000 words; Encounter: First Hand (first-hand accounts of contact with UFO phenomena and/or aliens), 500-2,500 words; News Section (news briefs and special aspects of UFO phenomena), 500-1,500 words; International Reports (UFO news from around the world) 500-2,000 words. Buys 15-20 mss/year. Send complete ms.

Fillers: Facts and newsbreaks. Buys 3-4/year. Pays $5-10.

Tips: "Our best submissions come from writers who have a working familiarity with the UFO subject and the research that has ensued in the modern UFO era (since 1947). But many potential contributors could also be those who have an abiding *private* fascination with UFOs along with exceptional writing skills! *UFO Magazine* is in constant need of comprehensive news-features on vital cases and/or issues concerning UFOs and related topics. The UFO subject is inextricably linked to the policies and practices of the U.S. military and intelligence agencies, so our magazine will venture into those sensitive avenues at times."

Automotive and Motorcycle

Publications in this section detail the maintenance, operation, performance, racing and judging of automobiles and recreational vehicles. Publications that treat vehicles as means of shelter instead of as a hobby or sport are classified in the Travel, Camping and Trailer category. Journals for service station operators and auto and motorcycle dealers are located in the Trade Auto and Truck section.

AMERICAN IRON MAGAZINE, TAM Communications Inc., 6 Prowitt St., Norwalk CT 06855. (203)855-0008. Fax: (203)852-9980. Interim Editor: Jack Daniels. 60% freelance written. Monthly magazine covering Harley-Davidson and Indian motorcycles, with a definite emphasis on Harleys. Circ. 80,000. Pays on publication. Publishes ms an average of 6 months after acceptance. Byline given. Query for electronic submissions. Reports in 3 weeks on queries. Sample copy $3.
Nonfiction: "Clean and non-offensive. Stories include bike features, touring stories, how-to tech stories with step-by-step photos, historical pieces, profiles, events, opinion and various topics of interest to the people who ride Harley-Davidsons." No fiction. Buys 60 mss/year. Pays $250 for touring articles with photos. Payment for other articles varies.
Photos: Submit color slides or large transparencies. No prints. Send SASE for return of photos.
Tips: "We're not looking for stories about the top 10 biker bars or do-it-yourself tattoos. We're looking for articles about motorcycling, the people and the lifestyle. If you understand the Harley mystique and can write well, you've got a good chance of being published."

AMERICAN MOTORCYCLIST, American Motorcyclist Association, P.O. Box 6114, Westerville OH 43081-6114. (614)891-2425. Executive Editor: Greg Harrison. For "enthusiastic motorcyclists, investing considerable time and money in the sport. We emphasize the motorcyclist, not the vehicle." Monthly magazine. Estab. 1942. Circ. 175,000. Pays on publication. Rights purchased vary with author and material. Pays 25-50% kill fee. Byline given. Query with SASE. Submit seasonal/holiday material 4 months in advance. Reports in 1 month. Free sample copy and writer's guidelines.
Nonfiction: How-to (different and/or unusual ways to use a motorcycle or have fun on one); historical (the heritage of motorcycling, particularly as it relates to the AMA); interviews (with interesting personalities in the world of motorcycling); photo feature (quality work on any aspect of motorcycling); and technical articles. No product evaluations or stories on motorcycling events not sanctioned by the AMA. Buys 20-25 mss/year. Query. Length: 500 words minimum. Pays minimum $6/published column inch.
Photos: Purchased with or without accompanying ms or on assignment. Captions required. Query. Pays $30 minimum/published photo.
Tips: "Accuracy and reliability are prime factors in our work with freelancers. We emphasize the rider, not the motorcycle itself. It's always best to query us first and the further in advance the better to allow for scheduling."

AMERICAN WOMAN MOTORSPORTS, American Woman Motorsports, 2830 Santa Monica Blvd., Santa Monica CA 90404. (310)829-0012. Fax: (310)453-8850. Publisher: Courtney Caldwell. Editor: Sue Elliott. 40% freelance written. Bimonthly magazine on women in automotive. "We are geared towards working women who are purchasing the 79 million vehicles today. Estab. 1988. Circ. 50,000. Pays on publication an average of 2 months after acceptance. Byline sometimes given. Buys first rights and second serial (reprint) rights or makes work-for-hire assignments. Submit seasonal/holiday material 4 months in advance. Previously published submissions OK. Send tearsheet or photocopy of article, including information about when and where the article previously appeared. For reprints, pays 50% of the amount paid for an original article. Query for electronic submissions. Reports in 2 months. Free sample copy.
Nonfiction: Humor, inspirational, interview/profile, new product, photo feature, travel and lifestyle. No articles depicting women in motorsports or professions that are degrading, negative or not upscale. Buys 30 mss/year. Send complete ms. Length 250-1,000 words. Pays 10¢/word for assigned articles; 7¢ for unsolicited articles. Sometimes pays expenses of writers on assignment.
Photos: Send photos with submission. Reviews contact sheets. Black and white or Kodachrome 64 preferred. Offers $10-50/photo. Captions, model releases and identification of subjects required. Buys all rights.
Columns/Departments: Lipservice (from readers); Tech Talk: (The Mall) new products; Tale End (News); 500-1,000 words.
Fillers: Anecdotes, facts, gags to be illustrated by cartoonist, newsbreaks and short humor. Buys 12/year. Length: 25-100 words. Negotiable.
Tips: "It helps if the writer is into motorcycles. It is a special sport. If he/she doesn't ride, he/she should have a positive point of view of motorcycling and be willing to learn more about the subject. We are a lifestyle type of publication more than a technical magazine. Positive attitudes wanted."

AUTOMOBILE, 38th Floor, 888 7th Ave., New York NY 10106. "Prefers not to share information."

‡**AUTOMOBILE QUARTERLY, The Connoisseur's Magazine of Motoring Today, Yesterday, and Tomorrow**, Kutztown Publishing Co., 15040 Kutztown Rd., Kutztown PA 19530. (215)683-3169. Publishing Director: Jonathan Stein. Managing Editor: Karla Rosenbusch. Contact: John Heilig, associate editor. 85% freelance written. Quarterly magazine covering "automotive history, hardcover, excellent photography." Estab. 1962. Circ. 17,000. **Pays on acceptance.** Publishes ms an average of 1 year after acceptance. Byline given. Buys first North American serial rights. Editorial lead time 9 months. Accepts simultaneous submissions. Reports in 2 weeks on queries; 2 months on mss. Sample copy $19.95.
Nonfiction: Essays, historical/nostalgic, photo feature and technical. Buys 25 mss/year. Query. Length: 5,000-8,000 words. Pays approximately 30¢/word. Sometimes pays expenses of writers on assignment.
Photos: State availability of photos with submission. Reviews 4 × 5, 35mm and 120 transparencies. Buys one-time rights.
Tips: "Study the publication."

BRACKET RACING USA, 299 Market St., Saddle Brook NJ 07662. (201)712-9300. Editor: Dale Wilson. Managing Editor: Peter Easton. Magazine published 8 times/year that covers bracket cars and bracket racing. Estab. 1989. Circ. 45,000. Pays on publication. Publishes ms 6 months after acceptance. Byline given. Buys first North American serial rights. Query for electronic submissions. Sample copy $3 for 9 × 12 SAE with 5 first class stamps.
Nonfiction: Automotive how-to and technical. Buys 35 mss/year. Query. Length: 500-1,500 words. Pays $150/magazine page for all articles. Sometimes pays expenses of writers on assignment.
Photos: Send photos with submission.

BRITISH CAR, P.O. Box 9099, Canoga Park CA 91309. (818)710-1234. Fax: (818)710-1877. Editor: Dave Destler. 50% freelance written. Bimonthly magazine covering British cars. "We focus upon the cars built in Britain, the people who buy them, drive them, collect them, love them. Writers must be among the aforementioned. Written by enthusiasts for enthusiasts." Estab. 1985. Circ. 30,000. Pays on publication. Publishes ms an average of 3 months after acceptance. Byline given. Buys all rights, unless other arrangements made. Submit seasonal/holiday material 4 months in advance. Query for electronic submissions. Reports in 1 month. Sample copy $4. Writer's guidelines for #10 SASE.
Nonfiction: Historical/nostalgic; how-to (on repair or restoration of a specific model or range of models, new technique or process); humor (based upon a realistic nonfiction situation); interview/profile (famous racer, designer, engineer, etc.); photo feature; and technical. Buys 30 mss/year. Send complete ms. "Include SASE if submission is to be returned." Length: 750-4,500 words. Pays $2-5/column inch for assigned articles; pays $2-3/column inch for unsolicited articles.
Photos: Send photos with submission. Reviews transparencies and prints. Offers $15-75/photo. Captions and identification of subjects required. Buys all rights, unless otherwise arranged.
Columns/Departments: Update (newsworthy briefs of interest, not too timely for bimonthly publication), approximately 50-175 words. Buys 20 mss/year. Send complete ms.
Tips: "Thorough familiarity of subject is essential. *British Car* is read by experts and enthusiasts who can see right through superficial research. Facts are important, and must be accurate. Writers should ask themselves 'I know I'm interested in this story, but will most of *British Car's* readers appreciate it?' "

CAA'S AUTOPINION ANNUAL, Canadian Automobile Association, 1775 Courtwood Crescent, Ottawa, Ontario K2C 3J2 Canada. (613)226-7631. Editor: David Steventon. 75% freelance written. Annual magazine covering new and used car purchasing. "Contains features relating to what's new in cars and automotive technology, and to the car buying process including: leasing and factors to consider (size, intended use of vehicle, towing, etc); new vehicle profiles; results of annual vehicle durability survey." Estab. 1988. Circ. 48,000. Pays on publication. Byline given. No kill fee. Buys all rights. Previously published submissions OK. Query for electronic submissions. Submission deadline Sept. 1 for publication Dec. 15.
Nonfiction: General interest (automotive), historical/nostalgic (auto), interview/profile, new product (automotive), and technical (automotive). Buys 5 mss/year. Query with or without published clips or send complete ms. Length: 2,500 words. Pays $250-500. Send photos with submission. Reviews transparencies. Offers no additional payment for photos accepted with ms. Captions, model releases and identification of subjects required. Buys one-time rights.
Tips: "Contact editor, submit clippings of recent work, verify material needed for next edition (topics, etc.)."

CAR AND DRIVER, 2002 Hogback Rd., Ann Arbor MI 48105. (313)971-3600. Editor-in-Chief: Csaba Csere. For auto enthusiasts; college-educated, professional, median 24-35 years of age. Monthly magazine. Estab. 1961. Circ. 1,000,000. **Pays on acceptance.** Rights purchased vary with author and material. Buys all rights or first North American serial rights.
Nonfiction: Non-anecdotal articles about automobiles, new and old. Automotive road tests, informational articles on cars and equipment, some satire and humor and personalities, past and present, in the automotive industry and automotive sports. "Treat readers as intellectual equals. Emphasis on people as well as hardware." Informational, humor, historical, think articles, and nostalgia. All road tests are staff-written. "Unso-

licited manuscripts are not accepted. Query letters must be addressed to the Query Editor. Rates are generous, but few manuscripts are purchased from outside."

Photos: Color slides and b&w photos sometimes purchased with accompanying mss.

• Ranked as one of the best markets for freelance writers in *Writer's Digest* magazine's annual "Top 100 Markets," January 1993.

Tips: "It is best to start off with an interesting query and to stay away from nuts-and-bolts ideas because that will be handled in-house or by an acknowledged expert. Our goal is to be absolutely without flaw in our presentation of automotive facts, but we strive to be every bit as entertaining as we are informative."

CAR AUDIO AND ELECTRONICS, Avcom Publishing, Suite 1600, 21700 Oxnard St., Woodland Hills CA 91367. (818)593-3900. Fax: (818)593-2274. Editor: William Neill. Managing Editor: Doug Newcomb. 80-90% freelance written. Monthly magazine on electronic products designed for cars. "We help people buy the best electronic products for their cars. The magazine is about electronics, how to buy, use and so on: *CA&E* explains complicated things in simple ways. Articles are accurate, easy, and fun." Estab. 1988. Circ. 122,000. **Pays on acceptance.** Publishes ms an average of 3-5 months after acceptance. Byline given. Buys all rights. Submit seasonal/holiday material 3-4 months in advance. Simultaneous submissions OK. Query for electronic submissions. Reports in 1 week on queries and mss. Sample copy $3.95 for 9 × 12 SAE with 4 first class stamps. Writer's guidelines for #10 SASE.

Nonfiction: How-to (buy electronics for your car), interview/profile, new product, opinion, photo feature and technical. Buys 60-70 mss/year. Query with or without published clips, or send complete ms. Length: 500-1,700 words. Pays $300-1,000.

Photos: Send photos with submission. Review transparencies, any size.

Tips: "Write clearly and knowledgeably about car electronics."

CAR CRAFT, Petersen Publishing Co., 8490 Sunset Blvd., Los Angeles CA 90069. (213)854-2320. Fax: (310)854-2263. Editor: John Baechtel. Monthly magazine for men and women, 18-34, "enthusiastic owners of 1949 and newer muscle cars." Circ. 400,000. Study past issues before making submissions or story suggestions. Pays generally on publication, on acceptance under special circumstances. Buys all rights. Buys 2-10 mss/year. Query.

Nonfiction: How-to articles ranging from the basics to fairly sophisticated automotive modifications. Drag racing feature stories and some general car features on modified late model automobiles. Especially interested in do-it-yourself automotive tips, suspension modifications, mileage improvers and even shop tips and homemade tools. Length: open. Pays $100-200/page.

Photos: Photos purchased with or without accompanying text. Captions suggested, but optional. Reviews 8 × 10 b&w glossy prints; 35mm or 2¼ × 2¼ color. Pays $30 for b&w, color negotiable. "Pay rate higher for complete story, i.e., photos, captions, headline, subtitle: the works, ready to go."

CHEVY HIGH PERFORMANCE, Petersen Publishing Co., 8490 Sunset Blvd., Los Angeles CA 90069. (310)854-2250. Editor: Mike Magda. Managing Editor: Laura Castellanos. 85% freelance written. Bimonthly magazine covering Chevrolet vehicles. "Covers all aspects of street, racing, restored high performance Chevrolet vehicles with heavy emphasis on technical modifications and quality photography." Estab. 1985. Circ. 125,000. Pays on acceptance. Byline given. Offers no kill fee. Buys all rights. Submit seasonal/holiday material 6 months in advance. Query for electronic submissions. Reports in 4 weeks. Sample copy for 9 × 12 SAE with 5 first class stamps.

Nonfiction: How-to, new product, photo feature, technical. "We need well-researched and photographed technical articles. Tell us how to make horse-power on a budget." Buys 20 mss/year. Query. Length: 500-2,000 words. Pays $150-1,000. Sometimes pays expenses of writers on assignment.

Photos: Send photos with submission. Reviews contact sheets, any transparencies and any prints. Offers no additional payment for photos accepted with ms. Model releases required. Buys all rights.

Columns/Departments: Buys 12 mss/year. Query. Length: 100-1,500. Pays $150-500.

Tips: "Writers must be aware of the 'street scene.' "

CLASSIC AUTO RESTORER, Fancy Publishing, Inc., P.O. Box 6050, Mission Viejo CA 92690-6050. (714)855-8822. Fax: (714)855-3045. Editor: Steve Kimball. 85% freelance written. Bimonthly magazine on auto restoration. "Our readers own old cars and they work on them. We help our readers by providing as much practical, how-to information as we can about restoration and old cars." Estab. 1988. Pays on publication. Publishes an average of 3 months after acceptance. Offers $50 kill fee. Buys first North American serial or one-time rights. Submit seasonal/holiday material 4 months in advance. Query for electronic submissions. Reports in 1 month on queries. Sample copy $5.50. Free writer's guidelines.

Nonfiction: How-to (auto restoration), new product, photo feature, technical and travel. Buys 60 mss/year. Query with or without published clips or send complete ms. Length: 200-5,000 words. Pays $100-500 for assigned articles; $75-500 for unsolicited articles.

Photos: Send photos with submission. Reviews contact sheets, transparencies and 5×7 prints. Offers no additional payment for photos accepted with ms.

Columns/Departments: Buys 12 mss/year. Send complete ms. Length: 400-1,000 words. Pays $75-200.

Tips: "Send a story. Include photos. Make it something that the magazine regularly uses. Do automotive how-tos. We need lots of them. We'll help you with them."

CLASSIC CAR DIGEST, Bemis Communication Group, Inc., 118 Pleasant St., Marblehead MA 01945. (617)639-3000. Editor: Nathan C. Ferrarelli. 50% freelance written. Quarterly magazine on classic car restoration for automobile restorers and collectors—semi-technical. Circ. 5,000. Pays on publication. Publishes ms an average of 3-6 months after acceptance. Byline given. Buys first rights. Reports in 3 months. Free sample copy and writer's guidelines.

Nonfiction: General interest, how-to (technical, about restoration), interview/profile and technical. "No fiction." Buys 10 mss/year. Query with published clips. Length: 1,500-4,000 words. Pays $150-500 for assigned articles; $100-200 for unsolicited articles. If writer has associated business, will offer free ad. Sometimes pays expenses of writers on assignment.

Photos: Send photos with submission. Reviews contact sheets and 5×7 prints. Offers $50 maximum/photo. Identification of subjects required. Buys one-time rights.

Columns/Departments: In Restoration (technical explanation) and Metalcrafting (side of each craft). Buys 8 mss/year. Send complete ms. Length: 500-1,000 words. Pays $150 maximum.

Tips: "Writer should be an avid enthusiast of classic cars and have an appreciation of craftsman's skills." Interviews with professional restorers and features about restoration facilities are areas most open to freelance writers.

CYCLE WORLD, Hachette Filipacchi Magazines, Inc., 1499 Monrovia Ave., Newport Beach CA 92663. (714)720-5300. Editor: David Edwards. 20% freelance written. Monthly magazine for active motorcyclists, "young, affluent, educated, very perceptive." Subject matter includes "road tests (staff-written), features on special bikes, customs, racers, racing events; technical and how-to features involving mechanical modifications." Circ. 360,000. **Pays on acceptance.** Publishes ms an average of 3 months after acceptance. Buys all rights. Query for electronic submissions. Reports in 2 weeks on queries; 1 month on mss. Sample copy $2.75. Writer's guidelines for #10 SASE.

Nonfiction: Buys informative, well-researched, technical, theory and how-to articles; interviews; profiles; humor; and historical pieces. Buys 20 mss/year. Query. Length: 1,000-2,000 words. Pays variable rates. Sometimes pays the expenses of writers on assignment.

Photos: Purchased with or without ms, or on assignment. Reviews contact sheets and transparencies. Pays $75 minimum. Buys one-time rights and reprint rights.

Tips: "Area most open to freelancers is short nonfiction features. They must contain positive and fun experiences regarding motorcycle travel, sport and lifestyle."

FORMULA, The International Autosport Magazine, 395 Matheson Blvd. E., Mississauga, Ontario L4Z 2H2 Canada. (416)890-1846. Fax: (416)890-5769. Publisher: Malcolm Elston. Managing Editor: Rene Fagnan. 80% freelance written. Magazine that covers motorsport (road racing). Ten issues/year. "Writers must have knowledge and enthusiasm regarding the subject." Estab. 1985. Circ. 25,000. Pays 45 days after release of issue. Byline given. Offers 50% kill fee. Buys first and international rights. Simultaneous and previously published submissions OK. Query for electronic submissions. Reports in 1 month on queries. Sample copy for 9×12 SAE with 3 IRCs.

Nonfiction: Interview/profile, photo feature, technical. Buys 150 mss/year. Query. Length: 750-2,000 words. Pays $150-1,000. Sometimes pays expenses of writers on assignment.

Photos: Send photos with submission. Reviews 35mm transparencies. Offers $25-40/photo. Captions and identification of subjects required. Buys one-time rights.

Columns/Departments: Buys 30 mss/year. Query. Length: 750-900 words. Pays $400-500.

Fiction: Humorous, fictionalized personal experience or observation pertaining to motorsport. Buys 5 mss/year. Query. Length: 500-1,500 words. Pays $100-500.

FOUR WHEELER MAGAZINE, 6728 Eton Ave., Canoga Park CA 91303. (818)992-4777. Fax: (818)992-4979. Editor: John Stewart. 20% freelance written. Works with a small number of new/unpublished writers each year. Emphasizes four-wheel-drive vehicles, competition and travel/adventure. Monthly 164 pages magazine. Estab. 1963. Circ. 355,466. Pays on publication. Publishes ms an average of 4 months after acceptance. Buys all rights. Submit seasonal/holiday material at least 4 months in advance. Query for electronic submissions. Writer's guidelines for #10 SASE.

Nonfiction: 4WD competition and travel/adventure articles, technical, how-tos, and vehicle features about unique four-wheel drives. "We like the adventure stories that bring four wheeling to life in word and photo: mud-running deserted logging roads, exploring remote, isolated trails, or hunting/fishing where the 4×4 is a necessity for success." See features by Gary Wescott and Matt Conrad for examples. Query with photos before sending complete ms. Length: 1,200-2,000 words; average 4-5 pages when published. Pays $100/page minimum for complete package.

Photos: Requires professional quality color slides and b&w prints for every article. Captions required. Prefers Kodachrome 64 or Fujichrome 50 in 35mm or 2¼ formats. "Action shots a must for all vehicle features and travel articles."

Tips: "Show us you know how to use a camera as well as the written word. The easiest way for a new writer/photographer to break in to our magazine is to read several issues of the magazine, then query with a short vehicle feature that will show his or her potential as a creative writer/photographer."

4-WHEEL & OFF-ROAD, Petersen Publishing Co., 8490 Sunset Blvd., Los Angeles CA 90069. (310)854-2360. Editor: Drew Hardin. Monthly magazine covering four-wheel-drive vehicles, "devoted to new-truck tests, buildups of custom 4×4s, coverage of 4WD racing, trail rides and other competitions." Circ. 330,000. **Pays on acceptance.** Publishes ms an average of 4 months after acceptance. Byline given. Pays 20% kill fee. Buys first North American serial rights or all rights. Submit seasonal/holiday material 4 months in advance. Reports in 3 weeks. Writer's guidelines for #10 SASE.

Nonfiction: How-to (on four-wheel-drive vehicles—engines, suspension, drive systems, etc.), new product, photo feature, technical and travel. Buys 12-16 mss/year. Send complete ms. Length: 1,000-2,500 words. Pays $200-600.

Photos: Send photos with submission. Reviews transparencies and b&w prints. Offers no additional payment for photos accepted with ms. Captions, model releases and identification of subjects required. Buys all rights.

Fillers: Anecdotes, facts, gags, newsbreaks and short humor. Buys 12-16/year. Length: 50-150 words. Pays $15-50.

Tips: "Attend 4×4 events, get to know the audience. Present material only after full research. Manuscripts should contain *all* of the facts pertinent to the story. Technical/how-to articles are most open to freelancers."

HIGH PERFORMANCE PONTIAC, CSK Publishing Co., 299 Market St., Saddle Brook NJ 07662. (201)712-9300. Editor: Richard A. Lentinello. Managing Editor: Peter Easton. Bimonthly magazine that covers Pontiac cars, events and technology. "Our writers must have a knowledge of automobiles in general, and of Pontiacs in particular." Estab. 1979. Circ. 45,000 nationwide. Pays on publication. Publishes ms an average of 3 months after acceptance. Byline given. Offers negotiable kill fee. Buys first North American serial rights. Query for electronic submissions. Reprints OK; send photocopy of article and information about when and where the article previously appeared. Length: 250-2,000 words. Pays $100-150/page for articles. Sometimes pays expenses of writers on assignment. Reports in 3 months. Sample copy $4.50.

Nonfiction: Historical/nostalgic, how-to (hands-on Pontiac technical articles, e.g., how to recover your GTO seats), interview/profile, new product, photo feature and technical. "We are not interested in articles about pre-'81 Pontiacs that have had Chevy engines installed (excluding Canadian Pontiacs, of course)." Buys 50 mss/year. Query with or without published clips or send complete ms.

Photos: Send photos with submission. Reviews contact sheets, negatives, transparencies and prints. Captions required. Buys one-time rights.

MOPAR MUSCLE, Dobbs Publishing Group, 3816 Industry Blvd., Lakeland FL 33811. (813)644-0449. Fax: (813)648-1187. Editor: Greg Rager. Managing Editor: Stephen Siegel. 25% freelance written. Bimonthly magazine covering Chrysler Corp. performance vehicles. "Our audience has a knowledge of and interest in Chrysler vehicles." Estab. 1987. Circ. 75,000. Pays within 30 days of publication. Byline given. Buys first rights. Submit seasonal/holiday material 6 months in advance. Query for electronic submissions. Reports in 2 weeks. Free sample copy and writer's guidelines.

Nonfiction: Historical/nostalgic, how-to/technical, humor, interview/profile, new product, personal experience, photo feature and technical. Buys 20-25 mss/year. Query with published clips. Sometimes pays expenses of writers on assignment.

Photos: Send photos with submission. Reviews contact sheets and transparencies. Model release required. Buys one-time rights.

Columns/Departments: Moparts (new products), 50 words; Mopar Scene (news for Chrysler devotees), length varies. Buys 20-25 mss/year. Query.

Fiction: Historical, humorous. Query.

MOTOR TREND, Petersen Publishing Co., 8490 Sunset Blvd., Los Angeles CA 90069. (213)854-2222. Editor: Jeff Karr. 5-10% freelance written. Prefers to work with published/established writers. Monthly magazine for automotive enthusiasts and general interest consumers. Circ. 900,000. Publishes ms an average of 3 months after acceptance. Buys all rights. "Fact-filled query suggested for all freelancers." Reports in 1 month.

Nonfiction: Automotive and related subjects that have national appeal. Emphasis on domestic and imported cars, road tests, driving impressions, auto classics, auto, travel, racing, and high-performance features for the enthusiast. Packed with facts. Freelancers should confine queries to photo-illustrated exotic drives and other feature material; road tests and related activity are handled inhouse.

Photos: Buys photos, particularly of prototype cars and assorted automotive matter. Pays $25-500 for transparencies.

MUSCLE CARS, CSK Publishing Co., 299 Market St., Saddlebrook NJ 07662. (201)712-9300. Editor: Jim Campisano. Managing Editor: Peter Easton. Bimonthly magazine that covers stock and modified muscle cars. Pays on publication. Byline given. Buys first North American serial rights.
Nonfiction: How-to (automotive) and technical. Buys 20 mss/year. Query. Length: 1,000-10,000 words. Pays $150/page for assigned articles.

MUSCLE MUSTANGS & FAST FORDS, CSK Publishing Co., 299 Market St., Saddlebrook NJ 07662. (201)712-9300. Editor: Steve Collison. Managing Editor: Peter Easton. 40% freelance written. Magazine published 9 times/year covering late model 5-liter Mustangs and other high-performance Fords. Estab. 1988. Circ. 45,000. Pays on publication. Publishes ms an average of 6 months after acceptance. Byline given. Buys first North American serial rights. Query for electronic submissions. Reports in 3 weeks on queries; 6 weeks on mss. Sample copy $3.50 for 9×12 SAE with 5 first class stamps. Free writer's guidelines.
Nonfiction: How-to (automotive) and technical (automotive). Buys 40 mss/year. Query. Length: 500-1,500 words. Pays $150/magazine page for all articles. Sometimes pays expenses of writers on assignment.
Photos: Send photos with submission.

‡**MUSTANG MONTHLY**, Dobbs Publications, Inc., P.O. Box 7157, Lakeland FL 33807. (813)646-5743. Editor: Tom Corcoran. Technical Editor: Mark Houlahan. 30% freelance written. Monthly magazine covering concours 1964½ through 1973 Ford Mustang, and mildly modified '80s and '90s Mustang. "Our average reader makes over $35,000 annually, and is 35 years of age." Estab. 1977. Circ. 85,000. Pays on publication. Publishes ms an average of 4 months after acceptance. Byline given. Buys first North American rights. No simultaneous submissions. Reports in 3 months on mss. Writers guidelines available.
Nonfiction: How-to and technical. Color car features. No seasonal, holiday, humor, fiction or first-person nostalgia material. Buys 25 mss/year. Query with or without published clips or send complete ms. Write for guidelines first. Length: 2,500 words maximum. Pays 15¢/word for first 500 words; 10¢/word to 2,500-limit. Generally uses ms within 6 months of acceptance.
Photos: Send photos with submission; photography will make or break articles. Reviews contact sheets, negatives and transparencies. No color prints. Offers $100/page color pro-rated to size, $25 minimum; $10/photo b&w, $25 minimum. Captions and model releases (on our forms) "required."
Tips: *"Mustang Monthly* needs color features on trophy-winning original Mustangs and well-researched b&w how-to and technical articles. Our format rarely varies. A strong knowledge of early Mustangs is essential."

NATIONAL DRAGSTER, Drag Racing's Leading News Weekly, National Hot Rod Association, 2035 Financial Way, Glendora CA 91740. (818)963-8475. Fax: (818)335-4307. Editor: Phil Burgess. Managing Editor: Vicky Walker. 20% freelance written. Weekly tabloid of NHRA drag racing. "Covers NHRA drag racing—race reports, news, performance industry news, hot racing rumors—for NHRA members. Membership included with subscription." Estab. 1960. Circ. 80,000. Pays on publication. Publishes ms 1 month after acceptance. Byline given. Buys all rights. Submit seasonal/holiday material 2 months in advance. Simultaneous submissions OK. Query for electronic submissions. Reports in 1 month. Free sample copy.
Nonfiction: General interest, historical/nostalgic, how-to, humor, interview/profile, new product, personal experience, photo feature and technical. Buys 20 mss/year. Query. Pay is negotiable. Sometimes pays expenses of writers on assignment.
Photos: State availability of photos with submission. Reviews 5×7 prints. Captions and identification of subjects required. Buys all rights.
Columns/Departments: On the Run (first-person written, ghost written by drag racers), 900-1,000 words. Buys 48 mss/year. Query. Pay is negotiable.
Tips: "Feature articles on interesting drag racing personalities or race cars are most open to freelancers."

ON TRACK, The Auto Racing Magazine of Record, OT Publishing, Inc., P.O. Box 8509, Fountain Valley CA 92728-8509. (714)966-1131. Fax: (714)556-9776. Editor: Tim Tuttle, Andrew Crask. 90% freelance written. Biweekly magazine on auto racing (no drag racing, sprint cars, etc.). Estab. 1981. Circ. 40,000. Pays on publication. Publishes ms an average of 2 months after acceptance. Byline given. Buys first North American serial rights. Query for electronic submissions. Reports on queries in 2 months. Sample copy $2.50. Free writer's guidelines.
Nonfiction: Interview/profile and technical. Stories about race drivers with quotes from driver. Buys 3-4 mss/year. Query with published clips or send complete ms. Length: 800-2,000 words. Pays $5.25/column inch. Sometimes pays expenses of writers on assignment.
Photos: State availability of photos with submission. Reviews 5×7 prints. Offers $12.50/photo. Captions and identification of subjects required. Buys one-time rights.
Columns/Departments: Inside Line (look at subjects affecting trends, safety rules, etc.), 850 words; Broadcast Booth (TV, radio), 850 words. Buys 40 mss/year. Send complete ms. Pays $5.25/column inch.

OPEN WHEEL MAGAZINE, General Media, Box 715, Ipswich MA 01938. (508)356-7030. Fax: (508)356-2492. Editor: Dick Berggren. 80% freelance written. Monthly magazine. *"OW* covers sprint cars, midgets, supermodifieds and Indy cars. *OW* is an enthusiast's publication that speaks to those deeply involved in oval track automobile racing in the United States and Canada. *OW*'s primary audience is a group of men and women actively engaged in competition at the present time, those who have recently been in competition and those who plan competition soon. That audience includes drivers, car owners, sponsors and crew members who represent perhaps 50-70% of our readership. The rest who read the magazine are those in the racing trade (parts manufacturers, track operators and officials) and serious fans who see 30 or more races per year." Circ. 150,000. Pays on publication. Publishes ms an average of 6 months after acceptance. Byline given. Buys all rights. Submit seasonal material 2 months in advance. Reports in 3 weeks on queries. Sample copy for 9 × 12 SAE with 7 first class stamps. Writer's guidelines for #10 SASE.

Nonfiction: General interest, historical/nostalgic, how-to, humor, interview/profile, new product, photo feature and technical. "We don't care for features that are a blow-by-blow chronology of events. The key word is interest. We want features which allow the reader to get to know the main figure very well. Our view of racing is positive. We don't think all is lost, that the sport is about to shut down and don't want stories that claim such to be the case, but we shoot straight and avoid whitewash." Buys 125 mss/year. Query with complete ms.

Photos: State availability of photos with submission. Reviews contact sheets, negatives, transparencies and prints. Buys one-time rights.

Fillers: Anecdotes, facts and short humor. Buys 100/year. Length: 1-3 pages, double-spaced. Pays $35.

Tips: "Virtually all our features are submitted without assignment. An author knows much better what's going on in his backyard than we do. We ask that you write to us before beginning a story theme. Judging of material is always a combination of a review of the story and its support illustrations. Therefore, we ask for photography to accompany the manuscript on first submission. We're especially in the market for tech."

‡**RIDER**, TL Enterprises, Inc., 29901 Agoura Rd., Agoura Hills CA 91301. (818)991-4980. Editor: Mark Tuttle Jr.. Managing Editor: Donya Carlson. Contact: Mark Tuttle, Jr., Editor. 50% freelance written. Monthly magazine on motorcycling. "*Rider* serves owners and enthusiasts of road and street motorcycling, focusing on touring, commuting, camping and general sport street riding." Estab. 1974. Circ. 140,000. Pays on publication. Publishes ms an average of 6-12 months after acceptance. Byline given. Offers 25% kill fee. Buys first North American serial rights. Editorial lead time 4 months. Submit seasonal material 6 months in advance. Query for electronic submissions. Reports in 2 months. Sample copy $2.50. Writer's guidelines for #10 SASE.

Nonfiction: General interest, historical/nostalgic, how-to (re: motorcycling), humor, interview/profile and personal experience. Does not want to see "fiction or articles on 'How I Began Motorcycling.' " Buys 30 mss/year. Query. Length: 500-1,500 words. Pays $100 minimum for unsolicited articles. Sometimes pays expenses of writers on assignment.

Photos: Send photos with submission. Reviews contact sheets, transparencies and 5 × 7 prints (b&w only). Offers no additional payment for photos accepted with ms. Captions required. Buys one-time rights.

Columns/Departments: Rides, Rallies & Clubs (favorite ride or rally), 800-1,000 words. Buys 15 mss/year. Query. Pays $100.

Tips: "We rarely accept manuscripts without photos (slides or b&w prints). Query first. Follow guidelines. We are most open to feature stories (must include excellent photography) and material for 'Rides, Rallies and Clubs.' Include information on routes, local attractions, restaurants and scenery in favorite ride submissions."

ROAD KING MAGAZINE, P.O. Box 250, Park Forest IL 60466. Fax: (708)481-1063. Editor-in-Chief: George Friend. Editor: Richard Vurva. 10% freelance written. Eager to work with new/unpublished writers. Bimonthly truck driver leisure reading magazine. Circ. 218,000. **Pays on acceptance.** Publishes ms an average of 2 months after acceptance. Usually buys all rights; sometimes buys first rights. Byline given "always on fiction—if requested on nonfiction." Submit seasonal/holiday material 3 months in advance. Reports in 6 months. Sample copy for 6 × 9 SAE with 4 first class stamps or get free sample copy at any Unocal 76 truck stop.

Nonfiction: Trucker slant or general interest, humor and photo feature. No articles on violence or sex. Name and quote release required. No queries. Submit complete ms. Length: 500-1,200 words. Pays $50-400.

Photos: Submit photos with accompanying ms. No additional payment for b&w contact sheets or 2¼ × 2¼ color transparencies. Captions preferred. Buys first rights. Model release required.

Fiction: Adventure, historical, humorous, mystery, rescue-type suspense and western. Especially about truckers. No stories on sex and violence. Buys 4 mss/year. Submit complete ms. Length: approximately 1,200 words. Pays up to $400. Writer should quote selling price with submission.

Fillers: Jokes, gags, anecdotes and short humor about truckers. Buys 20-25/year. Length: 50-500 words. Pays $5-100.

Tips: "No collect phone calls or postcard requests. Never phone for free copy as we will not handle such phone calls. We don't appreciate letters we have to answer. Do not submit manuscripts, art or photos using registered mail, certified mail or insured mail. Publisher will not accept such materials from the post office. Publisher will not discuss refusal with writer. Nothing personal, just legal. Do not write and ask if we would like such and such article or outline. We buy only from original and complete manuscripts submitted on speculation. Do not ask for writer's guidelines. See above and/or get a copy of the magazine and be familiar with our format before submitting anything. We are a trucker publication whose readers are often family members and sometimes Bible Belt. We refrain from violence, sex, nudity, etc."

STOCK CAR RACING MAGAZINE, General Media, Box 715, Ipswich MA 01938. Editor: Dick Berggren. 80% freelance written. Eager to work with new/unpublished writers. Monthly magazine for stock car racing fans and competitors. Circ. 400,000. Pays on publication. Publishes ms an average of 3 months after acceptance. Buys all rights. Byline given. Query for electronic submissions. Reports in 6 weeks. Free writer's guidelines.
Nonfiction: General interest, historical/nostalgic, how-to, humor, interviews, new product, photo features and technical. "Uses nonfiction on stock car drivers, cars and races. We are interested in the story behind the story in stock car racing. We want interesting profiles and colorful, nationally interesting features. We are looking for more technical articles, particularly in the area of street stocks and limited sportsman." Query with or without published clips or submit complete ms. Buys 50-200 mss/year. Length: 100-6,000 words. Pays up to $450.
Photos: State availability of photos. Pays $20 for 8 × 10 b&w photos; up to $250 for 35mm or larger transparencies. Captions required.
Fillers: Anecdotes and short humor. Buys 100 each year. Pays $35.
Tips: "We get more queries than stories. We just don't get as much material as we want to buy. We have more room for stories than ever before. We are an excellent market with 12 issues per year. Virtually all our features are submitted without assignment. An author knows much better what's going on in his backyard than we do. We ask that you write to us before beginning a story theme. If nobody is working on the theme you wish to pursue, we'd be glad to assign it to you if it fits our needs and you are the best person for the job. Judging of material is always a combination of a review of the story and its support illustration. Therefore, we ask for photography to accompany the manuscript on first submission."

‡SUPER CYCLE, LFP Inc., # 300, 9171 Wilshire Blvd., Beverly Hills CA 90210. (213)274-7684. Fax: (310)274-7985. Editor: Elliot Borin. 95% freelance written. Monthly magazine covering motorcycles—Harley-Davidson. "Motorcycle events, parties, fiction stories about bikers and motorcycle legislation, no foreign bike or 'bad-biker' stuff." Circ. 100,000. Pays on publication. Publishes ms an average of 6 months or longer after acceptance. Byline given. Offers no kill fee. Buys first rights. Submit seasonal/holiday material 6 months in advance. Query for electronic submissions. Reports in 2 months. Sample copy $4 for 9 × 12 SAE.
Nonfiction: Interview/profile (bike builder races, etc.), personal experience (bike rally), photo feature (super customized bike with model) and travel (motorcycling). "No foreign bikes, no poetry." Buys 25 mss/year. Query with or without published clips or send complete ms. Length: 200-1,500 words. Pays $200-400 for assigned articles; $200-300 for unsolicited articles. Pays in contributor copies or other premiums in trade for motorcycle painting, accessories, parts or work.
Photos: Send photos with submission. Reviews 2 × 2 transparencies, slides and 3 × 5 or 4 × 6 prints. Offers no additional payment for photos accepted with ms. Offers $35-50/photo with no ms. Model release required. Buys all rights.
Columns/Departments: Elliot Borin. Gearheads or Tech Tips (technical advice on motorcycles); Tattoo Time; and Parties, 100-1,000 words. Buys 25 mss/year. Send complete ms. Pays $200-400.
Fiction: Adventure, humorous, mystery, romance, science fiction, Vietnam, tattoo (must all pertain to bikers). "No stories about 'bad guy' bikers." Buys 12 mss/year. Send complete ms. Length: 1,000 words maximum. Pays $200-400.
Tips: "Writers must be literate; understand bikers; type; photograph; be better than the rest!"

SUPER FORD, Dobbs Publishing Group, 3816 Industry Blvd., Lakeland FL 33811-0322. (813)644-0449. Fax: (813)644-8373. Editor: Tom Wilson. Managing Editor: Steve Statham. 50% freelance written. Monthly magazine covering the Ford Motor Company automotive history and performance. Estab. 1987. Circ. 65,000. Pays on publication. Publishes ms an average of 5 months after acceptance. Byline given. Offers 20% kill fee. Buys one-time rights. Submit seasonal/holiday material 3 months in advance. Query for electronic submissions. Reports in 2 months. Free sample copy and writer's guidelines.
Nonfiction: Historical/nostalgic; how-to (automotive technical), interview/profile; new product; personal experience; photo features ("those on individual cars are our bread-and-butter"); and technical. We need more tech articles that are complete, in-depth and offer fresh information on Ford high-performance. Simple subjects areas desirable as complex stories. Buys 48 mss/year. Send complete ms. Length: 500-2,000 words. Pays $100-700 for unsolicited articles. Sometimes pays expenses of writers on assignment.
Photos: Reviews contact sheets and negatives and 2¼ × 2¼ transparencies. Soft box or umbrella lighting of b&w tech articles required. Offers $40/b&w photo, $150/color cover. Captions and identification of subjects required. Buys one-time rights.
Columns/Departments: Keepin' Track (Ford racing coverage), 50-1,000 words; In The Fast Lane (Ford automotive news), 100-200 words. Buys 15 mss/year. Query. Pays $50-150.
Tips: "We need more technical material. Our photography standards have risen."

VETTE MAGAZINE, CSK Publishing, Inc., 299 Market St., Saddle Brook NJ 07662-5312. (201)712-9300. Fax: (201)712-9899. Editor: D. Randy Riggs. Managing Editor: Peter Easton. 75% freelance written. Monthly magazine. All subjects related to the Corvette automobile. "Our readership is extremely knowledgeable about the subject of Corvettes. Therefore, writers must know the subject thoroughly and be good at fact checking." Estab. 1976. Circ. 65,000. Offers 50% kill fee. Buys first North American serial rights. Submit seasonal/holiday material 3 months in advance. Query for electronic submissions. Reports in 1 month on queries and mss. Sample copy for 9×12 SAE with 6 first class stamps. Writer's guidelines for #10 SASE.

Nonfiction: General interest, historical/nostalgic, how-to, interview/profile, new product, personal experience, photo feature, technical and travel. Buys 120 mss/year. Query with published clips. Length: 4pp-2,700 words. Pays $150-750 for assigned articles; $100-350 for unsolicited articles. Sometimes pays expenses of writers on assignment.

Photos: State availability of photos with submission. Reviews contact sheets. Offers no additional payment for photos accepted with ms. Captions and model releases required. Buys one-time rights.

Columns/Departments: Reviews (books/videos), 400-500 words. Buys 12 mss/year. Query. Pays $50-150.

Fiction: Adventure, fantasy and slice-of-life vignettes. Buys 2 mss/year. Query with published clips. Length: 400-2,500 words. Pays $100-500.

Aviation

Professional and private pilots and aviation enthusiasts read the publications in this section. Editors want material for audiences knowledgable about commercial aviation. Magazines for passengers of commercial airlines are grouped in the Inflight category. Technical aviation and space journals and publications for airport operators, aircraft dealers and others in aviation businesses are listed under Aviation and Space in the Trade section.

AIR & SPACE/SMITHSONIAN MAGAZINE, 10th Floor, 370 L'Enfant Promenade SW, Washington DC 20024-2518. (202)287-3733. Fax: (202)287-3163. Editor: George Larson. Managing Editor: Tom Huntington. 80% freelance written. Prefers to work with published/established writers. Bimonthly magazine covering aviation and aerospace for a non-technical audience. "Features are slanted to a technically curious, but not necessarily technically knowledgeable audience. We are looking for unique angles to aviation/aerospace stories, history, events, personalities, current and future technologies, that emphasize the human-interest aspect." Estab. 1985. Circ. 310,000. **Pays on acceptance.** Byline given. Offers kill fee. Buys first North American serial rights. Publishes reprints of previously published articles. Send photocopy of article, including information about when and where the article previously appeared. Reports in 2 months. Sample copy $3.50 for 9½×13 SASE. Free writer's guidelines.

Nonfiction: Book excerpts, essays, general interest (on aviation/aerospace), historical/nostalgic, how-to, humor, interview/profile, photo feature and technical. Buys 50 mss/year. Query with published clips. Length: 1,500-3,000 words. Pays $2,000 maximum. Pays the expenses of writers on assignment.

Photos: State availability of illustrations with submission. Reviews 35mm transparencies.

Columns/Departments: Above and Beyond (first person), 1,500-2,000 words; Flights and Fancy (whimsy), approximately 1,200 words; Oldies & Oddities (weird, wonderful or old), 1,200 words; Collections (profiles of unique museums), 1,200 words. Buys 25 mss/year. Query with published clips. Pays $1,000 maximum. Soundings (brief items, timely but not breaking news), 500-700 words. Pays $300.

Tips: "Soundings is the section most open to freelancers."

‡**AIR LINE PILOT,** Air Line Pilots Association, 535 Herndon Parkway, P.O. Box 1169, Herndon VA 22070. (703)689-4176. Editor: Esperison Martinez, Jr. 10% freelance written. Prefers to work with published/established writers; works with a small number of new/unpublished writers each year. Monthly magazine for airline pilots covering "commercial aviation industry information—economics, avionics, equipment, systems, safety—that affects a pilot's life in professional sense." Also includes information about management/labor relations trends, contract negotiations, etc. Estab. 1931. Circ. 60,000. **Pays on acceptance.** Publishes ms an average of 6 months after acceptance. Offers 50% kill fee. Buys all rights. Submit seasonal/holiday material 6 months in advance. Query for electronic submissions. Reports in 2 months. Sample copy $2. Writer's guidelines for #10 SASE.

Nonfiction: Humor, inspirational, photo feature and technical. "We are backlogged with historical submissions and prefer not to receive unsolicited submissions at this time." Buys 20 mss/year. Query with or without published clips, or send complete ms. Length: 700-3,000 words. Pays $200-600 for assigned articles; pays $50-600 for unsolicited articles.

Photos: Send photos with submission. Reviews contact sheets, 35mm transparencies and 8×10 prints. Offers $10-35/photo. Identification of subjects required. Buys one-time rights.

Tips: "For our feature section, we seek aviation industry information that affects the life of a professional airline pilot from a career standpoint. We also seek material that affects a pilot's life from a job security and work environment standpoint. Any airline pilot featured in an article must be an Air Line Pilot Association member in good standing."

BALLOON LIFE, Balloon Life Magazine, Inc., 2145 Dale Ave., Sacramento CA 95815-3632. (916)922-9648. Editor: Tom Hamilton. 75% freelance written. Monthly magazine for sport of hot air ballooning. Estab. 1986. Circ. 4,000. Pays on publication. Byline given. Offers 50-100% kill fee. Buys first North American serial or second serial (reprint) rights. Submit seasonal/holiday material 3-4 months in advance. Previously published submissions OK. Send photocopy of article of short story. For reprints, pays 100% of amount paid for original article. Query for electronic submissions. Reports in 3 weeks on queries; 1 month on mss. *Writer's Market* recommends allowing 2 months for reply. Sample copy for 9 × 12 SAE with $2 postage. Writer's guidelines for #10 SASE.

Nonfiction: Book excerpts, general interest, how-to (flying hot air balloons, equipment techniques), interview/profile, new product, letters to the editor and technical. Buys 150 mss/year. Query with or without published clips or send complete ms. Length: 800-5,000 words. Pays $50-75 for assigned articles; $25-50 for unsolicited articles. Sometimes pays expenses of writers on assignment.

Photos: Send photos with submission. Reviews transparencies and prints. Offers $15-50/photo. Identification of subjects required. Buys one-time rights.

Columns/Departments: Hangar Flying (real life flying experience that others can learn from), 800-1,500 words; Preflight (a news and information column), 100-500 words; and Logbook (recent balloon events — events that have taken place in last 3-4 months), 300-500 words. Buys 60 mss/year. Send complete ms. Pays $15-50.

Fiction: Humorous. Buys 3-5 mss/year. Send complete ms. Length: 800-1,500 words. Pays $50.

Tips: "This magazine slants toward the technical side of ballooning. We are interested in articles that help to educate and provide safety information. Also stories with manufacturers, important individuals and/or of historic events and technological advances important to ballooning. The magazine attempts to present articles that show 'how-to' (fly, business opportunities, weather, equipment). Both our Feature Stories section and Logbook section are where most mss are purchased."

CAREER PILOT, FAPA, 4959 Massachusetts Blvd., Atlanta GA 30337-6607. (404)997-8097. Editor: Teresa Greer. 80% freelance written. Monthly magazine covering aviation. "A career advisory magazine as a service to FAPA members. Readers largely are career pilots who are working toward their professional goals. Articles cover topics such as recent developments in aviation law and medicine, changes in the industry, job interview techniques and how to get pilot jobs." Estab. 1983. Circ. 16,500. Pays prior to publication. Publishes ms an average of 3-4 months after acceptance. Byline given. Offers 50% kill fee. Buys all rights. Simultaneous and previously published submissions OK. Query for electronic submissions. Reports in 3 months.

Nonfiction: How-to (get hired by an airline), interview/profile (aviation related) and personal experience (aviation related). Special issues: October — Corporate Aviation, January — Helicopters. "No humor, cartoons or fiction." Buys 60 mss/year. Query with clips or send complete ms. Length: 2,000-2,500 words. "Pays 18¢/word with $50 bonus for meeting deadlines." Sometimes pays expenses of writers on assignment. Reprints OK; send tearsheet of article, photocopy of article, typed ms with rights for sale noted or information about when and where the article previously appeared. Pays 50% of their fee for an original article.

Photos: State availability of photos with submission. Reviews prints. Offers no additional payment for photos accepted with ms. Captions and identification of subjects required.

Tips: "Send articles and clips that are aviation/business related. Express your interest in writing for our publication on a semi-regular basis."

FLYING, Hachette Filipacchi Magazine, Inc., 2nd Floor, 500 W. Putnam Ave., Greenwich CT 06830. (203)622-2700. Editor: J. "Mac" MacClellan. 10% freelance written. Monthly magazine. Circ. 322,096. **Pays on acceptance.** Publishes ms an average of 3 months after acceptance. Buys first North American serial rights, but with exclusivity for 2 years. Reports in 3 weeks on queries; 5 weeks on mss. "Writers should be pilots and know first-hand what they are writing about." Query with or without published clips or send complete ms. Length: 4 pages typeset maximum. Pay varies, $1,200 maximum.

GENERAL AVIATION NEWS & FLYER, N.W. Flyer, Inc., P.O. Box 98786, Tacoma WA 98498-0786. (206)588-1743. Fax: (206)588-4005. Editor: Dave Sclair. 30% freelance written. Prefers to work with published/established writers. Biweekly tabloid covering general aviation. Provides "coverage of aviation news, activities, regulations and politics of general and sport aviation with emphasis on timely features of interest to pilots and aircraft owners." Estab. 1949. Circ. 35,000. Pays 1 month after publication. Publishes ms an average of 3 months after acceptance. Byline given. Buys one-time and first North American serial rights; on occasion second serial (reprint) rights. Submit seasonal/holiday material 2 months in advance. Simultaneous queries and previously published submissions from noncompetitive publications OK but must be identified. Query for electronic submissions. Reports in 2 weeks on queries; 1 month on mss. Sample copy $3.50. Writer's and style guidelines for #10 SASE.

Nonfiction: Features of current interest about aviation businesses, developments at airports, new products and services, safety, flying technique and maintenance. "Good medium-length reports on current events — controversies at airports, problems with air traffic control, FAA, etc. We want solid news coverage of breaking stories." Query first on historical, nostalgic features and profiles/interviews. Many special sections throughout the year; send SASE for list. Buys 100 mss/year. Query or send complete ms. Length: 500-2,000 words. Pays up to $3/printed column inch maximum. Rarely pays the expenses of writers on assignment.

Photos: "Good pics a must." Send photos (b&w or color prints preferred, no slides) with ms. All photos must have complete captions and carry photographer's ID. Pays $10/b&w photo used.

Tips: "We always are looking for features on places to fly and interviews or features about people and businesses using airplanes in unusual ways. Travel features must include information on what to do once you've arrived, with addresses from which readers can get more information. Get direct quotations from the principals involved in the story. We want current, first-hand information."

PLANE AND PILOT, Werner Publishing Corp., Suite 1220, 12121 Wilshire Blvd., Los Angeles CA 90025. (310)820-1500. Fax: (310)826-5008. Editor: Steve Werner. Managing Editor: James Lawrence. 100% freelance written. Monthly magazine that covers general aviation. "We think a spirited, conversational writing style is most entertaining for our readers. We are read by private and corporate pilots, instructors, students, mechanics and technicians — everyone involved or interested in general aviation." Estab. 1964. Circ. 130,000. Pays on publication. Publishes ms an average of 3 months after acceptance. Byline given. Kill fee negotiable. Buys all rights. Publishes reprints of previously published articles. Send photocopy of article or typed ms with rights for sale noted. Include information about when and where the article previously appeared. For reprints, pays 50% of the amount paid for an original article. Submit seasonal/holiday material 4 months in advance. Query for electronic submissions. Reports in 3 months. Sample copy $2.95. Free writer's guidelines.

Nonfiction: Book excerpts, essays, general interest, how-to, humor, inspirational, new product, personal experience, technical, travel, pilot proficiency and pilot reports on aircraft. Buys 150 mss/year. Send complete ms. Length: 1,000-2,500 words. Pays $200-500. Pays expenses of writers on assignment.

Photos: Send photos with submission. Reviews transparencies and prints. Offers $50-300/photo. Captions and identification of subjects required. Buys all rights.

Columns/Departments: Associate Editor: Greta Guest. Readback (any newsworthy items on aircraft and/or people in aviation), 100-300 words; Flight I'll Never Forget (a particularly difficult or wonderful flight), 1,000-1,500 words; Jobs & Schools (a feature or an interesting school or program in aviation), 1,000-1,500 words; and Travel (any traveling done in piston-engine aircraft), 1,000-2,500 words. Buys 30 mss/year. Send complete ms. Length: 1,000-2,500 words. Pays $200-500.

PRIVATE PILOT, Fancy Publications Corp., P.O. Box 6050, Mission Viejo CA 92690-6050. (714)855-8822. Fax: (714)855-3450. Editor: Mary F. Silitch. 75% freelance written. Works with a small number of new/unpublished writers each year. For owner/pilots of private aircraft, for student pilots and others aspiring to attain additional ratings and experience. "We take a unique, but limited view within our field." Estab. 1964. Circ. 105,000. Buys first North American serial rights. Pays on publication. Publishes manuscript average of 6 months after acceptance. No simultaneous submissions. Query for electronic submissions. Reports in 2 months. Sample copy $4. Writer's guidelines for SASE.

Nonfiction: Material on techniques of flying, developments in aviation, product and specific airplane test reports, travel by aircraft, and development and use of airports. All must be related to general aviation field. Buys about 60-90 mss/year. Query. Length: 1,000-4,000 words. Pays $75-300.

Photos: Pays $50 for four-color prints or transparencies purchased with ms or on assignment. Pays $300 for color transparencies used on cover.

Tips: "Freelancer must know the subject about which he is writing and use good grammar; remember that we try to relate to the middle segment of the business/pleasure flying public. We see too many 'first flight' type of articles. Most writers do not do enough research on their subject. We would like to see more material on business-related flying, more on people involved in flying."

PROFESSIONAL PILOT, Queensmith Communications, 3014 Colvin St., Alexandria VA 22314. (703)370-0606. Fax: (703)370-7082. Editor: Clifton Stroud. 75% freelance written. Monthly magazine on major and regional airline, corporate, military and various other types of professional aviation. "Our readers are commercial pilots with highest ratings and the editorial content reflects their knowledge and experience." Estab. 1967. Circ. 35,000. **Pays on acceptance.** Publishes ms an average of 3 months after acceptance. Byline given. Kill fee negotiable. Buys all rights. Free sample copy.

Nonfiction: How-to (avionics and aircraft flight checks), humor, interview/profile, personal experience (if a lesson for professional pilots), photo feature and technical (avionics, weather, engines, aircraft). All issues have a theme such as regional airline operations, maintenance, jet aircraft, helicopters, etc. Buys 40 mss/year. Query. Length: 750-2,500. Pays $200-1,000. Sometimes pays expenses of writers on assignment.

Photos: Send photos with submission. Prefers transparencies. Offers no additional payment for photos accepted with ms. Captions and identification of subjects required. Buys all rights.

Columns/Departments: Pireps (aviation news), 300-500 words. Buys 12 mss/year. Query. Pays $100-250.

Tips: Query first. "Freelancer should have background in aviation that will make his articles believable to highly qualified pilots of commercial aircraft. We are placing a greater emphasis on airline operations, management and pilot concerns."

Business and Finance

Business publications give executives and consumers a range of information from local business news and trends to national overviews and laws that affect them. National and regional publications are listed below in separate categories. Magazines that have a technical slant are in the Trade section under Business Management, Finance or Management and Supervision categories.

National

‡BUSINESS, Omni Media, 2065 Cantu Court, Sarasota FL 34232. (813)378-9048. Editor: Deborah Robbins Millman. 60% freelance written. Bimonthly magazine for business. "We are a regional business magazine covering Sarasota and Manatee counties in Florida." Circ. 10,000. Pays on publication. Publishes ms an average of 2 months after acceptance. Byline given. Makes work-for-hire assignments. Editorial lead time 2 months. Submit seasonal material 2-3 months in advance. Query for electronic submissions. Prefers WordPerfect 5.0 5¼″ disks. Reports in 1 month on queries. Sample copy and writer's guidelines free on request.
Nonfiction: Book excerpts, essays, how-to, interview/profile, travel and business advice. No fiction. Buys 30-40 mss/year. Query with published clips. Length: 1,000-3,500 words. Pays $0-150. Pays with contributor's copies "if unsolicited article of interest for which we have not budgeted funds."
Photos: Send photos with submission. Offers no additional payment for photos accepted with ms in most cases but negotiates payment individually in some cases. Captions and identification of subjects required. Buys one-time rights.
Columns/Departments: Dollars & Sense (financial advice), 1,500-2,500 words. Buys 6 mss/year. Query with published clips. Pays $150.
Tips: "Send a resume and writing sample, plus any story ideas."

‡BUSINESS START-UPS, (formerly New Business Opportunities), Entrepreneur Group, Inc., 2392 Morse Ave., Irvine CA 92714. (714)261-2083. Editor: Rieva Lesonsky. 20-25% freelance written. Monthly magazine on small business. "Provides how-to information for starting a small business, running a small business during the 'early' years and profiles of entrepreneurs who have started successful small businesses." Estab. 1989. Circ. 210,000. **Pays on acceptance.** Byline given. Offers 20% kill fee. Buys first time international rights. Submit seasonal/holiday material 6 months in advance. Reports in 2 months on queries. Sample copy $3. Writer's guidelines for SASE. Please write: "Attn: Writer's Guidelines" on envelope.
Nonfiction: "We are especially seeking how-to articles for starting a small business. Please read the magazine and writer's guidelines first before querying." Interview/profiles on entrepreneurs. Query. Length: 1,800. Pays $300.
Photos: State availability of photos with submission. Identification of subjects required.

BUSINESS TODAY, Meridian International, Inc., P.O. Box 10010, Ogden UT 84409. (801)394-9446. 40% freelance written. Monthly magazine covering all aspects of business. Particularly interested in tips to small/medium business managers. **Pays on acceptance.** Publishes ms an average of 3 months after acceptance. Byline given. Buys first rights, second serial (reprint) rights and nonexclusive reprint rights. Reports in 2 months with SASE. Sample copy $1 for 9×12 SAE. Writer's guidelines for #10 SASE. All requests for samples and guidelines, and queries should be addressed Attn: Editorial Staff.
Nonfiction: General interest articles about employee relations, management principles, trends in finance, technology, ergonomics, and "how to do it better" stories. Articles covering up-to-date practical business information are welcome. Cover stories are often profiles of people who have expertise and success in a specific aspect of business. Buys 40 mss/year. Query. Length: 1,200-1,500 words. Pays 15¢/word for first rights plus non-exclusive reprint rights. Payment for second rights is 10¢/word.
Photos: Send photos with query. Reviews 35mm or larger transparencies and 5×7 or 8×10 color prints. Pays $35 for inside photo; $50 for cover photo. Captions, model releases and identification of subjects required.
Tips: "We're looking for meaty, hard-core business articles with practical applications. Profiles should be prominent business-people, preferably Fortune-500 league. The key is a well-written query letter that: 1) demonstrates that the subject of the article is tried-and-true and has national appeal, 2) shows that the article will have a clear, focused theme, 3) gives evidence that the writer/photographer is a professional, even if a beginner."

BUSINESS WEEK, McGraw Hill, 1221 Avenue of the Americas, New York NY 10020. Staff written. "Prefers not to share information."

CONSUMER SENSE, Consumer Sense Marketing, 177 Pine St., P.O. Box 2065, Natick MA 01760-0015. (508)653-2168. Editor: Ronald M. Weinberg. 30% freelance written. Quarterly company publication covering marketing issues. "Writers should address marketing issues in a direct manner with creative and practical considerations." Estab. 1990. Circ. 2,100. **Pays on acceptance.** Publishes an average of 6 months after acceptance. Byline sometimes given. Buys all rights. Reports in 1 month on queries; 6 weeks on mss. Sample copy and writer's guidelines $2.
Nonfiction: Inspirational, how-to, opinion and analytical. Buys 10-12 mss each year. Length: 800-1500 words. Pays $30-75 for articles.
Columns/Departments: By Example (how specific marketing challenges were successfully addressed by using accessible strategies and plans) and Hidden Markets (areas that offer plentiful marketing opportunities, but have not been fully explored: e.g., the home fitness market). Buys 1-3 mss/year. Query with published clips. Length: 800-1,200 words. Pays $30-75.
Fillers: Marketing Tips, buys 8-12/year. Pays $5-10.

D&B REPORTS, The Dun & Bradstreet Magazine for Small Business Management, Dun & Bradstreet, 24th Floor, 299 Park Ave., New York NY 10171. (212)593-6723. Editor: Patricia W. Hamilton. 10% freelance written. Works with a small number of new/unpublished writers each year. Bimonthly magazine for small business. "Articles should contain useful information that managers of small businesses can apply to their own companies. *D&B Reports* focuses on companies with $15 million in annual sales and under." Estab. 1954. Circ. 76,000. **Pays on acceptance.** Publishes ms an average of 2 months after acceptance. Byline given. Buys first North American serial rights. Query for electronic submissions. Reports in 1 month on manuscripts. Free sample copy and writer's guidelines.
Nonfiction: How-to (on management) and interview/profile (of successful entrepreneurs). Buys 5 mss/year. Query. Length: 1,500-2,500 words. Pays $500 minimum.
Photos: State availability of photos with submission. Identification of subjects required. Buys one-time rights.
Tips: "The area of our publication most open to freelancers is profiles of innovative companies and managers."

‡THE ECONOMIC MONITOR, The Charles B. McFadden Co., Inc., P.O. Box 2268, Winter Park FL 32790. (407)629-4548. Fax: (407)629-0762. 50% freelance written. Quarterly magazine on economics and national economic policy. "*The Economic Monitor* publishes articles that explain economic issues in lay terms. It observes and comments on national economic and social policy from a conservative free-market viewpoint." Estab. 1990. Circ. 500. Pays on publication. Publishes ms an average of 3 months after acceptance. Buys one-time rights. Editorial lead time 3 months. Accepts simultaneous and previously published submissions. Reports in 3 weeks on queries; 1 month on mss (prefer query first). Sample copy for 9 × 12 SAE with 2 first class stamps. Writer's guidelines for #10 SASE.
Nonfiction: Book excerpts, essays, expose, humor, interview/profile and opinion. "No opinion pieces that are not backed by research." Buys 12 mss/year. Query with published clips. Length: 500-2,500 words. Pays $50 minimum for assigned articles; $25 for unsolicited articles. Pays contributor copies "in addition to any cash stipend. Sometimes will pay in copies for unpublished or published book excerpts that the author can use for publicity/exposure."
Columns/Departments: The Press (media bias), 700-1,000 words. Buys 2 mss/year. Query with published clips. Pays $25-50.
Tips: "We are a small but growing magazine that eagerly seeks new conservative writers. Although we only offer small stipends at present, we are looking for material that is suitable for expansion into books and/or syndication. Anything we use must be well researched and backed by facts. We look for tight, well-written copy. We are particularly interested in these subjects: (1) liberal media bias; (2) effect of tax policy on gross domestic product; and (3) how government transfers the cost of its social programs to business."

ENTREPRENEUR MAGAZINE, 2392 Morse Ave., Irvine CA 92714. Fax: (714)755-4211. Editor: Rieva Lesonsky. 40% freelance written. "Readers are small business owners seeking information on running a better business." Circ. 360,000. **Pays on acceptance.** Publishes ms an average of 3-5 months after acceptance. Buys first international rights. Byline given. Submit seasonal/holiday material 6 months in advance of issue date. Reports in 2 months. Sample copy $3. Writer's guidelines for #10 SASE. Please write "Attn: Writer's Guidelines" on envelope.
  • Ranked as one of the best markets for freelance writers in *Writer's Digest* magazine's annual "Top 100 Markets," January 1993.

Nonfiction: How-to (information on running a business, profiles of unique entrepreneurs). Buys 60-70 mss/year. Query with clips of published work and SASE. Length: 200-2,000 words. Payment varies.

Photos: "We use color transparencies to illustrate articles. Please state availability with query." Uses standard color transparencies. Buys various rights. Model release required.

Tips: "Read several issues of the magazine! Study the feature articles. (Columns are not open to freelancers.) It's so exciting when a writer goes beyond the typical, flat "business magazine query" – how to write a press release, how to negotiate with vendors, etc. – and instead investigates a current trend and then develops a story on how that trend affects small business."

EXECUTIVE FEMALE, NAFE, 4th Floor, 127 W. 24th St., New York NY 10011-1914. (212)645-0770. Fax: (212)633-6489. Editor-in-Chief: Basia Hellwig. Executive Editor: Patti Watts. Assistant Managing Editor: Dorian Burden. Assistant Editor: Melissa Wahl. 60% freelance written. Bimonthly magazine emphasizing "useful career, business and financial information for the upwardly mobile female." 60% freelance written. Prefers to work with published/established writers. Estab. 1975. Circ. 200,000. Byline given. **Pays on acceptance.** Publishes ms an average of 2 months after acceptance. Submit seasonal/holiday material 6 months in advance. Buys first rights, second serial (reprint) rights to material originally published elsewhere. Previously published submissions OK. Reports in 2 months. Sample copy $2.50. Writer's guidelines for #10 SASE.

Nonfiction: "Articles on any aspect of career advancement and financial planning are welcomed." Needs how-tos for managers and articles about coping on the job, trends in the workplace, financial planning, trouble shooting, business communication, time and stress management, career goal-setting and get-ahead strategies. Written queries only. Submit photos with ms (b&w prints or transparencies) or include suggestions for artwork. Length: 800-2,000 words. Pays 50¢/word. Pays for local travel and telephone calls. Reprints OK; send photocopy of article, typed manuscript with rights for sale noted or information about when and where the article previously appeared. Pays 25% of their fee for an original article.

Columns/Departments: Your Money (savings, financial advice, economic trends, interesting tips); Managing Smart (tips on managing people, getting ahead); and Your Business (entrepreneurial stories). Buys 20 mss/year. Query with published clips or send complete ms. Length: 250-1,000 words. Pays 50¢/word.

FINANCIAL WORLD, Financial World Partners, 1328 Broadway, New York NY 10001. Staff written. "Prefers not to share information."

‡FUTURES MAGAZINE, The Magazine for Derivative Traders & Money Managers, Oster Communications, Suite 1150, 250 S. Wacker Dr., Chicago IL 60606. (312)977-0999. Editor: Ginger Szala. Managing Editor: Diane Glaser. Contact: Ginger Szala. 25% freelance written. Monthly magazine for financial and commodity markets. "*Futures Magazine* is written for institutional and individual traders, money managers, risk managers, brokers and investors who use the futures, options and derivatives markets. Articles focus on international financial, agricultural, energy, metals and stock index futures, options and derivative markets. Regular features: market analysis, price forecasts, trading strategies, profiles, news." Estab. 1972. Circ. 70,000. Pays on publication. Publishes ms an average of 3 months after acceptance, "depending on timing." Byline given. Buys all rights. Editorial lead time 3 months. Submit seasonal material 3 months in advance. Query for electronic submissions. Prefers Procom or WordPerfect. Reports in 1 month on queries. Sample copy and writer's guidelines free on request.

Nonfiction: Expose (market related), how-to (trade strategies), interview/profile (related to markets), new product and technical (computer, software). "*No* general pieces. We write for traders and sophisticated investors." Buys 14+ mss/year. Query with published clips. Length: 1,500-2,500 words. Pays 50¢-$1/word. Pays expenses of writers on assignment.

Photos: State availability of photos with submission. Offers no additional payment for photos accepted with ms. Identification of subjects required. Buys one-time rights.

Columns/Departments: Software Reviews (analysis of trading software), 600 words; Book Reviews (analysis of market-related books), 300 words; Trader Profile (interview with successful trader), 600 words. Buys 10 mss/year. Query with published clips. Pays 50¢-$1/word.

Tips: "Have an insider knowledge of how markets work, how futures and options are traded, what makes a trader/company successful using these markets. We are open to freelance submissions in Trader Profile, Book Reviews and Software Reviews."

I.B. (Independent Business), America's Small Business Magazine, Group IV Communications, Inc., #211, 875 S. Westlake Blvd., Westlake Village CA 91361. (805)496-6156. Editor: Daniel Kehrer. Editorial Director: Don Phillipson. 75% freelance written. Bimonthly magazine for small and independent business. "We publish only practical articles of interest to small business owners all across America; also some small business owner profiles." Estab. 1989. Circ. 630,000. **Pays on acceptance.** Publishes ms an average of 4 months after acceptance. Byline given. Offers 25% kill fee. First and non-exclusive reprint rights. Simultaneous queries OK. Reports in 3 months. Sample copy $4. Writer's guidelines for #10 SASE.

• Accepted articles must be submitted via disk or modem and must be Mac compatible.

Nonfiction: How-to, short interview/profile, new product and photo feature. No "generic" business articles, articles on big business or general articles on economic theory. Buys 80-100 mss/year. Query with bio/resume; do not send mss. Length: 1,000-2,000 words. Pays $500-1,500 for assigned articles. Pays expenses of writers on assignment.

Columns/Departments: Fast Track (short items on small business interests), 50-200 words. Tax Tactics, Small Business Computing, Marketing Moves, Ad-visor, Banking & Finance, Business Cost-Savers, all 500-1,500 words. Buys 40-50 mss/year. Query with resume and published clips. Pays $100-1,500.

Tips: "Talk to small business owners anywhere in America about what they want to read, what concerns or interests them in running a business. All areas open, but we use primarily professional business writers with top credentials in the field."

INCOME OPPORTUNITIES, IO Publications, 1500 Broadway, New York NY 10036-4015. (212)642-0600. Fax: (212)302-8269. Editor: Stephen Wagner. Managing Editor: Arthur Blougouras. 90% freelance written. Monthly magazine that covers small business. Estab. 1956. Circ. 425,000. **Pays on acceptance.** Publishes ms an average of 5 months after acceptance. Byline given. Buys second serial (reprint) or all rights and makes work-for-hire assignments. Submit seasonal/holiday material 6 months in advance. Query for electronic submissions. Reports in 3 weeks on queries, 1 month on mss. *Writer's Market* recommends allowing 2 months for reply. Free sample copy. Writer's guidelines for #10 SASE.

Nonfiction: How-to (start a small or home business) and new product (for mail order, flea market sales). Need freelance material for two home business issues. No purely inspirational articles. Buys 100 mss/year. Query. Length: 600-2,500 words. Pays $100-350. Sometimes pays expenses of writers on assignment.

Photos: Send photos with submission. Offers no additional payment for photos accepted with ms. Identification of subjects required. Buys all rights.

Tips: Areas most open to freelancers are "profiles of successful small-business operators. Details of how they started, start-up costs, how they operate, advertising methods, tools, materials, equipment needed, projected or actual earnings, advice to readers for success."

INDIVIDUAL INVESTOR, Financial Data Systems, Inc., 4th Floor, 38 E. 29th St., New York NY 10016-7911. (212)689-2777. Fax: (212)689-6663. Editor-in-Chief: Jonathan Steinberg. Editor: Gordon T. Anderson. 60% freelance written. Monthly magazine publishing "company profiles, designed to highlight possible stock investments for individuals. We also publish mutual fund profiles, investment advisory pieces, and a select number of broad features on topics related to the financial markets." Estab. 1981. Circ. 105,000. Pays on publication (within 30 days). Publishes ms an average of 1 month after acceptance. Byline given. Offers 40% kill fee. Buys all rights. Reports in 2 months. Query for electronic submissions. Free sample copy and writer's guidelines.

Nonfiction: Financial/business. Buys 50 mss/year. Query with published clips. Length: 1,200-1,500 words. Pays $350-450 for assigned articles.

Columns/Departments: Buys 50 mss/year. Query with published clips. Length: 1,200-1,500 words. Pays $350-450.

Tips: "Because we do not accept unsolicited articles, queries are essential. We are very open to freelancers, especially those who understand the stock market."

MONEY, Time & Life Bldg., Rockefeller Center, New York NY 10020. Staff written. "Prefers not to share information."

NATION'S BUSINESS, US Chamber of Commerce, 1615 H St., NW, Washington DC 20062-2000. (202)463-5650. Fax: (202)887-3437. Editor: Robert T. Gray. Managing Editor: Mary McElveen. 50% freelance written. Monthly magazine covering management of small businesses. Estab. 1912. Circ. 865,000. **Pays on acceptance.** Publishes ms an average of 6 months after acceptance. Byline given. Kill fee negotiable. Buys all rights. Query for electronic submissions. Reports in 1 month. Sample copy $2.50. Free writer's guidelines.

Nonfiction: Book excerpts, how-to, new product and personal experience. No opinion or corporate personnel. Buys 100 mss/year. Query. Length: 250-3,000 words. Pays $100-2,000. Sometimes pays expenses of writers on assignment.

‡OWNER-MANAGER, Ivy Holdings, Ltd., Suite 2411, 67 Wall St., New York NY 10005. (212)323-8056. Editor: Charles Riley II. Managing Editor: Jeff Deasy. Publisher: V. Ricasio. 20% freelance written. Bi-monthly magazine for business and enterprise. "Our readers are owners who manage their own companies. The editorial mission is to provide them with information to manage their businesses, but not merely to become better businessmen but fulfilled individuals as well." Estab. 1992. Circ. 10,000. Pays on publication. Publishes ms an average of 4 months after acceptance. Byline given. Offers 30% kill fee. Buys first rights or second serial rights. Editorial lead time 2 months. Submit seasonal material 3 months in advance. Accepts previously published submissions. Query for electronic submissions. Sample copy for 8½ × 11 SAE with 1 first class stamp. Writer's guidelines for #10 SASE.

Nonfiction: Book excerpts, essays, general interest, how-to (not detailed guide but why such actions are needed), interview/profile, opinion and technical. Buys 8 mss/year. Send complete ms. Length: 2,500-5,000 words. Pays $1,000 minimum for assigned articles, $350 minimum for unsolicited articles.

Photos: State availability of photos with submission. Reviews prints. Negotiates payment individually. Captions required. Buys one-time rights.

Columns/Departments: Buys 4 mss/year. Query. Pays $250-500.

Tips: "Cover stories are most open to freelancers."

PROFIT, The Magazine for Canadian Entrepreneurs, CB Media Limited, 2nd Floor, 70 The Esplanade, Toronto, Ontario M5E 1R2 Canada. (416)364-4760. Editor: Rick Spence. 80% freelance written. Quarterly magazine covering small and medium business. "We specialize in specific, useful information that helps our readers manage their businesses better. We want Canadian stories only." Estab. 1982. Circ. 110,000. **Pays on acceptance.** Publishes ms an average of 1-2 months after acceptance. Byline given. Kill fee varies. Buys first North American serial rights and database rights. Submit seasonal/holiday material 6 months in advance. Query for electronic submissions. Reports in 1 month on queries; 2-6 weeks on mss. Sample copy for 9 × 12 SAE with 84¢ postage (Canadian). Free writer's guidelines.

Nonfiction: How-to (business management tips), strategies and Canadian business profiles. Buys 50 mss/year. Query with published clips. Length: 800-2,000 words. Pays $500-2,000 (payment in Canadian dollars). Pays expenses of writers on assignment. State availability of photos with submission.

Columns/Departments: Innovators (interesting new Candian products, inventions or services), 200 words; Finance (info on raising capital in Canada), 700 words; Marketing (marketing strategies for independent business), 700 words. Buys 80 mss/year. Query with published clips. Length: 200-800 words. Pays $150-600 (Canadian dollars).

Tips: "We're wide open to freelancers with good ideas and some knowledge of business. Read the magazine and understand it before submitting your ideas."

TECHNICAL ANALYSIS OF STOCKS & COMMODITIES, The Trader's Magazine, Technical Analysis, Inc., 3517 SW Alaska St., Seattle WA 98126-2700. (206)938-0570. Publisher: Jack K. Hutson. 75% freelance written. Eager to work with new/unpublished writers. Magazine covers methods of investing and trading stocks, bonds and commodities (futures), options, mutual funds and precious metals. Estab. 1982. Circ. 40,000. Pays on publication. Publishes ms an average of 3 months after acceptance. Byline given. Offers 50% kill fee. Buys all rights; however, second serial (reprint) rights revert to the author, provided copyright credit is given. Previously published submissions OK. Query for electronic submissions. Reports in 3 weeks on queries; 1 month on mss. Sample copy $5. Writer's guidelines for #10 SASE.

Nonfiction: Thomas R. Hartle, editor. Reviews (new software or hardware that can make a trader's life easier, comparative reviews of software books, services, etc.); how-to (trade); technical (trading and software aids to trading); utilities (charting or computer programs, surveys, statistics or information to help the trader study or interpret market movements); and humor (unusual incidents of market occurrences, cartoons). "No newsletter-type, buy-sell recommendations. The article subject must relate to trading psychology, technical analysis, charting or a numerical technique used to trade securities or futures. Virtually requires graphics with every article." Buys 150 mss/year. Query with published clips if available or send complete ms. Length: 1,000-4,000 words. Pays $100-500. (Applies per inch base rate and premium rate—write for information). Sometimes pays expenses of writers on assignment.

Photos: Christine M. Morrison, photo editor. State availability of photos. Pays $20-150 for b&w or color negatives with prints or positive slides. Captions, model releases and identification of subjects required. Buys one-time and reprint rights.

Columns/Departments: Buys 100 mss/year. Query. Length: 800-1,600 words. Pays $50-300.

Fillers: Karen Webb, fillers editor. Jokes and cartoons on investment humor. Must relate to trading stocks, bonds, options, mutual funds or commodities. Buys 20/year. Length: 500 words. Pays $20-50.

Tips: "Describe how to use technical analysis, charting or computer work in day-to-day trading of stocks, bonds, mutual funds, options or commodities. A blow-by-blow account of how a trade was made, including the trader's thought processes, is, to our subscribers, the very best received story. One of our prime considerations is to instruct in a manner that the lay person can comprehend. We are not hyper-critical of writing style. The completeness and accuracy of submitted material are of the utmost consideration. Write for detailed writer's guidelines."

YOUR MONEY, Consumers Digest Inc., 5705 N. Lincoln Ave., Chicago IL 60659. (312)275-3590. Editor: Dennis Fertig. 75% freelance written. Bimonthly magazine on personal finance. "We cover the broad range of topics associated with personal finance—spending, saving, investing earning, etc." Estab. 1979. Circ. 250,000. **Pays on acceptance.** Publishes ms an average of 2 months after acceptance. Byline given. Offers 50% kill fee. Buys first rights and second serial (reprint) rights. Reports in 3 months on queries. Do not send computer disks. Sample copy and writer's guidelines for 9 × 12 SAE with $1 postage. Writer's guidelines for #10 SASE.

Nonfiction: How-to. "No first-person success stories or profiles of one company." Buys 25 mss/year. Send complete ms or query and clips. Include stamped, self-addressed postcard for more prompt response. Length: 1,500-2,500 words. Pays 30¢/word for assigned articles. Pays expenses of writers on assignment.

Tips: "Know the subject matter. Develop real sources in the investment community. Demonstrate a reader-friendly style that will help make the sometimes complicated subject of investing more accessible to the average person. Fill manuscripts with real-life examples of people who actually have done the kinds of things discussed within the ms—people we can later photograph."

Regional

ADCOM MAGAZINE New England's Own Advertising and Marketing Magazine, 18 Imperial Pl., Providence RI 02903. (401)751-6550. Fax: (401)751-6703. Editor: Karen Sullivan. 10% freelance written. Monthly magazine covering advertising, marketing, media and PR. "*Adcom Magazine* provides information and features on advertising, marketing, media, PR and related fields within New England. Primary freelance need: case studies and strategies. Readership: ad agencies, corporate advertising staff." Estab. 1976. Circ. 9,000. Pays 30 days after publication. Publishes ms an average of 2 months after acceptance. Byline given. No kill fee. Buys first rights or second serial (reprint) rights (send photocopy of article or typed ms with rights for sale noted). Submit seasonal/holiday material 3 months in advance. Simultaneous and previously published submissions OK. Query for electronic submissions. Reports in 1 month. Sample copy for 9 × 12 SAE with 6 first class stamps.

Nonfiction: How-to, opinion, strategies, case studies and industry overviews. Buys 10 mss/year. Query with published clips. Length: 500-3,000 words. Pays $75-350 for assigned articles; $25-50 for unsolicited articles.

Photos: State availability of photos with submission. Reviews contact sheets, transparencies and 5 × 7 prints. Offers $10-20/photo. Captions, model releases and identification of subjects required. Buys one-time rights.

Columns/Departments: Case Study (case study of a company's advertising/marketing program; must be a New England company), 1,200-3,000 words; Strategies ("how-to" or explanatory articles that relate to advertising, PR, marketing, direct marketing or media), 400-700 words; Industry Overview (an overview of marketing/advertising within specific industries in New England), 700-2,500 words. Buys 10 mss/year. Query with published clips. Length: 400-3,000 words. Pays $50-350.

Tips: "Call the editor. When she's not on deadline she's happy to brainstorm with prospective contributors. Best to send her a letter with clips first, though. Remember—submissions must have New England focus. Good luck!"

BOSTON BUSINESS JOURNAL, P&L Publications, 200 High St., Boston MA 02110-3036. (617)330-1000. Fax: (617)330-1016. Editor: Bennie DiNardo. 20% freelance written. Weekly newspaper covering business in Greater Boston. "Our audience is top managers at small, medium and Fortune 500 companies." Circ. 22,000. Pays on publication. Publishes ms an average of 2 weeks after acceptance. Byline given. Offers 50% kill fee. Buys all rights. Query for electronic submissions. Reports in 1 week on queries. Does not accept unsolicited mss.

Nonfiction: Freelancers used for special focus sections on hotels, health care, real estate, construction, computers and the office. Buys 50 mss/year. Query with published clips. Length: 800-1,000 words. Pays $155 for assigned articles.

Photos: State availability of photos with submission. Reviews 8 × 10 prints. Pays $40-55/photo. Identification of subjects required. Buys one-time and reprint rights.

Tips: "Look for hard news angle versus feature angle. Use 'numbers' liberally in the story. We prefer submissions on computer disk (call for specifics). We are only interested in local builders stories written by local writers."

BOULDER COUNTY BUSINESS REPORT, Suite D, 4885 Riverbend Rd., Boulder CO 80301-2617. (303)440-4950. Fax: (303)440-8954. Editor: Jerry W. Lewis. 75% freelance written. Prefers to work with published/established writers; works with a small number of new/unpublished writers each year. Monthly newspaper covering Boulder County business issues. Offers "news tailored to a monthly theme and read primarily by Colorado businesspeople and by some investors nationwide. Philosophy: Descriptive, well-written articles that reach behind the scene to examine area's business activity." Estab. 1982. Circ. 18,000. Pays on publication. Publishes ms an average of 1 month after acceptance. Byline given. Buys one-time rights and second serial (reprint) rights. Simultaneous queries OK. Query for electronic submissions. Reports in 1 month on queries; 2 weeks on mss. *Writer's Market* recommends allowing 2 months for reply. Sample copy $1.44.

Nonfiction: Interview/profile, new product, examination of competition in a particular line of business. "All our issues are written around one or two monthly themes. No articles are accepted in which the subject has not been pursued in depth and both sides of an issue presented in a writing style with flair." Buys 120 mss/year. Query with published clips. Length: 250-2,000 words. Pays $50-300.

Photos: State availability of photos with query letter. Reviews b&w contact sheets. Pays $10 maximum for b&w contact sheet. Identification of subjects required. Buys one-time rights and reprint rights.

Tips: "Must be able to localize a subject. In-depth articles are written by assignment. The freelancer located in the Colorado area has an excellent chance here."

‡**BUSINESS ATLANTA**, Communication Channels Inc., 6151 Powers Ferry Rd. NW, Atlanta GA 30339. (404)955-2500. Editor: John Sequerth. Managing Editor: Laurie Abbott. 75% freelance written. Monthly magazine. "As a consultant to Atlanta's top business executives, our aim is to enlighten our readers through crisp analysis of issues and trends." Estab. 1979. Circ. 37,000. Pays "upon publication of the issue for which the story was assigned—whether published or not." Publishes ms an average of 3 months after acceptance. Byline given. Offers 25% kill fee. Buys first rights and second serial (reprint) rights. Editorial lead time 3 months. Query for electronic submissions. Prefers Mac or IBM compatibles.

Nonfiction: How-to and interview/profile. "We don't accept any articles not assigned in advance by the editor." Buys 50 mss/year. Query with published clips. Length: 1,500-3,000 words. Pays $450 minimum. Pays expenses of writers on assignment.

Tips: "We appreciate writers with a level of expertise in particular subjects: banking/finance, high tech, real estate, hospitality/lodging, etc." Open to features only. Departments and columns are assigned to regular contributors.

BUSINESS NEW HAMPSHIRE MAGAZINE, Suite 201, 404 Chestnut St., Manchester NH 03101-1831. Editor: Robin Baskerville. 50% freelance written. Monthly magazine with focus on business, politics and people of New Hampshire. "Our audience consists of the owners and top managers of New Hampshire businesses." Estab. 1985. Circ. 13,000. Pays on publication. Publishes ms an average of 2 months after acceptance. Byline given. Writer's guidelines available to likely contributors.

Nonfiction: Features—how-to, interview/profile. Buys 24 mss/year. Query with published clips and resume. "No unsolicited ms; interested in local writers only." Length: 750-2,500 words. $75-250 for assigned articles.

Photos: Both b&w and color photos used. Pays $40-80. Buys one-time rights.

Tips: "I *always* want clips and resume with queries. Freelance stories are almost always assigned. Stories *must* be local to New Hampshire."

CALIFORNIA BUSINESS, Suite 700, 221 Main St., San Francisco CA 94105-1919. (415)543-8290. Fax: (415)543-8232. Editor: Umberto Tosi. 50% freelance written. Monthly business publication covering California. Includes Pacific rim and Mexico. Estab. 1965. Circ. 120,000. Pays on publication. Publishes ms an average of 3 months after acceptance. Byline given. Pays 15% kill fee. Buys first North American serial rights. Submit seasonal/holiday material 6 months in advance. Query for electronic submissions. Reports in 1 month. Sample copy for 9×12 SAE with 4 first class stamps. Writer's guidelines for #10 SASE.

Nonfiction: Book excerpts, expose, interview/profile. Buys 50 mss/year. Query. Length: 2,000-4,000 words. Pays $50-2,500 for assigned articles. Pays reasonable expenses of writers on assignment.

Photos: State availability of photos with submission. Reviews transparencies. Captions, model releases required. Buys one-time rights.

CORPORATE CLEVELAND, Business Journal Publishing Co., 3rd Floor, 1720 Euclid Ave., Cleveland OH 44115. (216)621-1644. Fax: (216)621-5918. Editor: Richard J. Osborne. Managing Editor: Robert G. Rosenbaum. 25% freelance written. Prefers to work with published/established writers based in Northeast Ohio. Monthly magazine covering general business topics. "*Corporate Cleveland* serves Northeast Ohio. Readers are business executives in the area engaged in manufacturing, agriculture, mining, construction, transportation, communications, utilities, retail and wholesale trade, services and government." Circ. 31,000. Pays for features on publication. Submit seasonal/holiday material 3-4 months in advance. Reports in 2 months. "Sample copy free to qualified writers."

Nonfiction: General interest, how-to, interview/profile, opinion and personal experience. "In all cases, write with the Northeast Ohio executive in mind. Stories should give readers useful information on business within the state, trends in management, ways to manage better or other developments that would affect them in their professional careers." Buys 14-20 mss/year. Query with published clips. Length: 800-2,500 words. Pays $75 minimum. Sometimes pays expenses of writers on assignment. All specifics must be negotiated in advance.

Photos: State availability of photos. Reviews b&w and color transparencies and prints. Captions and identification of subjects required. Buys variable rights.

Columns/Departments: News and People (profiles of business execs). Query with published clips. Length: 100-600 words. Pay varies.

Tips: "Features are most open to freelancers. Come up with new ideas or information for our readers: executives in manufacturing and service industries. Writers should be aware of the trend toward specialization in magazine publishing with strong emphasis on people in coverage."

‡**CRAIN'S DETROIT BUSINESS**, Crain Communications, Inc., 1400 Woodbridge, Detroit MI 48207-3187. (313)446-0460. Fax: (313)393-0997. Editor: Mary Kramer. Managing Editor: Dave Guilford. 20% freelance written. Weekly tabloid covering Detroit area businesses. "*Crain's Detroit Business* reports the activities of

local businesses. Our readers are mostly executives; many of them own their own companies. They read us to keep track of companies not often reported about in the daily press—privately held companies and small public companies. Our slant is hard news and news features. We do not report on the auto companies, but other businesses in Wayne, Oakland, Macomb, and Washtenaw counties are part of our turf." Estab. 1985. Circ. 35,000. Pays on publication. Byline given. Offers negotiable kill fee. Buys first rights, "the right to make the story available to the other 25 Crain publications and the right to circulate the story through the Crain News Service." Query for electronic submissions. Sample copy 50¢. Writer's guidelines for SASE.

Nonfiction: Cindy Goodaker, articles editor. No "how-tos, new product articles or fiction." Looking for local and statewide news. Buys 200 mss/year. Query. Length: 800 words average. Pays $6/inch and expenses for assigned articles. Pays $6/inch without expenses for unsolicited articles. Pays expenses of writers on assignment.

Tips: "What we are most interested in are specific news stories about local businesses. The fact that Widget Inc. is a great company is of no interest to us. However, if Widget Inc. introduced a new product six months ago and sales have gone up from $20 million to $30 million, then that's a story. The same is true if sales went down from $20 million to $10 million. I would strongly encourage interested writers to contact me directly. Although we don't have a blanket rule against unsolicited manuscripts, they are rarely usable. We are a general circulation publication, but we are narrowly focused. A writer not familiar with us would have trouble focusing the story properly. In addition, writers may not have a business relationship with the company they are writing about."

‡MEADOW'S GREATER NY BUSINESS, Meadow Publications Inc., 126 Library Lane, Mamaroneck NY 10543. (914)381-4740. Editor: Gayden Wren. 50% freelance written. Quarterly magazine for business in the Greater New York area. Audience is "CEOs and upper management of mid-to-large-sized companies in NY-NJ-CT tristate area. We aim to provide broad business coverage, with a special orientation toward the tristate area beyond Manhattan." Estab. 1993. Circ. 70,000. Pays on publication. Byline given. Buys first rights. Editorial lead time 4 months. Submit seasonal material 5 months in advance. Query for electronic submissions. Prefers Mac or ASCII format. Reports in 3 weeks on queries; 1 month on mss. *Writer's Market* recommends allowing 2 months for reply. Sample copy $3. Writer's guidelines for #10 SASE.

Nonfiction: Interview/profile, new product, opinion and business. Buys 10-20 mss/year. Query. Pays $100 minimum. Sometimes pays expenses of writers on assignment (limit agreed upon in advance).

Photos: State availability of photos with submission; send with submission. Reviews transparencies and prints. Negotiates payment individually. Captions, model release and identification of subjects required (when appropriate). Buys one-time rights.

Tips: "Write a letter asking for info."

METRO TORONTO BUSINESS JOURNAL, Metro Toronto Board of Trade, 1st Canadian Place, P.O. Box 60, Toronto Ontario M5X 1C1 Canada. (416)366-6811. Fax: (416)366-5620. Editor: Peter Carter. Managing Editor: Okey Chigbo. 90% freelance written. Monthly magazine on Toronto business. Circ. 41,000. **Pays on acceptance.** Offers 50% kill fee. Buys first North American serial rights. Reports in 2 weeks on queries; 1 week on mss. Sample copy for 9 × 12 SAE with 3 IRCs.

Nonfiction: Essays, expose, general interest, historical/nostalgic, humor, interview/profile, opinion, personal experience and photo feature. Buys 300 mss/year. Query. Length: 150-3,000 words. Pays $150-2,500 for assigned articles. Sometimes pays expenses of writers on assignment.

Photos: State availability of photos with submission. Reviews contact sheets. Captions required. Buys all rights.

Columns/Departments: City Business (Toronto related, innovative business ideas, personalities), 50-300 words; Landmarks (Toronto business landmarks, historic sites), 900 words. Buys 300 mss/year. Query. Pays $150-500.

MONEY SAVING IDEAS, The National Research Bureau Inc., 424 N. 3rd St., P.O. Box 1, Burlington IA 52601-0001. (319)752-5415. FAX (319)752-3421. Editor: Nancy Heinzel. 75% freelance written. Quarterly magazine that features money saving strategies. "We are interested in money saving tips on various subjects (insurance, travel, heating/cooling, buying a house, ways to cut costs and balance checkbooks). Our audience is mainly industrial and office workers." Estab. 1948. Pays on publication. Publishes ms an average of 1 year after acceptance. Byline given. Buys all rights. Sample copy and writers guidelines for #10 SAE with 2 first class stamps. Writer's guidelines for #10 SASE.

Nonfiction: How-to (save on grocery bills, heating/cooling bills, car expenses, insurance, travel). Query with or without published clips or send complete ms. Length: 500-700 words. Pays 4¢/word.

Tips: "Follow our writers guidelines. Keep articles to stated length, double spaced, neatly typed. If writer wishes rejected manuscript returned include SASE. Name, address and word length should appear on first page of ms."

‡OREGON BUSINESS, Oregon Business Media, Suite 407, 921 SW Morrison, Portland OR 97205. (503)223-0304. Editor: Kathy Dimond. 60% freelance written. Works with a small number of new/unpublished writers each year. Monthly magazine covering business in Oregon. Estab. 1981. Circ. 20,000. Pays on publication. Publishes ms an average of 3 months after acceptance. Byline given. Buys first rights. No simultaneous submissions or previously published submissions. Reports in 1 month. Sample copy for 9 × 12 SAE with 5 first class stamps.

Nonfiction: Statewide business magazine. Focus is on world trade, finance, family businesses, government regulations, and management issues. Geared to needs and interests of *Oregon* businesses and "helping Oregon companies grow." Virtually all freelance is assigned—query first. Buys 50 mss/year. Length: 600-2,000 words. Pays $100-400 depending on length of assignment.

Photos: Photo Editor: D.C. Jesse Burkhardt. "Always looking for new talent, and creativity—especially outside of Portland." Pays $75/assignment, and expenses.

ORLANDO MAGAZINE, Orlando Media Affiliates, P.O. Box 2207, Suite 130, 341 N. Maitland Ave., Orlando FL 32802-9999. (407)539-3939. Fax: (407)539-0533. 10% freelance written. Monthly magazine covering lifestyle, home and garden and business. Estab. 1946. Circ. 35,000. Pays on publication. Publishes ms an average of 2 months after acceptance. Byline given. Offers negotiable kill fee. Submit seasonal/holiday material 4-6 months in advance. Simultaneous submissions OK. Reports in 2 months. Free sample copy and writer's guidelines.

Nonfiction: Expose, how-to (business) and interview. Buys 12-15 mss/year. Send complete ms. Length: 1,000-2,500 words. Pays $100-450 for articles. "Looking for stories that locally reflect national trends in lifestyles, home and garden and business. Publish at least one issue-oriented story per month."

Photos: State availability of photos with submission. Reviews transparencies. Offers $5/photo. Captions and identification of subjects required. Buys one-time rights.

Columns/Departments: Sports, health, fitness, arts and virtually all business topics. All submissions should have local slant. Length: 1,200-1,500. Buys 12-15 mss/year. Pays $200-350.

ROCHESTER BUSINESS MAGAZINE, Rochester Business, Inc., 1600 Lyell Ave., Rochester NY 14606. (716)458-8280. Editor: Douglas Sprei. 25% freelance written. Monthly magazine. "*RBM* is a colorful tutorial business publication targeted specifically toward business owners and upper level managers in the Rochester metropolitan area. Our audience is comprised of upscale decision-makers with keen interest in the 'how-to' of business. Some features deal with lifestyle, golf, cultural focus, etc." Circ. 17,000. Pays on publication. Publishes ms an average of 6 months after acceptance. Byline given. Buys all rights. Previously published submissions OK. Reports in 1 month. Sample copy and writer's guidelines for SAE with 6 first class stamps.

Nonfiction: Essays, historical/nostalgic, how-to, humor, interview/profile and personal experience, all with business slant. Buys 12-24 mss/year. Query with published clips. Length: 1,500 words maximum. Pays $50-100.

Photos: State availability of photos with submission. Offers no additional payment for photos accepted with ms. Captions required.

VERMONT BUSINESS MAGAZINE, Lake Iroquois Publications, 2 Church St., Burlington VT 05401. (802)863-8038. Fax: (802)863-8069. Editor: Timothy McQuiston. 80% freelance written. Monthly tabloid covering business in Vermont. Circ. 16,000. Pays on publication. Publishes ms an average of 1 month after acceptance. Byline given. Offers kill fee. Publishes reprints of previously published articles. Send tearsheet of article or short story and information about when and where the article previously appeared. Not copyrighted. Buys one-time rights. Simultaneous submissions OK. Query for electronic submissions. Reports in 2 months. Sample copy for 11 × 14 SAE with 7 first-class stamps.

Nonfiction: Business trends and issues. Buys 200 mss/year. Query with published clips. Length: 800-1,800 words. Pays $50-150. Pays the expenses of writers on assignment.

Photos: Send photos with submission. Reviews contact sheets. Offers $10-35/photo. Identification of subjects required.

Tips: "Read daily papers and look for business angles for a follow-up article. We look for issue and trend articles rather than company or businessman profiles. Note: magazine accepts Vermont-specific material *only*. The articles *must* be about Vermont."

VICTORIA'S BUSINESS REPORT, Monday Publications Ltd., 1609 Blanshard St., Victoria, British Columbia V2X 2J5 Canada. (604)382-7777. Fax: (604)381-2662. Editor: Gery Lemon. 20% freelance written. Monthly magazine that covers Victoria business. "*Victoria's Business Report* focuses on business on Victoria and southern Vancouver Island." Pays on publication. Publishes ms an average of 2 months after acceptance. Byline given. Buys first North American serial rights. Simultaneous and previously published submissions OK. Query for electronic submissions. Reports in 3 weeks on queries. Sample copy $2.75.

Nonfiction: Length: 500-2,000 words. Pays $50-400 for assigned articles. Sometimes pays expenses of writers on assignment.

Photos: State availability of photos with submission. Offers $10-35/photo. Captions and identification of subjects required. Buys one-time rights.

Career, College and Alumni

Three types of magazines are listed in this section: university publications written for students, alumni and friends of a specific institution; publications about college life for students; and publications on career and job opportunities. Literary magazines published by colleges and universities are listed in the Literary and "Little" section.

THE BLACK COLLEGIAN, The Career & Self Development Magazine for African American Students, Black Collegiate Services, Inc., 1240 S. Broad St., New Orleans LA 70125. (504)821-5694. Fax: (504)821-5713. Editor: K. Kazi-Ferrouillet. 25% freelance written. Magazine for African-American college students and recent graduates with an interest in career and job information, African-American cultural awareness, personalities, history, trends and current events. Published bimonthly during school year (4 times/year). Estab. 1970. Circ. 121,000. Buys one-time rights. Byline given. Pays on publication. Submit seasonal and special interest material 2 months in advance of issue date Careers (September); Computers/Grad School and Travel/Summer programs (November); Engineering and Black History programs (January); Finance and Jobs (March). Reports in 2 months on queries; 3 months on mss. Sample copy $4 for 9 × 12 SAE. Writer's guidelines for #10 SASE.
Nonfiction: Material on careers, sports, black history, news analysis. Articles on problems and opportunities confronting African-American college students and recent graduates. Book excerpts, expose, general interest, historical/nostalgic, how-to (develop employability), opinion, personal experience, profile, inspirational and humor. Buys 40 mss/year (6 unsolicited). Query with published clips or send complete ms. Length: 500-1,500 words. Pays $50-500.
Photos: State availability of or send photos with query or ms. Black and white photos or color transparencies purchased with or without ms. 8 × 10 prints preferred. Captions, model releases and identification of subjects required. Pays $35/b&w; $50/color.

CAREER FOCUS, For Today's Professional, Communications Publishing Group, Inc., 250 Mark Twain Tower 106 W. 11th St., Kansas City MO 64105-1806. (816)221-4404. Editor: Georgia Clark. 40% freelance written. Monthly magazine "devoted to providing positive insight, information, guidance and motivation to assist Blacks and Hispanics (ages 21-40) in their career development and attainment of goals." Estab. 1988. Circ. 250,000. Pays on publication. Byline often given. Buys second serial (reprint) rights and makes work-for-hire assignments. Submit seasonal/holiday material 6 months in advance. Simultaneous and previously published submissions OK. Reports in 2 months. Sample copy for 9 × 12 SAE with 4 first class stamps. Writer's guidelines for #10 SASE.
Nonfiction: Book excerpts, general interest, historical, how-to, humor, inspirational, interview/profile, personal experience, photo feature, technical and travel. Length: 750-2,000 words. Pays $150-400 for assigned articles; 10¢/word for unsolicited articles. Sometimes pays expenses of writers on assignment.
Photos: State availability of photos with submission. Reviews transparencies. Pays $20-25/photo. Captions, model releases and identification of subjects required. Buys all rights.
Columns/Departments: Profiles (striving and successful Black and Hispanic young adult, ages 21-40). Buys 15 mss/year. Send complete ms. Length: 500-1,000 words. Pays $50-250.
Fiction: Adventure, ethnic, historical, humorous, mainstream and slice-of-life vignettes. Buys 3 mss/year. Send complete ms. Length: 1,500-5,000 words. Pays $100-400.
Poetry: Free verse. Buys 4/year. Length: 10-25 lines. Pays $10-50.
Fillers: Anecdotes, facts, gags to be illustrated by cartoonist, newsbreaks, short humor. Buys 10/year. Length: 25-250 words. Pays $25-100.
Tips: "For new writers: Submit full manuscript that is double-spaced; clean copy only. Need to have clippings and previously published works and resume. Should also tell when available to write. Most open to freelancers are profiles of successful and striving persons including photos. Profile must be of a Black or Hispanic adult living in the U.S. Include on first page of manuscript your name, address phone, Social Security number and number of words in article."

CAREER WOMAN, For Entry-Level and Professional Women, Equal Opportunity Publications, Inc., Suite 420, 150 Motor Parkway, Hauppauge NY 11788-5145. (516)273-8743. Fax: (516)273-8936. Editor: Eileen Nester. Estab. 1973. 80% freelance written. Works with new/unpublished writers each year. Magazine published 3 times/year (fall, winter, spring) covering career-guidance for college women. Strives to "bridge the gap between college life and the working world – with advice ranging from conducting an effective job search to surviving the first several years on the job to finding a balance between personal and professional lives." Audience is 60% college juniors and seniors, 40% working graduates. Circ. 10,500. Controlled circulation, distributed through college guidance and placement offices. Pays on publication. Publishes ms an average of 3-12 months after acceptance. Byline given. Buys first North American rights. Simultaneous queries and submissions OK. Reports in 2 months. Sample copy and writer's guidelines for 9 × 12 SAE with 5 first class stamps.
Nonfiction: "We want career-related articles describing for a college-educated woman the how-tos of obtaining a professional position and advancing her career." Looks for practical features detailing self-evaluation techniques, the job-search process and advice for succeeding on the job. Emphasizes role-model profiles of

successful career women. Needs manuscripts presenting information on professions offering opportunities to young women — especially the growth professions of the future. Special issues emphasize career opportunities for women in fields such as health care, communications, sales, marketing, banking, insurance, finance, science, engineering and computers. Query first.

Photos: Send with ms. Prefers 35mm color slides, but will accept b&w prints. Captions and identification of subjects required. Buys all rights.

Tips: "The best way to get published is to find a unique approach to common topics. Remember that you are addressing a group of women new to the workforce. They need advice on virtually every career-guidance topic."

‡**CAREERS & COLLEGES MAGAZINE,** E.M. Guild, Inc., 6th Floor, 989 Avenue of Americas, New York NY 10018. (212)563-4688. Editor: June Rogoznica. Senior Editor: Don Rauf. Contact: June Rogoznica. 85-95% freelance written. Quarterly magazine for education, careers and life choices for high school students. *"Careers & Colleges* is a magazine that believes in young people. It believes that they have the power — and responsibility — to shape their own futures. That is why each issue provides high school juniors and seniors with useful, thought-provoking reading on career choices, life values, higher education and other topics that will help them enjoy profitable and self-respecting work." Estab. 1980. Circ. 500,000. **Pays on acceptance.** Byline given. Offers 20% kill fee. Buys first North American serial rights. Editorial lead time 6 months. Submit seasonal material 6 months in advance. Reports in 1 month on queries. Sample copy for 9 × 12 SAE, 5 first class stamps and $2.50. Writer's guidelines free on request for #10 SASE.

Nonfiction: Book excerpts, how-to (job or college related) and interview/profile (teen role models). May publish a Spring issue on summer jobs and other employment opportunities for young adults. "No personal essays, life experiences or fiction." Buys 36-52 mss/year. Query with published clips. Length: 600-1,500 words. Pays $150 minimum. Sometimes pays expenses of writers on assignment (limit agreed upon in advance).

Photos: State availability of photos with submission. Negotiates payment individually. Buys one-time rights.

Columns/Departments: Money Wise (strategies and resources for financing education beyond high school), 600-800 words, and Career Watch (profiles of growth careers/interview plus statistics), 800 words. Buys 18-24 mss/year. Query or query with published clips. Pays $150-350.

Tips: "Be sure to request writer's guidelines. Follow guidelines specifically. No unsolicited manuscripts are accepted. Send a one-page query. Examine other teen magazines for current topic idea. Many opportunities exist in our career profile section — pay is low, but it is a good testing ground for us to gauge a writer's ability — strong performance here can lead to bigger articles. We are open to most material for our Career Watch section of career profiles. Query about growth careers that we have not covered in the past. (Consult magazine's Career Watch Index.)"

‡**CAREERS & MAJORS (for College Students),** Oxendine Publishing, Inc., 738 NW 23rd Ave., P.O. Box 14081, Gainesville FL 32609/32604-2081. (904)373-6907. Editor: W.H. "Butch" Oxendine Jr.. Managing Editor: Kay Quinn. 50% freelance written. Quarterly magazine for college careers and job opportunities. Estab. 1983. Circ. 17,000. Pays on publication. Publishes ms an average of 2-3 months after acceptance. Byline given. Buys all rights. Submit seasonal/holiday material 4 months in advance. Accepts simultaneous and previously published submissions. Query for electronic submissions. Prefers IBM. Reports in 1 month on queries. Sample copy for 8 × 11 SAE with 3 first class stamps. Writer's guidelines on request for SASE.

Nonfiction: How-to, humor, new product, opinion and other. "No lengthy individual profiles or articles without primary and secondary sources of attribution." Buys 10 mss/year. Query with published clips. Length: 250-1,000 words. Pays $35 maximum. Pays contributor copies to students or first-time writers.

Photos: State availability of photos with submission. Send photos with submission. Reviews contact sheets, negatives and transparencies; size "doesn't matter." Offers $50 maximum/photo. Captions, model releases and identification of subjects required. Buys all rights.

Columns/Departments: College Living (various aspects of college life, general short humor oriented to high school or college students), 250-1,000 words; From your Point of View (pro-con opinions on current issues), 1,000 words total. Buys 10 mss/year. Query. Length: 250-1,000 words. Pays $35 maximum.

Fillers: Facts, newsbreaks and short humor. Buys 10/year. Length: 100-500 words. Pays $35 maximum.

Tips: "Read other high school and college publications for current issues, interests. Send manuscripts or outlines for review. All sections open to freelance work. Always looking for lighter, humorous articles, as well as features on Florida colleges and universities, careers, jobs."

CARNEGIE MELLON MAGAZINE, Carnegie Mellon University, 5017 Forbes Ave., Pittsburgh PA 15213-3890. (412)268-2132. Fax: (412)268-6929. Editor: Ann Curran. Quarterly alumni publication covering university activities, alumni profiles, etc. Circ. 56,000. **Pays on acceptance.** Byline given. Not copyrighted. Reports in 1 month.

Nonfiction: Book reviews (faculty alumni), general interest, humor, interview/profile and photo feature. "We use general interest stories linked to Carnegie Mellon activities and research." No unsolicited mss. Buys 5 features and 5-10 alumni profiles/year. Query with published clips. Length: 800-2,000 words. Pays $100-400 or negotiable rate. Sample copy for 9 × 12 SAE and $2.

Poetry: Avant-garde or traditional. No previously published poetry. No payment.

CIRCLE K MAGAZINE, 3636 Woodview Trace, Indianapolis IN 46268-3196. Fax: (317)879-0204. Executive Editor: Nicholas K. Drake. 60% freelance written. "Our readership consists almost entirely of above-average college students interested in voluntary community service and leadership development. They are politically and socially aware and have a wide range of interests." Publishes 5 times/year. Circ. 15,000. **Pays on acceptance.** Normally buys first North American serial rights. Byline given. Submit seasonal/holiday material 6 months in advance. Reports in 1½-2 months. Sample copy and writer's guidelines for large SAE with 3 first class stamps.

Nonfiction: Articles published in *Circle K* are of two types—serious and light nonfiction. "We are interested in general interest articles on topics concerning college students and their lifestyles, as well as articles dealing with careers, community concerns and leadership development. No first person confessions, family histories or travel pieces." Query. Length: 1,700-2,200 words. Pays $225-400.

Photos: Purchased with accompanying ms. Captions required. Total purchase price for ms includes payment for photos.

Tips: "Query should indicate author's familiarity with the field and sources. Subject treatment must be objective and in-depth, and articles should include illustrative examples and quotes from persons involved in the subject or qualified to speak on it. We are open to working with new writers who present a good article idea and demonstrate that they've done their homework concerning the article subject itself, as well as concerning our magazine's style. We're interested in college-oriented trends, for example, entrepreneur schooling is now a major shift; rising censorship on campus; high-tech classrooms; virtual reality; music; leisure; and health issues."

COLLEGE MONTHLY, 40 Southbridge St., Worcester MA 01608. (508)753-2550. Editor: Maureen Castillo. Managing Editor: Randy Cohen. 25% freelance written. College lifestyle and entertainment magazine published 8 times/year. Estab. 1986. Circ. 73,000. Pays on publication. Byline given. Offers $5 kill fee. Buys one-time rights. Query for electronic submissions. Free sample copy and writer's guidelines for 9 × 12 SAE with 6 first class stamps.

Nonfiction: Humor, interview/profile, opinion, personal experience and travel. Query with published clips. Length: 500-2,000 words. Pays $25-100 for assigned articles; $5-25 for unsolicited articles. Sometimes pays the expenses of writers on assignment.

Photos: State availability of photos with submission. Offers no additional payment for photos accepted with ms. Caption required. Buys one-time rights.

Columns/Departments: Fashion (trends in the college market for clothes); Lifestyle (off-the-wall things students do); Sports (national sports and college); Politics (national level/hot social issues), all 500-750 words.

Fillers: Newsbreaks, short humor. Length: 100 words. Pays $5-25.

Tips: "We are looking for more fashion, education and sports articles."

COLLEGE PREVIEW, A Guide for College-Bound Students, Communications Publishing Group, 250 Mark Twain Tower, 106 W. 11th St., Kansas City MO 64105-1806. (816)221-4404. Fax: (816)221-1112. Editor: Georgia Clark. 40% freelance written. Quarterly educational and career source guide. "Contemporary guide designed to inform and motivate Black and Hispanic young adults, ages 16-21 years old about college preparation, career planning and life survival skills." Estab. 1985. Circ. 600,000. Pays on publication. Byline often given. Buys first serial and second serial (reprint) rights or makes work-for-hire assignments. Submit seasonal/holiday material 6 months in advance. Simultaneous and previously published submissions OK. Send photocopy of article or short story or typed ms with rights for sale noted. Include information about when and where the article previously appeared. For reprints, pays 50% of the amount paid for an original article. Reports in 2 months. Sample copy for 9 × 12 SAE with 4 first class stamps. Writer's guidelines for #10 SASE.

Nonfiction: Book excerpts or reviews, general interest, how-to (dealing with careers or education), humor, inspirational, interview/profile (celebrity or "up and coming" young adult), new product (as it relates to young adult market), personal experience, photo feature, technical and travel. Send complete ms. Length: 750-2,000 words. Pays $150-400 for assigned articles; 10¢/word for unsolicited articles. Sometimes pays expenses of writers on assignment.

Photos: State availability of photos with submission. Reviews transparencies. Offers $20-$25/photo. Captions, model releases and identification of subjects required. Will return photos—send SASE.

Columns/Departments: Profiles of Achievement (striving and successful minority young adults ages 16-35 in various careers). Buys 30 mss/year. Send complete ms. Length: 500-1,500. Pays 10¢/word.

Fiction: Adventure, ethnic, historical, humorous, mainstream and slice-of-life vignettes. Buys 3 mss/year. Send complete ms. Length: 1,000-5,000 words. Pays $100-400.

Poetry: Free verse. Buys 5 poems/year. Submit up to 5 poems at one time. Length: 10-25 lines. Pays $10-50.

Fillers: Anecdotes, facts, gags to be illustrated by cartoonist, newsbreaks, short humor. Buys 10/year. Length: 25-250 words. Pays $25-100.

Tips: "For new writers—send complete manuscript that is double spaced; clean copy only. If available, send clips of previously published works and resume. Should state when available to write. Include on first page of manuscript your name, address, phone, Social Security number, word count and SASE."

DIRECT AIM, A Resource Guide for Vocational/Technical Graduates, Communications Publishing Group, 250 Mark Twain Tower, 106 W. 11th St., Kansas City MO 64105-1806. (816)221-4404. Fax: (816)221-1112. Publisher: Georgia Clark. 40% freelance written. Quarterly educational and career source guide for Black and Hispanic college students at traditional, non-traditional, vocational and technical institutions. This magazine informs students about college survival skills and planning for a future in the professional world. Buys second serial (reprint) rights or makes work-for-hire assignments. Submit seasonal/holiday material 6 months in advance. Simultaneous, photocopied and previously published submissions OK. For reprints, send typed ms with rights for sale noted. Include information about when and where the article previously appeared. For reprints, pays 50% of the amount paid for an original article. Reports in 2 months. Sample copy for 9 × 12 SAE with 4 first class stamps. Writer's guidelines for #10 SASE.

Nonfiction: Book excerpts or reviews, general interest, how-to (dealing with careers or education), humor, inspirational, interview/profile (celebrity or "up and coming" young adult), new product (as it relates to young adult market), personal experience, photo feature, technical, travel. Query or send complete ms. Length: 750-2,000 words. Pays $150-400 for assigned articles; 10¢/word for unsolicited articles. Sometimes pays expenses of writers on assignment.

Photos: State availability of photos with submission. Reviews transparencies. Offers $20-25/photo. Captions, model releases and identification of subjects required. Will return photos.

Columns/Departments: Profiles of Achievement (striving and successful minority young adult age 18-35 in various technical careers). Buys 25 mss/year. Send complete ms. Length: 500-1,500. Pays $50-250.

Fiction: Publishes novel excerpts. Adventure, ethnic, historical, humorous, mainstream and slice-of-life vignettes. Buys 3 mss/year. Send complete ms. Length: 1,000-5,000 words. Pays $100-400.

Poetry: Free verse. Buys 5 poems/year. Submit up to 5 poems at one time. Length: 10-25 lines. Pays $10-50.

Fillers: Anecdotes, facts, gags to be illustrated by cartoonist, newsbreaks and short humor. Buys 30/year. Length: 25-250 words. Pays $25-100.

Tips: "For new writers—send complete manuscript that is double spaced; clean copy only. If available, send clips of previously published works and resume. Should state when available to write. Must include on first page of ms—name, address, phone, Social Security number and word count. Availability of photos enhances your chances."

EQUAL OPPORTUNITY, The Nation's Only Multi-Ethnic Recruitment Magazine for Black, Hispanic, Native American & Asian American College Grads, Equal Opportunity Publications, Inc., Suite 420, 150 Motor Pkwy., Hauppauge NY 11788-5145. (516)273-0066. Fax: (516)273-8936. Executive Editor: James Schneider. 50% freelance written. Prefers to work with published/established writers. Triannual magazine covering career guidance for minorities. "Our audience is 90% college juniors and seniors; 10% working graduates. An understanding of educational and career problems of minorities is essential." Estab. 1967. Circ. 15,000. Controlled circulation, distributed through college guidance and placement offices. Pays on publication. Publishes ms an average of 6 months after acceptance. Byline given. Buys first rights. Deadline dates: fall, June 10; winter, September 15; spring, January 1. Simultaneous queries and previously published submissions OK. Sample copy and writer's guidelines for 9 × 12 SAE with 5 first class stamps.

Nonfiction: Book excerpts and articles (job search techniques, role models); general interest (specific minority concerns); how-to (job-hunting skills, personal finance, better living, coping with discrimination); humor (student or career related); interview/profile (minority role models); opinion (problems of minorities); personal experience (professional and student study and career experiences); technical (on career fields offering opportunities for minorities); travel (on overseas job opportunities); and coverage of Black, Hispanic, Native American and Asian American interests. Special issues include career opportunities for minorities in industry and government in fields such as banking, insurance, finance, communications, sales, marketing, engineering, computers, military and defense. Query or send complete ms. Length: 1,000-1,500 words. Sometimes pays expenses of writers on assignment. Pays 10¢/word.

Photos: Prefers 35mm color slides and b&w. Captions and identification of subjects required. Buys all rights. Pays $15/photo use.

Tips: "Articles must be geared toward questions and answers faced by minority and women students."

ETC. MAGAZINE, Student Media—University of North Carolina at Charlotte, Cone University Center UNCC, Charlotte NC 28223-0001. (704)547-2146. Editor: Chip Drum. Semiannual magazine on collegiate lifestyle. "*Etc. Magazine* is a student publication serving the University of North Carolina at Charlotte that features general interest articles dealing with collegiate lifestyles." Estab. 1986. Circ. 5,000. Pays on publication. Byline given. Buys one-time rights. Previously published material OK. Reports in 6 months. Free sample copy and writer's guidelines.

Nonfiction: 2,000 word general interest cover story covering topical issues in university setting and 1,000 word general interest feature articles. Issue-oriented articles average 1,000 words. Pays up to $10 and contributor's copies.

Columns/Departments: Lifeline—helping students cope with stress and changes associated with college life; Skyline—highlighting university's important ties to the Charlotte community; Aspects—focusing on diverse ethnic groups which form large part of university community; Passport—interesting travel ideas for students on limited budgets. Length: 1,000 words. Pays up to $10 and contributor's copies.

Photos: State availability of or send photos with submission. Stipend of no more than $10 will be paid upon publication.

FIRST OPPORTUNITY, A Guide for Vocational/Technical Students, Communications Publishing Group, 250 Mark Twain Tower, 106 W. 11th St., Kansas City MO 64105-1806. (816)221-4404. Editor: Georgia Clark. 40% freelance written. Biannual resource publication focusing on advanced vocational/technical educational opportunities and career preparation for Black and Hispanic young adults, ages 16-21. Circ. 500,000. Pays on publication. Byline sometimes given. Buys second serial (reprint) rights or makes work-for-hire assignments. Submit seasonal/holiday material 6 months in advance. Simultaneous, photocopied and previously published submissions OK. For reprints send typed ms with rights for sale noted. Include information about when and where the article previously appeared. For reprints, pays 50% of the amount paid for an original article. Reports in 2 months. Sample copy for 9 × 12 SAE with 4 first class stamps. Writer's guidelines for #10 SASE.
Nonfiction: Book excerpts or reviews, general interest, how-to (dealing with careers or education), humor, inspirational, interview/profile (celebrity or "up and coming" young adult), new product (as it relates to young adult market), personal experience, photo feature, technical and travel. Length: 750-2,000 words. Pays $150-400 for assigned articles; 10¢/word for unsolicited articles. Sometimes pays expenses of writers on assignment.
Photos: State availability of photos with submission. Prefers transparencies. Offers $20-25/photo. Captions, model releases and identification of subjects required. Buys all rights.
Columns/Departments: Profiles of Achievement (striving and successful minority young adult, age 16-35 in various vocational or technical careers). Buys 15 mss/year. Send complete ms. Length: 500-1,500. Pays $50-250.
Fiction: Adventure, ethnic, historical, humorous, mainstream and slice-of-life vignettes. Buys 3 mss/year. Send complete ms. Length: 1,000-5,000 words. Pays $100-400.
Poetry: Free verse. Buys 5 poems/year. Submit up to 5 poems at one time. Length: 10-25 lines. Pays $10-50.
Fillers: Anecdotes, facts, gags to be illustrated by cartoonist, newsbreaks and short humor. Buys 10/year. Length: 25-250 words. Pays $25-100.
Tips: "For new writers—send complete manuscript that is double spaced; clean copy only. If available, send clippings of previously published works and resume. Should state when available to write. Include on first page your name, address, phone, Social Security number and word count in article. Photo availability is important."

FLORIDA LEADER, P.O. Box 14081, Gainesville FL 32604. (904)373-6907. Fax: (904)373-8120. Publisher: W.H. "Butch" Oxendine, Jr. Editor: Kay Quinn. Nearly 80% freelance written. Quarterly "college magazine, feature oriented, especially activities, events, interests and issues pertaining to college students." Estab. 1981. Circ. 27,000. Publishes ms an average of 2 months after acceptance. Byline given. Submit seasonal/holiday material 6 months in advance. Query for electronic submissions. Reports in 1 month on queries. Sample copy and writer's guidelines for 9 × 12 SAE with 5 first class stamps.
Nonfiction: How-to, humor, interview/profile, and feature—all Florida college related. Special issues include Careers and Majors (January and June); Florida Leader high school edition (August, January and May); Transfer (for community college transfers) (November and July); Returning Student (for nontraditional-age students) (July); and Student Leader, a national magazine for high school juniors and seniors devoted to leadership training (October and March) (pays double). Query. Length: 500 words or less. Payment varies. Sometimes pays expenses of writers on assignment.
Photos: State availability of photos with submission. Reviews negatives and transparencies. Captions, model releases and identification of subjects requested.

FORDHAM MAGAZINE, Fordham University, Suite 313, 113 W. 60th St., New York NY 10023. (212)636-6530. Fax: (212)765-2976. Editor: Michael Gates. 50% freelance written. Quarterly magazine on Fordham University and its alumni. "We use profiles of our alumni—e.g. actor Denzel Washington, author Mary Higgins Clark—and discuss how education influenced their careers." **Pays on acceptance.** Estab. 1966. Publishes ms an average of 6 months after acceptance. Byline given. Offers 25% kill fee. Submit seasonal/holiday material 6 months in advance. Previously published submissions OK. Reports in 2-3 months on queries; 3-4 months on mss. Sample copy for 9 × 12 SAE with 6 first class stamps. Writer's guidelines for SAE with 2 first class stamps.
Nonfiction: Book excerpts, essays, historical/nostalgic, interview/profile (alumni, faculty, students) and photo feature. All must be specific to Fordham University or its alumni. Buys 12 mss/year. Query with published clips. Length: 1,000-2,500. Pays $250-500 for assigned articles; $50-250 for unsolicited articles. Sometimes pays expenses of writers on assignment. Reprints OK; send photocopy of article and information about when and where the article appeared.
Photos: State availability of photos with submission. Reviews contact sheets, transparencies, prints. Offers additional payment for photos accepted with ms. Identification of subjects required.
Tips: "Research our alumni and see if there is a noted or interesting personality you might interview—someone who might live in your area."

JOURNEY, A Success Guide for College and Career Bound Students, Communications Publishing Group, 250 Mark Twain Tower, 106 W. 11th St., Kansas City MO 64105-1806. (816)221-4404. Fax: (816)221-1112. Editor: Georgia Clark. 40% freelance written. Biannual educational and career source guide for Asian-American high school and college students who have indicated a desire to pursue higher education through college, vocational and technical or proprietary schools. For students ages 16-25. Estab. 1982. Circ. 200,000. Pays on publication. Byline sometimes given. Buys second serial (reprint) rights or makes work-for-hire assignments. Submit seasonal/holiday material 6 months in advance. Simultaneous and previously published submissions OK. For reprints, send typed ms with rights for sale noted. Include information about when and where the article previously appeared. For reprints, pays 50% of the amount paid for an original article. Reports in 2 months. Sample copy for 9 × 12 SAE with 4 first class stamps. Writer's guidelines for #10 SASE.

Nonfiction: Book excerpts or reviews, general interest, how-to (dealing with careers or education), humor, inspirational, interview/profile (celebrity or "up and coming" young adult), new product (as it relates to young adult market), personal experience, photo feature, technical, travel and sports. First time writers with *Journey* must submit complete ms for consideration. Length: 750-2,000 words. Pays $150-400 for assigned articles; 10¢/word for unsolicited articles. Sometimes pays expenses of writers on assignment.

Photos: State availability of photos with submission. Prefers transparencies. Offers $20-25/photo. Captions, model releases and identification of subjects required. Buys all rights or one-time rights.

Columns/Departments: Profiles of Achievement (striving and successful minority young adult, age 16-35 in various careers). Buys 15 mss/year. Send complete ms. Length: 500-1,500. Pays $50-200.

Fiction: Publishes novel exerpts. Adventure, ethnic, historical, humorous, mainstream and slice-of-life vignettes. Buys 3 mss/year. Send complete ms. Length: 1,000-3,000 words. Pays $100-400.

Poetry: Free verse. Buys 5/year. Submit up to 5 poems at one time. Length: 10-25 lines. Pays $10-50.

Fillers: Anecdotes, facts, gags to be illustrated by cartoonist, newsbreaks, short humor. Buys 10/year. Length: 25-250 words. Pays $25-100.

Tips: "For new writers—must submit complete manuscript that is double spaced; clean copy only. If available, send clippings of previously published works and resume. Should state when available to write. Include on first page your name, address, phone, Social Security number and word count. Availability of photos enhances your chances. We desperately need more material dealing with concerns of Asian-American students."

MISSISSIPPI STATE ALUMNUS, Mississippi State University, Alumni Association, Editorial Office, P.O. Box 5328, Mississippi State MS 39762-5328. (601)325-3442. Fax: (601)325-7455. Editor: Allen Snow. Up to 10% freelance written. Works with small number of new/unpublished writers each year. Triannual magazine for well-educated and affluent audience emphasizing articles about Mississippi State graduates and former students. Estab. 1927. Circ. 57,000. Pays on publication. Publishes ms 6 months after acceptance. Buys one-time rights. Byline given. Simultaneous and previously published submissions OK. Reports in 6 weeks. Sample copy for 9 × 12 SAE with 5 first class stamps.

Nonfiction: Historical, informational, interview (with MSU grads), nostalgia (early days at MSU), personal experience and profile. Buys 1-3 mss/year. Send complete ms. Length: 500-2,000 words. Pays $50-100 (including photos, if used).

Photos: Offers no additional payment for photos purchased with accompanying ms. Captions required. Uses 5 × 7 and 8 × 10 b&w photos and color transparencies of any size.

Columns/Departments: Statements, "a section of the *Mississippi State Alumnus* that features briefs about alumni achievements and professional or business advancement. There is no payment for Statements briefs."

Tips: "All stories *must* be about Mississippi State University or its alumni. We're putting more emphasis on people and events on the campus—teaching, research and public service projects. But we're still eager to receive good stories about alumni in all parts of the world. We welcome articles about MSU grads in interesting occupations and have used stories on off-shore drillers, miners, horse trainers, etc. We also want profiles on prominent MSU alumni and have carried pieces on Senator John C. Stennis, author John Grisham, professional football players and coaches, and Eugene Butler, former editor-in-chief of *Progressive Farmer* magazine. We feature one or two alumni in each issue, alumni who have risen to prominence in their fields or who are engaged in unusual occupations. We're using more short features (500-700 words) to vary the length of our articles in each issue. We pay $25-50 for these, including one b&w photo."

NATIONAL FORUM: THE PHI KAPPA PHI JOURNAL, The Honor Society of Phi Kappa Phi, 216 Petrie Hall, Auburn University AL 36849. Editor: Stephen W. White. 20% freelance written. Prefers to work with published/established writers. Quarterly interdisciplinary, scholarly journal. "We are an interdisciplinary journal that publishes crisp, nontechnical analyses of issues of social and scientific concern as well as scholarly treatments of different aspects of culture." Circ. 120,000. Pays on publication. Query first. Publishes ms an average of 6 months after acceptance. Byline given. Buys exclusive rights with exceptions. Submit seasonal/holiday material 6 months in advance. Reports in 6 weeks on queries; 2 months on mss. Sample copy $2.75. Free writer's guidelines.

Nonfiction: General interest, interview/profile and opinion. No how-to or biographical articles. Each issue is devoted to the exploration of a particular theme. Query with clips of published work. Buys 5 unsolicited mss/year. Length: 1,500-2,000 words. Pays $50-200.

Photos: State availability of photos. Identification of subjects required. Buys all rights.
Columns/Departments: Educational Dilemmas of the 90s and Book Review section. Buys 8 mss/year for Educational Dilemmas, 40 book reviews. Length: Book reviews—400-800 words. Educational Dilemmas—1,500-1,800 words. Pays $15-25 for book reviews; $50/printed page, Educational Dilemmas.
Fiction: Humorous and short stories. No obscenity or excessive profanity. Buys 2-4 mss/year. Length: 1,500-1,800 words. Pays $50/printed page.
Poetry: No love poetry. Buys 20 mss/year. Submit 5 poems maximum. Prefers shorter poems. Prefers established poets. Include publication credentials in cover letter.

NOTRE DAME MAGAZINE, University of Notre Dame, Room 415, Administration Bldg., Notre Dame IN 46556-5602. (219)631-5335. Fax: (219)631-6947. Editor: Walton R. Collins. Managing Editor: Kerry Temple. 75% freelance written. Quarterly magazine covering news of Notre Dame and education and issues affecting the Roman Catholic Church. "We are interested in the moral, ethical and spiritual issues of the day and how Christians live in today's world. We are universal in scope, Catholic in viewpoint and serve Notre Dame alumni, friends and other constituencies." Estab. 1972. Circ. 110,000. **Pays on acceptance.** Publishes ms an average of 1 year after acceptance. Byline given. Kill fee negotiable. Buys first rights. Simultaneous queries OK. Query for electronic submissions. Reports in 1 month. Free sample copy.
Nonfiction: Opinion, personal experience, religion. "All articles must be of interest to Christian/Catholic readers who are well educated and active in their communities." Buys 35 mss/year. Query with clips of published work. Length: 600-3,000 words. Pays $500-1,500. Sometimes pays the expenses of writers on assignment.
Photos: State availability of photos. Reviews b&w contact sheets, transparencies and 8 × 10 prints. Model releases and identification of subjects required. Buys one-time rights.

OLD OREGON, The Magazine of the University of Oregon, University of Oregon, 101 Chapman Hall, Eugene OR 97403-1282. (503)346-5047. Fax: (503)346-2220. Editor: Tom Hager. Associate Editor: Mike Lee. 50% freelance written. Quarterly university magazine of people and ideas at the University of Oregon. Estab. 1919. Circ. 95,000. Pays on publication. Publishes ms an average of 3 months after acceptance. Byline given. Offers 20% kill fee. Buys first North American serial rights. Query for electronic submissions. Reports in 1 month. Sample copy for 9 × 12 SAE with 2 first class stamps.
Nonfiction: Northwest issues and culture from the perspective of UO alumni and faculty. Buys 30 mss/year. Query with published clips. Length: 500-2,500 words. Pays $50-250. Sometimes pays expenses of writers on assignment. Reprints OK; send photocopy of article and information about when and where the article previously appeared.
Photos: State availability of photos with submission. Reviews 8 × 10 prints. Offers $10-25/photo. Identification of subjects required. Buys one-time rights.
Tips: "Query with strong, colorful lead; clips."

PERSPECTIVES, Concepts for a career in communications, P.O. Box 515, Monroeville PA 15146-0515. (412)856-5024. Publisher/Editor: Loriann Hoff Oberlin. 5-10% freelance written. Newsletter published 10 times/year. "We cover communications careers (advertising, public relations, fiction and nonfiction writing, journalism, graphics) and speak to those making a living in communications careers (or studying to do just that) and to those seeking career information, writing assistance or practical advice from working professionals." Estab. 1990. **Pays on acceptance.** Publishes ms an average of 6 months after acceptance. Byline given. Buys one-time and second serial (reprint) rights. Submit seasonal/holiday material 9 months in advance. Previously published submissions OK. Send photocopy of article, including information about when and where the article previously appeared. For reprints, pays 50% of the amount paid for an original article. Reports in 1 month on queries; 6 weeks on mss. Sample copy $3 for #10 SASE. Make checks payable to: L.H. Oberlin, publisher.
Nonfiction: Book excerpts, how-to (study better, work smarter, get ahead or complete a communications-related task), interview/profile (mostly done inhouse) and brief tips to get ahead. Send complete ms with clips. Length: 30-350 words. Pays $5-20 (payment negotiated individually).
Columns/Departments: Business Briefs (practical tips to advance careers, make more money, write better, impress people, etc.), 30 words or less. Uses 50 mss/year. Send complete ms. Pays in portfolio copies for Business Briefs.
Tips: "Newsletter writing requires a keen ability to write clearly and concisely. Contributors *must* study newsletter and its style. Send for sample issues before submitting to me. Demonstrate that you understand the needs of entry-level communicators and beginning writers. Focus on ways readers can make money. Send for and study sample issues and follow directions (starting with a SASE and check payable to me). Beginning writers stand to gain the most from Perspectives. It offers great advice and lots of encouragement!"

‡THE PURDUE ALUMNUS, Purdue Alumni Association, Purdue Memorial Union 160, 101 N. Grant St., West Lafayette IN 47906-6212. (317)494-5184. Fax: (317)494-9179. Editor: Tim Newton. 75% freelance written. Prefers to work with published/established writers; works with small number of new/unpublished writers each year. Magazine published 9 times/year (except February, June, August) covering subjects of

interest to Purdue University alumni. Estab. 1912. Circ. 65,000. Pays on publication. Publishes ms an average of 2 months after acceptance. Byline given. Buys first rights and makes work-for-hire assignments. Submit seasonal/holiday material 6 months in advance. Simultaneous queries, and simultaneous and previously published submissions OK. Reports in 2 weeks on queries; 1 month on mss. Sample copy for 9 × 12 SAE with 2 first class stamps.
Nonfiction: Book excerpts, general interest, historical/nostalgic, humor, interview/profile and personal experience. Focus is on alumni campus news, issues and opinions of interest to 65,000 members of the Alumni Association. Feature style, primarily university-oriented. Issues relevant to education. Buys 12-20 mss/year. Length: 1,500-2,500 words. Pays $150-300. Sometimes pays expenses of writers on assignment.
Photos: State availability of photos. Reviews b&w contact sheet or 5 × 7 prints.
Tips: "We have 280,000 living, breathing Purdue alumni. If you can find a good story about one of them, we're interested. We use local freelancers to do campus places."

RIPON COLLEGE MAGAZINE, P.O. Box 248, Ripon WI 54971-0248. (414)748-8115. Fax: (414)748-9262. Editor: Loren J. Boone. 15% freelance written. "*Ripon College Magazine* is a quarterly publication that contains information relating to Ripon College and is mailed to alumni and friends of the college." Estab. 1851. Circ. 14,000. Pays on publication. Publishes ms an average of 3 months after acceptance. Byline given. Not copyrighted. Makes work-for-hire assignments. Query for electronic submissions. Reports in 2 weeks.
Nonfiction: Historical/nostalgic and interview/profile. Buys 4 mss/year. Query with or without published clips or send complete ms. Length: 250-1,000 words. Pays $25-350.
Photos: State availability of photos with submission. Reviews contact sheets. Offers additional payment for photos accepted with ms. Captions and model releases are required. Buys one-time rights.
Tips: "Story ideas must have a direct connection to Ripon College."

RUTGERS MAGAZINE, Rutgers University, Alexander Johnston Hall, New Brunswick NJ 08903. (908)932-7315. Editor: Eileen Garred. 50% freelance written. Quarterly university magazine of "general interest, but articles must have a Rutgers university or alumni tie-in." Circ. 134,000. **Pays on acceptance.** Publishes ms an average of 4 months after acceptance. Byline given. Pays 30-35% kill fee. Buys first North American serial rights. Submit seasonal/holiday material 6-8 months in advance. Query for electronic submissions. Reports in 1 month. Sample copy $3 for 9 × 12 SAE with 5 first class stamps.
Nonfiction: Book excerpts, essays, general interest, historical/nostalgic, humor, interview/profile, personal experience and photo feature. No articles without a Rutgers connection. Buys 15-20 mss/year. Query with published clips. Pays 25-40¢/word. Pays expenses of writers on assignment.
Photos: State availability of photos with submission. Payment varies. Identification of subjects required. Buys one-time rights.
Columns/Departments: Business, Money, Sports, Alumni Profiles (related to Rutgers), 1,200-1,800 words. Buys 6-8 mss/year. Query with published clips. Pays 25-40¢/word.
Tips: "Send ideas. We'll evaluate clips and topic for most appropriate use."

SCORECARD, Falsoft, Inc., 9509 US Highway 42, P.O. Box 385, Prospect KY 40059. (502)228-4492. Fax: (502)228-5121. Editor: John Crawley. 50% freelance written. Prefers to work with published/established writers. Weekly sports fan tabloid covering University of Louisville sports only. Estab. 1982. Circ. 7,500. Pays on publication. Publishes ms an average of 1 month after acceptance. Byline given. Buys first rights. Submit seasonal/holiday material 1 month in advance. Previously published submissions "rarely" OK. Reports in 2 weeks. Free sample copy and writer's guidelines.
Nonfiction: Assigned to contributing editors. Buys 100 mss/year. Query with published clips. Length: 750-1,500 words. Pays $20-50. Sometimes pays expenses of writers on assignment.
Photos: State availability of photos.
Columns/Departments: Notes Page (tidbits relevant to University of Louisville sports program or former players or teams). Buys 25 mss/year. Length: Approximately 100 words. Pay undetermined.
Tips: "Be very familiar with history and tradition of University of Louisville sports program. Contact us with story ideas. Know the subject."

SHIPMATE, U.S. Naval Academy Alumni Association Magazine, 247 King George St., Annapolis MD 21402-1306. (410)263-4469. Editor: Col. J.W. Hammond, Jr., USMC (retired). 100% freelance written. A magazine published 10 times a year by and for alumni of the U.S. Naval Academy. Estab. 1938. Circ. 35,500. Pays on publication. Byline given. Buys first North American serial rights. Submit seasonal/holiday material 10 months in advance. Reports in 1 week. Sample copy for 9 × 12 SAE with 6 first class stamps.
Nonfiction: Buys 50 mss/year. Send complete ms. Length: 2,000-7,500 words. Pays $100 for unsolicited articles.
Photos: Send photos with submission. Offers no additional payment for photos accepted with ms. Identification of subjects required. Buys one-time rights.
Tips: "The writer should be a Naval Academy alumnus (not necessarily a graduate) with first-hand experience of events in the Naval Service."

THE STUDENT, 127 9th Ave. N., Nashville TN 37234. Acting Editor: Cheryl Lewis. 10% freelance written. Works with a small number of new/unpublished writers each year. Publication of National Student Ministry Department of The Sunday School Board of the Southern Baptist Convention. Monthly magazine for college students focusing on freshman and sophomore levels. Estab. 1922. Circ. 40,000. Buys all rights. **Pays on acceptance.** Publishes ms an average of 10 months after acceptance. Mss should be double-spaced on white paper with 50-space line, 25 lines/page. Sources for quotes and statistics should be given for verification. Reports usually within 2 months. Sample copy and guidelines for 9 × 12 SAE with 3 first class stamps.

Nonfiction: Contemporary questions, problems, and issues facing college students viewed from a Christian perspective to develop high moral and ethical values. Cultivating interpersonal relationships, developing self-esteem, dealing with the academic struggle, coping with rejection, learning how to love and developing a personal relationship with Jesus Christ. Prefers complete ms rather than query. Length: 1,000 words maximum. Pays 5½¢/word after editing with reserved right to edit accepted material.

Fiction: Satire and parody on college life, humorous episodes; emphasize clean fun and the ability to grow and be uplifted through humor. Contemporary fiction involving student life, on campus as well as off. Length: 1,000 words. Pays 5½¢/word.

‡TEXAS ALCALDE, (formerly Alcalde), P.O. Box 7278, Austin TX 78713-7278. (512)471-3799. Fax: (512)471-8088. Editor: Ernestine Wheelock. 20% freelance written. Works with a small number of new/unpublished writers each year. Bimonthly magazine. Estab. 1913. Circ. 52,000. Pays on publication. Publishes ms an average of 6 months after acceptance. Buys all rights. Submit seasonal/holiday material 5 months in advance. Query for electronic submissions. Reports in 1 month. Sample copy for 8½ × 11 SAE with $1.30 postage. Writer's guidelines for #10 SASE.

Nonfiction: General interest; historical (University of Texas, research and faculty profile); humor (humorous Texas subjects); nostalgia (University of Texas traditions); profile (students, faculty, alumni); and technical (University of Texas research on a subject or product). No subjects lacking taste or quality, or not connected with the University of Texas. Buys 12 mss/year. Query. Length: 1,000-2,400 words. Pays according to importance of article.

‡TRANSFER (For Community College Students), Oxendine Publishing, Inc., 738 NW 23rd Ave., P.O. Box 14081, Gainesville FL 32609/32604-2081. (904)373-6907. Editor: W.H. "Butch" Oxendine Jr.. Managing Editor: Kay Quinn. 50% freelance written. Semiannual magazine "easing the transition from 2-year to 4-year schools." Estab. 1992. Circ. 20,000. Pays on publication. Publishes ms an average of 2-3 months after acceptance. Byline given. Buys all rights. Submit seasonal/holiday material 4 months in advance. Accepts previously published submissions. Query for electronic submissions. Prefers IBM. Reports in 1 month. Sample copy for 8 × 11 SAE with 3 first class stamps. Writer's guidelines for #10 SASE.

Nonfiction: How-to, humor, new product, opinion and other. "No lengthy individual's profiles, or articles without primary and secondary sources attribution." Buys 10 mss/year. Query. Length: 250-1,000 words. Pays $35 maximum. Pays with contributors copies to students or first-time writers.

Photos: State availability of or send photos with submission. Reviews contact sheets, negatives and transparencies. Offers $50 maximum/photo. Captions, model releases and identification of subjects required. Buys all rights.

Columns/Departments: Transfer Student Trials, 250-1,000 words; Finding Financial Aid, 250-1,000 words. Query. Pays $35 maximum.

Fillers: Facts, newsbreaks and short humor. Buys 10/year. Length: 100-500 words. Pays $35 maximum. "Read other high school and college publications for current issues, interests. Send manuscripts or outlines for review. All sections open to freelance work. Always looking for lighter, humorous articles, as well as features on Florida colleges and universities, careers, jobs."

VISIONS, A Success Guide for Native American Students, Communications Publishing Group, 250 Mark Twain Tower, 106 W. 11th St., Kansas City MO 64105-1806. (816)221-4404. Fax: (816)221-1112. Editor: Georgia Clark. 40% freelance written. Biannual education and career source guide designed for Native American students who want to pursue a higher education through colleges, vocational and technical schools or proprietary schools, to focus on insight, motivational and career planning informations. For young adults, ages 16-25. Circ. 100,000. Pays on publication. Byline sometimes given. Buys second serial (reprint) rights or makes work-for-hire assignments. Submit seasonal/holiday material 6 months in advance. Simultaneous, photocopied and previously published submissions OK. For reprints, send typed ms with rights for sale noted. Include information about when and where the article previously appeared. For reprints, pays 50% of the amount paid for an original article. Reports in 2 months. Sample copy for 9 × 12 SAE with 4 first class stamps. Writer's guidelines for #10 SASE.

Nonfiction: Book excerpts or reviews, general interest, how-to, humor, inspirational, interview/profile, new product, personal experience, photo feature, technical, travel and sports. Query or send complete ms. Length: 750-2,000 words. Pays $150-400 for assigned articles; 10¢/word for unsolicited articles. Sometimes pays expenses of writers on assignment.

Photos: State availability of photos with submission. Reviews transparencies. Offers $20-25/photo. Captions, model releases, and identification of subjects required. Buys all rights.

Columns/Departments: Profiles of Achievement (striving and successful Native American young adults, age 16-35, in various careers). Length: 500-1,500 words. Buys 15 mss/year. Send complete ms. Pays $50-250.

Fiction: Adventure, ethnic, historical, humorous, mainstream and slice-of-life vignettes. Buys 3 mss/year. Send complete ms. Length: 1,000-5,000 words. Pays $100-400.

Poetry: Free verse. Buys 5 poems/year. Submit up to 5 poems at one time. Length: 10-25 lines. Pays $10-50.

Fillers: Anecdotes, facts, gags to be illustrated by cartoonist, newsbreaks, short humor. Buys 10 fillers/year. Length: 25-250 words. Pays $25-100.

Tips: "For new writers—submit complete manuscript that is double spaced; clean copy only. If available, send clippings of previously published works and resume. Should state when available to write. Include on first page of manuscript your name, address, phone, Social Security number and word count. Availability of photos will enhance your chances."

WHAT MAKES PEOPLE SUCCESSFUL, The National Research Bureau, Inc., 424 N. 3rd St., P.O. Box 1, Burlington IA 52601-0001. (319)752-5415. Fax: (319)752-3421. Editor: Nancy Heinzel. Editorial Supervisor: Doris J. Ruschill. 75% freelance written. Eager to work with new/unpublished writers and works with a small number each year. Quarterly magazine. Estab. 1948. Pays on publication. Publishes ms an average of 1 year after acceptance. Buys all rights. Submit seasonal/holiday material 8 months in advance of issue date. Sample copy and writer's guidelines for #10 SAE with 2 first class stamps.

Nonfiction: How-to (be successful); general interest (personality, employee morale, guides to successful living, biographies of successful persons, etc.); experience; and opinion. No material on health. Buys 3-4 mss/issue. Query with outline. Length: 500-700 words. Pays 4¢/word.

Tips: Short articles (rather than major features) have a better chance of acceptance because all articles are short.

WPI JOURNAL, Worcester Polytechnic Institute, 100 Institute Rd., Worcester MA 01609-2280. Fax: (508)831-5604. Editor: Michael Dorsey. 20% freelance written. Quarterly alumni magazine covering science and engineering/education/business personalities for 20,000 alumni, primarily engineers, scientists, managers, national media. Estab. 1897. Circ. 24,500. Pays on publication. Publishes ms an average of 6 months after acceptance. Byline given. Buys one-time rights. Submit seasonal/holiday material 6 months in advance. Simultaneous queries, and simultaneous and previously published submissions OK. Query for electronic submissions. Requires hard copy also. Reports in 1 month on queries.

Nonfiction: Interview/profile (people in engineering, science); photo feature; and features on science, engineering and management. Query with published clips. Length: 1,000-4,000 words. Pays negotiable rate. Sometimes pays the expenses of writers on assignment.

Photos: State availability of photos with query or ms. Reviews b&w contact sheets. Pays negotiable rate. Captions required.

Tips: "Submit outline of story and/or ms of story idea or published work. Features are most open to freelancers. Keep in mind that this is an alumni magazine, so most articles focus on the college and its community."

Child Care and Parental Guidance

Readers of today's parenting magazines want more information on pregnancy, infancy, child development and parenting research. Child care magazines address these and other issues from many different perspectives. Some are general interest parenting magazines while others for child care providers combine care information with business tips. Other markets that buy articles about child care and the family are included in the Religious and Women's sections and in the Trade Education section. Publications for children can be found in the Juvenile section.

AMERICAN BABY MAGAZINE, For Expectant and New Parents, 475 Park Ave. S., New York NY 10016. (212)689-3600. Editor: Judith Nolte. 90% freelance written. Prefers to work with published/established writers; works with a small number of new/unpublished writers each year. Monthly magazine covering pregnancy, child care and parenting. "Our readership is composed of women in late pregnancy and early new motherhood. Most readers are first-time parents; some have older children. A simple, straightforward, clear approach is mandatory." Estab. 1938. Circ. 1,150,000. **Pays on acceptance.** Publishes ms an average of 6 months after acceptance. Byline given. Buys first North American serial rights. Submit seasonal holiday material 6 months in advance. Simultaneous and previously published submissions OK. Reprints OK; send tearsheet or photocopy of article and typed ms with rights for sale noted and information about when and where the article previously appeared. Pays 75% of their fee for an original article. Reports in 1 month on queries; 2 months on mss. Sample copy for 9 × 12 SAE with 6 first class stamps. Writer's guidelines for #10 SASE.

Nonfiction: Book excerpts, how-to (some aspect of pregnancy or child care), humor and personal experience. "No 'hearts and flowers' or fantasy pieces." Buys 60 mss/year. Query with published clips or send complete ms. Length: 1,000-2,500 words. Pays $350-1,000 for assigned articles; $300-500 for unsolicited articles. Pays the expenses of writers on assignment.

Photos: State availability of photos with submission. Reviews transparencies and prints. Model release and identification of subjects required. Buys one-time rights.

• Ranked as one of the best markets for freelance writers in *Writer's Digest* magazine's annual "Top 100 Markets," January 1993.

Tips: "Articles should either give 'how to' information on some aspect of pregnancy or child care, cover some common problem of child raising, along with solutions, give advice to the mother on some psychological or practical subject, or share an experience with some universal aspect of new parenthood."

‡ATLANTA PARENT/ATLANTA BABY, Capers for Kids Publications, Suite 506, 4330 Georgetown Square II, Atlanta GA 30338. (404)754-7599. Editor: Liz White. Managing Editor: Peggy Middendorf. 100% freelance written. Monthly tabloid covering parenting of children from birth – 14 years old. Offers "down-to-earth help for parents." Estab. 1983. Circ. 55,000. Pays on publication. Publishes ms 3 months after acceptance. Byline given. Buys one-time rights. Submit seasonal material 6 months in advance. Previously published submissions OK. Query for electronic submissions. Reports in 3 months. Sample copy $2.

Nonfiction: General interest, how-to, humor, interview/profile and travel. Special issues: Private school (January); Birthday parties (February); Camp (March/April); Maternity and Mothering (May); Child care (July); Back-to-school (August); Drugs (October); Holidays (November/December). Does not want first person accounts or philosophical discussions. Buys 60 mss/year. Query with or without published clips or send complete ms. Length: 700-2,100 words. Pays $15-30. Sometimes pays expenses of writers on assignment.

Photos: State availability of photos with submission and send photocopies. Reviews 3 × 5 photos "b&w preferably." Offers $5/photo. Buys one-time rights.

Columns/Departments: Pack up and go (travel), 700-1,500. Buys 8-10 mss/year. Send complete ms. Length: 700-1,500 words. Pays $15-30.

Tips: "Articles should be geared to problems or situations of families and parents. Should include down-to-earth tips and be clearly written. No philosophical discussions or first person narratives."

‡BABY CONNECTION NEWS JOURNAL, a newspaper for new and expectant families, Parent Education for Infant Development, Post Office Drawer 13320, San Antonio TX 78213. Editor: Gina Morris. Managing Editor: Ed Boyd. Editorial contact: Gina Morris. 100% freelance written. Quarterly newspaper/tabloid covering infant sensory development. Newspaper "explores issues of pregnancy, childbirth and specifically the infant's first year of development." Estab. 1986. Circ. 45,000. Pays on publication. Publishes ms an average of 6 months after acceptance. Byline given. Buys one-time rights. Editorial lead time 6-9 months. Submit seasonal material "anytime." Accepts simultaneous and previously published submissions. Reports in 2 months. Sample copy $1.80 for 10 × 13 SAE with 5 first class stamps.

Nonfiction: Essays, humor, inspirational, new product, personal experience. "No poetry. No weird, mystic, rambling articles. No harsh or judgemental articles." Buys 24 mss/year. Send complete ms. Length: 600-1,000 words. Pays $10. Sometimes pays contributor's copies "as an addition to payment."

Photos: State availability of photos with submission. Reviews contact sheets, negatives, and 4 × 6 prints. Offers $5-10/photo. Negotiates payment individually. Identification of subjects required. Buys one-time rights.

Columns/Departments: Baby Universe (news around the globe – infant related), 75-150 words; NewsNews-News (products new on the market for babies), 250-300 words. Buys 12 mss/year. Send complete ms. Pays $5-10.

Fiction: Adventure, humorous, romance, slice-of-life vignettes. "All articles with any slant must pertain to infancy issues." Buys 8-10 mss/year. Send complete ms. Length: 600-1,000 words. Pays $10.

Fillers: Anecdotes, facts, newsbreaks, short humor. Buys 36/year. Length: 40-180 words. Pays $5.

Tips: "State that your submission is via *Writer's Market* for special attention, be patient in allowing time for response. Always include brief bio with your submission – something that will endear you to our readers, male perspective encouraged. We prefer articles on infant development such as growth, stages, mental, social, physical, etc. Write as though you are in your kitchen talking to your best friend. Make a difference in our readers' lives, give emotional support, humor a big plus. Be personal and detailed."

A bullet introduces comments by the editor of
Writer's Market *indicating special information*
about the listing.

BAY AREA PARENT, The Santa Clara News Magazine, for Parents, Bay Area Publishing Group Inc., 401 "A" Alberto Way, Los Gatos CA 95032. Fax: (408)356-4903. Editor: Lynn Berardo. 80% freelance written. Works with locally-based published/established writers and some non-local writers. Monthly tabloid of resource information for parents and teachers. Circ 70,000. Pays on publication. Publishes ms an average of 3 months after acceptance. Byline given. Buys one-time rights. Submit seasonal/holiday material 3 months in advance. Simultaneous and previously published submissions OK. Query for electronic submissions. Sample copy for 9 × 12 SAE with 6 first class stamps. Writer's guidelines for #10 SASE.

Nonfiction: Book excerpts (related to our interest group); expose (health, psychology); historical/nostalgic ("History of Diapers"); how-to (related to kids/parenting); humor; interview/profile; photo feature; and travel (with kids, family). Special issues include Music (February); Art (March); Kid's Birthdays (April); Summer Camps (May); Family Fun (June); Pregnancy and Childbirth (July); Fashion (August); Health (September); and Mental Health (October). No opinion or religious articles. Buys 45-60 mss/year. Query or send complete ms. Length: 150-1,500 words. Pays 6¢/word. Sometimes pays expenses of writers on assignment.

Photos: State availability of photos. Prefers b&w contact sheets and/or 3 × 5 b&w prints. Pays $10-15. Model release required. Buys one-time rights.

Columns/Departments: Child Care, Family Travel, Birthday Party Ideas, Baby Page, Toddler Page, Adolescent Kids. Buys 36 mss/year. Send complete ms. Length: 400-1,200 words. Pays $20-75.

Fiction: Humorous.

Tips: "Submit new, fresh information concisely written and accurately researched. We also produce *Bay Area Baby Magazine,* a semiannual publication, and *Valley Parent.*"

‡**CHILD,** NY Times Co. Women's Magazine, 110 5th Ave., New York NY 10011. (212)463-1000. Editor: Freddi Greenberg. Executive Editor: Stephanie Wood. 95% freelance written. Monthly magazine for parenting. Estab. 1986. Circ. 575,000. **Pays on acceptance.** Byline given. Offers 25% kill fee. Buys first North American serial, first, one-time and second serial (reprint) rights. Editorial lead time 3 months. Submit seasonal material 6 months in advance. Accepts simultaneous submissions. Reports in 2 months. Sample copy $3.95. Writer's guidelines free on request.

Nonfiction: Book excerpts, general interest, interview/profile, new product and photo feature. No poetry. Query with published clips. Length: 250 words minimum. Payment negotiable. Pays expenses of writers on assignment.

Photos: State availability of photos with submission. Reviews transparencies. Negotiates payment individually. Buys one-time rights.

Columns/Departments: Deputy editor: Mary Beth Jordan. Love, Dad (fathers' perspective); Child of Mine (mothers' or fathers' perspective). Query with published clips.

● Ranked as one of the best markets for freelance writers in *Writer's Digest* magazine's annual "Top 100 Markets," January 1993.

CHRISTIAN PARENTING TODAY, Good Family Magazines, P.O. Box 850, 548 Sisters Parkway, Sisters OR 97759-0850. (503)549-8261. Editor: David Kopp. Managing Editor: Brad Lewis. 50% freelance written. Bimonthly magazine covering parenting today's children. "*Christian Parenting Today* is a positive, practical magazine that targets real needs of the contemporary family with authoritative articles based on fresh research and the timeless truths of the Bible. *CPT*'s readers represent the broad spectrum of Christians who seek intelligent answers to the new demands of parenting in the 90s." Estab. 1988. Circ. 250,000. Pays on acceptance or publication. Byline given. Buys first North American serial or second serial (reprint) rights. Send tearsheet or photocopy of article, or typed ms with rights for sale noted. Include information about when and where the article previously appeared. For reprints, pays 25% of the amount we paid for an original article. Submit seasonal/holiday material 6 months in advance. Query for electronic submissions. Reports in 2 months. Sample copy for 9 × 12 SASE with 5 first class stamps. Writer's guidelines for #10 SASE.

Nonfiction: Book excerpts, how-to, humor, inspirational and religious. Buys 50 mss/year. Query. Length: 750-2,000 words. Pays 15-25¢/word. Sometimes pays expenses of writers on assignment.

Photos: State availability of photos with submission. Do not submit photos without permission. Reviews transparencies. Model release required. Buys one-time rights.

Columns/Departments: Parent Exchange (family-tested parenting ideas from our readers), 25-100 words; Life In Our House (entertaining, true, humorous stories about your family), 25-100 words. Buys 120 mss/year. Send complete ms. Pays $25-40. No SASE required. Submissions become property of CPT.

Tips: "Our readers are active evangelical Christians from the broad spectrum of Protestant and Roman Catholic traditions. We are *not* interested in advocating any denominational bias. Our readers want authority, conciseness, problem-solving, entertainment, encouragement and surprise. They also require a clear biblical basis for advice. We are unable to acknowledge unsolicited mss without SASE."

EXPECTING, Gruner + Jahr USA Publishing, 685 3rd Ave., New York NY 10017. (212)878-8700. Editor: Evelyn Podsiadlo. 80% freelance written. Quarterly magazine covering pregnancy, birth and the newborn. "*Expecting* covers subjects that are of interest to expectant and new parents. Articles must be authoritative and reassuring." Estab. 1967. Circ. 1,300,000. **Pays on acceptance.** Byline given. No kill fee. Buys one-time rights. Submit seasonal/holiday material 6 months in advance. Reports in 1-2 months. Writer's guidelines for #10 SASE.

Nonfiction: Book excerpts, humor, personal experience, health, nutrition, and financial subjects related to pregnancy, birth and the newborn. "No essays or inspirational pieces." Buys 32 to 40 mss/year. Query with published clips. Length: 1,000-2,500 words. Pays $400-750 for assigned articles. Pays $300-600 for unsolicited articles.

Columns/Departments: Happenings (short, humorous anecdotes related to pregnancy, birth or new parenthood), 50-100 words; Your Turn (personal experience related to pregnancy, birth or new parenthood), 500-750 words. Buys 12-16 for Happenings; 2-3 for Your Turn. Send complete ms. "Happenings pays $25 on publication and mss are not returned. Your Turn pays $250 on acceptance and mss are returned."

Tips: "Much of the information in *Expecting* is health-related, so we prefer experienced health writers or writers who work well with doctors, nurses and other health professionals. Expertise in the areas of pregnancy, birth, and the newborn is also a plus. All areas of substance are open to freelancers. Articles must be authoritative."

‡**FAMILY TIMES,** Family Times, Inc., 1900 Super Fine Lane, Wilmington DE 19802. (802)575-0935. Editor: Alison Garber. Assistant Editor: Leigh Anne Perialas. 25% freelance written. Monthly tabloid for parenting. "Our targeted distribution is to parents via a controlled network of area schools, daycares, pediatricians and places where families congregate. We only want articles related to parenting, children's issues and enhancing family life." Estab. 1991. Circ. 50,000. Pays on publication. Publishes ms an average of 2 months after acceptance. Byline given. Buys one-time or second serial (reprint) rights. Editorial lead time 2 months. Submit seasonal material 2 months in advance. Accepts simultaneous and previously published submissions. Query for electronic submissions. Prefers Mac diskette. Reports in 1 month on mss. Sample copy for 3 first class stamps.

Nonfiction: Book excerpts, how-to parenting, inspirational, interview/profile, new product, opinion, personal experience, photo feature, travel, children and parenting. Schools—October; Camps—February; Maternity—July; Holiday—December; Fitness—March; Birthday—May; Back to School—August. Buys 48 mss/year. Send complete ms. Length: 350-1,200 words. Pays $30 minimum for assigned articles; $25 for unsolicited articles. Sometimes pays expenses of writers on assignment.

Photos: State availability of photos with submission. Negotiates payment individually. Identification of subjects required. Buys one-time rights.

Columns/Departments: Pays $25-50.

Tips: "Work with other members of PPA (Parenting Publications of America). Since we all share our writers and watch others' work. We pay little but you can sell the same story to 30+ other publications in different markets. We are most open to general features."

GROWING PARENT, Dunn & Hargitt, Inc., P.O. Box 620, Lafayette IN 47902-0620. (317)423-2624. Fax: (317)423-4495. Editor: Nancy Kleckner. 40-50% freelance written. Works with a small number of new/unpublished writers each year. "We do receive a lot of unsolicited submissions but have had excellent results in working with some unpublished writers. So, we're always happy to look at material and hope to find one or two jewels each year." Monthly newsletter which focuses on parents—the issues, problems, and choices they face as their children grow. "We want to look at the parent as an adult and help encourage his or her growth not only as a parent but as an individual." Estab. 1967. **Pays on acceptance.** Publishes ms an average of 6 months after acceptance. Byline given. Buys first North American serial rights; maintains exclusive rights for three months. Submit seasonal/holiday material 6 months in advance. Previously published submissions OK. Reports in 2 weeks. Sample copy and writer's guidelines for 5×8 SAE with 2 first class stamps.

Nonfiction: "We are looking for informational articles written in an easy-to-read, concise style. We would like to see articles that help parents deal with the stresses they face in everyday life—positive, upbeat, how-to-cope suggestions. We rarely use humorous pieces, fiction or personal experience articles. Writers should keep in mind that most of our readers have children under three years of age." Buys 15-20 mss/year. Query. Length: 1,000-1,500 words; will look at shorter pieces. Pays 8-10¢/word (depends on article). Reprints OK; send photocopy of article and information about when and where it previously appeared.

Tips: "Submit a very specific query letter with samples."

HEALTHY KIDS: BIRTH-3/HEALTHY KIDS: 4-10 YEARS, Cahners Publishing, 475 Park Ave. S., New York NY 10016-6902. (212)689-3600. Fax: (212)779-5790. Managing Editor: Ellen Wlody. 90% freelance written. Birth-3 published 4 times/year; 4-10 published 3 times/year. Both magazines cover children's health. Estab. 1989/1990. Circ. 1.5 million/2 million. **Pays on acceptance.** Byline given. Buys first rights. Submit seasonal/holiday material 6 months in advance. Reports in 1 month on queries. Free sample copy and writer's guidelines for SASE.

Nonfiction: How-to help your child develop as a person, keep safe, keep healthy and personal experience. No poetry, fiction, travel or product endorsement. Buys 30 mss/year. Query. Length: 1,500-2,000 words. Pays $500-1,000. Pays expenses of writers on assignment. Does not accept unsolicited mss.

Columns/Departments: Buys 30 mss/year. Query. Length: 1,500-2,000 words. Pays $500-1,000.

• Ranked as one of the best markets for freelance writers in *Writer's Digest* magazine's annual "Top 100 Markets," January 1993.

HOME EDUCATION MAGAZINE, P.O. Box 1083, Tonasket WA 98855-1083. Editors: Mark J. Hegener and Helen E. Hegener. 80% freelance written. Eager to work with new/unpublished writers each year. Bimonthly magazine covering home-based education. "We feature articles which address the concerns of parents who want to take a direct involvement in the education of their children—concerns such as socialization, how to find curriculums and materials, testing and evaluation, how to tell when your child is ready to begin reading, what to do when home schooling is difficult, teaching advanced subjects, etc." Estab. 1983. Circ. 5,500. Pays on publication. Publishes ms an average of 6 months after acceptance. Byline given. ("Please include a 30-50 word credit with your article.") Buys first North American serial, first, one-time, second serial (reprint) and simultaneous rights and makes work-for-hire assignments. Submit seasonal/holiday material 6 months in advance. Simultaneous and previously published submissions OK. Query for electronic submission requirements. Reports in 2 months. Sample copy $4.50. Writer's guidelines for #10 SASE.

Nonfiction: Book excerpts, essays, how-to (related to home schooling), humor, inspirational, interview/profile, personal experience, photo feature and technical. Buys 40-50 mss/year. Query with or without published clips, or send complete ms. Length: 750-3,500 words. Pays $10/final typeset page (about 750 words). Sometimes pays expenses of writers on assignment.

Photos: Send photos with submission. Reviews 5 × 7, 35mm prints and b&w snapshots. Write for photo rates. Identification of subjects required. Buys one-time rights.

Tips: "We would like to see how-to articles (that don't preach, just present options); articles on testing, accountability, working with the public schools, socialization, learning disabilities, resources, support groups, legislation and humor. We need answers to the questions that home schoolers ask."

HOME LIFE, Sunday School Board, 127 9th Ave. N., Nashville TN 37234. (615)251-2271. Editor-in-Chief: Charlie Warren. 50% freelance written. Prefers to work with published/established writers, but will work with new/unpublished writers. Monthly magazine emphasizing Christian marriage and Christian family life for married adults of all ages, but especially newlyweds and middle-aged marrieds. Estab. 1947. Circ. 625,000. **Pays on acceptance.** Publishes ms an average of 15 months after acceptance. Buys first, first North American serial and all rights. Byline given. Phone queries OK, but written queries preferred. Submit seasonal/holiday material 1 year in advance. Reports in 2 weeks for queries; 3 months for ms. Sample copy $1. Writer's guidelines for #10 SASE.

Nonfiction: How-to (good articles on marriage and family life); informational (about some current family-related issue of national significance such as "Television and the Christian Family" or "Whatever Happened to Family Worship?"); and personal experience (informed articles by people who have solved marriage and family problems in healthy, constructive ways). "No column material. We are not interested in material that will not in some way enrich Christian marriage or family life. We are interested in articles on fun family activities for a new department called Family Time." Buys 100-150 mss/year. Query or submit complete ms. Length: 600-1,800 words. Pays up to 5½¢/word.

Fiction: "Fiction should be family-related and should show a strong moral about how families face and solve problems constructively." Buys 12-20 mss/year. Submit complete ms. Length: 600-1,800 words. Pays up to 5½¢/word.

Tips: "Study the magazine to see our unique slant on Christian family life. We prefer a life-centered case study approach, rather than theoretical essays on family life. Our top priority is marriage enrichment material."

L.A. PARENT, The Magazine for Parents in Southern California, P.O. Box 3204, Burbank CA 91504. (818)846-0400. Fax: (818)841-4380. Editor: Jack Bierman. Managing Editor: David Jamieson. 80% freelance written. Prefers to work with published/established writers, but works with a small number of new/unpublished writers each year. Monthly tabloid covering parenting. Estab. 1980. Circ. 120,000. Pays on publication. Publishes ms an average of 4 months after acceptance. Byline given. Buys first rights and reprint rights. Submit seasonal/holiday material 3 months in advance. Simultaneous queries and previously published submissions OK. Query for electronic submissions. Reprints OK; send photocopy of article and information about when and where the article previously appeared. Pays 50% of their fee for an original article. Reports in 1 month. Sample copy and writer's guidelines $2 for 11 × 14 SAE with 5 first class stamps.

Nonfiction: David Jamieson, articles editor. General interest, how-to. "We focus on generic parenting for ages 0-10 and southern California activities for families, and do round-up pieces, i.e., a guide to private schools, fishing spots." Buys 60-75 mss/year. Query with clips of published work. Length: 700-1,200 words. Pays $250 plus expenses.

Tips: "We will be using more contemporary articles on parenting's challenges. If you can write for a 'city magazine' in tone and accuracy, you may write for us. The 'Baby Boom' has created a need for more generic parenting material."

For explanation of symbols, see the Key to Symbols and Abbreviations on page 72. For unfamiliar words, see the Glossary.

‡**LADIES' HOME JOURNAL PARENT'S DIGEST**, Meredith, 100 Park Ave., New York NY 10017. (212)351-3500. Editor: Mary Mohler. Magazine Editor: Carolyn B. Noyes. 75% freelance written. Quarterly magazine for childrearing and parenting. "This is a digest of materials that have previously appeared in books, newspapers or on the air." Estab. 1992. Circ. 400,000. **Pays on acceptance.** Byline given. Buys first North American serial, second serial (reprint) or all rights. Submit seasonal material 6 months in advance. Accepts previously published submissions. Reports in 6 weeks on queries.
Nonfiction: Book excerpts, essays, humor, new product and travel. Buys 50 mss/year. Query with published clips. Length: 250-2,500 words. Payment negotiable for previously published material. Sometimes pays expenses of writers on assignment (limit agreed upon in advance).
Photos: State availability of photos with submission. Negotiates payment individually. Model release and identification of subjects required.

LIVING WITH CHILDREN, Baptist Sunday School Board, 127 9th Ave. N., Nashville TN 37234. (615)251-2229. Fax: (615)251-3866. Contact Editor. 50% freelance written. Works with a small number of new/unpublished writers each year. Quarterly magazine covering parenting issues for parents of elementary-age children (ages 6 through 11). "Written and designed from a Christian perspective." Estab. 1892. Circ. 50,000. **Pays on acceptance.** Publishes ms an average of 2 years after acceptance. Byline given. "We generally buy all rights to mss; first serial rights on a limited basis (submit photocopy of article or short story and information about when and where the article previously appeared). First and reprint rights may be negotiated at a lower rate of pay." Submit seasonal/holiday material 1 year in advance. Previously published submissions (on limited basis) OK; send photocopy of article or short story, typed ms with rights for sale noted and information about when and where the article previously appeared. Pays 80% of their fee for an original article. Reports in 1 month on queries; 2 months on mss. Sample copy for 9 × 12 SAE with 4 first class stamps; free writer's guidelines.
Nonfiction: How-to (parent), humor, inspirational, personal experience, and articles on child development. No articles containing more than 15-20 lines quoted material. Buys 60 mss/year. Query or send complete ms (queries preferred). Length: 800-1,200 words. Pays 5½¢/word.
Photos: "Submission of photos with mss is strongly discouraged."
Fiction: Humorous (parent/child relationships) and religious. "We have very limited need for fiction." Buys maximum of 8 mss/year. Length: 800-1,200 words. Pays 5½¢/word.
Poetry: Light verse and inspirational. "We have limited need for poetry and buy only all rights." Buys 15 poems/year. Submit maximum 3 poems. Length: 4-30 lines. Pays $1.75 for 1-7 lines, plus $1.25 for each additional line; pays $5.40 for 8 lines or more plus 75¢ each additional line with $24 maximum.
Fillers: Jokes, anecdotes and short humor. Buys 15/year. Length: 100-400 words. Pays $5 minimum, 5½¢/word.
Tips: "Articles must deal with an issue of interest to parents. A mistake some writers make in articles for us is failing to write from a uniquely Christian perspective; that is very necessary for our periodicals. Material should be 800-1,200 in length. All sections, particularly articles, are open to freelance writers. Only regular features are assigned."

LIVING WITH PRESCHOOLERS, Baptist Sunday School Board, 127 9th Ave. N., Nashville TN 37234. (615)251-2229. Fax: (615)251-5058. Contact Editor. 50% freelance written. Works with a small number of new/unpublished writers each year. Quarterly magazine covering parenting issues for parents of preschoolers (infants through 5-year-olds). The magazine is "written and designed from a Christian perspective." Estab. 1892. Circ. 152,000. **Pays on acceptance.** Publishes ms an average of 2 years after acceptance. Byline given. "We generally buy all rights to manuscripts. First and reprint rights may be negotiated at a lower rate of pay." Submit seasonal/holiday material 2 years in advance. Previously published submissions (on limited basis) OK; OK; send photocopy of article or short story, typed ms with rights for sale noted and information about when and where the article previously appeared. Pays 80% of their fee for an original article. Reports in 1 month on queries; 2 months on mss. Sample copy for 9 × 12 SASE. Free writer's guidelines.
Nonfiction: How-to (parent), humor, inspirational, personal experience and articles on child development. No articles containing more than 15-20 lines quoted material. Buys 60 mss/year. Query or send complete ms (queries preferred). Length: 800-1,200 words. Pays 5½¢/word for mss offered on all-rights basis.
Photos: "Submission of photos with mss is strongly discouraged."
Fiction: Humorous (parent/child relationships) and religious. "We have very limited need for fiction." Buys maximum of 8 mss/year. Length: 800-1,200 words. Pays 5½¢/word.
Poetry: Light verse and inspirational. "We have limited need for poetry and buy only all rights." Buys 15 poems/year. Submit maximum 3 poems. Length: 4-30 lines. Pays $2.10 for 1-7 lines, plus $1.25 for each additional line; pays $5.40 for 8 lines or more plus 75¢ each additional line with $24 maximum.
Fillers: Jokes, anecdotes or short humor. Buys 15/year. Length: 100-400 words. Pays $10 minimum, 5½¢/word maximum.
Tips: "Articles must deal with an issue of interest to parents. A mistake some writers make in writing an article for us is failing to write from a uniquely Christian perspective; that is very necessary for our periodicals. Material should be up to 1,200 words in length. All sections, particularly articles, are open to freelance writers. Only regular features are assigned."

LONG ISLAND PARENTING NEWS, RDM Publishing, P.O. Box 214, Island Park NY 11558. (516)889-5510. Fax: (516)889-5513. Editor: Pat Simms-Elias. Managing Editor: Andrew Elias. 70% freelance written. Free community newspaper published monthly covering parenting, children and family issues. "A publication for concerned parents with active families and young children. Our slogan is: 'For parents who care to know.' " Estab. 1989. Circ. 40,000. Pays on publication. Publishes ms an average of 3 months after acceptance. Byline given. (Also 1-3 line bio, if appropriate.) Buys one-time rights. Simultaneous and previously published submissions OK. Reprints OK; send photocopy of article and information about when and where the article previously appeared. Pays 75-100% of their fee for an original article. Reports in 3 months. Sample copy $3 for 9 × 12 SAE with 5 first class stamps. Free writer's guidelines.

Nonfiction: Essays, general interest, humor, interview/profile, travel. Will need articles covering childcare, childbirth/maternity, schools, camps and back-to-school. Buys 20-30 mss/year. Query with or without published clips or send complete ms. Length: 350-2,000 words. Pays $25-150. "Sometimes trade article for advertising space." Sometimes pays expenses of writers on assignment.

Photos: Send photos with submission. Reviews 4 × 5 prints. Offers $5-50/photo. Captions required. Buys one-time rights.

Columns/Departments: Off The Shelf (book reviews); Fun & Games (toy and game reviews); KidVid (reviews of kids' video); The Beat (reviews of kids' music); Monitor (reviews of computer hardware and software for kids); Big Screen (reviews of kids' films); Soon Come (for expectant parents); Educaring (parenting info and advice); Something Special (for parents of kids with special needs); Growing Up (family health issues); On the Ball (sports for kids); Perspectives (essays on family life); Words Worth (storytelling); Getaway (family travel). Buys 20-30 mss/year. Send complete ms. Length: 500-1,000 words. Pays 25-150.

Fillers: Facts and newsbreaks. Buys 1-10/year. Length: 200-500. Pays $10-25.

METROKIDS MAGAZINE, The Resource for Parents and Children in the Delaware Valley, Kidstuff Publications, Inc., 2101 Spruce St., Philadelphia PA 19103. (215)735-7035. Fax: (215)735-1547. Editor: Nancy Lisagor. Managing Editor: Joan Horvath. 80% freelance written. Monthly tabloid that provides information for parents and kids in Philadelphia. Estab. 1990. Circ. 70,000. Pays on publication. Publishes ms an average of 10 months after acceptance. Byline given. Buys one-time rights. Submit seasonal/holiday material 4 months in advance. Previously published submissions OK. Publishes reprints of previously published articles or short stories. Wants to see tearsheet of article or short story and information about when and where the article previously appeared. For reprints, we pay 50-75% of the amount we pay for an original article. Query for electronic submissions. Reports in up to 8 months on queries. Sample copy for 9 × 12 SAE with 4 first class stamps. Writer's guidelines for #10 SASE.

Nonfiction: General interest, how-to, humor, new product and travel. "Each issue has a focus (for example: finance, extra-curricular lessons for kids, health and nutrition, new babies, birthdays, child care, etc.)." Buys 40 mss/year. Query with or without published clips. Length: 750 words maximum. Pays $1-50. Sometimes pays expenses of writers on assignment.

Photos: State availability of photos with submission. Captions are required. Buys one-time rights.

Columns/Departments: Away We Go (travel), 500 words; On Call (medical), 500 words; Book Beat (book reviews), 500 words; SOS (In search of software), 500 words. Buys 25 mss/year. Query. Pays $1-50.

Tips: "Send a query letter several months before a scheduled topical issue; then follow-up with a telephone call. We are interested in receiving feature articles (on specified topics) or material for our regular columns (which should have a regional/seasonal base)."

PARENTING MAGAZINE, 17th Floor, 301 Howard, San Francisco CA 94105. (415)546-7575. Fax: (415)546-0578. Managing Editor: Bruce Raskin. Editor: Steve Reddicliffe. Magazine published 10 times/year. "Edited for parents of children from birth to ten years old, with the most emphasis put on the under-sixes." Estab. 1987. **Pays on acceptance.** Byline given. Offers 25% kill fee. Buys first rights. Query for electronic submissions. Reports in 1-3 months. Sample copy $1.95 for 9 × 12 SAE with 5 first class stamps. Writer's guidelines for #10 SASE.

• Ranked as one of the best markets for freelance writers in *Writer's Digest* magazine's annual "Top 100 Markets," January 1993.

Nonfiction: Articles editor. Book excerpts, humor, investigative reports, personal experience and photo feature. Buys 20-30 features/year. Query with or without published clips or send complete ms. Length: 1,000-3,500 words. Pays $500-2,000. Sometimes pays expenses of writers on assignment.

Columns/Departments: News and Reviews (news items relating to children/family), 100-400 words; Ages and Stages (health, nutrition, new products and service stories), 100-500 words; Passages (parental rites of passage), 850 words; Up in Arms (opinion, 850 words). Buys 50-60 mss/year. Pays $50-500.

PARENTS CARE, PARENTS COUNT NEWSLETTER, P.O. Box 1563, Lancaster CA 93539. Editor: Marilyn Anita Dalrymple. 100% freelance written. Bimonthly newsletter for parents of addictive or disruptive children. "Writing must be done with empathy towards parents. No 'it's your fault' aimed at parent *or* child. Articles must contain message of 'I was there, and I survived,' or 'This helped me . . . .' " Estab. 1989. **Pays on acceptance.** Byline given. Buys one-time rights. Submit seasonal/holiday material 4 months in advance.

Simultaneous and previously published submissions OK. Reports in 2 months. Sample copy $1.70 for #10 SAE with 2 first class stamps. Writer's guidelines for #10 SASE.

Nonfiction: Humor, inspirational, personal experience and news updates concerning family/drugs. No how to be a "perfect parent," or raise a "perfect child." Length: 750 words maximum. Pays $2.50-7.50 for unsolicited articles.

Columns/Departments: Have You Read (book reviews); Have You Heard (audio/visual tapes); News Reports. Buys 18 mss/year. Length: 250 words. Send complete ms. Pays $2.50.

Poetry: Avant-garde, free verse, haiku, light verse, traditional. Buys 18/year. Submit maximum 5 poems. Length: 2-16 lines. Pays $2.50.

Fillers: Anecdotes, facts and newsbreaks. Length: 250 words maximum. Pays $2.50.

Tips: "Let me know you've been there, either as the child (addict), parent or professional who works with these families. Honesty is a must. Where technical data is concerned (laws, treatments, etc.), need verification. Freelancers are welcome to contribute to all departments."

PARENTS MAGAZINE, 685 3rd Ave., New York NY 10017. Fax: (212)867-4583. Editor-in-Chief: Ann Pleshette Murphy. 25% freelance written. Monthly. Estab. 1926. Circ. 1,740,000. **Pays on acceptance.** Publishes ms an average of 8 months after acceptance. Usually buys first serial or first North American serial rights; sometimes buys all rights. Pays 25% kill fee. Reports in approximately 6 weeks. Sample copy $2. Writer's guidelines for #10 SASE.

Nonfiction: "We are interested in well-documented articles on the development and behavior of preschool, school-age and adolescent children and their parents; good, practical guides to the routines of baby care; articles that offer professional insights into family and marriage relationships; reports of new trends and significant research findings in education and in mental and physical health; and articles encouraging informed citizen action on matters of social concern. Especially need articles on women's issues, pregnancy, birth, baby care and early childhood. We prefer a warm, colloquial style of writing, one which avoids the extremes of either slang or technical jargon. Anecdotes and examples should be used to illustrate points which can then be summed up by straight exposition." Query. Length: 2,500 words maximum. Payment varies. Sometimes pays the expenses of writers on assignment.

PARENTS' PRESS, The Monthly Newspaper for Bay Area Parents, 1454 Sixth St., Berkeley CA 94710. (510)524-1602. Editor: Dixie M. Jordan. Managing Editor: Deborah Haeseler. 50% freelance written. Monthly tabloid for parents. Estab. 1980. Circ. 75,000. Pays within two months of publication. Publishes ms an average of 6 months after acceptance. Kill fee varies (individually negotiated). Buys first, second serial (reprint) and almost always Northern California Exclusive rights. Submit seasonal material 8 months in advance. Reports in 2 months on queries; 3-4 months on mss. Sample copy $3. Writer's guidelines for #10 SASE.

Nonfiction: Book excerpts (family, children), how-to (parent, raise children, nutrition, health, etc.), humor (family life, children), interview/profile (of Bay Area residents, focus on their roles as parents), travel (family), family resources and family activities. "Annual issues include Pregnancy and Birth, Travel, Back-to-School, Children's Health. Write for planned topic or suggest one. We require a strong Bay Area focus where appropriate. Please don't send 'generic' stories. While we publish researched articles which spring from personal experience, we do not publish strictly personal essays. Please, no birth stories." Buys 30-50 mss/year. Query with or without published clips or send complete ms. Length: 300-3,000 words; 1,500-2,000 average. Pays $50-150 for assigned articles; $25-125 for unsolicited articles. Will negotiate fees for special projects written by Bay Area journalists. Reprints OK; send photocopy of article, typed ms with rights for sale noted and information about when and where the article previously appeared. Pays 10-25% of their fee for an original article.

Photos: State availability of photos with submission. Reviews prints, any size, b&w only. Offers $10-15/photo. Model release and identification of subject required. Buys one-time rights.

Columns/Departments: Books (reviews of parenting and children's books, preferably by San Francisco Bay Area authors, publishers). Buys 12-24 mss/year. Send complete ms. Length: 100-750 words. Pays $15-25.

Tips: "All sections of *Parents' Press* are open to freelancers, but we are protective of our regular columnists' turf (children's and women's health, infant and child behavior), so we ask writers to query if a topic has been addressed in the last three years. Best bets to break in are family activities, education, nutrition, family dynamics and issues. While we prefer articles written by experts, we welcome well-researched journalism."

PEDIATRICS FOR PARENTS, The Newsletter for Caring Parents, Pediatrics for Parents, Inc., P.O. Box 1069, Bangor ME 04402-1069. (207)942-6212. Fax: (207)947-3134. Editor: Richard J. Sagall, M.D. 20% freelance written. Eager to work with new/unpublished writers. Monthly newsletter covering medical aspects of rearing children and educating parents about children's health. Estab. 1981. Circ. 2,000. Pays on publication. Publishes ms an average of 3-4 months after acceptance. Byline given. Buys first North American serial rights, first and second rights to the same material, and second (reprint) rights to material originally published elsewhere. Rights always include right to publish article in our books on "Best of . . ." series. Submit seasonal/holiday material 6 months in advance. Simultaneous queries and previously published submissions OK. Query for electronic submissions. Reports in 1 month on queries; 6 weeks on mss. Sample copy $2. Writer's guidelines for #10 SAE with 2 first class stamps.

Nonfiction: Book reviews, how-to (feed healthy kids, exercise, practice wellness, etc.), new product and technical (explaining medical concepts in shirtsleeve language). No general parenting articles. Query with published clips or submit complete ms. Length: 25-1,000 words. Pays 2-5¢/edited word.

Columns/Departments: Book reviews, Please Send Me (material available to parents for free or at nominal cost) and Pedia-Tricks (medically-oriented parenting tips that work). Send complete ms. Pays $15-250. Pays 2¢/edited word.

Tips: "We are dedicated to taking the mystery out of medicine for young parents. Therefore, we write in clear and understandable language (but not simplistic language) to help people understand and deal intelligently with complex disease processes, treatments, prevention, wellness, etc. Our articles must be well researched and documented. Detailed references must always be attached to any article for documentation, but not for publication. We strongly urge freelancers to read one or two issues before writing."

‡SAN DIEGO FAMILY PRESS, San Diego County's Leading Resource for Parents & Educators Who Care!, P.O. Box 23960, San Diego CA 92193-0960. Editor: Sharon Bay. Contact: Dina Madruga, Assistant Editor. 75% freelance written. Monthly magazine for parenting and family issues. "*SDFP* strives to provide informative, educational articles emphasizing positive parenting for our typical readership of educated mothers, ages 25-45, with an upper-level income. Most articles are factual and practical, some are humor and personal experience. Editorial emphasis is uplifting and positive." Estab. 1983. Circ. 60,000. Pays on publication. Publishes ms an average of 5 months after acceptance. Byline given. Buys first, one-time or second serial (reprint) rights. Editorial lead time 1 month. Submit seasonal material 3 months in advance. Reports in 6-8 weeks on queries; 2-3 months on mss. Sample copy $3.50. Writer's guidelines for #10 SASE.

Nonfiction: How-to; parenting, new baby help, enhancing education, family activities, interview/profile (influential or noted persons or experts included in parenting or the welfare of children) and articles of specific interest to or regarding San Diego (for California) families/children/parents/educators. "No rambling, personal experience pieces." Buys 75 mss/year. Send complete ms. Length: 1,500 maximum words. Pays $1.25 per column inch. "Byline and contributor copies if writer prefers."

Photos: State availability of photos with submission. Reviews contact sheets and 3½×5 or 5×7 prints. Negotiates payment individually. Identification of subjects preferred. Buys one-time rights.

Columns/Departments: Kids' Books (topical book reviews), 800 words. Buys 12 mss/year. Query with published clips. Pays $1.25/column inch minimum.

Fillers: Facts and newsbreaks (specific to the family market). Buys 10/year. Length: 50-200 words. Pays $1.25 per column inch minimum, $25 maximum.

‡SEATTLE'S CHILD, #303, 2107 Elliott Ave., Seattle WA 98121. (206)441-0191. Editor: Ann Bergman. 85% freelance written. Works with a small number of new/unpublished writers each year. Monthly tabloid of articles related to being a parent of children age 12 and under directed to parents and professionals. Circ. 25,000. Pays on publication. Publishes ms an average of 6 months after acceptance. Byline given. Offers 50% kill fee. Buys first North American serial rights or all rights. Submit seasonal/holiday material 6 months in advance. Simultaneous queries and submissions OK. Publishes reprints of previously published articles. Send tearsheet of article or typed ms with rights for sale noted. Include information about when and where the article previously appeared. For reprints, pays 20% of the amount paid for an original article. Query for electronic submissions. Reports in 6 months on queries; 6 months on mss. Sample copy $1.50 for 10×13 SAE. Writer's guidelines for #10 SASE.

Nonfiction: Needs reports on political issues affecting families. Expose, general interest, historical/nostalgic, how-to, humor, interview/profile, new product, opinion, personal experience, travel, record, tape and book reviews, and educational and political reviews. Articles must relate to parents and parenting. Buys 120 mss/year. Send complete ms (preferred) or query with published clips. Length: 400-2,500 words. Pays 10¢/word.

Tips: "We prefer concise, critical writing and discourage overly sentimental pieces. Don't talk down to the audience. Consider that the audience is sophisticated and well-read."

SESAME STREET MAGAZINE, Parent's Guide, Children's Television Workshop, 1 Lincoln Plaza, New York NY 10023. (212)595-3456. Fax: (212)875-6105. Editor-in-Chief: Ira Wolfman. Executive Editor: Valerie Monroe. Senior Editors: Diane O'Connell and Susan Schneider. 80% freelance written. A ten-times-yearly magazine for parents of preschoolers. Circ. 1.2 million. **Pays on acceptance.** Byline given. Offers 33% kill fee. Buys all rights. Submit seasonal/holiday material 7 months in advance. Reprints OK; send typed ms with rights for sale noted and information about when and where the article previously appeared. Reports in 1 month on queries. Sample copy for 9×12 SAE with 6 first class stamps. Writer's guidelines for #10 SASE.

Nonfiction: Child development/parenting, how-to (practical tips for parents of preschoolers), interview/profile, personal experience, book excerpts, essays, photo feature and travel (with children). Buys 70 mss/year. Query with published clips, or send complete ms. Length: 500-2,000 words. Pays $300-2,000 for articles.

Photos: State availability of photos with submission. Model releases and identification of subjects required. Buys one-time rights or all rights.

THE SINGLE PARENT, Parents Without Partners, Inc., 8807 Colesville Rd., Silver Spring MD 20910-4346. (301)588-9354. Fax: (301)588-9216. Editor: Rene McDonald. 60% freelance written. Works with small number of new/unpublished writers each year. Bimonthly magazine emphasizing single parenting, family, divorce, widowhood and children. Distributed to members of Parents Without Partners, plus libraries, universities, psychologists, psychiatrists, subscribers, etc. Estab. 1957. Circ. 90,000. Pays on publication. Publishes ms an average of 9 months after acceptance. Buys one-time rights. Simultaneous and previously published submissions; send information about when and where the article previously appeared. For reprints, pays 100% of their fee for an original article. Reports in 3 months. Sample copy for 9×12 SAE with 5 first class stamps. Writer's guidelines for #10 SASE.

Nonfiction: Informational (parenting, legal issues, single parents in society, programs that work for single parents, children's problems); how-to (raise children alone, travel, find a new career, cope with life as a new or veteran single parent. No first-hand accounts of bitter legal battles with former spouses. No "poor me" articles. Buys 50 unsolicited mss/year. Query not required. Mss not returned unless SASE is enclosed. Length: 1,000-3,000 words. Payment $50-150, based on content, not length. Fillers to 500-700 words, $25-50.

Fiction: Publishes two short stories (800-1500 words)/issue for children. Stories may be aimed at any age group from toddlers through teens. Prefers stories about children in single parent households, coping with or learning from their situations. No anthropomorphics. Payment $35-75.

Columns/Departments: F.Y.I., for short news items, reports on research, tips on how to do things better, new products and Letters to Editor column.

Photos: Purchased with accompanying ms. Also uses freelance stock shots. Query. Pays negotiable rates. Model release required.

Tips: "Be familiar with our magazine and its readership before trying to write for us. We publish constructive, upbeat articles that present new ideas for coping with and solving the problems that confront single parents. Articles on origins of Halloween customs, tribal behavior in Ghana, or how to predict the weather have little likelihood of acceptance unless there is a clear tie-in to single parent issues."

TODAY'S FAMILY, 27 Empire Dr., St. Paul MN 55103. (612)227-4367. Managing Editor: Valerie Hockert. 65% freelance written. Bimonthly magazine that covers family social issues. Estab. 1991. Circ. 50,000. Pays on publication. Publishes ms 4 months after acceptance. Byline given. No kill fee. Buys first North American serial rights. Submit seasonal material 6 months in advance. Reports in 3 weeks on queries; 6 weeks on mss. Sample copy $4. Writer's guidelines for #10 SASE.

Nonfiction: General interest, how-to, interview/profile and educational. "No fiction or personal essays." Buys 50 mss/year. Query. Length: 750-1,200 words. "Payment for assigned articles is negotiable." Pays $10-50 for unsolicited articles. Sometimes pays expenses of writers on assignment.

Photos: State availability of photos with submission. Reviews contact sheets and transparencies. Offers $5 minimum/photo. Captions, model releases and identification of subjects required. Buys one-time rights.

Tips: "We like to see new ideas and new approaches to subjects of great concern to the family of today."

TWINS, The Magazine for Parents of Multiples, P.O. Box 12045, Overland Park KS 66282-2045. (913)722-1090. Fax: (913)722-1767. Editor-in-Chief: Barbara C. Unell. 100% freelance written. Eager to work with new/unpublished writers. Bimonthly international magazine designed to give professional guidance to help multiples, their parents and those professionals who care for them learn about twin facts and research. Estab. 1984. Circ. 53,000. Pays on publication. Publishes ms an average of 6 months after acceptance. Byline given. Buys all rights. Publishes reprints of previously published articles. Send tearsheet of article or typed ms with rights for sale noted. Include information about when and where the article previously appeared. Submit seasonal/holiday material 10 months in advance. Reports in 6 weeks on queries; 2 months on mss. Sample copy $5. Writer's guidelines for #10 SASE.

Nonfiction: Book excerpts, general interest, how-to, humor, interview/profile, personal experience and photo feature. "No articles that substitute the word 'twin' for 'child'—those that simply apply the same research to twins that applies to singletons without any facts backing up the reason to do so." Buys 150 mss/year. Query with or without published clips, or send complete ms. Length: 1,250-3,000 words. Payment varies; sometimes pays in contributor copies or premiums instead of cash. Sometimes pays the expenses of writers on assignment.

Photos: Send photos with submission. Reviews contact sheets, 4×5 transparencies and all size prints. Captions, model releases and identification of subjects required. Buys all rights.

Columns/Departments: Resources, Supertwins, Prematurity, Family Health, Twice as Funny, Double Focus (series from pregnancy through adolescence), Personal Perspective (first-person accounts of beliefs about a certain aspect of parenting multiples), Over the Back Fence (specific tips that have worked for the writer in raising multiples), Feelings on Fatherhood, Research, On Being Twins (first-person accounts of growing up as a twin), On Being Parents of Twins (first-person accounts of the experience of parenting twins), Double Takes (fun photographs of twins) and Education Matters. Buys 70 mss/year. Query with published clips. Length: 1,250-2,000 words. Payment varies.

Fillers: Anecdotes and short humor. Length: 75-750 words. Payment varies.

Tips: "Features and columns are both open to freelancers. Columnists write for *Twins* on a continuous basis, so the column becomes their column. We are looking for a wide variety of the latest, well-researched practical information. There is no other magazine of this type directed to this market. We are interested in personal interviews with celebrity twins or celebrity parents of twins, tips on rearing twins from experienced parents and/or twins themselves and reports on national and international research studies involving twins."

WORKING MOTHER MAGAZINE, Lang Communications, 230 Park Ave., New York NY 10169. (212)551-9500. Editor: Judsen Culbreth. Executive Editor: Mary McLaughlin. 90% freelance written. Prefers to work with published/established writers; works with a small number of new/unpublished writers each year. Monthly magazine for women who balance a career with the concerns of parenting. Circ. 850,000. **Pays on acceptance.** Publishes ms an average of 4 months after acceptance. Byline given. Buys first North American Serial and all rights. Pays 20% kill fee. Submit seasonal/holiday material 6 months in advance. Reports in 6 weeks. Sample copy $1.95. Writer's guidelines for SASE.

Nonfiction: Service, humor, child development, material pertinent to the working mother's predicament. Send query to attention of *Working Mother Magazine.* Buys 9-10 mss/issue. Length: 750-2,000 words. Pays $300-1,800. "We pay more to people who write for us regularly." Pays the expenses of writers on assignment.

• Ranked as one of the best markets for freelance writers in *Writer's Digest* magazine's annual "Top 100 Markets," January 1993.

Tips: "We are looking for pieces that help the reader. In other words, we don't simply report on a trend without discussing how it specifically affects our readers' lives and how they can handle the effects. Where can they look for help if necessary?"

Comic Books

Comic books aren't just for kids. Today, this medium also attracts a reader who is older and wants stories presented visually on a wide variety of topics. In addition, some instruction manuals, classics and other stories are being produced in a comic book format.

This doesn't mean you have to be an artist to write for comic books. Most of these publishers want to see a synopsis of one to two double-spaced pages. Be concise. Comics use few words and rely on graphics as well as words to forward the plot.

Once your synopsis is accepted, either an artist will draw the story from your plot, returning these pages to you for dialogue and captions, or you will be expected to write a script. Scripts run approximately 23 typewritten pages and include suggestions for artwork as well as dialogue. Try to imagine your story on actual comic book pages and divide your script accordingly. The average comic has six panels per page, with a maximum of 35 words per panel.

If you're submitting a proposal to Marvel, your story should center on an already established character. If you're dealing with an independent publisher, characters are often the property of their creators. Your proposal should be for a new series. Include a background sheet for main characters who will appear regularly, listing origins, weaknesses, powers or other information that will make your character unique. Indicate an overall theme or direction for your series. Submit story ideas for the first three issues. If you're really ambitious, you may also include a script for your first issue. As with all markets, read a sample copy before making a submission. The best markets may be those you currently read, so consider submitting to them even if they aren't listed in this section.

CARTOON WORLD, Dept. WM, P.O. Box 30367, Lincoln NE 68503. Editor: George Hartman. 100% freelance written. Works with published/established writers and a small number of new/unpublished writers each year. "Monthly newsletter for professional and amateur cartoonists who are serious and want to utilize new cartoon markets in each issue." Buys only from paid subscribers. Circ. 150-300. **Pays on acceptance.** Publishes ms an average of 2 months after acceptance. Byline given. Buys second (reprint) rights to material originally published elsewhere. Not copyrighted. Submit seasonal/holiday material 3 months in advance. Simultaneous submissions OK. Reports in 1 month. Sample copy $5.
Nonfiction: "We want only positive articles about the business of cartooning and gag writing." Buys 10 mss/year. Query. Length: 1,000 words. Pays $5/page.

COMICS SCENE, Starlog Group, 8th Floor, 475 Park Ave. S., New York NY 10016. (212)689-2830. Fax: (212)889-7933. Editor: David McDonnell. Magazine published 9 times/year on comic books, strips, cartoons, those who create them and TV/movie adaptations of both. Estab. 1981. Pays on publication. Byline given. Offers 25% kill fee. Buys all rights or second serial (reprint) rights. Submit seasonal/holiday material 6 months in advance. Absolutely *no* simultaneous submissions. Reports in 6 weeks on queries; 2 months on mss. Sample copy $5. Writer's guidelines for #10 SASE. *No* queries by phone for *any* reason whatsoever.
Nonfiction: Book excerpts, historical/nostalgic, interview/profile, new product, personal experience. Buys 90 mss/year. Query with published clips. Length: 750-3,500 words. Pays $150-250. Sidebars $50-75. Does *not* publish fiction or comics stories and strips. Rarely buys reprints.
Photos: State availability of photos and comic strip/book/animation artwork with submission. Reviews contact sheets, transparencies and 8×10 prints. Offers $10-25 for original photos. Captions, model releases, identification of subjects required. Buys all rights.
Columns/Departments: The Comics Reporter ("newsy" mini-interview with writer, director, producer of TV series/movie adaptations of comic books and strips). Buys 10-12 mss/year. Query with published clips. Length: 100-750 words. Pays $15-50.
Tips: "We *really* need coverage of independent comics companies' products and creators. We need interviews with specific comic strip creators. Most any writer can break in with interviews with hot comic book writers and artists (we really *need* more of the hot ones) — and with comic book creators who don't work for the big two companies. We do *not* want nostalgic items or interviews. Do not burden us with your own personal comic book stories or artwork. We don't have time to evaluate them and can't provide critiques or advice. Get interviews we can't get or haven't thought to pursue. Out-thinking overworked editors is an almost certain way to sell a story."

ECLIPSE COMICS, P.O. Box 1099, Forestville CA 95436. (707)887-1521. Publisher: Dean Mullaney. Editor-in-Chief: Catherine Yronwode. 100% freelance written. Works with a small number of new/unpublished writers each year. Publishers of various four-color comic books, graphic albums, and trading cards. "*Eclipse* publishes comic books with high-quality paper and color reproduction, geared toward the discriminating comic book fan and sold through the 'direct sales' specialty store market." Estab. 1978. Circ. varies (35,000-100,000). **Pays on acceptance** (net 1 month). Publishes ms an average of 6 months after acceptance. Byline given. Buys first North American serial rights, second serial (reprint) rights with additional payment, and first option on collection and non-exclusive rights to sell material to South American and European markets (with additional payments). Simultaneous queries and submissions OK. Reports in 2 months. Sample copy $2. Writer's guidelines for #10 SASE.
Fiction: "Most of our comics are fictional." Adventure, fantasy, mystery, science fiction and horror. "No sexually explicit material, please." Buys approximately 200 mss/year (mostly from established comics writers).
Tips: "At the present time we are publishing both adventure and super-heroic series but we are currently scheduling fewer 32-page periodical adventure comics and more 48-96 page graphic albums, some of which are nonfiction current events journalism in graphic format. We are moving into the arena of political and social commentary and current events in graphic form. We have also expanded our line of classic newspaper strip reprints and political satire non-sports trading cards sets. Because all of our comics are creator-owned, we do not buy fill-in plots or scripts for our periodicals. Plot synopsis less than a page can be submitted; we will select promising concepts for development into full script submissions. All full script submissions should

---

ALWAYS submit unsolicited manuscripts or queries with a self-addressed, stamped envelope (SASE) within your country or a self-addressed envelope with International Reply Coupons (IRC) purchased from the post office for other countries.

be written in comic book or 'screenplay' form for artists to illustrate. Writers who are already teamed with artists stand a better chance of selling material to us, but if necessary we'll find an artist. Our special needs at the moment are for heroic, character-oriented series with overtones of humanism, morality, political opinion, philosophical speculation and/or social commentary. Comic book adaptations (by the original authors) of previously published science fiction and horror short stories are definitely encouraged. Queries about current events/nonfiction albums and non-sports trading card sets should be discussed with us prior to a full-blown submission."

MARVEL COMICS, 387 Park Ave. S., New York NY 10016. (212)696-0808. Editor-in-Chief: Tom DeFalco. 99% freelance written. Publishes 60 comics and magazines/month, 6-12 graphic novels/year, and specials, storybooks, industrials, and paperbacks for all ages. Over 9 million copies sold/month. Pays a flat fee for most projects, plus a royalty type incentive based upon sales. Also works on advance/royalty basis on many projects. **Pays on acceptance.** Publishes ms an average of 6 months after acceptance. Byline given. Offers variable kill fee. Rights purchased depend upon format and material. Submit seasonal/holiday material 1 year in advance. Simultaneous submissions OK. Reports in 6 months. Writer's guidelines for #10 SASE. Additional guidelines on request.

Fiction: Super hero, action-adventure, science fiction, fantasy and other material. Only comics. Buys 600-800 mss/year. Query with brief plot synopses only. Do not send scripts, short stories or long outlines. A plot synopsis should be less than two typed pages; send two synopses at most. Pays expenses of writers on assignment.

• Marvel Comics no longer accepts unsolicited mss. Query with synopses.

Consumer Service and Business Opportunity

Some of these magazines are geared to investing earnings or starting a new business; others show how to make economical purchases. Publications for business executives and consumers interested in business topics are listed under Business and Finance. Those on how to run specific businesses are classified by category in the Trade section.

‡JERRY BUCHANAN'S INFO MARKETING REPORT, (formerly TOWERS Club, USA Newsletter), TOWERS Club Press, Inc., P.O. Box 2038, Vancouver WA 98668. (206)574-3084. Fax: (206)576-8969. Editor: Jerry Buchanan. 5-10% freelance written. Works with a small number of unpublished writers each year. Monthly of ten or more pages on entrepreneurial enterprises, reporting especially on self-publishing of how-to reports, books, audio and video tapes, seminars, etc. "By-passing big trade publishers and marketing your own work directly to consumer." (Mail order predominantly). Estab. 1974. Circ. 10,000. Pays on publication. Publishes ms an average of 2 months after acceptance. Byline given. Buys one-time rights. Fax submissions accepted of no more than 3 pages. Reports in 2 weeks. Sample copy $15 for 6×9 SASE.

Nonfiction: Expose (of mail order fraud); how-to (personal experience in self-publishing and marketing); book reviews of new self-published nonfiction how-to-do-it books (must include name and address of author). "Welcomes well-written articles of successful self-publishing/marketing ventures. Must be current, and preferably written by the person who actually did the work and reaped the rewards. There's very little we will not consider, *if* it pertains to unique money-making enterprises that can be operated from the home." Buys 10 mss/year. Send complete ms. Length: 500-1,500 words. Pays $150-250. Pays extra for b&w photo and bonus for excellence in longer manuscript.

Tips: "The most frequent mistake made by writers in completing an article for us is that they think they can simply rewrite a newspaper article and be accepted. That is only the start. We want them to find the article about a successful self-publishing enterprise, and then go out and interview the principal for a more detailed how-to article, including names and addresses. We prefer that writer actually interview a successful self-publisher. Articles should include how idea first came to subject; how they implemented and financed and promoted the project; how long it took to show a profit and some of the stumbling blocks they overcame; how many persons participated in the production and promotion; and how much money was invested (approximately) and other pertinent how-to elements of the story. Glossy photos (b&w) of principals at work in their offices will help sell article."

CHANGING TIMES, Kiplinger Personal Finance Magazine, 1729 H St. NW, Washington DC 20006. Editor: Ted Miller. Less than 10% freelance written. Prefers to work with published/established writers. Monthly magazine for general, adult audience interested in personal finance and consumer information. Estab. 1947. Circ. 1 million. **Pays on acceptance.** Publishes ms an average of 2 months after acceptance. Buys all rights. Reports in 1 month. Query for electronic submissions. Thorough documentation required for fact-checking.

Nonfiction: "Most material is staff-written, but we accept some freelance." Query with clips of published work. Pays expenses of writers on assignment.

Tips: "We are looking for a heavy emphasis on personal finance topics."

CONSUMERS DIGEST MAGAZINE, for People who Demand Value, Consumers Digest, Inc., 5705 N. Lincoln Ave., Chicago IL 60659. (312)275-3590. Editor: John K. Manos. 70% freelance written. Bimonthly magazine. "Practical advice on subjects of interest to consumers: products and services, automobiles, health, fitness, consumer legal affairs, personal money management, etc." Estab. 1959. Circ. 900,000. **Pays on acceptance.** Publishes ms an average of 3 months after acceptance. Byline given. Offers 50% kill fee. Buys all rights. Submit seasonal material 6 months in advance. Accepts simultaneous submissions. Query for electronic submissions. Reports in 6 weeks on queries; 3 months on mss. Sample copy for 9×12 SAE with 6 first class stamps. Free writer's guidelines.

Nonfiction: Elliott H. McCleary, articles editor. Expose, general interest, how-to (financial, purchasing), new product, travel, health, fitness. Buys 50 mss/year. Query with published clips. Length: 1,000-3,500 words. Pays $400-3,500 for assigned articles; $400-1,700 for unsolicited articles. Sometimes pays expenses of writers on assignment.

Photos: State availability of photos with submission. Reviews transparencies. Pays $100-500/photo. Captions, model releases and identification of subjects required. Buys all rights.

Columns/Departments: Mary S. Butler, column editor. Consumerscope (brief items of general interest to consumers—auto news, travel tips, the environment, smart shopping, news you can use). Buys 10 mss/year. Query. Length: 100-500 words. Pays $75-200.

Tips: "Keep the queries brief and tightly focused. Read our writer's guidelines first and request an index of past articles for trends and to avoid repeating subjects. Focus on subjects of broad national appeal. Stress personal expertise in proposed subject area."

ECONOMIC FACTS, The National Research Bureau, Inc., 424 N. 3rd St., P.O. Box 1, Burlington IA 52601-0001. (319)752-5415. Fax: (319)752-3421. Editor: Nancy Heinzel. Editorial Supervisor: Doris J. Ruschill. 75% freelance written. Eager to work with new/unpublished writers; works with a small number of new/unpublished writers each year. Published 4 times/year. Estab. 1948. Pays on publication. Publishes ms an average of 1 year after acceptance. Buys all rights. Byline given. Sample copy and writers guidelines for #10 SAE with 2 first class stamps.

Nonfiction: General interest (private enterprise, government data, graphs, taxes and health care). Buys 10 mss/year. Query with outline of article. Length: 500-700 words. Pays 4¢/word.

Contemporary Culture

These magazines combine politics, gossip, fashion and entertainment in a single package. Their approach to institutions is typically irreverent and the target is primarily a young adult audience. Although most of the magazines are centered in large metropolitan areas, some have a following throughout the country.

BOMB MAGAZINE, Artists Writers Actors Directors, New Art Publications, Suite 1002A, 594 Broadway, New York NY 10012. (212)431-3943. Editor-in-Chief: Betsy Sussler. 2% freelance accepted. Quarterly magazine covers literature, art, theater, film and music. "We are interested in interviews *between* professionals." Estab. 1981. Circ. 12,000. Pays on publication. Publishes ms an average of 6 months after acceptance. Byline given. Buys one-time rights. Reports in 4 months. Sample copy $5 with $2.90 postage.

Nonfiction: Book excerpts. "Literature *only*." Length: 250-5,000 words. Pays $100 minimum.

Photos: Offers $100 minimum/photo. Captions required. Buys one-time rights.

Fiction: Experimental and novel excerpts. "No commercial fiction." Buys 28 mss/year. Send complete ms. Length: 250-5,000. Pays $100 minimum.

Poetry: Editor: Roland Leguardi Laura. Avant-garde. Buys 10 poems/year. Submit maximum 6 poems. Pays $50 minimum.

BOSTON REVIEW, 33 Harrison Ave., Boston MA 02111. (617)350-5353. Fax: (617)350-6633. Editor: Josh Cohen. Managing Editor: Kim Cooper. 100% freelance written. Works with a small number of new/unpublished writers each year. Bimonthly magazine of the arts, politics and culture. Estab. 1975. Circ. 20,000. **Pays on acceptance.** Publishes ms an average of 3 months after acceptance. Buys first American serial rights. Byline given. Simultaneous submissions OK. Reports in 6 months. Sample copy $4. Writer's guidelines for #10 SASE.

Nonfiction: Critical essays and reviews, natural and social sciences, literature, music, painting, film and photography. Buys 20 unsolicited mss/year. Length: 1,000-3,000 words. Sometimes pays expenses of writers on assignment.

Fiction: Length: 2,000-4,000 words. Pays according to length and author, ranging from $50-200.

Poetry: Pays according to length and author.

Tips: "Short (500 words) color pieces for our 'Around Town' section are particularly difficult to find, so we are always on the look-out for them. Generally, we look for in-depth knowledge of an area, an original view of the material, and a presentation which makes these accessible to a sophisticated reader who will be looking for more and better articles which anticipate ideas and trends on the intellectual and cultural frontier."

CANADIAN DIMENSION, Dimension Publications Inc., #707-228 Notre Dame Ave., Winnipeg, Manitoba, R3B 1N7 Canada. Fax: (204)943-4617. 80% freelance written. Bimonthly magazine "that makes sense of the world. We bring a socialist perspective to bear on events across Canada and around the world. Our contributors provide in-depth coverage on popular movements, peace, labour, women, aboriginal justice, environment, third world and eastern Europe." Estab. 1963. Circ. 4,000. Pays on publication. Publishes ms an average of 6 months after acceptance. Copyrighted by CD after publication. Simultaneous submissions OK. Reports in 6 weeks on queries. Sample copy $1. Writer's guidelines for #10 SAE with IRC.

Nonfiction: Interview/profile, opinion, reviews, political commentary and analysis, journalistic style. Buys 8 mss/year. Length: 500-2,000 words. Pays $25-100.

‡COMMONWEAL A Review of Public Affairs, Religion, Literature and the Arts Published by Catholic Lay People, Commonweal Foundation, 15 Dutch St., New York NY 10038. Editor: Margaret O'Brien Steinfels. Managing Editor: Patrick Jordan. 20% freelance written. Biweekly "independent review of politics, literature, religion and the arts published by Catholic lay people. Audience with college education or an equivalent." Estab. 1924. Circ. 18,000. **Pays on acceptance.** Publishes ms an average of 3 months after acceptance. Byline given. Offers 25% kill fee. Submit seasonal material 2 months in advance. Sample copy and writer's guidelines free on request.

Nonfiction: Book excerpts, essays, general interest, historical/nostalgic, interview/profile, opinion, personal experience and religious. Buys 20 mss/year. Query with published clips. Length: 1,000-3,000 words. Pays $50.

Poetry: Rosemary Dean, poetry editor. Buys 40 poems/year. Pays 50¢ a line.

FRANCE TODAY, FrancePress Inc., 1051 Divisadero St., San Francisco CA 94115. (415)921-5100. Editor: Anne Prah-Perochon. Associate Publisher: Allyn Kaufmann. 90% freelance written. Tabloid covering contemporary France; published 10 times/year. "*France Today* is a feature publication on contemporary France including sociocultural analysis, business, trends, current events and travel." Estab. 1989. Circ. 7,500. Pays on publication. Publishes ms an average of 3-5 months after acceptance. Byline given. Buys first, first North American serial and second serial (reprint) rights. Submit seasonal/holiday material 4 months in advance. Simultaneous submissions OK. Reprints OK. Send tearsheet or photocopy of article. Include information about when and where the article previously appeared. Pays 50% of their fee for an original article. Reports in 3 months. Sample copy and writer's guidelines for 10×13 SAE with 3 first class stamps.

Nonfiction: Essays, expose, general interest, historical, humor, interview/profile, personal experience and travel. "No travel pieces about well-known tourist attractions." Buys 50% mss/year. Query with or without published clips or send complete ms. Length: 500-1,500 words. Pays $150-250. Pays expenses of writers on assignment "if actually assigned. Not for unsolicited pieces."

Photos: Offers $25-40/photo. Identification of subjects required. Buys one-time rights.

Columns/Departments: Letter from Paris (current issues, trends, tones of Paris), 1100 words; and En Route (itinerary of approx. 1,500 words including sidebar). Query with published clips and send complete ms. Length: 500-1,100 words. Pays $150-250.

‡GRAY AREAS, Examining The Gray Areas of Life, Gray Areas, Inc., P.O. Box 808, Broomall PA 19008-0808. (215)353-8238. Editor: Netta Gilboa. 33% freelance written. Quarterly magazine covering music, popular culture, technology and law. "We are interested in exploring all points of view about subjects which are illegal, potentially illegal, immoral and/or controversial." Estab. 1991. Circ. 10,000. Pays on publication. Publishes ms 3-6 months after acceptance. Buys first North American serial, one-time and second serial (reprint) rights. Previously published submissions OK. Send photocopy of article or short story. Include information about when and where the article previously appeared. For reprints, pays $25-50% of the amount paid for an original article. Editorial lead time 3-6 months. Query for electronic submissions. Reports in 1 month on queries. Sample copy $5.

Nonfiction: Book excerpts, essays, expose, general interviews/profile, opinion and personal experience. "No poetry, short stories or fiction." Query. Payment negotiable. "If we want it, we'll pay requested fees." Pays with contributor copies (if writer is a newcomer interested in building a portfolio).

Photos: State availability of photos with submission. Reviews prints only, any size. Negotiates payment individually. "We pay for one-time use of all photos published." Model releases and identification of subjects required. Buys one-time rights.

Columns/Departments: CD reviews (rock, pop, folk, world, etc., no classical), no limit; concert reviews (no classical, country or opera), no limit; "Would like to add regular columns on law, crime and AIDS." Query. Payment negotiable.

Tips: "1. We are actively looking for freelancers as we are new and writing most of *Gray Areas* ourselves. 2. We prefer letters to phone calls and will answer all letters within a week. 3. We use freelancers based on an ability to adhere to deadlines (which are loose as we are a quarterly) and based on their knowledge of our specialized subject matter. 4. We do not discriminate against freelancers for lack of prior publications, not having a computer or typewriter, etc. We need people with legal expertise, experience with criminals and/or law enforcement and with access to celebrities. We also need people whose tastes and political viewpoints differ from our own. Our readers have only one thing in common—an open mind. They want to read a broad spectrum of articles that disagree with each other."

HIGH TIMES, Trans High Corp., 5th Floor, 235 Park Ave. S., New York NY 10003-1405. (212)972-8484. Fax: (212)475-7604. Editor: Steve Hager. News Editor: Bill Weinberg. 75% freelance written. Monthly magazine covering marijuana and the counterculture. Circ. 250,000. Pays on publication. Byline given. Offers 20% kill fee. Buys one-time or all rights or makes work-for-hire assignments. Submit seasonal/holiday material 6 months in advance. Simultaneous submissions OK. Publishes reprints of previously published articles. Send tearsheet of article or typed manuscript with rights for sale noted. For reprints, pays in ad trade. Reports in 1 month on queries; 4 months on mss. Sample copy $5 and #10 SASE. Writer's guidelines for SASE.

Nonfiction: Book excerpts, expose, humor, interview/profile, new product, personal experience, photo feature and travel. Buys 30 mss/year. Send complete ms. Length: 1,000-10,000 words. Pays $150-400. Sometimes pays in trade for advertisements. Sometimes pays expenses of writers on assignment.

Photos: Malcolm Mackinnon, photo editor. Send photos with submission. Pays $50-300. Captions, model release and identification of subjects required. Buys all rights or one-time use.

Columns/Departments: Steve Bloom, music editor. Nate Eaton, cultivation editor. Peter Gorman, views editor. Drug related books; drug related news. Buys 10 mss/year. Query with published clips. Length: 100-2,000 words. Pays $25-300.

• No longer accepts fiction.

Fillers: Gags to be illustrated by cartoonist, newsbreaks and short humor. Buys 10/year. Length: 100-500 words. Pays $10-50. Cartoon Editor: John Holmstrom.

Tips: "All sections are open to good, professional writers."

SPY, Spy Corporation, 8th Floor, 5 Union Square W., New York NY 10003. (212)633-6550. Editor: K. Andersen. 50% freelance written. "*Spy* is a non-fiction satirical magazine published 10 times a year." Circ. 180,000. Pays on publication. Publishes ms an average of 3 months after acceptance. Byline given. Offers 25% kill fee. Buys first and second North American serial rights and non-exclusive anthology rights. Submit seasonal/holiday material 6 months in advance. Simultaneous submissions OK. Query for electronic submissions. Reports in 2 weeks on queries; 1 month on mss. Sample copy $4.

Nonfiction: James Collins, features editor. Jamie Malanowski, national editor (politics). Book excerpts, essays, expose, humor, interview/profile. Buys 100 mss/year. Query with published clips. Length: 200-4,000 words. Pays $50-3,000. Sometimes pays expenses of writers on assignment.

Photos: State availability of photos with submission. Reviews contact sheets. Offers $40-200/photo. Model release and identification of subjects required. Buys one-time rights.

UTNE READER, Suite 330, 1624 Harmon Place, Minneapolis MN 55403. Does *not* accept unsolicited material.

WOMEN & PERFORMANCE, A Journal of Feminist Theory, Women & Performance Project, Inc., NYV/TSOA, 6th Floor, 721 Broadway, New York NY 10003. (212)998-1625. Managing Editor: Judy C. Rosenthel. 100% freelance written. Semiannual newspaper for feminist theory and the performing arts. "Artists must have critical/theoretical slant and examine specific issues relating to feminism and performance." Estab. 1982. Circ. 1,300. Pays on publication. Publishes ms an average of 1 year after acceptance. Byline given. Buys one-time rights. Editorial lead time 6 months. Submit seasonal material 1 year in advance. Accepts simultaneous and previously pubilshed submissions. Query for electronic submissions. Prefers Macintosh or IBM programs. Reports in 2 weeks on queries; 6 months on mss. Sample copy $7. Writer's guidelines free on request.

Nonfiction: Jennifer Fink, assistant editor. Essays, interview/profile, play texts and reviews of performances. "We solicit critical/theatrical pieces; freelancers may submit reviews." Buys 20 mss/year. Query. Length: 800-3,000 words. Pays $10. "We don't pay for reviews except in 1 free copy."

Photos: Send photos with submission. Offers no additional payment for photos accepted with ms. Identification of subjects required. Buys one-time rights.

Columns/Departments: Judy Burns, reviews editor. Reviews (reviews of feminist performance), 1,000 words. Buys 12 mss/year. Query with published clips.

Fiction: Judy Burns. Play texts. "No plays without clear feminist focus." Buys 6 mss/year. Query with published clips. Length: 150-3,000.

Tips: "We are most open to material for the review section. Write clearly, with a feminist, theoretical focus — not an evaluation of how 'good' or 'bad' you think a performance is."

Detective and Crime

Fans of detective stories want to read accounts of actual criminal cases, detective work and espionage. The following magazines specialize in nonfiction, but a few buy some fiction. Markets specializing in crime fiction are listed under Mystery publications.

BACK CHANNELS, Kross Research & Publications, P.O. Box 9, Franklin Park NJ 08823-0009. (908)297-7923. Editor: Peter Kross. 90% freelance written. Quarterly magazine that covers espionage, conspiracies and history. "We publish nonfiction articles on: espionage, assassinations, conspiracies, historical pieces and book reviews." Pays on publication. Byline given. Offers $15 kill fee. Buys first North American serial rights. Submit seasonal material 6 months in advance. Accepts simultaneous submissions. Reports in 1 month. Sample copy $5 for 9 × 12 SAE with 4 first class stamps. Free writer's guidelines.

Nonfiction: Expose, historical/nostalgic and interview/profile. No fiction. No photos. Buys 20 mss/year. Query with or without published clips or send complete ms. Length: 1,000-1,200 words or 10 pages double spaced. Pays $25 for articles.

Fillers: Facts and newsbreaks. Buys 10/year. Length: 40-50 words. Pays $5.

Tips: "Read daily papers and books dealing with current events, historical and modern spying and conspiracies. We are looking for stories on Kennedy and King assassinations or current espionage cases. Will also accept book reviews."

DETECTIVE CASES, Detective Files Group, 1350 Sherbrooke St. W., Montreal, Quebec H3G 2T4 Canada. Editor-in-Chief: Dominick A. Merle. Bimonthly magazine. See *Detective Files*.

DETECTIVE DRAGNET, Detective Files Group, 1350 Sherbrooke St. W., Montreal, Quebec H3G 2T4 Canada. Editor-in-Chief: Dominick A. Merle. Bimonthly magazine; 72 pages. See *Detective Files*.

DETECTIVE FILES, Detective Files Group, 1350 Sherbrooke St. W., Montreal, Quebec H3G 2T4 Canada. Editor-in-Chief: Dominick A. Merle. Estab. 1930. 100% freelance written. Bimonthly magazine; 72 pages. **Pays on acceptance.** Publishes ms an average of 3-6 months after acceptance. Buys all rights. Reports in 1 month. Sample copy and writer's guidelines for SAE with IRCs.

Nonfiction: True crime stories. "Do a thorough job; don't double-sell (sell the same article to more than one market); deliver, and you can have a steady market. Neatness, clarity and pace will help you make the sale." Query. Length: 3,500-6,000 words. Pays $250-350.

Photos: Purchased with accompanying ms; no additional payment.

HEADQUARTERS DETECTIVE, Detective Files Group, 1350 Sherbrooke St. W., Montreal, Quebec H3G 2T4 Canada. Editor-in-Chief: Dominick A. Merle. Bimonthly magazine; 72 pages. See *Detective Files*.

INSIDE DETECTIVE, Official Detective Group, R.G.H. Publishing Corp., 460 W. 34th St., New York NY 10001. (212)947-6500. Editor-in-Chief: Rose Mandelsberg. Managing Editor: Christofer Pierson. Magazine published 7 times per year. Circ. 90,000. **Pays on acceptance.** Publishes ms an average of 3 months after acceptance. Byline given. Buys first rights and one-time world rights. Query for electronic submissions. Reports in 2 weeks. Free writer's guidelines.

Nonfiction: Buys 120 mss/year. Query. Pays $250. Length: 5,000-6,000 words (approx. 20 typed pages).

P. I. MAGAZINE, America's Private Investigation Journal, 755 Bronx, Toledo OH 43609. (419)382-0967. Editor: Bob Mackowiak. 75% freelance written. "Not a trade journal. Audience includes professional investigators and mystery/private eye fans. Estab. 1988. Circ. 1,500. Pays on publication. Publishes ms an average of 3 months after acceptance. Buys one-time rights. Submit seasonal/holiday material 3 months in advance. Simultaneous submissions OK. Reports in 3 months on queries; 4 months on mss. Sample copy $4.75.

Nonfiction: Interview/profile, personal experience and accounts of real cases. Buys 4-10 mss/year. Send complete ms. Length: 1,500+ words. Pays $25+ for unsolicited articles.

Photos: Send photos with submission. May offer additional payment for photos accepted with ms. Model releases and identification of subjects required. Buys one-time rights.

Tips: "The best way to get published in *P.I.* is to write a detailed story about a professional private detective's true-life case. With a switch to an all-true format as of our fifth anniversary, I need more and more accounts of true cases."

STARTLING DETECTIVE, Detective Files Group, 1350 Sherbrooke St. W., Montreal, Quebec H3G 2T4 Canada. Editor-in-Chief: Dominick A. Merle. Bimonthly magazine; 72 pages. See *Detective Files*.

TOP SECRET, (formerly *International Arts*), The International Group, 5139 S. Clarendon St., Detroit MI 48204-2923. Fax: (908)542-1266. Editor: Mr. Shannon Roxborough. 100% freelance written. Bimonthly newsletter covering private investigation, espionage, terrorism, privacy, communications and computer security and related topics. Estab. 1992. Circ. 5,000. **Pays on acceptance.** Publishes ms an average of 2 months after acceptance. Byline given. Buys all rights. Submit seasonal material 6 months in advance. Simultaneous submissions OK. Reports in 1 month. Sample copy $5 for SAE with 4 first class stamps. Writer's guidelines for #10 SASE.

Nonfiction: General interest, historical/nostalgic, how-to, interview/profile and photo feature. "No technical pieces." Buys 25-35 mss/year. Query with or without published clips or send complete ms. Length: 500-1,800 words. Pays $10-50 for assigned articles; $5-35 for unsolicited articles.

Photos: Send photos with submission. Reviews negatives and prints. Offers $1-10/photo. Captions required. Buys all rights.

Fillers: Buys 25-35/year. Length: 100-500 words. Pays $5-25.

Tips: "New and unpublished writers are especially welcome. Exotic and lesser-known subjects are welcomed. We buy all rights. We're interested in new trends or new ways of looking at old topics."

TRUE POLICE CASES, Detective Files Group, 1350 Sherbrooke St. W., Montreal, Quebec H3G 2T4 Canada. Editor-in-Chief: Dominick A. Merle. Bimonthly magazine; 72 pages. Buys all rights. See *Detective Files*.

Disabilities

These magazines are geared toward disabled persons and those who care for or teach them. A knowledge of disabilities and lifestyles is important for writers trying to break into this field; editors regularly discard material that does not have a realistic focus. Some of these magazines will accept manuscripts only from disabled persons or those with a background in caring for disabled persons.

ACCENT ON LIVING, P.O. Box 700, Bloomington IL 61702-0700. (309)378-2961. Fax: (309)378-4420. Editor: Betty Garee. 75% freelance written. Eager to work with new/unpublished writers. Quarterly magazine for physically disabled persons and rehabilitation professionals. Estab. 1956. Circ. 20,000. Buys first rights and second (reprint) rights. Byline usually given. Buys 50-60 unsolicited mss/year. Pays on publication. Publishes ms an average of 6 months after acceptance. Reports in 1 month. Sample copy and writer's guidelines $2.50 for #10 SAE with 7 first class stamps. Writer's guidelines for #10 SASE.

Nonfiction: Articles about new devices that would make a disabled person with limited physical mobility more independent; should include description, availability and photos. Medical breakthroughs for disabled people. Intelligent discussion articles on acceptance of physically disabled persons in normal living situations; topics may be architectural barriers, housing, transportation, educational or job opportunities, organizations, or other areas. How-to articles concerning everyday living, giving specific, helpful information so the reader can carry out the idea himself/herself. News articles about active disabled persons or groups. Good strong interviews. Vacations, accessible places to go, sports, organizations, humorous incidents, self improvement and sexual or personal adjustment—all related to physically handicapped persons. No religious-type articles. "We are looking for upbeat material." Query. Length: 250-1,000 words. Pays 10¢/word for article as it appears in magazine (after editing and/or condensing by staff).

Photos: Pays $10 minimum for b&w photos purchased with accompanying captions. Amount will depend on quality of photos and subject matter. Pays $50 and up for four-color slides used on cover. "We need good-quality transparencies or slides with submissions—or b&w photos."

Tips: "Ask a friend who is disabled to read your article before sending it to *Accent*. Make sure that he/she understands your major points and the sequence or procedure."

ARTHRITIS TODAY, Arthritis Foundation. 1314 Spring St. NW, Atlanta GA 30309. (404)872-7100. Fax: (404)872-8694. Editor: Cindy T. McDaniel. 70% freelance written. Bimonthly magazine about living with arthritis; latest in research/treatment. "*Arthritis Today* is written for the 37 million Americans who have arthritis and for the millions of others whose lives are touched by an arthritis-related disease. The editorial content is designed to help the person with arthritis live a more productive, independent and painfree life. The articles are upbeat and provide practical advice, information and inspiration." Estab. 1987. Circ. 500,000. Buys first North American serial rights but requires unlimited reprint rights in Arthritis Foundation publications. Submit seasonal/holiday material 6 months in advance. Simultaneous and previously published submissions OK. Reports in 1 month on queries; 2 months on mss. Sample copy for 9 × 11 SAE with 4 first class stamps. Writer's guidelines for #10 SASE.

Nonfiction: General interest, how-to (tips on any aspect of living with arthritis), inspirational, interview/profile, opinion, personal experience, photo feature, technical, personal finance, nutrition and travel. Buys 45 mss/year. Query with published clips. Length: 1,000-2,500. Pays $450-1,000. Sometimes pays expenses of writers on assignment. Reprints OK; send photocopy of article and information about when and where the article previously appeared. Pays 25-50% of their fee for an original article.

Photos: State availability of photos with submission. Reviews 3 × 5 transparencies and 5 × 7 prints. Offers $75-200/photo. Captions, model releases and identification of subjects required. Buys one-time or all rights.

Columns/Departments: Quick Takes (general news and information); Scientific Frontier (research news about arthritis), 200-600 words. Buys 16-20 mss/year. Query with published clips. Pays $250-400.

Fillers: Anecdotes, facts, newsbreaks and short humor. Buys 2-4/year. Length: 75-150 words. Pays $75-200.

Tips: "In addition to articles specifically about living with arthritis, we look for articles to appeal to an older audience on subjects such as travel, hobbies, general health, personal finance etc."

CAREERS & the disABLED, Equal Opportunity Publications, Suite 420, 150 Motor Pkwy., Hauppauge, NY 11788-5145. (516)273-0066. Fax: (516)273-8936. Executive Editor: James Schneider. 60% freelance written. Triannual career guidance magazine that is distributed through college campuses for disabled college students and professionals. Deadline dates: Fall, April 1; Winter, October 1; Spring, January 1. "The magazine offers role-model profiles and career guidance articles geared toward disabled college students and professionals." Pays on publication. Publishes ms an average of 6 months after acceptance. Estab. 1967. Circ. 15,000. Byline given. Buys first rights. Simultaneous and previously published submissions OK. Reports in 2 weeks. Sample copy and writer's guidelines for 9 × 12 SAE with 5 first class stamps.

Nonfiction: General interest, interview/profile, opinion and personal experience. Buys 15 mss/year. Query. Length: 1,000-1,500 words. Pays 10¢ per word. Sometimes pays the expenses of writers on assignment.

Photos: State availability of photos with submission. Reviews prints. Offers $15 per photo and/or color slides. Captions. Buys one-time rights.

Tips: "Be as targeted as possible. Role model profiles which offer advice to disabled college students are most needed."

CLOSING THE GAP, INC., P.O. Box 68, Henderson MN 56044-0068. (612)248-3294. Fax: (612)248-3810. Managing Editor: Paul M. Malchow. 40% freelance written. Eager to work with new/unpublished writers. Bimonthly tabloid covering microcomputers for handicapped readers and special education and rehabilitation professionals. "We focus on currently available products and procedures written for the layperson that incorporate microcomputers to enhance the educational opportunities and quality of life for persons with disabilities." Estab. 1982. Circ. 10,000. Pays on publication. Publishes ms an average of 2 months after acceptance. Byline given. Buys first serial rights. Simultaneous queries and submissions OK. Query for electronic submissions. Reports in 2 months. Sample copy and writer's guidelines for 9 × 12 SAE with 5 stamps.

Nonfiction: How-to (simple modifications to computers or programs to aid handicapped persons); interview/profile (users or developers of computers to aid handicapped persons); new product (computer products to aid handicapped persons); personal experience (by a handicapped person or on use of microcomputer to aid a handicapped person); articles of current research on projects on microcomputers to aid persons with disabilities; and articles that examine current legislation, social trends and new projects that deal with computer technology for persons with disabilities. No highly technical "computer hobbyist" pieces. Buys 25 mss/year. Query. Length: 500-2,000 words. Pays $25 and up (negotiable). "Many authors' material runs without financial compensation."

Tips: "Knowledge of the subject is vital, but freelancers do not need to be computer geniuses. Clarity is essential; articles must be able to be understood by a layperson. All departments are open to freelancers. We are looking for new ideas. If you saw it in some other computer publication, don't bother submitting. *CTG*'s emphasis is on increasing computer user skills in our area of interest, not developing hobbyist or technical skills. The most frequent mistakes made by writers in completing an article for us is that their submissions are too technical—they associate 'computer' with hobbyist, often their own perspective—and don't realize our readers are not hobbyists or hackers."

Always check the most recent copy of a magazine for the address and editor's name before you send in a query or manuscript.

DIABETES SELF-MANAGEMENT, R.A. Rapaport Publishing, Inc., Suite 800, 150 W. 22nd St., New York NY 10011-2421. (212)989-0200. Editor: James Hazlett. 20% freelance written. Bimonthly magazine about diabetes. "We publish how-to health care articles for motivated, intelligent readers who have diabetes and who are actively involved in their own health care management. All articles must have immediate application to their daily living." Estab. 1983. Circ. 265,000. Pays on publication. Publishes ms an average of 3 months after acceptance. Byline given. Offers 20% kill fee. Buys all rights. Submit seasonal/holiday material 6 months in advance. Query for electronic submissions. Reports in 1 month. Sample copy $3.50 for 9 × 12 SAE with 6 first class stamps. Writer's guidelines for #10 SASE.

Nonfiction: How-to (exercise, nutrition, diabetes self-care, product surveys), technical (reviews of products available, foods sold by brand name), travel (considerations and prep for people with diabetes). Buys 10-12 mss/year. Query with published clips. Length: 2,000-4,000 words. Pays $400-600 for assigned articles; $200-600 for unsolicited articles.

Tips: "The rule of thumb for any article we publish is that it must be clear, concise, useful and instructive, and it must have immediate application to the lives of our readers."

INDEPENDENT LIVING, Health Care ● Careers ● Lifestyles For People With Special Needs, Equal Opportunity Publications, Inc., Suite 420, 150 Motor Pkwy., Hauppauge NY 11788-5145. (516)273-8743. Fax: (516)273-8936. Editor: Anne Kelly. 75% freelance written. Quarterly magazine on home health care, rehabilitation and disability issues. "*Independent Living* magazine is written for persons with disabilities and the home care dealers, manufacturers, and health care professionals who serve their special needs." Estab. 1968. Circ. 35,000. Pays on publication. Byline given. Buys First North American serial rights. Reports in 3 months. Free sample copy and writer's guidelines.

Nonfiction: Essays, how-to, humor, inspirational, interview/profile, new product, opinion, personal experience, cartoons and travel. Buys 40 mss/year. Query. Length: 500-2,500 words. Pays 10¢/word.

Photos: Send photos with submission. Reviews prints. Offers $15/photo. Prefers 35mm color slides. Captions and identification of subjects required. Buys all rights.

Tips: "The best way to have a manuscript published is to first send a detailed query on a subject related to the home health care and independent lifestyles of persons who have disabilities. We also need articles on innovative ways that home health care dealers are meeting their clients needs, as well as profiles of people with disabilities who are successful in the workplace."

KALEIDOSCOPE: International Magazine of Literature, Fine Arts, and Disability, Kaleidoscope Press, 326 Locust St., Akron OH 44302-1876. Voice: (216)762-9755. Fax: (216)762-0912. Editor-in-Chief: Dr. Darshan Perusek. Estab. 1979. Subscribers include individuals, agencies and organizations that assist people with disabilities and many university and public libraries. Circ. 1,500. 75% freelance written. Eager to work with new/unpublished writers. Byline given. Publishes reprints of previously published articles or short stories. Send photocopy of article or short story. Include information about when and where the article previously appeared. Rights return to author upon publication. Appreciate work by established writers as well. Especially interested in work by writers with a disability. Features writers both with and without disabilities. Writers without a disability must limit themselves to our focus, while those with a disability may explore any topic (although we prefer original perspectives about experiences with disability). Submit photocopies with SASE for return of work. Please type submissions. All submissions should be accompanied by an autobiographical sketch. May include art or photos that enhance works, prefer black and white with high contrast. Reports back in 3 weeks, acceptance or rejection may take 6 months. Pays $10-125 plus 2 copies. Sample copy $4 prepaid. Guidelines free with SASE.

Nonfiction or Fiction: Publishes 8-14 ms/year. Maximum 5,000 words. Publishes novel excerpts. Personal experience essays, book reviews and articles related to disability. Short stories, excerpts. Traditional and experimental styles. Works should explore experiences with disability. Use people-first language.

Poetry: Limit 5 poems/submission. Publishes 12-20 poems/year. Do not get caught up in rhyme scheme. High quality with strong imagery and evocative language. Will review any style.

Tips: Inquire about future themes of upcoming issues. Sample copy very helpful. Works should not use stereotyping, patronizing or offending language about disability. We seek fresh imagery and thought-provoking language.

MAINSTREAM, Magazine of the Able-Disabled, Exploding Myths, Inc., 2973 Beech St., San Diego CA 92102. (619)234-3138. Editor: Cyndi Jones. Managing Editor: William Strothers. 100% freelance written. Eager to develop writers who have a disability. Magazine published 10 times/year (monthly except January and June) covering disability-related topics, written for active and upscale disabled consumers. Estab. 1975. Circ. 15,500. Pays on publication. Publishes ms an average of 3 months after acceptance. Byline given. Buys all rights. Submit seasonal/holiday material 4 months in advance. Reprints OK: send photocopy or tearsheet of article or short story, typed ms with rights for sale noted and information about when and where the article previously appeared. Payment varies. Reports in 4 months. Sample copy $4.25 or for 9 × 12 SAE with $3 and 6 first class stamps. Writer's guidelines for #10 SASE.

Nonfiction: Book excerpts, expose, how-to (daily independent living tips), humor, interview/profile, personal experience (dealing with problems/solutions), photo feature, technology, computers, travel, politics and legislation. "All must be disability-related, directed to disabled consumers." *NO* articles on " 'my favorite disabled character', 'my most inspirational disabled person', 'poster child stories.' " Buys 65 mss/year. Query with or without published clips and send complete ms. Length: 8-12 pages. Pays $100-150. May pay subscription if writer requests.

Photos: State availability of photos with submission. Reviews contact sheets, 1½×¾ transparencies and 5×7 or larger prints. Offers $20-25/b&w photo. Captions and identification of subjects required. Buys all rights.

Columns/Departments: Creative Solutions (unusual solutions to common aggravating problems); Personal Page (deals with personal relations: dating, meeting people). Buys 10 mss/year. Send complete ms. Length: 500-800 words. Pays $75. "We also are looking for disability rights cartoons."

Fiction: Humorous. Must be disability-related. Buys 4 mss/year. Send complete ms. Length: 800-1,200 words. Pays $75.

Tips: "It seems that politics and disability are becoming more important. Please include your phone number on cover page. We accept 5¼ or 3½" floppy discs—ASCII, Wordperfect, Wordstar-IBM."

‡**NEW MOBILITY**, Sam Maddox and Spinal Network, P.O. Box 4162, Boulder CO 80306. (303)449-5412. Contact: Jean Dobbs, Associate Editor. 40% freelance written. Bimonthly magazine for people who use wheelchairs. "*New Mobility* covers the lifestyles of *active* people with articles on health and medicine; sports, recreation and travel; equipment and technology; relationships, family and sexual issues; personalities; civil rights and legal issues. Writers should address issues with solid reporting and strong voice." Estab. 1989. Circ. 20,000. Pays on publication (10¢/word). Publishes ms an average of 6 months after acceptance. Byline given. Offers 50% kill fee. Buys first North American serial rights. Editorial lead time 6 months. Submit seasonal material 6 months in advance. Accepts simultaneous and previously published submissions (non-conflicting markets). Query for electronic submissions. Reports in 1 month on queries; 3 months on mss. Sample copy $5. Writer's guidelines for #10 SASE.

Nonfiction: Essays, expose, humor, interview/profile, new product, opinion, photo feature, travel and medical feature. "No inspirational tear-jerkers." Buys 30 mss/year. Query with 1-2 published clips. Length: 700-2,000 words. Pays 10¢/word. Sometimes pays expenses of writers on assignment.

Photos: State availability of photos with submission. Reviews contact sheets, transparencies and prints. Negotiates payment individually. Identification of subjects required. Buys one-time rights.

Columns/Departments: My Spin (opinion piece on disability-related topic), 700 words; Media (reviews of books, videos on disability), 300-400 words; People (personality profiles of people w/disabilities), 300-700 words. Buys 20 mss/year. Query with published clips. Send complete ms. Pays $30-70.

Tips: "Avoid 'courageous' or 'inspiring' tales of people who 'overcome' their disability. Writers don't have to be disabled to write for this magazine, but they should be familiar with the issues people with disabilities face. Most of our readers have disabilities, so write for this audience. We are most open to personality profiles, either for our short People department or as feature articles. In all of our departments, we like to see adventurous people, irreverent opinions and lively writing. Don't be afraid to let your *voice* come through."

PARAPLEGIA NEWS, Paralyzed Veterans of America, Suite 180, 2111 E. Highland Ave., Phoenix AZ 85016. (602)224-0500. Fax: (602)224-0507. Editor: Cliff Crase. Monthly magazine covering news and information for the wheelchair-user. "An official organ of the Paralyzed Veterans of America, *PN* is published in the interest of and for the benefit of paraplegics (civilians and veterans) all over the world. It is dedicated to the presentation of all news concerning paraplegics and wheelchair living." Estab. 1946. Circ. 25,000. Pays on publication. Publishes ms an average of 3 months after acceptance. Byline given. No kill fee. Buys first rights or second serial (reprint) rights. Submit seasonal/holiday material 4 months in advance. Simultaneous submissions OK. Publishes reprints of previously published articles. Send tearsheet, including information about when and where the article previously appeared. Query for electronic submissions. Reports in 1 month on queries; 2 weeks on mss. Free sample copy and writer's guidelines.

Nonfiction: Travel, accessible housing, employment of people with disabilities (wheelchair users). No fiction or poetry. Buys 5 mss/year. Query with or without published clips, or send complete ms. Length: 1,500-3,000 words. Pays $25-200. All authors receive 10-20 complimentary copies of issue. Sometimes pays the expenses of writers on assignment.

Photos: Send photos with submission. Reviews contact sheets, transparencies and 4×6 or larger prints. Offers $10-50/photo. Captions and identification of subjects required. Buys one-time rights.

Fillers: Newsbreaks and cartoons. Buys 25-50/year (cartoons only). Pays $10.

Tips: "Keep in mind that we do not write for all disabilities: wheelchair users only. We do not use condescending language in referring to people with disabilities (they are not victims, confined to a wheelchair, etc.). We are most open to feature articles. Include photos or illustrations. Best if wheelchair user in photos, to show how this article is applicable to them. Illustration OK, too. Write for a disabled audience."

PEOPLENET, "Where People Meet People," P.O. Box 897, Levittown NY 11756-1042. (516)579-4043. Editor: Robert Mauro. 10% freelance written. Triannual networking newsletter for *disabled* singles. "Covers relationships, mainly of disabled singles. I am looking for articles, poems and short shorts about disabled singles—people who want to meet people for friendship and romance." Estab. 1987. Circ. 200. **Pays on acceptance.** Publishes ms an average of 1 year after acceptance. Byline given. No kill fee. Buys first rights. Submit seasonal/holiday material 1 year in advance. Query for electronic submissions. Reports in 1 month. Sample copy $3 for #10 SAE with 52¢. Writer's guidelines for #10 SASE.

Nonfiction: How-to deal with (rejection, low self-esteem), humor, other (disabled singles and relationships). Does not want to see articles on "super-crips." Buys 1-3 mss/year. Send complete ms. Length: 500-750 words. Pays $5-7.50 plus 1 copy for unsolicited articles.

Columns/Departments: Dating Scene (ways and means and problems of dating), 500-750 words; and Coping Scene (coping with rejection, low self-esteem, low energy), 500-750 words. Buys 1-3 mss/year. Send complete ms. Length: 500-750 words. Pays $5-7.50.

Fiction: Experimental, fantasy, humorous, romance and slice-of-life vignettes. Does not want to see "anything that does not have a disabled character in it." Buys 1-3 mss/year. Send complete ms. Length: 500-1,000 words. Pays $5-10.

Poetry: Avant-garde, free verse, haiku, light verse and traditional. "Anything that is romantic. No "song lyrics" or "greeting card" poetry!" Buys 3-6 poems/year. Submit maximum 4 poems. Length: 4-20 lines. Pays $1-5.

Fillers: Gags, short humor. Buys 3-6 mss/year. Length: 100-500 words.

Tips: "We want *professionally* submitted pieces. I'd love to see some good cartoons on *the dilemmas of dating for the disabled*. All areas are open. But we want good material that will instruct, entertain and make a reader *think*."

SPORTS 'N SPOKES, The Magazine for Wheelchair Sports and Recreation, Paralyzed Veterans of America, Suite 180, 2111 E. Highland Ave., Phoenix AZ 85016-4702. (602)224-0500. Fax: (602)224-0507. Editor: Cliff Crase. Bimonthly magazine covering sports and recreation for the wheelchair user. "*Sports 'n Spokes* covers wheelchair competitive sports and recreation primarily for those with spinal cord injury, spina bifida, amputation and some congenital defects. Articles on wheelchair sports, recreation, equipment, personalities and related topics." Estab. 1975. Circ. 14,000. Pays on publication. Publishes ms an average of 5 months after acceptance. Byline given. No kill fee. Buys first rights or second serial (reprint) rights. Publishes reprints of previously published articles. Send tearsheet, including information about when and where the article previously appeared. Submit seasonal/holiday material 5 months in advance. Query for electronic submissions. Reports in 6 weeks on queries; 1 month on mss. Free sample copy and writer's guidelines.

Nonfiction: Survey of lightweight-wheelchair manufacturers, People in Sports (personal profile). No fiction, poetry or anything not relating to sports and recreation for the wheelchair-user. Buys 10 mss/year. Query with or without published clips, or send complete ms. Length: 1,500-3,000 words. Pays $25-200. All authors receive 10-20 complimentary copies of issue. Sometimes pays the expenses of writers on assignment.

Photos: Send photos with submission. Reviews negatives, transparencies and 4×6 or larger prints. Offers $10-50/photo. Captions and identification of subjects required. Buys one-time rights.

Fillers: Buys 20-30/year (cartoons only). Pays $10.

Tips: "Keep in mind that our readers are primarily wheelchair users. We do not use condescending language in referring to people with disabilities (they are not 'victims,' 'confined to a wheelchair,' etc.). Articles must have something to do with sports and recreation for the wheelchair user. We are most open to feature articles. Include photos or illustrations. Prefer wheelchair users shown in photos, showing how this article is applicable to them. Write for disabled audience."

Entertainment

This category's publications cover live, filmed or videotaped entertainment, including home video, TV, dance, theater and adult entertainment. In addition to celebrity interviews, most publications want solid reporting on trends and upcoming productions. Magazines in the Contemporary Culture section also use articles on entertainment. For those publications with an emphasis on music and musicians, see the Music section.

ANGLOFILE, British Entertainment & Pop Culture, The Goody Press, P.O. Box 33515, Decatur GA 30033. (404)633-5587. Editor: William P. King. Managing Editor: Leslie T. King. 15% freelance written. Bimonthly newsletter. "News and interviews on British entertainment, past and present, from an American point of view." Circ. 3,000. Pays on publication. Publishes ms an average of 6 months after acceptance. Byline given. Buys all rights. Reports in 2 months. Free sample copy.

Nonfiction: Articles Editor: Justin Stonehouse. Book excerpts, essays, historical/nostalgic, interview/profile, opinion, personal experience, photo feature, and travel. "No articles written for general audience." Buys 5/mss/year. Send complete ms. Length: 1,500 words. Pays $25-250.

Photos: Send photos with submission. Reviews prints. Offers $10-25/photo. Identification of subjects required. Buys all rights.

APPLAUSE, The Magazine of WHYY, Public Broadcast Publishers, Inc. and WHYY, Inc., WHYY/150 N. 6th St., Philadelphia PA 19106. (215)351-0539. Editor: Eileen Fisher. 70% freelance written. Monthly magazine covering public broadcast subjects, arts and regional culture. "*Applause* is designed for the Delaware Valley public broadcast subscriber. Style is sophisticated but lively. Emphasizes local and cultural." Estab. 1984. Circ. 145,000. Pays on publication. Byline given. Offers 20% kill fee. Buys first rights. Submit seasonal/holiday material 6 months in advance. Query; on-disc submissions preferred. Reports in 2 months. Free sample copy.

Nonfiction: Essays, general interest, historical/nostalgic, humor, interview/profile, photo feature. Buys 30-35 features/year. "Can send clips and description of writer's interests/specializations." Length: 1,500-2,000 words. Pays $400-500.

Columns/Departments: "Address by subject (Food Editor, etc.):" Books (reviews current major fiction and nonfiction releases), 1,500 words; Critic's Choice (monthly performing arts previews; generally use contributing editors), 500 words; Food & Wine, Smart $, Better Homes, Health (lifestyle topics covered in an informal style; by contributing editors), 11-1,200 words. Buys 150 mss/year. Query with published clips. Pays $300-350.

Fillers: Contact: Opening Lines Editor. Regional focus anecdotes, facts, short humor, short profiles. Buys 20-30/year. Length: 200-500 words. Pays $75-175.

Tips: "Start with an 'Opening Lines' or column query or, send clips with a list of your interests/specializations. We have a strong preference for local writers."

CINEASTE, America's Leading Magazine on the Art and Politics of the Cinema, Cineaste Publishers, Inc., #1320, 200 Park Ave. S., New York NY 10003. (212)982-1241. Managing Editor: Gary Crowdus. 50% freelance written. Quarterly magazine on motion pictures, offering "social and political perspective on the cinema." Estab. 1967. Circ. 8,000. Pays on publication. Publishes ms an average of 3 months after acceptance. Byline given. Offers 50% kill fee. Buys first North American serial rights. Reports in 3 weeks on queries; 1 month on mss. Sample copy $5. Writer's guidelines for #10 SASE.

Nonfiction: Essays, interview/profile, criticism. Buys 40-50 mss/year. Query with or without published clips, or send complete ms. Length: 3,000-6,000 words. Pays $20.

Photos: State availability of photos with submissions. Reviews prints. Offers no additional payment for photos accepted with ms. Identification of subjects required.

CINEFANTASTIQUE MAGAZINE, The review of horror, fantasy and science fiction films, P.O. Box 270, Oak Park IL 60303. (708)366-5566. Editor: Frederick S. Clarke. 100% freelance written. Willing to work with new/unpublished writers. Bimonthly magazine covering horror, fantasy and science fiction films. Estab. 1970. Circ. 60,000. Pays on publication. Publishes ms an average of 6 months after acceptance. Byline given. Buys all rights. Simultaneous queries OK. Reports in 2 months or longer. Sample copy $7 for 9 × 12 SAE. "Enclose SASE if you want your manuscript back."

Nonfiction: Historical/nostalgic (retrospects of film classics); interview/profile (film personalities); new product (new film projects); opinion (film reviews, critical essays); and technical (how films are made). Buys 100-125 mss/year. Query with published clips. Length: 1,000-10,000 words. Sometimes pays the expenses of writers on assignment.

Photos: State availability of photos with query letter or ms.

Tips: "Study the magazine to see the kinds of stories we publish. Develop original story suggestions; develop access to film industry personnel; submit reviews that show a perceptive point of view."

COMING ATTRACTIONS, Your Monthly Guide to Video Entertainment, Star Video L.P., 550 Grand St., Jersey City NJ 07302. (201)333-4600. Editor: Anne Sherber. 5% freelance written. Monthly entertainment magazine. "Highlights the best of video entertainment each month with synopses, humor columns and games." Estab. 1984. Circ. 428,958. Pays on publication. Publishes ms an average of 2 months after acceptance. Byline given. Makes work-for-hire assignments. Submit seasonal/holiday material 3 months in advance. Sample copy for 9 × 12 SAE with 4 first class stamps.

Nonfiction: Humor, interview/profile and new product. Buys 15 mss/year. Length: 500-1,000 words. Pays $25-200.

COUNTRY AMERICA, Meredith Publishing Corporation, 1716 Locust, Des Moines IA 50309-3023. (515)284-2910. Fax: (515)284-3035. Editor: Danita Allen. Managing Editor: Bill Eftink. Magazine covering country entertainment/lifestyle published 10 times/year. Estab. 1989. Circ. 1,000,000. **Pays on acceptance.** Byline given. Buys all rights (lifetime). Submit seasonal/holiday material 8 months in advance. Previously published submissions OK "if notified." Free writer's guidelines. Reports in 3 months.

Nonfiction: General interest, historical/nostalgic, how-to (home improvement), garden/food, interview/profile country music entertainers, photo feature and travel. Special Christmas, travel, wildlife/conservation, country music issues. Buys 130 mss/year. Query. Pays $100-1,000 for assigned articles. Sometimes pays expenses of writers on assignment.

Photos: State availability of photos with submission. Reviews contact sheets, negatives, 35mm transparencies. Offers $50-500/photo. Captions and identification of subjects required. Buys all rights.

Fillers: Short humor. Country curiosities that deal with animals, people, crafts, etc.

Tips: "Think visually. Our publication will be light on text and heavy on photos. Be general; this is a general interest publication meant to be read by every member of the family. We are a service-oriented publication; please stress how-to sidebars and include addresses and phone numbers to help readers find out more."

DANCE CONNECTION, 603, 815 1st St. SW, Calgary, Alberta T2P IN3 Canada. (403)263-3232 or (403)237-7327. Fax: (403)263-1707. Editor: Heather Elton. 75% freelance written. Published five times per year. Magazine devoted to dance with a broad editorial scope reflecting a deep commitment to a view of dance that embaces its diversity of style and function. Articles have ranged in subject matter from the role of dance in Plains Indian culture, to an inquest into the death of Giselle, to postmodern dance. Estab. 1983. Circ. 5,000. Pays on publication. Byline given. Buys first rights or second serial (reprint) rights. Submit seasonal material 3 months in advance. Simultaneous and previously published submissions OK. Send tearsheet or photocopy of article, including information about when and where the article previously appeared. For reprints, pays 50% of the smount paid for an original article. Query for electronic submissions. Sample copy for 9 × 12 SAE with 3 IRCs.

Nonfiction: A variety of writing styles including criticism, essay, exposé, general interest, historical/nostalgic, humor, opinion, interview, performance review, forum debate, literature and photo feature. Query with published clips, or send complete ms. Length 800-2,500 words. Pays $5-150.

Fiction: Literature and poetry relating to dance. No poems about ballet. Publishes novel excerpts.

Columns/Departments: Performance Reviews, Book Reviews, Dance News and Calendar.

DANCE MAGAZINE, 33 W. 60th St., New York NY 10023. (212)245-9050. Fax: (212)956-6487. Editor-in-Chief: Richard Philp. 25% freelance written. Monthly magazine covering dance. Estab. 1927. Circ. 51,000. Pays on publication. Byline given. Offers up to $150 kill fee (varies). Makes work-for-hire assignments. Submit seasonal/holiday material 4 months in advance. Reports in "weeks." Sample copy and writer's guidelines for 9 × 12 SASE.

Nonfiction: Interview/profile. Buys 50 mss/year. Query with published clips or send complete ms. Length: 300-2,000 words. Pays $15-350. Sometimes pays expenses of writers on assignment.

Photos: State availability of photos with submission. Reviews transparencies and prints. Offers $25-285/photo. Captions and identification of subjects required. Buys one-time rights.

Columns/Departments: Presstime News (topical, short articles on current dance world events) 75-400 words. Buys 40 mss/year. Query with published clips. Pays $20-75.

Tips: Writers must have "thorough knowledge of dance and take a sophisticated approach."

DRAMATICS MAGAZINE, International Thespian Society, 3368 Central Pkwy., Cincinnati OH 45225-2392. (513)559-1996. Editor-in-Chief: Donald Corathers. 70% freelance written. Works with small number of new/unpublished writers. For theater arts students, teachers and others interested in theater arts education. Magazine published monthly, September through May. Estab. 1929. Circ. 35,000. **Pays on acceptance.** Publishes ms an average of 3 months after acceptance. Buys first North American serial rights. Byline given. Submit seasonal/holiday material 3 months in advance. Simultaneous and previously published submissions OK. Query for electronic submissions. Reprints OK; send tearsheet of article or play or typed ms with rights for sale noted. Pays 50% of their fee for an original article. Reports in 3 months. Sample copy for 9 × 12 SAE with 5 first class stamps. Free writer's guidelines.

Nonfiction: How-to (technical theater, directing, acting, etc.), informational, interview, photo feature, humorous, profile and technical. Buys 30 mss/year. Submit complete ms. Length: 750-3,000 words. Pays $50-300. Rarely pays expenses of writers on assignment.

Photos: Purchased with accompanying ms. Uses b&w photos and transparencies. Query. Total purchase price for ms usually includes payment for photos.

Fiction: Drama (one-act and full-length plays). "No plays for children, Christmas plays or plays written with no attention paid to the conventions of theater." Prefers unpublished scripts that have been produced at least once. Buys 5-9 mss/year. Send complete ms. Pays $100-400.

Tips: "The best way to break in is to know our audience—drama students, teachers and others interested in theater—and to write for them. Writers who have some practical experience in theater, especially in technical areas, have a leg-up here, but we'll work with anybody who has a good idea. Some freelancers have become regular contributors. Others ignore style suggestions included in our writer's guidelines."

EAST END LIGHTS, The Quarterly Magazine for Elton John Fans ,Voice Communications Corp., P.O. Box 760, New Baltimore MI 48047. (313)949-7900. Fax: (313)949-2217. Editor: Tom Stanton. 70% freelance written. Quarterly magazine covering British rock star Elton John. "In one way or another, a story must relate to Elton John, his activities or associates (past and present). We appeal to discriminating Elton fans. No gushing fanzine material. No current concert reviews." Estab. 1990. Circ. 1,000. Pays 3 weeks after acceptance. Publishes ms an average of 2-3 months after acceptance. Byline given. Offers 100% kill fee. Buys first rights and second serial (reprint) rights. Submit seasonal material 2-3 months in advance. Reports in 2 months. Sample copy $2. Free writer's guidelines.

Nonfiction: Book excerpts, essays, expose, general interest, historical/nostalgic, humor and interview/profile. Buys 20 mss/year. Query with or without published clips or send complete ms. Length: 400-1,000 words. Pays $50-200 for assigned articles; $40-150 for unsolicited articles. Pays with contributor copies only if the writer requests. Sometimes pays the expenses of writers on assignment.

Photos: State availability of photos with submission. Reviews negatives and 5 × 7 prints. Offers $10-75/photo. Identification of subjects required. Buys one-time rights and all rights.

Columns/Departments: Clippings (non-wire references to Elton John in other publications), max. 200 words. Buys 12 mss/year. Send complete ms. Length: 50-200 words. Pays $10-20.

Tips: "Approach with a well-thought-out story idea. We'll provide direction. All areas equally open. We prefer interviews with Elton-related personalities—past or present. We are particularly interested in music/ memorabilia collecting of Elton material."

EMMY MAGAZINE, Academy of Television Arts & Sciences, 5220 Lankershin Blvd., N. Hollywood CA 91601-3109. (818)754-2800. Fax: (818)761-2827. Editor/Publisher: Hank Rieger. Managing Editor: Gail Polevoi. 100% freelance written. Prefers to work with published established writers. Bimonthly magazine on television for TV professionals and enthusiasts. Circ. 12,000. Pays on publication within 6 months. Publishes ms an average of 6 months after acceptance. Byline given. Offers 20% kill fee. Buys first North American serial rights. Reports in 1 month. Sample copy for 9 × 12 SAE with 6 first class stamps.

Nonfiction: Articles on issues, trends, and VIPs (especially those behind the scenes) in broadcast and cable TV; programming; new technology; and important international developments. "We require TV industry expertise and clear, lively writing." Length: 2,000 words. Pay $700-900. Pays some expenses of writers on assignment.

Columns/Departments: Most written by regulars, but newcomers can break into Below the Line, Viewpoint, or Innerviews. Length: 500-1,500 words, depending on department. Pays $250-600.

Tips: Study publication; query in writing with published clips. "No fanzine or academic approaches, please."

FANGORIA: Horror in Entertainment, Starlog Communications, Inc., 475 Park Ave. S., 8th Floor, New York NY 10016. (212)689-2830. Fax: (212)889-7933. Editor: Anthony Timpone. 95% freelance written. Works with a small number of new/unpublished writers each year. Published 10 times/year. Magazine covering horror films, TV projects, comics, videos and literature and those who create them. Estab. 1979. Pays on publication. Publishes ms an average of 3 months after acceptance. Byline given. Buys all rights. Submit seasonal/holiday material 6 months in advance. Simultaneous queries OK. Query for electronic submissions. Reports in 6 weeks. "We provide an assignment sheet (deadlines, info) to writers, thus authorizing queried stories that we're buying." Sample copy $4.95 with 10 × 13 SAE and 4 first class stamps; writers' guidelines for #10 SASE.

Nonfiction: Book excerpts, interview/profile of movie directors, makeup FX artists, screenwriters, producers, actors, noted horror novelists and others—with genre credits. No "think" pieces, opinion pieces, reviews (excluding books), or sub-theme overviews (i.e., vampire in the cinema). Buys 100 mss/year. Query with published clips. Length: 1,000-3,000 words. Pays $100-225. Rarely pays the expenses of writers on assignment. Avoids articles on science fiction films—see listing for sister magazine *Starlog* in *Writer's Market* science fiction magazine section.

Photos: State availability of photos. Reviews b&w and color prints and transparencies. "No separate payment for photos provided by film studios." Captions and identification of subjects required. Photo credit given. Buys all rights.

Columns/Departments: Monster Invasion (news about new film productions; must be exclusive, early information; also mini-interviews with filmmakers and novelists). Query with published clips. Length: 300-500 words. Pays $45-75.

Fiction: "We do *not* publish any fiction or poetry. *Don't* send any."

Tips: "Other than recommending that you study one or several copies of *Fangoria*, we can only describe it as a horror film magazine consisting primarily of interviews with technicians and filmmakers in the field. Be sure to stress the interview subjects' words—not your own opinions as much. We're very interested in small, independent filmmakers working outside of Hollywood. These people are usually more accessible to writers, and more cooperative. *Fangoria* is also sort of a *de facto* bible for youngsters interested in movie makeup careers and for young filmmakers. We are devoted only to *reel* horrors—the fakery of films, the imagery of the horror fiction of a Stephen King or a Clive Barker—*we do not* want nor would we *ever* publish articles on real-life horrors, murders, etc. A writer must *like* and *enjoy* horror films and horror fiction to work for us. If the photos in *Fangoria* disgust you, if the sight of (*stage*) blood repels you, if you feel 'superior' to horror (and its fans), you aren't a writer for us and we certainly aren't the market for you. In 1994, *Fangoria* will try for a lighter, irreverent, more 'Gonzo' tone, plus an expansion in horror comics coverage."

‡FILM QUARTERLY, University of California Press, Berkeley CA 94720. (510)601-9070. Fax: (510)601-9036. Editor: Ann Martin. 100% freelance written. Eager to work with new/unpublished writers. Quarterly. Buys all rights. Byline given. Pays on publication. Publishes ms an average of 3 months after acceptance. Query. Sample copy and writer's guidelines for SASE.

Nonfiction: Articles on style and structure in films, articles analyzing the work of important directors, historical articles on development of the film as art, reviews of current films and detailed analyses of classics and book reviews of film books. Must be familiar with the past and present of the art; must be competently, although not necessarily breezily, written; must deal with important problems of the art. "We write for people who like to think and talk seriously about films, as well as simply view them and enjoy them. We use no personality pieces or reportage pieces. Interviews usually work for us only when conducted by someone familiar with most of a filmmaker's work. (We don't use performer interviews.)" Length: 6,000 words maximum. Pay is about 2¢/word.

Tips: "*Film Quarterly* is a specialized academic journal of film criticism, though it is also a magazine (with pictures) sold in bookstores. It is read by film teachers, students, and die-hard movie buffs, so unless you fall into one of those categories, it is very hard to write for us. Currently, we are especially looking for material on independent, documentary, etc. films not written about in the national film reviewing columns."

JET, Johnson Publishing Co., 820 S. Michigan, Chicago IL 60605. Staff written. "Prefers not to share information."

‡KPBS On Air, San Diego's Guide to Public Broadcasting, KPBS-TV/FM, Suite 16, 5164 College Ave., San Diego CA 92115. Mailing address: KPBS Radio/TV, San Diego CA 92182-0527. (619)594-3766. Editor: Michael Good. 15% freelance written. Monthly magazine on public broadcasting programming and San Diego arts. "Our readers are very intelligent, sophisticated and rather mature. Your writing should be, too." Estab. 1970. Circ. 62,000. Pays on publication. Publishes ms an average of 1 month after acceptance. Byline given. Pays 50% kill fee. Not copyrighted. Buys first North American serial rights. Submit seasonal/holiday material 3 months in advance. Previously published submissions OK. Query for electronic submissions. Reports in 3 weeks. Sample copy for 9 × 12 SAE with 4 first class stamps.

Nonfiction: Interview/profile of PBS personalities and/or artists performing in S.D., opinion, profiles of public TV and radio personalities, backgrounds on upcoming programs. Nothing over 1,500 words. Buys 60 mss/year. Query with published clips. Length: 300-1,500 words. Pays 20¢/word. Sometimes pays expenses of writers on assignment

Photos: State availability of photos with submission. Reviews transparencies and 5 × 7 prints. Offers $30-300/photo. Identification of subjects required. Buys one-time rights.

Columns/Departments: On the Town (upcoming arts events in San Diego), 800 words; Short Takes (backgrounds on public TV shows), 500 words; Radio Notes (backgrounders on public radio shows), 500 words. Buys 35 mss/year. Query or query with published clips. Length: 300-800 words. Pays 20¢/word.

Tips: "Feature stories for national writers are most open to freelancers. Arts stories for San Diego writers are most open. Read the magazine, then talk to me."

MOVIE MARKETPLACE, World Publishing, 990 Grove St., Evanston IL 60201. (708)491-6440. Editor: Robert Meyers. 90% freelance written. Bimonthly magazine featuring video and movie subjects. Estab. 1987. Circ. 100,000. **Pays on acceptance.** Byline given. Offers $100 kill fee. Buys first North American serial rights. Submit seasonal/holiday material 6 months in advance. Simultaneous and previously published submissions OK. Reports in 3 weeks. Sample copy $2.50 for 9 × 11 SASE.

Nonfiction: Interview/profile and movie-video topics. Query with published clips. Length: 350 words, short; 750-900 words, long. Pays $100-200 for assigned articles.

Photos: State availability of or send photos (b&w only) with submission. Reviews contact sheets. Offers no additional payment for photos accepted with ms. Identification of subjects required. Buys first North American serial rights only.

NEW YORK/LONG ISLAND UPDATE, 151 Alkier St., Brentwood NY 11717. (516)435-8890. Fax: (516)435-8925. Editor: Cheryl Ann Meglio. Managing Editor: Allison A. Whitney. 60% freelance written. Monthly magazine covering "regional entertainment interests as well as national interests." Estab. 1980. Circ. 35,000. Pays on publication. Publishes ms an average of 4 months after acceptance. Byline given. Buys all rights. Submit seasonal/holiday material 4 months in advance. Query for electronic submissions. Reprints OK; send tearsheet or photocopy of article. Reports in 10 weeks on queries. Free sample copy and writer's guidelines.

Nonfiction: General interest, humor, interview/profile, new product and travel. Buys 60 mss/year. Query with published clips. Length: 250-1,500 words. Pays $25.

Columns/Departments: Nightcap (humor piece), 700 words. Query with published clips. Pays $25.

Fiction: Humorous. Buys 8 mss/year. Length: 700 maximum words. Pays $25 maximum.

PALMER VIDEO MAGAZINE, 1767 Morris Ave., Union NJ 07083. (908)686-3030. Fax: (908)686-2151. Editor: Susan Baar. 15% freelance written. Monthly magazine covering video and film related topics. "*The Palmer Video Magazine* is a 32-page magazine designed exclusively for Palmer Video members. It is both entertaining and informative as it pertains to film and video." Estab. 1983. Circ. 200,000. **Pays on acceptance.** Publishes ms 1 month after acceptance. Makes work-for-hire assignments. Submit seasonal/holiday material 2 months in advance. Simultaneous submissions OK. Publishes reprints of previously published articles. Send typed ms with rights for sale noted and information about when and where the article previously appeared. For reprints, pays 50% of the amount paid for an original article. Free sample copy and writer's guidelines.

Nonfiction: How-to (video related), interview/profile (film related) and technical (video related). Buys 40 mss/year. Query with published clips. Length: 500-2,000 words. Pays $50-200 for assigned articles.

Photos: State availability of photos with submission. Offers no additional payment for photos accepted with ms.

Columns/Departments: Profile (interviews of profiles on actors/directors, etc.), 1,000 words; Cinemascope (article pertaining to film genre), 1,000-2,000 words. Buys 40 mss/year. Query with published clips. Pays $50-200.

PEOPLE MAGAZINE, Time-Warner, Inc., Time & Life Bldg., Rockefeller Center, New York NY 10020. "Prefers not to share information."

PERFORMING ARTS MAGAZINE, 3539 Motor Ave., Los Angeles CA 90034. (310)839-8000. Editor: Dana Kitaj. 100% freelance written. Monthly magazine covering theater, music, dance, visual art. "We publish general pieces on the arts of a historical or 'current-events' nature." Estab. 1965. Circ. 700,000. Pays on publication. Publishes ms an average of 2 months after acceptance. Offers $150 kill fee. Buys one-time rights. Submit seasonal/holiday material 3 months in advance. Previously published submissions OK. Sample copy for 9 × 12 SASE.

Nonfiction: Book excerpts (on the Arts), general interest (theater, dance, opera), historical/nostalgic, interview/profile (performers, artists) and travel. No critical texts, religious, political essays or reviews. Buys 60 mss/year. Query with published clips. Length: 1,500-3,000 words. Pays $500-1,000. Sometimes pays expenses of writers on assignment.

Photos: State availability of photos with submission. Reviews transparencies. Offers no additional payment for photos accepted with ms. Buys one-time rights.

Tips: "Theater, dance and music on the West Coast are our main interests. Write broad information pieces or interviews."

THE PLAY MACHINE, P.O. Box 330507, Houston TX 77233-0507. Editor: Norman Clark Stewart Jr. 90% freelance written. Quarterly tabloid of recreation/adult play. Estab. 1990. Circ. 1,000. Pays on publication. Byline given. Buys first North American, one-time or second serial (reprint) rights. Submit seasonal/holiday material 8 months in advance. Simultaneous and previously published submissions OK. Reports in 8 months on mss. Sample copy for 9 × 12 SAE with 4 first class stamps. Writer's guidelines for #10 SAE with 2 first class stamps.

Nonfiction: How-to (play or have fun), humor (not satire—playful), interview/profile (with pranksters/jokers or genius in relation to fun), new product (recreational/hobby, etc.). Nothing that is not fun, playful or related to recreation—nothing serious. Buys 20-100 mss/year. Send complete ms. Length: 3,500 words maximum. Pays $50 maximum for unsolicited articles.

Photos: Send photos with submission. Offers no additional payment for photos accepted with ms. Model releases and identification of subjects required. Buys one-time rights.

Fillers: Anecdotes, facts, gags to be illustrated by cartoonist, short humor. Buys 200/year. Pays $5 maximum.

Tips: "Have fun writing the submissions."

PLAYBILL, Playbill Inc., 11th Floor, 52 Vanderbilt Ave., New York NY 10017. (212)557-5757. Editor-in-Chief: Joan Alleman. 50% freelance written. Monthly magazine covering NYC, Broadway and Off-Broadway theater. Estab. 1884. Circ. 1.43 million. **Pays on acceptance.** Publishes ms an average of 2 months after acceptance. Byline given. Buys all rights. Reports in 2 months.

Nonfiction: Book excerpts, humor, interview/profile, personal experience—must all be theater related. Buys approximately 10 mss/year. Query with published clips. Length: 1,500-1,800 words. Pays $250-500.

Photos: State availability of photos with submission. Offers no additional payment for photos accepted with ms. Identification of subjects required.

Fillers: Anecdotes, facts and short humor. Buys 10 mss/year. Length: 350-700 words. Pays $50-100. Must all be theater related.

SATELLITE ORBIT, Commtek Communications Corp., Suite 600, 8330 Boone Blvd., Vienna VA 22182. (703)827-0511. Fax: (703)356-6179. Publisher: David Wolford. Editor: Phillip Swann. 25% freelance written. Monthly magazine. **Pays on acceptance.** Publishes ms an average of 3 months after acceptance. Kill fee varies. Reports in 1 month.

Nonfiction: "Wants to see articles on satellite programming, equipment, television trends, sports and celebrity interviews." Query with published clips. Length: 700 words. Pay varies. Reprints OK.

SOAP OPERA DIGEST, News America, 45 W. 25 St., New York NY 10010. Editors: Lynn Leahey. Managing Editors: Jason Bonderoff, Roberta Caploe. 20% freelance written. Bimonthly magazine covering soap operas. "Extensive knowledge of daytime and prime time soap operas is required." Estab. 1975. Circ. 1,000,000. **Pays on acceptance.** Publishes ms an average of 3 months after acceptance. Byline given. Offers 30% kill fee. Buys first North American serial and second serial (reprint) rights. Submit seasonal/holiday material 4 months in advance. Reports in 1 month. Writer's guidelines for #10 SASE.
Nonfiction: Interview/profile. No essays. Buys 30 mss/year. Query with published clips. Length: 1,000-2,000 words. Pays $250-500 for assigned articles; $150-250 for unsolicited articles. Sometimes pays expenses of writers on assignment.
Photos: Offers no additional payment for photos accepted with ms. Buys all rights.

SOAP OPERA UPDATE, The Magazine of Stars and Stories, 270 Sylvan Ave., Englewood Cliffs NJ 07632. (201)569-6699. Fax: (201)569-2510. Editors: Dawn Mazzurco, Richard Spencer. 25% freelance written. Biweekly magazine on daytime serials. "We cover the world of soap operas with preview information, in-depth interviews and exclusive photos. Feature interviews, history, character sketches, events where soap stars are seen and participate." Estab. 1988. Pays on publication. Byline given. Buys first North American serial rights. Submit seasonal/holiday material 3 months in advance. Simultaneous submissions OK. Reports in 1 month.
Nonfiction: Humor, interview/profile. "Only articles directly about actors, shows or history of a soap opera." Buys 100 mss/year. Query with published clips. Length: 750-2,200 words. Pays $100-150. Sometimes pays expenses of writers on assignment.
Photos: State availability of photos with submission. Reviews transparencies. Offers $25. Captions and identification of subjects required. Buys all rights.
Tips: "Come up with fresh, new approaches to stories about soap operas and their people. Submit ideas and clips. Take a serious approach; don't talk down to the reader. All articles must be well written and the writer knowledgeable about his subject matter."

‡STORM MAGAZINE, Mature Entertainment, Storm Enterprises, Inc., 202 E. Main St., Reddick IL 60961. (815)365-2239. Editor: Dave A. Curl. 100% freelance written. Monthly magazine for indoor/outdoor entertainment. "We are not looking for articles or stories on the bad things in life. *Storm Magazine* wants fiction and nonfiction that is helpful to the reader, work that will challenge, humor with an edge. We seek a look at the finer things achieved through hard work and perseverance. Estab. 1993. Byline given. Offers 25% kill fee. Publication not copyrighted. Buys one-time rights. Editorial lead time 3 months. Submit seasonal material 3 months in advance. Simultaneous and previously published submissions OK. Reports in 2 weeks on queries; 1 month on mss.
Nonfiction: Book excerpts, essays, expose, general interest; how-to ("all kinds, mostly home and car"), humor, inspirational, interview/profile, new product, opinion, photo feature, technical and travel. "We will not accept religious or political propaganda. No X-rated material." Buys 50+ mss/year. Length: 3,000-5,000 words. Pays $1,200 minimum for assigned articles; $1,000 for unsolicited articles. Sometimes pays expenses of writers on assignment.
Photos: Send photos with submission. Reviews 3×5, 5×7 or 8×10 prints. Negotiates payment individually. Captions and identification of subjects required. Buys one-time rights.
Fiction: Adventure, erotica, experimental, fantasy, historical, horror, humorous, mainstream, mystery, science fiction, slice-of-life vignettes, suspense and western. "Accepts no X-rated material. No romance." Buys 50+ mss/year. Send complete ms. Length: 3,000-6,000 words. Pays $1,000 minimum.
Fillers: Anecdotes, facts, gags to be illustrated by cartoonist, newsbreaks and short humor. Pays $50-500.
Tips: "We are swayed by writers who present their work in a businesslike manner. *Storm* needs writers who are tuned in to the positives and pleasures of life. Gritty material is a turn off. *Storm Magazine* is entirely open to freelancers."

TV GUIDE, 1211 Avenue of the Americas, New York NY 10036. Editor (National Section): Barry Golson. Managing Editor: Jack Curry. 50% freelance written. Prefers to work with published/established writers but works with a small number of new/unpublished writers each year. Weekly. Circ. 14.5 million. Publishes ms an average of 1 month after acceptance.
Nonfiction: Wants offbeat articles about TV people and shows. This magazine is not interested in fan material. Also wants stories on the newest trends of television, but they must be written in clear, lively English. Study publication. Length: 1,000-2,000 words.
Photos: Uses professional high-quality photos, normally shot on assignment by photographers chosen by *TV Guide*. Prefers color. Pays $350 day rate against page rates—$450 for 2 pages or less.
● Ranked as one of the best markets for freelance writers in *Writer's Digest* magazine's annual "Top 100 Markets," January 1993.

VIDEO, 460 W. 34th St., New York NY 10001. (212)947-6500. Fax: (212)947-6727. Editor: James M. Barry. Managing Editor: Stan Pinkwas. 50% freelance written. Prefers to work with published/established writers; works with a small number of new/unpublished writers each year. Monthly magazine covering home video equipment, technology and prerecorded tapes. Circ. 450,000. **Pays on acceptance.** Publishes ms an average

of 3 months after acceptance. Byline given. Buys first North American serial rights. Query for electronic submissions. Reports in 3 weeks on queries; 1 month on mss. *Writer's Market* rcommends allowing 2 months for reply.
Nonfiction: Buys 50 mss/year. Query with published clips. Pays $300-1,000. Sometimes pays the expenses of writers on assignment.
Tips: The entire feature area is open to freelancers. Write a brilliant query and send samples of published articles.

‡**VIDEO MAGAZINE**, Reese Communications, 460 W. 34th St., New York NY 10001. (212)947-6500. Fax: (212)947-6727. Monthly magazine on home video in all its aspects. Estab. 1977. Circ. 450,000. **Pays on acceptance.** Publishes ms an average of 2-4 months after acceptance. Byline given. Buys first North American serial rights. Submit seasonal/holiday material 5 months in advance. Query for electronic submissions. Reports in 2-4 weeks on queries; 1-2 weeks on mss. Sample copy for 8×11 SAE.
Nonfiction: Jim Barry. Book excerpts (pre-publication galleys), how-to (editing and camera shooting), interview/profile, personal experience and technical. Buys 50-60 mss/year. Query with published clips. Length: 1,000-2,500 words. Pays $400-750 for assigned articles. Pays expenses of writers on assignment.
Photos: State availability of photos with submission. Captions, model releases and identification of subjects required. Buys one-time rights.
Columns/Departments: Camcorner (How-to shoot/edit home videos), 1,200 words; Technically Speaking (Technical aspects of home video gear), 1,200; and Gazette (Celebrity interviews/offbeat video applications), 200-500 words. Query with published clips. Length: 700-1,800 words. Pays $100-500.
Fillers: Brent Butterworth. Facts. Length: 100-200 words. Pays $25.

VIDEOMANIA, "The Video Collector's Newspaper," Legs Of Stone Publishing Co., P.O. Box 47, Princeton WI 54968-0047. Editor: Bob Katerzynske. 75% freelance written. Eager to work with new/unpublished writers. Monthly tabloid for the home video hobbyist. "Our readers are very much 'into' home video: they like reading about it—including both video hardware and software—98% also collect video (movies, vintage TV, etc.)." Estab. 1981. Circ. 5,000. Pays on publication. Publishes ms an average of 3 months after acceptance. Byline given. Buys all rights; may reassign. Submit seasonal/holiday material 6 months in advance. Reports in 1-3 months on mss. Reprints OK; send typed ms with rights for sale noted and information about when and where the article previously appeared. Pays 100% of their fee for an original article. Sample copy for 9×12 SAE with 9 first class stamps. Writer's guidelines for #10 SASE .
Nonfiction: Book excerpts, videotape and book reviews, expose, general interest, historical/nostalgic, how-to, humor, interview/profile, new product, opinion, personal experience, photo feature, technical and travel. "All articles should deal with video and/or film. We always have special holiday issues in November and December." No "*complicated*" technical pieces." Buys 24 mss/year. Send complete ms. Length: 500-800 words. Video reviews under 200 words. Pays $2.50 maximum. "Contributor copies also used for payment."
Photos: Send photos with submissions. Reviews contact sheets and 3×5 prints. Offers no additional payment for photos accepted with ms. Model releases and identification of subjects required. Buys all rights; may reassign.
Fiction: Adventure, horror and humorous. "We want short, video-related fiction only on an occasional basis. Since we aim for a general readership, we do not want any pornographic material." Buys 5 mss/year. Send complete ms. Length: 400 words. Pays $2.50 maximum plus copies.
Tips: "We want to offer more reviews and articles on offbeat, obscure and rare movies, videos and stars. Write in a plain, easy-to-understand style. We're not looking for a highhanded, knock-'em-dead writing style . . . just something good! We want more short video, film and book reviews by freelancers."

Ethnic/Minority

Ideas, interests and concerns of nationalities and religions are covered by publications in this category. General interest lifestyle magazines for these groups are also included. Many ethnic publications are locally-oriented or highly specialized and do not wish to be listed in a national publication such as *Writer's Market*. Query the editor of an ethnic publication with which you're familiar before submitting a manuscript, but do not consider these markets closed because they are not listed in this section. Additional markets for writing with an ethnic orientation are located in the following sections: Career, College and Alumni; Juvenile; Men's; Women's; and Teen and Young Adult.

AFRICAN-AMERICAN HERITAGE, Dellco Publishing Company, Suite 103, 8443 S. Crenshaw Blvd., Inglewood CA 90305. (213)752-3706. Editor: Dennis W. DeLoach. 30% freelance written. Quarterly magazine looking for "positive, informative, educational articles that build self-esteem, pride and an appreciation for the richness of culture and history." Estab. 1978. Circ. 25,000. Pays on publication. Publishes ms an average of 3-6 months after acceptance. Byline given. Offers 25% kill fee. Buys First North American serial, one-time or simultaneous rights. Submit seasonal/holiday material 6 months in advance. Simultaneous and previously published submissions OK. Reports in 1 month on queries; 2 months on mss. Sample copy for 9 × 12 SASE. Writer's guidelines for SAE with 4 first class stamps.

Nonfiction: Book excerpts, essays, general interest, historical/nostalgic, how-to, humor, inspirational, interview/profile, new product, opinion, personal experience, photo feature, religious and travel. Special issues: Black History Month (February). Buys 6 mss/year. Query. Length: 200-2,000 words. Pays $25-300 for assigned articles. Sometimes pays expenses of writers on assignment.

Photos: State availability of photos with submission. Reviews 5 × 7 prints. Offers no additional payment for photos accepted with ms. Identification of subject required. Buys one-time rights.

Columns/Departments: History (historical profiles); Commentary (letters to the editor); Interviews (personalities, unusual careers, positive experiences); Short Stories (well written, entertaining). Length: 2,000 words maximum. Buys 12 mss/year. Query. Pays $25-300.

Fiction: Adventure, ethnic, historical, humorous, mystery, religious, romance and slice-of-life vignettes. "No erotica, horror or fantasy." Buys 6 mss/year. Query. Length: 200-2,000 words. Pays $25-300.

Poetry: Avant-garde, free verse, Haiku, light verse and traditional. Buys 60 poems/year. Submit maximum 5 poems. Length: 4-36 lines. Pays $10-25.

Fillers: Anecdotes and facts. Buys 12/year. Length: 10-200 words. Pays $25-100.

AIM MAGAZINE, AIM Publishing Company, 7308 S. Eberhart Ave., Chicago IL 60619-1005. (312)874-6184. Editor: Ruth Apilado. Managing Editor: Dr. Myron Apilado. Estab. 1975. 75% freelance written. Works with a small number of new/unpublished writers each year. Quarterly magazine on social betterment that promotes racial harmony and peace for high school, college and general audience. Circ. 10,000. Pays on publication. Publishes ms an average of 3 months after acceptance. Offers 60% of contract as kill fee. Not copyrighted. Buys one-time rights. Submit seasonal/holiday material 6 months in advance. Simultaneous queries and submissions OK. Reports in 2 months on queries. Sample copy and writer's guidelines $4 for 9 × 12 SAE with 4 first class stamps.

Nonfiction: Expose (education); general interest (social significance); historical/nostalgic (Black or Indian); how-to (create a more equitable society); profile (one who is making social contributions to community); and book reviews and reviews of plays "that reflect our ethnic/minority orientation." No religious material. Buys 16 mss/year. Send complete ms. Length: 500-800 words. Pays $25-35.

Photos: Reviews b&w prints. Captions and identification of subjects required.

Fiction: Ethnic, historical, mainstream, and suspense. "Fiction that teaches the brotherhood of man." Buys 20 mss/year. Send complete ms. Length: 1,000-1,500 words. Pays $25-35.

Poetry: Avant-garde, free verse, light verse. No "preachy" poetry. Buys 20 poems/year. Submit maximum 5 poems. Length: 15-30 lines. Pays $3-5.

Fillers: Jokes, anecdotes and newsbreaks. Buys 30/year. Length: 50-100 words. Pays $5.

Tips: "Interview anyone of any age who unselfishly is making an unusual contribution to the lives of less fortunate individuals. Include photo and background of person. We look at the nations of the world as part of one family. Short stories and historical pieces about Blacks and Indians are the areas most open to freelancers. Subject matter of submission is of paramount concern for us rather than writing style. Articles and stories showing the similarity in the lives of people with different racial backgrounds are desired."

THE AMERICAN CITIZEN ITALIAN PRESS, 13681 V St., Omaha NE 68137. (402)896-0403. Fax: (402)895-7820. Publisher/Editor: Diana C. Failla. 80% freelance written. Quarterly newspaper of Italian-American news/stories. Estab. 1923. Circ. 8,490. Pays on publication. Publishes ms an average of 3 months after acceptance. Byline given. Not copyrighted. Buys first North American serial rights. Submit seasonal/holiday material 2 months in advance. Previously published submissions OK. Reports in 4 months. Sample copy for 10 × 13 SAE with $1.50 postage. Writer's guidelines for #10 SAE with 2 first class stamps.

Nonfiction: Book excerpts, general interest, historical/nostalgic, opinion, photo feature, celebrity pieces, travel, fashions, profiles and sports (Italian players). Query with published clips. Length: 400-600 words. Pays $15-25. Pays more for in-depth pieces.

For explanation of symbols, see the Key to Symbols and Abbreviations on page 72. For unfamiliar words, see the Glossary.

Photos: State availability of photos. Reviews b&w prints. Pays $5. Captions and identification of subjects required. Buys all rights.
Columns/Departments: Query.
Fiction: Query. Pays $15-20.
Poetry: Submit maximum 5 poems. Pays $5-10.
Tips: "Human interest stories are the most open to freelancers. We like work dealing with current issues involving those of Italian/American descent."

AMERICAN DANE, The Danish Brotherhood in America, 3717 Harney St., Omaha NE 68131-3844. (402)341-5049. Fax: (402)341-0830. Editor: Jerome L. Christensen. Managing Editor: Jennifer Denning-Kock. 50% freelance written. Prefers to work with published/established writers; works with a small number of new/unpublished writers each year. Monthly magazine of the Danish Brotherhood in America. All articles must have Danish ethnic flavor. Estab. 1916. Circ. 65,000. Pays on publication. Publishes ms an average of 1 year after acceptance. Byline given. Not copyrighted. Buys first rights. Submit seasonal/holiday material 1 year in advance. Reports in 2 weeks on queries. Sample copy for #10 SAE with 3 first class stamps. Writer's guidelines for #10 SASE.
Nonfiction: Historical, humor, inspirational, personal experience, photo feature and travel, all with a Danish flavor. Buys 12 mss/year. Query. Length: 1,500 words maximum. Pays $50 maximum for unsolicited articles.
Photos: Send photos with submission. Reviews prints. Offers no additional payment for photos accepted with ms. Captions and identification of subjects required. Buys one-time rights.
Fiction: Adventure, historical, humorous, mystery, romance and suspense, "all with a Danish flavor." Buys 6-12 mss/year. Query with published clips. Length: 1,500 words maximum. Pays $50 maximum.
Poetry: Traditional. Buys 1-6 poems/year. Submit maximum 6 poems. Pays $35 maximum.
Fillers: Anecdotes and short humor. Buys up to 12/year. Length: 300 words maximum. Pays $15 maximum.
Tips: "Feature articles are most open to freelancers. Reviews unsolicited manuscripts in August only."

AMERICAN VISIONS, The Magazine of Afro-American Culture, 2101 S Street, Washington DC 20008. (202)462-1779. Managing Editor: Joanne Harris. 75% freelance written. Bimonthly magazine on African-American art, culture and history. "Editorial is reportorial, current, objective, 'pop-scholarly'. Audience is ages 25-54, mostly black, college educated." Estab. 1986. Circ. 125,000. Pays 30 days after publication. Publishes mss an average of 2 months after acceptance. Byline given. Offers 25% kill fee. Buys first North American, one-time and second serial (reprint) rights. Submit seasonal/holiday material 5 months in advance. Simultaneous and previously published submissions OK. Query for electronic submissions. Reports in 2-3 months. Free sample copy and writer's guidelines with SASE.
Nonfiction: Book excerpts, general interest, historical/nostalgic, interview/profile, literature, photo feature and travel. Publishes travel supplements—domestic, Africa, Europe, Canada, Mexico. No fiction, poetry, personal experience or opinion. Buys about 60-70 mss/year. Query with or without published clips or send complete ms. Length: 500-2,500 words. Pays $100-600 for assigned articles; $100-400 for unsolicited articles. Sometimes pays expenses of writers on assignment.
Photos: State availability of photos with submission. Reviews contact sheets, 3×5 transparencies, and 3×5 or 8×10 prints. Offers $15 minimum. Identification of subjects required. Buys one-time rights.
Columns/Departments: Books, Cuisine, Film, Music, Profile and Travel, 750-1,750 words. Buys about 40 mss/year. Query or send complete ms. Pays $100-400.
Tips: "Little-known but terribly interesting information about black history and culture is desired. Aim at an upscale audience. Send ms with credentials." Looking for writers who are enthusiastic about their topics.

ARMENIAN INTERNATIONAL MAGAZINE, Suite 205, 207 S. Brand Blvd., Glendale CA 91204. (818)546-2246. Fax: (818)546-2283. Editor: Salpi H. Ghazarian. Managing Editor: Ishkhan Jinbashian. 75% freelance written. Monthly magazine about the Causasus and the global Armenian diaspora. "Special reports and features about politics, business, education, culture, profiles, etc." Estab. 1989. Circ. 30,000. Pays on publication. Publishes ms an average of 3 months after acceptance. Bylines sometimes given. Offers 20% kill fee. Buys all rights. Submit seasonal/holiday material 2 months in advance. Query for electronic submissions. Reports in 2 weeks on queries; 6 weeks on mss.
Nonfiction: General interest, historical, interview/profile, photo feature and travel. Buys 60 mss/year. Query with published clips. Length: 600-1,200 words. Pays $100-400 for assigned articles; $50-200 for unsolicited articles. Sometimes pays expenses of writers on assignment.
Photos: State availability of photos with submission. Reviews negatives, transparencies and prints. Offers $10-50/photo. Captions and identification of subjects required. Buys all rights.

THE B'NAI B'RITH INTERNATIONAL, JEWISH MONTHLY, 1640 Rhode Island Ave. NW, Washington DC 20036. (202)857-6645. Editor: Jeff Rubin. 50% freelance written. Magazine published 10 times/year covering Jewish affairs. Estab. 1886. Circ. 185,000. **Pays on acceptance.** Publishes ms an average of 5 months after acceptance. Byline given. Kill fee depends on rate of payment. Buys first North American serial rights. Submit seasonal/holiday material 6 months in advance. Query for electronic submissions. Reports in 2 weeks. Sample copy $2 for 9×13 SAE with 2 first class stamps. Free writer's guidelines.

Nonfiction: Book excerpts, essay, expose, general interest, historical, inspirational, interview/profile, photo feature and travel. Buys 40-50 mss/year. Query with published clips. Length: 750-3,000 words. Pays $50-750 for assigned articles; $50-500 for unsolicited articles. Sometimes pays expenses of writers on assignment.
Photos: State availability of photos with submission. Reviews contact sheets, 2×3 transparencies and prints. Payment depends on quality and type of photograph. Identification of subjects required. Buys one-time rights.
 • No longer publishes fiction.
Tips: "Writers should submit clips with their queries. The best way to break in to the *Jewish Monthly* is to submit a range of good story ideas accompanied by clips. We aim to establish relationships with writers and we tend to be loyal. All sections are equally open."

BRITISH HERITAGE, Cowles Magazines, 6405 Flank Dr., P.O. Box 8200, Harrisburg PA 17105-8200. (717)657-9555. Editor: Gail Huganir. Managing Editor: Bruce Heydt. 30% freelance written. Consumer magazine covering the United Kingdom. "*British Heritage* is for anglophiles. We cover places of interest in Great Britain, profiles of British historical figures, new British products, British foods and crafts." Estab. 1979. Circ. 100,000. **Pays on acceptance.** Bylines sometimes given. Buys all rights in most cases, sometimes first North American rights. Submit seasonal/holiday material 6 months in advance. Reports in 4 months. Sample copy $3.95 for SAE with 4 first class stamps. Free writer's guidelines.
Nonfiction: Historical, interview/profile and travel. No fiction. Buys 60 mss/year. Query. Length: 1,000 words. Pays $100-400 for assigned articles; $100-200 for unsolicited articles.
Photos: State availability of photos with submission. Pays $50-250 for photos. Identification of subjects required. Buys one-time rights.

CLASS, R.E. John-Sandy Ltd., 900 Broadway, New York NY 10003. (212)677-3055. Executive Editor: Constance M. Weaver. 25% freelance written. Monthly "general interest publication geared toward Caribbean, Latin and African Americans between ages 18 and 49." Estab. 1979. Circ. 250,000. Pays 45 days after publication. Byline given. Buys first North American serial and second serial (reprint) rights. Submit seasonal/holiday material 3 months in advance. Reports in 6 weeks. Sample copy for 9×12 SAE with 4 first class stamps. Writer's guidelines for #10 SASE.
Nonfiction: Expose, general interest, historical/nostalgic, interview/profile, religious and travel. Query with published clips. Length: 500-1,300 words. Pays 10¢/word maximum. Sometimes pays expenses of writers on assignment.
Photos: Send photos with submission. Offers no additional payment for photos accepted with ms. Captions, model releases and identification of subjects required. Buys all rights.
Columns/Departments: Length: 500-1,300 words. Pays 10¢/word maximum.
Poetry: Buys 10-20 poems/year. Submit maximum 5 poems. Pays $10 maximum.

CONGRESS MONTHLY, American Jewish Congress, 15 E. 84th St., New York NY 10028. (212)879-4500. Editor: Maier Deshell. 90% freelance written. Magazine published 7 times/year covering topics of concern to the American Jewish community representing a wide range of views. Distributed mainly to the members of the American Jewish Congress. "Readers are intellectual, Jewish, involved." Estab. 1933. Circ. 35,000. Pays on publication. Publishes ms an average of 3 months after acceptance. Byline given. Buys one-time rights. Submit seasonal/holiday material 2 months in advance. No previously published submissions. Reports in 2 months.
Nonfiction: General interest ("current topical issues geared toward our audience"). No technical material. Send complete ms. Length: 2,000 words maximum. Pays $100-150/article.
Photos: State availability of photos. Reviews b&w prints. "Photos are paid for with payment for ms."
Columns/Departments: Book, film, art and music reviews. Send complete ms. Length: 1,000 words maximum. Pays $100-150/article.

EBONY MAGAZINE, 820 S. Michigan Ave., Chicago IL 60605. (312)322-9200. Publisher: John H. Johnson. Executive Editor: Lerone Bennett, Jr. 10% freelance written. For Black readers of the US, Africa and the Caribbean. Monthly. Circ. 1.8 million. Buys first North American serial and all rights. Buys about 10 mss/year. Pays on publication. Publishes ms an average of 3 months after acceptance. Submit seasonal material 2 months in advance. Query. Reports in 1 month.
Nonfiction: Achievement and human interest stories about, or of concern to, Black readers. Interviews, profiles and humor pieces are bought. Length: 1,500 words maximum. "Study magazine and needs carefully. Perhaps one out of 50 submissions interests us. Most are totally irrelevant to our needs and are simply returned." Pays $200 minimum. Sometimes pays the expenses of writers on assignment.
Photos: Purchased with mss, and with captions only. Buys 8×10 glossy prints, color transparencies, 35mm color. Submit negatives and contact sheets when possible. Offers no additional payment for photos accepted with mss.

EMERGE, Black America's Newsmagazine, Emerge Communications, Inc., Suite 2200, 1700 N. Moore St., Arlington VA 22009. (703)875-0430. Fax: (703)516-6406. Editor: Geore E. Curry. Managing Editor: Florestine Purnell. 80% freelance written. African American news monthly. "*Emerge* is a general interest publication reporting on a wide variety of issues from health to sports to politics, almost anything that affects Black Americans. Our audience is comprised primarily of African Americans 25-49, individual income of $35,000, professional and college educated." Estab. 1989. Circ. 200,000. Pays on publication. Publishes ms an average of 3 months after acceptance. Byline given. 25% kill fee. Buys first North American serial rights. Submit seasonal material 6 months in advance. Query for electronic submissions. Reports in 5 weeks. Sample copy $3 for 9×12 SAE. Writer's guidelines for #10 SAE with 2 first class stamps.

Nonfiction: Essays, expose, general interest, historical/nostalgic, humor, interview/profile, technical, travel. "We are not interested in standard celebrity pieces that lack indepth reporting as well as analysis, or pieces dealing with interpersonal relationships." Query with published clips. Length: 150-2,000 words. Pays $35-1,500.

Photos: State availability of photos with submission. Reviews contact sheets. Negotiated payment. Captions, model releases, and indentification of subjects required. Buys one-time rights.

Columns/Departments: Query.

Tips: "If a writer doesn't have a completed ms, then he should mail a query letter with clips. No phone calls. First-time authors should be extremely sensitive to the *Emerge* style and fit within these guidelines as closely as possible. We do not like to re-write or re-edit pieces. We are a news monthly so articles must be written with a 3 month lead time in mind. If an assignment is given and another one is desired, writers must assist our research department during fact checking process and closing. Read at least 6 issues of the publication before submitting ideas."

EXITO, News and Sun Sentinel Company, #212, 8323 NW 12th St., Miami FL 33126. (305)597-5000. Editor: Humberto Cruz. 30% freelance written. Weekly tabloid that covers topics of general interest. "We reach bilingual, bicultural Hispanics, ages 25 to 54." Estab. 1991. Circ. 65,000. Pays on publication. Byline given. Buys one-time and second serial (reprint) rights. Submit seasonal/holiday material 6 months in advance. Accepts simultaneous submissions. Query for electronic submissions. Reports in 1 month. *Writer's Market* recommends allowing 2 months for reply. Sample copy for 9×12 SAE with 6 first class stamps.

Nonfiction: Christina Arencibia (for travel articles), Humberto Cruz (for general interest), Magaly Rubiera (for lifestyle, health). General interest, how-to, interview/profile, new product, religious and travel. Buys 200 mss/year. Query with or without published clips or send complete ms. Length: 1,700 words. Pays $75 for articles.

Photos: State availability of photos with submission. Reviews transparencies. Captions and identification of subjects required. Buys one-time rights.

Tips: *Exito* only accepts ms written in Spanish. "We are particularly interested in articles on travel."

GREATER PHOENIX JEWISH NEWS, Phoenix Jewish News, Inc., P.O. Box 26590, Phoenix AZ 85068-6590. (602)870-9470. Fax: (602)870-0426. Executive Editor: Flo Eckstein. Managing Editor: Leni Reiss. 5% freelance written. Prefers to work with published/established writers. Weekly tabloid covering subjects of interest to Jewish readers. Estab. 1948. Circ. 7,000. Publishes ms an average of 3 months after acceptance. Byline given. Submit seasonal/holiday material 3 months in advance. Simultaneous queries and simultaneous and previously published submissions OK. Send typed ms with rights for sale noted, including information about when and where the article previously appeared. Sample copy $1.

Nonfiction: General interest, issue analysis, interview/profile, opinion, personal experience, photo feature and travel. Special sections include Fashion and Health, House and Home, Back to School, Summer Camps, Party Planning, Bridal, Adult Lifestyles, Travel, Business and Finance, and Jewish Holidays. Send complete ms. Length: 1,000-2,500 words. Pays $15-50 for simultaneous rights; $1.50/column inch for first serial rights.

Photos: Send photos with query or ms. Pays $10 for 8×10 b&w prints. Captions required.

Tips: "We are looking for lifestyle and issue-oriented pieces of particular interest to Jewish readers. Our newspaper reaches across the religious, political, social and economic spectrum of Jewish residents in this burgeoning southwestern metropolitan area. We stay away from cute stories as well as ponderous submissions."

HADASSAH MAGAZINE, 50 W. 58th St., New York NY 10019. Executive Editor: Alan M. Tigay. 90% freelance written. Works with small number of new/unpublished writers each year. Monthly, except combined issues (June-July and August-September). Circ. 334,000. Buys first rights (with travel and family articles, buys all rights). Free sample copy and writer's guidelines with SASE.

Nonfiction: Primarily concerned with Israel, Jewish communities around the world and American civic affairs as relates to the Jewish community. "We are also open to art stories that explore trends in Jewish art, literature, theater, etc. Will not assign/commission a story to a first-time writer for Hadassah." Buys 10 unsolicited mss/year. No phone queries. Send query and writing samples. Length: 1,500-2,000 words. Pays $200-400, less for reviews. Sometimes pays the expenses of writers on assignment.

Photos: "We buy photos only to illustrate articles, with the exception of outstanding color from Israel which we use on our covers. We pay $175 and up for a suitable cover photo." Offers $50 for first photo; $35 for each additional. "Always interested in striking cover (color) photos, especially of Israel and Jerusalem."

Columns/Departments: "We have a Family column and a Travel column, but a query for topic or destination should be submitted first to make sure the area is of interest and the story follows our format."

Fiction: Contact Joan Michel. Short stories with strong plots and positive Jewish values. No personal memoirs, "schmaltzy" or women's magazine fiction. "We continue to buy very little fiction because of a backlog." Length: 3,000 words maximum. Pays $300 minimum. "Require proper size SASE."

Tips: "We are interested in reading articles that offer an American perspective on Jewish affairs (1,500 words). For example, a look at the presidential candidates from a Jewish perspective. Send query of topic first."

HERITAGE FLORIDA JEWISH NEWS, P.O. Box 300742, Fern Park FL 32730-0742. (407)834-8787. Fax: (407)834-8787. Associate Editor: N. Jill Hayflich. Publisher/Editor: Jeffrey Gaeser. 20% freelance written. Weekly tabloid on Jewish subjects of local, national and international scope, except for special issues. "Covers news of local, national and international scope of interest to Jewish readers and not likely to be found in other publications." Estab. 1976. Circ. 10,000. Pays on publication. Publishes ms an average of 2 months after acceptance. Byline given. Buys first North American serial, first, one-time, second serial (reprint) or simultaneous rights. Submit seasonal/holiday material 2 months in advance. Previously published submissions OK. Reports in 1 month. Sample copy $1 with 9 × 12 SASE.

Nonfiction: General interest, interview/profile, opinion, photo feature, religious and travel. "Especially needs articles for these annual issues: Rosh Hashanah, Financial, Chanukah, Celebration (wedding and bar mitzvah), Passover, Health and Fitness, Education and Travel. No fiction, poems, first-person experiences." Buys 50 mss/year. Send complete ms. Length: 500-1,000 words. Pays $15-25. Sometimes pays expenses of writers on assignment. Reprints OK; send typed ms with rights for sale noted. Pays $25 for reprints.

Photos: State availability of photos with submission. Reviews 5 × 7 prints. Offers $5/photo. Captions and identification of subjects required. Buys one-time rights.

THE HIGHLANDER, Angus J. Ray Associates, Inc., P.O. Box 397, Barrington IL 60011-0397. (708)382-1035. Editor: Angus J. Ray. Managing Editor: Ethyl Kennedy Ray. 50% freelance written. Works with a small number of new/unpublished writers each year. Bimonthly magazine covering Scottish history, clans, genealogy, travel/history, and Scottish/American activities. Estab. 1961. Circ. 40,000. **Pays on acceptance.** Publishes ms an average of 6 months after acceptance. Byline given. Buys first North American serial and second serial (reprint) rights to material originally published elsewhere. Submit seasonal/holiday material 6 months in advance. Previously published submissions OK. Reports in 1 month. Sample copy $2 for 9 × 12 SAE with 7 first class stamps. Free writer's guidelines.

Nonfiction: Historical/nostalgic. "No fiction; no articles unrelated to Scotland." Buys 50 mss/year. Query. Length: 750-2,000 words. Pays $75-150. Reprints OK; send tearsheet or photocopy of article. Pays 50% of their fee for an original article.

Photos: State availability of photos. Pays $5-10 for 8 × 10 b&w prints or transparencies. Reviews b&w contact sheets. Identification of subjects required. Buys one-time rights.

Tips: "Submit something that has appeared elsewhere."

HISPANIC, Suite 410, 111 Massachusetts Ave. NW, Washington DC 20001. (202)682-3000. Fax: (202)682-4091. Editor: Alfredo J. Estrada. 90% freelance written. Monthly magazine for the Hispanic community. "HISPANIC is a general interest, lifestyle, entertainment, upbeat, role model publication." Estab. 1987. Circ. 150,000. Pays on publication. Publishes ms an average of 4 months after acceptance. Byline given. Offers 25% kill fee. Buys all rights. Submit seasonal/holiday material 4 months in advance. Free sample copy and writer's guidelines.

Nonfiction: General interest, historical/nostalgic, humor, interview/profile, opinion, personal experience, photo feature and travel. Buys 200 mss/year. Query. Length: 50-3,000 words. Pays $50-600. Pays writers phone expenses, "but these must be cleared with editors first."

Photos: State availability of photos with submission. Reviews transparencies. Offers $25-600/photo. Captions, model releases and identification of subjects required. Buys one-time rights.

Columns/Departments: Forum (political opinion and analysis), cars, money, career, business and reviews. All columns are approximately 500 words but vary in fee.

HISPANIC BUSINESS, Hispanic Business, Inc., 360 S. Hope Ave., Santa Barbara CA 93105. (805)682-5843. Editor: Jesus Chavarria. Managing Editor: Janet Glasheen. 10% freelance written. Monthly trade magazine "written for and about Hispanic CEO's, managers and professionals." Estab. 1979. Circ. 165,000. Pays on publication. Byline given. Kill fee varies. Buys all rights. Submit seasonal/holiday material 3 months in advance. Query for electronic submissions. Reports in 2 weeks. Sample copy $5. Writer's guidelines $1.75 for #10 SASE.

Nonfiction: Interview/profile. Buys 25 mss/year. Query with published clips. Length: 750-3,000 words. Pays $225-900 for assigned articles; $195-780 for unsolicited articles. Sometimes pays the expenses of writers on assignment.

Photos: State availability of photos with submission. Reviews transparencies. Offers no additional payment for photos accepted with ms. Identification of subjects required. Buys all rights.
Tips: "We are looking for writers with close business ties to their local Hispanic community."

INSIDE, The Jewish Exponent Magazine, Jewish Federation of Greater Philadelphia, 226 S. 16th St., Philadelphia PA 19102. (215)893-5700. Fax: (215)546-3957. Editor: Jane Biberman. Managing Editor: Rochelle Nataloni. 95% freelance written (by assignment). Works with published/established writers and a small number of new/unpublished writers each year. Quarterly Jewish community magazine—for a general interest Jewish readership 25 years of age and older. Estab. 1979. Circ. 65,000. **Pays on acceptance.** Offers 15% kill fee. Publishes ms an average of 2 months after acceptance. Byline given. Buys first rights. Submit seasonal/holiday material 3 months in advance. Simultaneous queries OK. Reports in 2 weeks on queries; 3 weeks on mss. Sample copy $5 for 9×12 SAE. Writer's guidelines for #10 SASE.
Nonfiction: Book excerpts, general interest, historical/nostalgic, humor, interview/profile personal experience and religious. Philadelphia angle desirable. Buys 12 unsolicited mss/year. Query. Length: 1,000-3,500 words. Pays $100-1,000.
Photos: State availability of photos with submission. Offers $25. Identification of subjects required. Buys first rights.
Fiction: Short stories. Query.
Tips: "Personalities—very well known—and serious issues of concern to Jewish community needed."

JEWISH ACTION, Union of Orthodox Jewish Congregations of America, 18th Fl., 333 7th Ave., New York NY 10001-5072. (212)563-4000, ext. 146, 147. Fax: (212)564-9058. Editor: Charlotte Friedland. Assistant Editor: Deena Yellin. 80% freelance written. "Quarterly magazine offering a vibrant approach to Jewish issues, Orthodox lifestyle and values." Circ. 45,000. Pays 4-6 weeks after publication. Byline given. Submit seasonal/holiday material 4 months in advance. Reports in 3 months. Sample copy and guidelines for 9×12 SAE with 5 first class stamps.
Nonfiction: Current Jewish issues, history, biography, art, inspirational, humor, book reviews. Query with published clips. Length: 1,500-2,500 words. Pays $100-300 for assigned articles; $75-150 for unsolicited articles. Buys 30-40 mss/year.
Fiction: Must have relevance to Orthodox reader. Length: 1,000-2,000 words.
Poetry: Limited number accepted. Pays $25-75.
Columns/Departments: Student Voice (about Jewish life on campus); length: 1,000 words. Buys 4 mss/year. Jewish Living (section pertaining to holidays, contemporary Jewish practices); length: 1,000-1,500 words. Buys 10 mss/year.
Photos: Send photos with submission. Identification of subjects required.
Tips: "Remember that your reader is well-educated and has a strong commitment to Orthodox Judaism. Articles on the Holocaust, holidays, Israel and other common topics should offer a fresh insight."

‡LA RED/THE NET, The Hispanic Journal of Education, Floricanto Press, Suite 830, 16161 Ventura Blvd., Encino CA 91436. (818)990-1885. Editor: Giselle K. Cabello. 80% freelance written. Quarterly magazine on Hispanic issues, particularly education. Circ. 5,000. Pays 90 days after publication. Byline sometimes given. Buys all rights. Query for electronic submissions. Sample copy $5 for 9×12 SAE with $1.20 postage. Writer's guidelines for SAE with 50¢ postage.
Nonfiction: Hispanic issues. "No mainstream general articles." Buys 10 mss/year. Query or send complete ms. Length: 2,000-6,000 words. Pays $50-150 for assigned articles. $50 maximum for unsolicited articles. Sometimes pays writers with contributor copies or other premiums rather than cash on articles that are not very high interest.
Photos: Send photos with submission. Reviews 3½×1½ transparencies, 3×3 prints. Offers no additional payment for photos accepted with ms. Captions and identification of subjects required. Buys one-time rights.
Columns/Departments: Feature Review (a lengthy review of a high interest book) 3,000 words; Feature Article (a lengthy review on a high interest topic) 6,000 words. Buys 4 mss/year. Send complete ms. Pays $50-150.
Tips: "Take a high interest issue affecting Hispanics and write a well researched article; it must be informative; no jargon, please."

MIDSTREAM, A Monthly Jewish Review, 110 E. 59 St., New York NY 10022. Editor: Joel Carmichael. 90% freelance written. Works with a small number of new/unpublished writers each year. Monthly. Circ. 10,000. Buys first North American serial rights. Byline given. Pays after publication. Publishes ms an average of 6 months after acceptance. Reports in 2 months. Fiction guidelines for #10 SASE.
Nonfiction: "Articles offering a critical interpretation of the past, searching examination of the present, and affording a medium for independent opinion and creative cultural expression. Articles on the political and social scene in Israel, on Jews in Russia, the US and elsewhere; generally it helps to have a Zionist orientation." Buys historical and think pieces, primarily of Jewish and related content. Pays 5¢/word.

Fiction: Primarily of Jewish and related content. Pays 5¢/word.

Tips: "A book review is a good way to start. Send us a sample review or a clip, let us know your area of interest, suggest books you would like to review. For longer articles, give a brief account of your background or credentials in this field. Send query describing article or ms with cover letter. Since we are a monthly, we look for critical analysis rather than a 'journalistic' approach."

NA'AMAT WOMAN, Magazine of NA'AMAT USA, the Women's Labor Zionist Organization of America, NA'AMAT USA, 200 Madison Ave., New York NY 10016. (212)725-8010. Editor: Judith A. Sokoloff. 80% freelance written. Magazine published 5 times/year covering Jewish themes and issues; Israel; women's issues; Labor Zionism; and social, political and economic issues. Circ. 30,000. Pays on publication. Byline given. Not copyrighted. Buys first North American serial, one-time, first serial and second serial (reprint) rights to book excerpts and makes work-for-hire assignments. Reports in 2 months on queries, 2 months on mss. Writer's guidelines for SASE.

Nonfiction: Expose, general interest (Jewish), historical/nostalgic, interview/profile, opinion, personal experience, photo feature, travel (Israel), art and music. "All articles must be of particular interest to the Jewish community." Buys 35 mss/year. Query with clips of published work or send complete ms. Pays 10¢/word.

Photos: State availability of photos. Pays $10-30 for 4×5 or 5×7 prints. Captions and identification of subjects required. Buys one-time rights.

Columns/Departments: Film and book reviews with Jewish themes. Buys 20-25 mss/year. Query with clips of published work or send complete ms. Pays 10¢/word.

Fiction: Historical/nostalgic, humorous, women-oriented and novel excerpts. "Good intelligent fiction with Jewish slant. No maudlin nostalgia or trite humor." Buys 3 mss/year. Send complete ms. Length: 1,200-3,000 words. Pays 10¢/word.

NATIVE PEOPLES MAGAZINE, The Arts and Lifeways, Suite C-224, 5333 N. 7th St., Phoenix AZ 85014-2804. (602)252-2236. Fax: (602)265-3113. Editor: Gary Avey. Quarterly magazine on Native Americans. "The primary purpose of this magazine is to offer a sensitive portrayal of the arts and lifeways of native peoples of the Americas." Estab. 1987. Circ. 108,000. Pays on publication. Byline given. Buys one-time rights. Query for electronic submissions. Reports in 1 month on queries; 2 weeks on mss. Sample copy for 9×12 SAE with 5 first class stamps. Free writer's guidelines. "Extremely high quality reproduction with full-color throughout."

Nonfiction: Book excerpts, historical/nostalgic, interview/profile, personal experience and photo feature. Buys 35 mss/year. Query with published clips. Length: 1,400-2,000 words. Pays 25¢/word. Publishes nonfiction book excerpts.

Photos: State availability of photos with submission. Reviews transparencies (all formats). Offers $45-150 per page rates. Identification of subjects required. Buys one-time rights.

POLISH AMERICAN JOURNAL, Polonia's Voice, Panagraphics, Inc., 1275 Harlem Rd., Buffalo NY 14206-1980. (716)893-5771. Fax: (716)893-5783. Editor: Mark A. Kohan. Managing Editor: Paulette T. Kulbacki. 20% freelance written. Monthly tabloid for Polonia (Polish and Polish-American events, people, etc.). "Stories should be about Polish-Americans active in their community on either a local or national level. Prefer biographies/histories of these people or essays on their accomplishments." Estab. 1911. Circ. 20,000. Pays at end of publication quarter (March, June, Sept., Dec.). Publishes ms 3-4 months after acceptance. Byline given. Reports in 2 months. Offers $2 kill fee. Not copyrighted. Buys one-time rights. Submit seasonal/holiday material 3 months in advance. Previously published submissions OK. Query for electronic submissions. Sample copy for 9×12 SAE with 3 first class stamps.

Nonfiction: Expose (story on Polish-Americans), general interest (community news), historical/nostalgic (retrospectives on events), how-to (organize groups, etc.), interview/profile (background on local Pol-Ams), opinion (historical observations, anti-defamation, etc.), personal experience (growing up Polish-American). Special issues on Easter and Christmas celebrations—how practiced in other areas; travel to Poland, airfare and comparisons, etc.; salute to prominent Polish-American business leaders, clergy, media personalities, etc. Buys 6-8 mss/year. Query. Length: 200-1,000 words. Pays $10-25. Sometimes pays expenses of writers on assignment.

Photos: State availability of photos with submission. Reviews 8½×11 prints. Offers $2-7.50 per solicited photo. Identification of subjects required. Buys one-time rights.

Columns/Departments: Forum/Viewpoints (observations on recent decisions/events), 750 words maximum; culture (music/art developments), 750 words maximum; scholarships/studies (grants and programs available), 750 words maximum. Buys 6 mss/year. Query. Pays $10-25.

Fillers: Anecdotes, facts, gags to be illustrated by cartoonist, newsbreaks and short humor. Buys 10/year. Length: 50-250 words. Pays $2-10.

Tips: "We want articles which encourage people to participate and get involved with Polonia—from investments in Poland to 'how-to' pieces on egg dying. Travel stories will be returned unread. Freelancers who can provide light or humorous copy are most welcome."

‡SCANDINAVIAN REVIEW, The American-Scandinavian Foundation, 725 Park Ave., New York NY 10021. (212)879-9779. Editor: Adrienne Gynongy. 75% freelance written. Triannual magazine for contemporary Scandinavia. Audience: members, embassies, consulates, libraries. Slant: popular coverage of contemporary affairs in Scandanivia. Estab. 1913. Circ. 3,500. Pays on publication. Publishes ms 2 months after acceptance. Byline given. Buys first North American serial and second serial (reprint) rights. Editorial lead time 3 months. Submit seasonal material 3 months in advance. Previously published submissions OK. Query for electronic submissions. Reports in 6 weeks on queries. Sample copy and writer's guidelines free on request.

Nonfiction: General interest, interview/profile, photo feature and travel (must have Scandinavia as topic focus). Special issue on Scandinavian travel. *No pornography.* Buys 30 mss/year. Query with published clips. Length: 1,500-2,000 words. Pays $300 max. Pays contributor's copies (at writer's request).

Photos: State availability of photos with submission or send photos with submission. Reviews 3×5 transparencies or 3×5 prints. Pays $25-50/photo; negotiates payment individually. Captions required. Buys one-time rights.

THE UKRAINIAN WEEKLY, Ukrainian National Association, 30 Montgomery St., Jersey City NJ 07302-3821. (201)434-0237. Editor-in-Chief: Roma Hadzewycz. 30% freelance written (mostly by a corps of regular contributors). Weekly tabloid covering news and issues of concern to Ukrainian community, primarily in North America but also around the world, and events in Ukraine. "We have a news bureau in Kyyiv, capital of Ukraine." Estab. 1933. Circ. 11,000. Pays on publication. Publishes ms an average of 1-2 months after acceptance. Byline given. Buys first North American serial and second serial (reprint) rights or makes work-for-hire assignments. Submit seasonal/holiday material 1 month in advance. Reports in 1 month. Free sample copy for 9×12 SAE with 3 first class stamps.

Nonfiction: Book excerpts, essays, expose, general interest, historical/nostalgic, interview/profile, opinion, personal experience, photo feature and news events. Special issues include Easter, Christmas, anniversary of Ukrain's independence, August 24, 1991 (proclamation) and December 1, 1991 (referendum), student scholarships, anniversary of Chornobyl nuclear accident and year-end review of news. Buys 80 mss/year. Query with published clips. Length: 500-2,000 words. Pays $45-100 for assigned articles. Pays $25-100 for unsolicited articles. Sometimes pays the expenses of writers on assignment. Reprints OK; send information about when and where the article previously appeared. Pays 25-50% of their fee for an original article.

Photos: Send photos with submission. Reviews contact sheets, negatives and 3×5, 5×7 or 8×10 prints. Offers no additional payment for photos accepted with ms.

Columns/Departments: News & Views (commentary on news events), 500-1,000 words. Buys 10 mss/year. Query. Pays $25-50.

Tips: "Become acquainted with the Ukrainian community in the U.S. and Canada. The area of our publication most open to freelancers is community news—coverage of local events. We'll put more emphasis on events in Ukraine now that it has re-established its independence."

VISTA, The Hispanic Magazine (Florida), Suite 600, 999 Ponce de Leon Blvd., Coral Gables FL 33134. (305)442-2462. Fax: (305)443-7650. Editor: Renato Perez. 95% freelance written. Prefers to work with published/established writers. An English-language monthly directed at Hispanic Americans. Appears as a supplement to 36 newspapers across the country with a combined circulation of one million in cities with large Latin populations. Estab. 1985. Pays on publication. Publishes ms an average of 4 months after acceptance. Byline given. Offers 25% kill fee. Buys first rights. Submit seasonal/holiday material 6 months in advance. Reports in 2 weeks on queries; 1 month on mss. Sample copy and writer's guidelines for 3 first class stamps.

Nonfiction: General interest, historical, inspirational, interview/profile, opinion and travel. No articles without a Hispanic American angle. Buys 90 mss/year. Query with published clips. Length: 100-1,500 words. Pays $50-500. Sometimes pays the expenses of writers on assignment.

Photos: State availability of photos with submission. Reviews contact sheets, negatives, transparencies and prints. Negotiates payment. Identification of subjects required. Buys one-time rights.

Columns/Departments: Vistascopes and Newsnotes (Hispanic people in the news), 250 words; and Voices (personal views on matters affecting Hispanic Americans), 500 words. Buys 48 mss/year. Query with published clips. Length: 100-750 words. Pays $50-200.

Tips: "Be aware of topics and personalities of interest to Hispanic readers. We need profiles of Hispanic Americans in unusual or atypical roles and jobs. Anticipate events; profiles should tell the reader what the subject will be doing at the time of publication. Keep topics upbeat and positive: no stories on drugs, crimes. A light, breezy touch is needed for the profiles. Express your opinion in the Voices pages but be scrupulously impartial and accurate when writing articles of general interest."

Food and Drink

Magazines appealing to gourmets, health-conscious consumers and vegetarians are classified here. Journals aimed at food processing, manufacturing and retailing are in the Trade section. Many magazines in General Interest and Women's categories also buy articles on food topics.

BEST RECIPES MAGAZINE, Stauffer Magazine Group, 1503 SW 42nd St., Topeka KS 6609-1265. (913)274-4300. Editor-in-Chief: Roberta J. Peterson (*not* Robert). 20% freelance written. Bimonthly magazine with emphasis on recipes from a middle America perspective—*not* a high-income lifestyle or exotic cooking publication. Estab. 1987. Circ. 250,000. Pays on publication. Publishes average of 6 months after acceptance. Byline given. Buys first rights or makes work-for-hire assignments. Occasionally buys reprint rights if first publication was to extremely local or regional audience. Submit seasonal material nine months to one year in advance. Reports in 2 months on queries. Sample copy and writer's guidelines $4 for 11 × 14 SAE with 5 first class stamps.
Nonfiction: *Best Recipes* seeks articles about creative, interesting or famous people who cook or practical cooking advice, such as healthful ways to update grandma's recipes or adapting home cooking to the microwave. Top quality, professional color photography enhances acceptability of articles. Black and white line drawings also desirable for some stories, such as how-tos. Buys 8-10 mss a year. Length 800 words maximum. Pays $75 to $200 for unsolicited articles.
Tips: Do not send anything not related to foods, recipes, cooking tips. ALL stories (even tips, how-tos) should include practical, tested recipes.

BON APPETIT, America's Food and Entertaining Magazine, Knapp Communications Corporation, 6300 Wilshire Blvd., Los Angeles CA 70018-5202. (213)965-3600. Fax: (213)937-1206. Executive Editor: Barbara Fairchild. Editor-in-Chief: William J. Garry. 10% freelance written. Monthly magazine that covers fine food, restaurants and home entertaining. "*Bon Appetit* readers are upscale food enthusiasts and sophisticated travelers. They eat out often and entertain four to six times a month." Estab. 1975. Circ. 1,331,853. **Pays on acceptance.** Byline given. Negotiates rights. Submit seasonal/holiday material 1 year in advance. No simultaneous or previously published submissions. Reports in 6 weeks on queries. Writer's guidelines for #10 SASE.
Nonfiction: Travel (restaurant or food-related), food feature and dessert feature. "No cartoons, quizzes, poetry, historic food features or obscure food subjects." Buys 45 mss/year. Query with published clips. Length: 750-2,000 words. Pays $500-1,800. Sometimes pays expenses of writers on assignment.
Photos: Never send photos.
Tips: "We are most interested in receiving travel or restaurant stories from freelancers. They must have a good knowledge of food (as shown in accompanying clips) and a light, lively style with humor. Nothing long and pedantic please."

CHILE PEPPER, The Magazine of Spicy Foods, Out West Publishing Company, 5106 Grand NE, P.O. Box 80780, Albuquerque NM 87198-0780. (505)266-8322. Fax: (505)266-0141. 25-30% freelance written. Bimonthly magazine on spicy foods. "The magazine is devoted to spicy foods, and most articles include recipes. We have a very devoted readership who love their food hot!" Estab. 1986. Circ. 80,000. Pays on publication. Offers 50% kill fee. Buys first and second rights. Submit seasonal/holiday material 6 months in advance. Previously published submissions OK. Send tearsheet or photocopy of article. Include information about when and where the article previously appeared. Query for electronic submissions. Reports in 1 month on queries. Sample copy for 9 × 12 SAE with 5 first class stamps. Writer's guidelines for #10 SASE.
Nonfiction: Book excerpts (cookbooks), how-to (cooking and gardening with spicy foods), humor (having to do with spicy foods), new product (hot products), travel (having to do with spicy foods). Buys 20 mss/year. Query. Length: 1,000-3,000 words. Pays $150 minimum for assigned articles; $100 for unsolicited articles. Sometimes pays expenses of writers on assignment.
Photos: State availability of photos with submission. Reviews contact sheets, negatives, transparencies and prints. Offers $25 minimum/photo. Captions and identification of subjects required. Buys one-time rights.
Fillers: Newsbreaks, short humor. Buys 5/year. Length: 100 minimum. Pays $25 minimum.
Tips: "We're always interested in queries from *food* writers. Articles about spicy foods with six to eight recipes are just right."

COOKING LIGHT, The Magazine of Food and Fitness, Southern Living, Inc. P.O. Box 1748, Birmingham AL 35201-1681. (205)877-6000. Editor: Katherine M. Eakin. Managing Editor: Deborah G. Lowery. 75% freelance written. Bimonthly magazine on healthy recipes and fitness information. "*Cooking Light* is a positive approach to a healthier lifestyle. It's written for healthy people on regular diets who are counting calories or trying to make calories count toward better nutrition. Moderation, balance and variety are emphasized. The writing style is fresh, upbeat and encouraging, emphasizing that eating a balanced, varied, lower-calorie diet and exercising regularly do not have to be boring." Estab. 1987. Circ. 1,000,000. **Pays on acceptance.** Publishes

For information on setting your freelance fees, see How Much Should I Charge?

ms an average of 1 year after acceptance. Byline sometimes given. Offers 25% of original contract fee as kill fee. Buys all rights. Submit seasonal/holiday material 1 year in advance. Reports in 1 year.

Nonfiction: Personal experience on nutrition, healthy recipes, fitness/exercise. Buys 150 mss/year. Query with published clips. Length: 400-2,000 words. Pays $250-2,000 for assigned articles. Pays expenses of writers on assignment.

Columns/Departments: Profile (an incident or event that occurred in one's life that resulted in a total lifestyle change), 1,400 words; Children's Fitness (emphasis on prevention and intervention in regard to fitness, exercise, nutrition), 1,200 words; Taking Aim (a personal account of progression from desire to obstacle to achievement for incorporating exercise into one's routine schedule), 1,800 words; and Downfall (a humorous personal account of desire to obstacle to the continuing struggle to overcome a particular food habit or addiction), 700 words. Buys 30 mss/year. Query. Pays $300-2,000.

Tips: "Emphasis should be on achieving a healthier lifestyle through food, nutrition, fitness, exercise information. In submitting queries, include information on professional background. Food writers should include examples of healthy recipes which meet the guidelines of *Cooking Light*."

‡**EATING WELL, The Magazine of Food and Health,** Telemedia Communications (U.S.) Inc., Ferry Rd., Charlotte VT 05445. (802)425-3961. Editor: Scott Mowbray. Food Editor: Susan Stuck. 90% freelance written. Bimonthly magazine covering food and health. Estab. 1989. Circ. 525,000. Pays 45 days after acceptance. Publishes ms an average of 6 months after acceptance. Byline given. Offers 25% kill fee. Buys first North American serial and second serial (reprint) rights. Submit seasonal/holiday material 1 year in advance. Reports in 2 months.

Nonfiction: Scott Mowbray. Book excerpts, nutrition, cooking, interview/profile, food and travel. Query with published clips. Length: 2,000-4,000 words. Pays $1,500-3,500. Pays expenses of writers on assignment.

Photos: State availability of photos with submission. Reviews transparencies. Offers $50-250 per photo. Captions and identification of subjects required. Buys one-time rights.

Columns/Departments: Allison Cleary. Nutrition Letter (timely nutrition research news), 150-400 words; and Observer (current news in the food world), 150-400 words. Buys 60 mss/year. Query. Pays $200-300.

Tips: "We invite experienced, published science writers to do a broad range of in-depth, innovative food-health-nutrition features. Read the magazine first."

FOOD & WINE, American Express Publishing Corp., 1120 Avenue of the Americas, New York NY 10036. (212)382-5618. Editor: Mary Simons. Managing Editor: Warren Picower. Monthly magazine for "active people for whom eating, drinking, entertaining, dining out, travel and all the related equipment and trappings are central to their lifestyle." Estab. 1978. Circ. 800,000. **Pays on acceptance.** Byline given. Offers 25% kill fee. Buys first world rights. Submit seasonal/holiday material 9 months in advance. Query for electronic submissions. Reports in 3 weeks on queries; 2 weeks on mss. Sample copy $3. Writer's guidelines for #10 SASE.

Nonfiction: Essays, how-to, humor, kitchen and dining room design, and travel. Query with published clips. Buys 125 mss/year. Length: 1,000-3,000 words. Pays $800-2,000. Pays expenses of writers on assignment.

Photos: State availability of photos with submission. No unsolicited photos or art. Offers $100-450 page rate per photo. Model releases and identification of subjects required. Buys one-time rights.

Columns/Departments: What's New, Dining Out, The Hungry Traveler, Cooking Wisdom. Buys 120 mss/year. Query with published clips. Length: 800-3,000 words. Pays $800-2,000.

Tips: "Good service, good writing, up-to-date information, interesting article approach and appropriate point of view for *F&W*'s audience are important elements to keep in mind. Look over several recent issues before writing query."

GOURMET, 560 Lexington Ave., New York NY 10022. "Prefers not to share information."

‡**JOURNAL OF ITALIAN FOOD & WINE,** Suite 77, 609 W. 114th St., New York NY 10025. Editor: Robert DiLallo. Managing Editor: J. Mimser Woggins. 50% freelance written. Bimonthly magazine/newletter. Estab. 1991. Circ. 5,500. Pays on publication. Publishes ms 2-4 months after acceptance. Byline given. Offers 25% kill fee or $100. Buys all rights. Editorial lead time 2-6 months. Submit seasonal material 4 months in advance. Simultaneous submissions OK. Query for electronic submissions. Reports in 2 weeks on queries; 2 months on mss. Sample copy $4. Writer's guidelines for #10 SASE.

Nonfiction: Book excerpts, essays, historical, how-to (cooking Italian), humor, interview/profile, new product, photo feature and travel. Special Christmas issue. "No first person, 'I remember when the smell of my mother's cooking came wafting into my room,' or 'ethnic' humor." Buys 12-18 mss/year. Query. Length: 500-2,500. Pays $350 minimum for assigned articles; $250 minimum for unsolicited articles. Sometimes pays expenses of writers on assignment.

Photos: Send photos with submission. Reviews 5×7 prints. Offers $35-200 but negotiates payment individually. Captions, model releases and identification of subjects required. Buys all rights.

Columns/Departments: J. Mimser Woggins, managing editor. Nota Bene (short, short on Italian food or wine ideas), 125-250 words. Buys 5-7 mss/year. Send complete ms. Pays $20-75.

Fiction: Ethnic, historical, slice-of-life vignettes. Buys 6 mss/year. Query. Length: 500-1,500 words. Pays $100-300.

Poetry: J. Mimser Woggins, managing editor. Facts, gags to be illustrated by cartoonist, short humor, cartoons. Buys 15/year. Length: 50-200 words. Pays $10-50.

Tips: "Writers should ignore *all* other food magazines. Articles should be long on hard facts and well-edited *before* we get them. It costs too much in human resources to edit the basics. And, don't try to recycle old material to us. It will be tossed back immediately."

KASHRUS MAGAZINE, The Bimonthly for the Kosher Consumer and the Trade, Yeshiva Birkas Reuven, P.O. Box 204, Parkville Station, Brooklyn NY 11204. (718)336-8544. Editor: Rabbi Yosef Wikler. 25% freelance written. Prefers to work with published/established writers, but will work with new/unpublished writers. Bimonthly magazine covering kosher food industry and food production. Estab. 1980. Circ. 10,000. Pays on publication. Publishes ms an average of 2 months after acceptance. Byline given. Offers 50% kill fee. Buys first or second serial (reprint) rights. Submit seasonal/holiday material 2 months in advance. Simultaneous and previously published submissions OK. Prefers submissions in major word processing programs on disk with accompanying hard copy. Reports in 1 week on queries; 2 weeks on mss. *Writer's Market* recommends allowing 2 months for reply. Sample copy $2. Professional discount on subscription: $15/10 issues (regularly $27).

Nonfiction: General interest, interview/profile, new product, personal experience, photo feature, religious, technical and travel. Special issues feature; International Kosher Travel (October) and Passover (March). Buys 8-12 mss/year. Query with published clips. Length: 1,000-1,500 words. Pays $100-250 for assigned articles; pays up to $100 for unsolicited articles. Sometimes pays the expenses of writers on assignment. Reprints OK; send tearsheet or photocopy of article. Pays 25% of their fee for an original article.

Photos: State availability of photos with submission. Offers no additional payment for photos accepted with ms. Buys one-time rights.

Columns/Departments: Book Review (cook books, food technology, kosher food), 250-500 words; People in the News (interviews with kosher personalities), 1,000-1,500 words; Regional Kosher Supervision (report on kosher supervision in a city or community), 1,000-1,500 words; Food Technology (new technology or current technology with accompanying pictures), 1,000-1,500 words; Travel (international, national), must include Kosher information and Jewish communities, 1,000-1,500 words; and Regional Kosher Cooking, 1,000-1,500 words.Buys 8-12 mss/year. Query with published clips. Pays $50-250.

Tips: "*Kashrus Magazine* will do more writing on general food technology, production, and merchandising as well as human interest travelogs and regional writing in 1993 than we have done in the past. Areas most open to freelancers are interviews, food technology, regional reporting and travel. We welcome stories on the availability and quality of Kosher foods and services in communities across the US and throughout the world. Some of our best stories have been by non-Jewish writers about kosher observance in their region."

‡VEGETARIAN GOURMET, Chitra Publications, 2 Public Ave., Montrose PA 18801. (717)278-1984. Editor: Jessica Dubey. 75% freelance written. Quarterly magazine on vegetarian cooking. "An entertaining and practical how-to guide to cooking food that is delicious and healthful." Estab. 1991. Circ. 75,000. Pays on publication. Publishes ms an average of 1-3 months after acceptance. Byline given. Kill fee offered "depending on price ordinarily paid for accepted ms." Buys one-time rights and second serial (reprint) rights. Submit seasonal material 5-6 months in advance. Query for electronic submissions. Reports in 3 weeks on queries; 6 weeks on mss. Sample copy free on request. Writer's guidelines for #10 SASE.

Nonfiction: How-to (cooking), book and restaurant reviews. "No previously published or nonvegetarian material; no articles not directly related to food or cooking." Buys approximately 40 mss/year. Send complete ms. Length: 400-1,000 words. Pays $175-250. Sometimes pays expenses of writers on assignment.

Photos: Send photos with submission. Reviews 2¼ transparencies. Offers $25-50/photo. Captions required. Buys one-time rights.

Columns/Departments: International fare (vegetarian cuisine of a foreign country), 800 words; desserts (vegetarian dessert made with natural sweeteners), 800 words; extraordinary vegetables (introduce one or more less familiar vegetables), 800 words; entertainment (unique ways of entertaining with vegetarian food), 800 words; VG visits (profile of a vegetarian restaurant), 500-700 words; cook for kids (fun ideas for vegetarian meals for kids), 400-600 words; fast foods (dishes that can be made quickly with a particular food), 400-500 words. Buys 40 mss/year. Send complete ms. Pays $75-250.

Tips: "Submit a completed ms along with recipe blurbs, photos (if available) and information on less familiar ingredients (what they are and how to obtain them). Include useful cooking tips and nutritional value of food(s) you are writing about. All departments open to freelance."

THE WINE SPECTATOR, M. Shanken Communications, Inc., Opera Plaza, Suite 2014, 601 Van Ness Ave., San Francisco CA 94102-3200. (415)673-2040. Managing Editor: Jim Gordon. 20% freelance written. Prefers to work with published/established writers. Biweekly consumer news magazine covering wine. Estab. 1976. Circ. 120,000. Pays within 30 days of publication. Publishes ms an average of 2 months after acceptance. Byline given. Buys all rights and makes work-for-hire assignments. Submit seasonal/holiday material 4 months in advance. Query for electronic submissions. Reports in 3 months. Sample copy $2.50. Free writer's guidelines.

Nonfiction: General interest (news about wine or wine events); interview/profile (of wine, vintners, wineries); opinion; and photo feature. No "winery promotional pieces or articles by writers who lack sufficient knowledge to write below just surface data." Query. Length: 100-2,000 words average. Pays $50-500.

Photos: Send photos with ms. Pays $75 minimum for color transparencies. Captions, model releases and identification of subjects required. Buys all rights.

Tips: "A solid knowledge of wine is a must. Query letters essential, detailing the story idea. New, refreshing ideas which have not been covered before stand a good chance of acceptance. *The Wine Spectator* is a consumer-oriented *news magazine* but we are interested in some trade stories; brevity is essential."

WINE TIDINGS, Kylix Media Inc., #414, 5165 Sherbrooke St. W., Montreal, Quebec H4A 1T6 Canada. (514)481-5892. Fax: (514)481-9699. Publisher: Judy Rochester. Editor: Barbara Leslie. 90% freelance written. Works with small number of new/unpublished writers each year. Magazine published 8 times/year primarily for men with incomes of more than $50,000. "Covers anything happening on the wine scene in Canada." Circ. 25,000. Pays on publication. Publishes ms an average of 3-4 months after acceptance. Byline given. Buys all rights. Submit seasonal/holiday material 3 months in advance. Reports in 1 month.

Nonfiction: General interest, historical, humor, interview/profile, new product (and developments in the Canadian and US wine industries), opinion, personal experience, photo feature and travel (to wine-producing countries). "All must pertain to wine or wine-related topics and should reflect author's basic knowledge of and interest in wine." Buys 20-30 mss/year. Send complete ms. Length: 500-1,200 words. Pays $35-300.

Photos: "Are usually only accepted with accompanying articles. Occasional cover photos if an outstanding wine shot."

Games and Puzzles

These publications are written by and for game enthusiasts interested in both traditional games and word puzzles and newer role-playing adventure, computer and video games. Additional home video game publications are listed in the Entertainment section. Other puzzle markets may be found in the Juvenile section.

bePUZZLED, Mystery Jigsaw Puzzles, 45 Wintonbury Ave., Bloomfield CT 06002. (203)286-4222. Editor: Mary Ann Lombard. Managing Editor: Luci Seccareccia. 100% freelance written. Mystery jigsaw puzzle using short mystery stories published 2-4 times/year. Covers mystery, suspense, adventure for children and adults. Estab. 1987. Pays on completion. Publishes ms an average of 9 months after acceptance. Byline given (sometimes pen name required). Buys all rights. Submit seasonal/holiday material 9 months in advance. Simultaneous submissions OK. Reports in 2 weeks on queries; 3 months on mss. Free writer's guidelines with SASE.

Fiction: Luci Seccareccia. Adventure, humorous, mainstream, mystery, and suspense (*exact* subject within genre above is released to writers as available.) Buys 10 mss/year. Query. Length: 3,500-5,500 words. Pays $250-2,000.

Fillers: "Writers must follow submission format as outlined in writer's guidelines. We incorporate short mystery stories and jigsaw puzzles into a game where the clues to solve the mystery are cleverly hidden in both the short story and the puzzle picture. Writer must be able to integrate the clues in the written piece to these to appear in puzzle picture. Playing one of our games helps to clarify how we like to 'marry' the story clues and the visual clues in the puzzle."

CHESS LIFE, United States Chess Federation, 186 Route 9W, New Windsor NY 12553-7698. (914)562-8350. Fax: (914)561-2437. Editor: Glenn Petersen. 15% freelance written. Works with a small number of new/unpublished writers each year. Monthly magazine covering the chess world. Estab. 1939. Circ. 70,000. Pays variable fee. Publishes ms an average of 5 months after acceptance. Byline given. Offers kill fee. Buys first or negotiable rights. Submit seasonal/holiday material 8 months in advance. Simultaneous queries, and simultaneous and previously published submissions OK. Reports in 3 months. Sample copy and writer's guidelines for 9 × 11 SAE with 5 first class stamps.

Nonfiction: General interest, historical, interview/profile and technical—all must have some relation to chess. No "stories about personal experiences with chess." Buys 30-40 mss/year. Query with samples "if new to publication." Length: 3,000 words maximum. Sometimes pays the expenses of writers on assignment. Reprints OK; send typed ms with rights for sale noted and information about when and where the article previously appeared.

Photos: Reviews b&w contact sheets and prints, and color prints and slides. Captions, model releases and identification of subjects required. Buys all or negotiable rights.

Fiction: "Chess-related, high quality." Buys 2-3 mss/year. Pays variable fee.

Tips: "Articles must be written from an informed point of view—not from view of the curious amateur. Most of our writers are specialized in that they have sound credentials as chessplayers. Freelancers in major population areas (except New York and Los Angeles, which we already have covered) who are interested in short personality profiles and perhaps news reporting have the best opportunities. We're looking for more personality pieces on chessplayers around the country; not just the stars, but local masters, talented youths, and dedicated volunteers. Freelancers interested in such pieces might let us know of their interest and their range. Could be we know of an interesting story in their territory that needs covering."

COMPUTER GAMING WORLD, The Premier Computer Game Magazine, Golden Empire Publications, Inc., #260, 130 Chaparral Court, Anaheim CA 92808-2238. (714)283-3000. Fax: (714)283-3444. Editor: Johnny Wilson. 75% freelance written. Works with a small number of new/unpublished writers each year. Monthly magazine covering computer games. "*CGW* is read by an adult audience looking for detailed reviews and information on strategy, adventure and action games." Estab. 1981. Circ. 105,000. Pays on publication. Publishes ms an average of 3 months after acceptance. Byline given. Buys first rights. Submit seasonal/holiday material 4 months in advance. Electronic submissions preferred, but not required. Query first. Reports in 1 month. Sample copy $3.50. Free writer's guidelines.

Nonfiction: Reviews, strategy tips, industry insights. Buys 60 mss/year. Query. Length: 500-3,500 words. Pays $50-300. Sometimes pays the expenses of writers on assignment.

DRAGON MAGAZINE, TSR, Inc., P.O. Box 111, 201 Sheridan Springs Rd., Lake Geneva WI 53147-0111. (414)248-3625. Fax: (414)248-0389. Editor: Roger E. Moore. Associate Editor: Dale Donovan. Monthly magazine of fantasy and science-fiction role-playing games. 90% freelance written. Eager to work with published/established writers as well as new/unpublished writers. "Most of our readers are intelligent, imaginative teenage males." Estab. 1976. Circ. about 100,000, primarily across the United States, Canada and Great Britain. Byline given. Offers kill fee. Submit seasonal/holiday material 8 months in advance. Pays on publication for articles to which all rights are purchased; pays on acceptance for articles to which first/worldwide rights in English are purchased. Publishing dates vary from 1-24 months after acceptance. Sample copy $4.50. Writer's guidelines for #10 SAE with 1 first-class stamp or IRC.

Nonfiction: Articles on the hobby of science fiction and fantasy role-playing. No general articles on gaming hobby. "Our article needs are *very* specialized. Writers should be experienced in gaming hobby and role-playing. No strong sexual overtones or graphic depictions of violence." Buys 120 mss/year. Query. Length: 1,000-8,000 words. Pays $50-500 for assigned articles; $5-400 for unsolicited articles.

Fiction: Barbara G. Young, fiction editor. Fantasy only. "No strong sexual overtones or graphic depictions of violence." Buys 12 mss/year. Send complete ms. Length: 2,000-8,000 words. Pays 6-8¢/word.

Tips: "*Dragon Magazine* is *not* a periodical that the 'average reader' appreciates or understands. A writer must *be* a reader and must share the serious interest in gaming our readers possess."

‡GAME INFORMER MAGAZINE, for Video Game Enthusiasts, Sunrise Publications, 10120 West 76th St., Eden Prairie MN 55344. (612)946-7245. Editor: Elizabeth Olson. 10% freelance written. Bimonthly magazine for video game industry. Estab. 1991. Circ. 200,000. Pays on publication. Publishes ms an average of 3 months after acceptance. Byline given. Offers 50% kill fee. Buys first and one-time rights. Editorial lead time 3 months. Submit seasonal material 3-4 months in advance. Simultaneous submissions OK. Query for electronic submissions. Sample copy and writer's guidelines free on request.

Nonfiction: Essays, general interest, historical/nostalgic, how-to, interview/profile, new product, opinion, technical, game strategies. Publishes year-end tip and strategy guide (deadline mid-October). No game reviews. Buys 4 mss/year. Query with published clips. Length: 500-2,000 words. Pays $50 for assigned articles.

Photos: State availability of photos with submission. Reviews 2 × 2 transparencies and 3 × 5 prints. Negotiates payment individually. Identification of subjects required. Buys one-time rights.

Columns/Departments: Query. Pays $25-150.

Fillers: Facts, gags to be illustrated by cartoonist, newsbreaks. Buys 6/year. Length negotiable. Pay negotiable.

Tips: "We appreciate queries prior to manuscript submissions, as we prefer to assign articles or discuss them first. It is best to call with one or two story ideas in mind. We are a very topic-specific publication and look for writers with expertise in a given area. However, the writing style must be open and appeal to a broad age range. We often look for special interest or focus articles on a given aspect of the very dynamic industry that we cover. Technical hardware features or company profiles are also welcome."

GIANT CROSSWORDS, Scrambl-Gram, Inc., Puzzle Buffs International, 1772 State Road, Cuyahoga Falls OH 44223. (216)923-2397. Editor: C.R. Elum. 40% freelance written. Eager to work with new/unpublished writers. Quarterly crossword puzzle and word game magazine. Estab. 1970. **Pays on acceptance.** Publishes ms an average of 1 month after acceptance. No byline given. Buys all rights. Simultaneous queries OK. Reports in 1 month. "We offer constructors' kits, master grids, clue sheets and a 'how-to-make-crosswords' book for $37.50 postpaid." Send #10 SASE for details.
Nonfiction: Crosswords and word games only. Query. Pays according to size of puzzle and/or clues.
Tips: "We are expanding our syndication of original crosswords and our publishing schedule to include new titles and extra issues of current puzzle books."

‡**SCHOOL MATES**, United States Chess Federation, 186 Rte. 9W, New Windsor NY 12586. (914)562-8350. Editor: Jennie L. Simon. Contact: Beverly Byrne, editorial assistant. 10% freelance written. Bimonthly magazine of chess for the beginning (some intermediate) player. Includes instruction, player profiles, chess tournament coverage; listings. Estab. 1987. Circ. 13,800. Pays on publication. Publishes ms an average of 6 months after acceptance. Byline given. Publication copyrighted "but not filed with Library of Congress." Buys first rights. Editorial lead time 2 months. Submit seasonal material 2-3 months in advance. Accepts simultaneous submissions. Query for electronic submissions. Reports in "anywhere from 1 week to 6 months." Sample copy and writer's guidelines free on request.
Nonfiction: How-to, humor, personal experience (chess, but not "my first tournament"), photo feature, technical, travel and any other chess related item. "No poetry; no fiction; no sex, drugs, rock'n'roll." Buys 1-2 mss/year. Query. Length: 250-1,000 words. Pays $40/1,000 words. "We are not-for-profit; we try to make up for low payment rate with complimentary copies." Sometimes pays expenses of writers on assignment.
Photos: Send photos with submission. Reviews prints. Offers $25/photo for first time rights. Captions and identification of subjects required. Buys one-time rights, pays $15 for subsequent use.
Columns/Departments: Test Your Tactics/Winning Chess Tactics (explanation, with diagrams, of chess tactics; 8 diagrammed chess problems, e.g., "white to play and win in 2 moves"), 270 words; Basic Chess (chess instruction for beginners). Query with published clips. Pays $40/1,000 words.
Tips: "Know your subject; chess is technical and you can't fake it. Human interest stories on famous chess players or young chess players can be 'softer,' but always remember you are writing for children, and make it lively. We use the Frye readability scale (3rd-6th grade reading level), and items written on the appropriate reading level do stand out immediately! We are most open to human interest stories, puzzles, cartoons, photos. We are always looking for an unusual angle, e.g., (wild example) a kid who plays chess while surfing, or (more likely) a blind kid and how she plays chess with her specially-made chess pieces and board, etc."

General Interest

General interest magazines need writers who can appeal to a broad audience—teens and senior citizens, wealthy readers and the unemployed. Each magazine still has a personality that suits its audience—one that a writer should study before sending material to an editor. Other markets for general interest material are in these Consumer categories: Ethnic/Minority, Inflight, Men's, Regional and Women's. General interest magazines that are geared toward a specific group (such as doctors) are listed in Trade in their respective sections.

AMERICAN ATHEIST, American Atheist Press, P.O. Box 140195, Austin TX 78714-0195. (512)458-1244. Editor: R. Murray-O'Hair. Managing Editor: Jon Garth Murray. 20-40% freelance written. Quarterly magazine covering atheism and topics related to it and separation of State and Church. Estab.1959. Circ. 50,000. Publishes ms an average of 6 months after acceptance. Byline given. Buys one-time and all rights. Submit seasonal/holiday material 3 months in advance. Simultaneous queries and simultaneous and previously published submissions OK. Query for electronic submissions. Reprints OK; send typed ms with rights for sale noted and information about when and where the article previously appeared. Reports in 2 months on queries; 3 months on mss. Publishes ms an average of 6 months after acceptance. Sample copy and writer's guidelines for 9×12 SASE.
Nonfiction: Book excerpts, expose, general interest, historical, how-to, humor, interview/profile, opinion, personal experience and photo feature, but only as related to State/Church or atheism. "We receive a great many Bible criticism articles—and publish very few. We would advise writers not to send in such works. We are also interested in fiction with an atheistic slant." Buys 15 mss/year. Send complete ms. Length: 400-10,000 words. Pays in free subscription or 15 copies for first-time authors. Repeat authors paid $15/1,000 words. Sometimes pays the expenses of writers on assignment.

Columns/Departments: Atheism, Church/State separation, book reviews and humor. Send complete ms. Length: 400-10,000 words.

Poetry: Avant-garde, free verse, haiku, light verse and traditional. Submit unlimited poems. Length: open. Pays $10 per thousand words maximum.

Fillers: Jokes, short humor and newsbreaks. Length: 800 words maximum, only as related to State/Church separation or atheism.

Tips: "We are primarily interested in subjects which bear directly on atheism or issues of interest and importance to atheists. This includes articles on the atheist lifestyle, on problems that confront atheists, the history of atheism, personal experiences of atheists, separation of state and church, theopolitics and critiques of atheism in general and of particular religions. We are starting to have issues which focus on lifestyle topics relevant to atheism. We would like to receive more articles on current events and lifestyle issues."

THE AMERICAN LEGION MAGAZINE, P.O. Box 1055, Indianapolis IN 46206-1055. (317)635-8411. Editor: John Greenwald. Monthly. 95% freelance written. Prefers to work with published/established writers, but works with a small number of new/unpublished writers each year. Estab. 1919. Circ. 2.9 million. Buys first North American serial rights. Reports on submissions "promptly." **Pays on acceptance.** Publishes ms an average of 6 months after acceptance. Byline given. Sample copy for 9 × 12 SAE with 6 first class stamps. Writer's guidelines for #10 SASE.

• Ranked as one of the best markets for freelance writers in *Writer's Digest* magazine's annual "Top 100 Markets," January 1993.

Nonfiction: Query first, considers some unsolicited ms. Query should explain the subject or issue, article's angle and organization, writer's qualifications and experts to be interviewed. Well-reported articles or expert commentaries cover issues/trends in world/national affairs, contemporary problems, general interest, sharply-focused feature subjects. Monthly Q&A with national figures/experts. Few personality profiles. No regional topics. Buys 75 mss/year. Length: 1,000-2,000 words. Pays $600-2,000. Pays phone expenses of writers on assignment.

Photos: On assignment.

Tips: "Queries by new writers should include clips/background/expertise; no longer than 1½ pages. Submit suitable material showing you have read several issues. *The American Legion Magazine* considers itself 'the magazine for a strong America.' Reflect this theme (which includes economy, educational system, moral fiber, social issues, infrastructure, technology and national defense/security). We are a general interest, national magazine, not a strictly military magazine. No unsolicited jokes."

THE AMERICAN SCHOLAR, The Phi Beta Kappa Society, 1811 Q Street NW, Washington DC 20009-9974. (202)265-3808. Editor: Joseph Epstein. Managing Editor: Jean Stipicevic. 100% freelance written. Intellectual quarterly. "Our writers are specialists writing for the college educated public." Estab. 1932. Circ. 26,000. Pays after author has seen edited piece in galleys. Byline given. Offers 50% kill fee. Buys first rights. Submit seasonal/holiday material 6 months in advance. Reports in 2 weeks on queries; 2 months on ms. Sample copy $5.75. Writer's guidelines for #10 SASE.

Nonfiction: Book excerpts (prior to publication only), essays, historical/nostalgic, humor. Buys 40 mss/year. Query. Length: 3,000-5,000 words. Pays $500.

Columns/Departments: Buys 16 mss/year. Query. Length: 3,000-5,000 words. Pays $500.

Poetry: Sandra Costich, poetry editor. Buys 20/year. Submit maximum 3 poems. Length: 34-75 lines. Pays $50. "Write for guidelines."

Tips: "The section most open to freelancers is the book review section. Query and send samples of reviews written."

THE ATLANTIC, 745 Boylston St., Boston MA 02116. (617)536-9500. Editor: William Whitworth. Managing Editor: Cullen Murphy. Monthly magazine of arts and public affairs. Circ. 470,000. Pays on publication. Byline given. Buys first North American serial rights. Simultaneous submissions discouraged. Reporting time varies. All unsolicited mss must be accompanied by SASE.

Nonfiction: Book excerpts, essays, general interest, humor, personal experience, religious and travel. Query with or without published clips or send complete ms. Length: 1,000-6,000 words. Payment varies. Sometimes pays expenses of writers on assignment.

Fiction: C. Michael Curtis, fiction editor. Buys 15-18 mss/year. Send complete ms. Length: 2,000-6,000 words preferred. Payment varies.

Poetry: Peter Davison, poetry editor. Buys 40-60 poems/year.

• Writers should be aware that this is not a market for beginner's work (nonfiction and fiction), nor is it truly a market for intermediate work. Study this market before sending only your best, most professional work.

A BETTER LIFE FOR YOU, The National Research Bureau, Inc., 424 N. 3rd St., P.O. Box 1, Burlington IA 52601-0001. (319)752-5415. Fax: (319)752-3421. Editor: Nancy Heinzel. Editorial Supervisor: Doris J. Ruschill. 75% freelance written. Works with a small number of new/unpublished writers each year. Quarterly magazine. Estab. 1948. Pays on publication. Publishes ms an average of 1 year after acceptance. Buys all

rights. Submit seasonal/holiday material 7 months in advance of issue date. Previously published submissions OK. Sample copy and writer's guidelines for #10 SAE with 2 first class stamps.
Nonfiction: General interest (steps to better health, on-the-job attitudes); and how-to (perform better on the job, do home repair jobs, and keep up maintenance on a car). Buys 10-12 mss/year. Query or send outline. Length: 500-700 words. Pays 4¢/word.
Tips: "Writers have a better chance of breaking in at our publication with short articles."

CAPPER'S, Stauffer Communications, Inc., 1503 SW 42nd St., Topeka KS 66609-1265. (913)295-1108. Fax: (913)274-4305. Editor: Nancy Peavler. 25% freelance written. Works with a small number of new/unpublished writers each year. Biweekly tabloid emphasizing home and family for readers who live in small towns and on farms. Estab. 1879. Circ. 375,000. **Pays for poetry on acceptance;** articles on publication. Publishes ms an average of 6 months after acceptance. Buys first serial rights only. Submit seasonal/holiday material at least 2 months in advance. Reports in 3-4 months; 8-10 months for serialized novels. Sample copy 85¢. Writer's guidelines for #10 SASE.
Nonfiction: Historical (local museums, etc.), inspirational, nostalgia, travel (local slants) and people stories (accomplishments, collections, etc.). Buys 50 mss/year. Submit complete ms. Length: 700 words maximum. Pays $1.50/inch.
Photos: Purchased with accompanying ms. Submit prints. Pays $10-15 for 8×10 or 5×7 b&w glossy prints. Total purchase price for ms includes payment for photos. Limited market for color photos (35mm color slides); pays $30-40 each.
Columns/Departments: Heart of the Home (homemakers' letters, recipes, hints) and Hometown Heartbeat (descriptive). Submit complete ms. Length: 300 words maximum. Pays $1-7.
Fiction: "We buy very few fiction pieces—longer than short stories, shorter than novels." Adventure and romance mss. No explicit sex, violence or profanity. Buys 4-5 mss/year. Query. Pays $75-400 for 7,500-60,000 words.
Poetry: Free verse, haiku, light verse, traditional, nature and inspiration. "The poems that appear in *Capper's* are not too difficult to read. They're easy to grasp. We're looking for everyday events and down-to-earth themes." Buys 4-5/issue. Limit submissions to batches of 5-6. Length: 4-16 lines. Pays $5-10.
Tips: "Study a few issues of our publication. Most rejections are for material that is too long, unsuitable or out of character for our paper (too sexy, too much profanity, etc.). On occasion, we must cut material to fit column space."

THE CHRISTIAN SCIENCE MONITOR, 1 Norway St., Boston MA 02115. (617)450-2000. Contact: Submissions. International newspaper issued daily except Saturdays, Sundays and holidays in North America; weekly international edition. Circ. 110,000. Buys all newspaper rights worldwide for 3 months following publication. Buys limited number of mss, "top quality only." Publishes original (exclusive) material only. Pays on publication. Reports in 1 month. Submit complete original ms or letter of inquiry. Writer's guidelines for #10 SASE.
Nonfiction: Lawrence J. Goodrich, feature editor. In-depth features and essays. Please query by mail before sending mss. "Style should be bright but not cute, concise but thoroughly researched. Try to humanize news or feature writing so reader identifies with it. Avoid sensationalism, crime and disaster. Accent constructive, solution-oriented treatment of subjects." Home Forum page buys essays of 400-900 words. Pays $150 average. Education, people, books, food and science pages will consider articles not usually more than 800 words appropriate to respective subjects." Pays $150-200.
Poetry: Traditional, blank and free verse. Seeks non-religious poetry of high quality and of all lengths up to 75 lines. Pays $35-75 average.
Tips: "We prefer neatly typed originals. No handwritten copy. Enclosing an SAE and postage with ms is a must."

‡DESTINATION DISCOVERY The Magazine of the Discovery Channel, Discovery Publishing, Inc., 7700 Wisconsin Ave., Bethesda MD 20814. Editor: Rebecca Farwell. Managing Editor: Kathy H. Ely. Contact: Mike Carlewicz, Assistant Editor. 95% freelance written. Monthly magazine of general interest, inspired by television network. Estab. 1985. Circ. 200,000+. **Pays on acceptance.** Byline given. Offers 20% kill fee. Buys first North American serial rights. Editorial lead time 6 months. Simultaneous submissions OK. Query for electronic submissions. Prefers Microsoft Word or IBM Wordperfect. Reports in 2 months. Sample copy $2.50. Writer's guidelines free on request.
Nonfiction: Essays, expose, general interest, historical/nostalgic, interview/profile, personal experience, photo feature and travel. No poetry, fiction, humor, how-to articles or travelogues. Buys 100+ mss/year. Query with published clips. Length: 400-4,000 words. Pays 25¢/word minimum. "Variable w/experience and reporting." Sometimes pays expenses of writers on assignment (limit agreed upon in advance).
Photos: State availability of photos with submission. Reviews contact sheets, negatives, transparencies and prints. Negotiates payment individually. Identification of subjects required. Buys one-time rights.
Columns/Departments: Gary Parker, Associate Editor. Green Alert (environmental), 900 words; and Eureka! (science discoveries), 900 words. Buys 30+ mss/year. Query with published clips. Pays $400-900.
Tips: "All areas are open to freelancers, though newcomers usually start in our 'There & Back section, or on one of our columns."

DIVERSION, Hearst Professional Management, 60 E. 42nd St., New York NY 10165. All writing is commissioned. "Prefers not to share information."

‡**DOWN MEMORY LANE, Real People, Real Photographs, Real Memories**, 3816 Industry Blvd., Lakeland FL 33811. Editor: Lisa Ludy. Managing Editor: Adrian Hoff. Contact: Adrian Hoff. 80% freelance written. Bimonthly magazine of nostalgia. Estab. 1992. Circ. 35,000. Pays on publication. Publishes ms an average of 8 months after acceptance. Byline given. Offers 25% kill fee. Buys one-time, second serial (reprint) or simultaneous rights (in a non-competing market). Editorial lead time 5 months. Submit seasonal material 6 months in advance. Accepts previously published submissions. Reports in 3-4 months on mss. Sample copy $1.65 for 9×12 SAE. Writer's guidelines only available with sample copy.
Nonfiction: Essays, historical/nostalgic, humor, interview/profile, opinion, personal experience and photo feature. Special holiday issues include: Thanksgiving/Christmas, Easter, Grandparents Day, Mother's Day, Father's Day, Halloween and annual Summer Vacation issue. "Nothing without an obvious 30s to 60s focus. No drinking, smoking, sexcapades." Buys 175 mss/year. Send complete ms. Length: 75-800 words. Pays $75/published page. Sometimes pays expenses of writers on assignment (limit agreed upon in advance).
Photos: State availability of photos with submission. Reviews 35mm and larger transparencies and any size prints. Offers no additional payment for photos accepted with ms (included in page rate). Captions and identification of subjects required. Buys one-time rights.
Columns/Departments: Childhood Treasures (vintage toys, 30s thru 60s), pictorials/100 word lead paragraph with cutlines); For What It's Worth (mainstream collectibles (30s thru 60s), pictorials/100 word lead paragraph with cutlines); Photographs & Memories (vintage photos with brief first person anecdote), 50-150 words. Buys 50 mss/year. Send complete ms. Pays $75-125 (per page, depending on number of published pages).
Fillers: "Pictures a must." Anecdotes and short humor. Buys 200/year. Length: 50-150 words. Pays $25-75.
Tips: "We rarely buy manuscripts without pictures. Submitting material without reading the magazine is a waste of your time and ours. We will be glad to send a sample copy with guidelines for a 9×12 SASE with $1.65 postage. Due to a substantial backlog of feature-length manuscripts, we rarely purchase articles longer than 750 words. Manuscripts must be double spaced and typed on plain white paper. *First page* of manuscript should include name, address, daytime phone number and social security number. Pictures should be accompanied by basic cutline information, i.e. who, what, where, when. All sections and departments are open to freelancers. 'Photographs and Memories' offers best chance of acceptance."

EQUINOX: THE MAGAZINE OF CANADIAN DISCOVERY, Telemedia Communications, Inc., 7 Queen Victoria Rd., Camden East, Ontario K0K 1J0 Canada. (613)378-6661. Editor: Bart Robinson. Associate Editor: Jody Morgan. Bimonthly magazine "publishing in-depth profiles of people, places and wildlife to show readers the real stories behind subjects of general interest in the fields of science and geography." Estab. 1982. Circ. 175,000. **Pays on acceptance.** Byline given. Offers 50% kill fee. Buys first North American serial rights only. Submit seasonal queries 1 year in advance. Reports in 2 months. Sample copy $5 for #10 SAE with 48¢ Canadian postage. Writer's guidelines for #10 SASE.
Nonfiction: Book excerpts (occasionally), geography, science, art, natural history and environment. No travel articles. Buys 40 mss/year. Query. "Our biggest need is for science stories. We do not touch unsolicited feature manuscripts." Length: 5,000-10,000 words. Pays $1,750-3,000 negotiated.
Photos: Send photos with ms. Reviews color transparencies—must be of professional quality; no prints or negatives. Captions and identification of subjects required.
Columns/Departments: Nexus (current science that isn't covered by daily media) and Habitat (Canadian environmental stories not covered by daily media). Buys 80 mss/year. Query with clips of published work. Length: 200-800 words. Pays $250-500.
Tips: "Submit Habitat and Nexus ideas to us—the *only* route to a feature is through these departments if writers are untried."

FRIENDLY EXCHANGE, Meredith Publishing Services, 1912 Grand Ave., Des Moines IA 50309-3379. Publication Office: (515)284-2008. Editor: (702)786-7419. Editor: Adele Malott. 80% freelance written. Works with a small number of new/unpublished writers each year. Quarterly magazine for policyholders of Farmers Insurance Group of Companies exploring travel and leisure topics of interest to active families. "These are traditional families (median adult age 39) who live primarily in the area bounded by Ohio on the east and the Pacific Ocean on the west. New states added recently include Tennessee, Alabama, and Virginia." Estab. 1981. Circ. 5.6 million. **Pays on acceptance.** Publishes ms an average of 5 months after acceptance. Offers 25% kill fee. Buys all rights. Submit seasonal/holiday material 1 year in advance. Simultaneous queries OK. Query for electronic submissions. Reports in 2 months. Sample copy for 9×12 SAE with 5 first class stamps. Writer's guidelines for #10 SASE.
 • Ranked as one of the best markets for freelance writers in *Writer's Digest* magazine's annual "Top 100 Markets," January 1993.
Nonfiction: "Domestic travel and leisure topics of interest to the family can be addressed from many different perspectives, including health and safety, consumerism, heritage and education. Articles offer a service to readers and encourage them to take some positive action such as taking a trip. Style is colorful,

warm and inviting, making liberal use of anecdotes and quotes. The only first-person articles used are those assigned; all others in third person. Only domestic travel locations are considered. Buys 8 mss/issue. Query. Length: 600-1,800 words. Pays $300-800/article, plus agreed-upon expenses.

Photos: Jann Williams, art director. Pays $150-250 for 35mm color transparencies; and $50 for b&w prints. Cover photo payment negotiable. Pays on publication.

Columns/Departments: All columns and departments rely on reader-generated materials; none used from professional writers.

Tips: "We concentrate exclusively on the travel and leisure hours of our readers. Do not use destination approach in travel pieces—instead, for example, tell us about the people, activities, or events that make the location special. We prefer to go for a small slice rather than the whole pie, and we are just as interested in the cook who made it or the person who will be eating it as we are in the pie itself. Concentrate on what families can do together."

FUTURIFIC MAGAZINE, 150 Haven Ave., New York NY 10032. (212)297-0502. Editor-in-Chief: Balint Szent-Miklosy. 50-75% freelance written. Monthly. "Futurific, Inc. 'Foundation for Optimism,' is an independent, nonprofit organization set up in 1976 to study the future, and *Futurific Magazine* is its monthly report on findings. We report on what is coming in all areas of life from international affairs to the arts and sciences. Readership cuts across all income levels and includes leadership, in all areas of society." Estab. 1976. Circ. 10,000. Pays on publication. Publishes ms an average of 1 month after acceptance. Byline given in most cases. Buys one-time rights and will negotiate reprints. Reports within 1 month. Sample copy $5 for 9×12 SAE with 4 first class stamps. Writer's guidelines for #10 SASE.

Nonfiction: "All subjects must deal with the future: book, movie, theater and software reviews, general interest, how to forecast the future—seriously, humor, interview/profile, new product, photo feature and technical. *No historical, how-to, opinion or gloom and doom.*" Send complete ms. Length: 5,000 words maximum. Payment negotiable.

Photos: Send photos with ms. Reviews b&w prints. Pay negotiable. Identification of subjects required.

Columns/Departments: Medical breakthroughs, new products, inventions, book, movie, theater and software reviews, etc. "Anything that is new or about to be new." Send complete ms. Length: 5,000 words maximum.

Poetry: Avant-garde, free verse, haiku, light verse and traditional. "Must deal with the future. No gloom and doom or sad poetry." Buys 6/year. Submit unlimited number of poems. Length: open. Pays in copies.

Fillers: Clippings, jokes, gags, anecdotes, short humor, and newsbreaks. "Must deal with the future." Length: open. Pays in copies.

Tips: "It's not who you are, it's what you have to say that counts with us. We seek to maintain a light-hearted, professional look at forecasting. Be upbeat and *show a loving expectation for the marvels of human achievement*. Take any subject or concern you find in regular news magazines and extrapolate as to what the future will be. Use imagination. Get involved in the excitement of the international developments, social interaction. *Write the solution*—not the problem."

GRIT, America's Family Magazine, Stauffer Magazine Group, 1503 SW 42nd St., Topeka KS 66609-1265. (913)274-4300. Editor-in-Chief: Roberta J. Peterson (*not* Robert). 60% freelance written. Open to new writers. "*Grit* is Good News. As a wholesome, family-oriented magazine published for more than a century and distributed nationally. *Grit* is characterized by old-fashioned friendliness. *Grit*'s goal is to offer helpful and uplifting information in an appealing, interesting and readable manner. Our readers cherish family values and appreciate practical and innovative ideas. Many of them live in small town and rural areas across the country; others live in cities but share many of the values typical of small-town America. Estab. 1882. Circ. 400,000. Pays on publication. Publishes ms an average of 3 months after acceptance. Byline given. Buys first rights or makes work-for-hire assignments. Occasionally buys reprint rights if first publication was to extremely local or regional audience. Submit seasonal material 8 months in advance. Reports in 6 weeks on queries. Sample copy and writer's guidelines $2 for 11×14 SAE with 4 first class stamps.

Nonfiction: Most in need of cover stories (timely, newsworthy, but with a *Grit* angle); *Grit* People, Americana and human interest features, Home, Consumer, Health and Family and Friends stories. Each of these represents a specific department in the magazine; writers will best be able to successfully sell their work by becoming familiar with the publication. Pays 22¢ for *published* word for assigned articles (average $250-300 for a feature, more with photos), less for unsolicited mss or reprints. Main features run 1,000 to 1,500 words; department features average 800-1,000 words.

Fiction: Short stories, 2,500 words; may also purchase accompanying art if of high quality and appropriate. Send complete ms with SASE.

Photos: Professional quality photos (color slides) increase acceptability of articles. Black and white prints *required* with *Grit* People submissions. Photos: $40-175 each, dependent on quality, placement and color/b&w.

Tips: "With the exception of *Grit* People submissions, articles should be nationalized with several sources identified fully. Third-person accounts are preferred. Information in sidebar or graphic form is appropriate for many stories. *Grit* readers enjoy lists of tips, resources, or questions that help them understand the topic, for example, 5 ways to ... *Grit* stories should be helpful and conversational with an upbeat approach. Preferred to queries: Submit a list of brief but developed story ideas by department/feature along with a brief bio and examples of your published work."

HARPER'S MAGAZINE, 11th Floor, 666 Broadway, New York NY 10012. (212)614-6500. Fax: (212)228-5889. Editor: Lewis H. Lapham. 40% freelance written. Monthly magazine for well-educated, socially concerned, widely read men and women who value ideas and good writing. Estab. 1850. Circ. 205,000. Rights purchased vary with author and material. Publishes reprints of previously published articles. Send tearsheet or photocoy of article, or typed ms with rights for sale noted. Include information about when and where the article previously appeared. Pays negotiable kill fee. **Pays on acceptance.** Reports in 2 weeks. Publishes ms an average of 3 months after acceptance. Sample copy $2.95.
Nonfiction: "For writers working with agents or who will query first only, our requirements are: public affairs, literary, international and local reporting and humor." No interviews; no profiles. Complete ms and query must include SASE. No unsolicited poems will be accepted. Publishes one major report per issue. Length: 4,000-6,000 words. Publishes one major essay/issue. Length: 4,000-6,000 words. "These should be construed as topical essays on all manner of subjects (politics, the arts, crime, business, etc.) to which·the author can bring the force of passionately informed statement."
Fiction: Publishes one short story/month. Generally pays 50¢-$1/word.
Photos: Deborah Rust, Art Director. Occasionally purchased with mss; others by assignment. Pays $50-500.
   • Ranked as one of the best markets for freelance writers in *Writer's Digest* magazine's annual "Top 100 Markets," January 1993.

IDEALS MAGAZINE, Ideals Publishing, P.O. Box 140300, 565 Marriott Dr., Nashville TN 37214. (615)885-8270. Editor: Tim Hamling. 95% freelance written. Published 8 times a year. "Our readers are generally women over 50. The magazine is mainly light poetry and short articles with a nostalgic theme. Issues are seasonally oriented and thematic." Pays on publication. Publishes ms an average of 1 year after acceptance. Byline given. Buys one-time, North American serial and subsidiary rights. Submit seasonal/holiday material 8 months in advance. Simultaneous and previously published submissions OK. Send tearsheet or photocopy of article or short story and information about when and where the article previously appeared. Pays 100% of their fee for an original article. Reports in 3 months. Sample copy $3. Writer's guidelines for #10 SASE.
Nonfiction: Essays, historical/nostalgic, humor, inspirational and personal experience. "No down-beat articles or social concerns." Buys 20 mss/year. Query with or without published clips or send complete ms. Length: 500-800 words. Pays 10¢/word.
Photos: Send SASE for guidelines. Reviews transparencies and b&w prints. Offers no additional payment for photos accepted with ms. Captions, model releases and identification of subjects required. Buys one-time rights. Payment varies.
Fiction: Slice-of-life vignettes. Buys 10 mss/year. Query. Length: 500-800 words. Pays 10¢/word.
Poetry: Light verse and traditional. "No erotica or depressing poetry." Buys 250/year. Submit maximum 15 poems. Pays $10.
Tips: "Poetry is the area of our publication most open to freelancers. It must be oriented around a season or theme. The basic subject of *Ideals* is nostalgia, and poetry must be optimistic (how hard work builds character—not how bad the Depression was)."

‡KATY'S KAB, where cab driving becomes art form, Katy's Kab Publications, P.O. Box 3031, Anaheim CA 92801-3031. (714)935-1714. Editor: Katy Oviatt. Editorial contact: Noel Clancy, associate editor. 90% freelance written. Monthly magazine for taxicab drivers and passengers. Estab. 1992. Circ. 500. **Pays on acceptance.** Publishes ms an average of 2 months after acceptance. Byline given. Offers 50% kill fee; negotiable. "Copyright pending as of 3/13/93." Buys rights upon prior agreement or all rights. Editorial lead time 2-4 months. Submit seasonal material 6 months in advance. Simultaneous and previously published submissions OK. Reports in 2 months. Sample copy $2. Writer's guidelines for #10 SASE.
Nonfiction: Katy Oviatt, managing editor. Book excerpts, general interest, historical/nostalgic, how-to (self-protection, customer service, improve "people" skills, public service, handle difficult passengers, prevent drunk drivers), humor, inspirational, interview/profile, new product (taxi related), opinion, personal experience, photo feature, travel, consumer advice, "in memoriam", "cabbies who make a difference." "April is 'dispatcher appreciation'; May is 'peace officer appreciation'; November is 'customer appreciation'; and the usual seasonal events." No lengthy pieces. Buys 24-36 mss/year. Send complete ms. Length: 200-2,000 words. Pays $5-50. Pays contributor's copies upon request.
Photos: Send photos with submission. "Prefer 5×7 or smaller, any up to 8×10 prints; b&w works best." Offers no additional payment for photos accepted with ms. Negotiates payment individually. Captions, model releases, and identification of subjects required. Buys all rights unless otherwise negotiated.
Columns/Departments: From My Taxi (op-ed by guest cab drivers), 200-1,000 words; Critic's Choice (positive reviews of books, movies, music, theatre circuit, entertainment), 200-1,000 words; Tips on Tips (tells cab drivers how to earn bigger, better, tips—practical advice), 100-500 words. Buys 12-24 mss/year. Send complete ms. Pays $5-10.

Fiction: Juanita Wilcox, fiction editor. Adventure, condensed novels, experimental, fantasy, historical, horror (no gore), humorous, mainstream, mystery, novel excerpts, science fiction, serialized novels, slice-of-life vignettes, suspense, western. "No gratuitous violence; no minority or gender bashing (unless used in quotes by an ignorant character who suffers from his/her attitude in some way); no explicit sex; watch the foul language unless it's really necessary." Buys 12-24 mss/year. Send complete ms. Length: 200-2,000 words. Pays $5-50.

Poetry: Noel Clancy, associate editor. Free verse, haiku, light verse, traditional, "limerick of the month." Buys 24 poems/year. Submit maximum 10 poems. Length: 2-20 lines. Pays $2-5.

Fillers: Katy Oviatt, managing editor. Anecdotes, facts, gags to be illustrated by cartoonist, newsbreaks, short humor, trivia (short question and answer), puzzles, recipes, illustrated cartoons. Buys 36/year. Length varies. Pays $1-10.

Tips: "Keep material clean, and uplifting, whenever possible. *Katy's Kab* is decent enought for cab drivers to hand to their passengers as a public-relations gift. (We do have a use for grittier, more adult material, but not in the newsletter. Send adult material to our "anthology" department). No reply without SASE. We are most open to fiction! All genres are welcome, because we want to emulate the old pulp magazines from the fifties. We need lots of good short stories! No reply or return without SASE to *Katy's Kab*, P.O. Box 3031, Anaheim, CA 92803-3031."

KNOWLEDGE, Official Publication of the World Olympiads of Knowledge, Knowledge, Inc., 3863 Southwest Loop 820, S 100, Ft. Worth TX 76133-2076. (817)292-4272. Fax: (817)292-2893. Editor: Dr. O.A. Battista. Managing Editor: Elizabeth Ann Battista. 90% freelance written. Quarterly magazine for lay and professional audiences of all occupations. Estab. 1985. Circ. 3,000. Pays on publication. Publishes ms an average of 6 months after acceptance. Buys all rights. "We will reassign rights to a writer after a given period." Publishes reprints of previously published articles. Send photocopy of article. Byline given. Submit seasonal/holiday material 6 months in advance. Reports in 1 month. Sample copy $6. Writer's guidelines for #10 SASE.

Nonfiction: Informational—original new knowledge that will prove mentally or physically beneficial to all readers. Buys 30 unsolicited mss/year. Query. Length: 1,500-2,000 words maximum. Pays $100 minimum. Sometimes pays the expenses of writers on assignment.

Columns/Departments: Journal section uses maverick and speculative ideas that other magazines will not publish and reference. Payment is made, on publication, at the following minimum rates: Feature Articles $100. Why Don't They, $50; Salutes, $25; New Vignettes, $25; Quotes To Ponder, $10; and Facts, $5.

Tips: "The editors of *Knowledge* welcome submissions from contributors. Manuscripts and art material will be carefully considered but received *only* with the unequivocal understanding that the magazine will not be responsible for loss or injury. Material from a published source should have the publication's name, date and page number. Submissions cannot be acknowledged and will be returned only when accompanied by a SASE having adequate postage."

LEFTHANDER MAGAZINE, Lefthander International, P.O. Box 8249, Topeka KS 66608-0249. (913)234-2177. Managing Editor: Kim Kipers. 80% freelance written. Eager to work with new/unpublished writers. Bimonthly magazine for "lefthanded people of all ages and interests in 50 US states and 12 foreign countries. The one thing they have in common is an interest in lefthandedness." Estab. 1975. Circ. 26,000. Pays on publication. Publishes ms an average of 4 months after acceptance. Byline usually given. Offers 25% kill fee. Rights negotiable. Simultaneous queries OK. Reports on queries in 2 months. Sample copy $2 for 9×12 SAE. Writer's guidelines for #10 SASE.

Nonfiction: Interviews with famous lefthanders; features about lefthanders with interesting talents and occupations; how-to features (sports, crafts, hobbies for lefties); research on handedness and brain dominance; expose on discrimination against lefthanders in the work world; features on occupations and careers attracting lefties; education features relating to ambidextrous right brain teaching methods. Buys 50-60 mss/year. Length: 1,500-2,000 words for features. Pays $85-100. Buys 6 personal experience shorts/year. Pays $25. Pays expenses of writer on assignment. Query with SASE.

Photos: State availability of photos for features. Pays $10-15 for good b&w glossies. Rights negotiable.

Tips: "All material must have a lefthanded hook. We prefer quick, practical, self-help and self-awareness types of editorial content; keep it brief, light and of general interest. More of our space is devoted to shorter pieces. A good short piece gives us enough evidence of writer's style, which we like to have before assigning full-length features."

LEISURE WORLD, Ontario Motorist Publishing Company, 1215 Ovellette Ave., Box 580, Windsor, Ontario NX8 IJ3 Canada. (519)971-3208. Fax: (519)977-1197. Editor: Douglas O'Neil. 30% freelance written. Bimonthly magazine distributed to members of the Canadian Automobile Association in Southwestern Ontario and the Atlantic provinces. Editorial content is focused on travel, entertainment and leisure time pursuits of interest to CAA members." Estab. 1988. Circ. 318,000. Pays on publication. Publishes ms an average of 2 months after acceptance. Buys first rights and second serial (reprint) rights. Submit seasonal/holiday material 4 months in advance. Reprints OK; send information about when and where the article previously appeared. Pays 100% of original article fee for reprints. Reports in 2 months. Sample copy $2. Free writer's guidelines.

Nonfiction: Lifestyle, humor and travel. Buys 20 mss/year. Send complete ms. Length: 800-1,500 words. Pays $50-200.

Photos: Reviews negatives. Offers $40/photo. Captions and model releases required. Buys one-time rights.

Columns/Departments: Query with published clips. Length: 800 words. Pays $50-100.

Tips: "We are most interested in travel destination articles that offer a personal, subjective and positive point of view on international (including US) destinations. Good quality color slides are a must."

LIFE, Time & Life Bldg., Rockefeller Center, New York NY 10020. (212)522-1212. Managing Editor: Daniel Okrent. Articles: Assist Managing Editor: Jay D. Lovinger. 10% freelance written. Prefers to work with published/established writers; works with a small number of new/unpublished writers each year. Monthly general interest picture magazine for people of all ages, backgrounds and interests. Circ. 1.5 million. Average issue includes one short and one long text piece. **Pays on acceptance.** Publishes ms an average of 3 months after acceptance. Byline given. Buys first North American serial rights. Submit seasonal material 4 months in advance. Simultaneous submissions OK. Reports in 6 weeks.

 • Although this magazine is better known for its photos than its articles, the writing nonetheless is of exceptional quality.

Nonfiction: "We've done articles on anything in the world of interest to the general reader and on people of importance. It's extremely difficult to break in since we buy so few articles. Most of the magazine is pictures. We're looking for very high quality writing. We select writers whom we think match the subject they are writing about." Query with clips of previously published work. Length: 1,000-4,000 words.

‡LIFE TODAY, Looking in on life at its best, Grote Publishing, Suite 120, 2802 International Lane, Madison WI 53704. Editor: Rod Clark. 80% freelance written. Quarterly magazine covering general lifestyle. "Although many of our readers are 50-plus, we are looking for excellent writing that is not age-specific but targeted to a general adult readership. The *Life Today* editorial slant is toward opening gateways to experience, encouraging readers to look in on and participate in intellectual, spiritual and physical engagements presented through unique perspectives, often encompassing a non-nostalgic past, active present and a positive future." Estab. 1989. Circ. 125,000. Pays on publication. Publishes ms an average of 6 months after acceptance. Byline given. Buys first North American serial or second serial (reprint) rights; makes work-for-hire assignments. Editorial lead time 5 months. Submit seasonal material 6 months in advance. Simultaneous and previously published submissions OK. Query for electronic submissions. Reports in 3 months. Sample copy $3 for 9×12 SAE with 5 first class stamps. Writer's guidelines for #10 SASE.

Nonfiction: Book excerpts, essays, general interest, how-to (gardening, cooking, decorating, outdoor, enjoyment, etc.), humor, interview/profile, photo feature, technical (science & technology), travel, health, sports, arts and general finance. "We are not currently publishing fiction. Please do not submit nostalgia pieces. In travel articles, show us the landscape, not yourself—avoid heavy reliance on personal chronologies. If an essay is written from personal experience, make it universal, but unique in tone." Buys 20 mss/year. Query with published clips or send complete ms. Length: 600-2,500 words. Pays $375 minimum for assigned articles; $100 minimum for unsolicited articles, including reprints. Sometimes pays expenses of writers on assignment.

Photos: Send photos with submission. Reviews contact sheets, negatives, transparencies and prints no smaller than 5×7. Offers $50-300/photo. Negotiates payment individually. Model releases and identification of subjects required. Buys one-time rights.

Poetry: Open style—no limitations. "No 'cute' poems about growing older, please. Make sure the poem evokes deep feeling in someone other than the writer. Write in an accessible style." Buys very few. Submit maximum 5 poems. Length: 60 words maximum. Pays $50 minimum.

Tips: "Make it easy for us to make a decision on your submission. If the article is already written, submit the entire thing—with professional quality photos or photo/illustration sources if appropriate. If query, write part of it in the style you would write the article. Be sure to enclose clips. Also, don't send us 4,000 words when we ideally use articles of 1,500—do that editing yourself before you send it in. Send us something you would enjoy reading. If your article or idea has strong graphic possibilities all the better. In all areas, we try to emphasize exciting new directions or trends with a positive angle. Articles on health and medical issues and research must be founded in sound scientific method and include current, up-to-date data. You must be able to document your research. We also look for pieces that evoke comfort and curiosity: on food, nature, art and landscapes, for instance."

‡MONDO 2000, Fun City MegaMedia, P.O. Box 10171, Berkeley CA 94709. (510)845-9018. Editor: R.U. Sirius. Managing Editor: Andrew Hultkrans. Contact: Andrew Hultkrans. 75% freelance written. Quarterly magazine for cutting edge technology, music, arts, fashion. Estab. 1989. Circ. 80,000. Pays 1-2 months after *following* issue's publication. Byline given. Buys all rights. Editorial lead time 3 months. Submit seasonal material 2 months in advance. Query for electronic submissions. Reports in 2 weeks on queries; 1 month on mss. Sample copy $7. Writer's guidelines free on request.

Nonfiction: Book excerpts, essays, expose, how-to, humor, interview/profile, new product and technical. "No fiction, poetry, religious, nostalgic, "People" Magazine-type stories, personal experience or mainstream general interest." Query with published clips. Length: 650-3,900 words. Pays $32.50 minimum.

Photos: State availability of photos with submission. Reviews transparencies. Negotiates payment individually. Identification of subjects required. Buys all rights.

Columns/Departments: Contact: St. Jude Milhon, Senior Editor (510)540-8775. Street Tech (garage level, do it yourself high tech), 1,300 words and Reviews (books, software, film, computer games), 650-1,300 words. Buys 12 mss/year. Query with published clips. Pays $32.50 minimum, $130 maximum.

Tips: "Interviews, street tech, tech items, reviews are most open to freelancers. Must be *hot* — cutting edge, near future, non-mainstream, bizaare, intellectually stimulating, funny."

NATIONAL GEOGRAPHIC MAGAZINE, 17th and M St. NW, Washington DC 20036. (202)857-7000. Editor: William Graves. Approximately 50% freelance written. Prefers to work with published/established writers, but works with a small number of new/unpublished writers each year. Monthly magazine for members of the National Geographic Society. Estab. 1888. Circ. 9.5 million.

Nonfiction: *National Geographic* publishes general interest, illustrated articles on science, natural history, exploration politics and geographical regions. Almost half of the articles are staff-written. Of the freelance writers assigned, most are experts in their fields; the remainder are established professionals. Fewer than one percent of unsolicited queries result in assignments. Query (500 words) by letter, not by phone, to Senior Assistant Editor Robert Poole (Contract Writers). Do not send mss. Before querying, study recent issues and check a *Geographic Index* at a library since the magazine seldom returns to regions or subjects covered within the past ten years. Pays expenses of writers on assignment.

Photos: Photographers should query in care of the Illustration Division.

• Ranked as one of the best markets for freelance writers in *Writer's Digest* magazine's annual "Top 100 Markets," January 1993.

THE NEW YORKER, 20 W. 43rd St., New York NY 10036-7441. Editor: Tina Brown. Weekly. Estab. 1925. Circ. 600,000. Reports in 2 months. **Pays on acceptance.** Back issues $3.50.

Nonfiction, Fiction, Poetry and Fillers: Long fact pieces are usually staff-written. So is "Talk of the Town," although freelance submissions are considered. Pays good rates. Uses fiction, both serious and light. About 90% of the fillers come from contributors with or without taglines (extra pay if the tagline is used).

‡NOSTALGIA, A Sentimental State of Mind, Nostalgia Publications, P.O. Box 2224, Orangeburg SC 29116. Editor: Connie L. Martin. 100% freelance written. Semiannual magazine for poetry and true short stories. "True, personal experiences that relate faith, struggle, hope, success, failure and rising above problems common to all." Estab. 1986. Circ. 1,000. Pays on publication. Publishes ms an average 6-12 months after acceptance. Byline given. Buys one-time rights. Submit seasonal material 6 months in advance. Reports in 4-6 weeks on queries. Sample copy for $3. Writer's guidelines for #10 SASE.

Nonfiction: General interest, historical/nostalgic, humor, inspirational, opinion, personal experience, photo feature, religious and travel. Does not want to see "anything with profanity or sexual references." Buys 7-8 mss/year. Send complete ms. Length: 1,000 words. Pays $25 minimum. Pays contributor copies "if copies are preferred."

Photos: State availability of photos with submission. Offers no additional payment for photos with ms.

Poetry: Free verse, haiku, light verse, traditional and modern prose. "No ballads — no profanity — no sexual references." Submit 3 poems maximum. Length: 45-50 lines preferably. Pays $100. Semiannual Nostalgia Poetry Award.

‡OUT WEST, America's On the Road Newspaper, 10522 Brunswick Rd., Grass Valley CA 95945-9323. (916)477-9378. Editor: Chuck Woodbury. 30% freelance written. Quarterly tabloid for general audience. Estab. 1987. Circ. 12,000. Pays on acceptance or publication (negotiated). Byline given. Buys one-time or reprint rights. Submit seasonal/holiday material 4 months in advance. Simultaneous and previously published submissions OK. Send tearsheet or photocopy of article, or typed ms with rights for sale noted. Include information about when and where the article previously appeared. For reprints, pays 50-75% of the amount paid for an original article. Reports in 6 weeks. Sample copy $2. Writer's guidelines for #10 SASE.

Nonfiction: Essays, historical, humor, photo feature, profiles, travel, but always relating to the rural West. Readers are travelers and armchair travelers interested in what's along the back roads and old two-lane highways of the non-urban West. Articles about old cafes, motels, hotels, roadside trading posts, drive-in theaters, highways of yesteryear like Route 66 and good roadtrips are especially welcome. No foreign travel. Query or send complete ms. Length: 300-1,000 words. Pays $25-100.

Photos: Black and white only; prefers 5×7 or 8×10 prints. Buys stand-alone photos of funny things and signs along the road. Pays $5-30.

Columns/Departments: Western wildlife, roadfood, roadtrips, rural museums and attractions, tourist railroads, Alaska, Death Valley, ghost towns, western history, western tours and off-beat attractions. Length: 400-600 words. Pays $25-35.

Fillers: Anecdotes, short humor, unusual Western historical facts, funny small business slogans, cartoons, travel tips, book, video reviews. Length 25-150 words. Pays $5-20. Pays $2-12.

Tips: "It's very important to read the publication before submitting work. No how-to articles. Our West is not an RV or senior publication."

PARADE, Parade Publications, Inc., 750 3rd Ave., New York NY 10017. (212)573-7000. Editor: Walter Anderson. Weekly magazine for a general interest audience. 90% freelance written. Circ. 37 million. **Pays on acceptance.** Publishes ms an average of 3 months after acceptance. Kill fee varies in amount. Buys first North American serial rights. Reports in 5 weeks on queries. Writer's guidelines for #10 SAE.
Nonfiction: General interest (on health, trends, social issues, business or anything of interest to a broad general audience); interview/profile (of news figures, celebrities and people of national significance); and "provocative topical pieces of news value." Spot news events are not accepted, as *Parade* has a 6-week lead time. No fiction, fashion, travel, poetry, quizzes or fillers. Address single-page queries to Articles Correspondent. Length: 800-1,500 words. Pays $2,500 minimum. Pays expenses of writers on assignment.
Tips: "Send a well-researched, well-written query targeted to our market. Please, no phone queries. We're interested in well-written exclusive mss on topics of news interest. The most frequent mistake made by writers in completing an article for us is not adhering to the suggestions made by the editor when the article was assigned."

PEOPLE IN ACTION, Meridian International, Inc., Box 10010, Ogden UT 84409. (801)394-9446. 40% freelance written. Monthly inhouse magazine featuring personality profiles. **Pays on acceptance.** Publishes ms an average of 8 months after acceptance. Byline given. Buys first rights, second serial (reprint) rights and non-exclusive reprint rights. Simultaneous and previously published submissions OK. Query first. Reports in 2 months with SASE. Sample copy $1 for 9×12 SAE. Writer's guidelines for #10 SASE. All requests for sample copies, guidelines and queries should be addressed Attn: Editorial Staff.
Nonfiction: Personality profiles of nationally recognized celebrities in sports, entertainment and fine arts. "Celebrities must have positive values and make a contribution, beyond their good looks, to society. These are cover features—photogenic appeal needed." Buys 40 mss/year. Query. Length: 1,000-1,400 words. Pays 15¢/word for first rights plus non-exclusive reprint rights. Payment for second rights is 10¢/word.
Photos: Send photos with query. Pays $35/inside photo, $50/cover photo. Reviews 35mm or larger transparencies and 5×7 or 8×10 sharp color prints. Prefers transparencies. Captions, model releases and identification of subjects required.
Tips: "The key is a well-written query letter that: 1) demonstrates that the subject of the article has national appeal; 2) shows that a profile of the person interviewed will have a clear, focused theme; 3) gives evidence that the writer/photographer is a professional, even if a beginner."

READER'S DIGEST, Pleasantville NY 10570. Monthly. Circ. 16.5 million. Publishes general interest articles "as varied as all human experience." The *Digest* does not read or return unsolicited mss. Address proposals and tearsheets of published articles to the editors. Of articles published, half are original, written on assignment, and half are previously published articles. Pays $1,200/*Digest* page for World Digest rights (usually split 50/50 between original publisher and writer for reprints). Tearsheets of submitted article must include name of original publisher and date of publication.
Columns/Departments: "Original contributions become the property of *Reader's Digest* upon acceptance and payment. Life-in-these-United States contributions must be true, unpublished stories from one's own experience, revealing adult human nature, and providing appealing or humorous sidelights on the American scene." Length: 300 words maximum. Pays $400 on publication. True and unpublished stories are also solicited for Humor in Uniform, Campus Comedy and All in a Day's Work. Length: 300 words maximum. Pays $400 on publication. Towards More Picturesque Speech—the first contributor of each item used in this department is paid $50 for original material, $35 for reprints. Contributions should be dated, and the source must be given. For items used in Laughter, the Best Medicine, Personal Glimpses, Quotable Quotes, and elsewhere in the magazine payment is as follows; to the *first* contributor of each from a published source, $35. For original material, $30/*Digest* two-column line, with a minimum payment of $50. Send complete anecdotes to excerpt editor."
  • Ranked as one of the best markets for freelance writers in *Writer's Digest* magazine's annual "Top 100 Markets," January 1993.

READERS REVIEW, The National Research Bureau, Inc., 424 N. 3rd St., P.O. Box 1, Burlington IA 52601-0001. (319)752-5415. Fax: (319)752-3421. Editor: Nancy Heinzel. Editorial Supervisor: Doris J. Ruschill. 75% freelance written. Works with a small number of new/unpublished writers each year, and is eager to work with new/unpublished writers. Quarterly magazine. Estab. 1948. Pays on publication. Publishes ms an average of 1 year after acceptance. Buys all rights. Submit seasonal/holiday material 7 months in advance of issue date. Sample copy and writers guidelines for #10 SAE with 2 first class stamps.
Nonfiction: General interest (steps to better health, attitudes on the job); how-to (perform better on the job, do home repairs, car maintenance); and travel. Buys 10-12 mss/year. Query with outline or submit complete ms. Length: 500-700 words. Pays 4¢/word.
Tips: "Writers have a better chance of breaking in at our publication with short articles."

REAL PEOPLE, The Magazine of Celebrities and Interesting People, Main Street Publishing Co., Inc., 16th Floor, 950 3rd Ave. New York NY 10022-2705. (212)371-4932. Fax: (212)838-8420. Editor: Alex Polner. 75% freelance written. Bimonthly magazine for ages 35 and up focusing on celebs and show business, but also interesting people who might appeal to a national audience. Estab. 1988. Circ. 130,000. Pays on publication. Byline given. Pays 33% kill fee. Buys all rights. Submit seasonal/holiday material 6 months in advance. Reports within 1 month. Sample copy $3.50 for 8×11 SAE with 3 first class stamps. Writer's guidelines for #10 SASE.

Nonfiction: Book excerpts, interview/profile. Buys 80 mss/year. Query with published clips (and SAE). Length: 500-1,800 words. Pays $150-350 for assigned articles; $100-250 for unsolicited articles.

Columns/Departments: Newsworthy shorts—up to 200 words. Pays $25-50.

Photos: State availability of photos with submissions. Reviews 5×7 prints and/or slides. Offers no additional payment for photos accepted with ms. Captions, model releases and identification of subjects required. Buys one-time rights.

THE SATURDAY EVENING POST, The Saturday Evening Post Society, 1100 Waterway Blvd., Indianapolis IN 46202. (317)636-8881. Editor: Cory SerVaas, M.D. Managing Editor: Ted Kreiter. 30% freelance written. Bimonthly general interest, "family-oriented magazine focusing on physical fitness, preventive medicine." Estab. 1728. Circ. 570,000. Pays on publication. Publishes ms an average of 3 months after acceptance. Byline given. Buys second serial (reprint) and all rights. Submit seasonal/holiday material 4 months in advance. Simultaneous and previously published submissions OK. Query for electronic submissions. Reports in 1 month on queries; 6 weeks on mss. Writer's guidelines for #10 SASE.

Nonfiction: Book excerpts, general interest, how-to (gardening, home improvement), humor, interview/profile and travel. "No polifical articles or articles containing sexual innuendo or hypersophistication." Buys 50 mss/year. Query with or without published clips or send complete ms. Length: 750-2,500 words. Pays $100 minimum, negotiable maximum for assigned articles. Sometimes pays expenses of writers on assignment.

Photos: State availability of photos with submission. Reviews negatives and transparencies. Offers $50 minimum, negotiable maxmium per photo. Model release and identification required. Buys one-time or all rights.

Columns/Departments: Travel (destinations), 750-1,500. Buys 16 mss/year. Query with published clips or send complete ms. Length: 750-1,500 words. Pays $100 minimum, negotiable maximum.

Fiction: Jack Gramling, fiction editor. Historical, humorous, mainstream, mystery, science fiction and western. "No sexual innuendo or profane expletives." Send complete ms. Length: 1,000-2,500 words. Pays $150 minimum, negotiable maximum.

Poetry: Light verse.

Fillers: PostScripts Editor: Steve Pettinga. Anecdotes, short humor. Buys 200/year. Length 300 words. Pays $15.

Tips: "Areas most open to freelancers are PostScripts and Travel. For travel we like text-photo packages, pragmatic tips, side bars and safe rather than exotic destinations. Query by mail, not phone. Send clips."

SELECTED READING, The National Research Bureau, Inc., 424 N. 3rd St., P.O. Box 1, Burlington IA 52601-0001. (319)752-5415. Fax: (319)752-3421. Editor: Nancy Heinzel. Editorial Supervisor: Doris J. Ruschill. 75% freelance written. Works with a small number of new/unpublished writers each year. Quarterly magazine. Estab. 1948. Pays on publication. Publishes ms an average of 1 year after acceptance. Buys all rights. Submit seasonal/holiday material 7 months in advance of issue date. Sample copy and writer's guidelines for #10 SAE with 2 first class stamps.

Nonfiction: General interest (economics, health, safety, working relationships), how-to and travel (out-of-the way places). No material on car repair. Buys 10-12 mss/year. Query. Short outline or synopsis is best; lists of titles are no help. Length: 500-700 words. Pays 4¢/word.

Tips: "Writers have a better chance of breaking in at our publication with short articles."

SMITHSONIAN MAGAZINE, 900 Jefferson Dr., Washington DC 20560. Articles Editor: Marlane A. Liddell. 90% freelance written. Prefers to work with published/established writers. Monthly magazine for "associate members of the Smithsonian Institution; 85% with college education." Circ. 3 million. Buys first North American serial rights. "Payment for each article to be negotiated depending on our needs and the article's length and excellence." **Pays on acceptance.** Publishes ms an average of 6 months after acceptance. Submit seasonal material 3 months in advance. Reports in 2 months. Sample copy $3, % Judy Smith. Writer's guidelines for #10 SASE.

Nonfiction: "Our mandate from the Smithsonian Institution says we are to be interested in the same things which now interest or should interest the Institution: cultural and fine arts, history, natural sciences, hard sciences, etc." Query. Back Page humor: 750 words; full length article 3,500-4,500 words. Payment negotiable. Pays expenses of writers on assignment.

Photos: Purchased with or without ms and on assignment. Captions required. Pays $400/full color page.

• Ranked as one of the best markets for freelance writers in *Writer's Digest* magazine's annual "Top 100 Markets," January 1993.

SOUTHERN LIVING, Southern Progress Corp., 2100 Lakeshore Dr., Birmingham AL 35209. (205)877-6000. Editor: John A. Floyd, Jr. Managing Editor: Clay Nordan. Monthly magazine. Estab. 1966. **Pays on acceptance.** Publishes ms an average of 1 year after acceptance. Kill fee "varies with article." Buys all rights or other negotiated rights. Reports in 2½ months.

Nonfiction: Accepts unsolicited freelance only for essays about Southern life. Query with or without published clips, but prefers completed mss. Length: 500-900 words. Payment negotiated individually. Direct ms to Dianne Young, Features Editor.

SPECIAL REPORTS, Whittle Communications, 333 Main Ave., Knoxville TN 37902. "Prefers not to share information."
● Whittle is now channeling most of its editorial ventures into electronic publishing.

THE STAR, 660 White Plains Rd., Tarrytown NY 10591. (914)332-5000. Fax: (914)332-5043. Editor: Richard Kaplan. Executive Editor: Bill Ridley. Managing Editor: Steve LeGrice. 40% freelance written. Prefers to work with published/established writers. Weekly magazine "for every family; all the family—kids, teenagers, young parents and grandparents." Estab. 1974. Circ. 3.2 million. Publishes ms an average of 1 month after acceptance. Buys first North American serial, occasionally second serial book rights. Query for electronic submissions. Reports in 2 months. Pays expenses of writers on assignment.
Nonfiction: Expose (government waste, consumer, education, anything affecting family); general interest (human interest, consumerism, informational, family and women's interest); how-to (psychological, practical on all subjects affecting readers); interview (celebrity or human interest); new product; photo feature; profile (celebrity or national figure); health; medical; and diet. No first-person articles. Query or submit complete ms. Length: 500-1,000 words. Pays $50-1,500.
Photos: Alistair Duncan, Photo Editor. State availability of photos with query or ms. Pays $25-100 for 8 × 10 b&w glossy prints, contact sheets or negatives; $150-1,000 for 35mm color transparencies. Captions required. Buys one-time or all rights.

THE SUN, A Magazine of Ideas, The Sun Publishing Company, 107 N. Roberson St., Chapel Hill NC 27516. (919)942-5282. Fax: (919)932-3101. Editor: Sy Safransky. 90% freelance written. Monthly general interest magazine. "We are open to all kinds of writing, though we favor work of a personal nature." Estab. 1974. Circ. 20,000. Pays on publication. Publishes ms an average of 6 months after acceptance. Byline given. Buys first or one-time rights. Simultaneous and previously published submissions OK. Reports in 1 month on queries; 3-5 months on mss. Sample copy $3. Free writer's guidelines.
Nonfiction: Book excerpts, essays, expose, general interest, humor, interview/profile, opinion, personal experience, religious and travel. Buys 24 mss/year. Send complete ms. Length: 10,000 words maximum. Pays $100-200. "Complimentary subscription is given in addition to payment." Sometimes pays expenses of writers on assignment.
Photos: Send photos with submission. Reviews prints. Offers $25/photo. Model releases required. Buys one-time rights.
Fiction: Erotica, ethnic, experimental, historical, humorous, literary, mainstream, novel excerpts, religious, serialized novels. Buys 30 mss/year. Send complete ms. Length: 10,000 words maximum. Pays $100 for original fiction.
Poetry: Avant-garde, free verse, haiku and traditional. Buys 24 poems/year. Submit 6 poems maximum. Pays $25.

TIME, Time & Life Bldg., Rockefeller Center, New York NY 10020-1393. "Prefers not to share information."

WORLD'S FAIR, World's Fair, Inc., P.O. Box 339, Corte Madera CA 94976-0339. (415)924-6035. Editor: Alfred Heller. Less than 50% freelance written. Quarterly magazine covering fairs and expositions (past, present and future). "The people, politics and pageantry of world's fairs and thematic exhibitions; lively, good-humored articles of fact and analysis." Estab. 1981. Circ. 5,000. **Pays on acceptance.** Publishes ms an average of 3 months after acceptance. Byline given. Offers 50% kill fee. Buys all rights. Reports in 1 month. Sample copy and writer's guidelines for 9 × 12 SAE with 3 first class stamps.
Nonfiction: Informative articles, interview/profiles, photo features related to international fairs and world's-fair-caliber exhibits and exhibit technology. Buys 8-10 mss/year. Query with published clips. Length: 500-2,500 words. Pays $50-350. Sometimes pays expenses of writers on assignment.
Photos: State availability of photos or line drawings with submission. Reviews contact sheets and 8 × 10 b&w prints. Identification of subjects required. Buys one-time rights.
Tips: Looking for "correspondents in cities planning major expositions, in the US and abroad."

Health and Fitness

The magazines listed here specialize in covering health and fitness topics for a general audience. Many focus not as much on exercise as on general "healthy lifestyle" topics. Magazines covering health topics from a medical perspective are listed in the Medical category of Trade. Also see the Sports/Miscellaneous section where publications dealing with health and particular sports may be listed. For magazines that cover healthy eating, refer to the Food and Drink section. Many general interest publications are also potential markets for health or fitness articles.

AMERICAN HEALTH MAGAZINE, Fitness of Body and Mind, Reader's Digest Corp., 28 W. 23rd St., New York NY 10010. (212)366-8900. Editor: Carey Winfrey. Executive Editor: Judith Groch. 70% freelance written. 10 issues/year. General interest health magazine that covers both scientific and "lifestyle" aspects of health, including medicine, fitness, nutrition and psychology. Circ. 800,000. **Pays on acceptance.** Publishes ms an average of 4-6 months after acceptance. Byline or tagline given. Offers 25% kill fee. Buys first North American serial rights. Reports in 6 weeks. Sample copy $3. Writer's guidelines for #10 SASE.

Nonfiction: Mail to Editorial/Features. News-based articles usually with a service angle; well-written pieces with an investigative or unusual slant; humor; profiles (health or fitness related). No mechanical research reports, quick weight-loss plans or unproven treatments. "Stories should be written clearly, without jargon. Information should be new, authoritative and helpful to readers." Buys 60-70 mss/year (plus many more news items). Query with 2 clips of published work. Length: 1,000-3,000 words. Payment varies. Pays the expenses of writers on assignment.

Photos: Pays $100-600 for 35mm transparencies and 8 × 10 prints "depending on use." Captions and identification of subjects required. Buys one-time rights.

Columns/Departments: Mail to Editorial/News, Medicine, Fitness, Nutrition, The Mind, Family, Dental and Looking Good. Other news sections included from time to time. Buys about 300 mss/year. Query with clips of published work. Pays $150-250 upon acceptance.

• Ranked as one of the best markets for freelance writers in *Writer's Digest* magazine's annual "Top 100 Markets," January 1993.

Tips: "*American Health* has no fulltime staff writers; we rely on outside contributors for most of our articles. The magazine needs good ideas and good articles from experienced journalists and writers. Feature queries should be short (no longer than a page) and to the point. Give us a good angle and a paragraph of background. Queries only. We are not responsible for material not accompanied by a SASE."

BETTER HEALTH, Better Health Press, 1450 Chapel St., New Haven CT 06511-4440. (203)789-3972. Publishing Director: James F. Malerba. 75% freelance written. Prefers to work with published/established writers; will consider new/unpublished writers. Bimonthly magazine devoted to health and wellness issues, as opposed to medical issues. Estab. 1979. Circ. 175,000. Pays on publication. Byline given. Offers $75 kill fee. Buys first rights. Query first; do not send article. Sample copy $2.50. Writer's guidelines for #10 SASE.

Nonfiction: Wellness/prevention issues are of prime interest. New medical techniques or similar topics are not considered. No fillers, poems, quizzes, seasonal, heavy humor, inspirational or personal experience. Length: 2,000-2,500 words. Pays $200-500. Does not offer additional payment for photos, research costs, etc. No dot matrix.

Tips: "We look for upbeat health and wellness features of interest to a general audience, such as women's health issues, infertility, senior concerns and so forth. Absolutely no 'cute' humor or articles that are not well-researched through medical doctors at the Hospital of Saint Raphael (our parent organization), or similar authorities. Queries not accompanied with an SASE will be consigned to the wastebasket, unread."

BODYWISE, Magazine of Fitness, Diet, and Preventative Medicine, Prestige Publications, Inc., 4151 Knob Dr., Eagan MN 55122. (612)452-0571. Editor: Carla Waldemar. Managing Editor: Judy Soranno. 60% freelance written. Bimonthly magazine. "Articles should include what is *now* in fitness, diet, or medicine. Our audience is active adults ages 20-35 who want to take an active role in fitness and health." Estab. 1990. Circ. 200,000. Pays on publication. Byline given. Buys all rights. Publishes reprints of previously published articles. Send photocopy of article or typed ms with rights for sale noted. Include information about when and where the article previously appeared. Submit seasonal material 3 months in advance. Query for electronic submissions. Writer's guidelines for #10 SAE with 4 first class stamps.

Nonfiction: Book excerpts, general interest, how-to, inspirational, new product, exercise, nutrition, health discoveries; sidebars welcome. Length: 900-3,000 words. Pays $250-350/article. "*Bodywise* specials and *Today's Lifestyles* are short single subjects that offer authors the opportunity to submit or write on a work-for-hire single subject: fitness, health, diet and cookbooks. Books pay from $1,500-2,500. November focus of *Today's Lifestyles* will be '30 Day Shape Up!' " Query.

Photos: State availability of photos with submission. Reviews transparencies. Offers $100-350/photo. Buys one-time rights.

‡COUNTDOWN, Juvenile Diabetes Foundation, 432 Park Ave. S., New York NY 10016. (212)889-7575. Editor: Sandy Dylak. 75% freelance written. Quarterly magazine focusing on medical research. "*Countdown* is published for people interested in diabetes research. Written for a lay audience. Often, stories are interpretation of highly technical biomedical research." Estab. 1982. Circ. 150,000. **Pays on acceptance.** Byline given.

Buys first rights. Editorial lead time 3 months. Submit seasonal material 3 months in advance. Simultaneous and previously published submissions OK. Query for electronic submissions. Prefers disc—any format. Reports in 1 month. Sample copy free on request.
Nonfiction: Essays, general interest, how-to, interview/profile, new product and personal experience. "All articles must relate to diabetes. 95% published freelance stories are assigned." Buys 15 mss/year. Query with published clips. Length: 500-2,500 words. Pays $500 minimum for assigned articles. Pays expenses of writers on assignment.
Photos: State availability of photos with submission. Reviews transparencies and prints. Negotiates payment individually. Captions, model releases and identification of subjects required. Buys one-time rights.
Tips: "Knowledge of biomedical research, specifically immunology and genetics, is necessary. We are most open to feature stories and profiles."

FDA CONSUMER, 5600 Fishers Lane, Rockville MD 20857. (301)443-3220. Editor: Judith Levine Willis. 30% freelance written. Prefers to work with experienced health and medical writers. Monthly magazine for general public interested in health issues. January/February and July/August issues combined. A federal government publication (Food and Drug Administration). Circ. 28,000. Pays after acceptance. Publishes ms an average of 3 months after acceptance. Byline given. Not copyrighted. Pays 50% kill fee. "All rights must be assigned to the United States of America so that the articles may be reprinted without permission." Buys 15-20 freelance mss/year. "We cannot be responsible for any work by writer not agreed upon by prior contract." Free sample copy.
Nonfiction: "Upbeat feature articles of an educational nature about FDA regulated products and specific FDA programs and actions to protect the consumer's health and pocketbook. Articles based on health topics connected to food, drugs, medical devices, and other products regulated by FDA. All articles subject to clearance by the appropriate FDA experts as well as acceptance by the editor. All articles based on prior arrangement by contract." Length: 2,000-2,500 words. Pays $800-950 for "first-timers," $1,200 for those who have previously published in *FDA Consumer*. Pays phone and mailing expenses.
Photos: Black and white photos are purchased on assignment only.
Tips: "Besides reading the feature articles in *FDA Consumer*, a writer can best determine whether his/her style and expertise suit our needs by submitting a resume and clips; story suggestions are unnecessary as most are internally generated."

‡**HEALING JOURNAL,** Health Communication Research Institute, Inc., Suite 105, 1050 Fulton Ave., Sacramento CA 95825. Editor: Marlene M. von Friederichs-Fitzwater, Ph.D. 95% freelance written. Forum for health care professionals and patients dialogue. Quarterly magazine for health communication and health care. "The *Journal* is an attempt to improve healthcare by improving communication and is committed to creating healing relationships between and among healthcare professionals and patients." Estab. 1992. Circ. 7,500. Pays on publication. Byline given. Buys first North American serial rights and second serial (reprint) rights. Editorial lead time 2-3 months. Submit seasonal material 3 months in advance. Previously published submissions OK. Query for electronic submissions. Reports in 6 weeks on queries, 1-2 months on mss. Sample copy free on request.
Nonfiction: Book excerpts, essays, interview/profile, opinion, personal experience, photo feature, "all must be health-related—focus on relationships in health care. Nothing poorly written, no poorly conceived material—'New Age' or alternative health care material." Buys 25-30 mss/year. Send complete ms. Length: 1,500 words. Pays 10¢/word.
Photos: Send photos with submission. Reviews contact sheets, and 35mm slides or transparencies. Offers $10-25/photo. Identification of subjects required. Buys one-time rights.
Poetry: Avant-garde, free verse, haiku, traditional. "All must be health related or 'healing' focused." Buys 15-20 poems/year. Submit maximum 3 poems. Pays $10-35.
Tips: "You must read past issues to understand our purpose and philosophy."

HEALTH, Time Publishing Ventures, 18th Floor, 301 Howard St., San Francisco CA 94105. (415)512-9100. Editor: Eric Schrier. Send submissions to: Cassandra Wrightson, Editorial Assistant. 7 issues/year magazine of health, fitness, and nutrition. "Our readers are predominantly college-educated women in their 30s and 40s. Edited to focus not on illness, but on events, ideas and people." Estab. 1987. Circ. 900,000. **Pays on acceptance.** Byline given. 25% kill fee. Buys first North American serial rights. Submit seasonal material 5 months in advance. Accepts simultaneous submissions. Reports in 2 months on queries. Sample copy $5. Writer's guidelines for #10 SASE. "No phone calls, please."
Nonfiction: Cassandra Wrightson, editorial assistant. General interest, humor, inspirational, personal experience. "Articles should not be too narrow. They should offer practical advice and give clear explanations." Buys 50-60 mss/year. "No unsolicited manuscripts, please." Query with published clips. Length: 1,000-6,000 words. Pays $1,800-5,000 for assigned articles. Pays the expenses of writers on assignment.
Departments: Food, Drugs, Mind, Vanities, Fitness, Family. Length: 1,200-1,500 words. Buys 30 mss/year. Query with published clips. Pays $1,800.
• Ranked as one of the best markets for freelance writers in *Writer's Digest* magazine's annual "Top 100 Markets," January 1993.

Tips: "Keep the focus narrow and the appeal broad. A query that starts with an unusual local event and hooks it legitimately to some national trend or concern is bound to get our attention. Show, don't tell. Use quotes, examples and statistics to show why the topic is important and why the approach is workable. Freelancers have the best chance of getting published in departments."

LET'S LIVE MAGAZINE, Hilltopper Publications, Inc., 444 N. Larchmont Blvd., P.O. Box 74908, Los Angeles CA 90004-3030. (213)469-8379. Editor: Court van Rooten. Emphasizes nutrition. 15% freelance written. Works with a small number of new/unpublished writers each year. Monthly magazine. Estab. 1933. Circ. 140,000. Pays 1 month after publication. Publishes ms an average of 4 months after acceptance. Buys first world serial rights. Byline given. Submit seasonal/holiday material 6 months in advance. Reports in 2 months on queries; 3 months on mss. Sample copy $2.50 for 10 × 13 SAE with 6 first class stamps. Writer's guidelines for #10 SASE.
Nonfiction: General interest (effects of vitamins, minerals and nutrients in improvement of health or afflictions); historical (documentation of experiments or treatment establishing value of nutrients as boon to health); how-to (acquire strength and vitality, improve health of adults and/or children and prepare tasty health-food meals); interview (benefits of research in establishing prevention as key to good health); personal opinion (views of orthomolecular doctors or their patients on value of health foods toward maintaining good health); and profile (background and/or medical history of preventive medicine, M.D.s or Ph.D.s, in advancement of nutrition). Manuscripts must be well-researched, reliably documented and written in a clear, readable style. Buys 2-4 mss/issue. Query with published clips. Length: 1,000-1,200 words. Pays $150. Sometimes pays expenses of writers on assignment.
Photos: State availability of photos with ms. Pays $17.50 for 8 × 10 b&w glossy prints; $35 for 8 × 10 color prints and 35mm transparencies. Captions and model releases required.
Tips: "We want writers with experience in researching nonsurgical medical subjects and interviewing experts with the ability to simplify technical and clinical information for the layman. A captivating lead and structural flow are essential. The most frequent mistakes made by writers are in writing articles that are too technical; in poor style; written for the wrong audience (publication not thoroughly studied), or have unreliable documentation or overzealous faith in the topic reflected by flimsy research and inappropriate tone."

LISTEN MAGAZINE, Pacific Press Publishing Association, P.O. Box 7000, Boise ID 83707-1000. (208)465-2500. Fax: (208)465-2531. Editor: Lincoln Steed. Associate Editor: Glen Robinson. 75% freelance written. Works with a small number of new/unpublished writers each year. Monthly magazine specializing in drug prevention, presenting positive alternatives to various drug dependencies. "*Listen* is used in many high school classes and by professionals: medical personnel, counselors, law enforcement officers, educators, youth workers, etc." Circ. 70,000. Buys first rights for use in Listen, reprints and associated material. Byline given. **Pays on acceptance.** Publishes ms an average of 6 months after acceptance. Reprints OK; send tearsheet or photocopy of article and information about when and where it previously appeared. Pays 50% of original article fee for reprints. Reports in 3 months. Sample copy $1 for 9 × 12 SASE. Free writer's guidelines.
Nonfiction: Seeks articles that deal with causes of drug use such as poor self-concept, family relations, social skills or peer pressure. Especially interested in youth-slanted articles or personality interviews encouraging non-alcoholic and non-drug ways of life. Teenage point of view is essential. Popularized medical, legal and educational articles. Also seeks narratives which portray teens dealing with youth conflicts, especially those related to the use of or temptation to use harmful substances. Growth of the main character should be shown. "We don't want typical alcoholic story/skid-row bum, AA stories. We are also being inundated with drunk-driving accident stories. Unless yours is unique, consider another topic." Buys 15-20 unsolicited mss/year. Query. Length: 1,200-1,500 words. Pays 5-7¢/word. Sometimes pays the expenses of writers on assignment.
Photos: Purchased with accompanying ms. Captions required. Color photos preferred, but b&w acceptable.
Fillers: Word square/general puzzles are also considered. Pays $15.
Tips: "True stories are good, especially if they have a unique angle. Other authoritative articles need a fresh approach. In query, briefly summarize article idea and logic of why you feel it's good. Make sure you've read the magazine to understand our approach."

LONGEVITY, General Media International, Inc., 1965 Broadway, New York NY 10023-5965. (212)496-6100. Fax: (212)580-3693. Editor-in-Chief: Susan Millar Perry. Monthly magazine on medicine, health, fitness and life extension research. "*Longevity* is written for a baby-boomer audience who want to prolong their ability to lead a productive, vibrant, healthy life and to look as good as they feel at their best." Estab. 1989. Circ. 375,000. **Pays on acceptance.** Publishes ms an average of 2 months after acceptance. Byline given. Offers 25% kill fee. Makes work-for-hire assignments. Publishes reprints of previously published articles. Send typed ms with rights for sale noted and information about when and where the article previously appeared. Query for electronic submissions. Reports in 3 months. Sample copy for #10 SAE with 4 first class stamps.
Nonfiction: Consumer trends in anti-aging, new products and health. Query. Length: 150-2,000 words. Pays $100-2,500. Pays expenses of writers on assignment.
Columns/Departments: Antiaging News; Outer Limits; Looks Savers; Childwise; Air, Earth & Water; Marketing Youth; Medicine; The Intelligent Eater; Mind Body Spirit; Love & Longevity; In Shape; Long Life Ideas and Health Style Setters.

• Ranked as one of the best markets for freelance writers in *Writer's Digest* magazine's annual "Top 100 Markets," January 1993.

MASSAGE MAGAZINE, Keeping Those Who Touch—In Touch, Noah Publishing Co., P.O. Box 1500, Davis CA 95617-1500. (916)757-6033. Publisher: Robert Calvert. Managing Editor: Melissa B. Mower. 80% freelance written. Prefers to work with published/established writers, but works with a number of new/ unpublished writers each year. Bimonthly magazine on massage-bodywork and related healing arts. Circ. 45,000. Pays on publication. Publishes ms an average of 6 months after acceptance. Byline given. Buys first North American rights. Previously published submissions OK. Reports in 2 months on queries; 3 months on mss. Sample copy $5. Free writer's guidelines.
Nonfiction: General interest, historical/nostalgic, how-to, humor, experiential, inspirational, interview/profile, new product, photo feature, technical and travel. Length: 600-2,000 words. Pays $50-100 for assigned articles; $25-50 for unassigned. Sometimes pays the expenses of writers on assignment.
Photos: State availability of photos with submission. Offers $10-25/photo. Identification of subjects required. Buys one-time rights.
Columns/Departments: Touching Tales (experiential); Insurance; Table Talk (news briefs); Kneading Advice; Practice Building (business); In Touch with Associations (convention highlights); In Review/On Video (product, book, music and video reviews); Technique; Bodymind; and Convention Calendar (association convention listings). Length: 800-1,200 words. Pays $35-75.
Fillers: Anecdotes, facts, news briefs and short humor. Length: 100 words. Pays $25 maximum.

MEN'S FITNESS, Men's Fitness, Inc., 21100 Erwin St., Woodland Hills CA 91367. (818)884-6800. Executive Editor: Jim Rosenthal. Associate Editor: Matt Segal. 50% freelance written. Works with small number of new/unpublished writers each year. Monthly magazine for health-conscious men between the ages of 18 and 45. Provides reliable, entertaining guidance for the active male in all areas of lifestyle. Writers often share bylines with professional experts. Pays 1 month after acceptance. Publishes ms an average of 6 months after acceptance. Offers 20% kill fee. Buys all rights. Submit seasonal material 4 months in advance. Reports in 1 month. Writer's guidelines for 9 × 12 SAE. Query before sending ms.
Nonfiction: Service, informative, inspirational and scientific studies written for men. Few interviews or regional news unless extraordinary. Query with published clips. Buys 50 mss/year. Length: 2,000 words. Pays $400-1,000. Occasionally buys mss devoted to specific fitness programs, including exercises, e.g. 6-week chest workout, aerobic weight-training routine. Buys 10-15 mss/year. Pays $250-300.
Columns/Departments: Nutrition, Mind Fitness, Grooming, Sex, Prevention and Health. Length: 1,250-2,000 words. Buys 40-50 mss/year. Pays $400-500.
Tips: "Articles are welcomed in all facets of men's health; they must be well-researched, entertaining and intelligent."

MEN'S HEALTH, Rodale Press, 33 E. Minor St., Emmaus PA 18098. (215)967-5171. Fax: (215)967-8956. Editor: Michael Lafavore. Managing Editor: Steve Slon. 90% freelance written. Bimonthly magazine. "We publish health articles with a male slant. We take a broad view of health to encompass the physical and emotional." Circ. 675,000. **Pays on acceptance.** Publishes ms an average of 2 months after acceptance. Byline given. Offers 15% kill fee. Buys first North American serial or second serial (reprint) rights. Previously published submissions OK. Send tearsheet of article or typed ms with rights for sale noted and information about when and where the article previously appeared. Submit seasonal/holiday material 6-8 months in advance. Query for electronic submissions. Reports in 2 weeks. Sample copy $2.95 for SASE.
Nonfiction: Book excerpts, essays, expose, interview/profile, personal experience and travel. Buys 50 mss/ year. Query with published clips. Length: 100-2,000 words. Pays 25-50¢/word. Sometimes pays expenses of writers on assignment.
Photos: State availability of photos with submission. Offers no additional payment for photos accepted with ms. Model releases required. Buys one-time rights.
Columns/Departments: Eating Right (nutrition); Couples (relationships); Clinic (deals with a specific health problem) and Malegrams (short news items). Buys 10 mss/year. Query. Length: 800-1,000 words. Pays 25-60¢/word.
• Ranked as one of the best markets for freelance writers in *Writer's Digest* magazine's annual "Top 100 Markets," January 1993.

MUSCLE & FITNESS, Brute Enterprises Inc., 21100 Erwin St., Woodland Hills CA 91367. "Prefers not to share information."

MUSCLE MAG INTERNATIONAL, 6465 Airport Rd., Mississauga, Ontario L4U 1E4 Canada. Editor: Robert Kennedy. 80% freelance written. "We do not care if a writer is known or unknown; published or unpublished. We simply want good instructional articles on bodybuilding." Monthly magazine for 16- to 60-year-old men and women interested in physical fitness and overall body improvement. Estab. 1972. Circ. 20,000. Buys all rights. **Pays on acceptance.** Publishes ms an average of 4 months after acceptance. Byline given. Buys 200 mss/year. Sample copy $5 for 9 × 12 SAE. Reports in 1 month. Submit complete ms with IRCs.

Nonfiction: Articles on ideal physical proportions and importance of supplements in the diet, training for muscle size. Should be helpful and instructional and appeal to young men and women who want to live life in a vigorous and healthy style. "We would like to see articles for the physical culturist on new muscle building techniques or an article on fitness testing." Informational, how-to, personal experience, interview, profile, inspirational, humor, historical, expose, nostalgia, personal opinion, photo, spot news, new product and merchandising technique articles. "Also now actively looking for good instructional articles on Hardcore Fitness." Length: 1,200-1,600 words. Pays 10¢/word. Sometimes pays the expenses of writers on assignment.
Columns/Departments: Nutrition Talk (eating for top results) and Shaping Up (improving fitness and stamina). Length: 1,300 words. Pays 20¢/word.
Photos: Black and white and color photos are purchased with or without ms. Pays $20 for 8×10 glossy exercise photos; $20 for 8×10 b&w posing shots. Pays $200-400 for color cover and $30 for color used inside magazine (transparencies). More for "special" or "outstanding" work.
Fillers: Newsbreaks, puzzles, quotes of the champs. Length: open. Pays $5 minimum.
Tips: "The best way to break in is to seek out the muscle-building 'stars' and do in-depth interviews with biography in mind. Color training picture support essential. Writers have to make their articles informative in that readers can apply them to help gain bodybuilding success. Specific fitness articles should quote experts and/or use scientific studies to strengthen their theories."

‡NAUTILUS "America's Fitness Magazine," Nautilus International, 709 Power House Rd., Independence VA 24348. (703)773-2881. Contact: Amy Stoneman, Associate Editor. 95% freelance written. Quarterly magazine for fitness/wellness. "Editorial mission is guided toward educational, informative articles related to general wellness and the benefits of exercise. Special emphasis in many articles is geared toward strength training. Content includes medical columns, 'how-to' exercise articles, adventure/travel pieces, recipe columns and general, fitness-related subjects." Estab. 1992. Circ. 90,000. **Pays on acceptance.** Publishes ms an average of 4-5 months after acceptance. Buys first North American serial rights. Editorial lead time 6 months. Submit seasonal material 4-5 months in advance. Sample copy and writer's guidelines free on request.
Nonfiction: General interest, how-to, inspirational, interview/profile, opinion, personal experience. "No fiction." Buys 60 mss/year. Query with published clips. Length: 800-2,500 words. Pays $200 minimum. Sometimes pays expenses of writers on assignment.
Photos: State availability of photos with submission. Negotiates payment individually. Model releases and identification of subjects required.
Columns/Departments: Medical Q&A (exercise-related issues, medical problems), 800-1,500 words; Strength Training ("how-to" routines), 800-1,500 words. Buys 8-10 mss/year. Query with published clips. Pays $200-500.
Tips: "We appreciate any articles ideas, especially timely, innovative subjects related to fitness. Because virtually entire book is freelanced, opportunities are wide for authors. Articles generally are geared toward educational, informative nature."

NEW BODY, The Magazine of Health & Fitness, GCR Publishing Group, Inc., 34th Floor, 1700 Broadway, New York NY 10019. (212)541-7100. Editor: Nicole Dorsey. Managing Editor: Sandra Kosherick. 75% freelance written. Works with a small number of new/unpublished writers each year. Bimonthly magazine covering fitness and health for active young, middle-class women. Circ. 125,000. Pays on publication. Publishes ms an average of 6 months after acceptance. Byline given. Offers 20% kill fee. Buys all rights. Submit seasonal/holiday material 6 months in advance. Simultaneous submissions OK. Reports in 3 months.
Nonfiction: Health, exercise, psychology, relationships, diet, celebrities, and nutrition. Please no telephone queries. No articles on "How I do exercises." Buys 75 mss/year. Query with published clips. Length: 800-1,500 words. Pays $100-300 for assigned articles; $50-150 for unsolicited articles. Reprints OK; send tearsheet or photocopy of article and information about when and where the article previously appeared. Pays 50% of their fee for an original article. Publishes novel excerpts.
Photos: Reviews contact sheets, transparencies and prints. Model releases and identification of subjects required. Buys all rights.
Columns/Departments: How I Lost It. Readers can submit "before and after" success stories along with color slides or photos. Pays $100.
Tips: "We are moving toward more general interest women's material on relationships, emotional health, nutrition, etc. We look for a fresh angle—a new way to present the material. Celebrity profiles, fitness tips, and health news are good topics to consider. Make a clean statement of what your article is about, what it would cover—not why the article is important. We're interested in new ideas, new trends or new ways of looking at old topics."

NEW LIVING, Sports, Health & Fitness News That's Good For You, P.O. Box 1519, Stonybrook NY 11790. (516)981-7232. Fax: (516)585-4606. Editor: Christine Lynn Harvey. 20% freelance written. Monthly tabloid covering health, fitness and leisure sports. "*New Living* readers are mainstream, health conscious consumers who are also multi-sport fitness enthusiasts, not necessarily competitive athletes." Estab. 1991. Circ. 50,000. **Pays on acceptance.** Byline and bio notes given. 15% kill fee. Buys all rights or makes work-for-hire assignments. Submit seasonal material 2 months in advance. Query for electronic submissions. Sample copy $1.25 for 9 × 12 SAE. Editorial calendar for #10 SASE.

Nonfiction: General interest, how-to (health, fitness related), interview/profile (with sports and fitness personalities) and photo feature. "No articles referring to other books or articles." Buys 20 mss/year. Query with published clips. Length: 500-1,500 words. Pays $25-500 for assigned articles; $25-250 for unsolicited articles. Sometimes pays in contributor copies.

Photos: State availability of photos with submission. Offers $25/photo. Identification of subjects required. Buys all rights.

Columns/Departments: Golf, Tennis, Cycling, Running, Sports Medicine, Nutrition, Health, Recipes, Exercise tips and Beauty. Length: 100-500 words. Buys 150 mss/year. Query. Pays $25-100.

Fillers: Facts, gags to be illustrated by cartoonist. Buys 100/year. Length: 25-100 words. Pays $5-25.

Tips: "Query with samples of previously published clips first and tell us why the proposed article is worth publishing."

THE PHOENIX, Recovery, Renewal and Growth, 3307 14th Ave. S., Minneapolis MN 55407-2206. (612)722-1149. Editor: Rosanne Bane. Publisher: Fran Jackson. 100% freelance written. Monthly tabloid covering recovery and personal growth. Estab. 1981. Circ. 100,000. Pays on publication. Byline given. Offers 50% kill fee. Buys one-time rights or simultaneous rights. Query seasonal/holiday material 4 months in advance. Simultaneous and previously published submissions OK; send typed ms with rights for sale noted. Pays 25-50% of their fee for an original article. Query for electronic submissions. Sample copy, writer's guidelines and editorial calendar for 9 × 12 SAE with 4 first class stamps.

Nonfiction: Essays, how-to, humor, inspirational, interview/profile and opinion. Buys 60 mss/year. Query. Length: 800-2,000 words. Pays $35-150. Sometimes pays expenses of writers on assignment. Send photos with submission. Payment for photos accepted with ms. Identification of subjects required.

Tips: "We do work with new writers and have been delighted to help our writers grow into larger, better paying markets over the years. But please know who we are and who our readers are. Plea⊗, don't send an article about your cousin's 'recovery' from having her appendix removed. That isn't what we mean by 'recover.' Our readers are committed to personal and spiritual growth; many of them are members of 12 Step groups or other self-help programs. Their interests are usually beyond Stage I Recovery. (If you don't know what that means, you need to find out.) If you want to reach our audience, STUDY a sample copy, guidelines and editorial calendar first, then QUERY. Every other month the issue has a theme, for example, Healthy Sexuality, Parenting in Recovery or Recovery from Gambling Addition. Queries that address a theme have the best chance of being published. We emphasize articles/interviews that contain useful, practical information. Shorter pieces (800-1,000 words) are much easier to place. We are open to short, first-person stories of recovery and growth, but again, please take a look at the kinds of stories we've published in the past to get a feel for what we're looking for."

SHAPE MAGAZINE, Weider Health & Fitness, 21100 Erwin St., Woodland Hills CA 91367. (818)595-0593. Fax: (818)704-5734. Editor: Barbara Harris. 10% freelance written. Prefers to work with published/established writers, but will consider new/unpublished writers. Monthly magazine covering women's health and fitness. Estab. 1981. Circ. 800,000. Pays on publication. Publishes ms an average of 6 months after acceptance. Offers 33% kill fee. Buys all rights and reprint rights. Submit seasonal/holiday material 8 months in advance. Reports in 2 months. Sample copy for 9 × 12 SAE with 4 first class stamps.

Nonfiction: Book excerpts; expose (health, fitness related); how-to (get fit); interview/profile (of fit women); health/fitness; and humor. "We use some health and fitness articles written by professionals in their specific fields. No articles that haven't been queried first." Query with clips of published work. Length: 500-2,000 words. Pays negotiable fee. Pays expenses of writers on assignment.

SOBER TIMES, The Recovery Magazine, Sober Times Inc., 3601 30th St., San Diego CA 92104. (619)295-5377. Fax: (619)295-3030. Editor: J.S. Rudolf, Ph.D. Managing Editor: Milt Schwartz. 70% freelance written. Monthly tabloid on recovery from addictions. "*Sober Times* provides information about recovery from drug, alcohol and other addictive behavior, and it champions sober, sane and healthy lifestyles." Estab. 1987. Circ. 42,000. Pays on publication. Publishes ms an average of 2 months after acceptance. Byline given. Buys all rights and makes work-for-hire assignments. Submit seasonal/holiday material 3 months in advance. Reports in 2 months. Send SASE for writer's guidelines. Sample copy $3 for 9 × 12 SAE with 4 first class stamps.

Nonfiction: Essays, general interest, humor, interview/profile, opinion, personal experience and photo feature. "No fiction or poetry will be considered. No medical or psychological jargon." Buys 90 mss/year. Send complete ms. Length: 900-2,000 words. Pays $50+.

Photos: Send photos with submission. Reviews prints only. Offers no additional payment for photos accepted with ms. Identification of subjects required. Buys one-time rights.

Tips: "Send in finished ms with any prints. They will only be returned if accompanied by SASE. Most accepted articles are under 1,000 words. Celebrity interviews should focus on recovery from addiction."

TOTAL HEALTH, Body, Mind and Spirit, Trio Publications, Suite 300, 6001 Topanga Cyn Blvd., Woodland Hills CA 91367. (818)887-6484. Fax: (818)887-7960. Editor: Robert L. Smith. Managing Editor: Rosemary Hofer. Prefers to work with published/established writers. 80% freelance written. Bimonthly magazine covering fitness, diet (weight loss), nutrition and mental health—"a family magazine about wholeness." Estab. 1978. Circ. 90,000. Pays on publication. Publishes ms an average of 2 months after acceptance. Byline given. Buys all rights. Submit seasonal/holiday material 4 months in advance. Reports in 2 months. Sample copy $1 for 9 × 12 SAE with 5 first class stamps. Writer's guidelines for #10 SASE.
Nonfiction: Expose; how-to (pertaining to health and fitness) and religious (Judeo-Christian). Especially needs articles on skin and body care and power of positive thinking articles. No personal experience articles. Buys 48 mss/year. Send complete ms. Length: 1,500-2,000 words. Pays $50-75. Sometimes pays the expenses of writers on assignment.
Photos: State availability of photos with submission. Offers no additional payment for photos accepted with ms. Captions, model releases and identification of subjects required.
Tips: "Feature-length articles are most open to freelancers. We are looking for more self help, prevention articles."

VEGETARIAN JOURNAL, P.O. Box 1463, Baltimore MD 21203-1463. (410)366-VEGE. Editors: Charles Stahler and Debra Wasserman. Bimonthly journal on vegetarianism. "*Vegetarian* issues include health, nutrition, ethics and world hunger. Articles related to nutrition should be documented by established (mainstream) nutrition studies." Estab. 1982. Circ. 20,000. **Pays on acceptance.** Publishes ms an average of 5 months after acceptance. Byline given. Makes work-for-hire assignments. Submit seasonal/holiday material 6 months in advance. Reports in 1 month. Sample copy $3. Writer's guidelines for SASE.
Nonfiction: Book excerpts, expose, how-to, interview/profile, new products and travel. "At present we are only looking for in-depth articles on selected nutrition subjects from registered dietitians or M.D.'s. Please query with your background. Possibly some in-depth practical and researched articles from others. No miracle cures or use of supplements." Buys 1-5 mss/year. Query with or without published clips or send complete ms. Length: 2,500-8,250 words. Pays $100-300. Sometimes pays writers with contributor copies or other premiums "if not a specific agreed upon in-depth article." Sometimes pays the expenses of writers on assignment.
Photos: State availability of photos with submission. Reviews prints. Identification of subjects required. Buys one-time rights.
Poetry: Avant-garde, free verse, haiku, light verse, traditional. "Poetry should be related to vegetarianism, world hunger or animal rights. No graphic animal abuse. We do not want to see the word blood in any form." Pays in copies.
Tips: "We are most open to vegan-oriented medical professionals or vegetarian/animal rights activists who are new to freelancing."

VEGETARIAN TIMES, Box 570, Oak Park IL 60303. (708)848-8100. Fax: (708)848-8175. Managing Editor: Carol Wiley Lorente. 50% freelance written. Prefers to work with published/established writers; works with small number of new/unpublished writers each year. Monthly magazine. Circ. 300,000. Buys first serial or all rights. Byline given unless extensive revisions are required or material is incorporated into a larger article. **Pays on acceptance.** Publishes ms an average of 4 months after acceptance. Submit seasonal material 6 months in advance. Reports in 1 month. Query. Sample copy $3. Writer's guidelines for #10 SASE.
Nonfiction: Features articles that inform readers about how vegetarianism relates to diet, cooking, lifestyle, health, consumer choices, natural foods, environmental concerns and animal welfare. "All material should be well-documented and researched, and written in a sophisticated yet lively style." Informational, how-to, personal experience, interview, profile and investigative. Length: average 2,000 words. Pays flat rate of $100-1,000, sometimes higher, depending on length and difficulty of piece. Will also use 200-500-word items for news department. Sometimes pays expenses of writers on assignment.
Photos: Payment negotiated per photo.
Tips: "You don't have to be a vegetarian to write for *Vegetarian Times,* but it is VITAL that your article have a vegetarian slant. The best way to pick up that slant is to read several issues of the magazine (no doubt a tip you've heard over and over). We are very particular about the articles we run and thus tend to ask for rewrites. The best way to break in is by sending us your resume and a few samples; we generally first try out writers in our news section."
● See the interview with Carol Wiley Lorente that appears in the introduction to this section.

VIBRANT LIFE, A Magazine for Healthful Living, Review and Herald Publishing Assn., 55 W. Oak Ridge Dr., Hagerstown MD 21740-7390. (301)791-7000. Fax: (301)791-7012. Editor: Barbara Jackson-Hall. 20% freelance written. Enjoys working with published/established writers; works with a small number of new/unpublished writers each year. Bimonthly magazine covering health articles (especially from a prevention angle and with a Christian slant). Estab. 1849. Circ. 50,000. **Pays on acceptance.** "The average length of time between acceptance of a freelance-written manuscript and publication of the material depends upon the topics; some immediately used; others up to 2 years." Byline always given. Buys first serial, first North American serial, or sometimes second serial (reprint) rights. Reprints OK. Send tearsheet of article. For reprints, pays 50-75% of the amount paid for an original article. Submit seasonal/holiday material 6 months in advance. Reports in 2 months. Sample copy $1. Writer's guidelines for #10 SASE.

Nonfiction: Interview/profile (with personalities on health). "We seek practical articles promoting better health and a more fulfilled life. We especially like features on breakthroughs in medicine, and most aspects of health." Buys 20-25 mss/year. Send complete ms. Length: 750-1,800 words. Pays $125-250. Pays the expenses of writers on assignment.

Photos: Send photos with ms. Needs 35mm transparencies. Not interested in b&w photos.

Tips: "*Vibrant Life* is published for baby boomers, particularly women and young professionals, age 30-45. Articles must be written in an interesting, easy-to-read style. Information must be reliable; no faddism. We are more conservative than other magazines in our field. Request a sample copy, and study the magazine and writer's guidelines."

VIM & VIGOR, America's Family Health Magazine, Suite 11, 8805 N. 23rd Ave., Phoenix AZ 85021. (602)395-5850. Fax: (602)395-5853. Editor: Fred Petrovsky. 75% freelance written. Quarterly magazine covering health and healthcare. Estab. 1985. Circ. 850,000. **Pays on acceptance.** Publishes ms an average of 3 months after acceptance. Byline given. Buys all rights. Query for electronic submissions. Reports in 2 weeks on queries. Sample copy for 9 × 12 SAE with 8 first class stamps. Writer's guidelines for #10 SASE.

Nonfiction: Health, diseases and healthcare. "Don't send complete mss. All articles are assigned to freelance writers. Send samples of your style." Buys 4 mss/year. Query with published clips. Length: 2,000-4,000 words. Pays $450. Pays expenses of writers on assignment. Reprints OK; send photocopy of article and information about when and where the article previously appeared. Pays 50% of their fee for an original article.

Photos: State availability of photos with submission. Reviews contact sheets and any size transparencies. Offers no additional payment for photos accepted with ms. Captions, model releases and identification of subjects required. Buys one-time rights.

Tips: "We rarely accept suggested story ideas."

WEIGHT WATCHERS MAGAZINE, 11th Floor, 360 Lexington Ave., New York NY 10017. Fax: (212)687-4398. Editor-in-Chief: Lee Haiken. Health & Nutrition Editor: Susan Rees. Contact Managing Editor: Mary Novitsky. 80% freelance written. Works with a small number of new/unpublished writers each year. Monthly magazine for those interested in weight loss and weight maintenance through sensible eating and health/nutrition guidance. Estab. 1968. Circ. 1 million. Buys first North American serial rights only. **Pays on acceptance.** Publishes ms an average of 6 months after acceptance. Reports in 6 months. Sample copy and writer's guidelines $1.95 for 9 × 12 SAE.

● Ranked as one of the best markets for freelance writers in *Writer's Digest* magazine's annual "Top 100 Markets," January 1993.

Nonfiction: "We are interested in general health and medical articles; nutrition pieces based on documented research results; fitness stories that feature types of exercises that don't require special skills or excessive financial costs; and weight loss stories that focus on interesting people and situations. While our articles are authoritative, they are written in a light, upbeat style. A humorous tone is acceptable as long as it is in good taste. To expedite the fact-checking process, we require a second copy of your manuscript that is annotated in the margins with the telephone numbers of all interview subjects, with citations from such written sources as books, journal articles, magazines, newsletters, newspapers, or press releases. You must attach photocopies of these sources to the annotated manuscript with relevant passages highlighted and referenced to your margin notes. We will be happy to reimburse you for copying costs." Send detailed queries with published clips and SASE. No full-length mss; send feature ideas, as well as before-and-after weight loss story ideas dealing either with celebrities or "real people." Length: 750-1,000 words. Pays $250-500.

Tips: "Though we prefer working with established writers, *Weight Watchers Magazine* welcomes new writers as well. As long as your query is tightly written, shows style and attention to detail, and gives evidence that you are knowledgeable about your subject matter, we won't reject you out-of-hand just because you don't have three clips attached. When developing a story for us, keep in mind that we prefer interview subjects to be medical professionals with university appointments who have published in their field of expertise."

THE YOGA JOURNAL, California Yoga Teachers Association, 2054 University Ave., Berkeley CA 94704. (415)841-9200. Editor: Stephan Bodian. 75% freelance written. Bimonthly magazine covering yoga, holistic health, conscious living, spiritual practices and nutrition. "We reach a middle-class, educated audience interested in self-improvement and higher consciousness." Estab. 1975. Circ. 66,000. Pays on publication. Publishes ms an average of 6 months after acceptance. Byline given. Offers $50 kill fee. Buys first North American serial rights only. Reprints of previously published articles OK; submit tearsheet or photocopy of article and information about when and where the article previously appeared. Submit seasonal/holiday material 4 months in advance. Simultaneous queries OK. Reports in 3 months. Sample copy $3.50. Free writer's guidelines.

Nonfiction: Book excerpts; how-to (exercise, yoga, massage, etc.); inspirational (yoga or related); interview/profile; opinion; photo feature; and travel (if about yoga). "Yoga is our main concern, but our principal features in each issue highlight other New Age personalities and endeavors. Nothing too far-out and mystical. Prefer stories about Americans incorporating yoga, meditation, etc., into their normal lives." Buys 40 mss/year. Query. Length: 750-3,500 words. Pays $150-600.

Photos: Lawrence Watson, art director. Send photos with ms. Pays $200-300 for cover transparencies; $15-25 for 8×10 b&w prints. Model release (for cover only) and identification of subjects required. Buys one-time rights.

Columns/Departments: Forum; Cooking; Nutrition; Natural Body Care; Bodywork; Meditation; Well-Being; Psychology; Profiles; Music (reviews of New Age music); and Book Reviews. Buys 12-15 mss/year. Pays $50-150 for columns; $50-100 for book reviews.

Tips: "We always read submissions. We are very open to freelance material and want to encourage writers to submit to our magazine. We're looking for out-of-state contributors, particularly in the Midwest and East Coast."

YOUR HEALTH, Globe Communications Corp., 5401 NW Broken Sound Blvd., Boca Raton FL 33487. (407)997-7733. Editor: Susan Gregg. Associate Editor: Lisa Rappa. 70% freelance written. Semi-monthly magazine on health and fitness. "*Your Health* is a lay-person magazine covering the entire gamut of health, fitness and medicine." Estab. 1962. Circ. 50,000. Pays on publication. Byline given. Buys first North American serial and second serial (reprint) rights. Submit seasonal/holiday material 3 months in advance. Previously published submissions OK; send photocopy of article and information about when and where the article previously appeared. Reports in 1 month on queries; 6 weeks on mss. Free sample copy and writer's guidelines.

Nonfiction: Book excerpts, general interest, how-to (on general health and fitness topics), inspirational, interview/profile, medical breakthroughs, natural healing and alternative medicine and new products. "Give us something new and different." Buys 75-100 mss/year. Query with published clips or send complete ms. Length: 300-2,000 words. Pays $25-150.

Photos: Send photos with submission. Reviews contact sheets, negatives, transparencies and prints. Offers $50-100/photo. Captions, model releases and identification of subjects required. Buys one-time rights.

Tips: "Freelancers can best break in by offering us stories of national interest that we won't find through other channels, such as wire services. Well-written self-help articles, especially ones that focus on natural prevention and cures are always welcome."

YOUR HEALTH, Meridian International, Inc., Box 10010, Ogden UT 84409. (801)394-9446. 65% freelance written. Monthly in-house magazine covering personal health, customized with special imprint titles for various businesses, organizations and associations. "Articles should be timeless, noncontroversial, upscale and positive, and the subject matter should have national appeal." Circ. 40,000. **Pays on acceptance.** Publishes ms an average of 3 months after acceptance. Byline given. Buys first rights, second serial (reprint) and non-exclusive reprint rights. Simultaneous and previously published submissions OK. Reports in 2 months with SASE. Sample copy $1 for 9×12 SAE. Writer's guidelines for #10 SASE. (All requests for sample copies and guidelines and queries should be addressed to—Attention: Editorial Staff.)

Nonfiction: "Health care needs, particularly for mature reader. Medical technology; common maladies and survey of preventive or non-drug treatments; low-impact fitness activities; nutrition with recipes; positive aspects of hospital, nursing home, and home care by visiting nurse. Profiles on exceptional health care professionals or people coping with disability or illness. Photo support with healthy looking people is imperative. No chiropractic, acupuncture, podiatry or herbal treatments. Material must be endorsed by AMA or ADA. All articles are reviewed by a medical board for accuracy. Medical conclusions should be footnoted for fact-checking." Buys 40 mss/year. Query. Length: 1,000-1,200 words. Pays 15¢/word for first rights plus non-exclusive reprint rights. Payment for second rights is 10¢ word. Authors retain the right to resell material after it is printed by *Your Health*.

Photos: Send photos with query. Reviews 35mm and 2¼×2¼ transparencies and 5×7 or 8×10 color prints. Offers $35/inside photo and $50/cover photo. Captions, model releases and identification of subjects required.

Tips: "The key for the freelancer is a well-written query letter that demonstrates that the subject of the article has national appeal; establishes that any medical claims are based on interviews with experts and/or reliable documented sources; shows that the article will have a clear, focused theme; top-quality color photos; and gives evidence that the writer/photographer is a professional, even if a beginner. The best way to get started as a contributor to *Your Health* is to prove that you can submit a well-focused article, based on facts, along with a variety of beautiful color transparencies to illustrate the story. Material is reviewed by a medical board and must be approved by them."

YOUR HEALTH & FITNESS, General Learning Corp., 60 Revere Dr., Northbrook IL 60062-1563. (708)205-3000. Senior Editor: Carol Lezak. 90-95% freelance written. Prefers to work with published/established writers. Bimonthly magazine covering health and fitness. Needs "general, educational material on health, fitness and safety that can be read and understood easily by the layman." Estab. 1969. Circ. 1 million. Pays after publication. Publishes ms an average of 6 months after acceptance. No byline given. Offers 50% kill fee. Buys all rights. Submit seasonal/holiday material 6 months in advance.

Nonfiction: General interest. "All article topics assigned. No queries; if you're interested in writing for the magazine, send a cover letter, resume, curriculum vitae and writing samples. All topics are determined a year in advance of publication by editors; no unsolicited mss." Buys approximately 65 mss/year. Length: 350-1,400 words. Pays $100-700 for assigned articles. Sometimes pays the expenses of writers on assignment.

Photos: Offers no additional payment for photos accepted with ms.

Tips: "Write to a general audience that has only a surface knowledge of health and fitness topics. Possible subjects include exercise and fitness, psychology, nutrition, safety, disease, drug data, and health concerns."

History

Listed here are magazines and other periodicals written for historical collectors, genealogy enthusiasts, historic preservationists and researchers. Editors of history magazines look for fresh accounts of past events in a readable style. Some publications cover an era, such as the Civil War, or a region, while others specialize in historic preservation.

AMERICAN HERITAGE, 60 5th Ave., New York NY 10011. (212)206-5500. Fax: (212)620-2332. Editor: Richard Snow. 70% freelance written. Magazine published 8 times/year. Circ. 300,400. Usually buys first North American rights or all rights. Byline given. **Pays on acceptance.** Publishes ms an average of 6-12 months after acceptance. Before submitting material, "check our index to see whether we have already treated the subject." Submit seasonal material 1 year in advance. Reports in 1 month. Writer's guidelines for #10 SASE.

Nonfiction: Wants "historical articles by scholars or journalists intended for intelligent lay readers rather than for professional historians." Emphasis is on authenticity, accuracy and verve. "Interesting documents, photographs and drawings are always welcome. Query. Style should stress readability and accuracy." Buys 30 unsolicited mss/year. Length: 1,500-5,000 words. Sometimes pays the expenses of writers on assignment.

Tips: "We have over the years published quite a few 'firsts' from young writers whose historical knowledge, research methods and writing skills met our standards. The scope and ambition of a new writer tell us a lot about his or her future usefulness to us. A major article gives us a better idea of the writer's value. Everything depends on the quality of the material. We don't really care whether the author is 20 and unknown, or 80 and famous, or vice versa."

‡AMERICAN HISTORY ILLUSTRATED, P.O. Box 8200, Harrisburg PA 17105-8200. (717)657-9555. Fax: (717)657-9526. Editor: Ed Holm. 60% freelance written. "We are backlogged with submissions and prefer not to receive unsolicited complete mss at this time." Bimonthly magazine of cultural, social, military and political history published for a general audience. Estab. 1966. Circ. 160,000. **Pays on acceptance.** Byline given. Buys all rights. Query for electronic submissions. Reports in 10 weeks on queries. Writer's guidelines for #10 SASE. Sample copy and guidelines $4 (amount includes 3rd class postage) or $3.50 for 9 × 12 SAE with 4 first class stamps.

Nonfiction: Regular features include American Profiles (biographies of noteworthy historical figures); Artifacts (stories behind historical objects); Portfolio (pictorial features on artists, photographers and graphic subjects); Digging Up History (coverage of recent major archaeological and historical discoveries); and Testaments to the Past (living history articles on major restored historical sites). "Material is presented on a popular rather than a scholarly level." Writers are required to query before submitting ms. "Query letters should be limited to a concise 1-2 page proposal defining your article with an emphasis on its unique qualities." Buys 10-15 mss/year. Length: 1,000-5,000 words depending on type of article. Pays $200-1,000. Sometimes pays the expenses of writers on assignment.

Photos: Occasionally buys 8 × 10 glossy prints or color transparencies with mss; welcomes suggestions for illustrations. Pays for the reproduced color illustrations that the author provides.

Tips: "Key prerequisites for publication are thorough research and accurate presentation, precise English usage and sound organization, a lively style, and a high level of human interest. We are especially interested in publishing top-quality articles on significant American women, World War II, the Vietnam era and social/cultural history. Submissions received without return postage will not be considered or returned. Inappropriate materials include: fiction, book reviews, travelogues, personal/family narratives not of national significance, articles about collectibles/antiques, living artists, local/individual historic buildings/landmarks and articles of a current editorial nature."

AMERICA'S CIVIL WAR, Empire Press, Suite 300, 602 S. King St., Leesburg VA 22075. (703)771-9400. Editor: Roy Morris, Jr. 95% freelance written. Bimonthly magazine of "popular history and straight historical narrative for both the general reader and the Civil War buff." Estab. 1988. Circ. 125,000. Pays on publication. Publishes ms up to 2 years after acceptance. Byline given. Buys first North American serial rights. Query for electronic submissions. Reports in 3 months on queries; 6 months on mss. Sample copy $3.95. Writer's guidelines for #10 SASE.

Nonfiction: Book excerpts, historical, travel. No fiction or poetry. Buys 48 mss/year. Query. Length: 4,000 words maximum. Pays $300 maximum.

Photos: State availability of photos with submission. Payment for photos negotiable. Captions and identification of subjects required. Buys one-time rights.

Columns/Departments: Personality (probes); Ordnance (about weapons used); Commands (about units); and Travel (about appropriate historical sites). Buys 24 mss/year. Query. Length: 2,000 words. Pays up to $150.

ANCESTRY NEWSLETTER, Ancestry, Inc., P.O. Box 476, Salt Lake City UT 84110-0476. (801)531-1790. Fax: (801)531-1798. Editor: Loretto Szvcs. 95% freelance written. Eager to work with new/unpublished writers. Bimonthly newsletter covering genealogy and family history. "We publish practical, instructional and informative pieces specifically applicable to the field of genealogy. Our audience is the active genealogist, both hobbyist and professional." Estab. 1984. Circ. 8,200. Pays on publication. Publishes ms an average of 9 months after acceptance. Byline given. Buys first North American serial or all rights. Submit seasonal/holiday material 4 months in advance. Simultaneous submissions OK. Reports in 2 weeks. Sample copy and writer's guidelines for 9 × 12 SAE with 3 first class stamps.

Nonfiction: General interest (genealogical); historical; how-to (genealogical research techniques); instructional; and photo feature (genealogically related). No unpublished or published family histories, genealogies, the "story of my great-grandmother" or personal experiences. Buys 25-30 mss/year. Send complete ms. Length: 1,500-4,000 words. Pays $50.

Photos: Send photos with submission. Reviews contact sheets and 5 × 7 prints. Offers no additional payment for photos accepted with ms. Identification of subjects required. Buys one-time rights.

Tips: "You don't have to be famous, but you must know something about genealogy. Our readers crave any information which might assist them in their ancestral quest."

THE ARTILLERYMAN, Cutter & Locke, Inc., Publishers, RR 1 Box 36, Tunbridge VT 05077. (802)889-3500. Editor: C. Peter Jorgensen. 60% freelance written. Quarterly magazine covering antique artillery, fortifications and crew-served weapons 1750 to 1900 for competition shooters, collectors and living history reenactors using artillery. "Emphasis on Revolutionary War and Civil War but includes everyone interested in pre-1900 artillery and fortifications, preservation, construction of replicas, etc." Estab. 1979. Circ. 2,200. Pays on publication. Publishes ms an average of 6 months after acceptance. Byline given. Not copyrighted. Buys one-time rights. Simultaneous queries and simultaneous and previously published submissions OK. Reports in 3 weeks. Sample copy and writer's guidelines for 9 × 12 SAE with 4 first class stamps.

Nonfiction: Historical; how-to (reproduce ordnance equipment/sights/implements/tools/accessories, etc.); interview/profile; new product; opinion (must be accompanied by detailed background of writer and include references); personal experience; photo feature; technical (must have footnotes); and travel (where to find interesting antique cannon). Interested in "artillery *only*, for sophisticated readers. Not interested in other weapons, battles in general." Buys 24-30 mss/year. Send complete ms. Length: 300 words minimum. Pays $20-60. Sometimes pays the expenses of writers on assignment.

Photos: Send photos with ms. Pays $5 for 5 × 7 and larger b&w prints. Captions and identification of subjects required.

Tips: "We regularly use freelance contributions for Places-to-Visit, Cannon Safety, The Workshop and Unit Profiles departments. Also need pieces on unusual cannon or cannon with a known and unique history. To judge whether writing style and/or expertise will suit our needs, writers should ask themselves if they could knowledgably talk *artillery* with an expert. Subject matter is of more concern than writer's background."

CHICAGO HISTORY, The Magazine of the Chicago Historical Society, Chicago Historical Society, Clark St. at North Ave., Chicago IL 60614-6099. (312)642-4600. Fax: (312)266-2077. Acting Editor: Claudia Lamm Wood. Assistant Editor: Rosemary Adams. 100% freelance written. Works with a small number of new/unpublished writers each year. Triannual magazine covering Chicago history: cultural, political, economic, social and architectural. Estab. 1945. Circ. 9,500. Pays on publication. Publishes ms an average of 1 year after acceptance. Byline given. Buys all rights. Submit seasonal/holiday material 9 months in advance. Query for electronic submissions. Reports in 4 months. Sample copy $3.25 for 9 × 12 SAE with 3 first class stamps. Free writer's guidelines.

Nonfiction: Book excerpts, essays, historical and photo feature. Articles should be "analytical, informative, and directed at a popular audience with a special interest in history." No "cute" articles. Buys 8-12 mss/year. Query or send complete ms. Length: approximately 4,500 words. Pays $250.

For information on setting your freelance fees, see How Much Should I Charge?

Photos: State availability of photos with submission and submit photocopies. Would prefer no originals. Offers no additional payment for photos accepted with ms. Identification of subjects required.

Tips: "A freelancer can best break in by 1) calling to discuss an article idea with editor; and 2) submitting a detailed outline of proposed article. All sections of *Chicago History* are open to freelancers, but we suggest that authors do not undertake to write articles for the magazine unless they have considerable knowledge of the subject and are willing to research it in some detail. We require a footnoted manuscript, although we do not publish the notes."

CIVIL WAR TIMES ILLUSTRATED, P.O. Box 8200, Harrisburg PA 17105-8200. (717)657-9555. Fax: (717)657-9526. Editor: John E. Stanchak. 90% freelance written. Works with a small number of new/unpublished writers each year. Bimonthly magazine. Estab. 1961. Circ. 164,000. **Pays on acceptance.** Publishes ms an average of 12-18 months after acceptance. Buys all, first or one-time rights, or makes work-for-hire assignments. Submit seasonal/holiday material 1 year in advance. Query for electronic submissions. Reports in 2 weeks on queries; 4 months on mss. Sample copy $3. Free writer's guidelines.

Nonfiction: Profile, photo feature, and Civil War historical material. "Positively no fiction or poetry." Buys 20 freelance mss/year. Length: 2,500-5,000 words. Query. Pays $75-450. Sometimes pays the expenses of writers on assignment.

Photos: W. Douglas Shirk, art director. State availability of photos. Pays $5-50 for 8×10 b&w glossy prints and copies of Civil War photos; $400-500 for 4-color cover photos; and $100-250 for color photos for interior use.

Tips: "We're very open to new submissions. Query us after reading several back issues, then submit illustration and art possibilities along with the query letter for the best 'in.' Never base the narrative solely on family stories or accounts. Submissions must be written in a popular style but based on solid academic research. Manuscripts are required to have marginal source annotations."

GOOD OLD DAYS, America's Premier Nostalgia Magazine, House of White Birches, 306 E. Parr Rd., Berne IN 46711. (219)589-8741. Editor: Ken Tate. 75% freelance written. Monthly magazine of first person nostalgia, 1900-1955. "We look for strong narratives showing life as it was in the first half of this century. Our readership is comprised of nostalgia buffs, history enthusiasts and the people who actually lived and grew up in this era." Pays on publication. Publishes ms an average of 8 months after acceptance. Byline given. Buys all, first North American serial or one-time rights. Reprints OK; send photocopy of article and information about when and where the article previously appeared. Pays. 75% of their fee for an original article. Submit seasonal/holiday material 8 months in advance. Reports in 2 months. Sample copy $2. Writer's guidelines for #10 SASE.

Nonfiction: Historical/nostalgic, humor, interview/profile, personal experience, favorite food/recipes and photo features. Instructional (how to cane a chair, how to hand-bundle a shock of corn, etc.). Buys 300 mss/year. Query or send complete ms. Length: 1,000-1,800 words maximum. Pays 2-4¢/word or more, depending on quality and photos.

Photos: Send photos or photocopies of photos with submission. Offers $5/photo. Identification of subjects required. Buys one-time or all rights.

MEDIA HISTORY DIGEST, Media History Digest Corp., % *Editor and Publisher,* 11 W. 19th St., New York NY 10011-4234. Editor: Hiley H. Ward. 100% freelance written. Semiannual (will probably return to being quarterly) magazine. Estab. 1980. Circ. 2,000. Pays on publication. Publishes ms an average of 4 months after acceptance. Byline given. Buys first or second serial (reprint) rights. Submit seasonal/holiday material 8 months in advance. Previously published submissions OK. Reports in 4 months. Sample copy $3.75.

Nonfiction: Historical/nostalgic (media); humor (media history); and puzzles (media history). Buys 15 mss/year. Query. Length: 1,500-3,000 words. Pays $125 for assigned articles; $100 for unsolicited articles. Pays in contributor copies for articles prepared by university graduate students. Sometimes pays the expenses of writers on assignment.

Photos: Send photos with submission. Buys first or reprint rights.

Columns/Departments: Quiz Page (media history) and "Media Hysteria" (media history humor). Query. Pays $50-125 for humor; $25 for puzzles.

Fillers: Anecdotes and short humor on topics of media history.

Tips: "Send in-depth enterprising material targeted for our specialty—media history, pre-1970."

MILITARY HISTORY, Empire Press, #300, 602 S. King St. Leesburg VA 22075. (703)771-9400. Editor: C. Brian Kelly. 95% freelance written. Circ. 200,000. "We'll work with anyone, established or not, who can provide the goods and convince us as to its accuracy." Bimonthly magazine covering all military history of the world. "We strive to give the general reader accurate, highly readable, often narrative popular history, richly accompanied by period art." Pays on publication. Publishes ms 1-2 years after acceptance. Byline given. Buys all rights. Submit anniversary material 1 year in advance. Reports in 3 months on queries; 6 months on mss. Sample copy $3.95. Writer's guidelines for #10 SASE.

Nonfiction: Historical; interview (military figures of commanding interest); and personal experience (only occasionally). Buys 18 mss, plus 6 interviews/year. Query with published clips. "To propose an article, submit a short, self-explanatory query summarizing the story proposed, its highlights and/or significance. State also your own expertise, access to sources or proposed means of developing the pertinent information." Length: 4,000 words. Pays $400.

Columns/Departments: Espionage, weaponry, personality, travel (with military history of the place) and books—all relating to military history. Buys 24 mss/year. Query with published clips. Length: 2,000 words. Pays $200.

Tips: "We would like journalistically 'pure' submissions that adhere to basics, such as full name at first reference, same with rank, and definition of prior or related events, issues cited as context or obscure military 'hardware.' Read the magazine, discover our style, and avoid subjects already covered. Pick stories with strong art possibilities (*real* art and photos), send photocopies, tell us where to order the art. Avoid historical overview, focus upon an event with appropriate and accurate context. Provide bibliography. Tell the story in popular but elegant style."

OLD MILL NEWS, Society for the Preservation of Old Mills, 604 Ensley Dr., Rt. 29, Knoxville TN 37920. (615)577-7757. Editor: Michael LaForest. 40% freelance written. Quarterly magazine covering "water, wind, animal and steam power mills (usually grist mills)." Estab. 1972. Circ. 2,500. **Pays on acceptance.** Byline given. Buys first North American serial or first rights. Simultaneous submissions OK. Reports in 2 weeks. Sample copy $3.

Nonfiction: Historical and technical. "No poetry, recipes, mills converted to houses, commercial or alternative uses, nostalgia." Buys 8 mss/year. Query with or without published clips or send complete ms. Length: 400-1,000 words. Pays $15-50. Reprints OK; send typed ms with rights for sale noted and information about when and where the article previously appeared, if applicable. Original articles preferred.

Photos: Send photos with submission. "At least one recent photograph of subject is highly recommended." Uses b&w or color prints only; no transparencies. Offers $5-10/photo. Identification of subjects required. Buys one-time rights.

Fillers: Short humor. Buys 3-4/year. Length: 50-200 words. Pays $10 maximum.

Tips: "An interview with the mill owner/operator is usually necessary. Accurate presentation of the facts and good English are required."

OLD WEST, Western Periodicals, Inc., P.O. Box 2107, Stillwater OK 74076-2107. (405)743-3370. Fax: (405)743-3374. Editor: John Joerschke. Quarterly magazine. Byline given. See *True West.*

PERSIMMON HILL, 1700 NE 63rd St., Oklahoma City OK 73111. Fax: (405)478-4714. Editor: M.J. Van Deventer. 70% freelance written. Prefers to work with published/established writers; works with a small number of new/unpublished writers each year. Quarterly magazine for an audience interested in Western art, Western history, ranching and rodeo, including historians, artists, ranchers, art galleries, schools, and libraries. Publication of the National Cowboy Hall of Fame and Western Heritage Center. Estab. 1965. Circ. 15,000. Buys first rights. Byline given. Buys 15-20 mss/year. Pays on publication. Publishes ms an average of 6 months to 2 years after acceptance. Reports in 3 months. Sample copy $7 with 8 first class stamps. Writer's guidelines for #10 SASE.

Nonfiction: Historical and contemporary articles on famous Western figures connected with pioneering the American West, Western art, rodeo, cowboys, etc. (or biographies of such people), stories of Western flora and animal life and environmental subjects. "We want thoroughly researched and historically authentic material written in a popular style. May have a humorous approach to subject. No broad, sweeping, superficial pieces; i.e., the California Gold Rush or rehashed pieces on Billy the Kid, etc." Length: 1,500 words. Query with clips. Pays $100-250; special work negotiated.

Photos: Black and white glossy prints or color transparencies purchased with ms, or on assignment. Pays according to quality and importance for b&w and color photos. Suggested captions required.

Tips: "Excellent illustrations for articles are essential! No telephone queries."

‡PRESERVATION NEWS, National Trust for Historic Preservation, 1785 Massachusetts Ave. NW, Washington DC 20036. (202)673-4075. Executive Editor: Arnold M. Berke. 30% freelance written. Prefers to work with published/established writers. Monthly tabloid covering preservation of historic buildings in the US "We cover proposed or completed preservation projects and controversies involving historic buildings and districts. Most entries are news stories, features or opinion pieces." Circ. 200,000. Pays on publication. Publishes ms an average of 1 month after acceptance. Byline given. Offers variable kill fee. Buys one-time rights. Simultaneous queries OK. Reports in 2 months on queries. Sample copy $1 for 11 × 13 SAE with 56¢ postage.

Nonfiction: News, interview/profile, opinion, humor, personal experience, photo feature and travel. Buys 16 mss/year. Query with published clips. Length: 500-1,400 words. Pays $150-450. Sometimes pays the expenses of writers on assignment, but not long-distance travel.

Photos: State availability of photos with query or ms. Reviews b&w contact sheet, b&w/color prints and slides. Pays $25-100. Identification of subjects required. Credits given.

Columns/Departments: "We seek reporters who can give a historic preservation slant on development conflict throughout the United States. We also are looking for foreign coverage." Buys 8 mss/year. Query with published clips. Length: 800-1,400 words. Pays $150-450.

Tips: "Do not send or propose histories of buildings, descriptive accounts of cities or towns or long-winded treatises on any subjects. This is a *newspaper*. Proposals for coverage of fast-breaking events are especially welcome."

TIMELINE, Ohio Historical Society, 1982 Velma Ave., Columbus OH 43211-2497. (614)297-2360. Fax: (614)297-2411. Editor: Christopher S. Duckworth. 90% freelance written. Works with a small number of new/unpublished writers each year. Bimonthly magazine covering history, natural history, archaeology and fine and decorative arts. Estab. 1984. Circ. 17,500. **Pays on acceptance.** Publishes ms an average of 1 year after acceptance. Byline given. Offers $75 minimum kill fee. Buys first North American serial or all rights. Submit seasonal/holiday material 6 months in advance. Query for electronic submissions. Reports in 3 weeks on queries; 6 weeks on manuscripts. Sample copy $5 for 9 × 12 SAE. Writer's guidelines for #10 SASE.

Nonfiction: Book excerpts, essays, historical, profile (of individuals) and photo feature. Buys 22 mss/year. Query. Length: 500-6,000 words. Pays $100-900.

Photos: State availability of photos with submission. Will not consider submissions without ideas for illustration. Reviews contact sheets, transparencies and 8 × 10 prints. Captions, model releases, and identification of subjects required. Buys one-time rights.

Tips: "We want crisply written, authoritative narratives for the intelligent lay reader. An Ohio slant may strengthen a submission, but it is not indispensable. Contributors must know enough about their subject to explain it clearly and in an interesting fashion. We use high-quality illustration with all features. If appropriate illustration is unavailable, we can't use the feature. The writer who sends illustration ideas with a manuscript has an advantage, but an often-published illustration won't attract us."

TRACES OF INDIANA AND MIDWESTERN HISTORY, Indiana Historical Society, 315 W Ohio St., Indianapolis IN 46202-3299. (317)232-1884. Fax: (317)233-3109. Executive Editor: Thomas Mason. Managing Editor: Kent Calder. 80% freelance written. Quarterly magazine on Indiana and Midwestern history. Estab. 1989. Circ. 9,000. **Pays on acceptance.** Publishes ms an average of 6 months after acceptance. Byline given. Buys one-time rights. Submit seasonal/holiday material 1 year in advance. Previously published submissions OK. Reports in 3 months on mss. Sample copy $5 for 9 × 12 SAE with 6 first class stamps. Writer's guidelines for #10 SASE.

Nonfiction: Book excerpts, essays, historical/nostalgic and photo feature. Buys 20 mss/year. Send complete ms. Length: 2,000-3,000 words. Pays $100-500.

Photos: State availability of photos with submission. Reviews contact sheets, transparencies and prints. Pays "reasonable photographic expenses." Captions, model releases and identification of subjects required. Buys one-time rights.

Tips: "Freelancers should be aware of prerequisites for writing history in general and popular history in particular. Should have some awareness of other magazines of this type published by midwestern and western historical societies. Preference is given to subjects with an Indiana connection. Quality of potential illustration is also important."

TRUE WEST, Western Periodicals, Inc., P.O. Box 2107, Stillwater OK 74076-2107. (405)743-3370. Editor: John Joerschke. 100% freelance written. Works with a small number of new/unpublished writers each year. Magazine on Western American history before 1940. "We want reliable research on significant historical topics written in lively prose for an informed general audience." Estab. 1953. Circ. 30,000. **Pays on acceptance.** Publishes ms an average of 4 months after acceptance. Byline given. Buys first North American serial rights. Submit seasonal/holiday material 6 months in advance. Simultaneous queries OK. Reports in 1 month on queries; 2 months on mss. Sample copy $2 for 9 × 12 SAE. Writer's guidelines for #10 SASE.

Nonfiction: Historical/nostalgic, how-to, photo feature and travel. "We do not want rehashes of worn-out stories, historical fiction or history written in a fictional style." Buys 150 mss/year. Query. Length: 500-4,500 words. Pays 3-6¢/word.

Photos: Send photos with accompanying query or manuscript. Pays $10 for b&w prints. Identification of subjects required. Buys one-time rights.

Columns/Departments: Western Roundup—200-300-word short articles on historically oriented places to go and things to do in the West. Should include one b&w print. Buys 12-16 mss/year. Send complete ms. Pays $35.

Tips: "Do original research on fresh topics. Stay away from controversial subjects unless you are truly knowledgable in the field. Read our magazines and follow our guidelines. A freelancer is most likely to break in with us by submitting thoroughly researched, lively prose on relatively obscure topics. First person accounts rarely fill our needs."

VIKINGSHIP, P.O. Box 301, Chicago IL 60690-0301. (312)761-1888. Editor: W.R. Anderson. 25% freelance written. Quarterly historical newsletter "focusing on Medieval evidence of Norse Vikings in America." Estab. 1962. Circ. 1,240. **Pays on acceptance.** Byline sometimes given. Buys one-time rights. Previously published submissions OK; send tearsheet of article and information about when and where the article previously appeared. Reports in 2 weeks on queries. Sample copy $1 for #10 SAE with 2 first class stamps.
Nonfiction: Expose and general interest. "No rehash of textbook/encyclopedia data, which is generally known and largely false." Buys 3 mss/year. Query. Length: 100-2,000 words. Pays $10-200. Sometimes offers membership dues in lieu of small payment.
Photos: State availability of photos with submission. Reviews contact sheets and 5×7 prints. Offers $10/photo. Captions, model releases and identification of subjects required. Buys one-time rights.

VIRGINIA CAVALCADE, Virginia State Library and Archives, Richmond VA 23219-3491. (804)786-2312. Editor: Edward D.C. Campbell, Jr.. Quarterly magazine primarily for readers with an interest in Virginia history. 90% freelance written. "Both established and new writers are invited to submit articles." Estab. 1951. Circ. 9,000. Buys all rights. Byline given. **Pays on acceptance.** Publishes ms an average of 1 year after acceptance. Rarely considers simultaneous submissions. Submit seasonal material 18 months in advance. Reports in 6 weeks. Sample copy $3. Free writer's guidelines.
Nonfiction: "We welcome readable and factually accurate articles that are relevant to some phase of Virginia history. Art, architecture, literature, education, business, technology and transportation are all acceptable subjects, as well as political and military affairs. Articles must be based on thorough, scholarly research. We require foot- or endnotes but do not publish them. Any period from the age of exploration to the mid-20th century, and any geographical section or area of the state may be represented. Must deal with subjects that will appeal to a broad readership. Articles must be suitable for illustration, although it is not necessary that the author provide the pictures. If the author does have pertinent illustrations or knows their location, the editor appreciates information concerning them." Buys 12-15 mss/year. Query. Length: 3,500-4,500 words. Pays $100.
Photos: Uses 8×10 b&w glossy prints; transparencies should be at least 4×5.
Tips: "*Cavalcade* employs a narrative, anecdotal style. Too many submissions are written for an academic audience or are simply not sufficiently gripping."

‡WESTERN TALES, P.O. Box 33842, Granada Hills CA 91394. (818)881-6821. Editor: Dorman Nelson. Managing Editor: Mariann Kumke. Editor/Publisher: Dorman Nelson. 100% freelance written. Quarterly historical/western fiction literary magazine. Estab. 1993. Circ. 5,000 (1st printing). **Pays on acceptance.** Byline given. Buys first North American serial and/or second serial (reprint) rights. Publishes novel excerpts. Editorial lead time 6 months. Previously published submissions OK; send typed ms with rights for sale noted and information about when and where the article previously appeared. Reports in 2 weeks on queries; 2 months on mss. Sample copy $6. Writer's guidelines for #10 SASE.
Nonfiction: Book excerpts, general interest (western), historical/nostalgic, shorts and humor. Edgar Rice Burroughs issue; Women Western Writers' issue; individual Western Writers' issues; Native American Writers' issue. Buys up to 50 mss/year. Query or query with published clips. Pays $25.
Photos: Send photos with submission. Reviews contact sheets or 5×7 prints (no larger). Negotiates payment individually. Buys one-time rights. "Note: western oriented photos only."
Columns/Departments: Music (country/western/bluegrass reviews); Events (events around country—rodeos, pow-wows, round-ups etc.); and Review (review of western poetry—books, notes and writer's bios). Buys 12 each mss/year. Query. Negotiates payment.
Fiction: Adventure (western), historical, humorous (western), romance (western), slice-of-life vignettes, western. Buys 65 mss/year. Query or query with published clips or send complete ms. Pays $100-negotiable maximum.
Poetry: Western-flavor. Buys to 50 poems/year. Submit maximum 3 poems. Length to 20 lines. Pays $25-negotiable maximum.
Tips: "Write a good tale and send'er in! Note: The mainline is short western stories of fiction!"

WILD WEST, Empire Press, 602 S. King St. #300, Leesburg VA 22075. (703)771-9400. Editor: William M. Vogt. 95% freelance written. Bimonthly magazine on history of the American West. "*Wild West* covers the popular (narrative) history of the American West—events, trends, personalities, anything of general interest." Estab. 1988. Circ. 125,000. Pays on publication. Byline given. Buys all rights. Submit seasonal/holiday material 1 year in advance. Query for electronic submissions. Sample copy $3.95. Writer's guidelines for #10 SASE.
Nonfiction: Historical/nostalgic, humor and travel. No fiction or poetry—nothing current. Buys 24 mss/year. Query. Length: 4,000 words. Pays $300.
Photos: State availability of photos with submission. Captions and identification of subjects required. Buys one-time rights or all rights.
Columns/Departments: Travel; Gun Fighters & Lawmen; Personalities; Warriors & Chiefs; Artist West; and Books Reviews. Buys 16 mss/year. Length: 2,000. Pays $150 for departments, by the word for book reviews.

YESTERDAY'S MAGAZETTE, The Magazine of Memories, Independent Publishing Co., P.O. Box 15126, Sarasota FL 34277. Editor: Ned Burke. 95% freelance written. Bimonthly magazine of nostalgia. Estab. 1973. Circ. 2,500. Pays on publication. Publishes ms an average of 6 months after acceptance. Byline given. Buys first rights. Submit seasonal/holiday material 4 months in advance. Reports in 2 weeks on queries and mss. Sample copy $2 for 9 × 12 SAE with 4 first class stamps. Free writer's guidelines.

Nonfiction: General interest, historical/nostalgic, humor, inspirational, interview/profile ('yesterday' celebrities), opinion, personal experience, photo feature and photo. Special "Christmas" issue, deadline Nov. 15, featuring "My Favorite Christmas Memory." Plus special traditional poetry issue in May, deadline April 15. Buys 100 mss/year. Send complete ms. Length: 100-1,500 words. Pays $5-25 for unsolicited articles. Pays for most short articles, poems, etc.

Photos: Send photos with submission. Reviews 5 × 7 prints. Offers no additional payment for photos accepted with ms. Identification of subjects required. Buys one-time rights. "Write for details on our new 'Miss Yesterday' contest." SASE required.

Columns/Departments: The Way We Were (a look at certain period of time—40s, 50s, etc.); When I Was a Kid (childhood memories); In A Word (objects from the past—'ice box', etc.); and Yesterday Trivia (quiz on old movie stars, TV shows, etc.); all 300-750 words. Buys 12 mss/year. Send complete ms. Length: 500-750 words. Pays $5-10.

Fiction: Historical, humorous, slice-of-life vignettes. "No modern settings." Buys 4 mss/year. Send complete ms. Length: 750-2,500 words. Pays $5-25.

Poetry: Traditional. Nothing other than traditional. Buys 50 poems/year. Submit maximum 5 poems. Length: 4-32 lines. Pays $5 and/or contributor copies.

Fillers: Anecdotes, short humor. Buys 5/year. Length: 50-250 words. Pays $5 and/or contributor copies.

Tips: "We would like to see more 40s, 50s and 60s pieces, especially with photos. It's hard to reject any story with a good photo. All areas are open, especially 'Plain Folks Page' which uses letters, comments and opinions of readers."

Hobby and Craft

Magazines in this category range from home video to cross stitch. Craftspeople and hobbyists who read these magazines want new ideas while collectors need to know what is most valuable and why. They look to these magazines for inspiration and information. Publications covering antiques and miniatures are also listed here. Publications covering the business side of antiques and collectibles are listed in the Trade Art, Design and Collectibles section.

THE AMERICAN COLLECTORS JOURNAL, P.O. Box 407, Kewanee IL 61443-0407. (308)852-2602. Editor: Carol Savidge. 55% freelance written. Eager to work with new/unpublished writers. Bimonthly tabloid covering antiques and collectibles. Estab. 1963. Circ. 51,841. Pays on publication. Publishes ms an average of 8 months after acceptance. Byline given. Not copyrighted. Buys first North American serial rights. Submit seasonal/holiday material 6 months in advance. Reports in 1 month. Sample copy for 6 × 9 SAE with 4 first class stamps.

Nonfiction: Carol Harper, articles editor. General interest, interview/profile, photo feature and technical. Buys 12-20 mss/year. Query or send complete ms. Pays $10-35 for unsolicited articles.

Photos: Send photos with submission. Reviews 5 × 7 prints. Offers no additional payment for photos accepted with ms. Captions required. Buys one-time rights.

Tips: "We are looking for submissions with photos in all areas of collecting and antiquing, unusual collections, details on a particular kind of collecting or information on antiques."

AMERICAN WOODWORKER, Rodale Press, Inc., 33 E. Minor St., Emmaus PA 18098-0099. (215)967-5171. Fax: (215)967-8956. Editor: David Sloan. Managing Editor: Kevin Ireland. 70% freelance written. Bimonthly magazine. "*American Woodworker* is a how-to magazine edited for the woodworking enthusiast who wants to improve his/her skills. We strive to motivate, challenge and entertain." Estab. 1985. Circ. 270,000. Pays on publication. Publishes ms an average of 6 months after acceptance. Byline given. Offers $100 kill fee. Buys one-time and second serial (reprint) rights. Previously published articles OK. Send photocopy of article or typed ms with rights for sale noted. Submit seasonal material 8 months in advance. Query for electronic submissions. Reports in 2 weeks. Free sample copy and writer's guidelines.

Nonfiction: Essays, historical/nostalgic, how-to (woodworking projects and techniques), humor, inspirational, interview/profile, new product, personal experience, photo feature and technical. ("All articles must have woodworking theme.") Buys 30 mss/year. Query. Length: up to 2,500 words. Pay new authors base rate of $150/published page. Sometimes pays expenses of writers on assignment.

Photos: Send photos with submission. Reviews 35mm or larger transparencies. Offers no additional payment for photos accepted with ms. Model releases required. Buys one-time rights.

Columns/Departments: Final Pass (woodworking news and nonsense, 1,000 word max). Buys 10 mss/year. Send complete ms. Pays $100-300.

Poetry: Avant-garde, free verse, Haiku, light verse and traditional. "All poetry must have workworking or craftsmanship theme." Buys 1 poem/year. Submit maximum 5 poems. Pays $50-100.

Tips: "Reading the publication is the only real way to get a feel for the niche market *American Woodworker* represents and the needs and interests of our readers. Magazine editorial targets the serious woodworking enthusiast who wishes to improve his/her skills. Feature stories and articles most accessible for freelancers. Articles should be technically accurate, well organized and reflect the needs and interests of the amateur woodworking enthusiast."

ANTIQUE REVIEW, P.O. Box 538, Worthington OH 43085-0538. Editor: Charles Muller. (614)885-9757. Fax: (614)885-9762. 60% freelance written. Eager to work with new/unpublished writers. Monthly tabloid for an antique-oriented readership, "generally well-educated, interested in Early American furniture and decorative arts, as well as folk art." Monthly tabloid. Estab. 1975. Circ. 11,000. Pays on publication date assigned at time of purchase. Publishes ms an average of 3 months after acceptance. Buys first North American serial rights and second (reprint) rights to material originally published in dissimilar publications. Byline given. Phone queries OK. Reprints OK if not first printed in competitive publications. Send photocopy of article and information about where and when the article previously appeared. Pays 100% of original fee. Reports in 2 months. Free sample copy and writer's guidelines for #10 SASE.

Nonfiction: "The articles we desire concern history and production of furniture, pottery, china, and other quality Americana. In some cases, contemporary folk art items are acceptable. We are also interested in reporting on antiques shows and auctions with statements on conditions and prices. We do not want articles on contemporary collectibles." Buys 5-8 mss/issue. Query with clips of published work. Query should show "author's familiarity with antiques, an interest in the historical development of artifacts relating to early America and an awareness of antiques market." Length: 200-2,000 words. Pays $100-200. Sometimes pays the expenses of writers on assignment.

Photos: State availability of photos with query. Payment included in ms price. Uses 3×5 or larger glossy b&w prints. Color acceptable. Captions required. Articles with photographs receive preference.

Tips: "Give us a call and let us know of specific interests. We are more concerned with the background in antiques than in writing abilities. The writing can be edited, but the knowledge imparted is of primary interest. A frequent mistake is being too general, not becoming deeply involved in the topic and its research. We are interested in primary research into America's historic material culture."

THE ANTIQUE TRADER WEEKLY, P.O. Box 1050, Dubuque IA 52004-1050. (800)531-0880. Fax: (319)588-0888. Editor: Kyle D. Husfloen. 50% freelance written. Works with a small number of new/unpublished writers each year. Weekly newspaper for collectors and dealers in antiques and collectibles. Estab. 1957. Circ. 60,000. Publishes ms an average of 1 year after acceptance. Buys all rights. Payment at beginning of month following publication. Simultaneous submissions OK. Submit seasonal/holiday material 4 months in advance. Sample copy $1 for #10 SASE. Free writer's guidelines.

Nonfiction: "We invite authoritative and well-researched articles on all types of antiques and collectors' items and in-depth stories on specific types of antiques and collectibles. No human interest stories. We do not pay for brief information on new shops opening or other material printed as a service to the antiques hobby." Buys about 60 mss/year. Query or submit complete ms. Pays $25-100 for feature articles; $100-250 for feature cover stories.

Photos: Submit a liberal number of good b&w photos to accompany article. Uses 35mm slides for cover. Offers no additional payment for photos accompanying mss.

Tips: "Send concise, polite letter stating the topic to be covered in the story and the writer's qualifications. No 'cute' letters rambling on about some 'imaginative' story idea. Writers who have a concise yet readable style and know their topic are always appreciated. I am most interested in those who have personal collecting experience or can put together a knowledgable and informative feature after interviewing a serious collector/authority."

ANTIQUES & AUCTION NEWS, Route 230 West, P.O. Box 500, Mount Joy PA 17552. (717)653-1833, ext. 254. Editor: Doris Ann Johnson. Works with a very small number of new/unpublished writers each year. Weekly tabloid for dealers and buyers of antiques, nostalgics and collectibles, and those who follow antique shows, shops and auctions. Estab. 1969. Circ. 35,000. Pays on publication. Submit seasonal/holiday material 3 months in advance. Free sample copy available if you mention *Writer's Market*. Writer's guidelines for #10 SASE.

Nonfiction: "Our readers are interested in collectibles and antiques dating approximately from the Civil War to the present, originating in the US or western Europe. We will consider a few stories per year if they are well-written, slanted toward helping collectors, buyers, dealers and readers learn more about the field. This could be an historical perspective, a specific area of collecting, an especially interesting antique or unusual collection. Issues have included material on old Christmas ornaments, antique love tokens, collections of fans, pencils and pottery, and 'The Man from U.N.C.L.E.' books and magazines. Articles may be how-to, informational research, news and reporting and even an occasional photo feature." Call or write before submitting any manuscript. Length: 1,000 words or less preferred, but will consider up to 2,000 words. Pays $12.50 for articles without photos; $15 for articles with usable photos; $20 for front page. "We also accept an occasional short article—about one typed page, with a good photo—for which we will pay $7.50, $5 without photo."

Photos: Purchased as part of ms package. "We prefer b&w photos, usually of a single item against a simple background. Color photos can be used if there is good contrast between darks and lights." Captions required. Photos are returned.

BECKETT BASEBALL CARD MONTHLY, Statabase, Inc., Suite 200, 4887 Alpha Rd., Dallas TX 75244. (214)991-6657. Fax: (214)991-8930. Editor: Dr. James Beckett. Managing Editor: Jay Johnson. 85% freelance written. Monthly magazine on baseball card and sports memorabilia collecting. "Our readers expect our publication to be entertaining and informative. Our slant is that hobbies are fun and rewarding. Especially wanted are how-to-collect articles." Estab. 1984. Circ. 750,000. **Pays on acceptance.** Publishes ms an average of 4 months after acceptance. Byline given. Pays $50 kill fee. Buys first North American serial rights. Submit seasonal/holiday material 6 months in advance. "No simultaneous submissions, please!" Reports in 1 month. Sample copy $2.95. Free writer's guidelines.

Nonfiction: Book excerpts, historical/nostalgic, how-to, humor, interview/profile, new product, opinion, personal experience, photo feature and technical. Special issues include: February (spring training); April (season preview); July (All Star Game); August (Stay in School); and October (World Series). No articles that emphasize speculative prices and investments. Buys 145 mss/year. Send complete ms. Length: 300-1,500 words. Pays $100-400 for assigned articles; $50-200 for unsolicited articles. Sometimes pays expenses of writers on assignment.

Photos: Send photos with submission. Reviews 35mm transparencies, 5 × 7 or larger prints. Offers $10-300/photo. Captions, model releases and identification of subjects required. Buys one-time rights.

Fiction: Humorous only.

Tips: "A writer for *Becket Baseball Card Monthly* should be an avid sports fan and/or a collector with an enthusiasm for sharing his/her interests with others. Articles must be factual, but not overly statistic-laden. First person (not research) articles presenting the writer's personal experiences told with wit and humor, and emphasizing the stars of the game, are *always* wanted. Acceptable articles must be of interest to our two basic reader segments: teenaged boys and their middle-aged fathers who are re-experiencing a nostalgic renaissance of their own childhoods. Prospective writers should write down to neither group!"

BECKETT BASKETBALL MONTHLY, Statabase, Inc., Suite 200, 4887 Alpha Rd., Dallas TX 75244. (214)991-6657. Fax: (214)991-8930. Editor: Dr. James Beckett. Managing Editor: Jay Johnson. 85% freelance written. Monthly magazine on basketball card and sports memorabilia collecting. "Our readers expect our publication to be entertaining and informative. Our slant is that hobbies are fun and rewarding. Especially wanted are articles dealing directly with the hobby of basketball card collecting." Estab. 1990. Circ. 250,000. **Pays on acceptance.** Publishes ms an average of 4 months after acceptance. Byline given. Pays $50 kill fee. Buys first North American serial rights. Submit seasonal/holiday material 6 months in advance. "No simultaneous submissions, please!" Reports in 1 month. Sample copy $2.95. Free writer's guidelines.

Nonfiction: Book excerpts, historical/nostalgic, how-to, humor, interview/profile, new product, opinion, personal experience, photo feature and technical. Special issues include: February (All-Star Game, Stay in School); June (playoffs); and September (new card sets issued). No articles that emphasize speculative prices and investments. Buys 145 mss/year. Send complete ms. Length: 300-1,500 words. Pays $100-400 for assigned articles; $100-200 for unsolicited articles. Sometimes pays expenses of writers on assignment.

Photos: Send photos with submission. Reviews 35mm transparencies, 5 × 7 or larger prints. Offers $10-300/photo. Captions, model releases and identification of subjects required. Buys one-time rights.

Fiction: Humorous only.

Tips: "A writer for *Beckett Basketball Monthly* should be an avid sports fan and/or a collector with an enthusiasm for sharing his/her interests with others. Articles must be factual, but not overly statistic-laden. First person (not research) articles presenting the writer's personal experiences told with wit and humor, and emphasizing the stars of the game, are *always* wanted. Acceptable articles must be of interest to our two basic reader segments: late teenaged boys and their fathers who are re-experiencing a nostalgic renaissance of their own childhoods. Prospective writers should write down to neither group!"

BECKETT FOCUS ON FUTURE STARS, Statabase, Inc., Suite 200, 4887 Alpha Rd., Dallas TX 75244. (214)991-6657. Fax: (214)991-8930. Editor: Dr. James Beckett. Managing Editor: Jay Johnson. 85% freelance written. Monthly magazine offering superstar coverage of young, outstanding players in baseball (major-league rookies, minor league stars and college), basketball (college), football (college) and hockey (juniors and college), with an emphasis on collecting sports cards and memorabilia. "Our readers expect our publication to be entertaining and informative. Our slant is that hobbies are fun and rewarding. Especially wanted are how-to collect articles." Estab. 1991. Circ. 100,000. **Pays on acceptance.** Publishes ms an average of 4 months after acceptance. Byline given. Pays $50 kill fee. Buys first North American serial rights. Submit seasonal/holiday material 8 months in advance. "No simultaneous submissions, please!" Reports in 1 month. Sample copy $2.95. Free writer's guidelines.

Nonfiction: Book excerpts, historical/nostalgic, how-to, humor, interview/profile, new product, opinion, personal experience, photo feature and technical. Special issues include: January (card sets in review); February (Stay in School); June (Draft Special). No articles that emphasize speculative prices and investments on cards. Buys 145 mss/year. Send complete ms. Length: 300-1,500 words. Pays $100-400 for assigned articles; $50-200 for unsolicited articles. Sometimes pays expenses of writers on assignment.

Photos: Send photos with submission. Reviews 35mm transparencies, 5×7 or larger prints. Offers $25-300/photo. Captions, model releases and identification of subjects required. Buys one-time rights.

Fiction: Humorous only

Tips: "A writer for *Beckett Focus on Future Stars* should be an avid sports fan and/or a collector with an enthusiasm for sharing his/her interests with others. Articles must be factual, but not overly statistic-laden. First person (not research) articles presenting the writer's personal experiences told with wit and humor, and emphasizing the stars of the game, are *always* wanted. Acceptable articles must be of interest to our two basic reader segments: teenaged boys and their middle-aged fathers who are re-experiencing a nostalgic renaissance of their own childhoods. Prospective writers should write down to neither group!"

BECKETT FOOTBALL CARD MONTHLY, Statabase, Inc., Suite 200, 4887 Alpha Rd., Dallas TX 75244. (214)991-6657. Fax: (214)991-8930. Editor: Dr. James Beckett. Managing Editor: Jay Johnson. 85% freelance written. Monthly magazine on football card and sports memorabilia collecting. "Our readers expect our publication to be entertaining and informative. Our slant is that hobbies are fun and rewarding. Especially wanted are how-to collect articles." Estab. 1989. Circ. 250,000. **Pays on acceptance.** Publishes ms an average of 4 months after acceptance. Byline given. Pays $50 kill fee. Buys first North American serial rights. Submit seasonal/holiday material 6 months in advance. "No simultaneous submissions, please!" Reports in 1 month. Sample copy $2.95. Free writer's guidelines.

Nonfiction: Book excerpts, historical/nostalgic, how-to, humor, interview/profile, new product, opinion, personal experience, photo feature, technical. Special issues include: January (Super Bowl); February (Pro Bowl); April (NFL Draft); August (Stay in School issue); and September (Preview). No articles that emphasize speculative prices and investments. Buys 145 mss/year. Send complete ms. Length: 300-1,500 words. Pays $100-400 for assigned articles; $50-200 for unsolicited articles. Sometimes pays expenses of writers on assignment.

Photos: Send photos with submission. Reviews 35mm transparencies, 5×7 or larger prints. Offers $10-300/photo. Captions, model releases and identification of subjects required. Buys one-time rights.

Fiction: Humorous only.

Tips: "A writer for *Beckett Football Card Monthly* should be an avid sports fan and/or a collector with an enthusiasm for sharing his/her interests with others. Articles must be factual, but not overly statistic-laden. Acceptable articles must be of interest to our two basic reader segments: teenaged boys and their middle-aged fathers who are re-experiencing a nostalgic renaissance of their own childhoods. Prospective writers should write down to neither group!"

BECKETT HOCKEY MONTHLY, Statabase, Inc., Suite 200, 4887 Alpha Rd., Dallas TX 75244. (214)991-6657. Fax: (214)991-8930. Editor: Dr. James Beckett. Managing Editor: Jay Johnson. 85% freelance written. Monthly magazine on hockey, hockey card and memorabilia collecting. "Our readers expect our publication to be entertaining and informative. Our slant is that hobbies are for fun and rewarding. Especially wanted are how-to collect articles." Estab. 1990. Circ. 250,000. **Pays on acceptance.** Publishes ms an average of 3 months after acceptance. Byline given. Pays $50 kill fee. Buys first North American serial rights. Submit seasonal/holiday material 6 months in advance. "No simultaneous submissions, please!" Reports in 1 month. Sample copy $2.95. Free writer's guidelines.

Nonfiction: Book excerpts, historical/nostalgic, how-to, humor, interview/profile, new product, opinion, personal experience, photo feature and technical. Special issues include: February (All-Star Game); April (Stanley Cup Preview); June (Draft); and October (Season Preview). No articles that emphasize speculative prices and investments. Buys 145 mss/year. Send complete ms. Length: 300-1,500 words. Pays $100-400 for assigned articles; $50-200 for unsolicited articles. Sometimes pays expenses of writers on assignment.

Photos: Send photos with submission. Reviews 35mm transparencies, 5×7 or larger prints. Offers $10-300/photo. Captions, model releases and identification of subjects required. Buys one-time rights.

Fiction: Humorous only.

Tips: "A writer for *Beckett Hockey Monthly* should be an avid sports fan and/or a collector with an enthusiasm for sharing his/her interests with others. Articles must be factual, but not overly statistic-laden. Acceptable articles must be of interest to our two basic reader segments: teenaged boys and their middle-aged fathers who are re-experiencing a nostalgic renaissance of their own childhoods. Prospective writers should write down to neither group!"

THE BLADE MAGAZINE, BLADE TRADE, Blade Publications, P.O. Box 22007, Chattanooga TN 37422. Fax: (615)892-7254. Editor: Steve Shackleford. 90% freelance written. For knife enthusiasts who want to know as much as possible about quality knives and edged weapons. Publishes 8 issues/year. Estab. 1973. Pays on publication. Publishes ms an average of 6 months after acceptance. Buys all rights. Submit seasonal/holiday material 6 months in advance. Previously published submissions OK if not run in other knife publications. Reports in 2 months. Sample copy $3.25. Writer's guidelines for #10 SASE.

Nonfiction: How-to; historical (on knives and weapons); adventure on a knife theme; interview (knifemakers); celebrities who own knives; knives featured in movies with shots from the movie, etc.; new product; nostalgia; personal experience; photo feature; profile and technical. "We would also like to receive articles on knives in adventuresome life-saving situations." No poetry. Buys 75 unsolicited mss/year. "We evaluate complete manuscripts and make our decision on that basis." Length: 500-1,000 words, longer if content warrants it. Pays $150/story minimum; more for "better" writers. "We will pay top dollar in the knife market." Sometimes pays the expenses of writers on assignment. Reprints OK; send typed ms with rights for sale noted and information about when and where the article previously appeared. Pays 90% of their fee for an original article. Publishes novel excerpts.

Photos: Send photos with ms. Pays $5 for 8×10 b&w glossy prints, $25-75 for 35mm color transparencies. Captions required.

Tips: "We are always willing to read submissions from anyone who has read a few copies and studied the market. The ideal article for us is a piece bringing out the romance, legend, and love of man's oldest tool—the knife. We like articles that place knives in peoples' hands—in life saving situations, adventure modes, etc. (Nothing gory or with the knife as the villain). People and knives are good copy. We are getting more and better written articles from writers who are reading the publication beforehand. That makes for a harder sell for the quickie writer not willing to do his homework."

COINS, Krause Publications, 700 E. State St., Iola WI 54990-0001. (715)445-2214. Fax: (715)445-4087. Editor: Alan Herbert. 50% freelance written. Eager to work with new/unpublished writers. Monthly magazine about U.S. and foreign coins for all levels of collectors, investors and dealers. Estab. 1952. Circ. 71,000. Free sample copy and writer's guidelines.

Nonfiction: "We're looking for stories that are going to help coin collectors pursue their hobby in today's market. Stories should include what's available in the series being discussed, its value in today's market, and tips for buying that material." Buys 4 mss/issue. Query first. Length: 500-2,500 words. Pays 3¢/word to first-time contributors; fee negotiated for later articles.

Photos: Pays $5 minimum for b&w prints. Pays $25 minimum for 35mm transparencies used. Captions and model releases required. Buys first rights.

COLLECTOR EDITIONS, Collector Communications Corp., 170 5th Ave., New York NY 10010-5911. (212)989-8700. Fax: (212)645-8976. Editor: Joan Muyskens Pursley. 40% freelance written. Works with a small number of new/unpublished writers each year. Bimonthly magazine on porcelain and glass collectibles and limited-edition prints. "We specialize in contemporary (post-war ceramic and glass) collectibles, including reproductions, but also publish articles about antiques, if they are being reproduced today and are generally available." Estab. 1973. Circ. 75,000. Buys first North American serial rights. "First assignments are always done on a speculative basis." Pays within 30 days of acceptance. Publishes ms an average of 6 months after acceptance. Reports in 2 months. Sample copy $2. Writer's guidelines for #10 SASE.

Nonfiction: "Short features about collecting, written in tight, newsy style. We specialize in contemporary (postwar) collectibles. Values for pieces being written about should be included." Informational, interview, profile, exposé and nostalgia. Buys 15-20 mss/year. Query with sample photos. Length: 500-1,500 words. Pays $100-300. Sometimes pays expenses of writers on assignment.

Columns/Departments: Staff written; not interested in freelance columns.

Photos: B&w and color photos purchased with accompanying ms with no additional payment. Captions are required. "We want clear, distinct, full-frame images that say something."

Tips: "Unfamiliarity with the field is the most frequent mistake made by writers in completing an article for us."

COLLECTORS NEWS & THE ANTIQUE REPORTER, P.O. Box 156, Grundy Center IA 50638-0156. (319)824-6981. Fax: (319)824-3414. Editor: Linda Kruger. 20% freelance written. Estab. 1959. Works with a small number of new/unpublished writers each year. Monthly tabloid covering antiques, collectibles and nostalgic memorabilia. Circ. 13,000. Byline given. Pays on publication. Publishes ms an average of 1 year after acceptance. Buys first rights and makes work-for-hire assignments. Submit seasonal/holiday material 3 months in advance. Reports in 2 weeks on queries; 6 weeks on mss. Sample copy $2.50 for 9×12 SAE. Free writer's guidelines.

Nonfiction: General interest (any subject re: collectibles, antique to modern); historical/nostalgic (relating to collections or collectors); how-to (display your collection, care for, restore, appraise, locate, add to, etc.); interview/profile (covering individual collectors and their hobbies, unique or extensive; celebrity collectors, and limited edition artists); technical (in-depth analysis of a particular antique, collectible or collecting field); and travel (coverage of special interest or regional shows, seminars, conventions—or major antique shows, flea markets; places collectors can visit, tours they can take, museums, etc.). Special issues include January and June show/flea market issues and usual seasonal emphasis. Buys 100 mss/year. Query with sample of writing. Length: 900-1,200 words. Pays $1/column inch.

Photos: Reviews prints and slides. Payment for photos included in payment for ms. Captions required. Buys first rights.
Tips: Articles most open to freelancers are on farm/country/rural collectibles; celebrity collectors; collectors with unique and/or extensive collections; music collectibles; transportation collectibles; advertising collectibles; bottles; glass, china and silver; primitives; furniture; toys; black memorabilia; political collectibles; and movie memorabilia.

CRAFTS MAGAZINE, PJS Publications Inc., News Plaza, Box 1790, Peoria IL 61656. (309)682-6626. Fax: (309)682-7394. Editor: Judith Brossart. Monthly magazine. Circ. 400,000. **Pays on acceptance.** Publishes ms an average of 3 months after acceptance. Buys all rights. Reports in 1 month. "We do how-to only; we don't have special features in our magazine." Send query with photo or sketch first. Pays $75-300.

CRAFTS 'N' THINGS, Clapper Communications Companies, Suite 1000, 701 Lee St., Des Plaines IL 60016-4570. (708)297-7400. Fax: (708)297-8528. Editor: Julie Stephani. 80% freelance written. How-to and craft project magazine published 10 times/year. "We publish instruction for craft projects for beginners to intermediate level hobbyists." Estab. 1975. Circ. 300,000. Pays on publication. Publishes ms an average of 4 months after acceptance. Byline given. Offers $50 kill fee. Buys first, second serial (reprint) or all rights. Publishes reprints of previously published articles; send photocopy of article. Submit seasonal material 6 months in advance. Simultaneous submissions OK. Free sample copy and writer's guidelines.
Nonfiction: How-to (craft projects) and new product (for product review column). Send SASE for list of issue themes. Buys 240 mss/year. Send complete ms with photos and instructions. Pays $50-250. Offers listing exchange as a product source instead of payment in some cases.
Columns/Departments: Bright Ideas (original ideas for wroking better with crafts—hints and tips). Buys 30 mss/year. Send complete ms. Length: 25-50 words. Pays $20.
Tips: "Query for guidelines, themes and deadlines. How-to articles are best bet for freelancers."

‡CROSS STITCH SAMPLER, Sampler Publications, P.O. Box 413, Chester Heights PA 19017-0413. (215)358-9242. Fax: (215)358-9340. Editor: Deborah N. DeSimone. Quarterly magazine on needlework and counted thread. Estab. 1983. Circ. 118,000. Pays on publication. Publishes ms an average of 3 months after acceptance. Byline given. Buys all rights. Simultaneous and previously published submissions OK. Reprints OK; send typed ms with rights for sale noted and information about when and where the article previously appeared. Pays 50% of original article fee. Reports in 3 months. Sample copy for 9 × 12 SAE with 7 first class stamps.
Nonfiction: General interest, historical/nostalgic, inspirational, interview/profile, personal experience and photo feature. Buys 2-4 mss/year. Send complete ms. Pays $75-300.
Photos: Send photos with submission. Reviews contact sheets, 4 × 5 transparencies and 3 × 5 prints. Offers no additional payment for photos accepted with ms. Captions and identification of subjects required. Buys one-time rights.

CROSS-STITCH PLUS, House of White Birches, 306 E. Parr Rd., Berne IN 46711. (219)589-8741. Fax: (219)589-8093. Editor: Läna Schurb. 85% freelance written. Bimonthly magazine covering cross-stitch and, to a lesser degree, other needle crafts. "We print high-quality original cross-stitch designs of varying degrees of difficulty, aimed at novices and experienced needleworkers. We also feature, in each issue, one or two projects of another needle medium, designed to expand our readers' horizons." Estab. 1985. Circ. 75,000. Pays on publication. Byline given. Buys first rights, all rights, or makes work-for-hire assignments. Submit seasonal/holiday material 7 months in advance. Query for electronic submissions. Reports in 1 month. Sample copy $3. Writer's guidelines and editorial schedule for large SASE.
Tips: "A writer can best approach *Cross-Stitch Plus* by exhibiting excellence in their stitchery and by following our writer's guides (typed manuscripts, etc.). We are flexible and will work with beginners *if* their stitchery is good enough."

DECORATIVE ARTIST'S WORKBOOK, F&W Publications, Inc., 1507 Dana Ave., Cincinnati OH 45207-1005. Editor: Sandra Carpenter. Estab. 1987. 50% freelance written. Bimonthly magazine covering decorative painting projects and products of all sorts. Offers "straightforward, personal instruction in the techniques of decorative painting." Circ. 88,000. **Pays on acceptance.** Byline given. Offers 20% kill fee. Buys first North American serial rights. Submit seasonal/holiday material 8 months in advance. Reports in 1 month. Sample copy $3.65 for 9 × 12 SAE with 5 first class stamps.
Nonfiction: How-to (related to decorative painting projects), new products, techniques and artist profiles. Buys 30 mss/year. Query with slides or photos. Length: 1,200-1,800 words. Pays 10-12¢/word.
Photos: State availability of photos and slides with submission or send photos with submission. Reviews 35mm, 4 × 5 transparencies and quality photos. Offers no additional payment for photos accepted with ms. Captions required. Buys one-time rights.
Fillers: Anecdotes, facts and short humor. Buys 15/year. Length: 50-200 words. Pays $10-25.
Tips: "The more you know—and can prove you know—about decorative painting, crafting and home decor, the better your chances. I'm looking for experts in the field who, through their own experience, can artfully describe the techniques involved. How-to articles are most open to freelancers. Be sure to query with slides

or transparencies, and show that you understand the extensive graphic requirements for these pieces and are able to provide progressives—slides or illustrations that show works in progress."

DOLL WORLD The Magazine for Doll Lovers, House of White Birches, 306 E. Parr Rd., Berne IN 46711. (219)589-8741. Fax: (219)589-8093. Editor: Beth Schwartz. Associate Editor: Cary Raesner. 90% freelance written. Bimonthly magazine covering doll collecting, restoration. "Our readers collect dolls because they enjoy them. Some do as investments, but most consider them decorative." Estab. 1979. Circ. 85,000. Pays during mid-production. Byline given. Buys all rights. Submit seasonal/holiday material 1 year in advance. Simultaneous submissions OK. Reports in 2 weeks on queries. Sample copy $2.95. Writer's guidelines for SASE.
Nonfiction: Historical/nostalgic, how-to, interview/profile, technical and paper dolls. No articles about people and their doll collections. Query with or without published clips, or send complete ms. Length: 5,000 words maximum. Pays $50-250.
Photos: Send photos with submission. Offers no additional payment for photos accepted with article. Captions and identification of subjects required. Buys one-time or all rights.
Tips: "Choose a specific manufacturer and talk about his dolls or a specific doll—modern or antique—and explore its history and styles made."

DOLLS, The Collector's Magazine, Collector Communications Corp., 170 5th Ave., New York NY 10010-5911. (212)989-8700. Fax: (212)645-8976. Editor: Joan Muyskens Pursley. Managing Editor: Karen Bischoff. 75% freelance written. Works with a small number of new/unpublished writers each year. Magazine published 10 times/year covering doll collecting "for collectors of antique, contemporary manufacturer and artist dolls. We publish well-researched, professionally written articles illustrated with photographs of high quality, color or b&w." Estab. 1982. Circ. 115,000. Pays within 1 month of acceptance. Publishes ms an average of 6 months after acceptance. Byline given. "Almost all first manuscripts are on speculation. We rarely kill assigned stories, but fee would be about 33% of article fee." Buys first North American serial or second serial rights if piece has appeared in a non-competing publication. Send typed ms with rights for sale noted, including information about when and where the article previously appeared. For reprints, pays 50% of the amount paid for an original article. Submit seasonal/holiday material 6 months in advance. Reports in 2 months. Sample copy $2. Writer's guidelines for #10 SASE.
Nonfiction: Book excerpts; historical (with collecting angle); interview/profile (on doll artists); new product (just photos and captions; "we do not pay for these, but regard them as publicity"); technical (doll restoration advice by experts only); and travel (museums and collections around the world). "No sentimental, uninformed 'my doll collection' or 'my grandma's doll collection' stories or trade magazine-type stories on shops, etc. Our readers are knowledgable collectors." Query with clips. Length: 500-2,500 words. Pays $100-350. Sometimes pays expenses of writers on assignment.
Photos: Send photos with accompanying query or ms. Reviews 4×5 transparencies; 4×5 or 8×10 b&w prints and 35mm slides. "We do not buy photographs submitted without manuscripts unless we have assigned them; we pay for the manuscript/photos package in one fee." Captions required. Buys one-time rights.
Columns/Departments: Doll Views—a miscellany of news and views of the doll world includes reports on upcoming or recently held events. "*Not* the place for new dolls, auction prices or dates; we have regular contributors or staff assigned to those columns." Query with clips if available or send complete ms. Length: 200-500 words. Pays $25-75. Doll Views items are rarely bylined.
Fillers: "We don't use fillers but would consider them if we got something good. Hints on restoring, for example, or a nice illustration." Length: 500 words maximum. Pays $25-75.
Tips: "We need experts in the field who are also good writers. The most frequent mistake made by writers in completing an article assignment for us is being unfamiliar with the field; our readers are very knowledgeable. Freelancers who are not experts should know their particular story thoroughly and do background research to get the facts correct. Well-written queries from writers outside the NYC area are especially welcomed. Non-experts should stay away from technical or specific subjects (restoration, price trends). Short profiles of artists or a story of a local museum collection, with good photos, might catch our interest. Editors want to know they are getting something from a writer they cannot get from anyone else. Good writing should be a given, a starting point. After that, it's what you know."

EARLY AMERICAN LIFE, Cowles Magazines, Inc., P.O. Box 8200, Harrisburg PA 17105-8200. Fax: (717)657-9552. Editor: Frances Carnahan. 60% freelance written. Bimonthly magazine for "people who are interested in capturing the warmth and beauty of the 1600 to 1840 period and using it in their homes and lives today. They are interested in arts, crafts, travel, restoration and collecting." Estab. 1970. Circ. 150,000. Buys first North American serial rights. Buys 40 mss/year. **Pays on acceptance.** Publishes ms an average of 1 year after acceptance. Reports in 3 months. Sample copy and writer's guidelines for 9×12 SAE with 4 first class stamps. Query or submit complete ms with SASE.
Nonfiction: "Social history (the story of the people, not epic heroes and battles), travel to historic sites, country inns, antiques and reproductions, refinishing and restoration, architecture and decorating. We try to entertain as we inform. While we're always on the lookout for good pieces on any of our subjects, the 'travel to historic sites' theme is most frequently submitted. Would like to see more on how real people did something

great to their homes." Buys 40 mss/year. Query or submit complete ms. Length: 750-3,000 words. Pays $100-600. Pays expenses of writers on assignment.

Photos: Pays $10 for 5×7 (and up) b&w photos used with mss, minimum of $25 for color. Prefers 2¼×2¼ and up, but can work from 35mm.

Tips: "Our readers are eager for ideas on how to bring early America into their lives. Conceive a new approach to satisfy their related interests in arts, crafts, travel to historic sites, and especially in houses decorated in the early American style. Write to entertain and inform at the same time, and be prepared to help us with illustrations, or sources for them."

‡EDGES, The Official Publication of the American Blade Collectors Association, Blade Publications, P.O. Box 22207, Chattanooga TN 37421. Fax: (615)892-7254. Editor: J. Bruce Voyles. Quarterly magazine covering the knife business and knife collecting. Circ. 20,000. Pays on publication. Byline given. Buys all rights. Submit seasonal/holiday material 6 months in advance. Simultaneous queries and photocopied and previously published submissions OK "as long as they are exclusive to our market." Send photocopy of article, including information about when and where the article previously appeared. For reprints, pays 100% of the amount paid for an original article. Reports in 5 months. Acknowledges receipt of queries and ms in 2 months. Sample copy $1.

Nonfiction: "Emphasis on knife values with each story containing an extensive collector value chart with values on each knife." Book excerpts, expose, general interest, historical (well-researched), how-to, humor, new product, opinion, personal experience, photo feature and technical. "We look for articles on all aspects of the knife business, including technological advances, profiles, knife shows, and well-researched history. Ours is not a hard market to break into if the writer is willing to do a little research. To have a copy is almost a requirement." Buys 150 mss/year. Send complete ms. Length: 50-3,000 words "or more if material warrants additional length." Pays $150/story, minimum.

Photos: Story payment includes pictures. Captions and model release required (if persons are identifiable).

Fillers: Clippings, anecdotes and newsbreaks.

Tips: "If writers haven't studied the publication they shouldn't bother to submit an article. If they have studied it, we're an easy market to sell to." Buys 80% of the articles geared to "the knife business."

ELECTRONICS NOW, Gernsback Publications, Inc., 500 B Bi-County Blvd., Farmingdale NY 11735. (516)293-3000. Editor: Brian C. Fenton. 75% freelance written. Monthly magazine on electronics technology. "*Electronics Now* presents features on electronics technology and electronics construction." Estab. 1929. Circ. 175,000. **Pays on acceptance.** Publishes ms an average of 4 months after acceptance. Byline given. Buys all rights. Submit seasonal/holiday material 5-6 months in advance. Query for electronic submissions. Reports in 2 months on queries; 4 months on mss. Free sample copy and writer's guidelines.

Nonfiction: How-to (electronic project construction), humor (cartoons) and new product. Buys 150-200 mss/year. Send complete ms. Length: 1,000-10,000 words. Pays $200-800 for assigned articles; $100-800 for unsolicited articles.

Photos: Send photos with submission. Offers no additional payment for photos accepted with ms. Captions, model releases and identification of subjects required. Buys all rights.

FIBERARTS, The Magazine of Textiles, Altamont Press, 50 College St., Asheville NC 28801. (704)253-0467. Fax: (704)253-7952. Editor: Ann Batchelder. 100% freelance written. Eager to work with new/unpublished writers. Magazine appears 5 times/year, covering textiles as art and craft (weaving, quilting, surface design, stitchery, knitting, fashion, crochet, etc.) for textile artists, craftspeople, hobbyists, teachers, museum and gallery staffs, collectors and enthusiasts. Estab. 1975. Circ. 23,000. Pays 60 days after publication. Publishes ms an average of 4 months after acceptance. Byline given. Buys first rights. Editorial guidelines and style sheet available. Sample copy $4.50 for 10×12 SAE with 2 first class stamps. Writer's guidelines for #10 SAE with 2 first class stamps.

Nonfiction: Historical; artist interview/profile; opinion; photo feature; technical; education, trends; exhibition reviews; and textile news. Query. "Please be very specific about your proposal. Also an important consideration in accepting an article is the kind of photos—35mm slides and/or b&w glossies—that you can provide as illustration. We like to see photos in advance." Length: 250-2,000 words. Pays $40-300, depending on article. Rarely pays the expenses of writers on assignment or for photos.

Tips: "Our writers are very familiar with the textile field, and this is what we look for in a new writer. Familiarity with textile techniques, history or events determines clarity of an article more than a particular style of writing. The writer should also be familiar with *Fiberarts*, the magazine."

FINE WOODWORKING, The Taunton Press, P.O. Box 5506, Newtown CT 06470-5506. (203)426-8171. Fax: (203)426-3434. Editor: William Sampson. Bimonthly magazine on woodworking in the small shop. "All writers are also skilled woodworkers. It's more important that a contributor be a woodworker than a writer. Our editors (also woodworkers) will fix the words." Estab. 1975. Circ. 292,000. Pays on publication. Byline given. Kill fee varies; "editorial discretion." Buys first rights and rights to republish in anthologies and use in promo pieces. Submit seasonal/holiday material 6 months in advance. Simultaneous submissions OK. Query for electronic submissions. Reports in 2 months. Sample copy $5.50 with 10 first class stamps. Free writer's guidelines.

Nonfiction: How-to (woodworking). Buys 120 mss/year. "No specs—our editors would rather see more than less." Pays $150/magazine page. Sometimes pays expenses of writers on assignment.

Photos: Send photos with submission. Reviews contact sheets, negatives, transparencies and prints. Captions, model releases and identification of subjects required. Buys one-time rights.

Columns/Departments: Notes & Comment (topics of interest to woodworkers); Question & Answer (woodworking Q & A); Follow-Up (information on past articles/readers' comments); and Methods of Work (shop tips). Buys 400 items/year. Length varies. Pays $10-150/published page.

Tips: "Send for authors guidelines and follow them. Stories about woodworking reported by non-woodworkers *not* used. Our magazine is essentially reader-written by woodworkers."

FINESCALE MODELER, Kalmbach Publishing Co., 21027 Crossroads Circle, P.O. Box 1612, Waukesha WI 53187. (414)796-8776. Editor: Bob Hayden. 80% freelance written. Eager to work with new/unpublished writers. Magazine published 8 times/year "devoted to how-to-do-it modeling information for scale model builders who build non-operating aircraft, tanks, boats, automobiles, figures, dioramas, and science fiction and fantasy models." Circ. 80,000. **Pays on acceptance.** Publishes ms an average of 14 months after acceptance. Byline given. Buys all rights. Reports in 6 weeks on queries; 3 months on mss. Sample copy for 9 × 12 SAE with 3 first class stamps. Free writer's guidelines.

Nonfiction: How-to (build scale models); and technical (research information for building models). Query or send complete ms. Length: 750-3,000 words. Pays $30/published page minimum.

Photos: Send photos with ms. Pays $7.50 minimum for transparencies and $5 minimum for 5 × 7 b&w prints. Captions and identification of subjects required. Buys one-time rights.

Columns/Departments: *FSM* Showcase (photos plus description of model); and *FSM* Tips and Techniques (model building hints and tips). Buys 25-50 Tips and Techniques/year. Query or send complete ms. Length: 100-1,000 words. Pays $5-100.

Tips: "A freelancer can best break in first through hints and tips, then through feature articles. Most people who write for *FSM* are modelers first, writers second. This is a specialty magazine for a special, quite expert audience. Essentially, 99% of our writers will come from that audience."

HANDWOVEN, Interweave Press, 201 E. 4th St., Loveland CO 80537. (303)669-7672. Fax: (303)667-8317. Editor: Jean Scorgie. 75% freelance written. Bimonthly magazine (except July) covering handweaving, spinning and dyeing. Audience includes "practicing textile craftsmen. Article should show considerable depth of knowledge of subject, although tone should be informal and accessible." Estab. 1975. Circ. 35,000. Pays on publication. Publishes ms an average of 10 months after acceptance. Byline given. Pays 50% kill fee. Buys first North American serial rights. Simultaneous queries OK. Sample copy $4.50. Writer's guidelines for #10 SASE.

Nonfiction: Historical and how-to (on weaving and other craft techniques; specific items with instructions); and technical (on handweaving, spinning and dyeing technology). "All articles must contain a high level of in-depth information. Our readers are very knowledgeable about these subjects." Query. Length: 500-2,000 words. Pays $35-200.

Photos: State availability of photos. Identification of subjects required.

Tips: "We prefer work written by writers with an in-depth knowledge of weaving. We're particularly interested in articles about new weaving and spinning techniques as well as applying these techniques to finished products."

HOME MECHANIX, 2 Park Ave., New York NY 10016. (212)779-5000. Editor: Michael Chotiner. Contact: Natalie Posner. 50% freelance written. Prefers to work with published/established writers. "If it's good, and it fits the type of material we're currently publishing, we're interested, whether writer is new or experienced." Magazine, published 10 times/year, for the active home and car owner. "Articles emphasize an active, home-oriented lifestyle. Includes information useful for maintenance, repair and renovation to the home and family car. Information on how to buy, how to select products useful to homeowners/car owners. Emphasis in home-oriented articles is on good design, inventive solutions to styling and space problems, useful home-workshop projects." Estab. 1928. Circ. 1 million. **Pays on acceptance.** Publishes ms an average of 6 months after acceptance. Byline given. Buys first North American serial rights. Reports in 3 months. Query.

Nonfiction: Feature articles relating to homeowner/car owner, 1,500-2,500 words. "This may include personal home-renovation projects, professional advice on interior design, reports on different or unusual construction methods, energy-related subjects, outdoor/backyard projects, etc. No high-tech subjects such as aerospace, electronics, photography or military hardware. Most of our automotive features are written by experts in the field, but fillers, tips, how-to-repair, or modification articles on the family car are welcome. Articles on construction, tool use, refinishing techniques, etc., are also sought. Pays $300 minimum for features; fees based on number of printed pages, photos accompanying mss., etc." Pays expenses of writers on assignment.

Photos: Photos should accompany mss. Pays $600 and up for transparencies for cover. Inside color: $300/1 page, $500/2, $700/3, etc. Captions and model releases required.

• Ranked as one of the best markets for freelance writers in *Writer's Digest* magazine's annual "Top 100 Markets," January 1993.

Tips: "The most frequent mistake made by writers in completing an article assignment for *Home Mechanix* is not taking the time to understand its editorial focus and special needs."

THE HOME SHOP MACHINIST, 2779 Aero Park Dr., P.O. Box 1810, Traverse City MI 49685. (616)946-3712. Fax: (616)946-3289. Editor: Joe D. Rice. 95% freelance written. Bimonthly magazine covering machining and metalworking for the hobbyist. Circ. 24,500. Pays on publication. Publishes ms an average of 18 months after acceptance. Byline given. Buys first North American serial rights only. Simultaneous submissions OK. Reports in 2 months. Free sample copy and writer's guidelines for 9 × 12 SASE.

Nonfiction: How-to (projects designed to upgrade present shop equipment or hobby model projects that require machining) and technical (should pertain to metalworking, machining, drafting, layout, welding or foundry work for the hobbyist). No fiction. Buys 50 mss/year. Query or send complete ms. Length: open— "whatever it takes to do a thorough job." Pays $40/published page, plus $9/published photo; $70/page for camera-ready art; and $40 for b&w cover photo.

Photos: Send photos with ms. Pays $9-40 for 5 × 7 b&w prints. Captions and identification of subjects required.

Columns/Departments: Book Reviews; New Product Reviews; Micro-Machining; and Foundry. "Writer should become familiar with our magazine before submitting. Query first." Buys 25-30 mss/year. Length: 600-1,500 words. Pays $40-70/page.

Fillers: Machining tips/shortcuts. No news clippings. Buys 12-15/year. Length: 100-300 words. Pays $30-48.

Tips: "The writer should be experienced in the area of metalworking and machining; should be extremely thorough in explanations of methods, processes—always with an eye to safety; and should provide good quality b&w photos and/or clear drawings to aid in description. Visuals are of increasing importance to our readers. Carefully planned photos, drawings and charts will carry a submission to our magazine much farther along the path to publication."

JUGGLER'S WORLD, International Jugglers Association, Box 443, Davidson NC 28036. (704)892-1296. Fax: (704)892-2499. Editor: Bill Giduz. 25% freelance written. A quarterly magazine on juggling. "*Juggler's World* publishes news, feature articles, fiction and poetry that relates to juggling. We also encourage 'how-to' articles describing how to learn various juggling tricks." Circ. 3,500. **Pays on acceptance.** Publishes ms an average of 6 months after acceptance. Byline given. Buys all rights. Submit seasonal/holiday material 6 months in advance. Simultaneous and previously published submissions OK; send photocopy of article. For reprints, pays 50% of the amound paid for an original article. Query for electronic submissions. Reports in 1 week. Sample copy for 9 × 12 SAE with 5 first class stamps. Writer's guidelines for #10 SASE.

Nonfiction: Essays, general interest, historical/nostalgic, how-to, humor, interview/profile, opinion, personal experience, photo feature and travel. Buys 3 mss/year. Query. Length: 500-2,000 words. Pays $50-100 for assigned articles. Pays expenses of writers on assignment.

Photos: State availability of photos with submission. Reviews contact sheets, negatives and prints. Offers no additional payment for photos accepted with ms. Captions required. Buys one-time rights.

Fiction: Ken Letko, fiction editor. Adventure, fantasy, historical, humorous, science fiction and slice-of-life vignettes. Buys 2 mss/year. Query. Length: 250-1,000 words. Pays $25-50.

Tips: "The best approach is a feature article or an interview with a leading juggler. Article should include both human interest material (describe the performer as an individual) and technical juggling information to make clear to a knowledgeable audience the exact tricks and skits performed."

KITPLANES, For designers, builders and pilots of experimental aircraft, Fancy Publications, P.O. Box 6050, Mission Viejo CA 92690. (714)855-8822. Fax: (714)855-3045. Editor: Dave Martin. Associate Editor: Keith Beveridge. 70% freelance written. Eager to work with new/unpublished writers. Monthly magazine covering self-construction of private aircraft for pilots and builders. Estab. 1972. Circ. 75,000. Pays on publication. Publishes ms an average of 3 months after acceptance. Byline given. Offers negotiable kill fee. Buys first North American serial rights. Submit seasonal/holiday material 6 months in advance. Query for electronic submissions. Reports in 2 weeks on queries; 6 weeks on mss. Sample copy $3. Free writer's guidelines.

Nonfiction: How-to, interview/profile, new product, personal experience, photo feature, technical and general interest. "We are looking for articles on specific construction techniques, the use of tools, both hand and power, in aircraft building, the relative merits of various materials, conversions of engines from automobiles for aviation use, installation of instruments and electronics." No general-interest aviation articles, or "My First Solo" type of articles. Buys 80 mss/year. Query. Length: 500-5,000 words. Pays $100-400, including story photos.

Photos: Send photos with query or ms, or state availability of photos. Pays $250 for cover photos. Captions and identification of subjects required. Buys one-time rights.

Tips: "*Kitplanes* contains very specific information—a writer must be extremely knowledgeable in the field. Major features are entrusted only to known writers. I cannot emphasize enough that articles must be directed at the individual aircraft builder. We need more 'how-to' photo features in all areas of homebuilt aircraft."

THE LEATHER CRAFTERS JOURNAL, 4307 Oak Dr., Rhinelander WI 54501-9717. (715)362-5393. Editor: William R. Reis. Managing Editor: Dorothea Schulze. 100% freelance written. Bimonthly hobby and craft magazine. "Aid to craftsmen using leather as the base medium. All age groups and skill levels from beginners to master carvers and artisans." Estab. 1990. Circ. 6,000. Pays on publication. Publishes ms an average of 2 months after acceptance. Byline given. "All assigned articles subject to review for acceptance by editor." Buys first North American serial and second serial (reprint) rights. Submit seasonal/holiday material 6 months in advance. Simultaneous and previously published submissions OK. Reports in 1 month. Sample copy $4.50. Writer's guidelines for #10 SASE.

Nonfiction: How-to (crafts, arts and any other projects using leather). "I want only articles that include hands-on, step-by-step, how-to information." Buys 75 mss/year. Send complete ms. Length: 500-2,500 words. Pays $20-200 for assigned and $20-150 for unsolicited articles. Send good contrast color print photos and full size patterns and/or fullsize photo-carve patterns with submission. Lack of these reduces payment amount. Captions required. Reprints OK; send tearsheet or photocopy of article. Pays 50% of original article fee.

Columns/Departments: Beginners, Intermediate, Artists, Western Design, International Design and Letters (the open exchange of information between all peoples). Length: 500-2,500 on all. Buys 75 mss/year. Send complete ms. Pays 5¢/word.

Fillers: Anecdotes, facts, gags illustrated by cartoonist, newsbreaks. Length: 25-200 words. Pays $3-10.

Tips: "We want to work with people who understand and know leathercraft and are interested in passing on their knowledge to others. We would prefer to interview people who have achieved a high level in leathercraft skill."

‡LINN'S STAMP NEWS, Amos Press, 911 Vandemark Rd., P.O. Box 29, Sidney OH 45365. (513)498-0801. Fax: (513)498-0814. Editor: Michael Laurence. Managing Editor: Elaine Boughner. 50% freelance written. Weekly tabloid on the stamp collecting hobby. "All articles must be about philatelic collectibles." Estab. 1928. Circ. 75,000. Pays on publication. Publishes ms an average of 1 month after acceptance. Byline given. Buys first North American serial rights. Submit seasonal/holiday material 2 months in advance. Reports in 2 weeks on mss. Free sample copy. Writer's guidelines for #10 SAE with 2 first class stamps.

Nonfiction: General interest, historical/nostalgic, how-to, interview/profile and technical. "No articles merely giving information on background of stamp subject. Must have philatelic information included." Buys 300 mss/year. Send complete ms. Length: 500 words maximum. Pays $10-50. Rarely pays expenses of writers on assignment.

Photos: State availability of photos with submission. Prefers glossy b&w prints. Offers no additional payment for photos accepted with ms. Captions required. Buys all rights.

LIVE STEAM, Live Steam, Inc., 2779 Aero Park Dr., Box 629, Traverse City MI 49685. (616)946-3712. Fax: (616)946-3289. Editor: Joe D. Rice. 90% freelance written. Eager to work with new/unpublished writers. Bimonthly magazine covering steam-powered models and full-size engines (i.e., locomotives, traction, cars, boats, stationary, etc.) "Our readers are hobbyists, many of whom are building their engines from scratch. We are interested in anything that has to do with the world of live steam-powered machinery." Circ. 12,800. Pays on publication. Publishes ms an average of 18 months after acceptance. Byline given. Buys first North American serial rights only. Reports in 3 weeks. Free sample copy and writer's guidelines.

Nonfiction: Historical/nostalgic; how-to (build projects powered by steam); new product; personal experience; photo feature; and technical (must be within the context of steam-powered machinery or on machining techniques). No fiction. Buys 50 mss/year. Query or send complete ms. Length: 500-3,000 words. Pays $30/published page—$500 maximum. Sometimes pays the expenses of writers on assignment.

Photos: Send photos with ms. Pays $50/page of finished art. Pays $8 for 5×7 b&w prints; $40 for cover (color). Captions and identification of subjects required.

Columns/Departments: Steam traction engines, steamboats, stationary steam and steam autos. Buys 6-8 mss/year. Query. Length: 1,000-3,000 words. Pays $20-50.

Tips: "At least half of all our material is from the freelancer. Requesting a sample copy and author's guide will be a good place to start. The writer must be well-versed in the nature of live steam equipment and the hobby of scale modeling such equipment. Technical and historical accuracy is an absolute must. Often, good articles are weakened or spoiled by mediocre to poor quality photos. Freelancers must learn to take a *good* photograph."

‡LOOSE CHANGE, Mead Publishing Co., 1515 S. Commerce St., Las Vegas NV 89102-2703. (702)387-8750. Publisher: Daniel R. Mead. 5-10% freelance written. Eager to work with new/unpublished writers. Magazine covering gaming and coin-operated machines; published 10 times/year. Slot machines; trade stimulators; jukeboxes; gumball and peanut vendors; pinballs; scales, etc. "Our audience is predominantly male. Readers are all collectors or enthusiasts of coin-operated machines, particularly slot machines and jukeboxes. Subscribers are, in general, not heavy readers." Circ. 3,000. **Pays on acceptance.** Publishes ms an average of 2-3 months after acceptance. Byline given. Prefers to buy all rights, but also buys first and reprint rights. "We may allow author to reprint upon request in noncompetitive publications." Previously published submissions must be accompanied by complete list of previous sales, including sale dates. Query for electronic submissions. Reports in 1 month on queries; 6 weeks on mss. Sample copy $1.50. Writer's guidelines for #10 SASE.

Nonfiction: Historical/nostalgic, how-to, interview/profile, opinion, personal experience, photo feature and technical. "Articles illustrated with clear, black and white photos are always considered much more favorably than articles without photos (we have a picture-oriented audience). The writer must be knowledgable about subject matter because our readers are knowledgable and will spot inaccuracies." Buys up to 10 mss/year. Length: 900-6,000 words; 3,500-12,000 for cover stories. Pays $100 maximum, inside stories; $200 maximum, cover (feature) stories.

Photos: "Captions should tell a complete story without reference to the body text." Send photos with ms. Reviews 8 × 10 and 5 × 7 b&w glossy prints. Captions required. "Purchase price for articles includes payment for photos."

Fiction: "All fiction must have a gambling/coin-operated-machine angle. Very low emphasis is placed on fiction. Fiction must be exceptional to be acceptable to our readers." Buys maximum 4 mss/year. Send complete ms. Length: 800-2,500 words. Pays $60 maximum.

‡**LOST TREASURE, INC.,** P.O. Box 1589, Grove OK 74344. Managing Editor: Grace Michael. 75% freelance written. Monthly, bimonthly and annual magazines covering lost treasure. Estab. 1966. Circ. 55,000. Buys all rights. Byline given. Buys 225+ mss/year. Queries welcome. Length: 1,200-1,800 words. Pays on publication (4¢/word). No simultaneous submissions. Reports in 2 months. Queries welcome. Writers guidelines for #10 SASE. Sample copies (all three magazines) and guidelines for 10 × 13 SAE with $2.90 postage.

Nonfiction: 1)*Lost Treasure,* a monthly pubilcation, is composed of lost treasure stories, legends, folklore, and how-to articles. 2) *Treasure Facts,* a bimonthly publication, consists of how-to information for treasure hunters, treasure hunting club news, who's who in treasure hunting, tips, etc. 3) *Treasure Cache,* an annual publication, contains stories about documented treasure caches with a sidebar from the author telling the reader how-to search for the cache highlighted in the story.

Photos: Black and white glossy prints with mss help sell your story. $5/published photo. Cover photos pay $100/published photo; must be 35mm color slides, vertical. Captions required.

Tips: "We are only interested in treasures that can be found with metal detectors. Queries welcome but not required. If you write about famous treasures and lost mines, be sure we haven't used your selected topic recently and story must have a new slant or new information. Source documentation required. How-To's should cover some aspect of treasure hunting and how-to steps should be clearly defined. If you have a *Treasure Cache* story we will, if necessary, help the author with the sidebar telling how to search for the cache in the story."

‡**MAIL CALL, The Most Stirring Newsletter for Civil War Enthusiasts,** P.O. Box 5031, South Hackensack NJ 07606-5031. (201)296-0419. Managing Editor: Anna Pansini. Publisher: Chris Jackson. 25% freelance written. Bimonthly hobbyist newsletter covering Civil War in America "for Civil War enthusiasts interested in reading and writing first account impressions of soldiers, Union and Confederate, as well as today's reenactors and historians." Estab. 1990. Circ. 500. Pays on publication. Publishes ms 6-12 months after acceptance. Byline given "plus short bio or background." Offers 50% kill fee. Buys one-time rights. Editorial lead time 6 months. Submit seasonal material 6 months in advance. Simultaneous and previously published submissions OK. Send photocopy of article or typed ms with rights for sale noted. Include information about when and where the article previously appeared. For reprints, pays 25% of the amount paid for an original article. Reports in 2 months on queries; 4 months on mss. Sample copy for $2.50. Writer's guidelines for $5 (includes sample copy).

Nonfiction: Book excerpts, essays, exposé, general interest, historical/nostalgic, how-to, humor, inspirational, interview/profile, opinion, personal experience, religious, travel, poetry, song lyrics and quotes. "No stories which only touch or mention Civil War themes. We prefer articles where Civil War theme is central." Buys 10 mss/year. Query. Length: 500-5,000 words. Pays $25 minimum for assigned articles; $5 minimum for unsolicited articles. Pays contributor copies for anything other than personal experience." Sometimes pays expenses of writers on assignment.

Columns/Departments: Open Letters (personal experience). Buys 4 mss/year. Query. Pays $5-100.

Fiction: Adventure, condensed novels, ethnic, historical, horror, humorous, mainstream, novel excerpts, religious, romance, science fiction, slice-of-life vignettes, suspense, western and Civil War. Articles where Civil War theme is central. Buys 2 mss/year. Query. Length: 500-2,500 words. Pays copies to $50 maximum.

Poetry: Free verse, traditional. Buys 4 poems/year. Submit unlimited number of poems. Length: 2-100 lines. Pays $5-50.

Fillers: Anecdotes, facts, gags, illustrations, newsbreaks, short humor. Buys 5/year. Length: 10-500 words. Pays $5-25.

Tips: "Writers should be familiar with Civil War history, books or movies, music, sites, battlefields or reenacting."

MANUSCRIPTS, The Manuscript Society, Department of History, University of South Carolina, Columbia SC 29208. (803)777-6525. Editor: David R. Chesnutt. 10% freelance written. Quarterly magazine for collectors of autographs and manuscripts. Estab. 1948. Circ. 1,500. **Pays on acceptance.** Publishes ms an average of 6-18 months after acceptance. Byline given. Buys first publication rights. Query for electronic submissions. Reports in 2 weeks on queries; 1 month on mss. Sample copy for 6½ × 9½ SAE and 5 first class stamps.
Nonfiction: Historical, personal experience and photo feature. Buys 4-6 mss/year. Query. Length: 1,500-3,000 words. Pays $50-250 for unsolicited articles.
Photos: State availability of photos with submission. Reviews contact sheets and prints. Offers $15-30/photo. Captions and identification of subjects required. Buys one-time rights.
Tips: "The Society is a mix of autograph collectors, dealers and scholars who are interested in manuscripts. Good illustrations of manuscript material are essential. Unusual documents are most often the basis of articles. Scholarly apparatus may be used but is not required. Articles about significant collections of documents (or unusual collections) would be welcomed. Please query first."

MINIATURE QUILTS, Chitra Publications, 2 Public Ave., Montrose PA 18801. (717)278-1984. Fax: (717)278-2223. Editor: Patti Bachelder. 40% freelance written. Quarterly magazine on miniature quilts. "We seek patterns and articles of an instructional nature (all techniques), profiles of talented quiltmakers and informational articles on all aspects of miniature quilts. Miniature is defined as quilts made up of blocks smaller than five inches." Estab. 1990. Circ. 50,000. Pays on publication. Publishes ms an average of 6 months after acceptance. Byline given. Buys second serial (reprint) rights. Submit seasonal/holiday material 6-8 months in advance. Query for electronic submissions. Reports in 2 months on queries and mss. Free sample copy and writer's guidelines.
Columns/Departments: A Quilter's Dollhouse (patterns to scale); Loving Stitches (how-to for beginners, currently written by one writer); and Book and product reviews (focused on miniature quilts, currently written by one writer). Length: 800-1,600 words.
Photos: Send photos with submission. Reviews transparencies. Offers $20/photo. Captions, model releases and identification of subjects required. Buys all rights.
Tips: "Publication hinges on good photo quality. Query with ideas; send samples of prior work."

MINIATURES SHOWCASE, Kalmbach Publishing Co., 21027 Crossroads Circle, Waukesha WI 53186-1612. Fax: (414)796-1383. Editor: Geraldine Willems. 65% freelance written. Bimonthly about dollhouse miniatures. "We feature a different decorating theme each issue—our articles support the miniature room scene we focus on and features on private collections." Circ. 48,000. Pays on publication. Publishes ms an average of 3 months after acceptance. Byline given. Buys all rights. Submit seasonal/holiday material 4 months in advance. Query for electronic submissions. Reports in 1 month. Sample copy $4. Writer's guidelines for #10 SASE.
Nonfiction: Historical/social. Buys 12 mss/year. Query. Length: 100-1,500 words. Pays 10¢/word.
Photos: State availability of photos with submission. Reviews contact sheets, negatives, transparencies and 4-color prints only. Offers no additional payment for photos accepted with ms. Captions and identification of subjects required.
Tips: "Our articles are all assigned—a freelancer should query before sending in anything. Our features are open to freelancers—each issue deals with a different topic, often historical. We also feature private collections and need slides and brief articles on hobbyists."

MODEL RAILROADER, P.O. Box 1612, Waukesha WI 53187. Editor: Russell G. Larson. Monthly for hobbyists interested in scale model railroading. Buys exclusive rights. "Study publication before submitting material." Reports on submissions within 1 month.
Nonfiction: Wants construction articles on specific model railroad projects (structures, cars, locomotives, scenery, benchwork, etc.). Also photo stories showing model railroads. Query. First-hand knowledge of subject almost always necessary for acceptable slant. Pays base rate of $90/page.
Photos: Buys photos with detailed descriptive captions only. Pays $10 and up, depending on size and use. Pays double b&w rate for color; full color cover earns $200.

MODERN GOLD MINER AND TREASURE HUNTER, Modern Gold Miner's Association, Inc., 114 Druey Rd., P.O. Box 47, Happy Camp CA 96039-0047. (916)493-2062. Fax: (916)493-2095. Editor: Dave McCracken. Managing Editor: Gary Brooks. Bimonthly magazine on small-scale gold mining and treasure hunting. "We want interesting fact and fiction stories and articles about small-scale mining, treasure hunting, camping and the great outdoors." Estab. 1987. Circ. 50,000. Pays on publication. Buys all rights. Submit seasonal/holiday material 4 months in advance. Query for electronic submissions. Reprints OK; send tearsheets or photocopy of article and information about where and when it previously appeared. Pays 50% of original article fee. Reports in 2 weeks on queries. Sample copy for 9 × 12 SAE with $1.35 postage. Free writer's guidelines.
Nonfiction: How-to, humor, inspirational, interview/profile, new product, personal experience, photo feature and travel. "No promotional articles concerning industry products." Buys 125 mss/year. Send complete ms. Length: 1,500-2,500 words. Pays $25-150.

Photos: Send photos with submission. Reviews any size transparencies and prints. Pays $10-50/photo. Captions are required. Buys all rights.

Fiction: Adventure, experimental, fantasy, historical, horror, humorous, mystery, suspense and western.

Tips: "Our general readership is comprised mostly of individuals who are actively involved in gold mining and treasure hunting, or people who are interested in reading about others who are active and successful in the field. True stories of actual discoveries, along with good color photos—particularly of gold—are preferred. Also, valuable how-to information on new and workable field techniques, preferably accompanied by supporting illustrations and/or photos."

MONITORING TIMES, Grove Enterprises Inc., P.O. Box 98, Brasstown NC 28902-0098. (704)837-9200. Fax: (704)837-2216. Managing Editor: Rachel Baughn. Publisher: Robert Grove. 80% freelance written. Monthly magazine for radio hobbyists. Estab. 1982. Circ. 25,000. **Pays on acceptance.** Publishes ms an average of 2 months after acceptance. Byline given. Buys first North American serial rights. Submit seasonal/holiday material 4 months in advance. Simultaneous submissions OK. Reports in 1 month. Sample copy and writer's guidelines for 9×12 SAE with 9 first class stamps.

Nonfiction: General interest, how-to, humor, interview/profile, personal experience, photo feature and technical. Buys 275 mss/year. Query. Length: 1,000-2,500 words. Pays $150-200. Reprints OK; send photocopy of article and information about when and where the article previously appeared. Pays 25% of their fee for an original article.

Photos: State availability of photos with submission. Offers $10-25/photo. Captions required. Buys one-time rights.

Columns/Departments: "Query managing editor."

MOUNTAIN STATES COLLECTOR, Spree Publishing, P.O. Box 2525, Evergreen CO 80439. Fax: (303)674-1253. Editor: Carol Rudolph. Managing Editor: Peg DeStefano. 85% freelance written. Monthly tabloid covering antiques and collectibles. Estab. 1970. Circ. 10,000. Pays on publication. Publishes ms an average of 6 months after acceptance. Byline given. Buys first, one-time or second serial (reprint) rights. Submit seasonal/holiday material at least 3 months in advance. Simultaneous and previously published submissions OK; send typed ms with rights for sale noted. Pays 100% of their fee for an original article. Reports in 4 months. Sample copy for 9×12 SAE with 4 first class stamps. Writer's guidelines for #10 SASE.

Nonfiction: About antiques and/or collectibles—book excerpts, historical/nostalgic, how-to (collect), interview/profile (of collectors) and photo feature. Buys 75 mss/year. Query with or without published clips, or send complete ms. Length: 500-1,500 words. Pays $15. Sometimes pays the expenses of writers on assignment (mileage, phone—not long distance travel).

Photos: Send photos with submission. Reviews contact sheets, and 5×7 b&w prints. Offers $5/photo used. Captions preferred. Buys one-time rights.

Tips: "Writers should know their topics well or be prepared to do in-depth interviews with collectors. We prefer a down-home approach. We need articles on antiques, collectors and collections; how-to articles on collecting; how a collector can get started; or clubs for collectors. We would like to see more articles in 1994 with high-quality b&w photos."

NEEDLEPOINT PLUS, Counted Thread Designs, EGW Publishing, 1041 Shary Circle, Concord CA 94518. (510)671-9852. Editor: Judy Swager. Managing Editor: Wayne Lin. 90% freelance written. Bimonthly magazine "devoted exclusively to needlepoint and counted thread techniques. It is a full-color magazine with high quality projects for all levels of stitchers. Stitchers learn to work with traditional materials and stitches as well as new threads and techniques to create pillows, samplers, gifts, home and holiday decorations, and designs to wear." Estab. 1974. Circ. 30,000. Pays on publication. Publishes ms an average of 9 months after acceptance. Byline given. Offers $100 kill fee. Buys one-time rights. Submit seasonal material 1 year in advance. Reports in 4 months on queries; 4 months on mss. Sample copy $3.95. Free writer's guidelines.

Nonfiction: General interest, historical/nostalgic, how-to (stitch patterns, finish designs), inspirational, interview/profile, personal experience, photo feature, technical and travel. No cross stitch projects. Buys 42 mss/year. Query. Length: 100-2,000 words. Pays $50-75/printed page. Can exchange articles for ad space or contributor copies.

Photos: Send photos with submission. Reviews contact sheets, negatives, transparencies or prints. Captions and model releases required. Buys one-time rights.

THE NUMISMATIST, American Numismatic Association, 818 N. Cascade Ave., Colorado Springs CO 80903-3279. (719)632-2646. Fax: (719)634-4085. Editor/Publisher: Barbara Gregory. Monthly magazine "for collectors of coins, medals, tokens and paper money." Estab. 1888. Circ. 28,000. Pays on publication. Publishes ms an average of 1 year after acceptance. Byline given. Buys first North American serial or second serial (reprint) rights. Submit photocopy of article and information about when and where the article previously appeared. Submit seasonal/holiday material 1 year in advance. Previously published submissions OK. Reports in 2 months. Free sample copy and writer's guidelines for 9×12 SAE with 5 first class stamps.

Nonfiction: Essays, expose, general interest, historical/nostalgic, humor, interview/profile, new product, opinion, personal experience, photo feature and technical. No articles that are lengthy or non-numismatic. Buys 48-60 mss/year. Send complete ms. Length: 1,000-3,500 words. Pays "on rate-per-published-page basis." Sometimes pays the expenses of writers on assignment. Reprints OK; send tearsheet of article or typed ms with rights for sale noted, plus information about when and where the article previously appeared. Pays 100% of original article fee.

Photos: Send b&w photos with submission. Reviews contact sheets and 4×5 or 5×7 prints. Offers $2.50-5/photo. Captions and identification of subjects required. Buys one-time rights.

Columns/Departments: Buys 72 mss/year. Length: 775-2,000 words. "Pays negotiable flat fee per column."

NUTSHELL NEWS, For Creators and Collectors of Scale Miniatures, Kalmbach Publishing Co., 21027 Crossroads Circle, Waukesha WI 53187-9951. (414)796-8776. Fax: (414)796-1383. Editor: Sybil Harp. 50% freelance written. Monthly magazine covering dollhouse scale miniatures. "*Nutshell News* is aimed at serious, adult hobbyists. Our readers take their miniatures seriously and do not regard them as toys. We avoid 'cutesiness' and treat our subject as a serious art form and/or an engaging leisure interest." Estab. 1971. Circ. 35,000. Pays advance fee on acceptance and balance on publication. Byline given. Offers $25 kill fee. Buys all rights but will revert rights by agreement. Submit seasonal/holiday material 1 year in advance. Reports in 3 weeks on queries; 2 months on mss. Sample copy $3.50. Writer's guidelines for #10 SASE.

Nonfiction: How-to miniature projects in 1″, ½″, ¼″ scales, interview/profile (artisans or collectors), photo feature (dollhouses, collections, museums). Annual special issues: May—smaller scales annual (½″, ¼″ or smaller scales); and August—kitcrafting—customizing kits or commercial miniatures, a how-to issue. No articles on miniature shops or essays. Buys 120 mss/year. Query. Length: 1,000-1,500 words for features, how-to's may be longer. "Payment varies, but averages $150 for features, more for long how-to's." Sometimes pays expenses of writers on assignment.

Photos: Send photos with submission. Requires 35mm slides and larger, 3×5 prints. "Photos are paid for with manuscript. Seldom buy individual photos." Captions preferred; identification of subjects required. Buys all rights.

Tips: "It is essential that writers for *Nutshell News* be active miniaturists, or at least very knowledgeable about the hobby. Our readership is intensely interested in miniatures and will discern lack of knowledge or enthusiasm on the part of an author. A writer can best break in to *Nutshell News* by convincing me that he/she knows and is interested in miniatures, and by sending photos and/or clippings to substantiate that. Photographs are extremely important. They must be sharp and properly exposed to reveal details. For articles about subjects in the Chicago/Milwaukee area, we can usually send our staff photographer."

PAPER COLLECTORS MARKETPLACE, Watson Graphic Designs, Inc., P.O. Box 128, Scandinavia WI 54977-0128. (715)467-2379. Fax: (715)467-2243. Editor: Doug Watson. 100% freelance written. Monthly magazine on paper collectibles. "All articles must relate to the hobby in some form. Whenever possible values should be given for the collectibles mentioned in the article." Estab. 1987. Circ. 4,000. Pays on publication. Byline given. Offers 25% kill fee on commissioned articles. Buys first North American serial rights. Submit seasonal/holiday material 2 months in advance. Reports in 2 weeks. Free sample copy. Writer's guidelines for #10 SASE.

Nonfiction: Historical/nostalgic, how-to, photo feature and technical. Buys 60 mss/year. Query with published clips. Length: 1,000-2,000 words. Pays 3-5¢/word.

Photos: Send photos with submissions. Offers no additional payment for photos accepted with ms. Captions, model releases and identification of subjects required. Buys one-time rights.

THE PEN AND QUILL, Universal Autograph Collectors Club (UACC), P.O. Box 6181, Washington DC 20044-6181. (202)332-7388. Editor: Bob Erickson. 20% freelance written. Bimonthly magazine of autograph collecting. All articles must advance the hobby of autograph collecting in some manner. Estab. 1966. Circ. 1,800. Pays on publication. Publishes ms an average of 6 months after acceptance. Byline given. Buys first North American serial rights. Submit seasonal/holiday material 4 months in advance. Sample copy $5.

Nonfiction: General interest, historical/nostalgic, interview/profile. Buys 4 mss/year. Send complete ms. Length: 500-2,500 words. Pays $20-100.

Photos: Send photos with submission. Offers no additional payment for photos accepted with ms. Captions and identification of subjects required. Buys one-time rights.

POPULAR ELECTRONICS HOBBYIST'S HANDBOOK, Gernsback Publications, Inc., 500 B Bi-County Blvd., Farmingdale NY 11735-3918. (516)293-3000. Fax: (516)293-3115. Editor: Carl Laron. 75% freelance written. Annual magazine on hobby electronics. Estab. 1989. Circ. 87,625. **Pays on acceptance.** Byline given. Buys all rights. Submit seasonal/holiday material 5-6 months in advance. Query for electronic submissions. Reports in 2 weeks. Free sample copy and writer's guidelines for 9×12 SAE with 5 first class stamps.

Nonfiction: General interest, historical/nostalgic, how-to (build projects, fix consumer products, etc., all of which must be electronics oriented), photo feature and technical. "No product reviews!" Buys 50-60 mss/year. Send complete ms. Length: 1,000-5,000 words. Pays $100-500 for assigned articles; $100-500 for unsolicited articles.

Photos: Send photos with submission. "We want b&w glossy photos." Reviews 5×7 or 8×10 b&w prints. Offers no additional payment for photos accepted with ms. Captions and model releases are required. Buys all rights.
Tips: "Read the magazine. Know and understand the subject matter. Write it. Submit it."

POPULAR MECHANICS, Hearst Corp., 3rd Floor, 224 W. 57th St., New York NY 10019. (212)649-2000. Editor: Joe Oldham. Managing Editor: Deborah Frank. 50% freelance written. Monthly magazine on automotive, home improvement, science, boating, outdoors, electronics. "We are a men's service magazine that tries to address the diverse interests of today's male, providing him with information to improve the way he lives. We cover stories from do-it-yourself projects to technological advances in aerospace, military, automotive and so on." Estab. 1902. Circ. 1.6 million. **Pays on acceptance.** Publishes ms an average of 6 months after acceptance. Byline given. Offers 25% kill fee. Buys all rights. Submit seasonal/holiday material 6 months in advance. Query for electronic submissions. Reports in 2 weeks on queries; 1 month on mss. Sample copy and writer's guidelines for 9×12 SASE.
Nonfiction: General interest, how-to (shop projects, car fix-its), new product and technical. Special issues: January—Design and Engineering Awards; February—Boating Guide; April—Home Improvement Guide; May—Car Care Guide; October—Automotive Parts & Accessories Guide; and November—Woodworking Guide. No historical, editorial or critique pieces. Buys 24 mss/year. Query with or without published clips or send complete ms. Length: 500-3,000 words. Pays $500-1,500 maximum for assigned articles; $15-1,000 for unsolicited articles. Sometimes pays expenses of writers on assignment.
Photos: Send photos with submission. Reviews 5×7 transparencies and prints. Offers no additional payment for photos accepted with ms. Captions, model releases and identification of subjects required. Buys first and exclusive publication rights in the US during on-sale period of issue in which photos appear plus 90 days after.
Columns/Departments: New Cars (latest and hottest cars out of Detroit and Europe), Car Care (Maintenance basics, How It Works, Fix-Its and New products: send to Mike Allen. Electronics, Audio, Home Video, Computers, Photography: send to Frank Vizard. Boating (new equipment, how-tos, fishing tips), Outdoors (gear, vehicles, outdoor adventures): send to Joe Skorupa. Home & Shop Journal: send to Steve Willson. Science (latest developments), Tech Update (breakthroughs) and Aviation (sport aviation, homebuilt aircraft, new commercial aircraft, civil aeronautics): send to Abe Dane. All columns are about 1,000 words.

POPULAR WOODWORKING, EGW Publishing Co., 1320 Galaxy Way, Concord CA 94520. (510)671-9852. Fax: (510)671-0692. Editor: Robert C. Cook. 99% freelance written. Eager to work with new/unpublished writers. Bimonthly magazine covering woodworking. "Our readers are the woodworking hobbyist and small woodshop owner. Writers should have a knowledge of woodworking, or be able to communicate information gained from woodworkers." Estab. 1981. Circ. 284,000. Pays ½ on acceptance, and the balance plus five copies on publication. Publishes ms an average of 10-12 months after acceptance. Byline given. Buys first serial and second-time rights ("at our discretion"). Submit seasonal/holiday material 6 months in advance. Reports in 2 months. Sample copy and writer's guidelines $2.95 for 9×12 SAE with 6 first class stamps.
Nonfiction: How-to (on woodworking projects, with plans); humor (woodworking anecdotes); and technical (woodworking techniques). "No home-maintenance articles or stories about bloody accidents." Buys 120 mss/year. Query with or without published clips or send complete ms. Pays $500-1,000 for large, complex projects, and $100-500 for simpler projects and other features.
Photos: Send photos with submission. Reviews contact sheets, 4×5 transparencies, 5×7 glossy prints and 35mm color slides. Offers no additional payment for photos accepted with ms; $75 extra for cover photos only. Captions and identification of subjects required. Buys one-time rights.
Columns/Departments: Jig Journal (how to make special fixtures to help a tool do a task), 500-1,500 words. Buys 6 mss/year. Query.
Fillers: Anecdotes, facts, short humor and shop tips. Buys 15/year. Length: 50-500 words.
Tips: "Show a technical knowledge of woodworking. Sharp close-up color photos of a woodworker demonstrating a technique impress me. We really need project with plans articles. Describe the steps in making a piece of furniture (or other project). Provide a cutting list and a rough diagram (we can redraw). If the writer is not a woodworker, he should have help from a woodworker to make sure the technical information is correct."

QST, American Radio Relay League, Inc., 225 Main St., Newington CT 06111-1494. (203)666-1541. Fax: (203)665-7531. Editor: Mark Wilson. Contact Assistant Managing Editor: Kirk Kleinschmidt. 20% freelance written. Monthly magazine covering amateur radio, general interest, technical activities. "Ours are topics of interest to radio amateurs and persons in the electrical and communications fields." Estab. 1914. Circ. 165,000. Pays on publication. Publishes ms an average of 4 months after acceptance. Byline given. Buys all rights. Submit seasonal/holiday material 5 months in advance. Query for electronic submissions. Reports in 3 weeks on queries. Free sample copy and writer's guidelines for 10×13 SAE with 5 first class stamps.
Nonfiction: General interest, how-to, humor, new products, personal experience, photo feature, technical (anything to do with amateur radio). Buys 50 mss/year. Query with or without published clips, or send complete ms. Length: no minimum or maximum. Pays $50/published page. Sometimes pays expenses of writers on assignment.

Photos: Send photos with submission. Offers no additional payment for photos accepted with ms. Captions, model releases and identification of subjects required. Buys all rights.
Columns/Departments: Hints and Kinks (hints/time saving procedures/circuits/associated with amateur radio), 50-200 words. Buys 100 mss/year. Send complete ms. Pays $20.
Tips: "Write with an idea, ask for sample copy and writer's guide. Technical and general interest to amateur operators, communications and electronics are most open."

QUICK & EASY CRAFTS, For Today's Crafty Women, House of White Birches, 306 E. Parr Rd., Berne IN 46711. (219)589-8741. Fax: (219)589-8093. Editor: Beth Schwartz. 90% freelance written. Bimonthly magazine covering crafts that are upscale but easily and quickly done. "Our audience does not mind spending money on craft items to use in their projects but they don't have lots of time to spend." Estab. 1979. Circ. 380,000. Pays mid-production. Byline given. Buys all rights. Submit seasonal/holiday material 1 year in advance. Reports in 2 weeks on queries. Sample copy $2; free writer's guidelines.
Nonfiction: How-to. No profiles of other crafters. Buys 150 mss/year. Send complete ms. Pays $25-250.
Tips: "Send good, clear photo with ms. Manuscript should include complete instructions for project."

QUILT WORLD, House of White Birches, 306 E. Parr Rd., Berne IN 46711. (219)589-8741. Fax: (207)794-3290. Editor: Sandra L. Hatch. 100% freelance written. Works with a small number of new/unpublished writers each year. Bimonthly magazine covering quilting. "We publish articles on quilting techniques, profiles of quilters and coverage of quilt shows. Reader is 30-70 years old, midwestern." Circ. 130,000. Pays on publication. Publishes ms an average of 6 months after acceptance. Byline given. Buys all, first, one-time and second serial (reprint) rights. Submit seasonal/holiday material 9 months in advance. Previously published submissions OK; send photocopy of article and information about when and where itpreviously appeared. Query for electronic submissions. Reports in 1 month. Sample copy $3. Writer's guidelines for #10 SASE.
Nonfiction: How-to, interview/profile (quilters), technical, new product (quilt products) and photo feature. Buys 18-24 mss/year. Query. Length: open. Pays $35-100.
Photos: Send photos with submission. Reviews transparencies and prints. Offers $15/photo (except covers). Identification of subjects required. Buys all or one-time rights.
Tips: "Send list of previous articles published with resume and a SASE. List ideas which you plan to base your articles around."

‡QUILTER'S NEWSLETTER MAGAZINE, P.O. Box 394, Wheatridge CO 80033. Fax: (303)420-7358. Editor: Bonnie Leman. Monthly. Estab. 1969. Circ. 200,000. Buys first North American serial rights or second rights. Buys about 15 mss/year. Pays on publication, sometimes on acceptance. Reports in 5 weeks. Free sample copy.
Nonfiction: "We are interested in articles on the subject of quilts and quiltmakers *only*. We are not interested in anything relating to 'Grandma's Scrap Quilts' but could use fresh material." Submit complete ms. Pays 5¢/word minimum, usually more.
Photos: Additional payment for photos depends on quality.
Fillers: Related to quilts and quiltmakers only.
Tips: "Be specific, brief, and professional in tone. Study our magazine to learn the kind of thing we like. Send us material which fits into our format but which is different enough to be interesting. Realize that we think we're the best quilt magazine on the market and that we're aspiring to be even better, then send us the cream off the top of your quilt material."

‡QUILTING INTERNATIONAL, A Showcase of Collectible Quilts & Contemporary Fiber Art, All American Crafts, Inc., 243 Newton-Sparta Rd., Newton NJ 07860. (201)383-8080. Fax: (201)383-8133. Editorial Director: Camille Pomaco. Editor: Marion Buccieri. 50% freelance written. Bimonthly quilts and quilting magazine. "We feature articles that inform and inspire quilters and fabric artists, showcasing both pieced and appliqued items, antique and contemporary. Articles that emphasize international trends and exhibits in the expanding world of quilting as a fiber art are welcome." Estab. 1987. Pays on publication. Publishes ms an average of 6 months after acceptance. Byline given. Buys first North American serial rights. Editorial lead time 4 months. Submit seasonal/holiday material 6 months in advance. Reports in 6-8 weeks on queries. Sample copy for 9 × 12 SAE with 4 first class stamps. Free writer's guidelines for #10 SASE.
Nonfiction: Quilts and patterns; quilt exhibits, international and local quilt events, general interest, historical, how-to, inspirational, interview/profile, personal experience and photo feature (all as related to quilts and quilting). No poetry or fiction. Query. Length: 1,000-1500 words. Pays 10-15¢/word. Sometimes pays expenses of writers on assignment.
Photos: Send photos with submission. Reviews 4×5 transparencies or 3×5 prints. Pays $15-30. Captions required. Buys one-time rights.
Tips: "Good quality slides or chromes of beautiful quilts are highly desirable. We want articles about specific quilts and the quilters involved."

QUILTING TODAY MAGAZINE, The International Quilt Magazine, Chitra Publications, 2 Public Ave., Montrose PA 18801. (717)278-1984. Fax: (717)278-2223. Editor: Patti Bachelder. 80% freelance written. Bimonthly magazine on quilting, traditional and contemporary. "We seek articles that will cover one or two full pages (800 words each); informative to the general quilting public, present new ideas, interviews, instructional, etc." Estab. 1986. Circ. 90,000. Pays on publication. Publishes ms an average of 6 months after acceptance. Byline given. Buys second serial (reprint) rights and makes work-for-hire assignments. Submit seasonal/holiday material 6-8 months in advance. Query for electronic submissions. Reports in 1 month on queries; 2 months on mss. Free sample copy and writer's guidelines for 9 × 12 SAE with 6 first class stamps.

Nonfiction: Books excerpts, essays, how-to (for various quilting techniques), humor, interview/profile, new product, opinion, personal experience and photo feature. "No articles about family history related to a quilt or quilts unless the quilt is a masterpiece of color and design, impeccable workmanship." Buys 20-30 mss/ year. Query with or without published clips or send complete mss. Length: 800-1,600 words. Pays $50-75/ page. Sometimes pays expenses of writers on assignment.

Photos: Send photos with submission. Reviews 35mm slides and larger transparencies. Offers $20/photo. Captions, identification of subjects required. Buys all rights unless rented from a museum.

Columns/Departments: Book and product reviews, 300 words maximum. Quilters Lesson Book (instructional), 800-1,600 words. Buys 10-12 ms/year. Send complete ms. Pays up to $75/column.

Fiction: Fantasy, historical and humorous. Buys 1 mss/year. Send complete ms. Length: 300-1,600 words. Pays $50-75/page.

Tips: "Query with ideas; send samples of prior work so that we can assess and suggest assignment. Our publications appeal to traditional quilters (generally middle-aged) who use the patterns in each issue. Must have excellent photos."

RAILROAD MODEL CRAFTSMAN, Box 700, Newton NJ 07860. (201)383-3355. Fax: (201)383-4064. Editor: William C. Schaumburg. 75% freelance written. Works with a small number of new/unpublished writers each year. Monthly magazine for model railroad hobbyists, in all scales and gauges. Circ. 97,000. Buys all rights. Buys 50-100 mss/year. Pays on publication. Publishes ms an average of 9 months after acceptance. Submit seasonal material 6 months in advance. Sample copy $2. Writer's and photographer's guidelines for SASE.

Nonfiction: "How-to and descriptive model railroad features written by persons who did the work are preferred. Almost all our features and articles are written by active model railroaders. It is difficult for non-modelers to know how to approach writing for this field." Pays minimum of $1.75/column inch of copy ($50/page).

Photos: Purchased with or without mss. Buys sharp 8 × 10 glossy prints and 35mm or larger transparencies. Pays minimum of $10 for photos or $5/diagonal inch. $200 for covers, which must tie in with article in that issue. Caption information required.

Tips: "We would like to emphasize modeling based on actual prototypes of equipment and industries as well as prototype studies of them."

SCOTT STAMP MONTHLY, Amos Press, Inc., P.O. Box 828, 2280 Industrial Blvd., Sidney OH 45365-0828. Editor: Wayne L. Youngblood. 70% freelance written. Works with a small number of new/unpublished writers each year. Monthly magazine for stamp collectors, from the beginner to the sophisticated philatelist. "The *Scott Stamp Monthly* provides collectors with new Scott catalog numbers, entertaining and educational reading. All stories must primarily be about the stamps saved by collectors, and secondarily historical or topical." Estab. 1920. Circ. 22,000. Pays on publication. Publishes ms an average of 2-3 months after acceptance. Byline given. Buys first North American serial rights. Editorial lead time 2-3 months. Submit seasonal or holiday material at least 5 months in advance. Query for electronic submissions. Prefers ASCII-based, preferably Xy-write. Reports in 1-2 months. Sample copy for 9 × 12 SAE with 5 first class stamps. Writer's guidelines for #10 SASE.

Nonfiction: General interest, historical/nostalgic, how-to, opinion, personal experience, photo feature and technical (all must be stamp-related). "I do not want to see general articles that are only loosely tied to stamp collecting. This includes historical pieces tied to stamps only by illustration." Buys 65+ mss/year. Query with published clips. Length: 800-2,500 words. Pays $75 minimum.

Photos: Send photos with submission. Reviews contact sheets and 5 × 7 or larger prints. Offers no additional payment for photos accepted with ms. Buys one-time rights.

Columns: To Err is Divine (design errors on stamps), 30-40 words; and The Odd Lot (unusual or ironic stamp articles) 700-1,000 words. Buys 60 mss/year. Pays $25 for design errors, $75 maximum.

Fiction: Adventure, fantasy, historical and suspense. "No pat formulas. We rarely buy fiction and are very choosy about what we accept." Buys 2-3 mss/year. Query with published clips. Length: 800-2,500 words. Pays $75-125.

Fillers: Anecdotes and facts. Length: 50-600 words. Payment negotiable.

Tips: "I seriously doubt that anyone who is not a stamp collector will get material published. Articles must display an understanding of the hobby and a sensitivity to collectors' needs. I can't stress enough that articles should be primarily about the stamps themselves. We are more in need of features than anything else. Although not required, it would be most helpful for freelancers to frequently consult the Associated Press style book. This will result in fewer editorial changes, and a greater chance of acceptance."

SEW NEWS, The Fashion Magazine for People Who Sew, PJS Publications, Inc., News Plaza, P.O. Box 1790, Peoria IL 61656. (309)682-6626. Fax: (309)682-7394. Editor: Linda Turner Griepentrog. 90% freelance written. Works with a small number of new/unpublished writers each year. Monthly magazine covering fashion-sewing. "Our magazine is for the beginning home sewer to the professional dressmaker. It expresses the fun, creativity and excitement of sewing." Estab. 1980. Circ. 230,000. **Pays on acceptance.** Publishes ms an average of 6 months after acceptance. Byline given. Buys all rights. Submit seasonal/holiday material 6 months in advance. Reports in 2 months. Sample copy $3. Writer's guidelines for #10 SAE with 2 first class stamps.
Nonfiction: How-to (sewing techniques) and interview/profile (interesting personalities in home-sewing field). Buys 200-240 ms/year. Query with published clips if available. Length: 500-2,000 words. Pays $25-400. Rarely pays expenses of writers on assignment.
Photos: State availability of photos. Prefers b&w, color photographs or slides. Payment included in ms price. Identification of subjects required. Buys all rights.
Tips: "Query first with writing sample and outline of proposed story. Areas most open to freelancers are how-to and sewing techniques; give explicit, step-by-step instructions plus rough art."

SPIN-OFF, Interweave Press, 201 E. 4th St., Loveland CO 80537. (303)669-7672. Fax: (303)667-8317. Editor: Deborah Robson. 10-20% freelance written. Quarterly magazine covering handspinning, dyeing, techniques and projects for using handspun fibers. Audience includes "practicing textile/fiber craftsworkers. Article should show considerable depth of knowledge of subject, although the tone should be informal and accessible." Estab. 1975. Circ. 15,000. Pays on publication. Publishes ms an average of 1 year after acceptance. Byline given. Buys first North American serial rights. Sample copy $4.50 for 9 × 12 SAE. Writer's guidelines for #10 SAE with 2 first class stamps.
Nonfiction: Historical and how-to (spinning, and knitted, crocheted and woven projects from handspun fibers with instructions); interview/profile (of successful and/or interesting handspinners); and technical (on spinning, dyeing or fiber technology, use, properties). "All articles must contain a high level of in-depth information. Our readers are very knowledgable about these subjects." Query. Length: 2,000 words. Pays $15-100.
Photos: State availability of photos. Identification of subjects required.
Tips: "You should display knowledge of your subject, but you can tailor your article to reach beginning, intermediate or advanced spinners. Try for thoughtful organization, a personal informal style, and an article or series segment that is self-contained. New approaches to familiar topics are welcomed."

SPORTS COLLECTORS DIGEST, Krause Publications, 700 E. State St., Iola WI 54990. (715)445-2214. Fax: (715)445-4087. Editor: Tom Mortenson. 50% freelance written. Works with a small number of new/unpublished writers each year. Weekly sports memorabilia magazine. "We serve collectors of sports memorabilia — baseball cards, yearbooks, programs, autographs, jerseys, bats, balls, books, magazines, ticket stubs, etc." Estab. 1952. Circ. 52,000. Pays after publication. Publishes ms an average of 3 months after acceptance. Byline given. Buys first North American serial rights only. Submit seasonal/holiday material 3 months in advance. Simultaneous queries OK. Reprints OK; send tearsheet of article. Pays 100% of their fee for an original article. Reports in 5 weeks on queries; 2 months on mss. Free sample copy. Writer's guidelines for #10 SASE.
Nonfiction: General interest (new card issues, research on older sets); historical/nostalgic (old stadiums, old collectibles, etc.); how-to (buy cards, sell cards and other collectibles, display collectibles, ways to get autographs, jerseys and other memorabilia); interview/profile (well-known collectors, ball players — but must focus on collectibles); new product (new card sets); and personal experience ("what I collect and why"-type stories). No sports stories. "We are not competing with *The Sporting News*, *Sports Illustrated* or your daily paper. Sports collectibles only." Buys 100-200 mss/year. Query. Length: 300-3,000 words; prefers 1,000 words. Pays $50-125.
Photos: Unusual collectibles. State availability of photos. Pays $5-15 for b&w prints. Identification of subjects required. Buys all rights.
Columns/Departments: "We have all the columnists we need but welcome ideas for new columns." Buys 100-150 mss/year. Query. Length: 600-3,000 words. Pays $70-90.
Tips: "If you are a collector, you know what collectors are interested in. Write about it. No shallow, puff pieces; our readers are too smart for that. Only well-researched articles about sports memorabilia and collecting. Some sports nostalgia pieces are OK. Write only about the areas you know about."

STAMP COLLECTOR, For People Who Love Philately, Division of Van Dahl Publications, Capital Cities/ ABC, Inc., P.O. Box 10, Albany OR 97321-0006. (503)928-3569. Fax: (503)967-7262. Editor: Ken Palke. 70% freelance written. Weekly tabloid covering philately. "Stamp Collector is dedicated to promoting the growth and enjoyment of philately through the exchange of information and ideas. All shades of opinion are published to provide the widest possible view of the hobby." Estab. 1931. Circ. 18,500. Pays on publication. Byline given. Buys all rights. Submit seasonal/holiday material 1½ months in advance. Query for electronic submissions. Call for details. Reports in 2 months. Sample copy and writer's guidelines upon request for 9 × 12 SAE with 4 first class stamps.

Nonfiction: "No general articles on world history, world geography, lengthy articles about one particular stamp, puzzles, games, quizzes, etc." Buys 500 mss/year. Query. Pays $30-50. Sometimes pays the expenses of writers on assignment. Send photos, stamps or clear photocopies with submission. Buys all rights. Send SASE with unsolicited mss.

Columns/Departments: Guest Editorials, 1,000 words. Buys 15 mss/year. Send complete ms. Pays $30.

Tips: "Be a stamp collector or stamp dealer with some specific area of interest and/or expertise. Find a subject (stamps of a particular country, time period, designer, subject matter portrayed, printing method, etc.) that you are interested in and knowledgeable about, and in which our average reader would be interested. Our average reader is well-educated, intelligent, professional with diverse interests in postal services, printing methods, politics, geography, history, anthropology, economics, arts, etc."

STORYTELLING MAGAZINE, National Association for the Preservation and Perpetuation of Storytelling, P.O. Box 309, Jonesborough TN 37659. (615)753-2171. Editor: Mary C. Weaver. 80% freelance written. Quarterly magazine on storytelling, oral history and tradition, folklore. Estab. 1989. Circ. 8,000. Pays within 30 days of acceptance. Byline given. Offers 35% kill fee. Buys first North American serial and second serial (reprint) rights. Submit queries about seasonal/holiday material 6 months in advance. Simultaneous and previously published submissions OK; send photocopy of article and information about when and where the article previously appeared. Pays 100% of their fee for an original article. Query for electronic submissions. Reports in 2-4 months. Sample copy for 10×13 SAE with 6 first class stamps. Writer's guidelines for #10 SASE.

Nonfiction: Book excerpts, essays, general interest (within our subject matter), interview/profile, novel or interesting uses of storytelling, issues within the storytelling community. *No* fiction, poetry, how-tos, nostalgia or personal experiences. Buys 12 feature-length articles/year. Query with published clips. Length: 1,800-3,000 words. Pays $150-350. Pays expenses of writers on assignment.

Photos: State availability of photos with submission. Identification of subjects required. "We only rarely buy photos. Usually we borrow existing shots from interviewed subjects."

Columns/Departments: Gleanings (interesting ways performers, teachers, others are using the art of storytelling), 800 words; Profiles (storytellers, writers, other performers, teachers, ministers), 800 words; and Traditions (essay on roots of stories, folklore, myth, etc.), 800 words. Buys 28 mss/year. Query with published clips. Pays $65-100.

Tips: "Send clear, detailed queries. Keep the audience in mind. Most of our readers are teachers, librarians, and others in the helping professions who use storytelling in their work. Don't tell readers what they already know: that storytelling is enjoying a renaissance, that it can build children's creative skills, that ancient tales contain timeless psychological themes, etc. Gleanings and Profiles are most open to freelancers. Emphasize what's unique about the subject. My judgment of the writer's ability is based mostly on the quality of the query."

SUNSHINE ARTISTS, America's Art & Craft Show Magazine, Sunshine Artists USA Inc., 1736 N. Highway 427, Longwood FL 32750-3410. (407)332-4944. Editor: Kristine Petterson. Managing Editor: Merry Holden Mott. Monthly magazine covering art shows in the United States. "We are the premier marketing/reference magazine for those professional artists and photographers who earn their living through art shows nationwide. We list more than 4,000 shows annually, critique many of them and publish articles on marketing, selling and other issues of concern to professional artists." Circ. 14,000. Pays on publication. Publishes ms an average of 3 months after acceptance. Byline given. Buys first North American serial rights. Reports within one month on queries and manuscripts. Sample copy $5.

Nonfiction: "We have periodic openings for state reporters, a position that requires attending and reporting on art shows and festivals within an assigned state or region. Most reporters are full-time artists, but this is not required. We are also interested in articles of interest to artists who travel the art show circuit. Current topics include marketing, computers and RV living." No how-to. Buys 20 mss/year. Query of ms. Length: 550-2,000 words. Pays $50-150 for accepted articles.

Photos: State availability of photos with submission. Black and white photos only. Offers no additional payment for photos accepted with ms. Captions, model releases and identification of subjects required.

TEDDY BEAR REVIEW, Collector Communications Corp., 170 5th Ave., New York NY 10010. (212)989-8700. Managing Editor: Stephen L. Cronk. 75% freelance written. Works with a small number of new/unpublished writers each year. Bimonthly magazine on teddy bears. Estab. 1973. Pays 30 days after acceptance. Byline given. Buys first North American serial rights. Submit seasonal/holiday material 6 months in advance. Reports in 2 months. Sample copy and writer's guidelines $2 for 9×12 SAE.

Nonfiction: Book excerpts, historical, how-to and interview/profile. No nostalgia on childhood teddy bears. Buys 30-40 mss/year. Query with published clips. Length: 500-1,500 words. Pays $75-200. Sometimes pays the expenses of writers on assignment "if approved ahead of time."

Photos: Send photos with submission. Reviews transparencies and b&w prints. Offers no additional payment for photos accepted with ms. Captions required. Buys one-time rights.

Tips: "We are interested in good, professional writers around the country with a strong knowledge of teddy bears. Historical profile of bear companies, profiles of contemporary artists and knowledgeable reports on museum collections are of interest."

TRADITIONAL QUILTER, The Leading Teaching Mag for Creative Quilters, MSC Publishing Co., 243 Newton-Sparta Rd., Newton NJ 07860. (201)383-8080. Fax: (201)383-8133. Editorial Director: Camille Pomaco. Editor: Phyllis Barbieri. 45% freelance written. Bimonthly magazine on quilting. Estab. 1988. Pays on publication. Byline given. Buys first or all rights. Submit seasonal/holiday 6 months in advance. Reports in 2 months. Sample copy for 9×12 SAE with 4 first class stamps. Writer's guidelines for #10 SASE.

Nonfiction: Quilts and quilt patterns with instructions, quilt-related projects, historical/nostalgic, humor, interview/profile, opinion, personal experience, photo feature and travel—all quilt related. Query with published clips. Length: 350-1,000 words. Pays 7-10¢/word.

Photos: Send photos with submission. Reviews all size transparencies and prints. Offers $10-15/photo. Captions and identification of subjects required. Buys one-time or all rights.

Columns/Departments: Feature Teacher (qualified quilt teachers with teaching involved—with slides); Remnants (reports on conventions, history—humor); Profile (award-winning and interesting quilters); and Around the Quilting Frame (reports on quilting guild activities, shows, workshops, and retreats). Length: 1,000 words maximum. Pays 7-10¢/word.

Fillers: Anecdotes, facts, short humor. Buys 24/year. Length: 75-500 words. Pays 10-15¢/word.

TRADITIONAL QUILTWORKS, The Pattern Magazine for Creative Quilters, Chitra Publications, 2 Public Ave., Montrose PA 18801. (717)278-1984. Fax: (717)278-2223. Editor: Patti Bachelder. 60% freelance written. Bimonthly magazine on quilting. "We seek articles of an instructional nature, profiles of talented teachers, articles on the history of specific areas of quiltmaking (patterns, fiber, regional, etc.)." Estab. 1988. Circ. 90,000. Pays on publication. Publishes ms an average of 6 months after acceptance. Byline given. Buys second serial (reprint) rights. Submit seasonal/holiday material 6-8 months in advance. Query for electronic submissions. Reports in 2 months. Sample copy and writer's guidelines for 9×12 SASE with 6 first class stamps.

Nonfiction: Historical, instructional and quilting education. "No light-hearted entertainment." Buys 12-18 mss/year. Query with or without published clips, or send complete ms. Length: 1,600 words maximum. Pays $75/page.

Photos: Send photos with submission. Reviews transparencies (color). Offers $20 per photo. Captions, model releases and identification of subjects required. Buys all rights.

Tips: "Query with ideas; send samples of prior work so that we can assess and suggest assignment. Our publications appeal to traditional quilters, generally middle-aged and mostly who use the patterns in the magazine. Publication hinges on good photo quality."

TREASURE CHEST, The Information Source & Marketplace for Collectors and Dealers of Antiques and Collectibles, Venture Publishing Co., Suite 211A, 253 W. 72nd St., New York NY 10023. (212)496-2234. Editor: Howard E. Fischer. 100% freelance written. Monthly newspaper on antiques and collectibles. Estab. 1988. Circ. 50,000. Pays on publication. Publishes ms an average of 3 months after acceptance. Byline given. Buys first rights and second serial (reprint) rights. Previously published submissions OK. Reports in 2 months on mss. Sample copy for 9×12 SAE with $2. Writer's guidelines for #10 SASE.

Nonfiction: Expose, general interest, historical/nostalgic, how-to (detect reproductions, find new sources of items, etc.), humor, interview/profile, personal experience and photo feature. Primarily interested in feature articles on a specific field of collecting which includes a general overview of that field. Buys 20-35 mss/year. Send complete ms. Length: 700-1,000 words. Pays $20-30. Payment in contributor copies or other premiums negotiable.

Fillers: Anecdotes, facts, gags to be illustrated by cartoonist and short humor. Buys 12-30/year. Length: 100-350 words. Pays $5-10.

Tips: "Learn about your subject by interviewing experts—appraisers, curators, dealers."

‡**TREASURE DIVER,** Double Eagle Publishing, 31970 Yucaipa Blvd., Yucaipa CA 92399. (909)794-4612. Editor: Lee Chandler. Managing Editor: Jim Williams. Contact: Carol Spencer, Editor. 95% freelance written. Bimonthly magazine for treasure sites, detectors and dive equipment. "What is in the waters of the world and what to use to find it." Estab. 1970. Circ. 50,000. Pays on publication plus 30 days. Publishes ms an average of 4-10 months after acceptance. Byline given. Buys one-time, second serial rights or makes work-for-hire assignments. Editorial lead time 3½ months. Submit seasonal material 5 months in advance. Simultaneous submissions OK. Query for electronic submissions. Prefers IBM. Requires hard copy with electronic submission. Reports in 2 weeks on queries; 2 months on mss. Sample copy $1.45. Writer's guidelines free on request.

Nonfiction: Arthur P. Passanando, Publisher. Historical/nostalgic, how-to, humor, interview/profile, new product, personal experience, photo feature, technical and travel. "No fiction or non-hobby related material." Buys 250 mss/year. Query with published clips. Length: 1,500-20,000 words. Pays $35/pp minimum for assigned articles; $30/pp minimum for unsolicited articles. Sometimes pays expenses of writers on assignment. **Photos:** State availability of photos with submission. Reviews prints. Pays "same as page worth except covers." Model releases and identification of subjects required. Photos returned, only reprints of stories kept.

THE TRUMPETER, Croatian Philatelic Society, 1512 Lancelot, Borger TX 79007-6341. (806)273-7225. Editor: Eck Spahich. 80% freelance written. Eager to work with new/unpublished writers. Quarterly magazine covering stamps, coins, currency, military decorations and collectibles of the Balkans and central Europe. Estab. 1972. Circ. 800. Pays on publication. Publishes ms an average of 9 months after acceptance. Byline given. Buys first and one-time rights. Submit seasonal/holiday material 6 months in advance. Simultaneous submissions OK. Reports in 2 months. Sample copy $4. Writer's guidelines for #10 SASE.
Nonfiction: Book excerpts, general interest, historical/nostalgic, how-to (on detecting forged stamps, currency etc.) interview/profile, photo feature and travel. Buys 15-20 mss/year. Send complete ms. Length: 500-1,500 words. Pays $25-50 for assigned articles; $5-25 for unsolicited articles. Sometimes pays the expenses of writers on assignment. Reprints OK; send typed ms with rights for sale noted. Pays 50% of their fee for an original article.
Photos: State availability of photos with submission. Reviews 3×5 prints. Offers $5-10/photo. Captions and identification of subjects required. Buys one-time rights.
Columns/Departments: Book Reviews (stamps, coins, currency of Balkans), 200-400 words; and Forgeries (emphasis on pre-1945 period), 500-1,000 words. Buys 10 mss/year. Send complete ms. Length: 100-300 words. Pays $5-25.
Fillers: Facts. Buys 15-20/year. Length: 20-50 words. Pays $1-5.
Tips: "We desperately need features on Zara, Montenegro, Serbia, Bulgaria, Bosnia, Croatia, Romania and Laibach."

TUFF STUFF, The Nation's Favorite Trading Card Magazine, 2309 Hungary Rd., Richmond VA 23228. (804)266-0140. Fax: (804)266-1145. Editor: Tucker Freeman Smith. 40% freelance written. Monthly magazine covering sports memorabilia. "Our focus is on the sports memorabilia collecting hobby and the hobbyists. We like articles that balance the two to attract the largest audience possible." Estab. 1984. Pays on publication. Publishes ms an average of 3 months after acceptance. Byline given. Buys first and all rights. Submit seasonal/holiday material 4 months in advance. Simultaneous submissions OK. Send queries to the attention of Tucker Freeman Smith, Managing Editor. Reports in 3 months. Sample copy for 11×14 SAE with 10 first class stamps. Writers guidelines for #10 SASE.
Nonfiction: Historical/nostalgic, how-to, humor, interview/profile, new product and technical. No articles that do not somehow incorporate the sports memorabilia market. Buys 50 mss/year. Query with published clips. Length: 800-2,000 words. Pays $350-1,500 for assigned articles; $150-400 for unsolicited articles.
Photos: State availability of photos and other art with submission. Reviews 3×5 prints, slides. Offers no additional payment for photos accepted with ms. Buys first or all rights.
Fiction: Sports memorabilia–related considered. "Not interested in fiction that is not sports and/or collecting related." Buys 2 mss/year. Query with published clips. Length: 500-2,000 words. Pays $40-150.
Tips: "Collecting knowledge, well-researched and documented facts or stats a must. Nonfiction articles on sports and sports memorabilia collecting that share knowledge, give pointers, enlarge perspective and tell 'how-to' are most often in demand. We request published clips be sent with queries and/or simultaneous submissions. We offer some of the best freelance opportunities of any national newsstand magazine. Period."

VIDEOMAKER, Camcorders, Editing, Desktop Video, Audio and Video Production, Videomaker Inc., P.O. Box 4591, Chico CA 95927. (916)891-8410. Fax: (916)891-8443. Editor: Stephen Muratore. 75% freelance written. Monthly magazine on video production. "Our audience encompasses video camera users ranging from broadcast and cable TV producers to special-event videographers to video hobbyists . . . labeled professional, industrial, 'prosumer' and consumer. Editorial emphasis is on video*making* (production and exposure), *not* reviews of commercial videos. Personal video phenomenon is a young 'movement'; our readership is encouraged to participate — get in on the act, join the fun." Estab. 1986. Circ. 75,000. Pays on publication. Publishes ms an average of 4-6 months after acceptance. Byline given. Buys all rights. Submit seasonal/holiday material 6 months in advance. Simultaneous and previously published submissions OK. Query for electronic submissions. Reports in 3 months. Sample copy for 9×12 SAE with 9 first class stamps. Free writer's guidelines.
Nonfiction: How-to (tools, tips, techniques for better videomaking); interview/profile (notable videomakers); product probe (review of latest and greatest or innovative); personal experience (lessons to benefit other videomakers); and technical (state-of-the-art audio/video). Articles with comprehensive coverage of product line or aspect of videomaking preferred. Buys 70 mss/year. Query with or without published clips or send complete ms. Length: open. Pays $150-300, negotiable.

Photos: Send photos and/or other artwork with submissions. Reviews contact sheets, transparencies and prints. Captions required. Payment for photos accepted with ms included as package compensation. Buys one-time rights.

Columns/Departments: Computer Video (state-of-the-art products, applications, potentials for computer-video interface); Profile (highlights videomakers using medium in unique/worthwhile ways); Book/Tape Mode (brief reviews of current works pertaining to video production); Videocrafts (projects, gadgets, inventions for videomaking); Video for Hire (money-making opportunities); and Edit Points (tools and techniques for successful video editing). Buys 40 mss/year. Pays $35-200.

Fillers: Anecdotes, facts, cartoons, newsbreaks, short humor. Negotiable pay.

Tips: "Comprehensiveness a must. Article on shooting tips covers *all* angles. Buyer's guide to special-effect generators cites *all* models available. Magazine strives for an 'all-or-none' approach. Most topics covered once (twice tops) per year, so we must be thorough. Manuscript/photo package submissions helpful. *Video-maker* wants videomaking to be fulfilling and fun."

‡**VOGUE KNITTING,** Butterick Company, 161 6th Ave., New York NY 10013. Editor: Nancy J. Thomas. Managing Editor: Ruth Tobacco. 25% freelance written. Quarterly magazine that covers knitting. "High-fashioned magazine with projects for knitters of all levels. In-depth features on techniques, knitting around the world, interviews, bios and other articles of interest to well-informed readers." Estab. 1982. Circ. 200,000. **Pays on acceptance.** Publishes ms an average of 4 months after acceptance. Buys all rights. Editorial lead time 6 months. Submit seasonal material 6 months in advance. Accepts simultaneous submissions. Query for electronic submissions. Prefers IBM WordPerfect. Requires hard copy with electronic submission. Writer's guidelines free on request.

Nonfiction: Essays, general interest, historical/nostalgic, how-to, interview/profile, personal experience, photo feature, technical and travel. Buys 25 mss/year. Query. Length: 600-1,200 words. Pays $250 minimum for assigned; $250 minimum for unsolicited articles.

Photos: State availability of photos with submission. Reviews 3×5 transparencies. Negotiates payment individually. Captions, model releases and identification of subjects required. Buys all rights.

WEEKEND WOODCRAFTS, Easy Projects to Build & Finish, EGW International, 1041 Shary Circle, Concord CA 94518. (510)671-9852. Fax: (510)671-0692. Editor: Ben Green. Managing Editor: David F. Camp. Bimonthly magazine of woodworking and finishing. "*Weekend Woodcrafts* is the hobbyist's source for easy projects to build and finish." Estab. 1992. Circ. 140,000. **Pays on acceptance.** Publishes ms an average of 8 months after acceptance. No byline. Buys first North American serial rights. Editorial lead time 6 months. Submit seasonal material 6 months in advance. Reports in up to 2 months. Buys project designs only.

Tips: "Go through the magazine to get an idea of the type of project we're looking for."

WESTERN & EASTERN TREASURES, People's Publishing Co., Inc., P.O. Box 1095, Arcata CA 95521-1095. Fax: (707)822-0973. Editor: Rosemary Anderson. Monthly magazine emphasizing treasure hunting and metal detecting for all ages, entire range of education, coast-to-coast readership. 90% freelance written. Estab. 1966. Circ. 70,000. Pays on publication. Publishes ms an average of 1 year after acceptance. Buys all rights. Reports in 3 months. Sample copy and writer's guidelines $2 for 9×12 SAE with 8 first class stamps.

Nonfiction: How-to "hands on" use of metal detecting equipment, how to locate coins, jewelry and relics, prospect for gold, where to look for treasures, rocks and gems, etc., "first-person" experiences. "No purely historical manuscripts or manuscripts that require two-part segments or more." Buys 200 unsolicited mss/year. Submit complete ms. Length: maximum 1,500 words. Pays 2¢/word—negotiable.

Photos: Purchased with accompanying ms. Captions required. Submit b&w prints (preferred), color prints or 35mm Kodachrome transparencies. Pays $5 maximum for 3×5 and up b&w glossy prints; $50 and up for 35mm Kodachrome cover slides. Model releases required.

Tips: "The writer has a better chance of breaking in at our publication with short articles and fillers as these give the readers a chance to respond to the writer. The publisher relies heavily on reader reaction. Not adhering to word limit is the main mistake made by writers in completing an article for us. Writers must clearly cover the subjects described above in 1,500 words or less."

WOODSHOP NEWS, Soundings Publications Inc., 35 Pratt St., Essex CT 06426-1185. (203)767-8227. Fax: (203)767-1048. Editor: Ian C. Bowen. Senior Editor: Thomas Clark. 20% freelance written. Monthly tabloid "covering woodworking for professionals and hobbyists. Solid business news and features about woodworking companies. Feature stories about interesting amateur woodworkers. Some how-to articles." Estab. 1986. Circ. 100,000. Pays on publication. Publishes ms an average of 2 months after acceptance. Byline given. Offers 25% kill fee. Buys first North American serial rights. Submit seasonal/holiday material 4 months in advance. Simultaneous submissions OK. Query for electronic submissions. Reports in 3 weeks on queries; 1 month on mss. Free sample copy and writer's guidelines.

Nonfiction: How-to (query first), interview/profile, new product, opinion, personal experience and photo feature. No general interest profiles of "folksy" woodworkers. Buys 50-75 mss/year. Query with published clips. Length: 100-1,800 words. Pays $30-400 for assigned articles; $30-200 for unsolicited articles. Pays expenses of writers on assignment.

Photos: Send photos with submission. Reviews contact sheets and prints. Offers $20-35/photo. Captions and identification of subjects required. Buys one-time rights.

Columns/Departments: Pro Shop (business advice, marketing, employee relations, taxes etc. for the professional written by an established professional in the field); and Tech Talk (technical how-to, written by experts in the topic). Length: 1,200-1,500 words. Buys 24 mss/year. Query. Pays $200-350.

Tips: "The best way to start is a profile of a business or hobbyist woodworker in your area. Find a unique angle about the person or business and stress this as the theme of your article. Avoid a broad, general-interest theme that would be more appropriate to a daily newspaper. Our readers are woodworkers who want more depth and more specifics than would a general readership. If you are profiling a business, we need standard business information such as gross annual earnings/sales, customer base, product line and prices, marketing strategy, etc. Black and white 35 mm photos are a must. We need more freelance writers from the Mid-Atlantic, Midwest and West Coast."

WOODWORK, A magazine for all woodworkers, Ross Periodicals, P.O. Box 1529, Ross CA 94957. (415)382-0580. Fax: (415)382-0587. Editor: Graham Blackburn. Publisher: Tom Toldrian. 90% freelance written. Bimonthly magazine covering woodworking. "We are aiming at a broad audience of woodworkers, from the home enthusiast/hobbyist to more advanced." Estab. 1986. Circ. 100,000. Pays on publication. Byline given. Buys first North American serial and second serial (reprint) rights. Reports in 2 months. Sample copy $3 for 9 × 12 SAE with 6 first class stamps. Writer's guidelines for #10 SASE.

Nonfiction: How-to (simple or complex, making attractive furniture), interview/profile (of established woodworkers that make attractive furniture), photo feature (of interest to woodworkers) and technical (tools, techniques). "Do not send a how-to unless you are a woodworker." Buys 40 mss/year. Query first. Length: 1,500-3,000 words. Pays $150/published page. Reprints OK; send tearsheet or photocopy of article, typed ms with rights for sale noted and information about when and where the article previously appeared. Pays 25% of their fee for an original article.

Photos: Send photos with submission. Reviews 35mm slides. Offers no additional payment for photos accepted with ms. Captions and identification of subjects required. Buys one-time rights.

Columns/Departments: Feature articles 1,500-3,000 words. From non-woodworking freelancers, we use interview/profiles of established woodworkers. Bring out woodworker's philosophy about the craft, opinions about what is happening currently. Good photos of attractive furniture a must. Section on how-to desirable. Query with published clips. Pays $600-1,500 at $150 per published page.

Fillers: Anecdotes, facts, newsbreaks and short humor. Length: 1,000 words. Pays $150 maximum.

Tips: "If you are not a woodworker, the interview/profile is your best, really only chance. Good writing is essential as are good photos. The interview must be entertaining, but informative and pertinent to woodworkers' interests."

WORKBENCH, Suite 310, 700 W. 47th St., Kansas City MO 64112. (816)531-5730. Fax: (816)531-3873. Executive Editor: Robert N. Hoffman. 75% freelance written. Prefers to work with published/established writers; but works with a small number of new/unpublished writers each year. For woodworkers and home improvement do-it-yourselfers. Estab. 1957. Circ. 860,000. **Pays on acceptance.** Publishes ms an average of 1 year after acceptance. Byline given. Buys all rights. Reports in 3 months. Sample copy for 9 × 12 SAE with 6 first class stamps. Free writer's guidelines.

Nonfiction: "We have continued emphasis on do-it-yourself woodworking, home improvement and home maintenance projects. We provide in-progress photos, technical drawings and how-to text for all projects. We are very strong in woodworking, cabinetmaking and classic furniture construction. Projects range from simple toys to reproductions of furniture now in museums. We would like to receive woodworking projects that can be duplicated by both beginning do-it-yourselfers and advanced woodworkers." Query. Pays $175/published page or more depending on quality of submission. Additional payment for good color photos. "If you can consistently provide good material, including photos, your rates will go up and you will get assignments."

Columns/Departments: Shop Tips bring $25 with a line drawing and/or b&w photo.

Tips: "Our magazine focuses on woodworking, covering all levels of ability, and home improvement projects from the do-it-yourselfer's viewpoint, emphasizing the most up-to-date materials and procedures. We would like to receive articles on home improvements and remodeling, and/or simple contemporary furniture. We place a heavy emphasis on projects that are both functional and classic in design. We can photograph projects worthy for publication, so feel free to send snapshots."

YESTERYEAR, Yesteryear Publications, P.O. Box 2, Princeton WI 54968. (414)787-4808. Editor: Michael Jacobi. Prefers to work with published/established writers. For antique dealers and collectors, people interested in collecting just about anything. Monthly tabloid. Estab. 1976. Circ. 8,000. Pays on publication. Publishes ms an average of 3 months after acceptance. Buys one-time rights. Byline given. Submit seasonal/holiday material 3 months in advance. Simultaneous and previously published submissions OK; send photocopy of article and information about when and where the article previously appeared. Pays 100% of their fee for an original article. Reports in 1 month. Sample copy $2.

Nonfiction: General interest (basically, anything pertaining to antiques and collectible items); and how-to (refinishing antiques, how to collect). The more specific and detailed, the better. "We do not want personal experience or opinion articles." Buys 3 mss/year. Send complete ms. Pays $10-25.

Photos: Send photos with ms. Pays $5 for 5×7 b&w glossy or matte color prints. Captions preferred.

Home and Garden

Some magazines here concentrate on gardens; others on the how-to of interior design. Still others focus on homes and gardens in specific regions of the country. Be sure to read the publication to determine its focus before submitting a manuscript or query.

AMERICAN HORTICULTURIST, Publication of the American Horticultural Society, 7931 E. Blvd. Dr., Alexandria VA 22308-1300. (703)768-5700. Fax: (703)765-6032. Editor: Kathleen Fisher. 90% freelance written. Bimonthly magazine covering gardening. Estab. 1922. Circ. 25,000. Pays on publication. Publishes ms an average of 6 months after acceptance. Byline given. Offers 20% kill fee. Buys first North American serial rights. Submit seasonal/holiday material 6 months in advance. Query for electronic submissions. Reports in 3 months on queries. Sample copy $3. Free writer's guidelines.

Nonfiction: Book excerpts, historical, how-to (grow unusual plants, garden under difficult conditions), humor, interview/profile, personal experience and technical (explain science of horticulture to lay audience). Buys 30-40 mss/year. Query with published clips. Length: 1,000-2,500 words. Pays $100-400. Pays with contributor copies or other premiums when other horticultural organizations contribute articles.

Photos: State availability of photos with query. Pays $50-75/photo. Captions required. Buys one-time rights.

Tips: "We are read by sophisticated gardeners, but also want to interest beginning gardeners. Subjects should be unusual plants, recent breakthroughs in breeding, experts in the field, translated for lay readers."

ARCHITECTURAL DIGEST, Knapp Communications, 5900 Wilshire Blvd., Los Angeles CA 90036. "Prefers not to share information."

ATLANTA HOMES AND LIFESTYLES (formerly *Southern Homes*), Suite 580, 5775-B Glenridge Dr., Atlanta GA 30328. (404)252-6670. Fax: (404)252-6673. Editor: Barbara S. Tapp. 65% freelance written. Bimonthly magazine on shelter design, lifestyle in the home. "*Atlanta Homes and Lifestyles* is designed for the action-oriented, well-educated reader who enjoys his/her shelter, its design and construction, its environment, and living and entertaining in it." Estab. 1983. Pays on publication. Byline given. Publishes ms an average of 6 months after acceptance. Pays 25% kill fee. Buys all rights. Reprints OK; send tearsheet or photocopy of article and information about where and when it previously appeared. Pays 50% of original article fee for reprints. Reports in 3 months. Sample copy $3.50.

Nonfiction: Historical/nostalgic, interview/profile, new products, well-designed homes, antiques (then and now), photo features, gardens, local art, remodeling, food, preservation and entertaining. "We do not want articles outside respective market area, not written for magazine format, or that are excessively controversial, investigative or that cannot be appropriately illustrated with attractive photography." Buys 35 mss/year. Query with published clips. Length: 750-1,000 words. Pays $350 for features. Sometimes pays expenses of writers on assignment "if agreed upon in advance of assignment."

Photos: State availability of photos with submission; most photography is assigned. Reviews transparencies. Offers $40-50/photo. Captions, model releases, and identification of subjects required. Buys one-time rights.

Columns/Departments: Antiques, Quick Fix (simple remodeling ideas), Cheap Chic (stylish decorating that is easy on the wallet), Digging In (outdoor solutions from Atlanta's gardeners) and Big Fix (more extensive remodeling projects), Short Takes (news and finds about the people and products in home-related businesses in and around Atlanta), Home Eco, Home Tech, Real Estate News, Interior Elements (hot new furnishings on the market) and Weekender (long or short weekend getaway subjects). Query with published clips. Buys 25-30 mss/year. Length: 350-500 words. Pays $50-200.

BACKWOODS HOME MAGAZINE, INC., #213, 1257 Siskiyou Blvd., Ashland OR 97520. Editor: Dave Duffy. 80% freelance written. Bimonthly magazine covering house building, alternate energy, gardening, health and self-sufficiency. "We write for the person who values independence above all else. Our readers want to build their own homes, generate their own electricity, grow their own food and in general stand on their own two feet." Estab. 1989. Circ. 85,000. **Pays on acceptance.** Publishes ms an average of 2 months after acceptance. Byline given. Offers 15% kill fee. Buys first rights and second serial (reprint) rights or makes work-for-hire assignments. Submit seasonal/holiday material 6 months in advance. Previously published submissions OK. Query for electronic submissions. Reports in 2 weeks. Sample copy $2 for 9×12 SAE with 6 first class stamps. Writer's guidelines for #10 SASE.

Nonfiction: Historical/nostalgic, how-to (about country things, alternate energy), humor, interview/profile (of independent people), new product (alternate energy), personal experience, photo feature (about country things) and technical (about alternate energy production, building a house). "No opinion, expose or religious articles." Buys 50 mss/year. Query with or without published clips or send complete ms. Length: 300-3,000 words. Pays $15-100.

Photos: State availability of photos with submission. Reviews 3×5 or larger prints. Offers $5/photo. Identification of subjects required. Buys one-time rights.

Columns/Departments: Book Review (alternate energy/house building/gardening), 300-400 words; Recipes (country cooking), 150 words; Alternate Energy (solar cells, hydro, generator), 600-3,000 words; Gardening (organic), 600-1,800 words; Home Building (do-it-yourself), 600-2,800 words. Buys 30-40 mss/year. Send complete ms. Pays $15.

Poetry: Free verse, haiku, light verse and traditional. Buys 15 poems/year. Length: 3-25 lines. Pays $5.

Tips: "We insist on accuracy in nonfiction articles. Writers must know the subject. We are basically a country magazine that tries to show people how to do things that make country life more pleasant."

BETTER HOMES AND GARDENS, 1716 Locust St., Des Moines IA 50309-3023. (515)284-3000. Editor-in-Chief: Jean Lem Mon. Editor (Building): Joan McCloskey. Editor (Furnishings): Denise Caringer. Editor (Foods): Nancy Byal. Editor (Travel): Lois Naylor. Editor (Garden Outdoor Living): Doug Jimerson. Editor (Health & Education): Paul Krantz. Editor (Money Management, Automotive, Features): Margaret Daly. 10-15% freelance written. **Pays on acceptance.** Buys all rights. "We read all freelance articles, but much prefer to see a letter of query rather than a finished ms."

Nonfiction: Travel, education, health, cars, money management and home entertainment. "We do not deal with political subjects or with areas not connected with the home, community, and family." Pays rates "based on estimate of length, quality and importance." No poetry.

Tips: Direct queries to the department that best suits your story line.

CANADIAN WORKSHOP, The Do-It-Yourself Magazine, Camar Publications (1984) Inc., 130 Spy Court, Markham, Ontario L3R 5H6 Canada. (416)475-8440. Editor: Erina Kelly. 90% freelance written; half of these are assigned. Monthly magazine covering the "do-it-yourself" market including woodworking projects, renovation, restoration and maintenance. Circ. 130,000. Payment in two installments: half when received, half the month following. Byline given. Offers 50% kill fee. Rights are negotiated with the author. Submit seasonal/holiday material 6 months in advance. Reports in 4-6 weeks. Sample copy for 9×12 SASE. Writer's guidelines for #10 SASE.

Nonfiction: How-to (home maintenance, renovation projects, woodworking projects and features). Buys 40-60 mss/year. Query with clips of published work. Length: 1,500-2,500 words. Pays $800-1,200. Pays expenses of writers on assignment.

Photos: Send photos with ms. Payment for photos, transparencies negotiated with the author. Captions, model releases, and identification of subjects required.

Tips: "Freelancers must be aware of our magazine format. Products used in how-to articles must be readily available across Canada. Deadlines for articles are 4 months in advance of cover date. How-tos should be detailed enough for the amateur but appealing to the experienced."

COLONIAL HOMES, Hearst Corp., 28th Floor, 1700 Broadway, New York NY 10019. Staff written. "Prefers not to share information."

COLORADO HOMES & LIFESTYLES, 7009 S. Potomac St., Englewood CO 80112-4029. (303)397-7600. Fax: (303)397-7619. Editor: Anne McGregor Parsons. 50% freelance written. Bimonthly magazine covering Colorado homes and lifestyles for upper-middle-class and high income households as well as designers, decorators and architects. Circ. 30,000. **Pays on acceptance.** Publishes ms an average of 4 months after acceptance. Byline given. Buys all rights. Submit seasonal/holiday material 6 months in advance. Simultaneous queries OK. Query for electronic submissions. Reports in 3 months.

Nonfiction: Fine homes and furnishings, regional interior design trends, interesting personalities and lifestyles, gardening and plants—all with a Colorado slant. Buys 30 mss/year. Send complete ms. Length: 1,000-1,500 words. "For unique, well-researched feature stories, pay is $150-200. For regular departments, $125-140." Sometimes pays the expenses of writers on assignment.

Photos: Send photos with ms. Reviews 35mm, 4×5 and 2¼ color transparencies and b&w glossy prints. Identification of subjects required.

Tips: "The more interesting and unique the subject the better. A frequent mistake made by writers is failure to provide material with a style and slant appropriate for the magazine, due to poor understanding of the focus of the magazine."

COTTAGE LIFE, Quarto Communications, Suite 408, 111 Queen St. E., Toronto, Ontario M5C 1S2 Canada. (416)360-6880. Editor: Ann Vanderhoof. Managing Editor: David Zimmer. 80% freelance written. Bimonthly magazine covering cottaging in Ontario. "*Cottage Life* is written and designed for the people who own and spend time at cottages on Ontario's lakes." Estab. 1988. Circ. 75,000. **Pays on acceptance.** Publishes ms an average of 2 months after acceptance. Byline given. Buys first North American serial rights. Query for electronic submissions.

Nonfiction: Book excerpts, exposé, historical/nostalgic, how-to, humor, interview/profile, personal experience, photo feature and technical. Buys 90 mss/year. Query with published clips. Length: 150-3,500 words. Pays $100-2,200 for assigned articles. Pays $50-1,000 for unsolicited articles. Sometimes pays expenses of writers on assignment. Query first.

Columns/Departments: Cooking, Real Estate, Fishing, Nature, Watersports, Personal Experience and Issues. Length: 150-1200 words. Query with published clips. Pays $100-750.

COUNTRY HOME, Meredith Corp., Locust at 17th, Des Moines IA 50336. "Prefers not to share information."

COUNTRY LIVING, Hearst Corp., 224 W. 57th St., New York NY 10019. "Prefers not to share information."

DECORATING REMODELING, New York Times Company Magazine Group, 110 5th Ave., New York NY 10011. "Prefers not to share information."

‡FAMILY LIVING, The Trade Magazine for Homeowners, #448, 14742 Beach Blvd., La Mirada CA 90638. (714)632-9810. Editor: Marie Madera. 5% freelance written. Bimonthly magazine for the homeowner market. Estab. 1980. Circ. 1,000,000. Pays on publication. Byline given. Makes work-for-hire assignments. Submit seasonal/holiday material 4 months in advance. Simultaneous and previously published submissions OK. Sample copy $1.

Nonfiction: General interest, how-to, new product and travel. "No political or fiction material." Buys 1-2 mss/year. Query. Length: 100-600 words. Pays $50-150 for assigned articles. Sometimes pays the expenses of writers on assignments.

Photos: State availability of photos with submission. Offers no additional payment for photos accepted with ms. Identification of subjects required. Buys one-time rights.

FINE GARDENING, Taunton Press, 63 S. Main St., P.O. Box 5506, Newtown CT 06470-5506. 1-800-243-7252. Fax: (203)426-3434. Editor: Mark Kane. Bimonthly magazine on gardening. "Focus is broad subject of landscape and ornamental gardening, with secondary interest in food gardening. Articles written by avid gardeners—first person, hands-on-gardening experiences." Estab. 1988. Circ. 160,000. Pays on publication. Byline given. Buys first North American serial rights. Reports in 1 month. Free writer's guidelines.

Nonfiction: Book review, essays, how-to, opinion, personal experience and photo feature. Buys 50-60 mss/year. Query. Length: 1,000-3,000 words. Pays $150/page.

Photos: Send photos with submission. Reviews 35mm transparencies. Offers some additional payment for photos accepted with ms. Buys serial rights.

Columns/Department: Book reviews (on gardening); Gleanings (essays, stories, opinions, research); and Last Word (essays/serious, humorous, fact or fiction). Query. Length: 250-1,000 words. Pays $25-150.

Tips: "It's most important to have solid first-hand experience as a gardener. Tell us what you've done with your own landscape and plants."

FLOWER AND GARDEN MAGAZINE, Suite 310, 700 W. 47th St., Kansas City MO 64112. Fax: (816)531-3873. Editor: Kay Melchisedech Olson. 50% freelance written. Works with a small number of new/unpublished writers each year. Bimonthly picture magazine for home gardeners. Estab. 1957. Circ. 600,000. Buys first time nonexclusive reprint rights. Sometimes publishes reprints of previously published articles. Send typed ms with rights for sale noted, including information about when and where the article previously appeared. Byline given. **Pays on acceptance.** Publishes ms an average of 1 year after acceptance. Reports in 2 months. Sample copy $2.95 for 10×13 SAE. Writer's guidelines for #10 SASE.

Nonfiction: Interested in illustrated articles on how to do certain types of gardening and descriptive articles about individual plants. Flower arranging, landscape design, house plants and patio gardening are other aspects covered. "The approach we stress is practical (how-to-do-it, what-to-do-it-with). We emphasize plain talk, clarity and economy of words. An article should be tailored for a national audience." Buys 20-30 mss/year. Query. Length: 500-1,500 words. Rates vary depending on quality and kind of material.

Photos: Buys transparencies, 35mm and larger. Photos are paid for on publication.

Tips: "The prospective author needs good grounding in gardening practice and literature. Offer well-researched and well-written material appropriate to the experience level of our audience. Use botanical names as well as common. Photographs help sell the story. Describe special qualifications for writing the particular proposed subject."

THE HERB COMPANION, Interweave Press, 201 E. 4th St., Loveland CO 80537. (303)669-7672. Fax: (303)667-8317. Editor: Linda Ligon. Managing Editor: David Merrill. 80% freelance written. Bimonthly magazine about herbs: culture, history, culinary use, crafts and some medicinal. Audience includes a wide range of herb enthusiasts. Circ. 75,000. Pays on publication. Byline given. Buys first North American serial rights. Reports in 2 months. Query in writing. Length: 4-12 pages. Typical payment is $100/published page. Sample copy $4. Writer's guidelines for #10 SASE.

Photos: State availability of photos.

Tips: "Articles must show depth and working knowledge of the subject, though tone should be informal and accessible."

HERB QUARTERLY, P.O. Box 689, San Anselmo CA 94960-0689. Fax: (415)455-9541. Publisher: Linda Sparrowe. 80% freelance written. Quarterly magazine for herb enthusiasts. Estab. 1978. Circ. 25,000. Pays on publication. Publishes ms an average of 1 year after acceptance. Buys first North American serial and second (reprint) rights. Query for electronic submissions. Query letters recommended. Reports in 2 months. Sample copy $5 for 9×12 SASE. Writer's guidelines for #10 SASE.

Nonfiction: Gardening (landscaping, herb garden design, propagation, harvesting); medicinal and cosmetic use of herbs; crafts; cooking; historical (folklore, focused piece on particular period—*not* general survey); interview of a famous person involved with herbs or folksy herbalist; personal experience; and photo essay ("cover quality" 8×10 b&w or color prints). "We are particularly interested in herb garden design, contemporary or historical." No fiction. Send double-spaced ms. Length: 1,000-3,500 words. Pays $75.

Tips: "Our best submissions are narrowly focused on herbs with much practical information on cultivation and use for the experienced gardener."

HOME MAGAZINE, The Magazine of Remodeling and Decorating, 44th Floor, 1633 Broadway, New York NY 10019. Editor/Director: Gail Steves Dawson. 80% freelance written. Monthly magazine covering remodeling, decorating, architecture, entertaining, building and gardens. Circ. 1 million. **Pays on acceptance.** Publishes ms an average of 3-6 months after acceptance. Offers negotiable kill fee. Buys all rights. Submit seasonal/holiday material 6-13 months in advance. Free sample copy and writer's guidelines.

Nonfiction: Linda Lentz, articles editor. Essays, how-to, interview/profile, personal experience, photo feature and technical. Buys 100-120 mss/year. Query with published clips. Length: 500-1,500 words. Negotiates payment.

HOMES MAGAZINE, Homes Publishing Group, 178 Main St., Unionville, Ontario L3R 2G9 Canada. (416)479-4663. Editor: Risë Levy. 40% freelance written. Magazine published 8 times/year for new home buyers. "*Homes Magazine* is a new-home guide for the Greater Toronto/Ontario area." Estab. 1985. Circ. 100,000. Pays 30 days after publication. Publishes ms an average of 3 months after acceptance. Byline given. Offers 50% kill fee. Buys all rights (unless otherwise arranged). Publishes reprints of previously published articles or short stories. Send photocopy of article. For reprints, pays 10% of the amount paid for an original article. Submit seasonal/holiday material 4 months in advance. Query for electronic submissions. Free sample copy.

Nonfiction: Book excerpts, general interest, interview/profile, new product and photo feature. "We are looking for material for our anniversary issue (October) and for two issues of *Professional Renovation Magazine*. No fiction. Payment varies; please inquire.

Photos: State availability of or send photos with submission. Reviews transparencies and prints. Offers no additional payment for photos accepted with ms. Model releases and identification of subjects required. Buys one-time rights.

Tips: "Department columns are written by staff writers. Features are most often written by freelancers."

LOG HOME LIVING, Home Buyer Publications Inc., P.O. Box 220039, Chantilly VA 22022. (703)222-9411. Editor: Roland Sweet. Less than 20% freelance written. Bimonthly magazine "for people who own or are planning to build contemporary manufactured and handcrafted kit log homes. Our audience is comprised of married couples 35-50 years old." Estab. 1989. **Pays on acceptance.** Publishes ms an average of 6 months after acceptance. Byline given. Buys one-time rights. Submit seasonal/holiday material 9-12 months in advance. Reprints OK; send photocopy of article. Reports in 6 months. Sample copy $3.50. Writer's guidelines for #10 SASE.

Nonfiction: How-to (buy or build log home), interview/profile (log home owners), photo feature (log homes) and technical (design/decor topics). "We do not want historical/nostalgic material." Buys 4-6 mss/year. Query with published clips. Length: 750-1,500 words. Pays $100-500. Sometimes pays expenses of writers on assignment.

Photos: Send photos with submission. Reviews contact sheets, 2½×2½ transparencies and 5×7 prints. Offers $50-100/photo. Captions, model releases and identification of subjects required. Buys one-time rights.

Tips: "Owner profiles are most open to freelancers. Reveal how they planned for, designed and bought/built their dream home; how they decorated it; how they like it; advice for others thinking of buying."

MIDWEST LIVING, Meredith Corp., 1912 Grand Ave., Des Moines IA 50309. "Prefers not to share information."

‡**MUIR'S ORIGINAL LOG HOME GUIDE FOR BUILDERS & BUYERS,** Muir Publishing Company Inc., 164 Middle Creek Rd., Cosby TN 37722. (615)487-2256. Fax: (615)487-3249. Editor: Fred Dafoe. 65% freelance written. Quarterly magazine covering the buying and building of log homes. "We publish for persons who want to buy or build their own log home. Unlike conventional housing, it is possible for the average person

to build his/her own log home. Articles should aim at providing help in this or describe the experiences of someone who has built a log home." Estab. 1917. Circ. 170,000. Pays on publication. Publishes ms an average of 6 months after acceptance. Byline given. Buys first North American rights. Submit seasonal/holiday material 4 months in advance. Simultaneous queries, and simultaneous and previously published submissions OK ("writer should explain"). Send photocopy of article or typed ms with rights for sale noted. Include information about when and where the article previously appeared. For reprints, pays 50% of the amound paid for an original article. Query for electronic submissions. Reports in 2 weeks. Sample copy $3 (postage included). Writer's guidelines for SASE.

Nonfiction: General interest; historical/nostalgic (log home historic sites, restoration of old log structures); how-to (anything to do with building log homes); inspirational (sweat equity—encouraging people that they can build their own home for less cost); interview/profile (with persons who have built their own log homes); new product (or new company manufacturing log homes—check with us first); personal experience (author's own experience with building his own log home, with photos is ideal); photo feature (on log home decor, author or anyone else building his own log home); and technical (for "Techno-log" section: specific construction details, i.e., new log buding details, joining systems). Also, "would like photo/interview/profile stories on famous persons and their log homes—how they did it, where they got their logs, etc." Interested in log commercial structures. "Please no exaggeration—this is a truthful, back-to-basics type of magazine trying to help the person interested in log homes." Buys 25 mss/year. Query with clips of published work or send complete ms. "Prefer queries first with photo of subject house." Length: open. Pays 10-25¢/word, depending on quality.

Photos: Slides, transparencies or color prints, $5-50, depending on quality. "All payments are arranged with individual author/submitter." Captions and identification of subjects required. Buys first North American rights unless otherwise arranged.

Columns/Departments: Pro-Log (short news pieces of interest to the log-building world); Techno-Log (technical articles, i.e., solar energy systems; any illustrations welcome); Book-Log (book reviews only, on books related to log building and alternate energy; "check with us first"); Chrono-Log (features on historic log buildings); and Decor (practical information on how to finish and furnish a log house). Buys possible 50-75 mss/year. Query with clips of published work or send complete ms. Length: 100-1,000 words or more. "All payments are arranged with individual author/submitter." Enclose SASE.

Tips: "The writer may have a better chance of breaking in at our publication with short articles and fillers since writing well on log homes requires some prior knowledge of subject. The most frequent mistakes made by writers in completing an article assignment for us are not doing enough research or not having understanding of the subject; not people oriented enough; angled toward wrong audience. They don't study the publication before they submit manuscripts."

NATIONAL GARDENING, National Gardening Association, 180 Flynn Ave., Burlington VT 05401. (802)863-1308. Fax: (802)863-5962. Editor: Warren Schultz. Managing Editor: Vicky Congdon. 50% freelance written. Willing to work with new/unpublished writers. Bimonthly magazine covering all aspects of food gardening and ornamentals. "We publish not only how-to garden techniques, but also news that affects gardeners, like science advances. Detailed, experienced-based articles with carefully worked-out techniques for planting, growing, harvesting and using garden fruits and vegetables sought. Our material is for both experienced and beginning gardeners." Estab. 1978. Circ. 200,000. **Pays on acceptance.** Publishes ms an average of 9 months after acceptance. Byline given. Buys first serial and occasionally second (reprint) rights to material originally published elsewhere. Submit seasonal/holiday material 8 months in advance. Reports in 2 months. Sample copy for 9 × 12 SAE with 4 first class stamps. Writer's guidelines for #10 SASE.

Nonfiction: How-to, humor, inspirational, interview/profile, new product, pest patrol, opinion, personal experience, photo feature and technical. Buys 80-100 mss/year. Query first. Length: 500-3,000 words. Pays $30-500/article. Sometimes pays the expenses of writers on assignment; must have prior approval. Reprints OK; send tearsheet of article and information about when and where the article previously appeared. Pays 50% of their fee for an original article.

Photos: Vicky Congdon, Managing Editor. Send photos with ms. Pays $20-40 for b&w photos; $50 for color photos. Captions, model releases and identification of subjects required.

Tips: "Wordiness is a frequent mistake made by writers. Few writers understand how to write 'tight'. We have increased coverage of ornamentals, although primary focus will remain food gardening."

‡NEIL SPERRY'S GARDENS, The Definitive Word in Texas Horticulture, Gardens South, P.O. Box 864, 400 W. Louisiana St., McKinney TX 75069. (214)562-5050. Contact: Mike Goldman, Executive Editor. 80% freelance written. Ten issues/year magazine for gardening/landscaping. "We cover all facets of gardening in Texas: lawns, ornamentals, fruits and vegetables. Writers must exhibit strong knowledge of Texas horticulture." Estab. 1987. Circ. 25,400. Pays on publication. Publishes ms an average of 3 months after acceptance, with seasonal exceptions. Not copyrighted. Buys first North American serial rights. Editorial lead time 2 months. Submit seasonal material 4 months in advance. Query for electronic submissions. Reports in 1 month on queries. Sample copy free on request. Writer's guidelines for #10 SASE.

Nonfiction: How-to (new landscaping and garden techniques), interview/profile, photo feature, technical and travel. Buys 100-150 mss/year. Query with published clips. Length: 700-2,700 words. Pays $50 minimum. Sometimes pays expenses of writers on assignment.

Photos: Send photos with submission. Reviews contact sheets. Negotiates payment individually. Captions, model releases and identification of subjects required. Buys one-time rights. "All photos are color—no b&w accepted."

Columns/Departments: From the Bookshelf (reviews of garden books, especially Texas books), 800 words. Buys 10 mss/year. Query with published clips. Pays $25-150.

Tips: "If you garden in Texas, and it interests you, it interests us. Tell us how you perfected your landscape, or how you found that terrific new variety. Talk to experts—local nursery professionals and extension agents. Find out what they think is hot. Then tell us with clean, crisp writing. High-quality art material is not merely a bonus; it's mandatory. And think Texas. We are a freelance-oriented magazine. The field is wide open. Those that stand out find a new angle on an old problem, an off-beat personality profile, a can't-miss prospect. Keep your eyes and ears open. And remember, think Texas."

NORTHERN CALIFORNIA HOME AND GARDEN, Westar Media, 656 Bair Island Rd., Redwood City CA 94063. (415)368-8800. Fax: (415)368-6251. Editor: Ann Bertelsen. Senior Editor: Susannah Clark. 50% freelance written. Monthly magazine on architecture, interior decorating and gardening. Estab. 1987. Circ. about 70,000. Pays 90 days after acceptance. Publishes ms an average of 3 months after acceptance. Byline given. Offers 30% kill fee. Buys first North American serial and reprint rights. Submit seasonal/holiday material 5 months in advance. Simultaneous submissions and reprints OK. Send typed ms with rights for sale noted and information about when and where the article previously appeared. Reports in 1 month. Sample copy $3 for 8 × 10 SAE. Writer's guidelines for #10 SAE.

Nonfiction: Interview/profile on Northern Californian homeowner, architect or designer and a home or garden they own or designed; occasional food article with recipes; occasional features on furniture styles or designers. "Our June issue is devoted to remodeling; May is gardens. No lifestyle or technical articles on mundane topics." Buys 25 mss/year. Query with published clips. Length: 1,200-2,000 words. Pays $400-600. Sometimes pays expenses of writers on assignment. Pays 50% of commissioned article fee for reprints.

Photos: State availability of photos or send photos with submission. Reviews contact sheets, slides and 4 × 5 transparencies. Buys one-time rights. All photography/art assigned by art director.

Departments: Antiques; Real Estate; Elements (glasswork, concrete "coloring," "rescued" lumber, etc.); In the Garden; and How To. Query with published clips. Length: 1,200-1,500 words. Pays $150-250.

Tips: "The best approach for new freelancers is through departments. We hardly ever assign a feature to a freelancer that we don't know. Suggest several ideas but keep query letters to one page. You must be familiar with Northern California. Writers should speak to an upscale homeowner with a variety of interests in art and design."

ORGANIC GARDENING, Rodale Press, 33 E. Minor, Emmaus PA 18098. (215)967-5171. Managing Editor: Matt Damsker. 30% freelance written. Published 9 times/year. Pays between acceptance and publication. Buys all rights. Reports in 2 months on queries; 1 month on mss.

Nonfiction: "Our title says it all. We seem to put more emphasis on the gardening aspect." Query with published clips and outline. Pays 50¢/word.

SAN DIEGO HOME/GARDEN, Westward Press, Box 1471, San Diego CA 92112-1471. (714)233-4567. Fax: (619)233-1004. Editor: Peter Jensen. Senior Editor: Phyllis Van Doren. 50% freelance written. Works with a small number of new/unpublished writers each year. Monthly magazine covering homes, gardens, food and local travel for residents of San Diego city and county. Estab. 1979. Circ. 31,000. **Pays on acceptance.** Publishes ms an average of 3 months after acceptance. Byline given. Buys first North American serial rights only. Submit seasonal material 3 months in advance. Reports in 2 months. Sample copy $4.

Nonfiction: Residential architecture and interior design (San Diego-area homes only); remodeling (must be well-designed—little do-it-yourself); residential landscape design; furniture; other features oriented towards upscale readers interested in living the cultured good life in San Diego. Articles must have local angle. Buys up to 5 unsolicited mss/year. Query with published clips. Length: 700-2,000 words. Pays $50-350.

Tips: "No out-of-town, out-of-state subject material. Most freelance work is accepted from local writers. Gear stories to the unique quality of San Diego. We try to offer only information unique to San Diego—people, places, shops, resources, etc. We plan more food and entertaining-at-home articles and more articles on garden products. We also need more in-depth reports on major architecture, environmental, and social aspects of life in San Diego and the border area."

TEXAS GARDENER, The Magazine for Texas Gardeners, by Texas Gardeners, Suntex Communications, Inc., P.O. Box 9005, Waco TX 76714-9005. (817)772-1270. Editor: Chris S. Corby. 80% freelance written. Works with a small number of new/unpublished writers each year. Bimonthly magazine covering vegetable and fruit production, ornamentals and home landscape information for home gardeners in Texas. Estab. 1981. Circ. 37,000. Pays on publication. Publishes ms an average of 4 months after acceptance. Byline given. Buys first North American serial and all rights. Submit seasonal/holiday material 6 months in advance. Query for electronic submissions. Reports in 6 weeks. Sample copy $2.75 for SAE with 5 first class stamps. Writer's guidelines for #10 SASE.

Nonfiction: How-to, humor, interview/profile and photo feature. "We use feature articles that relate to Texas gardeners. We also like personality profiles on hobby gardeners and professional horticulturists who are doing something unique." Buys 50-100 mss/year. Query with clips of published work. Length: 800-2,400 words. Pays $50-200.

Photos: "We prefer superb color and b&w photos; 90% of photos used are color." State availability of photos. Pays negotiable rates for 2¼ or 35mm color transparencies and 8 × 10 b&w prints and contact sheets. Model release and identification of subjects required.

Tips: "First, be a Texan. Then come up with a good idea of interest to home gardeners in this state. Be specific. Stick to feature topics like 'How Alley Gardening Became a Texas Tradition.' Leave topics like 'How to Control Fire Blight' to the experts. High quality photos could make the difference. We would like to add several writers to our group of regular contributors and would make assignments on a regular basis. Fillers are easy to come up with in-house. We want good writers who can produce accurate and interesting copy. Frequent mistakes made by writers in completing an article assignment for us are that articles are not slanted toward Texas gardening, show inaccurate or too little gardening information or lack good writing style. We will be doing more 'people' features and articles on ornamentals."

YOUR HOME, Meridian International, Inc., Box 10010, Ogden UT 84409. (801)394-9446. 65% freelance written. Monthly in-house magazine covering home/garden subjects. **Pays on acceptance.** Publishes ms an average of 3 months after acceptance. Byline given. Buys first rights, second serial (reprint) rights and nonexclusive reprint rights. Eight-month lead time. Submit seasonal material 10 months in advance. Simultaneous and previously published submissions OK. Reports in 2 months with SASE. Sample copy $1 for 9 × 12 SAE. Writer's guidelines for #10 SASE. All requests for samples and guidelines and queries should be addressed Attn: Editorial Staff.

Nonfiction: General interest articles about fresh ideas in home decor, ranging from floor and wall coverings to home furnishings. Subject matter includes the latest in home construction (exteriors, interiors, building materials, design), the outdoors at home (landscaping, pools, patios, gardening), remodeling projects, home management, and home buying and selling. "No do-it-yourself pieces." Buys 40 mss/year. Length: 1,000-1,400 words. Pays 15¢/word for first rights plus nonexclusive reprint rights. Payment for second serial rights is 10¢/word.

Photos: Send phots with ms. Reviews 35mm or larger transparencies and 5 × 7 or 8 × 10 "sharp, professional-looking" color prints. Pays $35 for inside photo; pays $50 for cover photo. Captions, model releases and identification of subjects required.

Tips: "Always looking for upscale, universal pieces. No do-it-yourself articles. The key is a well-written query letter that: (1) demonstrates that the subject of the article is practical and useful and has national appeal; (2) shows that the article will have a clear, focused theme and will be based on interviews with experts; (3) outlines the availability (from the writer, a photographer or a PR source) of top-quality color photos. If you are a professional writer, send clips; we do also publish first-time writers."

Humor

Publications listed here specialize in gaglines or prose humor, some just for readers and others for performers or speakers. Other publications that use humor can be found in nearly every category in this book. Some have special needs for major humor pieces; some use humor as fillers; many others are interested in material that meets their ordinary fiction or nonfiction requirements but also has a humorous slant. The majority of humor articles must be submitted as complete manuscripts on speculation because editors usually can't know from a query whether or not the piece will be right for them.

‡FUNNY TIMES, A Monthly Humor Review, Funny Times, Inc., P.O. Box 18530, Cleveland Heights OH 44118. (216)371-8600. Editors: Raymond Lesser and Susan Wolpert. 10% freelance written. Monthly tabloid for humor. "*Funny Times* is a monthly review of America's funniest cartoonists and writers. We are the *Reader's Digest* of modern American humor with a progressive/peace oriented/environmental/politically activist slant." Estab. 1985. Circ. 43,000. Pays on publication. Publishes ms an average of 3 months after acceptance. Byline given. Buys one-time or second serial (reprint) rights. Editorial lead time 2 months. Accepts simultaneous and previously published submissions. Reports in 2 months on mss. Sample copy $2.50 for 9 × 12 SAE with 4 first class stamps. Writer's guidelines for #10 SASE.

Nonfiction: Essays (funny), humor, interview/profile, opinion (humorous), personal experience (absolutely funny). "We only publish humor or interviews with funny people (comedians, comic actors, cartoonists, etc.). Everything we publish is very funny. If your piece isn't extremely funny then don't bother to send it. Don't send us anything that's not outrageously funny. Don't send anything that other people haven't already read and told you they laughed so hard they peed their pants." Buys 36 mss/year. Send complete ms. Length: 1,000 words. Pays $20 minimum for unsolicited articles.

Fiction: Humorous. Buys 6 mss/year. Query with published clips. Length: 5,000 words. Pays $20-150.

Fillers: Short humor. Buys 6/year. Pays $20.

Tips: "Send us a small packet (1-3 items) of only your very funniest stuff. If this makes us laugh we'll be glad to ask for more. We particularly welcome previously published material that has been well-received elsewhere."

LAF!, Scher Maihem Publishing, Ltd., P.O. Box 313, Avilla IN 46710-0313. Editor: Julie Scher. Submissions Editor: Fran Glass. 100% freelance written. Monthly tabloid that features modern life humor for baby boomers. Estab. 1991. Circ. 500. Pays within 30 days of publication. Buys first or second serial (reprint) rights. Submit seasonal/holiday material 6 months in advance. No simultaneous submissions. Reports in 3 months on mss. Sample copy for 9 × 12 SASE with 2 first class stamps. Writer's guidelines for #10 SASE.

Nonfiction: Humor and cartoons. "No religious, political, sexually or racially offensive humor." Buys 60 mss/year. Send complete ms. Length: 200-500 words. Pays $5-15 for unsolicited articles.

Fiction: Humor and cartoons. "No religious, political, sexually or racially offensive humor. No poems." Buys 60 mss/year. Send complete ms. Length: 200-500 words. Pays $5-15.

Tips: "If your humor writing appeals to people ages 45 and younger who live in small towns and the suburbs, send it. Our audience is broad, so the writing and subject must have wide appeal. We highly suggest writers take a look at the magazine and guidelines first."

LATEST JOKES, P.O. Box 3304, Brooklyn NY 11202-0066. (718)855-5057. Editor: Robert Makinson. Estab. 1974. 20% freelance written. Monthly newsletter of humor for TV and radio personalities, comedians and professional speakers. **Pays on acceptance.** Byline given. Buys all rights. Submit seasonal/holiday material 3 months in advance. Reports in 1 month. Sample copy $3 and SASE.

Nonfiction: Humor (short jokes). No "stupid, obvious, non-funny vulgar humor. Jokes about human tragedy also unwelcome." Send complete ms. Pays $1-3/joke.

Fiction: Humorous jokes. Pays $1-3.

Poetry: Light verse (humorous). Submit maximum 3 poems at one time. Line length: 2-8 lines. Pays 25¢/line.

Tips: "No famous personality jokes. Clever statements are not enough. Be original and surprising."

MAD MAGAZINE, 485 Madison Ave., New York NY 10022. (212)752-7685. Editors: Nick Meglin and John Ficarra. 100% freelance written. Magazine published 8 times/year. Estab. 1952. Circ. 1 million. **Pays on acceptance.** Publishes ms an average of 6 months after acceptance. Byline given. Buys all rights. Submit seasonal/holiday material 6 months in advance. Reports in 6-10 weeks. Writer's guidelines for #10 SASE.

Nonfiction: Satire, parody. "We're always on the lookout for new ways to spoof and to poke fun at hot trends — music, computers, fashions, etc. We're *not* interested in formats we're already doing or have done to death like . . . 'you know you're a . . . when . . .' " Buys 400 ms yearly. Submit a premise with 3 or 4 examples of how you intend to carry it through, describing the action and visual content. Rough sketches not necessary. One-page gags: 2-8 panel cartoon continuities in the style and tradition of *MAD*. Pays minimum of $400/ *MAD* page. "*Don't* send riddles, advice columns, TV or movie satires, book manuscripts, articles about Alfred E. Neuman, poetry, essays, short stories or other text pieces."

Tips: "Have fun! Remember to think visually! Freelancers can best break in with nontopical material. Include SASE with each submission. Originality is prized. We like outrageous, silly and/or satirical humor."

NATIONAL LAMPOON, National Lampoon Inc., 10850 Wilshire Blvd., Los Angeles CA 02113. "Prefers not to share information."

SPEAKERS IDEA FILE, (formerly Current Comedy), 165 W. 47th St., New York NY 10036. Humor Editor: Gary Apple. For "business communicators of all types—politicians, CEO's, salespeople, teachers, toastmasters, etc." Pays on publication. Buys all rights. Writer's guidelines for SASE.

Fillers: "In our humor section, we publish funny one-liners and short jokes that public speakers can use in their presentations. These include jokes about news events, celebrities, trends, families, business, and finance. We also run jokes specifically geared toward the public speaking environment: jokes for beginning and ending a speech, introductions, hecklers, roasts, retirement, and so on." Pays $12/joke.

Tips: "The material that you send *must be original*. Do not send jokes you've heard somewhere, only truly funny jokes you've written yourself. Please submit no more than fifteen jokes at one time. Enclose a SASE for the return of your material."

WE ARE THE WEIRD, Briggs Museum of American Culture, P.O. Box 2002, Dallas TX 75221. Fax: (214)368-2310. Editor: Joe Bob Briggs. Assistant Editor: Tanja Lindstrom. 5% freelance written. Biweekly newsletter/fanzine covering Joe Bob Briggs, popular culture and film. "Radical humor in the spirit of syndicated columnist and TV personality Joe Bob Briggs." Estab. 1985. Circ. 3,500. Pays on publication. Publishes ms an average of 1 month after acceptance. Byline given. Buys first North American serial and second serial (reprint) rights. Submit seasonal/holiday material 2-3 months in advance. Simultaneous and previously published submissions OK. Query for electronic submissions. Sample copy for #10 SAE with 2 first class stamps.
Nonfiction: Essays, humor, opinion and personal experience. Buys 10 mss/year. Send complete ms. Length: 2,000 words maximum. Pays $25 maximum for unsolicited articles. Pays in contributor copies or other premiums when the writer requests it.
Photos: Send photos with submission. Offers $5-25/photo. Model releases and identification of subjects required. Buys all rights.
Fiction: Fantasy, horror, humorous and slice-of-life vignettes. Buys 5 mss/year. Send complete ms. Length: 2,000 maximum words. Pays $25 maximum.
Poetry: Avant-garde, free verse, Haiku, light verse and traditional. Buys 5 poems/year. Pays $25 maximum.
Fillers: Anecdotes, facts and short humor. Buys 5/year. Length: 25 words maximum.
Tips: "Anything that makes us laugh will get our attention. We are most open to poems or short essays (500 words or less). They should be humorous or deal with popular culture, especially the fields of movies, music and stand-up comedy."

Inflight

Most major inflight magazines cater to business travelers and vacationers who will be reading, during the flight, about the airline's destinations and other items of general interest. Airline mergers and acquisitions continue to decrease the number of magazines published in this area. Watch for airline announcements in the news and in ads and read the latest sample copies and writer's guidelines for current information.

‡ABOARD, North-South Net, Inc., Suite 220, 100 Almeria, Coral Gables FL 33134. (305)441-9744. Editor: Gloria Shanahan. 20% freelance written. Bimonthly magazine. Estab. 1976. Circ. 89,000. Pays on publication. Byline given. Buys one-time or simultaneous rights or makes work-for-hire assignments. Submit seasonal/holiday material 4 months in advance. Simultaneous and previously published submissions OK. Query for electronic submissions.
Nonfiction: General interest, historical/nostalgic, humor, new product, personal experience, photo feature, technical and travel. "No controversial or political material." Buys 50 mss/year. Length: 1,200-1,500 words. Pays $100-150. Sometimes pays expenses of writers on assignment.
Photos: Send photos with submission. Reviews transparencies. Offers no additional payment for photos accepted with ms. Offers $20 minimum/photo. Identification of subjects required. Buys one-time rights.
Fillers: Facts, short humor. Buys 6/year. Length: 800-1,200 words. Pays $100.
Tips: "Send article with photos. We need lots of travel material on Chile, Ecuador, Bolivia, El Salvador, Honduras, Peru, Guatemala and the Dominican Republic."

AMERICA WEST AIRLINES MAGAZINE, Skyword Marketing, Inc., Suite 240, 7500 N. Dreamy Draw Dr., Phoenix AZ 85020-4660. (602)997-7200. Editor: Michael Derr. 80% freelance written. Works with small number of new/unpublished writers each year. Monthly "general interest magazine, with substantial business editorial, emphasizing the western and southwestern U.S. Some Midwestern, Northwestern and Eastern subjects also appropriate. We look for innovative, newsworthy and unconventional subject matter." Estab. 1986. Query with published clips and SASE. Pays on publication. Publishes ms an average of 4 months after acceptance. Byline given. Offers 15% kill fee. Buys first North American rights. Submit seasonal/holiday material 6-8 months in advance. Simultaneous submissions OK, "if indicated as such." Query for electronic submissions. Reports in 1 month on queries; 5 weeks on mss. Sample copy $3. Writer's guidelines for 9 × 12 SAE with 3 first class stamps.
Nonfiction: General interest, creative leisure, profile, photo feature, science, sports, business issues, entrepreneurs, nature, arts, travel and trends. Also considers essays and humor. No puzzles, reviews or highly controversial features. Buys 130-140 mss/year. Length: 300-2,200. Pays $150-900. Pays some expenses.
Photos: State availability of original photography. Offers $50-250/photo. Captions, model releases and identification of subjects required. Buys one-time rights.
  • Ranked as one of the best markets for freelance writers in *Writer's Digest* magazine's annual "Top 100 Markets," January 1993.

AMERICAN WAY, P.O. Box 619640, Dallas/Fort Worth Airport TX 75261-9640. (817)967-1804. Fax: (817)967-1571. Editor: Doug Crichton. 98% freelance written. Prefers to work with published/established writers. Fortnightly inflight magazine for passengers flying with American Airlines. Estab. 1966. **Pays on acceptance.** Publishes ms an average of 4 months after acceptance. Buys first serial rights.
Nonfiction: Business and CEO profiles, the arts and entertainment, sports, personalities, technology, food, science, medicine and travel. "We are amenable to almost any subject that would be interesting, entertaining or useful to a passenger of American Airlines." Also humor, trivia, trends, and will consider a variety of ideas. Buys 450 mss/year. Query with published clips. Length: 1,000-4,000 words. Pays $850 and up. Usually pays the expenses of writers on assignment.
Fiction: Jeff Posey, editor. Length: 2,500 words maximum. Payment varies.

SKIES AMERICA PUBLISHING, Northwest Airlines World Traveler, Skies America Publishing Co., 7730 SW Mohawk, Tualatin OR 97062. (503)691-1955. Editor: Terri J. Wallo. Managing Editor: Kelly Kearns. 75% freelance written. Monthly magazine of business and leisure. Estab. 1969. Circ. 350,000. Pays on publication. Publishes ms an average of 2 months after acceptance. Byline given. Offers 100% kill fee. Buys first rights. Submit seasonal/holiday material 6 months in advance. Simultaneous submissions OK. Reports in 2 months. Sample copy $3 for 9×12 SASE. Writer's guidelines for #10 SASE.
Nonfiction: General interest, interview/profile, personal experience, photo feature and travel. No poetry, new product, controversial, fiction, religious or fillers. Buys 5 mss/year. Query. Length: 2,000-3,000 words. Pays $850-1,000. Pays expenses of writers on assignment.
Photos: State availability of photos with submission. Offers $200 maximum/photo. Captions and identification of subjects required. Buys one-time rights.
Tips: "Query letter only. No ms. No phone calls. Study structure of magazine. Freelancers have the best chance breaking in with articles on adventure sports, corporate profiles or sports profiles."

SKY, Inflight Magazine of Delta Air Lines, Halsey Publishing Co., 600 Corporate Dr., Ft. Lauderdale FL 33334. (305)776-0066. Editor: Lidia De Leon. Managing Editor: Barbara Whelehan. 90% freelance written. Monthly magazine. "Delta *SKY* is a general interest, nationally/internationally-oriented magazine with the main purpose to entertain and inform business and leisure travelers aboard Delta Air Lines." Estab. 1971. Circ. 500,000. **Pays on acceptance.** Publishes ms an average of 2 months after acceptance. Byline given. Offers 100% kill fee when cancellation is through no fault of the writer. Buys one-time rights. Submit seasonal/holiday material 9 months in advance. Simultaneous submissions OK. Query for electronic submissions. Reports in 1 month. Sample copy for 9×12 SAE. Writer's guidelines for #10 SASE.
 • Ranked as one of the best markets for freelance writers in *Writer's Digest* magazine's annual "Top 100 Markets," January 1993.
Nonfiction: General interest and photo feature. "No opinion, religious, reviews, poetry, fiction or fillers." Buys 200-250 mss/year. Query with published clips. Length: 1700-2500 words. Pays $500-700 for assigned articles; pays $400-500 for unsolicited articles. Pays expenses of writers on assignment.
Photos: State availability of photos with submission. Reviews 4×5 transparencies and 5×7 prints. Offers varying rates on photos. Captions, model releases and identification of subject required. Buys one-time rights.
Columns/Departments: Management (managerial techniques, methods of topical nature); Living (subjects of topical, contemporary interest); and Finance (personal finance, tips). Buys 50-60 mss/year. Query. Length: 1500-1700 words. Pays $300-450.
Tips: "Send a well detailed query tied in to one of the feature or column categories of the magazine. Since our lead times call for planning of editorial content 6-9 months in advance, that should also be kept in mind when proposing story ideas. All feature story and column/department categories are open to freelancers, with the exceptions of Travel (areas are predetermined by the airline) and the executive Profile Series (which is also predetermined)."

TRADEWIND, Caribbean Travel and Life, Inc., Suite 830, 8403 Colesville Rd., Silver Spring MD 20910. (301)588-2300. Editor: Norie Quintos Danyliw. 75% freelance written. Quarterly magazine covering destinations of ALM Antillean Airlines (Aruba, Bonaire, Curaçao, Jamaica, Guyana, Venezuela, Surinam, Cuba). "*TradeWind* is the inflight magazine for ALM Antillean Airlines, the airline of the Dutch Caribbean. We publish articles on travel to the Dutch Caribbean and other ALM destinations." Estab. 1987. Circ. 22,000. Pays on publication. Publishes ms an average of 4 months after acceptance. Byline given. Offers 25% kill fee. Buys first North American serial, one-time rights and second serial (reprint) rights. Submit seasonal material 6 months in advance. Simultaneous and previously published submissions OK. Query for electronic submissions. Reprints OK; send photocopy of article and information about when and where the article previously appeared. Pays 60% of their fee for an original article. Reports in 2 months. Sample copy for 9×12 SAE with 5 first class stamps. Writer's guidelines for #10 SASE.
Nonfiction: General interest (related to ALM destinations) and travel. "No superficial pieces, or pieces on destinations not on airline route." Buys 10 mss/year. Query with or without published clips, or send complete ms. Length: 800-1,000 words. Pays $35-200.

Photos: Send photos with submission. Reviews all sizes of transparencies. Offers $35-200/photo. Identification of subjects required. Buys one-time rights.

Columns/Departments: Panorama (short pieces on travel news, new books, tours), 400-600 words; and Sugar & Spice (food column on Caribbean food), 600-800 words. Buys 4 mss/year. Query with published clips or send complete ms. Pays $35-100.

Tips: "We are in particular need of story ideas on some of ALM's more exotic destinations: Caracas and Valencia, Venezuela; Georgetown, Guyana; Paramaribo, Surinam. Recent freelance pieces have been: Glassblowers of Caracas. Though our rates are on the low end, we're willing to work with new freelancers who have good ideas and skills."

USAIR MAGAZINE, Pace Communications, 1301 Carolina St., Greensboro NC 27401. (919)378-6065. Editor: Terri Barnes. Associate Editor: Julia Belcher. 95% freelance written. Works with published/established writers. Monthly general interest magazine published for airline passengers, many of whom are business travelers, male, with high incomes and college educations. Circ. 450,000. Pays before publication. Publishes ms an average of 4 months after acceptance. Buys first rights only. Submit seasonal material 4 months in advance. Reports in 1 month. Sample copy $5. Writer's guidelines for #10 SASE.

Nonfiction: Travel, business, sports, health, food, nature, the arts, science/technology and photography. Buys 125 mss/year. Send well-developed queries with clips of previously published work. Length: 1,500-2,800 words. Pays $500-1,000.

Photos: Send photos with ms. Pays $75-150/b&w print, depending on size; color from $100-250/print or slide. Captions preferred; model release required. Buys one-time rights.

Columns/Departments: Sports, food, health, business, living and science. Buys 8-10 mss/issue. Query. Length: 1,200-1,800 words. Pays $400-600.

Tips: "Send irresistible ideas and proof that you can write. It's great to get a clean manuscript from a good writer who has given me exactly what I asked for. Frequent mistakes are not following instructions, not delivering on time, etc. We do not accept telephone queries."

WASHINGTON FLYER MAGAZINE, #111, 11 Canal Center Plaza, Alexandria VA 22314. (703)739-9292. Editor: Brian T. Cook. Assistant Editors: Laurie McLaughlin, Stephen Soltis. 80% freelance written. Bimonthly in-airport magazine for business and pleasure travelers at Washington National and Washington Dulles International airports. "Primarily affluent, well-educated audience that flies frequently in and out of Washington DC." Estab. 1989. Circ. 160,620. **Pays on acceptance.** Byline given. Buys first North American rights. Submit seasonal/holiday material 4 months in advance. Query for electronic submissions. Reports in approximately 2½ months. Sample copy and writer's guidelines for 9 × 12 SAE with 9 first class stamps.

Nonfiction: General interest, historical/nostalgic, how-to, interview/profile and travel. Buys 30-40 mss/year. Query with published clips. Length: 500-1,500 words. Pays $100-600. Sometimes pays expenses of writers on assignment.

Photos: State availability of photos with submission. Reviews negatives and transparencies (almost always color). Will consider additional payment for top-quality photos accepted with ms. Identification of subjects required. Buys one-time rights.

Tips: "Know the Washington market and issues relating to frequent business/pleasure travelers as we move toward a global economy."

Juvenile

Just as children change and grow, so do juvenile magazines. Children's magazine editors stress that writers must read recent issues. This section lists publications for children ages 2-12. Magazines for young people 13-19 appear in the Teen and Young Adult category. Many of the following publications are produced by religious groups and, where possible, the specific denomination is given. A book of juvenile markets, *Children's Writer's and Illustrator's Market*, is available from Writer's Digest Books.

BOYS' LIFE, Boy Scouts of America, P.O. Box 152079, Irving TX 75015-2079. Executive Editor: Scott Stuckey. 75% freelance written. Prefers to work with published/established writers; works with small number of new/ unpublished writers each year. Monthly magazine covering activities of interest to all boys ages 8-18. Most readers are Scouts or Cub Scouts. Estab. 1911. Circ 1.3 million. **Pays on acceptance.** Publishes ms an average of 6-12 months after acceptance. Buys one-time rights. Reports in 4-6 weeks. Sample copy $2.50 for 9 × 12 SAE. Writer's guidelines for #10 SASE.

Nonfiction: Major articles run 750-1,500 words. Preferred length is about 1,000 words including sidebars and boxes. Pays minimum $500 for major article text. Uses strong photo features with about 500 words of text. Separate payment or assignment for photos. "Much better rates if you really know how to write for our market." Buys 60 major articles/year. Also needs how-to features and hobby and crafts ideas. "We pay top rates for ideas accompanied by sharp photos, clean diagrams, and short, clear instructions." Query first in writing. Buys 30-40 how-tos/year. Query all nonfiction ideas in writing. Pays expenses of writers on assignment. Also buys freelance comics pages and scripts. Query first in writing, not by phone.

Columns: "Food, Health, Pets, Bicycling and Magic Tricks are some of the columns for which we use 400-600 words of text. This is a good place to show us what you can do. Query first in writing." Pays $150 minimum. Buys 75-80 columns/year.

Fiction: Short stories 1,000-1,500 words; rarely longer. Send complete ms. w/SASE. Pays $500 minimum. Buys 15 short stories/year.

- Ranked as one of the best markets for freelance writers in *Writer's Digest* magazine's annual "Top 100 Markets," January 1993.

Tips: "We strongly recommend reading at least 12 issues of the magazine and learning something about the programs of the Boy Scouts of America before you submit queries. We are a good market for any writer willing to do the necessary homework."

‡CALLIOPE: The World History Magazine for Young People, Cobblestone Publishing, Inc., 7 School St., Peterborough NH 03458-1454. (603)924-7209. Fax: (603)924-7380. Editor-in-Chief: Carolyn P. Yoder. Editors: Rosalie and Charles Baker. 50% freelance written. Prefers to work with published/established writers. Magazine published 5 times/year covering world history through 1800 AD for 8- to 14-year-olds. Articles must relate to the issue's theme. Pays on publication. Byline given. Buys all rights. Simultaneous submissions OK. Previously published submissions rarely accepted. Sample copy $3.95 for 7½×10½ SAE with 5 first class stamps. Writer's guidelines for SASE.

Nonfiction: Essays, general interest, historical/nostalgic, how-to (activities), recipes, humor, interview/profile, personal experience, photo feature, technical and travel. Articles must relate to the theme. No religious, pornographic, biased or sophisticated submissions. Buys approximately 30-40 mss/year. Query with published clips. Feature articles 700-800 words. Pays 14-17¢ per printed word. Supplemental nonfiction 300-600 words. Pays 10-13¢ per printed word.

Photos: State availability of photos with submission. Reviews contact sheets, color slides and b&w prints. Buys one-time rights. Pays $15-50 for b&w (color cover negotiated).

Fiction: All fiction must be theme-related. Buys 10 mss/year. Query with published clips. Length: up to 800 words. Pays 10-17¢/word.

Poetry: Light verse and traditional. No religious or pornographic poetry or poetry not related to the theme. Submit maximum 1 poem. Pays on individual basis. Poetry, up to 100 lines.

Columns/Departments: Puzzles and Games (no word finds). Crossword and other word puzzles using the vocabulary of the issue's themes. Mazes and picture puzzles that relate to the theme. Pays on an individual basis.

Tips: "Writers must have an appreciation and understanding of world history. Writers must not condescend to our readers."

CHICKADEE MAGAZINE, For Young Children from *OWL*, The Young Naturalist Foundation, 56 The Esplanade, Suite 306, Toronto, Ontario M5E 1A7 Canada. (416)868-6001. Editor: Lizann Flatt. 25% freelance written. Magazine published 10 times/year (except July and August) for 3-9-year-olds. "We aim to interest young children in the world around them in an entertaining and lively way." Estab. 1979. Circ. 110,000 Canada and US. **Pays on acceptance.** Byline given. Buys all rights. Submit seasonal/holiday material up to 1 year in advance. Reports in 2 months. Sample copy $3.50 for SAE ($1 money order, no IRC's). Writer's guidelines for SAE.

Nonfiction: How-to (easy and unusual arts and crafts); personal experience (real children in real situations); and photo feature (wildlife features). No articles for older children; no religious or moralistic features.

Photos: Send photos with ms. Reviews 35mm transparencies. Identification of subjects required.

Fiction: Adventure (relating to the 3-9-year-old) and humor. No talking animal stories or religious articles. Send complete ms with $1 money order for handling and return postage. Pays $210 (US).

Tips: "A frequent mistake made by writers is trying to teach too much—not enough entertainment and fun."

CHILD LIFE, Children's Better Health Institute, P.O. Box 567, Indianapolis IN 46206-0567. (317)636-8881. Editor: Stan Zukowski. 90% freelance written. Monthly (except bimonthly January/February, April/May, July/August, October/November) magazine covering "general topics of interest to children—emphasis on health preferred but not necessary." Pays on publication. Publishes ms an average of 8 months after acceptance. Byline given. Buys all rights. Submit seasonal/holiday material 8 months in advance. Reports in 3 months. Sample copy $1.25. Writer's guidelines for #10 SASE.

Nonfiction: How-to (simple crafts), anything children might like—health topics preferred. Buys 20 mss/year. Send complete ms. Length: 400-1,000. Pays 10¢/word (approximately).

Photos: Send photos only with accompanying editorial material. Reviews transparencies and prints. Offers $25 for inside photo, $50 for front cover. Captions, model releases and identification of subjects required. Buys one-time rights.

Columns/Departments: Regular columns open to freelancers include "One World, Fun World: Games from the Global Village" and "Odd Jobs." Query for descriptions with #10 SASE.

Fiction: Adventure, fantasy, historical, humorous, multicultural, mystery, science fiction and suspense. All must be geared to children (9-11 years old). Buys 20-25 mss/year. Send complete ms. Length: 400-1,000 words. Pays 10¢/word (approximately).

Poetry: Free verse, haiku, light verse and traditional. No long "deep" poetry not suited for children. Buys 8 poems/year. Submit maximum 5 poems. Pays approximately $2.

Fillers: "Constant, ongoing demand for puzzles, games, mazes, etc." Variable pay.

Tips: "Present health-related items in an interesting, non-textbook manner. The approach to health fiction can be subtle—tell a good story first. We also consider non-health items—make them fresh and enjoyable for children."

CHILDREN'S DIGEST, Children's Better Health Institute, P.O. Box 567, Indianapolis IN 46206-0567. (317)636-8881. Editor: Elizabeth Rinck. 85% freelance written. Works with a small number of new/unpublished writers each year. Magazine published 8 times/year covering children's health for preteen children. Estab. 1950. Pays on publication. Publishes ms an average of 1 year after acceptance. Byline given. Buys all rights. Submit seasonal/holiday material 8 months in advance. Submit *only* complete mss. "No queries, please." Reports in 2 months. Sample copy $1.25. Writer's guidelines for #10 SASE.

Nonfiction: Historical, interview/profile (biographical), craft ideas, health, nutrition, fitness and sports. "We're especially interested in factual features that teach readers about fitness and sports or encourage them to develop better health habits. We are *not* interested in material that is simply rewritten from encyclopedias. We try to present our health material in a way that instructs *and* entertains the reader." Buys 15-20 mss/year. Send complete ms. Length: 500-1,200 words. Pays at least 10¢/word. Sometimes pays the expenses of writers on assignment.

Photos: State availability of full color or b&w photos. Payment varies. Model releases and identification of subjects required. Buys one-time rights.

Fiction: Adventure, humorous, mainstream and mystery. Stories should appeal to both boys and girls. "We need some stories that incorporate a health theme. However, we don't want stories that preach, preferring instead stories with implied morals. We like a light or humorous approach." Buys 15-20 mss/year. Length: 500-1,500 words. Pays at least 10¢/word.

Poetry: Pays $15 minimum.

Tips: "Many of our readers have working mothers and/or come from single-parent homes. We need more stories that reflect these changing times while communicating good values."

CHILDREN'S PLAYMATE, Children's Better Health Institute, P.O. Box 567, Indianapolis IN 46206-0567. (317)636-8881. Editor: Elizabeth Rinck. 75% freelance written. Eager to work with new/unpublished writers. "We are looking for articles, stories, and activities with a health, sports, fitness or nutritionally oriented theme. Primarily we are concerned with preventative medicine. We try to present our material in a positive light, and we try to incorporate humor and a light approach wherever possible without minimizing the seriousness of what we are saying." For children ages 6-8. Magazine published 8 times/year. Estab. 1928. Buys all rights. Byline given. Pays on publication. Publishes ms an average of 1 year after acceptance. Submit seasonal material 8 months in advance. Reports in 2 months. Sometimes may hold mss for up to 1 year, with author's permission. "Material will not be returned unless accompanied by a SAE and sufficient postage." Sample copy $1.25. Writer's guidelines for #10 SASE.

Nonfiction: 600 words maximum. "??A feature may be an interesting presentation on animals, people, events, objects or places, especially about good health, exercise, proper nutrition and safety. Include word count. Buys 30 mss/year. "We do not consider outlines. Reading the whole manuscript is the only way to give fair consideration. The editors cannot criticize, offer suggestions, or review unsolicited material that is not accepted." No queries. Pays up to 15¢/word.

Fiction: Short stories for beginning readers, not over 700 words. Seasonal stories with holiday themes. Humorous stories, unusual plots. "We are interested in stories about children in different cultures and stories about lesser-known holidays (not just Christmas, Thanksgiving, Halloween, Hanukkah)." Vocabulary suitable for ages 6-8. Submit complete ms. Pays up to 15¢/word. Include word count with stories.

Fillers: Puzzles, dot-to-dots, color-ins, hidden pictures and mazes. Buys 30 fillers/year. Payment varies.

Tips: Especially interested in stories, poems and articles about special holidays, customs and events.

‡**CLUBHOUSE, Your Story Hour**, P.O. Box 15, Berrien Springs MI 49103. (616)471-3701. Editor: Elaine Trumbo. 75% freelance written. Works with a small number of new/unpublished writers each year. Bimonthly magazine covering many subjects with Christian approach, though not associated with a church. "Stories and features for fun for 9-14 year-olds. Main objective: To provide a psychologically 'up' magazine that lets kids

know that they are acceptable, 'neat' people." Estab. 1951. Circ. 8,000. Pays on acceptance within about 6 months. Publishes ms an average of 1 year after acceptance. Byline given. Buys first serial rights or first North American serial rights, one-time rights, simultaneous rights, and second serial (reprint) rights. Simultaneous queries, and simultaneous and previously published submissions OK. Reports in 4-8 weeks. Sample copy for 6×9 SAE with 3 first class stamps. Writer's guidelines for #10 SASE.

Nonfiction: How-to (crafts), personal experience and recipes (without sugar or artificial flavors and colors). "No stories in which kids start out 'bad' and by peer or adult pressure or circumstances are changed into 'good' people." Send complete ms. Length: 750-800 words ($25); 1,000-1,200 words ($30); feature story, 1,200 words ($35).

Photos: Send photos with ms. Pays on publication according to published size. Buys one-time rights.

Columns/Departments: Body Shop (short stories or "ad" type material that is anti-smoking, drugs and alcohol and pro-good nutrition, etc.); and Jr. Detective (secret codes, word search, deduction problems, hidden pictures, etc.). Buys 12/year. Send complete ms. Length: 400 words maximum for Jr. Detective; 1,000 maximum for Body Shop. Pays $10-30.

Fiction: Adventure, historical, humorous and mainstream. "Stories should depict bravery, kindness, etc., without a preachy attitude." No science fiction, romance, confession or mystery. Cannot use Santa-elves, Halloween or Easter Bunny material. Buys 30 mss/year. Send query or complete ms (prefers ms). Length: 750-800 words ($20); 1,000-1,200 words ($30); lead story ($35).

Poetry: Free verse, light verse and traditional. Buys 6-10/year. Submit maximum 5 poems. Length: 4-24 lines. Pays $5-20.

Fillers: Cartoons. Buys 18/year. Pay $12 maximum.

Tips: "Send all material during March or April. (Not accepting material until April 1994.) By the middle of June acceptance or rejection notices will be sent. Material chosen will appear the following year. Basically, kids are more and more informed and aware of the world around them. This means that characters in stories for *Clubhouse* should not seem too simple, yet maintain the wonder and joy of youth."

‡COBBLESTONE: The History Magazine for Young People, Cobblestone Publishing, Inc., 7 School St., Peterborough NH 03458-1457. (603)924-7209. Fax: (603)924-7380. Editor-in-Chief: Carolyn P. Yoder. Editor: Samuel A. Mead. 100% (except letters and departments) freelance written (approximately 2 issues/year are by assignment only). Prefers to work with published/established writers. Monthly magazine (except July and August) covering American history for children ages 8-14. "Each issue presents a particular theme, from different angles, making it exciting as well as informative. Half of all subscriptions are for schools." Circ. 40,000. Pays on publication. Publishes ms an average of 4 months after acceptance. Byline given. Buys all rights or makes work-for-hire assignments. All material must relate to monthly theme. Simultaneous and previously published submissions OK. Sample copy $3.95 for 7½×10½ SAE with 5 first class stamps. Writer's guidelines for SASE.

Nonfiction: Historical/nostalgic, how-to, interview, plays, biography, recipes, activities and personal experience. "Request a copy of the writer's guidelines to find out specific issue themes in upcoming months." No material that editorializes rather than reports. Buys 5-8 mss/issue. Length: Feature articles 700-800 words. Pays 14-17¢/printed word. Supplemental nonfiction 300-600 words. Pays up to 10-13¢/printed word. Query with published clips, outline and bibliography.

Fiction: Adventure, historical, humorous and biographical fiction. "Has to be very strong and accurate." Buys 1-2 mss/issue. Length: up to 800 words. Request free editorial guidelines that explain upcoming issue themes and give query deadlines. "Message" must be smoothly integrated with the story. Query with written samples. Pays 10-17¢/printed word.

Poetry: Free verse, light verse and traditional. Submit maximum 2 poems. Length: up to 100 lines. Pays on an individual basis. Must relate to theme.

Columns/Departments: Puzzles and Games (no word finds). Crossword and other word puzzles using the vocabulary of the issue's theme. Mazes and picture puzzles that relate to the theme. Pays on an individual basis.

Tips: "All material is considered on the basis of merit and appropriateness to theme. Query should state idea for material simply, with rationale for why material is applicable to theme. Request writer's guidelines (includes themes and query deadlines) before submitting a query. Include SASE."

CRICKET, The Magazine for Children, Carus Publishing Co., P.O. Box 300, Peru IL 61354-0300. (815)224-6643. Editor-in-Chief: Marianne Carus. Monthly magazine. Estab. 1973. Circ. 120,000. Pays on publication. Byline given. Buys first publication rights in the English language. Submit seasonal/holiday material 1 year in advance. Previously published submissions OK; send typed ms with rights for sale noted, including information about when and where the article previously appeared. Reports in 3-4 months. Sample copy $2. Writer's guidelines for #10 SASE.

Nonfiction: Adventure, biography, foreign culture, geography, history, science, social science, sports, technology and travel. (A short bibliography is required for *all* nonfiction articles.) Send complete ms. Length: 200-1,200 words. Pays up to 25¢/word.

Fiction: Adventure, ethnic, fairy tales, fantasy, historical, humorous, mystery, novel excerpts, science fiction, suspense and western. No didactic, sex, religious or horror stories. Buys 24-36 mss/year. Send complete ms. Length: 200-1,500 words. Pays up to 25¢/word.

Poetry: Buys 8-10 poems/year. Length: 25 lines maximum. Pays up to $3/line on publication.

‡CRUSADER MAGAZINE, P.O. Box 7259, Grand Rapids MI 49510. Fax: (616)241-5558. Editor: G. Richard Broene. 40% freelance written. Works with a small number of new/unpublished writers each year. Magazine published 7 times/year. "*Crusader Magazine* shows boys (9-14) how God is at work in their lives and in the world around them." Estab. 1958. Circ. 14,000. Buys 20-25 mss/year. **Pays on acceptance.** Byline given. Publishes ms an average of 8 months after acceptance. Rights purchased vary with author and material; buys first serial, one-time, second serial (reprint) and simultaneous rights. Submit seasonal material (Christmas, Easter) at least 5 months in advance. Simultaneous submissions OK. Reports in 2 months. Sample copy and writer's guidelines for 9×12 SAE with 3 first class stamps.

Nonfiction: Articles about young boys' interests: sports, outdoor activities, bike riding, science, crafts, etc., and problems. Emphasis is on a Christian multi-racial perspective, but no simplistic moralisms. Informational, how-to, personal experience, interview, profile, inspirational and humor. Submit complete ms. Length: 500-1,500 words. Pays 2-5¢/word.

Photos: Pays $4-25 for b&w photos purchased with mss.

Fiction: "Considerable fiction is used. Fast-moving stories that appeal to a boy's sense of adventure or sense of humor are welcome. Avoid preachiness. Avoid simplistic answers to complicated problems. Avoid long dialogue and little action." Length: 900-1,500 words. Pays 2¢/word minimum.

Fillers: Uses short humor and any type of puzzles as fillers.

DISCOVERIES, 6401 The Paseo, Kansas City MO 64131. Editor: Latta Jo Knapp. Mostly freelance written. For boys and girls ages 8-9. Weekly. Estab. 1974. Publishes ms an average of 1 year after acceptance. Buys all rights. "Minimal comments on pre-printed form are made on rejected material." Reports in 1 month. Sample copy and guidelines for #10 SASE.

Fiction: Stories with Christian emphasis on high ideals, wholesome social relationships and activities, right choices, Sabbath observance, church loyalty and missions. *Discoveries* extends the Sunday School lesson with life-related stories of third and fourth grade children. Informal style. Submit complete ms. Length: 500-700 words. Pays 5¢/word.

DOLPHIN LOG, The Cousteau Society, Suite 402, 870 Greenbrier Circle, Chesapeake VA 23320-2641. (804)523-9335. Editor: Elizabeth Foley. 30-40% freelance written. Prefers to work with published/established writers; works with a small number of new/unpublished writers each year. Bimonthly nonfiction magazine covering marine biology, ecology, natural history and the environment. "*Dolphin Log* is an educational publication for children ages 7-15 offered by The Cousteau Society. Subject matter encompasses all areas that can be related to our global water system. The philosophy of the magazine is to delight, instruct and instill an environmental ethic and understanding of the interconnectedness of living organisms, including people." Estab. 1981. Circ. 100,000. Pays on publication. Publishes ms an average of 1 year after acceptance. Byline given. Buys one-time, reprint and translation rights. Reports in 2 months. Sample copy $2 for 9×12 SAE with 3 first class stamps. Writer's guidelines for SASE. (Make checks payable to The Cousteau Society.)

Nonfiction: General interest (per guidelines); how-to (water-related crafts or science); and photo feature (marine subject). "Of special interest are articles on specific marine creatures, and games involving an ocean/water-related theme which develop math, reading and comprehension skills. Experiments that can be conducted at home and demonstrate a phenomenon or principle of science are wanted as are clever crafts or art projects which also can be tied to an ocean theme. No 'talking' animals. First-person accounts are discouraged, as are fictional narratives and articles that address the reader." Buys 8-12 mss/year. Query or send complete ms. Length: 400-600 words. Pays $50-150.

Photos: Send photos with query or ms (duplicates only). Prefers underwater animals, water photos with children, photos that explain text. Pays $25-200/photo. Identification of subjects required. Buys one-time and translation rights.

Columns/Departments: Discovery (science experiments or crafts a young person can easily do at home), 50-250 words; and Creature Feature (lively article on one specific marine animal), 200-300 words. Buys 1 mss/year. Send complete ms. Pays $25-100.

Poetry: No "talking" animals or dark or religious themes. Buys 1-2 poems/year. Pays $10-100.

Tips: "Find a lively way to relate scientific facts to children without anthropomorphizing. We need to know material is accurate and current. Articles should feature an interesting marine creature and yet contain factual material that's fun to read. We will be increasingly interested in material that draws information from current scientific research."

THE FRIEND, 50 E. North Temple, Salt Lake City UT 84150. Managing Editor: Vivian Paulsen. 50% freelance written. Eager to work with new/unpublished writers as well as established writers. Appeals to children ages 3-11. Monthly publication of The Church of Jesus Christ of Latter-Day Saints. Circ. 235,000. **Pays on accep-**

tance. Buys all rights. Submit seasonal material 8 months in advance. Sample copy and writer's guidelines for 9 × 12 SAE with 4 first class stamps.

Nonfiction: Subjects of current interest, science, nature, pets, sports, foreign countries, and things to make and do. Special issues for Christmas and Easter. "Submit only complete ms — no queries, please." No simultaneous submissions. Length: 1,000 words maximum. Pays 9¢/word minimum.

Fiction: Seasonal and holiday stories and stories about other countries and their children. Wholesome and optimistic; high motive, plot and action. Character-building stories preferred. Length: 1,200 words maximum. Stories for younger children should not exceed 250 words. Pays 9¢/word minimum.

Poetry: Serious, humorous and holiday. Any form with child appeal. Pays $25.

Tips: "Do you remember how it feels to be a child? Can you write stories that appeal to children ages 3-11 in today's world? We're interested in stories with an international flavor and those that focus on present-day problems. Send material of high literary quality slanted to our editorial requirements. Let the child solve the problem — not some helpful, all-wise adult. No overt moralizing. Nonfiction should be creatively presented — not an array of facts strung together. Beware of being cutesy."

HIGH ADVENTURE, Gospel Publishing House, 1445 Boonville, Springfield MO 65802-1894. (417)862-2781, ext. 4178. Fax: (417)862-8558. Editor: Marshall Bruner. Eager to work with new/unpublished writers. Quarterly magazine "designed to provide boys with worthwhile, enjoyable, leisure reading; to challenge them in narrative form to higher ideals and greater spiritual dedication; and to perpetuate the spirit of the Royal Rangers program through stories, ideas and illustrations." Estab. 1971. Circ. 86,000. **Pays on acceptance.** Byline given. Buys one-time rights. Submit seasonal/holiday material 9 months in advance. Simultaneous queries, and simultaneous and previously published submissions OK; send typed ms with rights for sale noted. Reports in 1 month. Sample copy for 9 × 12 SAE with 3 first class stamps. Free writer's guidelines.

Nonfiction: Historical/nostalgic, how-to, humor, inspirational, sports, nature, current events and outdoor activities. Buys 25-50 mss/year. Query or send complete ms. Length: 800-1,200 words. Pays 3¢/word.

Photos: Reviews b&w negatives, color transparencies and prints. Identification of subjects required. Buys one-time rights.

Fiction: Adventure, historical, humorous, religious and western. Buys 25-50 mss/year. Send complete ms. Length: 1,000 words maximum. Pays 3¢/word.

Fillers: Jokes, gags and short humor. Pays $2-4 for jokes; $12-20 for cartoons; others vary.

HIGHLIGHTS FOR CHILDREN, 803 Church St., Honesdale PA 18431-1824. Fax: (717)253-0179. Editor: Kent L. Brown Jr. 80% freelance written. Magazine published 11 times/year for children ages 2-12. Estab. 1946. Circ. 2.8 million. **Pays on acceptance.** Buys all rights. Reports in about 2 months. Free sample copy. Writer's guidelines for #10 SASE.

Nonfiction: "We need articles on science, technology and nature written by persons with strong backgrounds in those fields. Contributions always welcomed from new writers, especially engineers, scientists, historians, teachers, etc., who can make useful, interesting facts accessible to children. Also writers who have lived abroad and can interpret the ways of life, especially of children, in other countries in ways that will foster world brotherhood. Sports material, biographies and articles of general interest to children. Direct, original approach, simple style, interesting content, not rewritten from encyclopedias. State background and qualifications for writing factual articles submitted. Include references or sources of information. Length: 800 words maximum. Pays $75 minimum. Also buys original party plans for children ages 7-12, clearly described in 300-800 words, including drawings or samples of items to be illustrated. Also, novel but tested ideas in crafts, with clear directions and made-up models. Projects must require only free or inexpensive, easy-to-obtain materials. Especially desirable if easy enough for early primary grades. Also, fingerplays with lots of action, easy for very young children to grasp and to dramatize. Avoid wordiness. We need creative-thinking puzzles that can be illustrated, optical illusions, brain teasers, games of physical agility and other 'fun' activities." Pays minimum $35 for party plans; $20 for crafts ideas; $25 for fingerplays.

Fiction: Unusual, meaningful stories appealing to both girls and boys, ages 2-12. "Vivid, full of action. Engaging plot, strong characterization, lively language." Prefers stories in which a child protagonist solves a dilemma through his or her own resources. Seeks stories that the child ages 8-12 will eagerly read, and the child ages 2-7 will begin to read and/or will like to hear when read aloud (400-800 words). "We publish stories in the suspense/adventure/mystery, fantasy and humor category, all requiring interesting plot and a number of illustration possiblities. Also need rebuses (picture stories 150 words or under), stories with urban settings, stories for beginning readers (100-400 words), sports and horse stories and retold folk tales. We also would like to see more material of 1-page length (300-500 words), both fiction and factual. War, crime and violence are taboo." Pays $65 minimum.

• Ranked as one of the best markets for freelance writers in *Writer's Digest* magazine's annual "Top 100 Markets," January 1993.

Tips: "We are pleased that many authors of children's literature report that their first published work was in the pages of *Highlights*. It is not our policy to consider fiction on the strength of the reputation of the author. We judge each submission on its own merits. With factual material, however, we do prefer that writers be authorities in their field or people with first-hand experience. In this manner we can avoid the encyclopedic article that merely restates information readily available elsewhere. We don't make assignments.

Query with simple letter to establish whether the nonfiction *subject* is likely to be of interest. A beginning writer should first become familiar with the type of material which *Highlights* publishes. Include special qualifications, if any, of author. Write for the child, not the editor."

HOPSCOTCH, The Magazine for Girls, Bluffton News Publishing & Printing Co., P.O. Box 164, Bluffton OH 45817-0164. (419)358-4610. Fax: (419)358-5027. Editor: Marilyn B. Edwards. 90% freelance written. Bimonthly magazine on basic subjects of interest to young girls. "*HOPSCOTCH* is a digest-size magazine with a four-color cover and two-color format inside. It is designed for girls ages 6 to 12 and features pets, crafts, hobbies, games, science, fiction, history, puzzles, careers, etc." Estab. 1989. Pays on publication. Byline given. Buys first and second rights. Submit seasonal/holiday material 6-8 months in advance. Simultaneous and previously published submissions OK. Reports in 3 weeks on queries; 1 month on mss. Sample copy $3. Writer's guidelines for #10 SASE.
Nonfiction: Book excerpts, general interest, historical/nostalgic, how-to (crafts), humor, inspirational, interview/profile, personal experience, pets, games, fiction, careers, sports, cooking. "No fashion, hairstyles, sex or dating articles." Buys 60 mss/year. Send complete ms. Length: 400-1,100 words. Pays $30-100.
Photos: Send photos with submission. Prefers b&w photos, but color photos accepted. Offers $7.50-10/photo. Captions, model releases and identification of subjects required. Buys one-time rights.
Columns/Departments: Science—nature, crafts, pets, cooking (basic), 400-1,000 words. Send complete ms. Pays $25-60.
Fiction: Adventure, fantasy, historical, humorous, mainstream, mystery, novel excerpts, suspense. Buys 15 mss/year. Send complete ms. Length: 600-1,000 words. Pays $30-70.
Poetry: Free verse, light verse and traditional. "No experimental or obscure poetry." Submit maximum 6 poems. Pays $10-30.
Tips: "Almost all sections are open to freelancers. Freelancers should remember that *HOPSCOTCH* is a bit old fashioned, appealing to *young* girls (6 to 12). We cherish nonfiction pieces that have a young girl or young girls directly involved in unusual and/or worthwhile activities. Any piece accompanied by decent photos stands an even better chance of being accepted."

HUMPTY DUMPTY'S MAGAZINE, Children's Better Health Institute, P.O. Box 567, Indianapolis IN 46206-0567. Editor: Christine French Clark. 90% freelance written. "We try not to be overly influenced by an author's credits, preferring instead to judge each submission on its own merit." Magazine published 8 times/year stressing health, nutrition, hygiene, exercise and safety for children ages 4-6. Combined issues: January/February, April/May, July/August, October/November. Pays on publication. Publishes ms at least 8 months after acceptance. Buys all rights (but will return one-time book rights if author has name of interested publisher and tentative date of publication). Submit seasonal material 8 months in advance. Reports in 3 months. Sample copy $1.25. Writer's guidelines for #10 SASE.
Nonfiction: "We are open to nonfiction on almost any age-appropriate subject, but we especially need material with a health theme—nutrition, safety, exercise, hygiene. We're looking for articles that encourage readers to develop better health habits without preaching. Very simple factual articles that creatively teach readers about their bodies. We use simple crafts, some with holiday themes. We also use several puzzles and activities in each issue—dot-to-dot, hidden pictures and other activities that promote following instructions, developing finger dexterity and working with numbers and letters. Submit complete ms. "Include number of words in manuscript and Social Security number." Length: 600 words maximum. Pays 10-20¢/word.
Fiction: "We use some stories in rhyme and a few easy-to-read stories for the beginning reader. All stories should work well as read alouds. Currently we need sports/fitness stories and seasonal stories with holiday themes. We use contemporary stories and fantasy, some employing a health theme. We try to present our health material in a positive light, incorporating humor and a light approach wherever possible. Avoid stereotyping. Characters in contemporary stories should be realistic and up-to-date. Remember, many of our readers have working mothers and/or come from single-parent homes. We need more stories that reflect these changing times but at the same time communicate good, wholesome values." Submit complete ms. "Include number of words in manuscript and Social Security number." Length: 600 words maximum. Pays 10-20¢/word.
Poetry: Short, simple poems. Pays $15 minimum.
Tips: "Writing for *Humpty Dumpty* is similar to writing picture book manuscripts. There must be a great economy of words. We strive for at least 50% art per page (in stories and articles), so space for text is limited. Because the illustrations are so important, stories should lend themselves well to visual imagery."

JACK AND JILL, Children's Better Health Institute, P.O. Box 567, Indianapolis IN 46206-0567. (317)636-8881. Editor: Steve Charles. 70% freelance written. Magazine published 8 times/year for children ages 7-10. Pays on publication. Publishes ms an average of 8 months after acceptance. Buys all rights. Byline given. Submit seasonal material 8 months in advance. Reports in 10 weeks. May hold material seriously being considered for up to 1 year. "Material will not be returned unless accompanied by SAE with sufficient postage." Sample copy $1.25. Writer's guidelines for #10 SASE.

Nonfiction: "Because we want to encourage youngsters to read for pleasure and for information, we are interested in material that will challenge a young child's intelligence *and* be enjoyable reading. Our emphasis is on good health, and we are in particular need of articles, stories, and activities with health, safety, exercise and nutrition themes. We try to present our health material in a positive light—incorporating humor and a light approach wherever possible without minimizing the seriousness of what we are saying." Straight factual articles are OK if they are short and interestingly written. "We would rather see, however, more creative alternatives to the straight factual article. For instance, we'd be interested in seeing a health message or facts presented in articles featuring positive role models for readers. Many of the personalities children admire—athletes, musicians, and film or TV stars—are fitness or nutrition buffs. Many have kicked drugs, alcohol or smoking habits and are outspoken about the dangers of these vices. Color slides, transparencies or b&w photos accompanying this type of article would greatly enhance salability." Buys 10-15 nonfiction mss/year. Length: 500-800 words. Pays a minimum of 10¢/word.

Photos: When appropriate, photos should accompany ms. Reviews sharp, contrasting b&w glossy prints. Sometimes uses color slides, transparencies or good color prints. Pays $20 for b&w, $35 for color, minimum of $50 for cover. Buys one-time rights.

Fiction: May include, but is not limited to, realistic stories, fantasy adventure—set in past, present or future. "All stories need a well-developed plot, action and incident. Humor is highly desirable. Stories that deal with a health theme need not have health as the primary subject." Length: 500-800 words (short stories). Pays 10¢/word minimum. Buys 20-25 mss/year.

Fillers: Puzzles (including various kinds of word and crossword puzzles), poems, games, science projects, and creative craft projects. Instructions for activities should be clearly and simply written and accompanied by models or diagram sketches. "We also have a need for recipes. Ingredients should be healthful; avoid sugar, salt, chocolate, red meat and fats as much as possible. In all material, avoid references to eating sugary foods, such as candy, cakes, cookies and soft drinks."

Tips: "We are constantly looking for new writers who can tell good stories with interesting slants—stories that are not full of out-dated and time-worn expressions. Our best authors are writers who know what today's children are like. Keep in mind that our readers are becoming 'computer literate', living in an age of rapidly developing technology. They are exploring career possibilities that may be new and unfamiliar to our generation. They are faced with tough decisions about drug and alcohol use. Many of them are latch-key children because both parents work or they come from single-parent homes. We need more stories and articles that reflect these changing times but that also communicate good, wholesome values. Obtain *current* issues of the magazines and *study* them to determine our present needs and editorial style."

KID CITY, Children's Television Workshop, 1 Lincoln Plaza, New York NY 10023. (212)595-3456. Editor-in-Chief: Maureen Hunter-Bone. Senior Editor: Lisa Rao. 10% freelance written. Works with small number of new/unpublished writers each year. Magazine published 10 times/year. "We are a humor/reading/activity magazine for children 6-10 years old." Estab. 1969. Circ. 350,000. **Pays on acceptance.** Publishes ms an average of 8 months after acceptance. Byline given. Offers 50% kill fee. Buys all rights. Submit seasonal/holiday material at least 6 months in advance. Simultaneous submissions OK. Reports in 6 weeks. Sample copy $1.50 for 9 × 12 SAE with 6 first class stamps.

Nonfiction: General interest, humor and photo feature. Buys 3-4 mss/year. Query with or without published clips or send complete ms. Length: 500 words maximum. Pays $25-350.

Photos: State availability of photos with submission. Model releases and identification of subjects required.

Fiction: Adventure, fantasy, historical, humorous, mystery and western. "No stories with heavily didactic, preachy moralistic messages or those whose main focus is child abuse, saying 'no,' divorce, etc." Buys 3 mss/year. Query or send complete ms. Length: 250-700 words. Pays $400 maximum.

Tips: "Just think about what you liked to read about when you were a kid and write it down. No stories about doggies, bunnies or kitties. No stories with heavy moral message. We're looking for more interesting items about *real* kids who have done something newsworthy or exceptional."

KID SPORTS, Southern Media Publishing Co., Suite 1800, 1101 Wilson Blvd., Arlington VA 22209. (703)276-3030. Editor: Stephen Hanks. 10% freelance written. Bimonthly sports magazine "geared to kids between the ages of 7-15. Writers need to keep our audience in mind." Estab. 1990. Circ. 100,000. Pays on publication. No byline. Buys all rights. Reports in 2 months on queries. Free sample copy and writer's guidelines.

Nonfiction: How-to, interview/profile. Query with published clips. Length: 500-3,000 words. Pays $200-400.

Photos: State availability of photos with submission. Reviews transparencies. Offers no additional payment for photos accepted with ms. Buys one-time rights.

LADYBUG, the Magazine for Young Children, Carus Publishing Co., P.O. Box 300, Peru IL 61354-0300. (815)224-6643. Editor-in-Chief: Marianne Carus. Associate Editor: Paula Morrow. Monthly general interest magazine for children (ages 2-6). "We look for quality writing—quality literature, no matter the subject." Estab. 1990. Circ. 130,000. Pays on publication. Byline given. All accepted manuscripts are published. Buys first publication rights in the English language. Submit seasonal/holiday material 1 year in advance. Simultaneous submissions OK. Do not query; send completed ms. Reports in 3 months. Sample copy $2. Writer's guidelines for #10 SASE.

Columns/Departments: Can You Do This?, 2-3 pages; The World Around You, 2-3 pages. Buys 35 mss/year. Send complete ms. Length: 250 maximum words. "Most *Ladybug* nonfiction is in the form of illustration. We'd like more simple science, how-things-work and behind-the-scenes on a preschool level. Maximum word length 250-300."

Fiction: Adventure, ethnic, fantasy, historical, humorous, mainstream and mystery. Buys 50 mss/year. Send complete ms. Length: 850 maximum words. Pays up to 25¢/word.

Poetry: Light verse, traditional, and humorous. Buys 20 poems/year. Submit *maximum* 5 poems. Length: 20 lines maximum. Pays up to $3/line.

Fillers: Anecdotes, facts and short humor. Buys 10/year. Length: 250 (approximately) maximum words. Pays up to 25¢/word. We welcome interactive activities: rebuses, up to 100 words; *original* fingerplays and action rhymes (up to 8 lines).

Tips: "Reread a ms *before* sending it in. The more polished a ms, the more likely it will be accepted. Be sure to keep within specified word limits. Study back issues before submitting to learn about the types of material we're looking for. Writing style is paramount. We look for rich, evocative language and a sense of joy or wonder. Remember that you're writing for preschoolers – be age-appropriate but not condescending. A story must hold enjoyment for both parent and child through repeated read-aloud sessions. Remember that we live in a multicultural world. People come in all colors, sizes, physical conditions and have special needs. Be inclusive!"

NOAH'S ARK, A Newspaper for Jewish Children, 7726 Portal, Houston TX 77071-1831. (713)771-7144. Editors: Debbie Israel Dubin and Linda Freedman Block. Monthly tabloid that "captures readers' interest and reinforces learning about Jewish history, holidays, laws and culture through articles, stories, recipes, games, crafts, projects, Hebrew column and more." For Jewish children, ages 6-12. Circ. 450,000. **Pays on acceptance.** Byline given. Buys first North American serial rights. Submit seasonal/holiday material 4 months in advance. Simultaneous submissions OK. Reports in 6 weeks on queries; 2 months on mss. Sample copy and writer's guidelines for #10 SASE.

Nonfiction: Historical/nostalgic, craft projects, recipes, humor and interview/profile. Send complete ms. Length: 350 words maximum. Usually pays 5¢/word.

Photos: State availability of photos with submission or send photos with submission. Offers no additional payment for photos accepted with ms. Identification of subjects required. Buys one-time rights.

Fiction: All must be of Jewish interest: historical, humorous, religious (Jewish) and slice-of-life vignettes. Any and all suitable for Jewish children. Buys 2-3 mss/year. Send complete ms. Length: 600 words maximum. Pays 5¢/word.

Poetry: Light verse and traditional. Buys 1 poem/year. Submit maximum 1 poem. Payment varies.

Fillers: All must be of Jewish interest: anecdotes, facts, gags, short humor and games. Buys 3-5/year. Payment varies.

Tips: "We're just looking for high quality material suitable for entertainment as well as supplemental religious school use." Encourages freelancers to take an "unusual approach to writing about holidays. All submissions must have Jewish content and positive Jewish values. Content should not be exclusively for an American audience."

ON THE LINE, Mennonite Publishing House, 616 Walnut Ave., Scottdale PA 15683-1999. (412)887-8500. Fax: (412)887-3111. Editor: Mary Clemens Meyer. 95% freelance written. Works with a small number of new/unpublished writers each year. Weekly magazine for children ages 10-14. Circ. 8,500. **Pays on acceptance.** Publishes ms an average of 1 year after acceptance. Byline given. Buys one-time rights. Submit seasonal/holiday material 6 months in advance. Simultaneous and previously published submissions OK. Reports in 1 month. Sample copy for 9×12 SAE with 2 first class stamps.

Nonfiction: How-to (things to make with easy-to-get materials); and informational (350-500 word articles on wonders of nature, people who have made outstanding contributions). Buys 95 unsolicited mss/year. Send complete ms. Length: 500-900 words. Pays $10-30.

Photos: Photos purchased with or without ms. Pays $10-25 for 8×10 b&w photos. Total purchase price for ms includes payment for photos.

Fiction: Adventure, humorous and religious. Buys 52 mss/year. Send complete ms. Length: 800-1,200 words. Pays 2-4¢/word.

Poetry: Light verse and religious. Length: 3-12 lines. Pays $5-15.

Tips: "Study the publication first. We need short well-written how-to and craft articles. Don't send query; we prefer to see the complete manuscript."

OWL MAGAZINE, The Discovery Magazine for Children, The Young Naturalist Foundation, 56 The Esplanade, Suite 306, Toronto, Ontario M5E 1A7 Canada. (416)868-6001. Fax: (416)868-6009. Editor: Debora Pearson. 25% freelance written. Works with small number of new writers each year. Magazine published 10 times/year (no July or August issues) covering science and nature. Aims to interest children in their environment through accurate, factual information about the world presented in an easy, lively style. Estab. 1976. Circ. 160,000. **Pays on acceptance.** Publishes ms an average of 3 months after acceptance. Byline given. Buys all rights. Submit seasonal/holiday material 1 year in advance. Reports in 10 weeks. Sample copy $4.28;

free writer's guidelines. Send SAE (large envelope if requesting sample copy) and a money order for $1 to cover postage (no stamps please).

Nonfiction: How-to (activities, crafts); personal experience (real life children in real situations); photo feature (natural science, international wildlife, and outdoor features); and science and environmental features. No problem stories with drugs, sex or moralistic views, or talking animal stories. Query with clips of published work.

Photos: State availability of photos. Reviews 35mm transparencies. Identification of subjects required. Send for photo package before submitting material.

Tips: "Write for editorial guidelines first. Review back issues of the magazine for content and style. Know your topic and approach it from an unusual perspective. Our magazine never talks down to children." Also publishes *Chickadee* for 4-9-year-olds.

POCKETS, The Upper Room, P.O. Box 189, Nashville TN 37202-0189. (615)340-7333. Fax: (615)340-7006. Editor: Janet R. McNish. Associate Editor: Lynn Gilliam. 50% freelance written. Eager to work with new/ unpublished writers. Monthly themed magazine (except January/February issue) covering children's and families spiritual formation. "We are a Christian, non-denominational publication for children 6 to 12 years of age." Estab. 1981. Circ. 70,000. **Pays on acceptance.** Byline given. Offers 4¢/word kill fee. Buys first North American serial rights. Submit seasonal/holiday material 1 year in advance. Reports in 10 weeks on mss. Sample copy for 7×9 SAE with 4 first class stamps. Writer's guidelines and themes for #10 SASE.

Nonfiction: Interview/profile, religious (retold scripture stories) and personal experience. List of themes for special issues available with SASE. No violence or romance. Buys 5 mss/year. Send complete ms. Length: 600-1,500 words. Pays 12¢/word. Reprints OK; send typed ms with rights for sale noted and information about where and when the article previously appeared.

Photos: Send photos with submission. Prefer no photos unless they accompany an article. Reviews contact sheets, transparencies and prints. Offers $25-50/photo. Buys one-time rights.

Columns/Departments: Refrigerator Door (poetry and prayer related to themes), 25 lines; Pocketsful of Love (family communications activities), 300 words; and Peacemakers at Work (profiles of people, particularly children, working for peace, justice and ecological concerns), 300-800 words. Buys 20 mss/year. Send complete ms. Pays 12¢/word; recipes $25.

Fiction: Adventure, ethnic and slice-of-life. "Stories should reflect the child's everyday experiences through a Christian approach. This is often more acceptable when stories are not preachy or overtly Christian." Buys 22 mss/year. Send complete ms. Length: 750-1,600 words. Pays 12¢/word and up.

Poetry: Buys 8 poems/year. Length: 4-25 lines. Pays $25-50.

Tips: "Theme stories, role models and retold scripture stories are most open to freelancers. Poetry is also open, but we rarely receive an acceptable poem. It's very helpful if writers send for our themes. These are *not* the same as writer's guidelines."

POWER AND LIGHT, 6401 The Paseo, Kansas City MO 64131. Fax: (816)333-4439. Editor: Beula Postlewait. Mostly freelance written. Weekly magazine for boys and girls ages 11-12 using WordAction Sunday School curriculum. Estab. 1992. Publishes ms an average of 1 year after acceptance. Buys multiple use rights. "Minimal comments on pre-printed form are made on rejected material." Reports in 1-3 months. Sample copy and guidelines for #10 SASE.

Fiction: Stories with Christian emphasis on high ideals, wholesome social relationships and activities, right choices, Sabbath observance, church loyalty and missions. Informal style. Submit complete ms. Length: 500-700 words. Pays 5¢/word.

Tips: "All themes and outcomes should conform to the theology and practices of the Church of the Nazarene."

R-A-D-A-R, 8121 Hamilton Ave., Cincinnati OH 45231. (513)931-4050. Editor: Margaret Williams. 75% freelance written. Prefers to work with published/established writers; works with a small number of new/ unpublished writers each year. Weekly for children in grades 3-6 in Christian Sunday schools. Estab. 1866 (publishing house). Rights purchased varies with author and material; prefers buying first serial rights, but will buy second (reprint) rights. Occasionally overstocked. **Pays on acceptance.** Publishes ms an average of 6-12 months after acceptance. Submit seasonal material 1 year in advance. Reports in 2 months. Free sample copy. Writer's guidelines for #10 SASE.

Nonfiction: Articles on hobbies and handicrafts, nature, famous people, seasonal subjects, etc., written from a Christian viewpoint. No articles about historical figures with an absence of religious implication. Length: 500-1,000 words. Pays 3-7¢/word maximum.

Fiction: Short stories of heroism, adventure, travel, mystery, animals and biography. "True or possible plots stressing clean, wholesome, Christian character-building ideas, but not preachy. Make prayer, church attendance and Christian living a natural part of the story. We correlate our fiction and other features with a definite Bible lesson. Writers who want to meet our needs should send for a theme list." No talking animal stories, science fiction, Halloween stories or first-person stories from an adult's viewpoint. Length: up to 1,000 words. Pays 3-7¢/word maximum.

RANGER RICK, National Wildlife Federation, 1400 16th St. NW, Washington DC 20036. (703)790-4274. Editor: Gerald Bishop. 40% freelance written. Works with a small number of new/unpublished writers each year. Monthly magazine for children from ages 6-12, with the greatest concentration in the 7-10 age bracket. Buys all world rights unless other arrangements made. Byline given "but occasionally, for very brief pieces, we will identify author by name at the end. Contributions to regular columns usually are not bylined." Estab. 1967. **Pays on acceptance.** Publishes ms an average of 18 months after acceptance. Reports in 6 weeks. "Anything written with a specific month in mind should be in our hands at least 10 months before that issue date." Writer's guidelines for #10 SASE.
Nonfiction: "Articles may be written on anything related to nature, conservation, the outdoors, environmental problems or natural science. Please avoid articles about animal rehabilitation, unless the species are endangered." Buys 25-35 unsolicited mss/year. Query. Pays from $50-575, depending on length, quality and content (maximum length, 900 words). Unless you are an expert in the field or are writing from direct personal experience, all factual information must be footnoted and backed up with current, reliable references.
Fiction: "Same categories as nonfiction plus fantasy and science fiction. The attributing of human qualities to animals is limited to our regular feature, 'The Adventures of Ranger Rick,' so please do not humanize wildlife. We discourage keeping wildlife as pets."
Photos: "Photographs, when used, are paid for separately. It is not necessary that illustrations accompany material."
Tips: "In your query letter, include details of what manuscript will cover; sample lead; evidence that you can write playfully and with great enthusiasm, conviction and excitement (formal, serious, dull queries indicate otherwise). Think of an exciting subject we haven't done recently, sell it effectively with query, and produce a manuscript of highest quality. Read past issues to learn successful styles and unique approaches to subjects."

SHOFAR Magazine, 43 Northcote Dr., Melville NY 11747-3924. (516)643-4598. Fax: (516)643-4598. Managing Editor: Gerald H. Grayson. 80-90% freelance written. Monthly children's magazine on Jewish subjects. Estab. 1984. Circ. 17,000. Pays on publication. Byline given. Buys one-time rights. Submit seasonal/holiday material 6 months in advance. Simultaneous submissions OK. Reports in 2 months. Sample copy and writer's guidelines for 9×12 SAE with 4 first class stamps.
Nonfiction: Dr. Gerald H. Grayson, publisher. Historical/nostalgic, humor, inspirational, interview/profile, personal experience, photo feature, religious and travel. Buys 15 mss/year. Send complete ms. Length: 750-1,000 words. Pays 7-10¢/word. Sometimes pays the expenses of writers on assignment.
Photos: State availability of photos with submission or send photos with submission. Offers $10-50/photo. Identification of subjects required. Buys one-time rights.
Fiction: Adventure, historical, humorous and religious. Buys 15 mss/year. Send complete ms. Length: 750-1,000 words. Pays 7-10¢/word.
Poetry: Free verse, light verse and traditional. Buys 4-5 poems/year. Length: 8-50 words. Pays 7-10¢/word.
Tips: "Submissions must be on a Jewish theme and should be geared to readers who are 8 to 12 years old."

SPARK!, Creative Fun for Kids, F&W Publications, Inc., 1507 Dana Ave., Cincinnati OH 45207-1005. (513)531-2222. Editorial Director: Michael Ward. Managing Editor: Beth Struck. 50% freelance written. Magazine published 9 times/year featuring art and writing projects that kids can do on their own or with minimal help from their parents. "*Spark!* is devoted to nurturing creativity, and literary and artistic growth in children ages 3-11." Estab. 1991. Circ. 100,000. **Pays on acceptance.** Byline given. Offers 20% kill fee. Buys first North American serial rights. Submit seasonal/holiday material 6 months in advance. Simultaneous and previously published submissions OK. Reports in 1 month. Sample copy $2.95 for 9×12 SAE with 5 first class stamps. Writer's guidelines for #10 SASE.
Nonfiction: How-to (step-by-step, easy-to-read instructions for subjects such as cartooning, drawing, edible food art, mixed media, new media, painting and printmaking). "No articles that don't take into account children's developmental skills and/or reading levels." Buys 40 mss/year. Query. Length: 350-500 words. Pays $50-250. Sometimes pays expenses of writers on assignment.
Photos: Freelancers should state availability of photos with submissions or send photos with submission. Reviews 4×5 transparencies and prints. Offers no additional payment for photos accepted with ms. Captions are required. Buys one-time rights.
Columns/Departments: Meet the Masters and Draw It!. Pays $150-200.
Fiction: "Finish the Adventure" (stories that have open-ended endings that allow kids to write their own conclusions).
Tips: "We're interested in working with children's writers and art educators who can help us reach our specialized audience. Established writers with a working knowledge of art and/or writing techniques are also encouraged to submit article ideas. Art-related features should include an introduction, list of materials and specific step-by-step instructions. Sidebars on related activities are encouraged. All projects must be accompanied by children's completed artwork."

SPORTS ILLUSTRATED FOR KIDS, Time-Warner, Time & Life Building, New York NY 10020. (212)522-5437. Fax: (212)522-0120. Managing Editor: Craig Neff. 50% freelance written. Monthly magazine on sports for children 8 years old and up. Content is divided 50/50 between sports as played by kids, and sports as played by professionals. Estab. 1989. **Pays on acceptance.** Publishes ms an average of 3 months after acceptance. Byline given. Offers 25% kill fee. Buys all rights. Sample copy $1.95. Writer's guidelines for SAE.

Nonfiction: Patricia Berry, Articles Editor. Games, general interest, how-to, humor, inspirational, interview/profile, photo feature and puzzles. Buys 30 mss/year. Query with published clips. Length: 100-1,500 words. Pays $75-1,000 for assigned articles; $75-800 for unsolicited articles. Pays expenses of writers on assignment.

Photos: State availability of photos with submission. Buys one-time rights.

Columns/Departments: The Worst Day I Ever Had (tells about day in pro athlete's life when all seemed hopeless), 500-600 words; Hotshots (young [8-15] athlete getting good things out of sports), 100-250 words; and Home Team (son, daughter, brother, sister of famous athlete), 500-600 words. Buys 30-40 mss/year. Query with published clips. Pays $75-600.

STONE SOUP, The Magazine by Children, Children's Art Foundation, P.O. Box 83, Santa Cruz CA 95063-0083. (408)426-5557. Fax: (408)426-1161. Editor: Ms. Gerry Mandel. 100% freelance written. Bimonthly magazine of writing and art by children, including fiction, poetry, book reviews, and art by children through age 13. Estab. 1973. Audience is children, teachers, parents, writers, artists. "We have a preference for writing and art based on real-life experiences; no formula stories or poems." Pays on publication. Publishes ms an average of 3 months after acceptance. Buys all rights. Submit seasonal/holiday material 6 months in advance. Reports in 2 weeks on queries; 1 month on mss. Sample copy $4. Free writer's guidelines.

Nonfiction: Book reviews. Buys 10 mss/year. Query. Pays $15 for assigned articles.

Fiction: Adventure, ethnic, experimental, fantasy, historical, humorous, mystery, science fiction, slice-of-life vignettes and suspense. "We do not like assignments or formula stories of any kind." Accepts 55 mss/year. Send complete ms. Pays $10 for stories. Authors also receive 2 copies and discounts on additional copies and on subscriptions.

Poetry: Avant-garde and free verse. Accepts 20 poems/year. Pays $10/poem. (Same discounts apply.)

Tips: "We can't emphasize enough how important it is to read a couple of issues of the magazine. We have a strong preference for writing on subjects that mean a lot to the author. If you feel strongly about something that happened to you or something you observed, use that feeling as the basis for your story or poem. Stories should have good descriptions, realistic dialogue and a point to make. In a poem, each word must be chosen carefully. Your poem should present a view of your subject and a way of using words that are special and all your own."

STORY FRIENDS, Mennonite Publishing House, 616 Walnut Ave., Scottdale PA 15683-1999. (412)887-8500. Fax: (412)887-3111. Editor: Marjorie Waybill. 80% freelance written. Monthly story paper in weekly parts for children ages 4-9. "*Story Friends* is planned to provide wholesome Christian reading for the 4- to 9-year-old. Practical life stories are included to teach moral values and remind the children that God is at work today. Activities introduce children to the Bible and its message for them." Estab. 1905. Circ. 10,000. **Pays on acceptance.** Publishes ms an average of 1 year after acceptance. Byline given. Publication not copyrighted. Buys one-time and second serial (reprint) rights. Submit seasonal/holiday material 6 months in advance. Simultaneous submissions and previously published material OK; send typed ms with rights for sale noted. Reports in 1 month. Sample copy for 9 × 12 SAE with 2 first class stamps. Writer's guidelines for #10 SASE.

Nonfiction: How-to (craft ideas for young children) and photo feature. Buys 20 mss/year. Send complete ms. Length: 300-500 words. Pays 3-5¢/word.

Photos: Send photos with submission. Reviews 8½ × 11 b&w prints. Offers $20-25/photo. Model releases required. Buys one-time rights.

Fiction: See writer's guidelines for *Story Friends*. Buys 50 mss/year. Send complete ms. Length: 300-800 words. Pays 3-5¢/word.

Poetry: Traditional. Buys 20 poems/year. Length: 4-16 lines. Pays $5-10/poem.

Tips: "Send stories that children from a variety of ethnic backgrounds can relate to; stories that deal with experiences similar to all children. For example, all children have fears but their fears may vary depending on where they live."

3-2-1 CONTACT, Children's Television Workshop, 1 Lincoln Plaza, New York NY 10023. (212)595-3456. Fax: (212)875-6105. Editor-in-Chief: Jonathan Rosenbloom. Editor: Curtis Slepian. 40% freelance written. Magazine published 10 times/year covering science and technology for children ages 8-14. Estab. 1979. Circ. 400,000. **Pays on acceptance.** Publishes ms an average of 6 months after acceptance. Buys all rights "with some exceptions." Submit seasonal material 8 months in advance. Simultaneous and previously published submissions OK if so indicated. Reports in 1 month. Sample copy $1.75 for 9 × 12 SAE with 2 first class stamps. Writer's guidelines for #10 SASE.

Nonfiction: General interest (space exploration, the human body, animals, computers and the new technology, current science issues); profile (of interesting scientists or children involved in science or with computers); photo feature (centered around a science theme); and role models of women and minority scientists. No articles on travel not related to science. Buys 5 unsolicited mss/year. Query with published clips. Length: 700-1,000 words. Pays $150-500. Sometimes pays expenses of writers on assignment.

Photos: Do *not* send photos on spec.

Tips: "I prefer a short query, without ms, that makes it clear that an article is interesting. When sending an article, include your telephone number. Don't call us, we'll call you. Many submissions we receive are more like college research papers than feature stories. We like articles in which writers have interviewed kids or scientists, or discovered exciting events with a scientific angle. Library research is necessary; but if that's all you're doing, you aren't giving us anything we can't get ourselves. If your story needs a bibliography, chances are, it's not right for us."

TOUCH, P.O. Box 7259, Grand Rapids MI 49510. Editor: Joanne Ilbrink. 80% freelance written. Prefers to work with published/established writers. Monthly magazine "to show girls ages 7-14 how God is at work in their lives and in the world around them. The May/June issue annually features material written by our readers." Estab. 1972. Circ. 15,500. **Pays on acceptance.** Publishes ms an average of 1 year after acceptance. Byline given. Buys second serial (reprint) and first North American serial rights. Submit seasonal/holiday material 9 months in advance. Simultaneous and previously published submissions OK. Reports in 2 months. Sample copy and writer's guidelines for 9 × 12 SAE with 3 first class stamps.

Nonfiction: How-to (crafts girls can make easily and inexpensively); informational (write for issue themes); humor (need much more); inspirational (seasonal and holiday); interview; multicultural materials; travel; personal experience (avoid the testimony approach); and photo feature (query first). "Because our magazine is published around a monthly theme, requesting the letter we send out twice a year to our established freelancers would be most helpful. We do not want easy solutions or quick character changes from bad to good. No pietistic characters. Constant mention of God is not necessary if the moral tone of the story is positive. We do not want stories that always have a good ending." Buys 36-45 unsolicited mss/year. Submit complete ms. Length: 100-1,000 words. Pays 2½-5¢/word, depending on the amount of editing.

Photos: Purchased with or without ms. Reviews 5 × 7 or 8 × 10 clear b&w glossy prints. Appreciate multicultural subjects. Pays $20-50 on publication.

Fiction: Adventure (that girls could experience in their hometowns or places they might realistically visit); humorous; mystery (believable only); romance (stories that deal with awakening awareness of boys are appreciated); suspense (can be serialized); and religious (nothing preachy). Buys 50 mss/year. Submit complete ms. Length: 300-1,000 words. Pays 2½-5¢/word.

Poetry: Free verse, haiku, light verse and traditional. Buys 10/year. Length: 30 lines maximum. Pays $5-15 minimum.

Fillers: Puzzles, short humor and cartoons. Buys 3/issue. Pays $7-15.

Tips: "Prefers not to see anything on the adult level, secular material or violence. Writers frequently oversimplify the articles and often write with a Pollyanna attitude. An author should be able to see his/her writing style as exciting and appealing to girls ages 7-14. The style can be fun, but also teach a truth. The subject should be current and important to *Touch* readers. We would like to receive material that features a multicultural slant."

TURTLE MAGAZINE FOR PRESCHOOL KIDS, Children's Better Health Institute, P.O. Box 567, Indianapolis IN 46206-0567. (317)636-8881. Editor: Christine French Clark. 90% freelance written. Monthly magazine (bimonthly January/February, April/May, July/August, October/November). General interest, interactive magazine with the purpose of helping preschoolers develop healthy minds and healthy bodies. Pays on publication. May hold manuscripts for up to 1 year before acceptance/publication. Byline given. Buys all rights. Submit seasonal/holiday material 8 months in advance. Reports in 10 weeks. Sample copy $1.25. Writer's guidelines for #10 SASE.

Nonfiction: "Uses very simple science experiments. Would like to see some short, simple nature articles—especially interested in subjects of gardening and environmental awareness."

Fiction: Fantasy, humorous and realistic stories. All should have single-focus story lines and work well as read-alouds. "Most of the stories we use will have a character-building bent, but they should not be preachy or overly moralistic. We are in constant need of stories that will help a preschooler grow to a greater appreciation of his/her body and what it can do; stories that encourage active, vigorous play; stories that teach fundamental lessons about good health without being too heavy-handed. We're no longer buying many stories about 'generic' turtles, as we now have PokeyToes, our own turtle character. All stories should 'move along' and lend themselves well to illustration. Writing should be energetic, enthusiastic and creative—like preschoolers themselves."

Market conditions are constantly changing! If this is 1995 or later, buy the newest edition of Writer's Market at your favorite bookstore or order directly from Writer's Digest Books.

Poetry: "We're especially looking for action rhymes to foster creative movement in preschoolers. We also use original finger plays, stories in rhyme and short verse."

Tips: "We are trying to include more material for our youngest readers. We'd like to see some well-executed ideas for teaching basic concepts to 2- and 3-year-olds. We're open to counting and alphabet stories, but they must be handled in a new, fresh way. All material must first be entertaining; otherwise all efforts to teach will be wasted."

VENTURE, Christian Service Brigade, P.O. Box 150, Wheaton IL 60189-0150. (708)665-0630. Editor: Deborah Christensen. 30% freelance written. Works with a small number of new/unpublished writers each year. Bimonthly company publication "published to support and compliment CSB's Stockade and Battalion programs. We aim to provide wholesome, entertaining reading for boys ages 10-15." Estab. 1959. Circ. 22,000. Pays on publication. Publishes ms an average of 6 months after acceptance, sometimes longer. Byline given. Offers $35 kill fee. Buys first North American serial, one-time and second serial (reprint) rights. Submit seasonal/holiday material 6 months in advance. Previously published submissions OK; send photocopy of article or short story or typed ms with rights for sale noted. Pays 5-6¢/word. Reports in 2 weeks. Sample copy $1.85 for 9×12 SAE with 4 first class stamps. Writer's guidelines for #10 SASE.

Nonfiction: General interest, humor, inspirational, interview/profile, personal experience, photo feature and religious. Buys 18-20 mss/year. Send complete ms. Length: 1,000-1,500 words. Pays $75-150 for assigned articles; $40-100 for unsolicited articles. Sometimes pays expenses of writers on assignment.

Photos: Send photos with submission. Reviews contact sheets and 5×7 prints. Offers $35-125/photo. Buys one-time rights.

Fiction: Adventure, humorous, mystery and religious. Buys 10-12 mss/year. Send complete ms. Length: 1,000-1,500 words. Pays $40-125.

Tips: "Talk to young boys. Find out the things that interest them and write about those things. We are looking for material relating to our theme: Building Men to Serve Christ. We prefer shorter (1,000 words) pieces. Writers *must* weave Christianity throughout the story in a natural way, without preaching or token prayers. How does a boy's faith in Christ influence the way he responds to a situation."

WONDER TIME, 6401 The Paseo, Kansas City MO 64131. (816)333-7000. Fax: (816)333-4439. Editor: Lois Perrigo. 75% freelance written. "Willing to read and consider appropriate freelance submissions." Published weekly by Church of the Nazarene for children ages 6-8. Estab. early 1900s. Pays on publication. Publishes ms an average of 1 year after acceptance. Byline given. Buys rights to reuse and all rights for curriculum assignments. Sample copy and writer's guidelines for 9×12 SAE with 2 first class stamps.

Fiction: Buys stories portraying Christian attitudes without being preachy. Uses stories for special days—stories teaching honesty, truthfulness, kindness, helpfulness or other important spiritual truths, and avoiding symbolism. Also, stories about real life problems children face today. "God should be spoken of as our Father who loves and cares for us; Jesus, as our Lord and Savior." Buys 52/mss year. Length: 250-350 words. Pays $25 on publication.

Poetry: Uses verse which has seasonal or Christian emphasis. Length: 4-8 lines. Pays 25¢/line, minimum $3.

Tips: "Any stories that allude to church doctrine must be in keeping with Nazarene beliefs. Any type of fantasy must be in good taste and easily recognizable."

Literary and "Little"

Fiction, poetry, essays, book reviews and scholarly criticism comprise the content of the magazines listed in this section. Some are published by colleges and universities, and many are regional in focus.

Everything about "little" literary magazines is different than other consumer magazines. Most carry few or no ads, and many do not even seek them. Circulations under 1,000 are common. And sales come more from the purchase of sample copies than from the newsstand.

The magazines listed in this section cannot compete with the pay rates and exposure of the high-circulation general interest magazines also publishing fiction and poetry. But most "little" literary magazines don't try. They are more apt to specialize in publishing certain kinds of fiction or poetry: traditional, experimental, works with a regional sensibility, or the fiction and poetry of new and younger writers. For that reason, and because fiction and poetry vary so widely in style, writers should *always* invest in the most recent copies of the magazines they aspire to publish in.

Many "little" literary magazines pay contributors only in copies of the issues in which their works appear. *Writer's Market* lists only those that pay their contributors in cash. However, *Novel & Short Story Writer's Market* includes nonpaying fiction markets, and has indepth information about fiction techniques and markets. The same is true of *Poet's Market* for nonpaying poetry markets (both books are published by Writer's Digest Books). There are also more literary opportunities listed in the Contests and Awards section.

ACM (Another Chicago Magazine), Left Field Press, 3709 N. Kenmore, Chicago IL 60613. Editor: Barry Silesky. 98% freelance written. Open to new/unpublished writers. Biannual literary journal. Estab. 1977. Circ. 2,500. **Pays on acceptance.** Publishes ms an average of 6 months after acceptance. Byline given. Buys first serial rights. Simultaneous queries and submissions OK. Reports in 10 weeks. Sample copy $7; writer's guidelines for #10 SASE.
Nonfiction: Interview (contemporary poets and fiction writers), essays (contemporary literature) and reviews of small press publications. Buys 5-6 mss/year. Query. Length: 1,000-20,000 words. Pays $5-25.
Fiction: Sharon Solwitz, fiction editor. Serious ethnic and experimental fiction. Buys 10-20 mss/year. Send complete ms. Length: 50-10,000 words. Pays $5-25.
Poetry: Serious poetry. No light verse or inspirational. Buys 50 poems/year. Length: 1-1,000 lines. Pays $5-25.

AGNI, Dept. WM, Boston University, 236 Bay State Rd., Boston, MA 02215. (617)353-5389. Editor: Askold Melnyczuk. Managing Editor: Jennifer Rose. Semiannual literary magazine. "*Agni* publishes poetry, fiction, essays and art portfolios. Also regularly publishes translations and is committed to featuring the work of emerging writers. We have published Derek Walcott, Joyce Carol Oates, Sharon Olds, John Updike, and many others, including then unknown writers: Sven Birkerts, Carolyn Chute, Tom Sleigh and Mary Morris." Estab. 1972. Circ. 1,500. Pays on publication. Publishes ms an average of 6 months after acceptance. Byline given. Buys first North American serial rights and rights to reprint in *Agni* anthology (with author's consent). Editorial lead time 6 months. Accepts simultaneous submissions. Reports in 2 weeks on queries; 1-4 months on mss. Sample copy $7. Writer's guidelines for #10 SASE.
Fiction: Short stories. Buys 6-12 mss/year. Send complete ms. Pays $20-150.
Poetry: Buys more than 140/year. Submit maximum 5 poems. Pays $20-150.
Tips: "We suggest writers read *Agni* first, and if they feel their work is compatible, send story or 1-5 poems for consideration. We read from October 1 through April 30. Manuscripts sent at other times will be returned unread."

ALASKA QUARTERLY REVIEW, College of Arts & Sciences, University of Alaska Anchorage, 3221 Providence Dr., Anchorage AK 99508. (907)786-4775. Executive Editor: Ronald Spatz. 100% freelance written. Prefers to work with published/established writers; eager to work with new/unpublished writers. Semiannual magazine publishing fiction and poetry, both traditional and experimental styles, literary criticism and reviews, with an emphasis on contemporary literature. Estab. 1982. Circ. 1,000. Pays honorariums on publication when funding permits. Publishes ms an average of 6 months after acceptance. Byline given. Buys first North American serial rights. Upon request, rights will be transferred back to author after publication. Reports in 4 months. Sample copy $4. Writer's guidelines for SASE.
Nonfiction: Essays, literary criticism, reviews and philosophy of literature. Buys 0-5 mss/year. Query. Length: 1,000-20,000 words. Pays $50-100 subject to funding; pays in copies and subscriptions when funding is limited.
Fiction: Experimental and traditional literary forms. No romance, children's or inspirational/religious. Publishes novel excerpts. Buys 20-26 mss/year. Send complete ms. Length: Up to 20,000 words. Pays $50-150 subject to funding; pays in contributor's copies and subscriptions when funding is limited.
Poetry: Thomas Sexton, Poetry Editor. Avant-garde, free verse, haiku and traditional. No light verse. Buys 10-30 poems/year. Submit maximum 10 poems. Pays $10-50 subject to availability of funds; pays in contributor's copies and subscriptions when funding is limited.
Tips: "All sections are open to freelancers. We rely exclusively on unsolicited manuscripts. *AQR* is a non-profit literary magazine and does not always have funds to pay authors."

AMBERGRIS, Dept. WM, P.O. Box 29919, Cincinnati OH 45229-0919. Editor: Mark Kissling. 75% freelance written. "*Ambergris* is a nonprofit annual dedicated to quality art and literature, and to fostering the emerging author and artist. *Ambergris* gives special but not exclusive consideration to Ohio authors and artists, and to works with Midwestern themes." Estab. 1987. Circ. 1,000. Pays on publication. Publishes ms an average of 8 months after acceptance. "Writers are notified on offer of acceptance if a ms is not to be published for a year or longer." Buys first North American serial rights and the right to reprint. Simultaneous submissions OK (if noted). No previously published submissions. Reports in 3 months, "longer if a ms is under serious consideration." Current issue for $4.95; sample copy for $3.95. Writer's guidelines for #10 SASE.

Nonfiction: "We are looking for literary essays, particularly essays with fictional elements: essays that read like fiction. No scholarly articles. We also publish one or two interviews with fiction writers in each issue." Buys 2-5 mss/year. Query with SASE for interviews; send complete ms with SASE for literary essays. Length: 1,000-5,000 words. Pays $5/published page, $50 maximum. Writers also receive two contributor's copies.

Fiction: Literary short stories and experimental short fiction. "No poetry, no genre fiction (mystery, romance, science fiction, fantasy, horror or western), nothing strictly for children or young adults, and no novel excerpts (unless the excerpt is unpublished and completely self-contained)." Buys 8-12 mss/year. Send complete ms with SASE. "We prefer works of 5,000 words or fewer." Pays $5/published page, $50 maximum. Writers also receive two contributor's copies.

• Sponsors annual short fiction award. See listing in Contests and Awards section or send #10 SASE for details.

Tips: *"Our reading period is August through April.* Manuscripts received in May, June and July will be returned unread, and then only if SASE is enclosed. We attempt to foster the emerging author, but we strongly encourage beginning writers and others not familiar with our format to invest in and *read a sample copy* before submitting work. There is simply no other way to determine what kind of fiction and essays this or any other literary magazine publishes without first reading an issue. *Ambergris* is a member of The Council of Literary Magazines and Presses and is read each year for *The Best American Short Stories, Prize Stories: The O. Henry Awards,* and *The Pushcart Prize."*

AMELIA MAGAZINE, Amelia Press, 329 E St., Bakersfield CA 93304. (805)323-4064. Editor: Frederick A. Raborg Jr. Estab. 1983. 100% freelance written. Eager to work with new/unpublished writers. *"Amelia* is a quarterly international magazine publishing the finest poetry and fiction available, along with expert criticism and reviews intended for all interested in contemporary literature. *Amelia* also publishes three supplements each year: *Cicada,* which publishes only high quality traditional or experimental haiku and senryu plus fiction, essays and cartoons pertaining to Japan; *SPSM&H,* which publishes the highest quality traditional and experimental sonnets available plus romantic fiction and essays pertaining to the sonnet; and the annual winner of the Charles William Duke long poem contest." Circ. 1,250. **Pays on acceptance.** Publishes ms an average of 6 months after acceptance. Byline given. Offers 50% kill fee. Buys first North American serial rights. Submit seasonal/holiday material 2 months in advance. Reports in 3 months on mss. Sample copy $7.95 (includes postage). Sample copy of any supplement $4.50. Writer's guidelines for #10 SASE.

• An eclectic magazine, open to greater variety of styles—especially genre and mainstream stories unsuitable for other literary magazines. Receptive to new writers.

Nonfiction: Historical/nostalgic (in the form of belles lettres); humor (in fiction or belles lettres); interview/profile (poets and fiction writers); opinion (on poetry and fiction only); personal experience (as it pertains to poetry or fiction in the form of belles lettres); travel (in the form of belles lettres only); and criticism and book reviews of poetry and small press fiction titles. "Nothing overtly slick in approach. Criticism pieces must have depth; belles lettres must offer important insights into the human scene." Buys 8 mss/year. Send complete ms. Length: 1,000-2,000 words. Pays $25 or by arrangement. Sometimes pays the expenses of writers on assignment.

Fiction: Adventure, book excerpts (original novel excerpts only), erotica (of a quality seen in Anais Nin or Henry Miller only), ethnic, experimental, fantasy, historical, horror, humorous, mainstream, mystery, novel excerpts, science fiction, suspense and western. "We would consider slick fiction of the quality seen in *Esquire* or *Vanity Fair* and more excellent submissions in the genres—science fiction, wit, Gothic horror, traditional romance, stories with complex *raisons d'être;* avant-garde ought to be truly avant-garde." No pornography ("good erotica is not the same thing"). Buys 24-36 mss/year. Send complete ms. Length: 1,000-5,000 words. Pays $35 or by arrangement for exceptional work.

Poetry: Avant-garde, free verse, haiku, light verse and traditional. "No patently religious or stereotypical newspaper poetry." Buys 100-160 poems/year depending on lengths. Prefers submission of at least 3 poems. Length: 3-100 lines. Pays $2-25; additional payment for exceptional work, usually by established professionals. *Cicada* pays $10 each to three "best of issue" poets; *SPSM&H* pays $14 to two "best of issue" sonnets; winner of the long poem contest receives $100 plus copies and publication.

Tips: *"Have something to say* and say it well. If you insist on waving flags or pushing your religion, then do it with subtlety and class. We enjoy a good cry from time to time, too, but sentimentality does not mean we want to see mush. Read our fiction carefully for depth of plot and characterization, then try very hard to improve on it. With the growth of quality in short fiction, we expect to find stories of lasting merit. I also

A bullet introduces comments by the editor of Writer's Market *indicating special information about the listing.*

hope to begin seeing more critical essays which, without sacrificing research, demonstrate a more entertaining obliqueness to the style sheets, more 'new journalism' than MLA. In poetry, we also often look for a good 'storyline' so to speak. Above all we want to feel a sense of honesty and value in every piece."

AMERICAN SHORT FICTION, University of Texas Press, University of Texas at Austin, Dept. of English, Austin TX 78712-1164. (512)471-1772. Editor: Laura Furman. 100% freelance written. Quarterly fiction magazine. "*American Short Fiction* carries fiction of all lengths up to and including the novella, and is aimed at a general readership. No special slant or philosophy is required in writing for our readers." Estab. 1990. **Pays on acceptance.** Publishes ms an average of 1 year after acceptance. Buys first serial rights. Reports in 4 months. Sample copy $7.95 plus $2 for foreign postage if necessary.
Fiction: "Stories are selected for their originality and craftsmanship. No condensed novels or slice-of-life vignettes, please." Publishes novel excerpts. Buys 20-30 mss/year. Send complete ms. Pays $500-1,000.
Tips: "Manuscripts are only accepted October 1-April 30."
• A magazine that is quickly gaining in national reputation, as evidenced by regular appearances in the prize anthologies. A finalist for the 1993 National Magazine Award in fiction. A very competitive and prestigious market.

THE AMERICAN VOICE, 332 W. Broadway, Louisville KY 40202. (502)562-0045. Editor: Frederick Smock. "We publish daring new writers along with the more radical work of established writers. Avant-garde, open-minded, feminist, pan-American." Circ. 2,000. Pays on publication. Publishes ms an average of 4 months after acceptance. Byline given. Buys first North American serial rights. Reports in 1 month on queries; 2 months on mss. Sample copy $5.
Nonfiction: Essays, opinion and criticism. Buys 40 mss/year. Send complete ms. Length: 10,000 words maximum. Pays $400/essay; $150 to translator.
Fiction: Buys 15 mss/year. Send complete ms. Pays $400/story; $150 to translator.
Poetry: Avant-garde and free verse. Buys 40 poems/year. Submit maximum 10 poems. Pays $150/poem; $75 to translator.
Tips: "We are looking only for vigorously original fiction, poetry and essays, from new and established writers, and will consider nothing that is in any way sexist, racist or homophobic."

ANTAEUS, 100 W. Broad St., Hopewell NJ 08525. Editor: Daniel Halpern. Semiannual literary magazine. Estab. 1970. Pays on publication. Publishes ms an average of 6 months after acceptance. Byline given. Buys first North American serial and trade edition reprint rights. Submit seasonal material 1 year in advance. Reports in 4 months. Sample copy $11.50. Writer's guidelines for #10 SASE.
Nonfiction: Essays, historical/nostalgic, interview/profile and travel. No book reviews. Buys up to 2 mss/year. Query with published clips. Pays $10/page. Pays in contributor copies or other premiums.
Photos: State availability of photos with submission. Offers no additional payment for photos accepted with ms. Buys one-time rights.
Fiction: Adventure, experimental, historical, humorous, mainstream, novel excerpts and science fiction. Buys 10-20 mss/year. Send complete ms. Pays $10/page.
Poetry: Avant-garde, free verse, haiku, light verse and traditional. Buys 20-60 poems/year. Pays $10/page.

ANTIETAM REVIEW, 3rd Floor, 82 W. Washington St., Hagerstown MD 21740-4804. (301)791-3132. Editors: Susanne Kass and Ann Knox. 100% freelance written. Annual magazine of fiction (short stories), poetry and b&w photography. Estab. 1982. Circ. 1,500. Pays on publication. Byline given. Reports in 2 months. Back issue $3.15; current issue $5.25. Writer's guidelines for SASE.
Fiction: Novel excerpts, short stories of a literary quality. No religious, romance, erotica, confession, horror or condensed novels. Buys 9 mss/year. Query or send complete ms. Length: 5,000 words. Pays $100.
Poetry: Crystal Brown. Avant-garde, free verse and traditional. Does not want to see haiku, religious and most rhyme. Buys 15-20 poems/year. Submit 5 poems maximum. Pays $20. "Writers must live in or be native of, Maryland, Pennsylvania, Delaware, Virginia, West Virginia or District of Columbia.

ANTIOCH REVIEW, P.O. Box 148, Yellow Springs OH 45387-0148. Editor: Robert S. Fogarty. Quarterly magazine for general, literary and academic audience. Estab. 1941. Buys all rights. Byline given. Pays on publication. Publishes ms an average of 10 months after acceptance. Reports in 2 months. Sample copy for $6. Writer's guidelines for #10 SASE.
Nonfiction: "Contemporary articles in the humanities and social sciences, politics, economics, literature and all areas of broad intellectual concern. Somewhat scholarly, but never pedantic in style, eschewing all professional jargon. Lively, distinctive prose insisted upon." Length: 2,000-8,000 words. Pays $15/published page.
Fiction: Quality fiction only, distinctive in style with fresh insights into the human condition. No science fiction, fantasy or confessions. Pays $15/published page.
Poetry: No light or inspirational verse. Contributors should be familiar with the magazine before submitting.

BAD HAIRCUT, #4, 1055 Adams St. SE, Olympia WA 98501-1443. Editors: Ray Goforth and Kim Goforth. 99% freelance written. Estab. 1987. Circ. 2,000. Pays on publication. Byline given. Buys first North American serial rights. Submit seasonal/holiday material 4 months in advance. Simultaneous and previously published submissions OK. Reports in 1 week on queries; 1 month on mss. *Writer's Market* recommends allowing 2 months for reply. Sample copy $4. Writer's guidelines for #10 SASE.

Nonfiction: Essays, expose (government), general interest, interview/profile (political leaders, activists), opinion and photo feature. No pornography or hate-oriented articles. Buys 6 mss/year. Query with or without published clips or send complete ms. Length: 500-2,500. Reprints OK; send typed ms with rights for sale noted. Pays copies and small cash amount. Sometimes pays writers with contributor copies or other premiums rather than a cash payment.

Fiction: Adventure, experimental, historical and science fiction. Buys 6 mss/year. Send complete ms. Length: 500-2,500 words. Pays $50 maximum (usually copies).

Poetry: Avant-garde and free verse. Buys 25 poems/year. Submit up to 10 poems at one time. Length: 1-30 lines. Pays with copies or small cash amount.

Fillers: Anecdotes, facts, newsbreaks. Buys 20 mss/year. Length: 7-100 words. Pays $2.

Tips: "There is a rising tide of activism—a caring for others and the common future we all share. Tap into this—let your heart guide you along the path to peace."

BLACK MOUNTAIN REVIEW, Lorien House, P.O. Box 1112, Black Mountain NC 28711-1112. (704)669-6211. Editor: David A. Wilson. 100% freelance written. Estab. 1969. Annual magazine covering literary figures. Each issue is dedicated to a writer. For example, #10 (1994) is on Carl Sandburg. Estab. 1987. Circ. 200. Byline given. Buys one-time rights. Previously published submissions OK. Reports in 1 week on queries, 1 month on mss. *Writer's Market* recommends allowing 2 months for reply. Sample copy for $6. Writer's guidelines for #10 SASE.

Nonfiction: Upcoming issues: #10 "On Carl Sandburg," #11 "On O. Henry." No violence, sex, or general material not related to the theme. Buys 3-4 mss/year. Query. Length: 500-2,000 words. Pays $15 or copies for articles. Reprints OK; send typed ms with rights for sale noted and information about when and where the article previously appeared. Pays 100% of their fee for an original article.

Photos: State availability of photos with submission. Reviews prints (5×7). Offers $5. Model release and identification of subjects required. Buys one-time rights.

Fiction: Buys 1-2 mss/year. Must relate to theme. Query. Length: 500-2,000 words. Pays $15 or copies.

Poetry: Poetry: On the theme *only*. Free verse, traditional. Buys 2 poems/year. Submit maximum 3 poems. Length: 60 lines maximum. Pays $5.

Tips: "Each issue is a specific theme, and by getting into some aspect of the theme, a writer has a very good chance of being published. The greatest problem is receiving general material which does not relate to the theme. A query first saves everyone time, energy and postage. Nonfiction is most needed, and well-researched material has the best chance of publication. Due to the tightening of finances. Payment may be in copies rather than dollars. Tell me your preference."

BLACK WARRIOR REVIEW, P.O. Box 2936, Tuscaloosa AL 35486-2936. (205)348-4518. Editor, volume 20: Leigh Ann Sockrider. Managing Editor: Mark Drew. 95% freelance written. Semiannual magazine of fiction and poetry. Estab. 1974. Circ. 2,000. Pays on publication. Publishes ms an average of 6 months after acceptance. Byline given. Buys first rights. Reports in 2 weeks on queries; 3 months on mss. Sample copy $6. Writer's guidelines for #10 SASE.

• Consistently excellent magazine. Edited and produced by students in the graduate writing program at University of Alabama so new editor every year. Placed a story in recent *Best American Short Stories* anthology.

Nonfiction: Interview/profile and book reviews. Buys 5 mss/year. Query or send complete ms. No limit on length. Payment varies. No nonfiction will be considered for vol. 20, No. 1.

Photos: State availability of photos with submission. Offers no additional payment for photos accepted with ms. Identification of subjects required. Buys one-time rights.

Fiction: Ashley Gibson, fiction editor. Buys 10 mss/year. Publishes novel excerpts. One story/chapter per envelope, please.

Poetry: Tom Geiger, poetry editor. Submit 3-6 poems. Long poems encouraged. Buys 50 poems/year.

Tips: "Read the *BWR* before submitting; editor changes each year. Send us your best work. Submissions of photos and/or artwork is encouraged. We sometimes choose unsolicited photos/artwork for the cover. Address all submissions to the appropriate genre editor."

Always check the most recent copy of a magazine for the address and editor's name before you send in a query or manuscript.

BOING-BOING, The World's Greatest Neurozine, #818, 11288 Ventura Blvd, Studio City CA 91604. (818)980-2009. Fax: (818)980-0902. Editor: Mark Frauenfelder. 50% freelance written. Quarterly magazine. "Exploring cyberpunk, fringe tech, altered consciousness, high weirdness and subculture curiosities." Estab. 1988. Circ. 15,000. Pays on publication. Buys one-time rights. Query for electronic submissions. Reprints OK; send photocopy of article or short story. Pays 100% of their fee for an original article. Reports in 3 weeks on queries; 2 months on mss. Sample copy $3.95. Writer's guidelines for #10 SASE.

• Unsolicited fiction and poetry is no longer accepted.

Nonfiction: Book excerpts, essays, expose, humor, interview/profile, new product, opinion, personal experience, technical (computer technology, brain toys), software, science fiction and book reviews. Buys 32 mss/year. Query with or without published clips or send complete ms. Length: 500-5,000 words. Pays 2-5¢/word.

Photos: State availability of photos with submission. Reviews prints. Offers $10 maximum/photo. Buys one-time rights.

Tips: "Scan computer bulletin boards to learn about cutting-edge developments in brain/mind research, computer technology, popular culture and science fiction. Read fanzines and attend lectures and workshops held by people with unusual ideas."

BOULEVARD, Opojaz, Inc., P.O. Box 30386, Philadelphia PA 19103-4326. Editor: Richard Burgin. 100% freelance written. Triannual literary magazine covering fiction, poetry and essays. "*Boulevard* is a diverse triquarterly literary magazine presenting original creative work by well-known authors, as well as by writers of exciting promise." Estab. 1985. Circ. 2,800. Pays on publication. Publishes ms an average of 3-12 months after acceptance. Byline given. Offers no kill fee. Buys first North American serial rights. Simultaneous submissions OK. Reports in 2 weeks on queries; 2 months on mss. Sample copy $6. Writer's guidelines for #10 SASE.

Nonfiction: Book excerpts, essays and interview/profile. "No pornography, science fiction, children's stories or westerns." Buys 8 mss/year. Send complete ms. Length: 8,000 words maximum. Pays $50-150 (sometimes higher).

Fiction: Confession, experimental, mainstream and novel excerpts. "We do not want erotica, science fiction, romance, western or children's stories." Buys 20 mss/year. Send complete ms. Length: 8,000 words maximum. Pays $50-150 (sometimes higher).

Poetry: Avant-garde, free verse, haiku and traditional. "Do not send us light verse." Buys 80 poems/year. Submit maximum 5 poems. Length: up to 200 lines. Pays $25-150 (sometimes higher).

Tips: "Read the magazine first. The work *Boulevard* publishes is generally recognized as among the finest in the country. We continue to seek more good literary or cultural essays. Send only your best work."

‡CANADIAN FICTION MAGAZINE, P.O. Box 1061, Kingston, Ontario K7L 4Y5 Canada. Editor: Geoffrey Hancock. Quarterly magazine. Publishes only Canadian fiction, short stories and novel excerpts. Circ. 1,800. Pays on publication. Buys first North American serial rights. Byline given. Reports in 6 weeks. Back issue $6; current issue $10 plus 7% tax (in Canadian funds).

Nonfiction: Interview (must have a definite purpose, both as biography and as a critical tool focusing on problems and techniques) and book reviews (Canadian fiction only). Looking for a critical series featuring speculation on the future of fiction. Buys 35 mss/year. Query. Length: 1,000-3,000 words. Pays $10/printed page plus 1-year subscription.

Photos: Purchased on assignment. Send prints. Pays $10 for 5×7 b&w glossy prints; $50 for cover. Model releases required.

Fiction: "No restrictions on subject matter or theme. We are open to experimental and speculative fiction as well as traditional forms. Style, content and form are the author's prerogative. Novellas and instant fiction also considered. We also publish self-contained sections of novel-in-progress and French-Canadian fiction in translation, as well as an annual special issue on a single author such as Mavis Gallant, Leon Rooke, Robert Harlow or Jane Rule. Please note that *CFM* is an anthology devoted *exclusively* to Canadian fiction. We publish only the works of writers and artists residing in Canada and Canadians living abroad." Pays $10/printed page.

Tips: "Prospective contributors must study several recent issues carefully. *CFM* is a serious professional literary magazine whose contributors include the finest writers in Canada."

CANADIAN LITERATURE, #223-2029 West Mall, University of British Columbia, Vancouver, British Columbia V6T 1Z2 Canada. Editor: W.H. New. 70% freelance written. Works with "both new and established writers depending on quality." Quarterly. Estab. 1959. Circ. 2,000. Not copyrighted. Buys first Canadian rights only. Pays on publication. Publishes ms an average of 2 years after acceptance. Reports in 1 month. *Writer's Market* recommends allowing 2 months for reply. Sample copy and writer's guidelines $15 (Canadian) for 7×10 SAE with $4.30 Canadian postage.

Nonfiction: Articles of high quality only on Canadian books and writers written in French or English. Articles should be scholarly and readable. Query "with a clear description of the project." Length: 2,000-5,500 words. Pays $5/printed page.

‡CATALYST, A Magazine of Heart & Mind, Catalyst, #400, 236 Forsyth St., Atlanta GA 30303. Managing Editor: Pearl Cleage. 99% freelance written. Semiannual literary magazine covering poetry, fiction, nonfiction. "*Catalyst* is committed to producing a high quality magazine that would stimulate both readers and writers and eventually have an impact on the 'worldwide flow of ideas.'" Estab. 1986. Circ. 5,000. Pays on publication. Publication not copyrighted. Buys simultaneous rights. Editorial lead time 6 months. Submit seasonal material 6 months in advance. Accepts simultaneous submissions. Reports in 3 months on queries. Sample copy $2.50 for #10 SASE. Writer's guidelines free on request.

Nonfiction: Book excerpts, essays, expose, general interest, humor, inspirational and personal experience. Buys 100 mss/year. Query. Length: 3,000 words maximum. Pays $100 minimum for assigned articles; $10 for unsolicited articles. "In addition to payment, contributors also receive 2 complimentary copies."

Photos: State availability of photos with submission. Reviews transparencies. Offers no additional payment for photos accepted with ms. Captions required. Buys all rights.

Fiction: Adventure, ethnic, fantasy, humorous, mainstream, romance, science fiction and serialized novels. Buys 75 mss/year. Query. Length: 3,000 words maximum. Pays $10-200.

Poetry: Avant-garde, free verse, light verse and traditional. Buys 50 poems/year. Length: 3,000 words maximum. Pays $10-100.

Tips: "Attend workshops, readings; take creative writing class; join a literary group; network. The entire magazine is open to all writers."

THE CHARITON REVIEW, Northeast Missouri State University, Kirksville MO 63501-9915. (816)785-4499. Fax: (816)785-4181. Editor: Jim Barnes. 100% freelance written. Semiannual (fall and spring) magazine covering contemporary fiction, poetry, translation and book reviews. Circ. 600. Pays on publication. Publishes ms an average of 6 months after acceptance. Byline given. Buys first North American serial rights. Reports in 1 week on queries; 2 weeks on mss. *Writer's Market* recommends allowing 2 months for reply. Sample copy $2.50 for 7×10 SAE with 4 first class stamps.

Nonfiction: Essays and essay reviews of books. Buys 2-5 mss/year. Send complete ms. Length: 1,000-5,000. Pays $15.

Fiction: Ethnic, experimental, mainstream, novel excerpts and traditional. "We are not interested in slick material." Buys 6-10 mss/year. Send complete ms. Length: 1,000-6,000 words. Pays $5/page.

Poetry: Avant-garde, free verse and traditional. Buys 50-55 poems/year. Submit maximum 5 poems. Length: open. Pays $5/page.

Tips: "Read *Chariton*. Know the difference between good literature and bad. Know what magazine might be interested in your work. We are not a trendy magazine. We publish only the best. All sections are open to freelancers. Know your market or you are wasting your time—and mine. Do *not* write for guidelines; the only guideline is excellence in all matters."

CHELSEA, Chelsea Associates, P.O. Box 5880, Grand Central Station, New York, NY 10163. (212)988-2276. Editor: Sonia Raiziss. 70% freelance written. Semiannual literary magazine. "We stress style, variety, originality. No special biases or requirements. Flexible attitudes, eclectic material. We take an active interest, as always, in cross-cultural exchanges, superior translations, and are leaning toward cosmopolitan, interdisciplinary techniques, but maintain no strictures against traditional modes." Estab. 1958. Circ. 1,350. Pays on publication. Publishes ms an average of 6 months after acceptance. Byline given. Buys first North American serial rights. Reports in 3 months on mss. Sample copy $5.

● Also sponsors a contest.

Nonfiction: Essays. Buys 6 mss/year. Send complete ms. Length: 6,000 words. Pays $5/page.

Fiction: Mainstream, literary. Buys 12 mss/year. Send complete ms. Length: 5-6,000 words. Pays $5/page.

Poetry: Avant-garde, free verse, traditional. Buys 60-75 poems/year. Pays $5/page.

CIMARRON REVIEW, Oklahoma State University, 205 Morrill Hall, OSU, Stillwater OK 74078. (405)744-9476. Editor: Gordon Weaver. Managing Editor: Deborah Bransford. 85% freelance written. Quarterly literary magazine. "We publish short fiction, poetry, and essays of serious literary quality by writers often published, seldom published and previously unpublished. We have no bias with respect to subject matter, form (traditional or experimental) or theme. Though we appeal to a general audience, many of our readers are writers themselves or members of a university community." Estab. 1967. Circ. 700. Pays on publication. Published ms and average of 1 year after acceptance. Byline given. Buys all rights (reprint permission freely granted on request). Reports in 1 week on queries; 2 months on mss. Sample copy $3 for 7×10 SASE. Writer's guidelines for #10 SASE.

Nonfiction: E.P. Walkiewicz, nonfiction editor, % Deborah Bransford. Essays, general interest, historical, interview/profile, opinion, personal experience, travel, literature and arts. "We are not interested in highly subjective personal reminiscences, obscure or arcane articles, or short, light 'human interest' pieces." Buys 9-12 mss/year. Send complete ms. Length: 1,000-7,500 words. Pays $50 plus one year's subscription.

Fiction: Mainstream and literary. No juvenile or genre fiction. Buys 12-17 mss/year. Send complete ms. Length: 1,250-7,000 words. Pays $50.

Poetry: Free verse and traditional. No haiku, light verse or experimental poems. Buys 55-70 poems/year. Submit maximum 6 poems. Pays $15/poem.

Tips: "For prose, submit legible, double-spaced typescript with name and address on manuscript. Enclose SASE and brief cover letter. For poetry, same standards apply, but single-spaced is conventional. Be familiar with high quality, contemporary mainstream writing. Evaluate your own work carefully."

CLOCKWATCH REVIEW, (A Journal of the Arts), Dept. of English, Illinois Wesleyan University, Bloomington IL 61702-2900. (309)556-3352. Editor: James Plath. 85% freelance written. Semiannual literary magazine. Estab. 1983. Circ. 1,400. **Pays on acceptance.** Byline given. Buys first North American serial rights. Submit seasonal/holiday material 6 months in advance. Reports in 1 month on queries; 2 months on mss. Sample copy $4. Writer's guidelines for #10 SASE.

Nonfiction: Literary essays, criticism (MLA style), and interviews with writers, musicians, artists. Buys 4 mss/year. Query with or without published clips. Length: 1,500-4,000 words. Pays up to $25.

Photos: State availability of photos with submission. Reviews contact sheets, negatives, transparencies. Offers no additional payment for photos accepted with ms. Buys one-time rights.

Fiction: Experimental, humorous, mainstream, novel excerpts. "Also literary quality genre stories that break the mold. No straight mystery, fantasy, sci-fi, romance or western." Buys 8 mss/year. Send complete ms. Length: 1,500-4,000 words. Pays $25.

Poetry: Avant-garde, free verse, light verse, traditional. Buys 30 poems/year. Submit maximum 6 poems. Length: 32 lines maximum. Pays $5.

CLOCKWISE An Urban Almanac, The Clockwork Press, 9611 Lorain Ave., Cleveland OH 44102-4751. Editor: James Guilford. 80% freelance written. Quarterly magazine. "Viewpoint, experience and the telling of the story (nonfiction or fiction) are what we are looking for. Capture the essence of living today—in the city, especially—and you'll catch our interest." Estab. 1991. Circ. 800. Pays on publication. Byline given. Buys one-time or second serial (reprint) rights. Editorial lead time 2 months. Submit seasonal material 6 months in advance. Accepts previously published submissions. Sample copy $1. Writer's guidelines for #10 SASE.

Nonfiction: Essays, general interest, historical/nostalgic, humor, interview/profile, and personal experience. "No scholarly dissertations loaded with footnotes, religious or technical discussions. Don't query." Send complete ms. Length: 2,000 maximum words. Pays $10 minimum.

Fiction: Fantasy, humorous, mainstream, mystery, science fiction and slice-of-life vignettes. Send complete ms.

Poetry: Free verse, Haiku, light verse and traditional. "No religious." Pays $5-10.

Fillers: Anecdotes, facts and short humor. Pays $5-10.

COLORADO REVIEW A Journal of Contemporary Literature, Dept. of English, Colorado State University, Ft. Collins CO 80523. (303)491-6428. Fiction Editor: David Milofsky. Biannual magazine of contemporary human experience and literature. "Our journal is dedicated to contemporary literature as a fine art; we print only the best writing we can find." Estab. 1977. Circ. 1,500. Pays on publication. Byline given. Buys first North American serial rights. Does not accept simultaneous submissions. Reports in 3 months. Sample copy $8. Writer's guidelines for #10 SASE.

Nonfiction: Essays, interviews with writers and poets, and literary essays on contemporary work. Send complete ms. Length: 2,000-4,000 words.

Fiction: "No formula writing. We want stories with believable characters we can care about in a language and a narrative style that is engaging, interesting." Length: 5,000 words maximum. Pays $5/printed page.

Poetry: "We print good poetry, regardless of its form." Buys 40-50 poems/year. Submit maximum 6 poems at a time. Length: 60 lines maximum. Pays $10/printed page.

CONFRONTATION, A Literary Journal, Long Island University, Brookville NY 11548. (516)299-2391. Editor: Martin Tucker. 75% freelance written. Semiannual literary magazine. "We are eclectic in our taste. Excellence of style is our dominant concern." Estab. 1968. Circ. 2,000. Pays on publication. Publishes ms an average of 6 months after acceptance. Byline given. "We rarely offer kill fee." Buys first North American serial, first, one-time or all rights. Simultaneous submissions OK. Reports in 3 weeks on queries; 2 months on mss. Sample copy $3.

• The editor of this magazine reports the backlog of material he had has eased somewhat. He is now more open to receiving stories and poems.

Nonfiction: Essays and personal experience. Buys 15 mss/year. Send complete ms. Length: 1,500-5,000 words. Pays $100-300 for assigned articles; $15-300 for unsolicited articles.

Photos: State availability of photos with submission. Offers no additional payment for photos accepted with ms. Buys one-time rights.

Fiction: Katherine Hill-Miller. Experimental, mainstream, science fiction and slice-of-life vignettes. "We judge on quality, so genre is open." Buys 60-75 mss/year. Send complete ms. Length 6,000 words maximum. Pays $25-250.

Poetry: Sandy McIntosh. Avant-garde, free verse, Haiku, light verse and traditional. Buys 60-75 poems/year. Submit maximum 6 poems. Length open. Pays $10-100.
Tips: "Most open to fiction and poetry."

THE CONNECTICUT POETRY REVIEW, P.O. Box 3783, New Haven CT 06525. Editors: J. Claire White and J. Wm. Chichetto. 100% freelance written. Annual poetry journal. Estab. 1981. Circ. 500. **Pays on acceptance.** Submit seasonal material 3 months in advance. Reports in 3 months. Sample copy $3.50. Writer's guidelines for #10 SASE.
Poetry: Avant-garde, free verse and traditional. "No previously published work. We have published Marge Piercy, Robert Peters, John Updike, Diane Wakoski and Odysseus Elytis, among others." Buys 25 poems/year. Submit maximum 5 poems. Length: 4-30 lines. Pays $5.

CRAZYHORSE, University of Arkansas at Little Rock, English Dept, UALR, 2801 S., Little Rock AR 72204-1099. (501)569-3160. Managing Editor: Zabelle Stodola. 100% freelance written. Semiannual literary magazine of poetry and fiction. Estab. 1960. Circ. 1,000. Pays on publication. Publishes ms an average of 1 year after acceptance. Reports in 4 months. Sample copy $5 for large SAE with 9 first class stamps.
Fiction: Judy Troy, fiction editor. Experimental and mainstream. "Serious quality fiction of any kind." Buys approximately 10 mss/year. Send complete ms. Pays $10/page. Offers $500 annual fiction prize.
Poetry: Ralph Burns, poetry editor. Traditional. Buys 50 poems/year. Pays $10/page. Offers $500 annual poetry prize.

THE CREAM CITY REVIEW, The University of Wisconsin-Milwaukee, English Dept., P.O. Box 413, UWM, Milwaukee WI 53201. Editor-in-Chief: Sandra Nelson. Poetry Editors: Aedan Hanley, Cynthia Belmont, Paul August. Fiction Editors: Patricia Montalbano, Kathleen Lester. Nonfiction Editor: Nancy Levy. 95% freelance written. Semiannual magazine of poetry, fiction and nonfiction. "61% of our readers are women. Most of our readers are college educated; 29% have doctoral degrees. Our focus is literary and we are interested in any poetry, fiction, or nonfiction that is well-crafted. All subjects are open. All styles are welcomed. No biases except quality." Estab. 1975. Circ. 2,000. Pays on publication. Byline given. "We include a lengthy contributor's note." Buys first rights. No reprints. Simultaneous submissions OK. Query for electronic submissions. Reports in 2 months, longer in summer. Sample copy $4.50. Writer's guidelines for #10 SASE.
Nonfiction: Essays, interview/profile, personal experience and literary reviews. Buys 20 mss/year. Send complete ms. Pays $5/page ($150 maximum) plus 2 contributor copies.
Photos: Send photos with submission. Reviews 5×7 or larger prints. Offers $5/photo plus 2 contributor copies.
Columns/Departments: Literary Review (poetry and fiction reviews), 2 pages. Buys 10 mss/year. Send complete ms. Pays $5/page, plus 2 contributor copies.
Fiction: Literary. Novel excerpts. Buys 16-20 mss/year. Send complete ms. Length: 1-30 pages. Pays $5/page ($150 maximum) plus 2 contributor's copies.
Poetry: Aedan Hanley, poetry editor. Avant-garde, free verse, haiku, traditional and literary. Buys 120 poems/year. Submit maximum 4-6 poems. Pays $5/page ($150 maximum) plus 2 contributor's copies.
Tips: "Of course go to the library or book store and read a little of us. No writer, famous or not, has an automatic in with our magazine. We look only at quality."

THE DENVER QUARTERLY, University of Denver, Dept. of English, Denver CO 80208. (303)871-2892. Editor: Donald Revell. 100% freelance written. Works with a small number of new/unpublished writers. Quarterly magazine for generally sophisticated readership. Estab. 1966. Circ. 1,000. Pays on publication. Publishes ms an average of 6-12 months after acceptance. Buys first North American serial rights. Reports in 3 months. Sample copy $5.
Nonfiction: "Most reviews are solicited; we do publish a few literary essays in each number. Use non-sexist language, please." Send complete ms. Pays $5/printed page.
Fiction: Buys 10 mss/year. Send complete ms. Pays $5/printed page.
Poetry: Buys 50 poems/year. Send poems. Pays $5/printed page.
Tips: "We decide on the basis of quality only. Prior publication is irrelevant. Promising material, even though rejected, may receive some personal comment from the editor; some material can be revised to meet our standards through such criticism. I receive more good stuff than *DQ* can accept, so there is some subjectivity and a good deal of luck involved in any final acceptance. *DQ* is becoming interested in issues of aesthetics and *lucid* perspectives and performances of the avant-garde. We are also interested in topics and translations in the literature of Eastern Europe. Please look at a *recent* issue before submitting. Reading unsolicited mss during academic year only; we do *not* read between May 15 and Sept. 15."

DESCANT, Descant Arts & Letters Foundation, P.O. Box 314, Station P, Toronto, Ontario M5S 2S8. (416)603-0223. Editor: Karen Mulhallen. Managing Editor: Elizabeth Mitchell. Quarterly literary journal. Estab. 1970. Circ. 1,200. Pays on publication. Publishes ms 8-16 months after acceptance. Editorial lead time

4 months. Submit seasonal material 4 months in advance. Query for electronic submissions. Sample copy $8. Writer's guidelines free on request.

Nonfiction: Book excerpts, essays historical/nostalgic, interview/profile, personal experience, photo feature and travel. Upcoming special issues include: First Nations (winter or spring 1993), Women in Film (winter or summer 1993). Query or send complete ms. Pays $100 honorarium plus one year's subscription. Sometimes pays the expenses of writers on assignment.

Photos: State availability of photos with submission. Reviews contact sheets and prints. Offers no additional payment for photos accepted with ms. Buys one-time rights.

Fiction: Send complete ms. Pays $100.

Poetry: Free verse, light verse and traditional. Submit maximum 10 poems. Pays $100.

Tips: "Familiarize yourself with our magazine before submitting."

EROTIC FICTION QUARTERLY, EFQ Publications, P.O. Box 424958, San Francisco CA 94142-4958. Editor: Richard Hiller. 100% freelance written. Small literary magazine (published irregularly) for thoughtful people interested in a variety of highly original and creative short fiction with sexual themes. Estab. 1983. **Pays on acceptance.** Byline given. Buys first rights. Reports in 1 month. Writer's guidelines for #10 SASE.

Fiction: "Heartfelt, intelligent erotica, any style. Also, stories—not necessarily erotic—about some aspect of authentic sexual experience. No standard pornography or men's magazine-type stories; no contrived or formula plots or gimmicks; no broad satire or parody. We do not publish poetry." Send complete ms. Length: 500-5,000 words, average 1,500 words. Pays $50 minimum.

Tips: "What we especially need and do not see enough of is truly interesting and original erotica, whether graphic or subtle, as well as literary-quality fiction that depends on sexual insight. No particular 'slant' is required. Stories should reflect real life, not media ideas."

EVENT, Douglas College, P.O. Box 2503, New Westminster, British Columbia V3L 5B2 Canada. Fax: (604)527-5095. Assistant Editor: Bonnie Bauder. 100% freelance written. Works with a small number of new/ unpublished writers each year. Triannual magazine (April, August and December) for "those interested in literature and writing." Estab. 1970. Circ. 1,000. Uses 80-100 mss/year. Small payment and contributor's copy only. Publishes ms an average of 6 months after acceptance. Buys first North American serial rights. Byline given. Reports in 4 months. Submit complete ms with IRCs.

Nonfiction: "High quality work." Reviews of Canadian books and essays.

Fiction: Short stories.

Poetry: Submit no more than ten poems at a time. "We are looking for high quality modern poetry."

FICTION QUARTERLY, *The Tampa Tribune,* P.O. Box 191, Tampa FL 33601. (813)272-7600. Editor: Rick Wilber. 75% freelance written. Quarterly newspaper fiction and poetry supplement. "We have a general newspaper readership, so we are touchy about explicit sex, rough language and the like." Estab. 1988. Circ. 400,000. Pays on publication. Byline given. Buys first North American serial rights. Reports in 1-6 months on mss.

Fiction: Adventure, confession, ethnic, experimental, fantasy, historical, horror, humorous, mainstream, mystery, novel excerpts, religious, romance, science fiction, slice-of-life vignettes, suspense and western. Buys 8-12 mss/year. Send complete ms. Length: 2,000-2,500 words. Pays $100-200.

Poetry: Free verse and narrative poetry. Buys 8-10 poems/year. Submit 4 or 5 poems maximum. Length: 20 lines maximum. Pays $40.

THE FIDDLEHEAD, University of New Brunswick, Campus House, P.O. Box 4400, Fredericton, New Brunswick E3B 5A3 Canada. (506)453-3501. Fax: (506)453-4599. Editor: Don MacKay. 90% freelance written. Eager to work with new/unpublished writers. Quarterly magazine covering poetry, short fiction and book reviews. Estab. 1945. Circ. 1,100. Pays on publication. Publishes ms an average of 1 year after acceptance. Not copyrighted. Buys first North American serial rights. Submit seasonal material 6 months in advance. Reports in 4 months. Sample copy $6.

Fiction: Diana Austin, Banny Belyear, Ted Colson, Linda McNutt, fiction editors. "Stories may be on any subject—acceptance is based on quality alone. Because the journal is heavily subsidized by the Canadian government, some preference is given to Canadian writers." Buys 24 mss/year. Pays $12/page.

Poetry: Robert Gibbs, Robert Hawkes, Don MacKay, Demetres Tryphonopoulos, poetry editors. "Poetry may be on any subject—acceptance is based on quality alone. Because the journal is heavily subsidized by the Canadian government, some preference is given to Canadian writers." Buys average of 60 poems/year. Submit maximum 10 poems. Pays $12/page; $100 maximum.

Tips: "Quality alone is the criterion for publication. Return postage (Canadian, or IRCs) should accompany all manuscripts."

FIELD MAGAZINE, Contemporary Poetry & Poetics, Rice Hall, Oberlin College, Oberlin OH 44074-1095. (216)775-8407/8. Fax: (216)775-8124. Editors: Stuart Friebert and David Young. Managing Editor: Dolorus Nevels. 25% freelance written. Semiannual magazine of poetry, poetry in translation, and essays on contem-

porary poetry by poets. Estab. 1969. Circ. 2,300. Pays on publication. Byline given. Buys first rights. Editorial lead time 6 months. Reports in 1 month on mss. Sample copy $6.
Poetry: Buys 100 poems/year. Submit maximum 10 poems. Pays $15 minimum/page.

FRANK: An International Journal of Contemporary Writing & Art, B.P. 29, Frank Books, 94301 Vincennes Cedex, France. (33)1-43-65-64-05. Fax: (33)1-43-65-33-02. Editor: David Applefield. 50% freelance written. Semiannual literary and arts magazine. "We are seeking writing that responds to the world—well-crafted but also conveys a sense of necessity. Work that takes risks and is non-ethnocentric." Estab. 1983. Circ. 4,000. Pays on publication. Publishes ms an average of 6 months after acceptance. Byline given. Buys one-time rights. Reports in 2 weeks on queries; 3 months on mss. Sample copy $8 from U.S. office: A-L Books, #305, 45 Newbury St., Boston MA 02116. Free writer's guidelines.
Nonfiction: Interview/profile. Buys 3 mss/year. Query. Length: 500-3,000 words. Pays $10-150 for assigned articles; $5/page plus two copies. Sometimes pays expenses of writers on assignment.
Photos: Send photos with submission. Reviews 8 × 10 prints. Offers $10-25/photo. Identification of subjects required. Buys one-time rights.
Fiction: Publishes novel excerpts, short stories, and other original forms of fiction.
Poetry: Avant-garde, translations and free verse. "No sentimental poetry." Buys 10-20 poems/year. Submit maximum 10 poems. Length: 1-200 lines. Pays $5-100.

‡**GASLIGHT, Tales of the Unsane**, Strait-Jacket Publications, P.O. Box 21, Cleveland MN 56017-0021. Editor: Melissa Gish. Estab. 1992. 90% freelance written. Triannual literary magazine covering science fiction, fantasy and horror. "We are a digest of highly imaginative fiction, poetry and artwork borne out of the darkest recessesof the creator's mind." Estab. 1992. Circ. 100. Pays on acceptance. Publishes ms an average of 4 months after acceptance. Byline given. Offers 100% kill fee. Buys first North American serial rights or one-time rights on reprints. Submit seasonal material 4 months in advance. Accepts simultaneous and previously published submissions. Send typed ms with rights for sale noted and information about when and where the article previously appeared. For reprints, pays 60% of the amount paid for an original article. Query for electronic submissions. Reports in 2 weeks on queries; 3-4 weeks on mss. Sample copy $4.25. Writer's guidelines for #10 SASE.
Nonfiction: Interview/profile. "We don't want anything not directly related to sci-fi, fantasy or horror." Buys 3 mss/year. Query. Length: up to 2,000 words. Pays $3-15. "Must query first." Sometimes pays expenses of writers on assignment (covers postage for interviews).
Fiction: Experimental, fantasy, horror, humorous (macabre), science fiction and suspense. Does not want to see "anything not related to sci-fi, fantasy or horror. No re-hashed monster movie plots. No sexism, racism, specism or degradation." Buys 35 mss/year. Send complete ms. Length: up to 3,000 words. Pays ¼-1¢/word.
Poetry: Avant-garde, free verse, light verse and traditional. Buys 45 poems/year. Submit maximum 5 poems. Length: 50 lines maximum. Pays up to $5. Pays in contributors copies for short poetry.
Fillers: Gags. Buys 3-6/year. Length: up to 25 words. Pays $3 maximum. Pays in contributors copies for artwork fillers.
Tips: "Consider the fantasy of Piers Anthony and be creative and imaginative. Nothing is too strange to be believable. Write horror from characters' perspective, not as an observer. Make us feel your terror and know your pain. We are most open to short short fiction (to 1,000 words). If you can tell a clear and believable tale in less than 1,000 words, you've got a better chance at getting in. We are eager to work with unpublished writers."

THE GETTYSBURG REVIEW, Gettysburg College, Gettysburg PA 17325. (717)337-6770. Editor: Peter Stitt. Managing Editor: Emily Ruark. Quarterly literary magazine. "Our concern is quality. Manuscripts submitted here should be extremely well written." Estab. 1988. Circ. 4,000. Pays on publication. Byline given. Buys first North American serial rights. Editorial lead time 6 months. Submit seasonal material 9 months in advance. Reports in 1 month on queries; 3 months on mss. Sample copy $7. Writer's guidelines for #10 SASE.
Nonfiction: Essays. Buys 20/year. Send complete ms. Length: 3,000-7,000. Pays $25/page.
Fiction: High quality, literary. Buys 20 ms/year. Send complete ms. Length: 2,000-7,000, Pays $25/page.
Poetry: Buys 50 poems/year. Submit maximum 3 poems. Pays $2/line.

‡**GRAHAM HOUSE REVIEW**, Colgate University Press, Box 5000, Hamilton NY 13346. (315)824-7271. Editors: Peter Balakian and Bruce Smith. Managing Editor: Ellen Walker. 100% freelance written. Annual magazine covering contemporary poetry/poetry in translation. "The editorial views of *GHR* are best described as eclectic; the editors do not identify with any particular styles or schools of thought. We take pride in discovering fine young poets and publishing neglected poets as well as established poets." Estab. 1976. Circ. approximately 300. Pays on publication. Publishes ms an average of 6-9 months after acceptance. Byline given. Buys first North American serial rights. Editorial lead time 1-2 months. Reports in 1-2 months on mss. Sample copy $7.50. Writer's guidelines free on request.
Nonfiction: Essays, interview/profile. "We pay $10/poem or $50/essay if funds from grants allow."

HANSON'S SYMPOSIUM, Hanson Publishing, 113 Merryman Ct., Annapolis MD 21401-4203. (410)626-0744. Editor: Eric Hanson. 50% freelance written. Annual literary magazine. Estab. 1988. Circ. 3,000. **Pays on acceptance.** Publishes ms an average of 8 months after acceptance. Byline given. Buys first North American serial or one-time rights. Reports in 2 months. Sample copy $6.

● This magazine is paying slightly more than it has in the past.

Nonfiction: Essays. Buys 8 mss/year. Send complete ms. Length: 1,000-5,000 words. Pays $50-200 for assigned articles; $50-150 for unsolicited articles. Sometimes pays expenses of writers on assignment.

Fiction: Erotica, experimental, fantasy, humorous and mainstream. Buys 15 mss/year. Send complete ms. Length: 1,500-8,000 words. Pays $50-200.

Poetry: Avant-garde, free verse and traditional. Buys 50 poems/year. Submit maximum 5 poems. Length: 4-100 lines. Pays $25-50.

Tips: "Due to the limited space in our publication, and due to its unique nature, we require that all writers interested in being published in *Hanson's Symposium* review a sample copy before submitting work."

‡HAWAI'I REVIEW, Board of Publications of the University of Hawai'i, 1733 Donaghho Rd., Dept. of English, UH, Honolulu HI 96822. (808)956-8548. Chief Editor: Tamara Moan. Managing Editor: Stacia Silva. 95% freelance written. Triannual literary magazine covering Hawaii themes or setting. "*Hawai'i Review* publishes all forms of literature, including (but not solely) works which focus on Hawai'i and the Pacific." Estab. 1973. Circ. 2,000. Pays on publication. Publishes ms an average of 6 months after acceptance. Byline given. Buys first North American serial rights. Editorial lead time 8 months. Submit seasonal material 8 months in advance. Accepts simultaneous submissions. Query for electronic submissions. Reports in 3 weeks on queries; 3-4 months on mss. Sample copy $5. Writer's guidelines for #10 SASE.

Nonfiction: Drew Kapp/Michele Viray, nonfiction co-editors. Book excerpts, essays, expose, historical/nostalgic, humor, interview/profile, opinion, personal experience, photo feature, travel and book reviews. Buys 20 mss/year. Send complete ms. Length: 750-7,000 words. Pays $10.

Photos: Send photos with submission. Reviews 8 × 10 prints. Offers $10-75/photo. Captions, model releases and identification of subjects required. Buys one-time rights.

Fiction: Carrie Hoshino/Michael McGinnis, fiction co-editors. Condensed novels, confession, ethnic, experimental, fantasy, historical, mainstream, novel excerpts and slice-of-life vignettes. Buys 30 mss/year. Send complete ms. Length: 250-7,000 words. Pays $10-75.

Poetry: Alan Aoki/Annie Fanning, poetry co-editors. Avant-garde, free verse, Haiku and traditional. Buys 150 poems/year. Submit maximum 5 poems. Length: 3-500 lines. Pays $10-75.

HIGH PLAINS LITERARY REVIEW, Suite 250, 180 Adams St., Denver CO 80206. (303)320-6828. Editor: Robert O. Greer, Jr. Managing Editor: Phyllis A. Harwell. 80% freelance written. Triannual literary magazine. "The *High Plains Literary Review* publishes short stories, essays, poetry, reviews and interviews, bridging the gap between commercial quarterlies and academic reviews." Estab. 1986. Circ. 1,200. Pays on publication. Byline given. Buys first North American serial rights. Simultaneous submissions OK. Reports in 12 weeks. Sample copy $4. Writer's guidelines for #10 SASE.

● Its unique editorial format—between commercial and academic—makes for lively reading. Could be good market for that "in between" story.

Nonfiction: Essays and reviews. Buys 20 mss/year. Send complete ms. Length: 10,000 words maximum. Pays $5/page.

Fiction: Ethnic, historical, humorous and mainstream. Buys 12 mss/year. Send complete ms. Length: 10,000 words maximum. Pays $5/page.

Poetry: Buys 45 poems/year. Pays $10/page.

THE HUDSON REVIEW, 684 Park Ave., New York NY 10021. Fax: (212)734-4177. Managing Editor: Ronald Koury. Quarterly. Estab. 1948. Pays on publication. Buys first world serial rights in English. Reports in 2 months.

Nonfiction: Articles, translations and reviews. Length: 8,000 words maximum.

Fiction: Uses "quality fiction." Length: 10,000 words maximum. Pays 2½¢/word.

Poetry: 50¢/line for poetry.

Tips: "Unsolicited mss will be read according to the following schedule: *Nonfiction:* Jan. 1-March 31, and Oct. 1-Dec. 31; *Poetry:* April 1-Sept. 30; *Fiction:* June 1-Nov. 30."

INDIANA REVIEW, Indiana University, 316 N. Jordan, Bloomington IN 47405. (812)855-3439. Editor: Gretchen Knapp. Associate Editor: Cara Diaconoff. 100% freelance written. Magazine published 2 times/year. "We publish fine innovative fiction and poetry. We're interested in energy, originality and careful attention to craft. While we publish many well-known writers, we also welcome new and emerging poets and fiction writers." Estab. 1982. Circ. 600. **Pays on acceptance.** Byline given. Buys first North American serial rights. Reports in 2 months. Sample copy $7. Free writer's guidelines.

Nonfiction: Essays. No pornographic or strictly academic articles dealing with the traditional canon. Buys 8 mss/year. Query. Length: 5,000 maximum. Pays $25-200.

Fiction: Experimental and mainstream. No pornography. Buys 18 mss/year. Send complete ms. Length: 250-15,000. Pays $5/page.

Poetry: Avant-garde and free verse. Prefers inventive and skillful writing. Buys 80 mss/year. Submit up to 5 poems at one time. Length: 5 lines minimum. Pays $5/page.

Tips: "Read us before you submit. Often reading is slower in summer months."

THE IOWA REVIEW, 369 EPB, The University of Iowa, Iowa City IA 52242. (319)335-0462. Fax: (319)335-2535. Editor: David Hamilton. Associate Editor: Mary Hussmann, with the help of colleagues, graduate assistants. Triannual magazine. Estab. 1970. Buys first serial rights. Reports in 3 months. Sample copy $6.

Nonfiction, Fiction and Poetry: "We publish essays, reviews, stories and poems and would like for our essays not always to be works of academic criticism." Buys 65-85 unsolicited mss/year. Submit complete ms with SASE. Pays $1/line for verse; $10/page for prose.

• This magazine's reading period is September-April.

IOWA WOMAN, Iowa Woman Endeavors, Inc., P.O. Box 680, Iowa City IA 52244-0680. Editor: Marianne Abel. Managing Editor: Rebecca Childers. Quarterly magazine of "award-winning fiction, poetry, essays, reviews, interviews and visual art by women everywhere. For readers of fine literature anywhere. As the publication of a nonprofit educational organization, we steer away from rhetoric and polemics." Estab. 1979. Circ. 2,500. Pays on publication. Publishes ms an average of 3 months after acceptance. Byline given. Buys first North American serial rights. Submit seasonal material 6-8 months in advance. Reports in 3 weeks on queries; 3 months on mss. Sample copy $6. Writer's guidelines for #10 SASE.

Nonfiction: Essays, historical, humor, interview/profile and personal experience. "No rhetorical slant on current political or environmental causes." Buys 16 mss/year. Query or send complete ms. Length: 2,000-6,000. Pays $5/page. Pays contributor copies if author prefers. Sometimes pays expenses of writers on assignment.

Photos: State availability of photos with submission or send photos with submission. Reviews contact sheets. Offers no additional payment for photos accepted with ms. Captions, model releases and identification of subjects required. Buys one time rights.

Columns/Departments: Under 21 (younger writers, any genre); As We Were (the good-?-!-old days); Crossings (culture shock in this society or others); First Person (a general category); Stopped Moments (incidents, environment, place); Genealogies (personal, historical, intergenerational); and New Writers (never before published, any genre). Buys 8-10 mss/year. Pays $5/page.

Fiction: Adventure, ethnic, experimental, fantasy, historical, humorous, mystery, science fiction, slice-of-life vignettes and women. "Nothing raunchy or maudlin." Buys 12 mss/year. Send complete ms. Length: 6,500 words maximum. Pays $5/page.

Poetry: Sandra Witt, poetry editor. Free verse and traditional. "No greeting card types or predictable rhymes or rhythms." Buys 25-40 poems/year. Submit maximum 5 poems. Pays $5/poem.

Tips: "We publish as many as 40 writers and artists each year for their first time and welcome new and emerging writers who submit quality work in any sector of the magazine. Submissions have a better chance through the year; don't necessarily wait for the annual writing contest which is quite competitive."

JAPANOPHILE, P.O. Box 223, Okemos MI 48864-0223. Editor: Earl Snodgrass. 80% freelance written. Works with a small number of new/unpublished writers each year. Quarterly magazine for literate people who are interested in Japanese culture anywhere in the world. Estab. 1974. Pays on publication. Publishes ms an average of 3 months after acceptance. Buys first North American serial rights. Previously published submissions OK. Reports in 3 months. Sample copy $4, postpaid. Writer's guidelines for #10 SASE.

Nonfiction: "We want material on Japanese culture in *North America or anywhere in the world,* even Japan. We want articles, preferably with pictures, about persons engaged in arts of Japanese origin: a Michigan naturalist who is a haiku poet, a potter who learned raku in Japan, a vivid 'I was there' account of a Go tournament in California. We would like to hear more about what it's like to be a Japanese in the US. Our particular slant is a certain kind of culture wherever it is in the world: Canada, the US, Europe, Japan. The culture includes flower arranging, haiku, sports, religion, art, photography, fiction, etc. It is important to study the magazine." Buys 8 mss/issue. Query preferred but not required. Length: 1,600 words maximum. Pays $8-20.

Photos: Pays $10-20 for 8×10 b&w glossy prints. "We prefer people pictures."

Fiction: Experimental, mainstream, mystery, adventure, humorous, romance and historical. Themes should relate to Japan or Japanese culture. Length: 1,000-6,000 words. Annual contest pays $100 to best short story (entry fee $5). Should include one or more Japanese and non-Japanese characters in each story.

• No longer considering science fiction.

Columns/Departments: Regular columns and features are Tokyo Topics and Japan in North America. "We also need columns about Japanese culture in various American cities." Query. Length: 1,000 words. Pays $20 maximum.

Poetry: Traditional, avant-garde and light verse related to Japanese culture or in a Japanese form such as haiku. Length: 3-50 lines. Pays $1-20.

Fillers: Newsbreaks, clippings and short humor of up to 200 words. Pays $1-5.

Tips: "We prefer to see more articles about Japanese culture in the US, Canada and Europe. Lack of convincing fact and detail is a frequent mistake."

THE JOURNAL, Ohio State University, 421 Denney Hall, 164 W. 17th Ave., Columbus OH 43210. (614)292-4076. Editors: Kathy Fagan and Michelle Herman. Associate Editor: Katherine Murphy. 100% freelance written. Semiannual literary magazine. "We're open to all forms; we tend to favor work that gives evidence of a mature and sophisticated sense of the language." Estab. 1972. Circ. 1,200. Pays on publication. Byline given. Buys first North American serial rights. Reports in 2 weeks on queries; 2 months on mss. Sample copy $5. Writer's guidelines for #10 SASE.

Nonfiction: Essays and interview/profile. Buys 2 mss/year. Query. Length: 2,000-4,000 words. Pays $25 maximum and contributor's copies.

Photos: State availability of photos with submission. Offers no additional payment for photos accepted with ms. Identification of subjects required. Buys one-time rights.

Columns/Departments: Reviews of contemporary poetry, 2,000-4,000 words. Buys 2 mss/year. Query. Pays $25.

Fiction: Novel excerpts and literary short stories.

Poetry: Avant-garde, free verse and traditional. Buys 100 poems/year. Submit maximum 5 poems/year. Pays $25.

‡LECTOR, The Hispanic Book Review Journal, Floricanto Press, Suite 830, 16161 Ventura Blvd., Encino CA 91436. (818)990-1885. Editor: Roberto Cabello-Argandona. Managing Editor: Giselle K. Cabello. 95% freelance written. Works with a small number of new/unpublished writers each year; eager to work with new/unpublished writers. Semiannual journal of US Hispanic cultural articles, Latin American literature and English reviews of books in Spanish (published in Spain, Central America and Latin America). "We desire cultural articles, particularly of Hispanic arts and literature, written for a popular level (as opposed to an academic level). Articles are to be nonsexist, nonracist." Circ. 3,000. Pays on publication. Publishes ms an averate of 6-12 months after acceptance. Byline given. Buys first rights or makes work-for-hire assignments. Photocopied submissions OK; previously published submissions sometimes accepted. Reports in 3 months. Sample copy $5. Writer's guidelines for #10 SASE.

Nonfiction: Interview/profile, photo feature and articles on art, literature and Latino small presses. No personal experience, religious or how-to. Buys 25 mss/year. "No unsolicited manuscripts; query us first." Length: 2,000-3,500 words. Pays $50-150. "Writers, along with payment, always get five copies of magazine."

Photos: Send photos with submission. Reviews contact sheets. Captions required. Buys one-time rights.

Columns/Departments: Publisher's Corner (covers publishing houses in Latin America or US [Latin]), 2,000-2,500 words; Perspective (cultural articles dealing with aspect of Hispanic art/literature), 2,500-3,500 words; Events in Profile (occasional column covering particular event in Chicano Studies), 1,500-2,000 words; Feature Review (in-depth review of particularly important published work), 2,500-3,000 words; Author's Corner (interview with recently published author), 1,500-2,000 words; and Inquiry (literary criticism), 2,000-2,500 words. Buys 15 mss/year. Query with published clips. Pays $50-150.

‡LINES IN THE SAND, LeSand Publications, 890 Southgate Ave., Daly City CA 94015-3741. Editor: Nina Z. Sanders. Managing Editor: Barbara J. Less. 100% freelance written. Bimonthly magazine. "Stories should be well-written, entertaining and suitable for all ages. Our readers range in age from seven to ninety. No particular slant or philosophy. We strive to have 'something for everybody.' " Estab. 1992. Circ. 125. Pays on publication. Publishes ms an average of 2-4 months after acceptance. Buys first North American serial or second serial (reprint) rights. Editorial lead time 2-4 months. Submit seasonal material 4 months in advance. Accepts simultaneous and previously published submissions. Reports in 4 months. Sample copy $3.50. Writer's guidelines for #10 SASE.

Fiction: Adventure, fantasy, horror, humorous, mainstream, mystery, science fiction, suspense, western and children/teen. "No erotica." Buys 50-60 mss/year. Send complete ms. Length: 100-2,000 words. Pays $3-10.

Poetry: Free verse, haiku, light verse and traditional. "No erotica and avant-garde." Buys 12 poems/year. Submit maximum 5 poems. Length: 4-25 lines. Pays $1-3.

Tips: "Use a fresh, original approach. Show, don't tell. Conform to guidelines. Stories should have some type of conflict. Use dialogue, when appropriate. The entire publication is open to freelancers."

LITERARY MAGAZINE REVIEW, English Dept., Kansas State University, Manhattan KS 66506. (913)532-6706. Editor: G.W. Clift. 98% freelance written. Quarterly literary magazine devoted almost exclusively to reviews of the current contents of small circulation serials publishing some fiction or poetry. "Most of our reviewers are recommended to us by third parties." Estab. 1981. Circ. 500. Pays on publication. Publishes ms an average of 1 month after acceptance. Byline given. Buys first rights. Query for electronic submissions. Reports in 2 weeks. *Writer's Market* recommends allowing 2 months for reply. Sample copy $4.

Nonfiction: Buys 60 mss/year. Query. Length: 1,500 words. Pays $25 maximum and two contributor's copies for assigned articles. Sometimes pays expenses of writers on assignment.

Photos: State availability of photos with submission. Identification of subjects required.

Tips: "Interested in omnibus reviews of magazines sharing some quality, editorial philosophy, or place of origin and in articles about literary magazine editing and the literary magazine scene."

LITERARY SKETCHES, P.O. Box 810571, Dallas TX 75381-0571. (214)243-8776. Editor: Olivia Murray Nichols. 33% freelance written. Willing to work with new/unpublished writers. Monthly newsletter for readers with literary interests of all ages. Estab. 1961. Circ 500. Byline given. Pays on publication. Publishes ms an average of 1 year after acceptance. Reports in 1 month. *Writer's Market* recommends allowing 2 months for reply. Sample copy for #10 SASE.

Nonfiction: Interviews of well-known writers and biographical material of more than common knowledge on past writers. Concise, informal style. Centennial pieces relating to a writer's birth, death or famous works. Buys 4-6 mss/year. Submit complete ms. Length: up to 1,000 words. Pays ½¢/word, plus copies.

Tips: "Articles need not be footnoted, but a list of sources should be submitted with the manuscript. We appreciate fillers of 100 words or less if they concern some little known information on an author or book."

LOST CREEK LETTERS, Lost Creek Publications, RR 2, Box 373A, Rushville MO 64484. Editor: Pamela Montgomery. 100% freelance written. Quarterly magazine. "We seek mature, thoughtful fiction, poetry and essays. Nothing trite, sentimental or didactic. We publish material on any subject. Our audience is generally college educated." Estab. 1988. Pays on publication. Publishes ms an average of 4 months after acceptance. Byline given. Buys one-time rights. Simultaneous and previously published submissions OK. No electronic submissions. Reports in 3 months. Sample copy $4 for 6×9 SAE with 3 first class stamps. Writer's guidelines for #10 SASE.

Nonfiction: Essays, humor. "No religious pieces, personal experience, inspirational articles or scholarly critical articles." Buys 50 mss/year. Send complete ms. Length: 500-2,500 words. Pays $5.

Fiction: Ethnic, experimental, fantasy, historical, humorous, mainstream, horror, slice-of-life vignettes and surrealism. "No religious or romance." Buys 8-10 mss/year. Send complete ms. Length: 200-3,000 words. Pays $5.

Poetry: Avant-garde, free verse, haiku and traditional. No "Hallmark card" poems or light verse. Looking for exceptional rhymed and metered poems. Buys 50-100 poems/year. Submit maximum 20 poems. Pays $2.

Tips: "Study literature which has withstood the test of time. Have something to say and say it once very well. Keep in mind our audience of college educated mature adults. *Send no cover letter and no credit lists, only the ms and SASE.* Above all, find out what a literary magazine is. We get many submissions that are totally unsuited for a litmag, wasting your precious writing time and a lot of expensive postage. Invest in a sample copy and share it with your writing friends, then submit material you believe to conform to our tastes."

THE MALAHAT REVIEW, The University of Victoria, P.O. Box 1700, Victoria, British Columbia V8W 2Y2 Canada. Contact: Editor. 100% freelance written. Eager to work with new/unpublished writers. Magazine published 4 times/year covering poetry, fiction, drama and criticism. Estab. 1967. Circ. 1,700. **Pays on acceptance.** Publishes ms up to 1 year after acceptance. Byline given. Offers 100% kill fee. Buys first serial rights. Reports in 2 weeks on queries; 3 months on mss. Sample copy $7.

Nonfiction: Interview/profile (literary/artistic). Buys 2 mss/year. Query first. Length: 1,000-8,000. Pays $35-175.

Photos: Pays $25 for b&w prints. Captions required. Pays $100 for color print used as cover.

Fiction: Buys 20 mss/year. Send complete ms. Length: no restriction. Pays $40/1,000 words.

Poetry: Avant-garde, free verse and traditional. Buys 100/year. Pays $25/page.

MANOA, A Pacific Journal of International Writing, University of Hawaii Press, 1733 Donaghho Rd., Honolulu HI 96822. (808)956-3070. Fax: (808)956-3083. Editors: Robert Shapard and Frank Stewart. Managing Editor: Darlaine Dudoit. Semiannual literary magazine. "No special slant. Just high quality literary fiction, poetry, essays, personal narrative. About half of each issue devoted to US writing, and half translations of new work from Pacific Rim nations. Our audience is primarily in the US, although expanding in Pacific Rim countries. US writing need not be confined to Pacific settings or subjects." Estab. 1989. Circ. 1,750. Pays on publication. Byline given. Buys first North American serial or non-exclusive, one-time reprint rights. Editorial lead time 6 months. Submit seasonal material 8 months in advance. Reports in 3 weeks on queries; 2 months on poetry mss, 4 months on fiction. Sample copy $7. Writer's guidelines free on request.

Nonfiction: Frank Stewart, editor. Book excerpts, essays, interview/profile, creative nonfiction or personal narrative related to literature or nature. No Pacific exotica. Buys 3-4 mss/year, excluding reviews. Query or send complete ms. Length: 1,000-5,000 words. Pays $25/printed page, plus contributor copies.

Fiction: Ian MacMillan, fiction editor. "We're potentially open to anything of literary quality, though usually not genre fiction as such." No Pacific exotica. Buys 12-18 mss/year in the US (excluding translation). Send complete ms. Length: 1,000-10,000. Pays $100-500 normally ($25/printed page).

Poetry: Frank Stewart, editor. No light verse. Buys 40-50 poems/year. Pays $25.

Tips: "Although we are a Pacific journal, we are a general interest U.S. literary journal, not limited to Pacific settings or subjects. We're more likely to be interested in a story (or poem) set in Tennessee than Tonga (if we run a story set in Tonga, it will probably be by a Tongan writer). Translations are least open to freelancers, since these are usually solicited by a special guest editor for a special feature."

THE MASSACHUSETTS REVIEW, Memorial Hall, University of Massachusetts, Amherst MA 01003. (413)545-2689. Editors: Mary Heath, Jules Chametzky and Paul Jenkins. Quarterly magazine. Pays on publication. Publishes ms 6-18 months after acceptance. Buys first North American serial rights. Reports in 3 months. Mss will not be returned unless accompanied by SASE. Sample copy $5 with 2 first class stamps.

Nonfiction: Articles on literary criticism, women, public affairs, art, philosophy, music and dance. Length: 6,500 words average. Pays $50.

Fiction: Short stories or chapters from novels when suitable for independent publication. Length: 25 pages maximum. Pays $50.

Poetry: 35¢/line or $10 minimum.

Tips: "No fiction manuscripts are considered from June to October."

MICHIGAN QUARTERLY REVIEW, 3032 Rackham Bldg., University of Michigan, Ann Arbor MI 48109-1070. Editor: Laurence Goldstein. 75% freelance written. Prefers to work with published/established writers. Quarterly. Estab. 1962. Circ. 2,000. Publishes ms an average of 1 year after acceptance. Pays on publication. Buys first serial rights. Reports in 2 months. Sample copy $2.50 with 2 first class stamps.

Nonfiction: "*MQR* is open to general articles directed at an intellectual audience. Essays ought to have a personal voice and engage a significant subject. Scholarship must be present as a foundation, but we are not interested in specialized essays directed only at professionals in the field. We prefer ruminative essays, written in a fresh style and which reach interesting conclusions. We also like memoirs and interviews with significant historical or cultural resonance." Length: 2,000-5,000 words. Pays $100-150, sometimes more.

Fiction and Poetry: No restrictions on subject matter or language. "We publish about 10 stories a year and are very selective. We like stories which are unusual in tone and structure, and innovative in language." Send complete ms. Pays $10/published page.

Tips: "Read the journal and assess the range of contents and the level of writing. We have no guidelines to offer or set expectations; every manuscript is judged on its unique qualities. On essays—query with a very thorough description of the argument and a copy of the first page. Watch for announcements of special issues, which are usually expanded issues and draw upon a lot of freelance writing. Be aware that this is a university quarterly that publishes a limited amount of fiction and poetry; that it is directed at an educated audience, one that has done a great deal of reading in all types of literature."

MID-AMERICAN REVIEW, Dept. of English, Bowling Green State University, Bowling Green OH 43403. (419)372-2725. Editor: George Looney. Willing to work with new/unpublished writers. Semiannual literary magazine of "the highest quality fiction, poetry and translations of contemporary poetry and fiction." Also publishes critical articles and book reviews of contemporary literature. Estab. 1972. Pays on publication. Publishes ms an average of 3-6 months after acceptance. Byline given. Buys one-time rights. Reports in 4 months. Current issue $5, back issues for $4; rare back issues $10.

Fiction: Character-oriented, literary. Buys 12 mss/year. Send complete ms; do not query. Pays $7/page up to $50.

Poetry: Strong imagery, strong sense of vision. Buys 60 poems/year. Pays $7/page up to $50.

Tips: "We are seeking translations of contemporary authors from all languages into English; submissions must include the original."

MODERN HAIKU, P.O. Box 1752, Madison WI 53701-1752. Editor: Robert Spiess. 90% freelance written. Triannual magazine of haiku. "*Modern Haiku* is the foremost international English language haiku journal. We are open to all schools of haiku but do not publish sentimental, pretty-pretty, striving-for-effect or to-startle work." Estab. 1969. Circ. 675. **Pays on acceptance.** Byline given. Buys first North American serial rights. Editorial lead time 3 months. Reports in 2 weeks. Sample copy $4.85.

Nonfiction: Essays. Buys 30 mss/year. Send complete ms. Pays $5/printed page.

Poetry: Haiku. "Send poems that can be recited in one breath length." Pays $1/haiku.

Tips: "A haiku is a poem written from the body's center of gravity, not from the head—written through the intelligence of the heart, not the mind. Forget the idea that a haiku must be 17 syllables; a haiku is an up-to-a-breath length *poem*, not an exercise in arithmetic."

ALWAYS enclose a self-addressed, stamped envelope (SASE) with all your queries and correspondence.

NEGATIVE CAPABILITY, 62 Ridgelawn Dr. E., Mobile AL 36608. Editor: Sue Walker. Managing Editor: Richard Beyer. 99% freelance written. Triannual literary journal. "Negative capability seeks work that lingers in the mind after the pages of the book have been closed. We want work that acts as an axe that breaks the frozen sea within us." Estab. 1981. Circ. 1,000. Pays on publication. Byline given. Buys first North American serial rights. Submit seasonal material 6 months in advance. Query for electronic submissions. Reports in 6 weeks on mss. Sample copy $5. Writer's guidelines free on request.

Nonfiction: Essays, general interest, humor, interview/profile, opinion, personal experience, photo feature and religious. Upcoming issue on literature and food: poems and stories related to eating and dining. Buys 6-8 mss/year. Send complete ms. Pays in contributor copies for nonfiction.

Photos: State availability of photos with submissions. Reviews 5 × 7 prints. Offers no additional payment for photos. Captions and identification of subjects required. Buys one-time rights.

Fiction: No pornography. Buys 30 mss/year. Pays $25.

Poetry: Avant-garde, free verse, haiku, light verse and traditional. Buys 100 poems/year. Submit maximum 5 poems.

Fillers: Anecdotes, gags to be illustrated by cartoonist, short humor.

NEW ENGLAND REVIEW, Middlebury College, Middlebury VT 05753. (802)388-3711, ext 5075. Editors: T.R. Hummer and Devon Jersild. Office Manager: Toni Best. 99% freelance written. Quarterly magazine covering contemporary literature. "We print a wide range of contemporary poetry, fiction, essays and reviews." Circ. 3,200. Pays on publication. Publishes ms an average of 6 months after acceptance. Byline given. Buys first-time rights. Reports in 2 months. Sample copy $7. For sample copy, write UPNE, 23 S. Main, Hanover, NH, 03755. Writer's guidelines for #10 SASE.

Nonfiction: Book excerpts, essays, general interest, humor and personal experience. Buys 10 mss/year. Send complete ms. Length: 500-6,000 words. Pays $10/page, $20 minimum.

Photos: Also accepts drawings, woodcuts and etchings. Send with submission. Reviews transparencies and prints. Offers $60 minimum for cover art. Captions and identification of subjects required. Buys one-time rights.

Fiction: Buys 30 mss/year. Send complete ms. Send one story at a time. Pays $10/page, $20 minimum.

Poetry: Buys 75 poems/year. Submit up to 6 at one time. Pays $10/page, $20 minimum.

Tips: "Read at least one issue to get an idea of our range, standards and style. Don't submit simultaneously to other publications. All sections are open. We look for writing that's intelligent, well-informed and well-crafted. We do not read during the summer (June 1 to September 1)."

● Formerly *New England Review/Breadloaf Quarterly*, this magazine is making fine strides in editorial content and focus under the editorship of T.R. Hummer, who made similar strides several years ago with the *Kenyon Review*.

THE NORTH AMERICAN REVIEW, University of Northern Iowa, Cedar Falls IA 50614-0516. (319)273-6455. Editor: Robley Wilson. 50% freelance written. Bimonthly. Circ. 5,000. Buys all rights for nonfiction and North American serial rights for fiction and poetry. Pays on publication. Publishes ms an average of 1 year after acceptance. Reports in 10 weeks. Sample copy $4.

● Now published six times per year rather than quarterly, this is one of the oldest and most prestigious literary magazines in the country. Also one of the most entertaining—and a tough market for the young writer.

Nonfiction: No restrictions, but most nonfiction is commissioned by magazine. Query. Rate of payment arranged.

Fiction: No restrictions; highest quality only. Length: open. Pays minimum $10/published page. Fiction department closed (no mss read) from April 1 to December 31. "Not reading prose until 1/1/94."

Poetry: Peter Cooley, department editor. No restrictions; highest quality only. Length: open. Pays 50¢/line minimum.

‡OASIS, P.O. Box 626, Largo FL 34649-0626. (813)587-9552. Editor/Publisher: Neal Storrs. 100% freelance written. Bimonthly magazine. "*Oasis* is not slanted toward any particular audience, unless it's an audience of people interested in what I hope will be high-quality contemporary fiction, nonfiction and poetry." Estab. 1992. Circ. 150. Pays on publication. Publishes ms an average of 2 months after acceptance. Byline given. Buys one-time rights. Editorial lead time 2 months. Accepts simultaneous and previously published submissions (in certain cases). Send photocopy of article or short story or typed ms with rights for sale noted and information about when and where the article previously appeared. For reprints, pays 100% of the amount paid for an original article. Query for electronic submissions. Reports in 2 weeks. Sample copy $4.95. Writer's guidelines for #10 SASE.

Nonfiction: Book excerpts, essays, expose, general interest, historical/nostalgic, humor and interview/profile. "No articles in which quality of writing is not a primary concern." Buys 8 mss/year. Send complete ms. Length: 1,000-7,000 words. Pays $15-50 for unsolicited articles.

Fiction: Mainstream. No children's. Buys 30 mss/year. Send complete ms. Length: 1,000-7,000 words. Pays $15-50.

Poetry: Avant-garde, free verse and haiku. Buys 30. Pays $5/poem.

Tips: "I prefer well-written prose and poetry that feels authentic as well as original. Doesn't everybody? Professionalism in packaging predisposes me to expect a better product, and it usually is. No specific tips: take your best shot and let it fly. And remember that I'm on your side; I want to love your submission as much as you want me to."

THE OHIO REVIEW, Ellis Hall, Ohio University, Athens OH 45701-2979. (614)593-1900. Editor: Wayne Dodd. 40% freelance written. Triannual magazine. "A balanced, informed engagement of contemporary American letters, with special emphasis on poetics." Circ. 2,000. Publishes ms an average of 8 months after acceptance. Rights acquired vary with author and material; usually buys first serial or first North American serial rights. Unsolicited material will be read only September-May. Reports in 10 weeks.

Nonfiction, Fiction and Poetry: Buys essays of general intellectual and special literary appeal. Not interested in narrowly focused scholarly articles. Seeks writing that is marked by clarity, liveliness and perspective. Interested in the best fiction and poetry. Submit complete ms. Buys 75 unsolicited mss/year. Pays minimum $5/page, plus copies.

Tips: "Make your query very brief, not gabby—one that describes some publishing history, but no extensive bibliographies. We publish mostly poetry—short fiction, some book reviews."

THE PARIS REVIEW, 45-39 171st Place, Flushing NY 11358. Submit mss to 541 E. 72nd St., New York NY 10021. Editor: George A. Plimpton. Quarterly. Buys all rights. Pays on publication. Reporting time varies. Address submissions to proper department. Sample copy $8. Writer's guidelines for #10 SASE (from Flushing Office). Reporting time can be 6 months or more.

Fiction: Study the publication. No length limit. Pays up to $600. Makes award of $1,000 in annual Aga Khan fiction contest. Awards $1,500 in John Train Humor Prize contest.

Poetry: Richard Howard, poetry editor. Study the publication. Pay varies according to length. $50 minimum. Awards $1,000 in Bernard F. Conners Poetry Prize contest.

● Still one of the top literary magazines in the country, but its commitment to discovering new writers and to literary irreverence and experimentation seems to be waning. Often very slow to respond on submissions. A tough market.

PIG IRON MAGAZINE, Pig Iron Press, P.O. Box 237, Youngstown OH 44501-0237. (216)747-6932. Editor-in-Chief: Jim Villani. 95% freelance written. Annual magazine emphasizing literature/art for writers, artists and intelligent lay audience interested in popular culture. Circ. 1,500. Buys one-time rights. Pays on publication. Publishes ms an average of 6-18 months after acceptance. Byline given. Previously published submissions OK. Reports in 3 months. Sample copy $4; writer's guidelines and current theme for #10 SASE.

Nonfiction: General interest, personal opinion, criticism, new journalism and lifestyle. Buys 3 mss/year. Query. Length: 8,000 words maximum. Pays $5/page minimum.

Photos: Submit photo material with query. Pays $5 minimum for 5×7 or 8×10 b&w glossy prints. Buys one-time rights.

Fiction: Narrative fiction, psychological fiction, environment, avant-garde, experimental, metafiction, satire and parody. Buys 4-12 mss/issue. Submit complete ms. Length: 8,000 words maximum. Pays $5 minimum.

Poetry: Avant-garde and free verse. Buys 25-50/issue. Submit in batches of 5 or less. Length: open. Pays $5 minimum.

Tips: "Looking for fiction and poetry that is sophisticated, elegant, mature and polished. Interested in literary works that are consistent with the fundamental characteristics of modern and contemporary literature, including works that address alienation, the unconscious, loss, despair and historical discontinuity."

THE PINEHURST JOURNAL, P.O. Box 360747, Milpitas CA 95036-0747. (510)440-9259. Editor: Michael K. McNamara. Contributing Editor: Kathleen M. McNamara. 90% freelance written. Quarterly magazine of distinctive fiction, nonfiction and poetry. "For an educated audience appreciative of polished, thought-provoking work. Audience is 25-75." Estab. 1990. Circ. 250. Pays on publication. Publishes ms an average of 1-4 months after acceptance. Byline given. Buys one-time rights. Submit seasonal/holiday material 6 months in advance. Simultaneous submissions OK, if identified as such. Offers 100% kill fee. Reports in 2 months. Sample copy $5. Writer's guidelines for #10 SASE.

Nonfiction: Book or theater reviews, essays, historical/nostalgic, profile or general interest. No Op-ed. Buys 2-4 mss/year. Query for reviews and profiles; otherwise send complete ms. Length: 1,500-3,500 words. Pays $5 plus 1 contributor copy. Needs b&w artwork, no photos. Pays 1 contributor copy for artwork.

Fiction: Experimental, light fantasy, gay, historical, horror, wry humor, lesbian, mainstream, mystery, slice-of-life and suspense. No formula romance or western. No hard sci-fi, occult, swords and sorcery, slasher, porno, travel or religious. Buys 60-70 mss/year. Send complete ms. Length: 750-4,000 words. Pays $5 plus 1 contributor copy.

Poetry: Avant-garde, free verse, haiku, light verse and traditional. Buys 90-110 poems/year. Submit maximum 6 poems. Length: 2-24 lines. Pays contributor copy.

Tips: "Try to make each word pull its own weight but not at the expense of warmth. Spend the extra 25 words, but don't overly embellish. Polish and punctuation are very important to us. Please enclose a 20-40 word bio. This can be publishing success or whatever you're comfortable with. All areas are equally open although nonfiction might be the hardest to crack because of the limited number of topics."

PLOUGHSHARES, Emerson College, Dept. M, 100 Beacon St., Boston MA 02116. Executive Director: DeWitt Henry. Triquarterly magazine for "readers of serious contemporary literature: students, educators, adult public." Circ. 4,500. Pays on publication. Publishes ms an average of 6 months after acceptance. Buys first North American serial rights. Reports in 5 months. Sample/back issue $6. Writer's guidelines for SASE. Reading period: August 1-April 1.

• A competitive and highly prestigious market. Rotating and guest editors make cracking the line-up even tougher, since it's difficult to know what is appropriate to send.

Nonfiction: Personal and literary essays. Length: 5,000 words maximum. Pays $50. Reviews (assigned). Length: 500 words maximum. Pays $10/page, $50 maximum.

Fiction: Literary and mainstream. Buys 25-35 unsolicited mss/year. Length: 300-6,000 words. Pays $10/page.

Poetry: Traditional forms, blank verse, free verse and avant-garde. Length: open. Pays $20/poem minimum, $10/page.

Tips: "Because of our policy of rotating editors, we suggest writers send a #10 SASE for guidelines on themes and reading periods before submitting."

POETRY, The Modern Poetry Association, 60 W. Walton St., Chicago IL 60610. (312)280-4870. Editor: Joseph Parisi. Managing Editor: Helen Lothrop Klaviter. 100% freelance written. Monthly poetry magazine. Estab. 1912. Circ. 7,500. Pays on publication. Byline given. Buys all rights. "Copyright assigned to author on request." Submit seasonal/holiday material 6 months in advance. Reports in 3 months. Sample copy $3.50. Writer's guidelines for #10 SASE.

Poetry: All styles and subject matter. Buys 180-250 poems/year. Submit maximum 4 poems. All lengths considered. Pays $2/line.

PRAIRIE FIRE, A Canadian Magazine of New Writing, Prairie Fire Press, Inc., Room 423, 100 Arthur St., Winnipeg, Manitoba R3B 1H3 Canada. Fax: (204)942-1555. Editor: Andris Taskans. 99% freelance written. Quarterly literary magazine. "Literary focus—poems, fiction, book reviews, primarily over-the-transom submissions and judged solely on quality; however, commissioned material is usually of a local interest. Most readers are Canadians, with locals predominant." Estab. 1978. Circ. 1,200. Pays on publication. Publishes ms an average of 6 months after acceptance (18 months for poetry). Offers $20-50 kill fee. Buys first North American serial rights. Editorial lead time 6 months. Reports in 2-4 months. Sample copy $7.95 (Canadian). Writer's guidelines for #10 SASE.

Nonfiction: Essays (literary), interview/profile (of authors), personal experience (writers' memoirs) and book reviews. "Upcoming special issue: New Native (or aboriginal) Canadian writing, September 1994. Deadline: April 1, 1994." Buys 40-60 mss/year. Query. Length: 200-4,000 words. Pays $40 minimum for articles. Sometimes pays expenses of writers on assignment.

Photos: State availability of photos with submission. Reviews contact sheets, transparencies and prints. Offers $25-50/photo. Captions and identification of subjects required. Buys one-time rights.

Fiction: Contact Fiction Reading Committee. Experimental, mainstream and novel excerpts. Buys 8-10 mss/year. Send complete ms. Length: 700-5,000 words. Pays $45 minimum (depends on length).

Poetry: Contact Poetry Reading Committee. Avant-garde and free verse. "No religious/sentimental poetry." Buys 60-80 poems/year. Submit maximum 6 poems. Pays $35 minimum (depends on length).

THE PRAIRIE JOURNAL of Canadian Literature, P.O. Box 61203, Brentwood Postal Services, 217K-3630 Brentwood Rd. NW, Calgary, Alberta T2L 2K6 Canada. Editor: A. Burke. 100% freelance written. Semiannual magazine of Canadian literature. Estab. 1983. Circ. 400. Pays on publication; "honorarium depends on grant." Byline given. Buys first North American serial rights. Reports 6 months. Sample copy $4 and IRCs.

Nonfiction: Interview/profile and scholarly. Buys 5 mss/year. Query with published clips. Include IRC. Pays $25-100 depending on length. Pays contributor copies or honoraria for literary work.

Photos: Send photocopies of photos with submission. Offers additional payment for photos accepted with ms. Identification of subjects required. Buys one-time rights.

Fiction: Literary. Buys 10 mss/year. Send complete ms.

Poetry: Avant-garde and free verse. Buys 10 poems/year. Submit maximum 6-10 poems.

Tips: "Commercial writers are advised to submit elsewhere. Art needed, b&w pen and ink drawings or good-quality photocopy. We are strictly small press editors interested in highly talented, serious artists. We are oversupplied with fiction but seek more high-quality poetry, especially the contemporary long poem or sequences from longer works."

PRISM INTERNATIONAL, Department of Creative Writing, Buch E462, 1866 Main Mall, University of British Columbia, Vancouver, British Columbia V6T 1Z1 Canada. Editor-in-Chief: Murray Logan. Executive Editor: Patricia Gabin. 100% freelance written. Eager to work with new/unpublished writers. Quarterly magazine emphasizing contemporary literature, including translations, for university and public libraries, and private subscribers. Estab. 1959. Circ. 1,000. Pays on publication. Publishes ms an average of 3 months after acceptance. Buys first North American serial rights. Reports in 3 months. Sample copy $5. Writer's guidelines for #10 SAE with 1 first class Canadian stamp (Canadian entries) or 1 IRC (US entries).
Nonfiction: *"Creative* nonfiction that reads like fiction." No reviews, tracts or scholarly essays.
Fiction: Zsuzsi Gartner, fiction editor. Experimental and traditional. Buys 3-5 mss/issue. Send complete ms. Length: 5,000 words maximum. Pays $20/printed page and 1-year subscription.
Poetry: Shannon Stewart, poetry editor. Avant-garde and traditional. Buys 30 poems/issue. Submit maximum 6 poems. Pays $20/printed page and 1-year subscription.
Drama: One-acts preferred. Pays $20/printed page and 1-year subscription.
Tips: "We are looking for new and exciting fiction. Excellence is still our number one criterion. As well as poetry, imaginative nonfiction and fiction, we are especially open to translations of all kinds, very short fiction pieces and drama which works well on the page."

QUEEN'S QUARTERLY, A Canadian Review, Queen's University, Kingston, Ontario K7L 3N6 Canada. (613)545-2667. Editor: Boris Castel. Estab. 1893. Quarterly magazine covering a wide variety of subjects, including science, humanities, arts and letters, politics and history for the educated reader. 15% freelance written. Circ. 3,000. Pays on publication. Publishes ms an average of 2-3 months after acceptance. Byline given. Buys first North American serial rights. Requires 1 double-spaced hard copy and 1 copy on disk in WordPerfect. Reports in 1 month on mss. *Writer's Market* recommends allowing 2 months for reply. Sample copy $6.50.
Fiction: Historical, humorous, mainstream and science fiction. Buys 8-12 mss/year. Send complete ms. Length: 4,000 words maximum. Pays $80-150.
• No longer accepting fantasy fiction.
Poetry: Avant-garde, free verse, haiku, light verse and traditional. No "sentimental, religious, or first efforts by unpublished writers." Buys 25/year. Submit maximum 6 poems. Length: open. Pays $20-35.
Tips: "Poetry and fiction are most open to freelancers. Don't send less than the best. No multiple submissions. No more than 6 poems or one story per submission. We buy very few freelance submissions."

RIVER STYX, Big River Association, 14 S. Euclid, St. Louis MO 63108. (314)361-0043. Triannual literary magazine. *"River Styx* publishes the highest quality fiction, poetry, interviews, essays and visual art. We are an internationally distributed multicultural literary magazine." Estab. 1975. Pays on publication. Publishes ms an average of 1 year after acceptance. Byline given. Buys one-time rights. Accepts simultaneous submissions if so noted. Reports in 4 months on mss. Sample copy $7. Writer's guidelines for #10 SASE.
Nonfiction: Essays, interview. Buys 2-5 mss/year. Send complete mss. Pays $8/page plus contributor copy.
Photos/Art: Send with submission. Reviews 5×7 or 8×10 b&w prints. Pays $8/page. Buys one-time rights.
Fiction: Mainstream and literary. Buys 6 mss/year. Send complete ms. Pays $8/page.
Poetry: Avant-garde, free verse and traditional. No religious. Buys 40-50 poems/year. Submit maximum 6 poems. Pays $8/page.

SHOOTING STAR REVIEW, Black Literary Magazine, Shooting Star Productions, Inc., 7123 Race St., Pittsburgh PA 15208-1423. (412)731-7464. Publisher: Sandra Gould Ford. 90% freelance written. Quarterly Black literary magazine. *"Shooting Star Review* employs the arts to increase understanding and appreciation of the Black experience." Circ. 1,500. Pays on publication. Publishes ms an average of 3-9 months after acceptance. Byline given. Buys first North American serial rights. Submit seasonal/holiday material 6 months in advance. Simultaneous submissions OK. Query for electronic submissions. Reports in 2 weeks on queries; 3 months on mss. Sample copy $3 for 9×12 SAE with 5 first class stamps. Writer's guidelines for SASE.
Nonfiction: Book excerpts, essays, historical/nostalgic, interview/profile, opinion, personal experience and photo feature. Each issue has a special theme. Buys 20 mss/year. Query. Length: 750-2,500 words. Pays $10-25 plus 2 contributor copies.
Photos: Send photos with submission. Reviews contact sheets, 35mm and 4×5 transparencies, and 5×7 and larger prints. Payment negotiated. Captions, model releases and identification of subjects required. Buys one-time rights.
Fiction: Historical, mainstream, novel excerpts and slice-of-life vignettes. Buys 20 mss/year. Send complete ms. Length: 3,500 words maximum. Pays $10-50 maximum plus 2 contributor copies.
Poetry: Avant-garde, free verse and traditional. Buys 40-60 poems/year. Submit maximum 6 poems at one time. Length: 50 lines maximum. Pays $10 maximum plus 2 contributor copies.
Tips: "Writers should keep in mind that *Shooting Star Review* regularly reprints classic fiction about the Black experience. From modern writers, we look for innovative, well structured, challenging, even controversial, creative writing. Short fiction is most open to freelancers. We get very excited about innovative subject treatment by writers who understand the elements of fine writing and demonstrate familiarity with the specific needs of short fiction."

SHORT FICTION BY WOMEN, Box 1276, Stuyvesant Station, New York NY 10009-1276. Editor: Rachel Whalen. 100% freelance written. Triannual literary magazine featuring fiction by women. Estab. 1991. Circ. 1,000. Pays on publication. Publishes ms an average of 4 months after acceptance. Byline given. Offers 100% kill fee. Buys first serial rights. No seasonal material. Simultaneous submissions OK. No reprints. Reports in 2 weeks on queries; 2 months on mss. "Reporting time may be longer if story is held for further consideration." Sample copy $6. Writer's guidelines for #10 SASE.

Fiction: Interested in all unpublished, top-quality short fiction: experimental, mainstream, novel excerpts, slice-of-life vignettes, gay and lesbian. "No horror, romance, mystery, erotica, religious or poetry." Buys 30-45 mss/year. Send complete ms. Length: 200-20,000 words. "Pay depends on length of work and funds available."

Tips: "*Short Fiction by Women* seeks superbly crafted fiction that somehow illuminates or translates our lives and world. Stories must be highly readable—they should grab the reader's interest and hold it, spellbound, until the last page. For examples of what works for us, writers should get a sample copy. All forms of short fiction are welcome: short stories, novel excerpts, short novels plays. Our special interest: works of more than 5,000 words."

SING HEAVENLY MUSE!, Women's Poetry and Prose, Sing Heavenly Muse! Inc., Box 13320, Minneapolis MN 55414. (612)822-8713. Assistant Editor: Ruth Berman. 100% freelance written. Annual journal of women's literature. Circ. 1,500. Pays on publication. Publishes ms an average of 1 year after acceptance. Byline given. Buys first North American serial rights. Reprints OK; send information about when and where the story previously appeared. Pays 100% of their fee for an original story. Reports in 3 months. Sample copy $4. Writer's guidelines for #10 SASE.

● Manuscripts that pass the first screening may be held longer.

Fiction: Women's literature, journal pieces, memoir and novel excerpts. Buys 15-20 mss/year. Length: 5,000 words maximum. Pays $15-25; contributors receive 2 free copies.

Poetry: Avant-garde, free verse, haiku, light verse and traditional. Accepts 75-100 poems/year. No limit on length. Pays $15-25.

Tips: "To meet our needs, writing must be feminist and women-centered. Reading periods vary. Issues are often related to a specific theme; writer should always query for guidelines and upcoming themes and reading periods before submitting manuscripts. We occasionally hold contests. Writers should query for contest guidelines."

THE SOUTHERN REVIEW, 43 Allen Hall, Louisiana State University, Baton Rouge LA 70803-5001. (504)388-5108. Fax: (504)388-5098. Editors: James Olney and Dave Smith. 75% freelance written. Works with a moderate number of new/unpublished writers each year. Quarterly magazine for academic, professional, literary, intellectual audience. Estab. 1965. Circ. 3,100. Buys first serial rights only. Byline given. Pays on publication. Publishes ms an average of 18 months after acceptance. No queries. Reports in 3 months. Sample copy $5. Writer's guidelines for #10 SASE.

Nonfiction: Essays with careful attention to craftsmanship, technique and to seriousness of subject matter. "Willing to publish experimental writing if it has a valid artistic purpose. Avoid extremism and sensationalism. Essays exhibit thoughtful and sometimes severe awareness of the necessity of literary standards in our time." Emphasis on contemporary literature, especially Southern culture and history. Minimum number of footnotes. Buys 25 mss/year. Length: 4,000-10,000 words. Pays $12/page for prose.

Fiction and Poetry: Short stories of lasting literary merit, with emphasis on style and technique. Length: 4,000-8,000 words. Pays $12/page for prose; $20/page for poetry.

SOUTHWEST REVIEW, 307 Fondren Library W., Box 374, Southern Methodist University, Dallas TX 75275-0374. (214)768-1036. Editor: Willard Spiegelman. 100% freelance written. Works with a small number of new/unpublished writers each year. Quarterly magazine for "adults and college graduates with literary interests and some interest in the Southwest, but subscribers are from all over America and some foreign countries." Circ. 1,500. Pays on publication. Publishes ms an average of 1 year after acceptance. Buys first North American serial rights. Byline given. Reports in up to 3 months. Sample copy $5.

Nonfiction: "Literary essays, social and political problems, history (especially Southwestern), folklore (especially Southwestern), the arts, etc. Articles should be appropriate for a literary quarterly; no feature stories. Critical articles should consider writer's whole body of work, not just one book. History should use new primary sources or new perspective, not syntheses of old material." Interviews with writers, historical articles. Query. Length: 3,500-7,000 words.

Fiction: No limitations on subject matter for fiction; high literary quality is only criterion. Prefers stories of experimental and mainstream. Submit complete ms. Length: 1,500-7,000 words. The John H. McGinnis Memorial Award of $1,000 made annually for fiction and nonfiction pieces that appeared in *SWR* during preceding year.

Poetry: No limitations on subject matter. Not particularly interested in broadly humorous, religious or sentimental poetry. Free verse, some avant-garde forms; open to all serious forms of poetry. "There are no arbitrary limits on length, but we find shorter poems are easier to fit into our format." The Elizabeth Matchett Stover Memorial Award of $150 made annually for a poem published in *SWR*.

Tips: "The most frequent mistakes we find in work that is submitted for consideration are lack of attention to grammar and syntax and little knowledge of the kind of thing we're looking for. Writers should look at a couple of issues before submitting."

SPECTRUM, Spectrum/Anna Maria College, Box 72-F, Sunset Lane, Paxton MA 01612-1198. (508)849-3450. Editor: Robert H. Goepfert. Managing Editor: Robert Lemieux. "*Spectrum* is a multidisciplinary national publication aimed particularly at scholarly generalists affiliated with small liberal arts colleges." Estab. 1985. Circ. 1,000. Pays on publication. Publishes ms an average of 6 months after acceptance. Byline given. Publication copyrighted. Buys first North American serial rights. Reports in 2 months. Sample copy $3. Writer's guidelines for #10 SASE.
Nonfiction: Essays, general interest, historical/nostalgic, inspirational, opinion and interdisciplinary. Buys 8 mss/year. Send complete ms. Length: 3,000-15,000 words. Pays $20 for unsolicited articles.
Photos: State availability of photos with submission. Black and white 8×10 prints only. Offers no additional payment for photos accepted with ms. Model releases and identification of subjects required. Buys one-time rights.
Columns/Departments: Reviews (books/recordings/audiovisual aids), 300-500 words; (educational computer software), up to 2,000 words. Buys 2 mss/year. Send complete ms. Length: 300-2,000 words. Pays $20.
Fiction: Ethnic, experimental, fantasy, historical, humorous, mainstream, romance and slice-of-life vignettes. "No erotica, mystery, western or science fiction." Buys 2 ms/year. Send complete ms. Length: 3,000 words. Pays $20.
Poetry: Avant-garde, free verse, light verse and traditional. No long poems (over 100 lines). Buys 8 poems/year. Submit maximum 6 poems.
Tips: "We welcome short fiction and poetry, as well as short- to medium-length articles that are interdisciplinary or that deal with one discipline in a manner accessible to the scholarly-generalist reader. Articles referring to or quoting work of other authors should be footnoted appropriately. All areas are equally open to freelancers. In general, originality and relative brevity are paramount, although we will occasionally publish longer works (e.g., articles) that explore ideas not subject to a briefer treatment."

THE SPIRIT THAT MOVES US, The Spirit That Moves Us Press, Inc., P.O. Box 820, Jackson Heights NY 11372-0820. (718)426-8788. Editor: Morty Sklar. Annual book of literary works. "We don't push any 'schools'; we're open to many styles and almost any subject matter. We favor work that expresses feeling, whether subtle or passionate. Every two years we publish *Editor's Choice: Fiction, Poetry & Art from the U.S. Small Press*, which consists of selections from nominations made by other small literary publishers. When writers see our open call for nominations for this anthology, they should encourage their publishers to nominate their and other people's work." Estab. 1975. Pays on publication. Publishes ms an average of 3 months after acceptance. Byline given. Buys first North American serial and/or second serial (reprint) rights. Accepts simultaneous submissions, if so noted, and previously published submissions (only for those collections that we specify). Reports in 2 weeks on queries; 2 months after deadline date on mss (nothing is accepted until everything is read). $5 for *15th Anniversary Issue*; $10 for *Editor's Choice* to readers of *Writer's Market*.
Nonfiction: Book excerpts, essays, interview/profile and personal experience. Upcoming special issues include: *Editor's Choice IV: Essays from the U.S. Small Press*, and *Phoenix: Stories, Essays & Poems from Ex-Drug-Addicts* (both to be published in 1994). Buys 20-30 mss for special issues. Query; "or if you've seen our call for mss and know the theme, send the ms." Length: 8,500 words maximum. Pays $15-25 and offers extra copies at 40% discount. Pays in contributor copies if so requested by author. "Royalty set-up for single-author books, with a cash advance."
Photos: Reviews contact sheets and 8×10 prints. Offers $15/photo; $100 for cover photos. Buys one-time rights. "Photos are considered for artistic merit, and not just illustrative function. All art that we use has to stand on its own."
Fiction: "Nothing slick or commercial." Buys 15-30 mss/year. Query; "or if you know our theme and time frame, send complete ms." Length: 8,500 words maximum. Pays $15-25.
Poetry: "Not interested in work that just tries to be smart, flashy, sensational; if it's technically skilled but conveys no feeling, we don't care about it for publication. We were the first US publisher to bring out a collection by the Czech poet Nobel Laureate of 1984 — and before he won the Nobel prize." Buys 50-100 poems/year. Pays $15 (depends on length and funding/sales obtained).
Tips: "Writers and visual artists should query first to see what we're working on if they haven't seen our latest call for mss in *Poets & Writers* magazine or elsewhere. Send #10 SASE for themes and time frames."

‡STAND MAGAZINE, 179 Wingrove Rd., Newcastle Upon Tyne NE4 9DA United Kingdom. (091)273-3280. Editors: Jon Silkin, Lorna Tracy, Rodney Pybus. Managing Editor: Philip Bomford. 99% freelance written. Quarterly magazine covering short fiction, poetry, criticism and reviews. "*Stand Magazine* was given this name because it was begun as a stand against apathy towards new writing and in social relations. Politically left of center, it has always shown a strong awareness of social injustices and emphasized the need for commitment on the part of the individual writer to his or her community." Estab. 1952. Circ. 4,500 worldwide. Pays on publication. Publishes ms an average of 2 years after acceptance. Byline given. Buys first rights. Editorial lead time 2 months. Reports in 1 week on queries; 1-2 months on mss. Sample cost $6.50. Writer's guidelines for sufficient number of IRCs.

Nonfiction: Essays, interview/profile, reviews of poetry/fiction. "Reviews are generally commissioned from known freelancers." Buys 8 mss/year. Query. Length: 200-5,000 words. Pays $30.

Fiction: "No genre fiction." Buys 8-10 mss/year. Send complete ms. Length: 8,000 words maximum. Pays $45/thousand words.

Poetry: Avant-garde, free verse, traditional. Buys 30-40 poems/year. Submit maximum 6 poems. Pays $45/poem.

Tips: "Poetry/fiction areas are most open to freelancers." Submissions should be accompanied by UK SAE or sufficient IRCs.

STORY, F&W Publications, Inc., 1507 Dana Ave., Cincinnati OH 45207-1005. (513)531-2222. Editor: Lois Rosenthal. 100% freelance written. Quarterly literary magazine of short fiction. "We want short stories and self-inclusive novel excerpts that are extremely well written. Our audience is sophisticated and accustomed to the finest imaginative writing by new and established writers." Estab. 1931. Circ. 30,000. **Pays on acceptance.** Byline given. Buys first North American serial rights. Reports in 1 month. Sample copy $5.95 for 7½×10½ SAE with 5 first class stamps. Writer's guidelines for #10 SASE.

 • This magazine won The National Magazine Award for Fiction in 1992.

Fiction: No genre fiction. Buys 40-50 mss/year. Send complete ms. Length: up to 8,000 words. Pays $400.

Tips: "No replies without SASE."

THE STRAIN, Premiere Interactive Arts Magazine, Box 330507, Houston TX 77233. (713)733-6042. Editor: Norman Clark Stewart Jr. 80% freelance written. Monthly literary compilation of photocopied mss. Estab. 1987. Circ. 200-1,000. Pays on publication. Publishes ms an average of 3 years after acceptance. Byline given. Buys first, one-time or second serial rights. Makes work-for-hire assignments. Submit seasonal/holiday material 4 months in advance. Previously published submissions OK. Reports in up to 2 years. Sample copy $5 for 9×12 SAE with 7 first class stamps. Writer's guidelines for #10 SAE with 2 first class stamps.

 • The primary purpose for this magazine is the exchange of ideas and criticism among its contributors and to develop or find material suitable for collections and anthologies.

Nonfiction: Alicia Alder, articles editor. Essays, expose, how-to, humor, photo feature, technical. Buys 2-20 mss/year. Send complete ms. Pays $5 minimum.

Photos: Send photos with submissions. Reviews transparencies and prints. Model releases and identification of subjects required. Buys one-time rights.

Columns/Departments: Charlie Mainze, editor. Multi-media performance art. Send complete ms. Pays $5 minimum.

Fiction: John Peterson, editor. Buys 1-35 mss/year. Send complete ms. Pays $5 minimum.

Poetry: Michael Bond, editor. Avant-garde, free verse, light verse and traditional. Buys 100. Submit maximum 5 poems. Pays $5 minimum.

TAMAQUA, Tamaqua Press, C120, Parkland College, 2400 W. Bradley Ave., Champaign IL 61821-1899. (217)351-2217. Fax: (217)351-2581. Editor-in-Chief: James McGowan. 100% freelance written. Semiannual magazine of literary and fine arts. "We are dedicated to being as open a forum as possible, publishing the best fiction, poetry, nonfiction, photography and artwork that we receive. We are particularly sensitive to emerging writers and artists." Estab. 1989. Circ. 2,000. Pays on publication. Byline given. Buys first North American serial rights. Simultaneous submissions OK. Query for electronic submissions. Reports in 3 weeks on queries; 3 months on mss. Sample copy $6 for 9×12 SAE with 7 first class stamps. Writer's guidelines for #10 SASE.

Nonfiction: Essays, historical/nostalgic, humor, opinion, personal experience, photo feature, travel and book reviews. Buys 6 mss/year. Query or send complete ms. Length: 10,000 words maximum. Pays $25-50.

Photos: State availability of photos with submission, or send photos with submission. Reviews contact sheets, transparencies and 5×5 and 6×10 prints. Offers $5-10/photo. Captions, model releases and identification of subjects required. Buys one-time rights.

Columns/Departments: Reviews (reviews/critiques/meditations on literary works, films, and art which go beyond the work itself. We seek personal/theoretical slant.), 2-10,000 words. Buys 2-6 mss/year. Query. Length: 1,000-10,000 words. Pays $25-50.

Fiction: "We are interested in all types of fiction, but we do not want to see stupid writing in any form." Buys 15 mss/year. Send complete ms. Length: 1-12,000 words. Pays $25-75.

Poetry: "We are interested in all types of poetry, but as in fiction, we do not want to see any stupid writing." Buys 125 poems/year. Pays $10-75.

Tips: "Nothing replaces knowledge of the market; hence, *study Tamaqua* and similar magazines to discern the difference between good, solid, intelligent literature and that which is not. All areas are equally open to freelancers."

TAMPA REVIEW, Humanities Division, University of Tampa, Tampa FL 33606-1490. (813)253-3333. Editor of Fiction: Andy Solomon, Box 135F. Editors of Poetry: Don Morrill, Box 115F; Kathy Van Spanckeren, Box 16F. 100% freelance written. Semiannual magazine of literary fiction and poetry. Estab. 1988. Circ. 5,000. Pays on publication. Publishes ms an average of 4 months after acceptance. Byline given. Buys first North American serial rights. Reports in 4 months on mss. Sample copy $10.
  • This magazine has increased its frequency from once to twice per year. The editors relate an increased demand for fiction and poetry.
Fiction: Mainstream and experimental. "We are far more concerned with quality than genre." Buys 8-10 mss/year. Send complete ms. Length: 1,000-6,000 words; slight preference for mss less than 20 pages. Pays $10/printed page.
Poetry: Buys 50 poems/year. Submit up to 5 poems at one time. Pays $10/printed page.

THEMA, Box 74109, Metairie LA 70033-4109. (504)887-1263. Editor: Virginia Howard. 100% freelance written. Quarterly literary magazine covering a different theme for each issue. "Journal is designed to stimulate creative thinking by challenging writers with unusual themes, such as "unrecognized at the airport" and "the Dreamland Café." Appeals to writers, teachers of creative writing and general reading audience." Estab. 1988. Circ. 350. **Pays on acceptance.** Byline given. Buys one-time rights. Reports in 2½ months on mss (after deadline for particular issue). Sample copy $5. Writer's guidelines for #10 SASE.
  • Query with SASE for upcoming themes.
Fiction: Adventure, ethnic, experimental, fantasy, historical, humorous, mainstream, mystery, religious, science fiction, slice-of-life vignettes, suspense and western. "No alternate lifestyle or erotica." Buys 48 mss/year. Send complete ms and *specify theme* for which it is intended. Pays $10-25.
Poetry: Avant-garde, free verse, haiku, light verse and traditional. No erotica. Buys 32 poems/year. Submit maximum 3 poems. Length: 4-50 lines. Pays $10.
Tips: "Be familiar with the themes. *Don't submit* unless you have an upcoming theme in mind. Specify the target theme on the first page of your manuscript or in a cover letter. Put your name on *first* page of manuscript only. (All submissions are judged in blind review after the deadline for a specified issue.) Most open to fiction and poetry. Don't be hasty when you consider a theme—mull it over and let it ferment in your mind. We appreciate interpretations that are carefully constructed, clever, subtle, well thought out."

THE THREEPENNY REVIEW, P.O. Box 9131, Berkeley CA 94709. (510)849-4545. Editor: Wendy Lesser. 100% freelance written. Works with small number of new/unpublished writers each year. Quarterly literary tabloid. "We are a general interest, national literary magazine with coverage of politics, the visual arts and the performing arts as well." Estab. 1980. Circ. 8,000. **Pays on acceptance.** Publishes ms an average of 1 year after acceptance. Byline given. Buys first North American serial rights. Reports in 1 month on queries; 2 months on mss. Sample copy $5 for 10 × 13 SAE with 5 first class stamps. Writer's guidelines for SASE.
Nonfiction: Essays, expose, historical, personal experience, book, film, theater, dance, music and art reviews. Buys 40 mss/year. Query with or without published clips or send complete ms. Length: 1,500-4,000 words. Pays $200.
Fiction: No fragmentary, sentimental fiction. Buys 10 mss/year. Send complete ms. Length: 800-4,000 words. Pays $200.
Poetry: Free verse and traditional. No poems "without capital letters or poems without a discernible subject." Buys 30 poems/year. Submit maximum 10 poems. Pays $100.
Tips: "Nonfiction (political articles, memoirs, reviews) is most open to freelancers."

‡TIMBERLINES, Lake City Writers' Forum, P.O. Box 34, Lake City CO 81235. Contact: Lynda Rivers. Estab. 1981. 100% freelance written. Annual magazine of short fiction, poetry, essays and creative nonfiction. Reviews mss from September through March. Deadline, March 1 for June publication. Likes nature/outdoor orientation, though not essential. Interested in new but capable writers. Reports in 6 months. SASE. Pays in copies. Sample copy $5.
Nonfiction: Essays and creative nonfiction. 2,500 words or less. Good writing with general appeal.
Fiction: 2,500 words or less. Well crafted. No theme restrictions, but well-written nature/outdoor stories will have an edge.
Poetry: Accessible but not trite; concise and concrete. Shorter poems have better chance because of space limitations. No rhymed doggerel.

TRIQUARTERLY, 2020 Ridge Ave., Northwestern University, Evanston IL 60208-4302. Editors: Reginald Gibbons and Susan Hahn. 70% freelance written. Eager to work with new/unpublished writers. Triannual magazine of fiction, poetry and essays, as well as artwork. Estab. 1964. Pays on publication. Publishes ms an average of 1 year after acceptance. Buys first serial and nonexclusive reprint rights. Reports in 3 months. Study magazine before submitting. Sample copy $4. Writer's guidelines for #10 SASE.
Nonfiction: Query before sending essays (no scholarly or critical essays except in special issues).
Fiction and Poetry: No prejudice against style or length of work; only seriousness and excellence are required. Buys 20-50 unsolicited mss/year. Pays $20/printed page.

UNIVERSITY OF WINDSOR REVIEW, Windsor, Ontario N9B 3P4 Canada. (519)253-4232. Editor: Joseph A. Quinn. Biannual for "the literate layman, the old common reader." Estab. 1965. Circ. 300. Buys first North American serial rights. Reports in 6 weeks. Sample copy $5 plus postage. Enclose SAE with IRCs.
Fiction: Alistair MacLeod, department editor. Publishes mainstream prose with open attitude toward themes. Length: 2,000-6,000 words. Pays $50.
Poetry: John Ditsky, department editor. Accepts traditional forms, blank verse, free verse and avant-garde. No epics. Pays $15.

WESTERN HUMANITIES REVIEW, University of Utah, Salt Lake City UT 84112-1107. (801)581-6070. Managing Editor: Kristoffer Jacobson. Quarterly magazine for educated readers. Circ. 1,200. **Pays on acceptance.** Publishes ms an average of 3-12 months after acceptance. Buys all rights. Simultaneous submissions OK. Reports in 3-5 months.
Nonfiction: Barry Weller, editor-in-chief. Authoritative, readable articles on literature, art, philosophy, current events, history, religion and anything in the humanities. Interdisciplinary articles encouraged. Departments on film and books. Buys 4-5 unsolicited mss/year. Pays $50-150.
Fiction: David Kranes, fiction editor. Any type, including experimental. Recent contributors include Robert Coover, Deborah Eisenberg, Chuck Rosenthal, Stephen Dixon, James McManus, Alan Singer, Cris Mazza, Norman Lavers and Francine Prose. Buys 8-12 mss/year. Send complete ms. Average payment $150.
Poetry: Richard Howard, poetry editor. Recent contributors include Allen Grossman, Joseph Brodsky, Daniel Halpern, Albert Goldbarth, Debora Greger, Jane Flanders, Lucie Brock-Broido and Jacqueline Osherow.
Tips: "Because of changes in our editorial staff, we urge familiarity with *recent* issues of the magazine. Inappropriate material will be returned without comment.

WILLOW SPRINGS, MS-1, Eastern Washington University, Cheney WA 99004. (509)458-6429. Editor: Nance Van Winckel. 100% freelance written. Semiannual literary magazine. "We publish quality contemporary poetry, fiction, nonfiction and works in translation." Estab. 1977. Circ. 1,000. Pays on publication. Publishes ms an average of 10 months after acceptance. Byline given. Buys all rights. Editorial lead time 2 months. Reports in 2 months. Sample copy $4.50. Writer's guidelines for #10 SASE.
Nonfiction: Essays. Buys 4 mss/year. Send complete ms. Pays $35.
Fiction: Literary fiction only. "No genre fiction, please." Buys 5-8 mss/year. Send complete ms. Pays $35 minimum.
Poetry: Avant-garde and free verse. "No haiku, light verse or religious." Buys 50-80 poems/year. Submit maximum 6 poems. Length: 12 pages maximum. Pays $10.
Tips: "Note: We do not read mss in June, July and August."
  • A magazine of growing reputation. Takes part in the AWP Intro Award program.

WITNESS, Oakland Community College, 27055 Orchard Lake Rd., Farmington Hills MI 48334. (313)471-7740. Editor: Peter Stine. 100% freelance written. Semiannual literary magazine. "*Witness* highlights the role of writer as witness. Alternate issues are thematic: holocaust, writings from prison, sixties, nature writing, sports in America, etc." Estab. 1987. Circ. 2,800. Pays on publication. Publishes ms an average of 1 year after acceptance. Byline given. Buys first North American serial rights. Editorial lead time 6 months. Accepts simultaneous submissions. Reports in 1 month on queries; 3 months on mss. Sample copy $5. Writer's guidelines free on request.
Nonfiction: Essays. Upcoming issue: Sports in America. Buys 10 mss/year. Send complete ms. Length: 1,000-8,000 words. Pays $6/page.
Fiction: Experimental, humorous, mainstream and literary. Buys 40 mss/year. Send complete ms. Length: 1,000-8,000 words. Pays $6/page.
Poetry: Avant-garde and traditional. Buys 15 poems/year. Submit maximum 4 poems. Pays $10/page.
  • A rising and energetic magazine. The frequent theme issues require more work from the writer in studying this market.

THE YALE REVIEW, P.O. Box 1902A Yale Station, New Haven CT 06520. Editor: J.D. McClatchy. Associate Editor: Wendy Wipprecht. Managing Editor: Ellen James. 20% freelance written. Buys first North American serial rights. Estab. 1911. Pays prior to publication. Publishes ms an average of 9 months after acceptance. "No writer's guidelines available. Consult back issues."
Nonfiction and Fiction: Authoritative discussions of politics, literature and the arts. Buys quality fiction. Length: 3,000-5,000 words. Pays $100-500.

YELLOW SILK: Journal of Erotic Arts, verygraphics, Box 6374, Albany CA 94706. (510)644-4188. Editor: Lily Pond. 90% freelance written. Prefers to work with published/established writers. Quarterly magazine of erotic literature and visual arts. "Editorial policy: All persuasions; no brutality. Our publication is artistic and literary, not pornographic or pandering. Humans are involved: heads, hearts and bodies – not just bodies alone; and the quality of the literature is as important as the erotic content." Circ. 16,000. Pays on publication. Publishes ms an average of 6 months after acceptance. Byline given. Buys all publication rights for one year, at which time they revert to author; and reprint and anthology rights for duration of copyright. Reports in 3 months on manuscripts. Sample copy $7.50.

Nonfiction: Book excerpts, essays, humor and reviews. "We often have theme issues, but non-regularly and usually not announced in advance. No pornography, romance-novel type writing, sex fantasies. No first-person accounts or blow-by-blow descriptions. No articles. No novels." Buys 5-10 mss/year. Send complete ms. All submissions should be typed, double-spaced, with name, address and phone number on each page; always enclose SASE. No specified length requirements. Pays $1/printed column inch, 3 contributor copies and subscription.

Photos: Photos may be submitted independently, not as illustration for submission. Reviews photocopies, contact sheets, transparencies and prints. We accept 4-color and b&w artwork. Offers varying payment for series of 8-20 used, plus copies. Buys one-time rights and reprint rights.

Columns/Departments: Reviews (book, movie, art, dance, food, music, anything). "Erotic content and how it's handled is focus of importance. Old or new does not matter. We want to bring readers information of what's out there." Buys 8-10 mss/year. Send complete ms or query. Pays $1/printed column inch plus copies.

Fiction: Erotica, including ethnic, experimental, fantasy, humorous, mainstream, novel excerpts and science fiction. See "Nonfiction." Buys 12-16 mss/year. Send complete ms. Pays $1/printed column inch, plus copies.

Poetry: Avant-garde, free verse, haiku, light verse and traditional. "No greeting-card poetry." Buys 80-100 poems/year. No limit on number of poems submitted, "but don't send book-length manuscripts." Pays .375¢/line, plus copies.

Tips: "The best way to get into *Yellow Silk* is produce excellent, well-crafted work that includes eros freshly, with strength of voice, beauty of language, and insight into character. I'll tell you what I'm sick of and have, unfortunately, been seeing more of lately: the products of 'How to Write Erotica' classes. This is not brilliant fiction; it is poorly written fantasy and not what I'm looking for."

ZYZZYVA, The Last Word: West Coast Writers & Artists, Suite 1400, 41 Sutter St., San Francisco CA 94104-4987. (415)255-1282. Fax: (415)255-1144. Editor: Howard Junker. 100% freelance written. Works with a small number of new/unpublished writers each year. Quarterly magazine. "We feature work by West Coast writers only. We are essentially a literary magazine, but of wide-ranging interests and a strong commitment to nonfiction." Estab. 1985. Circ. 4,000. **Pays on acceptance.** Publishes ms an average of 3 months after acceptance. Byline given. Buys first North American serial rights and one-time anthology rights. Reports in 1 week on queries; 1 month on mss. *Writer's Market* recommends allowing 2 months for reply. Sample copy $8.

Nonfiction: Book excerpts, general interest, historical/nostalgic, humor and personal experience. Buys 15 mss/year. Query. Length: open. Pays $50-250.

Fiction: Ethnic, experimental, humorous, mainstream and mystery. Buys 20 mss/year. Send complete ms. Length: open. Pays $50-250.

Poetry: Buys 20 poems/year. Submit maximum 5 poems. Length: 3-200 lines. Pays $50-250.

Men's

Men's magazines have been able to stabilize the downward spiral that affected them during the past several years, but few are prospering. Not many new magazines in this category have succeeded, but those that have are focusing either on information, service, sex, or fashion. Magazines that also use material slanted toward men can be found in Business and Finance, Relationships, Military and Sports sections.

BUXOM, America's No. 1 Big Tit Magazine, Man's World Publications, Inc., 10th Floor, 801 2nd Ave., New York NY 10017. (212)661-7878. Editor: Marc Medoff. 20% freelance written. Bimonthly magazine. "All material focuses on large-breasted women in an erotic, explicit and adult manner." Estab. 1989. Circ. 81,000. **Pays on acceptance.** Byline sometimes given. Offers 25% kill fee. Buys first North American serial rights. Submit seasonal material 6 months in advance. Accepts simultaneous and previously published submissions. Query for electronic submissions. Reports in 2 months. Sample copy for 9 × 12 SAE with 10 first class stamps. Writer's guidelines for #10 SASE.

Nonfiction: Essays, expose, how-to, humor, interview/profile, personal experience, photo feature and travel. Nothing non-sexual. Buys 5 mss/year. Send complete ms. Length:500-3,000 words. Pays $100-500. Sometimes pays in contributor copies (determined on a case-by-case basis). Sometimes pays expenses of writers on assignment.

Photos: Send photos with submission. Reviews 35 mm transparencies. Payment negotiable. Captions, model releases, and identification of subjects required, plus copy of photo IDs with dates of birth (models must be over 18). Buys one-time rights.

Columns/Departments: Fantasy Cum True (reader's sex fantasy w/pictures); Confessions (fiction); Swingers (reports on swingers' events, w/pictures); Live! (reports on erotic dancing w/pictures). Length: 500-3,000 words. Buys 6 mss/year. Send complete mss. Pays $100-500.

Fiction: Erotica and fantasy. Nothing non-sexual. Buys 6 mss/year. Send complete ms. Length: 500-3,000. Pays $100-500.

Tips: "Read competing magazines to know the market. Submit fiction with pictorials."

CHIC MAGAZINE, Larry Flynt Publications, Suite 300, 9171 Wilshire Blvd., Beverly Hills CA 90210-5530. Executive Editor: Doug Oliver. 40% freelance written. Monthly magazine for men, ages 20-35 years, college-educated and interested in current affairs, entertainment and sports. Estab. 1976. Circ. 90,000. Pays 1 month after acceptance. Publishes ms an average of 3 months after acceptance. Buys all rights. Pays 20% kill fee. Byline given unless writer requests otherwise. Reports in 2 months. Writer's guidelines for #10 SASE.

Nonfiction: Sex-related topics of current national interest; interview (off-beat personalities in news and entertainment); and celebrity profiles. Buys 12-18 mss/year. Query. Length: 3,000 words. Pays $750. Sometimes pays the expenses of writers on assignment.

Columns/Departments: Third Degree (short Q&As with unusual people), 2,000 words. Pays $350. My Confession (first-person sexual experiences), 1,000 words. Pays $25.

Fiction: Length: 3,000 words. Pays $500. "We buy stories with emphasis on erotic themes. These may be adventure, action, mystery, horror or humorous stories, but the tone and theme must involve sex and eroticism. The erotic nature of the story should not be subordinate to the characterizations and plot; the main graphically depicted sex slant should be 1½ pages in length, and must grow logically from the people and the plot, not be contrived or forced."

Tips: "We do not buy poetry or non-erotic science fiction. Refrain from stories with drug themes, sex with minors, male sexuality, incest and bestiality."

CLIMAX, America's No. 1 Couples Sex Magazine, Man's World Publications, Inc., 10th Floor, 801 2nd Ave., New York NY 10017. (212)661-7878. Editor: Marc Medoff. 20% freelance written. Bimonthly magazine. "We feature articles and pictorials about male-female sexual relations in an erotic, explicit and adult manner." Estab. 1990. Circ. 83,000. **Pays on acceptance.** Offers 25% kill fee. Buys first North American serial rights. Submit seasonal material 6 months in advance. Accepts simultaneous and previously published submissions. Query for electronic submissions. Reports in 2 months. Sample copy for 9 × 12 SAE with 10 first class stamps. Writer's guidelines for #10 SASE.

Nonfiction: Essays, expose, how-to, humor, interview/profile, personal experience, photo feature and travel. Nothing non-sexual. Buys 5 mss/year. Send complete ms. Length: 500-3,000 words. Pays $100-500. Sometimes pays in contributor copies (determined on a case-by-case basis). Sometimes pays the expenses of writers on assignment.

Photos: Send photos with submission. Reviews 35 mm transparencies. Negotiates payment. Captions, model releases, and identification of subjects required, plus a copy of photo IDs with dates of birth (models must be over 18). Buys one-time rights.

Columns/Departments: Fantasy Cum True (reader's sex fantasy w/pictures); Confessions (fiction); Swingers (reports on swingers' events w/pictures); Live! (reports on erotic dancing w/pictures). Length: 500-3,000 words. Buys 6 mss/year. Send complete ms. Pays $100-500.

Fiction: Erotica and fantasy. Nothing non-sexual. Buys 6 mss/year. Send complete ms. Length: 500-3,000 words. Pays $100-500.

Tips: "Read competing magazines. Submit fiction and pictorials."

COWBOY MAGAZINE, Range Writer, Inc., P.O. Box 126, LaVeta CO 81055-0126. (719)742-5250. Editor: Darrell Arnold. 80% freelance written. Quarterly magazine that covers all aspects of the cowboy lifestyle. "People who read our magazine are interested in cowboys. They want truth, not glorified, innacurate imaginings. If you've never worked on a ranch, or seen the West from horseback, you probably can't write for us." Estab. 1990. Circ. 15,500. Pays on publication. Publishes ms an average of 6 months after acceptance. Byline given. Buys first rights or one-time rights. Submit seasonal/holiday material 6 months in advance. Reports in 1 month on queries; 2 months on mss. Sample copy $4.50. Writer's guidelines for #10 SASE.

Nonfiction: Essays, expose, general interest, historical/nostalgic, humor, interview/profile, opinion and photo feature. "We are not another horse magazine. We don't want articles on horse care or horse training or horse shows. We do not want fiction except that pertaining to the life of a working cowboy." Buys 60 mss/year. Query. Length: 1,500 words maximum. Pays $200 maximum. Sometimes pays expenses of writers on assignment.

Photos: Send photos with submission. Reviews 5 × 7 prints. Offers $5/photo. Captions and identification of subjects required. Buys one-time rights.

Columns/Departments: Legacies (issues concerning the lives of cowboys and ranchers and others who value the use of public lands), 1,500 words. Buys 4 mss/year. Send complete ms. Pays $200 maximum.

Fiction: Historical, humorous, slice-of-life vignette and western. "No shoot-em-ups or romanticized visions of the West." Buys 4 mss/year. Send complete ms. Length: 1,500 words maximum. Pays $200 maximum.

Poetry: Traditional. "No verse that is not carefully rhymed, metered or constructed." Buys 4 poems/year. Submit maximum 5 poems. Length: 40 lines maximum. Pays $15 maximum.

Fillers: Facts, newsbreaks and short humor. Buys 4/year. Length: 200 words maximum. Pays $20 maximum.

Tips: "If you can write an honest, clear, account of some aspect of cowboy life, you can probably write for us. You must know the inside story on being a cowboy, on ranching life. You can do profiles of people who are cowboys or cowboy artists, or western (not country) musicians, or cowboy craftsmen. Don't make anything up. We can spot a phony. What we need the very most are articles about particular aspects of life as a working cowboy—how he does his work, where he lives, why he does it, etc. Good articles of this type are the hardest for us to get. They require spending some time on the ranch with a working cowboy or being one."

ESQUIRE, 250 W. 55th St., New York NY 10019. (212)459-7500. Editor-in-Chief: Terry McDonell. 99% freelance written. Monthly. Estab. 1933. **Pays on acceptance.** Publishes ms an average of 6 months after acceptance. Usually buys first serial rights. Reports in up to 2 months. "We depend chiefly on solicited contributions and material from literary agencies. We are unable to accept responsibility for unsolicited material." Query.

Nonfiction: Articles vary in length, but features usually average 2,000-5,000 words. Articles should be slanted for sophisticated, intelligent readers; however, not highbrow in the restrictive sense. Wide range of subject matter. Rates vary depending on length, quality, etc. Query. Sometimes pays expenses of writers on assignment.

Photos: Betsy Horan, photo editor. Payment depends on how photo is used. Guarantee on acceptance. Buys first periodical publication rights.

Fiction: L. Rust Hills, fiction editor. "Literary excellence is our only criterion." Discourages genre fiction (horror, science fiction, murder mystery, etc.), and does not use poetry. Length: about 1,000-6,000 words.

● Ranked as one of the best markets for freelance writers in *Writer's Digest* magazine's annual "Top 100 Markets," January 1993.

Tips: "The writer sometimes has a better chance of breaking in at *Esquire* with short, lesser-paying articles (rather than with major features) because we need more short pieces."

FLING, Relim Publishing Co., Inc., 550 Miller Ave., Mill Valley CA 94941. (415)383-5464. Editor: Arv Miller. Managing Editor: Ted Albert. 30% freelance written. Prefers to work with published/established writers. Bimonthly magazine in the men's sophisticate field. Young male audience of adults ages 18-34. Estab. 1957. Circ. 100,000. **Pays on acceptance.** Publishes ms an average of 6 months after acceptance. Buys first North American serial and second serial (reprint) rights; also makes work-for-hire assignments. Submit seasonal material 8 months in advance. Does not consider multiple submissions. Reports in 3 weeks on queries; 1 month on mss. Sample copy $5. Writer's guidelines for SASE.

Nonfiction: Expose; how-to (better relationships with women, better lovers); interview/profile; sports; finance; and taboo sex articles. Buys 15 mss/year. Query. Length: 1,500-3,000 words. Pays $150-350. Sometimes pays expenses of writers on assignment.

Photos: Send photos with query. Reviews 35mm color transparencies. Pays $10-25 for b&w; $20-35 for color. Model releases required. Buys one-time rights.

Columns/Departments: Buys 12 mss/year. Query or send complete ms. Length: 100-200 words. Pays $35-150.

Fiction: Sexually oriented, strong male-female relationship. Lots of written detail about female's abundant chest-size a must. No science fiction, western, plotless, private-eye, "dated" or adventure. Buys 10 mss/year. Send complete ms. Length: 2,000-3,000 words. Pays $135-200.

● No longer accepting fillers.

Tips: "Nonfiction and fiction are wide open areas to freelancers. Always query with one-page letter to the editor before proceeding with any writing. Also send a sample photocopy of published material, similar to suggestion."

FORUM, The International Journal of Human Relations, Penthouse International, 1965 Broadway, New York, NY 10023. (212)496-6100. Editor: V.K. McCarty. 100% freelance written. Works with small number of new/unpublished writers each year. Monthly magazine. "*Forum* is the only serious publication in the US to cover human sexuality in all its aspects for the layman—not only the erotic, but the medical, political, legal, etc." Circ. 300,000. **Pays on acceptance.** Publishes ms an average of 4-6 months after acceptance. Byline given. "Pseudonym mandatory for first-person sex stories." Offers 25% kill fee. Buys all rights. Submit seasonal/holiday material 6 months in advance. Query for electronic submissions. Reports in 1 month on queries.

Nonfiction: Book excerpts, personal experience and essays or articles on all aspects of sex and sexuality. Buys 12 mss/year. Query or send complete ms. Length: 2,000-3,000 words. Pays $800 and up.

Fiction: "Well-developed erotic fiction is considered. However, letters detailing sexual adventures are sent in by our readers, and we make no payment for them. We do not publish poetry. We are look for exciting erotic fiction dominated by stunningly memorable, highly explicit sex scenes. Will consider either third person or first person manuscripts." Pays $600 and up.

GALLERY MAGAZINE, Montcalm Publishing Corp., 401 Park Ave. S., New York NY 10016-8802. (212)779-8900. Fax: (212)725-7215. Editorial Director: Barry Janoff. Managing Editor: Rich Friedman. 50% freelance written. Prefers to work with published/established writers. Monthly magazine "focusing on features of interest to the young American man." Estab. 1972. Circ. 500,000. Pays 50% on acceptance, 50% on publication. Byline given. Pays 25% kill fee. Buys first North American serial rights; makes work-for-hire assignments. Submit seasonal/holiday material 6 months in advance. Reports in 1 month on queries; 2 months on mss. Sample copy $6.95 (add $2 for Canadian and foreign orders). Writer's guidelines for SASE.
Nonfiction: Investigative pieces, general interest, how-to, humor, interview, new products and profile. "We *do not* want to see pornographic articles." Buys 4-5 mss/issue. Query or send complete mss. Length: 1,000-3,000 words. Pays $300-2,000. "Special prices negotiated." Sometimes pays expenses of writers on assignment.
Photos: Send photos with accompanying mss. Pay varies for b&w or color contact sheets and negatives. Buys one-time rights. Captions preferred; model release required.
Fiction: Adventure, erotica (special guidelines available), experimental, humorous, mainstream, mystery and suspense. Buys 1 ms/issue. Send complete ms. Length: 1,000-3,000 words. Pays $350-500.

GENESIS, Jakel Corp., 20th Floor, 1776 Broadway, New York NY 10019. (212)265-3500. Fax: (212)265-8087. Editor: Michael Banka. 85% freelance written. Men's magazine published 13 times/year. "We are interested in headline and behind-the-headlines articles on sexual or controversial subjects of interest to men." Estab. 1973. Circ. 425,000. Pays 60 days after acceptance. Publishes ms an average of 3 months after acceptance. Byline given. Offers 25% kill fee. Buys second serial (reprint) and English worldwide rights (may revert to writer upon request). Submit seasonal material 6 months in advance. Simultaneous submissions OK. Reports in 3 months. Writer's guidelines for #10 SASE.
Nonfiction: Expose; humor; interview/profile; photo feature; erotica; film, music and book reviews; comment on contemporary relationships; and automotive. "With the exception of the entertainment reviews, one expose-style piece and one automotive piece/issue, all editorial in *Genesis* has a sexual orientation." Buys 60 mss/year. Query with published clips. First-time writers must submit ms on spec. Length: 1,500-2,000 words. Pays $300-700 for assigned articles; $100-500 for unsolicited articles.
Photos: State availability of photos with submission. Reviews transparencies (no fixed size requirements) and prints. Offers $50-100/photo. Model releases and identification of subjects required. Buys English worldwide and second serial (reprint) rights.
Columns/Departments: Film, music and book reviews, 500-750 words; 'On the Couch' (sexual confessions from woman's point of view), 750-1,000 words. Buys 65 mss/year. Query with published clips. First-time writers must submit ms on spec. Pays $75-350.
Tips: "Because we accept only a small number of nonsex-related articles, freelancers' best chance to break in is to write sex features or contribute to the entertainment pages. When writing about sexual issues or lifestyles, writers should offer their own opinions on the subject rather than provide drably objective overviews. First-person point-of-view is strongly recommended. Writing must be sexually explicit with a minimum amount of 'lead in.'"

‡GENT, "Home of the D-Cups," Dugent Publishing Corp., Suite 600, 2600 Douglas Rd., Coral Gables FL 33134. Managing Editor: Steve Dorfman. Contact: Steve Dorfman. 80% freelance written. Monthly magazine. Men's sophisticate with emphasis on big breasts. Estab. 1960. Circ. 150,000. Pays on publication. Byline given. Buys first North American serial or second serial (reprint) rights. Editorial lead time 8 months. Submit seasonal material 6 months in advance. Accepts previously published submissions. Reports in 2 weeks on queries; 3 months on mss. Sample copy $5. Writer's guidelines for #10 SASE.
Nonfiction: How-to ("anything sexually related") and personal experience ("any and all sexually related matters"). Buys 13 mss/year. Query. Length: 2,000-3,500 words. Pays $250.
Photos: Send photos with submission. Reviews 35mm transparencies. Negotiates payment individually. Model releases and identification of subjects required. Buys first North American with reprint rights.
Fiction: Erotica and fantasy. Buys 26 mss/year. Send complete ms. Length: 2,000-3,500 words. Pays $200-250.

GENTLEMEN'S QUARTERLY, Condé Nast, 350 Madison Ave., New York NY 10017. (212)880-8800. Editor-in-Chief: Arthur Cooper. Managing Editor: Martin Beiser. 60% freelance written. Circ. 700,000. Monthly magazine emphasizing fashion, general interest and service features for men ages 25-45 with a large discretionary income. **Pays on acceptance.** Byline given. Pays 25% kill fee. Submit seasonal/holiday material 6 months in advance. Reports in 1 month.
Nonfiction: Politics, personality profiles, lifestyles, trends, grooming, nutrition, health and fitness, sports, travel, money, investment and business matters. Buys 4-6 mss/issue. Query with published clips. Length: 1,500-4,000 words. Pay varies.
Columns/Departments: Martin Beiser, managing editor. Private Lives, Health and Games (sports). Query with published clips. Length: 1,000-2,500 words. Pay varies.
Tips: "Major features are usually assigned to well-established, known writers. Pieces are almost always solicited. The best way to break in is through the columns, especially Games, Health or Humor."

HEARTLAND USA, UST Publishing, P.O. Box 925, Hailey ID 83333-0925. (208)788-4500. Fax: (208)788-5098. Editor: Brad Pearson. Managing Editor: Clarence Stilwill. 50% freelance written. Quarterly magazine for working men. "*Heartland USA* is a general interest, lifestyle magazine for working men between the ages of 18 and 53. It covers spectator sports (primarily motor sports, football, baseball and basketball, hunting, fishing, how-to, travel, music, gardening, the environment, human interest, etc.), emphasizing the upbeat or humorous." Estab. 1991. Circ. 1,000,000. **Pays on acceptance.** Byline given. Offers 20% kill fee. Buys first North American serial and second serial (reprint) rights. Submit seasonal material 6 months in advance. Simultaneous and previously published submissions OK. Query for electronic submissions. Reprints OK; send tearsheet or photocopy of article, typed ms with rights for sale noted and information about when and where the article previously appeared. Pays 25% of their fee for an original article. Reports in 1 month on queries. Sample copy for 9 × 12 SAE with 10 first class stamps. Free writer's guidelines.
Nonfiction: Book excerpts, general interest, historical/nostalgic, how-to, humor, inspirational, interview/profile, new product, personal experience, photo feature, technical and travel. "No fiction or boring expository pieces." Buys 30 mss/year. Query with or without published clips or send complete ms. Length: 350-1,200 words. Pays 80¢ to $1/word for assigned articles; 25-80¢/word for unsolicited articles. Sometimes pays expenses of writers on assignment.
Photos: State availability of photos with submission. Reviews transparencies. Identification of subjects required. Buys one-time rights.
Tips: "Features with the possibility of strong photographic support are open to freelancers, as are our shorter departments. We look for a relaxed, jocular, easy-to-read style, and look favorably on the liberal use of anecdote or interesting quotations."

HIGH SOCIETY MAGAZINE, Drake Publishers, 801 2nd Ave., New York NY 10017. (212)661-7878/ Editor: Vincent Stevens. Managing Editor: Richard Hollander. 50% freelance written. Men's sophisticate magazine that emphasizes men's entertainment. "Everything of interest to the American male." Estab. 1976. Circ. 400,000. **Pays on acceptance.** Byline given. Offers $200 kill fee. Buys first North American serial rights. Submit seasonal material 6 months in advance. Accepts simultaneous submissions. Reports in 2 weeks on queries. Sample copy $2 for 9 × 12 SAE.
Nonfiction: Book excerpts, expose, general interest, interview/profile, photo feature. Buys 60 mss/year. Query with or without published clips, or send complete ms. Length: 1,500-3,000 words. Pays $300-800 for assigned articles; $200-500 for unsolicited articles. Sometimes pays expenses of writers on assignment.
Photos: Send photos with submission. Reviews 2¼ × 2¼ transparencies and 8 × 10 prints. Offers $200/photo. Captions, model releases and identification of subjects required. Buys one-time rights.
Columns/Departments: Private Passions (first person sexual accounts), 600 words; Bad Guys (crime related exposes), 1,800 words; and Sex & Music (biographies of female celebs in music business), 1,000 words. Buys 60 mss/year. Query with published clips. Pays $150-800.

HUSTLER BUSTY BEAUTIES, America's Breast Magazine, HG Publications, Inc., Suite 300, 9171 Wilshire Blvd., Beverly Hills CA 90210. (213)858-7100. Fax: (213)275-3857. Editor: N. Morgen Hagen. 40% freelance written. Men's monthly sophisticate magazine. "*Hustler Busty Beauties* is an adult title that showcases attractive large-breasted women with accompanying erotic fiction, reader letters, humor." Estab. 1988. Circ. 180,000. Pays on publication. Publishes ms an average of 3 months after acceptance. Byline given. Offers 25% kill fee. Buys all rights. Reports in 2 weeks on queries; 1 month on mss. Sample copy $6 for 9 × 12 SAE. Free writer's guidelines.
Columns/Departments: LewDDD Letters (erotic experiences involving large-breasted women from first-person point-of-view), 500-1,000 words. Buys 24-36 mss year. Send complete ms. Pays $50-75.
Fiction: Adventure, erotica, fantasy, humorous, mystery, science fiction and suspense. "No violent stories or stories without a bosomy female character." Buys 12 mss year. Send complete ms. Length: 750-2,500 words. Pays $250-500.
Jokes: Appropriate for audience. Pays $10-25.

‡NUGGET, Dugent Publishing Corp., Suite 600, 2600 Douglas Rd., Coral Gables FL 33134. Managing Editor: Nye Willden. Contact: Christopher James, editor-in-chief. 100% freelance written. Men's/adult magazine published 8 times a year covering fetish and kink. "Nugget is a one-of-a-kind publication which appeals to daring, open-minded adults who enjoy all forms of both kinky, alternative sex (catfighting, transvestism, fetishism, bi-sexuality, etc.) and conventional sex." Estab. 1960. Circ. 28,097. Pays on publication. Publishes ms an average of 1 year after acceptance. Byline given. Buys first North American serial rights. Editorial lead time 5 months. Submit seasonal material 1 year in advance. Accepts simultaneous submissions. Reports in 2 weeks on queries; 2 months on mss. Sample copy $3. Writer's guidelines free on request.

For explanation of symbols, see the Key to Symbols and Abbreviations on page 72. For unfamiliar words, see the Glossary.

Nonfiction: Interview/profile and sexual matters/trends (fetish and kink angle). Buys 4 mss/year. Query. Length: 2,000-3,000 words. Pays $200 minimum.

Photos: State availability of photos with submission. Reviews transparencies. Offers no additional payment for photos accepted with ms. Model releases required. Buys one-time rights.

Fiction: Erotica and fantasy. Buys 15 mss/year. Send complete ms. Length: 2,000-3,000 words. Pays $200-250.

Tips: "Most open to fiction submissions. (Follow writers' guidelines for suitable topics.)"

OPTIONS, AJA Publishing, P.O. Box 470, Port Chester NY 10573. (914)939-2111. Editor: Don Stone. Associate Editor: Diana Sheridan. Mostly freelance written. Sexually explicit magazine for and about bisexuals and homosexuals, published 10 times/year. "Articles, stories and letters about bisexuality. Positive approach. Safe-sex encounters unless the story clearly pre-dates the AIDS situation." Estab. 1977. Circ. 100,000. Pays on publication. Publishes mss an average of 10 months after acceptance. Byline given. Buys all rights. Submit seasonal material 8 months in advance; buys very little seasonal material. Reports in 3 weeks. Sample copy $2.95 for 6×9 SAE with 5 first class stamps. Writer's guidelines for SASE.

Nonfiction: Essays (occasional), how-to, humor, interview/profile, opinion and (especially) personal experience. All must be bisexually or gay related. Does not want "anything not bisexually/gay related, anything negative, anything opposed to safe sex, anything dry/boring/ponderous/pedantic. Write even serious topics informally if not lightly." Buys 70 mss/year. Send complete ms. Length: 2,000-3,000. Pays $100.

Photos: Reviews transparencies and prints. Pays $20 for b&w photos; $200 for full color. Black and white or color sets $150. Previously published photos acceptable.

Fiction: "We don't usually get enough true first-person stories and need to buy some from writers. They must be bisexual, usually man/man, hot and believable. They must not read like fiction." Buys 60 ms/year. Send complete ms. Length: 2,000-3,000. Pays $100.

Tips: "We use many more male/male pieces than female/female. Use only one serious article per issue. A serious/humorous approach is good here, but only if it's natural to you; don't make an effort for it. No longer buying 'letters'. We get enough real ones."

‡SCREW, P.O. Box 432, Old Chelsea Station, New York NY 10113. Managing Editor: Manny Neuhaus. 95% freelance written. Eager to work with new/unpublished writers. Weekly tabloid newspaper for a predominantly male, college-educated audience, 21-mid-40s. Estab. 1968. Circ. 125,000. Pays on publication. Publishes ms an average of 3 months after acceptance. Byline given. Buys all rights. Reports in 3 months. Free sample copy and writer's guidelines.

Nonfiction: "Sexually-related news, humor, how-to articles, first-person and true confessions. Frank and explicit treatment of all areas of sex; outrageous and irreverent attitudes combined with hard information, news and consumer reports. Our style is unique. Writers should check several recent issues." Buys 150-200 mss/year. Will also consider material for Letter From . . ., a consumer-oriented wrap-up of commercial sex scene in cities around the country; submit complete ms or query. Length: 1,000-3,000 words. Pays $100-250. Also, My Scene, a sexual true confession. Length: 1,000-2,500 words. Pays $40.

Photos: Reviews b&w glossy prints (8×10 or 11×14) purchased with or without manuscripts or on assignment. Pays $10-50.

Tips: "All mss get careful attention. Those written in *Screw* style on sexual topics have the best chance. I anticipate a need for more aggressive, insightful political humor."

THIGH HIGH, Luscious Legs, Feet and Asses, Man's World Publications, Inc., 10th Floor, 801 2nd Ave., New York NY 10017. (212)661-7878. 20% freelance written. Quarterly magazine. "All material focuses on foot and leg fetishes in an erotic, explicit and adult manner." Estab. 1991. Circ. 89,000. **Pays on acceptance.** Byline sometimes given. Offers 25% kill fee. Buys first North American serial rights. Submit seasonal material 6 months in advance. Accepts simultaneous and previously published submissions. Query for electronic submissions. Reports in 2 months. Sample copy for 9×12 SAE with 10 first class stamps. Writer's guidelines for #10 SASE.

Nonfiction: Essays, expose, how-to, humor, interview/profile, personal experience, photo feature and travel. Nothing non-sexual. Buys 5 mss/year. Send complete ms. Length: 500-3,000 words. Pays $100-500. Sometimes pays in contributor copies (determined on a case-by-case basis). Sometimes pays expenses of writers on assignment.

Photos: Send photos with submission. Reviews 35 mm transparencies. Negotiates payment. Captions, model releases and identification of subjects required, plus copy of photo IDs with dates of birth (models must be over 18). Buys one-time rights.

Columns/Departments: Fantasy Cum True (reader's sex fantasy w/pictures); The Other Cheek (fiction); Swingers (reports on swingers' events w/pictures); Live! (reports on erotic dancing w/pictures); and Fetish News (fetish events, foot and leg oriented news). Length: 500-3,000 words. Buys 6 mss/year. Send complete ms. Pays $100-500.

Fiction: Erotica and fantasy. Buys 6 mss/year. Send complete ms. Length: 500-3,000 words. Pays $100-500.
Tips: "Read competing magazines. Submit fiction with pictorials."

Military

These publications emphasize military or paramilitary subjects or other aspects of military life. Technical and semitechnical publications for military commanders, personnel and planners, as well as those for military families and civilians interested in Armed Forces activities are listed here. Publications covering military history can be found in the History section.

AMERICAN SURVIVAL GUIDE, McMullen & Yee Publishing, Inc., 774 S. Placentia Ave., Placentia CA 92670-6832. Editor: Jim Benson. 50% freelance written. Monthly magazine covering "self-reliance, defense, meeting day-to-day and possible future threats—survivalism for survivalists." Circ. 72,000. Pays on publication. Publishes ms up to 1 year after acceptance. Byline given. Submit seasonal material 5 months in advance. Sample copy $3.50. Writer's guidelines for SASE.
Nonfiction: Expose (political); how-to; interview/profile; personal experience (how I survived); photo feature (equipment and techniques related to survival in all possible situations); emergency medical; health and fitness; communications; transportation; food preservation; water purification; self-defense; terrorism; nuclear dangers; nutrition; tools; shelter; etc. "No general articles about how to survive. We want specifics and single subjects." Buys 60-100 mss/year. Query or send complete ms. Length: 1,500-2,000 words. Pays $140-350. Sometimes pays some expenses of writers on assignment.
Photos: Send photos with ms. "One of the most frequent mistakes made by writers in completing an article assignment for us is sending photo submissions that are inadequate." Captions, model releases and identification of subjects mandatory. Buys all rights.
Tips: "Prepare material of value to individuals who wish to sustain human life no matter what the circumstance. This magazine is a text and reference."

ARMY MAGAZINE, 2425 Wilson Blvd., Arlington VA 22201-3385. (703)841-4300. Fax: (703)525-9039. Editor-in-Chief: L. James Binder. Managing Editor: Mary Blake French. 70% freelance written. Prefers to work with published/established writers. Monthly magazine emphasizing military interests. Estab. 1904. Circ. 130,000. Pays on publication. Publishes ms an average of 5 months after acceptance. Buys all rights. Byline given except for back-up research. Submit seasonal/holiday material 3 months in advance. Sample copy and writer's guidelines for 9 × 12 SAE with $1 postage.
Nonfiction: Historical (military and original); humor (military feature-length articles and anecdotes); interview; new product; nostalgia; personal experience dealing especially with the most recent conflicts in which the US. Army has been involved (Desert Storm, Panama, Grenada); photo feature; profile; and technical. No rehashed history. "We would like to see more pieces about little-known episodes involving interesting military personalities. We especially want material lending itself to heavy, contributor-supplied photographic treatment. The first thing a contributor should recognize is that our readership is very savvy militarily. 'Gee-whiz' personal reminiscences get short shrift, unless they hold their own in a company in which long military service, heroism and unusual experiences are commonplace. At the same time, Army readers like a well-written story with a fresh slant, whether it is about an experience in a foxhole or the fortunes of a corps in battle." Buys 12 mss/issue. Submit complete ms. Length: 3,500 words, but shorter items, especially in 1,500 to 2,500 range, often have better chance of getting published. Pays 12-18¢/word.
Photos: Submit photo material with accompanying ms. Pays $25-50 for 8 × 10 b&w glossy prints; $50-350 for 8 × 10 color glossy prints or 2¼ × 2¼ transparencies; will also accept 35mm. Captions preferred. Buys all rights. Pays $35-50 for cartoon with strong military slant.
Columns/Departments: Military news, books, comment (*New Yorker*-type "Talk of the Town" items). Buys 8/issue. Submit complete ms. Length: 1,000 words. Pays $40-150.

ASIA-PACIFIC DEFENSE FORUM, Commander-in-Chief, U.S. Pacific Command, Box 13, Camp H.M. Smith HI 96861-5025. (808)477-0760/1454. Fax: (808)477-6247. Editor-in-Chief: Lt. Col. (Ret.) Paul R. Stankiewicz. Editor: Major Ricardo Finney. 12% (maximum) freelance written. Quarterly magazine for foreign military officers in 51 Asian-Pacific, Indian Ocean and other countries; all services—Army, Navy, Air Force and Marines. Secondary audience—government officials, media and academicians concerned with defense issues. "We seek to keep readers abreast of current status of US forces and of US national security policies in the Asia-Pacific area, and to enhance regional dialogue on military subjects." Estab. 1976. Circ. 34,000. **Pays on acceptance.** Publishes ms an average of 4 months after acceptance. Byline given. Buys simultaneous, second serial (reprint) or one-time rights. Simultaneous and previously published submissions OK; send tearsheet or photocopy of article and information about when and where the article previously appeared. Reports in

3 weeks on queries; at most 10 weeks on mss. Free sample copy and writer's guidelines (send self-addressed label).

Nonfiction: General interest (current type forces and weapons systems, strategic balance and regional security issues and Asian-Pacific armed forces); historical (rarely used); how-to (training, leadership, force employment procedures, organization); interview and personal experience (rarely used). "We do not want overly technical weapons/equipment descriptions, overly scholarly articles, controversial policy, or budget matters; nor do we seek discussion of in-house problem areas. We do not deal with military social life, base activities or PR-type personalities/job descriptions." Buys 2-4 mss/year. Query or send complete ms. Length: 1,000-3,000 words. Pays $100-300.

Photos: State availability of photos with query or ms. "We provide nearly all photos; however, we will consider good quality photos with manuscripts." Reviews color, b&w glossy prints or 35mm color transparencies. Offers no additional payment for photos accompanying mss. Photo credits given. Captions required. Buys one-time rights.

Tips: "Don't write in a flashy, Sunday supplement style. Our audience is relatively staid, and fact-oriented articles requiring a newspaper/journalistic approach are used more than a normal magazine style. Provide material that is truly foreign audience-oriented and easily illustrated with photos."

FAMILY MAGAZINE, The Magazine for Military Wives, 169 Lexington Ave., New York NY 10016. (212)545-9740. Editor: Barbara Ehrlich. 100% freelance written. Works with a small number of new/unpublished writers each year. Monthly magazine for military wives who are young parents, high school educated and move often. Estab. 1969. Circ. 545,000. Pays on publication. Publishes ms an average of 6-12 months after acceptance. Byline given. Buys first rights or second serial (reprint) rights. Submit seasonal/holiday material 6 months in advance. Simultaneous submissions OK. Reports in 6 weeks. Sample copy $1.25 for 9 × 12 SASE. Writer's guidelines for SASE.

Nonfiction: Humor, how-to, interview/profile, general interest, photo feature and travel, of interest to military wives. No romance or anything to do with getting a man or aging. Buys 50 mss/year. Query with clips. Length: 3,000 features. Pays $150-200.

Photos: Send photos with submissions. Reviews slides. Offers $50/photo. Captions helpful. Buys one-time rights.

LIFE IN THE TIMES, Army Times Publishing Co., Springfield VA 22159-0200. (703)750-8666. Fax: (703)750-8622. Editor: Margaret Roth. Managing Editor: Roger Hyneman. 30% freelance written. Willing to work with new/unpublished writers. Weekly lifestyle section of Army, Navy and Air Force Times covering current lifestyles and problems of career military families around the world. Circ. 305,000. **Pays on acceptance.** Publishes ms an average of 2 months after acceptance. Byline given. Buys first worldwide rights. Submit seasonal material 3 months in advance. Query for electronic submissions. Reports in about 1 month. Writer's guidelines for #10 SASE.

Nonfiction: Expose (current military); coping (families); interview/profile (military); personal experience (military only); and travel (of military interest). Buys about 200 mss/year. Query with published clips. Length: 500-2,000 words. Pays $100-275. Sometimes pays the expenses of writers on assignment.

• No longer publishes food articles. Also rejects generic articles unless they have a military angle.

Photos: State availability of photos or send photos with ms. Reviews 35mm color contact sheets and prints. Captions, model releases and identification of subjects required.

Tips: "In your query write a detailed description of story and how it will be told. A tentative lead is nice. A military angle is crucial. Just one good story 'breaks in' a freelancer. Follow the outline you propose in your query letter and humanize articles with quotes and examples."

MARINE CORPS GAZETTE, Professional Magazine for United States Marines, Marine Corps Association, P.O. Box 1775, Quantico VA 22134. (703)640-6161, (800)336-0291. Fax: (703)640-0823. Editor: Col. John E. Greenwood, USMC (Ret.). Managing Editor: Lt. Col. Steven M. Crittenden, USMC (Ret.). Less than 5% freelance written. "Will continue to welcome and respond to queries, but will be selective due to large backlog from Marine authors." Monthly magazine. "*Gazette* serves as a forum in which serving Marine officers exchange ideas and viewpoints on professional military matters." Estab. 1916. Circ. 37,900. Pays on publication. Publishes ms an average of 6 months after acceptance. Byline given. Buys all rights. Reprints OK; send tearsheet of article or typed ms with rights for sale noted and information about when and where the article previously appeared. Pays 100% of their fee for an original article. Reports in 3 weeks on queries; 2 months on mss. Free sample copy and writer's guidelines.

Nonfiction: Historical/nostalgic (Marine Corps operations only); and technical (Marine Corps related equipment). "The magazine is a professional journal oriented toward hard skills, factual treatment, technical detail—no market for lightweight puff pieces—analysis of doctrine, lessons learned goes well. A very strong Marine Corps background and influence are normally prerequisites for publication." Buys 4-5 mss/year from non-Marine Corps sources. Query or send complete ms. Length: 2,500-5,000 words. Pays $200-400.

Photos: "We welcome photos and charts." Payment for illustrative material included in payment forms. "Photos need not be original, nor have been taken by the author, but they must support the article."

Columns/Departments: Book Reviews (of interest and importance to Marines); and Ideas and Issues (an assortment of topical articles, e.g., opinion or argument, ideas of better ways to accomplish tasks, reports on weapons and equipment, strategies and tactics, etc., also short vignettes on history of Corps). Buys 60 book reviews/year; pays $25-50 plus book for 750-word book review. Buys 150 Ideas and Issues mss/year; pays $50-100 for these short features.

Tips: "Book reviews or short articles (500-1,500 words) on Marine Corps related hardware or technological development are the best way to break in. Sections/departments most open to freelancers are Book Reviews and Ideas & Issues sections—query first. We are not much of a market for those outside U.S. Marine Corps or who are not closely associated with current Marine activities."

MILITARY LIFESTYLE, Downey Communications, Inc., Suite 710, 4800 Montgomery Lane, Bethesda MD 20814-5341. (301)718-7600. Fax: (301)718-7652. Editor: Hope M. Daniels. 80% freelance written. Works with equal balance of published and unpublished writers. Published 10 times/year for military families in the US and overseas. Estab. 1969. Circ. 500,000. Pays on publication. Publishes ms an average of 4 months after acceptance. Buys first North American serial rights. Submit seasonal material at least 8 months in advance. Reports in approximately 3 months. Sample copy $1.50 for 9 × 12 SASE with adequate postage for a magazine. Writer's guidelines for #10 SASE.

Nonfiction: "All articles must have special interest for military families. General interest articles are OK if they reflect situations our readers can relate to." Food, entertaining, profiles, childraising, health, home decor, travel and finances. "Query letter should name sources, describe focus of article, use a few sample quotes from sources, indicate length, and should describe writer's own qualifications for doing the piece." Length: 1,000-1,500 words. Pays $400-750/article. Negotiates expenses on a case-by-case basis.

Photos: Purchased with accompanying ms and on assignment. Uses 35mm or larger transparencies. Captions and model releases are required. Query art director Judi Connelly.

Columns/Departments: Your View—personal experience pieces by military family members. Also, Your Pet, Your Money and Your Child. Query. Length: 800-1,200 words. Rates vary.

Fiction: Slice-of-life, family situation and contemporary tableaux. "Military family life or relationship themes only." Buys 6-8 mss/year. Query. Length: 1,200-1,500 words. Pays $500-600.

Tips: "We are a magazine for young military families. Our editorial attempts to enthusiastically to reflect that. Our ideal contributor is a military family member who can write. However, I'm always impressed by a writer who has analyzed the market and can suggest some possible new angles for us. Sensitivity to military issues is a must for our contributors, as is the ability to write good personality profiles and/or do thorough research about military family life. We don't purchase household hints, historical articles, poetry, WW II-era material or parenting advice that is too personal and limited only to the writer's own experience."

MILITARY REVIEW, U.S. Army Command and General Staff College, Fort Leavenworth KS 66027-6910. (913)684-5642. Fax: (913)684-2448. Editor-in-Chief: Ltc. Ronald N. Mazzia. 95% freelance written. Eager to work with new/unpublished writers. Monthly journal (printed in three languages: English, Spanish and Brazilian Portuguese), emphasizing the military for military officers, students and scholars. Estab. 1922. Circ. 27,000. Pays on publication. Publishes ms an average of 8 months after acceptance. Byline given. Buys first serial rights and reserves right to reprint for training purpose. Phone queries OK. Query for electronic submissions. Reports in 1 month. *Writer's Market* recommends allowing 2 months for reply. Writer's guidelines for #10 SASE.

Nonfiction: Operational level of war, military history, international affairs, tactics, strategy and book reviews. Buys 100-120 mss/year. Query. Length: 2,000-3,000 words. Pays $50-150.

Tips: "We need more articles from military personnel experienced in particular specialties. Examples: Tactics from a tactician, military engineering from an engineer, etc. By reading our publication, writers will quickly recognize our magazine as a forum for any topic of general interest to the US Army. They will also discover the style we prefer: concise and direct, in the active voice, with precision and clarity, and moving from the specific to the general."

OFF DUTY MAGAZINE, Suite C-2, 3303 Harbor Blvd., Costa Mesa CA 92626-1500. (714)549-7172. Fax: (714)549-4222. Editorial Director: Jim Shaw. Managing Editor: Gary Burch. 30% freelance written. Monthly magazine covering the leisure-time life of the military community. "Our audience is solely military members and their families; many of our articles could appear in other consumer magazines, but we always slant them toward the military; i.e. where to get a military discount when traveling." Estab. 1970. Circ. 662,000. **Pays on acceptance.** Publishes ms an average of 3 months after acceptance. Byline given. Buys one-time rights. Submit seasonal material at least 4 months in advance. Simultaneous submissions and reprints OK; send tearsheet or photocopy of article and information about when and where the article previously appeared. Reports in 2 months on queries. Sample copy for 9 × 12 SAE with 6 first class stamps. Writer's guidelines for SASE.

Nonfiction: Historical/nostalgic (military), humor (military), interview/profile (music and entertainment), travel, finance and lifestyle (with a military angle). "Nothing from somebody who does not know *Off Duty* and its needs." Buys 20 mss/year. Query. Length: 800-2,100 words. Pays $160-420 for assigned articles.

Photos: State availability of photos with submission. Reviews contact sheets and 35mm transparencies. Offers $75-200/photo. Captions and identification of subjects required. Buys one-time rights.

Tips: "Get to know the military community and its interests beyond the stereotypes. Travel—query with the idea of getting on our next year's editorial calendar. We choose our primary topics at least 6 months prior to its start."

OVERSEAS!, Military Consumer Today, Inc., Kolpingstr 1, 69172 Leimen, West Germany 011-49-6224-7060. Fax: 011-49-6224-70616. Editor: Greg Ballinger. Eager to work with new/unpublished writers. Monthly magazine. *"Overseas!* is aimed at the U.S. military in Europe. It is the leading military lifestyle magazine slanted toward living in Europe." Estab. 1973. Circ. 66,000. Pays on publication. Publishes ms an average of 3 months after acceptance. Byline given. Publishes photos, bio of new writers in editor's column. Offers kill fee depending on circumstances and writer. Buys one-time rights. Submit seasonal/holiday material at least 4 months in advance. Simultaneous queries and simultaneous and previously published submissions OK. Reports in 2 months. Sample copy for 9 × 12 SAE with 5 IRCs. Writer's guidelines for SAE and 1 IRC.

Nonfiction: General interest (lifestyle for men and other topics); interview/profile (music, personality interviews; current music stars); travel (European, first person adventure; write toward male audience). No articles that are drug- or sex-related. No cathedrals or museums of Europe stories. Query with or without published clips or send complete ms. Length: 750-2,000 words. Pays 10¢/word.

Photos: Photos must accompany travel articles—color slides.

Tips: "We would like more submissions on travel in Europe. Writing should be lively, interesting, with lots of good information. We anticipate a change in the length of articles. Articles will be shorter and livelier with more sidebars because readers don't have time to read longer articles."

PARAMETERS: U.S. Army War College Quarterly, U.S. Army War College, Carlisle Barracks PA 17013-5050. (717)245-4943. Editor: Col. John J. Madigan, U.S. Army Retired. 100% freelance written. Prefers to work with published/established writers or experts in the field. Readership consists of senior leadership of U.S. defense establishment, both uniformed and civilian, plus members of the media, government, industry and academia interested in national and international security affairs, military strategy, military leadership and management, art and science of warfare, and military history (provided it has contemporary relevance). Most readers possess a graduate degree. Estab. 1971. Circ. 11,000. Not copyrighted; unless copyrighted by author, articles may be reprinted with appropriate credits. Buys first serial rights. Byline given. Pays on publication. Publishes ms an average of 6 months after acceptance. Reports in 6 weeks. Free sample copy and writer's guidelines.

Nonfiction: Articles are preferred that deal with current security issues, employ critical analysis and provide solutions or recommendations. Liveliness and verve, consistent with scholarly integrity, appreciated. Theses, studies and academic course papers should be adapted to article form prior to submission. Documentation in complete endnotes. Submit complete ms. Length: 4,500 words average, preferably less. Pays $150 average (including visuals).

Tips: "Make it short; keep it interesting; get criticism and revise accordingly. Tackle a subject only if you are an authority."

THE RETIRED OFFICER MAGAZINE, 201 N. Washington St., Alexandria VA 22314-2539. (800)245-8762. Fax: (703)838-8179. Editor: Col. Charles D. Cooper, USAF-Ret. Managing Editor: Julia Leigh. 60% freelance written. Prefers to work with published/established writers. Monthly magazine for officers of the 7 uniformed services and their families. Estab. 1929. Circ. 380,000. **Pays on acceptance.** Publishes ms an average of 9-12 months after acceptance. Byline given. Buys first serial rights. Submit seasonal material (holiday stories with a military theme) at least 9-12 months in advance. Reports on material accepted for publication within 3 months. Sample copy and writer's guidelines for 9 × 12 SAE with 6 first class stamps.

Nonfiction: Current military/political affairs, health and wellness, recent military history, travel, second-career job opportunities and military family lifestyle. Also, upbeat articles on aging, issues pertinent to a retired military officer's milieu. "We rarely accept unsolicited mss. We look for detailed query letters with resume and sample clips attached. We do not publish poetry or fillers." Buys 48 mss/year. Length: 800-2,000 words. Pays up to $750.

Photos: Query with list of stock photo subjects. Reviews 8 × 10 b&w photos (normal halftone). Pays $20. Original slides or transparencies must be suitable for color separation. Pays up to $125 for inside color; up to $200 for cover.

Tips: "Our readers are 55-65. We never write about them as senior citizens, yet we look for upbeat stories that take into consideration the demographic characteristics of their age group. An author who can submit a complete package of story and photos is valuable to us."

SOLDIER OF FORTUNE, The Journal of Professional Adventurers, Omega Group, Ltd., P.O. Box 693, Boulder CO 80306-0693. (303)449-3750. Fax: (303)444-5617. Managing Editor: Tom Slizewski. Assistant Editor: Lynne Robertson. 50% freelance written. Monthly magazine covering military, paramilitary, police, combat subjects and action/adventure. "We are an action-oriented magazine; we cover combat hot spots around the world such as Afghanistan, El Salvador, Angola, etc. We also provide timely features on state-of-the-art weapons and equipment; elite military and police units; and historical military operations. Readership is primarily active-duty military, veterans and law enforcement." Estab. 1975. Circ. 175,000. Byline given. Offers 25% kill fee. Buys all rights; will negotiate. Will consider reprints (send tearsheet of article and information about when and where it previously appeared). For reprints, pays 100% of their fee for an original article. Submit seasonal material 5 months in advance. Reports in 3 weeks on queries; 1 month on mss. Sample copy $5. Writer's guidelines for #10 SASE. Send mss to articles editor; queries to managing editor.

Nonfiction: Expose; general interest; historical/nostalgic; how-to (on weapons and their skilled use); humor; profile; new product; personal experience; novel excerpts; photo feature ("number one on our list"); technical; travel; combat reports; military unit reports and solid Vietnam and Operation Desert Storm articles. "No 'How I won the war' pieces; no op-ed pieces *unless* they are fully and factually backgrounded; no knife articles (staff assignments only). *All* submitted articles should have good art; art will sell us on an article." Buys 75 mss/year. Query with or without published clips or send complete ms. Length: 2,000-3,000 words. Pays page rate of $150-250. Sometimes pays the expenses of writers on assignment.

Photos: Send photos with submission (copies only, no originals). Reviews contact sheets and transparencies. Offers no additional payment for photos accepted with ms. Pays $500 for cover photo. Captions and identification of subjects required. Buys one-time rights.

Columns/Departments: Address to articles editor. Combat craft (how-to military and police survival skills) and I Was There (first-person accounts of the arcane or unusual based in a combat or law enforcement environment), both 600-800 words. Buys 16 mss/year. Send complete ms. Length: 600-800 words. Combat craft pays $200; I was There $100.

Fillers: Bulletin Board editor. Newsbreaks; military/paramilitary related, "*has* to be documented." Length: 100-250 words. Pays $25.

Tips: "Submit a professionally prepared, complete package. All artwork with cutlines, double-spaced typed manuscript with 5¼" or 3½" IBM-compatible disc, if available, cover letter including synopsis of article, supporting documentation where applicable, etc. Manuscript must be factual; writers have to do their homework and get all their facts straight. One error means rejection. We will work with authors over the phone or by letter, tell them if their ideas have merit for an acceptable article, and help them fine-tune their work. I Was There is a good place for freelancers to start. Vietnam features, if carefully researched and art heavy, will always get a careful look. Combat reports, again, with good art, are number one in our book and stand the best chance of being accepted. Military unit reports from around the world are well received as are law enforcement articles (units, police in action). If you write for us, be complete and factual; pros read *Soldier of Fortune*, and are *very* quick to let us know if we (and the author) err. We will be Operation Desert Storm-oriented for years to come, in terms of first-person accounts and incisive combat reports. Read a current issue to see where we're taking the magazine in the 1990s."

VIETNAM, Empire Press, #300, 602 S. King St., Leesburg VA 22075. (703)771-9400. Editor: Colonel Harry G. Summers, Jr. Managing Editor: Kenneth Phillips. 80-90% freelance written. Quarterly magazine on military aspects of the Vietnam War. "Without debating the wisdom of U.S. involvement, pro or con, our objective is to tell the story of the military events, weaponry and personalities of the war, as it happened." Estab. 1988. Circ. 140,000. Pays on publication. Publishes ms up to 2 years after acceptance. Byline given. Buys all rights. Query for electronic submissions. Reports in 3 months on queries; 6 months on mss. Sample copy $3.95. Writer's guidelines for #10 SASE.

Nonfiction: Book excerpts (if original), historical, interview, personal/experience, military history. "Absolutely no fiction or poetry; we want straight history, as much personal narrative as possible, but not the gung-ho, shoot-em-up variety, either." Buys 50 mss/year. Query. Length: 4,000 words maximum. Pays $300 for features.

Photos: State availability of photos with submission. Pays up to $100/photo, depending on use. Identification of subjects required. Buys one-time rights.

Columns/Departments: Arsenal (about weapons used, all sides); Personality (profiles of the players, all sides), Fighting Forces (about various units or types of unites: air, sea, rescue); Perspectives. Query. Length: 2,000 words. Pays $150.

WORLD WAR II, Empire Press, #300, 602 S. King St., Leesburg VA 22075. (703)771-9400. Editor: Michael Haskew. Managing Editor: Kenneth Phillips. 95% freelance written. Prefers to work with published/established writers. Bimonthly magazine covering "military operations in World War II—events, personalities, strategy, national policy, etc." Estab. 1983. Circ. 200,000. Pays on publication. Publishes ms an average of 1-2 years after acceptance. Byline given. Buys all rights. Submit anniversary-related material 1 year in advance. Reports in 3 months on queries; 6 months or more on mss. Sample copy $4. Writer's guidelines for #10 SASE.

Nonfiction: World War II military history. No fiction. Buys 24 mss/year. Query. Length: 4,000 words. Pays $200.

Photos: State availability of art and photos with submission. (For photos and other art, send photocopies and cite sources. "We'll order.") Sometimes offers additional payment for photos accepted with ms. Captions and identification of subjects required. Buys one-time rights.

Columns/Department: Undercover (espionage, resistance, sabotage, intelligence gathering, behind the lines, etc.); Personalities (WW II personalities of interest); and Armaments (weapons, their use and development), all 2,000 words. Book reviews, 300-750 words. Buys 18 mss/year (plus book reviews). Query. Pays $100.
Tips: "List your sources and suggest further readings in standard format at the end of your piece—as a bibliography for our files in case of factual challenge or dispute. All submissions are on speculation. When the story's right, but the writing isn't, we'll pay a small research fee for use of the information in our own style and language."

Music

Music fans follow the latest music industry news in these publications. Types of music and musicians or specific instruments are the sole focus of some magazines. Publications geared to the music industry and professionals can be found in the Trade Music section. Additional music and dance markets are included in the Entertainment section.

THE ABSOLUTE SOUND, The Journal of The High End, P.O. Box 115, Sea Cliff NY 11579. (516)676-2830. Fax: (516)676-5469. Editor-in-Chief: Harry Pearson, Jr. Managing Editor: Frank Doris. 10% freelance written. Works with a small number of new/unpublished writers each year. Magazine published 8 times/year covering the music reproduction business, audio equipment and records for "up-scale, high tech men and women between the ages of 20 and 100, serious music lovers." Estab. 1973. Pays on publication. Byline given. Buys all rights. Reprints OK; send tearsheet or photocopy of article and information about when and where the article previously appeared. Pays 25-50% of their fee for an original article. Reports in 4 months. Query for electronic submissions. Sample copy $7.50.
Nonfiction: Expose (of bad commercial audio practices); interview/profile (famous recording engineers, famous conductors); new product (audio); opinion (audio and record reviews); and technical (how to improve your stereo system). Special Recordings issue. No puff pieces about industry. No newspaper clippings. Query with published clips. Length: 250-5,000 words. Pays $125-1,000. Sometimes pays the expenses of writers on assignment.
Columns/Departments: Audio Musings (satires) and Reports from Overseas (audio shows, celebrities, record companies). Buys 8 mss/year. Length: 250-750 words. Pays $125-200.
Tips: "Writers should know about audio, recordings and the engineering of same, as well as live music. The approach is *literate*, witty, investigative, good journalism."
• *The Absolute Sound* would like more industry reporting, as well as interviews with industry people. This magazine has increased its frequency from 6-8 issues/year. They report they need more queries.

AMERICAN SONGWRITER, 42 Music Square W., Nashville TN 37203-3206. (615)244-6065. Fax: (615)244-4314. Editor: Vernell Hackett. Managing Editor: Deborah Price. 30% freelance written. Bimonthly magazine, educating amateur songwriters while informing professionals. Estab. 1984. Circ. 4,000. Pays on publication. Publishes ms an average of 2 months after acceptance. Offers $10 kill fee. Buys first North American serial rights. Simultaneous submissions OK. Query for electronic submissions. Reprints OK; send photocopy of article or typed ms with rights for sale noted. Pays 50% of their fee for an original article. Reports in 2 months. Sample copy for $3. Writer's guidelines for SAE.
Nonfiction: General interest, interview/profile, new product and technical. "No fiction." Buys 20 mss/year. Query with published clips. Length: 300-1,200 words. Pays $25-50 for assigned articles.
Photos: State availability of photos with submission. Reviews 3×5 prints. Offers no additional payment for photos accepted with ms. Identification of subjects required. Buys one-time rights.

BAM, Rock and Video/the California Music Magazine, BAM Publications, 5470 Burkirk Ave., Pleasant Hill CA 94523. (510)934-3700. Editors: Steve Stolder and Bill Holdship. 60% freelance written. Biweekly tabloid. Circ. 110,000. Pays on publication. Publishes ms an average of 1 month after acceptance. Byline given. Offers negotiable kill fee. Buys first North American serial rights. Publishes reprints of previously pubished articles. Send typed ms with rights for sale noted. Include information about when and where the article previously appeared. For reprints, pays 100% of the amount paid for original article. Submit seasonal material 3 months in advance. Reports in 3 weeks. Sample copy $2.
Nonfiction: Book excerpts, interview/profiles, record reviews and new product reviews. Buys 100 mss/year. Query with published clips. Length: 1,500-5,000 words. Pays $40-300. Sometimes pays expenses of writers on assignment.
Tips: "*BAM*'s focus is on both the personality and the craft of musicians. Writers should concentrate on bringing out their subject's special traits and avoid bland, clichéd descriptions and quotes. Clear, crisp writing is essential. Many potential *BAM* writers try to be too clever and end up sounding stupid. Also, it helps to

have a clear focus. Many writers tend to ramble and simply string quotes together."

BANJO NEWSLETTER, P.O. Box 364, Greensboro MD 21639-0364. (410)482-6278. Editor: Don Nitchie. 10% freelance written. Monthly magazine covering the "instructional and historical treatment of the 5-string banjo. Covers all aspects of the instrument. Tablature is used for musical examples." Estab. 1973. Circ. 7,000. Pays on publication. Byline given. Buys one-time rights. Reprints OK; send typed ms with rights for sale noted and information about when and where the article previously appeared. Pays 100% of their fee for an original article. Query for electronic submissions. Reports in 1 month on queries. Sample copy for $1.
Nonfiction: Interviews with 5-string banjo players, banjo builders, shop owners, etc. No humorous fiction from anyone unfamiliar with the popular music field. Buys 6 mss/year. Query. Length: 500-4,000 words. Pays $20-100. Sometimes pays writers with contributor copies or other premiums "if that is what writer wants." Very seldom pays expenses of writers on assignment. "We can arrange for press tickets to musical events."
Photos: State availability of photos with submission. Reviews b&w prints. Offers $10-40/photo. Captions and identification of subjects required whenever possible. Buys one-time rights.
Columns/Departments: Buys 60 mss/year. Query. Length: 500-750 words. Payment varies.
Poetry: Don Nitchie, poetry editor: Rt. 1, Box 289, Chilwark MA 02535. Buys 2 poems/year. Submit maximum 1 poem at one time.
Tips: "The writer should be motivated by being a student of the 5-string banjo or interested in the folk or bluegrass music fields where 5-string banjo is featured. Writers should be able to read and write banjo tablature and know various musicians or others in the field."

BLUEGRASS UNLIMITED, Bluegrass Unlimited, Inc., P.O. Box 111, Broad Run VA 22014-0111. (703)349-8181. Fax: (703)341-0011. Editor: Peter V. Kuykendall. 80% freelance written. Prefers to work with published/established writers. Monthly magazine on bluegrass and old-time country music. Estab. 1966. Circ. 22,600. Pays on publication. Publishes ms an average of 4 months after acceptance. Byline given. Kill fee negotiated. Buys first North American serial, one-time, all rights and second serial (reprint) rights. Reprints OK; send typed ms with rights for sale noted and information about when and where the article previously appeared. Pays 70-80% of their fee for an original article. Submit seasonal material 4 months in advance. Reports in 2 weeks on queries; 2 months on mss. Free sample copy and writer's guidelines for #10 SASE.
Nonfiction: General interest, historical/nostalgic, how-to, interview/profile, personal experience, photo feature and travel. No "fan" style articles. Buys 75-80 mss/year. Query with or without published clips. No set word length. Pays 6-8¢/word.
Photos: State availability of photos or send photos with query. Reviews 35mm transparencies and 3×5, 5×7 and 8×10 b&w and color prints. Pays $50-150 for transparencies; $25-50 for b&w prints; and $50-150 for color prints. Identification of subjects required. Buys one-time rights and all rights.
Fiction: Ethnic and humorous. Buys 3-5 mss/year. Query. No set word length. Pays 6-8¢/word.
Tips: "We would prefer that articles be informational, based on personal experience or an interview with lots of quotes from subject, profile, humor, etc."

‡B-SIDE MAGAZINE, B-Side, P.O. Box 1860, Burlington NJ 08016. Editor: Carol L. Schutzbank. Managing Editor: Sandra A. Garcia. Contact: Carol L. Schutzbank. 60% freelance written. Bimonthly magazine covering music. "*B-Side* bridges the gap between home grown fanzines and slicker, more commercial publications." Estab. 1986. Pays on publication. Average publication of ms after acceptance varies. Byline given. Buys first rights. Editorial lead time varies. Accepts simultaneous submissions. Reports in 2-3 months. Sample copy $4. Writer's guidelines for #10 SAE with 2 first class stamps.
Nonfiction: General interest, interview/profile, new product, photo feature, reviews and live coverage. "Please be familiar with our magazine!" Number of mss purchased varies. Query with published clips. Length: varies. Payment varies according to category. Pays contributor copies for smaller pieces. Sometimes pays expenses of writers on assignment.
Photos: State availability of photos with submission. Reviews prints. Negotiates payment individually. Identification of subjects required. Buys one-time rights.
Columns/Departments: Spotlight (new and breaking artists), 500 words; Profile ("get to know" pieces), 750-1,000 words; Feature Reviews (in-depth interview), 1,000-3,000 words; and Reviews (video, book, live concert, release), varies. Payment "depends on piece."

‡CHORALE, Suite 15E, 30 5th Ave., New York NY 10011. (212)473-0568. Editor: Robert Schartoff. 50% freelance written. Monthly newsletter covering choral music. Estab. 1992. Circ. 1,000. Pays on publication. Byline given. Offers 100% kill fee. Publication not copyrighted. Buys all rights. Editorial lead time 1 month. Simultaneous and previously published submissions OK. Query for electronic submissions. Sample copy free on request.
Nonfiction: Book excerpts, essays, historical/nostalgic, how-to, humor, inspirational, interview/profile, new product, opinion, personal experience, photo feature, religious, technical and travel. Buys 30-35 mss/year. Query. Length: 300-1,000 words. Pays $25 minimum for assigned articles; $50 minimum for unsolicited articles. Sometimes pays expenses of writers on assignment.

Photos: State availability of photos with submission. Reviews prints. Negotiates payment individually. Identification of subjects required. Buys one-time rights.

Columns/Departments: CD Reviews (choral/new releases), 130-170 words; Concert Reviews (choral/new live concerts), 200-250 words; and Interviews (choral conductors, composers, etc.), 500-1,000. Buys 35 mss/year. Query. Pays $25-100.

Poetry: Free verse and traditional.

Fillers: Anecdotes, facts, newsbreaks and short humor.

Tips: "We are open to all new writers with an interest or passion for choral music . . . and with a thorough knowledge and understanding of music theory."

CLASSICAL MUSIC MAGAZINE, Suite 207, 121 Lakeshore Rd. E., Mississauga, Ontario L5G 1E5 Canada. Publisher: Anthony D. Copperthwaite. Associate Editor: C. Cooperthwaite. 90% freelance written. Prefers to work with published/established writers but works with a small number of new/unpublished writers each year. Magazine published 5 times/year. Estab. 1978. Circ. 10,000. Pays on publication. Publishes ms an average of 4 months after acceptance. Byline given. Buys first North American serial, one-time and second serial (reprint) rights. Submit seasonal material 4 months in advance. Previously published submissions (book excerpts) OK. Query for electronic submissions. Reports in 6 months. Sample copy and writer's guidelines $5 for 9×12 SAE.

Nonfiction: Interviews, personality profiles, book reviews, historical articles, some human interest stories. "All articles should pertain to the world of classical music. No academic analysis or short pieces of family experiences." Query with published clips; phone queries OK. Unsolicited articles will not be returned. Length: 500 words or less pays $35-75; 1,500-3,500 words pays $100-500 (Canadian funds). Sometimes pays expenses of writers on assignment.

Photos: Quality photos or illustrations purchased with article. No posed promotion photos. Captions required. Buys one-time rights with article.

Tips: "Send a sample of your writing with suggested subjects. A solidly researched historical article with source references, or an interview with photographs with a famous classical music personality are your best bets."

COUNTRY MUSIC, Silver Eagle Publishers, 329 Riverside Ave., Westport CT 06880. Staff written. "Prefers not to share information."

‡COUNTRY SONG ROUNDUP, Country Song Roundup, Inc., 63 Grand Ave., River Edge NJ 07661. (201)487-6124. Editor: Celeste R. Gomes. Assistant Editor: Jennifer Fusco-Giacobbe. Contact: Celeste R. Gomes. 10% freelance written. Monthly magazine covering country music. "Our music is for the country music fan and songwriter. The slant of our articles is on the music, the songs, the artistic side. At times, we cover the private side of an artist." Estab. 1940s. Circ. 200,000. Pays on publication. Publishes ms an average of 6 months after acceptance. Byline given. Offer 50% kill fee or $50. Buys first rights and second serial (reprint) rights. Editorial lead time 3 months. Submit seasonal material 6 months in advance. Query for electronic submissions. Reports in 2 weeks on queries; 2 months on mss. Sample copy: $2.95. Writer's guidelines for #10 SASE.

Nonfiction: Interview/profile of country artists. "No profiles on new artists—they're done inhouse. No personal experience articles, reviews of any kind or Question and Answer articles." Buys 25-30 mss/year. Query with published clips. Length: 1,000-1,200 words. Pays $100 minimum. "Besides regular fee ($100) a copy of the issue in which article appears is sent to the writer."

HIT PARADER, #220, 63 Grand Ave., River Edge NJ 07661. (210)487-6124. Editor: Andy Secher. Managing Editor: Anne Leighton. 5% freelance written. Monthly magazine covering heavy metal music. "We look for writers who have access to the biggest names in heavy metal music." Estab. 1948. Circ. 200,000. Pays on publication. Publishes ms an average of 4 months after acceptance. Byline given. Buys all rights. Submit seasonal material 4 months in advance. Reports in 2 months on queries. Sample copy for 9×12 SAE with 5 first class stamps.

Nonfiction: General interest and interview/profile. Buys 3-5 mss/year. Query with published clips. Length: 600-800 words. Pays $75-140. Lifestyle-oriented and hardball pieces. "Study and really know the bands to get new angles on story ideas."

Photos: Reviews transparencies, 5×7 and 8×10 b&w prints and Kodachrome 64 slides. Offers $25-200/photo. Buys one-time rights. "We don't work with new photographers."

Tips: "Interview big names in metal, get published in other publications. We don't take chances on new writers."

HOME & STUDIO RECORDING, The Magazine for the Recording Musician, Music Maker Publications, #200, 7318 Topanga Canyon Blvd., Canoga Park CA 91303-1242. (818)346-3404. Fax: (818)346-3597. Editor: Nick Batzdorf. 33% freelance written. Monthly magazine of technical and practical info to help musicians make better recordings. Estab. 1987. Circ. 40,000. Pays on publication. Publishes ms an average of 4 months after acceptance. Byline given. Buys first rights. Query for electronic submissions. Reports in 3 weeks on queries. Sample copy $2.95 for 9 × 12 SAE with 5 first class stamps. Writer's guidelines for #10 SASE.

Nonfiction: How-to, personal experience and technical. Buys 36 mss/year. Query. Length: up to 4,000 words. Pays $71.50-440.

Photos: State availability of photos with submission. Reviews contact sheets, negatives and transparencies. Offers no additional payment for photos accepted with ms. Buys one-time rights.

Tips: "Freelancer needs to have good knowledge of subject matter. Particularly interested in technical applications of equipment and recording techniques. We are also publishing new Spanish language version. We're interested in technical interviews with Latin American artists, recording engineers, etc. involved in recording—who are recognizable names."

ILLINOIS ENTERTAINER, Suite 150, 2250 E. Devon, Des Plaines IL 60018. (708)298-9333. Fax: (708)298-7973. Editor: Michael C. Harris. 95% freelance written. Prefers to work with published/established writers but open to new writers with "style." Monthly tabloid covering music and entertainment for consumers within 100-mile radius of Chicago. Estab. 1975. Circ. 80,000. Pays on publication. Publishes ms an average of 2 months after acceptance. Byline given. Offers 10% kill fee. Buys one-time rights. Simultaneous queries OK. Publishes reprints of previously published articles. Send tearsheet or photocopy of article, including information about when and where the article previously appeared. For reprints, pays 100% of the amount paid for an original article. Reports in 1 month on queries; 2 months on mss. Sample copy $5.

Nonfiction: Interview/profile (of entertainment figures). Buys 75 mss/year. Query with published clips. Length: 500-2,000 words. Pays $15-100. Sometimes pays expenses of writers on assignment.

Photos: State availability of photos. Pays $20-30 for 5 × 7 or 8 × 10 b&w prints; $125 for color cover photo, both on publication only. Captions and identification of subjects required.

Columns/Departments: Spins (record reviews stress record over band or genre). Buys 200 mss/year. Query with published clips. Length: 150-250 words. Pays $8-40.

Tips: "Send clips (published or unpublished) with phone number, and be patient. Full staff has seniority, but if you know the ins and outs of the entertainment biz, and can balance that knowledge with a broad sense of humor, then you'll have a chance. Also, *IE* is more interested in alternative music than the pop-pap you can hear/read about everywhere else."

INTERNATIONAL MUSICIAN, American Federation of Musicians, Suite 600, Paramount Building, 1501 Broadway, New York NY 10036. (212)869-1330. Fax: (212)302-4374. Editor: Stephen R. Sprague. Managing Editor: Jessica Roe. 10% freelance written. Prefers to work with published/established writers. Monthly magazine for professional musicians. Estab. 1900. **Pays on acceptance.** Publishes ms an average of 3 months after acceptance. Byline given. Reprints OK; send typed ms with rights for sale noted. Pays 60% of their fee for an original article. Reports in 3 months.

Nonfiction: Articles on prominent instrumentalists (classical, jazz, rock or country) who are members of the American Federation of Musicians. Send complete ms. Length: 1,500 words maximum.

JAZZ TIMES MAGAZINE America's Jazz Magazine, #303, 7961 Eastern Ave., Silver Spring MD 20910. Editor: Mike Joyce. 10% freelance written. Magazine published 10 times/year covering jazz. Estab. 1970. Circ. 71,000. Pays on publication. Publishes ms an average of 3 months after acceptance. Byline given. Offers 50% kill fee. Buys first rights. Editorial lead time 3-4 months. Submit seasonal material 4 months in advance. Query for electronic submissions. Sample copy $4. Writer's guidelines free on request.

Nonfiction: Interview/profile, reviews of CDS, books and videos. Query. Length: 250-2,000 words. Sometimes pays expenses of writers on assignment.

Photos: State availability of photos with submission. Reviews prints. Negotiates payment individually. Identification of subjects required. Buys one-time rights.

Tips: " We are interested in writers who are knowledgeable about jazz and who are already being published in newspapers or other music magazines. No beginners please. We are most open to CD reviews—Send clips. Get published in local papers or magazines first."

THE MISSISSIPPI RAG, "The Voice of Traditional Jazz and Ragtime," 6500 Nicollet Ave. S., Minneapolis MN 55423-1673. (612)861-2446 or (612)920-0312. Fax: (612)861-4621. Editor: Leslie Johnson. 70% freelance written. Works with small number of new/unpublished writers each year, "but most of our writers have been with us for years." Monthly tabloid covering traditional jazz and ragtime. Estab. 1973. Circ. 12,000. Pays on publication. Publishes ms an average of 4 months after acceptance. Byline given. Buys all rights, "but writer may negotiate if he wishes to use material later." Submit seasonal material 3 months in advance. Reports in 3 months. Sample copy and writer's guidelines for 9 × 12 SAE with 5 first class stamps.

Nonfiction: Historical, interview/profile, personal experience, photo features, current jazz and ragtime news, festival coverage, book, video and record reviews, gigs and festival listings. Reviews are always assigned. No "long-winded essays on jazz or superficial pieces on local ice cream social Dixieland bands." Buy 24-30 mss/year. Query with or without published clips or send complete ms. Length: 1,000-6,500 words. Pays 2¢/word.

Photos: Send photos with submission. Prefers b&w 5×7 or 8×10 prints. Offers $5 minimum/photo. Identification of subjects required. Buys one-time rights.

Columns/Departments: Book and Record reviews. Buys 60 assigned mss/year. Query with published clips. Pays 2¢/word.

Tips: "Become familiar with the jazz world. The *Rag* is read by musicians, jazz/ragtime writers, historians and jazz/ragtime buffs. We want articles that have depth — solid facts and a good basic grasp of jazz and/or ragtime history. Not for the novice jazz writer. Interviews with jazz and ragtime performers are most open to freelancers. It's wise to query first because we have already covered so many performers."

MODERN DRUMMER, 870 Pompton Ave., Cedar Grove NJ 07009. (201)239-4140. Fax: (201)239-7139. Editor-in-Chief: Ronald Spagnardi. Features Editor: William F. Miller. Managing Editor: Rick Van Horn. Monthly magazine for "student, semi-pro and professional drummers at all ages and levels of playing ability, with varied specialized interests within the field." 60% freelance written. Circ. 95,000. Pays on publication. Publishes ms an average of 3 months after acceptance. Buys all rights. Previously published submissions OK. Reports in 2 weeks. *Writer's Market* recommends allowing 2 months for reply. Sample copy $3.95. Free writer's guidelines.

Nonfiction: How-to, informational, interview, new product, personal experience and technical. "All submissions must appeal to the specialized interests of drummers." Buys 20-30 mss/year. Query or submit complete ms. Length: 5,000-8,000 words. Pays $200-500.

Photos: Purchased with accompanying ms. Reviews 8×10 b&w prints and color transparencies.

Columns/Departments: Jazz Drummers Workshop, Rock Perspectives, In The Studio, Show Drummers Seminar, Teachers Forum, Drum Soloist, The Jobbing Drummer, Strictly Technique, Book Reviews, Record Reviews, Video Reviews and Shop Talk. "Technical knowledge of area required for most columns." Buys 40-50 mss/year. Query or submit complete ms. Length: 500-2,500 words. Pays $25-150.

MUSICIAN, Billboard Publications, 11th Floor, 1515 Broadway, New York NY 10036. (212)536-5208. Editor: Bill Flanagan. Senior Editors: Matt Resnicoff, Charles Young and Mark Rowland. 85% freelance written. Monthly magazine covering contemporary music, especially rock, pop and jazz. Estab. 1976. Circ. 170,000. Pays on publication. Byline given. Offers kill fee of 25-33%. Buys first North American serial rights. Submit seasonal material 3 months in advance.

Nonfiction: All music-related: book excerpts, expose, historical, how-to (recording and performing), humor, interview/profile, new product and technical. Buys 150 mss/year. Query with published clips. Length: 300-10,000 words. Payment negotiable. Pays expenses of writers on assignment.

Photos: Assigns photo shoots. Uses some stock. Offers $50-300/photo.

Columns/Departments: Jazz (jazz artists or works), 1,000-5,000 words; Reviews (record reviews), 300-500 words; Faces (short, newsy stories), 300 words; and Working Musician (technical "trade" angles on musicians), 1,000-3,000 words. Query with published clips. Length 300-1,500 words.

Tips: "Be aware of special music writers' style; don't gush, be somewhat skeptical; get the best quotes you can and save the arcane criticism for reviews; know and apply Strunk and White; be interesting. Please send *published* clips; we don't want to be anyone's first publication. Our writing is considered excellent (in all modesty), even though we don't pay as much as we'd like. We recognize National Writers Union."

ONE SHOT, The Magazine of One-Hit Wonders, One Shot Enterprises, Contract Station 6, P.O. Box 145, Denver CO 80203. Editor: Steve Rosen. 80% freelance written. Eager to work with new/unpublished writers. "*One Shot* is dedicated to remembering now-obscure or under-appreciated performers of rock and related musics; expecially the one-hit wonders. Uses interviews, essays and journalism." Estab. 1986. Circ. 200. **Pays on acceptance.** Publishes ms up to 1 year after acceptance. Byline given. Buys one-time, second serial (reprint) or simultaneous rights, and makes work-for-hire assignments. Simultaneous and previously published submissions OK; send typed ms with rights for sale noted. Pays 75% of their fee for an original article. Reports in 1 month. Sample copy $3.50. Writer's guidelines for #10 SASE.

Nonfiction: Book excerpts, essays, expose, general interest, historical/nostalgic, interview/profile, opinion, personal experience and travel. No religious/inspirational articles. Buys 16 mss/year. Query. Length: 2,500 maximum words. Pays up to $100 for most articles, will pay more for longer features. Sometimes pays expenses of writers on assignment.

• This magazine only publishes journalism/essays related to rock 'n' roll one-hit wonders. It previously took journalism/fiction/essays/poetry related to all types of "neglected" rock 'n' roll.

Photos: State availability of photos with submission. Reviews contact sheets and 8½×11 prints. Offers additional payment for photos accepted with ms. Buys one-time rights.

Columns/Departments: Speak, Memory! (personal experiences with now-obscure rock, etc., performers); and Travel (update on a place that once figured in a rock song, or performer's career, such as "Hitsville USA" studios in Detroit). Buys 10 mss/year. Query with or without published clips or send complete ms. Length: 1,000 maximum words. Pays up to $100.

Tips: "*One Shot* needs 'Where are They Now' articles on one- or two-hit performers who were once popular. Those pieces should include interviews with the performer and others; and provide a sense of 'being there'. *One Shot* will pay for such stories. Just send me a note explaining your interests, and I'll respond with detailed suggestions. I won't disqualify anyone for not following procedures; I want to encourage a body of work on this topic."

‡**PLAYERS MAGAZINE**, P.E.G., Inc., P.O. Box 1867, Pinellas Park FL 34664. (813)578-1400. Editor: Bill Templeton. Managing Editor: Ron Boyko. 95% freelance written. Consumer publication. Biweekly free magazine for music. "Intelligent news, reviews and interviews about music and the people who make it." Estab. 1990. Circ. 30,000. Pays on publication. Byline given. Buys one-time, second serial (reprint) rights (not within market), simultaneous rights (not within market) or other rights (exclusive within market only). Submit seasonal material 6 weeks in advance. Accepts simultaneous, photocopied and previously published submissions. Query for electronic submissions. Sample copy $2. Call for writer's guidelines.
Nonfiction: Expose, interview/profile and music. Buys 150 mss/year. Query with published clips or send complete ms. Length: 200-2,500 words. Pays $20-50. Sometimes pays expenses of writers on assignment.
Photos: State availability of photos with submission. Reviews prints. Offers $10-20/photo. Captions and identification of subjects required. Buys one-time rights (exclusive within market only).
Columns/Departments: Jazzbeat/Bluesnotes (local and national talent), 600-2,000 words; Hard Report (metal/death metal, local and national), 600-1,000 words; and RadioRadio (local radio), 600-1,000 words. Buys 60 mss/year. Query. Pays $20-50.

PULSE!, Tower Records, 2500 Del Monte, Building C W, Sacramento CA 95691. (916)373-2450. Editor: Mike Farrace. Contact: Laurie MacIntosh. 60% freelance written. Works with a SMALL number of new/unpublished writers each year. Monthly magazine covering recorded music, film, video, video games and electronic hardware. Estab. 1983. Circ. 290,000. Pays on publication. Publishes ms an average of 3 months after acceptance. Byline given. Buys first serial rights. Reports in 5 weeks. Sample copy for 12 × 15 SAE with 8 first class stamps. Writer's guidelines for SASE.
Nonfiction: Feature stories and interview/profile (angled toward artist's taste in music, such as 10 favorite albums, first record ever bought, anecdotes about early record buying experiences). Always looking for concise news items and commentary about nonpopular musical genres. Buys 200-250 mss/year. Query or send complete ms. Length: 200-2,500 words. Pays $20-1,000. Sometimes pays expenses of writers on assignment.
Photos: State availability of photos. Transparencies preferred, but will also review b&w prints. Captions and identification of subjects required. Buys one-time rights.
Fillers: Newsbreaks.
Tips: "Break in with 200- to 400-word news-oriented stories on recording artists or on fast breaking, record-related news, personnel changes, unusual match-ups, reissues of great material. Any kind of music. The more obscure genres on independent labels are the hardest for us to cover, so they stand a good chance of being used. Remember, we are not only a magazine about records, but one that is owned by a record retailer."

RELIX MAGAZINE, Music for the Mind, P.O. Box 94, Brooklyn NY 11229. Editor: Toni A. Brown. Fax: (718)692-4345. 60% freelance written. Eager to work with new/unpublished writers. Bimonthly magazine covering rock 'n' roll music and specializing in Grateful Dead and other San Francisco and 60's related groups for readers ages 15-65. Estab. 1974. Circ. 60,000. Pays on publication. Publishes ms an average of 6 months after acceptance. Byline given. Buys all rights. Reports in 1 year. Sample copy $3.
Nonfiction: Historical/nostalgic, interview/profile, new product, personal experience, photo feature and technical. Special issues include year-end special. Query with published clips if available or send complete ms. Length open. Pays $1.75/column inch. Reprints OK; send typed ms with rights for sale noted and information about when and where the article previously appeared.
Fiction: Publishes novel excerpts.
Columns/Departments: Query with published clips, if available, or send complete ms. Pays variable rates.
Tips: "The most rewarding aspects of working with freelance writers are fresh writing and new outlooks."

THE $ENSIBLE SOUND, 403 Darwin Dr., Snyder NY 14226. (716)839-2199. Fax: (716)839-2264. Publisher: John A. Horan. 80% freelance written. Eager to work with new/unpublished writers. Quarterly magazine for "high fidelity enthusiasts, many having a high fidelity industry-related jobs." Circ. 9,300. **Pays on acceptance.** Publishes ms an average of 6 months after acceptance. Byline given. Buys all rights. Simultaneous and previously published submissions OK. Reports in 2 weeks. Sample copy $2, or free with writing sample, outline and ideas.
Nonfiction: Expose; how-to; general interest; humor; historical; interview (people in hi-fi business, manufacturers or retail); new product (all types of new audio equipment); nostalgia (articles and opinion on older equipment); personal experience (with various types of audio equipment); photo feature (on installation, or how-to tips); profile (of hi-fi equipment); and technical (pertaining to audio). "Subjective evaluations of hi-fi equipment make up 70% of our publication. We will accept 10/issue." Buys 8 mss/year. Submit outline. Pays $25 maximum. Pays expenses of writers on assignment.
Columns/Departments: Bits & Pieces (short items of interest to hi-fi hobbyists); Ramblings (do-it-yourself tips on bettering existing systems); and Record Reviews (of records which would be of interest to audiophiles and recordings of an unusual nature). Query. Length: 25-400 words. Pays $10/page.

SOUNDTRACK, The Journal of the Independent Music Association, SoundTrack Publishing, P.O. Box 609, Ringwood NJ 07456. (201)831-1317. Fax: (201)831-8672. Editor: Don Kulak. 60% freelance written. Bimonthly music and business magazine. Estab. 1988. Circ. 10,000. Pays on publication. Publishes ms an average of 2-3 months after acceptance. Byline sometimes given. Buys first and second serial (reprint) rights. Submit seasonal/holiday material 4 months in advance. Simultaneous and previously published submissions OK. Reports in 1 week on queries; 3 weeks on mss. *Writer's Market* recommends allowing 2 months for reply. Free sample copy and writer's guidelines for 9 × 12 SAE with $2 postage.

Nonfiction: Book excerpts, expose, how-to, interview/profile, opinion and technical. Buys 36 mss/year. Query with published clips. Length: 1,500-2,000 words.. Pays $50-200 for assigned articles. No unsolicited mss. Sometimes pays writers with contributor copies or other premiums rather than cash by "mutually beneficial agreement." Sometimes pays expenses of writers on assignment.

Photos: State availability of photos with submissions. Offers $10-20/photo. Buys all rights.

Columns/Departments: The Business of Music (promotion, distribution, forming a record label; alternative markets—film scores, jingles, etc.; how-to's on generating more income from own music); and Sound Input (in-depth and objective reporting on audio equipment and technology, emphasizing acoustical ramifications, also, cassette, record and CD manufacturing). Buys 24 mss/year. Query with published clips. Length: 1,500-2,000 words.

Tips: "Write a letter explaining background, interests, and areas of special study and what you hope to get out of writing for our publication. All sections are open to freelancers. Writing should be fluid and direct. When describing music, the writing should paint an aural picture with good use of metaphors, and not be overly critical or pretentious. Technical writing should be well documented."

STEREO REVIEW, Hachette Magazines, Inc., 1633 Broadway, New York NY 10019. (212)767-6000. Editor-in-Chief: Louise Boundas. Executive Editor: Michael Riggs. Classical Music Editor: Robert Ripps. Popular Music Editor: Steve Simels. 65% freelance written, almost entirely by established contributing editors, and on assignment. Monthly magazine. Estab. 1958. Circ. 500,000. **Pays on acceptance.** Publishes ms an average of 5 months after acceptance. Byline given. Buys first North American serial rights or all rights. Reports in 5 months. Sample copy for 9 × 12 SAE with 11 first class stamps.

Nonfiction: Equipment and music reviews, how-to-buy, how-to-use, stereo and interview/profile. Buys approximately 25 mss/year. Query with published clips. Length: 1,500-3,000 words. Pays $500-1,000 for assigned articles.

Tips: "Send proposals or outlines, rather than completed articles, along with published clips to establish writing ability. Publisher assumes no responsibility for return or safety of unsolicited art, photos or manuscripts."

TRADITION, Prairie Press, Box 438, Walnut IA 51577. (712)366-1136. Editor: Robert Everhart. 20% freelance written. Bimonthly magazine emphasizing traditional country music and other aspects of pioneer living. Circ. 2,500. Pays on publication. Not copyrighted. Byline given. Buys one-time rights. Submit seasonal/holiday material 6 months in advance. Simultaneous queries, and simultaneous and previously published submissions OK. Reports in 1 month. Sample copy $1.

Nonfiction: Historical (relating to country music); how-to (play, write, or perform country music); inspirational (on country gospel); interview (with traditional country performers); nostalgia (pioneer living); personal experience (country music); and travel (in connection with country music contests or festivals). Query. Length: 800-1,200 words. Pays $10-15.

Photos: State availability of photos with query. Payment included in ms price. Reviews 5 × 7 b&w prints. Captions and model releases required. Buys one-time rights.

Poetry: Free verse and traditional. Buys 4 poems/year. Length: 5-20 lines. Submit maximum 2 poems with SASE. Pays $2-5.

Fillers: Clippings, jokes and anecdotes. Buys 5/year. Length: 15-50 words. Pays $5-10.

Tips: "Material must be concerned with what we term 'real' country music as opposed to today's 'pop' country music. Freelancer must be knowledgable of the subject; many writers don't even know who the father of country music is, let alone write about him."

Mystery

These magazines buy fictional accounts of crime, detective work and mystery. Skim through other sections to identify markets for fiction; some will consider mysteries. For nonfiction crime markets, refer to the Detective section.

ALFRED HITCHCOCK MYSTERY MAGAZINE, Bantam Doubleday Dell, 1540 Broadway, New York NY 10036. Editor: Cathleen Jordan. Magazine published 13 times/year emphasizing mystery fiction. Circ. 225,000. **Pays on acceptance.** Byline given. Buys first rights, first anthology and foreign rights. Submit seasonal/holiday

material 7 months in advance. Reports in 2 months. Writer's guidelines for SASE.
Fiction: Original and well-written mystery and crime fiction. Length: up to 14,000 words.

ELLERY QUEEN'S MYSTERY MAGAZINE, Bantam Doubleday Dell, 1540 Broadway, New York NY 10036. Editor: Janet Hutchings. 100% freelance written. Magazine published 13 times/year. Estab. 1941. Circ. 279,000. **Pays on acceptance.** Publishes ms an average of 6 months after acceptance. Byline given. Buys first serial or second serial (reprint) rights. Simultaneous and previously published submissions OK. Reports in 2 months. Writer's guidelines for #10 SASE.
Fiction: Special consideration will be given to "anything timely and original. We publish every type of mystery: the suspense story, the psychological study, the private-eye story, the deductive puzzle—the gamut of crime and detection from the realistic (including stories of police procedure) to the more imaginative (including 'locked rooms' and impossible crimes). We always need detective stories, and do not want sex, sadism or sensationalism-for-the-sake-of-sensationalism." No gore or horror; seldom publishes parodies or pastiches. Buys up to 13 mss/issue. Length: 6,000 words maximum; occasionally higher but not often. Also buys 2-3 short novels/year of up to 17,000 words, by established authors and minute mysteries of 250 words. Pays 3-8¢/word.
Poetry: Short mystery verses and limericks. Length: 1 page, double-spaced maximum.
Tips: "We have a Department of First Stories to encourage writers whose fiction has never before been in print. We publish an average of 13 first stories every year."

Nature, Conservation and Ecology

These publications promote reader awareness of the natural environment, wildlife, nature preserves and ecosystems. Many of these "green magazines" also concentrate on recycling and related issues. They do not publish recreation or travel articles except as they relate to conservation or nature. Other markets for this kind of material can be found in the Regional; Sports; and Travel, Camping and Trailer categories, although magazines listed there require that nature or conservation articles be slanted to their specialized subject matter and audience. Some juvenile and teen publications also buy nature-related material for young audiences. For more information on recycling publications, turn to the Resources and Waste Reduction section in Trade.

‡**ALTERNATIVES,** P.O. Box 566822, Atlanta GA 30356. (404)973-1994. Editor: Rochel Haigh Blehr. 100% freelance written. Monthly newspaper of environmental/alternative health issues. Estab. 1989. Circ. 45,000. Pays on publication. Byline given. Buys first North American serial rights. Editorial lead time 1 month. Submit seasonal material 2 months in advance. Simultaneous submissions OK. Sample copy free on request. Writer's guidelines for #10 SASE.
Nonfiction: Environment. Buys 420 mss/year. Send complete ms. Length: 1,000-1,500 words. Pays $50 minimum for unsolicited articles.
Photos: State availability of or send photos with submission. Reviews 5 × 7 prints. Identification of subjects required.
Tips: "All submissions are read. They should be hard news AP style, with pros and cons. Topics must cover environment and alternative health. No personal opinion or personal agendas will be considered."

AMERICAN FORESTS, American Forests, 1516 P St. NW, Washington DC 20005. (202)667-3300. Fax: (202)667-7751. Editor: Bill Rooney. 70% freelance written. Bimonthly magazine "of trees and forests, published by a citizens' organization for the advancement of intelligent management and use of our forests, soil, water, wildlife and all other natural resources necessary for an environment of high quality." Estab. 1875. Circ. 30,000. **Pays on acceptance.** Publishes ms an average of 4-8 months after acceptance. Byline given. Buys one-time rights. Publishes reprints of previously published articles. Send tearsheet of article or typed ms with rights for sale noted. Include information about when and where the article previously appeared. For reprints, pays 70% of the amount paid for an original article. Written queries preferred. Submit seasonal material 5 months in advance. Reports in 3 months. Sample copy $1.20. Writer's guidelines for SASE.
Nonfiction: General interest, historical, how-to, humor and inspirational. All articles should emphasize trees, forests, forestry and related issues. Buys 7-10 mss/issue. Query. Length: 2,000 words. Pays $300-700.
Photos: State availability of photos. Offers no additional payment for photos accompanying ms. Uses 8 × 10 b&w glossy prints; 35mm or larger transparencies, originals only. Captions required. Buys one-time rights.
Tips: "Query should have honesty and information on photo support."

APPALACHIAN TRAILWAY NEWS, Appalachian Trail Conference, P.O. Box 807, Harpers Ferry WV 25425-0807. (304)535-6331. Fax: (304)535-2667. Editor: Judith Jenner. 50% freelance written. Bimonthly magazine. Estab. 1925. Circ. 26,000. **Pays on acceptance.** Byline given. Buys first North American serial or second serial (reprint) rights. Previously published submissions OK; send photocopy of article or typed ms with rights for sale noted or information about when and where the article previously appeared. Pays 30% of their fee for an original article. Reports in 2 months. Sample copy $2.50 includes guidelines. Writer's guidelines only for SASE.

● Articles must relate to Appalachian Trail.

Nonfiction: Essays, general interest, historical/nostalgic, how-to, humor, inspirational, interview/profile, photo feature, technical and travel. No poetry or religious materials. Buys 15-20 mss/year. Query with or without published clips or send complete ms. Length: 250-3,000 words. Pays $25-300. Pays expenses of writers on assignment. Publishes, but does not pay for "hiking reflections."

Photos: State availability of b&w photos with submission. Reviews contact sheets, negatives and 5 × 7 prints. Offers $25-125/photo. Identification of subjects required. Negotiates future use by Appalachian Trail Conference.

Tips: "Contributors should display an obvious knowledge of or interest in the Appalachian Trail. Those who live in the vicinity of the Trail may opt for an assigned story and should present credentials and subject of interest to the editor."

ARCHIPELAGO, The Society for Ocean Studies, P.O. Box 510266, Key Colony Beach FL 33051-0266. (305)743-6155. Editor: Robert O. Stafford. Managing Editor: Phil Edwards. Quarterly newsletter covering the oceans. "Our readers are educated, upscale laymen with an interest in marine matters. We run informative stories on just about any subject related to the sea." Estab. 1986. Circ. 200. Pays on publication. Publishes ms an average of 3 months after acceptance. Byline given. Buys first North American serial rights. Simultaneous submissions OK. Reports in 2 weeks. Sample copy and writer's guidelines for #10 SASE.

Nonfiction: "No high tech material with specialized jargon, highly localized interest or very broad subject matter." Buys 4-5 mss/year. Query. Length: 1,000-1,500 words. Pays $50.

Photos: State availability of photos with submission. Offers no additional payment for photos accepted with ms. Buys one-time rights.

Tips: "We are looking for general interest articles related to marine matters: oceanography, biology, chemistry, archaeology, history, meteorology, etc."

THE ATLANTIC SALMON JOURNAL, The Atlantic Salmon Federation, P.O. Box 429, St. Andrews, New Brunswick E0G 2X0 Canada. Fax: (506)529-4985. Editor: Harry Bruce. 50-68% freelance written. Works with a small number of new/unpublished writers each year. Quarterly magazine covering conservation efforts for the Atlantic salmon, catering to "affluent and responsive audience—the dedicated angler and conservationist." Circ. 15,000. Pays on publication. Publishes ms an average of 3-6 months after acceptance. Byline given. Buys first serial rights to articles and one-time rights to photos. Submit seasonal material 3 months in advance. Simultaneous queries and submissions OK. Query for electronic submissions. Reports in 2 months. Sample copy for 9 × 12 SAE with $1 (Canadian), or IRC. Free writer's guidelines.

Nonfiction: Expose, historical/nostalgic, how-to, humor, interview/profile, new product, opinion, personal experience, photo feature, technical, travel, conservation, cuisine, science, research and management. "We are seeking articles that are pertinent to the focus and purpose of our magazine, which is to inform and entertain our membership on all aspects of the Atlantic salmon and its environment, preservation and conservation." Buys 15-20 mss/year. Query with published clips and state availability of photos. Length: 1,500-2,500 words. Pays $200-400. Sometimes pays the expenses of writers on assignment.

Photos: State availability of photos with query. Pays $50 for 3 × 5 or 5 × 7 b&w prints; $50-100 for 2¼ × 3¼ or 35mm color slides. Captions and identification of subjects required.

Columns/Departments: Adventure Eating (cuisine) and First Person (nonfiction, anecdotal, from first-person viewpoint, can be humorous). Buys about 6 mss/year. Length: 1,000-1,500 words. Pays $150.

Fillers: Clippings, jokes, anecdotes and short humor. Length: 100-300 words average. Does not pay.

Tips: "Articles must reflect informed and up-to-date knowledge of Atlantic salmon. Writers need not be authorities, but research must be impeccable. Clear, concise writing is essential, and submissions must be typed. Anecdote, River Log and photo essays are most open to freelancers. The odds are that a writer without a background in outdoors writing and wildlife reporting will not have the 'informed' angle I'm looking for. Our readership is well-read and critical of simplification and generalization."

 A bullet introduces comments by the editor of Writer's Market *indicating special information about the listing.*

AUDUBON, The Magazine of the National Audubon Society, National Audubon Society, 700 Broadway, New York NY 10003-9501. Fax: (212)755-3752. Editor: Michael W. Robbins. 85% freelance written. Bimonthly magazine. Estab. 1887. Circ. 430,000. **Pays on acceptance.** Byline given. Buys first North American serial rights; second serial (reprint) rights on occasion. Query before submission. Reports in 3 months. Sample copy $4 for 9×12 SAE with 10 first class stamps. Writer's guidelines for #10 SASE.

Nonfiction: Essays, investigative, historical, humor, interview/profile, opinion, photo feature and book excerpts (well in advance of publication). Length: 250-4,000 words. Pays $250-4,000. Pays expenses of writers on assignment.

Photos: Query with photographic idea before submitting slides. Reviews 35mm transparencies. Offers page rates per photo on publication. Captions and identification of subjects required. Write for photo guidelines.

• Ranked as one of the best markets for freelance writers in *Writer's Digest* magazine's annual "Top 100 Markets," January 1993.

BIRD WATCHER'S DIGEST, Pardson Corp., P.O. Box 110, Marietta OH 45750. Editor: Mary Beacom Bowers. 60% freelance written. Works with a small number of new/unpublished writers each year. Bimonthly magazine covering natural history—birds and bird watching. "*BWD* is a nontechnical magazine interpreting ornithological material for amateur observers, including the knowledgable birder, the serious novice and the backyard bird watcher; we strive to provide good reading and good ornithology." Estab. 1978. Circ. 85,000. Pays on publication. Publishes ms an average of 1 year after acceptance. Byline given. Buys one-time, first serial and second serial (reprint) rights. Submit seasonal material 6 months in advance. Previously published submissions OK. Reports in 2 months. Sample copy $3. Writer's guidelines for #10 SASE.

Nonfiction: Book excerpts, how-to (relating to birds, feeding and attracting, etc.), humor, personal experience and travel (limited—we get many). "We are especially interested in fresh, lively accounts of closely observed bird behavior and displays and of bird watching experiences and expeditions. We often need material on less common species or on unusual or previously unreported behavior of common species." No articles on pet or caged birds; none on raising a baby bird. Buys 75-90 mss/year. Send complete ms. All submissions must be accompanied by SASE. Length: 600-3,500 words. Pays from $50.

Photos: Send photos with ms. Pays $10 minimum for b&w prints; $25 minimum for transparencies. Buys one-time rights.

Poetry: Avant-garde, free verse, light verse and traditional. No haiku. Buys 12-18 poems/year. Submit maximum 3 poems. Length 8-20 lines. Pays $10.

Tips: "We are aimed at an audience ranging from the backyard bird watcher to the very knowledgable birder; we include in each issue material that will appeal at various levels. We always strive for a good geographical spread, with material from every section of the country. We leave very technical matters to others, but we want facts and accuracy, depth and quality, directed at the veteran bird watcher and at the enthusiastic novice. We stress the joys and pleasures of bird watching, its environmental contribution, and its value for the individual and society."

BUZZWORM, The Environmental Journal, Buzzworm Inc., Suite 206, 2305 Canyon Blvd., Boulder CO 80302. (303)442-1969. Editor: Joseph E. Daniel. Managing Editor: Ilana Kotin. 50% freelance written. Bimonthly magazine. Estab. 1988. Circ. 100,000. Pays 2-3 months after off-sale date of publication. Byline given. Offers 10% kill fee. Buys first world serial, first or all rights. Submit seasonal material 6 months in advance. Reports in 3 months. Sample copy $5 for 9×11 SAE with 6 first class stamps. Writer's guidelines for #10 SASE. "Care is taken, but no responsibility accepted for unsolicited mss and photos."

Nonfiction: Book excerpts, essays, expose, interview/profile, photo feature and environmental. Buys 6-8 mss/year. Query with published clips. Length: 100-3,500 words. Pays $25-1,050 for assigned articles; $25-1,050 for unsolicited articles. Pays expenses of writers on assignment.

Photos: State availability of photos with submission. Offers additional payment for photos accepted and published. Captions, model releases and identification of subjects required. Buys one-time rights.

Columns/Departments: Buys 25 mss/year. Query with published clips. Length: 100-1,500 words. Pays $25-300.

Tips: "Know what has been covered, read the magazine and read the guidelines! Do not query over the phone. Do not call to see if we've received your mss."

‡E THE ENVIRONMENTAL MAGAZINE, Earth Action Network, P.O. Box 5098, Westport CT 06881. (203)854-5559. Editor: Doug Moss. Contact: Elissa Wolfson, managing editor. 80% freelance written. Bimonthly magazine on environmentalism. "*E Magazine* was formed for the purpose of acting as a clearinghouse of information, news and commentary on environmental issues." Estab. 1990. Circ. 75,000. Pays on publication. Byline given. Offers 50% kill fee. Buys first North American serial rights. Editorial lead time 3 months.

For information on setting your freelance fees, see How Much Should I Charge?

Submit seasonal material 3-6 months in advance. Accepts simultaneous submissions. Query for electronic submissions. Sample copy $4. Writer's guidelines for #10 SASE.

Nonfiction: Expose (environmental), how-to (the "Environmentalist" section), interview/profile, new product and opinion. No fiction or poetry. Buys 100 mss/year. Query with published clips. Length: 100-5,000 words. Pays 20¢/word, "negotiable on spec or free contributions are welcome." Sometimes pays telephone expenses of writers on assignment.

Photos: State availability or send photos with submission (if available). Reviews printed samples, e.g., magazine tearsheet, postcards, etc. to be kept on file. Negotiates payment individually. Identification of subjects required. Buys one-time rights.

Columns/Departments: In Brief/Currents (environmental news stories/trends), 450-1,000 words; Consumer News (environmentally sound products/trends), 1,200 or more words; Food and Health (ecological and health impacts of dietary choices), 1,200 or more words; the Environmentalist (how-to eco lifestyle tips), 1,000 or more words; Book Reviews (environmental books), 1,200 or more words; Interviews (environmental leaders), 2,000 words. Buys 100 mss/year. Query with published clips. Pays 20¢/word, "negotiable on spec or free contributions are welcome."

Tips: "Contact us to obtain writer's guidelines and back issues of our magazine. Tailor your query according to the department/section you feel it would be best suited for. Articles must be lively, well-researched, and relevant to a mainstream, national readership."

‡ENVIRONMENT, Heldref Publications, 1319 18th St. NW, Washington DC 20036-1802. Managing Editor: Barbara T. Richman. 2% freelance written. For scientists, business and government executives, teachers, citizens, high school and college students and teachers interested in environment or effects of technology and science in public affairs. Magazine published 10 times/year. Estab. 1958. Circ. 16,000. Buys all rights. Byline given. Pays on publication to professional writers. Publishes ms an average of 4 months after acceptance. Reports in 5 months. Query or submit 3 double-spaced copies of complete ms. Sample copy $4.50.

Nonfiction: Scientific and environmental material, and effects of technology on society. Preferred length: 4,000-5,000 words for full-length article. Pays $100-300, depending on material. Also accepts shorter articles (1,000-1,700 words) for "Overview" section. Pays $100. "All full-length articles must be annotated (referenced), and all conclusions must follow logically from the facts and arguments presented." Prefers articles centering around policy-oriented, public decision-making, scientific and technological issues.

HIGH COUNTRY NEWS, High Country Foundation, P.O. Box 1090, Paonia CO 81428. (303)527-4898. Editor: Betsy Marston. 80% freelance written. Works with a small number of new/unpublished writers each year. Biweekly tabloid covering environment and natural resource issues in the Rocky Mountain states for environmentalists, politicians, companies, college classes, government agencies, etc. Estab. 1970. Circ. 12,500. Pays on publication. Publishes ms an average of 2 months after acceptance. Byline given. Buys one-time rights. Reports in 1 month. Free sample copy and writer's guidelines.

Nonfiction: Reporting (local issues with regional importance); expose (government, corporate); interview/profile; opinion; personal experience; and centerspread photo feature. Special issues include those on states in the region. Buys 100 mss/year. Query. Length: 3,000 words maximum. Pays 10-15¢/word. Sometimes pays the expenses of writers on assignment.

Photos: Send photos with ms. Prefers b&w prints. Captions and identification of subjects required.

Poetry: Chip Rawlins, poetry editor, 67½ S. 500 W., Logan UT 84321. Avant-garde, free verse, haiku, light verse and traditional. Pays in contributor copies.

Tips: "We use a lot of freelance material, though very little from outside the Rockies. Start by writing a query letter."

INTERNATIONAL WILDLIFE, National Wildlife Federation, 8925 Leesburg Pike, Vienna VA 22184-0001. Editor: Jonathan Fisher. 85% freelance written. Prefers to work with published/established writers. Bimonthly for persons interested in natural history, outdoor adventure and the environment. Estab. 1971. Circ. 380,000. **Pays on acceptance.** Publishes ms an average of 4 months after acceptance. Usually buys all rights to text. "We are now assigning most articles but will consider detailed proposals for quality feature material of interest to a broad audience." Reports in 6 weeks. Writer's guidelines for #10 SASE.

Nonfiction: Focuses on world wildlife, environmental problems and peoples' relationship to the natural world as reflected in such issues as population control, pollution, resource utilization, food production, etc. Stories deal with non-US subjects. Especially interested in articles on animal behavior and other natural history, first-person experiences by scientists in the field, well-reported coverage of wildlife-status case studies which also raise broader themes about international conservation and timely issues. Query. Length: 2,000-2,500 words. Also in the market for short, 750-word "one pagers." Examine past issue for style and subject matter. Pays $1,500 minimum for long features. Sometimes pays expenses of writers on assignment.

Photos: Purchases top-quality color photos; prefers packages of related photos and text, but single shots of exceptional interest and sequences also considered. Prefers Kodachrome or Fujichrome transparencies. Buys one-time rights.

• Ranked as one of the best markets for freelance writers in *Writer's Digest* magazine's annual "Top 100 Markets," January 1993.

MICHIGAN NATURAL RESOURCES MAGAZINE, State of Michigan Department of Natural Resources, P.O. Box 30034, Lansing MI 48909. (517)373-9267. Managing Editor: Richard Morscheck. 80% freelance written. Works with a small number of new/unpublished writers each year. Bimonthly magazine covering natural resources in the Great Lakes area. Estab. 1931. Circ. 100,000. **Pays on acceptance.** Publishes ms an average of 9 months after acceptance. Byline given. Offers 100% kill fee. Buys first rights. Submit seasonal/holiday material 1 year in advance. Reports in 1 month. Sample copy $4 for 9 × 12 SAE. Writer's guidelines for #10 SASE.

• This magazine is relying more on freelance writers now than in the past.

Nonfiction: "All material must pertain to this region's natural resources: lakes, rivers, wildlife, flora and special features. No personal experience." Buys 30 mss/year. Query with clips of published work. Length: 1,000-3,000 words. Pays $150-400. Sometimes pays the expenses of writers on assignment.

Photos: Gijsbert (Nick) vanFrankenhuyzen, photo editor. "Photos submitted with an article can help sell it, but they must be of professional quality and razor sharp in focus." Send photos with ms. Pays $50-200 for 35mm transparencies; Fuji or Kodachrome preferred. Identification of subjects required. Buys one-time rights.

Tips: "We hope to exemplify why Michigan's natural resources are valuable to people and vice versa. We also strongly suggest that prospective writers familiarize themselves with past issues of the magazine before sending us material to review."

NATIONAL PARKS, 1776 Massachusetts Ave. NW, Washington DC 20036. (202)223-6722. Fax: (202)659-0650. Editor: Sue Dodge. 85% freelance written. Prefers to work with published/established writers. Bimonthly magazine for a highly educated audience interested in preservation of National Park System units, natural areas, and protection of wildlife habitat. Estab. 1919. Circ. 300,000. **Pays on acceptance.** Publishes ms an average of 5 months after acceptance. Buys first North American serial and second serial (reprint) rights. Reports in 10 weeks. Sample copy $3 for 9 × 12 SAE. Writer's guidelines for #10 SASE.

Nonfiction: Expose (on threats, wildlife problems in national parks); descriptive articles about new or proposed national parks and wilderness parks; natural history pieces describing park geology, wildlife or plants. All material must relate to national parks. No poetry, philosophical essays or first person narratives. "Queries are welcome, but unsolicited mss are not accepted." Length: 2,000-3,000 words. Pays $500-800.

Photos: $75-200 for transparencies. Captions required. Buys first North American serial rights.

• Ranked as one of the best markets for freelance writers in *Writer's Digest* magazine's annual "Top 100 Markets," January 1993.

NATIONAL WILDLIFE, National Wildlife Federation, 8925 Leesburg Pike, Vienna VA 22184-0001. (703)790-4524. Editor-in-Chief: Bob Strohm. Editor: Mark Wexler. 75% freelance written, "but assigns almost all material based on staff ideas. Assigns few unsolicited queries." Bimonthly magazine on wildlife, natural history and environment. "Our purpose is to promote wise use of the nation's natural resources and to conserve and protect wildlife and its habitat. We reach a broad audience that is largely interested in wildlife conservation and nature photography. We avoid too much scientific detail and prefer anecdotal, natural history material." Estab. 1963. Circ. 720,000. **Pays on acceptance.** Publishes ms an average of 1 year after acceptance. Offers 25% kill fee. Buys all rights. Submit seasonal material 8 months in advance. Reports in 6 weeks. Writer's guidelines for #10 SASE.

Nonfiction: General interest (2,500-word features on wildlife, new discoveries, behavior, or the environment); how-to (an outdoor or nature related activity); personal experience (outdoor adventure); photo feature (wildlife); and short 700-word features on an unusual individual or new scientific discovery relating to nature. Buys 50 mss/year. Query with or without published clips. Length: 750-2,500 words. Pays $500-2,000. Sometimes pays expenses of writers on assignment.

Photos: John Nuhn, photo editor. State availability of photos or send photos with query. Prefers Kodachrome or Fujichrome transparencies. Buys one-time rights.

• Ranked as one of the best markets for freelance writers in *Writer's Digest* magazine's annual "Top 100 Markets," January 1993.

Tips: "Writers can break in with us more readily by proposing subjects (initially) that will take only one or two pages in the magazine (short features)."

NATURAL HISTORY, Natural History Magazine, Central Park West at 79th St., New York NY 10024. Editor: Alan P. Ternes. 15% freelance written. Monthly magazine for well-educated, ecologically aware audience: professional people, scientists and scholars. Circ. 520,000. Pays on publication. Publishes ms an average of 3 months after acceptance. Byline given. Buys first serial rights and becomes agent for second serial (reprint) rights. Submit seasonal material at least 6 months in advance.

Nonfiction: Uses all types of scientific articles except chemistry and physics—emphasis is on the biological sciences and anthropology. Prefers professional scientists as authors. "We always want to see new research findings in almost all the branches of the natural sciences—anthropology, archeology, zoology and ornithology. We find that it is particularly difficult to get something new in herpetology (amphibians and reptiles) or entomology (insects), and we would like to see material in those fields. We lean heavily toward writers who are scientists. We expect high standards of writing and research. We favor an ecological slant in most of our pieces, but do not generally lobby for causes, environmental or other. The writer should have a deep knowledge of his subject, then submit original ideas either in query or by manuscript. Acceptance is more likely if article is accompanied by high-quality photographs." Buys 60 mss/year. Query or submit complete ms. Length: 1,500-3,000 words. Pays $750-1,000, plus additional payment for photos used.

Photos: Rarely uses 8 × 10 b&w glossy prints; pays $125/page maximum. Much color is used; pays $300 for inside and up to $500 for cover. Buys one-time rights.

Tips: "Learn about something in depth before you bother writing about it."

OUTDOOR AMERICA, Level B, 1401 Wilson Blvd., Arlington VA 22209-2318. (703)528-1818. Fax: (703)528-1836. Editor: Kristin Merriman. 30% freelance written. Prefers to work with published/established writers but is open to new writers who send complete manuscripts. Quarterly magazine about natural resource conservation and outdoor recreation for sports enthusiasts and local conservationists who are members of the Izaak Walton League. Estab. 1922. Circ. 58,000. Pays half on receipt of manuscript, half on publication. Publishes ms an average of 4 months after acceptance. Byline and brief biography given. Buys one-time North American rights, depending on arrangements with author. "Considers previously published material if there's not a lot of audience overlap." Query first. Submit seasonal material 6 months in advance. Reports in 1 month, often sooner. Sample copy $1.50 for 9 × 12 SAE. Writer's guidelines for SASE.

Nonfiction: "We are interested in thoroughly researched, well-written pieces on current natural resource and recreation issues of national importance (threats to water, fisheries, wildlife habitat, air, public lands, soil, etc.); articles on wildlife management controversies; and essays and humor pieces on outdoor recreation themes (fishing, hunting, camping, ethical outdoor behavior, etc.)." Length: 900-2,500 words. Payment: 20¢/word; 10¢/word for reprints (send typed ms with rights for sale noted and information about when and where the article previously appeared).

• The editor of this magazine would like to see more environmental, investigative, natural history and outdoor recreation queries.

Photos: Reviews 5 × 7 b&w glossy prints and 35mm and larger transparencies. Additional payment for photos with ms negotiated. Pays $225 for covers. Captions and model releases (for models under age 18) required. Buys one-time rights.

Tips: "Writers should obtain guidelines and sample issue *before* querying us. They will understand our needs and editorial focus much better if they've done this. Queries submitted without the writer having read the guidelines are *almost always* off base and almost always rejected."

PACIFIC DISCOVERY, California Academy of Sciences, Golden Gate Park, San Francisco CA 94118-4599. (415)750-7116. Fax: (415)750-7106. Editor: Keith Howell. 100% freelance written. Prefers to work with published/established writers. "Quarterly journal of nature and culture in California, the West, the Pacific and Pacific Rim countries read by scientists, naturalists, teachers, students, and others having a keen interest in knowing the natural world more thoroughly." Estab. 1948. Circ. 30,000. Buys first North American serial rights. Pays on publication. Query for electronic submissions. Reports within 2 months. Sample copy for 9 × 12 SAE with 5 first class stamps. Writer's guidelines for #10 SASE.

Nonfiction: "Subjects of articles include behavior and natural history of animals and plants, ecology, evolution, anthropology, geology, paleontology, biogeography, taxonomy and related topics in the natural sciences. Occasional articles are published on the history of natural science, exploration, astronomy and archaeology. Emphasis is on current research findings. Authors need not be scientists; however, all articles must be based, at least in part, on firsthand fieldwork. Accuracy is crucial." Query with 100-word summary of projected article for review before preparing finished ms. Length: 800-4,000 words. Pays 25¢/word.

Photos: Send photos with submission "even if an author judges that his own photos should not be reproduced. Referrals to professional photographers with coverage of the subject will be greatly appreciated." Reviews 35mm, 4 × 5 or other transparencies or 8 × 10 b&w glossy prints. Offers $75-175 and $200 for the cover. Buys one-time rights.

PJG MAGAZINE, For Garden and Bird Fanciers, Parrot Jungle and Gardens, 11000 SW 57th Ave., Miami FL 33156. (305)666-7834. Editor: Amy Jordan Smith. 10% freelance written. Semiannual magazine that covers aviculture and horticulture. "PJG is a publication of Parrot Jungle and Gardens, a landmark Miami bird sanctuary, wildlife habitat and botanical garden since 1936." Estab. 1988. Circ. 10,000. **Pays on acceptance.** Byline given. Buys first, one-time and second serial (reprint) rights or makes work-for-hire assignments. Submit seasonal material 1 year in advance. Reports in 2 weeks on queries; 2 months on mss. Sample copy $3 for 9 × 12 SAE with 4 first class stamps.

Nonfiction: General interest, how-to (must be slanted to the serious gardener or bird breeder) and technical. "No 'How I taught my Amazon to sing hymns' unless the bird is multilingual." Buys 6 mss/year. Query with or without published clips or send complete ms. Length: 250-1,500 words. Pay is negotiated.

Photos: State availability of photos with submission. Pays is negotiated. Model releases and identification of subjects required. Buys one-time rights.

Fillers: Anecdotes and facts. Buys 4/year. Length: 100 words maximum.

Tips: "We are interested in well-written articles by experienced aviculturists and gardeners."

SIERRA, 730 Polk St., San Francisco CA 94109. (415)923-5656. Fax: (415)776-4868. Editor-in-Chief: Jonathan F. King. Deputy Editor: Annie Stine. Senior Editors: Joan Hamilton, Reed McManus. Associate Editors: Mark Mardon and Paul Rauber. Managing Editor: Marc Lecurd. Works with a small number of new/unpublished writers each year. Bimonthly magazine emphasizing conservation and environmental politics for people who are well educated, activist, outdoor-oriented and politically well informed with a dedication to conservation. Estab. 1893. Circ. 500,000. **Pays on acceptance.** Publishes ms an average of 4 months after acceptance. Byline given. Buys first North American serial rights. Query for electronic submissions. Reports in 2 months.
Nonfiction: Expose (well-documented on environmental issues of national importance such as energy, wilderness, forests, etc.); general interest (well-researched nontechnical pieces on areas of particular environmental concern); historical (relevant to environmental concerns); how-to and equipment pieces (on camping, climbing, outdoor photography, etc.); photo feature (photo essays on threatened or scenic areas); and journalistic treatments of semi-technical topics (energy sources, wildlife management, land use, waste management, etc.). No "My trip to . . ." or "why we must save wildlife/nature" articles; no poetry or general superficial essays on environmentalism; no reporting on purely local environmental issues. Buys 5-6 mss/issue. Query with published clips. Length: 800-3,000 words. Pays $450-2,000. Pays limited expenses of writers on assignment.
Photos: Lacey Tuttle Brown, art and production manager. State availability of photos. Pays $300 maximum for transparencies; more for cover photos. Buys one-time rights.
● Ranked as one of the best markets for freelance writers in *Writer's Digest* magazine's annual "Top 100 Markets," January 1993.
Tips: "Queries should include an outline of how the topic would be covered and a mention of the political appropriateness and timeliness of the article. Statements of the writer's qualifications should be included."

SNOWY EGRET, The Fair Press, P.O. Box 9, Bowling Green IN 47833. (812)829-1910. Editors: Karl Barnebey and Michael Aycock. 95% freelance written. Semiannual magazine of natural history from literary, artistic, philosophical and historical perspectives. "We are interested in works that celebrate the abundance and beauty of nature, encourage a love and respect for the natural world, and examine the variety of ways through which human beings connect psychologically and spiritually with living things and landscape. Circ. 500. Pays on publication. Publishes ms an average of 1 year after acceptance. Buys first North American serial and one-time rights. Submit seasonal material 6 months in advance. Simultaneous submissions OK. Reports in 3 months. Sample copy $8 for 9 × 12 SAE. Writer's guidelines for 6 × 9 SASE.
Nonfiction: Essays, general interest, historical, interview/profile, opinion, personal experience and travel. "No topical, dated articles, highly scientific or technical pieces." Buys 20 mss/year. Send complete ms. Length: 500-10,000. Pays $2/page.
Fiction: Literary with natural history orientation. "No popular and genre fiction." Buys up to 10 mss/year. Send complete ms. Length: 500-10,000. Pays $2/page.
Poetry: Nature-oriented: avant-garde, free verse, haiku and traditional. Buys 20 poems/year. Pays $4/poem to $4/page.
Tips: "Make sure that all assertions, ideas, messages, etc. are thoroughly rooted in detailed observations and shared with the reader through description, dialogue and narrative. The reader needs to see what you've seen, live what you've lived. Whenever possible the subject shown should be allowed to carry its own message, to speak for itself. We look for book reviews, essays, poetry, fiction, conservation and environmental studies based on first-hand observations of plants and animals that show an awareness of detail and a thoroughgoing familiarity with the organisms or habitats in question."

SUMMIT, 1221 May St., Hood River OR 97031. Editor: John Harlin. 100% freelance written. Quarterly magazine covering mountain culture, environment and sport. "Sophisticated, inspired, introspective and passionate writing for an educated audience with high literary standards. The writing must relate to the mountain world, but this can be treated broadly." Estab. 1990. Pays 3 months prior to publication or on acceptance. Publishes ms an average of 3-9 months after acceptance. Byline given. Offers 25% kill fee. Buys first North American serial, first, second serial (reprint) or simultaneous rights. Submit seasonal material 3-12 months in advance. Simultaneous and previously published submissions OK. Send tearsheet or photocopy of article or short story, typed ms with rights for sale noted, and information about when and where the article previously appeared. Reports in 2 months. Sample copy $6 for 9 × 12 SAE with 10 first class stamps "or send $8 w/SAE and we'll stamp." Writer's guidelines for #10 SASE.
Nonfiction: Book excerpts, essays, expose, general interest, historical/nostalgic, humor, inspirational, interview/profile, opinion, personal experience, photo feature and travel. "No what-I-did stories that don't have strong literary content." Buys 30 mss/year. Query with or without published clips or send complete ms. Length: 500-5,000 words. Pays $50-800.
Photos: State availability of photos with query or ms. Send photos with submission. Reviews contact sheets, transparencies and prints. Offers $50-175/photo. $300 for cover. Identification of subjects required. Buys one-time rights.
Columns/Departments: Mountain Times and Scree (news and essays on mountain world), 50-1,500 words. Buys 25 mss/year. Query with published clips or send complete ms. Pays $50-300; and. The Summit Guide (mountain travel guide to destinations and techniques). Query stating fields of expertise. 50-1,500 words. Pays $50-700.

Fiction: Adventure, ethnic, experimental, historical, humorous and novel excerpts. Buys 1-4 mss/year. Send complete ms. Length: 500-5,000 words. Pays $200-800.

Poetry: Pays $50-200. Buys only occasionally. Must be mountain-related.

Fillers: Facts and short humor. Pays $50 minimum.

Tips: "If we don't know the writer, submitting complete manuscripts or partial manuscripts helps. Published clips help, but we distrust them because they've already been edited. Know the magazine, *know your subject* and *know your writing*. Mountain Times news pieces and essays can be about any place and anything in the mountain world but must be entertaining or provocative. Previously published material from non-competing magazines is welcome. Send published piece with date and source."

TRILOGY, The Magazine for Outdoor Enthusiasts, Trilogy Publishing, Inc., 310 Old E. Vine St., Lexington KY 40507-1534. (606)231-8522. Editor: Jon Klusmire. 75% freelance written. Bimonthly magazine that covers recreation, industry and the environment. Estab. 1989. Circ. 100,000. Pays on publication. Byline given. Buys first North American serial rights. Submit seasonal material 6 months in advance. Considers previously published submissions from non-competitive publications. Reports in 2 months on queries. Sample copy for $4.50. Writer's guidelines for #10 SASE.

Nonfiction: How-to (outdoor recreation), interview/profile, new product, opinion, personal experience, photo feature and technical. "We are only interested in material that is related to outdoor recreation, adventure travel, industry and the environment, and environmental topics." Buys 75 mss/year. Query with published clips. Length: 1,500-2,500 words. Pays $150-250.

Photos: State availability of photos with submission. Offers $50-250 per photo. Captions, model releases, identification of subjects required. Buys one-time rights.

Tips: "Get guidelines and send a query. Unsolicited mss go to the bottom of the pile."

WILDLIFE CONSERVATION MAGAZINE, New York Zoological Society, 185th St. and Southern Blvd., Bronx NY 10460-1068. (212)220-5121. Editor: Joan Downs. 90% freelance written. Bimonthly magazine covering wildlife. Estab. 1895. Circ. 141,858. **Pays on acceptance.** Publishes ms an average of 1 year or more after acceptance. Byline given. Buys first North American serial rights. Submit seasonal material 1 year in advance. Simultaneous submissions OK. Reports on 2 months on queries; 3 months on mss. Sample copy $2.95 for 9 × 12 SAE with 6 first class stamps. Writer's guidelines for SASE.

Nonfiction: Nancy Simmons, senior editor. Essays, personal experience and wildlife articles. No pet or any domestic animal stories. Buys 12 mss/year. Query. Length 1,500-2,500 words. Pays $750-3,000 for assigned articles; $500-1,000 for unsolicited articles.

Photos: State availability of photos with submission. Reviews transparencies. Buys one-time rights.

ZOO LIFE, Zoos, Aquariums, and Wildlife Parks, Ingle Publishing Co., 11661 San Vicente Blvd., Los Angeles CA 90049. (310)820-8841. Editor: Mary Batten. Managing Editor: Jody Ingle. 75% freelance written. "Quarterly magazine devoted to those readers interested in the conservation, education, research and captive-breeding efforts of zoos, aquariums and wildlife parks. Our articles appeal to educated adults as well as children; in short, to anyone who enjoys zoos and the animals in them." Estab. 1989. Circ. 80,000. Pays on publication. Publishes ms an average of 6 months after acceptance. Byline given. Buys one-time or second serial (reprint) rights. Submit seasonal material 1 year in advance. Accepts simultaneous and previously published submissions. Reports in 1 month on queries; 2 months on mss. Sample copy $3.95 for 9 × 12 SAE with 10 first class stamps. Free writer's guidelines.

Nonfiction: Book excerpts, essays, general interest, historical/nostalgic, how-to (photography), interview/profile, opinion, photo feature and travel. "Please, no general trips through a zoo exhibit; we prefer in-depth focus on a zoo animal, new research on animal behavior, exhibit, program, or personality." Buys 45 mss/year. Query with published clips. Length: 500-2,000 words. Pays $600 maximum for assigned articles.

Photos: State availability of photos with submission. Reviews 35mm or 4 × 5 transparencies. Payment negotiable. Identification of subjects required. Buys one-time rights.

Columns/Departments: Arkwatch (column devoted to zoos' captive-breeding programs), 1,200 words; Reviews (book, video reviews of relevant titles), 500-700 words; and Zoo Views (opinion, usually on conservation or zoo issues, usually written by professionals), 1,200 words. Buys 8 mss/year. Query with published clips. Length: 500-1,200 words. Pays $150-360.

Tips: "Querying with samples is the writer's best bet. Also, familiarity with the magazine and the articles it has *already* published is advised. We are looking for well-researched pieces featuring interviews with zoo experts or other authorities on animal conservation."

Personal Computers

Personal computer magazines continue to change and evolve. The most successful have a strong focus on a particular family of computers or widely-used applications and carefully target a specific type of computer use. Magazines serving MS-DOS and Macintosh families of computers are expected to grow, while new technology will also offer opportunities for new titles. Some of the magazines offer an online service for readers in which they can get the magazine alone or with a supplement on computer disk. Be sure you see the most recent issue of a magazine before submitting material.

AMAZING COMPUTING, PiM Publications, Inc., P.O. Box 2140, Fall River MA 02722-2140. (508)678-4200. Fax: (508)675-6002. Submissions Editor: Jeff Gamble. Managing Editor: Donald D. Hicks. 90% freelance written. Monthly magazine for the Commodore Amiga computer system user. Circ. 35,000. Pays on publication. Publishes ms an average of 2-4 months after acceptance. Byline given. Buys all rights. Query for electronic submissions. Reports in 2 months. Sample copy $5. Free writer's guidelines.
Nonfiction: How-to, new product, technical, reviews and tutorials. Buys 200 mss/year. Query. Length: 1,000 words minimum. Pays $65 minimum/page.
Photos: Send photos with submission. Reviews 4×6 prints. Offers $25/photo. Captions required. Buys all rights.
Columns/Departments: Reviews and Programs. Buys 100 mss/year. Query. Length: 1,000-3,000 words.

‡BYTE MAGAZINE, 1 Phoenix Mill Lane, Peterborough NH 03458. (603)924-9281. Editor: Dennis Allen. Monthly magazine covering personal computers for professional users of computers. 50% freelance written. Estab. 1975. Circ. 515,000. **Pays on acceptance.** Byline given. Buys all rights. Reports on rejections in 6 weeks; 3 months if accepted. Electronic submissions accepted, IBM or Macintosh compatible. Sample copy $3.50. Writer's guidelines for #10 SASE.
Nonfiction: News, reviews, and in-depth discussions of topics related to microcomputers or technology. Buys 160 mss/year. Query. Length: 1,500-5,000 words. Pay is $50-1,000+ for assigned articles; $500-750 for unassigned.
Tips: "Always interested in hearing from freelancers who are technically astute users of personal computers. Especially interested in stories on new computing technologies, from anywhere in the world. Read several issues of BYTE to see what we cover, and how we cover it. Read technical journals to stay on the cutting edge of new technology and trends. Send us a proposal with a short outline of an article explaining some new technology, software trend, and the relevance to advanced business users of personal computers. Our readers want accurate, useful, technical information; not fluff and meaningless data presented without insight or analysis."

COMPUTERCRAFT, The Practical Magazine for Personal Computers & Microcontrollers, CQ Communications, 76 N. Broadway, Hicksville NY 11801. (516)681-2922. Fax: (516)681-2926. 90% freelance written. Monthly magazine covering single-board computers, microcontrolled electronic devices, software, personal computers, electronic circuitry, construction projects and technology for readers with a technical affinity. Estab. 1984. Circ. 50,000. **Pays on acceptance.** Publishes ms an average of 3 months after acceptance. Byline given. Offers 25% kill fee. Buys first North American serial rights. Reports in 2 weeks on queries; 3 weeks on mss. *Writer's Market* recommends allowing 2 months for reply. Sample copy $1 for 9×12 SAE. Writer's guidelines for #10 SASE.
Nonfiction: How-to (construction projects, applications, computer enhancements, upgrading and troubleshooting); new product (reviews); opinion (experiences with computer products); and technical (features and tutorials: circuits, applications). "Articles must be technically accurate. Writing should be 'loose,' not textbookish." No long computer programs. Buys 125 mss/year. Query. Length: 500-4,000 words. Pays $90-150/published page. Sometimes pays expenses of writers on assignment.
Photos: Send photos with query or ms. Reviews transparencies and 5×7 b&w prints. Captions, model releases, and identification of subjects required. Buys first North American rights.
Tips: "The writer must have technical or applications acumen and well-researched material. Articles should reflect the latest products and technology. Sharp, interesting photos are helpful, as are rough, clean illustrations for re-drawing. Cover useful improvements to existing personal computers. Areas most open to freelancers include feature articles, technical tutorials, and projects to build. Some writers exhibit problems with longer pieces due to limited technical knowledge and/or poor organization. We can accept more short pieces. For electronic submissions, use Electronic mailbox, Computercraft, on MCI Mail."

GENEALOGICAL COMPUTING, Ancestry Inc., P.O. Box 476, Salt Lake City UT 84110. (801)531-1790. Fax: (801)531-1798. Editor: Dennis M. Sampson. 50% freelance written. Quarterly magazine on genealogy, using computers. Designed for genealogists who use computers for records management. "We publish articles on all types of computers: PC, Macintosh, Apple II, etc." Estab. 1981. Circ. 3,500. Pays on publication. Publishes ms an average of 4 months after acceptance. Byline given. Buys all rights. Query for electronic submissions. Reports in 2 months.

Nonfiction: New product, personal experience (with software), technical (telecommunications, data exchange, data base development) how-to, reviews, opinion and programming. "Articles on pure genealogy cannot be accepted; this also applies to straight computer technology." Query with outline/summary. Length: 1,000-4,000 words. Pays $100.

Tips: "We need how-to articles describing methods of managing genealogical information with your computer. We accept a *limited* number of pertinent BASIC programs or programming ideas for publication."

INCIDER/A+; Apple II/Macintosh, A+ Publishing, 80 Elm St., Peterborough NH 03458. (603)924-0100. Editor: Bill Kennedy. Executive Editor: Eileen Terrill. 50% freelance written. "*InCider/A+* is a magazine for Apple II and Macintosh computer users, dedicated to helping them get the most out of their hardware and software." Circ. 130,000. **Pays on acceptance.** Publishes ms an average of 5 months after acceptance. Byline given. Offers 50% kill fee. Buys all rights. Submit seasonal/holiday material 9 months in advance. Query for electronic submissions. Reports in 1 month.

Nonfiction: Paul Statt, articles editor. How-to (repair or use hardware, and how to build software); interview/profile (with software or hardware developer); technical (strictly limited to Apple II and Macintosh computers); and reviews of Apple II and Macintosh hardware and software. No fiction or poetry. Buys 18 mss/year. Query with published clips. Length: 200-2,500 words. Pays $100-1,000 for assigned articles; $25-500 for unsolicited articles. Sometimes pays the expenses of writers on assignment.

Photos: State availability of photos with submission. Offers no additional payment for photos accepted with ms.

Tips: "Reviews are most open to freelancers at *InCider*. In addition to 'read the magazine,' I would advice freelance reviewers to 'have an opinion.' A review should not explain how to use a product, or tell how the reviewer used it. The question is: 'What's it like to use it?' "

MICROpendium, Covering the TI99/4A, Myarc 9640 compatibles, Burns-Koloen Communications Inc., P.O. Box 1343, Round Rock TX 78680-1343. (512)255-1512. Editor: Laura Burns. 40% freelance written. Eager to work with new/unpublished writers. Monthly magazine for users of the "orphaned" TI99/4A. "We are interested in helping users get the most out of their home computers." Estab. 1984. Circ. 4,000. Pays on publication. Publishes ms an average of 2-3 months after acceptance. Byline given. Buys second serial rights. Publishes reprints of previously published articles. Send tearsheet or photocopy of article. Include information about when and where the article previously appeared. For reprints, payment varies. Query for electronic submission. Reports in 2 weeks on queries; 2 months on manuscripts. Sample copy and writer's guidelines for 9×12 SAE with 3 first class stamps.

Nonfiction: Book excerpts; how-to (computer applications); interview/profile (of computer "personalities," e.g. a software developer concentrating more on "how-to" than personality); and opinion (product reviews, hardware and software). Buys 30-50 mss/year. Query with or without published clips or send complete ms. "We can do some articles as a series if they are lengthy, yet worthwhile." Pays $10-150, depending on length. No pay for product announcements. Sometimes pays the expenses of writers on assignment.

Photos: Send photos with submission. Reviews contact sheets, negatives, transparencies, and prints (b&w preferred). Buys negotiable rights.

Columns/Departments: User Notes (tips and brief routines for the computer) 100 words and up. Buys 35-40 mss/year. Send complete ms. Pays $10.

Tips: "The area most open to freelancers is product reviews on hardware and software. The writer should be a sophisticated TI99/4A computer user. We are more interested in advising our readers of the availability of good products than in 'panning' poor ones. We are interested in coverage of the Geneve 9640 by Myarc. We are not at all interested in general computer or technology-related articles unrelated to TI or Myarc computers."

ONLINE ACCESS, The Magazine that Makes Modems Work, Chicago Fine Print, Inc., Suite 203, 920 N. Franklin, Chicago IL 60610. Fax: (312)573-0520. Editor-in-Chief: Tracy Weisman. Editor-at-Large: Len Strazewski. 90% freelance written. Magazine, guide and directory that covers the online computer industry for computer owners who use modems. Eight publications/year including four issues devoted to bulletin board systems. "Online Access is the largest circulation international magazine for people interested in learning about online services and commercial databases for both personal and business applications." Pays on publication. Publishes ms an average of 2 months after acceptance. Byline given. Offers $50 kill fee. Buys first rights or second serial (reprint) rights. Submit seasonal/holiday material 6 months in advance. "Query for electronic submissions." Reports in 1 month on queries; 3 weeks on mss. *Writer's Market* recommends allowing 2 months for reply. Sample copy $4.95.

Nonfiction: General interst (online industry); how-to (use a particular online service); humor; interview/profile (of major industry figures); new product (but *not* hardware!); opinion (about current online industry issues); personal experience (if relevant); and photo feature. "No overly technical pieces; no step-by-step guides to searching databases. Please don't write about your terrific new modem!" Query with published clips. Length: 1,500-2,500 words. Pays $100-500. Pays in contributor copies by mutual agreement before assignment is given. Sometimes pays expenses of writers on assignment.

Photos: State availability of photos with submission. Reviews 5×7 transparencies and prints. Offers no additional payment for photos accepted with ms. Captions, model releases and identification of subjects required. Buys one-time rights.

Tips: "We are seeking more articles about bulletin board systems."

PC, The Independent Guide to IBM-Standard Personal Computing, Ziff-Davis Publishing Co., 1 Park Ave., New York NY 10016. (212)503-5255. Fax: (212)503-5799. Editor-in-Chief: Michael J. Miller. Executive Editor/Hardware, PCs, Connectivity: Bill Howard. Executive Editor/Software, Trends: Robin Raskin. 75% freelance written. Prefers to work with published/established writers. Biweekly magazine for users/owners of IBM personal computers and compatible systems. Estab. 1965. **Pays on acceptance.** Publishes ms average of 4 months after acceptance. Byline given. Buys all rights. Electronic copy on floppy disk preferred. Reports in 2 months. Sample copy $5.

Nonfiction: How-to (software and hardware), technical, product evaluations and programs. Buys 800 mss/ year. Query, story proposals should be submitted to the executive editors. Length: 1,000-8,000 words. Sometimes pays expenses of writers on assignment.

Tips: "*PC Magazine* is a computer magazine for business people; however we also cover computer products for personal use (i.e. games and personal finance). We assign stories based on the latest product/technological developments in the micro-computer industry. In the coming year the hot topics will be OS/2, 80 486 chip technology and networking."

PC WORLD, PCW Communications, Inc., 501 2nd St., San Francisco CA 94107. (415)243-0500. Editor-in-Chief: Phil Lemmons. 60% freelance written. Monthly magazine covering IBM Personal Computers and compatibles. Circ. 901,000. **Pays on acceptance.** Byline given. Offers negotiable kill fee. Buys all rights. Query for electronic submissions. Free writer's guidelines.

Nonfiction: "*PC World* is composed of four departments: News, How-tos, Reviews and Features. Reviews critically and objectively analyzes new hardware and software. How-tos gives readers instructions for improving their PC productivity. Features help readers understand the impact of PC technology on their business lives. News keeps readers apprised of new products, trends and industry events." Articles must focus on the IBM PC or compatibles. Query with or without published clips or send complete ms. Buys 50 mss/year. Length: 1,500-2,500 words. Pays $50-2,000. Does not accept unsolicited mss.

Tips: "Familiarity with the IBM PC or technical knowledge about its operations—coupled with a solid understanding of business needs—often determines whether we accept a query. Send all queries to the attention of Proposals—Editorial Department."

PC WORLD LOTUS EDITION, Lotus Publishing Corp., Suite 300, 77 Franklin St., Boston MA 02110. Executive Editor: Eric Bender. Monthly magazine for Lotus users. Estab. 1985. Circ. 360,523. **Pays on acceptance.** Byline given. Offers 20% kill fee. Submit seasonal material 3 months in advance. Reports in 2 months. Free sample copy and writer's guidelines.

Nonfiction: Essays, how-to, new product and technical. Query with published clips and outline of subject. Length: 1,500-2,000 words. Pays $300-1,500. Sometimes pays expenses of writers on assignment.

Columns/Departments: Carrie Thomas, spreadsheet skills editor. Buys 12-20 mss/year. Query with published clips. Length: 600-1,500 words. Pays $300-1,500.

Tips: "Features sections are most open to freelancers."

PC/COMPUTING, Ziff-Davis Publishing Co., 20th Floor, 950 Tower Lane, Foster City CA 94404-2121. (415)578-7000. Fax: (415)578-7029. Executive Editors: Ron White and Charlotte D. Ziems. Monthly magazine on personal computing. Estab. 1988. Circ. 850,000. **Pays on acceptance.** Byline given. Offers negotiable kill fee. Makes work-for-hire assignments. Query for electronic submissions. Reports in 1 month. Sample copy $2.95. Writer's guidelines for #10 SASE.

Nonfiction: Book excerpts, how-to, new product and technical. Query with published clips. Payment negotiable. Sometimes pays expenses of writers on assignment.

Tips: "We're looking for helpful, specific information that appeals to advanced users of PCs. No novice material. Writers must be knowledgable about personal computers." Query the specific editor for each department. You may contact us by US mail or on MCI Mail as follows: Matt Lake, 473-9922, Help section; Sebastian Rupley, 501-3870, news and reviews; Scot Finnie, 496-1893, features editor. Either name or number can be used for the online address."

PCM, The Personal Computing Magazine for Tandy Computer Users, Falsoft, Inc., Falsoft Bldg., 9509 US Highway 42, Box 385, Prospect KY 40059. (502)228-4492. Fax: (502)228-5121. Editor: Lawrence C. Falk. Managing Editor: Sue Fomby. 75% freelance written. Monthly magazine for owners of the Tandy Model 100, 200 and 600 portable computer and the Tandy 1000, 1200, 2000, 3000, 4000 and 5000. Estab. 1983. Circ. 54,874. Pays on publication. Publishes ms an average of 3 months after acceptance. Byline given. Buys all rights and rights for disk service reprint. Submit seasonal material 4 months in advance. Query for electronic submissions. Reports in 2 months. Free writer's guidelines.

Nonfiction: Julie Hutchinson, submissions editor. "We prefer how-to articles with programs." No general interest material. Buys 80 mss/year. Send complete ms. "Do not query." Length: 300 words minimum. Pays $40-50/page.

Photos: State availability of photos. Rarely uses photos.

Tips: "At this time we are only interested in submissions for the Tandy MS-DOS and portable computers. Strong preference is given to submissions accompanied by brief program listings. All listings must be submitted on tape or disk as well as in hard copy form."

PUBLISH, The Art and Technology of Electronic Publishing, MultiMedia Communications, Inc., 501 2nd St., San Francisco CA 94107. (415)243-0600. Editor-in-Chief: Jake Widman. 50% freelance written. Monthly magazine on desktop publishing and presentations. Estab. 1986. Circ. 107,000. Pays on publication. Publishes ms an average of 4-5 months after acceptance. Byline given. Buys first international rights. Query for electronic submissions. Reports in 3 weeks. Writer's guidelines for #10 SASE.

Nonfiction: Book excerpts, product reviews, how-to (publishing topics), news, new products, technical tips. Buys 120 mss/year. Query with published clips. Length: 300-2,500 words. No unsolicited mss.

Photos: State availability of photos with submission. Reviews contact sheets. Captions and identification of subjects required.

SHAREWARE MAGAZINE, Software for the IBM & Compatible, PC-SIG, Inc., 1030-D, E. Duane Ave., Sunnyvale CA 94086-2600. (408)730-9291. Fax: (408)730-2107. Editor: Mike Callahan. Assistant Editor: Keely M. Swenson. 80% freelance written. Bimonthly magazine on shareware software. Estab. 1988. Circ. 100,000. Pays on publication. Publishes ms an average of 3-4 months after acceptance. Byline given. Buys first North American serial rights. Submit seasonal material 4 months in advance. Simultaneous and previously published submissions OK. Query for electronic submissions. Reports in 2 months. Sample copy and writer's guidelines for 9 × 12 SAE with 3 first class stamps.

Nonfiction: How-to (computers), humor, interview/profile, new product, personal experience, photo feature and technical. "No articles reviewing software not related to shareware." Buys 40 mss/year. Query with or without published clips, or send complete ms. Length: 1,200-6,000 words. Pays $50-800.

Photos: Send photos with submission. Reviews contact sheets. Payment for photos included in total payment for article. Captions, model releases and identification of subjects required. Buys one-time rights.

WORDPERFECT, THE MAGAZINE, WordPerfect Publishing Corp., 270 W. Center St., Orem UT 84057-4683. (801)226-5555. Fax: (801)226-8804. Editor-in-Chief: Clair F. Rees. Senior Editor: Lisa Bearnson. 70% freelance written. Monthly magazine of "how-to" articles for users of various WordPerfect computer software. Estab. 1988. Circ. 275,000. Publishes ms an average of 6-8 months after acceptance. Byline given. Negotiable kill fee. Buys first world rights. Submit seasonal/holiday material 8 months in advance. Query for electronic submissions only. Reports in 2 months. Sample copy for 9 × 12 SAE with 7 first class stamps. Free writer's guidelines.

Nonfiction: How-to, step-by-step applications (with keystrokes), humor, interview/company profile, new product and technical. "Easy-to-understand articles written with *minimum* jargon. Articles should provide readers good, useful information about word processing and other computer functions." Buys 120-160 mss/year. Query with or without published clips. Length: 800-1,800 words.

Photos: State availability of photos with submission. Reviews transparencies (35mm or larger). Offers no additional payment for photos accepted with ms. Captions and identification of subjects required. Buys one-time rights.

Columns/Departments: Macro Magic (WordPerfect macros), 1,000-1,400 words; Back to Basics (tips for beginners), 1,000-1,400 words; Final Keystrokes (humor), 800 words. Buys 90-120 mss/year. Query with published clips. Pays $400-700, on acceptance.

Tips: "Studying publication provides best information. We're looking for writers who can both inform *and* entertain our specialized group of readers."

Photography

Readers of these magazines use their cameras as a hobby and for weekend assignments. To write for these publications, you should have expertise in photography. Magazines geared to the professional photographer can be found in the Photography Trade section.

AMERICAN PHOTO, Hatchette Filipacchi Magazines, Inc., Dept. WM, 1633 Broadway, New York NY 10019. (212)767-6273. Editor: David Schonauer. Executive Editor: Sudie Redmond. Bimonthly magazine for advanced amateur, sophisticated general interest and professional photographers. **Pays on acceptance.** Byline given. Buys first North American serial rights. Sample copy $3.50. Writer's guidelines for #10 SASE.

Nonfiction: Length: 500-2,500 words. Query. Sometimes pays writers expenses on assignment (reasonable).
Columns/Departments: Buys 10-30 mss/year. Length: 700 words maximum.

‡**DARKROOM & CREATIVE CAMERA TECHNIQUES**, Preston Publications, Inc., P.O. Box 48312, 7800 Merrimac Ave., Niles IL 60714. (708)965-0566. Fax: (708)965-7639. Publisher: Seaton Preston. Editor: David Alan Jay. 85% freelance written. Bimonthly publication covering the most technical aspects of photography: photochemistry, lighting, optics, processing and printing, Zone System, special effects, sensitometry, etc. Aimed at advanced workers. Prefers to work with experienced photographer-writers; happy to work with excellent photographers whose writing skills are lacking. "Article conclusions often require experimental support." Estab. 1979. Circ. 45,000. Pays within about 2 weeks of publication. Publishes ms an average of 6 months after acceptance. Byline given. Buys one-time rights. Query for electronic submissions. Sample copy $4.50. Writer's guidelines with #10 SASE.
Nonfiction: Special interest articles within above listed topics; how-to, technical product reviews and photo features. Query or send complete ms. Length open, but most features run approximately 2,500 words or 3-4 magazine pages. Pays $100/published page for well-researched technical articles.
Photos: "Don't send photos with ms. Will request them at a later date." Ms payment includes payment for photos. Prefers transparencies and 8 × 10 b&w prints. Captions, model releases (where appropriate) and technical information required. Buys one-time rights.
Tips: "We like serious photographic articles with a creative or technical bent. Successful writers for our magazine are doing what they write about. Also, any ms that addresses a serious problem facing many photographers will get our immediate attention."

NATURE PHOTOGRAPHER, Nature Photographer Publishing Co., Inc., P.O. Box 2037, West Palm Beach FL 33402-2037. (407)586-7332. Fax: (407)586-9521. Editor: Evamarie Mathaey. 45% freelance written. Bimonthly magazine "emphasizing nature photography that uses low-impact techniques and ethics. Articles include how-to, travel to world-wide wilderness locations and how nature photography can be used to benefit the environment and environmental education of the public." Estab. 1990, Circ. 12,000. Pays on publication. Buys one-time rights. Submit seasonal material 8 months in advance. Accepts simultaneous and previously published submissions. Send photocopy of article, including information about when and where the article previously appeared. For reprints, pays 75% of the amount paid for an original article. Reports in 2 months. Sample copy for 9 × 12 SAE with 6 first class stamps. Writer's guidelines for #10 SASE.
Nonfiction: How-to (underwater, exposure, creative techniques, techniques to make photography easier, low-impact techniques, macro photography, large-format, wildlife), photo feature, technical and travel. No articles about photographing in zoos or on game farms. Buys 12-18 mss/year. Query with published clips or writing samples. Length: 750-2,500 words. Pays $75-150.
Photos: Send photos with submission. Reviews 35mm, 2¼ and 4 × 5 transparencies, 8 × 10 prints (b&w only). Offers no additional payment for photos accepted with ms. Identification of subjects required. Buys one-time rights.
Tips: "Query with original, well-thought out ideas and good writing samples. Make sure you send SASE. Areas most open to freelancers are travel, how-to and conservation. Must have good, solid research and knowledge of subject."

PICTURE PERFECT, Aquino Productions, Inc., Suite 206, 159 Main St., Box 15760, Stamford CT 06901-0760. (203)967-9952. Fax: (203)975-1119. Editor: Elaine Hallgren. Managing Editor: Andres Aquino. 50% freelance written. Bimonthly magazine covering photography in all its facets: fashion, commercial, travel, stock, creative, beauty. Estab. 1989. Circ. 140,000. Pays on publication. Publishes ms an average of 3 months after acceptance. Offers 50% kill fee. Buys first North American serial rights or all rights. Submit seasonal/holiday material 4 months in advance. Simultaneous submissions OK. Reports in 3 weeks on queries; 6 weeks on mss. Sample copy $4. Writer's guidelines for SAE and 2 first class stamps.
Nonfiction: Book excerpts, how-to, interview/profile, new product, personal experience, photo feature and travel. Buys 36-48 mss/year. Send complete ms. Length 250-1,500 words. Pays 20¢/word for assigned articles; 15¢/word for unsolicited articles. Sometimes pays expenses of writers on assignment.
Photos: Send photos with submission. Reviews b&w prints, 35mm slides, 2 × 2 transparencies. Offers $25/photo. Captions, model releases and identification of subjects required. Buys one-time rights or first North American rights.

POPULAR PHOTOGRAPHY, 1633 Broadway, New York NY 10019. "Prefers not to share information."

‡**PORTFOLIO, A Continuing-Education Program for the Serious Photographer**, Institute for Photographic Excellence, P.O. Box 3994, Walnut Creek CA 94598-3994. Director/Publisher: Robert Devere. 50% freelance written. Bimonthly journal covering photography. Estab. 1992. Circ. 5,000. **Pays on acceptance.** Byline given. Offers 25% kill fee. Buys first North American serial, first, one-time or simultaneous rights. Editorial lead time 3 months. Submit seasonal material 4 months in advance. Simultaneous and previously published submissions OK. Reports in 2 weeks on queries; 1 month on mss. *Writer's Market* recommends

allowing 2 months for reply. Sample copy $3 for 9 × 12 SAE with 4 first class stamps. Writer's guidelines for #10 SASE on request.

Nonfiction: How-to and photo feature. "Special issues are run one or two times a year. Writers should query about special issues." *No pornographic material.* Buys 12-15 mss/year. Query. Length: 750-1,500 words. Pays $100 minimum for assigned articles; $50 minimum for unsolicited articles.

Photos: State availability of photos with submission. Reviews contact sheets and 3½ × 5 to 8 × 10 prints. Offers $50/photo. Captions, model releases and identification of subjects required. Buys one-time rights.

Columns/Departments: Photo (how-to articles), 750-1,500 words; Legal (photography and the law), 750-1,500 words; and Marketing (promoting photography), 750-1,500 words. Buys 12-15 mss/year. Query. Pays $100-200.

‡**SHUTTERBUG MAGAZINE,** Patch Communications, 5211 S. Washington Ave., Titusville FL 32780. Editor: Bob Shell. Managing Editor: Bonnie Paulk. Contact: Bob Shell. 100% freelance written. Monthly magazine covering photography. "Provides how-to articles for advanced amateur to professional photographers." Estab. 1970. Circ. 100,000. Byline given. Buys first rights and second serial (reprint) rights. Editorial lead time 6 months. Submit seasonal material at least 6 months in advance. Previously published submissions OK. Reports in 6-8 weeks on queries. Sample copy free on request. Writer's guidelines for #10 SASE.

Nonfiction: Historical/nostalgia (photography), how-to (photography), humor, interview/profile, new product, photo feature and technical. "All photo related." *No unsolicited articles.* Buys 60 + mss/year. Query. Pays $300 minimum for assigned articles; $200 minimum for unsolicited articles. Pays expenses of writers on assignment.

Photos: Send photos with submission. Reviews any transparencies, 8 × 10 prints. Offers no additional payment for photos accepted with ms. Captions and model releases required. Buys one-time rights.

Tips: "Submit only material similar in style to that in our magazine. All sections open to freelancers."

WILDLIFE PHOTOGRAPHY, P.O. Box 224, Greenville PA 16125. (412)588-3492. Editor: Bob Noonan. 90% freelance written. Eager to work with new/unpublished writers. Bimonthly magazine "dedicated to the pursuit and capture of wildlife on film. Emphasis on how-to." Estab. 1985. Circ. 3,000. Pays on publication. Publishes ms an average of 1 year after acceptance. Byline given. Buys first, one-time or second serial (reprint) rights. Submit seasonal/holiday material 4 months in advance. Simultaneous and previously published submissions OK. Reports in 2 weeks on queries; 6 weeks on mss. Sample copy $2 for 9 × 12 SAE. Free writer's guidelines.

Nonfiction: Book excerpts; how-to (work with animals to take a good photo); interview/profile (of professionals); new product (of particular interest to wildlife photography); personal experience (with cameras in the field); and travel (where to find superb photo opportunities of plants and animals). No fiction or photography of pets, sports and scenery. Buys 30 mss/year. Query or send complete ms. Length: 500-3,000 words. Pays $30-100.

Photos: Send sharp photos with submission. Reviews contact sheets, negatives, transparencies and 5 × 7 prints as part of ms package. Photos accepted only with ms. Offers no additional payment for photos. Captions and identification of subjects required. Buys one-time rights.

Fillers: Anecdotes and facts. Buys 12/year. Length: 50-200 words. Pays $5-15.

Tips: "Give solid how-to info on how to photograph a specific species of wild animal. Send photos, not only of the subject, but of the photographer and his gear in action. The area of our publication most open to freelancers is feature articles."

Politics and World Affairs

These publications cover politics for the reader interested in current events. Other publications that will consider articles about politics and world affairs are listed under Business and Finance, Contemporary Culture, Regional and General Interest. For listings of publications geared toward the professional, see Government and Public Service and International Affairs in the Trade section.

THE ARIZONA UNCONSERVATIVE, Arizona's Progressive Voice, Vida Productions, P.O. Box 23683, Tempe AZ 85285. Editor: Aaron Heresi. 80% freelance written. Monthly newsletter for political/social/ethical awareness. "We enjoy hearing from writers who question conventional ideas and methods." Estab. 1991. Circ. 250. Pays on publication. Publishes ms an average of 1 month after acceptance. Byline given. Buys one-time rights. Submit seasonal material 2 months in advance. Simultaneous and previously published submissions OK; send typed ms with rights for sale noted and information about when and where the article previously appeared. Pays 50% of their fee for an original article.. Reports in 6 weeks. Sample copy $1. Writer's guidelines for #10 SASE.

Nonfiction: Expose, interview/profile, opinion and personal experience. "No articles that do not question or probe some issue or idea." Buys 36 mss/year. Send complete ms. Length: 10-500 words. Pays $1/100 printed words.

Fiction: C. Ehren Hay, fiction editor. Confession, ethnic, experimental, fantasy, humorous, science fiction, slice-of-life vignettes and gay/lesbian. "Nothing trite, cliché or mainstream." Buys 10 mss/year. Send complete ms. Length: 10-500 words. "We specialize in short shorts." Pays $1-5.

Poetry: C. Ehren Hay, poetry editor. Avant-garde, free verse and light verse. "No poetry in which the time spent trying to rhyme words outweighs the time spent trying to say something, or express a feeling." Buys 30 poems/year. Submit 3 poems maximum. Length: 1-50 lines. Pays $1-5.

Fillers: Facts and newsbreaks. Buys 20/year. Length: 10-300 words. Pays $1-3.

Tips: "Though centered in the metro-Phoenix area we are mostly interested in national issues. *The Arizona Unconservative* was developed as a forum for writers who keep a constant check on society. We question the direction of our country and would like you to do the same. All sections are extremely open to anyone who has something to say about life on Earth."

CALIFORNIA JOURNAL, 1714 Capitol Ave., Sacramento CA 95814. (916)444-2840. Editor: Richard Zeiger. Managing Editor: A.G. Block. 50% freelance written. Prefers to work with published/established writers. Monthly magazine that emphasizes analysis of California politics and government. Estab. 1970. Circ. 20,000. Pays on publication. Publishes ms an average of 2 months after acceptance. Byline given. Buys all rights. Query for electronic submissions. Writer's guidelines for #10 SASE.

Nonfiction: Profiles of state and local government and political analysis. No outright advocacy pieces. Buys 25 unsolicited mss/year. Query. Length: 900-3,000 words. Pays $150-500. Sometimes pays the expenses of writers on assignment.

CHURCH & STATE, Americans United for Separation of Church and State, 8120 Fenton St., Silver Spring MD 20910. (301)589-3707. Managing Editor: Joseph Conn. 10% freelance written. Prefers to work with published/established writers. Monthly magazine emphasizing religious liberty and church/state relations matters. Strongly advocates separation of church and state. Readership "includes the whole spectrum, but is predominantly Protestant and well-educated." Estab. 1947. Circ. 33,000. **Pays on acceptance.** Publishes ms an average of 2 months after acceptance. Buys all rights. Simultaneous and previously published submissions OK. Reports in 2 months. Sample copy and writer's guidelines for 9×12 SAE with 3 first class stamps.

Nonfiction: Expose, general interest, historical and interview. Buys 11 mss/year. Query. Length: 3,000 words maximum. Pays negotiable fee.

Photos: State availability of photos with query. Pays negotiable fee for b&w prints. Captions preferred. Buys one-time rights.

Tips: "We're looking for feature articles on underreported local church-state controversies. We also consider 'viewpoint' essays that offer a unique or personal take on church-state issues."

COMMONWEAL, A Review of Public Affairs, Religion, Literature and the Arts, Commonweal Foundation, 15 Dutch St., New York NY 10038. (212)732-0800. Editor: Margaret O'Brien Steinfels. Contact: Patrick Jordan, managing editor. Biweekly magazine. Estab. 1924. Circ. 18,000. **Pays on acceptance.** Byline given. Buys all rights. Submit seasonal material 2 months in advance. Reports in 2 months. Free sample copy.

Nonfiction: Essays, general interest, interview/profile, personal experience and religious. Buys 20 mss/year. Query with published clips. Length: 1,200-3,000 words. Pays $75-100.

Poetry: Rosemary Deen, poetry editor. Free verse and traditional. Buys 25-30 poems/year. Pays 50¢/line.

CURRENT WORLD LEADERS, Biography & News/Speeches & Reports, International Academy at Santa Barbara, Suite D, 800 Garden St., Santa Barbara CA 93101. (805)965-5010. Fax: (805)965-6071. Editorial Director: Thomas S. Garrison. 25% freelance written. Bimonthly magazine covering international and comparative politics. "We cover several perspectives for each issue topic. We welcome papers that present a particular point of view on current international political issues. Our main audience is college-level teachers and students." Estab. 1957. Pays on publication. Publishes ms an average of 4 months after acceptance. Byline given. No kill fee. Buys first rights. Simultaneous and previously published submissions OK. Query for electronic submissions. Reports in 3 weeks on queries. Free sample copy and writer's guidelines for 6×9 SAE with 5 first class stamps.

Nonfiction: Essays (political) and opinion (political). "No articles that do not have a political theme." Buys 3-5 mss/year. Length: 4,500-10,000 words. Pays $25-100.

• No longer seeking photos or photo features.

Tips: "Write and ask for our writers guidelines and our annual Call for Papers. Know your topic."

EMPIRE STATE REPORT, The magazine of politics and public policy in New York State, 16th Floor, 545 8th Ave., New York NY 10018. (212)239-9797. Fax: (212)564-0196. Editor: Alex Storozynski. 50% freelance written. Monthly magazine providing "timely political and public policy features for local and statewide public officials in New York State. Anything that would be of interest to them is of interest to us." Estab. 1983. Circ. 12,000. Pays 2 months after publication. Byline given. Buys first North American serial rights. Query for electronic submissions. Reports in 1 month on queries; 2 months on mss. Sample copy $3.50 with #10 SASE.

Nonfiction: Essays, expose, interview/profile and opinion. "Writers should send for our editorial calendar." Buys 48 mss/year. Query with published clips. Length: 750-3,000 words. Pays $35-400 for assigned articles. Sometimes pays expenses of writers on assignment.

Photos: State availability of photos with submission. Reviews any size prints. Offers $50-100/photo. Identification of subjects required. Buys one-time rights.

Columns/Departments: "Notes and Asides" (short gossip pieces about state politics), 200 words maximum; Perspective (opinion pieces), 750-800 words. Buys 24 mss/year. Query. Length: 750-1,000 words. Pays $50-100.

Tips: "Send us a query. If we are not already working on the idea, and if the query is well written, we might work something out with the writer. Writers have the best chance selling something for Notes and Asides."

EUROPE, #707, 2100 M St. NW, Washington DC 20037-1207. (202)862-9555. Fax: (202)429-1766. Editor: Robert Guttman. Managing Editor: Peter Gwin. 75% freelance written. Magazine published 10 times/year for anyone with a professional or personal interest in Europe and European/US relations. Estab. 1963. Circ. 25,000. Pays on publication. Publishes ms an average of 2 months after acceptance. Buys first serial and all rights. Submit seasonal material 3 months in advance. Reports in 4 months.

Nonfiction: Interested in current affairs (with emphasis on economics, business and politics), the Single Market and Europe's relations with the rest of the world. Publishes occasional cultural travel pieces, with European angle. "High quality writing a must. We publish articles that might be useful to people with a professional interest in Europe." Query or submit complete ms or article outline. Include résumé of author's background and qualifications. Length: 500-2,000 words. Pays $150-500.

• This magazine is accepting more freelance articles and has increased its pay rates for them. The editor is encouraging more queries.

Photos: Photos purchased with or without accompanying mss. Buys b&w and color. Pays $25-35 for b&w print, any size; $100 for inside use of transparencies; $450 for color used on cover; per job negotiable.

FREEDOM MAGAZINE, Church of Scientology, Suite 1200, 6331 Hollywood Blvd., Los Angeles CA 90028. (213)960-3500. Editor: Thomas G. Whittle. 20% freelance written. Monthly magazine "dedicated to investigative reporting in the public interest," with emphasis on hard news, current events and investigative reporting. Circ. 110,000. Pays on publication. Publishes ms an average of 3 months after acceptance. Rights purchased vary with author and material. Submit seasonal material 4 months in advance. Responds in 2-3 weeks. Sample copy on request.

Nonfiction: National and international news, investigative reporting and business news. Highlights individuals who are championing the cause of human rights in a special "Leaders in the Field of Human Rights" feature. Articles have exposed misconduct and abuses by officials in CIA, IRS and other agencies. Harmful effects of psychiatric drugs such as Prozac, Xanax and Valium have been examined in depth. Query with detailed outline, including statement of whether the information has appeared elsewhere. Enclosing clips of other stories you have published may help your chances of acceptance. Length: 800-3,000 words. Pays $100-250, occasionally more.

Photos: Send photos with submission. Color: 35mm slides but prefers 2¼×5 inch transparencies; b&w: 8×10 or 5×7 prints. Offers $20-100/photo. Captions required. Buys one-time rights.

THE FREEMAN, 30 S. Broadway, Irvington-on-Hudson NY 10533. (914)591-7230. Fax: (914)591-8910. Editor: John W. Robbins. 85% freelance written. Eager to work with new/unpublished writers. Monthly for "the layman and fairly advanced students of liberty." Estab. 1946. Byline given. Pays on publication. Buys all rights, including reprint rights. Publishes ms an average of 5 months after acceptance. Reprints OK; send tearsheet or photocopy of article and information about when and where the article previously appeared. Pays 50% of their fee for an original article. Sample copy for 7½×10½ SASE with 4 first class stamps.

Nonfiction: "We want nonfiction clearly analyzing and explaining various aspects of the free market, private enterprise, limited government philosophy. Though a necessary part of the literature of freedom is the exposure of collectivistic cliches and fallacies, our aim is to emphasize and explain the positive case for individual responsibility and choice in a free economy. Especially important, we believe, is the methodology of freedom—self-improvement, offered to others who are interested. We try to avoid name-calling and personality clashes and find satire of little use as an educational device. Ours is a scholarly analysis of the principles underlying a free market economy. No political strategy or tactics." Buys 100 mss/year. Length: 3,500 words maximum. Pays 10¢/word. Sometimes pays expenses of writers on assignment.

Tips: "It's most rewarding to find freelancers with new insights, fresh points of view. Facts, figures and quotations cited should be fully documented, to their original source, if possible."

THE NATION, 72 5th Ave., New York NY 10011. Fax: (212)463-9712. Editor: Victor Navasky. 75% freelance written. Works with a small number of new/unpublished writers each year. Weekly. Buys first serial rights. Query for electronic submissions. Free sample copy and writer's guidelines for 6×9 SASE.

Nonfiction: "We welcome all articles dealing with the social scene, from an independent perspective." Queries encouraged. Buys 100 mss/year. Length: 2,500 words maximum. Modest rates. Sometimes pays expenses of writers on assignment.

Tips: "We are firmly committed to reporting on the issues of labor, national politics, business, consumer affairs, environmental politics, civil liberties and foreign affairs."

NATIONAL REVIEW, National Review Inc., Dept. WM, 150 E. 35th St., New York NY 10016. (212)679-7330. Editor: John O'Sullivan. Managing Editor: Linda Bridges. 60% freelance written. Biweekly political and cultural journal of conservative opinion. "While we sometimes publish symposia including liberal or even leftist opinion, most of what we publish has a conservative or libertarian angle." Estab. 1955. Circ. 180,000. Pays on publication. Byline given. Offers 50% kill fee "on pieces definitely accepted." Buys first, one-time, second serial or simultaneous rights. Submit seasonal/holiday material 2 months in advance. Reports in 2 weeks on queries; 3 months on mss. Free sample copy.

Nonfiction: Mark Cunningham, articles editor. Essays, exposes (of government boondoggles), interview/profile and religious. No editorial-type pure opinion. Buys 130 mss/year. Query. Length: 500-3,000 words. Pays $100-1,000 for assigned articles; $100-600 for unsolicited articles. Sometimes pays expenses of writers on assignment.

Columns/Departments: Book reviews (conservative political where applicable) and arts pieces. Buys 130 mss/year. Query. Length: 800-1,200 words. Pays $225-300.

Tips: "Query—although if a writer already has a manuscript ready, he may as well send it in instead. We accept phone queries. Double-space manuscripts. For the book section, always query before sending manuscript. We expect a fairly conservative point of view, but don't want a lot of editorializing. And we prefer pieces that are a bit more essayistic than a standard newspaper report."

NEW JERSEY REPORTER, A Journal of Public Issues, The Center for Analysis of Public Issues, 16 Vandeventer Ave., Princeton NJ 19067. (609)924-9750. Fax: (609)924-0363. Managing Editor: Lee Seglem. 60% freelance written. Prefers to work with published/established writers but will consider submissions from others. Bimonthly magazine covering New Jersey politics, public affairs and public issues. "*New Jersey Reporter* is a hard-hitting and highly respected magazine published for people who take an active interest in New Jersey politics and public affairs, and who want to know more about what's going on than what newspapers and television newscasts are able to tell them. We publish a great variety of stories ranging from analysis to expose." Estab. 1970. Circ. 2,200. Pays on publication. Byline given. Buys all rights. Reports in 1 month. Sample copy available on request.

● This magazine is using more freelance writing now than ever before.

Nonfiction: Book excerpts, expose, interview/profile and opinion. "We like articles from specialists (in planning, politics, economics, corruption, etc.)—particularly if written by professional journalists—but we reject stories that do not read well because of jargon or too little attention to the actual writing of the piece. Our magazine is interesting as well as informative." Buys 18-25 mss/year. Query with published clips. Length: 1,800-4,500 words. Pays $100-500.

Tips: "Queries should be specific about how the prospective story is an issue that affects or will affect the people of New Jersey and its government. The writer's résumé should be included. Stories—unless they are specifically meant to be opinion—should come to a conclusion but avoid a 'holier than thou' or preachy tone. Allegations should be scrupulously substantiated. Our magazine represents a good opportunity for freelancers to acquire great clips. Our publication specializes in longer, more detailed, analytical features. The most frequent mistake made by writers in completing an article for us is too much personal opinion versus reasoned advocacy. We are less interested in opinion than in analysis based on sound reasoning and fact. *New Jersey Reporter* is a well-respected publication, and many of our writers go on to nationally respected newspapers and magazines."

THE PRAGMATIST, A Utilitarian Approach, P.O. Box 392, Forest Grove PA 18922-0392. Fax: (215)348-8006. Editor: Jorge Amador. Publisher: Hans G. Schroeder. 67% freelance written. Bimonthly magazine on politics and current affairs. "*The Pragmatist* is a free-market magazine with a social conscience. We explore the practical benefits of tolerance, civil liberties and the market order, with emphasis on helping the poor and the underprivileged." Estab. 1983. Circ. 1,250. Pays on publication. Publishes ms an average of 4 months after acceptance. Byline given. Publication not copyrighted "but will run copyright notice for individual author on request." Buys first rights and/or second serial (reprint) rights. Submit seasonal material 6 months in advance. Previously published submissions OK; send tearsheet or photocopy of article, or typed ms with rights for sale noted and information about when and where the article previously appeared. Pays 100% of their fee for an original article. Query for electronic submissions. Reports in 2 months. Sample copy $3 for 9×12 SAE with 3 first class stamps. Writer's guidelines for #10 SASE.

Nonfiction: Essays, humor and opinion. "*The Pragmatist* is solution-oriented. We seek facts and figures, not moralizing or abstract philosophy, and focus on the issues, not personalities. Recent articles have explored alternatives to socialized military defense and examined the hazards of drug prohibition." Buys 24 mss/year. Query with published clips or send complete ms. Length: 500-2,500 words. Pays 1¢/published word plus copies.
Columns/Departments: Book Review (history/current affairs, dealing with the dangers of power or the benefits of civil liberties and market relations). Buys 10-15 mss/year. Query with published clips or send complete ms. Length: 1,000-1,500 words. Pays 1¢/published word plus copies.
Fiction: "We use very little fiction, and then only if it makes a political point."
Tips: "We welcome new writers. Most of our authors are established, but the most important article criteria are clear writing and sound reasoning backed up by facts. Write for an educated lay audience, not first-graders or academics. Polite correspondence gets answered first. No phone calls, please. Don't get discouraged by initial rejections; keep working on your writing and your targeting."

THE PROGRESSIVE, 409 E. Main St., Madison WI 53703-2899. (608)257-4626. Fax: (608)257-3373. Editor: Erwin Knoll. 75% freelance written. Monthly. Estab. 1909. Pays on publication. Publishes ms an average of 6 weeks after acceptance. Byline given. Buys all rights. Reports in 1 month. Sample copy for 9 × 12 SAE with 4 first class stamps. Writer's guidelines for #10 SASE.
Nonfiction: Primarily interested in articles which interpret, from a progressive point of view, domestic and world affairs. Occasional lighter features. "*The Progressive* is a *political* publication. General-interest material is inappropriate." Query. Length: 3,000 words maximum. Pays $100-250.
Tips: "Display some familiarity with our magazine, its interests and concerns, its format and style. We want query letters that fully describe the proposed article without attempting to sell it—and that give an indication of the writer's competence to deal with the subject."

REASON MAGAZINE, Suite 400, 3415 S. Sepulveda Blvd., Los Angeles CA 90034-6060. (310)391-2245. Associate Editor: Jacob Sullum. 50% freelance written. "Strongly prefer experienced, published writers." Monthly public-affairs magazine with a classical liberal/libertarian perspective. Estab. 1968. Circ. 45,000. **Pays on acceptance.** Publishes ms an average of 2 months after acceptance. Rights purchased vary with author and material. Byline given. Offers kill fee by pre-arrangement. Query for electronic submissions. Reports in 2 months. Sample copy $3 for 9 × 12 SAE with 5 first class stamps.
Nonfiction: "*Reason* deals with social, economic and political issues, supporting both individual liberty and economic freedom. We are looking for politically sophisticated analysis, solid reporting and excellent writing. Authors should not submit mss without reviewing at least one recent issue." Query. Buys 50-70 mss/year. Length: 1,000-5,000 words. Sometimes pays expenses of writers on assignment.

SOUTHERN EXPOSURE, P.O. Box 531, Durham NC 27702. (919)419-8311. Contact: Editor. Quarterly journal for well educated Southerners of all ages interested in "left-liberal" political perspective and the South. Estab. 1970. Circ. 7,500. Pays on publication. Buys all rights. Offers kill fee. Byline given. Will consider simultaneous submissions. Submit seasonal material 6 months in advance. Reports in 3 months. "Query is appreciated, but not required." Sample copy $4. Writer's guidelines for #10 SASE.
Nonfiction: "Ours is one of the few publications about the South *not* aimed at business or upper-class people; it appeals to all segments of the population. *And,* it is used as a resource—sold as a magazine and then as a book—so it rarely becomes dated." Needs investigative articles about the following subjects as related to the South: politics, energy, institutional power from prisons to universities, women, labor, African-Americans and the economy. Informational interview, profile, historical, think articles, expose, opinion and book reviews. Length: 4,500 words maximum. Pays $50-200. Smaller fee for short items.
Photos: "Very rarely purchase photos, as we have a large number of photographers working for us." 8 × 10 b&w preferred; no color. Payment negotiable.
Tips: "Because we are publishing shorter issues on a quarterly basis, we are looking for clear and thoughtful writing, articles that relate specific experiences of individual Southerners or grass roots groups to larger issues."

‡TOWARD FREEDOM, A Progressive Perspective on World Events, Toward Freedom Inc., 209 College St., Burlington VT 05401. (802)658-2523. Editor: Kevin J. Kelley. 75% freelance written. Political journal published 8 times/year covering political/cultural analysis, focus on Third World and Europe. "*Toward Freedom* is an internationalist newsletter with a progressive perspective on political, cultural and environmental issues in the Third World and Europe. Also covers the United Nations, the Non-aligned Movement and US foreign policy." Byline given. Circ. 2,000. Pays on publication. Kill fee "rare–negotiable." Buys first North

The double dagger before a listing indicates that the listing is new in this edition. New markets are often more receptive to freelance submissions.

American serial and one-time rights. Editorial lead time 1 month. Query for electronic submissions. Reports in 2 weeks on queries; 1 month on mss. *Writer's Market* recommends allowing 2 months for reply. Sample copy $3. Writer's guidelines free on request.

Nonfiction: Book reviews, interview/profile, opinion, personal experience, travel, foreign political analysis and women's issues. Special issues in March: Women's Issue; and October: different focus each year. "No subjects not relevant to our focus; subjects limited to US interest; no religious, how-to or fiction. Buys 80-100 mss/year. Query. Length: 700-2,000 words. Pays 10¢/word for all used.

Photos: Send photos with submission, if available. Reviews any prints. Offers $25 maximum/photo. Identification of subjects required. Buys one-time rights.

Columns/Departments: Book Review (Third World/European writers; political), 800-1,000 words. Buys 8-10 mss/year. Query. Pays 10¢/word.

Tips: "Except for book or other reviews, writers must be knowledgable about country, political situation, foreign policy, etc., on which they are writing. Occasional cultural 'travelogues' accepted, especially those that would enlighten our readers about a foreign way of life. Writing must be professional."

‡**WASHINGTON MONTHLY,** The Washington Monthly Company, 1611 Connecticut Ave. NW, Washington DC 20009. Editor: Charles Peters. Managing Editor: David Segal. Contact: David Segal. 80% freelance written. Monthly magazine covering political commentary, Washington news. Estab. 1969. Circ. 30,000. Pays on publication. Publishss ms an average of 3-5 months after acceptance. Byline given. Buys all rights. Editorial lead time 1½ months. Submit seasonal material 2 months in advance. Query for electronic submissions. Reports in 1 week on queries; 1 month on mss. *Writer's Market* recommends allowing 2 months for reply. Sample copy $3.95 for SAE with 1 first class stamp. Writer's guidelines free on request.

Nonfiction: Book excerpts, essays, expose, historical/nostalgic, interview/profile, opinion, personal experience, "anything exposing frauds of government—interesting memos—government foibles." Buys 30 mss/year. Query. Length: 1,500-5,000 words. Pays 10¢/word.

Photos: State availability of photos with submission. Negotiates payment individually. Captions, model releases and identification of subjects required.

Fillers: Spidhar Tallapragada ('ST'), production manager. Anecdotes, facts, gags to be illustrated by cartoonist, newsbreaks and short humor. Accepted de gratis. Length: 15-100 words.

Tips: "Freelancers should read previous issues and articles of *The Washington Monthly* to gain an understanding of its journalistic purpose and intent."

WILSON QUARTERLY, Woodrow Wilson International Center for Scholars, Suite 704, 901 D Street SW, Washington DC 20024-2169. (202)287-3000. Editor: Jay Tolson. Managing Editor: James Carman. 25% freelance written. Scholarly magazine that "tries to present the world of scholarly thought and research to a non-academic, but educated audience." Recent articles have ranged from 'American Finance' to a profile of G.K. Chesterton." Estab. 1976. Circ. 70,000. Pays on publication. Byline given. Pays negotiable kill fee. Buys first rights. Publishes reprints of previously published articles. Send photocopy of article. For reprints, payment varies. Query for electronic submissions. Reports in 6 weeks. Sample copy $7.

Nonfiction: Scholarly research. No fiction, poetry, or academic theses. Buys 10 mss/year. Query. Length: 3,000 words. Pays $500-1,200 for assigned articles; $300-1,000 for unsolicited articles.

Photos: State availability of photos with submission. Offers no additional payment for photos accepted with ms. Captions, model releases and identification of subjects required. Buys one-time rights.

Columns/Departments: Current Books (freelance reviews; must query for assignment). Buys 20 mss/year. Query with published clips. Length: 300-500 words. Pays $20-100.

Tips "Independent essays are the best for freelancers. Writers should definitely read the magazine before submitting any article, and should query if at all possible. Often we reject manuscripts because they do not fit in with our editorial content or overlap with other articles already assigned. We are particularly interested in articles that contain new, independent scholarly research, but are written with a journalistic flavor."

WORLD MONITOR, The Christian Science Monitor Monthly, The Christian Science Publishing Society, 1 Norway St., Boston MA 02115. Editor: Earl W. Foell. "Does not accept unsolicited mss."

Psychology and Self-Improvement

These publications focus on psychological topics, how and why readers can improve their own outlooks, and how to understand people in general. Many General Interest, Men's and Women's publications also publish articles in these areas.

CELEBRATE LIFE, The Magazine of Positive Living, Unimedia Corp., P.O. Box 247, Indian Rocks Beach FL 34635. (813)595-4141. Co-Editors: Marty Johnson and Dorothy Maxwell. 75% freelance written. Quarterly magazine covering motivational, positive lifestyles. Estab. 1989. Circ. 25,000. Pays on publication. Publishes ms an average of 3 months after acceptance. Byline given. Buys first North American serial or all rights or make work-for-hire assignments. Submit seasonal/holiday material 6 months in advance. Simultaneous and previously published submissions OK "if notified." Query for electronic submissions. Reports in 2 months. Sample copy $2 for 9 × 12 SAE with 6 first class stamps. Writer's guidelines for #10 SASE.

Nonfiction: Interview/profile with professionals in healing, parapsychology, philosophy and leaders in spirituality. Also ecologically-oriented travel. "Each issue is thematic. This is an upbeat, positive publication." Query with or without published clips or send complete ms. Length: 400-2,000 words. Pays $25-75 for assigned articles. Complimentary copies to $25 or more for unsolicited material. "Rarely" pays expenses of writers on assignment.

Photos: State availability or send photos with submission. Reviews contact sheets, transparencies and prints. Captions, model releases and identification of subjects required. Buys one-time rights.

Columns/Departments: Books and Tapes (must be assigned), 100 words; Humor (new thought, reflections), 200 words. Query with published clips or send complete ms. Pays $10-20.

Poetry: Light verse. Submit maximum 3 poems. Length: 8-24 lines. Pays $5 maximum. "Usually for byline only."

Tips: "We are very specific about what we want in each upcoming issue. Read the magazine first. Nothing outside these parameters will fit. Interviews/profiles of leaders of positive change are wanted. We are currently backlogged with mss."

CHANGES MAGAZINE, the US Journal, Inc., 3201 SW 15th St., Deerfield Beach FL 33442-8190. (800)851-9100. Fax: (305)360-0034. Managing Editor: Jeffrey Laign. Associate Editor: Andrew Meacham. 10% freelance written. Bimonthly magazine covering self-help and recovery. "We want to help people to improve their lives." Estab. 1986. Circ. 100,000. Pays on publication. Publishes ms an average of 4 months after acceptance. Byline given. Pays $25 kill fee. Buys first North American serial rights. Submit seasonal material 6 months in advance. Simultaneous and previously published submissions discouraged. Query for electronic submissions. Reports in 2-4 months. Sample copy $3.75. Writer's guidelines for #10 SASE.

Nonfiction: Opinion, personal experience, recovery/therapy and investigative pieces. We must approve interviews. No religious material, self-advertisements or reviews of books. Buys 15-20 mss/year. Query. Length: 500-2,000 words. Pays 15¢/word. Pays poetry and personal experience pieces with contributor's copies or other premiums. Pays telephone expenses only.

Photos: State availability of photos with submission. Reviews 5 × 7 prints. Payment negotiable. Model releases required. Buys one-time rights.

Fiction: "Stories of triumph: We look for insightful fiction which casts the magazine's serious subjects in unique ways." Pays 15¢/word. Length: 2,000 words maximum.

Poetry: Avant-garde, free verse and light verse. Pays in contributor's copies.

Tips: "Query by mail, preferably. Show a willingness and skill for talking to a variety of sources, going to the library, tying in a current event, if applicable. Use a friendly, conversational style, but don't assume your readers are disinterested in the deeper aspects of your story."

‡THE HEALING WOMAN, The Monthly Newsletter for Women Survivors of Childhood Sexual Abuse, P.O. Box 3038, Moss Beach CA 94038. (415)728-0339. Fax: (415)728-0339. Editor: Margot Silk Forrest. 70% freelance written. Monthly newsletter covering recovery from childhood sexual abuse. "Submissions accepted only from writers with personal or professional experience with childhood sexual abuse. We are looking for intelligent, honest and compassionate articles on topics of interest to survivors. We also publish first-person stories, poetry, interviews and book reviews." Estab. 1992. Circ. 5,000. **Pays on acceptance.** Publishes ms an average of 2-5 months after acceptance. Byline given. Offers 50% kill fee. Buys first North American serial rights. Editorial lead time 2 months. Submit seasonal material 3-4 months in advance. Accepts previously published submissions. Query for electronic submissions. Reports in 2-3 weeks on queries. Writer's guidelines for #10 SAE with 2 first class stamps.

Nonfiction: Book excerpts, essays, general interest, interview/profile, opinion, personal experience. "No articles on topics with which the writer has not had first-hand experience. If you've been there, you can write about it for us. If not, don't write about it." Buys 30 mss/year. Query with published clips. Length: 300-1,500 words. Pays $25-50. "Pays in copies for poems, short first-person pieces." Sometimes pays expenses of writers on assignment.

Photos: State availability of photos with submission. Negotiates payment for photos individually. Identification of subjects required. Buys one-time rights.

Columns/Departments: Book Reviews (books or accounts of incest survivors, therapy for incest survivors), 500-600 words; and Survivors Speak Out (first-person stories of recovery), 300-500 words.

Poetry: No *long* poems preoccupied with painful aspects of sexual abuse. Buys 25 poems/year, but pays only in copies.

Tips: "Although our subject matter is painful, *The Healing Woman* is not about suffering—it's about healing. Our department called 'Survivors Speak Out' features short, honest, insightful first-person essays with a conversational tone. We are happy to work with unpublished writers in this department."

LOTUS, Journal for Personal Transformation, Lotus Inc., #500-137, 4032 S. Lamar Blvd., Austin TX 78704. (918)683-4560. Editor: Mary Nurrie Stearns. 20% freelance written. Quarterly magazine of personal and spiritual transformation. Estab. 1991. Circ. 21,300. Pays on publication. Publishes ms an average of 4 months after acceptance. Byline given. 25% kill fee. Buys first North American serial, first rights, one-time or second serial (reprint) rights. Submit seasonal material 4 months in advance. Simultaneous and previously published submissions OK. Query for electronic submissions. Reports in 6 weeks. Sample copy $5.95. Free writer's guidelines.
Nonfiction: Essays, inspirational, interview/profile and religious. Buys 8 mss/year. Send complete ms. Length: 500-5,000 words. Pays $50-500. Pays in contributor copies if requested.
Photos: Send photos with submission. Reviews contact sheets and 8×10 prints. Pays $15-85/photo. Buys one-time rights.
Columns/Departments: Reviews. "We review films and books that deal with personal and sprititual transformation." Length: 500-1250 words. Buys 16 mss/year. Send complete ms. Pays $25-100.
Tips: "We look for writings that are not dogmatic in content and that will appeal to individuals from most any religious background."

ROSICRUCIAN DIGEST, Rosicrucian Order, AMORC, Rosicrucian Park, San Jose CA 95191. (408)947-3600. Editor-in-Chief: Robin M. Thompson. 50% freelance written. Works with a small number of new/unpublished writers each year. Quarterly magazine emphasizing mysticism, science and the arts for "men and women of all ages, seeking answers to life's questions." Circ. 70,000. **Pays on acceptance.** Publishes ms an average of 5-6 months after acceptance. Buys first serial and second serial (reprint) rights. Byline given. Submit seasonal material 5 months in advance. Previously published submissions OK. Reports in 2 months. Free sample copy. Writer's guidelines for #10 SASE.
Nonfiction: How to deal with life—and all it brings us—in a positive and constructive way. Informational articles—new ideas and developments in science, the arts, philosophy and thought. Historical sketches, biographies, human interest, psychology, philosophical and inspirational articles. No religious, astrological or political material or articles promoting a particular group or system of thought. Buys variable amount of mss each year. Query. Length: 1,000-1,500 words. Pays 6¢/word.
Photos: Purchased with accompanying ms. Send prints. Pays $10/8×10 b&w glossy print.
Fillers: Short inspirational or uplifting (not religious) anecdotes or experiences. Buys 6/year. Query. Length: 22-250 words. Pays 2¢/word.
Tips: "We are looking for well-written articles with a positive, constructive approach to life in these trying times. This seems to be a time of indecision and apathy in many areas, and we are encouraged when we read an article that lets the reader know that he/she can get involved, take positive action, make a change in his/her life. We are also looking for articles about how other cultures outside our own deal with the big questions, problems, and changes in life, i.e., the questions of 'Who am I?' 'Where do I fit in?', the role of elders in passing on culture to new generations, philosophical aspects of other cultures that can help us grow today."

SCIENCE OF MIND MAGAZINE, 3251 W. 6th St., P.O. Box 75127, Los Angeles CA 90075. (213)388-2181. Editor: Kathy Juline. 30% freelance written. Monthly magazine that features articles on spirituality, self-help and inspiration. "Our publication centers on oneness of all life and spiritual empowerment through the application of science of mind principles." Pays on publication. Publishes ms an average of 5 months after acceptance. Byline given. Buys first North American serial rights. Submit seasonal material 6 months in advance. Reports in 1 month on queries; 6 weeks on mss. Free writer's guidelines.
Nonfiction: Book excerpts, inspirational, personal experience of science of mind and spiritual. Buys 35-45 mss/year. Query or send complete ms. Length: 750-2,000 words. Pays $25/printed page. Pays in contributors copies for some special features written by readers.
Photos: Reviews 35mm transparencies and 5×7 or 8×10 b&w prints. Buys one-time rights.
Poetry: Larry Barber, poetry editor. Inspirational and science of mind oriented. "We are not interested in poetry not related to science of mind principles." Buys 10-15 poems year. Length: 7-25 lines. Pays $25.
Tips: "We are interested in first person experiences of a spiritual nature having to do with the science of mind."

Regional

Many regional publications rely on staff-written material, but others accept work from freelance writers who live in or know the region. Some of these magazines are among the bestselling magazines in a particular area and are read carefully, so writers must be able to supply accurate, up-to-date material. The best regional publication to target with your submissions is usually the one in your hometown, whether it's a city or state magazine or a Sunday supplement in a newspaper. Since you are familiar with the region, it is easier to propose suitable story ideas.

Listed first are general interest magazines slanted toward residents of and visitors to a particular region. Next, regional publications are categorized alphabetically by state, followed by Canada. Publications that report on the business climate of a region are grouped in the regional division of the Business and Finance category. Recreation and travel publications specific to a geographical area are listed in the Travel, Camping and Trailer section. Keep in mind also that many regional publications specialize in specific areas, and are listed according to those sections. Regional publications are not listed if they only accept material from a select group of freelancers in their area or if they did not want to receive the number of queries and manuscripts a national listing would attract. If you know of a regional magazine that is not listed, approach it by asking for writer's guidelines before you send unsolicited material.

General

‡**THE APPALACHIAN LOG**, Appalachian Log Publishing Company, P.O. Box 20297, Charleston WV 25362. (304)342-5789. Editor: Ron Gregory. 40% freelance written. Monthly magazine covering southern Appalachia. "*The Appalachian Log* is dedicated to promoting the people and places of Southern Appalachia. We publish only 'positive' articles concerning our region. We are *not* interested in religious or political material." Estab. 1992. Circ. 5,000. Pays on publication. Publishes ms an average of 3 months after acceptance. Byline given. Offers 10% kill fee or $10. Not copyrighted. Buys first, one-time, second serial (reprint) or simultaneous rights. Editorial lead time 2 months. Submit seasonal material 2 months in advance. Simultaneous and previously published submissions OK. Query for electronic submissions. Reports in 2 weeks on queries; 2 months on mss. Sample copy $1.50. Writer's guidelines for #10 SASE.
Nonfiction: Book excerpts, essays, historical/nostalgic, humor, inspirational, interview/profile, personal experience, photo feature, travel and genealogy. Special issues include snow skiing in the Southern Appalachians, festivals in Southern Appalachia, whitewater rafting in Southern Appalachians. "No religious, expose or opinion pieces. (We are no longer interested in political/opinion articles.)" Buys 30 mss/year. Send complete ms. Length: 500 words minimum. Pays $50 minimum for assigned articles; $10 minimum for unsolicited articles. Sometimes pays expenses of writers on assignment.
Photos: State availability of photos with submission. Reviews contact sheets. Captions required. Buys one-time rights.
Columns/Departments: Betty Gregory, publisher. Family History (genealogy), 3,000 words. Buys 4 mss/year. Query. Pays $20-50.
Fiction: Condensed novels, historical, humorous, mainstream and slice-of-life vignettes. No religious or erotic material. Buys 10 mss/year. Send complete ms. Length: 500-5,000 words. Pays $25-200.
Poetry: Betty Gregory, publisher. Avant-garde, free verse, light verse and traditional. Buys 40 poems/year. Length: 10-80 lines. Pays $7.50-30.
Fillers: Anecdotes, facts and short humor. Buys 15/year. Length: 25-250 words. Pays $5-50.
Tips: "Cover letters that give some indication of the author's knowledge of our region are helpful. All articles and submissions should, likewise, display the author's familiarity with Southern Appalachia. Details—particularly nostalgic ones—must be authentic and correct. Fiction and nonfiction short stories or longer works that can be serialized appeal to us. Writers in this area should be clear in their storyline (no 'hidden' meanings) and should keep in mind that our magazine loves Southern Appalachia and its people."

BLUE RIDGE COUNTRY, Leisure Publishing, P.O. Box 21535, Roanoke VA 24018-1535. (703)989-6138. Fax: (703)989-7603. Editor: Kurt Rheinheimer. 75% freelance written. Bimonthly magazine on the Blue Ridge region from Maryland to Georgia. "The magazine is designed to celebrate the history, heritage and beauty of the Blue Ridge region. It is aimed at the adult, upscale readers who enjoy living or traveling in the mountain regions of Virginia, North Carolina, West Virginia, Maryland, Kentucky, Tennessee, South Carolina and Georgia." Estab. 1988. Circ. 70,000. Pays on publication. Publishes ms an average of 6-8 months after acceptance. Byline given. Offers $50 kill fee for commissioned pieces only. Buys first and second serial (reprint) rights. Submit seasonal material 6 months in advance. Query for electronic submissions. Reports in 2 months.

Sample copy for 9×12 SAE with 6 first class stamps. Writer's guidelines for #10 SASE.

Nonfiction: General interest, historical/nostalgic, interview/profile, personal experience, photo feature, travel and history. Buys 25-30 mss/year. Query with or without published clips or send complete ms. Length: 500-1,800 words. Pays $50-250 for assigned articles; $25-250 for unsolicited articles.

• This magazine is looking for more photo-essays and shorter pieces.

Photos: State availability of photos with submission. Prefers transparencies. Offers $10-25/photo and $100 for cover photo. Identification of subjects required. Buys all rights.

Columns/Departments: Country Roads (stories on people, events, ecology, history, antiques, books) and Mountain Living (profiles of cooks and their recipes, garden tips, weather info); 50-200 words. Buys 12-24 mss/year. Query. Pays $10-40.

Tips: "Freelancers needed for departmental shorts and 'macro' issues affecting whole region. Need field reporters from all areas of Blue Ridge region. Also, we need updates on the Blue Ridge Parkway, Appalachian Trail, national forests, ecological issues, preservation movements."

NORTHWEST PARKS & WILDLIFE, Spooner Industries Inc., P.O. Box 18000, Florence OR 97439-0130. (800)348-8401. Fax: (503)997-1124. Editor: Dave Peden. Managing Editor: Judy Fleagle. 80% freelance written. Bimonthly regional magazine for Oregon, Washington, Idaho, British Columbia, and occasionally Alaska, W. Montana and N. California. Estab. 1991. Circ. 20,000. Pays on publication. Publishes ms an average of 8-10 months after acceptance. Byline given. Offers 33% kill fee. Buys first North American serial rights. Submit seasonal material 6 months in advance. Query for electronic submissions. Reports in up to 2 months. Sample copy $4.50. Writer's guidelines for #10 SASE.

Nonfiction: General interest, interview/profile, personal experience, photo feature, wildlife and wilderness areas, and profiles of parks. "Any article not related to Pacific Northwest will be returned." Buys 100 mss/year. Query with published clips. Length: 500-2,000 words. Pays $50-350 plus 5 contributor's copies.

Photos: Send photos with submission. Reviews 35mm or larger transparencies and 3×5 or larger prints. Offers no additional payment for photos accepted with ms. Captions, model releases, photo credits and identification of subjects required. Buys one-time rights.

Fillers: Newsbreaks. Uses 45/year. Length: 300-500 words. No payment for fillers.

Tips: "Slant articles for readers not living in Pacific Northwest. Keep articles informative rather than travel oriented. Do give directions and contact information for 'GettingThere' section at end of article. An articulate query of one page is appreciated rather than a ms. Articles of 800-1,000 words with photos are easiest to fit in. Articles of 400 words with good horizontal photo are needed for back page section. Accurate captions and photo credits on separate sheet from photos are appreciated."

NOW AND THEN, Center for Appalachian Studies and Services, East Tennessee State University, P.O. Box 70556, Johnson City TN 37614-0556. (615)929-5348. Fax: (615)929-5348. Editor: Pat Arnow. 80% freelance written. Triannual regional magazine. Estab. 1984. Circ. 1,500. Pays on publication. Publishes ms an averge of 6 months after acceptance. Byline given. Buys one-time rights. Simultaneous submissions OK; send typed ms with rights for sale noted. Reports in 1 month on queries; 4 months on mss. Sample copy $3.50. Writer's guidelines for #10 SASE.

Nonfiction: Book excerpts, essays, historical, humor, interview/profile, personal experience and photo feature. "We do have a special focus in each issue—we've featured Appalachian Blacks, Cherokees, women, music and veterans. Write for future themes. Stereotypes (especially granny rocking on the front porch), generalizations, sentimental writing are rejected. It must have to do with Appalachia." Buys 8 mss/year. Query with or without published clips or send complete ms. Length: 2,500 words. Pays $15-60 for assigned articles; $10-60 for unsolicited articles. Sometimes pays expenses of writers on assignment.

Photos: Send photos with submission. Reviews contact sheets and prints. Sometimes can offer additional payment for photos accepted with ms. Captions, model releases and identification of subjects required. Buys one-time rights.

Fiction: Ethnic, experimental, historical, humorous, novel excerpts and slice-of-life vignettes. "Everything we publish has to be by or about Appalachians. No stereotypes, generalizations, or sentimentality." Buys 3 mss/year. Send complete ms. Length: 2,500 words maximum. Pays $10-50. Must have some relation to theme issues.

Poetry: Avant-garde and free verse. "Must have something to do with the Appalachian region. Avoid stereotypes, generalizations and sentimentality." Buys 30-35 poems/year. Pays 2 contributor's copies and a year subscription. Send no more than 5 poems at a time.

Tips: "Everything we publish has something to do with life in Appalachia present and past. Profiles of people living and working in the region, short stories that convey the reality of life in Appalachia (which can include malls, children who wear shoes and watch MTV) are the kinds of things we're looking for."

SUNDAY JOURNAL MAGAZINE, Providence Journal Co., 75 Fountain St., Providence RI 02902. (401)277-7349. Fax: (401)277-7346. Editor: Elliot Krieger. 50% freelance written. Weekly Sunday supplement magazine about news of Rhode Island and New England. Estab. 1946. Circ. 250,000. Pays on publication. Byline given. Buys first North American serial rights. Submit seasonal/holiday 3 months in advance. Simultaneous submissions OK. Publishes reprints of previously published articles. Send tearsheet or send typed ms with rights for sale noted. For reprints pays 50% of the amount paid for an original article. Query for electronic submissions. Reports in 1 month on queries.

Nonfiction: Book excerpts, expose, general interest, historical/nostalgic, interview/profile and photo feature. "We are strictly a regional news magazine." No fiction or poetry. Buys 100 mss/year. Query. Length: 250-5,000. Pays $50-500.

• This magazine is currently seeking more short pieces, containing less than 500 words.

Photos: State availability of photos with submission. Offers $25-100/photo. Captions and identification of subjects required.

Fiction: Accepts novel excerpts.

SUNSET, Sunset Publishing Corp., 80 Willow Rd., Menlo Park CA 94025-3691. "Prefers not to share information."

YANKEE, Yankee Publishing Inc., P.O. Box 520, Dublin NH 03444. (603)563-8111. Editor: Judson D. Hale, Sr.. Managing Editor: Tim Clark. 50% freelance written. Monthly magazine that features articles on New England. "Our mission is to express and perhaps, indirectly, preserve the New England culture—and to do so in an entertaining way. Our audience is national, and has one thing in common—they love New England." Estab. 1935. Circ. 700,000. Pays within 30 days of acceptance. Byline given. Offers 33% kill fee. Buys first rights. Submit seasonal material 5 months in advance. Simultaneous submissions and previously published submissions OK. Send tearsheet or photocopy of article or short story, typed ms with rights for sale noted and information about when and where the article previously appeared. For reprints pays 100% of the amount paid for an original article. Query for electronic submissions." Reports in 2 months on queries. Writer's guidelines for #10 SASE.

Nonfiction: Essays, general interest, historical/nostalgic, humor, interview/profile and personal experience. "No 'good old days' pieces, no dialect humor and nothing outside New England!" Buys 30 mss/year. Query with published clips. Length: 250-2,500 words. Pays $50-2,000 for assigned articles; $50-500 for unsolicited articles. Sometimes pays expenses of writers on assignment.

Photos: State availability of photos with submission. Reviews contact sheets and transparencies. Offers $50-150/photo. Identification of subjects required. Buys one-time rights.

Columns/Departments: New England Sampler (short bits on interesting people, anecdotes, lost and found), 100-400 words; Footnotes to History (unusual short history pieces), 400-500 words; Yankee's Home Companion (short pieces about home-related items), 100-400 words; and I Remember (nostalgia focused on specific incidents), 400-500 words. Buys 80 mss/year. Query with published clips. Pays $50-400.

Fiction: Edie Clark, fiction editor. "We publish high-quality literary fiction that explores human issues and concerns in a specific place—New England." Buys 6 mss/year. Send complete ms. Length: 500-2,500 words. Pays $1,000.

Poetry: Jean Burden, poetry editor. "We don't choose poetry by type. We look for the best. No inspirational, holiday-oriented, epic, limericks, etc." Buys 40 poems/year. Submit maximum 3 poems. Length: 2-20 lines. Pays $50.

• Ranked as one of the best markets for freelance writers in *Writer's Digest* magazine's annual "Top 100 Markets," January 1993.

Tips: "Submit lots of ideas. Don't censor yourself—let *us* decide whether an idea is good or bad. We might surprise you. Remember we've been publishing for 57 years, so chances are we've already done every 'classic' New England subject. Try to surprise us—it isn't easy. These departments are most open to freelancers: Footnote to History; Home Companion; I Remember. Study the ones we publish—the format should be apparent. Surprise us!"

Alabama

ALABAMA HERITAGE, University of Alabama, Box 870342, Tuscaloosa AL 35487-0342. (205)348-7467. Fax: (205)348-7434. Editor: Suzanne Wolfe. 50% freelance written. Quarterly magazine on Alabama history and culture. "*Alabama Heritage* is a nonprofit historical quarterly published by the University of Alabama for the intelligent lay reader. We are interested in lively, well written and thoroughly researched articles on Alabama/ Southern history and culture. Readability and accuracy are essential." Estab. 1986. Pays on publication. Byline given. Buys first rights and second serial (reprint) rights. Query for electronic submissions. Reports in 1 month. *Writer's Market* recommends allowing 2 months for reply. Sample copy $5. Writer's guidelines for #10 SASE.

Nonfiction: Historical. "We do not want fiction, poetry, book reviews, articles on current events or living artists and personal/family reminiscences." Buys 10 mss/year. Query. Length: 1,500-5,000 words. Pays $100 minimum. Also sends 10 copies to each author plus 1 year subscription.

Photos: Reviews contact sheets. Identification of subjects required. Buys one-time rights.

Tips: "Authors need to remember that we regard history as a fascinating subject, not as a dry recounting of dates and facts. Articles that are lively and engaging, in addition to being well researched, will find interested readers among our editors. No term papers, please. All areas of our magazine are open to freelance writers. Best approach is a written query."

‡**ALABAMA LIVING,** Alabama Rural Electric Assn., P.O. Box 244014, Montgomery AL 36124. (205)270-1454. Editor: Darryl Gates. 10% freelance written. Monthly magazine covering rural electric consumers. "Our magazine is an editorially balanced, informational and educational service to members of rural electric cooperatives. Our mix regularly includes Alabama history, nostalgia, gardening, outdoor and consumer pieces." Pays on publication. Publishes ms an average of 3 months after acceptance. Byline given. Publication is not copyrighted. Buys second serial (reprint) rights. Editorial lead time 3 months. Submit seasonal material 4 months in advance. Accepts simultaneous and previously published submissions. Reports in 1 month on queries. Sample copy free on request.
Nonfiction: Historical/nostalgic, rural-oriented. Buys 6 mss/year. Send complete ms (copy). Length: 300-750 words. Pays $100 minimum for assigned articles; $40 minimum for unsolicited articles.
Tips: "The best way to break into *Alabama Living* is to give us a bit of history or nostalgia about Alabama or the Southeast."

Alaska

ALASKA, The Magazine of Life on the Last Frontier, Suite 200, 808 E St., Anchorage AK 99501-9963. (907)272-6070. Fax: (907)272-2552. Editor: Tobin Morrison. Managing Editor: Nolan Hester. 80% freelance written. Eager to work with new/unpublished writers. Monthly magazine covering topics "uniquely Alaskan." Estab. 1935. Circ. 235,000. **Pays on acceptance.** Publishes ms an average of 6 months after acceptance. Byline given. Buys first or one-time rights. Submit seasonal material 1 year in advance. Query for electronic submissions. Reports in 2 months. Sample copy $3 for 9 × 12 SAE with 7 first class stamps. Writer's guidelines for #10 SASE.
Nonfiction: Historical/nostalgic, adventure, how-to (on anything Alaskan), humor, interview/profile, personal experience and photo feature. Also travel articles and Alaska destination stories. Does not accept fiction or poetry. Buys 60 mss/year. Query. Length: 100-2,500 words. Pays $100-1,250 depending upon length. Pays expenses of writers on assignment.
Photos: Send photos with submission. Reviews 35mm or larger transparencies. Captions and identification of subjects required.
Tips: "We are placing even more emphasis on natural history, adventure and profiles."
  • Ranked as one of the best markets for freelance writers in *Writer's Digest* magazine's annual "Top 100 Markets," January 1993.

Arizona

ARIZONA HIGHWAYS, 2039 W. Lewis Ave., Phoenix AZ 85009-9988. (602)258-6641. Fax: (602)254-4505. Managing Editor: Richard G. Stahl. 90% freelance written. Prefers to work with published/established writers. State-owned magazine designed to help attract tourists into and through the state. Estab. 1925. **Pays on acceptance.** Reports in up to 3 months. Writer's guidelines for SASE.
Nonfiction: Feature subjects include narratives and exposition dealing with history, anthropology, nature, wildlife, armchair travel, out of the way places, small towns, old west history, Indian arts and crafts, travel, etc. Travel articles are experience-based. All must be oriented toward Arizona and the Southwest. Buys 6 mss/issue. Buys first serial rights. Query with "a lead paragraph and brief outline of story. We deal with professionals only, so include list of current credits." Length: 600-2,000 words. Pays 35-55¢/word. Sometimes pays expenses of writers on assignment.
Photos: "We will use transparencies of 2¼, 4 × 5 or larger, and 35mm when they display exceptional quality or content. We prefer 35mm Kodachrome. Each transparency *must* be accompanied by information attached to each photograph: where, when, what. No photography will be reviewed by the editors unless the photographer's name appears on *each* and *every* transparency." Pays $80-350 for "selected" transparencies. Buys one-time rights.
Columns/Departments: New departments in the magazine include Focus on Nature, Along the Way, Back-Road Adventure, Legends of the Lost, Hike of the Month and Arizona Humor. "Back Road and Hikes also must be experience-based."
  • Ranked as one of the best markets for freelance writers in *Writer's Digest* magazine's annual "Top 100 Markets," January 1993.
Tips: "Writing must be of professional quality, warm, sincere, in-depth, well-peopled and accurate. Avoid themes that describe first trips to Arizona, the Grand Canyon, the desert, Colorado River running, etc. Emphasis is to be on Arizona adventure and romance as well as flora and fauna, when appropriate, and themes that can be photographed. Double check your manuscript for accuracy."

PHOENIX, Media America Corporation, #B-200, 5555 N. 7th Ave., Phoenix AZ 85013-1756. (602)207-3750. Fax: (602)207-3777. Editor/Publisher: Richard S. Vonier. Managing Editor: Beth Deveny. 70% freelance written. Monthly magazine covering southwest, state of Arizona, metro Phoenix. Estab. 1966. Circ. 50,000. Pays on acceptance or publication. Publishes ms an average of 5 months after acceptance. Byline given. Negotiable kill fee. Buys first North American serial rights and one-time rights. Submit seasonal material 4 months in advance. Simultaneous and previously published submissions OK; send photocopy of article, typed ms with rights for sale noted and information about when and where the article previously appeared. Pays 50% of their fee for an original article. Query for electronic submissions. Reports in 2 months. Sample copy $1.95 for 9 × 12 SAE with 5 first class stamps.
Nonfiction: Book excerpts, essays, investigative, general interest, historical/nostalgic, how-to, humor, inspirational, interview/profile, opinion, personal experience, photo feature, religious, technical, travel and other. "No material dealing with travel outside the region or other subjects that don't have an effect on the area." Buys 35-65 mss/year. Query with published clips. Pays $50-1,500 for assigned articles; $50-500 for unsolicited articles. Sometimes pays expenses of writers on assignment.
Photos: State availability of photos with submissions. Reviews contact sheets, negatives, transparencies and prints. Offers $25-100/photo. Captions, model releases and identification of subjects required. Buys one-time rights.
Tips: "We have no published guidelines. Articles should be of local or regional interest with vivid descriptions that put the reader in the story and present new information or a new way of looking at things. We are not afraid of opinion."

TUCSON LIFESTYLE, Citizen Publishing Company of Wisconsin, Inc., dba Old Pueblo Press, Suite 12, 7000 E. Tanque Verde Rd., Tucson AZ 85715-5318. (602)721-2929. Fax: (602)721-8665. Editor-in-Chief: Sue Giles. 90% freelance written. Prefers to work with published/established writers. Monthly magazine covering city-related events and topics. Estab. 1982. Circ. 27,000. **Pays on acceptance.** Publishes ms an average of 6 months after acceptance. Byline given. Buys first rights and second serial (reprint) rights. Submit seasonal material 1 year in advance. Previously published submissions OK. Send typed ms with rights for sale noted and information about when and where the article previously appeared. Pays 50% of their fee for an original article. Reports in 3 months. Sample copy $3.20. Free writer's guidelines.
Nonfiction: All stories need a Tucson angle. Historical/nostalgic, humor, interview/profile, personal experience, travel and local stories. Special Christmas issue (December). "We do not accept *anything* that does not pertain to Tucson or Arizona." Buys 100 mss/year. Query. Pays $50-300. Sometimes pays expenses of writers on assignment.
Photos: Reviews contact sheets, 2¼ × 2¼ transparencies and 5 × 7 prints. Offers $25-100/photo. Identification of subjects required. Buys one-time rights.
Columns/Departments: In Business—articles on Tucson businesses and business people; and Southwest Homes (environmental living in Tucson: homes, offices). Buys 36 mss/year. Query. Pays $100-200.
Tips: Features are most open to freelancers. " 'Style' is not of paramount importance; good, clean copy with interesting lead is a 'must.' "

California

BUZZ, The Talk of Los Angeles, Suite 450, 11835 W. Olympic Blvd., Los Angeles CA 90064-5000. (310)473-2721. Editor-in-Chief: Allan Mayer. 80% freelance written. Monthly magazine for Los Angeles. "We are looking for lively, provocative, insightful journalism, essays and fiction of and for Los Angeles." Estab. 1990. Circ. 75,000. Pays within 30 days of acceptance. Byline given. Offers 25% kill fee. Buys first North American serial rights. Submit seasonal material 4 months in advance. Query for electronic submissions. Reports in 2 months. Sample copy $2.50 for 10 × 13 SAE with 10 first class stamps.
Nonfiction: Greg Critser, deputy editor. Book excerpts, essays, general interest and interview/profile. "No satirical essays, book/movie/theater reviews or personal memoirs." Buys 30 mss/year. Query with published clips. Length: 2,500-4,000 words. Pays $2,000-5,000. Sometimes pays expenses of writers on assignment.
Photos: State availability of photos with submission. Photos are assigned separately. Model releases and identification of subjects required. Buys one-time rights.
Columns/Departments: Susan Gordon, senior editor. "What's the Buzz" (witty, "Talk of the Town"-like pieces on personalities, trends and events in L.A.), 300-1,000 words. Buys 60 mss/year. Query with published clips. Pays $200-1,000.
Fiction: Renee Vogel, fiction editor. "We are interested in any type fiction by L.A. writers, and in fiction relevant to L.A. by non-L.A.-based writers. No fiction that has no connection with L.A." Publishes novel excerpts. Buys 10 mss/year. Send complete ms. Length: 1,500-4,000 words. Pays $1,000-2,500.
- Ranked as one of the best markets for freelance writers in *Writer's Digest* magazine's annual "Top 100 Markets," January 1993.
Tips: "The 'What's the Buzz' section is the best place to break into *Buzz*. Freelancers should keep in mind that we're looking for national-quality works."

THE CITY, San Francisco's Magazine, All of US in De, Inc., Suite 312, 1095 Market St., San Francisco CA 94103. (415)252-1391. Fax: (415)252-7460. Editor: John Burks. Managing Editor: Wanda Hoberg. 65% freelance written. Monthly magazine covering San Francisco city and county. Estab. 1989. Circ. 30,000. Pays on publication. Publishes ms an average of 3 months after acceptance. Byline given. Buys first rights. Submit seasonal material 6 months in advance. Query for electronic submissions. Reports in 2 months. Sample copy for 8×10 SAE with 8 first class stamps. Writer's guidelines for #10 SASE.

Nonfiction: Expose, general interest, humor, interview/profile and photo feature. "We do not want to see anything not related to San Francisco, nor do we accept reviews." Buys 100 mss/year. Query with published clips. Length: 300-3,000 words. Pays $30-300 for assigned articles. Pays 10-30¢/published word.

Photos: State availability of photos with submission. Reviews contact sheets, all transparencies and all prints. Offers $35-150/photo. Model releases and identification of subjects required. Buys first rights.

Columns/Departments: Inside the City (San Francisco briefs—social, political, cultural, odd), 100-300 words; High Notes (San Francisco musical profiles), 100-1,000 words. Query with published clips. Length: 200-600 words. Pays $30-80.

Tips: "Send for writer's guidelines, then send written query. Follow up with phone call to managing editor, and be prepared to send manuscripts on a speculation basis. Be specific in queries. We expect the writer has contacted sources, estimated completion time, length, and knowledge of proposed topic. All areas open to freelancers on spec basis."

LOS ANGELES MAGAZINE, ABC/Capital Cities, 1888 Century Park East, Los Angeles CA 90067. (310)557-7569. Fax: (310)557-7517. Executive Editor: Rodger Claire. Editor: Lew Harris. 98% freelance written. Monthly magazine about southern California. "The primary editorial role of the magazine is to aid a literate, upscale audience in getting the most out of life in the Los Angeles area." Estab. 1960. Circ. 174,000. Pays on publication. Publishes ms an average of 4 months after acceptance. Byline given. Offers 30% kill fee. Buys first North American serial rights. Submit seasonal material 6 months in advance. Reports in 6 weeks. Sample copy $5. Writer's guidelines for #10 SASE.

Nonfiction: Book excerpts (about L.A. or by famous L.A. author); expose (any local issue); general interest; historical/nostalgic (about L.A. or Hollywood); and interview/profile (about L.A. person). Buys up to 100 mss/year. Query with published clips. Length: 250-3,500 words. Pays $50-2,000. Sometimes pays expenses of writers on assignment.

Photos: Nancie Clare, photo editor. State availability of photos.

Columns/Departments: Buys 170 mss/year. Query with published clips. Length: 250-1,200 words. Pays $50-600.

● Ranked as one of the best markets for freelance writers in *Writer's Digest* magazine's annual "Top 100 Markets," January 1993.

LOS ANGELES READER, Suite 301, 5550 Wilshire Blvd., Los Angeles CA 90036-3889. (213)965-7430. Fax: (213)933-0281. Editor: James Vowell. Managing Editor: Natalie Nichols. 85% freelance written. Weekly tabloid of features and reviews for "intelligent young Los Angelenos interested in politics, the arts and popular culture." Estab. 1978. Circ. 90,000. Pays on publication. Publishes ms an average of 3 weeks after acceptance. Byline given. Buys one-time rights. Reprints OK; send information about when and where the article previously appeared with electronic copy if available. Pays 50% of their fee for an original article. Query for electronic submissions. Reports in 2 months. Sample copy $1 for 9×12 SAE with 2 first class stamps.

Nonfiction: General interest, journalism, interview/profile, personal experience and photo features—all with strong local slant. Buys "scores" of mss/year. Send complete ms or query. Length: 200-3,500 words. Pays $25-300.

Tips: "Break in with submissions for our Cityside page which uses short (400-800 word) news items on Los Angeles happenings, personalities and trends. Try to have some conflict in submissions: 'x exists' is not as good a story as 'x is struggling with y over z.' We much prefer submissions in electronic form."

LOS ANGELES TIMES MAGAZINE, *Los Angeles Times*, Times Mirror Sq., Los Angeles CA 90053. (213)237-7000. Fax: (213)237-7386. Editor: Bret Israel. 50% freelance written. Weekly magazine of regional general interest. Circ. 1,164,388. Payment schedule varies. Publishes ms an average of 2 months after acceptance. Byline given. Buys first North American serial rights. Submit seasonal material 3 months in advance. Simultaneous queries and submissions OK. Reports in 1-2 months. Sample copy and writer's guidelines are free.

Nonfiction: General interest, investigative and narrative journalism, interview/profiles and reported essays. Covers California, the West, the nation and the world. Written queries only. Queries must include clips. Length: 2,500-4,500 words. Pays agreed upon expenses.

Photos: Query first. Reviews color transparencies and b&w prints. Payment varies. Captions, model releases and identification of subjects required. Buys one-time rights.

Tips: "Prospective contributors should know their subject well and be able to explain why a story merits publication. Previous national magazine writing experience preferred."

METRO, Metro Publishing Inc., 550 S. 1st St., San Jose CA 95113-2806. (408)298-8000. Editor: Dan Pulcrano. Managing Editor: Sharan Street. 35-50% freelance written. Weekly alternative newspaper. *"Metro* is for a sophisticated urban audience—stories must be more in-depth with an unusual slant not covered in daily newspapers." Estab. 1985. Circ. 80,000. Pays on publication from one week to two months. Byline given. Offers kill fee with assignment memorandum signed by editor. Buys first North American serial and second serial (reprint) rights—non-exclusive. Submit seasonal material 3 months in advance. Reprints OK. Send photocopy of article including information about when and where the article previously appeared. Pays $25-200 for reprints. Query for electronic submissions. Reports in 2 months on queries; 4 months on mss. Sample copy $3. Writer's guidelines for #10 SASE.

Nonfiction: Book excerpt, expose and interview/profile (particularly entertainment oriented). Some sort of local angle preferred. Special issues: Wedding Feature, Health and Fitness, Spring and Fall Fashion. Buys 75 mss/year. Query with published clips. Length: 500-4,000 words. Pays $50-500 for articles. Sometimes pays expenses of writers on assignment.

Photos: State availability of photos with submission. Reviews contact sheets, negatives, any size transparencies and prints. Offers $25-50/photo, more if used on cover. Captions, model releases and identification of subjects required. Buys one-time rights.

Columns/Departments: MetroMenu (copy related to food, dining out), 500-1,000 words; and MetroGuide (entertainment features, interviews), 500-1,500 words. Buys 100 mss/year. Query with published clips. Pays $25-75.

Tips: "Seasonal features are most likely to be published, but we take only the best stuff. Stories on local news events or national news events with a local angle will also be considered. Preferred submission format is Macintosh disk with accompanying printout."

ORANGE COAST MAGAZINE, The Magazine of Orange County, O.C.N.L., Inc., Suite B, 245-D Fischer Ave., Costa Mesa CA 92626. (714)545-1900. Fax: (714)545-1932. Editor: Erik Himmelsbach. Managing Editor: Lynn Beresford. 95% freelance written. Monthly magazine "designed to inform and enlighten the educated, upscale residents of Orange County, California; highly graphic and well-researched." Estab. 1974. Circ. 40,000. **Pays on acceptance.** Publishes ms an average of 4 months after acceptance. Byline given. Buys first serial rights. Submit seasonal material at least 6 months in advance. Simultaneous queries and submissions OK. Reports in 2 months. Sample copy $2.50 for 10×12 SAE with 8 first class stamps. Writer's guidelines for SASE.

Nonfiction: Expose (Orange County government, politics, business, crime); general interest (with Orange County focus); historical/nostalgic; guides to activities and services; interview/profile (prominent Orange County citizens); local sports; and travel. Special issues include Dining and Entertainment (March); Health and Fitness (January); Resort Guide (October); Home and Garden (June); and Holiday (December). Buys 100 mss/year. Query or send complete ms. Absolutely no phone queries. Length: 1,000-3,000 words. Pays $250 maximum.

Columns/Departments: Business statistics. Most departments are not open to freelancers. Buys 200 mss/year. Query or send complete ms. *Absolutely no phone queries.* Length: 1,000-2,000 words. Pays $100 maximum.

Fiction: Buys only under rare circumstances. Send complete ms. Length: 1,000-5,000 words. Pays $250.

Tips: "Most features are assigned to writers we've worked with before. Don't try to sell us 'generic' journalism. *Orange Coast* prefers articles with specific and unusual angles that in some way include Orange County. A lot of freelance writers ignore our Orange County focus. We get far too many generalized manuscripts."

PALM SPRINGS LIFE, Desert Publications, Inc., P.O. Box 2724, Palm Springs CA 92263-2724. (619)325-2333. Fax: (619)325-2333. Editor: Jamie Pricer. Estab. 1958. 30% freelance written. Monthly magazine covering "affluent resort/southern California/Coachella Valley. *Palm Springs Life* is a luxurious magazine aimed at the 'affluence' market. Surveys show that our readership has a median age of 50.1, a median household income of $190,000, a primary home worth $275,150 and a second home worth $190,500." Circ. 24,000. Pays on publication. Publishes ms an average of 3 months after acceptance. Byline given. Buys all rights (negotiable). Submit seasonal material 4 months in advance. Simultaneous and previously published submissions OK. Query for electronic submissions. Reports in 3 months. Sample copy $6.

Nonfiction: General interest, historical/nostalgic, humor, interview/profile, new product, photo feature and travel. Special issues include Real Estate (May); Home and Garden (May); Health (July); Desert Living Annual/Coachella Valley focus (September); Desert Progress (October); Arts & Culture (November) and Holiday Shopping (December). Query with published clips. Length: 700-1,200 words. Pays 20¢/word. Sometimes pays the expenses of writers on assignment.

● Increased focus on desert region and business writing opportunities.

Photos: Reviews 2¼×2¼, 4×5 and 35mm transparencies. Offers $50-500 (for cover). Captions, model releases and identification of subjects required.

Tips: "*Palm Springs Life* publishes articles about dining, fashion, food, wine, beauty, health, business, sports (especially tennis and golf) and the lifestyle of the powerful, rich and famous. We are always interested in new ways to enjoy wealth, display luxury and consume it. We want to hear what's 'in' and what's 'out,' what's new in Palm Springs and the Coachella Valley, and how to solve problems experienced by our readers."

‡PALO ALTO WEEKLY, Embarcadero Publishing Co., 703 High St., P.O. Box 1610, Palo Alto CA 94301. (415)326-8210. Editor: Tom Gibboney. 5% freelance written. Weekly tabloid focusing on local issues and local sources. Estab. 1979. Circ. 48,000. Pays on publication. Publishes ms an average of 1 month after acceptance. Byline given. Offers 50% kill fee. Buys first rights. Submit seasonal/holiday material 2 months in advance. Reports in 2 weeks. Sample copy for 9×12 SAE with 2 first class stamps.
Nonfiction: General interest, historical/nostalgic, interview/profile and photo feature. Together (weddings—mid February); Interiors (May, October). Nothing that is not local; no travel. Buys 25 mss/year. Query with published clips. Length: 700-1,000 words. Pays $25-40.
Photos: State availability of photos with submission. Reviews contact sheets and 5×7 prints. Offers $10 minimum/photo. Captions, model releases and identification of subjects required. Buys one-time rights.
Tips: "Writers have the best chance if they live within circulation area and know publication and area well. DON'T send generic, broad-based pieces. The most open sections are food, interiors and sports. Keep it LOCAL."

SACRAMENTO MAGAZINE, 4471 D St., Sacramento CA 95819. Fax: (916)452-6061. Editor: Karen Coe. Managing Editor: Krista Minard. 80-90% freelance written. Works with a small number of new/unpublished writers each year. Monthly magazine emphasizing a strong local angle on politics, local issues, human interest and consumer items for readers in the middle to high income brackets. Estab. 1975. Pays on publication. Publishes ms an average of 3 months after acceptance. Rights vary; generally buys first North American serial rights, rarely second serial (reprint) rights. Original mss only (no previously published submissions). Reports in 2 months. Sample copy $4.50. Writer's guidelines for #10 SASE.
Nonfiction: Local issues vital to Sacramento quality of life. Buys 5 unsolicited feature mss/year. Query first in writing. Length: 1,500-3,000 words, depending on author, subject matter and treatment. Sometimes pays expenses of writers on assignment.
Photos: State availability of photos. Payment varies depending on photographer, subject matter and treatment. Captions (including IDs, location and date) required. Buys one-time rights.
Columns/Departments: Business, home and garden, media, parenting, first person essays, regional travel, gourmet, profile, sports and city arts (1,000-1,800 words); and City Lights (250-400 words).

‡SAN FRANCISCO BAY GUARDIAN, 520 Hampshire St., San Francisco CA 94110. (415)255-3100. Editor/Publisher: Bruce Brugmann. 60% freelance written. Works with a small number of new/unpublished writers each year. Weekly news magazine specializing in investigative, consumer and lifestyle reporting for a sophisticated, urban audience. Circ. 135,000. Pays 1 month after publication. Publishes ms an average of 2 months after acceptance. Byline given. Buys 200 mss/year. Buys first rights. No simultaneous or multiple submissions. Query for electronic submissions.
Nonfiction: Jean Tepperman, senior news editor; Tommy Tompkins, seniors arts editor. Publishes "incisive local news stories, investigative reports, features, analysis and interpretation, how-to, consumer and entertainment reviews. Most stories have a Bay Area angle." Freelance material should have a "public interest advocacy journalism approach." Sometimes pays the expenses of writers on assignment.
Photos: Tracy Cox, art director. Purchased with or without mss.
Tips: "Work with our volunteer and intern projects in investigative, political and consumer reporting. We teach the techniques and send interns out to do investigative research. We like to talk to writers in our office before they begin doing a story."

SAN FRANCISCO FOCUS, The City Magazine for the San Francisco Bay Area, 2601 Mariposa St., San Francisco CA 94110-1400. (415)553-2800. Fax: (415)553-2470. Editor: Amy Rennert. Managing Editor: Rick Clogher. 80% freelance written. Prefers to work with published/established writers. Monthly city/regional magazine. Estab. 1968. Circ. 180,000. Pays on publication. Publishes ms an average of 2 months after acceptance. Byline given. Offers 25% kill fee. Buys one-time rights. Submit seasonal material 5 months in advance. Simultaneous queries OK. Query for electronic submissions. Reports in 2 months. Sample copy $2.50. Free writer's guidelines with SASE.
Nonfiction: Expose, interview/profile, the arts, politics, public issues, sports, consumer affairs and travel. All stories should relate in some way to the San Francisco Bay Area (travel excepted). Query with published clips. Length: 750-4,000 words. Pays $75-750. Sometimes pays the expenses of writers on assignment.

THE SAN GABRIEL VALLEY MAGAZINE, Miller Books, 2908 W. Valley Blvd., Alhambra CA 91803. (213)284-7607. Editor-in-Chief: Joseph Miller. 75% freelance written. Bimonthly magazine for middle- to upper-income people who dine out often at better restaurants in Los Angeles County. Estab. 1962. Circ. 3,400. Pays on publication. Publishes ms an average of 45 days after acceptance. Buys simultaneous, second serial (reprint) and one-time rights. Phone queries OK. Submit seasonal material 1 month in advance. Simultaneous submissions OK. Reports in 2 weeks. Sample copy $1.
Nonfiction: Expose (political); informational (restaurants in the Valley); inspirational (success stories and positive thinking); interview (successful people and how they made it); profile (political leaders in the San Gabriel Valley); and travel (places in the Valley). Interested in 500-word humor articles. Buys 18 unsolicited mss/year. Length: 500-10,000 words. Pays 5¢/word.

Columns/Departments: Restaurants, Education, Valley News and Valley Personality. Buys 2 mss/issue. Send complete ms. Length: 500-1,500 words. Pays 5¢/word.

Fiction: Historical (successful people) and western (articles about Los Angeles County). Buys 2 mss/issue. Send complete ms. Length: 500-10,000 words. Pays 5¢/word.

Tips: "Send us a good personal success story about a Valley or a California personality. We are also interested in articles on positive thinking."

VALLEY MAGAZINE, World of Communications, Inc., Suite 275, 16800 Devonshire St., Granada Hills CA 91344. (818)368-3353. Fax: (818)360-8079. Editor: Bonnie Steele. 90% freelance written. Monthly magazine covering topics and people of interest to the San Fernando, Santa Clarita, Simi, Conejo and San Gabriel Valleys. Estab. 1978. Circ. 40,000. Pays within 2 months of acceptance. Publishes ms an average of 3 months after acceptance. Byline given. Offers 20% kill fee. Buys first North American serial rights. Submit seasonal material 6 months in advance. Simultaneous and previously published submissions OK. Reports in 2 weeks. Sample copy $3 for 10×13 SAE. Writer's guidelines for #10 SASE.

Nonfiction: Book excerpts, education, business, essays, general interest, how-to, humor, interview/profile, personal experience and travel. "General interest articles range from health to business to personality profiles. There must be a Valley slant. Audience is upscale, mature professionals." Special issues include Dining, Travel, Health and Local Business. Buys 130 mss/year. Query with published clips. Length: 750-2,000 words. Pays $50-350 for assigned articles; $25-250 for unsolicited articles.

Photos: State availability of photos with submission. Reviews transparencies. Captions, model releases and identification of subjects required.

Colorado

ASPEN MAGAZINE, Ridge Publications, P.O. Box G3, Aspen CO 81612. (303)920-4040. Fax: (303)920-4044. Editor: Janet C. O'Grady. Managing Editor: Rebecca Levy. 85% freelance written. Bimonthly magazine covering Aspen and the Roaring Fork Valley. Estab. 1974. Circ. 16,000. Pays on publication. Byline given. Kill fee varies. Buys first North American serial rights. Query for electronic submissions. Sample copy for 9×12 SAE with 10 first class stamps. Writer's guidelines for #10 SASE.

Nonfiction: Essays, historical/nostalgic, interview/profile, new product, photo feature, travel, sports, outdoors and arts. "We do not publish general interest articles without an Aspen hook. We do not publish 'theme' (skiing in Aspen) or anniversary (40th year of Aspen Music Festival)." Buys 30-60 mss/year. Query with published clips. Length: 50-5,000 words. Pays $50-1,000. Sometimes pays expenses of writers on assignment.

Photos: State availability of photos with submission. Reviews contact sheets, negatives, transparencies and prints. Model release and identification of subjects required.

Columns/Departments: Discoveries (favorite spot, sense of place, enterprise, business, made in Aspen, crafts, then and now, history/present), 300-1,000. Query with published clips. Pays $50-150.

Connecticut

CONNECTICUT MAGAZINE, Communications International, 789 Reservoir Ave., Bridgeport CT 06606. (203)374-5488. Fax: (203)371-6561. Editor: Charles Monagan. Managing Editor: Dale Salm. 80% freelance written. Prefers to work with published/established writers who know the state and live/have lived here. Monthly magazine covering the state of Connecticut "for an affluent, sophisticated, suburban audience. We want only articles that pertain to living in Connecticut." Estab. 1971. Circ. 90,000. Pays on publication. Publishes ms an average of 3-4 months after acceptance. Byline given. Offers 20% kill fee. Buys first North American serial rights. Submit seasonal/holiday material 4 months in advance. Reports in 6 weeks on queries. Writer's guidelines for #10 SASE.

Nonfiction: Book excerpts, expose, general interest, interview/profile and other topics of service to Connecticut readers. No personal essays. Buys 50 mss/year. Query with published clips. Length: 2,500-4,200 words. Pays $600-1,200. Sometimes pays the expenses of writers on assignment.

Photos: State availability of photos with submission. Reviews contact sheets and transparencies. Offers $50 minimum/photo. Model releases and identification of subjects required. Buys one-time rights.

Columns/Departments: Business, Health, Politics, Connecticut Guide, Arts, Gardening, Environment, Education, People, Sports, Law and Courts, Media and From the Past. Buys 50 mss/year. Query with published clips. Length: 1,500-2,500 words. Pays $300-600.

Fillers: Around and About editor—Valerie Schroth, senior editor. Short pieces about trends, curiosities, interesting short subjects, etc. Buys 50/year. Length: 150-400 words. Pays $75.

Tips: "Make certain that your idea is not something that has been covered to death by the local press and can withstand a time lag of a few months. Freelancers can best break in with Around and About; find a Connecticut story that is offbeat and write it up in a fun, lighthearted, interesting manner. Again, we don't want something that has already received a lot of press."

METROPOLITAN HARTFORD, (formerly Hartford Monthly), 196 Trumbull St., Hartford CT 06103. (203)560-2699. Editor: Deborah Hornblow. 85% freelance written. Bimonthly magazine covering the Greater Hartford area. Estab. 1988. Circ. 20,000. Pays on publication. Publishes ms an average of 3 months after acceptance. Byline given. Offers 15% kill fee. Buys first North American serial rights. Submit seasonal material 6 months in advance. Reports in 1 month. Sample copy for 9 × 12 SAE with 6 first class stamps.
  • New editor, Deborah Hornblow has increased this magazine's coverage of the arts, politics, crime and personalities.
Nonfiction: Arts, lifestyle, politics, crime, interview/profile, expose, humor, essay, historical, personal experience and photo features. Buys 80-90 mss/year. Query with published clips. (Send complete ms only for "Lasting Impressions" page.) Length: 300-4,000 words. Pays $100-800. Sometimes pays expenses of writers on assignment. Special consideration given Connecticut writers.
Photos: State availability of or send photos with submission. Reviews transparencies and prints. Model releases and identification of subjects required. Buys one-time rights.
Fiction: "Invite all comers; especially interested in stories by or about native Nutmeggers or work set in Connecticut."

NORTHEAST MAGAZINE, *The Hartford Courant,* 285 Broad St., Hartford CT 06115-2510. (203)241-3700. Editor: Lary Bloom. 50% freelance written. Eager to work with new/unpublished writers. Weekly magazine for a Connecticut audience. Estab. 1982. Circ. 300,000. **Pays on acceptance.** Publishes ms an average of 10 months after acceptance. Byline given. Buys one-time rights. Reports in 3 months.
Nonfiction: General interest (has to have strong Connecticut tie-in); in-depth investigation of stories behind news (has to have strong Connecticut tie-in); historical/nostalgic; interview/profile (of famous or important people with Connecticut ties); and personal essays (humorous or anecdotal). No poetry. Buys 50 mss/year. Length: 750-2,500 words. Pays $200-1,500.
Photos: Most assigned; state availability of photos. "Do not send originals."
Fiction: Well-written, original short stories and (rarely) novel excerpts. Length: 750-1,500 words.
  • Ranked as one of the best markets for freelance writers in *Writer's Digest* magazine's annual "Top 100 Markets," January 1993.
Tips: "Less space available for all types of writing means our standards for acceptance will be much higher. We can only print 3-4 short stories a year."

District of Columbia

THE WASHINGTON POST, 1150 15th St. NW, Washington DC 20071. (202)334-7750. Travel Editor: Linda L. Halsey. 60% freelance written. Prefers to work with published/established writers. Weekly newspaper travel section (Sunday). Pays on publication. Publishes ms an average of 3-6 months after acceptance. Byline given. "We are now emphasizing staff-written articles as well as quality writing from other sources. Stories are rarely assigned; all material comes in on speculation; there is no fixed kill fee." Buys only first North American serial rights. Travel must not be subsidized in any way. Usually reports in 1 month. *Writer's Market* recommends allowing 2 months for reply.
Nonfiction: Emphasis is on travel writing with a strong sense of place, color, anecdote and history. Query with published clips. Length: 1,500-2,500 words, plus sidebar for practical information.
Photos: State availability of photos with ms.

THE WASHINGTON POST MAGAZINE, *The Washington Post,* 1150 15th St. NW, Washington DC 20071. Managing Editor: Linton Weeks. 40% freelance written. Prefers to work with published/established writers. Weekly magazine featuring articles of interest to Washington readers. Circ. 1.2 million (Sunday). Average issue includes 2 feature articles. **Pays on acceptance.** Publishes ms an average of 2 months after acceptance. Byline given. Buys all rights or first North American serial rights, depending on fee. Submit seasonal material 4 months in advance. Reports in 6 weeks. Sample copy for 9 × 12 SAE with 2 first class stamps.
Nonfiction: Controversial and consequential articles with a strong Washington angle. Query with published clips. Length: 1,500-6,500 words. Pays $100-up; competitive with major national magazine rates. Pays expenses of writers on assignment.
Photos: Reviews 4 × 5 or larger b&w glossy prints and 35mm or larger color transparencies. Model releases required.
Tips: "Always send SASE for return of material."
  • Ranked as one of the best markets for freelance writers in *Writer's Digest* magazine's annual "Top 100 Markets," January 1993.

THE WASHINGTONIAN MAGAZINE, Suite 200, 1828 L St. NW, Washington DC 20036-5169. Editor: John A. Limpert. Assistant Editor: Carrie Harper. 20% freelance written. Prefers to work with published/established writers who live in the Washington area. Monthly magazine for active, affluent and well-educated audience. Estab. 1965. Circ. 157,055. Buys first rights only. Pays on publication. Publishes ms an average of 2 months after acceptance. Simultaneous submissions OK. Reports in 2 months. Sample copy $4 for 9×12 SAE. Writer's guidelines for #10 SASE.

Nonfiction: *"The Washingtonian* is written for Washingtonians. The subject matter is anything we feel might interest people interested in the mind and manners of the city. The only thing we ask is thoughtfulness and that no subject be treated too reverently. Audience is literate. We assume considerable sophistication about the city and a sense of humor." Buys how-to, personal experience, interview/profile, humor, think pieces and exposes. Buys 75 mss/year. Length: 1,000-7,000 words; average feature 4,000 words. Pays 50¢/word. Sometimes pays the expenses of writers on assignment. Query or submit complete ms.

Photos: Photos rarely purchased with mss.

• Ranked as one of the best markets for freelance writers in *Writer's Digest* magazine's annual "Top 100 Markets," January 1993.

Florida

BOCA RATON MAGAZINE, JES Publishing, Suite 100, 6413 Congress Ave., Boca Raton FL 33487. (407)997-8683. Fax: (407)997-8909. Editor: Marie Speed. 70% freelance written. Bimonthly magazine covering Boca Raton lifestyles. "Ours is a lifestyle magazine devoted to the residents of South Florida, featuring fashion, interior design, food, people, places and issues that shape the affluent South Florida market." Estab. 1981. Circ. 20,000. **Pays on acceptance.** Publishes ms an average of 3 months after acceptance. Byline given. Offers $50 kill fee. Buys second serial (reprint) rights. Submit seasonal material 7 months in advance. Simultaneous submissions OK. Reprints OK; send tearsheet of article. Pays 50j% of their fee for an original article. Query for electronic submission. Reports in 1 month. Sample copy $3.50 for 10×13 SAE with 10 first class stamps. Writer's guidelines for #10 SASE.

• No longer publishes fiction.

Nonfiction: General interest, historical/nostalgic, humor, interview/profile, photo feature and travel. Query with or without published clips, or send complete ms. Length: 800-2,500 words. Pays $50-500 for assigned articles; $50-300 for unsolicited articles. Sometimes pays expenses of writers on assignment. Reprints OK; send tearsheet of article. Pays 50% of their fee for an original article.

Photos: State availability of photos with submission.

Columns/Departments: Body & Soul (health, fitness and beauty column, general interest), 1,000 words; Family Room (family and social interactions), 1,000 words; and Humor (South Florida topics), 600-1,200 words. Buys 6 mss/year. Query with published clips or send complete ms. Length: 600-1,500 words. Pays $50-250.

‡CREATIVE LOAFING/TAMPA, CL/Tampa, Inc., Suite 218, 402 Reo St., Tampa FL 33609. (819)286-1600. Editor: John Burciaga. 90% freelance written. Alternative newsweekly tabloid covering arts, news and entertainment. "We welcome feisty, irreverent, hard-hitting but responsible reportage and commentary on wide range of issues, for well-read audience ages 25-44." Estab. 1988. Circ. 70,000. Pays on publication. Byline given. Offers $25-50 kill fee. Buys first rights. Editorial lead time 1 month. Submit seasonal material 2-3 months in advance. Query for electronic submissions. Reports in 2 weeks on queries; 1 month on mss.

Nonfiction: Expose, interview/profile, opinion and photo feature. "No puff or promotional pieces." Buys 52 mss/year. Query with published clips or send complete ms. Length: 3,500-5,500. Pays $200 minimum. Sometimes pays expenses of writers on assignment.

Photos: State availability of photos with submission. Reviews 3×5 minimum prints. Offers $25-50/photo. Buys all rights.

Columns/Departments: Opinion (local, timely), 400 words; art review (local,timely), 600-800 words; perform/film (local, timely), 600-800 words. Buys 200 mss/year. Query with published clips or send complete ms. Pays $75-100.

‡FLORIDA KEYS MAGAZINE, Gibbons Publishing, Inc., P.O. Box 2921, Key Largo FL 33037. (800)273-1026. Editor: Gibbons D. Cline. Contact: Diane Thompson, associate editor. 75% freelance written. Bimonthly magazine for lifestyle in the Florida Keys. *"FKM* caters to full-time residents of the Florida Keys. These are people with a unique lifestyle and a rich, colorful history." Estab. 1978. Circ. 10,000. Pays on publication. Publishes ms an average of 4-6 months after acceptance. Byline given. Buys first North American serial, first or all rights. Editorial lead time 4-6 months. Submit seasonal material at least 6 months in advance. Query for electronic submissions. Reports in 3-4 weeks on queries; 1-3 months on mss. Sample copy for $2.50. Writer's guidelines free on request.

Nonfiction: General interest, historical/nostalgic, how-to (water sports, home improvement, gardening, crafts), humor, interview/profile (keys residents *only*) and travel. Special issues include Fantasy Fest-Key West (Halloween) and Real Estate. "No erotica or personal experiences in the Keys . . . please do not send stories regarding your Keys vacation!" Buys 20-30 mss/year. Query with published clips. Length: 500-2,000 words. Pays $2/column inch minimum.

Photos: State availability of photos with submissions. Reviews transparencies (any size), prints and slides. Offers no additional payment for photos accepted with ms. Model releases and identification of subjects required. Buys all rights.

Columns/Departments: Dining Guide (Keys recipes, restaurant reviews), 1,200 words; Eco-Watch (environmental issues in Florida Keys), 1,200 words; and Entertainment (reviews books, movies, music pertaining to Keys), 1,200 words. Buys 5-10 mss/year. Query with published clips. Pays $2/column inch.

Fillers: Trivia facts. Buys 5/year. Length: 100-800 words. Pays $2/column inch.

Tips: "It is difficult to write about Keys unless writer is resident of Monroe County, Florida, or frequent visitor. Must be familiar with unique atmosphere and lifestyle of Florida Keys. Request resume to be submitted with query and/or mss. If author is unfamiliar with Keys, massive research is suggested (strongly). We are most open to new and unusual angles on fishing, boating, diving, snorkeling, sailing, shelling, sunbathing and Keys special events. Health and environmental articles are welcome. Home & Garden and Arts & Crafts are easy to write with research."

‡**FLORIDA LIVING**, North Florida Publishing Co. Inc., Suite 6, 102 NE 10th Ave., Gainesville FL 32601. (904)372-8865. Editor: John Paul Jones. Managing Editor: Holly M. Hays. Monthly magazine covering Florida subjects for Floridians and would be Floridians. "We are a lifestyle magazine for Floridians and those interested in Florida. We have a rather large circulation outside of Florida." Estab. 1981. Circ. 22,000. Publishes ms an average of 3-6 months after acceptance. Byline given. No kill fee. Buys one-time rights. Submit seasonal/holiday material 3-12 months in advance. Writer's guidelines sent on request.

Nonfiction: General Florida interest, historical/nostalgic, interview/profile, personal experience, travel and out-of-the-way Florida places. Buys 50-60 mss/year. Query. Length: 500-1,500 words. Pays $25-200 for assigned articles; $25-100 for unsolicited articles.

Photos: Send photos with submission. Reviews 3 × 5 prints. Offers up to $10/photo. Captions required. Buys one-time rights.

Fiction: Historical. Buys 2-3 mss/year. Send complete ms. Length: 1,000-3,000 words. Pays $50-200.

FOLIO WEEKLY, Folio Publishing Inc., Suite 11, 9456 Phillips Highway, Jacksonville FL 32256. (904)260-9770. Fax: (904)260-9773. Editor: Tim Thornton. 50% freelance written. Weekly news and opinion tabloid. Estab 1987. Circ. 31,000. Pays on publication. Publishes ms an average of 1-2 months after acceptance. Byline given. Offers 50% kill fee. Buys first North American serial or second serial (reprint) rights or makes work-for-hire assignments. Submit seasonal material 4 months in advance. Simultaneous submissions OK. Reports in 1 month. Sample copy for 9 × 12 SAE.

Nonfiction: Buys 40 mss/year. Query with published clips. Length: 2,000-3,000 words. Pays $150-175 for assigned articles.

Photos: State availability of photos with submission. Offers $10/photo. Captions, model releases and identification of subjects required.

Columns/Departments: Backpage (locally oriented editorials), 900 words.

Tips: "*Folio* serves a concerned, bright, hip readership that's interested in the environment, politics and the arts. Good, clear, gripping writing is important, but it's more important to get the facts straight. Recent stories have dealt with mayoral politics, a housing development in a tidal swamp and computer sex. We're serious, but we have a sense of humor."

‡**HEARTLAND MAGAZINE, the ONLY magazine of Southcentral Florida**, Heartland Publishing Inc., 208 N. Circle, P.O. Box 1629, Sebring FL 33870. (813)385-7200. Editor: Audrey Vickers. 50% freelance written. Quarterly magazine covering regional, lifestyle. "Keep it simple for busy readers! Estab. 1987. Circ. 10,000 copies printed. Pays on publication. Byline given. Makes work-for-hire assignments. Submit seasonal material 3 months in advance. Simultaneous submissions OK. Query for electronic submissions. Reports in 2 weeks on queries. Free sample copy and writer's guidelines.

Nonfiction: General interest, historical/nostalgic, interview/profile, photo feature and travel. Fall—anniversary edition; winter—visitors guide. "No 'first person' articles." Buys 6-8 mss/year. Query. Length: 250-750. Pays $100-250 for assigned articles. Pays contributor copies in trade for services. Sometimes pays expenses of writers on assignment.

Photos: State availability of photos with submission. Reviews 8 × 10 prints. Offers $50-100/photo. Captions and identification of subjects required. Buys one-time rights.

Columns/Departments: In Season (Florida humor), Perspective (thoughtful topic-oriented), and In Times Like These (motivational), 250-500 words. Buys 12 mss/year. Query. Length: 250-500 words.

Tips: "Phone call to me personally with idea! We are most open to nonfiction articles, but columns are considered."

‡**ISLAND LIFE, The Enchanting Barrier Islands of Florida's Southwest Gulf Coast**, Island Life Publications, P.O. Box 929, Sanibel FL 33957. Editor: Joan Hooper. Editorial Associate: Susan Shores. 40% freelance written. Prefers to work with published/established writers, but works with a small number of new/unpublished writers each year. Quarterly magazine of the Barrier Islands Sanibel, Captiva, Marco, for upper-income residents and vacationers of Florida's Gulf Coast area. Estab. 1980. Circ. 20,000. Pays on publication.

Publishes ms an average of 1 year after acceptance. Byline given. Buys first serial and second serial (reprint) rights. Simultaneous queries and submissions OK. Reports in 1 month on queries; 3 months on mss.

Nonfiction: General interest, historical. "Travel and interview/profile done by staff. Our past use of freelance work has been heavily on Florida wildlife (plant and animal), Florida cuisine, and Florida parks and conservancies. We are a regional magazine. No fiction or first-person experiences. No poetry. Our editorial emphasis is on the history, culture, wildlife, art, scenic, sports, social and leisure activities of the area." Buys 10-20 mss/year. Query with ms and photos. Length: 500-1,500 words. Pays 3-8¢/word.

Photos: Send photos with ms. No additional payment. Captions, model releases, and identification of subjects required.

Tips: "Submissions are rejected, most often, when writer sends other than SW Florida focus."

‡**PALM BEACH ILLUSTRATED**, Palm Beach Media Group, 1016 N. Dixie Hwy., West Palm Beach FL 33401. (407)659-0210. Editor: Judy DiEdwardo. 80% freelance written. Magazine published 10 times/year for upscale lifestyle. Estab. 1952. Circ. 25,000. Pays on publication. Byline given. Buys first North American serial and/or second serial (reprint) rights. Editorial lead time 3 months. Submit seasonal material 3 months in advance. Simultaneous and previously published submissions OK. Query for electronic submissions. Reports in 2 months on queries. Writer's guidelines for #10 SASE.

Nonfiction: General interest, historical/nostalgic, humor, interview/profile, photo feature and travel. "No budget travel, please. Our readers travel to—and are interested in—the exotic places of the world." Buys 12-20 mss/year. Query with published clips. Length: 500-1,500 words. Pays $100 minimum. "Depends on the writer's circumstances."

Photos: Send photos with submission. Reviews transparencies. Offers no additional payment for photos accepted with ms. Captions, model releases and identification of subjects required. Buys one-time (exclusive use) rights.

Tips: "Read us first before submitting. Though we focus on the Palm Beach lifestyle, our readership has interests that are of national/international concern and interest. Travel, lifestyle, profiles, interviews are the top freelance-supported areas, however, we do consider submissions for other areas."

‡**PENSACOLA MAGAZINE**, PEC Printing and Publishing, 2101 W. Government St., Pensacola FL 32501. (904)438-5421. 100% freelance written. Monthly magazine for news about city of Pensacola. Estab. 1983. Pays on publication. Publishes ms an average of 2 months after acceptance. Byline given. Offers 25% kill fee. Buys one-time or second serial (reprint) rights or makes work-for-hire assignments. Editorial lead time 2 months. Submit seasonal material 3-4 months in advance. Simultaneous and previously published submissions OK. Query for electronic submissions. Reports in 3 weeks on queries; 1 month on mss. *Writer's Market* recommends allowing 2 months for reply. Sample copy $3.

Nonfiction: General interest, historical/nostalgic, humor, how-to, interview/profile (of Pensacola residents), photo feature and travel. Does not want to see anything other than travel or holiday material; rarely runs stories that don't relate to Pensacola. Buys 80 mss/year. Query with published clips. Length: 800-1,500 words. Pays 7¢/word.

Photos: State availability of photos with submission. Reviews contact sheets, transparencies and prints. Offers $25 minimum/photo. Negotiates payment individually. Captions, model releases and identification of subjects required. Buys one-time rights.

SENIOR VOICE OF FLORIDA, Florida's Leading Newspaper for Active Mature Adults, Suncoast Publishing Group, Suite E, 6281 39th St. N., Pinellas Park FL 34665. Publisher: Donna Castellanos. Editor: Nancy Yost. 25% freelance written. Prefers to work with published/established writers. Monthly newspaper for mature adults 50 years of age and over. Estab. 1981. Circ. 50,000. Pays on publication. Publishes ms an average of 3 months after acceptance. Byline given. Buys one-time rights. Submit seasonal material 3 months in advance. Simultaneous and previously published submissions OK. Reports in 2 months. Sample copy $1 for 10×13 SAE with 6 first class stamps.

Nonfiction: Expose, general interest, historical/nostalgic, how-to, humor, inspirational, interview/profile, opinion, photo feature, travel, health and finance, all slanted to a senior audience. Buys 10 mss/year. Query or send complete ms. Length: 300-600 words. Pays $15.

ALWAYS submit unsolicited manuscripts or queries with a self-addressed, stamped envelope (SASE) within your country or a self-addressed envelope with International Reply Coupons (IRC) purchased from the post office for other countries.

Photos: Send photos with submission. Reviews 3×5 color and 5×7 b&w prints. Identification of subjects required.

Columns/Departments: Travel (senior slant) and V.I.P. Profiles (mature adults). Buys 10 mss/year. Send complete ms. Length: 300-600 words. Pays $15.

Fillers: Anecdotes, facts, cartoons, gags to be illustrated by cartoonist and short humor. Buys 10/year. Length: 150-250 words. Pays $10.

Tips: "Our service area is the Florida Gulf Coast, an area with a high population of resident retirees and repeat visitors who are 50 plus. We are interested primarily in serving their needs. In writing for that readership, keep their interests in mind. What they are interested in, we are interested in. We like a clean, concise writing style. Photos are important."

SUNSHINE: THE MAGAZINE OF SOUTH FLORIDA, The Sun-Sentinel Co., 200 E. Las Olas Blvd., Fort Lauderdale FL 33301-2293. (305)356-4685. Editor: John Parkyn. 50% freelance written. Prefers to work with published/established writers, but works with a small number of new/unpublished writers each year. General interest Sunday magazine "for the *Sun-Sentinel's* 800,000 readers in South Florida." Circ. 340,000. Pays within 1 month of acceptance. Publishes ms an average of 2 months after acceptance. Byline given. Offers 25% kill fee for assigned material. Buys first serial rights or one-time rights in the state of Florida. Submit seasonal/holiday material 2 months in advance. Simultaneous queries, and simultaneous and previously published submissions OK. Send tearsheet or photocopy of article, or typed ms with rights for sale noted. Include information about when and where the article previously appeared. Reports in 2 weeks on queries; 1 month on mss. *Writer's Market* recommends allowing 2 months for reply. Free sample copy and writer's guidelines.

Nonfiction: General interest, interview/profile and travel. "Articles must be relevant to the interests of adults living in South Florida." Buys about 150 mss/year. Query with published clips. Length: 1,000-3,000 words; preferred length 2,000-2,500 words. Pays 20-25¢/word to $1,000 maximum.

Photos: State availability of photos. Pays negotiable rate for 35mm and 2¼ color slides and 8×10 b&w prints. Captions and identification of subjects required; model releases required for sensitive material. Buys one-time rights for the state of Florida.

Tips: "Do not phone, but do include your phone number on query letter. Keep your writing tight and concise—readers don't have the time to wade through masses of 'pretty' prose. We are always in the market for first-rate profiles, human-interest stories and travel stories (which usually spotlight destinations within easy access of South Florida, e.g. Southeastern US, Caribbean, Central America). Freelancers should also consider our 'First Person' feature, which describes personal experiences of unusual interest."

WATERFRONT NEWS, Ziegler Publishing Co., Inc., 1523 S. Andrews Ave., Ft. Lauderdale FL 33316-2507. (305)524-9450. Fax: (305)524-9464. Editor: John Ziegler. 75% freelance written. Monthly tabloid covering marine and boating topics for the Greater Ft. Lauderdale waterfront community. Estab. 1984. Circ. 42,000. Pays on publication. Publishes ms an average of 2 months after acceptance. Byline given. Buys first serial, second serial (reprint) rights or simultaneous rights in certain circumstances. Submit seasonal material 3 months in advance. Reprints OK; send information about when and where the article previously appared. Pays negotiable fee for reprints. Reports in 1 month on queries. *Writer's Market* recommends allowing 2 months for reply. Sample copy for 9×12 SAE with 4 first class stamps. Free writer's guidelines.

Nonfiction: Historical/nostalgic (nautical or Southern Florida); new marine products; opinion (on marine topics); technical (on marine topics); and marine travel. Buys 50 mss/year. Query with or without published clips or send complete ms. Length: 500-1,000 words. Pays $50-200 for assigned articles; $25-200 for unsolicited articles. Sometimes pays the expenses of writers on assignment.

Photos: State availability of photos or send photos with submission. Reviews contact sheets and 3×5 or larger prints. Offers $5/photo. Buys one-time rights.

Columns/Departments: Query with published clips. Length 500-1,000 words. Pays $25-100.

Fillers: Anecdotes, facts, nautical one-liners to be illustrated by cartoonist, newsbriefs and short humor. Buys 12/year. Length 100-500 words. Pays $10-200.

Tips: "Nonfiction marine, nautical or South Florida stories only. No fiction or poetry. Keep it under 1,000 words. Photos or illustrations help. Send for a sample copy of *Waterfront News* so you can acquaint yourself with our publication and our unique audience."

Hawaii

ALOHA, THE MAGAZINE OF HAWAII AND THE PACIFIC, Davick Publishing Co., # 309, 49 S. Hotel St., Honolulu HI 96813. (808)523-9871. Fax: (808)533-2055. Editor: Cheryl Tsutsumi. 50% freelance written. Bimonthly regional magazine of international interest. "Most of our readers do not live in Hawaii, although most readers have been to the Islands at least once. The magazine is directed primarily to residents of Hawaii in the belief that presenting material to an immediate critical audience will result in a true and accurate presentation that can be appreciated by everyone. *ALOHA* is not a tourist publication and is not geared to such a readership, although travelers will find it to be of great value." Estab. 1977. Circ. 65,000. Pays on publication. Publishes ms an average of 6 months after acceptance; unsolicited ms can take a year or more.

Byline given. Offers variable kill fee. Buys first rights. Submit seasonal material 1 year in advance. Reports in 2 months. Sample copy $2.95 for SASE. Free writer's guidelines.

Nonfiction: Book excerpts; historical/nostalgic (historical articles must be researched with bibliography); interview/profile; and photo features. Subjects include the arts, business, flora and fauna, people, sports, destinations, food, interiors and history of Hawaii. "We don't want stories of a tourist's experiences in Waikiki or odes to beautiful scenery. We don't want an outsider's impressions of Hawaii, written for outsiders." Buys 24 mss/year. Query with published clips. Length: 1,000-4,000 words. Pay ranges from $200-500. Sometimes pays expenses of writers on assignment.

Photos: State availability of photos with query. Pays $25 for b&w prints; prefers negatives and contact sheets. Pays $60 for 35mm (minimum size) color transparencies used inside; $125 for double-page bleeds; $175 for color transparencies used as cover art. "*ALOHA* features Beautiful Hawaii, a collection of photographs illustrating that theme, in every issue. A second photo essay by a sole photographer on a theme of his/her own choosing is also published occasionally. Queries are essential for the sole photographer essay." Model releases and identification of subjects required. Buys one-time rights.

Fiction: Ethnic and historical. "Fiction depicting a tourist's adventures in Waikiki is not what we're looking for. As a general statement, we welcome material reflecting the true Hawaiian experience." Buys 2 mss/year. Send complete ms. Length: 1,000-2,500 words. Pays $300.

Poetry: Haiku, light verse and traditional. No seasonal poetry or poetry related to other areas of the world. Buys 6 poems/year. Submit maximum 6 poems. Prefers "shorter poetry"—20 lines or less. Pays $30.

Tips: "Read *ALOHA*. Be meticulous in your research and have good illustrative material available to accompany your text."

HAWAII MAGAZINE, Fancy Publications, Inc., P.O. Box 6050, Mission Viejo CA 92690. (714)855-8822. Editor: Dennis Shattuck. Managing Editor: Julie Applebaum. 60% freelance written. Bimonthly magazine covering The Islands of Hawaii. "*Hawaii Magazine* is written for people all over the world who visit and enjoy the culture, people and places of the Hawaiian Islands." Estab. 1984. Circ. 65,000. Pays on publication. Byline given. Buys first North American serial rights. Submit seasonal material 6 months in advance. Query for electronic submissions. Reports in 1 month on queries; 6 weeks on mss. Sample copy $3.95. Free writer's guidelines.

Nonfiction: General interest, historical/nostalgic, how-to, interview/profile, personal experience, photo feature and travel. "No articles on the following: first trip to Hawaii—How I discovered the Islands, the Hula, Poi, or Luaus." Buys 66 mss/year. Query with or without published clips or send complete ms. Length: 4,000 words maximum. Pays $100-500 for assigned articles.

Photos: Send photos with submission. Reviews contact sheets and transparencies. Offers $25-150 per photo. Identification of subjects preferred. Buys one-time rights.

Columns/Departments: Backdoor Hawaii (humorous look at the islands), 800-1,200 words; Hopping the Islands (news, general interest items), 100-200 words. Buys 6-12 mss/year. Query. Length: 800-1,500 words. Pays $100-200.

Tips: "Freelancers must be knowledgeable about Island subjects, virtual authorities on them. We see far too many first-person, wonderful-experience types of gushing articles. We buy articles only from people who are thoroughly grounded in the subject on which they are writing."

HONOLULU, Honolulu Publishing Co., Ltd., 36 Merchant St., Honolulu HI 96813. (808)524-7400. Fax: (808)531-2306. Editor/Publisher: Ed Cassidy. Executive Editor: John Heckathorn. Managing Editor: Janice Otaguro. 20% freelance written. Prefers to work with published/established writers. Monthly magazine covering general interest topics relating to Hawaii. Estab. 1888. Circ. 75,000. **Pays on acceptance.** Publishes ms an average of 4 months after acceptance. Byline given. Buys first serial rights. Submit seasonal material 5 months in advance. Simultaneous queries and submissions OK. Reports in 2 months. Sample copy $2 for 9×12 SAE with 8 first class stamps. Free writer's guidelines.

Nonfiction: Expose, general interest, historical/nostalgic, and photo feature—all Hawaii-related. "We run regular features on fashion, interior design, Neighbor Island, travel, politics, dining and arts, plus other timely, provocative articles. No personal experience articles." Buys 10 mss/year. Query with published clips if available. Length: 2,000-4,000 words. Pays $500. Sometimes pays expenses of writers on assignment.

Photos: Teresa Black, photo editor. State availability of photos. Pays $15 maximum for b&w contact sheet; $25 maximum for 35mm transparencies. Captions and identification of subjects required. Buys one-time rights.

Columns/Departments: Calabash (light, "newsy," timely, humorous column on any Hawaii-related subject). Buys 15 mss/year. Query with published clips or send complete ms. Length: 250-1,000 words. Pays $35.

● This magazine is now requiring samples of previously published work.

Illinois

‡**CHICAGO LIFE,** Box 11311, Chicago IL 60611-0311. Editor: Pam Berns. 95% freelance written. Bimonthly magazine on Chicago life. Circ. 60,000. Pays on publication. Byline given. Kill fee varies. Submit seasonal/holiday material 8 months in advance. Simultaneous and previously published submissions OK. Reports in 3 months. Sample copy for 9×12 SAE with 7 first class stamps.

Nonfiction: Book excerpts, essays, expose, how-to, photo feature and travel. Buys 50 mss/year. Send complete ms. Length: 400-1,200 words. Pays $30 for unsolicited articles. Sometimes pays the expenses of writers on assignment.

Photos: Send photos with submission. Reviews contact sheets, negatives, transparencies and prints. Offers $15-30/photo. Buys one-time rights.

Columns/Departments: Law, Book Reviews, Travel and Fashion. Send complete ms. Length: 500 words. Pays $30.

Fillers: Facts. Pays $15-30.

Tips: "Please send finished work with visuals (photos, if possible). Topics open include travel, self improvement, how-to-do almost anything, entrepreneurs, how to get rich, beautiful, more well-informed."

CHICAGO MAGAZINE, 414 N. Orleans, Chicago IL 60610. Managing Editor: Joanne Trestrail. 40% freelance written. Prefers to work with published/established writers. Monthly magazine for an audience which is "95% from Chicago area; 90% college educated, upper income, overriding interests in the arts, politics, dining, good life in the city and suburbs. Most are in 25-50 age bracket, well-read and articulate." Circ. 210,000. Buys first serial rights. **Pays on acceptance.** Publishes ms an average of 6 months after acceptance. Submit seasonal material 4 months in advance. Reports in 2 weeks. Query; indicate "specifics, knowledge of city and market, and demonstrable access to sources." For sample copy, send $3 to Circulation Dept. Writer's guidelines for #10 SASE.

Nonfiction: "On themes relating to the quality of life in Chicago: past, present, and future." Writers should have "a general awareness that the readers will be concerned, influential longtime Chicagoans reading what the writer has to say about their city. We generally publish material too comprehensive for daily newspapers." Personal experience and think pieces, profiles, humor, spot news, historical articles and exposés. Buys about 50 mss/year. Length: 500-6,000 words. Pays $100-$2,500. Pays expenses of writers on assignment.

Photos: Reviews b&w glossy prints, 35mm color transparencies or color prints. Usually assigned separately, not acquired from writers.

Tips: "Submit detailed queries, be business-like and avoid clichéd ideas."

THE CHICAGO TRIBUNE MAGAZINE, Chicago Tribune Co., 435 N. Michigan Ave., Chicago IL 60611. (312)222-3573. Editor: Denis Gosselin. Managing Editor: John S. Wade. 50% freelance written. Weekly Sunday magazine. "We look for unique, compelling, all-researched, elequently written articles on subjects of general interest." Circ. 1.3 million. Pays on publication. Publishes ms an average of 2 months after acceptance. Offers $250 kill fee. Buys one-time rights. Submit seasonal/holiday material 6 months in advance. Query for electronic submissions. Reports in 1 month on queries; 6 weeks on mss.

Nonfiction: Book excerpts, expose, general interest, interview/profile, photo feature, technical and travel. Buys 35 mss/year. Query or send complete ms. Length: 2,500-4,000 words. Pays $750-1,000. Sometimes pays the expenses of writers on assignment.

Photos: State availability of photos with submission. Payment varies for photos. Captions and identification of subjects required. Buys one-time rights.

Columns/Departments: First Person (Chicago area subjects only, talking about their occupations), 1,000 words; Chicago Voices (present or former high-profile Chicago area residents with their observations on or reminiscences of the city of Chicago), 1,000 words. Buys 40 mss/year. Query. Pays $250.

HYPHEN MAGAZINE, Chicago's Magazine of the Arts, Shoestring Publications, Suite 6, 3458 W. Devon, Lincolnwood IL 60659. Editor: Eduardo Cruz Eusebio. Managing Editor: Kimberly Bagwill. 75% freelance written. Quarterly magazine of art, performing art, literature and the arts community in Chicago. Estab. 1991. Circ. 1,500. Pays on publication. Publishes ms an average of 4 months after acceptance. Buys first North American serial microform and anthology rights. Editorial lead time 8 months. Submit seasonal material 8 months in advance. Simultaneous and previously published submissions OK. Send typed ms with rights for sale noted and information about when and where the article previously appeared. For reprints, pays 100% of the amount paid for an original article. Query for electronic submissions. Reports in 1 month on queries; 4 months on mss. Sample copy $4.

Nonfiction: Book excerpts, essays, expose, general interest, humor, interview/profile, opinion and photo feature. Buys 12 mss/year. Query. Length: 3,500 words maximum. Pays expenses of writers on assignment, plus $10 minimum. Pays in subscription & copies if contributors prefer.

Photos: Send photos with submission. Reviews contact sheets and prints. Negotiates payment individually. Captions and model releases required. Buys one-time rights, microform and anthology rights.

Columns/Departments: Off the Bitten Track (food as an art form), 600 words; and Interviews (Chicago-area artists, writers, poets), 2,500 words. Buys 8 mss/year. Query. Pays $10-25, or with subscription and copies.

Fiction: Dave Mead and Margaret Lewis, fiction editors. Ethnic, experimental, humorous, mainstream, novel excerpts and serialized novels. Buys 12-16 mss/year. Send complete ms. Length: 7,000 words maximum. Pays $10-25 with subscription and copies.

Poetry: John Boyer, poetry editor. Avant-garde, free verse, haiku, light verse, traditional and slam. Buys 40 poems/year. Submit maximum 5 poems. Pays $5-15.

Tips: "We are looking for committed and vigorous writing from published and unpublished writers. We focus on the Chicago scene, but accept writing from elsewhere. Read the magazine and assess the level and range of writing, and never, ever send a first draft. In the coming year, we will need interviews, short stories, plays, screenplays, poetry and nonfiction. We offer no guidelines; just make it double spaced and legible."

NORTH SHORE, The Magazine of Chicago's North and Northwest Suburbs, PB Communications, 874 Green Bay Rd., Winnetka IL 60093. (708)441-7892. Publisher: Asher Birnbaum. Managing Editor: Karen Titus. 75% freelance written. Monthly magazine. "Our readers are a diverse lot, from middle-class communities to some of the country's wealthiest zip codes. But they all have one thing in common—our proximity to Chicago." Pays on publication. Publishes ms an average of 3 months after acceptance. Byline given. Offers 50% kill fee. Buys first North American serial rights. Submit seasonal material 5 months in advance. Previously published submissions OK. Reports in 2 months. Free writer's guidelines for #10 SASE.

Nonfiction: Book excerpts, expose, general interest, how-to, interview/profile, photo feature and travel. Special issues: Weddings—January, July; Fitness—February; Homes/Gardens—March, June, September, December; Weekend Travel—May; Nursing/Retirement Homes—August; Dining and Nightlife—October. Buys 50 mss/year. Query with published clips. Length: 500-4,000 words. Pays $100-800. Sometimes pays expenses of writers on assignment.

Photos: State availability of photos with submission. Reviews contact sheets, negatives, transparencies and prints. Offers $25-100/photo. Identification of subjects required. Buys one-time rights.

Columns/Departments: "Prelude" (shorter items of local interest), 200-500 words. Buys 12 mss/year. Query with published clips. Pays $50-100.

Tips: "We're always looking for something of local interest that's fresh and hasn't been reported elsewhere. Look for local angle. Offer us a story that's exclusive in the crowded Chicago-area media marketplace. Well-written feature stories have the best chance of being published. We cover all of Chicago's north and northwest suburbs together with some Chicago material, not just the North Shore."

Indiana

ARTS INDIANA, Arts Indiana, Inc. Suite 701, 47 S. Pennsylvania, Indianapolis IN 46204-3622. (317)632-7894. Fax: (317)632-7966. Editor: Richard J. Roberts. 95% freelance written. Monthly (September-June) magazine on artists and arts organizations working in Indiana—literary, visual and performing. Circ. 12,000. Pays on publication. Publishes ms an average of 3-6 months after acceptance. Byline given. Offers 50% kill fee. Buys first North American serial rights. Submit seasonal material 4 months in advance. Reports in 3 months. Free sample copy and writer's guidelines.

Nonfiction: Essays, historical/nostalgic, interview/profile, opinion, photo feature and interviews with reviews (Q & A format). "No straight news reportage." Query with published clips. Length: 1,000-3,000 words. Pays $50-250 for assigned articles; $50-150 for unsolicited articles. Complimentary one-year subscription is given in addition to cash payment. Sometimes pays expenses of writer on assignment.

Photos: Send photos with submission. Reviews 5×7 or larger prints. Offers no additional payment for photos accepted with ms. Captions and identification of subjects required. Buys one-time rights.

Tips: "We are looking for people-oriented and issue-oriented articles. Articles about people should reveal the artist's personality as well as describe his artwork. Contributing writers must reside in Indiana."

INDIANAPOLIS MONTHLY, Emmis Publishing Corp., Suite 1200, 950 N. Meridian St., Indianapolis IN 46204. (317)237-9288. Fax: (317)237-9496. Editor: Deborah Paul. Managing Editor: Sam Stall. 40% freelance written. Prefers to work with published/established writers. Monthly magazine of "upbeat material reflecting current trends. Heavy on lifestyle, homes and fashion. Material must be regional in appeal." Estab. 1977. Circ. 45,000. Pays on publication. Publishes ms an average of 2 months after acceptance. Byline given. Offers 50% kill fee in some cases. Buys first North American serial rights and makes work-for-hire assignments. Submit seasonal material 3 months in advance. Reports in 2 months. Sample copy $3.05 for 9×12 SAE. Writer's guidelines for #10 SASE.

Nonfiction: General interest, interview/profile and photo feature. No poetry, domestic humor or stories without a regional angle. "We prefer stories with a timely or topical angle or 'hook' as opposed to topics plucked out of thin air." Buys 50 mss/year. Query with published clips or send complete ms. Length: 200-5,000 words. Pays $50-500.

Photos: Send photos with submission. Reviews 35mm or 2¼ transparencies. Offers $50 minimum/photo. Identification of subjects required. Buys one-time rights.

Columns/Departments: Business (local made-goods); Sport (heroes, trendy sports); and Health (new specialties, technology); all 1,500 words. Buys 6-9 mss/year. Query with published clips or send complete mss. Pays $100-300.

Tips: "Monthly departments are open to freelancers. We also run monthly special sections—write for editorial special section lineups.

• This magazine will consider novel excerpts by local authors.

Kansas

KANSAS!, Kansas Department of Economic Development, Suite 1300, 700 SW Harrison, Topeka KS 66603-3957. (913)296-3479. Editor: Andrea Glenn. 90% freelance written. Quarterly magazine emphasizing Kansas "people and places for all ages, occupations and interests." Estab. 1945. Circ. 54,000. **Pays on acceptance.** Publishes ms an average of 1 year after acceptance. Byline given. Buys one-time rights. Submit seasonal material 8 months in advance. Reports in 2 months. Sample copy and writer's guidelines for 10×13 SAE with 3 first class stamps.
Nonfiction: General interest, interview, photo feature and travel. "Material must be Kansas-oriented and have good potential for color photographs. We feature stories about Kansas people, places and events that can be enjoyed by the general public. In other words, events must be open to the public, places also. People featured must have interesting crafts, etc. Query letter should clearly outline story in mind. I'm especially interested in Kansas freelancers who can supply their own photos." Length: 750-1,250 words. Pays $150-250. Sometimes pays expenses of writers on assignment.
Photos: "We are a full-color photo/manuscript publication." State availability of photos with query. Pays $50-75 (generally included in ms rate) for 35mm or larger format transparencies. Captions required.
Tips: "History and nostalgia stories do not fit into our format because they can't be illustrated well with color photography."

Kentucky

BACK HOME IN KENTUCKY, Greysmith Publishing Inc., P.O. Box 681629, Franklin TN 37068-1629. (615)794-4338. Fax: (615)790-6188. Managing Editor: Nanci P. Gregg. 50% freelance written. Bimonthly magazine covering Kentucky heritage, peoples, places, events. We reach Kentuckians and "displaced" Kentuckians living outside the state. Estab. 1977. Pays on publication. Publishes ms an average of 8 months after acceptance. Byline given. Buys first North American serial rights. Submit seasonal material 8 months in advance. Reprints OK; send tearsheet or photocopy of article and information about when and where the article previously appeared. Pays 25-50% of their fee for an original article. Query for electronic submissions. Reports in 2 months. Sample copy $2.50 for 9×12 SAE with 5 first class stamps. Writer's guidelines for #10 SASE.
Nonfiction: Historical (Kentucky related); how-to (might be gardening or crafts); interview/profile (noted or unusual Kentuckians); photo feature (Kentucky places and events); and travel (Kentucky places). No inspirational or religion—all must be Kentucky related. Buys 25 mss/year. Query with or without published clips or send complete ms. Length: 500-2,000 words. Pays $25-100 for assigned articles; $15-50 for unsolicited articles. "In addition to normal payment, writers receive 4 copies of issue containing their article and 1 year subscription." Sometimes pays expenses of writers on assignment.
Photos: Send photos with submission. Reviews transparencies and 5×7 prints. Offers no additional payment for photos accepted with ms. Model releases and identification of subjects required. Rights purchased depends on situation. Also looking for color transparencies for covers. Vertical format. Pays $50-150.
Columns/Departments: Kentucky travel, Kentucky crafts and Kentucky gardening. Buys 10-12 mss/year. Query with published clips. Length: 500-750 words. Pays $15-40.
Tips: "We recently purchased this magazine and are trying to organize and departmentalize its content. We work mostly with unpublished writers who have a feel for Kentucky—its people, places, events, etc. The areas most open to freelancers are travel—places in Kentucky, history, and profiles of interesting, unusual Kentuckians."

KENTUCKY LIVING, P.O. Box 32170, Louisville KY 40232-0170. (502)451-2430. Fax: (502)459-1611. Editor: Gary W. Luhr. Mostly freelance written. Prefers to work with published/established writers. Monthly feature magazine primarily for Kentucky residents. Estab. 1948. Circ. 380,000. **Pays on acceptance.** Publishes ms on average of 4-12 months after acceptance. Byline given. Buys first serial rights for Kentucky. Submit seasonal material at least 6 months in advance. Will consider previously published and simultaneous submissions (if previously published and/or submitted outside Kentucky). Reports in 2 weeks. Sample copy for 9×12 SAE with 4 first class stamps. Writer's guidelines for #10 SASE.
Nonfiction: Prefers Kentucky-related profiles (people, places or events), history, biography, recreation, travel, leisure or lifestyle articles or book excerpts. Buys 18-24 mss/year. Query or send complete ms. Pays $75 to $125 for "short" features (600-800 words) used in section known as "Kentucky Fare." For major articles (800-2,000 words) pays $150 to $350. Sometimes pays the expenses of writers on assignment.

Photos: State availability of or send photos with submission or advise as to availability. Reviews color slides and b&w prints. Identification of subjects required. Payment for photos included in payment for ms. Pays extra if photo used on cover.
Tips: "The quality of writing and reporting (factual, objective, thorough) is considered in setting payment price. We prefer well-documented pieces filled with quotes and anecdotes. Avoid boosterism. Well-researched, well-written feature articles, particularly on subjects of a serious nature, are given preference over light-weight material."

Louisiana

SUNDAY ADVOCATE MAGAZINE, P.O. Box 588, Baton Rouge LA 70821-0588. (504)383-1111, ext. 350. Fax: (504)388-0371. Newsfeatures Editor: Freda Yarbrough. 5% freelance written. "We are backlogged but still welcome submissions." Byline given. Estab. 1925. Pays on publication. Publishes ms up to 1 year after acceptance. Query for electronic submissions.
Nonfiction and Photos: Well-illustrated, short articles; must have local, area or Louisiana angle, in that order of preference. Also interested in travel pieces. Photos purchased with mss. Pays $100-200.
Tips: "Styles and subject matter may vary. Local interest is most important. No more than 4-5 typed, double-spaced pages."

Maine

ISLESBORO ISLAND NEWS, Islesboro Publishing, HCR 227, Islesboro ME 04848. (207)734-2262. Fax: (207)734-6515. Publisher: Agatha Cabaniss. 20% freelance written. Monthly tabloid on Penobscot Bay islands and people. Estab. 1985. **Pays on acceptance.** Byline given. Buys one-time rights. Sample copy $2. Writer's guidelines for #10 SAE with 3 first class stamps.
Nonfiction: Articles about contemporary issues on the islands, historical pieces, personality profiles, arts, lifestyles and businesses on the islands. Any story must have a definite Maine island connection. No travel pieces. Query or send complete ms. Pays $20-50.
Photos: State availability of photos with submission.
Tips: "Writers must know the Penobscot Bay Islands. We are not interested in pieces of a generic island nature unless they relate to development problems, or the viability of the islands as year round communities. We do not want 'vacation on a romantic island,' but we are interested in island historical pieces."

Maryland

‡BALTIMORE MAGAZINE, Suite 1000, 16 S. Calvert St., Baltimore MD 21202. (410)752-7375. Fax: (410)625-0280. Editor: Jonathan Witty. Managing Editor: Craig Stoltz. 30-40% freelance written. Monthly magazine covering the Baltimore area. "Pieces must address an educated, active, affluent reader and must have a very strong Baltimore angle." Estab. 1907. Circ. 50,000. Pays within 60 days of acceptance. Byline given. Offers 30% kill fee. Buys first rights. Submit seasonal/holiday material 4 months in advance. Query for electronic submissions. Reports in 2 months on queries; 2 weeks on assigned mss; 3 months on unsolicited mss. Sample copy $2.05 for 9×12 SAE with $2.40 postage. Writer's guidelines for a business-sized SASE.
Nonfiction: Mark Cohen. Book excerpt (Baltimore subject or Baltimore author); essays (Baltimore subject); expose (Baltimore subject); humor (Baltimore focus); interview/profile (w/Baltimorean); personal experience (Baltimore focus); photo feature; and travel (local and regional to Maryland *only*). "Nothing that lacks a strong Baltimore focus or angle." Query with published clips or send complete ms. Length: 200-4,500 words. Pays $25-2,500 for assigned articles; $25-500 for unsolicited articles. Sometimes pays expenses of writers on assignment.
Tips: "Writers who live in the Baltimore area can send resume and published clips to be considered for first assignment. Must show an understanding of writing that is suitable to an educated magazine reader and show ability to write with authority, describe scenes, help reader experience the subject. Too many writers send us newspaper-style articles, instead. We are seeking: 1) *Human interest features*—strong, even dramatic profiles of Baltimoreans of interest to our readers. 2) *First person accounts* of experience in Baltimore, or experiences of a Baltimore resident. 3) *Consumer*—according to our editorial needs, and with Baltimore sources."

CHESAPEAKE BAY MAGAZINE, 1819 Bay Ridge Ave., Annapolis MD 21403. (410)263-2662. Editor: Jean Waller. 40% freelance written. Works with a small number of new/unpublished writers each year. Monthly regional publication for "those who enjoy reading about the Chesapeake and its tributaries. Our readers are yachtsmen, boating families, fishermen, ecologists—anyone who is part of Chesapeake Bay life." Circ. 33,000. Pays on publication. Publishes ms an average of 10-14 months after acceptance. Buys first North American serial rights and all rights. Submit seasonal material 6-8 months in advance. Reports in 2 months. Sample copy $2.95. Writer's guidelines for SASE.

Nonfiction: "All material must be about the Chesapeake Bay area—land or water." How-to (fishing and sports pertinent to Chesapeake Bay); general interest; humor (welcomed, but don't send any "dumb boater" stories where common safety is ignored); historical; interviews (with interesting people who have contributed in some way to Chesapeake Bay life: authors, historians, sailors, oystermen, etc.); nostalgia (accurate, informative and well-paced—no maudlin ramblings about "the good old days"); personal experience (drawn from experiences in boating situations, adventures, events in our geographical area); photo feature (with accompanying ms); profile (on natives of Chesapeake Bay); technical (relating to boating, fishing); and Chesapeake Bay folklore. "We do not want material written by those unfamiliar with the Bay area, or general sea stories." Buys 25 unsolicited mss/year. Query or submit complete ms. Length: 1,000-2,500 words. Pays $100-150.

Photos: Chris Gill, art director. Submit photo material with ms. Reviews 8 × 10 b&w glossy prints and color transparencies. Pays $200 for 35mm, 2¼ × 2¼ or 4 × 5 color transparencies used for cover photos; $15-75 for color photo used inside. Captions and model releases required. Buys one-time rights with reprint permission.

Tips: "We are a regional publication entirely about the Chesapeake Bay and its tributaries. Our readers are true 'Bay' lovers, and look for stories written by others who obviously share this love. We are particularly interested in material from the Lower Bay (Virginia) area and the Upper Bay (Maryland/Delaware) area. We are looking for personal experience Chesapeake boating articles/stories, especially from power boaters."

MARYLAND MAGAZINE, 13th Floor, 100 S. Charles St., Baltimore MD 21201. (410)539-3100. Fax: (410)539-3188. Publisher: Gerry Hartung. Editorial Director: Michelle Scoville Burke. 95% freelance written. Prefers to work with published/established writers. Bimonthly magazine promoting the state of Maryland. Circ. 45,000. **Pays on acceptance.** Publishes ms 6-12 months after acceptance. Byline given. Offers 25% kill fee. Buys all rights. Submit seasonal/holiday material 1 year in advance. Send photocopy, including information about when and where the article previously appeared. For reprints, pays 50% of the amount paid for an original article. Reports in 3 months. Sample copy $3. Writer's guidelines for #10 SASE.

Nonfiction: General interest, historical/nostalgic, humor, interview/profile, photo feature and travel. Articles on any facet of Maryland life. No fiction or controversial material or any topic *not* dealing with the state of Maryland; no trendy topics, or one that has received much publicity elsewhere. Buys 48 mss/year. Query with published clips or send complete ms. Length: 300-2,200 words. Pays $200-600. Pays expenses of writers on assignment.

Tips: "All sections are open to freelancers. Thoroughly research your topic and give sources (when applicable)."

WARM WELCOMES MAGAZINE, Warm Welcomes Inc., P.O. Box 1066, Hagerstown MD 21741-1066. (301)797-9276. Editor: Winnie Wagaman. 25% freelance written. Monthly magazine that covers history, culture, events and people of the areas surrounding the state of Maryland. Our audience consists of upper- and middle-income professionals in Maryland, South Central Pennsylvania, Virginia, Washington, D.C. and West Virginia. Estab. 1989. Circ. 20,000. Pays on publication. Publishes ms an average of 3 months after acceptance. Byline given. Kill fee varies. Buys exclusive rights. Submit seasonal material 6 months in advance. Simultaneous submissions OK. Query for electronic submissions. Reports in 3 months. Sample copy for 6 × 9 SAE with 4 first class stamps. Writer's guidelines for #10 SASE.

Nonfiction: General interest, historical/nostalgic, interview/profile and travel (limited). "We accept only material related to our area's history, people and locations." Buys 12 mss/year. Query with or without published clips or send complete ms. Length: 600-1,200 words. Pays $25-75 for assigned articles; $25-50 for unsolicited articles.

Photos: Send photos with submission. Reviews contact sheets and 5 × 7 b&w prints. Pays $10-25. Identification of subjects required. Buys one-time rights.

Tips: "Writers can best approach our publication with a well-written query or ms pertaining to the area—something that shows they know their subject and the audience they are writing for. Interview/profile pieces have the best chance of being picked up for publication."

Massachusetts

BOSTON GLOBE MAGAZINE, *Boston Globe,* Boston MA 02107. Editor-in-Chief: Ms. Ande Zellman. Assistant Editor: Fiona Luis. 50% freelance written. Weekly magazine. Circ. 805,099. **Pays on acceptance.** Publishes ms an average of 2 months after acceptance. No reprints of any kind. Buys first serial rights. Submit seasonal material 3 months in advance. SASE must be included with ms or queries for return. Reports in 1 month. Sample copy for 9 × 12 SAE with 2 first class stamps.

Nonfiction: Expose (variety of issues including political, economic, scientific, medical and the arts); interview (not Q&A); profile; and book excerpts (first serial rights only). No travelogs. Buys up to 100 mss/year. Query. Length: 2,000-5,000 words. Payment negotiable.

Photos: Purchased with accompanying ms or on assignment. Reviews contact sheets. Pays standard rates according to size used. Captions required.

CAPE COD LIFE, Including Martha's Vineyard and Nantucket, Cape Cod Life, Inc., P.O. Box 767, Cataumet MA 02534-0767. (508)564-4466. Fax: (508)564-4470. Editor: Brian F. Shortsleeve. 80% freelance written. Bimonthly magazine focusing on "area lifestyle, history and culture, people and places, business and industry, and issues and answers." Readers are "year-round and summer residents of Cape Cod as well as non-residents who spend their leisure time on the Cape." Circ. 32,000. Pays 30 days after publication. Byline given. Offers 20% kill fee. Buys first North American serial rights or makes work-for-hire assignments. Submit seasonal/holiday material 6 months in advance. Simultaneous queries OK. Reports in 6 weeks on queries; 2 months on mss. Sample copy $3. Writer's guidelines for #10 SASE.

Nonfiction: General interest, historical, gardening, interview/profile, photo feature, travel, marine, nautical, nature, arts and antiques. Buys 20 mss/year. Query with or without published clips. Length: 1,000-4,000 words. Pays $100-400.

Photos: State availability of photos with query. Pays $7.50-20 for photos. Captions and identification of subjects required. Buys first rights with right to reprint.

Tips: "Freelancers submitting *quality* spec articles with a Cape Cod angle have a good chance at publication. We do like to see a wide selection of writer's clips before giving assignments. We accept more spec work written about Cape and Islands history than any other area."

‡PROVINCETOWN ARTS, Provincetown Arts, Inc., 650 Commercial St., Provincetown MA 02657. (508)487-3167. Editor; Christopher Busa. Managing Editor: Dean Albarelli. Contact: Christopher Busa. 90% freelance written. Annual magazine for contemporary art and writing. "*Provincetown Arts* focuses broadly on the artists and writers who inhabit or visit the Lower Cape, and seeks to stimulate creative activity and enhance public awareness of the cultural life of the nation's oldest continuous art colony. Drawing upon a 75-year tradition rich in visual art, literature, and theater, *Provincetown Arts* offers a unique blend of interviews, fiction, visual features, reporting, and poetry." Estab. 1985. Circ. 8,000. Pays on publication. Publishes ms an average of 4 months after acceptance. Offers 50% kill fee. Buys one-time and second serial (reprint) rights. Editorial lead time 4-6 months. Submit seasonal material 6 months in advance. Query for electronic submissions. Reports in 3 weeks on queries; 2 months on mss. Sample copy $5. Writer's guidelines for #10 SASE.

Nonfiction: Book excerpts, essays, humor and interview/profile. Buys 20 mss/year. Send complete ms. Length: 1,500-4,000 words. Pays $150 minimum for assigned articles; $125 minimum for unsolicited articles. Sometimes pays expenses of writers on assignment.

Photos: Send photos with submission. Reviews 8 × 10 prints. Offers $20-100/photo. Identification of subjects required. Buys one-time rights.

Fiction: Mainstream. Buys 7 mss/year. Send complete ms. Length: 500-5,000 words. Pays $75-300.

Poetry: Buys 25 poems/year. Submit maximum 3 poems. Pays $25-150.

WORCESTER MAGAZINE, P.O. Box 1000, Worcester MA 01614-1000. (617)799-0511. Editor: Paul Della Valle. 10% freelance written. Weekly tabloid emphasizing the central Massachusetts region. Estab. 1976. Circ. 30,000. **Pays on acceptance.** Publishes ms an average of 3 weeks after acceptance. Byline given. Buys all rights. Submit seasonal material 2 months in advance. No simultaneous submissions. Reports in 2 months. Sample copy $1 for 10 × 13 SAE with 6 first class stamps.

Nonfiction: Expose (area government, corporate); how-to (concerning the area, homes, vacations); interview (local); personal experience; opinion (local); and photo feature. No nonlocal stories. "We leave national and general topics to national and general publications." Buys 30 mss/year. Query with published clips. Length: 500-1,500 words. Pays $35-250.

Photos: State availability of photos with query. Pays $10 for b&w photos. Captions preferred; model release required. Buys all rights.

Michigan

‡ABOVE THE BRIDGE MAGAZINE, P.O. Box 416, Marquette MI 49855. Editor: Lynn DeLoughary St. Arnaud. 100% freelance written. Quarterly magazine on the Upper Peninsula of Michigan. "Most material, including fiction, has an Upper Peninsula of Michigan slant. Our readership is past and present Upper Peninsula residents." Circ. 2,000. Pays on publication. Publishes ms an average of 6 months after acceptance. Byline given. Buys one-time rights. Submit seasonal/holiday material 6 months in advance. Previously published submissions OK. Send typed ms with rights for sale noted, including information about when and where the article previously appeared. For reprints, pays 100% of the amount paid for an original article. Query for electronic submissions. Reports in 5 months. Sample copy $3.50. Writer's guidelines for #10 SASE.

Nonfiction: Book excerpts (books on Upper Peninsula or UP writer); essays; historical/nostalgic (UP); interview/profile (UP personality or business); personal experience; and photo feature (UP). Note: Travel by assignment only. "This is a family magazine; therefore, no material in poor taste." Buys 60 mss/year. Send complete ms. Length: 1,000-2,500 words. Pays 2¢/word.

Photos: Send photos with submission. Reviews prints (5×7 or larger). Offers $5 ($15-20 if used for cover). Captions, model releases and identification of subjects required. Buys one-time rights.
Fiction: Ethnic (UP heritage), humorous, mainstream and mystery. No horror or erotica. "Material set in UP has preference for publication. Accepts children's fiction." Buys 12 mss/year. Send complete ms. Length: 2,000 words (1,000 maximum for children's). Pays 2¢/word.
Poetry: Free verse, haiku, light verse and traditional. No erotica. Buys 20 poems/year. Shorter poetry preferred. Pays $5.
Fillers: Anecdotes and short humor. Buys 25/year. Length: 100-500 words. Pays 2¢/word maximum.
Tips: "Material on the shorter end of our requirements has a better chance for publication. We're very well-stocked at the moment. We can't use material by out-of-state writers with content not tied to Upper Peninsula of Michigan. Know the area and people, read the magazine. Most material received is too long. Stick to our guidelines. We love to publish well written material by previously unpublished writers."

ANN ARBOR OBSERVER, Ann Arbor Observer Company, 201 E. Catherine, Ann Arbor MI 48104. Fax: (313)769-3375. Editor: John Hilton. 50% freelance written. Works with a small number of new/unpublished writers each year. Monthly magazine featuring stories about people and events in Ann Arbor. Estab. 1976. Circ. 55,000. Pays on publication. Publishes ms an average of 2 months after acceptance. Byline given. Query for electronic submissions. Reports in 3 weeks on queries; "several months" on mss. Sample copy for 12½×15 SAE with $3 postage. Free writer's guidelines.
Nonfiction: Historical, investigative features, profiles and brief vignettes. Must pertain to Ann Arbor. Buys 75 mss/year. Length: 100-7,000 words. Pays up to $1,000/article. Sometimes pays expenses of writers on assignment.
Tips: "If you have an idea for a story, write a 100-200-word description telling us why the story is interesting. We are most open to intelligent, insightful features of up to 5,000 words about interesting aspects of life in Ann Arbor."

THE DETROIT FREE PRESS MAGAZINE, *The Detroit Free Press*, 321 W. Lafayette Blvd., Detroit MI 48231. (313)222-6558. Editor: Brian Dickerson. 20% freelance written. Prefers to work with published/established writers. Weekly magazine with a general newspaper readership; urban and suburban. Circ. 1.2 million. Pays within 6 weeks of publication. Publishes ms an average of 3 months after acceptance. Buys first or second serial rights. Byline given. Query for electronic submissions. Reports in 4 months. Mss are *not* returned.
Nonfiction: "Seeking quality magazine journalism on subjects of interest to Detroit and Michigan readers: trends, behavior, business and political intrigue, crime and cops, money, success and failure, sports, fascinating people, arts and entertainment. *DFP Magazine* is bright and cosmopolitan in tone. Most desired writing style is literate but casual—the way you'd like to read—and reporting must be unimpeachable." Buys 75-100 mss/year. Query or submit complete ms. "If possible, the letter should be held to one page. It should present topic, organizational technique and writing angle. It should demonstrate writing style and give some indication as to why the story would be of interest to us. It should not, however, be an extended sales pitch." Length: 1,000-5,000 words. Pays $150-2,500. Sometimes pays the expenses of writers on assignment.
Photos: Purchased with or without accompanying ms.

DETROIT MONTHLY, Crain Communications, 1400 Woodbridge, Detroit MI 48207. (313)446-6000. Fax: (313)446-1687. Editor: John Barron. 50% freelance written. Monthly magazine. "We are a city magazine for educated, reasonably well-to-do, intellectually curious Detroiters." Circ. 100,000. **Pays on acceptance.** Byline given. Offers negotiable kill fee. Buys first North American serial rights. Publishes reprints of previously published articles. Send tearsheet or photocopy of article. For reprints, pays 15-25% of the amount pays for an original article. Submit seasonal material 4 months in advance. Query for electronic submissions. Reports in 6 weeks.
Nonfiction: Book excerpts, expose and travel. Buys 25 mss/year. Query with published clips. Length: 1,000-5,000 words. Pays $100-1,200. Sometimes pays the expenses of writers on assignment.
Photos: State availability of photos with submission.

GRAND RAPIDS MAGAZINE, 549 Ottawa Ave. NW, Grand Rapids MI 49503-1444. (616)459-4545. Fax: (616)459-4800. Publisher: John H. Zwarensteyn. Editor: Carole Valade Smith. 70% freelance written. Eager to work with new writers. Monthly general feature magazine serving Western Michigan. Estab. 1964. Circ. 12,000. Pays on 15th of month of publication. Publishes ms an average of 4 months after acceptance. Buys first serial rights. Phone queries OK. Submit seasonal material 3 months in advance. Previously published submissions OK. Query for electronic submissions. Reports in 3 months. Sample copy $2 for 6 first class stamps.
　● This magazine is using fewer staff writers and more freelance writers than before.
Nonfiction: Western Michigan writers preferred. Western Michigan subjects only: government, labor, investigative, criminal justice, environment, health/medical, education, general interest, historical, interview/profile and nostalgia. Inspirational and personal experience pieces discouraged. No breezy, self-centered "human" pieces or "pieces not only light on style but light on hard information." Humor appreciated but must be specific to region. "If you live here, see the managing editor before you write. If you don't, send a query

letter with published clips, or phone." Length: 500-4,000 words. Pays $35-200. Sometimes pays the expenses of writers on assignment.

Photos: State availability of photos. Pays $25 minimum for 5×7 glossy print and $35 minimum for 35 or 120mm transparency. Captions and model releases required.

Tips: "Television has forced city/regional magazines to be less provincial and more broad-based in their approach. People's interests seem to be evening out from region to region. The subject matters should remain largely local, but national trends must be recognized in style and content. And we must *entertain* as well as inform."

MICHIGAN COUNTRY LINES, Michigan Electric Cooperative Association, 2859 Jolly Rd., Okemos MI 48864. (517)351-6322. Fax: (517)351-6396. Editor: Michael Buda. Managing Editor: Gail Knudtson. 10% freelance written. Bimonthly magazine covering rural Michigan. Estab. 1980. Circ. 170,000. Pays on publication. Publishes ms an average of 4 months after acceptance. Byline given. Buys one-time and second serial (reprint) rights. Submit seasonal material 3 months in advance. Query for electronic submissions. Reports in 2 months. Free sample copy.

Nonfiction: Personalities, how-to (rural living) and photo feature. No product or out-of-state. Buys 6 mss/year. Send complete ms. Length: 700-1,500 words. Pays $200 for assigned articles; $150 unsolicited articles. Pays expenses of writers on assignment.

Photos: Send photos with submission. Reviews contact sheets, 35mm transparencies and 3×5 prints. Offers $10-15/photo. Captions, model releases and identification of subjects required. Buys one-time rights.

Tips: "Features are most open to freelancers. We no longer need historical/nostalgic articles."

Minnesota

LAKE SUPERIOR MAGAZINE, Lake Superior Port Cities, Inc., P.O. Box 16417, Duluth MN 55816-0417. (218)722-5002. Fax: (218)722-4096. Editor: Paul L. Hayden. 60% freelance written. Works with a small number of new/unpublished writers each year. Bimonthly regional magazine covering contemporary and historic people, places and current events around Lake Superior. Estab. 1979. Circ. 20,000. Pays on publication. Publishes ms an average of 10 months after acceptance. Byline given. Offers $25 kill fee. Buys first North American serial and some second rights. Submit seasonal material 1 year in advance. Query for electronic submissions. Reports in 2 months. Sample copy $3.95 for 5 first class stamps. Writer's guidelines for #10 SASE.

Nonfiction: Book excerpts, general interest, historic/nostalgic, humor, interview/profile (local), personal experience, photo feature (local), travel (local), city profiles, regional business, some investigative. Buys 45 mss/year. Query with published clips. Length 300-2,200 words. Pays $80-400. Sometimes pays the expenses of writers on assignment.

Photos: Quality photography is our hallmark. State availability of photos with submission. Reviews contact sheets, 2×2 transparencies and 4×5 prints. Offers $20 for b&w and $35 for color. More for covers. Captions, model releases and identification of subjects required.

Columns/Departments: Current events and things to do (for Events Calendar section), short, under 300 words; Around The Circle (media reviews and short pieces on Lake Superior or Great Lakes environmental issues and themes and letters and short pieces on events and highlights of the Lake Superior Region), and I Remember (nostalgic lake-specific pieces), up to 1,100 words and up to 200 words; and Life Lines (single personality profile with b&w), up to 700 words. Other headings include Destinations, Nature, Wilderness Living, Heritage, Shipwreck, House For Sale. Buys 20 mss/year. Query with published clips. Pays $10-75.

Fiction: Ethnic, historic, humorous, mainstream, novel excerpts, slice-of-life vignettes and ghost stories. Must be regionally targeted in nature. Buys only 2-3 mss/year. Query with published clips. Length: 300-2,500 words. Pays $1-125.

Tips: "Well-researched queries are attended to. We actively seek queries from writers in Lake Superior communities. We prefer manuscripts to queries. Provide enough information on why the subject is important to the region and our readers, or why and how something is unique. We want details. The writer must have a thorough knowledge of the subject and how it relates to our region. We prefer a fresh, unused approach to the subject which provides the reader with an emotional involvement. Almost all of our articles feature quality photography, color or black and white. It is a prerequisite of all nonfiction. All submissions should include a *short* biography of author/photographer."

MPLS. ST. PAUL MAGAZINE, Suite 500, 220 S. 6th St., Pillsbury Center-South Tower, Minneapolis MN 55402. (612)339-7571. Fax: (612)339-5806. Editor: Brian Anderson. Executive Editor: Sylvia Paine. Managing Editor: Claude Peck. 70% freelance written. Monthly general interest magazine covering the metropolitan area of Minneapolis/St. Paul and aimed at college-educated professionals who enjoy living in the area and taking advantage of the cultural, entertainment and dining out opportunities. Reports on people and issues of importance to the community. Circ. 62,000. **Pays on acceptance.** Publishes ms an average of 3 months after acceptance. Byline given. Offers 25% kill fee. Buys first North American serial rights. Submit seasonal material 5 months in advance. Query for electronic submissions. Reports in 1 month. Sample copy $4.18.

Nonfiction: Book excerpts, general interest, historical/nostalgic, interview/profile (local), new product, photo feature (local) and travel (regional). Buys 200 mss/year. Query with published clips. Length: 1,000-4,000 words. Pays $100-1,200. Sometimes pays expenses of writers on assignment.
Photos: Chris Greco, photo editor.
Columns/Departments: Nostalgia—Minnesota historical; Home—interior design, local. Query with published clips. Length: 750-2,000 words. Pays $100-400.

Mississippi

MISSISSIPPI, Downhome Publications, 5 Lakeland Circle, P.O. Box 16445, Jackson MS 39216. (601)982-8418. Editor: Ann Becker. 95% freelance written. Bimonthly magazine "focuses almost exclusively on positive aspects of Mississippi—people, places, events." Estab. 1982. Circ. 25,000. Pays on publication. Publishes ms an average of 6 months after acceptance. Byline given. Offers $75 kill fee. Buys one-time rights. Submit seasonal material 1 year in advance. Query for electronic submissions. Reports in 3 months. Sample copy for $3.75. Writer's guidelines for #10 SASE.
Nonfiction: Essays, general interest, historical/nostalgic, interview/profile, personal experience, photo feature and travel. No essays on Southern accents or Southerners in the North. Buys 72 mss/year. Query with published clips. Length: 500-2,000 words. Pays $50-500.
Photos: Send photos with submission. Reviews contact sheets, 2¼ × 2¼ transparencies and 4 × 5 prints. Offers $25-100/photo. Captions, model releases and identification of subjects required. Buys one-time rights.
Columns/Departments: Travel, People, Music, Heritage, Sports, Business, Art, Outdoors, Homes and Gardens (focuses on Mississippi people, places or events), 1,500 words each. Buys 35 mss/year. Query with published clips. Length: 500-1,500 words. Pays $125.
Tips: "Query by mail. Query should give some idea of how story would read. Including a lead is good. Be patient. Be aware of past articles—we only feature a subject once. All departments are good starting points. Be sure subject has *state*wide interest. Be sure subject has good reputation in field."

Missouri

MISSOURI MAGAZINE, 9701 Gravois Rd., St. Louis MO 63123. (314)638-4050. Fax: (314)638-3880. Editor: Tony Nolan Adrignola. Quarterly magazine covering Missouri-oriented topics. "We prefer human-interest articles unique to Missouri—from historical pieces to profiles of people and places in Missouri today." Estab. 1974. Circ. 15,000. Pays on publication. Publishes ms an average of 9-18 months after acceptance. Byline given. Buys first rights. Publishes reprints of previously articles. Send tearsheet or photocopy of article. For reprints pays 50% of the amount paid for an original article. Submit seasonal material 6 months in advance. Simultaneous submissions OK. Query for electronic submissions. Reports in 1 month queries; 3 months on mss. Sample copy $4.95. Free writer's guidelines.
Nonfiction: General interest, historical/nostalgic, interview/profile, photo feature, travel, Missouri geology, natural history and wildlife. No fiction. Buys 28 mss/year. Send complete ms. Length: 1,500-3,000 words. Pays $150-300 for assigned articles; $75-200 for unsolicited articles. Sometimes pays in trade out with ads.
Photos: State availability of photos with submission. Reviews 2¼ × 2¼ transparencies. Offers $5-25/photo. Captions, model releases and identification of subjects required. Buys one-time rights.
Columns/Departments: Bed & Breakfast Review (reviews B&Bs in Missouri—unique, 'quality' establishments), 300 words; and Best Foot Forward (listing of exemplary establishments or services in Missouri), 50-100 words. Buys 28 mss/year. Send complete ms. Length 50-300 words. Pays $10-25.
Fillers: Facts. Buys 40/year. Length: 50-100 words. Pays $5-25.
Tips: "Send complete manuscript—professionally written with photos of excellent quality."

PITCH, Kansas City's News and Arts Weekly, Pitch Publishing, Inc., 3701 Summit, Kansas City MO 64111. (816)561-6061. Fax: (816)756-0502. Editor: Chuck Saults. 50% freelance written. Weekly alternative newspaper that covers arts, entertainment, politics and social and cultural awareness in Kansas City. Estab. 1980. Circ. 30,000. Pays on publication. Publishes ms an average of 2 months after acceptance. Kill fee negotiable. Buys first or one-time rights or makes work-for-hire assignments. Publishes reprints of previously published articles. Send photocopy of article. For reprints, pays 50% of the amount paid for an original article. Editorial lead time 1 month. Submit seasonal material 1 month in advance. *Query First!* Reports in 1 month on queries.
Nonfiction: Essays, expose, humor, interview/profile, opinion and photo feature. Buys 40-50 mss/year. Query with published clips. Length: 1,500-3,300. Pays $50 minimum. Sometimes pays expenses of writers on assignment (limit agreed upon in advance).
Photos: State availability of photos with submission. Reviews contact sheets. Offers no additional payment for photos accepted with ms. Captions and identification of subjects required. Buys one-time rights.
Tips: "Approach us with unusual angles on current political topics of responsible social documentary. Send well-written, clear, concise query with identifiable direction of proposed piece and SASE for reply or return. Previous publication in AAN paper a plus. We're looking for features and secondary features: current events

in visual and performing arts (include new trends, etc.); social issues (OK to have an opinion as long as facts are well-documented); liberal politics."

ST. LOUIS MAGAZINE, Box 88908, St. Louis MO 63118. (314)231-7200. Fax: (314)621-5031. Executive Editor: Tom Wolf. Editor: Ron Janecke. 50% freelance written. Monthly magazine about St. Louisans and St. Louis events. **Pays on acceptance.** Publishes ms an average of 2 months after acceptance. Byline given. Buys first rights and makes work-for-hire assignments. Submit seasonal/holiday material 4 months in advance. Reports in 2 months on queries; 3 months on mss.
Nonfiction: Historical, interview/profile, photo feature and travel. Query with published clips. Length: 250-4,000 words. Pays $25-500. Sometimes pays the expenses of writers on assignment.
Photos: State availability of photos with submission.
Columns/Departments: Travel, Arts, Health, Money, Sports and Entertaining. Buys 36 mss/year. Query with published clips. Length: 500-1,250 words. Pays $150 maximum.
Tips: "Columns and short articles are the best ways to break in."

‡SPRINGFIELD! MAGAZINE, Springfield Communications Inc., P.O. Box 4749, Springfield MO 65808-4749. (417)882-4917. Editor: Robert C. Glazier. 85% freelance written. Works with a small number of new/unpublished writers each year; eager to work with new/unpublished writers. Monthly magazine. "This is an extremely local and provincial magazine. No *general* interest articles." Estab. 1979. Circ. 10,000. Pays on publication. Publishes ms an average of 6 months after acceptance. Byline given. Buys first serial rights. Submit seasonal/holiday material 6-12 months in advance. Simultaneous queries OK. Reports in 3 months on queries; 6 months on mss. Sample copy $5 for 9½ × 12½ SAE.
Nonfiction: Book excerpts (by Springfield authors only); expose (local topics only); historical/nostalgic (top priority but must be local history); how-to (local interest only); humor (if local angle); interview/profile (needs more on females than on males); personal experience (local angle); photo feature (local photos); and travel (1 page per month). No material that could appeal to any other magazine anywhere else. Buys 150 mss/year. Query with published clips or send complete ms. Length: 500-5,000 words. Pays $25-250. Sometimes pays expenses of writers on assignment.
Photos: State availability of photos or send photos with query or ms. Reviews b&w and color contact sheets, 4×5 color transparencies, and 5×7 b&w prints. Pays $5-35 for b&w, $10-50 for color. Captions, model releases, and identification of subjects required. Buys one-time rights.
Columns/Departments: Buys 250 mss/year. Query or send complete ms. Length varies widely but usually 500-2,500 words.
Tips: "We prefer that a writer read eight or ten copies of our magazine prior to submitting any material for our consideration. The magazine's greatest need is for features which comment on these times in Springfield. We are overstocked with nostalgic pieces right now. We also are much in need of profiles about young women and men of distinction."

STL: The Art Of Living In St. Louis, St. Louis Regional Educational and Public Television Commission, 6996 Millbrook Blvd., St. Louis MO 63130-4944. (314)726-7685. Fax: (314)726-0677. Editor: Gayle R. McIntosh. Monthly magazine focusing on history, education, arts and culture of metropolitan area, including information on local public television station programming. Estab. 1991. Circ. 50,000. Pays on publication. Publishes ms an average of 2 months after acceptance. Byline given. Buys one-time rights. Submit seasonal material 4 months in advance. Simultaneous and previously published submissions OK; send photocopy of article or typed ms with rights for sale noted. Include information about when and where the article previously appeared. Pays 50% of their fee for an original article. Query for electronic submissions. Reports in 3 months on queries. Free sample copy for 9 × 12 SAE with 4 first class stamps.
Nonfiction: Book excerpts, historical/nostalgic, how-to (garden, home, cooking), interview/profile, personal experience and travel. Buys 20 mss/year. Query with published clips. Length: 1,000-2,500 words. Pays $75-300. Publishes novel excerpts occasionally, if by local writer or writer featured in PBS or local programming.
  • *STL* is using more local writers.
Photos: State availability of photos with submission. Offers no additional payment for photos accepted with ms. Identification of subjects required. Buys one-time rights.
Columns/Departments: Money, Travel, Health and Home every month. Epicure and Garden and quarterly. Must have *local* focus. Buys 44 mss/year. Query with published clips. Length: 500-750 words. Pays $50.

Montana

MONTANA MAGAZINE, American Geographic Publishing, P.O. Box 5630, Helena MT 59604-5630. (406)443-2842. Fax: (406)443-5480. 35% freelance written. Bimonthly "strictly Montana-oriented magazine that features community and personality profiles, contemporary issues, travel pieces." Estab. 1970. Circ. 69,000. Publishes ms an average of 8-12 months after acceptance. Byline given. Offers $50-100 kill fee on assigned stories only. Buys one-time rights. Submit seasonal material at least 6 months in advance. Simultaneous submissions OK; send information about when and where the article previously appeared. Pays 50% of their fee for an original article. Reports in 2 months. Sample copy $3; writer's guidelines for #10 SASE.

• This magazine is seeking more restaurant reviews and small town profiles.

Nonfiction: Essays, general interest, interview/profile, photo feature and travel. Special features on "summer and winter destination points. Query by January for summer material; July for winter material. No 'me and Joe' hiking and hunting tales; no blood-and-guts hunting stories; no poetry; no fiction; no sentimental essays. Buys 30 mss/year. Query. Length: 300-2,500 words. Pays $75-500 for assigned articles; pays $50-350 for unsolicited articles. Sometimes pays the expenses of writers on assignment.

Photos: Send photos with submission. Reviews contact sheets, 35mm or larger format transparencies; and 5×7 prints. Offers no additional payment for photos accepted with ms. Captions, model releases and identification of subjects required. Buys one-time rights.

Columns/Departments: Over the Weekend (destination points of interest to travelers, family weekends and exploring trips to take), 500-1,000 words plus b&w or color photo; Food and Lodging (great places to eat; interesting hotels, resorts, etc.), 700-1,000 words plus b&w or color photo; and Made in MT (successful cottage industries), 700-1,000 words plus b&w or color photo. Query. Pays $75-150.

Nevada

NEVADA MAGAZINE, 1800 E. Hwy. 50, Carson City NV 89710-0005. (702)687-5416. Fax: (702)687-6159. Publisher: Rich Moreno. Editor: David Moore. Contact: Carolyn Graham. 50% freelance written. Works with a small number of new/unpublished writers each year. Bimonthly magazine published by the state of Nevada to promote tourism in the state. Estab. 1936. Circ. 100,000. Pays on publication. Publishes ms an average of 6 months after acceptance. Byline given. Buys first North American serial rights. Phone queries OK. Submit seasonal material at least 6 months in advance. Query for electronic submissions. Word processing and page layout on Macintosh. Reports in 2 months. Sample copy $1. Free writer's guidelines.

Nonfiction: Nevada topics only. Historical, nostalgia, photo feature, people profile, recreational, travel and think pieces. "We welcome stories and photos on speculation." Buys 40 unsolicited mss/year. Submit complete ms or queries to Associate Editor, Carolyn Graham. Length: 500-2,000 words. Pays $75-300.

Photos: Paul AlLée, art director. Send photo material with accompanying ms. Pays $10-50 for 8×10 glossy prints; $15-75 for color transparencies. Name, address and caption should appear on each photo or slide. Buys one-time rights.

Tips: "Keep in mind that the magazine's purpose is to promote tourism in Nevada. Keys to higher payments are quality and editing effort (more than length). Send cover letter; no photocopies. We look for a light, enthusiastic tone of voice without being too cute; articles bolstered by amazing facts and thorough research; and unique angles on Nevada subjects."

New Jersey

ATLANTIC CITY MAGAZINE, P.O. Box 2100, Pleasantville NJ 08232-1924. (609)272-7900. Fax: (609)272-7910. Editor: Ken Weatherford. 80% freelance written. Works with small number of new/unpublished writers each year. Monthly regional magazine covering issues pertinent to the Jersey Shore area. Estab. 1978. Circ. 50,000. Pays on publication. Publishes ms an average of 4 months after acceptance. Byline given. Buys one-time rights. Offers variable kill fee. Reprints OK; send typed ms with rights for sale noted and information about when and where the article previously appeared. Pays 50% of their fee for an original article. Submit seasonal material 6 months in advance. Reports in 6 weeks. Sample copy $3 for 9×12 SAE with 6 first class stamps. Writer's guidelines for SASE.

Nonfiction: Entertainment, general interest, recreation, history, lifestyle, interview/profile, photo feature and trends. "No travel pieces or any article without a South Jersey shore area/Atlantic City slant." Query. Length: 100-3,000 words. Pays $50-700 for assigned articles; $50-500 for unsolicited articles. Sometimes pays the expenses of writers on assignment.

Photos: State availability of photos. Reviews contact sheets, negatives, 2¼×2¼ transparencies and 8×10 prints. Pay varies. Captions, model releases and identification of subjects required. Buys one-time rights.

Columns/Departments: Art, Business, Entertainment, Sports, Dining, History, Style and Real Estate. Query with published clips. Length: 500-2,000 words. Pays $150-400.

Tips: "Our readers are a broad base of local residents and visiting tourists. We need stories that will appeal to both audiences."

NEW JERSEY MONTHLY, P.O. Box 920, Morristown NJ 07963-0920. (201)539-8230. Editor: Jenny De Monte. 50% freelance written. Monthly magazine covering "almost anything that's New Jersey related." Estab. 1976. Circ. 81,081. Pays on completion of fact-checking. Byline given. Offers 10-30% kill fee. Buys first rights. Submit seasonal material 6 months in advance. Reports in 3 months. Sample copy $5.95 (⅝ Back Issue Dept.); writer's guidelines for #10 SASE.

Nonfiction: Book excerpts, essays, expose, general interest, historical, humor, interview/profile, opinion, personal experience and travel. Special issue features Dining Out (Feb. and Aug.); Real Estate (March); Home & Garden (April); Great Weekends (May); Shore Guide (June); Fall Getaways (Oct.); Holiday Shopping & Entertaining (Nov.). "No experience pieces from people who used to live in New Jersey or general pieces that have no New Jersey angle." Buys 96 mss/year. Query with published magazine clips and SASE. Length: 200-3,000 words. Pays 30¢/word and up. Pays reasonable expenses of writers on assignment with prior approval.

Photos: State availability of photos with submission. Payment negotiated. Identification of subjects and return postage required. "Submit dupes only. Drop off for portfolios on Wednesdays only. The magazine accepts no responsibility for unsolicited photography, artwork or cartoons." Buys exclusive first serial or one-time rights.

Columns/Departments: Business (company profile, trends, individual profiles); Health & Fitness (trends, personal experience, service); Home & Garden (homes, gardens, trends, profiles, etc.); and Travel (in and out-of-state). Buys 36 mss/year. Query with published clips. Length: 750-1,500 words. Pays 30¢ and up/word.

● Ranked as one of the best markets for freelance writers in *Writer's Digest* magazine's annual "Top 100 Markets," January 1993.

Tips: "To break in, we suggest contributing briefs to our front-of-the-book section, 'Upfront' (light, off-beat items, trends, people, things; short service items, such as the 10 best NJ-made ice creams; short issue-oriented items; gossip; media notes). We pay a flat fee, from $50-150."

THE SANDPAPER, Newsmagazine of the Jersey Shore, The SandPaper, Inc., 1816 Long Beach Blvd., Surf City NJ 08008-5461. (609)494-2034. Fax: (609)494-1437. Editor: Curt Travers. Freelance Submissions Editor: Gail Travers. 20% freelance written. Weekly tabloid covering subjects of interest to Jersey shore residents and visitors. "*The SandPaper* publishes three editions covering many of the Jersey Shore's finest resort communities including Long Beach Island, Cape May and Ocean City, New Jersey. Each issue includes a mix of news, human interest features, opinion columns and entertainment/calendar listings." Estab. 1976. Circ. 60,000. Pays on publication. Publishes ms an average of 1 month after acceptance. Byline given. Offers 100% kill fee. Buys first or all rights. Submit seasonal material 3 months in advance. Simultaneous and previously published submissions OK; send photocopy of article and information about when and where it previously appeared. Pays 25-50% of their fee for an original article.. Reports in 1 month. Sample copy for 9 × 12 SAE with 8 first class stamps.

Nonfiction: Essays, general interest, historical/nostalgic, humor, opinion and environmental submissions relating to the ocean, wetlands and pinelands. Must pertain to New Jersey shore locale. Also, arts and entertainment news and reviews if they have a Jersey shore angle. Buys 25 mss/year. Send complete ms. Length: 200-2,000 words. Pays $25-200. Sometimes pays the expenses of writers on assignment.

Photos: State availability of photos with submission. Offers $8-25/photo. Buys one-time or all rights.

Columns/Departments: SpeakEasy (opinion and slice-of-life; often humorous); and Commentary (forum for social science perspectives); both 500-1,500 words, preferably with local or Jersey shore angle. Buys 50 mss/year. Send complete ms. Pays $15-35.

Tips: "Anything of interest to sun worshippers, beach walkers, nature watchers, water sports lovers is of potential interest to us. There is an increasing coverage of environmental issues. The opinion page and columns are most open to freelancers. We are steadily increasing the amount of entertainment-related material in our publication. Articles on history of the shore area are always in demand."

New Mexico

NEW MEXICO MAGAZINE, Lew Wallace Bldg., 495 Old Santa Fe Trail, Santa Fe NM 87503. Editor-in-Chief: Emily Drabanski. Editor: Jon Bowman. Associate Editors: Walter K. Lopez, Camille Flores. 80% freelance written. Monthly magazine emphasizing New Mexico for a college-educated readership, above average income, interested in the Southwest. Estab. 1922. Circ. 125,000. **Pays on acceptance.** Publishes ms an average of 6 months to a year after acceptance. Buys first North American serial rights. Submit seasonal material one year in advance. Reports in 2 months. Sample copy $2.95. Free writer's guidelines.

Nonfiction: New Mexico subjects of interest to travelers. Historical, cultural, humorous and informational articles. "We are looking for more short, light and bright stories for the 'Asi Es Nuevo Mexico' section." No columns, cartoons, poetry or non-New Mexico subjects. Buys 5-7 mss/issue. Query with 3 published writing samples. Length: 250-2,000 words. Pays $100-450.

● This magazine rarely publishes reprints but sometimes publishes excerpts from novels and nonfiction books.

Photos: Purchased with accompanying ms or on assignment. Query or send contact sheet or transparencies. Pays $50-80 for 8 × 10 b&w glossy prints; $50-150 for 35mm—prefers Kodachrome. Photos should be in plastic-pocketed viewing sheets. Captions and model releases required. Mail photos to Art Director John Vaughan. Buys one-time rights.

Tips: "Send a superb short (300 words) manuscript on a little-known person, event, aspect of history or place to see in New Mexico. Faulty research will ruin a writer's chances for the future. Good style, good grammar. No generalized odes to the state or the Southwest. No sentimentalized, paternalistic views of Indians or Hispanics. No glib, gimmicky 'travel brochure' writing. No first-person vacation stories. We're always looking for well-researched pieces on unusual aspects of New Mexico history. Lively writing."

New York

ADIRONDACK LIFE, P.O. Box 97, Jay NY 12941-0097. Fax: (518)946-7461. Editor: Tom Hughes. 70% free-lance written. Prefers to work with published/established writers. Emphasizes the Adirondack region and the North Country of New York State in articles concerning outdoor activities, history, and natural history directly related to the Adirondacks. Publishes 7 issues/year, including special Annual Outdoor Guide. Estab. 1970. Circ. 50,000. Pays 30 days after acceptance. Publishes ms an average of 6 months after acceptance. Buys one-time rights. Byline given. Submit seasonal material 1 year in advance. Reports in 1 month. Sample copy for 9×12 SAE with 8 first class stamps. Writer's guidelines for #10 SASE.
Nonfiction: *"Adirondack Life* attempts to capture the unique flavor and ethos of the Adirondack mountains and North Country region through feature articles directly pertaining to the qualities of the area and through department articles examining specific aspects. Example: Barkeater: personal essay; Special Places: unique spots in the Adirondacks; Working: careers in the Adirondacks and Wilderness: environmental issues, personal experiences." Buys 20-25 unsolicited mss/year. Query. Length: for features, 5,000 words maximum; for departments, 1,800 words. Pays up to 25¢/word. Sometimes pays expenses of writers on assignment.
  • Also considers novel excerpts in its subject matter.
Photos: All photos must have been taken in the Adirondacks. Each issue contains a photo feature. Purchased with or without ms or on assignment. All photos must be identified as to subject or locale and must bear photographer's name. Submit color slides or b&w prints. Pays $25 for b&w prints; $50 for transparencies; $300 for cover (color only, vertical in format). Credit line given.
Tips: "We are looking for clear, concise, well-organized manuscripts, that are strictly Adirondack in subject."

BUFFALO SPREE MAGAZINE, Spree Publishing Co., Inc., Dept. WM, 4511 Harlem Rd., Buffalo NY 14226. (716)839-3405. Editor: Johanna V. Shotell. 90% freelance written. Quarterly literary, consumer-oriented, city magazine. Estab. 1967. Circ. 21,000. Pays on publication. Publishes ms an average of 6-12 months after acceptance. Byline given. Buys first North American serial rights. Submit seasonal material 9-12 months in advance. Reports in 6 months on mss. Sample copy $2 for 9×12 SAE with 9 first class stamps.
Nonfiction: Essays, interview/profile, historical/nostalgic, humor, personal experience and travel. Buys 50 mss/year. Send complete ms. Length: 600-2,000 words. Pays $100-150 for unsolicited articles.
Photos: State availability of photos with submission. Reviews prints (any size). Offers no additional payment for photos accepted with ms. Captions required. Buys one-time rights.
Fiction: Experimental, mainstream. "No pornographic or religious manuscripts." Buys 60 mss/year. Send complete ms. Length: 500-2,000 words. Pays $100-150.
Poetry: Janet Goldenberg, poetry editor. Buys 24 poems/year. Submit maximum 4 poems. Length: 50 lines maximum. Pays $25.

‡CITY LIMITS, City Limits Community Information Service, Inc., 40 Prince St., New York NY 10012. (212)925-9820. Fax: (212)996-3407. Editor: Andrew White. Associate Editor: Steve Mitra. 50% freelance written. Works with a small number of new/unpublished writers each year. Monthly magazine covering housing and related urban issues. "We cover news and issues in New York City as they relate to the city's poor, moderate and middle-income residents. We are advocacy journalists with a progressive or 'left' slant." Estab. 1976. Circ. 5,000. Pays on publication. Publishes ms an average of 1-2 months after acceptance. Byline given. Buys first North American serial, one-time, or second serial (reprint) rights. Query for electronic submissions. Reports in 3 weeks. Sample copy $2.
Nonfiction: Expose, interview/profile, opinion, hard news and community profile. "No fluff, no propaganda." Length: 600-2,500 words. Pays $50-150. Sometimes pays expenses of writers on assignment.
Photos: Reviews contact sheets and 5×7 prints. Offers $10-40/photo, cover only. Identification of subjects required. Buys one-time rights.
Columns/Departments: Short Term Notes (brief descriptions of programs, policies, events, etc.), 250-400 words; Book Reviews (housing, urban development, planning, etc.), 250-600 words; Pipeline (covers community organizations, new programs, government policies, etc.), 600-800 words; People (who are active in organizations, community groups, etc.), 600-800 words; and Organize (groups involved in housing, job programs, health care, etc.), 600-800 words. Buys 50-75 mss/year. Query with published clips or send complete ms. Pays $25-100.
Tips: "We are open to a wide range of story ideas in the community development field. If you don't have particular expertise in housing, urban planning etc., start with a community profile or pertinent book or film review. Short Term Notes is also good for anyone with reporting skills. We're looking for writing that is serious and informed but not academic or heavy handed."

HUDSON VALLEY MAGAZINE, Suburban Publishing, P.O. Box 429, Poughkeepsie NY 12602-3109. (914)485-7844. Fax: (914)485-5975. Editor: Susan Agrest. Monthly magazine. Estab. 1971. Circ. 27,000. Pays on publication. Byline given. Offers 25% kill fee. Buys first North American serial rights or first rights. Submit seasonal material 6 months in advance. Reprints OK; send tearsheet of article and information about when and where the article previously appeared. Pays 25% of their fee for an original article. Query for electronic submissions. Reports in 3 months. Sample copy $1 for 11×14 SAE with 4 first class stamps.
Nonfiction: Only articles related to the Hudson Valley. Book excerpts, expose, general interest, historical/nostalgic, how-to, humor, interview/profile, new product, opinion, photo feature, travel and business. Buys 150 mss/year. Query with published clips. Length: 300-3,500 words. Pays $25-800 for assigned articles.
Photos: State availability of photos with submission. Captions, model releases and identification of subjects required.
Columns/Departments: Open Season (advocacy/editorial); Environs (environmental); Pleasure Grounds; Charmed Places (homes); and Slice of Life (essays). Query with published clips. Length: 1,200-1,500 words. Pays $75-200.
Fiction: Novel excerpts accepted.
Fillers: Anecdotes, facts, gags to be illustrated by cartoonist, newsbreaks and short humor. Buys 36/year. Length: 300-500 words. Pays $25-50.
Tips: "Send a letter, resume, sample of best writing and queries. No manuscripts. Factual accuracy imperative."

NEW YORK MAGAZINE, News America Publishing, Inc., 755 2nd Ave., New York NY 10017-5998. (212)880-0700. Editor: Edward Kosner. Managing Editor: Peter Herbst. 25% freelance written. Weekly magazine focusing on current events in the New York metropolitan area. Circ. 433,813. **Pays on acceptance.** Offers 10% kill fee. Buys first North American serial rights. Submit seasonal material 2 months in advance. Reports in 1 month. Sample copy $3.50. Free writer's guidelines.
Nonfiction: Expose, general interest, profile, new product, personal experience and travel. Query. Pays 75¢-$1.25/word. Pays expenses of writers on assignment.
● Ranked as one of the best markets for freelance writers in *Writer's Digest* magazine's annual "Top 100 Markets," January 1993.
Tips: "Submit a detailed query to Peter Herbst, *New York*'s managing editor. If there is sufficient interest in the proposed piece, the article will be assigned."

NEWSDAY, Melville NY 11747-4250. Viewpoints Editor: Noel Rubinton. Opinion section of daily newspaper. Byline given. Estab. 1940.
Nonfiction: Seeks "opinion on current events, trends, issues—whether national or local, government or lifestyle. Must be timely, pertinent, articulate and opinionated. Preference for authors within the circulation area including New York City." Length: 700-800 words. Pays $150-200.
Tips: "It helps for prospective authors to be familiar with our paper and section."

‡SPOTLIGHT MAGAZINE, Meadown Publications Inc., 126 Library Lane, Mamaroneck NY 10543. (914)381-4740. 10% freelance written. Monthly magazine of general interest. Audience is "anyone who's literate in the NY-NJ-CT tristate area. We try to appeal to a broad audience throughout our publication area." Estab. 1977. Circ. 90,000. Pays on publication. Byline given. Buys first rights. Editorial lead time 3 months. Submit seasonal material 5 months in advance. Query for electronic submissions. Reports in 3 weeks on queries; 1 month on mss. *Writer's Market* recommends allowing 2 months for reply. Sample copy $3. Writer's guidelines for #10 SASE.
Nonfiction: Book excerpts, essays, expose, general interest, historical/nostalgic, how-to, humor, inspirational, interview/profile, new product, photo feature and travel. Publishes annual special-interest guides—Wedding—February and September; Dining—March: Home Design—April and October; Parenting—May; Travel—June and November; Health—July and January; Education—August; Holiday Gifts—December. Does not want to see fiction or poetry. Buys 5-10 mss/year. Query. Pays $50 minimum. Sometimes pays expenses of writers on assignment.
Photos: State availability of or send photos with submission. Reviews transparencies and prints. Negotiates payment individually. Captions, model releases and identification of subjects required (when appropriate). Buys one-time rights.
Columns/Departments: "Spotlight" (profiles), 600-750 words. Buys 3-5 mss/year. Query. Pays $75.
Tips: "Write a letter asking for info."

North Carolina

‡CHARLOTTE MAGAZINE, The New Charlotte Magazine, Inc., 6135 Park S. Dr., Charlotte NC 28210. (704)552-1530. Editor: Allan Maurer. 90% freelance written. Bimonthly magazine for Charlotte and regional NC lifestyles. "Though expanding, our current readership is largely female, 25-50. Our audience as a whole is urban, upscale, well-educated, and an admixture of native Charlotte or N. Carolinians and young, mobile professionals making a warmer life in the sunbelt." Estab. 1978. Circ. 20,000. Pays on publication. Publishes ms an average of 1-2 months after acceptance. Byline given. Buys first North American serial rights. Editorial lead time 2 months. Submit seasonal material 4 months in advance. Accepts simultaneous and previously published submissions. Query for electronic submissions. Reports in 2 weeks on queries. Sample copy for 9 × 12 SAE. Writer's guidelines for #10 SASE.

Nonfiction: Essays, expose, general interest, historical/nostalgic, how-to, humor, interview/profile, personal experience, photo feature and travel. "No generic how-to, pieces with no Charlotte or regional connection, humor with no Charlotte connection or syndicated (self or otherwise) material." Buys 30 mss/year. Query with published clips. Length: 750-2,500 words. Pays 12¢/word. Pays in contributor's copies "At request of the writers. Not usual, though it has happened." Sometimes pays expenses of writers on assignment.

Photos: State availability of photos with submission. Reviews transparencies and prints. Negotiates payment individually. Model releases and identification of subjects required. Buys one-time rights.

Columns/Departments: Essays (well written, humorous short essays on topics of interest to people who live in Charlotte), 750 words to 1,000 top. Pays 12¢/word minimum; negotiable.

Fiction: "We run fiction once a year in our summer reading issue." Buys 1-2 mss/year. Query.

Poetry: "We are considering poetry (short) by Charlotte poets only."

Tips: "For us, a strong feature idea is the best way to break in. New or interesting Charlotte or NC slants on travel, fashion, personalities, are sought constantly here."

THE STATE, Down Home in North Carolina, Suite 2200, 128 S. Tryon St., Charlotte NC 28202. Fax: (704)375-8129. Managing Editor: Scott Smith. 90% freelance written. Monthly. Circ. 21,000. Publishes ms an average of 6-12 months after acceptance. Byline given. No kill fee. Buys first serial rights. Pays on publication. Submit seasonal material 8-12 months in advance. Reports in 1 month. Sample copy $2.

Nonfiction: General articles about places, people, events, history, nostalgia and general interest in North Carolina. Emphasis on travel in North Carolina. Will use humor if related to region. Length: 700-2,000 words average. Pays $125-150 for assigned articles; $75-125 for unsolicited articles.

Photos: State availability of photos with submission. Reviews contact sheets and transparencies. Offers no additional payment for photos. Captions and identification of subjects required. Buys one-time rights.

Columns/Departments: The State We're In (newsbriefs about current events in NC; most have travel, historic or environmental slant) 150-500 words. Buys 5 mss/year. Pays $25.

Ohio

BEACON MAGAZINE, Akron Beacon Journal, P.O. Box 640, Akron OH 44309-0640. (216)996-3586. Editor: Ann Sheldon Mezger. 25% freelance written. Works with a small number of new/unpublished writers each year. Sunday newspaper magazine of general interest articles with a focus on Northeast Ohio. Circ. 225,000. Pays on publication. Publishes ms an average of 2 months after acceptance. Byline given. Offers 50% kill fee. Buys one-time, simultaneous and second serial (reprint) rights. Submit seasonal material 3 months in advance. Simultaneous queries, and simultaneous and previously published submissions OK; send typed ms with rights for sale noted and information about when and where the article previously appeared. Pays 50% of their fee for an original article. Reports in 1 month. Free sample copy and writer's guidelines.

Nonfiction: General interest, historical/nostalgic, short humor and interview/profile. Buys 50 mss/year. Query with or without published clips. Include Social Security number with story submission. Length: 500-3,000 words. Pays $75-500. Sometimes pays expenses of writers on assignment.

Photos: State availability of photos. Pays $25-50 for 35mm color transparencies and 8 × 10 b&w prints. Captions and identification of subjects required. Buys one-time rights.

BEND OF THE RIVER MAGAZINE, P.O. Box 39, Perrysburg OH 43552-0239. (419)874-7534. Fax: (419)874-1466. Publisher: R. Lee Raizk. 90% freelance written. Eager to work with new/unpublished writers. "We buy material that we like whether by an experienced writer or not." Monthly magazine for readers interested in Ohio history, antiques, etc. Estab. 1972. Circ. 4,000. Pays on publication. Publishes ms an average of 6 months after acceptance. Byline given. Buys one-time rights. Submit seasonal material 2 months in advance; deadline for holiday issue is October 15. Reports in up to 6 months. Sample copy $1.50.

Nonfiction: "We deal heavily in Northwestern Ohio history. We are looking for well-researched articles about local history and nostalgia. We'd like to see interviews with historical (Ohio) authorities; articles about grass roots farmers, famous people from Ohio like Doris Day, Gloria Steinem, etc. and preservation. Buys 75 unsolicited mss/year. Submit complete ms or send query. Length: 1,500 words. Pays $10-25.

Photos: Purchases b&w or color photos with accompanying mss. Pays $2 minimum. Captions required.

Tips: "Any Toledo area, well-researched history will be put on top of the heap. We like articles about historical topics treated in down-to-earth conversational tones. We pay a small amount but usually use our writers often and through the years. We're loyal."

CINCINNATI MAGAZINE, 409 Broadway, Cincinnati OH 45202. (513)421-4300. Editorial Director: Felix Winternitz. Homes Editor: Linda Vaccariello. Food Editor: Lilia F. Brady. Monthly magazine emphasizing Cincinnati living. Circ. 32,000. **Pays on acceptance.** Byline given. Buys first rights. Submit seasonal material 4 months in advance. Simultaneous **submissions** OK. Reports in 2 months.

Nonfiction: Profiles of Cincinnati celebrities, local business and trend stories. Buys 1 ms/issue. Query. Length: 2,000-4,000 words. Pays $150-400.

Columns/Departments: Cincinnati dining, media, arts and entertainment, people, politics and sports. Buys 2 mss/issue. Query. Length: 750-1,500 words. Pays $75-150.

Tips: "We do special features each month. January—Homes section; February—Dining out-restaurants; March—Health and Personal finance; April—Home and Fashion; May: Environment and Golf; June—Health; July—Food and Homes; August—Fashion; September—Homes; October—Best and Worst; November—Automotive Guide and Fashion; December: City guide. We also have a special issue in August where we feature a local fiction contest."

‡COLUMBUS MONTHLY, P.O. Box 29913, Columbus OH 43229-7513. (614)888-4567. Editor: Lenore E. Brown. 20-40% freelance written. Prefers to work with published/established writers. Monthly magazine emphasizing subjects specifically related to Columbus and central Ohio. Pays on publication. Publishes ms an average of 2 months after acceptance. Byline given. Buys all rights. Query for electronic submissions. Reports in 1 month. Sample copy $3.57.

Nonfiction: No humor, essays or first person material. "I like query letters which are well-written, indicate the author has some familiarity with *Columbus Monthly*, give me enough detail to make a decision and include at least a basic biography of the writer." Buys 4-5 unsolicited mss/year. Query. Length: 400-4,500 words. Pays $50-400. Sometimes pays the expenses of writers on assignment.

Photos: State availability of photos. Pay varies for b&w or color prints. Model release required.

Columns/Departments: Art, business, food and drink, movies, politics, sports and theatre. Buys 2-3 columns/issue. Query. Length: 1,000-2,000 words. Pays $100-175.

Tips: "It makes sense to start small—something for our City Journal section, perhaps. Stories for that section run between 400-1,000 words."

OHIO MAGAZINE, Ohio Magazine, Inc., Subsidiary of Dispatch Printing Co., 62 E. Broad St., Columbus OH 43215-3522. Contact: Editor. 40% freelance written. Works with a small number of new/unpublished writers each year. Monthly magazine emphasizing news and feature material of Ohio for an educated, urban and urbane readership. Estab. 1978. Circ. 100,000. Pays on publication. Publishes ms an average of 5 months after acceptance. Buys all, second serial (reprint), one-time, first North American serial or first serial rights. Byline given except on short articles appearing in sections. Submit seasonal material minimum 6 months in advance. Previously published submissions OK; send tearsheet or photocopy of article and information about when and where it previously appeared. Pays 50% of their fee for an original article. Reports in 2 months. Sample copy $3 for 9×12 SAE. Writer's guidelines for #10 SASE.

Nonfiction: Features: 2,000-8,000 words. Pays $800-1,400. Cover pieces $650-1,200. Sometimes pays expenses of writers on assignment.

Columns/Departments: Ohioans (should be offbeat with solid news interest; 1,000-2,000 words, pays $300-500); Business (covering business related news items, profiles of prominent people in business community, personal finance—all Ohio angle; 1,000 words and up, pays $300-500); and Environment (issues related to Ohio and Ohioans, 1,000-2,000 words, pays $400-700). Buys minimum 40 unsolicited mss/year.

Photos: Brooke Wenstrup, art director. Rate negotiable.

Tips: "Freelancers should send a brief prospectus if complete ms is not ready for submission. All articles should have a definite Ohio application. We need more columns and short features—especially original profile ideas."

PLAIN DEALER MAGAZINE, Plain Dealer Publishing Co., 1801 Superior Ave., Cleveland OH 44114. (216)344-4546. Fax: (216)694-6354. Contact: Editor. 50% freelance written. Weekly Sunday general interest newspaper magazine focusing on (but not limited to) Cleveland and Ohio. Circ. 550,000. Pays on publication. Publishes ms an average of 2-3 months after acceptance. Byline given. Buys first or one-time rights. Submit seasonal/holiday material 3 months in advance. Reports in 4 weeks on queries; 2 months on mss. Sample copy $1.

Nonfiction: Profiles, in-depth features, essays, expose, historical/nostalgic, humor, personal experience and travel. Buys 20 mss/year. Query with published clips or send complete ms. Manuscripts must be double-spaced and should include a daytime telephone number. Length: 800-3,000 words. Pays $150-500.

Photos: State availability of photos with submission. Buys one-time rights.

Fiction: Buys 6 mss/year. Send complete ms. Length: 1,000-3,000 words. Pays $150-400.

Tips: "We're always looking for good writers and good stories."

Oklahoma

OKLAHOMA TODAY, P.O. Box 53384, Oklahoma City OK 73152-9971. Fax: (405)521-3992. Editor: Jeanne M. Devlin. 80% freelance written. Works with a small number of new/unpublished writers each year. Bimonthly magazine covering people, places and things Oklahoman. "We are interested in showing off the best Oklahoma has to offer; we're pretty serious about our travel slant but regularly run history, nature and personality profiles." Estab. 1956. Circ. 45,000. **Pays on final acceptance.** Publishes ms an average of 6 months after acceptance. Byline given. Buys first serial rights. Submit seasonal material 1 year in advance "depending on photographic requirements." Simultaneous queries OK. Reprints OK; send tearsheet of article, or typed ms with rights for sale noted, and information about when and where the article previously appeared. Reports in 3 months. Sample copy $2.50 for 9 × 12 SASE. Writer's guidelines for #10 SASE.

Nonfiction: Book excerpts (pre-publication only, on Oklahoma topics); photo feature and travel (in Oklahoma). Buys 40-60 mss/year. Query with published clips; no phone queries. Length: 1,000-3,000 words. Pays $25-750.

• This market is seeking a variety of styles, from first person to essay.

Photos: High-quality transparencies, b&w prints. "We are especially interested in developing contacts with photographers who either live in Oklahoma or have shot here. Send samples and price range." Free photo guidelines with SASE. Pays $50-100 for b&w and $50-750 for color; reviews 2¼ and 35mm color transparencies. Model releases, identification of subjects and other information for captions required. Buys one-time rights plus right to use photos for promotional purposes.

Tips: "The best way to become a regular contributor to *Oklahoma Today* is to query us with one or more story ideas, each developed to give us an idea of your proposed slant. We're looking for *lively*, concise, well-researched and reported stories, stories that don't need to be heavily edited and are not newspaper style. We have a two-person editorial staff, and freelancers who can write and have done their homework get called again and again."

Oregon

CASCADES EAST, P.O. Box 5784, Bend OR 97708. (503)382-0127. Fax: (503)382-7057. Editor: Geoff Hill. 90% freelance written. Prefers to work with published/established writers. Quarterly magazine for "all ages as long as they are interested in outdoor recreation in central Oregon: fishing, hunting, sight-seeing, golf, tennis, hiking, bicycling, mountain climbing, backpacking, rockhounding, skiing, snowmobiling, etc." Estab. 1972. Circ. 10,000 (distributed throughout area resorts and motels and to subscribers). Pays on publication. Publishes ms an average of 6 months after acceptance. Buys all rights. Byline given. Submit seasonal material 6 months in advance. Reports in 2 months. Sample copy and writer's guidelines $4 for 9 × 12 SAE.

Nonfiction: General interest (first person experiences in outdoor central Oregon—with photos, can be dramatic, humorous or factual); historical (for feature, "Little Known Tales from Oregon History," with b&w photos); and personal experience (needed on outdoor subjects: dramatic, humorous or factual). "No articles that are too general, sight-seeing articles that come from a travel folder, or outdoor articles without the first-person approach." Buys 20-30 unsolicited mss/year. Query. Length: 1,000-3,000 words. Pays 3-10¢/word.

Photos: "Old photos will greatly enhance chances of selling a historical feature. First-person articles need b&w photos, also." Pays $10-25 for b&w; $15-100 for transparencies. Captions preferred. Buys one-time rights.

Tips: "Submit stories a year or so in advance of publication. We are seasonal and must plan editorials for summer '94 in the spring of '93, etc., in case seasonal photos are needed."

OREGON COAST, The Bi-Monthly Magazine of Coastal Living, 1525 12th St., Florence OR 97439-0130. (800)348-8401. Fax: (503)997-1124. Publisher & Creative Director: Alicia Spooner. Managing Editor: Judy Fleagle. 70% freelance written. Bimonthly magazine covering the Oregon Coast. Estab. 1982. Circ. 65,000. Pays on publication. Publishes ms an average of 8-10 months after acceptance. Byline given. Offers 33% kill fee. Buys first North American serial rights. Submit seasonal material 6 months in advance. Query for electronic submissions. Reports in 2 months. Sample copy $4.50. Writer's guidelines for #10 SASE.

Nonfiction: General interest, historical/nostalgic, humor, interview/profile, personal experience, photo feature, travel and nature as pertains to Oregon Coast. Buys 60 mss/year. Query with published clips. Length: 500-2,000 words. Pays $75-200 plus 5 contributor copies.

Photos: Send photos with submission. Reviews 35mm or larger transparencies and 3 × 5 or larger prints. Offers no additional payment for photos accepted with ms. Photo submissions with no ms for stand alone or cover photos. Captions, model releases, photo credits and identification of subjects required. Buys one-time rights.

Fillers: Newsbreaks (no-fee basis) and short articles. Buys 12/year. Length: 300-500 words. Pays $35-50.

Tips: "Slant article for readers who do not live at the Oregon Coast. At least one historical article is used in each issue. Manuscript/photo packages are preferred over mss with no photos. List photo credits and captions for each print or slide. Check all facts, proper names and numbers carefully in photo/ms packages."

Pennsylvania

PENNSYLVANIA, Pennsylvania Magazine Co., P.O. Box 576, Camp Hill PA 17001-0576. (717)761-6620. Editor: Albert E. Holliday. Managing Editor: Joan Holliday. 90% freelance written. Bimonthly magazine. Circ. 40,000. Pays on acceptance except for articles (by authors unknown to us) sent on speculation. Publishes ms an average of 6-12 months after acceptance. Byline given. Offers 25% kill fee. Buys first North American serial or one-time rights. Reprints OK; send tearsheet of article and information about when and where the article previously appeared. Pays 50% of their fee for an original article. Reports in 2 months. Sample copy $2.95. Writer's guidelines for #10 SASE.

Nonfiction: General interest, historical/nostalgic, photo feature and travel—all dealing with or related to Pennsylvania. Nothing on Amish topics, hunting or skiing. Buys 50-75 mss/year. Query. Length: 250-2,500 words. Pays $25-250. Sometimes pays the expenses of writers on assignment. All articles must be illustrated; send photocopies of possible illustrations with query or mss. *Will not consider without illustrations.*

Photos: Reviews 35mm and 2¼ color transparencies (no originals) and 5×7 to 8×10 color and b&w prints. Pays $15-50 for inside photos; up to $100 for covers. Captions required. Buys one-time rights.

Columns/Departments: Panorama—short items about people, unusual events; Made in Pennsylvania—short items about family and individually owned consumer-related businesses. Scrapbook (short historical items). All must be illustrated.

PHILADELPHIA MAGAZINE, Dept. WM, 1818 Market St., Philadelphia PA 19103. (215)564-7700. Editor: Eliot Kaplin. 40% freelance written. Prefers to work with published/established writers. Monthly magazine for sophisticated middle- and upper-income people in the Greater Philadelphia/South Jersey area. Circ. 152,272. **Pays on acceptance.** Publishes ms an average of 2 months after acceptance. Buys first serial rights. Pays 20% kill fee. Byline given. Reports in 1 month. Writer's guidelines for #10 SASE.

Nonfiction: Loren Seldman, articles editor. "Articles should have a strong Philadelphia (city and suburbs) focus but should avoid Philadelphia stereotypes—we've seen them all. Submit lifestyles, city survival, profiles of interesting people, business stories, music, the arts, sports and local politics, stressing the topical or unusual. Intelligent, entertaining essays on subjects of specific local interest. No puff pieces. We offer lots of latitude for style." Buys 50 mss/year. Length: 1,000-7,000 words. Pays $100-2,000. Sometimes pays expenses of writers on assignment.

PITTSBURGH MAGAZINE, QED Communications, Inc., 4802 5th Ave., Pittsburgh PA 15213. (412)622-1360. Fax: (412)622-7066. 60% freelance written. Prefers to work with published/established writers. "The magazine is purchased on newsstands and by subscription and is given to those who contribute $40 or more a year to public TV in western Pennsylvania." Estab. 1970. Circ. 65,000. Pays on publication. Publishes ms an average of 2 months after acceptance. Buys first North American serial rights and second serial (reprint) rights. Offers kill fee. Byline given. Submit seasonal material 6 months in advance. Query for electronic submissions. Reports in 2 months. Publishes ms an average of 2 months after acceptance. Sample copy $2 (old back issues).

Nonfiction: Expose, lifestyle, sports, informational, service, interview, nostalgia and profile. Query or send complete ms. Length: 2,500 words or less. Pays $100-1,200.

Photos: Query for photos. Model releases required. Sometimes pays the expenses of writers on assignment.

Columns/Departments: Art, cooking, dining, health, sports and theatre. "All must relate to Pittsburgh or tri-state area."

Rhode Island

RHODE ISLAND MONTHLY, Dept. WM, 18 Imperial Place, Providence RI 02903-4641. (401)421-2552. Fax: (401)831-5624. Editor: Dan Kaplan. Managing Editor: Vicki Sanders. 90% freelance written. Monthly magazine on Rhode Island living. Estab. 1988. Circ. 26,000. Pays on publication. Publishes ms an average of 2 months after acceptance. Byline given. Kill fee varies. Buys first rights. Submit seasonal material 4 months in advance. Query for electronic submissions. Sample copy $1.95 for 9×12 SAE with $1.20 postage.

Nonfiction: Profiles, human interest features, expose and photo feature. "We do not want material unrelated to Rhode Island." Buys 48 mss/year. Query with published clips. Length: 200-6,000 words. Pays $100-1,000. Pays expenses of writers on assignment for stories over $400.

Photos: State availability of photos with submission. Reviews contact sheets and 5×7 prints. Offers $50-200. Captions, model releases and identification of subjects required. Buys one-time rights.

South Carolina

CHARLESTON MAGAZINE, P.O. Box 21770, Charleston SC 29413-1770. (803)722-8018. Fax: (803)722-8116. Co-Editors: Louise F. Chase and Sally Topping Sun. Contributing Editor: Dawn Leggett. 95% freelance written. Monthly magazine covering the Lowcountry South Carolina, the South as a region. "Consumer magazine with a general focus each issue that reflects an essential element of Charleston life and Lowcountry living. Estab. 1987. Circ. 20,000. Pays on publication. Publishes ms an average of 3 months after acceptance. Byline given. Buys one-time rights. Submit seasonal material 4 months in advance. Simultaneous submissions and previously published submissions OK. Query for electronic submissions. Sample copies for 9×12 SAE with 5 first class stamps. Free writer's guidelines.

Nonfiction: Book excerpts, essays, expose, general interest, historical/nostalgic, humor, interview/profile, opinion, personal experience, photo feature and travel. "Each issue has a focus—these themes are listed in our writer's guidelines. Not interested in general interest articles. Must pertain to the Charleston area or, at their broadest scope, the South as a region." Buys 120 mss/year. Query with published clips. Length: 150-1,500 words. Pays 10¢/published word. Sometimes pays expenses of writers on assignment.

Photos: Send photos with submission if available. Reviews contact sheets, transparencies and slides. Offers $35 maximum/photo. Captions and identification of subjects required. Buys one-time rights.

Columns/Departments: Channel Markers (general interest) 50-1,200 words; Hindsight (historical perspectives and local Lowcountry interest) 1,000-1,200 words; First Person (profile—people of local interest) 1,000-1,200 words; Art (features a successful or innovative artist) 1,000-1,200; Architecture (renovations, restorations or new constructions of Lowcountry houses) 1,000-1,200; Sporting Life (humorous, adventurous tales of life outdoors) 1,000-1,200; Southern View (expanded editorial page in which a person expresses his or her view on the South) 750; and Food That Pleases (restaurant reviews) 1,000. Buys 90 mss/year. Query with published clips. Pays 3-10¢/word.

Tips: "Follow our writer's guidelines. Areas most open to freelancers are Columns/Departments and features. Should be of local or Southern interest."

SANDLAPPER, The Magazine of South Carolina, RPW Publishing Corp, P.O. Box 1108, Lexington SC 29071-1108. (803)359-9954. Fax: (803)957-8226. Editor: Robert P. Wilkins. Managing Editor: Daniel E. Harmon. 35% freelance written. Quarterly feature magazine focusing on the positive aspects of South Carolina. Estab. 1989. Circ. 5,000. Pays during the dateline period. Publishes ms an average of 4 months after acceptance. Byline given. Buys first North American serial rights and the right to reprint. Submit seasonal material 6 months in advance. Query for electronic submissions. Free writer's guidelines.

Nonfiction: Feature articles and photo essays about South Carolina's interesting people, places, cuisine, things to do. Occasional history articles. Query. Length: 600-5,000 words. Pays $50-500. Sometimes pays the expenses of writers on assignment.

Tips: "We're not interested in articles about topical issues, politics, crime or commercial ventures. Humorous angles are encouraged. Avoid first-person nostalgia and remembrances of places that no longer exist."

South Dakota

DAKOTA OUTDOORS, South Dakota, Hipple Publishing Co., P.O. Box 669, 333 W. Dakota Ave., Pierre SD 57501-0669. (605)224-7301. Fax: (605)224-9210. Editor: Kevin Hipple. 50% freelance written. Monthly magazine on Dakota outdoor life. Estab. 1975. Circ. 6,500. Pays on publication. Publishes ms an average of 2 months after acceptance. Byline given. Submit seasonal material 3 months in advance. Simultaneous and previously published submissions (if notified) OK; send photocopy of article, typed ms with rights for sale noted and information about when and where the article previously appeared. Pays 50% of their fee for an original article. Query for electronic submissions. Reports in 3 months. Sample copy for 9 × 12 SAE with 3 first class stamps.

Nonfiction: General interest, how-to, humor, interview/profile, new product, opinion, personal experience, photo feature and technical (all on outdoor topics—prefer in Dakotas). Buys 50 mss/year. Query with or without published clips, or send complete ms. Length: 200-1,000 words. Pays $5-50 for assigned articles; $40 maximum for unsolicited articles. Sometimes pays in contributor copies or other premiums (inquire).

Photos: Send photos with submission. Reviews 5 × 7 prints. Offers no additional payment for photos accepted with ms. Identification of subjects preferred. Buys one-time rights.

Fillers: Anecdotes, facts, gags to be illustrated by cartoonist, newsbreaks and short humor. Buys 10/year. Also publishes line drawings of fish and game. Prefers 5 × 7 prints.

Tips: "Submit samples of manuscript or previous works for consideration; photos or illustrations with manuscript are helpful."

Tennessee

MEMPHIS, MM Corporation, P.O. Box 256, Memphis TN 38101-0256. (901)521-9000. Fax: (901)521-0129. Editor: Tim Sampson. 60% freelance written. Works with a small number of new/unpublished writers. Estab. 1976. Circ. 21,917. Pays on publication. Publishes ms an average of 3 months after acceptance. Byline given. Buys first North American serial rights. Offers 20% kill fee. Simultaneous and previously published submissions OK; send photocopy of article, typed ms with rights for sale noted and information about when and where the article previously appeared. Reports in 2 months. Sample copy for 9 × 12 SAE with 9 first class stamps. Writer's guidelines for SASE.

Nonfiction: Expose, general interest, historical, how-to, humor, interview and profile. "Virtually all of our material has strong mid-South connections." Buys 25 freelance mss/year. Query or submit complete ms or published clips. Length: 500-5,000 words. Pays $50-500. Sometimes pays expenses of writers on assignment.

Tips: "The kinds of manuscripts we most need have a sense of story (i.e., plot, suspense, character), an abundance of evocative images to bring that story alive, and a sensitivity to issues at work in Memphis. The most frequent mistakes made by writers in completing an article for us are lack of focus, lack of organization, factual gaps and failure to capture the magazine's style. Tough investigative pieces would be especially welcomed."

Texas

‡ALERT TEXAN, The News Magazine For Texas, Suite 133-102, 8407 Bandera, San Antonio TX 78250. (512)695-8835. Editor: Franklin X. Dean. Contact: Wayland H. Griffith, editorial director. 95% freelance written. Monthly magazine covering news, information and entertainment. "*Alert Texan* is a positive reflection of Texas and Texans." Estab. 1990. Circ. 100,000. Pays on publication. Publishes ms 3-6 months after acceptance. Byline given. Buys first North American serial rights or makes work-for-hire assignments (occasionally). Editorial lead time 3 months. Submit seasonal material 6 months in advance. Simultaneous and previously published submissions OK. Query for electronic submissions "Apple computer *disks* only." Reports in 2 months. Sample copy for 9 × 12 SAE with 6 first class stamps. Writer's guidelines for #10 SASE.
Nonfiction: Expose, general interest, historical/nostalgic, how-to, humor, inspirational, interview/profile, new product, opinion, personal experience, photo feature, religious, travel and "anything relating to Texas/ Texas culture. No pornography; no biased, opinionated material; no poorly written or researched articles." Buys 200 mss/year. Query with published clips. Length: 400-3,000 words. Pays $50 minimum. Sometimes pays expenses of writers on assignment.
Photos: Send photos with submission. Reviews 2 × 2 transparencies. Negotiates payment individually. Captions, model releases and identificatin of subjects required. Buys one-time rights.
Columns/Departments: Buys 200 mss/year. Query. Pays $50-500.
Tips: "We love first-time, unpublished writers. We hate bad writing and purple prose. We want down-to-earth style, well researched work that will appeal to the widest possible range of readers. All departments are open to freelancers."

DALLAS LIFE MAGAZINE, Sunday Magazine of *The Dallas Morning News*, Communications Center, P.O. Box 655237, Dallas TX 75265. (214)977-8432. Managing Editor: Mike Maza. Weekly magazine. "We are a lively, topical, sometimes controversial city magazine devoted to informing, enlightening and entertaining our urban Sunbelt readers with material which is specifically relevant to Dallas lifestyles and interests." **Pays on acceptance.** Byline given. Buys first North American serial rights or simultaneous rights. Simultaneous queries and submissions OK ("if not competitive in our area"). Reports in 2 months.
Nonfiction: General interest, humor (short) and interview/profile. "All material must, repeat *must*, have a Dallas metropolitan area frame of reference." Special issues include: spring and fall home furnishings theme and travel. Buys 5-10 unsolicited mss/year. Query with published clips or send complete ms. Length: 1,200-3,000 words. Pays $350-1,200.

HOUSTON METROPOLITAN MAGAZINE, Houston Metropolitan Ltd., Dept WM, P.O. Box 25386, Houston TX 77265-5386. (713)524-3000. Editor: Chris Kelly. 85% freelance written. Monthly city magazine. Estab. 1974. Circ. 87,500. **Pays on acceptance.** Publishes ms an average of 3 months after acceptance. Byline given. Offers 25% kill fee. Buys first North American serial rights. Submit seasonal material 6 months in advance. Query for electronic submissions. Simultaneous submissions OK. Publishes reprints of previously published articles and short stories. For reprints, pays $500. Reports in 2 weeks on queries; 1 month on mss. *Writer's Market* recommends allowing 2 months for reply. Sample copy for 9 × 12 SAE with 8 first class stamps.
Nonfiction: Issue-oriented features, profiles, lifestyle/entertainment, food features, visual stories, and humorous features about Houston or Houstonians. Query with published clips or send complete ms. Length: 300-2,500 words. Pays $50-1,000.
Photos: Jeff Stanton, art director. State availability of photos with submission. Buys one-time rights. "Also assigns photographers at day or job rates."
Columns/Departments: Travel, Business, Dining, Habitat and City Stories. Must have strong Houston-area slant. Length: 300-500 words. Pays $50-800.
Tips: "Submit clips demonstrating strong writing and reporting skills with detailed queries, bearing in mind that this is a city magazine. Our intent is to be a lively, informative city book, addressing the issues and people who affect our lives objectively and fairly. But also with affection and, where suitable, a sense of humor. Only those familiar with the Houston metropolitan area should approach us."

> *Always check the most recent copy of a magazine for the address and editor's name before you send in a query or manuscript.*

TEXAS PARKS & WILDLIFE, Texas Parks and Wildlife Dept., 4200 Smith School Rd., Austin TX 78744. (512)389-4996. Fax: (512)389-4450. Editor: David Baxter. Managing Editor: Mary-Love Bigony. 80% freelance written. Monthly magazine featuring articles about Texas hunting, fishing, outdoor recreation, game and nongame wildlife, state parks, environmental issues. All articles must be about Texas. Estab. 1942. Circ. 180,000. **Pays on acceptance.** Publishes ms an average of 6 months after acceptance. Byline given. Kill fee determined by editor, usually $200-250. Buys first rights. Submit seasonal material 6 months in advance. Query for electronic submissions. Reports in 1 month on queries; 3 months on mss. Free sample copy and writer's guidelines.

Nonfiction: Jim Cox, articles editor. General interest (Texas only), historical/nostalgic, how-to (outdoor activities), interview/profile, photo feature and travel (state parks). Buys 60 mss/year. Query with published clips. Length: 250-2,500 words. Pays $500 maximum.

Photos: Send photos with submission. Reviews transparencies. Offers $60-150 maximum/photo. Captions and identification of subjects required. Buys one-time rights.

Columns/Departments: Outdoor Heritage Series (focus on an individual's commitment and contributions to the conservation of Texas's environment or wildlife), 500-1,000 words. Buys 6 mss/year. Query with published clips. Pays $100-300. Monthly departments: hunting and fishing, the environment, young naturalist, places to go. Maximum 1,000 words.

Tips: "Read outdoor pages of statewide newspapers to keep abreast of news items that can lead to story ideas. Feel free to include more than one story idea in one query letter. All areas are open to freelancers. All articles must have a Texas focus."

Utah

SALT LAKE CITY, Suite A, 1270 West 2320 S., Salt Lake City UT 84119. (801)975-1927. Fax: (801)975-1982. Editor: Margaret Traub-Aguirre. Managing Editor: Jane Chapman Martin. 60% freelance written. Bimonthly magazine. "Ours is a lifestyle magazine, focusing on the people, issues and places that make Utah and the Intermountain West unique. Our audience is mainly educated, affluent, ages 25-55. Our pieces are generally positive, or at the very least suggestive of solutions. Again, we focus heavily on people!" Estab. 1989. Circ. 15,000. Pays on publication. Publishes ms an average of 3-6 months after acceptance. Byline given. Offers $25 kill fee. Buys first North American serial or second serial (reprint) rights. Submit seasonal material 6 months in advance. Simultaneous and previously published submissions OK. Send typed ms with rights for sale noted. Query for electronic submissions. Reports in 6 weeks on mss. Free sample copy and writer's guidelines.

Nonfiction: Essays (health, family matters, financial); general interest; historical/nostalgic (pertaining to Utah and Intermountain West); humor; interview/profile (famous or powerful people associated with Utah business, politics, media); personal experience; photo feature (fashion available in Utah stores or cuisine of anywhere in world); and travel (anywhere exotic in the world). "No movie reviews or current news subjects, please." Buys 5 mss/year. Query with published clips or send complete ms. Length: 800-2,000 words. Pays $75-400 for assigned articles; $75-250 for unsolicited articles. "A major feature is negotiable."

Photos: State availability of photos with submission. Reviews transparencies (size not important). Captions, model releases and identification of subjects required. Payment and rights negotiable.

Columns/Departments: Up Close (standard personality profile) 1,200-1,500 words; Travel (exotic world travel/preferable to include excellent photography) 2,000 words; Q & A of famous person, 1,200-1,500 words; Executive Signature (profile, business slant of major Utah entrepeneur); and Food (recipes must be included) 1,000-1,500 words. Buys 5-10 mss/year. Query with published clips or send complete ms. Pays $75-250.

● No longer accepting unsolicited fiction and poetry. Also writing more articles in house.

Tips: "Well-written, neatly typed, well-researched, complete manuscripts that come across my desk are most likely to be published if they fit our format. They are a godsend! Writers have the best chance of selling us humor, eye-openers, family topics and small features on topics of general interest to Utahns and American western living. For example, we have covered mountainwest recreation, child abuse, education, earthquakes, air pollution and Native American issues."

UTAH HOLIDAY MAGAZINE, Cumming Communications Network, #200, 807 E. South Temple, Salt Lake City UT 84102. (801)532-3737. Fax: (801)532-3742. Editor: Barbara Cumming. Managing Editor: Mildred Evans. 100% freelance written. Monthly magazine on Utah-oriented subjects; newspapers do not print provocative opinion. Theatre, art and movie reviews. Estab. 1971. Circ. 10,000. Pays on 15th of month of publication. Byline given. Buys first North American serial rights. Submit seasonal material 3 months in advance. Query for electronic submissions. Reports in 3 weeks on queries. Sample copy for 10×12 SAE with 5 first class stamps. Writer's guidelines for #10 SASE.

Nonfiction: Essays, expose, interview/profile, opinion and personal experience. "No travel outside Utah, humor or personal essays." Buys 1 ms/year. Query with or without published clips or send complete ms. Length: 2,500-8,000 words. Pays $90-350 for assigned articles. Also pays in contributor copies or other premiums. Sometimes pays expenses of writers on assignment.

Photos: State availability of or send photos with submission. Reviews contact sheets and transparencies. Offers $15-70/photo. Identification of subjects required. Buys one-time rights.

Columns/Departments: Movie Reviews, Opera, Theatre, Ballet and Art (all slanted to current Utah productions), 1,500 words. Buys 10 mss/year. Query with published clips. Pays $90-120.

Vermont

VERMONT LIFE MAGAZINE, 6 Baldwin St., Montpelier VT 05602-2109. (802)828-3241. Editor-in-Chief: Thomas K. Slayton. 90% freelance written. Prefers to work with published/established writers. Quarterly magazine. Estab. 1946. Circ. 90,000. Publishes ms an average of 9 months after acceptance. Byline given. Offers kill fee. Buys first serial rights. Submit seasonal material 1 year in advance. Simultaneous queries, and simultaneous and previously published submissions OK. Reports in 1 month. *Writer's Market* recommends allowing 2 months for reply. Writer's guidelines for #10 SASE.

Nonfiction: Wants articles on today's Vermont, those which portray a typical or, if possible, unique aspect of the state or its people. Style should be literate, clear and concise. Subtle humor favored. No "Vermont clichés"—maple syrup, town meetings or stereotyped natives. Buys 60 mss/year. Query by letter essential. Length: 1,500 words average. Pays 20¢/word. Seldom pays expenses of writers on assignment.

Photos: Buys photographs with mss; buys seasonal photographs alone. Prefers b&w contact sheets to look at first on assigned material. Color submissions must be 4×5 or 35mm transparencies. Pays $75-150 inside color; $200 for cover. Gives assignments but only with experienced photographers. Query in writing. Captions, model releases, and identification of subjects required. Buys one-time rights, but often negotiates for re-use rights.

Tips: "Writers who read our magazine are given more consideration because they understand that we want authentic articles about Vermont. If a writer has a genuine working knowledge of Vermont, his or her work usually shows it. Vermont is changing and there is much concern here about what this state will be like in years ahead. It is a beautiful, environmentally sound place now and the vast majority of residents want to keep it so. Articles reflecting such concerns in an intelligent, authoritative, non-hysterical way will be given very careful consideration. The growth of tourism makes *Vermont Life* interested in intelligent articles about specific places in Vermont, their history and attractions to the traveling public."

VERMONT MAGAZINE, P.O. Box 288, Bristol VT 05443. (802)453-3200. Editor: John S. Rosenberg. Bimonthly magazine about Vermont. Estab. 1989. Buys first North American serial rights. Submit all material 5-6 months in advance; must query first. Query for electronic submissions. Reports in 2 weeks. *Writer's Market* recommends allowing 2 months for reply. Writer's guidelines for #10 SASE.

Nonfiction: Journalism and reporting, book excerpts, essays, expose, general interest, how-to, humor, interview/profile, photo feature and calendar. All material must be about contemporary Vermont. Buys 30 mss/year. Query with published clips. Length: 900-3,500 words. Pays $200-800. Sometimes pays expenses of writers on assignment. Rarely publishes reprints.

Photos: Send photos and illustrations to Steve Bradley, art director. Reviews contact sheets, 35mm transparencies and 8×10 b&w prints. Captions, model releases (if possible) and identification of subjects required. Buys one-time rights.

Fiction: Publishes novel excerpts (1/year, maximum).

Tips: "Our readers *know* their state well, and they know the 'real' Vermont can't be slipped inside a glib and glossy brochure. We're interested in serious journalism on major issues, plus coverage of arts, outdoors, living, nature, architecture."

Virginia

NOVASCOPE, Novascope, Inc., P.O. Box 1590, Middleburg VA 22117-1590. (703)687-3314. Fax: (703)687-4113. Editors: Mark Smith and Joy Smith. 75% freelance written. Monthly magazine on human interest, environmental issues, history and events pertinent to northern Virginia. Estab. 1985. Circ. 50,000. Pays on publication. Byline given. Buys first North American serial rights. Submit seasonal material 3 months in advance. Simultaneous submissions OK. Reports in 3 months. Free sample copy and writer's guidelines.

Nonfiction: General interest, historical and interview/profile, all pertinent to northern Virginia. Buys 50 mss/year. Query with published clips. Length: 1,000 words maximum. Pays $50 maximum for unsolicited articles.

Photos: State availability of photos with submission. Reviews 35mm transparencies. Offers $10 maximum/photo. Identification of subjects required. Buys one-time rights.

THE ROANOKER, Leisure Publishing Co., 3424 Brambleton Ave., P.O. Box 21535, Roanoke VA 24018. (703)989-6138. Fax: (703)989-7603. Editor: Kurt Rheinheimer. 75% freelance written. Works with a small number of new/unpublished writers each year. Magazine published 10 times/year covering people and events of Western Virginia. "*The Roanoker* is a general interest city magazine edited for the people of Roanoke,

Virginia and the surrounding area. Our readers are primarily upper-income, well-educated professionals between the ages of 35 and 60. Coverage ranges from hard news and consumer information to restaurant reviews and local history." Estab. 1974. Circ. 14,000. Pays on publication. Publishes ms an average of 4 months after acceptance. Byline given. Buys all rights; makes work-for-hire assignments. Submit seasonal material 4 months in advance. Simultaneous queries OK. Reports in 2 months. Sample copy $2 for 9×12 SAE with 5 first class stamps.

Nonfiction: Expose; historical/nostalgic; how-to (live better in western Virginia); interview/profile (of well-known area personalities); photo feature; and travel (Virginia and surrounding states). "Were looking for more photo feature stories based in western Virginia. We place special emphasis on consumer-related issues and how-to articles." Periodic special sections on fashion, real estate, media, banking, investing. Buys 60 mss/year. Query with published clips or send complete ms. Length: 1,400 words maximum. Pays $35-200.

• This magazine is looking for shorter pieces than before.

Photos: Send photos with ms. Reviews color transparencies. Pays $5-10 for 5×7 or 8×10 b&w prints; $10 maximum for 5×7 or 8×10 color prints. Captions and model releases required. Rights purchased vary.

Tips: "It helps if freelancer lives in the area. The most frequent mistake made by writers in completing an article for us is not having enough Roanoke-area focus: use of area experts, sources, slants, etc."

Washington

PACIFIC NORTHWEST, Adams Publishing of the Pacific Northwest, Suite 101, 701 Dexter Ave. N., Seattle WA 98109-4399. (206)284-1750. Fax: (206)284-2550. Editor: Ann Naumann. 80% freelance written. *"Pacific Northwest* is published 9 times/year, directed primarily at longtime residents of Oregon, Washington, Idaho, western Montana, Alaska, northern California, western Alberta and British Columbia." Estab. 1966. Circ. 76,581. Pays on publication. Publishes ms an average of 4 months after acceptance. Byline given. Offers kill fee. Buys first North American serial rights. Submit seasonal material 6 months in advance. Query for electronic submissions. Publishes reprints of previously published articles or short stories. Send photocopy of article or short story. Reports in 6 weeks. Sample copy $4. Free writer's guidelines.

Nonfiction: Book excerpts (Northwest), expose, general interest, interview/profile, personal experience, photo feature, travel, business and arts. No self-help. Buys 180 mss/year. Query with published clips. Length: 300-2,500 words. Pays $100-1,000 for assigned articles. Sometimes pays expenses of writers on assignment.

Photos: State availability of photos with submission. Reviews contact sheets. Offers $50-250/photo. Identification of subjects required. Buys one-time rights.

Columns/Departments: EcoHeroes (regional environmental leader profiles), 1,000 words; Gearing Up (outdoor activity how-to), 1,000 words; and Weekends (regional getaways), 500-1,200 words. Buys 90 mss/year. Query with published clips. Pays $150-300.

SEATTLE WEEKLY, Sasquatch Publishing, 1931 2nd Ave., Seattle WA 98101. (206)441-5555. Fax: (206)441-6213. Editor: David Brewster. 20% freelance written. Eager to work with new/unpublished writers, especially those in the region. Weekly tabloid covering arts, politics, food, business and books with local and regional emphasis. Estab. 1976. Circ. 34,000. Pays 1 week after publication. Publishes ms an average of 1 month after acceptance. Byline given. Offers variable kill fee. Buys first North American serial rights. Submit seasonal material minimum 2 months in advance. Simultaneous queries OK. Reports in 1 month. *Writer's Market* recommends allowing 2 months for reply. Sample copy $2. Writer's guidelines for #10 SASE.

Nonfiction: Book excerpts, expose, general interest, historical/nostalgic (Northwest), humor, interview/profile, opinion and arts-related essays. Buys 6-8 cover stories/year. Query with resume and published clips. Length: 700-4,000 words. Pays $75-800. Sometimes pays the expenses of writers on assignment.

Tips: "The *Seattle Weekly* publishes stories on Northwest politics and art, usually written by regional and local writers, for a mostly upscale, urban audience; writing is high-quality magazine style."

West Virginia

WONDERFUL WEST VIRGINIA, State of West Virginia Dept. of Natural Resources, Bldg. 3, 1900 Kanawha Blvd. E., State Capital Complex, Charleston WV 25305-0669. (304)558-9152. Editor: Nancy Clark. 95% freelance written. Monthly magazine of "general interest, show-piece quality, portraying a positive image of West Virginia, with emphasis on outdoor/natural resources subjects." Estab. 1970. Circ. 65,000. **Pays on acceptance.** Publishes ms an average of 24 months after acceptance. Byline given. Offers 5¢/word kill fee. Buys first or second rights. Submit seasonal material 6 months in advance. Reports in 3 months. Sample copy $3.25. Free writer's guidelines.

Nonfiction: General interest, natural resources, historical/nostalgic, photo feature and travel. "No outsider's views of West Virginia and its people; nothing negative or about poor, ignorant 'hillbilly' types of people or places. 'No Me and Joe hunting and fishing' stories." Buys 50 mss/year. Query. Length: 500-2,000 words. Pays $50-300.

• Looking especially for shorter articles (1,000 words or fewer).

Photos: Photos are taken by staff photographer, if feasible. Will consider photos with submission. Reviews 35mm or larger transparencies. Offers $75/color photo. Captions, model releases and identification of subjects required. Buys one-time rights.

Tips: "Read Guidelines for Writers. Write an article especially for readers who love West Virginia about an interesting place or event in West Virginia. Entire publication is open to freelancers. Need more stories on outdoor recreation (no hunting and fishing). We are only interested in articles from writers with a personal knowledge of West Virginia. We are presently scheduling stories into 1995 issues. Query us as to subject first."

Wisconsin

MILWAUKEE MAGAZINE, 312 E. Buffalo St., Milwaukee WI 53202. (414)273-1101. Fax: (414)273-0016. Editor: John Fennell. 40% freelance written. Monthly magazine covering Milwaukee and surrounding region. "We publish stories about Milwaukee, of service to Milwaukee-area residents and exploring the area's changing lifestyle, business, arts, politics and dining." Circ. 50,000. Pays on publication. Publishes an average of 2 months after acceptance. Byline given. Offers 20% kill fee. Buys first rights. Submit seasonal material 5-6 months in advance. Query for electronic submissions. Reports in 6 weeks on queries. *Writer's Market* recommends allowing 2 months for reply. Sample copy $4.

Nonfiction: Book excerpts, essays, expose, general interest, historical/nostalgic, interview/profile, photo feature, travel, food and dining and other services. "No articles without a strong Milwaukee or Wisconsin angle." Buys 30-50 mss/year. Query with published clips. Length: 1,500-5,000 words. Pays $600-1,000. Sometimes pays expenses of writers on assignment.

Photos: State availability of photos with submission. Reviews contact sheets, negatives, any transparencies and any prints. Offers no set rate per photo. Identification of subjects required. Buys one-time rights.

Columns/Departments: Steve Filmanowicz, departments editor. Insider (inside information on Milwaukee), 200-700 words. Buys 60 mss/year. Query with published clips. Pays $30-125.

Tips: "Pitch something for the Insider, or suggest a compelling profile we haven't already done and submit clips that prove you can do the job. The department most open is Insider. Think short, lively, offbeat, fresh, people-oriented."

WISCONSIN, *The Milwaukee Journal Magazine,* P.O. Box 661, Milwaukee WI 53201-0661. (414)224-2341. Fax: (414)224-2047. Editor: Alan Borsuk. 20% freelance written. Prefers to work with published/established writers. Weekly general interest magazine appealing to readers living in Wisconsin. Estab. 1969. Circ. 500,000. Pays on publication. Publishes ms an average of 4 months after acceptance. Byline given. Buys first serial rights. Submit seasonal material 4 months in advance. Simultaneous queries OK. Reports in 2 months on queries; 6 months on mss. Sample copy and writer's guidelines for 9 × 12 SAE with 2 first class stamps.

Nonfiction: Expose, general interest, humor, interview/profile, opinion, personal experience and photo feature, with Wisconsin angles in most cases. Buys 50 mss/year. Query. Length: 500-2,500 words. Pays $75-600. Sometimes pays expenses of writers on assignment.

Photos: State availability of photos.

Columns/Departments: Opinion, Humor and Essays. Buys 50 mss/year. Length: 300-1,000 words. Pays $100-200.

Tips: "We are primarily Wisconsin-oriented and are becoming more news-oriented."

WISCONSIN OUTDOOR JOURNAL, Krause Publications, 700 E. State St., Iola WI 54990-0001. (715)445-2214. Fax: (715)445-4087. Editor: Steve Heiting. 95% freelance written. Magazine published 8 times/year. "*Wisconsin Outdoor Journal* is more than a straight hook-and-bullet magazine. Though *WOJ* carries how-to and where-to information, it also prints narratives, nature features and state history pieces to give our readers a better appreciation of Wisconsin's outdoors." Estab. 1987. Circ. 45,000. **Pays on acceptance.** Byline given. Buys first North American serial rights. Submit seasonal material 1 year in advance. Reports in 6 weeks. *Writer's Market* recommends allowing 2 months for reply. Sample copy for 9 × 12 SAE with 7 first class stamps. Writer's guidelines for #10 SASE.

Nonfiction: Book excerpts, essays, historical/nostalgic, how-to, humor, interview/profile, personal experience and photo feature. Spring fishing and fall hunting annuals. No articles outside of the geographic boundaries of Wisconsin. Buys 80 mss/year. Query. Send complete ms. "Established writers may query, otherwise I prefer to see the complete ms." Length: 1,500-2,000 words. Pays $100-250.

Photos: Send photos with submission. Reviews 35mm transparencies. Offers no additional payment. Captions required. Buys one-time rights. Photos without mss pay from $10-150. Credit line given.

Fiction: Adventure, historical and humorous. "No eulogies of a good hunting dog." Buys 10 mss/year. Send complete ms. Length: 1,500-2,000 words. Pays $100-250.

Tips: "Writers need to know Wisconsin intimately—stories that appear as regionals in other magazines probably won't be printed within *WOJ*'s pages."

WISCONSIN TRAILS, P.O. Box 5650, Madison WI 53705-1056. (608)231-2444. Associate Editor: Patricia H. McKeown. 70% freelance written. Prefers to work with published/established writers. Bimonthly magazine for readers interested in Wisconsin; its contemporary issues, personalities, recreation, history, natural beauty and the arts. Estab. 1959. Circ. 55,000. Buys first serial rights, one-time rights occasionally. Pays on publication. Submit seasonal material at least 1 year in advance. Publishes ms an average of 6 months after acceptance. Byline given. Reports in 2 months. Sample copy for 9×12 SASE with 10 first class stamps. Writer's guidelines for #10 SASE.

Nonfiction: "Our articles focus on some aspect of Wisconsin life; an interesting town or event, a person or industry, history or the arts and especially outdoor recreation. We do not use first-person essays or biographies about people who were born in Wisconsin but made their fortunes elsewhere. No poetry. No articles that are too local for our regional audience, or articles about obvious places to visit in Wisconsin. We need more articles about the new and little-known." Buys 3 unsolicited mss/year. Query or send outline. Length: 1,000-3,000 words. Pays $150-500 (negotiable), depending on assignment length and quality. Sometimes pays expenses of writers on assignment.

Photos: Purchased with or without mss or on assignment. Uses 35mm transparencies; larger format OK. Color photos usually illustrate an activity, event, region or striking scenery. Prefer photos with people in scenery. Black and white photos usually illustrate a given article. Pays $50 each for b&w on publication. Pays $50-75 for inside color; $100-200 for covers. Captions preferred.

Tips: "We're looking for active articles about people, places, events and outdoor adventures in Wisconsin. We want to publish one in-depth article of state-wide interest or concern per issue, and several short (600-1,500 word) articles about short trips, recreational opportunities, restaurants, inns and cultural activities. We will be looking for more articles about out-of-the-way places in Wisconsin that are exceptional in some way."

Canada

CANADIAN GEOGRAPHIC, 39 McArthur Ave., Ottawa, Ontario K1L 8L9 Canada. (613)745-4629. Fax: (613)744-0947. Editor: Ian Darragh. Managing Editor: Eric Harris. 90% freelance written. Works with a small number of new/unpublished writers each year. Estab. 1930. Circ. 250,000. Bimonthly magazine. **Pays on acceptance.** Publishes ms an average of 3 months after acceptance. Buys first Canadian rights; interested only in first-time publication. Sample copy $3.95 (Canadian) for 9×12 SAE. Free writer's guidelines.

Nonfiction: Buys authoritative geographical articles, in the broad geographical sense, written for the average person, not for a scientific audience. Predominantly Canadian subjects by Canadian authors. Buys 30-45 mss/year. *Always query first in writing.* Length: 1,500-3,000 words. Pays 50¢/word minimum. Usual payment for articles ranges between $1,000-3,000. Higher fees reserved for commissioned articles. Sometimes pays the expenses of writers on assignment.

Photos: Pays $75-400 for color photos, depending on published size.

• Ranked as one of the best markets for freelance writers in *Writer's Digest* magazine's annual "Top 100 Markets," January 1993.

THE GEORGIA STRAIGHT, Vancouver Free Press Publishing Corp., 2nd Floor, 1235 W. Pender St., Vancouver, British Columbia V6E 2V6 Canada. (604)681-2000. Fax: (604)681-0272. Managing Editor: Charles Campbell. 90% freelance written. Weekly tabloid on arts, entertainment, lifestyle and civic issues. Estab. 1967. Circ. 85,000. Pays on publication. Byline given. Offers 75-100% kill fee. Buys first North American serial or second serial (reprint) rights. Simultaneous and previously published submissions OK; send typed ms with rights for sale noted and information about when and where the article previously appeared. Pays 50-100% of their fee for an original article. Reports in 1 month. *Writer's Market* recommends allowing 2 months for reply. Sample copy $1 for 9×12 SAE.

Nonfiction: General interest, humor, interview/profile, travel, and arts and entertainment. Buys 600 mss/year. Query with published clips. Length: 250-4,000 words. Pays $40-800. Sometimes pays expenses of writers on assignment.

Photos: Send photos with submission. Reviews, contact sheets, transparencies and 8×10 prints. Offers $35-150/photo. Captions, model releases and identification of subjects required. Buys one-time rights.

Tips: "Be aware of entertainment events in the Vancouver area and expansion of our news coverage. Most stories relate to those events. We don't return American mss because Canadian postage is not generally provided."

ONTARIO OUT OF DOORS, Dept. WM, 227 Front St. E., Toronto, Ontario M5A 1E8 Canada. (416)368-0185. Fax: (416)941-9113. Editor-in-Chief: Burton J. Myers. 80% freelance written. "We prefer a blend of both experienced and new writers." Magazine published 10 times/year emphasizing hunting, fishing, camping and conservation. Estab. 1968. Circ. 100,000. **Pays on acceptance.** Publishes ms an average of 6 months after acceptance. Buys first North American serial rights. Phone queries OK. Submit seasonal material 5 months in advance of issue date. Reports in 2 months. Sample copy and writer's guidelines for SASE; mention *Writer's Market* in request.

Nonfiction: Expose of conservation practices; how-to (improve your fishing and hunting skills); humor; photo feature (on wildlife); travel (where to find good fishing and hunting); and any news on Ontario. "Avoid 'Me and Joe' articles or funny family camping anecdotes." Buys 20-30 unsolicited mss/year. Query. Length: 150-3,500 words. Pays $35-500. Sometimes pays the expenses of writers on assignment.

Photos: Submit photo material with accompanying query. No additonal payment for b&w contact sheets and 35mm color transparencies. "Should a photo be used on the cover, an additional payment of $350-500 is made."

Fillers: Outdoor tips. Buys 100 mss/year. Length 20-50 words. Pays $15-35.

Tips: "It's rewarding for us to find a freelancer who reads and understands a set of writer's guidelines, but it is annoying when writers fail to submit supporting photography."

OTTAWA MAGAZINE, Ottawa Magazine Inc., 192 Bank St., Ottawa, Ontario K2P 1W8 Canada. (613)234-7751. Fax: (613)234-9226. Editor: Rosa Harris Adler. 80% freelance written. Prefers to work with published/established writers. Magazine published 9 times/year, covering life in Ottawa and environs. "*Ottawa Magazine* reflects the interest and lifestyles of its readers who tend to be married, ages 35-55, upwardly mobile and urban." Circ. 40,000. **Pays on acceptance.** Publishes ms an average of 6 months after acceptance. Byline given. "Kill fee depends on agreed-upon fee; very seldom used." Buys first North American serial and second serial (reprint) rights. Simultaneous queries and previously published submissions OK. Reports in 2 months. Sample copy $2.25.

Nonfiction: Book excerpts (by local authors or about regional issues); exposé (federal or regional government, education); general interest; interview/profile (on Ottawans who have established national or international reputations); photo feature (for recurring section called Freezeframe); and travel (recent examples are Brazil, Trinidad & Tobago, Copenhagen). "No articles better suited to a national or special interest publication." Buys 100 mss/year. Query with published clips. Length: 2,000-3,500 words. Pays $500/1,000 (Canadian).

Tips: "A phone call to our associate editor is the best way to assure that queries receive prompt attention. Once a query interests me the writer is assigned a detailed 'treatment' of the proposed piece which is used to determine viability of story. We will be concentrating on more issue-type stories with good, solid fact-researched base, also doing more fluffy pieces—best and worst of Ottawa—that sort of stuff. Harder for out-of-town writers to furnish. The writer should strive to inject a personal style and avoid newspaper-style reportage. *Ottawa Magazine* also doesn't stoop to boosterism and points out the bad along with the good. Good prospects for US writers are interiors (house and garden type), gardening (for Northern climate), leisure/lifestyles. Reprints OK."

WHERE VICTORIA/ESSENTIAL VICTORIA, Key Pacific Publishers Co. Ltd., 3rd Floor, 1001 Wharf St., Victoria, British Columbia V8W 1T6 Canada. (604)388-4324. Editor: S. Anne Peterson. 40% freelance written. Monthly magazine on Victoria and Vancouver Island. Estab. 1975. Circ. 30,000. Pays on publication. Publishes ms an average of 1-2 months after acceptance. Byline given. Buys first North American serial and all rights. Query for electronic submissions. Reprints OK; send photocopy of article and information about when and where the article previously appeared. Pays 75% of their fee for an original article. Reports in 3 months. Free sample copy.

Nonfiction: General interest and travel. Essential Victoria. Buys 30 mss/year. Query with published clips. Length: 500-2,500 words. Pays 20-40¢/word.

Photos: State availability of photos with submission. Reviews contact sheets, transparencies and prints. Offers $50-150/photo. Model releases and identification of subjects required. Buys one-time rights.

THE YUKON READER, World-Yukon Publications Ltd., P.O. Box 4306, Whitehorse, Yukon Y1A 3T3 Canada. (403)668-2355. Fax: (403)668-7953. Editor: Sam Holloway. 90% freelance written. Bimonthly magazine covering the Northwest (Alaska, Yukon, Northwest Territories and northern British Columbia). History and personality profiles. Estab. 1989. Circ. 17,000. Pays on publication. Byline given. Buys one-time rights. Simultaneous and previously published submissions OK. Reports in 3 weeks on queries; 2 months on mss. Electronic submissions preferred, IBM format; indicate wordprocessor used. Free sample copy.

Nonfiction: Book excerpts, expose, general interest, historical, nostalgic, humor, inspirational, interview/profile, personal experience, photo feature. Especially diary-type stories that happened in Alaska or the Yukon between 1850 and 1992. No free verse, poetry, political treatises. Buys 35 or 40 mss/year. Send complete ms. Length 500-6,000 words; $75-300 for unsolicited articles. Writers receive 15 copies, gold nugget and a check.

Photos: State availability of or send photos with submissions. Identification of subjects required. Buys one-time rights.

Relationships

These publications focus on lifestyles and relationships. They are read and often written by single people, gays and lesbians and those interested in these lifestyles or in alternative outlooks. They may offer writers a forum for unconventional views or serve as a voice for particular audiences or causes.

ATLANTA SINGLES MAGAZINE, Hudson Brooke Publishing, Inc., Suite 2, 1780 Century Circle, Atlanta GA 30359. (404)636-2260. Fax: (404)636-2366. Editor: Margaret Anthony. Associate Editor: Claire Barry. 10% freelance written. Works with a small number of new/unpublished writers each year. Bimonthly magazine for single, widowed or divorced adults, medium to high income level, many business and professionally oriented; single parents, ages 25 to 55. Estab. 1977. Circ. 15,000. Pays on publication. Publishes ms an average of 6 months after acceptance. Byline given. Buys one-time, second serial (reprint) and simultaneous rights. Submit seasonal material 6 months in advance. Simultaneous and previously published submissions OK; send tearsheet or photocopy of article. Pays 25-50% of their fee for an original article. Sample copy $2 for 8 × 10 SAE with 7 first class stamps. Writer's guidelines for #10 SASE.

Nonfiction: General interest, humor, personal experience, photo feature and travel. No fiction or pornography. Buys 5 mss/year. Send complete ms. Length: 600-1,200 words. Pays $50-150 for unsolicited articles; sometimes trades for personal ad.

Photos: Send photos with submission. Cover photos also considered. Reviews prints. Offers no additional payment for photos accepted with ms. Model releases and identification of subjects required. Buys one-time rights.

Columns/Departments: Will consider ideas. Query. Length: 600-800 words. Pays $50-150/column or department.

Tips: "We are open to articles on *any* subject that would be of interest to singles. For example, travel, autos, movies, love stories, fashion, investments, real estate, etc. Although singles are interested in topics like self-awareness, being single again, and dating, they are also interested in many of the same subjects that married people are, such as those listed."

BAY WINDOWS, New England's Largest Gay and Lesbian Newspaper, Bay Windows, Inc., 1523 Washington St., Boston MA 02118-2034. (617)266-6670. Fax: (617)266-5973. Editor: Jeff Epperly. Arts Editor: Ruby Kikel. 30-40% freelance written. Weekly newspaper of gay news and concerns. "*Bay Windows* covers predominantly news of New England, but will print non-local news and features depending on the newsworthiness of the story. We feature hard news, opinion, news analysis, arts reviews and interviews." Estab. 1983. Publishes ms within 2 months of acceptance, pays within 1 month of publication. Byline given. Offers 50% kill fee. Rights obtained varies, usually first serial rights. Simultaneous submissions accepted if other submissions are outside of New England. Submit seasonal material 3 months in advance. Reprints OK; send typed ms with rights for sale noted and information about when and where the article previously appeared. Pays 75% of their fee for an original article. Reports in 3 months. Sample copy $5. Writer's guidelines for #10 SASE.

Nonfiction: Hard news, general interest with a gay slant, interview/profile, opinion and photo features. Publishes 200 mss/year. Query with published clips or send complete ms. Length: 500-1,500 words. Pay varies: $25-100 news; $10-60 arts.

Photos: $25/published photo, b&w photos only. Model releases and identification of subjects required.

Columns/Departments: Film, music, dance, books, art. Length: 500-1,500 words. Buys 200 mss/year. Pays $10-100.

● Looking for more humor.

Poetry: All varieties. Publishes 50 poems per year. Length: 10-30 lines. No payment.

Tips: "Too much gay-oriented writing is laden with the clichés and catch phrases of the movement. Writers must have intimate knowledge of gay community; however, this should not mean that standard English usage is not required. We look for writers with new—even controversial perspectives on the lives of gay men and lesbians. While we assume gay is good, we will print stories which examine problems within the community and movement. No pornography or erotica."

‡DRUMMER, Desmodus, Inc., Box 410390, San Francisco CA 94141-0390. (415)252-1195. Fax: (415)252-9574. Editor: Marcus Wonacott. 80% freelance written. Gay male leather and related fetish erotica/news. Monthly magazine publishes "erotic aspects of leather and other masculine fetishes for gay men." Circ. 60,000. Pays on publication. Publishes ms an average of 3 months after acceptance. Byline given. Buys first North American serial rights or makes work-for-hire assignments. Submit seasonal/holiday material 9 months in advance. Previously published submissions OK. Reports in 1 month on queries; in 3 months on mss. Sample copy $6. Writer's guidelines for #10 SASE.

Nonfiction: Book excerpts, essays, historical/nostalgic, how-to, humor, interview/profile, new product, opinion, personal experience, photo feature, technical and travel. No feminine-slanted pieces. Buys 25 mss/year. Query with or without published clips or send complete ms. Length: 1,000-15,000 words. Pays $50-200 for assigned articles; $50-100 for unsolicited articles. Rarely pays expenses of writers on assignment.

Photos: Send photos with submission (photocopies OK). Reviews contact sheets and transparencies. Offers $10-100/photo. Model releases and identification of subjects required. Buys one-time rights or all rights.

Fiction: Adventure, erotica, ethnic, fantasy, historical, horror, humorous, mystery, novel excerpts, science fiction, slice-of-life vignettes, suspense and western. Must have gay "macho" erotic elements. Buys 60-75 mss/year. Send complete ms. Length: 1,000-20,000 words. Occasionally serializes stories. Pays $100.

Fillers: Anecdotes, facts, gags, cartoons and newsbreaks. Buys 50/year. Length: 10-100 words. pay $10-50.

Tips: "All they have to do is write—but they must be knowledgable about some aspect of the scene. While the magazine is aimed at gay men, we welcome contributions from straight men and from straight, bisexual and gay women who understand leather, s/m and kinky erotic fetishes. Fiction is most open to freelancers."

‡DUNGEON MASTER, Desmodus Inc., Box 410390, San Francisco CA 94141-0390. (415)252-1195. Fax: (415)252-9574. Editor: Anthony F. DeBlase. 50% freelance written. Quarterly magazine covering gay male erotic s/m. "Safety is emphasized. This is not a fantasy magazine but is for real how-to articles on equipment, techniques, etc." Circ. 6,000. Most articles are unpaid—except by complimentary subscriptions, ads, etc. Byline given. Buys first North American serial, one-time or simultaneous rights or makes work-for-hire assignments. Previously published submissions OK. Sample copy $5. Writer's guidelines for #10 SASE.

Nonfiction: Book excerpts, essays, historical/nostalgic, how-to (mainly), humor, interview/profile, new product, opinion, personal experience, photo feature (may be paid), technical, travel and safety. No fiction or unsafe practices. Buys 40 mss/year. Query with or without published clips or send complete ms. Length: no limit. Pays $25-200 for assigned articles. Usually pays writers with contributor copies or other premiums rather than a cash payment. Rarely pays expenses of writers on assignment.

Photos: Send photos with submission. Photocopies OK. Reviews contact sheets and transparencies. Offers $10-100/photo. Model releases and identification of subjects required. Buys one-time rights or all rights.

Fillers: Anecdotes, facts, gags to be illustrated and newbreaks. Buys 10/year. Pays $5-25.

Tips: "Must be knowledgable in specialized field. While the publication is aimed at gay men, submission by straight men and straight and gay women are welcome."

FIRST HAND, Experiences For Loving Men, Firsthand, Ltd., 310 Cedar Lane, Teaneck NJ 07666. (201)836-9177. Editor: Bob Harris. Publisher: Jackie Lewis. 75% freelance written. Eager to work with new/unpublished writers. Monthly magazine of homosexual erotica. Estab. 1980. Circ. 70,000. Pays 6 months after acceptance or on publication, whichever comes first. Publishes ms an average of 8 months after acceptance. Byline given. Buys all rights (exceptions made) and second serial (reprint) rights. Submit seasonal material 10 months in advance. Reports in 2 months. Sample copy $5. Writer's guidelines for #10 SASE.

Columns/Departments: Survival Kit (short nonfiction articles, up to 1,000 words, featuring practical information on safe sex practices, health, travel, psychology, law, fashion, and other advice/consumer/lifestyle topics of interest to gay or single men). "For this section, we sometimes also buy reprint rights to appropriate articles previously published in local gay newspapers around the country." Infotainment (short reviews up to 1,000 words on books, film, TV, video, theater, performance art, museums, etc.). Reviews must have a gay angle. Query. Pays $35-70, depending on length, if original; if reprint, pays half that rate.

Fiction: Erotic fiction up to 5,000 words, average 2,000-3,000 words. "We prefer fiction in the first person which is believable—stories based on the writer's actual experience have the best chance. We're not interested in stories which involve underage characters in sexual situations. Other taboos include bestiality, rape—except in prison stories, as rape is an unavoidable reality in prison—and heavy drug use. Writers with questions about what we can and cannot depict should write for our guidelines, which go into this in more detail. We print mostly self-contained stories; we will look at novel excerpts, but only if they stand on their own."

Poetry: Free verse and light verse. Buys 12/year. Submit maximum 5 poems. Length: 10-30 lines. Pays $25.

Tips: "*First Hand* is a very reader-oriented publication for gay men. Half of each issue is made up of letters from our readers describing their personal experiences, fantasies and feelings. Our readers are from all walks of life, all races and ethnic backgrounds, all classes, all religious and political affiliations, and so on. They are very diverse, and many live in far-flung rural areas or small towns; for some of them, our magazines are the primary source of contact with gay life, in some cases the only support for their gay identity. Our readers are very loyal and save every issue. We return that loyalty by trying to reflect their interests—for instance, by striving to avoid the exclusively big-city bias so common to national gay publications. So bear in mind the diversity of the audience when you write."

THE GUIDE, To Gay Travel, Entertainment, Politics and Sex, Fidelity Publishing, P.O. Box 593, Boston MA 02199-0593. (617)266-8557. Fax: (617)266-1125. Editor: French Wall. 50% freelance written. Monthly magazine on the gay and lesbian community. Estab. 1981. Circ. 30,000. **Pays on acceptance.** Publishes ms an average of 2 months after acceptance. Kill fee negotiable. Buys all rights. Submit seasonal material 2 months in advance. Simultaneous submissions OK. Reports in 3 months. Sample copy for 9 × 12 SAE with 8 first class stamps. Writer's guidelines for #10 SASE.

Nonfiction: Book excerpts (if yet unpublished), essays, expose, general interest, historical/nostalgic, humor, interview/profile, opinion, personal experience, photo feature and religious. Buys 24 mss/year. Query with or without published clips or send complete ms. Length: 500-5,000 words. Pays $50-180.

Photos: Send photos with submission. Reviews contact sheets. Offers no additional payment for photos accepted with ms (although sometimes negotiable). Captions, model releases, identification of subjects prefered; releases required sometimes. Buys one-time rights.

Tips: "Brevity, humor and militancy appreciated."

GUYS, First Hand Ltd., P.O. Box 1314, Teaneck NJ 07666-3441. (201)836-9177. Fax: (201)836-5055. Editor: William Spencer. 80% freelance written. Monthly magazine of erotica for gay men. "A positive, romantic approach to gay sex." Estab. 1988. Circ. 60,000. Pays on publication. Publishes ms an average of 1 year after acceptance. Byline given. Buys first North American serial or all rights. Submit seasonal material 10 months in advance. Reprints OK; send photocopy of article or short story or typed ms with rights for sale noted. Pays 50% of their fee for an original article. Reports in 2-6 months. Sample copy $5. Writer's guidelines for #10 SASE.

Columns/Departments: Starstruck (Hollywood with a gay angle), 1,250-1,500 words; and Point of View (op/ed), 1,000-1,500 words. Buys 12 mss/year. Query. Pays $75-100.

Fiction: Erotica. Buys 72 mss/year. Length: 1,000-10,000 words. Pays $75-250.

IN TOUCH FOR MEN, In Touch Publications International, Inc., 13122 Saticoy St., North Hollywood CA 91605-3402. (818)764-2288. Fax: (818)764-2307. Editor: D. DiFranco. 80% freelance written. Works with a small number of new/unpublished writers each year. Monthly magazine covering the gay male lifestyle, gay male humor and erotica. Estab. 1973. Circ. 70,000. Pays on publication. Byline given, pseudonym OK. Buys one-time rights. Simultaneous submissions OK. Reports in 2 months. Sample copy $5.95. Writer's guidelines for #10 SASE.

Nonfiction: Buys 36 mss/year. Send complete ms. Length: 3,000-3,500 words. Pays $25-75.
   • Needs more lifestyle features.

Photos: State availability of photos with submission. Reviews contact sheets, transparencies, and prints. Offers $35/photo. Captions, model releases and identification of subjects required. Buys one-time rights.

Fiction: Erotica, novel excerpts; all must be gay male erotica. Buys 36 mss/year. Send complete ms. Length: 3,000-3,500 words. Pays $75 maximum.

Fillers: Short humor. Buys 12/year. Length: 1,500-3,500 words. Pays $50-75.

Tips: "Our publication features male nude photos plus three fiction pieces, several articles, cartoons, humorous comments on items from the media, photo features. We try to present the positive aspects of the gay lifestyle, with an emphasis on humor. Humorous pieces may be erotic in nature. We are open to all submissions that fit our gay male format; the emphasis, however, is on humor and the upbeat. We receive many fiction manuscripts but not nearly enough articles and humor."

LAMBDA BOOK REPORT, A Review of Contemporary Gay and Lesbian Literature, Lambda Rising, Inc., 1625 Connecticut Ave. NW, Washington DC 20009-1013. (202)462-7924. Fax: (202)462-7257. Assistant Editor: Jim Marks. Managing Editor: Leslie Smith. 90% freelance written. Bimonthly magazine that covers gay/lesbian literature. "*Lambda Book Report* devotes its entire contents to the discussion of gay and lesbian books and authors. Any other submissions would be inappropriate." Estab. 1987. Circ. 11,000. Pays 30 days after publication. Byline given. Buys first rights. Query for electronic submissions. Reports in 1 month. *Writer's Market* recommends allowing 2 months for reply. Sample copy $3.95 for 9 × 12 SAE with 5 first class stamps. Free writer's guidelines.

Nonfiction: Book excerpts, essays (on gay literature), interview/profile (of authors) and book reviews. "No historical essays, fiction or poetry." Query with published clips. Length: 200-2,000 words. Pays $15-125 for assigned articles; $5-25 for unsolicited articles.

Photos: State availability of photos with submission. Reviews contact sheets. Offers $10-25/photo. Model releases required. Buys one-time rights.

Tips: "Assignments go to writers who query with 2-3 published book reviews and/or interviews. It is helpful if the writer is familiar with gay and lesbian literature and can write intelligently and objectively on the field. Review section is most open. Writers should demonstrate with clips their scope of knowledge, ability and interest in reviewing gay books."

‡LIBIDO, The Journal of Sex & Sensibility, Libido, Inc., 5318 N. Paulina St., Chicago IL 60640, Editor: Marianna Beck. Managing Editor: Jack Hafferkamp. 65% freelance written. Quarterly magazine covering literate erotica. "*Libido* is about sexuality. Orientation is not an issue, writing ability is. The aim is to enlighten as often as it is to arouse. Humor—sharp and smart—is important, so are safer sex contexts." Estab. 1988. Circ. 8,000. Pays on publication. Byline given. Kill fee "rare, but negotiable." Buys one-time or second serial (reprint) rights. Editorial lead time 3 months. Submit seasonal material 4 months in advance. Accepts previously published submissions. Reports in 3 months. Sample copy $7. Writer's guidelines for #10 SASE.

Nonfiction: Book excerpts, essays, historical/nostalgic, humor, personal experience, photo feature and travel. "No violence, sexism or misty memoirs." Buys 10-20 mss/year. Query. Length: 300-2,500 words. Pays $50 minimum for assigned articles; $15 minimum for unsolicited articles. Pays contributor copies "when money isn't an issue and copies or other considerations have equal or higher value." Sometimes pays expenses of writers on assignment.

Photos: Send photos with submission. Reviews contact sheets and 5×7 and 8×10 prints. Negotiates payment individually. Model releases required. Buys one-time rights.

Fiction: Erotica. Buys 10 mss/year. Send complete ms. Length: 800-2,500 words. Pays $20-50.

Poetry: Uses humorous short erotic poetry. No limericks. Buys 10 poems/year. Submit maximum 3 poems. Pays $15.

Tips: "Send us a manuscript—make it short, sharp and with a lead that makes us want to read. If we're not hooked by paragraph 4, we reject the ms."

METRO SINGLES LIFESTYLES, Metro Publications, Dept. WM, P.O. Box 28203, Kansas City MO 64118. (816)436-8424. Editor: Robert L. Huffstutter. 40% freelance written. Eager to work with new/unpublished writers and photographers. Bimonthly tabloid covering singles lifestyles. Estab. 1984. **Pays on acceptance.** Publishes ms an average of 2 months after acceptance. Byline given with photo optional. Buys one-time and second serial (reprint) rights. Submit seasonal material 3 months in advance. Reports in 6 weeks. Sample copy $3 for 9×12 SAE with 5 first class stamps.

Nonfiction: Essay, general interest, how-to (on meeting the ideal mate, recovering from divorce, etc.), inspirational, interview/profile, personal experience and photo feature. Buys 6-12 mss/year. Send complete ms. Length: 700-1,200 words. Pays $100 maximum for assigned articles; pays $20-50 for unsolicited articles. Will pay in copies or other if writer prefers.

Photos: Pays up to $100 for photo layouts (10-12 photos). Subject matter suggested includes swimwear fashion, recreational events, "day in the life of an American single," etc. Reviews 3×5 and 8×10 color or b&w prints. Model releases of close-up or fashion shots required. Buys one-time and reprint rights. **Pays on acceptance.**

Columns/Departments: Movie Reviews, Lifestyles, Singles Events, and Book Reviews (about singles), all 400-1,000 words. Buys 9-12 mss/year. Send complete ms. Pays $20-50.

Fiction: Confession, humorous, romance and slice-of-life vignettes. Buys 6-12 mss/year. Send complete ms. Length: 700-1,200 words. Pays $20-50.

Poetry: Free verse and light verse. Buys 40-60 poems/year. Submit maximum 3 poems. Length: 21 lines. Pays in complimentary copies and subscriptions for poetry. Byline given.

Tips: "A freelancer can best approach and break in to our publication with positive articles, photo features about singles and positive fiction about singles. Photos and short bios of singles (blue collar, white collar, and professional) at work needed. Photos and a few lines about singles enjoying recreation (swimming, sports, chess, etc.) always welcome. Color photos, close-up, are suitable."

MOM GUESS WHAT NEWSPAPER, 1725 L St., Sacramento CA 95814. (916)441-6397. Editor: Linda Birner. 80% freelance written. Works with small number of new/unpublished writers each year. Biweekly tabloid covering gay rights and gay lifestyles. Estab. 1978. Circ. 21,000. Publishes ms an average of 3 months after acceptance. Byline given. Buys all rights. Submit seasonal material 3 months in advance. Reports in 2 months. Sample copy $1. Writer's guidelines for 10×13 SAE with 4 first class stamps.

Nonfiction: Interview/profile and photo feature of international, national or local scope. Buys 8 mss/year. Query. Length: 200-1,500 words. Payment depends on article. Pays expenses of writers on special assignment.

Photos: State availability of photos with submission. Reviews 5×7 prints. Offers no additional payment for photos accepted with ms. Captions and identification of subjects required. Buys one-time rights.

Columns/Departments: News, Restaurants, Political, Health, and Film, Video and Book Reviews. Buys 12 mss/year. Query. Payment depends on article.

SINGLELIFE MAGAZINE, SingleLife Enterprises, Inc., 606 W. Wisconsin Ave., Milwaukee WI 53203-1992. (414)271-9700. Fax: (414)271-5263. Editor: Gail Levine. 40% freelance written. Prefers to work with published/established writers. Bimonthly magazine covering single lifestyles. Estab. 1982. Circ. 22,000. Pays on publication. Publishes ms an average of 4 months after acceptance. Byline given. Buys one-time second serial (reprint) and simultaneous rights. Submit seasonal material 4 months in advance. Simultaneous and previously published submissions OK. Reprints OK; send typed ms with rights for sale noted and information about when and where the article previously appeared. Pays 75% of their fee for an original article. Reports in 2 months. Sample copy and writer's guidelines for $3.50. Writer's guidelines for #10 SASE.

Nonfiction: Upbeat and in-depth articles on significant areas of interest to single people such as male/female relationships, travel, health, sports, food, single parenting, humor, finances, places to go and things to do. Prefers third person point of view and ms to query letter. "Our readers are between 25 and 50." Length: 1,000-1,500 words. Pays $60-100.

● No longer publishing fiction or poetry.

Tips: "The easiest way to get in is to write something humorous or insightful, or both."

THE WASHINGTON BLADE, Washington Blade, Inc., 1408 U St., NW, Washington DC 20009-3916. (202)797-7000. Fax: (202)797-7040. Senior Editor: Lisa M. Keen. 20% freelance written. Weekly news tabloid covering the gay/lesbian community. "Articles (subjects) should be written from or directed to a gay perspective." Estab. 1969. Circ. 40,500. Pays in 1 month. Publishes ms an average of 1 month after acceptance. Byline given. Offers $15 kill fee. Buys first North American serial rights. Submit seasonal material 1 month in

advance. Reports in 1 month. Sample copy and writer's guidelines for 9 × 12 SAE with 6 first class stamps.
Nonfiction: Expose (of government, private agency, church, etc., handling of gay-related issues); historical/ nostalgic; interview/profile (of gay community/political leaders; persons, gay or nongay, in positions to affect gay issues; outstanding achievers who happen to be gay; those who incorporate the gay lifestyle into their professions); photo feature (on a nationally or internationally historic gay event); and travel (on locales that welcome or cater to the gay traveler). *The Washington Blade* basically covers two areas: news and lifestyle. News coverage of D.C. metropolitan area gay community, local and federal government actions relating to gays, as well as national news of interest to gays. Section also includes features on current events. Special issues include annual gay pride issue (early June). No sexually explicit material. Articles of interest to the community must include and be written for both gay men and lesbians. Buys 30 mss/year, average. Query with published clips and resume. Length: 500-1,500 words. Pays 5-10¢/word. Sometimes pays the expenses of writers on assignment.
Photos: "A photo or graphic with feature/lifestyle articles is particularly important. Photos with news stories are appreciated." State availability of photos. Reviews b&w contact sheets and 5 × 7 glossy prints. Pays $25 minimum. Captions preferred; model releases required. On assignment, photographer paid mutually agreed upon fee, with expenses reimbursed. Publication retains all rights.
Tips: "Send good examples of your writing and know the paper before you submit a manuscript for publication. We get a lot of submissions which are entirely inappropriate. We're looking for more features, but fewer AIDS-related features. Greatest opportunity for freelancers resides in current events, features, interviews and book reviews."

‡**THE JAMES WHITE REVIEW, A Gay Men's Literary Quarterly,** P.O. Box 3356, Butler Quarter Station, Minneapolis MN 55403. Editor: Phil Willkie. Managing Editor: Bayne Holley. 100% freelance written. Quarterly tabloid covering gay men. Estab. 1983. Circ. 4,000. Byline given. Buys first North American serial rights. Editorial lead time 3 months. Submit seasonal material 3 months in advance. Query for electronic submissions. Reports in 3 months on queries. Sample copy $3. Writer's guidelines for #10 SASE.
Nonfiction: Book excerpts and essays. Buys 4 mss/year. Send complete ms. Length: 2,000 words maximum. Pays $50 minimum.
Photos: Send photos with submission. Reviews prints. Negotiates payment individually. Buys one-time rights.
Fiction: Confession, erotica, experimental, fantasy, historical, novel excerpts and serialized novels. Buys 20 mss/year. Send complete ms. Length: 2,000 words maximum. Pays $50 maximum.
Poetry: Cliff Mayhood, poetry editor. Avant-garde, free verse, light verse and traditional. Buys 80 poems/ year. Submit maximum 10 poems. Pays $20.

Religious

Religious magazines focus on a variety of subjects, styles and beliefs. Many are publishing articles relating to current affairs like AIDS, cults, or substance abuse. Fewer religious publications are considering poems and personal experience articles, but many emphasize special ministries to singles, seniors and deaf people. Such diversity makes reading each magazine essential for the writer hoping to break in. Educational and inspirational material of interest to church members, workers and leaders within a denomination or religion is needed by the publications in this category. Publications intended to assist professional religious workers in teaching and managing church affairs are classified in Church Administration and Ministry in the Trade section. Religious magazines for children and teenagers can be found in the Juvenile and Teen and Young Adult classifications. Other religious publications can be found in the Ethnic/Minority section as well.

AMERICA, 106 W. 56th St., New York NY 10019. (212)581-4640. Editor: Rev. George W. Hunt. Published weekly for adult, educated, largely Roman Catholic audience. Estab. 1909. **Pays on acceptance.** Byline given. Usually buys all rights. Reports in 3 weeks. Free writer's guidelines.
Nonfiction: "We publish a wide variety of material on politics, economics, ecology, and so forth. We are not a parochial publication, but almost all of our pieces make some moral or religious point. We are not interested in purely informational pieces or personal narratives which are self-contained and have no larger moral interest." Articles on literature, current political and social events. Length: 1,500-2,000 words. Pays $50-100.

Poetry: Length: 15-30 lines. Patrick Samway, S.J., poetry editor.

THE ANNALS OF SAINT ANNE DE BEAUPRE, Redemptorist Fathers, 9795 St. Anne Blvd., St. Anne De Beaupre, Quebec G0A 3C0 Canada. (418)827-4538. Fax: (418)827-4530. Editor: Bernard Mercier. Managing Editor: Roch Achard. 80% freelance written. Works with a small number of new/unpublished writers each year. Monthly magazine on religion. "Our aim is to promote devotion to St. Anne and Christian family values." Estab. 1878. Circ. 45,000. **Pays on acceptance.** Publishes ms an average of 1 year after acceptance. Byline given. Buys first North American serial rights. Submit seasonal material 2½ months in advance. Simultaneous queries OK. Reports in 2 weeks. Free sample copy and writer's guidelines.
Nonfiction: Expose, general interest, inspirational and personal experience. No articles without spiritual thrust. Buys 30 mss/year. Send complete ms. Length: 500-1,500 words. Pays 3-4¢/word.
Fiction: Religious. Buys 15 mss/year. Send complete ms. Length: 500-1,500 words. Pays 3-4¢/word.
Poetry: "Our poetry 'bank' is full and we will be not accepting any new items for the next year or so."
Tips: "Write something educational, inspirational, objective and uplifting. Reporting rather than analysis is simply not remarkable."

‡AREOPAGUS, A Living Encounter With Today's Religious World, Tao Fong Shan Christian Centre, P.O. Box 33, Shatin, New Territories, Hong Kong. (852)691-1904. Editor: John G. LeMond. Managing Editor: Eric Bosell. Contact: Editor. 75% freelance written. Quarterly magazine for interreligious dialogue. "*Areopagus* is a Christian periodical that seeks to engage its readers in a living encounter with today's religious world. Respecting the integrity of religious communities, *Areopagus* provides a forum for dialog between the good news of Jesus Christ and people of faith both in major world religious and new religious movements." Estab. 1987. Circ. 1,000. Pays on publication. Publishes ms an average of 6 months after acceptance. Offers 50% kill fee. Buys first rights. Editorial lead time 6 months. Submit seasonal material 6 months in advance. Accepts simultaneous and previously published submissions. Query for electronic submissions. Reports in 6 weeks on queries; 3 months on mss. Sample copy for $4. Writer's guidelines free on request.
Nonfiction: Book excerpts, essays and expose (all on religious themes), humor (of a religious nature), inspirational (interreligious encounter), interview/profile (w/religious figures), opinion (on religious subjects), personal experience (of spiritual journey), photo feature and religious. Issue themes under consideration: birth rites, death, family, sex, aging, suffering, war, hope, healing. "We are not interested in articles that seek to prove the superiority or inferiority of a particular religious tradition." Buys 40 mss/year. Send complete ms. Length: 1,000-5,000 words. Pays $50 minimum.
Photos: Send photos with submission. Offers $15-50/photo. Identification of subjects required. Buys one-time rights.
Columns/Departments: Getting to Know (objective description of major world religions), 4,000 words; Pilgrimage (stories of personal faith journies), 3,000 words; and People and Communities (description of faith communities), 3,000 words. Buys 30 mss/year. Send complete ms. Pays $50-100.
Poetry: Free verse, haiku, light verse and traditional. "Nothing about kittens or horses, unless they have had a significant religious experience." Buys 1 poem/year. Submit maximum 3 poems. Pays $15-50.
Fillers: Facts, newsbreaks. Buys 5/year. Length: 100-400 words. Pays $10-25.
Tips: "Articles that reflect a balanced approach to interreligious dialogue are the most likely candidates. Followers of all faiths are encouraged to write about personal experience. Articles about religious conspiracy and arcane religious conjecture are of little interest. Virtually all of our departments are open to freelancers. In general, we look for compassionate, direct and unself-conscious prose that reflects a writer firmly rooted in his or her own tradition but unafraid to encounter other traditions."

THE ASSOCIATE REFORMED PRESBYTERIAN, Associate Reformed Presbyterian General Synod, 1 Cleveland St., Greenville SC 29601-3696. (803)232-8297. Editor: Ben Johnston. 5% freelance written. Works with a small number of new/unpublished writers each year. Christian magazine serving a conservative, evangelical and Reformed denomination, most of whose members are in the Southeast U.S. Estab. 1976. Circ. 6,300. **Pays on acceptance.** Publishes ms an average of 4 months after acceptance. Byline given. Not copyrighted. Buys first, one-time, or second serial (reprint) rights. Submit seasonal material 4 months in advance. Simultaneous submissions and previously published submissions OK. Send tearsheet of article or short story, photocopy of article or short story, or typed ms with rights for sale noted and information about when and where the article previously appeared. For reprints, pays 100% of the amount paid for an original article. Reports in 1 month. Sample copy $1.50. Writer's guidelines for #10 SASE.
Nonfiction: Book excerpts, essays, inspirational, opinion, personal experience and religious. Buys 10-15 mss/year. Query. Length: 400-2,000 words. Pays $50 maximum.
Photos: State availability of photos with submission. Reviews 5×7 reprints. Offers $25 maximum/photo. Captions and identification of subjects required. Buys one-time rights.
Fiction: Religious and children's. Pays $50 maximum.
Tips: "Feature articles are the area of our publication most open to freelancers. Focus on a contemporary problem and offer Bible-based solutions to it. Provide information that would help a Christian struggling in his daily walk. Writers should understand that we are denominational, conservative, evangelical, Reformed

and Presbyterian. A writer who appreciates these nuances would stand a much better chance of being published here than one who does not."

BIBLICAL ILLUSTRATOR, The Sunday School Board, 127 9th Ave. N., Nashville TN 37234. Design Editor: James D. McLemore. "Articles are designed to coordinate with other Southern Baptist periodicals. Unsolicited mss are rarely applicable. Inquire first. Sample copy for 9 × 12 SAE with 3 first class stamps."

CATHOLIC NEAR EAST MAGAZINE, Catholic Near East Welfare Association, 1011 1st Ave., New York NY 10022-4195. (212)826-1480. Fax: (212)838-1344. Editor: Michael La Cività. 50% freelance written. Bimonthly magazine for a Catholic audience with interest in the Near East, particularly its current religious, cultural and political aspects. Circ. 100,000. **Pays on acceptance.** Publishes ms an average of 4 months after acceptance. Byline given. Buys all rights. Reports in 3 months. Sample copy and writer's guidelines for 7½ × 10½ SAE with 2 first class stamps.
Nonfiction: "Cultural, devotional, political, historical material on the Near East, with an emphasis on the Eastern Christian churches. Style should be simple, factual, concise. Articles must stem from personal acquaintance with subject matter, or thorough up-to-date research." Length: 1,200-1,800 words. Pays 20¢/word.
Photos: "Photographs to accompany manuscript are welcome; they should illustrate the people, places, ceremonies, etc. which are described in the article. We prefer color transparencies but occasionally use b&w. Pay varies depending on use – scale from $50-300."
Tips: "We are interested in current events in the regions listed above as they affect the cultural, political and religious lives of people and vice versa."

‡CHICAGO STUDIES, Box 665, Mundelein IL 60060. (708)566-1462. Editor: Rev. George J. Dyer. 50% freelance written. Triannual magazine for Roman Catholic priests and religious educators. Estab. 1962. Circ. 8,200. **Pays on acceptance.** Buys all rights. Reports in 2 months. Sample copy $5. Free writer's guidelines.
Nonfiction: Nontechnical discussion of theological, Biblical and ethical topics. Articles aimed at a nontechnical presentation of the contemporary scholarship in those fields. Submit complete ms. Buys 30 mss/year. Length: 3,000-4,000 words. Pays $35-100.

THE CHRISTIAN CENTURY, 407 S. Dearborn St., Chicago IL 60605-1150. (312)427-5380. Editor: James M. Wall. Senior Editors: Martin E. Marty and Dean Peerman. Managing Editor: David Heim. 70% freelance written. Eager to work with new/unpublished writers. Weekly magazine for ecumenically-minded, progressive church people, both clergy and lay. Circ. 37,000. Pays on publication. Publishes ms an average of 2 months after acceptance. Usually buys all rights. Reports in 2 months. Sample copy available for $2. All queries, mss should be accompanied by SASE.
Nonfiction: "We use articles dealing with social problems, ethical dilemmas, political issues, international affairs and the arts, as well as with theological and ecclesiastical matters. We focus on concerns that arise at the juncture between church and society, or church and culture." Query appreciated, but not essential. Length: 2,500 words maximum. Payment varies, but averages $30/page.

CHRISTIAN HOME & SCHOOL, Christian Schools International, 3350 East Paris Ave. SE, Grand Rapids MI 49512. (616)957-1070. Executive Editor: Gordon L. Bordewyk. Senior Editor: Roger Schmurr. 30% freelance written. Works with a small number of new/unpublished writers each year. Bimonthly magazine covering family life and Christian education. "For parents who support Christian education. We feature material on a wide range of topics of interest to parents." Estab. 1922. Pays on publication. Publishes ms an average of 4 months after acceptance. Byline given. Buys first North American serial rights. Submit seasonal material 4 months in advance. Simultaneous queries OK. Reports in 1 month. Sample copy for 9 × 12 SAE with 4 first class stamps. Writer's guidelines for #10 SASE.
Nonfiction: Book excerpts, interview/profile, opinion, personal experience and articles on parenting and school life. "We publish features on issues which affect the home and school and profiles on interesting individuals, providing that the profile appeals to our readers and is not a tribute or eulogy of that person." Buys 40 mss/year. Send complete ms. Length: 500-2,000 words. Pays $75-150. Sometimes pays the expenses of writers on assignment.
Photos: "If you have any b&w photos appropriate for your article, send them along."
Tips: "Features are the area most open to freelancers. We are publishing articles that deal with contemporary issues that affect parents. Use an informal easy-to-read style rather than a philosophical, academic tone. Try to incorporate vivid imagery and concrete, practical examples from real life."

‡CHRISTIAN READER, A Digest of the Best in Christian Reading, Christianity Today, 465 Gundersen Dr., Carol Stream IL 60188. (708)260-6200. Editor: Bonne Steffen. 80% freelance written. Bimonthly magazine for "evangelical Christian audience, especially women 35 and older." Estab. 1962. Circ. 200,000. **Pays on acceptance.** Byline given. Buys first North American serial, first or second serial (reprint) rights. Editorial lead time 6 months. Submit seasonal material 9 months in advance. Previously published submissions OK.

Reports in 6 months on mss; 1 month on queries. Sample copy for 5 × 8 SAE with 2 first class stamps. Writer's guidelines for #10 SASE.
Nonfiction: Book excerpts, humor, inspirational, personal experience and religious. Buys 120 mss/year. Query. Length: 500-1,500 words. Pays $100 minimum for unsolicited articles; $45 for reprinted articles. Pays expenses of writers on assignment.
Photos: State availability of photos with submission. Reviews 35mm 4 × 6 transparencies. Negotiates payment individually. Buys one-time rights.
Columns/Departments: Mary Ann Jeffreys, editorial coordinator. Lite Fare (adult church humor), 25-150 words; and Kids of the Kingdom (kids say and do funny things), 25-150 words; Rolling Down the Aisle (humorous wedding tales), 25-250 words. Buys 200 mss/year. Send complete ms. Pays $25.

CHRISTIAN SINGLE, Family Ministry Dept., Baptist Sunday School Board, 127 9th Ave. N., Nashville TN 37234. (615)251-4124. Editor: Stephen Felts. 30% freelance written. Prefers to work with published/established writers. Monthly "contemporary Christian magazine that seeks to give substantive information to singles for living the abundant life. It seeks to be constructive and creative in approach." Circ. 70,000. **Pays on acceptance.** Publishes ms 6-12 months after acceptance. Byline given. Buys all rights or makes work-for-hire assignments. Submit seasonal material 6 months in advance. Reports in 2 months. Reprints OK; send typed ms with rights for sale noted. Pays 75% of their fee for an original article. Sample copy and writer's guidelines for 9 × 12 SASE with 4 first class stamps.
Nonfiction: Humor (good, clean humor that applies to Christian singles); how-to (specific subjects which apply to singles); inspirational (of the personal experience type); high adventure personal experience (of single adults); photo feature (on outstanding Christian singles); financial articles targeted to single adults. Buys 60-75 unsolicited mss/year. Query with published clips. Length: 600-1,200 words. Pays 5½¢/word.
Fiction: "We are also looking for fiction suitable for our target audience."
Tips: "We are looking for people who experience single living from a positive, Christian perspective."

CHRISTIANITY & CRISIS, 537 W. 121st St., New York NY 10027. (212)662-5907. Editor: Leon Howell. Managing Editor: Vivian Lindermayer. 10% freelance written. Works with a small number of new/unpublished writers each year. Biweekly Protestant journal of opinion. "We are interested in foreign affairs, domestic, economic and social policy, and theological developments with social or ethical implications, e.g., feminist, black and liberation theologies. As an independent religious journal it is part of *C&C*'s function to discuss church policies from a detached and sometimes critical perspective. We carry no 'devotional' material but welcome solid contemplative reflections. Most subscribers are highly educated, well-informed." Estab. 1941. Circ. 14,000. Pays on publication. Publishes ms an average of 2 months after acceptance. Byline given. Offers variable kill fee. Submit seasonal material 2 months in advance. Simultaneous queries OK. Reports in 1 month. Sample copy $1.75 for 9 × 12 SAE with 2 first class stamps. Writer's guidelines for #10 SASE.
Nonfiction: Buys 150 mss/year. Query with or without published clips. Length: 1,000-4,000 words. Pays 3¢/word. Rarely pays expenses of writers on assignment.
Tips: "We have been publishing more international stories and need to build up reporting on US issues."

CHRISTIANITY TODAY, 465 Gundersen Dr., Carol Stream IL 60188-2498. Fax: (708)260-0114. 80% freelance written. Works with a small number of new/unpublished writers each year. Semimonthly magazine emphasizing orthodox, evangelical religion. Circ. 180,000. Publishes ms an average of 6 months after acceptance. Usually buys first serial rights. Submit seasonal material at least 8 months in advance. Reprints OK; send typed ms with rights for sale noted and information about when and where the article previously appeared. Pays 25% of their fee for an original article. Reports in 2 months. Sample copy and writer's guidelines for 9 × 12 SAE with 3 first class stamps.
Nonfiction: Theological, ethical, historical and informational (not merely inspirational). Buys 4 mss/issue. *Query only.* Unsolicited mss not accepted and not returned. Length: 1,000-4,000 words. Pays negotiable rates. Sometimes pays the expenses of writers on assignment.
   ● This magazine is swamped with mss about events in the former Soviet Union and Eastern Bloc. Queries on this subject must have unique angle as well as general appeal.
Columns/Departments: Church in Action (profiles of not-so-well-known Christians involved in significant or offbeat services). Buys 7 mss/year. Query only. Length: 900-1,000 words.
Tips: "We are developing more of our own manuscripts and requiring a much more professional quality of others. Queries without SASE will not be answered and manuscripts not containing SASE will not be returned."

CHRISTMAS, The Annual of Christmas Literature and Art, Augsburg Fortress Publishers, P.O. Box 1209, Minneapolis MN 55440. (612)330-3442. Editor: Kristine Oberg. 70-100% freelance written. "Annual literary magazine "that celebrates Christmas, focusing on the effect of God's love on the lives of people, and how it colors and shapes Christmas traditions and celebrations." Estab. 1931. **Pays on acceptance.** Byline given. Buys first rights, one-time rights and all rights; makes work-for-hire assignments. Submit seasonal material 18 months in advance (by March for the following year). Reports in 1 month on queries; 3 months on mss. Sample copy $12.95 plus postage. Contact customer service at (800)328-4648 for sample copy.

Nonfiction: Historical/nostalgic (on Christmas customs); inspirational, interview/profile, personal experience and travel. Focuses on family-oriented articles. Articles on art and music with Christmas relationships. Buys 3-4 mss/year. Query with published clips or send complete ms. Length: 2,000-3,000 words. Pays $300-450.

Photos: State availability of photos with submission. Reviews transparencies. Offers $15-100/photo. Captions and identification of subjects required. Buys one-time rights.

Fiction: Short stories with Christmas theme. "No stories of fictionalized characters at the Bethlehem stable. No Santas. Fiction should be true to the biblical heritage of Christmas without being didactic or preachy." Buys 3-4 mss/year. Send complete ms. Length: 1,500-5,000 words. Pays $300-450.

Poetry: Free verse, light verse and traditional. No poetry dealing with Santa Claus. Buys 2-3 poems/year. Submit maximum 3 poems. Pays $75-150.

CHRYSALIS, Journal of the Swedenborg Foundation, P.O. Box 549, West Chester PA 19381-0549. Send inquiries and mss directly to the editorial office: Route 1, Box 184, Dillwyn VA 23936. Editor: Carol S. Lawson. Managing Editor: Susanna van Rensselaer. 50% freelance written. Triannual literary magazine on spiritually related topics. *"It is very important to send for writer's guidelines and sample copies before submitting.* Content of fiction, articles, reviews, poetry, etc., should be directly focused on that issue's theme and directed to the educated, intellectually curious reader." Estab. 1985. Circ. 3,000. Pays at page-proof stage. Publishes ms an average of 9 months after acceptance. Byline given. Buys first rights and makes work-for-hire assignments. Reports in 1 month on queries; 2 months on mss. Sample copy and writer's guidelines $5 for 9 × 12 SAE. Writer's guidelines and copy deadlines for SASE.

Nonfiction: Essays and interview/profile. Upcoming Themes: Spring 1994: The Future of Religion; Summer 1994: Music; Autumn 1994: Order; Spring 1995: Invention; Summer 1995: Children and Education; Autumn 1995: Windows. Buys 15 mss/year. Query. Length: 750-2,500 words. Pays $50-250 for assigned articles; $50-150 for unsolicited articles.

Photos: Send suggestions for illustrations with submission. Offers no additional payment for photos accepted with ms. Captions and identification of subjects required. Buys original artwork for cover and inside copy; pays $25-150. Buys one-time rights.

Columns/Departments: Vital Issues (articles and material related to practical psychology, health, healing), 750-2,000 words; Patterns (philosophical inquiry into the underlying patterns found within reality), 750-2,000 words; Currents (articles and material on the fine and visionary arts); 750-2,000 words; and Fringe Benefits (book, film, art, video reviews relevant to *Chrysalis* subject matter), 350-500 words. Buys 12 mss/year. Length: 350-2,000. Pays $50-250.

Fiction: Phoebe Loughrey, fiction editor. Adventure, experimental, historical, mainstream, mystery and science fiction, related to theme of issue. Buys 6 mss/year. Query. Length: 500-2,500 words. Short fiction more likely to be published. Pays $50-150.

Poetry: Avante-garde and traditional *but not religious.* Buys 10 poems/year. Pays $25. Submit maximum 6.

THE CHURCH HERALD, 4500 60th St. SE, Grand Rapids MI 49512-9642. Editor: Jeffrey Japinga. Managing Editor: Christina Van Eyl. 5% freelance written. Prefers to work with published/established writers. Monthly magazine covering contemporary Christian life. *"The Church Herald* is the denominational publication of the Reformed Church in America, a Protestant denomination in the Presbyterian-Reformed family of churches. We will consider carefully researched and well-written articles on almost any subject, but they all must have a distinctively Christian perspective and have some connection with our intended denominational audience." Circ. 40,000. **Pays on acceptance.** Publishes ms an average of 3 months after acceptance. Byline given. Offers 50% kill fee. Buys first, one-time, second serial (reprint), simultaneous and all rights. Submit seasonal material 6 months in advance. Simultaneous and previously published submissions OK. Query for electronic submissions. Reports in 1 month on queries; 2 months on mss. Sample copy and writer's guidelines $2 for 9 × 12 SAE.

Nonfiction: Essays, general interest, humor, inspirational, personal experience and religious. Buys 30 mss/year. Queries only; unsolicited mss returned. Length: 400-1,500 words. Pays $50-200 for assigned articles. Pays $50-150 for unsolicited articles. Sometimes pays expenses of writers on assignment.

Photos: State availability of photos with submission. Reviews color transparencies and 8 × 10 b&w prints. Offers $25-50/photo. Model releases required. Buys one-time rights.

Fiction: Religious. "We consider good fiction written from a Christian perspective. Avoid pious sentimentality and obvious plots." Buys 5 mss/year. Send complete ms. Length: 400-1,500 words. Pays $45-120.

● No longer considering poetry.

Tips: "Research articles carefully. Superficial articles are immediately recognizable; they cannot be disguised by big words or professional jargon. Writers need not have personally experienced everything they write about, but they must have done careful research. Also, what our readers want are new solutions to recognized problems. If a writer doesn't have any, he or she should try another subject. Section most open to freelancers is feature articles."

COLUMBIA, 1 Columbus Plaza, New Haven CT 06507. Editor: Richard McMunn. Monthly magazine for Catholic families. Caters particularly to members of the Knights of Columbus. Estab. 1921. Circ. 1.5 million. **Pays on acceptance.** Buys first serial rights. Free sample copy and writer's guidelines.
Nonfiction and Photos: Fact articles directed to the Catholic layman and his family dealing with current events, social problems, Catholic apostolic activities, education, ecumenism, rearing a family, literature, science, arts, sports and leisure. Color glossy prints, transparencies or contact prints with negatives are required for illustration. Articles without ample illustrative material are not given consideration. Pays up to $500, including photos. Buys 30 mss/year. Query. Length: 1,000-1,500 words.

COMMENTS, From the Friends, P.O. Box 840, Stoughton MA 02072-0840. Editor: David A. Reed. 10% freelance written. Quarterly Christian newsletter written especially for "Jehovah's Witnesses, ex-Jehovah's Witnesses and persons concerned about Jehovah's Witness, relatives, friends, and neighbors." Estab. 1981. Circ. 1,500. Pays on publication. Publishes ms an average of 3 months after acceptance. Byline sometimes given. Buys second serial (reprint) and simultaneous rights. Submit seasonal/holiday material 4 months in advance. Simultaneous and previously published submissions OK. Pays 50% of their fee for an original article. Query for electronic submissions. Reports in 1 month on mss. *Writer's Market* recommends allowing 2 months for reply. Sample copy $1 for #10 SAE with 2 first class stamps. Writer's guidelines for #10 SAE with 2 first class stamps.
Nonfiction: Book excerpts, essays, expose, how-to (witnessing tips), humor, inspirational (aimed at JW's and ex-JW's *only*), interview/profile, personal experience, religious and book reviews of books on cults only. "No general religious material not written specifically for our unique readership." Buys 4 mss/year. Send complete ms. Length: 200-1,000 words. Pays $2-20. May pay with contributor copies rather than a cash payment "when a writer contributes an article as a gift to this ministry."
Columns/Departments: Witnessing Tips (brief, powerful and effective approaches), 250-300 words; and News Briefs (current events involving Jehovah's Witnesses and ex-Jehovah's Witnesses), 60-240 words. Buys 4 mss/year. Send complete ms. Length: 60-300 words. Pays $2-10.
Fillers: Facts, newsbreaks and quotes. Buys 4/year. Length: 10-50 words. Pays $1-5.
Tips: "Acquaint us with your background that qualifies you to write in this field. Write well-documented, germane articles in layman's language."

CONSCIENCE, A Newsjournal of Prochoice Catholic Opinion, Catholics for a Free Choice, Suite 301, 1436 U St. NW, Washington DC 20009-3997. (202)986-6093. Editor: Maggie Hume. 80% freelance written. Willing to work with new/unpublished writers. Quarterly newsjournal covering reproductive rights, specifically abortion rights in area of church, and church and government in U.S. and worldwide. "A feminist, prochoice perspective is a must, and knowledge of Christianity and specifically Catholicism is helpful." Circ. 12,000. Pays on publication. Publishes ms an average of 4 months after acceptance. Byline given. Buys first North American serial rights; makes work-for-hire assignments. Submit seasonal material 6 months in advance. Simultaneous queries and previously published submissions OK; send tearsheet or photocopy of article. Pays 20-30% of their fee for an original article. Query for electronic submissions. Reports in 2 months. Sample copy for 9×12 SASE with 98¢ postage. Writer's guidelines for #10 SASE.
● This magazine is increasingly international in focus.
Nonfiction: Book excerpts, interview/profile, opinion and personal experience. Especially needs material that recognizes the complexity of reproductive issues and decisions, and offers original, honest insight. Buys 8-12 mss/year. Query with published clips or send complete ms. Length: 1,000-3,500 words. Pays $25-150. "Writers should be aware that we are a nonprofit organization." Sometimes pays the expenses of writers on assignment.
Photos: State availability of photos with query or ms. Prefers b&w prints. Identification of subjects required.
Columns/Departments: Book reviews. Buys 6-10 mss/year. Send complete ms. Length: 600-1,200 words. Pays $25-50.
Fillers: Newsbreaks. Uses 6/year. Length: 100-300 words. $25-35.
Tips: "Say something new on the abortion issue. Thoughtful, well-researched and well-argued articles needed. The most frequent mistakes made by writers in completing an article for us are lack of originality and wordiness."

CORNERSTONE, Cornerstone Communications, Inc., 939 W. Wilson, Chicago IL 60640-5718. Editor: Dawn Herrin. Submissions Editor: Jennifer Ingerson. 10% freelance written. Eager to work with new/unpublished writers. Bimonthly magazine covering contemporary issues in the light of Evangelical Christianity. Estab. 1972. Circ. 50,000. Pays after publication. Byline given. Buys first serial rights. Submit seasonal material 6 months in advance. Simultaneous and previously published submissions OK. Manuscripts *not* returned. "Send copies, not originals. If work is considered for publication, we will contact." Reports in 8-12 weeks. Sample copy and writer's guidelines for 8½×11 envelope with 5 first class stamps.

Nonfiction: Essays, personal experience and religious. Buys 1-2 mss/year. Query. 2,700 words maximum. Pays negotiable rate, 8-10¢/word. Sometimes pays the expenses of writers on assignment.

Photos: Send photos with accompanying ms. Reviews 8 × 10 b&w and color prints and 35mm slides. Identification of subjects required. Buys negotiable rights.

Columns/Departments: Music (interview with artists, mainly rock, focusing on artist's world view and value system as expressed in his/her music); Current Events; Personalities; and Film and Book Reviews (focuses on meaning as compared and contrasted to biblical values). Buys 1-4 mss/year. Query. Length: 100-2,500 words (negotiable). Pays negotiable rate, 8-10¢/word.

Fiction: "Articles may express Christian world view but should not be unrealistic or 'syrupy.' Other than porn, the sky's the limit. We want fiction as creative as the Creator." Buys 1-4 mss/year. Send complete ms. Length: 250-2,500 words (negotiable). Pays negotiable rate, 8-10¢/word.

Poetry: Avant-garde, free verse, haiku, light verse and traditional. No limits *except* for epic poetry ("We've not the room!"). Buys 10-50 poems/year. Submit maximum 5 poems. Payment negotiated. 1-15 lines: $10. 16+ lines: $25.

Tips: "A display of creativity which expresses a biblical world view without clichés or cheap shots at non-Christians is the ideal. We are known as one of the most avant-garde magazines in the Christian market, yet attempt to express orthodox beliefs in language of the '90s. *Any* writer who does this may well be published by *Cornerstone*. Creative fiction is begging for more Christian participation. We anticipate such contributions gladly. Interviews where well-known personalities respond to the gospel are also strong publication possibilities."

THE COVENANT COMPANION, Covenant Publications of the Evangelical Covenant Church, 5101 N. Francisco Ave., Chicago IL 60625. (312)784-3000. Fax: (312)784-4366. Editor: James R. Hawkinson. 10-15% freelance written. "As the official monthly organ of The Evangelical Covenant Church, we seek to inform, stimulate and gather the denomination we serve by putting Covenants in touch with each other and assisting them in interpreting contemporary issues. We also seek to inform them on events in the church. Our background is evangelical and our emphasis is on Christian commitment and life." Circ. 23,500. Publishes ms an average of 2 months after acceptance. Byline given. Buys first or all rights. Submit seasonal material 4 months in advance. Simultaneous and previously published submissions OK. Query for electronic submissions. Sample copy $2.25 for 9 × 12 SASE. writer's guidelines for #10 SASE. Unused mss returned only if accompanied by SASE.

Nonfiction: Humor, inspirational and religious. Buys 20-25 mss/year. Send complete ms. Length: 500-2,000 words. Pays $15-50 for assigned articles; pays $15-35 for unsolicited articles.

Photos: Send photos with submissions. Reviews prints. Offers no additonal payment for photos accepted with ms. Identification of subjects required. Buys one-time rights.

Poetry: Traditional. Buys 10-15 poems/year. Submit maximum 10 poems. Pays $10-15.

Tips: "Seasonal articles related to church year and on national holidays are welcome."

DECISION, Billy Graham Evangelistic Association, 1300 Harmon Place, Minneapolis MN 55403-1988. (612)338-0500. Fax: (612)335-1299. Editor: Roger C. Palms. 25-40% freelance written. Works each year with small number of new/unpublished writers, as well as a solid stable of experienced writers. Magazine published 11 times/year, "to set forth to every reader the Good News of salvation in Jesus Christ with such vividness and clarity that he or she will be drawn to make a commitment to Christ; to encourage, teach and strengthen Christians." Estab. 1960. Circ. 1.8 million. Pays on publication. Byline given. Buys first rights and assigns work-for-hire manuscripts, articles, projects. Include telephone number with submission. Submit seasonal material 10 months in advance; other mss published up to 18 months after acceptance. Reports in 3 months on mss. Sample copy for 9 × 12 SAE with 4 first class stamps. Writer's guidelines for #10 SASE.

Nonfiction: How-to, motivational, personal experience and religious. "No personality-centered articles or articles which are issue-oriented or critical of denominations." Buys approximately 75 mss/year. Send complete ms. Length: 400-1,800 words. Pays $30-225. Pays expenses of writers on assignment.

Photos: State availability of photos with submission. Reviews prints. Captions, model releases and identification of subjects required. Buys one-time rights.

Poetry: Accepting submissions. Query.

Tips: "We are seeking personal conversion testimonies and personal experience articles which show how God intervened in a person's daily life and the way in which Scripture was applied to the experience in helping to solve the problem. The conversion testimonies describe in first person what author's life was like before he/she became a Christian, how he/she committed his/her life to Christ and what tangible difference He has made since that decision. We also are looking for vignettes on various aspects of personal evangelism. SASE required with submissions."

‡THE DOOR, Box 530, Yreka CA 96097. (916)842-2701. Contact: Bob Darden. (817)752-1468. 40% freelance written. Works with a small number of new/unpublished writers each year. Bimonthly magazine for men and women connected with the church. Circ. 11,000. Pays on publication. Publishes ms an average of 1 year after acceptance. Buys first rights. Publishes reprints of previously published articles. Send typed ms with rights for sale noted, including information about when and where the article previously appeared. Reports in 3 months.

Nonfiction: Satirical articles on church renewal, Christianity and organized religion. Few book reviews. Buys about 30 mss/year. Submit complete ms. Length: 1,500 words maximum, 750-1,000 preferred. Pays $60-200. Sometimes pays expenses of writers on assignments.

Tips: "We look for someone who is clever, on our wave length, and has some savvy about the evangelical church. We are very picky and highly selective. The writer has a better chance of breaking in with our publication with short articles and fillers since we are a bimonthly publication with numerous regular features and the magazine is only 36 pages. The most frequent mistake made by writers is that they do not understand satire. They see we are a humor magazine and consequently come off funny/cute (like *Reader's Digest*) rather than funny/satirical (like *National Lampoon*)."

EPISCOPAL LIFE, Episcopal Church in the United States, 815 2nd Ave., New York NY 10017. (212)922-5398. Editor: Jerrold F. Hames. Managing Editor: Edward P. Stannard. 35% freelance written. Monthly tabloid of news, information, viewpoints of Episcopal Church and ecumenical interest to Episcopalians in the US. Estab. 1990. Circ. 180,000. Pays on publication. Publishes ms an average of 2 months after acceptance. Byline given. Offers 50% kill fee. Buys one-time rights and makes work-for-hire assignments. Submit seasonal material 4 months in advance. Simultaneous and previously published submissions OK. Query for electronic submissions. Reports in 1 month. Free sample copy.

Nonfiction: Inspirational, interview/profile and religious. Needs freelance material for Christmas, Easter, education issue, book issue and environmental issue. No first-person articles. Buys 12 mss/year. Query with published clips. Length: 250-1,200 words. Pays $50-300. Pays expenses of writers on assignment.

Photos: State availability of photos with submission. Offers $50-75/photo. Identification of subjects required. Buys one-time rights.

Columns/Departments: Nan Cobbey, departments editor. Buys 36 mss/year. Query with published clips. Length: 300-600 words. Pays $35-75.

EVANGEL, Free Methodist Publishing House, P.O. Box 535002, Indianapolis IN 46253-5002. (317)244-3660. Fax: (317)244-1247. Editor: Vera Bethel. 100% freelance written. Weekly magazine. Estab. 1897. Circ. 26,000. Pays on publication. Publishes ms an average of 1 year after acceptance. Buys simultaneous, second serial (reprint) or one-time rights. Submit seasonal material 3 months in advance. Reports in 1 month. Sample copy and writer's guidelines for 6×9 SAE with 2 first class stamps.

Nonfiction: Interview (with ordinary person who is doing something extraordinary in his community, in service to others); profile (of missionary or one from similar service profession who is contributing significantly to society); and personal experience (finding a solution to a problem common to young adults; coping with handicapped child, for instance, or with a neighborhood problem. Story of how God-given strength or insight saved a situation). Buys 100 mss/year. Submit complete ms. Length: 300-1,000 words. Pays $10-25.

Photos: Purchased with accompanying ms. Captions required. Send prints. Pays $10 for 8×10 b&w glossy prints.

Fiction: Religious themes dealing with contemporary issues dealt with from a Christian frame of reference. Story must "go somewhere." Buys 50 mss/year. Submit complete ms. Length: 1,200 words. Pays $45.

Poetry: Free verse, haiku, light verse, traditional and religious. Buys 50 poems/year. Submit maximum 6 poems. Length: 4-24 lines. Pays $10.

Tips: "Seasonal material will get a second look (won't be rejected so easily). Write an attention grabbing lead followed by an article that says something worthwhile. Relate the lead to some of the universal needs of the reader—promise in that lead to help the reader in some way. Lack of SASE brands author as a nonprofessional; I seldom even bother to read the script." Prefers non-justified righthand margin.

EVANGELIZING TODAY'S CHILD, Child Evangelism Fellowship Inc., Box 348, Warrenton MO 63383-3420. (314)456-4321. Editor: Elsie Lippy. 75% freelance written. Prefers to work with published/established writers. Bimonthly magazine "for Sunday school teachers, Christian education leaders and children's workers in every phase of Christian ministry to children up to 12 years old. Our purpose is to equip Christians to win the world's children to Christ and disciple them." Estab. 1942. Circ. 22,000. Pays within 90 days of acceptance. Publishes ms an average of 6 months after acceptance. Byline given. Pays a kill fee if assigned. Buys first serial rights. Submit seasonal material 6 months in advance. Simultaneous queries OK. Reprints OK; send tearsheet of article. Pays 25% of their fee for an original article. Reports in 2 months. Sample copy for 9×12 SAE and 5 first class stamps; writer's guidelines for SASE.

Nonfiction: Unsolicited articles welcomed from writers with Christian education, training or current experience in working with children. Buys 25 mss/year. Query. Length: 1,200-1,500. Pays 8-10¢/word.

Photos: Submissions of photos on speculation accepted. Needs photos of children or related subjects. Pays $35 for 8×10 b&w glossy prints; $95 for inside color prints or transparencies; $125 for cover transparencies.

THE FAMILY—A Catholic perspective, Daughters of St. Paul, 50 St. Paul's Ave., Boston MA 02130. (617)522-8911. Editor: Sr. Mary Lea Hill. Monthly magazine on Catholic family life. "*The Family* magazine stresses the special place of the family within society as an irreplaceable center of life, love and faith. Articles on timely, pertinent issues help families approach today's challenges with a faith perspective and a spirit of commitment to the Gospel of Jesus Christ." Estab. 1952. Pays on publication. Publishes ms an average of 6 months after acceptance. Byline given. Buys first and second serial (reprint) rights. Reimbursement for reprints varies. Submit seasonal material 5 months in advance. Previously published submissions OK. Reports in 2 months. Sample copy $1.75 for 9 × 12 SAE with 5 first class stamps. Writer's guidelines for #10 SASE.

Nonfiction: Humor, inspirational, interview/profile, religious. Buys 70 mss/year. Send complete ms. Length: 500-1,500 words. Pays $50-125. Also may pay in contributor's copies.

Photos: Send photos with submission. Reviews 4 × 5 transparencies. Captions, model releases and identification of subjects required. Buys one-time rights.

Fiction: Humorous, religious, slice-of-life vignettes and family. Buys 12 mss/year. Send complete ms. Length: 1,000-2,000 words. Pays $50-125.

Fillers: Anecdotes, short humor. Buys 30/year. Length: 100-300 words. Pays $10-30.

‡**THE FAMILY DIGEST,** (formerly *Parish Family Digest*), P.O. Box 40137, Fort Wayne IN 46804. Editor: Corine B. Erlandson. 95% freelance written. Bimonthly magazine "geared to the life of the Catholic family, as well as the life of the Catholic parish." Estab. 1945. Circ. 150,000. **Pays on acceptance.** Publishes ms an average of 6-12 months after acceptance. Byline given. Buys first North American rights. Submit seasonal material 7 months in advance. Reports in 1 month. Sample copy and writer's guidelines for 6 × 9 SAE with 2 first class stamps.

Nonfiction: Family life, parish life, how-to, seasonal, inspirational and prayer life. Send ms with SASE. No poetry or fiction. Buys 55 unsolicited mss/year. Length: 750-1,100 words. Pays 5¢/word.

Photos: State availability of photos with ms. Pays $10 for preferably b&w prints. Buys one-time rights. Captions preferred; model releases required.

Fillers: Anecdotes and short humor. Buys 5/issue. Length: 100 words maximum.

Tips: "Prospective freelance contributors should be familiar with the publication, and the types of articles accepted and published. We rarely use reprints; we prefer fresh material that will hold up over time and is not tied to an event in the news. We are more oriented to families with kids and the problems such families face in the Church and society; in particular, the struggle to raise good Catholic kids in a secular society. Articles on family and parish life, including seasonal articles, how-to pieces, inspirational and humorous stories, will be gladly reviewed for possible publication."

GROUP MAGAZINE, P.O. Box 481, Loveland CO 80538. (303)669-3836. Fax: (303)669-3269. Editor: Rick Lawrence. Managing Editor: Cindy Parolini. 60% freelance written. Magazine published 8 times/year covering youth ministry. "Writers must be actively involved in youth ministry. Articles we accept are practical, not theoretical, and focused for local church youth workers." Estab. 1974. Circ. 57,000. **Pays on acceptance.** Publishes ms an average of 6 months after acceptance. Byline given. Offers $20 kill fee. Buys all rights. Submit seasonal material 7 months in advance. Reports in 1 month. Sample copy for 9 × 12 SAE with 3 first class stamps. Writer's guidelines for 9 × 12 SAE with 2 first class stamps.

Nonfiction: How-to (youth ministry issues). No personal testimony, theological or lecture-style articles. Buys 50-60 mss/year. Query. Length: 500-1,800 words. Pays $75-200. Sometimes pays for phone calls on agreement.

Photos: State availability of photos with submission. Model releases and identification of subjects required. Buys all rights.

GROWING CHURCHES, 127 9th Ave. N., Nashville TN 37234. (615)251-2485. Fax: (615)251-5091. Design Editor: David T. Seay. 30% freelance written. Works with new/unpublished writers. Quarterly magazine for Southern Baptist pastors, staff and volunteer church leaders. **Pays on acceptance.** Publishes ms an average of 1 year after acceptance. Byline given. Buys all rights. Free sample copy and writer's guidelines for SAE with 2 first class stamps.

Nonfiction: "This is a magazine that focuses on practical church growth ideas for Southern Baptists." Length: 1,200-1,800 words. Pays 5½¢/word.

Tips: "Send query letter. Articles must be targeted to Southern Baptist churches and their leaders. Type at 54 characters/line, 25 lines/page, double-spaced. Not responsible for manuscripts not accompanied by return postage."

GUIDEPOSTS MAGAZINE, 16 E. 34th St., New York NY 10016. Editor: Fulton Oursler, Jr. 30% freelance written. "Works with a small number of new/unpublished writers each year. *Guideposts* is an inspirational monthly magazine for people of all faiths, in which men and women from all walks of life tell in first-person narrative how they overcame obstacles, rose above failures, handled sorrow, learned to master themselves and became more effective people through faith in God." Estab. 1945. Publishes ms an "indefinite" number of months after acceptance. Pays 25% kill fee for assigned articles. "Most of our stories are ghosted articles, so the writer would not get a byline unless it was his/her own story." Buys all rights and second serial (reprint) rights.

Nonfiction and Fillers: Articles and features should be written in simple, anecdotal style with an emphasis on human interest. Short mss of approximately 250-750 words (pays $50-200) considered for such features as Quiet People and general one-page stories. Address short items to Rick Hamlin. For full-length mss, 750-

1,500 words, pays $200-400. All mss should be typed, double-spaced and accompanied by SASE. Annually awards scholarships to high school juniors and seniors in writing contest. Buys 40-60 unsolicited mss/year. Pays expenses of writers on assignment.

Tips: "Study the magazine before you try to write for it. Each story must make a single spiritual point. The freelancer would have the best chance of breaking in by aiming for a one- or two-page article. Sensitively written anecdotes are extremely useful. And it is much easier to just sit down and write them than to have to go through the process of preparing a query. They should be warm, well written, intelligent and upbeat. We like personal narratives that are true and have some universal relevance, but the religious element does not have to be driven home with a sledge hammer. A writer succeeds with us if he or she can write a true article in short-story form with scenes, drama, tension and a resolution of the problem presented."

HICALL, Gospel Publishing House, 1445 Boonville Ave., Springfield MO 65802-1894. (417)862-2781, ext. 4349. Editor: Deanna Harris. Mostly freelance written. Eager to work with new/unpublished writers. Weekly magazine, Assemblies of God denomination, of Christian fiction and articles for church-oriented teenagers, ages 12-17. Circ. 85,000. **Pays on acceptance.** Publishes ms an average of 15 months after acceptance. Byline given. Buys first North American serial, one-time, simultaneous and second serial (reprint) rights. Submit seasonal material 18 months in advance. Simultaneous and previously published submissions OK. Reports in 6 weeks. Sample copy for 9 × 12 SAE with 2 first class stamps. Writer's guidelines for #10 SASE.

Nonfiction: Book excerpts, historical, general interest, how-to (deal with various life problems), humor, inspirational and personal experience. Buys 80-100 mss/year. Send complete ms. Length: 500-1,500 words. Pays 2-3¢/word.

Photos: Photos purchased with or without accompanying ms. Pays $35/8 × 10 b&w glossy print; $50/35mm slide.

Fiction: Adventure, humorous, mystery, romance, suspense and religious. Buys 80-100 mss/year. Send complete ms. Length: 500-1,500 words. Pays 2-3¢/word.

Poetry: Free verse, light verse and traditional. Buys 30 poems/year. Length: 10-40 lines. Pays 25¢/line, minimum of $5. Buys first rights.

Fillers: Puzzles. Buys 10/year. Pays 2-3¢/word.

Tips: "We need more male-oriented stories, articles, etc."

‡HOME TIMES, A Good Little Newspaper, Neighbor News, Inc., P.O. Box 16096, West Palm Beach FL 33416. (407)439-3509. Editor: Dennis Lombard. Biweekly tabloid of conservative, pro-Christian news and views. "*Home Times* is a conservative newspaper written for the general public but with a pro-Christian, family-values slant. It is not religious or preachy." Estab. 1988. Circ. 10,000. Pays on publication. Byline given. Buys one-time rights. Editorial lead time 1 month. Submit seasonal material 1 month in advance. Accepts simultaneous and previously published submissions. Reports in 1 week. *Writer's Market* recommends allowing 2 months for reply. Sample copy $1 for 9 × 12 SASE with 3 stamps. Writer's guidelines for #10 SASE.

Nonfiction: Book excerpts, essays, general interest, historical/nostalgic, how-to, humor, inspirational, interview/profile, opinion, personal experience, photo feature, religious and travel. "Nothing preachy, moralistic, religious or with churchy slant." Buys 50 mss/year. Send complete ms. Length: to 900 maximum words. Pays $5 minimum. Pays contributor's copies on mutual agreement. Sometimes pays expenses of writers on assignment.

Photos: Send photos with submission. Reviews 4 × 5 prints. Offers $5-10/photo. Captions, model releases and identification of subjects required. Buys one-time rights.

Columns/Departments: Buys 50 mss/year. Send complete ms. Pays $5-15.

Fiction: Historical, humorous, mainstream, religious and issue-oriented contemporary. "Nothing preachy, moralistic." Buys 5 mss/year. Send complete ms. Length: 500-1,200 words. Pays $5-25.

Poetry: Free verse, light verse and traditional. Buys 10 poems/year. Submit maximum 3 poems. Length: 2-24 lines. Pays $5-10.

Fillers: Anecdotes, facts, newsbreaks and short humor. Uses 25/year. Length: to 100 words.

Tips: "We encourage new writers. We are different from ordinary news or religious publications. We strongly suggest you read guidelines and sample issues. (3 issues $3 and 9 × 12 SASE w/3 stamps; writer's subscription 12 issues plus 3 samples $9.) We are most open to material for new columns; journalists covering hard news in major news centers—with a Conservative slant."

THE JEWISH WEEKLY NEWS, Or V'Shalom, Inc., P.O. Box 1569, Springfield MA 01101-1569. (413)739-4771. Editor: Kenneth G. White. 25% freelance written. Jewish news and features, secular and non-secular; World Judaism; arts (New England based). Estab. 1945. Circ. 2,500. Pays on publication. Publishes ms an average of 2 months after acceptance. Byline given. Not copyrighted. Buys first North American serial rights and second serial (reprint) rights. Submit seasonal material 2 months in advance. Simultaneous and previously published submissions OK. Query for electronic submissions. Sample copy for 9 × 12 SAE with 5 first class stamps.

Nonfiction: Interview/profile, religious and travel. Special issues include Jewish New Year (September); Chanukah (December); Bridal (Winter/Fall); Bar/Bat Mitzvahs (May). Buys 61 mss/year. Query with published clips. Length: 300-1,000 words. Pays 50¢/inch.

Photos: Send photos with submission. Reviews 5 × 7 prints. Offers no additional payment for photos accepted with ms. Identification of subjects required.

● No longer seeking fiction.

Columns/Departments: Jewish Kitchen (Kosher recipes), 300-500 words. Buys 10 mss/year. Query with published clips. Length: 300-5,000 words. Pays 50¢/inch.

LIGHT AND LIFE MAGAZINE, Free Methodist Church of North America, P.O. Box 535002, Indianapolis IN 46253-5002. Fax: (317)244-1247. Editor: Bob Haslam. 35% freelance written. Works with a small number of new/unpublished writers each year. Monthly magazine emphasizing evangelical Christianity with Wesleyan slant for a cross section of adults. Estab. 1868. Circ. 33,000. Pays on publication. Publishes ms an average of 6 months after acceptance. Byline given. Prefers first serial rights; rarely buys second serial (reprint) rights. Submit seasonal material 6 months in advance. Reports in 6 weeks. Sample copy and guidelines $1.50. Writer's guidelines for SASE.

Nonfiction: "We need fresh, upbeat articles showing the average layperson how to be Christ-like at home, work and play." Submit complete ms. Buys 50-60 unsolicited ms/year. Pays 4¢/word. Length: 500-600 or 1,000-1,200 words.

Photos: Purchased without accompanying ms. Send prints or slides. Pays $5-35 for color or b&w photos.

LIGUORIAN, Liguori MO 63057-9999. Fax: (314)464-8449. Editor: Rev. Allan Weinert. Managing Editor: Francine M. O'Connor. 25% freelance written. Prefers to work with published/established writers. Monthly magazine for families with Catholic religious convictions. Estab. 1913. Circ. 430,000. **Pays on acceptance.** Byline given "except on short fillers and jokes." Buys all rights but will reassign rights to author *after* publication upon written request. Submit seasonal material 6 months in advance. Query for electronic submissions. Reports in up to 6 months. Sample copy and writer's guidelines for 6 × 9 SAE with 3 first class stamps.

Nonfiction: "Pastoral, practical and personal approach to the problems and challenges of people today. No travelogue approach or unresearched ventures into controversial areas. Also, no material found in secular publications—fad subjects that already get enough press, pop psychology, negative or put-down articles." Buys 60 unsolicited mss/year. Buys 12 fiction mss/year. Length: 400-2,000 words. Pays 10-12¢/word. Sometimes pays expenses of writers on assignment.

Photos: Photographs on assignment only unless submitted with and specific to article.

LIVE, 1445 Boonville Ave., Springfield MO 65802-1894. (417)862-2781. Fax: (417)862-8558. 100% freelance written. Works with several new/unpublished writers each year. Weekly magazine for adults in Assemblies of God Sunday schools. Circ. 160,000. **Pays on acceptance.** Publishes ms an average of 1 year after acceptance. Not copyrighted. Submit seasonal material 6 months in advance. "Do not mention Santa Claus, Halloween or Easter bunnies. Submissions held for consideration require more time." Publishes reprints of previously published articles or short stories. Send tearsheet of article or short story or typed ms with rights for sale noted and information about when and where the article previously appeared. Reports in up to 1 year. Free sample copy and writer's guidelines for 7½ × 10½ SAE and 2 first class stamps. Letters without SASE will not be answered.

Nonfiction: In the narrative mode emphasizing some phase of Christian living presented in a down-to-earth manner. Biography or missionary material using narrative techniques, but must include verification. Historical, scientific, nature, humorous material with spiritual lesson. "Be accurate in detail and factual material. Writing for Christian publications is a ministry. The spiritual emphasis must be an integral part of your material." Prefers not to see material on highly controversial subjects but would appreciate stories on contemporary issues and concerns (e.g. substance abuse, AIDS, euthanasia, cults, integrity, etc.). Buys about 12 mss/year. Length: 1,000-1,600 words. Pays 3¢/word for first serial rights; 2¢/word for second serial (reprint) rights, according to the value of the material and the amount of editorial work necessary.

Photos: Color photos or transparencies purchased with mss. Pay open.

Fiction: "Present believable characters working out their problems according to Bible principles; in other words, present Christianity in action without being preachy. The stories (fictional or true) should tell themselves without moral lessons tacked on. We want multinational, ethnic, urban and intercultural characters. Use action, suspense, humor! Stories should be true to life but not what we would feel is a sinful pattern for living. Stories should not put parents, teachers, ministers or other Christian workers in a bad light. Setting, plot and action should be realistic, with strong motivation. Characterize so that the people will live in your story. Construct your plot carefully so that each incident moves naturally and suspensefully toward crisis and conclusion. *An element of conflict is necessary in fiction.* We do not accept fiction based on incidents in the Bible." Length: 1,000-1,500 words. Buys 120 mss/year. Pays 3¢/word for first serial rights; 2¢/word for second serial (reprint) rights.

Poetry: Traditional, free verse and blank verse. Length: 12-20 lines. "Please do not send large numbers of poems at one time." Pays 25¢/line.

Fillers: Brief and humorous, usually containing an anecdote, and always with a strong evangelical emphasis. Length: 200-600 words.

LIVING WITH TEENAGERS, Baptist Sunday School Board, 127 9th Ave. N., Nashville TN 37234. (615)251-2273. Fax: (615)251-3866. Editor: Ellen Oldacre. 50-75% freelance written. Works with a number of new/unpublished writers each year. Quarterly magazine about teenagers for parents of teenagers. Estab. 1978. Circ. 50,000. Pays within 2 months of acceptance. Publishes ms an average of 18 months after acceptance. Buys all rights. Publishes reprints of previously published articles or short stories. Send photocopy of article or short story and information about when and where the article previously appeared. Submit seasonal material 1 year in advance. Reports in 2 months. Sample copy for 9 × 12 SAE with 4 first class stamps. Writer's guidelines for #10 SASE.

Nonfiction: "We are looking for a unique Christian element. We want a genuine insight into the teen/parent relationship." General interest (on communication, emotional problems, growing up, drugs and alcohol, leisure, sex education, spiritual growth, working teens and parents, money, family relationships and church relationships); inspirational; and personal experience. Buys 60 unsolicited mss/year. Query with clips of previously published work. Length: 600-2,000 words. Pays 5½¢/published word.

Fiction: Humorous and religious, but must relate to parent/teen relationship. "No stories from the teen's point of view." Buys 2 mss/issue. Query with clips of previously published work. Length: 600-2,000 words. Pays 5½¢/published word.

Poetry: Free verse, light verse, traditional and devotional inspirational; all must relate to parent/teen relationship. Buys 3 mss/issue. Submit 5 poems maximum. Length: 35 lines maximum. Pays $2.10 plus $1.25/line for 1-7 lines; $5.40 plus 75¢/line for 8 lines minimum.

Tips: "A writer can meet our needs if they have something to say to parents of teenagers concerning an issue the parents are confronting with the teenager."

THE LOOKOUT, 8121 Hamilton Ave., Cincinnati OH 45231-9981. (513)931-4050. Fax: (513)931-0904. Editor: Simon J. Dahlman. 50-60% freelance written. Eager to work with new/unpublished writers. Weekly magazine for Christian adults, with emphasis on spiritual growth through Sunday schools and small groups. Audience is mainly conservative Christians. Estab. 1894. **Pays on acceptance.** Publishes ms an average of 6 months after acceptance. Byline given. Buys first serial, one-time, second serial (reprint) or simultaneous rights. Simultaneous submissions OK. Reprints OK; send typed ms with rights for sale noted and information about when and where the article previously appeared. Pays 60% of their fee for an original article. Reports in 4 months, sometimes longer. Sample copy and writer's guidelines for 50¢. Guidelines only for #10 SASE.

Nonfiction: "Seeks stories about real people; items that are helpful in practical Christian living (how-to's); items that shed Biblical light on matters of contemporary controversy; and items that motivate, that lead the reader to ask, 'Why shouldn't I try that?' Articles should tell how real people are involved for Christ. In choosing topics, *The Lookout* considers timeliness, the church and national calendar, and the ability of the material to fit the above guidelines. Remember to aim at laymen." Submit complete ms. Length: 500-2,000 words. Pays 4-8¢/word. We also use inspirational short pieces. "About 400-700 words is a good length for these. Relate an incident that illustrates a point without preaching."

Fiction: "A short story is printed in many issues; it is usually between 1,200-2,000 words long and should be as true to life as possible while remaining inspirational and helpful. Use familiar settings and situations. Most often we use stories with a Christian slant." Pays 5-8¢/word.

Photos: Reviews b&w prints, 4 × 6 or larger. Pays $25-50. Pays $75-200 for color transparencies for covers and inside use. Needs photos of people, especially adults in a variety of settings. Send to Photo Editor, Standard Publishing, at the above address.

THE LUTHERAN, Magazine of the Evangelical Lutheran Church in America, Evangelical Lutheran Church in America, 8765 W. Higgins Rd., Chicago IL 60631-4183. (312)380-2540. Fax: (312)380-2751. Editor: Edgar R. Trexler. Managing Editor: Roger R. Kahle. 30% freelance written. Monthly magazine for "lay people in church. News and activities of the Evangelical Lutheran Church in America, news of the world of religion, ethical reflections on issues in society, personal Christian experience." Estab. 1988. Circ. 960,000. **Pays on acceptance.** Publishes ms an average of 3 months after acceptance. Byline given. Offers 50% kill fee. Buys first rights. Submit seasonal/holiday material 4 months in advance. Query for electronic submissions. Reports in 3 weeks on queries. Free sample copy and writer's guidelines.

Nonfiction: David L. Miller. Inspirational, interview/profile, personal experience, photo feature and religious. "No articles unrelated to the world of religion." Buys 40 mss/year. Query with published clips. Length: 300-2,000 words. Pays $400-1,000 for assigned articles; $50-400 for unsolicited articles. Pays expenses of writers on assignment.

Photos: Send photos with submission. Reviews contact sheets, transparencies and prints. Offers $50-175/photo. Captions and identification of subjects required. Buys one-time rights.

Columns/Departments: Lite Side (humor—church, religious), 25-100 words. Send complete ms. Length: 25-100 words. Pays $10.

Tips: "Writers have the best chance selling us feature articles."

LUTHERAN FORUM, P.O. Box 327, Delhi NY 13753. (607)746-7511. Editor: Dr. Leonard Klein. Works with a small number of new/unpublished writers each year. Quarterly review for church leadership, clerical and lay. Estab. 1914. Circ. 4,000. Pays on publication. Publishes ms an average of 6 months after acceptance.

Byline given. Rights purchased vary with author and material; buys all, first North American serial, second serial (reprint) and simultaneous rights. Will consider simultaneous submissions. Reports in 3 months or longer. Sample copy $1.50 for SAE with 5 first class stamps. Writer's guidelines for #10 SASE.

Nonfiction: Articles about important issues and developments in the church's institutional life and in its cultural/social setting. No purely devotional/inspirational material. Buys 2-3 mss/year. Query or submit complete ms. Length: 1,000-3,000 words. Informational, how-to, interview, profile, think articles and exposé. Length: 500-3,000 words.

Photos: Purchased with ms and only with captions. Prefers 4×5 prints. Pays $15 minimum.

THE LUTHERAN JOURNAL, 7317 Cahill Rd., Edina MN 55439-2081. Publisher: John W. Leykom. Editor: Rev. Armin U. Deye. Quarterly family magazine for Lutheran Church members, middle age and older. Estab. 1936. Circ. 136,000. Pays on publication. Byline given. Simultaneous submissions OK. Reports in 3 months. Sample copy for 9×12 SAE with 2 first class stamps.

Nonfiction: Inspirational, religious, human interest and historical articles. Interesting or unusual church projects. Informational, how-to, personal experience, interview, humor and think articles. Buys 25-30 mss/year. Submit complete ms. Length: 1,500 words maximum; occasionally 2,000 words. Pays 1-3¢/word.

Photos: Send b&w and color photos with accompanying ms. Captions required.

Fiction: Mainstream, religious and historical fiction. Must be suitable for church distribution. Length: 2,000 words maximum. Pays 1-1½¢/word.

Poetry: Traditional poetry, blank verse and free verse, related to subject matter.

MENNONITE BRETHREN HERALD, 3-169 Riverton Ave., Winnipeg, Manitoba R2L 2E5 Canada. (204)669-6575. Fax: (204)654-1865. Contact: Editor. 25% freelance written. Biweekly family publication "read mainly by people of the Mennonite faith, reaching a wide cross section of professional and occupational groups, but also including many homemakers. Readership includes people from both urban and rural communities." Estab. 1962. Circ. 14,000. Pays on publication. Publishes ms an average of 4-6 months after acceptance. Not copyrighted. Byline given. Sample copy $1 for 9×12 SAE with 2 IRCs. Reports in 6 months. Publishes reprints of previously published articles. Send photocopy of article or typed ms with rights for sale noted. Include information about when and where the article previously appeared.

Nonfiction: Articles with a Christian family orientation; youth directed, Christian faith and life, and current issues. Wants articles critiquing the values of a secular society, attempting to relate Christian living to the practical situations of daily living; showing how people have related their faith to their vocations. Length: 1,500 words. Pays $30-40. Pays the expenses of writers on assignment.

Photos: Photos purchased with mss; pays $10.

THE MESSENGER OF THE SACRED HEART, Apostleship of Prayer, 661 Greenwood Ave., Toronto, Ontario M4J 4B3 Canada. (416)466-1195. Editor: Rev. F.J. Power, S.J. Monthly magazine for "Canadian and US Catholics interested in developing a life of prayer and spirituality; stresses the great value of our ordinary actions and lives." 20% freelance written. Estab. 1891. Circ. 18,000. Buys first rights only. Byline given. **Pays on acceptance.** Submit seasonal material 5 months in advance. Reports in 1 month. Sample copy $1 for 7½×10½ SAE. Writer's guidelines for #10 SASE.

Fiction: Religious/inspirational. Stories about people, adventure, heroism, humor, drama. Buys 12 mss/year. Send complete ms with SAE and IRCs. Unsolicited mss, unaccompanied by return postage, will not be returned. Length: 750-1,500 words. Pays 4¢/word.

Tips: "Develop a story that sustains interest to the end. Do not preach, but use plot and characters to convey the message or theme. Aim to move the heart as well as the mind. Before sending, cut out unnecessary or unrelated words or sentences. If you can, add a light touch or a sense of humor to the story. Your ending should have impact, leaving a moral or faith message for the reader."

THE MIRACULOUS MEDAL, 475 E. Chelten Ave., Philadelphia PA 19144-5785. Fax: (215)848-1014. Editorial Director: Rev. John W. Gouldrick, C.M. 40% freelance written. Quarterly. Estab. 1915. **Pays on acceptance.** Publishes ms an average of 2 years after acceptance. Buys first North American serial rights. Buys articles only on special assignment. Reports in 3 months. Sample copy for 6×9 SAE with 2 first class stamps.

Fiction: Should not be pious or sermon-like. Wants good general fiction—not necessarily religious, but if religion is basic to the story, the writer should be sure of his facts. Only restriction is that subject matter and treatment must not conflict with Catholic teaching and practice. Can use seasonal material, Christmas stories. Length: 2,000 words maximum. Occasionally uses short-shorts from 750-1,250 words. Pays 2¢/word minimum.

Poetry: Maximum of 20 lines, preferably about the Virgin Mary or at least with religious slant. Pays 50¢/line minimum.

MOODY MAGAZINE, Moody Bible Institute, 820 N. LaSalle Blvd., Chicago IL 60610. (312)329-2163. Fax: (312)329-2149. Managing Editor: Andrew Scheer. 80% freelance written. Monthly magazine for evangelical Christianity. "Our readers are conservative, evangelical Christians highly active in their churches and concerned about applying their faith in daily living." Estab. 1900. Circ. 150,000. **Pays on acceptance.** Publishes ms an average of 6-9 months after acceptance. Byline given. Buys first North American serial rights. Submit seasonal material 9 months in advance. Query for electronic submissions. Unsolicited mss will be returned unread. Reports in 2 months. Sample copy for 10×13 SASE with 3 first class stamps. Writer's guidelines for #10 SASE.

Nonfiction: Personal narratives (on living the Christian life), a few reporting articles. Buys 80 mss/year. Query. Length: 750-2,000 words. Pays 15¢/word for queried articles; 20¢/word for assigned articles. Sometimes pays the expenses of writers on assignment.

Columns/Departments: First Person (the only article written for non-Christians; a personal conversion testimony written by the author [will accept 'as told to's']; the objective is to tell a person's testimony in such a way that the reader will understand the gospel and want to receive Christ as Savior), 800-1,000 words; and Just for Parents (provides practical anecdotal guidance for parents, solidly based on biblical principles), 1,300-1,500 words. Buys 22 mss/year. Query. Pays 15¢/word.

● Ranked as one of the best markets for freelance writers in *Writer's Digest* magazine's annual "Top 100 Markets," January 1993.

‡MY DAILY VISITOR, Our Sunday Visitor, Inc., 200 Noll Plaza, Huntington IN 46750. (219)356-8400. Editors: Catherine and William Odell. 99% freelance written. Bimonthly magazine of Scripture meditations based on the day's Catholic mass readings. Circ. 30,000. **Pays on acceptance.** Publishes ms an average of 6 months after acceptance. Byline given. Not copyrighted. Buys one-time rights. Reports in 2 months. Sample copy and writer's guidelines for #10 SAE with 2 first class stamps. "Guest editors write on assignment basis only."

Nonfiction: Inspirational, personal experience and religious. Buys 12 mss/year. Query with published clips. Length: 150-160 words times number of days in month. Pays $400 for one month (28-31) of meditations. Pays writers 25 gratis copies.

OBLATES, Missionary Association of Mary Immaculate, 15 S. 59th St., Belleville IL 62223-4694. (618)233-2238. Managing Editor: Jacqueline Lowery Corn. Manuscripts Editor: Priscilla Kurz. 30-50% freelance written. Prefers to work with published writers. Bimonthly inspirational magazine for Christians; audience mainly older adults. Circ. 500,000. **Pays on acceptance.** Usually publishes ms within 2 years after acceptance. Byline given. Buys first North American serial rights. Submit seasonal material 8 months in advance. Reports in 6 months. Sample copy and writer's guidelines for 6×9 or larger SAE with 2 first class stamps.

Nonfiction: Inspirational and personal experience with positive spiritual insights. No preachy, theological or research articles. Avoid current events and controversial topics. Send complete ms. Length: 500 words. Pays $80.

Poetry: Light verse—reverent, well written, perceptive, with traditional rhythm and rhyme. "Emphasis should be on inspiration, insight and relationship with God." Submit maximum 2 poems. Length: 8-16 lines. Pays $30.

Tips: "Our readership is made up mostly of mature Americans who are looking for comfort, encouragement, and a positive sense of applicable Christian direction to their lives. Focus on sharing of personal insight to problem (i.e. death or change), but must be positive, uplifting. We have well-defined needs for an established market, but are always on the lookout for exceptional work."

THE OTHER SIDE, 300 W. Apsley St., Philadelphia PA 19144-4285. Editor: Mark Olson. Managing Editor: Dee Dee Risher. Associate Editor: Doug Davidson. 50% freelance written. Prefers to work with published/established writers. Bimonthly magazine emphasizing "spiritual nurture, prophetic reflection, forgotten voices and artistic visions from a radical Christian perspective." Estab. 1965. Circ. 13,000. **Pays on acceptance.** Publishes ms an average of 6 months after acceptance. Byline given. Buys all or first serial rights. Query for electronic submissions. Reports in 3 months. Sample copy $4.50. Writer's guidelines for #10 SASE.

Nonfiction: Doug Davidson, associate editor. Current social, political and economic issues in the US and around the world: personality profiles, interpretative essays, interviews, how-to's, personal experiences, spiritual reflections, biblical interpretation and investigative reporting. "Articles must be lively, vivid and down-to-earth, with a radical faith-based Christian perspective." Length: 500-6,000 words. Pays $25-300. Sometimes pays expenses of writers on assignment.

Photos: Cathleen Benberg, art director. Photos or photo essays illustrating current social, political, or economic reality in the US and Third World. Especially interested in creative original art offering spiritual insight and/or fresh perspectives on contemporary issues. Pays $15-75 for b&w and $50-300 for color.

Fiction: Jennifer Wilkins, fiction editor. "Short stories, humor and satire conveying insights and situations that will be helpful to Christians with a radical commitment to peace and justice." Length: 300-4,000 words. Pays $25-250.

Poetry: Rod Jellema, poetry editor. "Short, creative poetry that will be thought-provoking and appealing to radical Christians who have a strong commitment to spirituality, peace and justice." Length: 3-50 lines. No more than 4 poems may be submitted at one time by any one author. Pays $15-20.

Tips: "We're looking for tightly written pieces (1,000-1,500 words) on interesting and unusual Christians (or Christian groups) who are putting their commitment to peace and social justice into action in creative and useful ways. We're also looking for provocative analytical and reflective pieces (1,000-4,000 words) dealing with contemporary social issues in the US and abroad."

OUR FAMILY, Oblate Fathers of St. Mary's Province, P.O. Box 249, Battleford, Saskatchewan S0M 0E0 Canada. (306)937-7771. Fax: (306)937-7644. Editor: Nestor Gregoire. 60% freelance written. Prefers to work with published/established writers. Monthly magazine for average family men and women with high school and early college education. Estab. 1949. Circ. 14,265. **Pays on acceptance.** Publishes ms an average of 6 months after acceptance. Byline given. Offers 100% kill fee. Generally purchases first North American serial rights; also buys all, simultaneous, second serial (reprint) or one-time rights. Submit seasonal material 4 months in advance. Simultaneous and previously published submissions OK. Reports in 1 month. *Writer's Market* recommends allowing 2 months for reply. Sample copy for 9 × 12 SAE and $2.50 postage. Writer's guidelines 49¢. Only Canadian postage or IRC useful in Canada.

Nonfiction: Humor (related to family life or husband/wife relations); inspirational (anything that depicts people responding to adverse conditions with courage, hope and love); personal experience (with religious dimensions); and photo feature (particularly in search of photo essays on human/religious themes and on persons whose lives are an inspiration to others). Phone queries OK. Buys 72-88 unsolicited mss/year. Pays expenses of writers on assignment.

Photos: Photos purchased with or without accompanying ms. Pays $35 for 5 × 7 or larger b&w glossy prints and color photos (which are converted into b&w). Offers additional payment for photos accepted with ms (payment for these photos varies according to their quality). Free photo spec sheet for SASE.

Poetry: Avant-garde, free verse, haiku, light verse and traditional. Buys 4-10 poems/issue. Length: 3-30 lines. Pays 75¢-$1/line. Must have a religious dimension.

Fillers: Jokes, gags, anecdotes and short humor. Buys 2-10/issue.

Tips: "Writers should ask themselves whether this is the kind of an article, poem, etc. that a busy housewife would pick up and read when she has a few moments of leisure. We are particularly looking for articles on the spirituality of marriage. We will be concentrating more on recent movements and developments in the church to help make people aware of the new church of which they are a part."

OUR SUNDAY VISITOR MAGAZINE, 200 Noll Plaza, Huntington IN 46750. (219)356-8400. Publisher: Robert P. Lockwood. Editor: Trish Hempel. 5% freelance written. Works with small number of new/unpublished writers each year. Weekly magazine for general Catholic audience. Circ. 150,000. **Pays on acceptance.** Publishes ms an average of 2 months after acceptance. Byline given. Submit seasonal material 2 months in advance. Query for electronic submissions. Reports in 3 weeks. Sample copy for #10 SASE.

Nonfiction: Catholic-related subjects. Should explain Catholic religious beliefs in articles of human interest, applying Catholic principles to current problems, Catholic profiles, etc. Payment varies depending on reputation of author, quality of work, and amount of research required. Buys 25 mss/year. Query. Length: 1,000-1,200 words. Minimum payment for features is $100. Pays expenses of writers on assignment.

Photos: Purchased with mss; with captions only. Reviews b&w glossy prints and transparencies. Pays minimum of $200/cover photo story; $125/b&w story; $25/color photo; $10/b&w photo.

PENTECOSTAL EVANGEL, The General Council of the Assemblies of God, 1445 Boonville, Springfield MO 65802-1894. (417)862-2781. Fax: (417)862-0416. Editor: Richard G. Champion. 33% freelance written. Works with a small number of new/unpublished writers each year. Weekly magazine emphasizing news of the Assemblies of God for members of the Assemblies and other Pentecostal and charismatic Christians. Estab. 1913. Circ. 270,000. **Pays on acceptance.** Publishes ms an average of 6 months after acceptance. Byline given. Buys first serial rights, a few second serial (reprint) or one-time rights. Submit seasonal material 6 months in advance. Reports in 3 months. Free sample copy and writer's guidelines.

Nonfiction: Informational (articles on homelife that convey Christian teachings), inspirational and personal experience. Buys 5 mss/issue. Send complete ms. Length: 500-1,200 words. Pays 8¢/word maximum. Sometimes pays the expenses of writers on assignment.

Photos: Photos purchased without accompanying ms. Pays $7.50-15 for 8 × 10 b&w glossy prints; $10-35 for 35mm or larger transparencies. Total purchase price for ms includes payment for photos.

Poetry: Religious and inspirational. Buys 1 poem/issue. Submit maximum 6 poems. Pays $25-50.

Tips: "Break in by writing up a personal experience. We publish first-person articles concerning spiritual experiences; that is, answers to prayer for help in a particular situation, of unusual conversions or healings through faith in Christ. All articles submitted to us should be related to religious life. We are Protestant, evangelical, Pentecostal, and any doctrines or practices portrayed should be in harmony with the official position of our denomination (Assemblies of God)."

THE PENTECOSTAL MESSENGER, Messenger Publishing House, P.O. Box 850, Joplin MO 64802-0850. (417)624-7050. Fax: (417)624-7102. Editor: Don Allen. Managing Editor: Peggy Lee Allen. 25% freelance written. Works with small number of new/unpublished writers each year. Monthly (excluding July) magazine covering Pentecostal Christianity. "*The Pentecostal Messenger* is the official organ of the Pentecostal Church of God. It goes to ministers and church members." Estab. 1919. Circ. 8,000. Pays on publication. Publishes ms an average of 6 months after acceptance. Byline given. Buys second serial (reprint) or simultaneous rights. Submit seasonal material 4 months in advance. Simultaneous and previously published submissions OK; send tearsheet or photocopy of article, or typed ms with rights for sale noted, and information about when and where the article previously appeared. Pays 100% of their fee for an original article. Reports in 1 month.

Sample copy for 9×12 SAE with 4 first class stamps. Free writer's guidelines.

Nonfiction: Inspirational, personal experience and religious. Buys 35 mss/year. Send complete ms. Length: 1,800 words. Pays 1½¢/word.

Photos: Send photos with submission. Reviews 2¼×2¼ transparencies and prints. Offers $10-25/photo. Captions and model releases required. Buys one-time rights.

Tips: "Articles need to be inspirational, informative, written from a positive viewpoint, and not extremely controversial."

PIME WORLD, 17330 Quincy St., Detroit MI 48221-2765. (313)342-4066. Managing Editor: Paul Witte. 10% freelance written. Monthly (except July and August) magazine emphasizing foreign missionary activities of the Catholic Church in Burma, India, Bangladesh, the Philippines, Hong Kong, Africa, etc., for an adult audience, interested in current issues in the missions. Audience is largely high school educated, conservative in both religion and politics." Estab. 1954. Circ. 27,500. Pays on publication. Publishes ms an average of 3 months after acceptance. Buys all rights. Byline given. Submit seasonal material 4 months in advance. Simultaneous submissions OK. Reports in 2 months.

Nonfiction: Informational and inspirational foreign missionary activities of the Catholic Church. Buys 5-10 unsolicited mss/year. Query or send complete ms. Length: 800-1,200 words. Pays 6¢/word.

Photos: Pays $5/color photo.

Tips: "Submit articles dealing with current issues of social justice, evangelization and pastoral work in Third World countries. Interviews of missionaries accepted. Good quality color photos greatly appreciated."

PRAIRIE MESSENGER, Catholic Journal, Benedictine Monks of St. Peter's Abbey, P.O. Box 190, Muenster, Saskatchewan S0K 2Y0 Canada. (306)682-5215. Fax: (306)682-5285. Editor: Andrew Britz. Associate Editor: Marian Noll. 10% freelance written. Weekly Catholic journal with strong emphasis on social justice, Third World and ecumenism. Estab. 1905. Circ. 9,600. Pays on publication. Publishes ms an average of 3 months after acceptance. Byline given. Offers 70% kill fee. Not copyrighted. Buys first North American serial, first, one-time, second serial (reprint) or simultaneous rights. Submit seasonal material 3 months in advance. Query for electronic submissions. Reports in 2 months. Sample copy and writers guidelines for 9×12 SAE with 80¢ Canadian postage or IRCs.

Nonfiction: Interview/profile, opinion and religious. "No articles on abortion or homosexuality." Buys 15 mss/year. Send complete ms. Length: 250-600 words. Pays $40-60. Sometimes pays expenses of writers on assignment.

Photos: Send photos with submission. Reviews 3×5 prints. Offers $10/photo. Captions required. Buys all rights.

PRESBYTERIAN RECORD, 50 Wynford Dr., Don Mills, Ontario M3C 1J7 Canada. (416)444-1111. Fax: (416)441-2825. 50% freelance written. Eager to work with new/unpublished writers. Monthly magazine for a church-oriented, family audience. Circ. 63,000. Pays on publication. Publishes ms an average of 4 months after acceptance. Buys first serial, one-time or simultaneous rights. Submit seasonal material 3 months in advance. Reports on ms accepted for publication in 2 months. Returns rejected material in 3 months. Sample copy and writer's guidelines for 9×12 SAE with $1 Canadian postage or IRCs.

Nonfiction: Material on religious themes. Check a copy of the magazine for style. Also personal experience, interview and inspirational material. No material solely or mainly American in context. When possible, photos should accompany manuscript; e.g., current events, historical events and biographies. Buys 15-20 unsolicited mss/year. Query. Length: 1,000-2,000 words. Pays $45-55 (Canadian). Sometimes pays expenses of writers on assignment.

Photos: Pays $15-20 for b&w glossy photos. Uses positive transparencies for cover. Pays $50. Captions required.

Tips: "There is a trend away from maudlin, first-person pieces redolent with tragedy and dripping with simplistic, pietistic conclusions."

PRESBYTERIAN SURVEY, Presbyterian Publishing House, Inc., 100 Witherspoon St., Louisville KY 40202-1396. (502)569-5637. Fax: (502)569-5018. Editor/Publisher: Ken Little. Managing Editor: Catherine Cottingham. Estab. 1867. 65% freelance written. Prefers to work with published/established writers. Denominational magazine published 10 times/year covering religion, denominational activities and public issues for members of the Presbyterian Church (U.S.A.). **Pays on scheduling for publication.** Publishes ms an average of 9 months after acceptance. Byline given. Buys first North American serial rights. Submit seasonal material 4 months in advance. Reprints OK; send typed ms with rights for sale noted and information about when and where the article previously appeared. Pays 75% of their fee for an original article. Reports in 2 weeks on queries; 1 month on mss. *Writer's Market* recommends allowing 2 months for reply. Sample copy and writer's guidelines available upon request.

Nonfiction: Inspirational and Presbyterian programs, issues, people; any subject from a Christian viewpoint. No secular subjects. Buys 20 mss/year. Send complete ms. Length: 800-1,500 words. Pays $75-100.

Photos: State availability of photos. Reviews color prints or transparencies and b&w prints. Pays $15-25 for b&w; $25-50 for color. Identification of subjects required. Buys one-time rights.

Columns/Departments: "The only column not by a regular columnist is an op ed page for readers of the magazine (As I See It)." Accepts 10 mss/year. Send complete ms. Length: 600-700 words. No payment.

PURPOSE, 616 Walnut Ave., Scottdale PA 15683-1999. (412)887-8500. Editor: James E. Horsch. 95% freelance written. Weekly magazine "for adults, young and old, general audience with varied interests. My readership is interested in seeing how Christianity works in difficult situations." Estab. 1908. Circ. 17,500. **Pays on acceptance.** Publishes ms an average of 8 months after acceptance. Byline given, including city, state/province. Buys one-time rights. Submit seasonal material 6 months in advance. Simultaneous submissions OK. Submit complete ms. Reports in 2 months. Sample copy and writer's guidelines for 6×9 SAE with 2 first class stamps.

Nonfiction: Inspirational stories from a Christian perspective. "I want stories that go to the core of human problems in family, business, politics, religion, gender and any other areas — and show how the Christian faith resolves them. I want material that's upbeat. *Purpose* is a magazine which conveys truth either through quality fiction or through articles that use the best story techniques. Our magazine accents Christian discipleship. Christianity affects all of life, and we expect our material to demonstrate this. I would like to see story-type articles about individuals, groups and organizations who are intelligently and effectively working at some of the great human problems such as hunger, poverty, international understanding, peace, justice, etc., because of their faith." Buys 175-200 mss/year. Submit complete ms. Length: 900 words maximum. Pays 5¢/word maximum. Buys one-time rights only.

Photos: Photos purchased with ms. Pays $5-15 for b&w (less for color), depending on quality. Must be sharp enough for reproduction; requires prints in all cases. Captions desired.

Fiction: Humorous, religious and historical fiction related to discipleship theme. "Produce the story with specificity so that it appears to take place somewhere and with real people. It should not be moralistic. Essays and how-to-do-it pieces must include a lot of anecdotal, life exposure examples."

Poetry: Traditional poetry, blank verse, free verse and light verse. Length: 12 lines maximum. Pays $5-15/poem depending on length and quality. Buys one-time rights only.

Fillers: Anecdotal items from 200-599 words. Pays 4¢/word maximum.

Tips: "We are looking for articles which show the Christian faith working at issues where people hurt; stories need to be told and presented professionally. Good photographs help place material with us."

QUEEN OF ALL HEARTS, Montfort Missionaries, 26 S. Saxon Ave., Bay Shore NY 11706-8993. (516)665-0726. Fax: (516)665-4349. Managing Editor: Roger Charest, S.M.M. 50% freelance written. Bimonthly magazine covering Marian doctrine and devotion. "Subject: Mary, Mother of Jesus, as seen in the sacred scriptures, tradition, history of the church, the early Christian writers, lives of the saints, poetry, art, music, spiritual writers, apparitions, shrines, ecumenism, etc." Estab. 1950. Circ. 5,000. **Pays on acceptance.** Publishes ms an average of 6 months after acceptance. Byline given. Not copyrighted. Submit seasonal material 6 months in advance. Reports in 2 months. Sample copy $2.50.

Nonfiction: Essays, inspirational, personal experience and religious. Buys 25 ms/year. Send complete ms. Length: 750-2,500 words. Pays $40-60. Sometimes pays writers in contributor copies or other premiums "by mutual agreement."

Photos: Send photos with submission. Reviews transparencies and prints. Offers variable payment per photo. Buys one-time rights.

Fiction: Religious. Buys 6 mss/year. Send complete ms. Length: 1,500-2,500 words. Pays $40-60.

Poetry: Joseph Tusiani, poetry editor. Free verse. Buys approximately 10 poems/year. Submit maximum of 2 poems at one time. Pays in contributor copies.

REVIEW FOR RELIGIOUS, Room 428, 3601 Lindell Blvd., St. Louis MO 63108-3393. (314)535-3048. Fax: (314)535-0601. Editor: David L. Fleming, S.J. 100% freelance written. Bimonthly magazine for Roman Catholic priests, brothers and sisters. Estab. 1942. Pays on publication. Publishes ms an average of 9 months after acceptance. Byline given. Buys first North American serial rights; rarely buys second serial (reprint) rights. Reports in 2 months.

Nonfiction: Articles on spiritual, liturgical and canonical matters only; not for general audience. Length: 2,000-8,000 words. Pays $6/page.

Tips: "The writer must know about religious life in the Catholic Church and be familiar with prayer, vows, community life and ministry."

ST. ANTHONY MESSENGER, 1615 Republic St., Cincinnati OH 45210-1298. Fax: (513)241-0399. Editor-in-Chief: Norman Perry. 55% freelance written. "Willing to work with new/unpublished writers if their writing is of a professional caliber." Monthly magazine for a national readership of Catholic families, most of which have children in grade school, high school or college. Circ. 334,926. **Pays on acceptance.** Publishes ms an average of 9 months after acceptance. Byline given. Buys first North American serial rights. Submit seasonal material 6 months in advance. Query for electronic submissions. Reports in 2 months. Sample copy and writer's guidelines for 9 × 12 SAE with 4 first class stamps.

Nonfiction: How-to (on psychological and spiritual growth, problems of parenting/better parenting, marriage problems/marriage enrichment); humor; informational; inspirational; interview; personal experience (if pertinent to our purpose); personal opinion (limited use; writer must have special qualifications for topic); and profile. Buys 35-50 mss/year. Length: 1,500-3,500 words. Pays 14¢/word. Sometimes pays the expenses of writers on assignment.

Fiction: Mainstream and religious. Buys 12 mss/year. Submit complete ms. Length: 2,000-3,000 words. Pays 14¢/word.

Tips: "The freelancer should ask why his or her proposed article would be appropriate for us, rather than for *Redbook* or *Saturday Review*. We treat human problems of all kinds, but from a religious perspective. We need more articles on prayer, scripture, Catholic worship. Get authoritative information (not merely library research); we want interviews with experts. Write in popular style. Word length is important."

ST. JOSEPH'S MESSENGER & ADVOCATE OF THE BLIND, Sisters of St. Joseph of Peace, St. Joseph's Home, P.O. Box 288, Jersey City NJ 07303-0288. Editor-in-Chief: Sister Ursula Maphet. 30% freelance written. Eager to work with new/unpublished writers. Quarterly magazine. Estab. 1898. Circ. 20,000. **Pays on acceptance.** Publishes ms an average of 3 months after acceptance. Buys first serial and second serial (reprint) rights; reassigns rights back to author after publication in return for credit line in next publication. Submit seasonal material 3 months in advance (no Christmas issue). Simultaneous and previously published submissions OK; send photocopy of article or short story or typed ms with rights for sale noted and information about when and where the article previously appeared. Pays 100% of their fee for an original article. Reports in 1 month. Sample copy and writer's guidelines for 9 × 12 SAE with 2 first class stamps.

Nonfiction: Humor, inspirational, nostalgia, personal opinion and personal experience. Buys 24 mss/year. Submit complete ms. Length: 300-1,500 words. Pays $3-15.

Fiction: Romance, suspense, mainstream and religious. Buys 30 mss/year. Submit complete ms. Length: 600-1,600 words. Pays $6-25.

Poetry: Light verse and traditional. Buys 25 poems/year. Submit maximum 10 poems. Length: 50-300 words. Pays $5-20.

Tips: "It's rewarding to know that someone is waiting to see freelancers' efforts rewarded by 'print'. It's annoying, however, to receive poor copy, shallow material or inane submissions. Human interest fiction, touching on current happenings, is what is most needed. We look for social issues woven into story form. We also seek non-preaching articles that carry a message that is positive."

‡SCP JOURNAL AND SCP Newsletter, Spiritual Counterfeits Project, P.O. Box 4308, Berkeley CA 94704-4308. (510)540-0300. Fax: (510)540-1107. Editors: Tal Brooke and Brooks Alexander. 5% freelance written. Prefers to work with published/established writers. "The *SCP Journal* and *SCP Newsletter* are quarterly publications that analyze new religious movements and spiritual trends from a Christian perspective. Their targeted audience is the educated lay reader." Estab. 1975. Circ. 16,500. Pays on publication. Publishes ms an average of 6 months after acceptance. Byline given. Simultaneous and previously published submissions OK after telephone inquiry.

Nonfiction: Book excerpts, essays, expose, interview/profile, opinion, personal experience and religious. Buys 10 mss/year. Query with published clips. Length: 2,500-3,500 words. Pays $20-35/typeset page.

Photos: State availability of photos with submission. Reviews contact sheets and prints. Offers no additional payment for photos accepted with ms. Captions, model releases and identification of subjects required. Buys one-time rights.

Tips: "The area of our publication most open to freelancers is reviews of books relevant to subjects covered by *SCP*. These should not exceed 6 typewritten, double-spaced pages, 1,500 words. Send samples of work that are relevant to the *SCP's* area of interest."

SEEK, Standard Publishing, 8121 Hamilton Ave., Cincinnati OH 45231. (513)931-4050, ext. 365. Editor: Eileen H. Wilmoth. 98% freelance written. Prefers to work with published/established writers. Quarterly Sunday school paper, in weekly issues for young and middle-aged adults who attend church and Bible classes. Circ. 45,000. **Pays on acceptance.** Publishes ms an average of 1 year after acceptance. Byline given. Buys first serial and second serial (reprint) rights. Submit seasonal material 1 year in advance. Reprints OK; send tearsheet of article or typed ms with rights for sale noted. Pays 50% of their fee for an original article. Reports in 3 months. Sample copy and writer's guidelines for 6 × 9 SAE with 2 first class stamps.

Nonfiction: "We look for articles that are warm, inspirational, devotional, of personal or human interest; that deal with controversial matters, timely issues of religious, ethical or moral nature, or first-person testimonies, true-to-life happenings, vignettes, emotional situations or problems; communication problems and examples of answered prayers. Article must deliver its point in a convincing manner but not be patronizing or preachy. It must appeal to either men or women, must be alive, vibrant, sparkling and have a title that demands the article be read. We always need stories about families, marriages, problems on campus and life testimonies." Buys 150-200 mss/year. Submit complete ms. Length: 400-1,200 words. Pays 5¢/word.

Photos: B&w photos purchased with or without mss. Pays $20 minimum for good 8 × 10 glossy prints.

Fiction: Religious fiction and religiously slanted historical and humorous fiction. No poetry. Length: 400-1,200 words. Pays 5¢/word.

Tips: "Submit mss which tell of faith in action or victorious Christian living as central theme. We select manuscripts as far as one year in advance of publication. Complimentary copies are sent to our published writers immediately following printing."

‡**SHARING THE VICTORY**, Fellowship of Christian Athletes, 8701 Leeds Rd., Kansas City MO 64129. (816)921-0909. Fax: (816)921-8755. Editor: John Dodderidge. Assistant Editor: Robyne Baker. Managing Editor: Don Hilkemeier. 60% freelance written. Prefers to work with published/established writers, but works with a growing number of new/unpublished writers each year. Monthly (September-May) magazine. "We seek to encourage and enable athletes and coaches at all levels to take their faith seriously on and off the 'field'." Estab. 1959. Circ. 50,000. Pays on publication. Publishes ms an average of 4 months after acceptance. Byline given. Buys first rights. Submit seasonal/holiday material 3 months in advance. Reports in 1 week on queries; 2 weeks on mss. *Writer's Market* recommends allowing 2 months for reply. Sample copy $1 for 9 × 12 SAE with 3 first class stamps. Free writer's guidelines for #10 SASE.

Nonfiction: Humor, inspirational, interview/profile (with "name" athletes and coaches solid in their faith), personal experience, and photo feature. No "sappy articles on 'I became a Christian and now I'm a winner.'" Buys 5-20 mss/year. Query. Length: 500-1,000 words. Pays $100-200 for unsolicited articles, more for the exceptional profile.

Photos: State availability of photos with submission. Reviews contact sheets. Pay depends on quality of photo but usually a minimum $100. Model releases required for "name" individuals. Buys one-time rights.

Poetry: Free verse. Buys 3 poems/year. Pays $50.

Tips: "Profiles and interviews of particular interest to coed athlete, primarily high school and college-age. Our graphics and editorial content appeal to youth. The area most open to freelancers is profiles on or interviews with well-known athletes or coaches (male, female, minorities) and offbeat but interscholastic team sports."

SIGNS OF THE TIMES, Pacific Press Publishing Association, P.O. Box 7000, Boise ID 83707. (208)465-2500. Fax: (208)465-2531. Editor: Greg Brothers. 40% freelance written. Works with a small number of new/unpublished writers each year. Monthly magazine on religion. "We are a Christian publication encouraging the general public to put into practice the principles of the Bible." Estab. 1874. Circ. 265,000. Pays on publication. Publishes ms an average of 8 months after acceptance. Byline given. Offers kill fee. Buys first North American serial rights and simultaneous rights. Submit seasonal material 8 months in advance. Simultaneous queries and submissions, and previously published submissions OK; send photocopy of article or typed ms with rights for sale noted. Pays 50% of their fee for an original article. Reports in 2 weeks on queries; 1 month on mss. *Writer's Market* recommends allowing 2 months for reply. Sample copy and writer's guidelines for 9 × 12 SAE with 3 first class stamps.

Nonfiction: General interest (home, marriage, health—interpret current events from a Biblical perspective); how-to (overcome depression, find one's identity, answer loneliness and guilt, face death triumphantly); inspirational (human interest pieces that highlight a Biblical principle); interview/profile; personal experience (overcome problems with God's help); and photo feature. "We want writers with a desire to share the good news of reconciliation with God. Articles should be people-oriented, well-researched and should have a sharp focus and include anecdotes." Buys 75 mss/year. Query with or without published clips or send complete ms. Length: 500-3,000 words. Pays $100-400. Sometimes pays the expenses of writers on assignment.

Photos: Merwin Stewart, photo editor. Send photos with query or ms. Reviews b&w contact sheets, 35mm color transparencies, 5 × 7 or 8 × 10 b&w prints. Pays $35-300 for transparencies; $20-50 for prints. Model releases and identification of subjects required (captions helpful). Buys one-time rights.

Tips: "One of the most frequent mistakes made by writers in completing an article assignment for us is trying to cover too much ground. Articles need focus, research and anecdotes. We don't want essays."

SISTERS TODAY, The Liturgical Press, St. John's Abbey, Collegeville MN 56321-2099. Editor-in-Chief: Sister Mary Anthony Wagner, O.S.B. Associate Editor: Sister Mary Elizabeth Mason, O.S.B. Review Editor: Sister Stefanie Weisgram, O.S.B. 80% freelance written. Prefers to work with published/established writers. Bimonthly magazine exploring the role of women and the Church, primarily. Circ. 8,000. Pays on publication. Publishes ms 1-2 years after acceptance. Byline given. Buys first rights. Submit seasonal material 4 months in advance. Reports in 3 months. Sample copy $3.

Nonfiction: How-to (pray, live in a religious community, exercise faith, hope, charity etc.), informational and inspirational. Also articles concerning religious renewal, community life, worship, and the role of sisters in the Church and in the world today. Buys 50-60 unsolicited mss/year. Query. Length: 500-2,500 words. Pays $5/printed page.

Poetry: Free verse, haiku, light verse and traditional. Buys 3 poems/issue. Submit maximum 4 poems. Pays $10.

Tips: "Some of the freelance material evidences the lack of familiarity with *Sisters Today*. We would prefer submitted articles not to exceed eight or nine pages."

SOCIAL JUSTICE REVIEW, 3835 Westminister Place, St. Louis MO 63108-3472. (314)371-1653. Contact: Rev. John H. Miller, C.S.C. 25% freelance written. Works with a small number of new/unpublished writers each year. Bimonthly. Estab. 1908. Publishes ms an average of 6-12 months after acceptance. Not copyrighted; "however special articles within the magazine may be copyrighted, or an occasional special issue has been copyrighted due to author's request." Buys first serial rights. Reprints OK; send typed ms with rights for sale noted and information about when and where the article previously appeared. Sample copy for 9 × 12 SAE with 3 first class stamps.

Nonfiction: Wants scholarly articles on society's economic, religious, social, intellectual and political problems with the aim of bringing Catholic social thinking to bear upon these problems. Query w/SASE. Length: 2,500-3,500 words. Pays about 2¢/word.

SPIRITUAL LIFE, 2131 Lincoln Rd. NE, Washington DC 20002-1199. (202)832-8489. Fax: (202)832-8967. Editor: Rev. Steven Payne, O.C.D. 80% freelance written. Prefers to work with published/established writers. Quarterly. "Largely Catholic, well-educated, serious readers. A few are non-Catholic or non-Christian." Circ. 12,000. **Pays on acceptance.** Publishes ms an average of 1 year after acceptance. Buys first North American serial rights. Reports in 6 weeks. Sample copy and writer's guidelines for 7 × 10 or larger SAE with 4 first class stamps.

Nonfiction: Serious articles of contemporary spirituality. High quality articles about our encounter with God in the present day world. Language of articles should be college level. Technical terminology, if used, should be clearly explained. Material should be presented in a positive manner. Sentimental articles or those dealing with specific devotional practices not accepted. Buys inspirational and think pieces. "Brief autobiographical information (present occupation, past occupations, books and articles published, etc.) should accompany article." No fiction or poetry. Buys 20 mss/year. Length: 3,000-5,000 words. Pays $50 minimum. "Five contributor's copies are sent to author on publication of article." Book reviews should be sent to Br. Edward O'Donnell, O.C.D.

STANDARD, Nazarene International Headquarters, 6401 The Paseo, Kansas City MO 64131. (816)333-7000, ext. 2555. Editor: Beth A. Watkins. 95% freelance written. Works with a small number of new/unpublished writers each year. Weekly inspirational paper with Christian reading for adults. Estab. 1938. Circ. 165,000. **Pays on acceptance.** Publishes ms an average of 15 months after acceptance. Byline given. Buys one-time rights and second serial (reprint) rights. Submit seasonal material 1 year in advance. Reports in 8-10 weeks. Free sample copy. Writer's guidelines for SAE with 2 first class stamps.

Nonfiction: How-to (grow spiritually), inspirational, social issues and personal experience (with an emphasis on spiritual growth). Buys 400 mss/year. Send complete ms. Length: 300-1,500 words. Pays 3½¢/word for first rights; 2¢/word for reprint rights.

Photos: Pays $25-45 for 8 × 10 b&w prints. Buys one-time rights. Accepts photos with ms.

Fiction: Adventure, religious, romance and suspense – all with a spiritual emphasis. Buys 400 mss/year. Send complete ms. Length: 500-1,500 words. Pays 3½¢/word for first rights; 2¢/word for reprint rights.

Poetry: Free verse, haiku, light verse and traditional. Buys 50 poems/year. Submit maximum 5 poems. Length: 50 lines maximum. Pays 25¢/line.

Fillers: Jokes, anecdotes and short humor. Buys 52/year. Length: 300 words maximum. Pays same as nonfiction and fiction.

Tips: "Articles should express Christian principles without being preachy. Setting, plot and characterization must be realistic. Fiction articles should be labeled 'Fiction' on the manuscript. True experience articles may be first person, 'as told to,' or third person."

SUN, Neighbor News, Inc., P.O. Box 16096, West Palm Beach FL 33416-6096. (407)439-3509. Editor: Dennis Lombard. 80% freelance written. Weekly tabloid covering home and family, singles, conservative Christian and Jewish views on world, national and local scales. Estab. 1988. Circ. 20,000. Pays on publication. Publishes ms an average of 2 months after acceptance. Byline given. No kill fee. Buys one-time and second serial (reprint) rights and makes work-for-hire assignments locally. Submit seasonal material 1 month in advance. Simultaneous and previously published submissions OK; send tearsheet or photocopy of article or short story or typed ms with rights for sale noted and information about when and where the article previously appeared. Pays 25-50% of their fee for an original article. Reports in 1 week on mss. *Writer's Market* recommends

---

For explanation of symbols, see the Key to Symbols and Abbreviations on page 72. For unfamiliar words, see the Glossary.

allowing 2 months for reply. No queries please! Sample copy and guidelines $1 for 9 × 12 SAE with 3 stamps; or (we suggest) three consecutive issues and guidelines $3 for 9 × 12 SAE with 3 stamps. Writer's guidelines for #10 SASE.

Nonfiction: Book excerpts, essays, how-to, humor, inspirational, interview/profile, opinion, personal experience, photo feature, religious. Buys 100 mss/year. Send complete ms. Length 500-1,000 words. Pays $5-25.

Photos: Send photos with submission. Reviews contact sheets and prints (any size). Offers $5-10/photo. Captions, model releases and identification of subjects required. Buys one-time rights only.

Columns/Departments: "Open to new column ideas." Buys 20 mss/year. Send complete ms. Length: 300-900 words. Pays $5-15.

Fiction: Humorous and religious. Buys 10 mss/year. Send complete ms. Length 300-1,200 words. Pays $5-25.

Poetry: Free verse, light verse and traditional. Buys 5-6 poems/year. Submit maximum 3 poems. Lines: 2-48 lines. Pays $5.

Fillers: "We accept and use but do not pay."

Tips: "We are very open to new writers. You must see and read the paper (we suggest three consecutive issues) to get the flavor of our conservative, Christian, Jewish, pro-family, pro-American slants. Writers have the best chance selling us Op Eds (200-500 words), personal experiences and fiction (religious but not preachy, doctrinal or denominational)."

SUNDAY DIGEST, David C. Cook Publishing Co., 850 N. Grove Ave., Elgin IL 60120. Editor: Christine Dallman. 75% freelance written. Prefers to work with established writers. Issued weekly to Christian adults in Sunday School. "*Sunday Digest* provides a combination of original articles and reprints, selected to help adult readers better understand the Christian faith, to keep them informed of issues within the Christian community, and to challenge them to a deeper personal commitment to Christ." Estab. 1886. **Pays on acceptance.** Publishes ms an average of 15 months after acceptance. Buys first or reprint rights. Reprints OK: send typed ms with rights for sale noted and information about when and where the article previously appeared. Pays 40-70% of their fee for an original article. Reports in 3 months. Sample copy and writer's guidelines for 6 × 9 SAE with 2 first class stamps.

Nonfiction: Needs articles applying the Christian faith to personal and social problems, articles on family life and church relationships, inspirational self-help, personal experience, how-to and interview articles preferred over fiction. Length: 400-1,700 words. Pays $40-200.

Fiction: Publishes novel excerpts (occasionally).

Tips: "It is crucial that the writer is committed to quality Christian communication with a crisp, clear writing style. Christian message should be woven in, not tacked on."

SUNDAY SCHOOL COUNSELOR, General Council of the Assemblies of God, 1445 Boonville, Springfield MO 65802-1894. (417)862-2781. Editor: Sylvia Lee. 60% freelance written. Works with small number of new/unpublished writers each year. Monthly magazine on religious education in the local church—the official Sunday school voice of the Assemblies of God channeling programs and help to local, primarily lay, leadership. Estab. 1939. Circ. 35,000. **Pays on acceptance.** Publishes ms an average of 9 months after acceptance. Byline given. Offers variable kill fee. Buys first North American serial, one-time, all, simultaneous, first serial or second serial (reprint) rights; makes work-for-hire assignments. Submit seasonal material 7 months in advance. Simultaneous and previously published submissions OK; send typed ms with rights for sale noted and information about when and where the article previously appeared. Pays 50% of their fee for an original article. Reports in 1 month. Free sample copy and writer's guidelines for SASE.

Nonfiction: How-to, inspirational, interview/profile, personal experience and photo feature. All related to religious education in the local church. Buys 100 mss/year. Send complete ms. Length: 300-1,800 words. Pays $25-150. Sometimes pays expenses of writers on assignment.

Photos: Send photos with ms. Reviews b&w and color prints. Model releases and identification of subjects required. Buys one-time rights.

• Looking for more photo-illustrated mss.

TEACHERS INTERACTION, A Magazine Church School Workers Grow By, Concordia Publishing House, 3558 S. Jefferson Ave., St. Louis MO 63118-3975. Editor: Jane Haas. 20% freelance written. Quarterly magazine (newsletter 7 times/year) of practical, inspirational, theological articles for volunteer church school teachers. Material must be true to the doctrines of the Lutheran Church—Missouri Synod. Estab. 1960. Circ. 20,400. Pays on publication. Publishes ms an average of 1 year after acceptance. Byline given. Buys first rights. Submit seasonal material 1 year in advance. Query for electronic submissions. Reports in 3 months on queries; 6 months on mss. Sample copy $1. Writer's guidelines for #10 SASE.

Nonfiction: How-to (practical help/ideas used successfully in own classroom); inspirational (to the church school worker—must be in accordance with LCMS doctrine); and personal experience (of a Sunday school classroom nature—growth). No theological articles. Buys 6 mss/year. Send complete ms. Length: 750-1,500 words.

• No longer buys reprints.

Fillers: Cartoons. Buys 14/year. "*Teachers Interaction* buys short items—activities and ideas planned and used successfully in a church school classroom." Buys 40/year. Length: 100 words maximum. Pays $10.

Tips: "Practical, or 'it happened to me' experiences articles would have the best chance. Also short items— ideas used in classrooms; seasonal and in conjunction with our Sunday school material, Our Life in Christ. Our format includes *all* volunteer church school teachers, Sunday school teachers, Vacation Bible School, and midweek teachers, as well as teachers of adult Bible studies."

THIS PEOPLE MAGAZINE, Exploring LDS issues and personalities, Utah Alliance Publishing Co., Box 2250, Salt Lake City UT 84110-2250. (801)581-0881. Fax: (801)581-0881. Editors: Scot Facer Proctor and Maurine Jensen Proctor. 75% freelance written. Quarterly magazine covering Mormon issues and personalities. "This magazine is aimed at Mormon readers and examines Mormon issues and people in an upbeat, problem-solving way." Estab. 1979. Circ. 20,000. Pays on publication. Publishes ms an average of 6 months after acceptance. Byline given. Offers 15% kill fee. Buys first rights. Submit seasonal material 6 months in advance. Query for electronic submissions. Reports in 2 months. Sample copy for 9×12 SAE with 4 first class stamps. Writer's guidelines for #10 SASE.

Nonfiction: Essays, historical/nostalgic, humor, inspirational, interview/profile, personal experience, photo feature and travel—all Mormon oriented. No poetry, cartoons, fiction. Buys 15-20 mss/year. Query with or without published clips, or send complete ms. Length: 1,000-3,500 words. Pays $150-400 for assigned articles; $100-400 for unsolicited articles. Sometimes pays expenses of writers on assignment.

Photos: State availability of photos with submission. Model releases and identification of subjects required. Buys all rights.

Tips: "I prefer query letters that include the first 6-8 paragraphs of an article plus an outline of the article. Clips and credits of previous publications are helpful."

THE UNITED CHURCH OBSERVER, 84 Pleasant Blvd., Toronto, Ontario M4J 2Z8 Canada. (416)960-8500. Fax: (416)960-8477. Editor: Muriel Duncan. 20% freelance written. Prefers to work with published/established writers. Monthly newsmagazine for people associated with The United Church of Canada. Deals primarily with events, trends and policies having religious significance. Most coverage is Canadian, but reports on international or world concerns will be considered. Pays on publication. Publishes ms an average of 4 months after acceptance. Byline usually given. Buys first serial rights and occasionally all rights.

Nonfiction: Occasional opinion features only. Extended coverage of major issues usually assigned to known writers. No opinion pieces or poetry. Submissions should be written as news, no more than 1,200 words length, accurate and well-researched. Queries preferred. Rates depend on subject, author and work involved. Pays expenses of writers on assignment "as negotiated."

Photos: Buys photographs with mss. B&w should be 5×7 minimum; color 35mm or larger format. Payment varies.

Tips: "The writer has a better chance of breaking in at our publication with short articles; this also allows us to try more freelancers. Include samples of previous *news* writing with query. Indicate ability and willingness to do research, and to evaluate that research. The most frequent mistakes made by writers in completing an article for us are organizational problems, lack of polished style, short on research, and a lack of inclusive language."

UNITY MAGAZINE, Unity School of Christianity, Unity Village MO 64065. Editor: Philip White. Associate Editor: Janet McNamara. 25% freelance written. Interested in working with authors who are skilled at writing in the metaphysical Christian/New Thought/spiritual development persuasion. Estab. 1889. Circ. 150,000. Pays on acceptance. Publishes ms an average of 1 year after acceptance. Byline given. Buys first North American serial rights. Sometimes publishes reprints of previously published articles. Send photocopy of article and information about when and where the article previously appeared. Submit seasonal material 9 months in advance. Query for electronic submissions. Reports in 6 weeks on queries; 2 months on mss. Free sample copy and writer's guidelines upon request.

Nonfiction: *Spiritual* self-help and personal experience, holistic health, prosperity, biblical interpretation, religious, inspirational. Buys 200 mss/year. Send complete ms. Length: 1,000-1,800 words. Pays 20¢/word.

Photos: State availability of photos with submission. Reviews transparencies and prints. Offers $35-200/ photo. Model releases and identification of subjects required. Buys one-time rights.

Poetry: Inspirational, religious and seasonal. Buys 100 poems/year. Submit maximum 5 poems. Length: 30 lines maximum. Pays $20 minimum.

 A bullet introduces comments by the editor of Writer's Market *indicating special information about the listing.*

THE UPPER ROOM, Daily Devotional Guide, P.O. Box 189, Nashville TN 37202-0189. (615)340-7252. Fax: (615)340-7006. Editor and Publisher: Janice T. Grana. Managing Editor: Mary Lou Redding. 95% freelance written. Eager to work with new/unpublished writers. Bimonthly magazine "offering a daily inspirational message which includes a Bible reading, text, prayer, 'Thought for the Day,' and suggestion for further prayer. Each day's meditation is written by a different person and is usually a personal witness about discovering meaning and power for Christian living through scripture study which illuminates daily life." Circ. 2.2 million (US); 385,000 outside US. Pays on publication. Publishes ms an average of 1 year after acceptance. Byline given. Buys first North American serial rights and translation rights. Submit seasonal material 14 months in advance. Manuscripts are not returned. If writers include a stamped, self addressed postcard, we will notify them that their writing has reached us. This does not imply acceptance or interest in purchase. Sample copy and writer's guidelines for SAE and 2 first-class stamps.

Nonfiction: Inspirational, personal experience and Bible-study insights. No poetry, lengthy "spiritual journey" stories. Buys 360 unsolicited mss/year. Send complete ms. Length: 250 words maximum. Pays $12.

Tips: "The best way to break into our magazine is to send a well-written manuscript that looks at the Christian faith in a fresh way. Standard stories and sermon illustrations are immediately rejected. We very much want to find new writers and welcome good material. We are particularly interested in meditations based on Old Testament characters and stories. Good repeat meditations can lead to work on longer assignments for our other publications, which pay more. A writer who can deal concretely with everyday situations, relate them to the Bible and spiritual truths, and write clear, direct prose should be able to write for *The Upper Room*. We want material that provides for more interaction on the part of the reader—meditation suggestions, journaling suggestions, space to reflect and link personal experience with the meditation for the day."

VIRTUE, The Christian Magazine for Women, P.O. Box 850, Sisters OR 97759-0850. (503)549-8261. Fax: (503)549-0153. Editor: Marlee Alex. Managing Editor: Jeanette Thomason. 75% freelance written. Works with small number of new/unpublished writers each year. Bimonthly magazine that "shows through features and columns the depth and variety of expression that can be given to femininty and faith." Estab. 1978. Circ. 175,000. Pays on acceptance or publication. Publishes ms an average of 4 months after acceptance. Byline given. Buys first North American serial rights. Submit seasonal material 9 months in advance. Reprints OK; send photocopy of article or short story and information about when and where the article previously appeared. For reprints, pays 25% of the amount paid for an original article. Reports in 6 weeks on queries; 2 months on mss. Sample copy 9×12 SAE with 5 first class stamps. Writer's guidelines for #10 SASE.

Nonfiction: Book excerpts, how-to, humor, inspirational, interview/profile, opinion, personal experience and religious. Buys 70 mss/year. Query. Length: 600-1,800 words. Pays 15-25¢/word. Sometimes pays the expenses of writers on assignment.

Photos: State availability of photos with submission.

Columns/Departments: In My Opinion (reader editorial); One Woman's Journal (personal experience); Equipped for Ministry (Christian service potpourri); Romancing the Home; and Real Men (women from a man's viewpoint). Buys 25 mss/year. Query. Length: 1,000-1,500. Pays 15-25¢/word.

Fiction: Humorous and religious. Buys 4-6 mss/year. Send complete ms. Length: 1,500-1,800 words. Pays 15-25¢/word.

Poetry: Free verse, haiku and traditional. Buys 7-10 poems/year. Submit maximum 3 poems. Length: 3-30 lines. Pays $15-50.

VISTA, Wesleyan Publishing House, P.O. Box 50434, Indianapolis IN 46250-0434. Editor: Brenda Bratton. 75% freelance written. Eager to work with new/unpublished writers—"quality writing a must, however." Weekly publication of The Wesleyan Church for adults. Estab. 1968. Circ. 40,000. **Pays on acceptance.** Publishes ms an average of 8 months after acceptance. Byline given. Not copyrighted. Buys first, simultaneous, second and reprint rights. Submit seasonal material 10 months in advance. Reports in 2 months. Sample copy for 9×12 SAE with 2 first class stamps. Writer's guidelines for #10 SASE.

Nonfiction: Testimonies, how-to's, humor, interviews and opinion pieces from conservative Christian perspective. Length: 500-700 words.

Photos: Pays $20-40 for 5×7 or 8×10 b&w glossy print: natural-looking close-ups of faces in various emotions, groups of people interacting. Various reader age groups should be considered.

Fiction: Believable, quality articles; no Sunday "soaps." Length: 800-1,200 words. Pays 2-4¢/word.

Tips: "Read the writer's guide carefully before submitting."

THE WESLEYAN ADVOCATE, The Wesleyan Publishing House, P.O. Box 50434, Indianapolis IN 46250-0434. (317)576-8156. Fax: (317)577-4397. Executive Editor: Dr. Norman G. Wilson. 50% freelance written. Monthly magazine of The Wesleyan Church. Estab. 1842. Circ. 20,000. Pays on publication. Publishes ms an average of 1 year after acceptance. Byline given. Buys first rights or simultaneous rights (prefers first rights). Submit seasonal material 6 months in advance. Simultaneous submissions OK. Reprints OK; send typed ms with rights for sale noted and information about when and where the article previously appeared. Pays 50% of their fee for an original article. Query for electronic submissions. Reports in 2 weeks. Sample copy for $2. Writer's guidelines for #10 SASE.

Nonfiction: Humor, inspirational and religious. Buys 50 mss/year. Send complete ms. Length: 250-650 words. Pays $10-40 for assigned articles; $5-25 for unsolicited articles.
Photos: Send photos with submission. Reviews transparencies. Buys one-time rights.
Tips: "Write for a guide."

‡**WOMAN'S TOUCH,** Assemblies of God Women's Ministries Department (GPH), 1445 Boonville, Springfield MO 65802-1894. (417)862-2781. Fax: (417)862-0503. Editor: Sandra Goodwin Clopine. Associate Editor: Aleda Swartzendruber. 75-90% freelance written. Willing to work with new/unpublished writers. Bimonthly inspirational magazine for women. "Articles and contents of the magazine should be compatible with Christian teachings as well as human interests. The audience is women, both homemakers and those who are career-oriented." Estab. 1977. Circ. 21,000. **Pays on acceptance.** Byline given. Buys one-time rights. Submit seasonal/holiday material 8 months in advance. Photocopied and previously published submissions OK; send photocopy of article or short story and information about when and where the article previously appeared. Reports in 3 weeks. Sample copy for 9½×11 SAE with 85¢ postage. Writer's guidelines for #10 SASE.
Nonfiction: General interest, how-to, inspirational, personal experience, religious and travel. Buys 75 mss/year. Send complete ms. Length: 500-1,000 words. Pays $10-35 for unsolicited articles.
Photos: State availability of photos with submission. Reviews negatives, transparencies and 4×6 prints. Offers no additional payment for photos accepted with ms. Identification of subjects required. Buys one-time rights.
Columns/Departments: A Creative Touch (special crafts, holiday decorations, family activities); and 'A Final Touch' for short human interest articles—home and family or career-oriented. Buys 10 mss/year. Query with published clips. Length: 80-500 words. Pays $20-35.
Poetry: Free verse, light verse and traditional. Buys 10 poems/year. Submit maximum 4 poems. Length: 4-50 lines. Pays $5-20.
Fillers: Facts. Buys 5/year. Length: 50-200. Pays $5-15.

‡**THE WORLD,** Unitarian Universalist Association, 25 Beacon St., Boston MA 02108. (617)742-2100. Editor: Linda Beyer. Contact: Sheila Jimenez, production manager. 50% freelance written. Bimonthly magazine covering religious education, spirituality, social consciousness, UUA projects and news, church communities, and personal philosophies of interesting people. "Purpose: to promote and inspire denominational self-reflection; to inform readers about the wide range of UU values, purposes, activities, aesthetics, and spiritual attitudes; and to educate readers about the history, personalities, and congregations that comprise UUism; to enhance its dual role of leadership and service to member congregations." Estab. 1987. Circ. 107,000. Pays on publication. Publishes ms an average of 1 year after acceptance. Byline given. Offers $300 kill fee. Buys one-time rights. Editorial lead time 3 months. Submit seasonal material 3 months in advance. Accepts previously published submissions. Query for electronic submissions. Reports in 2 months on queries; 3 months on mss. Sample copy and writer's guidelines for #10 SASE.
Nonfiction: Essays, historical/nostalgic (Unitarian or Universalist focus), inspirational, interview/profile (with UU), opinion, photo feature (of UU church or project), religious and travel. Buys 10 mss/year. Query with published clips. Length: 1,500-2,500 words. Pays $400 minimum for assigned articles; $250 for unsolicited articles. Sometimes pays expenses of writers on assignment.
Photos: State availability of photos with submission. Reviews contact sheets. Offers no additional payment for photos accepted with ms. Captions, model releases and identification of subjects required. Buys one-time rights.
Columns/Departments: Manuscript Editor: Jenna Leight. Among Ourselves (news, profiles, inspirational reports), 300-700 words; Book Reviews (liberal religion, social issues, politics), 600-800 words; Spotlight (social justice report, profile, feature), 650-850 words. Buys 15 mss/year. Query (profiles, book reviews) or send complete ms (news). Pays $75-250.
Tips: "Get to know your local congregation, find its uniqueness, tell its story. We don't have enough congregational profiles."

Retirement

Retirement magazines have changed to meet the active lifestyles of their readers. Editors dislike the kinds of stereotypes people have of the over-50 age group. More people are retiring in their 50s, while others are starting a business or traveling and pursuing hobbies. These publications give readers specialized information on health and fitness, medical research, finances and other topics of interest, as well as general articles on travel destinations and recreational activities.

ALIVE! A Magazine for Christian Senior Adults, Christian Seniors Fellowship, P.O. Box 46464, Cincinnati OH 45246-0464. (513)825-3681. Editor: J. David Lang. Office Editor: A. June Lang. 60% freelance written. Quarterly magazine for senior adults ages 55 and older. "We need timely articles about Christian seniors in vital, productive lifestyles, travels or ministries." Estab. 1988. Pays on publication. Byline given. Buys first or second serial (reprint) rights. Submit seasonal material 6 months in advance. Previously published submissions OK; send tearsheet or information about when and where the article previously appeared. Pays 60-75% of their fee for an original article. Reports in 6 weeks. Sample copy for 9 × 12 SAE with 2 first class stamps. Writer's guidelines for #10 SASE.

Nonfiction: General interest, humor, inspirational, interview/profile, photo feature, religious and travel. Buys 25 mss/year. Send complete ms. Length: 600-1,200 words. Pays $18-75. Organization membership may be deducted from payment at writer's request.

Photos: State availability of photos with submission. Offers $10-25. Model releases and identification of subjects required. Buys one-time rights.

Columns/Departments: Heart Medicine (humorous personal anecdotes; prefer grandparent/grandchild stories or anecdotes re: over 55 persons), 10-100 words; and Games n' Stuff (word games, puzzles, word search), 200-500 words. Buys 50 mss/year. Send complete ms. Pays $2-25.

Fiction: Adventure, humorous, religious, romance (if it fits age group), slice-of-life vignettes and motivational/inspirational. Buys 12 mss/year. Send complete ms. Length: 600-1,500 words. Pays $20-60.

Fillers: Anecdotes, facts, gags to be illustrated by cartoonist and short humor. Buys 15/year. Length: 50-500 words. Pays $2-15.

Tips: "Include SASE. If second rights, list where article has appeared and whether ms is to be returned or tossed."

FLORIDA RETIREMENT LIVING, Affordable Housing and Lifestyles for Active Adults, Gidder House Publishing, Inc., P.O. Box 161848, Altamonte Springs FL 32714. Editor: Dyeann Dummer. 20% freelance written. Monthly magazine directed toward the beginning retiree in an upbeat manner—unusual as well as typical Florida places, people, etc. Estab. 1946. Circ. 28,000. Pays on publication. Publishes ms an average of 3 months after acceptance. No kill fee. Buys first North American serial, first, one-time, second serial (reprint), simultaneous rights, all rights and/or makes work-for-hire assignments. Submit seasonal material 3 months in advance. Reprints OK. Query for electronic submissions. Reports in 3 weeks on queries. Free writer's guidelines. Sample copy $2.

Nonfiction: Historical/nostalgic, how-to (learn new skill as senior), humor, inspirational, interview/profile, new product, personal experience, photo feature and travel. Editorial calendar available on request. No negative or health related articles. Buys 30 mss/year. Query with or without published clips or send complete ms. Length: 750-1,250 words. Pays $100-150. Sometimes pays expenses of writers on assignment.

Photos: Send photos with submissions. Reviews transparencies and prints. Offers $5-25/photo. Model releases and identification of subjects required. Buys one-time rights or all rights.

Tips: "Look for the unusual, little known but interesting aspects of Florida living that seniors want or need to know about. Housing, finance and real estate are of primary interest."

‡FOURTH SEASON, Grass Roots Publishing, Inc., P.O. Box 1726, Stuart FL 34995. Editor: R.M. Touchberry. 20% freelance written. Monthly magazine. "We serve the retired community on Florida's treasure coast." Estab. 1989. Circ. 10,000. Pays on publication. Byline given. Buys first North American serial rights. Editorial lead time 2 months. Submit seasonal material 2 months in advance. Query for electronic submissions. Reports in 3 weeks on queries. Sample copy $1.25 for 9 × 11 SAE. Writer's guidelines for #10 SASE.

Nonfiction: Essays, general interest, historical/nostalgic (retirement related), inspirational, interview/profile and travel. No poetry. Buys 15-20 mss/year. Query. Length: 750-1,500 words. Pays $50 minimum.

Columns/Departments: Buys 60 mss/year. Query with published clips. Pays $40 minimum.

KEY HORIZONS, The Magazine For Your Best Years, Emmis Publishing Corp., Suite 1200, 950 N. Meridian St., Indianapolis IN 46204. Editor: Deborah Paul. Managing Editor: Joan Todd. 75% freelance written. Quarterly magazine for older adults, age 55+. "*Key Horizons* takes a positive approach to life, stressing the opportunities available to older adults." Estab. 1988. Circ. 200,000 (controlled circulation—sent to certain Blue Cross/Blue Shield policy holders in several states). Pays on publication. Publishes ms an average of 1-2 months after acceptance. Byline given. Offers $50 kill fee. Buys first North American serial rights. Submit seasonal material 4 months in advance. Query for electronic submissions. Reports in 1 month on queries; 2 months on mss. Free writer's guidelines.

Nonfiction: General interest, tips for better living, health, money and travel (national sources only). Buys 25-35 mss/year. Query with published clips or send complete ms. Length: 1,500-3,000 words. Pays $250-500.

Photos: State availability of photos with submission. Reviews 2¼ × 2¼ transparencies and 8 × 10 prints. Offers $25/photo. Captions and identification of subjects required. Buys one-time rights. Always looking for scenic parting shot. Payment negotiable.

Columns/Departments: Health, money, travel, gardening and food. (1,000 words). Like tips and sidebars. No nostalgia. Buys 12-16 mss/year. Query with published clips or send complete ms. Pays $300.

Tips: "Take an upbeat approach. View older adults as vital, productive, active people. We appreciate detailed, well-written query letters that show some preliminary research.

‡**LIFE TODAY, Looking in on life at its best,** Grote Publishing, Suite 120, 2802 International Lane, Madison WI 53704. Editor: Rod Clark. 80% freelance written. Quarterly magazine covering general lifestyle. "Although many of our readers are 50-plus, we are looking for excellent writing that is not age-specific but targeted to a general adult readership. The *Life Today* editorial slant is toward opening gateways to experience, encouraging readers to look in on and participate in intellectual, spiritual and physical engagements presented through unique perspectives, often encompassing a non-nostalgic past, active present and a positive future." Estab. 1989. Circ. 125,000. Pays on publication. Publishes ms an average of 6 months after acceptance. Byline given. Buys first North American serial or second serial (reprint) rights; makes work-for-hire assignments. Editorial lead time 5 months. Submit seasonal material 6 months in advance. Simultaneous and previously published submissions OK. Query for electronic submissions. Reports in 3 months. Sample copy $3 for 9×12 SAE with 5 first class stamps. Writer's guidelines for #10 SASE.

Nonfiction: Book excerpts, essays, general interest, how-to (gardening, cooking, decorating, outdoor, enjoyment, etc.), humor, interview/profile, photo feature, technical (science & technology), travel, health, sports, arts and general finance. "We are not currently publishing fiction. Please do not submit nostalgia pieces. In travel articles, show us the landscape, not yourself—avoid heavy reliance on personal chronologies. If an essay is written from personal experience, make it universal, but unique in tone." Buys 20 mss/year. Query with published clips or send complete ms. Length: 600-2,500 words. Pays $375 minimum for assigned articles; $100 minimum for unsolicited articles, including reprints. Sometimes pays expenses of writers on assignment.

Photos: Send photos with submission. Reviews contact sheets, negatives, transparencies and prints no smaller than 5×7. Offers $50-300/photo. Negotiates payment individually. Model releases and identification of subjects required. Buys one-time rights.

Poetry: Open style—no limitations. "No 'cute' poems about growing older, please. Make sure the poem evokes deep feeling in someone other than the writer. Write in an accessible style." Buys very few. Submit maximum 5 poems. Length: 60 words maximum. Pays $50 minimum.

Tips: "Make it easy for us to make a decision on your submission. If the article is already written, submit the entire thing—with professional quality photos or photo/illustration sources if appropriate. If query, write part of it in the style you would write the article. Be sure to enclose clips. Also, don't send us 4,000 words when we ideally use articles of 1,500—do that editing yourself before you send it in. Send us something you would enjoy reading. If your article or idea has strong graphic possibilities all the better. In all areas, we try to emphasize exciting new directions or trends with a positive angle. Articles on health and medical issues and research must be founded in sound scientific method and include current, up-to-date data. You must be able to document your research. We also look for pieces that evoke comfort and curiosity: on food, nature, art and landscapes, for instance."

‡**MATURE LIFESTYLES, The 50-plus News Magazine,** Media Publishing Group, Inc., #2-D, 15951 McGregor Blvd., Ft. Meyers FL 33908. (813)482-7969. Editor: Linda Kelley. 80% freelance written. Monthly tabloid. "Monthly tabloid size publication on newsprint with mag-style ad layout. All types of features that appeal to a 50-plus market, with emphasis on 50-65 age group." Estab. 1987. Circ. 130,000. Pays on publication. Publishes mss an average of 6-8 months after acceptance. Byline given. Buys one-time rights. Editorial lead time 2 months. Submit seasonal material 3 months in advance. Simultaneous and previously published submissions OK. Query for electronic submissions. Reports in 6 months on queries. Sample copy for 10×12 SAE.

Nonfiction: General interest, historical/nostalgic, how-to (handyman/cooking/recipes), humor, interview/profile, opinion, travel, fashion, 2nd/3rd careers, hobbies and grandparenting. No poetry. Buys 24 mss/year. Query. Length: 600-1,200 words. Pays $60 minimum for assigned articles; $35 for unsolicited articles.

Photos: Send photos with submission. Offers no additional payment for photos accepted with ms. Buys one-time rights.

Tips: "We are especially looking for articles that appeal to the pre-retiree or early retiree."

MATURE LIVING, A Christian Magazine for Senior Adults, Sunday School Board of the Southern Baptist Convention, 127 9th Ave. N., Nashville TN 37234. (615)251-2274. Editor: Al Shackleford. 70% freelance written. Monthly leisure reading magazine for senior adults 60 and older. Estab. 1892. Circ. 350,000. **Pays on acceptance.** Byline given. Buys all rights and sometimes one-time rights. Submit seasonal material 18 months in advance. Reports in 3 months. Sample copy for 9×12 SAE with 4 first class stamps. Writer's guidelines for #10 SASE.

Nonfiction: General interest, historical/nostalgic, how-to, humor, inspirational, interview/profile, personal experience, photo feature, crafts and travel. No pornography, profanity, occult, liquor, dancing, drugs, gambling. No book reviews. Buys 100 mss/year. Send complete ms. Length: 1,475 words maximum; prefers 950 words. Pays 5½¢/word (accepted).

Photos: State availability of photos with submission. Offers $10-15/photo. Pays on publication. Buys one-time rights.

Fiction: Humorous, mainstream and slice-of-life vignettes. No reference to liquor, dancing, drugs, gambling; no pornography, profanity or occult. Buys 12 mss/year. Send complete ms. Length: 900-1,475 words. Pays 5½¢/word.

Poetry: Light verse and traditional. Buys 50 poems/year. Submit 5 poems max. Length: open. Pays $5-24.

Fillers: Anecdotes, facts and short humor. Buys 15/issue. Length: 50 words maximum. Pays $5.

MATURE OUTLOOK, Meredith Corp., 1912 Grand Ave., Des Moines IA 50309-3379. Editor: Marjorie P. Groves, Ph.D. 80% freelance written. Bimonthly magazine and newsletter on travel, health, nutrition, money and garden for over-50 audience. They may or may *not* be retired. Circ. 925,000. **Pays on acceptance.** Publishes ms an average 6-7 months after acceptance. Byline given. Offers 20% kill fee. Buys all rights or makes work-for-hire assignments. Submit all material 9 months in advance. Query for electronic submissions. Reports in 2 weeks. Sample copy $1. Writer's guidelines for #10 SASE.

Nonfiction: How-to, health and fitness. No humor, personal experience or poetry. Buys 50-60 mss/year. Query with published clips. Length: 500-2,000 words. Pays $200-1,000 for assigned articles. Pays telephone expenses of writers on assignment.

Photos: State availability of photos with submission.

Tips: "Please query. Please don't call."

MATURE YEARS, 201 8th Ave. S., Nashville TN 37202-0801. Editor: Marvin W. Cropsey. 30% freelance written. Prefers to work with published/established writers. Quarterly magazine for retired persons and those facing retirement; persons seeking help on how to handle problems and privileges of retirement. **Pays on acceptance.** Publishes ms an average of 14 months after acceptance. Rights purchased vary with author and material; usually buys first North American serial rights. Submit seasonal material 14 months in advance. Publishes reprints of previously published articles. Send tearsheet or typed ms with rights for sale noted. Include information about when and where the article previously appeared. For reprints, pays 100% of the amount paid for an original article. Query for electronic submissions. Reports in 6 weeks. Sample copy $3.50 for 9 × 12 SAE. Writer's guidelines for #10 SASE.

Nonfiction: "*Mature Years* is different from the secular press in that we like material with a Christian and church orientation. Usually we prefer materials that have a happy, healthy outlook regarding aging. Advocacy (for older adults) articles are at times used; some are freelance submissions. We need articles dealing with many aspects of pre-retirement and retirement living, and short stories and leisure-time hobbies related to specific seasons. Give examples of how older persons, organizations and institutions are helping others. Writing should be of interest to older adults, with Christian emphasis, though not preachy and moralizing. No poking fun or mushy, sentimental articles. We treat retirement from the religious viewpoint. How-to, humor and travel are also considered." Buys 24 unsolicited mss/year. Submit complete ms (include SASE and Social Security number with submissions). Length: 1,200-2,000 words.

Photos: 8 × 10 color prints or transparencies purchased with ms or on assignment.

Fiction: "We buy fiction for adults. No children's stories and no stories about depressed situations of older adults." Length: 1,000-2,000 words. Payment varies, usually 4¢/word.

Tips: "We like writing to be meaty, timely, clear and concrete."

MODERN MATURITY, American Association of Retired Persons, 3200 E. Carson St., Lakewood CA 90712. (310)496-2277. Editor: J. Henry Fenwick. 50% freelance written. Prefers to work with published/established writers. Bimonthly magazine for readership of persons 50 years of age and over. Circ. 22.6 million. **Pays on acceptance.** Publishes ms an average of 6 months after acceptance. Byline given. Buys first North American serial rights. Submit seasonal material 6 months in advance. Query for electronic submissions. Reports in 10 weeks. Free sample copy and writer's guidelines.

Nonfiction: Careers, workplace, practical information in living, financial and legal matters, personal relationships and consumerism. Query first. *No unsolicited mss.* Length: up to 2,000 words. Pays up to $3,000. Sometimes pays expenses of writers on assignment.

Photos: Photos purchased with or without accompanying ms. Pays $250 and up for color and $150 and up for b&w.

Fiction: Very occasional short fiction.

Tips: "The most frequent mistake made in completing an article for us is poor follow-through with basic research. The outline is often more interesting than the finished piece. We do not accept unsolicited mss."

‡PARENT CARE, Newsletter for Children of Aging Parents, Parent Care Publications, Box 216, Bethany OK 73008. (405)787-7272. Editor: Betty Robertson. 75% freelance written. Monthly newsletter covering caring for aging parents. "*Parent Care* is a monthly newsletter for children of aging parents and those involved as caregivers for the older adult." Estab. 1991. Circ. 125. **Pays on acceptance.** Publishes ms an average of 3 months after acceptance. Byline given. Buys first, one-time, second serial (reprint) or simultaneous rights. Editorial lead time 3 months. Submit seasonal material 6 months in advance. Simultaneous and previously published submissions. Reports in 1 month on queries; 1-3 months on mss. Sample copy $2.50. Writer's guidelines for #10 SASE.

Nonfiction: Book excerpts, general interest, how-to, inspirational, new product, personal experience and religious. Buys 25-30 mss/year. Send complete ms. Length: 750-1,200 words. Pays $3 minimum for assigned articles.

Columns/Departments: What's Happening In Your World (personal caregiving experience), 750 words; and Pulse Check (devotion), 450 words.

Tips: "Research carefully; write about your own caregiving experiences."

SENIOR, California Senior Magazine, 3565 S. Higuera St., San Luis Obispo CA 93401. (805)544-8711. Fax: (805)544-4450. Editor: George Brand. 90% freelance written. Monthly magazine covering senior citizens to inform and entertain the "over-50" audience. Estab. 1982. Circ. 240,000. Pays on publication. Byline given. Publishes ms an average of 1 month after acceptance. Not copyrighted. Buys first or second rights. Submit seasonal material 2 months in advance. Reprints OK; send typed ms with rights for sale noted and information about when and where the article previously appeared. Pays 100% of their fee for an original article. Reports in 1 month. *Writer's Market* recommends allowing 2 months for reply. Sample copy for 9 × 12 SAE with 6 first class stamps. Writer's guidelines for SASE.

Nonfiction: Historical/nostalgic, humor, inspirational, personal experience and travel. Special issue features War Years (November); Christmas (December); and Travel (October, March). Buys 30-75 mss/year. Query. Length: 300-900 words. Pays $1.50/inch.

Photos: Send photos with submission. Reviews 8 × 10 b&w prints only. Offers $10-25/photo. Captions and identification of subjects required. Buys one-time rights.

Columns/Departments: Finance (investment), Taxes, Auto, Health. Lgth: 300-900 words. Pays $1.50/inch.

‡SENIOR MAGAZINE, Senior Inc., 3565 S. Higuera, San Luis Obispo CA 93401. (805)544-8711. 75% freelance written. Monthly magazine covering senior entertainment and information. Estab. 1982. Circ. 240,000. Byline given. Offers $30 kill fee. Not copyrighted. Buys first, second serial (reprint) or simultaneous rights or makes work-for-hire assignments. Editorial lead time 1 month. Submit seasonal material 3 months in advance. Simultaneous and previously published submissions OK. Reports in 3 weeks on queries; 1 month on mss. *Writer's Market* recommends allowing 2 months for reply. Sample copy for 9 × 12 SAE with $1.50 postage. Writer's guidelines for #10 SASE.

Nonfiction: Historical/nostalgic, interview/profile, personal experience and travel. Special issues: November—War years nostalgia; January—Travel; April—Travel. Buys 72 mss/year. Query. Length: 900-1,200 words. Pays $30-50 minimum for assigned articles; $15-30 minimum for unsolicited articles. Buys personality profiles on movie, television, sports and music stars. Has monthly "New Stuff" feature for new items to hit the retail market.

Photos: Send photos with submission. Reviews 5 × 7 transparencies and prints. Offers $15-25/photo. Captions and identification of subjects required.

Columns/Departments: Book Review (upbeat), 900-1,200 words; and Entertainment (profile), 900-1,200 words. Send complete ms.

Fiction: Adventure, historical, humorous, mystery, slice-of-life vignettes and suspense. "No science fiction, erotica or fantasy." Buys 12 mss/year. Send complete ms. Length: 1,500-2,150 words. Pays $100 Savings Bonds.

‡SENIOR SPOTLITE, Senior Spotlite Publications, 2840 Walton Creek Dr., Colorado Springs CO 80922. (719)591-9391. Fax: (719)591-5065. Publisher: Ed Ashby. 15% freelance written. Monthly tabloid for people over 50. "We are seeking anything of interest to seniors: health, travel, retirement, etc.; profiles of senior celebrities and remarkable seniors; outstanding hobbies, second careers, etc." Estab. 1986. Circ. 38,600. Pays on publication. Publishes ms an average of 3 months after acceptance. Byline given. Buys first rights or second serial (reprint) rights. Editorial lead time 3 months. Submit seasonal material 3-6 months in advance. Accepts simultaneous and previously published submissions. Query for electronic submissions. Reports in 1 month on queries; 2 months on mss. Sample copy $1 for 9 × 12 SAE with 2 first class stamps.

Nonfiction: Historical/nostalgic, humor, inspirational, personal experience, photo feature, religious and travel. "Nothing on the poor, helpless senior; our readers are active, full of life, self-sufficient." Buys 10 mss/year. Send complete ms. Length: 300-1,200 words. Pays $1/column inch.

Photos: Send photos with submission. Reviews prints. Offers no additional payment for photos accepted with ms. Captions, model releases and identification of subjects required. Buys one-time rights.

Tips: "Don't write about seniors, write to them. Forget your stereotypical nursing home resident. Remember, 60 used to be the threshold to old age. Now, it's 70!"

SENIOR WORLD NEWSMAGAZINE, Californian Publishing Co., P.O. Box 1565, El Cajon CA 92022. (619)593-2910. Executive Editor: Laura Impastato. Travel Editor: Jerry Goodrum. Entertainment Editor: Iris Neal. Health Editor: Doug Brunk. Lifestyle Editor: Sandra Pasqua. 5% freelance written. Prefers to work with published/established writers. Monthly tabloid newspaper for active older adults living in San Diego, Orange, Los Angeles, Riverside and San Bernardino counties. Estab. 1973. Circ. 500,000. Pays on publication. Buys first serial rights. Simultaneous submissions OK. Reports in 2 months. Sample copy $3. Free writer's guidelines.

Nonfiction: "We are looking for stories on health, stressing wellness and prevention; travel—international, domestic and how-to; profiles of senior celebrities and remarkable seniors; finance and investment tips for seniors; and interesting hobbies." Send query or complete ms. Length: 500-1,000 words. Pays $50-100.

Photos: State availability of photos with submission. Needs b&w with model release. Buys all rights to photos selected to run with a story.

Columns/Departments: Most of our columns are local or staff-written. We will consider a query on a column idea accompanied by a sample column.

Tips: "No pity the poor seniors material. Remember that we are primarily a news publication and that our content and style reflect that. Our readers are active, vital adults 55 years of age and older." No telephone queries.

SPECTRUM, For the Second Half of Your Life, (formerly *Senior Edition USA/Colorado* and *Colorado Old Times*), Suite 218, 1385 S. Colorado Blvd., Denver CO 80222-3312. (303)758-4040. Area Editor: Rose Beetem. 15% freelance written. Monthly tabloid. "Colorado newspaper for seniors (with national distribution) emphasizing legislation, opinion and advice columns, local and national news, features and local calendar aimed at over-55 community." Estab. 1972. Circ. 50,000. Pays on publication. Publishes ms an average of 6 months after acceptance. Byline given. Offer 25-50% kill fee for assigned stories only. Buys first North American serial rights and simultaneous rights. Submit seasonal material 3 months in advance. Reports in 3-6 months. Sample copy $1. Writer's guidelines for SASE.

Nonfiction: Historical/nostalgic, humor, opinion, personal experience and travel. Does not want "anything aimed at less than age 50-plus market; anything patronizing or condescending to seniors." Buys 3-6 mss/year. Buys over 70 mss/year in nostalgia. Query with or without published clips or send complete ms. Length: 50-1,000 words. (Note: Nostalgia length best under 800 words.) Pays $5-30 for assigned articles; $5-25 for unsolicited articles. Sometimes pays expenses of writers on assignment.

Photos: Send photos with submission (or photocopies of available pictures). Offers $3-10/photo. Identification of subjects required. Buys one-time rights.

Columns/Departments: Senior Overlook (opinions of seniors about anything they feel strongly about: finances, grandkids, love, life, social problems, etc. May be editorial, essay, prose or poetry). Buys 3-6 mss/year. Send complete ms. Length: 50-1,000 words. Pays $10 maximum.

• No longer seeking fillers.

Tips: Areas most open to freelancers are "Opinion: have a good, reasonable point backed with personal experience and/or researched data. Diatribes, vague or fuzzy logic or overworked themes not appreciated. Advice: solid information and generic articles accepted. We will not promote any product or business unless it is the only one in existence. Must be applicable to senior lifestyle."

‡**SUCCESSFUL RETIREMENT,** Grass Roots Publishing, 16th Floor, 950 3rd Ave., New York NY 10022. Editor: Marcia Vickers. 90% freelance written. Bimonthly magazine covering retirement. "Fun, upbeat, a youthful approach to retirement. No fuddy-duddyness. Our audience consists of "pretirees and retirees—average age 65. (No 'little old lady from Pasadena' stories)." Estab. 1993. Circ. 20,000. Pays on publication. Publishes ms an average of 3-4 months after acceptance. Byline given. Buys all rights. Editorial lead time 3-4 months. Submit seasonal material 6 months in advance. Query for electronic submissions. Reports in 2 months. Sample copy $3.50 (plus postage and handling). Writer's guidelines free on request.

Nonfiction: Health, historical/nostalgic, how-to, humor, inspirational, interview/profile, older celebrity profiles, relationships, travel, retirement locals and retirement life. "No lengthy, essay-type pieces or opinion pieces. Nothing negative or drab. Must pertain to retirement or aging." Buys 60 mss/year. Query with published clips. Length: 500-1,000 words. Pays $150 minimum.

Photos: State availability of photos with submission or send photos with submission. Identification of subjects required.

Columns/Departments: "Columns are written by staff writers. Query *only* if you have new column idea." Query with published clips. Pays $150-200.

Romance and Confession

Listed here are publications that need stories of romance ranging from ethnic and adventure to romantic intrigue and confession. Each magazine has a particular slant; some are written for young adults, others to family-oriented women. Some magazines also are interested in general interest nonfiction on related subjects.

BLACK SECRETS, Lexington Library Inc., 355 Lexington Ave., New York NY 10017. (212)973-3200. Fax: (212)986-5926. Editor: Tonia Shakespeare. See *Intimacy/Black Romance*.
Fiction: "This is our most romantic magazine of the five. We use one longer story between 20-24 pages for this book, and sometimes we feature it on the cover. Save your harsh, sleazy stories for another magazine. Give us your softest, dreamiest, most imaginative, most amorous story with a male love interest we can't help but fall in love with. Make sure your story has body and not just bodies. Our readers love romance, but they also require substance."
Tips: "Please request a sample and guidelines before submitting. Enclose a 9×12 SASE with 5 first class stamps."

BRONZE THRILLS, Lexington Library, Inc., 355 Lexington Ave., New York NY 10017. (212)973-3200. Fax: (212)986-5926. Editor: Tonia Shakespeare. Estab. 1982. See *Intimacy/Black Romance*.
Fiction: "Stories can be a bit more extraordinary and uninhibited than in the other magazines but still they have to be romantic. For example, we might buy a story about a woman who finds out her husband is a transsexual in *Bronze Thrills*, but not for *Jive* (our younger magazine). The stories for this magazine tend to have a harder, more adult edge of reality than the others."

INTIMACY/BLACK ROMANCE, 355 Lexington Ave., New York NY 10017. (212)973-3200. Fax: (212)986-5926. Editor: Tonia Shakespeare. 100% freelance written. Eager to work with new/unpublished writers. Bimonthly magazine of romance and love. Estab. 1982. Circ. 100,000. Pays on publication. Publishes ms an average of 6 months after acceptance. Byline given on articles only. Buys all rights. Submit seasonal material 6 months in advance. Reports in 2 months on queries; 6 months on mss. Sample copy for 9×12 SAE with 5 first class stamps. Writer's guidelines for #10 SASE.
Nonfiction: How-to (relating to romance and love) and feature articles on any aspect of relationships. Buys 100 mss/year. Query with published clips or send complete ms. Length: 750-1,250 words. Pays $100.
Photos: Send photos with submission. Reviews contact sheets, negatives, transparencies.
Fiction: Confession and romance. "I would not like to see anything that stereotypes Black people. Stories which are too sexual in content and lack romance are unacceptable." Buys 300 mss/year. Accepts stories which are a bit more romantic than those written for *Jive*, *Black Confessions* or *Bronze Thrills*. Send complete ms (4,000-5,000 words). Pays $75-100.
Tips: "I still get excited when I read a ms by an unpublished writer whose use of language is magical and fresh. I'm always looking for that diamond in the fire. Send us your *best* shot. Writers who are careless, sloppy and ungrammatical are an immediate turn-off for me. Please do your homework first. Is it the type of story we buy? Is it written in ms format? Does it make one want to read it?"

JIVE, Lexington Library, Inc., 355 Lexington Ave., New York NY 10017. (212)973-3200. Fax: (212)986-5926. Editor: Tonia Shakespeare. 100% freelance written. Eager to work with new/unpublished writers. Bimonthly magazine of romance and love. Estab. 1982. Circ. 100,000. Pays on publication. Publishes ms an average of 3 months after acceptance. Byline given on articles only. Buys all rights. Submit seasonal material 6 months in advance. Reports in 2 months on queries; 6 months on mss. Sample copy for 9×12 SASE with 5 first class stamps. Free writer's guidelines.
Nonfiction: How-to (relating to romance and love) and feature articles on any aspect of relationships. "We like our articles to have a down-to-earth flavor. They should be written in the spirit of sisterhood, fun and creativity. Come up with an original idea our readers may not have thought of but will be dying to try out." Buys 100 mss/year. Query with published clips or send complete ms. Length: 3-5 typed pages. Pays $100.
Columns/Departments: Fashion, health, beauty currently handled by assignment. Unsolicited articles will be returned.
Fiction: Confession and romance. "We would not like to see anything that stereotypes Black people. Stories which are too sexual in content and lack romance are unacceptable. However, all stories must contain one or two love scenes that are romantic, not lewd. All love scenes should not show the sex act, but should allude to it through the use of metaphors and tags." Buys 300 mss/year. Send complete ms (4,000-5,000 words). Pays $75-100.
Tips: "We are leaning toward more romantic writing styles as opposed to the more graphic stories of the past. Our audience is largely black teenagers. The stories should reinforce Black pride and should be geared toward teenage issues. Our philosophy is to show our experiences in as positive a light as possible without promoting any of the common stereotypes that are associated with Black men, lovemaking prowess, penile size, etc. Stereotypes of any kind are totally unacceptable. The fiction section which accepts romance stories and confession stories is most open to freelancers. Also, our special features section is very open. We would also like to see stories that are set outside the US (perhaps they could be set in the Caribbean, Europe, Africa, etc.) and themes that are reflective of things happening around us in the 90s—abortion, AIDS, alienation, surrogate mothers, etc. But we also like to see stories that transcend our contemporary problems and can give us a moment of pleasure, warmth, joy and relief. The characters should be anywhere from teenage to 30s but not the typical 'country bumpkin girl who was turned out by a big city pimp' type story. Please, writers who are not Black, research your story to be sure that it depicts Black people in a positive manner. Do not make a Black character a caricature of a non-Black character. Read contemporary Black

fiction to ensure that your dialogue and speech idioms are natural to the Black vernacular."

JIVE/BLACK CONFESSIONS, Lexington Library, Inc., 355 Lexington Ave., New York NY 10017. (212)973-3200. Fax: (212)986-5926. Editor: Tonia Shakespeare. Estab. 1982. See *Jive*.

MODERN ROMANCES, Sterling/Macfadden Partnership, 233 Park Ave. S., New York NY 10003. (212)979-4800. Editor: Cherie Clark King. 100% freelance written. Monthly magazine for family-oriented women, ages 18-65 years old. Circ. 200,000. Pays the last week of the month of issue. Buys all rights. Submit seasonal material at least 6 months in advance. Reports in 9-11 months. Writer's guidelines for #10 SASE.
Nonfiction and Fiction: Confession stories with reader identification and a strong emotional tone. No third-person material. Buys 12 mss/issue. Submit complete ms. Length: 2,500-12,000 words. Pays 5¢/word.
Poetry: Light, romantic poetry and seasonal/holiday subjects. Length: 24 lines maximum. Pay depends on merit.

TRUE CONFESSIONS, Macfadden Women's Group, 233 Park Ave. S., New York NY 10003. (212)979-4800. Editor: Pat Vitucci. 90% freelance written. Eager to work with new/unpublished writers. Monthly magazine for high-school-educated, blue-collar women, teens through maturity. Circ. 250,000. Buys all rights. Byline given on featured columns: My Man, The Feminine Side, Incredible But True, My Moment With God and You and Your Pet. Pays during the last week of month of issue. Publishes ms an average of 4 months after acceptance. Submit seasonal material 6 months in advance. Reports in 5 months.
Nonfiction and Fiction: Timely, exciting, emotional first-person stories on the problems that face today's women. The narrators should be sympathetic, and the situations they find themselves in should be intriguing, yet realistic. Many stories may have a strong romantic interest and a high moral tone; however, personal accounts or "confessions," no matter how controversial the topic, are encouraged and accepted. Careful study of a current issue is suggested. Length: 2,000-7,000 words; also book lengths of 8,000-10,000 words. Pays 5¢/word. Also publishes humor, poetry and mini-stories (1,200 words maximum). Submit complete ms. No simultaneous submissions. SASE required.

TRUE LOVE, Macfadden Women's Group, 233 Park Ave. S., New York NY 10003. (212)979-4800. Editor: Cynthia Di Martino. 100% freelance written. Monthly magazine for young, blue-collar women, teens through mid-30s. Confession stories based on true happenings, with reader identification and a strong emotional tone. Circ. 200,000. Pays the last week of the month of the issue. Buys all rights. Submit seasonal material 6 months in advance. No simultaneous submissions. Reports in 2 months. Sample copy $2 for 9×12 SAE. Writer's guidelines for #10 SASE.
Nonfiction and Fiction: Confessions, true love stories, problems and solutions, health problems, marital and child-rearing difficulties. Avoid graphic sex. Stories dealing with reality, current problems, everyday events, with emphasis on emotional impact. No stories written in third person. Buys 10 stories/issue. Submit complete ms; returned only with SAE and sufficient postage. Length: 2,000-10,000 words. Pays 3¢/word.
Columns/Departments: "The Life I Live," $100; "How I Know I'm In Love," 700 words or less; $75: "Pet Shop," $50.
Poetry: Light romantic poetry. Length: 24 lines maximum. Pay depends on merit.
Tips: "The story must appeal to the average blue-collar woman. It must deal with her problems and interests. Characters—especially the narrator—must be sympathetic. Focus is especially on teenagers, young working (or student) women."

‡TRUE ROMANCE, Sterling/Macfadden Partnership, 233 Park Ave. S., New York NY 10003. (212)979-4800. Fax: (212)979-7342. Editor: Pat Byrdsong. Monthly magazine. 100% freelance written. Readership primarily young, working class women, teens through mid-30's. Confession stories based on true happenings, with reader identification and strong emotional tone. No third-person material; no simultaneous submissions. Estab. 1923. Circ. 225,000. Pays 1 month after publication. Buys all rights. Submit seasonal/holiday material at least 6 months in advance. Reports in 5 months.
Nonfiction and Fiction: Confessions, true love stories; problems and solutions; dating and marital and child-rearing difficulties. Realistic stories dealing with current problems, everyday events, with strong emotional appeal. Buys 12 stories/issue. Submit complete ms. Length 1,500-7,500 words. Pays 3¢/word; slightly higher rates for short-shorts.
Poetry: Light romantic poetry. Buys 100/year. Length: 24 lines maximum. Pay depends on merit.
Tips: "A timely, well-written story that is told by a sympathetic narrator who sees the central problem through to a satisfying resolution is *all* important to break into *True Romance*. We are always looking for good emotional, identifiable stories."
  • Publisher has expressed an interest in stories with ethnic characters (i.e. Asians, Native-Americans, African-Americans, etc.) as long as the story is based in the United States or Canada.

‡TRUE STORY, Sterling/Macfadden Partnership, 233 Park Ave. S., New York NY 10003. (212)979-4800. Editor: Susan Weiner. 80% freelance written. Monthly magazine for young married, blue-collar women, 20-35; high school education; increasingly broad interests; home-oriented, but looking beyond the home for personal fulfillment. Circ. 1.7 million. Buys all rights. Byline given "on articles only." Pays 1 month after publication. Submit seasonal material 1 year in advance. Reports in approximately 8-12 months.

Nonfiction: Pays a flat rate for columns or departments, as announced in the magazine. Query for factual articles.

Fiction: "First-person stories covering all aspects of women's interests: love, marriage, family life, careers, social problems, etc. The best direction a new writer can be given is to carefully study several issues of the magazine; then submit a fresh, exciting, well-written true story. We have no taboos. It's the handling and believability that make the difference between a rejection and an acceptance." Buys about 125 full-length mss/year. Submit only complete mss for stories. Length: 1,500-10,000 words. Pays 5¢/word; $150 minimum.

Rural

Readers may be conservative or liberal, but these publications draw them together with a focus on rural lifestyles. Surprisingly, many readers are from urban centers who dream of or plan to build a house in the country.

ALBERTA FARM AND RANCH, Alberta's Foremost Rural Magazine, North Hill Publications, 4000 19th St. NE, Calgary, Alberta T2E 6P8 Canada. (403)250-6633. Fax: (403)291-0502. Editor: Michael Dumant. 10-30% freelance written. Monthly magazine covering rural and agricultural issues in Alberta. Estab. 1983. Circ. 80,288. Pays on publication. Publishes ms an average of 4 months after acceptance. Byline given. Buys First Canadian Rights. Submit seasonal material 6 months in advance. Reports in 2 months. Sample copy for 8 × 10 SAE with 2 first class Canadian stamps or 2 IRCs. Writer's guidelines for #10 SASE with Canadian postage or #10 SAE with 1 IRC.

Nonfiction: General interest, historical/nostalgic, politics, interview/profile, technical. "September's issue always features Women in Agriculture and related issues. No non-relevant articles or articles not of interest to rural Albertans." Buys 20-30 mss/year. Query with published clips. Length: 1,000-2,000 words. Pays $50-200 for assigned articles; $50-100 for unsolicited articles.

Photos: Reviews 4 × 6 prints. Offers $5-10/photo. Captions and identification of subjects required.

Columns/Departments: "Columnists work on annual contracts only."

Tips: "While *AF&R* seldom accepts unsolicited manuscripts, we always encourage writers to send in queries before going to the time and expense of completing a story. The best way to break into our magazine is with a unique story idea with specific interest to rural Albertans. Stories looking at unique personalities, insightful material on age-related issues and stories of issues concerning the family tend to fill most pages. For new writers trying to solicit their material with little publishing experience, I suggest the submission of typed mss in lieu of tearsheets. Caution: the fastest way to get a rejection is to spell words incorrectly or glaring grammatical errors. Also, superficial stories that do not entice reading or leave extensive informational gaps tend to be overlooked. I would rather see penned-in corrections than errors left unchecked."

COUNTRY JOURNAL, P.O. Box 8200, Harrisburg PA 17105. (717)657-9555. Fax: (717)657-9526. Editor: Peter V. Fossel. 90% freelance written. Works with a small number of new/unpublished writers each year. Bi-monthly magazine "providing pragmatic, useful information that will give the reader more control over his country life." Estab. 1974. Circ. 208,000. Average issue includes 6-8 feature articles and 10 departments. **Pays on acceptance.** Rates range from 20-40¢/word. Byline given. Buys first North American serial rights. Submit seasonal material 1 year in advance. Reports in 2 months. Sample copy $4. Writer's guidelines for SASE.

Nonfiction: Book excerpts; general interest; opinion (essays); profile (people who are outstanding in terms of country living); how-to; and issues affecting rural areas. Query with published clips and SASE. Length: 2,000-3,500 words. Pays 20-40¢/word.

Photos: Sheryl O'Connell, art director. State availability of photos. Reviews b&w contact sheets, 5 × 7 and 8 × 10 b&w glossy prints and 35mm or larger transparencies with SASE. Captions, model release and identification of subjects required. Buys one-time rights.

Columns/Departments: Sentinel (brief articles on country topics, how-tos, current events and updates). Buys 5 mss/issue. Query with published clips and SASE. Length: 200-400 words. Pays approximately $75.

Poetry: Free verse, light verse and traditional. Buys 1 poem/issue. Pays $50/poem. Include SASE.

• Ranked as one of the best markets for freelance writers in *Writer's Digest* magazine's annual "Top 100 Markets," January 1993.

Tips: "Be as specific in your query as possible and explain why you are qualified to write the piece (especially for how-to's and controversial subjects). The writer has a better chance of breaking in at our publication with short articles."

FARM FAMILY AMERICA, Fieldhagen Publishing, Inc., Suite 121, 333 On Sibley, St. Paul MN 55101. (612)292-1747. Editor: George Ashfield. 75% freelance written. Quarterly magazine published by American Cyanamid and written to the lifestyle, activities and travel interests of American farm families. Circ. 350,000.

Pays on acceptance. Publishes ms an average of 2 months after acceptance. Byline given. Offers 25% kill fee. Buys first rights or second serial (reprint) rights. Submit seasonal material 6 months in advance. Simultaneous submissions OK. Reports in 6 weeks. Writer's guidelines for #10 SASE.

Nonfiction: General interest and travel. Buys 24 mss/year. Query with published clips. Length: 1,000-1,800 words. Pays $300-650. Sometimes pays the expenses of writers on assignment.

Photos: State availability of photos with submission. Reviews 35mm transparencies and prints. Offers $160-700/photo. Model releases and identification of subjects required. Buys one-time rights.

‡FARM TIMES, 707 F St., Rupert ID 83350. (208)436-1111. Senior Editor: Doug Carlson. Managing Editor: Carol Whittom. Contact: Doug Carlson. 50% freelance written. Monthly tabloid for agriculture-farming/ranching. "*Farm Times* is 'dedicated to rural living.' Stories related to farming and ranching in the states of Idaho, Nevada, Utah, Wyoming and Oregon are our mainstay, but farmers and ranchers do more than just work. General, or human interest articles that appeal to rural readers, are often used." Estab. 1987. Circ. 90,000 (direct mail). Pays on publication. Byline given. Offers 100% kill fee "if submitted in acceptable form—writer's notes won't do it." Buys first rights. Editorial lead time 1 month. Submit seasonal material 2 months in advance. Query for electronic submissions. Reports in 2 weeks on queries. Sample copy and writer's guidelines free on request.

Nonfiction: Expose, general interest, historical/nostalgic, how-to, interview/profile, new product (few), opinion, and late breaking AG news. No humor, inspirational, essay, first person, personal experience or book excerpts. Buys 200 mss/year. Query with published clips. Send complete ms. Length: 600-800 words. Pays $1.25/column inch.

Photos: Send photos with submission. Reviews contact sheets with negatives, 35mm or larger transparencies and 5×7 or larger prints. Offers $5/b&w inside, $50/color cover. Captions, model releases and identification of subjects required. Buys one-time rights.

Column/Departments: Hoof Beats (horse care [technical]), 500-600 words; B Section Cover (winter months—travel [anywhere]), 600-1,200 words; B Section Cover (summer months—photo/essay [interesting people/places]) 600-1,200 words; Rural Religion (interesting churches/missions/religious activities) 600-800 words. Buys 12 mss/year. Query. Send complete ms. Pays $1.25/column inch.

Fillers: Anecdotes, facts, gags to be illustrated by cartoonist and newsbreaks. Buys 15/year. Length: 25-200 words. Pays $1.25/column inch.

Tips: "Query with a well-thought out idea that will appeal to rural readers. Phone queries OK. Of special interest is how environmental issues will affect farmers/ranchers, endangered species act, EPA, etc. We are also interested in features on specialty farming—mint, seed crops, unusual breeds of animals. All of *Farm Times* is a good market for freelancers, but Rural Religion is the best place to get started. Write tightly. Be sure of facts and names."

HAROWSMITH COUNTRY LIFE, Ferry Road, Charlotte VT 05445. (802)425-3961. Fax: (802)425-3307. Editor: John Barstow. Contact: Lisa Rathke. Bimonthly magazine covering country living, gardening, shelter, food and environmental issues. "*Harrowsmith Country Life* readers are generally college-educated country dwellers, looking for good information." Estab. 1986. Circ. 215,000. Pays 45 days after acceptance. Byline given. Offers 25% kill fee. Buys first North American serial rights. Reports in 2 months. Sample copy $4. Writer's guidelines for #10 SASE.

Nonfiction: Book excerpts, essays, expose (environmental issues), how-to (gardening/building), humor, interview/profile and opinion. Buys 36 mss/year. Query with published clips. Length: 500-5,000 words. Pays $500-1,500. Pays expenses of writers on assignment.

Photos: State availability of photos with submission. Reviews 35mm transparencies. Offers $100-325/photo. Model releases and identification of subjects required. Buys one-time rights.

Columns/Departments: Sourcebank (ideas, tips, tools, techniques relating to gardening, the environment, food, health), 50-400 words; and Gazette (brief news items). Buys 30 mss/year. Query with published clips. Length: 40-400 words. Pays $25-150.

Tips: "While main feature stories are open to freelancers, a good way for us to get to know the writer is through our Screed (essays), Sourcebank (tips and ideas) and Gazette (brief news items) departments. Articles should contain examples, quotations and anecdotes. They should be detailed and factual. Please submit material to Lisa Rathke, Assistant Editor."

THE MOTHER EARTH NEWS, Dept. WM, 5th Floor, 24 E. 23rd St., New York NY 10010. (212)260-7210. Editor: Owen Lipstein. Managing Editor: Matthew Scanlon. Mostly freelance written. Bimonthly magazine emphasizing "country living and country skills, for both long-time and would-be ruralites." Circ. 350,000. **Pays on acceptance.** Byline given. Submit seasonal material 5 months in advance. No handwritten mss. Reports within 3 months. Publishes ms an average of 6 months after acceptance. Sample copy $3. Writer's guidelines for #10 SASE with 2 first class stamps.

Nonfiction: How-to, home business, alternative energy systems, home building, home retrofit and home maintenance, energy-efficient structures, seasonal cooking, gardening and crafts. Buys 100-150 mss/year. Query. "A short, to-the-point paragraph is often enough. If it's a subject we don't need at all, we can answer immediately. If it tickles our imagination, we'll ask to take a look at the whole piece. No phone queries, please." Length: 300-3,000 words.

Photos: Purchased with accompanying ms. Send prints or transparencies. Uses 8×10 b&w glossies or any size color transparencies. Include type of film, speed and lighting used. Total purchase price for ms includes payment for photos. Captions and credits required.

Tips: "Probably the best way to break in is to study our magazine, digest our writer's guidelines, and send us a concise article illustrated with color transparencies that we can't resist. When folks query and we give a go-ahead on speculation, we often offer some suggestions. Failure to follow those suggestions can lose the sale for the author. We want articles that tell what real people are doing to take charge of their own lives. Articles should be well-documented and tightly written treatments of topics we haven't already covered. The critical thing is length, and our payment is by space, not word count. *No phone queries.*"

RURAL HERITAGE, 281 Dean Ridge Lane, Gainesboro TN 38562-9685. (615)268-0655. Editor: Gail Damerow. Publisher: Allan Damera. 98% freelance written. Willing to work with a small number of new/unpublished writers. Quarterly magazine devoted to the training and care of draft animals and other traditional country skills. Estab. 1975. Circ. 3,000. Pays on publication. Publishes ms an average of 6 months after acceptance. Byline given. Buys first World rights. Submit seasonal material 6 months in advance. Reports in 3 months. Sample copy $5.50. Writer's guidelines #10 SASE.

Nonfiction: How-to (all types of crafting and farming); interview/profile (especially people using draft animals); photo feature; and travel (emphasizing our theme, "rural heritage"). No articles on *modern* farming. Buys 100 mss/year. Query or send complete ms. Length: 500-1,500 words. Pays 5¢/word.

Photos: Send photos with ms (b&w 5×7 or larger.) No negatives. Pays $10. Captions and identification of subjects required. Buys one-time rights. Four covers/year, animals in harness $25.

Columns/Departments: Self-sufficiency (modern people preserving traditional American lifestyle), 500-1,500 words; Drafter's Features (draft horses and mules used for farming, horse shows and pulls—their care), 500-2,000 words; and Crafting (new designs and patterns), 500-1,500 words. Country Kids (descriptions of rural youngsters who have done [or are doing] remarkable things), 250-300 words. Buys 75 mss/year. Send complete ms. Pays 5¢/word."

Poetry: Traditional. Pays $5-25.

Fillers: Anecdotes and short humor. 500-900 words. Pays 5¢/word.

Tips: "Profiles/articles on draft horses and draft horse shows are always welcome."

RURALITE, P.O. Box 558, Forest Grove OR 97116-0558. (503)357-2105. Fax: (503)357-8615. Editor-in-Chief: Curtis Condon. Associate Editor: Walt Wentz. 80% freelance written. Works with new, unpublished writers "who have mastered the basics of good writing." Monthly magazine aimed at members of consumer-owned electric utilities throughout 9 western states, including Alaska. Publishes 54 regional editions. Estab. 1954. Circ. 265,000. Buys first rights, sometimes reprint rights. Send photocopy of article or typed ms with rights for sale noted and information about when and where the article previously appeared. For reprints, pays 50% of the amount paid for an original article. Rights may be reassigned. Byline given. **Pays on acceptance.** Query first; unsolicited manuscripts submitted without request rarely read by editors. Sample copy and writer's guidelines for 10×13 SAE with 4 first class stamps.

Nonfiction: Looking for well-written nonfiction, (occasional fiction piece) dealing primarily with human interest topics. Must have strong Northwest perspective and be sensitive to Northwest issues and attitudes. Wide range of topics possible, from energy-related subjects to little-known travel destinations to unusual businesses located in areas served by consumer-owned electric utilities. "About half of our readers are rural and small town residents; others are urban and suburban. Topics with an obvious 'big-city' focus not accepted. Family-related issues, Northwest history (no encyclopedia rewrites), people and events, unusual tidbits that tell the Northwest experience are best chances for a sale. Nostalgic, dripping sentimental pieces rejected out of hand." Buys 30-50 mss/yr. Length 800-2,000 words. Pays $140-400, quality photos may increase upper pay limit for "polished stories with impact."

Photos: "Illustrated stories are the key to a sale. Stories without art rarely make it, with the exception of humor pieces. Black and white prints, color slides, all formats, accepted with 'razor-sharp' focus. Fuzzy, low-contrast photos may lose the sale."

Tips: "We need solid writers and photographers who can relate to the Northwest attitude and convey that sensibility in their stories. Magazine is repositioning as regional four-color publication and will cover a wider range of topics. Recent coverage included regional health care (obstetrics); forest fire fighting; dog sled racing; finding a job in a recessionary economy. Look at a recent copy. We're looking for regular contributors to whom we can assign topics from our story list after they've proven their ability to deliver quality mss."

Science

These publications are published for laymen interested in technical and scientific developments and discoveries, applied science and technical or scientific hobbies. Publications of interest to the personal computer owner/user are listed in the Personal Computers section. Journals for scientists and engineers are listed in Trade in various sections.

AD ASTRA, 922 Pennsylvania Ave. SE, Washington DC 20003-2140. (202)543-3991. Fax: (202)546-4189. Editor-in-Chief: Richard Wagner. 80% freelance written. Bimonthly magazine covering the space program. "We publish non-technical, lively articles about all aspects of international space programs, from shuttle missions to planetary probes to plans for the future." Estab. 1989. Circ. 24,000. Pays on publication. Byline given. Buys first North American serial rights. Simultaneous and previously published submissions OK. Query for electronic submissions. Reports on queries when interested. Sample copy for 9 × 12 SASE; writer's guidelines for #10 SASE.
Nonfiction: Book excerpts, essays, expose, general interest, historical/nostalgic, interview/profile, opinion, personal experience, photo feature and technical. No science fiction or UFO stories. Query with published clips. Length: 1,200-3,000 words. Pays $100-200 for features.
Photos: State availability of photos with submission. Reviews 4 × 5 color transparencies and b&w prints. Negotiates payment. Identification of subjects required. Buys one-time rights.
Columns/Departments: Touchdown (opinion pieces). Query.
Tips: "Strongly prefer manuscripts to be accompanied by ASCII or Word Perfect 5.1 floppy disk."

ARCHAEOLOGY, Archaeological Institute of America, 135 William St., New York NY 10038. (212)732-5154. Fax: (212)732-5154. Editor: Peter A. Young. 5% freelance written. "We generally commission articles from professional archaeologists." Bimonthly magazine on archaeology. "The only magazine of its kind to bring worldwide archaeology to the attention of the general public." Estab. 1949. Circ. 150,000. Pays on publication. Byline given. Offers 25% kill fee. Buys first North American serial rights. Submit seasonal material 6 months in advance. Simultaneous submissions OK. Query preferred. Free sample copy and writer's guidelines.
Nonfiction: Essays and general interest. Buys 6 mss/year. Length: 1,000-3,000 words. Pays $750 maximum. Sometimes pays expenses of writers on assignment.
Photos: Send photos with submission.
  • Ranked as one of the best markets for freelance writers in *Writer's Digest* magazine's annual "Top 100 Markets," January 1993.

ASTRONOMY, Kalmbach Publishing, P.O. Box 1612, Waukesha WI 53187-1612. (414)796-8776. Fax: (414)796-1142. Editor: Robert Burnham. Managing Editor: Rhoda I. Sherwood. 75% freelance written. Monthly magazine covering astronomy—the science and hobby of. "Half of our magazine is for hobbyists (who may have little interest in the heavens in a scientific way); the other half is directed toward armchair astronomers who may be intrigued by the science." Estab. 1973. Circ. 170,000. **Pays on acceptance.** "We are governed by what is happening in the space program and the heavens. It can be up to a year before we publish a ms." Byline given. Buys first North American serial, one-time and all rights. Query for electronic submissions. Reports in 1 month on queries; 2 months on mss. Free writer's guidelines.
Nonfiction: Book excerpts, space and astronomy, how-to for astro hobbyists, humor (in the viewpoints column and about astro), new product, photo feature and technical. Buys 100-200 mss/year. Query. Length: 500-4,500 words. Pays $50-500.
Photos: Send photos with submission. Reviews transparencies and prints. Pays $25/photo. Captions, model releases and identification of subjects required.
Tips: "Submitting to *Astronomy* could be tough. (Take a look at how technical astronomy is.) But if someone is a physics teacher (or math or astronomy), he or she might want to study the magazine for a year to see the sorts of subjects and approaches we use and then submit a proposal."

THE ELECTRON, CIE Publishing, 1776 E. 17th St., Cleveland OH 44114-3679. (216)781-9400. Fax: (216)781-0331. Managing Editor: Michael E. Manning. 80% freelance written. Bimonthly tabloid on electronics and high technology. Estab. 1934. Circ. 50,000. Pays on publication. Publishes ms an average of 2 months after acceptance. Byline given. Buys all rights. Simultaneous queries and previously published submissions OK. Reports in 2 months. Free sample copy and writer's guidelines.
Nonfiction: Technical (tutorial and how-to), technology news and feature, photo feature and career/educational. All submissions must be electronics/technology-related. Query with letter/proposal and published clips. Pays $50-500.
Photos: State availability of photos. Reviews 8 × 10 and 5 × 7 b&w prints. Captions and identification of subjects required.
Tips: "We would like to receive educational electronics/technical articles. They must be written in a manner understandable to the beginning-intermediate electronics student. We are also seeking news/feature-type articles covering timely developments in high technology."

OMNI, Editorial Dept: Suite 205, 324 W. Wendover Ave., Greensboro NC 27408. Editor: Keith Ferrell. 75% freelance written. Prefers to work with published/established writers. Monthly magazine of the future covering science fact, fiction and fantasy for readers of all ages, backgrounds and interests. Estab. 1978. Circ. 700,000. Average issue includes 2-3 nonfiction feature articles and 1-2 fiction articles; also numerous columns. **Pays on acceptance.** Publishes ms an average of 5 months after acceptance. Offers 25% kill fee. Buys exclusive worldwide and exclusive first English rights and rights for *Omni* anthologies. Submit seasonal material 4-6 months in advance. Reports in 6 weeks. Free writer's guidelines with #10 SASE (request fiction or nonfiction).

Nonfiction: "Feature articles for *Omni* cover all branches of science with an emphasis on the future: What will this discovery or technique mean to us next year, in five years, or even by the year 2025? People want to know and understand what scientists are doing and how scientific research is affecting their lives and their future. *Omni* publishes articles about science in language that people can understand. We seek very knowledgeable science writers who are ready to work with scientists and futurists to produce articles that can inform, interest and entertain our readers with the opportunity to participate in many ground breaking studies." Send query/proposal. Length: 1,500-3,000 words. Pays $2,500-3,500, plus reasonable expenses.

Photos: Frank DeVino, graphic director. State availability of photos. Reviews 35mm slides and 4×5 transparencies.

Columns/Departments: Explorations (unusual travel or locations on Earth); Mind (psychiatry and psychology, neurology, the brain); Earth (environment); Space (technology); Arts (theatre, music, film, technology); Interview (of prominent person); Continuum (newsbreaks); Antimatter and UFO Update (unusual newsbreaks, paranormal); Stars (astronomy); Artificial Intelligence (computers, etc.); The Body (medical); Digs (anthropology, archaeology, paleontology, etc.); Books (technology, profiles); Transportation (technology); First Word (editorial commissioned, no queries); and Last Word (humor, submit ms, no queries). Query with clips of previously published work. Length: 750 words. Pays $750; $175 for Continuum and Antimatter items.

Fiction: Contact Ellen Datlow. Fantasy and science fiction. Publishes novel excerpts. Buys 2 mss/issue. Send complete ms. Length: 10,000 words maximum. Pays $1,250-2,000.

- Ranked as one of the best markets for freelance writers in *Writer's Digest* magazine's annual "Top 100 Markets," January 1993.

Tips: "To get an idea of the kinds of fiction we publish, check recent back issues of the magazine."

POPULAR SCIENCE, 2 Park Ave., New York NY 10016. (212)779-5000. Fax: (212)779-5468. Editor-in-Chief: Fred Abatemarco. Executive Editor: Jack Stepler. 50% freelance written. Prefers to work with published/ established writers. Monthly magazine for the well-educated adult, interested in science, technology, new products. Estab. 1872. Circ. 1.8 million. **Pays on acceptance.** Publishes ms an average of 4 months after acceptance. Byline given. Buys first North American serial rights only. Pays negotiable kill fee. Any electronic submission OK. Reports in 4 weeks. Query. Writer's guidelines for #10 SASE.

Nonfiction: "*Popular Science* is devoted to exploring (and explaining) to a nontechnical but knowledgable readership the technical world around us. We cover all of the sciences, engineering and technology, and above all, products. We are largely a 'thing'-oriented publication: things that fly or travel down a turnpike, or go on or under the sea, or cut wood, or reproduce music, or build buildings, or make pictures. We are especially focused on the new, the ingenious and the useful. Contributors should be as alert to the possibility of selling us pictures and short features as they are to major articles. Freelancers should study the magazine to see what we want and avoid irrelevant submissions." Buys several hundred mss/year. Uses mostly color photos. Pays expenses of writers on assignment.

- Ranked as one of the best markets for freelance writers in *Writer's Digest* magazine's annual "Top 100 Markets," January 1993.

Tips: "Probably the easiest way to break in here is by covering a news story in science and technology that we haven't heard about yet. We need people to be acting as scouts for us out there and we are willing to give the most leeway on these performances. We are interested in good, sharply focused ideas in all areas we cover. We prefer a vivid, journalistic style of writing, with the writer taking the reader along with him, showing the reader what he saw, through words. Please query first."

SCIENTIFIC AMERICAN, 415 Madison Ave., New York NY 10017. "Prefers not to share information."

21ST CENTURY SCIENCE & TECHNOLOGY, 21st Century Science Associates, P.O. Box 16285, Washington DC 20041. (703)777-7473. Editor: Carol White. Managing Editor: Marjorie Mazel Hecht. 10-20% freelance written. Quarterly magazine that covers frontier science and technology and science history. "We are interested in material that deals with progress." Estab. 1988. Circ. 30,000. Pays on publication. Byline given. Buys one-time rights and makes work-for-hire assignments. Simultaneous and previously published submissions OK. Send photocopy of article and information about when and where the article previously appeared. Query for electronic submissions. Reports in 6 weeks on queries. Sample copy for 9×12 SAE with 5 first class stamps.

Nonfiction: Book excerpts, expose (environmental hoaxes), historical, interview/profile, new product and technical (new scientific research, astronomy, cold fusion, fusion, space exploration, biophysics and advanced nuclear). Buys 5-6 mss/year. Query. Length: 500-6,000 words. Pays $100 minimum. We supply copies of issue in quantity.

Photos: State availability of photos with submission. Reviews contact sheets, transparencies and prints. Offers $25 minimum/photo. Captions, model releases and identification of subjects required. Buys one-time rights.

Science Fiction, Fantasy and Horror

These publications often publish experimental fiction and many are open to new writers. More information on these markets can be found in the Contests and Awards section under the Fiction heading.

ABERATIONS, A E Press, P.O. Box 8040, #13, 544 Ygnacio Valley Road, Walnut Creek CA 94596. (510)682-9662 or (510)825-4434. Editor-in-Chief/Publisher: Jon L. Herron. Managing Editor: Richard Blair. Monthly magazine of ADULT horror, science fiction and dark fantasy. "We emphasize our openness to the strange and different by the fact that even our name is an aberration. This is an 'in and out' adult publication—in your face and out on the edge." Estab. 1992. Circ. 1,500. Pays on publication. Publishes ms an average of 1 year after acceptance. Byline given. Buys first North American serial and one-time rights. Submit seasonal material 8 months in advance. Electronic submissions only after acceptance. Reports in 1 month on queries; 4 months on mss. Sample copy $5 postpaid. Writer's guidelines for #10 SASE.

Nonfiction: Contact: Jon L. Herron. "Interviews" with deceased madmen. "Prefer humorous, but you must pay attention to detail. Know your facts." Buys 12 mss/year. Send complete ms. Length: 1-3,000 words. Book, video, movie reviews (H/SF/F). Buys 70 mss/year. Send complete ms. Length: 350 words. Pays to $5 plus 1 copy for assigned articles; copies for unsolicited articles. Send ms with rights for sale noted.

Photos: Send photos with submission. Reviews 3×5 b&w prints *only*. Pays for photos in copy *only*. Model releases and subject identification required. Buys one-time rights.

Fiction: Contact: Richard Blair. Adult horror, science fiction, dark fantasy, mystery (with H/SF/F). "No formula stories. All must have sci-fi, horror, dark fantasy slant. Explicit sex, gore, profanity must be germane to the story. No work based on creation of others. We print stories other magazines are afraid to print." Buys 150 mss/year. Send complete ms. Length 500-8,000 words. Pays to $7 plus copy or copy(ies) only and discount for additional copies.

Poetry: Contact: Bobbie Sinha. Avant-garde, free verse, light verse and traditional. "No haiku, please." Buys 150 poems/year. Submit maximum 10 poems/mailing. Length: 4-100 lines. Pays $1 plus copy or copy(ies) *only*.

Tips: "Tell the tales that pulsate in the darkest corners of your mind, even though you believe no one would print them. Show us your aberrations. Submit original ideas. No formula stories. We cater to unpublished and underpublished writers. Writers have their best chance with nonfiction and poems."

ABORIGINAL SCIENCE FICTION, The 2nd Renaissance Foundation, P.O. Box 2449, Woburn MA 01888-0849. Editor: Charles C. Ryan. 99% freelance written. Quarterly science fiction magazine. "We publish short, lively and entertaining science fiction short stories and poems, accompanied by b&w illustrations." Estab. 1986. Circ. 23,000. Pays on publication. Publishes ms an average of 1 year after acceptance. Byline given. Buys first North American serial rights, non-exclusive options on other rights. Query for electronic submissions. Reports in 2-3 months. Sample copy $3.50 for 9×12 SAE with 4 first class stamps. Writer's guidelines for #10 SASE.

Fiction: Science fiction of all types. "We do not use fantasy, horror, sword and sorcery or *Twilight Zone* type stories." Buys 48 mss/year. Send complete ms. Length: 2,000-6,000 words. Pays $250. Send photocopy of short story.

Poetry: Science and science fiction. Buys 8-12 poems/year.

Tips: "Read science fiction novels and all the science fiction magazines. Do not rely on science fiction movies or TV. We are open to new fiction writers who are making a sincere effort."

‡ADVANCED WARNING! The Illustrated Anthology of Science Fiction and Fantasy, Graphic Image Press, Inc., P.O. Box 1109, Murray Hill Station, New York NY 10156-0604. Editor: Arnaldo Lopez. 95% freelance written. Literary magazine. Quarterly magazine covering science fiction and fantasy. "We're looking for quality science fiction and fantasy short stories and poems that can be enjoyed by adults and young adults alike, with no granitious profanity or graphic sex." Estab. 1992. **Pays on acceptance.** Publishes ms an average of 6 months after acceptance. Byline given. Buys first North American serial rights. Editorial lead time 6 months. Submit seasonal material 6 months in advance. Reports in 2-3 months on mss. Writer's guidelines for #10 SASE.

Fiction: Fantasy and science fiction. No horror, mystery or erotica. Buys 35 mss/year. Length: 1,200-7,000 words. Pays $100-300.

Poetry: Free verse, Haiku, light verse and traditional. Buys 8-12 poems/year. Submit maximum 4 poems. Length: 8-16 lines. Pays $75.

Tips: "Be professional in your submissions and don't forget your SASE! Please stick to our guidelines (which are available for SASE). We're publishing a magazine that can be enjoyed by readers of *all* ages; so gratuitous profanity or sex is a definite no-no!"

AMAZING STORIES, TSR, Inc., P.O. Box 111, Lake Geneva WI 53147-0111. (414)248-3625. Fax: (414)248-0389. Editor: Mr. Kim Mohan. 95% freelance written. Monthly magazine of science fiction, fantasy and horror short stories. "We are looking for stories and articles that truly live up to the magazine's name—imaginative, trend-setting, thought-provoking pieces of work that will hold a reader's attention and live in his or her memory long after the reading experience is over." Accepts ms submissions from new/unpublished writers as well as those with professional credentials. Circ. 15,000. **Pays on acceptance.** Publishes ms an average of 6 months after acceptance. Byline given. Buys first worldwide serial rights in the English language only; nonexclusive re-use option (with additional pay). No simultaneous or previously published submissions. Reports in 3 months. Sample copy $5. Writer's guidelines for #10 SASE.

Nonfiction: Science-fact articles of interest to science fiction audience; essays and opinion pieces by authorities in some area of science or speculative fiction. No true-life experiences, no "soap box" pieces about invalidated theories. Buys 6-12 mss/year. Query first, with published clips if available. Length: 1,000-5,000 words. Pays 10-12¢/word.

Fiction: Science fiction, contemporary and ethnic fantasy and horror. "We want science fiction stories to dominate the magazine's content, but will not turn away any well-written piece of speculative fiction. Horror has the best chance of selling if it has a science-fictional or fantastic setting. Stay away from predictable plot lines and rehashes of old themes—show us *new* ideas." Buys 100-120 mss/year. Send complete ms. Length: 1,000-25,000 words. Pays 6-10¢/word, with shorter stories earning higher rates.

Tips: "Although a large portion of each magazine is devoted to stories from established writers, we are also committed to finding new talent and being a place where unpublished authors can get a start. Nevertheless, we are *very* discriminating about what we purchase. Do not expect to succeed with cliché ideas, stereotypical characters or obtuse 'literary' rambling. Hard science fiction is especially in demand, but any such story must be based on a *plausible* extrapolation from real science. Be familiar with the magazine, and have a copy of our guidelines in hand, before sending us something to review."

ANALOG SCIENCE FICTION & FACT, Dell Magazines Fiction Group, 1540 Broadway, New York NY 10036. Editor: Dr. Stanley Schmidt. 100% freelance written. Eager to work with new/unpublished writers. For general future-minded audience. Monthly. Estab. 1930. Buys first North American serial and nonexclusive foreign serial rights. **Pays on acceptance.** Publishes ms an average of 10 months after acceptance. Byline given. Reports in 1 month. Sample copy $3 for 6×9 SASE with 5 first class stamps. Writer's guidelines for #10 SASE.

Nonfiction: Illustrated technical articles dealing with subjects of not only current but future interest, i.e., topics at the present frontiers of research whose likely future developments have implications of wide interest. Buys about 13 mss/year. Query. Length: 5,000 words. Pays 6¢/word.

Fiction: "Basically, we publish science fiction stories. That is, stories in which some aspect of future science or technology is so integral to the plot that, if that aspect were removed, the story would collapse. The science can be physical, sociological or psychological. The technology can be anything from electronic engineering to biogenetic engineering. But the stories must be strong and realistic, with believable people doing believable things—no matter how fantastic the background might be." Buys 60-100 unsolicited mss/year. Send complete ms of short fiction; query about serials. Length: 2,000-80,000 words. Pays 4¢/word for novels; 5-6¢/word for novelettes; 6-8¢/word for shorts under 7,500 words; $450-600 for intermediate lengths.

Tips: "In query give clear indication of central ideas and themes and general nature of story line—and what is distinctive or unusual about it. We have no hard-and-fast editorial guidelines, because science fiction is such a broad field that I don't want to inhibit a new writer's thinking by imposing 'Thou Shalt Not's.' Besides, a really good story can make an editor swallow his preconceived taboos. I want the best work I can get, regardless of who wrote it—and I need new writers. So I work closely with new writers who show definite promise, but of course it's impossible to do this with *every* new writer. No occult or fantasy."

ASIMOV'S SCIENCE FICTION, Dell Magazines Fiction Group, 1540 Broadway, New York NY 10036. (212)856-6400. Editor-in-Chief: Gardner Dozois. 98% freelance written. Works with a small number of new/unpublished writers each year. Published 13 times a year, including two double issues. Estab. 1977. Circ. 100,000. **Pays on acceptance.** Buys first North American serial and nonexclusive foreign serial rights; reprint rights occasionally. No simultaneous submissions. Reports in 6 weeks. Sample copy $3 for 6½×9½ SAE. Writer's guidelines for #10 SASE.

Nonfiction: Science. Query first.
Fiction: Science fiction primarily. Some fantasy and poetry. "It's best to read a great deal of material in the genre to avoid the use of some *very* old ideas." Buys 10 mss/issue. Submit complete ms. Length: 100-20,000 words. Pays 5-8¢/word except for novel serializations at 4¢/word.
Tips: "Query letters not wanted, except for nonfiction."

THE BARRELHOUSE, An Exercise Into the Unknown, 1600 Oak Creek Dr., Edmond OK 73034. Editor-in-Chief: Doug Coulson. Managing Editor: Rob Hibbard. Quarterly magazine of strange and speculative literatures. "Audience is wide. All ages. We try to challenge contemporary thought patterns through the utmost in imaginative writing. Have a statement, then communicate it with subtle class. Always remember the objective viewpoint. Much surrealism, dark fantasies, metaphorical, mythological extrapolations and suspense." Estab. 1992. Circ. 250. Pays on publication. Publishes ms an average of 1 year after acceptance. Byline given. Buys first North American serial or second serial (reprint) rights. Editorial lead time 4-6 months. Submit seasonal material 1 year in advance. Simultaneous submissions and previously published submissions OK; send tearsheet or photocopy of article or short story and typed ms with rights for sale noted. Include information about when and where the article previously appeared. For reprints, pays 25% of the amount paid for an original article. Reports in 1 month on queries; 3 months on mss. Sample copy $4.25. Writer's guidelines for #10 SASE.
Nonfiction: Interviews, reviews, historic/nostalgic, folklore, opinion, general interest on writing and essays (containing significant philosophical thought to some extent). Buys 10 mss/year. Query only if established. Length: 250-4,000 words. Pays $5-25 and copies. "Fortean: Work-for-hire tidbits of unexplained phenomena with source references, including name, date and page number. We are interested in really off-the-wall, strange happenings to use as sidebars on a regular basis; supernatural and/or odd and bizarre items, occult, or otherwise. Nothing solely pertaining to unsolved crimes. We will purchase all rights to these items, no byline given contributors. Maximum 100 words, average 25-50 words, explaining the occurrence in concise, straightforward, and entertaining terms. Payment $2.50-8 each (10¢/word, though we *mean* concise) plus one contributor's copy on acceptance. Accepts 15-30 mss/year. Real-life supernatural items only when clear and to the point within the required length and from reputable sources—not personal experience. Our editors are well-versed in this type of thing and will be extremely particular in our selections."
Fiction: Horror, adventure, erotica, ethnic, experimental, fantasy (light/dark), historical, humorous, mainstream, novel excerpts (only when they can stand on their own as stories), science fiction, slice-of-life vignettes, suspense, surrealism, satire, psychic/supernatural, occult and magical realism. "No porno." Buys 40-50 mss/year. Send complete ms. Length: 50-8,000 words. Pays $5-25 and copies.
Poetry: Avant-garde, free verse and haiku. "No light, sentimental verse. Nothing without meaning. Abstract, experimental easiest to use." Buys 20 poems/year. Submit maximum 10 poems. Length: 2 lines minimum. Pays $3-25 and copies.
Tips: "Authors should challenge existing thought patterns. We like alienation themes. We want topics that are in some way *unpublishable* in most markets. We like true surrealism. We like non-hardware science fiction. Dark fantasies, dark humor, satire also. Have a statement. Speculation is the thing at *The Barrelhouse*. Do not try to insist that your idea is the sole means in which to experience our surroundings. Use the art to communciate the idea in a desirable manner. Audience is wide. Believe in submissions. Craft is of the utmost importance."

MARION ZIMMER BRADLEY'S FANTASY MAGAZINE, P.O. Box 249, Berkeley CA 94701-0249. Editor: Marion Z. Bradley. 100% freelance written. Quarterly magazine of fantasy fiction. Estab. 1988. **Pays on acceptance.** Publishes ms an average of 1 year after acceptance. Byline given. Offers $25 kill fee. Buys first North American serial rights. Reports in 3 months. Sample copy $4.
Fiction: Fantasy. No science fiction, very little horror. Buys 55-60 mss/year. Send complete ms. Length: 300-7,500 words. Pays 3-10¢/word.
Tips: "Do not submit without first reading guidelines."

‡DEAD OF NIGHT MAGAZINE, Dead of Night Publications, Suite 228, 916 Shaker Rd., Longmeadow MA 01106-2416. Editor: Lin Stein. 90% freelance written. Semiannual April/October magazine. "Our readers enjoy horror, mystery, fantasy and sci-fi, and they also don't mind an 'old-fashioned' vampire or ghost story on occasion. Because of the genre mix in our magazine, we appeal to a wide readership." Estab. 1989. Circ. 300. Pays on publication. Publishes ms an average of 6-12 months after acceptance. Byline given. Offers 10% kill fee. Buys one-time rights. Editorial lead time 3 months. Submit seasonal material 6 months in advance. Reports in 3 weeks on queries; 1-2 months on mss. Sample copy $6.95 current issue; $2.50 back issue (subject to availability). Writer's guidelines for #10 SASE.
Nonfiction: Book excerpts, interview/profile and book/film reviews. Buys 8-10 mss/year. Send complete ms. Length: 350-1,800 words. Pays 2¢/word minimum.
Fiction: Fantasy, horror, mystery, novel excerpts and science fiction. Nothing non-genre. Buys 7-15 mss/year. Send complete ms. Length: 500-2,500 words. Pays 2-3¢/word.
Tips: "We are most open to fiction. (Most of our reviews are written by our contributing editors—on a regular basis, but freelancers may query.) For tips or hints, the best, of course, is to read the magazine! The second best is to at least read our guidelines, and the last tip is to try to present us with a horror/mystery/fantasy or

science fiction story that is fresh, original, and entertaining. If the story entertains the editors here, we'll buy it so our *readers* can enjoy it and be entertained by it as well."

FIGMENT, Tales from the Imagination, Figment Press, P.O. Box 3128, Moscow ID 83843-1806. Managing Editors: J.C. Hendee and Barb Hendee. Associate Editor: Mark Coen. 95% freelance written. Quarterly magazine of fiction in the genres of fantasy and science fiction. "We look for fiction set apart by solid characterization." Estab. 1989. Circ. 500. **Pays on acceptance.** Publishes ms an average of 5 months after acceptance. Byline given. Buys first North American serial rights. Submit seasonal material 9 months in advance. Reports in 2 weeks on queries; 2 months on mss. Sample copy $4 bulk; $5 first class. Writer's guidelines for #10 SASE.
Nonfiction: Genre-related essays, general interest, historical/nostalgic, humor, interview/profile and personal experience. Buys 4-8 mss/year. Query. Pays ½-2¢/per word, depending department/type; obtain guidelines for details.
Photos: State availability of photos with submission. Reviews contact sheets. Offers no additional payment for photos accepted with ms. Captions required.
Fiction: Experimental, fantasy, humorous, science fiction and slice-of-life-vignette. Never send artwork with stories; we assign artwork *after* a purchase. Buys 50 mss/year. Send complete ms. Length: 500-10,000 words. Pays ½-1¢/word.
Poetry: Free verse, haiku, light verse, traditional, sonnets, ballads, limericks, folk songs, epics. "We tend to be more formal in style than our competition." Buys 25 poems/year. Submit 5 maximum poems. Pays 15¢/line plus 2¢/word; $5 min.
Tips: "We look for highly-polished, well-crafted fiction. Strong characterization and a solid plot is a must. Never forget that fiction is by, for and about people. And lastly, it must always be entertaining. All areas are open to freelancers. We're always looking for new talent. Keep up the hard work—success in this business is a lot of hard work mixed with a bit of luck. Encourages disk submissions in most IBM compatible formats."

HAUNTS, Nightshade Publications, P.O. Box 3342, Providence RI 02906-0742. (401)781-9438. Fax: (401)943-0980. Editor: Joseph K. Cherkes. 98% freelance written. Prefers to work with published/established writers. "We are a literary quarterly geared to those fans of the 'pulp' magazines of the 30s, 40s and 50s, with tales of horror, the supernatural and the bizarre. We are trying to reach those in the 18-35 age group." Estab. 1984. Circ. 1,200. Pays on publication. Publishes ms an average of 1 year after acceptance. Byline given. Buys first North American serial rights. Reprints OK; send photocopy of article or short story. "Supports most major WP programs for IBM/PC. Send 5¼ or 3½ disk with work along with ms. Send work as both word processor format *and* ASCII text format." Reports in 3 weeks on queries; 3 months on mss. Sample copy $3.95 with 4 first class stamps. Writer's guidelines for #10 SASE.
Fiction: Fantasy, horror, novel excerpts and suspense. "No fiction involving blow-by-blow dismemberment, explicit sexual scenes or pure adventure." Buys 36 fiction mss/year. Query. Length: 1,500-8,000 words. Pays $5-50.
Poetry: Free verse, light verse and traditional. Buys 12-16 poems/year. Submit maximum 3 poems. Pays in contributor's copies.
Tips: "Market open from January 1 to December 1, inclusively. How the writer handles revisions often is a key to acceptance."

HOBSON'S CHOICE, The Starwind Press, P.O. Box 98, Ripley OH 45167-0098. (513)392-4549. Editors: David F. Powell and Susannah C. West. 75% freelance written. Eager to work with new/unpublished writers. Monthly magazine "for older teenagers and adults who have an interest in science and technology, and who also enjoy reading well-crafted science fiction and fantasy." Estab. 1974. Circ. 2,500. Pays on publication. Publishes ms an average of 1 year after acceptance. Byline given. Rights vary with author and material; negotiated with author. Usually first serial rights and second serial reprint rights (nonfiction). Query for electronic submissions. "We encourage disposable submissions; easier for us and easier for the author. Just enclose SASE for our response. Reprints OK; send photocopy of article or short story and information about when and where the article previously appeared. Pays 30% of their fee for an original article. We prefer non-simultaneous submissions." Reports in 3 months. Sample copy $2.25 for 9 × 12 SAE. Writer's guidelines for #10 SASE. "Tipsheet package for $1; contains all guidelines, tipsheets on science fiction writing, nonfiction science writing and submission etiquette."
Nonfiction: How-to (technological interest, e.g., how to build a robot eye, building your own radio receiver, etc.); interview/profile (of leaders in science and technology fields); and technical ("did you know" articles dealing with development of current technology). "No speculative articles, dealing with topics such as the Abominable Snowman, Bermuda Triangle, etc. At present, most nonfiction is staff-written or reprinted from other sources. We hope to use more freelance written work in the future." Query. Length: 1,000-7,000 words. Pays 1-4¢/word.
Photos: Send photos with accompanying query or ms. Reviews b&w contact sheets and prints. Model releases and identification of subjects required. "If photos are available, we prefer to purchase them as part of the written piece." Buys negotiable rights.

Fiction: Fantasy and science fiction. "No stories whose characters were created by others (e.g. Lovecraft, *Star Trek*, *Star Wars* characters, etc.)." Buys 15-20 mss/year. Send complete ms. Length: 2,000-10,000 words. Pays 1-4¢/word. "We prefer previously unpublished fiction. No query necessary. We don't publish horror, poetry, novel excerpts or serialized novels."

Tips: "Our need for nonfiction is greater than for fiction at present. Almost all our fiction and nonfiction is unsolicited. We rarely ask for rewrites, because we've found that rewrites are often disappointing; although the writer may have rewritten it to fix problems, he/she frequently changes parts we liked, too."

THE MAGAZINE OF FANTASY & SCIENCE FICTION, Mercury Press, P.O. Box 11526, Eugene OR 97440. Editor: Kristine Kathryn Rusch. 100% freelance written. Monthly fantasy fiction and science fiction magazine. Estab. 1949. Circ. 80,000. **Pays on acceptance.** Byline given. Buys first North American and foreign serial rights. Submit seasonal material 8 months in advance. Reports in 2 months. Writer's guidelines for #10 SASE.

Fiction: Fantasy, horror and science fiction. Send complete ms. Length: 2,000-20,000 words. Pays 5-7¢/word.

Tips: "We need more hard science fiction and humor."

MIDNIGHT ZOO, A E Press, #13, 544 Ygnacio Valley Road, Walnut Creek CA 94596. (510)682-9662 or (510)825-4434. Editor-in-Chief: Jon L. Herron. Monthly magazine of horror, sci-fi, fantasy and science fact. "All articles, stories and poems must have a H/SF/F slant. Science Fiction must be hard science. No explicit sex or gore. Audience 12-100+ years old." Estab. 1990. Circ. 3,000. Pays on publication. Publishes ms an average of 1 year after acceptance. Byline given. Buys first North American serial, one-time and second serial (reprint) rights. Submit seasonal material 8 months in advance. Previously published submissions OK; send typed ms with rights for sale noted. Reports in 1 month on queries; 4 months on mss. Sample copy $6 postpaid. Writer's guidelines for #10 SASE. Electronic submissions only after acceptance.

Nonfiction: Contact: Jon L. Herron. Book excerpts, essays, general interest (SF/H/F) humor, interview/profile (SF/H/F), new medical discoveries, new product, opinion, personal experience (psychic, occult, strange), technical (science), poetry and writer's interest. Length: 2,000 words. Book, video, movie reviews. Length 500 words. Buys 90 mss/year. Query with or without published clips or send complete ms. Length: 1,000-3,000 words. Pays $6 plus 1 copy for assigned articles; copies for unsolicited articles and reprints.

Photos: Send photos with submission. Reviews 3×5 b&w prints *only*. Pays for photos in copy *only*. Model releases and subject identification required. Buys one-time rights.

Columns/Departments: Contact: Jon L. Herron. Strange Happenings (occult, strange, supernatural, psychic, etc.), 1,000-2,000 words; Scientific Scene (hard science, new discoveries, etc) 1,000-2,000 words; Interviews (H/SF/F writers, artists, TV & movie stars, scientists), 2,000-4,000 words; and Writer's Corner (tips for writers), 1,000-1,500 words. Buys 90 mss/year. Query with published clips or send completed ms. Pays to $6 plus 1 copy or copy(ies) *only for short works*.

Fiction: Contact: Elizabeth Martin-Burk or Debbie Baker. Horror, science fiction, fantasy, mystery (with H/SF/F). "No formula stories. All must have sci-fi, horror, fantasy slant. No work based on creation of others." Buys 180 mss/year. Send complete ms. Length: 500-8,000 words. Pays to $12 plus copy of copy(ies) only.

Poetry: Contact: Bobbie Sinha. Avant-garde, free verse, light verse and traditional. "No haiku, please." Buys 150 poems/year. Submit maximum 10 poems/mailing. Length 4-100 lines. Pays $1-2 plus copy or copy(ies) *only*.

Fillers: Contact: Rus McLaughlin. Anecdotes, facts, gags to be illustrated by cartoonist, news breaks and short humor. Length: 20-1000 words. Pays copy(ies) *only*.

Tips: "Submit original ideas. No formula stories. We cater to unpublished and underpublished writers. Writers have their best chance with nonfiction and poems."

PANDORA, 2844 Grayson, Ferndale MI 48220. Editors: Meg MacDonald, Polly Vedder (art), Ruth Berman (poetry). 99% freelance written. Works with a number of new/unpublished writers each year. Semiannual anthology covering science fiction and fantasy. "We anticipate quarterly status in 1993/94." Estab. 1978. Circ. 500. Pays on publication. Publishes ms an average of 12-18 months after acceptance. Byline given. Buys first North American serial and second serial (reprint) rights; one-time rights on some poems. Reports in 3 months. Reprints OK; send typed ms with rights for sale noted and information about when and where the article previously appeared. Pays 100% of their fee for an original article. Sample copy $5, ($10 overseas). Writer's guidelines for #10 SASE. "International contributors, please use enough IRCs to cover return of manuscript or letter."

Fiction: "Query first! We may still be overstocked with fiction. *Unsolicited mss will be returned unread/unopened.*" Fantasy, science fiction. "No pun stories. No Lucifer or deals with the devil stories. Nothing X-rated (no vulgar language, gratuitous violence, sex, racisim, etc.). No inaccurate science and no horror of the chainsaw variety. Scary stories, ghost stories OK. No occult material, however." Buys 20 mss/year. Send complete ms. Length: under 6,000 words. Longer work must be exceptional. Pays 1-2¢/word.

Poetry: Contact Ruth Berman, poetry editor, 2809 Drew Ave. S., Minneapolis MN 55417. Buys 10-15 poems/year. Payment starts at $4. No romance, occult or horror. "Query first in 1994."

Tips: "We still want stories about characters our readers can sympathize with and care about. Then give them convincing, relevant problems that they must overcome. Stories about people and their difficulties, victories and losses are of more interest to us than stories about futuristic gadgets. What impact does the gadget have on society? *That's* what we want to know. Stories must have a point—not just a pun. Happy endings aren't necessary, but we urge authors to leave the reader with a sense that no matter the outcome, something has been accomplished between the first and last pages. *Reading our magazine is the best way to determine our needs, and we strongly recommend all contributors read at least one sample.* Always send for guidelines before submitting as well. We like to see whole stories, the shorter the better, and we will make attempts to respond personally with a critique. Stories which support the existence of a higher authority than God are welcome. We like fantasy and don't see enough of it. Highly descriptive, but not overwritten language is a plus. Take us on a magical journey—through time, through space, through the 'looking glass'—we want to see your work, and we want to publish as much as we can."

THE SCREAM FACTORY, The Magazine of Horrors, Past, Present, and Future, Deadline Press, 4884 Pepperwood Way, San Jose CA 95124-5218. Editors: Peter Enfantino, Bob Morrish and John Scoleri. 75% freelance written. Quarterly literary magazine about horror in films and literature. Estab. 1988. Circ. 2,000. **Pays on acceptance.** Publishes ms an average of 6 months after acceptance. Buys first North American serial rights. Submit seasonal material 6 months in advance. No simultaneous submissions or reprints. Reports in 2 weeks on queries, 1 month on ms. Sample copy $6 (please make checks payable to *The Scream Factory*). Writer's guidelines for #10 SASE.

Nonfiction: Essays, historical/nostalgic, interview/profile, new product and personal experience. Buys 35-50 mss/year. Query or send complete ms. Pays ½¢/word.

Photos: Send photos with submission. Reviews prints. Offers no additional payment for photos accepted with ms. Captions required. Buys one-time rights.

Columns/Departments: Book reviews of horror novels/collections; and Writer's Writing (what horror authors are currently working on).

Fillers: Facts and newsbreaks. Pays ½¢/word. Also small reviews (150-200 words). "Please query on these."

Tips: "Looking for reviews of horror fiction, especially the lesser known authors. News on the horror genre, interviews with horror authors and strong opinion pieces. No unsolicited fiction accepted."

THE SILVER WEB, Buzzcity Press, P.O. Box 38190, Tallahassee FL 32315. (904)385-8948. Editor: Ann Kennedy. Semiannual literary magazine that features science fiction, dark fantasy and horror. Estab. 1988. Circ. 500. **Pays on acceptance.** Byline given. Buys first North American serial, first, one-time or second serial (reprint) rights. Simultaneous submissions and previously published submissions OK. Query for electronic submissions. Reports in 1 month. Sample copy $5.75. Writer's guidelines for #10 SASE.

Nonfiction: Essays and opinion. Buys 4-8 mss/year. Query. Length: 500-8,000 words. Pays 1-3¢/word.

Photos: State availability of photos with submission. Reviews prints. Offers no additional payment for photos accepted with ms. Identification of subjects required. Buys one-time rights.

Fiction: Experimental, horror and science fiction. "We do not want to see typical storylines, endings or predictable revenge stories." Buys 20-25 mss/year. Send complete ms. Length: 500-8,000 words. Pays 1-3¢/word.

Poetry: Avant-garde, free verse and haiku. Buys 10-15/year. Submit maximum 5 poems. Pays $5-15.

Fillers: Gags to be illustrated by cartoonist and art fillers. Buys 10/year. Pays $2-5.

Tips: "Give us an unusual unpredictable story with strong, believable characters that we can care about. Surprise us with something unique. We do look for interviews with people in the field (writers, artists, filmmakers)."

STAR*LINE, Newsletter of the Science Fiction Poetry Association, 1412 NE 35th St., Ocala FL 34479. Editor: Margaret B. Simon. 95% freelance written. Eager to work with new/unpublished writers. Bimonthly newsletter covering science fiction, fantasy and horror poetry for association members. Estab. 1978. Circ. 200. Pays prior to publication. Byline given. Buys one-time rights. Submit seasonal material 3 months in advance. Reports in 1 month. Sample copy $1.50 for 6×9 SAE with 2 first class stamps. Writer's guidelines for #10 SASE.

Nonfiction: Articles must display familiarity with the genre. How to (write a poem); interview/profile (of science fiction, fantasy and horror poets); opinion (science fiction and poetics); and essays. Buys 4-6 mss/year. Send complete ms. Length: 500-2,000 words. Pays $1-5 plus complimentary copy.

Columns/Department: Pays 5¢/line plus 2¢/word. Reviews: 100-500 words, ¼¢/word. Articles: 500-2,500 words, ¼¢/word. Art: $1; reprint material acceptable. One copy to all contributors. Pays on publication for first North American serial rights with reversion of subsidiary rights on publication.

Poetry: Avant-garde, free verse, haiku, light verse and traditional. "Poetry must be related to speculative fiction subjects." Buys 60-80 poems/year. Submit maximum 3 poems. Length: 1-100 lines. Pays $1 for first 10 lines; 5¢/line thereafter plus complimentary copy.

Fillers: Speculative-oriented quotations—prose or poetic. Length: 10-50 words. Pays $1.

STARLOG MAGAZINE, The Science Fiction Universe, Starlog Group, 8th Floor, 475 Park Ave. S., New York NY 10016-1689. Editor: David McDonnell. 85% freelance written. Eager to work with new/unpublished writers. Monthly magazine covering "the science fiction-fantasy genre: its films, TV, books, art and personalities." Estab. 1976. "We concentrate on interviews with actors, directors, screenwriters, producers, special effects technicians and others. Be aware that 'sci-fi' and 'Trekkie' are seen as derogatory terms by our readers and by us." Pays on publication. Publishes ms an average of 4 months after acceptance. Byline given. Offers kill fee "only to mss *written* or interviews *done.*" Buys all rights and occasionally, second serial (reprint) rights to other material. Submit seasonal material 6 months in advance. No simultaneous submissions. Reports in 6 weeks. "We provide an assignment sheet and contract to *all* writers with deadline and other info, authorizing a queried piece." Sample copy $5. Writer's guidelines for #10 SASE.
Nonfiction: Interview/profile (actors, directors, screenwriters who've made science fiction films and science fiction novelists); photo features; retrospectives of famous SF films and TV series; coverage of science fiction fandom, etc. "We also sometimes cover SF/fantasy animation and comics." No personal opinion think pieces/essays. *No* first person. Avoids articles on horror films/creators. "We prefer article format as opposed to Q&A interviews." Buys 150 mss/year. Query first with published clips. "We prefer queries by mail. No phone calls. Ever!" Length: 500-3,000 words. Pays $35 (500-word pieces); $50-75 (sidebars); $125-250 (1,000-word plus pieces).
Photos: State availability of photos. Pays $10-25 for slide transparencies and 8 × 10 b&w prints depending on quality. "No separate payment for photos provided by film studios." Captions, model releases, identification of subjects and credit line on photos required. Photo credit given. Buys all rights.
Columns/Departments: Fan Network (articles on fandom and its aspects—mostly staff-written); Booklog (book reviews, $15 each, by assignment only); Medialog (news of upcoming science fiction films and TV projects); Videolog (videocassette and disk releases of genre interest, staff-written); and Gamelog (video, computer, role-playing games). Buys 80-100 reviews/year. Query with published clips. Length: 300-500 words. No kill fee.
Tips: "Absolutely *no fiction.* We do *not* publish it. We reject *ALL* fiction. And we throw away the fiction mss from writers who also *can't* be bothered to include SASES. Please do *NOT* send fiction! Nonfiction only please! A writer can best break in to *Starlog* by getting an unusual interview or by *out-thinking* us and coming up with something *new* on a current film or book. We are always looking for *new* angles on *Star Trek: The Next Generation, Deep Space Nine, Star Wars,* the original *Star Trek, Doctor Who* and seeking features on such series as *Starman, Beauty & the Beast, Lost in Space, Space 1999, Battlestar Galactica, The Twilight Zone, The Outer Limits.* Know your subject before you try us. Most full-length major assignments go to freelancers with whom we're already dealing. But if we like your clips and ideas, we'll be happy to give *you* a chance."

2 AM MAGAZINE, P.O. Box 6754, Rockford IL 61125-1754. Editor: Gretta M. Anderson. 95% freelance written. Quarterly magazine of fiction, poetry, articles and art for readers of fantasy, horror and science fiction. Estab. 1986. Circ. 1,500. **Pays on acceptance.** Publishes ms an average of 9 months after acceptance. Byline given. Buys first North American serial rights. Submit seasonal material 1 year in advance. Reports in 1 month on queries; 3 months on mss. Sample copy $5.95. Writer's guidelines for #10 SASE.
Nonfiction: How-to, interview/profile, opinion, also book reviews of horror, fantasy or SF recent releases. "No essays originally written for high school or college courses." Buys 5 mss/year. Query with or without published clips or send complete ms. Length: 500-2,000 words. Pay ½-1¢/word.
Photos: State availability of photos with submission. Offers no additional payment for photos accepted with ms. Identification of subjects required. Buys one-time rights.
Fiction: Fantasy, horror, mystery, science fiction and suspense. Buys 50 mss/year. Send complete ms. Length: 500-5,000 words. Pays ½-1¢/word.
Poetry: Free verse and traditional. "No haiku/zen or short poems without imagery." Buys 20 poems/year. Submit up to 5 poems at one time. Length: 5-100 lines. Pays $1-5.
Tips: "We are looking for taut, imaginative fiction. We need more reviews of horror novels. Please use proper manuscript format; all manuscripts must include a SASE to be considered. We suggest to Canadian and foreign writers that they send disposable manuscripts with one IRC and #10 SAE for response, if US postage stamps are unavailable to them."

Sports

A variety of sports magazines, from general interest to sports medicine, are covered in this section. For the convenience of writers who specialize in one or two areas of sport and outdoor writing, the publications are subcategorized by the sport or subject matter they emphasize. Publications in related categories (for example, Hunting and Fishing; Archery and Bowhunting) often buy similar material. Writers should read through this entire section to become familiar with the subcategories. Publications on horse breeding and hunting dogs are classified in the Animal section, while horse racing is listed here. Publications dealing with automobile or motorcycle racing can be found in the Automotive and Motorcycle category. Markets interested in articles on exercise and fitness are listed in the Health and Fitness section. Outdoor publications that promote the preservation of nature, placing only secondary emphasis on nature as a setting for sport, are in the Nature, Conservation and Ecology category. Regional magazines are frequently interested in sports material with a local angle. Camping publications are classified in the Travel, Camping and Trailer category.

Archery and Bowhunting

BOW AND ARROW HUNTING, Box HH/34249 Camino Capistrano, Capistrano Beach CA 92624. Editorial Director: Roger Combs. 80% freelance written. Eager to work with new/unpublished writers. Bimonthly magazine for bowhunters. **Pays on acceptance.** Publishes ms an average of 6 months after acceptance. Buys first serial rights. Byline given. Reports in 2 months. Query for electronic submissions—preferred. Author must have some knowledge of archery terms.
Nonfiction: Articles: bowhunting, techniques used by champs, how to make your own tackle and off-trail hunting tales. Likes a touch of humor in articles. "No dead animals or 'my first hunt.'" Also uses one technical and how-to article per issue. Submit complete ms. Length: 1,500-2,500 words. Pays $150-300.
Photos: Purchased as package with ms; 5×7 minimum. Pays $100 for cover chromes, 35mm or larger.
Tips: "Subject matter is more important than style—that's why we have editors and copy pencils. Good b&w photos are of primary importance. We staff-write our shorter pieces."

BOWHUNTER, The Magazine for the Hunting Archer, Cowles Magazines, 6405 Flank Dr., Harrisburg PA 17112-8200. (717)657-9555. Fax: (717)657-9552. Editor/Publisher: M.R. James. Editorial Director: Dave Canfield. Contact: Richard Cochran, managing editor. 85% freelance written. Bimonthly magazine (with two special issues) on hunting big and small game with bow and arrow. "We are a special interest publication, produced by bowhunters for bowhunters, covering all aspects of the sport. Material included in each issue is designed to entertain and inform readers, making them better bowhunters." Estab. 1971. Circ. 180,000. **Pays on acceptance.** Publishes ms an average of 10-12 months after acceptance. Byline given. Kill fee varies. Buys first North American serial and one-time rights. Submit seasonal material 8 months in advance. Reports in 1 month on queries; 5 weeks on mss. *Writer's Market* recommends allowing 2 months for reply. Sample copy $2. Free writer's guidelines.
Nonfiction: General interest, how-to, interview/profile, opinion, personal experience and photo feature. "We publish a special 'Big Game' issue each Fall (September) but need all material by mid-March. Our other annual publication, *Whitetail Bowhunter*, is staff written or by assignment only. We don't want articles that graphically deal with an animal's death. And, please, no articles written from the animal's viewpoint." Buys 100 plus mss/year. Query. Length: 250-2,000 words. Pays $500 maximum for assigned articles; $50-500 for unsolicited articles. Sometimes pays expenses of writers on assignment.
Photos: Send photos with submission. Reviews 35mm and 2¼×2¼ transparencies and 5×7 and 8×10 prints. Offers $35-200/photo. Captions required. Buys one-time rights.
Columns/Departments: Would You Believe (unusual or offbeat hunting experiences), 250-1,000 words. Buys 6-8 mss/year. Send complete ms. Pays $50-200.
Tips: "A writer must know bowhunting and be willing to share that knowledge. Writers should anticipate *all* questions a reader might ask, then answer them in the article itself or in an appropriate sidebar. Articles should be written with the reader foremost in mind; we won't be impressed by writers seeking to prove how good they are—either as writers or bowhunters. We care about the reader and don't need writers with 'I' trouble. Features are a good bet because most of our material comes from freelancers. The best advice is: Be yourself. Tell your story same as if sharing the experience around a campfire. Don't try to write like you think a writer writes."

BOWHUNTING WORLD, Ehlert Publishing Group, Suite 600, 601 Lakeshort Parkway, Minnetonka MN 55305-5215. (612)476-2200. Fax: (612)476-8065. Editor: Tim Dehn. Senior Editor: Mike Stroudlaud. Associate Editor: Tom Kacheroski. 70% freelance written. Monthly magazine for bowhunting and archery enthusiasts who participate in the sport year-round. Estab. 1951. Circ. 164,000. **Pays on acceptance.** Publishes manuscripts an average of 5 months after acceptance. Byline given. Buys first rights. Reports in 3 weeks on queries, 6 weeks on manuscripts. Sample copy for 9 × 12 SAE with 10 first class stamps. Free writer's and photographers guidelines.

Nonfiction: Hunting adventure, scouting and hunting how-to features (primarily from a first-person point of view), interview/profile pieces, historical articles, humor and do-it-yourself pieces. Buys 60 mss/year. Query or send complete ms. Length: 1,500-3,000 words. Pays from under $200 to over $500.

Photos: Send photos with submission. Reviews 35mm transparencies and b&w or color prints. Captions required. Buys one-time rights as part of package with ms. Send for separate photo guidelines. "We will also accept proof sheets and negs, returning any photos we do print and use to the author."

Tips: "We look for a combination of good writing and good information. Although we've expanded our focus in recent years to include all North American big and small game typically hunted with bow and arrow, nearly half the articles we buy are about bowhunting for deer. Many freelancers are submitting slides only because that allows magazines to reproduce photos in either b&w or color. Our experience shows that detail is lost converting the slides and that we typically buy additional freelance color to support the article. For that reason, we now encourage authors with access to high quality, b&w print developing services to send b&w illustrations with their packages."

INTERNATIONAL BOWHUNTER MAGAZINE, P.O. Box 67, Pillager MN 56473-0067. (218)746-3333. Fax: (218)746-3307. Editor: Johnny E. Boatner. 95% freelance written. Bimonthly magazine on bowhunting. "We are interested in any kind of articles that deal with bowhunting. We pride ourselves as a magazine written by hunter/writers, rather than writer/hunters. We are not interested in articles that just fill pages, we like each paragraph to say something." Estab. 1982. Circ. 57,000. Pays on publication. Publishes ms an average of 1 or 2 months after acceptance. Byline sometimes given. Buys first rights. Submit seasonal/holiday material 4 months in advance. Reports in 2 months. Free sample copy and writer's guidelines.

Nonfiction: Historical/nostalgic, how-to, humor, interview/profile, new product, personal experience, photo feature, technical and travel; all bowhunting and archery related. "No commercials of writers' pet products; no articles including bad ethics or gory, target archery." Buys 75 mss/year. Send complete ms. Length: 600-3,500 words. Pays $25 minimum for assigned articles; $25-150 for unsolicited articles. Sometimes pays in contributor copies or other premiums (trade ads for articles). Sometimes pays expenses of writers on assignments.

Photos: Send photos with submission. Reviews transparencies and prints. Don't send slides. Offers no additional payment for photos accepted with ms. Captions and identification of subjects required. Buys one-time rights.

Fiction: Adventure (bowhunting related) and historical (bowhunting). Send complete ms. Length: 600-3,500 words. Pays $25-150.

Fillers: Anecdotes, facts, gags to be illustrated by cartoonist, newsbreaks and short humor. Buys 10/year. Length: 100-500 words. Pays $10-25.

Tips: "We do mainly first person accounts as long as they relate to hunting with the bow and arrow. If you have a bowhunting story you want to tell, then type it up and send it in. We probably publish more first time writers than any other bowhunting magazine today. Keep the articles clean, entertaining and informative. We do a few how-tos, but mainly want articles about bowhunting and the great outdoors that relate to bowhunting."

Baseball and Softball

BALLS AND STRIKES, Amateur Softball Association, 2801 NE 50th St., Oklahoma City OK 73111. (405)424-5266. Fax: (405)424-3855. 20% freelance written. Works with a small number of new/unpublished writers each year. "Only national monthly magazine covering amateur softball." Circ. 300,000. Pays on publication. Publishes ms an average of 2 months after acceptance. Buys first rights. Byline given. Reports in 3 weeks. Free sample copy.

Nonfiction: General interest, historical/nostalgic, interview/profile and technical. Query. Length: 2-3 pages. Pays $50-75.

Tips: "We generally like shorter features because we try to get as many different features as possible in each issue."

‡SLO-PITCH NEWS, Varsity Publications, Inc., 6506 23rd Ave. NE, Seattle WA 98115. (206)524-8985. Editor: Dick Stephens. 10-25% freelance written. Monthly tabloid newspaper for slo-pitch softball. Focus on slo-pitch softball tournaments, teams, players and products/services for a national and western audience. Estab.

Market conditions are constantly changing! If this is 1995 or later, buy the newest edition of Writer's Market *at your favorite bookstore or order directly from Writer's Digest Books.*

1985. Circ. 25,000. Pays on publication. Byline given. Buys first North American serial and second serial (reprint) rights. Editorial lead time 3 months. Submit seasonal material 2 months in advance. Simultaneous and previously published submissions OK. Query for electronic submissions. Reports in 2 months on queries. Sample copy and writer's guidelines for #10 SASE.

Nonfiction: Book excerpts, essays, expose, general interest, historical/nostalgic, how-to, humor, inspirational, interview/profile, new product, opinion, personal experience, photo feature, travel and how-to (softball instructional). Special issues: Buyer's Guide (December); All-Star Edition (January). Buys 10 mss/year. Send complete ms. Length: 400-700 words. Pays $20 minimum. Pays contributor's copies "if piece was small enough, where payment wasn't expected."

Photos: Send photos with submission. Reviews 4×6 or 3×5 or larger prints. Offers $5-20/photo. Negotiates payment individually. Model releases and identification of subjects required. "depends on subject and focus."

Columns/Departments: Power Hitting (instructional softball), 500-600 words; numerous others on tournament coverage and administrative news. Buys 30 mss/year. Query with published clips. Send complete ms. Pays $10-30.

Fiction: "We don't solicit fiction often. No fluffy articles on sports." Buys 10 mss/year. Send complete ms. Length: 300-1,000 words. Pays $15-30.

Fillers: Anecdotes, facts, gags to be illustrated by cartoonist, newsbreaks and short humor. Buys 30/year. Length: 100-200 words. Pay negotiable.

Tips: "Send resume with clips and refs. Contact editor for further info. Background experience in softball is appreciated. We are most open to tournament/team profiles and reports. Stay within AP style and write to an adult softball audience."

Bicycling

BICYCLING, Rodale Press, Inc., 33 E. Minor St., Emmaus PA 18098. (215)967-5171. Fax: (215)967-8960. Editor and Publisher: James C. McCullagh. 20-25% freelance written. Prefers to work with published/established writers. Publishes 11 issues/year (10 monthly, 1 bimonthly); 104-250 pages. Estab. 1978. Circ. 385,000. **Pays on acceptance** or publication. Publishes ms an average of 6 months after acceptance. Byline given. Buys all rights. Submit seasonal/holiday material 5 months in advance. Query for electronic submissions. Sample copy $2.50. Writer's guidelines for #10 SASE.

Nonfiction: How-to (on all phases of bicycle touring, repair, maintenance, commuting, new products, clothing, riding technique, nutrition for cyclists, conditioning). Fitness is more important than ever. Also travel (bicycling must be central here); photo feature (on cycling events of national significance); and technical (component review—query). "We are strictly a bicycling magazine. We seek readable, clear, well-informed pieces. We rarely run articles that are pure humor or inspiration but a little of either might flavor even our most technical pieces. No poetry or fiction." Buys 1-2 unsolicited mss/issue. Send complete ms. Length: 1,500 words average. Pays $25-1,200. Sometimes pays expenses of writers on assignment.

Photos: State availability of photos with query letter or send photo material with ms. Pays $15-50 for b&w prints and $35-250 for transparencies. Captions preferred; model release required.

Fillers: Anecdotes and news items for Paceline section.

Tips: "We're alway seeking interesting accounts of cycling as a lifestyle."

BIKE MIDWEST MAGAZINE, Peter Wray, Publisher, P.O. Box 141287, Columbus OH 43214. (614)447-6559. 50% freelance written. Monthly tabloid on bicycling in Ohio, Michigan, Indiana, Kentucky, West Virginia and western Pennsylvania. "All aspects of adult bicycling covering both racing and recreational riding." Estab. 1987. Circ. 35,000. Pays on publication. Byline given. Buys first rights and second serial (reprint) rights. Send typed ms with rights for sale noted. Include information about when and where the article previously appeared. For reprints, pays 50% of the amount paid for an original article. Simultaneous submissions OK. Query for electronic submissions. Sample copy and writer's guidelines for 10×13 SAE with 75¢ postage. Writer's guidelines for #10 SASE.

Nonfiction: How-to (athletics), humor, interview/profile, new product, personal experience and photo feature but must have a regional angle; all bicycle-related. Buys 10 mss/year. Query. Length: 500-2,500 words. Pays $25-50. Sometimes pays expenses of writers on assignment.

Photos: Send photos with submission. Reviews contact sheets and 5×7 prints. Offers no additional payment for photos accepted with ms. Identification of subjects required. Buys one-time rights.

Tips: "Consult with editor. Looking for reports of racing/riding events, previews, interviews with personalities. We want regional stories. Inclusion of art is very important."

BIKEREPORT, Bikecentennial, Inc., The Bicycle Travel Association, Box 8308, Missoula MT 59807. (406)721-1776. Fax: (406)721-8754. Editor: Daniel D'Ambrosio. 75% freelance written. Works with a small number of new/unpublished writers each year. Bicycle touring magazine for Bikecentennial members published 9 times yearly. Circ. 30,000. Pays on publication. Publishes ms an average of 8 months after acceptance. Byline given. Include short bio with manuscript. Buys first serial rights. Submit seasonal/holiday material 3 months in advance. Simultaneous queries OK. Query for electronic submissions. Reports in 3 weeks on queries; 6

weeks on mss. Sample copy and guidelines for 9 × 12 SAE with 4 first class stamps.

Nonfiction: Historical/nostalgic (interesting spots along bike trails); how-to (bicycle); humor (touring); interview/profile (bicycle industry people); personal experience ("my favorite tour"); photo feature (bicycle); technical (bicycle); and travel ("my favorite tour"). Buys 20-25 mss/year. Query with published clips or send complete ms. Length: 800-2,500 words. Pays 3¢/word and up.

Photos: Bicycle, scenery and portraits. State availability of photos. Model releases and identification of subjects required.

Fiction: Adventure, experimental, historical and humorous. Not interested in anything that doesn't involve bicycles. Query with published clips or send complete ms. Length: 800-2,500 words. Pays 3¢/word and up.

CRANKMAIL, Cycling in Northern Ohio, 9611 Lorain Ave., Cleveland OH 44102-4751. Editor: James Guilford. Magazine published 10 times/year covering bicycling in all aspects. "Our publication serves the interests of bicycle enthusiasts . . . established, accomplished adult cyclists. These individuals are interested in reading about the sport of cycling, bicycles as transportation, ecological tie-ins, sports nutrition, the history and future of bicycles and bicycling." Estab. 1977. Circ. 1,000. Pays on publication. Byline given. Publication not copyrighted. Buys one-time or second serial (reprint) rights. Editorial lead time 1 month. Submit seasonal material 3 months in advance. Accepts previously published submissions. Sample copy $1. Writer's guidelines for #10 SASE.

Nonfiction: Essays, historical/nostalgic, how-to, humor, interview/profile, new product, personal experience, and technical. "No articles encouraging folks to start or get involved in bicycling—our readers are already cyclists." Send complete ms. "Don't query." Length: 2,500 words maximum. Pays $10 minimum for unsolicited articles.

Fillers: Anecdotes, facts, short humor and completed cartoons. Pays $5-10.

Tips: "Know what you're talking about. Our readers are intelligent, mostly established *adult* cyclists who subscribe to national bicycling publications."

CYCLING USA, The Official Publication of the U.S. Cycling Federation, One Olympic Plaza, Colorado Springs CO 80909. (719)578-4581. Fax: (719)578-4596. Editor: Steve Penny. Media and public relations assistant: Gina Fedash. 50% freelance written. Monthly magazine covering reportage and commentary on American bicycle racing, personalities and sports physiology, for USCF licensed cyclists. Circ. 32,000. Pays on publication. Publishes ms an average of 2 months after acceptance. Byline given. Simultaneous queries and previously published submissions OK. Reports in 2 weeks. Sample copy for 10 × 12 SAE with 2 first class stamps.

Nonfiction: How-to (train, prepare for a bike race), interview/profile, opinion, personal experience, photo feature, technical and race commentary on major cycling events. No comparative product evaluations. Buys 15 mss/year. Query with published clips. Length: 500-800 words. Pays 13¢/word.

Photos: State availability of photos. Pays $10-25 for 5 × 7 b&w prints; $100 for transparencies used as cover. Captions required. Buys one-time rights.

Tips: "A background in bicycle racing is important because the sport is somewhat insular, technical and complex. Most major articles are generated inhouse. Race reports are most open to freelancers. Be concise, informative and anecdotal. The most frequent mistake made by writers in completing an article for us is that it is too lengthy; our format is more compatible with shorter (500-800-word) articles than longer features."

‡DIRT RAG, A.K.A. Productions, 5732 3rd St., Verona PA 15147. (412)795-7495. Fax: (412)795-7439. Publisher: Maurice Tierney. Managing Editor: Elaine Tierney. 75% freelance written. Mountain biking magazine published 7 times/year. "Dirt Rag's style is much looser, fun and down to earth than mainstream (glossy) magazines on the same subject. We appeal to hard-core (serious) mountain bikers, and these people make our finest contributions. Avant-garde, humorous, off-beat, alternative." Estab. 1989. Circ. 5,000. Pays on publication. Byline given. No kill fee. Buys one-time rights. Simultaneous and previously published submissions OK. Query for electronic submissions. Sample copy for 5 first class stamps. Writer's guidelines for SASE.

Nonfiction: Book excerpts, essays, expose, general interest, historical/nostalgic, how-to (bike maintenance, bike technique), humor, interview/profile, new product, opinion, personal experience, photo feature, technical and travel (places to ride). Anything with mountain biking. Buys 24 mss/year. Query. Pays $15-75. Sometimes pays expenses of writers on assignment.

Photos: Send art or photos with or without submission. Reviews contact sheets and/or prints. Offers additional payment for photos accepted with ms. $75 b&w cover, $100 for color cover. $20 inside (b&w only). Captions required. Buys one-time rights. Always looking for good photography and art regardless of subject.

Columns/Departments: Place to Ride (must have map!), 500-2,000 words; Trialsin (coverage of the sport), 50-500 words; and Race Reports (coverage of race events), 50-250 words. Buys 14 mss/year. Query. Pays $10-50.

Fiction: Adventure, fantasy, historical, humorous, mainstream and slice-of-life vignettes. Buys 1-5 mss/year. Query. Pays $10-50.

Poetry: Avant-garde, free verse, light verse and traditional. Pays $10-25.

Fillers: Anecdotes, facts, gags, newsbreaks and short humor. Buys 20/year. Pays $0-50.

VELONEWS, The Journal of Competitive Cycling, 1830 55th St., Boulder CO 80301-2700. (303)440-0601. Fax: (303)444-6788. Managing Editor: Tim Johnson. 60% freelance written. Monthly tabloid September-February, biweekly March-August covering bicycle racing. Estab. 1972. Circ. 48,000. Pays on publication. Publishes ms an average of 1 month after acceptance. Byline given. Buys one-time rights. Simultaneous queries and submissions OK. Electronic submissions OK; call first. Reports in 3 weeks. Sample copy for 9×12 SAE with 7 first class stamps.

Nonfiction: In addition to race coverage, opportunities for freelancers include reviews (book and videos) and health-and-fitness departments. Buys 100 mss/year. Query. Length: 300-1,200 words. Pays 10¢/word minimum.

Photos: State availability of photos. Pays $16.50-50 for b&w prints. Pays $150 for color used on cover. Captions and identification of subjects required. Buys one-time rights.

Boating

BOAT PENNSYLVANIA, Pennsylvania Fish and Boat Commission, P.O. Box 67000, Harrisburg PA 17106-7000. (717)657-4518. Editor: Art Michaels. 80% freelance written. Quarterly magazine covering motorboating, sailing, canoeing, water skiing, kayaking and rafting in Pennsylvania. Prefers to work with published/established contributors, but works with a few unpublished writers and photographers every year. Pays 2 months after acceptance. Publishes ms an average of 8 months after acceptance. Byline given. Buys variable rights. Submit seasonal/holiday material 8 months in advance. Reprints OK; send typed ms with rights for sale noted. Reports in 2 weeks on queries; 2 months on mss. Sample copy for 9×12 SAE with 4 first class stamps. Writer's guidelines for #10 SASE. Query for electronic submission.

Nonfiction: How-to, technical and historical/nostalgic, all related to water sports in Pennsylvania. No saltwater fishing material. Buys 40 mss/year. Query. Length: 300-3,000 words. Pays $25-300.

Photos: Send photos with submission. Also reviews photos separately. Rights purchased and rates vary. Reviews 35mm and larger color transparencies and 8×10 b&w prints. Captions, model releases and identification of subjects required.

CANOE MAGAZINE, Canoe Associates, P.O. Box 3146, Kirkland WA 98083. (206)827-6363. Fax: (206)827-1893. Managing Editor: Jim Thompson. Editor: Dennis Stuhaug. 80-90% freelance written. Bimonthly magazine on canoeing, whitewater kayaking and sea kayaking. Estab. 1972. Circ. 60,000. Pays on publication. Publishes ms an average of 9-12 months after acceptance. Byline given. Buys right to reprint in annuals; author retains copyright. Submit seasonal/holiday material 4 months in advance. Reprints OK; send tearsheet or photocopy of article and information about where and when it previously appeared. Pays same for reprints as originals. Query for electronic submissions. Reports in 1 month. Sample copy and writer's guidelines for 9×12 SASE with 5 first class stamps.

Nonfiction: Essays, general interest, historical/nostalgic, how-to, humor, interview/profile, new product, opinion, personal experience, photo feature, technical and travel. Plans a special entry-level guide to canoeing and kayaking. No "trip diaries." Buys 60 mss/year. Query with or without published clips or send complete ms. Length: 500-2,200 words. Pays $5/column inch. Pays the expenses of writers on assignment.

Photos: State availability of or send photos with submission. "Good photos help sell a story." Reviews contact sheets, negatives, transparencies and prints. "Some activities we cover are canoeing, kayaking, canoe fishing, camping, canoe sailing or poling, backpacking (when compatible with the main activity) and occasionally inflatable boats. We are not interested in groups of people in rafts, photos showing disregard for the environment, gasoline-powered, multi-horsepower engines unless appropriate to the discussion, or unskilled persons taking extraordinary risks." Offers $50-150/photo. Model releases and identification of subjects occasionally required. Buys one-time rights.

Columns/Departments: Continuum (essay); Counter Currents (environmental) both 1,500 words; Put-In (short interesting articles); and Short Strokes (destinations), 1,000-1,500 words. Buys 60 mss/year. Pays $5/column inch.

Fiction: Uses very little fiction.

Fillers: Anecdotes, facts and newsbreaks. Buys 20/year. Length: 500-1,000 words. Pays $5/column inch.

Tips: "Start with Put-In articles (short featurettes) of approximately 500 words, book reviews, or short, unique equipment reviews. Or give us the best, most exciting article we've ever seen—with great photos. Short Strokes is also a good entry forum focusing on short trips on good waterways accessible to lots of people. Focusing more on technique and how-to articles."

CURRENTS, Voice of the National Organization for River Sports, 212 W. Cheyenne Mountain Blvd., Colorado Springs CO 80906. (719)579-8759. Fax: (719)576-6238. Editor: Greg Moore. 25% freelance written. Quarterly magazine covering whitewater river running (kayaking, rafting, river canoeing). Estab. 1979. Circ. 5,000. Pays on publication. Publishes ms an average of 6 months after acceptance. Byline given. Offers 25% kill fee. Buys first North American serial, first and one-time rights. Submit seasonal/holiday material 2 months in advance. Simultaneous queries, and simultaneous and previously published submissions OK. "Please let us know if this is a simultaneous submission or if the article has been previously published." Reports in 2 weeks on queries; 1 month on mss. *Writer's Market* recommends allowing 2 months for reply. Sample copy $1 for 9×12 SAE with 3 first class stamps. Writer's guidelines for #10 SASE.

Nonfiction: How-to (run rivers and fix equipment); in-depth reporting on river conservation and access issues and problems; humor (related to rivers); interview/profile (any interesting river runner); opinion; personal experience; technical; and travel (rivers in other countries). "We tell river runners about river conservation, river access, river equipment, how to do it, when, where, etc." No trip accounts without originality; no stories about "my first river trip." Buys 20 mss/year. Query with or without clips of published work. Length: 500-2,500 words. Pays $35-150.

Photos: State availability of photos. Pays $35-50. Reviews b&w or color prints or slides; b&w preferred. Captions and identification of subjects (if racing) required. Buys one-time rights. Captions must include names of the river and rapid.

Columns/Departments: Book and film reviews (river-related). Buys 5 mss/year. Query with or without clips of published work or send complete ms. Length: 100-500 words. Pays $25.

Fiction: Adventure (river). Buys 2 mss/year. Query. Length: 1,000-2,500 words. Pays $35-75. "Must be well-written, on well-known river and beyond the realm of possibility."

Fillers: Clippings, jokes, gags, anecdotes, short humor, newsbreaks. Buys 5/year. Length: 25-100 words. Pays $5-10.

Tips: "We need more material on river news—proposed dams, wild and scenic river studies, accidents, etc. If you can provide brief (300-500 words) on these subjects, you will have a good chance of being published. Material must be on whitewater rivers. Go to a famous river and investigate it; find out something we don't know—especially about rivers that are *not* in Colorado or adjacent states—we already know about the ones near us."

HEARTLAND BOATING, Inland Publications, Inc., P.O. Box 1067, Martin TN 38237-1067. (901)587-6791. Fax: (901)587-6893. Editor: Molly Lightfoot Blom. Estab. 1988. 50% freelance written. Bimonthly magazine on boating "devoted to both power and sail boating enthusiasts throughout middle America; houseboats are included. The focus is on the freshwater inland rivers and lakes of the Heartland; primarily the Tennessee, Cumberland, Ohio and Mississippi rivers and the Tennessee-Tombigbee Waterway. No Great Lakes or salt water material will be considered unless it applies to our area." Estab. 1988. Circ. 14,000. Pays on publication. Publishes ms an average of 3 months after acceptance. Byline given. Buys first North American serial and sometimes second serial (reprint) rights. Submit seasonal/holiday material 6 months in advance. Simultaneous submissions OK. Reprints OK; send tearsheet of article and information about where and when it previously appeared. Query for electronic submissions. Reports in 3 months. Sample copy $5. Free writer's guidelines.

Nonfiction: General interest, historical/nostalgic, how-to, humor, interview/profile, new product, personal experience, photo feature, technical and travel. Buys 40-60 mss/year. Prefers queries to unsolicited mss with or without published clips. Length: 800-2,000 words. Negotiates payment.

Photos: Send photos with query. Reviews contact sheets, transparencies. Buys one-time rights.

Columns/Departments: Buys 10 mss/year. Query. Negotiates payment.

JET SPORTS, The Official Publication of the International Jet Sports Boating Association, Pfanner Communications, Inc., Suite E, 1371 E. Warner Ave., Tustin CA 92680. (714)259-8240. Fax: (714)259-1502. Editor: Elyse M. Barrett. Estab. 1981. 25% freelance written. Quarterly magazine. "The magazine goes to members of IJSBA, new buyers of Kawasaki personal watercraft, selected newsstands nationwide and watercraft dealers. Slant is toward *active* sports enthusiasts, racing, performance-enhancement, adventure, home mechanic subjects." Circ. 42,000. Pays on publication. Publishes ms an average of 3 months after acceptance. Byline given. Offers 50% kill fee for assigned material *only.*. Buys first North American serial or one-time rights. Submit seasonal material 4 months in advance. Previously published submissions OK. Send tearsheet of article or typed ms with rights for sale noted. Include information about when and where the article previously appeared. For reprints, pays 50% of the amount paid for an original article. Query for electronic submissions. Reports in 6 weeks. Sample copy for 9×12 SAE with 7 first class stamps. Writer's guidelines for #10 SASE.

Nonfiction: Interview/profile, personal experience, photo feature, technical and travel. Holiday Buyers' Guide (expanded new product section), winter issue. Catalog special (advertorial), spring issue. World Finals report (spring issue). Buys 12 mss/year. Query with or without published clips or send complete ms. Length: 100-2,000 words. Pays $25-500. Sometimes pays expenses of writers on assignment.

Photos: Send photos with submission. Reviews contact sheets, 35mm transparencies and 5×7 prints. Offers $10-250/photo. Identification of subjects required. Buys one-time rights.

Columns/Departments: Starting Line (industry/business briefs, racer info); Legislative Lookout (state-by-state analysis of laws affecting personal watercraft); Club Scene (news of club activities nationwide); and Regional Racing (race announcements and results). Buys 40 mss/year. Send complete ms. Length: 50-150 words. Pays $25-100.

Fillers: Anecdotes and facts. Buys 3/year. Length: 150-500 words. Pays $15-55.

Tips: "Be a skilled watercraft rider, understand the industry, which is much like the motocross/motorcycle world, and query first! Write simply—some slang and jargon is OK. Departments most open to freelancers: Starting Line (inside scoop, latest rumors, good photos, hero/helper stories); Club Scene (timely notice of coming events or activities; detailed follow-ups); Legislative Lookout (local and state-wide happenings (closures of waterways to PWCs, laws proposed, actions by individuals and clubs to affect new regulations)."

LAKELAND BOATING, The magazine for Great Lakes boaters, O'Meara-Brown Publications, Suite 1220, 1560 Sherman Ave., Evanston IL 60201-4802. (708)869-5400. Fax: (708)869-5989. Editor: Sarah Wortham. 50% freelance written. Monthly magazine covering Great Lakes boating. Estab. 1945. Circ. 60,000. Pays on publication. Byline given. Buys first North American serial rights. Query for electronic submissions. Reports in 4 months. Sample copy $5.50 for 9×12 SAE with 6 first class stamps. Writer's guidelines for #10 SASE.

Nonfiction: Book excerpts, historical/nostalgic, how-to, interview/profile, personal experience, photo feature, technical and travel. No inspirational, religious, expose or poetry. Must relate to boating in Great Lakes. Buys 20-30 mss/year. Query. Length: 800-3,500 words. Pays $100-600 for assigned articles. Sometimes pays expenses of writers on assignment.

Photos: State availability of photos. Reviews transparencies; prefers 35mm. Captions required. Buys one-time rights.

Columns/Departments: Bosun's Locker (technical or how-to pieces on boating), 100-1,000 words. Buys 40 mss/year. Query. Pays $30-100.

OFFSHORE, Boating Magazine of the Northeast, Offshore Publications, Inc., 220-9 Reservoir St., Needham MA 02194. (617)449-6204. Editor: Herbert Gliick. Estab. 1976. 90% freelance written. Eager to work with new/unpublished writers. Monthly magazine covering boating and the coast from Maine to New Jersey. Circ. 35,000. **Pays on acceptance.** Publishes ms an average of 2 months after acceptance. Byline given. Offers negotiable kill fee. Buys first North American serial rights. Submit seasonal/holiday material 3 months in advance. Simultaneous queries, and simultaneous/previously published submissions OK. Send tearsheet of article or short story and information about when and where the article previously appeared. Pays $100 for reprints. Query for electronic submissions. Reports in 2 weeks. *Writer's Market* recommends allowing 2 months for reply. Sample copy for 10×13 SAE with 6 first class stamps. Writer's guidelines for #10 SASE.

Nonfiction: Articles on boats, boating, New York, New Jersey and New England coastal places and people. Coastal history of NJ, NY, CT, RI, MA, NH and ME. Thumbnail and/or outline of topic will elicit immediate response. Buys 90 mss/year. Query with writing sample or send complete ms. Length: 1,000-3,000 words. Pays 15¢/word and up.

Fiction: Boat related fiction.

Photos: Reviews 35mm slides only. For covers, pays $200 and up. Identification of subjects required. Buys one-time rights.

Tips: "Demonstrate familiarity with boats or region and ability to recognize subjects of interest to regional boat owners. Those subjects need not be boats. *Offshore* is serious but does not take itself as seriously as most national boating magazines. The most frequent mistake made by writers in completing an article for us is failing to build on a theme (what is the point of the story?)."

POWER BOATING CANADA, Unit 306, 2585 Skymark Ave., Mississauga, Ontario L4W 4L5 Canada. (416)624-8218. Editor: Pam Cottrell. 40% freelance written. Bimonthly magazine covering power boating. Estab. 1984. Circ. 50,000. Pays on publication. Publishes ms an average of 3 months after acceptance. Byline given. Not copyrighted. Buys first North American serial rights in English and French or second serial (reprint) rights. Simultaneous and previously published submissions OK. Query for electronic submissions.

Nonfiction: "Any articles related to the sport of power boating, especially boat tests." Travel (boating destinations). No personal anecdotes. Buys 20 mss/year. Query. Length: 1,000-2,500 words. Pays $150-300.

Photos: State availability of photos with submission. Send photos with submission. Reviews contact sheets, negatives, transparencies and prints. Offers no additional payment for photos accepted with ms. Identification of subjects required. Buys one-time rights.

SAIL, 275 Washington St., Newton MA 02158-1630. (617)964-3030. Fax: (617)964-8948. Editor: Patience Wales. Managing Editor: Amy Ullrich. 50% freelance written. Works with a small number of new/unpublished writers each year. Monthly magazine for audience that is "strictly sailors, average age 42, above average education." Estab. 1970. **Pays on acceptance.** Publishes ms an average of 10 months after acceptance. Buys first North American rights. Submit seasonal or special material at least 6 months in advance. Reprints OK; send tearsheet or photocopy of article or short story with information about when and where it previously appeared. Pays 50-75% of their fee for an original article. Reports in 10 weeks. Writer's guidelines for 1 first class stamp.

Nonfiction: Amy Ullrich, managing editor. Wants "articles on sailing: technical, techniques and feature stories." Interested in how-to, personal experience, distance cruising, destinations, technical aspects of boat construction and systems. "Generally emphasize the excitement of sail and the human, personal aspect. No logs." Special issues: "Cruising, chartering, fitting-out, special race (e.g., America's Cup), boat show." Buys

100 mss/year (freelance and commissioned). Length: 1,000-2,800 words. Pays $200-800. Sometimes pays the expenses of writers on assignment.

Photos: Offers additional payment for photos. Uses b&w glossy prints or Kodachrome 64 transparencies. Pays $600 if photo is used on the cover.

Tips: "Request an articles specification sheet."

SAILING WORLD, N.Y. Times Magazine Group, 5 John Clarke Rd., Newport RI 02840. Fax: (401)848-5048. Editor: John Burnham. 40% freelance written. Monthly magazine. Estab. 1962. Circ. 61,000. Pays on publication. Publishes ms an average of 4 months after acceptance. Buys first North American and world serial rights. Byline given. Query for electronic submissions. Reports in 3 months. Sample copy $5.

Nonfiction: How-to for racing and performance-oriented sailors, photo feature, profile, regatta reports and charter. No travelogs. Buys 5-10 unsolicited mss/year. Query. Length: 500-1,500 words. Pays $150-200/page text.

Tips: "Send query with outline and include your experience. The writer may have a better chance of breaking in with short articles and fillers such as regatta news reports from his or her own area."

SEA KAYAKER, Sea Kayaker, Inc., 6327 Seaview Ave. NW, Seattle WA 98107-2664. (206)789-1326. Fax: (206)789-6392. Editor: Christopher Cunningham. 80% freelance written. Works frequently with new/unpublished writers each year. Quarterly magazine on the sport of sea kayaking. Estab. 1984. Circ. 12,000. Pays on publication. Publishes ms an average of 6 months after acceptance. Byline given. Offers 10% kill fee. Buys first North American serial or second serial (reprint) rights. Submit seasonal material 6 months in advance. Reports in 2 months. Sample copy $4.60. Free writer's guidelines.

Nonfiction: Essays, historical, how-to (on making equipment), humor, profile, opinion, personal experience, technical and travel. Buys 40 mss/year. Query with or without published clips or send complete ms. Length: 750-4,000 words. Pays about 10¢/word. Sometimes pays the expenses of writers on assignment.

Photos: Send photos with submission. Reviews contact sheets. Offers $20-40/photo. Captions requested. Buys one-time rights.

Columns/Departments: History, Safety, Environment and Journey. Length: 750-4,000 words. Pays about 10¢/word.

Fiction: Kayak related adventure, fantasy, historical, humorous, mainstream and slice-of-life vignettes. Send complete ms. Length: 750-4,000 words. Pays about 10¢/word.

Tips: "We consider unsolicited mss that include a SASE, but we give greater priority to brief (several paragraphs) descriptions of proposed articles accompanied by at least two samples—published or unpublished—of your writing. Enclose a statement as to why you're qualified to write the piece and indicate whether photographs or illustrations are available to accompany the piece."

SOUTHERN BOATING MAGAZINE, The South's Largest Boating Magazine, Southern Boating & Yachting, Inc., 1766 Bay Rd., Miami Beach FL 33139-1414. (305)538-0700. Fax: (305)532-8657. Editor: Skip Allen, Sr. Editorial Director: Andree Conrad. 50% freelance written. Monthly magazine on cruising and fishing in the Southeastern US. "Our readers are long-time boat owners who spend a good deal of their time on the water. They have an interest in everything from diesel maintenance to one-design sailboat racing. Above all, they are interested in new and accurate information about cruising destinations." Estab. 1973. Circ. 26,000. Pays on publication. Publishes ms an average of 3-6 months after acceptance. Byline given. Buys first North American serial rights, first rights, or one-time rights. Some issues have themes. Submit seasonal/holiday material 4 months in advance. Simultaneous and previously published submissions OK. Query for electronic submissions. Sample copy $4. Writer's guidelines for #10 SASE.

Nonfiction: Book excerpts (occasionally), new products, photo features, technical and travel. "Write for editorial calendar. No personal experience or disasters aboard boats." Buys 50 ms/year. Query with or without published clips or send complete ms. Length: 750-2,500 words. Pays $100-200 for assigned articles; $75-150 for unsolicited articles. Sometimes pays expenses of writers on assignment.

Photos: Send photos with submission. Reviews transparencies (both slides and larger formats). Offers no additional payment for photos accepted with ms. Captions, model releases, and identification of subjects required. Buys one-time rights.

Tips: "Anyone who has plans to or has already taken a cruise in Southeastern or Carribean waters, and can adequately convey the kind of information other cruising yachtsmen need to decide whether they want to undertake a similar cruise, should contact us. We ask for excellent color pictures, preferably slides in Kodachrome or Fujichrome, 35mm or larger. We do not publish stories without photos. Maps are appreciated by all of our readers. Freelancers have the best chance with feature articles. We are also looking for writers with the ability to write technical information on engines, electronics and other topics of interest intelligibly."

WATERWAY GUIDE, Communication Channels, Inc., 6151 Powers Ferry Rd., NW, Atlanta GA 30339-2941. (404)955-2500. Fax: (404)955-0400. Associate Publisher: Judith Powers. 90% freelance written. Quarterly magazine on intracoastal waterway travel for recreational boats. "Writer must be knowledgable about navigation and the areas covered by the guide." Estab. 1947. Circ. 45,000. Pays on publication. Publishes ms an average of 3 months after acceptance. Byline given sometimes. Kill fee varies. Buys all rights. Reports in 3 month on queries; 4 months on mss. Sample copy $31.45 with $3 postage.

Nonfiction: Historical/nostalgic, how-to, photo feature, technical and travel. "No personal boating experiences." Buys 25 mss/year. Query with or without published clips or send complete ms. Length: 200 words minimum. Pays $50-3,000 for assigned articles. Pays in contributor copies or other premiums for helpful tips and useful information.

Photos: Send photos with submission. Reviews 3×5 prints. Offers $25/b&w photo, $600/color photos used on the cover. Identification of subjects required. Buys one-time rights.

Fillers: Facts. Buys 6/year. Length: 250-1,000 words. Pays $50-150.

Tips: "Must have on-the-water experience and be able to provide new and accurate information on geographic areas covered by *Waterway Guide*."

WOODENBOAT MAGAZINE, The Magazine for Wooden Boat Owners, Builders, and Designers, WoodenBoat Publications, Inc., P.O. Box 78, Brooklin ME 04616. (207)359-4651. Fax: (207)359-8920. Editor: Jon Wilson. Executive Editor: Jennifer Elliott. Senior Editor: Mike O'Brien. 50% freelance written. Works with a small number of new/unpublished writers each year. Bimonthly magazine for wooden boat owners, builders and designers. "We are devoted exclusively to the design, building, care, preservation, and use of wooden boats, both commercial and pleasure, old and new, sail and power. We work to convey quality, integrity and involvement in the creation and care of these craft, to entertain, inform, inspire, and to provide our varied readers with access to individuals who are deeply experienced in the world of wooden boats." Estab. 1974. Circ. 106,000. Pays on publication. Publishes ms an average of 1 year after acceptance. Byline given. Offers variable kill fee. Buys first North American serial rights. Simultaneous queries and submissions (with notification) and previously published submissions OK; send tearsheet or photocopy of article or typed wms with rights for sale noted with information about when and where the article previously appeared. Query for electronic submissions. Reports in 3 weeks on queries; 2 months on mss. Sample copy $4.50. Writer's guidelines for SASE.

Nonfiction: Technical (repair, restoration, maintenance, use, design and building wooden boats). No poetry, fiction. Buys 50 mss/year. Query with published clips. Length: 1,500-5,000 words. Pays $150-200/1,000 words. Sometimes pays expenses of writers on assignment.

Photos: Send photos with query. Negatives must be available. Pays $15-75 for b&w; $25-350 for color. Identification of subjects required. Buys one-time rights.

Columns/Departments: On the Waterfront pays for information on wooden boat-related events, projects, boatshop activities, etc. Buys 25/year. "We use the same columnists for each issue." Send complete information. Length: 250-1,000 words. Pays $5-50 for information.

Tips: "We appreciate a detailed, articulate query letter, accompanied by photos, that will give us a clear idea of what the author is proposing. We appreciate samples of previously published work. It is important for a prospective author to become familiar with our magazine first. It is extremely rare for us to make an assignment with a writer with whom we have not worked before. Most work is submitted on speculation. The most common failure is not exploring the subject material in enough depth."

YACHTING, Times Mirror Magazines Inc., 2 Park Ave., New York NY 10016-5695. (212)779-5300. Fax: (212)725-1035. Publishing Director: Oliver S. Moore III. Executive Editor: Charles Barthold. 50% freelance written. "The magazine is written and edited for experienced, knowledgable yachtsmen." Estab. 1907. Circ. 132,000. Pays on publication. Byline given. Buys first rights. Submit seasonal/holiday material 6 months in advance. Reports in 1 month.

Nonfiction: Book excerpts, personal experience, photo feature and travel. No cartoons, fiction, poetry. Query with published clips. Length: 250-2,000 words. Pays $250-1,000 for assigned articles. Pays expenses of writers on assignment.

Photos: Send photos with submission. Reviews 35mm transparencies. Offers some additional payment for photos accepted with ms. Captions, model releases and identification of subjects required.

Columns/Departments: Cruising Yachtsman (stories on cruising; contact Cynthia Taylor, senior editor); Racing Yachtsman (stories about sail or power racing; contact Ken Wooten); and Yacht Yard (how-to and technical pieces on yachts and their systems; contact Dennis Caprio, Senior editor). Buys 30 mss/year. Send complete ms. Length: 750 words maximum. Pays $250-500.

 • Ranked as one of the best markets for freelance writers in *Writer's Digest* magazine's annual "Top 100 Markets," January 1993.

Tips: "We require considerable expertise in our writing because our audience is experienced and knowledgable. Vivid descriptions of quaint anchorages and quainter natives are fine, but our readers want to know how the yachtsmen got there, too. They also want to know how their boats work."

Bowling

BOWLERS JOURNAL, Dept. WM, 200 S. Michigan Ave., Chicago IL 60604. (312)341-1110. Editor-in-Chief: Mort Luby. Managing Editor: Jim Dressel. 30% freelance written. Prefers to work with published/established writers; works with a small number of new/unpublished writers each year. Monthly magazine emphasizing bowling. Circ. 22,000. **Pays on acceptance.** Publishes ms an average of 2 months after acceptance. Buys all rights. Submit seasonal/holiday material 3 months in advance. Reports in 6 weeks. Sample copy $2.

Nonfiction: General interest (stories on top pros); historical (stories of old-time bowlers or bowling alleys); interview (top pros, men and women); and profile (top pros). "We publish some controversial matter, seek outspoken personalities. We reject material that is too general; that is, not written for high average bowlers and bowling proprietors who already know basics of playing the game and basics of operating a bowling alley." Buys 15-20 unsolicited mss/year. Query; phone queries OK. Length: 1,200-3,500 words. Pays $75-200.

Photos: State availability of photos with query. Pays $5-15 for 8×10 b&w prints; and $15-25 for 35mm or 2¼×2¼ color transparencies. Buys one-time rights.

BOWLING, Dept. WM, 5301 S. 76th St., Greendale WI 53129. (414)421-6400, ext. 230. Editor: Bill Vint. 15% freelance written. Bimonthly, official publication of the American Bowling Congress. Estab. 1934. Circ. 135,000. **Pays on acceptance.** Publishes ms an average of 2 months after acceptance. Byline given. Rights purchased vary with author and material; usually buys all rights. Reports in 1 month. Sample copy $2.50.

Nonfiction: "This is a specialized field and the average writer attempting the subject of bowling should be well-informed. However, anyone is free to submit material for approval." Wants articles about unusual ABC sanctioned leagues and tournaments, personalities, etc., featuring male bowlers. Nostalgia articles also considered. No first-person articles or material on history of bowling. Length: 500-1,200 words. Pays $100-300 per article. No poems, songs or fiction.

Photos: Pays $10-15/photo.

Tips: "Submit feature material on bowlers, generally amateurs competing in local leagues, or special events involving the game of bowling. Should have connection with ABC membership. Queries should be as detailed as possible so that we may get a clear idea of what the proposed story would be all about. It saves us time and the writer time. Samples of previously published material in the bowling or general sports field would help. Once we find a talented writer in a given area, we're likely to go back to him in the future. We're looking for good writers who can handle assignments professionally and promptly." No articles on professionals.

WOMAN BOWLER, 5301 S. 76th St., Greendale WI 53129. (414)421-9000. Fax: (414)421-3013. Editor: Jeffrey R. Nowak. 3% freelance written. Works with a small number of new/unpublished writers each year. Published 8 times/year, emphasizing bowling for women bowlers, ages 18-90. Circ. 120,000. Buys all rights. **Pays on acceptance.** Publishes ms an average of 3 months after acceptance. Byline given "except on occasion, when freelance article is used as part of a regular magazine department. When this occurs, it is discussed first with the author." Submit seasonal/holiday material 3 months in advance. Previously published submissions OK. Reports in 1 month. Free sample copy and writer's guidelines with SAE.

Nonfiction: Interview, profile and spot news. Buys 25 mss/year. Query. Length: 1,500 words maximum (unless by special assignment). Pays $25-100.

Photos: Purchased with accompanying ms. Query. Pays $25-100 for b&w glossy prints. Model releases and identification of subjects required.

Gambling

CASINO PLAYER, America's Premier Gaming Magazine, ACE Marketing, 2524 Arctic Ave., Atlantic City NJ 08401. Fax: (609)345-3469. Publisher: Glenn Fine. Editor: Roger Gros. 15% freelance written. Monthly magazine on casino gambling. "We cover any issue that would interest the gambler, from table games to sports betting, to slot machines. Articles should be light, entertaining and give tips on how to win." Estab. 1985. Circ. 210,000. Pays on publication. Byline not always given. Buys all rights. Submit seasonal/holiday material 3 months in advance. Reprints OK; send photocopy of article. Reports in 3 months. Sample copy $2 for 9×12 SAE with 5 first class stamps.

Nonfiction: How-to (win!) and new product (gaming equipment). "No articles dependent on statistics; no travelogues. First person gambling stories OK." Query with published clips. Length: 500-1,000 words. Pays $50-250 for assigned articles; $50-100 for unsolicited articles. Sometimes pays expenses of writers on assignment.

Photos: Send photos with submission. Reviews contact sheets and 5×7 prints. Offers $10/photo. Captions and identification of subjects required. Buys all rights.

Columns/Departments: Table Games (best ways to play, ratings); Slots (new machines, methods, casino policies); Nevada (what's new in state, properties); Tournaments (reports on gaming, tournaments); and Caribbean (gaming in the islands), all 500 words. Buys 10 mss/year. Query with published clips. Pays $50-100.

Fillers: Facts and gags to be illustrated by cartoonist. Buys 5/year. Length: 25-100 words. Pays $25-100.

Tips: "Writer must understand the gambler: why he gambles, what his motivations are. The spread of legalized gaming will be an increasingly important topic in the next year. Write as much to entertain as to inform. We try to give the reader information they will not find elsewhere."

‡WIN, Gambling Times Incorporated, Suite 215, 16760 Stagg St., Van Nuys CA 91406. (318)781-9355. Editor: Cecil Suzuki. Managing Editor: Dwight Chuman. Contact: C. Suzuki. 12% freelance written. Monthly magazine for gambling, entertainment, computers. Estab. 1979. Circ. 54,200. Pays on publication. Publishes ms an average of 3 months after acceptance. Byline given. Buys first North American serial rights. Editorial lead time 3 months. Submit seasonal material 3 months in advance. Simultaneous submissions OK. Query for electronic submissions. Reports in 6 weeks on queries; 2 months on mss. Sample copy and writer's guidelines with SASE.

Nonfiction: Book excerpts, essays, historical/nostalgic, how-to (casino games), interview/profile, new product, photo feature and technical. Buys 6 mss/year. Send complete ms. Length: 1,600-2,000 words. Pays $75 minimum for assigned articles. Sometimes "pays" contributors with travel, hotel rooms.

Photos: Send photos with submission. Reviews 4 × 5 transparencies and prints. Negotiates payment individually. Captions, model releases and identification of subjects required. Buys all rights.

Fiction: Fantasy, historical, science fiction and gambling subplots. No previously published fiction. Buys 12 mss/year. Send complete ms. Length: 1,200-2,500 words. Pay negotiable.

Fillers: Facts and newsbreaks. Buys 30/year. Length: 250-600 words. Pays $25 minimum.

WINNING!, NatCom, Inc., 15115 S. 76th East Ave., Bixby OK 74008-4147. (918)366-4441. Fax: (918)366-4439. Managing Editor: Jenny M. Kucera. 30% freelance written. Monthly newsletter covering contests, gaming/travel. "How-to-win articles addressing all aspects of legal gaming-casinos, high-stakes bingo, contests and sweepstakes and so on." Estab. 1976. Circ. 150,000. Pays 30 days after acceptance. Byline given. Buys first rights. No simultaneous submissions. Query for electronic submissions. Reports in 4-6 weeks on queries; 1 month on mss. *Writer's Market* recommends allowing 2 months for reply. Free sample copy for 9½ × 12 SAE with 3 first class stamps. Writer's guidelines for #10 SASE.

Nonfiction: How-to (gaming-casino, etc. bingo, sweepstakes and contests), winning tips, interview/profile, new product and travel. "No negative profiles of casino performers/how-to-cheat gaming articles"; no fiction or poetry. Buys 8-10 mss/year. Query. Length: 400-1,000 words. Pays $50-75 for articles; $5-25 for short items and fillers.

General Interest

‡CARIBBEAN SPORTS & TRAVEL, (formerly *Pleasure Boating Magazine*), Graphcom Publishing, Inc., Suite 107, 1995 NE 150th St., N. Miami FL 33181. (305)945-7403. Fax: (305)947-6410. Publisher: Robert Ulrich. Executive Editor: Kyle Stuart. 60% freelance written. Monthly magazine covering sports around The Bahamas and Caribbean. Estab. 1971. Circ. 25,000. Pays on publication. Publishes ms an average of 2 months after acceptance. Byline given. Kill fee varies. Buys first rights. Reports in 3 months on queries.

Nonfiction: General interest, sports, especially diving, fishing, golf and chartering. Buys 35-40 mss/year. Query with published clips. Length: 1,200-2,000 words. Pays $200 minimum; maximum amount varies. Sometimes pays the expenses of writers on assignment.

Photos: Send photos with submission. Reviews transparencies. Offers no additional payment for photos accepted with ms. Identification of subjects required. Buys one-time rights.

Tips: "Know the region we cover, offer fresh perspectives and be flexible with editors."

INSIDE SPORTS, Century Publishing Co., 990 Grove St., Evanston IL 60201. (708)491-6440. Editor-in-Chief: Vince Aversano. 90% freelance written. Monthly magazine. Circ. 675,000. Pays on publication. Publishes ms an average of 4 months after acceptance. Offers 100% kill fee. Rights are negotiated individually. Reports on queries and mss "as soon as we can; sometimes it will be the same day; sometimes it will be weeks."

Nonfiction: Query with or without published clips or send complete ms. Length of article and payment vary with each article and writer. "Please include a SASE with query/article."

• Ranked as one of the best markets for freelance writers in *Writer's Digest* magazine's annual "Top 100 Markets," January 1993.

OUTDOOR CANADA MAGAZINE, Suite 202, 703 Evans Ave., Toronto Ontario M9C 5E9 Canada. (416)695-0311. Fax: (416)695-0382. Editor-in-Chief: Teddi Brown. 90% freelance written. Works with a small number of new/unpublished writers each year. Magazine published 9 times/year emphasizing noncompetitive outdoor recreation in Canada *only*. Estab. 1972. Circ. 125,000. Pays on publication. Publishes ms an average of 6-8 months after acceptance. Buys first rights. Submit seasonal/holiday material 1 year in advance of issue date. Byline given. *Enclose SASE or IRCs or material will not be returned.* Reports in 1 month. *Writer's Market* recommends allowing 2 months for reply. Mention *Writer's Market* in request for editorial guidelines.

Nonfiction: Fishing, hunting, adventure, outdoor issues, exploring, outdoor destinations in Canada, some how-to. Buys 35-40 mss/year, usually with photos. Length: 1,000-2,500 words. Pays $100 and up.

Photos: Emphasize people in the outdoors. Pays $35-225 for 35mm transparencies; and $400/cover. Captions and model releases required.

Fillers: Short news pieces. Buys 70-80/year. Length: 200-500 words. Pays $6/printed inch.

OUTSIDE, Mariah Publications Corp., Dept. WM, 1165 N. Clark St., Chicago IL 60610. (312)951-0990. Editor: Mark Bryant. Managing Editor: Dan Ferrara. 90% freelance written. Monthly magazine on outdoor recreation and travel. "*Outside* is a monthly national magazine for active, educated, upscale adults who love the outdoors and are concerned about its preservation." Estab. 1977. Circ. 400,000. **Pays on acceptance.** Publishes ms an average of 3 months after acceptance. Byline given. Offers 25% kill fee. Buys first North American serial rights. Submit seasonal/holiday material 4-5 months in advance. Electronic submission OK for solicited materials; not for unsolicited. Reports in 6 weeks on queries; 2 months on mss. Sample copy $4 for 9×12 SAE with 9 first class stamps. Writer's guidelines for SASE.

Nonfiction: Book excerpts; essays; reports on the environment; outdoor sports and expeditions; general interest; how-to; humor; inspirational; interview/profile (major figures associated with sports, travel, environment, outdoor); opinion; personal experience (expeditions; trying out new sports); photo feature (outdoor photography); technical (reviews of equipment, how-to); and travel (adventure, sports-oriented travel). All should pertain to the outdoors: Bike section; Downhill Skiing; Cross-country Skiing; Adventure Travel. Do not want to see articles about sports that we don't cover (basketball, tennis, golf, etc.). Buys 40 mss/year. Query with published clips and SASE. Length: 1,500-4,000 words. Negotiates payment. Pays expenses of writers on assignment.

Photos: "Do not send photos; if we decide to use a freelancer's story, we may request to see the writer's photos." Reviews transparencies. Offers $180 minimum/photo. Captions and identification of subjects required. Buys one-time rights.

Columns/Departments: Dispatches, contact Alex Heard (news, events, short profiles relevant to outdoors), 200-1,000 words; Destinations, contact Kathy Martin, (places to explore, news, and tips for adventure travelers), 250-400 words; Review, contact Andrew Tilin, (evaluations of products), 200-1,500 words. Buys 180 mss/year. Query with published clips. Length: 200-2,000 words. Payment varies.

Tips: "Prospective writers should study the magazine before querying. Look at the magazine for our style, subject matter and standards." The departments are the best areas for freelancers to break in.

● Ranked as one of the best markets for freelance writers in *Writer's Digest* magazine's annual "Top 100 Markets," January 1993.

ROCKY MOUNTAIN SPORTS MAGAZINE, Sports & Fitness Publishing, 2025 Pearl St., Boulder CO 80302. (303)440-5111. Editor: Kathleen Gasperini. 50% freelance written. Monthly magazine of sports in the Rocky Mountain States and Canada. "*Rocky* is a magazine for sports-related lifestyles and activities. Our mission is to reflect and inspire the active lifestyle of Rocky Mountain residents." Estab. 1987. Circ. 45,000 Pays on publication. Publishes ms an average of 2 months after acceptance. Byline given. Offers 25% kill fee. Buys second serial (reprint) rights. Editorial lead time 1½ months. Submit seasonal material 2 months in advance. Previously published submissions OK. Query for electronic submissions. Reports in 3 weeks on queries; 2 months on mss. Sample copy and writer's guidelines for #10 SASE.

Nonfiction: Book excerpts, essays, expose, how-to: (no specific sports, trips, adventures), humor, inspirational, interview/profile, new product, opinion, personal experience, photo feature and travel. Special issues: Photo Annual (August); snowboarding (December); Alpine and Nordic (January and February); Mountain biking (April). No articles on football, baseball, basketball or other sports covered in-depth by newspapers. Buys 24 mss/year. Query with published clips. Length: 1,500 maximum words. Pays $150 minimum for assigned articles. Sometimes pays expenses of writers on assignment.

Photos: State availability of photos with submission. Reviews transparencies and prints. Offers $25-250/photo. Captions and identification of subjects required. Buys one-time rights.

Columns/Departments: Scree (short newsy items), 50-800 words; Photo Gallery (photos depicting nature and the spirit of sport); and High Altitude (essay on quirky topics related to Rockies). Buys 20 mss/year. Query. Pays $25-200.

Fiction: Adventure, experimental and humorous. "Nothing that isn't sport-related." Buys 5 mss/year. Query. Length: 250-1,500 words. Pays $50-200.

Fillers: Anecdotes, facts, gags to be illustrated by cartoonist, newsbreaks and short humor. Buys 20/year. Length: 10-200 words. Pays $25-75.

Tips: "Submit stories for the Scree section first."

SPORT, Petersen Publishing Co., 8490 Sunset Blvd., Los Angeles CA 90069. (310)854-6870. Contact: Cam Benty. 30% freelance written. Monthly magazine. **Pays on acceptance.** Publishes ms an average of 3 months after acceptance. Offers 25% kill fee. Buys first North American serial or all rights. Reports in 3 months.

Nonfiction: "Prefers to see articles on professional, big-time sports: basketball, football, baseball, with some boxing. The articles we buy must be contemporary pieces, not a history of sports or a particular sport." Query with published clips. Length: News briefs, 200-300 words; Departments, 1,400 words; Features, 1,500-3,000 words. Averages 50¢/word for articles.

THE SPORTING NEWS, Times Mirror Co., Dept. WM, 1212 N. Lindbergh Blvd., St. Louis MO 63132. (314)997-7111. Editor: John Rawlings. 50-60% freelance written. Weekly tabloid. Pays on publication. Publishes ms an average of 2-3 months after acceptance. Offers 50% kill fee. Buys first or one-time and second serial rights. Reports in 3 weeks.

Nonfiction: "Prefers to see trend stories, perspective stories, trend analysis of major spectator sports." Prefers to see complete ms, but may query with published clips. Length: 100-2,000 words. Pays $50-1,500.

SPORTS ILLUSTRATED, Time & Life Bld., Rockefeller Center, New York NY 10020-1393. "Prefers not to share information."

SPORTS PARADE, Meridian International, Inc., P.O. Box 10010, Odgen UT 84409. (801)394-9446. 65% freelance written. Works with a small number of new/unpublished writers each year. Monthly general interest sports magazine distributed by business and professional firms to employees, customers, clients, etc. Readers are predominantly upscale, mainstream, family oriented. **Pays on acceptance.** Publishes ms an average of 3 months after acceptance. Byline given. Buys first, second serial (reprint) and nonexclusive reprint rights. Simultaneous and previously published submissions OK. Reports in 2 months with SASE. Sample copy $1 for 9 × 12 SAE. Writer's guidelines for #10 SASE, Attn: Editorial Staff.
Nonfiction: General interest and interview/profile. "General interest articles covering the entire sports spectrum, personality profiles on top flight professional and amateur sports figures. We are looking for articles on well-known athletes in the top 10% of their field. We are still looking at articles and profiles of well-known celebrities. These are cover features; photogenic appeal is important." Buys 20 mss/year. Query. Length: 1,200-1,580 words. Pays 15¢/word. Pays 10¢/word for second rights.
Photos: Send with query or ms. Reviews 35mm or larger transparencies and 5 × 7 or 8 × 10 prints. Pays $35 for transparencies; $50 for cover. Captions and model releases required.
Tips: "I will be purchasing more articles based on personalities — today's stars. Celebrities must have positive values and be making a contribution to society. No nostalgic material."

WOMEN'S SPORTS & FITNESS MAGAZINE, Women's Sports & Fitness, Inc., 2025 Pearl St., Boulder CO 80302-5323. (303)440-5111. Fax: (303)440-3313. Editor: Marjorie McCloy. 90% freelance written. Works with a small number of new/unpublished writers each year. Magazine published 8 times/year emphasizing women's sports, fitness and health. Estab. 1974. Circ. 200,000. Pays on publication. Publishes ms an average of 3 months after acceptance. Buys first North American serial rights. Submit seasonal/holiday material 3 months in advance. Reports in 2 months. Sample copy $5 for 9 × 12 SAE. Writer's guidelines for #10 SASE.
  • Ranked as one of the best markets for freelance writers in *Writer's Digest* magazine's annual "Top 100 Markets," January 1993.
Nonfiction: Profile, service piece, interview, how-to, historical, personal experience, personal opinion and new product. "All articles should have the latest information from knowledgable sources. All must be of national interest to athletic women." Buys 5 mss/issue. Length: 500-1,500 words. Query with published clips. Pays $600-1,200 for features, including expenses.
Photos: State availability of photos. Pays about $50-300 for b&w prints; $50-500 for 35mm color transparencies. Buys one-time rights.
Columns/Departments: Buys 8-10/issue. Query with published clips. Length: 200-750 words. Pays $100-400.
Tips: "If the writer doesn't have published clips, best advice for breaking in is to concentrate on columns and departments (the Fast Breaks and Training Tips) first. Query letters should tell why our readers — active women (with an average age in the mid-thirties) who partake in sports or fitness activities six times a week — would want to read the article. We're especially attracted to articles with a new angle, fresh or difficult-to-get information. We go after the latest in health, nutrition and fitness research, or reports about lesser-known women in sports who are on the threshold of greatness. We also present profiles of the best athletes and teams. We want the profiles to give insight into the person as well as the athlete. We have a cadre of writers whom we've worked with regularly, but we are always looking for new writers."

Golf

GOLF DIGEST, Dept. WM, 5520 Park Ave., Trumbull CT 06611. (203)373-7000. Editor: Jerry Tarde. 30% freelance written. Monthly magazine emphasizing golfing. Circ. 1.45 million. **Pays on acceptance.** Publishes ms an average of 6 weeks after acceptance. Buys all rights. Byline given. Submit seasonal/holiday material 4 months in advance. Reports in 6 weeks.
Nonfiction: Lisa Sweet, editorial assistant. How-to, informational, historical, humor, inspirational, interview, nostalgia, opinion, profile, travel, new product, personal experience, photo feature and technical; "all on playing and otherwise enjoying the game of golf." Query. Length: 1,000-2,500 words.
Photos: Nick DiDio, art director. Purchased without accompanying ms. Pays $75-150 for 5 × 7 or 8 × 10 b&w prints; $100-300/35mm transparency. Model release required.
Poetry: Lois Hains, assistant editor. Light verse. Buys 1-2/issue. Length: 4-8 lines. Pays $50.
Fillers: Lois Hains, assistant editor. Jokes, gags, anecdotes and cutlines for cartoons. Buys 1-2/issue. Length: 2-6 lines. Pays $25-50.

‡GOLF ILLUSTRATED, Kachina Publications, Suite 250, 5050 N. 40th St., Phoenix AZ 85018. (602)955-0611. Editor: Mike Corcoran. Managing Editor: John Poinier. Contact: John Poinier. 15% freelance written. Monthly magazine for golf. "We cover everything and anything to do with golf, but we're not into the *politics* of the game. Humor, history, profiles of influential figures in golf, are the primary focus." Estab. 1983. Circ. 500,000. **Pays in 30 days upon acceptance.** Publishes ms an average of 3 months after acceptance. Byline given. Offers 20% kill fee. Buys first North American serial rights. Editorial lead time 2½ months. Submit seasonal material 3-6 months in advance. Query for electronic submissions. Reports in 1-2 months on queries. Writer's guidelines free on request.

Nonfiction: Historical/nostalgic, how-to (golf instruction), humor, interview/profile (golf figures), technical, travel (focus on golf) and golf equipment. "No opinion or politics." Buys 20 mss/year. Query. Length: 1,500-2,000 words. Pays $1/word minimum. Sometimes pays expenses of writers on assignment.

Photos: Negotiates payment individually. Identification of subjects required. Buys one-time rights.

Columns/Departments: Gallery Shots (humorous short pieces), 200-400 words. Buys 40 mss/year. Query. Pays $50-400.

Fiction: Humorous and slice-of-life vignettes. Buys 10 mss/year. Query. Length: 1,000-1,500 words. Pays $1/word minimum.

Poetry: Light verse. Buys 8 poems/year. Submit maximum 5 poems. Length: 10-20 lines. Pays $50-100.

Fillers: Anecdotes and short humor. Buys 20/year. Length: 50-200 words. Pays $50-200.

Tips: "Offer a unique perspective; short and sweet queries with SASE are appreciated. *Don't* call up every 2 weeks to find out when your story is going to be published. Be patient, we get lots of submissions and try our best to respond promptly. We are most open to humorous pieces—anything genuinely well-written."

GOLF MAGAZINE, Times Mirror Magazines, 2 Park Ave., New York NY 10016. (212)779-5000. Editor: James A. Frank. Senior Editors: David Barrett and Mike Purkey. 40% freelance written. Monthly magazine on golf, professional and amateur. Circ. 1.2 million. **Pays on acceptance.** Publishes ms an average of 4 months after acceptance. Byline sometimes given. Offers 20% kill fee. Buys first North American serial rights. Submit seasonal/holiday material 4 months in advance. Query for electronic submissions. Reports in 1 month on queries. *Writer's Market* recommends allowing 2 months for reply. Free writer's guidelines.

Nonfiction: General interest, historical/nostalgic, how-to, humor and interview/profile. Buys 10-20 mss/year. Query or query with published clips. Length: 100-2,500 words. Pays $100-2,500. Sometimes pays expenses of writers on assignment.

Photos: State availability of photos with submission or send photos with submission. Offers standard page rate. Captions, model releases and identification of subjects required. Buys one-time rights.

Columns/Departments: Buys 5-10 mss/year. Query with or without published clips or send complete ms. Length: 100-1,200 words. Pays $100-1,000.

Fillers: Newsbreaks and short humor. Buys 5-10/year. Length: 50-100 words. Pays $50-150.

Tips: "Be familiar with the magazine and with the game of golf."

GULF COAST GOLFER, Golfer Magazines, Inc., 9182 Old Katy Rd., Houston TX 77055. (713)464-0308. Fax: (713)464-0129. Editor: Steve Hunter. 30% freelance written. Prefers to work with published/established writers. Monthly magazine covering results of major area competition, data on upcoming tournaments, reports of new and improved golf courses, and how-to tips for active, competitive golfers in Texas Gulf Coast area. Estab. 1984. Circ. 30,000. Pays on publication. Publishes ms an average of 1 month after acceptance. Byline given. Buys one-time rights. Submit seasonal/holiday material 3 months in advance. Reports in 3 weeks. Sample copy for 10 × 13 SAE with 4 first class stamps. Free writer's guidelines.

Nonfiction: How-to, humor, interview/profile, personal experience and travel. Nothing outside of Gulf Coast area. Buys 20 mss/year. Query. Length: 500-1,500 words. Pays $50-250 for assigned articles.

Photos: Send photos with submission. Offers no additional payment for photos accepted with ms. Identification of subjects required.

Tips: "We publish mostly how-to, where-to articles. They're about people and events. We could use profiles of successful amateur and professional golfers—but only on a specific assignment basis. Most of the tour players already have been assigned to the staff or to freelancers. Do *not* approach people, schedule interviews, then tell us about it."

NORTH TEXAS GOLFER, Golfer Magazines, Inc., 9182 Old Katy Rd., Houston TX 77055. (713)464-0308. Fax: (713)464-0129. Editor: Steve Hunter. 30% freelance written. Monthly tabloid covering golf in North Texas. Emphasizes "grass roots coverage of regional golf course activities" and detailed, localized information on tournaments and competition in North Texas. Estab. 1986. Circ. 28,000. Pays on publication. Byline given. Buys one-time rights. Submit seasonal/holiday material 3 months in advance. Reports in 3 weeks. Sample copy for 9 × 12 SAE with 4 first class stamps.

Nonfiction: How-to, humor, interview/profile, personal experience and travel. Nothing outside of Texas. Buys 20 mss/year. Query. Length: 500-1,500 words. Pays $50-250 for assigned articles.

Photos: Send photos with submission. Offers no additional payment for photos accepted with ms. Identification of subjects required.

Tips: "We publish mostly how-to, where-to articles. They're about people and events in Texas only. We could use profiles of successful amateur and professional golfers in Texas—but only on a specific assignment basis. Most of the tour players already have been assigned to the staff or to freelancers. Do *not* approach people, schedule interviews, then tell us about it."

SCORE, Canada's Golf Magazine, Canadian Controlled Media Communications, 287 MacPherson Ave., Toronto, Ontario M4V 1A4 Canada. (416)928-2909. Fax: (416)928-1357. Managing Editor: Bob Weeks. 70% freelance written. Works with a small number of new/unpublished writers each year. Magazine published 7 times/year covering golf. "*Score* magazine provides seasonal coverage of the Canadian golf scene, professional, amateur, senior and junior golf for men and women golfers in Canada, the US and Europe through profiles, history, travel, editorial comment and instruction." Estab. 1982. Circ. 140,000 audited. **Pays on acceptance.** Byline given. Offers negotiable kill fee. Buys all rights and second serial (reprint) rights. Submit seasonal/holiday material 8 months in advance. Reports in 8 months. Sample copy $2 (Canadian) for 9 × 12 SAE with IRCs. Writer's guidelines for #10 SAE and IRC.

Nonfiction: Book excerpts (golf); historical/nostalgic (golf and golf characters); interview/profile (prominent golf professionals); photo feature (golf); and travel (golf destinations only). The yearly April/May issue includes tournament results from Canada, the U.S., Europe, Asia, Australia, etc., history, profile, and regular features. "No personal experience, technical, opinion or general-interest material. Most articles are by assignment only." Buys 25-30 mss/year. Query with published clips. Length: 700-3,500 words. Pays $200-1,500.

Photos: Send photos with query or ms. Pays $50-100 for 35mm color transparencies (positives) or $30 for 8 × 10 or 5 × 7 b&w prints. Captions, model release (if necessary), and identification of subjects required. Buys all rights.

Columns/Departments: Profile (historical or current golf personalities or characters); Great Moments ("Great Moments in Canadian Golf"—description of great single moments, usually game triumphs); New Equipment (Canadian availability only); Travel (golf destinations, including "hard" information such as greens fees, hotel accommodations, etc.); Instruction (by special assignment only; usually from teaching golf professionals); The Mental Game (psychology of the game, by special assignment only); and History (golf equipment collections and collectors, development of the game, legendary figures and events). Buys 17-20 mss/year. Query with published clips or send complete ms. Length: 700-1,700 words. Pays $140-400.

Tips: "Only writers with an extensive knowledge of golf and familiarity with the Canadian golf scene should query or submit in-depth work to *Score*. Many of our features are written by professional people who play the game for a living or work in the industry. All areas mentioned under Columns/Departments are open to freelancers. Most of our *major* features are done on assignment only."

Guns

GUN DIGEST, DBI Books, Inc., 4092 Commercial Ave., Northbrook IL 60062. (312)272-6310. Editor-in-Chief: Ken Warner. 50% freelance written. Prefers to work with published/established writers but works with a small number of new/unpublished writers each year. Annual journal covering guns and shooting. Estab. 1944. **Pays on acceptance.** Publishes ms an average of 20 months after acceptance. Byline given. Buys all rights. Reports in 1 month.

Nonfiction: Buys 50 mss/issue. Query. Length: 500-5,000 words. Pays $100-600; includes photos or illustration package from author.

Photos: State availability of photos with query letter. Reviews 8 × 10 b&w prints. Payment for photos included in payment for ms. Captions required.

Tips: Award of $1,000 to author of best article (juried) in each issue.

GUN WORLD, 34249 Camino Capistrano, Box HH, Capistrano Beach CA 92624. Editorial Director: Jack Lewis. 50% freelance written. Monthly magazine for ages that "range from mid-teens to mid-60s; many professional types who are interested in relaxation of hunting and shooting." Estab. 1960. Circ. 128,000. Buys 80-100 unsolicited mss/year. **Pays on acceptance.** Publishes ms an average of 6 months after acceptance. Buys first rights and sometimes all rights, but rights reassigned on request. Byline given. Submit seasonal material 5 months in advance. Query for electronic submissions. Reports in 6 weeks. Editorial requirements for #10 SASE.

Nonfiction: General subject matter consists of "well-rounded articles—not by amateurs—on shooting techniques, with anecdotes; hunting stories with tips and knowledge integrated. No poems or fiction. We like broad humor in our articles, so long as it does not reflect upon firearms safety. Most arms magazines are pretty deadly, and we feel shooting can be fun. Too much material aimed at pro-gun people. Most of this is staff-written and most shooters don't have to be told of their rights under the Constitution. We want articles on new developments; off-track inventions, novel military uses of arms; police armament and training techniques; do-it-yourself projects in this field." Buys informational, how-to, personal experience and nostalgia articles. Pays up to $300, sometimes more. Prefers electronic submissions.

Photos: Purchases photos with mss. Captions required. Wants 5×7 b&w photos. Sometimes pays the expenses of writers on assignment.

Tips: "The most frequent mistake made by writers in completing an article for us is surface writing with no real knowledge of the subject. To break in, offer an anecdote having to do with proposed copy."

GUNS & AMMO, Petersen Publishing Co., #204, 8490 Sunset Blvd., Los Angeles CA 90069. (213)854-2160. Editor: Red Bell. Managing Editor: Christine Potvin. 5% freelance written. Monthly magazine covering firearms. "Our readers are enthusiasts of handguns, rifles, shotguns and accessories." Circ. 600,000. **Pays on acceptance.** Publishes ms 6 months after acceptance. Byline given. Buys all rights. Submit seasonal material 6 months in advance. Query for electronic submissions. Writer's guidelines for #10 SASE.

Nonfiction: Opinion. Buys 12 mss/year. Send complete ms. Length: 1,000-2,500 words. Pays $125-500.

Photos: Send photos with submissions. Review 7×9 prints. Offers no additional payment for photos accepted with ms. Captions, model releases and identification of subjects required. Buys all rights.

Columns/Departments: RKBA (opinion column on right to keep and bear arms). Send complete ms. Length: 1,000-2,500 words. Pays $125-500.

‡GUNS MAGAZINE, Suite 200, 591 Camino de la Reina, San Diego CA 92108. (619)297-5352. Editor: Jerome Lee. 20% freelance written. Monthly magazine for firearms enthusiasts. Circ. 200,000. Pays on publication for first North American rights. Publishes manuscripts 4-6 months after acceptance. Writer's guidelines for SASE.

Nonfiction: Test reports on new firearms; round-up articles on firearms types; guns for specific purposes (hunting, target shooting, self-defense); custom gunmakers; and history of modern guns. Buys approximately 10 ms/year. Length: 1,000-2,500 words. Pays $100-350.

Photos: Major emphasis on quality photography. Additional payment of $50-200 for color, 4×5 or 2¼×2¼ preferred.

PETERSEN'S HANDGUNS for Sport & Defense, Petersen Publishing Co., #204, 8490 Sunset Blvd. Los Angeles CA 90069. (213)854-6891. Editor: Mr. Jan M. Libourel. Managing Editor: Karen Dunbar-Enzer. 60% freelance written. Monthly magazine covering handguns and handgun accessories. Estab. 1986. Circ. 150,000. **Pays on acceptance.** Byline given. No kill fee. Buys all rights. Reporting time varies. Free sample copy and writer's guidelines.

Nonfiction: General interest, historical, how-to, profile, new product and technical. "No articles not germane to established topics of magazine." Buys 50 mss/year. Send complete ms. Pays $300-500.

Photos: Send photos with submission. Reviews contact sheets and 5×7 prints. Offers no additional payment for photos accepted with ms. Captions, model releases and identification of subjects required. Buys all rights.

Tips: "Send manuscript after querying editor by telephone and establishing acceptability. We are most open to feature stories. Be guided by published examples appearing in the magazine."

Hockey

HOCKEY ILLUSTRATED, Lexington Library, Inc., 355 Lexington Ave., New York NY 10017. (212)973-3200. Fax: (212)986-5926. Editor: Stephen Ciacciarelli. 90% freelance written. Published 3 times in season. Magazine covering NHL hockey. "Upbeat stories on NHL superstars—aimed at hockey fans, predominantly a younger audience." **Pays on acceptance.** Publishes ms an average of 2 months after acceptance. Byline given. Buys first North American serial rights. Reports in 2 weeks. Sample copy $2.95 for 9×12 SAE with 3 first class stamps.

Nonfiction: Inspirational and interview/profile. Buys 40-50 mss/year. Query with or without published clips, or send complete ms. Length: 1,500-3,000 words. Pays $75-125.

Photos: State availability of photos with submission. Reviews transparencies and prints. Offers no additional payment for photos accepted with ms. Identification of subjects required. Buys one-time rights.

Horse Racing

THE BACKSTRETCH, 19899 W. 9 Mile Rd., Southfield MI 48075-3960. (313)354-3232. Fax: (313)354-3157. Editor: Harriet Randall. 50% freelance written. Works with a small number of new/unpublished writers each year. Bimonthly magazine for Thoroughbred horse trainers, owners, breeders, farm managers, track personnel, jockeys, grooms and racing fans who span the age range from very young to very old. Publication of United Thoroughbred Trainers of America, Inc. Estab. 1962. Circ. 12,000. Publishes ms an average of 3 months after acceptance. Reports in 3 months. Sample copy $3 for 9×12 SAE with 7 first class stamps.

Nonfiction: "*Backstretch* contains mostly general information. Articles deal with biographical material on trainers, owners, jockeys, horses, issues and trends within the industry, historical track articles, etc. Unless writer's material is related to Thoroughbreds and Thoroughbred racing, it should not be submitted. Opinion on Thoroughbreds should be qualified with expertise on the subject. Articles accepted on speculation basis — payment made after material is used. If not suitable, articles are returned if SASE is included. Articles that do not require printing by a specified date are preferred. There is no special length requirement and amount paid depends on material. It is advisable to include photos, if possible. Articles should be original copies and should state whether presented to any other magazine, or whether previously printed in any other magazine. Submit complete ms. We do not buy crossword puzzles, cartoons, newspaper clippings, poetry." Pays 50% of their original article fee for reprints.

THE QUARTER RACING JOURNAL, American Quarter Horse Association, P.O. Box 32470, Amarillo TX 79120. (806)376-4811. Editor: Jim Jennings. Executive Editor: Audie Rackley. 10% freelance written. Monthly magazine; the official racing voice of The American Quarter Horse Association. "We promote quarter horse racing. Articles include training, breeding, nutrition, sports medicine, health, history, etc." Estab. 1988. Circ. 12,000. **Pays on acceptance.** Publishes ms an average of 3 months after acceptance. Buys first North American serial rights. Submit seasonal/holiday material 3 months in advance. Reports in 1 month on queries. Free sample copy and writer's guidelines.
Nonfiction: Historical (must be on quarter horses or people associated with them), how-to (training), nutrition, health, breeding and opinion. "We welcome submissions year-round. No fiction." Query. Length: 700-2,500 words. Pays 7-9¢/word.
Photos: Send photos with submission. Offers no additional payment for photos accepted with ms. Captions and identification of subjects required.
Tips: "Query first — must be familiar with quarter horse racing and be knowledgable of the sport. If writing on nutrition, it must be applicable. Most open to features covering nutrition, health care. Use a knowledgable source with credentials."

SPUR, P.O. Box 85, Middleburg VA 22117. (703)687-6314. Fax: (703)687-3925. Editor: Cathy Laws. 80% freelance written. Prefers to work with published/established writers but works with a small number of new/unpublished writers each year. Bimonthly magazine covering thoroughbred horses and the people who are involved in the business and sports of flat racing, steeplechasing, hunter/jumper showing, dressage, driving, foxhunting and polo. Estab. 1964. Circ. 75,000. Pays on publication. Publishes ms an average of 3 months after acceptance. Byline given. Buys first North American rights. Reports in 1 month. Sample copy $5. Writer's guidelines for #10 SASE.
Nonfiction: Historical/nostalgic, personality profile, farm, special feature, travel and international stories. Buys 50 mss/year. Query with clips of published work, "or we will consider complete manuscripts." Length: 300-4,000 words. Payment negotiable. Sometimes pays the expenses of writers on assignment.
Photos: State availability of photos. Reviews color and b&w contact sheets. Captions, model releases and identification of subjects required.
Tips: "Writers must have a knowledge of horses, horse owners, breeding, training, racing, and riding — or the ability to obtain this knowledge from a subject."

Hunting and Fishing

ALABAMA GAME & FISH, Game & Fish Publications, Inc., P.O. Box 741, Marietta GA 30061. Editor: Jimmy Jacobs. See *Game & Fish Publications*.

AMERICAN HUNTER, Suite 1000, 470 Spring Park Pl., Herndon VA 22070. Editor: Tom Fulgham. 90% freelance written. For hunters who are members of the National Rifle Association. Circ. 1.3 million. Buys first North American serial rights. Byline given. Free sample copy for 9 × 12 SAE with 5 first class stamps. Writer's guidelines for #10 SASE.
Nonfiction: Factual material on all phases of hunting. Not interested in material on fishing or camping. Prefers queries. Length: 2,000-2,500 words. Pays $250-450.
Photos: No additional payment made for photos used with mss. Pays $25 for b&w photos purchased without accompanying mss. Pays $50-300 for color.

ARKANSAS SPORTSMAN, Game & Fish Publications, Inc., P.O. Box 741, Marietta GA 30061. (404)953-9222. Editor: Bob Borgwat. See *Game & Fish Publications*.

BASSMASTER MAGAZINE, B.A.S.S. Publications, 5845 Carmichael Pkwy., Montgomery AL 36117. (205)272-9530. Editor: Dave Precht. 80% freelance written. Prefers to work with published/established writers. Magazine published 10 issues/year about largemouth, smallmouth and spotted bass for dedicated beginning and advanced bass fishermen. Circ. 550,000. **Pays on acceptance.** Publication date of ms after acceptance "varies — seasonal material could take years"; average time is 8 months. Byline given. Buys all rights. Submit seasonal

material 6 months in advance. Reports in 1 month. Sample copy $2. Writer's guidelines for #10 SASE.
Nonfiction: Historical; interview (of knowledgable people in the sport); profile (outstanding fishermen); travel (where to go to fish for bass); how-to (catch bass and enjoy the outdoors); new product (reels, rods and bass boats); and conservation related to bass fishing."No 'Me and Joe go fishing' type articles." Query. Length: 400-2,100 words. Pays 20¢/word.
Columns/Departments: Short Cast/News & Views (upfront regular feature covering news-related events such as new state bass records, unusual bass fishing happenings, conservation, new products and editorial viewpoints); 250-400 words.
Photos: "We want a mixture of b&w and color photos." Pays $50 minimum for b&w prints. Pays $300-350 for color cover transparencies. Captions required; model releases preferred. Buys all rights.
Fillers: Anecdotes, short humor and newsbreaks. Buys 4-5 mss/issue. Length: 250-500 words. Pays $50-100.
Tips: "Editorial direction continues in the short, more direct how-to article. Compact, easy-to-read information is our objective. Shorter articles with good graphics, such as how-to diagrams, step-by-step instruction, etc., will enhance a writer's articles submitted to *Bassmaster Magazine*. The most frequent mistakes made by writers in completing an article for us are poor grammar, poor writing, poor organization and superficial research."

BC OUTDOORS, OP Publishing, 202-1132 Hamilton St., Vancouver, British Columbia V6B 2S2 Canada. (604)687-1581. Fax: (604)687-1925. Editor: George Will. 80% freelance written. Works with a small number of new/unpublished writers each year. Magazine published 8 times/year. covering fishing, camping, hunting and the environment of outdoor recreation. Estab. 1946. Circ. 42,000. **Pays on acceptance.** Pays ms an average of 3 months after acceptance. Byline given. Offers negotiable kill fee. Buys first North American serial rights. Query for electronic submissions. Reports in 1 month. Sample copy and writer's guidelines for 8×10 SAE with $2 postage.
Nonfiction: How-to (new or innovative articles on outdoor subjects); personal experience (outdoor adventure); and outdoor topics specific to British Columbia. "We would like to receive how-to, where-to features dealing with hunting and fishing in British Columbia and the Yukon." Buys 80-90 mss/year. Query. Length: 1,500-2,000 words. Pays $300-500. Sometimes pays the expenses of writers on assignment.
Photos: State availability of photos with query. Pays $25-75 on publication for 5×7 b&w prints; $35-150 for color contact sheets and 35mm transparencies. Captions and identification of subjects required. Buys one-time rights.
Tips: "Emphasis on environmental issues. Those pieces with a conservation component have a better chance of being published. Subject must be specific to British Columbia. We receive many manuscripts written by people who obviously do not know the magazine or market. The writer has a better chance of breaking in at our publication with short, lesser-paying articles and fillers, because we have a stable of regular writers in constant touch who produce most main features."

CALIFORNIA ANGLER, Great Outdoors Publishing, Inc., Suite 3-N, 1921 E. Carnegie Ave., Santa Ana CA 92705. (714)261-9779. Fax: (714)261-9853. Editor: Chuck Garrison. 90% freelance written. Monthly magazine devoted to the affluent, serious California angler. Circ. 30,000. Pays 1 month prior to publication. Publishes ms 4 months after acceptance. Byline given. Purchases one-time rights. Reprints OK; send tearsheet or photocopy of article, typed ms with rights for sale noted and information about when and where the article previously appeared. Pays 100% of their fee for an original article. Query for electronic submissions. Sample copy and writer's guidelines available upon request.
Nonfiction: How-to and where-to with emphasis on California destinations and techniques. Monthly stories on Baja, Mexico. Columns include: Travel, Tactics, Flyfishing, Beginner's Basics, Boating, Long-Range, Conservation, News, Baja Bite, Mexico Mainland and Bass. All open to freelancers. "We're working 6 months in advance so query accordingly. Pays $400 for a 2,000-2,500-word feature with 35mm transparencies and two short sidebars. Columns get $200 for 1,000-1,400 words. Illustrations requested and we buy 20 or more a year. Cover photos earn $300. Annual specials and themes include: Canada (January), Bass (February), Baja (September), Eastern Sierra (April), San Diego Long-Range (May), Alaska (December). We prefer first-hand stories that are well researched."
Photos: Send photos with submissions and queries, 35mm transparencies.
Tips: "We're always looking for talented writers. Remember, our name is *California Angler*, so the emphasis is on Golden State and Baja destinations. We also prefer to work with writers via CompuServe: 72010,3541."

CALIFORNIA GAME & FISH, Game & Fish Publications, Inc., Box 741, Marietta GA 30061. Editor: Burt Carey. See *Game & Fish Publications*.

FIELD & STREAM, 2 Park Ave., New York NY 10016. Fax: (212)725-3836. Editor: Duncan Barnes. 50% freelance written. Eager to work with new/unpublished writers. Monthly "broad-based service magazine for the hunter and fisherman. Editorial content ranges from very basic how-to stories detailing a useful technique or a device that sportsmen can make, to articles of penetrating depth about national hunting, fishing, and related activities. Also humor and personal essays, nostalgia and 'mood pieces' on the hunting or fishing experience." Estab. 1895. **Pays on acceptance.** Buys first rights. Byline given. Reports in 2 months. Query. Writer's guidelines for #10 SASE.

Nonfiction: Length: 1,500-2,000 words for features. Payment varies depending on the quality of work, importance of the article. Pays $800 and up for major features. *Field & Stream* also publishes regional sections with feature articles on hunting and fishing in specific areas of the country. The sections are geographically divided into East, Midwest, West and South, and appear 12 months a year. Reprints OK; send photocopy of article and information about when and where it previously appeared.

Photos: Prefers color photos to b&w. Query first with photos. When photos are purchased separately, pays $450 minimum for color. Buys first rights to photos.

Fillers: Buys "how it's done" fillers. Must be unusual or helpful subjects. Also buys "Field Guide" pieces, short articles on natural phenomena as specifically related to hunting and fishing; and "Myths and Misconceptions," short pieces debunking a commonly held belief about hunting and fishing.

- Ranked as one of the best markets for freelance writers in *Writer's Digest* magazine's annual "Top 100 Markets," January 1993.

FISHING WORLD, 51 Atlantic Ave., Floral Park NY 11001-2721. Fax: (516)437-6841. Editor: Scott Shane. 100% freelance written. Bimonthly. Estab. 1955. Circ. 250,000. **Pays on acceptance.** Buys first North American serial rights. Publishes ms an average of 6 months after acceptance. Reports in 3 weeks. Free sample copy. Writer's guidelines for #10 SASE.

Nonfiction: "Destination-oriented fishing feature articles should range from 1,200-1,500 words with the shorter preferred. A good selection of transparencies must accompany each submission. Subject matter should be a hot fishing site, either freshwater or salt. Where-to articles should be accompanied by sidebars covering how to make reservations and arrange transportation, how to get there, where to stay. Angling methods should be developed in clear detail, with accurate and useful information about tackle and boats." Pays $350. Brief queries accompanied by photos are preferred.

Photos: "Cover shots are purchased separately, rather than selected from those accompanying mss. The editor favors boat-fishing drama rather than serenity in selecting cover shots. Transparencies selected for cover use pay an additional $300."

Tips: Looking for "quality photography and more West Coast fishing. Send laundry list (5-10 ideas) of query ideas and recent samples of published works."

FLORIDA GAME & FISH, Game & Fish Publications, Inc., Box 741, Marietta GA 30061. (404)953-9222. Editor: Jimmy Jacobs. See *Game & Fish Publications*.

FLORIDA SPORTSMAN, Wickstrom Publishers Inc., 5901 SW 74 St., Miami FL 33143. (305)661-4222. Editor: Biff Lampton. 30% freelance written. Works with new/unpublished writers. Monthly magazine covering fishing, boating and related sports—Florida and Caribbean only. Circ. 100,000. **Pays on acceptance.** Publishes ms an average of 6 months after acceptance. Byline given. Offers 50% kill fee. Buys first North American serial rights. Submit seasonal/holiday material 6 months in advance. Reports in 1 week on queries; 1 month on mss. *Writer's Market* recommends allowing 2 months for reply. Free sample copy. Writer's guidelines for #10 SASE.

Nonfiction: Essays (environment or nature); how-to (fishing, hunting, boating); humor (outdoors angle); personal experience (in fishing, etc.); and technical (boats, tackle, etc., as particularly suitable for Florida specialties). "We use reader service pieces almost entirely—how-to, where-to, etc. One or two environmental pieces per issue as well. Writers *must* be Florida based, or have lengthy experience in Florida outdoors. All articles must have strong Florida emphasis. We do not want to see general how-to-fish-or-boat pieces which might well appear in a national or wide-regional magazine." Buys 40-60 mss/year. Query. Length: 2,000-3,000 words. Pays $300-400. Sometimes pays expenses of writers on assignment.

Photos: Send photos with submission. Reviews 35mm transparencies and 4×5 and larger prints. Offers no additional payment for photos accepted with ms. Buys one-time rights.

Tips: "Feature articles are most open to freelancers; however there is little chance of acceptance unless contributor is an accomplished and avid outdoorsman *and* a competent writer-photographer with considerable experience in Florida."

FLORIDA WILDLIFE, Florida Game & Fresh Water Fish Commission, 620 S. Meridian St., Tallahassee FL 32399-1600. (904)488-5563. Fax: (904)488-6988. Editor: Andrea H. Blount. About 30% freelance written. Bimonthly four-color state magazine covering hunting, natural history, fishing, endangered species and wildlife conservation. "In outdoor sporting articles we seek themes of wholesome recreation. In nature articles we seek Accuracy and conservation purpose." Estab. 1947. Circ. 29,000. Pays on publication. Publishes ms 2 months-2 years after acceptance. Byline given. Buys first North American serial and occasionally second serial (reprint) rights. Submit seasonal/holiday material 6 months in advance. Simultaneous queries, and simultaneous and previously published submissions OK. "Inform us if it is previously published work." Reports in 6 weeks on queries; variable on mss. Prefers photo/ms packages. Sample copy $1.25. Writer's/photographer's guidelines for SASE.

Nonfiction: General interest (bird watching, hiking, camping, boating); how-to (hunting and fishing); humor (wildlife related; no anthropomorphism); inspirational (conservation oriented); personal experience (wildlife, hunting, fishing, outdoors); photo feature (Florida species: game, nongame, botany); and technical (rarely purchased, but open to experts). "We buy general interest hunting, fishing and nature stories. No stories that humanize animals, or opinionated stories not based on confirmable facts." Buys 30-40 mss/year. Send slides/ms. Length: 500-1,500 words. Generally pays $50/published page; including use of photos.
Photos: State availability of photos with story query. Prefer 35mm color slides of hunting, fishing, and natural science series of Florida wildlife species. Pays $20-50 for inside photos; $100 for front cover photos, $50 for back cover. "We like short, specific captions." Buys one-time rights.
Fiction: "We rarely buy fiction, and then only if it is true to life and directly related to good sportsmanship and conservation. No fairy tales, erotica, profanity, or obscenity." Buys 2-3 mss/year. Send complete mss and label "fiction." Length: 500-1,200 words. Generally pays $50/published page.
Tips: "Read and study recent issues for subject matter, style and examples of our viewpoint, philosophy and treatment. We look for wholesome recreation, ethics, safety, and good outdoor experience more than bagging the game in our stories. We usually need well-written hunting and freshwater fishing articles that are entertaining and informative and that describe places to hunt and fish in Florida."

FLY FISHERMAN, Cowles Magazines Inc., P.O. Box 8200, Harrisburg PA 17105-8200. (717)657-9555. Fax: (717)657-9526. Editor and Publisher: John Randolph. Managing Editor: Philip Hanyok. 85-90% freelance written. Bimonthly magazine on fly fishing. Estab. 1969. Circ. 130,000. Reports in 2 months. Sample copy for 9×12 SAE with 7 first class stamps.

FUR-FISH-GAME, 2878 E. Main, Columbus OH 43209-9947. Editor: Mitch Cox. 65% freelance written. Works with a small number of new/unpublished writers each year. Monthly magazine for outdoorsmen of all ages who are interested in hunting, fishing, trapping, dogs, camping, conservation and related topics. Estab. 1900. Circ. 120,000. **Pays on acceptance.** Publishes ms an average of 7 months after acceptance. Byline given. Buys first serial rights or all rights. Reports in 2 months. Query. Sample copy $1 for 9×12 with SAE. Writer's guidelines for #10 SASE.
Nonfiction: "We are looking for informative, down-to-earth stories about hunting, fishing, trapping, dogs, camping, boating, conservation and related subjects. Nostalgic articles are also used. Many of our stories are 'how-to' and should appeal to small-town and rural readers who are true outdoorsmen. Some recent articles have told how to train a gun dog, catch big-water catfish, outfit a bowhunter and trap late-season muskrat. We also use personal experience stories and an occasional profile, such as an article about an old-time trapper. 'Where-to' stories are used occasionally if they have broad appeal." Length: 1,500-3,000 words. Pays $75-150 depending upon quality, photo support, and importance to magazine. Short filler stories pay $35-80.
Photos: Send photos with ms. Photos are part of ms package and receive no additional payment. Prefer b&w but color prints or transparencies OK. Prints can be 5×7 or 8×10. Captions required.
Tips: "We are always looking for quality articles that tell how to hunt or fish for game animals or birds that are popular with everyday outdoorsmen but often overlooked in other publications, such as catfish, bluegill, crappie, squirrel, rabbit, crows, etc. We also use articles on standard seasonal subjects such as deer and pheasant, but like to see a fresh approach or new technique. Trapping articles, especially instructional ones based on personal experience, are useful all year. Articles on gun dogs, ginseng and do-it-yourself projects are also popular with our readers. An assortment of photos and/or sketches greatly enhances any ms, and sidebars, where applicable, can also help."

GAME & FISH PUBLICATIONS, INC., Suite 110, 2250 Newmarket Parkway, Marietta GA 30067. (404)953-9222. Fax: (404)933-9510. Editorial Director: Ken Dunwoody. Publishes 30 different monthly outdoor magazines, each one covering the fishing and hunting opportunities in a particular state or region (see individual titles and editors). 90% freelance written. Estab. 1975. Total circ. 465,000. Pays 75 days prior to cover date of issue. Publishes ms an average of 6 months after acceptance. Byline given. Offers negotiable kill fee. Buys first North American serial rights. Submit seasonal material at least 8 months in advance. Editors prefer to hold queries until that season's material is assigned. Reports in 3 months on mss. Sample copy $2.50 for 9×12 SAE. writer's guidelines for #10 SASE.
Nonfiction: Prefer queries over unsolicited ms. Article lengths either 1,500 or 2,500 words. Pays separately for articles and accompanying photos. Manuscripts pay $125-250, cover photos $250, inside color $75 and b&w $25. Reviews transparencies and b&w prints. Prefers captions and identification of species/subjects. Buys one-time rights to photos. Reprints OK; send typed ms with rights for sale noted and information about when and where the article previously appeared. Pays 100% of their fee for an original article.
Fiction: Buys some humor and nostalgia stories pertaining to hunting and fishing. Pays $125-250. Length 1,500-2,500 words.
Tips: "Our readers are experienced anglers and hunters, and we try to provide them with useful, entertaining articles about where, when and how to enjoy the best hunting and fishing in their state or region. We also cover topics concerning game and fish management, conservation and environmental issues. Most articles should be aimed at outdoorsmen in one particular state. After familiarizing themselves with our magazine(s), writers should query the appropriate state editor (see individual listings) or send to Ken Dunwoody."

GEORGIA SPORTSMAN, Game & Fish Publications, Box 741, Marietta GA 30061. (404)953-9222. Editor: Jimmy Jacobs. See *Game & Fish Publications*.

GREAT PLAINS GAME & FISH, Game & Fish Publications, Box 741, Marietta GA 30061. (404)953-9222. Editor: Nick Gilmore. See *Game & Fish Publications*.

GULF COAST FISHERMAN, Harold Wells Gulf Coast Fisherman, Inc., 401 W. Main St., Port Lavaca TX 77979. (512)552-8864. Publisher/Editor: Gary M. Ralston. 95% freelance written. Quarterly magazine covering Gulf Coast saltwater fishing. "All editorial material is designed to expand the knowledge of the Gulf Coast angler and promote saltwater fishing in general." Estab. 1979. Circ 15,000. Pays on publication. Publishes ms an average of 2 months after acceptance. Byline given. Buys first North American serial rights. Submit seasonal/holiday material 2 months in advance. Query for electronic submissions. Reports in 1 month. *Writer's Market* recommends allowing 2 months for reply. Sample copy and writer's guidelines for 9 × 12 SAE with 5 first class stamps.
Nonfiction: How-to (any aspect relating to saltwater fishing that provides the reader specifics on use of tackle, boats, finding fish, etc.), interview/profile, new product, personal experience and technical. Buys 25 mss/year. Query with or without published clips or send complete ms. Length: 900-1,800 words. Pays $100-275.
Photos: State availability of photos with submission. Offers no additional payment for photos accepted with ms. Captions and identification of subjects required. Buys one-time rights.
Tips: "Features are the area of our publication most open to freelancers. Subject matter should concern some aspect of or be in relation to saltwater fishing in coastal bays or offshore. Prefers electronic submissions — 3½" Mac-compatible, or 5¼" DOS."

ILLINOIS GAME & FISH, Game & Fish Publications, Inc., Box 741, Marietta GA 30061. (404)953-9222. Editor: Bill Hartlage. See *Game & Fish Publications*.

INDIANA GAME & FISH, Game & Fish Publications, Inc., Box 741, Marietta GA 30061. (404)953-9222. Editor: Ken Freel. See *Game & Fish Publications*.

IOWA GAME & FISH, Game & Fish Publications, Inc., Box 741, Marietta GA 30061. (404)953-9222. Editor: Nick Gilmore. See *Game & Fish Publications*.

KENTUCKY GAME & FISH, Game & Fish Publications, Inc., Box 741, Marietta GA 30061. (404)953-9222. Editor: Bill Hartlage. See *Game & Fish Publications*.

LOUISIANA GAME & FISH, Game & Fish Publications, Inc., Box 741, Marietta GA 30061. (404)953-9222. Editor: Bob Borgwat. See *Game & Fish Publications*.

‡MARLIN, The International Sportfishing Magazine, Marlin Magazine, a division of World Publications, Inc., P.O. Box 12902, Pensacola FL 32576-2902. (904)434-5571. Fax: (904)433-6303. Editor: David Ritchie. 90% freelance written. Bimonthly magazine on big game fishing. "*Marlin* covers the sport of big game fishing (billfish, tuna, sharks, dorado and wahoo). Our readers are sophisticated, affluent and serious about their sport — they expect a high-class, well-written magazine that provides information and practical advice." Estab. 1982. Circ. 30,000. **Pays on acceptance for text,** on publication for photos. Publishes ms an average of 3 months after acceptance. Byline given. Buys first North American serial rights. Submit seasonal/holiday material 2-3 months in advance. Query for electronic submissions. Free sample copy and writer's guidelines.
Nonfiction: General interest, how-to (bait-rigging, tackle maintenance, etc.), new product, personal experience, photo feature, technical and travel. "No freshwater fishing stories. No 'me & Joe went fishing' stories, unless top quality writing." Buys 30-50 mss/year. Query with published clips. Length: 800-2,200 words. Pays $250-500.
Photos: State availability of photos with submission. Original slides, please. Offers $25-300/photo. $500 for a cover. Buys one-time rights.
Columns/Departments: Tournament Reports (reports on winners of major big game fishing tournaments), 300-600 words; and Blue Water Currents (news features), 300-900 words. Buys 25 mss/year. Query. Pays $100-250. Publishes reprints of previously published articles in news section only. Send photocopy of article, including information about when and where the article previously appeared. For reprints, pays 50-75% of the amount paid for an original article.

Always check the most recent copy of a magazine for the address and editor's name before you send in a query or manuscript.

Tips: "Tournament reports are a good way to break in to *Marlin*. Make them short but accurate, and provide photos of fishing action (*not* dead fish hanging up at the docks!). We always need how-tos and news items. Our destination pieces (travel stories) emphasize where and when to fish, but include information on where to stay also. For features: crisp, high action stories—nothing flowery or academic. Technical/how-to: concise and informational—specific details. News: Again, concise with good details—watch for legislation affecting big game fishing, outstanding catches, new clubs and organizations, new trends and conservation issues."

MICHIGAN OUT-OF-DOORS, P.O. Box 30235, Lansing MI 48909. (517)371-1041. Fax: (517)371-1505. Editor: Kenneth S. Lowe. 50% freelance written. Works with a small number of new/unpublished writers each year. Monthly magazine emphasizing outdoor recreation, especially hunting and fishing, conservation and environmental affairs. Estab. 1947. Circ. 130,000. **Pays on acceptance.** Publishes ms an average of 6 months after acceptance. Byline given. Buys first North American serial rights. Phone queries OK. Submit seasonal/holiday material 6 months in advance. Reports in 1 month. *Writer's Market* recommends allowing 2 months for reply. Sample copy $2. Free writer's guidelines.
Nonfiction: Expose, historical, how-to, informational, interview, nostalgia, personal experience, personal opinion, photo feature and profile. No humor or poetry. "Stories *must* have a Michigan slant unless they treat a subject of universal interest to our readers." Buys 8 mss/issue. Send complete ms. Length: 1,000-3,000 words. Pays $75 minimum for feature stories. Pays expenses of writers on assignment.
Photos: Purchased with or without accompanying ms. Pays $15 minimum for any size b&w glossy prints; $100 maximum for color (for cover). Offers no additional payment for photos accepted with accompanying ms. Buys one-time rights. Captions preferred.
Tips: "Top priority is placed on true accounts of personal adventures in the out-of-doors—well-written tales of very unusual incidents encountered while hunting, fishing, camping, hiking, etc. The most rewarding aspect of working with freelancers is realizing we had a part in their development. But it's annoying to respond to queries that never produce a manuscript."

MICHIGAN SPORTSMAN, Game & Fish Publications, Inc., Box 741, Marietta GA 30061. (404)953-9222. Editor: Dennis Schmidt. See *Game & Fish Publications*.

MID WEST OUTDOORS, Mid West Outdoors, Ltd., 111 Shore Drive, Hinsdale (Burr Ridge) IL 60521-5885. (708)887-7722. Fax: (708)887-1958. Editor: Gene Laulunen. Monthly tabloid emphasizing fishing, hunting, camping and boating. 100% freelance written. Estab. 1967. Circ. 43,814. Pays on publication. Buys simultaneous rights. Byline given. Submit seasonal material 2 months in advance. Simultaneous and previously published submissions OK. Reports in 3 weeks. Publishes ms an average of 3 months after acceptance. Sample copy $1. Writer's guidelines for #10 SASE.
Nonfiction: How-to (fishing, hunting, camping in the Midwest) and where-to-go (fishing, hunting, camping within 500 miles of Chicago). "We do not want to see any articles on 'my first fishing, hunting or camping experiences,' 'cleaning my tackle box,' 'tackle tune-up,' or 'catch and release.'" Buys 1,800 unsolicited mss/year. Send complete ms. Length: 1,000-1,500 words. Pays $15-30. Pays $25 for reprints.
Photos: Offers no additional payment for photos accompanying ms unless used as covers; uses b&w prints. Buys all rights. Captions required.
Columns/Departments: Fishing, Hunting. Open to suggestions for columns/departments. Send complete ms. Pays $25.
Tips: "Break in with a great unknown fishing hole or new technique within 500 miles of Chicago. Where, how, when and why. Know the type of publication you are sending material to."

MID-ATLANTIC GAME & FISH, Game & Fish Publications, Inc., Box 741, Marietta GA 30061. (404)953-9222. Editor: Ken Freel. See *Game & Fish Publications*.

MINNESOTA SPORTSMAN, Game & Fish Publications, Inc., Box 741, Marietta GA 30061. (404)953-9222. Editor: Dennis Schmidt. See *Game & Fish Publications*.

MISSISSIPPI GAME & FISH, Game & Fish Publications, Inc., Box 741, Marietta GA 30061. (404)953-9222. Editor: Bob Borgwat. See *Game & Fish Publications*.

MISSOURI GAME & FISH, Game & Fish Publications, Inc., Box 741, Marietta GA 30061. (404)953-9222. Editor: Bill Hartlage. See *Game & Fish Publications*.

MUSKY HUNTER MAGAZINE, Esox Publishing, Inc., #10, 2632 S. Packerland, Green Bay WI 54313. (414)496-0334. Fax: (414)496-0332. Editor: Joe Bucher. 90% freelance written. Bimonthly magazine on Musky fishing. "Serves the vertical market of Musky fishing enthusiasts. We're interested in how-to where-to articles." Estab. 1988. Circ. 18,000. Pays on publication. Publishes ms an average of 3 months after acceptance. Byline given. Buys first rights or one-time rights. Submit seasonal/holiday material 4 months in advance. Reports in 2 months. Sample copy for 9 × 12 SAE with 5 first class stamps. Writer's guidelines for #10 SASE.

Nonfiction: Historical/nostalgic (related only to Musky fishing), how-to (modify lures, boats and tackle for Musky fishing), personal experience (must be Musky fishing experience), technical (fishing equipment) and travel (to lakes and areas for Musky fishing). Buys 50 mss/year. Send complete ms. Length: 1,000-2,000 words. Pays $100-200 for assigned articles; $50-200 for unsolicited articles. Payment of contributor copies or other premiums negotiable.

Photos: Send photos with submission. Reviews 35mm transparencies and 3×5 prints. Offers no additional payment for photos accepted with ms. Identification of subjects required. Buys one-time rights.

NEW ENGLAND GAME & FISH, Game & Fish Publications, Inc., Box 741, Marietta GA 30061. (404)953-9222. Editor: Kim Leighton. See *Game & Fish Publications.*

NEW YORK GAME & FISH, Game & Fish Publications, Inc., Box 741, Marietta GA 30061. (404)953-9222. Editor: Kim Leighton. See *Game & Fish Publications.*

NORTH AMERICAN FISHERMAN, Official Publication of North American Fishing Club, Suite 260, 12301 Whitewater Dr., Minnetonka MN 55343. (612)936-0555. Publisher: Mark LaBarbera. Editor: Steve Pennaz. 75% freelance written. Bimonthly magazine on fresh- and saltwater fishing across North America. Estab. 1987. Circ. 375,000. **Pays on acceptance.** Publishes ms an average of 4 months after acceptance. Offers $150 kill fee. Buys first North American serial, one-time and all rights. Submit seasonal/holiday material 6 months in advance. Reports in 1 month. Sample copy $5 for 9×12 SAE with 6 first class stamps. Prefers written queries.

Nonfiction: How-to (species-specific information on how-to catch fish), news briefs on fishing from various state agencies and travel (where to information on first class fishing lodges). Buys 35-40 mss/year. Query by mail. Length: 700-2,100. Pays $100-500.

Photos: Send photos with submission. Additional payment made for photos accepted with ms. Captions and identification of subjects required. Buys one-time rights. Pays up to $200 for inside art, $500 for cover.

Fillers: Facts and newsbreaks. Buys 60/year. Length: 50-100. Pays $35-50.

• No longer accepts phone queries.

Tips: "We are looking for news briefs on important law changes, new lakes, etc. Areas most open for freelancers are: full-length features, cover photos and news briefs. Know what subject you are writing about. Our audience of avid fresh and saltwater anglers know how to fish and will see through weak or dated fishing information. Must be on cutting edge for material to be considered."

NORTH AMERICAN WHITETAIL, The Magazine Devoted to the Serious Trophy Deer Hunter, Game & Fish Publications, Inc., Suite 110, 2250 Newmarket Parkway, Marietta GA 30067. (404)953-9222. Fax: (404)933-9510. Editor: Gordon Whittington. 70% freelance written. Magazine published 8 times/year about hunting trophy-class white-tailed deer in North America, primarily the US. "We provide the serious hunter with highly sophisticated information about trophy-class whitetails and how, when and where to hunt them. We are not a general hunting magazine or a magazine for the very occasional deer hunter." Estab. 1982. Circ. 170,000. Pays 75 days prior to cover date of issue. Publishes ms an average of 6 months after acceptance. Byline given. Offers negotiable kill fee. Buys first North American serial rights. Submit seasonal/holiday material 10 months in advance. Reports in 3 months on mss. Editor prefers to keep queries on file, without notification, until the article can be assigned or author informs of prior sale. Sample copy $3 for 9×12 SAE with 7 first class stamps. Writer's guidelines for #10 SASE.

Nonfiction: How-to interview/profile. Buys 50 mss/year. Query. Length: 1,000-3,000 words. Pays $150-400.

Photos: Send photos with submission. Reviews 2×2 transparencies and 8×10 prints. Offers no additional payment for photos accepted with ms. Captions and identification of subjects required. Buys one-time rights.

Columns/Departments: Trails and Tails (nostalgic, humorous or other entertaining styles of deer-hunting material, fictional or nonfictional), 1,400 words. Buys 8 mss/year. Send complete ms. Pays $150.

Tips: "Our articles are written by persons who are deer hunters first, writers second. Our hard-core hunting audience can see through material produced by non-hunters or those with only marginal deer-hunting expertise. We have a continual need for expert profiles/interviews. Study the magazine to see what type of hunting expert it takes to qualify for our use, and look at how those articles have been directed by the writers. Good photography of the interviewee and his hunting results must accompany such pieces."

NORTH CAROLINA GAME & FISH, Game & Fish Publications, Inc., Box 741, Marietta GA 30061. (404)953-9222. Editor: Jeff Samsel. See *Game & Fish Publications.*

OHIO GAME & FISH, Game & Fish Publications, Inc., Box 741, Marietta GA 30061. (404)953-9222. Editor: Ken Freel. See *Game & Fish Publications.*

OHIO OUT-OF-DOORS, Redbird Publications, P.O. Box 117, St. Marys OH 45885. (419)394-3226. Editor/Publisher: John Andreoni. 40-50% freelance written. Monthly mgazine that covers outdoor activities and conservation issues. "We cover outdoors-related topics; the wise use of game and fish management; appreciation of the outdoors. Our readers are hunters, fishermen and conservationists." Estab. 1991. Circ. 4,000. Pays on publication. Byline given. Not copyrighted. Buys first North American serial rights. Submit seasonal/holiday material 4 months in advance. Previously published submissions OK. Send typed ms with rights for sale noted, including information about when and where the article previously appeared. Query for electronic submissions. Reports in 2 weeks on queries. Sample copy for 11×13 SAE with 4 first class stamps.

Nonfiction: Essays, general interest, historical/nostalgic, how-to (catch fish, make rods, learn to shoot or do anything outdoor oriented), humor, interview/profile, new product, opinion, photo feature, technical and travel. "We are looking for material on spring fishing, upland game, wildlife hunting, fishing for specifics, turkey hunting, deer hunting, morell hunting, boats, mushroom hunting, ice fishing and black powder guns. No 'Bob and me' or 'me and Joe' articles focusing on kill or catch." Buys 20 mss/year. *Query* only. Length: 500-2,000 words. Pays $25-50 for assigned articles.

Photos: State availability of photos or send photos with submission. Reviews 35mm vertical transparencies, 5×7 prints. Offers $5 for b&w, $10 for color and $25 for cover (one-time use vertical shot).

Columns/Departments: Buys 36 mss/year. *Query.* Length: 500-800 words. Pays $25 minimum.

Fiction: Adventure (outdoor slant), historical (outdoor slant) and humorous. Buys few mss/year. Query. Length: 500-2,000 words.

Tips: "Writers must sell publisher/editor with a query. Query should reflect writing style. Writers will have the best luck submitting material for features. Pick a specific topic, research well, quote authorities when possible and include a powerful, well-written lead."

OKLAHOMA GAME & FISH, Game & Fish Publications, Box 741, Marietta GA 30061. (404)953-9222. Fax: (404)933-9510. Editor: Nick Gilmore. See *Game & Fish Publications.*

OUTDOOR LIFE, Times Mirror Magazines, Inc., 2 Park Ave., New York NY 10016. (212)779-5000. Editor: Vin T. Sparano. Executive Editor: Gerald Bethge. 95% freelance written. Monthly magazine covering hunting and fishing. Estab. 1890. Circ. 1.5 million. **Pays on acceptance.** Publishes ms an average of 6-12 months after acceptance. Byline given. Buys first North American serial rights. Submit seasonal/holiday material 1 year in advance. Previously published submissions OK on occasion. Reports in 1 month on queries; 2 months on mss. Writer's guidelines for #10 SASE.

Nonfiction: Book excerpts, essays, how-to (must cover hunting, fishing or related outdoor activities), interview/profile, new product, personal experience, photo feature, technical and travel. No articles that are too general in scope—need to write specifically. Buys 400 mss/year. Query first; "photos are *very important.*" Length: 800-3,000 words. Pays $350-600 for 1,000-word features and regionals; $900-1,200 for 2,000-word or longer national features.

Photos: Send photos with submission. Reviews 35mm transparencies and 8×10 b&w prints. Offers variable payment. Captions and identification of subjects required. Buys one-time rights. "May offer to buy photos after first use if considered good and have potential to be used with other articles in the future (file photos)." Pays $100 for ¼ page color to $800 for 2-page spread in color; $1,000 for covers. All photos must be stamped with name and address.

Columns/Departments: This Happened to Me (true-to-life, personal outdoor adventure, harrowing experience), approximately 300 words. Buys 12 mss/year. Pays $50. Only those published will be notified.

Fillers: National and International newsbreaks (200 words maximum). Newsbreaks and do-it-yourself for hunters and fishermen. Buys unlimited number/year. Length: 1,000 words maximum. Payment varies.

 • Ranked as one of the best markets for freelance writers in *Writer's Digest* magazine's annual "Top 100 Markets," January 1993.

Tips: "It is best for freelancers to break in by writing features for one of the regional sections—East, Midwest, South, West. These are where-to-go oriented and run from 800-1,500 words. Writers must send one-page query with photos."

PENNSYLVANIA ANGLER, Pennsylvania Fish and Boat Commission, P.O. Box 67000, Harrisburg PA 17106-7000. (717)657-4518. CompuServe 76247, 624. Editor: Art Michaels. 80% freelance written. Prefers to work with published/established writers but works with a few unpublished writers every year. Monthly magazine covering fishing and related conservation topics in Pennsylvania. Circ. 50,000. Pays 2 months after acceptance. Publishes ms an average of 6 months after acceptance. Byline given. Rights purchased vary. Submit seasonal/holiday material 8 months in advance. Reprints OK; send typed ms with rights for sale noted. Query for electronic submission. Reports in 2 weeks on queries; 2 months on mss. Sample copy for 9×12 SAE with 4 first class stamps. Writer's guidelines for #10 SASE.

Nonfiction: How-to, where-to and technical. No saltwater or hunting material. Buys 120 mss/year. Query. Length: 500-3,000 words. Pays $25-300.

Photos: Send photos with submission. Reviews 35mm and larger transparencies and 8×10 b&w prints. Offers no additional payment for photos accepted with ms. Captions, model releases and identification of subjects required. Also reviews photos separately. Rights purchased and rates vary.

Tips: "Our mainstays are how-tos, where-tos and conservation pieces."

PENNSYLVANIA GAME & FISH, Game & Fish Publications, Inc., Box 741, Marietta GA 30061. (404)953-9222. Editor: Kim Leighton. See *Game & Fish Publications.*

PENNSYLVANIA GAME NEWS, Pennsylvania Game Commission, 2001 Elmerton Ave., Harrisburg PA 17110-9797. (717)787-3745. Editor: Bob Mitchell. 60% freelance written. Works with a small number of new/unpublished writers each year. "We have a large inventory; nevertheless, we read everything that comes in." Monthly magazine covering hunting and outdoors in Pennsylvania, emphasizing hunting and sportsmanship. Estab. 1930. Circ. 150,000. **Pays on acceptance.** Publishes ms an average of 10 months after acceptance. Byline given. Buys all rights; "we return unused rights after publication." Submit seasonal/holiday material 8 months in advance. Reports in 3 weeks on queries; 6 weeks on mss. Free sample copy and writer's guidelines.
Nonfiction: General interest and personal hunting experiences. "We consider material on any outdoor subject that can be done in Pennsylvania *except* fishing and boating." Buys 60 mss/year. Query. Length: 2,500 words maximum. Pays $250 maximum.
Photos: Send photos with submission. Offers $5-20/photo. Captions required. Buys all rights.
Fiction: Must deal with hunting or outdoors; no fishing. Buys very few mss/year. Send complete ms.
Tips: "True hunting experiences — 'me and Joe' stuff — are best chances for freelancers. Must take place in (or at least be applicable) to Pennsylvania."

PETERSEN'S HUNTING, Petersen's Publishing Co., 8490 Sunset Blvd., Los Angeles CA 90069. (310)854-2184. Editor: Craig Boddington. Managing Editor: Denise LaSalle. 40% freelance written. Works with a small number of new/unpublished writers each year. Monthly magazine covering sport hunting. "We are a 'how-to' magazine devoted to all facets of sport hunting, with the intent to make our readers more knowledgeable, more successful and safer hunters." Circ. 325,000. **Pays on acceptance.** Publishes ms an average of 9 months after acceptance. Byline given. Offers $50 kill fee. Buys all rights. Submit seasonal/holiday material 9 months in advance. Reports in 2 weeks. Free sample copy and writer's guidelines.
Nonfiction: General interest, historical/nostalgic, how-to (on hunting techniques), humor and travel. Special issues: Hunting Annual (August) and the Deer Hunting Annual (September). Buys 50 mss/year. Query. Length: 2,000-3,000 words. Pays $350 minimum.
Photos: Send photos with submission. Reviews 35mm transparencies and 8×10 b&w prints. Offers no additional payment for b&w photos accepted with ms; offers $50-250/color photo. Captions, model releases and identification of subjects required. Buys one-time rights.

ROCKY MOUNTAIN GAME & FISH, Game & Fish Publications, Inc., Box 741, Marietta GA 30061. Editor: Burt Carey. See *Game & Fish Publications.*

‡SAFARI MAGAZINE, The Journal of Big Game Hunting, Safari Club International, 4800 W. Gates Pass Rd., Tucson AZ 85745. (602)620-1220. Fax: (602)622-1205. Editor: William R. Quimby. 90% freelance written. Bimonthly club journal covering international big game hunting and wildlife conservation. Circ. 18,000. Pays on publication. Publishes ms an average of 12-18 months after acceptance. Byline given. Offers $100 kill fee. Buys all rights. Submit seasonal/holiday material 1 year in advance. Reports in 2 weeks on queries; up to 6 weeks on mss. Sample copy $4. Writer's guidelines for SAE.
Nonfiction: Doug Fulton; articles editor. Photo feature (wildlife) and technical (firearms, hunting techniques, etc.). Buys 48 mss/year. Query or send complete ms. Length: 1,500-2,500 words. Pays $200.
Photos: State availability of photos with query or ms, or send photos with query or ms. Payment depends on size in magazine. Pays $45 for b&w; $50-150 color. Captions, model releases and identification of subjects required. Buys one-time rights.
Tips: "Study the magazine. Send manuscripts and photo packages with query. Make it appeal to knowledgable, world-travelled big game hunters. Features on conservation contributions from big game hunters around the world are open to freelancers. We have enough stories on first-time African safaris and North American hunting. We need South American and Asian hunting stories, plus stories of hunting and conservation."

SALT WATER SPORTSMAN MAGAZINE, 280 Summer St., Boston MA 02210. (617)439-9977. Fax: (617)439-9357. Editor: Barry Gibson. Emphasizes saltwater fishing. 85% freelance written. Works with a small number of new/unpublished writers each year. Monthly magazine. Circ. 150,000. **Pays on acceptance.** Publishes ms an average of 5 months after acceptance. Byline given. Buys first North American serial rights. Offers 100% kill fee. Submit seasonal material 8 months in advance. Reports in 1 month. Sample copy and writer's guidelines for 9×12 SAE with $2.90 postage.
Nonfiction: How-to, personal experience, technical and travel (to fishing areas). "Readers want solid how-to, where-to information written in an enjoyable, easy-to-read style. Personal anecdotes help the reader identify with the writer." Prefers new slants and specific information. Query. "It is helpful if the writer states experience in salt water fishing and any previous related articles. We want one, possibly two well-explained ideas per query letter — not merely a listing. Good pictures with query often help sell the idea." Buys 100 mss/year. Length: 1,200-1,500 words. Pays $350 and up. Sometimes pays the expenses of writers on assignment. "A good way to break in with us is to submit short (800-1,000 words) where-to/how-to pieces for one of our three regional editions (Atlantic, Southern and Pacific) with a couple of b&w photos. Write Whit Griswold for regional guidelines."

Photos: Purchased with or without accompanying ms. Captions required. Uses 5×7 or 8×10 b&w prints and color slides. Pays $600 minimum for 35mm, 2¼×2¼ or 8×10 transparencies for cover. Offers additional payment for photos accepted with accompanying ms.

Columns/Departments: Sportsman's Workbench (how to make fishing or fishing-related boating equipment), 100 or more words.

Tips: "There are a lot of knowledgable fishermen/budding writers out there who could be valuable to us with a little coaching. Many don't think they can write a story for us, but they'd be surprised. We work with writers. Shorter articles that get to the point which are accompanied by good, sharp photos are hard for us to turn down. Having to delete unnecessary wordage—conversation, clichés, etc.—that writers feel is mandatory is annoying. Often they don't devote enough attention to specific fishing information."

SOUTH CAROLINA GAME & FISH, Game & Fish Publications, Inc., Box 741, Marietta GA 30061. (404)953-9222. Editor: Jeff Samsel. See *Game & Fish Publications.*

SOUTH CAROLINA WILDLIFE, P.O. Box 167, Rembert Dennis Bldg., Columbia SC 29202-0167. (803)734-3972. Editor: John Davis. Managing Editor: Linda Renshaw. Bimonthly magazine for South Carolinians interested in wildlife and outdoor activities. 75% freelance written. Estab. 1954. Circ. 69,000. Byline given. **Pays on acceptance.** Publishes ms an average of 6 months after acceptance. Buys first rights. Free sample copy. Reports in 2 months.

Nonfiction: Articles on outdoor South Carolina with an emphasis on preserving and protecting our natural resources. "Realize that the topic must be of interest to South Carolinians and that we must be able to justify using it in a publication published by the state wildlife department—so if it isn't directly about outdoor recreation, a certain plant or animal, it must be somehow related to the environment and conservation. Readers prefer a broad mix of outdoor related topics (articles that illustrate the beauty of South Carolina's outdoors and those that help the reader get more for his/her time, effort, and money spent in outdoor recreation). These two general areas are the ones we most need. Subjects vary a great deal in topic, area and style, but must all have a common ground in the outdoor resources and heritage of South Carolina. Review back issues and query with a one-page outline citing sources, giving ideas for photographs, explaining justification and giving an example of the first two paragraphs." Does not need any column material. Generally does not seek photographs. The publisher assumes no responsibility for unsolicited material. Buys 25-30 mss/year. Length: 1,000-3,000 words. Pays an average of $200-400/article depending upon length and subject matter.

Tips: "We need more writers in the outdoor field who take pride in the craft of writing and put a real effort toward originality and preciseness in their work. Query on a topic we haven't recently done. The most frequent mistakes made by writers in completing an article are failure to check details and go in-depth on a subject."

SOUTHERN OUTDOORS MAGAZINE, B.A.S.S. Publications, 5845 Carmichael Rd., Montgomery AL 36117. (205)277-3940. Editor: Larry Teague. Magazine published 9 times/year emphasizing Southern outdoor activities, including hunting, fishing, boating, shooting and camping. 90% freelance written. Prefers to work with published/established writers. Estab. 1952. Circ. 257,000. **Pays on acceptance.** Publishes ms an average of 6 months to 1 year after acceptance. Buys all rights. Reports in 1-2 months. Sample copy $2.50 for 9×12 SAE with 5 first class stamps.

Nonfiction: Articles should be service-oriented, helping the reader excel in outdoor sports. Emphasis is on techniques, trends and conservation. Some "where-to" features purchased on Southern hunting and fishing destinations. Buys 120 mss/year. Length: 2,500 words maximum. Sidebars are a selling point. Pays 15-20¢/word.

Photos: Usually purchased with mss. Pays $75 for 35mm transparencies without ms, $400 for covers.

Fillers: Humorous or thought-provoking pieces (1,500 words) appear in each issue's S.O. Essay department.

Tips: "It's easiest to break in with short articles. We buy very little first-person. Stories most likely to sell: outdoor medicine, bass fishing, deer hunting, other freshwater fishing, inshore saltwater fishing, bird and small-game hunting, shooting, camping and boating."

SPORT FISHING, The Magazine of Offshore Fishing, 330 W. Canton Ave., Winter Park FL 32803. (407)628-4802. Fax: (407)628-7061. Editor: Albia Dugger. Managing Editor: Dave Ferrell. 60% freelance written. Magazine covering offshore sport fishing. Estab. 1986. Circ. 85,000. Pays within 6 weeks of acceptance. Byline given. Offers $100 kill fee. Buys first North American serial or one-time rights. Submit seasonal/holiday material 2 months in advance. Simultaneous submission OK. Query for electronic submissions. Reports in 2 months. Free sample copy and writer's guidelines.

Nonfiction: How-to, all humor, new product, personal experience, photo feature, technical and travel; (all on sport fishing). Buys 32-40 mss/year. Query with or without published clips or send complete ms. Length: 1,500-4,500 words. Pays $150-600 for assigned articles.

Photos: Send photos with submission. Reviews transparencies. Offers $50-500/photo. Identification of subjects required. Buys one-time rights.
Columns/Departments: Fish Tales (humorous sport fishing anecdotes), 800-1,500 words; Rigging (how-to rigging for sport fishing), 800-1,500 words; and Technique (how-to technique for sport fishing), 800-1,500 words. Buys 8-24 mss/year. Send complete ms. Pays $200.

SPORTS AFIELD, 250 W. 55th St., New York NY 10019-5201. (212)649-4000. Editor-in-Chief: Tom Paugh. Executive Editor: Fred Kesting. 20% freelance written. Monthly magazine for people of all ages whose interests are centered around the out-of-doors (hunting and fishing) and related subjects. Estab. 1887. Circ. 515,444. Buys first North American serial rights for features. **Pays on acceptance.** Publishes ms an average of 6 months after acceptance. Byline given. "Our magazine is seasonal and material submitted should be in accordance. Fishing in spring and summer; hunting in the fall." Submit seasonal material 9 months in advance. Reports in 2 months. Query or submit complete ms. Writer's guidelines for 1 first class stamp.
Nonfiction: "Informative how-to articles with emphasis on product and service and personal experiences with good photos on hunting, fishing, camping, conservation, and environmental issues (limited where-to-go) related to hunting and fishing. We want first-class writing and reporting." Buys 15-17 unsolicited mss/year. Length: 500-2,500 words. "Pay scale: Self-contained 1-pager $500; a spread $800; three pagers $1,000; two spreads $1,200. Backcountry $800."
Photos: Buys photos with ms. "For photos without ms, duplicates of 35mm color transparencies preferred."
Fiction: Adventure, humor and nostalgia (if related to hunting and fishing).
Fillers: Send to *Almanac* editor. *Almanac* pays $10/column inch, with a minimum $25/item. For outdoor tips specifically for hunters, fishermen and campers, unusual, how-to and nature items. Payment on publication. Buys all rights.
Tips: "We seldom give assignments to other than staff. Top-quality 35mm slides to illustrate articles a must. Read a recent copy of *Sports Afield* so you know the market you're writing for. Ms *must* be available on disk."
  • Ranked as one of the best markets for freelance writers in *Writer's Digest* magazine's annual "Top 100 Markets," January 1993.

TENNESSEE SPORTSMAN, Game & Fish Publications, Box 741, Marietta GA 30061. (404)953-9222. Editor: Bill Hartlage. See *Game & Fish Publications*.

TEXAS SPORTSMAN, Game & Fish Publications, Inc., Box 741, Marietta GA 30061. (404)953-9222. Editor: Nick Gilmore. See *Game & Fish Publications*.

TRAPPER & PREDATOR CALLER, Krause Publications Inc., 700 E. State St., Iola WI 54990. (715)445-2214. Fax: (715)445-4087. Editor: Gordy Krahn. 90% freelance written. Monthly tabloid covers trapping, predator calling and muzzleloading. "Our editorial goal is to entertain and educate our readers with national and regional articles that promote trapping." Estab. 1975. Circ. 35,000. Pays on publication. Offers $50 kill fee. Buys first North American serial rights. Submit seasonal material 6 months in advance. Reports in 2 weeks. *Writer's Market* recommends allowing 2 months for reply. Free sample copy and writer's guidelines.
Nonfiction: How-to, humor, interview/profile, new product, opinion and personal experience. Buys 60 mss/year. Query with or without published clips or send complete ms. Length: 1,200-2,500 words. Pays $80-250 for assigned articles; $40-200 for unsolicited articles.
Photos: Send photos with submission. Reviews prints. Offers no additional payment for photos accepted with ms. Captions and identification of subjects required. Buys one-time rights.
Fillers: Facts, gags to be illustrated by cartoonist, newsbreaks and short humor. Buys 60/year. Length: 200-800 words. Pays $25-80.
Tips: "We are always looking for new ideas and fresh material on trapping, predator calling and black powder hunting."

TURKEY CALL, Wild Turkey Center, P.O. Box 530, Edgefield SC 29824-0530. (803)637-3106. Fax: (803)637-0034. Editor: Gene Smith. 50-60% freelance written. Eager to work with new/unpublished writers and photographers. Bimonthly educational magazine for members of the National Wild Turkey Federation. Estab. 1973. Circ. 65,000. Buys one-time rights. Byline given. **Pays on acceptance.** Publishes ms an average of 6 months after acceptance. Reports in 1 month. No queries necessary. Submit complete package. Wants original mss only. Sample copy $3 for 9 × 12 SAE. Writer's guidelines for #10 SASE.
Nonfiction: Feature articles dealing with the hunting and management of the American wild turkey. Must be accurate information and must appeal to national readership of turkey hunters and wildlife management experts. No poetry or first-person accounts of unremarkable hunting trips. May use some fiction that educates or entertains in a special way. Length: up to 3,000 words. Pays $35 for items, $65 for short fillers of 600-700 words, $200-350 for illustrated features.
Photos: "We want quality photos submitted with features." Art illustrations also acceptable. "We are using more and more inside color illustrations." For b&w, prefer 8 × 10 glossies, but 5 × 7 OK. Transparencies of any size are acceptable. No typical hunter-holding-dead-turkey photos or setups using mounted birds or domestic turkeys. Photos with how-to stories must make the techniques clear (example: how to make a turkey

call; how to sculpt or carve a bird in wood). Pays $20 minimum for one-time rights on b&w photos and simple art illustrations; up to $75 for inside color, reproduced any size. Most covers are donated. Any purchased are negotiated.

Tips: "The writer should simply keep in mind that the audience is 'expert' on wild turkey management, hunting, life history and restoration/conservation history. He/she *must know the subject*. We are buying more third-person, more fiction, more humor—in an attempt to avoid the 'predictability trap' of a single subject magazine."

VIRGINIA GAME & FISH, Game & Fish Publications, Inc., Box 741, Marietta GA 30061. (404)953-9222. Editor: Jeff Samsel. See *Game & Fish Publications.*

WASHINGTON-OREGON GAME & FISH, Game & Fish Publications, Inc., Box 741, Marietta GA 30061. Editor: Burt Carey. See *Game & Fish Publications.*

WEST VIRGINIA GAME & FISH, Game & Fish Publications, Inc., Box 741, Marietta GA 30061. (404)953-9222. Editor: Ken Freel. See *Game & Fish Publications.*

WESTERN SPORTSMAN, P.O. Box 737, Regina, Saskatchewan S4P 3A8 Canada. (306)352-2773. Fax: (306)565-2440. Editor: Roger Francis. 90% freelance written. Bimonthly magazine for fishermen, hunters, campers and others interested in outdoor recreation. "Note that our coverage area is Alberta, Saskatchewan and Manitoba." Estab. 1968. Circ. 29,000. Rights purchased vary with author and material. Usually buys first North American serial or second serial (reprint) rights. Publishes reprints of previously published articles. Send tearsheet of article or typed ms with rights for sale noted. Include information about when and where the article previously appeared. For reprints, pays 100% of the amount paid for an original article. Byline given. Pays on publication. Publishes ms an average of 6 months after acceptance. "We try to include as much information as possible on all subjects in each edition. Therefore, we often publish fishing articles in our winter issues along with a variety of winter stories. If material is dated, we would like to receive articles 4 months in advance of our publication date." Reports in 1 month. Sample copy $4 for 9×12 SAE with 4 IRCs (US). Free writer's guidelines with SASE.

Nonfiction: "It is necessary that all articles can identify with our coverage area. We are interested in mss from writers who have experienced an interesting fishing or hunting experience. We also publish other informational pieces as long as they relate to our coverage area. We are more interested in articles which tell about the average guy living on beans, guiding his own boat, stalking his game and generally doing his own thing in our part of Western Canada than a story describing a well-to-do outdoorsman traveling by motorhome, staying at an expensive lodge with guides doing everything for him except catching the fish or shooting the big game animal. The articles that are submitted to us need to be prepared in a knowledgable way and include more information than the actual fish catch or animal or bird kill. Discuss the terrain, the people involved on the trip, the water or weather conditions, the costs, the planning that went into the trip, the equipment and other data closely associated with the particular event. We're always looking for new writers." Buys 60 mss/year. Submit complete ms and SASE or IRCs. Length: 1,500-2,000 words. Pays up to $400. Sometimes pays the expenses of writers on assignment.

Photos: Photos purchased with ms with no additional payment. Also purchased without ms. Pays $30-50 for 5×7 or 8×10 b&w print; $175-250 for 35mm or larger transparency for front cover.

WISCONSIN SPORTSMAN, Game & Fish Publications, Inc., Box 741, Marietta GA 30061. Editor: Dennis Schmidt. See *Game & Fish Publications.*

Martial Arts

BLACK BELT, Rainbow Publications, Inc., 24715 Ave. Rockefeller, Valencia CA 91355. (805)257-4066. Fax: (805)257-3028. Executive Editor: Jim Coleman. 80-90% freelance written. Works with a small number of new/unpublished writers each year. Monthly magazine emphasizing martial arts for both practioner and layman. Estab. 1961. Circ. 100,000. Pays on publication. Publishes ms an average of 5 months after acceptance. Buys first North American serial rights, retains right to republish. Submit seasonal/holiday material 6 months in advance. Reports in 3 weeks.

Nonfiction: Expose, how-to, informational, interview, new product, personal experience, profile, technical and travel. Buys 8-9 mss/issue. Query or send complete ms. Length: 1,200 words minimum. Pays $100-300.

Photos: Very seldom buys photos without accompanying mss. Captions required. Total purchase price for ms includes payment for photos. Model releases required.

Fiction: Historical and modern day. Buys 1-2 mss/year. Query. Pays $100-150.

Tips: "We also publish an annual yearbook and special issues periodically. The yearbook includes our annual 'Black Belt Hall of Fame' inductees."

FIGHTING WOMAN NEWS, Martial Arts, Self-Defense, Combative Sports Quarterly, 6741 Tung Ave. W., Theodore AL 36582. Editor: Debra Pettis. Mostly freelance written. Prefers to work with published/established writers. Quarterly magazine for "adult women actually practicing martial arts with an average experience of 4+ years. Since our audience is also 80+ % college grads and 40% holders of advanced degrees we are an action magazine with footnotes. Our material is quite different from what is found in newsstand martial arts publications." Estab. 1975. Circ. 3,500. Pays on publication. "There is a backlog of poetry and fiction—hence a *very* long wait. A solid factual martial arts article would go out 'next issue' with trumpets and pipes." Byline given. Buys one-time rights. Submit seasonal/holiday material 6 months in advance. Simultaneous queries, simultaneous and previously published submissions OK; pays in copies for reprints. "For simultaneous and previously published we *must* be told about it." Query for electronic submissions. Reports "as soon as possible." Sample copy $3.50. Writer's guidelines for #10 SASE.

Nonfiction: Book excerpts, expose (e.g. discrimination against women in martial arts governing bodies); historical/nostalgic; how-to (martial arts, self-defense techniques); humor; inspirational (e.g., self-defense success stories); interview/profile ("we have assignments waiting for writers in this field"); new product; opinion; personal experience; photo feature; technical; and travel. Buys 6 mss/year. Query. Length: 1,000-3,000 words. Pays in copies, barter or $30 maximum. Some expenses negotiated, but not major costs such as planes or hotels.

Photos: State availability of photos with query or ms. Reviews "technically competent" b&w contact sheets and 8 × 10 b&w prints. "We negotiate photos and articles as a package. Sometimes expenses are negotiated. Captions and identification of subjects required. The need for releases depends on the situation."

Columns/Departments: News & Notes (short items relevant to our subject matter); Letters (substantive comment regarding previous issues); Sports Reports; and Reviews (of relevant materials in any medium). Query or send complete ms. Length: 100-1,000 words. Pays in copies or negotiates payment.

Fiction: Adventure, fantasy, historical and science fiction. "Any fiction must feature a woman skilled in martial arts." Buys 1 ms/year. Query. Length: 1,000-5,000 words. "We will consider serializing longer stories." Does not usually publish novel excerpts. Pays in copies or negotiates payment.

Poetry: "We'll look at all types. Must appeal to an audience of martial artists." Buys 3-4 poems/year. Length: open. Pays in copies or negotiates payment.

Tips: "First, read the magazine. Our major reason for rejecting articles is total unsuitability for our publication. The second most common reason for rejections is vagueness; we need the old Who, What, When, Where, Why and How and if your article doesn't have that save yourself the postage. Several articles returned by *FWN* have later shown up in other martial arts magazines and since they pay a lot more, you're better off trying them first unless an audience of literate, adult, female martial artists is what you're aiming at."

INSIDE KARATE, The Magazine for Today's Total Martial Artist, Unique Publications, 4201 Vanowen Pl., Burbank CA 91505. (818)845-2656. Fax: (818)845-7761. Editor: John Steven Soet. 90% freelance written. Works with a number of new/unpublished writers each year. Monthly magazine covering the martial arts. Circ. 120,000. Publishes ms an average of 3 months after acceptance. Byline given. Buys first North American serial rights. Reports in 3 weeks on queries; 6 weeks on mss. Sample copy $2.50 for 9 × 12 SAE with 5 first class stamps. Writer's guidelines for #10 SASE.

Nonfiction: Book excerpts, expose (of martial arts), historical/nostalgic, humor, interview/profile (with approval only), opinion, personal experience, photo feature and technical (with approval only). "*Inside Karate* seeks a balance of the following in each issue: tradition, history, glamour, profiles and/or interviews (both by assignment only), technical, philosophical and think pieces. Not interested in 'tough guys,' self-serving pieces, or movie-star wannabes." Buys 70 mss/year. Query. Length: 1,000-2,500 words; prefers 10-12 page mss. Pays $25-125.

Photos: Send photos with ms. Prefers 3 × 5 bordered b&w. Captions and identification of subjects required. Buys one-time rights.

Tips: "In our publication, writing style and/or expertise is not the determining factor. Beginning writers with martial arts expertise may submit. Trends in magazine publishing that freelance writers should be aware of include the use of less body copy, better (and interesting) photos to be run large with 'story' caps. If the photos are poor and the reader can't grasp the whole story by looking at photos and copy, forget it."

INSIDE KUNG-FU, The Ultimate In Martial Arts Coverage!, Unique Publications, 4201 Vanowen Pl., Burbank CA 91505. (818)845-2656. Fax: (818)845-7761. Editor: Dave Cater. 75% freelance written. Monthly magazine covering martial arts for those with "traditional, modern, athletic and intellectual tastes. The magazine slants toward little-known martial arts, and little-known aspects of established martial arts." Estab. 1973. Circ. 100,000. Pays on publication. Publishes ms an average of 6 months after acceptance. Byline given. Buys first North American serial rights. Submit seasonal/holiday material 4 months in advance. Simultaneous queries and submissions OK. Reprints OK, but does not pay for them. Send tearsheet of article or short story or typed ms with rights for sale noted and information about when and where the article previously appeared. Reports in 3 weeks on queries; 6 weeks on mss. Sample copy $2.95 for 9 × 12 SAE with 5 first class stamps. Writer's guidelines for #10 SASE.

Nonfiction: Expose (topics relating to the martial arts), historical/nostalgic, how-to (primarily technical materials), cultural/philosophical, interview/profile, personal experience, photo feature and technical. "Articles must be technically or historically accurate." No "sports coverage, first-person articles or articles which constitute personal aggrandizement." Buys 120 mss/year. Query or send complete ms. Length: 8-10 pages, typewritten and double-spaced.
Photos: Send photos with accompanying ms. Reviews b&w contact sheets, b&w negatives and 8 × 10 b&w prints. Offers no additional payment for photos. Captions and model release required.
Fiction: Adventure, historical, humorous, mystery and suspense. "Fiction must be short (1,000-2,000 words) and relate to the martial arts. We buy very few fiction pieces." Buys 2-3 mss/year.
Tips: "The writer may have a better chance of breaking in at our publication with short articles and fillers since smaller pieces allow us to gauge individual ability, but we're flexible – quality writers get published, period. The most frequent mistakes made by writers in completing an article for us are ignoring photo requirements and model releases (always number one – and who knows why? All requirements are spelled out in writer's guidelines)."

JOURNAL OF ASIAN MARTIAL ARTS, Via Media Publishing Co., 821 W. 24th St., Erie PA 16502-2523. (814)455-9517. Editor: Michael A. DeMarco. 90% freelance written. Quarterly magazine covering "all historical and cultural aspects related to Asian martial arts, offering a mature, well-rounded view of this uniquely fascinating subject. Although the journal treats the subject with academic accuracy (references at end), writing need not lose the reader!" Estab. 1991. Pays on publication. Publishes ms an average of 1 year after acceptance. Byline given. Buys first rights and second serial (reprint) rights. Submit seasonal/holiday material 6 months in advance. Query for electronic submissions. Reports in 1 month on queries; 2 months on mss. Sample copy for $10. Writer's guidelines for #10 SASE.
Nonfiction: Essays, expose, historical/nostalgic, how-to (martial art techniques and materials, e.g., weapons, symbols), interview/profile, personal experience, photo feature (place or person), religious, technical and travel. "All articles should be backed with solid, reliable reference material. No articles overburdened with technical/foreign/scholarly vocabulary, or material slanted as indirect advertising or for personal aggrandizement." Buys 30 mss/year. Query. Length: 2,000-10,000 words. Pays $150-500 for unsolicited articles.
Photos: State availability of photos with submission. Reviews contact sheets, negatives, transparencies and prints. Offers no additional payment for photos accepted with ms. Model releases and identification of subjects required. Buys one-time and reprint rights.
Columns/Departments: Location (city, area, specific site, Asian or Non-Asian, showing value for martial arts, researchers, history); and Media Review (film, book, stamps, music for aspects of academic and artistic interest). Buys 16 mss/year. Query. Length: 1,000-2,500 words. Pays $50-200.
Fiction: Adventure, historical, humorous, slice-of-life vignettes and translation. "We are not interested in material that does not focus on martial arts culture." Buys 2 mss/year. Query. Length: 2,000-10,000 words. Pays $100-500.
Poetry: Avant-garde, free verse, Haiku, light verse, traditional and translation. "No poetry that does not focus on martial art culture." Buys 4 poems/year. Submit maximum 10 poems. Pays $10-100.
Fillers: Anecdotes, facts, gags to be illustrated by cartoonist, newsbreaks, short humor. Buys 10/year. Length: 25-500 words. Pays $1-50.
Tips: "Always query before sending a ms. We are open to varied types of articles; most however require a strong academic grasp of Asian culture. For those not having this background, we suggest trying a museum review, or interview, where authorities can be questioned, quoted and provide supportive illustrations. We especially desire articles/reports from Asia, with photo illustrations, particularly of a martial art style, so readers can visually understand the unique attributes of that style, its applications, evolution, etc. 'Location' and media reports are special areas that writers may consider, especially if they live in a location of martial art significance."

‡KARATE/KUNG FU ILLUSTRATED, State of the Martial Arts, Rainbow Publications, P.O. Box 918, Santa Clarita CA 91380. (805)257-4066. Editor: David W. Clary. 80% freelance written. Bimonthly magazine for training and insights in the martial arts. "*KKI* specializes in open-hand, how-to articles for martial artists wanting to expand their repertoire. We publish style-specific technique pieces, as well as interviews and fiction. Everything must have a strong martial arts slant, however, and pertain to martial artists and their interests." Estab. 1969. Circ. 60,000. Pays on publication. Publishes ms an average of 3-4 months after acceptance. Byline given. Buys all rights, other rights (will negotiate) and makes work-for-hire assignments. Editorial lead time 3-4 months. Simultaneous submissions OK. Query for electronic submissions. Reports in 2-3 weeks on queries; 1 month on mss. *Writer's Market* recommends allowing 2 months for reply. Sample copy for $2.25. Writer's guidelines free on request.
Nonfiction: Expose, general interest, historical/nostalgic, how-to do specific martial arts techniques, humor, interview/profile, new product, photo feature, religious and technical. "We do not want to see articles on 3-year-old black belts, or 'masters' who can break a Buick in half while blindfolded. Query with any personality profiles or interview." Buys 45 mss/year. Query. Length: 1,000-5,000 words. Pays $100 minimum. "We sometimes offer a writer free ad space in lieu of payment, at his/her request." Sometimes pays expenses of writers on assignment.

Photos: State availability of photos with submission. Reviews 5×7 prints. Offers no additional payment for photos accepted with ms. Model releases and identification of subjects required. Buys one-time rights and reprint rights.

Columns/Departments: Faces (personality profiles, human interest stories), 200-500 words; Sport Karate News (tournament reports, breaking stories on professional fighters), 250-1,000 words. Buys 15 mss/year. Send complete ms. Pays $25-50.

Fiction: Adventure, historical, humorous and mainstream. "No erotica. No serializations." Buys 1-2 mss/year. Query. Length: 1,000-3,000 words. Pays $100-150.

Poetry: Free verse, haiku, light verse and traditional. Buys 1-2 poems/year. Submit maximum 3 poems. Length: 25 lines maximum. Pays $25.

Tips: "*KKI*'s strength is in its technique articles. Our best writers pick one element of a particular martial art, and then expound on it: The Punches of Shotokan Karate, for example. Find what makes an art unique, and explain it with words and pictures. We will consider *any* topic or article idea, as long as it is of interest to serious, long-time martial arts enthusiasts. Too many times writers submit articles that are of interest to beginning martial artists, but are not something more experienced practitioners would look for. The best way to break into the magazine is with a how-to article on martial arts techniques. Good writing, free of errors and knowledge of the subject matter, combined with GOOD black and white photos will almost always get our attention."

M.A. TRAINING, Rainbow Publications, P.O. Box 918, Santa Clarita CA 91380-9018. (805)257-4066. Fax: (805)257-3028. Contact: Marian K. Castinado. 75% freelance written. Works with many new/unpublished writers each year. Bimonthly magazine about martial arts training. Estab. 1961. Circ. 60,000. Pays on publication. Publishes ms an average of 6 months after acceptance. Buys all rights. Submit seasonal material 4 months in advance, but best to send query letter first. Reports in 2 months. Writer's guidelines for #10 SASE.

Nonfiction: How-to (training related features). Buys 30-40 unsolicited mss/year. Send query or complete ms. Length: 1,500-2,500 words. Pays $100.

Photos: State availability of photos. Most ms should be accompanied by photos. Reviews 5×7 and 8×10 b&w glossy prints. Can reproduce prints from negatives. Offers no additional payment for photos accepted with ms. Model releases required. Buys all rights. Photos not purchased without accompanying mss.

Tips: "I'm looking for how-to, nuts-and-bolts training stories which are martial arts related. Our magazine covers fitness and conditioning, not the martial arts techniques themselves."

Miscellaneous

NEW YORK OUTDOORS, 51 Atlantic Ave., Floral Park NY 11001. Fax: (516)437-6841. Editor: Gary P. Joyce. Associate Editor: Karen L. Silver. 100% freelance written. Estab. 1992. Published 10 times/year. Pays on publication. Buys first North American serial rights. Publishes ms an average of 6 months after acceptance. Reports in 2 weeks on queries. Writer's guidelines for #10 SASE.

Nonfiction: "*New York Outdoors* is dedicated to providing information to its readers about all outdoor participatory activities in New York and its surrounding states. Fishing, shooting, sports, paddlesports, camping, hiking, cycling, 'adventure' sports, etc." Length: 1,500-2,000 words. A good selection of transparencies must accompany submissions. Pays $250. Lead time 4 months. "Aside from accurate and interesting writing, provide source material for our readers who may wish to try the activity. We also have use for shorter pieces (to 500 words) on the same type of topics, but focusing on a single event, person, place or occurrence. These pay $50."

Tips: Would like to see more queries on "non-fishing/shooting sport" topic areas.

POLO, Polo Publications, Inc., 656 Quince Orchard Rd., Gaithersburg MD 20878-1472. (301)977-0200. Fax: (301)990-9015. Editor: Martha LeGrand. Contact Shelby Sadler, senior editor. Magazine published 10 times/year on polo—the sport and lifestyle. "Our readers are an affluent group. Most are well-educated, well-read and highly sophisticated." Circ. 6,500. **Pays on acceptance.** Publishes ms an average 4 months after acceptance. Kill fee varies. Buys first North American serial rights and makes work-for-hire assignments. Submit seasonal/holiday material 3 months in advance. Simultaneous submissions OK. Publishes reprints of previously published articles. Send tearsheet of article, including information about when and where the article previously appeared. For reprints, pays 50% of the amount paid for an original article. Reports in 3 months. Writer's guidelines for #10 SAE with 2 first class stamps.

Nonfiction: Shelby Sadler, senior editor. Historical/nostalgic, interview/profile, personal experience, photo feature, technical and travel. Buys 20 mss/year. Query with published clips or send complete ms. Length: 800-3,000 words. Pays $150-400 for assigned articles; $100-300 for unsolicited articles. Sometimes pays expenses of writers on assignment.

Photos: State availability of photos or send photos with submission. Reviews contact sheets, transparencies and prints. Offers $20-150/photo. Captions required. Buys one-time rights.

Columns/Departments: Yesteryears (historical pieces), 500 words; Profiles (clubs and players), 800-1,000 words. Buys 15 mss/year. Query with published clips. Pays $100-300.

Tips: "Query us on a personality or club profile or historic piece or, if you know the game, state availability to cover a tournament. Keep in mind that ours is a sophisticated, well-educated audience."

PRIME TIME SPORTS & FITNESS, GND Prime Time Publishing, P.O. Box 6097, Evanston IL 60204. (312)869-6434. Fax: (708)864-1206. Editor: Dennis A. Dorner. Managing Editor: Steven Ury. 80% freelance written. Eager to work with new/unpublished writers. Monthly magazine covering seasonal pro sports and racquet and health club sports and fitness. Estab. 1974. Circ. 35,000. Pays on publication. Publishes an average of 6 months after acceptance. Byline given. Buys all rights; will assign back to author in 85% of cases. Submit seasonal/holiday material 6 months in advance. Simultaneous and previously published submissions OK; send photocopy of article or short story, typed ms with rights for sale noted and information about when and where the article previously appeared. Pays 30-100% of their fee for an original article. Reports in 2-6 months. Sample copy for 10 × 12 SAE with 7 first class stamps.

Nonfiction: Book excerpts (fitness and health); expose (in tennis, fitness, racquetball, health clubs, diets); adult (slightly risqué and racy fitness); how-to (expert instructional pieces on any area of coverage); humor (large market for funny pieces on health clubs and fitness); inspirational (on how diet and exercise combine to bring you a better body, self); interview/profile; new product; opinion (only from recognized sources who know what they are talking about); personal experience (definitely—humor); photo feature (on related subjects); technical (on exercise and sport); travel (related to fitness, tennis camps, etc.); news reports (on racquetball, handball, tennis, running events). Special issues: Swimsuit and Resort Issue (March); Baseball Preview (April); Summer Fashion (July); Pro Football Preview (August); Fall Fashion (October); Ski Issue (November); Christmas Gifts and related articles (December). "We love short articles that get to the point. Nationally oriented big events and national championships. No articles on local-only tennis and racquetball tournaments without national appeal." Buys 150 mss/year. Length: 2,000 words maximum. Pays $20-150. Sometimes pays the expenses of writers on assignment.

Photos: Randy Lester, photo editor. Specifically looking for fashion photo features. Send photos with ms. Pays $5-75 for b&w prints. Captions, model releases and identification of subjects required. Buys all rights, "but returns 75% of photos to submitter."

Departments: Nancy Thomas, column/department editor. New Products; Fitness; Handball; Racquetball; and Tennis Newsletters; News & Capsule Summaries; Fashion Spot (photos of new fitness and bathing suits and ski equipment); and related subjects. Buys 100 mss/year. Send complete ms. Length: 50-250 words ("more if author has good handle to cover complete columns"). Pays $5-25.

Fiction: Judy Johnson, fiction editor. Erotica (if related to fitness club); fantasy (related to subjects); humorous (definite market); religious ("no God-is-my shepherd, but Body-is-God's-temple OK"); and romance (related subjects). "Upbeat stories are needed." Buys 20 mss/year. Send complete ms. Length: 500-2,500 words maximum. Pays $20-150.

Poetry: Free, Haiku, light verse and traditional on related subjects. Length: up to 150 words. Pays $10-25.

Tips: "Send us articles dealing with court club sports, exercise and nutrition that exemplify an upbeat 'you can do it' attitude. Pro sports previews 3-4 months ahead of their seasons are also needed. Good short fiction or humorous articles can break in. Expert knowledge of any related subject can bring assignments; any area is open. We consider everything as a potential article, but are turned off by credits, past work and degrees. We have a constant demand for well-written articles on instruction, health and trends in both. Other articles needed are professional sports training techniques, fad diets, tennis and fitness resorts, photo features with aerobic routines. A frequent mistake made by writers is length—articles are too long. When we assign an article, we want it newsy if it's news and opinion if opinion."

REFEREE, Referee Enterprises, Inc., P.O. Box 161, Franksville WI 53126-9987. (414)632-8855. Fax: (414)632-5460. Editor: Tom Hammill. 20-25% freelance written. Works with a small number of new/unpublished writers each year. Monthly magazine for well-educated, mostly 26- to 50-year-old male sports officials. Estab. 1976. Circ. 35,000. Pays on acceptance of completed ms. Publishes ms an average of 6 months after acceptance. Rights purchased varies. Submit seasonal/holiday material 6 months in advance. Previously published submissions OK; send photocopy of article and information about when and where it previously appeared. Pays 50% of their fee for an original article. Reports in 2 weeks. Sample copy for 10 × 13 SAE with 7 first class stamps. Writer's guidelines for #10 SASE.

Nonfiction: How-to, informational, humor, interview, profile, personal experience, photo feature and technical. Buys 54 mss/year. Query. Length: 700-3,000 words. Pays 4-10¢/word. "No general sports articles."

Photos: Purchased with or without accompanying ms or on assignment. Captions preferred. Send contact sheet, prints, negatives or transparencies. Pays $20 for each b&w used; $35 for each color used; $100 for color cover.

Columns/Departments: Law (legal aspects); Take Care (fitness, medical); Between the Lines (anecdotes); and Heads Up (psychology). Buys 24 mss/year. Query. Length: 200-800 words. Pays 4¢/word up to $100 maximum for regular columns.

Fillers: Jokes, gags, anecdotes, puzzles and referee shorts. Query. Length: 50-200 words. Pays 4¢/word in some cases; others offer only author credit lines.

Tips: "Queries with a specific idea appeal most to readers. Generally, we are looking more for feature writers, as we usually do our own shorter/filler-type material. It is helpful to obtain suitable photos to augment a story. Don't send fluff—we need hard-hitting, incisive material tailored just for our audience. Anything smacking of public relations is a no sale. Don't gloss over the material too lightly or fail to go in-depth looking for a quick sale (taking the avenue of least resistance)."

SIGNPOST FOR NORTHWEST TRAILS MAGAZINE, Suite 512, 1305 4th Ave., Seattle WA 98101-2401. Publisher: Washington Trails Association. Editor: Dan A. Nelson. 10% freelance written. "We will consider working with both previously published and unpublished freelancers." Monthly magazine about hiking, backpacking and similar trail-related activities, strictly from a Pacific Northwest viewpoint. Estab. 1966. Will consider any rights offered by author. Publishes ms an average of 6 months after acceptance. Reports in 2 months. Publishes reprints of previously published articles. Include information about when and where the article previously appeared. Query or submit complete ms. Writer's guidelines for #10 SASE.

Nonfiction and Photos: "Most material is donated by subscribers or is staff-written. Payment for purchased material is low, but a good way to break in to print and share your outdoor experiences."

Tips: "We cover only *self-propelled* backcountry sports and won't consider manuscripts about trail bikes, snowmobiles or power boats. We *are* interested in articles about modified and customized equipment, food and nutrition, and personal experiences in the Pacific NW backcountry."

SILENT SPORTS, Waupaca Publishing Co., P.O. Box 152, Waupaca WI 54981-9990. (715)258-5546. Fax: (715)258-8162. Editor: Greg Marr. 75% freelance written. Eager to work with new/unpublished writers. Monthly magazine on running, cycling, cross-country skiing, canoeing, camping, backpacking and hiking aimed at people in Wisconsin, Minnesota, northern Illinois and portions of Michigan and Iowa. "Not a coffee table magazine. Our readers are participants from rank amateur weekend athletes to highly competitive racers." Estab. 1984. Circ. 10,000. Pays on publication. Publishes ms an average of 3 months after acceptance. Byline given. Offers 20% kill fee. Buys one-time rights. Submit seasonal/holiday material 3 months in advance. Simultaneous queries and previously published submissions OK; send photocopy of article and/or typed ms with rights for sale noted plus information about when and where the article previously appeared. Reports in 2 months. Sample copy and writer's guidelines for 10×13 SAE with 6 first class stamps.

Nonfiction: General interest, how-to, interview/profile, opinion, technical and travel. First-person articles discouraged. Buys 25 mss/year. Query. Length: 2,500 words maximum. Pays $15-100. Sometimes pays expenses of writers on assignment.

Tips: "Where-to-go, how-to and personality profiles are areas most open to freelancers. Writers should keep in mind that this is a regional, Midwest-based publication."

SKYDIVING, 1725 N. Lexington Ave., DeLand FL 32724. (904)736-4793. Fax: (904)736-9786. Editor: Michael Truffer. 25% freelance written. Works with a small number of new/unpublished writers each year. Monthly tabloid featuring skydiving for sport parachutists, worldwide dealers and equipment manufacturers. Circ. 9,450. Average issue includes 3 feature articles and 3 columns of technical information. Pays on publication. Publishes ms an average of 3 months after acceptance. Byline given. Buys one-time rights. Simultaneous and previously published submissions OK, if so indicated. Query for electronic submissions. Reports in 1 month. *Writer's Market* recommends allowing 2 months for reply. Sample copy $2. Writer's guidelines for 9×12 SAE with 4 first class stamps.

Nonfiction: "Send us news and information on equipment, techniques, events and outstanding personalities who skydive. We want articles written by people who have a solid knowledge of parachuting." No personal experience or human-interest articles. Query. Length: 500-1,000 words. Pays $25-100. Sometimes pays the expenses of writers on assignment.

Photos: State availability of photos. Reviews 5×7 and larger b&w glossy prints. Offers no additional payment for photos accepted with ms. Captions required.

Fillers: Newsbreaks. Length: 100-200 words. Pays $25 minimum.

Tips: "The most frequent mistake made by writers in completing articles for us is that the writer isn't knowledgable about the sport of parachuting."

VOLLEYBALL MONTHLY, Straight Down Inc., Suite F, 1880 Santa Barbara, San Luis Obispo CA 93401. (805)541-2294. Fax: (805)541-2438. Editor: Jon Hastings. 25% freelance written. Monthly magazine covering volleyball. "National publication geared to players, coaches and fans of the sport of volleyball." Circ. 79,000. Pays on publication. Publishes ms an average of 2 months after acceptance. Byline given. Buys first rights. Submit seasonal material 4 months in advance. Reports in 2 weeks on queries. Sample copy and writer's guidelines for 9×12 SAE with $2.

Nonfiction: How-to, humor, interview/profile, personal experience, photo feature and travel. No "USC beat UCLA last week" articles. Buys 22 mss/year. Send complete ms. Length: 750-3,000 words. Pays $75-250 for assigned articles; $50-200 for unsolicited articles. Sometimes pays the expenses of writers on assignment.

Photos: State availability of or send photos with submission. Reviews transparencies and 8×10 prints. Offers $25-100/photo. Identification of subjects required. Buys one-time rights.

Columns/Departments: Buys 6 mss/year. Send complete ms. Length: 750-2,000 words. Pays $50-250.

Fiction: Buys 1-5 mss/year. Send complete ms. Pays $50-250.

Olympic Sports

INTERNATIONAL GYMNAST, Paul Ziert & Assoc., 225 Brooks St., Box 2450, Oceanside CA 92051-2450. (619)722-0030. Fax: (619)722-6208. Editor: Dwight Normile. 50% freelance written. Monthly magazine on gymnastics. "*IG* is dedicated to serving the gymnastics community with competition reports, personality profiles, training and coaching tips and innovations in the sport." Circ. 25,000. Pays on publication. Publishes ms an average of 3 months after acceptance. Byline given. Buys one-time rights. Submit seasonal/holiday material 3 months in advance. Sample copy $4.25. Writer's guidelines for #10 SASE.

Nonfiction: How-to (coaching/training/ business, i.e., running a club), interview/profile, opinion, photo feature (meets or training sites of interest, etc.), competition reports and technical. "Nothing unsuitable for young readers." Buys 25 mss/year. Send complete ms. Length: 500-2,250 words. Pays $15-25. Pays in contributor copies or other premiums when currency exchange is not feasible i.e., foreign residents.

Photos: Send photos with submission. Reviews transparencies and prints. Offers $5-40/photo published. Identification of subjects required. Buys one-time rights.

Columns/Departments: Innovations (new moves, new approaches, coaching tips); Nutrition (hints for the competitive gymnast); Dance (ways to improve gymnasts through dance, all types); Club Corner (business hints for club owners/new programs, etc.); and Book Reviews (reviews of new books pertaining to gymnastics). Buys 10 mss/year. Send complete ms. Length: 750-1,000. Pays $15-25.

Fiction: Humorous, anything pertaining to gymnastics, nothing inappropriate for young readers. Buys 1-2 ms/year. Send complete ms. Length: 1,500 words maximum. Pays $15-25.

Tips: "To *IG* readers, a lack of knowledge sticks out like a sore thumb. Writers are generally coaches, ex-gymnasts and 'hardcore' enthusiasts. Most open area would generally be competition reports. Be concise, but details are necessary when covering gymnastics. Again, thorough knowledge of the sport is indispensable."

INTERNATIONAL OLYMPIC LIFTER, IOL Publications, 3602 Eagle Rock, P.O. Box 65855, Los Angeles CA 90065. (213)257-8762. Editor: Bob Hise. 20% freelance written. Bimonthly magazine covering the Olympic sport of weightlifting. Estab. 1973. Circ. 10,000. Pays on publication. Publishes ms an average of 3 months after acceptance. Byline given. Offers $25 kill fee. Buys one-time rights or negotiable rights. Submit seasonal/holiday material 5 months in advance. Reports in 2 months. Sample copy $4. Writer's guidelines for 9×12 SAE with 5 first class stamps.

Nonfiction: Training articles, contest reports, diet—all related to Olympic weight lifting. Buys 4 mss/year. Query. Length: 250-2,000 words. Pays $25-100.

Photos: Action (competition and training). State availability of photos. Pays $1-5 for 5×7 b&w prints. Identification of subjects required.

Poetry: Dale Rhoades, poetry editor. Light verse, traditional—related to Olympic lifting. Buys 6-10 poems/year. Submit maximum 3 poems. Length: 12-24 lines. Pays $10-20.

Tips: "A writer must be acquainted with Olympic-style weight lifting. Since we are an international publication we do not tolerate ethnic, cultural, religious or political inclusions. Articles relating to AWA are readily accepted."

‡OLYMPIAN MAGAZINE, U.S. Olympic Committee, 1750 E. Boulder St., Colorado Springs CO 80909. (719)578-4529. Managing Editor: Frank Zang. 50% freelance written. Monthly magazine covering olympic sports and athletes. Estab. 1974. Circ. 50,000. Pays on publication. Byline given. Offers 100% kill fee. Query for electronic submissions. Free writer's guidelines.

Nonfiction: Photo feature, feature/profiles of athletes in Olympic sports. Query. Length: 1,200-2,000 words. Pays $300 for assigned articles. Sometimes pays expenses of writers on assignment.

Photos: State availability of photos with submission. Reviews transparencies and prints. Offers $50-250/photo. Captions, model releases and identification of subjects required. Buys one-time rights.

USA GYMNASTICS, United States Gymnastics Federation, Suite 300, 201 S. Capitol Ave., Pan American Plaza, Indianapolis IN 46225. (317)237-5050. Fax: (317)237-5069. Editor: Luan Peszek. 20% freelance written. Bimonthly magazine covering gymnastics—national and international competitions. Designed to educate readers on fitness, health, safety, technique, current topics, trends and personalities related to the gymnastics/fitness field. Readers are between the ages of 7 and 18, parents and coaches. Estab. 1981. Circ. 63,000. Pays on publication. Publishes ms an average of 3-4 months after acceptance. Byline given. Buys all rights. Submit seasonal/holiday material 4 months in advance. Simultaneous submissions OK. Publishes reprints of previously published articles. Reports in 2 months. Sample copy $5.

Nonfiction: General interest, how-to (related to fitness, health, gymnastics), inspirational, interview/profile, new product, opinion (Open Floor section) and photo feature. Buys 5 mss/year. Query. Length: 2,000 words maximum. Payment negotiated.

Photos: Send photos with submission. Offers no additional payment for photos accepted with ms. Identification of subjects required. Buys all rights.

Columns/Departments: Open Floor (opinions—regarding gymnastics/nutrition related topic), up to 1,000 words. Buys 2 mss/year. Query or send complete ms. No payment (articles donated—nonprofit organization).

Tips: "Any articles of interest to gymnasts (men, women and rhythmic gymnastics) coaches, judges and parents, are what we're looking for. This includes nutrition, toning, health, safety, current trends, gymnastics techniques, timing techniques etc. The sections most open to freelancers are Open Floor—opinions on topics related to gymnasts, and features on one of the above mentioned items."

Running

INSIDE TEXAS RUNNING, 9514 Bristlebrook Dr., Houston TX 77083. (713)498-3208. **Fax:** (713)879-9980. Editor: Joanne Schmidt. 50% freelance written. Monthly tabloid covering running, cycling and triathloning. "Our audience is made up of Texas runners and triathletes who may also be interested in cross training with biking and swimming." Estab. 1977. Circ. 10,000. **Pays on acceptance.** Publishes ms an average of 1-2 months after acceptance. Byline given. Buys first, one-time, second serial (reprint), exclusive Texas and all rights. Submit seasonal/holiday material 2 months in advance. Previously published submissions OK. Reprints OK; send photocopy of article. Pays 50% of their fee for an original article. Reports in 1 month on queries; 6 weeks on mss. Sample copy $1.50. Writer's guidelines for #10 SASE.

Nonfiction: Book excerpts, expose, historical/nostalgic, humor, interview/profile, opinion, photo feature, technical and travel. "We would like to receive controversial and detailed news pieces that cover both sides of an issue: for example, how a race director must deal with city government to put on an event. Problems seen by both sides including cost, traffic congestion, red tape, etc." No personal experience such as "Why I Love to Run," "How I Ran My First Marathon." Buys 18 mss/year. Query with published clips or send complete ms. Length: 500-2,500 words. Pays $100 maximum for assigned articles; $50 maximum for unsolicited articles. Sometimes pays the expenses of writers on assignment.

Photos: Send photos with submission. Offers $25 maximum/photo. Captions required. Buys one-time rights.

Tips: "We are looking for specific pieces that cite names, places, costs and references to additional information. Writers should be familiar with the sport and understand race strategies, etc. The basic who, what, where, when and how also applies. The best way to break in to our publication is to submit brief (3 or 4 paragraphs) write-ups on road races to be used in the Results section or submit fillers for our 'Texas Roundup' section."

NEW YORK RUNNING NEWS, New York Road Runners Club, 9 E. 89th St., New York NY 10128. (212)860-2280. **Fax:** (212)860-9754. Editor: Raleigh Mayer. Managing Editor: Don Mogelefsky. 75% freelance written. Bimonthly regional sports magazine covering running, racewalking, nutrition and fitness. Material should be of interest to members of the New York Road Runners Club. Estab. 1958. Circ. 45,000. Pays on publication. Time to publication varies. Byline given. Offers 33% kill fee. Buys first North American serial rights. Submit seasonal/holiday material 4 months in advance. Simultaneous and previously published submissions OK; send photocopy of article with information about when and where it previously appeared. Pays 25-50% of their fee for an original article. Reports in 2 months. Sample copy for $3. Writer's guidelines for #10 SASE.

Nonfiction: Running and marathon articles. Special issues include N.Y.C. Marathon (submissions in by August 1). No non-running stories. Buys 25 mss/year. Query. Length: 750-1,750 words. Pays $50-250. Pays documented expenses of writers on assignment.

Photos: Send photos with submission. Reviews 8 × 10 b&w prints. Offers $35-300/photo. Captions, model releases and identification of subjects required. Buys one-time rights.

Columns/Departments: Essay (running-related topics). Query. Length: 750 words. Pays $50-125.

• No longer accepts fiction.

Tips: "Be knowledgable about the sport of running. Write like a runner."

RUNNER'S WORLD, Rodale Press, 33 E. Minor St., Emmaus PA 18098. (215)967-5171. Senior Editor: Bob Wischnia. 10% freelance written. Monthly magazine on running, mainly long-distance running. "The magazine for and about distance running, training, health and fitness, injury precaution, race coverage, personalties of the sport." Estab. 1966. Circ. 450,000. Pays on publication. Publishes ms an average of 5-6 months after acceptance. Byline given. Buys one-time rights. Submit seasonal/holiday material 6 months in advance. Query for electronic submissions. Reports in 1 month. Writer's guidelines for #10 SASE.

Nonfiction: How-to (train, prevent injuries), interview/profile and personal experience. No "my first marathon" stories. No poetry. Buys 30 mss/year. Query. Pays the expenses of writers on assignment.
Photos: State availability of photos with submission. Identification of subjects required. Buys one-time rights.
Columns/Departments: Christina Negron. Finish Line (personal experience – humor); and Training Log (training of well-known runner). Buys 15 mss/year. Query.

Skiing and Snow Sports

AMERICAN SKATING WORLD, Independent Publication of the American Ice Skating Community, Business Communications Inc., 1816 Brownsville Rd., Pittsburgh PA 15210-3908. (412)885-7600. Fax: (412)885-7617. Editor: Robert A. Mock. Managing Editor: H. Kermit Jackson. 70% freelance written. Eager to work with new/unpublished writers. Monthly tabloid on figure skating. Estab. 1979. Circ. 15,000. Pays following publication. Publishes ms an average of 2-3 months after acceptance. Byline given. Buys first North American serial rights and occasionally second serial (reprint) rights. Submit seasonal/holiday material 3 months in advance. Reports in 3 months. Sample copy and writer's guidelines for $3.50.
Nonfiction: Expose; historical/nostalgic, how-to (technique in figure skating), humor, inspirational, interview/profile, new product, opinion, personal experience, photo feature, technical and travel. Special issues: recreational (July), classic skaters (August), annual fashion issue (September) and Industry (May). No fiction. AP Style Guidelines are the basic style source, but we are not bound by that convention. Short, snappy paragraphs desired. Buys 150 mss/year. Send complete ms. "Include phone number; response time longer without it." Length: 600-1,000 words. Pays $25-100.
Photos: Send photos with query or ms. Reviews transparencies and b&w prints. Pays $5 for b&w; $15 for color. Identification of subjects required. Buys all rights for b&w; one-time rights for color.
Columns/Departments: Buys 30 mss/year. Send complete ms. Length: 500-750 words. Pays $25-50.
Fillers: Clippings and anecdotes. No payment for fillers.
Tips: "Event coverage is most open to freelancers; confirm with managing editor to ensure event has not been assigned. We are drawing more extensively from non-US based writers. Questions are welcome; call managing editor EST, 10-4, Monday-Friday."

SKATING, United States Figure Skating Association, 20 1st St., Colorado Springs CO 80906-3697. (719)635-5200. Fax: (719)635-9548. Editor: Kim Mutchler. Monthly magazine (except August, September), official publication of the USFSA. Estab. 1923. Circ. 35,000. Pays on publication. Publishes ms an average of 3 months after acceptance. Buys all rights. Byline given.
Nonfiction: Historical, informational, interview, photo feature, historical biographies, profile (background and interests of national-caliber amateur skaters), technical and competition reports. Buys 4 mss/issue. All work by assignment.
Photos: Photos purchased with or without accompanying ms. Pays $15 for 8×10 or 5×7 b&w glossy prints and $35 for color prints or transparencies. Query.
Columns/Departments: Ice Abroad (competition results and report from outside the US); Book Reviews; and People. Buys 4 mss/issue. All work by assignment. Length: 500-2,000 words.
Tips: "We want writing by experienced persons knowledgable in the technical and artistic aspects of figure skating with a new outlook on the development of the sport. Knowledge and background in technical aspects of figure skating are essential to the quality of writing expected. We would also like to receive articles on former competitive skaters. No professional skater material."

SKI MAGAZINE, 2 Park Ave., New York NY 10016. (212)779-5000. Fax: (212)481-9261. Editor-in-Chief: Richard Needham. Editor: Steve Cohen. 15% freelance written. Monthly magazine on snow skiing. "*Ski* is a ski-lifestyle publication written and edited for recreational skiers. Its content is intended to help them ski better (technique), buy better (equipment and skiwear), and introduce them to new experiences, people and adventures." Estab. 1936. Circ. 430,000. **Pays on acceptance.** Publishes ms an average of 3 months after acceptance. Byline given. Offers 15% kill fee. Buys first North American serial rights. Submit seasonal/holiday material 8 months in advance. Reports in 1 month. Sample copy for 9×12 SAE with 5 first class stamps.
Nonfiction: Essays, historical/nostalgic, how-to, humor, interview/profile and personal experience. Buys 5-10 mss/year. Send complete ms. Length: 1,000-3,500 words. Pays $500-1,000 for assigned articles; $300-700 for unsolicited articles. Pays the expenses of writers on assignment.
Photos: Send photos with submission. Offers $75-300/photo. Captions, model releases and identification of subjects required. Buys one-time rights.
Columns/Departments: Ski Life (interesting people, events, oddities in skiing), 150-300 words; Going Places (items on new or unique places, deals or services available to skiers); and Take It From Us (special products or services available to skiers that are real values or out of the ordinary), 25-50 words.
Fillers: Facts and short humor. Buys 10/year. Length: 60-75 words. Pays $50-75.
  • Ranked as one of the best markets for freelance writers in *Writer's Digest* magazine's annual "Top 100 Markets," January 1993.

Tips: "Writers must have an extensive familiarity with the sport and know what concerns, interests and amuses skiers. Columns are most open to freelancers."

SKIING, Times Mirror Magazines, Inc., 2 Park Ave., New York NY 10016. "Prefers not to share information."

‡SNOWBOARDER, The Magazine, For Better Living Communications, P.O. Box 1028, Dana Point CA 92629. (714)496-5922. Editor: Douglas C. Palladini. Managing Editor: Steve Casimiro. 50% freelance written. Magazine published monthly during September-February covering snowboarding. Estab. 1987. Circ. 75,000. Pays on publication. Publishes ms an average of 4 months after acceptance. Byline given. 20% kill fee. Buys first North American serial rights. Query for electronic submissions. Reports in 1 month on queries. Sample copy $1 with 1 first class stamp. Free writer's guidelines.
Nonfiction: How-to, personal experience, photo feature, technical and travel. No fiction. Buys 7-10 mss/ year. Query with published clips. Length: 100-1,200 words. Pays $50-750. Sometimes pays expenses of writers on assignment.
Photos: State availability of photos with submissions. Reviews transparencies. Offers $50-600. Identification of subjects required. Buys one-time rights.

Soccer

SOCCER AMERICA, P.O. Box 23704, Oakland CA 94623. (510)528-5000. Fax: (510)528-5177. Managing Editor: Paul Kennedy. 10% freelance written. Works with a small number of new/unpublished writers each year. Weekly tabloid for a wide range of soccer enthusiasts. Estab. 1971. Circ. 25,000. Pays on publication. Publishes ms an average of 2 months after acceptance. Buys all rights. Byline given. Submit seasonal/holiday material 30 days in advance. Query for electronic submissions. Reports in 2 months. Sample copy and writer's guidelines $1.
Nonfiction: Expose (why a pro franchise isn't working right, etc.), historical, how-to, informational (news features), inspirational, interview, photo feature, profile and technical. "No 'Why I like soccer' articles in 1,000 words or less. It's been done. We are very much interested in articles for our 'special issues': fitness, travel, and college selection process." Buys 1-2 mss/issue. Query. Length: 200-1,500 words. Pays 50¢/inch minimum.
Photos: Photos purchased with or without accompanying ms or on assignment. Captions required. Pays $12 for 5×7 or larger b&w glossy prints. Query.
Tips: "Freelancers mean the addition of editorial vitality. New approaches and new minds can make a world of difference. But if they haven't familiarized themselves with the publication it is a total waste of my time and theirs."

YOUTH SOCCER NEWS, Varsity Publications, Inc., 6506 23rd Ave. NE, Seattle WA 98115. (206)524-8985. Editor: Dick Stephens. 10-25% freelance written. Monthly tabloid newspaper for US soccer with focus on youth. Focus on news tied to USYSA Youth Soccer, i.e., teams, tournaments, products in western states. Estab. 1985. Circ. 60,000. Pays on publication. Byline given. Buys first North American serial and second serial (reprint) rights. Editorial lead time 3 months. Submit seasonal material 2 months in advance. Simultaneous and previously published submissions OK. Query for electronic submissions. Reports in 2 months on queries. Sample copy and writer's guidelines for #10 SASE.
Nonfiction: Book excerpts, essays, expose, general interest, historical/nostalgic, how-to, humor, inspirational, interview/profile, new product, opinion, personal experience, photo feature, travel and how-to (soccer instruction). Buys 10 mss/year. Send complete ms. Length: 400-700 words. Pays $20 minimum. Pays contributor's copies "if piece was small enough, where payment wasn't expected."
Photos: Send photos with submission. Reviews 4×6 or 3×5 or larger prints. Offers $5-20/photo. Negotiates payment individually. Model releases and identification of subjects required. "depends on subject and focus."
Columns/Departments: Coaching Corner (instructional soccer), 500-600 words; numerous others on tournament coverage and administrative news. Buys 30 mss/year. Query with published clips. Send complete ms. Pays $10-30.
Fiction: "We don't solicit fiction often. No fluffy articles on sports." Buys 10 mss/year. Send complete ms. Length: 300-1,000 words. Pays $15-30.
Fillers: Anecdotes, facts, gags to be illustrated by cartoonist, newsbreaks and short humor. Buys 30/year. Length: 100-200 words. Pay negotiable.
Tips: "Send resume with clips and refs. Contact editor for further info. Background experience in soccer is appreciated. We are most open to tournament/team profiles and reports. Stay within AP style and write to an adult soccer audience."

Tennis

‡RACQUET, Heather & Pine, Inc., #1202, 42 W. 38th, New York NY 10018. (212)768-8360. Fax: (212)768-8365. Senior Editor: Karen Day. 30% freelance written. Bimonthly tennis/lifestyle magazine. "*Racquet* celebrates the lifestyle of tennis." Estab. 1978. Circ. 145,000. Pays on publication. Publishes ms an average of 2-

3 months after acceptance. Byline given. Offers negotiable kill fee. Rights purchased negotiable. Submit seasonal/holiday material 4-5 months in advance. Simultaneous submissions OK. Publishes reprints of previously published articles. Send tearsheet or photocopy of article. Query for electronic submissions. Reports in 1 month. *Writer's Market* recommends allowing 2 months for reply. Sample copy $4.

Nonfiction: Essays, expose, historical/nostalgic, humor, interview/profile, opinion, personal experience, travel. "No instruction or poetry." Buys 15-20 mss/year. Query. Length: 1,000-4,000 words. Pays $200-750 for assigned articles; $100-300 for unsolicited articles. Pays in contributor copies or other negotiable premiums. Sometime pays expenses of writers on assignment.

Photos: State availability of photos with submission. Offers no additional payment for photos accepted with ms. Rights negotiable.

Columns/Departments: "Courtside" (personal experience – fun facts), 500-2,000 words; and "Business of Tennis" (financial side of tennis and related industries), 2,000-2,500 words. Buys 5-10 mss/year. Query. Pays $100-300.

Fillers: Anecdotes and short humor. Buys 5/year. Length: 250-750 words. Pays $50-150.

Tips: "Get a copy, understand how we approach tennis, submit article written to style and follow-up. We are always looking for innovative or humorous ideas."

Water Sports

DIVER, Seagraphic Publications, Ltd., 10991 Shellbridge Way, Richmond, British Columbia V6X 3C6 Canada. (604)273-4333. Fax: (604)273-0813. Editor/Publisher: Peter Vassilopoulos. 75% freelance written. Magazine published 9 times/year emphasizing scuba diving, ocean science and technology (commercial and military diving) for a well-educated, outdoor-oriented readership. Circ. 20,000. Payment "follows publication." Buys first North American serial rights. Byline given. Query (by mail only). Submit seasonal/holiday material 3 months in advance of issue date. Send SAE with IRCs. Reports in 6 weeks. Publishes ms an average of 2 months after acceptance. "Articles are subject to being accepted for use in supplement issues on tabloid." Travel features considered only in September/October for use following year.

Nonfiction: How-to (underwater activities such as photography, etc.); general interest (underwater oriented); humor; historical (shipwrecks, treasure artifacts, archeological); interview (underwater personalities in all spheres – military, sports, scientific or commercial); personal experience (related to diving); photo feature (marine life); technical (related to oceanography, commercial/military diving, etc.); and travel (dive resorts). No subjective product reports. Buys 25 mss/year. Submit complete ms. Length: 800-1,500 words. Pays $2.50/column inch.

Photos: "Features are mostly those describing dive sites, experiences, etc. Photo features are reserved more as specials, while almost all articles must be well illustrated with color or b&w prints supplemented by color transparencies." Submit original photo material with accompanying ms. Pays $7 minimum for 5×7 or 8×10 b&w glossy prints; $15 minimum for 35mm color transparencies. Captions and model releases required. Buys one-time rights.

Columns/Departments: Book reviews. Submit complete ms. Length: 200 words maximum. Pays $2.50/column inch.

Fillers: Anecdotes, newsbreaks and short humor. Buys 8-10/year. Length: 50-150 words. Pays $2.50/column inch.

Tips: "It's rewarding finding a talented writer who can make ordinary topics come alive. But dealing with unsolicited manuscripts that don't even come close to being suitable for *Diver* is the most frustrating aspect of working with freelancers."

SCUBA TIMES, The Active Diver's Magazine, GBP, Inc., 14110 Perdido Key Dr., Pensacola FL 32507. (904)492-7805. Fax: (904)492-7805. Managing Editor: Fred D. Garth. Editor: Gwen Roland. 90% freelance written. Bimonthly magazine on scuba diving. Estab. 1979. Circ. 40,000. Pays on publication. Publishes ms an average of 6 months after acceptance. Byline given. Buys first North American serial rights. Publishes reprints of previously published articles. Send information about when and where the article previously appeared. For reprints, pays 100% of the amount paid for an original article. Submit seasonal material 1 year in advance. Query for electronic submissions. Reports in 6 weeks. Sample copy $3. Writer's guidelines for #10 SASE.

Nonfiction: How-to (advanced diving techniques such as technical, very deep, mixed gases, cave diving, wreck diving); humor; interview/profile (colorful characters in diving); personal experience (only if it is astounding); photo feature (creatures, places to dive); technical (physics, biology, medicine as it relates to diving); and travel (dive destinations). No beginner-level dive material. Buys 75 mss/year. Query with published clips or send complete ms. Length: 150 words for sidebars, 1,500 for major destination features. Pays $75/published page. Sometimes pays expenses of writers on assignment.

Photos: Send photos with submission. Reviews transparencies. Offers $25-75/page; $150/front cover photo. Captions and identification of subjects required. Buys one-time rights.

Columns/Departments: What a Wreck (informative guide to any wreck, old or new), 750 words; Creature Feature (one knock-out photo of a mysterious sea creature plus story of life cycle and circumstances that led to photo), 500 words; Last Watering Hole (great photos, usually topside, and story about a dive site so remote most divers will never go), 500 words and Advanced Diving (how-to and advanced techniques for expanding dive adventure), 750 words. Buys 60 mss/year. Query with published clips. Length; 500-1,000 words. Pays $25-75/page.

Fillers: " 'Free Flowing' sections allows writers to be creative, thought provoking as they contemplate diver's relationship to the marine world." Anecdotes and short humor. Buys 10/year. Length: 300-900 words. Pays $25-75/page.

Tips: "Be a diver. Everyone tries for the glamorous destination assignments, but it is easier to break into the columns, especially, 'Last Watering Hole,' 'What a Wreck' and 'Creature Feature.' Outstanding photos are a must. We will coax a good article out of a great photographer whose writing skills are not developed. Very little is written in-house. Diving freelancers are the heart and soul of *STM*. Unknowns receive as much consideration as the big names. Know what you are talking about and present it with a creative flair. Divers are often technical or scientific by profession or disposition and their writing lacks flow, power and grace. Make us *feel* those currents and *smell* the diesel from the yacht."

SKIN DIVER, Petersen Publishing Co., 8490 Sunset Blvd., Los Angeles CA 90069. (310)854-2960. Executive Editor: Bonnie J. Cardone. Group Operations Manager: Jim Warner. 85% freelance written. Eager to work with new writers. Monthly magazine on scuba diving. *"Skin Diver* offers broad coverage of all significant aspects of underwater activity in the areas of foreign and domestic travel, recreation, ocean exploration, scientific research, commercial diving and technological developments." Pays on publication. Publishes ms an average of 9 months after acceptance. Byline given. Buys one-time rights. Submit seasonal/holiday material 6 months in advance. No simultaneous submissions. Reports in 3 months. Writer's guidelines for #10 SASE.

Nonfiction: Personal experience, travel, local diving, adventure and wreck diving. No Caribbean travel; no "how I learned to dive." Buys 200 mss/year. Send complete ms. Length: 300-2,000 words, 1,200 preferred. Pays $50/published page.

Photos: Send photos with query or ms. Reviews 35mm transparencies and 8×10 prints. Pays $50/published page. Captions and identification of subjects required. Buys one-time rights.

Fillers: Newsbreaks and cartoons. Length: 300 words. Pays $25 for cartoons; $50/published page.

Tips: "Forget tropical travel articles and write about local diving sites, game diving, local and wreck diving."

SURFER, Surfer Publications, P.O. Box 1028, Dana Point CA 92629. (714)496-5922. Fax: (714)496-7849. Editor: Steve Hawk. Assistant Editor: Lisa Boelter. 20% freelance written. Monthly magazine "aimed at experts and beginners with strong emphasis on action surf photography." Estab. 1960. Circ. 110,000. Pays on publication. Byline given. Buys first North American serial rights. Submit seasonal/holiday material 6 months in advance. Simultaneous submissions OK. Query for electronic submissions. Reports in 2 months. Sample copy for $3.95 with 9×12 SASE. Writer's guidelines for #10 SASE.

Nonfiction: How-to (technique in surfing); humor; inspirational; interview/profile; opinion; personal experience (all surf-related); photo feature (action surf and surf travel); technical (surfboard design); and travel (surf exploration and discovery—photos required). Buys 30-50 mss/year. Query with or without published clips or send complete ms. Length: 500-2,500 words. Pays 15-20¢/word. Sometimes pays the expenses of writers on assignment.

Photos: Send photos with submission. Reviews 35mm negatives and transparencies. Buys 12-24 illustrations/year. Prices vary. Used for columns: Environment, Surf Docs and sometimes features. Send samples with SASE to Art Director. Offers $10-250/photo. Identification of subjects required. Buys one-time and reprint rights.

Columns/Departments: Environment (environmental concerns to surfers), 1,000-1,500 words; Surf Stories (personal experiences of surfing), 1,000-1,500 words; Reviews (surf-related movies, books), 500-1,000 words; and Sections (humorous surf-related items with b&w photos), 100-500 words. Buys 25-50 mss/year. Send complete ms. Pays 15-20¢/word.

Fiction: Surf-related adventure, fantasy, horror, humorous and science fiction. Buys 10 mss/year. Send complete ms. Length: 750-2,000 words. Pays 15-20¢/word.

Tips: "All sections are open to freelancers but interview/profiles are usually assigned. Try 'People Who Surf'—a good way to get a foot in the door. Stories must be authoritative and oriented to the hardcore surfer."

‡**THE WATER SKIER**, American Water Ski Association, 799 Overlook Dr., Winter Haven FL 33884. (813)324-4341. Editor: Greg Nixon. 60-70% freelance written. Seven times a year magazine for water skiing—all aspects of the sport. *"The Water Skier* is the official publication of the American Water Ski Association (AWSA), the national governing body for organized water skiing in the United States. The magazine has a controlled circulation and is available only to AWSA's membership, which is made up of 10,000 active competitive water skiers and 20,000 members who are supporting the sport. These supporting members may

participate in the sport but they don't compete. The editorial content of the magazine features distinctive and informative writing about the sport of water skiing only." Estab. 1951. Circ. 30,000. Byline given. Offers 30% kill fee. Buys all rights (no exceptions). Editorial lead time 3-4 months. Submit seasonal material 6 months in advance. Reports in 2 weeks on queries. Sample copy $1.25. Writer's guidelines for #10 SASE.

Nonfiction: Historical/nostalgic (has to pertain to water skiing), interview/profile (call for assignment), new product (boating and water ski equipment) and travel (water ski vacation destinations). Buys 10-15 mss/year. Query. Length: 1,500-3,000 words. Pays $125 minimum for assigned articles, $150 minimum for unsolicited articles.

Photos: State availability of photos with submission. Reviews contact sheets. Negotiates payment individually. Captions and identification of subjects required. Buys all rights.

Columns/Departments: Sports Science/Medicine (athlete conditioning, physical/mental training), 1,000-1,500 words; The Starting Dock (small news items about people and events in the sport), 400-500 words; and Waterways Issues (water skier's rights of access to waterways, environmental issues), 1,000-1,500 words. Query. Pays $75-125. Pay for columns negotiated individually with each writer.

Tips: "Contact the editor through a query letter (please no phone calls) with an idea. Avoid instruction, these articles are written by professionals. Concentrate on articles about the people of the sport. We are always looking for the interesting stories about people in the sport. Also, short news features which will make a reader say to himself, 'Hey, I didn't know that.' Keep in mind that the publication is highly specialized about the sport of water skiing." Most open to material for: feature articles (query editor with your idea), Sports/Science Medicine columns (query editor with ideas, looking for unique training or conditioning and method or sports rehabilitation), and The Starting Dock (interesting and unique news slants that are about the people and events in sport of water skiing).

‡WATERSKI MAGAZINE, The World's Leading Water Skiing Magazine, World Publications, 330 W. Canton Ave., Winter Park FL 32789. (407)628-4082. Associate Editor: Rob May. Managing Editor: Barb McCarter. Contact: Rob May. 25% freelance written. Magazine published 10 times/year for water skiing and related watersports. "*WaterSki* instructs, advises, enlightens, informs *and* creates an open forum for skiers around the world. It provides definitive information on instruction, products, people and travel destinations." Estab. 1978. Circ. 125,000. **Pays on acceptance.** Publishes ms an average of 4 months after acceptance. Offers 25% kill fee. Buys first North American serial and second serial (reprint) rights. Editorial lead time 2 months. Submit seasonal material 2 months in advance. Simultaneous submissions OK. Query for electronic submissions. Reports in 1 month on queries; 2 months on mss. Sample copy for 8½ × 11 SAE with 4 first class stamps. Writer's guidelines for #10 SASE.

Nonfiction: General interest, historical/nostalgic, how-to (water ski instruction boating-related), interview/profile, new product, photo feature, technical and travel. Does not want to see anything not directly related to the sport of water skiing. Buys 10 mss/year. Query with published clips. Length: 1,750-3,000 words. Pays $200 minimum for assigned articles. Pays other upon inability to meet author's pay request. Sometimes pays expenses of writers on assignment.

Photos: Send photos with submission. Reviews 2¼ × 2¼ transparencies, all slides. Negotiates payment individually. Identification of subjects required. Buys one-time rights on color, all rights on b&w.

Columns/Departments: Tech Talk (technical aspects of ski equipment), 750 words; Shortline (interesting news of the sport), 300 words; and Quick Tips (short instruction on water skiing and 500 words. Buys 10 mss/year. Query with published clips. Pays $75-125.

Fiction: Adventure, experimental, historical and humorous. Does not want to see anything not directly related to water skiing. Buys 10 mss/year. Query with published clips. Length: 1,750-4,000 words. Pays $200-300.

Fillers: Anecdotes, facts, gags to be illustrated by cartoonist, newsbreaks and short humor. Buys 15/year. Length: 200-500 words. Pays $75-125.

Tips: "I recommend a query call to see if there are any immediate openings in the calendar. Follow-up with a published submission (if applicable). Writers should have some interest in the sport, and understand its people, products and lifestyle. The features sections offer the most opportunity for freelancers. One requirement: It must have a positive, strong water skiing slant, whether it be personality, human interest, or travel."

Wrestling

WRESTLING WORLD, Lexington Library Inc., 355 Lexington Ave., New York NY 10017. (212)973-3200. Fax: (212)986-5926. Editor: Stephen Ciacciarelli. 100% freelance written. Bimonthly magazine for professional wrestling fans. We run profiles of top wrestlers and managers and articles on current topics of interest on the mat scene." Circ. 100,000. **Pays on acceptance.** Byline given. Buys first North American serial rights. Reports in 2 weeks. Sample copy $3 for SAE with 3 first class stamps.

Nonfiction: Interview/profile and photo feature. "No general think pieces." Buys 100 mss/year. Query with or without published clips or send complete ms. Length: 1,500-2,500 words. Pays $75-125.

Photos: State availability of photos with submision. Reviews 35mm transparencies and prints. Offers $25-50/photo package. Pays $50-150 for transparencies. Identification of subjects required. Buys one-time rights.

Tips: "Anything topical has the best chance of acceptance. Articles on those hard-to-reach wrestlers stand an excellent chance of acceptance."

Teen and Young Adult

The publications in this category are for young people ages 13-19. Publications for college students are listed in Career, College and Alumni. Those for younger children are listed in the Juvenile category.

BK NEWS, The Art of Being A Successful Entrepreneur, (formerly *Businessip*), Busines$ Kids, Suite 1080 East, 1300 I St., Washington DC 20005 (202)408-0699. Editor: Michael J. Holmes. 50% freelance written. Bimonthly tabloid for young entrepreneurs. "We look for stories about young entrepreneurs (under 20), how teens can become entrepreneurs, and useful information for effective business operation and management for young entrepreneurs." Estab. 1988. Circ. 75,000. Pays on publication. Publishes ms an average of 6 months after acceptance. Byline given (author listed as contributor). Buys all rights. Submit seasonal material 1 year in advance. Send complete ms. Free sample copy and writer's guidelines for #10 SAE with $1 in postage.

Nonfiction: How-to, interview/profile, new product and personal experience. "We are not interested in anything that does not pertain to young people in business." Buys 36 mss/year. Send complete ms with clips if possible. Length: 200-600 words. Pays 15¢/word.

Photos: Send photos with submission. Reviews contact sheets, 5 × 7 transparencies and 8 × 10 prints. Offers $5-10/photo. Captions, model releases and identification of subjects required. Buys all rights.

Columns/Departments: Buys 20 mss/year. Send complete ms. Length: 50-350 words. Pays 15¢/word.

Poetry: Avant-garde, free verse, Haiku, light verse and traditional. "We do not want to see anything that is inappropriate for young minds. Nothing unrelated to business." Pays $15-20.

Fillers: Cartoon, puzzles, games and news releases. Buys 12/year. Length: 25-100 words. Pays $10-50.

Tips: "For best chance of publication, write a feature story about a teen in business for themselves. Include photo."

‡CAMPUS LIFE, Christianity Today, Inc., 465 Gundersen Dr., Carol Stream IL 60188. (708)260-6200. Editor: Jim Long. Contact: Christopher Lutes, manuscripts editor. 35% freelance written. Magazine published ten times/year for the Christian life as it related to today's teen. "*Campus Life* is a magazine for high-school and college age teenagers. Our editorial slant is not overtly religious. The indirect style is intended to create a safety zone with our readers and to reflect our philosophy that God is interested in all of life. Therefore, we publish 'message stories' side by side with general interest, humor, etc." Estab. 1942. Circ. 120,000. **Pays on acceptance.** Publishes ms an average of 4-5 months after acceptance. Byline given. Offers 50% kill fee. Buys first and one-time rights. Editorial lead time 4 months. Submit seasonal material 4-5 months in advance. Simultaneous and previously published submissions OK. Reports in 3-5 weeks on queries; 1-2 months on mss. Sample copy $2 for 8 × 10 SAE with 3 first class stamps. Writer's guidelines for #10 SASE.

Nonfiction: Humor, personal experience and photo feature. The *Christian* college experience. Buys 10-20 mss/year. Query with published clips. Length: 250-2,500 words. Pays 10-20¢ minimum.

Photos: State availability of photos with submission. Reviews contact sheets, transparencies and 5 × 7 prints. Negotiates payment individually. Model release required. Buys one-time rights.

Columns/Departments: OnCampus (tips and information for today's student), 50-250 words; and Going for It (high school student who is doing something fun, exciting and/or interesting), 250-500 words. Buys 2-5 mss/year. Query with published clips. Pays $10-125.

Fiction: Buys 1-5 mss/year. Query. Length: 1,000-3,500 words. Pays 10-20¢/word.

Poetry: Free verse. "No material that does not 'communicate' to the average teenager." Buys 1-5 poems/year. Submit maximum 2 poems. Length: 5-20 lines. Pays $25-50.

Fillers: Anecdotes, facts and short humor. Buys 3-5/year. Length: 25-250 words. Pays $10-50.

Tips: "The best way to break in to *Campus Life* is through writing first-person or as-told-to first-person stories. But query first—with theme info, telling way this story would work for our audience. We are seeking humor: high school experiences with a "Dave Barry" flair, first-person, capturing a teen's everyday 'life lesson' experience."

‡CAREERS & COLLEGES, The Magazine for Today's Young Achievers, (formerly *Careers*), E.M. Guild, Inc., 1001 Avenue of the Americas, New York NY 10018. (212)354-8877. Fax: (212)354-8871. Editor: June Rogoznica. Estab. 1980. 75% freelance written. Works with a small number of new/unpublished writers each year. Quarterly magazine covering life-coping skills, career choices and educational opportunities for high school juniors and seniors. "*Careers & Colleges* is designed to offer a taste of the working world, new career opportunities, and stories covering the best ways to reach those opportunities—through education, etc." Circ. 500,000. Pays 30 days after acceptance. Publishes ms an average of 2-3 months after acceptance. Byline given. Offers 25% kill fee. Buys first North American serial rights. Submit seasonal/holiday material 6 months in advance. Sometimes accepts previously published submissions. Reports in 2 months on queries. Sample copy $2.50. Writer's guidelines for #10 SAE with 1 first class stamp.

Nonfiction: Book excerpts, how-to, interview/profile and humor. Buys 25 mss/year. Query with published clips. Length: 1,000-1,500 words. Pays $250-450. Sometimes pays the expenses of writers on assignment.

Photos: State availability of photos with submission. Reviews contact sheets and transparencies. Offers $100 minimum/photo. Captions, model releases, and identification of subjects required. Buys one-time rights.

Columns/Departments: Money Wise, College Hotline, Career Watch, Tech Talk and Get Involved. Buys 15 mss/year. Length: 1,000-1,500 words. Pays $250.

CHALLENGE, (formerly *Pioneer*), Baptist Brotherhood Commission, 1548 Poplar Ave., Memphis TN 38104. (901)272-2461. Editor: Jene Smith. 5% freelance written. Monthly magazine for "boys age 12-18 who are members of a missions organization in Southern Baptist churches." Circ. 35,000. Byline given. Pays on publication. Publishes ms an average of 6-8 months after acceptance. Buys simultaneous rights. Submit seasonal/holiday material 8 months in advance. Simultaneous submissions OK. Publishes reprints of previously published articles. Send tearsheet or photocopy of article or short story. Reports in 1 month. *Writer's Market* recommends allowing 2 months for reply. Sample copy and writer's guidelines for 9×12 SAE with $1.20 postage. Writer's guidelines only for #10 SASE.

Nonfiction: How-to (crafts, hobbies); informational (youth); inspirational (sports/entertainment personalities); and photo feature (sports, teen subjects). No "preachy" articles, fiction or excessive dialogue. Submit complete ms. Length: 500-800 words. Pays $20-50.

Photos: Purchased with accompanying ms or on assignment. Captions required. Query. Pays $10 for 8×10 b&w glossy prints.

Tips: "The writer has a better chance of breaking in at our publication with youth related articles (youth issues, and sports figures). Most topics are set years in advance. The most frequent mistake made by writers is sending us preachy articles. Aim for the mid- to older-teen instead of younger teen."

EXPLORING MAGAZINE, Boy Scouts of America, P.O. Box 152079, Irving TX 75015-2079. (214)580-2365. Fax: (214)580-2079. Executive Editor: Scott Daniels. 85% freelance written. Prefers to work with published/established writers. Magazine published 4 times/year—January, March, May, September—covering the co-ed teen-age Exploring program of the BSA. Estab. 1970. Circ. 350,000. **Pays on acceptance.** Publishes ms an average of 6 months after acceptance. Byline given. Buys first rights. Submit seasonal/holiday material 6 months in advance. Simultaneous queries OK. Reports in 1 month. *Writer's Market* recommends allowing 2 months for reply. Sample copy for 9×12 SAE with 4 first class stamps. Writer's guidelines for #10 SASE. Write for guidelines and "What is Exploring?" fact sheet.

Nonfiction: General interest: how-to (achieve outdoor skills, organize trips, meetings, etc.); interview/profile (of outstanding Explorer); and travel (backpacking or canoeing with Explorers). Buys 15-20 mss/year. Query with clips. Length: 800-1,600 words. Pays $350-500. Pays expenses of writers on assignment.

Photos: Brian Payne, photo editor. State availability of photos with query letter or ms. Reviews b&w contact sheets and 35mm transparencies. Captions required. Buys one-time rights.

Tips: "Contact the local Exploring Director in your area (listed in phone book white pages under Boy Scouts of America). Find out if there are some outstanding post activities going on and then query magazine editor in Irving, Texas. Strive for shorter texts, faster starts and stories that lend themselves to dramatic photographs."

‡FLORIDA LEADER, (for high school students), Oxendine Publishing, Inc., P.O. Box 14081, 738 NW 23rd Ave., Gainesville FL 32609/32604-2081. (904)373-6907. Editor: W.H. "Butch" Oxendine Jr. Managing Editor: Kay Quinn. Quarterly magazine covering high school and pre-college youth. Estab. 1983. Circ. 50,000. Pays on publication. Publishes ms an average of 2-3 months after acceptance. Buys all rights. Submit seasonal material 4 months in advance. Simultaneous and previously published submissions OK. Query for electronic submissions. Reports in 1 month on queries. Sample copy for 8×11 with 3 first class stamps. Writer's guidelines for #10 SASE.

Nonfiction: How-to, humor, new product and opinion. "No lengthy individual profiles or articles without primary and secondary sources of attribution." Length: 250-1,000 words. Pays $35 maximum. Pays students or first-time writers with contributor's copies.

Photos: Send photos with submission. Reviews contact sheets, negatives and transparencies. Offers $50/photo maximum. Captions, model releases and identification of subjects required. Buys all rights.

Columns/Departments: College Living (various aspects of college life, general short humor oriented to high school or college students), 250-1,000 words; From Your Point of View (pro-con opinions on current issues), 1,000 total. Buys 10 mss/year. Query. Length: 250-1,000 words. Pays $35 maximum.

Fillers: Facts, newsbreaks and short humor. Buys 10/year. Length: 100-500 words. Pays $35 maximum.

Tips: "Read other high school and college publications for current issues, interests. Send manuscripts or outlines for review. All sections open to freelance work. Always looking for lighter, humorous articles as well as features on Florida colleges and universities, careers, jobs."

‡FREEWAY, P.O. Box 632, Glen Ellyn IL 60138. Editor: Amy J. Cox. 80% freelance written. Eager to work with new/unpublished writers. Weekly magazine. Estab. 1967. Prefers one-time rights but buys some reprints. Purchases 100 mss/year. Byline given. Reports on material accepted for publication in 2 months. Publishes ms an average of 1 year after acceptance. Returns rejected material in 2 months. Free sample copy and writer's guidelines with SASE.

Nonfiction: "*FreeWay*'s greatest need is for personal experience stories showing how God has worked in teens' lives. Stories are best written in first-person, 'as told to' author. Incorporate specific details, anecdotes, and dialogue. Show, don't tell, how the subject thought and felt. Weave spiritual conflicts and prayers into entire manuscript; avoid tacked-on sermons and morals. Stories should show how God has helped the person resolve a problem or how God helped save a person from trying circumstances (1,000 words or less). Avoid stories about accident and illness; focus on events and emotions of everyday life. Short-short stories are needed as fillers. We also need self-help or how-to articles with practical Christian advice on daily living, and trend articles addressing secular fads from a Christian perspective. We do not use devotional material, or fictionalized Bible stories." Pays 6-10¢/word. Some poetry ($20-50).

Photos: Whenever possible, provide clear 8×10 or 5×7 b&w photos to accompany mss (or any other available photos). Payment is $5-30.

Fiction: "We use little fiction, unless it is allegory, parable or humor."

Tips: "Study our 'Tips to Writers' pamphlet and sample copy, then send complete ms. In your cover letter, include information about who you are, writing qualifications, and experience working with teens. Include SASE."

GUIDE, 55 W. Oak Ridge Dr., Hagerstown MD 21740. Fax: (301)791-7012. Editor: Jeannette Johnson. 50% freelance written. Works with a small number of new/unpublished writers each year. Weekly magazine journal for junior youth and early teens. "Its content reflects Christian beliefs and standards." Weekly magazine. Estab. 1953. Circ. 40,000. Buys first serial, simultaneous and second serial (reprint) rights. **Pays on acceptance.** Publishes ms an average of 6-9 months after acceptance. Byline given. Submit seasonal/holiday material 6 months in advance. Reprints OK; send typed ms with rights for sale noted and information about when and where the article previously appeared. Pays 50% of their fee for an original article. Reports in 3 weeks. Free sample copy.

Fiction: Wants stories of character-building and spiritual value. Should emphasize the positive aspects of living, obedience to parents, perseverance, kindness, etc. "We can always use Christian humor and 'drama in real life' stories that show God's protection, and seasonal stories—Christmas, Thanksgiving, special holidays. We do not use stories of hunting, fishing, trapping or spiritualism." Buys about 300 mss/year. Send complete ms (include word count and Social Security number). Length: up to 1,200 words. Pays 3-4¢/word.

Tips: "Typical topics we cover in a yearly cycle include choices (music, clothes, friends, diet); friend-making skills; school problems (cheating, peer pressure, new school); self-esteem; changes; sibling relationships; divorce; step-families; drugs; and communication. We often buy short fillers, and an author who does not fully understand our needs is more likely to sell with a short-short. Our target age is 10-14. Our most successful writers are those who present stories from the viewpoint of a young teen-ager, written in the active voice. Stories that sound like an adult's sentiments passing through a young person's lips are *not* what we're looking for. Use believable dialogue."

HIGH SCHOOL I.D., Pathway Press, 922 Montgomery Ave., P.O. Box 2250, Cleveland TN 37320-2250. (615)476-4512. Editor: Lance Colkmire. 6% freelance written. A weekly take-home paper emphasizing Christian living for high schoolers. **Pays on acceptance.** Estab. 1910. Publishes ms an average of 18 months after acceptance. Byline given. Buys first North American serial rights and one-time rights. Submit seasonal/holiday material 1 year in advance. Simultaneous and previously published submissions OK. Reports in 2 months. Free sample copy and writer's guidelines for SASE.

Nonfiction: Inspirational, interview/profile, personal experience and other nonfiction written from a Pentecostal perspective. "Our primary objective is to show how teens can live a Christian life in a secular world." Buys 3-5 mss/year. Length: 500-800 words. Pays 3-5¢/word.

Tips: "Write to conservative, pentecostal audience about current subjects involving young people today." Human interest stories, especially first-person experiences, are most open to freelancers.

KEYNOTER, Key Club International, 3636 Woodview Trace, Indianapolis IN 46268-3196. Executive Editor: Julie A. Carson. 65% freelance written. Works with a small number of new writers each year, but is eager to work with new/unpublished writers willing to adjust their writing styles to *Keynoter*'s needs. Monthly youth magazine (December/January combined issue), distributed to members of Key Club International, a high school service organization for young men and women. Estab. 1946. Circ. 137,000. **Pays on acceptance.** Publishes ms an average of 5 months after acceptance. Byline given. Buys first North American serial rights.

Submit seasonal/holiday material 7 months in advance. Simultaneous queries and submissions (if advised), and previously published submissions OK. Reports in 1 month. Sample copy for 9 × 12 SAE with 3 first class stamps. Writer's guidelines for #10 SASE.

Nonfiction: Book excerpts (included in articles); general interest (for intelligent teen audience); historical/nostalgic (generally not accepted); how-to (advice on how teens can enhance the quality of lives or communities); humor (accepted if adds to story); interview/profile (rarely purchased, "would have to be on/with an irresistible subject"); new product (affecting teens); photo feature (if subject is right); technical (understandable and interesting to teen audience); travel (must apply to club travel schedule); subjects that entertain and inform teens on topics that relate directly to their lives. "We would also like to receive self-help and school-related nonfiction on leadership, community service, and teen issues. *Please, no first-person confessions, fiction or articles that are written down to our teen readers.*" Buys 10-15 mss/year. Query. Length: 1,500-1,800 words. Pays $150-350. Sometimes pays the expenses of writers on assignment.

Photos: State availability of photos. Reviews b&w contact sheets and negatives. Identification of subjects required. Buys one-time rights. Payment for photos included in payment for ms.

Tips: "We want to see articles written with attention to style and detail that will enrich the world of teens. Articles must be thoroughly researched and must draw on interviews with nationally and internationally respected sources. Our readers are 13-18, mature and dedicated to community service. We are very committed to working with good writers, and if we see something we like in a well-written query, we'll try to work it through to publication."

THE MAGAZINE FOR CHRISTIAN YOUTH! The United Methodist Publishing House, 201 8th Ave. S., Box 801, Nashville TN 37202. (615)749-6319. Fax: (615)749-6078 or 749-6079. Editor: Anthony E. Peterson. Monthly magazine. Circ. 30,000. **Pays on acceptance.** Byline given. Buys one-time and all rights. Submit seasonal/holiday material 8-10 months in advance. Previously published submissions OK. Writer's guidelines for #10 SASE. Sample copy for 9 × 12 SAE with 5 first class stamps.

Nonfiction: Book excerpts; general interest; how-to (deal with problems teens have); humor (on issues that touch teens' lives); inspirational; interview/profile (well-known singers, musicians, actors, sports); personal experience; religious; and travel (include teen culture of another country). Buys 5 mss/year. Queries welcome. Length: 700-2,000 words. Pays $20-150 for assigned articles; 5¢/word for unsolicited articles.

Photos: State availability of photos with submission. Reviews transparencies and 8 × 10 prints. Offers $25-150/photo. Captions and model releases required. Buys one-time rights.

Fiction: From teens only: adventure, ethnic, fantasy, historical, humorous, mainstream, mystery, religious, romance, science fiction, suspense and western. No stories where the plot is too trite and predictable—or too preachy. Send complete ms. Length: 700-2,000 words. Pays 5¢/word.

Fillers: Cartoons, ideas newsbreaks, quizzes and short humor. Buys 6/year. Length: 50-200 words. Pays 5¢/word.

Tips: "Write to teens friend to friend. Treat instructional pieces with humor and grace, not judgmentally. Keep tone personal. Appreciate the wonders and joys of adolescent life."

 • Publisher is interested in hearing from teen writers.

THE NEW ERA, 50 E. North Temple, Salt Lake City UT 84150. (801)240-2951. Fax: (801)240-1727. Managing Editor: Richard M. Romney. 60% freelance written. "We work with both established writers and newcomers." Monthly magazine for young people of the Church of Jesus Christ of Latter-day Saints (Mormon), their church leaders and teachers. Estab. 1971. Circ. 200,000. **Pays on acceptance.** Publishes ms an average of 1 year after acceptance. Byline given. Buys all rights. Submit seasonal material 1 year in advance. Query for electronic submissions. Reports in 2 months. Sample copy $1 for 9 × 12 SAE with 2 first class stamps. Writer's guidelines for SASE.

Nonfiction: Material that shows how the Church of Jesus Christ of Latter-day Saints is relevant in the lives of young people today. Must capture the excitement of being a young Latter-day Saint. Special interest in the experiences of young Mormons in other countries. No general library research or formula pieces without the *New Era* slant and feel. Uses informational, how-to, personal experience, interview, profile, inspirational, humor, historical, think pieces, travel and spot news. Query preferred. Length: 150-2,000 words. Pays 3-12¢/word. *For Your Information* (news of young Mormons around the world). Pays expenses of writers on assignment.

Photos: Uses b&w photos and transparencies with mss. Payment depends on use in magazine, but begins at $10.

Fiction: Adventure, science fiction and humorous. Must relate to young Mormon audience. Pays minimum 3¢/word.

Poetry: Traditional forms, blank verse, free verse, light verse and all other forms. Must relate to editorial viewpoint. Pays minimum 25¢/line.

Tips: "The writer must be able to write from a Mormon point of view. We're especially looking for stories about successful family relationships. We anticipate using more staff-produced material. This means freelance quality will have to improve."

SEVENTEEN, 850 3rd Ave., New York NY 10022. Editor-in-Chief: Midge Richardson. Managing Editor: Roberta Anne Myers. 80% freelance written. Works with a small number of new/unpublished writers each year. Monthly. Circ. 1.9 million. Buys one-time rights for nonfiction and fiction by adult writers and work by teenagers. Pays 25% kill fee. **Pays on acceptance.** Publishes ms an average of 6 months after acceptance. Byline given. Reports in up to 3 months.

Nonfiction: Sarah Patton Duncan, articles editor. Articles and features of general interest to young women who are concerned with the development of their lives and the problems of the world around them; strong emphasis on topicality and helpfulness. Send brief outline and query, including a typical lead paragraph, summing up basic idea of article. Also likes to receive articles and features on speculation. Query with tearsheets or copies of published articles. Length: 1,200-2,000 words. Pays $50-150 for articles written by teenagers but more to established adult freelancers. Articles are commissioned after outlines are submitted and approved. Fees for commissioned articles $650-1,500. Sometimes pays the expenses of writers on assignment.

Photos: Margaret Kemp, art director. Photos usually by assignment only.

Fiction: Joe Bargmann, fiction editor. Thoughtful, well-written stories on subjects of interest to young women between the ages of 12 and 20. Avoid formula stories—"My sainted Granny," "My crush on Brad," etc.—no heavy moralizing or condescension of any sort. Humorous stories and mysteries are welcomed. Best lengths are 1,000-3,000 words. Pays $500-1,500.

Poetry: Contact Voice editor. By teenagers only. Pays $50. Submissions are nonreturnable unless accompanied by SASE.

Tips: "Writers have to ask themselves whether or not they feel they can find the right tone for a *Seventeen* article—a tone which is empathetic yet never patronizing; lively yet not superficial. Not all writers feel comfortable with, understand or like teenagers. If you don't like them, *Seventeen* is the wrong market for you. The best way for beginning teenage writers to crack the *Seventeen* lineup is for them to contribute suggestions and short pieces to the Voices section, a literary format which lends itself to just about every kind of writing: profiles, essays, exposes, reportage and book reviews."

STRAIGHT, Standard Publishing Co., 8121 Hamilton Ave., Cincinnati OH 45231-2323. (513)931-4050. Fax: (513)931-0904. Editor: Carla J. Crane. 90% freelance written. Estab. 1866 (publishing house). Weekly magazine (published quarterly) for "teens, age 13-19, from Christian backgrounds who generally receive this publication in their Sunday School classes or through subscriptions. **Pays on acceptance.** Publishes ms an average of 1 year after acceptance. Buys first rights, second serial (reprint) rights or simultaneous rights. Byline given. Submit seasonal/holiday material 1 year in advance. Previously published submissions OK. Send tearsheet of article or story. Reports in 2 months. Free sample copy. Writer's guidelines for #10 SAE with 2 first class stamps.

Nonfiction: Religious-oriented topics, teen interest (school, church, family, dating, sports, part-time jobs), humor, inspirational and personal experience. "We want articles that promote Christian values and ideals." No puzzles. Query or submit complete ms. Include Social Security number on ms. "We're buying more short pieces these days; 12 pages fill up much too quickly." Length: 800-1,500 words.

Fiction: Adventure, humorous, religious and suspense. "All fiction should have some message for the modern Christian teen. Fiction should deal with all subjects in a forthright manner, without being preachy and without talking down to teens. No tasteless manuscripts that promote anything adverse to the Bible's teachings." Submit complete ms. Length: 1,000-1,500 words. Pays 3-7¢/word.

Photos: May submit photos with ms. Pays $25-50 for 8 × 10 b&w glossy prints and $75-125 for color slides. Model releases should be available. Buys one-time rights.

● Ranked as one of the best markets for freelance writers in *Writer's Digest* magazine's annual "Top 100 Markets," January 1993.

Tips: "Don't be trite. Use unusual settings or problems. Use a lot of illustrations, a good balance of conversation, narration, and action. Style must be clear, fresh—no sermonettes or sickly-sweet fiction. Take a realistic approach to problems. Be willing to submit to editorial policies on doctrine; knowledge of the *Bible* a must. Also, be aware of teens today, and what they do. Language, clothing, and activities included in mss should be contemporary. We are becoming more and more selective about freelance material and the competition seems to be stiffer all the time."

‡STUDENT LEADER, (for college students), Oxendine Publishing Inc., P.O. Box 14081, 738 NW 23rd Ave., Gainesville FL 326091-32604. (904)373-6907. Editor: W.H. "Butch" Oxendine Jr.. Managing Editor: Kay Quinn. 50% freelance written. Semiannual magazine covering student government, leadership. Estab. 1993. Circ. 200,000. Pays on publication. Byline given. Buys all rights. Submit seasonal material 4 months in advance. Query for electronic submissions. Reports in 1 month on queries. Sample copy for #10 SAE with 3 first class stamps. Writer's guidelines for #10 SASE.

Nonfiction: How-to, humor, new product and opinion. "No lengthy individual profiles or articles without primary or secondary sources of attribution." Buys 10 mss/year. Query. Length: 250-1,000 words. Pays $35 maximum. Pays contributor copies to students or first-time writers.

Photos: State availability of or send photos with submission. Reviews contact sheets, negatives and transparencies. Offers $50 photo/maximum. Captions, model releases and identification of subjects required. Buys all rights.

Columns/Departments: Buys 10 mss/year. Query. Length: 250-1,000 words. Pays $35 maximum.

Fillers: Facts, newsbreaks and short humor. Buys 10/year. Length: 100 words minimum. Pays $35 maximum.

Tips: "Read other high school and college publications for current ideas, interests. Send outlines or manuscripts for review. All sections open to freelance work. Always looking for lighter, humorous articles, as well as features on colleges and universities, careers, jobs."

TEEN BEAT, MacFadden Holdings, 233 Park Ave. S., New York NY 10016. Staff written. "Prefers not to share information."

TEEN DREAM, Starline Publications, 63 Grand Ave., River Edge NJ 07661. (201)487-6124. Fax: (201)487-6390. Editor: Anne Raso. 20% freelance written. Bimonthly magazine of teen entertainment. Estab. 1988. Circ. 180,000. Pays on publication. Byline given. Offers 50% kill fee. Buys all rights. Submit seasonal/holiday material 3 months in advance. Reports in 2 months. Sample copy $3.

Nonfiction: Photo feature. No fiction or poetry; celebrity interviews exclusively. Buys 50 mss/year. "Call editor about ms." Length: 500-1,000 words. Pays $50-100 for assigned articles. Sometimes pays expenses of writers on assignment.

Photos: State availability of or send photos with submission. Reviews color slides and 8×10 b&w prints. Offers $25-125/photo. Captions required. Buys one-time rights.

'TEEN MAGAZINE, 8490 Sunset Blvd., Hollywood CA 90069. (212)854-2222. Editor: Roxanne Camron. 20-30% freelance written. Prefers to work with published/established writers. Monthly magazine for teenage girls. Circ. 1.1 million. Publishes ms an average of 6 months after acceptance. Buys all rights. Reports in 4 months. Sample copy and writer's guidelines for 9×12 SAE with $2.50.

Fiction: Dealing specifically with teenage girls and contemporary teen issues. Suspense, humorous and romance. "Young love is all right, but teens want to read about it in more relevant settings." Length: 2,500-4,000 words. Pays $100. Sometimes pays the expenses of writers on assignment.

Tips: "No fiction with explicit language, casual references to drugs, alcohol, sex, or smoking; no fiction with too depressing outcome."

‡TEENS TODAY, Church of the Nazarene, 6401 The Paseo, Kansas City MO 64131. (816)333-7000. Contact: Editor. 25% freelance written. Eager to work with new/unpublished writers. Weekly magazine for junior and senior high teens, to age 18, attending Church of the Nazarene Sunday School. Circ. 55,000. **Pays on acceptance.** Publishes ms an average of 14 months after acceptance. Byline given. Buys first and reprint rights. Submit seasonal/holiday material 10 months in advance. Simultaneous, photocopied and previously published submissions OK. Submissions not returned without SASE. Reports in 2 months. Sample copy and writer's guidelines 50¢ for SAE with 2 first class stamps.

Photos: Pays $10-30 for 8×10 b&w glossy prints.

Fiction: Adventure (if Christian principles are apparent), humorous, religious and romance (keep it clean). Buys 1 ms/issue. Send complete ms. Length: 1,000-1,500 words. Pays 3½¢/word, first rights; 3¢/word, second rights.

Tips: "We look for quality fiction dealing with teen issues: peers, self, parents, vocation, Christian truths related to life, etc. We do not condone dancing, drinking, drugs or premarital sex. Avoid overused themes."

WITH MAGAZINE, Faith and Life Press and Mennonite Publishing House, 722 Main St., P.O. Box 347, Newton KS 67114-0347. (316)283-5100. Coeditors: Eddy Hall, Carol Duerksen. 60% freelance written. Magazine for teenagers published 8 times/year. "We approach Christianity from an Anabaptist-Mennonite perspective. Our purpose is to disciple youth within congregations." Circ. 6,100. **Pays on acceptance.** Byline given. Buys one-time rights. Submit seasonal/holiday material 6 months in advance. Simultaneous and previously published submissions OK. Send typed ms with rights for sale noted, including information about when and where the article previously appeared. For reprints, pays 50% of the amount paid for an original article. Reports in 1 month on queries; 2 months on mss. Sample copy for 9×12 SAE with 4 first class stamps. Writer's guidelines and theme list for #10 SAE. Additional detailed guidelines for first person stories and/or how-to articles available for #10 SAE.

Nonfiction: Humor, personal experience, religious, how-to and youth. Buys 15 mss/year. Send complete ms. Length: 400-1,800 words. Pays 4¢/word for simultaneous rights; 2¢/word for reprint rights for unsolicited articles. Higher rates for first person stories and how-to articles written on assignment. (Query on these.)

Photos: Sometimes pays the expenses of writers on assignment. Send photos with submission. Reviews 8×10 b&w prints. Offers $10-50/photo. Identification of subjects required. Buys one-time rights.

Fiction: Humorous, religious, youth and parables. Buys 12 mss/year. Send complete ms. Length: 500-2,000 words. Payment same as nonfiction.

Poetry: Avant-garde, free verse, Haiku, light verse and traditional. Buys 20-25 poems. Pays $10-25.

Tips: "We're looking for more wholesome humor, not necessarily religious—fiction, nonfiction, cartoons, light verse. We're eager to see reprints from today's top writers for Christian teens."

YM, 685 3rd Ave., New York NY 10017. "Prefers not to share information."

‡YOU! MAGAZINE, The Alternative Youth Magazine, Veritas Communications Inc., #102, 29800 Agoura Rd., Agoura Hills CA 91301. (818)991-1813. Editor: Paul Lauer. Managing Editor: Tom Ehart. Contact: Tom Ehart. 50% freelance written. Monthly religious (Catholic) teen tabloid covering pop culture through the eyes of faith. Estab. 1987. Circ. 35,000 paid; 100,000 readership. Pays on publication. Publishes ms an average of 2 months after acceptance. Byline given. Buys one-time rights and second serial (reprint) rights. Editorial lead time 2 months. Submit seasonal material 4 months in advance. Simultaneous and previously published submsisions OK. Query for electronic submissions. Reports in 2 months on queries. Sample copy for 10×15 SAE with 5 first class stamps. Writer's guidelines free on request.
Nonfiction: Humor, inspirational, interview/profile, personal experience, religious and teen related social. "No adult material." Buys 25-50 mss/year. Query with published clips. Length: 100-1,600 words. Pays $10 minimum. Sometimes pays expenses of writers on assignment.
Photos: Send photos with submission. Reviews transparencies and 4×6 or 5×7 prints. Negotiates payment individually. Captions and identification of subjects required.
Columns/Departments: School (school issues facing teens), 350 words; Family (family issues facing teens), 350 words; and Friends (friends issues facing teens), 350 words. Buys 30 mss/year. Query with published clips. Pays $20-35.
Tips: "School, Family, Friends and Issues are open to freelancers. Give the problem with both positives and negatives and then offer solutions or ways in which Christian teens can deal with the situation from a faith perspective. Written in the language of teens!"

YOUNG SALVATIONIST, The Salvation Army, P.O. Box 269, Alexandria VA 22313-0269. . (703)684-5500. Fax: (703)684-5539. Editor: Capt. Lesa Salyer. 75% freelance written. Works with a small number of new/ unpublished writers each year. Monthly Christian magazine for high school teens. "Only material with a definite Christian emphasis or from a Christian perspective will be considered." Circ. 48,000. Pays on acceptance. Publishes ms an average of 10 months after acceptance. Byline given. Buys first North American serial, first, one-time or second serial (reprint) rights. Publishes reprints of previously published articles. Send tearsheet or photocopy of article or typed ms with rights for sale noted. Include information about when and where the article previously appeared. For reprints, pays 100% of the amount paid for an original article. Submit seasonal/holiday material 6 months in advance. Reports in 1 month. *Writer's Market* recommends allowing 2 months for reply. Sample copy for 9×12 SAE with 3 first class stamps. Writer's guidelines for #10 SASE.
Nonfiction: Inspirational, how-to, humor, interview/profile, personal experience, photo feature and religious. "Articles should deal with issues of relevance to teens today; avoid 'preachiness' or moralizing." Buys 60 mss/year. Send complete ms. Length: 500-1,200 words. Pays 10¢/word.
Fiction: Adventure, fantasy, humorous, religious, romance, science fiction—all from a Christian perspective. Length: 500-1,200 words. Pays 10¢/word.
Tips: "Study magazine, familiarize yourself with the unique 'Salvationist' perspective of *Young Salvationist*; learn a little about the Salvation Army; media, sports, sex and dating are strongest appeal."

YOUTH UPDATE, St. Anthony Messenger Press, 1615 Republic St., Cincinnati OH 45210-1289. (513)241-5615. Editor: Carol Ann Morrow. 90% freelance written. Monthly newsletter of faith life for teenagers, "designed to attract, instruct, guide and challenge Catholics of high school age by applying the Gospel to modern problems/situations." Circ. 35,000. Pays on acceptance. Publishes ms an average of 6 months after acceptance. Byline given. Reports in 2-3 months. Sample copy and writer's guidelines for #10 SASE.
Nonfiction: Inspirational, practical self-help and spiritual. Buys 12 mss/year. Query. Length: 2,200-2,300 words. Pays $350-400. Sometimes pays expenses of writers on assignment. No reprints.
Tips: "Query first!"

Travel, Camping and Trailer

Travel magazines give travelers indepth information about destinations, detailing the best places to go, attractions in the area and sites to see—but they also keep them up-to-date about potential negative aspects of these destinations. Publications in this category tell tourists and campers the where-tos and how-tos of travel. This category is extremely competitive, demanding quality writing, background information and professional photography. Each has its own slant and should be studied carefully before sending submissions.

ACCENT, Meridian International Inc., 1720 Washington, P.O. Box 10010, Ogden UT 84409. (801)394-9446. 60-70% freelance written. Works with a small number of new/unpublished writers each year. Monthly inhouse travel magazine distributed by various companies to employees, customers, stockholders, etc. "Readers are predominantly upscale, mainstream, family oriented." Circ. 110,000. **Pays on acceptance.** Publishes ms an average of 3 months after acceptance. Byline given. Buys first rights, second serial (reprint) and nonexclusive reprint rights. Simultaneous and previously published submissions OK. Reports in 2 months with SASE. Sample copy $1 for 9×12 SAE. Writer's guidelines for #10 SASE. Requests should be addressed Attn: Editorial Staff.
Nonfiction: "We want upbeat pieces slanted toward the average traveler, but we use some exotic travel. Resorts, cruises, hiking, camping, health retreats, historic sites, sports vacations, national or state forests and parks are all featured. No articles without original color photos." Buys 40 mss/year. Query. Length: 1,200 words. Pays 15¢/word.
Photos: Send color photos with ms. Pays $35 for color transparencies; $50 for cover. Captions and model releases required. Buys one-time rights. Review 35mm or larger transparencies and 5×7 or 8×10 color prints.
Tips: "Write about interesting places. We are inundated with queries for stories on California and the southeastern coast. Excellent color transparencies are essential. Most rejections are because of poor quality photography or the writer didn't study the market. We are using three times as many domestic pieces as foreign because of our readership. Avoid budget approaches and emphasize professionals who will take the worry out of your travel."

‡ADVENTURE FLORIDA, Gibbons Publishing, P.O. Box 22748, Ft. Lauderdale FL 33335, Editor: Gibbons D. Cline. Contact: Diane Thompson, associate editor. Annual magazine covering tourism and travel in Florida. "*Adventure Florida*, is a slick, glossy book with high quality art. Editorial must match quality of art, so book becomes tabletop keepsake, before and after vacation. We highlight tourism hotspots in major cities around Florida." Estab. 1987. Circ. 50,000. Pays on publication. Publishes ms 6-8 months after acceptance. Byline given. Buys all rights. Editorial lead time 8-12 months. Query for electronic submissions. Reports in 6-8 weeks on queries; 4-6 months on mss. Writer's guidelines free on request.
Nonfiction: Historical/nostalgic, travel and attractions. "We are seeking visitors' guide/tourism articles for following areas: Panhandle, (Pensacola, Ft. Walton Beach, Panama City, Tallahassee), Gainsville, Jacksonville, St. Augustine, Ft. Myers, Naples, Sarasota-Bradenton, Cape Canaveral-Cocoa Beach, Daytona Beach. Rentals—cars, accomodations, etc.—any city. Dining—any city. We don't want to see anything else—(vacation experiences especially, how-to, erotica, religious.)" Buys 5-10 mss/year. Query with published clips. Length: 800-2,500 words. Pays $2/column inch.
Photos: State availability of photos with submission. Reviews any size transparencies and prints and slides. Offers no additional payment for photos accepted with ms or negotiates payment individually. Model releases, identification of subjects required.
Fillers: Anecdotes (historical), and facts (trivia). Buys 3-5/year. Length: 50-600 words. Pays $2/column inch to $100.
Tips: "Do not write about a place to which you've never been. Please attach 1 page resume with query and/ or mss. We *only* want tourism-oriented articles pertaining to Florida. Nothing else is acceptable. Thorough research is advised. Please, no personal vacation experiences. We are most open to articles covering shopping, dining and attractions (especially in north and west Florida). Pick a city and detail: where to stay, what to do and see, where to eat, out-of-the-way places. Be *thorough*, don't suggest one place (no reviews), but cover as many attractions, for example, as are available in the area."

‡ADVENTURE WEST, America's Guide to Discovering the West, Ski West Publications, Inc., P.O. Box 3210, Incline Village NV 89450. (702)832-3700. Editor: Marianne Porter. Managing Editor: Katrina Veit. Contact: Marianne Porter, editor. 80% freelance written. Quarterly magazine covering adventure travel in the West. Estab. 1992. Circ. 150,000. Pays on publication. Publishes ms an average of 4-6 months after acceptance. Byline given. Offers 20% kill fee. Buys first North American serial rights. Editorial lead time 3 months. Submit seasonal material 5-6 months in advance. Simultaneous submissions OK. Reports in 6-8 weeks on queries; 2 months on mss. Sample copy $2.50. Writer's guidelines free on request.
Nonfiction: Historical/nostalgic, humor, interview/profile, personal experience, photo feature and travel. "We only publish adventure travel done in the West, including Alaska, Hawaii, western Canada and western Mexico." Buys 40 mss/year. Query with published clips. Length: 1,000-2,500 words. Pays $150-500. Sometimes pays expenses of writers on assignment.
Photos: Send photos with submission. Reviews transparencies and slides. Negotiates payment individually. Captions and identification of subjects required. "We need itemized list of photos submitted." Buys one-time rights.
Columns/Departments: Buys 40-48 mss/year. Query with published clips. Pays $150-450.
Fiction: Humorous and western. "We publish humorous experiences in the West; that is the only fiction we accept." Buys 4 mss/year. Query with published clips. Length: 1,000-1,500 words. Pays $270-450.
Poetry: Cowboy poetry. "We don't want to see anything *but* cowboy poetry." Buys 3-4 poems/year. Submit maximum 2 poems. Length: 30-60 lines. Pays $20-100.

Fillers: David Webster, events editor. Facts, gags to be illustrated by cartoonist and newsbreaks. Buys 12-20/year. Length: 50-100 words. Pays $150-300.

Tips: "We like exciting, inspirational first-person stories on adventure. If the query or the unsolicited ms grabs us, we will use it. Our writer's guidelines are comprehensive. Follow them."

AMOCO TRAVELER, K.L. Publications, Suite 105, 2001 Killebrew Dr., Bloomington MN 55425. Editor: Mary Lou Brooks. 80% freelance written. Quarterly magazine published for the Amoco Traveler Club. Circ. 55,000. Pays on acceptance by client. Byline given. Buys various rights. "This publication is a mix of original and reprinted material." Previously published submissions OK. Submit seasonal/holiday material 8 months in advance. Simultaneous submissions OK. Reports in 1 month. *Writer's Market* recommends allowing 2 months for reply. Sample copy for 9 × 12 SAE with 3 first class stamps. Writer's guidelines for #10 SASE.

Nonfiction: Focus is on US destinations by car, although occasionally will use a foreign destination. Traveler Roads showcases a North American city or area, its attractions, history and accomodations; Traveler Focus features a romantic, getaway destination for the armchair traveler; Traveler Weekends focuses on an activity-oriented destination. Length: 1,200-1,500 words. Pays $325-425 for originals; $100-150 for reprints.

Columns/Departments: Healthwise (travel-related health tips). Length: 500-600 words. Pays $175.

Photos: Reviews 35mm transparencies. No b&w. Pay varies.

‡ARUBA NIGHTS, Nights Publications, 1831 Rene Levesque Blvd. W., Montreal, Quebec H3H 1R4 Canada. Fax: (514)931-6273. Editor: Stephen Trotter. Managing Editor: Zelly Zuskin. Contact: Stephen Trotter, Editor. 80% freelance written. Destination lifestyle magazine. Annual magazine covering the Aruban vacation lifestyle experience. Estab. 1988. Circ. 185,000. **Pays on acceptance.** Publishes ms an average of 6-10 months after acceptance. Offers 15% kill fee. Buys first North American serial and first Caribbean rights. Editorial lead time 2 months. Query for electronic submissions. Reports in 2 weeks on queries; 1 month on mss. *Writer's Market* recommends allowing 2 months for reply. Sample copy $5. Writer's guidelines free on request.

Nonfiction: General interest, historical/nostalgic, how-to gamble, sail, etc., humor, inspirational, interview/profile, opinion, personal experience, photo feature, travel, Aruban culture, art, activities, entertainment and topics relative to vacationers in Aruba. "No negative pieces or stale rewrites." Buys 5-10 mss/year. Query with published clips. Length: 250-750 words. Pays $125-350 for assigned articles; $100-250 for unsolicited articles.

Photos: State availability with submission. Offers $25-100/photo. Captions, model releases and identification of subjects required. Buys one-time rights.

Tips: "Demonstrate your voice in your query letter. Focus on individual aspects of the Aruban lifestyle and vacation experience (e.g., art, gambling tips, windsurfing, a colorful local character, a personal experience, etc.), rather than generalized overviews. Provide an angle that will be entertaining to both vacationers and Arubans."

ASU TRAVEL GUIDE, ASU Travel Guide, Inc., 1525 E. Francisco Blvd., San Rafael CA 94901. (415)459-0300. Fax: (415)459-0494. Managing Editor: Christopher Gil. 80% freelance written. Quarterly guidebook covering international travel features and travel discounts for well-traveled airline employees. Estab. 1970. Circ. 60,000. Publishes ms an average of 4 months after acceptance. Byline given. Buys first North American serial rights, first and second rights to the same material, and second serial (reprint) rights to material originally published elsewhere; also makes work-for-hire assignments. Submit seasonal/holiday material 6 months in advance. Simultaneous queries and simultaneous and previously published submissions OK. Send tearsheet of article with information about when and where the article previously appeared. For reprints, pays 100% of the amount paid for an original article. Reports in 1 year. Sample copy available for 6½ × 9 SAE with $1.05 postage. Writer's guidelines for #10 SASE.

Nonfiction: International travel articles "similar to those run in consumer magazines. Not interested in amateur efforts from inexperienced travelers or personal experience articles that don't give useful information to other travelers." Buys 16 ms/year. Destination pieces only; no "Tips On Luggage" articles. Unsolicited mss or queries without SASE will not be acknowledged. No telephone queries. Length: 1,500-1,800 words. Pays $200.

Photos: "Interested in clear, high-contrast photos." Reviews 5 × 7 and 8 × 10 b&w or color prints. "Payment for photos is included in article price; photos from tourist offices are acceptable."

Tips: "Query with samples of travel writing and a list of places you've recently visited. We appreciate clean and simple style. Keep verbs in the active tense and involve the reader in what you write. Avoid 'cute' writing, coined words and stale cliches. The most frequent mistakes made by writers in completing an article for us are: 1) Lazy writing—using words to describe a place that could describe any destination such as 'there is so much to do in (fill in destination) that whole guidebooks have been written about it'; 2) Including fare and tour package information—our readers make arrangements through their own airline."

BACKPACKER, Rodale Press, Inc., 33 E. Minor St., Emmaus PA 18098-0099. (215)967-8296. Fax: (215)967-8960. Editor: John Viehman. Managing Editor: Tom Shealey. 25% freelance written. Magazine published 9 times/year covering wilderness travel. Estab. 1973. Circ. 210,000. **Pays on acceptance.** Byline given. Offers

25% kill fee. Buys one-time rights or all rights. Publishes reprints of previously published articles. Send tearsheet of article including information about when and where the article previously appeared. Reports in 2 months. Writer's guidelines for #10 SASE.

Nonfiction: Essays, expose, historical/nostalgic, how-to (expedition planner), humor, inspirational, interview/profile, new product, opinion, personal experience, technical and travel. No step-by-step accounts of what you did on your summer vacation—stories that chronicle every rest stop and gulp of water. Query with published clips and SASE. Length: 750-3,000 words. Pays $400. Sometimes pays (pre-determined) expenses of writers on assignment.

Photos: State availability of photos with submission. Amount varies—depends on size of photo used. Buys one-time rights.

Columns/Departments: "What we want are features that let us and the readers 'feel' the place, and experience your wonderment, excitement, disappointment or other emotions encountered 'out there.' If we feel like we've been there after reading your story, you've succeeded." Footnotes "News From All Over" (adventure, environment, wildlife, trails, techniques, organizations, special interests—well-written, entertaining, short, newsy item) 50-500 words; Geosphere (essay about some biological, psychological or scientific aspect of the natural world, often takes a philosophical approach, should offer the reader a fresh perspective on the natural world), 750-1,200 words; Body Language (in-the-field column) 750-1,200 words; Moveable Feast (food-related aspects of wilderness: nutrition, cooking techniques, recipes, products and gear), 500-750 words; Weekend Wilderness (three brief but detailed guides to wilderness areas, providing thorough trip-planning information, only enough anecdote to give a hint, then the where/when/hows) 500-750 words; Technique (ranging from beginner to expert focus, written by people with solid expertise, details ways to improve performance, how-to-do-it instructions, information on equipment manufacturers and places readers can go), 750-1,500 words; and Backcountry (personal perspectives, quirky and idiosyncratic, humorous critiques, manifestos and misadventures, interesting angle, lesson, revelation or moral), 750-1,200 words. Buys 25-50 mss/year. Query with published clips. Pays $25-350. No phone calls regarding story ideas. Written queries only.

Tips: "Our best advice is to read the publication—most freelancers don't know the magazine at all. The best way to break in is with an article for the Backcountry, Weekend Wilderness or Footnotes Department."

BAJA TIMES, Editorial Playas De Rosarito, S.A., P.O. Box 5577, Chula Vista CA 91912-5577. Fax: 01152-661-22366. Editor: John W. Utley. 90% freelance written. Monthly tourist and travel publication on Baja California, Mexico. "Oriented to the Baja California, Mexico aficionada—the tourist and those Americans who are living in Baja California or have their vacation homes there. Articles should be slanted to Baja." Estab. 1978. Pays on publication. Publishes ms an average of 8 months after acceptance. Byline given. Buys first rights. Publishes reprints of previously published articles. Send typed ms with rights for sale noted, including information about when and where the article previously appeared. For reprints, pays 100% of the amount paid for an original article. Submit seasonal/holiday material 4 months in advance. Reports in 3 months. Sample copy for 9×12 SAE with 5 first class stamps. Free writer's guidelines.

Nonfiction: General interest, historical/nostalgic, humor, personal experience, photo feature and travel. All with Baja California slant. "Nothing that describes any negative aspects of Mexico (bribes, bad police, etc.). We are a positive publication." Query with or without published clips or submit complete ms. Length: 750-1,600 words. Pays $50-100 for assigned articles; $35-50 for unsolicited articles. Sometimes pays expenses of writers on assignment.

Photos: Send photos with submission. Reviews 5×7 prints. Captions and identification of subjects required. Buys one-time rights.

Tips: "Take a chance—send in that Baja California related article. We guarantee to read them all. Over the years we have turned up some real winners from our writers—many who do not have substantial experience. The entire publication is open. We buy an average of 6 freelance each issue. Virtually any subject is acceptable as long as it has a Baja California slant. Remember Tijuana, Mexico (on the border with San Diego, CA) is the busiest border crossing in the world. We are always interested in material relating to Tijuana, Rosarito, Ensenada, San Felipe, La Paz."

CAMPING & RV MAGAZINE, Camping Voice of Midwest, P.O. Box 36, Iola WI 54945-0036. (715)445-4306. Fax: (715)445-4306. Editor: Craig Henrich. 75% freelance written. Monthly magazine on camping in the Midwest states. "We accept both casual and technical articles dealing with camping, and destination pieces from our coverage area." Estab. 1985. Circ. 25,000. Pays on publication. Publishes ms an average of 6 months after acceptance. Byline given. Buys first, one-time or second serial (reprint) rights. Submit seasonal/holiday material 3 months in advance. Previously published submissions OK; send typed ms with rights for sale noted and information about when and where the article previously appeared. Pays 100% of their fee for an original article. Reports in 6 months. Sample copy and writer's guidelines for #10 SAE with 8 first class stamps.

Nonfiction: General interest, how-to, personal experience, photo feature, technical and travel. "No articles of destinations out of our coverage area." Buys 60 mss/year. Send complete ms. Length: 1,000-2,000 words. Pays 5¢/word.

Photos: State availability of photos with submission. Reviews prints. Pays $5 per photo. Identification of subjects required. Buys one-time rights.

Columns/Departments: Living on Wheels; Camping Comforts; RV Wife; and Care of RV (hints, suggestions, general interest, technical, equipment care), 1,000 words. Buys 50 mss/year. Query. Pays 5¢/word.

Fillers: Anecdotes and facts. Buys 12/year. Length: 500-1,000 words. Pays 3-5¢/word.

Tips: "Write from a campground background—be knowledgable about how and where to camp as well as camping related activities."

CAMPING TODAY, Official Publication of National Campers & Hikers Association, 126 Hermitage Rd., Butler PA 16001-8509. (412)283-7401. Editors: DeWayne Johnston and June Johnston. 30% freelance written. Prefers to work with published/established writers. Monthly official membership publication of the NCHA, "the largest nonprofit family camping and RV organization in the United States and Canada. Members are heavily oriented toward RV travel, both weekend and extended vacations. A small segment is interested in hiking. Concentration is on member activities in chapters. Group is also interested in conservation and wildlife. The majority of members are retired." Estab. 1983. Circ. 25,000. Pays on publication. Publishes ms an average of 6 months after acceptance. Byline given. Buys one-time rights. Submit seasonal/holiday material 3 months in advance. Simultaneous and previously published submissions OK; send typed ms with rights for sale noted and information about when and where the article previously appeared. Pays 50% of their fee for an original article. Reports in 1 month. *Writer's Market* recommends allowing 2 months for reply. Sample copy and guidelines for 4 first class stamps. Writer's guidelines for #10 SASE.

Nonfiction: Travel (interesting places to visit by RV, camping); humor (camping or travel related, please, no "our first campout stories"); interview/profile (interesting campers); new products; and technical (RVs related). Buys 10-15 mss/year. Send complete ms with photos. Length: 750-2,000 words. Pays $50-150.

Photos: Send photos with ms. Need b&w or sharp color prints inside (we can make prints from slides) and vertical transparencies for cover. Captions required.

Tips: "Freelance material on RV travel, RV maintenance/safety, and items of general camping interest throughout the United States and Canada will receive special attention."

‡CANCÚN NIGHTS, Nights Publications, 1831 Rene Levesque Blvd. West, Montreal, Quebec H3H 1R4 Canada. Fax: (514)931-6273. Editor: Stephen Trotter. Managing Editor: Zelly Zuskin. Contact: Stephen Trotter, Editor. 80% freelance written. Destination lifestyle magazine. Semiannual magazine covering the Cancún vacation experience. Seeking "upbeat, entertaining lifestyle articles: colorful profiles of locals; lively features on culture, activities, night life, dining, special events, historical attractions, Mayan achievements; how-to features; humor. Our audience is the North American vacationer." Estab. 1991. Circ. 500,000. **Pays on acceptance.** Publishes ms an average of 6-10 months after acceptance. Offers 15% kill fee. Buys first North American serial rights and first Mexican rights. Editorial lead time 2 months. Query for electronic submissions. Reports 2 weeks on queries; 1 month on mss. *Writer's Market* recommends allowing 2 months for reply. Sample copy $5. Writer's guidelines free on request.

• This publisher is interested in hearing from Spanish writers who are familiar with Cancún.

Nonfiction: General interest, historical/nostalgic, how-to let vacationers get the most from their holiday, humor, inspirational, interview/profile, opinion, personal experience, photo feature, travel, local culture, art, activities, night life, and topics relative to vacationers in Cancún. Does not want to see negative pieces, stale rewrites. Buys 8-12 mss/year. Query with published clips. Length: 250-750 words. Pays $125-350 for assigned articles; $100-250 for unsolicited articles.

Photos: State availability of photos with submission. Reviews transparencies. Offers $25-100/photo. Captions, model releases and identification of subjects required. Buys one-time rights.

Tips: "Demonstrate your voice in your query letter. Focus on individual aspects of the Cancún lifestyle and vacation experience (e.g., art, history, snorkeling, fishing, a colorful local character, a personal experience, etc.), entertaining to both vacationers and residents."

CARIBBEAN TRAVEL AND LIFE, Suite 830, 8403 Colesville Rd., Silver Spring MD 20910. (301)588-2300. Editor-in-Chief: Veronica Gould Stoddart. 90% freelance written. Prefers to work with published/established writers. Bimonthly magazine covering travel to the Caribbean, Bahamas and Bermuda. Estab. 1985. Circ. 105,000. Pays on publication. Publishes ms an average of 3 months after acceptance. Byline given. Offers 25% kill fee. Buys first North American serial rights. Submit seasonal/holiday material 6 months in advance. Reports in 2 months. Sample copy for 9 × 12 SAE with 6 first class stamps. Writer's guidelines for #10 SASE.

Nonfiction: General interest, how-to, interview/profile, culture, personal experience and travel. No "guidebook rehashing; superficial destination pieces or critical exposes." Buys 30 mss/year. Query with published clips. Length: 2,000-2,500 words. Pays $550.

Photos: Send photos with submission. Reviews 35mm transparencies. Offers $75-400/photo. Captions and identification of subjects required. Buys one-time rights.

Columns/Departments: Resort Spotlight (in-depth review of luxury resort); Tradewinds (focus on one particular kind of water sport or sailing/cruising); Island Buys (best shopping for luxury goods, crafts, duty-free); Island Spice (best cuisine and/or restaurant reviews with recipes); all 1,000-1,500 words; Caribbeana (short items on great finds in travel, culture, and special attractions), 500 words. Buys 36 mss/year. Query with published clips or send complete ms. Length: 500-1,250 words. Pays $75-200.

Tips: "We are especially looking for stories with a personal touch and lively, entertaining anecdotes, as well as strong insight into people and places being covered. Writer should demonstrate why he/she is the best person to do that story based on extensive knowledge of the subject, frequent visits to destination, residence in destination, specialty in field."

CHEVY OUTDOORS, A Celebration of American Recreation and Leisure, The Aegis Group: Publishers, 30400 Van Dyke, Warren MI 48093. (313)574-9100. Editor: Michael Brudenell. 85% freelance written. Works with a small number of new/unpublished writers each year. Quarterly magazine covering outdoor recreation and adventure. Circ. 1 million. Pays on publication. Publishes ms an average of 3-6 months after acceptance. Offers 25% kill fee. Byline given. Buys first, one-time or second serial (reprint) rights. Submit seasonal/holiday material 6 months in advance. Simultaneous and previously published submissions OK. Reports in 6 weeks. Sample copy for 9×12 SAE with 5 first class stamps.

Nonfiction: Book excerpts; historical/nostalgic; how-to (on outdoor topics—camping, fishing, etc.); humor; interview/profile (on outdoors people, such as authorities in their fields); personal experience (must be outdoor or wilderness related); photo feature; technical (new technologies for campers, anglers, hunters, etc.); travel; and stories on new trends in outdoor recreation. "No exposés or negative articles; we like an upbeat, positive approach." Buys 50 mss/year. Query with published clips. Length: 200-1,500 words. Pays $100-750 for assigned articles; $100-500 for unsolicited articles. Sometimes pays the expenses of writers on assignment.

Photos: Send photos with submission. Reviews 35mm or larger transparencies. Offers $25-100/photo. Model releases and identification of subjects required. Buys one-time rights; sometimes all rights.

Columns/Departments: Outdoor Photography (how-tos by established photographers with national reputation in outdoor photography) and Outdoors People (profiles of notable outdoors enthusiasts or exceptional people who do work related to outdoor recreation). Buys 8-12 mss/year. Query with published clips. Length: 800-1,500 words. Pays $400-750.

Fillers: Anecdotes, facts and newsbreaks. Buys 25-30/year. Length: 25-200 words.

● Ranked as one of the best markets for freelance writers in *Writer's Digest* magazine's annual "Top 100 Markets," January 1993.

Tips: "Stories that are dynamic and active, and stories that focus on people will have a better chance of getting in. Focus queries tightly and look beyond the obvious. Use this as a touchstone—Is this a story that I would be compelled to read if I found it on a coffee table or in a waiting room? If the answer is 'yes,' we want to hear from you. Our features well is the best freelance target. Travel, personality profiles or activity features are probably the best ticket in. But the idea has to be fresh and original, and the copy has to sing. New or unpublished writers should write on topics with which they are *very* familiar; expertise can compensate for a lack of experience."

CHICAGO TRIBUNE, Travel Section, 435 N. Michigan Ave., Chicago IL 60611. (312)222-3999. Travel Editor: Randy Curwen. Weekly Sunday newspaper leisure travel section averaging 24 pages aimed at vacation travelers. Circ. 1.2 million. Pays on publication. Publishes ms an average of 1½ months after acceptance. Byline given. Buys one-time rights. Submit seasonal/holiday material 2 months in advance. Simultaneous submissions OK. Query for electronic submissions. Reports in 2 weeks. Sample copy for large SAE with $1.50 postage. Writer's guidelines for #10 SASE.

Nonfiction: Essays, general interest, historical/nostalgic, how-to (travel, pack), humor, opinion, personal experience, photo feature and travel. "There will be 16 special issues in the next 18 months." Buys 500 mss/year. Send complete ms. Length: 500-2,000 words. Pays $100-350.

Photos: State availability of photos with submission. Reviews 35mm transparencies and 8×10 or 5×7 prints. Offers $100/color photo; $25/b&w photo. $100 for cover photo. Captions required. Buys one-time rights.

Tips: "Be professional. Use a word processor. Make the reader want to go to the area being written about. Our Page 3 Reader is a travel essay, hopefully with humor, insight, tear jerking. A great read. Only 1% of mss make it."

‡COAST TO COAST MAGAZINE, 3601 Calle Tecate, Camarillo CA 93012. Editor: Valerie Rogers. Associate Editor: Kathleen McLaughlin. 80% freelance written. Magazine published 8 times/year for members of Coast to Coast Resorts. Estab. 1972. Circ. 300,000. **Pays on acceptance.** Publishes ms an average of 3 months after acceptance. Byline given. Offers 33% kill fee. Buys first North American serial rights. Submit seasonal/holiday material 5 months in advance. Query for electronic submissions. Reports in 1 month on queries; 2 months on mss. Sample copy $2 for 9×12 SASE.

Nonfiction: Book excerpts, essays, general interest, historical/nostalgic, how-to, humor, inspirational, interview/profile, new product, opinion, personal experience, photo feature, technical and travel. Buys 35 mss/year. Query with published clips or send complete ms. Length: 500-2,500 words. Pays $75-500.

Photos: Send photos with submission. Reviews transparencies. Offers $50-600/photo. Identification of subjects required. Buys one-time rights.

Tips: "Send published clips along with queries, or story ideas will not be considered."

CONDÉ NAST TRAVELER, 350 Madison Ave., New York NY 10017. "Prefers not to share information."

THE COOL TRAVELER, The Rome Cappucino Review, P.O. Box 11975, Philadelphia PA 19145-0275. (215)440-0592. Editor: Bob Moore. Managing Editor: MaryBeth Feeney. 100% freelance written. Quarterly publication covering travel. "We do not emphasize affluence but rather the experiences one has while traveling: romance, adventure, thrills, chills, etc. We have even published excerpts from diaries!" Estab. 1988. Circ. 750-1,250. Pays on publication. Publishes ms an average of 2-3 months after acceptance. Byline given. Buys one-time rights. Submit seasonal/holiday material 4 months in advance. Simultaneous and previously published submissions OK. Query for electronic submissions. Reports in 1 month "unless we like it—then it could be 4-6 months." Sample copy $3. Free writer's guidelines.

Nonfiction: Personal experience, travel and art history. Special issues: Christmas and International Festival. "We don't want a listing of names and prices but personal experiences and unusual experiences." Buys 10 mss/year. Send complete ms. Length: 1,500 words maximum. Pays $5-20 for unsolicited articles.

• Looking for more feature articles.

Columns/Departments: Seasonal (material pertaining to a certain time of year: like a winter festival or summer carnival), 1,500 words maximum. Women travel; environmental issues; cultural topics—race and ethnicity. Pays $5-20.

Poetry: Free verse, light verse and traditional. No poetry that is too sentimental. Buys 10 poems/year. Submit maximum 3 poems. Length: 5-75 lines. Pays $5-20.

Tips: "Writers should have firsthand knowledge and experience of their topic or topics and be able to give the reader a feeling of being there through cultural, artistic and visual references. All areas are open to freelancers. The same tips apply toward seasonal material. The writer should connote to the reader a feeling of personal experience through the usage of cultural, artistic and visual references."

CRUISE TRAVEL MAGAZINE, World Publishing Co., 990 Grove St., Evanston IL 60201-4370. (708)491-6440. Editor: Robert Meyers. Managing Editor: Charles Doherty. 95% freelance written. Bimonthly magazine on cruise travel. "This is a consumer-oriented travel publication covering the world of pleasure cruising on large cruise ships (with some coverage of smaller ships), including ports, travel tips, roundups." Estab. 1979. **Pays on acceptance.** Publishes ms an average of 5 months after acceptance. Byline given. Offers 50% kill fee. Buys first North American serial, one-time or second serial (reprint) rights. Simultaneous submissions OK; send tearsheet or photocopy of article and typed ms with rights for sale noted. Pays 50% of their fee for an original article. Reports in 1 month. *Writer's Market* recommends allowing 2 months for reply. Sample copy $3 for 9 × 12 SAE with 6 first class stamps. Writer's guidelines for #10 SASE.

Nonfiction: General interest, historical/nostalgic, interview/profile, personal experience, photo feature, travel. "No daily cruise 'diary', My First Cruise, etc." Buys 72 mss/year. Query with or without published clips or send complete ms. Length: 500-2,000 words. Pays $100-400.

Photos: Send photos with submission. Reviews transparencies and prints. "Must be color, 35m preferred (other format OK); color prints second choice." Offers no additional payment for photos accepted with ms "but pay more for well-illustrated ms." Captions and identification of subjects required. Buys one-time rights.

Fillers: Anecdotes, facts. Buys 3 mss/year. Length: 300-700 words. Pays $75-200.

Tips: "Do your homework. Know what we do and what sorts of things we publish. Know the cruise industry—we can't use novices. Good, sharp, bright color photography opens the door fast."

‡CURAÇAO NIGHTS, Nights Publications, 1831 Rene Levesque Blvd. West, Montreal, Quebec H3H 1R4 Canada. Fax: (514)931-6273. Editor: Stephen Trotter. Managing Editor: Zelly Zuskin. Contact: Stephen Trotter. 80% freelance written. Annual magazine covering the Curaçao vacation experience. "We are seeking upbeat, entertaining lifestyle articles; colorful profiles of locals; lively features on culture, activities, night life, dining, special events, gambling; how-to features; humor. Our audience is the North American vacationer." Estab. 1989. Circ. 155,000. **Pays on acceptance.** Publishes ms an average of 6-10 months after acceptance. Byline given. Offers 15% kill fee. Buys first North American and first Caribbean rights. Editorial lead time 2 months. Query for electronic submissions. Reports in 2 weeks on queries; 1 month on mss. *Writer's Market* recommends allowing 2 months for reply. Sample copy $5. Writer's guidelines free on request.

Nonfiction: General interest, historical/nostalgic, how-to help a vacationer get the most from their vacation, humor, inspirational, interview/profile, opinion, personal experience, photo feature, travel, local culture, art, activities, night life, and topics relative to vacationers in Curaçao. "No negative pieces or stale rewrites." Buys 5-10 mss/year. Query with published clips. Length: 250-750 words. Pays $125 minimum, $350 maximum for assigned articles; $100 minimum, $250 maximum for unsolicited articles.

Photos: State availability of photos with submission. Reviews transparencies. Offers $25-100/photo. Captions, model releases and identification of subjects required. Buys one-time rights.

Tips: "Demonstrate your voice in your query letter. Focus on individual aspects of the island lifestyle and vacation experience (e.g., art, gambling tips, windsurfing, a colorful local character, a personal experience, etc.), rather than generalized overviews. Provide an angle that will be entertaining to both vacationers and Curaçaoans."

ENDLESS VACATION, Endless Vacation, P.O. 80260, Indianapolis IN 46280-0260. (317)871-9504. Fax: (317)871-9507. Editor: Helen W. O'Guinn. Associate Editor: B. Ancil Davis. Prefers to work with published/ established writers. Bimonthly magazine covering travel destinations, activities and issues that enhance the lives of vacationers. Estab. 1974. Circ. 861,156. **Pays on acceptance.** Publishes ms an average of 6 months after acceptance. Byline given. Buys first North American serial rights. Simultaneous submissions OK; send tearsheet of article and typed ms with rights for sale noted and information about when and where the article previously appeared. For reprints, pays 25% of the amount paid for an original article. Publishes novel excerpts. Reports in 1 month. *Writer's Market* recommends allowing 2 months for reply. Sample copy $5 for 9 × 12 SAE with 3 first class stamps. Writer's guidelines for #10 SASE.
Nonfiction: Contact: Manuscript Editor. Buys 24 mss/year (approximately). Most are from established writers already published in *Endless Vacation. Accepts very few unsolicited pieces.* Query with published clips. Length: 1,000-2,000 words. Pays $500-1,000 for assigned articles; $250-800 for unsolicited articles. Sometimes pays the expenses of writers on assignment.
Photos: Reviews 4 × 5 transparencies and 35mm slides. Offers $100-500/photo. Model releases and identification of subjects required. Buys one-time rights.
Columns/Departments: Compleat Traveler (on travel news and service-related information); and Weekender (on domestic weekend vacation travel). Query with published clips. Length: 800-1,000 words. Pays $150-600. Sometimes pays the expenses of writers on assignment. Also news items for Facts, Fads and Fun Stuff column on travel news, products or problems. Length: 100-200 words. Pays $100/item.
● Ranked as one of the best markets for freelance writers in *Writer's Digest* magazine's annual "Top 100 Markets," January 1993.
Tips: "We will continue to focus on travel trends and resort destinations. Articles must be packed with pertinent facts and applicable how-tos. Information — addresses, phone numbers, dates of events, costs — must be current and accurate. We like to see a variety of stylistic approaches, but in all cases the lead must be strong. A writer should realize that we require first-hand knowledge of the subject and plenty of practical information. For further understanding of *Endless Vacation*'s direction, the writer should study the magazine and guidelines for writers."

FAMILY MOTOR COACHING, Official Publication of the Family Motor Coach Association, 8291 Clough Pike, Cincinnati OH 45244-2796. (513)474-3622. Fax: (513)474-2332. Editor: Pamela Wisby Kay. Associate Editor: Robbin Maue. 80% freelance written. "We prefer that writers be experienced RVers." Monthly magazine emphasizing travel by motorhome, motorhome mechanics, maintenance and other technical information. Estab. 1963. Circ. 50,000. **Pays on acceptance.** Publishes ms an average of 8 months after acceptance. Buys first North American serial rights. Byline given. Submit seasonal/holiday material 4 months in advance. Reports in 2 months. Sample copy $2.50. Writer's guidelines for #10 SASE.
Nonfiction: Motorhome travel (various areas of country accessible by motor coach), how-to (do it yourself motor home projects and modifications), bus conversions, humor, interview/profile, new product, technical and nostalgia. Buys 15-20 mss/issue. Query with published clips . Length: 1,000-2,000 words. Pays $100-500.
Photos: State availability of photos with query. Offers no additional payment for b&w contact sheets, 35mm or 2¼ × 2¼ color transparencies. Captions and model releases required. Prefers first North American serial rights but will consider one-hire rights on photos only.
Tips: "The greatest number of contributions we receive are travel; therefore, that area is the most competitive. However, it also represents the easiest way to break in to our publication. Articles should be written for those traveling by self-contained motor home. The destinations must be accessible to motor home travelers and any peculiar road conditions should be mentioned."

‡GIBBONS-HUMMS GUIDE, Florida Keys-Key West, Gibbons Publishing, Inc., P.O. Box 2921, Key Largo FL 33037. (800)273-1026. Editor: Gibbons D. Cline. Contact: Diane Thompson, associate editor. 15% freelance written. Quarterly magazine covering travel, tourism. Targeted to tourists and frequent visitors to Florida Keys (Monroe County, FL, from Key Largo to Key West). Estab. 1972. Circ. 55,000. Pays on publication. Publishes ms an average of 3-6 months after acceptance. Byline given. Buys all rights. Editorial lead time 4-6 months. Submit seasonal material at least 6 months in advance. Query for electronic submissions. Reports in 2-6 months on queries; 1-3 months on mss. Sample copy free on request. Writer's guidelines free on request.
Nonfiction: General interest, historical/nostalgic, how-to (water sports), humor, new product (marine related), technical (water sports) and travel. Special issues: Reefs and wrecks — highlighting artificial and natural reefs offshore for fishing diving and snorkeling enthusiasts; Vacation accommodations — condos, bed and breakfast inns, resorts, hotels, hostels, etc. "No religious or erotic material. Please, please, please — no stories about your vacation in the Keys!" Buys 5-10 mss/year. Query with published clips. Length: 500-1,500 words. Pays $2/column inch.
Photos: State availability of photos with submission. Reviews any size transparencies and prints and slides. Model releases and identification of subjects required. Buys all rights.
Columns/Departments: Fishing Digest (fishing hotspots, how-to, new equipment), 1,000 words; Keys Under the Seas (diving how-to, new equipment), 1,000 words; and Touring Highlights (attractions: Key West, Lower Keys, Marathon, Islamorada, Key Largo), 1,000 words. Buys 5 mss/year. Query with published clips. Pays $2/column inch to $100.

Fillers: Facts, trivia, puzzles—crossword or otherwise. Buys 3-5/year. Length: 100-800 words. Pays $2/column inch to $100.

Tips: "Please send resume with query and/or mss. It is helpful to visit Keys before trying to write about them. Get a feel for unique attitude, atmosphere and lifestyle in the Keys. Focus on things to do, like water sports. Try it, then write about it—but not from a personal experience angle. Find unique angles: strange characters, humorous anecdotes, etc. What makes *your* experience in the Keys different from everyone else's? Find a special bargain? Use new, state-of-the-art equipment? Met a 90-year-old grandmother who windsurfs? We're looking for the unusual."

‡**GREAT EXPEDITIONS**, P.O. Box 18036, Raleigh NC 27619; or P.O. Box 8000-411, Abbotsford, British Columbia V2S 6H1 Canada. Fax: (919)847-0780. Editor: George Kane. 90% freelance written. Eager to work with new/unpublished writers. Quarterly magazine covering "off-the-beaten-path" destinations, outdoor recreation, cultural discovery, budget travel, socially-responsible tourism and working abroad. Estab. 1978. Circ. 15,000. Pays on publication. Buys first and second (reprint) rights. Simultaneous queries, and simultaneous and previously published submissions OK. Send photocopy of article or typed ms with rights for sale noted. Include information about when and where the article previously appeared. Send SASE for return of article and photos. Reports in 2 months. Sample copy $4. Free writer's guidelines.

Nonfiction: Articles range from very adventurous (living with an isolated tribe in the Philippines) to mildly adventurous (Spanish language school vacations in Guatemala and Mexico). We also like to see "how-to" pieces for adventurous travelers (i.e., How to Sail Around the World for Free, Swapping Homes with Residents of Other Countries, How to Get in on an Archaeological Dig). Buys 30 mss/year. Pays $100 maximum. Length 1,000-3,000 words, average length 1,500 words; accepts shorter 200 word.

Photos: B&w photos, color prints or slides should be sent with article. Captions required.

Tips: "It's best to send for a sample copy for a first-hand look at the style of articles we are looking for. If possible, we appreciate practical information for travelers, either in the form of a sidebar or incorporated into the article, detailing how to get there, where to stay, specific costs, where to write for visas or travel information."

ISLANDS, An International Magazine, Islands Publishing Company, 3886 State St., Santa Barbara CA 93105-3112. Fax: (805)569-0349. Editor: Joan Tapper. 95% freelance written. Works with established writers. Bimonthly magazine covering islands throughout the world. "We cover accessible and once-in-a-lifetime islands from many different perspectives: travel, culture, lifestyle. We ask our authors to give us the essence of the island and do it with literary flair." Estab. 1981. Circ. 170,000. **Pays on acceptance.** Publishes ms an average of 8 months after acceptance. Byline given. Buys all rights. Query for electronic submissions. Reports in 1 month on queries; 6 weeks on ms. Sample copy $5.50. Writer's guidelines for #10 SASE.

Nonfiction: General interest, personal experience, photo feature and any island-related material. No service stories. "Each issue contains 3-4 feature articles of roughly 2,000-4,000 words, and 4-5 departments, each of which runs approximately 750-1,500 words. Any authors who wish to be commissioned should send a detailed proposal for an article, an estimate of costs (if applicable) and samples of previously published work." Buys 25 feature mss/year. "The majority of our manuscripts are commissioned." Query with published clips or send complete ms. Feature length: 2,000-4,000 words. Pays $800-3,000. Pays expenses of writers on assignment.

Photos: State availability or send photos with query or ms. Pays $75-300 for 35mm transparencies. "Fine color photography is a special attraction of *Islands*, and we look for superb composition, technical quality and editorial applicability." Label slides with name and address, include captions, and submit in protective plastic sleeves. Identification of subjects required. Buys one-time rights.

Columns/Departments: "Arts, Profiles, Nature, Sports, Lifestyle, Encounters and Island Hopping featurettes—all island related. Brief Logbook items should be highly focused on some specific aspect of islands." Buys 50 mss/year. Query with published clips. Length: 500-1,500 words. Pays $100-700.

 • Ranked as one of the best markets for freelance writers in *Writer's Digest* magazine's annual "Top 100 Markets," January 1993.

Tips: "A freelancer can best break in to our publication with short (500-1,000 word) departments or Logbooks that are highly focused on some aspect of island life, history, people, etc. Stay away from general, sweeping articles. We are always looking for topics for our Islanders and Logbook pieces. We will be using big name writers for major features; will continue to use newcomers and regulars for columns and departments."

JOURNAL OF CHRISTIAN CAMPING, Christian Camping International, P.O. Box 646, Wheaton IL 60189-0646. Fax: (708)462-0499. Editor: John Ashmen. Assistant Editor: Hollis Pippin. 75% freelance written. Prefers to work with published/established writers. Bimonthly magazine emphasizing the broad scope of organized camping with emphasis on Christian camping. "Leaders of youth camps and adult conferences read our magazine to get practical help in ways to run their camps." Estab. 1963. Circ. 6,000. Pays on publication. Publishes ms an average of 4 months after acceptance. Buys first rights. Byline given. Reprints OK; send photocopy of article and information about when and where the article previously appeared. Pays 50% of their fee for an original article. Reports in 1 month. Sample copy $2.50 for 9 × 12 SAE. Writer's guidelines for #10 SASE.

Nonfiction: General interest (trends in organized camping in general and Christian camping in particular); how-to (anything involved with organized camping from motivating staff, to programming, to record keeping, to camper follow-up); inspirational (limited use, but might be interested in practical applications of Scriptural principles to everyday situations in camping, no preaching); interview (with movers and shakers in camping and Christian camping in particular; submit a list of basic questions first); and opinion (write a letter to the editor). Buys 20-30 mss/year. Query required. Length: 600-1,200 words. Pays 10¢/word.

Photos: Send photos with ms. Pays $25-150 for 5×7 b&w contact sheet or print; price negotiable for 35mm color transparencies. Buys first rights.

Tips: "The most frequent mistake made by writers is that they send articles unrelated to our readers. Ask for our publication guidelines first."

LEISUREWAYS, Canada Wide Magazines Ltd., Suite 1707, 2 Carlton St., Toronto, Ontario M5B 1J3 Canada. (416)595-5007. Fax: (416)942-6308. Editor: Deborah Milton. 80% freelance written. Bimonthly member magazine for CAA covering travel and leisure. "*Leisureways* goes to 580,000 members of Canadian Automobile Association in Ontario. Primarily travel articles plus auto-related material." Circ. 580,000. **Pays on acceptance.** Byline given. Offers 50% kill fee. Buys all rights. Query for electronic submission. Free sample copy. Writer's guidelines for #10 SASE.
 • Remember to use Canadian stamps or IRCs.

Nonfiction: Interview/profile, photo feature and travel. Buys 70 mss/year. Query with published clips or send complete ms. Length: 300-1,800 words. Pays 50¢/word (Canadian).

Photos: State availability of photos with submission. Reviews 35mm or any transparencies. Offers no additional payment for photos accepted with ms. Captions and identification of subjects required. Buys first North American serial rights.

Columns/Departments: Great Cities (profile of major cities), 1,000 words; and Automotive (general interest), 500-1,500 words. Buys 25 mss/year. Query with published clips or send complete ms.

Tips: "We look for stories with interesting angles—a bit out of the ordinary. Travel pieces aimed at the mature traveler are particularly good for our readership. We have enough material for the next 6 issues."

THE MATURE TRAVELER, Travel Bonanzas for 49ers-Plus, GEM Publishing Group, Box 50820, Reno NV 89513-0820. (702)786-7419. Editor: Gene E. Malott. 30% freelance written. Monthly newsletter on senior citizen travel. Estab. 1984. Circ. 2,200. **Pays on acceptance.** Publishes ms an average of 3 months after acceptance. Byline given. Offers 25% kill fee. Buys one-time rights. Submit seasonal/holiday material 3 months in advance. Simultaneous and previously published submissions OK ("if we know about it"). Send tearsheet or photocopy of article and information about when and where the article previously appeared. Pays 40-50% of their fee for an original article. Reports in 3 weeks. Sample copy and guidelines $1 for #10 SAE with 52¢ postage. Writer's guidelines only for #10 SASE.

Nonfiction: Travel for seniors. "General travel and destination pieces should be senior-specific, aimed at 49ers+." Query. Length: 600-1,200 words. Pays $50-100.

Photos: State availability of photos with submission. Reviews contact sheets and b&w (only) prints. Captions required. Buys one-time rights.

Tips: "Read the guidelines and write stories to our readers' needs—not to the general public."

‡MEXICO EVENTS, A Traveler's Guide, Travel Mexico Magazine Group, P.O. Box 188037, Carlsbad CA 92009-0801. (619)929-0707. Group Editor: Katharine A. Diáz. Bimonthly magazine covering tourism and travel to Mexico. "*Mexico Events* focuses on promoting Mexico as a travel destination to readers in the United States and Canada. Our interest is in the many worlds of Mexico. We cover the people and cultures of Mexico with regular sections on food, history, ecotourism, language, walking tours, shopping guides, outdoor recreation and driving." Estab. 1992. Circ. 201,000. Pays on publication. Publishes ms an average of 1-2 months after acceptance. Byline given. Buys first rights. Editorial lead time 2-3 months. Submit seasonal material 4-5 months in advance. Query for electronic submissions. Reports in 2 weeks on queries; 1 month on mss. *Writer's Market* recommends allowing 2 months for reply. Sample copy for 10×13 SAE with 6 first class stamps. Writer's guidelines for #10 SASE.

Nonfiction: Travel—Mexico only. "We do not want articles that focus on other countries. We cover Mexico exclusively." Buys 75 mss/year. Query with published clips. Length: 400-1,200 words. Pays $100.

Photos: Send photos with submission. Reviews transparencies, slides. Offers $20-200/photo. Captions and identification of subjects required. Buys one-time rights.

Tips: "We are looking for writers who know Mexico and who have experience writing about that country. A positive attitude about Mexico is a plus. We do not recommend sending mss, but rather prefer that writers send query with published clips (that will be kept on file unless SASE enclosed) along with list of their area(s) of expertise with regard to Mexico. Our features and columns are all open to freelancers. We are most interested in new discoveries or new twists on familiar destinations in Mexico. But keep in mind that most of our articles are on assignment basis."

‡**MEXICO WEST**, Mexico West Travel Club, Inc., Suite 107, 3450 Bonita Rd., Chula Vista CA 91910. (619)585-3033. Fax: (619)421-6002. Publisher/Editor: Carolyn Files. 75% freelance written. Monthly newsletter on Baja California and Mexico as a travel destination. "Our readers are travelers to Mexico, and are interested in retirement, RV news and tours. They are knowledgable but are always looking for new places to see." Estab. 1975. Circ. 5,000. Pays on publication. Publishes an average of 2 months after acceptance. Byline given. Buys first North American serial rights. Submit seasonal/holiday material 3 months in advance. Previously published submissions OK. Free sample copy. Writer's guidelines for #10 SAE with 2 first class stamps.

Nonfiction: Historical, humor, interview, personal experience and travel. Buys 36-50 mss/year. Send complete ms. Length: 900-1,500 words. Pays $50.

Photos: State availability of photos with submission. Reviews 3×5 prints. Offers no additional payment for photos accepted with ms. Captions required. Buys one-time rights.

MOTORLAND, California State Automobile Assn., 150 Van Ness Ave., San Francisco CA 94101. "Prefers not to share information."

NEW YORK DAILY NEWS, Travel Section, 220 E. 42 St., New York NY 10017. (212)210-1699. Fax: (212)210-2203. Travel Editor: Gunna Biteé Dickson. 30% freelance written. Prefers to work with published/established writers. Weekly tabloid. Circ. 1.8 million. "We are the largest circulating newspaper travel section in the country and take all types of articles ranging from experiences to service oriented pieces that tell readers how to make a certain trip." Pays on publication. Publishes ms an average of 3 months after acceptance. Byline given. Submit seasonal/holiday material 4 months in advance. Query for electronic submissions. Reports "as soon as possible." Writer's guidelines for #10 SASE.

Nonfiction: General interest, historical/nostalgic, humor, inspirational, personal experience and travel. "Most of our articles involve practical trips that the average family can afford—even if it's one you can't afford every year. We put heavy emphasis on budget saving tips for all trips. We also run stories now and then for the Armchair Traveler, an exotic and usually expensive trip. We are looking for professional quality work from professional writers who know what they are doing. The pieces have to give information and be entertaining at the same time. No 'How I Spent My Summer Vacation' type articles. No PR hype." Buys 60 mss/year. Query with SASE. Length: 1,000 words maximum. Pays $75-200.

Photos: "Good pictures always help sell good stories." State availability of photos with ms. Reviews contact sheets and negatives. Captions and identification of subjects required. Buys all rights.

Columns/Departments: Short Hops is based on trips to places within a 300-mile radius of New York City. Length: 700-800 words. Travel Watch gives practical travel advice.

Tips: "A writer might have some luck gearing a specific destination to a news event or date: In Search of Irish Crafts in March, for example, but do it well in advance."

NORTHEAST OUTDOORS, Northeast Outdoors, Inc., P.O. Box 2180, Waterbury CT 06722-2180. (203)755-0158. Fax: (203)755-3480. Editorial Director: John Florian. 30% freelance written. Works with a small number of new/unpublished writers each year. Monthly tabloid covering family camping in the Northeastern US. Estab. 1968. Circ. 14,000. Pays on publication. Publishes ms an average of 8 months after acceptance. Byline given. Buys first rights and regional rights. Submit seasonal/holiday material 5 months in advance. Reprints OK; send typed ms with rights for sale noted and information about when and where the article previously appeared. Pays 50% of their fee for an original article. Query for electronic submissions. Reports in 2 weeks. *Writer's Market* recommends allowing 2 months for reply. Sample copy for 9×12 SAE with 6 first class stamps. Writer's guidelines for #10 SASE.

Nonfiction: How-to (camping); humor; new product (company and RV releases only); recreation vehicle and camping experiences in the Northeast; features about private (only) campgrounds and places to visit in the Northeast while RVing; personal experience; photo feature; and travel. "No diaries of trips, dog stories, or anything not camping and RV related." Length: 300-1,500 words. Pays $40-80 for articles with b&w photos; pays $30-75 for articles without art.

Photos: Send photos with submission. Reviews contact sheets and 5×7 prints or larger. Captions and identification of subjects required. Buys one-time rights.

Columns/Departments: Mealtime (campground cooking), 300-900 words. Buys 12 mss/year. Query or send complete ms. Length: 750-1,000 words. Pays $25-50.

Tips: "We most often need material on private campgrounds and attractions in New England. We are looking for upbeat, first-person stories about where to camp, what to do or see, and how to enjoy camping."

ALWAYS enclose a self-addressed, stamped envelope (SASE) with all your queries and correspondence.

ONTARIO MOTOR COACH REVIEW, Naylor Communications Ltd., 6th Floor, 920 Yonge St., Toronto, Ontario M4W 3C7 Canada. (416)961-1028. Fax: (416)924-4408. Editor: Greg Kero. 50% freelance written. Annual magazine on travel and tourist destinations. Estab 1970. Circ. 3,000. Pays 30 days from deadline. Byline given. Offers 33⅓% kill fee. Buys first North American serial rights and all rights. Submit seasonal/holiday material 2 months in advance. Simultaneous submissions OK; send photocopy of article and information about when and where the article previously appeared. Pays 80% of their fee for an original article. Query for electronic submissions. Reports in 6 weeks. *Writer's Market* recommends allowing 2 months for reply. Free sample copy and writer's guidelines.

Nonfiction: General interest, historical, interview/profile, new product, personal experience (related to motor coach travel), photo feature, technical and travel. Buys 5-10 mss/year. Query with published clips. Length: 500-3,000 words. Pays 20-25¢/word. Pays expenses of writers on assignment.

Photos: State availability of photos with submission. Reviews transparencies and prints. Offers $25-200/photo. Identification of subjects required.

RV TIMES MAGAZINE, Royal Productions, Inc., P.O. Box 6294, Richmond VA 23230-0294. (804)288-5653. Editor: Alice Posner Supple. 75% freelance written. Prefers to work with published/established writers; works with a small number of new/unpublished writers each year. Monthly except December. "We supply the camping public with articles and information on outdoor activities related to camping. Our audience is primarily families that own recreational vehicles." Estab. 1973. Circ. 35,000. Pays on publication. Publishes ms an average of 4-6 months after acceptance. Byline given. Buys one-time, second serial (reprint) or simultaneous rights. Submit seasonal/holiday material 2 months in advance. Simultaneous and previously published submissions OK; send typed ms with rights for sale noted and information about when and where the article previously appeared. Query for electronic submissions. Sample copy and writer's guidelines for 9 × 12 SAE with 7 first class stamps.

  • Reports only on acceptance. Allow 2 months for reply, if one is to come.

Nonfiction: How-to and travel; information on places to camp, "tourist related articles, places to go, things to see. Does not have to be camping related." Buys 80 mss/year. Query with or without published clips or send complete ms. Length: 500-2,000 words.

Photos: Always prefers "people" pictures as opposed to scenic. Buys one-time rights. Black and white, color prints, slides; prefer vertical format.

Tips: "All areas of *RV Times* are open to freelancers. We will look at all articles and consider for publication. Return of unsolicited mss is not guaranteed; however, every effort is made to return photos."

RV WEST MAGAZINE, Prescomm Media Inc., Suite I, 4133 Mohr Ave., Pleasanton CA 94566-4750. (510)426-3200. Fax: (510)426-1422. 85% freelance written. Works with a small number of new/unpublished writers each year. Monthly magazine for Western recreational vehicle owners. Estab. 1977. Circ. 90,000. Pays on publication. Publishes ms an average of 10 months after acceptance. Byline given. Buys one-time rights. Submit seasonal/holiday material 10 months in advance. Simultaneous and previously published submissions OK; send typed ms with rights for sale noted. Pays 100% of their fee for an original article. Query for electronic submissions. Reports in 2 months on queries; several months on mss. Free writer's guidelines.

Nonfiction: Historical/nostalgic; how-to (fix your RV); new product; personal experience (particularly travel); technical; and travel (destinations for RVs). No non-RV travel articles. Buys 36 mss/year. Query with or without published clips. Length: 750-2,000 words. Pays $1.50/inch.

Photos: Send photos with submissions. Reviews contact sheets, negatives, transparencies and prints. Prefers b&w prints. Offers $5 minimum/photo. Identification of subjects required.

Tips: "RV travel/destination stories are most open to freelancers. Include all information of value to RVers, and reasons why they would want to visit the location (13 Western states). Indicate best time frame for publication."

‡ST. MAARTEN NIGHTS, Nights Publications, 1831 Rene Levesque Blvd. West, Montreal, Quebec H3H 1R4 Canada. Fax: (514)931-6273. Editor: Stephen Trotter. Managing Editor: Zelly Zuskin. Contact: Stephen Trotter. 80% freelance written. Annual magazine covering the St. Maarten/St. Martin vacation experience seeking "upbeat entertaining lifestyle articles: colorful profiles of islanders; lively features on culture, activities, night life, dining, special events, gambling; how-to features; humor. Our audience is the North American vacationer." Estab. 1981. Circ. 200,000. **Pays on acceptance.** Publishes ms an average of 6-10 months after acceptance. Byline given. Offers 15% kill fee. Buys first North American serial and first Caribbean rights. Editorial lead time 2 month. Query for electronic submissions. Reports in 2 weeks on queries; 1 month on mss. *Writer's Market* recommends allowing 2 months for reply. Sample copy $5. Writer's guidelines free on request.

Nonfiction: General interest, historical/nostalgia, how-to (gamble), sail, etc., humor, inspirational, interview/profile, opinion, personal experience, photo feature, travel, local culture, art, activities, entertainment and topics relative to vacationers in St. Maarten/St. Martin. "No negative pieces or stale rewrites." Buys 5-10 mss/year. Query with published clips. Length: 250-750 words. Pays $125-350 for assigned articles; $100-250 for unsolicited articles.

Photos: State availability of photos with submission. Reviews transparencies. Offers $25-100/photo. Captions, model releases and identification of subjects required. Buys one-time rights.

TEXAS HIGHWAYS, Official Travel Magazine for the State of Texas, Texas Department of Transportation, Box 141009, Austin TX 78714-1009. (512)483-3675. Fax: (512)483-3672. Editor: Jack Lowry. Managing Editor: Rosemary Williams 85% freelance written. Prefers to work with published/established writers. Monthly tourist magazine covering travel and history for Texas only. **Pays on acceptance.** Publishes ms an average of 10 months after acceptance. Byline given. Offers $100 kill fee. Buys one-time rights. Submit seasonal/holiday material 1 year in advance. No simultaneous queries. Reports in 1 month on queries. Sample copy and writer's guidelines for 9 × 12 SAE with 3 first class stamps.

Nonfiction: Historical/nostalgic, photo feature and travel. Must be concerned with travel in Texas. Send material on "what to see, what to do, where to go in *Texas*." Material must be tourist-oriented. "No disaster features." Buys 75 mss/year. Query with published clips. Length: 1,000-2,000 words. Pays $400-1,000. Sometimes pays expenses of writers on assignment "after we have worked with them awhile."

Photos: Michael A. Murphy, photo editor. Send photos with query or ms. Pays upon publication $80 for less than half a page, $120 for half page, $170 for a full page, $400 for front cover, $300 for back cover. Accepts 35mm and large original color transparencies. Captions and identification of subjects required. Buys one-time rights.

• Ranked as one of the best markets for freelance writers in *Writer's Digest* magazine's annual "Top 100 Markets," January 1993.

‡TOURING AMERICA, Travel in the USA, Canada and Mexico, Fancy Publications, Inc., Box 6050, Mission Viejo CA 92690. (714)855-8822, ext. 410. Editor: Bob Carpenter. Managing Editor: Gene Booth. Contact: Gene Booth. 95% freelance written. Bimonthly magazine covering travel in North America. "Our niche is the trip story—from somewhere to somewhere—rather than destination pieces. We try to help the reader in planning the trip and while it is underway. The ideal piece would be on the seat beside the driver as the trip progresses. We aim for a family audience, professionals between 35-55 years." Estab. 1991. **Pays on acceptance.** Publishes ms an average of 6 months after acceptance. Byline given. Buys first North American serial and anthology rights. Editorial lead time 4 months. Submit seasonal material 6 months in advance ("after receiving go-ahead to write it.") Query for electronic submissions. Reports in 2-4 weeks on queries. Does not consider unsolicited mss. Sample copy $5.50 from Back Issue Dept. Writer's guidelines free on request for #10 SASE.

Nonfiction: General interest, historical/nostalgic, how-to travel successfully, humor, photo feature, technical and travel. "No 'My Last Vacation' pieces; no first person; no stories about resorts, specific hotels, restaurants, etc.; nothing with the first word 'Picture' or 'Imagine . . .'; no manuscripts without professional quality photography; no formula writing." Buys 60+ mss/year. Query. Query with published clips the first time. Length 1,000-1,800 words. Pays up to $750 "for accepted articles with photos and sidebars. Do not send unsolicited material!"

Photos: Send photos with submission. "We buy word-picture packages." Offers no additional payment for photos accepted with ms. Offers $25-125/photo (purchased separately.) "Cover photos $250-up." Captions, model releases (cover only) and identification of subjects required. "We always look at photos first to determine acceptance of article."

Columns/Departments: Picturing America (travel photography), 1,000-1,200 words plus sidebars; Alternative Travel (adventure, ecology, offbeat); 1,000-1,200 words plus sidebars. Buys 12 mss/year. Query. Pays $400 maximum.

Fillers: Facts. Buys 50-100/year. Length: 75-150 words with a selection of photos. Pays $25-75 for Travelers' Advisory items, One Last Snapshot.

Tips: "Have a dynamite lead—yank the reader right into the guts of the story. Tell a story—remember, a place description is not a travel story. Never have fewer than 12 tips or hints that will help the reader make the same trip easier and/or cheaper. Double check every name, address, phone number, admission charge, hour of operation before mailing in article. Always have two to four sidebars with the story. Do not write something for which you do not have professional color photography. Never ever submit a story to us that is going to another publisher at the time. Always write and send the article only after we respond to your query. Travelers' Advisory—a potpourri of short, interesting and engaging travel items—is the best place to start. Keep to 150 words or less with a couple of slides. All parts of the magazine are open, however. Just be jsure you 1) create excitement and 2) deliver maximum information in your manuscript."

TRANSITIONS ABROAD, P.O. Box 344, Amherst MA 01004-0344. (413)256-0373. Editor/Publisher: Prof. Clayton A. Hubbs. 80-90% freelance written. Eager to work with new/unpublished writers. Magazine resource for low-budget international travel with an educational or work component. Estab. 1977. Circ. 15,000. Pays on publication. Buys first rights and second (reprint) rights. Byline given. Written queries only. Reprints OK. Send typed ms with rights for sale noted including information about when and where the article previously appeared. For reprints, pays 100% of the amount paid for an original article. Reports in 2 months. Sample copy $3.50. Writer's guidelines and topics schedule for #10 SASE. Manuscript returned only with SASE.

Nonfiction: How-to (find courses, inexpensive lodging and travel); interview (information on specific areas and people); personal experience (evaluation of courses, special interest and study tours, economy travel); and travel (what to see and do in specific areas of the world, new learning and travel ideas). Foreign travel only. Few destination ("tourist") pieces. Emphasis on information and on interaction with people in host country. Buys 20 unsolicited mss/issue. Query with credentials. Length: 500-2,000 words. Pays $25-150. Include author's bio with submissions.

Photos: Send photos with ms. Pays $10-25 for prints (color acceptable, b&w preferred), $125 for covers (b&w only). Photos increase likelihood of acceptance. Buys one-time rights. Captions and ID on photos required.

Columns/Departments: Worldwide Travel Bargains (destinations, activities and accomodations for budget travelers—featured in every issue); Study/Travel Program Notes (evaluation of courses or programs); Traveler's Advisory/Resources (new information and ideas for offbeat independent travel); and Jobnotes (how to find it and what to expect). Buys 8/issue. Send complete ms. Length: 1,000 words maximum. Pays $20-50.

Fillers: Info Exchange (information, preferably first-hand—having to do with travel, particularly offbeat educational travel and work or study abroad). Buys 10/issue. Length: 1,000 words maximum. Pays $20-50.

Tips: "We like nuts and bolts stuff, practical information, especially on how to work, live and cut costs abroad. Our readers want usable information on planning their own travel itinerary. Be specific: names, addresses, current costs. We are particularly interested in educational travel and study abroad for adults and senior citizens. More and more readers want information not only on work but retirement possibilities. We have a new department on exchange programs, homestays, and study/tours for pre-college students. *Educational Travel Directory and Travel Planner* published each year in July provides descriptive listings of resources and information sources on work, study, and independent travel abroad along with study/travel programs abroad for adults."

TRAVEL À LA CARTE, 136 Walton St., Port Hope, Ontario L1A 1N5 Canada. (416)444-3633. (416)885-7202. Editor: Donna Carter. 70% freelance written. Bimonthly travel magazine. "Lighthearted entertaining articles on travel destinations worldwide, with a focus on the places and people visited. Our audience is travellers, airline, train and car." Pays on publication. Byline given. Offers no kill fee. Not copyrighted. Buys first North American and one-time rights. Submit seasonal/holiday material 4 months in advance. Simultaneous submissions OK. Free sample copy and writer's guidelines with SASE.

Nonfiction: Travel. Buys 25-30 mss/year. Query with published clips. Length: 1,500-2,000 words. Pays $125-275. Sometimes pays expenses of writers on assignment.

Photos: Send photos with submission. Reviews transparencies or slides. Offers no additional payment for photos accepted with ms. Identification of subjects required. Buys one-time rights.

Tips: "Send a list of travel destinations and samples of writing and photography. Do not send off-the-beaten path articles for destinations that require flight changes followed by train, canoe and treks to remote areas."

TRAVEL AMERICA, The U.S. Vacation Magazine, World Publishing Co., 990 Grove St., Evanston IL 60201-4370. (708)491-6440. Editor-in-Chief/Associate Publisher: Bob Meyers. Managing Editor: Randy Mink. 90% freelance written. Bimonthly magazine covering US vacation travel. Circ. 170,000. Byline given. Buys first North American serial rights. Submit seasonal/holiday material 6 months in advance. Previously published submissions acceptable, dependent upon publication—local or regional OK. Send photocopy of article, typed ms with rights for sale noted and information about when and where the article previously appeared. Pays 50% of their fee for an original article. Reports in 3 weeks on queries; 6 weeks on mss. *Writer's Market* recommends allowing 2 months for reply. Sample copy $3.50 for 9×12 SASE with 5 first class stamps.

Nonfiction: Primarily destination-oriented travel articles and resort/hotel profiles and roundups, but will consider essays, how-to, humor. "It is best to study current contents and query first." Buys 75 mss/year. Average length: 1,000 words. Pays $150-350.

Photos: Top-quality original color slides preferred. Captions required. Buys one-time rights. Prefers photo feature package (ms plus slides), but will purchase slides only to support a work in progress.

Columns/Departments: Travel Views (travel tips; service articles). Buys 6 mss/year. Query or send complete ms. Length: 800-1,500 words. Pays $125-200.

Tips: "Because we are heavily photo-oriented, superb slides are our foremost concern. The most successful approach is to send 2-3 sheets of slides with the query or complete ms. Include a list of other subjects you can provide as a photo feature package."

TRAVEL & LEISURE, American Express Publishing Corp., 1120 Ave. of the Americas, New York NY 10036. (212)382-5600. Editor-in-Chief: Nancy Novogrod. Executive Editor: Susan Crandell. Managing Editor: Maria Shaw. 80% freelance written. Monthly magazine. Circ. 1.2 million. **Pays on acceptance.** Byline given. Offers 25% kill fee. Buys first world and foreign edition rights. Reports in 3 weeks. *Writer's Market* recommends allowing 2 months for reply. Sample copy $5. Writer's guidelines for #10 SASE.

• Ranked as one of the best markets for freelance writers in *Writer's Digest* magazine's annual "Top 100 Markets," January 1993.

Nonfiction: Travel. Buys 200 mss/year. Query. Length open. Payment varies. Pays the expenses of writers on assignment.

Photos: Discourages submission of unsolicited transparencies. Payment varies. Captions required. Buys one-time rights.

Tips: "Read the magazine. Regional sections are best places to start."

TRAVEL NEWS, Travel Agents International, Inc., 15th Floor, 111 2nd Ave. NE, St. Petersburg FL 33701-3419. (813)895-8241. Fax: (813)894-6318. Editor: Matthew Wiseman. 40% freelance written. Monthly travel tabloid. "Travel stories written to praise a particular trip. We want readers to consider taking a trip themselves." Estab. 1982. Circ. 250,000. Pays on publication. Publishes ms an average of 2 months after acceptance. Byline given. Not copyrighted. Buys simultaneous rights. Submit seasonal/holiday material 4 months in advance. Simultaneous and previously published submissions OK; send typed ms with rights for sale noted. Reports in 6 weeks. *Writer's Market* recommends allowing 2 months for reply. Sample copy and writer's guidelines for 9 × 12 SAE with 4 first class stamps. No phone calls, please.

Nonfiction: Essays, general interest, historical/nostalgic, humor, new product, photo feature and travel. "Each issue focuses on one travel category. We will accept submissions anytime but prefer SASE for publication calendar. No negative articles that would discourage travel." Buys 30 mss/year. Query with or without published clips or send complete ms. Length: 500-1,500 words. Pays $20-200 for assigned articles; $10-125 for unsolicited articles.

Photos: State availability of photos with submission. Buys one-time rights.

Tips: "Send SASE for publication calendar, sample copy and submission requirements. Write well in advance of a trip to see what angle we would like the story to take. We will also review outlines."

TRAVEL PAPERS, Carousel Press/The Family Travel Guides Catalogue, P.O. Box 6061, Albany CA 94706-0061. (510)527-5849. Editor: Carole T. Meyers. 25% freelance written. Annual catalog covering family travel. "We publish articles that help families plan successful vacations. Helpful detail is important." Estab. 1987. Circ. 45,000. "We pay royalties on articles ordered by customers—once each year in January." Byline given. Author retains copyright. Buys second serial (reprint) rights. Previously published submissions OK. Send photocopy of article and information about when and where the article previously appeared. Reports in 1 month. *Writer's Market* recommends allowing 2 months for reply. Sample copy and writer's guidelines for #10 SAE with 2 first class stamps.

Nonfiction: Travel. Buys 10 mss/year. Send complete ms. Length: 1,000-2,500 words. Pays 10% royalty.

TRAVEL SMART, Communications House, Inc., Dobbs Ferry NY 10522. (914)693-4208. Editor/Publisher: H.J. Teison. Managing Editor: Nancy Dunnan. Covers information on "good-value travel." Monthly newsletter. Estab. 1976. Pays on publication. Buys all rights. Reports in 6 weeks. *Writer's Market* recommends allowing 2 months for reply. Sample copy and writer's guidelines for #10 SAE with 3 first class stamps.

Nonfiction: "Interested primarily in bargains or little-known deals on transportation, lodging, food, unusual destinations that are really good values. No destination stories on major Caribbean islands, London, New York, no travelogs, 'my vacation,' poetry, fillers. No photos or illustrations. Just hard facts. We are not part of 'Rosy fingers of dawn . . .' school." Write for guidelines, then query. Length: 100-1,500 words. Pays $150 maximum."

Tips: "When you travel, check out small hotels offering good prices, little known restaurants, and send us brief rundown (with prices, phone numbers, addresses). Information must be current. Include your phone number with submission, because we sometimes make immediate assignments."

VISTA/USA, P.O. Box 161, Convent Station NJ 07961-0161. (201)538-7600. Fax: (201)538-9509. Executive Editor: Kathleen M. Caccavale. Editor: Martha J. Mendez. 90% freelance written. Will consider ms submissions from unpublished writers. Quarterly magazine of Exxon Travel Club. "Our publication uses articles on North American areas. We strive to help our readers gain an in-depth understanding of cities, towns and areas as well as other aspects of American culture that affect the character of the nation." Estab. 1965. Circ. 800,000. **Pays on acceptance.** Publishes ms an average of 1 year after acceptance. Buys first North American serial rights. Query about seasonal subjects 18 months in advance. Reports in 6 weeks. *Writer's Market* recommends allowing 2 months for reply. Sample copy for 9 × 12 or larger SAE with 5 first class stamps. Writer's and photographer's guidelines for #10 SASE.

   • Ranked as one of the best markets for freelance writers in *Writer's Digest* magazine's annual "Top 100 Markets," January 1993.

Nonfiction: Geographically oriented articles on North America focused on the character of an area or place; photo essays (recent examples include slot canyons, sand sculptures, kites); and some articles dealing with nature, Americana, crafts and collecting. Usually one activity-oriented article per issue. "We buy feature articles on the US, Canada, Mexico and the Caribbean that appeal to a national audience and prefer that destination queries have a hook or angle to them that give us a clear, solid argument for covering the average subject 'soon' rather than 'anytime.' " No feature articles that mention driving or follow routes on a map. Uses 7-15 mss/issue. Query with outline and clips of previously published work. Length: 1,200-2,000 words. Pays $450 minimum for features. Pays the expenses of writers on assignment.

Columns/Departments: "MiniTrips are point to point or loop driving tours of from 50 to 350 miles covering a healthy variety of stops along the way. 'Close Focus' covers openings or changing aspects of major attractions, small or limited attractions not appropriate for a feature article (800-1,000 words). 'American Vignettes' covers anything travel related that also reveals a slice of American life, often with a light or humorous touch, such as asking directions from a cranky New Englander, or the phenomenon of vanity plates. 'Information Please' provides practical information on travel safety, and health trends, tips; a service column."

Photos: Contact: photo researcher. Send photos with ms. Pays $100 minimum for color transparencies. Captions preferred. Buys one-time rights.

Tips: "We are looking for readable pieces with good writing that will interest armchair travelers as much as readers who may want to visit the areas you write about. Queries about well-known destinations should have something new or different to say about them, a specific focus or angle. Articles should have definite themes and should give our readers an insight into the character and flavor of an area or topic. Stories about personal experiences must impart a sense of drama and excitement or have a strong human-interest angle. Stories about areas should communicate a strong sense of what it feels like to be there. Good use of anecdotes and quotes should be included. Study the articles in the magazine to understand how they are organized, how they present their subjects, the range of writing styles, and the specific types of subjects used. Afterwards, query with SASE and enclose samples of your best writing. We continue to seek department shorts and inventory articles of a general, nonseasonal nature (1,500 to 1,800 words)."

WESTERN RV NEWS, Suite B, 1350 SW Upland Dr., Portland OR 97221-2647. (503)222-1255. Fax: (503)222-1255. Editor: Elsie Hathaway. 75% freelance written. Monthly magazine for owners of recreational vehicles. Estab. 1966. Pays on publication. Publishes ms an average of 3-6 months after acceptance. Byline given. Buys first rights and second serial (reprint) rights. Simultaneous and previously published submissions OK; send typed ms with rights for sale noted and information about when and where the article previously appeared and photocopy of article if available. Pays 50-60% of their fee for an original article. Reports in 1 month. *Writer's Market* recommends allowing 2 months for reply. Sample copy and writer's guidelines for 9 × 12 SAE with 5 first class stamps. Guidelines for #10 SASE. Request to be put on free temporary mailing list for publication.

Nonfiction: How-to (RV oriented, purchasing considerations, maintenance); humor (RV experiences); new product (with ancillary interest to RV lifestyle); personal experiences (varying or unique RV lifestyles); technical (RV systems or hardware); and travel. "No articles without an RV slant." Buys 100 mss/year. Submit complete ms. Length: 250-1,200 words. Pays $15-100.

Photos: Send photos with submission. Prefer b&w. Offers $5-10/photo. Captions, model releases, and identification of subjects required. Buys one-time rights.

Fillers: Encourage anecdotes, RV related tips and short humor. Length: 50-250 words. Pays $5-25.

Tips: "Highlight the RV lifestyle! Western travel (primarily NW destinations) articles should include information about the availability of RV sites, dump stations, RV parking and accessibility. Thorough research and a pleasant, informative writing style are paramount. Technical, how-to, and new product writing is also of great interest to us. Photos definitely enhance the possibility of article acceptance."

Women's

Women have an incredible variety of publications available to them these days—about 50 appear on newsstands in an array of specialties. A number of titles in this area have been redesigned during the past year to compete in the crowded marketplace. Many have stopped publishing fiction and are focusing more on short, human interest nonfiction articles. Magazines that also use material slanted to women's interests can be found in the following categories: Business and Finance; Child Care and Parental Guidance; Contemporary Culture; Food and Drink; Health and Fitness; Hobby and Craft; Home and Garden; Relationships; Religious; Romance and Confession; and Sports.

ALLURE, Condé Nast, 350 Madison Ave., New York NY 10017. "Prefers not to share information."

AMERICAN WOMAN, GCR Publishing, 34th Floor, 1700 Broadway, New York NY 10019-5905. (212)541-7100. Fax: (212)245-1241. Editor: Lynn Varacalli. Managing Editor: Sandy Kosherick. 50% freelance written. Bimonthly magazine for "thirty-something women, mostly single, dealing with relationships and self-help." Estab. 1990. Circ. 200,000. Pays on publication. Publishes ms an average of 2 months after acceptance. Byline given. Offers 25% kill fee. Buys one-time and second serial (reprint) rights. Submit seasonal/holiday material

5 months in advance. Simultaneous and previously published submissions OK. Send information about when and where the article previously appeared. For reprints, pays 50% of the amount paid for an original article. Reports in 3 weeks. *Writer's Market* recommends allowing 2 months for reply. Sample copy for $2.50. Writer's guidelines for #10 SASE.

Nonfiction: Book excerpts, humor, inspirational, interview/profile, new product and personal experience. "No poetry, recipes or fiction." Buys 40 mss/year. Query with published clips. Length: 700-1,500 words. Pays $200-800 for assigned articles; $200-700 for unsolicited articles. Pays for phone, mailings, faxes and transportation costs of writers on assignment.

Photos: State availability of photos with submission. Reviews contact sheets, transparencies and prints. Offers $75-150/photo. Captions, model releases and identification of subjects required. Buys one-time rights.

Tips: "We are interested in stories of inspiration—women who have overcome obstacles in their lives, trends (new ideas in dating, relationships, places to go, new hot spots for meeting men), articles about women starting businesses (how to make more money, profile of an entrepreneur) and money-saving articles (on clothes, beauty, vacations, mail order, entertainment."

BRIDAL TRENDS, Meridian International, Inc., Box 10010, Ogden UT 84409-0010. (801)394-9446. 65% freelance written. Monthly magazine with useful articles for today's bride. Circ. 60,000. **Pays on acceptance.** Publishes ms an average of 10 months after acceptance. Byline given. Buys first, second serial (reprint) and nonexclusive reprint rights. Simultaneous and previously published submissions OK. Reports in 2 months with SASE. Sample copy $1 for 9×12 SAE. Writer's guidelines for #10 SASE. All requests for sample copies, guidelines and queries should be addressed Attn: Editorial Staff.

Nonfiction: "General interest articles about traditional and modern approaches to weddings. Topics include all aspects of ceremony and reception planning: flowers, invitations, catering, wedding apparel and fashion trends for the bride, groom, and other members of the wedding party, etc. Also featured are honeymoon destinations, how to build a relationship and keep romance alive, and adjusting to married life." Buys approximately 15 mss/year. Query. Length: 1,200 words. Pays 15¢/word for first rights plus nonexclusive reprint rights. Pays 10¢/word for second rights.

Photos: Send photos with query letter. Reviews 35mm or larger transparencies and 5×7 or 8×10 color prints. Pays $35 for inside photo. Captions, model release, and identification of subjects required.

Tips: "We publish articles that detail each aspect of wedding planning: invitations, choosing your flowers, deciding on the style of your wedding, and choosing a photographer and caterer. Emphasis is on the use of wedding consultants, gift registries, floral designers, caterers, travel agents, hotel and spa coordinators."

BRIDE'S, Condé Nast, 350 Madison Ave., New York NY 10017. (212)880-8535. Editor-in-Chief: Barbara D. Tober. 40% freelance written. Eager to work with new/unpublished writers. Bimonthly magazine for the first- or second-time bride, her family and friends, the groom and his family and friends. Circ. 400,000. **Pays on acceptance.** Publishes ms an average of 2 months after acceptance. Buys all rights. Also buys first and second serial rights for book excerpts on marriage, communication, finances. Offers 20% kill fee, depending on circumstances. Buys 40 unsolicited mss/year. Byline given. Reports in 2 months. Address mss to Features Department. Writer's guidelines for #10 SASE.

Nonfiction: "We want warm, personal articles, optimistic in tone, with help offered in a clear, specific way. All issues should be handled within the context of marriage. How-to features on all aspects of marriage: communications, in-laws, careers, money, sex, housing, housework, family planning, marriage after having a baby, religion, interfaith marriage, step-parenting, second marriage, reaffirmation of vows; informational articles on the realities of marriage, the changing roles of men and women, the kind of troubles in engagement that are likely to become big issues in marriage; stories from couples or marriage authorities that illustrate marital problems and solutions to men and women; book excerpts on marriage, communication, finances, sex; and how-to features on wedding planning that offer expert advice. Also success stories of marriages of long duration. We use first-person pieces and articles that are well researched, relying on quotes from authorities in the field, and anecdotes and dialogues from real couples. We publish first-person essays on provocative topics unique to marriage." Query or submit complete ms. Article outline preferred. Length: 1,000-3,000 words. Pays $300-800.

Columns/Departments: The Love column accepts reader love poems, for $25 each. The Something New section accepts reader wedding planning and craft ideas, pays $25.

Tips: "Since marriage rates are up, large, traditional weddings, personalized to reflect the couples' lifestyles, are back in style, and more women work than ever before, do *not* query us on just living together or becoming a stay-at-home wife after marriage. Send us a query or a well-written article that is both easy to read and offers real help for the bride or groom as she/he adjusts to her/his new role. No first-person narratives on wedding and reception planning, home furnishings, cooking, fashion, beauty, travel. We're interested in unusual ideas, experiences, and lifestyles. No 'I used baby pink rose buds' articles."

CHATELAINE, 777 Bay St., Toronto, Ontario M5W 1A7 Canada. (416)596-5425. Editor-in-Chief: Mildred Istona. 75% freelance written. Prefers to work with published/established writers. Monthly general-interest magazine for Canadian women, from age 20 and up. "*Chatelaine* is read by one woman in three across Canada, a readership that spans almost every age group but is concentrated among those 25 to 45 including homemakers and working women in all walks of life." Circ. over 1 million (combined English-French editions). **Pays on acceptance.** Byline given. Reports within 1 month. *Writer's Market* recommends allowing 2 months for reply. Sample copy $2. Free writer's guidelines.

Nonfiction: Ivor Shapiro, associate editor, articles. Submit an outline or query first. Full-length major pieces run from 1,500 to 2,500 words. Pays minimum $1,250 (Canadian) for acceptable major article. Buys first North American serial rights in English and French (the latter to cover possible use in *Chatelaine*'s sister French-language edition, edited in Montreal for French Canada). "We look for important national Canadian subjects, examining any and all facets of Canadian life, especially as they concern or interest women. Upfront columns include stories about relationships, health, nutrition, fitness and parents and kids. Submit outline first to Diane Merlevede, managing editor. All mss must be accompanied by a SASE (IRCs in lieu of stamps if sent from outside Canada)." Pays $350 for about 500 words.

Tips: "Features on beauty, food, fashion and home decorating are supplied by staff writers and editors, and unsolicited material is not considered."

● Ranked as one of the best markets for freelance writers in *Writer's Digest* magazine's annual "Top 100 Markets," January 1993.

COLABORER MAGAZINE, Woman's National Auxiliary Convention, Free Will Baptists, P.O. Box 5002, Antioch TN 37011-5002. Contact: Melissa Riddle. Estab. 1961. Unpublished articles, plays, poetry, programs and art related to Christian growth and evangelism for today's woman. Publishes reprints of previously published articles. Send typed ms with rights for sale noted and information about when and where the article previously appeared.

COMPLETE WOMAN, For All The Women You Are, Associated Publications, Inc., 1165 N. Clark, Chicago IL 60610. (312)266-8680. Editor: Bonnie L. Krueger. Managing Editor: Susan Handy. 90% freelance written. Bimonthly magazine of general interest for women. Areas of concern are love life, health, fitness, emotions, etc. Estab. 1980. Circ. 150,000. Pays on publication. Publishes ms an average of 5 months after acceptance. Byline given. Buys first North American serial, second serial (reprint) and simultaneous rights. Submit seasonal/holiday material 5 months in advance. Simultaneous submissions OK. Reprints OK; send tearsheet or photocopy of article or short story, or send typed ms with rights for sale noted and information about when and where the article previously appeared.

Reports in 2 months. Writer's guidelines for #10 SASE.

Nonfiction: Book excerpts, general interest, how-to, humor, inspirational, interview/profile, new product, personal experience and photo feature. "We like roundups, celebrity interviews and articles on what men want and need. Other topics should be centered on today's woman and her love life." Buys 60-100 mss/year. Query with or without published clips or send complete ms. Length: 800-2,000 words. Pays $80-400. Sometimes pays expenses of writers on assignment.

Photos: Send photos with submission. Reviews 2¼ or 35mm transparencies and 5×7 prints. Offers $35-75/photo. Captions, model releases and identification of subjects required. Buys one-time rights.

Poetry: Avant-garde, free verse, light verse and traditional. Nothing over 30 lines. Buys 50 poems/year. Submit maximum 5 poems. Pays $10.

COSMOPOLITAN, The Hearst Corp., 224 W. 57th St., New York NY 10019. Exec. Editor: Roberta Ashley. 90% freelance written. Monthly magazine for 18- to 35-year-old single, married, divorced women—all working. **Pays on acceptance.** Byline given. Offers 10-15% kill fee. Buys all magazine rights and occasionally negotiates first North American rights. Submit seasonal/holiday material 6 months in advance. Previously published submissions in minor publications OK. Reports in 1 week on queries; 3 weeks on mss. *Writer's Market* recommends allowing 2 months for reply. Sample copy $2.50. Writer's guidelines for #10 SASE.

Nonfiction: Book excerpts, how-to, humor, opinion, personal experience and anything of interest to young women. Buys 350 mss/year. Query with published clips or send complete ms. Length: 500-3,500 words. Pays expenses of writers on assignment.

Fiction: Betty Kelly. Condensed novels, humorous, novel excerpts, romance and original short stories with romantic plots. Buys 18 mss/year. Query. Length: 750-3,000 words.

Poetry: Free verse and light verse. Buys 30 poems/year. No maximum number. Length: 4-30 lines.

Fillers: Irene Copeland. Facts. Buys 240/year. Length: 300-1,000 words.

● Ranked as one of the best markets for freelance writers in *Writer's Digest* magazine's annual "Top 100 Markets," January 1993.

A bullet introduces comments by the editor of Writer's Market *indicating special information about the listing.*

COUNTRY WOMAN, Reiman Publications, P.O. Box 643, Milwaukee WI 53201. (414)423-0100. Managing Editor: Kathy Pohl. 75-85% written by readers. Willing to work with new/unpublished writers. Bimonthly magazine on the interests of country women. "*Country Woman* is for contemporary rural women of all ages and backgrounds and from all over the US and Canada. It includes a sampling of the diversity that makes up rural women's lives—love of home, family, farm, ranch, community, hobbies, enduring values, humor, attaining new skills and appreciating present, past and future all within the content of the lifestyle that surrounds country living." Estab. 1970. **Pays on acceptance.** Publishes ms an average of 1 year after acceptance. Byline given. Buys first North American serial, one-time and second serial (reprint) rights. Submit seasonal/holiday material 4-5 months in advance. Previously published submissions OK (on occasion). Reports in 2 months on queries; 2-3 months on mss. Sample copy $2. Writer's guidelines for #10 SASE.

Nonfiction: General interest, historical/nostalgic, how-to (crafts, community projects, decorative, antiquing, etc.), humor, inspirational, interview/profile, personal experience and photo/feature packages profiling interesting country women—all pertaining to a rural woman's interest. Articles must be written in a positive, light and entertaining manner. Query. Length: 1,000 words maximum.

Photos: Send color photos with query or ms. Reviews 35mm or 2¼ transparencies. Uses only excellent quality color photos. No b&w. "We pay for photo/feature packages." Captions, model releases and identification of subjects required. Buys one-time rights.

Columns/Departments: Why Farm Wives Age Fast (humor), I Remember When (nostalgia) and Country Decorating. Buys 10-12 mss/year (maximum). Query or send complete ms. Length: 500-1,000 words. Pays $75-125.

Fiction: Main character *must* be a country woman. All fiction must have a country setting. Fiction must have a positive, upbeat message. Includes fiction in every issue. Would buy more fiction if stories suitable for our audience were sent our way. Query or send complete ms. Length: 750-1,000 words. Pays $90-125.

Poetry: Traditional and light verse. "Poetry must have rhythm, rhyme and be country-related. Always looking for seasonal poetry." Buys 40 poems/year. Submit max. 6 poems. Length: 5-24 lines. Pays $10-25.

Tips: "We have recently broadened our focus to include 'country' women, not just women on farms and ranches. This allows freelancers a wider scope in material. Write as clearly and with as much zest and enthusiasm as possible. We love good quotes, supporting materials (names, places, etc.) and strong leads and closings. Readers relate strongly to where they live and the lifestyle they've chosen. They want to be informed and entertained, and that's just exactly why they subscribe. Readers are busy—not too busy to read—but when they do sit down, they want good writing, reliable information and something that feels like a reward. How-to, humor, personal experience and nostalgia are areas most open to freelancers. Profiles, to a certain degree, are also open. Be accurate and fresh in approach."

‡DAUGHTERS OF SARAH, The Magazine for Christian Feminists, Daughters of Sarah, 3801 N. Keeler, Chicago IL 60641. (312)736-3399. Editor: Reta Finger. Managing Editor: Sandra Volentine. Contact: Cathi Falsani, Assistant Editor. 85% freelance written. Quarterly magazine for "Christian feminism published by women calling for justice, mutuality, and reconciliation in the church and the world. We are a forum for a wide variety of viewpoints that are both Christian and feminist." Estab. 1974. Circ. 5,000. Pays on publication. Publishes ms an average of 3-4 months after acceptance. Byline given. Buys first North American serial and one-time rights. Editorial lead time 3 months. Submit seasonal material 3 months in advance. Simultaneous and previously published submissions OK. Reports in 2 months. Sample copy $3. Writer's guidelines for #10 SASE.

Nonfiction: Book excerpts, essays, expose, general interest, historical/nostalgic, humor, inspirational, interview/profile, opinion, personal experience and religious. "We are a thematic magazine. Each issue focuses on a specific theme. It is best to send for a theme list. We don't want to see anything *not* relating to women or women's issues and anything without Biblical or feminist perspective." Query. Length: 500-2,100 words. Pays $15/printed page minimum plus 3 copies.

Photos: Send photos with submission. Reviews 8 × 10 prints. Negotiates payment individually. Identification of subjects required. Buys one-time rights.

Columns/Departments: Reta Finger, editor. Segue (feminist women in conservative/mainline churches), 800 words; Bible as Feminist Pilgrim (Biblical exegesis/theological discourse), 1,000 words; and Women in Ministry (clergy women and lay women in ministry tell personal stories), 1,000 words. Buys 6 mss/year. Query. Pays $15-80.

Fiction: Confession, historical, humorous, religious and slice-of-life vignettes. Buys 2 mss/year. Query. Length: 600-2,000 words. Pays $15-80.

Poetry: Free verse and light verse. Buys 12/year. Submit 4 poems max. Length: 4-100 lines. Pays $15-45.

Fillers: Anecdotes, facts, gags to be illustrated by cartoonist, newsbreaks and short humor. Buys 2/year. Length: 50-450 words. Pays $15.

Tips: "Query, query, query! Our writer's guidelines are very helpful and speak to specific areas (and pet peeves) that will help you get published in *Daughters of Sarah.* Use inclusive language. Use a personal approach and avoid preaching academic-ese and issues not relating to women, feminism and Christianity. Our nonfiction area is most open. My greatest advice is to please send for our guidelines and themes and then please query first before sending a manuscript. Stick to issues relating to a specific theme."

ESSENCE, 1500 Broadway, New York NY 10036. Editor-in-Chief: Susan L. Taylor. Editor: Stephanie Stokes Oliver. Executive Editor: Valerie Wilson Wesley. Monthly magazine. Estab. 1970. Circ. 950,000. **Pays on acceptance.** Makes assignments on work-for-hire basis. 3 month lead time. Pays 25% kill fee. Byline given. Submit seasonal/holiday material 6 months in advance. Reports in 2 months. Sample copy $2. Free writer's guidelines.
  • Ranked as one of the best markets for freelance writers in *Writer's Digest* magazine's annual "Top 100 Markets," January 1993.
Nonfiction: Valerie Wilson Wesley, executive editor. "We're looking for articles that inspire and inform Black women. The topics we include in each issue are provocative. Every article should move the *Essence* woman emotionally and intellectually. We welcome queries from good writers on a wide range of topics; general interest, health and fitness, historical, how-to, humor, self-help, relationships, work, personality interview, personal experience, political issues, business and finances and personal opinion." Buys 200 mss/year. Query only; word length will be given upon assignment. Pays $500 minimum. Also publishes novel excerpts.
Photos: Marlowe Goodson, art director. State availability of photos with query. Pays $100 for b&w page; $300 for color page. Captions and model release required. "We particularly would like to see photographs for our travel section that feature Black travelers."
Columns/Departments: Query department editors: Contemporary Living (home, food, lifestyle, travel, consumer information): Andrea D. Pinkney; Arts: Gordon Chambers; Health & Working: Linda Villarosa; Money: Andrea D. Pinkney. Query only; word length will be given upon assignment. Pays $100 minimum.
Tips: "Please note that *Essence* no longer accepts unsolicited mss for fiction, poetry or nonfiction, except for the Brothers, Back Talk and Interiors columns. So please only send query letters for nonfiction story ideas."

FAMILY CIRCLE MAGAZINE, 110 5th Ave., New York NY 10011. (212)463-1000. Editor-in-Chief: Jacqueline Leo. 70% freelance written. Published 17 times/year. Usually buys all print rights. Offers 20% kill fee. Byline given. **Pays on acceptance.** "We are a national women's magazine which offers advice, fresh information and entertainment to women. Query should stress the unique aspects of an article and expert sources; we want articles that will help our readers or make a difference in how they live." Reports in 1 month.
Nonfiction: Susan Ungaro, deputy editor. Women's interest subjects such as family and personal relationships, children, physical and mental health, nutrition, self-improvement and profiles of ordinary women doing extraordinary things for her community or the nation from 'Women Who Make a Difference' series. "We look for well-written, well-reported stories told through interesting anecdotes and insightful writing. We want well-researched service journalism on all subjects." Query. Length: 1,000-2,500 words. Pays $1/word.
  • Ranked as one of the best markets for freelance writers in *Writer's Digest* magazine's annual "Top 100 Markets," January 1993.
Tips: "Query letters should be concise and to the point. Also, writers should keep close tabs on *Family Circle* and other women's magazines to avoid submitting recently run subject matter."

FIRST FOR WOMEN, Bauer Publishing Co., P.O. Box 1648, 270 Sylvan Ave., Englewood Cliffs NJ 07632. "Prefers not to share information."

GLAMOUR, Conde Nast, 350 Madison Ave., New York NY 10017. (212)880-8800. Editor-in-Chief: Ruth Whitney. 75% freelance written. Works with a small number of new/unpublished writers each year. Monthly magazine for college-educated women, 18-35 years old. Estab. 1939. Circ. 2.3 million. **Pays on acceptance.** Offers 20% kill fee. Publishes ms an average of 1 year after acceptance. Byline given. Reports in 2 months. Writer's guidelines for #10 SASE.
Nonfiction: Susan Pelzer, articles editor. "Editorial approach is 'how-to' with articles that are relevant in the areas of careers, health, psychology, interpersonal relationships, etc. We look for queries that are fresh and include a contemporary, timely angle. Fashion, beauty, travel, food and entertainment are all staff-written. We use 1,000-word opinion essays for our Viewpoint section. Our His/Hers column features generally stylish essays on relationships or comments on current mores by male and female writers in alternate months." Pays $1,000 for His/Hers mss; $500 for Viewpoint mss. Buys first North American serial rights. Buys 10-12 mss/issue. Query "with letter that is detailed, well-focused, well-organized, and documented with surveys, statistics and research; personal essays excepted." Short articles and essays (1,500-2,000 words) pay $1,000 and up; longer mss (2,500-3,000 words) pay $1,500 minimum. Sometimes pays the expenses of writers on assignment.
  • Ranked as one of the best markets for freelance writers in *Writer's Digest* magazine's annual "Top 100 Markets," January 1993.
Tips: "We're looking for sharply focused ideas by strong writers and are constantly raising our standards. We are interested in getting new writers, and we are approachable, mainly because our range of topics is so broad. We've increased our focus on male-female relationships."

GOOD HOUSEKEEPING, Hearst Corp., 959 8th Ave., New York NY 10019. (212)649-2000. Editor-in-Chief: John Mack Carter. Executive Editor: Mina Mulvey. Managing Editor: Mary Fiore. Prefers to work with published/established writers. Monthly magazine. Circ. 5 million. **Pays on acceptance.** Buys all rights. Pays

25% kill fee. Byline given. Submit seasonal/holiday material 6 months in advance. Reports in 6 weeks. *Writer's Market* recommends allowing 2 months for reply. Sample copy $2. Writer's guidelines for #10 SASE.

Nonfiction: Joan Thursh, articles editor. Phyllis Levy, book editor. Medical, informational, investigative, inspirational, interview, nostalgia, personal experience and profile. Buys 4-6 mss/issue. Query. Length: 1,500-2,500 words. Pays $1,500+ on acceptance for full articles from new writers. Regional Editor: Shirley Howard. Pays $250-350 for local interest and travel pieces of 2,000 words. Pays the expenses of writers on assignment.

Photos: Herbert Bleiweiss, art director. Photos purchased on assignment mostly. Some short photo features with captions. Pays $100-350 for b&w; $200-400 for color photos. Query. Model releases required.

Columns/Departments: Light Housekeeping & Fillers, edited by Rosemary Leonard. Humorous short-short prose and verse. Jokes, gags, anecdotes. Pays $25-50. The Better Way, edited by Erika Mark. Ideas and in-depth research. Query. Pays $250-500. "Mostly staff written; only outstanding ideas have a chance here."

Fiction: Lee Quarfoot, fiction editor. Uses romance fiction and condensations of novels that can appear in one issue. Looks for reader identification. "We get 1,500 unsolicited mss/month—includes poetry; a free-lancer's odds are overwhelming—but we do look at all submissions." Send complete mss. Manuscripts will not be returned. Only responds on acceptance. Length: 1,500 words (short-shorts); novel according to merit of material; average 5,000-word short stories. Pays $1,000 minimum for fiction short-shorts; $1,250 for short stories.

Poetry: Arleen Quarfoot, poetry editor. Light verse and traditional. "Presently overstocked." Poems used as fillers. Pays $5/line for poetry on acceptance.

Tips: "Always send an SASE. We prefer to see a query first. Do not send material on subjects already covered in-house by the Good Housekeeping Institute—these include food, beauty, needlework and crafts."

● Ranked as one of the best markets for freelance writers in *Writer's Digest* magazine's annual "Top 100 Markets," January 1993.

HOMEMAKER'S, Telemedia Publishing, 50 Holly St., Toronto, Ontario M1K 5W9 Canada. "Prefers not to share information."

THE JOYFUL WOMAN, For and About Bible-believing Women Who Want God's Best, The Joyful Woman Ministries, Inc., 118 Shannon Lake Circle, Greenville SC 29615-5402. (803)234-0289. Editor: Elizabeth Handford. 30% freelance written. Works with small number of new/unpublished writers each year. Bimonthly magazine covering the role of women in home and business. "*The Joyful Woman* hopes to encourage, stimulate, teach and develop the Christian woman to reach the full potential of her womanhood." Estab. 1978. Circ. 15,000. Pays on publication. Publishes ms an average of 4 months after acceptance. Byline given. Buys first and reprint rights. Send photocopy of article or short story. For reprints, pays 50% of the amount paid for an original article. Submit seasonal/holiday material 4 months in advance. Reports in 3 months. Sample copy $3 for 9×12 SAE with 4 first class stamps. Writer's guidelines for #10 SASE.

Nonfiction: Book excerpts, how-to (housekeeping, childrearing, career management, etc.); inspirational; interview/profile (of Christian women); and personal experience. "We publish material on every facet of the human experience, considering not just a woman's spiritual needs, but her emotional, physical, and intellectual needs and her ministry to others." Buys 60 mss/year. Query or send complete ms. Length: 700-2,500 words. Pays about 2¢/word.

Tips: "The philosophy of the woman's liberation movement tends to minimize the unique and important ministries God has in mind for a woman. We believe that being a woman and a Christian ought to be joyful and fulfilling personally and valuable to God, whatever her situation—career woman, wife, mother, daughter."

LADIES' HOME JOURNAL, Meredith Corporation, 100 Park Ave., New York NY 10017-5516. (212)953-7070. Publishing Director and Editor-in-Chief: Myrna Blyth. 50% freelance written. Monthly magazine focusing on issues of concern to women. Circ. 5 million. **Pays on acceptance.** Offers 25% kill fee. Rights bought vary with submission. Reports within 3 months on queries with SASE. Writer's guidelines for #10 SASE, attention: writer's guidelines.

Nonfiction: Submissions on the following subjects should be directed to the editor listed for each: Psychology/Relationships/Sex (Pam O'Brien, features and books editor); Medical/Health (Linda Troiano, health editor); Celebrities/Entertainment (Entertainment Editor); investigative reports and news-related features (articles and fiction editor, Jane Farrell); and travel stories (Linda Fears, senior editor). Query with published clips. Length: 1,500-3,000 words. Fees vary. Pays expenses of writers on assignment.

Photos: State availability of photos with submission. Offers variable payment for photos accepted with ms. Captions, model releases and identification of subjects required. Rights bought vary with submission. (*LHJ* arranges for its own photography almost all the time.)

Columns/Departments: Query the following editor or box for column ideas. A Woman Today (Box WR); Woman to Woman (Box WW); Parents' Journal (Mary Mohler, managing editor); Pet News (Shana Aborn, associate editor).

Fiction: Submit to Sarah McCraw, associate editor, books and fiction. Only short stories and novels submitted by an agent or publisher will be considered. Buys 12 mss/year. Does not accept poetry of any kind.

LADY'S CIRCLE, Lopez Publications, Inc., Suite 906, 152 Madison Ave., New York NY 10016. (212)689-3933. Fax: (212)725-2239. Editor: Mary F. Bemis. 50% freelance written. Bimonthly magazine for "midwestern homemakers, middle to low income. A large number of senior citizens read *Lady's Circle*." Estab. 1963. Circ. 200,000. Pays on publication. Byline given. Submit seasonal/holiday material 6 months in advance. Previously published submissions OK; send photocopy of article or short story or typed ms with rights for sale noted and information about when and where the article previously appeared. Pays 50% of their fee for an original article. Reports in 2 months on queries; 3 months on mss. Sample copy for 9 × 12 SAE with 5 first class stamps. Writer's guidelines for #10 SASE.
Nonfiction: Historical/nostalgic, how-to (crafts, cooking, hobbies), humor, inspirational, interview/profile, opinion and personal experience. No travel. Buys 50-75 mss/year. Query. Pays $125 for unsolicited articles. Sometimes pays expenses of writers on assignment.
 • Looking for more home decorating and craft submissions. No longer seeking fillers.
Photos: State availability of photos with submission. Reviews negatives, transparencies and prints. Offers $10/photo. Model releases and identification of subjects required.
Columns/Departments: Sound Off (pet peeves) 250 words; Readers' Cookbook (readers send in recipes); and Helpful Hints (hints for kitchen, house, etc.) 3-4 lines each. Send complete ms. Pays $5-10.
Fiction: Humorous, mainstream, romance and slice-of-life vignettes. Nothing experimental. No foul language. Buys 3 mss/year. Send complete ms. Pays $125.
Tips: "Write for guidelines. A good query is always appreciated. Fifty percent of our magazine is open to freelancers."

LEAR'S, Lear Publishing Inc., 655 Madison Ave., New York NY 10021. (212)888-0007. Editor-in-Chief: Caroline Miller. Articles Editor: Nelson W. Aldrich, Jr. Monthly magazine for women. Circ. 450,000. **Pays on acceptance.** Byline given. Offers 25% kill fee. Buys first North American serial rights. Reports in 2 months.
Nonfiction: Book excerpts, essays, general interest, interview/profile, opinion, personal experience and travel. Query with published clips. Length: 800-1,200 words. Pays $1/word.
Columns/Departments: Self-Center, Money & Worth, Health and Features. Query with published clips. Length: 800-1,000 words. Pays $1/word.

McCALL'S, 110 5th Ave., New York NY 10011-5603. (212)463-1000. Editor: Kate White. Executive Editor: Lynne Cusack. 90% freelance written. "Study recent issues. Our publication carefully and conscientiously services the needs of the woman reader—concentrating on matters that directly affect her life and offering information and understanding on subjects of personal importance to her." Monthly. Circ. 5 million. **Pays on acceptance.** Publishes ms an average of 6 months after acceptance. Offers 20% kill fee. Byline given. Buys exclusive or First North American rights. Reports in 2 months. Writer's guidelines for #10 SASE.
Nonfiction: No subject of wide public or personal interest is out of bounds for *McCall's* so long as it is appropriately treated. The editors are seeking meaningful stories of personal experience, fresh slants for self-help and relationship pieces, and well-researched articles and narratives dealing with social problems concerning readers. *McCall's* buys 200-300 articles/year, many in the 1,000- to 1,500-word length. Pays variable rates for nonfiction. Deputy Editor Lisel Eisenheimer is editor of nonfiction books, from which *McCall's* frequently publishes excerpts. These are on subjects of interest to women: personal narratives, celebrity biographies and autobiographies, etc. Almost all features on food, household equipment and management, fashion, beauty, building and decorating are staff-written. Query. "All mss must be submitted on speculation, and *McCall's* accepts no responsibility for unsolicited mss." Sometimes pays the expenses of writers on assignment.
Tips: "Except for humor, query first. Use the focus of our most recent issues as your guide. We don't encourage an idea unless we think we can use it." Preferred length: 1,000-2,000 words. Address submissions to executive editor unless otherwise specified.
 • No longer publishes fiction.

MADEMOISELLE, Conde Nast, 350 Madison Ave., New York NY 10017. (212)880-8559. Managing Editor: Joan Feeney. 95% freelance written. Prefers to work with published/established writers. Columns are written by columnists; "sometimes we give new writers a 'chance' on shorter, less complex assignments." Monthly magazine for women age 21-31. Circ 1.2 million. Buys first North American serial rights. **Pays on acceptance;** rates vary.
Nonfiction: Particular concentration on articles of interest to the intelligent young woman, including personal relationships, health, careers, trends, and current social problems. Send health queries to Jennifer Rapaport, associate editor. Send entertainment queries to Peter McQuaid, entertainment editor. Query with published clips and SAE. Length: 1,000 words.
Photos: Douglas Lloyd, art director. Commissioned work assigned according to needs. Photos of fashion, beauty, travel. Payment ranges from no-charge to an agreed rate of payment per shot, job series or page rate. Buys all rights. Pays on publication for photos.
Tips: "We are looking for timely, well-researched manuscripts."
 • *Mademoiselle* no longer publishes fiction. They offer no scholarships and accept no interns.

MIRABELLA, 200 Madison Ave., 8th Floor, New York NY 10016. "Prefers not to share information."

MODERN BRIDE, 249 W. 17th St., New York NY 10011. (212)337-7096. Editor: Cele Lalli. Managing Editor: Mary Ann Cavlin. **Pays on acceptance.** Offers 25% kill fee. Buys first periodical rights. Previously published submissions OK. Reports in 1 month.
Nonfiction: Book excerpts, general interest, how-to, personal experience. Buys 70 mss/year. Query with published clips. Length: 500-2,000 words. Pays $600-1,200.
Columns/Departments: Geri Bain, editor. Travel.
Poetry: Free verse, light verse and traditional. Buys very few. Submit maximum 6 poems.

  • Ranked as one of the best markets for freelance writers in *Writer's Digest* magazine's annual "Top 100 Markets," January 1993.

MS. MAGAZINE, Lang Communications, Inc., 7th Floor, 230 Park Ave., New York NY 10169-0799. (212)551-9595. Editor-in-Chief: Robin Morgan. Managing Editor: Barbara Findlen. Executive Editor: Marcia Gillespie. 75% freelance written. Bimonthly magazine on women's issues and news. Estab. 1972. Circ. 200,000. Pays on publication. Byline given. Offers 20% kill fee. Buys all rights. Submit seasonal material 6 months in advance. Reports in 2 months. Sample copy $5. Writer's guidelines for #10 SASE.
Nonfiction: International and national (US) news, the arts, books, popular culture, feminist theory and scholarship, ecofeminism, women's health, spirituality, and political and economic affairs. Photo essays. Runs fiction and poetry but does not accept, acknowledge, or return unsolicited fiction or poetry. Does not discuss queries on the phone. Query with published clips. Length: 300-3,000 words. Pays expenses of writers on assignment.
Photos: State availability of photos with submission. Model releases and identification of subjects required. Buys one-time rights.

NEW WOMAN MAGAZINE, A New Woman Is An Attitude, Not An Age, K-III Magazine Corporation, 215 Lexington Ave., New York NY 10016. (212)251-1500. Editor-in-Chief: Karen Walden. Managing Editor: Kathy L. Green. Monthly women's general interest/service magazine. "*New Woman* is edited for employed women who are eager to reach for new goals and to balance their personal and professional lives. The magazine's prime focus is on self-discovery, self-development and self-esteem." Estab. 1970. Circ. 1,390,630. **Pays on acceptance.** Byline given. Offers 20% kill fee. Buys first North American serial, first or one-time rights. Submit seasonal material 5 months in advance. Reports in 1 month. Writer's guidelines for #10 SASE.
Nonfiction: Essays, general interest, humor (from woman's experience viewpoint), inspirational, opinion and personal experience. "No fiction, poetry or straight travel pieces . . . travel must encompass a personal experience which leads to or adds to discovery, development and/or empowerment of a woman." 65% of mss from freelancers. Query with published clips. Length: 1,000-3,500 words. Pays $700-3,500. Sometimes pays expenses of writers on assignment.
Photos: State availability of photos with submission. Reviews contact sheets. Negotiates payment for photos. Model release and identification of subjects required. Buys one-time rights.
Fillers: Cartoons. Pays $225 on acceptance.
Tips: "Send a personal letter, with clippings of published work, telling us what you are interested in and want to write about, and your perceptions of *New Woman*. It counts when a writer loves the magazine and responds to it on a personal level. We look for originality, solid research, depth and a friendly, accessible style. Freelancers will have the best chances with feature articles on relationships or inspirational essays. Study and understand the 'voice' of *New Woman*: the magazine is friendly, helpful and accessible to its readership in all respects."

  • Ranked as one of the best markets for freelance writers in *Writer's Digest* magazine's annual "Top 100 Markets," January 1993.

RADIANCE, The Magazine for Large Women, Box 30246, Oakland CA 94604. (510)482-0680. Editor: Alice Ansfield. 95% freelance written. Quarterly magazine "that encourages and supports women *all* sizes of large to live fully now, to stop putting their lives on hold until they lose weight." Estab. 1984. Circ. 10,000. Pays on publication. Publishes ms an average of 3 months after acceptance. Byline given. Offers $25 kill fee. Buys one-time and second serial (reprint) rights. Submit seasonal/holiday material at least 6-8 months in advance. Previously published submissions OK. Query for electronic submissions. Reports in 2½-3 months. Sample copy $3.50. Writer's guidelines for #10 SASE.
Nonfiction: Book excerpts (related to large women), essays, expose, general interest, historical/nostalgic, how-to (on health/well-being/fashion/fitness, etc.), humor, inspirational, interview/profile, opinion, personal experience, photo feature and travel. "No diet successes or articles condemning people for being fat." Query with published clips. Length: 1,000-2,500 words. Pays $35-100. Sometimes pays writers with contributor copies or other premiums.

Photos: State availability of photos with submission. Offers $15-50/photo. Captions and identification of subjects preferred. Buys one-time rights.

Columns/Departments: Up Front and Personal (personal profiles of women from all areas of life); Health and Well-Being (physical/emotional well-being, self care, research); Images (designer interviews, color/style/fashion, features); Inner Journeys (spirituality, personal experiences, interviews); Perspectives (cultural and political aspects of being in a larger body); and On the Move (women active in all kinds of sports, physical activities). Buys 60 mss/year. Query with published clips. Length: 1,000-2,000 words. Pays $50-100.

Fiction: Condensed novels, ethnic, fantasy, historical, humorous, mainstream, novel excerpts, romance, science fiction, serialized novels and slice-of-life vignettes relating somehow to large women. "No woman-hates-self-till-meets-man'-type fiction!" Buys 15 mss/year. Query with published clips. **Length:** 800-1,500 words. Pays $35-100.

Poetry: Reflective, empowering, experiential. Related to women's feelings and experience, re: their bodies, self-esteem, acceptance. Buys 30 poems/year. Length: 4-45 lines. Pays $10-30.

Tips: "We welcome talented, sensitive, responsible, open-minded writers. We profile women from all walks of life who are all sizes of large, of all ages and from all ethnic groups and lifestyles. We welcome writers' ideas on interesting large women from across the US and abroad. We're an open, light-hearted magazine that's working to help women feel good about themselves now, whatever their body size. *Radiance* is one of the major forces working for size acceptance. We want articles to address all areas of vital importance in women's lives. Please read a copy of *Radiance* before writing for us."

REDBOOK MAGAZINE, 224 W. 57th St., New York NY 10019. Senior Editors: Diane Salvatore, Sally Lee. Health Editor: Toni Hope. Fiction Editor: Dawn Raffel. 90% freelance written. Monthly magazine. Estab. 1903. Circ. 3.2 million. **Pays on acceptance.** Publishes ms an average of 4-6 months after acceptance. Rights purchased vary with author and material. Reports in 3 months. Writer's guidelines for #10 SASE.
  • Ranked as one of the best markets for freelance writers in *Writer's Digest* magazine's annual "Top 100 Markets," January 1993.

Nonfiction: "*Redbook* addresses young mothers between the ages of 25 and 44. Most of our readers are married with children 12 and under; over 60 percent work outside the home. The articles entertain, educate and inspire our readers to confront challenging issues. Each article must be timely and be specific to *Redbook* readers' concerns. Article subjects of interest: social issues, parenting, sex, marriage, profiles, crime, money, psychology, and health. Please enclose sample of previously published work with articles or unsolicited manuscripts." Length: articles, 2,500-3,000 words; short articles, 1,000-1,500 words.

Columns/Departments: "We are interested in stories for the 'A Mother's Story' series offering the dramatic retelling of an experience involving you, your husband or child. For each 1,500-2,000 words accepted for publication as A Mother's Story, we pay $750. Manuscripts, accompanied by a 9×12 SASE, must be signed, and mailed to: A Mother's Story, c/o *Redbook Magazine.* Reports in 6 months. We also need stories for the back page Happy Endings column, stories of about 800 words that, just as the title suggests, end happily. See past issues for samples."

Fiction: "Of the 20,000 unsolicited manuscripts that we receive annually, we buy about 10 or more stories/year. We also find many more stories that are not necessarily suited to our needs but are good enough to warrant our encouraging the author to send others. *Redbook* looks for fresh, well-crafted stories that reflect some aspect of the experiences and interests of our readers; it's a good idea to read several issues to get a feel for what we buy. No unsolicited novels or novellas, please." Payment begins at $1,000 for short stories.

Tips: "Shorter, front-of-the-book features are usually easier to develop with first-time contributors, especially A Mother's Story and Happy Endings. We also buy short takes (250 words) for our You & Your Child opening page—succinct, charming advice-driven items. Most *Redbook* articles require solid research, full, well-developed anecdotes from on-the-record sources, and fresh, insightful quotes from established experts in a field that pass our 'reality check' test."

SELF, Conde Nast, 350 Madison Ave., New York NY 10017. (212)880-8834. Fax: (212)880-8110. Editor-in-Chief: Alexandra Penney. Managing Editor: Lisa Shelkin. 50% freelance written. "We prefer to work with writers—even relatively new ones—with a degree, training or practical experience in specialized areas from psychology to health to nutrition." Monthly magazine emphasizing self improvement of emotional and physical well-being for women of all ages. Circ. 1 million. Average issue includes 12-20 feature articles and 4-6 columns. **Pays on acceptance.** Publishes ms an average of 6 months after acceptance. Byline given. Offers 25% kill fee. Buys first North American serial rights. Submit seasonal material 4 months in advance. Simultaneous submissions OK. Reports in 1 month. *Writer's Market* recommends allowing 2 months for reply. Writer's guidelines for #10 SASE.

Nonfiction: Well-researched service articles on self improvement, health, careers, nutrition, fitness, fashion and beauty, medicine, male/female relationships and money. "We try to translate major developments and complex information in these areas into practical, personalized articles." Buys 6-10 mss/issue. Query with clips of previously published work. Length: 1,000-2,500 words. Pays $1,000-2,000. "We are always looking for any piece that has a psychological or behavioral side. We rely heavily on freelancers who can take an article on contraceptive research, for example, and add a psychological aspect to it. Everything should relate to the whole person." Pays the expenses of writers on assignment "with prior approval."

Photos: Submit to art director. State availability of photos. Reviews 5×7 b&w glossy prints.

Columns/Departments: Work (800-1,200 words on career topics); and Money (800-1,200 words on finance topics); others, such as Entertaining, Man's View. Buys 4-6 mss/issue. Query. Pays $800-2,000.

Tips: "Original ideas backed by research open our doors. We almost never risk blowing a major piece on an untried-by-us writer, especially since these ideas are usually staff-conceived. It's usually better for everyone to start small, where there's time and leeway for re-writes. The most frequent mistakes made by writers in completing an article for us are swiss-cheese research (holes all over it which the writer missed and has to go back and fill in) and/or not personalizing the information by applying it to the reader, but just reporting it."

TODAY'S CHRISTIAN WOMAN, 465 Gundersen Dr., Carol Stream IL 60188-2498. (708)260-6200. Fax: (708)260-0114. Editor: Julie A. Talerico. 25% freelance written. Works with a small number of new/unpublished writers each year. Bimonthly magazine for Christian women of all ages, single and married, homemakers and career women. Estab. 1979. Circ. 190,000. **Pays on acceptance.** Publishes ms an average of 3 months after acceptance. Byline given. Buys first rights only. Submit seasonal/holiday material 9 months in advance. Reports in 2 months. Sample copy $3.50. Writer's guidelines for #10 SASE.

Nonfiction: How-to, narrative and inspirational. Query only; no unsolicited mss. "The query should include article summary, purpose and reader value, author's qualifications, suggested length and date to send. Pays 15¢/word.

Tips: "Articles focus on the following relationships: marriage, parenting, self, spiritual life and friendship. All articles should be highly anecdotal, personal in tone, and universal in appeal."

VANITY FAIR, Conde Nast, 350 Madison Ave., New York NY 10017. "Prefers not to share information."

VICTORIA, Hearst Corp., 224 W. 57th St., New York NY 10019. "Prefers not to share information."

VOGUE, Conde Nast, 350 Madison Ave., New York NY 10017. "Prefers not to share information."

WEST COAST WOMAN, GDP Media, Inc., P.O. Box 3047, Sarasota FL 34230-3047. (813)954-3300. Editor: Kate Dowie. 50% freelance written. Biweekly tabloid for women on the west coast of Florida. *"West Coast Woman* is a lifestyle publication." Estab. 1988. Circ. 42,000. Pays on publication. Byline given. Offers 50% kill fee. Buys first or one-time rights. Submit seasonal/holiday material 2 months in advance. Sample copy $3.50. Writer's guidelines for #10 SASE.

Nonfiction: Real estate, gardening, how-to, health, beauty, book reviews, seniors, car care, home design, fitness, photo feature, technical, travel, sports, fashion, money/finance, nutrition, cooking, food/wine. "Special issues: Bridal issue (January), Health & Fitness (January), Careers (October), AIDS (November). No humor, slice-of-life, essays, poems, poetry or comics/cartoons." Buys 130 mss/year. Query with published clips. Length: 750-3,000 words. Pays $35-65 for 750 words. Also makes ad trades for promotional tie-ins.

Photos: State availability of photos with submission. Reviews contact sheets, 35mm transparencies. Model releases required. Buys one-time rights.

Columns/Departments: Money/Finance. Buys 130 mss/year. Query with published clips. Length: 750-3,000 words. Pays $35-65 for 750 words.

WOMAN'S DAY, 1633 Broadway, New York NY 10019. (212)767-6000. Articles Editor: Rebecca Greer. 75% or more of articles freelance written. 17 issues/year. Circ. 6 million. Pays negotiable kill fee. Byline given. **Pays on acceptance.** Reports in 1 month on queries. Submit detailed queries.

Nonfiction: Uses articles on all subjects of interest to women—marriage, family life, childrearing, education, homemaking, money management, careers, family health, work and leisure activities. Also interested in fresh, dramatic narratives of women's lives and concerns. "These must be lively and fascinating to read." Length: 500-2,500 words, depending on material. Payment varies depending on length, type, writer, and whether it's for regional or national use, but rates are high. Pays the expenses of writers on confirmed assignment. "We no longer accept unsolicited manuscripts—and can not return or be responsible for those that are sent to us."

Fillers: Neighbors and Tips to Share columns also pay $75/each for brief practical suggestions on homemaking, childrearing and relationships. Address to the editor of the appropriate section.

Tips: "Our primary need is for ideas with broad appeal that can be featured on the cover. We're buying more short pieces. Writers should consider Quick section which uses factual pieces of 100-300 words."

• Ranked as one of the best markets for freelance writers in *Writer's Digest* magazine's annual "Top 100 Markets," January 1993.

WOMAN'S WORLD, The Woman's Weekly, Heinrich Bauer North American, Inc., 270 Sylvan Ave., Englewood Cliffs NJ 07632. (201)569-0006. Editor-in-Chief: Dena Vane. 95% freelance written. Weekly magazine covering "controversial, dramatic, and human interest women's issues" for women across the nation. **Pays on acceptance.** Publishes ms an average of 4 months after acceptance. Byline given. Offers kill fee. Buys first North American serial rights. Submit seasonal/holiday material 4 months in advance. Simultaneous queries and simultaneous or previously published submissions OK. Reports in 6 weeks on queries; 2 months on mss. Writer's guidelines for #10 SASE.

Nonfiction: Well-researched material with "a hard-news edge and topics of national scope." Reports of 1,000-1,200 words, 200 word sidebar, on vital trends and major issues such as women and alcohol or teen suicide; dramatic, personal women's stories; articles on self-improvement, medicine and health topics; and the economics of home, career and daily life, pays $550. Features include In Real Life (true stories); Turning Point (in a woman's life); Families (highlighting strength of family or how unusual families deal with problems); True Love (tender, beautiful, touching and unusual love stories with happy endings). Other regular features are "Topics of the Week" (investigative news features with national scope, statistics, etc.); Scales of Justice (true stories of women and crime "if possible, presented with sympathetic attitude"); and Relationships (pop psychology or coping). Queries should be addressed to Johnene Granger. Pays telephone interview expenses.

Fiction: Jeanne Muchnick, fiction editor. Short story, romance and mainstream of 1,900 words and mini-mysteries of 1,000 words. "Each of our stories has a light romantic theme with a protagonist no older than 40. Each can be written from either a masculine or feminine point of view. Women characters may be single, married or divorced. Plots must be fast moving with vivid dialogue and action. The problems and dilemmas inherent in them should be contemporary and realistic, handled with warmth and feeling. The stories must have a positive resolution." Not interested in science fiction, fantasy, historical romance or foreign locales. No explicit sex, graphic language or seamy settings. Specify "short story" on envelope. Always enclose SASE. Reports in 2 months. No phone queries. Pays $1,000 on acceptance for North American serial rights for 6 months. "The 1,000 word mini-mysteries may feature either a 'whodunnit' or 'howdunnit' theme. The mystery may revolve around anything from a theft to murder. However, we are not interested in sordid or grotesque crimes. Emphasis should be on intricacies of plot rather than gratuitous violence. The story must include a resolution that clearly states the villain is getting his or her come-uppance." Submit complete mss. Specify "mini-mystery" on envelope. Enclose SASE. Stories slanted for a particular holiday should be sent at least 6 months in advance. No phone queries.

Photos: State availability of photos. "State photo leads. Photos are assigned to freelance photographers." Buys one-time rights.

Tips: "Come up with good queries. Short queries are best. We have a strong emphasis on well-researched material. Writers must send research with ms including book references and phone numbers for double checking. The most frequent mistakes made by writers in completing an article for us are sloppy, incomplete research, not writing to the format, and not studying the magazine carefully enough beforehand."

WOMEN'S CIRCLE, P.O. Box 299, Lynnfield MA 01940-0299. Editor: Marjorie Pearl. 100% freelance written. Bimonthly magazine for women of all ages. Buys all rights. **Pays on acceptance.** Byline given. Publishes ms an average of 6 months to 1 year after acceptance. Submit seasonal material 8 months in advance. Reports in 3 months. Sample copy $2. Writer's guidelines for #10 SASE.

Nonfiction: Especially interested in stories about successful, home-based female entrepreneurs with b&w photos or transparencies. Length: 1,000-2,000 words. Also interesting and unusual money-making ideas. Welcomes good quality crafts and how-to directions in any media—crochet, fabric, etc.

Consumer Magazines/Changes '93-'94

The following consumer publications were listed in the 1993 edition but do not have listings in this edition. The majority did not respond to our request to update their listings. If a reason was given for their exclusion, we have included it in parentheses after the listing.

AAA Going Places
AAA World
Adventure Road
Aegean Review
Africa Abroad
American Handgunner
American Matchcover Collectors Club
American Rifleman
Americas
Amicus Journal
Amigaworld
Amtrak Express
Anglo-American Spotlight (unable to contact)
Appaloosa Journal
Architectural Digest

Arizona Literary Review (unable to contact)
Arkansas Times
Asiapacific Travel
Axios
Baptist Leader
Barron's
Baseball Cards (asked to be deleted)
Better Nutrition for Today's Living (staff writers only)
Better World (ceased publication)
Beyond . . .
Bicycle Guide
Birder's World
Body Building Lifestyles

Boston Phoenix
Bostonia
Brennco Destinations
Bridal Crafts (ceased publication)
Bridal Guide
Brio (ceased publication)
Business to Business Magazine
Camera & Darkroom Magazine
Carolina Quarterly
Cat Companion (out of business)
Catholic Forester (no longer uses articles or stories)
CD Review
Changing Men
The Children's Album (ceased

publication)
Christian Herald
Collectors' Showcase
Columbus Bride & Groom Magazine (does not use freelancers)
Computoredge
Confident Living
Coral Springs Monthly/Plantation Monthly (unable to contact)
Creative Woodworks & Crafts (does not use freelancers)
Crisis Magazine
Cruising World
Crusader Magazine
Current Health
Currents (ceased publication)
"D" Magazine
Daily Meditation
Deer and Deer Hunting
Delaware Valley
Destination Washington
Discipleship Journal
The Diver
Dixie Gun Works Blackpowder Annual
Dog Fancy
Electric Consumer
Electronic Composition and Imaging
Entrepreneurial Woman (no longer publishing on regular basis)
Epoch
Erie & Chautauqua Magazine
The Evangelical Beacon
Exhibit
Expressions (out of business)
Facets of New York
Fantasy Baseball (does not use unsolicited material)
Farm & Ranch Living
Fifty-something Magazine
Final Frontier
Finger Lakes Magazine (unable to contact)
The Fisherman
Fishing and Hunting News
The Florida Horse
Food & Wine
Forbes Magazine
Forests & People (asked to be deleted)
The Gamut
Gem Show News
Genre
Georgia Journal
Gold Standard News (unable to contact)
Good Reading (out of business)
Great Lakes Fisherman
Great Lakes Sailor (out of business)
Greater Portland Magazine
Guitar Player Magazine
Guitar World
Gulfshore Life
Guns & Ammo Annual
Harrowsmith Magazine
Heddle Magazine
HG (ceased publication)
Hinduism Today

Hobo Jungle
Home & Away
Home Office Computing
Home
Hoof Beats
Horse Illustrated
Hot Rod
Illinois Magazine (out of business)
India Currents (does not pay)
Inner-view
Inside Hollywood (out of business)
Interlit (asked to be deleted)
International Arts (out of business)
Jabberwocky (unable to contact)
Jacksonville Magazine
Journal of Graphoanalysis
Junior Trails
Lake Effect
Lighthouse
Long Island Power & Sail
Louisiana Life Magazine
MacLean's
Madison Magazine
The Maine Sportsman
Memphis Business Journal (does not use freelance mss)
MHQ
Michigan Lviing
Mid-Atlantic Country
Military Images
Miniature Collector (magazine sold)
Modern Office (unable to contact)
Moneyworld (unable to contact)
Mother Jones Magazine
Motor Boating & Sailing
Music City News (asked to be deleted)
Music Express (unable to contact)
N.Y. Habitat Magazine
Nanny Times (out of business)
National Christian Reporter
National Lampoon
National Masters Running News (does not pay)
Natural Food & Farming
Navy Times
Near West Gazette
The New Renaissance
New York Antique Almanac (eliminated fine writing)
The New York Times Magazine
Newsday
Newsweek
North American Hunter
North Dakota REC/RTC
North-South
Northwest Travel
Oh! Idaho
Ohio Fisherman
On the Scene Magazine
The Onion (asked to be deleted)
Palm Beach Life
PC World
Peninsula Magazine
Pennsylvania Heritage

Penthouse
Personal Fitness and Weight Loss (ceased publication
Photo Traveler
Playboy
Playgirl
Policy Review
Popular Electronics
Portable 100
Postcard Collector
Powerboat Magazine
Prime Times
Prime
Quality Living (asked to be deleted)
Quantum (merging)
Quarry
R&R Shoppers News (ceased publication)
Reader's Digest (Canada)
Report on the Americas
The Reporter
Richmond Surroundings
Right On!
River City
Robb Report
Rockford Magazine
Running Times
Sagacity (asked to be deleted)
Sailaway
Sailing Magazine
Sea
Senior High I.D.
Sewanee Review
Shuttle Spindle & Dyepot
The Silly Club Rag
Site Sound (unable to contact)
680 Magazine
Snow Country
Snow Goer
Snowmobile Magazine
South Florida
Southern Links
Southern Prestigious Homes & Interiors (out of business)
Southern Saltwater Magazine
Southern Woman to Woman
Southwest Profile (asked to be deleted)
Spirit
Success Insight
Sun
Sunshine Magazine (out of business)
Swank
Swim Magazine
Tallahassee Magazine
Tampa Bay Life (unable to contact)
TDC
TDR
Team
Technology Review
The Tennessee Magazine
Tennis
Today's Times
Toronto Life
Tours & Resorts
Town and Country
Transcend
Travel Holiday
Travelore Report
Trip & Tour
Tropic Magazine

The Turkey Hunter (merged with Turkey & Turkey Hunting)
Turn-on Letters (out of business)
Undercurrent
United Methodist Reporter
University of Toronto Quarterly
Venture and Visions
Vermont Times
The Virginia Quarterly Review

Vital Christianity
Volkswagen World (does not use freelancers)
Voyager/Sun Scene (asked to be deleted)
The Walking Magazine (asked to be deleted)
Wang in the News
The Weekly News
West
Western Links
Western Outdoors

Western People
The Western Producer
Wine Enthusiast
Women & Guns
Women's Household Crochet
Women's Household
Wordperfect for Windows Magazine
Workbasket Magazine
The World & I
World Policy Journal
York Magazine

Trade, Technical and Professional Journals......... 680

Trade, Technical and Professional Journals

by Jack Neff

Though perhaps not as glamorous in the eyes of your friends and relatives as writing for *Harper's* or *Good Housekeeping*, publishing in trade periodicals provides, for many writers, something much more enticing than glamour — a good living. You won't find many trade publications paying $1/word and up. But you will find plenty of trade publications paying 15-50¢/word. Those rates let a reasonably hard-working writer make a decent living.

Trade journals offer another big economic advantage. By working for them, you can eliminate much of the time-consuming, costly process of pitching story ideas to new publications each month. Consumer publications often want a variety of voices, so it's harder to land repeat assignments. But trade journals are more loyal. They need writers with specialized knowledge, so it pays for them to cultivate a stable of writers rather than constantly bring newcomers up to speed.

Moreover, many trade journal editors regularly provide unsolicited assignments for freelance writers they know. And even if they don't, they're generally easier to approach with ideas than consumer editors. They usually don't have as many freelancers bombarding them with submissions so they tend to report more quickly on written queries or even approve phone queries from writers they know.

Trade writing requirements

Trade publications aren't for every writer. If you feel you're just slumming with trade journals until you can break into consumer publications, don't bother. Editors of trade publications expect no less research effort or writing quality than any other editors. If business or technical details bore you to death, this isn't the place for you, either. Readers and editors of trade publications don't let you gloss over the fine points. They want specific information they can put to use, not nice-sounding generalities.

Background or training in a trade or profession is a big plus for trade journal writers. But lack of previous experience in an industry doesn't necessarily

Jack Neff *is a Cincinnati-based freelance business writer who regularly contributes to publications in the food and woodworking industries as well as several other specialty publications. He is a contributing author to* The Writer's Essential Desk Reference *(Writer's Digest Books) and author of* Make Your Woodworking Pay for Itself *(Writer's Digest Books) and the* Designer's Guide to Making Money with Your Desktop Computer *(North Light Books).*

disqualify you. If your query shows you understand a subject and why the magazine's readers would be interested, you can make the sale. Trade editors realize that few writers have direct experience in the industries they cover, so they're often willing to help with background material, sources and questions to ask.

You research a trade publication the same way you do a consumer title. Look up its listing in this section to find out if the pay is in your ballpark and to glean tips that can help you develop ideas. Read several issues before you query, noting the style, format and any columns or departments into which your article might fit. At the same time, read for trends that can lend significance to your story idea.

Types of trade publications

Trade publications fall into two broad categories—news-oriented and feature-oriented. News-oriented publications are looking for breaking news stories, such as legislation, court cases, takeovers or major strategic moves by companies in the industry. They're usually dailies, weeklies or semi-monthlies. Feature-oriented publications are usually published monthly, bimonthly or quarterly and focus almost entirely on how-to stories and profiles. They may do trend stories—but it needs to be a bona fide, lasting trend and have at least one how-to sidebar.

All trade journals are interested in people or companies that have found better ways to do their jobs. Readers are looking for trends that will affect their careers and companies—or influence the decisions they make. They're interested in ways to make or save money. In short, trade publications cover the same things consumer business publications do—only for a particular industry.

As a writer it's best to specialize in a few industries. The more you learn about an industry, the easier it gets to come up with article ideas and know what will appeal to a trade journal's readers. Once you have the grasp of one industry, you can branch into related areas. For instance, an article about new environmental testing regulations for hazardous waste incinerators could, with some rewriting, go into a magazine for testing laboratories.

The easiest way to specialize is to draw from your own background or experience. Otherwise, your specialty may depend on chance. If a particular industry is strong in your region, it makes sense to follow it. Or you may learn of an innovative insurance plan and sell an article to an employee benefits magazine, then start developing other ideas for the same publication.

Finding the right market

The listings in this section are a good place to start in your search for trade markets. These journals are receptive to freelance submissions. There are

INSIDER REPORT

Trade magazine writers need to "walk the walk" and "talk the talk"

"The key difference between trade and consumer magazines that writers need to be aware of," says Steve Shapiro, editor of *Pacific Fishing*, "is that readers of trade magazines have a tremendous amount of expertise and a compelling interest in the subject matter. The reason is simple – they make their living by plying the craft that is the focus of the magazine."

Pacific Fishing is a monthly business magazine for commercial fishermen and others in the West Coast commercial fishing industry. Every month, Shapiro's readers expect to find interesting, technically correct articles and information that will help them do their jobs better.

Because of the expertise his readers bring to the magazine, they are *not* interested in basic information, Shapiro says. "This means they are looking to the magazine as a source of highly refined information or new insights on a well-known subject. We deal with all aspects of commercial fishing on the West Coast including catch, processing, markets, gear/boats, new technology and politics. Whereas a consumer magazine tends to identify trends of general interest and discuss them in lay terms, we need to generate discussion that is informative at an elevated level in order to meet our readers' needs."

Steve Shapiro

The practical result of having a subject-sophisticated readership is that trade magazines such as *Pacific Fishing* need writers who know the trade they are covering. "Readers of trade magazines want writers who evoke a sense of empathy with their vocation," says Shapiro, "writers who can 'walk the walk' and 'talk the talk.' This typically requires that the writer has some practical experience in the trade or at least is willing to get down and dirty in the field. I suppose that where a writer in a consumer magazine needs to have an air of authority over the subject matter, the trade writer needs an air of *authenticity* as well."

– *Mark Garvey*

many other trade and professional magazines; some are receptive to freelance queries but do not choose to have a listing because they prefer to work with writers who have industry experience. You can find listings for many publications in *The Business Publication Volume*, published by the Standard Rate and Data Service (SRDS). Updated monthly, it contains names and addresses of thousands of trade journals classified according to subject matter. SRDS designs its directory for ad buyers, so it doesn't cover the hundreds of specialty trade newsletters that don't accept advertising. *The Directory of Newsletters* (Oxbridge) and *Newsletters in Print* (Gale) are the best places to find these. Though many newsletters are entirely staff written, some welcome freelance submissions. Armed with their names and addresses, you can then write for sample copies and writer's guidelines.

For the most timely information on new magazine start-ups, monitor *Folio* and *Advertising Age*. Information about advertising page counts also can help you spot good markets in two ways. You can use the statistics to monitor which industries are flat and which are growing. Plus, you can look for publications with rapidly growing page counts. Their staffing probably hasn't kept pace with their ad pages and they may need freelance submissions in a hurry.

For information on additional trade publications not listed in *Writer's Market*, see Trade, Technical and Professional Journals/Changes '93-'94 at the end of this section.

Advertising, Marketing and PR

Trade journals for advertising executives, copywriters and marketing and public relations professionals are listed in this category. Those whose main focus is the advertising and marketing of specific products, such as home furnishings, are classified under individual product categories. Journals for sales personnel and general merchandisers can be found in the Selling and Merchandising category.

ADVERTISING AGE, Dept. WM, 740 N. Rush, Chicago IL 60611-2590. (312)649-5200. Managing Editor: Valerie Mackie. Managing Editor/Special Reports: Larry Edwards. Executive Editor: Dennis Chase. Deputy Editor: Larry Doherty. New York office: 220 E. 42 St., New York NY 10017. (212)210-0100. Editor: Fred Danzig. Currently staff-produced. Includes weekly sections devoted to one topic (i.e. marketing in Southern California, agribusiness/advertising, TV syndication trends). Little of this material is done freelance—on assignment only. Pays kill fee "based on hours spent plus expenses." Byline given "except short articles or contributions to a roundup."

AMERICAN DEMOGRAPHICS, American Demographics, Inc., P.O. Box 68, Ithaca NY 14851-0068. (607)273-6343. Fax: (607)273-3196. Editor-in-Chief: Brad Edmondson. Managing Editor: Nancy Ten Kate. Contact: Judith Waldrop, research editor. 25% freelance written. Works with a small number of new/unpublished writers each year. Monthly magazine for business executives, market researchers, media and communications people, public policymakers. Estab. 1978. Circ. 35,000. Pays on publication. Publishes ms an average of 6 months after acceptance. Buys all rights. Submit seasonal material 6 months in advance. Query for electronic submissions. Reports in 6 months. Include self-addressed stamped postcard for return word that ms arrived safely. Sample copy $5 for 9×11 SAE. Writer's guidelines for #10 SASE.
Nonfiction: General interest (on demographic trends, implications of changing demographics, profile of business using demographic data); and how-to (on the use of demographic techniques, psychographics, understand projections, data, apply demography to business and planning). No anecdotal material. Sometimes pays the expenses of writers on assignment.

Tips: "Writer should have clear understanding of specific population trends and their implications for business and planning. The most important thing a freelancer can do is to read the magazine and be familiar with its style and focus."

ART DIRECTION, Advertising Trade Publications, Inc., 6th Floor, 10 E. 39th St., New York NY 10016. (212)889-6500. Fax: (212)889-6104. Editor: Dan Barron. 10% freelance written. Prefers to work with published/established writers. Monthly magazine emphasizing advertising design for art directors of ad agencies (corporate, in-plant, editorial, freelance, etc.). Circ. 10,250. Pays on publication. Buys one-time rights. Reports in 3 months. Sample copy $4.50.
Nonfiction: How-to articles on advertising campaigns. Pays $100 minimum.

BARTER COMMUNIQUE, Full Circle Marketing Corp., Dept. WM, P.O. Box 2527, Sarasota FL 34236. (813)349-3300. Editor-in-Chief: Robert J. Murely. 100% freelance written. Semiannual tabloid emphasizing bartering for radio and TV station owners, cable TV, newspaper and magazine publishers and select travel and advertising agency presidents. Circ. 50,000. Pays on publication. Publishes ms an average of 3 months after acceptance. Rights purchased vary with author and material. Phone queries OK. Simultaneous and previously published submissions OK. Query for electronic submissions. Reports in 1 month. Free sample copy and writer's guidelines.
Nonfiction: Articles on "barter" (trading products, goods and services, primarily travel and advertising). Length: 1,000 words. "Would like to see travel mss on southeast US and the Bahamas, and unique articles on media of all kinds. Include photos where applicable. Not only manuscripts on barter for products, goods and services—primarily travel and media—but also excess inventory of business to business." Pays $30-50.
Tips: "Computer installation will improve our ability to communicate."

COMMUNICATIONS MANAGER, Practical Ideas and Methods for Publications, PR and Desktop Publishing Managers, Communications Concepts Inc., Dept. WM, P.O. Box 1608, Springfield VA 22151-0608. (703)425-7751. Editor/Publisher: Bill Londino. Monthly business to business newsletter that covers communications and publication production. "Our readers are busy communications, desktop publishing, PR and publication managers. They want useful, practical advice—succinctly delivered—on publication production and communications issues." Estab. 1984. Pays within 45 days. Publishes ms an average of 2 months after acceptance. Offers 50% kill fee. Buys all rights. Editorial lead time 2 months. Submit seasonal material 2 months in advance. Query for electronic submissions. Reports in 6 weeks on queries. Sample copy and writer's guidelines for #10 SAE with 52¢ postage.
Nonfiction: "Practical, short, well-researched how-to articles with source and ordering information for follow-up. We are open to ideas for special reports in the communication and publication production field." No humor, opinion, or inspirational items. Only interested in long articles if for special reports. Buys 150 mss/year. Query with published clips. Length: 50-300 words. Pays 15¢/word. Pays in contributor copies if requested by the writer. Sometimes pays expenses of writers on assignment.
Photos: State availability of photos with submission. Offers no additional payment for photos accepted with ms.
Columns/Departments: Quicktakes (communications resources, publication production), 50-200 words; PR & Marketing Strategy (practical steps for improving an organization's PR and marketing effectiveness), 200-350 words; Business Writing & Editing (writing and editing tips for non-professionals), 200-350 words. Buys 150 mss/year. Query with published clips. Pays 15¢/word.
Tips: "We enjoy working with writers who are accurate, have original ideas, and who verify their source information. Review recent issues of the magazine and editorial guidelines. We are most receptive to short items (100-300 words). Columns are most open to freelancers."
● This magazine uses material on how to write, edit and produce publications, not on how to get published.

THE COUNSELOR MAGAZINE, Advertising Specialty Institute, Dept. WM, NBS Bldg., 1120 Wheeler Way, Langhorne PA 19047-9981. (215)752-4200. Fax: (215)752-9758. Editor: Catherine Sigmund-Holnick. 25% freelance written. Monthly magazine for executives, both distributors and suppliers, in the ad specialty industry. Estab. 1954. Circ. 6,000. Pays on publication. Publishes ms an average of 3 months after acceptance. Buys first rights only. No phone queries. Submit seasonal material 4 months in advance. Simultaneous and previously published submissions OK. Reports in 3 months. Sample copy for 9 × 12 SAE with 3 first class stamps.
Nonfiction: How-to (promotional case histories); interview (with executives and government figures); profile (of executives); and articles on specific product categories. "Articles almost always have a specialty advertising slant and quotes from specialty advertising practitioners." Pays according to assigned length. Sometimes pays the expenses of writers on assignment.
Photos: State availability of photos. Black and white photos only. Prefers contact sheet(s) and 5 × 7 prints, or samples to be shot in-house. Offers some additional payment for original photos accepted with ms. Captions and model releases required. Buys one-time rights.

Tips: "If a writer shows promise, we can help him or her modify his style to suit our publication and provide leads. Writers must be willing to adapt or rewrite their material for a specific audience. If an article is suitable for 5 or 6 other publications, it's probably not suitable for us. The best way to break in is to write for *Imprint*, a quarterly publication we produce for the clients of ad specialty counselors."

IDENTITY For Specifiers and Customers of Sign and Corporate Graphics, ST Publications, Dept. WM, 407 Gilbert Ave., Cincinnati OH 45202. (513)421-2050. Fax: (513)421-5144. Editor: Lynn Baxter. 10% freelance written. Quarterly trade magazine on corporate identity. "We cover the design and implementation of corporate identity, sign programs and architectural graphics for environmental graphics designers, architects and their clients. We stress signage as a part of the total corporate identity program." Estab. 1988. Circ. 15,000. **Pays on acceptance.** Byline given. Offers 30% kill fee. Buys all rights. Query for electronic submissions. Reports in 2 weeks. Free sample copy and writer's guidelines for SASE.
Nonfiction: How-to, interview/profile, opinion and technical. "No histories or profiles of design firms or manufacturers." Buys 4-10 mss/year. Query with or without published clips or send complete ms. Length: 1,000-3,000 words. Pays $250-400. Sometimes pays expenses of writers on assignment.
Photos: Send photos with submission. Reviews 35mm to 4×5 transparencies. "We *sometimes* pay for photo rights from professional photographers." Identification of subjects required. Buys one-time rights.
Tips: "The best approach is a telephone or written query. Ours is a completely 4-color publication geared to a graphically sophisticated audience with professional photography and specific information about design solutions, fabrication and management of corporate identity programs. We prefer a case-history approach, but may accept some theoretical articles on use of corporate identity, value of signs, etc. Most open are feature stories written for designers (design, fabrication details) or buyers (value, costs, management of national programs). The more specific, the better. The more 'advertorial,' the less likely to be accepted. Unusual design solutions, unusual use of materials and breadth of design scope make stories more interesting."

IMPRINT, The Magazine of Specialty Advertising Ideas, Advertising Specialty Institute, Dept. WM, 1120 Wheeler Way, Langhorne PA 19047-9981. (215)752-4200. Managing Editor: Arn Bernstein. Editor: Catherine Sigmund-Holnick. 25% freelance written. Works with a small number of new/unpublished writers each year. Quarterly magazine covering specialty advertising. Estab. 1967. Circ. 60,000. Pays on final acceptance. Publishes ms an average of 6 months after acceptance. Byline given. Buys one-time rights. Submit seasonal material 6 months in advance. Simultaneous queries OK. Query for electronic submissions. Reports in 3 months. Sample copy for 9×12 SAE with 3 first class stamps.
Nonfiction: How-to (case histories of specialty advertising campaigns); and features (how ad specialties are distributed in promotions). "Emphasize effective use of specialty advertising. Avoid direct-buy situations. Stress the distributor's role in promotions. No generalized pieces on print, broadcast or outdoor advertising." Buys 10-12 mss/year. Query with published clips. Payment based on assigned length. "We pay authorized phone, postage, etc."
Photos: State availability of 5×7 b&w photos. Pays "some extra for *original* photos *only*." Captions, model releases and identification of subjects required.
Tips: "The predominant cause of misdirected articles is the fact that many new writers simply don't understand the medium of specialty advertising, or our target audience—end-users. Writers are urged to investigate the medium a bit before attempting an article or suggesting an idea for one. We can also provide additional leads and suggestions. All articles are specifically geared to specialty advertising (or premium) use."

MEDIA INC., Pacific Northwest media, marketing and creative services news, P.O. Box 24365, Seattle WA 98124-0365. (206)382-9220. Fax: (206)382-9437. Managing Editor: Paul Gargaro. 10% freelance written. Monthly tabloid covering Northwest US media, advertising, marketing and creative-service industries. "Audience is Northwest ad agencies, marketing professionals, media and creative-service professionals." Estab. 1987. Circ. 14,000. Byline given. Reports in 1 month. Sample copy for 9×12 SAE with 6 first class stamps.
Tips: "It is best if writers live in the Pacific Northwest and can report on local news and events in Media Inc.'s areas of business coverage."

MORE BUSINESS, 11 Wimbledon Court, Jericho NY 11753. Editor: Trudy Settel. 50% freelance written. Monthly magazine "selling publications material to business for consumer use (incentives, communication, public relations)—look for book ideas and manuscripts." Estab. 1975. Circ. 10,000. **Pays on acceptance.** Publishes ms an average of 1 month after acceptance. Buys all rights. Reports in 3 months. Sample copy for 9×12 SAE with 2 first class stamps.

ALWAYS enclose a self-addressed, stamped envelope (SASE) with all your queries and correspondence.

Nonfiction: General interest, how-to, vocational techniques, nostalgia, photo feature, profile and travel. Reviews new computer software. Buys 10-20 mss/year. Word length varies with article. Payment negotiable. Query. Pays $4,000-7,000 for book mss.

SIGNCRAFT, The Magazine for the Commercial Sign Shop, SignCraft Publishing Co., Inc., P.O. Box 06031, Fort Myers FL 33906. (813)939-4644. Editor: Tom McIltrot. 10% freelance written. Bimonthly magazine of the sign industry. "Like any trade magazine, we need material of direct benefit to our readers. We can't afford space for material of marginal interest." Estab. 1980. Circ. 20,500. Pays on publication. Publishes ms an average of 9 months after acceptance. Byline given. Offers negotiable kill fee. Buys first North American serial or all rights. Previously published submissions OK. Reports in 1 month. Sample copy and writer's guidelines $3.
Nonfiction: Interviews and profiles. "All articles should be directly related to quality commercial signs. If you are familiar with the sign trade, we'd like to hear from you." Buys 20 mss/year. Query with or without published clips. Length: 500-2,000 words. Pays up to $250.

SIGNS OF THE TIMES, The Industry Journal Since 1906, ST Publications, Dept. WM, 407 Gilbert Ave., Cincinnati OH 45202-2285. (513)421-2050. Fax: (513)421-5144. Editor: Wade Swormstedt. 15-30% freelance written. "We are willing to use more freelancers." Monthly magazine special buyer's guide between November and December issues. Estab. 1906. Circ. 18,000. Pays on publication. Publishes ms an average of 3 months after acceptance. Byline given. Buys variable rights. Simultaneous queries and simultaneous and previously published submissions OK. Reports in 3 months. Free sample copy and writer's guidelines for 9×12 SAE with 10 first class stamps.
Nonfiction: Historical/nostalgic (regarding the sign industry); how-to (carved signs, goldleaf, etc.); interview/profile (focusing on either a signshop or a specific project); photo feature (query first); and technical (sign engineering, etc.). Nothing "nonspecific on signs, an example being a photo essay on 'signs I've seen.' We are a trade journal with specific audience interests." Buys 15-20 mss/year. Query with clips. Pays $150-500. Sometimes pays the expenses of writers on assignment.
Photos: Send photos with ms. "Sign industry-related photos only. We sometimes accept photos with funny twists or misspellings."
Fillers: Open to queries; request rates.
  • This publication is looking for more business-related articles and short profiles.

VM & SD (Visual Merchandising and Store Design), ST Publications, 407 Gilbert Ave., Cincinnati OH 45202-2285. (513)421-2050. Fax: (513)421-5144. Editor: Janet Groeber. 30% freelance written. Monthly magazine emphasizing store design and merchandise presentation. Circ. 20,000. Pays on publication. Buys first and second rights to the same material. Simultaneous and previously published submissions OK. Reports in 1 month. Publishes ms an average of 3 months after acceptance. Sample copy $2.50 for 9×12 SAE.
Nonfiction: How-to (display); informational (store design, construction, merchandise presentation); interview (display directors and store owners, industry personalities); profile (new and remodeled stores); new product; photo feature (window display); and technical (store lighting, carpet, wallcoverings, fixtures). No "advertorials" that tout a single company's product or product line. Buys 24 mss/year. Query or submit complete ms. Length: 500-3,000 words. Pays $250-500.
Photos: Purchased with accompanying ms or on assignment.
Tips: "Be fashion and design conscious and reflect that in the article. Submit finished manuscripts with photos or slides always. Look for timely stories on department and specialty store visual merchandisers and store designers (profiles, methods, views on the industry, sales promotions and new store design or remodels), new store openings and innovative retail concepts."

Art, Design and Collectibles

The businesses of art, art administration, architecture, environmental/package design and antiques/collectibles are covered in these listings. Art-related topics for the general public are located in the Consumer Art and Architecture category. Antiques and collectibles magazines for enthusiasts are listed in Consumer Hobby and Craft. (Listings of markets looking for freelance artists to do artwork can be found in *Artist's Market* – see Other Books of Interest).

ANTIQUEWEEK, Mayhill Publications Inc., P.O. Box 90, Knightstown IN 46148-0090. (317)345-5133. Central Edition Editor: Tom Hoepf. Eastern Edition Editor: Connie Swaim. Genealogy Editor: Elsie Kilmer. 80% freelance written. Weekly tabloid on antiques, collectibles and genealogy. *AntiqueWeek* publishes two editions: Eastern and Central. "*AntiqueWeek* has a wide range of readership from dealers and auctioneers to collectors, both advanced and novice. Our readers demand accurate information presented in an entertaining style." Estab. 1968. Circ. 60,000. Pays on publication. Publishes ms an average of 1-2 months after acceptance. Byline given. Buys first and second serial (reprint) rights. Submit seasonal material 1 month in advance. Reports in 2 months. Free sample copy. Writer's guidelines for #10 SASE.

Nonfiction: Historical/nostalgic, how-to, interview/profile, opinion, personal experience, antique show and auction reports, feature articles on particular types of antiques and collectibles. Buys 400-500 mss/year. Query with or without published clips or send complete ms. Length: 1,000-2,000 words. Pays $25-150.

Photos: Send photos with submission. Reviews 3½×5 prints. Identification of subjects required. Buys one-time rights.

Columns/Departments: Insights (opinions on buying, selling and collecting antiques), 500-1,000 words; Your Ancestors (advice, information on locating sources for genealogists). Buys 150 mss/year. Query. Length: 500-1,500 words. Pays $25-50.

Tips: "Writers should know their topics thoroughly. Feature articles must be well-researched and clearly written. An interview and profile article with a knowledgeable collector might be the break for a first-time contributor. As we move toward the year 2000, there is much more interest in 20th-century collectibles. *Antiqueweek* also seeks articles that reflect the lasting popularity of traditional antiques."

APPLIED ARTS, Suite 324, 885 Don Mills Rd., Toronto, Ontario M3C 1V9 Canada. (416)510-0909. Fax: (416)510-0913. Editor: Peter Giffen. 70% freelance written. Magazine published 5 times/year covering graphic design, advertising, photography and illustration. Estab. 1986. Circ. 12,000. **Pays on acceptance.** Byline given. Buys first North American serial rights. Query for electronic submissions. Reports in 2 months on queries. Sample copy for 10×13 SAE with $1.70 Canadian postage or 4 IRCs.

Nonfiction: Interview/profile, opinion, photo feature, technical (computers and the applied arts) and trade articles about graphic design, advertising, photography and illustration. Buys 20-30 mss/year. Query with published clips. Length: 500-2,500 words. Pays 60¢ (Canadian)/word.

Photos: Offers no additional payment for photos accepted with ms. Buys one-time rights.

Tips: "It helps if writers have some familiarity with the communication arts field. Writers should include a solid selection of published articles. Writers have the best chance selling articles on graphic design and advertising. Take time to read back issues of the magazine before querying."

ART BUSINESS NEWS, Advanstar Communications Inc., P.O. Box 3837, Stamford CT 06905. (203)356-1745. Editor: Fergus Reid. Managing Editor: Sarah Seamark. 25% freelance written. Prefers to work with published/established writers. Monthly trade tabloid covering news relating to the art and picture framing industry. Circ. 30,000. Pays on publication. Publishes ms an average of 3 months after acceptance. Byline given. Buys first-time rights. Submit seasonal material 2 months in advance. Simultaneous submissions OK. Reports in 3 months. Sample copy $5 for 12×16 SAE.

Nonfiction: News in art and framing field; interview/marketing profiles (of dealers, publishers and suppliers in the art industry); new products; articles focusing on small business people—framers, art gallery management, art trends; and how-to (occasional article on "how-to frame" accepted). Buys 8-20 mss/year. Length: 1,000 words maximum. Query first. Pays $75-300. Sometimes pays the expenses of writers on assignment. Photography useful.

Tips: "We have more opportunity for shorter, hard news items and news features."

ARTS MANAGEMENT, 408 W. 57th St., New York NY 10019. (212)245-3850. Editor: A.H. Reiss. Magazine published 5 times/year for cultural institutions. 2% freelance written. Estab. 1962. Circ. 6,000. Pays on publication. Byline given. Buys all rights. Query. Reports in 2 months. Writer's guidelines for #10 SASE.

Nonfiction: Short articles, 400-900 words, tightly written, expository, explaining how art administrators solved problems in publicity, fund raising and general administration; actual case histories emphasizing the how-to. Also short articles on the economics and sociology of the arts and important trends in the nonprofit cultural field. Must be fact-filled, well-organized and without rhetoric. Pays 2-4¢/word. No photographs or pictures.

● Mostly staff-written; uses very little outside material.

CADALYST, Professional Management of AutoCAD Systems, P.O. Box 10460, Eugene OR 97440. (503)343-1200. Senior Editor: David Cohn. Editor: Sandy Lurins. Monthly trade journal covering AutoCAD (computer-aided design). Estab. 1984. Circ. 60,000. Pays on publication. Publishes ms an average of 3-6 months after acceptance. Byline given. Offers $100 kill fee. Buys first North American serial rights. Submit seasonal material 6 months in advance. Query for electronic submissions. Reports in 2 weeks on queries. Free writer's guidelines.

Nonfiction: Book excerpts (AutoCAD texts), expose, how-to (AutoCAD method articles, short tips), humor (AutoCAD person-in-the-trenches viewpoint), new product (press releases), opinion (guest editorial), personal experience, photo feature (Animator and other presentation graphics specific to AutoCAD), and technical (reviews of hardware and software). "No PR promotional articles on specific products or services." Buys 120 mss/year. Query. Length: 500-2,500 (can be longer for multiple product comparisons). Pays $100-1,000.

Photos: Send color photos with submission. Reviews negatives, transparencies ($2\frac{1}{4} \times 2\frac{1}{4}$), and prints ($8 \times 10$). Offers no additional payment for photos accepted with ms. Captions and identification of subjects required. Buys one-time rights.

Fillers: Anecdotes, facts, gags to be illustrated by cartoonist, newsbreaks and short humor. Buys 30/year. Length: 50-500 words. Pays $100-300.

Tips: "We are only interested in people with an AutoCAD background in architecture/engineering/industrial design/surveying/construction industry. We are more interested in technical content than style. All areas are open. Please telephone or E-mail us on CompuServe first so we can assign you an article or chat about your story proposals."

CALLIGRAPHY REVIEW, 1624 24th Ave. SW, Norman OK 73072. (405)364-8794. Fax: (405)364-8914. Publisher/Editor: Karyn L. Gilman. 98% freelance written. Eager to work with new/unpublished writers with calligraphic expertise and language skills. Quarterly magazine on calligraphy and related book arts, both historical and contemporary in nature. Estab. 1982. Circ. 5,500. Pays on publication. Publishes ms an average of 9 months after acceptance. Byline given. Offers 20% kill fee. Buys first rights. Publishes reprints of previously published articles. Send tearsheet or photocopy of article, or send typed ms with rights for sale noted. Include information about when and where the article previously appeared. For reprints, pays 25% of the amount paid for an original article. Query for electronic submissons. Reports in 3 months. Sample copy for 9×12 SAE with 7 first class stamps. Free writer's guidelines.

Nonfiction: Interview/profile, opinion, contemporary and historical. Buys 50 mss/year. Query with or without published clips or send complete ms. Length: 1,000-2,000 words. Pays $50-200 for assigned articles; $25-200 for unsolicited articles. Sometimes pays the expenses of writers on assignment.

Photos: State availability of photos with submission. Reviews contact sheets, negatives, transparencies and prints. Pays agreed upon cost. Captions and identification of subjects required. Buys one-time rights.

Columns/Departments: Book Reviews, Viewpoint (critical), 500-1,500 words; Ms. (discussion of manuscripts in collections), 1,000-2,000 words; and Profile (contemporary calligraphic figure), 1,000-2,000 words. Query. Pays $50-200.

Tips: "*Calligraphy Review*'s primary objective is to encourage the exchange of ideas on calligraphy, its past and present as well as trends for the future. Practical and conceptual treatments are welcomed, as are learning and teaching experiences. Third person is preferred, however first person will be considered if appropriate. Writer should realize that this is a specialized audience."

• The emphasis here is on articles of a critical nature specifically for this audience. They are looking for international coverage in particular.

‡CONFETTI, Bits & Pieces for Creative Communicators, Randall Publishing, Inc., P.O. Box 1426, 1425 Lunt Ave., Elk Grove Village IL 60007. (708)437-6604. Editor: Peg Carmack Short. Contact: Peg Short, Editor. Bimonthly magazine for graphic arts with emphasis on print media. Estab. 1988. Circ. 15,500. **Pays on acceptance.** Byline given. Buys one-time rights or makes work-for-hire assignments. Editorial lead time 2 months. Submit seasonal material 4 months in advance. Accepts previously published submissions. Query for electronic submissions. Reports in 4 months on mss; 1 month on queries. Sample copy and writer's guidelines free on request.

Nonfiction: Interview/profile and technical. "No articles directed to amateurs. Our audience is working graphic arts professionals. No 'how-to' articles. No gossipy profiles. Emphasis should be on artists' work." Buys 24-30 mss/year. Query with published clips. Length: 1,000-2,000 words. Pays $100 minimum for assigned articles. Will trade for display advertising in magazine. Sometimes pays expenses of writers on assignment.

Photos: State availability of photos with submission. Offers no additional payment for photos accepted with ms. Buys one-time rights.

Columns/Departments: Electronic Canvas (creating and working with desktop publishing), 1,200 words. Buys 6 mss/year. Query with or without published clips. Pays $100 minimum.

Tips: "Call us to discuss an idea for a story. If you are thinking of doing a profile on a particular artist, please send samples of artist's work. We are interested in profiling only top-quality artists, and acceptance of a story about an artist will depend as much on the quality of his/her work as on the quality of the story. We won't run a good story about a bad artist. Stories about successful work with DTP are always of interest, as are practical applications stories about DTP as long as they are not too product-oriented or too techie. Send us clips of your work and a brief resume. We are most open to material for 'Electronic Canvas'. We are always on the look-out for good stories to help artists integrate the new technology into their work. Just remember that our readers are artists and designers, not computer experts. The emphasis should be on how one can use these new tools to be more creative, not on how the new system works or on programming or gadgetry."

THE CRAFTS REPORT, The Newsmonthly for Crafts Professionals, The Crafts Report Publishing Company, P.O. Box 1992, Wilmington DE 19899. (302)656-2209. Editor: Marilyn Stevens. 50% freelance written. Monthly tabloid covering crafts industry. Estab. 1975. Circ. 20,000. Pays on publication. Publishes ms an average of 4 months after acceptance. Byline given. Offers $50 kill fee. Buys first North American serial, first rights, second serial (reprint) rights or makes work-for-hire assignments. Publishes reprints of previously published articles. Send tearsheet of article and information about when and where the article previously appeared. Pays $50/reprint. Editorial lead time 3 months. Submit seasonal material 6 months in advance. Reports in 8-10 weeks. Sample copy $3. Writer's guidelines for #10 SASE.

Nonfiction: Interview/profile, opinion, personal experience and small business tips. "No how-to (e.g. craft techniques) articles." Buys 80 mss/year. Query with published clips. Length: 400-2,000 words. Pays 12½¢/ word minimum for assigned articles; 3½¢/word minimum for unsolicited articles. Sometimes pays expenses of writers on assignment (limit agreed upon in advance).

Photos: Send photos with submission. Reviews transparencies and prints. Negotiates payment individually. Identification of subjects required. Buys one-time rights.

Columns/Departments: Money (small business advice for crafts professionals), 600-800 words; Craft and Trade Show Reviews (writers work from prepared questions), 300-700 words; Back-to-Basics (everything the new entrepreneur needs to know to start or grow a business), 600-800 words. Buys 20 mss/year. Query with published clips. Pays 3½-12½¢/published word.

HOW, The Bottomline Design Magazine, F&W Publications, Inc., 1507 Dana Ave., Cincinnati OH 45207-1005. (513)531-2222. Editor: Laurel Harper. 75% freelance written. Bimonthly graphic design and illustration business journal. "*HOW* gives a behind-the-scenes look at not only *how* the world's best graphic artists and illustrators conceive and create their work, but *why* they did it that way. We also focus on the *business* side of design—how to run a profitable studio." Estab. 1985. Circ. 35,000. **Pays on acceptance.** Byline given. Buys first North American serial rights. Query for electronic submissions. Reports in 6 weeks. Sample copy $8.50. Writer's guidelines for #10 SASE.

Nonfiction: Interview/profile, business tips and new products. Special issues—September/October: Self-Promotion Annual; November/December: Business Annual. No how-to articles for beginning artists or fine-art-oriented articles. Buys 40 mss/year. Query with published clips and samples of subject's work (artwork or design). Length: 1,200-1,500 words. Pays $250-600. Sometimes pays expenses of writers on assignment.

Photos: State availability of artwork with submission. Reviews 35mm or larger transparencies. May reimburse mechanical photo expenses. Captions are required. Buys one-time rights.

Columns/Departments: Marketplace (focuses on lucrative fields for designers/illustrators); and Production (ins, outs and tips on production). Buys 20 mss/year. Query with published clips. Length: 1,000-2,000 words. Pays $150-400.

Tips: "We look for writers who can recognize graphic designers on the cutting-edge of their industry, both creatively and business-wise. Writers must have an eye for detail, and be able to relay *HOW*'s step-by-step approach in an interesting, concise manner—without omitting any details. Showing you've done your homework on a subject—and that you can go beyond asking 'those same old questions'—will give you a big advantage."

MANHATTAN ARTS MAGAZINE, Renée Phillips Associates, Suite 26L, 200 East 72 St., New York NY 10021. (212)472-1660. Editor-in-Chief: Renée Phillips. Managing Editor: Michael Jason. 100% freelance written. Monthly magazine covering fine art. Audience is comprised of art professionals, artists and collectors. Educational, informative, easy-to-read style, making art more accessible. Highly promotional of new artists. Estab. 1983. Circ. 50,000. Pays on publication. Publishes ms an average of 1 month after acceptance. Byline given. Makes work for hire assignments. Submit seasonal material 3 months in advance. Simultaneous submissions OK. Reports in 3 months. Sample copy $4, payable to Renée Phillips Associates (no postage or envelope required).

Nonfiction: Book excerpts (art), essays (art world), general interest (collecting art), inspirational (artists success stories), interview/profile (major art leaders), new product (art supplies), technical (art business). Buys 100 mss/year. Query with published clips; all articles are assigned. Length: 150-500 words. Pays $25-50. New writers receive byline and promotion, art books. Sometimes pays expenses of writers on assignment.

Photos: Send photos with submission. Offers no additional payment for photos accepted with ms. Captions, model releases and identification of subjects required.

Columns/Departments: Reviews/Previews (art critiques of exhibitions in galleries and museums), 150-250 words; Artists/Profiles (features on major art leaders), 250-500 words; The New Collector (collectibles, interviews with dealers, collectors), 250-500 words; Artopia (inspirational features, success stories), 250-500 words; Art Books, Art Services, 150-500 words. Buys 100 mss/year. Query with published clips. Pays $25-50.

Tips: "A knowledge of the current, contemporary art scene is a must. An eye for emerging talent is an asset."

THE MIDATLANTIC ANTIQUES MAGAZINE, Monthly Guide to Antiques, Art, Auctions & Collectibles, The Henderson Daily Dispatch Company, Inc., P.O. Box 908, Henderson NC 27536-0908. (919)492-4001. Fax: (919)430-0125. Editor: Lydia Tucker. 65% freelance written. Monthly tabloid that covers antiques, art, auctions and collectibles. "The *MidAtlantic* is a monthly trade publication that reaches dealers, collectors, antique shows and auction houses primarily on the East Coast, but circulation includes 48 states and Europe." Estab. 1984. Circ. 12,000. Pays on publication. Byline given. Buys first rights. Submit seasonal material 6 months in advance. Reports in 1 month on queries; 2 months on mss. Sample copy and writer's guidelines for 10 × 13 SAE with 10 first class stamps.

Nonfiction: Book excerpts, historical/nostalgic, how-to (choose an antique to collect; how to sell your collection; how to identify market trends), interview/profile, personal experience, photo feature, and technical. Buys 60-75 mss/year. Query. Length: 800-2,000 words. Pays $50-125. Trade for advertising space. Rarely pays expenses of writers on assignment.

• The publisher needs writers to cover show and auction events.

Photos: Send photos with submission. Offers no additional payment for photos accepted with ms. Identification of subjects required. Buys one-time rights.

Tips: "Please contact by mail first, but a writer may call with specific ideas after initial contact. Looking for writers who have extensive knowledge in specific areas of antiques. Articles should be educational in nature. We are also interested in how-to articles, i.e., how to choose antiques to collect; how to sell your collection and get the most for it; looking for articles that focus on future market trends. We want writers who are active in the antiques business and can predict good investments. (Articles with photographs are given preference.) We are looking for people who are not only knowledgeable, but can write well."

PROGRESSIVE ARCHITECTURE, Dept. WM, P.O. Box 1361, Stamford CT 06904. Fax: (203)348-4023. Editor: John M. Dixon. Managing Editor: Valerie Kanter-Sisca. 5-10% freelance written. Prefers to work with published/established writers. Monthly. Estab. 1920. **Pays on acceptance.** Publishes ms an average of 4 months after acceptance. Buys all rights for use in architectural press. Query for electronic submissions. Reports in 4 months.

Nonfiction: "Articles of technical, professional interest devoted to architecture, interior design, and urban design and planning, and illustrated by photographs and architectural drawings. We also use technical articles which are prepared by technical authorities and would be beyond the scope of the lay writer. Practically all the material is professional, and most of it is prepared by writers in the field who are approached by the magazine for material." Pays $150-400. Sometimes pays the expenses of writers on assignment.

Photos: Buys one-time reproduction rights to b&w and color photos.

Auto and Truck

These publications are geared to automobile, motorcycle and truck dealers; professional truck drivers; service department personnel; or fleet operators. Publications for highway planners and traffic control experts are listed in the Government and Public Service category.

‡AFTERMARKET BUSINESS, Advanstar Communications, 7500 Old Oak Blvd., Cleveland OH 44130. Editor-in-Chief: Sandie Stambaugh-Cannon. 10% freelance written. Monthly tabloid for automotive aftermarket. Features articles devoted to the retail aftermarket; merchandising practices, business techniques, sales techniques, customer service. Estab. 1936. Circ. 23,526. Pays on publication. Byline given. Buys all rights and/or makes work-for-hire assignments. Editorial lead time 2 months. Accepts previously published submissions. Reports in 2 weeks on queries.

Nonfiction: Interview/profile and photo feature. November—publish Show Dailies at major trade show. Buys 3 mss/year. Query with published clips. Length: 2,000-4,000 words. Pays $300 minimum for assigned articles. Sometimes pays expenses of writers on assignment.

Photos: State availability of photos with submission. Reviews prints. Offers no additional payment for photos accepted with ms. Identification of subjects required. Buys all rights.

AUTO GLASS JOURNAL, Grawin Publications, Inc., Suite 101, 303 Harvard E., P.O. Box 12099, Seattle WA 98102-0099. (206)322-5120. Editor: Burton Winters. 10% freelance written. Prefers to work with published/established writers. Monthly magazine on auto glass replacement. International publication for the auto glass replacement industry. Includes step-by-step glass replacement procedures for current model cars and business management, industry news and trends. Estab. 1953. Circ. 5,700. **Pays on acceptance.** Publishes ms an average of 5 months after acceptance. No byline given. Buys all rights. Query for electronic submissions. Reports in 3 months. Sample copy for 6×9 SAE with 3 first class stamps. Writer's guidelines for #10 SASE.

Nonfiction: Articles relating to auto glass and general business management. Buys 12-20 mss/year. Query with published clips. Length: 1,000-3,000 words. Pays $50-200, with photos.

Photos: State availability of photos. Reviews b&w contact sheets and negatives. Payment included with ms. Captions required. Buys all rights.

THE BATTERY MAN, Independent Battery Manufacturers Association, Inc., 100 Larchwood Dr., Largo FL 34640-2811. (813)586-1409. Fax: (813)586-1400. Editor: Celwyn E. Hopkins. 20% freelance written. Monthly magazine emphasizing SLI battery manufacture, applications and new developments. Target audience: The entire, international industry that is involved in manufacturing, distributing and selling of batteries and battery-related products and technologies. Estab. 1959. Circ. 5,200. **Pays on acceptance.** Publishes ms an average of 4 months after acceptance. Submit seasonal material 2 months in advance. Simultaneous and previously published submissions OK. Query for electronic submissions. Reports in 2 months. Send SASE for return of ms.

Nonfiction: Technical articles on secondary, storage and industrial batteries; new developments in battery manufacturing; energy topics, such as Electric Vehicles, UPS, etc. are acceptable. Also publishes articles on alloys, metals, plastics, etc. and governmental and legislative concerns of the industry. Submit complete ms. Buys 15-20 unsolicited mss/year. Length: 750-2,000 words preferred. Pays 10¢/word. Photos accepted with article also, pays $10/photo.

Tips: "Most writers are not familiar enough with this industry to be able to furnish a feature article. They try to palm off something that they wrote for a hardware store, or a dry cleaner, by calling everything a 'battery store.' We receive a lot of manuscripts on taxes and tax information (such as US income tax) and on business management in general and managing a family-owned business. Since this is an international publication, we try to stay away from such subjects. US tax information is of no use or interest to overseas readers."

EASTERN AFTERMARKET JOURNAL, Stan Hubsher Inc., Dept. WM, P.O. Box 373, Cedarhurst NY 11516. (516)295-3680. Editor: Stan Hubsher. 100% freelance written. Bimonthly magazine for automotive parts wholesaler buyers at the warehouse and jobber level, on the Eastern seaboard. "Audience operates stores and warehouses that handle replacement parts for automobiles. No technical knowledge necessary. Profiles of owners/buyers, how they operate in highly competitive market that accounts for 40% of the entire country's aftermarket business." Estab. 1956. Circ. 9,500. Pays on publication. Buys all rights. Submit material 2 months in advance. Reports in 1 month. Sample copy and writer's guidelines for 9 × 12 SAE with 8 first class stamps.

Nonfiction: Buys 6-8 mss/year. Query. Length: 2,000 words. Pays $150 minimum to negotiable maximum. Sometimes pays expenses of writers on assignment.

Photos: Send photos with submission. Offers no additional payments for photos accepted with ms. Captions and identification of subjects required. Buys one-time rights.

Tips: "Freelancers must operate in Atlantic states or Pennsylvania and West Virginia only."

● This magazine has increased its geographical coverage and now covers territory from Maryland to Florida.

OVERDRIVE, The Magazine for the American Trucker, Randall Publishing Co./Overdrive, Inc., P.O. Box 3187, Tuscaloosa AL 35403-3187. (205)349-2990. Fax: (205)750-8070. Editor: G.C. Skipper. Managing Editor: Deborah Lockridge. 25% freelance written. Monthly magazine for independent truckers. Estab. 1961. Circ. 90,000. Pays on publication. Publishes ms an average of 2 months after acceptance. Byline given. 10% kill fee. Buys all North American rights. Reports in 2 months. Sample copy and writers' guidelines for 9 × 12 SASE.

Nonfiction: Essays, expose, how-to (truck maintainance and operation), interview/profile (successful independent truckers), personal experience, photo feature, technical. All must be related to independent trucker interest. Query with or without published clips or send complete ms. Length: 500-2,000 words. Pays $100-600 for assigned articles; $50-500 for unsolicited articles.

Photos: Send photos with submission. Reviews transparencies and 5 × 7 prints. Offers $25-50/photo. Identification of subjects required. Buys all rights.

Tips: "Talk to independent truckers. Develop a good knowledge of their concerns as small business owners, truck drivers and individuals. We prefer articles that quote experts, people in the industry and truckers to first-person expositions on a subject. Get straight facts. Look for good material on truck safety, on effects of government regulations, and on rates and business relationships between independent truckers, brokers, carriers and shippers."

● This magazine is buying fewer freelance mss—down from 30-25%.

REFRIGERATED TRANSPORTER, Tunnell Publications, P.O. Box 66010, Houston TX 77266. (713)523-8124. Editor: Gary Macklin. 5% freelance written. Monthly. Byline given. Pays on publication. Reports in 1 month.

Nonfiction: "Articles on fleet management and maintenance of vehicles, especially the refrigerated van and the refrigerating unit, shop tips, loading or handling systems—especially for frozen or refrigerated cargo, new equipment specifications, conversions of equipment for better handling or more efficient operations. Prefers articles with illustrations obtained from fleets operating refrigerated trucks or trailers." Pays variable rate, approximately $100/printed page.

‡SUCCESSFUL DEALER, Kona-Cal, Inc., Suite 300, 707 Lake Cook Rd., Deerfeld IL 60015. (708)498-3180. Editor: David Zaritz. Contact: Denise L. Rondini, Editorial Director. 20% freelance written. Bimonthly magazine for heavy-duty truck dealers' issues. "*Successful Dealer*'s primary readers are the principal owners of medium- and heavy-duty truck dealerships. Additional readers are the executives, managers and sales personnel employed by these dealerships." Estab. 1978. Circ. 17,500. **Pays on acceptance.** Publishes ms an average of 4 months after acceptance. Byline given. Buys first North American serial or second (reprint) rights. Editorial lead time 3 months. Reports in 2-3 weeks on queries. Sample copy and writer's guidelines free on request.

Nonfiction: General interest (industry trends/developments), how-to (operate more profitably), interview/profile (industry leaders) and technical (new developments in truck componentry). "We do not want single new product features; no opinion pieces." Buys 8 mss/year. Query. Length: 1,000-1,500 words. Pays $400 minimum for assigned articles or departments, $350 minimum for unsolicited articles. Sometimes pays expenses of writers on assignment.

Photos: Send photos with submission. Reviews contact sheets, negatives, transparencies and prints. Offers no additional payment for photos accepted with ms. Captions, model releases and identification of subjects required.

Tips: "It helps for the writer to be familiar with, if not the industry, then at least the subject of the article."

TOW-AGE, Kruza Kaleidoscopix, Inc., P.O. Box 389, Franklin MA 02038-0389. Editor: J. Kruza. For readers who run their own towing service business. 5% freelance written. Prefers to work with published/established writers. Published every 6 weeks. Estab. 1960. Circ. 18,000. Buys all rights; usually reassigns rights. **Pays on acceptance.** Simultaneous submissions OK. Reports in 1 month. Sample copy $3. Writer's guidelines for #10 SASE.

Nonfiction: Articles on business, legal and technical information for the towing industry. "Light reading material; short, with punch." Informational, how-to, personal, interview and profile. Buys about 18 mss/year. Query or submit complete ms. Length: 600-800 words. Pays $50-150. Spot news and successful business operations. Length: 300-800 words. Technical articles. Length: 400-1,000 words. Pays expenses of writers on assignment.

Photos: Black and white 8×10 photos purchased with or without mss, or on assignment. Pays $25 for first photo; $10 for each additional photo in series. Captions required.

‡TRUCK PARTS AND SERVICE, Kona Communications, Inc., Suite 300, 707 Lake Cook Rd., Deerfield IL 60015. Editor: David Zaritz. Managing Editor: Denise L. Rondini. Contact: David Zaritz. 20% freelance written. Monthly magazine for repair shops and distributors in heavy-duty trucking."Truck Parts and Service's primary readers are owners of truck parts distributorships and independent repair shops. Both types of businesses sell parts and repair service to fleet and individual owners of medium- to heavy-duty trucks as well as buses and trailers. Other readers include the executives, managers and sales personnel employed by the parts distributors and repair shops." Estab. 1966. Circ. 17,500. **Pays on acceptance.** Publishes ms an average of 4 months after acceptance. Byline given. Buys first North American serial or second serial (reprint) rights. Editorial lead time 3 months. Reports in 2-3 weeks on queries. Sample copy and writer's guidelines free on request.

Nonfiction: Denise L. Rondini. General interest (industry trends or developments); how-to (operate more profitably), interview/profile (industry leaders); and technical (new developments in truck components or repair and maintenance procedures). "We do not want single new product features; no opinion pieces." Buys 16 mss/year. Query. Length: 1,000-1,500 words. Pays $400 minimum for assigned articles, $350 for unsolicited articles. Sometimes pays expenses of writers on assignment.

Photos: Send photos with submission. Reviews contact sheets, negatives, transparencies and prints. Captions, model releases and identification of subjects required.

Tips: "It helps for the writer to be familiar with the subject of the article if not the business or industry itself."

TRUCK WORLD, Global Trade Publications Ltd., Dept. WM, #11, 106 E. 14th St., North Vancouver, British Columbia V7L 2N3 Canada. (604)984-2002. Fax: (604)984-2820. Managing Editor: Paul Young. Trade journal on the trucking industry. "*Truck World* is designed to reach people directly or indirectly employed in the Canadian trucking industry. Readers are generally assumed to have an understanding of the industry." Estab. 1984. Pays on publication. Publishes ms an average of 2 months after acceptance. Byline given. Buys first North American serial rights. Previously published submissions OK. Query for electronic submissions. Reports in 2 weeks on queries; 1 month on mss. *Writer's Market* recommends allowing 2 months for reply. Free sample copy with SASE.

Nonfiction: Humor, interview/profile, new product, photo feature and technical. "No personal trucking experiences. Stick to objective reporting on industry issues in Canada and the US." Buys 25 mss/year. Query with published clips. Length: 200-2,000 words. Pays $75-800. Pays expenses of writers on assignment.

Photos: State availability of photos or send photos with submission. Reviews 5×7 color or b&w prints. Offers no additional payment for photos accepted with ms. Captions and identification of subjects required. Buys one-time rights.

Columns/Departments: Finance (general pieces on finance and leasing relating to trucking industry), 500-1,000 words; Maintenance (general tips on trucking maintenance), 50-500 words; and Computers (latest in computer systems for trucking industry), 500-1,000 words. Buys 10 mss/year. Query with published clips. Pays $20-500.

Tips: "Potential contributors must have an awareness of the trucking industry. Do not attempt to write technical articles unless you have substantial knowledge in truck maintenance and operation."

UTILITY FLEET MANAGEMENT, The Equipment Magazine, Public Utilities Reports, Dept. WM, #200, 2111 Wilson Blvd., Arlington VA 22201-3060. (703)243-7000. Editor: Nancy Coe Bailey. 10% freelance written. Magazine published 8 times/year covering "investor-owned utilities, trucks and equipment fleets. *UFM* reaches utility fleet managers and their staffs, and the construction and maintenance employees who use the equipment. 80% of published material is about equipment: purchasing and maintaining." Estab. 1981. Circ. 6,000. **Pays on acceptance.** Publishes ms an average of 3 months after acceptance. Byline given. Buys all rights. Submit seasonal material 6 months in advance. Reports in 1 month on queries. Sample copy for 9×12 SAE with 5 first class stamps. Writer's guidelines for #10 SASE.
Nonfiction: How-to (i.e., new methods for recycling antifreeze; troubleshooting hydraulic systems; maintaining alternative fuel engines), interview/profile (leaders of large or innovative fleets), new product (if it's *really* new and intriguing), photo feature (want good photos of equipment in action). "No generic material. This is a technical publication and our readers want details. Not 'clean air engines are good' articles, but rather 'exactly how do they work?' " Buys 8 mss/year. Query. Length: 750-2,000 words. Pays $75 minimum for assigned articles; $75-300 for unsolicited articles. Technical/vendor "guest" writers are paid in contributor copies. Sometimes pays expenses of writers on assignment.
Photos: Reviews contact sheets, transparencies and prints. Offers no additional payment for photos accepted with ms. Identification of subjects required. Buys one-time rights.
Columns/Departments: Alternative Fuels/Vehicles (news, developments of alternative fuel vehicles—natural gas, electric, methanol, propane, etc.), 1,000 words; Management Forum (management techniques), 1,000 words; and Equipment Maintenance (technical tips on taking care of trucks and heavy equipment), 1,000 words. Buys 8 mss/year. Query. Pays $75-200.
Tips: "We need articles on equipment/truck selection and maintenance—things that will make a veteran fleet manager say, 'Wow, what a great idea!' Examples: A super truck big enough to hold another good-sized vehicle, with a complete rolling shop inside; an overhead crane that moves on tracks to 12 locations in a garage; tracked vehicles for emergency work that don't damage the environment."

VEHICLE LEASING TODAY, National Vehicle Leasing Association, Dept. WM, Suite 220, 3710 S. Robertson, P.O. Box 34579, Culver City CA 90232. (310)838-3170. Editor: Rodney Couts. 15% freelance written. Bimonthly magazine on vehicle leasing. "We cover critical issues for vehicle lessors, financial lending institutions, and computer software vendors with lessor programs." Estab. 1985. Circ. 6,000. Pays on publication. Publishes ms an average of 2 months after acceptance. Byline given. Negotiable kill fee. Buys one-time rights. Submit seasonal material 3 months in advance. Previously published submissions OK. Sample copy $5. Free writer's guidelines.
Nonfiction: How-to (anything relating to a vehicle lessor business), interview/profile, new product and technical. Buys 5 mss/year. Query. Length: 1,000-2,000 words. Pays $50-250 for assigned articles; $50-200 for unsolicited articles. Sometimes pays expenses of writers on assignment.
Photos: State availability of photos with submission. Reviews 5×7 prints. Offers no additional payment for photos accepted with ms. Model releases required. Buys one-time rights.
Columns/Departments: Financial Institutions, Lessor Issues, 500-1,000 words; New Products and Services, 500 words. Buys 3 mss/year. Send complete ms. Length: 300-1,000 words. Pays $25-100.

WARD'S AUTO WORLD, % 28 W. Adams, Detroit MI 48226. (313)962-4433. Fax: (313)962-4456. Editor-in-Chief: David C. Smith. Managing Editor: Marjorie A. Sorge. 10% freelance written. Prefers to work with published/established writers. Monthly magazine for top and middle management in all phases of auto industry. Also includes heavy-duty vehicle coverage. Estab. 1970. Circ. 100,000. Pays on publication. Kill fee varies. Byline given. Buys all rights. Phone queries OK. Query for electronic submissions. Reports in 1 month. Publishes ms an average of 1 month after acceptance. Sample copy and writer's guidelines for 8×10 SAE with 5 first class stamps.
Nonfiction: Expose, general interest, international automotive news, interview, new product and technical. Few consumer type articles. No "nostalgia or personal history stories (like 'My Favorite Car')." Buys 4-8 mss/year. Query. Length: 700-2,500 words. Pays $200-750. Sometimes pays the expenses of writers on assignment.
Photos: Assignment only.
Tips: "Don't send poetry, how-to and 'My Favorite Car' stuff. They don't stand a chance. This is a business newsmagazine and operates on a news basis just like any other newsmagazine. We like solid, logical, well-written pieces with *all* holes filled. Most surprises over the transom turn out to be exactly what we don't want. If you have questions, save yourself some headaches and use your phone."

Aviation and Space

In this section are journals for aviation business executives, airport operators and aviation technicians. Publications for professional and private pilots can be found in the Consumer Aviation section.

AG-PILOT INTERNATIONAL MAGAZINE, Graphics Plus, P.O. Box 1607, Mt. Vernon WA 98273-1607. (206)336-9737. Fax: (206)336-2506. Publisher: Tom J. Wood. Editor: Greg Skoglund. Monthly magazine emphasizing agricultural aerial application (crop dusting). "This is intended to be a fun-to-read, technical, as well as humorous, and serious publication for the ag pilot and operator. They are our primary target." 20% freelance written. Estab. 1978. Circ. 8,400. Pays on publication. Publishes ms an average of 3 months after acceptance. Buys all rights. Byline given unless writer requests name held. Reports in 1 month. Sample copy for 9 × 12 SAE with 7 first class stamps. Writer's guidelines for #10 SASE.

Nonfiction: Expose (of EPA, OSHA, FAA or any government function concerned with this industry), general interest, historical, interview (of well-known ag/aviation person), nostalgia, personal opinion, new product, personal experience and photo feature. "If we receive an article, in any area we have solicited, it is quite possible this person could contribute intermittently. The international input is what we desire. Industry-related material is a must. *No newspaper clippings.*" Send complete ms. Length: 800-1,500 words. Pays $50-200.

Photos: "We would like one color or b&w (5 × 7 preferred) with the manuscript, if applicable—it will help increase your chance of publication." Offers no additional payment for photos accepted with ms. Captions preferred, model release required.

Columns/Departments: International (of prime interest, crop dusting-related); Embryo Birdman (should be written, or appear to be written, by a beginner spray pilot); The Chopper Hopper (by anyone in the helicopter industry); Trouble Shooter (ag aircraft maintenance tips); and Catchin' The Corner (written by a person obviously skilled in the crop dusting field of experience or other interest-capturing material related to the industry). Send complete ms. Length: 800-1,500 words. Pays $25-100.

Poetry: Interested in all agri-aviation related poetry. Buys 1 poem/issue. Submit no more than 2 at one time. Maximum length: one 20 inch × 48 picas maximum. Pays $10-50.

Fillers: Short jokes, short humor and industry-related newsbreaks. Length: 10-100 words. Pays $5-20.

Tips: "Writers should be witty and knowledgeable about the crop dusting aviation world. Material *must* be agricultural/aviation-oriented. *Crop dusting or nothing!*"

‡CESSNA OWNER MAGAZINE, Jones Publishing, P.O. Box 337, 121 N. Main, Iola WI 54945. (715)445-5000. Editor: David Sakrison. 40-60% freelance written. Monthly magazine on Cessna single or twin engine aircraft/general aviation. "Ninety percent of our readers are pilots *and* aircraft owners. The aim of the magazine is to give them information to help them own and operate light aircraft safely and economically. Editorial content (product reviews, flight reports, safety, piloting skills, etc.) is aimed at *owners'* interest." Estab. 1975. Circ. 6,500. Pays on publication. Publishes ms an average of 6 months after acceptance. Byline given. Offers 25% kill fee. Buys one-time or second serial (reprint) rights. Editorial lead time 2 months. Submit seasonal material 2-3 months in advance. Simultaneous and previously published submissions OK. Query for electronic submissions. Reports in 1 month on queries; 3 months on mss. Sample copy and writer's guidelines free on request.

Nonfiction: Historical/nostalgic, how-to (maintenance, repairs, upgrades), humor, interview/profile (includes vendor profiles), new product and flight reports, opinion, personal experience, photo feature, technical (understanding aircraft systems), travel (by aircraft), safety, advanced ratings and pilot skills. Does not want to see: pilot/owner profiles; articles about first flight or learning to fly; articles about aircraft other than Cessnas; travel articles that don't involve airplanes. Buys 75 mss/year. Query with published clips or send complete ms. Length: 700-4,000 words. Pays 10¢/word minimum for assigned articles; 5¢/word for unsolicited articles. Sometimes pays expenses of writers on assignment.

Photos: Send photos with submission. Reviews 35mm transparencies and 3 × 5 or 5 × 7 (preferred) prints. Offers no additional payment for photos accepted with ms, or negotiates payment individually (under special circumstances). Identification of subjects required. Buys one-time rights or reprint rights on some.

Columns/Departments: On Final (short product reviews and industry news), 100-500 words; Destinations (short travel pieces, fly-in destinations), 100-1,000 words; Tail Feathers (humor, offbeat, history, esoterica), 1,000-1,500 words. Buys 10-20 mss/year. Send complete ms. Pays 5-10¢/word.

Tips: "Photos often make or break a story. Queries are appreciated, but we don't always have the time to respond. Writers should always follow a written query with a phone call. Press deadlines fall during the first 10-14 days of each month. Queries and calls between the 15th and 1st of each month get quicker, fuller attention. Best tip is to know the audience—owners and pilots of light aircraft."

‡PIPERS MAGAZINE, Jones Publishing, P.O. Box 337, 121 N. Main, Iola WI 54945. (715)445-5000. Editor: David Sakrison. 40-60% freelance written. Monthly magazine on Piper single or twin engine aircraft/general aviation. "Ninety percent of our readers are pilots *and* aircraft owners. The aim of the magazine is to give them information to help them own and operate light aircraft safely and economically. Editorial content (product reviews, flight reports, safety, piloting skills, etc.) is aimed at *owners'* interest." Estab. 1975. Circ. 6,500. Pays on publication. Publishes ms an average of 6 months after acceptance. Byline given. Offers 25% kill fee. Buys one-time or second serial (reprint) rights. Editorial lead time 2 months. Submit seasonal material 2-3 months in advance. Simultaneous and previously published submissions OK. Query for electronic submissions. Reports in 1 month on queries; 3 months on mss. Sample copy and writer's guidelines free on request.

Nonfiction: Historical/ nostalgic, how-to (maintenance, repairs, upgrades), humor, interview/profile (includes vendor profiles), new product and flight reports, opinion, personal experience, photo feature, technical (understanding aircraft systems), travel (by aircraft), safety, advanced ratings and pilot skills. Does not want to see: pilot/owner profiles; articles about first flight or learning to fly; articles about aircraft other than Pipers; travel articles that don't involve airplanes. Buys 75 mss/year. Query with published clips or send complete ms. Length: 700-4,000 words. Pays 10¢/word minimum for assigned articles; 5¢/word for unsolicited articles. Sometimes pays expenses of writers on assignment.

Photos: Send photos with submission. Reviews 35mm transparencies and 3×5 or 5×7 (preferred) prints. Offers no additional payment for photos accepted with ms. Negotiates payment individually (under special circumstances). Identification of subjects required. Buys one-time rights or reprint rights on some.

Columns/Departments: On final (short product reviews and industry news), 100-500 words; destinations (short travel pieces, fly-in destinations), 100-1,000 words; tail feathers (humor, offbeat, history, esoterica), 1,000-1,500 words. Buys 10-20 mss/year. Send complete ms. Pays 5-10¢/word.

Tips: "Photos often make or break a story. Queries are appreciated, but we don't always have the time to respond. Writers should always follow a written query with a phone call. Press deadlines fall during the first 10-14 days of each month. Queries and calls between the 15th and 1st of each month get quicker, fuller attention. Best tip is to know the audience—owners and pilots of light aircraft."

Beauty and Salon

LOOKING FIT, The Magazine for Health Conscious Tanning & Toning Centers, Virgo Publishing, Inc., Dept. WM, P.O. Box C-5400, Scottsdale AZ 85261. (602)990-1101. Fax: (602)990-0819. Editor: Nancy Bercaw. 15% freelance written. Monthly magazine on issues related to the indoor tanning and toning industries. "*Looking Fit* is interested in material dealing with any aspect of operating a tanning or toning salon. Preferred style is light whenever subject matter doesn't preclude it. Technical material should be written in a manner interesting and intelligible to the average salon operator." Estab. 1985. Circ. 28,000. Pays 1 month after publication. Byline given. Buys all rights. Submit seasonal material 3 months in advance. Simultaneous submissions OK. Query for electronic submissions. Reports in 3 months. Sample copy for 10×13 SAE with 9 first class stamps.

Nonfiction: How-to (operational—how to choose a location, buy equipment, etc.), humor, new product and technical. Buys 10-20 mss/year. Query with or without published clips or send complete ms. Length: 1,500-9,000 words. Pays $50-175 for assigned articles. Pays $50-150 for unsolicited articles.

Photos: Send photos with submission. Reviews contact sheets, 2×4 transparencies and 2×4 prints. Offers no additional payment for photos accepted with ms. Model releases and identification of subjects required.

Columns/Departments: Clublines (profiles of unusual/successful salons), 750-1,500 words; Profiles (profiles of unusual/successful manufacturers/distributors), 1,000-2,500 words. Buys 5-10 mss/year. Query or send complete ms. Length: 750-2,500 words. Pays $25-75.

Tips: "The best way to break in is to call or write with a good story idea. If it's workable, we'll have the writer do it. Unsolicited manuscripts are welcome, but may not fit into the magazine's goals. We're happy to offer direction or style angles by phone. In general, *Looking Fit* follows Associated Press style. Full-length (1,500-7,500 words) features are what we most often buy. For best results, contact us with story ideas and we can supply the names and numbers of industry contacts."

NAILS, Bobit Publishing, 2512 Artesia Blvd., Redondo Beach CA 90278. (310)376-8788. Editor: Cyndy Drummey. Managing Editor: Annie Gorton. 10% freelance written. Monthly magazine for the nail care industry. "*NAILS* seeks to educate its readers on new techniques and products, nail anatomy and health, customer relations, working safely with chemicals, salon sanitation, and the business aspects of working in or running a salon." Estab. 1983. Circ. 48,000. **Pays on acceptance.** Byline given. Buys all rights. Submit seasonal material 4 months in advance. Query for electronic submissions. Reports in 3 months on queries. Free sample copy. No writer's guidelines available.

Nonfiction: Historical/nostalgic, how-to, inspirational, interview/profile, personal experience, photo feature and technical. "No articles on one particular product, company profiles or articles slanted towards a particular company or manufacturer." Buys 20 mss/year. Query with published clips. Length: 1,200-3,000 words. Pays $100-400. Sometimes pays expenses of writers on assignment.

Photos: State availability of photos with submission. Reviews contact sheets, transparencies and prints (any standard size acceptable). Offers $50-200/photo. Captions, model releases and identification of subjects required. Buys all rights.

Tips: "Send clips and query; *do not send unsolicited manscripts*. We would like to see ideas for articles on a unique salon or a business article that focuses on a specific aspect or problem encountered when working in a salon. The Modern Nail Salon section, which profiles nail salons and full-service salons, is most open to freelancers. Focus on an innovative business idea or unique point of view. Articles from experts on specific business issues—insurance, handling difficult employees, cultivating clients—are encouraged."

Beverages and Bottling

Manufacturers, distributors and retailers of soft drinks and alcoholic beverages read these publications. Publications for bar and tavern operators and managers of restaurants are classified in the Hotels, Motels, Clubs, Resorts and Restaurants category.

AMERICAN BREWER, P.O. Box 510, Hayward CA 94543-0510. (415)538-9500 (a.m. only). Fax: (510)538-9500. Publisher: Bill Owens. 100% freelance written. Quarterly magazine covering micro-breweries. Estab. 1986. Circ. 6,000. Pays on publication. Publishes ms an average of 4 months after acceptance. Byline given. Buys one-time rights. Previously published submissions OK. Send tearsheet or photocopy of article. For reprints pays 30% of the amount paid for an original article. Reports in 2 weeks on queries. Sample copy $5.
Nonfiction: Humor, opinion and travel. Query. Length: 1,500-2,500 words. Pays $50-250 for assigned articles.

BEVERAGE WORLD, Keller International Publishing Corp., Dept. WM, 150 Great Neck Rd., Great Neck NY 11021. (516)829-9210. Editor: Larry Jabbonsky. Monthly magazine on the beverage industry. Estab. 1882. Circ. 35,000. **Pays on acceptance.** Publishes ms an average of 2 months after acceptance. Byline given. Buys all rights. Submit seasonal material 2 months in advance. Simultaneous submissions OK. Free sample copy and writer's guidelines.
Nonfiction: How-to (increase profit/sales), interview/profile and technical. Buys 15 mss/year. Query with published clips. Length: 1,000-2,500 words. Pays $200/listed page. Sometimes pays expenses of writers on assignment.
Photos: State availability of photos with submission. Reviews contact sheets. Captions required. Buys one-time rights.
Columns/Departments: Buys 5 mss/year. Query with published clips. Length: 750-1,000 words. Pay varies, $150/minimum.
Tips: "Requires background in beverage production and marketing. Business and/or technical writing experience *a must*. Do not call. This is a small staff that does not have much time for phone queries. Proof your queries carefully. Poor spelling/grammar is a turn-off."

LA BARRIQUE, Kylix Media Inc., Suite 414, 5165 Sherbrooke St. W., Montreal, Quebec H4A 1T6 Canada. (514)481-5892. Editor: Nicole Barette-Ryan. 20% freelance written. Magazine published 7 times/year on wine. "The magazine, *written in French*, covers wines of the world specially written for the province of Québec consumers and restaurant trade. It covers wine books, restaurants, vintage reports and European suppliers." Estab. 1972. Pays on publication. Publishes ms an average of 2 months after acceptance. Byline given. Buys first North American serial rights. Submit seasonal material 6 months in advance. Simultaneous submissions OK. Reports in 6 weeks on queries.
Nonfiction: General interest, how-to, humor, interview/profile, new product, opinion and travel. Knowledge of wines given primary consideration. Length: 500-1,500 words. Pays $25-100 for unsolicited articles.
Photos: Send photos with submission. Reviews transparencies and prints. Offers $25-100/photo. Identification of subjects required. Buys one-time rights.

‡MID-CONTINENT BOTTLER, Suite 218, 8575 W 110, Overland Park KS 66210. (913)469-8611. Fax: (913)469-8626. Publisher: Floyd E. Sageser. 5% freelance written. Prefers to work with published/established writers. Bimonthly magazine for "soft drink bottlers in the 20-state Midwestern area." Estab. 1970. Not copyrighted. **Pays on acceptance.** Publishes ms an average of 2 months after acceptance. Buys first rights only. Reports "immediately." Sample copy for 9 × 12 SAE with 10 first class stamps. Guidelines for #10 SASE.
Nonfiction: "Items of specific soft drink bottler interest with special emphasis on sales and merchandising techniques. Feature style desired." Buys 2-3 mss/year. Length: 2,000 words. Pays $15-100. Sometimes pays the expenses of writers on assignment.
Photos: Photos purchased with mss.

SOUTHERN BEVERAGE JOURNAL, Dept. WM, 13225 SW 88th Ave., Miami FL 33176. (305)233-7230. Fax: (305)252-2580. Editor: Jackie Preston. 60% freelance written. Works with a small number of new/unpublished writers each year. Monthly magazine for the alcohol beverage industry. Readers are personnel of bars, restaurants, package stores, night clubs, lounges and hotels—owners, managers and salespersons. Estab. 1945. Circ. 30,000. **Pays on acceptance.** Publishes ms an average of 4 months after acceptance. Byline given. Buys first rights. Publishes reprints of previously published articles. Send typed ms with rights for sale noted. Include information about when and where the article previously appeared. Submit seasonal material 4 months in advance. Query for electronic submissions. Reports in 1 month. *Writer's Market* recommends allowing 2 months for reply.

Nonfiction: General interest, historical, personal experience, interview/profile and success stories. Information on legislation (state) affecting alcohol beverage industry. No canned material. Buys 6 mss/year. Send complete ms. Length: 1,000-2,000 words. Pays 10¢/word for assigned articles.

Photos: State availability of photos with submission. Reviews 7×8 or 4×5 transparencies and 3×5 prints. Offers $15 maximum/photo. Identification of subjects required. Buys one-time rights.

Tips: "We are interested in legislation having to do with our industry and also views on trends, drinking and different beverages."

VINEYARD & WINERY MANAGEMENT, P.O. Box 231, Watkins Glen NY 14891. (607)535-7133. Fax: (607)535-2998. Editor: J. William Moffett. 80% freelance written. Bimonthly trade magazine of professional importance to grape growers, winemakers and winery sales and business people. Estab. 1975. Circ. 4,500. Pays on publication. Byline given. Buys first North American serial rights and occasionally simultaneous rights. Query for electronic submissions. Reports in 3 weeks on queries; 1 month on mss. *Writer's Market* recommends allowing 2 months for reply. Free sample copy. Writer's guidelines for #10 SASE.

Nonfiction: How-to, interview/profile and technical. Subjects are technical in nature and explore the various methods people in these career paths use to succeed, and also the equipment and techniques they use successfully. Business articles and management topics are also featured. The audience is national with western dominance. Buys 30 mss/year. Query. Length: 300-5,000 words. Pays $30-1,000. Pays some expenses of writers on some assignments.

Photos: State availability of photos with submission. Reviews contact sheets, negatives and transparencies. Identification of subjects required. "Black and white often purchased for $20 each to accompany story material; 35mm and/or 4×5 transparencies for $50 and up; 6/year of vineyard and/or winery scene related to story. Query."

Tips: "We're looking for long-term relationships with authors who know the business and write well. Electronic submissions preferred; query for formats."

• This publication no longer considers short fiction.

WINES & VINES, 1800 Lincoln Ave., San Rafael CA 94901-1298. Fax: (415)453-2517. Editor: Philip E. Hiaring. 10-20% freelance written. Works with a small number of new/unpublished writers each year. Monthly magazine for everyone concerned with the grape and wine industry including winemakers, wine merchants, growers, suppliers, consumers, etc. Estab. 1919. Circ. 4,500. Buy first North American serial or simultaneous rights. Publishes reprints of previously published articles. Send typed ms with rights for sale noted. Include information about when and where the article previously appeared. **Pays on acceptance.** Publishes ms an average of 3 months after acceptance. Special issues: Winetech, (January); Vineyard (February); State-of-the-Art (March); Brandy/specialty wines, (April); Export-import (May); Enological (June); Statistical (July); Merchandising (August); Marketing (September); Equipment and supplies (November); Champagne (December). Submit special issue material 3 months in advance. Reports in 2 months. Sample copy for 11×14 SAE with 7 first class stamps. Free writer's guidelines.

Nonfiction: Articles of interest to the trade. "These could be on grape growing in unusual areas; new winemaking techniques; wine marketing, retailing, etc." Interview, historical, spot news, merchandising techniques and technical. No stories with a strong consumer orientation as against trade orientation. Author should know the subject matter, i.e., know proper grape growing/winemaking terminology. Buys 3-4 ms/year. Query. Length: 1,000-2,500 words. Pays 5¢/word. Sometimes pays the expenses of writers on assignment.

Photos: Pays $10 for 4×5 or 8×10 b&w photos purchased with mss. Captions required.

Tips: "Ours is a trade magazine for professionals. Therefore, we do not use 'gee-whiz' wine articles."

Book and Bookstore

Publications for book trade professionals from publishers to bookstore operators are found in this section. Journals for professional writers are classified in the Journalism and Writing category.

BLOOMSBURY REVIEW, A Book Magazine, Owaissa Communications Co., Inc., Dept. WM, 1028 Bannock, Denver CO 80204. (303)892-0620. Fax: (303)892-5620. Publisher/Editor-in-chief: Tom Auer. Associate Publisher-Editor: Marilyn Auer. 75% freelance written. Tabloid published 8 times/year covering books and book-related matters. "We publish book reviews, interviews with writers and poets, literary essays and original poetry. Our audience consists of educated, literate, *non-specialized* readers." Estab. 1980. Circ. 50,000. Pays on publication. Publishes ms an average of 4 months after acceptance. Byline given. Buys first rights or one-time rights. Reports in 3 months. Reprints OK; send photocopy of article and information about when and where the article previously appeared. Pays 100% of their fee for an original article. Sample copy $4 for 9×12 SASE. Writer's guidelines for #10 SASE.

Nonfiction: Essays, interview/profile and book reviews. "Summer issue features reviews, etc. about the American West." No academic or religious articles. *"We do not publish fiction."* Buys 60 mss/year. Query with published clips or send complete ms. Length 800-1,500 words. Pays $10-20. Sometimes pays writers with contributor copies or other premiums "if writer agrees."

Photos: State availability of photos with submissions. Reviews prints. Offers no additional payment for photos accepted with ms. Buys one-time rights.

Columns/Departments: Book reviews and essays. Buys 6 mss/year. Query with published clips or send complete ms. Length: 500-1,500 words. Pays $10-20.

Poetry: Ray Gonzalez, poetry editor. Avant-garde, free verse, haiku, light verse and traditional. Buys 20 poems/year. Submit up to 5 poems at one time. Pays $5-10.

Tips: "We appreciate receiving published clips and/or completed manuscripts. Please—no rough drafts. Book reviews should be of new books (within 6 months of publication)."

THE FEMINIST BOOKSTORE NEWS, P.O. Box 882554, San Francisco CA 94188-2554. (415)626-1556. Editor: Carol Seajay. Managing Editor: Christine Chia. 10% freelance written. Works with a small number of new/unpublished writers each year. Bimonthly magazine covering feminist books and the women-in-print industry. *"Feminist Bookstore News* covers 'everything of interest' to the feminist bookstores, publishers and periodicals, books of interest and provides an overview of feminist publishing by mainstream publishers." Estab. 1976. Circ. 700. Pays on publication. Publishes ms an average of 2 months after acceptance. Byline sometimes given. Buys one-time rights. Simultaneous submissions OK. Reports in 3 weeks. Sample copy $6.

Nonfiction: Essays, expose, how-to (run a bookstore), new product, opinion and personal experience (in feminist book trade only). Special issues: Sidelines (July) and University Press (fall). No submissions that do not directly apply to the feminist book trade. Query with or without published clips or send complete ms. Length: 250-2,000 words. Pays in copies when appropriate.

Photos: State availability of photos with submission. Model release and identification of subjects required. Buys one-time rights.

Fillers: Anecdotes, facts, newsbreaks and short humor. Length: 100-400 words.

Tips: "The writer must have several years experience in the feminist book industry. We publish very little by anyone else."

THE HORN BOOK MAGAZINE, The Horn Book, Inc., Dept. WM, 14 Beacon St., Boston MA 02108. (617)227-1555. Editor: Anita Silvey. 25% freelance written. Prefers to work with published/established writers. Bimonthly magazine covering children's literature for librarians, booksellers, professors, and students of children's literature. Estab. 1924. Circ. 22,000. Pays on publication. Publishes ms an average of 4 months after acceptance. Byline given. Buys one-time rights. Submit seasonal material 6 months in advance. Simultaneous queries and submissions OK. Reports in 6 weeks on queries; 2 months on mss. Free sample copy. Writer's guidelines available upon request.

Nonfiction: Interview/profile (children's book authors and illustrators). Buys 20 mss/year. Query or send complete ms. Length: 1,000-2,800 words. Pays $25-250.

Tips: "Writers have a better chance of breaking in to our publication with a query letter on a specific article they want to write."

LOS ANGELES TIMES BOOK REVIEW, Times Mirror, Times Mirror Sq., Los Angeles CA 90053. (213)237-7778. Editor: Sonja Bolle. 70% freelance written. Weekly tabloid reviewing current books. Estab. 1881. Circ. 1.5 million. Pays on publication. Publishes ms an average of 3 weeks after acceptance. Byline given. Offers variable kill fee. Buys first North American serial rights. Accepts no unsolicited book reviews or requests for specific titles to review. "Query with published samples—book reviews or literary features." Buys 500 mss/year. Length: 200-1,500 words. Pays approx 35¢/word.

THE WOMEN'S REVIEW OF BOOKS, The Women's Review, Inc., Wellesley College, Wellesley MA 02181-8259. (617)283-2500. Editor: Linda Gardiner. Monthly newspaper. "Feminist review of recent trade and academic writing by and about women. Reviews recent nonfiction books, primarily." Estab. 1983. Circ. 14,000. Pays on publication. Publishes ms an average of 2 months after acceptance. Byline given. Offers $50 kill fee. Buys first North American serial rights. Editorial lead time 2 months. Query for electronic submissions. Reports in 2 months. Sample copy free on request.

Nonfiction: Book reviews only. No articles considered; no unsolicited mss. Only book review queries. Buys 200 mss/year. Query with published clips. Pays 10¢/word. Sometimes pays expenses of writers on assignment.

Tips: "Only experienced reviewers for national media are considered. Reviewers must have expertise in subject of book under review. Never send unsolicited manuscripts."

Brick, Glass and Ceramics

These publications are read by manufacturers, dealers and managers of brick, glass and ceramic retail businesses. Other publications related to glass and ceramics are listed in the Consumer Art and Architecture and Consumer Hobby and Craft sections.

AMERICAN GLASS REVIEW, P.O. Box 2147, Clifton NJ 07015-3517. (201)779-1600. Fax: (201)779-3242. Editor-in-Chief: Donald Doctorow. Managing Editor: Susan Grisham. 10% freelance written. Monthly magazine. Pays on publication. Estab. 1888. Byline given. Phone queries OK. Buys first rights. Publishes reprints of previously published articles; send tearsheet of article. For reprints, pays 10% of the amount paid for an original article. Submit seasonal material 2 months in advance of issue date. Reports in 2 months. Free sample copy and writer's guidelines; mention *Writer's Market* in request.
Nonfiction: Glass plant and glass manufacturing articles. Buys 3-4 mss/year. Query. Length: 1,500-3,000 words. Pays $200/printed page.
Photos: State availability of photos with query. No additional payment for b&w contact sheets. Captions preferred. Buys one-time rights.

GLASS MAGAZINE, For the Architectural Glass Industry, National Glass Association, Dept. WM, Suite 302, 8200 Greensboro Dr., McLean VA 22102-3881. (703)442-4890. Fax: (703)442-0630. Editor-in-Chief: Nicole Harris. 25% freelance written. Prefers to work with published/established writers. Monthly magazine covering the architectural glass industry. Circ. 16,500. **Pays on acceptance.** Publishes ms an average of 3-6 months after acceptance. Byline given. Kill fee varies. Buys first rights only. Reports in 2 months. Sample copy $5 for 9×12 SAE with 10 first class stamps. Free writer's guidelines.
Nonfiction: Interview/profile (of various glass businesses; profiles of industry people or glass business owners); and technical (about glazing processes). Buys 15 mss/year. Query with published clips. Length: 1,000 words minimum. Pays $150-300.
    • They are doing more inhouse writing; freelance cut by half.
Photos: State availability of photos.
Tips: "Do *not* send in general glass use stories. Research the industry first, then query."

Building Interiors

Owners, managers and sales personnel of floor covering, wall covering and remodeling businesses read the journals listed in this category. Interior design and architecture publications may be found in the Consumer Art, Design and Collectibles category. For journals aimed at other construction trades see the Construction and Contracting section.

ALUMI-NEWS, Work-4 Projects Ltd., Box 400, Victoria Station, Westmount, Québec H3Z 2V8 Canada. (514)489-4941. Fax: (514)489-5505. Publisher: Nachmi Artzy. 75% freelance written. Home renovation — exterior building products trade journal published 6 times/year. "We are dedicated to the grass roots of the industry: installers, dealers, contractors. We do not play up to our advertisers nor government." Estab. 1977. Circ. 18,000. Pays on publication. Byline usually given. Buys all rights. Simultaneous and previously published submissions OK. Free sample copy.
Nonfiction: Expose, how-to (pertaining to dealers — profit, production, or management); new product (exterior building products); technical and survey results (trends or products in our industry). Buys 12-24 mss/year. Query with published clips. Length: 200-2,000 words. Pays 10-20¢/word. Pays in contributor copies or other premiums if mutually suitable. Sometimes pays expenses of writers on assignment.
Photos: State availability of photos with submission. Reviews negatives, transparencies and prints. Pays $300 maximum per photo. Captions and identification of subjects required. Buys all rights.
Columns/Departments: Industry News (company profile: new location, product, personnel), 100-250 words; and Profiles (interviews), 1,000-2,500 words. Query with published clips. Length: 75-300 words. Pays 10-20¢/word.
Fillers: Facts and short humor. Length 5-50 words. Pays 10-20¢/word.
Tips: "Submit articles not found in *every* similar publication. Find a new angle; Canadian content."

‡PWC, Painting & Wallcovering Contractor, Finan Publishing Co. Inc., 8730 Big Bend Blvd., St. Louis MO 63119. (314)961-6644. Editor: Jeffery Beckner. 90% freelance written. Bimonthly magazine for painting and wallcovering contracting. "*PWC* provides news you can use: information helpful to the painting and wallcovering contractor in the here and now." Estab. 1928. Circ. 30,000. Pays 30 days after acceptance. Publishes ms an average of 1 month after acceptance. Byline given. Kill fee "to be determined on individual basis." Buys first North American serial rights. Editorial lead time 2 months. Submit seasonal material 2 months in advance. Simultaneous and previously published submissions OK. Query for electronic submissions; hard copy required. Reports in weeks. Sample copy free on request.

Nonfiction: Essays, expose, how-to (painting and wallcovering), interview/profile, new product, opinion and personal experience. Buys 40 mss/year. Query with published clips. Length: 1,500-2,500 words. Pays $300 minimum. Pays expenses of writers on assignment.

Photos: State availability of photos with submission. Send photos with submission. Reviews contact sheets, negatives, transparencies and prints. Offers no additional payment for photos accepted with ms. Identification of subjects required. Buys one-time and all rights.

Columns/Departments: (Anything of interest to the small businessman), 1,250 words. Buys 2 mss/year. Query with published clips. Pays $50-100.

Tips: "We almost always buy on an assignment basis. The way to break in is to send good clips, and I'll try and give you work."

REMODELING, Hanley-Wood, Inc., Suite 475, Dept. WM, 655 15th St. NW, Washington DC 20005. (202)737-0717. Fax: (202)737-2439. Editor: Wendy Jordan. 5% freelance written. Monthly magazine covering residential and light commercial remodeling. "We cover the best new ideas in remodeling design, business, construction and products." Estab. 1985. Circ. 98,000. Pays on publication. Publishes ms an average of 3 months after acceptance. Byline given. Offers 5¢/word kill fee. Buys first North American serial rights. Query for electronic submissions. Reports in 1 month. Free sample copy and writer's guidelines.

Nonfiction: Interview/profile, new product and technical. Buys 4 mss/year. Query with published clips. Length: 250-1,000 words. Pays 20¢/word. Sometimes pays the expenses of writers on assignment.

Photos: State availability of photos with submission. Reviews slides, 4×5 transparencies and 8×10 prints. Offers $25-100/photo. Captions, model releases and identification of subjects required. Buys one-time rights.

Tips: "The areas of our publication most open to freelancers are news and new product news."

REMODELING NEWS, DPH Communications, Inc., 2269 Saw Mill River Rd., Elmsford NY 10523. (914)347-3000. Editor: Liz Wagner. 80% freelance written. Monthly magazine covering professionally installed home remodeling and light construction. Estab. 1987. Circ. 82,000. Pays within 30 days of acceptance. Publishes ms an average of 3 months after acceptance. Byline given. Offers 25% kill fee. Buys First North American serial rights. Submit seasonal material 6 months in advance. Previously published submissions OK. Query for electronic submissions. Reports in 2 months. Free sample copy and writer's guidelines.

Nonfiction: How-to for professional remodelers, running a contracting business and remodeling products and materials. "Do not submit article for consumers or do-it-yourselfers." Query with published clips. Length: 600-3,000 words. Pays 20¢/word for assigned articles; $50-200 for reprints.

Photos: State availability of photos with submission. Reviews transparencies, slides or photos. Captions, model releases and identification of subjects required. Buys all rights.

Tips: "Articles must be geared toward professional contractors/remodelers, not do-it-yourselfers."

WALLS & CEILINGS, Dept. WM, 8602 N. 40th St., Tampa FL 33604. (813)989-9300. Fax: (813)980-3982. Editor: Greg Campbell. 20% freelance written. Monthly magazine for contractors involved in lathing and plastering, drywall, acoustics, fireproofing, curtain walls, movable partitions together with manufacturers, dealers, and architects. Estab. 1938. Circ. 20,000. Pays on publication. Byline given. Publishes ms an average of 4-6 months after acceptance. Buys all rights within trade. Submit seasonal material 4 months in advance. Accepts simultaneous and previously published submissions. Query for electronic submissions. Reports in 6 months. Sample copy for 9×12 SAE with $2 postage. Writer's guidelines for #10 SASE.

Nonfiction: How-to (drywall and plaster construction and business management) and technical. Buys 20 mss/year. Query or send complete ms. Length: 1,000-1,500 words. Pays $50-200. Sometimes pays the expenses of writers on assignment.

Photos: Send photos with submission. Reviews contact sheets, negatives, transparencies and prints. Photos required for ms acceptance, with captions and identification of subjects. Buys one-time rights.

Business Management

These publications cover trends, general theory and management practices for business owners and top-level business executives. Publications that use similar material but have a less technical slant are listed in the Consumer

Market conditions are constantly changing! If this is 1995 or later, buy the newest edition of Writer's Market at your favorite bookstore or order directly from Writer's Digest Books.

Business and Finance section. Journals for middle management, including supervisors and office managers, appear in the Management and Supervision section. Those for industrial plant managers are listed under Industrial Operations and under sections for specific industries, such as Machinery and Metal. Publications for office supply store operators are included in the Office Environment and Equipment section.

‡CHECKLIST, The International Magazine for Check Cashers, BKB Publications Inc., Suite 2030, 150 Nassau St., New York NY 10038. (212)267-7712. Editor: Charlene Komar Storey. 50% freelance written. Quarterly magazine for check cashing industry. "Material must be geared specifically to check cashers." Estab. 1989. Circ. 4,750. Pays on publication. Publishes ms an average of 3 months after acceptance. Byline given. Buys all rights. Editorial lead time 2 months. Accepts previously published submissions (if not published by a competitor). Query for electronic submissions. Reports in 1 month. Sample copy free on request.
Nonfiction: Interview/profile, technical and material of interest to check cashers, regulatory issues, marketing, etc. No consumer-oriented articles. Buys 20 mss/year. Query with published clips or send complete ms. Length: 500-3,000 words. Pays 10¢/word as published. Sometimes pays expenses of writers on assignment.
Photos: Send photos with submission. Reviews contact sheets, any transparencies or any prints. Negotiates payment individually. Captions and identification of subjects required. Buys all rights.
Tips: "Experienced business writers do best with us. An understanding of the check cashing industry is essential, as is knowledge of the approach required by a trade publication."

CHIEF EXECUTIVE, Dept. WM, 233 Park Ave. S., New York NY 10003. (212)979-4810. Fax: (212)979-4812. Editor: J.P. Donlon. Written by and for CEOs. Limited freelance opportunity. Published 9 times/year. Circ. 35,000. **Pays on acceptance.** Publishes ms an average of 2-3 months after acceptance. Byline given. Offers kill fee. Buys world serial rights. Free writer's guidelines.
Nonfiction: Query required for all departments. Unsolicited mss will not be returned. Pays $300-800. Pays previously agreed upon expenses of writers on assignment.
Photos: State availability of photos with submission. Reviews 4-color transparencies and slides. Offers $100/photo maximum. Captions required. Buys one-time rights.
Column/Departments: N.B. (profile of CEO/Chairman/President of mid- to large-size company), 400-500 words; Amenities, 1,000-1,500 words; CEO-At-Leisure, 1,000-1,500 words; and Business Travel (provides CEOs with *key names* and information on business/government inner network for city/area being visited—who to know to get things done), 1,000-1,500 words. Payment varies.

COMMUNICATION BRIEFINGS, Encoders, Inc., Dept. WM, Suite 110, 700 Black Horse Pike, Blackwood NJ 08012-1455. (609)232-6380. Fax: (609)232-8229. Executive Editor: Frank Grazian. 15% freelance written. Prefers to work with published/established writers. Monthly newsletter covering business communication and business management. "Most readers are in middle and upper management. They comprise public relations professionals, editors of company publications, marketing and advertising managers, fund raisers, directors of associations and foundations, school and college administrators, human resources professionals, and other middle managers who want to communicate better on the job." Estab. 1980. Circ. 46,000. **Pays on acceptance.** Publishes ms an average of 3 months after acceptance. Byline given sometimes on Bonus Items and on other items if idea originates with the writer. Buys one-time rights. Submit seasonal material 2 months in advance. Previously published submissions OK, "but must be rewritten to conform to our style." Reports in 1 month. Sample copy and writer's guidelines for #10 SAE and 2 first class stamps.
Nonfiction: "Most articles we buy are of the 'how-to' type. They consist of practical ideas, techniques and advice that readers can use to improve business communication and management. Areas covered: writing, speaking, listening, employee communication, human relations, public relations, interpersonal communication, persuasion, conducting meetings, advertising, marketing, fund raising, telephone techniques, teleconferencing, selling, improving publications, handling conflicts, negotiating, etc. Because half of our subscribers are in the nonprofit sector, articles that appeal to both profit and nonprofit organizations are given top priority." *Short Items:* Articles consisting of one or two brief tips that can stand alone. Length: 40-70 words. *Articles:* A collection of tips or ideas that offer a solution to a communication or management problem or that show a better way to communicate or manage. Examples: "How to produce slogans that work," "The wrong way to criticize employees," "Mistakes to avoid when leading a group discussion," and "5 ways to overcome writer's block." Length: 125-150 words. *Bonus Items:* In-depth pieces that probe one area of communication or management and cover it as thoroughly as possible. Examples: "Producing successful special events," "How to evaluate your newsletter," and "How to write to be understood." Length: 1,300 words. Buys 30-50 mss/year. Pays $15-35 for 40- to 150-word pieces; Bonus Items, $200. Pays the expenses of writers on assignment.

Tips: "Our readers are looking for specific, practical ideas and tips that will help them communicate better both within their organizations and with outside publics. Most ideas are rejected because they are too general or too elementary for our audience. Our style is down-to-earth and terse. We pack a lot of useful information into short articles. Our readers are busy executives and managers who want information dispatched quickly and without embroidery. We omit anecdotes, lengthy quotes and long-winded exposition. The writer has a better chance of breaking in at our publication with short articles and fillers since we buy only six major features (bonus items) a year. We require queries on longer items and bonus items. Writers may submit short tips (40-70 words) without querying. The most frequent mistakes made by writers completing an article for us are failure to master the style of our publication and to understand our readers' needs."

‡**CONVENE,** Professional Convention Meeting Assn., Suite 220, 100 Vestavia Office Pk., Birmingham AL 35216. (205)823-7262. Editor: Peter Shure. Managing Editor: Amy Cates Lyle. 50-60% freelance written. Monthly magazine on convention and meeting management. "Covers primarily how-to of all aspects of meeting/convention planning and management." Estab. 1986. Circ. 20,000. **Pays on acceptance.** Publishes ms an average of 3 months after acceptance. Byline given. Offers 50% kill fee. Publication not copyrighted. Buys all rights. Editorial lead time 2 months. Submit seasonal material 4 months in advance. Simultaneous and previously published submissions OK. Query for electronic submissions. Reports in 1 month. Sample copy $1 for SAE with 4 first class stamps.
Nonfiction: Book excerpts, essays, general interest, how-to, humor, interview/profile, opinion, personal experience, photo feature, technical and travel. Does not want to see anything not product-related. Buys 25 mss/year. Send complete ms. Length: 1,000-1,500 words. Pays $200 minimum for assigned articles. Pays expenses of writers on assignment.
Photos: State availability of photos with submission. Reviews contact sheets, transparencies and prints. Offers no additional payment for photos accepted with ms. Identification of subjects required. Buys one-time rights.
Columns/Departments: Food & Beverage (for group functions), 750 words; Hotel Industry (for group functions), 750 words; Travel Industry (for group functions), 750 words. Buys 50 mss/year. Send complete ms. Pays $200-400.
Tips: "Acquire an understanding of the industry."

‡**EARLY CHILDHOOD NEWS,** Peter Li, Inc., 330 Progress Rd., Dayton OH 45449. (513)847-5900. Fax: (513)847-5910. Editor: Janet Coburn. 75% freelance written. Bimonthly trade journal on child care centers. "Our publication is a news and service magazine for owners, directors and administrators of child care centers serving children from age 6 weeks to 2nd grade." Estab. 1988. Circ. 30,000. Pays on publication. Publishes ms an average of 3-4 months after acceptance. Copyright pending. Buys first rights. Submit seasonal/holiday material 5-6 months in advance. Query for electronic submissions. Sample copy $4 for 9 × 12 SAE with 2 first class stamps.
Nonfiction: How-to (how I solved a problem other center directors may face), interview/profile personal experience and business aspects of child care centers. "No articles directed at early childhood teachers or lesson plans." Buys 15 mss/year. Query with or without published clips or send complete ms. Length: 500-1,500 words. Pays $50-150.
Photos: Send photos with submission if available. Reviews 35mm and 4 × 5 transparencies and 5 × 7 prints. Captions, model releases and identification of subjects required. Buys one-time rights.
Fillers: Facts and newsbreaks. Length: 100-250 words. Pays $10-25.
Tips: "Send double-spaced typed mss and pay attention to grammar and punctuation. Enclose SASE for reply. No scholarly pieces with footnotes and bibliography. No activities/lesson plans for use with kids. We need short, easy-to-read articles written in popular style that give child care center owners information they can use right away to make their centers better, more effective, more efficient, etc. Feature stories and fillers are most open to freelancers. Be specific and concrete; use examples. Tightly focused topics are better than general 'The Day Care Dilemma' types."

FINANCIAL EXECUTIVE, Financial Executives Institute, 10 Madison Ave., Morristown NJ 07962-1938. Fax: (201)898-4649. Editor: Catherine M. Coult. Managing Editor: Robin L. Couch. 5% freelance written. Bi-monthly magazine for corporate financial management. "*Financial Executive* is published for senior financial executives of major corporations and explores corporate accounting and treasury related issues without being anti-business." Circ. 16,000. Pays on publication. Byline given. Buys all rights. Reports in 1 month on queries; 2 months on mss. Sample copy $5 for 9 × 12 SAE with 6 first class stamps. Writer's guidelines for #10 SASE.
Nonfiction: Interviews of senior financial executives involved in issues listed above. Also, pieces ghostwritten for financial executives. Accounting, finance and tax developments of interest to financial executives. Query with published clips. Length: 1,500-2,500 words. Pays $500-1,000.
Tips: "The query approach is best. (Address correspondence to Robin L. Couch.) We use business or financial articles that follow a *Wall Street Journal* approach—a fresh idea, with its significance (to financial executives), quotes, anecdotes and an interpretation or evaluation. Our content will follow developments in treasury management, information management, regulatory changes, tax legislation, Congressional hearings/legisla-

tion, re business and financial reporting. There is also interest in employee benefits, international business and impact of technology. We have very high journalistic standards."

MAY TRENDS, George S. May International Company, 303 S. Northwest Hwy., Park Ridge IL 60068-4255. (312)825-8806. Editor: John E. McArdle. 20% freelance written. Works with a small number of new/unpublished writers each year. Triannual free magazine for owners and managers of small and medium-sized businesses, hospitals and nursing homes, trade associations, Better Business Bureaus, educational institutions and newspapers. Estab. 1967. Circ. 30,000. Buys all rights. Byline given. Buys 10-15 mss/year. Pays on publication. Publishes ms an average of 6 months after acceptance. Returns rejected material immediately. Reports in 2 months. Sample copy for 9 × 12 SAE with 4 first class stamps.
Nonfiction: "We prefer articles dealing with how to solve problems of specific industries (manufacturers, wholesalers, retailers, service businesses, small hospitals and nursing homes) where contact has been made with key executives whose comments regarding their problems may be quoted. We want problem solving articles, *not* success stories that laud an individual company. We like articles that give the business manager concrete suggestions on how to deal with specific problems—i.e., '5 steps to solve . . .,' '6 key questions to ask when . . .,' and '4 tell-tale signs indicating . . .' Focus is on marketing, economic and technological trends that have an impact on medium- and small-sized businesses, not on the 'giants'; automobile dealers coping with existing dull markets; and contractors solving cost-inventory problems. Will consider material on successful business operations and merchandising techniques." Query or submit complete ms. Length: 2,000-3,000 words. Pays $150-250.
Tips: Query letter should tell "type of business and problems the article will deal with. We specialize in the problems of small (20-100 employees, $500,000-3,000,000 volume) businesses (manufacturing, wholesale, retail and service), plus medium and small healthcare facilities. We are now including nationally known writers in each issue—writers like the Vice Chairman of the Federal Reserve Bank, the US Secretary of the Treasury; names like George Bush and Malcolm Baldridge; titles like the Chairman of the Joint Committee on Accreditation of Hospitals; and Canadian Minister of Export. This places extra pressure on freelance writers to submit very good articles. Frequent mistakes: 1) Writing for big business, rather than small and 2) using language that is too academic."

THE MEETING MANAGER, Meeting Planners International, Suite 5018, 1950 Stemmons, Dallas TX 75207-3109. (214)712-7733. Fax: (214)712-7770. Editor: Tina Berres Filipski. 25% freelance written. Monthly association magazine for the meetings/hospitality/travel industries. Freelancers must have experience in meetings industry terminology, topics and issues. Estab. 1972. Circ. 10,500. **Pays on acceptance.** Byline given. Query. Reports in 2 months. Send SASE for sample and writer's guidelines.
Nonfiction: How-to, trends, interview/profile, personal development. Query with published clips. Length: 500-2,500 words. Pays $300-450.
Photos: State availability of photos with submission. Reviews contact sheets and transparencies. Offers no additional payment for photos accepted with ms. Captions required.

MINI-STORAGE MESSENGER, MiniCo Inc., Dept. WM, 2531 W. Dunlap Ave., Phoenix AZ 85021-2715. (800)824-6864. Director of Publishing: Randy Tipton. Managing Editor: Stefan Budricks. 50% freelance written. Monthly magazine on the self-storage industry. "We speak to self-storage owners, operators and managers, as well as those on the industry's fringes such as appraisers and bankers, architects, zoning officials, etc. We strive for balanced multi-source material with solid, practical information." Estab. 1975. Circ. 4,000. **Pays within 30 days of acceptance.** Publishes ms an average of 2 months after acceptance. Offers 25% kill fee. Buys first rights and second serial (reprint) rights. Reports in 1 month. Free sample copy and writer's guidelines.
Nonfiction: How-to (practical information on self-storage and related "storage" industries, e.g. boat, RV storage), interview/profile, new product, photo feature and technical. "One-source, first-person essays accepted." Buys 60 mss/year. Query with published clips. Length: 1,500-2,000 words. Pays $200-350. Payment includes the expenses of writers' phone bills.
Photos: State availability of photos with submission. Reviews transparencies (2¼ × 2¼). Offers $50-150/photo. Identification of subjects required. Buys all rights.
Columns/Departments: Construction (construction issues on self-storage, practical how-to information), 1,000 words; Operations (tips on successful operating techniques on self-storage), 1,000 words; Management (tips and trends in mini-storage management), 1,000 words; Marketing (tips and trends in mini-storage marketing), 1,000 words. Buys 50 mss/year. Query with published clips. Length: 1,000-1,200 words. Pays $200.
Tips: "Get to know self-storage industry or dig up something new about the industry or its people. We are very receptive to writers with their own strong ideas. Diligence and original research and sources are ways to impress us. New slants and story ideas will get our attention."

‡**PARTY & PAPER RETAILER,** 4Ward Corp, 70 New Canaan Ave., Norwalk CT 06850. (203)845-8020. Editor: Trisha McMahon Drain. 90% freelance written. Monthly magazine for party goods and fine stationery industry. Covers "every aspect of how to do business better for owners of party and paper retail shops. Tips and how-tos on display, marketing, success stories, advertising, operating costs, etc." Estab. 1985. Circ. 25,000.

Pays on publication. Offers 10% kill fee. Buys first North American serial rights. Editorial lead time 6 months. Submit seasonal material 6 months in advance. Accepts previously published submissions. Query for electronic submissions. Reports in 2 weeks. Sample copy $3.50

Nonfiction: Book excerpts and how-to (retailing related). No articles written in the first person. Buys 100 mss/year. Query with published clips. Length: 800-1,800 words. Pay "depends on topic, word count expertise, deadline." Pays expenses of writers on assignment.

Photos: State availability of photos with submission. Reviews transparencies. Negotiates payment individually. Captions and identification of subjects required. Buys one-time rights.

Columns/Departments: Shop Talk (successful party/stationery store profile), 1,800 words; Storekeeping (selling, employees, market, running store), 800 words; Cash Flow (anything finance related), 800 words. Buys 30 mss/year. Query with published clips. Pay varies.

RECORDS MANAGEMENT QUARTERLY, Association of Records Managers and Administrators, Inc., P.O. Box 4580, Silver Spring MD 20914-4580. Editor: Ira A. Penn, CRM, CSP. 10% freelance written. Eager to work with new/unpublished writers. Quarterly professional journal covering records and information management. Estab. 1967. Circ. 12,000. Pays on publication. Publishes ms an average of 6 months after acceptance. Byline given. Buys all rights. Simultaneous submissions OK. Reports in 1 month on mss. *Writer's Market* recommends allowing 2 months for reply. Sample copy $14. Free writer's guidelines.

Nonfiction: Professional articles covering theory, case studies, surveys, etc., on any aspect of records and information management. Buys 20-24 mss/year. Send complete ms. Length: 2,500 words minimum. Pays $50-200 "stipend"; no contract.

Photos: Send photos with ms. Does not pay extra for photos. Prefers b&w prints. Captions required.

Tips: "A writer *must* know our magazine. Most work is written by practitioners in the field. We use very little freelance writing, but we have had some and it's been good. A writer must have detailed knowledge of the subject he/she is writing about. Superficiality is not acceptable."

SECURITY DEALER, PTN Publishing Co., 445 Broad Hollow Rd., Melville NY 11747. (516)845-2700. Fax: (516)845-7109. Editor: Susan A. Brady. 25% freelance written. Monthly magazine for electronic alarm dealers; burglary and fire installers, with technical, business, sales and marketing information. Circ. 25,000. Pays 3 weeks after publication. Publishes ms an average of 4 months after acceptance. Byline sometimes given. Buys first North American serial rights. Simultaneous and previously published submissions OK. Prefer computer disk to accompany ms.

Nonfiction: How-to, interview/profile and technical. No consumer pieces. Query or send complete ms. Length: 1,000-3,000 words. Pays $300 for assigned articles; pays $100-200 for unsolicited articles. Sometimes pays the expenses of writers on assignment.

Photos: State availability of photos with submission. Reviews contact sheets and transparencies. Offers $25 additional payment for photos accepted with ms. Captions and identification of subjects required.

Columns/Departments: Closed Circuit TV, and Access Control (both on application, installation, new products), 500-1,000 words. Buys 25 mss/year. Query. Pays $100-150.

Tips: "The areas of our publication most open to freelancers are technical innovations, trends in the alarm industry and crime patterns as related to the business as well as business finance and management pieces."

SELF-EMPLOYED AMERICA, The News Publication for Your Small Business, National Association for the Self-Employed, P.O. Box 612067, DFW Airport TX 75261-2067. Editor: Karen C. Jones. 90% freelance written. Prefers to work with published/established writers. Bimonthly magazine for association members. "Keep in mind that the self-employed don't need business news tailored to meet needs of what government considers 'small business'. We reach those with few, if any, employees. Our readers are independent business owners going it alone—and in need of information." Estab. 1981. Circ. 300,000. Pays on publication. Byline given. Offers 10% kill fee. Buys full rights only and makes work-for-hire assignments. Publishes reprints of previously published articles. Send photocopy of article. Include information about when and where the article previously appeared. For reprints, pays 50% of the amount paid for an original article. Submit seasonal material 6 months in advance. Query for electronic submissions. Reports in 2 months on queries; 6 months on mss. Sample copy and writer's guidelines for 9 × 12 SAE with 3 first class stamps.

Nonfiction: Book excerpts, how-to and travel (how to save money on business travel or how to combine business and personal travel). "No big-business or how-to-claw-your-way-to-the-top stuff. Generally my readers are happy as small businesses." Buys 50-60 mss/year. Query with published clips. First article accepted many times on spec only. Length: 150-700 words. Pays $200-350 for assigned articles; $100-250 for unsolicited articles. Sometimes pays expenses of writers on assignment.

 The double dagger before a listing indicates that the listing is new in this edition. New markets are often more receptive to freelance submissions.

Photos: State availability of photos with submission. Reviews 3×5 prints. Offers $25-50/photo. Captions, model releases and identification required. Buys one-time rights.

Columns/Departments: Tax Tips. Send complete ms. Length: 200-300 words. Pays $50-100. Touch of Success profiles. Pays $70 for 125 words. Tight writing, concise.

Fillers: Anecdotes, facts, newsbreaks and short humor. Buys 50/year. Length: 75-125 words. Pays $25-50.

Tips: "Keep in mind reader demographics show 300,000 people with nothing in common except the desire to be independent. Be inventive with your subject matter proposed. We've covered the basics of small business already. Must quote knowledgeable sources in copy—these are not opinion pieces."

‡THE SERVICING DEALER, The Communications Group, Suite 090, 206 South Galena, Freeport IL 61032-5177. (815)232-5176. Fax: (815)232-1363. Editor: A.D. Horn. 15% freelance written. Magazine published 10 times/year on outdoor power equipment retailing and service. "Editorial is basic retail management oriented. Readers are servicing dealers of lawn and other outdoor power equipment. They're good mechanics but not-so-good businessmen." Estab. 1987. Circ. 24,000. Pays on publication. Publishes ms an average of 2 months after acceptance. Byline given. Buys one-time rights and exclusive rights within industry. Submit seasonal/holiday material 4 months in advance. Simultaneous and previously published submissions OK. Query for electronic submissions. Reports in 2 months. Sample copy $3. Writer's guidelines for #10 SASE.

Nonfiction: How-to (marketing, personnel management and financial management) and technical (dealing with small air-cooled engines and lawn equipment repair). Buys 6-10 mss/year. Query with published clips. Length: 600-1,200 words. Pays $150-300 for assigned articles; $50-250 for unsolicited articles. Sometimes pays expenses of writers on assignment.

Photos: Send photos with submission. Reviews contact sheets, transparencies and prints. Offers no additional payment for photos accepted with ms. Captions and identification of subjects required.

Columns/Departments: Sales Tips (basic sales methods and suggestions); Out Back (personnel management topics for small business); Greenbacks (financial management) and Ad-Visor (advertising and promotion for small business). Buys 7 mss/year. Query with published clips. Length: 450-675 words. Pays $50-250.

Tips: "Any prior knowledge of the outdoor power equipment industry, retail management topics, small engine repair is a plus. Read our magazine and other industry magazines. Small business management is a plus. Use electronic media to transfer directly into our Mac system. Give readers something they can walk away with and use the minute they put the magazine down."

SIGN BUSINESS, National Business Media Inc., 1008 Depot Hill Rd., P.O. Box 1416, Broomfield CO 80038-1416. (303)469-0424. Fax: (303)469-5730. Editor: Terence Wike. 25% freelance written. Trade journal on the sign industry—electric, commercial, architectural. "This is business-to-business writing; we try to produce news you can use, rather than human interest." Estab. 1985. Circ. 20,500. Pays on publication. Publishes ms an average of 2 months after acceptance. Byline given. Buys first North American serial rights. Publishes reprints of previously published articles. Send photocopy of article. For reprints pays 50% of the amount paid for an original article. Submit seasonal material 4 months in advance. Query for electronic submissions. Reports in 1 month. Sample copy $2.50. Writer's guidelines for #10 SASE.

Nonfiction: How-to (sign-painting techniques, new uses for computer cutters, plotters lettering styles); interview/profile (sign company execs, shop owners with *unusual* work etc.) and other (news on sign codes, legislation, unusual signs, etc.). "No humor, human interest, generic articles with sign replacing another industry, no first-person writing, no profiles of a sign shop just because someone nice runs the business." Buys 20 mss/year. Query with published clips. Length: 500-3,000 words. Pays $85-150.

Photos: Send photos with submission. Reviews 3×5 transparencies and 3×5 prints. Offers $5-10/photo. Identification of subjects required. Buys one-time rights and/or reprint rights.

Tips: "Find a sign shop, or sign company, and take some time to learn the business. The sign business is easily a $5 billion-plus industry every year in the United States, and we treat it like a business, not a hobby. If you see a sign that stops you in your tracks, find out who made it; if it's a one-in-10,000 kind of sign, chances are good we'll want to know more. Writing should be factual and avoid polysyllabic words that waste a reader's time. I'll work with writers who may not know the trade, but can write well."

WOMEN IN BUSINESS, The ABWA Co., Inc. 9100 Ward Parkway, Kansas City MO 64114-0728. (816)361-6621. Editor: Wendy Myers. 30% freelance written. Bimonthly magazine for members of the American Business Women's Association. "We publish articles of interest to the American working woman." Estab. 1949. Circ. 110,000. **Pays on acceptance.** Publishes ms an average of 2 months after acceptance. Byline given. Kill fee negotiable. Buys all rights. Submit seasonal material 4 months in advance. Reports in 1 week. *Writer's Market* recommends allowing 2 months for reply. Sample copy for 9×12 SAE with 4 first class stamps. Writer's guidelines for #10 SASE.

Nonfiction: "We cannot use success stories about individual businesswomen." Buys 30 mss/year. Query with published clips or send complete ms. Length: 1,000-3,000 words. Pays 15¢/word.

Photos: State availability of photos with submission. Offers no additional payment for photos accepted with ms. Identification of subjects required.

Columns/Departments: Holly Oeltjen, column/department editor. Money Wise (personal finance for women), 1,500 words; Health Scope (health topics for women); Career Smarts (advice for the up-and-coming woman manager); and It's Your Business (for women small business owners). Buys 18 mss/year. Query with

published clips or send complete ms. Length: 1,000-1,500 words. Pays 15¢/word.
Tips: "It would be very difficult to break into our columns. We have regular contributing freelance writers for those. But we are always on the lookout for good feature articles and writers. We are especially interested in writers who provide a fresh, new look to otherwise old topics, such as time management, etc."

Church Administration and Ministry

Publications in this section are written for clergy members, church leaders and teachers. Magazines for lay members and the general public are listed in the Consumer Religious section.

THE CHRISTIAN MINISTRY, The Christian Century Foundation, Suite 1405, 407 S. Dearborn St., Chicago IL 60605-1150. (312)427-5380. Editor: James M. Wall. Managing Editor: Mark R. Halton. 80% freelance written. Bimonthly magazine for parish clergy. "Most of our articles are written by parish clergy, describing parish situations. Our audience is comprised of mainline church ministers who are looking for practical ideas and insights concerning the ministry." Estab. 1969. Circ. 12,000. Pays on publication. Publishes ms an average of 6 months after acceptance. Byline given. Offers $20 kill fee. Buys all rights. Submit seasonal material 4 months in advance. Simultaneous submissions OK. Reports in 2 months. Sample copy $2.50 for 9 × 12 SAE with 4 first class stamps. Writer's guidelines for #10 SASE.
Nonfiction: Book excerpts (forthcoming books), essays, how-to (parish subjects), religious and preached sermons. No articles with footnotes or inspirational poetry. Buys 60 mss/year. Send complete ms. Length: 1,000-3,000 words. Pays $50-100 for assigned articles; $40-75 for unsolicited articles. Pays in contributor copies for book reviews.
Photos: State availability of photos with submission. Reviews 8 × 10 b&w prints. Offers $20-50/photo. Model releases preferred. Buys one-time rights.
Columns/Departments: Reflection on ministry (discusses an instance in which the author reflects on his or her practice of ministry), 2,500 words; From the Pulpit (preached sermons), 2,500 words. Buys 18 mss/year. Send complete ms. Length: 2,000-2,500 words. Pays $50-75.
Fillers: Newsbreaks and short humor. Buys 30/year. Length: 150-300 words. Pays $10.
Tips: "Send us finished manuscripts—not rough drafts. Freelancers have the best chance selling us articles on spec about issues affecting parish clergy."

CHURCH ADMINISTRATION, Dept. WM, 127 9th Ave. N., Nashville TN 37234. (615)251-2062. Fax: (615)251-3866. Editor: George Clark. 15% freelance written. Works with a small number of new/unpublished writers each year. Monthly magazine for Southern Baptist pastors, staff and volunteer church leaders. Uses limited amount of freelance material. Estab. 1953. **Pays on acceptance.** Publishes ms an average of 1 year after acceptance. Byline given. Buys all rights. Free sample copy and writer's guidelines for #10 SAE with 2 first class stamps.
Nonfiction: "Ours is a journal for effectiveness in ministry, including leadership, church programming, organizing, and staffing; administrative skills; church financing; church food services; church facilities; communication; and pastoral ministries and community needs." Length: 1,800-2,000 words. Pays 5½¢/word.
Tips: "Send query letter. Writers should be familiar with the organization and policy of Southern Baptist churches. Articles should be practical, how-to articles that meet genuine needs faced by leaders in SBC churches. Type at 54 characters per line, 25 lines per page, double-spaced. Send originals, not copies. Not responsible for manuscripts not accompanied by return postage."

CHURCH EDUCATOR, Creative Resources for Christian Educators, Educational Ministries, Inc., 165 Plaza Dr., Prescott AZ 86303-5549. (602)771-8601. Fax: (602)771-8621. Editor: Robert G. Davidson. Managing Editor: Linda S. Davidson. 80% freelance written. Works with a small number of new/unpublished writers each year. Monthly magazine covering religious education. Estab. 1976. Circ. 5,200. Pays on publication. Publishes ms an average of 4 months after acceptance. Byline given. Buys first rights. Submit seasonal material 4 months in advance. Simultaneous submissions OK. Publishes reprints of previously published articles. Send tearsheet, including information about when and where the article previously appeared. Reports in 3 months. Sample copy for 9 × 12 SAE with 3 first class stamps. Free writer's guidelines.
Nonfiction: General interest; how-to (crafts for church school) programs for church school, adult education study classes. "Our editorial lines are very middle of the road—mainline Protestant. We are not seeking extreme conservative or liberal theology pieces." No testimonials. Buys 100 mss/year. Send complete ms. Length: 100-2,000 words. Pays 3¢/word.
Fiction: Mainstream, religious and slice-of-life vignettes. Buys 15 mss/year. Send complete ms. Length: 100-2,000 words. Pays 3¢/word.
Tips: "Send the complete manuscript with a cover letter which gives a concise summary. We are looking for how-to articles related to Christian education. That would include most any program held in a church. Be straightforward and to the point—not flowery and wordy. We're especially interested in youth programs.

Give steps needed to carry out the program: preparation, starting the program, continuing the program, conclusion. List several discussion questions for each program."

CIRCUIT RIDER, A Journal for United Methodist Ministers, United Methodist Publishing House, P.O. Box 801, Nashville TN 37202-0801. (615)749-6137. Fax: (615)749-6079. Editor: Keith I. Pohl. Editorial Director: J. Richard Peck. 60% freelance written. Works with a small number of new/unpublished writers each year. Monthly magazine covering professional concerns of clergy. Estab. 1789. Circ. 40,000. **Pays on acceptance.** Publishes ms an average of 1 year after acceptance. Byline given. Buys all rights. Submit seasonal material 6 months in advance. Reports in 1 month. Sample copy for 9×12 SAE with 3 first class stamps. Writer's guidelines for #10 SASE.
Nonfiction: How-to (improve pastoral calling, preaching, counseling, administration, etc.). No personal experience articles; no interviews. Buys 50 mss/year. Send complete ms. Length: 600-2,000 words. Pays $30-150.
Photos: State availability of photos. Pays $25-100 for 8×10 b&w prints. Model release required. Buys one-time rights.
Tips: "Know the concerns of a United Methodist pastor. Be specific. Think of how you can help pastors."

LEADER, Board of Christian Education of the Church of God, P.O. Box 2458, Anderson IN 46018-2458. (317)642-0257. Fax: (317)642-0255 ext. 299. Editor: Joseph L. Cookston. 70% freelance written. Works with a small number of new/unpublished writers each year. Bimonthly magazine covering local Sunday school teaching and administrating, youth and children's work, worship, family life and other local church ministries. Estab. 1923. Circ. 4,000. Pays on publication. Publishes ms an average of 10 months after acceptance. Byline given. Buys first rights and second serial (reprint) rights. Submit seasonal material 6 months in advance. Simultaneous queries OK. Reports in 4 months. Sample copy and writer's guidelines for 9×12 SAE with 3 first class stamps.
Nonfiction: How-to, inspirational, personal experience, guidance for carrying out programs for special days, continuing ministries and short ministry ideas. No articles that are not specifically related to local church leadership. Buys 25 mss/year. Send complete ms, brief description of present interest in writing for church leaders, background and experience. Length: 300-800 words. Pays $10-30.
Tips: "How-to articles related to teaching, program development and personal teacher enrichment or growth, and program and teaching ideas are most open to freelancers."

LEADERSHIP, A Practical Journal for Church Leaders, Christianity Today, Inc., 465 Gundersen Dr., Carol Stream IL 60188. (312)260-6200. Editor: Marshall Shelley. 75% freelance written. Works with a small number of new/unpublished writers each year. Quarterly magazine covering church leadership. Writers must have a "knowledge of and sympathy for the unique expectations placed on pastors and local church leaders. Each article must support points by illustrating from real life experiences in local churches." Estab. 1980. Circ. 90,000. **Pays on acceptance.** Publishes ms an average of 6 months after acceptance. Byline given. Buys first North American serial rights. Submit seasonal material 6 months in advance. Previously published submissions OK. Reports in 6 weeks on queries; 2 months on mss. Sample copy $3. Free writer's guidelines.
Nonfiction: How-to, humor and personal experience. "No articles from writers who have never read our journal." Buys 50 mss/year. Send complete ms. Length: 100-5,000 words. Pays $30-300. Sometimes pays the expenses of writers on assignment.
Photos: State availability of photos with submission. Offers no additional payment for photos accepted with ms. Identification of subjects required. Buys one-time rights.
Columns/Departments: People in Print (book reviews with interview of author), 1,500 words. To Illustrate (short stories or analogies that illustrate a biblical principle), 100 words. Buys 25 mss/year. Send complete ms. Pays $25-100.

PASTORAL LIFE, Society of St. Paul, P.O. Box 595, Route 224, Canfield OH 44406-0595. Fax: (216)533-1076. Editor: Anthony Chenevey, SSP. 66% freelance written. Eager to work with new/unpublished writers. Monthly magazine emphasizing priests and those interested in pastoral ministry. Estab. 1953. Circ. 3,500. Buys first rights only. Byline given. Pays on publication. Publishes ms an average of 6 months after acceptance. Query with a outline before submitting ms. "New contributors are expected to include, in addition, a few lines of personal data that indicate academic and professional background." Reports in 1 month. Sample copy and writer's guidelines for 6×9 SAE with 4 first class stamps.
Nonfiction: "*Pastoral Life* is a professional review, principally designed to focus attention on current problems, needs, issues and all important activities related to all phases of pastoral work and life." Buys 30 unsolicited mss/year. Length: 2,000-3,400 words. Pays 4¢/word minimum.

THE PREACHER'S MAGAZINE, Nazarene Publishing House, E. 10814 Broadway, Spokane WA 99206-5003. Editor: Randal E. Denny. Assistant Editor: Cindy Osso. 15% freelance written. Works with a small number of new/unpublished writers each year. Quarterly magazine of seasonal/miscellaneous articles. "A resource for ministers; Wesleyan-Arminian in theological persuasion." Circ. 18,000. Pays on publication. Publishes ms an average of 9 months after acceptance. Byline given. Buys first serial, second serial (reprint) and simultaneous rights. Publishes reprints of previously published articles. Send photocopy of article or typed ms with rights for sale noted. Include information about when and where the article previously appeared. For reprints, pays 100% of the amount paid for an original article (3½¢/word). Submit seasonal material 9 months in advance. Simultaneous queries OK. Writer's guidelines for #10 SASE.

Nonfiction: How-to, humor, inspirational, opinion and personal experience, all relating to aspects of ministry. No articles that present problems without also presenting answers to them; things not relating to pastoral ministry. Buys 48 mss/year. Send complete ms. Length: 700-2,500 words. Pays 3½¢/word.

Photos: Send photos with ms. Reviews 35mm transparencies and 35mm b&w prints. Model release and identification of subjects required. Buys one-time rights.

Columns/Departments: Stories Preachers Tell Each Other (humorous).

Fiction: Publishes novel excerpts.

Fillers: Anecdotes and short humor. Buys 10/year. Length: 400 words maximum. Pays 3½¢/word.

Tips: "Writers for the *Preacher's Magazine* should have insight into the pastoral ministry, or expertise in a specialized area of ministry. Our magazine is a highly specialized publication aimed at the minister. Our goal is to assist, by both scholarly and practical articles, the modern-day minister in applying Biblical theological truths."

PREACHING, Preaching Resources, Inc., Dept. WM, 1529 Cesery Blvd., Jacksonville FL 32211. (904)743-5994. Editor: Dr. Michael Duduit. 75% freelance written. Bimonthly magazine for the preaching ministry. "All articles must deal with preaching. Most articles used offer practical assistance in preparation and delivery of sermons, generally from an evangelical stance." Estab. 1985. Circ. 10,000. Pays on publication. Publishes ms an average of 1 year after acceptance. Byline given. Buys first rights. Submit seasonal material 1 year in advance. Query for electronic submissions. Reports in 4 months. Sample copy $2.50 for 9 × 12 SAE with 8 first class stamps. Writer's guidelines for SASE.

Nonfiction: How-to (preparation and delivery of sermon, worship leadership). Special issues include Personal Computing in Preaching (September-October); materials/resources to assist in preparation of seasonal preaching (November-December, March-April). Buys 18-24 mss/year. Query. Length: 1,000-2,000 words. Pays $35-50.

Photos: Send photos with submission. Reviews prints. Offers no additional payment for photos accepted with ms. Captions, model releases and identification of subjects required. Buys one-time rights.

Fillers: Buys 10-15/year. "Buys only completed cartoons." Art must be related to preaching. Pays $25.

Tips: "Most desirable are practical, 'how-to' articles on preparation and delivery of sermons."

THE PRIEST, Our Sunday Visitor, Inc., 200 Noll Plaza, Huntington IN 46750. (219)356-8400. Fax: (219)356-8472. Editor: Father Owen F. Campion. Associate Editor: Robert A. Willems. 80% freelance written. Monthly magazine for the priesthood. "We run articles that will aid priests in their day-to-day ministry. Includes items on spirituality, counseling, administration, theology, personalities, the saints, etc." **Pays on acceptance.** Byline given. Publication not copyrighted. Buys first North American serial rights. Editorial lead time 3 months. Submit seasonal material at least 4 months in advance. Query for electronic submissions. Reports in 2 weeks on queries; 1 month on mss. *Writer's Market* recommends allowing 2 months for reply. Sample copy and writer's guidelines free on request.

Nonfiction: Essays, historical/nostalgic, humor, inspirational, interview/profile, opinion, personal experience, photo feature and religious. Buys 96 mss/year. Send complete ms. Length: 1,500-5,000 words. Pays $300 minimum for assigned articles; $50 minimum for unsolicited articles.

Photos: Send photos with submission. Reviews transparencies and prints. Negotiates payment individually. Captions and identification of subjects required. Buys one-time rights.

Columns/Departments: Viewpoint (whatever applies to priests and the Church), 1,000 words. Buys 36 mss/ year. Send complete ms. Pays $50-100.

Tips: "Say what you have to say in an interesting and informative manner and stop. Freelancers are most often published in 'Viewpoints.' Please do not stray from the magisterium of the Catholic Church."

YOUR CHURCH, Helping You With the Business of Ministry, Christianity Today, Inc., 465 Gundersen Dr., Carol Stream IL 60188. (708)260-6200. Editor: James Berkley. 70% freelance written. Bimonthly magazine for the business of today's church. "Articles pertain to the business aspects of ministry pastors are called upon to perform: administration, purchasing, management, technology, building, etc." Estab. 1954. Circ. 200,000. **Pays on acceptance.** Publishes ms an average of 4 months after acceptance. Byline given. Buys one-time rights. Submit seasonal material 5 months in advance. Simultaneous and previously published submissions OK. Submit photocopy of article and information about when and where the article previously appeared. Reports in 1 month on queries; 2 months on mss. Sample copy and writer's guidelines for 9 × 12 SAE with 5 first class stamps.

Nonfiction: How-to, new product and technical. Buys 12 mss/year. Send complete ms. Length: 900-1,500 words. Pays about 10¢/word. Pays 30% of their fee for an original article.

Photos: State availability of photos with submission. Reviews 4 × 5 transparencies and 5 × 7 or 8 × 10 prints. Offers no additional payment for photos accepted with ms. Captions, model releases and identification of subjects required. Buys one-time rights.

Tips: "The editorial is generally geared toward brief and helpful articles dealing with some form of church business. Concise, bulletted points from experts in the field are typical for our articles."

Clothing

APPAREL INDUSTRY MAGAZINE, Shore Communications, Dept. WM, Suite 200, 6255 Barfield Rd., Atlanta GA 30328-4300. Fax: (404)252-8831. Editor: Susan Hasty. Managing Editor: Colleen Moynahar. 30% freelance written. Monthly magazine for executive management in apparel companies with interests in new developments in apparel manufacturing, equipment, distribution and management. Estab. 1946. Circ. 18,700. Pays on publication. Publishes ms an average of 4 months after acceptance. Byline given. Buys first serial rights. Query for electronic submissions. Reports in 1 month. Sample copy $3. Writer's guidelines for #10 SASE.
Nonfiction: Articles dealing with equipment, manufacturing techniques, quality control, etc., related to the industry. "Use concise, precise language that is easy to read and understand. In other words, because the subjects are often technical, keep the language comprehensible. Material must be precisely related to the apparel industry. We are not a retail or fashion magazine." Buys 20 mss/year. Query. Length: 3,000 words maximum. Payment negotiated as part of assignment. Sometimes pays expenses of writers on assignment.
Photos: Pays $5/photo published with ms.
Tips: "Frequently articles are too general due to lack of industry-specific knowledge by the writer."
  • This magazine is only interested in freelance work from those with experience covering the apparel manufacturing industry.

ATI, America's Textiles International, Billian Publishing Co., 2100 Powers Ferry Rd., Atlanta GA 30339. (404)955-5656. Fax: (404)952-0669. Editor: Monte G. Plott. Associate Editor: Rolf Viertel. 10% freelance written. Monthly magazine covering "the business of textile, apparel and fiber industries with considerable technical focus on products and processes. No puff pieces pushing a particular product." Pays on publication. Byline sometimes given. Buys first North American serial rights. Query for electronic submissions.
Nonfiction: Technical, business. "No PR, just straight technical reports." Buys 10 mss/year. Query. Length: 500 words minimum. Pays $100/published page. Sometimes pays expenses of writers on assignment.
Photos: Send photos with submission. Reviews prints. Offers no additional payment for photos accepted with ms. Captions required. Buys one-time rights.

‡BOBBIN, Bobbin Blenheim Media Corp., 1110 Shop Rd., P.O. Box 1986, Columbia SC 29202-1986. (803)771-7500. Fax: (803)799-1461. Editor: Susan Black. 25% freelance written. Monthly magazine for CEO's and top management in apparel manufacturing companies. Circ. 9,500. Pays on publication. Byline given. Buys all rights. Reports in 6 weeks. Free sample copy and writer's guidelines.
Columns/Departments: Trade View, R&D, Network News, Partnerships, Personnel Management, Labor Forum, NON-Apparel Highlights, Fabric Notables.
Tips: "Articles should be written in a style appealing to busy top managers and should in some way foster thought or new ideas, or present solutions/alternatives to common industry problems/concerns. CEOs are most interested in quick read pieces that are also informative and substantive. Articles should not be based on opinions but should be developed through interviews with industry manufacturers, retailers or other experts, etc. Sidebars may be included to expand upon certain aspects within the article. If available, illustrations, graphs/charts, or photographs should accompany the article."

Coin-Operated Machines

AMERICAN COIN-OP, 500 N. Dearborn St., Chicago IL 60610-9988. (312)337-7700. Fax: (312)337-8654. Editor: Laurance Cohen. 30% freelance written. Monthly magazine for owners of coin-operated laundry and dry cleaning stores. Estab. 1960. Circ. 20,100. Rights purchased vary with author and material, but are exclusive to the field. Pays 2 weeks prior to publication. Publishes ms an average of 2 months after acceptance. Byline given. Reports as soon as possible; usually in 2 weeks. *Writer's Market* recommends allowing 2 months for reply. Free sample copy.
Nonfiction: "We emphasize store operation and use features on industry topics: utility use and conservation, maintenance, store management, customer service and advertising. A case study should emphasize how the store operator accomplished whatever he did—in a way that the reader can apply to his own operation. Manuscript should have a no-nonsense, business-like approach." Uses informational, how-to, interview, profile, think pieces and successful business operations articles. Length: 500-3,000 words. Pays 8¢/word minimum.

Photos: Pays $8 minimum for 5×7 b&w glossy photos purchased with mss. (Contact sheets with negatives preferred.)

Fillers: Newsbreaks and clippings. Pays $10 minimum.

Tips: "Query about subjects of current interest. Be observant of coin-operated laundries—how they are designed and equipped, how they serve customers and how (if) they advertise and promote their services. Most general articles are turned down because they are not aimed well enough at our audience. Most case histories are turned down because they lack practical purpose (nothing new or worth reporting). A frequent mistake is failure to follow up on an interesting point made by the interviewee—probably due to lack of knowledge about the industry."

PLAY METER MAGAZINE, Skybird Publishing Co., Inc., P.O. Box 24970, New Orleans LA 70184-9988. Fax: (504)488-7083. Publisher: Carol Lally. Editor: Valerie Cognevich. 25% freelance written. "We will work with new writers who are familiar with the amusement industry." Monthly trade magazine for owners/operators of coin-operated amusement machine companies, e.g., pinball machines, video games, arcade pieces, juke-boxes, etc. Estab. 1974. Circ. 6,000. Pays on publication. Publishes ms an average of 2 months after acceptance. Byline given. Buys all rights. Submit seasonal material 2 months in advance. Previously published submissions OK. Reports in 2 months on queries. Sample copy $5 for 10×12 SAE with 10 first class stamps. Free writer's guidelines.

Nonfiction: How-to (get better locations for machines, promote tournaments, evaluate profitability of route, etc.); interview (with industry leaders); and new product. "Our readers want to read about how they can make more money from their machines, how they can get better tax breaks, commissions, etc. Also no stories about *playing* pinball or video games. Also, submissions on video-game technology advances; technical pieces on troubleshooting videos, pinballs and novelty machines (all coin-operated); trade-show coverage (query); submissions on the pay-telephone industry. Our readers don't play the games per se; they buy the machines and make money from them." Buys 48 mss/year. Query or submit complete ms. Length: 250-3,000 words. Pays $30-215. Sometimes pays expenses of writers on assignment.

Photos: "The photography should have news value. We don't want 'stand 'em up-shoot 'em down' group shots." Pays $15 minimum for 5×7 or 8×10 b&w prints. Captions preferred. Buys all rights. Art returned on request.

Tips: "We need feature articles more than small news items or featurettes. Query first. We're interested in writers who either have a few years of reporting/feature-writing experience or who know the coin-operated amusement industry well but are relatively inexperienced writers."

VENDING TIMES, 545 8th Ave., New York NY 10018. Fax: (212)564-0196. Editor: Arthur E. Yohalem. Monthly magazine for operators of vending machines. Estab. 1960. Circ. 15,450. Pays on publication. Buys all rights. "We will discuss in detail the story requirements with the writer." Sample copy $4.

Nonfiction: Feature articles and news stories about vending operations; practical and important aspects of the business. "We are always willing to pay for good material." Query.

Confectionery and Snack Foods

These publications focus on the bakery, snack and candy industries. Journals for grocers, wholesalers and other food industry personnel are listed in Groceries and Food Products.

CANDY INDUSTRY, Advanstar Communications, Inc., Dept. WM, 7500 Old Oak Blvd., Cleveland OH 44130. (216)891-2612. Fax: (216)891-2651. Editor: Susan Tiffany. 5% freelance written. Prefers to work with published/established writers. Monthly magazine for confectionery manufacturers. Publishes ms an average of 4 months after acceptance. Buys all rights. Reports in 1 month. Writer's guidelines for #10 SASE.

Nonfiction: "Feature articles of interest to large scale candy manufacturers that deal with activities in the fields of production, packaging (including package design), merchandising; and financial news (sales figures, profits, earnings), advertising campaigns in all media, and promotional methods used to increase the sale or distribution of candy." Length: 1,000-1,250 words. Pays 15¢/word; "special rates on assignments."

Photos: "Good quality glossies with complete and accurate captions, in sizes not smaller than 5×7." Pays $15 for b&w; $20 for color.

Fillers: "Short news stories about the trade and anything related to candy." Pays 5¢/word; $1 for clippings.

PACIFIC BAKERS NEWS, 180 Mendell St., San Francisco CA 94124-1740. (415)826-2664. Publisher: C.W. Soward. 30% freelance written. Eager to work with new/unpublished writers. Monthly business newsletter for commercial bakeries in the western states. Estab. 1961. Pays on publication. No byline given; uses only one-paragraph news items.

Nonfiction: Uses bakery business reports and news about bakers. Buys only brief "boiled-down news items about bakers and bakeries operating only in Alaska, Hawaii, Pacific Coast and Rocky Mountain states. We welcome clippings. We need monthly news reports and clippings about the baking industry and the donut business. No pictures, jokes, poetry or cartoons." Length: 10-200 words. Pays 10¢/word for news and 6¢ for clips (words used).

Construction and Contracting

Builders, architects and contractors learn the latest industry news in these publications. Journals targeted to architects are also included in the Consumer Art and Architecture category. Those for specialists in the interior aspects of construction are listed under Building Interiors.

ACCESS CONTROL, Dept. WM, 6151 Powers Ferry Rd. NW, Atlanta GA 30339-2941. (404)955-2500. Editor: Greg Echols. 50% freelance written. Prefers to work with published/established writers. Monthly tabloid for end users and installers of access control equipment. Estab. 1955. Circ. 26,000. Pays on publication. Publishes ms an average of 2 months after acceptance. Buys all rights. Query for electronic submissions. Reports in 3 months. Sample copy for 8 × 10 SASE. Writer's guidelines for #10 SASE.
Nonfiction: Case histories, large-scale access control "systems approach" equipment installations. A format for these articles has been established. Query for details. Buys 10-12 unsolicited mss/year. Query. Length: 4,500 words maximum.
Columns/Departments: Also take technical or practical application features for following monthly columns dealing with perimeter security fencing and accessories, gate systems, sensor technology card access systems, and CCTV technology. Length: 1,000-2,000 words maximum.
Photos: Black and white 5 × 7 photos purchased with mss. Captions required.
Tips: "We will place more focus on access control installations."

AUTOMATED BUILDER, CMN Associates, Inc., P.O. Box 120, Carpinteria CA 93014-0120. (805)684-7659. Fax: (805)684-1765. Editor-in-Chief: Don Carlson. 15% freelance written. Monthly magazine specializing in management for industrialized (manufactured) housing and volume home builders. Estab. 1964. Circ. 25,000. **Pays on acceptance.** Publishes ms an average of 3 months after acceptance. Buys first North American serial rights. Phone queries OK. Reports in 2 weeks. *Writer's Market* recommends allowing 2 months for reply. Free sample copy and writer's guidelines.
Nonfiction: Case history articles on successful home building companies which may be 1) production (big volume) home builders; 2) mobile home manufacturers; 3) modular home manufacturers; 4) prefabricated (panelized) home manufacturers; 5) house component manufacturers; or 6) special unit (in-plant commercial building) manufacturers. Also uses interviews, photo features and technical articles. "No architect or plan 'dreams'. Housing projects must be built or under construction." Buys 15 mss/year. Query. Length: 500-1,000 words maximum. Pays $300 minimum.
Photos: Purchased with accompanying ms. Query. No additional payment. Wants 4 × 5, 5 × 7 or 8 × 10 b&w glossies or 35mm or larger color transparencies (35mm preferred). Captions required.
Tips: "Stories often are too long, too loose; we prefer 500 to 750 words. We prefer a phone query on feature articles. If accepted on query, article usually will not be rejected later."

CONSTRUCTION COMMENT, Naylor Communications Ltd., 6th Floor, 920 Yonge St., Toronto, Ontario M4W 3C7 Canada. (416)961-1028. Fax: (416)924-4408. Editor: Gregory Kero. 80% freelance written. Semian-nual magazine on construction industry in Ottawa. "*Construction Comment* reaches all members of the Ottawa Construction Association and most senior management of firms relating to the industry." Estab. 1970. Circ. 3,000. Pays 30 days after deadline. Byline given. Offers ⅓ kill fee. Buys first North American serial rights. Submit seasonal material 2 months in advance. Simultaneous submissions OK. Reprints OK; send tearsheet or photocopy of article and information about when and where the article previously appeared. Pays 80% of their fee for an original article. Query for electronic submissions. Reports in 6 weeks.
Nonfiction: General interest, historical, interview/profile, new product, photo feature and technical. "We publish a spring/summer issue and a fall/winter issue. Submit correspondingly or inquire two months ahead of these times." Buys 10 mss/year. Query with published clips. Length: 500-2,500 words. Pays 25¢/word. Pays expenses of writers on assignment.
Photos: State availability of photos with submission. Reviews transparencies and prints. Offers $25-200/photo. Identification of subjects required.
Tips: "Please send copies of work and a general query. I will respond as promptly as my deadlines allow. Company publications also include *Toronto Construction News,* a bimonthly magazine on construction industry in Toronto reaching all members of the Toronto Construction Association, and *The Generals,* a quarterly

magazine for general contractors in Ontario, reaching all members of the Ontario General Contractors Association."

COST CUTS, The Enterprise Foundation, Dept. WM, 500 American City Bldg., Columbia MD 21044. (410)964-1230. Editor: Peggy Armstrong. 25% freelance written. Bimonthly newsletter on rehabilitation of low-income housing. "As the construction arm of The Enterprise Foundation, the Rehab Work Group, which publishes *Cost Cuts*, seeks ways to reduce the cost of rehabbing and constructing low-income housing. *Cost Cuts* also informs of changes in federal policy, local and state efforts in low-income housing and pro bono work in this area. *Cost Cuts* is distributed nationally to rehab specialists, agencies and others involved in the production of low-income housing." Estab. 1983. Circ. 5,600. Pays on publication. Byline given. Buys one-time rights. Submit seasonal material 3 months in advance. Previously published submissions OK. Query for electronic submissions. Reports in 1 month. Sample copy for 9 × 12 SAE with 2 first class stamps. Writer's guidelines for #10 SASE.
Nonfiction: How-to, interview/profile, technical and international. "No personal experience of do-it-yourselfers in single-family homes. We want articles concerning high production of low-income housing." Buys 10-15 mss/year. Query with published clips. Length: 100-1,500 words. Pays $50-200 for assigned articles; $200 maximum for unsolicited articles. Sometimes pays expenses of writers on assignment.
Photos: Send photos with submission. Reviews contact sheets and 3 × 5 and 5 × 7 prints. Captions and identification of subjects required. Buys one-time rights.
Fillers: Facts and newsbreaks. Buys 20/year. Length: 100-500 words. Pays $25-50.
Tips: "The Foundation's mission is to see that all low-income people in the United States have the opportunity for fit and affordable housing within a generation and to move up and out of poverty into the mainstream of American life. Freelancers must be conscious of this context. Articles must include case studies of specific projects where costs have been cut. Charts of cost comparisons to show exactly where cuts were made are most helpful."

FINE HOMEBUILDING, The Taunton Press, Inc., Dept. WM, P.O. Box 5506, Newtown CT 06470. (203)426-8171. Editor: Kevin Ireton. Less than 5% freelance written. Bimonthly magazine covering house building, construction, design for builders, architects and serious amateurs. Estab. 1976. Circ. 245,000. Pays advance, balance on publication. Publishes ms an average of 6-12 months after acceptance. Byline given. Offers negotiable kill fee. Buys first rights and "use in books to be published." Query for electronic submissions. Reports "as soon as possible." Free writer's guidelines.
Nonfiction: Technical (techniques in design or construction process). Query. Length: 2,000-3,000 words. Pays $150-1,200.
Columns/Departments: Tools and Materials (products or techniques that are new or unusual); Great Moments in Building History (humorous, embarrassing, or otherwise noteworthy anecdotes); Reviews (short reviews of books on building or design); and Reports and Comment (essays, short reports on construction and architecture trends and developments). Query. Length: 300-1,000 words. Pays $50-250.

FLORIDA ARCHITECT, Florida Association of the American Institute of Architects, 104 E. Jefferson St., Tallahassee FL 32308. (904)222-7590. Editor: Diane Greer. 10% freelance written. Bimonthly magazine of "technical writing for a readership of professional architects." Estab. 1969. Circ. 6,500. Pays on publication. Publishes ms an average of 6 months after acceptance. Byline given. Buys one-time rights. Accepts simultaneous submissions and previously published submissions. Query for electronic submissions. Reports in 6 months. Free sample copy.
Nonfiction: Interview/profile, new product, opinion, photo feature, technical and travel. Buys 3 mss/year. Send complete ms. Length: 750-1,500 words. Pays $100-200.
Photos: State availability of photos or send photos with submission. Reviews 4 × 5 transparencies and 5 × 7 or 8 × 10 prints. Offers no additional payment for photos accepted with ms. Captions required. Buys one-time rights.
Columns/Departments: Viewpoint (an opinion by a professional in a field related to architecture, i.e., landscape, engineering, interiors), 750 words. Buys 3 mss/year. Send complete ms. Pays $100-200.

HOME BUILDER, Work-4 Projects Ltd., P.O. Box 400, Victoria Station, Westmount, Quebec H3Z 2V8 Canada. (514)489-4941. Fax: (514)489-5505. Publisher: Nachmi Artzy. Editor: Frank O'Brien. 80% freelance written. Magazine covers new home construction, published 6 times annually. "*Home Builder* reports on builders, architects, mortgage, sub-trades, associations and government. We keep the readers' concerns in the forefront, not the advertisers'." Estab. 1988. Circ. 16,000. Pays on publication. Publishes ms an average of 4 months after acceptance. Byline sometimes given. Buys all rights. Simultaneous submissions OK. Reports in 3 weeks on queries. Free sample copy.
Nonfiction: Exposé, how-to (builders, administration, production, etc.), interview/profile, new product and technical. Buys 20-30 mss/year. Query with published clips. Length: 100-500 words. Pays 10-20¢/word. Pays in contributor copies or other premiums "if suitable for both parties." Sometimes pays expenses of writers on assignment.

Photos: Send photos with submission. Reviews transparencies and prints. Offers expense-$300 per photo. Captions and identification of subjects required. Buys all rights.

Columns/Departments: Perspective (general news of importance to audience), 100-300 words; and Industry News (specific company information of relevance—not sales pitch), 75-300 words. Buys 20 mss/year. Query with published clips. Pays 10-20¢/word.

Fillers: Facts and gags. Buys 5/year. Length: 5-50 words. Pays 10¢/word-$25.

Tips: "Keep audience in mind. Give them something that will affect them, not something they will forget five minutes after reading it. Keep in mind Canadian content."

INLAND ARCHITECT, The Midwestern Building Arts Magazine, Inland Architect Press, P.O. Box 10394, Chicago IL 60610-0394. (312)321-0584. Fax: (312)321-9334. Senior Editor: Barbara K. Hower. 80% freelance written. Prefers to work with published/established writers. Bimonthly magazine covering architecture and urban planning. "*Inland Architect* is a critical journal covering architecture and design in the Midwest for an audience primarily of architects. *Inland* is open to all points of view, providing they are intelligently expressed and of relevance to architecture." Estab. 1957. Circ. 8,000. Pays on publication. Publishes ms an average of 2 months after acceptance. Byline given. Offers 50% kill fee. Buys first rights. Reports in 2 months. Sample copy $10 (includes shipping and handling).

Nonfiction: Book excerpts, essays, historical/nostalgic, interview/profile, criticism and photo feature of architecture. Every summer *Inland* focuses on a midwestern city, its architecture and urban design. Call to find out 1994 city. No new products, "how to run your office" or technical pieces. Buys 40 mss/year. Query with published clips or send complete ms. Length: 750-3,500 words. Pays $100-300 for assigned articles. Sometimes pays the expenses of writers on assignment.

Photos: Send photos with submission. Reviews 4×5 transparencies, slides and 8×10 prints. Offers no additional payment for photos accepted with ms. Identification of subjects required. Buys one-time rights.

Columns/Departments: Books (reviews of new publications on architecture, design, and occasionally, art), 250-1,000 words. Buys 10 mss/year. Query. Length: 250-1,000 words. Pays $50. Space (interiors), pays $125; Inlandscape (news of new/under construction projects), pays $125; and Earth (design projects with an emphasis on their environmental implications), pays $125.

Tips: "Propose to cover a lecture, to interview a certain architect, etc. Articles must be written for an audience primarily consisting of well-educated architects. If an author feels he has a 'hot' timely idea, a phone call is appreciated."

THE JOURNAL OF LIGHT CONSTRUCTION, Builderburg Group, Inc., RR2, Box 146, Richmond VT 05477. (802)434-4747. Fax: (802)434-4467. Editor: Steven Bliss. Managing Editor: Don Jackson. 50% freelance written. Monthly tabloid on residential and light-commercial construction/remodeling. "Most of our articles offer practical solutions to problems that small contractors face on the job site or in the office. For that reason, most of our authors have practical experience in construction. In fact, the accuracy of the information is more important to us than the quality of the writing." Estab. 1982. Pays on publication. Publishes ms an average of 4 months after acceptance. Byline given. Offers negotiable kill fee. Buys first North American serial and non-exclusive reprint rights. Query for electronic submissions. Sample copy $3. Writer's guidelines for SASE.

Nonfiction: How-to, new product and technical. Buys 40 mss/year. Query. Length: 1,300-2,500 words. Pays $150-400. Sometimes pays expenses of writers on assignment.

Photos: Send photos with submission. Reviews contact sheets, transparencies and prints. Offers additional payment for photos accepted with ms. Captions required. Buys first and non-exclusive reprint rights.

Columns/Departments: Eight-Penny News (news shorts in areas of business, technology, codes, human interest related to home construction), 300-1,000 words. Buys 12 mss/year. Send complete ms. Pays $50-200.

PACIFIC BUILDER & ENGINEER, Vernon Publications Inc., Suite 200, 3000 Northup Way, Bellevue WA 98004. (206)827-9900. Editor: Richard C. Bachus. Editorial Director: Michele Andrus Dill. 44% freelance written. Biweekly magazine covering non-residential construction in the Northwest and Alaska. "Our readers are construction contractors in Washington, Oregon, Idaho, Montana and Alaska. The feature stories in *PB&E* focus on ongoing construction projects in our coverage area. They address these questions: what is the most significant challenge to the general contractor? What innovative construction techniques or equipment are being used to overcome the challenges?" Estab. 1902. Circ. 14,500. Pays on publication. Publishes ms an average of 2 months after acceptance. Byline given. Buys first North American serial and second serial (reprint) rights. Editorial lead time 1½ months. Submit seasonal material 2 months in advance. Query for electronic submissions. Reports in 2 months on queries; 6 weeks on mss. Sample copy $7. Writer's guidelines for #10 SAE with 1 first class stamp.

Nonfiction: How-to, new product and photo feature. "No non-construction stories; residential construction articles; construction stories without a Northwest or Alaska angle." Buys 18 mss/year. Query with published clips. Length: 750-2,000 words. Pays $100. Sometimes pays expenses of writers on assignment.

Photos: State availability of photos with submission. Reviews contact sheets, transparencies. Offers $15-125/ photo. Captions and identification of subjects and equipment required. Buys one-time rights.

Tips: "Find an intriguing, ongoing construction project in our five-state region. Talk to the general contractor's project manager to see what he/she thinks is unusual, innovative or exciting about the project to builders. Then go ahead and query us. If we haven't already covered the project, there's a possibility that we may assign a feature. Be prepared to tour the site, put on a hard hat and get your boots dirty."

ROOFER MAGAZINE, D&H Publications, Suite 214, 6719 Winkler Rd., Ft. Myers FL 33919. (813)489-2929. Editor: Harry Megara. 10% freelance written. Eager to work with new/unpublished writers. Monthly magazine covering the roofing industry for roofing contractors. Estab. 1981. Circ. 18,500. Pays on publication. Publishes ms an average of 5 months after acceptance. Byline given. Buys first serial and second serial (reprint) rights. Submission must be exclusive to our field. Submit seasonal material 4 months in advance. Reports in 2 months. Sample copy and writer's guidelines for SAE with 6 first class stamps.
 • With an influx of material and reduction in staff, reporting times may run longer than stated.

Nonfiction: Profiles of roofing contractors (explicit guidelines available), humorous pieces; other ideas welcome. Buys 5-10 mss/year. Query in writing. Length: approximately 1,500 words. Pays $125-250 (average: $175).

Photos: Send photos with completed mss; color slides are preferred. Identification of subjects required. "We purchase photographs for specific needs, but those that accompany an article are not purchased separately. The price we pay in the article includes the use of the photos." Always searching for photos of unusual roofs or those with a humorous slant.

Tips: "Contractor profiles are our most frequent purchase from freelance writers and a favorite to our readers. Our guidelines explain exactly what we are looking for and should help freelancers select the right person to interview. We provide sample questions to ask about the topics we would like discussed the most. For those submitting queries about other articles, we prefer substantial articles (no fillers please). Slant articles toward roofing contractors. We have little use for generic articles that can appear in any business publication and give little consideration to such material submitted."

SHOPPING CENTER WORLD, Communication Channels Inc., 6151 Powers Ferry Rd., Atlanta GA 30339-2941. (404)955-2500. Fax: (404)955-0400. Editor: Teresa DeFranks. 75% freelance written. Prefers to work with published/established writers. A monthly magazine covering the shopping center industry. "Material is written with the shopping center developer, owner, manager and shopping center tenant in mind." Estab. 1972. Pays on publication. Publishes ms an average of 3 months after acceptance. Byline given. Buys all rights. Query for electronic submissions. Reports in 2 months. Sample copy $6.

Nonfiction: Interview/profile, new product, opinion, photo feature, and technical. Buys 50 mss/year. Query with published clips or send complete ms. Length: 750-3,000 words. Pays $75-500. Sometimes pays expenses of writers on assignment.

Photos: State availability of photos with submission. Reviews 4×5 transparencies and 35mm slides. Offers no additional payment for photos accepted with ms. Model releases and identification of subjects required. Buys one-time rights.

Tips: "We are always looking for talented writers to work on assignment. Send resumé and published clips. Writers with real estate writing and business backgrounds have a better chance. Product overviews, industry trends and state reviews are all freelance written on an assignment basis. Most assignments are made to those writers who are familiar with the magazine's subject matter and have already reviewed our editorial calendar of future topics."

SOUTHWEST CONTRACTOR, McGraw Hill Publishing Co., #1, 2050 E. University, Phoenix AZ 85034. (602)258-1641. Fax: (602)495-9407. Editor: Elaine M. Beall. 20% freelance written. Monthly magazine about construction industry/engineering and mining. "Problem-solving case histories of projects in Arizona, New Mexico, Nevada and West Texas emphasizing engineering, equipment, materials and people." Estab. 1938. Circ. 6,200. Pays on publication. Byline given. Buys first rights and makes work-for-hire assignments. Submit seasonal material 3 months in advance. Previously published submissions OK; send typed ms with rights for sale noted and information about when and where the article previously appeared. Does not pay for reprints. Reports in 2 months. Sample $3 for 9×12 SAE with 5 first class stamps. Writer's guidelines for #10 SASE.

Nonfiction: Interview/profile and technical. Buys 24 mss/year. Query. Length: 1,000-3,000 words. Pays $4/ column inch at 14 picas wide. Sometimes pays expenses of writers on assignment.

Photos: State availability of photos with submission. Reviews 3×5 prints. Offers $10 maximum/b&w photos; $75 color. Captions and identification of subjects required. Buys one-time rights.

Columns/Departments: People, Around Southwest (general construction activities), Association News (all associations involved with industry), Manufacturer's News, Legal News (construction only). Contracts awarded (construction only), Mining News.

Dental

DENTAL ECONOMICS, Penwell Publishing Co., P.O. Box 3408, Tulsa OK 74101. (918)835-3161. Fax: (918)831-9497. Publisher: Dick Hale. Senior Editor: Penny Anderson. 50% freelance written. Monthly dental trade journal. "Our readers are actively practicing dentists who look to us for current practice-building, practice-administrative and personal finance assistance." Estab. 1916. Circ. 110,000. **Pays on acceptance.** Publishes ms an average of 3-4 months after acceptance. Byline given. Buys first rights. Submit seasonal material 6 months in advance. Reports in 2 months. Free sample copy and writer's guidelines.

● This magazine reports it is buying fewer articles. They have a backlog of accepted pieces.

Nonfiction: General interest, how-to and new product. "No human interest and consumer-related stories." Buys 40 mss/year. Query. Length: 750-3,500 words. Pays $150-500 for assigned articles; pays $75-350 for unsolicited articles. Sometimes pays the expenses of writers on assignment.

Photos: State availability of photos with submission. Reviews contact sheets. Offers no additional payment for photos accepted with ms. Model releases and identification of subjects required. Buys one-time rights.

Columns/Departments: Ron Combs, editor. Tax Q&A (tax tips for dentists), 1,500 words; Capitolgram (late legislative news–dentistry), 750 words; and Dental Insurance, 750 words. Buys 36 mss/year. Pays $50-300.

Tips: "How-to articles on specific subjects such as practice-building, newsletters and collections should be relevant to a busy, solo-practice dentist."

PROOFS, The Magazine of Dental Sales and Marketing, PennWell Publishing Co., P.O. Box 3408, Tulsa OK 74101. (918)835-3161. Fax: (918)831-9497. Editor: Mary Elizabeth Good. 5% freelance written. Magazine published 10 times/year covering dental trade. "*Proofs* is the only publication of the dental trade. It reaches dental dealers, their respective sales forces and key marketing personnel of manufacturers. It publishes news of the industry (not the profession), personnel changes and articles on how to sell dental equipment and merchandise and services that can be provided to the dentist customer." Estab. 1917. Circ. 7,000. Pays on publication. Byline given. Buys first North American serial rights. Editorial lead time 1 month. Query for electronic submissions. Reports in 2 weeks on queries. Sample copy and writer's guidelines free on request.

Nonfiction: General interest, historical/nostalgic, how-to, interview/profile, opinion and personal experience. "No articles written for dentist readers." Buys 15 mss/year. Query or send complete ms. Length: 400-1,250. Pays $100-200.

Photos: Either state availability of photos with submission or send photos with submission. Reviews minimum size 3½×5 prints. Offers no additional payment for photos accepted with ms. Identification of subjects required. Buys one-time rights.

Tips: "Learn something about the dental industry and how it operates. We have no interest in manufacturers who sell only direct. We do not want information on products and how they work, but will take news items on manufacturers' promotions involving products. Most interested in stories on how to sell *in the dental industry*; industry personnel feel they are 'unique' and not like other industries. In many cases, this is true, but not entirely. We are most open to feature articles on selling, supply-house operations, providing service."

RDH, The National Magazine for Dental Hygiene Professionals, Stevens Publishing Corp., 225 N. New Rd., Waco TX 76710-2573. (817)776-9000. Editor: Kathleen Witherspoon. 65% freelance written. Monthly magazine covering information relevant to dental hygiene professionals as business-career oriented individuals. "Dental hygienists are highly trained, licensed professionals; most are women. They are concerned with ways to develop rewarding careers, give optimum service to patients and to grow both professionally and personally." Circ. 65,000. Usually pays 30 days after publication. Publishes ms an average of 8 months after acceptance. Byline given. Buys first serial rights. Reports in 2 weeks on queries; 2 months on mss. Sample copies and writer's guidelines available.

Nonfiction: Essays, general interest, interview/profile, personal experience, photo feature and technical. "We are interested in any topic that offers broad reader appeal, especially in the area of personal growth (communication, managing time, balancing career and personal life). No undocumented clinical or technical articles; how-it-feels-to-be-a-patient articles; product-oriented articles (unless in generic terms); anything cutesy-unprofessional." Length: 1,500-3,000 words. Pays $100-350 for assigned articles; $50-200 for unsolicited articles. Sometimes pays expenses of writers on assignment.

Photos: Covers are shot on location across US.

Tips: "Freelancers should have a feel for the concerns of today's business-career woman–and address those interests and concerns with practical, meaningful and even motivational messages. We want to see good-quality manuscripts on both personal growth and lifestyle topics. For clinical and/or technical topics, we prefer the writers be members of the dental profession. New approaches to old problems and dilemmas will always get a close look from our editors. *RDH* is also interested in manuscripts for our feature section. Other than clinical information, dental hygienists are interested in all sorts of topics–finances, personal growth, educational opportunities, business management, staff/employer relations, communication and motivation, office rapport and career options. Other than clinical/technical articles, *RDH* maintains an informal tone. Writing style can easily be accommodated to our format."

Drugs, Health Care and Medical Products

THE APOTHECARY, Health Care Marketing Services, P.O. Box AP, Los Altos CA 94023. (415)941-3955. Fax: (415)941-2303. Editor: Jerold Karabensh. Publication Director: Janet Goodman. Managing Editor: Susan Keller. 100% freelance written. Prefers to work with published/established writers who possess some knowledge of pharmacy and business/management topics. Quarterly magazine providing practical information to community retail pharmacists." Estab. 1888. Circ. 60,000. **Pays on acceptance.** Publishes ms an average of 5 months after acceptance. Byline given. Buys all rights. Submit seasonal material 8 months in advance. Simultaneous queries OK. Reports in up to 6 months. Sample copy for 9 × 12 SAE with 4 first class stamps. Writer's guidelines for #10 SASE.

Nonfiction: How-to (e.g., manage a pharmacy), opinion (of registered pharmacists), and health-related feature stories. "We publish only those general health articles with some practical application for the pharmacist as business person. No general articles not geared to our pharmacy readership; no fiction." Buys 4 mss/year. Query with published clips. Length: 750-3,000 words. Pays $100-300.

Columns/Departments: Commentary (views or issues relevant to the subject of pharmacy or to pharmacists). Send complete ms. Length: 750-1,000 words. "This section is unpaid; we will take submissions with byline."

Tips: "Submit material geared to the *pharmacist* as *business person.* Write according to our policy, i.e., business articles with emphasis on practical information for a community pharmacist. We suggest reading several back issues and following general feature story tone, depth, etc. Stay away from condescending use of language. Though our articles are written in simple style, they must reflect knowledge of the subject and reasonable respect for the readers' professionalism and intelligence."

‡CALIFORNIA PHARMACIST, California Pharmacists Association, Suite 300, 1112 I St., Sacramento CA 95814. (916)444-7811. Managing Editor: Bob Andosca. 25% freelance written. Monthly magazine covering pharmacy. Readers are mostly practicing pharmacists in California in various pharmacy settings. Strong, accurate and timely clinical articles, legal articles relating cases relative to pharmacy and legislative and administrative articles pertaining to California pharmacy. Estab. 1956. Circ. 7,000. Pays on publication. Publishes ms an average of 2 months after acceptance. Byline given. Offers 100% kill fee. Buys first rights. Editorial lead time 3 months. Submit seasonal material 3 months in advance. Reports in 3 weeks on queries. Sample copy and writer's guidelines free on request.

Nonfiction: Interview/profile, photo feature and technical. Buys 15 mss/year. Send complete ms. Length: 1,500-5,000 words. Pays $150.

Tips: "Pharmacy is dynamic and writers must be ahead of the news in order to produce timely and pertinent articles. Look at how today's news will create tomorrow's headlines. Strong clinical articles are most sought after. Other articles such as HIV/AIDS research and development, managed care and medicaid are important to us."

CANADIAN PHARMACEUTICAL JOURNAL, 1785 Alta Vista Dr., Ottawa, Ontario K1G 3Y6 Canada. (613)523-7877. Fax: (613)523-0445. Editor: Jane Dewar. Staff Writers: Andrew Reinboldt, Barbara Edie. Works with a small number of new/unpublished writers each year. Monthly journal for pharmacists. Estab. 1868. Circ. 13,300. Pays after editing. Publishes ms an average of 3-6 months after acceptance. Buys first serial rights. Reports in 2 months. Free sample copy and writer's guidelines.

Nonfiction: Relevant to Canadian pharmacy. Publishes continuing education, exposes (pharmacy practice, education and legislation); how-to (pharmacy business operations); historical (pharmacy practice, Canadian legislation, education). Length: 200-400 words (for news notices); 800-1,500 words (for articles). Query. Payment is contingent on value. Sometimes pays expenses of writers on assignment.

Photos: Color and b&w (5 × 7) glossies purchased with mss. Captions and model releases required.

Tips: "Query with complete description of proposed article, including topic, sources (in general), length, payment requested, suggested submission date, and whether photographs will be included. It is helpful if the writer has read a *recent* copy of the journal; we are glad to send one if required. References should be included where appropriate (this is vital where medical and scientific information is included). Send 3 copies of each manuscript. Author's degree and affiliations (if any) and writing background should be listed."

CONSULTANT PHARMACIST, American Society of Consultant Pharmacists, 1321 Duke St., Alexandria VA 22314-3563. (703)739-1300. Fax: (703)739-1500. Editor: L. Michael Posey. Assistant Editor: Joanne Kaldy. Production Manager: Catherine Burdette. 10% freelance written. Monthly journal on consultant pharmacy. "We do not promote drugs or companies but rather ideas and information." Circ. 11,200. **Pays on acceptance.** Publishes ms an average of 4 months after acceptance. Byline given. Buys first North American serial rights. Send disk with accepted article. Reports in 2 weeks. Sample copy for 9 × 12 SAE with 6 first class stamps. Writer's guidelines for #10 SASE.

Nonfiction: How-to (related to consultant pharmacy), interview/profile and technical. Buys 10 mss/year. Query with published clips. Length: 750-2,000 words. Pays $300-1,200. Sometimes pays expenses of writers on assignment.

Photos: Send photos with submission. Offers $100/photo session. Captions, model releases and identification of subjects required. Buys one-time rights.

Tips: "This journal is devoted to consultant pharmacy, so articles must relate to this field."

PHARMACY TIMES, Romaine Pierson Publishers, 80 Shore Rd., Port Washington NY 11050. (516)883-6350. Fax: (516)883-6609. Publisher: William J. Reynolds. Editor-in-Chief: Bruce Buckley. 15% freelance written. Monthly magazine providing clinical, educational and economic information to pharmacists. Estab. 1897. Circ. 97,000. Pays on publication. Publishes ms an average of 4 months after acceptance. Byline given. Buys one-time rights. Submit seasonal material 6 months in advance. Query for electronic submissions. Reports in 1 month on queries; 6 weeks on mss. Free sample copy and writer's guidelines.

Nonfiction: Interview/profile, new product, opinion, personal experience, photo feature, technical and travel. Buys 12-15 mss/year. Send complete ms. Length: 800-1,500 words. Pays $250-400 for assigned articles; $100-250 for unsolicited articles. Pays in contributor copies or other premiums "per author request or for reprinted material."

Photos: State availability of photos with submission. Reviews negatives and 3×5 prints. Offers no additional payment for photos accepted with ms. Captions, model releases and identification of subjects required. Buys one-time rights.

Education and Counseling

Professional educators, teachers, coaches and counselors—as well as other people involved in training and education—read the journals classified here. Many journals for educators are nonprofit forums for professional advancement; writers contribute articles in return for a byline and contributor's copies. *Writer's Market* includes only educational journals that pay freelancers for articles. Education-related publications for students are included in the Consumer Career, College and Alumni and Teen and Young Adult sections.

ARTS & ACTIVITIES, Publishers' Development Corporation, Dept. WM, Suite 200, 591 Camino de la Reina, San Diego CA 92108-9989. (619)297-5352. Fax: (619)297-5353. Managing Editor: Maryellen Bridge. 95% freelance written. Eager to work with new/unpublished writers. Monthly (except July and August) art education magazine covering art education at levels from preschool through college for educators and therapists engaged in arts and crafts education and training. Estab. 1932. Circ. 24,000. Pays on publication. Publishes ms an average of 6 months after acceptance. Byline given. Buys first North American serial rights. Submit seasonal material 4 months in advance. Reports in 3 months. Sample copy for 9×12 SAE with 8 first class stamps. Writer's guidelines for #10 SASE.

Nonfiction: Historical/nostalgic (arts, activities, history); how-to (classroom art experiences, artists' techniques); interview/profile (of artists); opinion (on arts activities curriculum, ideas on how to do things better); personal experience in the art classroom ("this ties in with the how-to, we like it to be *personal*, no recipe style"); and articles on exceptional art programs. Buys 50-80 mss/year. Length: 200-2,000 words. Pays $35-150.

 • Editors here are seeking more materials for upper elementary and secondary levels on printmaking, ceramics, 3-dimensional design and crafts.

Tips: "Frequently in unsolicited manuscripts, writers obviously have not studied the magazine to see what style of articles we publish. Send for a sample copy to familiarize yourself with our style and needs. The best way to find out if his/her writing style suits our needs is for the author to submit a manuscript on speculation."

‡THE EDUCATION CENTER, INC., The Mailbox (3 editions)—Magazines Division, 1607 Battleground Ave., Greensboro NC 27408. Senior Editors: Diane Badden, Primary edition (grades 1-3); Becky Andrews, Intermediate edition (grades 4-6); Karen Shelton, preschool/Kindergarten edition. 3 editions, 6 issues each. Ideas for preschool-grade 6 teachers. "Our audience is elementary (preschool to grade 6) teachers. We are looking for practical, creative, hands-on teaching ideas and tips as opposed to articles about education,. Must be educationally sound." **Pays on acceptance.** Editorial lead time varies up to one year. Reports in 2 months on queries. Query with resume showing teaching experience. Sample copy and writer's guidelines for 8½×11 SASE to qualified applicants.

Nonfiction: Educational-teacher directed. "We *absolutely* require that all writers have *at least* three years of *self-contained* classroom teaching experience, preferably recent, at the same grade level. Applicants may be excellent writers, but without the teaching experience, **will be** rejected." Pays $30/worksheet; $165/8-10 idea unit.

A bullet introduces comments by the editor of Writer's Market *indicating special information about the listing.*

EDUCATION IN FOCUS, Books for All Times, Inc., Box 2, Alexandria VA 22313. (703)548-0457. Editor: Joe David. Semiannual newsletter that covers educational issues. Pays on publication. Buys first, one-time and second serial (reprint) rights. Will negotiate rights to include articles in books. Accepts simultaneous submissions. Reports in 1 month. *Writer's Market* recommends allowing 2 months for reply.
Nonfiction: "We are looking for articles that expose the failures of public education and discuss the success of private education."

INSTRUCTOR MAGAZINE, Scholastic, Inc., 730 Broadway, New York NY 10003. Executive Editor: Debra Martorelli. Publishing Coordinator: Eryth Zecher. Eager to work with new/unpublished writers, "especially teachers." Monthly magazine emphasizing elementary education. Estab. 1891. Circ. 275,000. **Pays on acceptance.** Publishes ms an average of 1 year after acceptance. Byline given. Buys all rights. Submit seasonal material 6 months in advance. Query for electronic submissions. Reports in 1 month on queries; 2 months on mss. Sample copy $3. Writer's guidelines for SASE; mention *Writer's Market* in request.
Nonfiction: How-to articles on elementary classroom practice—practical suggestions and project reports. Occasionally publishes first-person accounts of classroom experiences. Buys 100 mss/year. Query. Length: 400-2,000 words. Pays $15-75 for short items; $125-400 for articles and features. Send all queries to Attention: manuscripts editor.
Photos: Send photos with submission. Reviews 4×5 transparencies and prints. Offers no additional payment for photos accepted with ms. Model releases and identification of subjects required. Buys all rights.
Columns/Departments: Idea Notebook (quick teacher tips and ideas); Planner (seasonal activities, bulletin boards and crafts); Primary Place (teaching ideas for primary grades); and Partnerships (teacher-initiated school/business partnerships). Buys 100 mss/year. Query with SASE. Length: 50-1,000 words. Pays $30-100.
Fiction: Occasionally buys plays and read-aloud stories for children. Length: 500-2,500 words. Pays $75-200.
Tips: "How-to articles should be kept practical, with concrete examples whenever possible. Writers should keep in mind that our audience is elementary teachers."

JOURNAL OF CAREER PLANNING & EMPLOYMENT, College Placement Council, Inc., Dept. WM, 62 Highland Ave., Bethlehem PA 18017. (215)868-1421. Fax: (215)868-0208. Associate Editor: Bill Beebe. 25% freelance written. Magazine published November, January, March and May for career development professionals who counsel and/or hire college students, graduating students, employees and job-changers. Estab. 1940. Circ. 4,200. **Pays on acceptance.** Publishes ms an average of 4 months after acceptance. Byline given. Buys first rights. Reports in 1 month on queries; 2 months on mss. Writer's guidelines for #10 SASE.
Nonfiction: How-to, interview/profile, new techniques/innovative practices and current issues in the field. *No articles that speak directly to job candidates.* Buys 7-10 mss/year. Query with published clips, or send complete ms or hard copy plus floppy disk. Length: 3,000-4,000 words. Pays up to $400.
Tips: "A freelancer can best break into our publication by sending query with clips of published work, by writing on topics that aim directly at the journal's audience—professionals in the college career planning, placement and recruitment field—and by using an easy-to-read, narrative style rather than a formal, thesis style. The area of our publication most open to freelancers is nonfiction feature articles only. Topics should directly relate to the career planning and employment of the college educated and should go beyond the basics of career planning, job hunting and hiring issues, since readers are well-versed in those basics."

LEARNING 94, 1111 Bethlehem Pike, Springhouse PA 19477-0908. Fax: (215)646-4399. Editor: Charlene F. Gaynor. Senior Editor: Jeanette Moss. 45% freelance written. Magazine published monthly during school year emphasizing elementary and junior high school education topics. Estab. 1972. Circ. 275,000. **Pays on acceptance.** Buys all rights. Submit seasonal material 9 months in advance. Reports in up to 4 months. Sample copy $3. Free writer's guidelines.
Nonfiction: "We publish manuscripts that describe innovative, practical teaching strategies." How-to (classroom management, specific lessons or units or activities for children—all at the elementary and junior high level—and hints for teaching in all curriculum areas); personal experience (from teachers in elementary and junior high schools); and profile (with teachers who are in unusual or innovative teaching situations). Strong interest in articles that deal with discipline, teaching strategy, motivation and working with parents. Buys 250 mss/year. Query. Length: 1,000-3,500 words. Pays $50-350.
● This magazine has become more selective; submissions must meet their format.
Tips: "We're looking for practical, teacher-tested ideas and strategies as well as first-hand personal accounts of dramatic successes—or failures—with a lesson to be drawn. No theoretical or academic papers. We're also interested in examples of especially creative classrooms and teachers. Emphasis on professionalism will increase: top teachers telling what they do best and others can also."

LOLLIPOPS, The Magazine for Early Childhood Educators, Good Apple, Inc., P.O. Box 299, Carthage IL 62321-0299. (212)357-3981. Fax: (212)357-3987. Editor: Donna Borst. 20% freelance written. Magazine published 5 times/year providing easy-to-use, hands-on practical teaching ideas and suggestions for early childhood education. Circ. 20,000. Pays on publication. Buys all rights. Submit seasonal material 6 months in advance. Sample copy for 9×12 SAE with 3 first class stamps. Writer's guidelines for #10 SASE.

Nonfiction: How-to (on creating usable teaching materials). Buys varying number of mss/year. Send complete ms. Length: 200-1,000 words. Pays $25-100 for assigned articles; $10-30 for unsolicited articles. Writer has choice of cash or Good Apple products worth twice the contract value.

Columns/Departments: Accepts material dealing with the solving of problems encountered by early childhood education. Buys varying number of mss/year. Pays $25-100.

Fiction: Adventure and fantasy (for young children).

Poetry: Light verse. Buys varying number of poems/year.

Tips: "I'm always looking for something that's new and different — something that works for teachers of young children. Seasonal materials are of special interest."

‡**MEDIA & METHODS**, American Society of Educators, 1429 Walnut St., Philadelphia PA 19102. (215)563-3501. Editor/Director: Michele Sokoloff. Bimonthly trade journal published during the school year about educational products, media technologies and programs for schools and universities. Readership: Librarians and media specialists. Estab. 1963. Circ. 40,000. Pays on publication. Publishes ms an average of 3 months after acceptance. Byline given. Buys first North American serial rights. Free sample copy and writer's guidelines.

Nonfiction: How-to, practical, new product, personal experience and technical. Must send query letter, outline or call editor. Do not send ms. Length: 600-1,200 words. Pays $75-200.

Photos: State availability of photos with submission. Reviews 3×5 prints. Offers no additional payment for photos accepted with ms. Captions and identification of subjects required. Buys one-time rights.

MEDIA PROFILES: The Health Sciences Edition, Olympic Media Information, P.O. Box 190, West Park NY 12493-0190. (914)384-6563. Publisher: Walt Carroll. 100% freelance written. Consists entirely of signed reviews of videos and films for healthcare education (no editorials or "articles"). Subscribers are medical and nursing libraries, colleges and universities where health sciences are taught. Serial, in magazine format, published quarterly. Estab. 1967. Circ. 1,000. Pays on publication. Publishes ms an average of 6 months after acceptance. Buys all rights. Buys 160 mss/year. Word processing (IBM) disk submissions preferred. "Sample copies and writer's guidelines sent on receipt of resume, background, and mention of subject areas you are interested (most qualified) in reviewing. Enclose $5 for writer's guidelines and sample issue. (Refunded with first payment upon publication)." Reports in 1 month. Query.

Nonfiction: "We are the only review publication devoted exclusively to evaluation of audiovisual aids for medical and health training. We have a highly specialized, definite format that must be followed in all cases. Samples should be seen by all means. Our writers should first have a background in health sciences; second, have some experience with audiovisuals; and third, follow our format precisely. Writers with advanced degrees and teaching affiliations with colleges and hospital education departments given preference. We are interested in reviews of media materials for nursing education, in-service education, continuing education, personnel training, patient education, patient care and medical problems. Currently seeking MDs, RNs, PhDs with clinical and technical expertise. Unsolicited mss not welcome. We will have videos sent directly to reviewers who accept the assignments." Pays $15/review.

MOMENTUM, National Catholic Educational Association, 1077 30th St. NW, Washington DC 20007-3852. Editor: Patricia Feistritzer. 10% freelance written. Quarterly magazine for Catholic administrators and teachers, some parents and students, in all levels of education (preschool, elementary, secondary, higher). Estab. 1970. Circ. 25,000. Pays on publication. Buys first serial rights. Reports in 3 months. Sample copy for 9×12 SASE.

Nonfiction: Articles concerned with educational philosophy, psychology, methodology, innovative programs, teacher training, research, financial and public relations programs and management systems — all applicable to nonpublic schools. Book reviews on educational/religious topics. Avoid general topics or topics applicable *only* to public education. "We look for a straightforward, journalistic style with emphasis on practical examples, as well as scholarly writing and statistics. All references must be footnoted, fully documented. Emphasis is on professionalism." Buys 28-36 mss/year. Length: 1,500-2,000 words. Pays 2¢/word.

‡**SCHOOL ARTS MAGAZINE**, 50 Portland St., Worcester MA 01608-9959. Fax: (508)753-3834. Editor: Kent Anderson. 85% freelance written. Magazine published monthly, September through May, serving arts and craft education profession, K-12, higher education and museum education programs. Written by and for art teachers. Estab. 1901. Pays on publication. Publishes ms an average of 3 months "if timely; if less pressing, can be 1 year or more" after acceptance. Buys first serial and second serial (reprint) rights. Reports in 3 months. Free sample copy and writer's guidelines.

Nonfiction: Articles on art and craft activities in schools. Should include description and photos of activity in progress, as well as examples of finished artwork. Query or send complete ms. Length: 600-1,400 words. Pays $20-100.

Tips: "We prefer articles on actual art projects or techniques done by students in actual classroom situations. Philosophical and theoretical aspects of art and art education are usually handled by our contributing editors. Our articles are reviewed and accepted on merit and each is tailored to meet our needs. Keep in mind that art teachers want practical tips, above all — more hands-on information than academic theory. Write your article with the accompanying photographs in hand." The most frequent mistakes made by writers are "bad visual material (photographs, drawings) submitted with articles, or a lack of complete descriptions of art processes; and no rationale behind programs or activities. Familiarity with the field of art education is essential."

‡**TEACHING THEATRE**, Educational Theatre Association, 3368 Central Pkwy., Cincinnati OH 45211. (513)559-1996. Editor: James Palmarini. 75% freelance written. Membership benefit of Teachers Education Association (part of ETA). Quarterly magazine covering education theater K-12, primary emphasis on secondary. "*Teaching Theatre* emphasizes the teaching, theory, philosophy issues that are of concern to teachers at the elementary, secondary, and—as they relate to teaching K-12 theater—college levels. We publish work that explains specific approaches to teaching (directing, acting, tech theater, etc.); advocates curriculum reform; or offers theories of theater education." Estab. 1989. Circ. 2,000. **Pays on acceptance.** Publishes ms an average of 3-6 months after acceptance. Byline given. Buys one-time rights. Editorial lead time 2 months. Submit seasonal material 3 months in advance. Accepts simultaneous and previously published submissions. Query for electronic submissions. Reports in 1 month on queries; 3 months on mss. Sample copy $2. Writer's guidelines for #10 SASE.
Nonfiction: Book excerpts, essays, how-to, interview/profile, opinion and technical theater. "*Teaching Theatre*'s audience is well-educated and most have considerable experience in their field; while *generalist* articles are not discouraged, it should be assumed that readers already *possess* basic skills." Buys 15 mss/year. Query. Pays $100 for published articles. "We generally pay cash and 5 copies of issue."
Photos: State availability of photos with submission. Reviews contact sheets, 5×7 and 8×10 transparencies, 5×7 and 8×10 prints. Offers no additional payment for photos accepted with ms.

TEACHING TODAY, 49 Primrose Blvd., Sherwood Park, Alberta T8H 1G1 Canada. (403)467-5273. Editor: Betty Ann Coderre. Publisher/Editor: Max Coderre. 90% freelance written. Educational magazine published 5 times/year. Estab. 1983. Circ. 8,000-10,000. Pays on publication. Publishes ms an average of 2 years after acceptance. Mss must be accompanied by SAE with IRCs for return. Byline given. Buys first rights, one-time or all rights. Simultaneous submissions OK. Reprints OK; send tearsheet, photocopy of article or typed ms with rights for sale noted. Information about when and where the article was previously published should be accompanied by permission from original publisher to reprint (if necessary). Pays 50% of above noted fee for "reprint" article. Query for electronic submissions. Reports in 10 weeks. Sample copy $3 (includes postage for US destinations, in Canada 84¢ postage); check or money order addressed to *Teaching Today*.
Nonfiction: How-to (related to teaching), humor (related to education), inspiration, personal experience (if related to teaching), communication skills and professional development (teacher). Buys 50-60 mss/year. Query with published clips. Length: 150-1,000 words. Pays $20-225 for assigned articles; $15-100 for unsolicited articles. Sometimes pays expenses of writers on assignment.
Photos: Send photos with submission. Reviews b&w or color 4×5, 3×5, or 4×6 prints; or 8×10 color (for cover only). Offers $15-100/photo. Model releases and identification of subjects required. Buys one-time rights.
Fillers: Anecdotes and gags to be illustrated by cartoonist. Buys 20/year. Length: 20-100 words. Pays $5-25.
Tips: "A freelancer can best break into our magazine with articles, cartoons, fillers related to education. Articles primarily that will *help* educators personally or professionally."

TEACHING/K-8, The Professional Magazine, Early Years, Inc., 7th Floor, 40 Richards Ave., Norwalk CT 06854-2319. (203)855-2650. Fax: (203)855-2656. Editor: Allen Raymond. Editorial Director: Patricia Broderick. 50% freelance written. "We prefer material from classroom teachers." Monthly magazine covering teaching of kindergarten through eighth grades. Estab. 1970. Pays on publication. Publishes ms an average of 7 months after acceptance. Byline given. Buys all rights. Submit seasonal material 6 months in advance. Reports in 2 months. Sample copy $3 for 9×12 SAE with 10 first class stamps. Writer's guidelines for #10 SASE.
Nonfiction: Classroom curriculum material. Send complete ms. Length: 1,200-1,500 words. Pays $35 maximum.
  • This magazine has a backlog of accepted mss.
Photos: Offers no additional payment for photos accepted with ms. Model releases and identification of subjects required.
Tips: "Manuscripts should be specifically oriented to a successful teaching strategy, idea, project or program. Broad overviews of programs or general theory manuscripts are not usually the type of material we select for publication. Because of the definitive learning level we cover (pre-school through grade eight) we try to avoid presenting general groups of unstructured ideas. We prefer classroom tested ideas and techniques."

TECH DIRECTIONS, (formerly *School Shop/Tech Directions*), Prakken Publications, Inc., P.O. Box 8623, Ann Arbor MI 48107-8623. Fax: (313)769-8383. Managing Editor: Paul J. Bamford. 100% freelance written. Eager to work with new/unpublished writers. Monthly (except June and July) magazine covering issues, trends and projects of interest to industrial, vocational, technical and technology educators at the secondary and postsecondary school levels. Estab. 1934. Circ. 45,000. Buys all rights. Pays on publication. Publishes ms an average of 8-12 months after acceptance. Byline given. Prefers authors who have direct connection with the field of industrial and/or technical education. Simultaneous queries and simultaneous and previously published submissions OK. Reprints OK; send photocopy of article and information about when and where the article previously appeared. Pays 100% of their fee for an original article. Reports in 2 months. Sample copy and writer's guidelines for 9 × 12 SAE with 3 first class stamps.

Nonfiction: Uses articles pertinent to the various teaching areas in industrial and technology education (woodwork, electronics, drafting, machine shop, graphic arts, computer training, etc.). "The outlook should be on innovation in educational programs, processes or projects that directly apply to the industrial/technical education area." Buys general interest, how-to, opinion, personal experience, technical and think pieces, interviews, humor, and coverage of new products. Buys 135 unsolicited mss/year. Length: 200-2,000 words. Pays $25-150.

Photos: Send photos with accompanying query or ms. Reviews b&w and color prints. Payment for photos included in payment for ms.

Columns/Departments: Tech-Niques (brief items which describe short-cuts or special procedures relevant to the technology or vocational education). Buys 30 mss/year. Send complete ms. Length: 20-100 words. Pays $15 minimum.

Tips: "We are most interested in articles written by industrial, vocational and technical educators about their class projects and their ideas about the field. We need more and more technology-related articles, especially written for the community college level."

TECHNOLOGY & LEARNING, Suite A4, 2169 Francisco Blvd. E., San Rafael CA 94901. Fax: (415)457-4379. Editor-in-Chief: Holly Brady. 50% freelance written. Works with a small number of new/unpublished writers each year. Monthly magazine published during school year emphasizing elementary through high school educational technology topics. Estab. 1980. Circ. 83,000. **Pays on acceptance.** Publishes ms an average of 8 months after acceptance. Buys all or first serial rights. Submit seasonal material 6 months in advance. Reports in 3 months. Sample copy for 8 × 10 SAE with 6 first class stamps. Writer's guidelines for #10 SASE.

Nonfiction: "We publish manuscripts that describe innovative ways of using technology in the classroom as well as articles that discuss controversial issues in computer education." Interviews, brief technology-related activity ideas and longer featurettes describing fully-developed and tested classroom ideas. Buys 50 mss/year. Query. Length: 500 words or less for classroom activities; 1,500-2,500 words for major articles. Pays $25 for activities; payment varies from $200 or more for articles. Educational Software Reviews are assigned through editorial offices. "If interested, send a letter telling us of your areas of interest and expertise as well as the microcomputer(s) and other equipment you have available to you." Pays $75/review. Pays expenses of writers on assignment.

Photos: State availability of photos with query.

Tips: "The talent that goes into writing our shorter hands-on pieces is different from that required for features (e.g., interviews, issues pieces, etc.) Write whatever taps your talent best. A frequent mistake is taking too 'novice' or too 'expert' an approach. You need to know our audience well and to understand how much they know about computers. Also, too many manuscripts lack a definite point of view or focus or opinion. We like pieces with clear, strong, well thought-out opinions."

TODAY'S CATHOLIC TEACHER, 330 Progress Rd., Dayton OH 45449. (513)847-5900. Fax: (513)847-5910. Editor: Stephen Brittan. 40% freelance written. Works with a small number of new/unpublished writers each year. For administrators, teachers and parents concerned with Catholic schools, both parochial and CCD. Estab. 1967. Circ. 60,000. Pays after publication. Publishes ms an average of 3 months after acceptance. Byline given. Buys all rights. Phone queries OK. Submit seasonal material 3 months in advance. Reports in 4 months. Sample copy $3. Writer's guidelines for #10 SASE; mention *Writer's Market* in request.

Nonfiction: How-to (based on experience, particularly for teachers to use in the classroom to supplement curriculum, philosophy with practical applications); interview (of practicing educators, educational leaders); personal experience (classroom happenings other educators can learn from); and a few profiles (of educational leaders). Buys 40-50 mss/year. Submit complete ms. Length: 800-2,000 words. Pays $15-175.

Photos: State availability of photos with ms. Offers no additional payment for 8 × 10 b&w glossy prints. Buys one-time rights. Captions preferred; model releases required.

Tips: "We prefer articles that are of interest or practical help to educators—teaching ideas, curriculum-related material, administration suggestions, resource guides, articles teachers can use in classroom to teach current topics, etc. We use many one-page features."

Electronics and Communication

These publications are edited for broadcast and telecommunications technicians and engineers, electrical engineers and electrical contractors. Included are journals for electronic equipment designers and operators who maintain electronic and telecommunication systems. Publications for appliance dealers can be found in Home Furnishings and Household Goods.

BROADCAST TECHNOLOGY, P.O. Box 420, Bolton, Ontario L7E 5T3 Canada. (416)857-6076. Fax: (416)857-6045. Editor-in-Chief: Doug Loney. 50% freelance written. Monthly (except August, December) magazine emphasizing broadcast engineering. Estab. 1975. Circ. 8,000. Pays on publication. Byline given. Buys all rights. Phone queries OK.
Nonfiction: Technical articles on developments in broadcast engineering, especially pertaining to Canada. Query. Length: 500-1,500 words. Pays $100-300.
Photos: Purchased with accompanying ms. Black and white or color. Captions required.
Tips: "Most of our outside writing is by regular contributors, usually employed full-time in broadcast engineering. The specialized nature of our magazine requires a specialized knowledge on the part of a writer."

BUSINESS RADIO, National Association of Business and Educational Radio, 1501 Duke St., Alexandria VA 22314-3450. (703)739-0300. Fax: (703)836-1608. Editor: A.E. Goetz. Managing Editor: Christine W. Byrum. 25% freelance written. Magazine published 10 times/year on mobile communications "for land mobile equipment users, dealers, service shop operators, manufacturers, communications technicians, paging and SMR system owners and operators. To acquaint members with the diversity of uses to which land mobile radio can be applied and to identify and discuss new and developing areas of RF technology and their application." Estab. 1965. Circ. 3,000. **Pays on acceptance.** Publishes ms an average of 3 months after acceptance. Byline given. Buys first rights. Query for electronic submissions. Reports in 3 months. Sample copy for 9 × 12 SAE with 5 first class stamps. Writer's guidelines for #10 SASE.
Nonfiction: General interest, interview/profile, new product, technical, and general small business or management articles all related to land mobile communications. Buys 5 mss/year. Query with or without published clips or send complete ms. Length: 1,500-2,200 words. Pays $100-300 for unsolicited articles. Sometimes pays expenses of writers on assignment.
Photos: Send photos with submission. Reviews contact sheets, negatives, transparencies and prints. Offers no additional payment for b&w photos accepted with ms. Captions, model releases and identification of subjects required. Buys one-time rights.
Columns/Departments: ShopTalk (small business, general management), 1,500-2,500 words. Buys 8 mss/year. Query or send complete ms. Pays $150-250.
Tips: "We are seeking writers who are knowledgeable in mobile communications and telecommunications to write in-depth user profiles and new technology pieces."

CABLE COMMUNICATIONS MAGAZINE, Canada's Authoritative International Cable Television Publication, Ter-Sat Media Publications Ltd., Dept. WM, 1421 Victoria St. N., Kitchener, Ontario N2B 3E4 Canada. (519)744-4111. Fax: (519)744-1261. Editor: Udo Salewsky. 33% freelance written. Prefers to work with published/established writers. Monthly magazine covering the cable television industry. Estab. 1934. Circ. 8,119. **Pays on acceptance.** Publishes ms an average of 2 months after acceptance. Byline given. Buys all rights. Submit seasonal material 1 month in advance. Query for electronic submissions. Reports in 2 weeks on queries; 1 month on mss. Sample copy for 9 × 12 SAE with $3.50 in IRCs. Free writer's guidelines.
Nonfiction: Expose, how-to, interview/profile, opinion, technical articles, and informed views and comments on topical, industry-related issues. Also, problem solving-related articles, new marketing and operating efficiency ideas. No fiction. Buys 50 mss/year. Query with published clips or send complete ms. Length: 1,000-4,000 words. Pays $250-1,000. Pays expenses of writers on assignment.
Columns/Departments: Buys 48 items/year. Query with published clips or send complete ms. Length: 1,000-1,500 words. Pays $250-375.
Tips: "Forward manuscript and personal resume. We don't need freelance writers for short articles and fillers. Break in with articles related to industry issues, events and new developments; analysis of current issues and events. Be able to interpret the meaning of new developments relative to the cable television industry and their potential impact on the industry from a growth opportunity as well as a competitive point of view. Material should be well supported by facts and data. Insufficient research and understanding of underlying issues are frequent mistakes."

COMMUNICATIONS QUARTERLY, P.O. Box 465, Barrington NH 03825. (603)664-2515. Fax: (603)664-2515. Publisher: Richard Ross. Editor: Terry Littlefield. 80% freelance written. Quarterly publication on theoretical and technical aspects of amateur radio and communication industry technology. Estab. 1990. Circ. 10,000. Pays on publication. Publishes ms an average of 6 months after acceptance. Byline given. Buys first rights. Query for electronic submissions. Reports in 1 month. Writer's guidelines for #10 SASE.
Nonfiction: "Interested in technical and theory pieces on all aspects of amateur radio and the communications industry. State-of-the-art developments are of particular interest to our readers. No human interest stories." Query or send complete ms. Pays $40/published page.

Photos: Send photos with submission. Reviews 5×7 b&w prints. Offers no additional payment for photos accepted with ms. Captions and identification of subjects required. Buys one-time rights.

Tips: "We are looking for writers with knowledge of the technical or theoretical aspects of the amateur radio and communication industries. Our readers are interested in state-of-the-art developments, high-tech construction projects and the theory behind the latest technologies."

ELECTRONIC SERVICING & TECHNOLOGY, CQ Communications, 76 N. Broadway, Hicksville NY 11801. (516)681-2922. Fax: (516)681-2926. Editorial Office: P.O. Box 12487, Overland Park KS 66282-2487. Phone/Fax: (913)492-4857. Editor: Conrad Persson. Associate Editor: Linda Romanello. 90% freelance written. Eager to work with new/unpublished writers. Monthly magazine for professional servicers and electronic enthusiasts who are interested in buying, building, installing and repairing consumer electronic equipment (audio, TV, video, microcomputers, electronic games, etc.). Estab. 1950. Circ. 38,000. **Pays on acceptance.** Publishes ms an average of 6 months after acceptance. Byline given. Buys all rights. Simultaneous queries OK. Publishes reprints of previously published articles. Send typed ms with rights for sale noted and information about when and where the article previously appeared. Reports in 2 weeks on queries; 1 month on mss. *Writer's Market* recommends allowing 2 months for reply. Sample copy and writer's guidelines for 9×12 SAE with 5 first class stamps.

Nonfiction: How-to (service, build, install and repair home entertainment; electronic testing and servicing equipment). "Explain the techniques used carefully so that even hobbyists can understand a how-to article." Buys 36 mss/year. Send complete ms. Length: 1,500 words minimum. Pays $100-300.

Photos: Send photos with ms. Reviews color and b&w transparencies and b&w prints. Captions and identification of subjects required. Buys all rights. Payment included in total ms package.

Columns/Departments: Linda Romanello, associate editor. Troubleshooting Tips: Buys 12 mss/year. Send complete ms. Pays $25.

Tips: "In order to write for *ES&T* it is almost essential that a writer have an electronics background: technician, engineer or serious hobbyist. Our readers want nuts-and-bolts information on electronics."

THE INDEPENDENT Film & Video Monthly, Foundation for Independent Video & Film, 9th Floor, 625 Broadway, New York NY 10012-2611. (212)473-3400. Fax: (212)677-8732. Editor: Patricia Thomson. 60% freelance written. Works with a small number of new/unpublished writers each year. Monthly magazine of practical information for producers of independent film and video with focus on low budget, art and documentary work. Estab. 1979. Circ. 18,000. Pays on publication. Publishes ms an average of 4 months after acceptance. Byline given. Buys first serial rights. Submit seasonal material 4 months in advance. Simultaneous queries OK. Query for electronic submissions. Reports in 3 months. Reprints OK; send tearsheet or photocopy of article, or typed ms with rights for sale noted, with information about when and where the article previously appeared. Pay varies. Sample copy for 9×12 SASE with 5 first class stamps.

Nonfiction: Book excerpts ("in our area"), how-to, technical (low-tech only), and theoretical/critical articles. No reviews. Buys 60 mss/year. Query with published clips. Length: 1,200-3,500 words. Pays $50-200.

Tips: "Since this is a specialized publication, we prefer to work with writers on short pieces first. Writers should be familiar with specific practical and theoretical issues concerning independent film and video."

INFORMATION TODAY, Learned Information Inc., 143 Old Marlton Pike, Medford NJ 08055-8750. (609)654-6266. Fax: (609)654-4309. Publisher: Thomas H. Hogan. Editor: Patricia Lane. 30% freelance written. Tabloid published 11 times/year for the users and producers of electronic information services. Estab. 1979. Circ. 10,000. Pays on publication. Publishes ms an average of 1-3 months after acceptance. Byline given. Buys first North American serial rights. Submit seasonal material 2 months in advance. Reports in 2 weeks. Sample copy and writer's guidelines for 9×12 SAE with 6 first class stamps.

Nonfiction: Book reviews; interview/profile and new product; technical (dealing with computerized information services); and articles on library technology, artificial intelligence, online databases and services, and integrated online library systems. We also cover software and optical publishing (CD-ROM and Multi Media). Buys approximately 25 mss/year. Query with published clips or send complete ms on speculation. Length: 500-1,500 words. Pays $90-220.

Photos: State availability of photos with submission.

Tips: "We look for clearly-written, informative articles dealing with the electronic delivery of information. Writing style should not be jargon-laden or heavily technical."

‡MICROWAVES & RF, 611 Route #46 W., Hasbrouck Heights NJ 07604. (201)393-6293. Fax: (201)393-6297. Chief Editor: Jack Browne. 20% freelance written. Monthly magazine emphasizing radio frequency design. "Qualified recipients are those individuals actively engaged in microwave and RF research, design, development, production and application engineering, engineering management, administration or purchasing departments in organizations and facilities where application and use of devices, systems and techniques involve frequencies from HF through visible light." Estab. 1962. Circ. 61,000. Pays on publication. Publishes ms an average of 6 months after acceptance. Buys all rights. Phone queries OK. Query for electronic submissions. Reports in 6 months. Free sample copy and writer's guidelines; mention *Writer's Market* in request.

Nonfiction: "We are interested in material on research and development in microwave and RF technology and economic news that affects the industry." How-to (circuit design), new product, opinion, and technical. Buys 10 mss/year. Query. Pays $100.

OUTSIDE PLANT, P.O. Box 183, Cary IL 60013-0183. (312)639-2200. Fax: (312)639-9542. Editor: John H. Saxtan. 50% freelance written. Prefers to work with published/established writers. Trade publication focusing exclusively on the outside plant segment of the telephone industry. Readers are end users and/or specifiers at Bell and independent operating companies, as well as long distance firms whose chief responsibilities are construction, maintenance, OSP planning and engineering. Readership also includes telephone contracting firms. Publishes an average of 12 issues/year. Estab. 1982. Circ. 18,000. Buys first rights. Pays on publication. Publishes ms an average of 3 months after acceptance. Reports in 2 months.

Nonfiction: Must deal specifically with outside plant construction, maintenance, planning and fleet vehicle subjects for the telephone industry. "Case history application articles profiling specific telephone projects are best. Also accepts trend features, tutorials, industry research and seminar presentations. Preferably, features should be bylined by someone at the telephone company profiled." Pays $35-50/published page, including photographs; pays $35 for cover photos.

Columns/Departments: OSP Tips & Advice (short nuts-and-bolts items on new or unusual work methods); and OSP Tommorrow (significant trends in outside plant), 300-600 word items. Pays $5-50. Other departments include new products, literature, vehicles and fiber optics.

Tips: "Submissions should include author bio demonstrating expertise in the subject area."

PRO SOUND NEWS, International News Magazine for the Professional Sound Production Industry, 2 Park Ave., New York NY 10016. (212)213-3444. Fax: (212)213-3484. Editor: Debra A. Pagan. 20% freelance written. Works with a small number of new/unpublished writers each year. Monthly tabloid covering the music recording, concert sound reinforcement, TV and film sound industry. Circ. 21,000. Pays on publication. Publishes ms an average of 1 month after acceptance. Byline given. Buys first serial rights. Simultaneous queries and previously published submissions OK. Query for electronic submissions. Reprints OK. Reports in 2 weeks.

Nonfiction: Query with published clips. Pays $200-300 for assigned articles (approximately 1,000 words). Sometimes pays the expenses of writers on assignment.

‡RADIO WORLD INTERNATIONAL, Industrial Marketing Advisory Services, Suite 310, 5827 Columbia Pike, Falls Church VA 22041. (703)998-7600. Fax: (703)998-2966. Editor: Alan Carter. Managing Editor: Charles Taylor. 50% freelance written. Monthly trade newspaper for radio broadcasting "covering radio station technology, regulatory news, business and management developments outside the US. Articles should be geared toward engineers, producers and managers." Estab. 1990. Circ. 20,000. Pays on publication. Byline given. Offers 50% kill fee. Buys serial rights. Query for electronic submissions. Reports in 3 weeks. Free sample copy and writer's guidelines.

Nonfiction: New products, technical, regulatory and management news. Programming trend pieces. Buys 100 mss/year. Query with published clips. Length: 750-1,000 words. Pays 20¢/word. Sometimes pays expenses of writers on assignment.

Photos: Send photos with submission. Captions and identification of subjects required. Buys all rights.

Columns/Departments: User reports (field reports from engineers on specific equipment); radio management; and studio/audio issues, 750-1,000 words. Buys 50/year. Query. Pays 20¢/word.

Fillers: Newsbreaks. Buys 50/year. Length: 100-500 words.

Tips: "Our news and feature sections are the best bets for freelancers. Focus on radio station operations and the state of the industry worldwide."

RADIO WORLD NEWSPAPER, Industrial Marketing Advisory Services, Suite 310, 5827 Columbia Pike, Falls Church VA 22041. (703)998-7600. Fax: (703)998-2966. Editor: Lucia Cobo. News Editor: John Gatski. 50% freelance written. Bimonthly newspaper on radio station technology and regulatory news. "Articles should be geared toward radio station engineers, producers, technical people and managers wishing to learn more about technical subjects. The approach should be more how-to than theoretical, although emerging technology may be approached in a more abstract way." Estab. 1976. Pays on publication. Publishes ms an average of 2 months after acceptance. Byline given. Buys first North American serial rights plus right to publish in monthly international and annual directory supplements. Submit seasonal material 2 months in advance. Query for electronic submissions. Reports in 2 months.

Nonfiction: Expose, historical/nostalgic, how-to (radio equipment maintenance and repair), humor, interview/profile, new product, opinion, personal experience, photo feature and technical. "No general financial, or vogue management concept pieces." Buys 24-40 mss/year. Query. Length: 750-1,250 words. Pays $75-200. Pays in contributor copies or other premiums "if they request it, and for one special feature called Workbench." Sometimes pays expenses of writers on assignment.

Photos: Send photos with submission. Reviews 3 × 5 or larger prints. Offers no additional payment for photos accepted with ms. Identification of subjects required. Buys one-time rights.
Columns/Departments: Mary Anne Dorsie, Buyers Guide editor. Buyers Guide User Reports (field reports from engineers on specific pieces of radio station equipment). Buys 100 mss/year. Query. Length: 750-1,250 words. Pays $25-125.
Fillers: Newsbreaks and short humor. Buys 6/year. Length: 500-1,000 words. Pays $25-75.
Tips: "I frequently assign articles by phone. Sometimes just a spark of an idea can lead to a story assignment or publication. The best way is to have some radio station experience and try to think of articles other readers would benefit from reading."

SATELLITE RETAILER, Triple D Publishing, Inc., Dept. WM, P.O. Box 2384, Shelby NC 28151-2384. (704)482-9673. Fax: (704)484-8558. Editor: David B. Melton. 75% freelance written. Monthly magazine covering home satellite TV. "We look for technical, how-to, marketing, sales, new products, product testing, and news for the satellite television dealer." Estab. 1981. Circ. 12,000. Pays on publication. Byline given. Offers 30% kill fee. Buys all rights. Submit seasonal material 3 months in advance. Simultaneous submissions OK. Query for electronic submissions. Reports in 2 months. Free sample copy and writer's guidelines.
Nonfiction: How-to, new product, personal experience, photo feature, technical. Buys 24 mss/year. Query with or without published clips or send complete ms. Length: 1,800-3,600 words. Pays $150-400. Sometimes pays expenses of writers on assignment.
Photos: Send photos with submission. Reviews contact sheets, transparencies (35mm or 4 × 5). Captions, model releases and identification of subjects required. Buys all rights.
Tips: "Familiarity with electronics and television delivery systems is a definite plus."

Energy and Utilities

People who supply power to homes, businesses and industry read the publications in this section. This category includes journals covering the electric power, natural gas, petroleum, solar and alternative energy industries.

ALTERNATIVE ENERGY RETAILER, Zackin Publications, Inc., P.O. Box 2180, Waterbury CT 06722-2180. (203)755-0158. Fax: (203)755-3480. Editorial Director: John Florian. 5% freelance written. Prefers to work with published/established writers. Monthly magazine on selling alternative energy products—chiefly solid fuel and gas-burning appliances. "We seek detailed how-to tips for retailers to improve business. Most freelance material purchased is about retailers and how they succeed." Estab. 1980. Circ. 10,000. Pays on publication. Publishes ms an average of 2 months after acceptance. Buys first North American serial rights. Submit seasonal material 4 months in advance. Reports in 2 weeks on queries. Sample copy for 9 × 12 SAE with 4 first class stamps. Writer's guidelines for #10 SASE.
Nonfiction: How-to (improve retail profits and business know-how) and interview/profile (of successful retailers in this field). No "general business articles not adapted to this industry." Buys 10 mss/year. Query. Length: 1,000 words. Pays $200.
Photos: State availability of photos. Pays $25-125 maximum for 5 × 7 b&w prints. Reviews color transparencies. Identification of subject required. Buys one-time rights.
Tips: "A freelancer can best break in to our publication with features about readers (retailers). Stick to details about what has made this person a success."
  • Submit articles that focus on market trends and successful sales techniques.

ELECTRICAL APPARATUS, The Magazine of the Electromechanical & Electronic Application & Maintenance, Barks Publications, Inc., 400 N. Michigan Ave., Chicago IL 60611-4198. (312)321-9440. Editorial Director: Elsie Dickson. Managing Editor: Kevin N. Jones. Monthly magazine for persons working in electrical and electronic maintenance, chiefly in industrial plants, who install and service electrical motors, transformers, generators, controls and related equipment. Estab. 1967. Circ. 17,000. **Pays on acceptance.** Publishes ms an average of 3 months after acceptance. Byline given. Buys all rights unless other arrangements made. Reports in 1 week on queries; 1 month on mss. *Writer's Market* recommends allowing 2 months for reply. Query for electronic submissions. Sample copy $4.
Nonfiction: Technical. Length: 1,500-2,500. Pays $250-500 for assigned articles plus authorized expenses.
  • Columns are now all staff-written.
Tips: "All feature articles are assigned to staff and contributing editors and correspondents. Professionals interested in appointments as contributing editors and correspondents should submit resume and article outlines, including illustration suggestions. Writers should be competent with a camera, which should be described in resumé. Technical expertise is absolutely necessary, preferably an E.E. degree, or practical experience. We are also book publishers and some of the material in *EA* is now in book form, bringing the authors royalties. Also publishes an annual directory, subtitled *ElectroMechanical Bench Reference.*"

‡NATIONAL PETROLEUM NEWS, 950 Lee St., Des Plaines IL 60016. (708)296-0770. Fax: (708)803-3328. Editor: Don Smith. 3% freelance written. Prefers to work with published/established writers. For businessmen who make their living in the oil marketing industry, either as company employees or through their own business operations. Monthly magazine. Estab. 1909. Circ. 14,000. Rights purchased vary with author and material. Usually buys all rights. Pays on acceptance if done on assignment. Publishes ms an average of 2 months after acceptance. "The occasional freelance copy we use is done on assignment." Query.

Nonfiction: Material related directly to developments and issues in the oil marketing industry and "how-to" and "what-with" case studies. "No unsolicited copy, especially with limited attribution regarding information in story." Buys 3-4 mss/year. Length: 2,000 words maximum. Pays $50-150/printed page. Sometimes pays the expenses of writers on assignment.

Photos: Pays $150/printed page. Payment for b&w photos "depends upon advance understanding."

PIPELINE & UNDERGROUND UTILITIES CONSTRUCTION, Oildom Publishing Co. of Texas, Inc., Box 22267, Houston TX 77027. Editor: Robert Carpenter. 5% freelance written. Prefers to work with published/established writers. Monthly magazine covering oil, gas, water and sewer pipeline construction for contractors and construction workers who build pipelines. Circ. 27,000. No byline given. Not copyrighted. Buys first North American serial rights. Publishes ms an average of 3 months after acceptance. Simultaneous queries OK. Reports in 2 weeks on queries; 3 weeks on mss. *Writer's Market* recommends allowing 2 months for reply. Sample copy $1 for 9×12 SAE.

Nonfiction: How-to. Query with published clips. Length: 1,500-2,500 words. Pays $100/printed page "unless unusual expenses are incurred in getting the story." Sometimes pays the expenses of writers on assignment.

Photos: Send photos with ms. Reviews 5×7 and 8×10 prints. Captions required. Buys one-time rights.

Tips: "We supply guidelines outlining information we need." The most frequent mistake made by writers in completing articles is unfamiliarity with the field.

PUBLIC POWER, Dept. WM, 2301 M St. NW, Washington DC 20037-1484. (202)467-2948. Editor/Publisher: Jeanne Wickline LaBella. 20% freelance written. Prefers to work with published/established writers. Bimonthly. Estab. 1942. **Pays on acceptance.** Publishes ms an average of 3 months after acceptance. Byline given. Query for electronic submissions. Free sample copy and writer's guidelines.

Nonfiction: Features on municipal and other local publicly owned electric systems. Pays 20¢/word on edited ms.

Photos: Uses b&w glossy and color slides.

RELAY MAGAZINE, Florida Municipal Electric Association, P.O. Box 10114, Tallahassee FL 32302-2114. (904)224-3314. Editor: Stephanie Wolanski. 5% freelance written. Monthly trade journal. "Must be electric utility oriented, or must address legislative issues of interest to us." Estab. 1957. Circ. 1,800. Pays on publication. Byline given. Publication not copyrighted. Buys first North American serial, one-time and second serial (reprint) rights. Publishes reprints of previously published articles. Send photocopy of article or typed ms with rights for sale noted. Include information about when and where article previously appeared. Pays 50-75% of the amount paid for an original article. Simultaneous submissions OK. Query for electronic submissions. Reports in 3 months. Free sample copy.

Nonfiction: Interview/profile, technical and electric innovations. No articles that haven't been pre-approved by query. Length: 3-6 pages double spaced. Pays $50.

Photos: State availability of photos with submission. Pay and rights purchased vary. Captions and identification of subjects required.

UTILITY AND TELEPHONE FLEETS, Practical Communications, Inc., 321 Cary Point Dr., P.O. Box 183, Cary IL 60013. (708)639-2200. Fax: (708)639-9542. Editor/Associate Publisher: Alan Richter. 10% freelance written. Magazine published 8 times/year for fleet managers and maintenance supervisors for electric gas and water utilities, telephone, interconnect and cable TV companies, public works departments and related contractors. "We seek case history/application features are also welcome." Circ. 18,000. Pays on publication. Publishes ms an average of 1 month after acceptance. Byline given. Offers 20% kill fee. Buys all rights. Submit seasonal material 2 months in advance. Reports in 2 weeks. Free sample copy and writer's guidelines.

Nonfiction: How-to (ways for performing fleet maintenance/improving management skills/vehicle tutorials), technical, case history/application features. No advertorials in which specific product or company is promoted. Buys 2-3 mss/year. Query with published clips. Length: 1,000-2,800 words. Pays $50/page.

Photos: Send photos with submission. Reviews contact sheets, negatives, transparencies (3×5) and prints (3×5). Offers no additional payment for photos accepted with ms. Captions required. Buys one-time rights.

Columns/Departments: Vehicle mManagement and Maintenance Tips (nuts-and-bolts items dealing with new or unusual methods for fleet management, maintenance and safety). Buys 2 mss/year. Query with published clips. Length: 100-400 words. Pays $25.

Tips: "Working with a utility or telephone company and gathering information about a construction, safety or fleet project is the best approach for a freelancer."

Engineering and Technology

Engineers and professionals with various specialties read the publications in this section. Publications for electrical, electronics and telecommunications engineers are classified separately under Electronics and Communication. Magazines for computer professionals are in the Information Systems section.

AMERICAN MACHINIST, Penton Publishing, Dept. WM, 1100 Superior Ave., Cleveland OH 44114. (216)696-7000. Editor: George Weimer. Monthly magazine about durable-goods manufacturing. Circ. 82,000. **Pays on acceptance.** Publishes ms an average of 4 months after acceptance. Sometimes byline given. Makes work-for-hire assignments. Query for electronic submissions. Reports in 2 months on queries; 3 months on mss. Free sample copy for SASE.
Nonfiction: Technical. Query with or without published clips or send complete ms. Length: 1,500-4,000 words. Pays $300-1,500. Pays the expenses of writers on assignment.
Photos: Send photos with submission. Offers no additional payment for photos accepted with ms. Buys all rights.
Tips: "Articles that are published are probably 85% engineering details. We're interested in feature articles on technology of manufacturing in the metalworking industries (automaking, aircraft, machinery, etc.). Aim at instructing a 45-year-old degreed mechanical engineer in a new method of making, say, a pump housing."

GRADUATING ENGINEER, Peterson's/COG Publishing, Dept. WM, Suite 560, 16030 Ventura Blvd., Encino CA 91436. (818)789-5371. Editor-in-Chief: Charlotte Chandler Thomas. 90% freelance written. Prefers to work with published/established writers. Magazine published September-March "to help graduating engineers make the transition from campus to the working world." Estab. 1979. Circ. 83,000. Pays 30 days after acceptance. Publishes ms an average of 2 months after acceptance. Byline given. Buys first North American serial rights. Publishes reprints of previously published articles. Send tearsheet or photocopy of article, or typed ms with rights for sale noted. Include information about when and where the article previously appeared. Writer's guidelines available.
Nonfiction: General interest (on management, human resources), career entry, interpersonal skills, job markets, careers and career trends. Special issues: Minority, Women and High Technology. Buys 100 mss/year. Query. Length: 2,000-3,000 words. Pays $300-700.
  • Graduating Engineer is using fewer freelance writers, and more inhouse.
Photos: State availability of photos, illustrations or charts. Reviews 35mm color transparencies, 8×10 b&w glossy prints. Captions and model release required.
Tips: "We're generating new types of editorial. We closely monitor economy here and abroad so that our editorial reflects economic, social and global trends."

HIGH TECHNOLOGY CAREERS, %Writers Connection, Suite 103, 275 Saratoga Ave., Santa Clara CA 95050-6664. (408)554-2090. Fax: (408)554-2099. Managing Editor: Meera Lester. 100% freelance written. Magazine published every six weeks focusing on high technology industries. "Articles must have a high technology tie-in and should be written in a positive and lively manner. The audience includes managers, engineers and other professionals working in the high technology industries." Circ. 348,000. Pays on publication. Publishes ms an average of 3 months after acceptance. Byline given. Offers 25% kill fee. Buys all rights. Query for electronic submissions. Reports in 2 months. Reprints OK; send tearsheet of article and information about when and where the article previously appeared. Payment individually negotiated. Sample copy for 9×12 SAE with $4 in stamps. Writer's guidelines for #10 SASE.
Nonfiction: General interest (with high-tech tie-in), technical. Publishes five regular 800-word columns (career-oriented) and two 1,200-word features each issue. Buys 50-60 mss/year. Query with or without published clips or send complete ms. Length: 1,000-1,200 words. Pays 17½¢/word. Sometimes pays expenses of writers on assignment.
Photos: State availability of photos with submission.

‡MACHINE DESIGN, Penton Publishing Inc., 1100 Superior Ave., Cleveland OH 44114-2543. (216)696-7000. Fax: (216)621-8469. Editor: Ronald Khol. Executive Editor: Lee Teschler. 1-2% freelance written. Works with a small number of new/unpublished writers each year. A bimonthly magazine covering technical developments in products or purchases of interest to the engineering community. Estab. 1929. Circ. 180,000. Pays on publication. Publishes ms an average of 2 months after acceptance. Byline given. Buys first rights. Reports in 2 months. Free sample copy.

Nonfiction: General interest; how-to (on using new equipment or processes); and new product. No non-technical submissions. Buys 10-15 mss/year. Query. Length and payment for articles must be negotiated in advance. Sometimes pays the expenses of writers on assignment.

  • *Machine Design* is currently working only with freelancers from Europe and the Far East; they are meeting domestic needs with their staff.

Photos: State availability of photos with submission. Offers negotiable payment. Captions, model releases, and identification of subjects required.

Columns/Departments: Design International (international news), captions; Backtalk (technical humor); and Personal Computers in Engineering (use of personal computers), both have negotiable word length. Buys 50-200 items/year. Query. Pays $20 minimum.

Tips: "The departments of our publication most open to freelancers are Back Talk, News Trends and Design International. Those without technical experience almost never send in adequate material."

MECHANICAL ENGINEERING, American Society of Mechanical Engineers, Dept. WM, 345 E. 47th St., New York NY 10017. (212)705-7782. Editor: Jay O'Leary. Managing Editor: John Falcioni. 30% freelance written. Monthly magazine on mechanical process and design. "We publish general interest articles for graduate mechanical engineers on high-tech topics." Circ. 135,000. **Pays on acceptance.** Sometimes byline given. Kill fee varies. Buys first rights. Submit seasonal material 4 months in advance. Reports in 6 weeks. Free writer's guidelines.

Nonfiction: Historical, interview/profile, new product, photo feature and technical. Buys 25 mss/year. Query with or without published clips or send complete ms. Length: 1,500-3,500 words. Pays $500-1,500.

Photos: Send photos with submission. Reviews transparencies and prints. Offers no additional payment for photos accepted with ms. Captions and identification of subjects required. Buys one-time rights.

MINORITY ENGINEER, An Equal Opportunity Career Publication for Professional and Graduating Minority Engineers, Equal Opportunity Publications, Inc., Suite 420, 150 Motor Parkway, Hauppauge NY 11788-5145. (516)273-0066. Fax: (516)273-8936. Executive Editor: James Schneider. 60% freelance written. Prefers to work with published/established writers. Quarterly magazine covering career guidance for minority engineering students and professional minority engineers. Estab. 1969. Circ. 16,000. Pays on publication. Publishes ms an average of 6 months after acceptance. Byline given. Buys first rights. "Deadline dates: fall, June 1; winter, September 15; spring, January 15; April/May, March 1." Simultaneous and previously published submissions OK. Sample copy and writer's guidelines for 9 × 12 SAE with 5 first class stamps.

Nonfiction: Book excerpts; articles (on job search techniques, role models); general interest (on specific minority engineering concerns); how-to (land a job, keep a job, etc.); interview/profile (minority engineer role models); new product (new career opportunities); opinion (problems of ethnic minorities); personal experience (student and career experiences); and technical (on career fields offering opportunities for minority engineers). "We're interested in articles dealing with career guidance and job opportunities for minority engineers." Query or send complete ms. Length: 1,000-1,500 words. Sometimes pays the expenses of writers on assignment. Pays 10¢/word.

Photos: Prefers 35mm color slides but will accept b&w. Captions and identification of subjects required. Buys all rights. Pays $15. Cartoons accepted. Pays $25.

Tips: "Articles should focus on career guidance, role model and industry prospects for minority engineers. Prefer articles related to careers, not politically or socially sensitive."

NATIONAL DEFENSE, American Defense Preparedness Association, Dept. WM, 2101 Wilson Blvd., Arlington VA 22201-3061. (703)522-1820. Fax: (703)522-1885. Editor: Robert Williams. Managing Editor: Vincent P. Grimes. Magazine published 10 times/year covering all facets of the North American defense industrial base. "Interest is on articles offering a sound analysis of new and ongoing patterns in procurement, research and development of new technology, and budgeting trends." Estab. 1920. Circ. 40,000. Pays on publication. Byline given. Buys all rights. Requires electronic submission. Reports in 1 month on queries. Free sample copy and writer's guidelines for SASE.

Nonfiction: Feature and photos. Buys 12-15 mss/year. Query first. Length: 1,500-2,000 words. Pays negotiated fees, up to $1,000. Pays expenses of writers on assignment "with prior arrangement."

Photos: Send photos with submission. Reviews contact sheets, negatives, transparencies and prints. Offers no additional payment for photos accepted with ms. Captions required. Buys all rights.

WOMAN ENGINEER, An Equal Opportunity Career Publication for Graduating Women and Experienced Professionals, Equal Opportunity Publications, Inc., Suite 420, 150 Motor Parkway, Hauppauge NY 11788-5145. (516)273-8743. Fax: (516)273-8936. Editor: Anne Kelly. 60% freelance written. Works with a small number of new/unpublished writers each year. Magazine published 4 times/year (fall, winter, spring, April/May) covering career guidance for women engineering students and professional women engineers. Estab. 1968. Circ. 16,000. Pays on publication. Publishes ms an average of 3-12 months after acceptance. Byline given. Buys First North American serial rights. Reports in 2 months. Free sample copy and writer's guidelines.

Nonfiction: "Interested in articles dealing with career guidance and job opportunities for women engineers. Looking for manuscripts showing how to land an engineering position and advance professionally. Wants features on job-search techniques, engineering disciplines offering career opportunities to women; companies with career advancement opportunities for women; problems facing women engineers and how to cope with such problems; and role-model profiles of successful women engineers, especially in government, military and defense-related industries." Query. Length: 1,000-2,500 words. Pays 10¢/word.

Photos: Prefers color slides but will accept b&w. Captions and identification of subjects required. Buys all rights. Pays $15.

Tips: "We will be looking for shorter manuscripts (800-1,000 words) on job-search techniques and first-person 'Personal Perspective.' "

Entertainment and the Arts

The business of the entertainment/amusement industry in arts, film, dance, theater, etc. is covered by these publications. Journals that focus on the people and equipment of various music specialties are listed in the Music section, while art and design business publications can be found in Art, Design and Collectibles. Entertainment publications for the general public can be found in the Consumer Entertainment section.

‡**AMUSEMENT BUSINESS**, Billboard Publications, Inc., P.O. Box 24970, Nashville TN 37202. (615)321-4269. Fax: (615)327-1575. Managing Editor: Lisa Zhito. 25% freelance written. Works with a small number of new/unpublished writers each year. Weekly tabloid emphasizing hard news of the amusement, sports business, and mass entertainment industry for top management. Circ. 15,000. Pays on publication. Publishes ms an average of 3 weeks after acceptance. Byline sometimes given; "it depends on the quality of the individual piece." Buys all rights. Submit seasonal/holiday material 3 weeks in advance. Phone queries OK. Sample copy for 11 × 14 SAE with 5 first class stamps.

Nonfiction: How-to (case history of successful advertising campaigns and promotions); interviews (with leaders in the areas we cover highlighting appropriate problems and issues of today, i.e. insurance, alcohol control, etc.). Likes lots of financial support data: grosses, profits, operating budgets and per-cap spending. Also needs lots of quotes. No personality pieces or interviews with stage stars. Publishes profiles of key industry leaders, but must be well-known within the entertainment industry. Buys 500-1,000 mss/year. Query. Length: 400-700 words.

Photos: State availability of photos with query. Captions and model release required. Buys all rights.

Columns/Departments: Auditorium Arenas; Fairs, Parks & Attractions; Food Concessions; Merchandise; Promotion; Shows (carnival and circus); Talent & touring; Management Changes; Sports; Profile; Eye On Legislation; Commentary and International News.

Tips: There will be more and more emphasis on financial reporting of areas covered. "Submission must contain the whys and whos, etc. and be strong enough that others in the same field will learn from it and not find it naive. We will be increasing story count while decreasing story length."

BILLBOARD, The International News Weekly of Music and Home Entertainment, Dept. WM, 1515 Broadway, New York NY 10036. (212)764-7300; or 5055 Wilshire Blvd., Beverly Hills CA 90036. (213)273-7040. Editor-in-Chief: Timothy White. L.A. Bureau Chief: Craig Rosen. Weekly music magazine. Pays on publication. Buys all rights.

Nonfiction: "Correspondents are appointed to send in spot amusement news covering phonograph record programming by broadcasters and record merchandising by retail dealers." Concert reviews, interviews with artists, and stories on video software (both rental and merchandising).

BOXOFFICE MAGAZINE, RLD Publishing Corp., Suite 100, 6640 Sunset Blvd., Hollywood CA 90028-7159. (213)465-1186. Fax: (213)465-5049. Editor: Harley W. Lond. 5% freelance written. Monthly business magazine about the motion picture industry for members of the film industry: theater owners, film producers, directors, financiers and allied industries. Estab. 1920. Circ. 10,000. Pays on publication. Publishes ms an average of 2-4 months after acceptance. Byline given. Buys one-time rights. Submit seasonal material 2 months in advance. Simultaneous and previously published submissions OK. Reprints OK; send tearsheet or photocopy of article and typed ms with rights for sale noted. Include information about when and where the article previously appeared. Pays 100% of their fee for original article. Reports in 3 months. Sample copy for 9 × 12 SAE with 6 first class stamps.

Nonfiction: Investigative, interview, profile, new product, photo feature and technical. "We are a general news magazine about the motion picture industry and are looking for stories about trends, developments, problems or opportunities facing the industry. Almost any story will be considered, including corporate profiles, but we don't want gossip or celebrity stuff." Query with published clips. Length: 1,500-2,500 words. Pays $100-150.

Photos: State availability of photos. Pays $10 maximum for 8×10 b&w prints. Captions required.

Tips: "Request a sample copy, indicating you read about *Boxoffice* in *Writer's Market*. Write a clear, comprehensive outline of the proposed story and enclose a resume and clip samples. We welcome new writers but don't want to be a classroom. Know how to write. We look for 'investigative' articles."

‡CALLBOARD, Monthly Theatre Trade Magazine, Theatre Bay Area, #402, 657 Mission St., San Francisco CA 94105. (415)957-1557. Editor: Belinda Taylor. 50% freelance written. Monthly magazine for theater. "We publish news, views, essays and features on the Northern California theater industry. We also include listings and job resources." Estab. 1976. Circ. 10,000. Pays on publication. Publishes ms an average of 3-4 months after acceptance. Byline given. Offers 50% kill fee. Buys first rights. Editorial lead time 1 month. Submit seasonal material 2 months in advance. Accepts simultaneous and previously published submissions. Query for electronic submissions. Reports in 1 month on queries. Sample copy $4.75.

Nonfiction: Book excerpts, essays, opinion, personal experience and technical (theater topics only). *No profiles of actors.* Buys 12-15 mss/year. Query with published clips. Length: 800-2,000 words. Pays $75 minimum for assigned articles. Pays other for unsolicited articles. Sometimes pays expenses of writers on assignment (phone calls and some travel).

Photos: State availability of photos with submission. Reviews contact sheets or 5×7 prints. Offers no additional payment for photos accepted with ms. Identification of subjects required. Buys one-time rights.

THE ELECTRIC WEENIE, Dept. WM, Box 2715, Quincy MA 02269. (617)749-6900 ext. 248. Fax: (617)749-3691. Publisher: Jerry Ellis. Editor: Paula Williams. Monthly magazine covering "primarily radio, for 'personalities' worldwide (however, mostly English speaking). We mail flyers mainly to radio people, but obviously no one is excepted if he/she wants a monthly supply of first-rate gags, one liners, zappers, etc." Estab. 1970. Circ. 800. Sample copy and writer's guidelines for #10 SASE.

Fillers: Jokes, gags, short humor, one liners, etc. "Short is the bottom line; if it's over two sentences, it's too long." Uses 300/month. Pays $2/gag used — higher price paid for quality material.

• *The Electric Weenie* is not accepting material at this time.

FUNWORLD, International Association of Amusement Parks & Attractions, 1448 Duke St., Alexandria VA 22314-3464. (703)836-4800. Fax: (703)836-4801. Editor: Rick Henderson. 50% freelance written. Monthly trade journal covering the amusement park industry. "Articles should be written for amusement park executives, not the public." Estab. 1986. Circ. 6,200. Pays on publication. Publishes ms an average of 2 months after acceptance. Byline given. Offers 30% kill fee. Buys all rights. Submit seasonal material 4 months in advance. Query for electronic submissions. Reports in 2 months on queries. Reprints OK; send typed ms with information about rights for sale and when and where the article previously appeared. Pays 20% of their fee for an original article. Sample copy $2.50. Free writer's guidelines.

Nonfiction: How-to, interview/profile, photo feature and technical. "No articles about industry suppliers." Buys 20 mss/year. Query with published clips. Length: 750-2,500 words. Pays $150-500 for assigned articles; $100-400 for unsolicited articles. Sometimes pays expenses of writers on assignment.

Photos: State availability of photos with submission or send photos with submission. Reviews 3×5 prints. Captions, model releases and identification of subjects required. Buys one-time rights.

Tips: "Writers should visit a small- to medium-sized park in their area and look for unique features or management styles that other park managers might like to read about. We want less fluff, more substance."

THE HOLLYWOOD REPORTER, 5055 Wilshire Blvd., Los Angeles CA 90036-4396. (213)469-8770. Fax: (213)525-2377. Publisher and Editor-in-Chief: Robert J. Dowling. Executive Editor: Alex Ben Block. Editor of Special Issues: Randall Tierney. 25% freelance written. Daily entertainment trade publication emphasizing in-depth analysis and news coverage of creative and business aspects of film, TV, theater and music production. Estab. 1930. Circ. 23,000. Publishes ms an average of 1 week after acceptance for daily; 1 month for special issues. Send queries first.

Tips: "Short articles fit our format best. The most frequent mistake made by writers in completing an article for us is that they are not familiar with our publication. We are a business publication; we don't want celebrity gossip."

‡LOCATION UPDATE, Suite 612, 6922 Hollywood Blvd., Hollywood CA 90028. (213)461-8887. Fax: (213)469-3711. Editor: Manley Witten. Monthly entertainment industry magazine covering all aspects of filming on location. "*Location Update* communicates the issues, trends, problems, solutions and business matters that affect productions working on location. Features include interviews with industry professionals, controversial issues, regional spotlights, hard-to-find or difficult locations, etc. Audience is made up of producers, directors, production managers, location managers — any person who works on location for film, TV, commercials and videos." Estab. 1985. Circ. 30,000. Pays on publication. Publishes ms an average of 2 months after acceptance. Byline given. Offers 25% kill fee.

Photos: State availability of photos with submission. Reviews contact sheets, 35mm, 2¼ × 2¼ transparencies and 8 × 10 prints. Offers no additional payment for photos accepted with ms. Identification of subjects required. Buys one-time rights.

Columns/Departments: Locations (hard to find or difficult locations and how to use them), 500-1,000 words; Supporting Roles (support services used on location: security companies, catering, etc.), 500-1,000 words; Newsreel (short news briefs on location-related issues), 250 words. Buys 25-30 mss/year. Query with published clips. Pays $25-100.

Tips: "The best way to break in is to query with story ideas and to be familiar with film, TV, video and commercials. Know the workings of the entertainment industry and the roles of producers, directors and location managers. Articles about locations are most open to freelance writers. Everything is a possible location for productions. Every state has a film commission that can help with who is where and how to go about using particular locations."

‡**MODEL & PERFORMER**, Aquino Productions, P.O. Box 15760, Stamford CT 06901. (203)967-9952. Editor: Andres Aquino. 40% freelance written. Monthly magazine on fashion modeling, entertainment (video, film). *"Model & Performer* covers the business of entertainment and fashion, including: performers, entertainers, dancers, actors, models, celebrities, agents, producers and managers, photographers; casting, TV, film, video, theater and show productions; plus creative support, stage facilities, services and products to the entertainment and fashion industries, trade shows and exhibits." Estab. 1991. Circ. 100,000. Pays on publication. Publishes ms an average of 2 months after acceptance. Byline given sometimes. Offers 50% kill fee. Buys first North American serial rights or all rights. Editorial lead time 3 months. Submit seasonal material 3 months in advance. Accepts simultaneous submissions. Reports in 6 weeks on queries; 2 months on mss. Sample copy $4. Writer's guidelines for 9 × 12 SAE with 6 first class stamps.

Nonfiction: General interest, how-to, interview/profile, photo feature and travel. Buys 24 mss/year. Send complete ms. Length: 300-1,500 words. Pays 10¢/word minimum for unsolicited articles.

Photos: Send photos with submission. Reviews 2 × 2 transparencies and 8 × 10 prints. Offers $10-25/photo. Captions, model release and identification of subjects required. Buys one-time rights or all rights.

Columns/Departments: Pays $25-50.

Tips: "Covers how-to articles: how to succeed in film, video, modeling. How to break into any aspect of the fashion and entertainment industries. Be specific. Send $4 for a sample and specific guidelines. Know the content of *Model & Performer.* We are most open to interviews with celebrities (with photos), and how-to articles."

STRIPPER MAGAZINE, Magazine for Exotic Dancing Industry, Dept. WM, Suite 140, 981 1st Ave., New York NY 10022. (212)832-2828. Fax: (212)832-4242. Managing Editor: Duncan Dexter. 75% freelance written. Magazine published 8 times/year covering the exotic dance industry. Estab. 1988. Circ. 20,000. Pays on publication. Publishes ms an average of 1 month after acceptance. Byline given. Offers 50% kill fee. Buys all rights. Submit seasonal material 3 months in advance. Simultaneous and previously published submissions OK. Query for electronic submissions. Reports in 1 month. Sample copy $5.

Nonfiction: Book excerpts, essays, expose, general interest, historical/nostalgic, how-to, humor, inspirational, interview/profile, new product, opinion, personal experience, photo feature, technical and travel (all related to exotic dancing). Buys 20 mss/year. Query. Length: 750-2,000 words. Pays 10¢/word. Pays in contributor copies or other premiums if requested. Pays expenses of writers on assignment.

Photos: State availability of photos with submission. Reviews contact sheets. Payment is "flexible." Model releases and identification of subjects required. Buys all rights.

‡**TOURIST ATTRACTIONS & PARKS MAGAZINE**, Kane Communications, Inc., Suite 210, 7000 Terminal Square, Upper Darby PA 19082. (215)734-2420. Fax: (215)734-2423. Editor: Sandy Meschkow. Magazine published 7 times/year covering mass entertainment and leisure facilities emphasizing management articles. Circ. 26,000. Reports in 3 weeks. Sample copy for 9 × 12 SAE with 6 first class stamps.

Nonfiction: Interview/profile and new product. Buys 10 mss/year. Query. Length: 1,000-2,500 words. Pays $50-250 for assigned articles; sometimes payment arranged individually with publisher. Sometimes pays expenses of writers on assignment.

Photos: State availability of photos with submission. Captions and model releases required.

Tips: "Inquire about covering trade shows for us, such as C.M.A."

Farm

The successful farm writer focuses on the business side of farming. For technical articles, editors feel writers should have a farm background or agricultural training, but there are opportunities for the general freelancer too. The following farm publications are divided into seven categories, each specializing in a different aspect of farming: agricultural equipment; crops and soil management; dairy farming; livestock; management; miscellaneous and regional.

Agricultural Equipment

CUSTOM APPLICATOR, Little Publications, Suite 540, 6263 Poplar Ave., Memphis TN 38119. (901)767-4020. Fax: (901)767-4026. Managing Editor: Henry Gantz. 50% freelance written. Works with a small number of new/unpublished writers each year. For "firms that sell and custom apply agricultural fertilizer and chemicals." Estab. 1957. Circ. 16,100. Pays on publication. Publishes ms an average of 2 months after acceptance. Buys all rights. Free sample copy and writer's guidelines.
Nonfiction: "We are looking for articles on custom application firms telling others how to better perform jobs of chemical application, develop new customers, handle credit, etc. Lack of a good idea or usable information will bring a rejection. Query is best. The editor can help you develop the story line regarding our specific needs." Length: 1,000-1,200 words "with 3 or 4 b&w glossy prints." Pays 20¢/word.
Photos: Accepts b&w glossy prints. "We will look at color slides for possible cover or inside use."
Tips: "We don't get enough shorter articles, so one that is well-written and informative could catch our eyes. Our readers want pragmatic information to help them run a more efficient business; they can't get that through a story filled with generalities."

Crops and Soil Management

ONION WORLD, Columbia Publishing, 2809A Fruitvale Blvd., P.O. Box 1467, Yakima WA 98907-1467. (509)248-2452. Fax: (509)248-4056. Editor: D. Brent Clement. 90% freelance written. Monthly magazine covering "the world of onion production and marketing" for onion growers and shippers. Estab. 1985. Circ. 5,500. Pays on publication. Publishes ms an average of 1 month after acceptance. Byline given. Not copyrighted. Buys first North American serial rights. Submit seasonal material 1 month in advance. Simultaneous submissions OK. Reports in 1 month. Reprints OK; send information about when and where the article previously appeared. Pays 50% of their fee for an original article. Sample copy for 9 × 12 SAE with 5 first class stamps.
Nonfiction: General interest, historical/nostalgic and interview/profile. Buys 60 mss/year. Query. Length: 1,200-1,500 words. Pays $75-150 for assigned articles.
Photos: Send photos with submission. Offers no additional payment for photos accepted with ms unless it's a cover shot. Captions and identification of subjects required. Buys all rights.
Tips: "Writers should be familiar with growing and marketing onions. We use a lot of feature stories on growers, shippers and others in the onion trade—what they are doing, their problems, solutions, marketing plans, etc."

SOYBEAN DIGEST, P.O. Box 411007, St. Louis MO 63141-1007. (314)576-2788. Fax: (314)576-2786. Editor: Gregg Hillyer. 75% freelance written. Works with a small number of new/unpublished writers each year. Monthly magazine (semi-monthly in February and March; bimonthly in May/June and August/September) emphasizing soybean production and marketing. Estab. 1940. Circ. 230,000. **Pays on acceptance.** Buys all rights. Byline given. Phone queries OK. Submit seasonal material 2 months in advance. Query for electronic submissions. Reports in 3 weeks. Sample copy $3; mention *Writer's Market* in request. Free writer's guidelines.
Nonfiction: How-to (soybean production and marketing) and new product (soybean production and marketing). Buys 100 mss/year. Query or submit complete ms. Length: 1,000 words. Pays $50-350. Sometimes pays the expenses of writers on assignment.
Photos: State availability of photos with query. Pays $25-100 for 5 × 7 or 8 × 10 b&w prints, $50-350 for 35mm color transparencies, and up to $600 for covers. Captions and/or ms required. Buys all rights.

Dairy Farming

BUTTER-FAT, Agrifoods International Cooperative Ltd., P.O. Box 9100, Vancouver, British Columbia V6B 4G4 Canada. (604)420-6611. Publications Editor: Grace Chadsey. Managing Editor: Carol A. Paulson. Eager to work with new/unpublished writers. 20% freelance written. Quarterly magazine emphasizing this dairy cooperative's processing and marketing operations for dairy farmers and dairy workers in British Columbia. Estab. 1923. Circ. 1,750. **Pays on acceptance.** Publishes ms an average of 8 months after acceptance. Byline given. Buys first rights and makes work-for-hire assignments. Phone queries preferred. Submit seasonal material 4 months in advance. Simultaneous and previously published submissions OK; send tearsheet of article and information about when and where the article previously appeared. For reprints, pays 50% of the amount paid for an original article. Reports in 1 week on queries; 2 months on mss. Free sample copy.

Nonfiction: Interview (character profile with industry leaders); British Columbian nostalgia; opinion (of industry leaders); and profile (of association members and employees).

Photos: Reviews 5×7 b&w negatives and contact sheets and color photos. Offers $10/published photo. Captions required. Buys all rights.

Columns/Departments: "We want articles on the people, products, business of producing, processing and marketing dairy foods in this province." Query first. Buys 2 mss/year. Length: approx. 1,000 words. Pays 7¢/word.

Fillers: Jokes, short humor, quotes, cartoons. Buys 5 mss/year. Pays $15.

Tips: "Make an appointment to come by and see us!"

THE DAIRYMAN, Dept. WM, P.O. Box 819, Corona CA 91718-0819. (714)735-2730. Fax: (714)735-2460. Editor: Dennis Halladay. 10% freelance written. Prefers to work with published/established writers. Monthly magazine dealing with large herd commercial dairy industry. Estab. 1922. Circ. 19,000. Pays on acceptance or publication. Publishes ms an average of 2-3 months after acceptance. Byline given. Buys first North American serial rights. Submit seasonal material 3 months in advance. Reprints OK: send information about when and where the article previously appeared. Pays 50% of their fee for an original article. Reports in 1 month. Sample copy for 9×12 SAE with 4 first class stamps.

Nonfiction: Humor, interview/profile, new product, opinion and industry analysis. Special issues: Computers (February); Herd Health (August); Feeds and Feeding (May); and Barns and Equipment (November). "No religion, nostalgia, politics or 'mom and pop' dairies." Query or send complete ms. Length: 300-5,000 words. Pays $100-300.

Photos: Send photos with query or ms. Reviews b&w contact sheets and 35mm or 2¼×2¼ transparencies. Pays $25 for b&w; $50-100 for color. Captions and identification of subjects required. Buys one-time rights.

● Photos are now a more critical part of story packages.

Tips: "Pretend you're an editor for a moment; would you want to buy a story without any artwork? Neither would I. Writers often don't know modern commercial dairying and they forget they're writing for an audience of *dairymen*. Publications are becoming more and more specialized. You've really got to know who you're writing for and why they're different."

Livestock

BEEF, The Webb Division, Intertec Publishing Corporation, 7900 International Dr., Minneapolis MN 55425-1563. (612)851-4668. Fax: (612)851-4600. Editor-in-Chief: Paul D. Andre. Managing Editor: Joe Roybal. 5% freelance written. Prefers to work with published/established writers. Monthly magazine for readers who have the same basic interest—making a living feeding cattle or running a cow herd. Estab. 1964. Circ. 107,000. **Pays on acceptance.** Publishes ms an'average of 4 months after acceptance. Buys all rights. Byline given. Submit seasonal material 3 months in advance. Reports in 2 months.

Nonfiction: How-to and informational articles on doing a better job of producing, feeding cattle, market building, managing and animal health practices. Material must deal with beef cattle only. Buys 8-10 mss/year. Query. Length: 500-2,000 words. Pays $25-300. Sometimes pays the expenses of writers on assignment. Articles and photos returned only if accompanied by SASE.

Photos: Black and white glossies (8×10) and color transparencies (35mm or 2¼×2¼) purchased with or without mss. Query or send contact sheet, captions and/or transparencies. Pays $10-50 for b&w; $25-100 for color. Model release required.

Tips: "Be completely knowledgeable about cattle feeding and cowherd operations. Know what makes a story. We want specifics, not a general roundup of an operation. Pick one angle and develop it fully. The most frequent mistake is not following instructions on an angle (or angles) to be developed."

‡THE BRAHMAN JOURNAL, Sagebrush Publishing Co., Inc., P.O. Box 220, Eddy TX 76524-0220. (817)859-5451. Editor: Joe Ed Brockett. 10% freelance written. Monthly magazine covering Brahman cattle. Estab. 1971. Circ. 6,000. Pays on publication. Publishes ms an average of 2 months after acceptance. Byline given. Not copyrighted. Buys first North American serial, one-time and second serial (reprint) rights or makes work-for-hire assignments. Submit seasonal/holiday material 3 months in advance. Previously published submissions OK; send typed ms with rights for sale noted. For reprints, pays 50% of the amount paid for an original article. Sample copy for 9×12 SAE with 5 first class stamps.

Nonfiction: General interest, historical/nostalgic and interview/profile. Special issues: Herd Bull (July) and Texas (October). Buys 3-4 mss/year. Query with published clips. Length: 1,200-3,000 words. Pays $100-250 for assigned articles.

Photos: Photos needed for article purchase. Send photos with submission. Reviews 4×5 prints. Offers no additional payment for photos accepted with ms. Captions required. Buys one-time rights.

FARM POND HARVEST, Dedicated to successful farm pond planning, construction, management and harvesting, Professional Sportsman's Publishing Company, 1390 N. 14500E Rd., Momence IL 60954-9420. (815)472-2686. Editor: Vic Johnson. Managing Editor: Joan Munyon. 75% freelance written. Quarterly magazine for fisheries. "Mainly informational for pond owners—we have many biologists, university libraries and government agencies on our subscription list." Estab. 1967. Pays on publication. Publishes ms an average of 1-3 months after acceptance. Byline given. Not copyrighted. Buys first rights or second serial (reprint) rights. Submit seasonal material 2 months in advance. Simultaneous and previously published submissions OK; send tearsheet, photocopy of article or typed ms with rights for sale noted and information about when and where the article previously appeared. Reports in 1 month. Sample copy for 9 × 12 SAE with 3 first class stamps.

Nonfiction: How-to (fisheries), personal experience, photo feature and technical. Buys 25 mss/year. Query with or without published clips or send complete ms. Length: 1,300-2,500 words. Pays $50-125 for assigned articles. Sometimes pays in free advertisement.

Photos: State availability of photos with submission. Reviews negatives and 5 × 7 prints. Usually offers no additional payment for photos accepted with ms, but sometimes pays $5 per photo. Buys one-time rights.

Columns/Departments: What's New (products—news bulletins—magazines—fishery field); Media Net (information pertaining to products/conventions, etc.); Ask Al (answers to questions from readers); and Cutting Bait (subscriber information). Buys 12 mss/year. Send complete ms.

Tips: Most open to freelancers are "how-to on planning, construction, management, fishing in farm ponds or small lakes. Personal experiences—some light-humorous articles accepted; also seasonal stories, winter, spring, summer or fall."

‡THE LAND, Minnesota's Ag Publication, Free Press Co., P.O. Box 3169, Mankato MN 56002. Editor: Randy Frahm. 50% freelance written. Weekly tabloid covering Minnesota agriculture. "We are interested in articles on farming in Minnesota. Although we're not tightly focused on any one type of farming, our articles must be of interest to farmers. In other words, will your article topic have an impact on people who live and work in rural areas?" Estab. 1976. Circ. 40,000. **Pays on acceptance.** Publishes ms an average of 3 months after acceptance. Byline given. Buys first North American serial rights. Editorial lead time 1 month. Submit seasonal material 2 months in advance. Reports in 3 weeks on queries; 2 months on mss. Sample copy free on request. Writer's guidelines for #10 SASE.

Nonfiction: General interest (Ag), how-to, interview/profile, personal experience and technical. Buys 15-40 mss/year. Query. Length: 500-1,500 words. Pays $25 minimum for assigned articles. Pays expenses of writers on assignment.

Photos: State availability of photos with submission. Reviews contact sheets. Negotiates payment individually. Buys one-time rights.

Tips: "Be enthused about rural Minnesota life and agriculture and be willing to work with our editors. We try to stress relevance." Most open to feature articles.

LLAMAS MAGAZINE, The International Camelid Journal, Clay Press, Inc., P.O. Box 100, Herald CA 95638. (209)223-0469. Fax: (209)223-0466. Editor: Cheryl Dal Porto. Magazine published 8 times per year covering llamas, alpacas, camels, vicunas and guanacos. Estab. 1979. Circ. 5,500. **Pays on acceptance.** Publishes ms an average of 4 months after acceptance. Byline given. Buys first rights, second serial (reprint) rights and makes work-for-hire assignments. Submit seasonal material 6 months in advance. Reports in 1 month. Reprints OK; send tearsheet of article and information about when and where the article previously appeared. Pays 50% of their fee for an original article. Free sample copy. Writer's guidelines for 8½ × 11 SAE with $2.90 postage.

Nonfiction: How-to (on anything related to raising llamas), humor, interview/profile, opinion, personal experience, photo feature and travel (to countries where there are camelids). "All articles must have a tie-in to one of the camelid species." Buys 30 mss/year. Query with published clips. Length: 1,000-5,000 words. Pays $50-300 for assigned articles; pays $50-150 for unsolicited articles. May pay new writers with contributor copies. Sometimes pays the expenses of writers on assignment.

Photos: State availability of photos or send photos with submission. Reviews transparencies and 5 × 7 prints. Offers $25-100/photo. Captions, model releases and identification of subjects required. Buys one-time rights.

Fillers: Anecdotes, gags and short humor. Buys 25/year. Length: 100-500 words. Pays $25-50.

Tips: "Get to know the llama folk in your area and query us with an idea. We are open to any and all ideas involving llamas, alpacas and the rest of the camelids. We are always looking for good photos. You must know about camelids to write for us."

NATIONAL CATTLEMEN, National Cattlemen's Association, 5420 S. Quebec St., Englewood CO 80111-1904. (303)694-0305. Editor: Scott R. Cooper. 15% freelance written. Monthly trade journal on the beef-cattle industry. "We deal extensively with animal health, price outlook, consumer demand for beef, costs of production, emerging technologies, developing export markets, marketing and risk management." Estab. 1898. Circ. 35,000. Pays on publication. Byline given. "Buys one-time rights but requires non-compete agreements." Sample copy for 9 × 12 SAE.

Nonfiction: How-to (cut costs of production, risk management strategies), new product (emerging technologies), opinion, and technical (emerging technologies, animal health, price outlook). Buys 20 mss/year. Query with published clips. Length: 1,300-1,500 words. Sidebars encouraged. Pays $300-400 for assigned articles.

• Buying more articles than last year.

Photos: Send photos with submission. Reviews negatives and transparencies. Identification of subjects required.

NATIONAL WOOL GROWER, American Sheep Industry Association, Inc., 6911 S. Yosemite St., Englewood CO 80112-1414. (303)771-3500. Editor: Janice Grauberger. 20% freelance written. Monthly trade journal covering sheep industry news. Estab. 1911. Circ. 21,500. Pays on publication. Byline sometimes given. Buys first rights and makes work-for-hire assignments. Submit seasonal material 3 months in advance. Free sample copy.

Nonfiction: How-to and interview/profile. Buys 15 mss/year. Query with or without published clips or send complete ms. Length: 1,000-5,000 words. Pays $150-200 for unsolicited articles.

Photos: Send photos with submission. Reviews transparencies and prints. Offers no additional payment for photos accepted with ms. Captions required. Buys one-time rights.

‡POLLED HEREFORD WORLD, 11020 NW Ambassador Dr., Kansas City MO 64153-2034. (816)891-8400. Fax: (816)891-8811. Editor: Ed Bible. 1% freelance written. Monthly magazine for "breeders of Polled Hereford cattle—about 80% registered breeders, 5% commercial cattle breeders; remainder are agribusinessmen in related fields." Estab. 1947. Circ. 10,000. Not copyrighted. Buys "no unsolicited mss at present." Pays on publication. Publishes ms an average of 2 months after acceptance. Submit seasonal material "as early as possible: 2 months preferred." Reports in 1 month. Query first for reports of events, activities and features. Free sample copy.

Nonfiction: "Features on registered or commercial Polled Hereford breeders. Some on related agricultural subjects (pastures, fences, feeds, buildings, etc.). Mostly technical in nature; some human interest. Our readers make their living with cattle, so write for an informed, mature audience." Buys informational articles, how-to's, personal experience articles, interviews, profiles, historical and think pieces, nostalgia, photo features, coverage of successful business operations, articles on merchandising techniques, and technical articles. Publishes reprints of previously published articles. Send tearsheet of article. Length: "varies with subject and content of feature." Pays about 5¢/word ("usually about 50¢/column inch, but can vary with the value of material").

Photos: Purchased with mss, sometimes purchased without mss, or on assignment; captions required. "Only good quality b&w glossies accepted; any size. Good color prints or transparencies." Pays $2 for b&w, $2-25 for color. Pays $50 for color covers.

SHEEP! MAGAZINE, Dept. WM, Rt. 1, Box 78, Helenville WI 53137. (414)593-8385. Fax: (414)593-8384. Editor: Dave Thompson. 50% freelance written. Prefers to work with published/established writers. Monthly magazine. "We're looking for clear, concise, useful information for sheep raisers who have a few sheep to a 1,000 ewe flock." Estab. 1980. Circ. 15,000. Pays on publication. Byline given. Offers $30 kill fee. Buys all rights. Makes work-for-hire assignments. Submit seasonal material 3 months in advance. Free sample copy and writer's guidelines.

Nonfiction: Book excerpts; information (on personalities and/or political, legal or environmental issues affecting the sheep industry); how-to (on innovative lamb and wool marketing and promotion techniques, efficient record-keeping systems or specific aspects of health and husbandry). Health and husbandry articles should be written by someone with extensive experience or appropriate credentials (i.e., a veterinarian or animal scientist); profiles (on experienced sheep producers who detail the economics and management of their operation); features (on small businesses that promote wool products and stories about local and regional sheep producer's groups and their activities); new products (of value to sheep producers; should be written by someone who has used them); and technical (on genetics, health and nutrition). First person narratives. Buys 80 mss/year. Query with published clips or send complete ms. Length: 750-2,500 words. Pays $45-250. Pays the expenses of writers on assignment.

Photos: "Color—vertical compositions of sheep and/or people—for our cover. Use only b&w inside magazine. B&w, 35mm photos or other visuals improve your chances of a sale." Pays $100 maximum for 35mm color transparencies; $20-50 for 5×7 b&w prints. Identification of subjects required. Buys all rights.

Tips: "Send us your best ideas and photos! We love good writing!"

Management

AGWAY COOPERATOR, P.O. Box 4933, Syracuse NY 13221-4933. (315)477-6231. Editor: Sue Zarins. 2% freelance written. Bimonthly magazine for farmers. Estab. 1964. **Pays on acceptance.** Publishes ms an average of 6 months after acceptance. Time between acceptance and publication varies considerably. Usually reports in 1 month. Free sample copy.

Nonfiction: Should deal with topics of farm or rural interest in the Northeastern US. Length: 1,200 words maximum. Pays $100-150, depending on length, illustrations.

Tips: "We prefer an Agway tie-in, if possible. Fillers don't fit into our format. We do not assign freelance articles."

FARM FUTURES, Dept. WM, Suite 160, 12400 Whitewater Dr., Minnetonka MN 55343. (612)931-0211. Editor-in-Chief: Claudia Waterloo. 40% freelance written. Eager to work with new/unpublished writers. Estab. 1973. Circ. 225,000. **Pays on acceptance.** Publishes ms an average of 2 months after acceptance. Byline given. Offers negotiable kill fee. Buys first rights only. Simultaneous submissions OK. Query for electronic submissions. Reports in 1 month. Free sample copy and writer's guidelines.

Nonfiction: Practical advice and insights into managing commercial farms, farm marketing how-to's, financial management, use of computers in agriculture and farmer profiles. Buys 45 mss/year. Query first; do not send unsolicited mss. Length: 250-2,000 words. Pays $35-400. Sometimes pays the expenses of writers on assignment.

Tips: "The writer has a better chance of breaking in at our publication with short articles and fillers since our style is very particular; our stories are written directly to farmers and must be extremely practical. It's a style most writers have to 'grow into.' The most frequent mistakes made by writers in completing an article for us are lack of thoroughness and good examples; language too lofty or convoluted; and lack of precision — inaccuracies. Our magazine is growing — we'll be needing more freelance material."

FARM JOURNAL, Dept. WM, 230 W. Washington Square, Philadelphia PA 19105. (215)829-4700. Editor: Earl Ainsworth. Published 13 times/year with many regional editions. Material bought for one or more editions depending upon where it fits. Buys all rights. Byline given "except when article is too short or too heavily rewritten to justify one." **Pays on acceptance.** Payment is the same regardless of editions in which the piece is used.

Nonfiction: Timeliness and seasonableness are very important. Material must be highly practical and should be helpful to as many farmers as possible. Farmers' experiences should apply to one or more of these 8 basic commodities: corn, wheat, milo, soybeans, cotton, dairy, beef and hogs. Technical material must be accurate. No farm nostalgia. Query to describe a new idea that farmers can use. Length: 500-1,500 words. Pays 10-20¢/published word.

Photos: Much in demand either separately or with short how-to material in picture stories and as illustrations for articles. Warm human-interest-pix for covers — activities on modern farms. For inside use, shots of home-made and handy ideas to get work done easier and faster, farm news photos, and pictures of farm people with interesting sidelines. In b&w, 8 × 10 glossies are preferred; color submissions should be 2¼ × 2¼ for the cover and 35mm for inside use. Pays $50 and up for b&w shot; $75 and up for color.

Tips: "*Farm Journal* now publishes in hundreds of editions reflecting geographic, demographic and economic sectors of the farm market."

‡FARM SUPPLY RETAILING, Quirk Enterprises, Inc., P.O. Box 23536, 6607 18th Ave. So., Minneapolis MN 55423. (612)861-8051. Editor: Joseph Rydholm. 30% freelance written. Monthly magazine for owners and managers of stores that sell farm hardware and supplies. "Our magazine is similar to the now-defunct *Farm Store.* Our readers are the owners and managers of stores that sell feed, seed, fertilizer, farm supplies and hardware and related items. Our editorial goal is to give them practical information they can use to make their stories better and more profitable. The main stories will be case history profiles of successful dealers and marketing-related articles tailored to farm store owners." Estab. 1993. Circ. 22,000. **Pays on acceptance.** Publishes ms an average of 3 months after acceptance. Byline given. Buys one-time rights. Editorial lead time 3 months. Submit seasonal material 4 months in advance. Accepts simultaneous and previously published submissions. Query for electronic submissions. Reports in 1 month on queries; 2 months on mss. Sample copy and writer's guidelines free on request.

Nonfiction: How-to, interview/profile (with successful agribusiness dealers), opinion (on controversial industry issues). Subjects must be business-oriented (taxes, credit, inventory, employee relations, etc.). "No self-serving pieces by motivational speakers/consultants or articles that don't pertain to our editorial focus." Buys 15 mss/year. Query with published clips. Length: 1,000-2,500 words. Pays $200 minimum for assigned articles, $150 minimum for unsolicited articles. Sometimes pays expenses of writers on assignment.

Photos: State availability of photos with submission. Reviews contact sheets, any size transparencies and prints. Offers $25-75/photo. Identification of subjects required. Buys one-time rights.

Tips: "We welcome articles from freelancers. Our greatest need is for profiles of successful dealers. Submit two or three b&w photos or color slides with the article. Length between 1,500-2,000 words. Our readers are curious about how other dealers run their operations. Articles should discuss the dealer's selling philosophies, the farming sectors (hog farming, soybean, corn, etc.) his or her customers work in, any companies or product lines he or she has had success with, and any promotional or marketing efforts (advertising, direct mail) that have been successful. We also need articles on various business-related topics such as store layout, displays, store appearance, customer relations, employee management. We will consider articles of a general business nature but the most desirable are those tailored to farm supply dealers."

FFA NEW HORIZONS, 5632 Mt. Vernon Memorial Highway, Alexandria VA 22309-0160. (703)360-3600. Fax: (703)360-5524. Associate Editor: Lawinna McGary. 20% freelance written. Prefers to work with published/ established writers. Bimonthly magazine for members of the National FFA Organization who are students of agriculture in high school, ranging in age from 14-21 years; major interest in careers in agriculture/agribusiness and other youth interest subjects. Circ. 400,000. **Pays on acceptance.** Publishes ms an average of 4 months after acceptance. Buys all rights. Byline given. Submit seasonal material 4 months in advance. Query for electronic submissions. Reports in 2 months. Free sample copy and writer's guidelines.

Nonfiction: How-to for youth (outdoor-type such as camping, hunting, fishing); and informational (getting money for college, farming; and other help for youth). Informational, personal experience and interviews are used only if FFA members or former members are involved. "Science-oriented material is being used more extensively as we broaden people's understanding of agriculture." Buys 15 unsolicited mss/year. Query or send complete ms. Length: 1,000 words maximum. Pays 10-15¢/word. Sometimes pays the expenses of writers on assignment.

Photos: Purchased with mss (5×7 or 8×10 b&w glossies; 35mm or larger color transparencies). Pays $15 for b&w; $30-40 for inside color; $100 for cover.

Tips: "Find an FFA member who has done something truly outstanding that will motivate and inspire others, or provide helpful information for a career in farming, ranching or agribusiness. We've increased emphasis on agriscience and marketing. We're accepting manuscripts now that are tighter and more concise. Get straight to the point."

FORD NEW HOLLAND NEWS, P.O. Box 1895, New Holland PA 17557. Fax: (717)355-3600. Editor: Gary Martin. 50% freelance written. Works with a small number of new/unpublished writers each year. Magazine on agriculture; published 8 times/year; designed to entertain and inform farm families. Estab. 1960. **Pays on acceptance.** Publishes ms an average of 9 months after acceptance. Byline given. Offers negotiable kill fee. Buys first North American serial rights, one-time rights and second serial (reprint) rights. Submit seasonal material 6 months in advance. Simultaneous queries and previously published submissions OK. Reports in 1 month. Sample copy and writer's guidelines for 9×12 SASE and 2 first class stamps.

Nonfiction: "We need strong photo support for articles of 1,200-1,700 words on farm management and farm human interest." Buys 40 mss/year. Query. Pays $400-600. Sometimes pays the expenses of writers on assignment.

Photos: Send photos with query when possible. Reviews color transparencies. Pays $50-300. Captions, model release and identification of subjects required. Buys one-time rights.

Tips: "We thrive on good article ideas from knowledgeable farm writers. The writer must have an emotional understanding of agriculture and the farm family and must demonstrate in the article an understanding of the unique economics that affect farming in North America. We want to know about the exceptional farm managers, those leading the way in agriculture. We want new efficiencies and technologies presented through the real-life experiences of farmers themselves. Use anecdotes freely. Successful writers keep in touch with the editor as they develop the article."

HIGH PLAINS JOURNAL, The Farmer's Paper, High Plains Publishers, Inc., P.O. Box 760, Dodge City KS 67801-0760. (316)227-7171. Editor: Galen Hubbs. 5% freelance written. Weekly tabloid with news, features and photos on all phases of farming and livestock production. Estab. 1884. Circ. 64,000. Pays on publication. Publishes ms an average of 1 month after acceptance. Byline given. Not copyrighted. Buys first serial rights. Submit seasonal material 1 month in advance. Simultaneous queries OK. Reports in 3 weeks on queries; 1 month on mss. *Writer's Market* recommends allowing 2 months for reply. Sample copy $2.

Nonfiction: General interest (agriculture), how-to; interview/profile (farmers or stockmen within the High Plains area) and photo feature (agricultural). No rewrites of USDA, extension or marketing association releases. Buys 10-20 mss/year. Query with published clips. Length: 10-40 inches. Pays $1/column inch. Sometimes pays the expenses of writers on assignment.

Photos: State availability of photos. Pays $5-10 for 4×5 b&w prints. Captions and complete identification of subjects required. Buys one-time rights.

Tips: "Limit submissions to agriculture. Stories should not have a critical time element. Stories should be informative with correct information. Use quotations and bring out the human aspects of the person featured in profiles. Stories are often too long or are too far from our circulation area to be beneficial."

PROGRESSIVE FARMER, Southern Progress Corp., Dept. WM, 2100 Lakeshore Dr., Birmingham AL 35209. (205)877-6419. Editor-in-Chief: Tom Curl. Editor: Jack Odle. 3% freelance written. Monthly agriculture trade journal. "Country people, farmers, ranchers are our audience." Estab. 1886. Circ. 865,000. **Pays on acceptance.** Publishes ms an average of 4 months after acceptance. Byline sometimes given. Buys all rights. Reports in 3 weeks. Free sample copy and writer's guidelines.

Nonfiction: How-to (agriculture and country related), humor (farm related) and technical (agriculture). Buys 30-50 mss/year. Query with published clips. Length: 2,000 words maximum. Pays $100 minimum. Sometimes pays expenses of writers on assignment.

Photos: Send photos with submission. Reviews negatives and transparencies. Payment negotiable. Captions and identification of subjects required. Rights depend on assignment.

Columns/Departments: Handy Devices (photos and short text on the little shop ideas that make farm work easier and rural living more enjoyable). Buys 70 mss/year. Send complete ms. Length: 20-75 words. Pays $50.

Tips: Query with ideas compatible with basic tone of magazine.

‡**SMALL FARM TODAY, The how-to magazine of alternative crops, livestock, and direct marketing,** (formerly *Missouri Farm Magazine*), Missouri Farm Publishing, Inc., Ridge Top Ranch, 3903 W. Ridge Trail Rd., Clark MO 65243-9525. (314)687-3525. Editor: Ron Macher. Bimonthly magazine "for small farmers and small-acreage landowners interested in diversification, direct marketing, alternative crops, horses, draft animals, small livestock, exotic and minor breeds, home-based businesses, gardening, vegetable and small fruit crops." Estab. 1984 as *Missouri Farm Magazine*. Circ. 12,000. Pays on publication. Publishes ms an average of 3 months after acceptance. Byline given. Buys first serial rights and nonexclusive reprint rights (right to reprint article in an anthology). Rarely buys reprints. Submit seasonal/holiday material 3 months in advance. Reports in 3 months. Sample copy $3. Writer's guidelines available.

Nonfiction: Practical and how-to (small farming, gardening, alternative crops/livestock). Query letters recommended. Length: 500-2,000 words. Pays $1.50 per column inch.

• In the past this magazine concentrated on articles that applied to Missouri farms. Now they have a national audience and need articles from all over the US.

Photos: Send photos with submission. Offers $6 for inside photos and $10 for cover photos. Captions required. Pays $4 for negatives or slides. Buys one-time rights and nonexclusive reprint rights (for anthologies).

Tips: "Topic must apply to the small farm or acreage. It helps to provide more practical and helpful information without the fluff."

SUCCESSFUL FARMING, Dept. WM, 1716 Locust St., Des Moines IA 50309-3023. (515)284-2826. Managing Editor: Gene Johnston. 3% freelance written. Prefers to work with published/established writers. Monthly magazine for farm families that make farming their business. Estab. 1902. Circ. 500,000. Buys all rights. **Pays on acceptance.** Publishes ms an average of 2 months after acceptance. Reports in 2 weeks. Sample copy for SAE with 5 first class stamps.

Nonfiction: Semi-technical articles on all aspects of farming, including production, business, country living and recreation with emphasis on how to apply this information to one's own farm family. Also articles on interesting farm people and activities. Buys 30 unsolicited mss/year. Query with outline. Length: 1,000 words maximum. Pays $250-600. Sometimes pays the expenses of writers on assignment.

Photos: Jim Galbraith, art director. Prefers color transparencies. Buys exclusive rights. Assignments are given, sometimes a guarantee, provided editors can be sure photos will be acceptable.

Tips: "A frequent mistake made by writers in completing articles is that the focus of the story is not narrow enough and does not include enough facts, examples, dollar signs and a geographic and industry perspective. Greatest need is for short articles and fillers that are specific and to the point."

‡**TODAY'S FARMER,** MFA Incorporated, 615 Locust, Columbia MO 65201. (314)876-5252. Editor: Chuck Lay. Managing Editor: Tom Montgomery. Contact: Chuck Lay. 50% freelance written. Company publication. Magazine published 10 times/year covering agriculture. "We are owned and published by MFA Incorporated, an agricultural cooperative. We examine techniques and issues that help farmers and ranchers better meet the challenges of the present and future." Estab. 1908. Circ. 46,000. **Pays on acceptance.** Publishes ms an average of 2 months after acceptance. Byline given. Offers 100% kill fee. Publication not copyrighted. Buys first North American serial rights. Editorial lead time 2 months. Submit seasonal material 3+ months in advance. Query for electronic submissions. Sample copy $1. Writer's guidelines "available by phone."

Nonfiction: How-to (ag technical), interview/profile, photo feature and technical. "No fiction, articles on MFA competitors, or subjects outside our trade territory (Missouri, Iowa, Arkansas)." Buys 30 mss/year. Query with published clips. Length: 1,000-2,000 words. Pays $200 minimum (features). Sometimes pays expenses of writers on assignment.

Photos: Send photos with submission. Reviews contact sheets. Negotiates payment individually. Identification of subjects required. Buys one-time rights.

Tips: "Freelancers can best approach us by knowing our audience (farmers/ranchers who are customers of MFA) and knowing their needs. We publish traditional agribusiness information that helps farmers do their jobs more effectively. Know the audience. We edit for length, AP style."

Miscellaneous

BEE CULTURE, (formerly *Gleanings in Bee Culture*), P.O. Box 706, Medina OH 44256-0706. Fax: (216)725-5624. Editor: Mr. Kim Flottum. 50% freelance written. Monthly magazine for beekeepers and those interested in the natural science of honey bees. Publishes environmentally oriented articles relating to honey bees or pollination. Estab. 1873. Buys first North American serial rights. Pays on both publication and acceptance. Publishes ms an average of 4 months after acceptance. Reports in 1 month. Reprints OK; send tearsheet or photocopy of article. Pays 100% of their fee for an original article. Sample copy for 9×12 SAE with 5 first class stamps. Free writer's guidelines.

Nonfiction: Interested in articles giving new ideas on managing bees. Also looking for articles on honey bee/environment connections or relationships. Also uses success stories about commercial beekeepers. No "how I began beekeeping" articles. No highly advanced, technical and scientific abstracts or impractical advice. Length: 2,000 word average. Pays $30-50/published page—on negotiation.

Photos: Sharp b&w photos (pertaining to honey bees, honey plants or related to story) purchased with mss. Can be any size, prints or enlargements, but 4×5 or larger preferred. Pays $7-10/picture.

Tips: "Do an interview story on commercial beekeepers who are cooperative enough to furnish accurate, factual information on their operations. Frequent mistakes made by writers in completing articles are that they are too general in nature and lack management knowledge."

Regional

AGRI-TIMES NORTHWEST, J/A Publishing Co., 206 S.E. Court, P.O. Box 189, Pendleton OR 97801. (503)276-7845. Fax: (503)276-7964. Editor: Virgil Rupp. Managing Editor: Jim Eardley. 50% freelance written. Weekly newspaper on agriculture in western Idaho, eastern Oregon and eastern Washington. "News, features about regional farmers/agribusiness *only.*" Estab. 1983. Circ. 5,200. Pays on 15th of month after publication. Publishes ms an average of 1 month after acceptance. Byline given. Buys one-time rights. Submit seasonal material 1 month in advance. Simultaneous and previously published submissions OK. Send typed ms with rights for sale noted and information about when and where the article previously appeared. For reprints, pays 100% of the amount paid for an original article. Reports in 1 month. Sample copy 50¢ for 8×10 SAE with 4 first class stamps. Writer's guidelines for #10 SASE.

Nonfiction: How-to (farming and ranching *regional*), humor (regional farming and ranching), interview/profile (regional farmers/ranchers), photo feature (regional agriculture) and technical (regional farming and ranching). Buys 100 mss/year. Query with or without published clips or send complete ms. Length: 750 words maximum. Pays 75¢/column inch.

Photos: Send photos with submission. Reviews contact sheets, negatives and prints. Offers $5-10/photo. Captions and identification of subjects required. Buys one-time rights.

Columns/Departments: Agri-Talk (quips, comments of farmers/ranchers). Buys 50 mss/year. Send complete ms. Length: 100 words maximum. Pays 75¢ per column inch.

Tips: "Focus on our region's agriculture. Be accurate."

FARMWEEK, Mayhill Publications, Inc., P.O. Box 90, Knightstown IN 46148-0900. (317)345-5133. Editor: Nancy Searfoss. Associate Editor: Scot E. Long. 5% freelance written. Weekly newspaper that covers agriculture in Indiana, Ohio and Kentucky. Estab. 1955. Circ. 28,000. Pays on publication. Byline given. Buys first rights. Submit seasonal material 1 month in advance. Simultaneous submissions OK. Reporting time varies; up to 1 year. Free sample copy and writer's guidelines.

Nonfiction: General interest (agriculture), interview/profile (ag leaders), new product and photo feature (Indiana, Ohio, Kentucky agriculture). "We don't want first-person accounts or articles from states outside Indiana, Kentucky, Ohio (unless of general interest to all farmers and agribusiness)." Query with published clips. Length: 500-1,500 words. Pays $50 maximum. Sometimes pays expenses of writers on assignment.

Photos: State availability of photos with submission. Reviews contact sheets and 4×5 and 5×7 prints. Offers $10 photo/maximum. Identification of subjects required. Buys one-time rights.

Tips: "We want feature stories about farmers and agribusiness operators in Indiana, Ohio and Kentucky. How do they operate their business? Keys to success, etc.? Best thing to do is call us first with idea, or write. Could also be a story about some pressing issue in agriculture nationally that affects farmers everywhere."

‡FLORIDA GROWER AND RANCHER, The only independent spokesman for all aspects of Florida agriculture, FGR, Inc., 1331 N. Mills Ave., Orlando FL 32803. (407)894-6522. Editor: Frank Garner. 25% freelance written. Monthly magazine covering all aspects of Florida agriculture. "The magazine is edited for the Florida farmer with commercial production interest in citrus, beef cattle, vegetables, dairy, field crops and other ag endeavors. Our goal is to provide articles which update and inform on such areas as production, ag financing, farm labor relations, technology, safety, education and regulation." Estab. 1907. Circ. 18,500. Pays on publication. Byline given. Buys all rights. Editorial lead time 2 months. Submit seasonal material 3 months in advance. Query for electronic submissions. Reports in 1 month. Sample copy for 9×12 SAE with 5 first class stamps. Writer's guidelines free on request.

Nonfiction: Interview/profile, photo feature and technical. Query with published clips. Length: 750-1,500 words. Pays 12¢/word.

Photos: Send photos with submission. Reviews contact sheets and prints. Offers $10/photo.

Columns/Departments: Query with published clips. Pays 12¢/word.

IOWA REC NEWS, Suite 48, 8525 Douglas, Urbandale IA 50322-2992. (515)276-5350. Editor: Jody Garlock. 5% freelance written. Monthly magazine emphasizing energy issues and human interest features for residents of rural Iowa. Estab. 1948. Circ. 116,000. Pays on publication. Publishes ms an average of 3 months after acceptance. Buys first serial and second serial (reprint) rights. Simultaneous and previously published submissions OK. Reprints OK; send information about when and where the article previously appeared. Reports in 2 months.

Nonfiction: General interest, historical, humor, rural lifestyle trends, energy awareness features and photo feature. Send complete ms.

Tips: "The easiest way to break into our magazine is: research a particular subject well, include appropriate attributions to establish credibility, authority and include a couple paragraphs about the author. Reading and knowing about rural people is important. Stories that touch the senses or can improve the lives of the readers are highly considered, as are those with a strong Iowa angle. We're also looking for good humor articles. Freelancers have the advantage of offering subject matter that existing staff may not be able to cover. Inclusion of nice photos is also a plus. The most frequent mistakes made by writers are: story too long, story too biased; no attribution to any source of info; and not relevant to electric consumers, rural living."

MAINE ORGANIC FARMER & GARDENER, Maine Organic Farmers & Gardeners Association, RR 2, Box 594, Lincolnville ME 04849. (207)763-3043. Editor: Jean English. 40% freelance written. Prefers to work with published/established local writers. Bimonthly magazine covering organic farming and gardening for urban and rural farmers and gardeners and nutrition-oriented, environmentally concerned readers. "*MOF&G* promotes and encourages sustainable agriculture and environmentally sound living. Our primary focus is organic farming, gardening and forestry, but we also deal with local, national and international agriculture, food and environmental issues." Estab. 1976. Circ. 10,000. Pays on publication. Publishes ms an average of 8 months after acceptance. Byline and bio given. Buys first North American serial, one-time, first serial or second serial (reprint) rights. Submit seasonal material 1 year in advance. Simultaneous queries and submissions OK. Reprints OK; send typed ms with rights for sale noted and information about when and where the article previously appeared; pays 50% of their fee for an original article. Reports in 2 months. Sample copy $2 for SAE with 7 first class stamps. Free writer's guidelines.

Nonfiction: Book reviews; how-to based on personal experience, research reports, or interviews. Profiles of farmers, gardeners, plants, weeds, insects, trees. Information on renewable energy, recycling, nutrition, health, non-toxic pest control, organic farm management and marketing. "We use profiles of New England organic farmers and gardeners and news reports (500-1,000 words) dealing with US/international sustainable ag research and development, rural development, recycling projects, environmental and agricultural problems and solutions, organic farms with broad impact, cooperatives and community projects." Buys 30 mss/year. Query with published clips or send complete ms. Length: 1,000-3,000 words. Pays $20-100.

Photos: State availability of b&w photos with query; send 3 × 5 b&w photos with ms. Captions, model releases and identification of subjects required. Buys one-time rights.

Tips: "We are a nonprofit organization. Our publication's primary mission is to inform and educate, but we also want readers to enjoy the articles."

N.D. REC/RTC MAGAZINE, N.D. Association of RECs, P.O. Box 727, Mandan ND 58554-0727. (701)663-6501. Fax: (701)663-3745. Editor: Kent Brick. 10% freelance written. Prefers to work with published/established writers. Monthly magazine covering rural electric program and rural North Dakota lifestyle. "Our magazine goes to the 70,000 North Dakota families who get their electricity from rural electric cooperatives. We cover rural lifestyle, energy conservation, agriculture, farm family news and other features of importance to this predominantly agrarian state. Of course, we represent the views of our statewide association." Estab. 1954. Circ. 74,000. Pays on publication; "**pays on acceptance for assigned features.**" Publishes ms average of 6 months after acceptance. Byline given. Buys first North American serial rights. Publishes reprints of previously published articles or short stories. Send photocopy of article or short story, or typed ms with rights for sale noted. For reprints, pays 25% of the amount paid for an original article. Submit seasonal material 6 months in advance. Simultaneous queries OK. Reports in 2 months. Sample copy for 9 × 12 SAE with 6 first class stamps.

Nonfiction: Expose (subjects of ND interest dealing with rural electric, agriculture, rural lifestyle); historical/nostalgic (ND events or people only); how-to (save energy, weatherize homes, etc.); interview/profile (on great leaders of the rural electric program, agriculture); and opinion (why family farms should be saved, etc.). Buys 10-12 mss/year. Pays $35-300. Pays expenses of writers on assignment.

Photos: "Good quality photos accompanying ms improve chances for sale."

Fiction: Historical. "No fiction that does not relate to our editorial goals." Buys 2-3 mss/year. Length: 400-1,200 words. Pays $35-150. Reprints novel excerpts.

Poetry: Jo Ann Winistorfer, managing editor. Buys 2-4 poems/year. Submit maximum 8 poems. Pays $5-50.

Tips: "Write about a North Dakotan—one of our members who has done something notable in the ag/energy/rural electric/rural lifestyle areas."

OHIO FARMER, 1350 W. 5th Ave., Columbus OH 43212. (614)486-9637. Editor: Tim White. 10% freelance written. Magazine published 15 issues/year (monthly April-December; biweekly January-March) for Ohio farmers and their families. Estab. 1848. Circ. 77,000. Usually buys all rights. Pays on publication. Publishes ms an average of 2 months after acceptance. Reports in 2 months. Query for electronic submissions. Sample copy $1 for SAE with 4 first class stamps. Free writer's guidelines.

Nonfiction: Technical and on-the-farm stories. Buys informational, how-to and personal experience. Buys 5 mss/year. Submit complete ms. Length: 600-700 words. Pays $100.

Photos: Photos purchased with ms with no additional payment, or without ms. Pays $5-25 for b&w; $35-100 for color; send 4×5 b&w glossies; and transparencies or 8×10 color prints.

Tips: "We are now doing more staff-written stories. We buy very little freelance material."

● This magazine is part of Farm Progress Co. state farm magazine group.

PENNSYLVANIA FARMER, Farm Progress Publications, 704 Lisburn Rd., Camp Hill PA 17011-0704. (717)761-6050. Editor: John Vogel. 10% freelance written. Monthly farm business magazine "oriented to providing readers with ideas to help their businesses and personal lives." Estab. 1877. Circ. 68,000. Pays on publication. Publishes ms an average of 3 months after acceptance. Byline sometimes given. Buys first-time rights. Submit seasonal material 3 months in advance. Simultaneous submissions OK. Reports in 1 month. Writer's guidelines for #10 SASE.

Nonfiction: Humor, inspirational and technical. No stories without a strong tie to Mid-Atlantic farming. Buys 15 mss/year. Query. Length: 500-1,000 words. Pays $50-150. Sometimes pays the expenses of writers on assignment.

Photos: Send photos with submission. Reviews 35mm transparencies. Pays $25-50 for each color photo accepted with ms. Captions and identification of subjects required. Buys one-time rights.

USAGRICULTURE, Webb Division/Intertec Publishing, 7900 International Dr., Minneapolis MN 55425. (612)851-9329. Fax: (612)851-4600. Editor: David Hest. Managing Editor: Norman Senjem. 20% freelance written. Magazine published 23 times/year covering agriculture in the upper Midwest (MN, SD, ND, IL, IA, NE, IN, MT) "providing timely, in-depth information on crop and livestock production. farm business, governmental affairs/policy and farm lifestyle." Estab. 1892. Circ. 250,000. **Pays on acceptance.** Byline given. Buys first rights or one-time rights. Query for electronic submissions. Reports in 1 month. Sample copy for self-addressed mailing label with $2.90 postage.

Nonfiction: "Trends affecting agriculture in the midwest; profiles of successful farmers and ranchers and how-to (make money farming/ranching in the upper midwest). Buys 25-50 mss/year. Query. Length: 300-1,200 words. Pays $100-700 for assigned articles; $100-300 for unsolicited articles. Sometimes pays expenses of writers on assignment.

Photos: Send photos with submission. Reviews contact sheets and transparencies. Offers no additional payment for photos accepted with ms. Captions and identification of subjects required. Buys one-time rights.

WYOMING RURAL ELECTRIC NEWS, P.O. Box 380, Casper WY 82602-0380. (307)234-6152. Editor: Karen Hepp. 25% freelance written. Monthly magazine for audience of small town residents, vacation-home owners, farmers and ranchers. Estab. 1950. Circ. 30,000. Not copyrighted. Byline given. Pays on publication. Publishes ms an average of 3 months after acceptance. Buys first serial rights. Submit seasonal material 2 months in advance. "Sometimes" buys reprints; pays 80-100% of their fee for an original article. Reports in up to 3 months. Sample copy for SAE with 3 first class stamps.

Nonfiction and Fiction: Wants energy-related material, "people" features, historical pieces about Wyoming and the West, and things of interest to Wyoming's rural people. Buys informational, humor, historical, nostalgia and photo mss. Submit complete ms. Buys 7 mss/year. Length for nonfiction and fiction: 800-1,500 words. Pays $15-45. Buys some western, humorous and historical fiction.

Photos: Photos purchased with accompanying ms with additional payment, or purchased without ms. Captions required. Pays up to $40 for cover photos. Color only.

Tips: "Study an issue or two of the magazine to become familiar with our focus and the type of freelance material we're using. We're always looking for *good* humor. Always looking for fresh, new writers, original perspectives. Submit entire manuscript. Don't submit a regionally set story from some other part of the country. Photos and illustrations (if appropriate) are always welcomed."

Finance

These magazines deal with banking, investment and financial management. Publications that use similar material but have a less technical slant are listed under the Consumer Business and Finance section.

THE BOTTOM LINE, The News and Information Publication for Canada's Financial Professionals, Bottom Line Publications Inc., Dept. WM, Suite 300, 204 Richmond St. W., Toronto, Ontario M5V 1V6 Canada. (416)598-5211. Fax: (416)474-9803. Editor: Mike Lewis. 35% freelance written. Monthly tabloid on accounting/ finance/ business. "Reaches 80% of all Canadian accountants. Information should be news/ commentary/analysis of issues or issues of interest to or about accountants." Estab. 1985. Circ. 48,000. Pays on publication. Publishes ms an average of 2 weeks to 4 months after acceptance. Byline given. Buys first rights. Query for electronic submissions. Reports in 2 months. Free sample copy for SASE.

Photos: State availability of photos with submission. Offers $50 photo/maximum. Buys one-time rights.
   • This magazine has reduced its freelance contribution during the past year.

CA MAGAZINE, 277 Wellington St., W., Toronto, Ontario M5S 3H2 Canada. Fax: (416)204-3409. Editor: Nelson Luscombe. Managing Editor: Jane Litchfield. 10% freelance written. Works with a small number of new/unpublished writers each year. Monthly magazine for accountants and financial managers. Estab. 1911. Circ. 67,000. Pays on publication for the article's copyright. Buys all rights. Publishes ms an average of 4 months after acceptance. Reports in 1 month. Free sample copy and writer's guidelines.

Nonfiction: Accounting, business, finance, management and taxation. Also, subject-related humor pieces and cartoons. "We accept whatever is relevant to our readership, no matter the origin as long as it meets our standards." Length: 1,500-3,500 words. Payment varies with qualification of writers. Sometimes pays the expenses of writers on assignment.

‡CREDIT UNION NEWS, The National Newspaper Serving the Fastest Growing Financial Institutions, BKB Publications Inc., Suite 2030, 150 Nassau St., New York NY 10038. (212)267-7707. Editor: Charlene Komar Storey. 30% freelance written. Biweekly newspaper tabloid for credit unions. "Material geared specifically to credit unions, from a business viewpoint only." Estab. 1981. Circ. 7,000. Pays 2 weeks after publication. Byline given. Buys all rights. Editorial lead time 2 weeks. Accepts previously published submissions (if not published by a competitor). Query for electronic submissions. Reports in 1 month. Sample copy free on request.

Nonfiction: Interview/profile, technical and credit union-oriented material—regulatory issues, marketing, etc. Credit & Debit Cards; Share Drafts; Investments; Electronic Filing; Travelers Checks; Mortgages; Data Processing; Asset/Liability Management; Building Design/Office Equipment. "No material that is *not* geared to credit union industry." Buys 250 mss/year. Query with published clips or send complete ms. Length: 500-2,000 words. Pays $5.50/published inch. Sometimes pays expenses of writers on assignment.

Photos: Send photos with submission. Reviews contact sheets and 5 × 7 prints. Negotiates payment individually. Captions and identification of subjects required. Buys all rights.

Tips: "Experienced newspaper writers do best with us. An understanding of the approach required by a trade publication is essential, as is a knowledge of the credit union industry."

‡EQUITIES MAGAZINE INC., (formerly *Equities*), Suites 5B and 5C, 145 E. 49th St., New York NY 10017. (212)832-7800. Editor: Robert J. Flaherty. 50% freelance written. Monthly magazine covering publicly owned middle market and emerging growth companies. "We are a financial magazine covering the fastest-growing companies in the world. We study the management of companies and act as critics reviewing their performances. We aspire to be 'The Shareholder's Friend'. We want to be a bridge between quality public companies and sophisticated investors." Estab. 1951. Circ. 15,000. Pays on publication. Publishes ms an average of 2 months after acceptance. Byline given. Buys first rights or reprint rights. Sample copy for 9 × 12 SAE with 5 first class stamps.

Nonfiction: New product and technical. Buys 30 mss/year. "We must know the writer first as we are careful about whom we publish. A letter of introduction with resume and clips is the best way to introduce yourself. Financial writing requires specialized knowledge and a feel for people as well, which can be a tough combination to find." Query with published clips. Length: 300-1,500 words. Pays $150-750 for assigned articles, more for very difficult or investigative pieces. Carries guest columns by famous money managers who are not writing for cash payments, but to showcase their ideas and approach. Pays expenses of writers on assignment.

Photos: Send photos with submission. Reviews contact sheets, negatives, transparencies and prints. Offers no additional payment for photos accepted with ms. Identification of subjects required.

Columns/Departments: Pays $25-75 for assigned items only.

Tips: "Anyone who enjoys analyzing a business and telling the story of the people who started it, or run it today, is a potential *Equities* contributor. But to protect our readers and ourselves, we are careful about who writes for us. Business writing is an exciting area and our stories reflect that. If a writer relies on numbers and percentages to tell his story, rather than the individuals involved, the result will be numbingly dull."

THE FEDERAL CREDIT UNION, National Association of Federal Credit Unions, P.O. Box 3769, Washington DC 20007-0269. (703)522-4770. Fax: (703)524-1082. Editor: Patrick M. Keefe. Managing Editor: Robin Johnston. 25% freelance written. "Looking for writer with financial, banking or credit union experience, but will work with inexperienced (unpublished) writers based on writing skill." Bimonthly magazine covering credit unions. Estab. 1967. Circ. 8,200. Pays on publication. Publishes ms an average of 3 months after acceptance. Byline sometimes given. Buys first North American serial rights. Submit seasonal material 5 months in advance. Simultaneous submissions OK. Query for electronic submissions. Reports in 2 months; must include SASE and correct postage. Sample copy for 10 × 13 SAE with 5 first class stamps. Writer's guidelines for #10 SASE.

Nonfiction: Query with published clips. Length: 1,200-2,000 words. Pays $200-600 for assigned articles.

Photos: Send photos with submission. Reviews 35mm transparencies and 5 × 7 prints. Offers no additional payment for photos accepted with ms. Model releases and identification of subjects required. Buys all rights.

Tips: "Provide resume or listing of experience pertinent to subject. Looking only for articles that focus on events in Congress and regulatory agencies."

‡FUTURES MAGAZINE, 219 Parkade, Cedar Falls IA 50613. (319)277-6341. Publisher: Merrill Oster. Editor-in-Chief: Ginger Szala. 20% freelance written. Monthly magazine for private, individual traders, brokers, exchange members, agribusinessmen, bankers, anyone with an interest in futures or options. Estab. 1972. Circ. 65,000. Buys all rights. Byline given. Pays on publication. Publishes ms an average of 6 months after acceptance. Reports in 1 month. Sample copy for 9 × 12 SAE with 8 first class stamps.

Nonfiction: Articles analyzing specific commodity futures and options trading strategies; fundamental and technical analysis of individual commodities and markets; interviews, book reviews, "success" stories; and news items. Material on new legislation affecting commodities, trading, any new trading strategy ("results must be able to be substantiated") and personalities. No "homespun" rules for trading and simplistic approaches to the commodities market. Treatment is always in-depth and broad. Informational, how-to, interview, profile, technical. "Articles should be written for a reader who has traded commodities for one year or more; should not talk down or hypothesize. Relatively complex material is acceptable." No get-rich-quick gimmicks, astrology articles or general, broad topics. "Writers must have solid knowledge of the magazine's specific emphasis and be able to communicate well." Buys 30-40 mss/year. Query or submit complete ms. Length: 1,500 words optimum. Pays $50-1,000, depending upon author's research and writing quality. "Rarely" pays the expenses of writers on assignment.

Tips: "Writers must have a solid understanding and appreciation for futures or options trading. We will have more financial and stock index features as well as new options contracts that will require special knowledge and experience. Trading techniques and corporate strategies involving futures/options will get more emphasis in the coming year."

‡ILLINOIS BANKER, Illinois Bankers Association, Suite 1111, 111 N. Canal St., Chicago IL 60606. (312)876-9900. Editor: Meg Bullock. Monthly magazine covering commercial banking. "*Illinois Banker* publishes articles that directly relate to commercial banking. Our audience is approximately 3,000 bankers and vendors related to the banking industry. The purpose of the publication is to educate and inform readers on major public policy issues affecting banking today, as well as provide new ideas that can be applied to day-to-day operations and management. Writers may not sell or promote a product or service." Estab. 1916. Circ. approx. 2,500. **Pays on acceptance.** Publishes ms an average of 3 months after acceptance. Byline given. Buys first North American serial rights. Editorial lead time 1½ months. Accepts simultaneous and previously published submissions. Query for electronic submissions. Sample copy and writer's guidelines free on request.

Nonfiction: Essays, historical/nostalgic, humor, inspirational, interview/profile, new product, opinion, personal experience, financially related. "It is *IBA* policy that writers do not sell or promote a particular product, service or organization within the content of an article written for publication." Buys 3-5 mss/year. Query. Length: 500-1,000 words. Pays $50 minimum for unsolicited articles.

Photos: State availability of photos with submission. Reviews contact sheets, negatives, transparencies and prints. Offers $25-50/photo. Negotiates payment individually. Captions and identification of subjects required. Buys one-time rights.

Fiction: Historical, humorous, mainstream, slife-of-life vignettes (financial). Buys 3 mss/year. Query. Length: 500-1,000 words. Pays $50-100.

Tips: "We appreciate that authors contact the editor before submitting articles to discuss topics. Articles published in *Illinois Banker* address current issues of key importance to the banking industry in Illinois. Our intention is to keep readers informed of the latest industry news, developments and trends, as well as provide necessary technical information. We publish articles on any topic that affects the banking industry, provided the content is in agreement with Association policy and position. Because we are a trade association, most articles need to be reviewed by an advisory committee before publication; therefore, the earlier they are submitted the better. Some recent topics include: agriculture, bank architecture, commercial and consumer credit, marketing, operations/cost control, security and technology. In addition, articles are also considered on the topics of economic development and business/banking trends in Illinois and the Midwest region."

INDEPENDENT BANKER, Independent Bankers Association of America, P.O. Box 267, Sauk Centre MN 56378-0267. Editor: David C. Bordewyk. 25% freelance written. Works with a number of new/unpublished writers each year. Monthly magazine targeting the CEOs of the nation's community banks. Estab. 1950. Circ. 10,000. Pays on publication. Publishes ms an average of 4 months after acceptance. Byline given. Not copyrighted. Buys all rights. Reports in 6 weeks. Sample copy and writer's guidelines for 9 × 12 SAE with 6 first class stamps.

Nonfiction: Features: interview/profile (example: a community bank's innovative economic development program), banking trends, how-to articles on bank operation and marketing issues. "Our editorial approach is predicated on two things: quality writing and an ability to give readers a sense of the people interviewed for a particular story. People enjoy reading about other people." Buys first-time rights; usually 15 mss/year. Publishes reprints of previously published articles. Send photocopy of article and information about when and where the article previously appeared. Sidebars welcome. No fiction. Query. Length: 1,500-2,500 words. Pays $250 maximum.

Photos: State availability of photos with submission. Uses color transparencies, color prints or b&w prints. Pays $5 for each published photo. Identification of subjects required. Buys one-time rights.

Columns/Departments: "Newslines," short general-interest items about banking and finance, and "Update," short pieces about community banks and bankers, such as a bank's unique home mortgage marketing program or an interesting personality in community banking. Items are 75-175 words in length. Byline given. Pays $25.

Tips: "The best way to get acquainted with us is by writing a short piece (75-175 words) for either our 'Newslines' or 'Update' departments. Since they are often read first, the accent is on crisp, clean writing that packs a punch. Our editorial content seeks to convey the strength of locally owned, locally managed community banks, and the need to protect America's diversified financial system. We are working to position *Independent Banker* as a writer's magazine that provides solid information for community bank CEOs in a creative, entertaining manner."

‡**PENSION WORLD,** Communication Channels, Inc., #200, 6151 Powers Ferry Rd. NW, Atlanta GA 30339-2941. (404)955-2500. Fax: (404)618-0348. Editor: Ed LaBorwit. 10% freelance written. Monthly magazine on pension investment and employee benefits. Estab. 1964. Circ. 28,146. Pays on pasteup. Byline given. Buys all rights. Submit seasonal/holiday material 4 months in advance. Reports in 2 weeks on queries; 3 weeks on mss. *Writer's Market* recommends allowing 2 months for reply. Free writer's guidelines.
Nonfiction: General interest, interview/profile, new product and opinion. Query with published clips. Length: 1,500-2,500 words.

‡**RESEARCH MAGAZINE, Ideas for Today's Investors,** Research Services, 2201 3rd St., San Francisco CA 94107. (415)621-0220. Editor: Anne Evers. 50% freelance written. Monthly business magazine of corporate profiles and subjects of interest to stockbrokers. Estab. 1977. Circ. 80,000. Pays on publication. Publishes ms an average of 2 months after acceptance. Byline given. Offers 20% kill fee. Buys first North American serial or second serial (reprint) rights. Query for electronic submissions. Reports in 1 month. Sample copy for 9 × 12 SAE with 4 first class stamps. Writer's guidelines for #10 SASE.
Nonfiction: How-to (sales tips), interview/profile, new product and financial products. Buys approximately 50 mss/year. Query with published clips. Length: 1,000-3,000 words. Pays $300-900. Sometimes pays expenses of writers on assignment.
Tips: "Only submit articles that fit our editorial policy and are appropriate for our audience. *Only the non-corporate profile section is open to freelancers.* We use local freelancers on a regular basis for corporate profiles."

Fishing

PACIFIC FISHING, Salmon Bay Communications, 1515 NW 51st St., Seattle WA 98107. (206)789-5333. Fax: (206)784-5545. Editor: Steve Shapiro. 75% freelance written. Eager to work with new/unpublished writers. Monthly business magazine for commercial fishermen and others in the West Coast commercial fishing industry. "*Pacific Fishing* views the fisherman as a small businessman and covers all aspects of the industry, including harvesting, processing and marketing." Estab. 1979. Circ. 11,000. Pays on publication. Publishes ms an average of 2 months after acceptance. Byline given. Offers 10-15% kill fee on assigned articles deemed unsuitable. Buys one-time rights. Reports in 2 months. Sample copy and writer's guidelines for 9 × 12 SAE with 10 first class stamps.
Nonfiction: Interview/profile and technical (usually with a business hook or slant). "Articles must be concerned specifically with *commercial* fishing. We view fishermen as small businessmen and professionals who are innovative and success-oriented. To appeal to this reader, *Pacific Fishing* offers four basic features: technical, how-to articles that give fisherman hands-on tips that will make their operation more efficient and profitable; practical, well-researched business articles discussing the dollars and cents of fishing, processing and marketing; profiles of a fisherman, processor or company with emphasis on practical business and technical areas; and in-depth analysis of political, social, fisheries management and resource issues that have a direct bearing on West Coast commercial fishermen." Buys 20 mss/year. Query noting whether photos are available, and enclosing samples of previous work. Length: 1,500-2,500 words. Pays 15¢/word. Sometimes pays the expenses of writers on assignment.

● Editors here are putting more focus on local and international seafood marketing.

Photos: "We need good, high-quality photography, especially color, of West Coast commercial fishing. We prefer 35mm color slides. Our rates are $150 for cover; $50-100 for inside color; $25-50 for b&w and $10 for table of contents."

Tips: "Because of the specialized nature of our audience, the editor strongly recommends that freelance writers query the magazine in writing with a proposal. We enjoy finding a writer who understands our editorial needs and satisfies those needs, a writer willing to work with an editor to make the article just right. Most of our shorter items are staff written. Our freelance budget is such that we get the most benefit by using it for feature material."

WESTCOAST FISHERMAN, Westcoast Publishing Ltd., 1496 West 72 Ave., Vancouver, British Columbia V6P 3C8 Canada. (604)266-8611. Editor: Peter Robson. 40% freelance written. Monthly trade journal covering commercial fishing in British Columbia. "We're a non-political, non-aligned magazine dedicated to the people in the B.C. commercial fishing industry. Our publication reflects and celebrates the individuals and communities that collectively constitute B.C. fishermen." Pays on publication. Publishes ms an average of 2-3 months after acceptance. Byline given. Buys first rights and one-time rights. Query for electronic submission. Reprints OK; send tearsheet or photocopy of article and information about when and where the article previously appeared.For reprint pays 50% of their fee for an original article. Publishes book excerpts. Reports in 2 months.

Nonfiction: Interview/profile, photo feature and technical. Buys 30-40 mss/year. Query with or without published clips or send complete ms. Length: 250-2,500 words. Pays $25-450.

Photos: Send photos with submission. Reviews contact sheets, negatives, 24×36 transparencies and 5×7 prints. Offers $5-100/photo. Identification of subjects required. Buys one-time rights.

Poetry: Avant-garde, free verse, haiku, light verse and traditional. "We use poetry written by or for West Coast fishermen." Buys 6 poems/year. Length: 1 page. Pay is same as editorial copy.

Florists, Nurseries and Landscaping

Readers of these publications are involved in growing, selling or caring for plants, flowers and trees. Magazines geared to consumers interested in gardening are listed in the Consumer Home and Garden section.

FLORIST, Florists' Transworld Delivery Association, 29200 Northwestern Hwy., P.O. Box 2227, Southfield MI 48037-2227. (313)355-9300. Editor-in-Chief: William P. Golden. Managing Editor: Barbara Koch. 5% freelance written. Monthly magazine for retail flower shop owners, managers and floral designers. Other readers include floriculture growers, wholesalers, researchers and teachers. Circ. 28,000. **Pays on acceptance.** Publishes ms an average of 2 months after acceptance. Buys one-time rights. Pays 10-25% kill fee. Byline given "unless the story needs a substantial rewrite." Submit seasonal material 4 months in advance. Simultaneous and previously published submissions OK. Reports in 1 month.

Nonfiction: Articles should pertain to marketing, merchandising, financial management or personnel management in a retail flower shop. Also, giftware, floral and interior design trends. No general interest, fiction or personal experience. Buys 5 unsolicited mss/year. Query with published clips. Length: 1,200-2,500 words. Pays $200-500.

Photos: State availability of photos with query. Pays $10-25 for 5×7 b&w photos or color transparencies. Buys one-time rights.

Tips: "Business management articles must deal specifically with retail flower shops and their unique merchandise and concerns. Send samples of published work with query. Suggest several ideas in query letter."

FLOWER NEWS, Dept. WM, 549 W. Randolph St., Chicago IL 60661. (312)236-8648. Fax: (312)236-8891. Editor: Rosemary C. Baldwin. Assistant Editor: Mary Hayes. Weekly newspaper for retail, wholesale florists, floral suppliers, supply jobbers and growers. Estab. 1946. Circ. 18,000. **Pays on acceptance.** Byline given. Submit seasonal material at least 2 months in advance. Previously published submissions OK. Reports "as soon as possible." Sample copy for 10×13 SAE with 10 first class stamps.

Nonfiction: How-to (increase business, set up a new shop, etc.; anything floral-related without being an individual shop story); informational (general articles of interest to industry); and technical (grower stories related to industry, but not individual grower stories). Submit complete ms. Length: 3-5 typed pages. Payment varies.

Photos: "We do not buy individual pictures. They may be enclosed with manuscript at regular manuscript rate (b&w only)."

‡**GROWERTALKS,** Ball Publishing, 335 N. River St., P.O Box 9, Batavia IL 60510. (708)208-9080. Managing Editor: Julie A. Martens. Contact: Bev Stelk, Editorial Assistant. 50% freelance written. Monthly magazine covering ornamental horticulture—primarily greenhouse flower growers. "*GrowerTalks* serves the commer-

cial greenhouse grower. Editorial emphasis is on floricultural crops: bedding plants, potted floral crops, foliage and fresh cut flowers. Our readers are growers, managers and owners." Estab. 1982. Circ. 10,500. Pays on publication. Publishes ms an average of 6 months after acceptance. Byline given. Buys first North American serial rights. Editorial lead time 4 months. Submit seasonal material 6 months in advance. Query for electronic submissions. Reports in 1 month. Sample copy and writer's guidelines free on request.

Nonfiction: How-to (time- or money-saving projects for professional flower/plant growers), interview/profile (ornamental horticulture growers), personal experience (of a grower), and technical (about growing process in greenhouse setting). "No articles that promote only one product." Buys 36 mss/year. Query. Length: 1,200-1,600 words. Pays $125 minimum for assigned articles, $75 minimum for unsolicited articles. Sometimes pays in other premiums or contributor copies.

Photos: State availability of photos with submission. Reviews 2½ × 2½ transparencies, slides and 3 × 5 prints. Negotiates payment individually. Captions, model releases and identification of subjects required. Buys one-time rights.

Tips: "Discuss magazine with ornamental horticulture growers to find out what topics that have or haven't appeared in the magazine interest them."

THE GROWING EDGE, New Moon Publishing Inc., Suite 201, 215 SW 2nd, P.O. Box 1027, Corvallis OR 97339-1027. (503)757-2511. Fax: (503)757-0028. Editor: Don Parker. 60% freelance written. Eager to work with new or unpublished writers. Quarterly magazine signature covering indoor and outdoor high-tech gardening techniques and tips. Estab. 1980. Circ. 40,000. Pays on publication. Publishes ms an average of 3 months after acceptance. Byline given. Buys first serial and reprint rights. Submit seasonal material at least 6 months in advance. Query for electronic submissions. Reports in 3 months. Sample copy $6.50. Writer's guidelines for #10 SASE.

Nonfiction: Book excerpts and reviews relating to high-tech gardening, general interest, how-to, interview/profile, personal experience and technical. Query first. Length: 500-2,500 words. Pays 10¢/word.

Photos: Pays $175/color cover photos; $25-50/inside photo. Pays on publication. Credit line given. Buys first and reprint rights.

Tips: Looking for information which will give the reader/gardener/farmer the "growing edge" in high-tech gardening and farming on topics such as hydroponics, high intensity grow lights, water conservation, drip irrigation, advanced organic fertilizers, new seed varieties and greenhouse cultivation.

‡ORNAMENTAL OUTLOOK, The Professional Magazine for the Professional Grower, FGR, Inc., 1331 N. Mills Ave., Orlando FL 32803. (407)894-6522. Editor: Rhonda Hunsinger. 75% freelance written. Magazine published 8 times/year covering ornamental horticulture. "*Ornamental Outlook* is written for commercial growers of ornamental plants in Florida. Our goal is to provide interesting and informative articles on such topics as production, legislation, safety, technology, pest control, water management and new varieties as they apply to Florida growers." Estab. 1991. Circ. 25,000. Pays on publication. Publishes ms an average of 4 months after acceptance. Byline given. Buys all rights. Editorial lead time 2 months. Submit seasonal material 3 months in advance. Query for electronic submissions. Reports in 1 month. Sample copy for 9 × 12 SAE with 5 first class stamps. Writer's guidelines free on request.

Nonfiction: Interview/profile, photo feature and technical. "No first-person articles. No word-for-word meeting transcripts or all-quote articles." Buys 50 mss/year. Query with published clips. Length: 750-1,000 words. Pays 12¢/word.

Photos: Send photos with submission. Reviews contact sheets, transparencies and prints. Offers $10-30/photo. Captions and identification of subjects required. Buys one-time rights.

Columns/Departments: Management (news that helps wholesale growers manage nursery), 750 words. Buys 10 mss/year. Query with published clips. Pays 12¢/word.

Tips: "I am most impressed by written queries that address specific subjects of interest to our audience. Our biggest demand is for features, about 1,000 words, that follow subjects listed on our editorial calendar (which is sent with guidelines)."

PRO, Helping Lawn Maintenance Firms Operate Profitably, Johnson Hill Press, Dept. WM, 1233 Janesville Ave., Ft. Atkinson WI 53538. (414)563-6388. Managing Editor: Karla Cuculi. 25% freelance written. Bimonthly tabloid on lawn maintenance firms. Estab. 1988. Circ. 40,000. Pays on publication. Byline given. Buys all rights. Submit seasonal material 6 months in advance. Reports in 1 month. Free sample copy and writer's guidelines.

Nonfiction: How-to (business management, employee management, marketing, advertising), interview/profile (successful lawn maintenance firms), new product and technical (equipment selection, use and care). Buys 12 mss/year. Query with or without published clips or send complete ms. Length: 500-1,400 words. Pays $10-300 for assigned articles; $10-200 for unassigned articles. Sometimes pays writers with contributor copies or other premiums rather than a cash payment. Pays expenses of writers on assignment.

Photos: Send photos with submission. Reviews negatives, transparencies and prints. Offers no additional payment for photos accepted with ms. Captions and identification of subjects required. Buys all rights.

Columns/Departments: Rx for Downtime (lawncare equipment preventive maintenance); Safety pen (safe equipment operation); In-gear (better procedures for bigger profits, employee productivity); Business management (business management techniques); and Ask the Computerman (business use of computers). Buys 24 mss/year. Query with published clips. Length: 500-1,400 words. Pays $10-100.

Tips: "Have experience in this industry. Query with article idea before writing article. Provide color photos with stories."

TURF MAGAZINE, P.O. Box 391, 50 Bay St., St. Johnsbury VT 05819. (802)748-8908. Fax: (802)748-1866. Editors and Publishers: Francis Carlet and Dan Hurley. Managing Editor: Susan J. Harlow. 60% freelance written. "Our readers are professional turf grass managers: superintendents of grounds for golf courses, cemeteries, athletic fields, parks, recreation fields, lawn care companies, landscape contractors/architects." Estab. 1977. Four regional editions: North, South, Central and West; with a combined national circulation of 74,000. Pays on publication. Byline given. Buys all rights or makes work-for-hire assignments. Submit seasonal material 2 months in advance. Reports in 3 months. Sample copy for 10 × 13 SAE with 8 first class stamps.

Nonfiction: How-to, interview/profile, opinion and technical. "We use on-the-job type interviews with good b&w photos that combine technical information with human interest. Buys 150 mss/year. Query with clips or send complete ms. Submissions on IBM disk preferred. Pays $100 for columns; $200 minimum for feature stories. Often pays the expenses of writers on assignment.

Photos: Send photos with ms. Payment for photos is included in payment for articles. Reviews b&w contact sheets and 8 × 10 b&w prints. Needs a variety of photos with the story. Also seeking color transparencies for cover.

Tips: "Good, accurate stories needing minimal editing, with art, are welcomed."

Government and Public Service

Listed here are journals for people who provide governmental services at the local, state or federal level or for those who work in franchised utilities. Journals for city managers, politicians, bureaucratic decision makers, civil servants, firefighters, police officers, public administrators, urban transit managers and utilities managers are listed in this section.

THE CALIFORNIA HIGHWAY PATROLMAN, California Association of Highway Patrolmen, 2030 V Street, Sacramento CA 95818-1730. (916)452-6751. Editor: Carol Perri. 80% freelance written. Monthly magazine covering CHP info; transportation; history of vehicles and/or transportation. "Our readers are either uniformed officers or pro-police oriented." Estab. 1937. Circ. 20,000. Pays on publication. Publishes ms an average of 6-9 months after acceptance. Byline given. Buys one-time rights. Submit seasonal material 6 months in advance. Simultaneous and previously published submissions OK; send information on where and when it was published. Query for electronic submissions. Reports in 1 month on queries; up to 3 months on mss. Sample copy for 9 × 12 SAE with 5 first class stamps. Writer's guidelines for #10 SASE.

Nonfiction: General interest, historical/nostalgic, humor, interview/profile, photo feature, technical and travel. "No 'how you felt when you received a ticket (or survived an accident)!' No fiction." Buys 80-100 mss/year. Query with or without published clips or send complete ms. Length: 750-3,000 words. Pays $50 minimum.

Photos: State availability of photos with submission. Send photos (or photocopies of available photos) with submission. Reviews prints. Offers $5/photo. Captions and identification of subjects required. Buys one-time rights.

‡CAMPAIGNS AND ELECTIONS, 1020 1511 K St., N.W., Washington DC 20005. (202)638-7788. Editor: Ron Faucheux. 80% freelance written. Magazine published 7 times/year covering US campaigns and elections; political professionals. Estab. 1981. Circ. 19,500. Pays on publication. Publishes ms an average of 2 months after acceptance. Byline given. Offers negotiable kill fee. Buys first North American serial rights. Accepts photocopied submissions. Query for electronic submissions. Reports in 1 weeks on queries; 3 weeks on mss. *Writer's Market* recommends allowing 2 months for reply. Sample copy for 9 × 12 SAE with 5 first class stamps. Free writer's guidelines.

Nonfiction: Book excerpts, general interest, how-to, humor/political, interview/profile/political, new product campaign industry, personal experience/political and technical/political-campaign industry. "Does not want to see anything not related to campaign industry. No 'issues,' i.e. abortion, health care, etc." Buys 12 mss/year. Query with or without published clips or send complete ms. Length: 400-2,800 words. Pays $25-1,000. Pays for brief 'news items.'

Photos: Send photos with submission. Reviews contact sheets, negatives, transparencies and 5×7 prints. Offers no additional payment for photos accepted with ms. Captions and identification of subjects required. Buys one-time rights.

Columns/Departments: Campaign Confidential (tales involving political professionals—unpublished information), 400 words; From the Field (from the campaign trail-hard, fast, unpublished), 200 words. Buys 15 mss/year. Query. Length: 200-400 words. Pays copies and $25 maximum.

Fillers: Anecdotes, short humor "must be political, true, unpublished." Buys 6/year. Length: 100-250 words. Pays copies and $25 maximum. "Call—discuss a topic. Understand we write for candidates, elected officials and the political professionals who support them, with how-to help, and case studies (always sought). Don't write news, don't interview slews of people—explain (for our target audience) how to develop a winning strategy for a narrow element of their campaign."

CANADIAN DEFENCE QUARTERLY, Revue Canadienne de Défense, Baxter Publications Inc., 310 Dupont St., Toronto, Ontario M5R 1V9 Canada. (416)968-7252. Fax: (416)968-2377. Editor: John Marteinson. 90% freelance written. Bimonthly professional journal on strategy, defense policy, military technology and history. "A professional journal for officers of the Canadian Forces and for the academic community working in Canadian foreign and defense affairs. Articles should have Canadian or NATO applicability." Estab. 1971. Pays on publication. Byline given. Offers $150 kill fee. Buys all rights. Simultaneous submissions OK. Reports in 2 months. Free sample copy and writer's guidelines.

Nonfiction: Historical, new product, opinion, technical and military strategy. Buys 36 mss/year. Query with or without published clips or send complete ms. Length: 2,500-4,000 words. Pays $150-300.

Photos: State availability of photos with submission. Offers no additional payment for photos accepted with ms. Buys one-time rights.

Tips: "Submit a well-written manuscript in a relevant field that demonstrates an original approach to the subject matter. Manuscripts *must* be double-spaced, with good margins."

CHIEF OF POLICE MAGAZINE, National Association of Chiefs of Police, 3801 Biscayne Blvd., Miami FL 33137. (305)573-0070. Editor-in-Chief: Jim Gordon. Bimonthly trade journal for law enforcement commanders (command ranks). Circ. 13,500. **Pays on acceptance.** Publishes ms an average of 4-6 months after acceptance. Byline given. Buys first rights. Submit seasonal material 6 months in advance. Simultaneous and previously published submissions OK. Reports in 2 weeks. Sample copy $3 for 9×12 SAE with 5 first class stamps. Writer's guidelines for #10 SASE.

Nonfiction: General interest, historical/nostalgic, how-to, humor, inspirational, interview/profile, new product, personal experience, photo feature, religious and technical. "We want stories about interesting police cases and stories on any law enforcement subject or program that is positive in nature. No expose types. Nothing anti-police." Buys 50 mss/year. Send complete ms. Length: 600-2,500 words. Pays $25-75 for assigned articles; $10-50 for unsolicited articles. Sometimes (when pre-requested) pays the expenses of writers on assignment.

Photos: Send photos with submission. Reviews 5×6 prints. Pays $5-10 for b&w; $10-25 for color. Captions required. Buys one-time rights.

Columns/Departments: New Police (police equipment shown and tests), 200-600 words. Buys 6 mss/year. Send complete ms. Pays $5-25.

Fillers: Anecdote, short humor and law-oriented cartoons. Buys 100/year. Length: 100-1,600 words. Pays $5-25.

Tips: "Writers need only contact law enforcement officers right in their own areas and we would be delighted. We want to recognize good commanding officers from sergeant and above who are involved with the community. Pictures of the subject or the department are essential and can be snapshots. We are looking for interviews with police chiefs and sheriffs on command level with photos."

FIREHOUSE MAGAZINE, PTN Publishing, Suite 21, 445 Broad Hollow Rd., Melville NY 11747. (516)845-2700. Fax: (516)845-7109. Editor-in-Chief: Barbara Dunleavy. 85% freelance written. Works with a small number of new/unpublished writers each year. Monthly magazine covering fire service. "*Firehouse* covers major fires nationwide, controversial issues and trends in the fire service, the latest firefighting equipment and methods of firefighting, historical fires, firefighting history and memorabilia. Fire-related books, firefighters with interesting avocations, fire safety education, hazardous materials incidents and the emergency medical services are also covered." Estab. 1976. Circ. 110,000. Pays on publication. Byline given. Exclusive submissions only. Query for electronic submissions. Reports in 1 month. Sample copy for 9×12 SAE with 7 first class stamps. Free writer's guidelines.

For explanation of symbols, see the Key to Symbols and Abbreviations on page 72. For unfamiliar words, see the Glossary.

Nonfiction: Book excerpts (of recent books on fire, EMS and hazardous materials); historical/nostalgic (great fires in history, fire collectibles, the fire service of yesteryear); how-to (fight certain kinds of fires, buy and maintain equipment, run a fire department); technical (on almost any phase of firefighting, techniques, equipment, training, administration); and trends (controversies in the fire service). No profiles of people or departments that are not unusual or innovative, reports of nonmajor fires, articles not slanted toward fire-fighters' interests. Buys 100 mss/year. Query with or without published clips or send complete ms. Length: 500-3,000 words. Pays $50-400 for assigned articles; $50-300 for unsolicited articles. Sometimes pays the expenses of writers on assignment.

Photos: Send photos with query or ms. Pays $15-45 for b&w prints; $20-200 for transparencies and color prints. Captions and identification of subjects required.

Columns/Departments: Training (effective methods); Book Reviews; Fire Safety (how departments teach fire safety to the public); Communicating (PR, dispatching); Arson (efforts to combat it). Buys 50 mss/year. Query or send complete ms. Length: 750-1,000 words. Pays $100-300.

Tips: "Read the magazine to get a full understanding of the subject matter, the writing style and the readers before sending a query or manuscript. Send photos with manuscript or indicate sources for photos. Be sure to focus articles on firefighters."

FOREIGN SERVICE JOURNAL, Dept. WM, 2101 E St. NW, Washington DC 20037-2990. (202)338-4045. Fax: (202)338-6820. Editor: Anne Stevenson-Yang. 80% freelance written. Monthly magazine for Foreign Service personnel and others interested in foreign affairs and related subjects. Estab. 1924. Pays on publication. Publishes ms an average of 3 months after acceptance. Byline given. Buys first North American serial rights. Reports in 1 month. Sample copy $3.50 for 10 × 12 SAE with 6 first class stamps.

Nonfiction: Uses articles on "diplomacy, professional concerns of the State Department and Foreign Service, diplomatic history and articles on Foreign Service experiences. Much of our material is contributed by those working in the profession. Informed outside contributions are welcomed, however." Query. Buys 5-10 unsolicited mss/year. Length: 1,000-4,000 words. Offers honoraria. Publishes novel excerpts.

● New columns are foreign vignettes and career issues.

Tips: "We're more likely to want your article if it has something to do with diplomacy or diplomats."

FOUNDATION NEWS MAGAZINE: Philanthropy and the Nonprofit Sector, Council on Foundations, Dept. WM, 1828 L St. NW, Washington DC 20036. (202)466-6512. Fax: (202)785-3926. Managing Editor: Jody Curtis. 70% freelance written. Prefers to work with published/established writers. Bimonthly magazine covering the world of philanthropy, nonprofit organizations and their relation to current events. Read by staff and executives of foundations, corporations, hospitals, colleges and universities and various nonprofit organizations. Circ. 13,000. **Pays on acceptance.** Publishes ms an average of 3 months after acceptance. Byline given. Offers negotiable kill fee. Not copyrighted. Buys all rights. Submit seasonal material 5 months in advance. Simultaneous queries and previously published submissions OK. Reports in 6 weeks.

Nonfiction: Book excerpts, expose, general interest, historical/nostalgic, how-to, interview/profile and photo feature. Submit written query; no telephone calls. Length: 2,000 words maximum. Pays $200-2,000. Pays expenses of writers on assignment.

Photos: State availability of photos with submission. Pays negotiable rates for b&w contact sheet and prints. Captions and identification of subjects required. Buys one-time rights; "some rare requests for second use."

Columns/Departments: Buys 12 mss/year. Query. Length: 900-2,000 words. Pays $250-750.

Tips: "We have a great interest in working with writers familiar with the nonprofit sector."

LAW AND ORDER, Hendon Co., 1000 Skokie Blvd., Wilmette IL 60091. (312)256-8555. Editor: Bruce W. Cameron. 90% freelance written. Prefers to work with published/established writers. Monthly magazine covering the administration and operation of law enforcement agencies, directed to police chiefs and supervisors. Estab. 1952. Circ. 30,000. Pays on publication. Publishes ms an average of 6 months after acceptance. Byline given. Buys first North American serial rights. Submit seasonal material 3 months in advance. No simultaneous queries. Query for electronic submissions. Can accept mss via CompuServe: #71171, 1344. Reports in 1 month. Sample copy for 9 × 12 SAE. Free writer's guidelines.

Nonfiction: General police interest; how-to (do specific police assignments); new product (how applied in police operation); and technical (specific police operation). Special issues: Buyers Guide (January); Communications (February); Training (March); International (April); Administration (May); Small Departments (June); Mobile Patrol (July); Equipment (August); Weapons (September); Police Science (November); and Community Relations (December). No articles dealing with courts (legal field) or convicted prisoners. No nostalgic, financial, travel or recreational material. Buys 100 mss/year. Length: 2,000-3,000 words. Pays 10¢/word for professional writers; 5¢/word for others.

Photos: Send photos with ms. Reviews transparencies and prints. Identification of subjects required. Buys all rights.

Tips: "*L&O* is a respected magazine that provides up-to-date information that chiefs can use. Writers must know their subject as it applies to this field. Case histories are well received. We are upgrading editorial quality—stories *must* show some understanding of the law enforcement field. A frequent mistake is not getting photographs to accompany article."

‡NATIONAL MINORITY POLITICS, Lionshare, Inc., Suite 3-296, 5757 Westheimer, Houston TX 77057. (713)444-4265. Editor: Gwenevere Daye Richardson. 5-10% freelance written. Monthly newsletter covering minority politics and urban affairs. "This publication's audience includes libraries, universities, political organizations, elected officials, lobbying groups, media outlets and individuals interested in minority political issues." Estab. 1988. Circ. 400. Pays on publication. Publishes ms an average of 1 month after acceptance. Byline given. Buys one-time rights. Editorial lead time 1 month. Submit seasonal material 2 months in advance. Simultaneous and previously published submissions OK. Query for electronic submissions. Reports in 2 weeks on queries. Sample copy and writer's guidelines free on request.

Nonfiction: Expose, interview/profile, opinion and features on political topics related to minority or urban affairs. Annual Political Directory, published each August. Buys 2-5 mss/year. Query with published clips. Length: 750-1,500 words. Pays $75 minimum for assigned articles, $50 minimum for unsolicited articles.

Columns/Departments: Featured Politico (minority politician of national prominence), 750 words; Editorial (timely political topic), 500 words; and Feature (timely political topic), 1,500 words. Buys 2-5 mss/year. Query with published clips. Pays $50-100.

Fillers: Gags to be illustrated by cartoonist and short humor. Pays $25-75.

Tips: "Submissions must be well-written, timely, have depth and take an angle not generally available in national newspapers and magazines. We are particularly interested in urban affairs and community development issues. We are most open to featured politico and feature articles or editorials."

9-1-1 MAGAZINE, Official Publications, Inc., 18201 Weston Pl., Tustin CA 92680. (714)544-7776. Fax: (714)838-9233. Editor: Alan Burton. 85% freelance written. Bimonthly magazine for knowledgeable emergency response personnel and those associated with those respective professions. "*9-1-1 Magazine* is published to provide information valuable to all those interested in this dangerous, exciting and rewarding profession." Estab. 1988. Circ. 30,000. Pays on publication. Publishes ms an average of 2 months after acceptance. Byline given. Offers 20% kill fee. Buys one-time and second serial (reprint) rights. Submit seasonal material well in advance. Simultaneous submissions OK. Query for electronic submissions. Reports in 2 months on queries; 3 months on mss. Must be accompanied by SASE if to be returned. Sample copy for 9 × 12 SAE with 5 first class stamps. Writer's guidelines for #10 SASE.

Nonfiction: Incident report, new product, photo feature and technical. Buys 10 mss/year. Send complete ms. "We prefer queries, but will look at manuscripts on speculation. Most positive responses to queries are considered on spec, but occasionally we will make assignments." Length: 1,000-2,500 words. Pays $100-300 for unsolicited articles.

Photos: Send photos with submission. Reviews color transparencies and prints. Offers $25-300/photo. Captions and identification of subjects required. Buys one-time rights.

Fillers: Cartoons. Buys 10/year. Pays $25-50.

Tips: "What we don't need are 'my first call' articles, or photography of a less-than-excellent quality. We seldom use poetry or fiction. *9-1-1 Magazine* is published for a knowledgable, up-scale audience. Our primary considerations in selecting material are: quality, appropriateness of material, brevity, knowledge of our readership, accuracy, accompanying photography, originality, wit and humor, a clear direction and vision, and proper use of the language."

PLANNING, American Planning Association, 1313 E. 60th St., Chicago IL 60637-2891. (312)955-9100. Editor: Sylvia Lewis. 25% freelance written. Monthly magazine emphasizing urban planning for adult, college-educated readers who are regional and urban planners in city, state or federal agencies or in private business or university faculty or students. Estab. 1972. Circ. 30,000. Pays on publication. Publishes ms an average of 3 months after acceptance. Buys all rights or first rights. Byline given. Previously published submissions OK. Reports in 2 months. Sample copy and writer's guidelines for 9 × 12 SAE with 5 first class stamps.

Nonfiction: Expose (on government or business, but on topics related to planning, housing, land use, zoning); general interest (trend stories on cities, land use, government); how-to (successful government or citizen efforts in planning; innovations; concepts that have been applied); and technical (detailed articles on the nitty-gritty of planning, zoning, transportation but no footnotes or mathematical models). Also needs news stories up to 400 words. "It's best to query with a fairly detailed, one-page letter. We'll consider any article that's well written and relevant to our audience. Articles have a better chance if they are timely and related to planning and land use and if they appeal to a national audience. All articles should be written in magazine feature style." Buys 2 features and 1 news story/issue. Length: 500-2,000 words. Pays $100-750. "We pay freelance writers and photographers only, not planners."

Photos: "We prefer that authors supply their own photos, but we sometimes take our own or arrange for them in other ways." State availability of photos. Pays $25 minimum for 8 × 10 matte or glossy prints and $200 for 4-color cover photos. Caption material required. Buys one-time rights.

POLICE, Hare Publications, 6300 Yarrow Dr., Carlsbad CA 92009-1597. (619)438-2511. Editor: Dan Burger. 90% freelance written. Monthly magazine covering topics related to law enforcement officers. "Our audience is primarily law enforcement personnel such as patrol officers, detectives and security police." Circ. 58,000. **Pays on acceptance.** Publishes ms an average of 6 months after acceptance. Buys all rights (returned to author

45 days after publication). Submit theme material 6 months in advance. Reports in 3 months. Sample copy $2. Writer's guidelines for #10 SAE with 2 first class stamps.

Nonfiction: General interest, interview/profile, new product, personal experience and technical. Buys 60 mss/year. Query or send complete ms. Length: 2,000-4,000 words. Pays $200-250 for unsolicited articles.

Photos: Send photos with submission. Reviews color transparencies. Captions required. Buys all rights.

Columns/Departments: The Beat (entertainment section — humor, fiction, first-person drama, professional tips); The Arsenal (weapons, ammunition and equipment used in the line of duty); and Officer Survival (theories, skills and techniques used by officers for street survival). Buys 75 mss/year. Query or send complete ms. Length: 1,500-2,500 words. Pays $75-250.

Tips: "You are writing for police officers — people who live a dangerous and stressful life. Study the editorial calendar — yours for the asking — and come up with an idea that fits into a specific issue. We are actively seeking talented writers."

‡POLICE AND SECURITY NEWS, Days Communications, Inc.. 15 Thatcher Rd., Quakertown PA 18951-2503. (215)538-1240. Fax: (215)538-1208. Editor: James Devery. 40% freelance written. Bimonthly tabloid on public law enforcement and private security. "Our publication is designed to provide educational and entertaining information directed toward management level. Technical information written for the expert in a manner that the non-expert can understand." Estab. 1985. Circ. 20,640. Pays on publication. Publishes ms an average of 2 months after acceptance. Byline given. Buys first North American serial rights. Submit seasonal/holiday material 2 months in advance. Simultaneous and previously published submissions OK. Free sample copy and writer's guidelines.

Nonfiction: Al Menear, articles editor. Expose, historical/nostalgic, how-to, humor, interview/profile, opinion, personal experience, photo feature and technical. Buys 12 mss/year. Query. Length: 200-4,000 words. Pays 10¢/word. Sometimes pays in trade-out of services.

Photos: State availability of photos with submission. Reviews prints (3 × 5). Offers $10-50/photo. Buys onetime rights.

Fillers: Facts, newsbreaks and short humor. Buys 6/year. Length: 200-2,000 words. Pays 10¢/word.

POLICE TIMES, American Federation of Police, 3801 Biscayne Blvd., Miami FL 33137. (305)573-0070. Fax: (305)573-9819. Editor-In-Chief: Jim Gordon. 80% freelance written. Eager to work with new/unpublished writers. Bimonthly tabloid covering "law enforcement (general topics) for men and women engaged in law enforcement and private security, and citizens who are law and order concerned." Circ. 55,000. **Pays on acceptance.** Publishes ms an average of 3-6 months after acceptance. Byline given. Buys second serial (reprint) rights. Submit seasonal material 4 months in advance. Simultaneous and previously published submissions OK. Sample copy $2.50 for 9 × 12 SAE with 3 first class stamps. Writer's guidelines for #10 SASE.

Nonfiction: Book excerpts; essays (on police science); expose (police corruption); general interest; historical/nostalgic; how-to; humor; interview/profile; new product; personal experience (with police); photo feature; and technical — all police-related. "We produce a special edition on police killed in the line of duty. It is mailed May 15 so copy must arrive six months in advance. Photos required." No anti-police materials. Buys 50 mss/year. Send complete ms. Length: 200-4,000 words. Pays $5-50 for assigned articles; $5-25 for unsolicited articles.

Photos: Send photos with submission. Reviews 5 × 6 prints. Offers $5-25/photo. Identification of subjects required. Buys all rights.

Columns/Departments: Legal Cases (lawsuits involving police actions); New Products (new items related to police services); and Awards (police heroism acts). Buys variable number of mss/year. Send complete ms. Length: 200-1,000 words. Pays $5-25.

Fillers: Anecdotes, facts, newsbreaks, cartoons and short humor. Buys 100/year. Length: 50-100 words. Pays $5-10. Fillers are usually humorous stories about police officer and citizen situations. Special stories on police cases, public corruptions, etc. are most open to freelancers.

SUPERINTENDENT'S PROFILE & POCKET EQUIPMENT DIRECTORY, Profile Publications, 220 Central Ave., P.O. Box 43, Dunkirk NY 14048-0043. (716)366-4774. Fax: (716)366-3626. Editor: Robert Dyment. 60% freelance written. Prefers to work with published/established writers. Monthly magazine covering "outstanding" town, village, county and city highway superintendents and Department of Public Works directors throughout New York state only. Estab. 1978. Circ. 2,600. Publishes ms an average of 4 months after acceptance. Pays within 90 days. Byline given for excellent material. Buys first rights. Publishes reprints of previously published articles. Send tearsheet of article. For reprints, pays 50% of the amount paid for an original article. Submit seasonal material 3 months in advance. Simultaneous queries OK. Reports in 2 months. Sample copy for 9 × 12 SAE with 4 first class stamps.

Nonfiction: Contact: John Powers. Interview/profile (of a highway superintendent or DPW director in NY state who has improved department operations through unique methods or equipment); and technical. Special issues include winter maintenance profiles. No fiction. Buys 20 mss/year. Query. Length: 1,500-2,000 words. Pays $150 for a full-length ms. "Pays more for excellent material. All manuscripts will be edited to fit our format and space limitations." Sometimes pays the expenses of writers on assignment.

Photos: Contact: John Powers. State availability of photos. Pays $5-10 for b&w contact sheets; also reviews 5×7 prints. Captions and identification of subjects required. Buys one-time rights.

Poetry: Buys poetry if it pertains to highway departments. Pays $5-15.

Tips: "We are a widely read and highly respected state-wide magazine, and although we can't pay high rates, we expect quality work. Too many freelance writers are going for the expose rather than the meat-and-potato type articles that will help readers. We use more major features than fillers. Writers should read sample copies first. We will be purchasing more material because our page numbers are increasing."

TRANSACTION/SOCIETY, Rutgers University, New Brunswick NJ 08903. (201)932-2280, ext. 83. Fax: (201)932-3138. Editor: Irving Louis Horowitz. Publisher: Mary E. Curtis. 10% freelance written. Prefers to work with published/established writers. Bimonthly magazine for social scientists (policymakers with training in sociology, political issues and economics). Estab. 1962. Circ. 45,000. Buys all rights. Byline given. Pays on publication. Publishes ms an average of 6 months after acceptance. No simultaneous submissions. Query for electronic submissions; "manual provided to authors." Reports in 3 months. Sample copy and writer's guidelines for 9×12 SAE with 5 first class stamps.

Nonfiction: Brigitte M. Goldstein, managing editor. "Articles of wide interest in areas of specific interest to the social science community. Must have an awareness of problems and issues in education, population and urbanization that are not widely reported. Articles on overpopulation, terrorism, international organizations. No general think pieces." Query. Payment for articles is made only if done on assignment. *No payment for unsolicited articles.*

Photos: Douglas Harper, photo editor. Pays $200 for photographic essays done on assignment or accepted for publication.

Tips: "Submit an article on a thoroughly unique subject, written with good literary quality. Present new ideas and research findings in a readable and useful manner. A frequent mistake is writing to satisfy a journal, rather than the intrinsic requirements of the story itself. Avoid posturing and editorializing."

YOUR VIRGINIA STATE TROOPER MAGAZINE, Virginia State Police Association, 6944 Forest Hill Ave., Richmond VA 23225. Editor: Rebecca V. Jackson. 60% freelance written. Triannual magazine covering police topics for troopers (state police), non-sworn members of the department and legislators. Estab. 1974. Circ. 5,000. **Pays on acceptance.** Publishes ms an average of 3 months after acceptance. Byline given. Buys first North American serial and all rights on assignments. Submit seasonal material 4 months in advance. Simultaneous submissions OK. Reprints OK; send typed ms with rights for sale noted and information about when and where the article previously appeared. For reprints pays 20% of their fee for an original article. Reports in 2 months.

Nonfiction: Expose (consumer or police-related); general interest; fitness/health; tourist (VA sites); financial planning (tax, estate planning tips); historical/nostalgic; how-to; book excerpts/reports (law enforcement related); humor, interview/profile (notable police figures); technical (radar) and other (recreation). Buys 55-60 mss/year. Query with clips or send complete ms. Length: 2,500 words. Pays $250 maximum/article (10¢/word). Sometimes pays expenses of writers on assignment. Does not send sample copies.

Photos: Send photos with ms. Pays $50 maximum for several 5×7 or 8×10 b&w glossy prints to accompany ms. Cutlines and model releases required. Buys one-time rights.

Cartoons: Send copies. Pays $20. Buys one-time rights. Buys 20 cartoons/year.

Fiction: Adventure, humorous, mystery, novel excerpts and suspense. Buys 3 mss/year. Send complete ms. Length: 2,500 words minimum. Pays $250 maximum (10¢/word) on acceptance.

Tips: In addition to items of interest to the VA State Police, general interest is stressed.

Groceries and Food Products

In this section are publications for grocers, food wholesalers, processors, warehouse owners, caterers, institutional managers and suppliers of grocery store equipment. See the section on Confectionery and Snack Foods for bakery and candy industry magazines.

CANADIAN GROCER, Maclean-Hunter Ltd., Maclean Hunter Building, 777 Bay St., Toronto, Ontario M5W 1A7 Canada. (416)596-5772. Editor: George H. Condon. Managing Editor: Simone Collier. 40% freelance written. Prefers to work with published/established writers. Monthly magazine about supermarketing and food retailing for Canadian chain and independent food store managers, owners, buyers, executives, food brokers, food processors and manufacturers. Estab. 1886. Circ 18,500. **Pays on acceptance.** Publishes an average of 2 months after acceptance. Byline given. Buys first Canadian rights. Publishes reprints of previously published articles. Send typed ms with rights for sale noted. Include information about when and where the article previously appeared. For reprints, pays 50% of the amount paid for an original article. Phone queries OK. Submit seasonal material 2 months in advance. Reports in 2 months. Sample copy $5.

Nonfiction: Interview (Canadian trendsetters in marketing, finance or food distribution); technical (store operations, equipment and finance); and news features on supermarkets. "Freelancers should be well versed on the supermarket industry. We don't want unsolicited material. Writers with business and/or finance expertise are preferred. Know the retail food industry and be able to write concisely and accurately on subjects relevant to our readers: food store managers, senior corporate executives, etc. A good example of an article would be 'How a dairy case realignment increased profits while reducing prices, inventory and stock-outs.' " Query with clips of previously published work. Pays 30¢/word. Pays the expenses of writers on assignment.

Photos: State availability of photos. Pays $10-25 for prints or slides. Captions preferred. Buys one-time rights.

Tips: "Suitable writers will be familiar with sales per square foot, merchandising mixes and direct product profitability."

‡CANDY WHOLESALER, American Wholesalers Marketers Association, 1128 16th St. NW, Washington DC 20036-4808. (202)463-2124. Publisher: Shelley Estersohn. Editor: Kevin Settlage. 35% freelance written. Monthly magazine for distributors of candy, tobacco, snacks, groceries and other convenience-store items. "*Candy Wholesaler* magazine is published to assist the candy/tobacco/snack food distributor in improving his business by providing a variety of relevant operational information. Serves as the voice of the distributor in the candy/tobacco/snack industry." Circ. 11,559. **Pays on acceptance.** Publishes ms an average of 4 months after acceptance. Byline given. Offers $50 kill fee. Buys all rights. Submit seasonal/holiday material 6 months in advance. Query for electronic submissions. Reports in 1 month. Sample copy for 9×12 SAE with 6 first class stamps.

Nonfiction: Historical/nostalgic, how-to (related to distribution), interview/profile, photo feature, technical (data processing) and (profiles of distribution films/or manufacturers). "No simplistic pieces with consumer focus that are financial, tax-related or legal." Buys 30-35 mss/year. Query with or without published clips, or send complete ms. Length: 8-12 double-spaced typewritten pages. Pays $750-1,000 for assigned articles. Pays $250-500 for unsolicited articles. Sometimes pays copies to industry members who author articles. Pays the expenses of writers on assignment.

Photos: Send photos with submission. Reviews contact sheets, transparencies and prints. Offers $5-10/photo. Captions and identification of subjects required. Buys all rights.

Fillers: Kevin Settlage, fillers editor. Anecdotes, facts and short humor. Length: 50-200 words. Pays $10-20.

Tips: "Talk to wholesalers about their business—how it works, what their problems are, etc. We need writers who understand this industry. Company profile feature stories are open to freelancers. Get into the nitty gritty of operations and management. Talk to several key people in the company."

CITRUS & VEGETABLE MAGAZINE, and the Florida Farmer, Suite 291, 4902 Eisenhower Blvd., Tampa FL 33634. Fax: (813)888-5290. Editor: Gordon Smith. Monthly magazine on the citrus and vegetable industries. Estab. 1938. Circ. 12,000. Pays on publication. Publishes ms an average of 1 month after acceptance. Byline given. Kill fee varies. Buys exclusive first rights. Reports in 2 months on queries. Free sample copy and writer's guidelines.

Nonfiction: Book excerpts (if pertinent to relevant agricultural issues), how-to (grower interest—cultivation practices, etc.), new product (of interest to Florida citrus or vegetable growers), personal experience and photo feature. Buys 50 mss/year. Query with published clips or send complete ms. Length: approx. 1,200 words. Pays about $200.

Photos: Send photos with submission. Reviews 5×7 prints. Prefers color slides. Offers $15/photo minimum. Captions and identification of subjects required. Buys first rights.

Columns/Departments: Citrus Summary (news to citrus industry in Florida: market trends, new product lines), and Vegetable Vignettes (new cultivars, anything on trends or developments within vegetable industry of Florida). Send complete ms.

Tips: "Show initiative—don't be afraid to call whomever you need to get your information for story together—accurately and with style. Submit ideas and/or completed ms well in advance. Focus on areas that have not been widely written about elsewhere in the press. Looking for fresh copy. Have something to sell and be convinced of its value. Become familiar with the key issues, key players in the citrus industry in Florida. Have a specific idea in mind for a news or feature story and try to submit manuscript at least 1 month in advance of publication."

FLORIDA GROCER, Florida Grocer Publications, Inc., P.O. Box 430760, South Miami FL 33243-0760. (305)441-1138. Fax: (305)661-6720. Editor: Dennis Kane. 5% freelance written. "*Florida Grocer* is a 16,000-circulation monthly trade newspaper, serving members of the Florida food industry. Our publication is edited for chain and independent food store owners and operators as well as members of allied industries." Estab.

For information on setting your freelance fees, see How Much Should I Charge?

1956. **Pays on acceptance.** Byline given. Buys all rights. Submit seasonal material 3 months in advance. Reports in 2 months. Sample copy for 10×14 SAE with 10 first class stamps.
Nonfiction: Book excerpts, expose, general interest, humor, features on supermarkets and their owners, new product, new equipment, photo feature and video. Buys variable number of mss/year. Query with or without published clips or send complete ms. Payment varies. Sometimes pays the expenses of writers on assignment.
Photos: State availability of photos with submission. Terms for payment on photos "included in terms of payment for assignment."
Tips: "We prefer feature articles on new stores (grand openings, etc.), store owners, operators; Florida-based food manufacturers, brokers, wholesalers, distributors, etc. We also publish a section in Spanish and also welcome the above types of materials in Spanish (Cuban)."

‡THE FOOD CHANNEL, America's Source For Food Trends, Noble Communications Co., 29th Floor, 515 N. State Chicago IL 60610. (312)644-4600. Editor: Christopher Wolf. Contact: Stacie Passon, managing editor. 30% freelance written. Biweekly newsletter covering food trends. "*The Food Channel* is published twice monthly by Noble & Associates, a food-focused advertising, promotional marketing and new product development company. It provides insight into emerging trends in the food and beverage industries and the implications for manufacturers, suppliers and consumers." Estab. 1988. Circ. 2,500. Pays on publication. Publishes ms an average of 2 months after acceptance. Byline given. Editorial lead time 2 months. Submit seasonal material 1 month in advance. Accepts simultaneous submissions. Query for electronic submissions. Sample copy and writer's guidelines free on request.
Nonfiction: General interest, interview/profile and new product. Length: 500-1,100 words. Pays 20¢/word.
Columns/Departments: Buys 15 mss/year. Query.
Tips: "We are most open to 500-1,100-word articles covering international trends and underground trends."

FOODSERVICE DIRECTOR, Bill Communications, 355 Park Ave. S., New York NY 10010. (212)592-6533. Fax: (212)592-6539. Editor: Walter J. Schruntek. Managing Editor: Karen Weisberg. 20% freelance written. Monthly tabloid on non-commercial foodservice operations for operators of kitchens and dining halls in schools, colleges, hospitals/health care, office and plant cafeterias, military, airline/transportation, correctional institutions. Estab. 1988. Circ. 45,000. Pays on publication. Byline given sometimes. Offers 25% kill fee. Buys all rights. Submit seasonal material 2-3 months in advance. Simultaneous submissions OK. Free sample copy.
Nonfiction: How-to, interview/profile. Buys 60-70 mss/year. Query with published clips. Length: 700-900 words. Pays $250-500. Sometimes pays the expenses of writers on assignment.
Photos: Send photos with submission. Reviews transparencies. Offers no additional payment for photos accepted with ms. Identification of subjects required. Buys all rights.
Columns/Departments: Equipment (case studies of kitchen/serving equipment in use), 700-900 words; Food (specific category studies per publication calendar), 750-900 words. Buys 20-30 mss/year. Query. Pays $150-250.

THE GOURMET RETAILER, #300, 3301 Ponce De Leon Blvd., Coral Gables FL 33134-7273. (305)446-3388. Executive Editor: Quinn Moore. 30% freelance written. Monthly magazine covering specialty foods and housewares. "Our readers are owners and managers of specialty food and upscale housewares retail units. Writers must know the trade exceptionally well and be research-oriented. Numerous interviews required for each article." Estab. 1979. Circ. 18,000. Pays on publication. Publishes ms an average of 3 months after acceptance. Byline sometimes given. No kill fee. Buys all rights. Submit seasonal material 6 months in advance. Query for electronic submissions. Reports in 2 months on queries. Free sample copy and writer's guidelines.
Nonfiction: Interview/profile (retail stores, manufacturers). "Do not send unsolicited manuscripts; queries only." Buys 12 mss/year. Query with published clips. Length: 1,500-2,200 words. Pays $500 for assigned articles plus pre-approved expenses such as phone and mail.
Photos: State availability of photos with submission. Reviews negatives, 5×7 transparencies, 8×10 prints. Offers $15-25/photo. Identification of subjects required. Buys one-time rights.
Tips: "I enjoy hearing from writers who are established in my industry and from very good writers who would like to break in. I am looking for profiles of specialty retailers. We are demanding. Last year we were NEAL Award finalists."

HEALTH FOODS BUSINESS, Howmark Publishing Corp., 567 Morris Ave., Elizabeth NJ 07208-9808. (908)353-7373. Fax: (908)353-8221. Editor: Gina Geslewitz. 40% freelance written. Eager to work with new/unpublished writers if competent and reliable. Monthly magazine for owners and managers of health food stores. Circ. 11,000. Pays on publication. Publishes ms an average of 4 months after acceptance. Buys first North American serial rights; "also exclusive rights in our trade field." Phone queries OK. "Query us about a good health food store in your area. We use many store profile stories." Simultaneous submissions OK if exclusive to their field. Reports in 2 months. Sample copy $3 for SAE with 8 first class stamps. Writer's guidelines for #10 SASE.

Nonfiction: Pays $100 and up for store profiles.

Photos: "Most articles must have photos included"; negatives and contact sheet OK. Captions required. No additional payment.

Tips: "A writer may find that submitting a letter with a sample article he/she believes to be closely related to articles read in our publication is the most expedient way to determine the appropriateness of his/her skills and expertise."

MINNESOTA GROCER, Serving the Upper Midwest Retail Food Industry, (formerly *Midwest Grocer*) Minnesota Grocers Council, Inc., 533 St. Clair Ave., St. Paul MN 55102-2859. (612)228-0973. Fax: (612)228-1949. Director of Communications: Randy Schubring. 25% freelance written. Bimonthly magazine on the retail grocery industry in Minnesota. Estab. 1951. Circ. 4,200. Pays on publication. Publishes ms an average of 1-2 months after acceptance. Byline given. Buys all rights. Submit seasonal material 3 months in advance. Previously published submissions OK. Reports in 2 months. Sample copy and writer's guidelines for 9 × 12 SAE with 4 first class stamps.

Nonfiction: How-to better market, display and sell food and other items in a grocery store. How to find new markets. Interview/profile and new products. Special issues: "We do an economic forecast in January/February issue." Buys 6 mss/year. Query with published clips. Length: 300-1,500 words. Pays $100-500 for assigned articles. Sometimes pays expenses of writers on assignment.

Photos: State availability of photos with submission. Reviews contact sheets and 5 × 7 prints. Captions, model releases and identification of subjects required. Buys all rights.

Columns/Departments: Query with published clips.

Tips: "The best way to be considered for a freelance assignment is first and foremost to have a crisp, journalistic writing style on clips. Second it is very helpful to have a knowledge of the issues and trends in the grocery industry. Because we are a regional trade publication, it is crucial that articles be localized to Minnesota or the Upper Midwest."

PRODUCE NEWS, 2185 Lemoine Ave., Fort Lee NJ 07024-6003. Fax: (201)592-0809. Editor: Gordon Hochberg. 10-15% freelance written. Works with a small number of new/unpublished writers each year. Weekly magazine for commercial growers and shippers, receivers and distributors of fresh fruits and vegetables, including chain store produce buyers and merchandisers. Estab. 1897. Circ. 10,000. Pays on publication. Publishes ms an average of 2 weeks after acceptance. Deadline is Monday afternoon before Thursday press day. Reports in 1 month. Sample copy and writer's guidelines for 10 × 13 SAE with 4 first class stamps.

Nonfiction: News stories (about the produce industry). Buys profiles, spot news, coverage of successful business operations and articles on merchandising techniques. Query. Pays minimum of $1/column inch for original material. Sometimes pays the expenses of writers on assignment.

Photos: B&w glossies. Pays $8-10 for each one used.

Tips: "Stories should be trade-oriented, not consumer-oriented. As our circulation grows in the next year, we are interested in stories and news articles from all fresh fruit-growing areas of the country."

• This publication looks for stringers in specific areas of the country to cover the produce business.

QUICK FROZEN FOODS INTERNATIONAL, E.W. Williams Publishing Co., Dept. WM, Suite 305, 2125 Center Ave., Fort Lee NJ 07024-5898. (201)592-7007. Fax: (201)592-7171. Editor: John M. Saulnier. 20% freelance written. Works with a small number of new/unpublished writers each year. Quarterly magazine covering frozen foods around the world—"every phase of frozen food manufacture, retailing, food service, brokerage, transport, warehousing, merchandising. Especially interested in stories from Europe, Asia and emerging nations." Circ. 13,700. Pays on publication. Publishes ms an average of 3 months after acceptance. Byline given. Offers kill fee; "if satisfactory, we will pay promised amount. If bungled, half." Buys all rights, but will relinquish any rights requested. Submit seasonal material 6 months in advance. Sample copy $8.

Nonfiction: Book excerpts, general interest, historical/nostalgic, interview/profile, new product (from overseas), personal experience, photo feature, technical and travel. No articles peripheral to frozen food industry such as taxes, insurance, government regulation, safety, etc. Buys 20-30 mss/year. Query or send complete ms. Length: 500-4,000 words. Pays 5¢/word or by arrangement. "We will reimburse postage on articles ordered from overseas." Sometimes pays the expenses of writers on assignment.

Photos: "We prefer photos with all articles." State availability of photos or send photos with accompanying ms. Pays $10 for 5 × 7 b&w prints (contact sheet if many shots). Captions and identification of subject required. Buys all rights. Release on request.

Columns/Departments: News or analysis of frozen foods abroad. Buys 20 columns/year. Query. Length: 500-1,500 words. Pays by arrangement.

Fillers: Newsbreaks. Length: 100-500 words. Pays $5-20.

Tips: "We are primarily interested in feature materials (1,000-3,000 words with pictures). We are now devoting more space to frozen food company developments in Pacific Rim and East European countries. Stories on frozen food merchandising and retailing in foreign supermarket chains in Europe, Japan and Australia/New Zealand are welcome. National frozen food production profiles are also in demand worldwide. A frequent mistake is submitting general interest material instead of specific industry-related stories."

THE WISCONSIN GROCER, Wisconsin Grocers Association, Suite 203, 802 W. Broadway, Madison WI 53713-1899. (608)222-4515. Eager to work with new/unpublished writers. Bimonthly magazine covering grocery industry of Wisconsin. Estab. 1900. Circ. 1,500. Pays on publication. Publishes ms an average of 3 months after acceptance. Byline given. Not copyrighted. Buys first North American serial, second serial (reprint) or simultaneous rights. Submit seasonal material 5 months in advance. Simultaneous submissions OK. Reprints OK; send photocopy of article with information about when and where the article previously appeared. Reports in 2 weeks on queries; 2 months on mss. Sample copy for 9 × 12 SAE with 3 first class stamps.
Nonfiction: How-to (money management, employee training/relations, store design, promotional ideas); interview/profile (of WGA members and Wisconsin politicians only); opinion; technical (store design or equipment). No articles about grocers or companies not affiliated with the WGA. Buys 6 mss/year. Query. Length: 500-2,000 words. Pays $15 minimum. Pays in copies if the writer works for a manufacturer or distributor of goods or services relevant to the grocery industry, or if a political viewpoint is expressed.
Photos: Send photos with submission. Reviews 5 × 7 prints. Offers no additional payment for photos accepted with ms. Identification of subjects required. Buys one-time rights.
Columns/Departments: Security (anti-shoplifting, vendor thefts, employee theft, burglary); Employee Relations (screening, training, management); Customer Relations (better service, corporate-community relations, buying trends); Money Management (DPP programs, bookkeeping, grocery—specific computer applications); Merchandising (promotional or advertising ideas); all 1,000 words. Buys 6 mss/year. Query. Length: 500-1,500 words.
Fillers: Facts and newsbreaks. Buys 6/year. Length: 50-250 words.
Tips: "How-tos are especially strong with our readers. They want to know how to increase sales and cut costs. Cover new management techniques, promotional ideas, customer services and industry trends."

Hardware

Journals for general and specialized hardware wholesalers and retailers are listed in this section. Journals specializing in hardware for a certain trade, such as plumbing or automotive supplies, are classified with other publications for that trade.

HARDWARE AGE, Chilton Co., Dept. WM, 1 Chilton Way, Radnor PA 19089. (215)964-4275. Editor-in-Chief: Terry Gallagher. Managing Editor: Rick Carter. 2% freelance written. Monthly magazine emphasizing retailing, distribution and merchandising of hardware and building materials. Circ. 71,000. Buys first North American serial rights. No guarantee of byline. Simultaneous and previously published submissions OK, if exclusive in the field. Reports in 2 months. Sample copy $1; mention *Writer's Market* in request.
Nonfiction: Rick Carter, managing editor. How-to more profitably run a hardware store or a department within a store. "We particularly want stories on local hardware stores and home improvement centers, with photos. Stories should concentrate on one particular aspect of how the retailer in question has been successful." Also wants technical pieces (will consider stories on retail accounting, inventory management and business management by qualified writers). Buys 1-5 unsolicited mss/year. Submit complete ms. Length: 1,500-3,000 words. Pays $100-400.
Photos: "We like store features with b&w photos. Usually use b&w for small freelance features." Send photos with ms. Pays $25 for 4 × 5 glossy b&w prints. Captions preferred. Buys one-time rights.
Columns/Departments: Retailers' Business Tips; Wholesalers' Business Tips; and Moneysaving Tips. Query or submit complete ms. Length: 1,000-1,250 words. Pays $100-150. Open to suggestions for new columns/departments.

Home Furnishings and Household Goods

Readers rely on these publications to learn more about new products and trends in the home furnishings and appliance trade. Magazines for consumers interested in home furnishings are listed in the Consumer Home and Garden section.

APPLIANCE SERVICE NEWS, 110 W. Saint Charles Rd., P.O. Box 789, Lombard IL 60148-0789. Editor: William Wingstedt. Monthly "newspaper style" publication for professional service people whose main interest is repairing major and/or portable household appliances. Their jobs consist of service shop owner, service manager or service technician. Estab. 1950. Circ. 51,000. Buys all rights. Byline given. Pays on publication. Will consider simultaneous submissions. Reports in about 1 month. Sample copy $2.

Nonfiction: James Hodl, associate editor. "Our main interest is in technical articles about appliances and their repair. Material should be written in a straightforward, easy-to-understand style. It should be crisp and interesting, with high informational content. Our main interest is in the major and portable appliance repair field. We are not interested in retail sales." Query. Pays $200-300/feature.

Photos: Pays $20 for b&w photos used with ms. Captions required.

CHINA GLASS & TABLEWARE, Doctorow Communications, Inc., P.O. Box 2147, Clifton NJ 07015. (201)779-1600. Fax: (201)779-3242. Editor-in-Chief: Amy Stavis. 60% freelance written. Works with a small number of new/unpublished writers each year. Monthly magazine for buyers, merchandise managers and specialty store owners who deal in tableware, dinnerware, glassware, flatware and other tabletop accessories. Estab. 1892. Pays on publication. Publishes ms an average of 3-4 months after acceptance. Buys one-time rights. Byline given. Phone queries OK. Submit seasonal material 3 months in advance. Reports in 3 months. Sample copy and writer's guidelines for 9 × 12 SAE; mention *Writer's Market* in request.

Nonfiction: General interest (on store successes, reasons for a store's business track record); interview (personalities of store owners, how they cope with industry problems, why they are in tableware); and technical (on the business aspects of retailing china, glassware and flatware). "Bridal registry material always welcomed." No articles on how-to or gift shops. Buys 2-3 mss/issue. Query. Length: 1,500-3,000 words. Pays $60/page. Sometimes pays the expenses of writers on assignment.

Photos: State availability of photos with query. No additional payment for b&w or color contact sheets. Captions required. Buys first serial rights.

Tips: "Show imagination in the query; have a good angle on a story that makes it unique from the competition's coverage and requires less work on the editor's part for rewriting a snappy beginning."

FLOORING MAGAZINE, Williamsport Plaza, Suite 213, 398 W. Bagley Rd., Berea OH 44017. (216)243-7757. Fax: (216)243-7759. Editor: Mark S. Kuhar. 10-20% freelance written. Prefers to work with published/established writers. Monthly magazine for floor covering retailers, wholesalers, contractors, specifiers and designers. Estab. 1931. Circ. 25,000. Pays on publication. Publishes ms an average of 3 months after acceptance. Byline given. Buys all rights. Query for electronic submissions. "Send letter with writing sample to be placed in our freelance contact file." Editorial calendar available on request. Send #10 SASE.

Nonfiction: "Mostly staff written. Buys a small number of manuscripts throughout the year. Needs writers with 35mm photography skills for local assignments. Study our editorial calender and send a concise query."

HAPPI, (*Household and Personal Products Industry*), 17 S. Franklin Turnpike, P.O. Box 555, Ramsey NJ 07446-0555. Fax: (201)825-0553. Editor: Tom Branna. 5% freelance written. Magazine for "manufacturers of soaps, detergents, cosmetics and toiletries, waxes and polishes, insecticides, and aerosols." Estab. 1964. Circ. 18,000. Not copyrighted. Pays on publication. Publishes ms an average of 2 months after acceptance. Submit seasonal material 2 months in advance. Reports in 1 month.

Nonfiction: "Technical and semi-technical articles on manufacturing, distribution, marketing, new products, plant stories, etc., of the industries served. Some knowledge of the field is essential in writing for us." Buys informational interview, photo feature, spot news, coverage of successful business operations, new product articles, coverage of merchandising techniques and technical articles. No articles slanted toward consumers. Query with published clips. Buys 3 to 4 mss a year. Length: 500-2,000 words. Pays $25-300. Sometimes pays expenses of writers on assignment.

Photos: Black and white 5 × 7 or 8 × 10 glossies purchased with mss. Pays $10.

Tips: "The most frequent mistakes made by writers are unfamiliarity with our audience and our industry; slanting articles toward consumers rather than to industry members."

HOME LIGHTING & ACCESSORIES, P.O. Box 2147, Clifton NJ 07015. (201)779-1600. Fax: (201)779-3242. Editor: Peter Wulff. 2-5% freelance written. Prefers to work with published/established writers. Monthly magazine for lighting stores/departments. Estab. 1923. Circ. 10,000. Pays on publication. Publishes ms an average of 4-6 months after acceptance. Buys all rights. Submit seasonal material 6 months in advance. Reports in 2 months. Sample copy for 9 × 12 SAE with 4 first class stamps.

Nonfiction: Interview (with lighting retailers); personal experience (as a businessperson involved with lighting); profile (of a successful lighting retailer/lamp buyer); and technical (concerning lighting or lighting design). Buys less than 6 mss/year. Query. Pays $60/published page. Sometimes pays the expenses of writers on assignment.

Photos: State availability of photos with query. Offers no additional payment for 5 × 7 or 8 × 10 b&w glossy prints. Pays additional $90 for color transparencies used on cover. Captions required.

Tips: "We don't need fillers—only features."

Hospitals, Nursing and Nursing Homes

In this section are journals for medical and nonmedical nursing home personnel, clinical and hospital staffs and medical laboratory technicians and managers. Journals publishing technical material on medical research and information for physicians in private practice are listed in the Medical category.

AMERICAN JOURNAL OF NURSING, 555 W. 57th St., New York NY 10019-2961. (212)582-8820. Editor: Mary B. Mallison, RN. 2% freelance written. Eager to work with new/unpublished writers. Monthly magazine covering nursing and health care. Estab. 1900. Circ. 235,000. Pays on publication. Publishes ms an average of 6 months after acceptance. Byline given. Simultaneous queries OK. Reports in 3 weeks on queries, 3 months on mss. Sample copy $4. Free writer's guidelines.
Nonfiction: How-to, satire, new product, opinion, personal experience, photo feature and technical. No material other than nursing care and nursing issues. "Nurse authors mostly accepted for publication." Query. Length: 1,000-1,500 words. Payment negotiable. Pays the expenses of writers on assignment.
Photos: Forbes Linkhorn, art director. Reviews b&w and color transparencies and prints. Model release and identification of subjects required. Buys variable rights.
Columns/Departments: Buys 20 mss/year. Query with or without clips of published work.

HOSPITAL RISK MANAGEMENT, American Health Consultants, P.O. Box 740059, Atlanta GA 30374. (404)262-7436. Fax: (404)262-7837. Editor: Cheli Brown. 10% freelance written. Monthly newsletter on health care risk management. Estab. 1977. Circ. 2,500. Pays on publication. Publishes ms an average of 2 months after acceptance. Byline given. Buys all rights. Reports in 3 months. Free sample copy.
Nonfiction: How-to (pertaining to hospitals' legal liability management). We need informative articles written by experts in the field that aren't boring, on topics concerning hospital safety, insurance for hospitals and reducing legal risk. Nothing analytical. Buys 10-12 mss/year. Query. Length: 1,500 words. Pays $50-150 or free subscription.

NURSEWEEK, California's Largest Newspaper and Career Guide for Nurses, California Nursing Review, 1156-C Aster Ave., Sunnyvale CA 94086. (408)249-5877. Editor: Clarice Hutchison. 25% freelance written. Biweekly nursing newspaper for greater L.A. and S.F. areas with six additional statewide issues throughout year. Estab. 1989. Circ. 80,000 metro; 210,000+ statewide. Pays on publication. Byline given. Offers kill fee, which may vary, depending on the situation. Buys all rights. Submit seasonal material 6 months in advance. Query for electronic submissions. Reports in 3 months. Sample copy and writer's guidelines for 9×12 SAE with 2 first class stamps.
Nonfiction: News, workplace, socio-economic, historical/nostalgic, humor, inspirational, interview/profile, personal experience, technical (continuing education articles) and travel, all nursing related. "Open to new ideas. No articles unrelated to nursing." Buys 120 mss/year. Query with published clips. Length: 300-2,500 words. Pays $100-500 for assigned articles; $75-300 for unsolicited articles. Pays expenses of writers on assignment.
Photos: State availability of photos with submission. Reviews transparencies and 3×5 prints. Captions, model releases and identification of subjects required; no exceptions. Buys one-time rights.
Columns/Departments: After Hours (what nurses do in their off hours); Newsmaker (profile of a distinguished nurse), 1,500-2,000 words. Buys 40 mss/year. Query with published clips. Pays $100-300.
Tips: "Query the editor. Keep the audience in mind; different than consumer health publications. Strongly urge writers to read several issues before inquiring. Features and news items relevant to registered nurses are the best areas for the freelancer to break in."

NURSING94, Springhouse Corporation, P.O. Box 908, 1111 Bethlehem Pike, Springhouse PA 19477-0908. (215)646-8700. Fax: (215)653-0826. Editor: Maryanne Wagner. Managing Editor: Jane Benner. 100% freelance written by nurses. Monthly magazine on the nursing field. "Our articles are written by nurses for nurses; we look for practical advice for the working nurse that reflects the author's experience." Estab. 1971. Circ. 500,000. Pays on publication. Publishes ms an average of 12-18 months after acceptance. Byline given. Offers 50% kill fee. Buys all rights. Submit seasonal material 6-8 months in advance. Query for electronic submissions. Reports in 2 weeks on queries; 3 months on mss. Sample copy for $3 with 9×12 SAE. "Call Pat Wolf for free writers' guidelines."
Nonfiction: Book excerpts, expose, how-to (specifically as applies to nursing field), inspirational, new product, opinion, personal experience and photo feature. No articles from patients' point of view, humor articles, poetry, etc. Buys 100 mss/year. Query. Length: 100 words minimum. Pays $50-400.
Photos: State availability of photos with submission. Offers no additional payment for photos accepted with ms. Model releases required. Buys all rights.

Hotels, Motels, Clubs, Resorts and Restaurants

These publications offer trade tips and advice to hotel, club, resort and restaurant managers, owners and operators. Journals for manufacturers and distributors of bar and beverage supplies are listed in the Beverages and Bottling section.

BARTENDER MAGAZINE, Foley Publishing, P.O. Box 158, Liberty Corner NJ 07938. (908)766-6006. Fax: (908)766-6607. Publisher: Raymond P. Foley. Editor: Jaclyn M. Wilson. Quarterly magazine emphasizing liquor and bartending for bartenders, tavern owners and owners of restaurants with full-service liquor licenses. 100% freelance written. Prefers to work with published/established writers; eager to work with new/ unpublished writers. Circ. 140,000. Pays on publication. Publishes ms an average of 3 months after acceptance. Buys first serial, first North American serial, one-time, second serial (reprint), all and simultaneous US rights. Byline given. Submit seasonal material 3 months in advance. Simultaneous and previously published submissions OK. Send tearsheet of article. For reprints, pays 50% of the amount paid for an original article. Reports in 2 months. Sample copies for 9×12 SAE with 9 first class stamps.
Nonfiction: General interest, historical, how-to, humor, interview (with famous bartenders or ex-bartenders); new products, nostalgia, personal experience, unique bars, opinion, new techniques, new drinking trends, photo feature, profile, travel and bar sports or bar magic tricks. Send complete ms. Length: 100-1,000 words.
Photos: Send photos with ms. Pays $7.50-50 for 8×10 b&w glossy prints; $10-75 for 8×10 color glossy prints. Caption preferred and model release required.
Columns/Departments: Bar of the Month; Bartender of the Month; Drink of the Month; New Drink Ideas; Bar Sports; Quiz; Bar Art; Wine Cellar; Tips from the Top (from prominent figures in the liquor industry); One For The Road (travel); Collectors (bar or liquor-related items); Photo Essays. Query. Length: 200-1,000 words. Pays $50-200.
Fillers: Clippings, jokes, gags, anecdotes, short humor, newsbreaks and anything relating to bartending and the liquor industry. Length: 25-100 words. Pays $5-25.
Tips: "To break in, absolutely make sure that your work will be of interest to all bartenders across the country. Your style of writing should reflect the audience you are addressing. The most frequent mistake made by writers in completing an article for us is using the wrong subject."

CASINO JOURNAL, Casino Journal Publishing Group, 2524 Arctic Ave., Atlantic City NJ 08401. (609)344-9000. Fax: (609)345-3469. Editor: Roger Gros. Estab. 1984. 20% freelance written. Monthly magazine that covers specific technical aspects of the casino industry. Pays on publication. Publishes ms an average of 2 months after acceptance. Byline given. Buys all rights. Submit seasonal material 4 months in advance. Query for electronic submissions. Reports in 3 months. Sample copy $2 for SAE with 6 first class stamps.
Nonfiction: Interview/profile, new product, photo feature and technical. "No first-person gambling stories." Buys 25-30 mss/year. Query with or without published clips or send complete ms. Length: 500-2,500 words. Pays $75-150 for assigned articles. "If author has product to sell, we run ad."
Photos: State availability of photos with submission. Reviews contact sheets, transparencies and prints. Offers $10-25/photo. Captions, model releases and identification of subjects required. Buys one-time rights.

FLORIDA HOTEL & MOTEL JOURNAL, The Official Publication of the Florida Hotel & Motel Association, Accommodations, Inc., P.O. Box 1529, Tallahassee FL 32302-1529. (904)224-2888. Editor: Mrs. Jayleen Woods. 10% freelance written. Prefers to work with published/established writers. Monthly magazine for managers in the lodging industry (every licensed hotel, motel and resort in Florida). Estab. 1978. Circ. 7,000. Pays on publication. Publishes ms an average of 2 months after acceptance. Byline given. Offers $50 kill fee. Buys all rights and makes work-for-hire assignments. Submit seasonal material 2 months in advance. Reports in 4-6 weeks. Sample copy and writer's guidelines for 9×12 SAE with 7 first class stamps.
Nonfiction: General interest (business, finance, taxes); historical/nostalgic (old Florida hotel reminiscences); how-to (improve management, housekeeping procedures, guest services, security and coping with common hotel problems); humor (hotel-related anecdotes); inspirational (succeeding where others have failed); interview/profile (of unusual hotel personalities); new product (industry-related and non brand preferential); photo feature (queries only); technical (emerging patterns of hotel accounting, telephone systems, etc.); travel (transportation and tourism trends only—no scenics or site visits); and property renovations and maintenance techniques. "We would like to run more humorous anecdotes on hotel happenings than we're presently receiving." Buys 10-12 mss/year. Query with proposed topic and clips of published work. Length: 750-2,500 words. Pays $75-250 "depending on type of article and amount of research." Sometimes pays the expenses of writers on assignment.
Photos: Send photos with ms. Pays $25-100 for 4×5 color transparencies; $10-15 for 5×7 b&w prints. Captions, model release and identification of subjects required.
Tips: "We prefer feature stories on properties or personalities holding current membership in the Florida Hotel and Motel Association. Membership and/or leadership brochures are available (SASE) on request. We're open to articles showing how hotel management copes with energy systems, repairs, renovations, new guest needs and expectations. The writer may have a better chance of breaking in at our publication with

short articles and fillers because the better a writer is at the art of condensation, the better his/her feature articles are likely to be."

FLORIDA RESTAURATEUR, Florida Restaurant Association, 2441 Hollywood Blvd., Hollywood FL 33020-6623. (305)921-6300. Fax: (305)925-6381. Editor: Hugh P. (Mickey) McLinden. 15% freelance written. Monthly magazine for food service and restaurant owners and managers—"deals with trends, legislation, training, sanitation, new products, spot news." Estab. 1946. Circ. 26,331. Pays on publication. Publishes ms an average of 1 month after acceptance. Byline given. Buys one-time rights. Submit seasonal material 3 months in advance. Simultaneous submissions OK. Publishes reprints of previously published articles. Send photocopy of article and typed ms with rights for sale noted. Include information about when and where the article previously appeared. For reprints, pays 25% of the amount paid for an original article. Reports in 3 weeks on queries; 1 month on mss. *Writer's Market* recommends allowing 2 months for reply.
Nonfiction: How-to, general interest, interview/profile, new product, personal experience and technical. Query. Length: 500-2,000 words. Pays $200-300 for assigned articles; $150-250 for unsolicited articles.
Photos: State availability of photos with submission. Reviews transparencies and 5×7 prints. Offers $50-250/photo. Model releases and identification of subjects required. Buys one-time rights.

FOOD & SERVICE, Texas Restaurant Association, P.O. Box 1429, Austin TX 78767-1429. (512)472-3666 (in Texas, 1-800-395-2872). Fax: (512)472-2777. Editor: Julie Stephen Sherrier. 50% freelance written. Magazine published 11 times/year providing business solutions to Texas restaurant owners and operators. Estab. 1941. Circ. 5,700. **Pays on acceptance.** Written queries required. Reports in 1 month. Byline given. Not copyrighted. Buys first rights. Simultaneous queries, photocopied submissions OK. No previously published submissions. Query for electronic submissions. Sample copy and editorial calendar for 11×14 SAE with 6 first class stamps. Free writer's guidelines.
Nonfiction: Features must provide business solutions to problems in the restaurant and food service industries. Topics vary but always have business slant; usually particular to Texas. No restaurant critiques, human interest stories or seasonal copy. Quote members of the Texas Restaurant Association; substantiate with facts and examples. Query. Length: 2,000-2,500 words, features; shorter articles sometimes used; product releases, 300-word maximum. Payment rates vary.
Photos: State availability of photos, but photos usually assigned.

INNKEEPING WORLD, P.O. Box 84108, Seattle WA 98124. Fax: (206)362-7847. Editor/Publisher: Charles Nolte. 75% freelance written. Eager to work with new/unpublished writers. Magazine published 10 times/year emphasizing the hotel industry worldwide. Published 10 times a year. Estab. 1979. Circ. 2,000. **Pays on acceptance.** Publishes ms an average of 2 months after acceptance. Buys all rights. No byline. Submit seasonal material 1 month in advance. Reports in 1 month. Sample copy and writer's guidelines for 9×12 SAE with 3 first class stamps.
Nonfiction: Managing—interviews with successful hotel managers of large and/or famous hotels/resorts (600-1,200 words); Marketing—interviews with hotel marketing executives on successful promotions/case histories (300-1,000 words); Sales Promotion—innovative programs for increasing business (100-600 words); Food Service—outstanding hotel restaurants, menus and merchandising concepts (300-1,000 words); and Guest Relations—guest service programs, management philosophies relative to guests (200-800 words). Pays $100 minimum or 20¢/word (whichever is greater) for main topics. Other topics—advertising, cutting expenses, guest comfort, hospitality, ideas, reports and trends, special guestrooms, staff relations. Length: 50-500 words. Pays 20¢/word. "If a writer asks a hotel for a complimentary room, the article will not be accepted, nor will *Innkeeping World* accept future articles from the writer."
Tips: "We need more in-depth reporting on successful sales promotions—results-oriented information."

LODGING HOSPITALITY MAGAZINE, Penton Publishing, 1100 Superior Ave., Cleveland OH 44114-2543. (216)696-7000. Fax: (216)696-7658. Editor: Edward Watkins. 10% freelance written. Prefers to work with published/established writers. Monthly magazine covering the lodging industry. "Our purpose is to inform lodging management of trends and events which will affect their properties and the way they do business. Audience: owners and managers of hotels, motels, resorts." Estab. 1949. Circ. 50,000. **Pays on acceptance.** Publishes ms an average of 2 months after acceptance. Byline given. Buys first rights. Reports in 2 months.
Nonfiction: General interest, how-to, interview/profile and travel. Special issues: renovation (April); financing (May), technology (June), franchising (July), renovation (September) and human resources (October). "We do *not* want personal reviews of hotels visited by writer, or travel pieces. All articles are geared to hotel executives to help them in their business." Buys 25 mss/year. Query. Length: 700-2,000 words. Pays $150-600. Sometimes pays the expenses of writers on assignment.
Photos: State availability of photos with submission. Reviews contact sheets and transparencies. Offers no additional payment for photos accepted with ms. Captions and identification of subjects required. Buys one-time rights.
Columns/Departments: *Strategies*, all one-page reports of 700 words. Buys 10 mss/year. Query. Pays $150-250.

RESTAURANT HOSPITALITY, Penton Publishing, 1100 Superior Ave., Cleveland OH 44114. (216)696-7000. Fax: (216)696-0836. Editor-in-Chief: Michael DeLuca. 10% freelance written. Works exclusively with published/established writers. Monthly magazine covering the foodservice industry for owners and operators of independent restaurants, hotel foodservices, executives of national and regional restaurant chains. Estab. 1919. Circ. 100,000. Average issue includes 5-10 features. **Pays on acceptance.** Publishes ms an average of 3 months after acceptance. Byline given. Buys first North American serial rights. Reports in 2 months. Sample copy for 9 × 12 SAE with 10 first class stamps.

• *Restaurant Hospitality* is accepting fewer stories.

Nonfiction: General interest (articles that advise operators how to run their operations profitably and efficiently), interview (with operators) and profile. Stories on psychology, consumer behavior, managerial problems and solutions, design elements. No restaurant reviews. Buys 20-30 mss/year. Query with clips of previously published work and a short bio. Length: 500-1,500 words. Pays $125/published page. Pays the expenses of writers on assignment.

Photos: Send color photos with ms. Captions required.

Tips: "We would like to receive queries for articles on food and management trends. We need new angles on old stories, and we like to see pieces on emerging trends and technologies in the restaurant industry. Our readers don't want to read how to open a restaurant or why John Smith is so successful."

‡**THE SUCCESSFUL HOTEL MARKETER, The Newsletter of Profit-Building Ideas for the Lodging Industry**, (incorporating *Motel/Hotel Insider*), Magna Publications, Inc., 2718 Dryden Dr., Madison WI 53704-3006. (608)249-2455. Fax: (608)249-0355. Editor: Tim Kelley. 10% freelance written. "The newsletter is a high-priced, monthly publication that offers practical, useful, innovative and transferable marketing strategies and success stories to its lodging industry audience. It has no advertising, its articles are brief and targeted. Its checklists, interviews, how-to and perspective pieces are all tightly written to save the reader's valuable time." Estab. 1971. Publishes ms an average of 2 months after acceptance. Byline given. Offers 25% kill fee. Buys first North American serial rights. Submit seasonal material 4 months in advance. Query for electronic submissions. Sample copy $6. Writer's guidelines for 6 × 9 SASE.

Nonfiction: Query or send complete ms. Length: 175-400 words: pays $75-125; 400-650 words: pays $125-200; 650-800 words: pays $200-300.

Tips: "This newsletter's audience is very knowledgeable about the industry, hungry for fresh marketing ideas and at the same time tends to know all the well-publicized promotional strategies in vogue. It is our mission to find the unpublished ones, by building contacts with creative hotel marketers around the country. Therefore, we welcome sophisticated hotel marketing information: articles, interviews or checklists on new promotional packages, dos and don'ts, marketing for new properties and renovations, successful strategies by B&B's, etc."

VACATION INDUSTRY REVIEW, Worldex Corp., P.O. Box 431920, South Miami FL 33243-1920. (305)666-1861, ext. 7022. Fax: (305)665-2546. Editor: George Leposky. 20% freelance written. Prefers to work with published/established writers. Quarterly magazine covering leisure lodgings (timeshare resorts, fractionals, and other types of vacation ownership properties). Estab. 1982. Circ. 15,000. Pays on publication. Publishes ms an average of 3-6 months after acceptance. Byline given. Buys all rights and makes work-for-hire assignments. Submit seasonal material 6 months in advance. Query for electronic submissions. Reports in 1 month. Writer's guidelines for #10 SASE.

Nonfiction: How-to, interview/profile, new product, opinion, personal experience, technical and travel. No consumer travel or non-vacation real-estate material. Buys 8-10 mss/year. Query with published clips. Length: 1,000-2,500 words. Pays 20¢/word. Pays the expenses of writers on assignment, if previously arranged.

Photos: Send photos with submission. Reviews contact sheets, 35mm transparencies, and 5 × 7 or larger prints. Offers no additional payment for photos accepted with ms. Captions and identification of subjects required. Buys one-time rights.

Tips: "We want articles about the business aspects of the vacation industry: entrepreneurship, project financing, design and construction, sales and marketing, operations, management—in short, anything that will help our readers plan, build, sell, and run a quality vacation property that satisfies the owners/guests and earns a profit for the developer and marketer. Our destination pieces are trade-oriented, reporting the status of tourism and the development of various kinds of vacation ownership facilities in a city, region, or country. You can discuss things to see and do in the context of a resort located near an attraction, but that shouldn't be the main focus or reason for the article. We're also interested in owners associations at vacation ownership resorts (not residential condos). Prefers electronic submissions. Query for details."

‡**THE WISCONSIN RESTAURATEUR**, Wisconsin Restaurant Association, #300, 31 S. Henry, Madison WI 53703. (608)251-3663. Fax: (608)251-3666. Editor: Jan La Rue. 20% freelance written. Eager to work with new/unpublished writers. Monthly magazine (December/January combined) emphasizing restaurant industry, particularly Wisconsin, for restaurateurs, hospitals, institutions, food service students, etc. Estab. 1933. Circ. 4,000. **Pays on acceptance, or publication, varies.** Publishes ms an average of 6 months after acceptance. Buys all rights or first rights. Editorial lead time 2 months. Pays 10% kill fee or $10. Byline given. Phone queries OK. Submit seasonal/holiday material 3 months in advance. Previously published submissions OK;

send tearsheet of article or short story and information about when and where it previously appeared. Reports in 3 weeks. Sample copy and writer's guidelines for 9 × 12 SASE.

Nonfiction: Book excerpts, historical/nostalgia, how-to, humor, inspirational interview/profile, new product, opinion, personal experience and photo feature articles. "All must relate to foodservice. Need more in-depth articles. No features on nonmember restaurants." Buys 6 mss/year. Query with "copyright clearance information and a note about the writer in general." Length: 1,000-5,000 words. Pays $100 minimum for assigned articles; $25 minimum for unsolicited articles. Pays other than cash payment when requested.

Photos: Fiction and how-to mss stand a better chance for publication if photos are submitted. State availability of photos; send photocopies. Pays $5-10 for b&w 8 × 10 glossy prints. Model release required. Buys one-time rights; varies.

Columns/Departments: Opinion, Guest Editorial. Buys 2/year. Query. Length 500-1,500 words. Pays $20-100.

Fiction: Experimental, historical, humorous stories and slice-of-life vignettes—related to foodservice only. "No romance or anything biased." Buys 4 mss/year. Query. Length: 1,000-5,000 words. Pays $10-50.

Poetry: Uses all types of poetry, but must have foodservice as subject. Does not want to see "anything expressing bad attitude." Buys 6/year. Submit maximum 3 poems. Length: 25 lines maximum. Pays $5-50.

Fillers: Clippings, jokes, gags to be illustrated by cartoonist, newsbreaks, facts, anecdotes and short humor. No puzzles or games. Buys 6/year. Length: 100 words maximum. Pays $5-15.

Tips: "Most open to features, stand alone articles and fillers."

Industrial Operations

Industrial plant managers, executives, distributors and buyers read these journals. Some industrial management journals are also listed under the names of specific industries. Publications for industrial supervisors are listed in Management and Supervision.

CHEMICAL BUSINESS, Schnell Publishing Company, 80 Broad St., New York NY 10004-2203. (212)248-4177. Fax: (212)248-4901. Editor: Arthur R. Kavaler. Executive Editor: J. Robert Warren. 90% freelance written. Monthly magazine covering chemicals and related process industries such as plastics, paints, some minerals, essential oils, soaps, detergents. Publishes features on the industry, management, financial (Wall Street), marketing, shipping and storage, labor, engineering, environment, research, international and company profiles. Estab. 1979. Circ. 36,000. **Pays on acceptance.** Publishes ms an average of 3 months after acceptance. Byline given. Offers $100 kill fee. Buys all rights. Query for electronic submissions. Reports in 1 month. Free sample copy and writer's guidelines.

● Starting with the April 1993 issue, *Chemical Business* converted to a report-letter format and provides managerial-style articles on issues of interest to executives in the chemical process industries. Rates ($500 for assigned articles plus expenses and a $100 kill fee) remained unchanged, as did most other particulars, but fewer freelance pieces are used (2-3 per issue or 23-36 per year). Freelance mss are, thus, being cut back by nearly half.

Nonfiction: Chemical industry-targeted ideas only; no how-to articles. Publishes only assigned articles. Call before submitting article ideas. Query. Length: 1,200-1,500 words. Pays $500 for assigned articles. Pays the expenses of writers on assignment.

Photos: Send photos with submission. Reviews contact sheets, negatives and 35mm or 70mm ("almost any size") transparencies. No pay for company photos; offers $10-25/photo taken by writer. Model releases required. Buys all rights.

COMPRESSED AIR, 253 E. Washington Ave., Washington NJ 07882-2495. Editor/Publications Manager: S.M. Parkhill. 75% freelance written. Magazine published 8 times/year emphasizing applied technology and industrial management subjects for engineers and managers. Estab. 1896. Circ. 145,000. Buys all rights. Publishes ms an average of 6 months after acceptance. Reports in 6 weeks. Free sample copy; mention *Writer's Market* in request.

Nonfiction: "Articles must be reviewed by experts in the field." Buys 56 mss/year. Query with published clips. Pays negotiable fee. Sometimes pays expenses of writers on assignment.

Photos: State availability of photos in query. Payment for slides, transparencies and glossy prints is included in total purchase price. Captions required. Buys all rights.

Tips: "We are presently looking for freelancers with a track record in industrial/technology/management writing. Editorial schedule is developed in the summer before the publication year and relies heavily on article ideas from contributors. Resume and samples help. Writers with access to authorities preferred; and prefer interviews over library research. The magazine's name doesn't reflect its contents. We suggest writers request sample copies."

INDUSTRIAL FABRIC PRODUCTS REVIEW, Industrial Fabrics Association International, Suite 800, 345 Cedar St., St. Paul MN 55101. (612)222-2508. Fax: (612)222-8215. Senior Editor: Sue Hagen. 100% staff- and industry-written. Monthly magazine covering industrial textiles and products made from them for company owners, salespersons and researchers in a variety of industrial textile areas. Estab. 1915. Circ. 10,000. Pays on publication. Publishes ms an average of 2 months after acceptance. Byline given. Buys all rights. Simultaneous queries OK if outside the same market of readers. Reports in 1 month.

Nonfiction: Technical, marketing and other topics related to any aspect of industrial fabric industry from fiber to finished fabric product. Special issues include new products, industrial products and equipment. No historical or apparel-oriented articles. Buys 10-15 mss/year. Query with phone number. Length: 1,200-3,000 words.

Tips: "We encourage freelancers to learn our industry and make regular, solicited contributions to the magazine. We no longer buy photography."

MANUFACTURING SYSTEMS, The Management Magazine of Integrated Manufacturing, Hitchcock Publishing Co., 191 S. Gary Ave., Carol Stream IL 60188. (708)665-1000. Fax: (708)462-2225 (staff). Editor: Tom Inglesby. Senior Editor: Kevin Parker. Managing Editor: Barbara Dutton. Associate Editor: Carol Smith. 10-15% freelance written. Monthly magazine covering computers/information in manufacturing for upper and middle-level management in manufacturing companies. Estab. 1982. Circ. 115,000. **Pays on acceptance.** Publishes ms an average of 4 months after acceptance. Byline given. Offers 35% kill fee on assignments. Buys all rights. Publishes reprints of previously published articles. Send typed ms with rights for sale noted; include information about when and where the article previously appeared. For reprints,pays 60% of the amount paid for an original article. Simultaneous submissions OK. Exclusive submissions receive more consideration. Query for electronic submissions. Reports in 2 months. Free sample copy and writer's guidelines.

Nonfiction: Book excerpts, essays, general interest, interview/profile, new product, opinion, technical, case history—applications of system. "Each issue emphasizes some aspect of manufacturing. Editorial schedule available, usually in September, for next year." Buys 6-8 mss/year. Query with or without published clips or send complete ms. Length: 500-2,500 words. Pays $150-600 for assigned articles; $50/published page for unsolicited articles. Sometimes pays limited, pre-authorized expenses of writers on assignment.

Photos: State availability of photos with submission. Reviews contact sheets, negatives, 2×2 and larger transparencies and 5×7 and larger prints. Offers no additional payment for photos accepted with ms. Captions and identification of subjects required. Buys one-time rights.

Columns/Departments: Forum (VIP-to-VIP, bylined by manufacturing executive), 1,000-1,500 words. Buys 1-2 mss/year. Query. Sometimes pays $100-200. "These are *rarely* paid for but we'd consider ghost written pieces bylined by 'name.' "

Tips: "We are moving more toward personal management issues and away from technical articles—how to manage, not what tools are available. Check out success stories of companies winning against overseas competition in international marketplace. New trends in manufacturing include application of artificial intelligence (expert systems); standards for computer systems, networks, operating systems; computer trends, trade, taxes; movement toward lights-out factory (no human workers) in Japan and some US industries; desire to be like Japanese in management style; more computer power in smaller boxes. Features are the most open area. We will be happy to provide market information, reader profile and writer's guidelines on request. We are moving to 'require' submission in electronic form—diskette, MCI-mail. Rekeying ms into our word processing system is more work (and cost)."

PLANT, Dept. WM, 777 Bay St., Toronto, Ontario M5W 1A7 Canada. (416)596-5776. Fax: (416)596-5552. Editor: Ron Richardson. 10% freelance written. Prefers to work with published/established writers. Bimonthly magazine for Canadian plant managers and engineers. Estab. 1940. Circ. 42,000. **Pays on acceptance.** Publishes ms an average of 2 months after acceptance. Buys first Canadian rights. Reports in 3 weeks. Free sample copy.

Nonfiction: How-to, technical and management technique articles. Must have Canadian slant. No generic articles that appear to be rewritten from textbooks. Buys fewer than 20 unsolicited mss/year. Query. Pays 28¢/word minimum. Pays the expenses of writers on assignment.

 • *Plant* is seeking submission which display greater technical knowledge about computers in industry.

Photos: State availability of photos with query. Pays $60 for b&w prints; $100 for 2¼×2¼ or 35mm transparencies. Captions required. Buys one-time rights.

Tips: "Increased emphasis on the use of computers and programmable controls in manufacturing will affect the types of freelance material we buy. Read the magazine. Know the Canadian readers' special needs. Case histories and interviews only—no theoretical pieces. We have gone to tabloid-size format, and this means shorter (about 800-word) features."

Always check the most recent copy of a magazine for the address and editor's name before you send in a query or manuscript.

QUALITY ASSURANCE BULLETIN, Bureau of Business Practice, 24 Rope Ferry Rd., Waterford CT 06386. (800)243-0876. Fax: (203)434-3078. 80% freelance written. Biweekly newsletter for quality assurance supervisors and managers and general middle to top management. **Pays on acceptance.** No byline given. Buys all rights. Reports in 2 weeks on queries; 1 month on mss. *Writer's Market* recommends allowing 2 months for reply. Free sample copy and writer's guidelines.
Nonfiction: Interview and articles with a strong how-to slant that make use of direct quotes whenever possible. Query before writing your article. Length: 800-1,500 words. Pays 8-15¢/word.
Tips: "Write for freelancer guidelines and follow them closely."

QUALITY DIGEST, QCI International, P.O. Box 1503, 1425 Vista Way, Red Bluff CA 96080-1503. (916)527-8875. Editor: Scott M. Paton. 75% freelance written. Monthly trade magazine covering quality improvement. Estab. 1981. Circ. 20,000. **Pays on acceptance.** Byline given. Buys all rights. Submit seasonal material 4 months in advance. Accepts simultaneous and previously published submissions. Query for electronic submissions. Reports in 2 months. Free sample copy and writer's guidelines.
Nonfiction: Book excerpts, how-to implement quality programs, etc., interview/profile, opinion, personal experience and technical. Buys 25 mss/year. Query with or without published clips or send complete ms. Length: 1,000-6,000 words. Pays $25-350. Pays with contributor copies or other premiums for unsolicited mss. Sometimes pays expenses of writers on assignment.
Photos: Send photos with submission. Reviews any size prints. Offers no additional payment for photos accepted with ms. Captions, model releases and identification of subjects required. Buys one-time rights.
Tips: "Please be specific in your articles. Explain what the problem was, how it was solved and what the benefits are. Tell the reader how the technique described will benefit him or her."

WEIGHING & MEASUREMENT, Key Markets Publishing Co., P.O. Box 5867, Rockford IL 61125. (815)229-1818. Fax: (815)229-4086. Editor: David M. Mathieu. Bimonthly magazine for users of industrial scales and meters. Estab. 1914. Circ. 15,000. **Pays on acceptance.** Buys all rights. Pays 20% kill fee. Byline given. Reports in 2 weeks. Sample copy $2.
Nonfiction: Interview (with presidents of companies); personal opinion (guest editorials on government involvement in business, etc.); profile (about users of weighing and measurement equipment); and technical. Buys 25 mss/year. Query on technical articles; submit complete ms for general interest material. Length: 750-1,500 words. Pays $125-200.

Information Systems

These publications give computer professionals more data about their field. Consumer computer publications are listed under Personal Computers.

‡**COMPUTER GRAPHICS WORLD,** Penn Well Publishing Company, One Technology Park Dr., Westford MA 01886. (508)392-2166. Editor: Stephen Porter. Managing Editor: Audrey Doyle. 60% freelance written. Monthly magazine covering computer graphics. "*Computer Graphics World* specializes in covering computer-aided 3D modeling, animation technologies and visualization and their uses in engineering, science and entertainment applications." Estab. 1978. Circ. 70,000. **Pays on acceptance.** Publishes ms an average of 2 months after acceptance. Byline given. Offers 25% kill fee. Buys all rights. Editorial lead time 3 months. Submit seasonal material 3 months in advance. Reports in 2 months. Sample copy and writer's guidelines free on request.
Nonfiction: General interest, how-to (how-to create quality models and animations), interview/profile, new product, opinion, technical and user application stories. "We do not want to run articles that are geared to computer programmers. Our focus as a magazine is on end-users involved in specific applications." Buys 40 mss/year. Query with published clips. Length: 1,200-3,000 words. Pays $500 minimum. Sometimes pays expenses of writers on assignment.
Columns/Departments: Output (offers personal opinion on relevant issue), 700 words; Reviews (offers hands-on review of important new products), 750 words; and Application Stories (highlights a unique use of the technology by a single user), 800 words. Buys 60 mss/year. Query with published clips. Pays $100-500.
Tips: "Freelance writers will be most successful if they have some familiarity with computers and know how to write from an end-user perspective. They do not need to be computer experts, but they do have to understand how to explain the impact of the technology and the applications in which an end-user is involved. Both our feature section and our application story section are quite open to freelancers. The trick to winning acceptance for your story is to have a well-developed idea that highlights a fascinating new trend or development in computer graphics technology or profiles a unique and fascinating use of the technology by a single user or a specific class of users."

DBMS, Miller Freeman, Inc., Dept. WM, 411 Borel Ave., San Mateo CA 94402-32522. (415)358-9500. Managing Editor: Kathleen O'Connor. 60% freelance written. Monthly magazine covering database applications and technology. "Our readers are database developers, consultants, VARs, programmers in MIS/DP departments and serious users." Estab. 1988. Circ. 55,000. **Pays on acceptance.** Publishes ms 3 months after acceptance. Byline given. Offers 33% kill fee. Buys all rights. Query for electronic submissions. Reports in 6 weeks on queries. Samply copy for 9 × 12 SAE with 8 first class stamps.

Nonfiction: Technical. Buys 40-50 mss/year. Query with published clips. Length: 750-6,000 words. Pays $800.

Photos: Send photos with submission. Offers no additional payment for photos accepted with ms. Captions, model releases and identification of subjects required. Buys all rights.

Tips: "New writers should submit clear, concise queries of specific article subjects and ideas. *Read the magazine* to get a feel for what articles we publish. This magazine is written for a highly technical computer database developer, consultant and user readership. We need technical features that inform this audience of new trends, software, hardware and techniques, including source code, screen caps and procedures."

‡DR. DOBB'S JOURNAL, Miller Freeman Inc., 411 Borel Ave., San Mateo CA 94402. (415)358-9500. Editor-in-Chief: Jon Erickson. Managing Editor: Tami Zemel. Contact: Jon Erickson. 65% freelance written. Monthly magazine covering software for the professional programmer. Estab. 1976. Circ. 100,000+. Pays on publication. Publishes ms an average of 15 months after acceptance. Byline given. Offers $50 kill fee. Buys first North American serial rights. Editorial lead time 3 months. Query for electronic submissions. Writer's guidelines free on request.

Nonfiction: New product and technical (hi-end software). "No self-serving articles from companies." Buys approximately 200 mss/year. Query. Length: 2,500-3,000 words. Pay negotiable. Sometimes pays expenses of writers on assignment.

Photos: State availability of photos with submission. Reviews contact sheets, negatives and transparencies. Negotiates payment individually. Buys one-time rights.

Tips: "*DDJ* covers C, assembly language, C++, Pascal, Moderator-2. *DDJ* also covers DOS, UNIX, OS/2, and System 7.0."

‡FLEXLINES, Data Access Corp., 14000 SW 199 Ave., Miami FL 33186. (305)238-0012. Managing Editor: Beverly Horning-Gore. 20% freelance written. Bimonthly magazine covering Data Flex software. "Publication is for users, developers and sellers of Data Flex software." Estab. 1984. Circ. 10,000. Pays on publication. Publishes ms an average of 2 months after acceptance. Byline given. Negotiable kill fee. Buys all rights. Query for electronic submissions. Reports in 2 weeks. Sample copy and writer's guidelines free on request.

Nonfiction: New product, technical (about Data Flex). Buys 15 mss/year. Send complete ms. Length: 1,000-5,000 words. Pays $100-250. Sometimes pays expenses of writers on assignment.

Photos: Send photos with submission. Reviews prints (any). Offers no additional payment for photos accepted with ms. Captions and model releases required. Buys one-time rights.

Tips: "Know Data Flex as an expert."

‡HP/APOLLO WORKSTATION, Publications and Communications, Inc., 12416 Hymeadow Dr., Austin TX 78750. (512)250-9023. Editor: Larry Storer. Managing Editor: John Mitchell. 40% freelance written. Monthly magazine covering news for Hewlett-Packard/Apollo Workstation computer users. "We provide detailed and useful information for engineers, scientists and technical managers on trends, products, services and market news about HP and Apollo Workstation computers." Estab. 1985. Circ. 18,000. Pays on publication. Publishes ms an average of 2-3 months after acceptance. Byline given. Buys one-time rights. Editorial lead time 2 months. Query for electronic submissions. Reports in 2 weeks on queries; 1 month on mss. *Writer's Market* recommends allowing 2 months for reply. Sample copy and writer's guidelines free on request.

Nonfiction: How-to, new product and technical. Buys 12-15 mss/year. Send complete ms. Length: 1,500 words maximum. Pays $200 minimum for assigned articles, $150 minimum for unsolicited articles.

Photos: State availability of photos with submission. Offers no additional payment for photos accepted with ms.

Tips: "This is as niche as the computer market writer can get. If you don't know H-P Workstations and the software and peripherals they require, pass by. If you do, call and let's talk. We can fit your interests into a story that will work for the readership by chatting rather than written correspondence. We accept good, balanced site profiles and technical articles most from freelancers. Site profiles should be unique (HP computers at the White House, using them to run housing projects, etc.). Technical pieces explain how aspects of the system work, or how to make new office configurations (networks, different vendor's computers) work."

‡ID SYSTEMS, The Magazine of Automatic Data Collection, Helmers Publishing, Inc.. 174 Concord St., Peterborough NH 03458. (603)924-9631. Fax: (603)924-7408. Editor: Deborah Navas. Managing Editor: Margaret Mary Langen. 30% freelance written. Monthly magazine about automatic identification technologies. Circ. 68,000. **Pays on acceptance.** Byline given. Buys all rights. Query for electronic submissions. Reports in 2 months on queries. Free sample copy and writer's guidelines.

Nonfiction: Application stories and technical tutorials. "We want articles we have assigned, not spec articles." Buys 20/year. Query with published clips. Length: 1,500 words. Pays $300.

Photos: Send photos with submission. Reviews contact sheets, transparencies (35mm) and prints. Offers no additional payment for photos accepted with ms. Identification of subjects required. Rights vary article to article.

Tips: "Send letter, resume and clips. If background is appropriate, we will contact writer as needed. We give detailed instructions."

NETWORK WORLD, Network World Publishing, Dept. WM, 161 Worcester Rd., Framingham MA 01701. (508)875-6400. Fax: (508)820-3467. Editor: John Gallant. Features Editor: Charles Bruno. 25% freelance written. Weekly tabloid covering data, voice and video communications networks (including news and features on communications management, hardware and software, services, education, technology and industry trends) for senior technical managers at large companies. Estab. 1986. Circ. 150,000. **Pays on acceptance.** Byline given. Offers negotiable kill fee. Buys all rights. Submit all material 2 months in advance. Query for electronic submissions. Reports in 3 weeks. Free sample copy and writer's guidelines.

Nonfiction: Expose, general interest, how-to (build a strong communications staff, evaluate vendors, choose a value-added network service), humor, interview/profile, opinion and technical. Editorial calendar available. "Our readers are users: avoid vendor-oriented material." Buys 100-150 mss/year. Query with published clips. Length: 500-2,500 words. Pays $600 minimum—negotiable maximum for assigned or unsolicited articles.

Photos: Send photos with submission. Reviews 35mm, 2¼ and 4×5 transparencies and b&w prints (prefers 8×10 but can use 5×7). Captions, model releases and identification of subjects required. Buys one-time rights.

Tips: "We look for accessible treatments of technological, managerial or regulatory trends. It's OK to dig into technical issues as long as the article doesn't read like an engineering document. Feature section is most open to freelancers. Be informative, stimulating, controversial and technically accurate."

SOFTWARE MANAGEMENT NEWS, (formerly *Software Maintenance News*), Suite 5F, 141 Saint Mark's Place, Staten Island NY 10301. (718)816-5522. Fax: (718)816-9038. Editor: Nicholas Zvegintzov. 50% freelance written. Bimonthly magazine covering software maintenance. Estab. 1983. Circ. 4,000. Pays on publication. Publishes ms an average of 3 months after acceptance. Byline given. Buys one-time rights. Simultaneous submissions OK. Query for electronic submissions. Reports in 1 week. Free sample copy.

Nonfiction: New product, technical. "No how-to or user stories." Buys 12 mss/year. Query or send complete ms. Length: 100-2,400 words. Pays about 4¢/word.

Photos: State availability of photos with submission. Offers no additional payment for photos accepted with ms. Captions required. Buys one-time rights.

Fiction: We *are* looking for fiction. Must be about software. Buys 1 ms/year. Query or send complete ms. Length: 600-2,400 words. Pays about 4¢/word.

Poetry: Haiku, light verse. Must be about software! Buys 2 poems/year. Pays about 4¢/word.

Tips: "Call first. Show familiarity with field."

UNIFORUM MONTHLY, Uniforum Association, 2901 Tasman Dr., Santa Clara CA 95054-1179. (408)986-8840. Fax: (408)986-1645. Publications Director: Richard Shippee. Managing Editor: Susan Bryant. 80% freelance writtten. Monthly trade journal covering UNIX and open systems. "Writers must have a sound knowledge of the UNIX operating system." Estab. 1981. Circ. 12,000. **Pays on acceptance.** Publishes ms an average of 2 months after acceptance. Byline given. Offers 30% kill fee. Buys all rights. Query for electronic submissions. Reports in 2 months. Free sample copy and writer's guidelines.

Nonfiction: Interview/profile, opinion and technical. Buys 35 mss/year. Query with or without published clips. Length: 1,000-3,500 words. Pays $0-1,200. Sometimes pays in other premiums or contributors copies "when article is written by industry member." Pays expenses of writers on assignment. International writers ⸱ actively sought.

Photos: Send photos with submission. "Photos are required with ms, but offers no additional payment." Buys one-time rights.

Columns/Departments: Career Corner (career tips), 700-800 words; UAR Update, 700-800 words. Federal Watch, 700-800 words. Buys 12 mss/year. Query. Pays $0-250.

UNIX WORLD, McGraw-Hill's Magazine of Open Systems Computing, McGraw-Hill Inc., 1900 O'Farrell St., San Mateo CA 94403. (415)513-6800. Fax: (415)513-6986. Managing Editor: David Diamond. 30% freelance written. Monthly magazine directed to people who use, make or sell UNIX products, particularly in an open systems environment. Readers are employed in management, engineering and software development. Estab. 1978. Circ. 94,000. **Pays on acceptance.** A rewrite is usually required. Publishes ms an average of 4 months after acceptance. Byline given. Offers kill fee. Buys all rights. Electronic submissions only. Reports in 1 month. Sample copy $3. Writer's guidelines sent. Ask for editorial calendar so query can be tailored to the magazine's need; send SASE with 2 first class stamps.

Nonfiction: Increasingly looks for articles on how end-users are using UNIX in an open system environment (strategies). Also needs vendor strategy stories, industry personality profiles and industry trend articles. Tutorials (technical articles on the UNIX system or the C language); new products; technical overviews; and product reviews. Query by phone or with cover letter and published clips. Length: 1,500-3,000 words. Pays $100-2,000. Sometimes pays the expenses of writers on assignment.

Tips: "We have shifted more toward a business and commercial focus. The best way to get an acceptance on an article is to consult our editorial calendar and tailor a pitch to a particular story."

Insurance

BUSINESS & HEALTH, Solutions in Managed Care, Medical Economics Publishing Co., 5 Paragon Dr., Montvale NJ 07645. (201)358-7208. Fax: (201)573-1045. Editor: Joe Burns. Managing Editor: Cindy Cordero. 90% freelance written. Magazine published 14 times/year covering health care for employers offering benefits for workers. "*B&H* carries articles about how employers can cut their health care costs and improve the quality of care they provide to workers. We also write about health care policy at the federal, state and local levels." Estab. 1983. Circ. 40,000. **Pays on acceptance.** Publishes ms an average of 2 months after acceptance. Byline given. Offers 20% kill fee. Buys all rights. Editorial lead time 3 months. Submit seasonal material 4 months in advance. Query for electronic submissions. Reports in 1 month on queries; 2 months on mss. Sample copy for 9×12 SAE with 6 first class stamps. Writer's guidelines for #10 SASE.
Nonfiction: How-to (cut health care benefits costs). "No articles that do not include a cost-benefit analysis." Buys 150 mss/year. Query with published clips. Length: 2,000-3,500 words. Pays $800-1,200 for articles. Pays expenses of writers on assignment.
Columns/Departments: State Report (state health care reform measures), 1,000-2,000 words; Law Report (legal issues in employee health care), 1,000-2,000 words; and Coalition Report (efforts by employer coalitions to cut costs), 1,000-3,000 words. Buys 42 mss/year. Query with published clips. Pays $500-1,000.
Tips: "Please read and follow writer's guidelines, which include examples of well written articles that have been published in *B&H*. Readers approach articles from a business point of view and want to see an evaluation of the costs versus the benefits of all strategies discussed. Include plenty of charts, graphs and tables supporting the strategy discussed. Use plenty of cost-benefit analysis data."

‡COMPASS, Marine Office of America Corporation (MOAC), 180 Maiden Lane, New York NY 10038. (212)440-7735. Editor: David R. Thompson. 100% freelance written. Prefers to work with published/established writers. Semiannual magazine of the Marine Office of America Corporation distributed in the US and overseas to persons in marine insurance (agents, brokers, risk managers), government authorities and employees. Estab. 1955. Circ. 8,000. Pays half on acceptance, half on publication. Publishes ms an average of 6 months after acceptance. Byline given. Offers $750 kill fee on mss accepted for publication, but subsequently cancelled. Offers $250 kill fee on solicited ms rejected for publication. Not copyrighted. Buys first North American serial rights. Does not accept previously published work, unsolicited mss or works of fiction. Query first. Simultaneous queries OK. Query for electronic submissions. Reports in 2 months on queries. Free sample copy and writer's guidelines.
Nonfiction: General interest, historical/nostalgic and technical. US or overseas locale. "Historical/nostalgia should relate to ships, trains, airplanes, balloons, bridges, sea and land expeditions, marine archeology, seaports and transportation of all types. General interest includes marine and transportation subjects; fishing industry; farming; outdoor occupations; environmental topics such as dams, irrigation projects, water conservations, inland waterways; space travel and satellites. Articles must have human interest. Technical articles may cover energy exploration and development—offshore oil and gas drilling, developing new sources of electric power and solar energy; usages of coal, water and wind to generate electric power; special cargo handling such as containerization on land and sea; salvage; shipbuilding; bridge or tunnel construction. Articles must not be overly technical and should have strong reader interest." No book excerpts, first-person, exposes, how-to, or opinion. Buys 8 mss/year. Query with published clips. Length: 1,500-2,000 words. Pays $1,500 maximum. Sometimes pays the expenses of writers on assignment.
Photos: Robert A. Cooney, photo editor. (212)546-2471. State availability of photos. Reviews b&w and transparencies and prints. Captions and identification of subjects required. Buys one-time rights.
Tips: "We want profiles of individuals connected with marine, energy, and transportation fields who are unusual. Send a brief outline of the story idea to editor mentioning also the availability of photographs in b&w and color. All articles must be thoroughly researched and original. Articles should have human interest through the device of interviews. We only publish full-length articles—no fillers."

FLORIDA UNDERWRITER, National Underwriter Company, Suite 213, 9887 Gandy Blvd. N., St. Petersburg FL 33702-2488. (813)576-1101. Fax: (813)577-7424. Editor: James E. Seymour. Managing Editor: Garry Baumgartner. 20% freelance written. Monthly magazine about insurance. "*Florida Underwriter* covers insurance for Florida insurance professionals: producers, executives, risk managers, employee benefit administrators. We want material about any insurance line, Life & Health or Property & Casualty, but *must* have a Florida tag—Florida authors preferred." Estab. 1984. Circ. 10,000. Pays on publication. Publishes ms an average of 2-3 months after acceptance. Byline given. Buys all rights. Submit seasonal material 3 months in advance. Simultaneous and previously published submissions OK (notification of other submission, publications required). Query for electronic submissions. Reports in 1 month. Free sample copy and writer's guidelines.

Nonfiction: Essay, expose, historical/nostalgic, how-to, interview/profile, new product, opinion and technical. "We don't want articles that aren't about insurance for insurance people or those that lack Florida angle. No puff pieces. Note: Most non-inhouse pieces are contributed gratis by industry experts." Buys 6 mss/year. Query with or without published clips or send complete ms. Length: 500-1,500 words. Pays $50-150 for assigned articles; $25-100 for unsolicited articles. "Industry experts contribute in return for exposure." Sometimes pays expenses of writers on assignment.

Photos: State availability of photos with submission. Send photos with submission. Reviews 5×7 prints. Offers no additional payment for photos accepted with ms. Identification of subjects required.

GEICO DIRECT, K.L. Publications, Suite 105, 2001 Killebrew Dr., Bloomington MN 55425-1879. Editor: Patricia Burke. 60% freelance written. Semiannual magazine published for the Government Employees Insurance Company (GEICO) policyholders. Estab. 1988. Circ. 1.5 million. Pays on acceptance by client. Byline given. Buys first North American serial rights. Query for electronic submissions. Reports in 2 months.
Nonfiction: Americana, home and auto safety, car care, financial, lifestyle and travel. Query with published clips. Length: 1,000 words. Pays $350-600.
Photos: Reviews 35mm transparencies. Payment varies.
Columns/Departments: Moneywise, 50+, Your Car. Query with published clips. Length: 500-600 words. Pays $175-350.
Tips: "We prefer work from published/established writers, especially those with specialized knowledge of the insurance industry, safety issues and automotive topics."

THE LEADER, Fireman's Fund Insurance Co., 777 San Marin Dr., Novato CA 94998-0000. (415)899-2109. Fax: (415)899-2126. Editor/Communications Manager: Jim Toland. 70% freelance written. Quarterly magazine on insurance. "*The Leader* contains articles and information for Fireman's Fund employees and retirees about special projects, employees and offices nationwide—emphasizing the business of insurance and the unique people who work for the company." Estab. 1863. **Pays on acceptance.** Publishes ms an average of 3 months after acceptance. Simultaneous submissions OK. Publishes reprints of previously published articles; send tearsheet or photocopy of article and typed ms with rights for sale noted. Reports in 1 month on mss. *Writer's Market* recommends allowing 2 months for reply. Free sample copy.
Nonfiction: Interview/profile, new products and employees involved in positive activities in the insurance industry and in the communities where company offices are located. Query with published clips. Length: 200-2,500 words. Pays $100-500.
Photos: Reviews contact sheets and prints. Sometimes buys color slides. Offers $50-75/photo for b&w, up to $250 for color. Buys one-time rights.
Tips: "It helps to work in the insurance business and/or know people at Fireman's Fund. Writers with business reporting experience are usually most successful—though we've published many first-time writers. Research the local Fireman's Fund branch office (not sales agents who are independents). Look for newsworthy topics. Strong journalism and reporting skills are greatly appreciated."

PROFESSIONAL AGENT MAGAZINE, The magazine of the National Association of Professional Insurance Agents, 400 N. Washington St., Alexandria VA 22314-9345. (703)836-9340; (703)836-9345 after 5 pm Eastern time. Fax: (703)836-1279. Editor: Alan Prochoroff. 85% freelance written. Monthly magazine covering insurance/small business for independent insurance agents, legislators, regulators and others in the industry. Estab. 1936. Circ. 30,000. **Pays on acceptance.** Publishes ms an average of 2 months after acceptance. Byline given. Buys exclusive rights in the industry. Prefers electronic submissions. Reports in 3 months. Sample copy and writer's guidelines for 9×12 SAE with 5 first class stamps.
Nonfiction: Management for independent insurance agents. Buys 24-30 mss/year. Query with published clips or send complete ms. Length: 2,000-4,000 words. Pays $650-1,250. Pays fax and long-distance telephone expenses of writers on assignment.
Tips: "All work is assigned. No writing on spec. We prefer to work with established magazine writers who are familiar with business and/or the insurance industry, particularly from an agent's perspective. Always looking to add to our stable of regular contributors. Query by phone or letter; send clips or mss and include SASE. We prefer submissions by modem or disk (Mac or 3.5″ IBM), with hard copy accompanying by mail."

Jewelry

THE DIAMOND REGISTRY BULLETIN, #806, 580 5th Ave., New York NY 10036. (212)575-0444. Fax: (212)575-0722. Editor-in-Chief: Joseph Schlussel. 50% freelance written. Monthly newsletter. Estab. 1969. Pays on publication. Buys all rights. Submit seasonal material 1 month in advance. Simultaneous and previously published submissions OK. Reports in 3 weeks. Sample copy $5.
Nonfiction: Prevention advice (on crimes against jewelers); how-to (ways to increase sales in diamonds, improve security, etc.); and interview (of interest to diamond dealers or jewelers). Submit complete ms. Length: 50-500 words. Pays $75-150.

Tips: "We seek ideas to increase sales of diamonds."

THE ENGRAVERS JOURNAL, 26 Summit St., P.O. Box 318, Brighton MI 48116. (313)229-5725. Fax: (313)229-8320. Co-Publisher: Michael J. Davis. Managing Editor: Rosemary Farrell. 15% freelance written. "We are eager to work with published/established writers as well as new/unpublished writers." Magazine published 10 times/year covering the recognition and identification industry (engraving, marking devices, awards, jewelry, and signage.) "We provide practical information for the education and advancement of our readers, mainly retail business owners." Estab. 1975. **Pays on acceptance.** Publishes ms an average of 1 year after acceptance. Byline given "only if writer is recognized authority." Buys all rights (usually). Query with published clips and resume. Previously published submissions OK. Query for electronic submissions. Reports in 2 weeks. Free writer's guidelines; sample copy to "those who send writing samples with inquiry."

Nonfiction: General interest (industry-related); how-to (small business subjects, increase sales, develop new markets, use new sales techniques, etc.); interview/profile; new product; photo feature (a particularly outstanding signage system); and technical. No general overviews of the industry. Buys 12 mss/year. Query with writing samples "published or not," or "send samples and resume to be considered for assignments on speculation." Length: 1,000-5,000 words. Pays $75-250, depending on writer's skill and expertise in handling subject.

Photos: Send photos with query. Reviews 8×10 prints. Pays variable rate. Captions, model release and identification of subjects required.

Tips: "Articles should always be down to earth, practical and thoroughly cover the subject with authority. We do not want the 'textbook' writing approach, vagueness, or theory—our readers look to us for sound practical information."

FASHION ACCESSORIES, S.C.M. Publications, Inc., 65 W. Main St., Bergenfield NJ 07621-1696. (201)384-3336. Fax: (201)384-6776. Managing Editor: Samuel Mendelson. Monthly newspaper covering costume or fashion jewelry. "Serves the manufacturers, manufacturers' sales reps, importers and exporters who sell exclusively through the wholesale level in ladies' fashion jewlery, men's jewelry, gifts and boutiques and related novelties." Estab. 1951. Circ. 8,000. **Pays on acceptance.** Byline given. Not copyrighted. Buys first rights. Submit seasonal material 3 months in advance. Sample copy $2 for 9×12 SAE with 4 first class stamps.

Nonfiction: Essays, general interest, historical/nostalgic, how-to, humor, interview/profile, new product and travel. Buys 20 mss/year. Query with published clips. Length: 1,000-2,000 words. Pays $100-300. Sometimes pays the expenses of writers on assignment.

Photos: Send photos with submission. Reviews 4×5 prints. Offers no additional payment for photos accepted with ms. Identification of subjects required. Buys one-time rights.

Columns/Departments: Fashion Report (interviews and reports of fashion news), 1,000-2,000 words.

Tips: "We are interested in anything that will be of interest to costume jewelry buyers at the wholesale level."

Journalism and Writing

Journalism and writing magazines cover both the business and creative sides of writing. Writing publications offer inspiration and support for professional and beginning writers. Although there are many valuable writing publications that do not pay, we only have space to list those writing publications that pay for articles.

‡**AMERICAN JOURNALISM REVIEW,** (formerly Washington Journalism Review), University of Maryland College of Journalism, Suite 310, 4716 Pontiac St., College Park MD 20740. (301)513-0001. Fax: (301)441-9495. Editor: Rem Rieder. Contact: Elliott Negin, managing editor. 90% freelance written. Magazine published 10 times/year covering journalism. "*AJR* reports on the business, ethics and problems of the new media." Estab. 1977. Circ. 25,000. Pays on publication. Publishes ms an average of 2 months after acceptance. Byline given. Offers 25% kill fee. Buys first North American serial rights and second serial (reprint) rights. Editorial lead time 2-3 months. Submit seasonal material 3-4 months in advance. Query for electronic submissions. Reports in 1 month. Please read a copy before sending queries. Sample copy $4.50.

Nonfiction: Analysis of media coverage, book excerpts, essays, expose, humor and interview/profile. Buys 100 mss/year. Query with published clips. Length: 500-5,000 words. Pays 20¢/word minimum. Pays expenses of writers on assignment.

Photos: "We only use commissioned photos."

Fillers: Contact: Chip Rowe, Associate Editor. Buys 100/year. Length: 5-30 words. Pays $25. "*AJR*'s 'Take 2' column prints humorous headlines and short excerpts from articles."

BOOK DEALERS WORLD, North American Bookdealers Exchange, P.O. Box 606, Cottage Grove OR 97424. (503)942-7455. Editorial Director: Al Galasso. Senior Editor: Judy Wiggins. 50% freelance written. Quarterly magazine covering writing, self-publishing and marketing books by mail. Circ. 20,000. Pays on publication. Publishes ms an average of 3 months after acceptance. Byline given. Buys first serial and second serial (reprint) rights. Simultaneous and previously published submissions OK. Reports in 1 month. Sample copy $3.

Nonfiction: Book excerpts (writing, mail order, direct mail, publishing); how-to (home business by mail, advertising); and interview/profile (of successful self-publishers). Positive articles on self-publishing, new writing angles, marketing, etc. Buys 10 mss/year. Send complete ms. Length: 1,000-1,500 words. Pays $25-50.

Columns/Departments: Print Perspective (about new magazines and newsletters); Small Press Scene (news about small press activities); and Self-Publisher Profile (on successful self-publishers and their marketing strategy). Buys 20 mss/year. Send complete ms. Length: 250-1,000 words. Pays $5-20.

Fillers: Fillers concerning writing, publishing or books. Buys 6/year. Length: 100-250 words. Pays $3-10.

Tips: "Query first. Get a sample copy of the magazine."

‡BOOK WRITERS MARKET LETTER, Archer Publications, P.O. Box 158, Mount Joy PA 17552. (717)653-6000. Editor: George Sheldon. 50% freelance written. Monthly newsletter covering writing and books. "We are not a general writing publication. Our focus is exclusively for the book writer. Estab. 1990. Circ. 2,000. **Pays on acceptance.** Byline given. Offers 50% kill fee. Buys first North American serial rights. Editorial lead time 3 months. Submit seasonal material 3 months in advance. Accepts simultaneous submissions. Query for electronic submissions. Reports in 1 month on mss. *Writer's Market* recommends allowing 2 months for reply. Sample copy and writer's guidelines for #10 SASE.

Nonfiction: Expose, general interest, "how-to market books and manuscripts", interview/profile and new product. "We do a special issue each spring on agents." "No writer "suddenly-made-it" success stories; nothing rewritten from another writer's magazine." Buys 36 mss/year. Query with published clips. Length: up to 1,500 maximum words. Pays 20¢/word maximum for assigned articles; 10¢/word maximum for unsolicited articles. "We give a free 3 month subscription in addition to payment." Sometimes pays expenses of writers on assignment.

Photos: Send photos with submission. Reviews contact sheets and 5 × 7 prints. Negotiates payment individually. Captions, model releases and identification of subjects required. Buys one-time rights.

Columns/Departments: Interview (an interview with an agent, acquisitions editor), 1,200 words. Buys 12 mss/year. Query with published clips. Pays $100-200.

Fillers: Newsbreaks. Buys 12/year ("more, if they were submitted"). Pays 10¢/word.

Tips: "Be professional: No handwritten inquiries, please! Get to know our publication, and follow our formula. Too much of what has been submitted in the past was wordy—we are a newsletter, and a well-written, tightly worded piece always works best for us. We really need more how-to articles. Our readers want step-by-step info on how they can make more money as a book writer, how to get more publicity, how to sell more books, how to get booked on Oprah always works for us. We are a publication for both new book writers and experienced authors.

BYLINE, P.O. Box 130596, Edmond OK 73013-0001. (405)348-5591. Executive Editor/Publisher: Marcia Preston. Managing Editor: Kathryn Fanning. 80-90% freelance written. Eager to work with new/unpublished writers. Monthly magazine for writers and poets. "We stress encouragement of beginning writers." Estab. 1981. Publishes ms an average of 3 months after acceptance. Byline given. Buys first North American serial rights. Reports in 2 months. Sample copy $3.50 postpaid. Writer's guidelines for #10 SASE.

Nonfiction: How-to, humor, inspirational, personal experience, *all* connected with writing and selling. Read magazine for special departments. Buys approximately 72 mss/year. Prefers queries; will read complete mss. Length: 1,500-2,000 words. Usual rate for features is $50; **pays on acceptance.** Needs short humor on writing (300-600 words). Pays $15-25 on acceptance.

Fiction: General fiction of high quality. Send complete ms: 2,000-3,000 words preferred. Pays $50 on acceptance.

Poetry: Any style, on a writing theme. Preferred length: 4-30 lines. Pays $5-10 on acceptance, plus free issue.

CANADIAN AUTHOR, Canadian Authors Association, Suite 500, 275 Slater St., Ottawa, Ontario K1P 5H9 Canada. Contact: Editor. 95% freelance written. Prefers to work with published/established writers. Quarterly magazine "for writers—all ages, all levels of experience." Estab. 1919. Circ. 3,000. Pays on publication. Publishes ms an average of 6 months after acceptance. Buys first Canadian rights. Byline given. Written queries only. Sample copy $5. Writer's guidelines for #10 SAE and IRC.

Nonfiction: How-to (on writing, selling; the specifics of the different genres—what they are and how to write them); informational (the writing scene—who's who and what's what); interview (with writers, mainly leading ones, but also those with a story that can help others write and sell more often); and opinion. No personal, lightweight writing experiences; no fillers. Query with immediate pinpointing of topic, length (if ms is ready) and writer's background. Length: 1,000-2,500 words. Pays $30/printed page.

Photos: "We're after an interesting-looking magazine, and graphics are a decided help." State availability of photos with query. Offers $10/photo for b&w photos accepted with ms. Buys one-time rights.

Poetry: High quality. "Major poets publish with us—others need to be as good." Buys 60 poems/year. Pays $15.

Tips: "We dislike material that condescends to its reader and articles that advocate an adversarial approach to writer/editor relationships. We agree that there is a time and place for such an approach, but good sense should prevail. If the writer is writing to a Canadian freelance writer, the work will likely fall within our range of interest."

CANADIAN WRITER'S JOURNAL, Gordon M. Smart Publications, P.O. Box 6618, Depot 1, Victoria, British Columbia V8P 5N7 Canada. (604)477-8807. Editor: Gordon M. Smart. Accepts well-written articles by inexperienced writers. Quarterly magazine for writers. Estab. 1985. Circ. 350. 75% freelance written. Pays on publication, an average of 3-9 months after acceptance. Byline given. Reprints OK; send typed ms with rights for sale noted and information about when and where the article previously appeared. For reprints, pays 100% of their fee for an original article. Reports in 2 months. Sample copy $3 with $1 postage. Writer's guidelines for #10 SAE and IRC. Pays about $5 (Canadian) per published magazine page.

Nonfiction: How-to articles for writers. Buys 50-55 mss/year. Query optional. Length: 500-1,200 words.

Fiction: Occasional short story to 1,000 words. Requirements currently being met by annual contest.

Poetry: Short poems or extracts used as part of articles on the writing of poetry. Annual poetry contest commencing in 1993.

Tips: "We prefer short, tightly written, informative how-to articles. US writers note that US postage cannot be used to mail from Canada. Obtain Canadian stamps, use IRCs or send small amounts in cash."

COLUMBIA JOURNALISM REVIEW, 700 Journalism Bldg., Columbia University, New York NY 10027. (212)854-1881. Fax: (212)854-8580. Managing Editor: Gloria Cooper. Estab. 1960. "We welcome queries concerning media issues and performance. *CJR* also publishes book reviews. We emphasize in-depth reporting, critical analysis and good writing. All queries are read by editors."

THE COMICS JOURNAL, The Magazine of News and Criticism, Fantagraphics, Inc., 7563 Lake City Way, Seattle WA 98115. (206)524-1967. Managing Editor: Carole Sobocinski. Editor: Gary Groth. 90% freelance written. Monthly magazine covering the comic book industry. "Comic books can appeal intellectually and emotionally to an adult audience, and can express ideas of which other media are inherently incapable." Estab. 1975. Circ. 15,000. Pays on publication. Publishes ms an average of 2 months after acceptance. Byline given. Buys first rights. Submit seasonal material 5 months in advance. Reports in 2 months. Sample copy $3.50 for 9×12 SAE with 7 first class stamps.

Nonfiction: Essays, news, expose, historical, interview/profile, opinion and magazine reviews. Buys 120 mss/year. Send complete ms. Length: 500-3,000 words. Pays 1.5¢/word; writers may request trade for merchandise. Pays the expenses of writers on assignment.

Photos: Send photos with submission. Offers additional payment for photos accepted with ms. Identification of subjects required. Buys one-time rights.

Columns/Departments: Opening Shots (brief commentary, often humorous), 1,000 words; Newswatch (in-depth reporting on the industry, US and foreign news); The Comics Library (graphic review); and Ethics (examining the ethics of the comic book industry), both 3,000 words. Buys 60 mss/year. Send complete ms. Pays 1.5¢/word; more for news items.

Tips: "Have an intelligent, sophisticated, critical approach to writing about comic books."

‡**CROSS & QUILL, Christian Writers Newsletter**, Christian Writers Fellowship International, The Word Center, P.O. Box 730, DeLand FL 32721-0730. Editor: Mary Harwell Sayler. 40% freelance written. Bi-monthly newsletter covering writing and marketing mss for publication. "Our publication informs, encourages, and instructs Christian writers and editors. We want only manuscripts that have them in mind." Estab. 1976. **Pays on acceptance.** Publishes ms an average of 6-12 months after acceptance. Byline given. Offers 100% kill fee. Buys first North American serial, second serial (reprint) or first rights. Editorial lead time 2-4 months. Submit seasonal material 6 months in advance. Accepts previously published submissions "if specified." Reports in 2-3 weeks on queries; 1 month on mss. *Writer's Market* recommends allowing 2 months for reply. Sample copy $3. Writer's guidelines for #10 SASE.

Nonfiction: How-to write, market, and promote work; humor as relates to writers; technical tips on pc's and software. "In our November/December issue each year, our "Marketlines" column by Sandy Brooks features Christian writing conferences for the upcoming year. Our January/February issue focuses on the recepients of our annual Koala Awards. We don't want any material for beginners since we have our Personalized Study Program units from which to draw. Also, we want manuscripts that treat editors positively." Buys 6-18 mss/year. Send complete ms. Length: 100-500 words. Pays $5-25. "We pay in coupons applicable toward annual CWFI dues or toward ms critique by our very well-published staff."

Columns/Departments: Bytes and PC's (tips on using computer in writing), 100-500 words. Buys up to 6 mss/year. Send complete ms. Pays $5-25.
Poetry: Free verse, Haiku, light verse and traditional. "We want only poems that are specifically for writers." Buys 6-18 poems/year. Submit maximum 3 poems. Length: 2-8 lines. Pays $5-10.
Fillers: Facts, newsbreaks and short humor. "All must be of immediate use to writers." Buys 4-24/year. Length: 50-250 words. Pays $5-10.
Tips: "Tell us what worked for you in writing, selling and promoting your manuscripts. Keep our professional readers in mind so they'll have a take-away they can use in their work. Write tightly and offer specific suggestions we can number or bullet point. Humor is appreciated, especially in 4-line poems with a snappy ending. Be sure to state what rights you offer us, and tell us where and when a piece has seen print. Our interviews with professional writers, 'Marketlines,' and inspirational pieces (except poems) are staff-written. We welcome freelance material (with SASE) for other areas of the concise informational sections of our newsletter."

EDITOR & PUBLISHER, 11 W. 19th St., New York NY 10011-4234. Fax: (212)929-1259. Editor: Robert U. Brown. Managing Editor: John Consoli. 10% freelance written. Weekly magazine for newspaper publishers, editors, executives, employees and others in communications, marketing, advertising, etc. Circ. 29,000. Pays on publication. Publishes ms an average of 2 weeks after acceptance. Buys first serial rights. Sample copy $1.
Nonfiction: Uses newspaper business articles and news items; also newspaper personality features and printing technology. Query.

THE EDITORIAL EYE, Focusing on Publications Standards and Practices, EEI, Suite 200, 66 Canal Center Plaza, Alexandria VA 22314-5507. (703)683-0683. Fax: (703)683-4915. Editor: Linda B. Jorgensen. 5% freelance written. Prefers to work with published, established and working professional editors and writers. Monthly professional newsletter on editorial subjects: writing, editing, graphic design, production, quality control and levels of editing. "Our readers are professional publications people. Use journalistic style but avoid overly general topics and facile prescriptions. Our review process is vigorous." Circ. 3,000. **Pays on acceptance.** Publishes ms an average of 3-6 months after acceptance. Byline given. Buys first North American serial rights. "We retain the right to use articles in our training division and in an anthology of collected articles." Reports in 3 months. Sample copy and guidelines for #10 SAE with 2 first class stamps.
Nonfiction: Editorial and production problems, issues, standards, practices and techniques; publication management; publishing technology; writing, style, grammar and usage, and neologisms. No word games, vocabulary building, language puzzles or poetry!! Buys 12-20 mss/year. Query. Length: 300-1,200. Pays $50-200.
Tips: "We seek mostly lead articles written by people in the publications field about the practice of publications work. Our style is journalistic with a light touch (not cute). We are interested in submissions on the craft of editing, levels of editing, writing and editing aided by computer, publications management, lexicography, usages, quality control, resources, and interviews with nonfiction writers and editors. Our back issue list provides a good idea of the kinds of articles we run."

EDITORS' FORUM, Editors' Forum Publishing Company, P.O. Box 411806, Kansas City MO 64141-1806. (913)384-2552. Managing Editor: William R. Brinton. 50% freelance written. Prefers to work with published/established writers but works with a small number of new/unpublished writers each year. Monthly newsletter geared toward communicators, particularly those involved in the editing and publication of newsletters and company publications. Estab. 1980. Circ. 1,200. Pays on publication. Publishes ms an average of 4 months after acceptance. Byline given. Offers 25% kill fee. Buys first North American serial and second serial (reprint) rights or makes work-for-hire assignments. Previously published submissions OK, depending on content. Reports in 1 month on queries. Sample copy for 9×12 SAE with 2 first class stamps. Writer's guidelines for #10 SASE.
Nonfiction: How-to on editing and writing, etc. "With the advent of computer publishing, *EF* is running a regular high tech column on desktop publishing, software, etc. We can use articles on the latest techniques in computer publishing. Not interested in anything that does not have a direct effect on writing and editing newsletters. This is a how-to newsletter." Buys 22 mss/year. Query. Length: 250-500 words. Pays $20/page maximum.
Photos: State availability of photos/illustrations with submission. Reviews contact sheets. Offers $5/photo. Captions, model releases and identification of subjects required. Buys one-time rights.
Tips: "We are necessarily interested in articles pertaining to the newsletter business. That would include articles involving writing skills, layout and makeup, the use of pictures and other graphics to brighten up our reader's publication, and an occasional article on how to put out a good publication inexpensively."

FREELANCE WRITER'S REPORT, CNW Publishing, Maple Ridge Rd., North Sandwich NH 03259. (603)284-6367. Fax: (603)284-6648. Editor: Dana K. Cassell. 35% freelance written. Prefers to work with published/established writers. Monthly newsletter covering writing and marketing advice for established freelance writers. Estab. 1982. Pays on publication. Publishes ms an average of 6 months after acceptance. Byline given.

Buys one-time rights. Submit seasonal material 2 months in advance. Simultaneous queries, and simultaneous and previously published submissions OK. Reports in 1 month. Sample copy for 9 × 12 envelope with 3 first class stamps. No writer's guidelines; refer to this listing.
Nonfiction: Book excerpts (on writing profession); how-to (market, write, research); interview (of writers or editors); new product (only those pertaining to writers); photojournalism; promotion and administration of a writing business. No humor, fiction or poetry. Buys 72 mss/year. Query or send complete ms. Length: 500 words maximum. Pays 10¢/edited word to subscribers; non-subscribers receive a trade-out subscription equal to 10¢/edited word.
Tips: "Write in terse newsletter style, eliminate flowery adjectives and edit mercilessly. Send something that will help writers increase profits from writing output—must be a proven method. We're targeting more to the established writer, less to the beginner."

HOUSEWIFE-WRITER'S FORUM, P.O. Box 780, Lyman WY 82937. (307)786-4513. Editor: Diane Wolverton. 90% freelance written. Bimonthly newsletter and literary magazine for women writers. "We are a support network and writer's group on paper directed to the unique needs of women who write and juggle home life." Estab. 1988. Circ. 1,500. **Pays on acceptance.** Publishes ms an average of 6-12 months after acceptance. Byline given. Buys first North American serial rights. Submit seasonal material 6 months in advance. Simultaneous and previously published submissions sometimes used. Reports in 1 month on queries; 3 months on mss. Sample copy $3. Writer's guidelines for #10 SASE.
Nonfiction: Essays, how-to, humor, interview/profile, opinion, personal experience. Buys 60-100 mss/year. Query with or without published clips. Length: 2,000 words maximum, 1,000-1,500 words preferred. Pays 1¢ per word.
Columns/Departments: Confessions of Housewife-Writers (essays pertaining to our lives as women and writers. Buys 30-40 mss/year. Send complete ms. Length: 250-750 words. Pays 1¢/word.
Fiction: Bob Haynie, fiction editor. Confession, experimental, fantasy, historical, horror, humorous, mainstream, mystery, romance, science fiction, slice-of-life vignettes and suspense. No pornography. Buys 12-15 mss/year. Send complete ms. Length: 2,000 words maximum. Pays 1¢/word.
Poetry: Avant-garde, free verse, haiku, light verse, traditional and humorous. Buys 30-60 poems/year. Submit maximum 5 poems at one time. 45 lines max. Pays $2 maximum.
Fillers: Anecdotes, facts, short humor, hints on writing and running a home. Length: 25-300 words. Pays $2 maximum.
Tips: "Our tone is warm, nurturing and supportive to writers in all stages of their writing careers. We favor how-to articles on writing and getting published and would like to see more profiles of writers who have achieved some degree of success. Our 'Confessions' department is for all the fun, interesting, funny, tragic, unbelievable things that happen to you as a Housewife-Writer."

THE ILLINOIS PUBLISHER, Illinois Press Association, 701 South Grand Ave., West, Springfield IL 62704. (217)523-5092. Fax: (217)523-5103. Editor: David Porter. 75% freelance written. Quarterly magazine covering newspapers, especially Illinois. "We have a sophisticated, statewide audience that includes lawmakers, judges and other community leaders as well as publishers and editors of Illinois newspapers. Humor must be well done and be relative to topic." Estab. 1917. Circ. 2,000. **Pays on acceptance.** Publishes ms an average of 10 months after acceptance. Byline given. Offers 20% kill fee. Buys serial rights, all rights or makes work-for-hire assignments. Submit seasonal material 6 months in advance. Simultaneous and previously published submissions OK. Include information about when and where the article previously appeared. Query for electronic submissions. Reports in 3 months. Sample copy $2. Writer's guidelines for SASE.
Nonfiction: Essays, historical/nostalgic, how-to (anything relating to newspapers, production or editorial or advertising), humor, interview/profile, opinion, personal experience, photo feature, technical. No poetry. Buys 12-14 mss/year. Query with published clips. Length: 500-3,000 words. Pays $75-175 for assigned articles; $50-100 for unsolicited articles. Sometimes pays expenses of writers on assignment.
Photos: State availability of photos with submission. Offers no additional payment for photos accepted with ms. Model releases and identification of subjects required.
Columns/Departments: Initial Insights (current, often first-person accounts about newspaper trends—recycling, First Amendment, etc.), 500 words; Parting Shots (like Initial Insights but often tongue-in-cheek), 500 words; On the Law (current legal issues pertaining to newspapers), 500 words. Buys 10-12 mss/year. Send complete ms. Length: 450-600 words. Pays copies. "We are in need of 'On the Law' columns. Will pay $50 plus copies."
Tips: "We try to utilize Illinois writers, especially those affiliated with a newspaper. Other writers are encouraged, though. Remember that newspaper writers are not like other types of writers, and probably more than half of our readers are not writers. Stories about the craft of writing without a strong newspaper angle will be rejected."

NEW WRITER'S MAGAZINE, Sarasota Bay Publishing, P.O. Box 5976, Sarasota FL 34277-5976. (813)953-7903. Editor: George J. Haborak. 95% freelance written. Bimonthly magazine for new writers. *"New Writer's Magazine* believes that *all* writers are *new* writers in that each of us can learn from one another. So, we reach *pro* and non-pro alike." Estab. 1986. Circ. 5,000. Pays on publication. Byline given. Buys first rights. Reports in 2 weeks on queries; 1 month on mss. *Writer's Market* recommends allowing 2 months for reply. Sample copy $3. Writer's guidelines for #10 SASE.

Nonfiction: General interest, how-to (for new writers), humor, interview/profile, opinion and personal experience (with *pro* writer). Buys 50 mss/year. Send complete ms. Length: 300-1,000 words. Pays $5-50 for assigned and unsolicited articles.

Photos: Send photos with submission. Reviews 5 × 7 prints. Offers no additional payment for photos accepted with ms. Captions required.

Fiction: Experimental, historical, humorous, mainstream and slice-of-life vignettes. "Again, we do *not* want anything that does not have a tie-in with the writing life or writers in general." Buys 2-6 mss/year. "We offer a special fiction contest held each year with cash prizes." Send complete ms. Length: 750-1,000 words. Pays $5-20.

Poetry: Free verse, light verse and traditional. Does not want anything *not* for writers. Buys 10-20 poems/year. Submit maximum 3 poems. Length: 8-20 lines. Pays $5 maximum.

Fillers: Anecdotes, facts, newsbreaks and short humor. Buys 5-15/year. Length: 20-100 words. Pays $5 maximum. Cartoons, writing lifestyle slant. Buys 20-30/year. Pays $10 maximum. Buys 5-15/year. Length: 20-100 words. Pays $5 maximum.

Tips: "Any article *with photos* has a good chance, especially an *up close & personal* interview with an established professional writer offering advice, etc."

RISING STAR, 47 Byledge Rd., Manchester NH 03104. (603)623-9796. Editor: Scott E. Green. 50% freelance written. Bimonthly newsletter on science fiction and fantasy markets for writers and artists. Estab. 1980. Circ. 150. Pays on publication. Publishes ms an average of 3 months after acceptance. Byline given. Not copyrighted. Buys first rights. Simultaneous submissions OK. Publishes reprints of previously published articles. Send photocopy of article; include information about when and where the article previously appeared. For reprints, pays $5. Reports in 1 month on queries. Sample copy $1.50 for #10 SASE. Free writer's guidelines. Subscription $7.50 for 6 issues, payable to Scott Green.

Nonfiction: Book excerpts, essays, interview/profile and opinion. Buys 8 mss/year. Query. Length: 500-900 words. Pays $3 minimum.

ST. LOUIS JOURNALISM REVIEW, 8380 Olive Blvd., St. Louis MO 63132. (314)991-1699. Fax: (314)997-1898. Editor/Publisher: Charles L. Klotzer. 50% freelance written. Prefers to work with published/established writers. Monthly tabloid newspaper critiquing St. Louis media, print, broadcasting, TV and cable primarily by working journalists and others. Also covers issues not covered adequately by dailies. Occasionally buys articles on national media criticism. Estab. 1970. Circ. 5,500. Buys all rights. Byline given. Sample copy $2.50.

Nonfiction: "We buy material which analyzes, critically, St. Louis metro area media and, less frequently, national media institutions, personalities or trends." No taboos. Pays the expenses of writers on assignment subject to prior approval.

SCAVENGER'S NEWSLETTER, 519 Ellinwood, Osage City KS 66523-1329. (913)528-3538. Editor: Janet Fox. 15% freelance written. Eager to work with new/unpublished writers. Monthly newsletter covering markets for science fiction/fantasy/horror/mystery materials especially with regard to the small press. Estab. 1984. Circ. 1,000. Publishes ms an average of 8 months after acceptance. Byline given. Not copyrighted. Places copyright symbol on title page; rights revert to contributor on publication. Buys one-time rights. Simultaneous and previously published submissions OK; send information about when and where the article previously appeared. For reprints, pays 100% of their fee for an original article. Reports within 1 month. Sample copy $2. Writer's guidelines for #10 SASE.

Nonfiction: Essays, general interest, how-to (write, sell, publish SF/fantasy/horror/mystery), humor, interview/profile (writers, artists in the field) and opinion. Buys 12-15 mss/year. Send complete ms. Length: 1,000 words maximum. **Pays on acceptance, $4.**

Poetry: Avant-garde, free verse, haiku and traditional. All related to science fiction/fantasy/horror/mystery genres. Buys 48 poems/year. Submit maximum 3 poems. Length: 10 lines maximum. **Pays on acceptance, $2.**

Tips: "Because this is a small publication, it has occasional overstocks. We're especially looking for SF/fantasy/horror/mystery commentary as opposed to writer's how-to's."

SCIENCE FICTION CHRONICLE, P.O. Box 2730, Brooklyn NY 11202-0056. (718)643-9011. Editor: Andrew Porter. 3% freelance written. Works with a small number of new/unpublished writers each year. Monthly magazine about science fiction, fantasy and horror publishing for readers, editors, writers, et al., who are interested in keeping up with the latest developments and news. Publication also includes market reports, UK news, letters, reviews, columns. Estab. 1979. Circ. 6,000. Buys first serial rights. Pays on publication. Publishes ms an average of 2 months after acceptance. Submit seasonal material 4 months in advance. Reports in up to 3 months. Sample copy for 9 × 12 SAE with 5 first class stamps.

Nonfiction: New product and photo feature. No articles about UFOs, or "news we reported six months ago." Buys 10 unsolicited mss/year. Send complete ms. Length: 200-500 words. Pays 3-5¢/word.

Photos: Send photos with ms. Pays $5-15 for 4×5 and 8×10 b&w prints. Captions preferred. Buys one-time rights.

Tips: "News of publishers, booksellers and software related to SF, fantasy and horror is most needed from freelancers. *No fiction*. This is a news magazine, like *Publishers Weekly* or *Writer's Digest*. (I still get 10-20 story mss a year, which are returned, unread.)"

SMALL PRESS, The Magazine of Independent Publishing, Small Press Inc., Kymbolde Way, Wakefield RI 02879-1915. Fax: (401)789-3793. Editor: Wendy Reid Crisp. 90% freelance written. Quarterly magazine on independent publishers/independent publishing. "The writers and reviewers of *Small Press*, in cooperation with the publishers, editors, booksellers and trade participants, work to create a periodical that affirms and nurtures independent-press publishing and that epitomizes the ideology and strength of our industry." Estab. 1983. Circ. 10,000. Pays on publication. Publishes ms an average of 2-6 months after acceptance. Byline given. Makes work-for-hire assignments. Submit seasonal material 3-6 months in advance. "While *Small Press* does, occasionally, reprint articles, we strive to publish only original material; articles of particular relevance to the trade are accepted on other bases with the editor's approval." Query for electronic submissions. Reports in 6 weeks on queries; 2 months on mss. Sample copy $4. Writer's guidelines for #10 SASE.

Nonfiction: Essays, general interest to the trade, how-to (practical applications), interview/profile, new product, technical, use of computers, legal/financial strategies, promotion and marketing. "Interested parties should write for an editorial calendar. Such a calendar is available upon request, and there is no charge. Editorial agenda is fixed to a degree, but certain items are subject to change. NO FICTION!! I prefer not to receive blind submissions. Please inquire before mailing. Articles of a strictly personal nature—not genre-oriented—are discouraged. Articles must relate to the independent-press industry." Buys 10-12 mss/year. Query with published clips or send complete ms. Length: 250-4,000 words. Pays $45-65/page. Book reviewers receive only the title sent for review and a copy of the issue in which the review appears. Sometimes pays expenses of writers on assignment.

Photos: Send photos with submission. Offers no additional payment for photos accepted with ms. Captions, model releases and identification of subjects required.

Columns/Departments: "Columns are assigned to contributing editors. Only practical and advisory trade articles are available to freelance writers at this time." Practical and advisory articles on technical, legal, financial, promotional strategies (e.g., marketing to independent bookstores, tax advice for publishers, non-traditional marketing techniques, implementation of graphics with computer systems, etc.), 250-2,000 words. Buys 30-50 mss/year. Query with published clips. Send complete ms. Pays $45-65/page.

Fillers: Facts and newsbreaks. Buys 6/year. Length: 250-1,500 words. Pays $65 maximum.

Tips: "Please familiarize yourself with the independent-press industry. I neither want nor need writers who have neither knowledge nor appreciation of the industry *Small Press* serves. Writing skills are not sufficient qualification. Genre-oriented articles are sought and preferred. Filler articles on a variety of subjects of practical advice to the trade are the most open to freelance writers. I am amenable to submissions of feature articles relating to publishers, inventories, traditional and desktop-publishing systems, trade events (London Book Fair, Frankfurt, ABA, etc.), publishing trends, regional pieces (with a direct relationship to the independent-press industry), production issues, business-oriented advice, promotion and marketing strategies, interviews with industry participants."

SMALL PRESS REVIEW, P.O. Box 100, Paradise CA 95967. Editor: Len Fulton. Monthly for "people interested in small presses and magazines, current trends and data; many libraries." Circ. 3,500. Byline given. "Query if you're unsure." Reports in 2 months. Free sample copy.

Nonfiction: News, short reviews, photos, short articles on small magazines and presses. Uses how-to, personal experience, interview, profile, spot news, historical, think, photo, and coverage of merchandising techniques. Accepts 50-200 mss/year. Length: 100-200 words.

THE WRITER, 120 Boylston St., Boston MA 02116-4615. Editor-in-Chief/Publisher: Sylvia K. Burack. 20-25% freelance written. Prefers to buy work of published/established writers. Monthly. Estab. 1887. **Pays on acceptance.** Publishes ms an average of 6-8 months after acceptance. Buys first serial rights. Sample copy $3.

Nonfiction: Practical articles for writers on how to write for publication, and how and where to market manuscripts in various fields. Will consider all submissions promptly. No assignments. Length: 2,000 words maximum.

Tips: "New types of publications and our continually updated market listings in all fields will determine changes of focus and fact."

WRITERS CONNECTION, Suite 103, 275 Saratoga Ave., Santa Clara CA 95050-6664. (408)554-2090. Editor: Jan Stiles. 60% freelance written. Works with new/unpublished writers each year. Monthly newsletter covering writing and publishing. Estab. 1983. Circ. 2,500. Pays in services on acceptance or in cash on publication. Publishes ms an average of 8 months after acceptance for articles; much less for column updates. Byline given on articles. Buys first serial or second serial (reprint) rights. Submit seasonal material 4 months in advance. Simultaneous queries and submissions OK; send typed ms with rights for sale noted and information about when and where the article previously appeared. For reprints, pays 50-60% of their fee for an original article. Prefers complete ms. Reports in 2 months. Sample copy $5 postpaid. Writer's guidelines for #10 SASE.

Nonfiction: Book excerpts (on writing/publishing); how-to (write and publish, market your writing); interview/profile (editors, agents, writers and publishers with how-to or marketing slant); new product occasionally (books, videotapes, software etc., on writing and publishing); and writing for business and technical fields. "All types of writing from technical to romance novels and article writing are treated." No personal experience without a strong how-to slant. Buys 25-32 mss/year. Length: 800-1,800 words. Pays $25-75 on publication, or in certificates, on acceptance, for $50 to $150 toward WC membership and/or conferences.

Columns/Departments: Markets, contests, events, etc., are staff-written. Send information or announcements 6 weeks in advance of issue date for free listings in our newsletter; space available basis.

Tips: "We are currently seeking how-to articles that will benefit writers working for business and high-tech companies. The focus for these articles should appeal to the working professional writer. Also, find and report on new markets where freelancers can break in. Provide new techniques, ideas or perspectives for writing fiction or nonfiction; present your ideas in a lively, but practical style. No parodies or sarcasm, please. And no why-I-have-to-write or how-I-faced-writer's-block essays. We see (and return) far too many of these."

WRITER'S DIGEST, 1507 Dana Ave., Cincinnati OH 45207. (513)531-2222. Submissions Editor: Angela Terez. 90% freelance written. Monthly magazine about writing and publishing. "Our readers write fiction, poetry, nonfiction, plays and all kinds of creative writing. They're interested in improving their writing skills, improving their sales ability, and finding new outlets for their talents." Estab. 1921. Circ. 225,000. **Pays on acceptance.** Publishes ms an average of 1 year after acceptance. Buys first North American serial rights for one-time editorial use, microfilm/microfiche use and magazine promotional use. Pays 20% kill fee. Byline given. Submit seasonal material 8 months in advance. Previously published submissions OK; send tearsheet or photocopy of article, noting rights for sale and when and where the article previously appeared. Query for electronic submissions. "We're able to use electronic submissions only for accepted pieces and will discuss details if we buy your work. We'll accept computer printout submissions, of course—but they *must* be readable. We strongly recommend letter-quality. If you don't want your manuscript returned, indicate that on the first page of the manuscript or in a cover letter." Reports in 2-4 weeks. Sample copy $3. Writer's guidelines for #10 SASE.

• *Writer's Digest* was ranked as one of the best freelance markets in *Writer's Digest Magazine* annual "Top 100 Markets," January 1993.

Nonfiction: "Our mainstay is the how-to article—that is, an article telling how to write and sell more of what you write. For instance, how to write compelling leads and conclusions, how to improve your character descriptions, how to become more efficient and productive. We like plenty of examples, anecdotes and $$$ in our articles—so other writers can actually see what's been done successfully by the author of a particular piece. We like our articles to speak directly to the reader through the use of the first-person voice. Don't submit an article on what five book editors say about writing mysteries. Instead, submit an article on how you cracked the mystery market and how our readers can do the same. But don't limit the article to your experiences; include the opinions of those five editors to give your article increased depth and authority." General interest (about writing); how-to (writing and marketing techniques that work); humor (short pieces); inspirational; interview and profile (query first); new product; and personal experience (marketing and freelancing experiences). "We can always use articles on fiction and nonfiction technique, and solid articles on poetry or scriptwriting are always welcome. No articles titled 'So You Want to Be a Writer,' and no first-person pieces that ramble without giving a lesson or something readers can learn from in the sharing of the story." Buys 90-100 mss/year. Queries are preferred, but complete mss are OK. Length: 500-3,000 words. Pays 10¢/word minimum. Sometimes pays expenses of writers on assignment.

Photos: Used only with interviews and profiles. State availability of photos or send contact sheet with ms. Captions required.

Columns/Departments: Chronicle (first-person narratives about the writing life; length: 1,200-1,500 words); The Writing Life (length: 50-800 words); and Tip Sheet (short items that offer solutions to writing- and freelance business-related problems that writers commonly face). Buys approximately 200 articles/year for Writing Life and Tip Sheet sections. Send complete ms.

Poetry: Light verse about "the writing life"—joys and frustrations of writing. "We are also considering poetry other than short light verse—but related to writing, publishing, other poets and authors, etc." Buys 2-3/issue. Submit poems in batches of 1-8. Length: 2-20 lines. Pays $10-50/poem.

Fillers: Anecdotes and short humor, primarily for use in The Writing Life column. Uses up to 4/issue. Length: 50-250 words.

WRITER'S FORUM, Writer's Digest School, 1507 Dana Ave., Cincinnati OH 45207. (513)531-2222. Editor: Tom Clark. 100% freelance written. Quarterly newsletter covering writing techniques, marketing and inspiration for students of courses in fiction and nonfiction writing offered by Writer's Digest School. Estab. 1970. Circ. 13,000. **Pays on acceptance.** Publishes ms an average of 6 months after acceptance. Byline given. Buys first serial and second serial (reprint) rights. Submit seasonal/holiday material 4 months in advance. Simultaneous and previously published submissions OK. Query for electronic submissions. Reports in 4-6 weeks. Free sample copy.

Nonfiction: How-to (write or market short stories, or articles, novels and nonfiction books) and inspirational articles that will motivate beginning writers. Buys 12 mss/year. Prefers complete mss to queries. "If you prefer to query, please do so by mail, not phone." Length: 500-1,000 words. Pays $10-25.

WRITER'S GUIDELINES: A Roundtable for Writers and Editors, P.O. Box 608, Pittsburg MO 65724. Editor: Susan Salaki. 97% freelance written. Bimonthly roundtable forum for writers and editors. "We are interested in what writers on both sides of the desk have to say about the craft of writing." Estab. 1988. Circ. 1,000. Pays on publication. Byline given. Rights to the original work revert to contributors after publication. Reports in 1 month. Sample copy $4. Writer's guidelines and themes for upcoming issues for #10 SAE with 3 first class stamps.

Nonfiction: General interest, historical articles on writers/writing, psychological aspects of being a writer, how-to, interview/profile, personal experience, humor and fillers. Buys 20 mss/year. Prefer disposable photocopy submissions complete with SASE. May use both sides of each sheet of paper to save postage costs. Include SASE with all correspondence. Length: 800-1,000 words. Pay varies from copies to up to $10.

Poetry: Short poetry, any form, having to do with writing or editing. Submit minimum of 3 poems. Pays 1 copy. Length: up to 20 lines "unless it is exceptional."

Fillers: Facts about writing or writers, short humor and cartoons, "wide-open to any facts of interest to writers or editors." No payment for fillers.

Tips: "If you believe what you have to say about writing or editing has needed to be said for some time now, then I'm interested. If you say it well, I'll buy it. This is a unique publication in that we offer original guidelines for over 300 magazine and book publishers and because of this service, writers and editors are linked in a new and exciting way—as correspondents. Articles that help to bridge the gap which has existed between these two professions have the best chance of being accepted. Publishing background does not matter. Include a short biography and cover letter with your submissions."

WRITER'S INFO, Box 1870, Hayden ID 83835-1870. Editor: Linda Hutton. 90% freelance written. Eager to work with new/unpublished writers. Monthly newsletter on writing. "We provide helpful tips and advice to writers, both beginners and old pros." Estab. 1981. Circ. 200. **Pays on acceptance.** Publishes ms an average of 6 months after acceptance. Byline given. Buys first North American serial rights and second serial (reprint) rights. Submit seasonal material 9 months in advance. Simultaneous queries and submissions OK. Reports in 1 month. Sample copy for #10 SAE and 2 first class stamps. Writer's guidelines for #10 SASE.

Nonfiction: How-to, humor and personal experience, all related to writing. No interviews or re-hashes of articles published in other writers magazines. Buys 50-75 mss/year. Send complete ms. Length: 300 words. Pays $1-10. Reprints OK; send tearsheet or photocopy of article or short story and information about when and where the article previously appeared. Does not pay for reprints.

Poetry: Free verse, light verse and traditional. No avant-garde or shaped poetry. Buys 40-50/year. Submit maximum 6 poems. Length: 4-20 lines. Pays $1-10.

Fillers: Jokes, anecdotes and short humor. Buys 3-4/year. Length: 100 words maximum. Pays $1-10.

Tips: "Tell us a system that worked for you to make a sale or inspired you to write. All departments are open to freelancers. We especially need 200-word mss on My First Sale for which we pay $2 on acceptance. Please do not telephone for information. We will no longer mail guidelines or sample copies on telephone requests— SASEs only."

WRITER'S JOURNAL, Minnesota Ink, Inc., 27 Empire Dr., St. Paul MN 55103. (612)225-1306. Publisher/ Managing Editor: Valerie Hockert. Poetry Editor: Esther M. Leiper. 40% freelance written. Monthly. Circ. 45,000. Pays on publication. Publishes ms an average of 4 months after acceptance. Byline given. Buys first North American serial rights. Submit seasonal material 6 months in advance. Simultaneous queries OK. Query for electronic submissions. Reports in 1 month on queries; 6 weeks on mss. Sample copy $4. Writer's guidelines for #10 SASE.

Nonfiction: How-to (on the business and approach to writing); motivational; interview/profile; opinion. "*Writer's Journal* publishes articles on style, technique, editing methods, copy writing, research, writing of news releases, writing news stories and features, creative writing, grammar reviews, marketing, the business aspects of writing, copyright law and legal advice for writers/editors, independent book publishing, interview techniques, and more." Also articles on the use of computers by writers and a book review section. Buys 30-40 mss/year. Send complete ms. Length: 700-1,000 words. Pays to $50.

Poetry: Avant-garde, free verse, haiku, light verse and traditional. "The *Writer's Journal* runs two poetry contests each year in the spring and fall: Winner, 2nd, 3rd place and 10 honorable mentions." Buys 20-30 poems/year. Submit maximum 5 poems. Length: 25 lines maximum. Pays 25¢ line.

Tips: "Articles must be *well* written and slanted toward the business (or commitment) of writing and/or being a writer. Interviews with established writers should be in-depth, particularly reporting interviewee's philosophy on writing, how he or she got started, etc." The *Writer's Journal* now incorporates Minnesota Ink. Minnesota Ink is 100% freelance written and contains fiction and poetry.

WRITERS OPEN FORUM, Bristol Publishing, P.O. Box 516, Tracyton WA 98393. Editorial Director: Sandra E. Haven. 90% freelance written. Bimonthly publication designed to publish aspiring writers' stories, essays, and articles and to forward resulting critiques from readers. Estab. 1990. Buys first rights. Byline and brief bio given. No poetry. Also offers a column of tips from readers and information of interest to writers. Submit mss with SASE, cover letter, clear copies (not originals as notations may be made prior to return). No multiple or simultaneous submissions. Reports in 6 weeks. Guidelines and contest information available for SASE. Sample copy $3; subscription $14.

Nonfiction: Any subject (except on the subject of writing) suitable for a general audience. Mss published will be open to critiques by readers. Length: 2,000 word max. Pays $5 on acceptance plus 1 copy. Send complete ms.

Columns/Departments: Writer to Writer: tips on writing sent in by writers (max. 300 words) and Perspectives: one essay published per issue that offers a writer's personal, philosophic and/or humorous perspective (max. 500 words). Pays in 1 contributor copy. Send complete ms; mark for intended column.

Fiction: Any genre (no slice-of-life, violence, graphic sex or experimental formats). Stories published will be open to critiques by readers. Send complete ms. Book excerpts considered if they are so marked and within our fiction limits (include brief overview of book). Length: 2,000 words maximum. **Pays on acceptance, $5,** plus 1 copy.

Tips: "Shorter manuscripts have greater chance of acceptance. In stories we like definite plots and resolutions resulting from the main character's action and/or decision. Essays need to make a statement (not just ramble) and offer personal experiences to both back up the point and create reader empathy. Articles need a clear intention, strong opening, good information or examples and a conclusion. Always include a cover letter telling us a bit about yourself and your manuscript's intended audience (children's story, technical article, whatever). All sincere submissions (clean copy, guidelines followed, cover letter included) receive a personal reply; all subscriber submissions receive a brief critique."

WRITER'S YEARBOOK, 1507 Dana Ave., Cincinnati OH 45207. Submissions Editor: Angela Terez. 90% freelance written. Newsstand annual for freelance writers, journalists and teachers of creative writing. "Please note that the *Yearbook* is currently using a 'best of' format. That is, we are reprinting the best writing about writing published in the last year: articles, fiction and book excerpts. The *Yearbook* now uses little original material, so do not submit queries or original manuscripts. We will, however, consider already-published material for possible inclusion." Estab. 1929. Buys reprint rights; send tearsheet or photocopy of article, noting rights for sale and when and where the article previously appeared. Pays 20% kill fee. Byline given. **Pays on acceptance.** Publishes ms an average of 6 months after acceptance. "If you don't want your manuscript returned, indicate that on the first page of the manuscript or in a cover letter."

Nonfiction: "In reprints, we want articles that reflect the current state of writing in America: trends, inside information and money-saving and money-making ideas for the freelance writer. We try to touch on the various facets of writing in each issue of the *Yearbook* — from fiction to poetry to playwriting, and any other endeavor a writer can pursue. How-to articles — that is, articles that explain in detail how to do something — are very important to us. For example, you could explain how to establish mood in fiction, how to improve interviewing techniques, how to write for and sell to specialty magazines, or how to construct and market a good poem. We are also interested in the writer's spare time — what she/he does to retreat occasionally from the writing wars; where and how to refuel and replenish the writing spirit. 'How Beats the Heart of a Writer' features interest us, if written warmly, in the first person, by a writer who has had considerable success. We also want interviews or profiles of well-known bestselling authors, always with good pictures. Articles on writing techniques that are effective today are always welcome. We provide how-to features and information to help our readers become more skilled at writing and successful at selling their writing." Buys 15-20 mss (reprints only)/year. Length: 750-4,500 words. Pays 2½¢/word minimum.

Photos: Interviews and profiles must be accompanied by high-quality photos. Reviews b&w photos only, depending on use. Captions required.

WRITING CONCEPTS, The Newsletter on Writing & Editing, Communications Concepts, Inc., Dept. WM, P.O. Box 1608, Springfield VA 22151-0608. Editor/Publisher: Bill Londino. Monthly business to business newsletter of writing and editing. "Our readers are experienced professionals who want specific, practical advice on how to do a better job writing and editing." Estab. 1990. Pays within 45 days of acceptance. Publishes ms an average of 2 months after acceptance. Byline sometimes given. Offers 50% kill fee. Buys all rights. Editorial lead time 2 months. Submit seasonal material 2 months in advance. Query for electronic submissions. Reports in 6 weeks on queries. Sample copy and writer's guidelines for #10 SASE with 52¢ postage.

● *Writing Concepts* does *not* use material on how to get published.

Nonfiction: "Practical, short, well-researched, how-to articles with source and ordering information for follow-up. We are open to ideas for special reports in the communications and publication production field. No humor, opinion, inspirational items. No long articles, except special reports." Buys 60 mss/year. Query with published clips. Length: 50-600 words. Pays 15¢/word. Pays in contributor copies if requested by writer. Sometimes pays expenses of writers on assignment.

Photos: State availability of photos with submission. Offers no additional payment for photos accepted with ms.

Columns/Departments: Quick Takes (useful sources, style tips, writing techniques, electronic editing, free-lancing), 50-200 words; Electronic Editing (trends and techniques for editing on computer), 300-600 words; Writing Techniques (practical how-to advice), 300-600 words. Buys 60 mss/year. Query with published clips. Pays 15¢/word.

Tips: "We enjoy working with writers who are accurate, have original ideas and who verify their source information. The best submission advice is to review recent issues and editorial guidelines. We are most receptive to short items (100-400 words), provided they offer practical advice on the craft of writing and editing. Columns are most open to freelancers."

Law

While all of these publications deal with topics of interest to attorneys, each has a particular slant. Be sure that your subject is geared to a specific market — lawyers in a single region, law students, paralegals, etc. Publications for law enforcement personnel are listed under Government and Public Service.

ABA JOURNAL, American Bar Association, Dept. WM, 6th Floor, 750 N. Lake Shore Dr., Chicago IL 60611. (312)988-5000. Fax: (312)988-6014. Editor: Gary A. Hengstler. Managing Editor: Robert Yates. 35% freelance written. Prefers to work with published/established writers. Monthly magazine covering law and lawyers. "The content of the *Journal* is designed to appeal to the association's diverse membership with emphasis on the general practitioner." Circ. 400,000. **Pays on acceptance.** Publishes ms an average of 2 months after acceptance. Byline given. "Editor works with writer until article is in acceptable form." Buys all rights. Submit seasonal material 3 months in advance. Simultaneous queries and submissions OK. Query for electronic submissions. Reports in 1 month. Free sample copy and writer's guidelines.

Nonfiction: Book excerpts, general interest (legal), how-to (law practice techniques), interview/profile (law firms and prominent individuals) and technical (legal trends). "The emphasis of the *Journal* is on the practical problems faced by lawyers in general practice and how those problems can be overcome. Articles should emphasize the practical rather than the theoretical or esoteric. Writers should avoid the style of law reviews, academic journals or legal briefs and should write in an informal, journalistic style. Short quotations from people and specific examples of your point will improve an article." Special issues have featured women and minorities in the legal profession. Buys 30 mss/year. Query with published clips or send complete ms. Length: 3,000 words. Pays $1,000-2,000. Pays expenses of writers on assignment.

Tips: "Write to us with a specific idea in mind and spell out how the subject would be covered. Full-length profiles and feature articles are always needed. We look for practical information. If *The New York Times* or *Wall Street Journal* would like your style, so will we."

THE ALTMAN WEIL PENSA REPORT TO LEGAL MANAGEMENT, Altman Weil Pensa Publications, P.O. Box 625, Newtown Square PA 19073. (215)359-9900. Fax: (215)359-0467. Editor: Linda Diehl. 15-20% freelance written. Works with a small number of new/unpublished writers each year. Monthly newsletter covering law office purchases (equipment, insurance services, space, etc.), technology and law office management. Estab. 1974. Circ. 2,200. Pays on publication. Publishes ms an average of 3-6 months after acceptance. Byline given. Buys all rights; sometimes second serial (reprint) rights. Previously published submissions OK; send typed ms with rights for sale noted plus diskette, and information about when and where the article previously appeared. Query for electronic submissions. Reports in 1 month on queries; 2-3 months on mss. Sample copy for #10 SASE.

Nonfiction: How-to (buy, use, repair), interview/profile and new product. Buys 12 mss/year. Query. Submit a sample of previous writing. Length: 500-2,500 words. Pays $125/published page.

BARRISTER, American Bar Association Press, 750 N. Lake Shore Dr., Chicago IL 60611-4403. (312)988-6047. Fax: (312)988-6281. Editor: Vicki Quade. 60% freelance written. Prefers to work with published/established writers. Quarterly magazine for young lawyers who are members of the American Bar Association concerned about practice of law, career trends, public service, social issues, personalities. Estab. 1971. Circ. 175,000. **Pays on acceptance.** Publishes ms an average of 3-6 months after acceptance. Buys first serial rights. Query for electronic submissions. Reports in 2 months. Sample copy $5.

Nonfiction: "All areas of law are fair game, but stories should have a young lawyer tie-in. Readers interested in career stories (such as what to do when you lose your job), social issues (such as free speech and hate crimes), and personality profiles of innovative or prominent young lawyers. Rarely use humor. No political opinion pieces." Length: 2,500-3,000 words; pays $600-750 and reasonable expenses. Must query with outline. Buys 12 mss/year. Special summer issue features "20 Young Lawyers Whose Work Makes a Difference," 700-1,000 words; $250 payment. Buys 15 mss/year. Query.

Photos: Gina Wilson, photo editor. Black and white photos and color transparencies purchased without accompanying ms. Pays $35-150.

Tips: "The biggest mistake writers make is to think of us as a law review journal. We are a general interest magazine with a focus on young lawyers. We want cutting-edge topics written in a crisp journalistic style."

CALIFORNIA LAWYER, Dept. WM, 1210 Fox Plaza, 1390 Market St., San Francisco CA 94102. (415)252-0500. Editor: Ray Reynolds. Managing Editor: Tom Brom. 80% freelance written. Monthly magazine of law-related articles and general interest subjects of appeal to lawyers and judges. Estab. 1928. Circ. 135,000. **Pays on acceptance.** Publishes ms an average of 3 months after acceptance. Byline given. Buys first rights; publishes only original material. Simultaneous queries and submissions OK. Reports in 2 weeks on queries; 3 weeks on mss. *Writer's Market* recommends allowing 2 months for reply. Sample copy and writer's guidelines on request with SASE.

Nonfiction: General interest, new and feature articles on law-related topics. "We are interested in concise, well-written and well-researched articles on recent trends in the legal profession, legal aspects of issues of current concern, as well as general interest articles of potential appeal and benefit to the state's lawyers. We would like to see a description or outline of your proposed idea, including a list of possible sources." Buys 36 mss/year. Query with published clips if available. Length: 500-3,000 words. Pays $200-1,500.

Photos: Cristina Taccone, photo editor. State availability of photos with query letter or manuscript. Reviews prints. Identification of subjects and releases required.

Columns/Departments: Legal Technology, Law Office Management, Marketing, Ethics, Books. Query with published clips if available. Length: 750-1,500 words. Pays $200-600.

THE DOCKET, National Association of Legal Secretaries, Suite 550, 2250 E. 73rd St., Tulsa OK 74103-4503. (918)493-3540. Editor: Ellen Sue Blakey. 10% freelance written. Bimonthly magazine that covers continuing legal education for legal support staff. "*The Docket* is written and edited for legal secretaries, legal assistants and other non-attorney personnel. Feature articles address general trends and emerging issues in the legal field, provide practical information to achieve proficiency in the delivery of legal services, and offer techniques for career growth and fulfillment." Circ. 20,000. Pays on publication. Publishes ms an average of 3-6 months after acceptance. Byline given. Offers 25-35% of original commission fee as kill fee. Buys first North American serial rights. Simultaneous and previously published submissions OK. Reports in 4 months. Sample copy for 9 × 12 SAE with 2 first class stamps.

Nonfiction: How-to (enhance the delivery of legal services or any aspect thereof), new product (must be a service or equipment used in a legal office), personal experience (legal related) and technical (legal services and equipment). Buys 10-15 mss/year. Query about specific subjects/articles or send complete ms. Length: 500-2,500 words. Pays $50-250.

• Articles are shorter and material must be timely and news-oriented.

Photos: State availability of photos with submission. Reviews contact sheets, negatives, transparencies and prints. Buys one-time rights.

LAW PRACTICE MANAGEMENT—the Magazine of the Section of Law Practice Management of the American Bar Association, P.O. Box 11418, Columbia SC 29211-1418. Managing Editor/Art Director: Delmar L. Roberts. Editorial contact for freelance submissions: Robert M. Greene, Esq., Articles Editor, Phillips, Lytle, et al., 3400 Marine Midland Ctr., Buffalo NY 14203. 10% freelance written. Magazine published 8 times/year for the practicing lawyer and law practice administrator. Estab. 1975. Circ. 23,004 (BPA). Rights purchased vary with author and material. Usually buys all rights. Byline given. Pays on publication. Publishes ms an average of 8 months after acceptance. Query. Sample copy $7 (make check payable to American Bar Association). Free writer's guidelines. Returns rejected material in 3 months, if requested.

Nonfiction: "We assist the practicing lawyer in operating and managing his or her office by providing relevant articles and departments written in a readable and informative style. Editorial content is intended to aid the lawyer by conveying management methods that will allow him or her to provide legal services to clients in a prompt and efficient manner at reasonable cost. Typical topics of articles include fees and billing; client/lawyer relations; computer hardware/software; mergers; retirement/disability; marketing; compensation of partners and associates; legal data base research; and use of paralegals." No elementary articles on a whole field of technology, such as, "why you need computers in the law office." Pays $100-400.

Photos: Pays $50-60 for b&w photos purchased with mss; $50-100/color; $200-300/cover transparencies.

Tips: "We have a theme for each issue with two to three articles relating to the theme. We also publish thematic issues occasionally in which an entire issue is devoted to a single topic. The March and November/December issues each year are devoted to law practice technology."

THE LAWYER'S PC, A Newsletter for Lawyers Using Personal Computers, Shepard's/McGraw-Hill, Inc., P.O. Box 1108, Lexington SC 29071-1108. (803)359-9941. Editor: Robert P. Wilkins. Managing Editor: Daniel E. Harmon. 50% freelance written. Biweekly newsletter covering computerized law firms. "Our readers are lawyers who want to be told how a particular microcomputer program or type of program is being applied to a legal office task, such as timekeeping, litigation support, etc." Estab. 1983. Circ. 4,500. Pays end of the month of publication. Publishes ms an average of 1-2 months after acceptance. Byline given. Buys first North

American serial rights and the right to reprint. Submit seasonal material 5 months in advance. Query for electronic submissions. Reports in 1 month on queries; 4 months on mss. Sample copy for 9×12 SAE with 3 first class stamps. Free writer's guidelines.

Nonfiction: How-to (applications articles on law office computerization) and software reviews written by lawyers who have no compromising interests. No general articles on why lawyers need computers or reviews of products written by public relations representatives or vending consultants. Buys 30-35 mss/year. Query. Length: 500-2,500 words. Pays $25-125. Sometimes pays the expenses of writers on assignment.

Tips: "Most of our writers are lawyers. If you're not a lawyer, you need to at least understand why general business software may not work well in a law firm. If you understand lawyers' specific computer problems, write an article describing how to solve one of those problems, and we'd like to see it."

THE LAWYERS WEEKLY, The Newspaper for the Legal Profession in Canada, Butterworth (Canada) Inc., Suite 300, 204 Richmond St. West, Toronto Ontario M5V 1V6 Canada. (416)598-5211. Fax: (416)598-5659. Editor: Don Brillinger. 20% freelance written. "We will work with any *talented* writer of whatever experience level." Tabloid published 48 times/year covering law and legal affairs for a "sophisticated up-market readership of lawyers." Estab. 1983. Circ. 41,000. Pays on publication. Publishes ms within 1 month after acceptance. Byline given. Offers 50% kill fee. Usually buys all rights. Submit seasonal material 6 weeks in advance. Simultaneous queries and submissions OK. Query for electronic submissions. Reports in 1 month. Sample copy $7 (Canadian) with 9×12 SAE.

Nonfiction: Expose, general interest (law), how-to (professional), humor, interview/profile (lawyers and judges), opinion, technical, news and case comments. "We try to wrap up the week's legal events and issues in a snappy informal package with lots of visual punch. We especially like news stories with photos or illustrations. We are always interested in feature or newsfeature articles involving current legal issues, but contributors should keep in mind our audience is trained in *English/Canadian common law*—not US law. That means most US-focused stories will generally not be accepted. Special Christmas issue. No routine court reporting or fake news stories about commercial products. Buys 200-300 mss/year. Query or send complete ms. Length: 700-1,500 words. Payment negotiable. Payment in Canadian dollars. Sometimes pays the expenses of writers on assignment.

Photos: State availability of photos with query letter or ms. Reviews b&w and color contact sheets, negatives and 5×7 prints. Identification of subjects required. Buys one-time rights.

Fillers: Clippings and newsbreaks. Length: 50-200 words. Pays $10 minimum.

Tips: "Freelancers can best break into our publication by submitting news, features, and accounts of unusual or bizarre legal events. A frequent mistake made by writers is forgetting that our audience is intelligent and learned in law. They don't need the word 'plaintiff' explained to them." No unsolicited mss returned without SASE (or IRC to US or non-Canadian destinations). "No US postage on SASEs, please!"

‡LAWYERS WEEKLY USA, Lawyers Weekly Publications, 41 West St., Boston MA 02111. (617)451-7300. Editor: Robert Ambrogi. Contact: Michelle Bates Deakin, Associate Editor. Biweekly newspaper covering the legal profession. Estab. 1993. **Pays on acceptance.** Publishes ms an average of 1 month after acceptance. Byline given. Buys all rights. Simultaneous submissions OK. Query for electronic submissions. Reports in 1 month. Sample copy 9×12 SAE with 2 first class stamps. Writer's guidelines for SASE.

Nonfiction: How-to (articles about law practice and law office management), humor, interview/profile and opinion. Query with published clips. Length: 250-2,000 words. Pay negotiable. Sometimes pays expenses of writers on assignment.

Tips: "Writers should be familiar with the specific concerns of lawyers practicing in small to mid-sized law firms and tailor their stories to them. We are most open to news stories about local legal issues of national relevance, and how-to stories about law office management, marketing, and legal technology."

‡LEGAL ASSISTANT TODAY, James Publishing, Inc., Suite E, 3520 Cadillac Ave., Costa Mesa CA 92626. (714)755-5450. Fax: (714)556-4133. Editor-in-Chief: Leanne Cazares. Executive Editor: Debra Tillinghast. Bimonthly magazine covering information for paralegals/legal assistants. "Our magazine is geared toward all legal assistants/paralegals throughout the country, regardless of specialty (litigation, corporate, bankruptcy, environmental law, etc.). It covers news in the profession, paralegal profiles, how-to articles to help paralegals do their jobs more effectively, career and salary information, and features about paralegals' involvement in current events." Estab. 1983. Circ. 17,000. **Pays on acceptance.** Publishes ms an average of 3 months after acceptance. Byline given. Offers 33% kill fee. Buys first North American serial or all rights, "depends, but usually we buy all; negotiable." Editorial lead time 2½ months. Submit seasonal material 3 months in advance. Accepts simultaneous submissions. Reports in 2 weeks on queries; 2 months on mss. Sample copy free on request. Writer's guidelines free on request—usually given by phone.

Nonfiction: Expose, general interest, how-to for paralegals, humor, interview/profile of paralegals, new product for law office, opinion on legal topics (paralegal), personal experience of paralegals on the job, photo feature of paralegal and news for paralegals. "Each issue has a theme: litigation support, research and discovery, corporate services. Since ours is a national magazine, we limit regional or local stories (except for the news)." Buys 24 mss/year. Query with published clips. Length: 2,000-4,000 words. (News, profiles shorter.) Pays $500 minimum for assigned articles, $400 minimum for unsolicited articles. "Pays if negotiated per assignment; pay can be *substantially* more depending on experience and length and quality of manuscript." Pays expenses of writers on assignment.

• Publisher is interested in seeing investigative pieces.

Photos: Send photos with submission. Reviews any size prints. Negotiates payment individually. Identification of subjects required. Buys one-time rights.

Columns/Departments: "We accept no columns from freelance writers as yet, but are open to ideas."

Fillers: Anecdotes, facts, newsbreaks and short humor "pertaining to paralegals." Pay negotiated.

Tips: "We prefer writers with previous experience working in a law office or writing for legal publications who have some understanding of what paralegals would find interesting or useful. Writers must understand our audience. There is some opportunity for investigative journalism as well as the usual features, profiles and news. The magazine is still evolving, so we are open to ideas. If you are a great writer who can interview effectively, and really dig into the topic to grab the readers' attention, we need you! We are open to ideas (queries), but also assign selected topics: News: brief, hard news topics regarding paralegals (or trend pieces on the profession.); Profiles: paralegals who've worked on fascinating cases, etc.; Current events/stories: human interest or current events in which paralegals are involved; Features: presents information to help paralegals advance in their careers."

THE NATIONAL LAW JOURNAL, New York Law Publishing Company, Dept. WM, 111 8th Ave., New York NY 10011. (212)741-8300. Editor: Doreen Weisenhaus. Managing Editor: Fred Strasser. 25-50% freelance written. Weekly newspaper for the legal profession. Estab. 1978. Circ. 50,000. Pays on publication. Publishes ms an average of 1 month after acceptance. Byline given. Kill fee varies. Buys all rights. Simultaneous queries OK. Query for electronic submissions. Reports in 3 weeks on queries; 5 weeks on mss. Sample copy $2 for 9 × 12 SAE with 2 first class stamps.

Nonfiction: News, expose (on subjects of interest to lawyers); interview/profile (of lawyers or judges of note), nonfiction book excerpts. "The bulk of our freelance articles are short, spot-news stories on local court decisions, lawsuits and lawyers; often, these come from legal affairs writers on local newspapers. Pay range: $25-150. We also buy longer pieces, 1,500-2,000-word profiles of prominent lawyers or legal trend stories. No articles without a legal angle, but we like to see good, idiomatic writing, mostly free of legal jargon." Buys 50-100 mss/year. Query with published clips or send complete ms. Pays $500. Sometimes pays the expenses of writers on assignment.

Columns/Departments: "For those who are not covering legal affairs on a regular basis, a good way into *The National Law Journal* is through our Exhibit A feature. Every week we print a sort of reporter's notebook on some proceeding currently underway in a courtroom or a short profile. The feature is stylistically and thematically quite flexible — we've even run pieces about lawyers' hangouts, mini-travelogues, and television reviews. It runs about 1,800 words and pays $250. We also use op-ed pieces on subjects of legal interest, many of which come from freelancers. Writers interested in doing an op-ed piece should query first." Pays $150.

THE PENNSYLVANIA LAWYER, Pennsylvania Bar Association, 100 South St., P.O. Box 186, Harrisburg PA 17108-0186. (717)238-6715. Executive Editor: Marcy Carey Mallory. Managing Editor: Donald C. Sarvey. 25% freelance written. Prefers to work with published/established writers. Magazine published 6 times/year as a service to the legal profession. Estab. 1895. Circ. 27,000. **Pays on acceptance.** Publishes ms an average of 3-6 months after acceptance. Byline given. Buys negotiable serial rights; generally first rights, occasionally one-time rights or second serial (reprint) rights. Submit seasonal material 6 months in advance. Simultaneous submissions are discouraged. Reports in 6 weeks. Free sample copy and writer's guidelines for #10 SAE with 3 first class stamps.

Nonfiction: General interest, how-to, interview/profile, new product, law-practice management and personal experience. All features *must* relate in some way to Pennsylvania lawyers or the practice of law in Pennsylvania. Buys 10-12 mss/year. Query. Length: 600-1,500 words. Pays $75-350. Sometimes pays the expenses of writers on assignment.

THE PERFECT LAWYER, A Newsletter for Lawyers Using WordPerfect Products, Shepard's/McGraw-Hill Inc., P.O. Box 1108, Lexington SC 29071-1108. (803)359-9941. Editor: Robert P. Wilkins. Associate Editor: Daniel E. Harmon. 50% freelance written. Monthly newsletter covering the use of WordPerfect Corporation-related products in law offices. Estab. 1990. Circ. 4,500. Pays at end of the month after publication. Publishes ms an average of 2-3 months after acceptance. Byline given. Buys first North American serial rights, electronic rights and the right to reprint. Submit seasonal material 5 months in advance. Query for electronic submissions. Reports in 4 months. Sample copy for 9 × 12 SAE with 4 first class stamps. Free writer's guidelines.

Nonfiction: How-to computer articles. Must be law office-specific. Occasional reviews of WordPerfect-related products for law firms. Buys 25-35 mss/year. Query. Length: 500-2,500 words. Pays $25-200. Sometimes pays expenses of writers on assignment.

Tips: "Writers should understand the specific computer needs of law firms. Our readers are interested in how to solve office automation problems with computers and WordPerfect or related software products."

SHEPARD'S ELDER CARE/LAW NEWSLETTER, Shepard's/McGraw-Hill, Inc., P.O. Box 1108, Lexington SC 29071-1108. (803)359-9941. Editor: Robert P. Wilkins. Managing Editor: Daniel E. Harmon. Associate Editor: Aida Rogers. 40% freelance written. Monthly newsletter for lawyers and other professionals who work with older clients, focusing on legal and related issues of concern to the aging community. Estab. 1991. Pays end of the month of publication. Publishes ms an average of 2 months after acceptance. Byline given. Buys first North American serial rights, electronic rights and reprint rights. Submit seasonal material 5 months in advance. Query for electronic submissions. Reports in 1 month on queries; 2 months on mss. Reprints OK. Pay negotiable. Sample copy for 9 × 12 SAE with 3 first class stamps. Free writer's guidelines.
Nonfiction: Informational articles about legal issues, pending and new legislation, organizations and other resources of interest to lawyers who work with aging clients and their families. Query. Pays $25-200.

STUDENT LAWYER, American Bar Association, 750 N. Lake Shore Dr., Chicago IL 60611. (312)988-6048. Editor: Sarah Hoban. Managing Editor: Miriam R. Krasno. 95% freelance written. Works with a small number of new/unpublished writers each year. Monthly (September-May) magazine. Estab. 1972. Circ. 35,000. Pays on publication. Buys first serial and second serial (reprint) rights. Publishes reprints of previously published articles. Send tearsheet of article, typed ms with rights for sale noted and information about when and where the article previously appeared. For reprints, pays 25-50% of the amount paid for an original article. Pays negotiable kill fee. Byline given. Submit seasonal material 4 months in advance. Reports in 6 weeks. Publishes ms an average of 3 months after acceptance. Sample copy $4. Free writer's guidelines.
Nonfiction: Features cover legal education and careers and social/legal subjects. The magazine also publishes profiles (prominent persons in law-related fields); opinion (on matters of current legal interest); essays (on legal affairs); interviews; and photo features. Query. Length: 3,000-5,000 words. Pays $250-800 for main features. Covers some writer's expenses.
Columns/Departments: Briefly (short stories on unusual and interesting developments in the law); Legal Aids (unusual approaches and programs connected to teaching law students and lawyers); Esq. (brief profiles of people in the law); End Note (short pieces on a variety of topics; can be humorous, educational, outrageous); Pro Se (opinion slot for authors to wax eloquent on legal issues, civil rights conflicts, the state of the union); and Et Al. (column for short features that fit none of the above categories). Buys 4-8 mss/issue. Length: 250-1,000 words. Pays $75-250.
Fiction: "We buy fiction only when it is very good and deals with issues of law in the contemporary world or offers insights into the inner workings of lawyers. No mystery, poetry or science fiction accepted."
Tips: "*Student Lawyer* actively seeks good new writers. Legal training definitely not essential; writing talent is. The writer should not think we are a law review; we are a feature magazine with the law (in the broadest sense) as the common denominator. Past articles concerned gay rights, prison reform, the media, pornography, capital punishment and drug education. Find issues of national scope and interest to write about; be aware of subjects the magazine—and other media—have already covered and propose something new. Write clearly and well."

Leather Goods

SHOE RETAILING TODAY, National Shoe Retailers Association, Suite 255, 9861 Broken Land Pkwy., Columbia MD 21046-1151. (410)381-8282. Fax: (410)381-1167. Editor: Cynthia Emmel. 10% freelance written. Bimonthly newsletter covering footwear/accessory industry. Looks for articles that are "informative, educational, but with wit, interest and creativity. I hate dry, dusty articles." Estab. 1972. Circ. 4,000-5,000. Byline given. Buys one-time rights. Submit seasonal material 3 months in advance. Reprints OK; send photocopy of article. For reprints, pays 50% of their fee for an original article. Reports in 3 months. Sample copy and writer's guidelines for 9 × 12 SAE with 2 first class stamps.
Nonfiction: How-to, interview/profile, new product and technical. January and July are shoe show issues. Buys 6 mss/year. Length: 500 words. Pays $50-100 for assigned articles. Pays up to $200 for "full-fledged research—1,000 words or more on assigned articles."
Photos: State availability of photos with submission. Offers no additional payment for photos accepted with ms. Buys one-time rights.
Columns/Departments: Query. Pays $50-125.
Tips: "We are a trade magazine/newsletter for the footwear industry. Any information pertaining to our market is helpful: advertising/display/how-tos."

SHOE SERVICE, SSIA Service Corp., 5024-R Campbell Blvd., Baltimore MD 21236. (410)931-8100. Fax: (410)931-8111. Editor: Mitchell Lebovic. 25% freelance written. "We want well-written articles, whether they come from new or established writers." Monthly magazine for business people who own and operate small shoe repair shops. Estab. 1921. Circ. 8,000. Pays on publication. Publishes ms an average of 3 months after acceptance. Byline given. Buys first serial, first North American serial and one-time rights. Submit seasonal material 3 months in advance. Simultaneous queries and previously published submissions OK. Reports in 6 weeks. Sample copy $2 for 9 × 12 SAE.

Nonfiction: How-to (run a profitable shop); interview/profile (of an outstanding or unusual person on shoe repair); and business articles (particularly about small business practices in a service/retail shop). Buys 12-24 mss/year. Query with published clips or send complete ms. Length: 500-2,000 words. Pays 5¢/word.

Photos: "Quality photos will help sell an article." State availability of photos. Pays $10-30 for 8×10 b&w prints. Uses some color photos, but mostly uses b&w glossies. Captions, model release and identification of subjects required.

Tips: "Visit some shoe repair shops to get an idea of the kind of person who reads *Shoe Service*. Profiles are the easiest to sell to us if you can find a repairer we think is unusual."

Library Science

Librarians read these journals for advice on promotion and management of libraries, library and book trade issues and information access and transfer. Be aware of current issues such as censorship, declines in funding and government information policies. For journals on the book trade see Book and Bookstore.

AMERICAN LIBRARIES, 50 E. Huron St., Chicago IL 60611. (312)280-4216. Fax: (312)440-0901. Editor: Thomas Gaughan. Senior Editor: Gordon Flagg. 10-20% freelance written. Works with a small number of new/unpublished writers each year. Magazine published 11 times/year for librarians. "A highly literate audience. They are for the most part practicing professionals with a down-to-earth interest in people and current trends." Estab. 1907. Circ. 55,000. Buys first North American serial rights. Publishes ms an average of 4 months after acceptance. Pays negotiable kill fee. Byline given. Submit seasonal material 6 months in advance. Reports in 10 weeks.

Nonfiction: "Material reflecting the special and current interests of the library profession. Nonlibrarians should browse recent journals in the field, available on request in medium-sized and large libraries everywhere. Topic and/or approach must be fresh, vital or highly entertaining. Library memoirs and stereotyped stories about old maids, overdue books, fines, etc., are unacceptable. Our first concern is with the American Library Association's activities and how they relate to the 55,000 reader/members. Tough for an outsider to write on this topic, but not to supplement it with short, offbeat or significant library stories and features." No fillers. Buys 2-6 freelance mss/year. Pays $15 for news tips used, and $25-300 for briefs and articles.

Photos: "Will look at color transparencies and bright color prints for inside and cover use." Pays $50-200 for photos.

Tips: "You can break in with a sparkling, 300-word report on a true, offbeat library event, use of new technology, or with an exciting color photo and caption. Though stories on public libraries are always of interest, we especially need arresting material on academic and school libraries."

CHURCH MEDIA LIBRARY MAGAZINE, 127 9th Ave. N., Nashville TN 37234. (615)251-2752. Editor: Floyd B. Simpson. Quarterly magazine for adult leaders in church organizations and people interested in library work (especially church library work). Estab. 1891. Circ. 16,000. Pays on publication. Buys all, first serial and second serial (reprint) rights. Byline given. Phone queries OK. Submit seasonal material 14 months in advance. Previously published submissions OK. Reports in 1 month. Free sample copy and writer's guidelines.

Nonfiction: "We are primarily interested in articles that relate to the development of church libraries in providing media and services to support the total program of a church and in meeting individual needs. We publish how-to accounts of services provided, promotional ideas, exciting things that have happened as a result of implementing an idea or service; human interest stories that are library-related; and media training (teaching and learning with a media mix). Articles should be practical for church library staffs and for teachers and other leaders of the church." Buys 10-15 mss/issue. Query. Pays 5½¢/word.

THE LIBRARY IMAGINATION PAPER, Carol Bryan Imagines, 1000 Byus Dr., Charleston WV 25311-1310. (304)345-2378. 30% freelance written. Quarterly newspaper covering public relations education for librarians. Clip art included in each issue. Estab. 1978. Circ. 3,000. Pays on publication. Publishes ms an average of 6 months after acceptance. Byline given. Buys one-time rights. Submit seasonal material 3 months in advance. Simultaneous submissions OK. Reprints OK; send tearsheet or photocopy of article and information about when and where the article previously appeared. Reports in 2 months. Sample copy $5. Writer's guidelines for SASE.

Nonfiction: How-to (on "all aspects of good library public relations—both mental tips and hands-on methods. We need how-to and tips pieces on all aspects of PR, for library subscribers—both school and public libraries. In the past we've featured pieces on taking good photos, promoting an anniversary celebration, working with printers, and producing a slide show.") No articles on "what the library means to me." Buys 4-

6 mss/year. Query with or without published clips, or send complete ms. Length: 600 or 2,200 words. Pays $25 or $50.

Photos: Send photos with submission. Reviews 5×7 prints. Offers $5/photo. Captions required. Buys one-time rights.

Tips: "Someone who has worked in the library field and has first-hand knowledge of library PR needs, methods and processes will do far better with us. Our readers are people who cannot be written down to—but their library training has not always incorporated enough preparation for handling promotion, publicity and the public."

LIBRARY JOURNAL, Dept. WM, 249 W. 17th St., New York NY 10011. (212)645-9700. Editor-in-Chief: John N. Berry III. 60% freelance written by librarians. Eager to work with new/unpublished writers. Magazine published 20 times/year for librarians (academic, public, special). Circ. 30,000. Buys all rights. Pays on publication. Publishes ms an average of 12-18 months after acceptance. "Our response time is slow, but improving."

Nonfiction: *"Library Journal* is a professional magazine for librarians. Freelancers are most often rejected because they are not librarians or they submit one of the following types of article: 'A wonderful, warm, concerned, loving librarian who started me on the road to good reading and success'; 'How I became rich, famous, and successful by using my public library'; 'Libraries are the most wonderful and important institutions in our society, because they have all of the knowledge of mankind—praise them.' We need material of greater sophistication, government information, dealing with issues related to the transfer of information, access to it, or related phenomena. (Currently hot are copyright, censorship, the decline in funding for public institutions, the local politics of libraries, trusteeship, US government information policy, etc.)" Professional articles on criticism, censorship, professional concerns, library activities, historical articles, information technology, automation and management, and spot news. Outlook should be from librarian's point of view. Buys 50-65 unsolicited mss/year. Submit complete ms. Length: 1,500-2,000 words. Pays $50-350. Sometimes pays the expenses of writers on assignment.

Photos: Payment for b&w or color glossy photos purchased without accompanying mss is $35. Must be at least 5×7. Captions required.

Tips: "We're increasingly interested in material on library management, public sector fundraising, and information policy."

WILSON LIBRARY BULLETIN, Dept. WM, 950 University Ave., Bronx NY 10452. (718)588-8400 ext. 2245. Fax: (718)681-1511. Editor: Grace Anne A. DeCandido. 75% freelance written. Monthly (September-June) for professional librarians and those interested in the book and library worlds. Estab. 1914. Circ. 13,000. Pays on publication. Publishes ms an average of 2 months after acceptance. Buys first North American serial rights. Sample copies may be seen on request in most libraries. "Manuscript must be original copy, double-spaced; additional photocopy is appreciated." Deadlines are a minimum 2 months before publication. Reports in 10 weeks. Free sample copy and writer's guidelines.

Nonfiction: Uses articles "of interest to librarians and information professionals throughout the nation and around the world. Style must be lively, readable and sophisticated, with appeal to modern professionals; facts must be thoroughly researched. Subjects range from the political to the comic in the world of media and libraries, with an emphasis on the human as well as the technical aspects of any story. No condescension: no library stereotypes." Prefers material from practicing librarians. Buys 20 mss/year. Send complete ms. Length: 2,500-3,500 words. Pays about $100-400, "depending on the substance of article and its importance to readers." Sometimes pays the expenses of writers on assignment.

Tips: "The best way you can break in is with a first-rate black-and-white or color photo and caption information on a library, library service or librarian who departs completely from all stereotypes and the commonplace. Libraries have changed. You'd better first discover how."

Lumber

NORTHERN LOGGER AND TIMBER PROCESSOR, Northeastern Loggers' Association, Dept WM, P.O. Box 69, Old Forge NY 13420. (315)369-3078. Fax: (315)369-3736. Editor: Eric A. Johnson. 40% freelance written. Monthly magazine of the forest industry in the northern US (Maine to Minnesota and south to Virginia and Missouri). "We are not a purely technical journal, but are more information oriented." Estab. 1952. Circ. 13,600. Pays on publication. Publishes ms an average of 3 months after acceptance. Byline given. Buys all rights. Submit seasonal material 3 months in advance. Previously published submissions OK. Reports in 2 weeks. Free sample copy and writer's guidelines.

Nonfiction: Expose, general interest, historical/nostalgic, how-to, interview/profile, new product and opinion. "We only buy feature articles, and those should contain some technical or historical material relating to the forest products industry." Buys 12-15 mss/year. Query. Length: 500-2,500 words. Pays $50-250.

Photos: Send photos with ms. Pays $35 for 35mm color transparencies; $15 for 5×7 b&w prints. Captions and identification of subjects required.

Tips: "We accept most any subject dealing with this part of the country's forestindustry, from historical to logging, firewood and timber processing."

SOUTHERN LUMBERMAN, Greysmith Publishing, Inc., P.O. Box 681629, Franklin TN 37068-1629. (615)791-1961. Fax: (615)790-6188. Editor: Nanci P. Gregg. 20-30% freelance written. Works with a small number of new/unpublished writers each year. Monthly trade journal for the sawmill industry. Estab. 1881. Circ. 12,000. Pays on publication. Publishes ms an average of 3 months after acceptance. Byline given. Not copyrighted. Buys first North American rights. Submit seasonal material 6 months in advance. Query for electonic submissions. Reprints OK; send tearsheet or photocopy of article and information about when and where the article previously appeared. For reprints, pays 25-50% of fee paid for an original article. Reports in 1 month on queries; 2 months on mss. Sample copy $2 for 9×12 SAE with 5 first class stamps. Writer's guidelines for #10 SASE.

Nonfiction: How to sawmill better, interview/profile, equipment analysis, technical. Sawmill features. Buys 10-15 mss/year. Query with or without published clips, or send complete ms. Length: 500-2,000 words. Pays $150-350 for assigned articles; pays $100-250 for unsolicited articles. Sometimes pays the expenses of writers on assignment.

Photos: Send photos with submission. Reviews transparencies and 4×5 b&w prints. Offers $10-25/photo. Captions and identification of subjects required.

Tips: "Like most, we appreciate a clearly-worded query listing merits of suggested story—what it will tel lour readers they need/want to know. We want quotes, we want opinions to make others discuss the article. Best hing? Find an interesting sawmill operation owner and start asking questions—I bet a story idea develops. We need b&w photos too. Most open is what we call the Sweethart Mill stories. We publish at least one per month, and hope to be printing two or more monthly in the immediate future. Find a sawmill operator and ask questions—what's he doing bigger, better, different. We're interested in new facilities, better marketing, improved production."

Machinery and Metal

AUTOMATIC MACHINING, 100 Seneca Ave., Rochester NY 14621. (716)338-1522. Editor: Donald E. Wood. For metalworking technical management. Buys all rights. Byline given.

Nonfiction: "This is not a market for the average freelancer. A personal knowledge of the trade is essential. Articles deal in depth with specific job operations on automatic screw machines, chucking machines, high production metal turning lathes and cold heading machines. Part prints, tooling layouts always required, plus written agreement of source to publish the material. Without personal background in operation of this type of equipment, freelancers are wasting time. No material researched from library sources." Query. Length: 4 double-spaced pages."

CUTTING TOOL ENGINEERING, Suite 395, 400 Skokie Blvd, Northbrook IL 60062. (708)498-9100. Fax: (708)559-4444. Publisher: John William Roberts. 25% freelance written. Prefers to work with published/established writers. Magazine published 9 times/year for metalworking industry executives and engineers concerned with the metal-cutting/metal and material removal/abrasive machining function in metalworking. Circ. 36,303. Pays on publication. Publishes ms an average of 6 months after acceptance. Byline given. Buys all rights. Query for electronic submissions. Write to the publisher before querying or submitting ms. Free sample copy.

Nonfiction: "Intelligently written articles on specific applications of all types of metal cutting tools, mills, drills, reamers, etc. Articles must contain all information related to the operation, such as feeds and speeds, materials machined, etc. Should be tersely written, in-depth treatment. In the Annual Diamond/Superabrasive Directory, published in June, we cover the use of diamond/superabrasive cutting tools and diamond/superabrasive grinding wheels." Length: 1,000-2,500 words. Payment varies.

Photos: Purchased with mss. Color or b&w 8×10 glossies preferred.

Tips: "The most frequent mistake made by writers in submitting an article for us is that they don't know the market."

‡**FABRICATOR, Ornamental & Miscellaneous Metal**, National Ornamental & Miscellaneous Metals Assoc., #E, 804-10 Main St., Forest Park GA 30050. Editor: Todd Daniel. 20% freelance written. Bimonthly magazine covering ornamental metalwork. "Any 'business' stories published must contain an angle specific to this industry." Estab. 1959. Circ. 8,000. **Pays on acceptance.** Byline given. Publication not copyrighted. Buys one-time rights. Editorial lead time 2 months. Submit seasonal material 2 months in advance. Simultaneous and previously published submissions OK. Query for electronic submissions. Reports in 6 weeks on queries. Sample copy for #10 SASE. Writer's guidelines $1.

Nonfiction: How-to, humor, interview/profile, personal experience, photo feature and technical. "Nothing in a Q&A format." Buys 3-6 mss/year. Query. Length: 1,300-2,000 words. Pays $150 minumum for assigned articles, $125 minimum for unsolicited articles. "Many write for publicity." Sometimes pays expenses of writers on assignment.

Photos: State availability of photos with submission. Reviews contact sheets, negatives, transparencies and prints. Offers no additional payment for photos acepted with ms. Model releases required. Buys one-time rights.

Tips: "Don't write articles in passive voice."

MODERN MACHINE SHOP, 6600 Clough Pike, Cincinnati OH 45244-4090. (513)231-8020. Fax: (513)231-2818. Executive Editor: Mark Albert. 25% freelance written. Monthly. Estab. 1928. Pays 1 month following acceptance. Publishes ms an average of 6 months after acceptance. Byline given. Query for electronic submissions. Reports in one month. Call for a sample copy. Writer's guidelines for #10 SASE.
Nonfiction: Uses articles dealing with all phases of metalworking, manufacturing and machine shop work, with photos. No general articles. "Ours is an industrial publication, and contributing authors should have a working knowledge of the metalworking industry. "We regularly use contributions from machine shop owners, engineers, other technical experts, and suppliers to the metalworking industry. Almost all of these contributors pursue these projects to promote their own commercial interests. " Buys 10 unsolicited mss/year. Query. Length: 1,000-3,500 words. Pays current market rate.
Tips: "The use of articles relating to computers in manufacturing is growing."

NICKEL, The magazine devoted to nickel and its applications, Nickel Development Institute, Suite 510, 214 King St. W., Toronto, Ontario M5H 3S6 Canada. (416)591-7999. Editor: James S. Borland. 30% freelance written. Quarterly magazine covering the metal nickel and all of its applications. Estab. 1985. Circ. 30,000. **Pays on acceptance.** Publishes ms an average of 3 months after acceptance. Byline given. Reports in 1 month. Buys first rights. Publishes reprints of previously published articles. Send tearsheet of article, or send typed ms with rights for sale noted. Include information about when and where the article previously appeared. For reprints, pays 50% of the amount paid for an original article. Free sample copies and writer's guidelines from Nickel Development Institute Librarian.
Nonfiction: Semi-technical. Buys 20 mss/year. Query. Length: 50-1,000 words. Pays competitive rates, by negotiation. Sometimes pays expenses of writers on assignment.
Photos: State availability of photos (uses color transparencies only) with submission. Offers competitive rates by negotiation. Captions, model releases and identification of subjects required.
Tips: "Write to Librarian, Nickel Development Institute, for two free copies of *Nickel* and study them. Know something about nickel's 300,000 end uses. Be at home in writing semitechnical material. Then query the editor with a story idea in a one-page letter—no fax queries or phone calls. Complete magazine is open, except Technical Literature column."

Maintenance and Safety

CLEANING BUSINESS, 1512 Western Ave., P.O. Box 1273, Seattle WA 98111. (206)622-4241. Fax: (206)622-6876. Publisher: William R. Griffin. Associate Editor: Jim Saunders. 80% freelance written. Quarterly magazine covering technical and management information relating to cleaning and self-employment. "We cater to those who are self-employed in any facet of the cleaning and maintenance industry and seek to be top professionals in their field. *Cleaning Business* is published for self-employed cleaning professionals, specifically carpet, upholstery and drapery cleaners; janitorial and maid services; window washers; odor, water and fire damage restoration contractors. Our readership is small but select. We seek concise, factual articles, realistic but definitely upbeat." Circ. 6,000. Pays 1 month after publication. Publishes ms an average of 3 months after acceptance. Byline given. Buys first serial, second serial (reprint) and all rights or makes work-for-hire assignments. Submit seasonal material 6 months in advance. Simultaneous queries and previously published work (rarely) OK. Reports in 3 months. Sample copy $3 for 8 × 10 SAE with 3 first class stamps. Writer's guidelines for #10 SASE.
Nonfiction: Expose (safety/health business practices); how-to (on cleaning, maintenance, small business management); humor (clean jokes, cartoons); interview/profile; new product (must be unusual to rate full article—mostly obtained from manufacturers); opinion; personal experience; and technical. Special issues: "What's New?" (February). No "wordy articles written off the top of the head, obviously without research, and needing more editing time than was spent on writing." Buys 40 mss/year. Query with or without published clips. Length: 500-3,000 words. Pays $5-80. ("Pay depends on amount of work, research and polishing put into article much more than on length.") Pays expenses of writers on assignment with prior approval only.
Photos: State availability of photos or send photos with ms. Pays $5-25 for "smallish" b&w prints. Captions, model release and identification of subjects required. Buys one-time rights and reprint rights. "Magazine size is 8½ × 11—photos need to be proportionate. Also seeks full-color photos of relevant subjects for cover."
Columns/Departments: "Ten regular columnists now sell four columns per year to us. We are interested in adding Safety & Health and Fire Restoration columns (related to cleaning and maintenance industry). We are also open to other suggestions—send query." Buys 36 columns/year; department information obtained at no cost. Query with or without published clips. Length: 500-1,500 words. Pays $15-85.
Fillers: Jokes, gags, anecdotes, short humor, newsbreaks and cartoons. Buys 40/year. Length: 3-200 words. Pays $1-20.
Tips: "We are constantly seeking quality freelancers from all parts of the country. A freelancer can best break in to our publication with fairly technical articles on how to do specific cleaning/maintenance jobs; interviews with top professionals covering this and how they manage their business; and personal experience.

Our readers demand concise, accurate information. Don't ramble. Write only about what you know and/or have researched. Editors don't have time to rewrite your rough draft. Organize and polish before submitting."

CLEANING MANAGEMENT, The Magazine for Today's Building Cleaning Maintenance/Housekeeping Executive, National Trade Publications, Inc., 13 Century Hill Dr., Latham NY 12110-2197. (518)783-1281. Fax: (518)783-1386. Editor: Thomas H. Williams. Monthly national trade magazine covering building cleaning maintenance/housekeeping operations in larger institutions such as hotels, schools, hospitals, office buildings, industrial plants, recreational and religious buildings, shopping centers, airports, etc. Articles must be aimed at managers of on-site building/facility cleaning staffs or owners/managers of contract cleaning companies. Estab. 1963. Circ. 45,000. Pays on publication, with invoice. Byline given. Buys all rights. Reports in 2 weeks. Sample copy and writer's guidelines for 9 × 12 SAE with 8 first class stamps.
Nonfiction: Articles on: how-to discussions of custodial operations/cleaning tasks; the organization of cleaning tasks on an institution-wide basis; recruitment, training, motivation and supervision of building cleaning employees; the cleaning of buildings or facilities of unusual size, type, design, construction or notoriety; interesting case studies; or advice for the successful operation of a contract cleaning business. Buys 6-12 mss/year. Length: 800-1,500 words. Pays $50-250. Please query.
Photos: State availability of photos. Prefer color or b&w prints, rates negotiable. Captions, model releases and identification of subjects required.
Tips: Chances of acceptance are directly proportional to the article's relevance to the professional, on-the-job needs and interests of custodial managers or contract building cleaners.

‡OCCUPATIONAL HEALTH & SAFETY, Stevens Publishing Corporation, P.O. Box 2573, Waco TX 76702. Editor: Mark Hartley. Associate Editor: Teri Lynn Eisma. 30% freelance written. Monthly magazine covering workplace safety and health issues. "*Occupational Health & Safety* is a business magazine whose editorial promotes the understanding and control of occupational illness, injury and hazardous exposure in the workplace. The mission of *Occupational Health & Safety*, as a professional publication, is to serve the market's editorial and advertising needs by consistently providing the industrial and corporate workplace with this field's definitive source of reliable information, which is useful in decreasing worker risk while increasing job productivity." Estab. 1932. Circ. 83,000. Pays on publication. Publishes ms an average of 3 months after acceptance. Byline given. Offers 25% kill fee. Buys first North American serial rights. Editorial lead time 3 months. Query for electronic submissions. Reports in 2 months on mss; 1 month on queries; "manuscripts are reviewed by editorial board 50-75% of time." Sample copy free on request "by calling Customer Service Department or fax request to (817)776-9018 attn: Customer Service." Writer's guidelines and editorial calendar free on request.
Nonfiction: How-to (implement safety programs in a company, for example); interview/profile (of innovative people in safety field); and technical. "No humor (particularly cartoons) or personal experience." Buys 20-30 mss/year. Query. Length: 1,000-3,000 words. Pays $300 minimum for assigned articles, $100 minimum for unsolicited articles. Seldom pays in other premiums or contributor copies, "but it's negotiable." Sometimes pays expenses of writers on assignment.
Photos: State availability of photos with submission. Reviews negatives. Negotiates payment individually. Model releases and identification of subjects required. Buys one-time rights.
Tips: "The magazine's readers are typically mid-level management, engineers or professional safety consultants. They all face increasing pressure to comply with a myriad of federal regulations. Any information that helps them perform their jobs more easily will be bought. We are most open to feature articles. If you have good contacts with local industry, keep an eye out for innovative programs that minimize the risk of injury or illness to workers."

PEST CONTROL MAGAZINE, 7500 Old Oak Blvd., Cleveland OH 44130. (216)243-8100. Fax: (216)891-2675. Editor: Tom Johnson. Monthly magazine for professional pest control operators and sanitarians. Estab. 1933. Circ. 15,000. Buys all rights. Buys 12 mss/year. Pays on publication. Submit seasonal material 2 months in advance. Reports in 1 month. Query or submit complete ms.
Nonfiction: Business tips, unique control situations, personal experience (stories about 1-man operations and their problems) articles. Must have trade or business orientation. No general information type of articles desired. Buys 3 unsolicited mss/year. Length: 1,000 words. Pays $150-500 minimum. Regular columns use material oriented to this profession. Length: 2,000 words.
Photos: No additional payment for photos used with mss. Pays $50-150 for 8 × 10 color or transparencies.

SAFETY COMPLIANCE LETTER, with OSHA Highlights, Bureau of Business Practice, 24 Rope Ferry Rd., Waterford CT 06386. (203)442-4365. Editor: Shelley Wolf. Managing Editor: Many Schantz. 80% freelance written. Bimonthly newsletter covering occupational safety and health. Publishes interview-based how-to and success stories for personnel in charge of safety and health in manufacturing/industrial environments. Circ. 8,000. Pays on acceptance after editing. Publishes ms an average of 3-6 months after acceptance. No byline given. Buys all rights. Submit seasonal material 4 months in advance. Reports in 1 week on queries; 1 month on mss. *Writer's Market* recommends allowing 2 months for reply. Free sample copy and writer's guidelines.

Nonfiction: How-to implement a particular occupational safety/health program, changes in OSHA regulations, and examples of exceptional safety/health programs. Only accepts articles that are based on an interview with a safety manager, safety consultant, occupational physician, or OSHA expert. Buys 48 mss/year. Query. Length: 750-1,200 words. Pays 10¢-15¢/word.

SANITARY MAINTENANCE, Trade Press Publishing Co., Dept. WM, 2100 W. Florist Ave., Milwaukee WI 53209-3799. (414)228-7701. Fax: (414)228-1134. Managing Editor: Austin Weber. Associate Editor: Susan M. Netz. 15-20% freelance written. Prefers to work with published/established writers, although all will be considered. Monthly magazine for the sanitary supply and paper industry covering "trends; offering information concerning the operations of janitor supply distributors and paper merchants; and helping distributors in the development of sales personnel." Estab. 1943. Circ. 18,000. Pays on publication. Publishes ms an average of 2 months after acceptance. Byline given. Buys first North American serial rights. Query for electronic submissions. Reports in 1 month. Free sample copy and writer's guidelines.
Nonfiction: How-to (improve sales, profitability as it applies to distributors) and technical. No product application stories. Buys 12-15 mss/year. Query with published clips. Length: 2,000 words. Pays $300-400.
Photos: State availability of photos with query letter or ms. Reviews 5 × 7 prints. Payment for photos included in payment for ms. Identification of subjects required.
Tips: Articles on wholesaling/distribution management issues are open to freelancers.

SECURITY SALES, Management Resource for the Professional Installing Dealer, Bobit Publishing, 2512 Artesia Blvd., Redondo Beach CA 90278. (310)376-8788. Editor: Jason Knott. Managing Editor: Patty Gallagher. 5% freelance written. Monthly magazine that covers the security industry. "Editorial covers technology, management and marketing designed to help installing security dealers improve their businesses. Closed-circuit TV, burglary and fire equipment, and access control systems are main topics." Estab. 1979. Circ. 22,000. Pays on publication. Publishes ms an average of 3-6 months after acceptance. Byline sometimes given. Buys all rights. Editorial lead time 2 months. Submit seasonal material 4 months in advance. Query for electronic submissions. Accepts simultaneous submissions. Sample copy free on request.
Nonfiction: How-to and technical. "No generic business operations articles. Submissions must be specific to security and contain interviews with installing dealers." Buys 3-6 mss/year. Send complete ms. Length: 800-1,500 words. Pays $50 minimum.
Photos: Send photos with submission. Reviews prints. Offers no additional payment for photos accepted with ms. Captions, model releases and identification of subjects required.
Tips: "Case studies of specific security installations with photos and diagrams are needed. Interview dealers who installed system and ask how they solved specific problems, why they chose certain equipment, cost of job, etc."

UTILITY CONSTRUCTION AND MAINTENANCE, Practical Communications, Inc., 321 Cary Point Dr., P.O. Box 183, Cary IL 60013-0183. (708)639-2200. Fax: (708)639-9542. Editor: Alan Richter. 5% freelance written. Quarterly magazine for equipment managers and maintenance supervisors for electric, gas and water utilities; interconnect and cable TV companies, public works departments and related contractors. "We seek case history/application features covering specific equipment management and maintenance projects/installations. Instructional/tutorial features are also welcome." Circ. 25,000. Pays on publication. Publishes ms an average of 1 month after acceptance. Byline given. 20% kill fee. Buys all rights. Publishes reprints of previously published articles. Send tearsheet or photocopy of article and information about when and where the article previously appeared. Submit seasonal material 2 months in advance. Reports in 2 weeks. Free sample copy and writer's guidelines.
Nonfiction: How-to (ways for performing fleet maintenance/improving management skills/vehicle tutorials), technical, case history/application features. No advertorials in which specific product or company is promoted. Buys 2-3 ms/year. Query with published clips. Length: 1,000-2,800 words. Pays $50/page.
Photos: Send photos with submission. Reviews contact sheets, negatives, tranparencies (3×5) and prints (3×5). Offers no additional payment for photos accepted with ms. Captions required. Buys one-time rights.

Management and Supervision

This category includes trade journals for middle management business and industrial managers, including supervisors and office managers. Journals for business executives and owners are classified under Business Management. Those for industrial plant managers are listed in Industrial Operations.

CONSTRUCTION SUPERVISION & SAFETY LETTER, (CL) Bureau of Business Practice, Dept. WM, 24 Rope Ferry Rd., Waterford CT 06386. (201)592-2831. Editor: Barry Richardson. 80% freelance written. "We're willing to work with a few new writers if they're willing to follow guidelines carefully." Semimonthly newsletter emphasizing all aspects of construction supervision. Buys all rights. Publishes ms an average of 4 months after acceptance. Phone queries OK. Submit seasonal material at least 4 months in advance. Reports in 6 weeks. Free sample copy and writer's guidelines.

Nonfiction: Publishes solid interviews with construction managers or supervisors on how to improve a single aspect of the supervisor's job. Buys 50 unsolicited mss/year. Length: 360-750 words. Pays 15¢/word.

Tips: "A writer should call before he or she does anything. We like to spend a few minutes on the phone exchanging information. We have a new design and no longer use photographs."

EMPLOYEE RELATIONS AND HUMAN RESOURCES BULLETIN, Bureau of Business Practice, 24 Rope Ferry Rd., Waterford CT 06386. Fax: (203)434-3078, CompuServe E-mail 70303, 2324. Senior Editor: Barbara Kelsey. 40% freelance written. Works with a small number of new/unpublished writers each year. Semi-monthly newsletter for personnel, human resources and employee relations managers on the executive level. Estab. 1940. Circ. 8,000. **Pays on acceptance.** Publishes ms an average of 3 months after acceptance. Buys all rights. No byline. Phone queries OK. Submit seasonal material 6 months in advance. Reports in 1 month. Free sample copy and writer's guidelines.

Nonfiction: Interviews about all types of business and industry such as banks, insurance companies, public utilities, airlines, consulting firms, etc. Interviewee should be a high level company officer – human resources executive, president, industrial relations manager, etc. Writer must get signed release from person interviewed showing that article has been read and approved by him/her, before submission. Some subjects for interviews might be productivity improvement, communications, compensation, labor relations, safety and health, grievance handling, human relations techniques and problems, etc. No general opinions and/or philosophy of good employee relations or general good motivation/morale material. Buys 2 mss/issue. Query is mandatory. Length: 2,000-2,500 words. Pays 8-18¢/word after editing. Sometimes pays the telephone expenses of writers on assignment. Modem transmission available by prior arrangement with editor.

HUMAN RESOURCE EXECUTIVE, Axon Group, 747 Dresher Rd., P.O. Box 980, Dept. 500, Dresher PA 19044. (215)784-0860. Editor: David Shadovitz. 30% freelance written. Monthly magazine for human resource professionals/executives. "The magazine serves the information needs of chief human resource executives in companies, government agencies and nonprofit institutions with 500 or more employees." Estab. 1987. Circ. 45,000. **Pays on acceptance.** Publishes ms an average of 2 months after acceptance. Byline given. Offers 50% kill fee on assigned stories. Buys first rights and second serial (reprint) rights. Query for electronic submissions. Reports in 1 month. Sample copy for 10 × 13 SAE with 2 first class stamps. Writer's guidelines for #10 SAE with 1 first class stamp.

Nonfiction: Book excerpts, interview/profile. Buys 16 mss/year. Query with published clips. Length: 1,700-2,400 words. Pays $200-700. Sometimes pays expenses of writers on assignment.

Photos: State availability of photos with submission. Reviews contact sheets. Offers no additional payment for photos accepted with ms. Identification of subjects required. Buys first and repeat rights.

INDUSTRY WEEK, The Management Magazine for Industry, Penton Publishing Inc., Dept. WM, 1100 Superior Ave., Cleveland OH 44114-2543. (216)696-7000. Fax: (216)696-7670. Managing Editor: Dale W. Sommer. 15% freelance written. Industrial management magazine published on the first and third Monday of each month. "*Industry Week* is designed to help its audience – mid- and upper-level managers in industry – manage and lead their organizations better. Every article should address this editorial mission." Estab. 1921. Circ. 288,000. **Pays on acceptance.** Publishes ms an average of 2-4 months after acceptance. Byline given. Buys first North American serial rights. Reports in 1 month. Free sample copy and writer's guidelines. "An SAE speeds replies."

Nonfiction: Interview/profile. "Any article submitted to *Industry Week* should be consistent with its mission. We suggest authors contact us before submitting anything." Buys 15-20 mss/year. Query with or without published clips or send complete ms. Length: 750-2,500 words. Pays $350 minimum. "We pay *routine* expenses; we do *not* pay for travel unless arranged in advance."

Photos: State availability of photos with submission or send photo with submission. Reviews contact sheets, transparencies and prints. Payment arranged individually. Captions and identification of subjects required. Buys one-time rights.

Tips: "Become familiar with *Industry Week*. We're after articles about managing in industry, period. While we do not use freelancers too often, we do use some. The stories we accept are written with an understanding of our audience, and mission. We prefer multi-source stories that offer lessons for all managers in industry."

MANAGE, 2210 Arbor Blvd., Dayton OH 45439. (513)294-0421. Fax: (513)294-2374. Editor-in-Chief: Douglas E. Shaw. 60% freelance written. Works with a small number of new/unpublished writers each year. Quarterly magazine for first-line and middle management and scientific/technical managers. Estab. 1925.

ALWAYS enclose a self-addressed, stamped envelope (SASE) with all your queries and correspondence.

Circ. 65,000. **Pays on acceptance.** Publishes ms an average of 6 months after acceptance. Buys North American magazine rights with reprint privileges; book rights remain with the author. Reports in 3 months. Sample copy and writer's guidelines for 9×12 SAE with 3 first class stamps.

Nonfiction: "All material published by *Manage* is in some way management oriented. Most articles concern one or more of the following categories: communications, executive abilities, human relations, job status, leadership, motivation and productivity and professionalism. Articles should be specific and tell the manager how to apply the information to his job immediately. Be sure to include pertinent examples, and back up statements with facts. *Manage* does not want essays or academic reports, but interesting, well-written and practical articles for and about management." Buys 6 mss/issue. Phone queries OK. Submit complete ms. Length: 600-1,200 words. Pays 5¢/word.

Tips: "Keep current on management subjects; submit timely work. Include word count on first page of ms."

PERSONNEL MANAGER'S LETTER, (formerly *Personnel Advisory Bulletin*), Bureau of Business Practice, 24 Rope Ferry Rd., Waterford CT 06386. (203)442-4365, ext. 778. Editor: Jill Whitney. 75% freelance written. Eager to work with new/unpublished writers. Semimonthly newsletter emphasizing all aspects of personnel practices for personnel managers in all types and sizes of companies, both white collar and industrial. **Pays on acceptance.** Publishes ms an average of 5 months after acceptance. Buys all rights. Submit seasonal material 4 months in advance. Reports in 1 month. Sample copy and writer's guidelines for 10×13 SAE with 2 first class stamps.

Nonfiction: Interviews with personnel managers or human resource professionals on topics of current interest in the personnel field. Buys 30 mss/year. Query with brief, specific outline. Length: 800-1,500 words.

Tips: "We're looking for concrete, practical material on how to solve problems. We're providing information about trends and developments in the field. We don't want filler copy. It's very easy to break in. Include your phone number with your query so we can discuss the topic. Send for guidelines first, though, so we can have a coherent conversation."

PRODUCTION MANAGEMENT BULLETIN, (formerly *Production Supervisor's Bulletin*), Bureau of Business Practice, 24 Rope Ferry Rd., Waterford CT 06386. (800)243-0876. Fax: (203)434-3078. 75% freelance written. Biweekly newsletter for production/manufacturing managers primarily. "Articles are meant to address a common workplace issue faced by such managers (absenteeism, low productivity, improving quality, ensuring safety, etc.) and explain how readers may deal with the issue. **Pays on acceptance.** Publishes ms an average of 4 months after acceptance. Byline not given. Buys all rights. Reports in 2 weeks on queries; 3 weeks on mss. *Writer's Market* recommends allowing 2 months for reply. Free sample copy and writer's guidelines.

Nonfiction: How-to (on managing people, solving workplace problems, improving productivity). No high-level articles aimed at upper management. Buys 60-70 mss/year. Query. Length: 800-1,500 words. Pays 9-15¢/word.

Tips: Freelancers may call the editor at (800)243-0876. Prospective writers are strongly urged to send for writer's guidelines. Sections of publication most open to freelancers are lead story; inside stories (generally 3 to 4 per issue); and Production Management Clinic (in every other issue). Include concrete, how-to steps for dealing effectively with the topic at hand.

SALES MANAGER'S BULLETIN, The Bureau of Business Practice, 24 Rope Ferry Rd., Waterford CT 06386. Fax: (203)434-3078. Editor: Paulette S. Kitchens. 33% freelance written. Prefers to work with published/established writers. Semimonthly newsletter for sales managers and salespeople interested in getting into sales management. Estab. 1917. **Pays on acceptance.** Publishes ms an average of 3-6 months after acceptance. Written queries only except from regulars. Submit seasonal material 6 months in advance. Original interview-based material only. Buys all rights. Reports in 1 month. Sample copy and writer's guidelines only when request is accompanied by SAE with 2 first class stamps.

Nonfiction: How-to (motivate salespeople, cut costs, create territories, etc.); interview (with working sales managers who use innovative techniques); and technical (marketing stories based on interviews with experts). No articles on territory management, saving fuel in the field, or public speaking skills. Break into this publication by reading the guidelines and sample issue. Follow the directions closely and chances for acceptance go up dramatically. One easy way to start is with an interview article ("Here's what sales executives have to say about . . ."). Query is vital to acceptance: "Send a simple note explaining briefly the subject matter, the interviewees, slant, length, and date of expected completion, accompanied by a SASE." Does not accept unqueried mss. Length: 800-1,200 words. Pays 10-15¢/word.

Tips: "Freelancers should always request samples and writer's guidelines, accompanied by SASE. Requests without SASE are discarded immediately. Examine the sample, and don't try to improve on our style. Write as we write. Don't 'jump around' from point to point and don't submit articles that are too chatty and with not enough real information. The more time a writer can save the editors, the greater his or her chance of a sale and repeated sales, when queries may not be necessary any longer. We will focus more on selling more product, meeting intense competition, while spending less money to do it."

SECURITY MANAGEMENT BULLETIN: Protecting Property, People & Assets, Bureau of Business Practice, 24 Rope Ferry Rd., Waterford CT 06386. Editor: Alex Vaughn. 75% freelance written. Eager to work with new/unpublished writers. Semimonthly newsletter emphasizing security for industry. "All material should be slanted toward security directors, primarily industrial, retail and service businesses, but others as well." Circ. 3,000. **Pays on acceptance.** Buys all rights. Phone queries OK. Reports in 2 weeks. Free sample copy and writer's guidelines.

Nonfiction: Interview (with security professionals only). "Articles should be tight and specific. They should deal with new security techniques or new twists on old ones." Buys 2-5 mss/issue. Query. Length: 750-1,000 words. Pays 15¢/word.

SUPERVISION, 424 N. 3rd St., P.O. Box 1, Burlington IA 52601-0001. Fax: (319)752-3421. Publisher: Michael S. Darnall. Editorial Supervisor: Doris J. Ruschill. Editor: Barbara Boeding. 95% freelance written. Monthly magazine for first-line foremen, supervisors and office managers. Estab. 1939. Circ. 4,200. Pays on publication. Publishes ms an average of 6 months after acceptance. Buys all rights. Reports in 1 month. Sample copy and writer's guidelines for 9 × 12 SAE with 4 first class stamps; mention *Writer's Market* in request.

Nonfiction: How-to (cope with supervisory problems, discipline, absenteeism, safety, productivity, goal setting, etc.); and personal experience (unusual success story of foreman or supervisor). No sexist material written from only a male viewpoint. Include biography and/or byline with ms submissions. Author photos requested. Buys 12 mss/issue. Query. Length: 1,500-1,800 words. Pays 4¢/word.

Tips: "Following AP stylebook would be helpful." Uses no advertising. Send correspondence to Editor.

SUPERVISOR'S BULLETIN, Bureau of Business Practice, 24 Rope Ferry Rd., Waterford CT 06386-0001. (203)442-4365. Fax: (203)434-3078. Editor: Carl Thunberg. 50-75% freelance written. "We work with both new and established writers, and are always looking for fresh talent." Bimonthly newsletter for manufacturing supervisors wishing to improve their managerial skills. Estab. 1915. **Pays on acceptance.** Publishes ms an average of 3 months after acceptance. No byline given. Buys all rights. Reports in 2 weeks on queries; 6 weeks on mss. Free sample copy and writer's guidelines.

Nonfiction: How-to (solve a supervisory problem on the job or avoid litigation); and interview (of top-notch supervisors or experts who can give advice on supervisory issues). Sample topics could include: how to increase productivity, cut costs, achieve better teamwork, and step-by-step approaches to problem-solving. No filler or non-interview based copy. Buys 72 mss/year. Query first. "Strongly urge writers to study guidelines and samples." Length: 750-1,000 words. Pays 12-18¢/word.

Tips: "We need interview-based articles that emphasize direct quotes. Define a problem and show how the supervisor solved it. Write in a light, conversational style, talking directly to supervisors who can benefit from putting the interviewee's tips into practice."

UTILITY SUPERVISION, Bureau of Business Practice, 24 Rope Ferry Rd., Waterford CT 06386. (203)739-0169. Editor: Winifred Bonney. 80% freelance written. "We're willing to work with a few new writers if they're willing to follow guidelines carefully." Semimonthly newsletter emphasizing all aspects of utility supervision. **Pays on acceptance.** Publishes ms an average of 4 months after acceptance. Buys all rights. Phone queries OK. Submit seasonal material 4 months in advance. Reports in 6 weeks. Free sample copy and writer's guidelines.

Nonfiction: Publishes how-to (interview on a single aspect of supervision with utility manager/supervisor concentrating on how reader/supervisor can improve in that area). Buys 50 mss/year. Query. Length: 360-750 words. Pays 15¢/word.

• Photos are no longer accepted with mss.

Tips: "A writer should call before he or she does anything. I like to spend a few minutes on the phone exchanging information."

WAREHOUSING SUPERVISOR'S BULLETIN, Bureau of Business Practice, 24 Rope Ferry Rd., Waterford CT 06386. (203)442-4365. Fax: (203)434-3078. Editor: April L. Katz. 75-90% freelance written. "We work with a wide variety of writers, and are always looking for fresh talent." Biweekly newsletter covering traffic, materials handling and distribution for warehouse supervisors "interested in becoming more effective on the job." **Pays on acceptance.** Publishes ms an average of 3 months after acceptance. No byline given. Buys all rights. Reports in 2 weeks on queries; 6 weeks on mss. Free sample copy and writer's guidelines.

Nonfiction: How-to (increase efficiency, control or cut costs, cut absenteeism or tardiness, increase productivity, raise morale); and interview (of warehouse supervisors or managers who have solved problems on the job). No noninterview articles, textbook-like descriptions, union references or advertising of products. Buys 50 mss/year. Query. "A resume and sample of work are helpful." Length: 1,580-2,900 words. Pays 10-15¢/word. Sometimes pays the expenses of writers on assignment.

Tips: "All articles must be interview-based and emphasize how-to information. They should also include a reference to the interviewee's company (location, size, products, function of the interviewee's department and number of employees under his control). Focus articles on one problem, and get the interviewee to pinpoint the best way to solve it. Write in a light, conversational style, talking directly to warehouse supervisors who can benefit from putting the interviewee's tips into practice."

Marine and Maritime Industries

CHARTER INDUSTRY, The Management Magazine for the Charter Industry, Charter Industry Services, Inc., 43 Kindred St., P.O. Box 375, Stuart FL 34995-0375. (407)288-1066. Editor: Paul McElroy. 50% freelance written. Bimonthly trade journal that covers legislative and industry issues. "*CI* is not a consumer 'Let's go on a fishing trip' publication, but is a business publication for people in the charter business, including sportfishing, diving, excursion and sailing charters." Estab. 1985. Circ. 10,750. Pays on publication. Byline given. No kill fee. Buys all rights and makes work-for-hire assignments. Reports in 2 weeks on queries. Sample copy for 9×12 SAE with 6 first class stamps. Writer's guidelines for #10 SAE with 2 first class stamps.

Nonfiction: Historical/nostalgic, how-to, humor, inspirational, interview/profile and opinion. No fishing stories. Buys 24 mss/year. Query with published clips. Length: 800-2,000 words. Pays $75-150. Sometimes pays expenses of writers on assignment.

Photos: State availability of photos with submission or send photos with submission. Reviews 5×7 prints. Offers no additional payment for photos accepted with ms. Captions, model releases and identification of subjects required. Buys one-time rights.

Columns/Departments: Taxes, Legal and Photography. Buys 12 mss/year. Query. Length: 600 words.

Tips: "Writers should know that the readers are professional captains who depend upon their boats and the sea to make their living. They demand the writer know the subject and the application to the industry. Those without knowledge of the industry should save their postage." Areas most open to freelancers are "personal profiles of sucessful charter captains and charter ports. We have guidelines for articles on both subjects. Most freelancer submissions are rejected because they don't do their homework properly. Our readers are tough taskmasters. Don't try to fool them!"

MARINE BUSINESS JOURNAL, The Voice of the Marine Industries Nationwide, 1766 Bay Rd., Miami Beach FL 33139. (305)538-0700. Editorial Director: Andree Conrad. Executive Editor: John W. Wooldridge. 25% freelance written. Bimonthly tabloid that covers the recreational boating industry. "*The Marine Business Journal* is aimed at boating dealers, distributors and manufacturers, naval architects, yacht brokers, marina owners and builders, marine electronics dealers, distributors and manufacturers, and anyone involved in the US marine industry. Articles cover news, new product technology and public affairs affecting the industry." Estab. 1986. Circ. 26,000. Pays on publication. Publishes ms an average of 1 month after acceptance. Byline given. Buys first North American serial, one-time or second serial (reprint rights). Query for electronic submissions. Reports in 2 weeks on queries. Sample copy $2.50 for 9×12 SAE with 7 first class stamps. Writer's guidelines for #10 SASE.

Nonfiction: "Send query before sending ms." Buys 20 mss/year. Query with published clips. Length: 500-2,000 words. Pays $100-200 for assigned articles. Sometimes pays expenses of writers on assignment.

Photos: State availability of photos with submission. Reviews 35mm or larger transparencies and 5×7 prints. Offers $25-50/photo. Captions, model releases and identification of subjects required. Buys one-time rights.

Tips: "Query with clips. It's a highly specialized field, written for professionals by professionals, almost all on assignment or by staff."

NORTHERN AQUACULTURE, Harrison House Publishers, 4611 William Head Rd., Victoria, British Columbia V9B 5T7 Canada. (604)478-9209. Fax: (604)478-1184. Editor: Peter Chettleburgh. 50% freelance written. Works with a small number of new/unpublished writers each year. Bimonthly magazine covering aquaculture in Canada and the northern US. Estab. 1985. Circ. 4,000. Pays on publication. Publishes ms an average of 3 months after acceptance. Byline given. Buys first North American serial rights. Submit seasonal material 5 months in advance. Reports in 3 weeks. Free sample copy for 9×12 SAE with $2 IRCs. Free writer's guidelines.

Nonfiction: How-to, interview/profile, new product, opinion and photo feature. Buys 20-24 mss/year. Query. Length: 200-1,500 words. Pays 10-20¢/word for assigned articles; pays 10-15¢/word for unsolicited articles. May pay writers with contributor copies if writer requests. Sometimes pays the expenses of writers on assignment.

Photos: Send photos with submission. Reviews 5×7 prints. Captions required. Buys one-time rights.

PROCEEDINGS, Dept. WM, U.S. Naval Institute, Annapolis MD 21402. (410)268-6110. Editor: Fred H. Rainbow. Managing Editor: John G. Miller. 95% freelance written. Eager to work with new/published writers. Monthly magazine covering naval and maritime subjects. Circ. 100,000. **Pays on acceptance.** Publishes ms an average of 5 months after acceptance. Byline given. Buys all rights. Submit seasonal material 3 months in advance. Reports in 2 weeks on queries; 1 month on mss. *Writer's Market* recommends allowing 2 months for reply. Free sample copy and writer's guidelines.

Nonfiction: Essays, expose, general interest, historical/nostalgic, how-to (related to sea service professional subjects), humor, interview/profile, new product, opinion, personal experience, photo feature and technical. "*Proceedings* is an unofficial, open forum for the discussion of naval and maritime topics." Special issues: International Navies (March) and Naval Review (May). Buys 250 mss/year. Query or send complete ms. Length: up to 3,500 words. Pays $50-600. Sometimes pays writers with contributor copies or other premiums "if author desires." Sometimes pays the expenses of writers on assignment.

Photos: Send photos with submission. Reviews contact sheets, negatives, transparencies and prints. Offers $10-100/photo. Buys one-time rights.

Columns/Departments: Book Reviews, Nobody Asked Me But . . ., and Crossword Puzzles (all with naval or maritime slants), all 500-2,000 words. Buys 90 mss/year. Query. Pays $50-200.

Fiction: Adventure, historical and humorous. Buys 4 mss/year. Query. Length: 500-3,000 words. Pays $50-600.

Fillers: Anecdotes. Buys 50/year. Length: 1,000 words maximum. Pays $25-150.

Tips: "Write about something you know about, either from first-hand experience or based on primary source material. Our letters to the editor column is most open to freelancers."

SEA'S INDUSTRY WEST, The Western Marine Industry Magazine, Duncan McIntosh Co. Inc., Suite C, 2nd Floor, 17782 Cowan, Irvine CA 92714. (714)660-6150. Fax: (714)660-6172. Managing Editor: John Vigor. 30% freelance written. Quarterly magazine covering recreational boating industry in the 13 western states. "*Sea's Industry West* covers news and trends that directly affect the western marine industry. Articles are aimed directly at industry professionals, offering them the information they need to make the most of their business." Estab. 1991. Circ. 12,375. **Pays on acceptance.** Publishes ms an average of 2 months after acceptance. Byline given. Buys first North American serial or second serial (reprint) rights. Query for electronic submissions. Reports in 1 month on queries; 6 weeks on mss. Sample copy and writer's guidelines for SASE.

Nonfiction: Interview/profile, new product, West Coast industry trend features. "No cartoons, poetry, fiction or features aimed at consumers instead of marine business people." Buys 25 mss/year. Query with published clips or send complete ms. Length: 250-2,000 words. Pays $35-275. "Some expenses covered if requested in advance, in writing."

Photos: State availability of photos with submission or send photos with submission. Reviews any size color transparencies. Offers $35-250/photo. Identification of subjects required. Buys one-time rights.

Columns/Departments: Business Briefs (short news items about changes, developments at Western marine companies); Legislative Update (new bills, laws and court decisions affecting the marine industry in the West); New Products (boating accessories and services available for sale by Western marine distributors/retailers). Query with published clips or send complete ms. Length: 250 words. Pays $35.

WORKBOAT, P.O. Box 1348, Mandeville LA 70470. (504)626-0298. Fax: (504)624-5801. Editor: Don Nelson. 60% freelance written. Bimonthly magazine on all working boats: commerical inland and near shore. Target work boat owners, boat captains, operators, service companies and related businesses. Estab. 1943. Pays on acceptance or publication. Publishes ms average of 2 months after acceptance. Byline given. Offers negotiable kill fee. Buys first rights. Query for electronic submissions. Sample copy $3 for 9 × 12 SAE. Writer's guidelines for #10 SASE.

Nonfiction: General interest, how-to, interview/profile and technical. Query with or without published clips. Sometimes pays expenses of writers on assignment.

Photos: State availability of photos with submission. Reviews contact sheets and transparencies, prefers color. Pay negotiable. Identification of subjects required. Buys one-time rights.

Tips: "Learn all you can about tugs, barges, supply boats, passenger vessels (excursion and ferry), dredges, fire boats, patrol boats and any vessel doing business on America's inland waterways, harbors and close to shore. Also, familiarity with issues affecting the maritime industry is a plus."

Medical

Through these journals physicians, therapists and mental health professionals learn how other professionals help their patients and manage their medical practices. Publications for nurses, laboratory technicians and other medical personnel are listed in the Hospitals, Nursing and Nursing Home section. Publications for drug store managers and drug wholesalers and retailers, as well as hospital equipment suppliers, are listed with Drugs, Health Care and Medical Products. Publications for consumers that report trends in the medical field are found in the Consumer Health and Fitness categories.

AMERICAN MEDICAL NEWS, American Medical Association, Dept. WM, 515 N. State St., Chicago IL 60610. (312)464-4429. Editor: Barbara Bolsen. 5-10% freelance written. "Prefers writers already interested in the health care field—not clinical medicine." Weekly tabloid providing nonclinical information for physicians—information on socio-economic, political and other developments in medicine. "*AMN* is a specialized publication circulating to physicians, covering subjects touching upon their profession, practices and personal lives. This is a well-educated, highly sophisticated audience." Circ. 375,000 physicians. **Pays on acceptance.** Publishes ms an average of 2 months after acceptance. Byline given. Offers variable kill fee. Buys first North American rights. Simultaneous queries OK. Reports in 1 month. Sample copy for 9×12 SAE with 2 first class stamps. Free writer's guidelines.

CARDIOLOGY WORLD NEWS, Medical Publishing Enterprises, P.O. Box 1548, Marco Island FL 33969. (813)394-0400. Editor: John H. Lavin. 75% freelance written. Prefers to work with published/established writers. Monthly magazine covering cardiology and the cardiovascular system. "We need short news articles *for doctors* on any aspect of our field—diagnosis, treatment, risk factors, etc." Estab. 1985. **Pays on acceptance.** Publishes ms an average of 2 months after acceptance. Byline given "for special reports and feature-length articles." Offers 20% kill fee. Buys first North American serial rights. Query for electronic submissions. Reports in 2 months. Sample copy $1. Free writer's guidelines with #10 SASE.
Nonfiction: New product and technical (clinical). No fiction, fillers, profiles of doctors or poetry. Query with published clips. Length: 250-1,500 words. Pays $50-300; $50/column for news articles. Pays expenses of writers on assignment.
Photos: State availability of photos with query. Pays $50/published photo. Rough captions, model release and identification of subjects required. Buys one-time rights.
Tips: "Submit written news articles of 250-500 words on speculation with basic source material (not interview notes) for fact-checking. We demand clinical or writing expertise for full-length feature. Clinical cardiology conventions/symposia are the best source of news and feature articles."

CINCINNATI MEDICINE, Academy of Medicine, 320 Broadway, Cincinnati OH 45234-9506. (513)421-7010. Fax: (513)721-4378. Executive Editor: Pamela G. Fairbanks. Managing Editor: Rhonda Tepe. 40-50% freelance written. Works with a small number of new/unpublished writers each year. Quarterly membership magazine for the Academy of Medicine of Cincinnati covering socio-economic and political factors that affect the practice of medicine in Cincinnati. For example: Effects of Medicare changes on local physicians and patients. (Ninety-nine percent of our readers are Cincinnati physicians.) Estab. 1978. Circ. 3,500. **Pays on acceptance.** Publishes ms an average of 3-6 months after acceptance. Byline given. Makes work-for-hire assignments. Reprints OK; send photocopy of article and information about when and where the article previously appeared. Pays negotiable rate. Reports in 6 weeks on queries; 3 months on mss. Sample copy $3 for 9×12 SAE with 9 first class stamps. Writer's guidelines for #10 SASE.
Nonfiction: Historical/nostalgic (history of, or reminiscences about, medicine in Cincinnati); interview/profile (of medical leaders in Cincinnati); and opinion (opinion pieces on controversial medico-legal and medico-ethical issues). "We do not accept scientific/research articles." Buys 10-12 mss/year. Query with published clips or send complete ms. Length: 800-1,500 words. Pays $125-300.
Photos: State availability of photos with query or ms. Captions and identification of subjects required. Buys one-time rights.
Tips: Send published clips. "We emphasize solid reporting and accurate, well-balanced analysis."

‡**DOCTORS SHOPPER**, Marketing Communications, Inc., 1086 Remsen Ave., Brooklyn NY 11236. (718)257-8484. Fax: (718)257-8845. Publisher: Ralph Selitzer. 35% freelance written. Quarterly magazine on medical business, travel, finances, lifestyle articles for doctors. Circ. 211,000. Pays on publication. Byline given. Buys one-time rights. Submit seasonal/holiday material 6 months in advance. Previously published submissions OK. Reports in 1 month. Free sample copy for 9×12 SAE with 12 first class stamps. Writer's guidelines for #10 SASE.
Nonfiction: General interest, new product, photo feature, technical, travel and financial. Buys 8 mss/year. Send complete ms. Length: 250-2,000 words. Pays $250-500 for assigned articles; $125-250 for unsolicited articles.
Photos: State availability of photos with submission. Reviews contact sheets and 2×2 transparencies. Offers no additional payment for photos accepted with ms. Captions, model releases and identification of subjects required. Buys one-time rights.
Columns/Departments: CME Travel (travel articles for doctors attending continuing education conferences), 500-1,000 words. Buys 4 mss/year. Pays $125-250.
Fillers: Anecdotes, facts, gags to be illustrated by cartoonist, all *medical*. Buys 8/year. Length: 100-500 words. Pays $25-50.
Tips: "Contribute self-help articles for physicians on serving patients better, running a more efficient practice, enjoying leisure time, travel, etc. Travel articles, new medical office methods, actual physician case histories are areas most open to freelancers."

EMERGENCY, The Journal of Emergency Services, 6300 Yarrow Dr., Carlsbad CA 92009-1597. (619)438-2511. Fax: (619)931-5809. Editor: Rhonda L. Foster. 100% freelance written. Works with a small number of new/unpublished writers each year. Monthly magazine covering pre-hospital emergency care. "Our readership is primarily composed of EMTs, paramedics and other EMS personnel. We prefer a professional, semi-technical approach to pre-hospital subjects." Estab. 1969. Circ. 29,000. **Pays on acceptance.** Publishes ms an average of 4 months after acceptance. Byline given. Buys all rights (revert back to author after 3 months). Submit seasonal material 6 months in advance. Reports in 2-3 months. Sample copy $3. Writer's guidelines for #10 SASE.

Nonfiction: Semi-technical expose, how-to (on treating pre-hospital emergency patients), interview/profile, new techniques, opinion and photo feature. "We do not publish cartoons, term papers, product promotions disguised as articles or overly technical manuscripts." Buys 60 mss/year. Query with published clips. Length 1,500-3,000 words. Pays $100-300.

Photos: Send photos with submission. Reviews color transparencies and b&w prints. Photos accepted with mss increase payment. Offers $30/photo without ms; $100 for cover photos. Captions and identification of subjects required.

Columns/Departments: Open Forum (opinion page for EMS professionals), 500 words; Skills Primer (basic skills, how-to with photos), 1,000-2,000 words; and Drug Watch (focus on one particular drug a month). Buys 10 mss/year. Query first. Pays $50-250.

Fillers: Facts and newsbreaks. Buys 10/year. Length: no more than 500 words. Pays $0-75.

Tips: "Writing style for features and departments should be knowledgeable and lively with a clear theme or story line to maintain reader interest and enhance comprehension. The biggest problem we encounter is dull, lifeless term-paper-style writing with nothing to pique reader interest. Keep in mind we are not a textbook. Accompanying photos are a plus.We appreciate a short, one paragraph biography on the author."

FACETS, American Medical Association Auxiliary, Inc., 515 N. State St., Chicago IL 60610. (312)464-4470. Fax: (312)464-4184. Editor: Kathleen T. Jordan. 25% freelance written. Works with both established and new writers. Bimonthly magazine for physicians' spouses. Estab. 1965. Circ. 90,000. **Pays on acceptance.** Publishes ms an average of 6 months after acceptance. Buys first rights. Simultaneous and previously published submissions OK. Reports in 2 months. Sample copy and writer's guidelines for 9 × 12 SAE with 2 first class stamps.

Nonfiction: All articles must be related to the experiences of physicians' spouses. Current health issues; financial topics, physicians' family circumstances, business management and volunteer leadership how-to's. Buys 12 mss/year. Query with clear outline of article—what points will be made, what conclusions drawn, what sources will be used. No personal experience or personality stories. Length: 1,000-2,500 words. Pays $300-800. Pays expenses of writers on assignment.

Photos: State availability of photos with query. Uses 8 × 10 glossy b&w prints and 2¼ × 2¼ transparencies.

Tips: Uses "articles only on specified topical matter with good sources, not hearsay or personal opinion. Since we use only nonfiction and have a limited readership, we must relate factual material."

FITNESS MANAGEMENT, Issues and solutions for fitness services, Leisure Publications, Inc., Suite 110, 215 S. Highway 101, P.O. Box 1198, Solana Beach CA 92075-0910. (619)481-4155. Fax: (619)481-4228. Editor: Edward H. Pitts. 50% freelance written. Monthly magazine covering commercial, corporate and community fitness centers. "Readers are owners, managers and program directors of physical fitness facilities. *FM* helps them run their enterprises safely, efficiently and profitably. Ethical and professional positions in health, nutrition, sports medicine, management, etc., are consistent with those of established national bodies." Estab. 1985. Circ. 21,000. Pays on publication. Publishes ms an average of 5 months after acceptance. Byline given. Pays 50% kill fee. Buys all rights. Submit seasonal material 6 months in advance. Query for electronic submissions. Reports in 3 months. Sample copy $5. Writer's guidelines for #10 SASE.

Nonfiction: Book excerpts (prepublication), how-to (manage fitness center and program), new product (no pay), photo feature (facilities/programs), technical and other (news of fitness research and major happenings in fitness industry). No exercise instructions or general ideas without examples of fitness businesses that have used them successfully. Buys 50 mss/year. Query. Length: 750-2,000 words. Pays $60-300 for assigned articles; up to $300 for unsolicited articles. Pays expenses of writers on assignment.

Photos: Send photos with submission. Reviews contact sheets, 2 × 2 and 4 × 5 transparencies; prefers glossy prints, 5 × 7 to 8 × 10. Offers $10-25/photo. Captions and model releases required.

Tips: "We seek writers who are expert in a business or science field related to the fitness-service industry or who are experienced in the industry. Be current with the state of the art/science in business and fitness and communicate it in human terms (avoid intimidating academic language; tell the story of how this was learned and/or cite examples of quotes of people who have applied the knowledge successfully)."

GERIATRIC CONSULTANT, Medical Publishing Enterprises, P.O. Box 1548, Marco Island FL 33969. (813)394-0400. Editor: John H. Lavin. 70% freelance written. Prefers to work with published/established writers. Bimonthly magazine for physicians covering medical care of the elderly. "We're a clinical magazine directed to doctors and physician assistants. All articles must *help* these health professionals to help their elderly patients. We're too tough a market for nonmedical beginners." Estab. 1982. Circ. 97,500. **Pays on**

acceptance. Publishes ms an average of 3-6 months after acceptance. Byline given. Offers 20% kill fee. Buys first North American serial rights. Simultaneous queries OK. Query for electronic submissions. Reports in 1 month. Sample copy $1. Writer's guidelines for #10 SASE.

Nonfiction: How-to (diagnosis and treatment of health problems of the elderly) and technical/clinical. No fiction or articles directed to a lay audience. Buys 20 mss/year. Query. Length: 750-3,000 words. Pays $200-400 for features; $50-100 for 250-word-plus news articles. Pays expenses of writers on assignment.

Photos: State availability of photos. (Photos are not required.) Model release and identification of subjects required. Buys one-time rights.

Tips: "Many medical meetings are now held in the field of geriatric care. These offer potential sources and subjects for us."

HEALTH SYSTEMS REVIEW, P.O. Box 8708, Little Rock AR 72217-8708. (501)661-9555. Fax: (501)663-4903. Editor: John Herrmann. 5% freelance written. Bimonthly trade journal on health care issues and health care politics (federal and state). *"Health Systems Review* publishes articles concerning the politics of health care, covers legislative activities and broad grass roots stories involving particular hospitals or organizations and their problems/solutions. Goes to health care managers, executives, to all members of the Congress, its staffs, the Administration and staff." Estab. 1967. Circ. 30,000. **Pays on acceptance.** Byline given. Buys first North American serial rights and second serial (reprint) rights. Publishes reprints of previously published articles. Send tearsheet of article. Submit seasonal material 6 months in advance. Simultaneous submissions OK. Query for electronic submissions. Reports in 1 week on queries; 1 month on mss. *Writer's Market* recommends allowing 2 months for reply. Sample copy for 9×12 SAE with 5 first class stamps.

Nonfiction: Essays, interview/profile, opinion and personal experience. "No articles about health care or medical procedures. No new products pieces. No articles about health care and the stock market." Buys 2-4 mss/year. Query with published clips. Length: 1,500-3,500 words. Pays $200. "Articles by health care leaders, members of Congress and staff and legal columns generally not paid." Pays expenses of writers on assignment.

Photos: Send photos with submission. Reviews contact sheets, transparencies and prints. Offers no additional payment for photos accepted with ms. Captions and identification of subjects required. Buys one-time rights.

Columns/Departments: Jennifer L. Smith. Health Care Financing (business issues in health care), 1,500-3,500 words; Health Law Perspectives (written in-house); and Supply Side (health care suppliers news update), 1,500-3,500 words. Buys 2 mss/year. Query with published clips. Pays $100-200.

Tips: "Health care reform measures; a good large multi-hospital group business story (failure or success); good contacts with state or federal senators and representatives and/or their staff members for close-ups, profiles. No writing in supply side that sells the supplier or its products but, rather, how it sees current issues from its perspective."

‡HMO MAGAZINE, Directions in Managed Health Care, Group Health Association of America, Suite 600, 1129 20th St., NW, Washington DC 20036. (202)778-3250. Editor: Susan Pisano. Contact: Lisa Lopez, managing editor. 35% freelance written. Bimonthly magazine for news and analysis of the health maintenance organization (HMO) industry. *"HMO Magazine* is geared toward senior administrative and medical managers in HMOs. Articles must succinctly and clearly define issues of concern or news to the HMO industry. Articles must ask 'why' and 'how' and answer with examples. Articles should inform and generate interest and discussion about topics on anything from medical management to regulatory issues." Estab. 1990. Circ. 6,000. Pays 30 days within acceptance of article in final form. Publishes ms an average of 2 months after acceptance. Byline given. Offers 30% kill fee. Buys all rights. Editorial lead time 2 months. Submit seasonal material 2 months in advance. Simultaneous submissions OK. Query for electronic submissions. Reports in 1 month on queries. Sample copy and writer's guidelnes free on request.

Nonfiction: How-to (how industry professionals can better operate their health plans) and opinion. "We do not accept any articles relating to clinical health issues, such as nutrition or any general health topics that do not address issues of concern to HMO administrators; nor do we accept stories that promote products." Buys 20 mss/year. Query. Length: 1,800-2,500 words. Pays 40¢/word minimum for assigned articles, 35¢/word minimum for unsolicited articles. Pays phone expenses of writers on assignment.

Photos: State availability of photos with submission. Reviews contact sheets. Offers no additional payment for photos accepted with ms. Buys all rights.

Columns/Departments: Washington File (health policy issues relating to HMOs and managed health care), 1,800 words; Preventive Care (case study or discussion of public health HMOs), 1,800 words; The Market (market niches for HMOs—with examples), 1,800 words. Buys 6 mss/year. Query with published clips. Pays 35-50¢/word.

Tips: "Follow the current health care debate. Much of what the Clinton Administration proposes will definitely impact the HMO industry. Look for HMO success stories in your community; we like to include case studies on everything from medical management to regulatory issues so that our readers can learn from their colleagues. Our readers are members of our trade association and look for advice and news. Topics relating to the quality and cost benefits of HMOs are the ones most frequently assigned to writers, whether a feature or department. For example, a recent story on 'The High Price of Compliance' relating to costs associated with not complying with prescription advice, got a lot of reader interest. The writer interviewed a number of experts inside and outside the HMO field."

JEMS, The Journal of Emergency Medical Services, Jems Communications, Suite 200, 1947 Camino Vida Roble, Carlsbad CA 92008-2789. (619)431-9797. Fax: (619)431-8176. Executive Editor: Keith Griffiths. Managing Editor: Tara Regan. 25% freelance written. Monthly magazine for emergency medical services— all phases. The journal is directed to the personnel who serve the emergency medicine industry: paramedics, EMTs, emergency physicians and nurses, administrators, EMS consultants, etc. Estab. 1980. Circ. 35,000. Pays on publication. Publishes ms an average of 3-6 months after acceptance. Byline given. Buys all North American serial rights. Submit seasonal material 6 months in advance. Query for electronic submissions. Reports in 2 months. Free sample copy and writer's guidelines.
Nonfiction: Essays, general interest, how-to (prehospital care), continuing education, humor, interview/ profile, new product, opinion, photo feature, technical. Buys 18 mss/year. Query. Length: 900-3,600 words. Pays $150-350.
  • *Jems* has an increased need for investigative reporters who can cover system politics, trends and product concerns.
Photos: State availability of photos with submission. Offers no additional payment for photos accepted with ms. Buys one-time rights.
Columns/Departments: Teacher Talk (directed toward EMS instructors), 2,400 words; Pediatric Notebook (emergency care of the child), 2,400 words; Manager's Forum (EMS administrators), 1,500-2,000 words; and First Person (personal accounts of life in EMS).
Tips: Feature articles are most open to freelancers. We have guidelines available upon request and, of course, manuscripts must be geared toward our specific EMS audience.

THE JOURNAL, Addiction Research Foundation of Ontario, 33 Russell St., Toronto, Ontario M5S 2S1 Canada. (416)595-6053. Fax: (416)595-6036. Editor: Anne MacLennan. Managing Editor: Elda Hauschildt. 50% freelance written. Prefers to work with published/established writers. Monthly tabloid covering addictions and related fields around the world. "*The Journal* alerts professionals in the addictions and related fields or disciplines to news events, issues, opinions and developments of potential interest and/or significance to them in their work, and provides them an informed context in which to judge developments in their own specialty/geographical areas." Circ. 12,000. Pays on publication. Publishes ms an average of 3 months after acceptance. Byline given. Kill fee negotiable. Not copyrighted. Buys first serial and second serial (reprint) rights. Reports in 2 months on queries; 3 months on mss. Sample copy and writer's guidelines for 9 × 12 SAE.
Nonfiction: Only. Query with published clips or send complete ms. Length: 1,000 words maximum. Pays 26¢/word minimum. Sometimes pays the expenses of writers on assignment.
Photos: Elda Hauschildt, managing editor. State availability of photos. Pays $25 and up for 5 × 7 or 8 × 10 b&w prints. Captions, model release, and identification of subjects required. Buys one-time rights.
Columns/Departments: Under contract.
Tips: "A freelancer can best break in with our publication with six years reporting experience, preferably with medical/science writing background. We rarely use untried writers."

MD MAGAZINE, MD Publications, 14th Floor, 55 5th Ave., New York NY 10003-4301. (212)477-2727. Managing Editor: Helen Smith. 40% freelance written. Monthly magazine that is distributed nationally to physicians. "*MD* is a cultural/lifestyle magazine for physicians. It covers medicine, science, art, travel, social issues, books, technology, history, theater, biography, music and sports—the world outside the doctor's office. It does not cover clinical subjects." Estab. 1957. Circ. 125,000. Pays on publication. Publishes ms 3 months after acceptance. Byline given. Offers 33% kill fee. Buys first North American serial rights. Submit seasonal material 4 months in advance. Query for electronic submissions. Reports in 2 months. Sample copy for 9 × 12 SAE with 5 first class stamps. Writer's guidelines for #10 SASE.
Nonfiction: General interest, historical, interview/profile, photo feature and travel. "No articles on clinical medicine or problems of running a medical practice." Buys 45 mss/year. Query only or query with published clips. Length: 750-3,000 words. Pays $250-3,000. Sometimes pays expenses of writers on assignment.
Photos: State availability of photos with submission. Offers no additional payment for photos accepted with ms. Captions, model releases and identification of subjects required. Buys one-time rights.
Tips: "Our purview is broad, but our approach is particular: we seek to portray the world the way a doctor sees it. We focus particularly on the doctor-reader's concerns. We look *through* the physicians' eyes—from their perspective—we don't just present material *for* them. All nonfiction areas are open to freelancers. The level of information should not be elementary—articles should be written with a sophisticated, demanding audience in mind."

MEDICAL ECONOMICS, Medical Economics Publishing, 5 Paragon Dr., Montvale NJ 07645-1742. (201)358-7200. Editor: Stephen K. Murata. Managing Editor: Larry Frederick. Less than 10% freelance written. Biweekly magazine covering topics of nonclinical interest to office-based private physicians (MDs and DOs only). "We publish practice/management and personal/finance advice for office-based MDs and osteopaths." Circ. 175,000. **Pays on acceptance.** Publishes ms an average of 3 months after acceptance. Byline given. Offers

25% of full article fee as kill fee. Buys all rights and first serial rights. Reports in 2 months on queries; 3 weeks on mss. *Writer's Market* recommends allowing 2 months for reply. Sample copy $5 for 9 × 12 SASE.
Nonfiction: Contact Lilian Fine, chief of Outside Copy Division. How-to (office and personnel management, personal-money management); personal experience (only involving MDs or DOs in private practice); and travel (how-to articles). No clinical articles, hobby articles, personality profiles or office design articles. Query with published clips. Length: 1,500-3,000 words. Pays $750-1,800. "The payment level is decided at the time go-ahead is given after query."
Tips: "How-to articles should fully describe techniques, goals, options and caveats—in terms that are clear and *realistic* for the average physician. Use of anecdotal examples to support major points is crucial. Our full-time staff is quite large, and therefore we buy only freelance articles that are not already assigned to staff writers. This puts a premium on unusual and appealing subjects."

THE NEW PHYSICIAN, 1890 Preston White Dr., Reston VA 22091-4325. Contact: Editor. 50% freelance written. Magazine published 9 times/year for medical students, interns and residents. Circ. 30,000. Buys first serial rights. **Pays on acceptance.** Publishes features an average of 2 months after acceptance. Will consider simultaneous submissions. Publishes reprints of previously published articles. Include information about when and where the article previously appeared. Reports in 2 months. Sample copy for 10 × 13 SAE with 5 first class stamps. Writer's guidelines for SASE.
Nonfiction: Articles on social, political, economic issues in medicine/medical education. Buys about 12 features/year. Query or send complete ms. Length: 800-3,500 words. Pays $100-1,000 with higher fees for selected pieces. Pays expenses of writers on assignment.
Tips: "Although we are published by an association (the American Medical Student Association), we are not a 'house organ.' We are a professional magazine for readers with a progressive view on health care issues and a particular interest in improving the health care system. Our readers demand sophistication on the issues we cover. Freelancers should be willing to look deeply into the issues in question and not be satisfied with a cursory review of those issues."

THE NEW YORK DOCTOR, Chase Communications, Dept. WM, P.O. Box 9001, Mt. Vernon NY 10552-9001. (914)699-2020. Fax: (914)664-1503. Editor: Francine Silverman. Monthly news and city magazine for physicians in the five boroughs, Long Island and Westchester. "Our magazine covers AIDS, medical ethics, malpractice and legislative issues affecting New York-area doctors." Estab. 1985. Circ. 15,000. **Pays on acceptance.** Byline given. No kill fee. Buys first North American serial or second rights. Query for electronic submissions. Reports in 1 month on mss. *Writer's Market* recommends allowing 2 months for reply. Sample copy for 8 × 10 SAE with 3 first class stamps.
Nonfiction: "We do not want anything too clinical or technical." Accepts very little freelance material. Buys 35-60 mss/year. Query with published clips. Length: 250-1,500 words. Pays $25-350 for assigned articles.
Photos: State availability of photos with submission. Reviews contact sheets, negatives and prints. Payment varies. Captions and identification of subjects required.
Columns/Departments: Inside-talk (hospitals, government, pharmaceutical companies); Medicare; The Environment/Medical Waste Management; After Hours (New York area physicians' hobbies, lifestyles); Recruitment (trends at hospitals, managed-care companies, pharmaceutical companies); Malpractice; Office Labs; Op-Ed (by health-care experts); Research (human-interest behind the effort); and Book Review.

THE PHYSICIAN AND SPORTSMEDICINE, McGraw-Hill, 4530 W. 77th St., Edina MN 55435. (612)835-3222. Features Editor: Amber Stenger. Managing Editor: Terry Monahan. 30% freelance written. Prefers to work with published/established writers. Monthly magazine covering medical aspects of sports and exercise. "We publish articles that are of practical, clinical interest to our physician audience." Estab. 1973. Circ. 130,000. **Pays on acceptance.** Publishes ms an average of 4 months after acceptance. Byline given. Generally buys all rights. Reports in 2 months. Sample copy $6. Writer's guidelines for #10 SASE.
Nonfiction: New developments and issues in sports medicine. Query. Length: 250-2,500 words. Pays $150-1,200.
  • This publication has started relying more on writers with medical or technical reporting experience.
Photos: Bernadette Gerten, photo editor. State availability of photos. Buys one-time rights.

PHYSICIAN'S MANAGEMENT, Advanstar Communications, 7500 Old Oak Blvd., Cleveland OH 44130-3511. (216)243-8100. Fax: (216)891-2683. Editor-in-Chief: Bob Feigenbaum. Prefers to work with published/established writers. Monthly magazine emphasizes finances, investments, malpractice, socioeconomic issues, estate and retirement planning, small office administration, practice management, computers and taxes for primary care physicians in private practice. Estab. 1960. Circ. 120,000. **Pays on acceptance.** Publishes ms an average of 6 months after acceptance. Buys first North American rights. Submit seasonal material 5 months in advance. Query for electronic submissions. Reports in 1 month. Sample copy $4. Writer's guidelines for #10 SASE.
Nonfiction: *"Physician's Management* is a practice management/economic publication, not a clinical one." Publishes how-to articles (limited to medical practice management); informational (when relevant to audience); and personal experience articles (if written by a physician). No fiction, clinical material or satire that

portrays MD in an unfavorable light; or soap opera, "real-life" articles. Length: 2,000-2,500 words. Query with SASE. Pays $125/3-column printed page. Use of charts, tables, graphs, sidebars and photos strongly encouraged. Sometimes pays expenses of writers on assignment.

Tips: "Talk to doctors first about their practices, financial interests, and day-to-day nonclinical problems and then query us. Also, the ability to write a concise, well-structured and well-researched magazine article is essential. Freelancers who think like patients fail with us. Those who can think like MDs are successful."

PHYSICIANS' TRAVEL & MEETING GUIDE, Cahners Publishing Company, Dept. WM, 249 W. 17th St., New York NY 10011. (212)463-6405. Editor: Bea Riemschneider. Managing Editor: Susann Tepperberg. 70% freelance written. Monthly magazine that covers continuing medical education and travel. *Physicians' Travel & Meeting Guide* supplies continuing medical education events listings, education features and extensive travel coverage of international and national destinations. Circ. 190,000. **Pays on acceptance.** Byline given. Buys first North American serial rights. Submit seasonal material 4-6 months in advance. Reports in 3 months.
Nonfiction: Photo feature and travel. Buys 25-30 mss/year. Query with published clips. Length: 450-3,000 words. Pays $150-1,000 for assigned articles.
Photos: State availability of photos with submission. Send photos with submission. Reviews 35mm or 4×5 transparencies. Captions and identification of subjects required. Buys one-time rights.

PODIATRY MANAGEMENT, P.O. Box 50, Island Station NY 10044. (212)355-5216. Fax: (212)486-7706. Publisher: Scott C. Borowsky. Editor: Barry Block, DPM, J.D. Managing Editor: Martin Kruth. Magazine published 9 times/year for practicing podiatrists. "Aims to help the doctor of podiatric medicine to build a bigger, more successful practice, to conserve and invest his money, to keep him posted on the economic, legal and sociological changes that affect him." Estab. 1982. Circ. 13,000. Pays on publication. Byline given. Buys first North American serial and second serial (reprint) rights. Submit seasonal material 4 months in advance. Simultaneous queries, and simultaneous and previously published submissions OK. Reprints OK; send photocopy of article. For reprints, pays 20-50% of their fee for an original article. Reports in 2 weeks. Sample copy $3 with 9×12 SAE. Writer's guidelines for #10 SASE.
Nonfiction: General interest (taxes, investments, estate planning, recreation, hobbies); how-to (establish and collect fees, practice management, organize office routines, supervise office assistants, handle patient relations); interview/profile about interesting or well-known podiatrists; and personal experience. "These subjects are the mainstay of the magazine, but offbeat articles and humor are always welcome." Send tax and financial articles to Martin Kruth, 5 Wagon Hill Lane, Avon, CT 06001. Buys 25 mss/year. Query. Length: 1,000-2,500 words. Pays $150-600.
Photos: State availability of photos. Pays $15 for b&w contact sheet. Buys one-time rights.

PRIVATE PRACTICE, P.O. Box 890547, Oklahoma City OK 73189-0547. Fax: (405)692-4446. Executive Editor: Brian Sherman. Estab. 1968. 60% freelance written. Eager to work with new/unpublished writers. Monthly magazine for medical doctors in private practice. Buys first North American serial rights. "If an article is assigned, it is paid for in full, used or killed." Byline given "except if it was completely rewritten or a considerable amount of additional material is added to the article." Pays on publication. Publishes ms an average of 6 months after acceptance. Query. Reports in 2 weeks. Free sample copy and writer's guidelines.
Nonfiction: "Articles that indicate importance of maintaining freedom of medical practice or which detail outside interferences in the practice of medicine, including research, hospital operation, drug manufacture, etc. Straight reporting style. No cliches, no scare words, no flowery phrases to cover up poor reporting. Stories must be actual, factual, precise and correct. Copy should be lively and easy to read." Length: up to 2,500 words. Pays "usual minimum $150." Publishes reprints of previously published articles. Send photocopy of article.
Photos: Photos purchased with mss only. Black and white glossies, 8×10. Payment "depends on quality, relevancy of material, etc."
Tips: "The article we are most likely to buy will be a straight report on some situation where the freedom to practice medicine has been enhanced, or where it has been intruded on to the detriment of good health."

RESCUE, Jems Communications, P.O. Box 2789, Carlsbad CA 92018-2789. (619)431-9797. Fax: (619)431-8176. Managing Editor: Jeff Lucia. 60% freelance written. Bimonthly magazine covering both the technical side and excitement of being a rescuer. Estab. 1988. Circ. 25,000. Pays on publication. Byline given. Buys first North American and one-time rights. Submit seasonal material 6 months in advance. Query for electronic submissions (prefers diskette to accompany ms). Reports in 3 weeks on queries; 2 months on mss. Sample copy and writer's guidelines for 9×12 SAE with 5 first class stamps.
Nonfiction: Book excerpts, how-to, humor, new product, opinion, photo feature and technical. Special issues: Vehicle Extrication, rescue training, mass-casualty incidents, water rescue and wilderness rescue. No hazardous material incidents, "I was saved by a ranger" articles. Buys 15-20 mss/year. Query with or without published clips or send complete ms. Length: 1,000-3,000 words. Pays $125-250. Sometimes pays the expenses of writers on assignment.

Photos: Send photos with submission. Reviews contact sheets, negatives, 2×2 and 35mm transparencies and 5×7 prints. Offers $50-125/photo. Buys one-time rights.

Tips: "Read our magazine, spend some time with a rescue team. We focus on all aspects of rescue, including vehicle extrication, rope rescue, disaster training, search and rescue, collapse rescue, and mountain rescue in addition to specialized rescue. Emphasis on techniques and new technology, with color photos as support."

‡**SECOND SOURCE IMAGING, The Medical Imaging Equipment Magazine,** Second Source Publications, Inc., P.O. Box 930, 207 High Point Ave., Portsmouth RI 02871. (401)633-7470. Editor: Jack Spears. Managing Editor: Michael Buller. Contact: Michael Buller, Managing Editor. 5% freelance written. Monthly magazine covering diagnostic imaging equipment. "Our editorial statement is to provide cost-effective solutions to the maintenance and management of diagnostic imaging equipment. Articles should address this." Estab. 1986. Circ. 12,000. **Pays on acceptance.** Publishes ms an average of 2 months after acceptance. Byline given. Offers 50% kill fee. Buys all rights. Editorial lead time two 2 months. Responds to query letters "as soon as possible, but best to follow up query with phone call." Sample copy $10 prepaid. Writer's guidelines for #10 SASE.

Nonfiction: Interview/profile and technical. "No general interest/human interest stories about healthcare. Articles *must* deal with our industry-diagnostic imaging." Buys 6 mss/year. Query with published clips. Length: 1,500-2,500 words. Pays approximately 20¢/word. Sometimes pays expenses of writers on assignment.

Photos: State availability of photos with submission. Reviews negatives. Offers no additional payment for photos accepted with ms "unless assigned separately." Model releases and identification of subjects required. Buys all rights.

Tips: "Send a letter with an interesting story idea that is applicable to our industry, diagnostic imaging. Then follow up with a phone call. Areas most open to freelancers are feature and technology. You don't have to be an engineer or doctor but you have to know how to talk and listen to them."

STRATEGIC HEALTH CARE MARKETING, Health Care Communications, 11 Heritage Ln., P.O. Box 594, Rye NY 10580. (914)967-6741. Editor: Michele von Dambrowski. 60% freelance written. Prefers to work with published/established writers. "Will only work with unpublished writer on a 'stringer' basis initially." Monthly newsletter covering health care services marketing in a wide range of settings including hospitals and medical group practices, home health services and ambulatory care centers, emphasizing strategies and techniques employed within the health care field and relevant applications from other service industries. Estab. 1984. Pays on publication. Publishes ms an average of 2 months after acceptance. Byline given. Offers 25% kill fee. Buys first North American serial rights. Reports in 1 month. Sample copy for 9×12 SAE with 3 first class stamps. Guidelines sent with sample copy only.

Nonfiction: How-to, interview/profile, new product and technical. Buys 35 mss/year. Query with published clips. No unsolicited mss accepted. Length: 700-2,000 words. Pays $100-400. Sometimes pays the expenses of writers on assignment with prior authorization.

Photos: State availability of photos with submissions. (Photos, unless necessary for subject explanation, are rarely used.) Reviews contact sheets. Offers $10-30/photo. Captions and model releases required. Buys one-time rights.

Tips: "Writers with prior experience on business beat for newspaper or newsletter will do well. This is not a consumer publication—the writer with knowledge of both health care and marketing will excel. Interviews or profiles are most open to freelancers. Absolutely no unsolicited manuscripts; any received will be returned or discarded unread."

Music

Publications for musicians and for the recording industry are listed in this section. Other professional performing arts publications are classified under Entertainment and the Arts. Magazines featuring music industry news for the general public are listed in the Consumer Entertainment and Music sections. (Markets for songwriters can be found in *Songwriter's Market*—see Other Books of Interest).

THE INSTRUMENTALIST, Instrumentalist Publishing Company, Dept. WM, 200 Northfield Rd., Northfield IL 60093. (708)446-5000. Fax: (708)446-6263. Senior Editor: Catherine Sell. Approximately 95% freelance written. Monthly magazine covering instrumental music education for school band and orchestra directors, as well as performers and students. Estab. 1944. Circ. 22,000. Pays on publication. Publishes ms an average of 6-9 months after acceptance. Byline given. Buys all rights "but willing to permit authors to sell articles again to noncompeting publications." Submit seasonal material 6 months in advance. Reports in 1 month. Sample copy $2.50 for 9×12 SAE. Free writer's guidelines.

Nonfiction: Book excerpts (rarely); essays (on occasion); general interest (on occasion, music); historical/nostalgic (music); how-to (teach, repair instruments); humor (on occasion); interview/profile (performers, conductors, composers); opinion; personal experience; photo feature; and travel. Buys 100 mss/year. Send complete ms. Length: 750-1,750 words. Pays $30-45/published page.
Photos: State availability of photos with submission. Reviews slides and 5×7 prints (photo guidelines available upon request). Payment varies. Captions and identification of subjects required. Buys variable rights.
Columns/Departments: Personal Perspective (opinions on issues facing music educators), 500-750 words; Idea Exchange ('how-tos' from educators), 250-500 words. Send complete ms. Length: 250-500 words. Pays $30-45.
Fillers: Anecdotes and short humor. Buys 5/year. Length: 250 words maximum. Pays $25-45.
Tips: "Know the music education field, specifically band and orchestra. Interviews with performers should focus on the person's contribution to education and opinions about it. We are interested in interviews and features that focus on ideas rather than on personalities. Writers must have a strong educational background in classical music."

OPERA NEWS, Metropolitan Opera Guild, Inc., 70 Lincoln Center Plaza, New York NY 10023-6593. (212)769-7080. Fax: (212)769-7007. Editor: Patrick J. Smith. Managing Editor: Brian Kellow. 75% freelance written. Magazine (monthly May-November, biweekly December-April) for people interested in opera; the opera professional as well as the opera audience. Estab. 1936. Circ. 120,000. Pays on publication. Publishes ms an average of 4 months after acceptance. Byline given. Buys first serial rights only. Query for electronic submissions. Sample copy $4.
Nonfiction: Most articles are commissioned in advance. Monthly issues feature articles on various aspects of opera worldwide; biweekly issues contain articles related to the broadcasts from the Metropolitan Opera. Emphasis is on high quality writing and an intellectual interest to the opera-oriented public. Informational, personal experience, interview, profile, historical, think pieces, personal opinion and opera reviews. "Also willing to consider quality fiction and poetry on opera-related themes though acceptance is rare." Query; no telephone inquiries. Length: 1,500-2,800 words. Pays $450-1,000. Sometimes pays the expenses of writers on assignment.
Photos: State availability of photos with submission. Buys one-time rights.
Columns/Departments: Buys 24 mss/year.

‡**STUDIO SOUND, and Broadcast Engineering,** Spotlight Publications, Ludgate House, 245 Blackfriars Rd., London SE1 9UR United Kingdom. (+)71-620-3636. Editor: Tim Goodyer. Assistant Editor: Julian Mitchell. 80% freelance written. Monthly magazine covering professional audio and recording. Covers "all matters relating to pro audio—music recording, music for pictures, post production—reviews and feature articles." Circ. 20,000 worldwide. Pays on publication. Byline given. Offers 20% kill fee. Buys first rights. Editorial lead time 3 months. Simultaneous submissions OK. Query for electronic submissions.
Nonfiction: Historical/nostalgic, how-to, interview/profile, new product, opinion, personal experience and photo feature. No company profiles. Buys 80 mss/year. Send complete ms. Length: 850-4,000 words. Pays $150 minimum. Sometimes pays expenses of writers on assignment.
Photos: State availability of photos with submission. Reviews 35mm transparencies and 5×7 prints. Negotiates payment individually. Identification of subjects required. Buys one-time rights.

Office Environment and Equipment

MODERN OFFICE TECHNOLOGY, Penton Publishing, Dept. WM, 1100 Superior Ave., Cleveland OH 44114. (216)696-7000. Fax: (216)696-7658. Associate Publisher and Editorial Director: John Dykeman. Editor: Lura K. Romei. Production Manager: Gina Runyon. 5-10% freelance written. Monthly magazine covering office automation for corporate management and personnel, financial management, administrative and operating management, systems and information management, managers and supervisors of support personnel and purchasing. Estab. 1956. Circ. 150,000. Pays on publication. Publishes ms an average of 6 months after acceptance. Byline given. Buys first and one-time rights. Query for electronic submissions. Reports in 6 weeks. Reprints OK; send photocopy of article, typed ms with rights for sale noted and information about when and where the article previously appeared. Sample copy and writer's guidelines for 9×12 SAE with 4 first class stamps.
Nonfiction: New product, opinion and technical. Query with or without published clips or send complete ms. Length: open. Pays $300-600 for assigned articles; $250-400 for unsolicited articles. Pays expenses of writers on assignment.
Photos: Send photos with submission. Reviews contact sheets, 4×5 transparencies and prints. Additional payment for photos accepted with ms. Consult editorial director. Captions and identification of subjects required. Buys one-time rights.
Tips: "Submitted material should alway present topics and ideas, on issues that are clearly and concisely defined. Material should describe problems and solution. Writer should describe benefits to reader in tangible results whenever possible."

‡**THE SECRETARY**, Stratton Publishing & Marketing, Inc., Suite 706, 2800 Shirlington Rd., Arlington VA 22206. Publisher: Debra J. Stratton. Managing Editor: Tracy Fellin Savidge. 90% freelance written. Magazine published 9 times/year covering the secretarial profession. Estab. 1946. Circ. 44,000. Pays on acceptance or "mostly unpaid." Publishes ms an average of 6 months after acceptance. Byline given. Kill fee negotiable. Buys first rights. Editorial lead time 3 months. Submit seasonal material 5 months in advance. Simultaneous and previously published submissions OK. Query for electronic submissions. Reports in 1 month. Sample copy $3 through (816)891-6600 ext. 235. Writer's guidelines free on request through publishing office.

Nonfiction: Book excerpts, general interest, how-to (buy and use office equipment, advance career, etc.), interview/profile, new product and personal experience. Buys 6-10 mss/year. Query. Length: 2,000 words. Pays $250 minimum for assigned articles; $0-75 minimum for unsolicited articles. Pays expenses of writers on assignment.

Photos: Send photos with submission. Reviews transparencies and prints. Offers no additional payment for photos accepted with ms. Identification of subjects required. Buys one-time rights.

Columns/Departments: Product News (new office products, non promotional), 500 words maximum; Random Input (general interest—career, woman's, workplace issues), 500 words maximum; First Person (first-hand experiences from secretaries), 800 words. Send complete ms.

Tips: "We're in search of articles addressing financial management; computer hardware and software; workplace issues; international business topics. Must be appropriate to secretaries."

Paper

BOXBOARD CONTAINERS, Maclean Hunter Publishing Co., Dept. WM, 29 N. Wacker Dr., Chicago IL 60606-3298. (312)726-2802. Fax: (312)726-2574. Executive Editor: Charles Huck. Editor: Greg Kishbaugh. Monthly magazine covering box and carton manufacturing for corrugated box, folding carton, setup box manufacturers internationally emphasizing technology and management. Circ. 14,000. Pays on publication. Byline given. Buys first North American serial rights. Submit seasonal material 2 months in advance. Query for electronic submissions. Reports in 1 month. Free sample copy.

Nonfiction: How-to, interview/profile, new product, opinion, personal experience, photo feature and technical. Buys 10 mss/year. Query. Length: 2,000-6,000 words. Pays $75-350 for assigned articles; $50-200 for unsolicited articles. Sometimes pays the expenses of writers on assignment.

Photos: Send photos with submission. Reviews 35mm, 4×5 and 6×6 transparencies and 8×10 prints. Offers no additional payment for photos accepted with ms. Captions, model releases and identification of subjects required. Buys one-time rights.

Tips: Features are most open to freelancers.

MARI/BOARD CONVERTING NEWS, The Package Converting Magazine of Latin America, EXM, Suite 9, 3086 Hwy. 27, Kendall Park NJ 08824. (908)422-8200. Fax: (908)422-8780. Editor: Keith Sickafoose. Managing Editor: Max Jaramillo. 40% freelance written. Quarterly magazine that covers the corrugated industry, especially for Latin America. "We publish for a professional and business audience." Estab. 1990. Circ. 2,500. Pays on publication. Byline given. Buys first rights. Simultaneous and previously published submissions OK. Query for electronic submissions. Reports in 2 months on mss. Free sample copy.

Nonfiction: Interview/profile, new product and technical. Buys 10 mss/year. Send complete ms. Length: 600-900 words. Pays $150/article.

Photos: State availability or send photos with submission. Offers no additional payment for photos accepted with ms. Identification of subjects required. Buys one-time rights.

Tips: "We are looking for stories geared toward the Latin American corrugated board industry: business, personal interviews, technical innovations. Can be written in either Spanish or English; we will do translations. If the story is technical, give it a slant to fit the context of Latin America."

‡**PULP & PAPER CANADA**, Southam Business Communications Inc., Suite 410, 3300 Côte Vertu, St. Laurent, Quebec H4R 2B7 Canada. (514)339-1399. Fax: (514)339-1396. Editor/Associate Publisher: Peter N. Williamson. Managing Editor: Susan Stevenson. 5% freelance written. Prefers to work with published/established writers. Monthly magazine. Estab. 1903. Circ. 9,309. **Pays on acceptance.** Publishes ms "as soon as possible" after acceptance. Byline given. Offers kill fee according to prior agreement. Buys first North American serial rights. Reports in 1 month. Free sample copy and writer's guidelines.

Nonfiction: How-to (related to processes and procedures in the industry); interview/profile (of Canadian leaders in pulp and paper industry); and technical (relevant to modern pulp and/or paper industry). No fillers, short industry news items, or product news items. Buys 10 mss/year. Query first with published clips or send complete ms. Articles with photographs (b&w glossy) or other good quality illustrations will get priority review. Length: maximum 1,500 words (with photos). Pays $160 (Canadian funds)/published page, including photos, graphics, charts, etc.

Tips: "Any return postage must be in either Canadian stamps or International Reply Coupons *only*."

Pets

Listed here are publications for professionals in the pet industry—pet product wholesalers, manufacturers, suppliers, and retailers, and owners of pet specialty stores, grooming businesses, aquarium retailers and those interested in the pet fish industry. The Veterinary section lists journals for animal health professionals. Publications for pet owners are listed in the Consumer Animal section.

GROOM & BOARD, Incorporating "Groomers Gazette Kennel News," H.H. Backer Associates Inc., Suite 200, 20 E. Jackson Blvd., Chicago IL 60604. (312)663-4040. Fax: (312)663-5676. Editor: Karen Long MacLeod. 10% freelance written. Magazine published 9 times/year about grooming and boarding pets. "*Groom & Board* is the only national trade publication for pet-care professionals, including pet groomers, boarding kennel operators and service-oriented veterinarians. It provides news, technical articles and features to help them operate their businesses more successfully." Estab. 1980. Circ. 17,968. **Pays on acceptance.** Publishes ms an average of 6 months after acceptance. Byline given. Buys first North American serial, one-time, all rights or exclusive to industry. Query for electronic submissions. Reprints OK; send tearsheet of article, typed ms with rights for sale noted and information about when and where the article previously appeared. Reports in 6 months. Sample copy $2.50 plus $3.50 shipping and handling (total $6). Writer's guidelines for #10 SASE.
Nonfiction: How-to (groom specific breeds of pets, run business, etc.), interview/profile (successful grooming and/or kennel operations) and technical. "We do not want consumer-oriented articles or stories about a single animal (animal heroes, grief, etc.)." Buys 3-6 mss/year. Query with published clips or send complete ms. Length: 1,000-3,000 words. Pays $90-500 for assigned articles; $65-150 for unsolicited articles. Sometimes pays expenses of writers on assignment.
Photos: Reviews transparencies and 5×7 b&w glossy prints. Offers $8/photo (negotiable). Captions and identification of subjects required. Buys one-time rights.

PET AGE, The Magazine for the Professional Retailer, H.H. Backer Associates, Inc., Suite 200, 20 E. Jackson Blvd., Chicago IL 60604. (312)663-4040. Fax: (312)663-5676. Editor: Karen Long MacLeod. 20-40% freelance written. Prefers to work with published/established writers. Monthly magazine for pet/pet supplies retailers, covering the complete pet industry. Estab. 1971. Circ. 18,121. **Pays on acceptance.** Publishes ms an average of 6 months after acceptance. Byline given. Buys first North American serial, one-time, all or exclusive industry rights. Submit seasonal material 6 months in advance. Query for electronic submissions. Reprints OK; send tearsheet of article, typed ms with rights for sale noted and information about when and where the article previously appeared. Reports in 4 months on queries; 2 months on mss. Sample copy $2.50 plus $3.50 shipping and handling (total $6). Writer's guidelines for #10 SASE.
Nonfiction: Book excerpts, profile (of a successful, well-run pet retail operation), how-to and technical— all trade-related. Query first with published clips. Buys 6-12 mss/year. "Query as to the name and location of a pet operation you wish to profile and why it would make a good feature. No general retailing articles or consumer-oriented pet articles." Length: 1,000-3,000 words. Pays $100-500 for assigned articles; $65-150 for unsolicited articles. Sometimes pays the expenses of writers on assignment.
Photos: Reviews 5×7 b&w glossy prints and color transparencies. Captions and identification of subjects required. Offers $8/photo (negotiable). Buys one-time rights.
Tips: "This is a business publication for busy people, and must be very informative in easy-to-read, concise style. The type of article we purchase most frequently is the pet shop profile, a story about an interesting/successful pet shop. We need queries on these (we get references on the individual shop from our sources in the industry). We supply typical questions to writers when we answer their queries. Articles about animal care or business practices should have the pet-retail angle or cover issues specific to this industry."

THE PET DEALER, Howmark Publishing Corp., 567 Morris Ave., Elizabeth NJ 07208-1995. (908)353-7373. Fax: (908)353-8221. Editor: Gina Geslewitz. 70% freelance written. Prefers to work with published/established writers, but is eager to work with new/published writers. "We want writers who are good reporters and clear communicators with a fine command of the English language." Monthly magazine emphasizing merchandising, marketing and management for owners and managers of pet specialty stores, departments, and pet groomers and their suppliers. Estab. 1949. Circ. 17,500. Pays on publication. "May be many months between acceptance of a manuscript and publication." Byline given. Submit seasonal material 4 months in advance. Reprints OK; send typed ms with rights for sale noted and information about when and where the article previously appeared. For reprints, pays 1-10% of their fee for an original article. Reports in 3 months.

Sample copy $5 for 8×10 SAE with 10 first class stamps. Queries without SASE will not be answered.

Nonfiction: How-to (store operations, administration, merchandising, marketing, management, promotion and purchasing). Consumer pet articles—lost pets, best pets, humane themes—*not* welcome. "We *are* interested in helping—dog, cat, monkey, whatever stories tie in with the human/animal bond. Emphasis is on *trade* merchandising and marketing of pets and supplies." Buys 2-4 unsolicited mss/year. Length: 800-1,500 words. Pays $40-100.

Photos: Submit undeveloped photo material with ms. No additional payment for 5×7 b&w glossy prints. Buys one-time rights. Will give photo credit for photography students. Also seeking cover art: original illustrated animal portraits (paid).

Fillers: "Will publish poetry and cartoons (unpaid) as fillers."

Tips: "We're interested in store profiles outside the New York, New Jersey, Connecticut and Pennsylvania metro areas. Photos are of key importance and should include a storefront shot. Articles focus on new techniques in merchandising or promotion, and overall trends in the Pet Industry. Want to see more articles from retailers and veterinarians with retail operations. Submit query letter first, with writing background summarized; include samples. We seek one-to-one, interview-type features on retail pet store merchandising. Indicate the availability of the proposed article, and your willingness to submit on exclusive or first-in-the-trade-field basis."

‡PET PRODUCT NEWS & PSM, Fancy Publishing, P.O. Box 6050, Mission Viejo CA 92690. (714)855-8822. Editor: John Chadwell. 90% freelance written. Monthly magazine for retail pet stores. "*PPN&PSM* covers business/legal and economic issues of importance to small business owners of pet retail stores, as well as product information and animal care issues. We're looking for straightforward articles on the proper care of dogs, cats, birds, fish and exotics (reptiles, hamsters, etc.) as information the retailers can pass on to new pet owners." Estab. 1947. Circ. 18,000. Pays on publication. Byline given. Offers 50% kill fee or $100. Buys first North American serial rights. Editorial lead time 3 months. Submit seasonal material 4 months in advance. Query for electronic submissions. Reports in 2 weeks on queries. Sample copy $4.50. Writer's guidelines free on request.

Nonfiction: General interest, how-to, interview/profile, new product, photo feature and technical. "No cute animal stories or those directed at the pet owner." buys 150 mss/year. Query. Length: 500-2,000 words. Pays $175-350. Sometimes pays expenses of writers on assignment.

Columns/Departments: Dog & Cat (products and care of), 1,500-2,000 words; Fish & Bird (products and care of), 1,500-2,000 words; Exotics (products and care of), 1,500-2,000 words. Buys 120 mss/year. Query. Send complete ms. Pays $175-350.

Tips: "Be more than just an animal lover. You have to know about health, nutrition and care. Product articles are told in both an informative and entertaining style. Go into pet stores, talk to the owners and see what they need to know to be better business people in general, who have to deal with everything from balancing the books, free trade agreements and animal right activists. All sections are open, but you have to be extremely knowledgeable on the topic, be it taxes, management, profit building, products, nutrition, animal care or marketing."

Photography Trade

Journals for professional photographers are listed in this section. Magazines for the general public interested in photography techniques are in the Consumer Photography section. (For listings of markets for freelance photography use *Photographer's Market*—see Other Books of Interest).

AMERICAN CINEMATOGRAPHER, A.S.C. Holding Corp., P.O. Box 2230, Hollywood CA 90078-2230. (213)969-4333. Fax: (213)876-4973. Editor: David Heuring. 50% freelance written. Monthly international journal of film and video production techniques "addressed to creative, managerial and technical people in all aspects of production. Its function is to disseminate practical information about the creative use of film and video equipment, and it strives to maintain a balance between technical sophistication and accessibility." Estab. 1919. Circ. 30,000. Pays on publication. Buys all rights. Submit one-page proposal. Writer's guidelines for #10 SASE.

Nonfiction: Stephen Pizzello, associate editor. Descriptions of new equipment and techniques or accounts of specific productions involving unique problems or techniques; historical articles detailing the production of a classic film, the work of a pioneer or legendary cinematographer or the development of a significant technique or type of equipment. Also discussions of the aesthetic principles involved in production techniques. Pays according to position and worth. Negotiable.

Photos: Black and white and color purchased with mss. No additional payment.

Tips: "No unsolicited articles. Do not call. Doesn't matter whether you are published or new. Queries must describe writer's qualifications and include writing samples."

PHOTO LAB MANAGEMENT, PLM Publishing, Inc., 1312 Lincoln Blvd., Santa Monica CA 90401. (310)451-1344. Fax: (310)395-9058. Editor: Carolyn Ryan. Associate Editor: Arthur Stern. 75% freelance written. Monthly magazine covering process chemistries and equipment, digital imaging, and marketing/administration for photo lab owners, managers and management personnel. Estab. 1979. Circ. 21,000. Pays on publication. Publishes ms an average of 3 months after acceptance. Byline and brief bio given. Buys first North American serial rights. Query for electronic submissions. Reports on queries in 6 weeks. Sample copy and writer's guidelines for #10 SAE with 3 first class stamps.

Nonfiction: Personal experience (lab manager); technical; and management or administration. Buys 40-50 mss/year. Query with brief biography. Length: 1,200-1,800 words. Payment negotiable.

Photos: Reviews 35mm color transparencies and 4-color prints suitable for cover. "We're looking for outstanding cover shots of photofinishing images."

Tips: "Our departments are written inhouse and we don't use 'fillers'. Send a query if you have some background in the industry or have a specific news story relating to photo processing or digital imaging. This industry is changing quickly due to computer technology, so articles must be cutting edge. Business management articles must focus on a photo lab approach and not be generic. Writers must have photofinishing knowledge."

PHOTO MARKETING, Photo Marketing Assocation Intl., 3000 Picture Place, Jackson MI 49201-8853. (517)788-8100. Fax: (517)788-8371. Director, Publications: Margaret Hooks. 2% freelance written. Monthly magazine for photo industry retailers, finishers and suppliers. "Articles must be specific to the photo industry and cannot be authored by anyone who writes for other magazines in the photo industry. We provide management information on a variety of topics as well as profiles of successful photo businesses and analyses of current issues in the industry." Estab. 1925. Circ. 22,000. **Pays on acceptance.** Publishes ms an average of 2 months after acceptance. Byline given. Buys one-time rights and exclusive photo magazine rights. Simultaneous submissions OK. Reports in 2 months. Free sample copy. Writer's guidelines for #10 SASE.

Nonfiction: Interview/profile (anonymous consumer shops for equipment); personal experience (interviews with photo retailers); technical (photofinishing lab equipment); and new technology (still electronic video). Buys 5 mss/year. Send complete ms. Length: 1,000-2,300 words. Pays $150-350.

Photos: State availability of photos with submission. Reviews negatives, 5×7 transparencies and prints. Offers $25-35/photo. Buys one-time rights.

Columns/Departments: Anonymous Consumer (anonymous shopper shops for equipment at photo stores), 1,800 words. Buys 5 mss/year. Query with published clips. Length: 1,800 words. Pays up to $200.

Tips: "All main sections use freelance material: business tips, promotion ideas, employee concerns, advertising, co-op, marketing. But they must be geared to and have direct quotes from members of the association."

● *Photo Marketing* has less need for freelancers this year.

THE PHOTO REVIEW, 301 Hill Ave., Langhorne PA 19047-2819. (215)757-8921. Editor: Stephen Perloff. 50% freelance written. Quarterly magazine on photography with reviews, interviews and articles on art photography. Estab. 1976. Circ. 1,200. Pays on publication. Publishes ms an average of 3 months after acceptance. Byline given. Buys one-time rights. Simultaneous and previously published submissions OK. Reports in 1 month on queries; 2 months on mss. Sample copy for 9×12 SAE with 6 first class stamps. Writer's guidelines for #10 SASE.

Nonfiction: Essays, historical/nostalgic, interview/profile and opinion. No how-to articles. Buys 10-15 mss/year. Query. Pays $25-200.

Photos: Send photos with submission. Reviews 8×10 prints. Offers no additional payment for photos accepted with ms. Captions and identification of subjects required. Buys one-time rights.

PHOTOLETTER, PhotoSource International, Pine Lake Farm, Osceola WI 54020. (715)248-3800. Fax: (715)248-7394. Editor: Lynette Walters. Managing Editor: H.T. White. 10% freelance written. A monthly newsletter on marketing photographs. "The *Photoletter* pairs photobuyers with photographers' collections." Estab. 1976. Circ. 780. **Pays on acceptance.** Publishes ms an average of 6 months after acceptance. Byline given. Buys one-time rights and simultaneous rights. Submit seasonal material 3 months in advance. Simultaneous and previously published submissions OK. Query for electronic submissions. Reports in 2 weeks on queries. Sample copy $3. Writer's guidelines for #10 SASE.

Nonfiction: How-to market photos and personal experience in marketing photos. "Our readers expect advice in how-to articles." No submissions that do not deal with selling photos. Buys 6 mss/year. Query. Length: 300-850 words. Pays $50-100 for unsolicited articles.

Columns/Departments: Jeri Engh, columns department editor. "We welcome column ideas." Length: 350 words. Pays $45-75.

Fillers: Facts. Buys 20/year. Length: 30-50 words. Pays $10.

Tips: "Columns are most open to freelancers. Bring an *expertise* on marketing photos or some other aspect of aid to small business persons."

PROFESSIONAL PHOTOGRAPHER, The Business Magazine of Professional Photography, Professional Photographers of America, Inc., 1090 Executive Way, Des Plaines IL 60018-1587. (708)299-8161. Fax: (708)299-2685. Editor: Alfred DeBat. 80% freelance written. Monthly magazine of professional portrait, wedding, commercial, corporate and industrial photography. Describes the technical and business sides of professional photography—successful photo techniques, money-making business tips, legal considerations, selling to new markets, and descriptions of tough assignments and how completed. Estab. 1907. Circ. 32,000. Publishes ms an average of 6-9 months after acceptance. Byline given. Buys one-time rights. Submit seasonal material 6 months in advance. Simultaneous queries and previously published submissions OK. Reports in 2 months. Sample copy $5. Free writer's guidelines.
Nonfiction: How-to. Professional photographic techniques: How I solved this difficult assignment, How I increased my photo sales, How to buy a studio, run a photo business, etc. Special issues: Wedding Photography (February); Portrait Photography (April); Commercial Photography (May); and Corporate Photography (August). Buys 8-10 ms/issue. Query. Length: 1,000-3,000 words. "We seldom pay, as most writers are PP of A members and pro photographers who want recognition for their professional skills, publicity, etc."
Photos: State availability of photos. Reviews color transparencies and 8×10 unmounted prints. Captions and model release required. Buys one-time rights.
Tips: "We have an increased interest in electronic imaging and computer manipulation of images in professional photography."

THE RANGEFINDER, 1312 Lincoln Blvd., Santa Monica CA 90406. (310)451-8506. Fax: (310)395-9058. Editor: Arthur C. Stern. Associate Editor: Sandi Messana. Monthly magazine emphasizing professional photography. Circ. 50,000. Pays on publication. Publishes ms an average of 6-9 months after acceptance. Byline given. Buys first North American serial rights. Phone queries OK. Submit seasonal material 4 months in advance. Reports in 6 weeks. Sample copy $3.50. Writer's guidelines for SASE.
Nonfiction: How-to (solve a photographic problem; such as new techniques in lighting, new poses or set-ups); profile; and technical. "Articles should contain practical, solid information. Issues should be covered in-depth. Look thoroughly into the topic." Buys 5-7 mss/issue. Query with outline. Length: 800-1,200 words. Pays $60/published page.
Photos: State availability of photos with query. Captions preferred; model release required.
Tips: "Exhibit knowledge of photography. Introduce yourself with a well-written letter and a great story idea."

SHOOTER'S RAG, The Practical Photographic Gazette, Havelin Communications, P.O. Box 8509, Asheville NC 28814. (704)254-6700. Editor: Michael Havelin. 50-70% freelance written. Quarterly magazine covering photography and electronic imaging. "*Shooter's Rag* is a magazine for the productive photographer, whether amateur, semi-pro or full-time professional. Our magazine is designed to provide information on shooting techniques, electronic imaging, photographer's legal issues and ethics, marketing, interviews, reviews and photographic adventures." Estab. 1992. Circ. 2,500. Pays on publication. Publishes ms an average of 2-6 months after acceptance. Byline given. Buys one-time rights. Submit seasonal material 6 months in advance. Accepts simultaneous submissions. Query for electronic submissions. Reports in 1 month. Sample copy $3. Writer's guidelines for #10 SASE.
Nonfiction: Book excerpts, essays, historical/nostalgic, how-to (varied photographic techniques), humor (in photographic experience), interview/profile, new product, opinion, personal experience, photo feature, technical, travel and investigative. "We are open to all photo-related material." Buys 6-14 mss/year. Query with or without clips. Length: 500-2,000 words. Pays 5¢/word minimum. Sometimes pays expenses of writers on assignment.
Photos: State availability of photos with submission. Reviews contact sheets, all size transparencies, 8×10 b&w prints. Package price for text and photos. Captions, model releases and identification of subjects required. Buys one-time rights.
Columns/Departments: Columns are written on a contract basis. Buys 8-16 mss/year. Query with published clips. Length: 500-2,000 words. Pays 5¢/word minimum.
Fiction: Photo related stories. Query with published clips. Length: 500-2,000 words. Pays 5¢/word minimum.
Fillers: Anecdotes, facts, cartoons, newsbreaks and short humor. Length: 25-150 words. Pays 5¢/word minimum.
Tips: "We are open to all sorts of well written, articulate, factually accurate and concise articles on photography-related subjects."

Plumbing, Heating, Air Conditioning and Refrigeration

DISTRIBUTOR, The Voice of Wholesaling, Technical Reporting Corp., Dept. WM, #300, 651 Washington St., Chicago IL 60661. (312)993-0929. Managing Editor: Mary Dolan. 30% freelance written. Prefers to work with published/established writers. Bimonthly magazine for heating, ventilating, air conditioning and refrigeration wholesalers. Editorial material shows "executive wholesalers how they can run better businesses and cope with personal and business problems." Circ. 17,000. Pays on publication. Publishes ms an average of 1 month after acceptance. Byline sometimes given. Buys one-time rights. Submit seasonal material 3 months in advance. "We want material exclusive to the field (industry)." Query for information on electronic submissions. Reports in 1 month. Sample copy $4.

Nonfiction: How-to (run a better business, cope with problems) and interview/profile (the wholesalers). No flippant or general approaches. Buys 6 mss/year. Query with or without published clips or send complete ms. Length: 1,000-2,000 words. Pays $100-200 (10¢/word). Sometimes pays the expenses of writers on assignment.

Photos: State availability of photos or send photos with query or ms. Pays $5 minimum. Captions and identification of subjects required.

Tips: "Know the industry—come up with a different angle on an industry subject (one we haven't dealt with in a long time). Wholesale ideas and top-quality business management articles are most open to freelancers."

SNIPS MAGAZINE, 1949 N. Cornell Ave., Melrose Park IL 60160. (708)544-3870. Fax: (708)544-3884. Editor: Nick Carter. 2% freelance written. Monthly magazine for sheet metal, warm air heating, ventilating, air conditioning and roofing contractors. Estab. 1932. Publishes ms an average of 3 months after acceptance. Buys all rights. "Write for detailed list of requirements before submitting any work."

Nonfiction: Material should deal with information about contractors who do sheet metal, warm air heating, air conditioning, ventilation and roofing work; also about successful advertising campaigns conducted by these contractors and the results. Length: "prefers stories to run less than 1,000 words unless on special assignment." Pays 5¢/word for first 500 words, 2¢/word thereafter.

Photos: Pays $5 each for small snapshot pictures, $10 each for usable 8×10 pictures.

Printing

CANADIAN PRINTER, Maclean Hunter Ltd., Dept. WM, 777 Bay St., Toronto, Ontario M5W 1A7 Canada. (416)596-5884. Fax: (416)596-5965. Editor: Nick Hancock. Assistant Editor: Stephan Forbes. 30% freelance written. Monthly magazine for printing and the allied industries. "*Canadian Printer* wants technical matter on graphic arts, printing, binding, typesetting, packaging, specialty production and trends in technology. Circ. 13,000. Pays on publication. Publishes ms an average of 1-3 months after acceptance. Byline given. Buys first North American serial rights. Reports in 6 months. Sample copy for 9×12 SAE and 2 IRCs.

Nonfiction: Technical. "We do not want US plant articles—this is a Canadian magazine." Buys 30-40 mss/year. Query or send complete ms. Length: 400-1,600 words. Pays $120-500 Canadian. Pays expenses of writers on assignment "on prior arrangement."

Photos: Send photos with submission. Reviews 4×5 prints. Offers $50 per photo. Captions and identification of subjects required. Buys one-time rights.

HIGH VOLUME PRINTING, Innes Publishing Co., P.O. Box 368, Northbrook IL 60062-2319. (708)564-5940. Fax: (708)564-8361. Editor: Catherine M. Stanulis. Estab. 1982. 35% freelance written. Eager to work with new/unpublished writers. Bimonthly magazine for book, magazine printers, large commercial printing plants with 20 or more employees. Aimed at telling the reader what he needs to know to print more efficiently and more profitably. Circ. 41,000. Pays on publication. Publishes ms an average of 9 months after acceptance. Byline given. Buys first and second serial rights. Simultaneous queries OK. Query for electronic submissions. Publishes reprints of previously published articles from noncompetitive or regional publications only. Send photocopy of article along with information about when and where the article previously appeared. Pays 50% of their fee for an original article. Reports in 2 months. Writer's guidelines, sample articles provided.

Nonfiction: How-to (printing production techniques); new product (printing, auxiliary equipment, plant equipment); photo feature (case histories featuring unique equipment); technical (printing product research and development); shipping; and publishing distribution methods. No product puff.

● Printing industry/technology knowledge is a *must!*

Buys 12 mss/year. Query. Length: 700-3,000 words. Pays $50-300.

Photos: Send photos with ms. Pays $25-150 for any size color transparencies and prints. Captions, model release, and identification of subjects required.

Tips: "Feature articles covering actual installations and industry trends are most open to freelancers. Be familiar with the industry, spend time in the field, and attend industry meetings and trade shows where equipment is displayed. We would also like to receive clips and shorts about printing mergers."

Market conditions are constantly changing! If this is 1995 or later, buy the newest edition of Writer's Market *at your favorite bookstore or order directly from Writer's Digest Books.*

PRINT & GRAPHICS, 1432 Duke St., Alexandria VA 22314. (703)683-8800. Fax: (703)683-8807. Publisher: Geoff Lindsay. 10% freelance written. Eager to work with new/unpublished writers. Monthly tabloid of the commercial printing industry for owners and executives of graphic arts firms. Circ. 20,000. **Pays on acceptance.** Publishes ms an average of 2 months after acceptance. Byline given. Buys one-time rights. Simultaneous queries, and simultaneous and previously published submissions OK. For previously published article, send photocopy of article. Electronic submissions OK via standard protocols, but requires hard copy also. Reports in 1 week. Sample copy $2.

Nonfiction: Book excerpts, historical/nostalgic, how-to, interview/profile, new product, opinion, personal experience, photo feature and technical. "All articles should relate to graphic arts management or production." Buys 20 mss/year. Query with published clips. Length: 750-2,000 words. Pays $100-250.

Photos: State availability of photos. Pays $25-75 for 5×7 b&w prints. Captions and identification of subjects required.

QUICK PRINTING, The Information Source for Commercial Copyshops and Printshops, Coast Publishing, Dept. WM, 1680 SW Bayshore Blvd., Port St. Lucie FL 34984. (407)879-6666. Fax: (407)879-7388. Publisher: K.J. Moran. Editor: Bob Hall. 50% freelance written. Monthly magazine covering the quick printing industry. "Our articles tell quick printers how they can be more profitable. We want figures to illustrate points made." Estab. 1977. Circ. 57,000. **Pays on acceptance.** Publishes ms an average of 4 months after acceptance. Byline given. Buys first North American serial or all rights. Submit seasonal material 6 months in advance. Rarely uses previously published submissions. Query for electronic submissions. Reports in 1 month. Sample copy $3 for 9×12 SAE with 7 first class stamps. Writer's guidelines for #10 SASE.

Nonfiction: How-to (on marketing products better or accomplishing more with equipment); new product; opinion (on the quick printing industry); personal experience (from which others can learn); and technical (on printing). No generic business articles, or articles on larger printing applications. Buys 75 mss/year. Send complete ms. Length: 1,500-3,000 words. Pays $150 and up.

Photos: State availability of photos with submission. Reviews transparencies and prints. Offers no payment for photos. Captions and identification of subjects required.

Columns/Departments: Viewpoint/Counterpoint (opinion on the industry); QP Profile (shop profiles with a marketing slant); Management (how to handle employees and/or business strategies); and Marketing Impressions, all 500-1,500 words. Buys 10 mss/year. Send complete ms. Pays $75.

Tips: "The use of electronic publishing systems by quick printers is of increasing interest. Show a knowledge of the industry. Try visiting your local quick printer for an afternoon to get to know about us. When your articles make a point, back it up with examples, statistics, and dollar figures. We need good material in all areas, but avoid the shop profile. Technical articles are most needed, but they must be accurate. No puff pieces for a certain industry supplier."

SCREEN PRINTING, 407 Gilbert Ave., Cincinnati OH 45202-2285. (513)421-2050. Fax: (513)421-5144. Editor: Steve Duccilli. 30% freelance written. Works with a small number of new/unpublished writers each year. Monthly magazine for the screen printing industry, including screen printers (commercial, industrial and captive shops), suppliers and manufacturers, ad agencies and allied professions. Estab. 1953. Circ. 15,000. Pays on publication. Publishes ms an average of 3-4 months after acceptance. Byline given. Buys all rights. Reporting time varies. Sample copies available for sale through circulation department. Writer's guidelines for SAE.

Nonfiction: "Because the screen printing industry is a specialized but diverse trade, we do not publish general interest articles with no pertinence to our readers. Subject matter is open, but should fall into one of four categories—technology, management, profile, or news. Features in all categories must identify the relevance of the subject matter to our readership. Technology articles must be informative, thorough, and objective—no promotional or 'advertorial' pieces accepted. Management articles may cover broader business or industry specific issues, but they must address the screen printer's unique needs. Profiles may cover serigraphers, outstanding shops, unique jobs and projects, or industry personalities; they should be in-depth features, not PR puff pieces, that clearly show the human interest or business relevance of the subject. News pieces should be timely (reprints from non-industry publications will be considered) and must cover an event or topic of industry concern." Buys 6-10 mss/year. Query. Unsolicited mss not returned. Length: 1,500-3,500 words. Pays minimum of $200 for major features. Sometimes pays the expenses of writers on assignment.

• There's an increasing emphasis here on personality features and coverage of fine art screen printers.

Photos: Cover photos negotiable; b&w or color. Published material becomes the property of the magazine.

Tips: "If the author has a working knowledge of screen printing, assignments are more readily available. General management articles are rarely used."

Real Estate

‡**AREA DEVELOPMENT MAGAZINE**, 400 Post Ave., Westbury NY 11590. (516)338-0900. Editor-in-Chief: Tom Bergeron. 50% freelance written. Prefers to work with published/established writers. Monthly magazine emphasizing corporate facility planning and site selection for industrial chief executives worldwide. Estab.

1964. Circ. 34,000. Pays following publication. Publishes ms an average of 2 months after acceptance. Buys first rights only. Byline given. Free sample copy. Writer's guidelines for #10 SASE.

Nonfiction: How-to (experiences in site selection and all other aspects of corporate facility planning); historical (if it deals with corporate facility planning); interview (corporate executives and industrial developers); and related areas of site selection and facility planning such as taxes, labor, government, energy, architecture and finance. Buys 100 mss/yr. Query. Pays $50-60/ms page; rates for illustrations depend on quality and printed size. Sometimes pays the expenses of writers on assignment.

Photos: State availability of photos with query. Prefer 8×10 or 5×7 b&w glossy prints or color transparencies—35mm OK. Captions preferred.

Tips: "Articles must be accurate, objective (no puffery) and useful to our industrial executive readers. Avoid any discussion of the merits or disadvantages of any particular areas or communities. Writers should realize we serve an intelligent and busy readership—they should avoid 'cute' allegories and get right to the point."

BUSINESS FACILITIES, Group C Communications, Inc., 121 Monmouth St., P.O. Box 2060, Red Bank NJ 07701. (908)842-7433. Fax: (908)758-6634. Editor: Eric Peterson. Managing Editor: Mary Lou Lang. 20% freelance written. Prefers to work with published/established writers. A monthly magazine covering corporate expansion, economic development and commercial and industrial real estate. "Our audience consists of corporate site selectors and real estate people; our editorial coverage is aimed at providing news and trends on the plant location and corporate expansion field." Estab. 1967. Circ. 40,000. Pays on publication. Publishes ms an average of 2 months after acceptance. Byline given. Buys all rights. Reports in 2 weeks. Sample copy and writer's guidelines for SASE.

• Magazine is currently overstocked, and for the near future will be accepting fewer pieces.

Nonfiction: General interest, how-to, interview/profile and personal experience. No news shorts or clippings; feature material only. Buys 12-15 mss/year. Query. Length: 1,000-3,000 words. Pays $200-1,000 for assigned articles, pays $200-600 for unsolicited articles. Sometimes pays the expenses of writers on assignment.

Photos: State availability of photos with submission. Reviews contact sheets, transparencies and 8×10 prints. Payment negotiable. Captions and identification of subjects required. Buys one-time rights.

Tips: "First, remember that our reader is a corporate executive responsible for his company's expansion and/or relocation decisions and our writers have to get inside that person's head in order to provide him with something that's helpful in his decision-making process. And second, the biggest turnoff is a telephone query. We're too busy to accept them and must require that all queries be put in writing. Submit major feature articles only; all news departments, fillers, etc., are staff prepared. A writer should be aware that our style is not necessarily dry and business-like. We tend to be more casual and a writer should look for that aspect of our approach."

FINANCIAL FREEDOM REPORT QUARTERLY, 2450 Fort Union Blvd., Salt Lake City UT 84121-9961. (801)943-1280. Fax: (801)942-7489. Chairman of the Board: Mark O. Haroldsen. Managing Editor: Carolyn Tice. 25% freelance written. Eager to work with new/unpublished writers. Quarterly magazine for "professional and nonprofessional investors and would-be investors in real estate—real estate brokers, insurance companies, investment planners, truck drivers, housewives, doctors, architects, contractors, etc. The magazine's content is presently expanding to interest and inform the readers about other ways to put their money to work for them." Estab. 1976. Circ. 50,000. Pays on publication. Publishes ms an average of 3 months after acceptance. Buys all rights. Phone queries OK. Simultaneous submissions OK. Query for electronic submissions. Reports in 2 months. Sample copy $5.

Nonfiction: How-to (find real estate bargains, finance property, use of leverage, managing property, developing market trends, goal setting, motivational) and interviews (success stories of those who have relied on own initiative and determination in real estate market or related fields). Buys 10 unsolicited mss/year. Query with clips of published work or submit complete ms. Length: 1,500-3,000 words. Pays 5-10¢/word. Sometimes pays the expenses of writers on assignment.

Photos: Send photos with ms. Uses 8×10 b&w or color matte prints. Captions required.

Tips: "We would like to find several specialized writers in our field of real estate investments. A writer must have had some hands-on experience in the real estate field."

JOURNAL OF PROPERTY MANAGEMENT, Institute of Real Estate Management, P.O. Box 109025, Chicago IL 60610-9025. (312)329-6058. Fax: (312)661-0217. Executive Editor: Mariwyn Evans. 30% freelance written. Bimonthly magazine covering real estate management and development. "The *Journal* has a feature/information slant designed to educate readers in the application of new techniques and to keep them abreast of current industry trends." Circ. 19,500. **Pays on acceptance.** Publishes ms an average of 3 months after acceptance. Byline given. Buys all rights. Simultaneous submissions OK. Query for electronic submissions. Reprints OK: send photocopy of article and information about when and where the article prevously appeared. Reports in 6 weeks on queries; 1 month on mss. *Writer's Market* recommends allowing 2 months for reply. Free sample copy and writer's guidelines.

• This journal wants more "nuts-and-bolts" articles.

GET YOUR WORK INTO THE RIGHT BUYERS' HANDS!

You work hard... and your hard work deserves to be seen by the right buyers. But with the constant changes in the industry, it's not always easy to know who those buyers are. That's why you'll want to keep up-to-date and on top with the most current edition of this indispensable market guide.

Totally Updated Each Year

Keep ahead of the changes by ordering *1995 Writer's Market* today. You'll save the frustration of getting manuscripts returned in the mail, stamped MOVED: ADDRESS UNKNOWN. And of NOT submitting your work to new listings because you don't know they exist. All you have to do to order the upcoming 1995 edition is complete the attached post card and return it with your payment or charge card information. Order now, and there's one thing that won't change from your *1994 Writer's Market* - the price! That's right, we'll send you the 1995 edition for just $26.95. *1995 Writer's Market* will be published and ready for shipment in September 1994.

Don't let another opportunity slip by…get a jump on the industry with the help of *1995 Writer's Market*. Order today! You deserve it!

(See other side for more books to help you get published)

To order, drop this postpaid card in the mail.

☐ **Yes!** I want the most current edition of *Writer's Market*. Please send me the 1995 edition at the 1994 price - $26.95.* (NOTE: *1995 Writer's Market* will be ready for shipment in September 1994.) #10385

Also send me these books to help me get published:

_____(#10363) 1994 Guide to Literary Agents & Art/Photo Reps $18.95 $16.10* (available 2/94)

_____(#10361) 1994 Novel & Short Story Writer's Market $19.95 $16.95* (available 2/94)

_____(#45060) 1994 Novel & Short Story Wrtr's Mkt AND 1994 Literary Agents 2-book set
SPECIAL PRICE $32.00 * (available 2/94)

_____(#10283) This Business of Writing $19.95 $16.95* (available NOW)

_____(#10369) The Complete Guide to Magazine Article Writing $17.95 $15.25* (available NOW)

_____(#10314) How to Write Fast $17.95 $15.25* (available NOW)

*Plus postage and handling: $3.00 for one book or set, $1.00 for each additional book or set. Ohio residents add $5^{1}/2$% sales tax.

Credit card orders call toll-free 1-800-289-0963

☐ Payment enclosed (Slip this card and your payment into an envelope)

☐ Please charge my: ☐ Visa ☐ MasterCard

Account #_____ Exp. Date _____

Signature _____ Phone ( ) _____

Name _____

Address _____

City _____ State _____ Zip_____

(This offer expires May 1, 1995)

| 30-Day Money Back Guarantee |

W WRITER'S DIGEST BOOKS
Writer's Digest Books
1507 Dana Avenue
Cincinnati, OH 45207

6402

SAVE UP TO $6.90

NEW! 1994 Guide to Literary Agents & Art/Photo Reps

Literary agents can open publishers' doors for you! This directory (now in its 3rd year) is better than ever with over 500 listings, plus answers to the most-often-asked questions about reps in 10 articles written by professionals in the field. 240 pages/ $18.95 $16.10/paperback/available 2/94

NEW! 1994 Novel & Short Story Writer's Market

Are you a fiction writer? This directory offers marketing information on 1,900 fiction publishers, plus helpful articles and interviews with professionals to help you sell your novel or short story. 624 pages/$19.95 $16.95/paperback/ available 2/94

Order both 1994 Guide to Literary Agents AND 1994 Novel & Short Story Writer's Market and Save $6.90 on the 2-Book Set! SPECIAL PRICE $32.00

This Business of Writing

The perfect companion to *Writer's Market!* If you're serious about making money with your writing, you have to think of your writing as a business. This book is a fun-to-read guide filled with practical advice and anecdotes on building a successful - and profitable - writing career. 256 pages/$19.95 $16.95/hardcover

NEW! The Complete Guide to Magazine Article Writing

Covers the essentials of non-fiction writing — primarily article writing for magazines and newspapers. Explains what elements articles must have in order to be clean, effective... and salable. 256 pages/$17.95 $15.25/hardcover/available NOW

Use coupon on other side to order today!

BUSINESS REPLY MAIL

FIRST CLASS MAIL   PERMIT NO. 17   CINCINNATI OHIO

POSTAGE PAID BY ADDRESSEE

NO POSTAGE
NECESSARY
IF MAILED
IN THE
UNITED STATES

WRITER'S DIGEST BOOKS

1507 DANA AVENUE
CINCINNATI OH 45207-9965

Nonfiction: How-to, interview, technical (building systems/computers), demographic shifts in business employment and buying patterns, marketing. "No non-real estate subjects, personality or company, humor." Buys 8-12 mss/year. Query with published clips. Length: 1,500-4,000 words. Sometimes pays the expenses of writers on assignment.

Photos: State availability of photos with submission. Reviews contact sheets. May offer additional payment for photos accepted with ms. Model releases and identification of subjects required. Buys one-time rights.

Columns/Departments: Martha Schindler, associate editor. Insurance Insights, Tax Issues, Investment and Finance Insights and Legal Issues. Buys 6-8 mss/year. Query. Length: 750-1,500 words.

‡**PLANTS SITES & PARKS, The Corporate Advisor for Relocation Strategies**, BPI Communications Inc., Suite 201, 10100 West Sample Rd., Coral Springs FL 33065. (800)753-2660. Editor: Ken Ibold. 35% freelance written. Bimonthly magazine covering business, especially as it involves site locations. Estab. 1974. Circ. 37,500. **Pays on acceptance.** Publishes ms an average of 1 month after acceptance. Byline given. Negotiable kill fee. Buys all rights. Editorial lead time 3-4 months. Reports in 1 month on queries. Sample copy and writer's guidelines free on request.

Nonfiction: Book excerpts, real estate, labor, industry, finance topics geared toward manufacturing executives. Buys 25-30 mss/year (total for features *and* columns/departments). Query with published clips. Length: 1,000-7,000 words. Pays $300 minimum for assigned articles. Pays expenses of writers on assignment.

Photos: State availability of photos with submission. Negotiates payment individually. Captions required. Rights negotiable.

Columns/Departments: Regional Review (profile business climate of each state), 3,000-5,000 words; Industry Outlook (trend stories on specific industries), 5,000-7,500 words; Global Market (business outlook for specific overseas areas), 2,000-5,000 words. Buys 25-30 mss/year (total for columns/departments and features). Query with published clips. Pays $300-2,000.

‡**REALTOR® MAGAZINE**, Network Publications, P.O. Box 100001, Lawrenceville GA 30236. (404)962-7220. Editor: Tim Darnell. 40% freelance written. Monthly magazine covering Atlanta residential real estate. "Our goal is to provide information to real estate agents enabling them to become more profitable in their businesses. We are issues-oriented, and we are particularly interested in real estate market trends." Estab. 1986. Circ. 17,000. Pays on publication. Publishes ms an average of 2 months after acceptance. Byline given. Buys all rights. Editorial lead time 3 months. Submit seasonal material 4 months in advance. Reports in 2 weeks on queries. Sample copy and writer's guidelines free on request.

Nonfiction: How-to, inspirational, interview/profile, personal experience, photo feature and technical. No humor or historical/nostalgic pieces. Buys 16 mss/year. Query. Query with published clips. Length: 1,000-3,000 words. Pays $100 minimum for assigned articles. Sometimes pays expenses of writers on assignment (limit agreed upon in advance).

Photos: State availability of photos with submission. Reviews 4×6 transparencies, 4 color slides and 3×5 prints. Offers no additional payment for photos accepted with ms. Captions and identification of subjects required. Buys all rights.

Columns/Departments: Countdown to 96 (Olympics coverage), 750 words. Buys 12 mss/year. Query with published clips. Pays $75.

Resources and Waste Reduction

GROUND WATER AGE, National Trade Publications, 13 Century Hill Dr., Latham NY 12110-2197. (518)783-1281. Managing Editor: Roslyn Scheib Dahl. Monthly magazine covering water well drilling and pump installation. Estab. 1981. Circ. 14,000. **Pays on acceptance.** Publishes ms an average of 3-4 months after acceptance. Byline given. Buys first North American serial rights. Submit seasonal material 6 months in advance. Reports in 1 month on queries; 2 months on mss. Sample copy for 9×12 SAE with 10 first class stamps.

Nonfiction: Historical/nostalgic, interview/profile, new product, photo feature and technical. Buys 1-5 mss/year. Query with published clips. Length: 750-3,000 words. Pays $50-350 for assigned articles; $50-250 for unsolicited articles. "Trades articles for advertising, on occasion and when desirable."

Photos: State availability of photos with submission. "We need quality photos of water well drillers, monitoring well contractors or pump installers in action, on the job." Reviews contact sheets, negatives, transparencies and prints. Offers no additional payment for photos accepted with ms. Identification of subjects required. Buys one-time rights.

Columns/Departments: Technically Speaking (technical, how-to aspects of water well or monitoring well drilling and technical aspects of water well pumps, tanks, valves and piping for domestic well systems); Business Strategies (business topics for improving productivity, marketing, etc.), 300-1,000 words. Buys 1-5 mss/year. Query first by phone or mail. Pays $50-150.

THE PUMPER, COLE Publishing Inc., Drawer 220, Three Lakes WI 54562-0220. (715)546-3347. President: Robert J. Kendall. Production Manager: Ken Lowther. 50% freelance written. Eager to work with new/unpublished writers. Monthly tabloid covering the liquid waste hauling industry (portable toilet renters, septic tank pumpers, industrial waste haulers, chemical waste haulers, oil field haulers, and hazardous waste haulers). "Our publication is read by companies that handle liquid waste and manufacturers of equipment." Estab. 1979. Circ. 15,000. Pays on publication. Publishes ms an average of 1 month after acceptance. Byline given. Buys first serial rights. Publishes reprints of previously published articles. Send tearsheet or photocopy of article, or send typed ms with rights for sale noted. Include information about when and where the article previously appeared. For reprints, pays 100% of the amount paid for an original article. Submit seasonal material 3 months in advance. Simultaneous queries, and simultaneous and previously published submissions OK. Query for electronic submissions. Reports in 2 months. Free sample copy and writer's guidelines.

Nonfiction: Expose (government regulations, industry problems, trends, public attitudes, etc.); general interest (state association meetings, conventions, etc.); how-to (related to industry, e.g., how to incorporate septage or municipal waste into farm fields, how to process waste, etc.); humor (related to industry, especially septic tank pumpers or portable toilet renters); interview/profile (including descriptions of business statistics, type of equipment, etc.); new product; personal experience; photo feature; and technical (especially reports on research projects related to disposal). "We are looking for quality articles that will be of interest to our readers; length is not important. We publish trade journals. We need articles that deal with the trade. Studies on land application of sanitary waste are of great interest." Query or send complete ms. Pays 7½¢/word.

Photos: Send photos with query or ms. Pays $15 for b&w and color prints that are used. No negatives. "We need good contrast." Captions "suggested" and model release required. Buys one-time rights.

Tips: "Material must pertain to liquid waste-related industries listed above. We hope to expand the editorial content of our monthly publications. We also have publications for sewer and drain cleaners with the same format as *The Pumper*; however, *The Cleaner* has a circulation of 18,000. We are looking for the same type of articles and pay is the same."

RECYCLING TODAY, Municipal Market Edition, GIE Inc., Dept. WM, 4012 Bridge Ave., Cleveland OH 44113. (216)961-4130. Editor: John Bruening. 25% freelance written. Monthly trade magazine covering recycling programs for municipalities. *Recycling Today* serves recycling coordinators at the state, county and municipal levels, as well as private companies providing information and services to government. Estab. 1990. Circ. 15,000. Pays on publication. Publishes ms an average of 2 months after acceptance. Byline given. No kill fee. Buys all rights (will reassign). Submit seasonal material 3 months in advance. Simultaneous submissions OK. Sample copy for 9×12 SAE with 6 first class stamps.

Nonfiction: Profiles of innovative recycling programs, solutions to current recycling challenges. Buys 40 mss/year. Query with published clips. Length: 2,000-3,000 words. Pays $200-300. Sometimes pays expenses of writers on assignment.

Photos: Send photos with submission. Reviews contact sheets, 2×3 slide or transparencies or 3×5 prints. Offers no additional payment for photos accepted with ms. Captions and identification of subjects required. Buys all rights (will reassign).

RESOURCE RECYCLING, North America's Recycling Journal, Resource Recycling, Inc., Dept. WM, P.O. Box 10540, Portland OR 97210-0540. (503)227-1319. Fax: (503)227-6135. Editor-in-Chief: Jerry Powell. Editor: Meg Lynch. 5% freelance written. Eager to work with new/unpublished writers. Monthly trade journal covering post-consumer recycling of paper, plastics, metals, glass and other materials. Estab. 1982. Circ. 14,000. Pays on publication. Publishes ms an average of 3-9 months after acceptance. Byline given. Buys first rights. Simultaneous submissions OK. Query for electronic submissions. Reports in 2 months on queries. Reprints OK; send tearsheet of article and information about when and where the article previously appeared. Pays 100% of their fee for an original article. Sample copy and writer's guidelines for 9×12 SAE with 7 first class stamps.

Nonfiction: "No non-technical or opinion pieces." Buys 10-15 mss/year. Query with published clips. Length: 1,200-1,800 words. Pays $300-350. Pays with contributor copies "if writers are more interested in professional recognition than financial compensation." Sometimes pays the expenses of writers on assignment.

Photos: State availability of photos with submission. Reviews contact sheets, negatives and prints. Offers $5-50. Identification of subjects required. Buys one-time rights.

Tips: "Overviews of one recycling aspect in one state (e.g., oil recycling in Alabama) will receive attention. We will increase coverage of source reduction and yard waste composting."

Selling and Merchandising

Sales personnel and merchandisers interested in how to sell and market products successfully consult these journals. Publications in nearly every category of Trade also buy sales-related materials if they are slanted to the product or industry with which they deal.

THE AMERICAN SALESMAN, 424 N. 3rd St., P.O. Box 1, Burlington IA 52601-0001. Fax: (319)752-3421. Publisher: Michael S. Darnall. Editorial Supervisor: Doris J. Ruschill. Editor: Barbara Boeding. 95% freelance written. Prefers to work with published/established writers, but works with a small number of new/ unpublished writers each year. Monthly magazine for distribution through company sales representatives. Estab. 1955. Circ. 1,500. Pays on publication. Publishes ms an average of 4 months after acceptance. Buys all rights. Reports in 4 months. Sample copy and writer's guidelines for 6½ × 9½ SAE with 3 first class stamps; mention *Writer's Market* in request.
Nonfiction: Sales seminars, customer service and follow-up, closing sales, sales presentations, handling objections, competition, telephone usage and correspondence, managing territory and new innovative sales concepts. No sexist material, illustration written from a salesperson's viewpoint. No ms dealing with supervisory problems. Length: 900-1,200 words. Pays 3¢/word. Uses no advertising. Follow AP Stylebook. Include biography and/or byline with ms submissions. Author photos used. Send correspondence to Editor.

ART & CRAFTS RETAILER, (formerly *Art Material Trade News*), Communication Channels Inc., 6151 Powers Ferry Rd., NW, Atlanta GA 30339-2941. (404)955-2500. Editor: Ben Johnson. 50% freelance written. Works with a small number of new/unpublished writers each year. Bimonthly magazine on art and craft materials. "Our editorial thrust is to bring art and craft retailers, distributors and manufacturers information they can use in their everyday operations." Estab. 1949. Circ. 12,000. Pays on publication. Publishes ms an average of 3 months after acceptance. Buys first serial rights. Submit seasonal material 3 months in advance. Reports in 6 months. Sample copy for 9 × 12 SAE with 4 first class stamps. Writer's guidelines for #10 SASE.
Nonfiction: How-to (sell, retail/wholesale employee management, advertising programs); interview/profile (within industry); and technical (commercial art drafting/engineering). "We encourage a strong narrative style where possible. We publish an editorial 'theme' calendar at the beginning of each year." Buys 15-30 mss/year. Query with published clips. Length: 1,000-3,000 words (prefers 2,000 words). Pays $75-300.
Photos: State availability of photos. Pays $10 maximum for b&w contact sheets. Identification of subjects required.

ASD/AMD TRADE NEWS, Associated Surplus Dealers/Associated Merchandise Dealers, 2525 Ocean Park Blvd., Santa Monica CA 90405-5201. (310)396-6006. Fax: (310)399-2662. Editor: Jay Hammeran. 75% freelance written. Monthly trade newspaper on trade shows and areas of interest to surplus/merchandise dealers. "Many of our readers have small, family-owned businesses." Estab. 1967. Circ. 80,000. Pays on publication. Publishes ms an average of 1-2 months after acceptance. Byline given. Negotiable kill fee. Buys all rights. Submit seasonal material 3 months in advance. Simultaneous submissions OK. Publishes reprints of previously published articles. Send photocopy of article or typed ms with rights for sale noted and information about when and where the article previously appeared. For reprints, pays 100% of the amount paid for an original article. Query for electronic submissions. Reports in 2 weeks on queries; 2 months on mss. Free sample copy and writer's guidelines.
Nonfiction: How-to (merchandise a store more effectively, buy and sell products), interview/profile (dealers/ owners), personal experience (of dealers and merchandisers), photo feature (ASD/AMD trade shows), and general business articles of interest. "February and August are the largest issues of the year. We generally need more freelance material for those two issues. No articles that are solely self-promotion pieces or straight editorials. We also need articles that tell a small business owner/manager how to handle legal issues, personnel questions and business matters, such as accounting." Buys 100 mss/year. Query with or without published clips, or send complete ms. Length: 500-1,250 words. Pays $50-100. Pays expenses of writers on assignment.
Photos: State availability of photos with submission. Reviews 3½ × 5 prints. Payment depends on whether photos were assigned or not. Identification of subjects required. Buys all rights.
Columns/Departments: Business & News Briefs (summarizes important news/business news affecting small businesses/dealers/merchandisers), 500 words; ASD Profile (interview with successful dealer), 1,000-1,250 words; Merchandising Tips (how to better merchandise a business), 750-1,000 words. Legal, Finance, Marketing, Advertising, Personnel sections: 1,000 words. Buys 70 mss/year. Query or send complete ms. Pays $50-100.
Fillers: Facts and newsbreaks. Buys 10/year. Length: 50-300 words. Pays $25-45.
Tips: "Talk to retailers. Find out what their concerns are, and the types of wholesalers/merchandisers they deal with. Write articles to meet those needs. It's as simple as that. The entire publication is open to freelance writers who can write good articles. We're now more sectionalized. We especially need articles that are of use or interest to very small businesses (1-10 employees). We need new looks at the cities in which we hold trade shows (Las Vegas, Atlantic City, Reno and Dallas.)"

BALLOONS AND PARTIES TODAY MAGAZINE, The Original Balloon Magazine of New-Fashioned Ideas, Festivities Publications, 1205 W. Forsyth St., Jacksonville FL 32204. (904)634-1902. Fax: (904)633-8764. Publisher: Debra Paulk. Editor: April Anderson. 10% freelance written. Monthly international trade journal for professional party decorators and for gift delivery businesses. Estab. 1986. Circ. 15,000. Pays on publication. Publishes ms an average of 3 months after acceptance. Byline given. Buys one-time rights. Submit seasonal material 6 months in advance. Query for electronic submissions. Reports in 6 weeks on queries; 6 weeks on mss. Sample copy for 9 × 12 SAE with $2.40 in postage.

Nonfiction: Interview/profile, photo feature, technical, craft. Buys 24 mss/year. Query with or without published clips or send complete ms. Length: 500-1,500 words. Pays $100-300 for assigned articles; $50-200 for unsolicited articles. Sometimes pays expenses of writers on assignment.

Photos: Send photos with submission. Reviews 2×2 transparencies and 3×5 prints. Pays $10/photo accepted with ms (designs, arrangements, decorations only—no payment for new products). Captions, model releases and identification of subjects required. Buys one-time rights.

Columns/Departments: Great Ideas (craft projects using balloons, large scale decorations), 200-500 words. Send full manuscript with photos. Pays $10/photo.

Tips: "Show unusual, lavish, and outstanding examples of balloon sculpture, design and decorating. Offer specific how-to information. Be positive and motivational in style."

BEDROOM MAGAZINE, Bobit Publishing, 2512 Artesia Blvd., Redondo Beach CA 90278-3210. (310)376-8788. Fax: (310)376-9043. Editor: Kathy Knoles. 10% freelance written. Prefers to work with published/established writers. Monthly magazine covering bedroom furniture, mattresses, linens and accessories for specialty shop owners, buyers, furniture stores, sleep shops and bedroom furniture manufacturers, distributors. Estab. 1983. Circ. 19,200. Pays on publication. Publishes ms an average of 2 months after acceptance. Byline given. Buys first rights or second serial (reprint) rights. Submit seasonal material 3 months in advance. Reprints OK; send tearsheet of article or typed manuscript with rights for sale noted and information about when and where the article previously appeared. For reprints, pays 50% of fee paid for an original article. Reports in 1 month. Sample copy for 10×13 SAE with 5 first class stamps.

Nonfiction: Book excerpts, historical/nostalgic, how-to (business management, display techniques, merchandising tips), humor (if in good taste), interview/profile, new product, personal experience, photo feature, technical and general features depicting bedroom furniture and accessories in a positive way. No articles depicting furniture or mattresses in a negative manner. Query with published clips. Length: 1,000-5,000 words. Pays $60-250 for assigned articles; pays $50-200 for unsolicited articles. Sometimes pays the expenses of writers on assignment.

Photos: Send photos with submission. Reviews contact sheets, transparencies and 8×10 prints. Offers $25-100/photo. Captions and identification of subjects required. Buys one-time rights.

Tips: "We need profiles on successful bedroom furniture retailers in all parts of the country. Most of our freelance articles concern store management. Stores that do an excellent job with display and promotions are of special interest when accompanied by good photos. We need articles on obtaining credit, display techniques, merchandising, how to be a successful salesperson, attracting new customers, creating effective advertising, how to put together an attractive store window display, hiring employees, etc. Anything that could benefit a salesperson or store owner."

● Writers who can do dealer profiles and also take good photos to accompany the article will find this market open.

CANADIAN COMPUTER DEALER NEWS, Plesman Publication Ltd., 2005 Sheppard Ave. E., 4th Floor, Willowdale, Ontario M2J 5B1 Canada. (416)497-9562. Fax: (416)497-9427. Editor: Sean Stokes. 10% freelance written. Biweekly newspaper about computer channels for retailers, resellers, vendors and consultants. Circ. 10,000. Pays on publication. Publishes ms an average of 1 month after acceptance. Byline given. Offers kill fee. Buys first North American serial rights. Submit seasonal material 2 months in advance. Free sample copy and writer's guidelines.

Nonfiction: Expose, how-to (market computers effectively, establish advertising budgets or choose a PR firm), interview/profile, new product, personal experience (applications) and other. Buys 250 mss/year. Query with published clips or send complete ms. Length: 600-1,000 words. Pays $300-600 for assigned articles.

Photos: Send photos with submission. Reviews 3×5 color prints. Identification of subjects required.

Columns/Departments: Dealer Report (profile of Canadian computer dealer), 800 words; Distribution (profile of Canadian computer distributor), 800 words; VAR Tracks (profile of a Canadian VAR *or* of vendors VAR program), 800 words; and Vendor Update (profile of a Canadian computer vendor), 800 words. Buys 50 mss/year. Query with published clips. Pays $300.

Tips: "If freelancer is familiar with the computer industry, he might call to discuss story ideas. The writer would then be asked to send a more detailed outline. Editor might suggest contacts, sources, if necessary."

CASUAL LIVING, Columbia Communications, 370 Lexington Ave., New York NY 10017. (212)532-9290. Fax: (212)779-8345. Editor: Eileen Robinson Smith. Monthly magazine covering outdoor furniture for outdoor furniture specialists, including retailers, mass merchandisers and department store buyers. Estab. 1957. Circ. 14,000. Pays on publication. Buys first North American serial rights. Publishes reprints of previously published articles. Send tearsheet of article along with information about when and where the article previously appeared. Submit seasonal material 2 months in advance. Reports in 1 month. Sample copy for 9×12 SAE with 2 first class stamps.

Nonfiction: Interview/profile (case histories of retailers in the industry), new product, opinion and technical. Buys 7-8 mss/year. Query with clips, then follow up with phone call. Length: 1,000 words average. Pays $150-350.

Photos: State availability of photos with query letter or ms. Reviews b&w contact sheets and color prints. Payment for photos usually a package deal with ms. Buys all rights.

Tips: "Know the industry, trades and fashions, and what makes a successful retailer."

CHRISTIAN RETAILING, Strang Communications, 600 Rinehart Road, Lake Mary FL 32746. (407)333-0600. Editor: Brian Peterson. 60% freelance written. Monthly magazine covering issues and products of interest to Christian vendors and retail stores. "Our editorial is geared to help retailers run a successful business. We do this with product information, industry news and feature articles." Estab. 1958. Circ. 9,500. Pays on publication. Publishes ms an average of 5 months after acceptance. Bylines sometimes given. Kill fee varies with writer, length of article. Buys all rights. Submit seasonal material 5 months in advance. Previously published submissions OK. Reports in 2 months. Sample copy $3. Writer's guidelines for #10 SASE.

Nonfiction: How-to (any articles on running a retail business—books, gifts, music, video, clothing of interest to Christians), new product, religious, technical. Buys 36 mss/year. Send complete ms. Length: 700-2,300 words. Pays 12¢/word minimum for assigned articles; 10¢/word minimum for unsolicited articles. Sometimes pays expenses of writers on assignment.

Photos: State availability of photos with submission. Reviews contact sheets, transparencies (any) and prints (any). Usually offers no additional payment for photos accepted with ms. Captions required. Buys one-time rights.

Columns/Departments: Book News; Music Notes; Video Talk; Gift Rap. Pays 12¢/word minimum; no maximum.

Fillers: Anecdotes, facts, gags to be illustrated by cartoonist, short humor. Buys 5/year. Length: 50-300 words. Pays 12¢/word minimum.

Tips: "Visit Christian bookstores and see what they're doing—the products they carry, the issues that concern them. Then write about it!"

‡FOREIGN TRADE, A Survival Tool For World Traders, Defense & Diplomacy Inc., Suite 200, 6849 Old Dominion Dr., McLean VA 22101-3705. (703)448-1338. Editor: Russell W. Goodman. 50% freelance written. Magazine published 10 times/year covering international trade. *"Foreign Trade* publishes practical, 'News You can Use' articles on international trade for readers worldwide who specialize in importing, exporting and manufacturing." Estab. 1991. Circ. 15,000. Pays on publication. Publishes ms an average of 1 month after acceptance. Byline given. Buys all rights. Editorial lead time 2 months. Reports in 1 week on queries.

Nonfiction: How-to (break into certain markets) and travel. Buys 200 mss/year. Query with published clips. Length: 300-800 words. Pays $150 minimum.

Columns/Departments: Trade Briefs (articles on trading with certain countries), 300-800 words; Financing Deals (financial aspects of importing/exporting), 300-800 words. Buys 200 mss/year. Query with published clips. Pays $150-400.

Tips: "Writers approaching us should have practical experience in trading, banking, government regulations *or* experience in business writing. We are most open to trade briefs—articles should be short, precise, practical about specific trading opportunities."

GIFT BASKET REVIEW, Festivities Publications, 1205 W. Forsyth St., Jacksonville FL 32204. (904)634-1902. Fax: (904)633-8764. Publisher: Debra Paulk. Editor: Elizabeth Skelton. 25% freelance written. Monthly magazine for gourmet food and gift basket retailers. "Our readers are creative small business entrepreneurs. Many are women who start their business out of their homes and eventually branch into retail." Estab. 1990. Circ. 19,000. Pays on publication. Publishes ms an average of 3 months after acceptance. Byline given. Buys one-time rights. Submit seasonal material 9 months in advance. Accepts simultaneous and previously published submissions. Reports in 2 months.

Nonfiction: How-to (how to give a corporate presentation, negotiate a lease, etc.), photo feature and technical. "No personal profiles or general experience." Buys 6-8 mss/year. Send complete ms. Length: 500-2,000 words. Pays 10¢/word. Sometimes pays expenses of writers on assignment.

Photos: Send photos with submission. Reviews contact sheets, negatives, 2×2 transparencies and 3×5 prints. Offers $10/photo minimum. Model releases and identification of subjects required. Buys one-time rights.

Columns/Departments: Corporate Talk (deals with obtaining corporate clients), 1,500 words; In the Storefront (emphasis on small business owners with a retail storefront), 1,500 words; and On the Homefront (specifically for home-based entrepreneurs), 1,500 words. Buys 12 mss/year. Send complete ms. Pays 10¢/word.

Fillers: Anecdotes, facts, gags to be illustrated by cartoonist, newsbreaks and short humor. Length: 300 words maximum. Pays 10¢/word.

Tips: "Freelancers can best approach us by attending the various conventions (including our annual Jubilee convention) involving gift basket, floral and gourmet foods. Become involved with these businesses. All departments are open to freelancers. Be very specific with concrete tips and creative marketing ideas. Don't generalize. Don't tell us to take an ad in the yellow pages, tell us how to write an ad to promote a small creative business."

INFO FRANCHISE NEWSLETTER, P.O. Box 670, 9 Duke St., St. Catharines, Ontario L2R 6W8 Canada or P.O. Box 550, 728 Center St., Lewiston NY 14092-0550. (716)754-4669. Editor-in-Chief: E.L. Dixon, Jr. Managing Editor: Denise Muir. Monthly newsletter. Estab. 1977. Circ. 5,000. Pays on publication. Buys all rights. Reports in 1 month.
Nonfiction: Expose, how-to, informational, interview, profile, new product, personal experience and technical. "We are particularly interested in receiving articles regarding franchise legislation, franchise litigation, franchise success stories, and new franchises. Both American and Canadian items are of interest. We do not want to receive any information which is not fully documented or articles which could have appeared in any newspaper or magazine in North America. An author with a legal background who could comment upon such things as arbitration and franchising or class actions and franchising, would be of great interest to us."

PROFESSIONAL SELLING, 24 Rope Ferry Rd., Waterford CT 06386. (203)442-4365. Fax: (203)434-3078. Editor: Paulette S. Kitchens. 33% freelance written. Prefers to work with published/established writers. Bimonthly newsletter in two sections for sales professionals covering industrial, wholesale, high-tech and financial services sales. "*Professional Selling* provides field sales personnel with both the basics and current information that can help them better perform the sales function." Estab. 1917. **Pays on acceptance.** Publishes ms an average of 4-6 months after acceptance. No byline given. Buys all rights. Submit seasonal material 6 months in advance. Reports in 1 month. Sample copy and writer's guidelines for #10 SAE with 2 first class stamps.
Nonfiction: How-to (successful sales techniques); and interview/profile (interview-based articles). "We buy only interview-based material." Buys 12-15 mss/year. No unsolicited manuscripts; written queries only. Length: 1,000-1,200 words.
Tips: "*Professional Selling* includes a 4-page clinic devoted to a single topic of major importance to sales professionals. Only the lead article for each section is open to freelancers. Lead article must be based on an interview with an actual sales professional. Freelancers may occasionally interview sales managers, but the slant must be toward field sales, *not* management."

‡**SPECIAL EVENTS NEWS,** ST Century Marketing, 7250C Westfield Ave., Pennsauken NJ 08110. (609)488-5255. Contact: Maria King. 20% freelance written. Monthly tabloid covering special events across North America, including festivals, fairs, auto shows, home shows, trade shows, etc. There are 21 categories of shows/events that are covered. Byline given. Buys first rights. Submit seasonal material 3 months in advance. Photocopied and previously published submissions OK. Free sample copy and writers guidelines.
Nonfiction: How-to, interview/profile, event review and new product. Special issues include an annual event directory and semiannual flea market directory. No submissions unrelated to selling at events. Query. Length: 400-750 words. Pays $2.50/column inch.
Photos: Send photos with submission. Reviews contact sheets. Offers $10/photo. Captions required. Buys one-time rights.
Columns/Departments: 5 columns monthly (must deal with background of event, vendors or unique facets of industry in North America). Query with published clips. Length: 400-700 words. Pays $3/column inch.

Sport Trade

Retailers and wholesalers of sports equipment and operators of recreation programs read these journals. Magazines about general and specific sports are classified in the Consumer Sports section.

‡**ACTION SPORTS,** Miller Freeman, Inc., 31652 2nd Ave., South Laguna CA 92625. (714)499-5374. Editor: Sada Valov. 75% freelance written. Magazine published 9 times/year covering surf, snowboard, swim, skate retailers. "We publish in the interests of the growth and development of specialty sport retailers and related lifestyles and apparel." Estab. 1979. Circ. 15,000. **Pays on acceptance.** Publishes ms an average of 2 months after acceptance. Byline given. Offers 25% kill fee. Buys all rights and other rights (negotiable). Editorial lead time 3-4 months. Simultaneous submissions OK. Query for electronic submissions. Reports in 2 weeks on queries; 1 month on mss. *Writer's Market* recommends allowing 2 months for reply. Sample copy free on request.
Nonfiction: General interest, historical/nostalgic, how-to, interview/profile, new product (all related to industry) and technical (related to sports covered). How-to related to business management for specialty store employers/owners. "No general interest not related to our specific sports, which include skateboarding, surfing, snowboarding." Buys 120 mss/year. Query with published clips. Length: 100-2,000 words. Pays $75 minimum (dependent upon length). Sometimes pays expenses of writers on assignment.

Photos: State availability of photos with submission. Reviews transparencies. Negotiates payment individually. Buys one-time rights.

Columns/Departments: Snowboarding (new product information, etc.), 500-750 words; Swimwear (trend reports, profiles, etc.), 500-750 words; Surfing (manufacture related stories), 500-750 words. Buys 40 mss/ year. Query with published clips. Pays $100-300.

Fillers: Facts, Buys 5/year. Length: 50 maximum words. Pays $25-100.

Tips: "The author should be versed in the surf-related industry including snowboarding, skateboard. Also important is a sound knowledge of business. Our magazine goes directly to retailers—and they need to know how to survive in today's economy. It's best if potential writers first send in a resume and some writing samples. Follow-up with a phone call, and the editors can make an evaluation of their abilities. We're especially interested in writers from areas other than California, namely New York and Hawaii."

AMERICAN FIREARMS INDUSTRY, AFI Communications Group, Inc., 2455 E. Sunrise Blvd., 9th Floor, Ft. Lauderdale FL 33304-3118. Fax: (305)561-4129. 10% freelance written. "Work with writers specifically in the firearms trade." Monthly magazine specializing in the sporting arms trade. Estab. 1973. Circ. 30,000. Pays on publication. Publishes ms an average of 1 month after acceptance. Buys all rights. Reports in 2 weeks.

Nonfiction: R.A. Lesmeister, articles editor. Publishes informational, technical and new product articles. No general firearms subjects. Query. Length: 900-1,500 words. Pays $150-300. Sometimes pays the expenses of writers on assignment.

Photos: Reviews 8×10 b&w glossy prints. Manuscript price includes payment for photos.

AMERICAN FITNESS, Suite 200, 15250 Ventura Blvd., Sherman Oaks CA 91403. (818)905-0040. Fax: (818)990-5468. Editor-at-Large: Peg Jordan, R.N. Managing Editor: Rhonda J. Wilson. 75% freelance written. Eager to work with new/unpublished writers. Bimonthly magazine covering exercise and fitness, health and nutrition. "We need timely, in-depth, informative articles on health, fitness, aerobic exercise, sports nutrition, sports medicine and physiology." Circ. 25,100. Pays 4-6 weeks after publication. Publishes ms an average of 6 months after acceptance. Byline given. Buys first North American serial and simultaneous rights (in some cases). Submit seasonal material 4 months in advance. Simultaneous queries and simultaneous and previously published submissions OK. Query for electronic submissions. Reports in 6 weeks. Sample copy $1 for SAE with 6 first class stamps. Writer's guidelines for SAE.

Nonfiction: Women's health and fitness issues (pregnancy, family, pre- and post-natal, menopause and eating disorders); expose (on nutritional gimmickry); historical/nostalgic (history of various athletic events); inspirational (sports leader's motivational pieces); interview/profile (fitness figures); new product (plus equipment review); personal experience (successful fitness story); photo feature (on exercise, fitness, new sport); youth and senior fitness and travel (spas that cater to fitness industry). No articles on unsound nutritional practices, popular trends or unsafe exercise gimmicks. Buys 18-25 mss/year. Query. Length: 800-1,800 words. Pays $80-140. Sometimes pays expenses of writers on assignment.

Photos: Sports, action, fitness, aquatic aerobics, aerobic competitions and exercise classes. "We are especially interested in photos of high-adrenalin sports like rock climbing and mountain biking." Pays $10 for b&w prints; $35 for transparencies. Captions, model release, and identification of subjects required. Buys one-time rights; other rights purchased depend on use of photo.

Columns/Departments: Adventure (treks, trails and global challenges); strength (the latest breakthroughs in weight training) and clubscene (profiles and highlights of the fitness club industry). Query with published clips or send complete ms. Length: 800-1,000 words. Pays $80-100.

Fillers: Cartoons, clippings, jokes, short humor and newsbreaks. Buys 12/year. Length: 75-200 words. Pays $35.

Tips: "Cover an athletic event, get a unique angle, provide accurate and interesting findings, and write in a lively, intelligent manner. We are looking for new health and fitness reporters and writers. *AF* is a good place for first-time authors or for regularly published authors who want to sell spin-offs or reprints."

‡AQUA, The Business Magazine for Spa and Pool Professionals, AB Publications, 1846 Hoffman St., Madison WI 53704. (608)836-9470. Editor: Alan E. Sanderfoot. Managing Editor: Elissa Sard Pollack. Contact: Alan E.Sanderfoot. 20% freelance written. Monthly magazine covering swimming pools and spas. "*AQUA* is written for spa and pool dealers to help them improve their retail operations and increase their profitability." Estab. 1973. Circ. 15,000. Pays on publication. Byline given. Offers 25% kill fee. Buys first North American serial rights. Editorial lead time 2½ months. Submit seasonal material 2½ months in advance. Accepts simultaneous and previously published submissions. Query for electronic submissions. Reports in 2 weeks on queries; 1 month on mss. *Writer's Market* recommends allowing 2 months for reply. Sample copy free on request.

Nonfiction: Book excerpts, how-to, interview/profile, new product, opinion, photo feature and technical. No consumer-oriented lifestyle pieces. Buys 36 mss/year. Query with published clips. Length:1,500-2,500 words. Pays $300 minimum for assigned articles, $150 minimum for unsolicited articles. Sometimes pays expenses of writers on assignment (limit agreed upon in advance).

Photos: Send photos with submission. Reviews 3×5 prints. Negotiates payment individually. Captions and identification of subjects required. Buys one-time rights.
Columns/Departments: Sales (retail sales suggestions for spa and pool dealers), 1,000 words; Management (management tips for small retail businesses), 1,000 words; Tech Notes (technical column on some aspect of pool/spa construction or maintenance), 1,000 words. Buys 36 mss/year. Send complete ms. Pays $50 minimum.
Tips: "Read the magazine, learn about pool and spa construction, and understand retailing. We are most open to profiles—find pool/spa dealers with a unique approach to retailing and highlight that in a query."

BICYCLE BUSINESS JOURNAL, 1904 Wenneca, P.O. Box 1570, Fort Worth TX 76101. Fax: (817)870-0341. Editor: Rix Quinn. Works with a small number of new/unpublished writers each year. 10% freelance written. Monthly. Circ. 10,000. **Pays on acceptance.** Publishes ms an average of 3 months after acceptance. Buys all rights. Reprints OK; send typed manuscript with rights for sale noted and information about when and where the article previously appeared. Pays same fee as for an original article. Reports in 2 months. Sample copy for 9×12 SAE with 6 first class stamps.
Nonfiction: Stories about dealers who service what they sell, emphasizing progressive, successful sales ideas in the face of rising costs and increased competition. Length: 750 words. Sometimes pays the expenses of writers on assignment.
Photos: B&w or color glossy photo a must; vertical photo preferred. Query.

‡BOWLING PROPRIETOR, Bowling Proprietors' Association of America, P.O. Box 5802, Arlington TX 76017. (817)649-5105. Editor: Daniel W. Burgess. 5% freelance written. Monthly magazine covering bowling industry. "We cover the business of bowling, from the perspective of the owners and operators of bowling *centers* (not alleys)." Estab. 1954. Circ. 5,000. Pays on publication. Publishes ms an average of 2 months after acceptance. Byline sometimes given. Offers 50% kill fee. Buys first North American serial rights. Editorial lead time 2 months. Submit seasonal material 4 months in advance. Accepts simultaneous submissions. Query for electronic submissions. Reports in 6 weeks on queries. Sample copy free on request.
Nonfiction: Book excerpts, how-to, interview/profile, new product, opinion, technical and business angles, i.e.: marketing, customer service. "No 50s, 60s nostalgia pieces." Buys 2 mss/year. Query with published clips. Length: 500-1,200 words. Pays $300 minimum for assigned articles, $100 minimum for unsolicited articles. Sometimes pays in contributor copies or other premiums for "unsolicited, mutually beneficial articles." Sometimes pays expenses of writers on assignment (limit agreed upon in advance).
Photos: State availability of photos with submission. Reviews contact sheets, 35mm transparencies, 5×7 or 8×10 prints. Negotiates payment individually. Captions and identification of subjects required. Buys one-time rights.
Columns/Departments: News Notes (regular news items of the industry), 250 words. Buys 1 ms/year. Send complete ms. Pays $10-50.

‡EQ RETAILER, An Equestrian Publication, Equine Markets Inc., Suite 200, dBCM-4487 N. Mesa, El Paso TX 79902. (915)532-4117. Editor: Brad Cooper. Contact: Michelle Brown, managing editor. 30% freelance written. Quarterly magazine covering equestrian news and marketing information. Estab. 1992. Circ. 14,000. Pays on publication. Publishes ms an average of 3 months after acceptance. Byline given. Offers 25% kill fee. Buys one-time, second serial (reprint) rights or simultaneous rights. Editorial lead time 3 months. Submit seasonal material 6 months in advance. Accepts simultaneous and previously published submissions (if noted). Reports in 3 months on mss; 2 months on queries. Sample copy and writer's guidelines free on request.
Nonfiction: How-to (sell/market, make money on equestrian store sales), interview/profile, new product and photo feature. "No puff pieces." Buys 6 mss/year. Query with published clips. Length: 500-3500 words. Pays $200 minimum for assigned articles. Sometimes pays expenses of writers on assignment (limit agreed upon in advance).
Photos: State availability of photos with submission. Reviews contact sheets. Negotiates payment individually. Captions, model releases and identification of subjects requierd. Buys one-time rights.
Tips: "We want hard-hitting equestrian-related, sales-oriented topics. Also 'how to' make more money as a retailer/small business person. Major features—Engineering approach—'10 ways to make more money by _____.' Reader must be able to put down the magazine and say, 'I just learned something I can turn into profit.'"

IDEA TODAY, The International Association of Fitness Professionals, Dept. WM, Suite 204, 6190 Cornerstone Court E., San Diego CA 92121. (619)535-8979. Editor: Patricia A. Ryan. Executive Editor: Mary Monroe. 70% freelance written. Magazine published 10 times/year for the dance-exercise and personal training industry. "All articles must be geared to fitness professionals—aerobics instructors, one-to-one trainers and studio and health club owners—covering topics such as aerobics, nutrition, injury prevention, entrepreneurship in fitness, fitness-oriented research and exercise programs." Estab. 1984. Circ. 20,000. **Pays on acceptance.** Publishes ms an average of 4 months after acceptance. Byline given. Buys all rights. Simultaneous submissions OK. Reports in 2 months on queries. Sample copy $4.

Nonfiction: How-to, technical. No general information on fitness; our readers are pros who need detailed information. Buys 15 mss/year. Query. Length: 1,000-3,000 words. Pays $100-300.

Photos: State availability of photos with submission. Offers no additional payment for photos with ms. Model releases required. Buys all rights.

Columns/Departments: Exercise Science (detailed, specific info; must be written by expert), 750-1,500 words; Industry News (short reports on research, programs and conferences), 150-300 words; and Fitness Handout (exercise and nutrition info for participants), 750 words. Buys 80 mss/year. Query. Length: 150-1,500 words. Pays varies.

Tips: "We don't accept fitness information for the consumer audience on topics such as why exercise is good for you. Writers who have specific knowledge of, or experience working in the fitness industry have an edge."

‡**THE INTERNATIONAL SADDLERY AND APPAREL JOURNAL,** Equine Excellence Management Group, P.O. Box 3039, Berea KY 40403-3039. (606)986-4644. Fax: (606)986-1770. Editor: Pamela R. Harrell. 25% freelance written. Monthly magazine on the US equine trade. Estab. 1987. Circ. 15,000. Pays on publication. Byline given. Offers negotiable kill fee. Buys first North American serial rights. Reports in 1 month on queries. Sample copy and writer's guidelines $4.

Nonfiction: Expose (business-oriented), how-to (should be useable business information), interview/profile (with industry people). We are not a "backyard," casual interest horse magazine. No fiction. Buys 60 mss/year. Query with published clips. Length: 1,000-2,500 words. Payment based on piece and the information and value of the article. Rarely pays expenses of writers on assignment.

Photos: State availability or send photos with submissions. Reviews 3½ × 5 prints. Offers $5-15/photo (negotiable). Captions or model releases required. Buys one-time rights.

Columns/Departments: International (overseas, business interest pieces), 1,000 words; Retail Marketing (articles that give tack shop retailers information about marketing products), 1,000 words. Buys 10 mss/year. Query with published clips.

Tips: "Read *SAJ* and other trade publications. Understand that we serve the professional business community, including: tack shops, feed stores, gift shops, veterinarians, farriers and manufacturers. People in the equine trade are like other business-people; they have employees, need insurance, travel, own computers, advertise and want pertinent business information."

POOL & SPA NEWS, Leisure Publications, 3923 W. 6th St., Los Angeles CA 90020-4290. (213)385-3926. Fax: (213)383-1152. Editor-in-Chief: Jim McCloskey. 15-20% freelance written. Semimonthly magazine emphasizing news of the swimming pool and spa industry for pool builders, pool retail stores and pool service firms. Estab. 1960. Circ. 17,000. Pays on publication. Publishes ms an average of 1-2 months after acceptance. Buys all rights. Query for electronic submissions. Reports in 2 weeks. Sample copy $5 for 9 × 12 SAE with 10 first class stamps.

Nonfiction: Interview, new product, profile and technical. Phone queries OK. Length: 500-2,000 words. Pays 5-14¢/word. Pays expenses of writers on assignment.

Photos: Pays $10/b&w photo used.

PROFESSIONAL BOATBUILDER MAGAZINE, WoodenBoat Publications Inc., P.O. Box 78, Naskeag Rd., Brooklin ME 04616-0078. (207)359-4651. Fax: (207)359-8920. Editor: Chris Cornell. 75% freelance written. Bimonthly magazine for boat building companies, repair yards, naval architects, and marine surveyors. Estab. 1989. Circ. 20,000. Pays 45 days after acceptance. Byline given. Offers 20% kill fee. Buys first North American serial rights. Publishes reprints of previously published articles. Send tearsheet of article, or send typed ms with rights for sale noted. Include information about when and where article previously appeared. For reprints, pays 50% of fee paid for an original article. Reports in 2 months. Free sample copy and writer's guidelines.

Nonfiction: How-to, new product, opinion, technical. No information better directed to consumers. Buys 20 mss/year. Query with or without published clips or send complete ms. Length: 1,000-4,000 words. Pays 20¢/word. Sometimes pays expenses of writers on assignment.

Photos: State availability of photos with submission. Reviews transparencies and 8 × 10 b&w prints. Offers $15-200/photo; $350 for color cover. Identification of subjects and full captions required. Buys one-time rights.

Columns/Departments: Barbara Walsh, managing editor. Tools of the Trade (new tools/materials/machinery of interest to boatbuilders), 100-500 words. Buys 10 mss/year. Query with published clips. Pays $25-100.

PRORODEO SPORTS NEWS, Professional Rodeo Cowboys Association, 101 Pro Rodeo Dr., Colorado Springs CO 80919-9989. (719)593-8840. Fax: (719)593-8235. Editor: Kendra Santos. Biweekly tabloid that covers PRCA Rodeo. "The *Prorodeo Sports News* is the official publication of the PRCA, covering cowboys, stock contractors, contract members and general rodeo-related news about the PRCA membership and PRCA sponsors. We do not print material about any non-sanctioned rodeo event, or other rodeo associations." Estab. 1952. Circ. 35,000. Pays on publication. Publishes ms 1 month after acceptance. Byline given. Submit seasonal material 2 months in advance. Sample copy for 8 × 10 SAE with 4 first class stamps. Free writer's guidelines.

Nonfiction: Interview/profile and photo feature. Buys 15 mss/year. Query. Length: 1,500 words maximum. Pays $50-100. Sometimes pays expenses of writers on assignment.

Photos: Send photos with submission. Reviews negatives and 5×7 and 8×10 prints. Offers $15-85/photo. Identification of subjects required.

Tips: "Feature stories written about PRCA cowboys will always be considered for publication. Along with feature stories on PRCA members, I foresee the *Prorodeo Sports News* printing more articles about rodeo sponsorship and creative rodeo promotions. Like all professional sports, PRCA rodeo is a business. The *Prorodeo Sports News* will reflect the business aspect of professional rodeo, as well as cover the people who make it all happen."

SWIMMING POOL/SPA AGE, Communication Channels, Inc., Suite 200, 6151 Powers Ferry Rd., Atlanta GA 30339. (404)955-2500. Fax: (404)955-0400. Editor: Terri Simmons. 30% freelance written. Works with a small number of new/unpublished writers each year. Monthly tabloid emphasizing pool, spa and hot tub industry. Estab. 1926. Circ. 17,500. Pays on publication. Publishes ms an average of 3 months after acceptance. Buys all rights. Submit seasonal material 3 months in advance. Query for electronic submissions.

Nonfiction: How-to (installation techniques, service and repairs, tips, etc.); interview (with people and groups within the industry); photo feature (pool/spa/tub construction or special use); technical (should be prepared with expert within the industry); industry news; and market research reports. Also, comparison articles exploring the same type of products produced by numerous manufacturers. Buys 1-3 unsolicited mss/year. Query. Length: 250-2,500 words. Pays 10¢/word. Sometimes pays the expenses of writers on assignment.

Photos: Purchased with accompanying ms or on assignment. Query or send contact sheet. Will accept 35mm transparencies of good quality. Captions required.

Tips: "If a writer can produce easily understood technical articles containing unbiased, hard facts, we are definitely interested. We will be concentrating on technical and how-to articles because that's what our readers want."

‡TENNIS BUYER'S GUIDE, New York Times Magazine Group, 5520 Park Ave., Trumbull CT 06611-0395. (203)373-7232. Fax: (203)373-7033. Editor: Sandra Dolbow. 5% freelance written. A bimonthly tabloid on the tennis industry. "We publish for the tennis retailer. We favor a business angle, providing information that will make our readers better tennis professionals and better business people." Estab. 1985. Circ. 11,000. Pays on publication. Publishes ms an average of 3 months after acceptance. Byline given. Offers 15% kill fee. Buys one-time rights. Submit seasonal/holiday material 6 months in advance. Simultaneous submissions OK. Reports in 6 weeks on queries.

Nonfiction: How-to, interview/profile, new product, photo feature, technical and travel. No professional tennis tour articles. Buys 8 mss/year. Send complete ms. Length: 500-2,000 words. Pays $75-300 for assigned articles. Pays $50-300 for unsolicited articles. Sometimes pays the expenses of writers on assignment.

Photos: Reviews transparencies and prints (35mm). Captions, model releases and identification of subjects required. Buys one-time rights.

Tips: "Express an interest in and knowledge of tennis or a business management field and an understanding of retail business."

THOROUGHBRED TIMES, Thoroughbred Publications, Inc., Suite 101, 801 Corporate Dr., P.O. Box 8237, Lexington KY 40533. (606)223-9800. Editor: Mark Simon. 10% freelance written. Weekly tabloid that covers thoroughbred racing and breeding. "Articles are written for professionals who breed and/or race thoroughbreds at tracks in the US. Articles must help owners and breeders understand racing to show profit." Estab. 1985. Circ. 21,000. Pays on publication. Publishes ms an average of 1 month after acceptance. Byline given. Offers 50% kill fee. Buys all rights. Submit seasonal material 2 months in advance. Query for electronic submissions. Reports in 2 weeks. Free sample copy.

Nonfiction: General interest, historical/nostalgic, interview/profile, technical. Buys 52 mss/year. Query. Length: 500-2,500 words. Pays 10-20¢/word. Sometimes pays expenses of writers on assignment.

Photos: State availability of photos with submission. Reviews prints. Offers $25/photo. Identification of subjects required. Buys one-time rights.

Tips: "We are looking for farm stories and profiles of owners, breeders, jockeys and trainers."

WOODALL'S CAMPGROUND MANAGEMENT, Woodall Publishing Co., 28167 N. Keith Dr., Lake Forest IL 60045-4528. (708)362-6700. Editor: Mike Byrnes. 10% freelance written. Monthly tabloid covering campground management and operation for managers of private and public campgrounds throughout the US. Estab. 1970. Circ. 10,000. Pays after publication. Publishes ms an average of 8 months after acceptance. Byline given. Buys all rights. Will reassign rights to author upon written request. Submit seasonal material 4

The double dagger before a listing indicates that the listing is new in this edition. New markets are often more receptive to freelance submissions.

months in advance. Simultaneous queries OK. Reports in 1 month on queries; 2 months on mss. Free sample copy and writer's guidelines.

Nonfiction: How-to, interview/profile and technical. "Our articles tell our readers how to maintain their resources, manage personnel and guests, market, develop new campground areas and activities, and interrelate with the major tourism organizations within their areas. 'Improvement' and 'profit' are the two key words." Buys 14 mss/year. Query. Length: 500 words minimum. Pays $50-200.

Photos: Send contact sheets and negatives. "We pay for each photo used."

Tips: "The best type of story to break in with is a case history approach about how a campground improved its maintenance, physical plant or profitability."

Stone, Quarry and Mining

COAL PEOPLE MAGAZINE, Al Skinner Productions, Dept. WM, 629 Virginia St. W., P.O. Box 6247, Charleston WV 25362. (304)342-4129. Fax: (304)343-3124. Editor/Publisher: Al Skinner. 50% freelance written. Monthly magazine with stories about coal people, towns and history. "Most stories are about people or historical—either narrative or biographical on all levels of coal people, past and present—from coal execs down to grass roots miners. Most stories are upbeat—showing warmth of family or success from underground up!" Estab. 1976. Circ. 11,000. Pays on publication. Publishes ms an average of 3 months after acceptance. Byline given. Buys first rights, second serial (reprint) rights and makes work-for-hire assignments. Will buy rewrites of previously published material. Submit seasonal material 2 months in advance. Reports in 3 months. Sample copy for 9 × 12 SAE with 10 first class stamps.

Nonfiction: Book excerpts (and film if related to coal), historical/nostalgic (coal towns, people, lifestyles), humor (including anecdotes and cartoons), interview/profile (for coal personalities), personal experience (as relates to coal mining), photo feature (on old coal towns, people, past and present). January issue every year is calendar issue for more than 300 annual coal shows, association meetings, etc. July issue is always surface mining/reclamation award issue. December issue is Christmas in Coal Country issue. No poetry, no fiction or environmental attacks on the coal industry. Buys 32 mss/year. Query with published clips. Length: 5,000 words. Pays $50.

Photos: Send photos with submission. Reviews contact sheets, transparencies, and 5 × 7 prints. Captions and identification of subjects required. Buys one-time rights and one-time reprint rights.

Columns/Departments: Editorials—anything to do with current coal issues (non-paid); Mine'ing Our Business (bull pen column—gossip—humorous anecdotes), Coal Show Coverage (freelance photojournalist coverage of any coal function across the US). Buys 10 mss/year. Query. Length: 300-500 words. Pays $5.

Fillers: Anecdotes. Buys 10/year. Length: 300 words. Pays $5.

Tips: "We are looking for good feature articles on coal people, towns, companies—past and present, color slides (for possible cover use) and b&w photos to complement stories. Could also use a few news writers to take photos and do journalistic coverage on coal events across the country. Slant stories more toward people and less on historical. More faces and names than old town, company store photos. Include more quotes from people who lived these moments!" The following geographical areas are covered: Eastern Canada; Mexico; Europe; China; Russia; Poland; Australia; as well as US states Alabama, Tennessee, Virginia, Washington, Oregon, North and South Dakota, Arizona, Colorado, Alaska and Wyoming.

DIMENSIONAL STONE, Dimensional Stone Institute, Inc., Dept. WM, Suite 400, 20335 Ventura Blvd., Woodland Hills CA 91364. (818)704-5555. Fax: (818)704-6500. Editor: John Maynard. 25% freelance written. Monthly magazine covering dimensional stone use for managers of producers, importers, contractors, fabricators and specifiers of dimensional stone. Estab. 1979. Circ. 15,849. Pays on publication. Publishes ms an average of 2 months after acceptance. Byline given. Buys first rights or second serial (reprint) rights. Reports in 1 month. Reprints OK; send tearsheet of article and information about when and where the article previously appeared. Pays 50% of their fee for an original article. Sample copy for 9 × 12 SAE with 11 first class stamps. Writer's guidelines for #10 SASE.

Nonfiction: Interview/profile and technical, only on users of dimensional stone. Buys 6-7 mss/year. Send complete ms. Length: 1,000-3,000 words. Pays $100 maximum. Sometimes pays the expenses of writers on assignment.

Photos: Send photos with submission. Reviews any size prints. Offers no additional payment for photos accepted with ms. Identification of subjects required.

Tips: "Articles on outstanding uses of dimensional stone are most open to freelancers."

GOLD PROSPECTOR, Gold Prospectors Association of America, Dept. WM, P.O. Box 507, Bonsall CA 92003. (909)699-4749. Editor-in-Chief: George Massie. Managing Editor: Perry Massie. Production Editor: Tom Kraak. 60% freelance written. Eager to work with new/unpublished writers. Bimonthly magazine covering gold prospecting and mining. "*Gold Prospector* magazine is the official publication of the Gold Prospectors Association of America. The GPAA is an international organization of more than 25,000 members who are interested in recreational prospecting and mining. Our primary audience is people of all ages who like to take their prospecting gear with them on their weekend camping trips, and fishing and hunting trips. Our readers are interested not only in prospecting, but camping, fishing, hunting, skiing, backpacking, etc. We try to carry stories in each issue pertaining to subjects besides prospecting." Estab. 1965. Circ. 50,000. Pays on publication. Publishes ms an average of 6 months after acceptance. Byline given. Buys first North American serial and second serial (reprint) rights. Submit seasonal/holiday material 6 months in advance. Simultaneous queries and previously published submissions OK. Reports in 6 weeks. Sample copy $2. Writer's guidelines for #10 SASE.

Nonfiction: Historical/nostalgic, how-to (prospecting techniques, equipment building, etc.), humor, new product, personal experience, technical and travel. "One of our publishing beliefs is that our audience would rather experience life than watch it on television—that they would like to take a rough and tumble chance with the sheer adventure of taking gold from the ground or river after it has perhaps lain there for a million years. Even if they don't, they seem to enjoy reading about those who do in the pages of *Gold Prospector* magazine." Buys 75-100 mss/year. Query with or without published clips if available or send complete ms. Length: 1,000-3,000 words. Pays 75¢/column inch (photos and illustrations are measured the same as type).

Photos: State availability of photos with query or ms. Pays 75¢/column inch for photos, transparencies or reflective art. Buys all rights.

Tips: "Articles must be slanted to interest a prospector, miner, or treasure hunter. For example, a first-aid article could address possible mining accidents. Any subject can be so tailored."

MINE REGULATION REPORTER, Pasha Publications, #1000, 1616 N. Fort Myer Dr., Arlington VA 22209. (703)528-1244. Editor: Ellen Smith. 30% freelance written. Biweekly newsletter covering health, safety and environmental issues that relate to mine operations. Estab. 1989. Pays on publication. Publishes ms an average of 1 week after acceptance. Offers $25 kill fee. Buys all rights. Simultaneous submissions OK. Query for electronic submissions, which are preferred. Free sample copy.

Nonfiction: Interview/profile, new product, technical. Buys 2 mss/year. Query. Pays $12.50/published inch—minimum 5 inches. Sometimes pays expenses of writers on assignment.

Tips: "Just give us the facts." Stories wanted on safety, health or environmental issues, such as in the mining industry.

STONE REVIEW, National Stone Association, 1415 Elliot Place NW, Washington DC 20007-2506. (202)342-1100. Fax: (202)342-0702. Editor: Frank Atlee. Bimonthly magazine covering quarrying and supplying of crushed stone, "designed to be a communications forum for the crushed stone industry. Publishes information on industry technology, trends, developments and concerns. Audience are quarry operations/management, and manufacturers of equipment, suppliers of services to the industry." Estab. 1985. Circ. 4,000. Pays on publication. Publishes ms an average of 3 months after acceptance. Byline given. Negotiable kill fee. Buys one-time rights. Simultaneous submissions OK. Reprints OK; send tearsheet, photocopy or typed ms with information about when and where the article previously appeared. Payment negotiable. Reports in 1 month. Sample copy for 9 × 12 SAE with 3 first class stamps.

Nonfiction: Technical. Query with or without published clips or send complete ms. Length: 1,000-2,500 words. "Note: We have no budget for freelance material, but I'm willing to secure payment for right material."

Photos: State availability of photos with query, then send photos with submission. Reviews contact sheets, negatives, transparencies and prints. Offers no additional payment for photos accepted with ms. Identification of subjects required. Buys one-time rights.

Tips: "At this point, most features are written by contributors in the industry, but I'd like to open it up. Articles on unique equipment, applications, etc. are good, as are those reporting on trends (e.g., there is a strong push on now for environmentally sound operations). Also interested in stories on family-run operations involving three or more generations."

STONE WORLD, Tradelink Publishing Company, Suite 205, 1 Kalisa Way, Paramus NJ 07652. (201)599-0136. Fax: (201)599-2378. Editor: John Sailer. Associate Editor: Susan Springstead. Monthly magazine on natural building stone for producers and users of granite, marble, limestone, slate, sandstone, onyx and other natural stone products. Estab. 1984. Circ. 16,000. Pays on publication. Publishes ms an average of 6 months after acceptance. Byline given. Buys first rights or second serial (reprint) rights. Submit seasonal material 6 months in advance. Reprints OK; send photocopy of article. Pays 100% of their fee for an original article. Reports in 2 months. Sample copy for $10.

Nonfiction: How-to (fabricate and/or install natural building stone), interview/profile, photo feature, technical, architectural design, artistic stone uses, statistics, factory profile, equipment profile and trade show review. Buys 25 mss/year. Query with or without published clips or send complete ms. Length: 600-3,000 words. Pays $115/page. Pays the expenses of writers on assignment.

Photos: State availability of photos with submission. Reviews transparencies and prints. Pays $10/photo accepted with ms. Captions and identification of subjects required. Buys one-time rights.

Columns/Departments: News (pertaining to stone or design community); New Literature (brochures, catalogs, books, videos, etc. about stone); New Products (stone products); New Equipment (equipment and machinery for working with stone); Calendar (dates and locations of events in stone and design communities). Query or send complete ms. Length: 300-600 words. Pays $4/inch.

Tips: "Articles about architectural stone design accompanied by professional color photographs and quotes from designing firms are often published, as are articles about new techniques of quarrying and/or fabricating natural building stone."

Toy, Novelty and Hobby

Publications focusing on the toy and hobby industry are listed in this section. For magazines for hobbyists see the Consumer Hobby and Craft section.

PLAYTHINGS, Geyer-McAllister, 51 Madison Ave., New York NY 10010-1675. (212)689-4411. Fax: (212)683-7929. Editor: Frank Reysen, Jr. Executive Editor: Eugene Gilligan. 20-30% freelance written. Monthly merchandising magazine covering toys and hobbies aimed mainly at mass market toy retailers. Estab. 1903. Circ. 15,000. **Pays on acceptance.** Publishes ms an average of 3 months after acceptance. Byline sometimes given. Buys one-time rights. Submit seasonal material 3 months in advance. Simultaneous submissions OK. Reports in 1 month. Free sample copy and writer's guidelines.
Nonfiction: Interview/profile, photo feature and retail profiles of toy and hobby stores and chains. Annual directory published in May. Buys 10 mss/year. Query. Length: 900-2,500 words. Pays $100-350. Sometimes pays the expenses of writers on assignment.
Photos: Send photos with submission. Captions and identification of subjects required. Buys one-time rights.
Columns/Departments: Buys 5 mss/year. Query. Pays $100-200.

‡**SOUVENIRS & NOVELTIES MAGAZINE,** Kane Communications, Inc., Suite 210, 7000 Terminal Square, Upper Darby PA 19082. President: Scott Borowsky. Editor: Sandy Meschkow. Magazine published 7 times/year for resort and gift industry. Circ. 27,000. Pays on publication. Byline given. Buys all rights. Reports in 3 weeks. Sample copy for 6×9 SAE with 5 first class stamps.
Nonfiction: Interview/profile and new product. Buys 6 mss/year. Query. Length: 700-1,500 words. Pays $25-175 for assigned articles. Sometimes pays the expenses of writers on assignment.
Photos: State availability of photos with submission. Captions, model releases and identification of subjects required.

THE STAMP WHOLESALER, P.O. Box 706, Albany OR 97321-0006. (503)928-4484. Fax: (503)967-7262. Managing Editor: Carol Ann Lysek. 80% freelance written. Newspaper published 28 times/year for philatelic businesspeople; many are part-time and/or retired from other work. Estab. 1937. Circ. 4,700. Pays on publication. Byline given. Buys all rights. Reports in 1 month. Free sample copy and writer's guidelines.
Nonfiction: "Focus on how-to, general business techniques, computer how-to for business, stamp business trends and history, specialty aspects of the stamp business i.e., auctions, catalogs, postal history, cinderellas, approvals, mail order, opinion pieces. The articles must be directed specifically to stamp dealers. Most of our writers are stamp dealers themselves." Buys 120 ms/year. Submit complete ms. Length: 1,000-2,000 words. Pays $35 and up/article.
Tips: "Send queries on business stories or stamp dealer profiles. We need stories to help dealers make and save money. We also buy cartoons on stamp dealer topics. We especially need business profiles of stamp dealers located in various parts of the country. We pay $250 for these, but we expect an in-depth, facts and figures business article with color pictures in return. We are also looking for writers who can write about computers in a way that is relevant to small business stamp dealers."

Transportation

These publications are for professional movers and people involved in transportation of goods. For magazines focusing on trucking see also Auto and Truck.

BUS WORLD, Magazine of Buses and Bus Systems, Stauss Publications, P.O. Box 39, Woodland Hills CA 91365-0039. (818)710-0208. Editor: Ed Stauss. 25% freelance written. Quarterly trade journal covering the transit and intercity bus industries. Estab. 1978. Circ. 5,000. Pays on publication. Reports in 1 month. Sample copy with writer's guidelines $2.
Photos: "We buy photos with manuscripts under one payment."
Fillers: Cartoons. Buys 4-6/year. Pays $10.
Tips: "No tourist or travelog viewpoints. Be employed in or have a good understanding of the bus industry. Be enthusiastic about buses—their history and future. Acceptable material will be held until used and will not be returned unless requested by sender. Unacceptable and excess material will be returned only if accompanied by suitable SASE."

INBOUND LOGISTICS, Thomas Publishing Co., Dept. WM, 8th Floor, 5 Penn Plaza, New York NY 10001. (212)629-1560. Fax: (212)629-1584. Publisher: Keith Biondo. Editor: Felicia Stratton. 50% freelance written. Prefers to work with published/established writers. Monthly magazine covering the transportation industry. "*Inbound Logistics* is distributed to people who buy, specify, or recommend inbound freight transportation services and equipment. The editorial matter provides basic explanations of inbound freight transportation, directory listings, how-to technical information, trends and developments affecting inbound freight movements, and expository, case history feature stories." Estab. 1980. Circ. 46,000. Pays on publication. Publishes ms an average of 3 months after acceptance. Byline given. Buys all rights. Simultaneous queries and submissions OK. Reports in 2 months. Reprints OK: send tearsheet of article and information about when and where the article previously appeared. Pays 20% of their fee for an original article. Sample copy and writer's guidelines for 9×12 SAE with 5 first class stamps.
Nonfiction: How-to (basic help for purchasing agents and traffic managers) and interview/profile (purchasing and transportation professionals). Buys 20 mss/year. Query with published clips. Length: 750-1,000 words. Pays $100-400. Pays expenses of writers on assignment.
Photos: Chelsea Michaels, photo editor. State availability of photos with query. Pays $100-500 for b&w contact sheets, negatives, transparencies and prints; $250-500 for color contact sheets, negative transparencies and prints. Captions and identification of subjects required.
Columns/Departments: Viewpoint (discusses current opinions on transportation topics). Query with published clips.
Tips: "Have a sound knowledge of the transportation industry; educational how-to articles get our attention."

THE PRIVATE CARRIER, Private Carrier Conference, Inc., Suite 720, 1320 Braddock Place, Alexandria VA 22314-1649. (703)683-1300. Fax: (703)683-1217. Editor: Don Tepper. 20% freelance written. Monthly magazine on freight transportation. "*The Private Carrier* is the national publication for private fleet managers. Its goal is to help them manage their private fleets and their other transportation activities as efficiently and cost-effectively as possible." Circ. 16,000. Pays on publication. Publishes ms an average of 2 months after acceptance. Byline given. Offers $100 maximum kill fee. "We buy first rights and retain right for reprint. However, after publication, writer may use/sell article as he/she sees fit." Submit seasonal material 3 months in advance. Reprints OK; send photocopy of article and typed manuscript with rights for sale noted. Pays 50% of their fee for an original article. Reports in 3 months. Sample copy for 9×12 SAE with 4 first class stamps.
Nonfiction: Expose, interview/profile, opinion and photo feature. Buys 10 mss/year. Query. Length: 1,000-3,000 words. Pays $100-250. Sometimes pays the expenses of writers on assignment.
Photos: Send photos with submission. Reviews transparencies (35mm) and prints (5×7 or 8×10). Offers no additional payment for photos accepted with ms. When necessary model releases and identification of subjects required. Buys one-time rights.
Columns/Departments: Computer Briefs (computer software for transportation); On The Road (humorous true items dealing with transportation); and Picture This (humorous photos dealing with transportation). Send complete ms. Length: 100-300 words. Pays $10-50.
Tips: "Tailor articles to our readers. Writing style is less important than clean, well-written copy. We love good photos or articles that lend themselves to good illustrations. We like the slightly off-beat, unconventional or novel way to look at subjects. Articles for whatever department that profile how a private fleet solved a problem (i.e., computers, drivers, maintenance, etc.). The structure is: 1) company identifies a problem, 2) evaluates options, 3) selects a solution, and 4) evaluates its choice."

‡**SHIPPING DIGEST, The National Shipping Weekly of Export Transportation,** Geyer McAllister Publications Inc., 51 Madison Ave., New York NY 10010. (212)689-4411. Fax: (212)683-7929. Editor: Maria Reines. 20% freelance written. Weekly magazine that covers ocean, surface, air transportation, ports, intermodal and EDI. "Read by executives responsible for exporting US goods to foreign markets. Emphasis is on services offered by ocean, surface and air carriers, their development and trends; port developments; trade agreements; government regulation; electronic data interchange." Pays on publication. Publishes ms an average of 1 month after acceptance. Byline given. Buys first rights. Reports in 1 month. Free sample copy and writers guidelines.
Nonfiction: Interview/profile. Query. Length: 800-1,500 words. Pays $125-300.
Photos: State availability of photos with submission. Reviews contact sheets and 5×7 prints. Offers no payment for photos accepted with ms. Identification of subjects required. Buys one-time rights.

Travel

Travel professionals read these publications to keep up with trends, tours and changes in transportation. Magazines about vacations and travel for the general public are listed in the Consumer Travel section.

BUS TOURS MAGAZINE, The Magazine of Bus Tours and Long Distance Charters, National Bus Trader, Inc., 9698 W. Judson Rd., Polo IL 61064-9015. (815)946-2341. Fax: (815)946-2347. Editor: Larry Plachno. Editorial Assistant: Carol Merbach. 80% freelance written. Eager to work with new/unpublished writers. Bimonthly magazine for bus companies and tour brokers who design or sell bus tours. Estab. 1979. Circ. 9,306. Pays as arranged. Publishes ms an average of 6 months after acceptance. Byline given. Not copyrighted. Buys rights as arranged. Submit seasonal material 9 months in advance. Simultaneous queries OK. Reports in 1 month. Sample copy and writer's guidelines for 9 × 12 SAE.

Nonfiction: Historical/nostalgic, how-to, humor, interview/profile, new product, professional, personal experience and travel; all on bus tours. Buys 10 mss/year. Query. Length: open. Pays negotiable fee.

Photos: State availability of photos. Reviews 35mm transparencies and 6 × 9 or 8 × 10 prints. Caption, model release and identification of subjects required.

Columns/Departments: Bus Tour Marketing; and Buses and the Law. Buys 15-20 mss/year. Query. Length: 1-1½ pages.

Tips: "Most of our feature articles are written by freelancers under contract from local convention and tourism bureaus. Specifications sent on request. Writers should query local bureaus regarding their interest. Writer need not have extensive background and knowledge of bus tours."

‡MEXICO UPDATE, For the North American travel industry, Travel Mexico Magazine Group, P.O. Box 188037, Carlsbad CA 92009-0801. (619)929-0707. Group Editor: Katharine A. Diáz. 50% freelance written. Bimonthly magazine covering tourism and travel to Mexico. "*Mexico Update* focuses on keeping travel professionals in the US and Canada up to date on the travel industry in Mexico. Our goal is to help them better sell Mexico as a travel destination to their clients. Target: travel agents; wholesalers; tour operators; incentive, meeting and convention planners; etc." Estab. 1992. Circ. 41,000. Pays on publication. Publishes ms an average of 1-2 months after acceptance. Byline given. Buys first rights. Editorial lead time 2-3 months. Submit seasonal material 4-5 months in advance. Query for electronic submissions. Reports in 2 weeks on queries; 1 month on mss. *Writer's Market* recommends allowing 2 months for reply. Sample copy for 10 × 13 SAE with 6 first class stamps. Writer's guidelines for #10 SASE.

Nonfiction: Travel and Mexico only from trade angle. "We do not want articles that focus on any other topic than Mexico." Buys 35 mss/year. Query with published clips. Length: 400-1,200 words. Pays $100 minimum.

Photos: Send photos with submission. Reviews transparencies and slides. Offers $20-200/photo. Captions and identification of subjects required. Buys one-time rights.

Tips: "We are looking for writers who have had experience writing about the travel trade—specifically Mexico. Freelancers should have intimate knowledge of Mexico's travel industry infrastructure, key players within the industry, organizations and associations, hotels and other travel service providers. Because we work only on assignment it's best to send query with published clips (that will be kept on file unless SASE enclosed) that establish writer's expertise."

NATIONAL BUS TRADER, The Magazine of Bus Equipment for the United States and Canada, 9698 W. Judson Rd., Polo IL 61064-9015. (815)946-2341. Fax: (815)946-2347. Editor: Larry Plachno. 25% freelance written. Eager to work with new/unpublished writers. Monthly magazine for manufacturers, dealers and owners of buses and motor coaches. Estab. 1977. Circ. 7,354. Pays on either acceptance or publication. Publishes ms an average of 3 months after acceptance. Byline given. Not copyrighted. Buys rights "as required by writer." Simultaneous queries, simultaneous and previously published submissions OK. Reports in 1 month. Sample copy for 9 × 12 SAE.

Nonfiction: Historical/nostalgic (on old buses); how-to (maintenance repair); new products; photo feature; and technical (aspects of mechanical operation of buses). "We are finding that more and more firms and agencies are hiring freelancers to write articles to our specifications. We are more likely to run them if someone else pays." No material that does *not* pertain to bus tours or bus equipment. Buys 3-5 unsolicited mss/year. Query. Length varies. Pays variable rate. Sometimes pays the expenses of writers on assignment.

Photos: State availability of photos. Reviews 5 × 7 or 8 × 10 prints and 35mm transparencies. Captions, model release and identification of subjects required.

Columns/Departments: Bus maintenance; Buses and the Law; Regulations; and Bus of the Month. Buys 20-30 mss/year. Query. Length: 250-400 words. Pays variable rate.

Tips: "We are a very technical magazine. Writers should submit qualifications showing extensive background in bus vehicles. We're very interested in well-researched articles on older bus models and manufacturers, or current converted coaches. We would like to receive history of individual bus models prior to 1953 and history of GMC 'new look' models. Write or phone editors with article concept or outline for comments and approval."

RV BUSINESS, TL Enterprises, Inc., 29901 Agoura Rd., Agoura CA 91301. (818)991-4980. Fax: (818)991-8102. Editor: Katherine Sharma. 60% freelance written. Prefers to work with published/established writers. Monthly magazine covering the recreational vehicle and allied industries for people in the RV industry—dealers, manufacturers, suppliers and finance experts. Estab. 1950. Circ. 19,000. **Pays on acceptance.** Publishes ms an average of 2 months after acceptance. Byline given. Offers 50% kill fee. Buys first North

American serial rights. Submit seasonal material 6 months in advance. Query for electronic submissions. Reports in 2 months. Sample copy for 9×12 SAE with 5 first class stamps.

Nonfiction: Technical, financial, legal or marketing issues; how-to (deal with any specific aspect of the RV business); specifics and verification of statistics required—must be factual; and technical (photos required, 4-color preferred). General business articles may be considered. Buys 50 mss/year. Query with published clips. Send complete ms—"but only read on speculation." Length: 1,000-1,500 words. Pays variable rate up to $500. Sometimes pays expenses of writers on assignment.

Photos: State availability of photos with query or send photos with ms. Reviews 35mm transparencies and 8×10 b&w prints. Captions, model release, and identification of subjects required. Buys one-time or all rights; unused photos returned.

Columns/Departments: Guest editorial; News (50-500 words maximum, b&w photos appreciated); and RV People (color photos/4-color transparencies; this section lends itself to fun, upbeat copy). Buys 100-120 mss/year. Query or send complete ms. Pays $25-200 "depending on where used and importance."

Tips: "Query. Phone OK; letter preferable. Send one or several ideas and a few lines letting us know how you plan to treat it/them. We are always looking for good authors knowledgable in the RV industry or related industries. Change of editorial focus requires more articles that are brief, factual, hard hitting, business oriented and in-depth. Will work with promising writers, published or unpublished."

‡**SPECIALTY TRAVEL INDEX**, Alpine Hansen, #313, 305 San Anselmo Ave., San Anselmo CA 94960. (415)459-4900. Editor: C. Steen Hansen. Managing Editor: Barbara Bell. Contact: C. Steen Hansen. 90% freelance written. Semiannual magazine covering adventure and special interest travel. Estab. 1980. Circ. 45,000. Pays on publication. Byline given. Buys one-time rights. Editorial lead time 3 months. Submit seasonal material 3 months in advance. Accepts previously published submissions. Query for electronic submissions. Sample copy and writer's guidelines free on request.

Nonfiction: How-to, new product, personal experience, photo feature and travel. Buys 15 mss/year. Query. Length: 1,000 words. Pays $200 minimum.

Photos: State availability of photos with submission. Reviews 35mm transparencies and 5×7 prints. Negotiates payment individually. Captions and identification of subjects required.

STAR SERVICE, Reed Travel Group, 500 Plaza Dr., Secaucus NJ 07096-3602. (201)902-2000. Fax: (201)902-7989. Publisher: Steven R. Gordon. "Eager to work with new/unpublished writers as well as those working from a home base abroad, planning trips that would allow time for hotel reporting, or living in major ports for cruise ships." Worldwide guide to accommodations and cruise ships founded in 1960 (as *Sloane Travel Agency Reports*) and sold to travel agencies on subscription basis. Pays 15 days after publication. Buys all rights. Query should include details on writer's experience in travel and writing, clips, specific forthcoming travel plans, and how much time would be available for hotel or ship inspections. Buys 5,000 reports/year. Pays $18/report used. Sponsored trips are acceptable. General query statement should precede electronic submission. Reports in 3 months. Writer's guidelines and list of available assignments for #10 SASE.

Nonfiction: Objective, critical evaluations of hotels and cruise ships suitable for international travelers, based on personal inspections. Freelance correspondents ordinarily are assigned to update an entire state or country. "Assignment involves on-site inspections of all hotels and cruise ships we review; revising and updating published reports; and reviewing new properties. Qualities needed are thoroughness, precision, perseverance and keen judgment. Solid research skills and powers of observation are crucial. Travel and travel writing experience are highly desirable. Reviews must be colorful, clear, and documented with hotel's brochure, rate sheet, etc. We accept no hotel advertising or payment for listings, so reviews should dispense praise and criticism where deserved."

Tips: "We may require sample hotel or cruise reports on facilities near freelancer's hometown before giving the first assignment. No byline because of sensitive nature of reviews."

‡**TRAVELAGE WEST**, Official Airline Guides, Inc., # 460, 49 Stevenson St., San Francisco CA 94105. Managing Editor: Robert Carlsen. 5% freelance written. Prefers to work with published/established writers. Weekly magazine for travel agency sales counselors in the western US and Canada. Estab. 1969. Circ. 35,000. Pays on publication. Publishes ms an average of 1 month after acceptance. Byline given. Buys all rights. Offers kill fee. Submit seasonal/holiday material 2 months in advance. Query for electronic submissions. Reports in 6 months. Free writer's guidelines.

Nonfiction: Travel. "No promotional approach or any hint of do-it-yourself travel. Emphasis is on news, not description. No static descriptions of places, particularly resort hotels." Buys 40 mss/year. Query. Length: 1,000 words maximum. Pays $2/column inch.

Tips: "Query should be a straightforward description of the proposed story, including (1) an indication of the news angle, no matter how tenuous, and (2) a recognition by the author that we run a trade magazine for travel agents, not a consumer book. I am particularly turned off by letters that try to get me all worked up about the 'beauty' or excitement of some place. Authors planning to travel might discuss with us a proposed angle before they go; otherwise their chances of gathering the right information are slim."

Veterinary

NEW METHODS, The Journal of Animal Health Technology, Dept. WM, P.O. Box 22605, San Francisco CA 94122-0605. (415)664-3469. Managing Editor: Ronald S. Lippert, AHT. Monthly "educational and informational newsletter about animal health technology." Estab. 1976. Circ. 5,600. Pays on publication. Byline given. Buys simultaneous rights. Submit seasonal material 2 months in advance. Simultaneous submissions OK. Reports in 1 month. Reprints OK; send photocopy of article and information about when and where the article previously appeared. Sample copy for $2.90. Writer's guidelines for #10 SASE.
Nonfiction: How-to (technical), new product and technical. Buys 1 ms/year. Query. Pays in contributor copies or other premiums. Sometimes pays expenses of writers on assignment.
Photos: State availability of photos with submission. Reviews contact sheets. Offers variable payment. Captions, model releases and identification of subjects required. Buys one-time rights.
Columns/Departments: Buys 12 mss/year. Query. Length and payment variable.
Poetry: We do not want unrelated subject matter, very long or abstract poetry. Buys 2 poems/year. Submit maximum 1 poem. Length and payment variable.
Fillers: Facts and newsbreaks. Buys 12/year.
Tips: "Contact *New Methods* in writing with an SASE before writing or submitting any finished material; ideas first. Could use individual(s) to write and submit press releases."

VETERINARY ECONOMICS MAGAZINE, 9073 Lenexa Dr., Lenexa KS 66215. (913)492-4300. Fax: (913)492-4157. Editor: Rebecca R. Turner. Senior Associate Editor: Renée Anderson. 75% freelance written. Prefers to work with published/established writers but will work with several new/unpublished writers each year. Monthly business magazine for all practicing veterinarians in the US. Estab. 1960. Buys exclusive rights in the field. Pays on publication. Publishes ms 3-6 months after acceptance. Reports in 4 months. Free sample copy and writer's guidelines.
Nonfiction: Publishes non-clinical articles on business and management techniques that will strengthen a veterinarian's private practice. Also interested in articles on financial problems, employee relations, marketing and similar subjects of particular interest to business owners. "We look for carefully researched articles that are specifically directed to our field." Pays negotiable rates. Pays expenses of writers on assignment.
Tips: "Our articles focus on nuts-and-bolts practice management techniques prescribed by experts in the practice management field and applied by successful veterinarians. Articles must be useful and appeal to a broad section of our readers."

Trade, Technical and Professional Journals/ Changes '93-'94

The following trade publications were listed in the 1993 edition but do not have listings in this edition of *Writer's Market*. The majority did not respond to our request to update their listings or return a questionnaire for a new listing. If a reason was given for their exclusion, we have included it in parentheses after the listing.

AB Bookman's Weekly
American Mover
The Appraisers Standard
Archery Business
Atlantic Construction
Atunc Newsletter
Automatic Merchandiser
Automotive Executive
Bank Human Resources Report
Bank Technology Report
Beef Today (no longer uses unknown writers)
Brake & Front End
Brilliant Ideas for Publishers
Builder Insider
Bus Ride
Cablecaster

Canadian Forest Industries (publication sold)
Canadian Machinery & Metalworking
Chain Saw Age
Childbirth Instructor
The Church Musician
Consumer Lending Report
Cottonwood Monthly (ceased publication)
CPI Purchasing
The Crafts Report
Dealer Communicator
Design Management
DG Review (unable to contact)
Dixie Contractor
Educational Dealer
Emergency Librarian

Farm Show Magazine
Farm Store (out of business)
Florida Forum
Focus
Food & Drug Packaging
The Future, Now
Golf Course News
Grassroots Fundraising Journal
Heating, Plumbing, Air Conditioning
Hog Farm Management (ceased publication)
Hospital Supervisor's Bulletin (out of business)
Incentive
Interior Landscape
Jobber Topics
Laser Focus World Magazine

Meeting News
Middle Eastern Dancer
Miniatures Dealer Magazine (out of business)
National Utility Contractor
New England Farm Bulletin & Garden Gazette
New England Farmer
Nostalgia World
NSGA Retail Focus
The Paralegal
Pest Management
Professional Stained Glass

Profitable Games (ceased publication)
PTN
Retailer and Marketing News
Retailing News (unable to contact)
Sales & Marketing Manager Canada
Secondary Marketing Executive
Ski Business
Snack Food (no longer uses freelance work)

Southern Motor Cargo
Southern Shipper
Southwest Real Estate News
Surgical Rounds (does not use freelancers)
Texas Architect
Textile World
Training
Victimology
Workstation
The Writer's Nook News

Scriptwriting

by Kerry Cox

The call was like so many others we get at the offices of *The Hollywood Script-writer* newsletter. Maybe just a little more desperate.

"Look, I flew all the way to Hollywood from England just to sell my story to a movie producer, and I can't even get anyone to talk to me! I'm supposed to fly back in two days, I've got to hurry! Can you help?"

"Sure," I answered. "First, grab your swimsuit and go lie on the beach and enjoy your last two days in L.A. Then, fly back to England and spend the next few months turning your story idea into a script. When you're finished, write another one. After that, send them around to some friends who you feel can be objective, and ask for their comments. If any of those friends happen to be writers or actors, all the better. Listen to their comments, and if any of them seem useful, rewrite the scripts. If those two scripts still aren't the very best work you can do, write two more. When you finally have two scripts you're proud of, then and only then are you ready to take a stab at marketing—finding an agent, contacting independent producers, etc."

The point is, there are certain procedures to follow in order to become a professional scriptwriter, just as there are prescribed steps to becoming a doctor, lawyer or accountant. As an aspiring scriptwriter, it's imperative that you are cognizant of these ground rules. If you think Hollywood producers are just sitting around waiting for some unknown to wander in with the next Great Idea, you're deluding yourself. What they ARE sitting around for is a Great Writer with a Great Idea, and the only way to prove that person is you is with a Great Script.

As you pursue the market listings that follow, keep that in mind. If you don't already have two terrific sitcom spec scripts (scripts written "on specula-tion," or, simply put, for free), two wonderful feature-length scripts, or even a couple of great educational or corporate video scripts you can use to show you're a professional and a master of the craft. . .then follow the advice I gave to that English fellow.

Write first. Then market.

Kerry Cox *is a Los Angeles writer with more than 11 years of experience in television, motion picture, theater and business/educational scriptwriting. He's the co-author (with Jurgen Wolff) of* Successful Scriptwriting *(Writer's Digest Books) and is editor and publisher of* Hollywood Scriptwriter, *a newsletter for scriptwriters throughout the U.S. and Canada.*

Business and educational writing

Take all the movies produced last year, lump them together with all the television shows that made it on the air, and you probably still wouldn't come close to the amount of industrial, corporate and educational material produced in film, video or multi-image format. This lucrative market is often overlooked by scriptwriters with their sights set on the silver screen, but the fact is that it can be a good source of steady income while you exercise your creative muscles and hone your craft.

Whether for training, sales, motivation, entertainment or a plethora of other uses, this is a medium that has become more and more sophisticated every year. Audiences are "TV-wise" — that is, they expect top-quality production anytime something appears on a screen. Unfortunately, it's the rare industrial or education show that boasts a big-league budget, so it's often up to the writer to make up the difference by injecting the script with originality, humor, drama or a unique concept.

For the most part, scripts are written in the two-column video format. There is software available that will automize this formatting for you, and many word processing programs can be manipulated to handle it as well. If you don't have a computer, just divide the page into Video and Audio columns; Video on the left, Audio on the right. Video instructions and shot descriptions are single-spaced on the left (usually all caps), while dialogue and narration is double-spaced on the right (usually upper and lower-case). A page of script will equal roughly 45 seconds of running time, but this could vary quite a bit.

Many larger companies have inhouse writers/producers, but smaller companies rely exclusively on freelance production teams. Your best approach as a freelancer is to try and hook up with a small production company that specializes in this kind of work, while at the same time introducing yourself to the inhouse supervisors so they'll know who to turn to when they need help with overload.

Don't forget advertising agencies as a possible source for this kind of work. Very often their clients call on them for help in producing training or business-related shows, and it's not common for agencies to have anyone on staff to handle this kind of work. This puts you in the position of a consultant, which can be a very lucrative position indeed.

Budgets are typically tight and are usually set in stone. You should have a rough idea of the production's budget before writing the script and work closely with the producer to be sure your script is shootable.

Your fee will vary according to the aforementioned budgets, but some things to keep in mind are: the number of drafts you'll do (three is the norm); the number of meetings you'll have to attend; the intended length of the show;

the intended use of the show; how much research is involved; and how long it will take you to write the script. A general rule of thumb is to charge a minimum—say, $500—and go up from there based on the above factors. A fee of $2,000 for a 10-minute meeting opener is not at all excessive.

A good way to keep up with the business is through the International Television Association, which has local chapters throughout the U.S. Many of those chapters run a job hotline updating current opportunities.

For information on more business and educational scriptwriting markets, see Scriptwriting Markets/Changes '93-'94 at the end of the Screenwriting section.

‡ABS ENTERPRISES, (formerly ABS & Associates), P.O. Box 5127, Evanston IL 60204. (708)982-1414. President: Alan Soell. "We produce material for all levels of corporate, medical, cable and educational institutions for the purposes of training and development, marketing and meeting presentations. We also are developing programming for the broadcast areas." 75% freelance written. "We work with a core of three to five freelance writers from development to final drafts." All scripts published are unagented submissions. Buys all rights. Accepts previously produced material. Reports in 2 weeks on queries.
Needs: Videotape, multimedia, realia, slides, tapes and cassettes, and television shows/series. Currently interested in "sports instructional series that could be produced for the consumer market on tennis, gymnastics, bowling, golf, aerobics, health and fitness, cross-country skiing and cycling. Also motivational and self-improvement type videos and film ideas to be produced. These could cover all ages '6-60'; and from professional to blue collar jobs. These two areas should be 30 minutes and be timeless in approach for long shelf life. Sports audience, age 25-45; home improvement, 25-65. Cable TV needs include the two groups of programming detailed here. We are also looking for documentary work on current issues, nuclear power, solar power, urban development, senior citizens—but with a new approach." Query or submit synopsis/ outline and resume. Pays by contractual agreement.
Tips: "I am looking for innovative approaches to old problems that just don't go away. The approach should be simple and direct so there is immediate audience identification with the presentation. I also like to see a sense of humor used. Trends in the audiovisual field include interactive video with disk—for training purposes."

ADVANTAGE MEDIA INC., Suite 102, 21356 Nordhoff St., Chatsworth CA 91311. (818)700-0504. Vice President: Susan Cherno. Estab. 1983. Audience is "all employees, including supervisory and management staff; generic audiences; medium-large companies, educational institutions, government, healthcare, insurance, financial." Works with 1-2 writers/year. Buys exclusive rights for distribution. Accepts previously produced material (exclusive distribution only). Reports in 1 month on quries. Free catalog. Submit synopsis/outline, completed script or resume. Usually pays flat fee for writing. Negotiable by project.
Needs: Videotapes. "Generic settings, rainbow mix of characters. Topics: change, motivation, diversity, quality, safety, customer service. 20 mins. max. Documentary if points are clear or skill-building 'how to'. Must make a point for teaching purposes."
Tips: Training programs must appeal to a diverse audience but be 'TV quality'. They must teach, as well as be somewhat entertaining. Must hold interest. Should present the problem, but solve it and not leave the audience hanging or to solve it themsvles. Must stay realistic, believable and be fast-paced. I think there will be a need for even more types of video-based materials for a growing need for training within organizations.

ARNOLD AND ASSOCIATES PRODUCTIONS, INC., 1204 16th Ave. S., Nashville TN 37212. (615)329-2800. President: John Arnold. Executive Producers: Deirdre Say, James W. Morris and Peter Dutton. Produces material for the general public (entertainment/motion pictures) and for corporate clients (employees/customers/consumers). Buys 10-15 scripts/year. Works with 3 writers/year. Buys all rights. Accepts previously produced material OK. Reports in 1 month.
Needs: Films (35mm) and videotape. Looking for "upscale image and marketing programs." Dramatic writing for "name narrators and post scored original music; and motion picture. $5-6 million dollar budget. Dramatic or horror." Query with samples or submit completed script. Makes outright purchase of $1,000.
Tips: Looking for "upscale writers who understand corporate image production, and motion picture writers who understand story and dialogue."

A/V CONCEPTS CORP., 30 Montauk Blvd., Oakdale NY 11769-1431. (516)567-7227. Fax: (516)567-8745. Contact: P. Solimene or L. Solimene. Produces material for elementary-high school students, either on grade level or in remedial situations. Estab. 1971. 100% freelance written. Buys 25 scripts/year from unpublished/

unproduced writers. Employs video, book and personal computer media. Reports on outline in 1 month; on final scripts in 6 weeks. Buys all rights. Sample copy for 9 × 12 SAE with 5 first class stamps.

Needs: Interested in original educational computer (disk-based) software programs for Apple +, 48k. Main concentration in language arts, mathematics and reading. "Manuscripts must be written using our lists of vocabulary words and meet our readability formula requirements. Specific guidelines are devised for each level. Length of manuscript and subjects will vary according to grade level for which material is prepared. Basically, we want material that will motivate people to read." Pays $300 and up.

Tips: "Writers must be highly creative and highly disciplined. We are interested in high interest/low readability materials."

SAMUEL R. BLATE ASSOCIATES, 10331 Watkins Mill Dr., Gaithersburg MD 20879-2935. (301)840-2248. President: Samuel R. Blate. Produces audiovisual and educational material for business, education, institutions, state and federal governments. "We work with 2 *local* writers per year on a per project basis—it varies as to business conditions and demand." Buys first rights when possible. Query for electronic submissions. Reports in 1 month. SASE for return.

Needs: Scripts on technical subjects. Query with samples. SASE for return. Payment "depends on type of contract with principal client." Pays expenses of writers on assignment.

Tips: "Writers must have a strong track record of technical and aesthetic excellence. Clarity is not next to divinity—it is above it."

BOSUSTOW MEDIA GROUP, Suite 100, 1245 16th St., Santa Monica CA 90404-1239. (310)315-3459. Owner: Tee Bosustow. Estab. 1983. Produces material for corporate, PBS and home video clients. Reports in 2 weeks on queries.

Needs: Tapes, cassettes and videotapes. "Unfortunately, no one style, etc. exists. We produce a variety of products." Submit synopsis/outline and resume only. Pays agreed upon fee.

‡CAMBRIDGE EDUCATIONAL, 90 MacCorkle Ave. SW, South Charleston WV 25303. Production Staff: Charlotte Angel or Matt Clark. Estab. 1983. Audience is junior high/high schools, vocational schools, libraries, guidance centers. Buys 18-24 scripts/year. Works with 12-18 writers/year. Buys all rights. "Samples are kept for file reference." Reports only if interested. Free catalog. Query with synopsis, resume or writing sample ("excerpt from a previous script, preferably"). Makes outright purchase of $2,000-4,000.

Needs: Charts and videotapes. Educational programming suitable for junior high and high school age groups (classroom viewing and library reference). "Programs range from 20-35 minutes in length. Each should have a fresh approach for how-to's, awareness, and introductions to various subject matters. Subjects range from guidance, home economics, parenting, health, and vocational to social studies, fine arts, music, and business."

Tips: "We are looking for a new slant on some standard educational topics, as well as more contemporary issues. We want a fresh approach. Remember how boring it was when you were forced to watch educational videos in the classroom?

‡CINEBAR PRODUCTIONS INC., 714 Thimble Shoals Blvd., Newport News VA 23606. (804)873-3232. Vice President-Production: William R. Ball. Estab. 1987. Audience is general—documentary. Buys 6-10 scripts/year. Works with 4-8 writers/year. Buys all rights. Accepts previously produced material. Reports in 1 month. Query with synopsis or resume. Pay negotiable.

Needs: Videotapes. "We produce historical documentaries, museum special use programs, artist bios and arts programs."

Tips: "Stick to your field—know what you are writing about as if you had lived it."

COMPRO PRODUCTIONS, Suite 114, 2080 Peachtree Ind. Court, Atlanta GA 30341. (404)455-1943. Fax: (404)455-3356. Producers: Nels Anderson and Steve Brinson. Estab. 1977. Audience is general public and specific business audience. Buys 10-25 scripts/year. Buys all rights. No previously produced material. No unsolicited material; submissions will not be returned because "all work is contracted."

Needs: "We solicit writers for corporate films/video in the areas of training, point purchase, sales, how-to, benefit programs, resorts and colleges." Produces 16-35mm films and videotapes. Query with samples. Makes outright purchase or pays cost/minute.

EDUCATIONAL IMAGES LTD., P.O. Box 3456, Elmira NY 14905. (607)732-1090. Executive Director: Dr. Charles R. Belinky. Produces material (videos, sound filmstrips, multimedia kits and slide sets) for schools, kindergarten through college and graduate school, public libraries, parks, nature centers, etc. Also produces science-related software material. Buys 50 scripts/year. Buys all AV rights. Free catalog.

Needs: Videos, slide sets and filmstrips on science, natural history, anthropology and social studies. "We are looking primarily for complete AV programs; we will consider slide collections to add to our files. This requires high quality, factual text and pictures." Query with a meaningful sample of proposed program. Pays $150 minimum.

Tips: The writer/photographer is given high consideration. "Once we express interest, follow up. Potential contributors lose many sales to us by not following up on initial query. Don't waste our time and yours if you can't deliver. The market seems to be shifting to greater popularity of video and computer software formats."

EDUCATIONAL VIDEO NETWORK, 1401 19th St., Huntsville TX 77340. (409)295-5767. President: Dr. Kenneth L. Russell. Executive Editor: Gary Edmondson. Produces material for junior high, senior high, college and university audiences. Buys "perhaps 20 scripts/year." Buys all rights or pays royalty on gross retail and wholesale. Accepts previously produced material. Reports in 1 week on queries; 1 month on submissions. Free catalog and writer's guidelines.
Needs: "Video for educational purposes. Query. Royalty varies.
Tips: Looks for writers with the "ability to write and illustrate for educational purposes. Schools are asking for more curriculum oriented live-action video."

EFFECTIVE COMMUNICATION ARTS, INC., 221 W. 57th St., New York NY 10019-2137. (212)333-5656. Fax: (212)333-7748. Vice President: W.J. Comcowich. Estab. 1965. Produces films, videotapes and interactive multimedia for physicians, nurses and medical personnel. Prefers to work with published/established writers. 80% freelance written. Buys approximately 20 scripts/year. Query for electronic submissions. Buys all rights. Reports in 1 month.
Needs: Multimedia kits, television shows/series, videotape presentations and interactive videodisks. Currently producing about 15 videotapes for medical audiences; 6 interactive disks for medical audience; 3 interactive disks for point-of-purchase. Submit complete script and resume. Makes outright purchase. Pays expenses of writers on assignment.
Tips: "Interactive design skills are increasingly important."

EURO COMMUNICATION ENTERTAINMENT GROUP, 223 Strand St., Santa Monica CA 90405. (213)399-1101. Producer: Liliane Pelzman. Estab. 1983. Produces material for all ages. Buys all rights. No previously published material. Does not return submissions.
Needs: Pays royalty in accordance with Writers Guild standards.

HAYES SCHOOL PUBLISHING CO., INC., 321 Pennwood Ave., Wilkinsburg PA 15221-3398. (412)371-2373. Fax: (412)371-6408. President: Clair N. Hayes, III. Estab. 1940. Produces material for school teachers and principals, elementary through high school. Also produces charts, workbooks, teacher's handbooks, posters, bulletin board material and reproducible blackline masters (grades K-12). 25% freelance written. Prefers to work with published/established writers. Buys 5-10 scripts/year from unpublished/unproduced writers. 100% of scripts produced are unagented submissions. Buys all rights. Query for electronic submissions. Reports in 3 months. Catalog for SAE with 3 first class stamps. Writer's guidelines for #10 SAE with 2 first class stamps.
Needs: Educational material only. Particularly interested in educational material for elementary school level. Query. Pays $25 minimum.

‡IMAGE INNOVATIONS, INC., Suite 201, 29 Clyde Rd., Somerset NJ 08873. President: Mark A. Else. Estab. 1974. Produces material for business, education and general audiences. 50% freelance written. "Credentials and reputation important." Commissions 5-10 scripts/year for clients. All scripts produced are unagented submissions. Reports in 2 weeks. Buys all rights.
Needs: Subject topics include education, sales, public relations and technical. Produces hi-image 1" and ½" Betacam video and tapes and cassettes. Query with samples. Pays in outright purchase of $1,000-5,000. Sometimes pays the expenses of writers on assignment.

‡INSTRUCTIONAL/COMMUNICATIONS TECHNOLOGY, 10 Stepan Place, Huntington Station NY 11746. President: Stanford Taylor. Produces material for educational audience. Works with 100-200 computer programs annually. Works with 2-3 writers/year. Buys all rights. Accepts previously produced material. Reports in 1 month on queries; 1-2 months on submissions. Free catalog. Query with synopsis. Pays 2-6% royalty of list.
Needs: Videotapes, multimedia kits, silent filmstrips, tapes and cassettes. Reading improvement selections for secondary/adult market—reading levels 1-8, mature interests, 1,000-2,000 words with comprehensive questions and guides for re-reading.

‡JACOBY/STORM PRODUCTIONS INC., 22 Crescent Rd., Westport CT 06880. (203)227-2220. Contact: Doris Storm. Produces material for corporations, schools, TV. Works with 4-6 writers annually. Buys all rights. No previously produced material. Reports in 2 weeks.
Needs: "Short dramatic films on business subjects, educational films at all levels, sales and corporate image films." Produces 16mm films, slides, tapes and cassettes, videotapes and videodisks. Query. Usually makes outright purchase.
Tips: "Prefers local people. Looks for experience, creativity, dependability, attention to detail, enthusiasm for project, ability to interface with client. Wants creative approaches to material."

‡KOLMOR VISIONS (KMV), 1 Bank St., Stamford CT 06901. (203)325-2978. Executive Producer: Tom Moore. Estab. 1982. Corporate audience. Buys 2-4 scripts/year. Works with 10-12 writers/year. Buys all rights. Accepts previously produced material. Reports in 2 months on queries; 6 months on submissions. Query with synopsis. Pays 10% royalty.
Needs: Videotapes. "We are developing 'how to' and educational programs for cable and sale. 'Over 60' and children programming ideas usually receive the most attention. Next area of interest—environmental safety."

‡LOCKWOOD FILMS, 365 Ontario St., London, Ontario N5W 3W6 Canada. (519)434-6006. President: Nancy Johnson. Estab. 1974. Audience is corporate, education, general broadcast. Works with 5-6 writers/year. Buys all rights. No previously produced material. Reports in 2 months on queries. Submit query with synopsis, resume or sample scripts. Negotiated fee.
Needs: Videotapes and multimedia kits. Seeking education programs for elementary and high school students; corporate videos for training, orientation, sales promotion (length from 10-30 minutes); television documentary/general interest/entertainment.
Tips: "Potential contributors should have a fax machine."

MARSH MEDIA, P.O. Box 8082, Shawnee Mission KS 66208. (816)523-1059. Fax: (816)333-7421. President: Joan K. Marsh. Estab. 1969. Produces software and video and filmstrips for elementary and junior/senior high school students. Also publishes books for children. 100% freelance written. Works with a small number of new/unpublished writers each year. Buys 8-16 scripts/year. All scripts produced are unagented submissions. Buys all rights.
Needs: 50-frame; 15-minute scripts for video or sound filmstrips; book texts to our format. Pays by outright purchase. $1,000/text.
Tips: "We are seeking texts for childrens' books written to our guidelines only. Send SASE for guidelines."

‡MOTIVATION MEDIA, INC., 1245 Milwaukee Ave., Glenview IL 60025-2499. (708)297-4740. Fax: (708)297-6829. Creative Director: Ken Lewis. Produces customized meeting, training and marketing material for presentation to salespeople, customers, corporate/industrial employees and distributors. 90% freelance written. Buys 50 scripts/year. Prefers to work with published/established writers. All scripts produced are unagented submissions. Buys all rights. Reports in 1 month.
Needs: Material for all audiovisual media—particularly marketing-oriented (sales training, sales promotional, sales motivational) material. Produces 16mm films, multimedia sales meeting programs, videotapes, cassettes and slide sets. Software should be AV oriented. Query with samples and resumé. Pays $150-5,000. Pays the expenses of writers on assignment.

OMNI PRODUCTIONS, 655 West Carmel Dr., Carmel IN 46032-2500. (317)844-6664. Vice President: Dr. Sandra M. Long. Estab. 1976. Produces commercial, training, educational and documentary material. Buys all rights.
Needs: "Educational, documentary, commercial, training, motivational." Produces slides, video shows, multi-image and videotapes. Query. Makes outright purchase.
Tips: "Must have experience as writer and have examples of work. Examples need to include print copy and finished copy of videotape if possible. A resume with educational background, general work experience and experience as a writer must be included. Especially interested in documentary-style writing. Writers' payment varies, depending on amount of research needed, complexity of project, length of production and other factors."

ONE ON ONE COMPUTER TRAINING, (formerly Fliptrack Learning Systems), Division of Mosaic Media, Inc., Suite 100, 2055 Army Trail Rd., Addison IL 60101-9961. (708)628-0500. Fax: (708)628-0550. Publisher: F. Lee McFadden. Contact: Natalie Young. Estab. 1976. Produces training courses for microcomputers and business software. Works with a small number of new/unpublished writers each year. 35% freelance written. Buys 3-5 courses/year; 1-2 from unpublished/unproduced writers. All courses published are unagented submissions. Works with 3-5 writers/year. Buys all rights. Query for electronic submissions. Reports in 3 weeks. Free product literature; sample copy for 9×12 SAE.
Needs: Training courses on how to use personal computers/software, primarily audio geared to the adult student in a business setting and usually to the beginning/intermediate user; also some courses at advanced levels. Primarily audio, also some reference manuals, other training formats for personal computers considered. Query with resume and samples if available. Pays negotiable royalty or makes outright purchase.
Tips: "We prefer to work with Chicago-area writers with strong teaching/training backgrounds and experience with microcomputers. Writers from other regions are also welcome."

‡PALARDO PRODUCTIONS, Suite 4, 1807 Taft Ave., Hollywood CA 90028. (213)469-8991. Director: Paul Ardolino. Estab. 1971. Produces material for youth ages 13-35. Buys 3-4 scripts/year. Buys all rights. Reports in 2 weeks on queries; 1 month on mss.

Needs: Multimedia kits, tapes and cassettes, videotapes. "We are seeking ideas relating to virtual reality, comedy scripts involving technology and coming of age; rock'n'roll bios." Submit synopsis/outline and resume. Pays in accordance with Writers Guild standards.
Tips: "Do not send a complete script—only synopsis of 4 pages or less *first.*"

PHOTO COMMUNICATION SERVICES, INC., P.O. Box 508, Acme MI 49601. (616)922-3050. President: Lynn Jackson. Produces commercial, industrial, sales, training material etc. 95% freelance written. No scripts from unpublished/unproduced writers. 100% of scripts produced are unagented submissions. Buys all rights and first serial rights. Query for electronic submissions. Reports in 1 month.
Needs: Multimedia kits, slides, tapes and cassettes, and video presentations. Primarily interested in 35mm multimedia and video. Query with samples or submit completed script and résumé. Pays in outright purchase or by agreement.

‡PICTURE ENTERTAINMENT CORPORATION, (formerly Lee Caplin Productions), Suite 505, 9595 Wilshire Blvd., Beverly Hills CA 90212. (310)858-8300. President/CEO: Lee Caplin. Vice President Development: Sonia Mintz. Produces feature films for theatrical audience and TV audience. Buys 2 scripts/year, works with 10 writers/year. Buys all rights. Reports on submissions in 2 months.
Needs: Films (35mm) and videotapes. Feature scripts 100-120 pp. Submit completed script. Pays "on a deal by deal basis/some WGA, some not."
Tips: "Don't send derivative standard material. Emphasis on unique plot and characters, realistic dialogue. *Discourage* period pieces, over-the-top comedy, graphic sex/violence, SciFi. *Encourage* action, action/comedy, thriller, thriller/comedy."

‡PREMIER FILM, VIDEO & RECORDING CORP., 3033 Locust, St. Louis MO 63103. (314)531-3555. Marketing Manager: Donna Blue. Estab. 1940. "Audience varies—educational/entertainment." Buys 2-3 scripts/year. Works with 2-3 writers/year. Buys first rights. Accepts previously produced material. "We will return any submissions we have requested." Reports in 1-2 month. Submit resume. Pays in accordance with Writer's Guild standards (other arrangements may be discussed).
Needs: Videotapes, filmstrips, sound, tapes and cassettes.

‡CHARLES RAPP ENTERPRISES, INC., 1650 Broadway, New York NY 10019. (212)247-6646. President: Howard Rapp. Estab. 1954. Produces materials for firms and buyers. Works with 5 writers/year. "Work as personal manager/agent in sales." Accepts previously produced material. Reports in 1 month on queries; 2 months on submissions. Submit resume or sample of writing. Pays in accordance with Writer's Guild standards.
Needs: Videotapes.

BILL RASE PRODUCTIONS, INC., 955 Venture Ct., Sacramento CA 95825. (916)929-9181. Fax: (916)929-4751. President: Bill Rase. Produces material for business education and mass audience. Buys about 20 scripts/year. Buys all rights. Reports "when an assignment is available."
Needs: Produces multimedia, slides, cassettes and video productions. Submit resume and sample page or two of script, and description of expertise. Pays negotiable rate in 30 days.
Tips: "Call and ask for Bill Rase or Esther Marcroft personally. Must be within 100 miles and thoroughly professional."

SPENCER PRODUCTIONS, INC., 234 5th Ave., New York NY 10001. (212)697-5895. General Manager: Bruce Spencer. Executive Producer: Alan Abel. Produces material for high school students, college students and adults. Occasionally uses freelance writers with considerable talent. Reports in 1 month. Catalog for #10 SASE.
Needs: 16mm films, prerecorded tapes and cassettes. Satirical material only. Query. Pay is negotiable.

TALCO PRODUCTIONS, 279 E. 44th St., New York NY 10017-4336. (212)697-4015. President: Alan Lawrence. Vice President: Marty Holberton. Produces variety of material for TV, radio, business, trade associations, nonprofit organizations, etc. Audiences range from young children to senior citizens. 20-40% freelance written. Buys scripts from published/produced writers only. Buys all rights. No previously published material. Reports in 3 weeks on queries. *Does not accept unsolicited mss.*
Needs: Films (16, 35mm), slides, radio tapes and cassettes and videotape. "We maintain a file of writers and call on those with experience in the same general category as the project in production. We do not accept unsolicited manuscripts. We prefer to receive a writer's resume listing credits. If his/her background merits, we will be in touch when a project seems right." Makes outright purchase/project and in accordance with

ALWAYS enclose a self-addressed, stamped envelope (SASE) with all your queries and correspondence.

Writers Guild standards (when appropriate). Sometimes pays the expenses of writers on assignment.
Tips: "Concentration is now in TV productions. Production budgets will be tighter. *Productions will be of shorter length to save money.*"

‡**ED TAR ASSOCIATES, INC.**, 230 Venice Way, Venice CA 90291. (310)306-2195. Fax: (310)306-0654. Estab. 1972. Audience is dealers, salespeople, public. Buys all rights. No previously produced material. Makes outright purchase.
Needs: Films (16, 35mm), videotapes, filmstrips, slides, tapes and cassettes. "We are constantly looking for *experienced* writers of corporate, product and live show scripts. (We do not consider writers of 30 second commercials or PR press releases for our work.) Send a resume and samples. Track record of proven writing for a variety of corporate clients a must."

TEL-AIR INTERESTS, INC., 1755 NE 149th St., Miami FL 33181. (305)944-3268. President: Grant H. Gravitt. Produces material for groups and theatrical and TV audiences. Buys all rights. Submit resume.
Needs: Documentary films on education, travel and sports. Produces films and videotape. Makes outright purchase.

TRI VIDEO TELEPRODUCTION—Lake Tahoe, P.O. Box 8822, Incline Village NV 89452-8822. (702)323-6868. Production Manager: Beth Davidson. Produces material primarily for corporate targets (their sales, marketing and training clients). Works with 1-2 writers each year developing contracted material. Buys all rights or negotiable rights. No previously produced material. Does not return material unless requested.
Needs: "Will have a need for writing contract projects; would consider other projects which are either sold to a client and need a producer, or which the writer wishes to sell and have produced. In all cases, corporate sales, marketing and training materials in the fields of health and the environment." Produces only in videotape format. Query. Makes outright purchase in accordance with Writers Guild standards.
Tips: "Our strength is production skills, graphics and animation. We seldom sell projects so if your project needs to be sold, we are the wrong avenue!"

TROLL ASSOCIATES, 100 Corporate Dr., Mahwah NJ 07430. (201)529-4000. Contact: M. Schecter. Produces material for elementary and high school students. Buys approximately 200 scripts/year. Buys all rights. Reports in 3 weeks. Free catalog.
Needs: Produces multimedia kits, tapes and cassettes, and (mainly) books. Query or submit outline/synopsis. Pays royalty or makes outright purchase.

‡**VISUAL HORIZONS**, 180 Metro Park, Rochester NY 14623. (716)424-5300. Fax: (716)424-5313. President: Stanley Feingold. Produces material for general audiences. Buys 5 programs/year. Reports in 5 months. Free catalog, 48 pages.
Needs: Business, medical and general subjects. Produces silent and sound filmstrips, multimedia kits, slide sets and videotapes. Query with samples. Payment negotiable.

Playwriting

It's said that scriptwriting is a visual medium, but in the case of playwriting that's not entirely true. Nowhere is The Word held in such high esteem as when writing for the stage, which is one reason writers love the theater. Here, the writer is king, and changes are supposed to be made only with the permission of the writer. In fact, as Canadian playwright Peter Colley once told *The Hollywood Scriptwriter*, "It's the only place where a writer has so much power he or she can actually close a production down if it isn't following the script." That's the kind of power film and television writers can only dream of.

Breaking in as a playwright means becoming involved in local theater. There's simply no other way to get a good feel for what can and can't be done, what works and doesn't work, how a production budget is spent, and what logistics are involved in staging a scene. In this way you'll also become acquainted with the artistic director or dramaturg of the theater, which is the best way to get your script considered for production.

Writing for local theater means you must write scripts with few characters, limited set and lighting demands and simple props. Avoid staging requirements that could be problematic, such as fistfights, fast wardrobe changes or difficult physical action.

The idea is to get a production of your work done on a local level and progress to larger and larger theaters. In fact, this avenue has been traveled recently by writers who eventually want to put plays on the screen as films; the already mentioned Colley is a prime example, having now seen three of his plays go before the lens.

Playwrights must use perseverance and ingenuity to get their plays produced since agents will only handle established writers. The positive side to this, though, is that the doors of local theaters are always open to anyone who wants to help, and if you'll put some time in at a theater, you stand a good chance of getting a staged reading if your work is up to par.

The pay? Well, you won't get rich right away, that's for sure. Most times you'll be getting a percentage of the house, at least in the early going. But once your play establishes itself, you want to get it published through a play publisher. That way it's being marketed for you, and the royalties come in from all over the country—or even the world. Just ask Colley, who remembers fondly the time he walked out to his mailbox a few months after he'd heard an American theater in Germany was producing one of his plays, and found a check for $12,000! As he happily says, "Royalties are God's gift to writers."

There tends to be a lot of turnover in the smaller theaters, so you'll want to keep up with the industry through such trade publications as The Dramatists Guild Newsletter, 234 W. 44th St., New York NY 10036 and *Dramalogue*, P.O. Box 38771, Hollywood CA 90038.

For information on more playwriting markets, see Scriptwriting Markets/ Changes '93-'94 at the end of the Screenwriting section.

A.D. PLAYERS, 2710 W. Alabama, Houston TX 77098-2106. (713)526-2721. Artistic Director: Jeannette Clift George. Estab. 1967. Produces 4-6 plays/year. Professional Christian Theater Company. "Productions include 4-6 Grace Theater Series shows and 4 Nancy Calhoun Paulson Children's Theatre Series shows, 2-3 staged readings and 10-12 Repertory Series shows on tour. The mainstage performance area is a proscenium stage with minimal wing space and no fly space; the children's theater space is in the round. Tour performance arenas vary from auditoriums and theaters to gymnasiums/cafetoriums and churches. Audiences for each series include adults and children, some with church affiliation." Query with synopsis only. Send materials to Martha Doolittle, Dramaturg/literary manager. Reports in 2-12 months. Payment terms negotiable.
Needs: "One-act and full-length plays, any style, reflecting God's reality in everyday life. Seasonal plays, any length, and short pieces (up to 1 hour) especially needed." Write to the Literary Manager for specific script submittal guidelines. No unsolicited mss.
 • A.D. Players is interested in seeing more children's material.
Tips: "Because of our specific signature as a Christian repertory company we would not be interested in plays that have no reference to the reality of God or man's search for spiritual significance in his world."

ACTORS' STOCK COMPANY, 3884 Van Ness Lane, Dallas TX 75220. (214)353-9916. Artistic Director: Keith Oncale. Estab. 1988. Produces 3-4 plays/year. We stage semi-professional productions to a young adult to middle-aged general audience. Query with synopsis. Reports in 3 months. No rights purchased except reading privileges. Pays royalty.

Needs: Two and three act plays, covering a wide variety of styles, but with fewer than 12 cast members. Our average staging facilities are 100 seat houses or smaller.
Tips: "Trends today reflect a return to comic realism that comments on our society without commenting on the play itself."

ACTORS THEATRE OF LOUISVILLE, 316 W. Main St., Louisville KY 40202-4218. (502)584-1265. Producing Director: Jon Jory. Estab. 1964. Produces approximately 30 new plays of varying lengths/year. Professional productions are performed for subscription audience from diverse backgrounds. Agented submissions only for full-length plays; open submissions to National Ten-Minute Play Contest. (Plays ten pages or less.) Reports in 6-9 months on submissions, mostly in the fall. Buys variable rights. Offers variable royalty.
Needs: "We are interested in full-length, one-act and ten-minute plays and in plays of ideas, language, humor, experiment and passion."

ALBUNDEGUS ALL-STARS, 709 13th St., Greeley CO 80631. Artistic Director: Michael Baczuk. Estab. 1989. Produces 4-6 plays/year. Query with SASE or submit complete ms with synopsis and SASE. Reports in 4 months. Buys exclusive rights in Colorado area for 6 months; rights returned to author after this period. Pays $5-15/performance.
Needs: "We're not concerned about genre, style or topic so long as it's well written. Prefer play length no longer than 2 hours and not less than 15 minutes. Cast size of no more than 8. Try to keep the set and props simple."
Tips: "Though we want to encourage and present the works of Colorado playwrights, we also present plays from writers outside Colorado. We present everything from plays for children to hard-edged social issues."

‡ALLEY THEATRE, 615 Texas Ave., Houston TX 77002. Literary Director: Christopher Baker. A resident professional theatre: large stage seating 824; arena stage seating 296.
Needs: Plays and musicals, adaptations and translations. Makes variable royalty arrangements. No unsolicited scripts accepted, professional recommendation only. Reports in 6 months. Produces 10 plays/year.

AMELIA MAGAZINE, 329 "E" St., Bakersfield CA 93304. (805)323-4064. Editor: Frederick A. Raborg, Jr. Estab. 1983. Publishes 1 play/year. Submit complete ms. Reports in 2 months. Buys first North American serial rights only. Pays $150 plus publication as winner of annual Frank McClure One-Act Play Award.
• See this magazine's listing in the Consumer, Literary and "Little" section for more information.
Needs: "Plays with virtually any theme or concept. We look for excellence within the one-act, 45 minutes running time format. We welcome the avant garde and experimental. We do not object to the erotic, though not pornographic. Fewer plays are being produced on Broadway, but the regionals seem to be picking up the slack. That means fewer equity stages and more equity waivers."

‡AMERICAN REPERTORY THEATRE, 64 Brattle St., Cambridge MA 02138. (617)495-2668. Artistic Director: Robert Brustein. Estab. 1966. Publishes 8 plays/year. Plays are performed by a professional company for a Boston/Cambridge audience. Query with synopsis or agented submission. Reports in 2 weeks on synopses, 3 months on scripts. Buys single production rights only.
Needs: "We are seeking good plays. We prefer imaginative plays which stay away from kitchen sink realism. 'Message' plays are rarely good ones." No more than 12 in cast.
Tips: "We don't want to see conventional commercial fare. Too many scripts for the stage are transposed TV fare. Avoid smart gags every 2 minutes and exploitation of hot topical issues. The poetry of the stage is our main aesthetic interest. A fleshing-out of our contemporary dream life is one way to describe a good play. We are *mainly* looking for good plays."

AMERICAN STAGE FESTIVAL, P.O. Box 225, Milford NH 03055-0225. Producing Director: Matthew Parent. Estab. 1975. "The ASF is a central New England professional theater (professional equity company) with a 3-month summer season (June-August)" for audience of all ages, interests, education and sophistication levels. Query with synopsis. Produces 20% musicals, 80% nonmusicals. Five are mainstage and ten are children's productions; 40% are originals. Royalty option and subsequent amount of gross: optional. Reports in 6 months.
Needs: "The Festival can do comedies, musicals and dramas. However, the most frequent problems are bolder language and action than a general mixed audience will accept. Prefer not to produce plays with strictly urban themes. We have a 40-foot proscenium stage with 30-foot wings, but no fly system. Festival plays are chosen to present scale and opportunities for scenic and costume projects far beyond the 'summer theater' type of play." Length: mainstage: 2-3 acts; children's productions: 50 minutes.
Tips: Writers could improve submissions with "dramatic action, complexity, subplot and a unique statement. Try to get a staged reading of the script before submitting the play to us. Our audiences prefer plays that deal with human problems presented in a conventional manner."

AN CLAIDHEAMH SOLUIS/CELTIC ARTS CENTER, P.O. Box 20630, Los Angeles CA 90006-0630. (213)462-6844. Artistic Director: Sean Walsh. Estab. 1985. Produces 6 plays/year. Equity waiver. Query with synopsis. Reports in 6 months. Rights acquired vary. Pays $25-50.

Needs: Scripts of Celtic interest (Scottish, Welsh, Irish, Cornish, Manx, Breton). "This can apply to writer's background or subject matter. We are particularly concerned with works that relate to the survival of ethnic cultures and traditions, especially those in danger of extinction."

‡ARAN PRESS, 1320 S. Third St., Louisville KY 40208. (502)636-0115. Editor/Publisher: Tom Eagan. Estab. 1983. Audience is professional, community, college, university, summer stock and dinner theaters. Query. Reports in 1-2 weeks on submissions. Contracts for publication and play production. Pays 10% book royalty and 50% production royalty.
Tips: No children's plays. "Tip to writers of plays: don't. Write novels, nonfiction, whatever, but don't write plays. If you *must* write plays, and you can't get published by one of the other publishers, send us an inquiry. If you care for what we have to offer, welcome aboard."

ARKANSAS REPERTORY THEATRE, P.O. Box 110, Little Rock AR 72203-0110. (501)378-0445. Literary Manager: Brad Mooy. Estab. 1976. Produces 11 full productions each season (7 on the MainStage, 3 on the SecondStage and 1 Educational Tour). We also produce staged readings and Celebrity Playreadings plus workshop productions. One MainStage show tours the country and the Educational tour is regional. Query with synopsis. Reports in up to 3 months. Rights purchased vary. Pays royalty or per performance; "this also varies per show."
Needs: "We produce an ecclectic season, with musicals, comedies, dramas and at least one original premiere per season."

‡ARROW ROCK LYCEUM, Main St., Arrow Rock MO 65320. (816)837-3311. Artistic Director: Michael Bollinger. Produces 8 plays/year. "The Lyceum's 33rd summer repertory season in the historic village of Arrow Rock, MO, will open in a beautiful new $700,000 expansion featuring new stage, auditorium, lobby/archive space and more. The season consists of 7 plays in rotating rep, with a professional acting company selected from national auditions." Query with synopsis throughout year. Enclose SASE for reply. Also sponsors the National Playwrights Contest. "Lyceum and original artistic staff to get future credit, and Lyceum to retain 5% of author's gross commissions for first 5 years only. Lyceum either commissions w/separate deals, or simply pays a flat fee to National Playwrights Contest winners, which also receive full-scale world premiere."
Needs: The repertory season includes seven diverse plays, including musicals, classic, comedy, drama, world premiere. Generally each season will feature one world premiere, contest winner or a commissioned work. "I would suggest plays with casts not exceeding 12, and one set, or rather open space with various locales."
Tips: "Who knows—if it works, anything can go! However, keeping budgets in mind, etc., works that have a bit of flexibility are best—could be produced with all 20 characters, or could be produced with six actors doubling supporting roles. Also, keep the set in mind. Generally two or three realistic sets in one play could hinder original chances; one set or open staging could help. I do feel it is important for professional theaters to be 'theatrical creators' as well as mere 'consumers'!"

ART CRAFT PUBLISHING CO., 233 Dows Bldg., Box 1058, Cedar Rapids IA 52406-1058. (319)364-6311. Fax: (319)364-1771. Publisher: C. McMullen. Publishes plays and musicals for the junior and senior high school market. Query with synopsis or submit complete ms. Reports in 2 months. Acquires amateur rights only. Makes outright purchase or pays royalty.
Needs: One- and three-acts—preferably comedies or mystery comedies. Also publishes musicals. Currently needs plays with a larger number of characters for production within churches and schools. Prefers one-set plays. No "material with the normal 'taboos'—controversial material."

ART EXTENSIONS THEATRE, 11144 Weddington, N. Hollywood CA 91601. (818)760-8675. Artistic Director: Maureen Kennedy Samuels. Estab. 1989. Produces 2 plays/year. Equity waiver productions for general audiences. Query with synopsis or submit complete ms. Reports in 2 months. Buys rights to produce play for 6-week run. Pays 2-10% royalty.
Needs: One acts, full-length plays and musicals: Comedy or drama particularly interested in plays with strong female characters, plays with dance. Staging should be one set and as simple as possible.
Tips: "We have been receiving a lot of submissions in which the plots, characters and dialogue sound too much like a soap opera or situation comedy. Above all there is too much talk that does not move the action or develop characters. We are looking for theater pieces with three elements: 1)real, well-developed characters, 2)dialogue that is real, poetic and moves the play along and 3)subjects and plots with a bite or

Market conditions are constantly changing! If this is 1995 or later, buy the newest edition of Writer's Market *at your favorite bookstore or order directly from* Writer's Digest Books.

edge to them. In other words, we are looking for a play that can stand on its own as a piece of literature."

ARTREACH TOURING THEATRE, 3074 Madison Rd., Cincinnati OH 45209. (513)871-2300. Fax: (513)871-2501. Director: Kathryn Schultz Miller. Produces 6 plays/year to be performed nationally in theaters and schools. "We are a professional company. Our audience is primarily young people in schools and their families." Submit complete ms. Reports in 3 months. Buys exclusive right to produce for 9 months. Pays $10/show (approximately 1,000 total performances through the year).
Needs: Plays for children and adolescents. Serious, intelligent plays about contemporary life or history/legend. "Limited sets and props. Can use scripts with only 3 actors; 45 minutes long. Should be appropriate for touring." No clichéd approaches, camp or musicals.
Tips: "We look for opportunities to create innovative stage effects using few props, and we like scripts with good acting opportunities."

ASOLO THEATRE COMPANY, (formerly Asolo Center for the Performing Arts), 5555 N. Tamiami Tr., Sarasota FL 34243. (813)351-9010. Contact: Literary Manager. Produces 8 plays/year. 20% freelance written. 100% of scripts produced are unagented submissions. A LORT theater with an intimate performing space. Works with 2-4 unpublished/unproduced writers annually. "We do not accept unsolicited scripts. Writers must send us a letter and 1 page synopsis and one page of dialogue with self-addressed stamped envelope." Reports in 8 months. Negotiates rights and payment.
Needs: Play must be *full length*. "We do not restrict ourselves to any particular genre or style—generally we do a good mix of classical and modern works."

BAILIWICK REPERTORY, Dept. WM, 1225 W. Belmont Ave., Chicago IL 60657-3205. (312)883-1090. Artistic Director: David Zak. Estab. 1982. Produces: 5 mainstage plays (classic and newly comissioned) each year (submit by Nov. 1); 5 new full-length in New Directions series; 50 1-act in annual Directors Festival (submit by Dec. 1); pride performance series (gay and lesbian plays, poetry), includes one-act, poetry, workshops, and staged adaptations of prose. Submit by Oct. 1. Our audience is a typical Chicago market. Our plays are highly theatrical and politically aware. One acts should be submitted *before* Dec. 1. (One-act play fest runs March-April). Reports in 3 months. Pays 8% royalty.
Needs: We need daring scripts that break the mold. Large cast or musicals are OK. Creative staging solutions are a must.
Tips: "Know the rules, then break them creatively and *boldly*! *Please send SASE for manuscript submission guidelines before you submit.*"

BAKER'S PLAYS PUBLISHING CO., Dept. WM, 100 Chauncy St., Boston MA 02111. (617)482-1280. Fax: (617)482-7613. Editor: John B. Welch. Estab. 1845. 80% freelance written. Plays performed by amateur groups, high schools, children's theater, churches and community theater groups. 90% of scripts are unagented submissions. Works with 2-3 unpublished/unproduced writers annually. Submit complete script. Submit complete cassette of music with musical submissions. Publishes 18-25 straight plays and musicals, all originals. Pay varies; outright purchase price to split in production fees. Reports in 4 months.
Needs: "We are finding strong support in our new division—plays for young adults featuring contemporary issue-oriented dramatic pieces for high school production."
   • Send SASE for information on Baker's Plays High School Playwriting Contest.

MARY BALDWIN COLLEGE THEATRE, Mary Baldwin College, Staunton VA 24401. (703)887-7192. Artistic Director: Terry K. Southerington. Estab. 1842. Produces 5 plays/year. 10% freelance written. 75% of scripts are unagented submissions. Works with 0-1 unpublished/unproduced writer annually. An undergraduate women's college theater with an audience of students, faculty, staff and local community (adult, conservative). Query with synopsis. Query for electronic submissions. Reports in 1 year. Buys performance rights only. Pays $10-50/performance.
Needs: Full-length and short comedies, tragedies, musical plays, particularly for young women actresses, dealing with women's issues both contemporary and historical. Experimental/studio theater not suitable for heavy sets. Cast should emphasize women. No heavy sex; minimal explicit language.
Tips: "A perfect play for us has several roles for young women, few male roles, minimal production demands, a concentration on issues relevant to contemporary society, and elegant writing and structure."

BARTER THEATRE, P.O. Box 867, Abingdon VA 24210-0867. (703)628-2281. Artistic Director: Richard Rose. Estab. 1933. Produces 10 plays/year. Play performed in residency at our two facilities, a 400-seat proscenium theater and a smaller 150-seat thrust theater. "Our plays are intended for diversified audiences of all ages." Submit synopsis and dialogue sample only to: Tina Jeffers, Company Manager. Reports in 3-6 months. Royalty negotiable.
Needs: "We are looking for good plays, comedies and dramas, that entertain and are relevant; plays that comment on the times and mankind; plays that are universal. We prefer casts of 4-12, single or unit set."

BERKSHIRE PUBLIC THEATRE, 30 Union St., P.O. Box 860, Pittsfield MA 01202-0860. (413)445-4631. Fax: (413)445-4640. Artistic Director: Frank Bessell. Literary Manager: Linda Austin. Estab. 1976. Produces 10 plays/year. Year-round regional theater. Professional, non-Equity. Special interests: Contemporary issues; works dealing with ethics and morality; global concerns. Send resume, production history of the work, character break-down, synopsis, ten pages of dialogue, and self-addressed, stamped postcard for our response. Reports in 2 months on queries; 1 year on ms. Various payment arrangements.

‡BILINGUAL FOUNDATION OF THE ARTS, #19, 421 N. Ave., Los Angeles CA 90031. (213)225-4044. Fax: (213)225-1250. Artistic Director: Margarita Galban. Estab. 1973. Produces 3-5 plays plus 9-10 staged readings/year. "Productions are presented at home theater in Los Angeles, California. Our audiences are largely Hispanic and all productions are performed in English and Spanish. The Bilingual Foundation of the Arts produces plays in order to promote the rich heritage of Hispanic history and culture. Though our plays must be Hispanic in theme, we reach out to the entire community." Submit complete ms. Reports in 3-6 months. Rights negotiable. Pays royalty.
Needs: "Plays must be Hispanic in theme. Comedy, drama, light musical, children's theater, etc. are accepted for consideration. Theater is 99-seater, no fly space."

BOARSHEAD THEATER, 425 S. Grand Ave., Lansing MI 48933. (517)484-7800. Artistic Director: John Peakes. Estab. 1966. Produces 7-9 plays/year. Mainstage Actors' Equity Association company; also Youth Theater—touring to schools by our intern company. Query with synopsis, cast list (with descriptions), 5-10 pages of representative dialogue, SASE postcard. "Reports on query and synopsis in 1 week. Full manuscripts (when requested by us) in 4-8 months." Pays royalty.
Needs: Thrust stage. Cast usually 8 or less; ocassionally up to 12-14. Prefer staging which depends on theatricality rather than multiple sets.

CALIFORNIA THEATER CENTER, P.O. Box 2007, Sunnyvale CA 94110. (408)245-2978. Literary Manager: Will Huddleston. Estab. 1976. Produces 15 plays/year. Plays are for young audiences in both our home theater and for tour. Query and synopsis. Reports in 6 months. We negotiate a set fee.
Needs: All plays must be suitable for young audiences, must be under one hour in length. Cast sizes vary. Sets must be able to tour easily.

CAPITAL REPERTORY COMPANY, Dept. WM, P.O. Box 399, Albany NY 12201. (518)462-4531. Artistic Director: Bruce Bouchard. Estab. 1981. Produces 6 plays/year. "Plays are performed in LORT D 299 seat thrust house. Subscriber audience leans towards the more adventurous side of the mainstream." Query with synopsis plus first 15 pages. Agented submissions only for whole ms. Reports in 8 months. "We seek 5 years of subsidiary rights for premiere productions." Pays royalty.
Needs: "We are looking for contemporary material, comedies and dramas. No farce. We seek plays with elevated language which place the dramatic focus on the actor and the words. We love plays that are theatrical and can be served by the kind of spectacle which can be created in a small room. We also look for plays of thematic size and sweep. Plays under 6 have the best shot. Cast must be fewer than 10."
Tips: Send theatrical plays of ideas with compelling people in compelling situations. The plays, even if they depict past events, should help our audience consider and refine their sense of who they are as individuals and a society. Today, there is too much TV and film onstage. Playwrights must rediscover the essences of the theatrical imagination. Pay more attention to the voice in your cover letter and synopsis if you send unsolicited material. Send us the first 15 pages of the play. If we like it, and get the idea, we'll want to see more. Keep seeing plays, and keep writing."

CENTER STAGE, 700 N. Calvert St., Baltimore MD 21202-3686. (410)685-3200. Dramaturg: James Magruder. Estab. 1963. Produces 6-8 plays/year. "Professional LORT 'B' company; audience is both subscription and single-ticket. Wide-ranging audience profile." Query with synopsis, 10 sample pages, and resumé or submit through agent. Reports in 3 months. Rights and payment negotiated.
Needs: Produces "dramas and comedies, occasional musicals. No restrictions on topics or styles, though experimental work is encouraged. No one-act plays. Casts over 12 would give us pause. Be inventive, theatrical, not precious; we like plays with vigorous language and stage image. Domestic naturalism is discouraged; strong thematic, political, or social interests are encouraged."
Tips: "We are interested in reading adaptations and translations as well as original work."

CENTER THEATER, 1346 W. Devon Ave., Chicago IL 60660. (312)508-0200. Artistic Director: Daniel S. LaMorte. Estab. 1984. Produces approximately 13 plays/year. "We run professional productions in our Chicago 'off-Loop' theaters for a diverse audience. We also hold an international play contest annually. For more info send SASE to Dale Calandra, Literary Manager." *Agented submissions only.* Reports in 2 months.

THE CHANGING SCENE THEATER, 1527½ Champa St., Denver CO 80202. Director: Alfred Brooks. Contact: Maxine Munt. Year-round productions in theater space. Cast may be made up of both professional and amateur actors. For public audience; age varies, but mostly youthful and interested in taking a chance on new and/or experimental works. No limit to subject matter or story themes. Emphasis is on the innovative. "Also, we require that the playwright be present for at least one performance of his work, if not for the entire rehearsal period. We have a small stage area, but are able to convert to round, semi-round or environmental. Prefer to do plays with limited sets and props." Two-act and three-act.

Needs: Produces 8-10 original nonmusicals/year; all are originals. 90% freelance written. 65% of scripts produced are unagented submissions. Works with 3-4 unpublished/unproduced writers annually. "We do not pay royalties or sign contracts with playwrights. We function on a performance-share basis of payment. Our theater seats 76; the first 50 seats go to the theater; the balance is divided among the participants in the production. The performance-share process is based on the entire production run and not determined by individual performances. We do not copyright our plays." Send complete script. Reporting time varies; usually several months.

Recent Production: *Oh Revoir Mirabeau* by Mark Dunn.

Tips: "We are experimental: open to young artists who want to test their talents and open to experienced artists who want to test new ideas/explore new techniques. Dare to write 'strange and wonderful' well-thought-out scripts. We want upbeat ones. Consider that we have a small performance area when submitting."

‡CHARLOTTE REPERTORY THEATRE, 2040 Charlotte Plaza, Charlotte NC 28244. (704)375-4796. Fax: (704)375-9462. Literary Manager: Claudia Carter Covington. Litarary Associate: Carol Bellamy. Estab. 1976. Produces 13 plays/year. "We are a not for profit regional theater." Submit complete ms. Reports in 2-3 months. Writers receive free plane fare and housing for festival. SASE.

Needs: "Need full length, not previously professionally produced, non-musical scripts." "No limitations in cast, props, staging, etc."

‡CHILDREN'S STORY SCRIPTS, Baymax Productions, Suite 130, 2219 W. Olive Ave., Burbank CA 91506. (818)563-6105. Fax: (818)563-2968. Editor: Deedra Bebout. Estab. 1990. Publishes 5-15 scripts/year. "Our audience consists of children, grades K-8 (5-13 year olds)." Send complete ms with SASE. Reports in 1 month. Licenses all rights to story; author retains copyright. Pays graduated royalty based on sales.

Needs: We will publish almost any topic. Stories with a purpose that can be discussed afterwards work well. Stories that dovetail with classroom studies also work well. Scripts blend narration and dialogue. They are not meant to be memorized. Cast is stationary, readers theater-style.

Tips: "The scripts are not like theatrical scripts. They read like prose. If a writer shows promise, we'll work with him. Our most important goal is to benefit children. Send #10 SASE for guidelines with samples."

‡CHILDSPLAY, INC., P.O. Box 517, Tempe AZ 85280. (602)350-8101. Artistic Director: David P. Saar. Estab. 1978. Produces 5-6 plays/year. "Professional: Touring and inhouse productions for youth and family audiences." Submit complete ms. Reports in 6 months. "On commissioned work we hold a small percentage of royalties for 3-5 years." Pays royalty or pays $20-35/performance (touring) or pays $3-8,000 commission.

Needs: Seeking *theatrical* plays on a wide range of comtemporary topics. Touring shows: 5-6 actors; van-size. Inhouse: 6-10 actors; no technical limitations."

Tips: No traditionally handled fairy tales. "Theater for young people is growing up and is able to speak to youth and adults. The material *must* respect the artistry of the theater and the intelligence of our audience."

CINCINNATI PLAYHOUSE IN THE PARK, Dept. WM, P.O. Box 6537, Cincinnati OH 45206-0537. (513)345-2242. Fax: (513)345-2254. Contact: Artistic Associate. Estab. 1960. Produces 2 original works, 8 or 9 previously produced plays. "Nonprofit LORT theater, producing in two spaces—a 629-seat thrust stage and a 220-seat three/sided arena. The audience is a broad cross-section of people from all over the Ohio, Kentucky and Indiana areas, from varied educational and financial bases." Write for guidelines for the Lois and Richard Rosenthal New Play Prize.

CIRCUIT PLAYHOUSE/PLAYHOUSE ON THE SQUARE, 51 S. Cooper, Memphis TN 38104. (901)725-0776. Artistic Director: Jackie Nichols. Produces 16 plays/year. 100% freelance written. Professional plays performed for the Memphis/Mid-South area. Member of the Theatre Communications Group. 100% are unagented submissions. Works with 1 unpublished/unproduced writer annually. A play contest is held each fall. Submit complete ms. Reports in 6 months. Buys "percentage of royalty rights for 2 years." Pays $500.

Needs: All types; limited to single or unit sets. Cast of 20 or fewer.

Tips: "Each play is read by three readers through the extended length of time a script is kept. Preference is given to scripts for the southeastern region of the US."

CITIARTS THEATRE, 1950 Parkside Dr., Concord CA 94519-2578. (510)671-3065. Fax: (510)676-5726. Contact: Richard Elliott. Estab. 1978. Produces 9 plays/year. Professional production during subscription season (August-June). Approximate yearly audience of 49,000, San Francisco Bay Area. Submit complete ms with SASE and resume. Reports in 6 months. "Obtains negotiable, various rights." Pays negotiable royalty.

Needs: "We need smaller (9 person or less) musicals (or revues with a plot), contemporary dramas dealing with urban issues and contemporary comedy—all styles. We have no flyspace, and prefer unit or platform sets, using 9 people or less."

Tips: "Besides conventional and mainstream theater pieces, we are seeking thoughtful, carefully composed works incorporating performance art, with strong narrative, blends of different styles. We accept scripts year-round, with the preference being between November and February of each year."

‡**CITY THEATRE COMPANY**, 57 S. 13th St., Pittsburgh PA 15203. Fax: (412)431-5535. Producing Director: Marc Masterson. Produces 5 full productions/year. "We are a small professional theater, operating under an Equity contract, and committed to plays of ideas and substance relevant to contemporary American values and cultures. Our seasons are innovative and challenging, both artistically and socially. We perform in a 225-seat thrust or proscenium stage, playing usually 7 times a week, each production running 1 month or more. We have a committed audience following." Query with synopsis or submit through agent. Obtains no rights. Pays 5-6% royalty. Reports in 6 months.
Needs: "No limits on style or subject, but we are most interested in theatrical plays that have something to say about the way we live. No light comedies or TV-issue dramas." Normal cast limit is 7. Plays must be appropriate for small space without flies.
Tips: "Our emphasis is on new and recent American plays."

I.E. CLARK, INC., Saint John's Rd., P.O. Box 246, Schulenburg TX 78956-0246. (409)743-3232. Contact: Carol Drabek. Estab. 1956. Publishes 15 plays/year for educational theater, children's theater, religious theater, regional professional theater and amateur community theater. 20% freelance written. 3-4 scripts published/year are unagented submissions. Works with 2-3 unpublished writers annually. Submit complete ms, one at a time. Manuscript will not be returned without SASE. Reports in 3-6 months. Buys all available rights; "we serve as an agency as well as a publisher." Pays standard book and performance royalty, "the amount and percentages dependent upon type and marketability of play." Catalog $2. Writer's guidelines for #10 SASE.
Needs: "We are interested in plays of all types—short or long. Audiotapes of music or videotapes of a performance are requested with submissions of musicals. We require that a play has been produced (directed by someone other than the author); photos, videos, and reviews of the production are helpful. No limitations in cast, props, staging, etc. Plays with only one or two characters are difficult to sell. We insist on literary quality. We like plays that give new interpretations and understanding of human nature. Correct spelling, punctuation and grammar (befitting the characters, of course) impress our editors."
Tips: "Entertainment value and a sense of moral responsibility seem to be returning as essential qualities of a good play script. The era of glorifying the negative elements of society seems to be fading rapidly. Literary quality, entertainment value and good craftsmanship rank in that order as the characteristics of a good script in our opinion. 'Literary quality' means that the play must—in beautiful, distinctive, and un-trite language—say something; preferably something new and important concerning man's relations with his fellow man; and these 'lessons in living' must be presented in an intelligent, believable and creative manner. Plays for children's theater are tending more toward realism and childhood problems rather than fantasy or dramatization of fairy tales."

THE CLEVELAND PLAY HOUSE, Dept. WM, 8500 Euclid Ave., Cleveland OH 44106. (216)795-7010. Fax: (216)795-7005. Artistic Director: Josephine R. Abady. Literary Manager: Roger T. Danforth. Produces 12 plays/year. Resident LORT theater. Audience: subscribers and single ticket buyers; three different theaters with different audience needs/requirements: 160-experimental, 499 and 615-mainstage subscription theaters. Agented submissions only. Reports in 6 months. Negotiated rights. Pay negotiable.
Needs: Full length; emphasis on American realism; all styles and topics given full consideration, however. Musicals also welcome.
Tips: "No translations of foreign works. No previously produced works that received national attention."

CLEVELAND PUBLIC THEATRE, 6415 Detroit Ave., Cleveland OH 44102. (216)631-2727. Artistic Director: James A. Levin. Estab. 1982. Produces 6 (full production) plays annually. Also sponsors Festival of New Plays. 150-seat alternative performance space. "Our audience believes that art touches your heart and your nerve endings." Query with synopsis for full season. Rights negotiable. Pays $15-100/performance.
Needs: Poetic, experimental, avant-garde, political, multicultural works that need a stage (not a camera); interdisciplinary cutting-edge work (dance/performance art/music/visual); works that stretch or explode the imagination and conventional boundaries. "We are a 150-seat black box with no fly space. We are low-budget—imagination must substitute for dollars."
Tips: "No conventional comedies, musicals, adaptations, children's plays—if you think Samuel French would love it, we probably won't. No TV sitcoms or soaps masquerading as theater. Theater is *not* TV or films. Learn the impact of what live bodies do to an audience in the same room. We are particularly interested in artists from our region who can grow with us on a longterm basis."

COLONY STUDIO THEATRE, 1944 Riverside Dr., Los Angeles CA 90039. New play selection committee: Judith Goldstein. Produces 4 mainstage productions and 4 workshop productions/year. Professional 99-seat theater with thrust stage. Casts from a resident company of professional actors. No unsolicited scripts.

Submission guidelines for #10 SASE. Reports in 6 months on mss. Negotiated rights. Royalties for each performance.
Needs: "Full length (90-120 minutes) with a cast of 2-10. No musicals or experimental works.
Tips: "A polished script is the mark of a skilled writer. Submissions should be in professional (centered) format."

CONTEMPORARY DRAMA SERVICE, Meriwether Publishing Ltd., P.O. Box 7710, Colorado Springs CO 80933. (303)594-4422. Fax: (719)594-9916. Editor-in-Chief: Arthur Zapel. Associate Editors: Theodore Zapel and Rhonda Wray. Estab. 1969. Publishes 50-60 plays/year. "We publish for the secondary school market and colleges. We also publish for mainline liturgical churches—drama activities for church holidays, youth activities and fundraising entertainments. These may be plays or drama-related books." Query with synopsis or submit complete ms. Reports in 6 weeks or less. Obtains either amateur or all rights. Pays 10% royalty or outright negotiated purchase.
Needs: "Most of the plays we publish are one-acts, 15 to 45 minutes in length. We occasionally publish full-length three-act plays. We prefer comedies in the longer plays. Musical plays must have name appeal either by prestige author, prestige title adaptation or performance on Broadway or TV. Comedy sketches, mono-logues and 2-character plays are welcomed. We prefer simple staging appropriate to high school, college or church performance. We like playwrights who see the world positively and with a sense of humor. Offbeat themes and treatments are accepted if the playwright can sustain a light touch and not take himself or herself too seriously. In documentary or religious plays we look for good research and authenticity. We are publishing more textbooks on the theatrical arts than trade books."

THE COTERIE, 2450 Grand Ave., Kansas City MO 64108-2520. (816)474-6785. Fax: (816)474-6785. Artistic Director: Jeff Church. Estab. 1979. Produces 7-8 plays/year. "Plays produced at Hallmark's Crown Center in downtown Kansas City in the Coterie's resident theater (capacity 240). A typical performance run is one month in length." Submit query with synopsis or complete ms only if an established playwright in youth theater field. Reports in 2-4 months. "We retain some rights on commissioned plays." Pays royalty, per performance and flat fee.
Needs: "We produce plays which are universal in appeal; they may be original or adaptations of classic or contemporary literature. Typically, not more than 12 in a cast—prefer 5-9 in size. No fly space or wing space."
Tips: "No couch plays. Prefer plays by seasoned writers who have established reputations. Groundbreaking and exciting scripts from the youth theater field welcome. It's prefectly fine if your play is a little off center." Trends in the field that writers should be mindful of: "Make certain your submitted play to us is *very* theatrical and not cinematic. Writers need to see how far the field of youth and family theater has come—the interesting new areas we're going—before sending us your query or manuscript."

CREATIVE PRODUCTIONS, INC., 2 Beaver Pl., Aberdeen NJ 07747. (908)566-6985. Artistic Director: Walter L. Born. Produces 2 musicals/year. Non-equity, year-round productions. "We use musicals with folks with disabilities and the older performers in addition to 'normal' performers, for the broad spectrum of viewers." Query with synopsis. Reports in 2 weeks. Buys rights to perform play for specified number of performances. Pays $75-150/performance.
Needs: Musicals about people with disabilities where they are actually used as performers; unusual subjects out of ordinary human experiences plus music. Limitations: Cast: maximum 12, sets can't "fly," facilities are schools, no mammoth sets and multiple scene changes.
Tips: No blue material, pornographic, obscene language. Submit info on any performances plus pix of set and actors in costume. Demo tape (musicals); list of references on users of their material to confirm bio info.

CREEDE REPERTORY THEATRE, P.O. Box 269, Creede CO 81130-0269. (719)658-2541. Artistic Director: Richard Baxter. Estab. 1966. Produces 6 plays/year. Plays performed for a summer audience. Submit query and synopsis. Reports in 1 year. Royalties negotiated with each author—paid on a per performance basis.
Needs: One-act children's scripts. Special consideration given to plays focusing on the cultures and history of the American West and Southwest.
Tips: "No avant garde or experimental work. We seek new adaptations of classical or older works as well as original scripts."

‡**DELAWARE THEATRE COMPANY**, 200 Water St., Wilmington DE 19801-5030. (302)594-1104. Artistic Director: Cleveland Morris. Estab. 1978. Produces 5 plays/year. 10% freelance written. "Plays are performed as part of a five-play subscription season in a 300-seat auditorium. Professional actors, directors and designers are engaged. The season is intended for a general audience." 10% of scripts are unagented submissions. Works with 1 unpublished/unproduced writer every two years. Query with synopsis. Reports in 6 months. Buys variable rights. Pays 5% (variable) royalty.
Needs: "We present comedies, dramas, tragedies and musicals. All works must be full length and fit in with a season composed of standards and classics. All works have a strong literary element. Plays showing a flair for language and a strong involvement with the interests of classical humanism are of greatest interest. Single-

set, small-cast works are likeliest for consideration." Recent trend toward "more economical productions."

DENVER CENTER THEATRE COMPANY, 1050 13th St., Denver CO 80204. (303)893-4200. Fax: (303)893-2860. Artistic Director: Donovan Marley. Estab. 1979. Produces 12 plays/year. "Denver Center Theater Company produces an annual New Plays Festival, entitled US West TheatreFest. Up to 8 new scripts are rehearsed and presented in staged readings; up to 4 are presented in full production." Submission guidelines for SASE. TheatreFest submittals must be previously unproduced. DCTC negotiates for production rights on scripts selected for full presentation but does not hold rights on TheatreFest scripts. Royalty to be negotiated.
Needs: Full-length unproduced scripts. "We do not accept one-acts, adaptations, or children's plays."

DISCOVERY '94, Paul Mellon Arts Center, P.O. Box 788, Wallingford CT 06492. (203)269-1113. Artistic Director: Terrence Ortwein. Estab. 1984. Produces 3 plays/year. "Choate Rosemary Hall in Wallingford, Connecticut, will host its 10th summer theater program committed to the discovery and development of new scripts written specifically for secondary school production. Students with an interest in theater from around the country will join directors and writers-in-residence in order to rehearse and perform new works in July. Playwrights will have the opportunity to hear, see and rewrite their scripts during three-week residencies. Public workshop performances will provide audience reactions to the works-in-progress and will enable the playwrights to further develop their scripts for future productions." Submit complete ms. Playwrights selected must agree to be in residence at Choate Rosemary Hall the last 3½ weeks in July. Room, board and a $700 stipend will be given each playwright selected. The workshop productions, script-in-hand so that the playwright will have every opportunity to rewrite during every step of his or her *discovery*, will be the responsibility of Choate Rosemary Hall.
Tips: "The content should appeal strongly and directly to teenagers. Although all the characters don't have to be teenagers, the actors will be. In most high schools, more girls than boys participate in drama. Most high schools have limited technical resources and limited budgets. Although we will look at full-length scripts, the real need and interest is in the one-act and hour-length play. This program is established to help playwrights develop scripts, not to produce already finished scripts. *Only unproduced and unpublished scripts may be submitted.*" Submission date: March 1, 1994. Notification: May 1, 1994. Include SASE for returns.

DORSET THEATRE FESTIVAL, Box 519, Dorset VT 05251-0519. (802)867-2223. Artistic Director: Jill Charles. Estab. 1976. Produces 5 plays/year, one of which is a new work. "Our plays will be performed in our Equity summer stock theatre and are intended for a sophisticated community." Agented submissions only. Reports in 3-6 months. Rights and compensation arranged on an individual basis.
Needs: "We are looking for full length contemporary American comedy or drama. We are limited to a cast of 6."
Tips: "Language and subject matter appropriate to general audience."

DRAMATICS MAGAZINE, Dept. WM, 3368 Central Pkwy., Cincinnati OH 45225. (513)559-1996. Editor: Don Corathers. Estab. 1929. Publishes 5 plays/year. For high school theater students and teachers. Submit complete ms. Reports in 2 months. Buys first North American serial rights only. Purchases one-time publication rights only for $100-400.
Needs: "We are seeking one-acts to full-lengths that can be produced in an educational theater setting. We don't publish musicals."
Tips: "No melodrama, farce, children's theater, or cheap knock-offs of TV sit-coms to movies. Fewer writers are taking the time to learn the conventions of theater—what makes a piece work on stage, as opposed to film and television—and their scripts show it."

ELDRIDGE PUBLISHING CO., P.O. Box 216, Franklin OH 45005-0216. (513)746-6531. Fax: (800)453-5179. Editor: Nancy Vorhis. Estab. 1906. Publishes 35-40 new plays/year for middle school, junior high, senior high, church and community audience. Query with synopsis (acceptable) or submit complete ms (preferred). Please send cassette tapes with any operettas. Reports in 2 months. Buys all rights. Pays 50% royalties and 10% copy sales. Outright purchase from $200-500. Writer's guidelines for #10 SASE.
Needs: "We are most interested in full-length plays and musicals for our school and community theater market. Prefer large, flexible casts, if possible. Nothing lower than junior high level, please. We always love comedies but also look for serious, high caliber plays reflective of today's sophisticated students. We also need one-acts and plays for children's theater. In addition, in our religious market we're always searching for Christmas and Easter plays."

 The double dagger before a listing indicates that the listing is new in this edition. New markets are often more receptive to freelance submissions.

Tips: "Submissions are welcomed at any time but during our fall season; response will definitely take 2 months. Authors are paid royalties twice a year. They receive complimentary copies of their published plays, the annual catalog and 50% discount if buying additional copies."

THE EMPTY SPACE, P.O. Box 1748, Seattle WA 98111-1748. (206)587-3737. Artistic Director: Eddie Levi Lee. Estab. 1970. Produces 6 plays/year. 100% freelance written. Professional plays for subscriber base and single ticket Seattle audience. One script/year is unagented submission. Works with 5-6 unpublished/unproduced writers annually. Query with synopsis before sending script. Response in 5 months. LOA theater.
Needs: "Other things besides linear, narrative realism, but we are interested in that as well. No restriction on subject matter. Generally we opt for broader, more farcical comedies and harder-edged, uncompromising dramas. We like to go places we've never been before."

ENCORE PERFORMANCE PUBLISHING, P.O. Box 692, Orem UT 84059. (801)225-0605. Editor: Michael C. Perry. Estab. 1979. Publishes 20-50 plays/year. "Our audience consists of all ages with emphasis on the family; educational institutions from elementary through college/university, community theaters and professional theaters." Query with synopsis. Reports in 2 weeks on queries; 3 months on mss. Pays 50% performance royalty; 10% book royalty.
Needs: "We are looking for plays with strong message about or for families, plays with young actors among cast, any length, all genres. We prefer scripts with at least close or equal male/female roles, could lean to more female roles." Plays must have had at least 2 fully staged productions. Unproduced plays can be read with letter of recomendation accompanying the query.
Tips: "No performance art pieces or plays with overtly sexual themes or language. Looking for adaptations of Twain and other American authors."

THE ENSEMBLE STUDIO THEATRE, 549 W. 52nd St., New York NY 10019. (212)247-4982. Fax: (212)664-0041. Artistic Director: Curt Dempster. Estab. 1971. Produces 250 projects annually for off-off Broadway developmental theater. 100-seat house, 60-seat workshop space. Do not fax ms or résumés. Submit complete ms. Reports in 3 months. Standard production contract: mini contract with Actors' Equity Association or letter of agreement. Pays $80-1,000.
Needs: Full-lengths and one-acts with strong dramatic actions and situations. No musicals, verse-dramas or elaborate costume dramas.
Tips: Submit work September through April. "We are dedicated to developing new American plays."

ENSEMBLE THEATRE OF CINCINNATI, 1127 Vine St., Cincinnati OH 45210. (513)421-3556. Artistic Director: David A. White II. Estab. 1986. Produces 6 plays/year. "ETC is a franchised theater of the Actors' Equity Association. Our audiences tend to be serious theater people, with an interest in new works." Submit complete ms. Reports in 3 months. Pays 7% royalty or $1,000-10,000 outright purchase.
Needs: "We have discovered that good comedies are hard to come by. We are also interested in socially relevant material. We prefer a simple set with 6 or fewer actors."
Tips: "No AIDS or 'thirtysomething' material."

FAIRFIELD COUNTY, (formerly Boston Post Road Stage Company), 25 Powers Court., Westport CT 06880. (203)227-1290. Artistic Director: Burry Fredrik. Produces 6 plays/year. "LOA (Equity) theater playing to audiences in Fairfield County. Audiences are adult, seniors and interested students." Also has an outreach program for schools. Submit complete ms. Reports in 6 months. Right to produce a 4-week run of the play with an option for several months following conclusion of run to explore further production possibilities. Pays 4-5% royalty.
Needs: Off-Broadway in Connecticut. Emphasis on originality of script. "We will take risks if the play is good. We produce a wide range of plays, comedy, drama, musical (small). Budgetary considerations are our limitations. Maximum seven characters; we prefer fewer, however. We are eligible for grants to develop new plays if something were to strike us which was more expensive than our budget would allow."
Tips: "We're tired of NYC apartment tirades and moot-point 'true' biographies. No obviously large cast or panoramic history plays. The dramatic structure of a play must stimulate an audience. Foul language acceptable only when inherent to the dramatic situation. No headline plays that cannot transcend the ordinary details of everyday life; even a 'slice-of-life' play must inform us about life, not just illustrate it."

FLORIDA STUDIO THEATRE, 1241 N. Palm Ave., Sarasota FL 34236. (813)366-9017. New plays director: Steve Ramay. Produces 4 established and 3 new plays/year. "FST is a professional not-for-profit theater." Plays are produced in 165-seat theater for a subscription audience (primarily). FST operates under a small professional theater contract of Actor's Equity. Query with synopsis. Reports in 2 months on queries; 7 months on mss. Pays $200 for workshop production of new script.
Needs: Contemporary plays ("courageous and innovative"). Prefers casts of no more than 8 and single sets.

‡**THE FREELANCE PRESS,** P.O. Box 548, Dover MA 02030-2207. (508)785-1260. Managing Editor: Narcissa Campion. Estab. 1984. Publishes 4 plays/year for children/young adults. Submit complete ms and SASE. Reports in 3-4 months. Pays 2-3% royalty. Pays 10% of the price of each script and score.

Needs: "Publish original musical theater for young people, dealing with issues of importance to them, also adapt 'classics' into musicals for 8-16-year-old age groups to perform." Large cast; flexible, simple staging and props.

SAMUEL FRENCH, INC., 45 W. 25th St., New York NY 10010-2751. Fax: (212)206-1429. Editor: Lawrence Harbison. "We publish about 50-60 new titles/year. We are the world's largest publisher of plays. 10-20% are unagented submissions. In addition to publishing plays, we occasionally act as agents in the placement of plays for professional production—eventually in New York. Pays on royalty basis. Submit complete ms (bound). Always type your play in the standard, accepted stageplay ms format used by all professional playwrights in the US. If in doubt, send $4 to the attention of Lawrence Harbison for a copy of 'Guidelines.' We require a minimum of 2 months to report."
Needs: "We are willing at all times to read the work of freelancers. Our markets prefer simple-to-stage, light, happy romantic comedies or mysteries with a good complement of female roles. No puppet plays; no adaptations of public domain children's stories; no verse plays; no large-cast historical (costume) plays; no seasonal plays; no television, film or radio scripts."

GEORGE STREET PLAYHOUSE, 9 Livingston Ave., New Brunswick NJ 08901. (908)846-2895. Producing Director: Gregory Hurst. Literary Manager: Wendy Liscow. Produces 7 plays/year. Professional regional theater (LORT C). No unsolicited scripts. Professional recommendation only. Reports on scripts in 8-12 months on mss.
Needs: Full-length dramas, comedies and musicals that present a fresh perspective on society and challenge expectations of theatricality. Prefers cast size under 9. We also present 40-minute social issue plays appropriate for touring to school-age children. Cast size limited to 4 actors.
Tips: "We present a series of 6 staged readings each year. We produce up to 4 new plays and 1 new musical each season. We have a strong interest in receiving work from minority writers."

GEORGETOWN PRODUCTIONS, 7 Park Ave., New York NY 10016-4330. Producer: Gerald van de Vorst. Literary Manager: George Grec. Estab. 1972. Produces 1-2 plays/year for a general audience. Works with 2-3 unpublished/unproduced writers annually. Submit complete ms only. Reports in 2 weeks. Standard Dramatists Guild contract.
Needs: Prefers plays with small casts and not demanding more than one set. Interested in new unconventional scripts dealing with contemporary issues, comedies, mysteries, musicals or dramas. No first drafts, outlines or one-act plays.
Tips: "The current trend is toward light entertainment, as opposed to meaningful or serious plays."

‡THE GOODMAN THEATRE, 200 S. Columbus Ave., Chicago IL 60603. (312)443-3811. Artistic Director: Robert Falls. Estab. 1925. Produces 9 plays/year. "The Goodman is a professional, not-for-profit theater producing both a mainstage and studio series for its subscription-based audience. The Goodman does not accept unsolicited scripts from playwrights or agents, nor will it respond to synopses of plays submitted by playwrights, unless accompanied by a stamped, self-addressed postcard. The Goodman may request plays to be submitted for production consideration after receiving a letter of inquiry or telephone call from recognized literary agents or producing organizations." Reports in 6 months. Buys variable rights. Pay is variable.
Needs: Full-length plays, translations, musicals; special interest in social or political themes.

GREATWORKS PLAY SERVICE, P.O. Box 3148, Shell Beach CA 93448-3148. (805)773-3419. Editor: Richard Sharp. Publishes 30 plays/year. All professional, community theatre and college; some high school. Query with synopsis. Reports in 1 month on queries; 1 year on mss. Buys exclusive rights to publish and represent play for purposes/leasing production rights. Pays variable royalty. Submissions with SASE returned.
Needs: "We limit ourselves to translations from other languages and adaptation for the stage from other forms—especially recognized works of literature. No material that has not already been produced."

‡GRETNA THEATRE, P.O. Box 578, Mt. Gretna PA 17064. (717)964-3322. Producing Director: Al Franklin. Estab. 1977. Produces 1 new play/year. "Plays are performed at a professional equity theater during summer for a conservative audience." Query with synopsis. "Include character breakdown with script's production history, plus 5 pages." Reports in 4-6 weeks. Rights negotiated. Royalty negotiated (6-12%).
Needs: "We produce full length plays for a conservative, summer audience—subject, language, content important; comedy is popular." Cast of 10 limit—simple settings best.
Tips: "No one acts, musicals, *heavy* drama or poorly written work."

‡THE GROUP (Seattle Group Theatre), 305 Harrison St., Seattle WA 98109. (206)441-9480. Artistic Director: Tim Bond. (Submit to Nancy Griffiths, Dramaturg, Literary Manager). Estab. 1978. Produces 6 plays and 3 workshop productions/year. "Plays are performed in our 197-seat theater—The Carlton Playhouse. Intended for a multi-ethnic audience. Professional, year-round theater." Query with synopsis, sample pages of dialogue and SASE for reply. Reports in 6-8 weeks. Rights obtained vary per production. Royalty varies.

Needs: "We look for scripts suitable for multi-ethnic casting that deal with social, cultural and political issues relevant to the world today."
Tips: *No phone calls.*

HARTFORD STAGE COMPANY, 50 Church St., Hartford CT 06103. (203)525-5601. Artistic Director: Mark Lamos. Contact: John Dias, literary associate. Estab. 1964. Produces 6 plays/year. Professional regional theater with subscriber base. Query with synopsis. Reports in 8 months. Buys only one-time production rights. Pays royalty.
Needs: Full-length plays, translations, adaptations. Limitations are figured on a per-season, rather than per-script basis.
Tips: No one-acts or work for children.

HEUER PUBLISHING CO., 233 Dows Bldg., Box 248, Cedar Rapids IA 52406-0248. (319)364-6311. Fax: (319)364-1771. Owner/Editor: C. Emmett McMullen. Publishes plays and musicals for junior and senior high school and church groups. Query with synopsis or submit complete ms. Reports in 2 months. Purchases amateur rights only. Pays royalty or cash.
Needs: "One- and three-act plays suitable for school production. Preferably comedy or mystery comedy. All material should be of the capabilities of high school actors. We prefer material with one set. No special day material or material with controversial subject matter."

HILBERRY THEATRE, 95 W. Hancock, Detroit MI 48202. (313)577-3508. Artistic Director, Wayne State Playwrights' Workshop: Joe Calarco. Estab. 1962. Produces 7 plays/year. Plays performed in the metro Detroit area for educated, mature audience. Query with synopsis and 10 pages of dialogue. Reports on queries in 1 month, fall and winter. Pays royalty.
Needs: "Hilberry is a theater which produces classical plays as well as modern and new material. We need plays for large casts (20 actors). Our acting company consists of 14 men and 6 women."
Tips: "Plays with strong narratives are especially desirable. Our theater is a 530 seat open stage which produces 7 plays (150 plus performances) to approximately 90% capacity over a 9 month season (September-May). Subscriptions account for 70% of the audience."

‡HIPPODROME STATE THEATRE, 25 SE 2nd Place, Gainesville FL 32601. (904)373-5968. Artistic Director: Mary Hausch. Estab. 1973. Produces 6 productions, (4 new play readings). Plays are performed on one main stage (268 seats) for a subscriber audience. Query with synopsis and resume. Reports in 6-8 months. Pay negotiable.
Needs: "We accept plays of any genre or subject matter. We're looking for *good writing* and fresh, original voices. Cast should not exceed 10; staging flexible, but should be appropriate for thrust stage."
Tips: No plays that are derivative of contemporary playwrights. "Writers should stay true to their taste and vision and forget about what audiences or producers might want to see. The more evidence a writer has that he/she is serious and committed to playwriting, the better chance he/she has at our reading their script."

‡HONOLULU THEATRE FOR YOUTH, 2846 Ualena St., Honolulu HI 96819. (808)839-9885. Fax: (808)839-7018. Artistic Director: Pam Sterling. Produces 6 plays/year. 50% freelance written. Plays are professional productions in Hawaii, primarily for young audiences (ages 2 to 20). 80% of scripts are unagented submissions. Works with 2 unpublished/unproduced writers annually. Reports in 4 months. Buys negotiable rights.
Needs: Contemporary subjects of concern/interest to young people; adaptations of literary classics; fantasy including space, fairy tales, myth and legend. "HTY wants well-written plays, 60-90 minutes in length, that have something worthwhile to say and that will stretch the talents of professional adult actors." Cast not exceeding 8; *no* technical extravaganzas; *no* full-orchestra musicals; simple sets and props, costumes can be elaborate. No plays to be enacted by children or camp versions of popular fairytales. Query with synopsis. Pays $1,000-2,500.
Tips: "Young people are intelligent and perceptive; if anything, more so than lots of adults, and if they are to become fans and eventual supporters of good theater, they must see good theater while they are young. Trends on the American stage that freelance writers should be aware of include a growing awareness that we are living in a world community. We must learn to share and understand other people and other cultures."

HORIZON THEATRE COMPANY, P.O. Box 5376, Station E, Atlanta GA 30307. (404)584-7450. Artistic Director: Lisa Adler. Estab. 1983. Produces 4 plays/year. Professional productions. Query with synopsis and resume. Reports in 1-2 years. Buys rights to produce in Atlanta area. Pays 6-8% royalty or $50-75/performance.
Needs: "We produce contemporary plays with realistic base, but which utilize heightened visual or language elements. Interested in comedy, satire, plays that are entertaining and topical, but also thought provoking. Also particular interest in plays by women or with Southern themes." No more than 10 in cast.
Tips: "No plays about being in theater or film; no plays without hope; no plays that include playwrights as leading characters; no all-male casts; no plays with all older (50 plus) characters."

WILLIAM E. HUNT, 801 West End Ave., New York NY 10025. Estab. 1947. Producer/Director: William E. Hunt. Interested in reading scripts for stock production, off-Broadway and even Broadway production. "Small cast, youth-oriented, meaningful, technically adventuresome; serious, funny, far-out. Must be about people first, ideas second. No political or social tracts." No one-act, anti-Black, anti-Semitic or anti-gay plays. "I do not want 1920, 1930 or 1940 plays disguised as modern by 'modern' language. I do not want plays with 24 characters, plays with 150 costumes, plays about symbols instead of people. I do not want plays that are really movie or television scripts." Works with 2-3 unpublished/unproduced writers annually. Pays royalties on production. Off-Broadway, 5%; on Broadway, 5%, 7½% and 10%, based on gross. No royalty paid if play is selected for a showcase production. Reports in "a few weeks." Must have SASE or script will not be returned.
Tips: "Production costs and weekly running costs in the legitimate theater are so high today that no play (or it is the very rare play) with more than six characters and more than one set, by a novice playwright, is likely to be produced unless that playwright will either put up or raise the money him or herself for the production."

INVISIBLE THEATRE, 1400 N. 1st Ave., Tucson AZ 85719. (602)882-9721. Artistic Director: Susan Claassen. Literary Manager: Deborah Dickey. Estab. 1971. Produces 5-7 plays/year. 10% freelance written. Semiprofessional regional theater for liberal, college-educated audiences. Plays performed in 78-seat non-Equity theater with small production budget. Works with 1-5 unpublished/unproduced writers annually. No unsolicited scripts; script must be accompanied by recommendation from theater professional. Reports in 6 months. Buys non-professional rights. Royalty paid.
Needs: "Two-act plays, generally contemporary, some historical, comedies, drama, small musicals, wide range of topics. Limited to plays with small casts of 10 or less, strong female roles, simple sets, minimal props." No large musicals, complex set designs, casts larger than 10.
Tips: "Trends in the American stage that will affect the types of scripts we accept include social issues — social conscience — i.e. South Africa, coming to terms with elderly parents, overcoming effects of disease, family relationships, things that the average person can relate to and think about. Challenges we can all relate to, common experiences, because people enjoy people. Our audiences include some older, somewhat conservative, members (although *not* rigid or dogmatic) as well as younger, more liberal groups. We try to have broad appeal — mixing experimental with comedy and drama throughout the year."

JEWEL BOX THEATRE, 3700 N. Walker, Oklahoma City OK 73118-7099. (405)521-1786. Artistic Director: Charles Tweed. Estab. 1988. Produces 6 plays/year. Amateur productions. For 3,000 season subscribers and general public. Submit complete ms. Reports in 4 months. "We would like to have first production rights and 'premiere' the play at Jewel Box Theatre." Pays $500 contest prize.
Needs: "Write theater for entry form during September-October. We produce dramas, comedies and musicals. Only two- or three-act plays can be accepted. Our theater is in-the-round, so we adapt plays accordingly." Deadline: middle of January.

JEWISH REPERTORY THEATRE, 1395 Lexington Ave., New York NY 10128. (212)415-5550. Artistic Director: Ran Avni. Associate Director: Edward M. Cohen. Estab. 1974. Produces 4 plays, 15 readings/year. New York City professional off-Broadway production. Submit complete ms. Reports in 1 month. First production/option to move to Broadway or off-Broadway. Pays royalty.
Needs: Full-length only. Straight plays and musicals. Must have some connection to Jewish life, characters, history. Maximum 7 characters. Limited technical facilities.
Tips: No biblical plays.

KUMU KAHUA, 1770 East-West Rd., Honolulu HI 96822-2366. (808)956-2588. Managing Director: Dennis Carroll. Estab. 1971. Produces 4 productions, 4 public readings/year. "Plays performed at various theaters for community audiences." Submit complete ms. Reports in 3 months. Royalty is $35/performance; usually 10 performances of each production.
Needs: "Plays must have some interest for local audiences, preferably by being set in Hawaii or dealing with some aspect of the Hawaiian experience. Prefer small cast, with simple staging demands."
Tips: "We need time to evaluate scripts (our response time is 3 months)."

‡LAGUNA PLAYHOUSE, 606 Laguna Canyon Rd., Laguna Beach CA 92651. (714)497-5900, ext. 206. Artistic Director: Andrew Barnicle. Estab. 1922. Produces 10 plays/year. Amateur with Equity Guest Artists: 5 mainstage (9,000 subscribers); Amateur: 5 youth theater (1,500 subscribers). Submit complete ms. Reports in 2-6 months. Pay negotiable. Royalty negotiable.
Needs: Seeking full-length plays: comedy, drama, classical, musical youth theater.
Tips: "We are committed to one full production of an original play every other season."

LILLENAS PUBLISHING CO., P.O. Box 419527, Kansas City MO 64141-6527. (816)931-1900. Fax: (816)753-4071. Editor: Paul M. Miller. "We publish on two levels: (1) Program Builders — seasonal and topical collections of recitations, sketches, dialogues and short plays; (2) Drama Resources. These assume more than one format: (a) full length scripts, (b) one-acts, shorter plays and sketches all by one author, (c) collection of short plays and sketches by various authors. All program and play resources are produced with local church and Christian school in mind. Therefore there are taboos." Queries are encouraged, but synopses and complete mss are read. "First rights are purchased for Program Builder manuscripts. For our line of Drama Resources, we purchase all print rights, but this is negotiable." Writer's guidelines for #10 SASE. Reports in 3 months.

• This publisher has added a line of full-length plays for school and dinner theater use; wholesome entertainment—not religious.

Needs: 98% of Program Builder materials are freelance written. Manuscripts selected for these publications are outright purchases; verse is 25 cents/line, prose (play scripts) are $5/double-spaced page. "Lillenas Drama Resources is a line of play scripts that are, for the most part, written by professionals with experience in production as well as writing. However, while we do read unsolicited manuscripts, more than half of what we publish is written by experienced authors whom we have already published." Drama Resources (whether full-length scripts, one-acts, or sketches) are paid on a 10% royalty. There are no advances.

Tips: "All plays need to be presented in standard play script format. We welcome a summary statement of each play. Purpose statements are always desirable. Approximate playing time, cast and prop lists, etc. are important to include. We are interested in fully scripted traditional plays, reader's theater scripts, choral speaking pieces. Contemporary settings generally have it over Biblical settings. Christmas and Easter scripts must have a bit of a twist. Secular approaches to these seasons (Santas, Easter bunnies, and so on), are not considered. We sell our product in 10,000 Christian bookstores and by catalog. We are probably in the forefront as a publisher of religious drama resources."

LIVE OAK THEATRE, 311 Nueces St., Austin TX 78701. (512)472-5143. Artistic Director: Don Toner. Literary Manager: Amparo Garcia. Estab. 1982. Professional theatre that produces 2 plays/season. "Live Oak has a history of producing works of Texas and southern topics. Well-crafted, new American plays that are strongly theatrical." Query with synopsis and 10 pages of dialogue. Reports in 1 month on queries; 6 months on mss. Pays royalty.

Needs: Full-length, one-acts, translations, adaptations, musicals, plays for young audiences. Guidelines for #10 SASE.

Tips: Also sponsors annual new play awards. Guidelines for #10 SASE after August 1.

MAD RIVER THEATER WORKS, P.O. Box 248, W. Liberty OH 43357-0248. (513)465-6751. Fax: (513)465-3914. Artistic Director: Jeff Hooper. Estab. 1978. Produces 3 plays/year. "Mad River is a professional company. We present over 150 performances each year at colleges, universities and in small towns, for a broad, multigenerational audience. Our intended audience is primarily rural." Query with synopsis. Reports in 2 months. Buys exclusive production rights for a limited time. Pays negotiable royalty.

Needs: "We primarily produce works that deal with rural themes and/or issues. A small cast is most likely to be accepted. As a touring company, simple technical requirements are also a factor."

Tips: "We reach out to many different kinds of people, particularly audiences in rural areas without other access to professional theater. We seek to challenge, as well as entertain, and present works which can speak to conservative individuals as well as seasoned theatergoers."

‡MAGIC THEATRE, INC., Bldg. D, Fort Mason, San Francisco CA 94123. (415)441-8001. Artistic Director: Larry Eilenberg. Estab. 1966. Produces 7 plays/year. Regional theater. Query with synopsis. Reports in 4 months. Pays royalty or per performance fee.

Needs: "Plays that are innovative in theme and/or craft, cutting-edge political concerns, intelligent comedy. Full-length only, strong commitment to multicultural work

• Magic Theatre has all new artistic leadership.

Tips: "Not interested in classics, conventional approaches and cannot produce large-cast plays."

MANHATTAN THEATRE CLUB, 453 W. 16th St., New York NY 10011-5896. Director of Play Development: Kate Loewald. Produces 8 plays/year. Two-theater arts complex classified as off-Broadway, using professional actors. No unsolicited scripts. Query with synopsis. Reports in 6 months. Contract terms negotiable.

Needs: "We present a wide range of new work, from this country and abroad, to a subscription audience. We want plays about contemporary problems and people. Comedies are welcome. Heavy set shows or multiple detailed sets are discouraged. We present shows with casts of not more than 15; average cast is 8. No skits."

MERRIMACK REPERTORY THEATRE, Dept. WM, P.O. Box 228, Lowell MA 01853-0228. (508)454-6324. Artistic Director: David G. Kent. Estab. 1979. Produces 7 plays/year. Professional LORT D. Agented submissions and letters of inquiry only. Reports in 6 months.

Needs: All styles and genres. "We are a small 386-seat theater—with a modest budget. Plays should be good stories, with strong dialogue, real situations and human concerns. Especially interested in plays about American life and culture."

MERRY-GO-ROUND PLAYHOUSE, INC., P.O. Box 506, Auburn NY 13021. (315)255-1305. Artistic Director: Edward Sayles. Estab. 1958. Produces 10 plays/year. Childrens touring company—throughout US and Canada. Summer Musical—refurbished carousel; seating 325. Submit complete ms. Reports in 3 months. Rights negotiable. Pays 8-15% royalty or $20-35/performance.
Needs: Childrens musicals, fairy tales, educational and social minded plays, adult play readings, musical theater. Prefers cast of no more than 4, props and staging needs to be flexible for touring.
Tips: "We look at and consider any and all material—particularly self-esteem and multicultural themes."

MILL MOUNTAIN THEATRE, Market Square, Center in Square, Roanoke VA 24011-1437. (703)342-5730. Executive Director: Jere Lee Hodgin. Literary Manager: Jo Weinstein. Produces 8 established plays, 10 new one-acts and 2 new full-length plays/year. "Some of the professional productions will be on the main stage and some in our alternative theater B. We no longer accept full-length unsolicited scripts." Send letter, synopsis and 10 pages of sample dialogue. Reports in 8 months. Payment negotiable on individual play. Send SASE for guidelines; cast limit 15 for play and 24 for musicals. Do not include loose stamps or money.
Needs: "We are interested in plays with racially mixed casts, but not to the exclusion of others. We are constantly seeking one-act plays for 'Centerpieces', our Lunch Time Program of Script-in-Hand Productions. Playing time should be between 25-35 minutes. Cast limit 6."
Tips: "Subject matter and character variations are open, but gratuitous language and acts are not acceptable. A play based on large amounts of topical reference or humor has a very short life. Be sure you have written a play and not a film script."

MILWAUKEE PUBLIC THEATRE, P.O. Box 07147, Milwaukee WI 53207. Artistic Director: Michael Moynihan. Estab. 1971. Produces 3-5 plays/year. Professional productions performed in theaters and outdoors for general audiences, family and children. Query with synopsis. Reports in 1 year. Buys one-time rights. Payment varies with writer/production.
Needs: Fast moving, topical, with a good plot, highly theatrical style, reasonable cast size (1-8 actors). Interested in regional-local, political themes, satire. Must have unit sets.
Tips: "No plays about playwrights or actors."

‡MIXED BLOOD THEATRE COMPANY, 1501 S. 4th St., Minneapolis MN 55454. (612)338-0937. Artistic Director: Jack Reuler. Estab. 1975. Produces 5 plays/year. Equity productions in 200-seat theater. "Professional main stage production for adult audiences." Query with synopsis only. No unsolicited scripts unless intended for "Mixed Blood Versus America Annual Playwriting Contest. We pay for production and retain no rights beyond that. Payment varies. Playwright receives a guaranteed fee plus a percentage of the gate. Our payments to writers are competitive."
Needs: Seeking "well-written stories with characters we care about."
Tips: "We are currently seeking to establish an ongoing relationship with one or more film production companies in Hollywood for the purpose of referring appropriate scripts—with the playwright's permission—for consideration as possible film projects."

MODERN INTERNATIONAL DRAMA, Theater Dept., SUNY, P.O. Box 6000, Binghamton NY 13902-6000. (607)777-2704. Managing Editor: George E. Wellwarth. Estab. 1967. Publishes 5-6 plays/year. "Audience is academic and professional." Query with synopsis or submit complete ms. Reports in 2 months. "Rights remain with author and translator." Pays 3 complimentary copies.
Needs: Publishes plays of ideas; 20th century; any style and any length; *translations of previously untranslated plays from any language only.*
Tips: "No popular theater."

THE MUNY STUDENT THEATRE, (formerly The Muny/Student Theatre Project), 560 Trinity Ave., St. Louis MO 63130. (314)862-1255. Fax: (314)863-7761. Artistic Director: Christopher Limber. Estab. 1979. "One of the most comprehensive theater education programs in Missouri." Touring Company tours 3 shows to schools in the St. Louis metropolitan area, outstate Missouri and southern Illinois (grades 4-8 and 7-12). Professional staff of storytellers. Two mainstage family shows/year. Query with synopsis. Reports in 3 months. Pays 4-8% royalty.
Needs: 45-minute shows that enhance academic curriculum, promote creative exploration of topics and present socially relevant themes. "We prefer a cast of 5 for touring productions. Sets must be minimal."

MUSICAL THEATRE WORKS, INC., Dept. WM, 4th Floor, 440 Lafayette St., New York NY 10003-6919. (212)677-0040. Artistic Director: Anthony Stimac. Estab. 1983. "MTW develops scripts from informal to staged readings. When the project is deemed ready for the public, a showcase is set up for commercial interest. MTW musicals are professionally produced and presented in an off-Broadway New York City theater and intended for a well-rounded, sophisticated, theater-going audience. Additionally, 50% of all MTW MainStage productions have gone on to engagements on Broadway and in 12 states across the country." Submit complete ms with audiotape. Reports in 2 months. Buys 1% future gross; on fully-produced works. Pays negotiable royalty.

Needs: "MTW only produces full-length works of musical theater and is interested not only in those classically written, but has a keen interest in works which expand the boundaries and subject matter of the artform. MTW is a small, but prolific, organization with a limited budget. It is, therefore, necessary to limit production costs."

Tips: "The dramatic stage of recent years has successfully interpreted societal problems of the day, while the musical theater has grown in spectacle and foregone substance. Since the musical theater traditionally incorporated large themes and issues it is imperative that we now marry these two ideas—large themes and current issues—to the form. Send a neat, clean, typewritten manuscript with a well marked, clear audiotape, produced as professionally as possible, to the attention of the Literary Manager."

NATIONAL MUSIC THEATER CONFERENCE, EUGENE O'NEILL THEATER CENTER, Suite 901, 234 W. 44th St., New York NY 10036. (212)382-2790. Fax: (212)921-5538. Artistic Director: Paulette Haupt. Estab. 1978. Paying audiences drawn from local residents, New York and regional theater professionals and others. Conference takes place each August at center in Waterford, Connecticut. Application guidelines for #10 SASE after September 15. Application deadline: February 1 (subject to change). Pays stipend plus room and board during conference.

Needs: "We develop new music theater works of all forms, traditional and non-traditional. Singing must play a dominant role. Works are given minimally staged readings, script in hand, no props or lighting, piano only."

Tips: Works not considered eligible are those that have been fully produced by a professional company and adapted works for which rights have not been obtained. Writers and composers must be US citizens or permanent residents.

NECESSARY ANGEL THEATRE, Suite #201, 490 Adelaide St. W., Toronto, Ontario M5V 1T2 Canada. (416)365-0406. Fax: (416)363-8702. Dramaturg: D. D. Kugler. Estab. 1978. Produces 2 plays/year. Plays are Equity productions in various Toronto theaters and performance spaces for an urban audience between 20-55 years of age. Submit synopsis only. It will not be returned. Reports in 6 months. Pays 10% royalty.

Needs: "We are open to new theatrical ideas, environmental pieces, unusual acting styles and large casts. The usual financial constraints exist, but they have never eliminated a work to which we felt a strong commitment." No "TV-influenced sit-coms or melodramas."

THE NEW CONSERVATORY CHILDREN'S THEATRE COMPANY AND SCHOOL, New Conservatory Theatre Center, 25 Van Ness, Lower Level, San Francisco CA 94102. (415)861-4814. Fax: (415)861-6988. Artistic Director: Ed Decker. Produces 4-5 plays/year. "The New Conservatory is a children's theater school (ages 4-19) and operates year-round. Each year we produce several plays, for which the older students (usually 10 and up) audition. These are presented to the general public at the New Conservatory Theatre Center in San Francisco (50-150 seats). Our audience is approximately age 5-adult." Query with synopsis. Reports in 3 months. Royalty negotiable.

Needs: "We emphasize works in which children play *children*, and prefer relevant and controversial subjects, although we also do musicals. We have a commitment to new plays. Examples of our shows are: Mary Gail's *Nobody Home* (world premiere; about latchkey kids); Brian Kral's *Special Class* (about disabled kids); and *The Inner Circle*, by Patricia Loughrey (commissioned scripts about AIDS prevention for kids). As we are a nonprofit group on limited budget, we tend not to have elaborate staging; however, our staff is inventive—includes choreographer and composer. Write innovative theater that explores topics of concern/interest to young people, that takes risks. We concentrate more on ensemble than individual roles, too. We do *not* want to see fairy tales or trite rehashings of things children have seen/heard since the age of 2. See theater as education, rather than 'children being cute'."

Tips: "It is important for young people and their families to explore and confront issues relevant to growing up in the 90s. Theater is a marvelous teaching tool that can educate while it entertains."

NEW PLAYS INCORPORATED, Dept. WM, P.O. Box 5074, Charlottesville VA 22905-5074. (804)979-2777. Publisher: Patricia Whitton. Estab. 1964. Publishes an average of 4 plays/year. Publishes for producers of plays for young audiences and teachers in college courses on child drama. Query with synopsis. Reports in 2 months. Agent for amateur and semi-professional productions, exclusive agency for script sales. Pays 50% royalty on productions; 10% on script sales. Free catalog.

Needs: Plays for young audiences with something innovative in form and content. Length: usually 45-90 minutes. "Should be suitable for performance by adults for young audiences." No skits, assembly programs, improvisations or unproduced mss.

NEW PLAYWRIGHTS' PROGRAM, The University of Alabama, P.O. Box 870239, Tuscaloosa AL 35487-0239. (205)348-9032. Director and Dramaturg: Dr. Paul C. Castagno. Endowed by Gallaway fund, estab. 1982. Produces at least 1 new play/year. Mainstage and second stage. Collaborations with Stillman College and Theatre Tuscaloosa, University Theatre, The University of Alabama. Submit complete ms. Playwrights may submit potential workshop ideas for consideration. Reports in 3-6 months. Accepts scripts in various forms: new dramaturgy to traditional. Also radio plays. If you are a recent MFA playwriting graduate (within one year) you may be given consideration for ACTF productions. Send SASE. Stipends competitive with or exceed most contests.

NEW TUNERS THEATRE, 1225 W. Belmont Ave., Chicago IL 60657. (312)929-7287. Literary Manager: Allan Chambers. Produces 1-3 new musicals/year. 66% developed in our Making Tuners workshop. "Some scripts produced are unagented submissions. Plays performed in 3 small off-Loop theater seating 148 for a general theater audience, urban/suburban mix. Submit synopsis, cover letter and cassette selections of the score, if available. Reports in 2 months. Next step is script and score (reports in 6 months). "Submit first, we'll negotiate later." Pays 5-10% of gross. "Authors are given a stipend to cover a residency of at least 2 weeks."
Needs: "We're interested in all forms of musical theater including more innovative styles. Our production capabilities are limited by the lack of space, but we're very creative and authors should submit anyway. The smaller the cast, the better. We are especially interested in scripts using a younger (35 and under) ensemble of actors. We mostly look for authors who are interested in developing their script through workshops, rehearsals and production. No casts over 12. No one-man shows."
Tips: "Freelance writers should be aware that musical theater can be more serious. The work of Sondheim and others who follow demonstrates clearly that musical comedy can be ambitious and can treat mature themes in a relevant way. We would like to see the musical theater articulating something about the world around us, rather than merely diverting an audience's attention from that world."

NEW YORK SHAKESPEARE FESTIVAL/PUBLIC THEATER, Dept. WM, 425 Lafayette St., New York NY 10003. (212)598-7100. Artistic Director: George C. Wolfe. Literary Manager: Jason Fogelson. Estab. 1954. Interested in plays, musicals, translations, adaptations. No restriction as to style, form, subject matter. Produces classics, new American and international works year-round at the Public Theater complex housing 5 theaters (100-300 seat capacity): Newman, Anspacher, Shiva, LuEsther Hall, Martinson. Also at Delacorte 2,100-seat amphitheater in Central Park. Transfers to Broadway, film and television. Unsolicited and unagented submissions accepted. All scripts: include cast of characters with age and brief description; musical works: submit cassette with at least 3 songs. Standard options and production agreements. Response in 4 months. Include SASE with all submissions.

NEW YORK STATE THEATRE INSTITUTE, P.O. Box 28, Troy NY 12181-0028. (518)274-3200. Fax: (518)274-3815. Producing Director: Patricia B. Snyder. Produces 4-5 plays/year. Professional regional productions for adult and family audiences. Query with synopsis. Reports in 3 months. Pay varies.

NEW YORK THEATRE WORKSHOP, 18th Floor, 220 W. 42 St., New York NY 10036-7211. (212)302-7737. Fax: (212)391-9875. Artistic Director: James C. Nicola. Literary Associate: Christopher Grabowski. Estab. 1979. Produces 3-4 full productions; approximately 50 readings/year. Plays are performed off-Broadway, Equity LOA contract theater. Audience is New York theater-going audience and theater professionals. Query with synopsis and 10 page sample scene. Reports in 5 months. Option to produce commercially; percentage of box office gross from commercial productions and percentage of author's net subsidiary rights within specified time limit from our original production. Pays fee because of limited run, with additional royalty payments; for extensions; $1,500-2,000 fee range.
Needs: Full-length plays, one-acts, translations/adaptations, music theater pieces; proposals for performance projects. Large issues, socially relevant issues, innovative form and language, minority issues. Plays utilizing more than 8 actors usually require outside funding.
Tips: No overtly commercial, traditional, Broadway-type "musicals."

THE NORTH CAROLINA BLACK REPERTORY COMPANY, Dept. WM, P.O. Box 95, Winston-Salem NC 27102. (919)723-2266. Artistic Director: Larry Leon Hamlin. Estab. 1979. Produces 4-6 plays/year. Plays produced primarily in North Carolina, New York City, and the North and Southeast. Submit complete ms. Reports in 5 months. Obtains negotiable rights. Negotiable payment.
Needs: "Full-length plays and musicals: mostly African-American with special interest in historical or contemporary *statement* genre. A cast of 10 would be a comfortable limit; we discourage multiple sets."
Tips: "The best time to submit manuscript is between September and February."

ODYSSEY THEATRE ENSEMBLE, 2055 S. Sepulveda Blvd., Los Angeles CA 90025. (310)477-2055. Literary Manager: Jan Lewis. Estab. 1969. Produces 10 plays/year. Plays performed in a 3-theater facility. "All three theaters are Equity 99-seat theater plan. We have a subscription audience of 2,000 who subscribe to a six-play main season and a 3-4 play lab season, and are offered a discount on our remaining non-subscription plays. Remaining seats are sold to the general public." Query with resume, synopsis, cast breakdown and 8-10 pages of sample dialogue. Scripts must be securely bound. Reports in 1 month on queries; 6 months on mss. Buys negotiable rights. Pays 5-7% royalty. "We will *not* return scripts without SASE."
Needs: "Full-length plays only with either an innovative form and/or provocative subject matter. We desire highly theatrical pieces that explore possibilities of the live theater experience. We are seeking full-length musicals and some plays with smaller casts (2-4). We are not reading one-act plays or light situation comedies.

We are seeking Hispanic material for our resident Hispanic unit as well as plays from all cultures and ethnicities."

OLD GLOBE THEATRE, P.O. Box 2171, San Diego CA 92112-2171. (619)231-1941. Literary Manager: Raúl Moncada. Produces 12 plays/year. "We are a LORT B+ institution with 3 theaters: 581-seat mainstage, 225-seat arena, 621-seat outdoor. Our plays are produced for a single-ticket and subscription audience of 250,000 patrons from a large cross-section of southern California, and including visitors from throughout the US." Submit complete ms through agent only. One-page query or synopsis if not represented. Reports in 3-10 months. Buys negotiable rights. Royalty varies.
Needs: "We are looking for plays of strong literary and theatrical merit, works that display an accomplished sense of craft, and pieces that present a detailed cultural vision. All submissions must be full-length plays or musicals."

EUGENE O'NEILL THEATER CENTER'S NATIONAL PLAYWRIGHTS CONFERENCE and NEW DRAMA FOR MEDIA PROJECT, Suite 901, 234 W. 44th St., New York NY 10036. (212)382-2790. Artistic Director: Lloyd Richards. Administrator: Lori Robishaw. Estab. 1965. Develops staged readings of 9-12 stage plays, 2-3 screenplays or teleplays/year. "We accept unsolicited mss with no prejudice toward either represented or unrepresented writers. Our theater is located in Waterford, Connecticut, and we operate under an Equity LORT contract. We have 3 theaters: Barn—250 seats, Amphitheater—300 seats, Instant Theater—150 seats. Submission guidelines for #10 SASE in the fall. Complete bound, unproduced, original plays are eligible (no adaptations). Decision by late April. Pays stipend plus room, board and transportation. We accept script submissions from Sept. 15-Dec. 1 of each year. Conference takes place during four weeks in July each summer."
• Scripts are selected on the basis of talent, not commercial potential.
Needs: "We use modular sets for all plays, minimal lighting, minimal props and no costumes. We do script-in-hand readings with professional actors and directors. Our focus is on new play/playwright development."

THE OPEN EYE: NEW STAGINGS, 270 W. 89th St., New York NY 10024-1705. (212)769-4143. Fax: (212)595-0336. Artistic Director: Amie Brockway. Estab. 1972. Produces 3 full-length plays/year plus a Lab series. "The Open Eye is a professional, Equity LOA and TYA 115-seat, off-off Broadway theater. Our audiences include a broad spectrum of ages and backgrounds." Submit complete ms in clean, bound copy with SASE for its return. Reports in 6 months. Playwright fee for mainstage varies.
Needs: "New Stagings is particularly interested in one-act and full-length plays that take full advantage of the live performance situation. We especially like plays that appeal to young people and adults alike."

OREGON SHAKESPEARE FESTIVAL ASSOCIATION, P.O. Box 158, Ashland OR 97520. (503)482-2111. Associate Director/Play Development: Cynthia White. Estab. 1935. Produces 16 plays/year. The Angus Bowmer Theater has a thrust stage and seats 600. The Black Swan is an experimental space and seats 150; The Elizabethan Outdoor Theatre seats 1,200 (stages almost exclusively Shakespearean productions there—mid-June through September). OSFA also produces a separate five-play season at the Portland Center for The Performing Arts in a 900-seat proscenium theater. Producing director of OSFA Portland Center Stage: Dennis Bigelow. Query with synopsis, resume and 10 pages of dialogue from unsolicited sources. Complete mss from agents only. Reports in 9 months. Negotiates individually for rights with the playwright's agent. "Most plays run within our 10-month season for 6-10 months, so royalties are paid accordingly."
Needs: "A broad range of classic and contemporary scripts. One or two fairly new scripts/season. Also a play readings series which focuses on new work. Plays must fit into our 10-month rotating repertory season. Black Swan shows usually limited to 10 actors." No one-acts or musicals. Submissions from women and minority writers are strongly encouraged.
Tips: "Send your work through an agent if possible. Send the best examples of your work rather than all of it. Don't become impatient or discouraged if it takes 6 months or more for a response. Don't expect detailed critiques with rejections. I want to see plays with heart and soul, intelligence, humor and wit. We're seeking plays with characters that *live*—that exist as living beings, not simply mouthpieces for particular positions. Try to avoid TV writing (i.e., cliche situations, dialogue, characters, unless it's specifically for broad comic purposes. I also think theater is a place for the *word*. So, the word first, then spectacle and high-tech effects."

‡ORGANIC THEATER COMPANY, 3319 N. Clark, Chicago IL 60657. (312)327-2427. Artistic Committee of 5 people. Estab. 1969. Produces 8 plays/year. AEA, CAT and non-equity. Query with synopsis and 10 page sample. Reports in 1-3 weeks on queries. Negotiable royalty. Send inquiries to Literary Manager.
Needs: "We are seeking full-length or long one acts—challenging plays that fully explore the theatrical medium; strong visual and physical potential (unproduced works only). No kitchen sink realism. Know your medium! Don't send a TV script to a theater."

PENNSYLVANIA STAGE COMPANY, Dept. WM, 837 Linden St., Allentown PA 18101. (215)434-6110. Artistic Director: Peter Wrenn-Meleck. Estab. 1980. Produces 7 plays and musicals/year. "We are a LORT D theater and our season runs from October through June. The large majority of our audience comes from the

Lehigh Valley. Our audience consists largely of adults. We also offer special student and senior citizen matinees." Query with synopsis; also would like a character breakdown and SASE or postcard. Reports in 3 months for scripts; 1 month for synopsis. Payment negotiable.

Needs: "The PSC produces full-length plays and musicals that are innovative and imaginative and that broaden our understanding of ourselves and society. Looking for wide range of styles and topics." Prefers 8 characters or fewer for plays and musicals.

Tips: "Works presented at the Stage Company have a passion for being presented now, should be entertaining and meaningful to our local community, and perpetuate our theatrical and literary heritage. We do not want to limit our options in achieving this artistic mission. No one-acts and material that contains grossly offensive language. We appreciate also receiving a sample of dialogue with the synopsis. We have a staged reading program where a director, actors and the playwright work together during an intensive 3-day rehearsal period. A discussion with the audience follows the staged reading."

‡PERSEVERANCE THEATRE, 914 3rd St., Douglas AK 99801. (907)364-2421. Artistic Director: Molly Smith. Produces 5 mainstage, 2-3 second stage plays/year. Professional productions, Southeast Alaska. Primarily Juneau audiences; occasional tours to other places. Query with synopsis, no unsolicited mss. Reports in 6 months. Pays $25-50/performance.

Tips: "We are producing very few original pieces from writers outside of Alaska. Because of that, we are reading few new plays."

‡PHILADELPHIA DRAMA GUILD, 100 N. 17th St., Philadelphia PA 19103. (215)563-7530. Artistic Director: Mary B. Robinson. Produces 5 plays/year. Professional productions performed at the 900 seat Zellerbach Theatre. Submit query and synopsis. Reports in 4 months. Pays royalty.

Needs: "We produce full-length plays that speak to our diverse Philadelphia audience."

Tips: "We do not produce one acts or works-in-progress."

PIER ONE THEATRE, P.O. Box 894, Homer AK 99603. (907)235-7333. Artistic Director: Lance Petersen. Estab. 1973. Produces 5-8 plays/year. "Plays to various audiences for various plays—e.g. children's, senior citizens, adult, family, etc. Plays are produced on Kemai Peninsula." Submit complete ms. Reports in 2 months. Pays $25-125/performance.

Needs: "No restrictions—willing to read *all* genres." No stock reviews, hillbilly or sit-coms.

Tips: "There are slightly increased opportunities for new works. Don't start your play with a telephone conversation. New plays ought to be risky business; they ought to be something the playwright feels is terribly important."

PIONEER DRAMA SERVICE, INC., P.O. Box 22555, Denver CO 80222-0555. (303)759-4297. Fax: (303)759-0475. Publisher: Steven Fendrich. Estab. 1963. 10% freelance written. Plays are performed by high school, junior high and adult groups, colleges, churches and recreation programs for audiences of all ages. "We are one of the largest full-service play publishers in the country in that we handle straight plays, musicals, children's theater and melodrama." Publishes 15 plays/year; 20% musicals and 80% straight plays. Query only; no unsolicited mss. Buys all rights. Reports in 2 months. Pays on royalty basis with some outright purchase. All submissions automatically entered in Shubert Fendrich Memorial Playwriting Contest. Contest guidelines for SASE.

Needs: "We use the standard two-act format, two-act musicals, religious drama, comedies, mysteries, drama, melodrama and plays for children's theater (plays to be done by adult actors for children). We are looking for more plays dealing with the problems of teens." Length: two-act musicals and comedies, up to 90 minutes; children's theater, 1 hour. Prefer many female roles, one simple set. Currently overstocked on one-act plays.

□PLAYERS PRESS, INC., P.O. Box 1132, Studio City CA 91614-0132. Senior Editor: Robert W. Gordon. "We deal in all entertainment areas and handle publishable works for film and television as well as theater. Performing arts books, plays and musicals. All plays must be in stage format for publication." Also produces scripts for video and material for cable television. 80% freelance written. 20-30 scripts/year are unagented submissions; 5-15 books are also unagented. Works with 1-10 unpublished/unproduced writers annually. Query. "Include one #10 SASE, reviews and proof of production. All play submissions must have been produced and should include a flyer and/or program with dates of performance." Reports in 3 months on queries; 1 year on mss. Buys negotiable rights. "We prefer all area rights." Pays variable royalty "according to area; approximately 10-75% of gross receipts." Also pays in outright purchase of $100-25,000 or $5-5,000/performance.

Needs: "We prefer comedies, musicals and children's theater, but are open to all genres. We will rework the ms after acceptance. We are interested in the quality, not the format. Performing Arts Books that deal with theater how-to are of strong interest."

Tips: "Send only material requested. Do not telephone."

PLAYS, The Drama Magazine for Young People, 120 Boylston St., Boston MA 02116-4615. Editor: Sylvia K. Burack. Estab. 1941. Publishes approximately 75 one-act plays and dramatic program material each school year to be performed by junior and senior high, middle grades, lower grades. Mss should follow the general style of *Plays*. Stage directions should not be typed in capital letters or underlined. No incorrect grammar or dialect. Desired lengths for mss are: junior and senior high—18-20 double-spaced ms pages (25 to 30 minutes playing time); middle grades—10 to 15 pages (15 to 20 minutes playing time); lower grades—6 to 10 pages (8 to 15 minutes playing time). Pays "good rates on acceptance." Query first for adaptations. Reports in 2-3 weeks. Sample copy $3.50; send SASE for mss specification sheet.

Needs: "Can use comedies, farces, melodramas, skits, mysteries and dramas, plays for holidays and other special occasions, such as Book Week; adaptations of classic stories and fables; historical plays; plays about black history and heroes; puppet plays; folk and fairy tales; creative dramatics; and plays for conservation, ecology or human rights programs."

THE PLAYWRIGHTS' CENTER'S PLAYLABS, 2301 Franklin Ave. E., Minneapolis MN 55406. (612)332-7481. Director of Public Relations: Lisa Stevens. Estab. 1971. "Playlabs is a 2-week developmental workshop for new plays. The program is held in Minneapolis and is open by script competition. It is an intensive two-week workshop focusing on the development of a script and the playwright. Four-six new plays are given rehearsed public readings at the site of the workshop." Announcements of playwrights by April 15. Playwrights receive honoraria, travel expenses, room and board.

Needs: "We are interested in playwrights with talent, ambitions for a sustained career in theater and scripts which could benefit from an intensive developmental process involving professional dramaturgs, directors and actors. US citizens or permanent residents, only. Participants must attend all or part of conference depending on the length of their workshop. No previously produced or published materials. Send SASE after Oct. 1 for application. Submission deadline: Dec. 1.

Tips: "We do not buy scripts or produce them. We are a service organization that provides programs for developmental work on scripts for members."

PLAYWRIGHTS PREVIEW PRODUCTIONS, #304, 1160 5th Ave., New York NY 10029. Artistic Director: Frances Hill. Literary Manager: David Sheppard. Estab. 1983. Produces 4-6 plays/year. Professional productions off or off off-Broadway, 1 production Kennedy Center—throughout the year. General audience. Submit complete ms. Reports in 4 months. If produced, option for 6 months. Pays royalty.

Needs: Both one-act and full-length; generally one set or styled playing dual. Good imaginative, creative writing. Cast limited to 3-7.

Tips: "We tend to reject 'living-room' plays. We look for imaginative settings. Be creative and interesting with intellectual content. All submissions should be bound."

PLAYWRIGHTS THEATRE OF NEW JERSEY, 33 Green Village Rd., Madison NJ 07940. (201)514-1787. Artistic Director: John Pietrowski. Associate Artistic Director: Michele Ortlip. Estab. 1986. Produces 1 production, 5 staged readings and 10 sit-down readings/year. "We operate under a letter of agreement (LOA with LORT Rules) with Actors' Equity Association for all productions. Readings are held under a staged reading code." Submit complete ms. Short bio and production history required. Reports in 3 months. "For productions we ask the playwright to sign an agreement that gives us exclusive rights to the play for the production period and for 30 days following. After the 30 days we give the rights back with no strings attached, except for commercial productions. We ask that our developmental work be acknowledged in any other professional productions." Pays $250 for productions, $150 for staged readings.

Needs: Any style or length; full-length, one-acts, musicals.

Tips: "We are looking for plays in the early stages of development—plays that take on important personal and social issues in a theatrical manner."

PRIMARY STAGES COMPANY, INC., 584 9th Ave., New York NY 10036. (212)333-7471. Artistic Director: Casey Childs. Estab. 1983. Produces 4 plays, 3 workshops, over 100 readings/year. All plays are produced professionally off-Broadway at the 45th Street Theatre, 354 West 45th St. Query with synopsis. Reports in 3 months. "If Primary Stages produces the play, we ask for the right to move it for up to 6 months after the closing performance." Writers paid "same as the actors."

Needs: "We are looking for highly theatrical works that were written exclusively with the stage in mind. We do not want TV scripts or strictly realistic plays."

Tips: No "living room plays, disease-of-the-week plays, back-porch plays, father/son work-it-all-out-plays, etc."

QUAIGH THEATRE, 205 W. 89th St., New York NY 10024-1868. (212)787-0862. Artistic Director: Will Lieberson. Estab. 1973. Produces 4 major productions/year. Off off-Broadway. Query with synopsis. Reports in 1 month on queries; 6 months on mss. Rights differ on each script. Pays variable royalty.

Tips: "No plays on familiar subjects done in a familiar way. Plays need action as well as words. Plays are not meant for public reading. If they work as readings they really are rotten plays."

THE QUARTZ THEATRE, 392 Taylor, Ashland OR 97520-3058. (503)482-8119. Artistic Director: Dr. Robert Spira. Estab. 1973. Produces several video films/year. Send 3-page dialogue and personal bio. Reports in 2 weeks. Pays 5% royalty after expenses.

Needs: "Any length, any subject, with or without music. We seek playwrights with a flair for language and theatrical imagination."

Tips: "We look at anything. We do not do second productions unless substantial rewriting is involved. Our theater is a stepping stone to further production. Our playwrights are usually well-read in comparative religion, philosophy, psychology, and have a comprehensive grasp of human problems. We seek the 'self-indulgent' playwright who pleases him/herself first of all."

THE ROAD COMPANY, P.O. Box 5278 EKS, Johnson City TN 37603-5278. (615)926-7726. Literary Manager: Christine Murdock. Estab. 1975. Produces 3 plays/year. "Our professional productions are intended for a general adult audience." Query with synopsis. Reports in 4 months. Pays royalty. "When we do new plays we generally try to have the playwright in residence during rehearsal for 3-4 weeks for about $1,000 plus room and board."

Needs: "We like plays that experiment with form, that challenge, inform and entertain. We are a small ensemble based company. We look for smaller cast shows of 4-6."

Tips: "We are always looking for 2-character (male/female) plays. We are interested in plays set in the South. We are most interested in new work that deals with new forms. We write our own plays using improvisational techniques which we then tour throughout the Southeast. When funding permits, we include one of our own new plays in our home season."

SHAW FESTIVAL THEATRE, P.O. Box 774, Niagara-on-the-Lake, Ontario L0S 1J0 Canada. Fax: (416)468-5438. Artistic Director: Christopher Newton. Estab. 1962. Produces 9 plays/year. "Professional summer festival operating three theaters (Festival: 861 seats; Court House: 349 seats; and Royal George: 353 seats). We also host some music and some winter rentals. Mandate is based on the works of G.B. Shaw and his contemporaries. We prefer to hold rights for Canada and northeastern US, also potential to tour." Pays 5-6% royalty. Submit with SASE or SAE and IRCs, depending on country of origin.

Needs: "We operate an acting ensemble of up to 75 actors; this includes 14 actor/singers and we have sophisticated production facilities. During the summer season (April-October) the Academy of the Shaw Festival organizes several workshops of new Canadian plays."

THE SHAZZAM PRODUCTION COMPANY, 418 Pier Ave., Santa Monica CA 90405. Artistic Director: Edward Blackoff. Estab. 1980. Produces 2 plays/year. Equity-waiver productions for adult audience. Query with complete ms and synopsis. Reports in 2 months. Obtains negotiable rights. Pays $15-25/performance.

Needs: "Full-length plays dealing with important contemporary social and political human issues. Limit of 2 sets and requiring no more than 12 actors. No musicals or drawing-room farces."

AUDREY SKIRBALL-KENIS THEATRE, Suite 304, 9478 W. Olympic Blvd., Beverly Hills CA 90212. (213)284-8965. Program Director: Dennis Clontz. Estab. 1989. Produces 40 stage readings and workshop productions/year. "We utilize 3 theater facilities in the Los Angeles area with professional director and casts. Our stage readings and workshop productions are offered year-round. Our audience is the general public *and* theater professionals." Query with synopsis. Reports in 3-4 months. Obtains no rights. Pays $100 for stage readings; $500 for workshop productions.

Needs: "We need full-length original plays that have not been produced in the Los Angeles area and from which the playwright would benefit from a stage reading or workshop production as a means to either further develop the play or attract possible producing entities."

Tips: "No screenplays disguised as stage plays or domestic dramas about dysfunctional families. We are a nonprofit organization dedicated to new plays and playwrights. We do not produce plays for commercial runs, nor do we request any future commitment from the playwright should their play find a production by virtue of our stage reading or workshop programs."

SOUTH COAST REPERTORY, P.O. Box 2197, Costa Mesa CA 92628-1197. (714)957-2602. Fax: (714)545-0391. Dramaturg: Jerry Patch. Literary Manager: John Glore. Estab. 1964. Produces 6 plays/year on mainstage, 5 on second stage. Professional nonprofit theater; a member of LORT and TCG. "We operate in our own facility which houses a 507-seat mainstage theater and a 161-seat second stage theater. We have a combined subscription audience of 21,000." Query with synopsis; mss considered if submitted by agent. Reports in 4 months. Acquires negotiable rights. Pays negotiable royalty.

Needs: "We produce full-lengths. We prefer well written plays that address contemporary concerns and are dramaturgically innovative. A play whose cast is larger than 15-20 will need to be extremely compelling and its cast size must be justifiable."

Tips: "We don't look for a writer to write for us — he or she should write for him or herself. We look for honesty and a fresh voice. We're not likely to be interested in writers who are mindful of *any* trends. Originality and craftsmanship are the most important qualities we look for."

SOUTHERN APPALACHIAN REPERTORY THEATRE (SART), Mars Hill College, P.O. Box 620, Mars Hill NC 28754-0620. (704)689-1384. Artistic Director: James W. Thomas. Asst. Managing Director: Jan W. Blalock. Estab. 1975. Produces 5 plays/year. "Since 1975 the Southern Appalachian Repertory Theatre has produced

848 performances of 92 plays and played to over 116,000 patrons in the 152-seat Owen Theatre on the Mars Hill College campus. The theater's goals are quality, adventurous programming and integrity, both in artistic form and in the treatment of various aspects of the human condition. SART is a professional summer theater company whose audiences range from students to senior citizens." Also conducts an annual Southern Appalachian Playwrights' Conference in which five playwrights are invited for informal readings of their new scripts. Deadline for submission is October 1 and conference is held the last weekend in January. If script is selected for production during the summer season, an honorarium is paid to the playwright in the amount of $500. Please enclose SASE for return of script.

Needs: "Since 1975, one of SART's goals has been to produce at least one original play each summer season. To date, 28 original scripts have been produced. Plays by southern Appalachian playwrights or about southern Appalachia are preferred, but by no means exclusively. Complete new scripts welcomed."

STAGE ONE: The Louisville Children's Theatre, 425 W. Market St., Louisville KY 40202-3300. (502)589-5946. Fax: (502)589-5779. Producing Director: Moses Goldberg. Estab. 1946. Produces 6-7 plays/year. 20% freelance written. 15-20% of scripts produced are unagented submissions (excluding work of playwright-in-residence). Plays performed by an Equity company for young audiences ages 4-18; usually does different plays for different age groups within that range. Submit complete ms. Reports in 4 months. Pays negotiable royalty or $25-50/performance.

Needs: "Good plays for young audiences of all types: adventure, fantasy, realism, serious problem plays about growing up or family entertainment. Cast: ideally, 10 or less. Honest, visual potentiality, worthwhile story and characters are necessary. An awareness of children and their schooling is a plus. No campy material or anything condescending to children. No musicals unless they are fairly limited in orchestration."

STAGE WEST, 1024B W. 7th, Fort Worth TX 76102. (812)332-6238. Artistic Director: Jerry Russell. Estab. 1979. Produces 8 plays/year. "We stage professional productions at our own theater for a mixed general audience." Query with synopsis. Reports in 3-6 months. Rights are negotiable. Pays 7% royalty.

Needs: "We want full-length plays that are accessible to a mainstream audience but possess traits that are highly theatrical. Cast size of 10 or less and single or unit set are desired."

CHARLES STILWILL, Managing Artistic Director, Community Playhouse, P.O. Box 433, Waterloo IA 50704-0433. (319)235-0367. Estab. 1917. Plays performed by Waterloo Community Playhouse with a volunteer cast. Produces 11 plays (6 adult, 5 children's); 1-2 musicals and 9-10 nonmusicals/year; 1-3 originals. 17% freelance written. Most scripts produced are unagented submissions. Works with 1-3 unpublished/unproduced writers annually. "We are one of few community theaters with a commitment to new scripts. We do at least 1 and have done as many as 4/year. We have 4,300 season members. Average attendance is 3,000. We do a wide variety of plays. Our public isn't going to accept nudity, too much sex, too much strong language. We don't have enough Black actors to do all-Black shows. Theater has done plays with as few as 2 characters, and as many as 98. "On the main stage, we usually pay between $400 and $500. We also produce children's theater. Submit complete ms. Please, no loose pages. Reports negatively within 1 year, but acceptance sometimes takes longer because we try to fit a wanted script into the balanced season. We sometimes hold a script longer than a year if we like it but cannot immediately find the right slot for it. We just did the world premier of *Grace Under Pressure* which was written in 1984 and last year we did the midwest premiere of *Even in Laughter* which was written in 1981. November 93 we will do the World Premiere of *The Ninth Step* which we have had for over three years."

Needs: "For our Children's Theater and our Adult Biannual Holiday (Christmas) show, we are looking for good adaptations of name children's stories or very good shows that don't necessarily have a name. We produce children's theater with both adult and child actors."

TACOMA ACTORS GUILD, Jones Building, 6th Floor, 901 Broadway Plaza, Tacoma WA 98402. (206)272-3107. Artistic Director: Bruce K. Sevy. Estab. 1978. Produces 6-7 plays/year. Plays perfomed at Theatre On The Plaza. Audience consists of playgoers in the south Puget Sound region. Query with synopsis. Reports in 6 weeks on queries; 1 year on mss. Rights negotiable. Pays negotiable royalty or makes outright purchase of $500 minimum.

Needs: "Full length. Single or simple set. Modest cast (2-7). Comedy, drama, musical. Our budgets are modest."

Tips: "No extreme language, violence, nudity, sexual situations. We don't do a *lot* of new work so opportunities are limited."

TADA!, 120 W. 28th St., New York NY 10001. (212)627-1732. Artistic Director: Janine Nina Trevens. Estab. 1984. Produces 2-4 plays/year. "TADA! produces original musicals and plays performed by children at our 95-seat theater. Productions are for family audiences." Submit complete ms and tape, if musical. Reports in 3 months. Pays 5% royalty or commission fee (varies).

Needs: "Generally pieces run from 45 to 70 minutes. Must be enjoyed by children and adults and performed by a cast of children ages 6-17."

Tips: "No redone fairy tales or pieces where children are expected to play adults. Be careful not to condescend when writing for children's theater."

THE TEN-MINUTE MUSICALS PROJECT, P.O. Box 461194, West Hollywood CA 90046. (213)656-8751. Producer: Michael Koppy. Estab. 1987. Produces 1-10 plays/year. "Plays performed in Equity regional theaters in the US and Canada." Submit complete ms, lead sheets and cassette. Deadline August 31st annually; notification by December 15 annually. Buys performance rights. Pays $250 royalty advance upon selection, against equal share of performance royalties when produced. Submission guidelines for #10 SASE.
Needs: "We are looking for complete short stage musicals playing between 7-14 minutes. Limit cast to 10 (5 women, 5 men). No fairy tales or works based on contemporary news events."

THEATER ARTISTS OF MARIN, P.O. Box 150473, San Rafael CA 94915. (415)454-2380. Artistic Director: Charles Brousse. Estab. 1980. Produces 3 plays/year. Professional showcase productions for a general adult audience. Submit complete ms. Reports in 3 months. Assists in marketing to other theaters.
Needs: "All types of scripts: comedy, drama, farce. Prefers contemporary setting, with some relevance to current issues in American society. Will also consider 'small musicals,' reviews or plays with music." No children's shows, domestic sitcoms, one-man shows or commercial thrillers.

THE THEATER OF NECESSITY, 11702 Webercrest, Houston TX 77048. (713)733-6042. Artistic Director: Philbert Plumb. Estab. 1981. Produces 4 plays/year. Our plays are produced in a small professional theater. Submit complete ms. Reports in 1 year. Buys performance rights. Pays standard royalties based on size of house for small productions or individual contracts for large productions (average $500/run). "We usually keep mss on file unless we are certain we will never use script." Send SASE for script and #10 SASE for response.
Needs: "Any play in a recognizable genre must be superlative in form and intensity. Experimental plays are given an easier read. We move to larger venue if the play warrants the expense."

THEATRE & COMPANY, 20 Queen St. N., Kitchener, Ontario N2H 2G8 Canada. Artistic Director: Stuart Scadron-Wattles. Literary Manager: Wes Wikkerink. Estab. 1988. Produces 4 plays/year. Semi-professional productions for a general audience. Query with synopsis and SAE with IRCs. Reports in 3 months. Pays $50-100/performance.
Needs: "One-act or full-length; comedy or drama; musical or straight; written from or compatible with a biblical world view." No cast above 10; prefers unit staging. Looking for small cast (less than 5) ensemble comedies.
Tips: Looks for "non-religious writing from a biblical world view for an audience which loves the theater. Avoid current trends toward shorter scenes. Playwrights should be aware that they are writing for the stage — not television. We encourage audience interaction, using an acting ensemble trained in improvisation."

THEATRE DE LA JEUNE LUNE, P.O. Box 582176, Minneapolis MN 55458-2176. (612)332-3968. Artistic Directors: Barbra Berlovitz Desbois, Vincent Garcieux, Robert Rosen, Dominique Serrand. Estab. 1979. Produces 2-3 plays/year. Professional nonprofit company producing September-May for general audience. Query with synopsis. Reports in 3 months. Pays royalty or per performance. No unsolicited mss, please.
Needs: "All subject matter considered, although plays with universal themes are desired; plays that concern people of today. We are constantly looking for plays with large casts. Generally *not* interested in plays with 1-4 characters. No psychological drama or plays that are written alone in a room without the input of outside vitality and life."
Tips: "We are an acting company that takes plays and makes them ours; this could mean cutting a script or not heeding a writer's stage directions. We are committed to the performance in front of the audience as the goal of all the contributing factors; therefore, the actors' voice is extremely important."

THEATRE ON THE MOVE, Dept. WM, 1000 Murray Ross Parkway, North York, Ontario M3J 2P3 Canada. (416)665-8824. Artistic Director: Anne Hines. Produces 4 plays/year for families and young audiences — elementary and high schools and special venues (museums, etc.). Uses professional, adult, union actors. Query with synopsis or complete ms. Reports in 3 months. Acquires exclusive rights to Ontario, usually for a minimum of 1 year. Pays royalty or commission for works-in-progress.
Needs: Musicals or dramas for small casts (limit 4 actors) which deal with current topics of interest to children and families. Uncomplicated, "tourable" sets.
Tips: "Our shows have to educate the audience about some aspect of modern life, as well as entertain. The trend is away from fairy tales, etc."

THEATRE VIRGINIA, 2800 Grove Ave., Richmond VA 23221-2466. Artistic Director: William Gregg. Estab. 1955. Produces 5-8, publishes 0-2 new plays/year. Query with synopsis and 15 page sample. Solicitations in 1 month for initial query, 3-8 months if ms is submitted. Rights negotiaged. Payment negotiated.

For information on setting your freelance fees, see How Much Should I Charge?

Needs: No one-acts; no children's theater.

‡THEATRE WEST, 3333 Cahuenga W., Los Angeles CA 90068. Contact: Artistic Board. Estab. 1962. Produces 6 plays/year. "99 seat waiver productions in our theater. Audiences are primarily young urban professionals." Submit ms, resume and letter requesting membership. Reports in 2 months. Buys 5% of writer's share of sale to another media. Pays royalty "based on gross box office—equal to all other participants."
Needs: Uses minimalistic scenery.
Tips: "TW is a dues-paying membership company. Only members can submit plays for production. So you must seek membership prior to action for a production."

THEATREWORKS, University of Colorado, P.O. Box 7150, Colorado Springs CO 80933-7150. (719)593-3232. Fax: (719)593-3362. Producing Director: Whit Andrews. Estab. 1975. Produces 4 full-length plays/year and 2 new one-acts. "New full-length plays produced on an irregular basis. Casts are semi-professional and plays are produced at the university." Query with synopsis. No unsolicited mss. One-act plays are accepted as Playwrights' Forum competition entries. Submit complete ms. Deadline: Dec. 1; winners announced March 1. Two one-act competition winners receive full production, cash awards and travel allowances. Acquires exclusive regional option for duration of production. Full rights revert to author upon closing. Pays $300-1,200.
Needs: Full-lengths and one-acts—no restrictions on subject. "Cast size should not exceed 20; stage area is small with limited wing and fly space. Theatreworks is interested in the exploration of new and inventive theatrical work. Points are scored by imaginative use of visual image and bold approach to subject." No melodrama or children's plays.
Tips: "Too often, new plays seem far too derivative of television and film writing. We think theater is a medium which an author must specifically attack. The standard three-act form would appear to be obsolescent. Economy, brevity and innovation are favorably received."

THEATREWORKS/USA, 890 Broadway, New York NY 10003. (212)677-5959. Artistic Director: Jay Harnick. Literary Manager: Barbara Pasternack. Produces 3 new musical plays/season. Produces professional musicals and plays that primarily tour (TYA contract) but also play at an off-Broadway theater for a young audience. Query with synopsis or sample song. Reports in 8 months. Buys all rights. Pays 6% royalty; offers $1,500 advance against future royalties for new, commissioned plays.
Needs: Musicals and plays with music for children. Historical/biographical themes (ages 8-15), classic literature, fairy tales, and issue-oriented themes and material suitable for young people ages 5-12. Five person cast, minimal lighting. "We like well-crafted shows with good dramatic structure—a protagonist who wants something specific, an antagonist, a problem to be solved—character development, tension, climax, etc. No Saturday Afternoon Special-type shows, shows with nothing to say or 'kiddie' theater shows or fractured fairy tales. We do not address high school audiences."
Tips: "Writing for kids is just like writing for adults—only better (clearer, cleaner). Kids will not sit still for unnecessary exposition and overblown prose. Long monologues, soliloquies and 'I Am' songs and ballads should be avoided. Television, movies and video make the world of entertainment highly competitive. We've noticed lately how well popular children's titles, contemporary and in public domain, sell. We are very interested in acquiring adaptations of this type of material."

UNIVERSITY OF MINNESOTA, DULUTH THEATRE, 10 University Dr., Duluth MN 55812-2496. (218)726-8562. Department Head: Jon Berry. Estab. 1974. Produces 8 plays/year at the University Theatre, American College Theatre Festival and the Minnesota Repertory Theatre (summer). Query with synopsis only. Acquires performance rights. Pays $35-100/performance.
Needs: All genres. Prefers younger casting requirements and single set or unit setting shows. No previously produced work or one-act plays.
Tips: "We are a very active undergraduate theater program that is very interested in producing new work. We frequently produce new plays for the American College Theatre Festival in which there are several major playwriting awards."

THE UNUSUAL CABARET, 14½ Mt. Desert St., Bar Harbor ME 04609. (207)288-3306. (Phone *only* June through mid-October.) Artistic Director: Gina Kaufmann. Estab. 1990. "Our audience tends to be youthful (25-50) and educated. They are tourists from all over the world, as well as dedicated, local regulars." Produces 3 plays/year. Reports on submissions in 3 months. "We produce two musical scripts and one non-musical script every season. Scripts must be 45 to 75 minutes in length and require no more than 8 actors. Our space is intimate, with minimal technical capacity. We always strive for the unusual in format and subject matter, without sacrificing accessibility." Submit completed ms (with tape, if applicable). Pays 10-12% royalty.
Tips: "As a true cabaret in the tradition of the Chat Noir and Cabaret Voltaire, we attempt to narrow or even eliminate the distance between spectator and performer, so pervasive in elitist or high art. We look for non-naturalistic scripts which are simultaneously challenging and playful. We encourage writers to be involved in the actual production process."

VIRGINIA STAGE COMPANY, P.O. Box 3770, Norfolk VA 23514-3770. (804)627-6988. Fax: (804)628-5958. Literary Manager: Jefferson H. Lindquist. Estab. 1979. VSC is a LORT C-1 theatre serving Southeastern Virginia audiences. Performing spaces are mainstage (700-seat) theatre with proscenium stage, and a 99-seat second stage, the Virginia Theatre Laboratory. Produces 4-6 plays/year. Accepts and encourages unsolicited scripts—especially from playwrights residing in Virginia. Submission time: January-April. Responds in 6 months. Scripts returned to author/agent only if postage is included.
Needs: Full-length plays, and musicals with tapes only. "Interested in poetic drama and comedy—no kitchen sink plays."

WALNUT STREET THEATRE, 9th and Walnut Streets, Philadelphia PA 19107. (215)574-3550. Executive Director: Bernard Havard. Literary Manager: Alexa Kelly. Estab. 1809. Produces 5 mainstage and 4 studio plays/year. "Our plays are performed in our own space. WST has 3 theaters—a proscenium (mainstage), 1,052 seats; 2 studios, 79-99 seats. We have a subscription audience, second largest in the nation." Query with synopsis and 10 pages. Reports in 5 months. Rights negotiated per project. Pays royalty (negotiated per project) or outright purchase.
Needs: "Full-length dramas and comedies, musicals, translations, adaptations and revues. The studio plays must be small cast, simple sets."
Tips: "We will consider anything. Bear in mind that on the mainstage we look for plays with mass appeal, Broadway-style. The studio spaces are our off-Broadway. No children's plays. Our mainstage audience goes for work that is entertaining and light. Our studio season is when we look for plays that have bite and are more provocative."

WEST COAST ENSEMBLE, P.O. Box 38728, Los Angeles CA 90038. (213)871-8673. Artistic Director: Les Hanson. Estab. 1982. Produces 6 plays/year. Plays will be performed in one of our two theaters in Hollywood. Submit complete ms. Reports in 6 months. Obtains the exclusive rights in southern California to present the play for the period specified. All ownership and rights remain with the playwright. Pays $25-45/performance. Writers guidelines for #10 SASE.
Needs: Prefers a cast of 6-12.
Tips: "Submit the ms in acceptable dramatic script format."

WESTBETH THEATRE CENTER, INC., 151 Bank St., New York NY 10014-2049. (212)691-2272. Fax: (212)924-7185. Producing Director: Arnold Engelman. Literary Manager: Steven Bloom. Estab. 1977. Produces 10 readings and 6 productions/year. Professional off-Broadway theater. Submit complete ms with SASE. Responds in 4 months. Obtains rights to produce as showcase with option to enter into full option agreement.
Needs: "Contemporary full-length plays. Production values (i.e., set, costumes, etc.) should be kept to a minimum." No period pieces. Limit 10 actors; doubling explained.

THE ANN WHITE THEATRE, 5266 Gate Lake Rd., Fort Lauderdale FL 33319. (305)772-4371. Artistic Director: Ann White. Estab. 1984. Produces 6 plays/year. "Alternative theater, professional productions for mature audiences. Plays performed in various settings: libraries, theaters, colleges and universities, hotels and dinner theaters." Conducts annual playwrights' competition and festival. Submit mss August-November 15 for productions in spring. SASE for guidelines. Winning playwright receives $500 and production by The Ann White Theatre.
Tips: "We are always interested in plays that focus on contemporary issues."

THE WOMEN'S PROJECT AND PRODUCTIONS, 7 W. 63rd St., New York NY 10023-7102. (212)873-3040. Artistic Director: Julia Miles. Estab. 1978. Produces 3 plays/year. Professional off-Broadway productions. Query with synopsis and 10 sample pages of dialogue. Reports in 1 month on queries.
Needs: "We are looking for full-length plays, written by women."

WOOLLY MAMMOTH THEATRE COMPANY, Dept. WM, 1401 Church St. NW, Washington DC 20005. (202)393-3939. Artistic Director: Howard Shalwitz. Literary Manager: Jim Byrnes. Produces 5 plays/year. 50% freelance written. Produces professional productions for the general public in Washington, DC. 2-3 scripts/year are unagented submissions. Works with 1-2 unpublished/unproduced writers annually. Accepts unsolicited scripts. Reports in 3 months on scripts; very interesting scripts often take much longer. Buys first- and second- class production rights. Pays 5% royalty.
Needs: "We look only for plays that are highly unusual in some way. Also interested in multicultural projects. Apart from an innovative approach, there is no formula. One-acts are not used." Cast limit of 8.

‡**WORCESTER FOOTHILLS THEATRE COMPANY**, 074 Worcester Center, 100 Front St., Worcester MA 01608. (508)754-3314. Artistic Director: Marc P. Smith. Estab. 1974. Produces 7 plays/year. Full time professional theater, general audience. Query with synopsis. Reports in 3 weeks. Pays royalty.

Needs: "Produce plays for general audience. No gratuitous violence, sex or language. Prefer cast under 10 and single set. 30′ proscenium with apron but no fly space."

Screenwriting

A person with no medical experience at all probably wouldn't dream of walking into an emergency room at the local hospital, watching an operation or two and then saying, "Heck, I can do better than that." After all, it takes years of education, training and experience to become a skilled surgeon.

Yet, it is entirely commonplace for someone with no writing experience at all to watch a movie or television show and come away saying, "Heck, I can do better than that." And since all you need to start is pencil and paper — unlike the aspiring surgeon, who must somehow find willing patients — the aspiring screenwriter begins. And probably fails.

The reason? Screenwriting is a craft, an art and a business, and unless you are committed to learning, practicing and perfecting the skills necessary to write a good script, you will not be able to rise above the intense competition and claim the potentially huge rewards.

And make no mistake about it, there is plenty of competition from amateurs and professionals alike. In order to deal with the daily influx of scripts, both solicited and unsolicited, producers and agents have set up some ground rules to try and save everybody wasted time and effort.

Number 1: If submitting to a production company, include a standard release form (a sample form you can use is included in *Successful Scriptwriting*, published by Writer's Digest Books, and is occasionally reprinted in *The Hollywood Scriptwriter*).

Number 2: Always include a SASE. Your script will never, ever be returned unless you provide a postage-paid envelope.

Number 3: Allow a minimum of a month before writing a follow-up letter. It takes at least this long for an agent or producer to wade through the stack of scripts and get to yours.

Number 4: Take "no" for an answer and move on. Agents and producers do not have time to critique your script or listen to your arguments about why they should take another look at it. Write a thank you letter and try the next on the list.

Number 5: Don't send your script. That is, until you've received an OK as a result of a query letter. Most of the time unsolicited submissions will be returned unread.

Your query letter should be concise, no more than a page. It should contain a one-paragraph synopsis of your story and any credits you may have. If you don't have any, don't mention it. If your background is important to the script (for instance, if you'd written *In the Line of Fire*, you'd want it known that you were a bodyguard or worked in Washington DC security) be sure to include it. Enclose a SASE, and refer to Numbers 3-5.

If your script is requested, be sure it's written in the proper format. If you don't know the difference between feature format and sitcom format, find out. There are plenty of books on the subject. Don't use fancy binding, artistic fonts or illustrated covers. Just sandwich 90-120 pages between two pieces of 80 lb. stock, punch three holes through the lot and fasten with two brass fasteners. Don't put the title of the script on the front; make your first page a title page, complete with name, address and phone number.

You'll be sending what's known as a "spec" script, one written on speculation. It should be an original feature (movie length) or a television script based on a current show. Don't send TV scripts based on original concepts; they won't be read. On the feature side, don't send sequels, that is, scripts that rely on existing characters. Those won't get read either.

There are any number of books out there that focus on the art, craft and business of screenwriting, and you should read as many as you can. Also, stay in touch with the day-to-day doings of the industry through the trade papers such as *Daily Variety* (Suite 120, 5700 Wilshire Blvd., Los Angeles CA 90036) or *Hollywood Reporter* (6715 Sunset Blvd., Hollywood CA 90028), and keep up with tips from top professionals and agents through specialty newsletters such as *The Hollywood Scriptwriter* (#385-WM, 1626 N. Wilcox, Hollywood CA 90028; 818-991-3096).

If the road seems long and hard sometimes, be comforted by the experiences of writers like Michael Blake, who struggled for more than 20 years before seeing *Dances with Wolves* capture the heart of the movie-going public and win an Academy Award. In fact, when Blake got the call to write the screenplay for his book, he had given up on his dream and was working as a cook at a Chinese restaurant in New Mexico.

The call can come at any time, but you have to be ready. Know your craft, know your art and understand the business. That way when opportunity knocks, you'll be ready.

For information on more screenwriting markets, see Scriptwriting Markets/ Changes '93-'94 at the end of this section.

‡AFA FILM PRODUCTIONS, P.O. Box 3662, Santa Clara CA 95055. Producer: Adeeb Barsoum. Estab. 1981. Produces material for the general public. Buys 6 scripts/year. Works with 5 writers/year. Buys all rights. SASE. Reports in 2 months. Free catalog. Submit complete ms. Pays in accordance with Writer's Guild standards.
Needs: Films (35mm) and videotapes.
Tips: "We use all materials for all subjects. We have a special interest in material for video."

ALLIED ARTISTS, INC., Suite 377, 859 N. Hollywood Way, Burbank CA 91505. (818)594-4089. Vice President, Development: John Nichols. Estab. 1990. Produces material for broadcast and cable television, home video and theater. Buys 3-5 scripts/year. Works with 10-20 writers/year. Buys first rights or all rights. Accepts previously produced material. Reports in 2 months on queries; 3 months on mss. Submit synopsis/outline. Pays in accordance with Writer's Guild standards (amount and method negotiable).

Needs: Films (16 and 35mm) and videotapes. Social issue TV special (30-60 minutes); special interest home video topics; instruction and entertainment; positive values feature screenplays.
Tips: "We are looking for positive, up-lifting dramatic stories involving real people situations. Future trend is for more reality-based programming, as well as interactive television programs for viewer participation."

‡ANGEL FILMS, 967 Hwy. 40, New Franklin MO 65274-9778. (314)698-3900. Fax: 9314)698-3900. Vice President Production: Matthew Eastman. Estab. 1980. Produces material for feature films, television. Buys 10 scripts/year. Works with 20 writers/year. Buys all rights. Accepts previously published material (if rights available). Reports in 1 months on queries; 1-2 months on mss. Catalog for #10 SAE with 2 first class stamps. Query with synopsis. Makes outright purchase "depending upon budget for project. Our company is a low budget producer which means people get paid fairly, but don't get rich."
Needs: Films (35mm) and videotapes. "We are looking for projects that can be used to produce feature film and television feature films and series work. These would be in the areas of action adventure, comedy, horror, thriller, science fiction, animation for children."
Tips: "Don't copy others. Try to be original. Don't overwork your idea. As far as trends are concerned, don't pay attention to what is 'in'. By the time it get to us it will most likely be on the way 'out.' And if you can't let your own grandmother read it, don't send it. If you wish material returned, enclose proper postage with all submissions."

ANGEL'S TOUCH PRODUCTIONS, 10445 Chandler Blvd., North Hollywood CA 91601. Director of Development: Phil Nemy. Professional screenplays and teleplays. Send script and/or synopsis. Reports in 6 months. Rights negotiated between production company and author. Payment negotiated.
Needs: All types, all genres, only full-length teleplays and screenplays—no one-acts.
Tips: "We are now only seeking feature film screenplays, television screenplays, episodic and sitcom teleplays."

‡ASKA FILM PRODUCTIONS, Suite 211, 1600 De Lorimier, Montreal, Quebec H2K 3W5 Canada. Story Editor: Natalya Rybina. Estab. 1979. Buys 2 scripts/year. Works with 2 writers/year. Buys all rights. Accepts previously produced material. Reports in 1 month. Submit completed ms. Pays in accordance with Writer's Guild standards.
Needs: Films (35mm).

‡BIG STAR MOTION PICTURES LTD., #201, 13025 Yonge St., Richmond Hill, Ontario L4E 1Z5 Canada. (416)720-9825. Contact: Frank A. Deluca. Estab. 1991. Buys 5 scripts/year. Works with 5-10 writers/year. Reports in 1 month on queries; 2 months on mss. Submit synopsis. "We deal with each situation differently and work on a project by project basis."
Needs: Films (35mm). "We are very active in all medias, but are primarily looking for television projects, cable, network, etc. True life situations are of special interest for M.O.W."

TONY BILL PRODUCTIONS, 73 Market St., Venice CA 90291. (310)396-5937. Contact: Deborah Gauthier. Estab. 1969. Produces feature films. Buys 2-3 scripts/year. Works with 4-5 writers/year. Reports in 2 months. Submit synopsis/Outline. Pays in accordance with Writer's Guild standards or option.
Needs: 35mm films.

‡BRADYCO PRODUCTIONS, #202, 127 Broadway, Santa Monica CA 90401. (310)394-4701. President: Bradley F. Richardson. Estab. 1989. Produces feature films via major studios. Produces 1-5/year. Buys all rights. SASE. Reports in 2 months on queries; 6 months on submissions.
Needs: 35mm film. Query with synopsis. Pays in accordance with Writers Guild standanrds.
Tips: "No sci-fi, no horror, no exploitation."

‡THE BROOKLYN BRIDGE PEOPLE, 5460 White Oak, Encino CA 91316. (818)986-3813. Producer: Bert Steinberger. Estab. 1991. Produces material for all audiences. Buys 2 scripts/year. Works with 2 writers/year. Buys all rights. Accepts previously produced material. Reports in 1 month. Query. Pays in accordance with Writer's Guild standards.
Needs: Films (35mm). "Original screenplays only!"

‡DAVID BROOKS PRODUCTIONS, % Citadel Pictures, 11340 W. Olympic Blvd., Los Angeles CA 90064. "Citadel is owned by Time/Warner." Produces material for TV movies. Buys 15 scripts/year. Buys film/TV rights. No previously produced material. Reports in 1-2 months. Query with synopsis. Pays option agreements.
Needs: TV movies, scripts or true stories. No treatments or novels.

‡ANTHONY CARDOZA ENTERPRISES, Box 4163, North Hollywood CA 71617. (818)985-5550. President: Anthony Cardoza. Produces material for "theater, TV and home." Buys one screenplay/year. Buys all rights. No previously produced material. Reports in 6 months.
Needs: Feature films. Submit completed ms. Makes outright purchase.

‡**THE CHICAGO BOARD OF RABBIS BROADCASTING COMMISSION,** 1 S. Franklin St., Chicago IL 60606-4694. (312)444-2896. Fax: (312)855-2474. Director of Broadcasting: Mindy Soble. "Television scripts are requested for *The Magic Door*, a children's program produced in conjunction with CBS's WBBM-TV 2 in Chicago." Four scripts/television season. Buys all rights. Reports in 1 month. Writers guidelines for #10 SASE.

Needs: "*Magic Door Television Theatre* is an anthology series of 4 specials/year designed for broadcast on weekends around the 5 p.m. hour. The target audience is 12 years of age, however the material should be viable for the whole family to enjoy. It is Jewish in content, yet universal in scope. Each episode should be built on an idea anchored in a Jewish value. While the perspective is Jewish, such topics as family, education, adversity, tradition, etc. are obviously not exclusive to the Jewish purview. We seek material rooted in Jewish thought, yet characterized by a "pro-social" message. This anthology series is television theater. It is designed to look like theater and we hope to capitalize on the elements characteristic of theater such as focused use of language, interior space, condensed time and vivid characterizations. The series is produced on videotape in a TV studio which lends itself to this style. We want scripts that are highly stylized and expressionistic. For the young target audience humor is an important element in each script. Each half hour episode stands on its own and is wholly unrelated to other episodes in the series. Submit synopsis/outline, resume or a complete ms with the right to reject. Makes outright purchase of $400.

Tips: "A Judaic background is helpful, yet not critical. Writing for children is key. We prefer to use Chicago writers, as script rewrites are paramount and routine."

‡**CLARK PRODUCTIONS, INC.,** P.O. Box 773, Balboa CA 92661. President: Mr. Clark. Estab. 1987. General audience. Buys 1 script/year. Works with 4 writers/year. Buys first rights. No previously produced material. Reports in 6 months. Submit synopsis/outline. Pays in accordance with Writer's Guild standards.

Needs: "We will rewrite existing screenplay (if owned). We did full length motion picture *The Ralph DePalma Story*."

CORNERSTONE PRODUCTIONS, #600, 6290 Sunset Blvd., Hollywood CA 90028-8710. (213)871-2255. Fax: (213)871-1627. Development Executive: John Burlein. Estab. 1969. Produces material for the Disney Channel, After School Specials, network TV movies and cable movies (USA, HBO, etc.). Buys 2 scripts/year. Works with 4 writers/year. Buys all rights. Reports in 1 month on queries; 2 months on mss. Query with SASE. Pays in accordance with Writer's Guild standards. Payment negotiable.

Needs: "We are currently seeking completed screenplays or treatments."

CUTTING EDGE PRODUCTIONS, 2026 Federal Ave., Los Angeles CA 90025. (310)478-8700. President: Tom Forsythe. Estab. 1982. We are looking for full length feature film scripts for theatrical release. We buy 5 scripts/year. Buys film, TV and allied rights. Reports in 1 month on mss.

Needs: Screenplays should be in standard format, approximately 120 pages. Query with synopsis. Pays in accordance with Writers Guild standards.

Tips: "Recognize that film distribution is becoming centralized by the major studios who only buy screenplays that are $20 million ideas. Before starting a script ask yourself: Is this a $20 million idea? Always ask yourself if you would watch the story you're telling. The smash hit mentality dominates feature production. Despite films like *Driving Miss Daisy*, hard-edged films continue to be the rule. We only respond to submissions accompanied by SASE."

‡**DAWBER & COMPANY, INC.,** Suite 4200, 25505 W. 12 Mile Rd., Southfield MI 48034. Creative Director: Andrew Dahl. Estab. 1976. General audience. "*We do not accept unsolicited material.*" Buys 2-3 scripts/year. Works with 1-2 writers/year. Buys all rights. No previously produced material. Submissions are presented personally by agents. Does not respond to queries; returns submissions without opening. Submit through WGA-approved agent. Pays in accordance with Writer's Guild standards.

Needs: Films (35 and 70mm) and videotapes. Needs entertainment shorts. "Style, etc. varies with venue."

Tips: "Do not send unsolicited material."

‡**HARRY DELIGTER PRODUCTIONS,** 3866 Keeshen Dr., Los Angeles CA 90066. (310)398-4949. President: Harry DeLigter. We have a theatrical motion pictures and television audience. Buys film, TV, worldwide and all media rights. Reports only if interested.

Needs: Films, scripts and videotapes. Query with synopsis and SASE.

Tips: "Remember we're offering entertainment. Upbeat, uplifting themes inventively presented reach bigger audiences. A sense of humor and good characters are important. Fragmented market means we're competing even more for audiences. Pitch/synopsis should include a simple to grasp one-line hook that might attract audiences in advertisement or in film trailers."

‡**DOOMSDAY STUDIOS LIMITED,** 212 James. St., Ottawa, Ontario K1R 5M7 **Canada.** (613)230-9769. President: Ramona Macdonald. Estab. 1978. Audience is theaters. Works with 5 screenplays/year. Rights variable. No previously produced material. Reporting time "variable. We are usually backed up with material." Submit synopsis/outline. Pay "variable, according to budget and financing of each project."

Needs: Films (16mm and 35mm).
Tips: "We are always on the lookout for cutting-edge material that can be independently produced and is suitable for marketing internationally. We are not interested in anything which 'reminds us' of something we have previously seen. We do not wish to see material which is exploitative or pornographic. We are especially 'open' to material from minority groups."

EARTH TRACKS PRODUCTIONS, (formerly Blazing Productions, Inc.), Suite 286, 4809 Ave. N., Brooklyn NY 11234. Contact: David Krinsky. Estab. 1985. Produces material for "major and independent studios." Buys 1-3 scripts/year. Buys all rights. No books, no treatments, no articles. *Only* completed movie and television movie scripts. Reports in 6 weeks on queries.
Needs: Commercial, well written, high concept scripts in the drama, comedy, action and thriller genres. No other scripts. Query with one-page synopsis. No treatments. Include SASE. *Do not send any scripts unless requested.*
Tips: "Can always use a *good* comedy. Writers should be flexible and open to suggestions. Material with interest (in writing) from a known actor/director is a *major plus* in the consideration of the material. We also need sexy thrillers. Any submissions of more than 2 pages will *not* be read or returned."
● This producer notes a high rate of inappropriate submissions. Please read and follow his guidelines carefully.

ENTERTAINMENT PRODUCTIONS, INC., Suite 744, 2210 Wilshire Blvd., Santa Monica CA 90403. (310)456-3143. Producer: Edward Coe. Estab. 1971. Produces films for theatrical and television (worldwide) distribution. Reports in 1 month (only if SASE is enclosed for reply and/or return of material). Contact: Story Editor.
Needs: Screenplays. Only unencumbered originals. Query with synopsis. Makes outright purchase for all rights. Price negotiated on a project-by-project basis. Writer's release in any form will be acceptable.
Tips: "State why script has great potential."

‡FINE ART PRODUCTIONS, 67 Maple St., Newburgh NY 12550. (914)561-5866. Contact: Richie Suraci. Estab. 1992. Produces material for all genres. Buys variable number of scripts/year. Works with variable number of writers/year. Buys first rights, all rights, "varies with project. Negotiable." Accepts previously produced material. Reports in 3-6 months. Catalog for 8½ × 11 envelope and 52¢ postage. Query with synopsis, outline, script and resume. "Everything is negotiable by project, varies per project."
Needs: Charts, film loops (all formats), films (all formats), kinescopes, microfilm, videotapes, multimedia kits, phonograph records, silent and sound filmstrips, teaching machine programs, overhead transparencies, slides, study prints, tapes and cassettes and models. "Looking for all genres. Submit or we won't know it exists."

‡FURMAN FILMS, INC., P.O. Box 1769, Venice CA 90291-1769. (213)306-2700. Fax: (310)306-2754. Vice President: Norma Doane. Estab. 1967. Produces material for the general public. Buys 2-3 scripts/year. Buys all rights. No previously produced material. Reports in 2 weeks on queries; 6 weeks on submissions.
Needs: Films (16mm) and videotapes. Looking for general film and video projects—8-30 minutes; corporate. Also looking for TV series—60 minutes each. Query or query with synopsis. Pays in accordance with Writers Guild standards.

‡GOODMAN ASSOCIATES, INC., 718 S. 22nd St., Philadelphia PA 19146. President: Robert Goodman. Estab. 1985. "Each project is targeted to a specific audience." Buys 1-5 scripts/year. Works with 1-3 writers/year. Buys all rights. No previously produced material. Reports in 1 month. Query with synopsis, resume, reply card. "Payment varies according to the project. Dramatic is different than a market project."
Needs: Films (16mm) and videotapes. "We work on projects for specific audiences and would be interested in dramatic or documentary proposals."

INTERNATIONAL HOME ENTERTAINMENT INC., Suite 350, 1440 Veteran Ave., Los Angeles CA 90024. (213)460-4545. Assistant to the President: Jed Leland, Jr. Estab. 1976. Buys first rights. Reports in 2 months. Query. Pays in accordance with Writers Guild standards. *No unsolicited mss.*

‡JAG ENTERTAINMENT, 4508 Noeline Ave., Encino CA 91436. President/CEO: Jo-Ann Geffen. Estab. 1992. Produces material for TV/film, audience ages 18-40. Works with "many" writers/year. Buys all rights. No previously produced material. Reports in 1 month on queries; 2+ months on mss. Submit synopsis/outline, complete ms and resume.
Needs: "Features, TV movies only; reality shows OK." Looking for "female/character driven pieces. True stories are particularly interesting."

‡JEF FILMS, 143 Hickory Hill Circle, Osterville MA 02655. (508)428-7198. President: Jeffrey H. Aikman. Estab. 1973. "Feature films primarily geared for teens through adults." Buys 12 scripts/year. Buys all rights. Accepts previously published material. Reports in 3 months. Catalog for #10 SASE. Query with synopsis. Makes outright purchase, "amount dependent on style length, budget of project, experience of writer."

Needs: Films (35mm) and videotapes. Feature films in the dramatic, science fiction, erotic thriller, screwball comedy fields.
Tips: "Keep trying. We get 75-100 scripts/week, we will work with first-time writers, especially for quirky/offbeat materials. More needs for erotic thrillers, good dramatic stories featuring strong character actors."

‡KJD TELEPRODUCTIONS, 30 Whyte Dr., Voorhees NJ 08043. (609)751-3500. President: Larry Scott. Estab. 1989. Broadcast audience. Buys 6 scripts/year. Works with 3 writers/year. Buys all rights. No previously produced material. Reports in 1 month. Free catalog. Query. Makes outright purchase.
Needs: Films, videotapes and multimedia kits.

‡KN'K PRODUCTIONS INC., 12386 Ridge Circle, Los Angeles CA 90049. (310)471-3608. Creative Director: Katharine Kramer. Estab. 1992. "Looking for film material with strong roles for mature women (ages 40-55 etc.). Also roles for young women and potential movie musicals, message movies." Buys 4 scripts/year. Works with 4 writers/year. Buys all rights. No previously produced material. Reports in 3 months on queries; 2 months on mss. Catalog for #10 SASE. Submit synopsis, complete ms and resume. Pays in accordance with Writer's Guild standards or partnership.
Needs: Multimedia kits.
Tips: "We are seeking inspirational true/life stories such as women overcoming obstacles, human growth, movie musicals."

LAWSON PRODUCTIONS LTD., 2 Clarendon Close, London W2 2NS England. (071)706-3111. Managing Director: Sarah Lawson. *No freelance submissions except through agents.*

‡LIGHTVIEW ENTERTAINMENT, Suite 802, 11659 Santa Monica Blvd., Los Angeles CA 90025. (310)820-1929. Producer: Laura McCorkindale. Estab. 1991. Buys 20 scripts/year. Buys all rights. Send synopsis of screenplay. If interested, will contact directly via telephone and ask for screenplay. Pay negotiable.
Needs: Screenplays for feature films—smaller budget, independent films and big budget studio films.
Tips: "We are looking for all types of screenplays, all budget ranges and all genres, but are especially are drawn to material that enlightens and entertains."

LUCASFILM, LTD., P.O. Box 2009, San Rafael CA 94912. *Does not accept unsolicited material.*

▢LEE MAGID PRODUCTIONS, P.O. Box 532, Malibu CA 90265. (213)463-5998. President: Lee Magid. Produces material for all markets: adult, commercial—even musicals. 90% freelance written. 70% of scripts produced are unagented submissions. Works with "many" unpublished/unproduced writers. Buys all rights or will negotiate. No previously produced material. Does not return unsolicited material.
Needs: Films, sound filmstrips, phonograph records, television shows/series and videotape presentations. Currently interested in film material, either for video (television) or theatrical. "We deal with cable networks, producers, live-stage productions, etc." Works with musicals for cable TV. Prefers musical forms for video comedy. Submit synopsis/outline and resume. Pays in royalty, in accordance with Writers Guild standards, makes outright purchase or individual arrangement depending on author.
Tips: "We're interested in comedy material. Forget drug-related scripts."

‡MARS PRODUCTIONS CORPORATION, 10215 Riverside Dr., Toluca Lake CA 91602. (818)980-8011. Executive Assistant: Julia Fakhouri. Estab. 1969. Produces family and action films. Buys 3 scripts/year. Works with 5 writers/year. Buys all rights, options. No previously produced material. Reports in 1 month. Query with synopsis. Submit synopsis/outline. Makes outright purchase "depending on the project."
Needs: Film (35mm).
Tips: "Follow the standard script format. I do not like too much detail of action or details of camera angles."

▢MEDIACOM DEVELOPMENT CORP., P.O. Box 1926, Simi Valley CA 93062. (818)594-4089. Director/Program Development: Felix Girard. Estab. 1978. 80% freelance written. Buys 10-20 scripts annually from unpublished/unproduced writers. 50% of scripts produced are unagented submissions. Query with samples. Reports in 1 month. Buys all rights or first rights.
Needs: Produces charts, sound filmstrips, 16mm films, multimedia kits, overhead transparencies, tapes and cassettes, slides and videotape with programmed instructional print materials, broadcast and cable television programs. Publishes software ("programmed instruction training courses"). Negotiates payment depending on project.

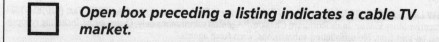

Open box preceding a listing indicates a cable TV market.

Tips: "Send short samples of work. Especially interested in flexibility to meet clients' demands, creativity in treatment of precise subject matter. We are looking for good, fresh projects (both special and series) for cable and pay television markets. A trend in the audiovisual field that freelance writers should be aware of is the move toward more interactive video disk/computer CRT delivery of training materials for corporate markets."

MERIWETHER PUBLISHING LTD. (Contemporary Drama Service), Dept. WM, 885 Elkton Dr., Colorado Springs CO 80907-3557. President: Mark Zapel. Executive Editor: Arthur L. Zapel. Estab. 1969. "We publish how-to materials in book and video formats. We are interested in materials for high school and college level students only. Our Contemporary Drama Service division publishes 60-70 plays/year." 80% written by unpublished writers. Buys 40-60 scripts/year from unpublished/unproduced writers. 90% of scripts are unagented submissions. Reports in 1 month on queries; 2 months on full-length mss. Query with synopsis/outline, resume of credits, sample of style and SASE. Catalog available for $2 postage. Offers 10% royalty or makes outright purchase.
Needs: Book mss on theatrical arts subjects. Christian children's activity book mss also accepted. We will consider elementary level religious materials and plays, but no elementary level children's secular plays. Query. Pays royalty; sometimes makes outright purchase.
Tips: "We publish a wide variety of speech contest materials for high school students. We are publishing more reader's theater scripts and musicals based on classic literature or popular TV shows, provided the writer includes letter of clearance from the copyright owner. Our educational books are sold to teachers and students at college and high school levels. Our religious books are sold to youth activity directors, pastors and choir directors. Our trade books are directed at the public with a sense of humor. Another group of buyers is the professional theater, radio and TV category."

THE MERRYWOOD STUDIO, 137 E. 38th St., New York NY 10016-2650. Creative Director: Raul daSilva. 20% freelance written. Estab. 1984. Produces animated motion pictures for entertainment audiences. No children's material sought or produced.
Needs: Proprietary material only. Human potential themes woven into highly entertaining drama, high adventure, comedy. This is a new market for animation with only precedent in the illustrated novels published in France and Japan. Cannot handle unsolicited mail/scripts and will not return mail. Open to *agented* submissions of credit sheets, concepts and synopses only. Profit sharing depending upon value of concept and writer's following. Will pay at least Writer's Guild scale or better, plus expenses.
Tips: "This is not a market for beginning writers. Established, professional work with highly unusual and original themes is sought. If you love writing, it will show and we will recognize it and reward it in every way you can imagine. We are not a 'factory' and work on a very high level of excellence."

METRO-GOLDWYN-MAYER INC. COMMUNICATIONS, (formerly MGM-Pathe Communications), 10000 W. Washington Blvd., Culver City CA 90232. Feature Story Coordinator: Mike Jones. Buys all rights. Pays in accordance with Writer's Guild standards.
Tips: "We do not accept unsolicited material. Please do not submit to us unless you have a WGA signatory agent. That agent should make contact with us first."

MONAREX HOLLYWOOD CORPORATION, 9421½ West Pico Blvd., Los Angeles CA 90035. (310)552-1069. Fax: (310)552-1724. President: Chris D. Nebe. Estab. 1978. Producers of theatrical and television motion pictures and miniseries; also international distributors. Buys 5-6 scripts/year. Buys all rights. Reports in 2 months.
Needs: Films (35mm) and videotapes. "We are seeking action, adventure, comedy and character-oriented love stories, dance, horror and dramatic screenplays." Submit synopsis/outline and complete ms with SASE. Pays in accordance with Writer's Guild standards.
Tips: "We look for exciting visuals with strong characters and a unique plot."

‡NEW & UNIQUE VIDEOS, 2336 Sumac Dr., San Diego CA 92105. (619)282-6126. Creative Director: Candace Love. Estab. 1982. General TV and videotape audiences. Buys 10-15 scripts/year. Buys first rights, all rights. No previously produced material. Reports in 1-2 months. Catalog for #10 SASE. Query with synopsis. Makes outright purchase, negotiable.
Needs: Videotapes.
Tips: "We are seeking unique slants on interesting topics in 60-90 minute special-interest videotape format. The sky's the limit. Imagination and passion, not to mention humor are pluses. Titles produced include 'Massage for Relaxation' and 'Ultimate Mountain Biking.' Be positive and let your fun side come out. Trends: We are moving toward 'moving pictures' (i.e. video, computers, CD-Rom, etc.) in a big way as book sales diminish. If writers can adapt to the changes, their work will always be in demand."

NEW LINE PRODUCTIONS, Suite 200, 116 N. Robertson Blvd., Los Angeles CA 90048. Fax: (310)854-1824. Executive Story Editor: Janis Rothbard Chaskin. "Agented submissions only. Query letter, including synopsis, must be sent first. No unsolicited submissions, even from agents."

PACE FILMS, INC., 411 E. 53rd St., PHC, New York NY 10022. (212)755-5486. President: R. Vanderbes. Estab. 1965. Produces material for a general theatrical audience. Buys all rights. Reports in 2 months.
Needs: Theatrical motion pictures. Produces and distributes 35mm motion pictures for theatrical, TV and videocassettes. Query with synopsis/outline and writing background/credits. Completed ms should be submitted together with an outline and SASE. Pays in accordance with Writer's Guild standards.

‡**PAPILLON PRODUCTIONS,** 1712 Anacapa St., Santa Barbara CA 93101. (805)569-0733. President: Emmanuel Itier. Estab. 1989. Produces material for any audience. Buys 2 scripts/year. Works with 4 writers/year. Buys all rights. Accepts previously produced material. Reports in 1 month. Free catalog. Submit complete ms and resume. Pays in accordance with Writers Guild standards.
Needs: Films. "We are seeking any screenplay for full-length motion pictures."
Tips: "Be patient but aggressive enough to keep people interested in your screenplay."

PARALLEL PICTURES, P.O. Box 985B, Hollywood CA 90078. New Projects Executive: Rick Tyler. Estab. 1988. "For a general audience, ages 16-45; depends on project. We produce for domestic as well as overseas audiences." Works with 3 writers/year. Buys all rights. No previously published material. Reports in 2 months on queries; 6 months on mss.
Needs: Films (35mm). "We are looking for feature-length screenplays—action, comedy, low budget. We accept all genres—very openminded. We love rare and new ideas." Submit a short synopsis of your script or project with a release form. Makes outright purchase.
Tips: "Take risks. I see too many replicas and poor development. If I don't see a plan of action or direction by the first 30 pages, something is wrong. Plots make the movie. That doesn't mean having many plots. You can keep it simple. Also, 80 pages is not feature length. Please bind all material. We won't look at a script made up of loose papers. Don't call us. We will call you."

□ **TOM PARKER MOTION PICTURES,** #285, 3491 S. Bristol, Santa Anna CA 92704. (714)545-2887. Fax: (714)545-9775. President: Tom Parker. Produces and distributes feature-length motion pictures worldwide (Member AFMA) for theatrical, home video, pay and free TV. Also produces short subject "special interest films (30, 45, 60 minutes). Works with 5-10 scripts/year. Previously produced and distributed "Amazing Love Secret" (R), "Amorous Adventures of Ricky D." (R), and "The Sturgis Story" (R). Reports within 3 months. "Follow the instructions herein and do not phone for info or to inquire about your script."
Needs: Complete ms *only* for low budget (under $1 million) "R" or "PG" rated action/thriller, action/adventure, comedy, adult romance (R), sex comedy (R), family action/adventure to be filmed in 35mm film for the theatrical and home video market (do not send TV movie scripts, series, teleplays, stage plays). *Very limited dialogue.* Scripts should be action-oriented and fully described. Screen stories or scripts OK, but no camera angles please. No heavy drama, documentaries, social commentaries, dope stories, weird or horror. Violence or sex OK, but must be well motivated with strong story line. Submit synopsis and description of characters with finished scripts. Makes outright purchase: $5,000-25,000. Will consider participation, co-production.
Tips: "Absolutely will not return scripts or report on rejected scripts unless accompanied by SASE."

‡**POP/ART FILM FACTORY,** #215, 513 Wilshire Blvd., Santa Monica CA 90401. Contact: Daniel Zirilli. Estab. 1990. Produces material for "all audiences/features films." Reports in 2 months. Query with synopsis. Pays on per project basis.
Needs: Film (35mm) and multimedia kits. "We are interested in producing 1 feature length film—$2 million budget or less. Hard-edged, independent."
Tips: "Be original. Do not play it safe."

PULSAR FILM CORPORATION, Dept. WM, P.O. Box 353, Fairfield IA 52556. (515)472-0301. Executive Director: Chip Hoyt. Estab. 1979. "We produce family entertainment material." Buys all rights or options. Reports in 2 weeks on queries; 6 weeks on submissions.
Needs: Films (30 minutes-2 hours). "We are interested in 30 page sci-fi scripts that are upbeat or humorous with a spiritual angle." Query with synopsis and SASE, then submit completed script with SASE. Pays in accordance with Writer's Guild standards. Material is optioned first.
Tips: "No horror, S&M or heavy sexual themes. We are interested in light-hearted or upbeat short scripts with space characters interacting with earth people. Scripts should contain some esoteric element or spiritual themes. These days, scripts should be very polished (needing only minor changes). They should be character driven and should feature characters that are very well developed."

‡**THE PUPPETOON STUDIOS,** P.O. Box 2019, Beverly Hills CA 90213. Producer/Director: Arnold Leibovit. Estab. 1987. "Broad audience." Works with 5 writers/year. Buys all rights. Reports in 1 month on queries; 2 months on mss. Query with synopsis. Submit complete ms. "A Submission Release *must* be included with all queries. Produced and directed 'The Puppetoon Movie.' SASE required for return of all materials—otherwise they will not be returned." Pays in accordance with Writer's Guild standards.

Needs: Films (35mm). "We are seeking animation properties including presentation drawings and character designs. The more detailed drawings with animation scripts the better."

‡**RED HOTS ENTERTAINMENT**, 813 N. Cordova St., Burbank CA 91505-2924. Vice President Development: Dan Pomeroy/Chip Miller. Estab. 1990. Buys 3 scripts/year. Works with 6-8 writers/year. Buys first rights, all rights, "short and long term options, as well." No previously produced material. Reports in 2-3 weeks on queries; 1-2 months on mss. Query with synopsis or submit complete ms ("writer's choice"). Pays in accordance with Writer's Guild standards. "Negotiable on writer's previous credits, etc."
Needs: Film loops (16mm), films (35mm), videotapes. "We are a feature film and television production company and have no audiovisual material needs."
Tips: "Best advice possible: originality, uniqueness, write from your instincts and *don't* follow trends."

THE SHELDON/POST COMPANY, 1437 Rising Glen Rd., Los Angeles CA 90069. (213)467-7989. Producers: David Sheldon and Ira Post. Estab. 1980. "We produce movies and series for television and theatrical motion pictures. Have contracts with Paramount Pictures, Hearst Entertainment, Citadel Entertainment and Columbia Pictures." Options and acquires all rights. Reports in 1 month. Query with synopsis. Pays in accordance with Writers Guild standards. No advance payments.
Needs: "We look for true stories, strong women's stories, suspense thrillers, action-adventure—scripts or treatments."
Tips: "Write realistic stories with good characters."

SOUTH FORK PRODUCTIONS, P.O. Box 1935, Santa Monica CA 90406-1935. Producer: Jerry Burke. Estab. 1980. Produces material for TV and film. Buys 2 scripts/year. Works with 4 writers/year. Buys all rights. No previously produced material. Send synopsis/outline and motion picture treatments, plus previous credits. Do not send completed script. Pays in accordance with Writers Guild Standards.
Needs: Films (16 and 35 mm) and videotapes.
Tips: "Follow established formats for treatments. SASE for return."

TALKING RINGS ENTERTAINMENT, P.O. Box 2019, Beverly Hills CA 90213-2019. President and Artistic Director: Arnold Leibovit. Estab. 1988. "We produce material for motion pictures and television." Buys 2 scripts/year. Works with 5 writers/year. Buys first rights or all rights. Reports on submissions in 2 months. Only send completed scripts. No treatments. Send complete ms with SASE and Submission Release if not agent. Pays in accordance with Writers Guild standards.
Needs: 35mm films and videotapes.

‡□ **TELEVISION PRODUCTION SERVICES CORP.**, Box 1233, Edison NJ 08818. (201)287-3626. Executive Director/Producer: R.S. Burks. Produces corporate and video music materials for major market distributor networks, etc. Buys 50-100 scripts/year. Buys all rights. Reports in 2 weeks.
Needs: "We do corporate and video music for record companies, ATT, HBO networks and commercials. We use treatments of story ideas from the groups' management. We also do commercials for over-the-air broadcast and cable. We are now doing internal in-house video for display on disk or internally distributed channels, and need good script writers." Submit synopsis/outline or complete ms and resume; *include SASE for response or materials will not be returned.*
Tips: Looks for rewrite flexibility and availability. "We have the capability of transmission electronically over the phone modem to our printer or directly onto disk for storage. We commission or contract out all scripts."

UNIFILMS, INC., 22931 Sycamore Creek Dr., Valencia CA 91354-2050. (805)297-2000. Vice President, Development: Jack Adams. Estab. 1984. We buy 0-5 scripts/year. Reports in 2 weeks on queries.
Needs: Feature films *only*. We are looking for feature film screenplays, current format, 100-120 pages long; commercial but not stupid, dramatic but not "artsy," funny but not puerile. Query with synopsis and SASE. "We do not accept unsolicited scripts. Save your postage; if you send us a script we'll return it unopened."
Tips: "If you've taken classes, read books, attended seminars and writers workshops all concerned with scriptwriting and read hundreds of produced studio screenplays *prior* to seeing the film and you're still convinced you've got a wonderful script, we might want to see it. If you've got someone else in the entertainment industry to recommend your script, we might be more interested in seeing it. But if you waste our time with a project that's not yet ready to be seen, we're not going to react well. Your first draft is not usually the draft you're going to show to the industry. *Get a professional opinion first*, then rewrite before you submit to us. Very few people care about synopses, outlines or treatments for sales consideration. THE SCRIPT is the basic blueprint, and everyone in the country is working on a script. Ideas are a dime a dozen. If you can *execute* that idea well and get people *excited* about that idea, you've got something. But most writers are wanna-bes, who submit scripts that need a lot more work just to get to the "promising" stage. Scripts are *always* rewritten. If you can't convince us you're a *writer*, we don't care. But if you *can* write and you've got a *second* idea we might talk."

VIDEO-VISIONS, #1, 126 N. Almont Dr., Beverly Hills CA 90211. (213)275-3658. Executive Producer: Christine Peres-Peña. Estab. 1986. "We produce material for children, Spanish audiences, PBS audience and young male audiences (ages 17-35). Buys 2-5 scripts/year. Buys all rights. Reports in 1 month on queries; 2 months on mss. Catalog for 9×12 SAE.

Needs: Films (16 and 35mm) and videotapes. "We need children's programming for the Hispanic market and cartoons, educational programs (30 minutes)—fast action entertainment (1½ or 2 hours)." Submit complete ms. Makes outright purchase of $500-5,000 in accordance with Writers Guild standards.

Tips: "We are looking for original ideas that are entertaining, educational and meaningful with morals and principles. We are also interested in explorations into the inner layers of society (the mind, the heart, etc.). There are many opportunities becoming available with the growth of the Hispanic market and its rich culture."

‡**VISION FILMS**, 4626 Lemona Ave., Sherman Oaks CA 91403. (818)784-1702. President: Stephen Rocha. Estab. 1989. "Worldwide audience." Buys 1 script/year. Works with 1 writer/year. Buys all rights. No previously produced material. Reports in 1 month on queries; 1 month on mss. Submit synopsis/outline with resume and information about where project has been previously pitched. Makes outright purchase $1,000 minimum, Writers Guild standards, with co-production opportunities.

Needs: Films (35mm) and videotapes. Seeking 1) entertaining documentary 1 hour television program specials with worldwide appeal; 2) movies with Hispanic appeal; 3) movies with special effects (under 5 million dollar budget).

Tips: "We are currently producing 18-part series for The Discovery Channel entitled *Movie Magic* about special effects."

Scriptwriting Markets/Changes '93-94

The following scriptwriting markets were listed in the 1993 edition but do not have listings in this edition of *Writer's Market*. The majority did not respond to our request to update their listing or return a questionnaire for a new listing. If a reason was given for their exclusion, we have included it in parentheses after the listing name.

The Allagash Group
The American Place Theatre
American Stage
Benenson Productions
Bristol Riverside Theatre
Carey-It-Off Productions
The Chamba Organization
Cine/Design Films, Inc.
Clearvue, Inc.
Comark
Continental Filme Productions, Corp.
The Cricket Theatre
Cronus International Entertainment, Inc.
Delta Max Productions
The Dramatic Publishing Co.
East West Players
Educational Insights
Glasnost Pictures, Inc.
The Goldstein Co. (too many

inappropriate submissions)
Great American History Theatre
Edward D. Hansen, Inc.
Impulse Theatre Co. (no longer accepting scripts)
International Home Entertainment, Inc.
Intiman Theatre Co.
Kimbo Educational-United Sound Arts, Inc. (asked to be deleted)
Marathon Entertainment Producers
Milwaukee Repertory Theater
Mirimar Enterprises
Missouri Repertory Theatre
Northlight Theatre
Oldcastle Theatre Co.
The Passage Theater
Philadelphia Festival Theatre

for New Plays
Playwrights Horizons
Pulse Productions (unable to contact)
Radio Repertory Co.
Rhythms Productions
Southeast Playwrights Project (unable to contact)
Target Canada Productions
Theater Ludicrum, Inc.
Theatre Calgary
Bob Thomas Productions
Trinity Square Ensemble
Undermain Theatre (does not accept unsolicited scripts)
Unicorn Theatre
Unity Pictures Corp. (does not accept unsolicited scripts)
The Wilma Theater

Syndicates

Newspapers are in for tough times in the coming years. For various reasons — ranging from the emergence of interactive video systems to the fact that today's young adults (tomorrow's newspaper subscribers) tend to read papers infrequently — newspaper circulation is expected to drop steadily over the next half dozen years. Lower circulation means lower ad rates which mean lower profits. In order to remain viable and compete effectively for readers and ad dollars, newspapers will have to keep up with trends in information technology, work harder than ever at selling their product to the consumer — and become accustomed to operating on lower profit margins.

As the number of daily newspapers diminishes, the syndication industry is becoming more and more competitive. Coveted spots in sports, humor and political commentary are held by big name columnists such as Peter Gammons, Dave Barry and Anna Quindlen. And multitudes of aspiring writers wait in the wings, hoping one of these heavy hitters will move on to something else and leave the spotlight open.

Although this may seem discouraging, there are in fact many areas in which less known writers are syndicated. As consumer interests and lifestyles change, new doors are being opened for innovative writers who can cover fitness; recycling/environmental issues; money-saving tips; and how-to material such as woodworking, gardening and cooking.

Most syndicates distribute a variety of columns, cartoons and features. Although the larger ones are usually only interested in running ongoing material, smaller ones often accept short features and one-shots in addition to continuous columns. One-shot features tend to be longer than columns and can be tied to a news peg or event. Specialized syndicates — those that deal with a single area such as business — often sell to magazines, trade journals and other business publications as well as to newspapers.

The winning combination

In presenting yourself and your work, take note that most syndicated columnists start out writing for local newspapers. Many begin as staff writers, develop a following in a particular area, and are then picked up by a syndicate. Before approaching a syndicate, write for a paper in your area. Be sure to develop a good collection of clips that you feel is representative of your best writing.

New ideas are paramount to syndication. Sure, you'll want to study the popular columnists to see how their pieces are structured (most are short—from 500-750 words—and really pack a punch), but don't make the mistake of imitating a well-known columnist. Syndicates are looking for original material that is timely, salable and original. Do not submit a column to a syndicate on a subject it already covers. The more unique the topic, the greater your chances of having it picked up. Most importantly, be sure to choose a topic that interests you and one you know well.

Approaching markets

Most syndicates prefer a query letter and about six sample columns or writing samples and a SASE. You may also want to include a client list and business card if available. If you have a particular area of expertise that is pertinent to your submission, be sure to mention this in your letter and back it up by sending related material. For highly specialized or technical matter, provide some credentials to show you are qualified to handle the topic.

In essence, syndicates act as agents or brokers for the material they handle. Writing material is usually sold as a package. The syndicate will promote and market the work to newspapers (and sometimes to magazines) and will keep careful records of sales. Writers usually receive 40-60% of gross receipts. Some syndicates may also pay a small salary or flat fee for one-shot items.

Syndicates usually aquire all rights to accepted material, although a few are now offering writers and artists the option of retaining ownership. In selling all rights, writers give up ownership and future use of their creations. Consequently, sale of all rights is not the best deal for writers, and has been the reason many choose to work with syndicates that buy less restrictive rights. Before signing a contract with a syndicate, you may want to go over the terms with an attorney or with an agent who has a background in law. The best contracts will usually offer the writer a percentage of gross receipts (as opposed to net receipts) and will not bind the writer for longer than five years.

The self-syndication option

Many writers choose to self-syndicate. This route allows you to retain all rights, and gives you the freedom of a business owner. But as a self-syndicated writer, you must also act as your own manager, marketing team and sales force. You must develop mailing lists, and a pricing, billing and collections structure.

Payment is usually negotiated on a case-by-case basis. Small newspapers may offer only $10-20 per column, but larger papers may pay much more (for more information on pay rates, see How Much Should I Charge? on page 46.). The number of papers you deal with is only limited by your marketing budget and your tenacity.

If you self-syndicate you should be aware that some newspapers are not

Competition for syndication slots is formidable

Anita Tobias is not so sure the predicted decline in newspaper circulation will take place. "Actually, as our society on the whole ages, I believe circulation will increase, since older people are more likely to be newspaper readers," says Tobias, Vice President and General Manager of Creators Syndicate. "What has occurred over the past few years is a decline in the number of newspapers."

The effect, Tobias says, of that drop in the number of papers is that the competition for syndication will be tougher than ever. "Only the best will be offered syndication contracts," she says, "and of those, only a percentage will succeed."

Writers hoping for a slot with Creators Syndicate should send tearsheets or clips if the columns have been published, and double-spaced, typed and num-

Anita Tobias

bered pages if not. Tobias recommends sending between eight and ten sample columns. "At this time," says Tobias, "we are not accepting articles for one-time publication within the United States. Right now, we deal strictly with contract features such as weekly or biweekly political, business or lifestyle columns.

"A good candidate for syndication," she says, "will be someone who already has exposure of some kind. Success in a related field, or even a completely different area, can be enormously helpful. Of course, the column must be of national interest, original and well written. The key to succeeding remains unchanged: Be the best."

copyrighted, so you should copyright your own material. It's less expensive to copyright columns as a collection than individually. For more information on copyright procedures, see Copyrighting Your Writing in the Business of Writing section.

Additional information on newspaper markets can be found in *The Gale Directory of Publications* (available in most libraries). The *Editor & Publisher Syndicate Directory* (11 W. 19th St., New York NY 10011) has a list of syndicates, contact names and features; the weekly magazine, *Editor & Publisher*, also has news articles about syndicates and can provide you with information about changes and events in the industry.

INSIDER REPORT

Doing it yourself

Mark Powell would like to be a syndicated newspaper columnist. Until that happens, though, he is not sitting on his hands waiting for the phone to ring. Powell has been successful in placing his op-ed columns in over 60 newspapers. He has sold newspaper and magazine feature articles and he does radio news reports and commentary. And he has done it all on his own; Powell is self-distributed.

Mark Powell

"I've gotten all my publications by dealing directly with the newspapers I've published in," he says. Though he does hope to be syndicated some day, Powell is not optimistic about the opportunities currently available with the syndicates. "It is a very tough market to crack. For an individual freelancer to achieve syndication, he has to, one, be writing something sufficiently unique that the syndicate is not already publishing something like it, and two, be writing something that is marketable to a wide demographic audience—or, conversely, something narrow enough to appeal to a sizable niche market."

He markets his work energetically, and Powell's not one to simply send off an article and wait patiently to hear the result. "I send the piece itself and a bio. And I follow up on the phone. Sometimes I'll even precede the piece by placing a call to engage the editor—to get him or her expecting it. You can't be afraid of making a pest of yourself to editors. You'll never get anywhere if you're afraid to risk rejection.

"I have a two-stage plan," Powell says. "I would like to hook up as a columnist or editor at a major paper. Then I would like to achieve syndication. I see the former as a prerequisite to the latter. It's virtually impossible to get a syndication deal unless you're an established writer working steadily on a paper."

For information on syndicates not included in *Writer's Market*, see Syndicates/Changes '93-'94 at the end of this section.

ALLIED FEATURE SYNDICATE, Dept. WM, P.O. Drawer 48, Joplin MO 64802-0048. (417)673-2860. Editor: Robert J. Blanset. Contact: Irene Blanset. Estab. 1940. 70% written by writers on contract; 30% freelance by writers on a one-time basis. Works with 36 writers/year. Works with 30 previously unpublished writers/year. Syndicates to newspapers (60%); magazines (30%); in-house organs (10%). Submissions will be returned "only on request." Reports in 6 weeks. Buys all rights.
Needs: Buys news articles, cartoon strips, panels and features. Must be directly related to business, electronics, human resources, computers or quality and test design. All other non-related materials will be rejected and returned to sender if SASE is included. Query with clips of published work. Pays 50% author's percentage "after production costs" or 5¢/word. Currently syndicates "A Little Prayer," by Mary Alice Bennett (religious filler); "Murphy's Law of Electronics," by Nic Frising (cartoon panel); "Selling in the Year 2000," by Dick Meza (marketing column).
Tips: "Allied Feature Syndicate is one of very few agencies syndicating electronics manufacturing targeted materials and information."

‡AMERICA INTERNATIONAL SYNDICATE, 1324 N. 3rd St., St. Joseph MO 64501. (816)233-8190. Fax: (816)279-9315. Executive Director: Gerald A. Bennett. Associate Director (London office): Paul Eisler. 100% freelance written by cartoonists on contract. "We sell to newspapers, trade magazines, puzzle books and comic books." Reports in 6 weeks. Buys all rights.

Needs: Short fictional crime story "You Are The Detective" for magazines, books and comics; also comic strips of adventure, western or family type. Children's features and games also needed. Scientific or unusual features with art and written text needed. Send 6-8 samples with SASE. Pays 50% of gross sales. Currently syndication features: "Alfonso," "Silent Sam," "Tex Benson," "Buccaneers," "Figment," "Adventures in Nature" (comic strips). Panel features are "Stacey," "Girls," "The Edge," "Kids & Pets," and "Odds & Ends."

Tips: "Keep the art simple and uncluttered as possible. Know your subject and strive for humor. We have a need for uncaptioned cartoon panels and strips at present time."

AMERICAN NEWS FEATURES SYNDICATE, P.O. Box 46004, Bedford OH 44146-0004. (216)232-7771. Managing Editor: Christopher Wyatt. Estab. 1988. Syndicates one-shot feature articles to a wide variety of newspapers throughout the country.

Needs: "We are unusual in that we pay for ideas as well as for writing an article. We are only interested in stories that have been covered before in another publication. We must know and see the source. We are not seeking "original" story ideas. We take stories/ideas that have already been written about – usually at the local level – and then write a feature for a national audience. We are constantly on the lookout for articles that have appeared in local papers that might have national appeal. You must send us a good photocopy of the article. If interested, we will either pay for the idea outright or assign the article. We are looking for government waste, how-to, profile/interview, human interest, consumerism, women's interest, medical, especially breakthrough, celebrities, inspirational." No first person or fiction and absolutely no continuing series, columns or cartoons." Pays $35-200 for an idea; up to $400 for a 1,000-word article. Idea and writer's guidelines request *must* include SASE. Reports in 1 month.

Tips: "The best way to make an impression with us is to read our guidelines. We need articles that are newsy, breezy, emotional, and can be written with a punchy lead. *Forget* ideas/articles that have appeared in major magazines, newspapers, wire service stories such as AP, UPI or the tabloids. But if it happened in your town and was covered only by the local paper, then you have a real shot. Be sure to include your name, address and daytime phone number on the back of the photocopy. Do not send us completed mss. If you want the article/idea returned you must include a SASE."

AMERIPRESS/AMERIPRENSA (Latin America and Spain), P.O. Box 8443, Virginia Beach VA 23450-8443. (804)471-0110. Editors: Russ Mathena and Rene Lopez-Perez. Estab. 1991. 100% from freelancers, 50% by writers on a one-time basis. 20% photos. Syndicates to magazines and newspapers. Send all material on IBM ASCII diskettes with hard copy. Reports in 1-2 months. All rights, first North American serial or second (reprints) rights.

Needs: Magazine and newspaper features, news items and sexuality articles considered. Single (one-shot) features and article series on spec only. Spanish and English (translations 10% less). Query or submit complete ms on IBM ASCII diskette w/hard copy. If you want your material returned, send SASE. Pays 50% author's percentage for articles with all expenses from syndicate share. 60% for photos. "We are working more closely with foreign as well as the domestic market. We have good relations with European, Japanese and New Zealand syndicates as well."

AMPERSAND COMMUNICATIONS, 2311 S. Bayshore Dr., Miami FL 33133-4728. (305)285-2200. Editor: George Leposky. Estab. 1982. 100% written by writers on contract. "We syndicate only our own material at present, but we will consider working with others whose material is exceptionally good. Novices need not contact us." Syndicates to magazines and newspapers. Query for electronic submissions. Reports in up to 4 months. Buys all rights. Writer's guidelines $2 for SASE.

Needs: Newspaper columns, travel, business, science and health, regional cuisine, natural foods, environment; typically 500-750 words, rarely up to 1,500 words. Material from other writers must complement, not compete with, our own travel, business, environment, health and home improvement columns. Query with clips of published work and submit complete ms – samples of proposal columns. Pays 50% of net after production. "Note: For columns requiring photos, the writer must supply to us the required number of images and quantity of each image at his/her expense. We are not in the photo duplication business and will not provide this service." Currently syndicates Traveling the South, by George and Rosalie Leposky (travel); Business Insights, by Lincoln Avery (business); Food for Thought (cooking) by Rosalie Leposky; HealthScan, by George Leposky (health); EnviroScan, by George Leposky (environment); House and Home, by Lynne Avery (home improvement).

Tips: "Be an *excruciatingly* good writer; good alone isn't enough. Find a niche that doesn't seem to be covered. Do research to cover your topics in-depth, but in few words. The reader's attention span is shriveling, and so are ad lineage and column inches available for syndicated features."

‡ARKIN MAGAZINE SYNDICATE INC., Suite A8, 300 Bayview Dr., N. Miami Beach FL 33160-4747. Editor: Joseph Arkin. Estab. 1958. 20% freelance written by writers on contract; 70% freelance written by writers on a one-time basis. "We regularly purchase articles from several freelancers for syndication in trade and professional magazines." Previously published submissions OK, "if all rights haven't been sold." Reports in 3 weeks. Buys all North American magazine and newspaper rights.

Needs: Magazine articles (nonfiction, 750-2,200 words), directly relating to business problems common to several different types of businesses and photos (purchased with written material). "We are in dire need of the 'how-to' business article." Will not consider article series. Submit complete ms; "SASE required with all submissions." Pays 3-10¢/word; $5-10 for photos; "actually, line drawings are preferred instead of photos." **Pays on acceptance.**

Tips: "Study a representative group of trade magazines to learn style, needs and other facets of the field."

ARTHUR'S INTERNATIONAL, Suite 28-88, 101 S. Rainbow, Las Vegas NV 89128. (702)255-7866. Editor: Marvin C. Arthur. Syndicates to newspapers and magazines. Reports in 1 week. "SASE must be enclosed." Buys all rights.

Needs: Fillers, magazine columns, magazine features, newspaper columns, newspaper features and news items. "We specialize in timely nonfiction and historical stories, and columns, preferably the unusual. We utilize humor. Travel stories utilized in 'World Traveler.' " Buys one-shot features and article series. "Since the majority of what we utilize is column or short story length, it is better to submit the article so as to expedite consideration and reply. Do not send any lengthy mss." Pays 50% of net sales, salary on some contracted work and flat rate on commissioned work. Currently syndicates Marv, by Marvin C. Arthur (informative, humorous, commentary); Humoresque, by Don Alexander (humorous); and World Spotlight, by Don Kampel (commentary).

Tips: "We do not use cartoons but we are open for fine illustrators."

BUDDY BASCH FEATURE SYNDICATE, 771 West End Ave., New York NY 10025-5572. (212)666-2300. Editor/Publisher: Buddy Basch. Estab. 1965. 10% written by writers on contract; 2% freelance written by writers on a one-time basis. Buys 10 features/year; works with 3-4 previously unpublished writers annually. Syndicates to print media: newspapers, magazines, giveaways, house organs, etc. Reports in 3 weeks. Buys first North American serial rights.

• Most stories are done inhouse.

Needs: Magazine features, newspaper features, and one-shot ideas that are really different. "Try to make them unusual, unique, real 'stoppers,' not the usual stuff." Will consider one-shots and article series on travel, entertainment, human interest—"the latter, a wide umbrella that makes people stop and read the piece. Different, unusual and unique are the key words, not what the *writer* thinks is, but which have been done nine million times before." Query. Pays 20-50% commission. Additional payment for photos $10-50. Currently syndicates It Takes a Woman by Frances Scott (woman's feature), Travel Whirl, Scramble Steps (puzzle) and others.

Tips: "Never mind what your mother, fiancé or friend thinks is good. If it has been done before and is old hat, it has no chance. Do some research and see if there are a dozen similar items in the press. Don't just try a very close 'switch' on them. You don't fool anyone with this. There are fewer and fewer newspapers, with more and more people vying for the available space. But there's *always* room for a really good, *different* feature or story. Trouble is few writers (amateurs especially) know a good piece, I'm sorry to say. Read *Writer's Market*, carefully, noting which syndicate might be interested in the type of feature you are submitting. That will save you time and money."

CHRONICLE FEATURES, Dept. WM, Suite 1011, 870 Market St., San Francisco CA 94102. (415)777-7212. General Manager: Stuart Dodds. Contact: Jean W. Arnold. Buys 3 features/year. Syndicates to daily newspapers in the US and Canada with representation overseas. Reports in 2 months.

Needs: Newspaper columns and features. "In choosing a column subject, the writer should be guided by the concerns and aspirations of today's newspaper reader. We look for originality of expression and, in special fields of interest, exceptional expertise." Preferred length: 500-700 words. Submit complete ms. Pays 50% revenue from syndication. Offers no additional payment for photos or artwork accompanying ms. Currently syndicates Bizarro, by Dan Piraro (cartoon panel); Earthweek, by Steve Newman (planetary diary); Home Entertainment, by Harry Somerfield (audiovisual equipment advice and reviews); and Streetwise, by Herb Greenberg (up-to-the-minute business column).

Tips: "We are seeking features that will be ongoing enterprises, not single articles or news releases. Examples of a proposed feature are more welcome than a query letter describing it. Please conduct all correspondence by mail rather than by telephone."

CONTINENTAL FEATURES/CONTINENTAL NEWS SERVICE, Suite 265, 341 W. Broadway, San Diego CA 92101-3802. (619)492-8696. Editor: Gary P. Salamone. Estab. 1981. 100% written by writers on contract; 30% freelance written by writers on a one-time basis. "Writers who offer the kind and quality of writing we seek stand an equal chance regardless of experience." Syndicates to the print media. Reports in 1 month. Writer's guidelines for #10 SASE.

Needs: Magazine and newspaper features. "Feature material should fit the equivalent of one-quarter to one-half standard newspaper page, and Continental News considers an ultra-liberal or ultra-conservative slant inappropriate." Query. Pays 70% author's percentage. Currently syndicates News and Comment by Charles Hampton Savage (general news commentary/analysis); Continental Viewpoint, by staff; Portfolio, by William F. Pike (cartoon/caricature art); FreedomWatch, by Glenn Church; Travelers Checks by Anne Hattes; Middle East Cable, by Mike Maggio; and InVideo by Harley Lond.

• This syndicate is now considering submissions for children's features.

Tips: "Continental News seeks country profiles/background articles that pertain to foreign countries. Writers who possess such specific knowledge/personal experience stand an excellent chance of acceptance, provided they can focus the political, economic and social issues. We welcome them to submit their proposals. We foresee the possibility of diversifying our feature package by representing writers and feature creators on more one-shot projects."

‡**CRAFT PATTERNS, INC.,** 3545 Stern Ave., St. Charles IL 60174. (708)584-3334. Marketing Rep: Marsha Sidmore. Estab. 1940. 25% written by writers on contract. Buys 1 feature/year. Works with 2 writers/year. Syndicates to newspapers. Query for electronic submissions. Reports in 2 months. Buys all rights. Query with clips of published work.

Needs: Fillers and newspaper features. Pay negotiable. Currently syndicates "Project-of-the-Week," by Woodley Smith (woodworking project feature); "Home Design-of-the-Week," by M. Sidmore (home plan feature).

CREATE-A-CRAFT, P.O. Box 330008, Ft. Worth TX 76163. (817)292-1855. Contact: Editor. Estab. 1967. 5% written by writers on contract; 50% freelance written. Buys 5 features/year. Works with 3 writers/year. Works with 3 new previously unpublished writers/year. Syndicates to magazines and newspapers. Reports in 4 months. Submissions will not be returned. Buys all rights. Writer's guidelines $2.50 for #10 SASE. Prefers agented submissions only (submit complete ms).

Needs: Magazine columns and features, newspaper columns and features. "Looking for material on appraising, art, decorative arts, politics (how politics affect art only); 400-2,000 words. Comics must be in strip form only." Pays $6-10 flat hourly rate (depending on project). All work is work-for-hire. Currently syndicates Appraisals by Abramson (appraisal column); Those Characters from Cowtown (cartoon); Rojo (cartoon); Golden Gourmets (cartoon); Gallant Gators (cartoon). Author is always listed as Create-A-Craft (no byline given).

Tips: "Know the market you are writing for."

CREATIVE SYNDICATION SERVICES, P.O. Box 40, Eureka MO 63025-0040. (314)938-9116. Fax: (314)343-0966. Editor: Debra Holly. Estab. 1977. 10% written by writers on contract; 50% freelance written by writers on a one-time basis. Syndicates to magazines, newspapers and radio. Query for electronic submissions. Reports in 1 month. Buys all rights. Currently syndicates The Weekend Workshop, by Ed Baldwin; Woodcrafting, by Ed Baldwin; and Classified Clippers, a feature exclusive for the Classified Section of newspapers.

Tips: "We are looking for writers who do crafts, woodworking, needle-crafts and sewing."

CREATORS SYNDICATE, INC., Suite 700, 5777 W. Century Blvd., Los Angeles CA 90045. (213)337-7003. Vice President/General Manager: Anita Tobias. Estab. 1987. Syndicates to newspapers. Reports in 1-2 months. Buys negotiable rights. Writer's guidelines for #10 SASE.

Needs: Newspaper columns and features. Query with clips of published work or submit complete ms. Author's percentage: 50%. Currently syndicates Ann Landers (advice), Harris Poll, Walter E. Williams, Mona Charen, Percy Ross and Thomas Sowell (columns), B.C. and Wizard of Id (comic strips) and Herblock (editorial cartoon).

Tips: "Syndication is very competitive. Writing regularly for your local newspaper is a good start."

CRICKET COMMUNICATIONS, INC., P.O. Box 527, Ardmore PA 19003-0527. (215)789-2480. Editor: J.D. Krickett. Estab. 1975. 10% written by writers on contract; 10% freelance written by writers on a one-time basis. Works with 2-3 previously unpublished writers annually. Syndicates to trade magazines and newspapers. Reports in 1 month. Buys all rights.

Needs: Magazine columns and features, newspaper columns and features, and news items—all tax and financial-oriented (700-1,500 words); also newspaper columns, features and news items directed to small business. Query with clips of published work. Pays $50-500. Currently syndicates Hobby/Business, by Mark E. Battersby (tax and financial); Farm Taxes, by various authors; and Small Business Taxes, by Mark E. Battersby.

CROWN SYNDICATE, INC., P.O. Box 99126, Seattle WA 98199. President: L.M. Boyd. Estab. 1967. Buys countless trivia items. Syndicates to newspapers, radio. Reports in 1 month. Buys first North American serial rights. Free writer's guidelines.

Needs: Filler material used weekly, items for trivia column (format guidelines sent on request). Pays $1-5/ item, depending on how it's used, i.e., trivia or filler service. Offers no additional payment for photos accompanying ms. Currently syndicates columns and puzzle panels.

‡**DANY NEWS SERVICE**, 22 Lesley Dr., Syosset NY 11791. Editor: David Nydick. Estab. 1962. Buys 10% from freelancers. Buys 30 features/year (from freelancers). Syndicates to newspapers. Reports in 1 month. Buys all rights. Submit complete ms.
Needs: Newspaper columns, newspaper features, how-to (help your child). Pays $50 minimum guarantee. "You, Your Child and School," "You, Your Child and Sports," and "You, Your Child and Entertainment," (how-to help your child).

EDITORIAL CONSULTANT SERVICE, P.O. Box 524, West Hempstead NY 11552. (516)565-6332. Editorial Director: Arthur A. Ingoglia. Estab. 1964. 40% written by writers on contract; 25% freelance written by writers on a one-time basis. "We work with 75 writers in the US and Canada." Previously published writers only. Adds about 5 new columnists/year. Syndicates material to an average of 60 newspapers, magazines, automotive trade and consumer publications, and radio stations with circulation of 50,000-575,000. Buys all rights. Writer's guidelines for #10 SASE. Reports in 1 month.
Needs: Magazine and newspaper columns and features, news items and radio broadcast material. Prefers carefully documented material with automotive slant. Also considers automotive trade features. Will consider article series. No horoscope, child care, lovelorn or pet care. Query. Author's percentage varies; usually averages 50%. Additional payment for 8 × 10 b&w and color photos accepted with ms. Submit 2-3 columns. Currently syndicates Let's Talk About Your Car, by R. Hite.
Tips: "Emphasis is placed on articles and columns with an automotive slant. We prefer consumer-oriented features, how to save money on your car, what every woman should know about her car, how to get more miles per gallon, etc."

ENTERTAINMENT NEWS SYNDICATE, 155 East 55th St., New York NY 10022. (212)223-1821. Fax: (212)223-3737. Editor: Lee Canaan. Estab. 1970. 10% written by writers on contract. Syndicates to newspapers and magazines. Reports in 1 month. Buys all rights. Free writer's guidelines.
Needs: Fillers, magazine and newspaper features, and news on travel and entertainment. No single (one-shot) features. Query. Payment negotiable. Currently syndicates Cruise Callings, Hotels & Spas and Tour Treats, by L. Canaan (column).

EUROPA PRESS NEWS SERVICE, Clasificador 5, Tajamar Providencia, Santiago, Chile. (562)235-2902 or (562)235-1584. Fax: (562)235-1731. Editor: Maria Marta Raggio. Estab. 1963. 50% freelance written by writers on a one-time basis. Syndicates to magazines and newspapers. Reports in 3 months. Buys second serial rights for Latin America and other customers in Europe, Far East. Publishes reprints of previously published articles. Send tearsheet of article. For reprints, pays 50% of the amount paid for an original article.
Needs: Magazine features (science, technology, celebrities: interviews with candid shots), newspaper features, recipes, handiworks, etc. with color photos. Buys one-shot features and article series. "Travel, adventure, human-interest stories with pictures. Query with clips of published work or submit complete ms. Pays 50% author's percentage. Currently syndicates Moda al dia, by Claudia Moda (color photo with captions); Household Advice, by Penny Orchard (column with illustrations); and The World Today, by London Express (articles with b&w pictures).
Tips: "We are seeking good, up-to-date articles about technology, science, medicine, business, marketing; also, interviews with celebrities in show business, politics, sports preferably with color photos. Do not submit travel articles unless with colour transparencies."

‡**FNA NEWS**, P.O. Box 11999, Salt Lake City UT 84147. (801)355-1901. Editor: R.N. Goldberger. 5% written by writers on contract; 95% freelance written by writers on one-time basis. Works with 10 freelance writers/ year. Syndicates to magazines and newspapers. Usually reports in 7 months. Sometimes buys all rights, first North American serial rights or second serial (reprint) rights.
Needs: High quality fillers, magazine columns, magazine features, newspaper columns, newspaper features, news items, great photographs and radio broadcast material. Buys one-shot features and articles series. Query with unpublished clips. Payment negotiated separately.
Tips: "Be very clear. Do not use unnecessary words. Write to be comfortably read. Remember people have just too much to read." Also offers a private writing consultation service and newsletter, newspaper and magazine design services.

FOTOPRESS, INDEPENDENT NEWS SERVICE INTERNATIONAL, Box 1268, Station Q, Toronto, Ontario M4T 2P4 Canada. (416)841-1065. Fax: (416)841-2283. Executive Editor: John Milan Kubik. Estab. 1983. 50% written by writers on contract; 25% freelance written by writers on a one-time basis. Works with 30% previously unpublished writers. Syndicates to domestic and international magazines, newspapers, radio, TV stations and motion picture industry. Reports in 6 weeks. Buys variable rights. Writer's guidelines for $3 in IRCs.

Needs: Fillers, magazine columns, magazine features, newspaper columns, newspaper features, news items, radio broadcast material, documentary, the environment, travel and art. Buys one-shot and article series for international politics, scientists, celebrities and religious leaders. Query or submit complete ms. Pays 50-75% author's percentage. Offers $5-150 for accompanying ms.
Tips: "We need all subjects from 500-3,000 words. Photos are purchased with or without features. All writers are regarded respectfully—their success is our success."

(GABRIEL) GRAPHICS NEWS BUREAU, P.O. Box 38, Madison Square Station, New York NY 10010. (212)254-8863. Cable: NOLNOEL, NY. Editor: J. G. Bumberg. 25% freelance written by writers on contract; 50% freelance written by writers on one-time basis. Custom-syndicates for clients to selected weeklies, suburbans and small dailies. Reports in 1 month. Buys all rights for clients' packages. Writer's guidelines for SASE.
Needs: Magazine features, newspaper columns, fillers and features and news items for PR clients, custom packages. Pays 15% from client. Also has consulting/conceptualizing services in communications/graphics/management.

GENERAL NEWS SYNDICATE, 1600 Broadway, New York NY 10019. (212)956-1189. Editor: Richard Falk. Estab. 1940. 25% written by writers on contract; 12% freelance written by writers on a one-time basis. Works with 12 writers/year; average of 5 previously unpublished writers/year. Syndicates to an average of 12 newspaper and radio outlets averaging 20 million circulation; buys theater and show business people columns (mostly New York theater pieces). Reports on *accepted* material in 3 weeks. Buys one-time rights.
Needs: Entertainment-related material.
Tips: Looking for "short copy (250-500 words)."

GSM FEATURES, P.O. Box 104, Oradell NJ 07649-0104. (201)385-2000. Editorial Director: Bob Nesoff. Estab. 1968. 100% written by writers on contract. Buys 300 pieces/year. Syndicates to newspapers. Reports in 1 month. Buys first North American serial rights. Writer's guidelines for SASE.
Needs: Newspaper columns and features. Does not purchase single (one-shot) features. Query only with SASE. Pays flat rate $25-100. Currently syndicates Traveling, by Bob and Sandy Nesoff (weekly travel column); Cooking, by Janine Draizin (recipes); Powder Trails, by Wendy Naimaister and Barbara Thorson (18-30 year old audience ski column); Books, by Ross Warren (book review column); Skiing by Bob Nesoff (weekly ski column); The Scene, by Karen Michelle (weekly youth column 17-25 year old audience); Wine & Dine, by Gail Gerson (weekly restaurant column); Stage & Screen, by Ed Curtis, Hollywood & Broadway Insider Info Reviews of Movies & Stage, (weekly column).
Tips: "Trend toward more family-oriented and less expensive activities."

HISPANIC LINK NEWS SERVICE, 1420 N St. NW, Washington DC 20005. (202)234-0280. Fax: (202)234-4090. Publisher: Charles A. Ericksen. Editor: Jonathan Higuera. Estab. 1980. 50% freelance written by writers on contract; 50% freelance written by writers on a one-time basis. Buys 156 columns and features/year. Works with 50 writers/year; 5 previously unpublished writers. Syndicates to 100 newspapers and magazines with circulations ranging from 5,000 to 300,000. Reports in up to 1 month. Buys second serial (reprint) or negotiable rights. For reprints, send photocopy of article. Pays 100% of the amount paid for an original article ($25 for guest columns). Free writer's guidelines.
Needs: Newspaper columns and features. One-shot features and article series. "We prefer 650-700 word op/ed analysis or new features geared to a general national audience, but focus on issue or subject of particular interest to Hispanic Americans. Some longer pieces accepted occasionally." Query or submit complete ms. Pays $25-100. Currently syndicates Hispanic Link, by various authors (opinion and/or feature columns).
Tips: "We would especially like to get topical material and vignettes relating to Hispanic presence and progress in the United States. Provide insights on Hispanic experience geared to a general audience. Of the columns we accept, 85 to 90% are authored by Hispanics; the Link presents Hispanic viewpoints and showcases Hispanic writing talent through its subscribing newspapers and magazines. Copy should be submitted in English. We syndicate in English and Spanish."

HOLLYWOOD INSIDE SYNDICATE, P.O. Box 49957, Los Angeles CA 90049-0957. (909)678-6237. Fax: (909)678-6237. Editor: John Austin. Estab. 1968. 10% written by writers on contract; 40% freelance written by writers on a one-time basis. Purchases entertainment-oriented mss for syndication to newspapers in San Francisco, Philadelphia, Detroit, Montreal, London, Sydney, Manila, South Africa, etc. Previously published submissions OK, if published in the U.S. and Canada only. Reports in 3 months.
Needs: News items (column items concerning entertainment—motion picture—personalities and jet setters for syndicated column; 750-800 words). Also considers series of 1,500-word articles; "suggest descriptive query first. We are also looking for off-beat travel pieces (with pictures) but not on areas covered extensively in the Sunday supplements; not luxury cruise liners but lower cost cruises. We also syndicate nonfiction book subjects—sex, travel, etc., to overseas markets. No fiction. Must have b&w photos with submissions if possible." Also require 1,500-word celebrity profiles on internationally recognized celebrities. We stress *internationally*." Query or submit complete ms. Currently syndicates Books of the Week column and "Celebri-Quotes" "Movie Trivia Quiz," "Hollywood Inside."

Tips: "Study the entertainment pages of Sunday (and daily) newspapers to see the type of specialized material we deal in. Perhaps we are different from other syndicates, but we deal with celebrities. No 'I' journalism such as 'when I spoke to Cloris Leachman.' Many freelancers submit material from the 'dinner theater' and summer stock circuit of 'gossip type' items from what they have observed about the 'stars' or featured players in these productions—how they act off stage, who they romance, etc. We use this material."

INTERPRESS OF LONDON AND NEW YORK, 400 Madison Ave., New York NY 10017-1909. (212)832-2839. Editor: Jeffrey Blyth. Estab. 1971. 50% freelance written by writers on contract; 50% freelance written by writers on a one-time basis. Works with 3-6 previously unpublished writers/year. Buys British and European rights mostly, but can handle world rights. Previously published submissions OK "for overseas." Pays on publication or agreement of sale. Reports in 2 weeks.
Needs: "Unusual nonfiction stories and photos for British and European press. Picture stories, for example, on such 'Americana' as a 5-year-old evangelist; the 800-pound 'con-man'; the nude-male calendar; tallest girl in the world; interviews with pop celebrities such as Madonna, Michael Jackson, Bill Cosby, Tom Selleck, Cher, Priscilla Presley, Bette Middler, Eddie Murphy, Liza Minelli; also news of stars on top TV shows; cult subjects such as voodoo, college fads, anything amusing or offbeat. Extracts from books such as Earl Wilson's *Show Business Laid Bare*, inside-Hollywood type series ('Secrets of the Stuntmen'). Real life adventure dramas ('Three Months in an Open Boat,' 'The Air Crash Cannibals of the Andes'). No length limits—short or long, but not too long. Query or submit complete ms. Payment varies; depending on whether material is original, or world rights. Pays top rates, up to several thousand dollars, for exclusive material."
Photos: Purchased with or without features. Captions required. Standard size prints. Pay $50-100, but no limit on exclusive material.
Tips: "Be alert to the unusual story in your area—the sort that interests the American tabloids (and also the European press)."

INTERSTATE NEWS SERVICE, 237 S. Clark Ave., St. Louis MO 63135. (314)522-1300. Editor: Michael J. Olds. Estab. 1985. "Interstate acts as the local news bureau for newspapers that are too small to operate their own state capital bureau." Buys all rights and makes work-for-hire assignments. Call for information.
Needs: Independent news reporters on long-term contract to open new state capital bureaus. Must be experienced news reporters to write stories with hard news emphasis, concentrating on local delegations, tax money and local issues. Query with clips of published work. Negotiates with writers under contract. "Interstate News is interested in contracting with reporters in Colorado, Indiana, Ohio, Pennsylvania, Michigan and Minnesota."
Tips: "We do not buy unsolicited mss."

JODI JILL FEATURES, Suite 321, 1705 14th St., Boulder CO 80302-1200. Art/Writer Editor: Carol Handz. Estab. 1985. 40-60% written by writers on contract; 25% freelance written by writers on a one-time basis. Buys 10 features/year. Works with 20 writers/year. Works with 5 new previously unpublished writers/year. Syndicates to magazines, newspapers, weekly shoppers. Reports in 1 month. Buys first North American serial rights. Free writer's guidelines. Submit complete ms with SASE.
Needs: Fillers (cartoons and 500-word articles), newspaper columns (500-750 words on general topics), puzzles. "We purchase mostly puzzles, visual and word, that can be made into quarter page inserts. These features can be for children or adults. They are placed in weekly papers." Pays 45% author's percentage of gross for columns. Pays $10 flat rate per paper for single features. Pays $17-150 for photos. Currently syndicates Brain Baffler, by Jodi Jill (puzzle); Minor Cartoon, by various artists every week (cartoons); Mirage, by Jodi Jill (puzzle).
Tips: "A writer will only succeed by promotion of his/her own work. Beating your own drum is tough, but it is better than not eating. Keep trying and you will be a success in syndication. And finally, send us your column—we are looking for some great material."

‡A.D. KAHN, INC., 35336 Spring Hill, Farmington Hills MI 48331-2044. (318)355-4100. Fax: (313)356-4344. Contact: A. David Kahn. Estab. 1960. Syndicates to newspapers. Reports in 1-3 months.
Needs: Newspaper features, comics and cartoons. Currently syndicates Say What You See, by A. David Kahn (puzzle); Picture This, by Monte Nagler (photography).

ALWAYS submit unsolicited manuscripts or queries with a self-addressed, stamped envelope (SASE) within your country or a self-addressed envelope with International Reply Coupons (IRC) purchased from the post office for other countries.

KING FEATURES SYNDICATE, INC., Dept. WM, 235 E. 45th St., New York NY 10017. (212)455-4000. Executive Editor: Paul Eberhard. Syndicates on-going columns to newspapers. Submit brief cover letter with six samples of column. Reports in 2 weeks by letter. No single articles.
Needs: "We are looking for original ideas for columns and first-rate writing."
Tips: "Check *Editor & Publisher Annual Directory of Syndicated Services* before you submit a column idea."

LANDMARK DESIGNS, INC., P.O. Box 2307, Eugene OR 97402. (503)345-3429. President: Jim McAlexander. Estab. 1977. 99% written by writers on contract; 1% freelance written by writers on a one-time basis. Buys 60 features/year. Works with 3 writers/year. Works with 2 previously unpublished writers/year. Syndicates to newspapers. Query for electronic submissions. Reports in 3 months. Buys all rights. Writer's guidelines for #10 SASE. Query with clips of published work.
Needs: Newspaper features. Purchases one shot features and article series. Pays flat rate. Currently syndicates Landmark Designs, Designer Homes and Today's Homes.

LEW LITTLE ENTERPRISES, INC., Box 850, Borrego Springs CA 92004. (619)767-3148. Editor: Lewis A. Little. Estab. 1986. 100% written by writers on contract. Buys 2-3 features/year. Works with 300-400 writers/year. Works with 200 previously unpublished writers/year. Syndicates to newspapers. Reports in 1 month. Buys all rights. Writer's guidelines for #10 SASE. "For cartoon features, I prefer that writers, after receiving my guidelines, submit an outline and about 12 finished and rough samples."
Needs: Newspaper columns and features. "I specialize in the development of comics." No one-shot features. All contracts vary and all terms negotiable. Currently syndicates The Fusco Brothers, by J.C. Duffy (comic strip); Sibling Revelry, by Man Martin (comic strip); Brainstormers, by Mike Smith (comic strip).

LOS ANGELES TIMES SYNDICATE, Times Mirror Square, Los Angeles CA 90053. (213)237-7987. Vice President and General Manager: Steven Christensen. Special Articles Editor: Dan O'Toole. Syndicates to US and worldwide markets. Usually buys first North American serial rights and world rights, but rights purchased can vary. Submit seasonal material 6 weeks in advance. Material ranges from 800-2,000 words.
Needs: Reviews continuing columns and comic strips for US and foreign markets. Send columns and comic strips to Steven Christensen. Also reviews single articles, series, magazine reprints, and book serials; send these submissions to Dan O'Toole. Send complete ms. Pays 50% commission. Currently syndicates Art Buchwald, Dr. Henry Kissinger, Dr. Jeane Kirkpatrick, William Pfaff and Paul Conrad.
Tips: "We're dealing with fewer undiscovered writers but still do review material."

‡MEGALO MEDIA, P.O. Box 678, Syosset NY 11791. (212)535-6811. Editor: J. Baxter Newgate. Estab. 1972. 50% written by writers on contract; 50% freelance written by writers on a one-time basis. Works with 5 previously unpublished writers/year. Syndicates to newspapers. Query for electronic submissions. Reports in 1 month. Buys all rights. Free writer's guidelines.
Needs: Crossword puzzles. Buys one-shot features. Submit complete ms. Pays flat rate of $150 for Sunday puzzle. Currently syndicates National Challenge, by J. Baxter Newgate (crossword puzzle); Crossword Puzzle, by J. Baxter Newgate.

NATIONAL NEWS BUREAU, P.O. Box 43039, Philadelphia PA 19129-0628. (215)546-8088. Editor: Harry Jay Katz. "We work with more than 200 writers and buy over 1,000 stories/year." Syndicates to more than 500 publications. Reports in 2 weeks. Buys all rights. Writer's guidelines for 9 × 12 SAE with 3 first class stamps.
Needs: Newspaper features; "we do many reviews and celebrity interviews. Only original, assigned material." One-shot features and article series; film reviews, etc. Query with clips. Pays $5-200 flat rate. Offers $5-200 additional payment for photos accompanying ms.

NEW LIVING, P.O. Box 1519, Stony Brook NY 11790. (516)981-7232. Publisher: Christine Lynn Harvey. Estab. 1991. 20% written by freelancers under contract; 5% on one-time basis. Buys 20 features/year. Works with 20 writers/year. Works with 5 previously unpublished writers/year. Syndicates to magazines, newspapers, radio, 900 phone lines. Query for electronic submissions. Reports in 6 months. Buys all rights. Query with clips of published work. Writer's guidelines for #10 SASE.
Needs: Magazine and newspaper columns, news items, fillers, magazine and newspaper features, radio broadcast material. Purchases single (one shot) features and article series. "Looking for articles on health and fitness (nutrition, healthy recipes, sports medicine, exercise tips, running, tennis, golf, bowling, aerobics, cycling, swimming, cross-training, watersports, travel, medical advice)." Pays minimum guarantee of $25 or flat rate of $100, or salary of $5,000/year. Also offers to list author's business affiliation, address, and phone number in article. Currently syndicates: Golf, by Mike Hebron; Tennis, by Adam Cooper; Swimming, by Stephen Tarpinian.
Photos: Offers $25-100 for photos accepted with ms.
Tips: "Be highly qualified in the area that you are writing about. If you are going to write a medical column, you must be a doctor, or at least affiliated with a nationally recognized medical organization."

NEW YORK TIMES SYNDICATION SALES CORP., Dept. WM, 130 5th Ave., New York NY 10011. (212)645-3000. Fax: (212)645-3949. Executive Editor: Gloria Anderson. Syndicates numerous one-shot articles. Buys second serial (reprint) rights or all rights.
Needs: Magazine and newspaper features. "On syndicated articles, payment to author is varied. We only consider articles that have been previously published." Photos are welcome with articles.
Tips: "Topics should cover universal markets and either be by a well-known writer or have an off-beat quality. Quizzes are welcomed if well researched."

NEWS FLASH INTERNATIONAL, INC., Division of the Observer Newspapers, 2262 Centre Ave., Bellmore NY 11710-3400. (516)679-9888. Editor: Jackson B. Pokress. Estab. 1960. 25% written by writers on contract; 25% freelance written by writers on a one-time basis. Supplies material to Observer newspapers and overseas publications. Works with 10-20 previously unpublished writers annually. "Contact editor prior to submission to allow for space if article is newsworthy." Pays on publication. Reports in 2 months.
Nonfiction: "We have been supplying a 'ready-for-camera' sports page (tabloid size) complete with column and current sports photos on a weekly basis to many newspapers on Long Island, as well as pictures and written material to publications in England and Canada. Payment for assignments is based on the article. Payments vary from $20 for a feature of 800 words. Our sports stories feature in-depth reporting as well as book reviews on this subject. We are always in the market for good photos, sharp and clear, action photos of boxing, wrestling, football, baseball and hockey. We cover all major league ball parks during the baseball and football seasons. We are accredited to the Mets, Yanks, Jets and Giants. During the winter we cover basketball and hockey and all sports events at the Nassau Coliseum."
Photos: Purchased on assignment; captions required. Uses "good quality 8×10 b&w glossy prints; good choice of angles and lenses." Pays $7.50 minimum for b&w photos.
Tips: "Submit articles which are fresh in their approach on a regular basis with good quality black and white glossy photos if possible; include samples of work. We prefer well-researched, documented stories with quotes where possible. We are interested in profiles and bios on woman athletes. There is a big interest in this in the foreign market. Women's boxing, volleyball and basketball are major interests."

NEWSPAPER ENTERPRISE ASSOCIATION, INC., Dept. WM, 200 Park Ave., New York NY 10166-0079. (212)692-3700. Director, International Newspaper Operations: Sidney Goldberg. Deputy Editorial Director: Diana Loevy. Director of Comic Art: Sarah Gillespie. 100% written by writers on contract. "We provide a comprehensive package of features to mostly small- and medium-sized newspapers." Reports in 6 weeks. Buys all rights.
Needs: "Any column we purchase must fill a need in our feature lineup and must have appeal for a wide variety of people in all parts of the country. We are most interested in lively writing. We are also interested in features that are not merely copies of other features already on the market. The writer must know his or her subject. Any writer who has a feature that meets all of those requirements should send a few copies of the feature to us, along with his or her plans for the column and some background material on the writer." Current columnists include Bob Walters, Bob Wagman, Hodding Carter, III, Chuck Stone, Dr. Peter Gott, Tom Tiede, Ben Wattenberg and William Rusher. Current comics include Born Loser, Frank & Ernest, Eek & Meek, Kit 'n' Carlyle, Berry's World, Arlo and Janis, and Snafu.
Tips: "We get enormous numbers of proposals for first person columns—slice of life material with lots of anecdotes. While many of these columns are big successes in local newspapers, it's been our experience that they are extremely difficult to sell nationally. Most papers seem to prefer to buy this sort of column from a talented local writer."

OCEANIC PRESS SERVICE, #106, 1030 Calle Cordillera, San Clemente CA 92673. (714)498-7227. Editor: Peter Carbone. Estab. 1956. 40% written by writers on contract; 25% freelance written by writers on a one-time basis. Buys approximately 300 features/year. Works with 35 writers/year. Works with 9 previously unpublished writers/year. Syndicates to magazines, newspapers, radio and merchandising. Query for electronic submissions. Reports in 1 month. Buys all rights or second serial (reprint) rights. Writer's guidelines $2. Query with clips of published work.
Needs: Fiction, magazine columns and features, newspaper columns and features, radio broadcast material, interview with celebrities and pictures, book excerpts. Purchases single (one shot) features and article series. Pays 50% author's percentage for articles and photos. Currently syndicates Better English by D.C. William (educational); Brain Twisters, by J. Cloony (puzzle); Fit for Life, by Sheila Cluff (fitness).
Tips: "Write for a world market. Features on family, celebrities, computers and jobs have the best chances. Interviews and quizzes are easiest to sell."

‡PACIFIC NEWS SERVICE, Room 506, 450 Mission St., San Francisco CA 94105-2505. (415)243-4364. Fax: (415)243-0815. Editor: Sandy Close. Estab. 1970. 50% written by writers on contract; 50% freelance written by writers on a one-time basis. Buys 200 articles/year. "We use about 10% of all submissions." Syndicates to magazines and newspapers. Reports in 2 weeks. Buys first North American rights. Writer's guidelines for SASE.

Needs: Newspaper and news features (700-900 words). Buys one-shot features. Query with clips of published work or submit complete ms. Pays flat rate of $100-150. "We do not regularly syndicate *anyone*. We distribute individual articles daily via wire, then compile weekly packet."

‡**ROYAL FEATURES**, P.O. Box 58174, Houston TX 77258. (713)280-0777. Executive Director: Fay W. Henry. Estab. 1984. 80% written by writers on contract; 10% freelance written by writers on one-time basis. Syndicates to magazines and newspapers. Reports in 2 months. Buys all rights or first North American serial rights.
Needs: Magazine and newspaper columns and features. Buys one-shot features and article series. Query with or without published clips. Send SASE with unsolicited queries or materials. Pays authors percentage, 40-60%.

SENIOR WIRE, Clear Mountain Communications, 2377 Elm St., Denver CO 80207. (303)355-3882. Editor: Allison St. Claire. Estab. 1988. 100% freelance written. Monthly news, information and feature syndication service to various senior publications, general interest publications, and companies interested in senior market. Circulation nationwide, varies per article depending on which articles are bought for publication. Pays 50% of fee for each use of manuscript (fees range from $5-50). Pays on publication. Buys first North American serial rights and simultaneous rights. Submit seasonal/holiday material 3 months in advance. Prefers manuscripts; queries only with SASE. No payment for photos but they help increase sales. Reports in up to 2 months. Writer's guidelines $1 for SASE. Query for electronic submissions. Please indicate on top of ms if available on 3½" or 5¼" floppy disk or by modem.
Needs: Does not want "anything aimed at less than age 55-plus market; anything patronizing or condescending to seniors." Manuscripts requested include: seasonal features, especially those with a nostalgic angle (750-1,000 words); older celebrity profiles, photos required (900-1,100 words); travel tips (no more than 500-750 words); personal travel experiences as a mature traveler, photos are a must (1,000 words); humorous fillers or poems (100-500 words); or miscellaneous other material of universal interest to seniors. Accepts 12 mss in each category/year, 25-50 fillers/year.
Tips: "All areas open to freelancers. Sometimes give assignments to proven, reliable freelancers whose work has sold well through the syndication. Want fresh approach to senior issues, overworked themes not appreciated. Solid informational and generic articles accepted. We will not promote any product or business unless it is the only one in existence. Must be applicable to senior lifestyle."

SINGER MEDIA CORPORATION, Seaview Business Park, Unit #106, 1030 Calle Cordillera, San Clemente CA 92673-6234. (714)498-7227. Fax: (714)498-2162. Editors: Helen J. Lee and Kurt Singer. Estab. 1940. 25% written by writers on contract; 25% freelance written by writers on a one-time basis. Syndicates to magazines, newspapers, cassettes and book publishers. Reports in 3 weeks. Rights negotiable, world rights preferred. Writer's guidelines $2 for #10 SAE.
Needs: Puzzles, quizzes, interviews, entertainment and psychology features, cartoons, books for serialization and foreign reprints. Syndicates one-shot features and article series on celebrities. Query with clips of published work. Pays 50% author's percentage. Currently syndicates Solve a Crime, by B. Gordon (mystery puzzle) and Hollywood Gossip, by June Finletter (entertainment).
Tips: "Good interviews with celebrities, men/women relations, business and job-related features have a good chance with us. Aim at world distribution and therefore have a universal approach."

THE SOUTHAM SYNDICATE, Suite 512, 151 Sparks St., Ottawa, Ontario K1P 5E3 Canada. (416)222-8000. Editor: Beth Burgess. Estab. 1986. 90% written by writers on contract; 5% freelance written by writers on a one-time basis. Buys 10 features/year. Works with 3-4 previously unpublished writers/year. Syndicates to newspapers. Query for electronic submissions. Reports in 2 months. Buys Canadian rights.
Needs: Fillers (400-500 words), newspaper columns (700-800 words, self help) and newspaper features (1,000 words). Buys one-shot features and article series. Query with clips of published work. Pays 50% author's percentage. Currently syndicates Claire Hoy, William Johnson, Ben Wicks and David Suzuki.

SYNDICATED FICTION PROJECT, P.O. Box 15650, Washington DC 20003. Director: Caroline Marshall. Estab. 1982. 100% freelance written by writers on a one-time basis. Buys 40-50 short stories/year (short fiction of 2,500 words or less). Outlets: newspapers, literary magazines, inc. The quarterly *American Short Fiction*, and radio (NPR, BBC). Receives submissions in January *only* each year; replies by late May. Buys all rights for 3 years.
Needs: Fiction (short stories of 2,500 words or fewer). Submit complete ms (Jan. only). "Please send #10 SASE to Project for guidelines first." Pays flat rate of $500 for purchase of rights, $100/print publication thereafter, $100 if used in print or audio anthology.
Tips: "We're looking for stories of exceptional quality that have a 'high narrative profile' (principally because they work best on radio)."

SYNDICATED NEWS SERVICE, 232 Post Ave., Rochester NY 14619. (716)328-2144. Fax: (716)328-7018. Editor: Frank Judge. Estab. 1982. 50% written by writers on contract. Buys 10-20 features/year. Works with 10-15 previously unpublished writers/year. Syndicates to newspapers and magazines (weekly, daily and

monthly). Reports in 6 months. Buys all rights. Writers guidelines for SASE.
Needs: Fiction, fillers, magazine columns and features, newspaper columns and features and news items. "Please send submissions in manuscript form with finished art if applicable." Does not purchase single (one-shot) features. Submit complete ms. Author's percentage 50% of gross sales. Currently syndicates Filmbriefs by Frank Judge (entertainment), Windows by Paul Murphy (computer) and Mind & Body by Dr. Julian Whitaker (health).

‡**TEENAGE CORNER, INC.,** 70-540 Gardenia Ct., Rancho Mirage CA 92270. President: Mrs. David J. Lavin. Buys 122 items/year for use in newspapers. Submit complete ms. Reports in 1 week. Material is not copyrighted.
Needs: 500-word newspaper features. Pays $25.

TRIBUNE MEDIA SERVICES, 64 E. Concord St., Orlando FL 32801. (407)420-6200. Chairman: Robert S. Reed. President: David D. Williams. Editor: Michael Argirion. Syndicates to newspapers. Reports in 1 month. Buys all rights, first North American serial rights or second serial (reprint) rights.
Needs: Newspaper columns, comic strips. Query with published clips. Currently syndicates the columns of Mike Royko, Bob Greene, Andy Rooney and Marilyn Beck; and cartoons of Jeff MacNelly and Don Wright.

UNITED FEATURE SYNDICATE, 200 Park Ave., New York NY 10166-0079. (212)692-3700. Executive Editor: Diana Loevy. Director International Newspaper Operations: Sidney Goldberg. Director of Comic Art: Sarah Gillespie. 100% contract writers. Supplies features to 1,700 US newspapers, plus Canadian and other international papers. Works with published writers. Query with 4-6 samples and SASE. Reports in 2 months.
Needs: Current columnists include Jack Anderson, Judith Martin, Donald Lambro, Martin Sloane, June Reinisch. Comic strips include Peanuts, Garfield, Nancy, Drabble, Marmaduke, Rose is Rose and Robotman. Standard syndication contracts are offered for columns and comic strips.
Tips: "We buy the kind of writing similar to other major syndicates—varied material, well-known writers. The best way to break in to the syndicate market is for writers to latch on with a major newspaper and to develop a following. Also, cultivate new areas and try to anticipate trends."

UNITED MEDIA, Dept. WM, 200 Park Ave., New York NY 10166. (212)692-3700. Deputy Editorial Director: Diana Loevy. VP Director of Comic Art: Sarah Gillespie. 100% written by writers on contract. Syndicates to newspapers. Reports in 6 weeks. Writer's guidelines for #10 SASE.
Needs: Newspaper columns and newspaper features. Query with photocopied clips of published work. "Authors under contract have negotiable terms." Currently syndicates Miss Manners, by Judith Martin (etiquette); Dr. Gott, by Peter Gott, M.D. (medical), Supermarket Shopper, by Martin Sloane (coupon clipping advice), Jack Anderson and Michael Binstein (investigative reporting).
Tips: "We include tips in our guidelines. We buy very few of the hundreds of submissions we see monthly. We are looking for the different feature as opposed to new slants on established columns."

UNIVERSAL PRESS SYNDICATE, Dept. WM, 4900 Main St., Kansas City MO 64112. (816)932-6600. Estab. 1970. Buys syndication rights. Reports normally in 1 month. Return postage required.
Nonfiction: Looking for features—columns for daily and weekly newspapers. Distributes one-shot articles (profiles, lifestyle pieces, etc). "Any material suitable for syndication in daily newspapers." Currently handling James J. Kilpatrick, Dear Abby, Erma Bombeck and others. Payment varies according to contract.

WASHINGTON POST WRITERS GROUP, 1150 15th St. NW, Washington DC 20071-9200. (202)334-6375. Editorial Director/General Manager: Alan Shearer. Estab. 1973. Currently syndicates 32 features (columns and cartoons). News syndicate that provides features for newspapers nationwide. Reports in 3 weeks. Buys all rights.
Needs: Newspaper columns (editorial, lifestyle, humor), and newspaper features (comic strips, political cartoons). Query with clips of published work and samples of proposed column. Currently syndicates George F. Will column (editorial), Ellen Goodman column (editorial), David Broder column (editorial), William Raspberry column (editorial) and Jane Bryant Quinn column (financial). Writers Group will not consider single (freelance) articles or stories.
Tips: "The Washington Post Writers Group will review editorial page and lifestyle page columns, as well as political cartoons and comic strips. Probably will not consider games, puzzles, or similar features. Send sample columns and cartoons or comic strips (photocopies—no original artwork, please) to the attention of Alan Shearer, editorial director. Enclose a SASE for the return and response."

WHITEGATE FEATURES SYNDICATE, 71 Faunce Dr., Providence RI 02906. (401)274-2149. Contact: Eve Green. Editor: Ed Isaac. Estab. 1987. Buys 100% of material from freelance writers. Syndicates to newspapers; planning to begin selling to magazines and radio. Query for electronic submissions. Reports in 3 months. Buys all rights.

Needs: Fiction for Sunday newspaper magazines; magazine columns and features, newspaper columns and features, cartoon strips. Buys one-shots and article series. Query with clips of published work. For cartoon strips, submit samples. Pays 50% author's percentage on columns. Additional payment for photos accepted with ms. Currently syndicates Indoor Gardening, by Jane Adler; Looking Great, by Gloria Lintermans; Strong Style, by Hope Strong; On Marriage and Divorce, by Dr. Melvyn A. Berke.

Tips: "Please aim for a topic that is fresh. Newspapers seem to want short text pieces, 400-800 words. We prefer *not* to return materials. Enclose self-addressed, stamped postcard for reply. We like to know a little about author's or cartoonist's background. We prefer people who have already been published. Please send material to Eve Green."

WORLD NEWS SYNDICATE, LTD., P.O. Box 419, Hollywood CA 90078-0419. Fax: (818)398-9624-0419. Managing Editor: Laurie James. Estab. 1965. Syndicates to newspapers. Reports in 1 month. Buys first North American serial rights. Query with published clips. "We're looking for short columns, featurettes, home, medical, entertainment-interest, music, TV, films. Nothing over 500-600 words."

Needs: Fillers and newspaper columns. Pays 45-50% author's percentage.

Syndicates/Changes '93-'94

The following syndicates were listed in the 1993 edition but do not have listings in this edition of *Writer's Market*. The majority did not respond to our request to update their listings or return a questionnaire for a new listing. If a reason was given for their exclusion, we have included it in parentheses after the listing name.

American Newspaper Syndicate (ceased publication)
Continuum Broadcasting Network/Metro News Fea

tures, Inc.
Hyde Park Media
Intermedia News and Feature Service

International Photo News
Kainos Press
World Features Syndicate

Greeting Cards & Gift Ideas

Many card buyers would rather spend the entire afternoon in a store looking for the perfect sentiment than suffer the agony of writing a message. And greeting card companies are now making it possible for consumers to find *exactly* what they're looking for—to say *exactly* what they want to say—with a card. Cards are not just for holidays and birthdays anymore; on the contrary, they cover all of life's major (and not so major) events.

In fact, nearly 50% of all first class mail now consists of greeting cards. And, of course, card manufacturers rely on writers to supply them with enough skillfully crafted sentiments to meet the demand. The perfect greeting card verse is one that will appeal to a large audience, yet will make each buyer feel that the card was written exclusively for him or her.

Three greeting card companies continue to dominate this industry; together, American Greetings, Hallmark and Gibson Greetings supply about 80% of all cards sold. The other 20% are published by hundreds of companies who have found success mainly by not competing head to head with the big three but by choosing instead to pursue niche markets—regional and special-interest markets that the big three either cannot or do not supply.

A professional approach to markets

As markets become more focused, it's important to keep current on specific company needs. Familiarize yourself with the differences among lines of cards by visiting card racks. Ask retailers which lines are selling best. You may also find it helpful to read trade magazines such as *Greetings* and *Party and Paper Retailer*. These publications will keep you apprised of changes and events within the field, including seminars and trade shows.

Once you find a card line that appeals to you, write to the company and request its market list, catalog or submission guidelines (usually available for a SASE or a small fee). This information will help you determine whether or not your ideas are appropriate for that market.

Submission procedures vary among greeting card publishers, depending on the size and nature of the company. Keep in mind that many companies (especially the large ones) will not review your writing samples until you've signed and returned their disclosure contract or submission agreement, assuring them that your material is original and has not been submitted elsewhere.

Some editors prefer to see individual card ideas on 3 × 5 cards, while others prefer to receive a number of complete ideas on 8½ × 11 bond paper. Be sure to put your best pieces at the top of the stack. Most editors do not want to see artwork unless it is professional, but they do appreciate conceptual suggestions for design elements. If your verse depends on an illustration to make its point or if you have an idea for a unique card shape or foldout, include a dummy card with your writing samples.

The usual submission includes from 5 to 15 card ideas and an accompanying cover letter, plus mechanical dummy cards, if necessary. Some editors also like to receive a résumé, client list and business card. Some do not. Be sure to check the listings and the company's writer's guidelines for such specifications before submitting material.

Payment for greeting card verse varies, but most firms pay per card or per idea; a handful pay small royalties. Some companies prefer to test a card first and will pay a small fee for a test card idea. In some instances, a company may even purchase an idea and never use it.

Greeting card companies will also buy ideas for gift products and may plan to use card material for a number of subsequent items. Licensing—the sale of rights to a particular character for a variety of products from mugs to T-shirts—is a growing part of the greetings industry. Because of this, however, note that most card companies buy all rights. We now include in this section markets for licensed product lines such as mugs, bumper stickers, buttons, posters and the like.

Managing your submissions

Because you will be sending out many samples, you may want to label each sample. Establish a master card for each verse idea and record where and when each was sent and whether it was rejected or purchased. Keep all cards sent to one company in a batch and give each batch a number. Write this number on the back of your return SASE to help you match up your verses as they are returned.

For more information on greeting card companies not listed in *Writer's Market*, see Greeting Card & Gift Ideas/Changes '93-'94 at the end of this section.

AMBERLEY GREETING CARD CO., 11510 Goldcoast Dr., Cincinnati OH 45249-1695. (513)489-2775. Editor: Ned Stern. Estab. 1966. 90% freelance written. Bought 200 freelance ideas/samples last year. Reports in 1 month. Material copyrighted. Buys all rights. **Pays on acceptance.** Writer's guidelines for #10 SASE. Market list is regularly revised.
Needs: "Original, easy to understand, belly-laugh or outrageous humor. We sell to the 'masses, not the classes' so keep it simple and to the point. Humor accepted in all captions, including general birthday, family birthday, get well, anniversary, thank you, friendship, etc. No seasonal or non-humorous material needed or considered this year. Pays $150/card idea."
Tips: "Send SASE for our writer's guidelines before submitting. Amberley publishes humorous specialty lines in addition to a complete conventional line that is accented with humor. Since humor is our specialty, we are highly selective. Be sure that a SASE with the correct US postage is included with your material. Otherwise it will not be returned."

INSIDER REPORT

Careful study of markets can pay off

Nan Stine has worked at Current, Inc. since 1979, after a 5-year stint with Hallmark Cards. As Creative Writing Manager at Current, overseeing three "very busy" inhouse writers, Nan sometimes looks to outside talent to get the job done. She is in a position to know what sells and how freelancers can work most effectively with greeting card companies.

Nan Stine

She says many freelancers make two mistakes: First, they fail to educate themselves sufficiently about the needs of the markets they are attempting to sell to. Since Current, Inc. publishes cards that the customer buys in "assortments," the sentiments Current wants must be *generally* sendable. "That is," says Stine, "they must be appropriate to send to a wide number of people." Second, much of the unsolicited work Stine sees fails to rise above the ordinary.

She wants to be surprised by seeing fresh treatments. "I get way too many 'easy' sentiments," she says. "I mean the kind that are 'fine' because they're so similar to everything else on the market. What I need from you is a reason to buy—a creative spark that will distinguish your copy from the other 200 submissions I've received during the month."

The best way to familiarize yourself with the needs of a particular market, says Stine, is simply to ask. "Always send a self-addressed stamped envelope, and ask for our editorial guidelines and needs list. It won't do you any good to send me 50 St. Patrick's Day cards when we don't carry them. Always ask for a catalog and study the types of cards and the types of copy we offer. Try to get a feel for our customer. Obviously, if you send me something off-color or about nuclear physics, your chances of getting a sale are diminished."

AMCAL, 2500 Bisso Lane, Building 500, Concord CA 94520-4845. (510)689-9930. Product Development Manager: Jennifer DeCristoforo. Estab. 1975. 80% freelance written. Receives 100 submissions annually; buys 20 freelance ideas/samples per year. Reports in 1 month. Rights negotiable. **Pays on acceptance.** Writer's guidelines for SASE.
Needs: Conventional, informal, sensitive and light-hearted lines. Prefers generally unrhymed. Submit 12 ideas/batch.
Other Product Lines: Calendars and gift products.
Tips: "Our target audience is female, ages 20-50. Direct, thoughtful sentiments sell the best. Generally short."

AMERICAN GREETINGS, Dept. WM, 10500 American Rd., Cleveland OH 44144. (216)252-7300. Creative Recruitment Dept: Lynne Shlonsky. No unsolicited material. "We like to receive a letter of inquiry describing education or experience, or a resume first. We will then screen those applicants and request samples from those that interest us." Reports in 3 months. Buys all rights. **Pays on acceptance.** Guidelines for #10 SASE.
Tips: "Our target audience is the mass-market retail crowd, so we generally purchase the more conventional forms of verse, prose and humorous writing."

ARGUS COMMUNICATIONS, 200 E. Bethany, Allen TX 75002-3804. (214)248-6300. Fax: (214)727-2175. Editorial Coordinator: Lori Potter. 90% freelance written. Primarily interested in material for posters. Reports in 2 months. Buys all rights. **Pays on acceptance.** Submission guidelines available for #10 SASE.
Needs: Posters for teachers to place in their classrooms that are positive, motivational, inspirational, thought-provoking and success oriented. Also poster editorial related to specific subjects such as: math, science, reading, English, health etc. Also posters for teenagers ages 13-18 humorously captioned with brief text reflecting current trends, lifestyles and attitudes."
Other Product Lines: Greeting cards, postcards and calendars.
Tips: "Keep in mind that poster editorial is an at-a-glance message that is succinct and memorable. Our posters capture your attention with a creative mixture of humorous, dynamic and motivational editorial. We encourage you to be funny, to be inspirational, but also to be brief. Please indicate the market your submission is for on the outside of your envelope."

BLUE MOUNTAIN ARTS, INC., Dept. WM, P.O. Box 1007, Boulder CO 80306-1007. Contact: Editorial Staff. Estab. 1971. Buys 50-75 items/year. Reports in 6-8 months. **Pays on acceptance.**
Needs: "Primarily need sensitive and sensible writings about love, friendships, families, philosophies, etc.—written with originality and universal appeal." Also poems and writings for specific holidays (Christmas, Valentine's Day, etc.), and special occasions, such as birthdays, get well, and sympathy. Seasonal writings should be submitted at least 4 months prior to the actual holiday. For worldwide, exclusive rights we pay $200/poem; for one-time use in anthology, we pay $25.
Other Product Lines: Calendars, gift books and greeting books. Payment varies.
Tips: "Get a feel for the Blue Mountain Arts line prior to submitting material. Our needs differ from other card publishers; the majority of the material we publish does not rhyme, as we prefer instead a more honest, person-to-person style. Have a specific person or personal experience in mind as you write. We use sensitive poetry and prose on the deep significance and meaning of life and relationships. We do not wish to receive books, unless you are interested in having portions excerpted for greeting cards. A very limited amount of freelance material is selected each year, either for publication on a notecard or in a gift anthology, and the selection prospects are highly competitive. But new material is always welcome and each manuscript is given serious consideration."

BLUE SKY, 10600 Markison Rd., Dallas TX 75087. (214)553-8686. President: Van Walker. Estab. 1984. 10% freelance written. Receives 60 submissions/year; bought 10 ideas/samples last year. Submit seasonal/holiday material 10 months in advance. Reports in 1 month. Material not copyrighted. Pays royalty on sales volume. Free writer's guidelines/market list. Market list is regularly revised.
Needs: Children's cards. Submit 12 ideas/batch.

BRILLIANT ENTERPRISES, 117 W. Valerio St., Santa Barbara CA 93101-2927. President: Ashleigh Brilliant. Buys all rights. Submit words and art in black on 3½ × 3½ horizontal, thin white paper in batches of no more than 15. Reports "usually in 2 weeks." Catalog and sample set for $2.
Needs: Postcards. Messages should be "of a highly original nature, emphasizing subtlety, simplicity, insight, wit, profundity, beauty and felicity of expression. Accompanying art should be in the nature of oblique commentary or decoration rather than direct illustration. Messages should be of universal appeal, capable of being appreciated by all types of people and of being easily translated into other languages. Because our line of cards is highly unconventional, it is essential that freelancers study it before submitting. No topical references or subjects limited to American culture or puns." Limit of 17 words/card. Pays $50 for "complete ready-to-print word and picture design."

THE CALLIGRAPHY COLLECTION INC., 2604 NW 74th Place, Gainesville FL 32606-1237. (904)375-8530. Fax: (904)374-9957. Editor: Katy Fischer. Reports in 6 months. Buys all rights. Pays on publication.
Needs: "Ours is a line of framed prints of watercolors with calligraphy." Conventional, humorous, informal, inspirational, sensitivity and soft line. Prefers unrhymed verse, but will consider rhymed. Submit 3 ideas/batch. Pays $50-100/framed print idea.
Other Product Lines: Gift books, greeting books and plaques.
Tips: Sayings for friendship are difficult to get. Bestsellers are humorous, sentimental and inspirational ideas—such as for wedding and family and friends. "Our audience is women 20 to 50 years of age. Write something they would like to give or receive as a lasting gift."

COMSTOCK CARDS, Suite 15, 600 S. Rock, Reno NV 89502-4115. Fax: (702)856-9406. Owner: Patti P.Wolf. Art Director: David Delacroix. Estab. 1986. 35% freelance written. Receives 500 submissions annually; buys 50 freelance ideas/samples per year. Submit seasonal/holiday material 1 year in advance. Reports in 5 weeks. Buys all rights. **Pays on acceptance.** Writer's guidelines/market list for SASE. Market list issued one time only.
Needs: Humorous, informal, invitations and "puns, put-downs, put-ons, outrageous humor aimed at a sophisticated, adult female audience. Also risque cartoon cards. No conventional, soft line or sensitivity hearts and flowers, etc." Pays $50-75/card idea, negotiable.

Other Product Lines: Notepads, cartoon cards, invitations.

Tips: "Always keep holiday occasions in mind and personal me-to-you expressions that relate to today's occurrences. Ideas must be simple and concisely delivered. A combination of strong image and strong gag line make a successful greeting card. Consumers relate to themes of work, sex and friendship combined with current social, political and economic issues."

CONTEMPORARY DESIGNS, 213 Main St., Gilbert IA 50105. (515)232-5188. Fax: (515)232-3380. Editor: S. Abelson. Estab. 1977. 90% freelance written. Submit seasonal/holiday material 1 year in advance. Reports in 1 month. Buys all rights. **Pays on acceptance.**

Needs: Short humorous copy for memo pads, mugs, etc.

Other Product Lines: Quote and gift books, mugs, tote bags, aprons and pillow cases.

CONTENOVA GIFTS, P.O. Box 69130, Postal Station K, Vancouver, British Columbia V5K 4W4 Canada. (604)253-4444. Fax: (604)253-4014. Creative Director: Jeff Sinclair. Estab. 1965. 100% freelance written. Receives an estimated 15,000 submissions annually. Submit ideas on 3×5 cards or small mock-ups in batches of 10-15. Buys world rights. **Pays on acceptance.** Current needs list for SAE and IRC.

Needs: Humorous. Both risqué and nonrisqué for mugs. "Short gags with good punch work best." Birthday, belated birthday, get well, anniversary, thank you, congratulations, miss you, new job, etc. Seasonal ideas needed for Christmas, Valentine's Day, Mother's Day, Father's Day. Pays $50.

Tips: "No longer using drinking themes. Put together your best ideas and submit them. One great idea sent is much better than 20 poor ideas filling an envelope. We are always searching for new writers who can produce quality work. You need not be previously published. Our audience is 18-65 — the full mug consumers. We do *not* use poetry."

‡COUNTRY TOONS, 2148 Strombury Dr., Nashville TN 37076. Vice President, Development: Paul Burns. Estab. 1991. 25-50% freelance written. Receives 10 submissions/year. Reports in 1 month. Rights bought negotiable. Pays on publication.

Needs: Informal, inspirational and humorous. Prefers unrhymed verse ideas. Submit 12 ideas/batch.

Other Product Lines: Post cards ($20-50) and T-shirts ($20-50).

Tips: "Our target market is country music fans. Therefore, consider their wants as far as humorous verses or tag lines for T-shirts to be purchased on sight at a retail outlet."

CREATE-A-CRAFT, P.O. Box 330008, Fort Worth TX 76163-0008. (817)292-1855. Estab. 1967. 5% freelance written. Receives 300 submissions annually; buys 2 freelance ideas/samples per year. Submit seasonal/holiday material 1 year in advance. "No phone calls from freelancers accepted. We deal through agents only. Submissions not returned even if accompanied by SASE — not enough staff to take time to package up returns." Buys all rights. Sample greeting cards $2.50 for #10 SASE.

Needs: Announcements, conventional, humorous, juvenile and studio. "Payment depends upon the assignment, amount of work involved, and production costs involved in project."

Tips: No unsolicited material. "Send letter of inquiry describing education and experience, or resumé with one sample first. We will screen applicants and request samples from those who interest us."

‡N.J. CROCE CO., 466-A W. Arrow Hwy., San Dimas CA 91773. (714)599-8467. Estab. 1981. 5% freelance written. Receives 5 submissions annually; buys 1 idea/year. Reports in 1 month. Pays royalties based on sales.

Needs: Humorous and cutting edge.

Other Product Lines: Bumper stickers, gift books, bendables, mugs, T-shirts, key rings, earrings and stickers.

Tips: "We are not a greeting card company. We do humor T-shirts, novelty gifts and gift books. We are always interested in new material."

CURRENT, INC., Box 2559, Colorado Springs CO 80901-2559. (719)594-4100. Supervisor, Creative Writing: Nan Roloff Stine. Estab. 1950. 5-10% freelance written. Receives an estimated 1,500 submissions annually; bought 180 freelance sentiments or mss last year. Submit seasonal/holiday material 18 months in advance. Reports in 2 months. Buys all rights. **Pays on acceptance.** "Flat fee only; no royalty." Writer's guidelines for #10 SASE.

Needs: Humorous. All occasion and woman-to-woman cards; short 1-2 line puns for all occasions not too risque; short children's stories. Pays $50/sentiment.

Tips: "We are primarily looking for original humor of all forms, except risque, off-color sentiments. 99% of our customers are women and 80% of them are married and have children under the age of 18. Writers need to keep in mind that this is the audience we are trying to reach. We pick up trends and create our own. We suggest that writers keep abreast of what's selling at retail. Don't send traditional short prose sentiments or off-color humor because we *don't* buy it. Read our direct mail catalog."

‡DESIGN DESIGN INC., P.O. Box 2266, Grand Rapids MI 49501-2266. Fax: (616)774-4020. President: Don Kallil. Estab. 1985. 100% freelance written. Receives 450 submissions/year. Submit seasonal/holiday material 1 year in advance. Reports in 2 months. Buys all rights. Pays on publication. Free writer's guidelines on request.

Needs: Announcements, informal, juvenile, conventional, sensitivity, seasonal, humorous and invitations. Prefers unrhymed verse. Submit 12 ideas/batch.
Tips: "All ages of adults is our target audience. No risque material."

DIGRESSIONS, INC., 44 Old Pomona Rd., Suffern NY 10901. (914)354-0816. Vice President: Lenore Benowitz. Estab. 1989. 25% freelance written. Receives 500 submissions annually; bought 25 ideas/samples last year. Submit seasonal/holiday material 6 months in advance. Reports in 1 month. Buys all first time rights. Pays on publication. Writer's guidelines/market list for #10 SASE.
Needs: Announcements, informal, juvenile, holidays, humorous and invitations. Prefers unrhymed verse ideas. Submit 10 ideas/batch.
Tips: Seeking humorous material. Target audience: 20-50 years old.

EPHEMERA, INC., P.O. Box 490, Phoenix OR 97535. Contact: Editor. Estab. 1979. 90% freelance written. Receives 20,000 submissions/year; bought 200 ideas/samples last year. Reports in 2½ months. Buys all rights. Pays on publication. Writer's guidelines/market list for #10 SASE. Market list issued one time only.
Needs: Button ideas: "original, provocative, irreverent and outrageously funny slogans for buttons sold in card and gift shops, bookstores, record shops, political and gay shops, adult stores, amusement parks etc.!" Pays $25/slogan.

FOTOFOLIO, INC., 536 Broadway, New York NY 10012. (212)226-0923. Fax: (212)226-0072. Editors: Julie Galant and Ron Schick. Estab. 1976. Submit seasonal/holiday material one year in advance (visuals only). Reports in 1 month. Pays on publication.
Other Product Lines: Postcards, notecards, posters.
Tips: "We specialize in high quality fine art photography."

FULLMOON CREATIONS INC., 81 S. Main St., Doylestown PA 18901. (215)345-1233. Editor: Lisa Gingras. Estab. 1986. 30-80% freelance written. Buys 10 freelance works/year. Reports in 1 month. Pays on publication. Market list is regularly revised.
Needs: Announcements, humorous, inspirational, creative.
Other Product Lines: Promotions.

GALLANT GREETINGS, Dept. WM, 2654 W. Medill, Chicago IL 60647. Editorial Coordinator: Carolyn McDilda. Fax: (312)489-1860. 90% freelance written. Bought 500 freelance ideas/samples last year. Reports in 1 month. Buys world greeting card rights. Pays 60-90 days after acceptance. Writer's guidelines for SASE.
Needs: Announcements, conventional, humorous, informal, inspirational, invitations, juvenile and studio. Submit 20 cards in one batch.
Tips: "Greeting cards should and do move with the times, and sometimes writers don't. Keep aware of what is going on around you."

GIBSON GREETINGS, 2100 Section Rd., Cincinnati OH 45237. "Prefers not to share information."

HALLMARK CARDS, INC., P.O. Box 419580, Mail Drop 216, Kansas City MO 64141-6580. Contact Carol King for submission agreement and guidelines. Include SASE; no samples. Reports in 2 months. Not currently soliciting new writers or sentiments. Work is on assignment basis, working from "needs lists" only. "Most needs are met by large writing staff; freelancers must show exceptional originality and stylings not available from in-house employees, and must have previous sentiment writing experience."

MARIAN HEATH GREETING CARDS, INC., Dept. WM, 9 Kendrick Rd., Wareham MA 02571. Art Director: Susan H. Bint. Estab. 1942. Not accepting any unsolicited material. Submit seasonal/holiday material 6 months in advance. *No* Christmas material. Reports in 1 month. Material not copyrighted. **Pays on acceptance.** Free writer's guidelines/market list. Market list is issued one time only.
Needs: Conventional, humorous, inspirational, sensitivity, soft line. Uses both rhymed and unrhymed verse ideas. Submit 2 ideas/batch.
Tips: "Send birthday—especially family categories and get-well material."

IMAGINE, Dept. WM, 21431 Stans Lane, Laguna Beach CA 92651. (714)497-1800. Contact/Owners: John Stuhr/Nan Goin. Estab. 1982. 50% freelance written. Receives 150 submissions/year; bought 75 ideas/samples last year. Submit seasonal/holiday material 1 year in advance. Reports in 1 month. Material not copyrighted. Time of payment varies. Free writer's guidelines/market list. Market list is regularly revised.

ALWAYS enclose a self-addressed, stamped envelope (SASE) with all your queries and correspondence.

Needs: "We are open to all ideas." Submit 12 ideas/batch.
Other Product Lines: Bumper stickers, gift books, greeting books, plaques, postcards, promotions, puzzles, greeting cards and humorous slogans. Pays $25 and up.

KIMBERLEY ENTERPRISES, INC., 15029 S. Figueroa St., Gardena CA 90248-1721. (310)538-1331. Fax: (310)538-2045. Vice President: M. Hernandez. Estab. 1979. 15% freelance written. Receives less than 100 submissions annually; buys 12 ideas/year. Submit seasonal material 9 months in advance. Reports in up to 3 months. Material not copyrighted. Pays on acceptance. Market list available on mailing list basis.
Needs: Announcements, conventional, inspirational and invitations. Send 12 ideas maximum.
Other Product Lines: Plaques. Pays $10-250.
Tips: "The primary future interest for the company is in the plaque line, with an emphasis on inspirational or conventional appeal."

LIFE GREETINGS, Dept. WM, Box 468, Little Compton RI 02837. (401)635-8535. Editor: Kathy Brennan. 50% freelance written. Bought 400 samples in past year. Submit seasonal/holiday material 6 months in advance. Reports in 2 weeks. Buys all rights. **Pays on acceptance.** Free guidelines sheet.
Needs: Humorous, inspirational, sensitivity.
Tips: Our cards are marketed mainly through Christian bookstores.

‡MAILAWAYS, P.O. Box 782, Tavares FL 32778-0782. (904)742-8196. Editor: Gene Chambers. Estab. 1992. Submit seasonal/holiday material 3 months in advance. Reports in 1 month. Material "not yet copyrighted, but will be." Rights negotiable. **Pays on acceptance.** Writer's guidelines for #10 SAE with 2 first class stamps. Market list issued one time only.
Needs: Inspirational, sensitivity and experimental poetry. Prefers either rhymed or unrhymed verse. Submit 5 ideas/batch.
Other Product Lines: Gift books ($10, negotiable) and greeting books ($10, negotiable).
Tips: "What sells best is the *short*, inspirational verse, rhymed or not, upbeat but with an emotional *jolt* of familiar feeling. Audience is both the average person *and* the *sensitive soul.*"

MALENA PRODUCTIONS, INC., P.O. Box 14483, Ft. Lauderdale FL 33302-4483. Contact: Helena Steiner-Hornsteyn. Estab. 1985. 20% freelance written. Receives 500 submissions/year; bought 5 ideas/samples last year. Also needs new cartoon/comic strip writers. Submit seasonal/holiday material 8 months in advance. Reports in 1 month. Usually buys all rights. **Pays on acceptance.**
Needs: Humorous, informal, inspirational and Christmas/holiday. Submit 10 ideas/batch.
Tips: "We sell high-end cards with cute design and modern approach. Our audience is yuppies and preppies (youth in their twenties) and professionals up to fifty."

NEW BOUNDARY DESIGNS, INC., 1453 Park Rd., Chanhassen MN 55317. (612)474-0924. Fax: (612)474-9525. Marketing Manager: Chuck Schneider. Estab. 1979. 5% freelance written. Receives 100 submissions annually; buys 9 freelance ideas/samples per year. Submit seasonal/holiday material 1 year in advance. Reports in 6 months. Pays on publication.
Needs: Traditional, inspirational, juvenile and sensitivity. Prefers unrhymed verse.

OATMEAL STUDIOS, P.O. Box 138W3, Rochester VT 05767. (802)767-3171. Creative Director: Helene Lehrer. Estab. 1979. 85% freelance written. Buys 200-300 greeting card lines/year. **Pays on acceptance.** Reports within 2 months. Current market list for #10 SASE.
Needs: Birthday, friendship, anniversary, get well cards, etc. Also Christmas, Chanukah, Mother's Day, Father's Day, Easter, Valentine's Day, etc. Will review concepts. Humorous material (clever and *very* funny) year-round. "Humor, conversational in tone and format, sells best for us." Prefers unrhymed contemporary humor. Current pay schedule available with guidelines.
Other Product Lines: Notepads.
Tips: "The greeting card market has become more competitive with a greater need for creative and original ideas. We are looking for writers who can communicate situations, thoughts, and relationships in a funny way and apply them to a birthday, get well, etc., greeting and we are willing to work with them in targeting our style. We will be looking for material that says something funny about life in a new way."

OUTREACH PUBLICATIONS, P.O. Box 1010, Siloam Springs AR 72761. (501)524-9381. Editor: David Taylor. Estab. 1971. Submit seasonal/holiday material 1 year in advance. Reports in 2 months. **Pays on acceptance.** Guidelines for #10 SASE.
Needs: Calendars, announcements, invitations, all major seasonal and special days, all major everyday cards—birthday, anniversary, get well, friendship, etc. Material must be usable for the Christian market.
Tips: "Study our line, DaySpring Greeting Cards, before submitting. We are looking for sentiments with relational, inspirational messages that minister love and encouragement to the receiver." Prefer unrhymed verse.

‡**P.S. GREETINGS/FANTUS PAPER PRODUCTS,** 4459 W. Division St., Chicago IL 60641. (312)384-0909. Art Director: Kevin Lahvic. Receives 60 submissions/year. Reports in 5 months. "Buys worldwide exclusive rights." Pays after receipt of signed release requested upon acceptance. Writer's guidelines for #10 SASE. "We issue no market list—we are open to all types of submissions except for risque."
Needs: Informal, juvenile, studio, conventional, inspirational, sensitivity, humorous and soft line. Submit no more than 20 ideas/batch.
Tips: "We have a need for all types of verses from humorous to short and snappy to long and sentimental. Sentimental verse works well for seasonal cards such as Valentine's Day, Mother's Day and Christmas. We do not use risque verse. Platonic friendship and romantic friendship cards are always in demand. Only submissions with an SASE will be returned."

‡**PAINTED HEARTS & FRIENDS,** 1222 N. Fair Oaks Ave., Pasadena CA 91103. Sales Manager: Richard Crawford. Estab. 1988. 6% freelance written. Receives "many" submissions annually; bought 21 ideas/samples last year—"we're just starting." Submit seasonal/holiday material 10 months in advance. Reports back "usually very quickly." Some material copyrighted. **Pays on acceptance.**
Needs: Announcements, informal, juvenile, conventional, inspirational, sensitivity, humorous, invitations and soft line.
Other Product Lines: Calendars, gift books and greeting books.
Tips: "We look for simple quotes—very direct, great quotes. No off-color."

PARAMOUNT CARDS INC., Dept. WM, P.O. Box 6546, Providence RI 02940-6546. (401)726-0800. Contact: Editorial Freelance Coordinator. Estab. 1906. Buys 200 greeting card ideas/year. Submit seasonal/material at least 6 months in advance. Reports in 1 month. Buys all rights. **Pays on acceptance.** Writer's guidelines for SASE.
Needs: All types of conventional verses. Fresh, inventive humorous verses, especially family birthday cards. Would also like to see more conversational prose, especially in family titles such as Mother, Father, Sister, Husband, Wife, etc. Submit in batches of 10-15. Does not want tired, formulaic rhymes.
Tips: "Study the market! Go to your local card shops and analyze what you see. Ask the storekeepers which cards are selling. Then apply what you've learned to your own writing. The best cards (and we buy only the best) will have mass appeal and yet, in the consumer's eyes, will read as though they were created exclusively for her. A feminine touch is important, as 90% of all greeting cards are purchased by women."

‡**C.M. PAULA COMPANY,** 7773 School Rd., Cincinnati OH 45249. Contact: Editorial Supervisor. Estab. 1958. 10% freelance written. Receives 100 submissions/year. "We purchase both per idea or set fee per project." Submit seasonal/holiday material 1 year in advance. Reports in 4-6 weeks. Buys all rights. **Pays on acceptance.** Writer's guidelines for SASE. Market list issued one time only.
Product Lines: Plaques, key rings, magnets, stationery pads, coffee mugs, collectible plates, dimensional statues and awards.
Tips: "Our needs range from inspirational verse and prose to cute sayings and light humor (nothing risqué). A writer can get a quick idea of the variety of copy we use by looking over our store displays. Please note— we do not publish greeting cards."

PEACOCK PAPERS INC., 273 Summer St., Boston MA 02210. Fax: (617)423-3717. Contact: Mia Miranda, New Product Manager. Estab. 1982. 85% of material is freelance written. Receives 1,000 submissions/year; bought 100 ideas/samples last year. Submit seasonal/holiday material 10 months in advance. Reports in 3 months. Buys all rights. **Pays on acceptance.** Writer's guidelines/market list for #10 SASE. Market list is regularly revised.
Needs: Prefers unrhymed verse. Submit ideas on 8½×11 paper, double spaced.
Other Product Lines: Also produces soft goods (T-shirts, night shirts, boxer shorts, women's bikinis), ceramic mugs, lapel and jumbo buttons, key tags, gift bags (all sizes). Pays $50 for first product use; $25 for second; $12.50 for additional uses.
Tips: Best-selling lines for us are ones that capture current events/themes, witty or humorous thoughts with current themes, age-related lines and series (however, they must be up-beat and must relate to a broad group of people). We do not accept risque, off-color lines nor do we purchase greeting card copy."

PLUM GRAPHICS INC., P.O. Box 136, Prince Station, New York NY 10012. (212)966-2573. Editor: Yvette Cohen. Estab. 1983. 100% freelance written. Bought 21 samples last year. Does not return samples unless accompanied by SASE. Reports in 3-4 months. Buys greeting card and stationery rights. Pays on publication. Guidelines sheet for SASE. "Sent out about twice a year in conjunction with the development of new cards."
Needs: Humorous. "We don't want general submissions. We want them to relate to our next line." Prefers unrhymed verse. Greeting cards pay $40.
Tips: "Sell to all ages. Humor is always appreciated. Wants short to-the-point lines."

PORTAL PUBLICATIONS, 770 Tamalpias Dr., Corte Madera CA 94925. (415)924-5652. Contact: Scott Graham. Estab. 1954. 50% freelance written. Receives 200 submissions annually; buys 100 freelance ideas/samples per year. Reports in 3 months. Pays on publication. "Please send an example of your work so that we may keep it on file. If in the future, we have a need for writers for our greeting cards or other products we will contact you."
Needs: Conventional, humorous, informal, soft line and studio. Also copy for humorous and inspirational posters. Prefers unrhymed verse. Submit 12 ideas/batch.
Other Product Lines: Calendars and posters.
Tips: "Upscale, cute, humorous cards for bookstores and college bookstores."

RED FARM STUDIO, 1135 Roosevelt Ave., P.O. Box 347, Pawtucket RI 02862-0347. Creative Director: Lisa Harter Saunders. Estab. 1965. 100% freelance written. Receives "thousands" of submissions annually; buys 100 ideas/samples per year. Reports in 2 months. Buys exclusive publishing rights. **Pays on acceptance; within 1 month.** Market list for #10 SASE. Market list issued one time only.
Needs: Conventional, humorous and Christmas ("our only seasonal line") cards. "We are looking for straight forward, sincere sentiments, both serious and humorous. No family headings. Usually no longer than 4 lines." Submit any number of ideas/samples per batch. Pays $3/line of copy. Prose, short and long.
Tips: "We pride ourselves on a premier nautical line of everyday greeting cards and Christmas boxed cards as well as our traditional lines."

ROCKSHOTS, INC., 632 Broadway, New York NY 10012. (212)420-1400. Fax: (212)353-8756. Editor: Bob Vesce. Estab. 1979. "We buy 75 greeting card verse (or gag) lines annually." Submit seasonal/holiday material 1 year in advance. Reports in 2 months. Buys rights for greeting-card use. Writer's guidelines for SASE.
Needs: Humorous ("should be off-the-wall, as outrageous as possible, preferably for sophisticated buyer"); soft line; combination of sexy and humorous come-on type greeting ("sentimental is not our style"); and insult cards ("looking for cute insults"). No sentimental or conventional material. "Card gag can adopt a sentimental style, then take an ironic twist and end on an off-beat note." Submit no more than 10 card ideas/samples per batch. Send to attention: Submissions. Pays $50/gagline. Prefers gag lines on 8×11 paper with name, address, and phone and social security numbers in right corner, or individually on 3×5 cards.
Tips: "Think of a concept that would normally be too outrageous to use, give it a cute and clever wording to make it drop-dead funny and you will have commercialized a non-commercial message. It's always good to mix sex and humor. Our emphasis is definitely on the erotic. Hard-core eroticism is difficult for the general public to handle on greeting cards. The trend is toward 'light' sexy humor, even cute sexy humor. 'Cute' has always sold cards, and it's a good word to think of even with the most sophisticated, crazy ideas. 80% of our audience is female. Remember that your gag line will be illustrated by a photographer. So try to think visually. If no visual is needed, the gag line *can* stand alone, but we generally prefer some visual representation. It is a very good idea to preview our cards at your local store if this is possible to give you a feeling of our style."

‡RULE 62 STUDIO, 61535 S. Hwy. 97 9-156, Bend OR 97702. Contact: Bruno Marlova. Estab. 1992. 10% freelance written. Buys all rights. Pays on publication. Writer's guidelines/market list for SASE.
Needs: Very humorous pertaining to recovery issues.
Other Product Lines: Bumper stickers ($10-100), postcards ($10-100) and posters ($10-100).
Tips: "We are interested only in very funny postcards, posters, bumper stickers pertaining to 12-step and other recovery groups. Example: Caption reads "Admitted we were powerless over our addictions, that our lives had become unmanageable. Picture: man standing at one of several urinals looking to his left where urinal is being used by a giant yellow bird. IDEAS FOR PICTURE ONLY. WE EXECUTE ILLUSTRATION."

SANGAMON, INC., P.O. Box 410, Taylorville IL 62568. (217)824-2261. Contact: Editorial Department. Estab. 1931. 90% freelance written. Reports in 3 months. Buys all rights. **Pays on acceptance.** Writer's guidelines or market list for SASE. Market list is regularly revised.
Needs: Conventional, humorous, inspirational, juvenile, sensitivity and studio. "We offer a balance of many styles. We'd like to see more conversational prose styles for the conventional lines." Submit 15 ideas maximum/batch.
Other Product Lines: Calendars and promotions.
Tips: "We only request submissions based on background and writing experience. We work 12-18 months ahead of a season and only accept material on assignment."

Market conditions are constantly changing! If this is 1995 or later, buy the newest edition of Writer's Market *at your favorite bookstore or order directly from Writer's Digest Books.*

SCOTT CARDS INC., P.O. Box 906, Newbury Park CA 91319. President: Larry Templeman. Estab. 1985. 95% freelance written. Buys 75 freelance ideas/samples per year. Not printing seasonal/holiday cards at present. Reports in 5 months. **Pays on acceptance.** Writer's guidelines/brochure for #10 SAE and 2 first class stamps.
Needs: Conventional, humorous and sensitivity.
Tips: "New ways to say 'I love you' always sell if they aren't corny or too obvious. Humor helps, especially if there is a twist. We are looking for non-traditional sentiments that are sensitive, timely and sophisticated. Our cards have a distinct flavor, so before submitting your work, write for our guidelines and sample brochure."

‡SECOND NATURE INC., 7700 Cherry Creek S. Dr., Denver CO 80231. (303)671-8466. Marketing Director: Deborah Devore. Estab. 1988. 25% freelance written. Submit seasonal/holiday material 9 months in advance. Reports in 4 months. Pays on publication. Free writer's guidelines.
Needs: Informal, sensitivity, humorous and soft line. Prefers unrhymed verse ideas. Submit 6 ideas/batch.
Tips: "Audience is contemporary, fun. Age: mid-twenties to fifties. Friendship cards, encouragement."

‡SECOND NATURE LTD., 10 Malton Rd., London W10 5UP England. (800)233-0092. Editor: Rod Shrager. Estab. 1980. Submit seasonal/holiday material 18 months in advance. Reports in 6 weeks. **Pays on acceptance.** Market list is regularly revised.
Needs: Humorous, informal, inspirational and soft line. Rhymed and unrhymed verse OK.

SILVER VISIONS, P.O. Box 49, Newton Highlands MA 02161. (617)244-9504. Editor: B. Kaufman. Estab. 1981. Submit seasonal/holiday material 9 months-1 year in advance. Reports in 6 months. Pays on publication. Guidelines for SASE.
Needs: Humorous, humorous Jewish, contemporary occasion for photography line. "Copy must work with a photograph; in other words, submit copy that can be illustrated photographically. Send 10-16 card ideas/batch.

‡SNAFU DESIGNS, Box 16643, St. Paul MN 55116. (612)646-6118. Editor: Scott F. Austin. Estab. 1985. Reports in 6 weeks. Buys all rights. **Pays on acceptance.** "Before we send you our guidelines, please send us something that is representative of your sense of humor (include a SASE). We will send you our guidelines if we feel your humor is consistent with ours."
Needs: Humorous, informal, birthday, friendship, thank you, anniversary, congratulations, get well and new baby. Prefers unrhymed verse. Submit no more than 10 ideas/batch. Pays $75/idea.
Tips: "We use clever ideas that are simple and concisely delivered and are aimed at a sophisticated adult audience. Off-the-wall humor that pokes fun at the human condition. Please do not submit anything cute."

SUNRISE PUBLICATIONS, INC., P.O. Box 4699, Bloomington IN 47402-4699. (812)336-9900. Contact: Editorial Coordinator. Estab. 1973. 10% freelance written. Receives an estimated 1,500 submissions annually; bought 50 freelance ideas/samples last year. Reports in 2 months. **Pays on acceptance.** Free writer's guidelines. Market list is regularly revised.
Needs: Conventional, humorous and informal. No "off-color humor or lengthy poetry." Prefers unrhymed verses/ideas. "Generally, we like short one- or two-line captions, sincere or clever. Our customers prefer this to lengthy rhymed verse. Longer copy is used but should be conversational. Submit ideas for birthday, get well, friendship, wedding, baby congrats, sympathy, thinking of you, anniversary, belated birthday, thank you, fun and love. We also have strong seasonal lines that use traditional, humorous and inspirational verses. These seasons include Christmas, Valentine's Day, Easter, Mother's Day, Father's Day, Graduation, Halloween and Thanksgiving." Payment varies.
Tips: "Think always of the sending situation and both the person buying the card and its intended recipient."

‡TLC GREETINGS, 615 McCall Rd., Manhattan KS 66502. (913)776-4041. Fax: (913)776-4041, ext. 232. Creative Director: Michele Johnson. Estab. 1987. 80% freelance written. We buy approximately 25 ideas/samples per month. Submit seasonal/holiday material 6 months in advance. Reports in 1 month. Buys rights to the purchased idea/sentiment. **Pays on acceptance.** Writer's guidelines/market list for any size SAE and 2 first class stamps. Market list is regularly revised; available to writer on mailing list basis.
Needs: Studio, humorous, invitations and soft line. Prefers unrhymed verse. Submit 30 ideas/batch.
Other Product Lines: Mugs, note pads, posters, gift bags and greeting books. ("Our minimum is $35; maximum we negotiate.")
Tips: "Our target audience is women. What sells well for us are cards that are humorous (light humor). We do not use risque, although we're beginning to use more cards that are a little biting (making fun of the recipient). Also expanding into the male audience, by looking at sports/leisure related activities. Interest also in college humor."

TRISAR, INC., 121 Old Springs Rd., Anaheim CA 92808. (714)282-2626. Editor: Randy Harris. Estab. 1979. 10% freelance written. Buys 36 freelance ideas/samples per year. Submit seasonal/holiday material 9 months in advance. Reports in 3 months. **Pays on acceptance.** Writers guidelines for legal size SASE. (No catalogs).

Needs: Humorous, studio and age-related adult feelings about turning 40, 50, 60; sport and hobby themes; seasonal oriented themes. Prefers unrhymed verse and one-liners.

Other Product Lines: T-shirts, mugs and buttons.

Tips: "Our market is 'over the hill' themes and birthdays for adults turning 30, 40, 50 and retirement, etc. Thoughts on growing older but not wanting to grow up. We are especially looking for humor concerning turning 50."

VAGABOND CREATIONS, INC., 2560 Lance Dr., Dayton OH 45409. (513)298-1124. Editor: George F. Stanley, Jr. 10% freelance written. Buys 10-15 ideas annually. Submit seasonal/holiday material 6 months in advance. Reports in 1 week. Buys all rights. Ideas sometimes copyrighted. **Pays on acceptance.** Writer's guidelines for #10 SASE. Market list issued one time only.

Needs: Cute, humorous greeting cards (illustrations and copy) often with animated animals or objects in people-situations with short, subtle tie-in message on inside page only. No poetry. Pays $15-25/card idea.

VINTAGE IMAGES, (formerly Wildwood Design Group), P.O. Box 228, Lorton VA 22199. (703)550-1881. Editor: Brian Smolens. Estab. 1986. Not accepting freelance material at this time. Reports in 3 months. Buys all rights. Pays on publication. Writer's guidelines/market list for 9 × 12 SAE with 3 first class stamps.

Needs: Humorous only. "We supply pictures—caption *must* be written to match." Also developing new architectural and travel series.

Other Product Lines: Post cards ($20) and posters ($25-50).

WARNER PRESS, PUBLISHERS, P.O. Box 2499, 1200 E. 5th St., Anderson IN 46018. Product Editor: Robin Fogle. 50% freelance written. Reports in 5 weeks. Buys all rights. **Pays on acceptance.** Must send #10 SASE for guidelines before submitting.

Needs: Religious themes; sensitive prose and inspirational verse for boxed cards, posters, calendars. Pays $20-35. Also accepts ideas for coloring and activity books.

‡WEEDN DESIGN, 3rd Floor, 925 De La Vina., Santa Barbara CA 93101. (805)564-6905. Traffic Coordinator: Shellie Anderson. Estab. 1986. 5% freelance written. Receives 20 submissions/year. Submit seasonal/holiday material 2 years in advance. Reports in 1 month. Buys licensing rights. Pays on royalty basis.

Needs: Inspirational, sensivity and soft line. Prefers unrhymed verse. Submit 10-15 ideas/batch.

Other Product Lines: Calendars, gift books, greeting books and posters. "Payment is based on royalties, not bought outright."

Tips: "Most of our cards and books are written by in-house writers, mainly Flavia, our most well known property. Audience is 18-55-year-old caring women. Products marketed worldwide, strong inspirational following."

WEST GRAPHICS, 238 Capp St., San Francisco CA 94110-1212. (415)621-4641. Fax: (415)621-8613. Art Director: Tom Drew. Estab. 1980. 60% freelance written. Receives 1,000 submissions annually; buys 200 freelance ideas/samples per year. Reports in 2 months. Buys greeting card rights. Pays 30 days after publication. Writer's guidelines/market list for #10 SASE.

Needs: Humorous and studio. Prefers unrhymed verse. Submit 10-30 ideas/batch. Pays $100.

Other Product Lines: Notepads, gift bags.

Tips: "The majority of our audience are women in their 30s and 40s, so ideas should be targeted to issues they care about: relationships, sex, aging, success, money, crime, etc. We're looking for fresh, humorous ideas on the cutting edge."

CAROL WILSON FINE ARTS, INC., P.O. Box 17394, Portland OR 97217-1810. Fax: (503)287-2217. Editor: Gary Spector. Estab. 1983. 90% freelance written. Receives thousands of submissions annually; buys 100 freelance ideas/samples per year. Submit seasonal/holiday material 1 year in advance. Reports in 2 months. Buys negotiable rights. Pays on acceptance or publication depending on type of agreement. Writer's guidelines/market list for #10 SASE.

Needs: Humorous and unrhymed. Pays $50-100/card idea. "Royalties could be considered for a body of work."

Other Product Lines: Post cards.

Tips: "We are looking for laugh-out-loud, unusual and clever ideas for greeting cards. All occasions are needed but birthday cards are needed most of all. It's OK to be outrageous or risque. Cards should be 'personal.' Ask yourself—is this a card that someone would buy for a specific person?"

Greeting Cards & Gift Ideas/Changes '93-'94

The following greeting card publishers were listed in the 1993 edition but do not have listings in this edition of *Writer's Market*. The majority did not respond to our request to update their listings or return a questionnaire for a new listing. If a reason was given for their exclusion, we have included it in parentheses after the listing name.

Dancing Frog Graphics

Digressions (asked to be deleted)

Innovisions (does not use freelance work)

Popshots, Inc.

Potpourri Press (does not use freelance work)

Quality Artworks

Silver Visions

These Three, Inc.

Resources

Contests and Awards

The contests and awards listed in this section are arranged alphabetically by subject. Nonfiction writers can turn immediately to nonfiction awards listed alphabetically by the name of the contest or award. The same is true for fiction writers, poets, playwrights and screenwriters, journalists, children's writers and translators. You'll also find general book awards, miscellaneous awards, arts council and foundation fellowships, and multiple category contests.

New contests and awards are announced in various writer's publications nearly every day. However, many lose their funding or fold—and sponsoring magazines go out of business just as often. We have contacted the organizations whose contests and awards are listed here with the understanding that they are valid through 1994. If you are using this section in 1995 or later, keep in mind that much of the contest information listed here will not be current. Requirements such as entry fees change, as do deadlines, addresses and contact names.

To make sure you have all the information you need about a particular contest, always send a self-addressed, stamped, business-sized envelope (#10 SASE) to the contact person in the listing before entering a contest. The listings in this section are brief, and many contests have lengthy, specific rules and requirements that we could not include in our limited space. A response with rules and guidelines will not only provide specific instructions, it will also confirm that the award is still being offered.

When you receive a set of guidelines, you will see that some contests are not for some writers. The writer's age, previous publication, geographic location and the length of the work are common matters of eligibility. Read the requirements carefully to ensure you don't enter a contest for which you are not qualified. You should also be aware that every year, more and more contests, especially those sponsored by "little" literary magazines, are charging entry fees.

Contest and award competition is very strong. While a literary magazine may publish 10 short stories in an issue, only one will win the prize in a contest. Give yourself the best chance of winning by sending only your best work. There is always a percentage of manuscripts a contest judge or award director casts off immediately as unpolished, amateurish or wholly unsuitable for the competition.

To avoid first-round rejection, make certain that you and your work qualify in every way for the award. Some contests are more specific than others. There are many contests and awards for a "best poem," but some award only the best lyric poem, sonnet or haiku.

Winning a contest or award can launch a successful writing career. Take a professional approach by doing a little extra research. Find out who the previous winner of the award was by investing in a sample copy of the magazine in which the prize-winning article, poem or short story appeared. Attend the staged reading of an award-winning play. Your extra effort will be to your advantage in competition with writers who simply submit blindly.

If a contest or award requires nomination by your publisher, ask your publisher to nominate you. Many welcome the opportunity to promote a work (beyond their own, conventional means) they've published. Just be sure the publisher has plenty of time before the deadline to nominate your work.

Further information on funding for writers is available at most large public libraries. See the *Annual Register of Grant Support* (National Register Publishing Co., 3004 Glenview Rd., Wilmette IL 60091); *Foundations and Grants to Individuals* (Foundation Center, 79 5th Ave., New York NY 10003) and *Grants and Awards Available to American Writers* (PEN American Center, 568 Broadway, New York NY 10012). For more listings of contests and awards for fiction writers, see *Novel & Short Story Writer's Market. Poet's Market* lists contests and awards available to poets. *Children's Writer's & Illustrator's Market* has a section of contests and awards as well (all three published by Writer's Digest Books). Two more good sources for literary contests are *Poets & Writers* (72 Spring St., New York NY 10012), and the *Associated Writing Programs Newsletter* (Old Dominion University, Norfolk VA 23529). Journalists should look into the annual Journalism Awards Issue of *Editor & Publisher* magazine (11 W. 19th St., New York NY 10011), published in the last week of December. Playwrights should be aware of the newsletter put out by The Dramatists Guild, (234 W. 44th St., New York NY 10036).

For more information on contests and awards not listed in *Writer's Market*, see Contests and Awards/Changes '93-'94 at the end of this section.

General

THE ATHENAEUM OF PHILADELPHIA LITERARY AWARD, The Athenaeum of Philadelphia, 219 S. 6th St., Philadelphia PA 19106-3794. (215)925-2688. Award Director: Lea C. Sherk. Estab. 1949. Nominated book by a Philadelphia resident. Deadline: Dec. 31.

‡CALIFORNIA LITERATURE AWARDS, The Commonwealth Club of California, 595 Market St., San Francisco CA 94105. (415)597-6700. Fax: (415)597-6729. Contest/Award Director: Annie Hayflick. Estab. 1931. Offered annually. Previously published submissions must have appeared in print between 1/1/93 and 12/31/

93. "Purpose of award is the encouragement and production of literature in California. Categories include: fiction, nonfiction, poetry, first novel, juvenile ages up to 10, juvenile 11-16, notable contribution to publishing and California." Deadline: Jan. 30. Contest/award rules and entry forms available for SASE. Can be nominated by publisher as well. Prize: "Medals to be awarded at publicized event." Judged by jury of academics and peers. "Work must be authored by California resident (or must have been a resident at time of publication)."

THE CHRISTOPHER AWARD, The Christophers, 12 E. 48th St., New York NY 10017. (212)759-4050. Award Director: Peggy Flanagan. Estab. 1949. Outstanding books published during the calendar year that "affirm the highest values of the human spirit."

COMMONWEALTH CLUB OF CALIFORNIA BOOK AWARDS, 595 Market St., San Francisco CA 94105. (415)597-6700. Contact: Book Awards Jury. Previously published books from each year. "For books of exceptional literary merit by a California resident." Deadline Jan. 31. Guidelines for #10 SASE. Prizes: gold and silver medals.

EDITORS' BOOK AWARD, Pushcart Press, P.O. Box 380, Wainscott NY 11975. (516)324-9300. President: Bill Henderson. Unpublished books. Deadline: Sept. 15. "All manuscripts must be nominated by an editor in a publishing house."

FAW LITERARY AWARD, Friends of American Writers, 506 Rose Ave., Des Plaines IL 60016. Contact: Vivian Mortensen. Previously published books. Author must be a resident (or have previously been a resident for approximately 5 years) of AR, IL, IN, IA, KS, MI, MN, MS, ND, NE, OH, SD or WI; or the locale of the book must be in the region above. Author shall not have published more than 3 books under his own and/or pen name. Submit: Jan. 1-Dec. 31.

JERUSALEM PRIZE, Jerusalem International Book Fair, Binyaney Ha'ooma, P.O. Box 6001, Jerusalem Israel 91060. (02)528556. Fax: (02)243144. "Biennial competition for which authors must be nominated. Winner receives $5,000 and citation, and becomes a guest of Jerusalem Book Fair." Contest is judged by a jury of three (Israeli professors, authors, dignitaries). "Any writer can be nominated. The prize, however, is awarded to an internationally recognized author whose works express the idea of the freedom of man in society."

MINNESOTA VOICES PROJECT COMPETITION, New Rivers Press, #910, 420 N. 5th St., Minneapolis MN 55401. (612)339-7114. Editor/Publisher: C.W. Truesdale. Annual award for new and emerging writers of poetry, prose, essays, and memoirs (as well as other forms of creative prose) from Wisconsin, Minnesota, Iowa and the Dakotas, to be published in book form for the first time. Deadline: April 1. Send SASE for guidelines and necessary entry form.

NATIONAL BOOK AWARDS, National Book Foundation, Attn: National Book Awards, 260 5th Ave., Room 904, New York NY 10001. (212)685-0261. Executive Director: Neil Baldwin. Fiction, nonfiction and poetry—books by American authors. "Publishers must enter the books." Deadlines: July 15 (entry forms); July 31 (books). Charges $100 fee.

‡NEW WRITING AWARD, New Writing, Box 1812, Amherst NY 14226-7812. Contest/Award Director: Sam Meade. Offered annually for unpublished work. "Purpose is to award the best of *new* writing. We accept short stories, poems, plays, novels, essays, films and emergent forms. All are considered for the award based on originality. Charges $10 first entry; $5 additional—no limit. Prize: Monetary award and possible publication. Judged by editors of magazine. "We are looking for new, interesting and experimental work."

OHIOANA BOOK AWARDS, Ohioana Library Association, 65 S. Front St., Room 1105, Columbus OH 43215. (614)466-3831. Editor: Barbara Maslekoff. Estab. 1929. Books published within the past 12 months by Ohioans or about Ohio and Ohioans. Submit two copies of book on publication.

PEN CENTER WEST LITERARY AWARDS, PEN Center West, 672 S. Lafayette Park Place, #41, Los Angeles CA 90057. (213)365-8500. Fax: (213)365-9616. Estab. 1952. Awards and $500 cash prizes offered for work published in previous calendar year. Deadline: 4 copies must be received by Dec. 31. Open to writers living west of the Mississippi River. Award categories: fiction, nonfiction, poetry, drama, children's literature, screenplay, journalism, translation.

PEN PUBLISHER CITATION, PEN American Center, 568 Broadway, New York NY 10012. (212)334-1660. Fax: (212)334-2181. Contact: Pamela Pearce. "Awarded every two years to a publisher who has throughout his career, given distinctive and continuous service." Nominated by the PEN Executive Board.

PULITZER PRIZES, The Pulitzer Prize Board, 702 Journalism, Columbia University, New York NY 10027. (212)854-3841. Estab. 1917. Awards for journalism in U.S. newspapers (published daily or weekly), and in literature, drama and music by Americans. Deadline: Feb. 1 (journalism); March 1 (music and drama); July 1 and Nov. 1 (letters).

SAINT LOUIS LITERARY AWARD, Associates of Saint Louis University Libraries, 40 N. Kingshighway, St. Louis MO 63108-1392. (314)361-1616. Fax: (314)361-0812. Estab. 1967. Annual award. Works are nominated by committee.

THE CARL SANDBURG LITERARY ARTS AWARDS, The Friends of the Chicago Public Library, 400 S. State St., 9S-7, Chicago IL 60605. (312)747-4907. Estab. 1979. Chicago (and metropolitan area) writers of published fiction, nonfiction, poetry and children's literature. Deadline for submission: August 1.

SMALL PRESS PUBLISHER OF THE YEAR, Quality Books Inc., 918 Sherwood Dr., Lake Bluff IL 60044-2204. (312)295-2010. Fax: (708)295-1556. Contact: Amy Mascillino. Estab. 1964. "Each year a publisher is named that publishes titles we stock and has demonstrated ability to produce a timely and topical title, suitable for libraries. This publisher attains 'quality bestseller status and supports their distributor.'" Title must have been selected for stocking by Quality Books Inc. QBI is the principal nationwide distributor of small press titles to libraries.

SOCIETY OF MIDLAND AUTHORS AWARD, Society of Midland Authors, % Bowman, 152 N. Scoville, Oak Park IL 60302-2642. (708)383-7568. President: Jim Bowman. Award offered annually for previously published (between Jan. 1 and Dec. 31) work. "Award for best work by writers of the 12 Midwestern states: Illinois, Indiana, Iowa, Kansas, Michigan, Minnesota, Missouri, Nebraska, North Dakota, South Dakota, Wisconsin, Ohio and the stimulation of creative literary effort. 7 categories: poetry, adult fiction, adult nonfiction, biography, juvenile fiction, juvenile nonfiction, drama." Deadline: Jan. 15. SASE for award guidelines. Money and plaque given at annual dinner, Drake Hotel, Chicago, in May.

TOWSON STATE UNIVERSITY PRIZE FOR LITERATURE, College of Liberal Arts, Towson State University, Towson MD 21204-7097. (410)830-2128. Award Director: Dean Annette Chappell. Estab. 1979. Book or book-length manuscript that has been accepted for publication, written by a Maryland author of no more than 40 years of age. Deadline: May 15.

‡SAUL VIENER PRIZE, American Jewish Historical Society, 2 Thornton Rd., Waltham MA 02154. Contest/Award Director: Hasia R. Diner. Offered every two years for previously published (within 2 year period) work. "Award for outstanding scholarly work in American Jewish history." Deadline: Feb. 15. Write/call Hasia Diner. Prize: $500. Open to any writer.

WHITING WRITERS' AWARDS, Mrs. Giles Whiting Foundation, Rm. 3500, 30 Rockefeller Plaza, New York NY 10112. Director: Gerald Freund. "The Foundation gives annually $30,000 each to up to ten writers of poetry, fiction, nonfiction and plays. The awards place special emphasis on exceptionally promising emerging talent." Direct applications and informal nominations are not accepted by the Foundation.

H.W. WILSON LIBRARY PERIODICAL AWARD, donated by H.W. Wilson Company, administered by the American Library Association, 50 E. Huron, Chicago IL 60611. (800)545-2433. For a periodical published by a local, state or regional library, library group, or association in U.S. or Canada which has made an outstanding contribution to librarianship. (This excludes publications of ALA, CLA and their divisions.) All issues for the calendar year prior to the presentation of the award will be judged on the basis of sustained excellence in both content and format, with consideration being given to both purpose and budget.

WORLD FANTASY AWARDS ASSOCIATION, 5 Winding Brook Dr., #1B, Guilderland NY 12084-9719. President: Peter Dennis Pautz. Estab. 1975. Previously published work recommended by previous convention attendees in several categories, including life achievement, novel, novella, short story, anthology, collection, artist, special award-pro and special award non-pro. Deadline: July 1. Works are recommended by attendees

---

The double dagger before a listing indicates that the listing is new in this edition. New markets are often more receptive to freelance submissions.

of previous two years' conventions, and a panel of judges. Winners are determined by vote of the panel.

Nonfiction

AAAS PRIZE FOR BEHAVIORAL SCIENCE RESEARCH, American Association for the Advancement of Science, Directorate for Education and Human Resources Programs, 11th Floor, 1333 H. St. NW, Washington DC 20005. Anthropology/psychology/social sciences/sociology. Published in peer-reviewed journals only since Jan. 1, 1993. Deadline: July 1, 1994.

‡ANNUAL PERSONAL ESSAY CONTEST, Belles Lettres: A Review of Books by Women, 11151 Captain's Walk Ct., North Potomac MD 20878. (301)294-0278. Fax: (301)294-0023. Contest/Award Director: Suzanne Berne. Send entries to her at 120 Bellevue Rd., Watertown MA 02172. Offered annually for unpublished work. "Purpose is to promote excellence in personal essay writing." Entries accepted Jan.1-July 31 of each year. Contest rules and entry forms available for SASE. Charges $20. This entitles writer to 1 year's subscription to *Belles Lettres*. Current subscribers may enter for free." Prize: $500. Judged by Faye Moskowitz, author of *A Leak in the Heart, Whoever Finds This . . . I Love You*, and *And The Bridge Is Love*. "Rights revert to author after piece is published, except for anthology inclusions." Open to women only.

VINCENT ASTOR MEMORIAL LEADERSHIP ESSAY CONTEST, U.S. Naval Institute, 118 Maryland Ave., Annapolis MD 21402-5035. (410)268-6110. Fax: (410)269-7940. Award Director: James A. Barber, Jr. Essays on the topic of leadership (junior officers and officer trainees). Deadline: Feb. 15.

ARLEIGH BURKE ESSAY CONTEST, U.S. Naval Institute, 118 Maryland Ave., Annapolis MD 21402-5035. (410)268-6110. Fax: (410)269-7940. Award Director: James A. Barber, Jr. Estab. 1873. Essay that advances professional, literary or scientific knowledge of the naval and maritime services. Deadline: Dec. 1.

‡CLIFFORD PRIZE, American Society for 18th Century Studies, Computer Center 108, Utah State University, Logan UT 84322-3730. (801)750-4065. Fax: (801)750-4065. Executive Secretary: Dr. Jeffrey Smitten. Offered annually for previously published (between July 1992 and June 1993) work. Award is for "the best nominated article, an outstanding study of some aspect of 18th-century culture, interesting to any 18th-century specialist, regardless of discipline." Deadline: Feb. 1, 1994. Award rules and entry form available for SASE. Prize: $500, certificate from ASECS. Judged by committee of distinguished members. Winners must be society members.

MORTON N. COHEN AWARD, Modern Language Association of America, 10 Astor Pl., New York NY 10003-6981. (212)475-9500. Fax: (212)477-9863. Director: Richard Brod. Estab. 1989. Awarded in odd numbered years for a previously published distinguished edition of letters. Prize: $1,000. Guidelines for #10 SASE. Deadline: May 1.

DE LA TORRE BUENO PRIZE, Dance Perspectives Foundation, %85 Ford Ave., Fords NJ 08863. (908)738-7598. Fax: (908)548-2642. Contact: Barbara Palfy. Open to writers or their publishers who have published an original book of dance scholarship within the previous year. Deadline: Jan. 15.

DEXTER PRIZE, Society for the History of Technology, Dept. of Social Sciences, Michigan Tech Univ., 1400 Townsend Dr., Houghton MI 49931-1295. (906)487-2459. Fax: (906)487-2468. Contact: Society Secretary. Estab. 1968. Previously published (previous three years: for 1993—1990 to 1992). "Award given to the best book in the history of technology." Deadline: April 15. SASE for guidelines. Prize: $2,000 and a plaque from the Dexter Chemical Company.

GORDON W. DILLON/RICHARD C. PETERSON MEMORIAL ESSAY PRIZE, American Orchid Society, Inc., 6000 S. Olive Ave., West Palm Beach FL 33405-0654. (407)585-8666. Fax: (407)585-0654. Contact: James Watson. Estab. 1985. "To honor the memory of two outstanding former editors of the *American Orchid Society Bulletin*. Annual themes of the essay competitions are announced by the Editor of the *A.O.S. Bulletin* in the May issue. Themes in past years have included Orchid Culture, Orchids in Nature and Orchids in Use. The contest is open to all individuals with the exception of A.O.S. employees and their immediate families."

‡DOG WRITER'S ASSOCIATION OF AMERICA ANNUAL WRITING CONTEST, Suite 142, 3018 J St., Sacramento CA 95816. Competition Chair: Gina Spadafori. Previously published writing, photography, graphic arts and videotapes about dogs—their rearing, training, care and all aspects of companionship. For material published from Oct. 1 through Sept. 30. Deadline: Oct. 1. Charges $10 fee.

THE RALPH WALDO EMERSON AWARD, The Phi Beta Kappa Society, 1811 Q St. NW, Washington DC 20009. (202)265-3808. Contact: Administrator, Phi Beta Kappa Book Awards. Studies of the intellectual and cultural condition of man published in the U.S. during the 12-month period preceding the entry deadline, and submitted by the publisher. Books must have been published between May 1, 1992 and April 30, 1993. Deadline: April 30. Author must be a US citizen or resident.

DAVID W. AND BEATRICE C. EVANS BIOGRAPHY AWARD, Mountain West Center for Regional Studies, Utah Sate University, University Hill, Logan UT 84322-0735. (801)750-3630. Fax: (801)750-1092. Contact: F. Ross Peterson or Shannon R. Hoskins. Estab. 1986. Submissions to be published or unpublished. To encourage the writing of biography about people who have played a role in Mormon Country. (Not the religion, the country: Intermountain West with parts of Southwestern Canada and Northwestern Mexico.) Deadline: Dec. 31, 1993. Publishers or author may nominate book. Criteria for consideration: Work must be a biography or autobiography on "Mormon Country"; must be submitted for consideration for publication year's award; new editions or reprints are not eligible; manuscripts are accepted. Submit 6 copies.

GEORGE FREEDLEY MEMORIAL AWARD, Theatre Library Association, New York Public Library at Lincoln Center, 111 Amsterdam Ave., New York NY 10023. (212)870-1644. Fax: (212)787-3852. Contact: Award Committee Chair. Estab. 1968. Published books related to theater. Deadline: Feb. 1.

THE CHRISTIAN GAUSS AWARD, The Phi Beta Kappa Society, 1811 Q St. NW, Washington DC 20009. (202)265-3808. Contact: Administrator, Phi Beta Kappa Book Awards. Estab. 1950. Works of literary criticism or scholarship published in the U.S. during the 12-month period preceding the entry deadline, and submitted by the publisher. Books must have been published between May 1, 1992 and April 30, 1993. Deadline: April 30. Author must be a US citizen or resident.

‡LOUIS GOTTSCHALK PRIZE 1993, American Society for 18th Century Studies, Computer Center 108, Utah State University, Logan UT 84322-3730. (801)750-4065. Fax: (801)750-4065. Executive Secretary: Jeffrey Smitten. Offered annually for previously published (between Jan. 1993 and Dec. 1993) work. Purpose is "to award outstanding historical or critical study on the 18th century. Louis Gottschalk (1899-1975), second president of ASECS, President of the American Historical Association and for many years Distinguished Service Professor at the University of Chicago, exemplified in his scholarship the humanistic ideals which this award is meant to encourage." Deadline: Nov. 15, 1993. Award rules and entry form available for SASE. "Publisher must send in 5 copies for contest." No entry fee. Winners must be members of the society. Prize: $1,000 and certificate from ASECS. Judged by committee of distinguished members. "Winners must be society members ($15-35 dues)."

CLARENCE HARING PRIZE, American Historical Association, 400 A St. SE, Washington DC 20003. Contact: Executive Assistant. Awarded quinquennially for the best work by a Latin American scholar in Latin American history. Cash award is $500. Deadline: May 15.

ANSON JONES AWARD, % Texas Medical Association, 401 W. 15th St., Austin TX 78701-1680. (512)370-1390. Estab. 1957. Health (Texas newspaper, magazine—trade, commercial, association, chamber or company—radio, TV and Spanish language). Deadline: Jan. 15.

KATHERINE SINGER KOVACS PRIZE, Modern Language Association of America, 10 Astor Pl, New York NY 10003-6981. (212)475-9500. Fax: (212)477-9863. Director: Richard Brod. Estab. 1990. Annual award for previously published book in English on Latin American or Spanish literatures and cultures. Guidelines for #10 SASE. Prize: $1,000. Deadline: May 1.

JOSEPH W. LIPPINCOTT AWARD, Donated by Joseph W. Lippincott, Jr., Administered by the American Library Association Awards Committee, 50 E. Huron, Chicago IL 60611. (312)280-2518. "To a librarian for distinguished service to the profession of librarianship, such service to include outstanding participation in the activities of professional library associations, notable published professional writing, or other significant activity on behalf of the profession and its aim."

LITERARY NONFICTION WRITERS' PROJECT GRANTS, NC Arts Council, Dept. of Cultural Resources, Raleigh NC 27601-2807. (919)733-2111. Literature Director: Deborah McGill. Annual grant "to recognize the literary value of nonfiction and to encourage the artistic growth of the state's writers of nonfiction." Write for guidelines. Writer must have been a resident of North Carolina for at least a year and may not be enrolled in any degree-granting program at the time of application. Deadline: Feb. 1.

LOFT CREATIVE NONFICTION RESIDENCY PROGRAM, The Loft, Pratt Community Center, 66 Malcolm Ave., S.E., Minneapolis MN 55414-3551. Attn: Assoc. Program Director. Estab. 1974. Opportunity to work in month-long seminar with resident writer and cash award to six creative nonfiction writers. "Must live close enough to Minneapolis to participate fully." Deadline: April (subject to change).

JAMES RUSSELL LOWELL PRIZE, Modern Language Association of America, 10 Astor Pl., New York NY 10003-6981. (212)475-9500. Fax: (212)477-9863. Director: Richard Brod. Annual award for previously published literary, linguistic study, or critical edition or biography. Open to MLA members only. Guidelines for #10 SASE. Prize: $1,000. Deadline: March 1.

McLEMORE PRIZE, Mississippi Historical Society, P.O. Box 571, Jackson MS 39205-0571. (601)359-6850. Fax: (601)359-6905. Contact: Secretary/Treasurer. Estab. 1902. Scholarly book on a topic in Mississippi history/biography published in the year of competition. Deadline: Jan. 1.

HOWARD R. MARRARO PRIZE, Modern Language Association of America, 10 Astor Pl., New York NY 10003-6981. (212)475-9500. Fax: (212)477-9863. Director: Richard Brod. Awarded in even numbered years for previously published books or essays on any phase of Italian literature or comparative literature involving Italian. Open to MLA members only. Guidelines for #10 SASE. Prize: $750. Deadline: May 1.

THE MAYFLOWER SOCIETY CUP COMPETITION, North Carolina Literary and Historical Association, 109 E. Jones St., Raleigh NC 27601-2807. (919)733-7305. Contact: Award Director. Previously published nonfiction by a North Carolina resident. Deadline: July 15.

KENNETH W. MILDENBERGER PRIZE, Modern Language Association of America, 10 Astor Pl., New York NY 10003-6981. (212)475-9500. Fax: (212)477-9863. Director: Richard Brod. Annual award for previously published research in the field of teaching foreign languages and literatures. Guidelines for #10 SASE. Prize: $500. Deadline: May 1.

MLA PRIZE FOR INDEPENDENT SCHOLARS, Modern Language Association of America, 10 Astor Pl., New York NY 10003-6981. (212)475-9500. Fax: (212)477-9863. Director: Richard Brod. Annual award for previously published book or article in the field of English or another modern language literature. Guidelines and application form for #10 SASE. Prize. $1,000. Deadline: May 1.

‡ROBERT T. MORSE WRITERS AWARD, American Psychiatric Association, 1400 K Street, NW, Washington DC 20005. (202)682-6220. Contact: Media Coordinator. Offered annually for work previously published (between January 1 and December 31 of preceding year). "To recognize the outstanding achievement and excellence in media coverage of mental illnesses and psychiatric treatment for significant contribution(s) to public understanding of these illnesses and the treatments available to those who suffer from the illnesses." Deadline: January. "Deadline is first few days of January, exact day depends on what day Jan. 1 falls on." Contest/award rules and entry forms available on request. "Entries can be self-nominated, by organization or by a District Branch of the APA." Prize: A $1,000 honorarium and an engraved plaque. "Entries are accepted from national and local news writers or groups of writers who have covered the mental health/ illness field or who have written an exemplary article or special series of articles. The entry(s) must be intended for the general public and must address pertinent mental health or mental illness issues and the *role of psychiatry within these issues.*"

‡GEORGE JEAN NATHAN AWARD FOR DRAMATIC CRITICISM, Cornell University, Dept. of English, Goldwin Smith Hall, Ithaca NY 14853. (607)255-6801. Contact: Chair, Dept. of English. Offered annually for previously published works. "Awarded to the American who has written the best piece of drama criticism during the theatrical year (July 1 to June 30), whether it is an article, an essay, treatise or book." Rules and entry forms available for SASE. Prize: $5,000. "Winner also receives a silver medallion and a certificate symbolic of, and attesting to, the award." "Only published work may be submitted, and the author must be an American citizen."

NATIONAL JEWISH BOOK AWARD—AUTOBIOGRAPHY/MEMOIR, Sandra Brand and Arik Weintraub Award, 15 E. 26th St., New York NY 10010. (212)532-4949. Director: Paula G. Gottlieb. Given to an author of an autobiography or a memoir of the life of a Jewish person.

NATIONAL JEWISH BOOK AWARD—CONTEMPORARY JEWISH LIFE, The Ronald Lauder Foundation Award, 15 E. 26th St., New York NY 10010. (212)532-4949. Contact: Paula G. Gottlieb. Nonfiction work dealing with the sociology of modern Jewish life.

NATIONAL JEWISH BOOK AWARD—HOLOCAUST, Leon Jolson Award, Jewish Book Council, 15 E. 26th St., New York NY 10010. (212)532-4949. Contact: Paula G. Gottlieb. Nonfiction book concerning the Holocaust. Deadline: Nov. 20.

NATIONAL JEWISH BOOK AWARD—ISRAEL, Morris J. and Betty Kaplun Memorial Award, Jewish Book Council, 15 E. 26th St., New York NY 10010. (212)532-4949. Director: Paula G. Gottlieb. Nonfiction work about the State of Israel. Deadline: Nov. 20.

NATIONAL JEWISH BOOK AWARD—JEWISH HISTORY, Gerrard and Ella Berman Award, Jewish Book Council, 15 E. 26th St., New York NY 10010. (212)532-4949. Director: Paula G. Gottlieb. Book of Jewish history. Deadline: Nov. 20.

NATIONAL JEWISH BOOK AWARD—JEWISH THOUGHT, Jewish Book Council, 15 E. 26th St., New York NY 10010. (212)532-4949. Director: Paula G. Gottlieb. Book dealing with some aspect of Jewish thought, past or present. Deadline: Nov. 20.

NATIONAL JEWISH BOOK AWARD—SCHOLARSHIP, Sarah H. and Julius Kushner Memorial Award, Jewish Book Council, 15 E. 26th St., New York NY 10010. (212)532-4949. Director: Paula G. Gottlieb. Book which makes an original contribution to Jewish learning. Deadline: Nov. 20.

NATIONAL JEWISH BOOK AWARD—VISUAL ARTS, Anonymous Award, Jewish Book Council, 15 E. 26th St., New York NY 10010. (212)532-4949. Director: Paula G. Gottlieb. Book about Jewish art. Deadline: Nov. 20.

NATIONAL WRITERS CLUB ARTICLES AND ESSAYS CONTEST, The National Writers Club, Suite 424, 1450 S. Havana, Aurora CO 80012. (303)751-7844. Fax: (303)751-8593. Director: Sandy Whelchel. Annual contest "to encourage writers in this creative form and to recognize those who excel in nonfiction writing." $11 entry fee. Prizes: $200, $100, $50. Rules and entry forms available for #10 SASE.

‡**THE FREDERIC W. NESS BOOK AWARD**, Assn. of American Colleges, 1818 R St. NW, Washington DC 20009. (202)387-3760. Fax: (202)265-9532. Exec. Asst. to the President: Peggy Neal. Offered annually for previously published (between July 1 and June 30 of the year in which it is being considered) work. "Each year the Frederic W. Ness Book Award Committee of the Association of American Colleges recognizes books which contribute to the understanding and improvement of liberal education." Deadline: Aug. 15. Contest/ award rules and entry forms available for SASE. "Writers may nominate their own work; however, we send letters of invitation to publishers to nominate qualified books." Recognition: Presentation at the association's annual meeting and $1,000. (Transportation and one night hotel for meeting are also provided.)

ALLAN NEVINS PRIZE, Society of American Historians, 2 Butler Library, Columbia University, New York NY 10027. Sec./Treas.: Professor Mark Carnes. American history (nominated doctoral dissertations on arts, literature, science and American biographies). Deadline: January 15. Prize: $1,000, certificate and publication.

‡**NEW JERSEY HUMANITIES BOOK AWARD**, New Jersey Committee for the Humanities (NJCH), Suite 602, 390 George St., New Brunswick NJ 08901-2019. (908)932-7726. Fax: (908)932-1179. Coordinator: Erica Mosner. Offered annually for previously published (between Jan. 1 and Dec. 31) work. Purpose is "to honor a New Jersey author by virtue of birth, residence, or occupation, and to bring more exposure to humanities books that stimulate curiosity and enrich the general public's understanding of their world." Deadline: "Usually Feb. 1." Contest/award rules and entry forms available for SASE. "Publisher only must nominate the book, but author can call us and we will send the information directly to their publisher." Prize: $1,000 for the author, $2,000 pro forma marketing award to publisher, and title distributed to up to 100 libraries throughout New Jersey. Judged by NJCH's Book Award Committee.

NEW YORK STATE HISTORICAL ASSOCIATION MANUSCRIPT AWARD, P.O. Box 800, Cooperstown NY 13326-0800. (607)547-2508. Director of Publications: Dr. Wendell Tripp. Estab. 1973. Unpublished book-length monograph on New York State history. Deadline: Feb. 20.

NORTH AMERICAN INDIAN PROSE AWARD, University of Nebraska Press, 327 Nebraska Hall, Lincoln NE 68588-0520. Contact: Award Director. "A publication prize for the best new work by an American Indian writer. The award-winning ms will be published by the University of Nebraska Press. The author will receive a $1,000 advance." Send #10 SASE for guidelines. Deadline: July 1.

ELI M. OBOLER MEMORIAL AWARD, American Library Association's Intellectual Freedom Round Table, 50 E. Huron St., Chicago IL 60611. (312)280-4224. Contact: Chairman. "Award offered every two years to the author of an article (including a review), a series of thematically connected articles, a book, or a manual published on the local, state or national level, in English or in English translation. The works to be considered must have as their central concern one or more issues, events, questions or controversies in the area of intellectual freedom, including matters of ethical, political, or social concern related to intellectual freedom. The work for which the award is granted must have been published within the *two-year* period ending the December prior to the ALA Annual Conference at which it is granted." Deadline: Dec. 1.

FRANCIS PARKMAN PRIZE, Society of American Historians, 2 Butler Library, Columbia University, New York NY 10027. (212)854-2221. Contact: Professor Mark Carnes. Colonial or national US history book. Deadline: Jan. 15. Prize: $1,000, bronze medal and certificates to author and publisher.

Discover the Best New Fiction Published in America

Subscribe to STORY, the award-winning magazine that made literary history by first publishing the short fiction of Salinger, Capote, Mailer and scores more.

Relaunched just three years ago, STORY has continued the tradition, winning the distinguished National Magazine Award, being named by *Library Journal* as one of the best new launches in '89 and captivating more readers than the combined circulation of the next three

best selling literaries in America.

We invite you to join the growing circle of literary aficionados who in each issue discover the excitement and challenge of memorable short stories.

"STORY is one of the most attractive and consistently readable magazines of its kind. Its contents are wonderfully varied and scrupulously edited."
— Joyce Carol Oates

Introductory Subscription Invitation

☐ I accept! Please enter my one-year subscription and send me the next four quarterly issues for just $19. I save 20% off the single copy price!

☐ Payment enclosed. (*Thank you!*)   ☐ Please bill me.

☐ Charge my ☐ VISA ☐ MC

Card Number_____

Exp. _____

Signature _____

NAME_____

ADDRESS_____ APT._____

CITY_____ STATE_____ ZIP_____

VNWM0

STORY

National Magazine Award for Fiction

*Outside U.S. add $7 (includes GST in Canada) and remit in U.S. funds.

MY 100% RISK-FREE GUARANTEE:
If I'm ever dissatisfied with STORY for any reason, I may cancel and receive a full refund for all unmailed issues.

"...firmly committed to discovering and showcasing the best new voices in American fiction."

— Richard Currey

Today STORY maintains its tradition of recognizing fresh new writing talent. Each handsomely-bound collection will introduce you to brilliant new authors who promise to be the literary greats of tomorrow, just as it introduced the world to the first works of Salinger, Capote, Mailer, and others.

Be on hand for the next STORY discovery, and start your subscription to the most widely circulated literary magazine published in America.

BUSINESS REPLY MAIL

FIRST CLASS MAIL   PERMIT NO. 156   HARLAN, IOWA

POSTAGE WILL BE PAID BY ADDRESSEE

STORY

PO BOX 5068
HARLAN IA 51593-2568

No Postage
Necessary
If Mailed
In The
United States

PEN/JERARD FUND, PEN American Center, 568 Broadway, New York NY 10012. (212)334-1660. Fax: (212)334-2181. Contact: John Morrone. Estab. 1986. Biennial grant of $4,000 for American woman writer of nonfiction for a booklength work in progress in odd-numbered years. Next award: 1995. Deadline: Jan. 15.

PEN/MARTHA ALBRAND AWARD FOR NONFICTION, PEN American Center, 568 Broadway, New York NY 10012. (212)334-1660. Fax: (212)334-2181. Coordinator: John Morrone. For a first-published book of general nonfiction distinguished by qualities of literary and stylistic excellence. Eligible books must have been published in the calendar year under consideration. Authors must be American citizens or permanent residents. Although there are no restrictions on the subject matter of titles submitted, non-literary books will not be considered. Books should be of adult nonfiction for the general or academic reader. Deadline: Dec. 31. Publishers, agents and authors themselves must submit *three* copies of each eligible title. $1,000 prize.

PEN/SPIELVOGEL-DIAMONSTEIN AWARD, PEN American Center, 568 Broadway, New York NY 10012. (212)334-1660. Fax: (212)334-2181. Coordinator: John Morrone. "For the best previously unpublished collection of essays on any subject by an American writer. The $5,000 prize is awarded to preserve the dignity and esteem that the essay form imparts to literature. Authors must be American citizens or permanent residents. The essays included in books submitted may have been previously published in magazines, journals or anthologies, but must not have collectively appeared before in book form. Books will be judged on the basis of the literary character and distinction of the writing. *Four* copies of each eligible title may be submitted by publishers, agents, or the authors themselves. Deadline: Dec. 31.

PHI BETA KAPPA AWARD IN SCIENCE, The Phi Beta Kappa Society, 1811 Q St. NW, Washington DC 20009. (202)265-3808. Contact: Administrator, Phi Beta Kappa Book Awards. Estab. 1959. Interpretations of the physical or biological sciences or mathematics published in the U.S. during the 12-month period preceding the entry deadline, and submitted by the publisher. Books must have been published between May 1, 1992 and April 30, 1993. Books that are exclusively histories of science are *not* eligible, nor are biographies of scientists in which a narrative emphasis predominates. Works of fiction are not eligible. Deadline: April 30. Author must be a US citizen or resident.

PHI BETA KAPPA BOOK AWARDS, The Phi Beta Kappa Society, 1811 Q St. NW, Washington DC 20009. (202)265-3808. Contact: Linda Surles. Estab. 1776. "Annual award to recognize and honor outstanding scholarly books published in the United States in the fields of the humanities, the social sciences, and the natural sciences and mathematics." Books must have been published between May 1, 1992 and April 30, 1993. Deadline: April 30. "Authors may request information, however it is requested that books be submitted by the publisher." Entries must be the works of authors who are US citizens or residents.

THE BARBARA SAVAGE "MILES FROM NOWHERE" MEMORIAL AWARD, The Mountaineers Books, Suite 107, 1011 SW Klickitat Way, Seattle WA 98134. (206)223-6303. Award Director: Donna DeShazo. Award offered for previously unpublished book-length nonfiction. Acceptable subjects include personal narratives involving hiking, mountain climbing, bicycling, paddle sports, skiing, snowshoeing, nature, conservation, ecology and adventure travel not involving public transport. Guidelines for 9 × 12 SASE. Prize: $3,000 cash award, a $12,000 guaranteed advance against royalties and publication by The Mountaineers.

‡ALDO AND JEANNE SCAGLIONE PRIZE IN COMPARATIVE LITERARY STUDIES, Modern Language Association of America, 10 Astor Place, New York NY 10003-6981. (212)614-6406. Director of Special Projects: Richard Brod. Offered for previously published (in the year preceding award) work. Award is for outstanding scholarly work in the field of comparative literary studies that involve at least two languages. Prize: Check for $1,000 and an engrossed certificate. Judged by committee of the Modern Language Association of America. "Writer must be a member of the MLA. Works of scholarship, literary history, literary criticism and literary theory are eligible. Books that are primarily translations are not."

‡ALDO AND JEANNE SCAGLIONE PRIZE IN FRENCH AND FRANCOPHONE STUDIES, 10 Astor Place, New York NY 10003-6981. (212)614-6406. Director of Special Projects: Richard Brod. Offered for previously published (the year preceding that of the awarding) work. Award is for an outstanding scholarly work in the field of French or francophone linguistic or literary studies. Prize: A check for $1,000 and an engrossed certificate. Judged by a committee of the Modern Language Association. Writer must be a member of the MLA. Works of scholarship, literary history, literary criticism and literary theory are eligible; books that are primarily translations are not.

MINA P. SHAUGHNESSY PRIZE, Modern Language Association of America, 10 Astor Pl., New York NY 10003-6981. (212)475-9500. Fax: (212)477-9863. Director: Richard Brod. Annual award for research publication (book or article) in the field of teaching English language and literature. Guidelines for #10 SASE. Prize: $500. Deadline: May 1.

‡**THE JOHN BEN SNOW PRIZE,** Syracuse University Press, 1600 Jamesville Ave., Syracuse NY 13244. (315)443-5534. Fax: (315)443-5545. Contact: Director. Offered annually for unpublished submissions. The John Ben Snow Prize, inaugurated in 1978, is given annually by Syracuse University Press to the author of a nonfiction manuscript dealing with some aspect of New York State. The purpose of the award is to encourage the writing of books of genuine significance and literary distinction that will augment knowledge of New York State and appreciation for its unique physical, historical and cultural characteristics. A manuscript based on direct, personal experience will receive the same consideration as one relying on scholarly research. The criteria are authenticity, accuracy, readability and importance. Deadline: Dec. 31. Prize: $1,500 to the author as advance against royalties and publication by Syracuse University Press. Send for contest rules and entry forms.

BRYANT SPANN MEMORIAL PRIZE, History Dept., Indiana State University, Terre Haute IN 47809. Estab. 1980. Social criticism in the tradition of Eugene V. Debs. Deadline: April 30. Send SASE for guidelines. SASE also required with submissions. Prize: $1,000.

THE TEN BEST "CENSORED" STORIES OF 1994, Project Censored—Sonoma State University, Rohnert Park CA 94928. (707)664-2500. Fax: (707)664-2505. Award Director: Carl Jensen, Ph.D. Estab. 1976. Current published, nonfiction stories of national social significance that have been overlooked or under-reported by the news media. Deadline: Nov. 1.

THE THEATRE LIBRARY ASSOCIATION AWARD, Theatre Library Association, New York Public Library at Lincoln Center, 111 Amsterdam Ave., New York NY 10023. (212)870-1640. Fax: (212)787-3852. Awards Committee Chair: Stephen M. Vallillo. Estab. 1973. Book published in the United States in the field of recorded performance, including motion pictures and television. Deadline: Feb. 1.

WHITNEY-CARNEGIE AWARD, American Library Association Publishing Services, 50 E. Huron, Chicago IL 60611-2795. (312)280-5416. Fax: (312)944-8741. Contact: Director of Publishing. Submissions to be unpublished. "The grants are awarded to individuals for the preparation of bibliographic aids for research. The aids must be aimed at a scholarly audience but have a general applicability. Products prepared under this project must be offered to ALA Publishing Services for first consideration." Maximum award: $5,000. Deadline: Sept. 1.

Fiction

AIM MAGAZINE SHORT STORY CONTEST, P.O. Box 20554, Chicago IL 60620-0554. (312)874-6184. Publisher: Ruth Apilado. Estab. 1975. Unpublished short stories (4,000 words maximum) "promoting brotherhood among people and cultures." Deadline: Aug. 15.

AMBERGRIS ANNUAL FICTION AWARD, *Ambergris* Magazine, P.O. Box 29919, Cincinnati OH 45229-0919. Editor: Mark Kissling. Estab. 1988. "Recognizes and rewards excellence in short fiction." Prefers works of 5,000 words or fewer. Winner is chosen from all works submitted during the year. Writer's guidelines for #10 SASE. Award: $100 and nomination to *The Pushcart Prize.*

ANVIL PRESS INTERNATIONAL 3-DAY NOVEL WRITING CONTEST, Anvil Press, 15-2414 Main St., Vancouver, British Columbia V5T 3E3 Canada. (604)876-8710. Contact: Brian Kaufman. Estab. 1972. Best novel written in three days; specifically, over the Labor Day weekend. Entrants return finished novels to Anvil Press for judging. Registration deadline: Friday before Labor Day weekend. Send SASE (IRC if from the US) for details. Charges $15 fee.

‡**RAYMOND CARVER SHORT STORY CONTEST,** English Department, Humboldt State University, Arcata CA 95521. Coordinator: Kim T. Halliday. Offered annually for unpublished work. Deadline: Nov. 1. Contest/ award rules and entry forms available for SASE. Charges $7.50 fee. "First prize—$500 plus publication in *Toyon*, Humboldt State University's literary magazine. Second prize—$250. Previous year's judges include Deena Metzger, James D. Houston, Gary Fisketjon." Contest open to any writer living in the US.

‡**JAMES FENIMORE COOPER PRIZE,** Society of American Historians, New York Library, Columbia University, New York NY 10027. (212)854-2221. Contact: Professor Mark Carnes. Historical novel on an American theme. Deadline: Jan. 15. Prize $1,000 and certificates to author or publisher.

ROBERT L. FISH MEMORIAL AWARD, Mystery Writers of America, Inc., 6th Floor, 17 E. 47th St., New York NY 10017. (212)888-8171. Contact: Priscilla Ridgway. Annual award for the best first mystery or suspense short story published during the previous year. Deadline: Dec. 1.

‡THE HEEKIN GROUP FOUNDATION FICTION FELLOWSHIPS, The Heekin Group Foundation, P.O. Box 1534, Sisters OR 97759. (503)548-4147. Contest/Award Director: Sarah Heekin Redfield. Offered annually for unpublished works. "James J. Fellowship for the Novel in Progress, Tara Fellowship for Short Fiction; both fellowships are awarded to beginning career writers for assistance in their literary pursuits." Deadline: Dec. 15. Contest rules and entry form available for SASE. Charges $15 for short fiction, $20 for Novel in Progress; $25 dual entry. Prize: James J. Fellowship: $10,000; Tara Fellowship: $5,000. Previously judged by GrayWolf Press (final round). "Fellowship competition is open to all begininng career writers, those writers who are still unpublished in the novel and those writers who are either unpublished in short fiction or have had three or fewer short fiction pieces published."

DRUE HEINZ LITERATURE PRIZE, University of Pittsburgh Press, 127 N. Bellefield Ave., Pittsburgh PA 15260. (412)624-4111. Fax: (412)624-7380. Series Editor: Ed Ochester. Estab. 1936. Collection of short fiction. Award open to writers who have published a book-length collection of fiction or a miñimum of three short stories or novellas in commercial magazines or literary journals of national distribution. We are unable to return any manuscripts for this contest. Write for complete submission guidelines. Submit: July-August.

ERNEST HEMINGWAY FOUNDATION AWARD, PEN American Center, 568 Broadway, New York NY 10012. Contact: John Morrone. First-published novel or short story collection by an American author. Submit 3 copies. Deadline: Dec. 31.

HEMINGWAY SHORT STORY COMPETITION, Hemingway Days Festival, P.O. Box 4045, Key West FL 33041-4045. (305)294-4440. Coordinator: Lorian Hemingway. Estab. 1981. Unpublished short stories. Deadline: early July. Charges $10 fee. Send SASE for rules, specific deadline, and entry form. Prizes: $1,000 cash (first prize); two $500 runner-up awards.

L. RON HUBBARD'S WRITERS OF THE FUTURE CONTEST, P.O. Box 1630, Los Angeles CA 90078-1630. (213)466-3310. Award Director: Rachel Denk. Estab. 1983. Unpublished science fiction and fantasy. Send #10 SASE for guidelines.

INTERNATIONAL IMITATION HEMINGWAY COMPETITION, PEN Center West, Suite 41, 672 S. Lafayette Park Pl., Los Angeles CA 90057. Fax: (213)365-9616. Unpublished one-page (500 words) parody of Hemingway. Deadline: February 1. Winner receives roundtrip transportation for two to Florence, Italy and dinner at Harry's Bar & American Grill in Florence. Ten finalists are published in *American Way* Magazine.

LAWRENCE FOUNDATION AWARD, *Prairie Schooner*, 201 Andrews, University of Nebraska, Lincoln NE 68588-0334. (402)472-3191. Fax: (402)472-4636. Editor: Hilda Raz. Estab. 1978. Annual award for the best short story published in *Prairie Schooner*. Winner announced in the spring issue of the following year. Prize: $1,500. The Lawrence Foundation is a charitable trust located in New York City.

LINES IN THE SAND SHORT FICTION CONTEST, LeSand Publications, 1252 Terra Nova Blvd., Pacifica CA 94044. (415)355-9069. Associate Editor: Barbara J. Less. Annual contest. Purpose: "to encourage the writing of good, short fiction." Deadline: Oct. 31. Guidelines for #10 SASE. Charges $5 fee. Prizes: $50-first; $25-second; $10-third, plus publication in January/February Awards edition.

‡MID-LIST PRESS FIRST NOVEL SERIES AWARD, Mid-List Press, 4324-12th Ave. S., Minneapolis MN 55407-3218. (612)822-3733. Acquisitions Editor: Maria Ahrens. Offered annually for unpublished works. "The purpose is to locate and publish quality manuscripts by first-time writers, particularly those mid-list titles that major publishers may be rejecting." Deadline: February 1. Contest/award rules and entry forms available for SASE. *Applicants should write, not call, for guidelines.* Charges $10 fee. Prize: First Novel: $1,000 plus publication. Judged by "the regular readers and editors of Mid-List Press; editors and publishers make final decisions." Open to any writer who has never published a *novel*.

MILITARY LIFESTYLE FICTION CONTEST, *Military Lifestyle Magazine*, Suite 710, 4800 Montgomery Lane, Bethesda MD 20814-5341. (301)718-7600. Fax: (301)718-7652. Editor-in-Chief: Hope M. Daniels. Estab. 1969. Annual award for short stories featuring U.S. military servicemembers and/or military families. Write to request current year's theme and rules, usually available by Jan. 1. Deadline: March 31.

‡MILKWEED NATIONAL FICTION PRIZE, Milkweed Editions, Suite 400, 1st Ave. N., Minneapolis MN 55401. (612)332-3192. Fax: (612)332-6248. Annual award for unpublished works. "Milkweed is looking for a novel, novella, or a collection of short stories. Manuscripts should be of high literary quality and must be double-spaced and between 150-400 pages in length." Deadline: July 15. *Must* request contest guidelines, send SASE. Charges $5 reading fee. Prize: Publication by Milkweed Editions and a cash advance of $3,000 against royalties. "Entry must be written in English. Contest is open to writers who have previously published a book of fiction or 3 short stories (or novellas) in magazines/journals with national distribution." Catalog available on request for 3 first class stamps.

MINNESOTA INK FICTION CONTEST, Minnesota Ink, Inc., 27 Empire Dr., St. Paul MN 55103. (612)225-1306. Contact: Valerie Hockert. Previously unpublished fiction. Deadline: Dec. 31. Charges $5 fee.

NATIONAL JEWISH BOOK AWARD—FICTION, The Arete Foundation Award, 15 E. 26th St., New York NY 10010. (212)532-4949. Director: Paula G. Gottlieb. Jewish fiction (novel or short story collection). Deadline: Nov. 20.

NEGATIVE CAPABILITY SHORT FICTION CONTEST, *Negative Capability*, 62 Ridgelawn Dr. E, Mobile AL 36608-6116. (205)460-6146. Contact: Sue Walker. Estab. 1981. Previously unpublished short fiction."To recognize and support fiction writers." Deadline Dec. 1. Guidelines for #10 SASE. Reading fee $10 per story. Prize: $1,000 plus publication.

CHARLES H. AND N. MILDRED NILON EXCELLENCE IN MINORITY FICTION AWARD, University of Colorado at Boulder and Fiction Collective Two, University of Colorado, Campus Box 494, Boulder CO 80309-0494. Contact: Beth Partin. Estab. 1989. Unpublished book-length fiction, 200 pages minimum. Only mss from protected racial and ethnic minority authors will be considered.

THE FLANNERY O'CONNOR AWARD FOR SHORT FICTION, The University of Georgia Press, 330 Research Drive, Athens GA 30602-4901. (706)369-6130. Fax: (706)369-6131. Series Editor: Charles East. Editorial Assistant: Laura Sutton. Estab. 1981. Submission period: June-July 31. Charges $10 fee. Mss will not be returned. Mss must be 175-250 pages long. Authors do not have to be previously published. Send SASE for complete guidelines.

FRANK O'CONNOR PRIZE FOR FICTION, *Descant*, Texas Christian University, P.O. Box 32872, Fort Worth TX 76129-1000. (817)921-7240. Estab. 1984. An annual award for the best short story in the *Descant* volume; writer of the story receives a $500 prize given through the magazine by an anonymous donor.

‡ONE-ACT PLAYWRITING COMPETITION, Warehouse Theatre Co., Stephens College, Columbia MO 65215. (314)876-7194. Contact: Artistic Director of Warehouse Theatre. Offered annually for unpublished work. "Playwrights are encouraged to submit plays which are by, for, and about women." Deadline: Jan.1. Contest/award rules and entry forms available for SASE. Charges $8 fee. Prize: "a $200 award, and the winning manuscript will be produced by the Warehouse Theatre Co." Judged by Warehouse Theatre Company's Artistic Director and individuals of the board, staff, and Stephens faculty. "The winning playwright awards the Warehouse Theatre Company the right to produce the winning play." Playwright must be a student of graduate, undergraduate, or high school level.

EDGAR ALLAN POE AWARD, Mystery Writers of America, Inc., 17 E. 47th St., New York NY 10017. (212)888-8171. Contact: Priscilla Ridgway. Entries must be copyrighted or produced/published in the year they are submitted. Deadline: Dec. 1. Entries for the book categories are usually submitted by the publisher but may be submitted by the author or his agent.

QUARTERLY WEST NOVELLA COMPETITION, *Quarterly West*, 317 Olpin Union, University of Utah, Salt Lake City UT 84112. (801)581-3938. Estab. 1976. Award given every two years for two unpublished novellas. Send SASE for guidelines. Deadline: Dec. 31 of even-numbered years.

SIR WALTER RALEIGH AWARD, North Carolina Literary and Historical Association, 109 E. Jones St., Raleigh NC 27601-2807. (919)733-7305. Awards Coordinator: Freda Brittain. Previously published fiction by a North Carolina resident. Deadline: July 15.

‡HAROLD U. RIBALOW AWARD, Hadassah WZOA (Administered by *Hadassah Magazine*, 50 W. 58th St., New York NY 10019. Editor: Alan Tigay. Offered annually. Award for an English-language book of fiction on a Jewish theme. "Books *published* between January 1 and December 31 in a calendar year will be eligible for that year's award. The award for a given year will be made the following year." Deadline: March. Prize: $1,000. "Award is for a published book and therefore submitted by the publisher."

SEVENTEEN MAGAZINE FICTION CONTEST, 850 3rd Ave., New York NY 10022. Estab. 1948. Previously unpublished short stories from writers 13-21 years old. Deadline: April 30th. Send SASE for more information.

SFWA NEBULA AWARDS, Science-Fiction and Fantasy Writers of America, Inc., 5 Winding Brook Dr. #1B, Guilderland NY 12084-9719. Estab. 1966. Science fiction or fantasy in the categories of novel, novella, novelette and short story recommended by members.

SHORT STORY CONTEST, *Japanophile*, P.O. Box 223, Okemos MI 48864-0223. (517)669-2109. Contact: Earl Snodgrass. Annual award for unpublished short stories "that lead to a better understanding of Japanese culture. We prefer a setting in Japan and at least one Japanese and one non-Japanese character." Entry fee: $5. Deadline: Dec. 31.

JOHN SIMMONS SHORT FICTION AWARD and IOWA SHORT FICTION AWARDS, Department of English, University of Iowa. English-Philosophy Building, Iowa City IA 52242-1408. Previously unpublished fiction. Two awards and publications. Guidelines for #10 SASE. Deadline: Aug. 1-Sept. 30.

‡THE SOUTHERN REVIEW/LOUISIANA STATE UNIVERSITY SHORT FICTION AWARD, Louisiana State University, 43 Allen Hall, Baton Rouge LA 70803. (504)388-5108. Selection Committee Chairman: Jim Bennett. First collection of short stories by an American published in the US during previous year. Deadline: Jan. 31. A publisher or an author may submit an entry by mailing two copies of the collection to *The Southern Review* Short Fiction Award.

THE STAND MAGAZINE SHORT STORY COMPETITION, *Stand Magazine* and the Cheltenham Festival of Literature, 179 Wingrove Rd., Newcastle on Tyne, NE4 9DA United Kingdom. (091)-2733280. Contact: Editors of *Stand Magazine*. "This competition is an open international contest for unpublished writing in the English language intended to foster a wider interest in the short story as a literary form and to promote and encourage excellent writing in it." Deadline: March. "Please note that intending entrants enquiring from outside the U.K. should send International Reply Coupons, not stamps from their own countries. In lieu of an entry fee we ask for a minimum donation of £3.50 or $7 U.S. per story entered." Editorial inquiries should be made with SASE to: Daniel Schenker and Amanda Kay, Route #2, Box 122-B, Lacey's Spring AL 35754.

EDWARD LEWIS WALLANT BOOK AWARD, Mrs. Irving Waltman, 3 Brighton Rd., West Hartford CT 06117. Published fiction with significance for the American Jew (novel or short stories) by an American writer. Book must have been published during current year. Deadline: Dec. 31.

WASHINGTON PRIZE FOR FICTION, Larry Kaltman Literary Agency, 1301 S. Scott St., Arlington VA 22204-4656. (703)920-3771. Estab. 1989. Fiction, previously unpublished, of at least 65,000 words. Deadline: Nov. 30. Charges $25 fee. Prizes: $2,000, $1,000 and $500.

WELLSPRING'S SHORT FICTION CONTEST, 770 Tonkawa Rd., Long Lake MN 55356-9233. (612)471-9259. Contest Director: Maureen LaJoy. Estab. 1988. Contest offered twice annually for previously unpublished short fiction. "To encourage the writing of well-crafted and plotted, meaningful short fiction." Deadlines Jan. 1 and July 1. Guidelines for #10 SASE. Charges $5 fee. Prizes: $100, $75, $25.

WORLD'S BEST SHORT SHORT STORY CONTEST, English Department, Writing Program, Florida State University, Tallahassee FL 32306. (904)644-4230. Contact: Jerome Stern. Estab. 1986. Annual award for unpublished short short story (no more than 250 words). Send #10 SASE for rules. Deadline: Feb. 15. Prize $100.

WRITERS' JOURNAL ANNUAL SHORT STORY CONTEST, Minnesota Ink, Inc., 27 Empire Dr., St. Paul MN 55103. (612)225-1306. Contact: Valerie Hockert. Estab. 1987. Previously unpublished short stories. Deadline: May 31. Charges $5 per entry.

Poetry

JOHN WILLIAMS ANDREWS NARRATIVE POETRY CONTEST, *Poet Lore*, The Writer's Center, 4508 Walsh St., Bethesda MD 20815. (301)654-8664. "Annual contest for unpublished narrative poems of 100 lines or more." Deadline: November 30. Prize includes $350 and publication in *Poet Lore*. "*Poet Lore* has first publication rights for poems submitted. All rights revert to the author after publication in *Poet Lore*."

‡ANHINGA PRIZE FOR POETRY, Anhinga Press, P.O. Box 10595, Tallahassee FL 32302. (904)575-5592. Fax: (904)224-5127. Contact: Rick Campbell. Offered annually. "We publish a book-length collection of poetry by an author who has not published more than one book of poetry. We use a well-known independent judge." Manuscripts accepted Jan. 1-Mar. 15. Contest/award rules available for SASE. Charges $15 fee. Prize: $1,500 and publication. "Open to any writer writing in English."

‡ANNUAL INTERNATIONAL NARRATIVE CONTEST, Poets and Patrons, Inc., 1725 N. Patton, Arlington Hts. IL 60004. Contact: Richard Calisch. Unpublished poetry. Deadline: Sept. 1. Prizes: $75, 1st prize; $25, 2nd.

ANNUAL POETRY CONTEST, National Federation of State Poetry Societies, 3520 State Rt. 56, Mechanicsburg OH 43044. (513)834-2666. Chairman: Amy Jo Zook. Estab. 1959. Previously unpublished poetry. "There are fifty categories. Entrant must have flyer to see them all." Deadline March 15. Guidelines for #10 SASE. Charges entry fees. See guidelines for fees and prizes.

ARKANSAS POETRY AWARD, The University of Arkansas Press, 201 Ozark Ave., Fayetteville AR 72701. (501)575-3246. Fax: (501)575-6044. Award Director: Carolyn Brt. Estab. 1990. Previously unpublished full-length poetry manuscript. The purpose is to recognize living U.S. poets whose works have not been previously published or accepted for publication in book form and thus forward the Press's stated mission of "disseminating the fruits of creative activity." Deadline May 1. Guidelines for #10 SASE. Award: publication of the collection by the University of Arkansas Press.

GORDON BARBER MEMORIAL AWARD, Poetry Society of America, 15 Gramercy Park S., New York NY 10003. (212)254-9628. Contact: Award Director. "For a poem of exceptional merit or character." Send #10 SASE for guidelines. Deadline: Dec. 22. Members only. Award: $200.

GEORGE BOGIN MEMORIAL AWARD, Poetry Society of America, 15 Gramercy Park S., New York NY 10003. (212) 254-9628. Contact: Award Director. "For a selection of 4 or 5 poems that reflects the encounter of the ordinary and the extraordinary, uses language in an original way, and takes a stand against oppression in any of its forms." Send #10 SASE for guidelines. Deadline: Dec. 22. Charges $5 fee.

BRITTINGHAM PRIZE IN POETRY, University of Wisconsin Press, 114 N. Murray St., Madison WI 53715. Contest Director: Ronald Wallace. Estab. 1985. Unpublished book-length manuscript of original poetry. Submissions must be *received* by the press *during* the month of September (postmark is irrelevant) and must be accompanied by a SASE for contest results. Prize is $1,000 and publication of winning ms. Guidelines for #10 SASE. Manuscripts will *not* be returned. Charges $15 fee, payable to University of Wisconsin Press. Results in February.

‡BUCKNELL SEMINAR FOR YOUNGER POETS, Stadler Center for Poetry, Bucknell University, Lewisburg PA 17837. (717)524-1853. Contact: John Wheatcroft. Offered annually. "The Seminar provides an extended opportunity for undergraduates to write and to be guided by established poets. It balances private time for writing, disciplined learning, and camaraderie among the ten Fellows selected." Deadline: March 1. Contest/award rules available for SASE. Prize: Ten fellowships that provide tuition, room, board, and spaces for writing. Fellows are responsible for their own transportation. The Seminar is four weeks long. Only students from American colleges who have completed their sophomore, junior, or senior years are eligible to apply.

WITTER BYNNER FOUNDATION FOR POETRY, INC. GRANTS, 105 E. Marcy St. Suite 118, Santa Fe NM 87501. (505)988-3251. Executive Director: Steven D. Schwartz. Estab. 1972. Grants for poetry and poetry-related projects. Deadline: Feb. 1. Only nonprofit organizations are eligible to apply.

GERALD CABLE POETRY CHAPBOOK COMPETITION, *Silverfish Review,* P.O. Box 3541, Eugene OR 97403-0541. (503)344-5060. Editor: Rodger Moody. Previously published poems and simultaneous submissions are acceptable. All entrants will receive a copy of the winning chapbook. Purpose is to publish a poetry chapbook by a deserving author. Submit mss during Aug. and Sept. Send #10 SASE for guidelines. Reading fee $7.50. Prize: $100 and 25 copies (press run of 750).

GERTRUDE B. CLAYTOR MEMORIAL AWARD, Poetry Society of America, 15 Gramercy Park S., New York NY 10003. (212)254-9628. Contact: Award Director. Poem in any form on the American scene or character. Send #10 SASE for guidelines. Deadline: Dec. 22. Members only. Award: $250.

CLEVELAND STATE UNIVERSITY POETRY CENTER PRIZE, Cleveland State University Poetry Center, Cleveland OH 44115. (216)687-3986. Fax: (216)687-9366. Editor: Leonard Trawick. Estab. 1962. To identify, reward and publish the best unpublished book-length poetry manuscript submitted. Submissions accepted only Dec.-Feb. Deadline: Postmarked on or before March 1. Charges $10 fee. "Submission implies willingness to sign contract for publication if manuscript wins." $1,000 prize for best manuscript. Two of the other finalist manuscripts are also published for standard royalty (no prize). Send SASE for guidelines and entry form.

COLLEGIATE POETRY CONTEST, *The Lyric,* 307 Dunton Dr. SW, Blacksburg VA 24060. Editor: Leslie Mellichamp. Estab. 1921. Unpublished poems (36 lines or less) by fulltime undergraduates in U.S. or Canadian colleges. Winners receive one-time cash awards of $25 to $200. Deadline: June 1. Send #10 SASE for rules.

COMPUWRITE, The Writers Alliance, 12 Skylark Lane, Stony Brook NY 11790. Contest Director: Kiel Stuart. Estab. 1982. Previously unpublished poems. "We want an expressive, clever poem (up to 30 lines) on the act of writing with a personal computer." Deadline Jan. 15. Guidelines for #10 SASE. Charges $2 per poem. First prize: publication plus a software package with at least $100 retail value.

GUSTAV DAVIDSON MEMORIAL AWARD, Poetry Society of America, 15 Gramercy Park S., New York NY 10003. (212)254-9628. Contact: Award Director. Sonnet or sequence in traditional forms. Send #10 SASE for guidelines. Deadline: Dec. 22. Members only. Award: $500.

MARY CAROLYN DAVIES MEMORIAL AWARD, Poetry Society of America, 15 Gramercy Park S., New York NY 10003. (212)254-9628. Contact: Award Director. Unpublished poem suitable for setting to music. Send #10 SASE for guidelines. Deadline: December 22. Members only. Award: $250.

BILLEE MURRAY DENNY POETRY CONTEST, Lincoln College, 300 Keokuk St., Lincoln IL 62656. Contest Administrator: Valecia Crisafulli. Estab. 1981. Unpublished poetry. Deadline: May 31. Charges $2 fee per poem (limit 3). Enclose #10 SASE with request for entry form.

MARIE LOUISE D'ESTERNAUX POETRY CONTEST, Brooklyn Poetry Circle, #3U, 2550 Independence Ave., Bronx NY 10463. Contact: Ruth M. Fowler. "Annual contest for previously unpublished poetry. The purpose of the contest is to encourage young people to study poetry, to write poetry and to enrich themselves and others." Deadline: April 15. Send #10 SASE for contest rules. First Prize: $50; Second Prize: $25.

ALICE FAY DI CASTAGNOLA AWARD, Poetry Society of America, 15 Gramercy Park S., New York NY 10003. (212)254-9628. Contact: Award Director. Manuscript in progress: poetry, prose (on poetry) or verse-drama. Send #10 SASE for guidelines. Deadline: Dec. 22. Members only. Award: $2,000.

"DISCOVERY"/THE NATION, The Unterberg Poetry Center of the 92nd Street YM-YWHA, 1395 Lexington Ave., New York NY 10128. (212)415-5760. Estab. 1973. Open to poets who have not published a book of poems (chapbooks, self-published books included). Deadline: Early February. Write or call for competition guidelines.

THE EIGHTH MOUNTAIN POETRY PRIZE, The Eighth Mountain Press, 624 SE 29th Ave., Portland OR 97214-3026. (503)233-3936. Contact: Ruth Gundle. Estab. 1987. "Biennial prize for a book-length manuscript by a woman writer. Poems may be considered if submission is termed 'collected' or 'selected'. Award is judged by a nationally recognized woman poet." Buys all rights. Entries must be post-marked in January of even-numbered years. Guidelines for #10 SASE. $15 entry fee. Prize consists of $1,000 advance against royalties and publication in the prize series.

EVE OF ST. AGNES POETRY COMPETITION, *Negative Capability*, 62 Ridgelawn Dr. E, Mobile AL 36608-6116. (205)460-6146. Contact: Sue Walker. Estab. 1981. Previously unpublished poetry. "To recognize and support poets." Deadline Jan. 15. Guidelines for #10 SASE. Charges $3 per poem. Prize: $1,000 plus publication.

NORMA FARBER FIRST BOOK AWARD, Poetry Society of America, 15 Gramercy Park S., New York NY 10003. (212)254-9628. Contact: Award Director. Book of original poetry submitted by the publisher. Deadline: Dec. 22. Award: $1,000.

THE 49th PARALLEL POETRY CONTEST, The Signpost Press Inc., 1007 Queen St., Bellingham WA 98226. (206)734-9781. Contest Director: Knute Skinner. Estab. 1977. Unpublished poetry. Submission period: Sept. 15-Dec. 1. Charges $3/poem. Anyone submitting 3 or more poems will receive a complimentary 1-year subscription to *The Bellingham Review*. Awards: $150, first prize; $100, second prize; $50, third prize.

GROLIER POETRY PRIZE, Grolier Poetry Book Shop, Inc. & Ellen LaForge Memorial Poetry Foundation, Inc., 6 Plympton St., Cambridge MA 02138. (617)547-4648. Fax: (617)547-4230. Contact: Ms. Louisa Solano. Estab. 1973. Previously unpublished work. The primary purpose of the prize is to encourage and recognize developing writers. Open to all poets who have not published with either a vanity, small press, trade, or chapbook of poetry. Deadline: April 15. SASE for guidelines. Charges $5 fee. Prize: honorarium of $150 for two poets. Also 4 poems of each winner will be chosen for publication in the Grolier Poetry Prize Annual.

THE CHESTER H. JONES FOUNDATION NATIONAL POETRY COMPETITION, P.O. Box 498, Chardon OH 44024-9996. Estab. 1982. An annual competition for persons in the U.S., Canada and U.S. citizens living abroad. Winning poems plus others, called "commendations," are published in a chapbook available from the foundation. Deadline: March 31. Charges $2 for first poem, then $1 for each succeeding poem up to 10. Maximum 10 entries, no more than 32 lines each; must be unpublished.

THE JUNIPER PRIZE, University of Massachusetts, Amherst MA 01003. (413)545-2217. Contact: Bruce Wilcox. Estab. 1964. First book of poetry. Deadline: Sept. 30. Charges $10 fee.

LAMONT POETRY SELECTION, The Academy of American Poets, Suite 1208, 584 Broadway, New York NY 10012-3250. (212)427-5665. Award Director: Beth McCabe. Second book of unpublished poems by an American citizen, submitted by publisher in manuscript form. Deadline: April 30. Contact the Academy office for guidelines and official entry form.

THE PETER I.B. LAVAN YOUNGER POETS AWARD, The Academy of American Poets, Suite 1208, 584 Broadway, New York NY 10012. (212)274-0343. American poets 40 years old or younger who have published at least one full-length collection of poetry. Recipients are selected by the Academy's Chancellors. No applications.

ELIAS LIEBERMAN STUDENT POETRY AWARD, Poetry Society of America, 15 Gramercy Park S., New York NY 10003. (212)254-9628. Contact: Award Director. Unpublished poem by student (grades 9-12). Poet must reside in the US or its territories. Send #10 SASE for guidelines. Deadline: Dec. 22. Charges $5 fee.

THE RUTH LILLY POETRY PRIZE, The Modern Poetry Association and The American Council for the Arts, 60 W. Walton St., Chicago IL 60610-3380. Contact: Joseph Parisi. Estab. 1986. Annual prize to poet "whose accomplishments in the field of poetry warrant extraordinary recognition." No applicants or nominations are accepted. Deadline varies.

LOUISIANA LITERATURE PRIZE FOR POETRY, *Louisiana Literature*, P.O. Box 792, Southeastern Louisiana University, Hammond LA 70403. Contest Director: Dr. David Hanson. Estab. 1987. Unpublished poetry. Deadline: Feb. 15. Write for rules. Prize: $400. Entries considered for publication.

AMY LOWELL POETRY TRAVELING SCHOLARSHIP, % Choate, Hall & Stewart, Exchange Place, 35th Floor, Boston MA 02109-2891. (617)227-5020. Fax: (617)227-7566. Award Director: F. Davis Dassori, Jr., Trustee. "Annual award to support an American-born poet whose work would benefit from a year spent outside of North America." Deadline: Oct. 15. Guidelines for #10 SASE. Prize: $28,000 (amount varies as it is a portion of income of a portfolio) to be paid in quarterly installments.

THE LENORE MARSHALL/NATION PRIZE FOR POETRY, The New Hope Foundation and *The Nation* Magazine, 72 5th Ave., New York NY 10011. (212)242-8400. Administrator: Peter Meyer. Book of poems published in the United States during the previous year and nominated by the publisher. Cash award of $10,000. Deadline: June 1. Books must be submitted *directly* to judges. Query *The Nation* for addresses of judges.

MINNESOTA INK SEMI-ANNUAL POETRY CONTEST, Minnesota Ink, Inc., 27 Empire Dr., St. Paul MN 55103. (612)225-1306. Contact: Anthoney Stomski. Offered winter and summer. Unpublished poets. Deadlines: Feb. 28; Aug. 15. Charges $2 for first poem; $1 each poem thereafter.

MIRRORS INTERNATIONAL TANKA AWARD, AHA Books, P.O. Box 1250, Gualala CA 95445-1250. (707)882-2226. Editor: Jane Reichhold. Estab. 1988. "The purpose of the contest is to acquaint writers with the Japanese poetry form, tanka. By choosing 31 winners for publication in a chapbook, it is hoped that standards and examples will be set, re-evaluated, changed and enlarged. The genre is one of Japan's oldest, but the newest to English." Deadline: Nov. 30. Guidelines for #10 SASE. Maximum 10 entries: no fee. Send SASE for winners list. 31 winning entries published in *Tanka Splendor*, which is given to the winners and then goes on sale for up to 3 years by AHA Books distribution.

MISSISSIPPI VALLEY NON-PROFIT POETRY CONTEST, P.O. Box 3188, Rock Island IL 61204-3188. (309)788-8041. Director: Sue Katz. Estab. 1971. Unpublished poetry: adult general, student division, Mississippi Valley, senior citizen, religious, rhyming, humorous, haiku, history and ethnic. Deadline: Sept. 15. Charges $5 to enter contest; $3 for students. Up to 5 poems may be submitted with a limit of 50 lines per poem.

ALWAYS submit unsolicited manuscripts or queries with a self-addressed, stamped envelope (SASE) within your country or a self-addressed envelope with International Reply Coupons (IRC) purchased from the post office for other countries.

MORSE POETRY PRIZE, Northeastern University English Deptment, 406 Holmes Hall, Boston MA 02115. (617)437-2512. Contact: Guy Rotella. Previously published poetry, book-length mss. Charges $10/entry. Prize: Publication of mss by Northeastern University Press and a $500 cash award.

NATIONAL LOOKING GLASS POETRY CHAPBOOK COMPETITION, *Pudding Magazine*, 60 N. Main St., Johnstown OH 43031. (614)967-6060. Contest Director: Jennifer Bosveld. "To publish a collection of poems that represents our magazine's editorial slant: Applied Poetry. Poems might be themed or not." Deadline: June 30. Guidelines for #10 SASE. Charges $9 fee. Prize: $100 and publication of the book.

NATIONAL POETRY COMPETITION, 22 Betterton St., London WC2H 9BU England. 071-240-4810. Fax: 071-240-4818. Contest Organizer: Betty Redpath. Annual contest for unpublished poetry. Deadline: First week of November. Guidelines available for 6×9 SAE with 2 IRC's. Charges entry fee. 1st Prize £3,000; 2nd Prize; 3rd Prize plus 10 runner-up prizes. All winning poems are published in an anthology.

NATIONAL POETRY SERIES, P.O. Box G, Hopewell NJ 08525-0046. Coordinator: Tom Thompson. Estab. 1978. Annual prize for previously unpublished poetry in book form. "Our goal is to publish 5 books of poetry annually through a series of participating publishers." Open competition, Jan. 1-Feb. 15, annually. Guidelines for #10 SASE. Charges $15 fee. "Manuscripts cannot be returned." Award: book publication.

NATIONAL WRITERS CLUB POETRY CONTEST, The National Writers Club, Suite 424, 1450 S. Havana, Aurora CO 80012. (303)751-7844. Fax:(303)751-8593. Director: Sandy Whelchel. Annual contest "to encourage the writing of poetry, an important form of individual expression but with a limited commercial market." $7 entry fee. Prizes: 1st, $100, $50, $25, $15, $10. Rules and entry forms available for #10 SASE.

GUY OWEN POETRY PRIZE, *Southern Poetry Review*, English Dept. UNCC, Charlotte NC 28223. (704)547-4309. Contest/Award Director: Ken McLaurin and Lucinda Grey. Annual award for unpublished poetry. Award is given annually for the best poem submitted in an open competition. Given in memory of Guy Owen, a poet, fiction writer and founder of *Southern Poetry Review*. Submit in April only. Send SASE for guidelines. Charges $8 fee that includes one year subscription to *SPR* to begin with the fall issue, containing the winning poem. Prize: $500 and publication in *SPR*.

PANHANDLER POETRY CHAPBOOK COMPETITION, *The Panhandler Magazine*, English Dept., University of West Florida, Pensacola FL 32514-5751. (904)474-2923. Editor: Michael Yots. Estab. 1979. Individual poems may have been published. To honor excellence in the writing of short collections of poetry. Two winning manuscripts are published each year. Submit between Oct. 15 and Jan. 15. Charges $7 (includes copy of winning chapbooks).

‡PEOPLE'S VOICE POETRY CONTEST, People's Voice Press, P.O. Box 318, Allentown NJ 08501. Contact: Editor. Offered twice a year for unpublished work. Dedicated to publishing the voices of Americans (traditional and non-traditional) as they speak through the language of poetry. "We especially encourage new writers, people who would not necessarily be considered professional writers, but who love to write." Deadline: April 30, 1994; August 31, 1994. "August and April of every year." Contest/award rules for SASE. Charges $5 reading fee. Prizes: $1,000-First; $500-Second; $50-Honorable Mention(s) and publication. Judged by established poets, singer/songwriters, literary representatives and publishers throughout the country. Contest open to all writers.

PETERLOO POETS OPEN POETRY COMPETITION, 2 Kelly Gardens, Calstock, Cornwall PL18 9SA UK. Contact: Lynn Chambers. "Annual competition for new (unpublished) poetry." Deadline: March 1. Entry fee indicated on rules/entry form. Awards consist of cash prizes and publication. Sponsored by Marks & Spencer plc.

‡PN MAGAZINE 12-TONE POEM CONTEST, (formerly Elizabeth Bartlett Award), *PN Magazine*, P.O. Box 24, Zephyrhills FL 33539-0024. Editor: June Owens. For best 12-tone poem. No fee. Award $25 from Elizabeth Bartlett for single best entry, and publication in *PN Magazine*. Send SASE for guidelines.

THE POETRY CENTER BOOK AWARD, The Poetry Center, San Francisco State University, 1600 Holloway Ave., San Francisco CA 94132. (415)338-2227. Award Director: Karen Clark. Estab. 1980. Previously published books of poetry and chapbooks, appearing in year of the prize. "Prize given for an extraordinary book of American poetry." Deadline Dec. 31. Guidelines for #10 SASE. Charges $10/book. Prize: $500 and an invitation to read in The Poetry Center Reading Series.

POETRY CONTEST, The Poet Band Co., P.O. Box 2648, Newport News VA 23609-0648. (804)826-8994. Director: Arthur C. Ford. Estab. 1984. Send a maximum of 5 poems. Enclose $1.00 for reading fee. Use rhyme and non-rhyming verse. Maximum lines: 40. Prose maximum: 200-300 words. Allow 4 weeks for response. Sample copy $3. Send SASE for more information. Quarterly newsletter (*The Pen*) issued March, June, September and December.

POETRY MAGAZINE POETRY AWARDS, 60 W. Walton St., Chicago IL 60610. (312)280-4870. Editor: Joseph Parisi. Estab. 1912. All poems already published in *Poetry* during the year are automatically considered for annual prizes.

PRAIRIE SCHOONER STROUSSE AWARD, *Prairie Schooner*, 201 Andrews, University of Nebraska, Lincoln NE 68588-0334. (402)472-3191. Fax: (402)472-4636. Editor: Hilda Raz. Estab. 1977. Annual award given for the best poem or group of poems published in *Prairie Schooner*. Winner announced in the spring issue of the following year. Prize $500.

THE BYRON HERBERT REECE INTERNATIONAL POETRY AWARDS, Georgia State Poetry Society, Inc., 1590 Riderwood Court, Decatur GA 30033. (404)633-1647. Contest Director: Betty Lou Gore. Estab. 1987. Previously unpublished poetry. "To honor the late Georgia poet, Byron Herbert Reece." Deadline in January. Guidelines for #10 SASE. Charges $5 for the first poem; $1 for each additional poem. Prizes: First: $250, Second: $100, Third: $50.

ROANOKE-CHOWAN AWARD FOR POETRY, North Carolina Literary and Historical Association, 109 E. Jones St., Raleigh NC 27601-2807. (919)733-7305. Previously published poetry by a resident of North Carolina. Deadline: July 15.

NICHOLAS ROERICH POETRY PRIZE, Story Line Press, Three Oaks Farm, Brownsville OR 97327-9718. (503)466-5352. Contact: Joseph Bednarik. First full-length book of poetry. Any writer who has not published a full-length collection of poetry (48 pages or more) in English is eligible to apply. Deadline: Oct. 15. Charges $15 fee.

SNAKE NATION PRESS'S ANNUAL POETRY CONTEST, Snake Nation Press, 110 #2 W. Force St., Valdosta GA 31601. (912)219-8334. Contest Director: Roberta George. Annual contest. Purpose is to give a wider audience to readable, understandable poetry. Deadline: Sept. 1. Rules for #10 SASE. Charges $10 fee. Prize consists of $500, 20 copies and distribution. Open to everyone.

EDWARD STANLEY AWARD, *Prairie Schooner*, 201 Andrews, University of Nebraska, Lincoln NE 68588-0334. (402)472-3191. Fax: (402)472-4636. Editor: Hilda Raz. Annual award for poems published in *Prairie Schooner*. Winner announced in the spring issue of the following year. Prize: $300.

THE AGNES LYNCH STARRETT POETRY PRIZE, University of Pittsburgh Press, 127 N. Bellefield Ave., Pittsburgh PA 15260. (412)624-4111. Fax: (412)624-7380. Series Editor: Ed Ochester. Estab. 1936. First book of poetry for poets who have not had a full-length book published. Deadline: March and April only. Write for complete guidelines for manuscript submission.

ELIZABETH MATCHETT STOVER MEMORIAL AWARD, *Southwest Review*, 307 Fondren Library W., P.O. Box 374, SMU, Dallas TX 75275-0374. (214)373-7440. For the best poem or group of poems that appeared in the magazine during the previous year.

TROIKA COMPETITION, (formerly Goodman Award), Thorntree Press, 547 Hawthorn Ln., Winnetka IL 60093. (708)446-8099. Contact: Eloise Bradley Fink. Estab. 1985. Imagery is important. Mss considered Jan. 1-Feb. 14, in *odd-numbered years*. "We will be selecting three poets for our next *Troika*. Contestants are asked to submit a stapled group of ten pages of *un*published poetry, single or double spaced, photocopied, with a $4 reader's fee. Manuscripts will not be returned."

DANIEL VAROUJAN AWARD, New England Poetry Club, Box 308, Sudbury MA 01776. Contact: Diana DerHovanessian. Unpublished poems in duplicate. Send SASE for rules. Deadline: June 30. Annually. Charges $2 per poem; no charge for New England Poetry Club members and students. $500 for a poem in any form, not a translation. Worthy of Daniel Varoujan, Armenian poet killed by the Turks in the 1915 genocide.

VERVE POETRY CONTEST, *VERVE* Magazine, P.O. Box 3205, Simi Valley CA 93093. Contest Director: Ron Reichick. Estab. 1989. Contest offered three times annually for previously unpublished poetry. "Fund raiser for *VERVE* Magazine which receives no grants and has no ties with any institutions." Deadlines: March 1, July 1 and Nov. 1. Guidelines for #10 SASE. Charges $2 per poem. Prizes: First, $100; Second $50; Third $25; (plus publication and copy of issue).

WILLIAM CARLOS WILLIAMS AWARD, Poetry Society of America, 15 Gramercy Park S., New York NY 10003. (212)254-9628. Contact: Award Director. Small press, nonprofit, or university press book of poetry submitted by publisher. Deadline: Dec. 22. Award: $1,250.

ROBERT H. WINNER MEMORIAL AWARD, Poetry Society of America, 15 Gramercy Park S., New York NY 10003. (212)254-9628. Contact: Award Director. "For a poet whose first book appeared when he was almost 50, recognizing and rewarding the work of someone in midlife. Open to poets over 40, still unpublished or with one book." Send #10 SASE for guidelines. Charges $5 fee. Deadline: Dec. 22. Award: $2,500.

WINTER POETRY COMPETITION, Still Waters Press, 112 W. Duerer St., Galloway Township NJ 08201-9402. Contest Director: Shirley A. Warren. Guidelines for #10 SASE. Charges $10 fee. Deadline: Sept. 30.

ZUZU'S PETALS POETRY CONTEST, *Zuzu's Petals Quarterly*, P.O. Box 4476, Allentown PA 18105-4476. (215)821-1324. Editor: T. Dunn. Contest offered 4 times per year for previously unpublished poetry. Deadlines: March 1, June 1, Sept. 1, Dec. 1. Guidelines for #10 SASE. Charges $1 per poem. Prize: top 3 winners share 40% of "Zuzu's" proceeds. All entries are automatically considered for publication.

Playwriting and Scriptwriting

‡**ANNUAL ONE ACT PLAYWRITING COMPETITION,** The Little Theatre of Alexandria, 600 Wolf St., Alexandria VA 22314. (703)683-5778. Chairman: Anne Flinn. Offered annually for unpublished work. Purpose is "to encourage playwrights to submit original work for review and evaluation to determine the three top winners." Deadline: March 31. Guidelines for SASE. Prize: 1st $350, 2nd $250, 3rd $150. Judged by "an experienced committee of readers, competent to review the literary value of the play." Submit scripts after Nov. 2.

‡**ASIAN AMERICAN PLAYWRIGHTS' CONTEST,** Northwest Asian American Theatre, 409 7th Ave. S., Seattle WA 98104. (206)340-1445. Offered annually for unpublished work. "The purpose of the award is to encourage Asian American playwrights and playwrights of Asian American themes to develop their craft. The 'theme' of each year's contest varies. Past years have included Asian American comedies, one-acts and shows for youth. Works must never have had a full production." Deadline: Feb. 15, 1994. Annual deadline "varies slightly depending on the panelists' time frame." Contest/award rules and entry forms available for SASE. Prize: a cash award and a workshop production. Judged by a local panel of theater artists and staff. "If a play is chosen as the winner, the theater gets a one-year option on the rights to give the play its world premiere." Contest is open to any writer. "The only criteria is that the themes must be relevant to Asian Americans if the playwright is not Asian American and the work must never have been fully produced before."

THE BEVERLY HILLS THEATRE GUILD-JULIE HARRIS PLAYWRIGHT AWARD COMPETITION, 2815 N. Beachwood Drive, Los Angeles CA 90068. (213)465-2703. Playwright Award Coordinator: Marcella Meharg. Estab. 1978. Original full-length plays, unpublished, unproduced and not currently under option. Application required, available upon request with SASE. Submissions accepted with applications from August 1 thru annual deadline of Nov. 1.

CALIFORNIA PLAYWRIGHTS COMPETITION, South Coast Repertory, P.O. Box 2197, Costa Mesa CA 92628. (714)957-2602. Contact: John Glore. Estab. 1988. Previously unpublished and unproduced submissions. Deadline: TBA. Guidelines and application form available after September 1; writers must phone or write for complete guidelines and application form. Prize: $5,000 first prize; $3,000 second prize. "Writer must maintain principal residence in California."

CALIFORNIA YOUNG PLAYWRIGHTS CONTEST, The Playwright Project, Suite 215, 1450 Frazee Rd., San Diego CA 92108. (619)298-9242. Contest/Award Director: Deborah Salzer. Annual contest for previously unpublished plays by young writers. Purpose is "to stimulate young people to create dramatic works, and to nurture promising young writers (under age 19)." Deadline: April 1. Send 9 × 12 SASE for contest rules and entry forms. Award consists of "professional production of 3-5 winning plays at the Old Globe Theatre in San Diego, plus royalty. All entrants receive detailed evaluation letter." Judged by theater professionals in the Southern California area. "Scripts must be a minimum of 10 standard typewritten pages. Writers must be California residents under age 19 as of the deadline date."

CEC JACKIE WHITE MEMORIAL NATIONAL CHILDREN'S PLAYWRITING CONTEST, Columbia Entertainment Company, 309 Parkade Blvd., Columbia MO 65202. (314)874-5628. Contact: Betsy Phillips. Estab. 1988. Annual award for "top notch unpublished scripts for theater school use, to challenge and expand the talents of our students, ages 10-15. The entry should be a full length play with speaking roles for 20 to 30 characters of all ages and with at least 10 roles developed in some detail." Deadline: June 30. Production and some travel expenses for 1st and 2nd place winners, plus cash award for 1st place. Send SASE for full guidelines. Entrants receive written evaluation of work. $10 registration fee.

CELEBRATION OF ONE-ACTS, West Coast Ensemble, P.O. Box 38728, Los Angeles CA 90038-5306. Artistic Director: Les Hanson. Estab. 1984. Unpublished (in Southern California) one-act plays. Deadline: Nov. 15. "Up to 3 submissions allowed for each playwright." Casts should be no more than 6 and plays no longer than 35 minutes.

JANE CHAMBERS PLAYWRITING AWARD, Women and Theatre Program of Association for Theatre in Higher Education (WTP/ATHE). c/o Tori Haring-Smith, English Dept., Box 1852, Brown University, Providence RI 02912. Director: Tori Haring-Smith. Estab. 1983. "Purpose is to recognize a woman playwright who has written a play with a feminist perspective, a majority of roles for women, and which experiments with the dramatic form." Deadline: Feb. 15. Rules available for #10 SASE. Award is $1,000, plus travel expenses, and reading at the WTP/ATHE national conference in August. Student award is $100. "Writer must be female. A recommendation from a theatre professional is helpful, but not required."

‡**CLEVELAND PUBLIC THEATRE FESTIVAL OF NEW PLAYS**, Cleveland Public Theatre, 6415 Detroit Ave., Cleveland OH 44102. (216)631-2727. Contest/Award Director: James A. Levin. Annual festival that recognizes new, previously unpublished playwrights. Charges $10 reading fee. Deadline: Sept. 30.

‡**COE COLLEGE PLAYWRITING FESTIVAL**, Coe College, 1220 1st Ave. NE., Cedar Rapids IA 52402. (319)399-8689. Contact: Susan Wolverton. Offered every 2 years for unpublished work. Next festival: 94-95. Purpose is "to provide a venue for new works for the stage. There is usually a theme for the festival. We are interested in full length productions, *not* one acts or musicals." Contest/award rules and entry forms available for SASE. Prize: "$325, plus one-week residency as guest artist with airfare, room and board provided." Judges are a select committee of professionals. "There are no specific criteria although a current resume is requested."

THE CHRISTOPHER COLUMBUS SCREENPLAY DISCOVERY AWARDS, #600, 433 N. Camden Dr., Beverly Hills CA 90210. (310)288-1988. Fax: (310)475-0193. Monthly and annual contest. Purpose is "to discover new screenplay writers." Deadline: Dec. 1. $45 entry fee. Prize consists of "options up to $10,000, plus professional development guidance and access to agents, producers, and studios." Judged by reputable industry professionals (producers, development executives, story analysts). Writer must give option to purchase if selected.

‡**CUNNINGHAM PRIZE FOR PLAYWRITING**, The Theatre School, DePaul University, 2135 N. Kenmore, Chicago IL 60614. (312)362-6150. Fax: (312)362-5453. Contact: Lisa A. Quinn. Offered annually for either previously published or unpublished work. Purpose is "to recognize and encourage the writing of dramatic works which affirm the centrality of religion, broadly defined, and the human quest for meaning, truth and community." Deadline: Sept. 1. Contest/award rules and entry forms available for SASE. Prize: $5,000. Judged by "a panel of distinguised citizens including members of the faculty of DePaul University, representatives of the Cunningham Prize Advisory Commitee, critics and others from the theater professions, charied by John Ransford Watts, dean of the Theater School." Open to writers whose usual residence or base of operations is in the Chicago area.

DAYTON PLAYHOUSE FUTURE FEST, The Dayton Playhouse, 1301 E. Siebenthaler Ave., Dayton OH 45414. (513)277-0144. Managing Director: Jim Payne. "3 plays selected for full productions, 3 for readings at July 1994 Future Fest weekend; possible travel, room and board to attend rehearsals; judges view full productions and select winners of $1,000 1st prize, $500 for two runner-ups." Send SASE for guidelines. Deadline: Sept. 30.

DRURY COLLEGE ONE-ACT PLAY CONTEST, Drury College, 900 N. Benton Ave., Springfield MO 65802-3344. (417)865-8731. Contact: Sandy Asher. Estab. 1986. Contest is offered every two years, even years only. Plays must be unpublished and professionally unproduced. One play per playwright. Deadline: Dec. 1. Send SASE for complete guidelines. Winning plays receive special recommendation to The Open Eye: New Stagings, an off-Broadway theater in New York City.

EMERGING PLAYWRIGHT AWARD, Playwrights Preview Productions, 1160 5th Ave. #304, New York NY 10029. (212)289-2168. Contact: David Sheppard. Submissions required to be unpublished. Awards are announced in the spring/fall. Submissions accepted year-round.

‡**FAMILY ONE-ACT PLAY FESTIVAL**, Theatre With A Message/Last Minute Productions, P.O. Box 22551, Nashville TN 37202. (615)780-3777. Fax: (615)758-3399. Contact: Don Breedwell. Offered annually for unpublished work. Purpose is "promoting/encouraging family-oriented entertainment using theater. Musicals, dramas or comedies are welcomed!" Deadline: Feb. 1. Contest/award rules and entry forms available for SASE. Cash Award: 1st $250; 2nd $150; 3rd $100; possible production. Judged by "panel of judges selected

annually from nationwide venues." Winner must grant performance rights for 6 months from awards date, plus must be identified as winner in contest for 5 years. "Any writer/playwright who meets the entry criteria is eligible."

‡FMCT'S BIENNIAL PLAYWRIGHTS COMPETITION (MID-WEST), Fargo-Moorhead Community Theatre, P.O. Box 644, Fargo ND 58107-0644. (701)235-1901. Contact: Bruce Tinker. Estab. 1988. Contest offered every two years (next contest will be held 1993-94). Submissions required to be unpublished. Deadline: July 1.

FUND FOR NEW AMERICAN PLAYS, J.F. Kennedy Ctr., American Express & President's Committee on Arts & Humanities, % Kennedy Center, Washington DC 20566. (202)416-8024. Fax: (202)416-8026. Program Director: Sophy Burnham. Previously unproduced work. "Program objectives: to encourage playwrights to write, and nonprofit professional theaters to produce, new American plays; to ease the financial burdens of nonprofit professional theater organizations producing new plays; to provide a playwright with a better production of the play than the producing theater would normally be able to accomplish." Deadline: April 1 (date changes from year to year). "Writers or nonprofit theater organizations can mail in name and address to be placed on the mailing list." Prize: $10,000 for playwrights and grants to theaters according to need. A few encouragement grants of $2,500 are given to promising playwrights at the discretion of the FUND. Applications only through the producing theater.

JOHN GASSNER MEMORIAL PLAYWRITING AWARD, The New England Theatre Conference, Dept. of Theatre, 337 Ryder Hall, Northeastern University, 360 Huntington Ave., Boston MA 02115. (617)424-9275. Estab. 1952. Unpublished one-act plays. Guidelines for #10 SASE. Deadline: April 15. Charges $10 fee; free for members of New England Theatre Conference.

‡GEVA PLAYWRIGHTS AWARD, GeVa Theatre, 75 Woodbury Blvd., Rochester NY 14607. (716)232-1366. Fax: (716)232-4031. Festival Director: Anthony Zerbe. Award estab. 1990. Offered annually for plays which have not been professionally produced. "REFLECTIONS A New Plays Festival is produced as the sixth and final production of the GeVa Theatre season. Three American world premieres are presented in rotating repertory." The submissions deadline is subject to the GeVa Calendar which varies year to year. "If the play has not been professionally produced, the playwright should send the script with a SASE to: REFLECTIONS '94 A New Plays Festival, at the GeVa address." Prize: $5,000 plus royalties. "As long as the play has not had a professional production any writer can submit his or her play. Works that have had professional readings or workshops are eligible."

‡GREAT PLATTE RIVER PLAYWRIGHTS FESTIVAL, University of Nebraska at Kearney, Theatre Department, 905 W. 25th St., Kearney NE 68849. (308)234-8406. Fax: (308)234-8157. Contact: Charles Davies. Unpublished submissions. "Purpose of award is to develop original dramas and encourage playwrights to work in regional settings. There are five catagories: 1) Adult; 2) Youth (Adolescent); 3) Children's; 4) Musical Theater; 5) Native American. Entries may be drama or comedy." Deadline: March 15. Awards: $500-First, $300-Second, $200-Third, plus free lodging and a travel stipend. "The Festival reserves the rights to development and premiere production of the winning plays without payment of royalties." Contest open to entry by any writer "provided that the writer submits playscripts to be performed on stage—works in progress also acceptable. Works involving the Great Plains will be most favored. More than one entry may be submitted."

HENRICO THEATRE COMPANY ONE-ACT PLAYWRITING COMPETITION, Henrico Theatre Company, P.O. Box 27032, Richmond VA 23273. (804)672-5100. Fax: (804)672-5284. Contest/Award Director: J. Larkin Brown. Annual competition for previously unpublished plays. Purpose is "to produce new dramatic works in one-act form. Award also for plays/musicals with a Christmas theme." Deadline: Sept. 15. Send SASE for rules and entry forms. Prizes are: One Act $250; Runner up $125; Christmas Show $250. All winning entries are produced; videotape sent to author. Judged by H.T.C. Playreading Committee. "Scripts with small casts and simpler sets given preference. Controversial themes should be avoided."

‡HIGH SCHOOL PLAYWRITING CONTEST, Baker's Plays, 100 Chauncy St., Boston MA 02111. (617)482-1280. Fax: (617)482-7613. Contest Director: Raymond Pape. Annual contest for previously unpublished plays. "We must continue to commit ourselves to the future of American Theater by encouraging and supporting those who are its cornerstone: young playwrights." Deadline is usually the last week of January. Guidelines for #10 SASE. Prizes: 1st place: $500, and the play will be published under *Best Plays from the High School* series by Baker's Plays; 2nd place: $250 and an Honorable Mention; Third place: $100 and an Honorable Mention. "Open to any high school student. Plays must be accompanied by the signature of a sponsoring high school drama or English teacher, and it is recommended that the play receive a production or a public reading prior to the submission."

INNER CITY CULTURAL CENTER'S NATIONAL SHORT PLAY COMPETITION, Inner City Cultural Center, 1605 N. Ivar St., Los Angeles CA 90028. (213)962-2102. Contact: C. Bernard Jackson. Offered annually. Submissions to be unpublished. Deadline: June. Charges $35. "All entries are presented live before an audience and jurors who are professionals in the arts and entertainment industry. Writer is responsible for preparation of submission for presentation."

JEWEL BOX THEATRE PLAYWRIGHTING COMPETITION, Jewel Box Theatre, 3700 N. Walker, Oklahoma City OK 73118-7099. (405)521-1786. Contact: Charles Tweed. Only two or three acts accepted. Deadline: Jan. 15. Prize: $500.

MARC A. KLEIN PLAYWRITING AWARD FOR STUDENTS, Department of Theater Arts, Case Western Reserve University, 10900 Euclid Ave., Cleveland OH 44106-7077. (216)368-2858. Chair, Reading Committee: John Orlock. Estab. 1975. Unpublished, professionally unproduced full-length play, or substantial one-act play by student in American college or university. Deadline: May 15.

LEE KORF PLAYWRITING AWARDS, The Original Theatre Works, Cerritos College, 11110 Alondra, Norwalk CA 90650. (310)924-2100. Fax: (310)860-9680. Contact: Gloria Manriquez. Estab. 1984. Award for previously published or unpublished plays. Deadline: Jan. 1. "All plays—no special criteria—theater pieces, musicals." $750 royalty award and full-scale production during summer theater.

KUMU KAHUA/UHM THEATRE DEPARTMENT PLAYWRITING CONTEST, Kumu Kahua/UHM Theatre Dept., 1770 East-West Rd., Honolulu HI 96822. (808)956-7677. Contact: Dennis Carroll. Annual award for unpublished plays in two divisions: one for Hawaiian themes, one for residents of Hawaii only. Deadline: Jan. 1.

LOVE CREEK ANNUAL SHORT PLAY FESTIVAL, Love Creek Productions, % Granville, 47 El Dorado Place, Weehawken NJ 07087-7004. Festival Manager: Cynthia Granville. Annual festival for unpublished plays, unproduced in New York in the previous year. "We believe that a script is incomplete as a work of art until it is performed. As an encouragement to playwrights and an enrichment opportunity for Love Creek's over 150 member artists, administrators and technicians, we have therefore established the Festival as a playwriting competition in which scripts are judged on their merits in performance." Deadline: Sept. 30. Guidelines for #10 SASE. "Finalists receive a mini-showcase production in New York City—winner receives $300 prize."

LOVE CREEK MINI FESTIVALS, Love Creek Productions, % Granville, 47 El Dorado Place, Weehawken NJ 07087-7004. Festival Literary Manager: Cynthia Granville. "The Mini Festivals are an outgrowth of our annual Short Play Festival in which we produce scripts concerning a particular issue or theme which our artistic staff selects according to current needs, interests and concerns of both our members and playwrights submitting to our Short Play Festival throughout the year." Guidelines for #10 SASE. Finalists receive a mini-showcase production in New York City. Winner receives a $200 prize. Upcoming theme is Gay and Lesbian Perspectives. Deadline: Sept. 30.

DENNIS McINTYRE PLAYWRITING AWARD, Philadelphia Festival Theatre for New Plays, 3900 Chestnut St., Philadelphia PA 19104-3105. (215)222-5000. Literary Manager: Michael Hollinger. Annual award for previously unproduced plays. Purpose is "to encourage emerging playwrights of conscience examining society's ills with honest scrutiny." Deadline: ongoing. No longer accepts unsolicited scripts. Submit synopsis, resumé and 10 pages of sample dialogue with query. Prize includes production or staged reading plus cash prize (determined annually), plus residency during rehearsal period.

McLAREN MEMORIAL COMEDY PLAYWRITING COMPETITION, Midland Community Theatre, 2000 W. Wadley, Midland TX 79705. (915)682-2544. Fax: (915)682-6136. Contact: Mary Lou Cassidy. Estab. 1946. Contest offered annually for unpublished work. "Entry must be a comedy. Can be one- or two-act. Number of characters or subject is not limited. Make us laugh." Deadline: Jan. 31. Entry fee: $5. Rules and entry form for #10 SASE. Prize: $400, Reader's Theatre Performance, airfare and hotel for 1 week rehearsal and performance.

MAXIM MAZUMDAR NEW PLAY COMPETITION, Alleyway Theatre, One Curtain Up Alley, Buffalo NY 14202-1911. (716)852-2266. Dramaturg: Joyce Stilson. Annual competition. Full Length—not less than 90 minutes, no more than 10 performers. One-Act—less than 60 minutes, no more than 6 performers. Deadline: Sept. 1. Finalists announced Jan. 1. "Playwrights may submit work directly. There is no entry form. Annual playwright's fee is $5. Please specify if submission is to be included in competition." Prizes: full length—$400, travel plus lodging, production and royalties; one-act—$100, production plus royalties. "Alleyway Theatre must receive first production credit in subsequent printings and productions."

MID-SOUTH PLAYWRIGHT CONTEST, Playhouse on the Square, 51 S. Cooper, Memphis TN 38104. Contact: Jackie Nichols. Submissions required to be unproduced. Deadline: April 1. Contest/award rules and entry forms for SASE. Prize: $500 plus production. "Playwrights from the South will be given preference. South is defined as the following states: Alabama, Arkansas, Florida, Georgia, Kentucky, Louisiana, Mississippi, Missouri, North Carolina, South Carolina, Tennessee, Texas, Virginia and West Virginia. This means we will read all shows and when final decisions are made, every other aspect of the play being equal, will name a Southern author."

MILL MOUNTAIN THEATRE NEW PLAY COMPETITION, Mill Mountain Theatre, Center in the Square, 1 Market Sq., Roanoke VA 24011-1437. (703)342-5730. Literary Manager: Jo Weinstein. Estab. 1985. Previously unpublished and unproduced plays for up to 10 cast members. Deadline: Jan. 1. Send SASE for guidelines.

MINORITY SCREENWRITERS DEVELOPMENT AND PROMOTIONAL PROGRAM, Writers Workshop, P.O. Box 69799, Los Angeles CA 90069-0799. (213)933-9232. Fax: (213)933-7642. Founder/Director: Willard Rodgers. Estab. 1990. Previously unproduced scripts. "To bring ethnic minority writers to the attention of the motion picture industry, where they are severely under represented." Deadline varies. Guidelines for #10 SASE. Charges $25 fee. Prize: $500 and exposure to the motion picture industry.

MIXED BLOOD VERSUS AMERICA, Mixed Blood Theatre Company, 1501 S. 4th St., Minneapolis MN 55454. (612)338-0984. Contact: David B. Kunz. Estab. 1983. Theater Co. estab. 1975. "Mixed Blood Versus America encourages and seeks out the emerging playwright. Mixed Blood is not necessarily looking for scripts that have multi-racial casts, rather good scripts that will be cast with the best actors available." Open to all playwrights who have had at least one of their works produced or workshopped (either professionally or educationally). Only unpublished, unproduced plays are eligible for contest. Limit two submissions per playwright. No translations or adaptations. Send SASE for guidelines. Deadline: March 15, 1994.

MRTW ANNUAL RADIO SCRIPT CONTEST, Midwest Radio Theatre Workshop, 915 E. Broadway, Columbia MO 65201. (314)874-5676. Contact: Diane Huneke. Estab. 1979. "The purpose of the award is to encourage the writing of radio scripts and to showcase both established and emerging radio playwrights. Some winning works are produced for radio and all winning works are published in the annual MRTW Scriptbook. Our scriptbook is the only one of it's kind in this country." Deadline: Nov. 15. Rules and entry form for SASE. "A cash award of $800 is split among the top 2-4 entries, depending on recommendation of the jurors. Winners receive free workshop registration. Those who receive honorable mention, as well as award-winning plays, are included in the scriptbook; a total of 10-16 are published annually. We acquire the right to publish the script in the scriptbook, which is distributed at cost, and the right to produce the script for air; all other rights retained by the author."

MULTICULTURAL THEATRE WORKS SERIES, (formerly Multicultural Playwrights Festival), Seattle Group Theatre, 305 Harrison St., Seattle WA 98109. (206)441-9480. Estab. 1984. Related one-act, full-length translations, adaptations and plays for young audiences. Musicals are not eligible. "New works, by culturally diverse playwrights, focusing on contemporary social, political and cultural issues relevant to the world community. Submission packet should include query, sample pages of dialogue, synopsis and an SASE for reply. Full manuscript submitted by solicitation only." Honorarium, airfare and housing. Submission period: ongoing.

NATIONAL ONE-ACT PLAYWRITING COMPETITION, Little Theatre of Alexandria, 600 Wolfe St., Alexandria VA 22314. (703)683-5778. Contact: Chairman Playreading Committee. Estab. 1978. To encourage original writing for theatre. Submissions must be original, unpublished, unproduced one-act stage plays. Deadline: March 31. Send SASE for guidelines. Prize: $350 first; $250 second; $150 third.

NATIONAL PLAY AWARD, National Repertory Theatre Foundation, Suite 405, 630 N. Grand Ave., Los Angeles CA 90012. Contact: Michael Dewell. Offered every two years. "Award is for unproduced original full-length play—no translations, adaptations, musicals." Send SASE for guidelines. Prize: $7,500 grant to writer.

NATIONAL PLAYWRIGHTS' AWARD, Unicorn Theatre, 3820 Main St., Kansas City MO 64111. (816)531-7529. Literary Manager: Lisa J. Church. Offered annually for previously unproduced work. "We produce contemporary original scripts, preferring scripts that deal with social concerns. However, we accept (and have produced) comedies." Send SASE for guidelines. Prize: $1,000 in royalty/prize fee and a mainstage production at the Unicorn as part of its regular season.

NATIONAL TEN-MINUTE PLAY CONTEST, Actors Theatre of Louisville, 316 W. Main St., Louisville KY 40202-4218. (502)584-1265. Literary Manager: Michael Bigelow Dixon. Estab. 1989. Previously unproduced (professionally) ten-minute plays (10 pages or less). "Entries must *not* have had an Equity or Equity-waiver production." Deadline: Dec. 1.

NEW AMERICAN COMEDY FESTIVAL, Ukiah Players Theatre, 1041 Low Gap Rd., Ukiah CA 95482-3766. (707)462-1210. Contact: Catherine Babcock Magruder. Estab. 1988. Offered every two years. "NAC seeks to develop unpublished, unproduced full-length comedies. It is a 2-week workshop for two 'winning' playwrights who come to Ukiah to rework their plays with Ukiah Players Theatre directors and guest dramaturg as local actors rehearse them daily. Both plays are given staged readings at the Ukiah Playhouse for two weekends. Playwrights must be interested in and willing to *develop* their plays during festival." Send SASE for rules and entry forms. $500 cash award. Playwrights provided with travel (up to $400), and $25 per day as well as housing. Entries are judged by a core group of Ukiah Players Theatre directors and tech staff as well as NAC's guest dramaturg. Deadline: Dec. 31.

NEW PLAY COMPETITION, Contemporary Arts Center, P.O. Box 30498, New Orleans LA 70190-3908. (504)523-1216. Fax: (504)528-3828. Contact: Theater Manager. Estab. 1986. Plays may not have had a professional production. Annual competition "to discover previously unproduced dramatic material. Play may have been workshopped or staged in an amateur production or reading. Previously submitted, ineligible, unless significantly changed. Writers must be resident of Alabama, Arkansas, Georgia, Louisiana or Mississippi. Full-length only. Limit two scripts per writer. Deadline: Nov. 1. Rules and entry form available for SASE. Prizes: $500 first; staged reading of first, second and third. Judged by "independent professional juror."

NEW PLAY GRANT, Women in Theatre, P.O. Box 3718, Hollywood CA 90078. (213)465-5567. Award Director: Sally Shore. "Annual grant to encourage the production of new plays written by emerging female playwrights." Deadline: November. Award: $1,000. "Contest is open to producing theaters, theater groups or independent producers planning a Los Angeles production of the work. Playwrights *cannot* apply directly."

NEW PLAYWRIGHTS COMPETITION, The Ann White Theatre, 5266 Gate Lake Road, Ft. Lauderdale FL 33319. (305)722-4371. Director: Ann White. Annual award for previously unpublished full-length play scripts. Award: $500 and production by the Ann White Theatre. Competition opens Aug. 1. Deadline Nov. 15.

NEW WORKS COMPETITION, Ferndale Repertory Theatre, P.O. Box 892, Ferndale CA 95536-0892. (707)725-4636. Artistic Director: Clinton Rebik. Annual competition for unpublished plays. Purpose is "to encourage the development of new theatrical scripts; and to showcase the talents of these artists in production." Deadline: Oct. 15. Send SASE for rules and entry guidelines. "Prize is $250 royalty for 8 performances; plus a set of all publicity and promotional materials and photos." Theater has rights for first eight performances (and will reimburse $250 for privilege); all subsequent rights revert to author.

DON AND GEE NICHOLL FELLOWSHIPS IN SCREENWRITING, Academy of Motion Picture Arts & Sciences, 8949 Wilshire Blvd., Beverly Hills CA 90211-1972. (310)247-3059. Director: Greg Beal. Estab. 1985. Unproduced screenplays; up to five $25,000 fellowships awarded each year. Deadline: May 1. Charges $25 fee. Send SASE for application form.

‡OFF-OFF-BROADWAY ORIGINAL SHORT PLAY FESTIVAL, Love Creek Productions, 21-44 45th Ave., 04, Long Island City NY 11101. Contact: William Talbot. Offered annually for unpublished work. "The Festival was developed in 1976 to bolster those theater companies and schools who offer workshops, programs and instruction in playwriting. It proposes to encourage them by offering them and their playwrights the opportunity of having their plays seen by new audiences and critics, and of having them reviewed for publication." Deadline: March/April. Contest/award rules and entry forms available for SASE. Work must be nominated by a theater, school or workshop. Prize: "Presentation on NY stage before NY audiences and critics. Publication of selected plays by Samuel French Inc." Judged by members of NYC critics' circles. "No individual writer may enter on his/her own initiative. Entries must come from theater companies, professional schools or colleges which foster playwriting by conducting classes, workshops or similar programs of assistance to playwrights."

OGLEBAY INSTITUTE TOWNGATE THEATRE PLAYWRITING CONTEST, Oglebay Institute, Oglebay Park, Wheeling WV 26003. (304)242-4200. Fax: (304)242-4203. Annual contest for unpublished works. Deadline: Jan. 1. Contest rules and entry form for SASE. Prize: $300, limited-run production of play. "All full-length *non-musical* plays that have never been professionally produced or published are eligible."

‡ONE-ACT FAMILY PLAY FESTIVAL, Last Minute Productions/Theatre With A Message, P.O. Box 22551, Nashville TN 37202. (615)780-3777. Fax: (615)758-3399. Contact: Don Breedwell. Offered annually for unpublished work. "Family oriented material, medium cast, running 45 minutes or less, simple sets." Deadline: Feb. 1st. Contest/award rules and entry forms available for SASE. Prizes: 1st $250; 2nd $150; 3rd $100; plus production at Festival in August. "All writers are encouraged. Material must be for and about family."

‡ORIGINAL PLAYWRITING AWARD COMPETITION, Theatre Dept. of Elmira College, Elmira NY 14901. (607)735-1981. Contact: Prof. Amnon Kabatchnik. Offered every two years for unpublished work. Purpose is "to encourage the development of quality plays for the theater. Also provides students with the opportunity to mount an original work." Deadline: June 1. "The contest is offered every two years; therefore, the deadline date is June 1 of every other year, the next deadline being 1994." Contest/award rules and entry forms available for SASE. Prize: $1,000 cash and a full-scale production at Elmira College. Judged by screening committee headed by Amnon Kabatchnik, Artistic Director of Elmira College Theatre Department. "With the exception of a World Premiere Production at Elmira College, no other rights are acquired." Open to any writer.

‡ROBERT J. PICKERING AWARD FOR PLAYWRIGHTING EXCELLENCE, Coldwater Community Theater, % 89 Division, Coldwater MI 49036. (517)279-7963. Committee Chairperson: J. Richard Colbeck. Previously unproduced monetarily. "To encourage playwrights to submit their work, to present a previously unproduced play in full production." Deadline: end of year. Guidelines for #10 SASE. Prize: 1st prize, $200, 2nd prize $50, 3rd prize, $25. "We reserve right to produce winning manuscript."

‡PLAYWRIGHTING FELLOWSHIP, Women in Theatre, P.O. Box 3718, Hollywood CA 90078. (213)465-5567. Contact: Sally Shore. Annual contest for unpublished plays "to promote women playwrights." Deadline: Mar. 31. Rules and entry forms for SASE. Charges $10 for members, $25 for non-members. Prize: $300 fellowship, celebrity staged reading. "Open to women playwrights only. Must be full-length play, not previously produced."

PLAYWRIGHTS' CENTER JEROME PLAYWRIGHT-IN-RESIDENCE FELLOWSHIP, The Playwrights' Center, 2301 Franklin Ave. E, Minneapolis MN 55406. (612)332-7481. Estab. 1976. To provide emerging playwrights with funds and services to aid them in the development of their craft. Deadline: Nov. 7, 1994. Open to playwrights only—may not have had more than 2 different fully staged productions of their works by professional theaters. Must spend fellowship year in Minnesota at Playwrights' Center. US citizens only.

PLAYWRIGHTS' CENTER McKNIGHT FELLOWSHIP, The Playwrights' Center, 2301 Franklin Ave. E, Minneapolis MN 55406. (612)332-7481. Estab. 1982. Recognition of playwrights whose work has made a significant impact on the contemporary theater. Deadline: Dec. 15. Open to playwrights only. Must have had a minimum of two different fully staged productions by professional theaters. Must spend 1 month at Playwrights' Center. US citizens or permanent residents only.

THE PLAYWRIGHTS' CENTER PLAYLABS, (formerly The Playwrights' Center Midwest Playlabs), The Playwrights' Center, 2301 Franklin Ave. E, Minneapolis MN 55406. (612)332-7481. Assists in the development of unproduced or unpublished new plays. Deadline: Dec. 1. Playwrights only; and must be available for entire pre-conference and conference.

PLAYWRIGHTS' FORUM AWARDS, Theatreworks/Colorado, P.O. Box 7150, Colorado Springs CO 80933-7150. (719)593-3232. Fax: (719)593-3362. Producing Director: Whit Andrews. Estab. 1981. Submissions unpublished and unproduced. To recognize excellence in playwriting in the one-act form. Deadline: Dec. 1.

‡PLAYWRIGHTS PROJECT, Suite 215, 1450 Frazee Rd., San Diego CA 92108. (619)298-9242. Contact: Deborah Salzer. Estab. 1985. For Californians under 19 years of age. Every writer receives an individualized script critique if requested in cover letter; selected scripts receive professional productions. Deadline varies from May to June. Request for poster is sufficient. For California residents under 19 years of age.

PLAYWRITING COMPETITION FOR YOUNG AUDIENCES, Indiana University-Purdue University at Indianapolis, Young Audiences Playwriting Competition, 525 N. Blackford St., Indianapolis IN 46202-3120. (317)274-2095. Contact: Literary Manager. Previously unpublished plays for young audiences through high school. Send SASE for guidelines and submission form. Biennial competition held in the even year (i.e. 1994, 1996, etc.).

‡THE RCI FESTIVAL OF EMERGING AMERICAN THEATRE, (formerly The Festival of Emerging American Theatre), The Phoenix Theatre, 749 N. Park Ave., Indianapolis IN 46202. (317)635-7529. Contact: Bryan Fonseca. Annual playwriting competition. Deadline: Mar. 30.

THE LOIS AND RICHARD ROSENTHAL NEW PLAY PRIZE, Cincinnati Playhouse in the Park, Box 6537, Cincinnati OH 45206. (513)345-2242. Contact: Artistic Associate. Unpublished plays. "Scripts must not have received a full-scale professional production." Deadline: Oct. 15-Feb. 1.

‡SHENANDOAH PLAYWRIGHTS RETREAT, ShenanArts, Inc., Rt. 5, Box 167F, Staunton VA 24401. (703)248-1868. Fax: (703)248-1868. Program Director: Robert Graham Small. Offered annually. "Shenandoah exists to provide young and established playwrights with a challenging, stimulating environment to test and develop new work." Deadline: March 1. Award application form available for SASE. "The writers, each on fellowship, work in close and intensive collaboration with dramaturgs, directors and the acting company. What occurs is a simultaneous 'on-the-feet/on-the-page' exploration of each play, culminating in a staged reading and company response."

SHIRAS INSTITUTE/MILDRED & ALBERT PANOWSKI PLAYWRITING AWARD, Forest A. Roberts Theatre, Northern Michigan University, Marquette MI 49855-5364. (906)227-2553. Award Director: Dr. James A. Panowski. Estab. 1978. Unpublished, unproduced plays. Scripts must be *received* on or before Nov. 20.

SHUBERT FENDRICH MEMORIAL PLAYWRITING CONTEST, Pioneer Drama Service, P.O. Box 22555, Denver CO 80222. (303)759-4297. Fax: (303)759-0475. Contest/Award Director: Steven Fendrich. Annual contest for previously produced, but unpublished plays. Deadline: March 1. Prize is publication with $1,000 advance in royalty. "All rights to work are obtained by Pioneer. All submitted work must be produced prior to submission."

SIERRA REPERTORY THEATRE, P.O. Box 3030, Sonora CA 95370. (209)532-3120. Estab. 1980. Full-length plays. Deadline: August 31.

DOROTHY SILVER PLAYWRITING COMPETITION, Jewish Community Center, 3505 Mayfield Rd., Cleveland Heights OH 44118. (216)382-4000, ext. 275. Fax: (216)382-5401. Contact: Elaine Rembrandt. Estab. 1948. All entries must be original works, not previously produced, suitable for a full-length presentation; directly concerned with the Jewish experience. Deadline: Dec. 15. Cash award plus staged reading.

SUSAN SMITH BLACKBURN PRIZE, 3239 Avalon Place, Houston TX 77019. (713)654-4484. Fax: (713)654-8184. Director: Emilie S. Kilgore. Annual prize for woman playwright for full-length play written in English. Winner receives $5,000 and signed de Kooning print; second prize, $1,000. Other finalists $500 each. Deadline: Sept. 20. Nomination by artistic directors or theater professionals only.

SOUTH CAROLINA PLAYWRIGHTS FESTIVAL, Trustus Theatre, P.O. Box 11721, Columbia SC 29211. (803)771-9153. Literary Manager: Joyce T. Tromsness. Estab. 1989. Offered annually for previously unpublished work. "Full-length plays accepted. No musicals, cast limit 8." Accepts plays Jan. 1-Mar. 1. Contact by phone between 1-6 pm. Prize: 1st place $500, full production, travel and housing for rehearsals; 2nd place $250 plus staged reading.

SOUTHEASTERN THEATRE CONFERENCE NEW PLAY PROJECT, Department of Theatre, University of Alabama, P.O. Box 870239, Tuscaloosa AL 35487-0239. (205)348-9032. Chair: Dr. Paul Castagno. Annual contest dedicated to discovery, development and publicizing of worthy unproduced plays and playwrights. Eligibility limited to members of 10 state SETC Region: AL, FL, GA, KY, MS, NC, SC, TN, VA, WV. Submit: Mar. 15-June 1. Bound full-length or related one-acts under single cover (one submission only). SASE stapled to back cover. Guidelines available upon request. Prize is $1,000, staged reading at SETC Convention, expenses paid trip to convention and preferred consideration for National Playwrights Conference.

SOUTHERN PLAYWRIGHTS COMPETITION, Center for Southern Studies/Jacksonville State University, Pelham Rd., Jacksonville AL 36265. (205)782-5411. Fax: (205)782-5291. Contact: Steven J. Whitton. Estab. 1988. Offered annually for previously unpublished/unproduced work. "The Center for Southern Studies seeks to identify and encourage the best of Southern Playwrighting." Deadline: Feb. 15. Send SASE for contest guidelines. Prize: $1,000 and a production of the play. Playwrights must be native to or resident of AL, AR, FL, GA, KY, LA, MS, NC, SC, TN, TX, VA, or WV.

SOUTHERN PLAYWRITING COMPETITION, Festival of Southern Theatre, Dept. of Theatre Arts, Univ. of Mississippi, University MS 38677. (601)232-5816. Contact: Scott McCoy. Estab. 1985. Competition for unpublished and unproduced original full-length scripts for the theatre by a Southern writer or a work with a markedly Southern theme. Deadline: Dec. 1. Two or three winners annually are awarded $1,000 each and full professional production. Selections announced Feb. 15.

MARVIN TAYLOR PLAYWRITING AWARD, Sierra Repertory Theatre, P.O. Box 3030, Sonora CA 95370-3030. (209)532-3120. Producing Director: Dennis C. Jones. Estab. 1980. Full-length plays. Deadline: Aug. 31.

THEATRE MEMPHIS NEW PLAY COMPETITION, Theatre Memphis, P.O. Box 240117, Memphis TN 38124-0117. (901)682-8323. Estab. 1983. Chairman, New Play Competition: Kim Ford. Award offered every 3 years "to promote new playwrights' works and new works by established playwrights." No musicals or one-acts. Bound scripts only. Deadline for script entry: July 1, 1996. Include SASE if scripts are to be returned.

• This competition runs in a 3-year cycle.

‡TRANSLATION COMMISSIONS, National Theater Translation Fund, Box 355 Casta, Cuny Grad Ctr., 33 W. 42nd St., New York NY 10036. (212)642-2657. Fax: (212)642-2642. Contact: Executive Director. Offered annually. "The National Theater Translation Fund encourages the translation of foreign plays into stageworthy American English." Deadline: Oct. 15. Contest/award rules and entry forms available for SASE. Prize:

$4,000. Judged by a peer panel. Requires a statement of the rights to the work proposed for translation that states if work is in public domain; if rights have been obtained from author or author's representatives, or if translator is in process of obtaining rights. "Competition is open to translators who have completed a previous translation of a full length work. Translators with letters of recommendation from theater artistic directors or literary managers expressing interest in translator's work for production, workshop or staged reading will receive special consideration."

UNIVERSITY OF ALABAMA NEW PLAYWRIGHTS PROGRAM, P.O. Box 870239, Tuscaloosa AL 35487-0239. (205)348-9032. Director and Dramaturg: Dr. Paul C. Castagno. Estab. 1982. Full-length plays for mainstage; experimental plays for B stage. Workshops and radio plays can be proposed. Queries responded to quickly. Stipends competitive with, or exceed most contests. Development process includes readings, visitations, and possible complete productions with faculty director and dramaturg. Send SASE for rules and entry forms. Up to 6 months assessment time.

‡US WEST THEATREFEST, (formerly U.S. West Fest), Denver Center Theatre Company, 1050 13th St., Denver CO 80204. (303)893-4000. Fax: (303)893-2860. Program Director: Tom Szentgyorgyi, associate artistic director for new play development. Offered annually for unproduced work. "The US West TheatreFest is a new play program. We accept submissions of unproduced, full-length plays. Up to eight scripts are selected for developmental readings each year; up to four scripts are then chosen from among the plays read for production the following year." Deadline: Dec. 1. Send SASE for submission guidelines. Playwrights chosen for readings are given transportation to and from the TheatreFest, housing during it, and a stipend.

VERY SPECIAL ARTS YOUNG PLAYWRIGHTS PROGRAM, Very Special Arts, Education Office, The John F. Kennedy Center for the Performing Arts, Washington D.C. 20566. (202)628-2800. Fax: (202)737-0725. Contact: National Programs, Young Playwrights Programs. Annual contest for unpublished plays by teens. "Students between the ages of 12 and 18 may write a script that incorporates some aspect of disability." Deadline: mid-April. Write for rules and entry forms. Winning play produced at The John F. Kennedy Center for the Performing Arts Theater Lab. "Very Special Arts retains the rights to make the script available to other organizations for educational purposes." Contestants must be 12-18 years of age.

THEODORE WARD PRIZE FOR PLAYWRITING, Columbia College Theater/Music Center, 72 E. 11th St., Chicago IL 60605-1996. Contact: Chuck Smith. Estab. 1985. "To uncover and identify new unpublished African-American plays that are promising and produceable." Deadline: August 1. All rights for music or biographies must be secured prior to submission. All entrants must be of African-American descent and residing within the U.S. Only one completed script per playwright will be accepted.

‡L. ARNOLD WEISSBERGER PLAYWRITING COMPETITION, New Dramatists, Inc., 424 W. 44th St., New York NY 10036. (212)757-6960. Fax: (212)265-4738. Contest/Award Director: Paul A. Slee. Estab. 1984. Offered annually. No publication required; plays must be previously unproduced. "The L. Arnold Weissberger Award is a cash prize that recognizes a previously unproduced new play by a playwright with any level of experience. The $5,000 prize is awarded annually, and the competition is judged by professional theater critics. The selection criteria were established by L. Arnold Weissberger, a theatrical attorney, who sought to discover a 'well-made play.' " Deadline: May 31. Applications accepted between Sept. 15 of the previous year and May 31, the deadline, for an award announcement the following May. Contest/award rules and entry form available for SASE. Prize: $5,000 and a public staged reading of the prize-winning play. "No special criteria or nominating process required. 'The play's the thing.' " Send SASE for guidelines.

WEST COAST ENSEMBLE FULL-PLAY COMPETITION, CELEBRATION OF ONE-ACTS, West Coast Ensemble, P.O. Box 38728, Los Angeles CA 90038. Artistic Director: Les Hanson. Estab. 1982. Unpublished (in Southern California) plays. No musicals or children's plays for full-play competition. No restrictions on subject matter. Deadline: Nov. 15 for one-act plays; Dec. 31 for full-length plays.

‡WHITE BIRD ANNUAL PLAYWRITING CONTEST, White Bird Productions, Inc., P.O. Box 20233, Columbus Circle Station, New York NY 10023. (718)788-5984. Contact: Kathryn Dickinson. Offered annually for unpublished work. Purpose is "to award the two best one-act or full-length plays (non-musical) that best deal with an environmental theme, topic or event." Deadline: Feb. 15, 1994. Contest/award rules and entry forms available for SASE. Prize: "For 1993 $200 honorarium and a NYC staged reading." Judged by literary committee. Contest open to all playwrights.

WICHITA STATE UNIVERSITY PLAYWRITING CONTEST, Wichita State University Theatre, WSU, Box 31, Wichita KS 67208-1595. (316)689-3185. Contest Director: Professor Bela Kiralyfalvi. Estab. 1974. Two or three short, unpublished, unproduced plays or full-length plays of at least 90 minutes in playing time. No restriction on style or subject. Award: production of winning play (ACTF) and expenses paid trip for playwright to see final rehearsals and/or performances. Contestants must be graduate or undergraduate students in a U.S. college or university.

‡YOUNG PLAYWRIGHTS FESTIVAL, Young Playwrights Inc., Suite 906, 321 W. 44th St., New York NY 10036. (212)307-1140. Fax: (212)307-1454. Artistic Director: Nancy Quinn. Offered annually for unpublished work. Only stage plays accepted for submission (no musicals, screenplays or adaptations). "Writers age 18 and younger are invited to send scripts for consideration in the annual Young Playwrights Festival. Winning plays will be performed in professional Off Broadway production." Deadline: Oct. 1. Contest/award rules and entry forms available for SASE. Entrants must be 18 or younger on July 1 of the year of contest.

‡ANNA ZORNIO MEMORIAL THEATRE FOR YOUTH PLAYWRITING AWARD, U of NH Theatre In Education Program /TRY, Paul Creative Arts, Durham NH 03824. (603)862-3288. Contact: Peggy Rae Johnson. Purpose: To bring quality unpublished plays & musicals (45 minutes-1 hour in length) to elementary to middle school audiences. Deadline: Apr. 15. Production guaranteed, award of $250.

Journalism

AAAS-WESTINGHOUSE SCIENCE JOURNALISM AWARDS, American Association for the Advancement of Science, 1333 H St. NW, Washington DC 20005. (202)326-6440. Fax: (202)789-0455. Contact: Nan Broadbent. Annual award for previously published work (between July 1, 1992 and June 30, 1993). "Purpose is to reward excellence in reporting on science and its applications in daily newspapers with circulation over 100,000; newspapers with circulation under 100,000; general circulation magazines; radio; television." Deadline: July 13. Award: $2,500, plaque, trip to AAAS Annual Meeting.

AMERICAN SPEECH-LANGUAGE-HEARING ASSOCIATION (ASHA), NATIONAL MEDIA AWARDS, 10801 Rockville Pike, Rockville MD 20852-3279. (301)897-5700. Fax: (301)571-0457. Estab. 1925. Speech-language pathology and audiology (radio, TV, newspaper, magazine). Deadline: June 30.

AMY WRITING AWARDS, The Amy Foundation, P.O. Box 16091, Lansing MI 48901. (517)323-6233. President: James Russell. Estab. 1985. Articles communicating Biblical truth previously published in the secular media. Deadline: Jan. 31.

HOWARD W. BLAKESLEE AWARDS, American Heart Association, 7272 Greenville Ave., Dallas TX 75231. (214)706-1173. Fax: (214)706-1551. Award Director: Howard L. Lewis. Managing Editor: Vicki Graff. Estab. 1952. Offered annually for work previously published between Jan. 1 and Dec. 31 of preceding calendar year. Purpose is "to recognize outstanding medical/science journalism in the US that has contributed to the public's knowledge and understanding of heart and blood vessel disease." Print or broadcast reports on cardiovascular diseases published during preceding calendar year. Deadline: Feb. 1. Contest/award rules and entry forms available for SASE "or call (214)706-1173 and ask for an entry form." Prize: Plaque and $1,000 honorarium. Entry must have been published or broadcast in mass media publication/program during preceding calendar year. Advertising/PSA material not accepted."

THE HEYWOOD BROUN AWARD, The Newspaper Guild (AFL-CIO, CLC), 8611 2nd Ave., Silver Spring MD 20910. (301)585-2990. Contact: David J. Eisen. Previously published (between Jan. 1 and Dec. 31) work. Deadline: approx. Jan. 8. Rules for SASE available in November. Prize: $2,000 and a Guild citation. "Entries become the property of the award committee unless return is requested." Contest open to news writers, broadcasters, cartoonists, etc."

RUSSELL L. CECIL ARTHRITIS MEDICAL JOURNALISM AWARDS, Arthritis Foundation, 1314 Spring St. NW, Atlanta GA 30309-9901. (404)872-7100. Fax: (404)872-0457. Contact: Lisa M. Newbern. Estab. 1956. News stories, articles and radio/TV scripts on the subject of arthritis and the Arthritis Foundation published or broadcast for general circulation during the previous calendar year. Deadline: Feb. 15.

HARRY CHAPIN MEDIA AWARDS, (formerly World Hunger Media Awards), World Hunger Year, 21st Floor, 505 8th Ave., New York NY 10018-6582. (212)629-8850. Fax: (212)465-9274. Coordinator: Peter Mann. Critical issues of domestic and world hunger, poverty and development (newspaper, periodical, TV, radio, photojournalism, books). Cash prizes, $1,000-2,500. Deadline: Feb. 15.

THE GREAT AMERICAN TENNIS WRITING AWARDS, *Tennis Week*, 124 E. 40th St., New York NY 10016. (212)808-4750. Fax: (212)983-6302. Publisher: Eugene L. Scott. Estab. 1986. Category 1: unpublished manuscript by an aspiring journalist with no previous national byline. Category 2: unpublished manuscript by a non-tennis journalist. Category 3: unpublished manuscript by a tennis journalist. Categories 4-6: published articles and one award to a book. Deadline: Dec. 15.

SIDNEY HILLMAN PRIZE AWARD, Sidney Hillman Foundation, Inc., 15 Union Square, New York NY 10003. (212)242-0700. Executive Director: Joyce D. Miller. Awards Coordinator: Mary Contini. Estab. 1946. Social/economic themes related to ideals of Sidney Hillman (daily or periodical journalism, nonfiction, radio and TV). Deadline: Jan. 15.

DARRELL BOB HOUSTON PRIZE, 1931 2nd Ave., Seattle WA 98101. (206)441-6238. Journalism published within the previous year in Washington State which shows "some soul, some color, some grace, robustness, mirth and generosity," to honor the memory of writer Darrell Bob Houston. Contact for exact deadline date (usually in May).

THE ROY W. HOWARD AWARDS, Scripps Howard Foundation, P.O. Box 5380, Cincinnati OH 45201. (513)977-3035. Estab. 1972. Public service reporting by a daily newspaper in the US or its territories. Fact sheet available in fall of year.

INTERNATIONAL READING ASSOCIATION PRINT MEDIA AWARD, International Reading Association, P.O. Box 8139, Newark DE 19714-8139. (302)731-1600 ext. 215. Fax: (302)731-1057. Contact: Cindy Kirkpatrick. Estab. 1956. Reports by professional journalists from newspapers, magazines and wire services on reading and literacy activities and programs. Deadline: Jan. 15.

ROBERT F. KENNEDY JOURNALISM AWARDS, 1206 30th St., NW., Washington DC 20007. (202)333-1880. Fax: (202)333-4903. Director: Erin Scully. Estab. 1968. Previously published entries on problems of the disadvantaged. Deadline: last Friday of January.

DONALD E. KEYHOE JOURNALISM AWARD, Fund for UFO Research, P.O. Box 277, Mt. Rainier MD 20712. (703)684-6032. Fax: (703)684-6032. Contact: Executive Committee, Fund for UFO Research. Estab. 1979. Annual awards for the best article or story published or broadcast in a newspaper, magazine, TV or radio news outlet during the previous calendar year. Separate awards for print and broadcast media. Also makes unscheduled cash awards for published works on UFO phenomena research or public education.

THE EDWARD J. MEEMAN AWARDS, The Scripps Howard Foundation, P.O. Box 5380, Cincinnati OH 45201. (513)977-3035. Estab. 1967. Environmental reporting by a daily newspaper in the US or its territories. Fact sheet available in fall of the year.

MENCKEN AWARDS, Free Press Association, P.O. Box 15548, Columbus OH 43215. FPA Executive Director: Michael Grossberg. Estab. 1981. Honoring defense of human rights and individual liberties, or exposés of governmental abuses of power. Categories: News Story or Investigative Report, Feature Story or Essay/Review, Editorial or Op-Ed Column, Editorial Cartoon, Book, and Defense of First Amendment. Entries *must* have been published or broadcast during previous calendar year. Deadline: April 1 (for work from previous year). Fee: $4 per entry. Late deadline May 1 with extra fee. *Must* send SASE for entry form.

FRANK LUTHER MOTT-KAPPA TAU ALPHA RESEARCH AWARD IN JOURNALISM, University of Missouri, School of Journalism, Columbia MO 65205. (314)882-7685. Executive Director, Central Office: Dr. Keith Sanders. For "best researched book in journalism." 5 copies required. No forms required. Deadline: Jan. 15. Award: $1,000.

NATIONAL AWARDS FOR EDUCATION REPORTING, Education Writers Association, 1001 Connecticut Ave. NW, Washington DC 20036. (202)429-9680. Fax: (202)872-4016. Submissions to be previously published, previous year. There are 17 categories; write for more information. Deadline: mid-January. Charges $30 for first entry, $20 for each additional.

ALICIA PATTERSON JOURNALISM FELLOWSHIP, Alicia Patterson Foundation, Suite 1250, 1001 Pennsylvania Ave. NW, Washington DC 20004. (202)393-5995. Contact: Margaret Engel. Offered annually for previously published submissions. Purpose is "to give 5-7 print journalists a year of in-depth research and reporting. Applicants must have 5 years of professional print journalism experience and be U.S. citizens. Fellows write 4 magazine-length pieces for the *Alicia Patterson Reporter*, a quarterly magazine, during their fellowship year. Fellows must take a year's leave from their jobs, but may do other freelance articles during the year." Deadline: Oct. 1. SASE not required for contest guidelines. "Journalists should write or call for applications." Prize: $30,000 stipend for calendar year.

ERNIE PYLE AWARD, Scripps Howard Foundation, P.O. Box 5380, Cincinnati OH 45201. (513)977-3035. Estab. 1953. Human-interest reporting by a newspaper man or woman for work published in a daily newspaper in the US or its territories. Fact sheet available in fall of the year.

THE CHARLES M. SCHULZ AWARD, Scripps Howard Foundation, P.O. Box 5380, Cincinnati OH 45201. (513)977-3035. Estab. 1980. For a student cartoonist at a college newspaper or magazine. Fact sheet available in fall of the year.

SCIENCE IN SOCIETY JOURNALISM AWARDS, National Association of Science Writers, Box 294, Greenlawn NY 11740. (516)757-5664. Contact: Diane McGurgan. Newspaper, magazine and broadcast science writing. Deadline: (postmarked) July 1 for work published June 1-May 31 of previous year.

CHARLES E. SCRIPPS AWARD, Scripps Howard Foundation, P.O. Box 5380, Cincinnati OH 45201. (513)977-3035. Estab. 1986. Combatting illiteracy, by a daily newspaper, television, cable and/or radio station in the US or its territories. Fact sheet available in fall of the year.

THE EDWARD WILLIS SCRIPPS AWARD, Scripps Howard Foundation, P.O. Box 5380, Cincinnati OH 45201. (513)977-3035. Estab. 1976. Service to the First Amendment by a daily newspaper in the US or its territories. Fact sheet available in fall of the year.

SPECIAL LIBRARIES ASSOCIATION PUBLIC RELATIONS AWARD, Special Libraries Association, 1700 18th St., NW, Washington DC 20009-2508. (202)234-4700. Fax: (202)265-9317. Director, Communications: Mark Serepca. Estab. 1987. SLA's Public Relations Award is presented to a writer who develops an outstanding feature story on the special libraries profession published previous calendar year. The article must appear in a general-circulation magazine or newspaper. Library journal magazine articles or submissions from librarians are not eligible. Deadline: Dec. 31.

I.F STONE AWARD FOR STUDENT JOURNALISM, The Nation Institute, 72 5th Ave., New York NY 10011. (212)242-8400. Director: Peter Meyer. Annual award "to recognize excellence in student journalism." Open to undergraduate students in U.S. colleges. Award: $1,000, plus publication. Deadline: June 30.

THE WALKER STONE AWARDS, Scripps Howard Foundation, P.O. Box 5380, Cincinnati OH 45201. (513)977-3035. Estab. 1973. Editorial writing by a daily newspaper man or woman, published in the US or its territories. Fact sheet available in fall of the year.

TRAVEL JOURNALISM AWARDS, Hawaii Visitors Bureau, Suite 801, 2270 Kalakaua Ave., Honolulu HI 96815. (808)924-0213. Fax: (808)924-2120. Contact: Cari Ly Costanzo. Annual award for travel journalism. Send #10 SAE with 2 first class stamps for complete rules and guidelines. Deadline: July 10.

Writing for Children and Young Adults

JANE ADDAMS CHILDREN'S BOOK AWARD, Jane Addams Peace Association and Women's International League for Peace and Freedom, 980 Lincoln Pl., Boulder CO 80302-7234. Award Director: Jean Gore. Estab. 1953. Book published previous year that promotes peace, social justice, and the equality of the sexes and races. Deadline: April 1.

AMERICAN ASSOCIATION OF UNIVERSITY WOMEN AWARD, NORTH CAROLINA DIVISION, North Carolina Literary and Historical Association, 109 E. Jones St., Raleigh NC 27601-2807. (919)733-7305. Awards Coordinator: Freda Brittain. Previously published juvenile literature by a North Carolina resident. Deadline: July 15.

IRMA S. AND JAMES H. BLACK AWARD, Bank Street College of Education, 610 W. 112th St., New York NY 10025. (212)222-6700. Award Director: Linda Greengrass. Annual award. Estab. 1972. Purpose of the award: "The award is given each spring for a book for young children, published in the previous year, for excellence of both text and illustrations." Entries must have been published during the previous calendar year. Deadline for entries: January after book is published.

BOSTON GLOBE-HORN BOOK AWARD, *The Boston Globe*, 135 Morissey Blvd, Boston MA 02107. Offered annually for previously published work. One award for original fiction or poetry, one for a picture book and one for nonfiction. Publisher submits entry. Prize: $500 in each category.

‡MARGUERITE DE ANGELI PRIZE, Doubleday Books for Young Readers, 1540 Broadway, New York NY 10036. (212)354-6500. Fax: (212)782-9698. Offered annually for unpublished work. "Submissions should consist of a fiction manuscript suitable for readers 7-10 years of age that concerns the diversity of the American experience, either contemporary or historical." Write for details. Contest/award rules and entry forms available for SASE. Prize includes a book contract with a cash advance.

DELACORTE PRESS PRIZE FOR A FIRST YOUNG ADULT NOVEL, Delacorte Press, 1540 Broadway, New York NY 10036. (212)354-6500. Estab. 1983. Previously unpublished young adult fiction. Submissions: Labor Day through December 31 only. Send SASE for complete rules.

DON FREEMAN MEMORIAL GRANT-IN-AID, Society of Children's Book Writers and Illustrators, #106, 22736 Vandowen St., West Hills CA 91307. To enable picture-book artists to further their understanding, training and/or work. Members only. Deadline: Feb. 15. Grants: $1,000 and $500 runner-up grant.

FRIENDS OF AMERICAN WRITERS YOUNG PEOPLE'S LITERATURE AWARDS, Apt. 2609, 900 N. Lake Shore Dr., Chicago IL 60611. (312)280-0736. Chair: Mrs. Patricia R. Mose. Estab. 1960. "Annual awards for children's books that were published in the past year. Entry must be first, second or third children's book published by the author. The author must be a resident or native of AR, IL, IN, IA, KS, MI, MN, MO, NE, ND, OH, SD or WI or story can be *set* in one of these states. No poetry." Prize consists of cash (no less than $400 each) to 2 writers; certificates to publishers. Send SASE for guidelines. Deadline: Dec. 31.

GOLDEN KITE AWARDS, Society of Children's Book Writers and Illustrators (SCBWI), Suite 106, 22736 Vanowen St., West Hills CA 91307. (818)888-8760. Coordinator: Sue Alexander. Estab. 1973. Calendar year published children's fiction, nonfiction and picture illustration books by a SCBWI member. Deadline: Dec. 15.

HIGHLIGHTS FOR CHILDREN FICTION CONTEST, *Highlights for Children*, 803 Church St., Honesdale PA 18431-1824. Editor: Kent L. Brown Jr. Estab. 1946. Stories for children ages 2-12; category varies each year. Write for guidelines. Stories should be limited to 900 words for older readers, 600 words for younger readers. No crime or violence, please. Specify that your manuscript is a contest entry. All entries must be postmarked between Jan. 1 and Feb. 28.

INTERNATIONAL READING ASSOCIATION CHILDREN'S BOOK AWARD, International Reading Association, P.O. Box 8139, 800 Barksdale Rd., Newark DE 19714-8139. (302)731-1600 ext. 215. Given for a first or second book, either fiction or nonfiction, by an author who shows unusual promise in the children's book field. Two categories: younger readers, ages 4-10; older readers, ages 10-16+. Deadline: Dec 1.

‡MILKWEED PRIZE FOR CHILDREN'S LITERATURE, Milkweed Editions, Suite 400, 1st Ave. N., Minneapolis MN 55401. (612)332-3192. Fax: (612)332-6248. Annual prize for unpublished works. "Milkweed is looking for children's novels and biographies for readers in the 8-14 age group. Manuscripts should be of high literary quality and should embody humane values that contribute to cultural understanding." Deadline: March 15. Charges $5 reading fee. Prize: Publication by Milkweed *must* request contest guidelines (send SASE), or risk having entry disqualified. Editions and a cash advance of $3,000 against royalties. "Entry must be English language. Contest is open to writers who have previously published a book of fiction or nonfiction for children or adults, or a minimum of 3 short stories or articles in magazines for children or adults." Catalog available on request for 2 first class stamps.

NATIONAL JEWISH BOOK AWARD—CHILDREN'S LITERATURE, (The Barbara Cohen Memorial Award), Jewish Book Council, 15 E. 26th St., New York NY 10010. (212)532-4949. Director: Paula G. Gottlieb. Children's book on Jewish theme. Deadline: Nov. 20.

NATIONAL JEWISH BOOK AWARD—CHILDREN'S PICTURE BOOK, Marcia and Louis Posner Award, Jewish Book Council, 15 E. 26th St., New York NY 10010. (212)532-4949. Director: Paula G. Gottlieb. Author and illustrator of a children's book on a Jewish theme. Deadline: Nov. 20.

SCOTT O'DELL AWARD FOR HISTORICAL FICTION, 1418 E. 57th St., Chicago IL 60637. (312)752-7880. Director: Zena Sutherland. Estab. 1981. Historical fiction book for children set in the Americas. Entries must have been published during previous year. Deadline: Dec. 31.

PEN/NORMA KLEIN AWARD, PEN American Center, 568 Broadway, New York NY 10012. (212)334-1660. Fax: (212)334-2181. Contact: John Morrone. "Recognizes an emerging voice of literary merit among American writers of children's fiction." *Candidates may not nominate themselves.* Deadline for nominations: Jan. 31, 1995. (Awarded biennially.) Guidelines for #10 SASE. Award is $3,000.

TEXAS BLUEBONNET AWARD, Texas Library Association's Texas Association of School Librarians and Children's Round Table, Suite 401, 3355 Bee Cave Rd., Austin TX 78746. (512)328-1518. Contact: Patricia Smith. Published books for children recommended by librarians, teachers and students.

WORK-IN-PROGRESS GRANT, Society of Children's Book Writers and Illustrators and Judy Blume, #106, 22736 Vanowen St., West Hills CA 91307. Write *SCBWI* at preceding address. Two grants—one designated specifically for a contemporary novel for young people—to assist SCBWI members in the completion of a specific project. Deadline: June 1.

Translation

AMERICAN-SCANDINAVIAN FOUNDATION/TRANSLATION PRIZE, American-Scandinavian Foundation, 725 Park Ave., New York NY 10021. (212)879-9779. Fax: (212)249-3444. Contact: Publishing Division. Contemporary Scandinavian fiction and poetry translations. Deadline: June 1. Award: $2,000, bronze medallion, publication of an excerpt in the *Scandinavian Review*.

PIERRE-FRANÇOIS CAILLÉ MEMORIAL MEDAL, Fédération Internationale des Traducteurs (FIT), Heiveldstraat 245, Sint-Amandsberg/Gent Belgium B9040. (32)91283971. Fax: (32-91)283971. Contact: Council of FIT. "Medal is given every three years to individuals who have earned outstanding merit in promoting the standing and reputation of the translation profession on an international level. Deadline is two months before congress." Recipients receive medal and diploma.

KAREL ČAPEK TRANSLATION REWARD, Fédération International des Traducteurs (FIT), Heiveldstraat 245, Sint-Amandsberg/Gent Belgium B9040. (32)941283971. Fax: (32-91)283971. Contact: FIT Council. "The purpose of this contest is to promote the literary translation of works written in languages of limited diffusion. Contest runs every three years. Deadline is six months prior to the opening of FIT's triannual congress in August 1993." SASE. Prize consists of a medal and diploma. The contest is judged by an international jury of five members, appointed by the FIT Committee for LLD Translation and approved by the Executive Committee of FIT. Translators must be nominated by a Member Society of FIT.

‡FRENCH-AMERICAN FOUNDATION TRANSLATION PRIZE, 41 E. 72nd St., New York NY 10021. (212)288-4400. Fax: (212)288-4769. Contact: Deborah Levy. Offered annually for works published during the current year. Must appear in print between January 1 and December 31 of the current year. "For the best translation of a prose work from French to English (no poetry, reference, technical or children's books)." Deadline: July 1. "The *publisher* must submit two copies of the English translation and one copy of the original French to the French-American Foundation by July 1. If the book is not yet published, galleys are acceptable." Prize: $5,000 to the translator.

‡LEWIS GALANTIÈRE PRIZE FOR LITERARY TRANSLATION, American Translators Association, 3818 N. Ridgeview Rd., Arlington VA 22207. Chair: Breon Mitchell. Award offered in even years recognizing the "outstanding translation of a previously published work from languages other than German published in the United States." Deadline: April 15.

GERMAN PRIZE FOR LITERARY TRANSLATION, American Translators Association, 3818 N. Ridgeview Rd., Arlington VA 22207. (914)941-1500. Chair: Breon Mitchell. Prize offered in odd-numbered years. Submissions must be previously published and have appeared in print during the 2 previous years. "Recognizes outstanding translations of a literary work from German published in the United States." Deadline April 15.

JOHN GLASSCO TRANSLATION PRIZE, Literary Translators' Association of Canada, Association des traducteurs et traductrices du Canada, 3492, rue Lavel, Montréal, Québec H2X 3C8 Canada. Estab. 1981. Annual award for a translator's *first* book-length literary translation into French or English, published in Canada during the previous calendar year. The translator must be a Canadian citizen or landed immigrant. Eligible genres include fiction, creative nonfiction, poetry, published plays, children's books. Deadline: January 15. Write for application form. Award: $500.

PEN MEDAL FOR TRANSLATION, PEN American Center, 568 Broadway, New York NY 10012. (212)334-1660. Fax: (212)334-2181. Contact: John Morrone. Translators nominated by the PEN Translation Committee. Given every 3 years. Next award: 1994.

PEN/BOOK-OF-THE-MONTH CLUB TRANSLATION PRIZE, PEN American Center, 568 Broadway, New York NY 10012. Contact: John Morrone. One award to a literary book-length translation into English published in 1993. (No technical, scientific or reference.) Deadline: Dec. 31.

RENATO POGGIOLI TRANSLATION AWARD, PEN American Center, 568 Broadway, New York NY 10012. (212)334-1660. Fax: (212)334-2181. Contact: John Morrone. "Given to encourage a beginning and promising translator who is working on a first book-length translation from Italian into English." Deadline: Jan. 15.

THE TRANSLATION CENTER AWARDS, The Translation Center, 412 Dodge Hall, Columbia University, New York NY 10027. (212)854-2305. Fax: (212)749-0397. Executive Director: Frank MacShane. Awards are grants to a translator for an outstanding translation of a substantial part of a book length literary work from other languages into English. Deadline: Jan. 15. Award: $500-2,500. "In addition, the translation center publishes a biannual journal of foreign literature in translation. One year subscription is $18. Address all submission and subscription queries to the address above."

‡TRANSLATION COMMISSIONS, National Theater Translation Fund, Box 355 Casta, Cuny Grad Ctr., 33 W. 42nd St., New York NY 10036. (212)642-2657. Fax: (212)642-2642. Contact: Executive Director. Offered annually. "The National Theater Translation Fund encourages the translation of foreign plays into stageworthy American English." Deadline: Oct. 15. Call or write for guidelines. Prize: $4,000. Judged by a peer panel. Requires a statement of the rights to the work proposed for translation that states if work is in public domain; if rights have been obtained from author or author's representatives, or if translator is in process of obtaining rights. "Competition is open to translators who have completed a previous translation of a full length work.

Translators with letters of recommendation from theater artistic directors or literary managers expressing interest in translator's work for production, workshop or staged reading will receive special consideration."

Multiple Writing Areas

AKRON MANUSCRIPT CLUB WRITER'S CONTEST, Akron Manuscript Club & Akron University, P.O. Box 1011, Cuyahoga Falls OH 44223. (216)923-2094. Contact: M.M. Lopiccolo. "Annual contest for previously unpublished stories. The purpose of the contest is to provide critique, encouragement and some financial help to authors in six categories." Deadline is always some time in April. Rules and entry forms available for #10 SASE. "Entry fee varies according to whether applicant is mail-in or conference attendant." First prize: $100; Second prize: $50; Third prize: $25. "May vary according to funding."

AMELIA STUDENT AWARD, *Amelia Magazine*, 329 E St., Bakersfield CA 93304. (805)323-4064. Editor: Frederick A. Raborg, Jr. Previously unpublished poems, essays and short stories by high school students, 1 entry per student; each entry should be signed by parent, guardian *or* teacher to verify originality. Deadline: May 15.

ARIZONA AUTHORS' ASSOCIATION ANNUAL NATIONAL LITERARY CONTEST, Arizona Authors' Association, Suite 117WM, 3509 E. Shea Blvd., Phoenix AZ 85028-3339. (602)942-4240. Contact: Gerry Benninger. Previously unpublished poetry, short stories, essays. Deadline: July 29. Charges $6 for poetry; $9 for short stories and essays.

AWP ANNUAL AWARD SERIES, Associated Writing Programs, Old Dominion University, Norfolk VA 23529-0079. (804)683-3839. Contact: Beth Jarock. Annual award series for book length mss in poetry, short fiction, nonfiction and novel. Deadline: Feb. 28. Charges $10 per ms.

BEST OF HOUSEWIFE-WRITER'S FORUM: THE CONTESTED WILLS TO WRITE, *Housewife-Writer's Forum*, P.O. Box 780, Lyman WY 82937-0780. (307)786-4513. Contest Director: Diane Wolverton. Estab. 1988. Unpublished prose and poetry categories. Deadline: May 15. Charges $4 for prose; $2 for poetry.

BLACK WARRIOR REVIEW LITERARY AWARDS, *Black Warrior Review*, P.O. Box 2936, Tuscaloosa AL 35486-2936. (205)348-4518. Estab. 1974. Submit work for possible publication to the appropriate genre editor. Awarded annually. Purpose is "to award $500 each to a poet and fiction writer for outstanding work published in the *BWR*. All poetry and fiction appearing in the *BWR* is considered for that volume's award; we treat submissions for the contest as submissions for publication in the *BWR*." Contest/award rules and entry form for SASE. Winners are announced in the Fall/Winter issue.

BYLINE MAGAZINE CONTESTS, P.O. Box 130596, Edmond OK 73013. (405)348-5591. Publisher: Marcia Preston. Estab. 1981. Unpublished short stories, poems and other categories. Several categories offered each month which are open to anyone. Deadline on annual award, which is for subscribers only, Dec. 1. Send #10 SASE for information. Charges fee of $5 for short story; $2 for poems on annual award.

CALIFORNIA WRITERS' CLUB CONFERENCE CONTEST, 2214 Derby St., Berkeley CA 94705. (510)841-1217. Unpublished adult fiction (short stories), adult fiction (novels), adult nonfiction, juvenile fiction or nonfiction, poetry and scripts. "Our conference is biennial, next being in 1995." Deadline: varies in spring. Charges fee.

CANADIAN AUTHOR STUDENT CREATIVE WRITING AWARDS, Canadian Authors Association, Suite 500, 275 Slater St., Ottawa, Ontario K1P 5H9 Canada. Contact: Contest Editor of Canadian Author. Contest is to encourage creative writing of unpublished fiction, nonfiction and poetry at the secondary school level. Deadline: March 22, 1993. Must purchase fall or winter issue of magazine and use tearsheet entry form. Must be secondary school student and nominated by his/her instructor, who may only nominate one student. Prizes of $100 in each category (with matching prize to instructor). Also a $500 scholarship. Send SAE and 1 IRC for guidelines.

BILL CASEY AWARD, *San José Studies*, San José State University, San José CA 95192-0090. (408)924-4476. Editors: John Engell (fiction and poetry) and D. Mesher (nonfiction). Estab. 1975. Offered annually. Best published article, short story or poem in previous volume of *San José Studies*. Prize: $100 and full-page notice in spring issue of the following year.

THE CHELSEA AWARDS FOR POETRY AND SHORT FICTION, % Richard Foerster, Associate Editor, P.O. Box 1040, York Beach ME 03910. Previously unpublished submissions. "Two prizes awarded for the best work of short fiction and for the best group of 4-6 poems selected by the editors in anonymous competitions." Deadline: June 15 for fiction; Dec. 15 for poetry. Send SASE for guidelines. Charges $10 (entrants will receive a free subscription to *Chelsea*). Checks made payable to Chelsea Associates, Inc. Prize: $500; winning entries published in *Chelsea*. Include a SASE for notification of competition results. Manuscripts will not be returned. *Note:* General submissions and other business should be addressed to the editor at *Chelsea*, P.O. Box 5880, Grand Central Station, New York NY 10163.

‡CHICAGO FOUNDATION FOR LITERATURE AWARDS, Friends of Literature, P.O. Box 31486, Chicago IL 60631-0486. (312)792-2756. Fax: (312)792-9797. Contact: James W. Conklin. Offered annually for previously published (between 1/1/93 and 12/31/93) work. Purpose is "to recognize authors with a Chicago 'connection,' either born and/or raised here or have lived here at some time in their lives. Categories include fiction, nonfiction and poetry. Newly published writers of promise are given special consideration." Deadline: Jan. 15. Contest/award rules and entry forms available for SASE. Prize: cash and plaque. Judged by the board of directors of Friends of Literature.

CHICANO/LATINO LITERARY CONTEST, Dept. of Spanish and Portuguese, UCI, Irvine CA 92717. (714)856-8429. Contact: Juan Bruce-Novoa or Rosilie Herrández. Estab. 1974. "To promote the dissemination of unpublished Chicano/Latino literature, and to encourage its development. The call for entries will be genre specific, rotating through four categories: poetry (1993), drama (1994), novel (1995) and short story (1996)." Deadline: April 30. "Interested parties may write for entry procedures." The contest is open to all citizens or permanent residents of the United States.

EATON LITERARY ASSOCIATES LITERARY AWARDS PROGRAM, P.O. Box 49795, Sarasota FL 34230-6795. (813)366-6589. Vice President: Richard Lawrence. Estab. 1984. Previously unpublished short stories and book-length manuscripts. Deadline: March 31 (short story); Aug. 31 (book length). Prize amounts: $500 short story; $2,500 book length.

EYSTER PRIZE, *New Delta Review*, % Department of English, Louisiana State University, Baton Rouge LA 70803-5001. (504)388-4079. Editors: Catherine Williamson, Randi Gray, Nicola Mason. Estab. 1983. Semiannual award for best works of poetry and fiction in each issue. Deadline: March 1, spring/summer issue; Sept. 1, fall/winter issue.

VIRGINIA FAULKNER AWARD FOR EXCELLENCE IN WRITING, *Prairie Schooner*, 201 Andrews, University of Nebraska, Lincoln NE 68588-0334. (402)472-3191. Editor: Hilda Raz. Estab. 1988. All genres eligible for consideration. The winning piece must have been published in *Prairie Schooner* during that calendar year. Prize: $1,000.

FEMINIST WRITERS' CONTEST, Dept. WD, P.O. Box 2440, Des Plaines IL 60018. Contact: Clara Johnson for rules; SASE required. Estab. 1990. Categories: Fiction and nonfiction (5,000 or fewer words). Work should reflect feminist perspectives (should not endorse or promote sexism, racism, ageism, anti-lesbianism, etc.) Deadline: Aug. 30. Charge $10 fee. Cash awards.

FLORIDA STATE WRITING COMPETITION, Florida Freelance Writers Association, Contest Administrator, Maple Ridge Rd., North Sandwich NH 03259. Annual contest. Deadline: March 15. Subject areas include: adult articles, adult short stories, writing for children, poetry. Rules and entry forms available for #10 SASE. Entry fees vary, depending on subject area. *Note: Do not send entries to FFWA office.*

FOLIO, Department of Literature, American University, Washington DC 20016. Estab. 1984. Fiction, poetry, essays, interviews and b&w artwork. "We look for quality work and award an annual prize for best poem and best story published per year." Published twice annually. Manuscripts read Sept.-March 15.

‡MILES FRANKLIN LITERARY AWARD, Arts Management Pty. Ltd., 180 Goulburn St., Darlinghurst, NSW 2010 Australia. Annual award for work published for the first time the year preceding award. "The award is for a novel or play which presents Australian life in any of its phases. Biographies, collections of short stories or children's books are *not* eligible for the award." Deadline: Jan. 31. Contest/award rules and entry form for #10 SAE and 1 IRC. Prize: $25,000 (Australian). "This award is open to writers of any nationality. However, the novel or play must be about Australian life."

‡FRIENDS OF AMERICAN WRITERS AWARDS, Friends of American Writers, 506 Rose Ave., Des Plaines IL 60616. (312)827-8339. Contest/Award Directors: Vivian Mortensen (adult) and Patricia R. Mose (juvenile), #2609, 900 N. Lake Shore Dr., Chicago IL 60611. (312)280-0736. Annual award for submissions published between Jan. 1 and Dec. 31 of each year. Two categories: adult literature and young people's literature, fiction or nonfiction of literary quality. Deadline: Dec. 31. $1,500 for 1st adult award and $1,000 2nd adult award. Juvenile $700 1st and $400 2nd. Send #10 SASE for rules and entry forms.

‡GREAT LAKES COLLEGES ASSOCIATION NEW WRITERS AWARDS, English Department, Wabash College, Crawfordsville IN 47933. Director: Marc Hudson. (317)364-4232. Estab. 1970. Entries must have appeared between February and subsequent January of year submitted. Award given each year to the best *first*

book of poetry and fiction submitted by publishers. "To encourage writers of previously published poetry and fiction whose publishers consider their work especially meritorious and to bring those writers together with the students and faculty of the twelve sponsoring colleges of the GLCA to their mutual benefit." Deadline: Feb. 28/29. "Publishers must nominate the works to be considered and may do so by sending *four copies* of the nominated work together with a statement assuring the author will accept the prize under the terms stipulated in the official contest announcement."

THE GREENSBORO REVIEW LITERARY AWARD IN FICTION AND POETRY, *The Greensboro Review*, English Department, UNCG, Greensboro NC 27412-5001. (919)334-5459. Fax: (919)334-3281. Editor: Jim Clark. Estab. 1966. Annual award for fiction and poetry; recognizes the best work published in the winter issue of *The Greensboro Review*. Deadline: Sept. 15. Sample copy $4.

HACKNEY LITERARY AWARDS, *Writing Today*, Box A-3/Birmingham-Southern College, Birmingham AL 35254. (205)226-4921. Contact: Special Events Office. Annual award for unpublished novel, short story and poetry. Deadline: Sept. 30 for novels and Dec. 31 for short stories and poetry. Send SASE for guidelines.

‡HOPEWELL REVIEW, Arts Indiana, Inc., Suite 701, 47 S. Pennsylvania St., Indianapolis IN 46204. (317)632-7894. Publisher and CEO: Ann M. Stack. Editor: Michael Wilkerson. An annual collection of fiction and poetry by Indiana writers. It is distributed with September issue of *Arts Indiana* magazine to over 8,000 members of the not-for-profit arts service organization. Approximately 7 short stories and 35 poems are printed, and 2 $500 Awards of Excellence are given, one in fiction and one in poetry. Poetry Juror: Rginald Gibbons; Fiction Juror: Jonathan Galassi. Deadline: March 1. SASE for guidelines. $150 for each accepted short story and $35 for each poem. Writers must be Indiana residents and at least 18 years of age.

KANSAS QUARTERLY/KANSAS ARTS COMMISSION AWARDS, SEATON AWARDS, Department of English, Kansas State University, Manhattan KS 66506. (913)532-6716. Editor: Ben Nyberg, et al. Estab. 1968. *KQ/KAC* awards for poetry and fiction published in *KQ*; Seaton awards for Kansas writers whose poetry, fiction and prose appear in *KQ*.

‡ROBERT F. KENNEDY BOOK AWARD, 1206 30th St. NW, Washington DC 20007. (202)333-1880. Executive Director: Phil Johnston. Estab. 1980. Fiction or nonfiction published in the US in 1993. Book which reflects "concern for the poor and the powerless, justice, the conviction that society must assure all young people a fair chance and faith that a free democracy can act to remedy disparities of power and opportunity." Deadline: Jan. 3. Charges $25 entry fee. Contact Merrill Warschoff for more information.

JACK KEROUAC LITERARY PRIZE, Lowell Historic Preservation Commission, Suite 310, 222 Merrimack St., Lowell MA 01852. (508)458-7653. Annual award for unpublished nonfiction, fiction and poetry. Send SASE for guidelines. Deadline: July 30, 1993.

ROSE LEFCOWITZ PRIZES, *Poet Lore*, The Writer's Center, 4508 Walsh St., Bethesda MD 20815. (301)654-8664. "Annual award for previously unpublished poetry or criticism. The prizes go to the single best poem and piece of critical prose to appear in a given volume of *Poet Lore*. Rules for #10 SASE. Prizes include $150 for each winner (1 winner for poetry; 1 for prose). Rights revert to the author after first publication in *Poet Lore*. "Only poems and prose that appear in a volume of *Poet Lore* are considered. A poem or piece of critical prose must first appear in the magazine before it will be considered for the Prize."

LINDEN LANE MAGAZINE ENGLISH-LANGUAGE POETRY CONTEST, Linden Lane Magazine & Press, Inc., P.O. Box 2384, Princeton NJ 08543-2384. Editor: Belkis Cuza Male. Unpublished Spanish and English poetry, short story and essay prizes. Deadline: October 15. For guidelines send SASE. Charges $12 fee.

HUGH J. LUKE AWARD, *Prairie Schooner*, 201 Andrews, University of Nebraska, Lincoln NE 68588-0334. (402)472-3191. Fax: (402)472-4636. Editor: Hilda Raz. Annual award for work published in *Prairie Schooner*. Winner announced in the spring issue of the following year. Prize: $250.

‡MASTERS LITERARY AWARDS, Center Press, P.O. Box 16452, Encino CA 91416-6452. (818)377-4301. Contact: Jana Cain. Offered annually and quarterly for work previously published—within 2 years—(preferred) and unpublished work (accepted). 1-Fiction: 15 page, max.; 2-Poetry: 5 pages or 150 lines, max.; 3-Nonfiction: 10 page, max. Deadlines: March 15, June 15th, Aug. 15th, Dec. 15. Contest/award rules and entry forms available for SASE. Charges reading fee. Prize: one quarterly prize of $500 *and* one annual of $1,500. Judged by "three anonymous experts chosen yearly from literary and publishing field." Center Press retains 'one time publishing' rights to selected winners. Open to all writers.

MATURE WOMEN SCHOLARSHIP AWARD, The National League of American PEN Women, Inc., 1300 17th St. NW, Washington DC 20036. (202)785-1997. Offered every two years on even numbered years to women 35 and over. Classifications include: art, letters, music composition. Rules available after August. $8 entry fee. Award is $1,000 in each classification.

THE MENTOR AWARD, *Mentor Newsletter,* P.O. Box 4382, Overland Park KS 66204-0382. Award Director: Maureen Waters. Estab. 1989. Award offered quarterly. "To promote and encourage mentoring through feature articles, essays, book/movie reviews, interviews or short stories." Deadlines: March 31, June 30, Sept. 30, Dec. 31. Guidelines for #10 SASE. Charges $4 fee. Writer must be 16 years old.

‡**MIDLAND AUTHORS AWARD,** Society of Midland Authors, SASE % Bowman, 152 N. Scoville, Oak Park IL 60302. (708)383-7568. Estab. 1915. Annual awards for published or produced drama, fiction, nonfiction, poetry, biography, children's fiction and children's nonfiction. Authors must reside in the states of Illinois, Indiana, Iowa, Kansas, Michigan, Minnesota, Missouri, Nebraska, North Dakota, South Dakota, Wisconsin or Ohio. Deadline: Jan. 15.

‡**THE NEBRASKA REVIEW AWARDS IN FICTION AND POETRY,** *The Nebraska Review,* ASH 215, University of Nebraska-Omaha, Omaha NE 68182-0324. (402)554-2771. Contact: Susan Aizenberg (poetry) and James Reed (fiction). Estab. 1973. Previously unpublished fiction and a poem or group of poems. Deadline: Nov. 30.

NEUSTADT INTERNATIONAL PRIZE FOR LITERATURE, 110 Monnet Hall, Norman OK 73019. (405)325-4531. Estab. 1969. Previously published fiction, poetry and drama. Nominations are made only by members of the jury, which changes every two years.

NEW LETTERS LITERARY AWARDS, University of Missouri-Kansas City, Kansas City MO 64110-2499. Fax: (816)235-2611. Awards Coordinator: Glenda McCrary. Estab. 1986. Unpublished fiction, poetry and essays. Deadline: May 15. Finalists are notified the middle of August; winners announced the third week in September. Charges $10 fee per entry. Send SASE for guidelines.

NIMROD, ARTS AND HUMANITIES COUNCIL OF TULSA PRIZES, 2210 South Main, Tulsa OK 74114. (918)584-3333. Editor: Francine Ringold. Unpublished fiction (Katherine Anne Porter prize) and poetry (Pablo Neruda Prize). Deadline: April 17. Fee $10, for which you receive an issue of *Nimrod.* (Writers entering both fiction and poetry contest need only pay once.) Send #10 SASE for complete guidelines. Sample copies are $5 for an older issue, $7 for a recent issue.

‡**FELIX POLLAK/CHRIS O'MALLEY PRIZES IN POETRY AND FICTION,** *The Madison Review,* Dept. of English, 600 N. Park St., Madison WI 53706. (608)263-3374. Director: Ronald Kuka. Offered annually for previously unpublished work. "The Felix Pollak contest awards $500 to the best poems submitted, out of a field of around 500 submissions yearly. The purpose of the prize is to award good poets. Submissions must consist of three poems. The Chris O'Malley prize in fiction is awarded to the best piece of fiction." Deadline: Sept. 30. Prize: poetry $500; fiction $500; plus publication in the spring issue of *The Madison Review.* All contest entries are considered as submissions to *The Madison Review,* the literary journal sponsoring the contest. No simultaneous submissions to other publications. There is a reading fee of $2 for each entry in both the Pollak and O'Malley contests."

PRAIRIE SCHOONER BERNICE SLOTE AWARD, *Prairie Schooner,* 201 Andrews, University of Nebraska, Lincoln NE 68588-0334. (402)472-3191. Fax: (402)472-4636. Editor: Hilda Raz. Estab. 1984. Annual award for the best work by a beginning writer published in *Prairie Schooner.* Winner announced in the spring issue of the following year. Prize: $500.

PRAIRIE SCHOONER READERS' CHOICE AWARDS, *Prairie Schooner,* 201 Andrews, University of Nebraska, Lincoln NE 68588-0334. (402)472-3191. Fax: (402)472-4636. Editor: Hilda Raz. Annual awards for work published in *Prairie Schooner.* Winners announced in the spring issue of the following year. Prize: $250 each. Several Readers' Choice Awards are given each year.

‡**QRL POETRY SERIES,** *Quarterly Review of Literature,* 26 Haslet Ave., Princeton NJ 08540. (609)921-6976. Contact: Renée Weiss. An open competition that awards $1,000, plus 100 copies and publication to each winner for a book of miscellaneous poems, a single long poem, a poetic play, a book of translation. Submission May and October *only.* $20 subscription to the series. Send SASE for complete information.

QUINCY WRITER'S GUILD ANNUAL CREATIVE WRITING CONTEST, Quincy Writer's Guild, c/o Natalie Miller Rotunda, P.O. Box 112, Quincy IL 62306-0112. (217)223-3117. Categories include: poetry, short story, fiction and Clara (pen name works only in any of above categories). Opens: Feb. 15. Deadline: April 15. Entry fees: $2 per poem; $3 for Clara; $4 for short stories and articles. "No identification should appear on manuscripts, but should be on a separate 3x5 card attached to the entry with name, address, phone number, word count, and title of work." Previously unpublished work. Cash prizes. Guidelines for SASE.

‡**READER RITER POLL,** *Affaire de Coeur,* 1555 Washington Ave., San Leandro CA 94577. (415)357-5665. Director: Barbara N. Keenan. Awards for previously published material in 12 categories appearing in magazine. Deadline: March 15.

RHYME TIME CREATIVE WRITING COMPETITION, *Rhyme Time*, P.O. Box 2907, Decatur IL 62526. Award Director: Linda Hutton. Estab. 1981. Annual no-fee contest. Submit one typed poem, any style, any length. One winner will receive $25; one runner-up will receive a year's subscription to *Rhyme Time*. No poems will be published. Include an SASE and submit before November 1.

MARY ROBERTS RINEHART FUND, English Department, George Mason University, 4400 University Dr., Fairfax VA 22030-4444. (703)993-1185. Contact: Roger Lathbury. Grants by nomination to unpublished creative writers for fiction, poetry, drama, biography, autobiography or history with a strong narrative quality. Submissions are accepted for fiction and poetry in odd years, and nonfiction and drama in even years. Deadline: Nov. 30.

ROBERTS WRITING AWARDS, H.G. Roberts Foundation, Inc., P.O. Box 1868, Pittsburg KS 66762. (316)231-2998. Contact: Stephen Meats. Estab. 1988. Competitions in unpublished poetry, short fiction, and informal essays. No limitations on subject matter or form. Deadline: Sept. 15. Charges $6 for 1-5 poems; additional poems $1 each. Short fiction, essays, $6 each. Open to English language works by any writers. Send SASE for guidelines and entry form.

SONORA REVIEW ANNUAL LITERARY AWARDS, *Sonora Review*, English Department, University of Arizona, Tucson AZ 85721. "For the best previously unpublished poetry, fiction and nonfiction." Awards: $150 and $50 and publication in *Sonora Review*. Deadlines: Send work from August 1 to January 20. Poetry mss must be less than 12 pages, fiction/nonfiction no more than 8,000 words. No formal application form is required; regular submission guidelines apply. Guidelines for #10 SASE. For samples, send $5.

SOUTHWEST REVIEW AWARDS, Southern Methodist University, 307 Fondren Library West, P.O. Box 0374, Dallas TX 75275-0374. (214)768-1036. Annual awards for fiction, nonfiction and poetry published in the magazine. "The $1,000 John H. McGinnis Memorial Award is given each year for fiction and nonfiction that has been published in the *Southwest Review* in the previous year. Stories or articles are not submitted directly for the award, but simply for publication in the magazine. The Elizabeth Matchett Stover Award, an annual prize of $150, is awarded to the author of the best poem or group of poems published in the magazine during the preceding year."

SUCARNOCHEE REVIEW POETRY/FICTION AWARD, *The Sucarnochee Review*, Station 22, Livingston University, Livingston AL 35470. (205)652-9661. Contest/Award Director: Joe Taylor. Annual contest for previously unpublished work. No deadlines. "We roll over entries for subsequent issues. Send work to magazine; all submissions are automatically considered for competition. Multiple submissions OK." Prize consists of publication, 3 copies of magazine and $50.

WESTERN MAGAZINE AWARDS, Western Magazine Awards Foundation, 3898 Hillcrest Ave., Vancouver, British Columbia V7R 4B6 Canada. (604)984-7525. Fax: (604)985-6262. Contact: Tina Baird. "Annual awards for previously published magazine work. Entries must have appeared in print between January 1 and December 31 of previous calendar year. Entry categories include business, culture and science, technology and medicine, entertainment, fiction, political issues, and much more. Write or phone for rules and entry forms. Deadline: Feb. 1. Entry fee: $18 for work in magazines with circulation under 20,000; $24 for work in magazines with circulation over 20,000. $500 award. Applicant must be a Canadian citizen or a landed immigrant, or a full-time resident of Canada. The work must have been published in a magazine whose main editorial office is in Western Canada, the NW Territories and Yukon.

‡**WRITERS AT WORK FELLOWSHIP COMPETITION**, Writers at Work, P.O. Box 1146, Centerville UT 84014-5146. (801)292-9285. Contact: Barry Scholl. Offered annually for unpublished work. Contest is for short story or novel excerpts and poetry. Deadline: Mar. 15. Contest/award rules and entry forms available for SASE. "Call (801)292-9285." Charges fee. Write for current information. "Only the $10 fee is required for consideration. Short stories or novel excerpts must be no longer than 20 double-spaced pages (one story per entry only). Poetry submissions are limited to 6 poems, 20 pages maximum."

WRITER'S DIGEST WRITING COMPETITION, *Writer's Digest* Magazine, 1507 Dana Ave., Cincinnati OH 45207-9966. (513)531-2222. Fax: (513)531-2902. Contest Director: Alice P. Buening. Contest in 62nd year. Submissions to be unpublished. Send #10 SASE for guidelines. Deadline: May 31.

Arts Councils and Foundations

‡**ARTIST ASSISTANCE FELLOWSHIP**, Minnesota State Arts Board, 432 Summit Ave., St. Paul MN 55102. (612)297-2603. Fax: (612)297-4304. Artist Assistance Program Associate: Karen Mueller. Annual fellowships of $6,000 to be used for time, materials, living expenses. Literary categories include prose, poetry and theater arts (playwriting and screenwriting). Applicants must be Minnesota residents. Deadline: Late September.

‡**ARTIST FELLOWSHIPS**, Washington State Arts Commission, P.O. Box 42675, Olympia WA 98504-2675. (206)753-3858. Program Manager: Mary Frye. Offered every two years for either previously published or unpublished work. Purpose is to give support to generative artists to pursue their work—fellowship. Deadline: Fall (varies), "depends upon budget/staff constraints." Contest/award guidelines and application forms available on request. Prize: $5,000 fellowship. Judged by peer panel. "Artists must have 5 years professional experience, no students. Must prove WA state residency."

‡**ARTIST PROJECTS**, Rhode Island State Council on the Arts, Suite 103, 95 Cedar St., Providence RI 02903. (401)277-3880. Fax: (401)521-1351. Contact: Dawn Dunley Roch. Previously published or unpublished submissions. "Artist Project grants enable an artist to create new work and/or complete works-in-progress by providing direct financial assistance. By encouraging significant development in the work of an individual artist, these grants recognize the central contribution artists make to the creative environment of Rhode Island." Deadline: October 1. Send 9×12 SASE for guidelines. Prize: non-matching grants of $1,500-4,000. Open only to RI residents, age 18 or older. Students not eligible. Consult program director.

ARTISTS FELLOWSHIP GRANTS, Oregon Arts Commission, 550 Airport Rd. SE, Salem OR 97310. (503)378-3625. Assistant Director: Vincent K. Dunn. Award offered every two years. "Grants for advancement in the field of literature." Deadline: Sept. 1, 1994; only offered in even numbered years. Contact Oregon Arts Commission for details. Prize: $3,000 fellowships. Open only to Oregon residents. Students are not eligible.

ARTIST'S FELLOWSHIPS, New York Foundation for the Arts, 155 Ave. of the Americas, New York NY 10013-2206. (212)366-6900 ext. 217. Contact: Penelope Dannenberg. "Artists' Fellowships are cash grants of $7,000 awarded in 15 disciplines on a bi-annual rotation. Fiction and Playwriting/Screenwriting will be the literature disciplines under review in 1993-1994. Awards are based upon the recommendations of peer panels and are not project support. The fellowship may be used by each recipient as she/he sees fit. All applicants must be 18 years of age and a New York resident for 2 years prior to the time of application. Call for application in July. Deadlines will be in October. Results announced in May. The New York Foundation for the Arts supports artists at all stages of their careers and from diverse backgrounds."

‡**ARTS RECOGNITION AND TALENT SEARCH**, National Foundation for Advancement in the Arts, 3915 Biscayne Blvd., Miami FL 33137. (305)573-0490. Fax: (305)573-4870. President: Dr. William Banchs. Estab. 1981. For achievements in dance, music, theater, visual arts and writing. Students fill in and return the application, available at every public and private high school around the nation. Deadline: early-June 1, regular-October 1. Charges $25 registration fee.

ASSISTANCE TO ESTABLISHED WRITERS, Nova Scotia Dept. of Tourism and Culture, Cultural Affairs Division, P.O. Box 456, Halifax, Nova Scotia B3J 2R5 Canada. (902)424-6389. Fax: (902)424-2668. Offered twice annually for unpublished submissions. "Objective: To assist the professional writer with the costs of completing the research or manuscript preparation for a project in which a trade publisher has expressed serious interest." Deadline: April 1 and October 1. Prize: Maximum of $2,000 Canadian. Applicant must be a Canadian citizen or landed immigrant and must have had their principal residence in Nova Scotia for 12 consecutive months at the time of application. Applicant must be an experienced writer who writes for print or broadcast media, film or stage, who has been consistently published and/or produced in the media.

‡**ASSOCIATESHIP**, Rocky Mountain Women's Institute, 7150 Montview Blvd., Denver CO 80220. (303)871-6923. Fax: (303)871-6897. Contact: Cindy Stone. Offered annually for unpublished works. "The mission of the Rocky Mountain Women's Institute is to promote the intellectual and artistic accomplishment of women by creating a supportive community of artists, writers, and scholars." Deadline: March 15. Contest/award rules and forms available for SASE. Charges $5 fee. Prize: $1,000 stipend, office studio space and support services. Must live within commuting distance of Denver.

GEORGE BENNETT FELLOWSHIP, Phillips Exeter Academy, Exeter NH 03833-1104. Estab. 1968. Annual award of stipend, room and board "to provide time and freedom from material considerations to a person seriously contemplating or pursuing a career as a writer. Applicants should have a manuscript in progress which they intend to complete during the fellowship period." Send SASE for application form and details. Deadline: Dec. 1. Charges $5 fee. Residence at the Academy during the Fellowship period required.

BRODY ARTS FUND FELLOWSHIP, California Community Foundation, Suite 2400, 606 S. Olive St., Los Angeles CA 90014-1526. (213)413-4042. Fax: (213)629-4782. "The Brody Arts Fund is designed to serve the needs of emerging artists and arts organizations, especially those rooted in the diverse, multi-cultural communities of Los Angeles. The fellowship program rotates annually between 3 main subsections of the arts. Literary artists will be considered in 1994. Applicants must reside in Los Angeles County. Students not eligible."

BUNTING FELLOWSHIP, Radcliffe College, 34 Concord Ave., Cambridge MA 02138. (617)495-8212. Fax:(617)495-8136. Contact: Fellowships Coordinator. "Fellowship programs are designed to support women of exceptional promise and demonstrated accomplishment who wish to pursue independent work in academic and professional fields and in the creative arts. Projects with public policy applications are especially encouraged. Applications will be judged on the quality and significance of the proposed project, the applicant's record of accomplishment, and on the difference the fellowship might make in advancing the applicant's career." Deadline varies. Call or write for application. Award is $30,000 stipend, plus office space and access to most resources at Harvard University and Radcliffe College. "The competition for writers is very high. We discourage writers who have not had publications or demonstrated level of accomplishment."

BUSH ARTIST FELLOWSHIPS, The Bush Foundation, E-900 First Natl. Bank Bldg., 332 Minnesota St., St. Paul MN 55101. (612)227-5222. Contact: Sally F. Dixon. Award for Minnesota, North Dakota, South Dakota, and western Wisconsin residents "to buy 6-18 months of time for the applicant to do his/her own work." Up to 15 fellowships annually. $26,000 stipend each plus additional $7,000 for production and travel. Deadline: mid Nov.

‡CAREER OPPORTUNITY GRANTS, Minnesota State Arts Board, 432 Summit Ave., St. Paul MN 55102. (612)297-2603. Fax: (612)297-4304. Artist Assistance Program Associate: Karen Mueller. Award offered three times a year. "Career Opportunity grants ranging from $100 to $1,000 may be used to support unique, concrete opportunities that may significantly enhance an artist's work or career." Applications accepted in fiction, creative nonfiction, poetry, playwriting, screenwriting. Applicants must be Minnesota residents. Deadlines in August, December, April.

COMMONWEALTH OF PENNSYLVANIA COUNCIL ON THE ARTS LITERATURE FELLOWSHIPS, 216 Finance Bldg., Harrisburg PA 17120. (717)787-6883. Award Director: Marcia D. Salvatore. Estab. 1966. Fellowships for Pennsylvania writers of fiction and poetry. Deadline: Oct 1.

‡CREATIVE ARTISTS GRANT, Arts Foundation of Michigan, 2164 Penobscot Building, 645 Griswold St., Detroit MI 48226. (313)964-2244. Individual Artist Coordinator: Ann Treadwell. Grants of up to $7,000 for Michigan creative artists. Deadline: April. Check yearly for specific deadline.

CREATIVITY FELLOWSHIP, Northwood University Alden B. Dow Creativity Center, Midland MI 48640-2398. (517)837-4478. Award Director: Carol B. Coppage. Ten-week summer residency for individuals in any field who wish to pursue a new and different creative idea that has the potential of impact in that field. No accommodations for family/pets. Deadline: Dec. 31.

‡DIVERSE VISIONS REGIONAL GRANTS PROGRAM, Intermedia Arts, 425 Ontario St. SE, Minneapolis MN 55414. (612)627-4444. Director of Artist Programs: Al Kosters. Estab. 1986. Regional (IA, KS, MN, NE, ND, SD, WI) interdisciplinary grants. Deadline: spring

‡DORLAND MOUNTAIN ARTS COLONY RESIDENCIES, Dorland Mountain Arts Colony, P.O. Box 6, Temecula CA 92593. (909)676-5039. Contact: Admissions Secretary. Offered every 6 months for previously published or unpublished work. "Dorland Mountain Colony's Artist residencies are awarded semi-annually to writers, artists, composers whose work passes review by a committee of established artists in the appropriate discipline." Deadline: March 1, September 1. Contest/award rules and entry forms available for SASE. Prize: 2-week to 2-month residencies at Dorland; "small cabin donations are asked of accepted artists." Contest is open to any writer.

‡FELLOWSHIP IN LITERATURE, Rhode Island State Council on the Arts, Suite 103, 95 Cedar St., Providence RI 02903. (401)277-3880. Contact: Dawn Dunley Roch. Previously published or unpublished submissions. "Fellowships encourage the creative development of artists by enabling them to set aside time to pursue their work and achieve specific career goals. Fellowships provide funds for the purchase of materials and supplies." Deadline: April 1. Send 9 × 12 SASE with 75¢ postage for guidelines. Prize: $5,000 fellowship. Open only to RI residents, age 18 or older. Students not eligible. Consult program director.

FELLOWSHIP-LITERATURE, Alabama State Council on the Arts, 1 Dexter Ave., Montgomery AL 36130. (205)242-4076. Fax: (205)240-3269. Contact: Randy Shoults. Previously published or unpublished. "To set aside time to create and to improve skills." Deadline: May 1. Guidelines available. Prize: $10,000 or $5,000. Two year Alabama residency requirement. Literature Fellowship offered on alternate, even numbered years.

FELLOWSHIP/NEW JERSEY STATE COUNCIL ON THE ARTS, New Jersey State Council on the Arts, CN806, Trenton NJ 08625. (609)292-6130. Executive Director: Barbara F. Russo. Annual prose, poetry, playwriting in literature awards for New Jersey residents. Deadline: March.

FELLOWSHIPS TO ASSIST RESEARCH AND ARTISTIC CREATION, John Simon Guggenheim Memorial Foundation, 90 Park Ave., New York NY 10016. (212)687-4470. Annual. The fellowships assist scholars and artists to engage in research in any field of knowledge and creation in any of the arts, under the freest possible conditions and irrespective of race, color, or creed.

WILLIAM FLANAGAN MEMORIAL CREATIVE PERSONS CENTER, Edward F. Albee Foundation, 14 Harrison St., New York NY 10013. (212)226-2020. Annual contest/award. Either previously published or unpublished. One month residency at "The Barn" in Montauk, New York offers writers privacy and a peaceful atmosphere in which to work. Deadline: April 1. Prize: Room only; writers pay for food and travel expenses. Judging by panel of qualified professionals.

‡**FLORIDA INDIVIDUAL ARTIST FELLOWSHIPS,** Florida Department of State, Bureau of Grants Services, Division of Cultural Affairs, The Capitol, Tallahassee FL 32399-0250. (904)487-2980. Director: Peyton Fearington. Fellowship for Florida writers only. Award: $5,000 each for fiction, poetry and children's literature. Deadline: mid-February.

‡**FULBRIGHT SCHOLAR PROGRAM,** Council for International Exchange of Scholars, Suite 5M, 3007 Tilden St. NW, Washington DC 20008. (202)686-7877. Estab. 1947. Grants for faculty and professionals. "Approximately 1,000 awards are offered annually in virtually all academic disciplines for university lecturing or research in over 120 countries. The opportunity for multicountry research also exists in many areas. Grant duration ranges from 2 months to an academic year." Deadline: August 1, all world areas. Eligibility criteria include U.S. citizenship at the time of application; M.F.A., Ph.D or equivalent professional qualifications; for lecturing awards, university teaching experience.

GAP (GRANTS FOR ARTIST PROJECTS); FELLOWSHIP, Artist Trust, Suite 415, 1402 3rd Ave, Seattle WA 98101-2118. (206)467-8734. Fax: (206)467-9633. Executive Director: Marschel Paul. Fellowship offered as announced. Either published or unpublished works. "The GAP is awarded to 30-50 artists, including writers, per year. The award is meant to help finance a specific project, which can be in very early stages or near completion. The Fellowship is awarded to eight artists per year; the award is made on the basis of work of the past five years. It is 'no-strings-attached' funding." Send SASE for guidelines. Prize: GAP: up to $1,000. Fellowship: $5,000. Full-time students not eligible. *Only Washington state residents are eligible.*

GOVERNOR GENERAL'S LITERARY AWARDS, Canada Council, Writing and Publishing Section, 99 Metcalfe St., P.O. Box 1047, Ottawa, Ontario K1P 5V8 Canada. (613)598-4376. Contact: Writing and Publishing Officer. "Awards are given annually to the best English-language and French-language work in each of the seven categories of fiction, nonfiction, poetry, drama, translation children's literature (text) and children's literature (illustration). Books must be first-edition trade books which have been written, translated or illustrated by Canadian citizens or permanent residents of Canada and published in Canada or abroad during the previous year. In the case of translation, the original work must also be a Canadian-authored title. Books must be submitted by publishers and accompanied by a Publisher's Submission Form, which is available from the Writing and Publishing Section." Deadline: Aug. 31.

‡**IDAHO WRITER-IN-RESIDENCE,** Idaho Commission on the Arts, 304 W. State, Boise ID 83720. (208)334-2119. Program Coordinator: Diane Josophy Peavey. Estab. 1982. Offered every 2 years for previously published (within previous 5 years) or unpublished work. Award of $10,000 for an Idaho writer, who over the two-year period reads his/her work throughout the state to increase the appreciation for literature." Deadline: spring, 1993; 1995; dates change. Criteria and procedures information for SASE. Open to any Idaho writer.

ILLINOIS ARTS COUNCIL ARTISTS FELLOWSHIP, (formerly Artists Fellowship), State of Illinois Center, Suite 10-500, 100 W. Randolph, Chicago IL 60601. (312)814-6750. Contact: Director of Communication Arts. Offered every two years for previously published or unpublished work. "Submitted work must have been completed no more than 4 years prior to deadline. Artists fellowships are awarded to Illinois artists of exceptional talent to enable them to pursue their artistic goals; fellowships are offered in poetry and prose (fiction and craetive nonfiction)." Deadline: September 1. "Interested Illinois writers should write or call for information." Prize: $500 finalist award; $5,000 or $10,000 Artist's Fellowship. "Writer must be Illinois resident and not a degree-seeking student. Applicants for Poetry Fellowship can submit up to 15 pages of work in manuscript; prose fellowship applicants can submit up to 30 pages of work in manuscript."

‡**INDIVIDUAL ARTIST FELLOWSHIP,** Oregon Arts Commission, 550 Airport Rd. SE, Salem OR 97310. (503)378-3625. Contact: Assistant Director. Offered every two years (even years only). "Fellowships reward achievement in the field of literature." Deadline: Sept. 1st. Send SASE for application and instructions. Prize: $3,000. "Writers must be Oregon residents 18 years and older. Degree candidate students not eligible."

INDIVIDUAL ARTIST FELLOWSHIP AWARD, Montana Arts Council, Suite 252, 316 North Park Ave., Helena MT 59620. (406)444-6430. Contact: Martha Sprague. Award made every year to *Montana residents only.* Deadline: April 30.

INDIVIDUAL ARTIST PROGRAM, Wisconsin Arts Board, 101 E. Wilson St., 1st Floor, Madison WI 53703. (608)266-0190. Annual fellowships and grants for Wisconsin residents. Deadline: Sept. 15.

INDIVIDUAL ARTISTS FELLOWSHIPS, Nebraska Arts Council, 3838 Davenport St., Omaha NE 68131-2329. (402)595-2122. Fax: (402)595-2334. Contact: Suzanne Wise. Offered every two years (literature alternates with performing arts). Previously unpublished work preferred, not mandated. "The Individual Artists Fellowship program recognizes exemplary achievements by originating artists in their fields of endeavor and supports the contributions made by Nebraska artists to the quality of life in this state." Deadline: Nov. 1. "Generally, master awards are $3,000-4,000 and merit awards are $1,000-2,000. Funds available are announced in September prior to the deadline." Must be a resident of Nebraska for at least two years prior to submission date; 18 years of age; not enrolled in an undergraduate, graduate or certificate-granting program in English, creative writing, literature, or related field.

ISLAND LITERARY AWARDS, Prince Edward Island Council of the Arts, P.O. Box 2234, Chardottetown, Prince Edward Island C1A 8B9 Canada. (902)368-4410. Award Director: Judy K. MacDonald. Previously unpublished works. Offers 5 awards; poetry, short fiction, feature article, children's literature and student writing. Deadline Feb. 15. Guidelines for #10 SAE with 1 IRC. Charges $5 fee. *Available to residents of PEI only.*

‡JOSEPH HENRY JACKSON/JAMES D. PHELAN LITERARY AWARDS, The San Francisco Foundation, Administered by Intersection for the Arts, 446 Valencia St., San Francisco CA 94103. (415)626-2787. Awards Coordinator: Adrienne Krug. Jackson Award: unpublished, work-in-progress—fiction (novel or short story), nonfiction or poetry by author age 20-35, with 3-year consecutive residency in N. California or Nevada prior to submission. Phelan: unpublished, work-in-progress fiction, nonfiction, short story, poetry or drama by California-born author age 20-35. Deadline: Jan. 30.

‡JURIED COMPETITION, Florida Literary Foundation, 2516 Ridge Ave., Sarasota FL 34235. (813)957-1281. Fax: (813)954-5083. Contest Director: Patrick J. Powers. Previously unpublished poetry, fiction and nonfiction. "Will accept previously published poetry if poet has copyright." Deadlines June 30 and Jan. 30. Guidelines for #10 SASE. Donation requested. Prize: Publication; copies.

‡EZRA JACK KEATS MEMORIAL FELLOWSHIP, Ezra Jack Keats Foundation (funding) awarded through Kerlan Collection, University of Minnesota, 109 Walter Library 117 Pleasant St. SE., Minneapolis MN 55455. (612)624-4576. Curator, Kerlan Collection: Karen Hoyle. Offered annually. "Purpose is to award a talented writer and/or illustrator of children's books who wishes to use Kerlan Collection for the furtherance of his or her artistic development." Deadline: early May. Application materials or further information for SASE. Prize: $1,500 for travel to study at Kerlan Collection. Judged by a committee of 4-5 members from varying colleges at University of Minnesota and outside the University. "Special consideration will be given to someone who would find it difficult to finance the visit to the Kerlan Collection."

KENTUCKY ARTS COUNCILS FELLOWSHIPS IN WRITING, Kentucky Arts Council, 31 Fountain Place, Frankfort KY 40601. (502)564-3757. Fax: (502)564-2839. Contact: Irwin Pickett. Award offered every two years (even numbered years) for previously published or unpublished work for development/artist's work. Deadline: September every other year (in even numbered years). Rules and entry form for SASE (3 months before deadline). Award: $5,000. Must be Kentucky resident.

LITERARY ARTS PROGRAMS, (formerly Literary Arts Awards), Arts Branch, Dept of Municipalities, Culture and Housing, P.O. Box 6000, Fredericton, New Brunswick E3B 5H1 Canada. (506)453-2555. Fax: (506)453-2416. Contact: Arts Branch. Annual awards: Excellence Award, Creation Grant, Artist-in-Residence program, and travel program. *Available to New Brunswick residents only. (Must have resided in NB 2 of past 4 years.)*

THE GERALD LOEB AWARDS, The John E. Anderson Graduate School of Management at UCLA, 405 Hilgard Ave., Los Angeles CA 90024-1481. (310)206-1877. Fax: (310)206-9830. Contact: Office of Communications. Previously published during the previous calendar year. "To recognize writers who make significant contributions to the understanding of business, finance and the economy." Deadline: Feb. 15 "unless it lands

Market conditions are constantly changing! If this is 1995 or later, buy the newest edition of Writer's Market *at your favorite bookstore or order directly from* Writer's Digest Books.

on a holiday." Charges $20 fee per entry. Winners in each category receive $1,000. Honorable mentions, when awarded, receive $500.

LOFT-McKNIGHT WRITERS AWARD, The Loft, Pratt Community Center, 66 Malcolm Ave., S.E., Minneapolis MN 55414-3551. Attn: Assoc. Program Director. Eight awards of $7,500 and two awards of distinction at $10,500 each for Minnesota writers of poetry and creative prose. Deadline: November.

LOFT-MENTOR SERIES, The Loft, Pratt Community Center, 66 Malcolm Ave. S.E., Minneapolis MN 55414-3551. Attn: Assoc. Program Director. Estab. 1974. Opportunity to work with four nationally known writers and small stipend available to 8 winning poets and fiction writers. "Must live close enough to Minneapolis to participate fully in the series." Deadline: May.

MARIN INDIVIDUAL ARTISTS GRANTS, Marin Arts Council, 251 N. San Pedro Rd., San Rafael CA 94903. (415)499-8350. Contact: Beky Carter. "Frequency of award depends on funding source. Open to Marin residents only. No students. Categories include poetry, playwriting, art for youth, fiction/creative prose and screenwriting. Submit works completed in last 2 years only. Unrestricted fellowships based on the quality of the work submitted." Deadlines: usually end of Jan. or March. Rules and entry forms for SASE. Awards grants amounting between $2,000-10,000.

WALTER RUMSEY MARVIN GRANT, Ohioana Library Association, Suite 1105, 65 S. Front St., Columbus OH 43215. (614)466-3831. Director: Linda Hengst. Award given every 2 years, (even years). Applicant must have been born in Ohio or have lived in Ohio for 5 years or more, must be 30 years of age or younger, and not have published a book. Deadline Jan. 31.

‡**MONEY FOR WOMEN,** Barbara Deming Memorial Fund, Inc., P.O. Box 40-1043, Brooklyn NY 11240-1043. Contact: Pam McAllister. "Small grants to individual feminists in the arts (musicians, artists, dancers, writers, poets, photographers, playwrights, filmmakers) whose work addresses women's concerns and/or speaks for peace and justice from a feminist perspective." Deadline: Dec. 31/June 30. Rules and entry forms for SASE. Prize: Grants up to $1,000: "The Fund does *not* give educational assistance, monies for personal study or loans, monies for dissertation or research projects, grants for group projects, business ventures, or emergency funds for hardships." Open to individual feminists in the arts. Applicants must be citizens of the US or Canada.

LA NAPOULE RESIDENCY, North Carolina Arts Council, Dept. of Cultural Resources, Raleigh NC 27601-2807. (919)733-2111. Contact: Deborah McGill. "To provide an international experience and time to work for writers who live in North Carolina." Deadline: Feb. 1. Write for guidelines. The grant supports a 3-month stay for one writer of fiction, poetry, or literary nonfiction at the La Napoule Foundation in southern France; round trip air fare; room and board; materials subsidy of $500; $1,000 for additional living expenses. Writer must have been a resident of the state for at least a year prior to application and may not be enrolled in a degree-granting program.

NATIONAL ENDOWMENT FOR THE ARTS: ARTS ADMINISTRATION FELLOWS PROGRAM/FELLOWSHIP, National Endowment for the Arts, 1100 Pennsylvania Ave., NW, Washington DC 20506. (202)682-5786. Fax: (202)682-5610. Contact: Anya Nykyforiak. Estab. 1973. Offered three times each year: Spring, Summer and Fall. "The Arts Administration Fellowships are for arts managers and administrators in the non-profit literary publishing field or writers' centers. Fellows come to the NEA for an 11-week residency to acquire an overview of this Federal agency's operations. Deadline: Jan./April/July. Guidelines may be requested by letter or telephone.

NEW HAMPSHIRE INDIVIDUAL ARTISTS' FELLOWSHIPS, New Hampshire State Council on the Arts, 40 N. Main St., Concord NH 03301-4974. (603)271-2789. Coordinator: Audrey V. Sylvester. Previously published entries of not more than 5 years since completion. "To recognize artistic excellence and professional commitment." Deadline: July 1. Contest/award rules and entry forms available with SASE or call for application. Prize: up to $3,000. Applicant must be over 18; not enrolled as full-time student; have resided in NH for at least one year prior to application and may not have been a fellow in preceding year.

NEW YORK STATE WRITER IN RESIDENCE PROGRAM, New York State Council on the Arts, 915 Broadway, New York NY 10010. (212)387-7020. Contact: Literature Program Director. Biannual residency program. "In addition to rewarding the writers' work, residencies are awarded to give writers a chance to work with a nonprofit organization in a community setting." Deadline: March 1. "Award consists of an $8,000 stipend for a 6 month residency." Applications are judged by a panel of writers, administrators, and translators. Applicant must be nominated by a New York state nonprofit organization.

‡**PALENVILLE INTERARTS COLONY RESIDENCY PROGRAM,** June-Sept. 30: 2 Bond St., New York NY 10012, (212)254-4614; or Oct. 1-May 30: P.O. Box 59, Palenville NY 12463 (518)678-3332. Contact: Joanna Sherman/Patrick Sciarratta. Offered annually. "Competitive residency program offers room or cabin for

writers to work in a creative, unpressured environment free from distractions. Residencies, partially or fully subsidized, available between May 1 and Sept. 30." Deadline: April 20, "usually between April 1 and 30th annually." Information and application form available for SASE. Charges $10 application fee. Prize: partially or fully subsidized residencies. Judged by panel of artists in each discipline. "Writing panel is one person, changes every other year." "Writer should have 3 years professional experience – but acceptance is based on quality of submitted sample writing, primarily. Open to playwrights, poets, etc. etc. Emerging writers welcome to apply."

PRIX ALVINE-BELISLE, ASTED, 1030 Cherrier, Bureau 505, Montreal, Quebec H2L 1H9 Canada. Fax: (514)521-9561. Agent: Johanne Petel. Estab. 1974. French-Canadian literature for children submitted by the publisher.

‡RESIDENCY, Millay Colony for the Arts, Steepletop, P.O. Box 3, Austerlitz NY 12017. (518)392-3103. Exec. Director: Ann-Ellen Lesser. Offered to fiction writers, poets and playwrights of talent. In-office deadlines: Feb. 1 for June-September; May 1 for October-January, Sept. 1 for February-May. Write or call for brochure and application form. Prize: one-month residency, room and board and studio. Open to writers, composers and visual artists.

STEGNER FELLOWSHIP, Stanford Creative Writing Program, Stanford University, Stanford CA 94305-2087. (415)723-2637. Contact: Prof. Nancy Packer. Estab. 1955. Annual fellowships include all tuition costs and a living stipend (four in fiction and four in poetry) for writers to come to Stanford for a period of two years to attend workshop to develop their particular writing. Deadline: Jan. 1. Charges $20 fee.

‡STUDENT RESEARCH GRANT, the Society for the Scientific Study of Sex, Box 208, Mount Vernon IA 52314. (319)895-8407. Fax: (319)895-6203. Contact: Naomi McCormick, Ph.D. Offered twice a year for unpublished works. "The student research grant award is granted twice yearly to help support graduate student research on a variety of sexually related topics." Deadline: February 1 and September 1. Rules and entry forms for SASE. Prize: $500. "Only open to students pursuing graduate study."

UCROSS FOUNDATION RESIDENCY, 2836 U.S. Highway 14-16E, Clearmont WY 82835. (307)737-2291. Fax: (307)737-2322. Contact: Elizabeth Guheen. 8 concurrent positions open for artists-in-residence in various disciplines (includes writers, visual artists, music, humanities) extending from 2 weeks-2 months. No charge for room, board or studio space. Deadline: March 1 for August-December program; Oct. 1 for January-May program.

U.S. RESIDENCIES, (formerly Headlands Residency), North Carolina Arts Council, Dept. of Cultural Resources, Raleigh NC 27601-2807. (919)733-2111. Contact: Deborah McGill. "To provide writers an opportunity for concentrated work in new settings and in the company of diverse artists from across the country. The council sponsors these residencies in partnership with established residency centers. Residency periods range from one to two months. All grants include transportation, room, and full or partial board. An additional stipend may be available. At certain centers families may be welcome. Deadline varies. Write for guidelines. Writer must have been a resident of N.C. for at least a year prior to application and may not be enrolled in a degree-granting program."

‡VERMONT COUNCIL ON THE ARTS, 136 State St., Drawer 33, Montpelier VT 05633-6001. (802)828-329. Fax: (802)828-3233. Contact: *Cornelia Carey, Grants Officer. Offered annually. Deadline: March 1, 1993 for Poetry Fellowship applications; Spring 1994 deadline for Theater Arts (includes playwrighting); Spring 1995 deadline for Fiction and Nonfiction. Previously published or unpublished works. "Project Grants are for specific projects of writers (poetry, playwrights, fiction, nonfiction) as well as not-for-profit presses. Fellowships are awarded in recognition of artistic accomplishment." Deadline: March 1. Artist development grants provide technical assistance for Vermont writers. Rolling deadline. Write or call for entry information. Prize: up to $3,000 for projects; $3,500 for fellowships. "Both programs are open to Vermont residents only."

‡WALDEN RESIDENCY FELLOWSHIPS, Northwest Writing Institute, Campus Box 100, Lewis & Clark College, Portland OR 97219. (503)768-7745. Fax: (503)768-7715. Offered annually for previously published or unpublished work. Purpose is "to provide a quiet, remote work space for Oregon writers who are working on a project." Deadline: late November. Send SASE for information and application form. Prize: 6- to 8-week residencies (3 per year) in a cabin in Southern Oregon. Utilities and partial board are included. "The sponsor and two other writers form a committee to judge the applications and select recipients." Writer must be from Oregon.

WRITER-IN-RESIDENCE PROGRAM, The Syvenna Foundation, Rt 1, Box 193, Linden TX 75563-9738. (903)835-8252. Associate Director: Barbara Carroll. Opportunity for beginning and intermediate women writers to have a cottage rent and utilities free for 2 or 3 months to pursue their craft. Four terms available each year. A $300/month stipend is also provided. All types of writing are considered. Deadlines: Aug. 1, Oct. 1, Dec. 1, April 1. Send SASE for application and guidelines.

WRITERS FELLOWSHIPS, NC Arts Council, Dept. of Cultural Resources, Raleigh NC 27601-2807. (919)733-2111. Literature Director: Deborah McGill. Offered annually. "To serve writers of fiction and poetry in North Carolina and to recognize the contribution they make to this state's creative environment." Deadline: Feb. 1. Write for guidelines. We offer four $8,000 grants each year. Writer must have been a resident of NC for at least a year and may not be enrolled in any degree-granting program at the time of application.

WRITERS' SCHOLARSHIP, North Carolina Arts Council, Dept. of Cultural Resources, Raleigh NC 27601-2807. (919)733-2111. Literature Director: Deborah McGill. These competitive grants are available on six weeks' notice from July 1 through March 30. "To provide writers of fiction, poetry and literary nonfiction who have a record of literary accomplishment with opportunities for research or enrichment." Deadline: April 1. Write for guidelines. "We budget $1,500 each year for grants of up to $500." Writer must have a certain amount of work in print (see guidelines), must have been a resident of NC for at least a year, and may not be enrolled in any degree-granting program at the time of application.

Miscellaneous

AJL REFERENCE BOOK AWARD, Association of Jewish Libraries, National Foundation for Jewish Culture, 330 7th Ave., 21st Floor, New York NY 10001. (216)381-6440. Outstanding reference book published during the previous year in the field of Jewish studies.

AMWA MEDICAL BOOK AWARDS COMPETITION, American Medical Writers Association, 9650 Rockville Pike, Bethesda MD 20814. (301)493-0003. Contact: Book Awards Committee. Previously published and must have appeared in print previous year. Contest is to honor the best medical book published in the previous year in each of three categories: Books for Physicians, Books for Allied Health Professionals and Trade Books. Deadline April 1. Charges $10 fee.

‡ANIMAL RIGHTS WRITING AWARD, 421 South State St., Clarks Summit PA 18411. Contact: Helen Jones, Chairperson. Offered annually for previously published works. "Awarded to the author of an exceptionally meritorious book or article which advances the cause of animal rights. Works will be judged for content and literary excellence." Prize: $500 and plaque. "Nominations may be made by anyone providing the work has been published in the English language. Suggested divisions are: novel, book length nonfiction, children's book, article. Three copies of the work shall be submitted to the ISAR, with a cover letter stating author, date of publication, and name of person or entity submitting. If no submission is considered deserving, an award will not be given in that division. Special awards may be given at the discretion of the judges."

BEST OF HOUSEWIFE WRITER'S FORUM AND YOUR WRITING LIFE DREAM CONTEST, *Housewife Writer's Forum*, P.O. Box 780, Lyman WY 82937-0780. (307)786-4513. Contest/Award Director: Diane Wolverton. "Best of" annually; "Your Writing Life" semi-annually. Contest for unpublished submissions. Deadline: "Best of" May 15. "Your Writing Life" Jan. 30 and July 30. "Best of" charges $4 prose/$2 poetry fee. "Your Writing Life" charges $2 fee. Prizes for Best of: $30/$20/$10; Your Writing Life: $20/$10/$5. Send SASE for guidelines.

BOWLING WRITING COMPETITION, American Bowling Congress Publications, 5301 S. 76th St., Greendale WI 53129-1127. Fax: (414)421-1194. Director: Rory Gillespie, Publications Manager. Estab. 1935. Feature, editorial and news all relating to the sport of bowling. Deadline: December 1.

GAVEL AWARDS, American Bar Association, 750 N. Lake Shore Dr., Chicago IL 60611. (312)988-6137. Fax: (312)988-5865. Contact: Peggy O'Carroll. Estab. 1957. Previously published, performed or broadcast works that promote "public understanding of the American system of law and justice." Deadline: Feb. 1.

GOLF WRITER'S CONTEST, Golf Course Superintendents Association of America, GCSAA, 1421 Research Park Dr., Lawrence KS 66049-3859. Fax: (913)832-4466. Public Relations Manager: Scott Smith. Previously published work pertaining to golf course superintendents. Must be a member of Golf Writers Association of America.

HARVARD OAKS CAREER GUIDANCE AWARD, #1681, 208 S. LaSalle, Chicago IL 60604. Award Director: William A. Potter. "Quarterly award to writers of published articles covering relevant topics in career selection and job search strategies." Deadlines: March 31, June 30, Sept. 30, Dec. 31. Guidelines for #10 SASE.

LANDMARK EDITIONS AWARDS FOR STUDENTS, Landmark Editions, Inc., P.O. Box 4469, Kansas City MO 64127-0469. (816)241-4919. Editorial Director: Nan Thatch. Annual awards for students aged 6-19. Accepts mss written and illustrated by students. Guidelines for #10 SAE with 2 first class stamps. Entry fee $1.

STEPHEN LEACOCK MEMORIAL AWARD FOR HUMOUR, Stephen Leacock Associates, P.O. Box 854, Orillia, Ontario L3V 6K8 Canada. (705)325-6546. Contest Director: Jean Dickson. Estab. 1947. For a book of humor published in previous year by a Canadian author. Include 10 books each entry and a b&w photo with bio. Deadline: Dec. 31. Charges $25 fee. Prize: Stephen Leacock Memorial Medal and J.P. Wiser cash award of $3,500.

‡LOUDEST LAF! LAUREL, *Laf!,* Scher Maihem Publishing Ltd., P.O. Box 313, Avilla IN 46710-0313. Contact: Fran Glass. "To encourage the writing of excellent short humor (600 words or less), and develop great humorists in the tradition of Mark Twain." Deadline: June 1, 1994. Contest/award rules and entry forms available for #10 SASE. Charges $6—includes a one-year subscription to *Laf!,* a bi-monthly humor magloid. Prize: $100 first prize. Top six will be published in Jan/Feb '95 awards edition of *Laf!*

THE ORVIS WILDBRANCH GRANT, The Orvis Company, Inc., Historic Route 7A, Manchester VT 05254. (802)362-3622. Fax: (802)362-0089. Tuition, room, board to Wildbranch Writer's Workshop in Vermont. Submit 5 copies of unpublished ms related to nature, conservation or the outdoors. Deadline: March 1.

PEN WRITING AWARDS FOR PRISONERS, PEN American Center, 568 Broadway, New York NY 10012. (212)334-1660. Fax: (212)334-2181. Contact: Pamela Pearce."Awarded to the authors of the best poetry, plays, short fiction and nonfiction received from prison writers in the U.S." Deadline variable.

WESTERN HERITAGE AWARD, National Cowboy Hall of Fame & Western Heritage Center, 1700 NE 63rd, Oklahoma City OK 73111. (405)478-2250 ext. 221. Contact: Dana Sullivant. Annual award for excellence in representation of great stories of the American West. Competition includes seven literary categories: Nonfiction; Western Novel; Juvenile Book; Art Book; Short Story; Poetry Book; and Magazine Article. Works published between January 1 and December 31 of the applicable calendar year. Deadline for entries: December 31.

Contests and Awards/Changes '93-'94

The following contests were listed in the 1993 edition but do not have listings in this edition of *Writer's Market*. The majority did not respond to our request to update their listings or return a questionnaire for a new listing. If a reason was given for their exclusion, we have included it in parentheses after the listing name.

Organizations of Interest

As markets become more competitive, contacts have become increasingly important for freelancers who need an added edge. Professional organizations on both local and national levels can be very helpful in this capacity. They often provide valuable opportunities for networking, information about new developments in the industry, and guidance in business or legal matters.

The majority of organizations listed here publish newsletters and other materials that can provide you with useful information for your writing career. Some even provide such opportunities as conferences and referral services.

Keep in mind that numerous local organizations and writers' clubs also exist, and can provide occasions for networking in your own area. You can usually find information about such groups in your local library or through an area college writing program.

Some of the following national organizations have branches or chapters in different cities across the country. Write to the organization for information about their membership requirements, individual chapters and programs for writers.

American Book Producers Association
Suite 604, 160 5th Ave.
New York NY 10010-7000

American Medical Writers Association
9650 Rockville Pike
Bethesda MD 20814-3998

American Society of Journalists & Authors
Suite 302, 1501 Broadway
New York NY 10036

American Translators Association
Suite 903, 1735 Jefferson Davis Highway
Arlington VA 22202-3413

Associated Writing Programs
Old Dominion University
Norfolk VA 23529-0079

Association of Authors Representatives
3rd Floor, 10 Astor Pl.
New York NY 10003

Association of Desk-Top Publishers
#800, 4677 30th St.
San Diego CA 92116-3245

The Authors & Artists Resource Center
P.O. Box 64785
Tucson AZ 85740-1785

The Authors Guild
330 W. 42nd St.
New York NY 10036

The Authors League of America
29th Floor, 330 W. 42nd St.
New York NY 10036

Copywriters Council of America
Linick Bldg. 102, 7 Putter Lane
Middle Island NY 11953-0102

Council of Authors & Journalists
% Uncle Remus Regional Library System
1131 East Ave.
Madison GA 30650

Council of Literary Magazines & Presses
Suite 3C, 154 Christopher St.
New York NY 10014

The Dramatists Guild
234 W. 44th St.
New York NY 10036

Editorial Freelancers Association
Room 9R, 36 E. 23rd St.,
New York NY 10159-2050

Education Writers Association
Suite 310, 1001 Connecticut Ave. NW
Washington DC 20036

Freelance Editorial Association
P.O. Box 835
Cambridge MA 02238

International Association of Business Communicators
Suite 600, 1 Hallidie Plaza
San Francisco CA 94102

International Association of Crime Writers Inc., North American Branch
JAF Box 1500
New York NY 10116

International Television Association
6311 N. O'Connor Rd., Lock Box 51
Irving TX 75039

International Women's Writing Guild
Box 810, Gracie Station
New York NY 10028

Mystery Writers of America
6th Floor, 17 E. 47th St.
New York NY 10017

National Association of Science Writers
Box 294
Greenlawn NY 11740

National Writers Club
Suite 424, 1450 S. Havana
Aurora CO 80012

National Writers Union
Room 203, 873 Broadway
New York NY 10003

PEN American Center
568 Broadway
New York NY 10012

Poetry Society of America
15 Grammercy Park
New York NY 10003

Poets & Writers
72 Spring St.
New York NY 10012

Publication Services Guild
P.O. Box 19663
Atlanta GA 30325

Public Relations Society of America
33 Irving Place
New York NY 10003

Romance Writers of America
Suite 315, 13700 Veterans Memorial Dr.
Houston TX 77014

Science-Fiction Fantasy Writers of America
Suite 1B, 5 Winding Brook Dr.
Guilderland NY 12084

Society of American Business Editors & Writers
% Janine Latus-Musick
University of Missouri
P.O. Box 838
Columbia MO 65205

Society of American Travel Writers
Suite 500, 1155 Connecticut Ave. NW
Washington DC 20036

Society of Children's Book Writers
P.O. Box 66296
Mar Vista Station
Los Angeles CA 90066

Society of Professional Journalists
16 S. Jackson
Greencastle IN 46135

Volunteer Lawyers for the Arts
6th Floor, 1 E. 53rd St.
New York NY 10022

Women in Communications
Suite 417, 2101 Wilson Blvd.
Arlington VA 22201

Writers Alliance
Box 2014
Setauket NY 11733

Writers Connection
Suite 180, 1601 Saratoga-Sunnyvale Rd.
Cupertino CA 95014

Writers Guild of America (East)
555 W. 57th St.
New York NY 10019

Writers Guild of America (West)
8955 Beverly Blvd.
West Hollywood CA 90048

Publications of Interest

In addition to newsletters and publications from local and national organizations, there are trade publications, books, and directories which offer valuable information to help in writing, in marketing your manuscripts and in understanding the business side of publishing. Some also list employment agencies that specialize in placing publishing professionals, and some announce actual freelance opportunities.

Trade magazines

ADVERTISING AGE, Crain Communications, 220 E. 42nd St., New York NY 10017. *Weekly magazine covering advertising in magazines, trade journals and business.*

DAILY VARIETY, Daily Variety Ltd./Cahners Publishing Co., 5700 Wilshire Blvd., Los Angeles CA 90036. *Trade publication on the entertainment industry, with helpful information for screenwriters.*

EDITOR & PUBLISHER, The Editor & Publisher Co., 11 W. 19th St., New York NY 10011. *Weekly magazine covering the newspaper publishing industry.*

FOLIO, Cowles Business Media, P.O. Box 4949, Stamford CT 06907-0949. *Monthly magazine covering the magazine publishing industry.*

GREETINGS MAGAZINE, MacKay Publishing Corp., 309 5th Ave., New York NY 10016. *Monthly magazine covering the greeting card industry.*

HORN BOOK MAGAZINE, 14 Beacon St., Boston MA 02108. *Bimonthly magazine that covers children's literature.*

PARTY & PAPER RETAILER, 4Ward Corp., 70 New Canaan Ave., Norwalk CT 06850. *Monthly magazine covering the greeting card and gift industry.*

POETS & WRITERS, 72 Spring St., New York NY 10012. *Monthly magazine, primarily for literary writers and poets.*

PUBLISHERS WEEKLY, 249 W. 17th St., New York NY 10011. *Weekly magazine covering the book publishing industry.*

SCIENCE FICTION CHRONICLE, P.O. Box 2730, Brooklyn NY 11202-0056. *Monthly magazine for science fiction, fantasy and horror writers.*

WASHINGTON JOURNALISM REVIEW, Suite 310, 4716 Pontiac St., College Park MD 20740-2493. *10 issues/year magazine for journalists and communications professionals.*

THE WRITER, 120 Boylston St., Boston MA 02116. *Monthly writers' magazine.*

WRITER'S DIGEST, 1507 Dana Ave., Cincinnati OH 45207. *Monthly writers' magazine.*

Books and directories

AV MARKET PLACE, R.R. Bowker, A Reed Reference Publishing Co., 121 Chanlon Rd., New Providence NJ 07974.

THE COMPLETE BOOK OF SCRIPTWRITING, by J. Michael Straczynski, Writer's Digest Books, 1507 Dana Ave., Cincinnati OH 45207.

THE COMPLETE GUIDE TO SELF PUBLISHING, by Marilyn and Tom Ross, Writer's Digest Books, 1507 Dana Ave., Cincinnati OH 45207.

COPYRIGHT HANDBOOK, R.R. Bowker, A Reed Reference Publishing Co., 121 Chanlon Rd., New Providence NJ 07974.

DIRECTORY OF EDITORIAL RESOURCES, Editorial Experts Inc., Suite 200, 66 Canal Center Plaza, Alexandria VA 22314-1538.

DRAMATISTS SOURCEBOOK, edited by Angela E. Mitchell and Gilliam Richards, Theatre Communications Group, Inc., 355 Lexington Ave., New York NY 10017.

1994 GUIDE TO LITERARY AGENTS & ART/PHOTO REPS, edited by Kirsten Holm, Writer's Digest Books, 1507 Dana Ave., Cincinnati OH 45207. (Available March, 1994.)

THE GUIDE TO WRITERS CONFERENCES, ShawGuides, Suite 1406, 625 Biltmore Way, Coral Gables FL 33134.

HOW TO WRITE IRRESISTIBLE QUERY LETTERS, by Lisa Collier Cool, Writer's Digest Books, 1507 Dana Ave., Cincinnati OH 45207.

THE INSIDER'S GUIDE TO BOOK EDITORS, PUBLISHERS & LITERARY AGENTS, by Jeff Herman, Prima Communications Inc., Box 1260, Rocklin CA 95677-1260.

INTERNATIONAL DIRECTORY OF LITTLE MAGAZINES & SMALL PRESSES, edited by Len Fulton, Dustbooks, P.O. Box 100, Paradise CA 95967.

LITERARY MARKET PLACE and INTERNATIONAL LITERARY MARKET PLACE, R.R. Bowker, A Reed Reference Publishing Co., 121 Chanlon Rd., New Providence NJ 07974.

PROFESSIONAL WRITER'S GUIDE, edited by Donald Bower and James Lee Young, National Writers Press, Suite 424, 1450 S. Havana, Aurora CO 80012.

STANDARD DIRECTORY OF ADVERTISING AGENCIES, 3004 Glenview Rd., Wilmette IL 60091.

THE WRITER'S GUIDE TO SELF-PROMOTION AND PUBLICITY, by Elane Feldman, Writer's Digest Books, 1507 Dana Ave., Cincinnati OH 45207.

THE WRITER'S LEGAL COMPANION, by Brad Bunnin and Peter Beren, Addison-Wesley, 1 Jacob Way, Reading MA 01867.

WRITING TOOLS: Essential Software for Anyone Who Writes with a PC, by Hy Bender; Random House Electronic Publishing, 201 E. 50 St., New York NY 10022.

Glossary

Key to symbols and abbreviations is on page 72.

Advance. A sum of money a publisher pays a writer prior to the publication of a book. It is usually paid in installments, such as one-half on signing the contract; one-half on delivery of a complete and satisfactory manuscript. The advance is paid against the royalty money that will be earned by the book.

Advertorial. Advertising presented in such a way as to resemble editorial material. Information may be the same as that contained in an editorial feature, but it is paid for or supplied by an advertiser and the word "advertisement" appears at the top of the page.

All rights. See Rights and the Writer in the Minding the Details article.

Anthology. A collection of selected writings by various authors or a gathering of works by one author.

Assignment. Editor asks a writer to produce a specific article for a certain price to be paid upon completion.

Auction. Publishers sometimes bid for the acquisition of a book manuscript that has excellent sales prospects. The bids are for the amount of the author's advance, advertising and promotional expenses, royalty percentage, etc.

B&W. Abbreviation for black and white photographs.

Backlist. A publisher's list of its books that were not published during the current season, but that are still in print.

Belles lettres. A term used to describe fine or literary writing—writing more to entertain than to inform or instruct.

Bimonthly. Every two months. See also *semimonthly*.

Bionote. A sentence or brief paragraph about the writer. Also called a "bio," it can appear at the bottom of the first or last page of a writer's article or short story or on a contributor's page.

Biweekly. Every two weeks.

Boilerplate. A standardized contract. When an editor says "our standard contract," he means the boilerplate with no changes. Writers should be aware that most authors and/or agents make many changes on the boilerplate.

Book auction. Selling the rights (e.g. paperback, movie, etc.) of a hardback book to the highest bidder. A publisher or agent may initiate the auction.

Book packager. Draws all elements of a book together, from the initial concept to writing and marketing strategies, then sells the book package to a book publisher and/or movie producer. Also known as book producer or book developer.

Business size envelope. Also known as a #10 envelope, it is the standard size used in sending business correspondence.

Byline. Name of the author appearing with the published piece.

Category fiction. A term used to include all various labels attached to types of fiction. See also *genre*.

Chapbook. A small booklet, usually paperback, of poetry, ballads or tales.

Clean copy. A manuscript free of errors, cross-outs, wrinkles or smudges.

Clips. Samples, usually from newspapers or magazines, of your *published* work.

Coffee table book. An oversize book, heavily illustrated..

Column inch. The amount of space contained in one inch of a typeset column.

Commercial novels. Novels designed to appeal to a broad audience. These are often broken down into categories such as western, mystery and romance. See also *genre*.

Commissioned work. See *assignment*.

Concept. A statement that summarizes a screenplay or teleplay—before the outline or treatment is written.

Contributor's copies. Copies of the issues of magazines sent to the author in which the author's work appears.

Cooperative publishing. See *co-publishing*.

Co-publishing. Arrangement where author and publisher share publication costs and profits of a book. Also known as *cooperative publishing*. See also *subsidy publisher*.

Copyediting. Editing a manuscript for grammar, punctuation and printing style, not subject content.

Copyright. A means to protect an author's work. See Copyrighting Your Writing in the Minding the Details section.

Cover letter. A brief letter, accompanying a complete manuscript, especially useful if responding to an editor's request for a manuscript. A cover letter may also accompany a book proposal. A cover letter is *not* a query letter; see Targeting Your Ideas in the Getting Published section.

Derivative works. A work that has been translated, adapted, abridged, condensed, annotated or otherwise produced by altering a previously created work. Before producing a derivative work, it is necessary to secure the written permission of the author or copyright owner of the original piece.

Desktop publishing. A publishing system designed for a personal computer. The system is capable of typesetting, some illustration, layout, design and printing—so that the final piece can be distributed and/or sold.

Disk. A round, flat magnetic plate on which computer data may be stored.

Docudrama. A fictional film rendition of recent newsmaking events and people.

Dot-matrix. Printed type where individual characters are composed of a matrix or pattern of tiny dots. Near letter quality (see *NLQ*) dot-matrix submissions are generally acceptable to editors.

Electronic submission. A submission made by modem or on computer disk.

El-hi. Elementary to high school.

Epigram. A short, witty sometimes paradoxical saying.

Erotica. Fiction or art that is sexually oriented.

Fair use. A provision of the copyright law that says short passages from copyrighted material may be used without infringing on the owner's rights.

Fanzine. A noncommercial, small circulation magazine dealing with fantasy or science fiction literature and art.

FAX. A communication system used to transmit documents over telephone lines.

Feature. An article giving the reader information of human interest rather than news. Also used by magazines to indicate a lead article or distinctive department.

Filler. A short item used by an editor to "fill" out a newspaper column or magazine page. It could be a timeless news item, a joke, an anecdote, some light verse or short humor, puzzle, etc.

First chapter novel. A book for children that is roughly the size of an adult novel's first chapter.

First North American serial rights. See Rights and the Writer in the Minding the Details article.

Formula story. Familiar theme treated in a predictable plot structure—such as boy meets girl, boy loses girl, boy gets girl.

Galleys. The first typeset version of a manuscript that has not yet been divided into pages.

Genre. Refers either to a general classification of writing, such as the novel or the poem, or to the categories within those classifications, such as the problem novel or the sonnet. Genre fiction describes commercial novels, such as mysteries, romances and science fiction. Also called category fiction.

Ghostwriter. A writer who puts into literary form an article, speech, story or book based on another person's ideas or knowledge.

Glossy. A black and white photograph with a shiny surface as opposed to one with a nonshiny matte finish.

Gothic novel. A fiction category or genre in which the central character is usually a beautiful young girl, the setting an old mansion or castle, and there is a handsome hero and a real menace, either natural or supernatural.

Graphic novel. An adaptation of a novel in graphic form, long comic strip or heavily illustrated story, of 40 pages or more, produced in paperback form.

Hard copy. The printed copy of a computer's output.

Hardware. All the mechanically-integrated components of a computer that are not software. Circuit boards, transistors and the machines that are the actual computer are the hardware.

Hi-Lo. Abbreviation for high interest, low reading level, as pertains mostly to beginning adult readers.

Honorarium. Token payment—small amount of money, or a byline and copies of the publication.

Illustrations. May be photographs, old engravings, artwork. Usually paid for separately from the manuscript. See also *package sale*.

Imprint. Name applied to a publisher's specific line or lines of books (e.g., Anchor Books is an imprint of Doubleday).

Interactive fiction. Works of fiction in book or computer software format in which the reader determines the path the story will take. The reader chooses from several alternatives at the end of a "chapter," and thus determines the structure of the story. Interactive fiction features multiple plots and endings.

Invasion of privacy. Writing about persons (even though truthfully) without their consent.

Kill fee. Fee for a complete article that was assigned but which was subsequently cancelled.

Lead time. The time between the acquisition of a manuscript by an editor and its actual publication.

Letter-quality submission. Computer printout that looks typewritten.

Libel. A false accusation or any published statement or presentation that tends to expose another to public contempt, ridicule, etc. Defenses are truth; fair comment on a matter of public interest; and privileged communication—such as a report of legal proceedings or client's communication to a lawyer.

List royalty. A royalty payment based on a percentage of a book's retail (or "list") price. Compare *net royalty*.

Little magazine. Publications of limited circulation, usually on literary or political subject matter.

LORT. An acronym for League of Resident Theatres. Letters from A to D follow LORT and designate the size of the theater.

Magalog. Mail order catalog with how-to articles pertaining to the items for sale..

Mainstream fiction. Fiction that transcends popular novel categories such as mystery, romance and science fiction. Using conventional methods, this kind of fiction tells stories about people and their conflicts with greater depth of characterization, background, etc., than the more narrowly focused genre novels.

Mass market. Nonspecialized books of wide appeal directed toward an extremely large audience. Smaller and more cheaply produced than trade paperbacks, they are found in many non-bookstore outlets, such as drug stores, supermarkets, etc.

Microcomputer. A small computer system capable of performing various specific tasks with data it receives. Personal computers are microcomputers.

Midlist. Those titles on a publisher's list that are not expected to be big sellers, but are expected to have limited sales. Midlist books are mainstream, not literary, scholarly or genre, and are usually written by new or unknown writers.

Model release. A paper signed by the subject of a photograph (or the subject's guardian, if a juvenile) giving the photographer permission to use the photograph, editorially or for advertising purposes or for some specific purpose as stated.

Modem. A small electrical box that plugs into the serial card of a computer, used to transmit data from one computer to another, usually via telephone lines.

Monograph. A detailed and documented scholarly study concerning a single subject.

MOW. Movie of the week.

Multiple submissions. Sending more than one poem, gag or greeting card idea at the same time. This term is often used synonymously with simultaneous submission.

Net royalty. A royalty payment based on the amount of money a book publisher receives on the sale of a book after booksellers' discounts, special sales discounts and returns. Compare *list royalty*.

Newsbreak. A brief, late-breaking news story added to the front page of a newspaper at press time or a magazine news item of importance to readers.

NLQ. Near letter-quality print required by some editors for computer printout submissions. See also *dot-matrix*.

Novelette. A short novel, or a long short story; 7,000 to 15,000 words approximately. Also known as a novella.

Novelization. A novel created from the script of a popular movie, usually called movie "tie-ins" and published in paperback.

Offprint. Copies of an author's article taken "out of issue" before a magazine is bound and given to the author in lieu of monetary payment. An offprint could be used by the writer as a published writing sample.

On spec. An editor expresses an interest in a proposed article idea and agrees to consider the finished piece for publication "on speculation." The editor is under no obligation to buy the finished manuscript.

One-shot feature. As applies to syndicates, single feature article for syndicate to sell; as contrasted with article series or regular columns syndicated.

One-time rights. See Rights and the Writer in the Minding the Details article.

Outline. A summary of a book's contents in five to 15 double-spaced pages; often in the form of chapter headings with a descriptive sentence or two under each one to show the scope of the book. A screenplay's or teleplay's outline is a scene-by-scene narrative description of the story (10-15 pages for a ½-hour teleplay; 15-25 pages for a 1-hour teleplay; 25-40 pages for a 90-minute teleplay; 40-60 pages for a 2-hour feature film or teleplay).

Over-the-transom. Describes the submission of unsolicited material by a freelance writer.

Package sale. The editor buys manuscript and photos as a "package" and pays for them with one check.

Page rate. Some magazines pay for material at a fixed rate per published page, rather than per word.

Parallel submission. A strategy of developing several articles from one unit of research for submission to similar magazines. This strategy differs from simultaneous or multiple submission, where the same article is marketed to several magazines at the same time.

Payment on acceptance. The editor sends you a check for your article, story or poem as soon as he decides to publish it.

Payment on publication. The editor doesn't send you a check for your material until it is published.

Pen name. The use of a name other than your legal name on articles, stories or books when you wish to remain anonymous. Simply notify your post office and bank that you are using the name so that you'll receive mail and/or checks in that name. Also called a pseudonym.

Photo feature. Feature in which the emphasis is on the photographs rather than on accompanying written material.

Plagiarism. Passing off as one's own the expression of ideas and words of another writer.

Potboiler. Refers to writing projects a freelance writer does to "keep the pot boiling" while working on major articles—quick projects to bring in money with little time or effort. These may be fillers such as anecdotes or how-to tips, but could be short articles or stories.

Proofreading. Close reading and correction of a manuscript's typographical errors.

Proscenium. The area of the stage in front of the curtain.

Prospectus. A preliminary written description of a book or article, usually one page in length.

Pseudonym. See *pen name*.

Public domain. Material that was either never copyrighted or whose copyright term has expired.

Query. A letter to an editor intended to raise interest in an article you propose to write.

Rebus. Stories, quips, puzzles, etc., in juvenile magazines that convey words or syllables with pictures, objects or symbols whose names resemble the sounds of intended words.

Release. A statement that your idea is original, has never been sold to anyone else and that you are selling the negotiated rights to the idea upon payment.

Remainders. Copies of a book that are slow to sell and can be purchased from the publisher at a reduced price. Depending on the author's book contract, a reduced royalty or no royalty is paid on remainder books.

Reporting time. The time it takes for an editor to report to the author on his/her query or manuscript.

Reprint rights. See Rights and the Writer in the Minding the Details article.

Round-up article. Comments from, or interviews with, a number of celebrities or experts on a single theme.

Royalties, standard hardcover book. 10% of the retail price on the first 5,000 copies sold; 12½% on the next 5,000; 15% thereafter.

Royalties, standard mass paperback book. 4 to 8% of the retail price on the first 150,000 copies sold.

Royalties, trade paperback book. No less than 6% of list price on the first 20,000 copies; 7½% thereafter.

Scanning. A process through which letter-quality printed text (see *NLQ*) or artwork is read by a computer scanner and converted into workable data.

Screenplay. Script for a film intended to be shown in theaters.

Self-publishing. In this arrangement, the author keeps all income derived from the book, but he pays for its manufacturing, production and marketing.

Semimonthly. Twice per month.

Semiweekly. Twice per week.

Serial. Published periodically, such as a newspaper or magazine.

Sidebar. A feature presented as a companion to a straight news report (or main magazine article) giving sidelights on human-interest aspects or sometimes elucidating just one aspect of the story.

Similar submission. See *parallel submission*.

Simultaneous submissions. Sending the same article, story or poem to several publishers at the same time. Some publishers refuse to consider such submissions. No simultaneous submissions should be made without stating the fact in your letter.

Slant. The approach or style of a story or article that will appeal to readers of a specific magazine. For example, a magazine may always use stories with an upbeat ending.

Slice-of-life vignette. A short fiction piece intended to realistically depict an interesting moment of everyday living.

Slides. Usually called transparencies by editors looking for color photographs.

Slush pile. The stack of unsolicited or misdirected manuscripts received by an editor or book publisher.

Software. Computer programs and related manuals.

Speculation. The editor agrees to look at the author's manuscript with no assurance that it will be bought.

Style. The way in which something is written—for example, short, punchy sentences or flowing narrative.

Subsidiary rights. All those rights, other than book publishing rights included in a book contract—such as paperback, book club, movie rights, etc.

Subsidy publisher. A book publisher who charges the author for the cost to typeset and print his book, the jacket, etc. as opposed to a royalty publisher who pays the author. .

Syndication rights. See Rights and the Writer in the Minding the Details article.

Synopsis. A brief summary of a story, novel or play. As part of a book proposal, it is a comprehensive summary condensed in a page or page and a half, single-spaced. See also *outline*.

Tabloid. Newspaper format publication on about half the size of the regular newspaper page, such as the *National Enquirer*.

Tagline. A caption for a photo or a comment added to a filler.

Tearsheet. Page from a magazine or newspaper containing your printed story, article, poem or ad.

Trade. Either a hardcover or paperback book; subject matter frequently concerns a special interest. Books are directed toward the layperson rather than the professional.

Transparencies. Positive color slides; not color prints.

Treatment. Synopsis of a television or film script (40-60 pages for a 2-hour feature film or teleplay).

Unsolicited manuscript. A story, article, poem or book that an editor did not specifically ask to see.

User friendly. Easy to handle and use. Refers to computer hardware and software designed with the user in mind.

Vanity publisher. See *subsidy publisher*.

Word processor. A computer program, used in lieu of a typewriter, that allows for easy, flexible manipulation and output of printed copy.

Work-for-hire. See Copyrighting Your Writing in the Minding the Details article.

YA. Young adult books.

Book Publishers Subject Index

This Index will help you find publishers that consider books on specific subjects—the subjects you choose to write about. Remember that a publisher may be listed here under a general subject category such as Art and Architecture, while the company publishes *only* art history or how-to books. Be sure to consult each company's detailed individual listing, its book catalog and several of its books before you send your query or proposal. The page number of the detailed listed is provided for your convenience.

Fiction

Adventure. Actaeon 245; Archives 87; Atheneum Children's 89; Avanyu 90; Avon 90; Avon Flare 90; Bantam 92; Bethel 95; Black Tie 266; British American 101; Caitlin 229; Camelot 104; Carol 106; Cave 107; Clarion 112; Cool Hand 116; Council for Indian Education 117; Davenport 119; Dutton Children's 124; Fine 128; Greene 277; Gryphon 134; Harian 253; HarperCollins 135; Hendrick-Long 138; Holiday House 139; Jesperson 234; Kar-Ben Copies 150; Little, Brown Children's 155; Lodestar 156; Longmeadow 157; Mountaineers 166; New Victoria 170; North Country 257; Permanent/Second Chance 178; Pippin 180; Players 181; Presidio 183; QED 259; Québec/Amérique 238; Random House 187; Random House Juvenile 188; Rising Tide 189; Rubicon 238; St. Clair 191; Scribner's 194; Sierra Club 195; Simon & Pierre 239; Soho Press 197; SouthPark 198; Southwest 198; Turnstone 240; Vandamere 217; Vista 261; Walker and Co. 219; Warren 219; Wayfinder 220; Wilderness 222; Willowisp 223; Woodsong 261; Worldwide 243; Zebra and Pinnacle 226; Whitman 221.

Erotica. Archives 87; Asylum Arts 246; Black Tie 266; Caradium 105; Carroll & Graf 106; Circlet 111; Gay Sunshine and Leyland 130; Masefield 257; Merry Men 270; New Victoria 170; Press Gang 237; Rising Tide 189; Vandamere 217; Zebra and Pinnacle 226.

Ethnic. Actaeon 245; Another Chicago 265; Arcade 87; Arsenal Pulp 228; Asian Humanities 88; Atheneum Children's 89; Avon Flare 90; Bottom Dog 266; Branden 100; Charlesbridge 109; China 110; Coffee House 114; Colonial 114; Coteau 231; Council for Indian Education 117; Cuff 231; Eastern Caribbean 267; Faber & Faber 126; Four Walls Eight Windows 129; Gay Sunshine and Leyland 130; Greene 277; Guernica 232; Herald 233; Holiday House 139; Interlink 146; Kar-Ben Copies 150; Lincoln Springs 269; Lodestar 156; Lollipop Power 269; Longmeadow 157; Northland 171; Oolichan 235; Permanent/Second Chance, The 178; Players 181; QED 259; Sakura 272; Soho 197; Spinsters Ink 199; Stemmer House 201; Theytus 239; Turnstone 240; University of Illinois 212; Vesta 242; Warren 219; Weigl 242.

Experimental. Asylum Arts 246; Atheneum Children's 89; Beach Holme 228; British American 101; Buddha Rose 102; China 110; Coach House 230; Faber & Faber 126; Four Walls Eight Windows 129; Gay Sunshine and Leyland 130; Goose Lane 232; Harian 253; Lintel 269; Masefield 257; New Directions 169; Oolichan 235; Players Inc. 181; QED 259; Quarry 186; Random House 187; Rutgers 190; Scots Plaid 272; Smith 196; Theytus 239; Turnstone 240; University of Illinois 212; Woodsong 261; Xenos 225; York 243.

Fantasy. Ace 81; Actaeon 245; Atheneum Children's 89; Avon 90; Baen 91; Bantam 92; British American 101; Camelot 104; Carol 106; Carroll & Graf 106; Circlet Press 111; Crossway 118; Davenport 119; Del Rey 121; Delta Sales 250; Dragon's Den 267; Dutton Children's 124; Fine 128; Gryphon 134; HarperCollins 135; Holiday House 139; Hollow Earth 140; Intervarsity 147; Kar-Ben Copies 150; Lion 155; Little, Brown Children's

From the publishers of <u>Writer's</u> <u>Digest</u> and *<u>Writer's</u> <u>Market</u>*

Go One-On-One
With a Published Author

Are you serious about learning to write better? Getting published? Getting paid for what you write? If you're dedicated to your writing, **Writer's Digest School** can put you on the fast track to writing success.

You'll Study With A Professional

Writer's Digest School offers you more than textbooks and assignments. As a student you'll correspond <u>directly with a professional writer</u> who is currently writing **and selling** the kind of material that you want to write. You'll learn from a pro who knows from personal experience what it takes to get a manuscript written and published. A writer who can guide you as you work to achieve the same thing. A true mentor.

Work On Your Novel, Short Story,
Nonfiction Book, Or Article

Writer's Digest School offers six courses: The Novel Writing Workshop, the Nonfiction Book Workshop, Writing to Sell Fiction (Short Stories), Writing to Sell Nonfiction (Articles), the Science Fiction and Fantasy Workshops and the Mystery Writing Workshops. Each course is described on the reverse side.

If you're serious about your writing, you owe it to yourself to check out **Writer's Digest School**. Mail the coupon below today for FREE information! Or call **1-800-759-0963**. (Outside the U.S., call (513) 531-2222.) Writer's Digest School, 1507 Dana Avenue, Cincinnati, Ohio 45207-1005.

Reg. #73-0409H

Send Me Free Information!

I want to write and sell with the help of the professionals at **Writer's Digest School**. Send me free information about the course I've checked below:

☐ Novel Writing Workshop   ☐ Writing to Sell Fiction (Short Stories)
☐ Nonfiction Book Workshop   ☐ Writing to Sell Nonfiction (Articles)
☐ Science Fiction & Fantasy Workshops   ☐ Mystery Writing Workshops

Name _____

Address _____

City _____ State _____ Zip + 4 _____

Phone: (Day) (_____) _____ (Eve.) (_____) _____

Mail this card today! No postage needed.
Or Call **1-800-759-0963** for free information today.

IWMXXXX4

There are six **Writer's Digest School** courses to help you write better and sell more:

Novel Writing Workshop. A professional novelist helps you iron out your plot, develop your main characters, write the background for your novel, and complete the opening scene and a summary of your novel's complete story. You'll even identify potential publishers and write a query letter.

Nonfiction Book Workshop. You'll work with your mentor to create a book proposal that you can send directly to a publisher. You'll develop and refine your book idea, write a chapter-by-chapter outline of your subject, line up your sources of information, write sample chapters, and complete your query letter.

Writing to Sell Fiction. Learn the basics of writing/selling short stories: plotting, characterization, dialogue, theme, conflict, and other elements of a marketable short story. Course includes writing assignments and one complete short story.

Writing to Sell Nonfiction. Master the fundamentals of writing/selling nonfiction articles: finding article ideas, conducting interviews, writing effective query letters and attention-getting leads, targeting your articles to the right publication, and other important elements of a salable article. Course includes writing assignments and one complete article manuscript (and its revision).

Science Fiction and Fantasy Workshops. Explore the exciting world of science fiction and fantasy with one of our professional science fiction writers as your guide. Besides improving your general writing skills, you'll learn the special techniques of creating worlds, science and magic, shaping time and place. And how to get published in this world. Choose Short Story or Novel Writing.

Mystery Writing Workshops. With the personal attention, experience and advice from a professional, published mystery writer, you'll uncover the secrets of writing suspenseful, involving mysteries. In addition to learning the genre's special techniques like how to drop red herrings, when and where to plant critical clues and what to keep hidden from your reader, you'll continue to improve your general writing skills that will lay a critical foundation for your story. Choose Short Story or Novel Writing.

Mail this card today for **FREE** information!

NO POSTAGE
NECESSARY
IF MAILED
IN THE
UNITED STATES

BUSINESS REPLY MAIL

FIRST CLASS MAIL   PERMIT NO. 17   CINCINNATI, OHIO

POSTAGE WILL BE PAID BY ADDRESSEE

Writer's Digest School
1507 DANA AVENUE
CINCINNATI OH 45207-9965

York 278; Morrow Junior 165; Nightwood 235; Northland 171; Orca 236; Parachute 279; Peachtree 177; Peguis 236; Pelican 177; Philomel 179; Piccadilly 179; Pippin 180; Prairie 237; Québeç/Amérique 238; Rubicon 238; St. Paul 191; Scribner's 194; Seacoast 272; Sevgo 194; Soundprints 197; Speech Bin 199; Spheric 273; Sunbelt 203; Tambourine 205; Thistledown 239; Tidewater 208; Tundra 240; Walker 219; Warren 219; Weigl 242; Weiss 279; Whitman 221; Willowisp 223.

Literary. Actaeon 245; Another Chicago 265; Applezaba 87; Arcade 87; Archives 87; Arsenal 228; Asylum Arts 246; Bantam 92; Black Moss 228; Black Sparrow 96; Black Tie 266; Bottom Dog 266; British American 101; Buddha Rose 102; Calyx 266; Capra 104; Carol 106; Carroll & Graf 106; Catbird 107; Cave 107; Center Press 108; China 110; Cleis 113; Coach House 230; Coffee House 114; Coteau Books 231; Creative Arts 249; E.M. 267; Eastern Caribbean 267; Eriksson 126; Fine 128; Four Walls Eight Windows 129; Goose Lane 232; Graywolf 133; Greene 277; Hampton Roads 253; Harper-Collins 135; Herald Press Canada 233; HMS 233; Hollow Earth 140; Hounslow 233; Howells 141; Lawrence 152; Lincoln Springs 269; Little, Brown and Co. 155; Longstreet 157; Louisiana State 158; Mercury 235; New Directions 169; New Rivers 170; NeWest 235; Nightshade 271; Oolichan 235; Orca Book 236; Overlook 174; Peachtree 177; Permanent/Second Chance 178; Pineapple 180; Poseidon 182; Press Gang 237; Puckerbrush 271; QED 259; Quarry 186; Québec/Amérique 238; Rising Tide 189; Rubicon 238; Rutgers 190; Scots Plaid 272; Simon & Pierre 239; Smith 196; Soho Press 197; Southern Methodist 198; Stemmer House 201; Stone Bridge 273; Stormline 273; Theytus 239; Thistledown 239; Three Continents 207; Turnstone 240; UCLA-American Indian 274; University of Arkansas, The 211; University of North Texas 214; University of Pittsburgh 214; Vesta 242; Willowisp 223; Xenos 225; Zebra and Pinnacle 226; Zoland 226.

Mainstream/Contemporary. Academy Chicago 80; Actaeon 245; Arcade 87; Atheneum Children's 89; Avalon 90; Avon Flare 90; Bantam 92; Barn Owl 266; Beach Holme 228; Berkley 94; Branden 100; British American 101; Caitlin 230; Camelot 104; Capra 104; Carroll & Graf 106; Citadel 112; Cool Hand 116; Coteau 231; Crossway 118; Cuff 231; Delancey 267; Dickens 267; Down East 123; E.M. 267; Edicones 251; Faber & Faber 126; Fawcett Juniper 127; Fine 128; Greene 277; Hampton Roads 253; Harian 253; Howells House 141; International 147; Intervarsity 147; Jesperson 234; Lincoln Springs 269; Little, Brown 155; Lodestar 156; Longmeadow 157; Longstreet 157; Mercury 235; Morrow 165; N.A.L. Dutton 167; Norton 172; Orca 236; Pantheon 175; Peachtree 177; Pelican 177; Permanent/Second Chance 178; Perspectives 178; Pineapple 180; Players 181; Poseidon 182; QED 259; Québec/Amérique 238; Random House 187; Rising Tide 189; Rubicon 238; St. Clair 191; Sierra Club 195; Simon & Pierre 239; Simon & Schuster 195; Soho 197; Stemmer House 201; Sunbelt 203; Ticknor & Fields 208; Turnstone 240; University of Illinois 212; University of Iowa 212; University Press of Mississippi 216; Villard 218; Vista 261; Willowisp 223; Woodsong 261; Xenos 225; Zebra and Pinnacle 226.

Military/War. Naval Institute 168; Presidio 183; Sunflower 203.

Mystery. Academy Chicago 80; Accord 81; Actaeon 245; Arcade 87; Atheneum Children's 89; Avalon 90; Avon 90; Avon Flare 90; Baker 91; Bantam 92; Berkley 94; Book Creations 276; British American 101; Camelot 104; Carol 106; Carroll & Graf 106; Cave 107; Clarion 112; Cool Hand 116; Council for Indian Education 117; Countryman 117; Delta 250; Dickens 267; Doubleday 123; Dragon's Den 267; Fine 128; Four Walls Eight Windows 129; Gay Sunshine and Leyland 130; Gryphon 134; HarperCollins 135; Harvest House 136; Hendrick-Long 138; Holiday House 139; Hollow Earth 140; Intervarsity 147; Jesperson 234; Lincoln Springs 269; Little, Brown Children's 155; Lodestar 156; Longmeadow 157; Mega-Books of New York, Inc. 278; Mysterious 167; Naiad Press, The 167; New Victoria 170; North Country 257; Permanent/Second Chance 178; Pippin 180; Players, Inc. 181; Pocket 181; Presidio 183; QED 259; Random House 187; Random House, Juvenile 188; Rising Tide 189; Scholastic 193; Scribner's 194; Simon & Pierre 239; Soho 197; Southwest 198; Turnstone 240; Vandamere 217; Vista 261; Walker 219; Wayfinder 220; Whitman 221; Willowisp 223; Woodsong 261; Zebra and Pinnacle 226.

Occult. Archives 87; Colonial 114; Hampton Roads 253; Llewellyn 155; Longmeadow 157; Masefield 257; Rising Tide 189; Southwest 198; Space and Time 273; Zebra and Pinnacle 226.

Picture Books. Center 108; Charlesbridge 109; Children's 110; Chronicle 111; Cobblehill 113; Colonial 114; Concordia 115; Coteau 231; Council for Indian Education 117; Farrar, Straus and Giroux 127; Grosset & Dunlap 133; Harcourt Brace 135; Herald Press

Canada 233; Holiday House 139; Interlink 146; Little, Brown, Children's 155; Lodestar 156; Lothrop, Lee & Shepard 158; Lucas-Evans 278; Orca Book 236; Philomel 179; Pippin 180; Quarry 186; Québec/Amérique 238; Random House, Juvenile 188; Rubicon 238; Scribner's Sons 194; Tambourine 205; Tundra 240; Warren 219; Wayfinder 220; Weiss 279; Whitman 221; Willowisp 223; Xenos 225.

Plays. Anchorage 86; Asylum Arts 246; Colonial 114; Coteau 231; Drama 123; Eastern Caribbean 267; Illuminations 268; Meriwether 162; Piccadilly 179; Players 181; Playwrights Canada 237; Scots Plaid 272; Simon & Pierre 239; Tambra 273; Xenos 225.

Poetry (including chapbooks). Acme 265; Ahsahta 265; Applezaba 87; Asian Humanities 88; Asylum Arts 246; Black Hat 247; Black Moss 228; Black Tie 266; Blue Dolphin, Inc. 97; Boyds Mills 99; British American 101; Browndeer 102; Buddha Rose 102; Caitlin 230; Calyx 266; Chatham 109; Christopher 248; Cleveland State 113; Colonial 114; Council for Indian Education 117; Creative with Words 267; Daniel 119; Dante 119; Dusty Dog 267; Edicones 251; Ford-Brown 268; Guernica 232; High Plains 139; HMS 233; Illuminations 268; Inverted-A, 269; Alice James 269; Laughing Bear 269; Lintel 269; Louisiana State University 158; Mercury 235; Morrow 165; Netherlandic 235; New Directions 169; New Rivers 170; Nightshade 271; Oolichan 235; Orchises 173; Papier-Mache 271; Perivale 271; Press Gang 237; Proclaim 258; Puckerbrush 271; QED 259; Quarry 186; Red Apple 259; Signature 195; Simon & Pierre 239; Smith 96; Sono Nis 239; Spinsters Ink 199; Star Books 200; Starbooks 260; Still Waters 201; Systems 204; Texas Tech 206; Theytus Books 239; Thistledown 239; Three Continents 207; Turnstone 240; UCLA-American Indian Studies 274; University of Arkansas, The 211; University of California 211; University of Iowa 212; University of Massachusetts 212; University of North Texas 214; University of Pittsburgh 214; University of Scranton 215; Vehicule 241; Vesta Publications 242; Vista Publishing 261; Whole Notes 274; Wolsak and Wynn 243; Xenos 225.

Regional. Beach Holme 228; John F. Blair 96; Borealis 229; Bottom Dog 266; Cuff 231; Down East 123; Eastern Caribbean 267; Faber & Faber 126; Interlink 146; Nightshade 271; Northland 171; Peachtree 177; Pelican 177; Philomel 179; Prairie 237; South Wind 198; Sunstone 203; Texas Christian University 206; Thistledown 239; Tidewater 208; University of Maine 212; University Press of New England 217; Vista 218.

Religious. A.R.E. 79; ACTA 81; Actaeon 245; Archives 87; Bethel 95; Bookcraft 98; Branden 100; British American 101; Broadman & Holman 101; China 110; Concordia 115; Cool Hand 116; Crossway 118; Friends United 130; Greene 277; Harvest House 136; Hensley 138; Herald 138; Herald 233; Intervarsity 147; Kar-Ben Copies 150; Masefield 257; Thomas Nelson 168; Players 181; Resource 259; St. Paul 191; Shaw 194; Signature 195; Southwest 198; Standard 200; Star 200; Theytus 239; Tyndale 209; Victor 217.

Romance. Actaeon 245; Atheneum Children's 89; Avalon 90; Avon 90; Avon Flare 90; Bantam 92; Berkley 94; Book Creations 276; Branden 100; British American 101; Doubleday 123; Harian 253; Harlequin 232; Herald Press Canada 233; Jesperson 234; Leisure 153; Lincoln Springs 269; Meteor 162; New Victoria 170; North Country 257; Players 181; Pocket 181; Rising Tide 189; Scholastic 193; Silhouette 195; Southwest 198; Walker 219; Willowisp 223; Woodsong Inc. 261; Zebra and Pinnacle 226.

Science Fiction. Ace 81; Actaeon 245; Atheneum Children's 89; Avon 90; Baen 91; Bantam 92; Beach Holme 228; Carol 106; Carroll & Graf 106; Circlet 111; Crossway 118; Del Rey 121; Delta 250; Dragon's Den 267; Fine 128; Gay Sunshine and Leyland 130; Gryphon 134; HarperCollins 135; Holiday House 139; Hollow Earth 140; Intervarsity 147; Inverted-A 269; Little, Brown Children's 155; Lodestar 156; Merry Men 270; New Victoria 170; Players Press 181; Pocket Books 181; QED 259; Québec/Amérique 238; Random House, Juvenile 188; Scribner's 194; Smith 196; Southwest 198; Space and Time 273; TOR 209; TSR 209; Walker 219; Willowisp 223; Woodsong 261; Xenos 225.

Short Story Collections. Actaeon 245; Another Chicago 265; Applezaba 87; Arcade 87; Arsenal Pulp 228; Asylum Arts 246; Black Moss 228; Black Sparrow 96; Bottom Dog 266; British American 101; Caitlin 230; Calyx 266; Capra 104; Center 108; Chronicle 111; Circlet 111; Coach House 230; Coffee House 114; Colonial 114; Coteau 231; Council for Indian Education 117; Creative with Words 267; Daniel 119; Dutton Children's 124; E.M. 267; Faber & Faber 126; Gay Sunshine and Leyland 130; Goose Lane 232; Graywolf 133; Greene 277; Harian 253; Herald Press Canada 233; Independence 268; Indiana Historical 269; Interlink 146; International 147; Inverted-A 269; Jesperson 234; Lincoln Springs Press 269; Little, Brown And Company, Children's Book Division 155;

Louisiana State University Press 158; Mercury 235; Naiad 167; New Directions 169; New Rivers 170; NeWest 235; Oolichan 235; Press Gang 237; QED 259; Québec/Amérique 238; Resource 259; Simon & Pierre 238; Southern Methodist 198; Star 200; Still Waters 201; Turnstone 240; University of Arkansas 211; University of Illinois 212; University of Missouri 213; University of North Texas 214; Vista 261; Willowisp 223; Xenos 225; Zebra and Pinnacle 226; Zoland 226.

Suspense. Accord 81; Actaeon 245; Arcade 87; Atheneum Children's 89; Avon 90; Avon Flare 90; Bantam 92; Berkley 94; Bethel 95; British American 101; Camelot 104; Carroll & Graf 106; Clarion 112; Cool Hand 116; Doubleday 123; Fine 128; Gryphon 134; Harlequin 232; HarperCollins 135; Holiday House 139; Hounslow 233; Little, Brown Children's 155; Lodestar 156; Longmeadow 157; Mysterious 167; North Country 257; Permanent/Second Chance 178; Pippin 180; Players 181; Pocket 181; QED 259; Random House 187; Random House, Juvenile 188; Rising Tide 189; Scribner's 194; Soho 197; Southwest 198; TOR 209; Vandamere 217; Vista 261; Walker 219; Willowisp 223; Woodsong 261; Zebra and Pinnacle 226.

Western. Actaeon 245; Atheneum Children's 89; Avalon 90; Avanyu 90; Avon 90; Bantam 92; Berkley 94; Book Creations 276; Council for Indian Education 117; Doubleday 123; Evans 126; Fine 128; HarperCollins 135; Hendrick-Long, Inc. 138; Holiday House 139; Lodestar 156; Longmeadow 157; New Victoria 170; Players 181; Pocket 181; Southwest 198; Sunflower 203; Walker 219; Woodsong 261; Zebra and Pinnacle 226.

Young Adult. Actaeon 245; Archway/Minstrel 88; Bantam 92; Beach Holme 228; Bethel 95; Boyds Mills 99; Browndeer 102; Caitlin 230; Cobblehill 113; Colonial 114; Creative with Words 267; Crossway 118; Eastern Caribbean 267; Farrar, Straus and Giroux 127; Harcourt Brace 135; Herald 138; Herald Press Canada 233; Houghton Mifflin 141; Jesperson 234; Jones University 149; Lerner 153; Lion 155; Little, Brown, Children's 155; Lodestar 156; Longmeadow 157; Lucas-Evans 278; McElderry 159; Mega-Books 278; Morrow 165; Nelson 168; Parachute Press 279; Philomel 179; Québec/Amérique 238; Random House Juvenile 188; Rubicon 238; Scholastic 193; Simon & Pierre 239; Spheric House 273; Star 200; Tambourine 205; Texas Christian University 206; Thistledown 239; Tundra 240; Weiss 279; Wilderness Adventure 222; Willowisp 223; Zebra and Pinnacle 226.

Nonfiction

Agriculture/Horticulture. Camden House 230; Camino 104; Dorling Kindersley 123; Godine 132; Hartley & Marks 136; Haworth 137; Interstate 255; Iowa State University 148; Kumarian 256; Lyons & Burford 159; Maupin House 270; Michigan State University 163; Pruett 185; Purdue 186; Stipes 202; Storey/Garden Way 202; Sunflower 203; Timber 208; University of Idaho 211; University of Alaska 210; University of Nebraska 213; University of North Texas 214; Warren 219; Whitman 221; Windward 223; Woodbridge 224.

Alternative Lifestyles. Luramedia 159; Sterling 201.

Americana. Actaeon 245; Alaska Northwest 82; Ancestry 86; Atheneum Children's 89; Avanyu 90; B&B 92; Bantam 92; Blair 96; Boston Mills 229; Bottom Dog 266; Bowling Green State University 99; Branden 100; Brevet 100; California State University 103; Camino 104; Capstone 105; Carol 106; Carpenter 276; Cave 107; Caxton 107; Christopher 248; Clarion 112; Clark 248; Clear Light 112; Creative 118; Crown 118; Denali 122; Devin-Adair 250; Down East 123; Durst 124; Eastern National Park 125; Elliott & Clark 125; Eriksson 126; Faber & Faber 126; Filter 252; Glenbridge 131; Globe Pequot 131; Godine 132; Golden 132; Greene 277; Hancock House 135; Harian 253; HarperCollins 135; Herald 138; Heyday 139; High Plains 139; Hope Publishing House 254; Howells 141; International 147; Jordan 255; Knowledge 151; Laing 278; Lehigh University 153; Lerner 153; Lexikos 154; Library Research 154; Lifetime 154; Lincoln Springs 269; Little, Brown Children's 155; Longmeadow 157; Longstreet 157; Lorien House 269; Lyons & Burford 159; McDonald & Woodward 159; McFarland 159; Madison House 160; Media/Midgard 162; Meyerbooks 270; Monitor 164; Mosaic 270; Mountain Press 166; Mustang 166; Mystic Seaport 270; New England 169; Oregon Historical Society 173; Pacific 175; Pelican 177; Peter Pauper 178; Pruett 185; Purdue University 186; Push/Pull 186; Quarry 186; Ragged Mountain 187; Red Apple 259; Rutgers University 190; Sachem 279; Sand River 272; Schiffer 193; Signature 195; Smith 196; Stemmer House 201; Sunbelt 203; Sunflower 203; T.F.H. 204; Texas Christian University 206;

Texas Tech University 206; Transaction 260; University of Idaho 211; University of Alaska 210; University of Arkansas 211; University of Illinois 212; University of Nebraska 213; University of North Carolina 214; University of North Texas 214; University of Oklahoma 214; University of Pennsylvania 214; University of Tennessee 215; University Press of Kentucky 216; University Press of Mississippi 216; University Press of New England 217; Utah State University 217; Vandamere 217; Vesta 242; Washington State 220; Wayfinder 220; Westernlore 221; Wieser & Wieser 280; Wilderness Adventure 222; Ye Galleon 262.

Animals. Actaeon 245; Alpine 246; Archway/Minstrel 88; Atheneum Children's 89; Barron's 93; Beaver Pond 247; Bergh 247; Blockbuster 96; Boxwood 99; Camden House 230; Canadian Plains 230; Capra 104; Capstone 105; Carol 106; Carolrhoda 106; Cave 107; Charles 248; Christopher 248; Cool Hand 116; Crown 118; Denlingers 122; Doral 122; Dorling Kindersley 123; Dutton Children's 124; Eriksson 126; Faber & Faber 126; Half Halt 134; Harmony House 253; HarperCollins 135; Hay 137; Homestead 140; Hounslow 233; Iowa State University 148; Jesperson 234; Jones University Press 49; Kesend 150; Krieger 152; Lifetime 154; Lone Pine 234; Longmeadow 157; Lyons & Burford 159; McDonald & Woodward 159; Millbrook 163; Mosaic Press 270; Northland 171; Parachute 279; Pineapple 180; Pippin 180; Plexus 181; Pruett 185; Random House Juvenile 188; Rocky Top 189; Sandhill Crane 192; Scribner's 194; Sierra 195; Soundprints 197; Stemmer House 201; Sterling 201; Storey/Garden Way 202; T.F.H. 279; Texas Tech 206; Trafalgar Square 274; University of Alaska 210; Warren 219; Wheetley 279; Whitman 221; Wilderness Adventure 222; Williamson 222; Willowisp 223; Wilshire 223; Windward 223; Xenos 225.

Anthropology/Archaelogy. Actaeon 245; Alaska Northwest 82; American Media 246; American 85; Avanyu 90; Bantam 92; Baywood 93; Beacon 93; Blue Dolphin 97; Bowling Green 99; Broadview 229; Buddha Rose 102; Cambridge 103; Cave 107; Clear Light 112; Council for Indian Education 117; Denali 122; Eagle's View 124; Filter 252; Hope 254; Howells House 141; Inner Traditions 145; Insight 145; Johnson 149; Kent State 150; Kodansha America 151; Kumarian 256; Lerner 153; Lone Pine 234; Louisiana State University 158; Lucent 158; McDonald & Woodward 159; Marketscope 161; Masefield 257; Milkweed 163; Millbrook 163; Minnesota Historical Society 164; Northland 171; Outcrop 236; Pax 271; Pendaya 177; Pennsylvania Historical 177; Pruett 185; Rhombus 272; Routledge 189; Rutgers University 190; Scots Plaid 272; Stanford 200; Sunflower 203; UCLA-American Indian 274; University of Idaho 211; University of Alabama 210; University of Alaska 210; University of Arizona 211; University of Iowa 212; University of Michigan 213; University of Nevada 213; University of New Mexico 213; University of Pennsylvania 214; University of Pittsburgh 214; University of Tennessee, The 215; University of Texas 215; University Press of Kentucky 216; Vista 218; Westernlore·221; Wheetley 279; White Cliffs 221; Whitman 221; Xenos 225.

Art/Architecture. Alaska Northwest 82; Allworth 83; American Press 85; Architectural 87; Art Direction 88; Ashgate 246; Asian Humanities 88; Atheneum Children's 89; Avanyu 90; Barron's 93; Bowling Green 99; Branden 100; Broadview 229; Buddha Rose 102; California State 103; Calyx 266; Cambridge 103; Camino 104; Capra 104; Carol 106; Carolrhoda 106; Center 108; Chicago Review 109; China 110; Christopher 248; Chronicle 111; Clarkson Potter 112; Clear Light 112; Coach House 230; Consultant 115; Cool Hand 116; Crisp 118; Crown 118; Davenport 119; Davis 120; Dorling Kindersley 123; Dunburn 231; Durst 124; Elliott & Clark 125; Eriksson 126; Excalibur 267; Fairleigh Dickinson 127; Family Album 127; Fitzhenry & Whiteside 232; Four Walls Eight Windows 129; Gallerie 252; Godine 132; Goose Lane 232; Greene 277; Guernica 232; HarperCollins 135; Hartley & Marks 136; High Plains 139; Hollow Earth 140; Holmes & Meier 140; Homestead 140; Hounslow 233; Howells House 141; Hudson Hills 141; Inner Traditions 145; Insight 145; Interlink 146; Intervarsity 147; Italica 148; Jordan 255; Kent State 150; Kodansha 151; Lang 256; Lehigh 153; Lerner 153; Little, Brown Children's 155; Locust Hill 156; Lone Pine 234; Longmeadow 157; Louisiana State 158; Loyola 158; Lyons & Burford 159; McFarland & Company 159; Mercury 235; Meriwether 162; Milkweed 163; Minnesota Historical 164; Morrow 165; Mosaic 270; Museum of Northern Arizona 166; Mystic Seaport 270; NeWest 235; North Light 171; Northland 171; Oregon Historical 173; Overlook 174; PBC 176; Peachtree 177; Pendaya 177; Pennsylvania Historical and 177; Phanes 179; Pickering 179; Pickwick 258; Preservation 183; Press at California State 183; Princeton Architectural 258; Professional 184; Quarry 186; Random House 187; Resource 259; Retail 279; Sasquatch 193; Schiffer 193; Simon &

Schuster 195; Smith 196; Sound View 273; ST 199; Stemmer House 201; Sterling 201; Sunstone 203; TAB 204; Tenth Avenue 279; Texas Tech 206; University of Alaska 210; University of Alberta 240; University of California 211; University of Massachusetts 212; University of Missouri 213; University of New Mexico 213; University of Pennsylvania 214; University of Pittsburgh 214; University of Scranton 215; University of Tennessee 215; University of Texas 215; University Press of America 216; University Press of New England 217; Virginia State Library 274; Walch 219; Warren 219; Washington State 220; Western/Journal 261; Wheetley 279; Whitman 221; Whitson 222; Xenos 225; Zoland Inc. 226.

Astrology/Psychic/New age. Astro 246; Bear 93; Blue Dolphin 97; Cassandra 106; Delphi 121; E.J.M. 267; Hampton Roads 253; Harper 135; Hay House 137; Humanics 142; In Print 268; Llewellyn 155; Masefield 257; New Horizons 270; Newcastle 170; Sterling 201; Theosophical 207.

Audiocassettes. Accelerated 80; Bantam 92; Humanics 142; Interstate 255; NASW 167; Rainbow 187; Schirmer 193; Stemmer House 201; Walch 219.

Autobiography. Berkley 94; Biddle 266; Carolina Wren 266; Clarkson Potter 112; Cottage 267; Daniel 119; Diskotech 267; E.M. 267; Greene 277; Permanent/Second Chance 178; Poseidon 182; Soho 197; Xenos 225; Zondervan 226.

Bibliographies. Borgo 98; Family Album 127; Gryphon 134; Klein B. 151; Locust Hill 156; Scarecrow 193; Whitson 222.

Biography. American Eagle 84; American Media 246; American Nurses 85; APU 265; Arcade 87; Architectural 87; Archives 87; Arsenal 228; Atheneum Children's 89; Atheneum 90; Avanyu 90; Avon 90; Bantam 92; Beach Holme 228; Bergh 247; Berkley 94; Binford & Mort 247; Blackbirch, Inc. 276; Blair 96; Blue Dolphin 97; Bonus 98; Borgo 98; Bowling Green 99; Boxwood 99; Branden 100; Brassey's (US) 100; British American 101; Broadview 229; Caitlin 230; California State 103; Cambridge 103; Camino 104; Canadian Plains 230; Capra 104; Carol 106; Carolina Wren 266; Carolrhoda 106; Carpenter 276; Carroll & Graf 106; Catholic University of America 107; Cave 107; Chelsea Green 109; China 110; Christopher 248; Citadel 112; Clarion 112; Clark 248; Clarkson Potter 112; Clear Light 112; Colonial 114; Consortium 249; Contemporary Books 116; Cool Hand 116; Council for Indian Education 117; Creative Arts 249; Creative 118; Cross Cultural 118; Crown 118; Cuff 231; Daniel 119; Dante 119; Davidson 120; Dawson 120; Death Valley 121; Dee 121; Discipleship 122; Discovery 250; Diskotech 267; Dunburn 231; Dutton Children's 124; E.J.M. 267; E.M. 267; Eastern Caribbean 267; Eastern National Park 125; Edicones 251; Elliott & Clark 125; Enslow 126; Eriksson 126; Faber & Faber 126; Family Album 127; Feminist Press 128; Fine 128; Fitzhenry & Whiteside 232; Friends 130; Gallaudet 130; Giniger 277; Godine 132; Goose Lane 232; Great Northwest 133; Guernica 232; Hancock House 135; Harper 135; HarperCollins 135; Hastings House 136; Hay House 137; Hendrick-Long 138; High Plains 139; HMS 233; Holmes & Meier 140; Homestead 140; Hope 254; Hounslow 233; Howells 141; Huntington 143; In Print 268; Independence 268; Indiana Historical 269; Insight Books 145; International 147; Italica 148; Jesperson 234; Jones University 149; Jordan 255; Kent State 150; Kesend 150; Kodansha 151; Laing 278; Lamppost 278; Lang Publishing 256; Lawrence Books 152; Lawrence Inc. 152; Lee & Low 269; Lehigh 153; Lerner 153; Library Research 154; Lifetime 154; Lion 155; Little, Brown 155; Lone Pine 234; Longmeadow 157; Longstreet House 257; Longstreet Press, Inc. 157; Louisiana State 158; Loyola 158; Lucent 158; McDonald & Woodward 159; Madison 160; Madison House 160; Marketscope 161; Media Forum 161; Media/Midgard 162; Mercury 235; Mid-List 270; Minnesota Historical 164; Monitor 164; Morrow 165; Mosaic 270; Motorbooks 165; Mystic Seaport 270; N.A.L. Dutton 167; National Press 167; Naval Institute 168; New England 169; New Leaf 169; New Victoria 170; North Country 257; Oolichan 235; Orca 236; Orchises 173; Oregon Historical 173; Oregon State 174; Outcrop 236; Overlook 174; Pacific Press 175; Pandora 236; Parenting 176; Partners 271; Pelican 177; Pennsylvania Historical 177; Permanent/Second Chance 178; Piccadilly 179; Pineapple 180; Pippin 180; Plexus 181; Pocket 181; Poseidon 182; Press at California State 183; Press Gang 237; Prima 184; Pruett 185; Purdue 186; QED 259; Quill 187; Ragged Mountain 187; Random House 187; Random House Juvenile 188; Red Apple 259; Rhombus 272; Rutgers 190; Rutledge Hill 190; St. Paul 191; Sandlapper 192; Schirmer 193; Scots Plaid 272; Scribner's 194; Sevgo 194; Signature 195; Simon & Pierre 239; Simon & Schuster 195; Sky 196; Smith 196; Soho 197; Sono Nis 239; South Wind 198; Southern Methodist 198; Star Books 200; Stemmer House 201; Sunbelt Media 203;

Coffee Table Book. American Media 246; Arsenal Pulp 228; Bantam 92; Bentley 94; Blockbuster 96; Bonus 98; Brassey's (US) 100; California State 103; Canadian Plains 230; Caxton 107; China 110; Chronicle 111; Clear Light 112; Cool Hand 116; Death Valley 121; Dorling Kindersley 123; Dunburn 231; Elliott & Clark 125; Giniger 277; Godine 132; Greene 277; Harian 253; Harmony House 253; Hastings 136; Herald Press Canada 233; Homestead 140; Hounslow 233; Howells House 141; Ideals 143; Imagine 143; Inner Traditions 145; Interlink 146; Laing 278; Lark 152; Lexikos 154; Lifetime 154; Longmeadow 157; Longstreet 157; McDonald & Woodward 159; Minnesota Historical 164; Museum of Northern Arizona 166; North Country 257; Northword 172; Pelican 177; Pendaya 177; Pennsylvania Historical 177; Press at California State 183; Quarry 186; Schiffer 193; Sky 196; T.F.H. Books Inc. 204; T.F.H. Publications 279; Taylor 205; Texas Tech 206; Theytus 239; University of North Texas 214; Voyageur 218; Wieser & Wieser 280; WRS 225; Zoland 226.

Communications. Longman 157; TAB 204; Tiare 208; Univelt 210; Vestal 217.

Community/Public Affairs. Madison 160; Pfeiffer 179; Russell Sage 190; University of Alabama 210.

Computers/Electronic. Actaeon 245; Amacom 83; American Eagle 84; And 86; Arcsoft 88; Bantam 92; Baywood 93; Boyd & Fraser 99; Branden 100; Career 105; Carol 106; Compute 115; Duke 123; Gifted Education 131; Grapevine 132; Hollow Earth 140; IEEE 254; Industrial 144; Jain 148; Jamenair 269; Laing 278; Lerner 153; Lifetime 154; Lucent 158; Microtrend 163; MIS 164; Noyes 172; O'Reilly 174; Orion 257; Osborne/McGraw-Hill 174; Peachpit 176; Prentice Hall Canada, Inc. 237; PSI 185; Q.E.D. 186; R&E 259; Resolution 272; San Francisco 191; Slawson 196; Sourcebooks 197; Sterling 201; Sybex 204; Systemsware 273; TAB 204; Teachers College 205; Tiare 208; University of North Texas 214; Waite 218; Walch, 219; Wheetley 279; White Cliffs 221; Whitman 221.

Consumer Affairs. Almar Press 83; And 86; Benjamin 94; Consumer Reports 116; International Foundation 146; Menasha 162; NAR 270.

Cooking/Foods/Nutrition. A.R.E. 79; Actaeon 245; Alaska Northwest 82; American 246; Applezaba 87; Arcade 87; Archives 87; Atheneum Children's 89; Avery 90; Bantam 92; Barron's 93; Benjamin 94; Bergh Publishing, Inc. 247; Better Homes and Gardens 95; Blockbuster 96; Blue Dolphin 97; Bonus 98; Book Creations 276; Briarcliff 247; Bristol 101; British American 101; Caitlin 230; Cambridge 103; Camden House 230; Camino 104; Carol 106; Cassandra 106; Chicago Review 109; China 110; Christopher 248; Chronicle 111; Chronimed 111; Clarkson Potter 112; Clear Light 112; Colonial 114; Consumer Reports 116; Contemporary Books 116; Cool Hand 116; Countryman 117; Crossing 118; Crown 118; David 119; Dorling Kindersley 123; Durst 124; Edicones 251; Eriksson 126; Evans 126; Facts On File 127; Fiesta City Publishers 268; Filter 252; Fine 128; Fisher 128; Four Walls Eight Windows 129; Gem Guides 130; Globe Pequot 131; GMS 268; Godine 132; Gulf 252; Hampton Roads 253; Harian 253; Harmony House 253; HarperCollins 135; Harvard Common 136; Hastings House 136; Hawkes 253; Haworth 137; Hay House 137; Herald Press Canada 233; Hillbrook 268; Hounslow 233; Howell 141; Info Net 255; Inner Traditions 145; Interlink 146; Jain 148; Jesperson 234; Jordan 255; Kodansha America 151; Laing 278; Lamppost 278; Lark 152; Lerner 153; Lifetime 154; Little, Brown 155; Little, Brown Children's 155; Longmeadow 157; Longstreet 157; Lyons & Burford 159; McGraw-Hill Ryerson 234; Maverick 161; Meadowbrook 161; Media Forum 161; Meyerbooks 270; Minnesota Historical 164; Morrow 165; Mosaic 270; National 167; Nordicpress 171; Northland 171; Outcrop 236; Pacific Press 175; Parachute 279; Peachtree 177; Pelican 177; Pennsylvania Historical 177; Pocket Books 181; Prentice-Hall Canada 237; Price Stern Sloan 183; Prima 184; Pruett 185; QED 259; Ragged Mountain 187; R&E 259; Random House 187; Red Apple 259; RedBrick 271; Richboro 189; Rutledge Hill 190; Sand River 272; Sandlapper 192; Sasquatch 193; Sevgo 194; Spheric House 273; Stemmer House 201; Storey/Garden Way 202; Sunbelt 203; Systems 204; Ten Speed 205; Tidewater 208; Times 208; Twin Peaks 209; University of North Carolina 214; Vista 218; Voyageur 218; Warren 219; Westport 221; Wheetley 279; Whitman 221; Wieser & Wieser 280; Williamson 222; Windward 223; Wine Appreciation 223; Woodbridge 224; Woodsong 261; Yankee 225.

Counseling/Career Guidance. Accelerated Development 80; Almar 83; Career 105; Ferguson 128; Garrett Park 130; Graduate 252; Harvard Common 136; Jamenair 269; Jist Works 149; NASW 167; National Textbook 167; Octameron 172; Peterson's 179;

Feminism. Chicago Review 109; Crossing 118; Feminist Press 128; Firebrand 128; New Victoria 170; Publishers 185; Times Change 274; Vehicule 241.

Film/Cinema/Stage. Applause 87; Borgo 98; Citadel 112; Dee 121; Drama 123; Fairleigh Dickinson 127; Focal 129; Guernica 232; Imagine 143; Indiana University 144; Knowledge Industry 151; Lone Eagle 156; Love Child 158; McFarland 159; Media Forum 161; Meriwether 162; New York Zoetrope 170; Overlook 174; Piccadilly 179; Players 181; Press at California State 183; Scarecrow 193; Schirmer 193; Teachers College 205; Theatre Arts 207; University of Michigan 213; University of Texas 215; University Press of America 216; Vestal Press 217.

Gardening. Actaeon 245; Better Homes and Gardens 95; Briarcliff Press 247; Camden House 230; Camino Books 104; Capra 104; Chanticleer 276; Chicago 109; China 110; Chronicle 111; Dorling Kindersley 123; Elliott & Clark 125; Fisher 128; Globe Pequot 131; Godine 132; Gulf 252; Hartley & Marks 136; Hay House 137; HMS 233; Howell 141; Interlink 146; Jones University 149; Jordan 255; Kodansha America 151; Lamppost 278; Lark 152; Lifetime 154; Lone Pine 234; Longstreet 157; Lyons & Burford 159; NAR 270; Naturegraph 270; Pineapple 180; Pruett 185; Richboro 189; Sasquatch 193; Stackpole 200; Storey/Garden Way 202; Taylor 205; Ten Speed 205; Timber 208; University of North Carolina 214; Vandamere 217; Warren 219; Whitman 221; Wieser & Wieser 280; Williamson Co. 222; Windward 223; Woodbridge 224.

Gay/Lesbian. Actaeon 245; Bantam 92; Barn Owl 266; Beacon 93; Calyx 266; Carol 106; Carolina Wren 266; Cleis 113; Crossing 118; Feminist Press 128; Firebrand 128; Gallerie 252; Gay Sunshine and Leyland 130; Gylantic 134; Haworth 137; Hay House 137; Insight 145; Little, Brown Children's 155; Madwoman 269; Masefield 257; New Victoria 170; Press Gang 237; Publishers 185; Rising Tide 189; Routledge 189; Rutgers 190; Signature 195; South End 197; Starbooks 260; Volcano 274.

General Nonfiction. American Psychiatric 85; Arcade 87; Atheneum 90; Avon Flare 90; Bandb 276; Beacon 93; Biddle 266; Brett 266; Broadview 229; Delancey 267; Evans 126; Fawcett Juniper 127; Frost 277; Indiana University 144; Inverted-A 269; Johnson 149; Kent State 150; Knopf 151; Lang 256; Leisure 153; Lothrop, Lee & Shepard 158; Mills & Sanderson 163; Morrow 165; Netherlandic 235; New England 278; NewSage 270; Norton 172; Pacific 175; Pantheon 176; Peachtree 177; Pippin 180; Pocket 181; Potentials 182; Rainbow 187; S.P.I. 260; Scholastic 193; Shaw 194; Silvercat 272; Ticknor & Fields 208; University of Calgary 241; Villard 218; Writer's Digest 224.

Government/Politics. Actaeon 245; America West 83; American Media 246; American Press 85; Arcade 87; Ashgate 246; Atheneum 90; Atheneum Children's 89; Avon 90; Bandanna 92; Bantam 92; Bergh 247; Bonus 98; Borgo 98; Branden 100; Brassey's (US) 100; British American 101; Broadview 229; Buddha Rose 102; C Q 102; California State 103; Camino 104; Canadian Plains 230; Catholic University 107; Cato 107; Center for Learning 108; Chelsea Green 109; China 110; Christopher 248; Cleis 113; Colonial 114; Cool Hand 116; CQ 102; Cross Cultural 118; Crown 118; Cuff 231; Davidson 120; Dee 121; Denali 122; Devin-Adair 250; East Coast 124; Eastern Caribbean 267; Edicones 251; Eriksson 126; Fairleigh Dickinson 127; Feminist Press 128; Four Walls Eight Windows 129; FPMI 129; Frost 277; Glenbridge 131; Greene 277; Guernica 232; HarperCollins 135; Health Administration 137; Holmes & Meier 140; Hope 254; Howells House 141; Humanities 254; Huntington House 143; ILR 143; Indiana University 144; Initiatives 144; Insight 145; Intercultural 145; Interlink 146; International 147; Kodansha America 151; Kumarian 256; Lang 56; Lerner 153; Library Research 154; Lincoln Springs 269; Lone Pine 234; Longman 157; Longmeadow 157; Loompanics 157; Louisiana State 158; Lucent 158; Madison House 160; Masefield 257; Mercury 235; Michigan State 163; Milkweed 163; Millbrook 163; N.A.L. Dutton 167; NAR 270; National Press 167; NeWest 235; Noble 171; Oolichan 235; Oregon Historical 173; Outcrop 236; Pelican 177; Pennsylvania Historical 177; Poseidon 182; Praeger 182; Prentice-Hall Canada 237; Press at California State 183; Prima 184; Probe 271; Publishers 185; Purdue 186; Québec/Amérique 238; R&E 259; Reidmore 238; Rhombus 272; Riverdale 189; Routledge 189; Russell Sage 190; Rutgers 190; Sachem 279; Social Science Education 196; South End 197; Stanford 200; Sunflower 203; Teachers College 205; Temple 205; Theytus 239; Thunder's Mouth 208; Transaction 261; Trend 209; UCLA-American Indian 274; University of Alabama 210; University of Alaska 210; University of Alberta 240; University of Arkansas 211; University of Illinois 212; University of Michigan 213; University of Missouri 213; University of North Carolina 214; University of North Texas 214; University of Ottawa 241; University of Pittsburgh 214; University Press, Kentucky 216;

University Press of Mississippi 216; University Press of New England 217; Utah State 217; Vehicule 241; Vesta 242; Vista 218; Walch 219; Washington State 220; Watts 220; Wayfinder 220; Western/Journal 261; Wheetley 279; Xenos 225.

Health/Medicine. A.R.E. 79; Accelerated Development 80; Acorn 265; Actaeon 245; Almar 83; America West 83; American Hospital 84; American Nurses 85; American Press 85; American Veterinary 86; Atheneum Children's 89; Avery 90; Avon 90; Bantam 92; Barron's Educational Series, Inc. 93; Baywood 93; Benjamin 94; Berkley 94; Biddle 266; Blue Dolphin 97; Blue Poppy 97; Bonus Books 98; Book Creations 276; Branden 100; Briarcliff 247; Broadview 229; Cambridge 103; Carol 106; Cassandra 106; Cato 107; Charles 248; Christopher 248; Chronicle 111; Chronimed 111; Cleaning Consultant 248; Consortium 249; Consumer Reports 116; Contemporary 116; Cool Hand 116; Crisp 118; Crossing 118; Crown 118; Deaconess 120; Devin-Adair 250; Dimi 267; Dorling Kindersley 123; Elysium Growth 125; Eriksson 126; Evans 126; Facts On File 127; Feminist Press 128; Ferguson 128; Fisher 128; Fitzhenry & Whiteside 232; Frost Associates 277; Gallaudet 130; Giniger 277; Government Institutes 132; Gylantic 134; Hampton Roads 253; HarperCollins 135; Hartley & Marks 136; Harvard Common, The 136; Hastings House 136; Hawkes 253; Haworth 137; Hay House 137; Health Administration 137; Hope 254; Hounslow 233; Human Kinetics 142; Humanics 142; Hunter House 254; Information Resources 144; Inner Traditions 145; Insight 145; International Foundation of Employee Benefit Plans 146; International Information 146; International Medical 146; Iowa State University 148; Ishiyaku Euroamerica 148; Jain 148; Jones University 149; Jordan 255; Kesend 150; Knowledge 151; Krieger 152; Laing 278; Lamppost 278; Lawrence 152; Lerner 153; Lifetime 154; Llewellyn 155; Longmeadow 157; Luramedia 159; McFarland 159; McGuinn & McGuire 160; M&H 160; Marketscope 161; Masefield 257; Maupin House 270; Menasha Ridge 162; Metamorphous 162; Meyerbooks 270; Mid-List 270; Millbrook 163; Mosaic 270; NAR 270; NASW 167; Naturegraph 270; Neal-Schuman 168; New Readers 169; Newcastle 170; Nordicpress 171; Olson & Co., C. 271; Oryx 174; Pacific 175; Parkside 176; Pax 271; Pelican 177; Perspectives 178; Plenum 181; Popular Medicine 271; Precept 183; Prentice-Hall Canada 237; Prentice Hall Canada, School 237; Press Gang 237; Prima 184; Proclaim Publishing 258; Québec/Amérique 238; R&E 259; Random House 187; Rocky Top 189; Rutgers 190; San Francisco 191; Scribner's 194; Sierra Club 195; Skidmore-Roth 260; South End 197; Southern Methodist 198; Speech Bin 199; Spheric House 273; Sterling 201; Stillpoint 202; Sunflower 203; Taylor 205; Temple 205; Ten Speed 205; Texas Tech 206; Theosophical 207; Thorsons 240; Times 208; Transaction 261; Twin Peaks 209; Ulysses 210; University of Alaska 210; University of Pennsylvania 214; University of Pittsburgh 214; VGM Career Horizons 217; Vista Inc. 261; Volcano 274; Walch 219; Walker 219; Wall & Emerson 242; Warren 219; Waterfront 274; Weiser 220; Wheetley 279; Whitman 221; Wieser & Wieser 280; Williamson 222; Wingbow Press 224; Woodbine House 224; Woodbridge Press 224; Woodland Health 224; WRS 225; Yes 262; YMAA 274; Zebra and Pinnacle 226.

Hi-Lo. Cambridge 103; National Textbook 167; New Readers 169; Prolingua 185; University of Michigan 213.

History. Academy Chicago 80; Accord 81; Actaeon 245; Alaska Northwest 82; American Media 246; American Press 85; Ancestry 86; Appalachian Mountain Club 87; Arcade 87; Architectural 87; Arsenal Pulp 228; Atheneum 90; Atheneum Children's 89; Avanyu 90; Avery 90; Avon 90; Bandanna 92; B&B 92; Beach Holme 228; Behrman House 94; Biddle 266; Binford & Mort 247; Blair 96; Borgo 98; Boston Mills 229; Bowling Green 99; Boxwood 99; Branden 100; Brassey's (US) 100; Brevet 100; British American 101; Broadview 229; Buddha Rose 102; Caitlin 230; Cambridge 103; Camden House 104; Camino 104; Canadian Plains Research 230; Capstone 105; Carol 106; Carolrhoda 106; Carpenter 276; Carroll & Graf 106; Catholic University of America 107; Cave 107; Center for Learning 108; Chatham 109; China 110; Christopher 248; Citadel 112; Clarion 112; Clark 248; Clear Light 112; Colonial 114; Cool Hand 116; Coteau 231; Cottage 267; Council for Indian Education 117; Countryman Press 117; Creative 118; Cross Cultural 118; Crossway 118; Crown 118; Cuff 231; Dante University of America 119; Davidson 120; Dawson 120; Death Valley Natural History 121; Dee 121; Denali 122; Devin-Adair 250; Discipleship 122; Discovery 250; Down East 123; Drama 123; Dunburn 231; Dutton Children's 124; Eagle's View 124; Eastern National Park & Monument 125; Eerdmans 251; Elliott & Clark 125; Eriksson 126; Faber & Faber 126; Facts on File 127; Fairleigh Dickinson 127; Family Album 127; Feminist Press 128; Fine 128;

Fitzhenry & Whiteside 232; Flores 128; Four Walls Eight Windows 129; Friends United 130; Frost 277; Gallaudet 130; Giniger 277; Glenbridge 131; Globe Pequot 131; Goose Lane 232; Greene 277; Guernica 232; Gylantic 134; Hancock House 135; HarperCollins 135; Hawkes 253; Heart of the Lakes 253; Herald Press Canada 233; Herald Publishing House 138; Heritage 139; Heyday 139; High Plains 139; Hippocrene 139; HMS 233; Holmes & Meier 140; Homestead 140; Hounslow 233; Howell Inc. 141; Howells House 141; Humanities 254; ICS 143; ILR 143; Indiana University 144; Info Net 255; Inner Traditions 145; Interlink 146; International Marine 146; International Publishers 147; Intervarsity 147; Iowa State 148; Italica 148; Jesperson 234; Johnson 149; Jones University 149; Jordan 255; Kent State 150; Kesend 150; Kinseeker 151; Kodansha America 151; Krieger 152; Laing 278; Lang 256; Lehigh 153; Lerner 153; Lexikos 154; Library Research 154; Lincoln Springs 269; Litle, Brown 155; Little, Brown Children's 155; Little, Brown and Co., Inc. 155; Longman 157; Longmeadow 157; Longstreet House 257; Longstreet Press 157; Lorien 269; Louisiana State 158; Loyola 158; Lucent 158; McDonald & Woodward 159; McFarland 159; McGuinn & McGuire 160; Madison 160; Madison House 160; Marabou 270; Masefield 257; Maverick 161; Media/Midgard 162; Mercury 235; Meyerbooks 270; Michigan State 163; Milkweed 163; Millbrook 163; Minnesota Historical 164; Morehouse 165; Morrow 165; Mosaic 270; Motorbooks 165; Mountain 166; Mountaineers 166; Mystic Seaport 270; National 167; Nautical & Aviation 168; Naval Institute 168; New England 169; New Victoria 170; NeWest 235; Noble 171; Northern Illinois 171; Northland 171; Oddo 173; Oolichan 235; Orca 236; Oregon Historical 173; Oregon State University 174; Outcrop 236; Overlook 174; Peachtree 177; Pelican 177; Pennsylvania Historical 177; Permanent/Second Chance 178; Phanes 179; Pickering 180; Pickwick 258; Pineapple 180; Pippin 180; Poseidon 182; Praeger 182; Prentice Hall Canada, School 237; Preservation 183; Presidio 183; Press at California State 183; Primer 271; Pruett 185; Publishers Associates 185; Publishers Syndication 271; Purdue 186; Push/Pull 186; Quarry 186; Quill 187; R&E 259; Random 187; Red Apple 259; Reidmore 238; Riverdale 189; Rockbridge 272; Routledge 189; Russell Sage 190; Rutgers 190; Sachem 279; St. Bede's 191; Sand River 272; Sandlapper 192; Sasquatch 192; Schiffer 193; Scots Plaid 272; Scribner's 194; Sevgo 194; Sierra 195; Signature 195; Simon & Schuster 195; Smith 196; Social Science Education 196; Sono Nis 239; South End 197; South Wind 198; Southern Methodist 198; Stanford 200; Stemmer House 201; Sterling 201; Stone Wall 273; Sunbelt 203; Sunflower 203; Sunstone 203; Teachers College 205; Temple 205; Texas A&M 206; Texas Tech 206; Texas Western 206; Theytus 239; Three Continents 207; Tidewater 208; Times 208; Transaction 260; Transportation Trails 209; Trend 209; UCLA-American Indian Studies 274; University of Idaho 211; University of Alabama 210; University of Alaska 210; University of Alberta The 240; University of Arkansas 211; University of California 211; University of Illinois 212; University of Iowa 212; University of Maine 212; University of Manitoba 241; University of Massachusetts 212; University of Michigan 213; University of Missouri 213; University of Nebraska 213; University of Nevada 213; University of New Mexico 213; University of North Carolina 214; University of North Texas 214; University of Oklahoma 214; University of Ottawa 241; University of Pennsylvania 214; University of Pittsburgh 214; University of Tennessee 215; University of Texas 215; University Press of America 216; University Press of Kentucky 216; University Press of Mississippi 216; University Press of New England 217; Utah State 217; Vandamere 217; Vehicule 241; Vestal 217; Virginia State Library 274; Vista 218; Walch 219; Walker 219; Ward Hill 219; Warren 219; Washington State 220; Watts 220; Wayfinder 220; Western/Journal 261; Western Tanager 274; Westernlore 221; Wheetley 279; Wieser & Wieser 280; Wilderness Adventure 222; Xenos 225; Ye Galleon 262; Zondervan 226; Whitman 221.

Hobby. Actaeon 245; Almar 83; Ancestry 86; Arcsoft 88; Atheneum Children's 89; Bale 91; Beaver Pond 247; Benjamin The 94; Betterway 95; Camden House 230; C&T 104; Capstone 105; Carstens 106; Collector 114; Cool Hand 116; Council for Indian Education 117; Crown 118; Dorling Kindersley 123; Dunburn 231; Durst 124; E.M. 267; Eagle's View 124; Eriksson 126; Facts on File 127; Filter 252; Gem 131; Gryphon 134; Hawkes Inc. 253; Info Net 255; Interweave 148; Jordan 255; Kalmbach 150; Kesend 150; Klein 151; Lark 152; Lifetime 154; Little, Brown Children's 155; Longmeadow 157; Lyons & Burford 159; Maverick 161; Menasha Ridge 162; Millbrook 163; Mosaic 270; Mustang 166; NAR 270; Push/Pull 186; Ragged Mountain 187; Rocky Top 189; Schiffer 193; Sky 196; Sono Nis 239; SouthPark 198; Stackpole 200; Sterling 201; Storey/Garden Way 202; Success 203; T.F.H. 204; Twin Peaks 209; University of North Carolina 214;

Vestal 217; Warren 219; Wieser & Wieser 280; Williamson 222; Woodsong 261.

House and Home. Better Homes and Gardens 95; Bookworks 276; Brighton 101; Taylor 205; Williamson 222.

How-To. AASLH 79; Abbott, Langer 80; Accent 81; Accord 81; Actaeon 245; Allen 82; Allworth 83; Almar 83; Alpine 246; Amacom 83; American Correctional 84; American Nurses 85; Amherst 86; Ancestry 86; Andrews and McMeel 86; Appalachian Mountain Club Books 87; Archives 87; Aronson 88; Art Direction 88; Atheneum Children's 89; Auto 266; Avery 90; Avon 90; Bantam 92; Beaver Pond 247; Benjamin 94; Bentley 94; Berkley 94; Better Homes and Gardens 95; Betterway 95; Bicycle 96; Blackbirch 276; Blockbuster, Inc. 96; Blue Bird 97; Blue Dolphin 97; Bonus 98; Bookworks 276; Briarcliff 247; Brick House 100; Brighton 101; British American 101; Business News 102; Calgre 103; Cambridge Educational 103; Camden House 230; Camino 104; C&T 104; Capra 104; Caradium 105; Cardoza 105; Career Advancement 248; Carol 106; Cassandra 106; CCC 108; Center 108; Charles 248; Chicago Review 109; China 110; Chosen 111; Christopher 248; Church Growth 111; Clarkson Potter 112; Cleaning Consultant 248; College Board 114; Concordia 115; Consultant 115; Consumer Reports 116; Contemporary 116; Cool Hand 116; Cornell Maritime 116; Council for Indian Education 117; Countryman 117; Craftsman 117; Crisp 118; Crossing 118; Crown 118; David 119; Dearborn Financial 120; Delta 250; Denlingers 122; Devin-Adair 250; Devyn 122; Dickens 267; Diskotech 267; Doral 122; Dorling Kindersley 123; Duke 123; Dunamis 250; Durst 124; E.M. 267; Eagle's View 124; East Coast 124; Education 251; Eriksson 126; Fiesta City 268; Filter 252; Flores 129; Focal 129; Focus on the Family 129; Gay Sunshine and Leyland 130; Gifted Education 131; Global 131; Globe Pequot 131; GMS 268; Grapevine 132; Graphic Arts Technical 133; Great Northwest 133; Gryphon House 134; Half Halt 134; Hamilton 135; Hampton Roads 253; Hancock House 135; Harper 135; HarperCollins 135; Hartley & Marks 136; Harvard Common 136; Harvest House 136; Hastings House 136; Hawkes 253; Hay House 137; Heritage 139; Heyday 139; Hillbrook 268; HMS 233; Hollow Earth 140; Home Education 140; Hope 253; Hounslow 233; Human Kinetics 142; Imagine 143; In Print 268; Info Net 255; Initiatives 145; Insight 145; Intercultural 145; Interlink 146; International Information 146; International Wealth 147; Interweave 148; Jain 148; Jamenair 269; Jist Works 149; Jordan 255; Kalmbach 150; Kesend 150; Klein 151; Knowledge Book 151; Laing 278; Lamppost 278; Lark 152; LAWCO 269; Liberty Bell 269; Library Research 154; Lifetime 154; Little, Brown and Co. 55; Llewellyn 155; Lone Eagle 156; Lone Pine 234; Longmeadow 157; Loompanics 157; Lorien 269; Love Child 158; McDonald & Woodward 159; McGraw-Hill Ryerson 234; McGuinn & McGuire 160; Marketscope 161; Masefield 257; Maupin House 270; Maverick 161; Meadowbrook 161; Media/Midgard 162; Menasha Ridge 162; Meriwether 162; Metamorphous 162; Mid-List 270; Morrow 165; Mother Courage 165; Motorbooks 165; Mountaineers 166; Mustang 166; Mystic Seaport 270; Naturegraph 270; Neal-Schuman 168; New England 169; Newcastle 170; Nordicpress 171; North Light 171; Northword 172; Olson 271; Optimus 271; Orchises 173; Orion 257; Pacific Boating 257; Pacific Press 175; Paladin 175; Partners 271; Peachpit 176; Pelican 177; Pennsylvania Historical 177; Perspectives 178; Peterson's 179; Piccadilly 179; Pickering 180; Pineapple 180; PMN 258; Prima 184; Princeton 184; Probus 184; ProStar 259; PSI 185; Push/Pull 186; QED 259; Ragged Mountain 187; Rainbow 187; R&E 259; Resource 259; Richboro 189; Rocky Top 189; S.P.I. 260; Schiffer 193; Scots Plaid 272; Self-Counsel 238; Sevgo 194; Shorewood 272; Sierra 195; Sky 196; SouthPark 198; Southwest 198; Speech Bin 199; Spheric House 273; ST 199; Standard 200; Sterling 201; Still Waters 201; Stoeger 202; Stone Wall 273; Stoneydale 202; Storey Communications/Garden Way 202; Success 203; Sunstone 203; Systems 204; T.F.H. Books 204; T.F.H. Publications 279; TAB 204; Tambra 273; Ten Speed 205; Tenth Avenue Editions 279; Theytus 239; Thomas 207; Tiare 208; Twin Peaks 209; UCLA-American Indian Studies Center 274; University of Alberta 240; Vista 261; Waite 218; Ward Hill 219; Wasatch 274; Waterfront 274; Weiser 220; Wilderness Adventure 222; Wilderness Press 222; Williamson 222; Wilshire 223; Windsor 223; Windward 223; Wine Appreciation 223; Woodsong 261; Writer's Digest 224; Yankee 225; Yes International 262; Zebra and Pinnacle 226.

Humanities. Asian Humanities 88; Borgo 98; Duquesne 124; Feminist Press 128; Free 130; Gifted Education 131; Indiana 144; Lang 256; Riverdale 189; Roxbury 190; Southern Illinois 198; Stanford 200; University of Arkansas 211; Whitson 222; Zondervan 226.

Humor. Acme 265; Actaeon 245; Andrews and McMeel 86; Arsenal Pulp 228; Atheneum Children's 89; Bale 91; Bantam 92; Blue Dolphin 97; British American 101; Camino

104; Carol 106; Catbird 107; CCC 108; Citadel 112; Clarion 112; Clarkson Potter 112; Clear Light 112; Colonial 114; Compcare 115; Contemporary 116; Cool Hand 116; Council for Indian Education 117; Crown 118; CSS 249; Cuff 231; Dawson 120; Delta 250; E.J.M. 267; Edicones 251; Eriksson 126; Fine 128; Friends United 130; Godine. 132; Harian 253; HarperCollins 135; Hastings House 136; Hay House. 137; Hillbrook House 268; Hounslow 233; Jesperson 234; Jordan 255; Knowledge 151; Lamppost 278; Longmeadow 157; Longstreet Inc. 157; Marketscope 161; Media Forum 161; Meriwether 162; Mosaic 270; Mustang 166; Orchises 173; Paladin 175; Pax 271; Peachtree 177; Pelican 177; Peter Pauper 178; Piccadilly 179; Pippin 180; Press Gang 237; Price Stern Sloan 183; Push/Pull 186; QED 259; Quarry 186; Ragged Mountain 187; R&E 259; Random House 187; Random House, Juvenile 187; Red Apple 259; Rutledge Hill 190; S.P.I. 260; Sandlapper 192; Scots Plaid 272; Signature 195; Star 200; Sterling 201; Still Waters 201; Success 203; Systems 204; Woodsong 261; Yankee 225; Zebra and Pinnacle 226.

Illustrated book. Actaeon 245; American Nurses 85; Atheneum Children's 89; Avanyu 90; Bandanna 92; Bantam 92; Bear 93; Bergh 247; Betterway 95; Blackbirch 276; Boston Mills 229; Branden 100; Canadian Plains Research 230; C&T 104; Carol 106; Chanticleer 276; Charlesbridge 109; Chatham 109; Cleaning Consultant 248; Coach House 230; Colonial 114; Cool Hand 116; Council for Indian Education 117; Davis 120; Discovery Enterprises 250; Dorling Kindersley 123; Elysium Growth 125; Flores 129; Giniger 277; Godine 132; Goose Lane 232; Graphic Arts Center 132; Greene Communications 277; Hampton Roads 252; Harmony House 253; Harvest House 136; Herald Press Canada 233; Holiday House 139; Homestead 140; Hounslow 233; Howell Press, Inc. 141; Howells House 141; Imagine 143; Indiana Historical Society 269; Inner Traditions 145; Interlink 146; Jesperson 234; Jordan 255; Kesend 150; Laing 278; Lamppost 278; Lark 152; Lexikos 154; Lifetime 154; Longmeadow 157; Longstreet 157; Lothrop, Lee & Shepard 158; McDonald & Woodward 159; Meadowbrook 161; Metamorphous 162; Milkweed 163; Minnesota Historical 164; Mosaic 270; Mountain Automation 270; New England 169; Northword 172; Orca 236; Pelican 177; Pendaya 177; Pennsylvania Historical 178; Philomel 179; Pickering 180; Pippin 180; Pogo 182; Press Gang 237; Princeton Architectural 258; Proclaim 258; Pruett 185; Push/Pull 186; Quarry 186; Québec/Amérique 238; Ragged Mountain 187; R&E 259; Random House 187; Random House, Juvenile 188; Sandlapper 192; Schiffer 193; Sky 196; Smith 196; Soundprints 197; South Wind 98; Speech Bin 199; Stemmer House 201; Sunbelt 203; Sunflower 203; T.F.H. 279; Tenth Avenue Editions 279; Texas Tech 206; Theytus 239; Tidewater 208; UAHC 261; University of New Mexico 213; Warren 219; Wayfinder 220; Wilderness Adventure 222; Willowisp 223; Windward 223; Woodsong 261; Xenos 225.

Juvenile books. Abingdon 80; Actaeon 245; Appalachian Mountain 87; Arcade 87; Archives 87; Archway/Minstrel 88; Atheneum Children's 89; Baker 91; B&B 92; Bantam 92; Barron's 93; Beach Holme 228; Beacon 93; Behrman House 94; Bergh 247; Blackbirch 276; Bookcraft 98; Boyds Mills 99; Branden 100; Browndeer 102; Cambridge 103; Camino 104; C&T 104; Capstone 105; Carolrhoda 106; Carpenter 276; Centering 108; Charlesbridge 109; Chicago Review 109; Children's 110; China 110; Clarion 112; Clarkson Potter 112; Cobblehill 113; Colonial 114; Concordia 115; Council for Indian Education 117; Davenport 119; Death Valley Natural History 121; Denison 122; Dickens 267; Discovery 250; Doral 122; Dunburn 231; Dutton Children's 124; Eastern National Park 125; Enslow 126; Feminist Press 128; Fiesta City 268; Fitzhenry & Whiteside 232; Focus on the Family 129; Free Spirit 268; Friends United 130; Global 131; Godine 132; Greenhaven 133; Grosset & Dunlap 133; Gryphon House 268; Harcourt Brace 135; Harvest House 136; Hastings House 136; Hay House 137; Hendrick-Long 138; Herald Press 138; Herald Press Canada 233; Holiday House 139; Homestead 140; Hope 254; Houghton Mifflin 141; Huntington House 143; Incentive 144; Interlink 146; Jones University 149; Jordan Enterprises 255; Kar-Ben Copies 150; Knowledge Book 151; Laing 278; Lamppost 278; Lark 152; Lee & Low 269; Lerner 153; Lion 155; Little, Brown Children's 155; Lodestar 156; Lone Pine 234; Longmeadow 157; Lothrop 158; Lucas-Evans 278; Lucent 158; McElderry 159; Marlor 161; Meadowbrook 161; Millbrook 163; Morehouse 165; Morrow 165; Morrow Junior 165; Nightwood 235; Northword 172; Oddo 173; Orca 236; Oregon Historical 173; Pacific 175; Parachute 279; Parenting 176; Peachtree 177; Pelican 177; Perspectives 178; Philomel 179; Pippin 180; Players 181; Preservation 183; Price Stern Sloan 183; Proclaim 258; Quarry 186; Québec/Amérique 238; Random House, Juvenile 188; Red Apple 259; Review and Herald 188; Rubicon 238; St. Paul

191; Sandlapper 192; Sasquatch 193; Scholastic Professional 194; Scribner's 194; Sierra Club 195; SkippingStone 273; Soundprints 197; South Wind 198; Speech Bin 199; Spheric House 273; Standard 200; Star 200; Stemmer House 201; Sterling 201; Storey/ Garden Way 202; Sunbelt 203; T.F.H. 204; Tambourine 205; Tenth Avenue Editions 279; Texas Christian 206; Tidewater 208; Tyndale House 209; UAHC 261; Victor 217; Volcano 274; Voyageur 218; Walker 219; Ward Hill 219; Warren 219; Waterfront 274; Weiss 279; Whitman 221; Williamson 222; Willowisp 223; Windward 223; Woodsong 261; Zondervan 226.

Labor/Management. Abbott, Langer 80; BNA 97; Brevet 100; Drama 123; FPMI 129; Gulf 252; Hamilton Institute 135; Health Administration 137; ILR 143; Intercultural 145; International 147; Pfeiffer 179; Temple 205.

Language and Literature. Actaeon 245; Anchorage 86; Asian Humanities 88; Bandanna 92; Bantam 92; Barron's Educational 93; Black Sparrow 96; Bowling Green 99; British American 101; Broadview 229; California State 103; Calyx 266; Capra 104; Carolina Wren 266; Catholic University of America 107; Center for Learning 108; Center 108; China 110; Clarion 112; Clarkson Potter 112; Coach House 230; College Board 114; Colonial 114; Consortium 249; Coteau 231; Cottonwood 117; Creative Arts 249; Creative with Words 267; Crossing 118; Daniel 119; Dante University of America 119; Davidson 120; Dee 121; Dunburn 231; Education Center 125; Facts on File, Inc. 127; Family Album 127; Feminist Press 128; Ford-Brown 268; Four Walls Eight Windows 129; Frost Associates 277; Gallaudet 130; Goose Lane 232; Graywolf 133; Greene 277; Gryphon 134; Guernica 232; Harian 253; Herald Canada 233; Hippocrene 139; HMS 233; Hope House 254; Insight 145; Interlink 146; Intervarsity 147; Italica 148; Jesperson 234; Jordan 255; Kent State 150; Kodansha America 151; Lang 256; Lehigh 153; Lerner 153; Lincoln Springs 269; Locust Hill 156; Longman 157; Longmeadow 157; Longstreet 157; Louisiana State 158; Mercury 235; Michigan State 163; Milkweed 163; Modern Language 164; National Textbook 167; New Readers 169; Nightshade 271; NTC 172; Oddo 173; Oolichan 235; Oregon State 174; Pandemic 175; Peguis 236; Perivale 271; Pippin 180; Prentice Hall Canada, School 237; Press Gang 237; Proclaim 258; Prolingua 185; Purdue 186; Quarry 186; Québec/Amérique 238; Roxbury 190; Rubicon 238; Rutgers 190; Sakura 272; Sand River 272; Scots Plaid 272; Simon & Pierre 239; SkippingStone 273; Smith 196; Southern Methodist 198; Spheric House 273; Stanford 200; Still Waters 201; Stone Bridge 273; Sunflower 203; Texas Tech 206; Three Continents 207; UCLA-American Indian Studies Center 274; University of Idaho 211; University of Alabama 210; University of Alaska 210; University of California 211; University of Illinois 212; University of Iowa 212; University of Michigan 213; University of Nebraska 213; University of Nevada 213; University of North Carolina 214; University of North Texas 214; University of Oklahoma 214; University of Ottawa 241; University of Pennsylvania 214; University of Pennsylvania 214; University of Pittsburgh 214; University of Scranton 215; University of Texas 215; University Press of America 216; University Press of Kentucky 216; University Press of Mississippi 216; Utah State University 217; Vehicule 241; Vesta 242; Vista 218; Walch 219; Warren 219; Wheatley 279; Writer's Digest 224; Xenos 225; York 243; Zoland 226.

Law. Almar 83; American Bar Association 84; Banks-Baldwin 92; BNA 97; Catbird 107; Durst 124; East Coast 124; Government Institutes 132; Hamilton Institute 135; Lawyers & Judges 153; Liberty Bell 269; Library Research 154; Monitor 164; Professional 184; Temple University 205; Transaction 260; Trend 209; University of Michigan 213; University of North Carolina 214; University of Pennsylvania 214.

Literary Criticism. Accord 81; Barron's Educational 93; Borgo 98; Coach House 230; Dunburn 231; ECW 231; Fairleigh Dickinson 127; Firebrand 128; Holmes & Meier 140; Lang 256; Loyola 158; Mysterious 167; Northern Illinois 171; Purdue 186; Routledge 189; Stanford 200; Texas Christian 206; Three Continents 207; University of Alabama 210; University of Arkansas 211; University of Massachusetts 212; University of Michigan 213; University of Missouri 213; University of Tennessee 215; University Press of Mississippi 216; Xenos 225; York 243.

Marine Subjects. Binford & Mort 247; Cornell Maritime 116; Howell 141; International Marine 146; Maverick 161; Mystic Seaport 270; ProStar 259; Sono Nis 239; TAB 204; Transportation 209; Wescott Cove 221.

Military/War. Actaeon 245; American Eagle 84; American Media 246; Avery 90; Avon 90; B&B 92; Bantam 92; Blair 96; Brassey's (US) 100; Cato 107; Crown 118; Eastern National Park 125; Fairleigh Dickinson 127; Fine 128; Flores 129; Harmony House 253;

Hippocrene 139; HMS 233; Hope 254; Howell Press 141; Howells House 141; Jesperson Ltd. 234; Lifetime 154; Lincoln Springs 269; Longmeadow 157; Longstreet House 257; Louisiana State 158; Lucent 158; McGraw-Hill Ryerson 234; Nautical & Aviation 168; Naval Institute 168; Paladin 175; PMN 258; Praeger 182; Presidio 183; Publishers Syndication 271; Quill 187; Reference Service 188; Sachem Inc. 279; Schiffer 193; Sevgo 194; South End 197; Stackpole 200; Sterling 201; Sunbelt 203; Sunflower 203; Texas A&M 206; University of Idaho 211; University of Alaska 210; University of North Texas 214; Vandamere 217; Vanwell 241; Virginia State Library 274; Wieser & Wieser 280; Zebra and Pinnacle 226.

Money/Finance. Actaeon 245; Allen 82; Almar 83; American Media 246; Ashgate 246; Bale 91; Bantam 92; Better Homes and Gardens 95; Blockbuster 96; Blue Horizon 247; Bonus 98; Briarcliff 247; Brick House 100; Broadview 229; Cambridge Educational 103; Caradium 105; Career Advancement Center 248; Carol 106; Cato 107; Center 108; Consumer Reports 116; Contemporary 116; Crisp 118; Dearborn Financial 120; Flores, J. 129; Focus on the Family 129; Gylantic 134; Hampton Roads 253; Hancock House 135; Harvard Common 136; Hay House 137; Hensley 138; Herald, Canada 233; Hounslow 233; Initiatives 145; Insight 145; International Information 146; International Wealth Success 147; Jain 148; Jordan Enterprises 255; Lamppost 278; Lerner 153; Lifetime 154; Longmeadow 157; McGraw-Hill Ryerson 234; Marketscope 161; NAR 270; National 167; NavPress 168; Pax 271; Pilot 180; PMN 258; Probus 184; PSI Research 185; QED 259; R&E 259; Shorewood 272; Sourcebooks 197; Success 203; Sunflower University 203; Technical Analysis of Stocks & Commodities 273; Ten Speed 205; United Resource 210; Vesta 242; Wheetley 279; Windsor 223; Zebra and Pinnacle 226.

Music and Dance. Actaeon 245; American Catholic 84; American 85; And 86; Atheneum Children's 89; Bantam 92; Betterway 95; Bold Strummer 98; Branden 100; California State University 103; Cambridge University 103; Carol 106; Carolrhoda 106; Centerstream 109; Colonial 114; Consortium 249; Cool Hand 116; Creative Arts 249; Dance Horizons 118; Davenport 119; Discipleship Resources 122; Drama Book 123; Faber & Faber 126; Fairleigh Dickinson University 127; Feminist Press at the City University of New York, The 128; Fiesta City 268; Glenbridge 131; Greene 277; Guernica Editions 232; HarperCollins 135; Indiana University 144; Inner Traditions International 145; Jesperson 234; Jordan Enterprises 255; Krieger 152; Lang 256; Lerner 153; Locust Hill 156; Longmeadow 157; Louisiana State University 158; McFarland & Company 159; Mercury 235; Meriwether 162; Mosaic Press Miniature 270; Pelican 177; Pendragon 258; Phanes 179; Press At California State University, Fresno, The 183; Prima 184; Princeton 184; Push/Pull/Press 186; Quill 187; R&E 259; Random House 187; Resource 259; San Francisco 191; Scarecrow 193; Schirmer 193; Simon & Pierre 238; South End 197; Stipes 202; Sunflower University 203; Tenth Avenue Editions 279; Texas Tech University 206; Timber 208; Transaction 261; University of Illinois 212; University of Michigan 213; University of Pittsburgh 214; University Press of America 216; University Press of New England 217; Vestal 217; Walch 219; Walker and Co. 219; Warren 219; Weiser 220; Wheetley 279; White Cliffs Media 221; Writer's Digest 224.

Nature and Environment. Actaeon 245; Alaska Northwest 82; Appalachian Mountain Club 87; Arcade 87; Atheneum Children's 89; Avery 90; Backcountry 91; B&B 92, 266; Baywood 93; Beacon 93; Bear and Co. 93; Beaver Pond 247; Binford & Mort 247; Blackbirch Graphics 276; Blair 96; Blue Dolphin 97; BNA 97; Boxwood 99; Brick House 100; Broadview 229; Buddha Rose 102; Camden House 230; Canadian Plains Research Center 230; Capra 104; Carol 105; Carolrhoda 106; Cave 107; Chanticleer 276; Charlesbridge 109; Chelsea Green 109; China Books & Periodicals 110; Chronicle 111; Clarion 112; Clarkson Potter 112; Clear Light 112; Cool Hand 116; Council for Indian Education 117; Countryman 117; Crown 118; Death Valley Natural History 121; Devin-Adair 250; Discipleship Resources 122; Dorling Kindersley 123; Down East 123; Dunamis House 250; Dutton Children's 124; Eastern National Park & Monument 125; Elliott & Clark 125; Elysium Growth 125; Eriksson 126; Facts on File 127; Four Walls Eight Windows 129; Gem Guides 130; Global Press Works 131; Godine 132; Goose Lane Editions 232; Government 132; Grosset & Dunlap 133; Hancock House 135; Harmony House 253; HarperCollins 135; Hartley & Marks 136; Hay House 137; Herald Canada 233; Heyday 139; High Plains 139; Homestead 140; Hope 254; Hunter House 254; Inner Traditions International 145; Insight 145; Interlink 146; Jain 148; Jesperson 234; Johnson 149; Jones University 149; Jordan Enterprises 255; Kesend 150; Kodansha America 151; Kumarian 256; Lark 152; Lawrence Books 152; Lawrence 152; Lerner 153; Lexikos 154;

Lifetime 154; Little, Brown And Company, Children's Book Division 155; Llewellyn 155; Lone Pine 234; Longmeadow 157; Longstreet 157; Lorien House 269; Lucent 158; Luramedia 159; Lyons & Burford 159; McDonald & Woodward 159; McGuinn & McGuire 160; Marketscope 161; Maverick 161; Meyerbooks 270; Milkweed Editions 163; Millbrook 163; Mosaic Press Miniature 270; Mountain 166; Mountaineers 166; Museum of Northern Arizona 166; Naturegraph 270; Nature's Design 270; New England 169; Nightshade 270; Noble 171; North Country 257; Northland 171; Northword 172; Noyes Data 172; Oddo 173; Olson & Co. 271; Orca 236; Oregon Historical Society 173; Oregon State University 174; Outcrop, The Northern 236; Pacific Press 175; Pennsylvania Historical and Museum Commission 177; Phanes 179; Pineapple 180; Pippin 180; Plexus 181; Primer 271; Pruett 185; Ragged Mountain 187; R&E 259; Random House, Juvenile 188; Review and Herald 188; Rhombus 272; Rocky Top 189; Rutgers University 190; Sandhill Crane Nature 192; Sasquatch 193; Scots Plaid 272; Scribner's Sons, Charles 194; Sierra Club 195; Sky 196; Smith, Publisher, Gibbs 196; Soundprints 197; South End 197; South Wind 198; Stemmer House 201; Sterling 201; Stillpoint 202; Stipes 202; Stone Wall 273; Storey Communications/Garden Way 202; Sunbelt Media 203; Sunflower University 203; T.F.H. 204; Taylor 205; Ten Speed 205; Texas A&M University 206; Texas Tech University 206; Thorsons 240; Timber 208; Times Change 274; University Of Idaho 211; University of Alaska 210; University of Alberta 240; University of Arizona 211; University of Arkansas 211; University of California 211; University of Nebraska 213; University of North Carolina 214; University of North Texas 214; University of Ottawa 241; University of Texas 215; University Press of Colorado 216; University Press of Mississippi 216; University Press of New England 217; VGM Career Horizons 217; Voyageur 218; Walker and Co. 219; Warren 219; Wasatch 274; Washington State University 220; Waterfront 274; Wayfinder 220; Wheetley 279; Whitman and Co. 221; Wieser & Wieser 280; Wilderness Adventure 222; Wilderness 222; Williamson 222; Willowisp 223; Windward 223; Yankee 225; Zoland 226.

Philosophy. A.R.E. 79; Actaeon 245; Ashgate 246; Asian Humanities 88; Atheneum Children's 89; Baker Book House 91; Bandanna 92; Bantam 92; Beacon 93; Boxwood 99; Broadview 229; Buddha Rose 102; Carol 106; Cassandra 106; Catholic University of America 107; Center 108; Christopher 248; Clear Light 112; Colonial 114; Cool Hand 116; Cross Cultural 118; Davidson 120; Eastern Caribbean 267; Edicones Universal 251; Eerdmans 251; Elysium Growth 125; Facts on File 127; Fairleigh Dickinson University 127; Gallerie 252; Gifted Education 131; Glenbridge 131; Guernica Editions 232; Harper San Francisco 135; HarperCollins 135; Hay 137; Hope 254; Humanities Press International 254; Indiana University 144; Inner Traditions International 145; Intercultural 145; International 147; Intervarsity 147; Italica 148; Jordan Enterprises 255; Kodansha America 151; Krieger 152; Lang 256; Larson 152; Lifetime 154; Locust Hill 156; Lone Pine 234; Louisiana State University 158; Masefield 257; Michigan State University 163; Noble 171; Northern Illinois University 171; Open Court 173; Paulist 176; Pax 271; Phanes 179; Praeger 182; Purdue University 186; Push/Pull/Press 186; R&E 259; Rocky Top 189; Routledge 189; St. Bede's 191; Savant Garde Workshop 272; Scots Plaid 272; Sierra Club 195; Simon & Schuster 195; South End 197; Southwest of Arizona 198; Teachers College 205; Temple University 205; Theosophical 207; Theytus 239; Transaction 261; University of Alberta 240; University of Illinois 212; University of Massachusetts 212; University of Ottawa 241; University of Pittsburgh 214; University of Scranton 215; University Press of America 216; Vesta 242; Wall & Emerson 242; Washington State University 220; Weiser 220; Wheetley 279; Woodsong Graphics 261; Xenos 225; Yes International 262.

Photography. Actaeon 245; Allworth 83; Amherst Media 86; Atheneum Children's 89; Avanyu 90; Beaver Pond 247; Bowling Green State University Popular 99; Branden 100; Caitlin 230; Camden House 230; Carstens 106; Cave 107; Center 108; Chronicle 111; Clarion 112; Clarkson Potter 112; Clear Light 112; Consultant 115; Crown 118; Cuff 231; Devin-Adair 250; Dorling Kindersley 123; Elliott & Clark 125; Elysium Growth 125; Focal 129; Goose Lane Editions 232; Harmony 253; Hollow Earth 140; Homestead 140; Hounslow 233; Howells 141; Hudson Hills 141; Jordan Enterprises 255; Lone Pine 234; Longstreet 157; Louisiana State University 158; Milkweed Editions 163; Minnesota Historical Society 164; Motorbooks International 165; Northland 171; NTC 172; Oregon Historical Society 173; Orion Research 257; Pendaya 177; Pennsylvania Historical and Museum Commission 177; Quarry 186; Ragged Mountain 187; Random House 187; Sierra Club 195; Sky 196; Stormline 273; Sunflower University 203; Temple University

205; Tenth Avenue Editions 279; University of Iowa 212; University of Nebraska 213; University of New Mexico 213; Voyageur 218; Wayfinder 220; Whitman and Co. 221; Wieser & Wieser 280; Writer's Digest 224; Zoland 226.

Psychology. A.R.E. 79; Accelerated Development 80; Actaeon 245; American Nurses 85; American 85; And 86; Aquarian 228; Aronson 88; Asian Humanities 88; Atheneum Children's 89; Atheneum 90; Avon 90; Baker Book House 91; Bantam 92; Baywood 93; Blue Dolphin 97; Boxwood 99; British American 101; Broadview 229; Buddha Rose 102; Cambridge University 103; Carol 106; Carroll & Graf 106; Cassandra 106; Charles 248; Christopher House 248; Chronimed 111; Citadel 112; Colonial 114; Compcare 115; Conari 115; Consortium 249; Contemporary 116; Cool Hand 116; Crown 118; Deaconess 120; Delta Sales 250; Dimi 267; Edicones Universal 251; Education 251; Eerdmans 251; Elysium Growth 125; Eriksson 126; Facts on File 127; Fairleigh Dickinson University 127; Free Spirit 268; Frost 277; Gallaudet University 130; Gifted Education 131; Glenbridge 131; Greene Communications 277; Guernica Editions 232; Harper San Francisco 135; HarperCollins 135; Hartley & Marks 136; Hastings House 136; Hawkes 253; Haworth 137; Hay House 137; Health Communications 137; Herald Press Canada 233; Hope House 254; Human Kinetics 142; Human Services 142; Humanics 142; Hunter House 254; Inner Traditions International 145; Insight 145; Intercultural 145; International Information 146; Intervarsity 147; Ishiyaku Euroamerica 148; Jordan Enterprises 255; Kodansha America 151; Krieger 152; Lang 256; Larson 152; Lawrence 152; Libra 256; Lifetime 154; Llewellyn 155; Locust Hill 156; Longmeadow 157; Lorien House 269; Luramedia 159; Masefield 257; Metamorphous 162; Mother Courage 165; N.A.L. Dutton 167; National 167; Newcastle 170; Open Court 173; Parkside 176; Pax 271; Perspectives 178; Plenum 181; Poseidon 182; Praeger 182; Prima 184; Push/Pull/Press 186; Quill 187; R&E 259; Riverdale 189; Routledge 189; Russell Sage Foundation 190; St. Paul Books and Media 191; Scots Plaid 272; Self-Counsel 238; Stanford University 200; Theosophical House 207; Thorsons 240; Transaction 261; University of Nebraska 213; University Press of America 216; University Press of New England 217; Victor 218; Vista 261; Walch 219; Wall & Emerson 242; Washington State University 220; Weiser 220; Westport 221; Wheetley 279; Williamson 222; Wilshire 223; Wingbow 224; Woodbridge 224; Woodsong Graphics 261; WRS 225; Xenos 225; Yes International 262.

Real Estate. Contemporary 116; Dearborn Financial 120; Government 132; PMN 258.

Recreation. Accord 81; Acorn 265; Actaeon 245; Alaska Northwest 82; Appalachian Mountain Club 87; Atheneum Children's 89; Backcountry 91; Beaver Pond 247; Betterway 95; Bicycle 96; Binford & Mort 247; Bonus 98; Book Creations 276; British American 101; Cambridge Educational 103; Camden House 230; Capra 104; Cardoza 105; Carol 106; Cave 107; Chatham 109; Chicago Review 109; Chronicle 111; Cool Hand Communications 116; Council for Indian Education 117; Countryman 117; Crown 118; Denali 122; Discipleship Resources 122; Dorling Kindersley 123; Down East 123; Dunamis House 250; Elysium Growth 125; Enslow 126; Eriksson 126; Facts on File 127; Falcon Press 252; Gem Guides 131; Globe Pequot 131; Hancock House 135; Harian Creative 253; Hay House 137; Herald Press Canada 233; Heyday 139; Human Kinetics 142; Info Net 255; Johnson 149; Jordan Enterprises 255; Kalmbach 150; Little, Brown And Company, Children's 155; Lone Pine 234; Longmeadow 157; McFarland & Company 159; Marketscope 161; Maverick 161; Menasha Ridge 162; Meriwether 162; Mountaineers 166; Mustang 166; NAR 270; New York Niche 170; Nordicpress 171; Optimus 271; Orca 236; Pacific Boating Almanac 257; Peachtree 177; Pelican 177; Piccadilly 179; ProStar 259; Pruett 185; Ragged Mountain 187; Random House, Juvenile Books 188; Riverdale 189; Sasquatch 193; Sierra Club 195; South Wind 198; SouthPark 198; Sterling 201; Stipes 202; Sunflower University 203; Ten Speed 205; Twin Peaks 209; University of Idaho 211; Vandamere 17; Voyageur 218; Wasatch 274; Wayfinder 220; Western Tanager 274; Wheetley 279; Whitman and Co. 221; Wieser & Wieser 280; Wilderness 222; Wilshire 223; Windward 223; World Leisure 274; WRS 225.

Reference. AASLH 79; Abbott, Langer & Associates 80; Accelerated Development 80; Accord 81; Actaeon 245; Allworth 83; Amacom 83; American Correctional 84; American Hospital 84; American Library 85; American Media 246; American Nurses 85; American Psychiatric 85; American Veterinary 86; Ancestry 86; Andrews and McMeel 86; Appalachian Mountain Club 87; APU 265; Architectural Book 87; Archives 87; Aronson 88; Ashgate 246; Asian Humanities 88; Avanyu 90; Avery 90; Backcountry 91; Baker Book House 91; B&B 92; Banks-Baldwin Law 92; Behrman House 94; Bethel 95; Betterway 95; Binford & Mort 247; Blackbirch Graphics 276; Blue Bird 97; BNA 97;

Borgo 98; Bowling Green State University Popular 99; Branden 100; Brassey's (US) 100; Brick House 100; Broadview 229; Broadway 101; Buddha Rose 102; Business News 102; CQ 102; Calgre 103; Cambridge University 103; Camden House 104; Camden House 230; Caradium 105; Cardoza 105; Carpenter House 276; Catbird 107; Christopher 248; Clark Co. 248; Cleaning Consultant Services 248; College Board 114; Compute 115; Consultant 115; Consumer Reports 116; Contemporary 116; Coteau 231; Crown 118; Cuff 231; Dante University Of America 119; David 119; Dearborn Financial 120; Delphi 121; Denali 122; Doral 122; Dorling Kindersley 123; Drama 123; Dunburn 231; Durst 124; Dustbooks 124; East Coast 124; ECW 231; Edicones Universal 251; Eerdmans 251; Enslow 126; Evans and Co. 126; Facts on File 127; Fairleigh Dickinson University 127; Ferguson 128; Focal 129; Friends United 130; Garrett Park 130; Giniger 277; Glenbridge 131; Government 132; Graduate 252; Graphic Arts Technical Foundation 133; Gryphon 134; Gulf 252; Harper San Francisco 135; HarperCollins 135; Harvard Common 136; Harvest House 136; Hastings House 136; Haworth 137; Hay House 137; Health Administration 137; Herald Press Canada 233; Heritage 139; Heyday 139; Hippocrene 139; Hollow Earth 140; Holmes & Meier 140; Homestead 140; Hope 254; HRD 141; Human Kinetics 142; Hunter 142; IEEE 254; Imagine 143; Indiana Historical Society 269; Indiana University 144; Industrial 144; Info Net 255; Information Resources 144; Initiatives 145; Intercultural 145; International Foundation Of Employee Benefit Plans 146; International Information 146; International Medical 146; International 147; Ishiyaku Euroamerica 148; Jesperson 234; Jist Works 149; Jordan Enterprises 255; Kinseeker 151; Klein 151; Krieger 152; Laing 278; Lang 256; Lawyers & Judges 153; Leadership 153; Lehigh University 153; Libraries Unlimited 154; Library Research 154; Lifetime 154; Locust Hill 156; Lone Eagle 156; Longmeadow 157; Longstreet 157; Loompanics Unlimited 157; Love Child 158; McFarland & Company 159; McGraw-Hill Ryerson 234; Madison Books 160; Madison House 160; Maupin House 270; Maverick 161; Meadowbrook 161; Media Forum International 161; Media/Midgard 162; Menasha Ridge 162; Meriwether 162; Metamorphous 162; Meyerbooks 270; Michigan State University 163; Minnesota Historical Society 164; Monitor 164; Museum of Northern Arizona 166; Mysterious 167; Mystic Seaport Museum 270; Nautical & Aviation 168; Neal-Schuman 168; Nelson 168; New York Zoetrope 170; NTC 172; Octameron 172; Ohio Biological Survey 271; Orchises 173; Oregon Historical Society 173; Orion Research 257; Oryx 174; Our Sunday Visitor 174; Outcrop, The Northern 236; Pacific 175; Pandemic International 175; Pandora 236; Partners in Publishing 271; Peachpit 176; Pendragon 258; Pennsylvania Historical and Museum Commission 177; Pineapple 180; Plexus 181; PMN 258; Pocket 181; Precept 183; Princeton 184; Professional 184; Prolingua 185; PSI Research 185; Quarry 186; Québec/Amérique 238; Quill 187; Rainbow 187; R&E 259; Reference Service 188; Resolution Business 272; Rocky Top 189; Routledge 189; Rubicon 238; Rutledge Hill 190; Sachem 279; Sandhill Crane Nature 192; Sandlapper 192; Scarecrow 193; Schiffer 193; Schirmer 193; Shorewood 272; Simon & Pierre 239; Sky 196; Sono Nis 239; Sound View 273; Sourcebooks 197; Speech Bin 199; ST 199; Standard 200; Sterling 201; Stoeger 202; Sunflower University 203; T.F.H. 279; TAB 204; Ten Speed 205; Thomas 207; Tidewater 208; Transaction 261; Trend 209; Twin Peaks 209; UCLA-American Indian Studies Center 274; University Of Idaho 211; University of Alaska 210; University of Alberta 240; University of Illinois 212; University of Michigan 213; University of North Texas 214; University of Ottawa 241; University of Pittsburgh 214; University Press of Kentucky 216; University Press of New England 217; Utah State University 217; Vesta 242; Victor 218; Virginia State Library and Archives 274; Vista 261; Waite 218; Walker and Co. 219; Wall & Emerson 242; Wayfinder 220; Wingbow 224; Woodbine House 224; Woodsong Graphics 261; Xenos 225; York 243; Zondervan House 226.

Regional. Actaeon 245; Alaska Northwest 82; Almar 83; Appalachian Mountain Club 87; APU 265; Arsenal Pulp 228; Avanyu 90; Beach Holme 228; Binford & Mort 247; Blair, John F. 96; Borealis 229; Boston Mills 229; Bottom Dog 266; Bowling Green State University 99; Boxwood 99; Brick House 100; British American 101; Caddo Gap 103; Caitlin 230; Camino 104; Canadian Plains 230; Capra 104; Carol 106; Cave 107; Caxton Printers 107; Chatham 109; Chicago Review 109; Chronicle 111; Clear Light 112; Colonial 114; Coteau 231; Countryman 117; Creative Arts 249; Creative 118; Cuff Harry 231; Davidson, Harlan 120; Dawson, W.S. 120; Death Valley Natural History Association 121; Denali 122; Down East 123; Dunamis House 250; Dunburn 231; ECW 231; Eerdmans, William B. 251; Faber & Faber 126; Family Album 127; Filter 252; Fitzhenry

& Whiteside 232; Gem Guides 131; Globe Pequot 131; Golden West 132; Great Northwest 133; Greene Communications 277; Guernica Editions 232; Gulf 252; Hampton Roads 253; Hancock House 135; Harian Creative 253; Heart of the Lakes 253; Hemingway Western Studies Series 268; Hendrick-Long 138; Herald 138; Heritage 139; Heyday 139; High Plains 139; Hunter 142; Indiana Historical Society 269; Indiana University 144; Jesperson 234; Johnson 149; Jordan Enterprises 255; Kent State University 150; Kinseeker 151; Lahontan Images 269; Lerner 153; Lexikos 154; Lifetime 154; Longmeadow 157; Longstreet House 257; Longstreet Press, Inc. 157; Louisiana State University 158; McGraw-Hill Ryerson Limited 234; Marketscope 161; Maupin House 270; Maverick 161; Media/Midgard 162; Milkweed Editions 163; Minnesota Historical Society 164; Moon 164; Mountain Press 166; Museum of Northern Arizona 166; National Press 167; Netherlandic 235; New England Press 169; New York Niche 170; Nightshade 271; Nightwood Editions 235; North Country 257; Northern Illinois University 171; Northland 171; Oolichan 235; Orca 236; Oregon Historical Society 173; Oregon State University 174; Overlook 174; Pacific Books 175; Pelican 177; Pennsylvania Historical and Museum Commission 177; Pickering 180; Prentice-Hall Canada 237; Primer 271; Pruett 185; Purdue University 186; Quarry 186; R&E 259; Renaissance House 188; Resolution Business 271; Rhombus 272; Rutgers University 190; Sand River 272; Sandlapper 192; Sasquatch 193; Schiffer 193; Scots Plaid 272; Seacoast of New England 272; Sevgo 194; Signature 195; Smith, Publisher, Gibbs 196; Sono Nis 239; South Wind 198; Southern Methodist University 198; Southwest of Arizona 198; Stormline 273; Sunbelt Media 203; Sunflower University 203; Sunstone 203; Syracuse University 204; Temple University 205; Texas A&M University 206; Texas Christian University 206; Texas Tech University 206; Texas Western 206; Tidewater 208; Timber 208; Trend 209; Umbrella 210; University of Idaho 211; University of Alaska 210; University of Alberta 240; University of Arizona 211; University of Iowa 212; University of Maine 212; University of Manitoba 241; University of Michigan 213; University of Missouri 213; University of Nevada 213; University of North Texas 214; University of Oklahoma 214; University of Pittsburgh 214; University of Scranton 215; University of Tennessee 215; University of Texas 215; University Press of Colorado 216; University Press of Mississippi 216; University Press of New England 217; Utah State University 217; Valiant 274; Vandamere 217; Vanwell 241; Vehicule 241; Vestal 217; Vista 218; Voyageur 218; Wasatch 274; Washington State University 220; Wayfinder 220; Western/Journal 261; Western Tanager 274; Westernlore 221; Westport 221; Wheetley 279; Wilderness Adventure 222; Yankee 225; Yes International 262; Zoland 226.

Religion. A.R.E. 79; Abingdon 80; Accent 81; ACTA 81; Aglow 81; Alban Institue 82; American Catholic 84; And Books 86; Anima 265; Aquarian 228; Aronson, Inc., Jason 88; Ashgate 246; Asian Humanities 88; Atheneum Children's 89; Baker Book House 91; Bantam 92; Beacon Press 93; Beacon Hill Press of Kansas City 93; Bear 93; Behrman 94; Berkley 94; Bethel 95; Blockbuster 96; Blue Dolphin 97; Bookcraft 98; Bowling Green State University 99; Broadman & Holman 101; Buddha Rose 102; Cassandra 106; Catholic University of America 107; Center For Learning 108; China Books & Periodicals 110; Chosen Books 111; Christopher Publishing House 248; Church Growth 111; College Press 249; Concordia 115; Cross Cultural 118; Crossway 118; CSS 249; David, Jonathan 119; Delphi 121; Discipleship Resources 122; Eerdmans, William B. 251; Facts on File 127; Franciscan 268; Friends United 130; Greene Communications 277; Guernica Editions 232; HarperCollins 135; Harvest House 136; Haworth 137; Hay 137; Hendrickson 138; Hensley, Virgil W. 138; Herald 138; Herald Press Canada 233; Herald Publishing House 138; Hollow Earth 140; Holmes & Meier 140; Hope 254; ICS 143; Indiana University 144; Inner Traditions International 145; Interlink 146; Intervarsity 147; Italica 148; Jesperson 234; Jordan Enterprises 255; Judson 149; Kodansha America 151; Kumarian 256; Lang, Peter 256; Larson/PBPF 152; Lifetime 154; Lion 155; Locust Hill 156; Loyola University 158; Luramedia 159; Marketscope 161; Masefield 257; Meriwether 162; Michigan State University 163; Morehouse 165; Morrow, William 165; National 270; NavPress 168; Nelson, Thomas 168; New Leaf 169; Newcastle 170; Oolichan 235; Open Court 173; Our Sunday Visitor 174; Pacific 175; Paulist 176; Pelican 177; Peter Pauper 178; Phanes 179; Pickwick 258; Pilgrim 180; PMN 258; Probe 271; Proclaim 258; Publishers Associates 185; Purdue University 186; Random House 187; Religious Education 188; Resource 259; Review and Herald 188; S.P.I. 260; St. Anthony Messenger 190; St. Bede's 191; St. Paul 191; Servant 194; Shaw, Harold 194; Signature 195; Standard 200; Star 200; Stillpoint 202; Sunflower University 203;

Theosophical 207; Tyndale House 209; UAHC 261; University of Alabama 210; University of Manitoba 241; University of North Carolina 214; University of Ottawa 241; University of Scranton 215; University of Tennessee 215; University Press of America. 216; Vesta 242; Victor 218; Weiser, Samuel 220; Wheetley 279; Whitman, Albert 221; Xenos 225; Zondervan 226; Harper San Francisco 135.

Scholarly. Baywood 93; Beacon 93; BNA 97; Cambridge University 103; Canadian Plains Research Center 230; Cross Cultural 118; Dante University Of America 119; Fairleigh Dickinson University 127; Gallaudet University 130; Hemingway Western Studies Series 268; Humanities 254; Kent State University 150; Knopf, Alfred A. 151; Lang, Peter 256; Lehigh University 153; McFarland & Company 159; Michigan State University 163; Modern Language Association of America 164; Nelson-Hall 169; Oise 235; Oregon State University 174; Pacific 175; Pendragon 258; Pickwick 258; Pilgrim 180; Press at California State University, Fresno 183; Publishers Associates 185; Purdue University 186; Religious Education 188; Riverdale 189; Scarecrow 193; Schirmer 193; Southern Illinois University 198; Stanford University 200; Temple University 205; Texas Christian University 206; Texas Tech University 206; Texas Western 206; Three Continents 207; Transaction 261; University of Alabama 210; University of Alaska 210; University of Alberta 240; University of Arizona 211; University of Calgary 241; University of California Los Angeles Center for Afro-American Studies 274; University of California 211; University of Illinois 212; University of Maine 212; University of Manitoba 241; University of Missouri 213; University of New Mexico 213; University of North Carolina 214; University of Ottawa 241; University of Pennsylvania 214; University of Pittsburgh 214; University of Scranton 215; University of Tennessee 215; University of Texas 215; University Press of America 216; University Press of Colorado 216; University Press of Kentucky 216; University Press of Mississippi 216; Utah State University 217; Washington State University 220; Westernlore 221; Whitson 222; York 243.

Science/Technology. Actaeon 245; Alaska Northwest 82; American Astonautical 83; American Eagle 84; American Nurses 85; American Press 85; American Veterinary, Inc. 86; Amherst Media 86; Arcsoft 88; B&B 92; Bantam 92; Bear 93; Boxwood 99; Buddha Rose 102; Cambridge University 103; Capstone 105; Carol 106; Cave 107; Charlesbridge 109; Chicago Review 109; College Board 114; Colonial 114; Consortium 249; Crown 118; Dutton Children's 124; Enslow 126; Focal 129; Four Walls Eight Windows 129; Gifted Education 131; Grapevine 132; Grosset & Dunlap 133; Gulf 252; HarperCollins 135; Hay 137; Helix 268; Howells 141; HRD 141; IEEE 254; Industrial 144; Insight 145; International Information 146; Interstate 255; Iowa State University 148; Johnson 149; Jordan Enterprises 255; Kalmbach 150; Knowledge 151; Kodansha America 151; Krieger 152; Laing 278; Lehigh University 153; Lerner 153; Little, Brown/Children's Book 155; Little, Brown 155; Locust Hill 156; Longmeadow 157; Lorien 269; Lucent 158; Lyons & Burford 159; McDonald & Woodward 159; McGuinn & McGuire 160; Metamorphous 162; Mid-List 270; Millbrook 163; Mountain 166; Museum of Northern Arizona 166; N A L Dutton 167; Naturegraph 270; New Readers 169; Noyes Data 172; Oddo 173; Oregon State University 174; Outcrop, The Northern 236; Phanes 179; Pippin 180; Plenum 181; Plexus 181; Precept 183; Prentice-Hall Canada 237; Prentice Hall Canada, School 237; Purdue University 186; Quill 187; Rainbow 187; R&E 259; Random House, Juvenile 187; Rocky Top 189; Rutgers University 190; St. Clair 191; San Francisco 191; Scribner's Sons, Charles 194; Sierra Club 195; Simon & Schuster 195; Sky 196; South End 197; Stanford University 200; Sterling 201; Stipes 202; Sunflower University 203; TAB 204; Ten Speed 205; Texas Tech University 206; Theosophical 207; Times 208; Transaction 261; Univelt 210; University of Alaska 210; University of Arizona 211; University of Pennsylvania 214; University of Texas 215; University Press of New England 217; Walch, J. Weston 219; Walker 219; Wall & Emerson 242; Warren 219; Watts, Franklin 220; Western/Journal 261; Wheetley 279; Whitman, Albert 221; Willowisp 223; Windward 223; WRS 225; Xenos 225.

Self-Help. A.R.E. 79; Accent 81; Actaeon 245; Aegis 265; Aglow 81; Allen 82; Almar 83; Amacom 83; Atheneum Children's 89; Avon 90; Baker 91; Bantam 92; Benjamin 94; Betterway 95; Blackbirch Graphics 276; Blockbuster 96; Blue Dolphin 97; Blue Poppy 97; Book Creations 276; British American 101; Broadview 229; Buddha Rose 102; Calgre 103; Cambridge Educational 103; Capra 104; Caradium 105; Career Advancement Center 248; Carol 106; Cassandra 106; CCC 108; Centering Corp. 108; Challenger 266; Charles 248; China Books 110; Chosen Books 111; Christopher 248; Chronimed 111; Clarkson Potter 112; Cleaning Consultant Services 248; Cliffs Notes 113; College Board

114; Colonial 114; Compcare 115; Conari 115; Consortium 249; Consumer Reports 116; Contemporary 116; Cool Hand Communications 116; Crisp 118; Crown 118; CSS 249; David, Jonathan 119; Deaconess 120; Delta Sales 250; Devyn 122; E.J.M. 267; Elliott & Clark 125; Elysium Growth 125; Eriksson, Paul S. 126; Fine, Donald I. 128; Fisher 128; Flores, J. 129; Focus on the Family 129; Free Spirit 268; Giniger , K S 277; Global 131; Grapevine 132; Greene 277; Hampton Roads 253; Hancock House 135; Harian Creative 253; Harper San Francisco 135; HarperCollins 135; Hartley & Marks 136; Harvard Common 136; Harvest House 136; Hastings 136; Hawkes 253; Hay House 137; Health 137; Herald Press 138; Herald Press Canada 233; Herald Publishing House 138; Hillbrook 268; Hounslow 233; Human Kinetics 142; Human Services Institute 142; Humanics 142; Humdinger 142; Hunter House 254; Huntington 143; Info Net 255; Initiatives 144; Inner Traditions 145; Insight 145; Intercultural 145; International Information Associates 146; International Wealth Success 147; Jain 148; Jamenair 269; Jist Works 149; Jordan Enterprises 255; Kesend, Michael 150; Klein, B. 151; Lamppost 278; Lifetime 154; Llewellyn 155; Longmeadow 157; Loompanics Unlimited 157; Luramedia 159; McDonald & Woodward 159; McGraw-Hill Ryerson Limited 234; McGuinn & McGuire 160; Marketscope 161; Masefield 257; Maupin House 270; Media/Midgard 162; Menasha Ridge 162; Metamorphous 162; Meyerbooks 270; Mid-List 270; Mills & Sanderson 163; Mother Courage 165; Mustang 166; N.A.L. Dutton 167; National Press 167; Nelson, Thomas 168; New Leaf 169; Newcastle 170; Nordicpress 171; Optimus 271; Our Sunday Visitor 174; Pacific Press 175; Parkside 176; Partners in Publishing 271; Paulist 176; Pax 271; Pelican 177; Perspectives 178; Peterson's 179; Piccadilly 179; Pickering 179; PMN 258; Press Gang 237; Prima 184; Princeton 184; Proclaim 258; PSI Research 185; QED 259; Québec/Amérique 238; Rainbow 187; R&E 259; Random 187; Rocky Top 189; Rutledge Hill 190; St. Paul 191; Scribner's Sons, Charles 194; Self-Counsel 238; Shaw, Harold 194; Shorewood 272; SouthPark 198; Southwest Publishing Company of Arizona 198; Spinsters Ink 199; Star Books 200; Stillpoint 202; Success 203; Systems 204; Tambra 273; Ten Speed 205; Theosophical 207; Thorsons 240; Twin Peaks 209; Tyndale House 209; Ulysses Travel 240; Victor 218; Vista 261; Volcano 274; Waite Group 218; Walker 219; Weiser, Samuel 220; Western/Journal 261; Wilshire 223; Wingbow 224; Woodbridge 224; Woodsong Graphics 261; World Leisure 274; WRS 225; Yes International 262; Zondervan 226.

Social Sciences. B&B 266; Borgo 98; C Q Press 102; Duquesne University 124; Eerdmans, William B. 251; Feminist Press at the City University of New York 128; Free Press 130; Independence 268; Indiana Historical Society 269; Indiana University 144; Insight 145; International 147; Lang, Peter 256; Longman 157; Nelson-Hall 169; New Readers 169; Northern Illinois University 171; Oddo 173; Plenum 181; Prentice Hall Canada, School 237; Riverdale 189; Routledge 189; Roxbury 190; Social Science Education Consortium 196; Southern Illinois University 198; Stanford University 200; Teachers College 205; University of California 211; University of Missouri 213; Walch, J. Weston 219; Whitson 222.

Sociology. Actaeon 245; American Press 85; Arsenal Pulp 228; Ashgate 246; Atheneum Children's 89; Avanyu 90; Baker 91; Bantam 92; Baywood 93; Blue Bird Bowling Green State University Popular 99; Branden 100; Buddha Rose 102; Canadian Plains Research Center 230; Capra 104; Cato Institute 107; Charles Press 248; Child Welfare League Of America 110; China 110; Christopher 248; Cleis 113; Coach House 230; Colonial 114; Compcare 115; Cool Hand 116; Cross Cultural 118; Cuff, Harry 231; Davidson, Harlan 120; Deaconess 120; Edicones Universal 251; Eerdmans, William B. 251; Elysium Growth 125; Enslow 126; Eriksson, Paul S. 126; Faber & Faber. 126; Fairleigh Dickinson University 127; Feminist Press at the City University of New York 128; Gallaudet University 130; Glenbridge 131; HarperCollins 135; Haworth 136; Hay 137; Health Administration 137; Holmes & Meier 140; Hope House Publishing 254; Howells House 141; Humanics 142; Humanities 254; ILR 143; Insight 145; Intercultural 145; Intervarsity 147; Jordan Enterprises 255; Kodansha America 151; Kumarian 256; Lang, Peter 256; Libra 256; Lincoln Springs 269; Longman 157; Longmeadow 157; McFarland 159; Madison 160; Marketscope 161; Masefield 257; Mercury 235; Metamorphous 162; Mother Courage 165; NASW 167; Noble 171; Pendragon 258; Perspectives 178; Plenum 181; Praeger 182; Purdue University 186; Push/Pull/Press 186; R&E 259; Random 187; Riverdale 189; Roxbury 190; Russell Sage Foundation 190; Rutgers University 190; Scots Plaid 272; South End 197; Stanford University 200; Sunflower University 203; Teachers College 205; Temple University 205; Thomas 207; Transaction 260; Twin

271; Orchises 173; O'Reilly & Associates 174; Osborne/McGraw-Hill 174; Pacific Boating Almanac 257; Pacific 175; Partners in Publishing 271; Peachpit 176; Pennsylvania Historical and Museum Commission 177; PMN 258; Precept 183; Probus 184; Professional 184; ProStar 259; Q.E.D. 186; Québec/Amérique 238; Ragged Mountain 187; R&E 259; Religious Education 188; Retail Reporting 279; Riverdale 189; Rocky Top 189; San Francisco 191; Sandhill Crane Nature 192; SAS Institute 192; Skidmore-Roth 260; Sky 196; Slawson Communications 196; Sourcebooks 197; Spheric House 273; St ST 199; Sterling 201; Stipes 202; Sybex 204; Systems 204; Systemsware 273; T.F.H. 279; TAB 204; Texas Tech University 206; Texas Western 206; Tiare 208; Transaction 260; Univelt 210; University Of Idaho 211; University of Alaska 210; University of Alberta 240; Vestal 217; Waite Group 218; Western/Journal 261; Wheetley 279; Windsor 223.

Textbook. AASLH 79; Abingdon 80; Accelerated Development 80; Actaeon 245; Amacom 83; American Correctional Association 84; American Eagle 84; American Hospital 84; American Nurses 85; American Press 85; American Psychiatric 85; American Veterinary 86; Anchorage 86; Anima 265; APU 265; Art Direction 88; Ashgate 246; Asian Humanities 88; Avery 90; Baker 91; Bandanna 92; Barron's Educational Series 93; Beacon Hill Press of Kansas City 93; Behrman 94; Blue Poppy 97; Bowling Green State University 99; Boxwood 99; Boyd & Fraser 99; Branden 100; Brassey's (US) 100; Broadman & Holman 101; Broadview 229; Buddha Rose 102; Business News 102; C Q 102; Cambridge University 103; Canadian Plains Research Center 230; Career 105; Carpenter 276; Charlesbridge 109; China 110; Christopher 248; Church Growth Institute 111; Cleaning Consultant Services 248; Cliffs Notes 113; College Press 249; Colonial 114; Consortium 249; Corwin 117; Cottonwood 117; Cuff, Harry 231; Davidson, Harlan 120; Dearborn Financial 120; Death Valley Natural History Association 121; Discovery Enterprises 250; Drama 123; Duke 123; Eastern Caribbean Institute 267; Education Associates 251; Eerdmans, William B. 251; Elysium Growth 125; ETC 126; Fitzhenry & Whiteside 232; Focal 129; Free 130; Friends United 130; Frost Associates, Helena 277; Glenbridge 131; Grapevine 132; Graphic Arts Technical Foundation 133; Haworth 136; Health Administration 137; Herald Press Canada 233; Hope Publishing House 254; Howells House 141; Human Kinetics 142; IEEE 254; Information Resources 144; Intercultural 145; International Foundation Of Employee Benefit Plans 146; International Information Associates 146; International Medical 146; International 147; Interstate 255; Intervarsity 147; Iowa State University 148; Ishiyaku Euroamerica. 148; Jesperson 234; Jist Works 149; Jordan Enterprises 255; Krieger 152; Laing Communications 278; Leadership 153; Libraries Unlimited 154; Longman 157; Loyola University 158; Madison House 160; Masefield 257; Media/Midgard 162; Meriwether 162; Metal Powder Industries Federation 270; Metamorphous 162; NASW 167; National Textbook 167; Neal-Schuman 168; Nelson-Hall 169; New York Zoetrope 170; NTC 172; Oddo 173; Ohio Biological Survey 271; Oise 235; Open Court 173; Orchises 173; Orion Research 257; Pacific Boating Almanac 257; Pacific Books 175; Pacific Press 175; Partners in Publishing 271; Paulist 176; PMN 258; Precept 183; Prentice-Hall Canada 237; Prentice Hall Canada, School 237; Press Gang 237; Princeton Architectural 258; Princeton 184; Probe 271; Proclaim 258; Professional 184; Prolingua Associates 185; ProStar 259; Pruett 185; PSI Research 185; Publishers Associates 185; R&E 259; Reidmore 238; Religious Education 188; Riverdale 189; Routledge 189; Roxbury 190; Rubicon 238; Rutgers University 190; St. Bede's 191; San Francisco 191; Sandhill Crane Nature 192; Sandlapper 192; SAS Institute 192; Schiffer 193; Schirmer 193; Scots Plaid 272; Sevgo 194; Skidmore-Roth 260; SkippingStone 273; Sky Publishing 196; Sourcebooks 197; Speech Bin 199; Spheric House 273; ST 199; Stanford University 200; Stipes 202; Stone Bridge 273; Systems 204; Systemsware 273; T.F.H. 279; Theytus 239; Thomas 207; Transaction 261; Trend Book 209; UAHC 261; University of Idaho 211; University of Alaska 210; University of Alberta 240; University of Michigan 213; University of Ottawa 241; University of Pittsburgh 214; University Press of America 216; Utah State University 217; VGM Career Horizons 217; Vista 261; Wall & Emerson 242; Warren 219; Watts, Franklin 220; Weigl Educational 242; Wheetley 279; White Cliffs Media 221; Xenos 225; York 243; Zondervan 226.

Translation. Actaeon 245; Alaska Northwest 82; Architectural Book 87; Arcsoft 88; Asian Humanities 88; Bandanna 92; Barron's Educational Series 93; Blue Dolphin 97; Briarcliff 247; Calyx 266; Chatham 109; China 110; Citadel 112; Clarkson Potter 112; Cleis 113; Colonial 114; Dante University Of America 119; Davis 120; Devin-Adair 250; Drama 123; Edicones Universal 251; ETC 126; Feminist Press at the City University of

New York 128; Free Press 130; Goose Lane Editions 232; Guernica Editions 232; Hartley & Marks 136; Harvard Common 136; Holmes & Meier 140; Hope Publishing House 254; Hounslow 233; Howells House 141; Indiana University 144; Intercultural 145; Intervarsity 147; Iowa State University 148; Italica 148; Jesperson 234; Johnson 149; Jordan Enterprises 255; Kodansha America 151; Lang, Peter 256; Motorbooks International 165; Mountaineers 166; Oolichan 235; Pacific Books 175; Paulist 176; Pickwick 258; Resource Publications 259; St. Bede's 191; Scots Plaid 272; Stone Bridge 273; Theosophical 207; Three Continents 207; Timber 208; Transaction 260; University of Alabama 210; University of Alaska 210; University of California 211; University of Massachusetts 212; University of Nebraska 213; University of Ottawa 241; University of Texas 215; Vesta 242; Wheetley 279; Xenos 225; Zoland 226; Auto Book 266; Bentley, Robert 94; Boston Mills 229; Carstens 106; Consumer Reports 116; Fisher 128; Golden West 132; Howell 141; Iowa State University 148; McGraw-Hill Ryerson Limited 234; Motorbooks International 165; Schiffer 193; Sono Nis 239; TAB Books 204; Transportation Trails 209; University of Iowa 212; Ward Hill 219.

Travel. Academy Chicago 80; Actaeon 245; Alaska Northwest 82; Almar 83; Appalachian Mountain Club 87; Arcade 87; Atheneum Children's 89; Bantam 92; Barron's Educational Series 93; Bicycle 96; Binford & Mort 247; Blair, John F. 96; Briarcliff 247; British American 101; Broadview 229; Buddha Rose 102; Camden House 230; Camino 104; Capstone 105; Cardoza 105; Carol 106; Carousel 266; Catbird 107; Cave 107; Chatham 109; Chelsea Green 109; China 110; Christopher 248; Chronicle 111; Compass American Guides 114; Cool Hand Communications 116; Countryman 117; Denali 122; Devin-Adair 250; Dorling Kindersley 123; Eerdmans, William B. 251; Elysium Growth 125; Eriksson, Paul S. 126; Falcon 252; Filter 252; Four Walls Eight Windows 129; Gem Guides 131; Giniger, K S 277; Globe Pequot 131; Gulf 252; HarperCollins 135; Harvard Common 136; Hastings House 136; Heyday Books 139; High Plains 139; Hippocrene 139; Hollow Earth 140; Homestead 140; Hope Publishing House 254; Hounslow 233; Hunter 142; Info Net 255; Intercultural 145; Interlink 146; Italica 148; Johnson 149; Jordan Enterprises 255; Kesend, Michael 150; Kodansha America 151; Lifetime 154; Lone Pine 234; Lonely Planet 156; Longmeadow 157; Lyons & Burford 159; McDonald & Woodward 159; Marlor 161; Maupin House 270; Maverick 161; Meadowbrook 161; Menasha Ridge 162; Moon 164; Mosaic Press Miniature 270; Mountain 166; Mountaineers 166; Mustang 166; Nature's Design 270; NTC 172; Orca 236; Outcrop 236; Pandemic International 175; Passport 176; Peachtree 177; Pelican 177; Pendaya 177; Pennsylvania Historical and Museum Commission 177; Pilot 180; Prima 184; Primer 271; Push/Pull/Press 186; Ragged Mountain 187; Rainbow 187; R&E 259; RedBrick 271; Renaissance House 188; Rhombus 272; Riverdale 189; Rockbridge 272; Sasquatch 193; Scots Plaid 272; Sierra Club 195; Soho 197; South Wind 198; SouthPark 198; Stone Bridge 273; Stone Wall 273; Trend Book 209; Twin Peaks 209; Ulysses 210; Ulysses Travel 240; Umbrella 210; Vandamere 217; Vista 218; Voyageur 218; Wasatch 274; Wayfinder 220; Wescott Cove 221; Whitman, Albert 221; Wieser & Wieser 280; Wilderness Adventure 222; Wine Appreciation Guild 223; World Leisure 274; Yankee 225; Zoland 226.

Women's Issues/Studies. Actaeon 245; American Nurses 85; Baker 91; Bandanna 92; Barn Owl 266; Baywood 93; Beacon 93; Blackbirch Graphics 276; Blue Poppy 97; Bonus 98; Bowling Green State University 99; Broadview 229; Calyx 266; C&T 104; Carol 106; China 110; Cleis 113; Clothespin Fever 267; Conari 115; Contemporary 116; Coteau 231; Crossing 118; Davidson, Harlan 120; Delphi 121; Fairleigh Dickinson University 127; Feminist Press at the City University of New York 128; Focus on the Family 129; Gallerie 252; Goose Lane Editions 232; Greene Communications 277; Gylantic 134; Harvest House 136; Haworth 137; Hay 137; Hensley, Virgil W. 138; Holmes & Meier 140; Hope Publishing House 254; Human Services Institute 142; ILR 143; Indiana University 144; Inner Traditions International 145; Insight 145; Interlink 146; International 147; Jordan Enterprises 255; Kumarian 256; Lamppost 278; Lifetime 154; Lincoln Springs 269; Llewellyn 155; Locust Hill 156; Longmeadow 157; Longstreet 157; Lucent 158; Luramedia 159; McFarland 159; McGuinn & McGuire 160; Mercury 235; Milkweed Editions 163; Minnesota Historical Society 164; NavPress 168; Noble 171; Open Court 173; Oregon Historical Society 173; Pandora 236; Papier-Mache 271; Praeger 182; Press Gang 237; Proclaim 258; Publishers Associates 185; R&E 259; Reference Service 188; Routledge 189; Russell Sage Foundation 190; Rutgers University 190; Scarecrow 193; Signature 195; South End 197; Spinsters Ink 199; Still Waters 201; Sunflower University

General Index

Can't find a listing? Check the end of each section: Book Publishers, page 280; Consumer Publications, page 676; Trade Journals, page 827; Scriptwriting Markets, page 871; Syndicates, page 886; Greeting Card Publishers, page 898; and Contests, page 943.

Other Books of Interest

Annual Market Directories

Save 15% on the following
Writer's Digest Books Annual Directories!

Maximize your chances of selling your work with these market directories that offer up-to-date listings of markets for your books, articles, stories, novels, poems, gags, photos, designs, illustrations, and more. Each listing gives contact name and address, details on the type(s) of work they're seeking, pay/royalty rates, and submission requirements, to help you target your work to the best prospects.

Children's Writer's & Illustrator's Market, edited by Christine Martin (paper) $19.95
Guide to Literary Agents & Art/Photo Reps, edited by Kirsten Holm (paper) $18.95
Novel & Short Story Writer's Market, edited by Robin Gee (paper) $19.95
Mystery Writer's Marketplace and Sourcebook, edited by Donna Collingwood $17.95
Photographer's Market, edited by Michael Willins $22.95
Poet's Market, edited by Michael J. Bugeja and Christine Martin $19.95
Songwriter's Market, edited by Cindy Laufenberg $19.95
Market Guide for Young Writers, by Kathy Henderson $16.95
Writer's Market, edited by Mark Garvey $26.95

To receive your **15% discount** on any of the above listed Market Books, simply mention **#6299** when phoning in your order to toll-free **1-800-289-0963**.

General Writing Books
Discovering the Writer Within, by Bruce Ballenger & Barry Lane $18.95
Getting the Words Right: How to Rewrite, Edit and Revise, by Theodore A. Rees Cheney (paper) $12.95
How to Write Fast While Writing Well, by David Fryxell $17.95
How to Write with the Skill of a Master and the Genius of a Child, by Marshall J. Cook $18.95
Make Your Words Work, by Gary Provost $8.99
Shift Your Writing Career into High Gear, by Gene Perret $16.95
The 30-Minute Writer: How to Write and Sell Short Pieces, by Connie Emerson $17.95
30 Steps to Becoming a Writer, by Scott Edelstein $16.95
The 29 Most Common Writing Mistakes & How to Avoid Them, by Judy Delton (paper) $9.95
The Writer's Essential Desk Reference, edited by Glenda Neff $19.95
Write Tight: How to Keep Your Prose Sharp, Focused and Concise, by William Brohaugh $16.95
Writing as a Road to Self-Discovery, by Barry Lane $16.95

Nonfiction Writing
How to Do Leaflets, Newsletters, & Newspapers, by Nancy Brigham (paper) $14.95
How to Write Irresistible Query Letters, by Lisa Collier Cool (paper) $10.95
The Complete Guide to Magazine Article Writing, by John M. Wilson $17.95
The Writer's Complete Guide to Conducting Interviews, by Michael Schumacher $14.95
Writing Articles From the Heart: How to Write & Sell Your Life Experiences, by Marjorie Holmes $16.95

Fiction Writing
Beginnings, Middles and Ends, by Nancy Kress $13.95
Characters & Viewpoint, by Orson Scott Card $13.95
The Complete Guide to Writing Fiction, by Barnaby Conrad $18.95
Dialogue, by Lewis Turco $13.95
Manuscript Submission, by Scott Edelsteinn $13.95
Plot, by Ansen Dibell $13.95
Scene and Structure, by Jack Bickham $14.95
Theme and Strategy, by Ronald B. Tobias $13.95
20 Master Plots (And How to Build Them)), by Ronald B. Tobias $16.95

The Writing Business
The Complete Guide to Self-Publishing, by Tom & Marilyn Ross (paper) $18.95
How You Can Make $25,000 a Year Writing, by Nancy Edmonds Hanson (paper) $14.95
This Business of Writing, by Gregg Levoy $19.95

To order directly from the publisher, include $3.00 postage and handling for 1 book and $1.00 for each additional book. Allow 30 days for delivery.

Writer's Digest Books
1507 Dana Avenue, Cincinnati, Ohio 45207
Credit card orders call TOLL-FREE 1-800-289-0963

Stock is limited on some titles; prices subject to change without notice.
Write to this same address for information on *Writer's Digest* magazine, *Story* magazine, Writer's Digest Book Club, Writer's Digest School, and Writer's Digest Criticism Service.

Canadian Postage by the Page

The following chart is for the convenience of Canadian writers sending domestic mail and American writers sending an SAE with International Reply Coupons (IRCs) or Canadian stamps for return of a manuscript from a Canadian publisher.

For complete postage assistance, use in conjunction with the U.S. Postage by the Page (see inside front cover). Remember that manuscripts returning from the U.S. to Canada will take a U.S. stamped envelope although the original manuscript was sent with Canadian postage. The reverse applies to return envelopes sent by American writers to Canada; they must be accompanied with IRCs or Canadian postage.

In a #10 envelope, you can have up to five pages for 43¢ (on manuscripts within Canada) or 49¢ (on manuscripts going to the U.S.). If you enclose a SASE, four pages is the limit. If you use 10×13 envelopes, send one page less than indicated on the chart.

IRC's are worth 49¢ Canadian postage but cost 95¢ to buy in the U.S. (Hint to U.S. writers: If you live near the border or have a friend in Canada, stock up on Canadian stamps. Not only are they more convenient than IRCs, they are cheaper.)

Canada Post designations for types of mail are:

Standard Letter Mail — Minimum size: 9cm × 14cm (3⁹⁄₁₆×5½"); Maximum size: 15cm × 24.5cm (5⅞ ×9⅝"); Maximum thickness: 5mm (³⁄₁₆")

Oversize Letter Mail (Exceeds any measurement for Standard) — Maximum size: 27cm ×38cm (10⅞ ×15"); Maximum thickness: 2cm (¹³⁄₁₆")

International Letter Mail — Minimum size: 9cm × 14cm (3⅝ × 5½"); Maximum size: Length + width + depth 90cm (36"); Greatest dimension must not exceed 60cm (24")

Insurance: To U.S. —65¢ for each $100 coverage to the maximum coverage of $1,000. Within Canada —$1 for first $100 coverage; 45¢ for each additional $100 coverage to a maximum coverage of $1,000. International —65¢ for each $100 coverage to the maximum coverage allowed by country of destination.

Registered Mail: $2.95 plus postage (air or surface — Canadian destination). Legal proof of mailing provided. No indemnity coverage. International destination: $5.15 plus postage. Fee includes fixed indemnity of $40.

Security Registered Mail: Within Canada —$5.15 for the first $250 indemnity; 43¢ for each additional $100 to a maximum of $5,000. (Plus appropriate postage.)* To U.S. —$5.15 for the first $100 indemnity; 43¢ for each additional $100 to a maximum of $1,000. (Plus appropriate postage.)

* Acknowledgement of receipt (Canadian or U.S. destination) 85¢ at time of mailing or $1.50 after mailing.